Literary Terms

(Continued on back end page)

Literature

An Introduction to Critical Reading

Literature

An Introduction to Critical Reading

Lee A. Jacobus
University of Connecticut

Prentice Hall, Upper Saddle River, New Jersey 07458

Library of Congress Cataloging-in-Publication Data

Acquisitions Editor: Maggie Barbieri
Editorial/production supervisor: Mary P. Rottino
Interior design: Eileen Burke
Cover design: Carol Anson
Cover art: Jenny Okun
Manufacturing Buyer: Mary Ann Gloriande

© 1996, by Prentice-Hall, Inc.
Simon & Schuster/A Viacom Company
Upper Saddle River, New Jersey 07458

Acknowledgments–Continued on page 1901–

Continued on page 1901–

INTERPRETING LITERATURE

Robert Frost. "Fire and Ice" from The Poetry of Robert Frost edited by Edward Connery Lathem. Copyright 1916, 1923, 1930, 1934, 1939, (c) 1969 by Henry Holt and Company, Inc. Copyright 1936, 1944, 1951, (c)1956, 1958, 1960, 1962 by Robert Frost. Copyright (c) 1964, 1967 by Lesley Frost Ballantine. Reprinted by permission of Henry Holt and Company, Inc.
Nikki Giovanni. "Master Charge Blues" from *Re:creation by* Nikki Giovanni. Copyright (c)1970 by Nikki Giovanni. Reprinted by permission of the author.

Printed in the United States of America
10 9 8 7 6 5 4 3 2 1

ISBN 0-13-282633-X

PRENTICE-HALL INTERNATIONAL (UK) LIMITED, *London*
PRENTICE-HALL OF AUSTRALIA PTY. LIMITED, *Sydney*
PRENTICE-HALL CANADA INC., *Toronto*
PRENTICE-HALL HISPANOAMERICANA, S.A., *Mexico*
PRENTICE-HALL OF INDIA PRIVATE LIMITED, *New Delhi*
PRENTICE-HALL OF JAPAN, INC., *Tokyo*
SIMON & SCHUSTER ASIA PTE. LTD., *Singapore*
Edirora Prentice-Hall do Brasil, Ltda., *Rio de Janiero*

*This book is dedicated to
my teachers,
David Krause and Edwin Hoenig*

$\mathscr{B}$rief $\mathscr{C}$ontents

ONTENTS

An Album of Short Fiction   **167**

8   Interpreting Poetry   644

An Album of Poems   663

REFACE

Literature: An Introduction to Critical Reading reflects the ways in which literature is taught in classrooms around the world today. It assumes a wide range of possible critical approaches and avoids forcing literature into a limited or limiting perspective. You will find here opportunities to develop New Critical formalist strategies of reading, as well as feminist, psychoanalytic, historicist, economic, political, cultural, ethnic, response criticism, and other modes as well. The selections engage the interest of the modern student while offering a remarkable range of nationalities, historical periods, and authors: canonical, marginalized, and contemporary. The collection includes 48 short stories, 372 poems, and 19 plays.

CLOSE READING

The primary strategy used in this book is traditional close reading. However, it is used not as an end in itself. Close reading is preliminary to any discussion of a text. The primary goal of reading in this book is interpretation. Therefore, close reading begins the process and enlightened criticism completes it. In this sense, the book encourages us to consider what is truly important in any given work of literature, regardless of its genre. Instead of demanding that a given work be examined only for its treatment of character, its development of imagery, its attention to setting, or its elaboration of theme, I have chosen works that excite ideas first, then yield to an examination of its elements as appropriate. I emphasize elements rather than a given element because, while each genre has an individual chapter discussing the elements most appropriate to it, my concern is how the elements intersect, complement one another, and ultimately serve a higher literary purpose: to make a lasting statement. Interpretation cannot be limited to accounting for the separable elements of literature, but must move on to dealing with the purposes they serve.

CRITICAL READING

The first section of the book begins with a chapter titled *Interpreting Literature*. It gives a step-by-step approach to the practice of interpretation, using a short work of literature and employing a wide variety of strategies, such as feminist, reader response, historicist, political, and formalist, demonstrating that many works of literature can be fruitfully examined from more than one critical standpoint. The chapter emphasizes critical reading by employing a technique of observation and questioning that helps open the work to interpretation. Each strategy of reading produces more and more insight into the work. Interpretation always implies a search for meaning, and the approach used in this book emphasizes the fact that meaning is negotiated by analysis and reflection.

WRITING ABOUT LITERATURE

The second chapter, *Writing About Literature*, provides a process approach to close reading resulting in a written essay. Pre-writing techniques such as listing, brainstorming, clustering, and freewriting prove useful for the purposes of interpreting literature. Discussions of outlining, drafting, and revising result in the production of two sample essays written from different critical perspectives on a single work, Percy Bysshe Shelley's "Ozymandias." For those courses in which writing instruction is not paramount, this chapter will help students develop material for class discussion and for critical reading of texts.

Later chapters, *Interpreting Short Fiction, Interpreting Poetry*, and *Interpreting Drama* each examine a specimen text: William Faulkner's "A Rose for Emily," Robert Frost's "Birches," and Susan Glaspell's *Suppressed Desires*. In each case the chapters provide a model of close reading and a range of interpretations involving formalist, feminist, psychoanalytic, reader response, and other methods. And each chapter attends to the special concerns and demands of the genre and its elements. In each chapter interpretation results in a short written essay, usually combining two or more critical strategies.

These chapters follow the pattern of Chapter 2, Writing About Literature and end with a sample essay. Again, if your emphasis is not on writing, these chapters will serve as models of interpretation and discussion. The step-by-step illustration of critical method will be of value regardless of the use to which you put the chapter.

ENJOYING LITERATURE

The ultimate goal of readers of literature is to enjoy what they read. Like most instructors, I believe it is important to understand what is read in order to enjoy it. Some works of literature are enjoyable because they provide a special delight. Chapter 3, Enjoying Short Fiction, Chapter 6, Enjoying Poetry, and Chapter 9, Enjoying Drama, all focus on literary works that provide delight to most readers for a large number of reasons, from humor to wordplay and pleasant sounds. Enjoyment is an important goal for all of us in regard to literature, and each genre has its special pleasures. The samples in these chapters are chosen for their immediacy and appeal.

THE ELEMENTS OF LITERATURE

Historically, introduction to literature courses have emphasized the elements: setting, character, plot, point of view, irony, tone, attitude, figurative language, form, and theme, among others. In this book a single chapter introduces these elements for each genre in a way that is both thorough and efficient. Students will find appropriate opportunity to discuss and observe these elements in action as well as to consider how they intersect and cooperate. These chapters: 4. Elements of Short Fiction, 7. Elements of Poetry, and 10. Elements of Drama provide a large number of sample texts which use specific elements effectively, but the book is not designed around the elements. The elements must be understood in order to establish a useful discourse about literature, but they serve a larger function in grounding the student in preparation for interpreting literary works in each of the major genres.

EXPANDING THE CANON

Debates regarding the canon of literary works have encouraged modern readers to look beyond the immediate horizons of "authorized" writers and to consider works that may be unfamiliar, innovative, challenging, and responsive to the needs of a wide variety of audiences. Some fresh faces are apparent in the section on short fiction: Bharati Mukherjee, Becky Birtha, Scott Bradfield, Sandra Cisneros, Raymond Carver, Richard Ford, Louise Erdrich, Alice Munro, and Tim O'Brien. They appear alongside more traditional writers such as Anton Chekhov, James Joyce, Ralph Ellison, Doris Lessing, Virginia Woolf, Margaret Atwood, Katherine Mansfield, and Eudora Welty.

Among the poets who may be new discoveries to many readers are Carol Rumens, Andrew Hudgins, Walter McDonald, Judith Rodriguez, Peter Meinke, Gerald Costanzo, William Carpenter, Patricia Goedicke, Philip Dacey, Marilyn Waniek, Margaret Gibson, Agha Shalid Ali, Lynda Hull, Henri Coulette, Judith Rodriguez, Juanita Casey, Marilyn Chin, Mazisi Kunene, Lorna Goodison, Mekeel McBride, Alurista, Fily-Dabo Sissoko, and many more. In the poetry album you will find a sampling of Chicano and Chicana poets, Native American poets, poets of the Harlem Renaissance, and African poets in translation. In addition you will find a generous sampling of Imagist poets and of individual poets such as Emily Dickinson, Robert Frost, Langston Hughes, and William Butler Yeats. In the section on drama, you will find classic plays such as Sophocles' *Oedipus Rex*, Shakespeare's *Hamlet*, Molière's *The Misanthrope*, Strindberg's *Miss Julie*, Ibsen's *A Doll House* and *Hedda Gabler*, Arthur Miller's *Death of a Salesman*, and Tennessee Williams' *The Glass Menagerie*. But you will also find contemporary playwrights' work, such as Woody Allen's *Death Knocks*, Tina Howe's *Teeth*, Athol Fugard's *MASTER HAROLD . . . and the boys*, John Guare's *Six Degrees of Separation*, Manuel Puig's *Kiss of the Spider Woman*, August

Wilson's *Fences*, and Paula Vogel's moving AIDS play on the death of her brother, *The Baltimore Waltz*.

CRITICAL WINDOWS

Throughout each of the albums of stories, poems, and plays, critical windows establish specific concerns that should interest a reader in each of the genres. Their purpose is to clarify important critical issues, point the way to authors concerned with the issues, and focus the discussion of the issues. *Fiction and the Canon* introduces the issues surrounding canon formation and the debate that currently involves the attention of readers. *Fiction and the Reader* discusses response criticism and its role in reading intelligently. *Fiction and Politics* raises issues regarding works that have a political valence, while *Freud and Fiction, Feminist Fiction, Fiction and Culture,* and *History and Fiction* all cite specific works that profit from consideration of their contexts. Each of these windows precedes a story that it will specially illuminate. And each window contains a brief bibliography to help and encourage students to do further reading.

Special critical windows in the poetry section range from *Chicano Poetry, Poems in Translation: African Poets,* and *Poetry and Feminism* to *Romantic Poetry, Modernism and Its Practitioners, The Long Poem, Poetic School: The Imagists,* and *Background: Yeats and Byzantium.* In the section on drama you will find such windows as *Types, Stereotypes, and Archetypes; Politics, Ethnicity, and Drama; Feminist Drama;* and *Freud, Oedipus, and Drama.* Each of these windows offers opportunities for exploration of critical issues that concern to-day's readers.

The albums are presented alphabetically by author. A good many of the poets are represented generously, either by offering a number of their poems, or, in many cases, by offering a poem that is somewhat longer than usual for anthologies of this kind. Longer poems give students useful experience in part because they can see an idea develop and flower, and the pleasure of reading the poem grows in the imagination. Poems such as Robert Hayden's "Middle Passage," Ann Sexton's, "Red Riding Hood," and "Snow White and the Seven Dwarfs," and Dolores Kendrick's "Leah: In Freedom" are extraordinary performances.

Authors in Depth

In the case of each genre, one author is developed in depth, offering a range of that author's work for examination along with a commentary that can be used to develop a detailed understanding of that author. Eudora Welty has three stories and several commentaries by Welty herself and critics who have thought carefully about her work. The same is true for Sylvia Plath, who has twelve poems and three passages from journals and letters, that shed light on her as a writer. Henrik Ibsen's work is also presented in depth, with *A Doll House* and *Hedda Gabler.* The plays are followed by commentaries by Ibsen,

Bernard Shaw, and Janet Achurch, who played the role of Nora. In the case of each of these writers, the materials presented are sufficient to sustain an original interpretation of their work. They also help students understand the dimensions of a writer's life, which is not possible when reading only one or two examples from a life's work.

INSTRUCTOR'S MANUAL

An extensive instructor's manual of more than 500 pages distills my own philosophy of teaching literature. It offers a range of important resources, such as sample syllabi, video and audio recordings of writers in the collection, and detailed treatments of all the works in the text. Each story, poem, and play has questions for close reading appropriate for in-class discussion, or which can be given to students to use on their own. A second set of questions for critical interpretation helps engage the student in interpretive consideration of the work. These questions can be used for directing class discussion or for assignments in writing. They are open-ended questions designed to stimulate discussion, not close it down.

Every work in each album has a commentary on the author and the value for the classroom of the story, poem, or play. In addition, every piece in the albums has a sample of interpretations from the most appropriate critical approaches, such as formalist, psychoanalytic, feminist, cultural, and others. I was assisted in the preparation of the manual by four experienced Teaching Assistants working toward their doctorates at the University of Connecticut. They all have extensive experience teaching Introduction to Literature. My charge to them was to produce commentary and material that would be especially useful to Teaching Assistants, especially to those who might be teaching for the first time. With their early experiences close at hand, Catherine Nevil Parker, Julie Pfeiffer, Marianne Sadowski, and Mary Ann Reimann produced an unusually valuable guide to the use of this book. My own contributions to the manual supplement theirs in every section. They are based on my more than thirty years experience in the classroom teaching Introduction to Literature and related courses. I have aimed to anticipate problems in teaching specific works as well as to provide interesting and controversial readings of important works throughout the book. Further, I added to and developed their original commentaries in order to provide extensive material for the experienced teacher.

AN INTRODUCTION TO THEORY IN THE CLASSROOM

In addition to the Instructor's Manual, a separate volume of essays, *Teaching Literature: A Collection of Essays on Theory and Practice*, on the subject of teaching Introduction to Literature is available to teachers using of this book.

This volume includes up-to-date essays written by a wide range of contemporary teachers recording their views on the role theory has in today's classroom. Among the essays are: Stephen Booth, *The Function of Criticism at the Present Time and All Others*; Jo Keroes, *Half Someone Else's: Theories, Stories, and the Conversation of Literature*; Steven Mailloux, *The Institutional Rhetoric of Literary Criticism*; Steven Lynn, *A Passage Into Critical Theory*; Robert Scholes, *Is There a Fish in this Text?*; Richard Marius, *Reflections on the Freshman English Course*; William R. Schroeder, *A Teachable Theory of Interpretation*; Edward Hirsch, from *Validity in Interpretation*; Nan Johnson, *Reader Response and the* Pathos *Principle*; Jane Tompkins, *The Reader in History: The Changing Shape of Literary Response*; Deanne Bogdan, *From the Inside Out: On First Teaching Women's Literature and Feminist Criticism.*

These teachers discuss teaching from a practical point of view and aim to help all of us who hope to make the study of literature a significant experience for our students. The essays explore current practice, demonstrating the ways in which literature is being taught across the country now that so many interpretive avenues are available.

ACKNOWLEDGMENTS

The people who contributed to this book are so numerous that I am bound to omit some who have made important contributions. First, I must thank Sharon Jacobus who first mentioned this project to Prentice-Hall. Then, I must mention Kate Morgan, my first enthusiastic editor, and Phil Miller, who saw the need for this book. Tony English has been both friend and supporter of the project. Joyce Perkins, my development editor, was its champion and persistent enthusiast, and the stalwart throughout. Alison Reeves guided me expertly through a number of problematic challenges. Marlane Miriello brought considerable grace and insight into the book in its last stages of development and helped me improve it substantially. Finally, my editor and in some ways soulmate, Maggie Barbieri, has shown me the best in college publishing: seriousness, honor, insight, and fun.

My indebtedness to my students is very great. Not only do I owe a great deal to the legion of students in my Introduction to Literature courses, but also to the graduate students who spent time responding to the issues raised in this book. I especially owe a debt of gratitude to Nevil, Julie, Marianne, and Mary Ann, whose excitement at the prospect of finally having a book they could teach from and be true to their understanding of how we interpret literature was inspiring to me at every turn. James Anderson deserves special mention for help in editing the essays on teaching literature. Amy Page helped with numerous details along the way, including the index and glossary.

But in addition to students who contributed to the book, I must thank many colleagues. Regina Barreca was helpful in more ways than I can count, and perhaps most importantly in my inclusion of some of her suggestions for stories and poems. Michael Meyer was extraordinarily generous in his suggestions for the book and for his subtle analysis of the questions of canon formation. Brenda Murphy and George Monteiro gave me support and fellowship. Annie Charters stimulated me with good conversation. Tom Recchio's positive response to the project was especially encouraging. Sylvan Barnet, extraordinary teacher and scholar, saved me some grief. As always, many colleagues listened to my ideas and gave me good advice: A. Harris Fairbanks, Lynn Bloom, Tom Recchio, Margaret Gibson, Donna Hollenberg, Robert Hazenfratz, Margaret Higonnet, and Samuel Pickering are some of them. I also profited from comments by many friends at other universities.

Special mention goes to Jenny Okun, whose photograph provided the cover for this book. Her work is original, inspired, and moving. She once welcomed a group of my students to her London studio for a memorable discussion of the art of photography.

In the end, of course, I owe an immense debt to Joanna Jacobus, who has seen a number of large projects to completion with me, and whose enthusiasm for this one bouyed me throughout.

Lee A. Jacobus

Introduction

What Is Literature?

What is literature? Nobody has found a universally satisfactory answer to that question. Many people would agree that literature is words artfully arranged to stimulate feelings and impart understanding. Some would also agree that literature can be grouped into three genres: fiction, poetry, and drama. Other kinds of nonfiction prose, such as essays, diaries, journals, newspaper articles, histories, crime reports, wills, deeds, insurance policies, advertisements, and genealogical trees, are at times considered literature too, though some people would exclude all nonfiction prose, including the essay. The criterion used for this book is that a work of literature must both entertain and enlighten the reader; most other kinds of writing, by contrast, aim only at enlightenment. The fiction, poetry, and drama in this collection fulfill those two purposes.

Throughout history, we have valued literature because we believe that the writer is unusually sensitive: in touch with life in a special way and therefore capable of making us more aware ourselves. The writer's skills at metaphor and imagery are highly developed versions of the same skills we all have. The same is true of the whole bag of tricks used to create people and feelings, places and circumstances that educate our imagination. Literature expands our life because it derives from an enlarged sensibility that is deep and informative. It shows us how rich our world is, how filled with potential we are, and how keen the drama of our life is.

This education succeeds, however, only because it is fused with entertainment of some kind. Whatever else literature does, its primary goal is to give us pleasure. In a short story, we enjoy being taken out of ourselves into other worlds and being given insight into other places, other people, and other ways of living—even when those worlds seem troubled. Likewise, we are amused by witty language, surprised by sharp images, and moved by beautiful sounds and rhythms. It is this element of pleasure which captures us in literature, whatever important "message" the author might have. Some writers inform us about how the world works and what is important ethically, but no reader will pay much attention if the writing is not engaging. For example,

> "Double, double toil and trouble
> Fire burn and cauldron bubble"

does not have a great deal of specific meaning or instruction, but in the context of *Macbeth* and spoken by the three witches, the expression becomes almost magical.

Literature, then, does all these things—

- It gives us a special awareness of what we already know.
- It tells us what we don't already know.
- It moves our feelings.
- It gives us pleasure.
- It puts us in another world.
- It uses language in especially powerful ways.

Knowing what literature can do can help you decide whether a specific work is literature. The main question to ask, however, is whether the work tells you something and at the same time delights you; if it does, it is literature.

1

Interpreting Literature

WHAT IS INTERPRETATION?

Literature has many meanings; interpretation is the exploration of those meanings. When responding to a work of literature, people draw on their own understanding, background, and observations. Interpreting literature is nothing more complicated than making those responses available for examination: setting them forth for comparison, discussion, and development. Close reading—the observation of detail, special use of language, and patterns of repetition—not only begins the process but is the basis of interpretation. Interpretive techniques can illuminate a wide variety of values important to the writer and the work itself. Consequently, this book emphasizes a range of interpretive strategies that apply to most literature most of the time. The strategies of formalist New Criticism, psychoanalytic interpretation, and reader response, feminist, political-economic, cultural, and historicist interpretation are all important approaches which the student of literature can use to achieve greater insight into a work of literature.

THE IMPORTANCE OF INTERPRETATION

Interpretation is the exploration of significance. In some works this significance seems clear at first reading; in other works it may seem completely obscure. Obviously, literature that is not self-evident must be interpreted carefully; however, even works that seem clear on first reading can benefit from a deeper consideration because they can have subtle implications that may be uncovered only after more reflection. All literature rewards interpretation by delivering insights into its art.

When you interpret a text—

- You gain a deeper understanding of literature and enjoy it in proportion to your understanding.
- Your interpretation helps others discover what they may have missed or not understood.
- Your interpretation establishes your view of a text's meaning. Since literature can mean many things to many people, your analysis may be unique.

CLOSE READING

Interpretion begins with close reading. In this process, you note specific uses of language, such as imagery, symbols, repeated terms, patterns of expression, the tone of the speaker, and the main ideas the writer introduces. Whether close reading takes the form of writing, discussion, or silent observation, it should be based on a careful questioning of the text. The following pages introduce several different strategies for interpretation, all of which depend on a close reading.

Among other things, close reading requires that you—

- Take the text seriously enough to study it: to read and reread it.
- Search for details that might otherwise go unobserved.
- Examine the text for special words and terms—and refer to the dictionary to be sure of their meaning when necessary.
- Look for symbolic uses of language that might not be evident from a quick reading.
- Ask why certain patterns of behavior or patterns of words repeat themselves: What does their repetition signify?
- Note allusions to other literature.
- Develop and work to answer questions about the text.

Your personal experience helps you interpret a literary text in a slightly different way than anyone else; likewise, others notice details that you might not—everyone has insights and limitations as a reader. Partly because everyone has a unique perspective, the works in this book yield many interpretations. At the same time, however, the value of your interpretation still depends on how well it supports the text. In other words, it has to be convincing.

Any interpretation of Robert Frost's "Fire and Ice" first calls for a close reading.

Robert Frost   (1874–1963)
FIRE AND ICE   1923

Some say the world will end in fire,
Some say in ice.
From what I've tasted of desire
I hold with those who favor fire.
But if it had to perish twice,   5
I think I know enough of hate
To say that for destruction ice
Is also great
And would suffice.

A close reading uncovers important details and questions like these.

- The poem implies that the world can be destroyed by fire or ice.
- The narrator sees fire and ice as opposing forces.
- Are fire and ice symbols?
- The narrator links fire to desire and ice to hate.
- Has the narrator experienced both desire and hate?
- The destruction of the world by fire seems to be an allusion to the Bible, which promised Noah that the next time the world was destroyed it would be by fire.
- The poem uses three rhyme sounds: "-ice" (*ice, twice, suffice*); "-ire" (*fire, desire, fire*); "-ate" (*hate, great*).
- Who uses the power of fire and ice?

An interpretation of "Fire and Ice" begins by taking into account some or all of the questions and observations uncovered by this reading. At first, fire and ice seem to be gigantic forces of nature that could destroy the planet. But the third line brings these forces down to their human equivalents: to a personal experience with desire, which is compared to fire, and to hate, which is compared to ice. The lines that follow, which explore the potential for destruction by ice, also explore the human emotion of hate. Soon it becomes clear that people are the sources of fire and ice, desire and hate. We realize that Frost has used the forces of fire and ice symbolically to say that human emotions are overwhelming in their power, especially their power to destroy. Frost tells us that the emotions of desire and hate have the power to destroy the world.

THE PROCESS OF INTERPRETATION

The details from a close reading must be brought into an interpretation as evidence to support your views. For example, here is a brief interpretation that grows out of the close reading above.

> "Fire and Ice" is a warning to all of us not to permit our emotions to be ungoverned. Robert Frost reminds us that "Some say the world will end in fire" but that ice too "would suffice" to destroy it. We know that a holocaust or an ice age could destroy the world, but he points to something more subtle by symbolically linking fire to desire—such as human lust. He says, "I hold with those who favor fire." But he also symbolically links ice with hate, which can be as destructive as desire, although in a different way. By reminding us of God's biblical promise to Noah that the world will be destroyed by fire, not by water again, Frost suggests that the destruction of the world will depend on our moral behavior. Therefore, controlling desire and hate will be a matter of great importance to the human race.

Close reading examines details; interpretation aims to establish the overall meaning of a work. A work of literature may be interpreted in a number of ways, but some interpretations are more convincing than others. This interpretation of "Fire and Ice" is not the only possible one. Other interpretations might depend on information outside the poem. For example, if you discovered evidence that Frost wrote in response to a long-term hostility with his wife during which he feared lust might destroy his personal world, your interpretation of the poem might change. Suppose, however, that as an animal rights activist you interpret the poem as telling people not to wear fur coats. The first thing you'd hear is, "Where are the textual references to animals, furs, or clothing? Where is anything that points to animal rights?" Even if you suggested in your close reading that *fire* really means "fur" and *ice* really means "eyes," it is unlikely that such an interpretation would be convincing to anyone else. The evidence drawn from a close reading overwhelmingly points in directions other than those needed to support an animal rights interpretation.

Now consider this interpretation.

> Frost's poem "Fire and Ice" is about a person's struggle in the kitchen, trying to cook dinner against great odds. Frost tells us that some say they can never create a perfect meal to satisfy their "desire." With the stove, they can apply the "fire" to the meal, even if it has been frozen in "ice" in the "hate"-ful freezer so that it would not "perish." They "desire" a meal that is "great," but the fact is that they "hate" cooking and would not care if the world ended with the destruction of the stove or the refrigerator. Either way would "suffice."

Unlike the animal rights interpreter, this reader uses specific terms from the poem to back up the interpretation. You may consider this interpretation unconvincing, but to make the writer realize how unconvincing it is, you would have to create your own interpretation, explaining that "fire" and "ice" are metaphors representing larger issues than a struggle with a kitchen stove and a refrigerator-freezer (neither of which is mentioned in the poem). If you feel this is not a kitchen lyric but a poem about more cosmic concerns, your work is cut out for you.

One strategy is to go back to the poem and remind the interpreter that Frost starts out talking not about kitchens but about the way the world will end. He chooses the extremes of fire and ice because the Bible tells us after Noah's voyage in Genesis that the world was destroyed by a flood but that the next time destruction will be by fire. On the other hand, some scientists are worried that our civilization may perish in a new ice age. Now, to make a case for this larger interpretation, you might need some specialized knowledge about what the Bible says and what the scientists say. Interpretations profit from bringing many kinds of knowledge to bear on a piece of literature because all literature intersects with life. Even without specialized knowledge, you can always challenge the kitchen interpreter by pointing out that Frost talks about the world, not the kitchen.

For the sake of argument, suppose the interpreter finds plausible evidence to support the kitchen metaphor as well as the destruction of the world. If the interpretation accounts for all the important elements in the poem—and that is a big *if*—then you would find yourself able, and probably willing, to accept it. The same should be true of your own interpretations. You must demonstrate how all the details support your interpretation.

Interpretation and the Author's Intention

Writers sometimes have a clear intention in writing a story, poem, or play. However, many times the work itself does not reveal the author's intention— it may even seem to contradict its apparent intention. The truth is, we cannot know the author's intention. Once, when Robert Browning was asked what a line from one of his poems meant, he said, "When I wrote that line both I and God knew what I meant. Now, God only knows." William Faulkner, responded to a similar question about a story by saying he "was so corned up" when he wrote his piece that he could not be expected to know what he intended.

Some critics assume that the work reveals its own intention, even when it may contradict what the author said about it. Often a difference exists between what we intend a statement to mean and what our audience interprets it to mean. The question is, which takes precedence, interpretation or intention? If interpretation takes precedence, then the job of interpreting a work of literature is very important.

Interpretation and the Search for Meaning

To many people meaning is "in" a work of literature. But modern literary studies quarrel with that view. All works of literature, whether spoken words or printed words, are composed of signs that readers interpret. When a storyteller says, "Marvin walked down the dark hallway," each of us supplies a somewhat different image, a somewhat longer or shorter hallway, a somewhat larger or smaller Marvin. Until we read them, those words have neither a person nor a hallway in them. Were those words to appear here in Chinese, you would realize how important is the reader's role in creating meaning from signs and symbols.

Nonetheless, when we understand the words, they control the meaning we derive from them. For example, most readers reading the words about Marvin would have a general image of a man (not a taxicab) walking down a dark hallway (not a boulevard). Because we know that some interpretations are unconvincing, such as the idea that animal rights is the subject of "Fire and Ice," we also know that every literary text restricts meaning to some extent.

INTERPRETIVE STRATEGIES

Most interpretations are primarily text based, reader based, or context based. **Text-based interpretations** assume that the meaning is "in" the text and that the critic's job is to find it. **Reader-based interpretation** assumes that the meaning of the text is created by the reader in the act of reading. **Context-based interpretations** consider the text in relation to biographical, historical, and cultural information. They assume that the meaning of the text is not exclusively in the text or in the reader but is affected by the relationship of text and reader to the cultural issues surrounding the creation of the text, its present circumstances, or the cultural circumstances of the reader.

Text-based Interpretations

The text-based strategy of **formalism** examines the interrelationship of the formal elements of a text, such as theme, plot, setting, characterization, the expression of ideas, special use of language, metaphor, tone, rhyme, meter, and all other stylistic qualities. The formalist is especially interested in **irony**, the use of language that says one thing but means another. Sarcasm is one form of irony. In literature, we often see tragic irony, in which characters sometimes achieve their dearest wish only to find that it destroys them. For example, Oedipus discovers that the killer of Laius is himself.

A widely known formalist method is **New Criticism**, which examines texts for their unity and tries to show how each detail contributes to a unified overall meaning. **Psychoanalytic Criticism** is also text based when it centers on an examination of symbols, including symbolic relationships between characters, such as those that resemble mother and son or father and daughter. (Pyschoanalytic interpretations become context based when they begin to focus on the author's life, which is outside the text, not in it.)

The Formalist Approach: New Criticism   Developed in the 1940s, **New Criticism** continues to be one of the strong intellectual forces in modern thought. The following list describes some of its purer forms.

Issues of New Criticism

- A work of literature should be considered as an object independent of the author's intention or biography.
- The response of the reader is not part of the work of literature and therefore should not figure in its interpretation.
- Political, sociological, religious, or moral issues outside the work do not affect its meaning. Therefore, they do not enter into the act of interpretation.
- Because works of literature aim for organic unity, one goal of interpretation is demonstrating how every element and detail helps achieve that unity.
- Patterns of imagery, such as light and dark, sun and moon, and other repetition of details observed during close reading, often provide the basis of interpretation.
- The most interesting literary effects usually involve tension produced by irony, ambiguity, paradox, and wit.

Today, most practitioners relax enough to admit that history and ideas outside the work can sometimes influence our reading. However, the ideal of the work as an object separate from the reader's apprehension remains. In New Criticism, it is especially important to separate the reader's response from the work. For example, that you may be saddened or frightened by a poem is irrelevant to an interpretation of its unity or the relationship of its imagery to its theme.

Psychoanalytic Criticism   Literature has always had a psychological dimension, and **psychoanalytic criticism** pays special attention to it. Hamlet's psychology has fascinated audiences for three hundred years. Relations between parents and children have always been important in both psychology and literature. The way characters cope with sexual awareness, an important stage in psychological development, is a major theme in most stories of growing up. Even the most ancient epic literature has revealed insights into personality and psychology for almost every generation of readers. Literature and psychology were connected before psychology became a science.

Acknowledging this significant connection in *The Interpretation of Dreams*, Sigmund Freud (1856–1939), the founder of psychoanalysis, explained that literature such as the story of Oedipus in *Oedipus Rex* gives insights into the subconscious, the aspect of the mind that speaks to us in dreams.

The foundation of Freud's theories about human psychology is that the mind has three parts: the ego, or conscious personality; the superego, which monitors and censors desires unacceptable to the ego; and the id, which contains dark sexual desires that would destroy society if they were let loose. Sexuality, according to Freud, is at the heart of most human behavior, whether the individual is conscious or unconscious of this motivation. The ego, the conscious part of the mind, communicates in language. The subconscious mind, the superego and the id, communicates only in symbols. Freudian psychoanalysis puts important emphasis on the symbols of dreams as clues to an individual's psychology.

Many psychoanalytic critics apply Freudian theory to literary works. Looking for a work's repressed sexual content, for example, such critics consider telephone poles, steeples, rifles, pencils, cigars, and zeppelins to be symbols for the penis, and dark, damp caves, forests, interiors of houses, unknown locations on a map, and the unknown in general to be symbols of the vagina.

Issues of Psychoanalytic Criticism

- Part of the critic's job is to reconcile sexual symbols with the theme of the work.
- A central concern is to find signs of restricted emotional development.
- A close reading takes special interest in recurrent sexual symbols, dreams, and evidence of repressed feelings directing the action of characters or the author.
- A close reading examines the narrative for its manifest meaning—what it apparently means—and its latent meaning—what it really means to the subconscious. Casual accidents, such as mistakes in language, therefore take on important significance.
- An important function is to discover patterns of behavior central to Freudian theory, such as complexes and neuroses. The critic tries to reveal subconscious motivations that characters (and untrained readers) do not notice.

Psychoanalytic criticism has been applied most to works written after 1910, the authors of which were likely to have absorbed some of Freud's ideas even though they may not have read his works. At first glance it may seem inappropriate to apply Freudian theory to works by writers who predated Freud. However, if Freud's ideas accurately describe human psychology, their relevance is not time bound. If Freud was right, a Freudian interpretation of Shakespeare's *Hamlet* is as legitimate as one of Susan Glaspell's play *Suppressed Desires*.

Reader-Based Interpretation

Reader Response Criticism   **Response criticism** is based on the reactions of the reader to the work of literature. Because the work causes responses, examining those responses delivers insight into the work. The reader's accumulated experience always affects his or her response. For instance, someone who has never seen a Frankenstein movie will respond very differently to Mary Shelley's novel *Frankenstein* than will a person who has seen the film with Boris Karloff and Elsa Lanchester.

Issues of Reader Response Criticism
- The work of literature is not an object separate from the reader; in a sense it does not exist until it is read. The reader's response is the most important part of the interpretive act.
- We can learn about a work of literature by seeing how readers in different ages responded to it. The history of the work includes a history of readers' responses.
- The reader supplies what the literary text omits, which can include the physical appearance of characters, the sensory experience of events, and a variety of unspoken background information, such as what it means to be male, female, young, old, sick, or well. The ability of the reader to supply that information affects the interpretation.
- Because readers are different, there are many responses to the same work of literature, each valuable because each provides insights for interpreting a literary work.
- Readers tend to fall into what reader response critic Stanley Fish calls "interpretive communities," groups of people who respond similarly. For example, readers who respond to the cosmic issues in Frost's "Fire and Ice" constitute one community, and those who do not perceive the cosmic issues form another community.
- A close reading notes the kinds of reactions the author seems to expect from the reader, and the kinds that the reader really gives.
- A close reading also takes into account what changes in attitude the author has caused in the reader as the reader progresses through the work. To what use does the author put those changes?

Since specific elements in a work of literature—such as metaphors, word choice, and images—affect readers in specific ways, the reader response critic examines the elements for the response they demand. One obvious value of the reader response strategy is that, since virtually all readers have some response to a work of literature, everyone has a place from which to begin an interpretation. In addition, this interpretive strategy helps explain why the meanings of texts—whose words remain the same—change over the years.

Context-based Interpretations

The contexts in which a literary text's author, the text itself, and/or its reader exist can inform context-based interpretations. **Feminist criticism** examines gender issues within and outside texts; **political-economic criticism** examines economic and political issues; **cultural criticism** examines African-American, Asian-American, native American, Hispanic, and other cultural issues. **Historicism** and **New Historicism** aim to place the text in a historical context, thereby showing its meaning in a new light.

Close reading by context-based critics is often preceded by special preparation, such as collecting historical or political information or information about ethnic groups, cultural values, or other cultural issues.

Feminist Criticism Interpretive strategies developed by feminist critics are context based since they take into consideration the social circumstances surrounding the creation and the reading of a text. **Feminist criticism** focuses on aspects of literature that have often been ignored by male authors, male readers, or male critics. The feminist interpretation examines gender distinctions implied in the roles that women play or are expected to play. The extent to which women have been oppressed by the expectations of a society—illustrated, for example, in Charlotte Perkins Gilman's story "The Yellow Wallpaper"—becomes a major interpretive issue.

Certain feminist critics have argued that the ways in which men and women use language differ. Some of them suggest that men perceive women's language as being less logical, more intuitive, and more difficult to follow. Therefore, men do not credit women's use of language and force women either to adopt the masculine use of language or be ignored. Feminist critics, whatever their special interest, examine literature for language that oppresses women. Because feminists assume that society is patriarchal (male-dominated), they also look for assumptions of male dominance in works of literature.

Issues of Feminist Criticism

- One function of close reading is to find language oppositions: *sun/moon; powerful/weak; light/dark; logical/intuitive; calm/hysterical; active/passive; rational/emotional; master/slave; intellectuality/sensitivity; dominating/ nurturing; self/other.* The first word in each of these pairings is culturally associated with male dominance; the second is associated with female passivity.

- Exposing subconscious patriarchal assumptions in literature reveals hitherto unexpected themes in a work.

- Features such as unusual awareness of the female body, maternity, natural cycles, madness, witchery, the demonic, and disease are important to explore.

- A reevaluation of literature written when male dominance was taken for granted is implicit.

Like most current schools of criticism, feminist criticism "borrows" from other interpretive strategies. For example, feminist critics are interested in a reader's responses. They also use techniques of New Criticism to connect patterns that produce meanings that might be otherwise unnoticed. However, unlike New Critics, they do not insist that the work must be read alone, without reference to anything outside itself. Feminist critics value psychoanalytic techniques as well as those of the historical critic, particularly in regard to examining the condition of women when a work was written.

Political-Economic Criticism   Although not every piece of literature highlights political and economic issues, every piece of literature does reflect a certain political economy, and this is the focus of **political-economic criticism.** These critics are especially interested in the relation of individual characters to their society, especially the class system that holds their society together. **Marxist criticism** focuses on the class struggle between the bourgeoisie, those who control capital and the means of production, and the proletariat, those who do the work. Marxists examine literature for its position on the exploitation of the poor by the rich. Often that means looking for signs of indifference on the part of the author or the characters.

Generally, the interpretive strategy emphasizing political and economic issues looks closely at the level of awareness shown by the literature. For example, in many plays the characters may have no observable occupation—one wonders how they can live in comfort and yet do nothing to earn their position. Comedies often ignore the basic issues of making a living because they seem insignificant in relation to the action of the drama. But the political and economic perspective attempts to establish a balance and produce an interpretation sensitive to the realities that most people have to face.

Issues of Political-Economic Criticism

- Economic circumstances in a work of literature receive close scrutiny for signs of economic exploitation.
- The literary work reflects the economic social order that produces it; therefore, writers are expected to reflect their class concerns.
- The text, the author, and the reader's responses are all susceptible to analysis because all three reveal attitudes toward the bourgeoisie (upper-middle class) and the proletariat (workers).
- Contradictions and exaggerations of character, description, or language in a piece of literature are sometimes taken as implied critiques of the economic order.
- Colonialism, whether implicit or overt, becomes a significant subject of analysis.
- The study of the class struggle reveals itself in literature.

Because most literature assumes the appropriateness of the economic circumstances of its time, political and economic interpretations often come up with surprises. For example, in *Robinson Crusoe* Daniel Defoe does not comment on the exploitation of Crusoe's servant, Friday. From the political perspective, however, exploitation is a key issue because Crusoe represents the colonial European who lands on a foreign shore and forces the native population to support and serve while learning the exploiter's language. Crusoe makes no effort to learn Friday's language—nor does he even bother to learn his name—because there is no economic advantage in doing so. Perhaps without intending to, Defoe has represented the general attitude of English society in his own time toward colonial exploitation of people in other countries. This kind of political-economic criticism calls our attention to politics and economics as moral issues in literature.

Cultural Criticism Since the 1960s **cultural criticism** has called attention to issues involving the special provinces of Asian, Latino, Chicano, and African-American literary experience that are not taken into account by traditional critical methods. For example, the rhythms and styles of American jazz have influenced poets such as Langston Hughes and Nikki Giovanni. Themes of nostalgia for the loss of older ways of life inform Chicano literature. For Chicanos, Aztlán (northern Mexico and southwestern United States) is the homeland. Asian writers have explored family structures, traditions, and other distinguishing features that mark their culture. Louise Erdrich, Carter Revard, and other native Americans sometimes focus on their knowledge of life both within and apart from the larger American culture.

Like feminist criticism, cultural criticism focuses on a specific segment of society. For example, it often examines works by writers of a particular ethnic group. Larger cultural issues such as apartheid, prejudice, and the effects of colonialism on the colony and the colonizer are also considered important.

Likewise, lesbian and homosexual criticism examine issues relating to lesbians and homosexuals that might otherwise be unnoticed, such as prejudice against their lifestyles. In addition, certain works, such as Becky Birtha's short story "Johnnieruth," contain explicit lesbian themes, which need examination on their own terms rather than on terms dictated by the assumptions of a heterosexual majority.

Issues of Cultural Criticism
- Both stated and unstated cultural issues in literature are to be examined.
- Black English, Chicano bilingualism, and the special uses of language by ethnic groups are examined as special sources of literary power.
- The role of art and music in literature is of special importance.
- Folk tales have a special cultural significance in many works.
- Gender roles and gender expectations relevant to gay and lesbian characters can be the focus of interpretation.

Cultural criticism shares many interests with other critical schools, such as the political-economic concern for oppression and the feminist concern for male domination. However, you need not be a member of a specific cultural group to use cultural interpretive strategies any more than you need to be a feminist, Marxist, or psychoanalyst to use those interpretive strategies. Although the methods of cultural criticism are context based, since they examine the cultural context of the literature, the text is very important in itself. Thus the cultural critic often uses formalist interpretive strategies, such as searching for irony, patterns of imagery, and revealing uses of language within the cultural context.

Historicism and New Historicism   Before the 1940s, historical criticism, or **historicism**, was concerned with factual historical matters surrounding the literary text: When was the work written? What are the author's dates? What sovereigns or political leaders were in place when the work was published? This school of thought was a prime target of the New Critics, who led a revolt in literature in the 1930s and 1940s to encourage study of the work of literature, not its historical period.

New Historicism shows how a greater understanding of a work can develop when its cultural, political, sociological, and ideological context—in effect, its cultural history—is known. The New Historicist might search out the general writings prevalent in 1923, when Frost's "Fire and Ice" was published. In 1923, five years after the end of World War I, the world was still reeling from the destruction of war and the deaths of many millions. The extent to which "Fire and Ice" was affected by the mood of the times could be an interesting clue to its meaning. The New Historicist links a work to the culture of its time.

Issues of Historical Approaches to Criticism

- Every work of literature profits from being read in a context of its own historical culture.
- A social era—its assumptions, limitations, aspirations, and values—affects its literature, becoming part of its meaning, and therefore affects our interpretation.
- Understanding intellectual trends and scientific, psychological, economic, and political theories of the time is essential to interpretation.
- Details about the life of the author can be relevant to an interpretation.
- The study of history is a primary preparation for interpreting any work of literature.

Historical approaches to literature involve and reward research and reading in the period associated with the work of literature. If, for example, you have studied the history of the court of Queen Elizabeth in 1600–1601, when *Hamlet* was produced, knowing that it was filled with intrigue and uncertainty because Elizabeth was old, frail, quarrelsome, and threatened by rebellion, you would interpret *Hamlet* much differently than someone who lacks this historical knowledge. Instead of appearing to be only about revenge, the play opens up to reveal a layer of meaning about royal succession, Shakespeare perhaps reflecting England's uncertainty as to who would succeed Queen Elizabeth.

Combining Interpretive Strategies

Methods of interpretation are not always absolutely distinct from one another. In practice, feminist critics often use psychoanalytic techniques, and political-economic critics may rely on formalist New Critical techniques for support. Interestingly, these interpretive strategies feed one another. A text-based reading will find elements in the text that need to be accounted for in a formalist strategy and then interpret those elements. A reader-based approach will find details in the text to which the reader must respond and then interpret the responses. A context-based approach will find biographical, cultural, or historical details in and relating to the text and then interpret them. No one of these approaches needs to be kept separate from others that may be useful to you.

USING INTERPRETING STRATEGIES

The following brief interpretations of Nikki Giovanni's "Master Charge Blues" show the extraordinary resources of the poem and the interests and outcomes of various interpretive strategies. The interpretations result from the different kinds of questions that are implied in each strategy. All strategies begin with a close reading of the text; some add the reader's response; others add cultural considerations. As you read this section, you will discover that your own interpretation of the poem differs from these because you bring a different experience to Nikki Giovanni's poem.

For the sake of illustration, these interpretations make an effort to avoid combining strategies. In practice, however, you can and will mix the strategies to produce a personal interpretation.

Nikki Giovanni   (b. 1943)
MASTER CHARGE BLUES   1970

> its wednesday night baby
> and i'm all alone
> wednesday night baby
> and i'm all alone

sitting with myself   5
waiting for the telephone

wanted you baby
but you said you had to go
wanted you yeah
but you said you had to go   10
called your best friend
but he can't come 'cross no more

did you ever go to bed
at the end of a busy day
look over and see the smooth   15
where your hump usta lay
feminine odor and no reason why
asked the lord to help me
he shook his head "not i"

but i'm a modern woman baby   20
ain't gonna let this get me down
i'm a modern woman
ain't gonna let this get me down
gonna take my master charge
and get everything in town   25

A Formalist Interpretation: New Criticism

The repetition of phrases, such as "wanted you baby / but you said you had to go / wanted you yeah / but you said you had to go," identifies the form of the poem as a song. The title tells us that it is a blues song, which means that it will focus on some kind of personal complaint. However, the blues usually expresses a personal slight, and sometimes the slight is the result of deeper social injustice. Here, the complaint is that "a modern woman" has been rebuffed by her man, and she wants to do something about it.

The New Critic, who often searches for irony, will find it in this poem in a number of ways. For example, this modern woman uses a modern aggressive approach and a modern instrument, the telephone, but she still cannot get what she needs. After being disappointed by her lover, she is modern enough to call her absent lover's best friend, only to find "he can't come 'cross no more." (She has apparently called him before.) The irony lies in the failure of the woman's modernity: it does not produce sexual satisfaction. She has gone so far as to ask "the lord to help me," but he does nothing. She has got herself sexually excited (or perfumed): "feminine odor and no reason why." Ironically, this modern woman, if she cannot get what she really wants, can take out her sexual frustration in a bout of shopping: "get everything in town." But again ironically, buying everything in town is not going to solve her problem or give her anything more than temporary satisfaction. In this sense, the poem is an appropriate blues song: her actions may increase the modern woman's unhappiness.

A Psychoanalytic Interpretation

The psychoanalytic critic finds this a congenial poem because it focuses on the basic Freudian question of channeling the sexual drive in ways that are acceptable to society. This poem is sexual, and the rhythms of sex are implied in the chanted repetition of critical lines like "wanted you baby." Even the word *baby* has a sexual value in this poem. The allusion to the bed and "where your hump usta lay" contains obvious sexual meaning. The bed is there, but the bed is painfully empty. All that is left is the imprint of a body, a memory of sexuality.

This "modern woman" has no channel for these powerful sexual energies. We know she must repress her energies because "you said you had to go." Yet we know that such energies cannot long remain unexpressed, or else she will become neurotic. Therefore, she emblematically seizes a phallic instrument: the master charge with (if it is a MasterCard) its emblem of male sex. Finally, she finds an acceptable channel for sexual energies in shopping.

A Reader Response Interpretation

A blues song often invites the listener to share the emotional mood associated with the blues. In order to do the same, this poem must establish the narrator as someone who is worthy of the reader's sympathy. A reader who is not sympathetic will respond differently than a reader who is. Thus a reader's personal values may become involved in a response to the poem. For example, a reader who does not approve of the narrator's being sexually assertive might want to interpret this poem in terms of what it lacks: a stable relationship with a man, for example. The detail of calling "your best friend" implies that at this point any man will do. Some readers may be shocked by this detail, and their interpretation of the poem will emphasize that shock. Another response might be to compare a personal recollection of romantic disappointment with the feelings expressed in this poem. It is possible that many readers have gone shopping as a substitute for romance. Is this a triumph over adversity, or a surrender to the materialism of shopping? A reader's response to the situation explored in the poem will affect his or her interpretation of this point. Important questions to explore include: How does Nikki Giovanni present this woman? Does she seem like a loser or a winner? How many responses are possible?

A Feminist Interpretation

A feminist interpretation would see this unnamed woman as a victim of a male-dominated social order that forces her to question her self-sufficiency. Her culture has lied to her by making her think that as a modern woman she is incomplete without a man. The telephone's failure to produce a lover produces instead an expression of feminine willpower: "ain't gonna let this get me down." She has been let down by men, including the patriarchal "lord" who "shook his head 'not i'" when she asked for help. The male world has turned against her in a big way.

The modern woman's decision to turn this moment into a triumph even after the Lord turns her down is a testament to the power of woman. She takes special pleasure in her "feminine odor" and turns the emblem of male domination—"*master* charge"—into an instrument to get back at the men who let her down.

A Political-Economic Interpretation

The political-economic critic sees economic issues at the center of the poem. The master card is a symbol of oppression because it invites the proletariat, including this woman, to spend money it does not have. Then, once the money has been spent, those who control its source demand repayment with interest, a typical capitalist strategy. The capitalist has the money and lends it to the woman so she can "get everything in town." But soon a reckoning will come. Society, by encouraging her to spend her money impetuously in response to her frustration, exploits this "modern woman." Her master card is an all too convenient instrument of exploitation. Those who control the master card do not work: their capital earns money for them. The woman, on the other hand, does work (she comes home "at the end of a busy day") but does not get the satisfaction she needs. Ironically, she thinks that by using a credit card she will get back at the men in her life, but the reality is that society exploits her by providing her with this dangerous instrument of self-oppression.

A Cultural Interpretation

The *master* in *master card* has obvious negative connotations for any cultural critic sensitive to issues of slavery and domination. This woman, whether she knows it or not, is dominated by the economic realities of her life. The blues is a form developed by African-American musicians, and Nikki Giovanni is African-American. The modern woman in the poem sounds like Bessie Smith, a famous African-American blues singer (see her poem "Empty Bed Blues" in the Poetry section), and may be herself African-American. The blues, which often portrays disappointment, is an African-American art describing the African-American experience, and this poem celebrates this woman's victory of character, something common to most blues tunes.

A Historical Interpretation

The emphasis on the concept of "modern" immediately tips off the historical critic. This poem establishes a New Historicist position regarding romance and courtship by referring to modern instruments such as the telephone and the Mastercard. Understanding the poem may well depend on understanding what the credit card permits the woman in the poem to do. For example, if it is her own credit card and she has earned enough money to pay for her bills, then the card will give her pleasure. If, on the other hand, she is borrowing on the card, then she may have the later grief associated with debt. Finally, if the card is owned by the man she cannot contact, then her purchases may be a form of revenge.

On the other hand, the historicist may also wish to probe into the personal history of Nikki Giovanni. If her biography were available, and she or her biographer were able to supply enough details about this poem to show that it is a personal statement, the poem could be interpreted in relation to a specific event in her life.

A Final Point

The short stories, poems, plays, and essays you read in this book can be interpreted using most of the strategies introduced in this chapter. Your choice will depend on the individual work and on your personal experience. However, keep in mind that it is possible to combine these strategies and produce an interesting interpretation. The approach you use will depend on what you bring to the work and what interpretive strategies you find most congenial to your thinking.

2

Writing About Literature

THE IMPORTANCE OF WRITING
ABOUT LITERATURE

Writing helps you establish, clarify, and communicate your interpretations of literature. Not all readers of Nikki Giovanni's "Master Charge Blues" would have thought of the psychological or economic issues uncovered in the previous chapter. Such interpretations developed from special points of view naturally expand everyone's sensitivity to the function of various issues in the poem. Your writing will, in turn, do that for others. In addition, it will clarify your own ideas and insights and make them more useful to you.

DEVELOPING INSIGHTS

Writing about literature begins with finding critical insights to help make your interpretation original and useful. One such insight might be the sudden awareness that Robert Frost's "Fire and Ice" is not a poem about the natural physics of hot and cold but about the human emotions of anger and hatred, which we associate with hot and cold. Insights begin with questions developed from a close reading. As you ask questions about details, your insights will lead you to a deeper understanding of the piece of literature and signal the possibility that you are on to something.

Sometimes you develop insights almost automatically when you read a piece of literature. But other times, a story, play, or poem will be resistant to your reading. The following tips can help you in either case because they give you a system for freeing up your powers of observation.

- Assume that most details in the work will add up to a meaning that may not be obvious. Ask questions about each detail: How does it relate to details that follow it or details that come before? What significance do the details seem to have? What effect do the details have on you?

- Look for repeated words, phrases, or actions. Ask yourself: Why do these details repeat themselves? What possible meanings could they have?

- Note patterns of repetition: of similar characters, similar behavior, imagery, language, and action. Ask yourself if the patterns could add up to something meaningful.

- Examine your responses and trust them. Why do certain characters make you feel uneasy? Why do others win your sympathy?

- Study details or situations that you do not immediately understand and note what they might possibly mean to the overall work.

- Learn by watching and listening. In your discussions about literature, notice what kinds of insights other people develop and what they make of them. Keep track of the kinds of questions they seem to ask and ask them yourself.

Beginning with Close Reading

The insights that will guide you toward your interpretation of a work begin with close reading, through which you try to account for the details within the literary text. To demonstrate, let's consider the following poem.

Percy Bysshe Shelley   (1792–1822)
OZYMANDIAS   1818

> I met a traveller from an antique land
> Who said: Two vast and trunkless legs of stone
> Stand in the desert . . . Near them, on the sand,
> Half sunk, a shattered visage lies, whose frown,
> And wrinkled lip, and sneer of cold command,   5
> Tell that its sculptor well those passions read
> Which yet survive, stamped on these lifeless things,
> The hand that mocked them, and the heart that fed:
> And on the pedestal these words appear:
> "My name is Ozymandias, king of kings: 10
> Look on my works, ye Mighty, and despair!"
> Nothing beside remains. Round the decay
> Of that colossal wreck, boundless and bare
> The lone and level sands stretch far away.

Questions for close reading depend on the poem, not on background or other considerations. You should formulate these questions as you read and reread. Later, you can learn the background of the poem.

Questions for Close Reading

1. What is "Ozymandias"? Is it a person or a place?
2. Who is speaking in the poem?
3. What antique land is being spoken about?
4. What does the traveler describe? Why are the legs "trunkless"? Why is the visage shattered?
5. The expression on the face is a sneer. What does that tell us about the person?
6. Whose is the "hand that mocked them"? What did it mock?
7. What is the meaning of the words on the pedestal? Is there a difference in their meaning today and when they were originally written?
8. Why is there nothing around the "colossal wreck"? Why is important to know that the "sands stretch far away"?

Not all these questions may be answered right away. They come from a line-by-line reading of the poem that tries to puzzle out the main issues. Some of the questions can be answered relatively easily. For example, the name Ozymandias refers to a person. The pedestal tells us that he was a mighty king, but the fact that the statue that was on the pedestal lies shattered on the ground also tells us that the greatness of the king did not live after him. The king's power, implied in the sneer of command that the sculptor carved into the stone of the statue, has disappeared. He was not as powerful as he thought. The statue is colossal, but it is a wreck, and the works of the king have long since gone. Certain other questions, such as what antique land is referred to and who is speaking, may be held off until more work is done on the poem. Close reading is only a beginning in interpreting literature.

Taking Notes and Summarizing

During your first readings of a work such as "Ozymandias," your best preparation for writing is to underline the key phrases and words and jot down questions or observations in the margins. Use the margins to keep track of what you think is important for understanding. Once you have underlined key passages, you can then make notes and summarize the work's main ideas. Here is a sample summary with notes about what the reader needs to do to make fuller sense of the poem.

```
What seems to be going on here is that the poet heard about an
"antique land"—probably Egypt—where there's a broken statue. The
word visage is interesting—means face. Look it up. This is a tough
```

face, like a dictator or something. It sounds as if he looks mean. But it's broken now. The statue is shattered and "nothing . . . remains." All you see is desert. So this guy's empire is wasted. But there's that inscription where he says he's "king of kings." So there's a contradiction here and that's probably the point of the poem. Time destroys things, even when they're made out of stone— even big stone, like this, which is supposed to be "colossal." But that's all there is to it. This guy tells the poet he saw the broken statue and then the empty sand. I guess that's the point. I should look up Ozymandias in an encyclopedia. What I don't understand is what the line means, "The hand that mocked them, and the heart that fed." I also wonder what the things are that "yet survive."

Keeping a Response Journal

One way to track the responses you give to a literary work is to use a response journal. For best results, date the journal entries so you can see what happens when you go over the work again. Here is a sample from a **response journal** on "Ozymandias." Notice that one of the responses comes after a class discussion of the poem.

Sept. 22. This poem makes me a little scared because it talks about the way things get ruined. Like whole cultures. If this is about Egypt, then it makes sense. There are these great statues in the desert there and once the Egyptians dominated the world. But that's all gone. And the point of this seems to be that if they can be destroyed, so can we. Or at least that's what it says to me. It's scary.

Sept. 24. We talked about the poem in class. I was surprised because one person said the poem made her feel relieved. That didn't make sense to me, but she said she was relieved because the king was probably a bad guy. She got that from the sneer and the frown on his face. Anyone who would leave a monument behind like that to tell everyone how great he was has to be strange. Anyway, she was relieved because the poem made her realize that people like that are wrong when they think their empire will last forever. Better things take its place. We didn't talk about the hand and the heart. I should have asked.

Sept. 27. I want to write about this one. I don't feel relieved. Or maybe in a way I do, about the tyrant being destroyed. In class we said his real name is Ramses II and he's supposed to be the pharaoh who booted out Moses in Exodus in the Bible. In those days they didn't have nuclear weapons. We do. We could destroy our civilization in an instant. Ozymandias. The point is that you feel secure when your society seems dominant, like now for us. But nothing lasts forever. Like we said in class, the Egyptians, then the Greeks, then the Romans, every empire goes down the tubes. What we said, it's kind of ironic. That's what I realized, that the whole point of the poem was ironic. Here's this big deal pharaoh, or whatever, saying his works are fantastic, when they are totally blown away. It's a tough poem when you break it down.

Whether extensive or brief, a response can be a starting point for writing about a work of literature. The focus of the last journal entry above is on irony, a contrast between what is said and what is understood: Ozymandias's boast echoes uselessly in the middle of a wasteland. Because irony is one of the favorite topics of formalist New Criticism, this journal already gives the writer a hint about one critical strategy that would be appropriate for the poem. The writer's concern about the destruction of civilization also provides an excellent beginning for a reader response approach. And talking about Egypt and wondering about the reign of Ozymandias suggest a historical approach. Studying the history of that age might produce many critical insights for interpreting this poem. Thus already three possible approaches spring to mind from these journal entries.

THE PROCESS OF WRITING AN INTERPRETIVE ESSAY: PREWRITING

Writing implies a process of discovering material and gathering, organizing, and polishing it until you have a presentable essay. Underlining, taking notes, summarizing, and keeping a response journal to generate ideas to come back to later are **prewriting** techniques. Others include freewriting, brainstorming, and listing, which also produce useful insights, often so much material that you may need to discard several promising topics as you focus on one.

Freewriting, Brainstorming, and Listing

Freewriting, brainstorming, and listing work best at high speed because speed neutralizes the normal self-censorship that can make writing difficult. In these stages of the writing process you can forget about punctuation, spelling, accuracy, and all the details that count in your final essay. The less you censor, the more you will find that ideas emerge, ideas you didn't know you had.

- Prewriting techniques work best right after you have read or reread the work you wish to write about.
- Speed is an essential part of these techniques because it frees up the normal restrictions we place on ourselves.
- These techniques produce garbage as well as diamonds. After freewriting or listing, sift through and pick out the diamonds—the most useful critical insights.
- Don't censor yourself. Anything you produce in the prewriting stage is potentially valuable. Remember, at this stage be totally open-minded.

Freewriting is best done with a time limit. The following example was produced with a stopwatch in one minute. The writer wrote as fast as possible. The mistakes were left as is.

```
wrinkled lip gross. this visage thing. then trunkless what is
trunkless about the legs. how can the legs standt isf they are
brokenwreck and sand plenty of sand the sculptor must have had to
deal with this guy he sculpted maybe he got killed in the act but
he saw something did Oz. like this sculpture maybe would I like it
```

Brainstorming implies speed, too. But it also implies saying anything, no matter how unrelated it may seem at the time. Brainstorming was first used in industry: people sat around a table saying the first thing that came to their mind, usually in response to what was said by someone else. That method works. It also works when one person does it, bouncing one insight off another. After the session you sift through to find the most useful insights. Here are the results of a one-minute brainstorming on "Ozymandias."

```
travelers cover a big distance
they see places we can't
bring back ideas
expand horizons
innovation
do they tell the truth?
they like to tell stories
the thing is that nothing is here
this traveler was going where?
```

```
people travel in Egypt even today
people see ruins all the time there
ruins tell us about ourselves
ruins are always broken
that makes them interesting
who broke these statues
were they people who knew Ozymandias?
statue breakers are iconoclasts
the traveler is an iconoclast maybe
not just broken, but decayed
decay means something special
stone doesn't decay
what decays?
```

The brainstorming session begins with a concern for the traveler, then moves to a concern for the statues and how they got broken. This session produced different material than the response journal or the freewriting session. It also produced apparently unrelated ideas, such as the reflection on decay, which at first seems irrelevant because stone does not decay. But that raises the question: What decays? Answering that question could provide the focus of an interpretive essay.

A third prewriting method, **listing**, connects or collects ideas together. As in freewriting and brainstorming, work fast, do not censor yourself, and let the ideas flow freely. Aim to list all related ideas that you develop in response to the work. Begin with a word or phrase from the poem. List everything you can think of that relates to it, and when you see that you have begun another "subject," start a new list. If you need to go back to the poem for a new word or phrase to start a new list with, then do it. The list here was generated in two minutes.

```
1                           2
pedestal                    colossal
standing                    huge, so vast
nothing stands              the waste is huge
falling from a pedestal     sand stretches forever
a crash                     nothing
a collapse                  vast nothingness
a cracking up
smashing from a height
```

3	4
frown is a sneer	despair
wrinkled lip, a sneer	this is the point: give up hope
Oz. sneered at the gods	ironic—who has hope?
He's like the Greeks who sneered	
at the gods and fell	Oz. had hope, maybe faith
Oz. deserves his fate	faith in his empire
	to lose faith = despair

Narrowing the Topic

These prewriting techniques have produced more than enough material to begin shaping an interpretive essay. Each technique has provided material that can be narrowed down to a useful topic. Here are the possibilities that have been suggested by the prewriting.

Taking Notes and Summarizing The best focus is on the contradiction built into the inscription in contrast with the emptiness of the sand stretching around. The questions concerning what "yet survive[s]" and what the hand and heart mean are good points to develop.

Keeping a Response Journal The response journal focuses on the fate of Ozymandias's huge empire as a model for the fate of our own society. Empires do not live forever, even those carved in stone. Whether the world should be glad or sad about the destruction of the empire of Ozymandias is also important.

Freewriting The freewriting centers on the role of the sculptor. Did he purposely reveal Ozymandias's weaknesses of character? What did Ozymandias's own people know about him?

Brainstorming A concern for the statue breakers links with a concern for the stories travelers tell. The traveler is a historian whose tale of broken statues makes him an *iconoclast* ("breaker of statues"). An iconoclast, according to the dictionary, has no respect for authority, and this traveler has no respect for Ozymandias's authority.

Listing New issues come into play with listing. The pedestal suggests an elevation, and one cannot have a fall without an elevation: you have to go up before you can go down. Therefore, the pedestal is a symbol. The wrinkled lips suggest disdainful sneering, a challenging of the gods, which usually comes before a tragic fall. Did Ozymandias insult the gods and tempt fate by making colossal statues of himself?

Trying Out Interpretive Strategies

The interpretive strategies discussed in the last chapter can be brought into play, either singly or in combination, with most works of literature. The material developed during prewriting suggests a number of useful interpretive strategies for "Ozymandias." Here are a few possibilities.

Formalist/New Critical   Formalists focus on tensions within the poem, such as those relating to the ironic contrast of the boastful inscription on the pedestal and the level sands that stretch far away. The formalist interpretation would then focus on such contrasts, a number of which have been discovered in the prewriting stages: the traveler and the listener; hope and despair; the surviving passions on "lifeless things"; the nothingness that the traveler saw and the empire that was supposed to be there.

Reader Response   The response journal helps here. A reader response interpretation could focus on the way the poem makes us uneasy about the survival of our own culture. Shelley might be trying to tell us that we have less reason to be confident that our culture will survive than Ozymandias did. Like his, our culture could be swallowed up by the sands of time. The reader response interpretation would use as support details in the poem that intensify such a response. It could also describe the feelings that the poem draws on for its power.

Psychoanalytic   A psychoanalytic interpretation might begin with biographical information about the issues that were pressing on Shelley in 1817–1818 when the poem was written. For one thing, Harriet, his first wife, whom he married in 1811, committed suicide in London on December 10, 1816. Shelley had run off with Mary Wollstonecraft in 1814, and he married her on December 30, 1816. Another close friend, Fanny Imlay, killed herself in 1816 as well. Around the time the poem was written, Shelley was sick and a daughter died in infancy. Shelley was worried that his work was a failure and that he would leave nothing to posterity. Such anxieties could express themselves in this poem. The best biography of Shelley, by Newman Ivey White, discusses these issues in depth. Biographical details could produce insights into the significance of the poem.

Historicist   Since history is, in a way, part of the subject of the poem, a historicist approach is possible. The first thing to do, in addition to the prewriting exercise, is to look up the history of this poem in a biography of Shelley or in Thomas Hutchinson's notes in the Oxford edition of Shelley's poetry. Hutchinson's notes reveal that Shelley found the quoted inscription in *The Historical Library* by Greek historian Diodorus Siculus, who lived near the time of Christ. Diodorus said that the largest statue he saw in Egypt had the inscription "I am Ozymandias, king of kings; if anyone wishes to know what

I am and where I lie, let him surpass me in some of my exploits." The Egyptian name for Ozymandias was Ramses, who was a hard-bitten warrior and part of a dynasty of eleven Egyptian pharaohs. Research into the social assumptions of Egypt of the time of Ramses II (1200 B.C.) could help an interpretation using historicist techniques. Research into the recent defeat of Napoleon in 1814 would also bring useful insights into Shelley's political fears of a modern tyranny in Europe.

Other critical strategies might be used to interpret this poem, but these four approaches are probably the most useful ones, given the poem and the material that prewriting has developed.

Developing a Thesis

A **thesis** states the position you propose to argue in your essay. It helps you clarify your thinking. You can develop it in the prewriting stage, in your first draft, or even later.

- A thesis makes an interpretive claim that needs to be defended.
- You can find the subject of your claim in your prewriting materials. Examine them for insights that could be the core of your essay.
- Determine your best argument by observing what you say about the literary work throughout your prewriting. Choose among your observations for the position you can best defend.
- In your thesis state a position that you will defend by a close reading of the text.

Here are some sample theses built from the prewriting material gathered above and keyed to interpretive strategies:

Formalist   The power of "Ozymandias" depends on irony. Ozymandias's boastful claim contrasts ironically with the reality of his broken statue lying in a desert wasteland.

Reader Response   "Ozymandias" is frightening because the same destruction of a civilization described in the poem can take place now to our own civilization.

Psychoanalytic   Shelley may have been unconsciously fretting over sexual guilt and his own potential failure as a poet when he wrote this poem.

Historicist   Shelley's poem criticizes the staying power and influence of Ozymandias, a real king whose empire was built on terror and fear.

Theses like these samples help define the limits of your essay. They also clarify your purposes and reveal your direction in interpreting the poem. They clarify your aim because they give you something to prove. A good thesis states your purpose and implies how you are going to achieve it.

PRINCIPLES OF EVIDENCE

Backing Up Your Thesis with Details from the Text

A thesis is one thing; backing it up is another. If you say, for instance, that the most significant element in "Ozymandias" is the irony implied in the boast on a pedestal of a destroyed statue of a destroyed king, then your obligation is to back up that thesis. You do so by referring to the text of the poem and interpreting it to show how it emphasizes irony. The text is the most important source of evidence for an interpretive claim. For example, you can point to these instances of irony in the poem.

> the legs "Stand in the desert," but ironically there is no body on them
>
> the "visage" of the statue has a "sneer of cold command," but it is "shattered"
>
> "passions" survive on "lifeless things"
>
> the statue is gigantic but totally alone in the desert
>
> the inscription "on the pedestal" makes a claim that is mocked by the emptiness of the "lone and level sands"

The greatest irony is that there are no "works" to "look on" except for the gigantic statue broken into fragments. Making a claim for the importance of irony in the poem will best be defended by going to the text and finding instances of irony and analyzing them.

Assume, for example, that you begin with the following thesis.

```
Shelley emphasizes the irony of finding such a colossal statue on
the empty desert by focusing on the "visage" in a kind of movie
close-up.
```

A sample interpretation beginning with the above statement and centering on its irony follows.

```
Shelley emphasizes the irony of finding such a colossal statue on
the empty desert by focusing on the "visage" in a kind of movie
close-up. He says the "visage" of the statue has a "sneer of cold
command," and then says it is "shattered." Calling it a visage is
```

especially ironic. A king would have a visage, for instance. So
when he says "visage," we get the picture of something that is
really great and impressive. But this visage is shattered, and
Shelley is telling us that everything Ozymandias stood for is
shattered, too. There is nothing left of all the greatness that he
boasts about. The terrific frown that everybody feared is broken
down, just like his whole empire.

The quoted words in the paragraph above are details drawn from the text. An
interpretation usually uses quotations sparingly, but such details communicate your ideas and keep you close to the text and its issues. If you do not account for details in the text, you risk the possibility of wandering off in a general ramble. Keep your attention on the poem by showing how the details
clarify your thesis.

Finding Patterns, Implications, Silent Gestures, Codes, and Subtleties

Underlining and taking notes as you read a poem or other piece of literature
help keep track of details that should eventually suggest a pattern. Patterns
usually add up to meaning and provide material to interpret. But the details
imply more than they say outright. The shattering of the visage implies a loss
of face, just as the "trunkless legs" imply that no body is there: nobody is visible here, only a gesture. The shards of the statue are silent gestures telling us
that Ozymandias's ambition was thwarted by history. We cannot actually look
at his works anymore, but we can think that our own cultural achievements
may be destroyed as Ozymandias's were.

The "frown," "wrinkled lip," and "sneer" on the face are codes for
tyranny. The tyrant or dictator rarely smiles. Usually the dictator shows displeasure and maintains a look designed to instill fear in people. The words
vast and *colossal* are codes for the scope of Ozymandias's rule, but they are
neutralized by the equally powerful code words for nothingness: *boundless
and bare* and *lone and level*. These codes need interpretation. They suggest
that natural forces somehow destroyed the unnatural tyranny of Ozymandias
and, along with it, his empire. Those who fear that our culture may perish as
did Ozymandias's can take heart from these codes. They seem to imply that
as long as our culture avoids tyranny and the sneering power of the dictator,
we may avoid the fate of destruction.

However, none of this is said directly in the poem. In order to say it, you
need to fill in the poem's silences. The poem gives you the code for tyranny,
then shows you the boast of the tyrant, then points to the barren landscape.
But it does no more. It does not tell you that you must beware or that tyrants
come to a bad end. You sense those things from interpreting the details and

seeing how they form patterns. Filling in the silences is the most interesting part of the job of interpretation.

USING OUTSIDE SOURCES

Ordinarily, your only source will be the work of literature you are interpreting. For a research essay, however, critical essays, letters or journal entries from your author, a biography, or historical documents can all be important sources. In this book, you will find critical and biographical sources about the authors who are treated in depth. These sources of information can place a work in a new light to help you interpret it in new ways.

Finding Available Sources

Background sources are available for most authors. Many biographies center on economic or psychological issues and could be useful for political-economic or psychoanalytic interpretations. Some authors wrote extensive journals or letters that have been collected and published. These may provide insight into the circumstances under which a work was written. Some writers have commented on their work in interviews. The *Paris Review Interviews* (available in most libraries) includes many modern writers, beginning in the 1960s. All these can help in the study of any work of literature.

Your library will be the best source for available biographies of your author. Look up your author's name in the catalog for holdings, especially journals or letters. Also go to the shelves where your author's works are held, and study the books there. First you will find works by your author, then next to them critical and biographical discussions. Browsing on the shelves supplements the computer or card catalog, which does not always tell everything important about your author.

More specific studies can help you focus on a work such as "Ozymandias." The Modern Language Association publishes an *Annual Bibliography* keyed to literature according to its language, its nation, its historical period, its author, and then its title. You can look up *English, England, Nineteenth Century, Shelley,* and *Ozymandias* to find out what has been written in a given year on the poem. Or you can go to a library that subscribes to the *MLA Bibliography* on CD-ROM and do a computer search that will list all that has been written since 1963. The search will produce a list of critical essays, some of which may be available in your library's holdings of critical journals. You would not need to read more than a few of those available, and your best strategy is to read the most modern essay first, then read back in time. The following example is the result of a search that specified two fields: Author: Shelley; Title: Ozymandias.

```
1 HUM
Nablow, Ralph A.
Shelley, Ozymandias, and Volney's Les ruines
Notes and Queries v36 p172-3 June '89

SUBJECTS COVERED:
Antiquities in literature
Shelley, Percy Bysshe: 1792-1822/Sources
Volney, Constantin Francois de Chasseboeuf:comte de:
1757-1820/Influence


2 HUM
Fruman, Norman
Ozymandias and the reconciliation of opposites
Studies in the Literary Imagination v19  p71-87  Fall '86

SUBJECTS COVERED:
Imagination
Criticism
Polarity in literature
Coleridge, Samual Taylor:1772-1834


3 HUM Freedman, William
Postponement and perspectives in Shelley's Ozymandias
Studies in Romanticism v25  p63-73 Spring '86

SUBJECTS COVERED:
Travel in literature
Perspective (Philosophy)
Sculpture in literature
Shelley, Percy Bysshe:1792-1822


4 HUM
Siegal, Mark
Ozymandias melancholia:  the nature of parody in Woody Allen's
Stardust memories
Literature/Film Quarterly v13  no2  p77-84  '85
i'l

SUBJECTS COVERED:
Parody
Allen, Woody


5 HUM
Janowitz, Anne
Shelley's monument to Ozymandias
Philological Quarterly v63  p477-91  Fall '84

SUBJECTS COVERED:
Sonnets, English
Antiquities in literature
Sculpture in literature
Egypt/Antiquities
Egypt in literature
Monuments
Shelley, Percy Bysshe:1792-1822


6 HUM
Quinn, Mary A.
Ozymandias as Shelley's rejoinder to Peacock's Palmyra
English Language Notes v21  p48-56  June '84

SUBJECTS COVERED:
Antiquities in literature
Shelley, Percy Bysshe:1792-1822/Sources
Peacock,  Thomas Love:1785-1866/Influence


7 HUM
Marks, Sally
My name is Ozymandias:  the Kaiser in exile
Central European History  v16  p122-70  June  '83

SUBJECTS COVERED:
World War,  1914-1918/Peace
World War,  1914-1918/Netherlands
Exiles
William: II:German Emperor:1859-1941
```

Gathering and Using Sources

As you conduct research, be sure to record in a research notebook all the sources you want to consult. Include in each entry the information you will need when you compile a Works Cited list for your essay. (See p. 42–45 in this book or refer to the *MLA Handbook for Writers of Research Papers*, 3rd ed., by Joseph Gibaldi and Walter S. Achtert for more about creating a Works Cited list of sources.) Here is an example of how to write an entry for an article in your research notebook.

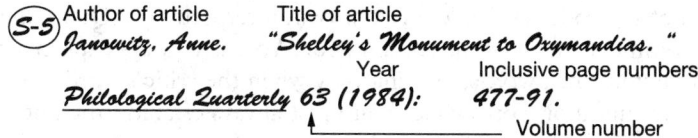

Here is an example of how to write an entry for a book in your research notebook.

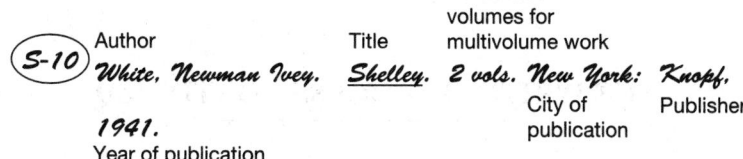

When you find an article you want to read, photocopy it, and then assign it and its listing in your research notebook a number or letter (S-5 and S-10 in the examples). Write this source identification code on every page of the photocopy. Make sure the article's page numbers show up on the photocopy; if they don't, write them in. When you read the photocopy, you can underline the important passages. (Never underline the library's copy of an article.)

When you use a book source, you will probably have to take notes, as opposed to photocopying. Use the identification number (or letter) you assign to the source on every note card or page of notes you take. Also put the source's page number(s) for the material covered on each page of notes or every note card that you write. For a multivolume work, like the White source above, include the volume number too.

Perhaps most important, *always* put quotation marks around the source's words in your notes. Write the page number in the source right after the closing quotation mark.

All these details about the identification-number system, taking notes, clearly noting page and volume numbers, and carefully distinguishing a source's words from yours will help you document the use you make of sources' words and ideas in your essay.

If your library does not have a source you want, interlibrary loan can often supply it. You can underline these articles (they are photocopies) and take notes from loaned books.

Make every effort to consult worthwhile sources. When using a book written about your author, make sure it was published by a reliable university or commercial press and that it is up to date. Look for a balanced view, one that is not obviously biased and that supports its argument with logically sound evidence. Although most sources you find will be reliable, occasionally one may be eccentric. If in doubt, ask your instructor's opinion.

Be moderate in quoting from your sources. If you quote extensively, you will reduce the room available for your own interpretation. Quote the most telling comment, the most important issue. You can always explain a critic's opinion in your own words, quoting only when the critic's words are particularly economical or worthwhile. You must always establish the importance of a citation. Even the critic will need some interpretation. One mistake some writers make is leaving the critic's words there without comment, as if they settled everything. In fact, they rarely do. Your commentary and explanation are essential. (See p. 40 for advice on handling punctuation, format, and documentation of source material in your essays.)

THE WRITING PROCESS CONTINUED

Outlining

The prewriting stage—brainstorming, listing, freewriting, and other methods—helps you free yourself up to produce a first draft of an essay. If you produce a useful list or if you see that your freewriting is taking you in a useful direction, one of the best things you can do early on is prepare an outline. It need not be absolutely detailed, but it should guide you in structuring the essay. Decide what goes where: what parts of a story, poem, or play will be discussed, and what your discussion angle will be.

The following brief outline depends on the response journal and prewriting assignments that directed the writer to combine formalist and historicist interpretive strategies.

```
The Shattered Visage: Irony in "Ozymandias"
I. Background: who Ozymandias was
   A. Ramses II
      1. Statue in the British Museum
      2. Taken from Napoleon after Waterloo
   B. Current politics (maybe)
```

```
II.  Competition to write a sonnet
  A. Horace Smith
  B. Shelley's best sonnet
III. Shelley emphasizes irony
  A. Ironic boast of Ozymandias
  B. The sneer on the broken face
IV.  How irony fits in with current affairs
  A. Napoleon defeated
  B. Maybe an end to tyranny
```

Since it is "approximate," this outline can be kept flexible. It does not have too much detail, and it can change as you write drafts. When you read the essay (at the end of this chapter), you will see that this outline is dynamic and that it changed with the essay. Most of the material in the outline appears in the essay, but not all of it is where the author thought it would go when she constructed the outline. Your own style will dictate how you may want to outline your essay; just remember that an outline is a guide intended to change. Think of an outline as a form of planning. Make it as detailed as you need it, but do not let it constrain your imagination.

Drafting and Revising

Once you have settled on the best approach and have set up an outline that will serve you, the next step is to begin drafting. **Drafting** means writing an early version of the essay. Generally, writers try to get a rough draft at first so that they can rethink their purposes and strategies. If you do your planning well, your rough draft may be close to your final version. However, you must not miss the opportunity to rearrange sentences or sections of your first draft. Whether you use a computer or a ballpoint pen, you can always profit from **revising**: rethinking your organization and looking for ways to sharpen your focus and put the emphasis where it belongs.

Revision Issues
- Check to see if your overall argument needs revision. You may find yourself beginning with one thesis but discovering that the evidence points you in a new direction. If that happens, revise your first draft to take your revised thesis into account. Revise your thesis statement.
- Outline your first draft to discover what additions you will need. Compare the new outline with the old to see if you have accounted for everything you wanted to.
- Before writing the final draft, make a new outline. Try to follow it closely and profit from the discoveries you made in your first draft.

- Do not let your first draft cramp your style. If you are writing a short essay, do not be afraid to discard sections and redo them. Remember that a second draft has the advantage of the first: you know more about what you want to say and how to say it.

Drafting and revising present important opportunities for making your essay strong and effective. Do not hand in a retyped first draft. Even excellent essays profit from revision.

Editing

Editing an essay is different from revising it. Revision implies making major, structural changes; editing implies making stylistic changes. When editing your essay, whether the first, second, or later draft, aim for establishing your authority as a writer. Look for chances to use the strongest verbs, the clearest sentences, the best-organized paragraphs possible. Always avoid jargon, overly technical language designed to impress somebody. Look for the simplest way to say what you mean. Test sentences by saying them out loud. Ask yourself if this is the way you would express this sentence to a parent or to a friend. Think of your audience when you write. Ask yourself whether a willing reader can hope to understand your points. If possible, have a friend read your essay and comment on it.

Editing Issues

- Strengthen verbs. Usually a first draft overdoes the verb *to be*. Look for and highlight all occurrences of *is, are, was, will be,* and *were*. When you revise each sentence, find ways to eliminate those weak verbs and substitute action verbs. Use *to be* only when it presents the simplest, most essential way to say what you want. Eliminate weak verbs in this way: *Original*: Calling it a visage is especially ironic. A king would have a visage, for instance. So when he says "visage," we get the picture of something that is really great and impressive. But this visage is shattered. *Revision*: *Visage* is ironic. We picture the face of a king, not the shattered remains Shelley describes.
- Avoid passive voice. First drafts often suffer from this problem. Here is a common example of passive voice: "In Wasserman's article, *it is stated* that Shelley was depressed in 1816." A revision to active tense is shorter and stronger: "Wasserman *says* that Shelley was depressed in 1816."
- Avoid redundancy. First-draft jitters may make you say the same thing twice. Expressions such as "the poet Shelley" or "the literary critic Earl Wasserman" are all too common. Context makes clear that one is a poet and the other a critic. The same is true of an expression such as "in the play *Hamlet*." You can just write "in *Hamlet*" and be well understood. Search for redundancies and root them out.

- Shorten sentences and say things clearly. First drafts often produce long, tangled sentences because they try to say too many things at once. Break down long sentences and revise them for clarity. Vary sentence lengths in your final draft, but avoid overloading sentences with more than one topic.

- Double-check spelling, look for typos, and repair basic grammatical glitches such as faulty subject-verb agreement, sentence fragments, dangling references, and unnecessary shifts of tense, person, or perspective. Remember to use the present tense when you write about a literary *text* ("Shelley *says* the 'visage' of the statue *has* a 'sneer of cold command' ").

- Prepare a clean copy of this final, edited draft, and proofread it carefully. Uncorrected typos, misspellings, and other careless errors drain away some of your authority as a writer and critic.

The Interpretive Essay's Structure

Interpretive essays come in many sizes. Usually, an essay will be three, five, or sometimes even ten pages long. For the sake of this discussion, we have assumed an essay of three typed pages length, the size of the sample essays at the end of this chapter. In typescript that would be about seven hundred fifty words. But no matter how long the essay is, its structure will conform to most of the following requirements.

- The essay begins with a title that indicates your subject.

- The first paragraph presents your thesis (argument) and reveals the direction your essay will take.

- The body of the essay contains the bulk of your interpretation. Each paragraph develops an aspect of your main thesis and works out the details of the argument.

- Quotations from the text of the story, play, or poem establish your views and give you a chance for interpretive commentary.

- Sources, either quoted or alluded to, may back up your position and allow you opportunity for interpretation and further commentary.

- Your last paragraph or paragraphs are your conclusion. They draw your argument to a close and sum up or restate your position.

These suggestions can help you fashion a strong essay. But they are only suggestions and should not be regarded as absolute. Your ultimate goal is always to offer an original and interesting interpretation of a text *that engages your attention*. There will be times when you will follow the suggestions above closely, and other times when you will veer from them. Your judgment and the suggestions of your instructor will guide you.

THE MECHANICS OF QUOTATION
AND DOCUMENTATION

When you write about a literary text, one of the main strategies you use to provide evidence for your interpretation is quoting the text itself. When you use sources in addition to the literary text, you incorporate some of their ideas into your essay, quoting, paraphrasing, or summarizing them. In this section you will find advice about the mechanics of quotation, as well as MLA guidelines for documenting the uses you make of other writers' words and ideas.

Quoting from a Literary Text

In writing about a work of literature, you usually need to quote words, phrases, passages, or lines of verse from it. These quotations represent a portion of your evidence and offer you the opportunity to make your own commentary and analysis—two aspects of your interpretation.

Incorporating Short Quotations   Quotations shorter than forty words of prose and four lines of poetry can be put in quotation marks and incorporated into your own sentences.

```
When Shelley said, "I met a traveller from an antique land," he
implied that the traveller was also old.
```

Separate two or three lines of quoted poetry with a slash mark. Type a space on each side of this line-dividing slash.

```
With its first words, "I met a traveller from an antique land / Who
said: Two vast and trunkless legs of stone / Stand in the desert,"
the poem conveys an impersonal, faceless impression.
```

Setting Off Long Quotations   Quotations of more than forty words of prose and quotations of four or more lines of poetry should be visually set off from your words. Start a new line for the quotation, and, if your instructor wants you to follow MLA style guidelines, indent each line ten spaces from the left. Then start another new line for your own words after the end of the quotation. Don't use quotation marks around a set-off quotation.

```
With its first words, the poem creates an impersonal, faceless
impression:
              I met a traveller from an antique land
              Who said: Two vast and trunkless legs of stone
              Stand in the desert . . . Near them, on the sand,
              Half sunk, a shattered visage lies, . . .
```

```
But the appearance of a "face" immediately changes the mood from
impersonal to ominous.
```

Documenting Quotations from a Literary Text

Unless your instructor gives you other instructions, you don't have to give publication information about a literary text you are writing about. If you are quoting from a long poem or play, however, giving location information for the quotation itself can be a courtesy to your readers. When omitting words from a quotation, use an ellipsis, three periods with a space separating each:

```
"'My name is Ozymandias . . . Look on my works, . . . and
despair!' "
```

When omitting a sentence in an ellipsis, use four periods with a space separating each. The fourth period is the final punctuation mark:

```
"in the desert. . . . these lifeless things."
```

When ending a quotation with an omission, also use four periods:

```
"in the desert. . . ."
```

When quoting poetry and omitting a line or more, use a full line of spaced periods:

```
I met a traveller from an ancient land

. . . . . . . . . . . . . . . . . . . .

The lone and level sands stretch far away.
```

When quoting from a long poem, put the line numbers in parentheses—two spaces from the last word in a set-off quotation or one space after the closing quotation mark of a short quotation. For *Paradise Lost* by John Milton, for example, (X. 123–37) at the end of a quotation means that the quoted material is lines 123 to 137 in Book X.

Quoting from a play usually involves citing the act, scene, and line numbers, especially in the works of Shakespeare or other verse playwrights. Here is that famous line from *Hamlet*: "To be, or not to be—that is the question" (III.i.56). The parenthetical information means that the quotation is from act III, Scene i, line 56. In prose plays, give act, scene, and page number. Note that the parenthetical information for this short quotation comes *after* the quotation marks but *before* the closing period. If this were a set-off quotation, the parentheses would follow the concluding period as well.

```
To be, or not to be—that is the question:
Whether 'tis nobler in the mind to suffer
The slings and arrows of outrageous fortune
Or to take arms against a sea of troubles
And by opposing end them. . . .  (III.i.56-60)
```

Compiling a Works Cited List

MLA (Modern Language Association) documentation format is standard for all student research papers on literature.[1] The main purpose of this format is to provide a simple, reliable method for citing sources that you rely on when writing an interpretive essay. The method uses references, often parenthetical, that direct readers to a list that appears at the end of your essay, on a separate page, usually headed *Works Cited*. These are the articles and books that you actually quote, paraphrase, or summarize in your text, apart from the literary text you are interpreting. If you read articles or books that you do not refer to but feel your reader should know about, you include them in a separate list named *Works Consulted*. That list comes after the Works Cited list. The Works Cited list makes it possible for you to refer to a book or article in a parenthetical shorthand of the kind illustrated in examples in the next section and in the student papers on "Ozymandias." Here is a Works Cited list for an essay on "Ozymandias."

Works Cited

Holmes, Richard. <u>Shelley: The Pursuit</u>. London: Weidenfeld, 1974.

Janowitz, Anne. "Shelley's Monument to Ozymandias."

    <u>Philological Quarterly</u> 63 (1984): 477-91.

"Ramses." <u>Encyclopedia Britannica: Macropaedia</u>. 1986 ed.

"Shelley in Bloomsbury." <u>Smithsonian Magazine</u> June 1988: 64-73.

Thomas Hutchinson, ed. <u>Poems of Percy Bysshe Shelley</u>. Rev. G. M.

    Matthews. Oxford: Oxford UP, 1970.

Wasserman, Earl. "Shelley's Crisis." <u>Shelley: A Collection of</u>

    <u>Critical Essays</u>. Ed. George Ridenour. Englewood Cliffs:

    Prentice, 1965. 77-80.

White, Newman Ivey. <u>Shelley</u>. 2 vols. New York: Knopf, 1941.

Works Consulted

Fruman, Norman. "Ozymandias and the Reconciliation of

    Opposites." <u>Studies in the Literary Imagination</u> 19.3 (1986):

    71-87.

Yeats, W. B. "The Philosophy of Shelley's Poetry." <u>Essays</u>.

London:

    Macmillan, 1924.

---

[1]Published books, including this one, often follow the style outlined by the *Chicago Manual of Style*.

Important Features of Works Cited Lists

- Works are alphabetized, by the last name of the author. If the author's name is unknown, use the title of the work.

- Each entry uses a hanging indentation: the first line is flush left, and every succeeding line is indented five spaces.

- Periods end each segment of the citation: Author (or editor). Title of book or article. Journal title. Volume number and other information (if an article). Place of publication: Publisher, date (if a book). Date is in parentheses if you cite an article, followed by colon (:) and pages (see Janowitz entry on p. 44).

- Book titles are underlined; names of journals are underlined. Articles are in quotation marks. The general rule is that anything of book length is underlined, whereas anything normally included in a book (such as a chapter) uses quotation marks (see Wasserman entry above: note both article and book titles).

- Short forms and abbreviations are used for publishers' names, such as Simon for *Simon & Schuster* and UP for *University Press*.

- When a second work by an author is listed, three hyphens and a period: ---. are used instead of repeating the name.

  Holmes, Richard. <u>Shelley: The Pursuit</u>. London: Weidenfeld, 1974.

  ---. <u>Coleridge: Early Visions</u>. New York: Viking, 1990.

- For magazines, include month of publication (see "Shelley in Bloomsbury" on p. 44), not the volume number.

- When a journal paginates continuously throughout a given year—as when, for example, volume 15, number 1 (1993), begins with page 1; volume 15, number 2 (1993), with page 221; and volume 15, number 3 (1993), with page 345—you need not cite the individual issue number (see Janowitz entry on p. 44).

- When the journal begins new pagination with each issue within a volume, then cite the volume, issue number, and pagination (see Fruman entry above).

- For encyclopedia articles, include the date of the edition (see "Ramses" entry above).

A fuller discussion of these details is available in the *MLA Handbook for Writers of Research Papers*, 3rd ed., by Joseph Gibaldi and Walter S. Achtert, published by the Modern Language Association of America in 1988 and widely available in college bookstores. It covers all the possible problems you might face in citing any sources.

Citing Works in Your Essay in MLA Style

A few examples here and the student papers on "Ozymandias" show the basic principles of citing works in your own essays to support your points as you write. The rule is, keep it simple. Use parentheses to supply the important information that will allow readers to find the source in your Works Cited list. The following examples rely on the Works Cited list in the preceding section.

When you mention the author's name in your text, include volume (if necessary) and page reference in parentheses:

```
Newman Ivey White says that Shelley had eye trouble when he wrote
"Ozymandias" (2: 321).
```

When you do not mention the author's name in your text, include it in parentheses along with the volume and page reference:

```
Apparently, Shelley played a great deal of chess around the time he
wrote "Ozymandias" (White 2: 323).
```

Note that no comma comes after the author's name, the colon separates volume and page number, and you do not need "p." to indicate the page reference.

When you want to note that more than one author cites an important detail, use this form:

```
(Holmes 316; Yeats 110).
```

And if you need to refer to an author who has more than one title in your Works Cited list, use a short form of the title to indicate which book you are referring to:

```
(Hutchinson, Poem 331).
```

(If you used the author's name in your sentence, then you only need the title and page number.)

When in doubt, be sure to use the simplest, most economical means of citing a reference. Thus if there is no author of a piece, use the key word of the title:

```
("Shelley" 15).
```

Similarly, for an encyclopedia article, use the key term of the article as you would the author's name, and no page numbers:

```
("Ramses").
```

When you need to consult outside sources in your interpretive essays, use the clearest and most reliable method. Do not let your sources overwhelm you. Question them, use them sparingly, and be sure to go beyond them with your own commentary. Do not let them limit your imagination in regard to the work you interpret.

DETAILS OF MANUSCRIPT PREPARATION

A well-presented manuscript is more important than you may realize. When you demonstrate that you understand the formalities and conventions of an essay that needs sources, you convince your instructor of your seriousness. If you do not use sources, then a neatly typed—or carefully handwritten—essay makes the job of reading and commenting on your work much easier. If your instructor doesn't give you special manuscript format guidelines, you can safely follow these.

- Begin the first page about one-third down, with your name, course name, and instructor's name at the right. Your instructor's name is important because if the paper is lost it will be returned more quickly to your instructor than to you. In order to minimize the risk of loss, be sure to photocopy any essay you hand in. A typical first page would begin something like this.

Betsy Bisberg

English 109-07

Mr. Jacobus

     The Shattered Visage: Irony in "Ozymandias"
     Percy Bysshe Shelley's "Ozymandias," "the finest sonnet
he ever wrote" (Holmes 410), is ironic in many ways. One of the
most interesting things about Shelley's poem is that it was written
in a competition with another poet, Horace Smith (Reiman 47-49).
Both had been to the British Museum to see the Egyptian

- Leave margins of approximately 1 to 1 1/2 inches on the left so that your instructor can offer useful comments.
- Number each page except the first in the upper right corner.
- When you type, double-space so that comments and corrections can be inserted between the lines. If you handwrite, ask your instructor whether the essay should be single- or double-spaced.
- Do not crowd your pages. Leave comfortable margins on the top, bottom, and right.

- Proofread your essays before handing them in. Make sure that you have done everything to avoid handing in essays with typos, with misspellings (especially of the names of your author or instructor), or with omissions that you could have caught if you were vigilant.

SAMPLE ESSAYS

Both of the following essays on Shelley's "Ozymandias" were developed from the prewriting and planning efforts shown above. The first essay uses outside sources and joins a New Critical formalist method with a historicist approach. The second, which did not consult outside sources except for class discussion, uses a reader response approach. Both essays offer a distinct interpretation of the poem.

A Formalist/Historicist Interpretation Using Sources

Betsy Bisberg

English 109-07

Mr. Jacobus

The Shattered Visage: Irony in "Ozymandias"

The power of Percy Bysshe Shelley's "Ozymandias," "the finest sonnet he ever wrote" (Holmes 410), depends on irony. The boast "Look on my works, ye Mighty, and despair!" contrasts ironically with the reality of his broken statue lying in a desert wasteland. Shelley's poem was written in a competition with another poet, Horace Smith (Reiman 47-49). Both had been to the British Museum to see the Egyptian statues brought there in 1817 by the British after the defeat of Napoleon in Egypt. "Among these . . . the massive figure of Ramses II . . . perhaps the most famous of all Egyptian fragments . . ." (Holmes 410). Holmes tells us that Shelley imagined the traveller and the setting for his poem. But he did not have to imagine the statue, since its fragments rested near where he lived and he saw them whenever he wanted. In its way that was also an irony. Ramses II could not prevent these huge statues from being carted off like souvenirs. Ozymandias would not have been able to imagine a time when his statue could be carted away.

Shelley did not like tyrants, and Ramses II was a tyrant in ancient Egypt. A warlike general, he caused great turmoil in the world. According to the <u>Encyclopedia Britannica</u> he was probably the pharaoh who caused Moses to leave on the exodus from Egypt. Ironically, the statue of Ramses was brought to London after the British defeated a modern tyrant, Napoleon, at Waterloo. In 1817, when Shelley saw the fragments of this huge statue, the world could breathe easier because both tyrants were defeated (Holmes 409).

Shelley really focused on the ironic boasts of all tyrants when he wrote his poem. Shelley says the "visage" of the statue has a "sneer of cold command," and then says it is "shattered." He emphasizes the irony of finding such a colossal statue on the empty desert by focusing on the "visage" in a kind of movie close-up. Calling it a visage is especially ironic. A king would have a visage, for instance. So when he says "visage," we get the picture of something that is really great and impressive. But this visage is shattered and Shelley says everything Ozymandias stood for is shattered, too. There is nothing left of all the greatness that he boasts about. The terrific frown that everybody feared is broken down, just like his whole empire.

The writing on the pedestal is: "My name is Ozymandias, king of kings: / Look on my works, ye Mighty, and despair!" The irony here is plain. There are no works, except for the statue, and it is broken. Everything else is gone. The writing on the real statue Shelley saw is pretty much the same: "I am Ozymandias, king of kings; if anyone wishes to know what I am and where I lie, let him surpass me in some of my exploits" (Hutchinson 121). Hutchinson says Shelley probably got this from reading the Greek historian Diodorus Siculus, who was probably the model for the "ancient traveller" of the first line. In either case, the writing adds to the irony, especially the way Shelley changes it. He changes it to include the idea of despair. We are supposed to look on all these mighty works and despair.

Telling us to despair means we should automatically give up hope. Well, maybe we would have when this statue was standing. And maybe that is what Ramses II wanted Moses and the Hebrews to do in the Bible. The only way not to give up hope, though, is to have faith. Moses had faith. Ozymandias had faith in his empire, but it was like his statue. It was built out of stone and it broke.

Works Cited

Holmes, Richard. <u>Shelley: The Pursuit</u>. London: Weidenfeld, 1974.

Hutchinson, Thomas, ed. <u>Poems of Percy Bysshe Shelley</u>. Rev. G. M.
    Matthews. Oxford: Oxford UP, 1970.

"Ramses." <u>Encyclopedia Britannica: Macropaedia</u>. 1986 ed.

Reiman, Donald. <u>Percy Bysshe Shelley</u>. New York: Twayne, 1969.

Works Consulted

Janowitz, Anne. "Shelley's Monument to Ozymandias."
    <u>Philological Quarterly</u> 63 (1984): 477-91.

Ridenour, George, ed. <u>Shelley: A Collection of Critical Essays</u>.
    Englewood Cliffs: Prentice, 1965.

White, Newman Ivey. <u>Shelley</u>. 2 vols. New York: Knopf, 1941.

Yeats, W. B. "The Philosophy of Shelley's Poetry." <u>Essays</u>.
    London: Macmillan, 1924.

A Reader Response Interpretation

Louis Mendes

English 109-07

Mr. Jacobus

"Ozymandias": What the Future Holds

When I first read this poem I could not help but feel a
little frightened for the future. Shelley tells us about a "king of
kings" whose great empire now lies around in ruins. I have seen
pictures of the sphinx and the pyramids and some of the big statues
still in the desert in Egypt, and the way Shelley describes things,
"The lone and level sands stretch far away," gives you the feeling
that there is nothing here but emptiness where there was once a
gigantic civilization.

In class, when we talked about it I could not agree that
the poem should make us feel better because Ozymandias is dead and
gone. I agree that the sneer on the "visage" means he was a tough
guy, a mean ruler. And maybe it is true that the empire he led was
cruel in a lot of ways. But you also have to admit that those great
things they built, and the good things they had, like cities and
high culture, were impressive. Even now the pyramids impress people
from around the world, so the ancient Egyptians must have had a
fantastic organization to get them built. Someone said that the

culture the Egyptians put together was imitated by the Greeks and even the Romans and maybe some of what they were doing is even still being done by our culture. But in a way that makes me worried.

I am not sure Shelley wanted me to worry about civilization going under, but I think it is possible. I mean, he uses words like decay, wreck, bare, and lifeless for a reason. He wants to get us worked up about this statue. The notes to the poem say that "the hand that mocked them" refers to the hand of the sculptor who made the lips into a sneer and the expression into a frown. "The heart that fed" is supposed to be the heart of Ozymandias because he ate it all up as if it was praise. Here Ozymandias thought he was leader of an empire that was going to be around forever. But it is gone.

That scares me. The Egyptians are gone, and they were once mighty. The Greeks were great and so were the Romans. They all conquered the world but everything they built is more or less gone. Look at Greece and Italy today. And what about our culture? We build a lot of monuments, too. The Statue of Liberty, the Sears Tower, and the Space Needle, to mention only three pretty big things. You could include the Golden Gate Bridge in San Francisco, and the new tunnel from England to France. These are great monuments and you could write the same kind of thing on them that Ozymandias wrote on his statue. You can imagine all of them "half sunk" and "shattered."

What the poem makes me think of is the possibility that our civilization will destroy itself. With the threats of global warming, general pollution, the ozone layer depletion, and nuclear war, we could probably destroy our civilization much faster than Ozymandias's civilization went. We could wipe ourselves out in an instant. That is scary. In ancient Egypt it was a big operation to break up statues that were gigantic like the one Shelley describes. They did it, but it took lots of time. We can do it too, and it would take no time at all. Then, when you think of it, how could there be "a traveller from an antique land" telling anyone about us? There would be no way. There could never be another Shelley, any more than there could be a poem like this written in the future.

So what gets me worried is the thought that if we let our civilization disappear the way Ozymandias did, there will be no way anyone would hear about it. There would be no future if we destroy life on the planet. The sands that stretch away in this poem will stretch away on the earth, but there will not be anyone to see them and report back. That is the bottom line in this poem, and it is one of the scariest poems I have read.

Short Fiction

3

Enjoying Short Fiction

WHAT IS SHORT FICTION?

Like definitions of *literature*, no definition of **short fiction** can satisfy every-one. Still, some qualities of short fiction can be identified. For one, short fiction is prose storytelling whose incidents are deeply revealing of human val-ues. No length limits have ever been settled on; the stories in this collection range easily from two pages to dozens of pages. Usually, the reader's sense of satisfaction signals the completion of a story, but you will find that some of the following stories purposely deny you a sense of satisfaction in order to bring you to a point of reflection and questioning. Such stories invite you to round them out in your mind.

No one knows the origins of storytelling, but it began early in human history. In dreams may lie the beginnings of storytelling because people seem to have a universal impulse to tell others their dreams. Or perhaps dreams are the product, not the origin, of fiction. Some dreams have a narrative plot, character, action, setting, and language. They often follow the action/ad-venture, science fiction, mystery, or other style of narratives found in short fiction. Freud assumed a connection between literature and dreams and felt that literature reflected the subconscious.

Both "The Pot of Basil" and "Two Cents," in this chapter, have dream-like qualities. In the first story, one character appears to the heroine as a ghost, as if in a dream. In the second story, people behave as if they are detached from themselves—somewhat the way that the "you" in your dreams is de-tached from the "you" in life. We can say that dreams are interactive with fic-tion. They may have helped produce it, and in some ways they help sustain it. Scientists tell us we need to dream in order to retain our sanity. If that is true, we may also need fiction to help us maintain a balanced inner life.

For many of us, stories help to form personal values and personal identity. Childhood stories are often moral tales designed to awaken an awareness that we are not alone in the universe, that we have responsibilities to others. They even have the effect of clarifying our sense of ourselves. An influential contemporary literary critic, Stephen J. Greenblatt, tells us this about himself:

> My earliest recollections of "having an identity" or "being a self" are bound up with story-telling—narrating my own life or having it narrated for me by my mother. I suppose that I usually used the personal pronoun "I" in telling my own stories and that my mother used my name, but the heart of the initial experience of selfhood lay in the stories, not in the unequivocal, unmediated possession of an identity.[1]

Greenblatt also remembered going through a terrible period in his life in which he began to "narrate" his existence, saying to himself such things as "He's sitting down, now. He's opening his book." Such behavior gives you an idea of how powerful the typical narrative style of short fiction can become. Ultimately, Greenblatt recognizes one of the most important qualities of fiction: "Pleasure is an important part of my sense of literature—that is, part both of my own response . . . and of what I most wish to understand."

INTERPRETING A STORY FROM *THE DECAMERON*

Some people think of the short story as a modern, virtually American invention. The stories and theorizing of Nathaniel Hawthorne (1804–1864) and Edgar Allan Poe (1809–1849) are so influential that such a view is almost supportable. However, the impulse to tell stories is ancient. Among the most important innovators of the short story is Giovanni Boccaccio (1313–1375), whose *Decameron* was designed carefully, almost like a piece of architecture. "I shall narrate a hundred stories or fables or parables or histories or whatever you choose to call them, recited in ten days by a worthy band of seven ladies and three young men, who assembled together during the plague which recently took such heavy toll of life." For ten days, while cloistered away from an epidemic of the Black Death in 1348, these ten young aristocrats tell stories for one another's enjoyment. The hundred stories, some very brief, delve into psychology, inquire into the manners and mores of their culture, and expose the hypocrisy of such institutions as the church, families, and professional societies. Although they are set in the 1300s in Florence, Italy, they are recognizably modern. They touch upon other nations and cultures, such as

---

[1]*Learning to Curse* (New York: Routledge, 1990), 6.

the Arabic world, which traded with Florence. Their universality shows up in the fact that numerous cultures have raided the stories and adapted them for their own. Like all great literature, they speak to a universal audience.

"The Pot of Basil" is the fifth story of the fourth day, told by Filomena, who was moved to tell it after hearing the love story that preceded hers. Often retold, this story was popular among the Romantic poets of the early nineteenth century.

Giovanni Boccaccio   (1313–1375)
THE POT OF BASIL   1353

Translated by G. H. McWilliam

When Elissa's story came to an end, the king bestowed a few words of praise upon it and then called upon Filomena to speak next. Being quite overcome with compassion for the hapless Gerbino and his lady-love, she fetched a deep sigh, then began as follows:

This story of mine, fair ladies, will not be about people of so lofty a rank as those of whom Elissa has been speaking, but possibly it will prove to be no less touching, and I was reminded of it by the mention that has just been made of Messina, which was where it all happened.

In Messina, there once lived three brothers, all of them merchants who had been left very rich after the death of their father, whose native town was San Gemignano. They had a sister called Lisabetta, but for some reason or other they had failed to bestow her in marriage, despite the fact that she was uncommonly gracious and beautiful.

In one of their trading establishments, the three brothers employed a young Pisan named Lorenzo, who planned and directed all their operations, and who, being rather dashing and handsomely proportioned, had often attracted the gaze of Lisabetta. Having noticed more than once that she had grown exceedingly fond of him, Lorenzo abandoned all his other amours and began in like fashion to set his own heart on winning Lisabetta. And since they were equally in love with each other, before very long they gratified their dearest wishes, taking care not to be discovered.

In this way, their love continued to prosper, much to their common enjoy-   5
ment and pleasure. They did everything they could to keep the affair a secret, but one night, as Lisabetta was making her way to Lorenzo's sleeping-quarters, she was observed, without knowing it, by her eldest brother. The discovery greatly distressed him, but being a young man of some intelligence, and not wishing to do anything that would bring discredit upon his family, he neither spoke nor made a move, but spent the whole of the night applying his mind to various sides of the matter.

Next morning he described to his brothers what he had seen of Lisabetta and Lorenzo the night before, and the three of them talked the thing over at considerable length. Being determined that the affair should leave no stain upon the reputation either of themselves or of their sister, he decided that they must pass it over in silence and pretend to have neither seen nor heard anything until such time as it was safe and convenient for them to rid themselves of this ignominy before it got out of hand.

Abiding by this decision, the three brothers jested and chatted with Lorenzo in their usual manner, until one day they pretended they were all going off on a pleasure-trip to the country, and took Lorenzo with them. They bided their time, and on reaching a very remote and lonely spot, they took Lorenzo off his guard, murdered him, and buried his corpse. No one had witnessed the deed, and on their return to Messina they put it about that they had sent Lorenzo away on a trading assignment, being all the more readily believed as they had done this so often before.

Lorenzo's continued absence weighed heavily upon Lisabetta, who kept asking her brothers, in anxious tones, what had become of him, and eventually her questioning became so persistent that one of her brothers rounded on her, and said:

"What is the meaning of this? What business do you have with Lorenzo, that you should be asking so many questions about him? If you go on pestering us, we shall give you the answer you deserve."

From then on, the young woman, who was sad and miserable and full of   10 strange forebodings, refrained from asking questions. But at night she would repeatedly utter his name in a heart-rending voice and beseech him to come to her, and from time to time she would burst into tears because of his failure to return. Nothing would restore her spirits, and meanwhile she simply went on waiting.

One night, however, after crying so much over Lorenzo's absence that she eventually cried herself off to sleep, he appeared to her in a dream, pallid-looking and all dishevelled, his clothes tattered and decaying, and it seemed to her that he said:

"Ah, Lisabetta, you do nothing but call to me and bemoan my long absence, and you cruelly reprove me with your tears. Hence I must tell you that I can never return, because on the day that you saw me for the last time, I was murdered by your brothers."

He then described the place where they had buried him, told her not to call to him or wait for him any longer, and disappeared.

Having woken up, believing that what she had seen was true, the young woman wept bitterly. And when she arose next morning, she resolved to go to the place and seek confirmation of what she had seen in her sleep. She dared not mention the apparition to her brothers, but obtained their permission to make a brief trip to the country for pleasure, taking with her a maidservant who had once acted as her go-between and was privy to all her affairs. She immediately set out, and on reaching the spot, swept aside some dead leaves and started to excavate a section of the ground that appeared to have been disturbed. Nor did she have to dig very deep before she uncovered her poor lover's body, which, showing no sign as yet of decomposition or decay, proved all too clearly that her vision had been true. She was the saddest woman alive, but knowing that this was no time for weeping, and seeing that it was impossible for her to take away his whole body (as she would dearly have wished), she laid it to rest in a more appropriate spot, then severed the head from the shoulders as best she could and enveloped it in a towel. This she handed into her maidservant's keeping whilst she covered over the remainder of the corpse with soil, and then they returned home, having completed the whole of their task unobserved.

Taking the head to her room, she locked herself in and cried bitterly, weeping so profusely that she saturated it with her tears, at the same time implanting a thousand kisses upon it. Then she wrapped the head in a piece of rich cloth, and laid it in a large and elegant pot, of the sort in which basil or marjoram is grown. She next covered it with soil, in which she planted several sprigs of the finest Salernitan basil, and never watered them except with essence of roses or orange-blossom, or with her own teardrops. She took to sitting permanently beside this pot and gazing lovingly at it, concentrating the whole of her desire upon it because it was where her beloved Lorenzo lay concealed. And after gazing raptly for a long while upon it, she would bend over it and begin to cry, and her weeping never ceased until the whole of the basil was wet with her tears.

Because of the long and unceasing care that was lavished upon it, and also because the soil was enriched by the decomposing head inside the pot, the basil grew very thick and exceedingly fragrant. The young woman constantly followed this same routine, and from time to time she attracted the attention of her neighbors. And as they had heard her brothers expressing their concern at the decline in her good looks and the way in which her eyes appeared to have sunk into their sockets, they told them what they had seen, adding:

"We have noticed that she follows the same routine every day."

The brothers discovered for themselves that this was so, and having reproached her once or twice without the slightest effect, they caused the pot to be secretly removed from her room. When she found that it was missing, she kept asking for it over and over again, and because they would not restore it to her she sobbed and cried without a pause until eventually she fell seriously ill. And from her bed of sickness she would call for nothing else except her pot of basil.

The young men were astonished by the persistence of her entreaties, and decided to examine its contents. Having shaken out the soil, they saw the cloth and found the decomposing head inside it, still sufficiently intact for them to recognize it as Lorenzo's from the curls of his hair. This discovery greatly amazed them, and they were afraid lest people should come to know what had happened. So they buried the head, and without breathing a word to anyone, having wound up their affairs in Messina, they left the city and went to live in Naples.

The girl went on weeping and demanding her pot of basil, until eventually she cried herself to death, thus bringing her ill-fated love to an end. But after due process of time, many people came to know of the affair, and one of them composed the song which can still be heard to this day:

> Whoever it was,
> Whoever the villain
> That stole my pot of herbs, etc.

Analyzing the Story

The next chapter explains the elements of fiction—those qualities of the story that are interesting to isolate and analyze: setting and mood, character and psychology, style and theme, plot and structure, point of view, and irony and tone—in detail. "The Pot of Basil" includes each of these elements despite its being so short. The following brief list suggests only some immediate ways the elements figure in an interpretation.

Setting and Mood   The story does not provide extensive discussions of the setting, the place and time of the action. However, a dark mood, the atmosphere or feelings evoked by the setting, pervades the narrative, especially in regard to the brothers and their behavior.

Character and Psychology   Characters can be fully developed, with recognizable psychological depth, or they can be undeveloped sketches. The characters in this story are sketches: the wicked and self-centered brothers, the innocent and lovelorn Lisabetta, and the industrious, attractive Lorenzo. A single act complicates the psychology of the story immensely: Lisabetta's placing the head of Lorenzo in the pot of basil. This act may imply Lisabetta's insanity.

Style and Theme   The style, the special use of language, is plain; a major theme, or main idea, is that of thwarted love.

Plot   The plot or unraveling of the action is simple enough that Boccaccio summarizes it in a few lines at the beginning. But the central action, placing the head in the basil pot, is anything but simple. It leads us to marvel at the gesture and to wonder what it might mean.

Point of View   The point of view—the control of the story by its teller—is detached. Filomena, the narrator or storyteller, does not interject her evaluation of the story into its telling.

Irony and Tone   The story is told straightforwardly, without irony, or the sense that we are to treat the action as other than what it seems to be, and its tone, the author's attitude toward the subject, seems sincere, however sad the tale itself may be.

Using Interpretive Strategies

Although the individual elements of this story are not extensively developed, and although characterization and plot are limited, the interpretive opportunities are rich and various.

The formalist approach would concentrate on images that recur in the story, such as the burial of Lorenzo. First, his love for Lisabetta is "buried" because Lisabetta cannot tell her brothers of her love. She loves Lorenzo in secret. Yet her secret is "uncovered." Once Lorenzo is killed and his corpse secretly buried, his ghost "uncovers" the truth about his disappearance. After Lisabetta discovers Lorenzo's body, she gives his head a proper "burial" in a pot of basil. The herb basil has been an emblem of love since ancient times, so Lisabetta is burying her love in several senses. The word *basil* (as an unabridged dictionary tells us) is derived from *basileus*, which means both king and serpent. The serpent is a phallic emblem (also medicinal), perhaps implying Lisabetta's loss of virginity. Finally, taking Lorenzo from her a second time, the brothers bury not only Lisabetta's love (and her emotional life) but kill her from grief in the process. The brothers had buried Lisabetta earlier by not permitting her to marry "for some reason or other." Burial becomes a metaphor for control.

A psychoanalytic critic would find this story rich with significance, especially since Lisabetta suffered from a nervous disorder that caused her brothers to express "their concern at the decline in her good looks and the way in which her eyes appeared to have sunk into their sockets." She also behaved in a compulsive fashion when she "constantly followed this same routine" and "attracted the attention of her neighbors." On the one hand, the psychoanalytic critic might focus attention first on the efforts of the brothers to repress Lisabetta's libido, her natural sexual instincts, then second on her own efforts to prevent the brothers' knowledge of her affair with Lorenzo. On the other hand, potting the head of her lover may be an emblem of Lisabetta's own madness. Her sexuality has been repressed once more, and she has sublimated it (given it expression) into the watering and tending of the pot of basil, whose growth now depends on her tears. Her joy is converted into grief by her brothers' repression and there is no healthy outlet that will bring her back to sanity.

The brothers themselves are perverse. They seem to have no love at all in their lives. Even their love for Lisabetta is totally absent. The one brother who speaks to her behaves threateningly, like a vicious tyrant. They are engaged in some form of banking or trade and seem to have sublimated their emotions into a worship of money and position. Their "reputation" takes precedence over any sensitive regard for their sister. They have become sadistic and vicious.

Boccaccio anticipated the reader response approach. When she begins the story, Filomena is "quite overcome with compassion" from hearing the story preceding hers. She suspects that her story might "prove to be no less touching." The three brothers behave like the older sisters of Cinderella. They control Lisabetta and seem unwilling to permit her to have her own life. Such a situation demands an emotional response, especially from those young and in love. Furthermore, the story itself is filled with emotion. Lisabetta cries so much over the loss of Lorenzo that "her weeping never ceased until the whole of the basil was wet with her tears." The story centers on the grief of its main character, who "eventually cried herself to death." However, you may also respond to another emotion: the sense of injustice that you may feel for the fact that the brothers never pay for their terrible behavior. For some readers, that may translate into outrage. Boccaccio, by telling the story matter-of-factly, permits our emotions to take their own shape.

Feminist critics might see in this story an emblem of the brutal dispossession of women. The brothers represent the establishment that exploits women by forcing them into marriages of family or political convenience. The father is dead, but the responsibility for the family falls not on Lisabetta's shoulders but on those of her brothers, who clearly dominate her in every way. They virtually ignore her presence until she threatens their reputation. Her reputation, which is also at stake, is significant only insofar as it might receive a "stain" that would reflect badly on them.

Even Lorenzo falls short in living up to a position of responsibility. He "planned and directed all [the brothers'] operations," yet he seduced her with no mention of the possibility of marriage—which would have saved her honor—nor with any thought of declaring himself to her brothers, which would have preserved the possibility of a totally honorable conclusion. Despite his love for her, Lorenzo profits from her lack of power and her suppression as a woman. Lisabetta's powerlessness is pathetically represented by her quiet grief over the potted head of her beloved. She cannot complain to her brothers; "she locked herself in and cried bitterly." Her grief is the grief of all women dominated by men whose values are determined by family reputation and who regard women as inferior.

In sympathy with the feminist critic, the political-economic or Marxist critic will see Lisabetta as an economic counter. She must marry in a way that enhances the economic status of the family organization. The family itself is identified in terms of "their trading establishment," and the brothers—not Lisabetta—were "merchants who had been left very rich after the death of their father." Money is at the core of the brothers' behavior. Lorenzo may run the business, but he is a Pisan who, apart from being an outsider, is a mere employee, someone from a lower class than Lisabetta. The class distinction keeps Lorenzo from declaring his love in the open. It forces him to sneak behind the backs of the brothers. Although he is good enough to work for them and even, in the manner of servants, to live in their huge household, he is not good enough to merit Lisabetta's hand. The Marxist critic could justifiably see this as a story rooted deep in the class struggle of an emerging merchant-dominated Renaissance Italy. The dominant values are those of the emerging European middle class, the bourgeoisie for whom appearances and "what the neighbors think" are of great importance.

The historicist might begin by examining Italian marriage documents from the fourteenth century to uncover the obligations of one spouse to another at that time. The historicist might also be interested in studying documents of indenture—which fix the responsibilities of young people working for established businesses. It is entirely possible that Lorenzo is indentured to the brothers, in which case he would not have been free either to marry Lisabetta or to sleep with her even if he intended to marry her in the future. In the absence of documents, the historicist would learn something about the history of fourteenth-century Italy to discover as much as possible about the relative position of merchants. Recent studies of everyday life can shed light on what Lisabetta's expectations might have been, or what Lorenzo's opportunities may have been. If Lorenzo is an opportunist—someone who is using Lisabetta for his own purposes to advance his position—then the historical situation could shed light on the nature of his motivations. Reconstructing historical circumstances could be appropriate for you if you have studied Italian history.

BEGINNING WITH CLOSE READING

The following story by the Quebec writer Suzanne Jacob shows how much can be accomplished in a page or so. Jacob's stories, characteristically short and intense, are emblems of modern ritual and therefore sometimes mysterious. But once they begin to come clear, they show themselves as full, satisfying, and pleasing. "Two Cents," published in 1989, is recognizably contemporary, but certain aspects are also primeval—referring us to our prehistory—and therefore jarring.

Suzanne Jacob   (contemp.)
TWO CENTS   1989

Translated by Susanna Finnell

They understood each other. There would be no crying. No tears. There would be no trial, no accounting. Neither one brought accusations: they understood each other.

They invited the few friends with whom they had shared their lives for nine years. The man oiled the two rifles, the woman inspected the photo and chose the place. They started walking.

Drizzle settled softly on the event. Everyone knew Mount Baldy. Everyone knew the Piperock, they knew where to go. As they got closer, their hair seemed to turn a little greyer. Very far away, a train whistled. Someone suggested that it would have been better to have gone in the direction of Envy River. The speaker stumbled over a stump and forgot his suggestion. Everyone gathered dead branches found on the way. That was part of the agreement. The man passed around the flask filled with liquor. No one refused a drink.

They knew the rites and understood the ceremony. They had been initiated to the songs of the monks at a very early age. They built up the fire until it reached new growth on the pine branches. The woman was crouching. The rifle between her legs looked like a soft old animal. As always, the man stood sideways, breathing. This assured the others that he was absent despite appearances.

When the moment came to present the offerings, the friends broke into an old song. Now you could see the dove in its white cage. Everyone was thrilled. The cage was put down near the fire and everyone was hypnotized by the flames. Stupid little things that surfaced in their minds, very ordinary things, resolved

5

themselves, melting away in the heat. They chose not to remember anything, none of the innumerable ecstasies, none of the thresholds crossed. Nothing, by choice they were remembering nothing. In the middle of their forest, they consented absolutely to the evidence of the present.

The man and the woman aimed their rifles. They trusted each other. There was only one bullet and there was no way of knowing which weapon fired the shot that split the fog, the cage and the bird with the necklace. No one ever tried to figure it out.

They went their separate ways. They met children who were running yelling: "We heard shooting!"

They got back to their downtown offices and continued to read the same newspapers without being moved.

Much later, the man met the woman in a tobacco shop. She said she was two cents short for her pack of Camels. The man had them.

Brief as it is, "Two Cents" is a subtle story. It has a clear plot and identifiable but nameless characters. The action of the story is direct and uncomplicated, but nothing explicit seems to emerge from it. The setting is perhaps as rich in detail as any aspect of the story, but it, too, is purposely made imprecise, especially since the time of the action is uncertain.

A close reading begins with some important questions:

- What actually happens in the story?
- Why does the story focus on one woman and one man?
- What is implied by the contrast between the woodsy setting of "Piperock" and the "downtown offices" to which people return?
- The story calls the action a "ritual." What kind of ritual could it be?
- Is the reference to the initiation and the "songs of the monks" a clue to the ritual?
- The dove, an emblem of peace, must be a symbol here. But of what?
- Why is it important that neither the man nor the woman knows which bullet kills the dove? And why does no one ever ask?
- Does the fact that we are told at the beginning, "There would be no trial, no accounting" imply that the action of the story is questionable or possibly outside the normal moral boundaries of these people?

The following close reading answers the questions raised above. It could become the basis of a formalist, New Critical interpretation by demonstrating how the details cohere to produce a sense of unity and how they are all connected significantly to one another. However, this close reading is essentially unfinished. It could also be the basis for a psychological, feminist, or even political-economic interpretation of the story.

This seems to be a story of an infrequently performed ritual centering on a man and woman who appear to act for the community. By focusing on one man and one woman, the story implies that the ritual is shared equally by both genders. They are both given guns, and in the end they both aim and fire at a dove wearing a symbolic necklace. The necklace implies it is a valued and special bird, and since this is a frequently repeated ritual ("They knew the rites and understood the ceremony"), the dove must be a sacrifice. The ritual takes place in the woods, implying that it is primitive, perhaps seen as related to nature. The closeness of the man and woman in the woods is contrasted by their distance from one another in "downtown," where their only interaction occurs when the man helps the woman out when she is two cents short for her pack of Camels.

This ritual must have religious overtones: "the moment came to present the offerings." Religious sacrifices of "offerings" are common enough in primitive tribes and in the Bible. The ritual in the story is fully understood, performed regularly but not frequently, and involves religious "songs of the monks," which they learned "at a very early age" when they were "initiated." While it is happening all they think about are the "stupid little things that surfaced in their minds." "They consented absolutely to the evidence of the present." Because this is a religious event, they will not have to worry about a "trial" even if they are taking the life of an innocent bird. Since they do not know exactly who killed the bird, it is impossible to single out one of them for trial anyway. If both were prosecuted, one innocent person would be found guilty, making trial impossible even if this were not a familiar religious ritual.

The dove may be a symbol of peace or innocence. It must die for the good of the order of people. Yet no one must be responsible for its death because then the act would be individual rather than collective. All the people who gather at Piperock have an investment in the action of the man and the woman. They act not just for themselves but for the community.

After the ritual, no one thinks much about it. "They went their separate ways. . . . They got back to their downtown offices and continued to read the same newspapers without being moved." So whatever the ritual is, once it is performed it does not weigh on the minds of the man and the woman. They hardly keep the memory of meeting by the pine fire where everyone was "hypnotized by the flames."

Back in the larger community the man and woman have no contact with each other. They apparently go about their work; their only important contact was for the purposes of enacting the ritual. In the community of "downtown offices" they meet only in a tobacco shop—an emblem of petty vice—where the woman smokes a rather powerful cigarette: Camels. The two cents the man helps her out with seems to suggest the depth of his "responsibility" to her outside the setting of ritual sacrifice.

If the dove is a symbol for Christ—the dove is usually the sign of the third person of the Trinity—then the necklace may be a kind of rosary. The ritual might stand for a version of the mass—although a mockery of it—and the essential indifference of the people in their offices after the ritual reveals the separateness of the people from their religious beliefs. As the story implies, they do nothing different when participating in a religious ritual. They read the same papers but do nothing. They are unmoved and content to smoke their Camels. Their faith seems no more important than the "two cents" of the final lines.

MEANING: IMPLIED AND EXPLICIT

Stories such as "Two Cents" imply their meaning rather than state it. However, **fables** (stories using animals with recognizable human qualities), such as those by Aesop or La Fontaine, usually end with a moral tag that contains the meaning of the fable just in case you did not get it.

Aesop   (c. 6th century B.C.)
THE ROOSTER AND THE PRECIOUS GEM

Jacobus recension from Caxton

As a rooster was searching for seeds and corn in his dunghill one day, he uncovered a precious glittering gem and looked at it startled. "Aha! You are a fair and precious gem lying here in the filth, glittering like the sun. If only a woman who desires such gems were here to find you, she should pick you up and place you on her finger and show you all about to the great acclaim of the multitude of ladies. But, alas! It is I who have found you, and you must know that I, a rooster, have nothing to do with such things as precious gems. I cannot do you any good, and there is certainly no good you can do for me." This fable, said Aesop to those who will read his book, intends you to understand the rooster is like a fool who has no intelligence, no wisdom because, like the rooster who sees a precious gem and can make no use of it, the fool will read this precious book and have no understanding of it.

At first you might think that having the meaning stated outright is better than having it implied. But in fact the opposite is true. If a short story were like a fable of Aesop, with a moral, then it would be like a disposable flashlight. You could use it, but it would not last. Good short stories last. Reread the fable above and note that once you get the message there is no need to go back over it again. A fable of Aesop is useful for teaching morals to children. All children will get the same message: end of interpretation. However, with a good short story no two people will get precisely the same message: beginning of interpretation.

The story whose meaning is stated outright will not hold your interest long enough for you to read it twice. The more the meaning is implied, the more essential is your own act of interpretation. What, for example, is the meaning of "The Pot of Basil"? If you expect meaning to be reducible to a moral tag, you may find it difficult to accept the answer that the meaning of the story is in your interpretation. Just as you realize your interpretation is likely to account for only part of the meaning of the story, so you realize that the meaning of a successful story is virtually limitless.

The meaning of a short story is inherent in your interpretation, my interpretation, and those of all its readers. There is no ideal collective interpretation that then represents its real meaning. Instead, there are many separable interpretations that may group together to produce what Stanley Fish has called "communities of interpretation." One community of interpreters may think, for example, that "Two Cents" concerns a quasi-religious ritual that, performed mindlessly, shows us how detached people are from their religious roots. Another community of interpreters may think that it shows that religious practice hides primitive acts of violence, sublimating them so they do not interfere with business in the "downtown offices." Yet another community of interpreters will see the story as having nothing to do with religion at all. Formalist critics may constitute an interpretive community. They approach short stories in similar ways, using similar techniques. Yet they too can disagree on important issues of interpretation. The same is true of psychoanalytic, reader response, feminist, historicist, and political-economic critics. Although they may seem to start in much the same place and apply much the same methods, and although they may constitute an interpretive community, their interpretations will differ sharply. In interpretation there is always room for disagreement.

4

Elements of Short Fiction

WHY THE ELEMENTS ARE IMPORTANT

Preparing yourself to interpret a short story involves thinking about what makes a short story work. If part of your responsibility in close reading involves examining details, then in any but a very brief story the details could soon become so overwhelming that a single close reading could become almost a life's work. Therefore, you need to focus on the most important details. A close reading accounts for setting, character, theme, plot, style, action, and other important elements. By identifying those elements and by understanding how they work, you prepare yourself to read closely and interpret well. When you read a short story, all these elements function together. For the sake of analysis, the following stories highlight only a few of those elements at a time so that their function can be examined more closely. The last story demonstrates the elements in action together.

THE ELEMENTS OF FICTION

We will focus on twelve elements and their effects.

Setting and Mood   **Setting** refers to the environment, the physical place and time, in which the story takes place. In Boccaccio's "The Pot of Basil," it is the environment of Renaissance Italy in the town of Messina. The **mood**—the feelings communicated by the setting—is usually established by description. In Boccaccio the mood is dark and uneasy, communicated by shadowy description.

Character and Psychology   In Boccaccio's story, the **characters** play recognizable roles: the young suitor, the young girl in love, the evil brothers. Beyond that their psychological nature is revealed in terms of their action, and especially in terms of Lisabetta's grieving over the pot of basil. In "Two Cents" the characters are nameless in order to emphasize their ordinariness. In some works characters possess a psychological complexity resembling our own. Hamlet, for instance, is one of literature's most psychologically complex characters.

Style and Theme   **Style** refers to artistic decisions in language and narrative techniques. Writers usually develop distinctive personal styles. All stories are about something and therefore have one or more **themes**. One theme of "The Pot of Basil" is frustrated love. One theme of "Two Cents" could be the ritual of sacrifice and what it means in the modern world.

Plot and Narrative Structure   The **plot** is a sequence of actions whose shape produces a clear impression and whose ending implies a sense of finality. Everyday life has no plot, which may be why we value carefully plotted fiction. The ending of "The Pot of Basil" produces a sense of satisfaction, even if we are disappointed that Lisabetta must die of grief, because it seems inevitable given the beginning of the story. Stories without a structured plot have characters in action, but the action is much like the life we live ourselves. Plotless stories are often called **"slice of life" stories** because they seem to slice out some moments of the character's life and present them to us as they seem to have been lived. Such stories attempt to achieve the impression of artlessness.

Point of View   The question of **point of view** is, Who tells the story? Do you trust the narrator's accuracy? "The Pot of Basil" is narrated by Filomena, about whom you know little. Filomena is not involved in the action of Lisabetta's story, so you can presume she tells things objectively. "Two Cents" is told from a detached point of view by an unnamed narrator who knows everything about the characters and the action. The narrator of "Two Cents" controls everything in the story, including your reactions.

Irony and Tone   Some stories are meant to be ironic: they say one thing, but mean another. You recognize irony by observing the language in which the story is told. In a few cases, you may not be able to tell whether the writer is being sincere or ironic. "Two Cents" may be such a story. Is Suzanne Jacob describing an ironic sacrifice, or is it a serious religious ritual? The **tone** of a story may reveal an author's attitude toward characters or their values. The tone of these stories suggests sympathy for the characters. In some stories the tone is judgmental; in others it is neutral.

Which Elements Are Important?

Most stories possess all the basic elements of short fiction. However, some stories, such as F. Scott Fitzgerald's "Babylon Revisited," emphasize character more than plot. Mysteries and adventure stories, such as Scott Bradfield's "The Dream of the Wolf," depend more on plot. Kate Chopin's "The Story of an Hour" emphasizes action, the death of a husband, and a character's subsequent psychological reaction. In all these stories both character and plot are important, but one may take precedence over the other.

Consequently, one job is to decide which elements are most interesting to talk about in any story you decide to interpret. When you find that character is most important or most challenging, then your discussion may center on character. Other times setting and mood or point of view will provide you with most of your opportunities.

The Elements Working Together

Examining the elements separately helps develop a sensitivity to their function. However, it can also give you the illusion that every story has only one element worth looking at. It can also suggest that the individual elements are somehow more important than the whole story. The last story in the following group, Bharati Mukherjee's "Jasmine," shows how you can take into account the interaction of several elements in a story.

Interpretations are usually based on a range of elements and rarely on one. After all, it is extremely difficult to talk about the plot of *Hamlet* as if it were separate from the character of Hamlet or even separate from the setting of the court of Denmark. In addition, since irony is common in Hamlet's speeches to Polonius, Rosenkrantz, Guildenstern, and most of the other characters except for Horatio, one could hardly interpret the play well by ignoring it. The same is true for short stories. Considering the elements separately is a convenience, but nothing more.

SETTING AND MOOD

Stories happen in times and places that evoke feelings associated with history or locale, the physical environment. Historical settings often depend on specialized knowledge of a given period. Very few modern readers will have much specific knowledge of the period of time in which Boccaccio's "The Pot of Basil" took place. The Renaissance is to most of us simply an older time when economic and social structures were recognizable but very different from today. Social structures were more fixed: one born into the peasantry stayed a peasant, aristocrats had privileges, and merchants were only beginning to have influence. More than that we really do not need to know. But even this much gives us great insight into "The Pot of Basil."

Edgar Allan Poe's "The Masque of the Red Death" suggests a similar historical time because its chief character is a prince who behaves as if he has unlimited power. The Renaissance experienced plague—the Black Death—in recurring epidemics that sometimes wiped away a third of the population at a stroke. The locale of Prince Prospero's court is crucial to the story, and thus the reader must be aware that courts similar to the court of Denmark in *Hamlet* were the center of power and influence. Law, religion, and military power all resided at court. Courtiers dressed brilliantly, spoke brilliantly, and threw magnificent parties.

The power of Poe's story lies in the fact that the Red Death is so democratic that it will not excuse such privileged persons. The setting of the story is "the deep seclusion of one of [Prince Prospero's] castellated abbeys." An abbey is a residence for monks and clerics, those who pray and read and retire from the world. Most of Poe's readers associated abbeys with mysterious goings-on.

Poe depends on our having enough associations historically and architecturally to respond to his descriptions of time and place, which establish the setting. However, beyond these Poe also presents us with more immediate and palpable descriptions. One is of the word *masque*, which is unusual and exotic. Poe translates it several times: it is a masked ball and a masquerade. In other words, it is a party, like Halloween, in which everyone is disguised. The disguises, extravagant and amusing, challenge the imagination of the courtiers in a huge, self-indulgent entertainment.

The architecture of the abbey, with its Gothic windows and its seven apartments (rooms) is one of the most carefully described aspects of the setting. Since all the action takes place inside the abbey, Poe describes each of the rooms carefully. He emphasizes details that imply another age: tapestries, candelabra, stained glass, tripods, braziers, and casements. He also emphasizes the colors of these apartments: one is dominated by blue, another by purple, and the next ones by green, orange, white, violet, and finally black.

The setting affects us through Poe's powerful visual description, which makes us aware of special colors, exotic furniture, and materials. Poe also appeals to our sense of touch when he reminds us that the black velvet tapestries fall in heavy folds: we feel the heaviness. He appeals to our sense of sound by describing musicians and introducing the "gigantic clock of ebony" with its "monotonous clang." As Poe says, "It was a voluptuous scene," meaning it awakens the sensual part of ourselves. Setting is presented to us in sensory terms designed to affect our emotional response to locale and its circumstances. Poe is a master of such responses.

Edgar Allan Poe   (1809–1849)

Edgar Allan Poe's brief but intense and unhappy life was marked by early insecurity. His family was English but lived in Ireland before emigrating to Maryland. His parents died when he was two, and he was adopted by John Allan and his wife, who went to England and sent Poe to school. After they returned to America in 1826, Poe went to the University of Virginia, distinguishing himself with drinking, gambling, and what some called neurotic behavior. After the university his relationship with John Allan deteriorated. Poe joined the army and was recommended to West Point. But there he began his lifelong alcoholism and was not only court-martialed but also disowned by his adoptive father. He made his living as a writer, winning several prizes for short stories and poems. He was a brilliant theorist of poetry and fiction, and his work has been read continuously since his death.

THE MASQUE OF THE RED DEATH

The "Red Death" had long devastated the country. No pestilence had ever been so fatal, or so hideous. Blood was its Avatar and its seal—the redness and the horror of blood. There were sharp pains, and sudden dizziness, and then profuse bleeding at the pores, with dissolution. The scarlet stains upon the body and especially upon the face of the victim, were the pest ban which shut him out from the aid and from the sympathy of his fellow-men. And the whole seizure, progress and termination of the disease, were the incidents of half an hour.

But the Prince Prospero was happy and dauntless and sagacious. When his dominions were half depopulated, he summoned to his presence a thousand hale and light-hearted friends from among the knights and dames of his court, and with these retired to the deep seclusion of one of his castellated abbeys. This was an extensive and magnificent structure, the creation of the prince's own eccentric yet august taste. A strong and lofty wall girdled it in. This wall had gates of iron. The courtiers, having entered, brought furnaces and massy hammers and welded the bolts. They resolved to leave means neither of ingress or egress to the sudden impulses of despair or of frenzy from within. The abbey was amply provisioned. With such precautions the courtiers might bid defiance to contagion. The external world could take care of itself. In the meantime it was folly to grieve, or to think. The prince had provided all the appliances of pleasure. There were buffoons, there were improvisatori,° there were ballet-dancers, there were musicians, there was Beauty, there was wine. All these and security were within. Without was the "Red Death."

It was toward the close of the fifth or sixth month of his seclusion, and while the pestilence raged most furiously abroad, that the Prince Prospero entertained his thousand friends at a masked ball of the most unusual magnificence.

It was a voluptuous scene, that masquerade. But first let me tell of the rooms in which it was held. There were seven—an imperial suite. In many palaces, however, such suites form a long and straight vista, while the folding doors slide back nearly to the walls on either hand, so that the view of the whole extent is scarcely impeded. Here the case was very different; as might have been expected from the duke's love of the bizarre. The apartments were so irregularly disposed that the vision embraced but little more than one at a time. There was a sharp turn at every twenty or thirty yards, and at each turn a novel effect. To the right and left, in

---

improvisatori: Actors who improvised comedies.

the middle of each wall, a tall and narrow Gothic window looked out upon a closed corridor which pursued the windings of the suite. These windows were of stained glass whose color varied in accordance with the prevailing hue of the decorations of the chamber into which it opened. That at the eastern extremity was hung, for example, in blue—and vividly blue were its windows. The second chamber was purple in its ornaments and tapestries, and here the panes were purple. The third was green throughout, and so were the casements. The fourth was furnished and lighted with orange—the fifth with white—the sixth with violet. The seventh apartment was closely shrouded in black velvet tapestries that hung all over the ceiling and down the walls, falling in heavy folds upon a carpet of the same material and hue. But in this chamber only, the color of the windows failed to correspond with the decorations. The panes here were scarlet—a deep blood color. Now in no one of the seven apartments was there any lamp or candelabrum, amid the profusion of golden ornaments that lay scattered to and fro or depended from the roof. There was no light of any kind emanating from lamp or candle within the suite of chambers. But in the corridors that followed the suite, there stood, opposite to each window, a heavy tripod, bearing a brazier of fire that projected its rays through the tinted glass and so glaringly illumined the room. And thus were produced a multitude of gaudy and fantastic appearances. But in the western or black chamber the effect of the fire-light that streamed upon the dark hangings through the blood-tinted panes, was ghastly in the extreme, and produced so wild a look upon the countenances of those who entered, that there were few of the company bold enough to set foot within its precincts at all.

It was in this apartment, also, that there stood against the western wall, a gigantic clock of ebony. Its pendulum swung to and fro with a dull, heavy, monotonous clang; and when the minute-hand made the circuit of the face, and the hour was to be stricken, there came from the brazen lungs of the clock a sound which was clear and loud and deep and exceedingly musical, but of so peculiar a note and emphasis that, at each lapse of an hour, the musicians of the orchestra were constrained to pause, momentarily, in their performance, to harken to the sound; and thus the waltzers perforce ceased their evolutions; and there was a brief disconcert of the whole gay company; and, while the chimes of the clock yet rang, it was observed that the giddiest grew pale, and the more aged and sedate passed their hands over their brows as if in confused reverie or meditation. But when the echoes had fully ceased, a light laughter at once pervaded the assembly; the musicians looked at each other and smiled as if at their own nervousness and folly, and made whispering vows, each to the other, that the next chiming of the clock should produce in them no similar emotion; and then, after the lapse of sixty minutes (which embrace three thousand and six hundred seconds of the Time that flies), there came yet another chiming of the clock, and then were the same disconcert and tremulousness and meditation as before.

But, in spite of these things, it was a gay and magnificent revel. The tastes of the duke were peculiar. He had a fine eye for colors and effects. He disregarded the *decora* of mere fashion. His plans were bold and fiery, and his conceptions glowed with barbaric luster. There are some who would have thought him mad. His followers felt that he was not. It was necessary to hear and see and touch him to be *sure* that he was not.

He had directed, in great part, the moveable embellishments of the seven chambers, upon occasion of this great fête; and it was his own guiding taste which had given character to the masqueraders. Be sure they were grotesque. There were much glare and glitter and piquancy and phantasm—much of what has been since seen in "Hernani."° There were arabesque figures with unsuited limbs and appointments. There were delirious fancies such as the madman fashions. There was much of the beautiful, much of the wanton, much of the bizarre, something of the terrible, and not a little of that which might have excited disgust. To and fro in the seven chambers there stalked, in fact, a multitude of dreams. And these—the dreams—writhed in and about, taking hue from the rooms, and causing the wild music of the orchestra to seem as the echo of their steps. And, anon, there strikes the ebony clock which stands in the hall of the velvet. And then, for a moment, all is still, and all is silent save the voice of the clock. The dreams are stiff-frozen as they stand. But the echoes of the chime die away—they have endured but an instant—and a light, half-subdued laughter floats after them as they depart. And now again the music swells, and the dreams live, and writhe to and fro more merrily than ever, taking hue from the many tinted windows through which stream the rays from the tripods. But to the chamber which lies most westwardly of the seven, there are now none of the maskers who venture: for the night is waning away; and there flows a ruddier light through the blood-colored panes; and the blackness of the sable drapery appals; and to him whose foot falls upon the sable carpet, there comes from the near clock of ebony a muffled peal more solemnly emphatic than any which reaches *their* ears who indulge in the more remote gaieties of the other apartments.

But these other apartments were densely crowded, and in them beat feverishly the heart of life. And the revel went whirlingly on, until at length there commenced the sounding of midnight upon the clock. And then the music ceased, as I have told; and the evolutions of the waltzers were quieted; and there was an uneasy cessation of all things as before. But now there were twelve strokes to be sounded by the bell of the clock; and thus it happened, perhaps, that more of thought crept, with more of time, into the meditations of the thoughtful among those who revelled. And thus, too, it happened, perhaps, that before the last echoes of the last chime had utterly sunk into silence, there were many individuals in the crowd who had found leisure to become aware of the presence of a masked figure which had arrested the attention of no single individual before. And the rumor of this new presence having spread itself whisperingly around, there arose at length from the whole company a buzz, or murmur, expressive of disapprobation and surprise—then, finally, of terror, of horror, and of disgust.

In an assembly of phantasms such as I have painted, it may well be supposed that no ordinary appearance could have excited such sensation. In truth the masquerade license of the night was nearly unlimited; but the figure in question had out-Heroded Herod,° and gone beyond the bounds of even the prince's indefinite decorum. There are chords in the hearts of the most reckless which cannot be touched without emotion. Even with the utterly lost, to whom life and death are equally jests, there are matters of which no jest can be made. The whole company, indeed, seemed now deeply to feel that in the costume and bearing of the stranger neither wit nor propriety existed. The figure was tall and gaunt, and

---

"*Hernani*": A political novel (1830) by Victor Hugo (1802–1885), later dramatized in an opera.
Herod: Ruler of Galilee who sentenced Jesus of Nazareth to crucifixion.

shrouded from head to foot in the habiliments of the grave. The mask which concealed the visage was made so nearly to resemble the countenance of a stiffened corpse that the closest scrutiny must have had difficulty in detecting the cheat. And yet all this might have been endured, if not approved, by the mad revellers around. But the mummer had gone so far as to assume the type of the Red Death. His vesture was dabbled in *blood*—and his broad brow, with all the features of the face, was besprinkled with the scarlet horror.

When the eyes of Prince Prospero fell upon this spectral image (which with   10
a slow and solemn movement, as if more fully to sustain its rôle, stalked to and fro among the waltzers) he was seen to be convulsed, in the first moment with a strong shudder either of terror or distaste; but, in the next, his brow reddened with rage.

"Who dares?" he demanded hoarsely of the courtiers who stood near him— "who dares insult us with this blasphemous mockery? Seize him and unmask him— that we may know whom we have to hang at sunrise, from the battlements!"

It was in the eastern or blue chamber in which stood the Prince Prospero as he uttered these words. They rang throughout the seven rooms loudly and clearly—for the prince was a bold and robust man, and the music had become hushed at the waving of his hand.

It was in the blue room where stood the prince, with a group of pale courtiers by his side. At first, as he spoke, there was a slight rushing movement of this group in the direction of the intruder, who at the moment was also near at hand, and now, with deliberate and stately step, made closer approach to the speaker. But from a certain nameless awe with which the mad assumptions of the mummer had inspired the whole party, there were found none who put forth hand to seize him; so that, unimpeded, he passed within a yard of the prince's person; and, while the vast assembly, as if with one impulse, shrank from the centers of the rooms to the walls, he made his way uninterruptedly, but with the same solemn and measured step which had distinguished him from the first, through the blue chamber to the purple—through the purple to the green—through the green to the orange— through this again to the white—and even thence to the violet, ere a decided movement had been made to arrest him. It was then, however, that the Prince Prospero, maddening with rage and the shame of his own momentary cowardice, rushed hurriedly through the six chambers, while none followed him on account of a deadly terror that had seized upon all. He bore aloft a drawn dagger, and had approached, in rapid impetuosity, to within three or four feet of the retreating figure, when the latter, having attained the extremity of the velvet apartment, turned suddenly and confronted his pursuer. There was a sharp cry—and the dagger dropped gleaming upon the sable carpet, upon which, instantly afterwards, fell prostrate in death the Prince Prospero. Then, summoning the wild courage of despair, a throng of the revellers at once threw themselves into the black apartment, and, seizing the mummer, whose tall figure stood erect and motionless within the shadow of the ebony clock, gasped in unutterable horror at finding the grave-cerements and corpse-like mask which they handled with so violent a rudeness, untenanted by any tangible form.

And now was acknowledged the presence of the Red Death. He had come like a thief in the night. And one by one dropped the revellers in the blood-bedewed halls of their revel, and died each in the despairing posture of his fall. And the life of the ebony clock went out with that of the last of the gay. And the flames of the tripods expired. And Darkness and Decay and the Red Death held illimitable dominion over all.

Questions for Close Reading for Setting and Mood

1. How do the visible signs of the Red Death—"profuse bleeding," and "scarlet horror"—contribute to the setting of the story? Which senses does Poe appeal to in order to make us aware of the Red Death's power?
2. The final room in which Prospero encounters the Red Death is described as velvet. How does Poe make a velvet room seem especially frightening?
3. What effects do you perceive in the procession of Prospero from one colored room to another? How expressive or symbolic are the colors?
4. How effective was the masquerade costume of the Red Death?
5. What does the clock add to the power of the story?
6. Why does Poe emphasize that the orchestra plays waltzes?
7. What details of language contribute most powerfully to the setting?
8. Is the "mummer" who portrays the Red Death literally the Red Death, or is he one of the "thousand hale and light-hearted friends" who took sick?

Questions for Interpretation

New Critical

1. Prospero's name means, "I Prosper." Poe uses it ironically (since he obviously does not prosper) for effect. What ironies are implied in the setting of the story? In what ways is the overall point of the story ironic?

Psychoanalytic

2. In what ways does the architectural setting contribute to a nightmarelike quality of the story? Is the invading disease to be thought of as a masculine spermlike thing penetrating a female host? Is the architecture of the abbey to be thought of as symbolically female? What forces does Prospero seem to be attempting to repress in his own mind? What realities can he not face?

Reader Response

3. Establish as much as possible the range of responses that you find yourself giving the story. What are your strongest responses? How much of your response is given to the setting? What is your range of responses to the situation Prospero and his courtiers find themselves in and their decision to retreat from the world? In what ways do your responses lead you toward a final judgment of Prospero and his behavior? Does Poe make good use of anticipation and fright? Is this a horror story?

Feminist

4. Abbeys were segregated by sex. Most of them were foundations for monks, some for nuns. The men in the church generally controlled the operation of all abbeys. However, Prospero's abbey was never used by a religious order: it was "the creation of the prince's own eccentric yet august taste." What would be the feminist view of this mock-religious architecture? Does it suggest that Prospero has a gender bias, or does he treat men and women equally?

Political-Economic

5. Half the population has been killed. The courtiers, who control the wealth of the community, withdraw to pursue pleasure in face of almost certain death. A Marxist critic would point out that these aristocrats live off the work of the peasants and give them nothing back. The setting permits the aristocrats to extend their pleasure for five or six months. From the point of view of the larger community, is this desirable or undesirable behavior? Does the setting help us reach an answer to that question?

Historicist

6. In the Renaissance, abbeys were places where men and women retired to spend their time in spiritual meditation. They were often wealthy and self-sufficient and played only a small part in the larger society. Courtiers, by contrast, were power brokers in a secular world. Why do Prince Prospero and the courtiers retire to an abbey? What benefit do they expect? Does the mock-religious setting imply that their retirement is an immoral act? Or does it imply that Prospero thought of himself as especially moral?

CHARACTER AND PSYCHOLOGY

Character is often the central focus of a story, as in Eudora Welty's Phoenix in "A Warm Path," a psychologically powerful portrait of a child. Some characters, such as Hamlet, are **round**, or psychologically developed, and other characters, such as Lorenzo, are **flat**, or psychologically undeveloped. Some characters, such as Prince Prospero in "The Masque of the Red Death," are **static**: they do not change in the course of the story. Others, such as Imogen Keel and Father Tim Buckley of Seán O'Faoláin's "Falling Rocks, Narrowing Road, Cul-de-Sac, Stop," are **dynamic**: they change.

Stock characters are common types we recognize: a gossip who tells tales about people, a soldier who brags about his exploits, a mean stepmother, a young idler. The wicked brothers in "The Pot of Basil" are stock characters who parallel the wicked sisters in "Cinderella." Both Lisabetta and Lorenzo are, on one level, stock characters: young lovers foiled by their elders.

Characters reveal themselves mainly through their actions and reflections. Boccaccio shows us Lisabetta first as a daring young woman becoming the lover of the man she wants to marry. After he is dead, we see her weeping over her lover's head until she is driven mad. Yet we never learn the details of her thoughts and feelings, such as how she can tolerate the injustices of her brothers. Were she a psychologically developed character, we would learn more about her reflections: her thoughts and her inner life. As it is, we know only her actions. Similarly, the actions of the characters in "Two Cents" show us all we are permitted to know about them. In Seán O'Faoláin's story, by contrast, we learn much about the characters through both their inner thoughts and actions. Finally, some authors restrict what they show us and develop character by simply *telling* us what they are like. Poe does this with Prospero: "But the Prince Prospero was happy and dauntless and sagacious."

The main character in a short story is called the **protagonist**. Some people use the term **hero** or **heroine**, but the protagonist, especially in modern fiction, is often not heroic. For example, O'Faoláin begins "Falling Rocks, Narrowing Road, Cul-de-Sac, Stop" with the description of his protagonist, Morgan Myles, who is a perfect example of an antihero. In his discussion of modern fiction, *The Vanishing Hero* (1957), O'Faoláin defines the **antihero** as one who lacks the self-confidence and certainty of the traditional hero. Morgan Myles lacks almost all the qualities normally associated with the hero: he is not brave, dynamic, decisive, charming, resourceful, or brilliant. Instead, he is a poet and librarian, very self-absorbed and finicky. His assistant, Marianne Simcox, is "a frail, long-legged, neurotically efficient, gushingly idealistic, ladylike (that is to say, Protestant) young woman," as the narrator tells us. Myles is called a "Catholic cad," which reminds us that O'Faoláin is Irish and the story set in Ireland, where the labels Protestant and Catholic are like road signs: "Falling Rocks . . . Stop."

Dr. Francis Breen does not practice medicine at all. He has studied neurology in Vienna—where the great Sigmund Freud lived—and becomes involved in the story only when Morgan Myles comes to him with a boil under his tongue. Breen's motivation for not practicing medicine is boredom; his motivation for treating Morgan is his interest in poetry. O'Faoláin had read Freud's *Interpretation of Dreams*, and he knew that Freud told a story about a serious boil that caused him to dream in odd ways.

Father Tim Buckley becomes a pal of Breen and Myles, and the three of them go off on picnics and listen to Buckley lecture on chastity. Buckley is an expert on Freudian psychology, and he explains such things as "the sexual significance of pocket watches" and reminds us that their little group is latently homosexual.

When Frau Keel and her daughter Imogen Keel show up, they overwhelm the three bachelors with their female heterosexuality. The three men reveal themselves to be more inhibited than the women, and the women lead the entire group astray. Since one of the main themes of the story concerns psychoanalysis, characters analyze one another. Objects of interest become sexual symbols, a common characteristic of Freudianism.

O'Faoláin, who knew a great deal about Freud, plays with psychology in this story. His characters are round: rich and complex in part because he gives them time to develop. Even a minor character, Dolly Lynch, the housekeeper, is complex and real. Most of the characters surprise us at the end of the story because O'Faoláin wants us to realize that they are capable of change.

Seán O'Faoláin   (1900–1991)

Long the dean of Irish short story writers, Seán O'Faoláin was educated in Ireland and fought in the Irish Civil War in 1921. His experience sharpened his understanding of the political circumstances of Ireland. He knew most of the important literary figures of his generation, including many he mentions in his story, such as T. S. Eliot and W. B. Yeats. Some of his best work as a short story writer came in a period spanning four decades: A Nest of Simple Folk *(1933),* The Heat of the Sun *(1966), and* Foreign Affairs and Other Stories *(1976).*

The Freudianism in "Falling Rocks, Narrowing Road, Cul-de-Sac, Stop" is partly tongue-in-cheek but also partly serious. Like playwright Susan Glaspell in Suppressed Desires, *O'Faoláin has fun while also illuminating Freud. The character Morgan Myles was interesting enough to O'Faoláin that he permitted him to appear in a number of other stories.*

FALLING ROCKS, NARROWING ROAD, CUL-DE-SAC, STOP   1976

The day Morgan Myles arrived in L—— as the new county librarian he got a painful boil under his tongue. All that week he was too busy settling into his new quarters to do anything about it beyond dribbling over his mother's hand mirror into a mouth as pink and black as a hotel bathroom. Otherwise he kept working off the pain and discomfort of it in outbursts of temper with his assistant, Marianne Simcox, a frail, long-legged, neurotically efficient, gushingly idealistic, ladylike (that is to say, Protestant) young woman whom he hated and bullied from the first moment he met her. This, however, could have been because of his cautious fear of her virginal attractiveness.

On his fourth day in the job he was so rude to her that she turned on him, called him a Catholic cad, and fled sobbing behind the stacks. For fifteen minutes he went about his work humming with satisfaction at having broken her ladylike ways; but when she failed to come trotting to his next roar of command, he went tearing around the stacks in a fury looking for her. He was horrified to find her sitting on the floor of the Arts Section still crying into her mouse-sized handkerchief. With a groan of self-disgust he sat on the floor beside her, put his arm around her shoulder, rocked her as gently as if she was a kid of twelve, told her he was a bastard out of hell, that she was the most efficient assistant he had ever had in his life and that from this time on they would be doing marvellous things together with "our library." When she had calmed, she apologized for being so rude, and thanked him so formally, and so courteously, and in such a ladylike accent that he decided that she was a born bitch and went off home in a towering temper to his mother who, seeing the state her dear boy was in, said, "Wisha, Morgan love, why don't you take that gumboil of yours to a doctor and show it to him. You're not your natural nice self at all. You're as cranky as a bag of cats with it."

At the word "doctor" Morgan went pale with fear, bared his teeth like a five-barred gate and snarled that he had no intention of going next nor nigh any doctor in this one-horse town. "Anyway," he roared, "I hate all doctors. Without exception of age or sex. Cods and bluffers they are, the whole lot of them. And you know well that all any doctor ever wants to do with any patient is to take X-rays of his insides, order him into hospital, take the clothes down off of him, stick a syringe into his backside and before the poor fathead knows where he is there'll be half a dozen fellows in white nightshirts sawing away at him like a dead pig. It's just a gumboil. It doesn't bother me one bit. I've had dozens of them in my time. It's merely an Act of God. Like an earthquake, or a crick in the neck. It will pass."

But it did not pass. It went on burning and smarting until one windy sun-struck afternoon in his second week when he was streeling miserably along the Dublin Road, about a mile beyond the town's last untidy lot, beside its last unfinished suburban terrace. About every ten minutes or so, the clouds opened and the sun flicked and vanished. He held the collar of his baggy, tweed overcoat humped about his neck. His tongue was trying to double back acrobatically to his uvula. Feeling as lost and forlorn as the grey heron he saw across the road standing by the edge of a wrinkled loch, he halted to compose. "*O long-legged bird by your ruffled lake/ Alone as I, as bleak of eye, opaque . . .*" As what? He unguardedly rubbed his under-tongue on a sharp tooth, cursed, the sun winked, and he was confronted by one of destiny's infinite options. It was his moment of strength, of romance, of glamor, of youth, of sunshine on a strange shore. A blink of sunlight fell on a brass plate fastened to the red-brick gate pillar beside him, DR. FRANCIS BREEN.

The gate was lined with sheet metal. Right and left of it there was a high cut-stone wall backing on a coppice of rain-black macrocarpa that extended over the grassgrown border of the road. The house was not visible. He squeaked the gate open, peered timidly up a short curved avenue at it, all in red brick, tall, turreted and baywindowed. An empty-looking conservatory hooped against one side of it (intended, presumably, for the cultivation of rare orchids). Along the other side, a long veranda (intended, doubtless, to shelter Doctor Francis Breen from Ireland's burning tropical sun). He opened his mouth wide as he gazed, probed with his finger for the sore spot, and found it.

It did not look like a house where anybody would start cutting anybody up. It did not look like a doctor's house at all. It looked more like a gentleman's residence. Although he did remember the American visitor to Dublin who said to him that every Irish surgery looked as if it had been furnished by Dr. Watson for Sherlock Holmes. As he cautiously entered the avenue he observed that the gate bore a perpendicular column of five warning signs in blue lettering on white enamel. NO DOGS. NO CANVASSERS. NO HAWKERS. NO CIRCULARS. SHUT THE GATE. He advanced on the house, his fists clenched inside his overcoat pockets, his eyebrows lifted to indicate his contempt for all doctors. Twice on the way to the front door he paused, as if to admire the grounds, really to assure himself that no dog had failed to read the NO DOGS sign: a born cityman,

5

he feared all living animals. He was very fond of them in poetry. He took the final step upward to the stained glass door, stretched out his index finger, to tip, to tempt, to test, to press the brass bellknob. (An enamel sign beneath it said, TRADESMEN TO THE REAR.) His mother had spoken of a deficiency. She had also mentioned pills. He would ask this sawbones for a pill, or for a soothing bottle. He would not remove his shirt for him. And he would positively refuse to let down his pants. "Where," he foresaw himself roaring, "do you think I have this boil?"

A shadow appeared behind the door. He looked speculatively over his glasses at the servant who partly opened it. She was grey and settled, but not old, dressed in black bombazine, wearing a white starched apron with shoulder frills. When he asked for the doctor she immediately flung the door wide open as if she had been eagerly expecting him for years and years; then, limping eagerly ahead of him, dot and carry one down a softly upholstered corridor, she showed him into what she called "the dachtar's sargery," quacking all about "what an ahful co-eld dayeh it iss Gad bliss itt" in what he had already scornfully come to recognize as the ducks' dialect of this sodden, mist-shotten dung-heap of the Shannon's delta.

Left to himself he had time only to be disturbed by the sight of one, two, three barometers side by side on the wall, and one, two, three, four clocks side by side on the mantelpiece; relieved by an opposite wall lined with books; and enchanted by a dozen daintily tinted lithographs of flying moths and half a dozen hanging glass cases displaying wide-winged butterflies pinned against blue skies, when the door was slammed open by a tall, straight, white-haired, handsome, military-looking man, his temper at boiling point, his voice of the barrack-square, the knuckles of his fist white on the doorknob as if he were as eager to throw out his visitor as his Bombazine had been to welcome him in. Morgan noted that his eyes were quiet as a novice of nuns, and that his words were as polite, and remembered hearing somewhere that when the Duke of Wellington gave his order for the final charge at Waterloo his words to his equerry had been, "The Duke of Wellington presents his compliments to Field Marshal von Blücher and begs him to be so kind as to charge like blazes."

"Well, sir?" the doctor was saying. "Would you be so kind as to tell me what you mean by entering my house in this cavalier fashion? Are you an insurance salesman? Are you distributing circulars? Are you promoting the Encyclopaedia Britannica? Are you a hawker? A huckster? A Jehovah's Witness?"

At these words Morgan's eyes spread to the rims of his lake-size glasses. He felt a heavenly sunlight flooding the entire room. He raised two palms of exultant joy. More than any other gift of life, more than drink, food, girls, books, nicotine, coffee, music, more even than poetry and his old mother (whom he thought of, and saw through, as if she were a stained glass image of the Mother of God), he adored all cranks, fanatics, eccentrics and near-lunatics, always provided that they did not impinge on his personal comfort, in which case he would draw a line across them as fast as a butcher cuts off a chicken's head. More than any other human type he despised all men of good character, all solid citizens, all well-behaved social men, all mixers, joiners, hearty fellows and jolly good chaps, always provided that he did not require their assistance in his profession as librarian, in which case he would cajole them and lard them and lick them like a pander, while utterly despising himself, and his job, for having to tolerate such bores for one moment. But, here, before his eyes was a figure of purest gold. If there were any other such splendid crackpots in L—— then this was heaven, nor was he ever to be out of it.

"But," he protested gaily, "you are a doctor! I have a gumboil! We are the perfect match."

The old man moaned as if he had been shot through by an arrow of pain.

"It is true that I am, by letters patent, a man licensed to practice the crude invention called medicine. But I have never practiced, I have never desired to practice and I never do intend to practice medicine. I know very well, sir, what you want me to do. You want me to look down your throat with an electric torch and make some such solemn, stupid and meaningless remark as 'You have a streptococcal infection.' Well," he protested, "I will do nothing of the kind for you. Why should I? It might be only a symptom. Next week you might turn up with rheumatic heart disease, or a latent kidney disease, as people with strep throats have been known to do. You talk airily of a gumboil. You may well be living in a fool's paradise, sir. Even supposing I were to swab strep out of your throat and grow it on a culture medium, what would that tell me about the terrible, manifold, creeping, subtle, lethal disease-processes that may be going on at this moment in the recesses of your body as part of that strep infection, or set off by it? The only thing I, or any other doctor—bluffers and liars that we all are—could honestly say to you would be the usual evasion. 'Gargle with this bottle three times a day and come back in a week.' By which time Nature or God would have in any case cured you without our alleged assistance. I know the whole bag of tricks from the Hippocratic collection, the treatises of Galen and the Canon of Avicenna° down. I suppose you imagine that I spent all my years in Dublin and Vienna studying medicine. I spent them studying medicos. I am a neurologist. Or I was a neurologist until I found that what true medicine means is true magic. Do you know how to remove a wart? You must wait on the roadway to the cemetery until a funeral passes, and say, 'Corpse, corpse, take away my wart.' And your wart will go, sir! That is true medicine. I believe in miracles because I have seen them happen. I believe in God, prayer, the imagination, the destiny of the Irish, our bottomless racial memory—and in nothing else."

Morgan's left hand was circling his belly in search of manifold, creeping, secret diseases.

"But, surely to God, doctor," he whined, "medical science can do *something*   15 for a gumboil?"

"Aha! I know what you're up to now. X-rays! That's the mumbo-jumbo every patient wants. And neither will I suggest, as you would probably like me to suggest, that you should go to hospital. All you would do there would be either to pass your infection to some other patient or pick up his infection from him. I will have nothing to do with you, sir. And please keep your distance. I don't want your beastly infection. If you want to mess about with your gumboil you will have to go to a doctor. If you wish me to pray for your gumboil I will pray for it. But I refuse to let you or anybody else turn me into the sort of mountebank who pretends he can cure any tradesman's sore toe or any clerk's carbuncle in one second with a stroke of his pen and a nostrum from the chemist's shop. Good afternoon to you, sir. You are now in the hands of God!"

Galen . . . Canon of Avicenna: These are the ancient medical treatises that guide modern medical philosophy.

Morgan, stung by arrogance and enraged by fear, roared back a line fit for his memoirs.

"And good afternoon to you, sir! From one who is neither clerk nor trades-man, higgler nor hawker, huckster nor hounddog but, by God's grace, a poet whose poems will live long after," hand waving, "your butterflies have been de-voured by the jaws of your moths."

The old man's rage vanished like a ghost at cockcrow. He closed the door gently behind him.

"A poet?" he asked quietly. "Now, this is most interesting." Courteously he   20
indicated a chair. "Won't you sit down? Your name is?"

"Morgan Myles," Morgan Myles boomed as if he were a majordomo an-nouncing Lord Byron.

"Mine is Francis Breen. Yours is more euphonious. I can see it already on your first book of verses. But a poet should have three names. Like American politicians. Percy Bysshe Shelley. George Gordon Byron. Thomas Stearns Eliot. William Butler Yeats. Ella Wheeler Wilcox. Richard Milhous Nixon. You have a second name? Taken at your Confirmation? Arthur? There we have it! *First Poems.* By Morgan Arthur Myles!"

Morgan, like most men who are adept at flattering others, could never re-sist flattery himself. He waggled his bottom like a dog. His grin was coy but cock-sure. Three minutes later the doctor was tenderly parting his lips and illuminat-ing the inside of his mouth. He extinguished the torch. He lifted his eyes and smiled into Morgan's.

"Well, Doc?" Morgan asked fearfully. "What did you see there?"

"You are not even," his new-found friend smiled, "about to give birth to a   25
couplet. Just a blister." He sat to his desk. "I will give you a prescription for a gargle. Rinse your mouth with this three times a day. And come back to me in a week. But if you wish to get better sooner come sooner, any evening for a drink and a chat. I have no friends in L——."

"Nor have I!"

Within a week they were bosom cronies.

From start to finish it was a ridiculous friendship. Indeed, from that day on-ward, to the many of us who saw them every day after lunch walking along O'Connell Street arm in arm like father and son, or nose to nose like an ageing ward boss with a young disciple, it seemed an unnatural business. Can the east wind, we asked one another in wonder, lie down with the west wind? A cormorant mate with a herring? A heron with a hare? An end with a beginning? We gave their beautiful friendship three months. As a matter of fact we were only two years and eleven months out.

Even to look at they were a mismatch: the doctor straight and spare as a spear, radiating propriety from every spiky bone of his body, as short of step as a woman, and as carefully dressed from his wide-brimmed bowler hat to the rub-ber tip of his mottled, gold-headed malacca cane; the poet striding beside him; halting only to swirl his flabby tweeds; his splendid hydrocephalic head stretched behind his neck like a balloon; his myopic eyes glaring at the clouds over the roofs through the thick lenses of his glasses; a waterfall of black hair permanently frozen over his left eye; his big teeth laughing, his big voice booming, he looked for all the world like a peasant Yeats in a poor state of health. The only one of us who managed to produce any sort of explanation was our amateur psychiatrist, Father Tim Buckley, and we never took him seriously anyway. He said, with an episcopal *sprinkle me O Lord with hyssop* wave of his hand, "They have invented one another."

Now, we knew from experience that there was only one way to handle Tim 30 Buckley. If he said some fellow was a homosexual because he had fallen in love with his hobbyhorse when he was five you had to say at once, "But, Tim, why did he fall in love with his hobbyhorse when he was five?" If he said that it was because the poor chap hated his mother and loved his father you had to say, at once, "But, Tim, why did he hate his ma and love his da?" If he then said that it was natural for every child to prefer one parent to another, you had to say at once, "But, Tim, why . . ." And so on until he lost his temper and shut up. This time, however, he was ready for our counterattack.

"They have invented one another," he said, "for mutual support because they are both silently screaming for freedom. Now what is the form of slavery from which all human beings most want to be free?"

"Sex," we conceded, to save time, knowing our man.

"Passion!" he amended. "For this agony there are only three solutions. The first is sin, which," he grinned, "I am informed on the best authority is highly agreeable but involves an awful waste of time. I mean if you could hang a girl up in the closet every time you were finished with her that would be very convenient, but. Then there is marriage, which as Shaw said is the perfect combination of maximum temptation and maximum opportunity. And there is celibacy of which, I can say with authority, as the only member of the present company who knows anything at all about it, that it bestows on man the qualified freedom of a besieged city where one sometimes has to eat rats. Of our two friendly friends the older man needs approval for his lifelong celibacy. The younger man needs encouragement to sustain his own. Or so they have chosen to imagine. In fact neither of them really believes in celibacy at all. Each has not only invented the other. He has invented himself."

Our silence was prolonged.

"Very well," he surrendered. "In that case thicken your own plot!" 35

Of course, we who had known Frank Breen closely ever since we were kids together in L⸺ , knew that there was nothing mysterious about him: he had simply always been a bit balmy, even as a four-eyed kid. When his parents sent him to school in England we saw much less of him; still less when he went to Dublin for his MB, and from there on to Austria for his MD. After he came back to L⸺ to settle down for life in the old Breen house on the Dublin Road on the death of his father, old Doctor Frank, and of his mother, we hardly saw him at all. We knew about him only by hearsay, chiefly through the gossip of his housekeeper, Dolly Lynch, passed on to Claire Coogan, Father Tim Buckley's housekeeper, and gleefully passed on by him to the whole town.

That was how the town first heard that the brass plate on his gate pillar—his father's, well polished by chamois and dulled by weather—would never again mean that there was a doctor behind it; about his four clocks and his three barometers; about his collection of moths and butterflies; about the rope ladder he had coiled in a red metal box under every bedroom window; about his bed always set two feet from the wall lest a bit of cornice should fall on his head during the night;

about the way he looked under the stairs for hidden thieves every night before going to bed; that his gold-knobbed malacca cane contained a sword; that he never arrived at the railway station less than half an hour before his train left; that he hung his pyjamas on a clothes hanger; had handmade wooden trees for every pair of his handmade boots; that he liked to have his bootlaces washed and ironed; that his vest-pocket watch told the time, the date, the day, the year, the points of the compass, and contained an alarm buzzer that he was always setting to remind him of something important he wanted to do later on, but whose nature he could never remember when the buzzer hummed over his left gut—very much the way a wife will leave her wedding ring at night on her dressing table to remind her in the morning of something that by then she has incontinently forgotten.

So! A bit odd. Every club in the world must have elderly members like him— intelligent and successful men of whose oddities the secretary will know one, the headwaiter another, the bartender a third, their fellow members smile at a fourth. It is only their families, or if they live for a long time in a small town their towns- folk who will, between them, know the lot. Frank Breen might have gone on in his harmless, bumbling way to the end of his life if that brass plate of his had not winked at Morgan Myles, and if Father Tim Buckley—was he jealous?—had not decided to play God.

Not that we ever called him "Father Tim Buckley." He was too close to us, too like one of ourselves for that. We called him Tim Buckley, or Tim, or even if the whiskey was fluming, Bucky. He was not at all like the usual Irish priest who is as warm as toast and as friendly and understanding as a brother until you come to the sixth commandment, and there is an end to him. Tim was like a man who had dropped off an international plane at Shannon; not a Spencer Tracy priest from downtown Manhattan, all cigar and white cuffs, parish computer and portable typewriter, fists and feet, and there is the end to him; perhaps more like an unfrocked priest from Bolivia or Brazil, so ungentlemanly in his manners as to have given acute pain to an Evelyn Waugh and so cheerful in spite of his scars as to have shocked a Graham Greene;° or still more like, among all other alterna- tives, a French workers' priest from Liège; or in other words, as far as we were concerned, the right man in the right place and as far as the bishop was concerned, a total disaster. He was handsome, ruddy and full-blooded in a sensual way, al- ready so heavy in his middle thirties that he had the belly, the chins and (when he lost his temper) something of the voracity of Rodin's ferocious statue of Balzac in his dressing gown; but he was most himself when his leaden-lidded eyes glis- tened with laughter, and his tiny mouth, crushed between the peonies of his cheeks, reminded you of a small boy whistling after his dog, or of some young fellow saucily making a kiss-mouth across the street to his girl. His hobby was psychoanalysis.

His analysis of the doctor was characteristic. He first pointed out to us, over   40 a glass of malt, the sexual significance of pocket watches, so often fondled and rubbed between the fingers. He merely shrugged at the idea of ladders unfold- ing from red containers, and said that swords being in sword sticks needed no

---

Greene: Spencer Tracy (1900–1967), American actor who often played a Catholic priest; Evelyn Waugh (1903–1966) and Graham Greene (1904–1992) were popular Catholic nov- elists.

comment. Clocks and barometers were merely extensions of pocket watches. (The wristwatch, he assured us, was one of the great sexual revolutions of our age—it brought everything out in the open.) But, above all, he begged us to give due attention to Frank Breen's mother complex—evident in his love of seclusion behind womblike walls, dark trees, a masked gate; and any man must have a terrible hate for his father who mockingly leaves his father's brass plate on a pillar outside his home while publicly refusing to follow his father's profession inside it. ("By the way, can we ignore that NO DOGS sign?") The looking for thieves under the stairs at night, he confessed, puzzled him for the moment. Early arrival for trains was an obvious sign of mental insecurity. "Though, God knows," laughing in his fat, "any man who doesn't feel mentally insecure in the modern world must be out of his mind." As for this beautiful friendship, that was a classical case of Narcissism: the older man in love with an image of his own lost and lonely youth.

"Any questions?"

No wonder he was the favorite confessor of all the nubile girls in town, not (or not only) because they thought him handsome but because he was always happy to give them the most disturbing explanations for their simplest misdemeanors. "I kissed a boy at a dance, Father," they would say to some other priest and, as he boredly bade them say three Hail Marys for their penance, they would hear the dark slide of the confessional move dismissively across their faces. Not so with Father Tim! He would lean his cheek against the grille and whisper, "Now, my dear child, in itself a kiss is an innocent and beautiful act. Therefore the only reason prompting you to confess it as a sin must refer to the manner in which the kiss was given and the spirit in which it was received, and in this you may be very wise. Because, of course, when we say *kiss*, or *lips*, we may—one never knows for certain—be thinking of something quite different . . ." His penitents would leave his box with their faces glowing, and their eyes dazed. One said that he made her feel like a Magdalen with long floating hair. Another said he made her want to go round L—— wearing a dark veil. A third (who was certain to come to a bad end) said he had revealed to her the *splendeurs et misères de l'amour*. And a fourth, clasping her palms with delight, giggled that he was her Saint Rasputin.

We who met him in our homes, with a glass in his fist and his Roman collar thrown aside, did not worry about what he told our daughters. We had long since accepted him as an honest, innocent, unworldly man who seemed to know a lot about sex-in-the-head—and was always very entertaining about it—but who knew sweet damn all about love-in-the-bed, not to mention love at about eleven o'-clock at night when your five kids are asleep and the two of you are so edgy from adding up the household accounts that by the time you have decided once again that the case is hopeless all "to go to bed" means is to go sound asleep. But we did worry about him. He was so outspoken, so trustful of every stranger, had as little guard over his tongue as a sailor ashore, that we could foresee the day when his bishop would become so sick of getting anonymous letters about him that he would shanghai him to some remote punishment-curacy on the backside of Slievenamuck.

We would try to frighten him into caution by telling him that he would end up there, exiled to some spot so insignificant that it would not be marked even on one of those nostalgic one-inch-to-the-mile British Ordnance maps of 1899 that still—indifferent to the effects of time and history, of gunshot and revolution—record every burned out constabulary barracks, destroyed mansion, abandoned branch-railway, eighteenth century "inn," disused blacksmith's hovel, silenced windmill, rook-echoing granary or "R.C. Chapel," where, we would tell him, is where our brave Bucky would then be, in a baldface presbytery, altitude 1750 feet, serving a cement-faced chapel, beside an anonymous crossroads, without a tree in sight for ten miles, stuck for life as curator, nurse and slave of some senile parish priest. He would just raise his voice to spit scorn at us; like the night he gobbled us up in a rage:—

"And," he roared, "if I can't say what I think how the hell am I going to   45
live? Am I free or am I not free? Am I to lie down in the dust and be gagged and handcuffed like a slave? Do ye want me to spend my whole life watching out for traffic signs? Falling rocks! Narrowing Road! Cul-de-sac! Stop! My God, are ye men or are ye mice?"

"Mice!" we roared back with one jovial voice and dispelled the tension in laughter so loud that my wife looked up in fright at the ceiling and said, "Sssh! Ye bastards! If ye wake the kids I'll make every one of ye walk the floor with them in yeer arms till three in the morning. Or do ye think ye're starting another revolution in yeer old age?"

"We could do worse," Tim smiled into his double chin.

Whenever he smiled like that you could see the traffic signs lying right and left of him like idols overthrown.

It was a Sunday afternoon in May. The little island was deserted. He was lying on the sunwarmed grass between the other two, all three on their backs, in a row, their hats on their faces. They were neither asleep nor awake. They were breathing as softly as the lake at their feet. They had driven at their ease that morning to the east side of the lake past the small village of Mountshannon, now looking even smaller across the level water, rowed to the island (Tim Buckley at the oars), delighted to find every hillocky green horizon slowly bubbling with cumulus clouds. They had inspected the island's three ruined churches, knee-deep in nettles and fern, and its tenth-century Round Tower that had stood against the morning sun as dark as a factory chimney. They had photographed the ruins, and one another, and then sat near the lake and the boat to discuss the excellent lunch that Dolly Lynch always prepared for "the young maaaster" on these Sunday outings: her cold chicken and salad, her handmade mayonnaise, her own brown bread and butter, the bottle of Liebfraumilch that Frank had hung by a string in the lake to cool while they explored the island, her double roasted French coffee, flavored, the way the maaaster always liked it, with chicory and a suspicion of cognac. It was half an hour since they had lain back to sleep. So far everything about the outing had been perfect. No wonder Morgan had jackknifed out of bed that morning at eight o'clock, and Frank Breen wakened with a smile of special satisfaction.

Before Morgan came, exactly two years and eleven months ago, it had been   50
the doctor's custom, at the first call of the cuckoo, to take off now and again (though never too often to establish a precedent), on especially fine Sundays like this, with Father Timothy Buckley in Father Timothy's roomy secondhand Peugeot—Frank did not drive—in search of moths and butterflies, or to inspect the last four walls, perhaps the last three walls, of some eighth-century Hiberno-Romanesque churchlet, or the rotting molar of some Norman castle smelling of

cow dung, purple mallow, meadowsweet and the woodsmoke of the last tinkers who had camped there. After Morgan came he had begun to drive off every fine Sunday with Morgan in Morgan's little Ford Prefect. Still, *noblesse oblige*, and also if the journey promised to be a rather long one, he had about twice a year suggested to Morgan that they might invite Father Timothy to join them; and Tim had always come, observing with amusement that they indulgently allowed him to bring his own car, and that they would, after loud protestations, allow him to do all the driving, and that he also had to persuade them forcibly to allow him to pack the luggage on the seat beside him, so as to leave plenty of room—at this point they would all three laugh with the frankest irony—for their lordships' bottoms in the soft and roomy rear of the Peugeot. This luggage consisted of Frank's two butterfly nets, in case one broke, three binoculars and three cameras, one for each, two umbrellas for himself and Morgan, the bulging lunch basket for them all, two foam-rubber cushions, one for his poor old back, one for Morgan's poor young back, and a leather-backed carriage rug so that the dear boy should not feel the cold of the grass going up through him while he was eating his lunch and enjoying—as he was now enjoying—his afternoon siesta.

Retired, each one, into his own secret shell of sleep, they all three looked as dead as they would look in fifteen years' time in one of the photographs they had just taken of themselves. The day had stopped. The film of the climbing towers of clouds had stopped. The lake was silent. The few birds and the three cows they had seen on the island were dozing. Thinking had stopped. Their three egos had stopped. Folk tales say that when a man is asleep on the grass like that, a tiny lizard may creep into his mouth, devour his tongue and usurp its power. After about an hour of silence and dozing some such lizard spoke from the priest's mouth. Afterwards he said that he had been dreaming of the island's hermits, and of what he called the shortitude and latitude of life, and of how soon it stops, and that those two selfish bastards beside him were egotistical sinners, too concerned with their comfort as adolescents to assert their dignity as men. "And I?" he thought with a start, and woke.

"In Dublin last month," his lizard said hollowly into his hat, "I saw a girl on a horse on a concrete street."

"What?" Morgan asked drowsily, without stirring.

"A girl on a horse," Tim said, removing his hat, and beholding the glorious blue sky. "It was the most pathetic sight I ever saw."

"Why pathetic?" Morgan asked, removing his hat and seeing the blue Pacific 55 sweep into his ken.

"She was riding on a concrete street, dressed as if she was riding to hounds. The fantasy of it was pathetic. Miles away from green fields. But all the girls are gone mad on horses nowadays. I wish somebody would tell them that all they're doing is giving the world a beautiful example of sexual transference. They have simply transferred their natural desire for a man to a four-legged brute."

"Balderdash," said Morgan, and put back his hat as Frank patiently lifted his to ask the blueness what all the poor girls who haven't got horses do to inform the public of their adolescent desires.

"They have cars," Tim said, and sat up slowly, the better to do battle. Morgan sat up abruptly.

"So," he demanded, "every time I drive a car I become a homosexual?"

Tim considered the matter judicially. 60

"Possibly," he agreed. "But not necessarily. There are male cars for women, and female cars for men. For women? Clubman, Escort, Rover, Consort, Jaguar, Triumph. Fill 'em up and drive them at seventy miles an hour! What fun! For men? Giulietta. Whose Romeo? Morris Minor. The word means moor—symbolical desire for a small negress. Mercedes? Actually that is Mrs. Benz's name. Also means Our Lady of Mercy. Symbolical desire for a large virgin. Ford Consul? Consuela, Our Lady of Consolations. Volvo? Vulva. Volkswagen. Double V. Symbolical . . ."

"Well of all the filthy minds!" Morgan roared.

The doctor sat up with a sigh. His siesta was ruined. His anger was hot upon his humor and his honor.

"I do think, Father Timothy, that you, as a priest of God . . ."

Tim scrambled to his feet, high above him, black as a winetun° against the   65
pale sheen of the lake.

"A priest, a presbyter, an elder, a sheikh, an old man, a minister, a pastor of sheep? What does that mean? Something superior, elegant, stainless and remote from life like yourself and Master Poet here? An angel, a seraph, a saint, a mystic, a eunuch, a cherubim, a morning star? Do I look like it? Or like a man fat from eating too much, wheezy from smoking too much, sick and tired from trying to do the job he was called on to do? A priest of God is a man with a bum and a belly, and everything that hangs out of a belly or cleaves it, with the same appetites and desires, thirsts and hungers as the men and women, the boys and the girls he lives and works with. It may be very nice for you to look at us before the altar in Saint Jude's all dressed up in our golden robes, swinging a censer, and to think, 'There is heavenly power, there is magic.' But I have no power. I'm nothing alone. I merely pretend to a power that is an eternity beyond me. When I was in Rome, as a student, a priest in Southern Italy went mad, ran down to the bakery to turn the whole night's baking into the body of God, and from there to the wine factory to turn every flask and vat of flowing wine into the blood of the Lord. But did he? Of course not. Alone he hadn't the power to make a leaf of basil grow. But I will pretend to any boy or girl who is troubled or in misery that I have all the power in heaven to cure them, do mumbo-jumbo, wave hands, say hocus pocus, anything if it will only give them peace. And if that doesn't work I tell them the truth."

"You are shouting, Father," Doctor Frank said coldly.

Tim controlled himself. He sat down again. He laughed.

"Ye don't want to hear the truth. Too busy romanticizing, repressing, rationalizing, running away, when everybody knows the pair of ye think of nothing but women from morning to night! Your moths, Frank, that come out in the twilight, your easy girls, your lights o' love, fluttering against your windowpanes? Do you want me to believe that you never wish you could open the window to let one in? I saw you, Morgan, the other day in the library fawning over that unfortunate virgin Simcox, and a child could see what was in the minds of the pair of ye. And what do you think she thinks she's doing every time she goes out to the yard to wash the backside of your car with suds and water? Why don't you be a man, Morgan, and face up to it—one day you'll have to be spliced. It's the common fate of all mankind."

winetun: Wine barrel.

"It hasn't been yours, Father," Frank snapped.   70

"Because I took a vow and kept to it, logically."

"Pfoo!" Morgan snarled at him. "You know damned well that logic has as much to do with marriage as it has with music."

Tim looked at him with the air of a small boy who is thinking what fun it would be to shove his Auntie Kitty down the farmyard well.

"You know," he said slyly, "you should ask Fräulein Keel about that the next time she is playing the Appassionata for you," and was delighted to observe the slow blush that climbed up Morgan's face and the black frown that drew down the doctor's eyebrows. The silence of his companions hummed. He leaned back.

It was about two months ago since Frau Keel had come to L—— with her   75
daughter Imogen and her husband Georg, an electrical engineer in charge of a new German factory at the Shannon Free Airport complex. He was about fifty and a Roman Catholic, which was presumably why he had been chosen for this Irish job. His wife was much younger; blonde, handsome, curlyheaded, well-corseted, with long-lashed eyes like a cow. Hera-eyed,° Morgan said; dopey, Frank said; false lashes, Tim Buckley said. She was broad of bosom and bottom, strong-legged as a peasant and as heavy-shouldered, one of those abundant, self-indul-gent, flesh-folding bodies that Rubens so loved to paint in their pink skin. Imogen was quite different; small, black-avised,° black-haired, her skin like a bit of burned cork. She was a *belle laide°* of such intensity, so packed and powerful with femi-ninity that you felt that if you were to touch her with one finger she would hoop her back and spring her arms around you like a trap. Morgan had met her in the library, let her talk about music, found himself invited by her mother to hear her play, and unwisely boasted about it to Tim Buckley.

In the sullen silence he heard the lake sucking the stones of the beach. The clouds were less bright. The doctor said primly that he wanted to try his hand with his butterfly net. Morgan said gruffly that he wanted to take some more pic-tures before the sun went down. Together they walked away across the island. Tim reached for his breviary and began to read the office of the day. "Let us then be like newborn children hungry for the fresh milk . . ."

The delicate India paper of his breviary whispered each time he turned a page. Presently a drop of rain splashed on his knuckles. He looked about him. The sun still touched the island but nowhere else. The lake hissed at the shore. He stood on a rock but could see no sign of his companions. Were they colloguing with the seventh century? He packed the lunch basket, rolled up the rugs, loaded the cargo, sat in the stern of the boat, opened an umbrella, lit his pipe and waited. He was sick of them. No doubt when slaves fall in love they feel more free . . .

They returned slowly and silently. Little was said as he rowed them to the mainland, and less on the way back to L—— because the rain became a cloud-burst, and he was alone peering into it. On previous excursions he had always been invited to dine with them. He knew he would not be this evening: a snub that Morgan aggravated by assuring him that they must all meet soon again "on a more propitious occasion." He gave them a cheerful goodbye and drove off along the rain-dancing asphalt. To the devil with their four-course dinner. His

---

Hera-eyed: Hera, wife of Zeus, had huge eyes. *black-avised*: Possessing a dark complexion. *belle laide*: Beautiful woman.

freedom was more important to him. Anyway there were a dozen houses in town where the wife would be delighted to give him a plate of bacon and eggs.

Frank said nothing until he had poured their usual aperitif—a stout dollop of malt.

"That," he said as he handed the glass of whiskey to Morgan deep in the   80
best armchair on the side of the turf fire, "is probably the last time we shall meet his reverence socially."

Morgan looked portentously over his glasses at the fire.

"A terrible feeling sometimes assails me," he said, smacking each sibilant, "that Timothy John Buckley has a coarse streak in him."

Frank took the opposite armchair.

"I would call it a grave lack of tact. Even presuming that La Keel has not already told him that she is a patient of mine."

"Imogen?" said Morgan, sitting straight up. "Good God! Is there something   85
wrong with her?"

"Imogen? Oh, you mean the child? I was referring to the mother."

Morgan sat back.

"Oh, and what's wrong with that old battle-axe? Are you beginning to take patients?"

Frank frowned.

"I have done my best to avoid it. The lady, and her husband, ever since they   90
heard that I studied neurology in Vienna, have been very persistent. As for what is wrong, I should not, ethically speaking as a doctor, discuss the affairs of any patient but, in this case, I think I may safely speak to you about the matter. Aye. Because I can trust you. And Bee. Because there is nothing whatsoever wrong with the lady."

"Then why did she come to consult you?"

Frank answered this one even more stiffly.

"She speaks of her cycles."

Morgan, like an old lady crossing a muddy road, ventured between the pools of his inborn prudishness, his poetic fastidiousness and his natural curiosity:—

"Do you by any chance mean she has some sort of what they call woman   95
trouble?"

"If you mean the menopause, Madame Keel is much too young for that. She means emotional cycles. Elation-depression. Vitality-debility. Exultation-despair. The usual manic-depressive syndrome. She says that ever since she came to Ireland she has been melancholy."

"Jaysus! Sure, aren't we all melancholy in Ireland? What I'd say that one needs is a few good balls of malt every day or a dose or two of cod liver oil. If I were you, Frank, I'd pack her off about her business."

The doctor's body stirred restively.

"I have made several efforts to detach myself. She insists that I give her comfort."

Morgan looked over his glasses at his friend.   100

"And what kind of comfort would that be?" he asked cautiously.

"That," his friend said, a trifle smugly, "is scarcely for me to say."

Morgan glared into his glass. For a moment he wished Bucky was there to crash through the ROAD NARROWS sign, the CUL-DE-SAC, the FALLING ROCKS.

"It is a compliment to you," he said soapily.

"I take small pride in it, Morgan. Especially since she tells me that she also 105 gets great comfort from her pastor."

Morgan rose to his feet, dark as a thundercloud, or as a Jove who had not shaved for a week.

"What pastor?" he demanded in his deepest basso.

"You have guessed it. Our companion of today. The Reverend Timothy Buckley. He also gives great comfort to Herr Keel. And to the girl. He holds sessions."

Jehovah's thunder-rumble rolled.

"Sessions?" 110

"It is apparently the latest American-Dutch ecumenical idea. Group confessions."

"The man," Morgan boomed, "must be mad! He is worse than mad. Who was it called him Rasputin? He was born to be hanged! Or shot! Or poisoned! That man is e-e-e-evil. Frank! You must stop this monstrous folly at once. Think of the effect on that innocent poor child."

"I have no intention whatsoever of interfering," Frank fluttered. "It's a family affair. I have no least right to interfere. And I suspect she is not in the least innocent. And she is not a child. She is eighteen."

"Frank!" Morgan roared. "Have you NO principles?"

A mistake. It is not a nice question to be asked by anybody. Suppose Morgan 115 had been asked by somebody if he had any principles himself! How does any of us know what his principles are? Nobody wants to have to start outlining his principles at a word of command.

"I begin to fear," Frank said huffily, "that in all this you are not thinking of me, nor of Frau Keel, nor of Herr Keel, nor of my principles, nor of any principles whatever but solely of the sexual attractions of Fräulein Keel. She has hairy legs. A well-known sign of potency."

At which moment of dead silence Dolly Lynch opened the door, put in her flushed face and in her slow, flat, obsequious Shannon voice, said, "Dinner is i-now-eh sarvedeh, Dachter." Her employer glared at her. Why was she looking so flushed? The foul creature had probably been outside the door for the last three minutes listening to the rising voices. By tomorrow the thing would be all over the town.

They entered the dining room in silence. She served them in silence. When she went out they maintained silence, or said small polite things like, "This spring lamb is very tender," or "Forced rhubarb?" The silences were so heavy that Morgan felt obliged to retail the entire life of Monteverdi. Immediately after the coffee, in the drawing room, he said he had better go home to his mother, and, with fulsome thanks for a splendid lunch and a marvellous dinner, he left his friend to his pipe and, if he had any, his principles.

Morgan did not drive directly to his cottage on the Ennis Road. He drove to the library, extracted from the music section a biography of Monteverdi and drove to the Keels' flat in O'Connell Square. It was Frau Keel, majestic as Brünnhilde, who opened the door, received the book as if it were a ticket of admission and invited him to come in. To his annoyance he found Buckley half-filling a settee, winking cheerfully at him, smoking a cigar, a coffee in his paw, a large brandy on a small table beside him. Herr Keel sat beside him, enjoying the same pleasures. Through the dining room door he caught a glimpse of Imogen with her back to him, clearing the dinner table, her oily black hair coiled as usual on either side of her cheeks. As she leaned over the table he saw the dimpled backs of her knees. She was not wearing stockings. The dark down on her legs suggested the untamed forests of the north.

"Aha!" Herr Keel cried, in (for so ponderous a man) his always surprising 120 countertenor. "It is Mister Myles. You are most welcome. May I offer you a coffee and a good German cigar? We had just begun a most interesting session."

Morgan beamed and bowed ingratiatingly. He almost clicked his heels in his desire to show his pleasure and to conceal the frightening thought:—"Is this one of Bucky's sessions?" He beamed as he received the cigar and a brandy from Herr Keel, who bowed in return. He bowed as he accepted a coffee from Frau Keel who beamed in return before she went back to her own place on a small sofa of the sort that the French—so he found out next day from a History of Furniture—call a *canapé*, where she was presently joined by Imogen. Thereafter he found that whenever he glanced (shyly) at Frau Keel she was staring anxiously and intently at Buckley, and whenever he glanced (shyly) at Imogen she was looking at himself with a tiny smile of what, crestfallen, he took to be amusement until she raised her hairy eyebrows and slowly shook her midnight head, and he heard a beautiful noise like a bomb exploding inside his chest at the thought that this black sprite was either giving him sympathy or asking sympathy from him. Either would be delightful. But, then, her eyebrows suddenly plunged, she shook her head threateningly, her smile curled, anger and disapproval sullied her already dark eyes.

"As I was saying," Father Tim was saying, magisterially waving his cigar, "if adultery is both a positive fact and a relative term, so is marriage. After all, marriage is much more than what The Master of the Sentences called a *conjunctio viri et mulieris.*° It is also a union of sympathy and interest, heart and soul. Without these marriage becomes licensed adultery."

"I agree," Frau Keel sighed. "But no woman ever got a divorce for that reason."

Buckley pursed his little mouth into a provocative smile. "In fact people do divorce for that very reason. Only they call it mental cruelty."

"Alas," said Brünnhilde, "according to our church, there is no such sin as 125 mental cruelty and therefore there is no divorce."

"There are papal annulments," Herr Keel said to her coldly, "if you are interested in such things."

"I am very interested," she said to him as frigidly, which was not the kind of warm domestic conversation that Morgan had read about in books.

"You were about to tell us, Father Tim," Imogen said, "what you consider unarguable grounds for the annulment of a marriage."

Sickeningly Buckley beamed at the girl; fawningly she beamed back. *She!* The Hyrcanian tigress! Had this obese sensualist mesmerized the whole lot of them? But he could not, as Buckley calmly began to enumerate the impediments to true wedlock, center his mind on what was being said, so dumbfounded was he to find

conjunctio viri et mulieris: A joining together of men and women.

that nobody but himself seemed to be forming images of the hideous realities of what he now heard. All he could do was to gulp his brandy, as any man of the world might in such circumstances, and struggle to keep his eyes from Imogen's hirsute legs. (Where had he read that Charles XII had a woman in his army whose beard was two feet long?)

"It is not," Buckley said, "a true marriage if it has been preceded by rape. It 130 is not a true marriage if either or both parties are certifiable lunatics. It is not," here he glanced at Keel, "a genuine marriage if the father marries the daughter," smiling at Imogen, "or if the sister marries the brother. It is not marriage if by error either party marries the wrong person, which can happen when a number of people are being married simultaneously. If either party has previously murdered the wife or husband of the other party it is not really a very good marriage. Nor if either party persuades the other party into adultery beforehand by a promise of marriage afterwards. It is not marriage if the male party is impotent both antecedently and perpetually. Nor if a Christian marries a Jew or other heathen . . ."

At which point they all started talking together, Imogen declaring passionately, "I would marry a Jew if I damn well wanted to," and Georg Keel demanding, "How can you prove impotency?", and Frau Keel protesting with ringed fingers, "Kein Juden! Kein Juden!",° Buckley laughingly crying out, "I agree, I agree," and Morgan wailing that it was all bureaucratic balderdash, all quashed suddenly into silence by the prolonged ringing of the doorbell. Keel glanced at his watch and said testily, "Who on earth . . .?" Imogen, unwilling to lose a fraction of the fight, rushed to the door and led in the latecomer. It was the doctor.

Morgan had to admire his comportment. Though he must have been much taken aback to see all his problems personified before him, the old boy did not falter for a moment in his poise and manners. He formally apologized for his late call to Frau Keel, who revealed her delight in his visit by swiftly patting her hair as she passed a mirror, making him sit beside her, fluttering to Imogen to sit beside Morgan, and yielding him a brandy glass between her palms as if it were a chalice. He accepted it graciously, he did not allow it to pass over him, he bowed like a cardinal, he relaxed into the company, legs crossed, as easily as if he were the host and they his guests. Morgan observed that the cuffs of his trousers were wet. He had walked here in the rain. He must be feeling greatly upset.

"Are you a friend of this dirty old doctor?" Imogen whispered rapidly to Morgan.

"I know him slightly. I like you very much, Imogen."

"He is a vurm!" she whispered balefully. "You are another vurm. You both 135 turned Father Tim from the door without a meal."

"Neither," said Tim, resuming control, "is it a marriage if it is clandestine, that is, performed secretly."

"I would marry in secret if I wanted to," like a shot from Imogen.

"It wasn't my house," Morgan whispered. "I wanted him to stay."

"What does 'secret' mean?" Keel asked petulantly.

"I know you lie," she whispered.   140

"It means failing to inform your parish priest."

"That's more bureaucratic fiddlesticks!" Morgan said, and an electric shock ran up his thigh when Imogen patted it approvingly.

Kein Juden: No Jews.

"So," Tim said dryly to him, "the Empress Josephine thought, but her failure to obey the regulation meant that the Pope was able to allow the Emperor to eject her from his bed and marry again."

"Then," Keel agreed, "it is a wise precaution."

"It's bosh!" Morgan declared. "And cruel bosh."   145

"Good man!" said Imogen, and gave him another shock, while Frau Keel turned inquiringly to her pastor who said that the rule might be useful to prevent bigamy but was really no reason for dissolving a marriage, whereat she said, "Then it is bosh!" and her husband, outraged, proclaimed, "In my house I will allow nobody to say I am defending bosh!"

She waved him aside, clasped her paws, beamed at Father Timothy and cried, "And now, for adultery!"

"Alas, Madame, adultery by either party is not sufficient cause to annul a marriage."

"So we women are trapped!"

"While you men," charged Imogen, glaring around her, "can freely go your 150 adulterous ways."

The doctor intervened mildly.

"Happily none of this concerns anybody in this room."

"How do you know what concerns me?" she challenged, jumping to her feet, her gripped fists by her lean flanks, her prowlike nose pointing about her like a setter. "I, Imogen Keel, now, at this moment, vant to commit adultery with somebody in this room."

Morgan covered his face in his hands. O God! The confessions! She means me. What shall I say? That I want to kiss her knees?

"Imogen!" Keel blazed at her. "I will not permit this. In delicacy! Not to 155 say, in politeness!"

"Please, Georg!" his wife screamed. "Not again!" She turned to the company. "Always I hear this appeal to politeness and delicacy. It is an excuse. It is an evasion. It is an alibi."

"Aha!" Imogen proclaimed, one hand throwing towards her father's throat an imaginary flag or dagger. "But he has always been excellent at alibis."

Keel slammed his empty brandy glass on the coffee table so hard that its stem snapped. "How fiery she is!" Morgan thought. What a heroic way she has of rearing her head back to the left and lifting her opposite eyebrow to the right. A girl like that would fight for her man to her death—or, if he betrayed her, to his. Has she, he wondered, hair on her back? Father Tim, amused by the whole scene, was saying tactfully but teasingly, "Imogen, there is one other injustice to women that you must hear about. It is that you will in most countries not be permitted to marry, no matter how much you protest, until you have arrived at the age of twelve and your beloved at the age of fourteen."

She burst into laughter. They all laughed with relief.

"Finally," he said tristfully, "priests may not marry at all."   160

"They are nevertheless doing so," the girl commented pertly.

He looked at her, seemed to consider saying something, drank the last drop of his coffee, and did not say it. Frau Keel said it for him, compassionately.

"Only by giving up their priesthood."

"Or more," he agreed in a subdued voice.

"The whole caboodle," Imogen mocked.   165

They talked a little about current examples of priests who had given up everything. The subject trailed away. Keel looked at the window. "Rain," he sighed,
in so weary a voice that the doctor at once rose, and all the others with him. As
the group dissolved towards the entrance hall of the apartment Morgan found
himself trailing behind with Imogen.

"What have you against the doctor?" he asked her.

"He is just like my father. And I hate my father. The only good thing I say
about your doctor is that he helps my mother to put up with my father."

He must drive old Frank home—he must go on helping Frau Keel; they must
talk about the best way to handle Buckley in future; they must have Georg Keel
on one of their excursions; if the girl was lonely perhaps Keel would like to bring
her with them. She was a superb, a wonderful, a marvellous girl, so heroic, so
wild, so passionate. The very first thing they must do was to have Buckley to dinner, and maybe Buckley would bring the girl with him . . . Just then he heard
Frank ask Keel if it was too late for them to have a brief word together before he
left. If this meant the old fool was falling back on some ridiculous, bloody point
of principle about treating Frau Keel . . . As he was making his way towards his
friend to offer him a lift home Frau Keel absently shook his hand, handed him his
hat, opened the door, bade him good night and the door closed on her voice suggesting to Imogen to drive the good Father to his presbytery in her little car. A
minute later he was in the street cursing.

There was not a soul in sight. The rain hung like vests around the lamplights   170
of O'Connell Street. When his car refused to start his rage boiled against that stupid cow Marianne Simcox who must have let water (or something) get into the
petrol. After many fruitless zizzings from the starter he saw Imogen's little blue
car with the priest aboard shoot past in a wake of spray. More zizzings, more
pulling at the choke, a long rest to deflood the carburetor and the engine roared
into life, just as Keel's Mercedes, with the doc aboard, vanished through the rain
towards the bridge and the Dublin road. He circled wildly, followed their tail-
lights, halted twenty yards behind them outside Frank's house, dowsed his lights,
saw him get out and Keel drive away. He ran forward to where Frank was unlocking his iron gate, and clutched his arm beseechingly.

"Frank! I simply must talk to you about Buckley. What is he doing to all
those people? What is he doing to that Imogen girl? For God's sake what's going on in that Keel family? I won't sleep a wink unless you tell me all you know
about them."

The doctor marvelled at him for a moment and then returned to his unlocking.

"I do not feel disposed," he said in his haughtiest voice, holding the gate six
inches ajar for the length of his reply, "to discuss such matters at twelve o'clock at
night, on an open road, under a downpour of rain, and all the less so since, so far
as I can see, nothing is, as you so peculiarly put it, 'going on' that is of any interest to me. Everything seems perfectly normal and in order in the Keel family, except that Herr Keel is a total idiot who seems unable to control his wife, that she
seems to me to have developed a most unseemly sexual interest in Father Timothy
Buckley, that she is intent on divorcing her husband, that their daughter, who is
both impertinent and feckless, is a nymphomaniac, who has quite obviously decided to seduce you, and that I am very glad to say that I need never again lay eyes
on them for the rest of my natural life. And, now, sir, goodnight to you."

With which he entered his drive, banged the metalled gate behind him, and his wet footsteps died into a voice from his front door wailing, "Oh, dachtar, dachtar! Wait for me! I have the umberella here for you. You'll be dhrowneded all together with that aaahful rain . . ."

Morgan spat on the gate, turned and raced for his car, which resolutely re- 175 fused to start. He implored it until its exhausted starter died into the silence of a final click. He got out, kicked its door soundly, and then overwhelmed by all the revelations he had just heard, especially the one about Imogen and himself, he walked home through the empty streets of L——, singing love songs from the *Barber* and *Don Giovanni*° at the top of his voice to the summer rain.

One of the more pleasantly disconcerting things about wilful man is that his most table-thumping decisions rarely conclude the matter in hand. There is always time for a further option. Every score is no better than half-time. *Viz:*—

1. That July our poor, dear friend Tim Buckley left us for a chin-pimple of a village called Four Noughts (the vulgarization of a Gaelic word meaning Stark Naked) on the backside of Slievenamuck.° We loyally cursed His Lordship the bishop, while feeling that he had had no option. For weeks the dogs in the streets had been barking, "Im-o-gen Keel." At the farewell party Tim assured us that the bish had neither hand, act nor part in it. He had himself asked His Lordship for a transfer. He asked us to pray for him. He said sadly that he believed he was gone beyond it. The die was cast, the Rubicon° crossed, it was the Ides of March,° and so forth and so on.

One effect of this event (Dolly Lynch reporting, after her usual survey of her master's wastepaper basket) was that Mister Myles had been invited to dinner with the dachtar at his earliest convenience.

2. That August we heard that Frau Keel was claiming a separation from her husband *a mensa et a thoro*;° that she was also applying for a papal annulment of her marriage on the ground of his impotence, which meant that she was ready to swear that Imogen was not his child. Herr Keel, we gathered, had knocked her down, broken one of her ribs with a kick and left for Stuttgart swearing that he would foil her if it cost him his last deutschmark.

Mister Myles was by now dining every week with the doctor, who was also 180 (Dolly Lynch's knuckle suspended outside the dining room door) seeing Frau Keel regularly, who (Dolly Lynch's hand on the doorknob) was also in constant consultation, through Imogen, with Father Tim Buckley in his exile on Slievenamuck.

3. That September Tim Buckley disappeared from Four Noughts, Imogen Keel disappeared from the Keel flat, and both were reported to have been seen at Shannon Airport boarding a plane for Stockholm. This blow brought us down. Tim's way of living life had been to tell us how to live it. Now that he was starting to live it himself he was no better than any of us. He was the only one of us who had both faced and been free of the world of men, of women, of children,

---

Barber and *Don Giovanni*: *Barber of Seville* and *Don Giovanni,* comic operas by Mozart. *Slievenamuck*: Literally, garbage hill.   *Rubicon*: A river that Caesar crossed to begin a major war.   *Ides of March*: March 15, the day the seer foretold that Caesar would be killed.   *a mensa et a thoro*: Legal term meaning a separation from bed and board, an action preliminary to formal divorce.

of the flesh. Now we knew that it cannot be done. You must not put your toe into the sea if you do not want to swim in it.

Myles was by now dining with Frank Breen three times a week, friendship glued by gossip.

4.   October. Dreadful news from Stuttgart. Herr Keel had accidentally killed himself while cleaning a shotgun. When the news came Morgan was having tea with Frau Keel. She collapsed, calling for the doctor. Morgan drove at once to Frank's house and brought him back to her. For the rest of that month Myles was dining every night with the doctor.

5.   By November Dolly Lynch reported that Mister Myles had stopped dining with the doctor, but Mrs. Keel, she spat, was coming as often as "tree taimes every bluddy wee-uk." When we heard this we looked at one another. Our eyes said, "Could it be possible?" We asked Morgan. He was in no doubt about it.

"Buckley was right!" he stormed. "The man is a sexual maniac! A libertine!   185 A corrupter of women! A traitor and a liar. As that foolish woman will discover before the year is out."

It was a spring wedding, and the reception was one of the gayest, most crowded, most lavish the town had ever seen. The metal sheeting was gone from the gate, the cypresses cut down, the warning signs inside the gate removed, the brass plate removed, the conservatory packed with flowers, the only drink served was champagne. The doctor became Frank to every Tom and Harry. For the first time we found out that his wife's name was Victorine. With his hair tinted he looked ten years younger. Long before the reception ended he was going around whispering to everybody, as a dead secret, that Victorine was expecting.

6.   Morgan, naturally, did not attend the wedding. He took off for the day with Marianne Simcox, and they have since been taking off every fine Sunday in her red Mustang, together with Morgan's mother, in search of faceless churchlets in fallow fields where the only sound is the munching of cattle. His mother prepares the lunch. Marianne reads out his own poems to him. They both feed him like a child with titbits from their fingers. But who knows the outcome of any mortal thing? Buckley—there is no denying it—had a point when he insisted that man's most ingenious invention is man, that to create others we must first imagine ourselves, and that to keep us from wandering, or wondering, in some other direction where a greater truth may lie, we set up all sorts of roadblocks and traffic signals. Morgan has told his Marianne that he has always admired the virginal type. It is enough to put any girl off her stroke. A wink of a brass plate in a country road set him off on one tack. A wink from her might set him off on another. What should she do? Obey his traffic signs, or acknowledge the truth—that he is a born liar—and start showing him a glimpse of thigh?

Heaven help the women of the world, always wondering what the blazes their men's next graven image will be.

Questions for Close Reading for Character and Psychology

1. O'Faoláin tells us that Marianne Simcox cries into a "mouse-sized handkerchief." How do you respond to her after reading that description?
2. How does Myles's initial reaction to doctors, on the first two pages of the story, help establish our expectations of what Dr. Francis Breen will be like?

3. What descriptive passage is most effective in characterizing Dr. Breen before we meet him?

4. Which is the best character analysis performed by another character in this story? Why?

5. The narrator says of Morgan Myles and Breen: "even to look at they were a mismatch." What personality traits match or do not match among these characters?

6. Deep in the story, the narrator explains that he grew up with Frank Breen and that "he had simply always been a bit balmy." What evidence does the story give us that the narrator is right?

7. Imogen Keel is very direct—scandalously direct. What are the most important ways in which she differs from Myles, Breen, and Buckley? How does her contrasting character help illuminate their characters?

Questions for Interpretation

New Critical

1. What is the meaning of the title of the story? What road signs do these characters see in their own life, and to what extent do they abide by them? How can they be interpreted as helping to guide the development of character? Does the story say we must abide by such signs?

2. Do you feel the story arises from the personality of the characters, or from their situations? What drives this story: character or circumstance?

Psychoanalytic

3. The Freudian view suggests that people's unconscious desires motivate them. The libido—the sexual drive—is ordinarily controlled by the superego, the mind's censor. The ego expresses itself in a balance of these forces. To what extent are the characters motivated by unconscious desires? What happens when some of the desires become conscious?

4. Imogen Keel is not a repressed character. She states openly near the end of the story, "I . . . vant to commit adultery with somebody in this room!" In what ways could this story be said to be a conflict between repression and expression of desires?

5. What does Imogen's hairiness symbolize?

Reader Response

5. What responses do you have to individual characters in the story? List each character and the response you give to him or her. Who do you like, and who do you find yourself disliking? How do your responses to individual characters affect your interpretation of the entire story? Is it clear that O'Faoláin controls your responses in order to achieve an overall effect?

Feminist

6. Morgan Myles begins the story with Marianne Simcox and ends it with her planning picnics with "Morgan's mother, in search of faceless church-lets in fallow fields." Is Morgan Myles the protagonist in the story? Do the men in the story treat the women unfairly? Is the story sexist?

7. Does the fact that Morgan Myles is a mama's boy explain the final out-come of the story? Does he have a psychological problem rooted in gen-der confusion?

STYLE AND THEME

Style: Formal, Informal, and Ornamented

Style includes all the verbal qualities of a short story. Therefore, you could isolate virtually any interesting use of language and claim it is a key to un-derstanding the style of a story. For example, you might feel that the style of "The Masque of the Red Death" is dominated by sensuous description, em-phasizing colors, light and darkness, and architectural details. You might feel that the **informal style** of everyday conversation is one of the most charm-ing aspects of O'Faoláin's story. Some stories impress you with their **formal style**: use of uncommon words, and long sentences. Poe's language is formal, not conversational: telling us that "Prince Prospero was happy and dauntless and sagacious" is exact, and quite unlike anything we would say. It gives us the feeling of being removed from this scene, as if it all happened long ago in a distant place. Most of the stories in the album reflect a modern infor-mality. However, each in its way uses so many different stylistic choices that you cannot state simply what its style is.

Ornamented styles are those formal or informal styles that depend on special techniques for their success.

- *Metaphor*   A **metaphor** implies much more than it says, usually through a strong image. For example, when O'Faoláin refers to Marianne Simcox's "mouse-sized handkerchief" he implies that she is herself mousy. In that same story, Morgan Myles's mother points to the effects of his gumboil: "You're as cranky as a bag of cats." These comparisons are metaphoric (the second is technically a simile) and marvelous because they are so un-expected. They enrich the story for us while also pointing toward some of its deeper meaning.

- *Imagery*   **Images** are rich descriptions that make a strong appeal to our senses of sight, sound, touch, taste, and smell. Occasionally an image will appeal to more than one sense, such as Cheever's reference to cordite— the smell left over after explosions, which, as he uses it, invokes not only a smell but also a sound.

- *Patterns of repetition*   The repetition of Prince Prospero passing from one carefully described apartment to the next is patterned carefully so as to build up suspense. In Cheever's "The Swimmer," we find a curious pattern of repetition right from the first, but it is in the repetition of dialogue: "I *drank* too much last night"; "I *drank* too much"; "we all *drank* too much"; "I *drank* too much of that claret." That message repeats itself through the story, along with the description of one swimming pool after another. We learn that these repetitions—almost refrains—are central to the story's significance.

Theme and Variations

The theme of a short story is its subject matter—what it is about. Until you have given the story a close reading and begun your interpretation, you may not know what that theme is. The theme of "The Pot of Basil" is so complex that probably no two readers will agree on what it is. You might feel that the theme is love confounded by Lisabetta's dominant, insensitive, and criminal brothers. Other readers may emphasize the theme of the feminine response of madness as a technique for coping with a cruel masculine world. If you perceive the theme of this story as rooted in grief, you may imagine many variations on that theme, all relevant to the story. Most stories have several themes. Writers make conscious decisions about most stylistic possibilities; they think they know what their story is about (its theme), but often they find that they, too, have to interpret what they have written to discover their theme.

John Cheever has been praised for writing on the theme of suburban American life. Certainly "The Swimmer" is about suburban New York, with its wealth, privilege, social snobbery, and its indulgences. Neddy Merrill fits the scene perfectly, with his concerns about drinking, about what kind of stroke he uses in the pool, about what distinguishes each of the neighbors whose pools he swims through on his way home. He is conversant about pools, tennis, golf, houses, and investments, although he thinks it vulgar to talk about money. He thinks of himself not only as acceptable but as several rungs up the social ladder.

Neddy lives in a world of illusion. He drinks vastly too much. His scheme of swimming home is at first comical but ultimately mad. His neighbors—and his mistress—regard him with horror. We are left with the question of whether he ever comes to understand reality. "The Swimmer" treats a range of themes all connected by the lifestyle and perceptions of Neddy Merrill, who begins the story with one hand "around a glass of gin."

John Cheever (1912–1982)

For much of his later life, John Cheever drank compulsively—enough to ruin his relationship with his family. Even with psychiatric help, he found it impossible to change his habits. "The Swimmer," with its suburban locale and its compulsive drinking, comes from The Stories of John Cheever *(1964). His first collection,* The Way Some People Live, *was published in 1942, but his reputation was solidified by* The Enormous Radio and Other Stories *(1953).* Collected Stories *was published in 1978. His journals are painfully honest, almost ruthless in their self-judgment. They show a writer tortured by his own weaknesses but aware of every breath he took, every gesture he made, and every hesitation on the part of others. He was an astonishing observer of his own life.*

THE SWIMMER 1964

It was one of those midsummer Sundays when everyone sits around saying, "I *drank* too much last night." You might have heard it whispered by the parishioners leaving church, heard it from the lips of the priest himself, struggling with his cassock in the *vestiarium,*° heard it from the golf links and the tennis courts, heard it from the wildlife preserve where the leader of the Audubon group was suffering from a terrible hangover. "I *drank* too much," said Donald Westerhazy. "We all *drank* too much," said Lucinda Merrill. "It must have been the wine," said Helen Westerhazy. "I *drank* too much of that claret."

This was at the edge of the Westerhazys' pool. The pool, fed by an artesian well with a high iron content, was a pale shade of green. It was a fine day. In the west there was a massive stand of cumulus cloud so like a city seen from a distance—from the bow of an approaching ship—that it might have had a name. Lisbon. Hackensack. The sun was hot. Neddy Merrill sat by the green water, one hand in it, one around a glass of gin. He was a slender man—he seemed to have the especial slenderness of youth—and while he was far from young he had slid down his banister that morning and given the bronze backside of Aphrodite° on the hall table a smack, as he jogged toward the smell of coffee in his dining room. He might have been compared to a summer's day, particularly the last hours of one, and while he lacked a tennis racket or a sail bag the impression was definitely one of youth, sport, and clement weather. He had been swimming and now he was breathing deeply, stertorously as if he could gulp into his lungs the components of that moment, the heat of the sun, the intenseness of his pleasure. It all seemed to flow into his chest. His own house stood in Bullet Park, eight miles to the south, where his four beautiful daughters would have had their lunch and might be playing tennis. Then it occurred to him that by taking a dogleg to the southwest he could reach his home by water.

His life was not confining and the delight he took in this observation could not be explained by its suggestion of escape. He seemed to see, with a cartographer's eye, that string of swimming pools, that quasi-subterranean stream that curved across the county. He had made a discovery, a contribution to modern geography; he would name the stream Lucinda after his wife. He was not a practical joker nor was he a fool but he was determinedly original and had a vague and modest idea of himself as a legendary figure. The day was beautiful and it seemed to him that a long swim might enlarge and celebrate its beauty.

He took off a sweater that was hung over his shoulders and dove in. He had an inexplicable contempt for men who did not hurl themselves into pools. He

---

vestiarium: Dressing Room. *Aphrodite:* Venus.

swam a choppy crawl, breathing either with every stroke or every fourth stroke and counting somewhere well in the back of his mind the one-two one-two of a flutter kick. It was not a serviceable stroke for long distances but the domestication of swimming had saddled the sport with some customs and in his part of the world a crawl was customary. To be embraced and sustained by the light green water was less a pleasure, it seemed, than the resumption of a natural condition, and he would have liked to swim without trunks, but this was not possible, considering his project. He hoisted himself up on the far curb—he never used the ladder—and started across the lawn. When Lucinda asked where he was going he said he was going to swim home.

The only maps and charts he had to go by were remembered or imaginary but these were clear enough. First there were the Grahams, the Hammers, the Lears, the Howlands, and the Crosscups. He would cross Ditmar Street to the Bunkers and come, after a short portage, to the Levys, the Welchers, and the public pool in Lancaster. Then there were the Hallorans, the Sachses, the Biswangers, Shirley Adams, the Gilmartins, and the Clydes. The day was lovely, and that he lived in a world so generously supplied with water seemed like a clemency, a beneficence. His heart was high and he ran across the grass. Making his way home by an uncommon route gave him the feeling that he was a pilgrim, an explorer, a man with a destiny, and he knew that he would find friends all along the way; friends would line the banks of the Lucinda River.

He went through a hedge that separated the Westerhazys' land from the Grahams', walked under some flowering apple trees, passed the shed that housed their pump and filter, and came out at the Grahams' pool. "Why, Neddy," Mrs. Graham said, "what a marvelous surprise. I've been trying to get you on the phone all morning. Here, let me get you a drink." He saw then, like any explorer, that the hospitable customs and traditions of the natives would have to be handled with diplomacy if he was ever going to reach his destination. He did not want to mystify or seem rude to the Grahams nor did he have the time to linger there. He swam the length of their pool and joined them in the sun and was rescued, a few minutes later, by the arrival of two carloads of friends from Connecticut. During the uproarious reunions he was able to slip away. He went down by the front of the Grahams' house, stepped over a thorny hedge, and crossed a vacant lot to the Hammers'. Mrs. Hammer, looking up from her roses, saw him swim by although she wasn't quite sure who it was. The Lears heard him splashing past the open windows of their living room. The Howlands and the Crosscups were away. After leaving the Howlands' he crossed Ditmar Street and started for the Bunkers', where he could hear, even at that distance, the noise of a party.

The water refracted the sound of voices and laughter and seemed to suspend it in midair. The Bunkers' pool was on a rise and he climbed some stairs to a terrace where twenty-five or thirty men and women were drinking. The only person in the water was Rusty Towers, who floated there on a rubber raft. Oh, how bonny and lush were the banks of the Lucinda River! Prosperous men and women gathered by the sapphire-colored waters while caterer's men in white coats passed them cold gin. Overhead a red de Haviland trainer was circling around and around and around in the sky with something like the glee of a child in a swing. Ned felt a passing affection for the scene, a tenderness for the gathering, as if it was something he might touch. In the distance he heard thunder. As soon as Enid Bunker saw him she began to scream: "Oh, look who's here! What a marvelous surprise!

When Lucinda said that you couldn't come I thought I'd *die*." She made her way to him through the crowd, and when they had finished kissing she led him to the bar, a progress that was slowed by the fact that he stopped to kiss eight or ten other women and shake the hands of as many men. A smiling bartender he had seen at a hundred parties gave him a gin and tonic and he stood by the bar for a moment, anxious not to get stuck in any conversation that would delay his voyage. When he seemed about to be surrounded he dove in and swam close to the side to avoid colliding with Rusty's raft. At the far end of the pool he bypassed the Tomlinsons with a broad smile and jogged up the garden path. The gravel cut his feet but this was the only unpleasantness. The party was confined to the pool, and as he went toward the house he heard the brilliant, watery sound of voices fade, heard the noise of a radio from the Bunkers' kitchen, where someone was listening to a ball game. Sunday afternoon. He made his way through the parked cars and down the grassy border of their driveway to Alewives Lane. He did not want to be seen on the road in his bathing trunks but there was no traffic and he made the short distance to the Levys' driveway, marked with a PRIVATE PROPERTY sign and a green tube for *The New York Times*. All the doors and windows of the big house were open but there were no signs of life; not even a dog barked. He went around the side of the house to the pool and saw that the Levys had only recently left. Glasses and bottles and dishes of nuts were on a table at the deep end, where there was a bathhouse or gazebo, hung with Japanese lanterns. After swimming the pool he got himself a glass and poured a drink. It was his fourth or fifth drink and he had swum nearly half the length of the Lucinda River. He felt tired, clean, and pleased at that moment to be alone; pleased with everything.

It would storm. The stand of cumulus cloud—that city—had risen and darkened, and while he sat there he heard the percussiveness of thunder again. The de Haviland trainer was still circling overhead and it seemed to Ned that he could almost hear the pilot laugh with pleasure in the afternoon; but when there was another peal of thunder he took off for home. A train whistle blew and he wondered what time it had gotten to be. Four? Five? He thought of the provincial station at that hour, where a waiter, his tuxedo concealed by a raincoat, a dwarf with some flowers wrapped in newspaper, and a woman who had been crying would be waiting for the local. It was suddenly growing dark; it was that moment when the pin-headed birds seem to organize their song into some acute and knowledgeable recognition of the storm's approach. Then there was a fine noise of rushing water from the crown of an oak at his back, as if a spigot there had been turned. Then the noise of fountains came from the crowns of all the tall trees. Why did he love storms, what was the meaning of his excitement when the door sprang open and the rain wind fled rudely up the stairs, why had the simple task of shutting the windows of an old house seemed fitting and urgent, why did the first watery notes of a storm wind have for him the unmistakable sound of good news, cheer, glad tidings? Then there was an explosion, a smell of cordite, and rain lashed the Japanese lanterns that Mrs. Levy had bought in Kyoto the year before last, or was it the year before that?

He stayed in the Levys' gazebo until the storm had passed. The rain had cooled the air and he shivered. The force of the wind had stripped a maple of its red and yellow leaves and scattered them over the grass and the water. Since it was midsummer the tree must be blighted, and yet he felt a peculiar sadness at this sign of autumn. He braced his shoulders, emptied his glass, and started for the Welchers' pool. This meant crossing the Lindleys' riding ring and he was surprised to find it overgrown with grass and all the jumps dismantled. He wondered if the Lindleys had sold their horses or gone away for the summer and put them out to board. He seemed to remember having heard something about the Lindleys and their horses but the memory was unclear. On he went, barefoot through the wet grass, to the Welchers', where he found their pool was dry.

This breach in his chain of water disappointed him absurdly, and he felt like some explorer who seeks a torrential headwater and finds a dead stream. He was disappointed and mystified. It was common enough to go away for the summer but no one ever drained his pool. The Welchers had definitely gone away. The pool furniture was folded, stacked, and covered with a tarpaulin. The bathhouse was locked. All the windows of the house were shut, and when he went around to the driveway in front he saw a FOR SALE sign nailed to a tree. When had he last heard from the Welchers—when, that is, had he and Lucinda last regretted an invitation to dine with them? It seemed only a week or so ago. Was his memory failing or had he so disciplined it in the repression of unpleasant facts that he had damaged his sense of the truth? Then in the distance he heard the sound of a tennis game. This cheered him, cleared away all his apprehensions and let him regard the overcast sky and the cold air with indifference. This was the day that Neddy Merrill swam across the county. That was the day! He started off then for his most difficult portage. 10

Had you gone for a Sunday afternoon ride that day you might have seen him, close to naked, standing on the shoulders of Route 424, waiting for a chance to cross. You might have wondered if he was the victim of foul play, had his car broken down, or was he merely a fool. Standing barefoot in the deposits of the highway—beer cans, rags, and blowout patches—exposed to all kinds of ridicule, he seemed pitiful. He had known when he started that this was a part of his journey—it had been on his maps—but confronted with the lines of traffic, worming through the summery light, he found himself unprepared. He was laughed at, jeered at, a beer can was thrown at him, and he had no dignity or humor to bring to the situation. He could have gone back, back to the Westerhazys', where Lucinda would still be sitting in the sun. He had signed nothing, vowed nothing, pledged nothing, not even to himself. Why, believing as he did, that all human obduracy was susceptible to common sense, was he unable to turn back? Why was he determined to complete his journey even if it meant putting his life in danger? At what point had this prank, this joke, this piece of horseplay become serious? He could not go back, he could not even recall with any clearness the green water at the Westerhazys', the sense of inhaling the day's components, the friendly and relaxed voices saying that they had *drunk* too much. In the space of an hour, more or less, he had covered a distance that made his return impossible.

An old man, tooling down the highway at fifteen miles an hour, let him get to the middle of the road, where there was a grass divider. Here he was exposed to the ridicule of the northbound traffic, but after ten or fifteen minutes he was able to cross. From here he had only a short walk to the Recreation Center at the edge of the village of Lancaster, where there were some handball courts and a public pool.

The effect of the water on voices, the illusion of brilliance and suspense, was the same here as it had been at the Bunkers' but the sounds here were louder, harsher, and more shrill, and as soon as he entered the crowded enclosure he was confronted with regimentation. "ALL SWIMMERS MUST TAKE A SHOWER BEFORE USING THE POOL. ALL SWIMMERS MUST USE THE FOOTBATH. ALL SWIMMERS MUST WEAR THEIR IDENTIFICATION DISKS." He took a shower, washed his feet in a cloudy and bitter solution, and made his way to the edge of the water. It stank of chlorine and looked to him like a sink. A pair of lifeguards in a pair of towers blew police whistles at what seemed to be regular intervals and abused the swimmers through a public address system. Neddy remembered the sapphire water at the Bunkers' with longing and thought that he might contaminate himself—damage his own prosperousness and charm—by swimming in this murk, but he reminded himself that he was an explorer, a pilgrim, and that this was merely a stagnant bend in the Lucinda River. He dove, scowling with distaste, into the chlorine and had to swim with his head above water to avoid collisions, but even so he was bumped into, splashed, and jostled. When he got to the shallow end both lifeguards were shouting at him: "Hey, you, you without the identification disk, get outa the water." He did, but they had no way of pursuing him and he went through the reek of suntan oil and chlorine out through the hurricane fence and passed the handball courts. By crossing the road he entered the wooded part of the Halloran estate. The woods were not cleared and the footing was treacherous and difficult until he reached the lawn and the clipped beech hedge that encircled their pool.

The Hallorans were friends, an elderly couple of enormous wealth who seemed to bask in the suspicion that they might be Communists. They were zealous reformers but they were not Communists, and yet when they were accused, as they sometimes were, of subversion, it seemed to gratify and excite them. Their beech hedge was yellow and he guessed this had been blighted like the Levys' maple. He called hullo, hullo, to warn the Hallorans of his approach, to palliate his invasion of their privacy. The Hallorans, for reasons that had never been explained to him, did not wear bathing suits. No explanations were in order, really. Their nakedness was a detail in their uncompromising zeal for reform and he stepped politely out of his trunks before he went through the opening in the hedge.

Mrs. Halloran, a stout woman with white hair and a serene face, was reading the *Times*. Mr. Halloran was taking beech leaves out of the water with a scoop. They seemed not surprised or displeased to see him. Their pool was perhaps the oldest in the country, a fieldstone rectangle, fed by a brook. It had no filter or pump and its waters were the opaque gold of the stream.   15

"I'm swimming across the county," Ned said.

"Why, I didn't know one could," exclaimed Mrs. Halloran.

"Well, I've made it from the Westerhazys'," Ned said. "That must be about four miles."

He left his trunks at the deep end, walked to the shallow end, and swam this stretch. As he was pulling himself out of the water he heard Mrs. Halloran say, "We've been *terribly* sorry to hear about all your misfortunes, Neddy."

"My misfortunes?" Ned asked. "I don't know what you mean."   20

"Why, we heard that you'd sold the house and that your poor children . . ."

"I don't recall having sold the house," Ned said, "and the girls are at home."

"Yes," Mrs. Halloran sighed. "Yes . . ." Her voice filled the air with an unseasonable melancholy and Ned spoke briskly. "Thank you for the swim."

"Well, have a nice trip," said Mrs. Halloran.

Beyond the hedge he pulled on his trunks and fastened them. They were 25 loose and he wondered if, during the space of an afternoon, he could have lost some weight. He was cold and he was tired and the naked Hallorans and their dark water had depressed him. The swim was too much for his strength but how could he have guessed this, sliding down the banister that morning and sitting in the Westerhazys' sun? His arms were lame. His legs felt rubbery and ached at the joints. The worst of it was the cold in his bones and the feeling that he might never be warm again. Leaves were falling down around him and he smelled wood smoke on the wind. Who would be burning wood at this time of year?

He needed a drink. Whiskey would warm him, pick him up, carry him through the last of his journey, refresh his feeling that it was original and valorous to swim across the county. Channel swimmers took brandy. He needed a stimulant. He crossed the lawn in front of the Hallorans' house and went down a little path to where they had built a house for their only daughter, Helen, and her husband, Eric Sachs. The Sachses' pool was small and he found Helen and her husband there.

"Oh, *Neddy*," Helen said. "Did you lunch at Mother's?"

"Not *really*," Ned said. "I *did* stop to see your parents." This seemed to be explanation enough. "I'm terribly sorry to break in on you like this but I've taken a chill and I wonder if you'd give me a drink."

"Why, I'd *love* to," Helen said, "but there hasn't been anything in this house to drink since Eric's operation. That was three years ago."

Was he losing his memory, had his gift for concealing painful facts let him 30 forget that he had sold his house, that his children were in trouble, and that his friend had been ill? His eyes slipped from Eric's face to his abdomen, where he saw three pale, sutured scars, two of them at least a foot long. Gone was his navel, and what, Neddy thought, would the roving hand, bed-checking one's gifts at 3 A.M., make of a belly with no navel, no link to birth, this breach in the succession?

"I'm sure you can get a drink at the Biswangers'," Helen said. "They're having an enormous do. You can hear it from here. Listen!"

She raised her head and from across the road, the lawns, the gardens, the woods, the fields, he heard again the brilliant noise of voices over water. "Well, I'll get wet," he said, still feeling that he had no freedom of choice about his means of travel. He dove into the Sachses' cold water and, gasping, close to drowning, made his way from one end of the pool to the other. "Lucinda and I want *terribly* to see you," he said over his shoulder, his face set toward the Biswangers'. "We're sorry it's been so long and we'll call you *very* soon."

He crossed some fields to the Biswangers' and the sounds of revelry there. They would be honored to give him a drink, they would be happy to give him a drink. The Biswangers invited him and Lucinda for dinner four times a year, six weeks in advance. They were always rebuffed and yet they continued to send out their invitations, unwilling to comprehend the rigid and undemocratic realities of their society. They were the sort of people who discussed the price of things at cocktails, exchanged market tips during dinner, and after dinner told dirty stories to mixed company. They did not belong to Neddy's set—they were not even on Lucinda's Christmas-card list. He went toward their pool with feelings of indifference, charity, and some unease, since it seemed to be getting dark and these were the longest days of the year. The party when he joined it was noisy and large. Grace Biswanger was the kind of hostess who asked the optometrist, the veterinarian, the real-estate dealer, and the dentist. No one was swimming and the twilight, reflected on the water of the pool, had a wintry gleam. There was a bar and he started for this. When Grace Biswanger saw him she came toward him, not affectionately as he had every right to expect, but bellicosely.

"Why, this party has everything," she said loudly, "including a gate crasher."

She could not deal him a social blow—there was no question about this and he did not flinch. "As a gate crasher," he asked politely, "do I rate a drink?" 35

"Suit yourself," she said. "You don't seem to pay much attention to invitations."

She turned her back on him and joined some guests, and he went to the bar and ordered a whiskey. The bartender served him but he served him rudely. His was a world in which the caterer's men kept the social score, and to be rebuffed by a part-time barkeep meant that he had suffered some loss of social esteem. Or perhaps the man was new and uninformed. Then he heard Grace at his back say: "They went for broke overnight—nothing but income—and he showed up drunk one Sunday and asked us to loan him five thousand dollars. . . ." She was always talking about money. It was worse than eating your peas off a knife. He dove into the pool, swam its length and went away.

The next pool on his list, the last but two, belonged to his old mistress, Shirley Adams. If he had suffered any injuries at the Biswangers' they would be cured here. Love—sexual roughhouse in fact—was the supreme elixir, the pain killer, the brightly colored pill that would put the spring back into his step, the joy of life in his heart. They had had an affair last week, last month, last year. He couldn't remember. It was he who had broken it off, his was the upper hand, and he stepped through the gate of the wall that surrounded her pool with nothing so considered as self-confidence. It seemed in a way to be his pool, as the lover, particularly the illicit lover, enjoys the possessions of his mistress with an authority unknown to holy matrimony. She was there, her hair the color of brass, but her figure, at the edge of the lighted, cerulean water, excited in him no profound memories. It had been, he thought, a lighthearted affair, although she had wept when he broke it off. She seemed confused to see him and he wondered if she was still wounded. Would she, God forbid, weep again?

"What do you want?" she asked.

"I'm swimming across the county." 40

"Good Christ. Will you ever grow up?"

"What's the matter?"

"If you've come here for money," she said, "I won't give you another cent."

"You could give me a drink."

"I could but I won't. I'm not alone." 45

"Well, I'm on my way."

He dove in and swam the pool, but when he tried to haul himself up onto the curb he found that the strength in his arms and shoulders had gone, and he paddled to the ladder and climbed out. Looking over his shoulder he saw, in the lighted bathhouse, a young man. Going out onto the dark lawn he smelled chrysanthemums or marigolds—some stubborn autumnal fragrance—on the night air, strong as gas. Looking overhead he saw that the stars had come out, but why should he seem to see Andromeda, Cepheus, and Cassiopeia? What had become of the constellations of midsummer? He began to cry.

It was probably the first time in his adult life that he had ever cried, certainly the first time in his life that he had ever felt so miserable, cold, tired, and bewildered. He could not understand the rudeness of the caterer's barkeep or the rudeness of a mistress who had come to him on her knees and showered his trousers with tears. He had swum too long, he had been immersed too long, and his nose and his throat were sore from the water. What he needed then was a drink, some company, and some clean, dry clothes, and while he could have cut directly across the road to his home he went on to the Gilmartins' pool. Here, for the first time in his life, he did not dive but went down the steps into the icy water and swam a hobbled sidestroke that he might have learned as a youth. He staggered with fatigue on his way to the Clydes' and paddled the length of their pool, stopping again and again with his hand on the curb to rest. He climbed up the ladder and wondered if he had the strength to get home. He had done what he wanted, he had swum the county, but he was so stupefied with exhaustion that his triumph seemed vague. Stooped, holding on to the gateposts for support, he turned up the driveway of his own house.

The place was dark. Was it so late that they had all gone to bed? Had Lucinda stayed at the Westerhazys' for supper? Had the girls joined her there or gone someplace else? Hadn't they agreed, as they usually did on Sunday, to regret all their invitations and stay at home? He tried the garage doors to see what cars were in but the doors were locked and rust came off the handles onto his hands. Going toward the house, he saw that the force of the thunderstorm had knocked one of the rain gutters loose. It hung down over the front door like an umbrella rib, but it could be fixed in the morning. The house was locked, and he thought that the stupid cook or the stupid maid must have locked the place up until he remembered that it had been some time since they had employed a maid or a cook. He shouted, pounded on the door, tried to force it with his shoulder, and then, looking in at the windows, saw that the place was empty.

Questions for Close Reading for Style and Theme

Note: questions relating to theme immediately get you into interpretation, so some of these questions can also apply to the interpretation of the whole story.

1. Is the style of the story informal (conversational) or formal?
2. In the second paragraph, Cheever says that Neddy Merrill "might have been compared to a summer's day, particularly the last hours of one." Is this a stylistic or thematic detail? In what ways does this metaphoric comparison give us a glimpse of the theme of the story?
3. Early in the story, Neddy sees the gathering cumulus clouds, and "in the distance he heard thunder." How do Cheever's images of the clouds and the weather prepare us for the ending of the story?
4. The descriptions of the Bunkers' crowded pool and the Levys' empty pool contrast sharply with that of the public pool. Which images, appealing to which senses, most effectively establish the contrast that Neddy feels?
5. At one point Neddy thinks with pride, "This was the day that Neddy Merrill swam across the county." Cheever uses the metaphor of swimming from

swimming pool to swimming pool to comment on the journey of Neddy's life. How does it begin to reveal the theme or themes of the story?

6. How does the way people speak to Neddy when he begins his swim differ from the way they speak at the end? Are the differences stylistic?

Questions for Interpretation

New Critical

1. Examine the imagery of weather, sky, flowers, and nature in the story. How does Cheever use this imagery to reveal the inner nature of Neddy Merrill and the quality of his life? What does the imagery reveal? Cheever commented that the imagery of the constellations near the end of the story was crucial to its understanding. Neddy looks up "to see Andromeda, Cepheus, and Cassiopeia." He asks, "What had become of the constellations of midsummer?" Why does he cry—for the first time in his adult life—when he realizes that summer is gone and the winter constellations have appeared? What is their metaphoric significance?

Psychoanalytic

2. At one point Neddy's mistress snaps at him, "Good Christ. Will you ever grow up?" What feelings does Neddy have about love or sex? Is his naming the string of swimming pools "Lucinda River" a hint about his psychological problems? What emotional needs does Neddy have? What seem to be his emotional inadequacies? Why does his ex-mistress worry about his ever growing up? Are swimming pools sexual symbols?

Reader Response

3. What response do you have toward Neddy Merrill? How do stylistic and thematic aspects of the story contribute toward your responses to the lifestyle portrayed in the story? Do you respond positively to any character who appears in the story? How does the central importance of drinking, to Neddy and his friends, affect you?

Feminist

4. In what sense are the genders expected to play specific roles in Neddy's society? Are women equal partners in the society? Does Neddy expect them to be equal or want them to be equal? How strong are the characters Cheever creates? Is Neddy comfortable in the gender role that society has assigned him? What metaphors in the story convince you one way or the other? What feminist themes emerge from the metaphors in the story?

Political-Economic

5. The style of the story reveals Neddy as sophisticated, judgmental, and snobbish. His friends are wealthy, but the only characters who work in the story are caterers, bartenders, and servants. How might you interpret

Neddy's story taking into account the apparent economic inequities he accepts as okay? Does Neddy exploit the laborers in the story? Is the story a critique of a life of privilege?

PLOT AND NARRATIVE STRUCTURE

Plot in short fiction implies a sequence of actions that hold together by virtue of their causing and shaping the actions that follow. Morgan Myles's boil leads him to Dr. Breen, thence to Father Tim and their afternoons of conversation. All of Father Tim's lectures on psychology seem to have prepared him to run off with Imogen Keel, although the reader might be only aware of that in hindsight. Causality distinguishes carefully plotted stories because the actions seem to logically cause what follows. Certain narrative structures either omit or mute causality to produce a random effect, partly to emphasize the apparent randomness of reality.

Narratives take many shapes. Here are three of the most common.

- *Chronological* Most stories are **chronological** in that the action follows linear time. As in "The Pot of Basil," events are told to us in the same order as they happen in time.
- *Flashback* Many modern stories use a popular film technique: the **flashback**. This technique involves a narrative whose present-time action is interrupted to narrate selected past actions. O'Faoláin's story uses that technique.
- *Nonlinear* Some modern stories defy time and continuity, using instead **nonlinear** action. John Cheever's "The Swimmer" appears at first to be linear and continuous, but soon you realize that it began in the summer and ended in the winter, and Neddy Merrill has lost touch with time and reality. Modern authors who use magical realism, a technique blending realistic details with events that seem impossible (such as Lorenzo's speaking to Lisabetta after death), find this technique useful because it adds to the mystery. Time is fragmented, the sequence of events is fractured, and the reader is responsible for piecing things together.

The plots of short stories have many qualities in common, even if each of them is unique. For example, many stories begin *in medias res*—in the middle of things—and in order to bring us up to date with what has happened, the author must provide exposition. Exposition tells us what has happened so far—at least enough so we can read the story intelligently. "The Swimmer" begins with a paragraph that tells us that "it was one of those midsummer Sundays when everyone sits around saying, 'I *drank* too much last night.'" And the rest of the paragraph fills us in on the usual "scene" before Neddy Merrill enters swimming. Similarly, when Poe opens his story by saying, "The 'Red Death' had long devastated the country," and goes on to speak of the Avatar of blood, he begins the exposition necessary to understand what is about to happen.

The well-plotted story depends also on conflict between the protagonist and the antagonist. The **antagonist**—the villain—is either a character or an abstract force that restricts the action of the protagonist. The conflict may be direct, indirect, or merely threatened. In "The Masque of the Red Death" the protagonist is Prince Prospero and the antagonist is the Red Death, the plague that Prospero thinks he can avoid. The conflict between Prospero and the Red Death is threatened from the first line of the story, and its presence builds suspense. Suspense depends upon the anticipation of how the plot will develop. Will Prospero avoid the Red Death? Will the masquers all die? Will Neddy realize he is doing something destructive? Suspense is often part of the **rising action**: the buildup of tension and decription of action that precedes the climax. The **climax** is the point of greatest emotional intensity in the story, and it may take many forms. In Poe's story the climax comes when Prince Prospero races through the carefully described rooms with a "drawn dagger" to kill the uninvited mummer only to fall instantly dead. In "The Swimmer" the climax comes when Neddy is described rudely as a "gate crasher." The suspense in "The Swimmer" builds from swimming pool to swimming pool because the resolution of the action—the **denouement**—is anything but clear. Few readers could predict the story's outcome. The denouement in "The Masque of the Red Death" coincides with the climax and the death of the first masquer. The denouement in "The Swimmer" comes when Neddy for the "first time in his adult life" begins to cry. His tears imply that he finally understands the painful limitations of his life.

Suspense is built in part by the use of **foreshadowing**. Foreshadowing hints at what is to come, but does so without giving away the ending of the story. Poe's references to "the Time that flies" and his intense descriptions all act as foreshadowing of some impending doom. This is especially true in his descriptions of each room, ending with the black room. In "Falling Rocks, Narrowing Road, Cul-de-Sac, Stop," the sexual symbolism in Father Tim's discussions acts as a foreshadowing of the unexpected outcome of the action. Father Tim's running off with Imogen makes better sense when the story is reread for the hints the foreshadowing gives of its resolution.

Katherine Anne Porter's "The Jilting of Granny Weatherall" begins *in medias res* and is told almost entirely in flashback. You are given a frame to work from: Granny is on her deathbed and her daughter Cornelia and Doctor Harry are with her. Other children arrive. But Granny, in whose mind the entire story takes place, thinks about the past. The exposition reveals that one event in her life has risen to the surface above all others: the day long ago when her fiancé, George, left her standing—jilted—in front of the priest at the altar.

As she is dying that one day takes precedence over the rest of her life. She says repeatedly that she would never trade John, the man she married, for anyone and that he gave her far better children than she expected. But despite that she can think of almost nothing but the day she was jilted.

Porter narrates the events of the day in flashback, interrupted by the occasional demands of father and Cornelia and Granny's irritable responses. Granny remembers the names of everyone, including the priest who was to marry her. The memory of the event is broken now and then by Granny's realization that death is upon her and that she needs to make some specific bequests of land and amethysts.

Typical of some, but not all, flashback narratives, "The Jilting of Granny Weatherall" tells two stories: the events in present time, and the events of past time. In present time her children are slowly gathering by her bed, but in past time she is a young girl facing the most humiliating and painful experience of her life. At the end of the story, the two narratives seem to come to one point: the past and the present suddenly and mysteriously merge.

Katherine Anne Porter   (1890–1980)

Katherine Anne Porter was a Texan who spent most of her life in Greenwich Village, Mexico, and Europe. She worked as a newspaper woman and traveled in Mexico at the end of its revolution. She lectured to supplement a meager income until her novel, Ship of Fools, *was published in 1962; money from the sale of the film rights freed Porter financially. After her first collection of stories,* Flowering Judas *(1930), appeared, critics saw her as a master of the craft of short fiction. Most of the stories in the collection concern Mexico and revolution, but on a deeper level they treat the themes of disillusion and loss of innocence, especially on the part of a young American woman, a character in the title story. Porter's* Collected Stories *(1964) is regarded as her major work.*

THE JILTING OF GRANNY WEATHERALL   1930

She flicked her wrist neatly out of Doctor Harry's pudgy careful fingers and pulled the sheet up to her chin. The brat ought to be in knee breeches. Doctoring around the country with spectacles on his nose! "Get along now, take your schoolbooks and go. There's nothing wrong with me."

Doctor Harry spread a warm paw like a cushion on her forehead where the forked green vein danced and made her eyelids twitch. "Now, now, be a good girl, and we'll have you up in no time."

"That's no way to speak to a woman nearly eighty years old just because she's down. I'd have you respect your elders, young man."

"Well, Missy, excuse me." Doctor Harry patted her cheek. "But I've got to warn you, haven't I? You're a marvel, but you must be careful or you're going to be good and sorry."

"Don't tell me what I'm going to be. I'm on my feet now, morally speaking. It's Cornelia. I had to go to bed to get rid of her." 5

Her bones felt loose, and floated around in her skin, and Doctor Harry floated like a balloon around the foot of the bed. He floated and pulled down his waistcoat and swung his glasses on a cord. "Well, stay where you are, it certainly can't hurt you."

"Get along and doctor your sick," said Granny Weatherall. "Leave a well woman alone. I'll call for you when I want you. . . . Where were you forty years ago when I pulled through milk-leg and double pneumonia? You weren't even born. Don't let Cornelia lead you on," she shouted, because Doctor Harry appeared to float up to the ceiling and out. "I pay my own bills, and I don't throw my money away on nonsense!"

She meant to wave good-by, but it was too much trouble. Her eyes closed of themselves, it was like a dark curtain drawn around the bed. The pillow rose and floated under her, pleasant as a hammock in a light wind. She listened to the leaves rustling outside the window. No, somebody was swishing newspapers: no, Cornelia and Doctor Harry were whispering together. She leaped broad awake, thinking they whispered in her ear.

"She was never like this, *never* like this!" "Well, what can we expect?" "Yes, eighty years old. . . ."

Well, and what if she was? She still had ears. It was like Cornelia to whisper   10 around doors. She always kept things secret in such a public way. She was always being tactful and kind. Cornelia was dutiful; that was the trouble with her. Dutiful and good: "So good and dutiful," said Granny, "and I'd like to spank her." She saw herself spanking Cornelia and making a fine job of it.

"What'd you say, Mother?"

Granny felt her face tying up in hard knots.

"Can't a body think, I'd like to know?"

"I thought you might want something."

"I do. I want a lot of things. First off, go away and don't whisper."   15

She lay and drowsed, hoping in her sleep that the children would keep out and let her rest a minute. It had been a long day. Not that she was tired. It was always pleasant to snatch a minute now and then. There was always so much to be done, let me see: tomorrow.

Tomorrow was far away and there was nothing to trouble about. Things were finished somehow when the time came; thank God there was always a little margin over for peace: then a person could spread out the plan of life and tuck in the edges orderly. It was good to have everything clean and folded away, with the hair brushes and tonic bottles sitting straight on the white embroidered linen: the day started without fuss and the pantry shelves laid out with rows of jelly glasses and brown jugs and white stone-china jars with blue whirligigs and words painted on them: coffee, tea, sugar, ginger, cinnamon, allspice: and the bronze clock with the lion on top nicely dusted off. The dust that lion could collect in twenty-four hours! The box in the attic with all those letters tied up, well, she'd have to go through that tomorrow. All those letters—George's letters and John's letters and her letters to them both—lying around for the children to find afterwards made her uneasy. Yes, that would be tomorrow's business. No use to let them know how silly she had been once.

While she was rummaging around she found death in her mind and it felt clammy and unfamiliar. She had spent so much time preparing for death there was no need for bringing it up again. Let it take care of itself now. When she was sixty she had felt very old, finished, and went around making farewell trips to see her children and grandchildren, with a secret in her mind: This is the very last of your mother, children! Then she made her will and came down with a long fever. That was all just a notion like a lot of other things, but it was lucky too, for she had once for all got over the idea of dying for a long time. Now she couldn't be worried. She hoped she had better sense now. Her father had lived to be one hundred and two years old and had drunk a noggin of strong hot toddy on his last birthday. He told the reporters it was his daily habit, and he owed his long life to that. He had made quite a scandal and was very pleased about it. She believed she'd just plague Cornelia a little.

"Cornelia! Cornelia!" No footsteps, but a sudden hand on her cheek. "Bless you, where have you been?"

"Here, Mother."

"Well, Cornelia, I want a noggin of hot toddy." 20

"Are you cold, darling?"

"I'm chilly, Cornelia. Lying in bed stops the circulation. I must have told you that a thousand times."

Well, she could just hear Cornelia telling her husband that Mother was getting a little childish and they'd have to humor her. The thing that most annoyed her was that Cornelia thought she was deaf, dumb, and blind. Little hasty glances and tiny gestures tossed around her and over her head saying, "Don't cross her, let her have her way, she's eighty years old," and she sitting there as if she lived in a thin glass cage. Sometimes Granny almost made up her mind to pack up and move back to her own house where nobody could remind her every minute that she was old. Wait, wait, Cornelia, till your own children whisper behind your back!

In her day she had kept a better house and had got more work done. She 25 wasn't too old yet for Lydia to be driving eighty miles for advice when one of the children jumped the track, and Jimmy still dropped in and talked things over: "Now, Mammy, you've a good business head, I want to know what you think of this? . . ." Old. Cornelia couldn't change the furniture around without asking. Little things, little things! They had been so sweet when they were little. Granny wished the old days were back again with the children young and everything to be done over. It had been a hard pull, but not too much for her. When she thought of all the food she had cooked, and all the clothes she had cut and sewed, and all the gardens she had made—well, the children showed it. There they were, made out of her, and they couldn't get away from that. Sometimes she wanted to see John again and point to them and say, Well, I didn't do so badly, did I? But that would have to wait. That was for tomorrow. She used to think of him as a man, but now all the children were older than their father, and he would be a child beside her if she saw him now. It seemed strange and there was something wrong in the idea. Why, he couldn't possibly recognize her. She had fenced in a hundred acres once, digging the post holes herself and clamping the wires with just a negro boy to help. That changed a woman. John would be looking for a young woman with the peaked Spanish comb in her hair and the painted fan. Digging post holes changed a woman. Riding country roads in the winter when women had their babies was another thing: sitting up nights with sick horses and sick negroes and sick children and hardly ever losing one. John, I hardly ever lost one of them! John would see that in a minute, that would be something he could understand, she wouldn't have to explain anything!

It made her feel like rolling up her sleeves and putting the whole place to rights again. No matter if Cornelia was determined to be everywhere at once, there were a great many things left undone on this place. She would start to-morrow and do them. It was good to be strong enough for everything, even if all you made melted and changed and slipped under your hands, so that by the time you finished you almost forgot what you were working for. What was it I set out to do? she asked herself intently, but she could not remember. A fog rose over the valley, she saw it marching across the creek swallowing the trees and moving up the hill like an army of ghosts. Soon it would be at the near edge of the or-chard, and then it was time to go in and light the lamps. Come in, children, don't stay out in the night air.

Lighting the lamps had been beautiful. The children huddled up to her and breathed like little calves waiting at the bars in the twilight. Their eyes fol-lowed the match and watched the flame rise and settle in a blue curve, then they moved away from her. The lamp was lit, they didn't have to be scared and hang on to mother any more. Never, never, never more. God, for all my life I thank Thee. Without Thee, my God, I could never have done it. Hail, Mary, full of grace.

I want you to pick all the fruit this year and see that nothing is wasted. There's always someone who can use it. Don't let good things rot for want of using. You waste life when you waste good food. Don't let things get lost. It's bitter to lose things. Now, don't let me get to thinking, not when I am tired and taking a lit-tle nap before supper. . . .

The pillow rose about her shoulders and pressed against her heart and the memory was being squeezed out of it: oh, push down the pillow, somebody: it would smother her if she tried to hold it. Such a fresh breeze blowing and such a green day with no threats in it. But he had not come, just the same. What does a woman do when she has put on the white veil and set out the white cake for a man and he doesn't come? She tried to remember. No, I swear he never harmed me but in that. He never harmed me but in that . . . and what if he did? There was the day, the day, but a whirl of dark smoke rose and covered it, crept up and over into the bright field where everything was planted so carefully in orderly rows. That was hell, she knew hell when she saw it. For sixty years she had prayed against remembering him and against losing her soul in the deep pit of hell, and now the two things were mingled in one and the thought of him was a smoky cloud from hell that moved and crept in her head when she had just got rid of Doctor Harry and was trying to rest a minute. Wounded vanity, Ellen, said a sharp voice in the top of her mind. Don't let your wounded vanity get the upper hand of you. Plenty of girls get jilted. You were jilted, weren't you? Then stand up to it. Her eyelids wavered and let in streamers of blue-gray light like tissue paper over her eyes. She must get up and pull the shades down or she'd never sleep. She was in bed again and the shades were not down. How could that happen? Better turn over, hide from the light, sleeping in the light gave you nightmares. "Mother, how do you feel now?" and a stinging wetness on her forehead. But I don't like having my face washed in cold water!

Hapsy? George? Lydia? Jimmy? No, Cornelia, and her features were swollen and full of little puddles. "They're coming, darling, they'll all be here soon." Go wash your face, child, you look funny.

Instead of obeying, Cornelia knelt down and put her head on the pillow. She seemed to be talking but there was no sound. "Well, are you tongue-tied? Whose birthday is it? Are you going to give a party?"

Cornelia's mouth moved urgently in strange shapes. "Don't do that, you bother me, daughter."

"Oh, no, Mother. Oh, no. . . ."

Nonsense. It was strange about children. They disputed your every word. "No what, Cornelia?"

"Here's Doctor Harry."

"I won't see that boy again. He just left five minutes ago."

"That was this morning, Mother. It's night now. Here's the nurse."

"This is Doctor Harry, Mrs. Weatherall. I never saw you look so young and happy!"

"Ah, I'll never be young again—but I'd be happy if they'd let me lie in peace and get rested."

She thought she spoke up loudly, but no one answered. A warm weight on her forehead, a warm bracelet on her wrist, and a breeze went on whispering, trying to tell her something. A shuffle of leaves in the everlasting hand of God. He blew on them and they danced and rattled. "Mother, don't mind, we're going to give you a little hypodermic." "Look here, daughter, how do ants get in this bed? I saw sugar ants yesterday." Did you send for Hapsy too?

It was Hapsy she really wanted. She had to go a long way back through a great many rooms to find Hapsy standing with a baby on her arm. She seemed to herself to be Hapsy also, and the baby on Hapsy's arm was Hapsy and himself and herself, all at once, and there was no surprise in the meeting. Then Hapsy melted from within and turned flimsy as gray gauze and the baby was a gauzy shadow, and Hapsy came up close and said, "I thought you'd never come," and looked at her very searchingly and said, "You haven't changed a bit!" They leaned forward to kiss, when Cornelia began whispering from a long way off, "Oh, is there anything you want to tell me? Is there anything I can do for you?"

Yes, she had changed her mind after sixty years and she would like to see George. I want you to find George. Find him and be sure to tell him I forgot him. I want him to know I had my husband just the same and my children and my house like any other woman. A good house too and a good husband that I loved and fine children out of him. Better than I hoped for even. Tell him I was given back everything he took away and more. Oh, no, oh, God, no, there was something else besides the house and the man and the children. Oh, surely they were not all? What was it? Something not given back. . . . Her breath crowded down under her ribs and grew into a monstrous frightening shape with cutting edges; it bored up into her head, and the agony was unbelievable: Yes, John, get the doctor now, no more talk, my time has come.

When this one was born it should be the last. The last. It should have been born first, for it was the one she had truly wanted. Everything came in good time. Nothing left out, left over. She was strong, in three days she would be as well as ever. Better. A woman needed milk in her to have her full health.

"Mother, do you hear me?"

"I've been telling you—"

"Mother, Father Connolly's here."

"I went to Holy Communion only last week. Tell him I'm not so sinful as all that."

"Father just wants to speak to you."

He could speak as much as he pleased. It was like him to drop in and inquire about her soul as if it were a teething baby, and then stay on for a cup of tea and a round of cards and gossip. He always had a funny story of some sort, usually about an Irishman who made his little mistakes and confessed them, and the point lay in some absurd thing he would blurt out in the confessional showing his struggles between native piety and original sin. Granny felt easy about her soul. Cornelia, where are your manners? Give Father Connolly a chair. She had her secret comfortable understanding with a few favorite saints who cleared a straight road to God for her. All as surely signed and sealed as the papers for the new Forty Acres. Forever . . . heirs and assigns forever. Since the day the wedding cake was not cut, but thrown out and wasted. The whole bottom dropped out of the world, and there she was blind and sweating with nothing under her feet and the walls falling away.

His hand had caught her under the breast, she had not fallen, there was the 50 freshly polished floor with the green rug on it, just as before. He had cursed like a sailor's parrot and said, "I'll kill him for you." Don't lay a hand on him, for my sake leave something to God. "Now, Ellen, you must believe what I tell you. . . ."

So there was nothing, nothing to worry about any more, except sometimes in the night one of the children screamed in a nightmare, and they both hustled out shaking and hunting for the matches and calling, "There, wait a minute, here we are!" John, get the doctor now, Hapsy's time has come. But there was Hapsy standing by the bed in a white cap. "Cornelia, tell Hapsy to take off her cap. I can't see her plain."

Her eyes opened very wide and the room stood out like a picture she had seen somewhere. Dark colors with the shadows rising towards the ceiling in long angles. The tall black dresser gleamed with nothing on it but John's picture, enlarged from a little one, with John's eyes very black when they should have been blue. You never saw him, so how do you know how he looked? But the man insisted the copy was perfect, it was very rich and handsome. For a picture, yes, but it's not my husband. The table by the bed had a linen cover and a candle and a crucifix. The light was blue from Cornelia's silk lampshades. No sort of light at all, just frippery. You had to live forty years with kerosene lamps to appreciate honest electricity. She felt very strong and she saw Doctor Harry with a rosy nimbus around him.

"You look like a saint, Doctor Harry, and I vow that's as near as you'll ever come to it."

"She's saying something."

"I heard you, Cornelia. What's all this carrying on?"   55

"Father Connolly's saying—"

Cornelia's voice staggered and bumped like a cart in a bad road. It rounded corners and turned back again and arrived nowhere. Granny stepped up in the cart very lightly and reached for the reins, but a man sat beside her and she knew him by his hands, driving the cart. She did not look in his face, for she knew without seeing, but looked instead down the road where the trees leaned over and bowed to each other and a thousand birds were singing a Mass. She felt like singing too, but she put her hand in the bosom of her dress and pulled out a rosary, and Father Connolly murmured Latin in a very solemn voice and tickled her feet. My God, will you stop that nonsense? I'm a married woman. What if he did run away and leave me to face the priest by myself? I found another a whole world better. I wouldn't have exchanged my husband for anybody except St. Michael himself, and you may tell him that for me with a thank you in the bargain.

Light flashed on her closed eyelids, and a deep roaring shook her. Cornelia, is that lightning? I hear thunder. There's going to be a storm. Close all the windows. Call the children in. . . . "Mother, here we are, all of us." "Is that you, Hapsy?" "Oh, no, I'm Lydia. We drove as fast as we could." Their faces drifted above her, drifted away. The rosary fell out of her hands and Lydia put it back. Jimmy tried to help, their hands fumbled together, and Granny closed two fingers around Jimmy's thumb. Beads wouldn't do, it must be something alive. She was so amazed her thoughts ran round and round. So, my dear Lord, this is my death and I wasn't even thinking about it. My children have come to see me die. But I can't, it's not time. Oh, I always hated surprises. I wanted to give Cornelia the amethyst set—Cornelia, you're to have the amethyst set, but Hapsy's to wear it when she wants, and, Doctor Harry, do shut up. Nobody sent for you. Oh, my dear Lord, do wait a minute. I meant to do something about the Forty Acres, Jimmy doesn't need it and Lydia will later on, with that worthless husband of hers. I meant to finish the altar cloth and send six bottles of wine to Sister Borgia for her dyspepsia. I want to send six bottles of wine to Sister Borgia, Father Connolly, now don't let me forget.

Cornelia's voice made short turns and tilted over and crashed. "Oh, Mother, oh, Mother, oh, Mother. . . ."

"I'm not going, Cornelia. I'm taken by surprise. I can't go."   60

You'll see Hapsy again. What about her? "I thought you'd never come." Granny made a long journey outward, looking for Hapsy. What if I don't find her? What then? Her heart sank down and down, there was no bottom to death, she couldn't come to the end of it. The blue light from Cornelia's lampshade drew into a tiny point in the center of her brain, it flickered and winked like an eye, quietly it fluttered and dwindled. Granny lay curled down within herself, amazed and watchful, staring at the point of light that was herself, her body was now only a deeper mass of shadow in an endless darkness and this darkness would curl around the light and swallow it up. God, give a sign!

For the second time there was no sign. Again no bridegroom and the priest in the house. She could not remember any other sorrow because this grief wiped them all away. Oh, no, there's nothing more cruel than this—I'll never forgive it. She stretched herself with a deep breath and blew out the light.

Questions for Close Reading for Plot and Narrative Structure

1. When do you first realize that the narrative is of Granny Weatherall dying? What information about her has been imparted by the exposition up to that point?
2. What kind of person was Granny Weatherall when she was young? What does she reveal about herself in her ruminations?
3. Religion takes an important role in the story: "Without Thee, my God, I could never have done it. Hail, Mary, full of grace." During the rising action, what do you learn about Granny's sense of religion?
4. Granny's sense of time is not accurate. What does Porter do to help us see how distorted time has become for her? Why does it matter that time is not clear and distinct to her? How does her sense of time affect the pacing of the plot?

5. Do you think Hapsy is among the children at the bedside, or is she dead? In one paragraph near the end of the story, Granny thinks, "Hapsy's time has come." Did she die?
6. Does the story have a climax? Does it have a denouement?
7. Is Granny Weatherall's name symbolic?

Questions for Interpretation

New Critical

1. The last paragraphs of the story seem to narrate Granny's death journey. She is looking for Hapsy but does not find her. At the end of the next to last paragraph she seems panicky and says, "God, give a sign!" What does Porter imply when she says, "For the second time there was no sign. Again no bridegroom and the priest in the house"? What would the second jilting of Granny Weatherall amount to?

Psychoanalytic

2. Granny Weatherall lost her first love at the altar and seems never to have been able to cope with the loss. Is there evidence, either in the structure of the narrative or in the imagery of the story, to suggest that she suffers from an emotional trauma or shock caused by not having been able to deal with her feelings? Why would an incident fifty years earlier not have been resolved? How might that lack of resolution have affected her?

Reader Response

3. Does the flashback technique of narration intensify this story, or do you feel it is a distraction? Is it used in a way that evokes a clear range of responses from you? Do you find yourself positively impressed by Granny Weatherall? What are her positive and her negative qualities?

Feminist

4. How would a feminist critic approach this story? Granny Weatherall was left embarrassed at the altar by George. As she speaks she reveals that her fulfillment as a woman came from being a wife and mother. Does the resolution of this story contradict or support feminist desires for independence?

Cultural

5. Examine the story for its religious images. Do they produce suspense? What senses do they appeal to, and in what way are they religious? Are the images a form of foreshadowing? Granny Weatherall thinks about religion much of the time. Do you see her as truly and deeply religious? Does the narrative itself suggest a religious progress of any kind? Could the story be said to be religious?

POINT OF VIEW

Every story is told by a **narrator**, who is created by the author and usually different from the author's voice. The narrator controls the story by talking from a particular **point of view**. Points of view have traditionally been classed as first person, second person, and third person; however, as we shall see, such a classification only begins to describe the mystery of storytelling.

- **First-Person Narrator**   In this strategy, the story is told from the point of view of "I," as in Charles Boxter's "Gryphon." The I-narrator may be part of the action or an observer. As readers, we cannot know or witness anything the narrator does not tell us. We therefore share all the limitations of the narrator. This technique has the advantage of a sharp and precise focus. Moreover, you feel part of the story because the narrator's "I" echoes the "I" already in your own mind.

- **Second-Person Narrator**   This narrator speaks directly to the reader: "You walk in the room and what do you see? It's Mullins again, and you say, 'Out. I've done with him.'" This point of view is rare primarily because it is artificial and self-conscious. It seems to invite identification on the part of the reader with the narrator, but it often fails.

- **Third-Person Narrator**   This is the most common narrative style, illustrated by John Cheever's "The Swimmer": "His life was not confining and the delight he took in this observation could not be explained by its suggestion of escape." Third-person narration permits the author to be **omniscient** (all-knowing) when necessary but also to bring the focus tightly in on the central character by limiting observation only to what that character could possibly witness or recall. One emotional effect of the technique is the acceptance of the authority of the narrator. In essence, the narrator *sounds* like the author.

One of the most significant aspects of point of view is whether it is restricted or unrestricted. This question is important regardless of which point of view is used. The **restricted narrator** does not know everything but restricts his or her observations about thought and feeling to one central character or to a limited physical area, such as the space in which the characters act. When the narrator is the same as a character in the story, this point of view usually respects the character's limitations: the narrator can tell us only what the character knows. Many first-person narrators are restricted in this way, such as the narrator in "Gryphon," who is limited by what a fourth-grader would observe. However, third-person narration can also be restricted. John Cheever uses the third person *he* to narrate "The Swimmer," but he stays very close to Neddy, and what we know of him is restricted to what Neddy Merrill knows and thinks. Nor does the narrator make any value judgment about Neddy; that is left to us.

The **unrestricted narrator**—usually called omniscient—often resembles the voice of the author and tells us many things: this narrator knows what the characters think, what they say when they are out of sight and hearing, and what they feel. Often this narrator also steps back to comment on the behavior of the characters. Unrestricted narration is usually third person but not always. The voice in Poe's "The Masque of the Red Death" is first person but still seems omniscient: "No pestilence had ever been so fatal, or so hideous." This narrator knows more than any single character; he is an observer, not an actor, and by assuming an authoritative voice appears to speak on behalf of Poe himself. A more traditional, third-person omniscient narration is used by Filomena in "The Pot of Basil"; compared with the character Lisabetta, she is totally unrestricted. However, within the larger group of tales she is only one narrator, and therefore her knowledge may be more restricted than Boccaccio's. Boccaccio may be trying to say something about her character to us, but only a reading of the entire *Decameron* could verify that guess.

Another way of describing narrators is to say that they are reliable or unreliable. The **reliable narrator** can be counted on to know the truth and to reveal it to the reader. The **unreliable narrator** is a character in the story who may tell the truth or not but, like any other character, is beset with limitations and personal prejudices that color his or her values and point of view. The narrators in "The Masque of the Red Death" and in "The Jilting of Granny Weatherall" appear reliable: we can believe what they tell us. However, the mysterious narrator in "Falling Rocks, Narrowing Road, Cul-de-Sac, Stop" is not as reliable. Our initial assumption that the narrative voice is omniscient changes when we read "many of us who saw them." Suddenly we realize that the narrator is restricted and may be telling only part of the truth. We need not believe his every word because his point of view is limited by the same prejudices that mark any character in the story.

Traditionally, older stories are often told from the point of view of a narrative voice that resembles the author. In other words, that voice is totally authoritative. This is true of Poe's narrator. To an extent the same is true of the narrator in Seán O'Faoláin's story. In the beginning, the reader may notice that the narrator appears briefly as judgmental and restricted, but the story continues in such a way as to give the impression that the narrative is third-person objective and omniscient. In the last few pages, however, the narrator reveals that he is a character living in the same town with Morgan Myles and the rest of the cast of characters. O'Faoláin mixes his narrative technique to take advantage of the virtues of both kinds of narrative stance. He uses a kind of sleight of hand by permitting his narrator to tell the story from an omniscient point of view: he tells us many details, thoughts, and conversations that only a character on the spot could know, and we know that the narrator is often not present in the scenes he narrates. The reason for doing this is to permit the reader to accept what is told as if it came from the authority of the author. Only later is the reader alerted enough to arouse appropriate skepticism about the details of the story. In relation to the psychoanalytic character of the story, this leaves us with a narrative that needs to be analyzed; it is equivalent to a dream that a psychoanalyst would interpret in order to gain insight into the character of the dreamer. By interposing a narrator of the sort that reveals himself at the end of the story, O'Faoláin shifts the insights into the storyteller away from himself and onto the unnamed narrator. Such a switch is often found in contemporary stories, and its presence makes the job of interpreting point of view much more interesting than it might at first seem.

The narrator of Charles Baxter's "Gryphon" is a fourth-grader who watches in awe the performance of his substitute teacher. How much can you trust the narrative of the average fourth-grader? Perhaps this fourth-grader is above average, but he is still a young child. On the other hand, if the narrator were completely restricted to this point of view, the narrative might include limited grammar and vocabulary and other limitations appropriate to the imagination of a fourth-grader. Thus Baxter is really looking back at an earlier time and telling a story of childhood from the point of view of a mature person remembering the distant past. In that way an author can get around the obvious limitations of a child's point of view.

A final question is whether the narrator takes a subjective or objective stance. The **subjective narrator** is given to expressing personal quirks, animosities, and limitations, as in the first-person narrator in "Gryphon." The boy tells us, "'hope you feel better tomorrow, Mr. Hibler,' Bobby Kryzanowicz, the faultless brown-noser said, and I heard Carol Peterson's evil giggle." Such a narrator makes judgments about characters and events and expects you to accept them. If you feel the narrator is unreliable, you may reject them entirely. The **objective narrator**, on the other hand, seems to present a totally neutral interpretation of events and therefore does not make judgments about characters. For that reason, "Two Cents" by Suzanne Jacob might appear mysterious to you. The third-person objective narrator does not permit you to know what the characters think or feel. You must interpret them objectively, from an emotional distance.

One special form of narration, the **stream-of-consciousness technique**, has become extremely flexible in the hands of modern writers. It recreates the interior of a character's mind so you know and feel what the character knows and feels directly. You learn to think as the character thinks. Katherine Anne Porter's "The Jilting of Granny Weatherall" uses stream of consciousness. However, Porter mixes the point of view in that story by beginning in third person, "She flicked her wrist . . .," and then entering Granny Weatherall's mind after a page, "Tomorrow was far away and there was nothing to trouble about." We learn about the jilting in Granny's recollections, but the point of view shifts from a nameless narrator who tells us what is happening now to the interior of Granny's mind to tell us what happened before and how Granny feels about what happened. The nameless narrator is not a character in the action and is therefore presumably reliable and objective. This mix of narrative point of view is common in early experiments with the stream of consciousness technique.

"Gryphon" provides us with special pleasures because we see the action through the eyes of the fourth-grader telling the story. The setting and mood of the grade school classroom dominate the story, and the distance that usually separates the fourth-grader from the teacher is deliciously present. Thus Miss Ferenczi becomes even more exotic than she might be were you to meet her in person.

Charles Baxter   (b. 1947)

Charles Baxter teaches at Wayne State University in Detroit. His short story collections, Harmony of the World *(1984) and* Through the Safety Net *(1985), from which "Gryphon" is taken, have won important writing awards and have caught the attention of both writers and critics. Some of his work falls into the genre of horror stories. The* New York Times *critic Michiko Kakutani has said, Baxter "makes his characters' fears palpable to the reader by slowly drawing us into their day-to-day routines and making us see things through their eyes." That is certainly the case in "Gryphon," which pulls us into the strange yet familiar world of the fourth grade.*

GRYPHON   1986

On Wednesday afternoon, between the geography lesson on ancient Egypt's hand-operated irrigation system and an art project that involved drawing a model city next to a mountain, our fourth-grade teacher, Mr. Hibler, developed a cough. This cough began with a series of muffled throat clearings and progressed to propulsive noises contained within Mr. Hibler's closed mouth. "Listen to him," Carol Peterson whispered to me. "He's gonna blow up." Mr. Hibler's laughter—dazed and infrequent—sounded a bit like his cough, but as we worked on our model cities we would look up, thinking he was enjoying a joke, and see Mr. Hibler's face turning red, his cheeks puffed out. This was not laughter. Twice he bent over, and his loose tie, like a plumb line, hung down straight from his neck as he exploded himself into a Kleenex. He would excuse himself, then go on coughing. "I'll bet you a dime," Carol Peterson whispered, "we get a substitute tomorrow."

Carol sat at the desk in front of mine and was a bad person—when she thought no one was looking she would blow her nose on notebook paper, then crumble it up and throw it into the wastebasket—but at times of crisis she spoke the truth. I knew I'd lose the dime.

"No deal," I said.

When Mr. Hibler stood us up in formation at the door just prior to the final bell, he was almost incapable of speech. "I'm sorry, boys and girls," he said. "I seem to be coming down with something."

"I hope you feel better tomorrow, Mr. Hibler," Bobby Kryzanowicz, the faultless brown-noser said, and I heard Carol Peterson's evil giggle. Then Mr. Hibler opened the door and we walked out to the buses, a clique of us starting noisily to hawk and cough as soon as we thought we were a few feet beyond Mr. Hibler's earshot.

5

Five Oaks being a rural community, and in Michigan, the supply of substitute teachers was limited to the town's unemployed community college graduates, a pool of about four mothers. These ladies fluttered, provided easeful class days, and nervously covered material we had mastered weeks earlier. Therefore it was a surprise when a woman we had never seen came into the class the next day, carrying a purple purse, a checkerboard lunchbox, and a few books. She put the books on one side of Mr. Hibler's desk and the lunchbox on the other, next to the Voice of Music phonograph. Three of us in the back of the room were playing with Heever, the chameleon that lived in the terrarium and on one of the plastic drapes, when she walked in.

She clapped her hands at us. "Little boys," she said, "why are you bent over together like that?" She didn't wait for us to answer. "Are you tormenting an animal? Put it back. Please sit down at your desks. I want no cabals this time of the day." We just stared at her. "Boys," she repeated, "I asked you to sit down."

I put the chameleon in his terrarium and felt my way to my desk, never taking my eyes off the woman. With white and green chalk, she had started to draw a tree on the left side of the blackboard. She didn't look usual. Furthermore, her tree was outsized, disproportionate, for some reason.

"This room needs a tree," she said, with one line drawing the suggestion of a leaf. "A large, leafy, shady, deciduous . . . oak."

Her fine, light hair had been done up in what I would learn years later was   10 called a chignon, and she wore gold-rimmed glasses whose lenses seemed to have the faintest blue tint. Harold Knardahl, who sat across from me, whispered "Mars," and I nodded slowly, savoring the imminent weirdness of the day. The substitute drew another branch with an extravagant arm gesture, then turned around and said, "Good morning. I don't believe I said good morning to all you yet."

Facing us, she was no special age—an adult is an adult—but her face had two prominent lines, descending vertically from the sides of her mouth to her chin. I knew where I had seen those lines before: *Pinocchio.* They were marionette lines. "You may stare at me," she said to us, as a few more kids from the last bus came into the room, their eyes fixed on her, "for a few more seconds, until the bell rings. Then I will permit no more staring. Looking I will permit. Staring, no. It is impolite to stare, and a sign of bad breeding. You cannot make a social effort while staring."

Harold Knardahl did not glance at me, or nudge, but I heard him whisper "Mars" again, trying to get more mileage out of his single joke with the kids who had just come in.

When everyone was seated, the substitute teacher finished her tree, put down her chalk fastidiously on the phonograph, brushed her hands, and faced us. "Good morning," she said. "I am Miss Ferenczi, your teacher for the day. I am fairly new to your community, and I don't believe any of you know me. I will therefore start by telling you a story about myself."

While we settled back, she launched into her tale. She said her grandfather had been a Hungarian prince; her mother had been born in some place called Flanders, had been a pianist, and had played concerts for people Miss Ferenczi referred to as "crowned heads." She gave us a knowing look. "Grieg," she said, "the Norwegian master, wrote a concerto for piano that was," she paused, "my mother's triumph at her debut concert in London." Her eyes searched the ceiling. Our eyes followed. Nothing up there but ceiling tile. "For reasons that I shall not go into, my family's fortunes took us to Detroit, then north to dreadful Saginaw, and now here I am in Five Oaks, as your substitute teacher, for today, Thursday, October the eleventh. I believe it will be a good day: All the forecasts coincide. We shall start with your reading lesson. Take out your reading book. I believe it is called *Broad Horizons,* or something along those lines."

Jeannie Vermeesch raised her hand. Miss Ferenzi nodded at her. "Mr. Hibler   15 always starts the day with the Pledge of Allegiance," Jeannie whined.

"Oh, does he? In that case," Miss Ferenczi said, "you must know it *very* well by now, and we certainly need not spend our time on it. No, no allegiance pledging on the premises today, by my reckoning. Not with so much sunlight coming into the room. A pledge does not suit my mood." She glanced at her watch. "Time *is* flying. Take out *Broad Horizons.*"

She disappointed us by giving us an ordinary lesson, complete with vocabulary word drills, comprehension questions, and recitation. She didn't seem to care for the material, however. She sighed every few minutes and rubbed her glasses with a frilly perfumed handkerchief that she withdrew, magician style, from her left sleeve.

After reading we moved on to arithmetic. It was my favorite time of the morning, when the lazy autumn sunlight dazzled its way through ribbons of clouds past the windows on the east side of the classroom, and crept across the linoleum floor. On the playground the first group of children, the kindergartners, were running on the quack grass just beyond the monkey bars. We were doing multiplication tables. Miss Ferenczi had made John Wazny stand up at his desk in the front row. He was supposed to go through the tables of six. From where I was sitting, I could smell the Vitalis soaked into John's plastered hair. He was doing fine until he came to six times eleven and six times twelve. "Six times eleven," he said, "is sixty-eight. Six times twelve is . . . ." He put his fingers to his head, quickly and secretly sniffed his fingertips, and said, "seventy-two." Then he sat down.

"Fine," Miss Ferenczi said. "Well now. That was very good."

"Miss Ferenczi!" One of the Eddy twins was waving her hand desperately in   20 the air. "Miss Ferenczi! Miss Ferenczi!"

"Yes?"

"John said that six times eleven is sixty-eight and you said he was right!"

"*Did* I?" She gazed at the class with a jolly look breaking across her marionette's face. "Did I say that? Well, what *is* six times eleven?"

"It's sixty-six!"

She nodded. "Yes. So it is. But, and I know some people will not entirely   25 agree with me, at some times it is sixty-eight."

"When? When is it sixty-eight?"

We were all waiting.

"In higher mathematics, which you children do not yet understand, six times eleven can be considered to be sixty-eight." She laughed through her nose. "In higher mathematics numbers are . . . more fluid. The only thing a number does is contain a certain amount of something. Think of water. A cup is not the only way to measure a certain amount of water, is it?" We were staring, shaking our heads. "You could use saucepans or thimbles. In either case, the water *would be the same.* Perhaps," she started again, "it would be better for you to think that six times eleven is sixty-eight only when I am in the room."

"Why is it sixty-eight," Mark Poole asked, "when you're in the room?"

"Because it's more interesting that way," she said, smiling very rapidly behind 30
her blue-tinted glasses. "Besides, I'm your substitute teacher, am I not?" We all
nodded. "Well, then, think of six times eleven equals sixty-eight as a substitute fact."

"A substitute fact?"

"Yes." Then she looked at us carefully. "Do you think," she asked, "that
anyone is going to be hurt by a substitute fact?"

We looked back at her.

"Will the plants on the windowsill be hurt?" We glanced at them. There were
sensitive plants thriving in a green plastic tray, and several wilted ferns in small
clay pots. "Your dogs and cats, or your moms and dads?" She waited. "So," she
concluded, "what's the problem?"

"But it's wrong," Janice Weber said, "isn't it?" 35

"What's your name, young lady?"

"Janice Weber."

"And you think it's wrong, Janice?"

"I was just asking."

"Well, all right. You were just asking. I think we've spent enough time on 40
this matter by now, don't you, class? You are free to think what you like. When
your teacher, Mr. Hibler, returns, six times eleven will be sixty-six again, you can
rest assured. And it will be that for the rest of your lives in Five Oaks. Too bad,
eh?" She raised her eyebrows and glinted herself at us. "But for now, it wasn't.
So much for that. Let us go to your assigned problems for today, as painstakingly
outlined, I see, in Mr. Hibler's lesson plan. Take out a sheet of paper and write
your names in the upper left-hand corner."

For the next half hour we did the rest of our arithmetic problems. We handed
them in and went on to spelling, my worst subject. Spelling always came before
lunch. We were taking spelling dictation and looking at the clock. "Thorough,"
Miss Ferenczi said. "Boundary." She walked in the aisles between the desks, holding the spelling book open and looking down at our papers. "Balcony." I clutched
my pencil. Somehow, the way she said those words, they seemed foreign,
Hungarian, mis-voweled and mis-consonanted. I stared down at what I had
spelled. *Balconie.* I turned my pencil upside down and erased my mistake. *Balconey.*
That looked better, but still incorrect. I cursed the world of spelling and tried
erasing it again and saw the paper beginning to wear away. *Balkony.* Suddenly I
felt a hand on my shoulder.

"I don't like that word either," Miss Ferenczi whispered, bent over, her
mouth near my ear. "It's ugly. My feeling is, if you don't like a word, you don't
have to use it." She straightened up, leaving behind a slight odor of Clorets.

At lunchtime we went out to get our trays of sloppy joes, peaches in heavy
syrup, coconut cookies, and milk, and brought them back to the classroom, where
Miss Ferenczi was sitting at the desk, eating a brown sticky thing she had unwrapped from tightly rubber-banded wax paper. "Miss Ferenczi," I said, raising
my hand. "You don't have to eat with us. You can eat with the other teachers.
There's a teachers' lounge," I ended up, "next to the principal's office."

"No, thank you," she said. "I prefer it here."

"We've got a room monitor," I said. "Mrs. Eddy." I pointed to where Mrs. 45
Eddy, Joyce and Judy's mother, sat silently at the back of the room, doing her
knitting.

"That's fine," Miss Ferenczi said. "But I shall continue to eat here, with you children. I prefer it," she repeated.

"How come?" Wayne Razmer asked without raising his hand.

"I talked with the other teachers before class this morning," Miss Ferenczi said, biting into her brown food. "There was a great rattling of the words for the fewness of ideas. I didn't care for their brand of hilarity. I don't like ditto machine jokes."

"Oh," Wayne said.

"What's that you're eating?" Maxine Sylvester asked, twitching her nose. "Is it food?"   50

"It most certainly *is* food. It's a stuffed fig. I had to drive almost down to Detroit to get it. I also bought some smoked sturgeon. And this," she said, lifting some green leaves out of her lunchbox, "is raw spinach, cleaned this morning before I came out here to the Garfield-Murry school."

"Why're you eating raw spinach?" Maxine asked.

"It's good for you," Miss Ferenczi said. "More stimulating than soda pop or smelling salts." I bit into my sloppy joe and stared blankly out the window. An almost invisible moon was faintly silvered in the daytime autumn sky. "As far as food is concerned," Miss Ferenczi was saying, "you have to shuffle the pack. Mix it up. Too many people eat . . . well, never mind."

"Miss Ferenczi," Carol Peterson said, "what are we going to do this afternoon?"

"Well," she said, looking down at Mr. Hibler's lesson plan, "I see that your   55
teacher, Mr. Hibler, has you scheduled for a unit on the Egyptians." Carol groaned. "Yessss," Miss Ferenczi continued, "that is what we will do: the Egyptians. A remarkable people. Almost as remarkable as the Americans. But not quite." She lowered her head, did her quick smile, and went back to eating her spinach.

After noon recess we came back into the classroom and saw that Miss Ferenczi had drawn a pyramid on the blackboard, close to her oak tree. Some of us who had been playing baseball were messing around in the back of the room, dropping the bats and the gloves into the playground box, and I think that Ray Schontzeler had just slugged me when I heard Miss Ferenczi's high-pitched voice quavering with emotion. "Boys," she said, "come to order right this minute and take your seats. I do not wish to waste a minute of class time. Take out your geography books." We trudged to our desks and, still sweating, pulled out *Distant Lands and Their People*. "Turn to page forty-two." She waited for thirty seconds, then looked over at Kelly Munger. "Young man," she said, "why are you still fossicking in your desk?"

Kelly looked as if his foot had been stepped on. "Why am I what?"

"Why are you . . . burrowing in your desk like that?"

"I'm lookin' for the book, Miss Ferenczi."

Bobby Kryzanowicz, the faultless brown-noser who sat in the first row by   60
choice, softly said, "His name is Kelly Munger. He can't ever find his stuff. He always does that."

"I don't care what his name is, especially after lunch," Miss Ferenczi said. "*Where is your book?*"

"I just found it." Kelly was peering into his desk and with both hands pulled at the book, shoveling along in front of it several pencils and crayons, which fell into his lap and then to the floor.

"I hate a mess," Miss Ferenczi said. "I hate a mess in a desk or a mind. It's . . . unsanitary. You wouldn't want your house at home to look like your desk at school, now, would you?" She didn't wait for an answer. "I should think not. A house at home should be as neat as human hands can make it. What were we talking about? Egypt. Page forty-two. I note from Mr. Hibler's lesson plan that you have been discussing the modes of Egyptian irrigation. Interesting, in my view, but not so interesting as what we are about to cover. The pyramids and Egyptian slave labor. A plus on one side, a minus on the other." We had our books open to page forty-two, where there was a picture of a pyramid, but Miss Ferenczi wasn't looking at the book. Instead, she was staring at some object just outside the window.

"Pyramids," Miss Ferenczi said, still looking past the window. "I want you to think about the pyramids. And what was inside. The bodies of the pharaohs, of course, and their attendant treasures. Scrolls. Perhaps," Miss Ferenczi said, with something gleeful but unsmiling in her face, "these scrolls were novels for the pharaohs, helping them to pass the time in their long voyage through the centuries. But then, I am joking." I was looking at the lines on Miss Ferenczi's face. "Pyramids," Miss Ferenczi went on, "were the repositories of special cosmic powers. The nature of a pyramid is to guide cosmic energy forces into a concentrated point. The Egyptians knew that; we have generally forgotten it. Did you know," she asked, walking to the side of the room so that she was standing by the coat closet, "that George Washington had Egyptian blood, from his grandmother? Certain features of the Constitution of the United States are notable for their Egyptian ideas."

Without glancing down at the book, she began to talk about the movement of souls in Egyptian religion. She said that when people die, their souls return to Earth in the form of carpenter ants or walnut trees, depending on how they behaved—"well or ill"—in life. She said that the Egyptians believed that people act the way they do because of magnetism produced by tidal forces in the solar system, forces produced by the sun and by its "planetary ally," Jupiter. Jupiter, she said, was a planet, as we had been told, but had "certain properties of stars." She was speaking very fast. She said that the Egyptians were great explorers and conquerors. She said that the greatest of all the conquerors, Genghis Khan, had had forty horses and forty young women killed on the site of his grave. We listened. No one tried to stop her. "I myself have been in Egypt," she said, "and have witnessed much dust and many brutalities." She said that an old man in Egypt who worked for a circus had personally shown her an animal in a cage, a monster, half bird and half lion. She said that this monster was called a gryphon and that she had heard about them but never seen them until she traveled to the outskirts of Cairo. She said that Egyptian astronomers had discovered the planet Saturn, but had not seen its rings. She said that the Egyptians were the first to discover that dogs, when they are ill, will not drink from rivers, but wait for rain, and hold their jaws open to catch it.

"She lies."

We were on the school bus home. I was sitting next to Carl Whiteside, who had bad breath and a huge collection of marbles. We were arguing. Carl thought she was lying. I said she wasn't, probably.

"I didn't believe that stuff about the bird," Carl said, "and what she told us about the pyramids? I didn't believe that either. She didn't know what she was talking about."

"Oh yeah?" I had liked her. She was strange. I thought I could nail him. "If she was lying," I said, "what'd she say that was a lie?"

"Six times eleven isn't sixty-eight. It isn't ever. It's sixty-six, I know for a   70 fact."

"She said so. She admitted it. What else did she lie about?"

"I don't know," he said. "Stuff."

"What stuff?"

"Well." He swung his legs back and forth. "You ever see an animal that was half lion and half bird?" He crossed his arms. "It sounded real fakey to me."

"It could happen," I said. I had to improvise, to outrage him. "I read in this   75 newspaper my mom bought in the IGA about this scientist, this mad scientist in the Swiss Alps, and he's been putting genes and chromosomes and stuff together in test tubes, and he combined a human being and a hamster." I waited, for effect. "It's called a humster."

"You never." Carl was staring at me, his mouth open, his terrible bad breath making its way toward me. "What newspaper was it?"

"The *National Enquirer*," I said, "that they sell next to the cash registers." When I saw his look of recognition, I knew I had bested him. "And this mad scientist," I said, "his name was, um, Dr. Frankenbush." I realized belatedly that this name was a mistake and waited for Carl to notice its resemblance to the name of the other famous mad master of permutations, but he only sat there.

"A man and a hamster?" He was staring at me, squinting, his mouth opening in distaste. "Jeez. What'd it look like?"

When the bus reached my stop, I took off down our dirt road and ran up through the back yard, kicking the tire swing for good luck. I dropped my books on the back steps so I could hug and kiss our dog, Mr. Selby. Then I hurried inside. I could smell Brussels sprouts cooking, my unfavorite vegetable. My mother was washing other vegetables in the kitchen sink, and my baby brother was hollering in his yellow playpen on the kitchen floor.

"Hi, Mom," I said, hopping around the playpen to kiss her. "Guess what?"   80 "I have no idea."

"We had this substitute today, Miss Ferenczi, and I'd never seen her before, and she had all these stories and ideas and stuff."

"Well. That's good." My mother looked out the window behind the sink, her eyes on the pine woods west of our house. Her face and hairstyle always reminded other people of Betty Crocker, whose picture was framed inside a gigantic spoon on the side of the Bisquick box; to me, though, my mother's face just looked white. "Listen, Tommy," she said, "go upstairs and pick your clothes off the bathroom floor, then go outside to the shed and put the shovel and ax away that your father left outside this morning."

"She said that six times eleven was sometimes sixty-eight!" I said. "And she said she once saw a monster that was half lion and half bird." I waited. "In Egypt, she said."

"Did you hear me?" my mother asked, raising her arm to wipe her forehead   85
with the back of her hand. "You have chores to do."

"I know," I said. "I was just telling you about the substitute."

"It's very interesting," my mother said, quickly glancing down at me, "and
we can talk about it later when your father gets home. But right now you have
some work to do."

"Okay, Mom." I took a cookie out of the jar on the counter and was about
to go outside when I had a thought. I ran into the living room, pulled out a dictionary next to the TV stand, and opened it to the G's. *Gryphon:* "variant of griffin." *Griffin:* "a fabulous beast with the head and wings of an eagle and the body
of a lion." Fabulous was right. I shouted with triumph and ran outside to put my
father's tools back in their place.

Miss Ferenczi was back the next day, slightly altered. She had pulled her hair
down and twisted it into pigtails, with red rubber bands holding them tight one
inch from the ends. She was wearing a green blouse and pink scarf, making her
difficult to look at for a full class day. This time there was no pretense of doing a
reading lesson or moving on to arithmetic. As soon as the bell rang, she simply
began to talk.

She talked for forty minutes straight. There seemed to be less connection   90
between her ideas, but the ideas themselves were, as the dictionary would say,
fabulous. She said she had heard of a huge jewel, in what she called the Antipodes,
that was so brilliant that when the light shone into it at a certain angle it would
blind whoever was looking at its center. She said that the biggest diamond in the
world was cursed and had killed everyone who owned it, and that by a trick of
fate it was called the Hope diamond. Diamonds are magic, she said, and this is
why women wear them on their fingers, as a sign of the magic of womanhood.
Men have strength, Miss Ferenczi said, but no true magic. That is why men fall
in love with women but women do not fall in love with men: they just love being loved. George Washington had died because of a mistake he made about a
diamond. Washington was not the first *true* President, but she did not say who
was. In some places in the world, she said, men and women still live in the trees
and eat monkeys for breakfast. Their doctors are magicians. At the bottom of the
sea are creatures thin as pancakes which have never been studied by scientists because when you take them up to the air, the fish explode.

There was not a sound in the classroom, except for Miss Ferenczi's voice,
and Donna DeShano's coughing. No one even went to the bathroom.

Beethoven, she said, had not been deaf; it was a trick to make himself famous, and it worked. As she talked, Miss Ferenczi's pigtails swung back and forth.
There are trees in the world, she said, that eat meat: their leaves are sticky and
close up on bugs like hands. She lifted her hands and brought them together,
palm to palm. Venus, which most people think is the next closest planet to the
sun, is not always closer, and, besides, it is the planet of greatest mystery because
of its thick cloud cover. "I know what lies underneath those clouds," Miss Ferenczi
said, and waited. After the silence, she said, "Angels. Angels live under those
clouds." She said that angels were not invisible to everyone and were in fact smarter
than most people. They did not dress in robes as was often claimed but instead
wore formal evening clothes, as if they were about to attend a concert. Often angels *do* attend concerts and sit in the aisles where, she said, most people pay no

attention to them. She said the most terrible angel had the shape of the Sphinx: "There is no running away from that one," she said. She said that unquenchable fires burn just under the surface of the earth in Ohio, and that the baby Mozart fainted dead away in his cradle when he first heard the sound of a trumpet. She said that someone named Narzim al Harrardim was the greatest writer who ever lived. She said that planets control behavior, and anyone conceived during a solar eclipse would be born with webbed feet.

"I know you children like to hear these things," she said, "these secrets, and that is why I am telling you all this." We nodded. It was better than doing comprehension questions for the readings in *Broad Horizons.*

"I will tell you one more story," she said, "and then we will have to do arithmetic." She leaned over, and her voice grew soft. "There is no death," she said. "You must never be afraid. Never. That which is, cannot die. It will change into different earthly and unearthly elements, but I know this as sure as I stand here in front of you, and I swear it: you must not be afraid. I have seen this truth with these eyes. I know it because in a dream God kissed me. Here." And she pointed with her right index finger to the side of her head, below the mouth, where the vertical lines were carved into her skin.

Absent-mindedly we all did our arithmetic problems. At recess the class was out on the playground, but no one was playing. We were all standing in small groups, talking about Miss Ferenczi. We didn't know if she was crazy, or what. I looked out beyond the playground, at the rusted cars piled in a small heap behind a clump of sumac, and I wanted to see shapes there, approaching me. 95

On the way home, Carl sat next to me again. He didn't say much, and I didn't either. At last he turned to me. "You know what she said about the leaves that close up on bugs?"

"Huh?"

"The leaves," Carl insisted. "The meat-eating plants. I know it's true. I saw it on television. The leaves have this icky glue that the plants have got smeared all over them and the insects can't get off 'cause they're stuck. I saw it." He seemed demoralized. "She's tellin' the truth."

"Yeah."

"You think she's seen all those angels?" 100

I shrugged.

"I don't think she has," Carl informed me. "I think she made that part up."

"There's a tree," I suddenly said. I was looking out the window at the farms along County Road H. I knew every barn, every broken windmill, every fence, every anhydrous ammonia tank, by heart. "There's a tree that's . . . that I've seen . . . ."

"Don't you try to do it," Carl said. "You'll just sound like a jerk."

I kissed my mother. She was standing in front of the stove. "How was your day?" she asked. 105

"Fine."

"Did you have Miss Ferenczi again?"

"Yeah."

"Well?"

"She was fine. Mom," I asked, "can I go to my room?" 110

"No," she said, "not until you've gone out to the vegetable garden and picked me a few tomatoes." She glanced at the sky. "I think it's going to rain. Skedaddle and do it now. Then you come back inside and watch your brother for a few minutes while I go upstairs. I need to clean up before dinner." She looked down at me. "You're looking a little pale, Tommy." She touched the back of her hand to my forehead and I felt her diamond ring against my skin. "Do you feel all right?"

"I'm fine," I said, and went out to pick the tomatoes.

Coughing mutedly, Mr. Hibler was back the next day, slipping lozenges into his mouth when his back was turned at forty-five-minute intervals and asking us how much of the prepared lesson plan Miss Ferenczi had followed. Edith Atwater took the responsibility for the class of explaining to Mr. Hibler that the substitute hadn't always done exactly what he would have done, but we had worked hard even though she talked a lot. About what? he asked. All kinds of things, Edith said. I sort of forgot. To our relief, Mr. Hibler seemed not at all interested in what Miss Ferenczi had said to fill the day. He probably thought it was woman's talk; unserious and not suited for school. It was enough that he had a pile of arithmetic problems from us to correct.

For the next month, the sumac turned a distracting red in the field, and the sun traveled toward the southern sky, so that its rays reached Mr. Hibler's Halloween display on the bulletin board in the back of the room, fading the scarecrow with a pumpkin head from orange to tan. Every three days I measured how much farther the sun had moved toward the southern horizon by making small marks with my black Crayola on the north wall, ant-sized marks only I knew were there, inching west.

And then in early December, four days after the first permanent snowfall,   115 she appeared again in our classroom. The minute she came in the door, I felt my heart begin to pound. Once again, she was different: this time, her hair hung straight down and seemed hardly to have been combed. She hadn't brought her lunchbox with her, but she was carrying what seemed to be a small box. She greeted all of us and talked about the weather. Donna DeShano had to remind her to take her overcoat off.

When the bell to start the day finally rang, Miss Ferenczi looked out at all of us and said, "Children, I have enjoyed your company in the past, and today I am going to reward you." She held up the small box. "Do you know what this is?" She waited. "Of course you don't. It is a tarot pack."

Edith Atwater raised her hand. "What's a tarot pack, Miss Ferenczi?"

"It is used to tell fortunes," she said. "And that is what I shall do this morning. I shall tell your fortunes, as I have been taught to do."

"What's fortune?" Bobby Kryzanowicz asked.

"The future, young man. I shall tell you what your future will be. I can't do   120 your whole future, of course. I shall have to limit myself to the five-card system, the wands, cups, swords, pentacles, and the higher arcanes. Now who wants to be first?"

There was a long silence. Then Carol Peterson raised her hand.

"All right," Miss Ferenczi said. She divided the pack into five smaller packs and walked back to Carol's desk, in front of mine. "Pick one card from each of these packs," she said. I saw that Carol had a four of cups, a six of swords, but I couldn't see the other cards. Miss Ferenczi studied the cards on Carol's desk for a minute. "Not bad," she said. "I do not see much higher education. Probably an early marriage. Many children. There's something bleak and dreary here, but I can't tell what. Perhaps just the tasks of a housewife life. I think you'll do very well, for the most part." She smiled at Carol, a smile with a certain lack of interest. "Who wants to be next?"

Carl Whiteside raised his hand slowly.

"Yes," Miss Ferenczi said, "let's do a boy." She walked over to where Carl sat. After he picked his five cards, she gazed at them for a long time. "Travel," she said. "Much distant travel. You might go into the Army. Not too much romantic interest here. A late marriage, if at all. Squabbles. But the Sun is in your major arcana, here, yes, that's a very good card." She giggled. "Maybe a good life."

Next I raised my hand, and she told me my future. She did the same with   125
Bobby Kryzanowicz. Kelly Munger, Edith Atwater, and Kim Foor. Then she came to Wayne Razmer. He picked his five cards, and I could see that the Death card was one of them.

"What's your name?" Miss Ferenczi asked.

"Wayne."

"Well, Wayne," she said, you will undergo a *great* metamorphosis, the greatest, before you become an adult. Your earthly element will leap away, into thin air, you sweet boy. This card, this nine of swords here, tells of suffering and desolation. And this ten of wands, well, that's certainly a heavy load."

"What about this one?" Wayne pointed to the Death card.

"That one? That one means you will die soon, my dear." She gathered up   130
the cards. We were all looking at Wayne. "But do not fear," she said. "It's not really death, so much as change." She put the cards on Mr. Hibler's desk. "And now, let's do some arithmetic."

At lunchtime Wayne went to Mr. Faegre, the principal, and told him what Miss Ferenczi had done. During the noon recess, we saw Miss Ferenczi drive out of the parking lot in her green Rambler. I stood under the slide, listening to the other kids coasting down and landing in the little depressive bowl at the bottom. I was kicking stones and tugging at my hair right up to the moment when I saw Wayne come out to the playground. He smiled, the dead fool, and with the fingers of his right hand he was showing everyone how he had told on Miss Ferenczi.

I made my way toward Wayne, pushing myself past two girls from another class. He was watching me with his little pinhead eyes.

"You told," I shouted at him. "She was just kidding."

"She shouldn't have," he shouted back. "We were supposed to be doing arithmetic."

"She just scared you," I said. "You're a chicken. You're a chicken, Wayne.   135
You are. Scared of a little card," I singsonged.

Wayne fell at me, his two fists hammering down on my nose. I gave him a good one in the stomach and then I tried for his head. Aiming my fist, I saw that he was crying. I slugged him.

"She was right," I yelled. "She was always right! She told the truth!" Other kids were whooping. "You were just scared, that's all!"

And then large hands pulled at us, and it was my turn to speak to Mr. Faegre.

In the afternoon Miss Ferenczi was gone, and my nose was stuffed with cotton clotted with blood, and my lip had swelled, and our class had been combined with Mrs. Mantei's sixth-grade class for a crowded afternoon science unit on insect life in ditches and swamps. I knew where Mrs. Mantei lived: she had a new house trailer just down the road from us, at the Clearwater Park. She was no mystery. Somehow she and Mr. Bodine, the other fourth-grade teacher, had managed to fit forty-five desks into the room. Kelly Munger asked if Miss Ferenczi had been arrested, and Mrs. Mantei said no, of course not. All that afternoon, until the buses came to pick us up, we learned about field crickets and two-striped grasshoppers, water bugs, cicadas, mosquitoes, flies, and moths. We learned about insects' hard outer shell, the exoskeleton, and the usual parts of the mouth, including the labrum, mandible, maxilla, and glossa. We learned about compound eyes and the four-stage metamorphosis from egg to larva to pupa to adult. We learned something, but not much, about mating. Mrs. Mantei drew, very skillfully, the internal anatomy of the grasshopper on the blackboard. We learned about the dance of the honeybee, directing other bees in the hive to pollen. We found out about which insects were pests to man, and which were not. On lined white pieces of paper we made lists of insects we might actually see, then a list of insects too small to be clearly visible, such as fleas; Mrs. Mantei said that our assignment would be to memorize these lists for the next day, when Mr. Hibler would certainly return and test us on our knowledge.

Questions for Close Reading for Point of View

1. Does the narrator sound like a typical fourth-grader? Can you believe that the narrator is a fourth-grader during the telling of this story, or did the narrator recall the events much later?
2. What picture do you get of Miss Ferenczi through the eyes of the narrator? What do you observe about her that the narrator does not?
3. Is the narrative technique omniscient or limited? Does the narrative seem subjective or objective?
4. Is the narrator reliable or not? How would you support either position?
5. How much do you know about the narrator? How would you characterize him?

Questions for Interpretation

New Critical

1. The story seems to comment on the nature of truth when Miss Ferenczi talks about facts and substitute facts. Mrs. Mantei talks about insects and provides the students with lists to memorize at the end of class. What kind of facts are they, and how do they differ from Miss Ferenzci's? Which is more scientific? Which is more truthful? What comment does the story make on these distinctions? To what extent is the story itself a fact or substitute fact?

Psychoanalytic

2. To what extent is Miss Ferenczi's behavior typical of the teachers you had in the fourth grade? Is it possible that she is mentally unbalanced? If so, what is the narrator's reaction to her odd behavior? For example, she disregards accuracy in spelling and mathematics and she eats lunch with the children. She tells them that God kissed her. Is the gryphon a symbol of madness? Why is the detail of the mad scientist introduced? Was she wrong to tell Wayne he would die?

Reader Response

3. How do you react to Miss Ferenczi? Does the narrator give enough information for you to make a judgment distinct from his? Would you have done what Wayne did at the end of the story if Miss Ferenczi had told your fortune and implied that you would die young? How do you react to a teacher who says there are substitute facts?

4. Consider your own experiences in grade school with substitute teachers. To what extent does this story rely upon your knowledge and your range of responses to the memory of fourth grade for its success? What unspoken playground ethics are at work in the story? Would someone who did not attend a grade school miss anything crucial to understanding this story?

Feminist

5. The pool of substitute teachers consists of four housewives who went to community college. The narrator's regular teacher is a man. Do the students treat a woman substitute with the same respect they would a man substitute? Is Miss Ferenczi a feminist?

Cultural

6. Is there a marked social or cultural difference between Miss Ferenczi and the community she serves in the school? What differences of attitude and outlook seem to exist between them? Education can appeal to the world of facts or to the world of imagination, or both. What position does Miss Ferenczi take toward facts and imagination? Is it shared by the community? What does she awaken in the narrator that his earlier teachers did not?

IRONY AND TONE

When Bobby Kryzanowicz told Mr. Hibler to "feel better tomorrow" in "Gryphon," he was using sarcasm, a form of **verbal irony**. When Carol Peterson laughed at him she indicated that she "got" the irony. Sarcasm, like all verbal irony, depends on diction—the proper choice of words to achieve a given effect. One particularly delightful use of verbal irony occurs at the end of "Falling Rocks, Narrowing Road, Cul-de-Sac, Stop," when the narrator tells us that Morgan Myles and Marianne Simcox "have since been taking off every fine Sunday in her red Mustang, together with Morgan's mother, in search of faceless churchlets in fallow fields where the only sound is the munching of cattle. His mother prepares the lunch." The narrator tells us this and at the same time reveals that he—as narrator—may be critical of the goings-on of Morgan Myles, Dr. Breen, and Father Tim.

However, irony goes far beyond sarcasm and attention to diction. **Dramatic irony**—irony built into the characters' actions and not just their words—depends upon a contradiction of expectations. Characters expect one thing and get another. When Father Tim goes off with Imogen, after all his lectures about celibacy, we witness an ironic action (though some of us might have guessed it). James Thurber's "The Secret Life of Walter Mitty" is itself an ironic action, since the real Walter Mitty is a henpecked Mr. Milquetoast, while his fantasy life casts him as a heroic star in dangerous scenarios. Dramatic irony can be, as in the case of Father Tim and Walter Mitty, **comic irony**. We are amused or laugh at the circumstances of the story. **Tragic irony** has the opposite effect. For example, it is a tragic irony that Prince Prospero walls himself in to avoid the Red Death and then actually pursues the uninvited guest—who *is* the Red Death—and is the first to die. We may not feel a sense of grief because we do not respect Prospero, but from Prospero's point of view the action is tragic. "The Pot of Basil" contains several tragic ironies: Lisabetta ironically ends up with her lover, but the very fact that she has him near her drives her insane. From the point of view of the brothers, their action may have been designed to protect the honor of their sister, but has resulted in her madness. Such ironic contradictions are common not only to drama but to short fiction as well.

Tone is the author's attitude to the subject of the story. One wonders, for example, at the apparently neutral and nonjudgmental tone of John Cheever in "The Swimmer." We know that Neddy Merrill is much like many people Cheever knew and lived with. His tone reveals an understanding, a concern, but nonetheless we ultimately become aware of the shallowness of Neddy's life. Cheever's narrator maintains a neutral tone that guides us but does not force us to a conclusion. The tone of the unnamed narrator in Seán O'Faoláin's story is judgmental and ironic, especially at the end of the story. The uncertain tone of the narrator of "Gryphon" results from the disjunction between the way a teacher is expected to behave and the way Mrs. Ferenczi actually does behave. The boy's tone is respectful but clearly confused. He is not in a position to make a value judgment the way his parents can.

James Thurber's tone in "The Secret Life of Walter Mitty" is complicated. You might rightly ask whether Thurber approved of Walter Mitty. Did he like the character or despise him? Since Thurber never says one way or the other, you need to decide on the basis of your interpretation of the story. The same is true for his attitude toward Walter Mitty's wife. In what sense is he judgmental of her? Does he like her or despise her? Thurber's tone is steady throughout the story, and his use of irony is constant, subtle, and intriguing.

However, Thurber also leaves you plenty of room to make up your own mind about the characters and the situation.

James Thurber (1894–1961)

James Thurber lost an eye as a child playing William Tell with his brother, and even though his good eye slowly deteriorated, he wrote and cartooned late into his life. Some of his best-known books are My Life and Hard Times *(1933),* Thurber Country: A New Collection of Pieces about People *(1952),* Further Fables for Our Times *(1956), and* Vintage Thurber *(1963). A play,* A Thurber Carnival *(1960), was among several produced on Broadway. Thurber made people laugh, but he always wondered what people thought was funny. John Updike, who knew him at the* New Yorker, *said, "Thurber's genius was to make of our despair a humorous fable." "The Secret Life of Walter Mitty" was published in* My World and Welcome to It *(1942), after Thurber had become blind. Carl Lindner said of this story that Thurber "touched upon one of the major themes in American literature—the conflict between individual and society."*

THE SECRET LIFE OF WALTER MITTY   1942

"We're going through!" The Commander's voice was like thin ice breaking. He wore his full-dress uniform, with the heavily braided white cap pulled down rakishly over one cold grey eye. "We can't make it, sir. It's spoiling for a hurricane, if you ask me." "I'm not asking you, Lieutenant Berg," said the Commander. "Throw on the power lights! Rev her up to 8,500! We're going through!" The pounding of the cylinders increased: ta-pocketa-pocketa-pocketa-*pocketa-pocketa*. The Commander stared at the ice forming on the pilot window. He walked over and twisted a row of complicated dials. "Switch on No. 8 auxiliary!" he shouted. "Switch on No. 8 auxiliary!" repeated Lieutenant Berg. "Full strength in No. 3 turret!" shouted the Commander. "Full strength in No. 3 turret!" The crew, bending to their various tasks in the huge, hurtling eight-engined Navy hydroplane, looked at each other and grinned. "The Old Man'll get us through," they said to one another. "The Old Man ain't afraid of Hell!" . . .

"Not so fast! You're driving too fast!" said Mrs Mitty. "What are you driving so fast for?"

"Hmm?" said Walter Mitty. He looked at his wife, in the seat beside him, with shocked astonishment. She seemed grossly unfamiliar, like a strange woman who had yelled at him in a crowd. "You were up to fifty-five," she said. "You know I don't like to go more than forty. You were up to fifty-five." Walter Mitty drove on toward Waterbury in silence, the roaring of the SN202 through the worst storm in twenty years of Navy flying fading in the remote, intimate airways of his mind. "You're tensed up again," said Mrs Mitty. "It's one of your days. I wish you'd let Dr. Renshaw look you over."

Walter Mitty stopped the car in front of the building where his wife went to have her hair done. "Remember to get those overshoes while I'm having my hair done," she said. "I don't need overshoes," said Mitty. She put her mirror back into her bag. "We've been all through that," she said, getting out of the car.

"You're not a young man any longer." He raced the engine a little. "Why don't you wear your gloves? Have you lost your gloves?" Walter Mitty reached in a pocket and brought out the gloves. He put them on, but after she had turned and gone into the building and he had driven on to a red light, he took them off again. "Pick it up, brother!" snapped a cop as the light changed, and Mitty hastily pulled on his gloves and lurched ahead. He drove around the streets aimlessly for a time, and then he drove past the hospital on his way to the parking lot.

. . . "It's the millionaire banker, Wellington McMillan," said the pretty nurse. 5 "Yes?" said Walter Mitty, removing his gloves slowly. "Who has the case?" "Dr. Renshaw and Dr. Benbow, but there are two specialists here, Dr. Remington from New York and Mr. Pritchard-Mitford from London. He flew over." A door opened down a long, cool corridor and Dr. Renshaw came out. He looked distraught and haggard. "Hello, Mitty," he said. "We're having the devil's own time with McMillan, the millionaire banker and close personal friend of Roosevelt. Obstreosis of the ductal tract. Tertiary. Wish you'd take a look at him." "Glad to," said Mitty.

In the operating room there were whispered introductions: "Dr. Remington, Dr. Mitty. Mr. Pritchard-Mitford, Dr. Mitty." "I've read your book on strep-tothricosis," said Pritchard-Mitford, shaking hands. "A brilliant performance, sir." "Thank you," said Walter Mitty. "Didn't know you were in the States, Mitty," grumbled Remington. "Coals to Newcastle, bringing Mitford and me up here for a tertiary." "You are very kind," said Mitty. A huge, complicated machine, connected to the operating table, with many tubes and wires, began at this moment to go pocketa-pocketa-pocketa. "The new anesthetizer is giving way!" shouted an intern. "There is no one in the East who knows how to fix it!" "Quiet, man!" said Mitty, in a low, cool voice. He sprang to the machine, which was now going pocketa-pocketa-queep-pocketa-queep. He began fingering delicately a row of glistening dials. "Give me a fountain pen!" he snapped. Someone handed him a fountain pen. He pulled a faulty piston out of the machine and inserted the pen in its place. "That will hold for ten minutes," he said. "Get on with the operation." A nurse hurried over and whispered to Renshaw, and Mitty saw the man turn pale. "Coreopsis has set in," said Renshaw nervously. "If you would take over, Mitty?" Mitty looked at him and at the craven figure of Benbow, who drank, and at the grave, uncertain faces of the two great specialists. "If you wish," he said. They slipped a white gown on him; he adjusted a mask and drew on thin gloves; nurses handed him shining . . .

"Back it up, Mac! Look out for that Buick!" Walter Mitty jammed on the brakes. "Wrong lane, Mac," said the parking-lot attendant, looking at Mitty closely. "Gee. Yeh," muttered Mitty. He began cautiously to back out of the lane marked "Exit Only." "Leave her sit there," said the attendant. "I'll put her away." Mitty got out of the car. "Hey, better leave the key." "Oh," said Mitty, handing the man the ignition key. The attendant vaulted into the car, backed it up with insolent skill, and put it where it belonged.

They're so damn cocky, thought Walter Mitty, walking along Main Street; they think they know everything. Once he had tried to take his chains off, outside New Milford, and he had got them wound around the axles. A man had had to come out in a wrecking car and unwind them, a young, grinning garageman. Since then Mrs Mitty always made him drive to a garage to have the chains taken off. The next time, he thought, I'll wear my right arm in a sling; they won't grin at me then. I'll have my right arm in a sling and they'll see I couldn't possibly take the chains off myself. He kicked at the slush on the sidewalk. "Overshoes," he said to himself, and he began looking for a shoe store.

When he came out into the street again, with the overshoes in a box under his arm, Walter Mitty began to wonder what the other thing was his wife had told him to get. She had told him, twice, before they set out from their house for Waterbury. In a way he hated these weekly trips to town—he was always getting something wrong. Kleenex, he thought, Squibb's, razor blades? No. Toothpaste, toothbrush, bicarbonate, carborundum, initiative and referendum? He gave it up. But she would remember it. "Where's the what's-its-name?" she would ask. "Don't tell me you forgot the what's-its-name." A newsboy went by shouting something about the Waterbury trial.

. . . "Perhaps this will refresh your memory." The District Attorney suddenly   10
thrust a heavy automatic at the quiet figure on the witness stand. "Have you ever seen this before?" Walter Mitty took the gun and examined it expertly. "This is my Webley-Vickers 50.80," he said calmly. An excited buzz ran around the courtroom. The Judge rapped for order. "You are a crack shot with any sort of firearms, I believe?" said the District Attorney, insinuatingly. "Objection!" shouted Mitty's attorney. "We have shown that the defendant could not have fired the shot. We have shown that he wore his right arm in a sling on the night of the fourteenth of July." Walter Mitty raised his hand briefly and the bickering attorneys were stilled. "With any known make of gun," he said evenly, "I could have killed Gregory Fitzhurst at three hundred feet *with my left hand*." Pandemonium broke loose in the courtroom. A woman's scream rose above the bedlam and suddenly a lovely, dark-haired girl was in Walter Mitty's arms. The District Attorney struck at her savagely. Without rising from his chair, Mitty let the man have it on the point of the chin. "You miserable cur!" . . . .

"Puppy biscuit," said Walter Mitty. He stopped walking and the buildings of Waterbury rose up out of the misty courtroom and surrounded him again. A woman who was passing laughed. "He said 'Puppy biscuit'," she said to her companion. "That man said 'Puppy biscuit' to himself." Walter Mitty hurried on. He went into an A. & P., not the first one he came to but a smaller one farther up the street. "I want some biscuit for small, young dogs," he said to the clerk. "Any special brand, sir?" The greatest pistol shot in the world thought a moment. "It says 'Puppies Bark for It' on the box," said Walter Mitty.

His wife would be through at the hairdresser's in fifteen minutes, Mitty saw in looking at his watch, unless they had trouble drying it; sometimes they had trouble drying it. She didn't like to get to the hotel first; she would want him to be there waiting for her as usual. He found a big leather chair in the lobby, facing a window, and he put the overshoes and the puppy biscuit on the floor beside it. He picked up an old copy of *Liberty* and sank down into the chair. "Can Germany Conquer the World Through the Air?" Walter Mitty looked at the pictures of bombing planes and of ruined streets.

. . . "The cannonading has got the wind up in young Raleigh, sir," said the sergeant. Captain Mitty looked up at him through tousled hair. "Get him to bed," he said wearily. "With the others. I'll fly alone." "But you can't, sir," said the sergeant anxiously. "It takes two men to handle that bomber and the Archies are pounding hell out of the air. Von Richtman's circus is between here and Saulier."

"Somebody's got to get that ammunition dump," said Mitty. "I'm going over. Spot of brandy?" He poured a drink for the sergeant and one for himself. War thundered and whined around the dugout and battered at the door. There was a rending of wood and splinters flew through the room. "A bit of a near thing," said Captain Mitty carelessly. "The box barrage is closing in," said the sergeant. "We only live once, Sergeant," said Mitty, with his faint, fleeting smile. "Or do we?" He poured another brandy and tossed it off. "I never see a man could hold his brandy like you, sir," said the sergeant. "Begging your pardon, sir." Captain Mitty stood up and strapped on his huge Webley-Vickers automatic. "It's forty kilometers through hell, sir," said the sergeant. Mitty finished one last brandy. "After all," he said softly, "what isn't?" The pounding of the cannon increased; there was the rat-tat-tatting of machine guns, and from somewhere came the menacing pocketa-pocketa-pocketa of the new flame-throwers. Walter Mitty walked to the door of the dugout humming "Auprès de Ma Blonde." He turned and waved to the sergeant. "Cheerio!" he said. . . .

Something struck his shoulder. "I've been looking all over this hotel for you," said Mrs. Mitty. "Why do you have to hide in this old chair? How did you expect me to find you?" "Things close in," said Walter Mitty vaguely. "What?" Mrs. Mitty said. "Did you get the what's-its-name? The puppy biscuit? What's in that box?" "Overshoes," said Mitty. "Couldn't you have put them on in the store?" "I was thinking," said Walter Mitty. "Does it ever occur to you that I am sometimes thinking?" She looked at him. "I'm going to take your temperature when I get you home," she said.

They went out through the revolving doors that made a faintly derisive 15 whistling sound when you pushed them. It was two blocks to the parking lot. At the drugstore on the corner she said, "Wait here for me. I forgot something. I won't be a minute." She was more than a minute. Walter Mitty lighted a cigarette. It began to rain, rain with sleet in it. He stood up against the wall of the drugstore, smoking. . . . He put his shoulders back and his heels together. "To hell with the handkerchief," said Walter Mitty scornfully. He took one last drag on his cigarette and snapped it away. Then, with that faint, fleeting smile playing about his lips, he faced the firing squad; erect and motionless, proud and disdainful, Walter Mitty the Undefeated, inscrutable to the last.

Questions for Close Reading for Irony and Tone

1. How would you describe the tone of the passages that are part of Mitty's fantasy world? Is it despairing? Hopeful? Realistic? How might fantasies such as his originate?
2. How can you tell when Thurber switches from fantasy to reality? Since Thurber never says that he is shifting gears, how can a reader be sure which is which? Can you imagine a reader becoming confused?
3. Why is the disjunction between the real Walter Mitty and the fantasized Walter Mitty ironic? Is the irony obvious?
4. The story has been praised for its excellent use of associational psychology: Mitty hears an expression or a sound and by means of association constructs a fantasy. Find examples of such transformations in the story and discuss the way they work.

5. How does Mitty think he appears to other people? What other people—
outside his fantasies—does he mention or think about? How do people in
his fantasy life regard him? How do people in real life regard him?

Questions for Interpretation

New Critical

1. The power of the story depends on the ironic contrast between Mitty's
real and fantasized worlds. What point does Thurber make about that contrast? Does Thurber comment on modern life as you know it, or is it only
a comment on Walter Mitty?
2. What is Thurber's attitude toward Walter Mitty? Is he sympathetic, hostile, critical, forgiving, contemptuous? What is his attitude toward Walter
Mitty's wife? Does Thurber imply a causal relationship between the circumstances of Mitty's real world and his fantasy world?

Psychoanalytic

3. Is Walter Mitty insane? He lives part of the time in a totally unreal world.
Could that be an acceptable definition of insanity? Do you feel that Walter
Mitty has a psychological problem? What comment does Thurber make
on the condition of Mitty's mental health? Do his fantasies seem to be
health producing or do they seem psychologically destructive?

Reader Response

4. Do you find yourself pleased or displeased by the irony and tone of this
story? Do you think your reaction would be shared by many other readers, or are the sources of your pleasure or displeasure personal? How do
you react to a character who spends so much of his life fantasizing? How
do you think Thurber expected you to respond to his character?

Feminist

5. How might a feminist interpret this story? Is the portrait of a henpecked
husband a gesture of antifeminism? Why are all his fantasies so overtly macho? Is he dominated by his wife?

Historicist

6. This story generated a great deal of discussion in magazines and papers,
enough that people thought of Walter Mitty as an identifiable "type." Is
it still true that people live fantasy lives of the kind Mitty enjoys? How different are today's fantasies from those of the period of this story (just before World War II)? Do you think Walter Mitty is a "type" today?

SEEING THE ELEMENTS WORK TOGETHER

Examining one element of a short story constrains you by a limitation you may not have chosen. For example, you may have wanted to ignore point of view in Charles Baxter's "Gryphon" in favor of discussing its theme or the psychology of its characters. You may have wanted to discuss the setting of "The Swimmer" instead of focusing on style and theme. Or you may have wanted to talk about several elements rather than just one in relation to all the stories. Well, the good news is that interpretations of short fiction offer you a wide range of choices. You can discuss all or none of the elements of the short story as you like.

When a story impresses you as good, something has caused it to do so. Your responses are caused not by one element but rather by a combination. A good interpretation of a short story may therefore move from setting to character to theme to style and tone and back again at will. Great short stories succeed because all their elements work together and create a powerful effect. Bharati Mukherjee's "Jasmine" is such a story. The setting is economical, the characters are rich and complex, and the style imparts subtle contrasts, some of them ironic, with the thematic concerns of a young woman making her way in a strange and unexpected world. The straightforward action is told with no flashbacks, and the point of view is consistent with the most conventional storytelling techniques. Conventional simplicities add to the richness and complexity of the story because they help us contrast the simplicity of certain characters' perceptions with the enormous subtleties of the environment.

"Jasmine," told from a third-person point of view, never veers from what Jasmine saw, thought, and experienced. The reader sees the world through her eyes because the narrative stays entirely within her sphere of understanding; it is restricted. The setting is recognizable to any contemporary North American, especially one who has visited large cities like Detroit or who has experienced college towns like Ann Arbor. However, the experiences are unusual because of the perceptions of the character, for whom they are exotic. Jasmine is an East Indian who had been living in Trinidad and who has now come to the United States through Canada. She is illegal. She is also eager and excited by her opportunities.

Bharati Mukherjee   (b. 1940)

Born in Calcutta, India, Bharati Mukherjee came to the United States when she was twenty one and then moved in 1968 to Canada. Partly in reaction to prejudice against Indians in Canada, she returned to the United States in 1980 and became a permanent resident. Mukherjee has written several novels: The Tiger's Daughter *(1972);* Wife *(1975); and* Jasmine *(1989), which further treats the character in this story. Her short stories are collected in* Darkness *(1980) and* The Middleman and Other Stories *(1988). She has also written some personal*

reminiscences, Days and Nights in Calcutta *and* The Sorrow and the Terror.
Mukherjee is a powerful writer in the early stages of her career.

JASMINE   1988

Jasmine came to Detroit from Port-of-Spain, Trinidad, by way of Canada.
She crossed the border at Windsor in the back of a gray van loaded with mattresses and box springs. The plan was for her to hide in an empty mattress box if
she heard the driver say, "All bad weather seems to come down from Canada,
doesn't it?" to the customs man. But she didn't have to crawl into a box and hold
her breath. The customs man didn't ask to look in.

The driver let her off at a scary intersection on Woodward Avenue and gave
her instructions on how to get to the Plantations Motel in Southfield. The trick
was to keep changing vehicles, he said. That threw off the immigration guys real
quick.

Jasmine took money for cab fare out of the pocket of the great big raincoat
that the van driver had given her. The raincoat looked like something that nuns
in Port-of-Spain sold in church bazaars. Jasmine was glad to have a coat with wool
lining, though; and anyway, who would know in Detroit that she was Dr. Vassanji's
daughter?

All the bills in her hand looked the same. She would have to be careful when
she paid the cabdriver. Money in Detroit wasn't pretty the way it was back home,
or even in Canada, but she liked this money better. Why should money be pretty,
like a picture? Pretty money is only good for putting on your walls maybe. The
dollar bills felt businesslike, serious. Back home at work, she used to count out
thousands of Trinidad dollars every day and not even think of them as real. Real
money was worn and green, American dollars. Holding the bills in her fist on a
street corner meant she had made it in okay. She'd outsmarted the guys at the
border. Now it was up to her to use her wits to do something with her life. As
her Daddy kept saying, "Girl, is opportunity come only once." The girls she'd
worked with at the bank in Port-of-Spain had gone green as bananas when she'd
walked in with her ticket on Air Canada. Trinidad was too tiny. That was the trouble. Trinidad was an island stuck in the middle of nowhere. What kind of place
was that for a girl with ambition?

The Plantations Motel was run by a family of Trinidad Indians who had come   5
from the tuppenny-ha'penny° country town, Chaguanas. The Daboos were nobodies back home. They were lucky, that's all. They'd gotten here before the rush
and bought up a motel and an ice cream parlor. Jasmine felt very superior when
she saw Mr. Daboo in the motel's reception area. He was a pumpkin-shaped man
with very black skin and Elvis Presley sideburns turning white. They looked like
earmuffs. Mrs. Daboo was a bumpkin, too; short, fat, flapping around in house
slippers. The Daboo daughters seemed very American, though. They didn't seem
to know that they were nobodies, and kept looking at her and giggling.

She knew she would be short of cash for a great long while. Besides, she
wasn't sure she wanted to wear bright leather boots and leotards like Viola and
Loretta. The smartest move she could make would be to put a down payment on

---

tupenny-ha'penny: Equivalent in American slang to nickel-dime.

a husband. Her Daddy had told her to talk to the Daboos first chance. The Daboos ran a service fixing up illegals with islanders who had made it in legally. Daddy had paid three thousand back in Trinidad, with the Daboos and the mattress man getting part of it. They should throw in a good-earning husband for that kind of money.

The Daboos asked her to keep books for them and to clean the rooms in the new wing, and she could stay in 16B as long as she liked. They showed her 16B. They said she could cook her own roti;° Mr. Daboo would bring in a stove, two gas rings that you could fold up in a metal box. The room was quite grand, Jasmine thought. It had a double bed, a TV, a pink sink and matching bathtub. Mrs. Daboo said Jasmine wasn't the big-city Port-of-Spain type she'd expected. Mr. Daboo said that he wanted her to stay because it was nice to have a neat, cheerful person around. It wasn't a bad deal, better than stories she'd heard about Trinidad girls in the States.

All day every day except Sundays Jasmine worked. There wasn't just the bookkeeping and the cleaning up. Mr. Daboo had her working on the match-up marriage service. Jasmine's job was to check up on social security cards, call clients' bosses for references, and make sure credit information wasn't false. Dermatologists and engineers living in Bloomfield Hills, store owners on Canfield and Woodward: she treated them all as potential liars. One of the first things she learned was that Ann Arbor was a magic word. A boy goes to Ann Arbor and gets an education, and all the barriers come crashing down. So Ann Arbor was the place to be.

She didn't mind the work. She was learning about Detroit, every side of it. Sunday mornings she helped unload packing crates of Caribbean spices in a shop on the next block. For the first time in her life, she was working for a black man, an African. So what if the boss was black? This was a new life, and she wanted to learn everything. Her Sunday boss, Mr. Anthony, was a courtly, Christian, churchgoing man, and paid her the only wages she had in her pocket. Viola and Loretta, for all their fancy American ways, wouldn't go out with blacks.

One Friday afternoon she was writing up the credit info on a Guyanese   10 Muslim who worked in an assembly plant when Loretta said that enough was enough and that there was no need for Jasmine to be her father's drudge.

"Is time to have fun," Viola said. "We're going to Ann Arbor."

Jasmine filed the sheet on the Guyanese man who probably now would never get a wife and got her raincoat. Loretta's boyfriend had a Cadillac parked out front. It was the longest car Jasmine had ever been in and louder than a country bus. Viola's boyfriend got out of the front seat. "Oh, oh, sweet things," he said to Jasmine. "Get in front." He was a talker. She'd learned that much from working on the matrimonial match-ups. She didn't believe him for a second when he said that there were dudes out there dying to ask her out.

Loretta's boyfriend said, "You have eyes I could leap into, girl."

Jasmine knew he was just talking. They sounded like Port-of-Spain boys of three years ago. It didn't surprise her that these Trinidad country boys in Detroit were still behind the times, even of Port-of-Spain. She sat very stiff between the two men, hands on her purse. The Daboo girls laughed in the back seat.

roti: A kind of bread.

On the highway the girls told her about the reggae night in Ann Arbor. Kevin   15
and the Krazee Islanders. Malcolm's Lovers. All the big reggae groups in the Midwest
were converging for the West Indian Students Association fall bash. The ticket didn't
come cheap but Jasmine wouldn't let the fellows pay. She wasn't that kind of girl.

The reggae and steel drums brought out the old Jasmine. The rum punch,
the dancing, the dreadlocks, the whole combination. She hadn't heard real music since she got to Detroit, where music was supposed to be so famous. The
Daboo girls kept turning on rock stuff in the motel lobby whenever their father
left the area. She hadn't danced, really *danced*, since she'd left home. It felt so
good to dance. She felt hot and sweaty and sexy. The boys at the dance were more
than sweet talkers; they moved with assurance and spoke of their futures in
America. The bartender gave her two free drinks and said, "Is ready when you
are, girl." She ignored him but she felt all hot and good deep inside. She knew
Ann Arbor was a special place.

When it was time to pile back into Loretta's boyfriend's Cadillac, she just
couldn't face going back to the Plantations Motel and to the Daboos with their
accounting books and messy files.

"I don't know what happen, girl," she said to Loretta. "I feel all crazy inside. Maybe is time for me to pursue higher studies in this town."

"This Ann Arbor, girl, they don't just take you off the street. It *cost* like hell."

She spent the night on a bashed-up sofa in the Student Union. She was a   20
well-dressed, respectable girl, and she didn't expect anyone to question her right
to sleep on the furniture. Many others were doing the same thing. In the morning, a boy in an army parka showed her the way to the Placement Office. He was
a big, blond, clumsy boy, not bad-looking except for the blond eyelashes. He
didn't scare her, as did most Americans. She let him buy her a Coke and a hotdog. That evening she had a job with the Moffitts.

Bill Moffitt taught molecular biology and Lara Hatch-Moffitt, his wife, was
a performance artist. A performance artist, said Lara, was very different from being an actress, though Jasmine still didn't understand what the difference might
be. The Moffitts had a little girl, Muffin, whom Jasmine was to look after, though
for the first few months she might have to help out with the housework and the
cooking because Lara said she was deep into performance rehearsals. That was all
right with her, Jasmine said, maybe a little too quickly. She explained she came
from a big family and was used to heavy-duty cooking and cleaning. This wasn't
the time to say anything about Ram, the family servant. Americans like the Moffitts
wouldn't understand about keeping servants. Ram and she weren't in similar situations. Here mother's helpers, which is what Lara had called her—Americans
were good with words to cover their shame—seemed to be as good as anyone.

Lara showed her the room she would have all to herself in the finished basement. There was a big, old TV, not in color like the motel's and a portable typewriter on a desk which Lara said she would find handy when it came time to turn
in her term papers. Jasmine didn't say anything about not being a student. She
was a student of life, wasn't she? There was a scary moment after they'd discussed
what she could expect as salary, which was three times more than anything Mr.
Daboo was supposed to pay her but hadn't. She thought Bill Moffitt was going
to ask her about her visa or her green card number and social security. But all Bill
did was smile and smile at her—he had a wide, pink, baby face—and play with a
button on his corduroy jacket. The button would need sewing back on, firmly.

Lara said, "I think I'm going to like you, Jasmine. You have a something about you. A something real special. I'll just bet you've acted, haven't you?" The idea amused her, but she merely smiled and accepted Lara's hug. The interview was over.

Then Bill opened a bottle of Soave and told stories about camping in northern Michigan. He'd been raised there. Jasmine didn't see the point in sleeping in tents; the woods sounded cold and wild and creepy. But she said, "Is exactly what I want to try out come summer, man. Campin and huntin."

Lara asked about Port-of-Spain. There was nothing to tell about her hometown that wouldn't shame her in front of nice white American folk like the Moffitts. The place was shabby, the people were grasping and cheating and lying and life was full of despair and drink and wanting. But by the time she finished, the island sounded romantic. Lara said, "It wouldn't surprise me one bit if you were a writer, Jasmine." 25

Ann Arbor was a huge small town. She couldn't imagine any kind of school the size of the University of Michigan. She meant to sign up for courses in the spring. Bill brought home a catalogue bigger than the phonebook for all of Trinidad. The university had courses in everything. It would be hard to choose; she'd have to get help from Bill. He wasn't like a professor, not the ones back home where even high school teachers called themselves professors and acted like little potentates. He wore blue jeans and thick sweaters with holes in the elbows and used phrases like "in vitro" as he watched her curry up fish. Dr. Parveen back home—he called himself "doctor" when everybody knew he didn't have even a Master's degree—was never seen without his cotton jacket which had gotten really ratty at the cuffs and lapel edges. She hadn't learned anything in the two years she'd put into college. She'd learned more from working in the bank for two months than she had at college. It was the assistant manager, Personal Loans Department, Mr. Singh, who had turned her on to the Daboos and to smooth, bargain-priced emigration.

Jasmine liked Lara. Lara was easygoing. She didn't spend the time she had between rehearsals telling Jasmine how to cook and clean American-style. Mrs. Daboo did that in 16B. Mrs. Daboo would barge in with a plate of stale samosas and snoop around giving free advice on how mainstream Americans did things. As if she were dumb or something! As if she couldn't keep her own eyes open and make her mind up for herself. Sunday mornings she had to share the butcher-block workspace in the kitchen with Bill. He made the Sunday brunch from new recipes in *Gourmet* and *Cuisine*. Jasmine hadn't seen a man cook who didn't have to or wasn't getting paid to do it. Things were topsy-turvy in the Moffitt house. Lara went on two- and three-day road trips and Bill stayed home. But even her Daddy, who'd never poured himself a cup of tea, wouldn't put Bill down as a woman. The mornings Bill tried out something complicated, a Cajun shrimp, sausage, and beans dish, for instance, Jasmine skipped church services. The Moffitts didn't go to church, though they seemed to be good Christians. They just didn't talk church talk, which suited her fine.

Two months passed. Jasmine knew she was lucky to have found a small, clean, friendly family like the Moffitts to build her new life around. "Man!" she'd exclaim as she vacuumed the wide-plank wood floors or ironed (Lara wore pure silk or pure cotton). "In this country Jesus givin out good luck only!" By this time they knew she wasn't a student, but they didn't care and said they wouldn't report her. They never asked if she was illegal on top of it.

To savor her new sense of being a happy, lucky person, she would put herself through a series of "what ifs": what if Mr. Singh in Port-of-Spain hadn't turned her on to the Daboos and loaned her two thousand! What if she'd been ugly like the Mintoo girl and the manager hadn't even offered! What if the customs man had unlocked the door of the van! Her Daddy liked to say, "You is a helluva girl, Jasmine."

"Thank you, Jesus," Jasmine said, as she carried on.   30

Christmas Day the Moffitts treated her just like family. They gave her a red cashmere sweater with a V neck so deep it made her blush. If Lara had worn it, her bosom wouldn't hang out like melons. For the holiday weekend Bill drove her to the Daboos in Detroit. "You work too hard," Bill said to her. "Learn to be more selfish. Come on, throw your weight around." She'd rather not have spent time with the Daboos, but that first afternoon of the interview she'd told Bill and Lara that Mr. Daboo was her mother's first cousin. She had thought it shameful in those days to have no papers, no family, no roots. Now Loretta and Viola in tight, bright pants seemed trashy like girls at Two-Johnny Bissoondath's Bar back home. She was stuck with the story of the Daboos being family. Village bumpkins, ha! She would break out. Soon.

Jasmine had Bill drop her off at the RenCen. The Plantations Motel, in fact, the whole Riverfront area, was too seamy. She'd managed to cut herself off mentally from anything too islandy. She loved her Daddy and Mummy, but she didn't think of them that often anymore. Mummy had expected her to be homesick and come flying right back home. "Is blowin sweat-of-brow money is what you doin, Pa," Mummy had scolded. She loved them, but she'd become her own person. That something that Lara said: "I am my own person."

The Daboos acted thrilled to see her back. "What you drinkin, Jasmine girl?" Mr. Daboo kept asking. "You drinkin sherry or what?" Pouring her little glasses of sherry instead of rum was a sure sign he thought she had become whitefolk-fancy. The Daboo sisters were very friendly, but Jasmine considered them too wild. Both Loretta and Viola had changed boyfriends. Both were seeing black men they'd danced with in Ann Arbor. Each night at bedtime, Mr. Daboo cried. "In Trinidad we stayin we side, they stayin they side. Here, everything mixed up. Is helluva confusion, no?"

On New Year's Eve the Daboo girls and their black friends went to a dance. Mr. and Mrs. Daboo and Jasmine watched TV for a while. Then Mr. Daboo got out a brooch from his pocket and pinned it on Jasmine's red sweater. It was a Christmasy brooch, a miniature sleigh loaded down with snowed-on mistletoe. Before she could pull away, he kissed her on the lips. "Good luck for the New Year!" he said. She lifted her head and saw tears. "Is year for dreams comin true."

Jasmine started to cry, too. There was nothing wrong, but Mr. Daboo, Mrs.   35
Daboo, she, everybody was crying.

What for? This is where she wanted to be. She'd spent some damned uncomfortable times with the assistant manager to get approval for her loan. She thought of Daddy. He would be playing poker and fanning himself with a magazine. Her married sisters would be rolling out the dough for stacks and stacks of roti, and Mummy would be steamed purple from stirring the big pot of goat curry on the stove. She missed them. But. It felt strange to think of anyone celebrating New Year's Eve in summery clothes.

In March Lara and her performing group went on the road. Jasmine knew that the group didn't work from scripts. The group didn't use a stage, either; instead, it took over supermarkets, senior citizens' centers, and school halls, without notice. Jasmine didn't understand the performance world. But she was glad that Lara said, "I'm not going to lay a guilt trip on myself. Muffie's in super hands," before she left.

Muffie didn't need much looking after. She played Trivial Pursuit all day, usually pretending to be two persons, sometimes Jasmine, whose accent she could imitate. Since Jasmine didn't know any of the answers, she couldn't help. Muffie was a quiet, precocious child with see-through blue eyes like her dad's, and red braids. In the early evenings Jasmine cooked supper, something special she hadn't forgotten from her island days. After supper she and Muffie watched some TV, and Bill read. When Muffie went to bed, Bill and she sat together for a bit with their glasses of Soave. Bill, Muffie, and she were a family, almost.

Down in her basement room that late, dark winter, she had trouble sleeping. She wanted to stay awake and think of Bill. Even when she fell asleep it didn't feel like sleep because Bill came barging into her dreams in his funny, loose-jointed, clumsy way. It was mad to think of him all the time, and stupid and sinful; but she couldn't help it. Whenever she put back a book he'd taken off the shelf to read or whenever she put his clothes through the washer and dryer, she felt sick in a giddy, wonderful way. When Lara came back things would get back to normal. Meantime she wanted the performance group miles away.

Lara called in at least twice a week. She said things like, "We've finally obliterated the margin between realspace and performancespace." Jasmine filled her in on Muffie's doings and the mail. Bill always closed with, "I love you. We miss you, hon." 40

One night after Lara had called—she was in Lincoln, Nebraska—Bill said to Jasmine, "Let's dance."

She hadn't danced since the reggae night she'd had too many rum punches. Her toes began to throb and clench. She untied her apron and the fraying, knotted-up laces of her running shoes.

Bill went around the downstairs rooms turning down lights. "We need atmosphere," he said. He got a small, tidy fire going in the living room grate and pulled the Turkish scatter rug closer to it. Lara didn't like anybody walking on the Turkish rug, but Bill meant to have his way. The hissing logs, the plants in the dimmed light, the thick patterned rug: everything was changed. This wasn't the room she cleaned every day.

He stood close to her. She smoothed her skirt down with both hands.

"I want you to choose the record," he said. 45

"I don't know your music."

She brought her hand high to his face. His skin was baby smooth.

"I want *you* to pick," he said. "You are your own person now."

"You got island music?"

He laughed, "What do you think?" The stereo was in a cabinet with albums 50
packed tight alphabetically into the bottom three shelves. "Calypso has not been a force in my life."

She couldn't help laughing. "Calypso? Oh, man." She pulled dust jackets out at random. Lara's records. The Flying Lizards. The Violent Fems. There was so much still to pick up on!

"This one," she said, finally.

He took the record out of her hand. "God! he laughed. "Lara must have found this in a garage sale!" He laid the old record on the turntable. It was "Music for Lovers," something the nuns had taught her to foxtrot to way back in Port-of-Spain.

They danced so close that she could feel his heart heaving and crashing against her head. She liked it, she liked it very much. She didn't care what happened.

"Come on," Bill whispered. "If it feels right, do it." He began to take her   55
clothes off.

"Don't, Bill," she pleaded.

"Come on, baby," he whispered again. "You're a blossom, a flower."

He took off his fisherman's knit pullover, the corduroy pants, the blue shorts. She kept pace. She'd never had such an effect on a man. He nearly flung his socks and Adidas into the fire. "You feel so good," he said. "You smell so good. You're really something, flower of Trinidad."

"Flower of Ann Arbor," she said, "not Trinidad."

She felt so good she was dizzy. She'd never felt this good on the island where   60
men did this all the time, and girls went along with it always for favors. You couldn't feel really good in a nothing place. She was thinking this as they made love on the Turkish carpet in front of the fire: she was a bright, pretty girl with no visa, no papers, and no birth certificate. No nothing other than what she wanted to invent and tell. She was a girl rushing wildly into the future.

His hand moved up her throat and forced her lips apart and it felt so good, so right, that she forgot all the dreariness of her new life and gave herself up to it.

Questions for Close Reading

1. Jasmine's entrance into Detroit was illegal. What was her emotional state upon entry? Did she feel guilty? Should she? How does the initial setting contribute to her feelings? How do you respond to her arrival?

2. What was Jasmine's background before she arrived in Detroit? What was her attitude toward herself in relation to the society around her?

3. Is Jasmine ambitious? What is her relationship to the Daboos? What does she mean when she thinks, "The Daboos were nobodies back home"? How do the Daboos treat her?

4. Jasmine thinks room 16B is "quite grand." How do you react to the setting of 16B? Does Mukherjee rely on irony for effect here?

5. How do the characters react to those of other races? What is Jasmine's attitude toward blacks? Toward whites? Toward other Indians? Is racial prejudice a major theme of the story?

6. In what ways is the contrast between Lara Hatch-Moffitt and Jasmine ironic? Why does Jasmine think, "Things were topsy-turvy in the Moffitt house"? Is she right?

7. One of the central themes of the story is the disjunction between traditional Indian social style and the American style of the Moffitts. What chief distinctions does Jasmine notice? Is the disjunction ironic?

8. What stylistic contrasts in the use of language do you feel are most important in the story? What are the major differences in the ways in which different people speak? What do the differences add to the story?

Questions for Interpretation

New Critical

1. How appropriate is the restricted third-person point of view to the telling of Jasmine's story? Is the action of the story more satisfying because of the point of view, or less satisfying? How effective is this point of view for revealing Jasmine's personality? What overall effect does this point of view have on making you understand her emotional and moral circumstances?

2. At the end of the story, as Bill undresses Jasmine, he says, "If it feels right, do it." This is an ethical statement. What has Jasmine done throughout the story to prepare her to accept and act upon that statement? Has Bill's ethical view always been one Jasmine could share? When, in the story, does she seem to have begun accepting it? Does the story make a judgment in approval or disapproval of this ethical view? Is Bill's comment ironic or sincere? Is the story ironic?

Reader Response

3. Are you sympathetic or unsympathetic to Jasmine and her situation? Does she do things that annoy you? Or please you? How do you feel about Bill and Lara Moffitt? Are your responses to them positive or not? What about the Daboos and their daughters, Viola and Loretta? To what extent are your sympathies controlled by Jasmine's experiences? To what extent are your sympathies controlled by your own views on illegal immigrants?

Feminist

4. What is the position of women in the story? How many different women are important in the story? What are their approximate ages? What is expected of them, and how free or independent are they? Are women oppressed in "Jasmine"? Is Jasmine oppressed? Was Jasmine right in going along with Bill's seduction at the end of the story? What does it mean to say, "She was a girl rushing wildly into the future"? Does Bill exploit Jasmine?

Cultural

5. One theme of the story is emigration—a theme common to much of Mukherjee's writing. What significance does the story have for us regarding emigration to America, especially of nonwhites? What cultural disjunctions does Jasmine experience? What does Jasmine mean by the reference to "all the dreariness of her new life" on the last page of the story?

5

Interpreting Short Fiction

BEGINNING WITH CLOSE READING

This chapter offers you further practice in interpretation. Your first reading of William Faulkner's "A Rose for Emily" should be slow and primarily for enjoyment. During your second reading underline passages that reveal some of the important details and ideas in the story. Every reader will underline different passages, but the purpose of underlining is to keep track of ideas you think are important. You may want to consider identifying the important elements in the story and establishing what their function may be.

When you read "A Rose for Emily" the second time, note the town's opinions of Miss Emily and her family, her father's role in her life, and her environment. Keep track of details of point of view, important themes, and significant characters. Everything you notice is important. You may compare your observations with the sample close reading and interpretations that follow.

William Faulkner   (1897–1962)

William Faulkner, who won the Nobel Prize for literature in 1950, worked on a newspaper in New Orleans after World War I but soon returned to his native Oxford, Mississippi, where he spent most of his life writing. He created Yoknapatawpha, an imaginary Mississippi county, for the setting of most of his stories. Colonel Sartoris, mentioned in "A Rose for Emily," figures in several stories and novels set in Yoknapatawpha, and lives through the post–Civil War era, a period of American history that fascinated Faulkner. Faulkner's most important books are The Sound and the Fury *(1929),* As I Lay Dying *(1930),*

Sanctuary *(1931),* Light in August *(1932),* Absalom, Absalom! *(1936), and*
The Hamlet *(1940). His short stories are usually direct and less complex than his*
novels, but they are also informed by the history of the American south.

"A ROSE FOR EMILY"   1924

I

When Miss Emily Grierson died, our whole town went to her funeral: the
men through a sort of respectful affection for a fallen monument, the women
mostly out of curiosity to see the inside of her house, which no one save an old
manservant—a combined gardener and cook—had seen in at least ten years.

It was a big, squarish frame house that had once been white, decorated with
cupolas and spires and scrolled balconies in the heavily lightsome style of the seventies, set on what had once been our most select street. But garages and cotton gins had encroached and obliterated even the august names of that neighborhood; only Miss Emily's house was left, lifting its stubborn and coquettish
decay above the cotton wagons and the gasoline pumps—an eyesore among eyesores. And now Miss Emily had gone to join the representatives of those august
names where they lay in the cedar-bemused cemetery among the ranked and
anonymous graves of Union and Confederate soldiers who fell at the battle of
Jefferson.

Alive, Miss Emily had been a tradition, a duty, and a care; a sort of hereditary obligation upon the town, dating from that day in 1894 when Colonel
Sartoris, the mayor—he who fathered the edict that no Negro woman should appear on the streets without an apron—remitted her taxes, the dispensation dating from the death of her father on into perpetuity. Not that Miss Emily would
have accepted charity. Colonel Sartoris invented an involved tale to the effect that
Miss Emily's father had loaned money to the town, which the town, as a matter
of business, preferred this way of repaying. Only a man of Colonel Sartoris' generation and thought could have invented it, and only a woman could have believed it.

When the next generation, with its more modern ideas, became mayors and
aldermen, this arrangement created some little dissatisfaction. On the first of the
year they mailed her a tax notice. February came, and there was no reply. They
wrote her a formal letter, asking her to call at the sheriff's office at her convenience. A week later the mayor wrote her himself, offering to call or to send his
car for her, and received in reply a note on paper of an archaic shape, in a thin,
flowing calligraphy in faded ink, to the effect that she no longer went out at all.
The tax notice was also enclosed, without comment.

They called a special meeting of the Board of Aldermen. A deputation waited   5
upon her, knocked at the door through which no visitor had passed since she
ceased giving china-painting lessons eight or ten years earlier. They were admitted by the old Negro into a dim hall from which a stairway mounted into still
more shadow. It smelled of dust and disuse—a close, dank smell. The Negro led
them into the parlor. It was furnished in heavy, leather-covered furniture. When
the Negro opened the blinds of one window, they could see that the leather was
cracked; and when they sat down, a faint dust rose sluggishly about their thighs,

spinning with slow motes in the single sun–ray. On a tarnished gilt easel before the fireplace stood a crayon portrait of Miss Emily's father.

They rose when she entered—a small, fat woman in black, with a thin gold chain descending to her waist and vanishing into her belt, leaning on an ebony cane with a tarnished gold head. Her skeleton was small and spare; perhaps that was why what would have been merely plumpness in another was obesity in her. She looked bloated, like a body long submerged in motionless water, and of that pallid hue. Her eyes, lost in the fatty ridges of her face, looked like two small pieces of coal pressed into a lump of dough as they moved from one face to another while the visitors stated their errand.

She did not ask them to sit. She just stood in the door and listened quietly until the spokesman came to a stumbling halt. Then they could hear the invisible watch ticking at the end of the gold chain.

Her voice was dry and cold. "I have no taxes in Jefferson. Colonel Sartoris explained it to me. Perhaps one of you can gain access to the city records and satisfy yourselves."

"But we have. We are the city authorities, Miss Emily. Didn't you get a notice from the sheriff, signed by him?"

"I received a paper, yes," Miss Emily said. "Perhaps he considers himself the   10
sheriff . . . I have no taxes in Jefferson."

"But there is nothing on the books to show that, you see. We must go by the—"

"See Colonel Sartoris. I have no taxes in Jefferson."

"But, Miss Emily—"

"See Colonel Sartoris." (Colonel Sartoris had been dead almost ten years.) "I have no taxes in Jefferson. Tobe!" The Negro appeared. "Show these gentlemen out."

II

So she vanquished them, horse and foot, just as she had vanquished their fa-   15
thers thirty years before about the smell. That was two years after her father's death and a short time after her sweetheart—the one we believed would marry her—had deserted her. After her father's death she went out very little; after her sweetheart went away, people hardly saw her at all. A few of the ladies had the temerity to call, but were not received, and the only sign of life about the place was the Negro man—a young man then—going in and out with a market basket.

"Just as if a man—any man—could keep a kitchen properly," the ladies said; so they were not surprised when the smell developed. It was another link between the gross, teeming world and the high and mighty Griersons.

A neighbor, a woman, complained to the mayor, Judge Stevens, eighty years old.

"But what will you have me do about it, madam?" he said.

"Why, send her word to stop it," the woman said. "Isn't there a law?"

"I'm sure that won't be necessary," Judge Stevens said. "It's probably just   20
a snake or a rat that nigger of hers killed in the yard. I'll speak to him about it."

The next day he received two more complaints, one from a man who came in diffident deprecation. "We really must do something about it, Judge. I'd be the last one in the world to bother Miss Emily, but we've got to do something."

That night the Board of Aldermen met—three graybeards and one younger man, a member of the rising generation.

"It's simple enough," he said. "Send her word to have her place cleaned up. Give her a certain time to do it in, and if she don't . . . ."

"Dammit, sir," Judge Stevens said, "will you accuse a lady to her face of smelling bad?"

So the next night, after midnight, four men crossed Miss Emily's lawn and slunk about the house like burglars, sniffing along the base of the brickwork and at the cellar openings while one of them performed a regular sowing motion with his hand out of a sack slung from his shoulder. They broke open the cellar door and sprinkled lime there, and in all the outbuildings. As they recrossed the lawn, a window that had been dark was lighted and Miss Emily sat in it, the light behind her, and her upright torso motionless as that of an idol. They crept quietly across the lawn and into the shadow of the locusts that lined the street. After a week or two the smell went away.

That was when people had begun to feel really sorry for her. People in our town, remembering how old lady Wyatt, her great-aunt, had gone completely crazy at last, believed that the Griersons held themselves a little too high for what they really were. None of the young men were quite good enough to Miss Emily and such. We had long thought of them as a tableau; Miss Emily a slender figure in white in the background, her father a spraddled silhouette in the foreground, his back to her and clutching a horsewhip, the two of them framed by the back-flung front door. So when she got to be thirty and was still single, we were not pleased exactly, but vindicated; even with insanity in the family she wouldn't have turned down all of her chances if they had really materialized.

When her father died, it got about that the house was all that was left to her; and in a way, people were glad. At last they could pity Miss Emily. Being left alone, and a pauper, she had become humanized. Now she too would know the old thrill and the old despair of a penny more or less.

The day after his death all the ladies prepared to call at the house and offer condolence and aid, as is our custom. Miss Emily met them at the door, dressed as usual and with no trace of grief on her face. She told them that her father was not dead. She did that for three days, with the ministers calling on her, and the doctors, trying to persuade her to let them dispose of the body. Just as they were about to resort to law and force, she broke down, and they buried her father quickly.

We did not say she was crazy then. We believed she had to do that. We remembered all the young men her father had driven away, and we knew that with nothing left, she would have to cling to that which had robbed her, as people will.

III

She was sick for a long time. When we saw her again, her hair was cut short, making her look like a girl, with a vague resemblance to those angels in colored church windows—sort of tragic and serene.

The town had just let the contracts for paving the sidewalks, and in the summer after her father's death they began the work. The construction company came with niggers and mules and machinery, and a foreman named Homer Barron, a Yankee—a big, dark, ready man, with a big voice and eyes lighter than his face.

The little boys would follow in groups to hear him cuss the niggers, and the niggers singing in time to the rise and fall of picks. Pretty soon he knew everybody in town. Whenever you heard a lot of laughing anywhere about the square, Homer Barron would be in the center of the group. Presently we began to see him and Miss Emily on Sunday afternoons driving in the yellow-wheeled buggy and the matched team of bays from the livery stable.

At first we were glad that Miss Emily would have an interest, because the ladies all said, "Of course a Grierson would not think seriously of a Northerner, a day laborer." But there were still others, older people, who said that even grief could not cause a real lady to forget *noblesse oblige*°—without calling it *noblesse oblige*. They just said, "Poor Emily. Her kinsfolk should come to her." She had some kin in Alabama; but years ago her father had fallen out with them over the estate of old lady Wyatt, the crazy woman, and there was no communication between the two families. They had not even been represented at the funeral.

And as soon as the old people said, "Poor Emily," the whispering began. "Do you suppose it's really so?" they said to one another. "Of course it is. What else could . . . ." This behind their hands; rustling of craned silk and satin behind jalousies closed upon the sun of Sunday afternoon as the thin, swift clop-clop-clop of the matched team passed: "Poor Emily."

She carried her head high enough—even when we believed that she was fallen. It was as if she demanded more than ever the recognition of her dignity as the last Grierson; as if it had wanted that touch of earthiness to reaffirm her imperviousness. Like when she bought the rat poison, the arsenic. That was over a year after they had begun to say "Poor Emily," and while the two female cousins were visiting her.

"I want some poison," she said to the druggist. She was over thirty then, still a slight woman, though thinner than usual, with cold, haughty black eyes in a face the flesh of which was strained across the temples and about the eye-sockets as you imagine a lighthouse-keeper's face ought to look. "I want some poison," she said.

"Yes, Miss Emily. What kind? For rats and such? I'd recom—"   35
"I want the best you have. I don't care what kind."
The druggist named several. "They'll kill anything up to an elephant. But what you want is—"
"Arsenic," Miss Emily said. "Is that a good one?"
"Is . . . arsenic? Yes, ma'am. But what you want—"
"I want arsenic."   40
The druggist looked down at her. She looked back at him, erect, her face like a strained flag. "Why, of course," the druggist said. "If that's what you want. But the law requires you to tell what you are going to use it for."

Miss Emily just stared at him, her head tilted back in order to look him eye for eye, until he looked away and went and got the arsenic and wrapped it up. The Negro delivery boy brought her the package; the druggist didn't come back. When she opened the package at home there was written on the box, under the skull and bones: "For rats."

---

noblesse oblige: The obligations of the "upper classes" to look after the poor, now regarded as evidence of snobbery.

IV

So the next day we all said, "She will kill herself"; and we said it would be the best thing. When she had first begun to be seen with Homer Barron, we had said, "She will marry him." Then we said, "She will persuade him yet," because Homer himself had remarked—he liked men, and it was known that he drank with the younger men in the Elks' Club—that he was not a marrying man. Later we said, "Poor Emily" behind the jalousies as they passed on Sunday afternoon in the glittering buggy, Miss Emily with her head high and Homer Barron with his hat cocked and a cigar in his teeth, reins and whip in a yellow glove.

Then some of the ladies began to say that it was a disgrace to the town and a bad example to the young people. The men did not want to interfere, but at last the ladies forced the Baptist minister—Miss Emily's people were Episcopal—to call upon her. He would never divulge what happened during that interview, but he refused to go back again. The next Sunday they again drove about the streets, and the following day the minister's wife wrote to Miss Emily's relations in Alabama.

So she had blood-kin under her roof again and we sat back to watch de-   45 velopments. At first nothing happened. Then we were sure that they were to be married. We learned that Miss Emily had been to the jeweler's and ordered a man's toilet set in silver, with the letters H. B. on each piece. Two days later we learned that she had bought a complete outfit of men's clothing, including a nightshirt, and we said, "They are married." We were really glad. We were glad because the two female cousins were even more Grierson than Miss Emily had ever been.

So we were not surprised when Homer Barron—the streets had been finished some time since—was gone. We were a little disappointed that there was not a public blowing-off, but we believed that he had gone on to prepare for Miss Emily's coming, or to give her a chance to get rid of the cousins. (By that time it was a cabal, and we were all Miss Emily's allies to help circumvent the cousins.) Sure enough, after another week they departed. And, as we had expected all along, within three days Homer Barron was back in town. A neighbor saw the Negro man admit him at the kitchen door at dusk one evening.

And that was the last we saw of Homer Barron. And of Miss Emily for some time. The Negro man went in and out with the market basket, but the front door remained closed. Now and then we would see her at a window for a moment, as the men did that night when they sprinkled the lime, but for almost six months she did not appear on the streets. Then we knew that this was to be expected too; as if that quality of her father which had thwarted her woman's life so many times had been too virulent and too furious to die.

When we next saw Miss Emily, she had grown fat and her hair was turning gray. During the next few years it grew grayer and grayer until it attained an even pepper-and-salt iron-gray, when it ceased turning. Up to the day of her death at seventy-four it was still that vigorous iron-gray, like the hair of an active man.

From that time on her front door remained closed, save for a period of six or seven years, when she was about forty, during which she gave lessons in china-painting. She fitted up a studio in one of the downstairs rooms, where the daughters and granddaughters of Colonel Sartoris' contemporaries were sent to her with the same regularity and in the same spirit that they were sent to church on Sundays with a twenty-five cent piece for the collection plate. Meanwhile her taxes had been remitted.

Then the newer generation became the backbone and the spirit of the town, and the painting pupils grew up and fell away and did not send their children to her with boxes of color and tedious brushes and pictures cut from the ladies' magazines. The front door closed upon the last one and remained closed for good. When the town got free postal delivery, Miss Emily alone refused to let them fasten the metal numbers above her door and attach a mailbox to it. She would not listen to them.

Daily, monthly, yearly we watched the Negro grow grayer and more stooped, going in and out with the market basket. Each December we sent her a tax notice, which would be returned by the post office a week later, unclaimed. Now and then we would see her in one of the downstairs windows—she had evidently shut up the top floor of the house—like the carven torso of an idol in a niche, looking or not looking at us, we could never tell which. Thus she passed from generation to generation—dear, inescapable, impervious, tranquil, and perverse.

And so she died. Fell ill in the house filled with dust and shadows, with only a doddering Negro man to wait on her. We did not even know she was sick; we had long since given up trying to get any information from the Negro. He talked to no one, probably not even to her, for his voice had grown harsh and rusty, as if from disuse.

She died in one of the downstairs rooms, in a heavy walnut bed with a curtain, her gray head propped on a pillow yellow and moldy with age and lack of sunlight.

V

The Negro met the first of the ladies at the front door and let them in, with their hushed, sibilant voices and their quick, curious glances, and then he disappeared. He walked right through the house and out the back and was not seen again.

The two female cousins came at once. They held the funeral on the second day, with the town coming to look at Miss Emily beneath a mass of bought flowers, with the crayon face of her father musing profoundly above the bier and the ladies sibilant and macabre; and the very old men—some in their brushed Confederate uniforms—on the porch and the lawn, talking of Miss Emily as if she had been a contemporary of theirs, believing that they had danced with her and courted her perhaps, confusing time with its mathematical progression, as the old do, to whom all the past is not a diminishing road but, instead, a huge meadow which no winter ever quite touches, divided from them now by the narrow bottle-neck of the most recent decade of years.

Already we knew that there was one room in that region above stairs which no one had seen in forty years, and which would have to be forced. They waited until Miss Emily was decently in the ground before they opened it.

The violence of breaking down the door seemed to fill this room with pervading dust. A thin, acrid pall as of the tomb seemed to lie everywhere upon this room decked and furnished as for a bridal: upon the valence curtains of faded rose color, upon the rose-shaded lights, upon the dressing table, upon the delicate array of crystal and the man's toilet things backed with tarnished silver, silver so tarnished that the monogram was obscured. Among them lay a collar and tie, as if they had just been removed, which, lifted, left upon the surface a pale crescent in the dust. Upon a chair hung the suit, carefully folded; beneath it the two mute shoes and the discarded socks.

The man himself lay in the bed.

For a long while we just stood there, looking down at the profound and fleshless grin. The body had apparently once lain in the attitude of an embrace, but now the long sleep that outlasts love, that conquers even the grimace of love, had cuckolded him. What was left of him, rotted beneath what was left of the nightshirt, had become inextricable from the bed in which he lay; and upon him and upon the pillow beside him lay that even coating of the patient and biding dust.

Then we noticed that in the second pillow was the indentation of a head. 60 One of us lifted something from it, and leaning forward, that faint and invisible dust dry and acrid in the nostrils, we saw a long strand of iron-gray hair.

Responses for an Interpretation

Close-reading fiction usually involves taking note of details that may be of significance to an interpretation. Many such details show up in underlining, and making a list of important details helps in the first stages of interpreting a story. Here is one list of important details in "A Rose for Emily."

```
The whole town went to Miss Emily's funeral
No one had seen the inside of the house for ten years—except "the old
    Negro"
Miss Emily lived in a run-down section, but her house had once been
    nice
When she was alive, she was a "hereditary obligation upon the town"
Colonel Sartoris "remitted her taxes" in a way that did not seem to
    be charity
She was "a small, fat woman in black"—she was "bloated" as if
    "submerged"
When the next generation came to explain the taxes she told them to
    see Colonel Sartoris
Emily had dealt with the authorities before about "the smell" after
    her lover had "deserted her"
City officials spread lime to counter the smell, which went away in
    about a week
People felt sorry for Miss Emily; they also thought the Griersons
    were a little too high and mighty
There was insanity in the family
```

No man was good enough for her; her father stood in the door with a
    horsewhip

For three days she refused to believe her father was dead, then she
    "relented" and "they buried her father quickly"

People remembered "all the young men her father had driven away"

She was sick for a long time

Homer Barron was a Yankee foreman of a construction company who
    would "cuss the niggers" working for him building streets

People thought Miss Emily was too good for a Yankee like Barron

Miss Emily and Homer Barron were seen together and caused some talk

She bought poison without having to explain what it was for

People thought she would kill herself

Homer had remarked "that he was not a marrying man"

Two cousins were called in by the town to get her to marry Homer

Miss Emily bought Homer "a man's toilet set in silver, with the
    letters H. B." engraved on them, apparently anticipating
    marriage

Homer Barron then disappeared; no one was surprised

When he came back to the house, Homer disappeared entirely

For six months Miss Emily did not appear on the streets

People thought that the "quality of her father which had thwarted
    her woman's life so many times had been too virulent and too
    furious to die"

Over the years her hair had become iron-gray

For a period of six years she gave china-painting lessons

"She passed from generation to generation—dear, inescapable,
    impervious, tranquil, and perverse"

When she died no one knew she had been sick

The Negro let the ladies in the house, then disappeared out the
    back never to be seen again

The two cousins appeared; people knew there was one room in the
    house that was locked for forty years and would "have to be
    forced"

When they broke the door in the room was like a "tomb"

The room was "furnished as for a bridal"; the toilet set was there,
    tarnished

Homer Barron's body "in the attitude of an embrace" lay on the bed

A "long strand of iron-gray hair" lay on the pillow beside the body

A STUDENT INTERPRETATION

The following entries from a response journal were written after the list of details above.

Oct. 14. In some ways this is a creepy story. Miss Emily is some kind of pillar of the community, or her family is. But the house is decaying and there's dust everywhere. Her father is a problem. Nobody is good enough for her to marry, so he keeps all the men away. What's the problem? Why is she so tied down? I wouldn't let my father do that to me. But he wouldn't try, so there's a big difference.

Oct. 17. I reread the story. The whole town protects Miss Emily. I think that's a key to the story. They know she can't pay her taxes, but they cook up a scheme so she doesn't have to. When the new people come in as "aldermen" she stands them down, a lot like her father would have. She's got iron-gray hair, but there's some iron in her, too. She's got enough strength to keep the town in line, but she can't get Homer Barron. He's not the kind of man her father would have liked. In fact, he's supposed to be below her in society. Some people think that way today, but it seems weird to me. Then there is the ending. It's like out of a horror movie. This corpse is on the bed, and she has been laying next to it. Wow. It's creepy.

Oct. 18. I wonder if she killed her father, too. The story doesn't say, but she pretended he wasn't dead. She must have pretended Homer Barron wasn't dead, too. Or could she just be totally crazy? The way she got the poison—doesn't seem like someone crazy. She seems to just want Homer to stick around. She wasn't going to lose him.

After keeping a response journal, this writer tried some freewriting, concentrating on the question of how the town regarded the Grierson family.

Freewriting

Some people thought that the Griersons were too "high and mighty" in the way they thought about themselves. They looked down on people. But the town in the old days thought they were pretty

important. Colonel Sartoris protected Miss Emily—even lied to her
to save her the embarrassment of not being able to pay her taxes.
She inherited almost nothing from her father, just the house. So
she had no real status at all. Because she is so strong she's able
to go on as if she really did have some kind of important position.
But she can't even hold on to a loud day laborer like Homer. He
seemed interested, but he wasn't the marrying type. Okay. So the
point is she does what she has to do to survive, at least in her
own mind. She wanted to get married, and in a weird way she did.
People in the town must have known something was wrong when she got
poison and there was that smell after Homer disappeared. How come
they didn't investigate? She couldn't get away with that today.

By now, the writer saw a connection between the way the town treated
Miss Emily and the decay that attacked her family. She began to think that
the story was symbolic, and therefore she prepared to write a formalist interpretation, emphasizing the symbolic meaning of Miss Emily to the people of
Jefferson. The writer wrote some thoughts down in search of a thesis that
would guide the entire essay, but she also hoped that some of the paragraphs
of the finished essay would develop from some of these statements.

Miss Emily is probably a symbol for the South. In a way, she
represents the South's honor because she kept herself away from
committing to change. The town of Jefferson took a special interest
in Miss Emily because her family was distinguished in its history.
When she was alive, she had been "a tradition, a duty, a care." The
town tried its best to preserve her dignity because in a way it was
preserving its own dignity at the same time. What they did not seem
to see—and neither did she—is that the times were changing.

Miss Emily was the last member of the Grierson family. She had
no children because her father did not think there was anyone good
enough for her to marry. As a result, the entire family came down
to two distant cousins and this one "small, fat woman."

The neighborhood decayed over the years until what was once a
nice area was run down and her house was "an eyesore among
eyesores." Miss Emily never went out, so she did not notice.

Miss Emily must have been frustrated all her life, with her
father keeping the men away, and with her inability to keep hold of
Homer Barron. The only man in her life at the end was the old Negro

who cooked for her. He disappeared as soon as she died, almost as
if her death had released him.

With this much material, the writer decided to make an outline and then
write an interpretation.

Outline: "Why Jefferson Protected Miss Emily"
I. How the town felt about the Griersons
  A. What they thought of her father
  B. How they thought about her
    1. Why they thought she was high and mighty
II. Miss Emily as a symbol of the South in decline
  A. Why she was a tradition and duty for the town
  B. The feelings of the gossips in town
  C. The decay of the house and neighborhood
  D. The Negro servant
III. What Homer Barron meant to Miss Emily
  A. His character
    1. His social status
    2. What he was like
  B. Her frustration
IV. The marriage of Emily and Homer
  A. The bridal "tomb"

Sample Essay: An Interpretation

Susan Warther
English 109
Paper 3
Mr. Jacobus

Why Jefferson Protected Miss Emily: "The Fallen Monument"
    Jefferson protected Miss Emily because she was a symbol for
the whole town. She was more than just a person in Jefferson. She
was an institution. When she died "our whole town went to her
funeral." Most old women who die alone have almost no one at their
funeral, so Faulkner is telling us that Miss Emily was very
special. The men in town went to her funeral because she was like
"a fallen monument," but the women went because they were curious
about seeing the "inside of her house."

In the 1890s the town still regarded the family highly.
Emily's father was a figure people remembered. He stood in the
"back-flung front door" with a whip in his hand as a kind of signal
to people to watch out. The town was curious about Emily because,
even though there was insanity in the family, they expected she
would get married. She might have if her father had not been so
mean to her suitors. He kept up appearances as if they were
wealthy, even when he knew they were poor. When he died, she did
the same.

Faulkner describes Miss Emily as "a tradition, a duty,
and a care; a sort of hereditary obligation on the town." Because
she was the last of the Griersons (with the exception of her
distant cousins), Colonel Sartoris cooked up the scheme of her not
paying taxes. Otherwise she would lose the house and become a
pauper. But even more important, the town would lose some of its
own tradition. The cemetery she is buried in holds the graves of
"Union and Confederate soldiers who fell at the battle of
Jefferson," so it is clear that during the Civil War this was an
important place.

Like Miss Emily and her house, Jefferson seems to have
decayed. Nothing is mentioned in the story about positive changes
in town. "Garages and cotton gins" have taken over, but the fact
that the younger aldermen are so worried about Miss Emily's taxes
tells us that it is no longer a prosperous town. The great families
whose names are on the streets are all gone. When Miss Emily dies,
the town symbolically loses part of its tradition. That is what we
learn when some of the men at Miss Emily's funeral show up in Civil
War uniforms. They carried on that tradition for a long time. They
are like Miss Emily.

The Yankee Homer Barron may stand for signs of change. He
came into town to pave sidewalks and he was popular with most
people. The town was horrified when they realized Miss Emily was
interested in him. They thought she would be above taking up with a
Yankee "day laborer." They felt pity for her, and when she bought
the poison they "said it would be the best thing" if she used it to
commit suicide. But she did not. She killed Homer Barron instead.

People in Jefferson seemed to think they could interfere
with the way Miss Emily lived her life. They called Emily's cousins
to tell them that she was "a bad example to the young people"

because she was seen in public with Homer but was not married. The
town ladies sent in the minister, but Miss Emily must have told him
off. Finally the cousins came to enforce tradition. Emily then
bought the silver toilet set and the man's suit. Homer Barron
returned after the cousins left, but he probably did not plan to
stay. He was not the marrying kind.

The bridal "tomb" was furnished with rose-colored
curtains. The dust was like the dust of tradition. The air was
stifling, and Homer's body, in its nightshirt, with its "attitude
of an embrace," implies that when he held Miss Emily he was holding
a dead tradition, a tradition that killed him, too.

Jefferson protected Miss Emily, but it stifled her, too.
It was overprotective. The people were curious about her and
thought it was best for her to keep the tradition of the family and
the town. In the end she became a frustrated old maid who killed
her lover to preserve her honor. The most painful thing about the
story is imagining Miss Emily sleeping next to the corpse of a man
nobody thought was good enough for her when he was alive. It is
almost like a modern horror movie.

Further Strategies for Interpretation

Susan Warther's essay on "A Rose for Emily" combines two interpretive strategies. The first is a formalist strategy, emphasizing the symbolic element in the
story. The second is the reader's response to the story, her sense that it was
almost like a modern horror movie. The symbolic reading centered on the
image of Miss Emily as a "fallen monument." That image related closely to
the concept of her being "a tradition, a duty, and a care." The repeated pattern of decay in Miss Emily's house and in the town of Jefferson provided a
link to show how the town's own traditions were symbolically connected with
those of her family. The writer responded negatively to the people of Jefferson
interfering in Miss Emily's life. She interpreted their interference as causing
Miss Emily to give in to tradition. That meant killing Homer Barron and
keeping him in a "bridal tomb" for the rest of her life.

Other interpretive strategies could have been used for discussing important issues in "A Rose for Emily."

Psychoanalytic   Insanity enters the story early: "People in our town" remembered "how old lady Wyatt, her great-aunt, had gone completely crazy at last."
When, earlier, Miss Emily is referred to as "a sort of hereditary obligation" of the
town, the theme of hereditary insanity is made explicit. But that theme is introduced by the narrator, who, as part of the town, may be unreliable. More impor-

tant are the images of Miss Emily's father standing in the doorway—blocking the doorway—with his whip in his hand. He becomes the repressive father, much like the repressive brothers in "The Pot of Basil," but once he dies, the town essentially takes over his repressive role. When Miss Emily is attracted to Homer Barron—as everyone else is—she is harshly judged by the town for bad behavior. She is made to feel guilty, which possibly leads her to buy poison while her "female cousins were visiting her." The pressures of her cousins, "who were even more Grierson than Miss Emily had ever been," eventually break her down. Her murder of Homer Barron and her creation of a bridal tomb are direct results of the psychological pressures that both family and society put upon her.

Feminist   Miss Emily is without power to direct her life for only one reason: she is a woman. In Jefferson, women must conform to the "rules." When she refuses—by being seen in public with a social inferior, Homer Barron—the town puts pressure on her. They expect her to conform to tradition and marry, even if Barron is beneath her and not the marrying kind. When Emily bought the poison she may have intended to use it on herself. The townspeople pitied her and began to think she would be better off dead. The town feared her father and would never have acted toward him as it did toward her. The town thinks it is "caring" for Miss Emily, but it is actually coercing her into behaving as it thinks she must. In other words, the town expects her to relinquish her freedom and surrender to tradition and duty because she is a woman.

Cultural   Colonel Sartoris treats Miss Emily in a special way: he appears to be benevolent on the surface, but he actually causes harm, much as he does when he puts forth "the edict that no Negro woman should appear on the streets without an apron." Jefferson was part of the Confederacy, which among other things fought to preserve the tradition of slavery. That it has not entirely forsaken its tradition is central to the whole story and completely evident in the Confederate uniforms worn at Miss Emily's funeral. Even Homer Barron, the Yankee, would "cuss the niggers," so his views parallel Jefferson's. The unnamed Negro man who remains with Miss Emily is like a shadow. He cooks, he admits people to the house, and he does the marketing and other chores. He behaves like a traditional slave. After a while he "talked to no one, probably not even to her, for his voice had grown harsh and rusty, as if from disuse." Miss Emily is like a "fallen monument," but until she falls entirely, this man is like her slave. After her death, he lets "the first of the ladies" in and then "walked right through the house and out the back and was not seen again." Her death frees him.

These suggestions cover only a few possibilities. You could develop more by considering economic issues as well as different formalist or other approaches based on details other than those suggested here. You can begin to appreciate how many possibilities for interpretation exist in a story like "A Rose for Emily." Most fine short stories permit multiple interpretations, each of which enriches our understanding and appreciation.

An Album of Short Fiction

Isabel Allende   (b. 1942)

Isabel Allende was born in Lima, Peru. Her father was a Chilean diplomat stationed there, but she grew up in Santiago, Chile, and considered herself thoroughly Chilean. Her father's brother, Salvatore Allende, the socialist president of Chile, was eventually murdered in a coup, and Isabel was forced into exile, much of it in Venezuela. Nevertheless, she considers herself a Latin American, and her writing looks back to her family home and the magical elements of her childhood. She is remarkable for having established herself, Alexander Coleman has said, as "the first woman to join what has heretofore been an exclusive male club of Latin American novelists."

The magical element that frequently appears in Allende's work may have been drawn from experiences with her fortune-telling grandmother, who held séances when Isabel was a child. Isabel's first important novel is The House of the Spirits *(1982), which began as a memoir designed to keep the memory of her grandmother alive. When she finished the novel she found enormous prejudice against her on the part of publishers, who would not take her seriously as a woman. Of Love and Shadows (1984) concerns the mission of a female journalist, Irene Beltrán, in a country controlled by the military and in which people suddenly disappear. The novel has been criticized for its political polemic, but also praised for its honesty. Eva Luna (1988) is a rambling novel about a half-Indian, half-European orphan who finds her way in a crowded city partly on the strength of her storytelling. The selections that follow are from* The Stories of Eva Luna *(1991). They represent a sequel to the novel and they reveal the storytelling virtuosity for which there is little room in the novel* Eva Luna.

167

WALIMAI   1991

Translated by Margaret Sayers Peden

The name given me by my father is Walimai, which in the tongue of our brothers in the north means "wind." I can tell it to you, since now you are like my own daughter and you have my permission to call my name, although only when we are among family. The names of persons and living creatures demand respect, because when we speak them we touch their heart and become a part of their life force. This is how we blood kinsmen greet each other. I cannot understand the ease with which the white ones call each others' names, with no fear; not only does it show a lack of respect, it can also lead to grave danger. I have noted that these persons speak unthinkingly, not realizing that to speak is also to be. Word and gesture are man's thought. We should not speak without reason; this I have taught my sons and daughters, but they do not always listen to my counsel. Long ago, taboos and traditions were respected. My grandfathers, and the grandfathers of my grandfathers, received all necessary knowledge from their grandfathers. Nothing changed. A man with a good memory could recall every teaching he had received and thus knew what to do in any situation. But then came the white ones speaking against the wisdom of the grandfathers, and pushing us off our land. We move always deeper into the jungle, but always they overtake us; sometimes years pass, but finally they come again, and we must destroy our planted fields, put our children on our back, bind our animals, and depart. So it has been as long as I have memory: leave everything, and run away like mice—not like the mighty warriors and gods who inhabited these lands in days of old. Some of our young are curious about the whites, and while we travel deeper into the forest to continue to live as our ancestors did, others undertake a different path. We think of those who leave as if they were dead, because very few return, and those who do have changed so that we cannot recognize them as kinsmen.

They tell that in the years before I came into the world not enough women were born to our people, and thus my father had to travel long roads to seek a wife from a different tribe. He journeyed through the forests, following the marks of others who had traveled that route before him and for the same purpose and returned with women not of our blood. After much traveling, when my father had begun to lose hope of finding a life companion, he saw a girl standing by a tall waterfall, a river that fell from the sky. Staying some distance away, in order not to frighten her, he spoke to her in the tone that hunters use to calm their prey, and explained his need to marry her. She made signs that he might come near, studied him openly, and must have been pleased by the face of the traveler, because she decided that the idea of marriage was not a rash one. My father had to work for his father-in-law until he paid for the woman's value. After they had fulfilled the rituals of marriage, they made the return journey to our village.

I grew up with my brothers and sisters beneath the canopies of tall trees, never seeing the sun. Sometimes a wounded tree would fall, leaving an opening in the thick dome of the forest; at those times we saw the blue eye of the sky. My father and mother told me stories; they sang songs to me, and taught me what a man must know to survive alone, with nothing but his bow and his arrows. I was free. We, the Children of the Moon, cannot live unless we are free. When we are closed inside walls or bars we collapse inward; we become blind and deaf, and in a few days our spirit detaches itself from the bones of our chest and abandons us. At those times we become like miserable beasts and, almost always, we prefer to die. That is why our houses have no walls, only a sloped roof to stop the wind and shed the rain; beneath it we hang our hammocks close together, because we like to listen to the dreams of the women and the children and feel the breath of the monkeys and dogs and pigs that sleep beneath the same shelter. In the earliest times we lived in the jungles without knowing that there was a world beyond the cliffs and rivers. Friends came to visit from other tribes, and told us rumors of Boa Vista and El Plantanal, of the white ones and their customs, but we believed these were only stories to make us laugh. I reached manhood, and my turn came to find a wife, but I decided to wait, because I liked being with the bachelors; we were happy, and lived well. Even so, I could not devote myself solely to games and resting as the others did, because my family is very large: brothers and sisters, cousins, nieces and nephews, many mouths to feed, and much work for a hunter.

One day a group of the pale men came to our village. They hunted with powder, from far away, without skill or courage; they could not climb a tree or spear a fish in the water; they moved clumsily through the jungle, they were always getting tangled in their packs, their weapons, even their own feet. They did not clothe themselves in air, as we do, but wore wet and stinking clothing; they were dirty and they did not know the laws of decency, but they insisted on telling us of their knowledge and their gods. We compared them with what we had been told about the white men, and we verified the truth of that gossip. Soon we realized that these men were not missionaries, or soldiers or rubber collectors: they were mad. They wanted the land; they wanted to carry away the wood; they were also searching for stones. We explained that the jungle is not something to be tossed over your shoulder and transported like a dead bird, but they did not want to hear our arguments. They made camp near our village. Each one of them was like a wind of catastrophe; he destroyed everything he touched; he left a trail of waste behind him; he disturbed animals and people. At first we obeyed the laws of courtesy, and pleased them, because they were our guests; but they were never satisfied, they wanted always more, until, weary of their games, we declared war with all traditional ceremonies. They are not good warriors; they are easily frightened and their fragile skullbones could not withstand the clubbing we gave them. Afterward we abandoned our village and we journeyed to the east where the forest is impenetrable, traveling for long stretches through the tops of the trees so their companions could not find us. We had been told that they are vengeful, and that for each one of them who dies, even in fair battle, they are capable of eliminating an entire tribe, including the children. We discovered a place to establish a new village. It was not as good—the women had to walk hours to find clean water—but we stayed there because we believed that no one would come so far to search for us. A year later I was far from our village following the track of a puma, when I approached too near a camp of soldiers. I was tired, and had not eaten in several days; for this reason, I used poor judgment. Instead of turning back when I glimpsed the strangers, I lay down to rest. The soldiers caught me. They did not mention the men we had clubbed to death. In fact, they asked me nothing; perhaps they did not know those men or did not know that I am Walimai. They pressed me into work with the rubber collectors, with many men from other tribes, men they had dressed in trousers and driven to work with no thought for their wishes. The rubber demands much care, and there were not enough people to do the work; that was why they forced us. That was a time without freedom, and I do not want to speak of it. I stayed only to see whether I could learn any-thing, but from the beginning I knew I would return to my people. Nothing can long hold a warrior against his will.

We worked from sun to sun, some bleeding the trees to drain their life drop by drop, others cooking the liquid to thicken it and form it into great balls. The air outdoors was sick with the stench of the burned sap, and the air indoors in the sleeping quarters foul with the sweat of the men. No one could draw a deep breath in that place. They gave us maize to eat, and bananas, and the strange contents of some cans, which I never tasted, because nothing good for humans can grow in tins. At one end of the camp they had built a large hut where they kept the women. After two weeks of working with the raw rubber, the boss handed me a slip of paper and sent me where the women were. He also gave me a cup of liquor, which I turned out on the ground, because I have seen how that water destroys a man's good sense. I stood in line with the others. I was the last, and when it came my turn to enter the hut, the sun had gone down and night begun, with its clamor of frogs and parrots.

She was of the tribe of the Ila, the people of gentle heart, from which the most delicate girls come. Some men travel months on end to find the Ila; they take them gifts and hunt for them in the hope of obtaining one of their women. She looked like a lizard lying there, but I recognized her because my mother, too, was an Ila woman. She lay naked on her straw mat, tied by one ankle to a chain staked in the ground, sluggish, as if she had breathed in the *yopo* of the acacia; she had the smell of sick dogs, and she was wet with the dew of all the men who had covered her before me. She was the size of a young boy, and her bones clicked like small stones in the river. The Ila women remove all their bodily hair, even their eyelashes; they adorn their ears with feathers and flowers; they thrust pol-ished sticks through their cheeks and nose; they paint designs over all their body in the reds of the annatto, the deep purple of the palm, and the black of carbon. But she had none of that. I placed my machete on the ground, and greeted her as a sister, imitating some songbirds and the sound of rivers. She did not respond. I pounded her chest, to see whether her spirit still resonated in her rib cage, but there was no echo; her soul was very weak and could not answer me. Kneeling beside her, I gave her water to drink and spoke to her in my mother's tongue. She opened her eyes, and stared at me a long time. I understood.

First of all, I washed myself without wasting the clean water. I took a good draft into my mouth and sprinkled it in small streams onto my hands, which I rubbed carefully and then wet to clean my face. I did the same with her, to cleanse the men's dew from her body. I removed the trousers the boss had given me. From a cord at my waist hung my sticks for making fire, the tips of arrows, my roll of tobacco, my wooden knife with a rat's tooth in the point, and a bag of strong leather in which I carried a small amount of curare. I spread a bit of that paste on the point of my knife, bent over the woman and, with the poisoned in-strument, opened a small cut in her neck. Life is a gift from the gods. The hunter kills to feed his family; he tries not to eat the flesh of his prey but prefers to eat what another hunter offers him. At times, tragically, a man kills another in war, but he never harms a woman or a child. She looked at me with large eyes yellow

5

as honey, and I thought she tried to smile, gratefully. For her I had violated the first taboo of the Children of the Moon, and I would have to pay for my shame with many labors of expiation. I held my ear to her mouth, and she murmured her name. I repeated it twice in my mind to be very sure, but did not speak it aloud; it is not good to mention the dead or disturb their peace, and she was already dead even though her heart still beat. Soon I saw the muscles of her belly, her chest, her arms stiffen with paralysis; she stopped breathing, and changed color. A sigh escaped her, and her body died without a struggle, as small creatures die.

Immediately, I felt her spirit leave through her nostrils and enter mine, anchoring itself to my breastbone. All her weight fell upon me, and I had to struggle to get to my feet. I moved very slowly, as if I were under water. I arranged her body in the position of the last rest, with her knees touching her chin. I bound her with fibers from the mat, then made a mound with the rest of the straw and used my sticks to make fire. When I saw that the fire was blazing intensely, I left the hut slowly, laboriously climbed the camp fence—because she kept dragging me down—and walked into the forest. I had reached the first trees when I heard the alarm bells.

I walked all the first day without stopping. On the second day I fashioned a bow and arrows so I could hunt for her, and for myself as well. The warrior who bears the weight of another human life must fast for ten days; in this way the spirit of the dead one grows weak; finally it lets go and journeys to the land of souls. If the warrior does not do this, the spirit grows fat on the food it is fed and grows inside the man until it suffocates him. I have seen men of great courage die this way. But before I fulfilled those conditions, I had to lead the spirit of the Ila woman into the thickest jungle where she would never be found. I ate very little, barely enough not to kill her a second time. Each mouthful tasted like spoiled meat, and every sip of water was bitter, but I forced myself to swallow, to nourish the two of us. For one complete cycle of the moon I traveled deep into the jungle, carrying inside me the soul of the woman who weighed more each day. We spoke often. The tongue of the Ila is uninhibited and resounds beneath the trees with a long echo. We communicated singing, with our body, with our eyes, our waist, our feet. I repeated to her the legends I had learned from my mother and my father; I told her my past, and she told me of the first part of her life, when she was a happy girl playing with her brothers and sisters, rolling in the mud and swinging from the high branches. Out of courtesy, she did not mention her recent past of misfortune and humiliation. I caught a white bird; I plucked the finest feathers and made adornments for her ears. At night I kept a small fire burning so she would not be cold, and so jaguars or serpents would not disturb her sleep. I bathed her in the river with care, rubbing her with ash and crushed flowers, to take away her bad memories.

Finally one day we reached the perfect spot, and had no further excuse to continue walking. There the jungle was so dense that in places I had to open a path by slashing the undergrowth with my machete, even my teeth, and we had to speak in a low voice to not alter the silence of time. I chose a place near a thread of water; I put up a roof of leaves and made a hammock for her from three long strips of bark. With my knife I shaved my head and began my fast.

During the time we had walked together the woman and I had come to love one another so much that we did not want to part; but man does not control life, 10

not even his own, and so I had to fulfill my obligation. For many days, I took nothing in my mouth except a few sips of water. As I grew weak, she slipped from my
embrace, and her spirit, ever more ethereal, did not weigh upon me as before. After
five days, while I dozed, she took her first steps, but she was not ready to continue
her journey alone, and she returned to me. She repeated those brief travels on several occasions, each time venturing a little farther. The sorrow of her parting was as
terrible as a deep burn, and I had to call on all the courage I had learned from my
father not to call her name aloud and bring her back to me forever. After twelve
days I dreamed that she was flying like a toucan above the treetops, and I awakened
feeling very light, and wanting to weep. She was gone. I picked up my weapons and
walked for many hours until I reached a branch of the river. I walked into the water up to my waist; I speared a small fish with a sharp stick and swallowed it whole,
scales, tail, and all. I immediately vomited it up with a little blood; it was as it should
be. I was not sad now. I had learned that sometimes death is more powerful than
love. Then I went to hunt, so I would not return to my village with empty hands.

Margaret Atwood   (b. 1939)

*Margaret Atwood is one of Canada's most visible writers, having produced more
than ten volumes of poetry, six novels, and many short stories. She has also written
plays and distinguished herself as a cartoonist and illustrator. Her novel* Surfacing
*(1972), based on her experience working as a girl in summer camps in Canada,
expresses some of her concerns with nature and the wilderness. Educated at the
University of Toronto and Radcliffe College of Harvard University, she has taught
creative writing at York University and the University of Toronto. Her life has
been filled with passionate involvements with various causes, some of which have
surfaced in her books.* Lady Oracle *(1976) parodies her own work and some of the
themes in her life.* The Handmaid's Tale *(1985), her best-known work, develops,
in a twenty-first-century fantasy, many of the feminist themes of her prose and
poetry. Her short stories appear in two volumes,* Dancing Girls *(1977) and*
Bluebeard's Egg *(1983), in which the following story appears.*

SIGNIFICANT MOMENTS IN THE LIFE OF
MY MOTHER   1983

When my mother was very small, someone gave her a basket of baby chicks
for Easter. They all died.

"I didn't know you weren't supposed to pick them up," says my mother.
"Poor little things. I laid them out in a row on a board, with their little legs sticking out straight as pokers, and wept over them. I'd loved them to death."

Possibly this story is meant by my mother to illustrate her own stupidity, and
also her sentimentality. We are to understand she wouldn't do such a thing now.

Possibly it's a commentary on the nature of love; though, knowing my
mother, this is unlikely.

My mother's father was a country doctor. In the days before cars he drove   5
a team of horses and a buggy around his territory, and in the days before snow

ploughs he drove a team and a sleigh, through blizzards and rainstorms and in the middle of the night, to arrive at houses lit with oil lamps where water would be boiling on the wood range and flannel sheets warming on the plate rack, to deliver babies who would subsequently be named after him. His office was in the house, and as a child my mother would witness people arriving at the office door, which was reached through the front porch, clutching parts of themselves— thumbs, fingers, toes, ears, noses—which had accidentally been cut off, pressing these severed parts to the raw stumps of their bodies as if they could be stuck there like dough, in the mostly vain hope that my grandfather would be able to sew them back on, heal the gashes made in them by axes, saws, knives, and fate.

My mother and her younger sister would loiter near the closed office door until shooed away. From behind it would come groans, muffled screams, cries for help. For my mother, hospitals have never been glamorous places, and illness offers no respite or holiday. "Never get sick," she says, and means it. She hardly ever does.

Once, though, she almost died. It was when her appendix burst. My grandfather had to do the operation. He said later that he shouldn't have been the person to do it: his hands were shaking too much. This is one of the few admissions of weakness on his part that my mother has ever reported. Mostly he is portrayed as severe and in charge of things. "We all respected him, though," she says. "He was widely respected." (This is a word which has slipped a little in the scale since my mother's youth. It used to outrank *love*.)

It was someone else who told me the story of my grandfather's muskrat farm: how he and one of my mother's uncles fenced in the swamp at the back of their property and invested my mother's maiden aunt's savings in muskrats. The idea was that these muskrats would multiply and eventually be made into muskrat coats, but an adjoining apple farmer washed his spraying equipment upstream, and the muskrats were all killed by the poison, as dead as doornails. This was during the Depression, and it was no joke.

When they were young—this can cover almost anything these days, but I put it at seven or eight—my mother and her sister had a tree house, where they spent some of their time playing dolls' tea parties and so forth. One day they found a box of sweet little bottles outside my grandfather's dispensary. The bottles were being thrown out, and my mother (who has always hated waste) appropriated them for use in their dolls' house. The bottles were full of yellow liquid, which they left in because it looked so pretty. It turned out that these were urine samples.

"We got Hail Columbia° for that," says my mother. "But what did we know?"   10

My mother's family lived in a large white house near an apple orchard, in Nova Scotia. There was a barn and a carriage-house; in the kitchen there was a pantry. My mother can remember the days before commercial bakeries, when flour came in barrels and all the bread was made at home. She can remember the first radio broadcast she ever heard, which was a singing commercial about socks.

In this house there were many rooms. Although I have been there, although I have seen the house with my own eyes, I still don't know how many. Parts of it were closed off, or so it seemed; there were back staircases. Passages led elsewhere.

We got Hail Columbia: An old-fashioned way of saying "We got hell."

Five children lived in it, two parents, a hired man and a hired girl, whose names and faces kept changing. The structure of the house was hierarchical, with my grandfather at the top, but its secret life—the life of pie crusts, clean sheets, the box of rags in the linen closet, the loaves in the oven—was female. The house, and all the objects in it, crackled with static electricity; undertows washed through it, the air was heavy with things that were known but not spoken. Like a hollow log, a drum, a church, it amplified, so that conversations whispered in it sixty years ago can be half-heard even today.

In this house you had to stay at the table until you had eaten everything on your plate. "'Think of the starving Armenians,' mother used to say," says my mother. "I didn't see how eating my bread crusts was going to help them out one jot."

It was in this house that I first saw a stalk of oats in a vase, each oat wrapped in the precious silver paper which had been carefully saved from a chocolate box. I thought it was the most wonderful thing I had ever seen, and began saving silver paper myself. But I never got around to wrapping the oats, and in any case I didn't know how. Like many other art forms of vanished civilizations, the techniques for this one have been lost and cannot quite be duplicated.

"We had oranges at Christmas," says my mother. "They came all the way   15
from Florida; they were very expensive. That was the big treat: to find an orange in the toe of your stocking. It's funny to remember how good they tasted, now."

When she was sixteen, my mother had hair so long she could sit on it. Women were bobbing their hair by then; it was getting to be the twenties. My mother's hair was giving her headaches, she says, but my grandfather, who was very strict, forbade her to cut it. She waited until one Saturday when she knew he had an appointment with the dentist.

"In those days there was no freezing," says my mother. "The drill was worked with a foot pedal, and it went *grind, grind, grind.* The dentist himself had brown teeth: he chewed tobacco, and he would spit the tobacco juice into a spittoon while he was working on your teeth."

Here my mother, who is good mimic, imitates the sounds of the drill and the tobacco juice: "*Rrrrr! Rrrrr! Rrrrr! Phtt! Rrrrr! Rrrrr! Rrrrr! Phtt!* It was always sheer agony. It was a heaven-sent salvation when gas came in."

My mother went into the dentist's office, where my grandfather was sitting in the chair, white with pain. She asked him if she could have her hair cut. He said she could do anything in tarnation° as long as she would get out of there and stop pestering him.

"So I went out straight away and had it all chopped off," says my mother   20
jauntily. "He was furious afterwards, but what could he do? He'd given his word."

My own hair reposes in a cardboard box in a steamer° trunk in my mother's cellar, where I picture it becoming duller and more brittle with each passing year, and possibly moth-eaten; by now it will look like the faded wreaths of hair in Victorian funeral jewellery. Or it may have developed a dry mildew; inside its tissue-paper wrappings it glows faintly, in the darkness of the trunk. I suspect my mother has forgotten it's in there. It was cut off, much to my relief, when I was twelve and my sister was born. Before that it was in long curls: "Otherwise," says

tarnation: Damnation.   *steamer*: Ship.

my mother, "it would have been just one big snarl." My mother combed it by winding it around her index finger every morning, but when she was in the hospital my father couldn't cope. "He couldn't get it around his stubby fingers," says my mother. My father looks down at his fingers. They are indeed broad compared with my mother's long elegant ones, which she calls boney. He smiles a pussycat smile.

So it was that my hair was sheared off. I sat in the chair in my first beauty parlor and watched it falling, like handfuls of cobwebs, down over my shoulders. From within it my head began to emerge, smaller, denser, my face more angular. I aged five years in fifteen minutes. I knew I could go home now and try out lipstick.

"Your father was upset about it," says my mother, with an air of collusion. She doesn't say this when my father is present. We smile, over the odd reactions of men to hair.

I used to think that my mother, in her earlier days, led a life of sustained hilarity and hair-raising adventure. (That was before I realized that she never put in the long stretches of uneventful time that must have made up much of her life: the stories were just the punctuation.) Horses ran away with her, men offered to, she was continually falling out of trees or off the ridgepoles of barns, or nearly being swept out to sea in rip-tides; or, in a more minor vein, suffering acute embarrassment in trying circumstances.

Churches were especially dangerous. "There was a guest preacher one Sunday," she says. "Of course we had to go to church every Sunday. There he was, in full career, preaching hellfire and damnation"—she pounds an invisible pulpit—"and his full set of false teeth shot out of his mouth—*phoop!*—just like that. Well, he didn't miss a stride. He stuck his hand up and caught them and popped them back into his mouth, and he kept right on, condemning us all to eternal torment. The pew was shaking! The tears were rolling down our faces, and the worst of it was, we were in the front pew, he was looking right at us. But of course we couldn't laugh out loud: father would have given us Hail Columbia." 25

Other people's parlors were booby-trapped for her; so were any and all formal social occasions. Zippers sprang apart on her clothes in strategic places, hats were unreliable. The shortage of real elastic during the war demanded constant alertness: underpants then had buttons, and were more taboo and therefore more significant than they are now. "There you would be," she says, "right on the street, and before you knew it they'd be down around your galoshes. The way to do was to step out of them with one foot, then kick them up with your other foot and whip them into your purse. I got quite good at it."

This particular story is told only to a few, but other stories are for general consumption. When she tells them, my mother's face turns to rubber. She takes all the parts, adds the sound effects, waves her hands around in the air. Her eyes gleam, sometimes a little wickedly, for although my mother is sweet and old and a lady, she avoids being a sweet old lady. When people are in danger of mistaking her for one, she flings in something from left field; she refuses to be taken for granted.

But my mother cannot be duped into telling stories when she doesn't want to. If you prompt her, she becomes self-conscious and clams up. Or she will laugh and go out into the kitchen, and shortly after that you will hear the whir of the

Mixmaster. Long ago I gave up attempting to make her do tricks at parties. In gatherings of unknown people, she merely listens intently, her head tilted a little, smiling a smile of glazed politeness. The secret is to wait and see what she will say afterwards.

At the age of seventeen my mother went to the Normal School in Truro. This name—"Normal School"—once held a certain magic for me. I thought it had something to do with learning to be normal, which possibly it did, because really it was where you used to go to learn how to be a schoolteacher. Subsequently my mother taught in a one-room school house not far from her home. She rode her horse to and from the school house every day, and saved up the money she earned and sent herself to university with it. My grandfather wouldn't send her: he said she was too frivolous-minded. She liked ice-skating and dancing too much for his taste.

At Normal School my mother boarded with a family that contained several 30 sons in more or less the same age group as the girl boarders. They all ate around a huge dining-room table (which I pictured as being of dark wood, with heavy carved legs, but covered always with a white linen tablecloth), with the mother and father presiding, one at each end. I saw them both as large and pink and beaming.

"The boys were great jokers," says my mother. "They were always up to something." This was desirable in boys: to be great jokers, to be always up to something. My mother adds a key sentence: "We had a lot of fun."

Having fun has always been high on my mother's agenda. She has as much fun as possible, but what she means by this phrase cannot be understood without making an adjustment, an allowance for the great gulf across which this phrase must travel before it reaches us. It comes from another world, which, like the stars that originally sent out the light we see hesitating in the sky above us these nights, may be or is already gone. It is possible to reconstruct the facts of this world—the furniture, the clothing, the ornaments on the mantelpiece, the jugs and basins and even the chamber pots in the bedrooms, but not the emotions, not with the same exactness. So much that is now known and felt must be excluded.

This was a world in which guileless flirtation was possible, because there were many things that were simply not done by nice girls, and more girls were nice then. To fall from niceness was to fall not only from grace: sexual acts, by girls at any rate, had financial consequences. Life was more joyful and innocent then, and at the same time permeated with guilt and terror, or at least the occasions for them, on the most daily level. It was like the Japanese haiku: a limited form, rigid in its perimeters, within which an astonishing freedom was possible.

There are photographs of my mother at this time, taken with three or four other girls, linked arm in arm or with their arms thrown jestingly around each other's necks. Behind them, beyond the sea or the hills or whatever is in the background, is a world already hurtling towards ruin, unknown to them: the theory of relativity has been discovered, acid is accumulating at the roots of trees, the bull-frogs are doomed. But they smile with something that from this distance you could almost call gallantry, their right legs thrust forward in parody of a chorus line.

One of the great amusements for the girl boarders and the sons of the fam- 35 ily was amateur theatre. Young people—they were called "young people"—frequently performed in plays which were put on in the church basement. My mother was a regular actor. (I have a stack of the scripts somewhere about the house, yellowing little booklets with my mother's parts checked in pencil. They are all comedies, and all impenetrable.) "There was no television then," says my mother. "You made your own fun."

For one of these plays a cat was required, and my mother and one of the sons borrowed the family cat. They put it into a canvas bag and drove to the rehearsal (there were cars by then), with my mother holding the cat on her lap. The cat, which must have been frightened, wet itself copiously, through the canvas bag and all over my mother's skirt. At the same time it made the most astonishingly bad smell.

"I was ready to sink through the floorboards," says my mother. "But what could I do? All I could do was sit there. In those days things like that"—she means cat pee, or pee of any sort—"were not mentioned." She means in mixed company.

I think of my mother driven through the night, skirts dripping, overcome with shame, the young man beside her staring straight ahead, pretending not to notice anything. They both feel that this act of unmentionable urination has been done, not by the cat, but by my mother. And so they continue, in a straight line that takes them over the Atlantic and past the curvature of the earth, out through the moon's orbit and into the dark reaches beyond.

Meanwhile, back on earth, my mother says: "I had to throw the skirt out. It was a good skirt, too, but nothing could get rid of the smell."

"I only heard your father swear once," says my mother. My mother herself   40 never swears. When she comes to a place in a story in which swearing is called for, she says "dad-ratted" or "blankety-blank."

"It was when he mashed his thumb, when he was sinking the well, for the pump." This story, I know, takes place before I was born, up north, where there is nothing underneath the trees and their sheddings but sand and bedrock. The well was for a hand pump, which in turn was for the first of the many cabins and houses my parents built together. But since I witnessed later wells being sunk and later hand pumps being installed, I know how it's done. There's a pipe with a point at one end. You pound it into the ground with a sledge hammer, and as it goes down you screw other lengths of pipe onto it, until you hit drinkable water. To keep from ruining the thread on the top end, you hold a block of wood between the sledge hammer and the pipe. Better, you get someone else to hold it for you. This is how my father mashed his thumb: he was doing both the holding and the hammering himself.

"It swelled up like a radish," says my mother. "He had to make a hole in the nail, with his toad-sticker, to ease the pressure. The blood spurted out like pips from a lemon. Later on the whole nail turned purple and black and dropped off. Luckily he grew another one. They say you only get two chances. When he did it though, he turned the air blue for yards around. I didn't even know he knew those words. I don't know where he picked them up." She speaks as if these words are a minor contagious disease, like chicken pox.

Here my father looks modestly down at his plate. For him, there are two worlds: one containing ladies, in which you do not use certain expressions, and another one—consisting of logging camps and other haunts of his youth, and of gatherings of acceptable sorts of men—in which you do. To let the men's world slip over verbally into the ladies' would reveal you as a mannerless boor, but to carry the ladies' world over into the men's brands you a prig and maybe even a pansy. This is the word for it. All of this is well understood between them.

This story illustrates several things: that my father is no pansy, for one; and that my mother behaved properly by being suitably shocked. But my mother's eyes shine with delight while she tells this story. Secretly, she thinks it funny that my father got caught out, even if only once. The thumbnail that fell off is, in any significant way, long forgotten.

There are some stories which my mother does not tell when there are men   45
present: never at dinner, never at parties. She tells them to women only, usually in the kitchen, when they or we are helping with the dishes or shelling peas, or taking the tops and tails off the string beans, or husking corn. She tells them in a lowered voice, without moving her hands around in the air, and they contain no sound effects. These are stories of romantic betrayals, unwanted pregnancies, illnesses of various horrible kinds, marital infidelities, mental breakdowns, tragic suicides, unpleasant lingering deaths. They are not rich in detail or embroidered with incident: they are stark and factual. The women, their own hands moving among the dirty dishes or the husks of vegetables, nod solemnly.

Some of these stories, it is understood, are not to be passed on to my father, because they would upset him. It is well known that women can deal with this sort of thing better than men can. Men are not to be told anything they might find too painful; the secret depths of human nature, the sordid physicalities, might overwhelm or damage them. For instance, men often faint at the sight of their own blood, to which they are not accustomed. For this reason you should never stand behind one in the line at the Red Cross donor clinic. Men, for some mysterious reason, find life more difficult than women do. (My mother believes this, despite the female bodies, trapped, diseased, disappearing, or abandoned, that litter her stories.) Men must be allowed to play in the sandbox of their choice, as happily as they can, without disturbance; otherwise they get cranky and won't eat their dinners. There are all kinds of things that men are simply not equipped to understand, so why expect it of them? Not everyone shares this belief about men; nevertheless, it has its uses.

"She dug up the shrubs from around the house," says my mother. This story is about a shattered marriage: serious business. My mother's eyes widen. The other women lean forward. "All she left him were the shower curtains." There is a collective sigh, an expelling of breath. My father enters the kitchen, wondering when the tea will be ready, and the women close ranks, turning to him their deceptive blankly smiling faces. Soon afterwards, my mother emerges from the kitchen, carrying the tea pot, and sets it down on the table in its ritual place.

"I remember the time we almost died," says my mother. Many of her stories begin this way. When she is in a certain mood, we are to understand that our lives have been preserved only by a series of amazing coincidences and strokes of luck; otherwise the entire family, individually or collectively, would be dead as doornails. These stories, in addition to producing adrenalin, serve to reinforce our sense of gratitude. There is the time we almost went over a waterfall, in a canoe, in a fog; the time we almost got caught in a forest fire; the time my father almost got squashed, before my mother's very eyes, by a ridgepole he was lifting into place; the time my brother almost got struck by a bolt of lightning, which went by him so close it knocked him down. "You could hear it sizzle," says my mother.

This is the story of the hay wagon. "Your father was driving," says my mother, "at the speed he usually goes." We read between the lines: *too fast.* "You kids were in the back." I can remember this day, so I can remember how old I was, how old my brother was. We were old enough to think it was funny to annoy my father by singing popular songs of a type he disliked, such as "Mockingbird Hill"; or perhaps we were imitating bagpipe music by holding our noses and humming, while hitting our Adam's apples with the edges of our hands. When we became too irritating my father would say, "Pipe down." We weren't old enough to know that his irritation could be real: we thought it was part of the game.

"We were going down a steep hill," my mother continues, "when a hay   50
wagon pulled out right across the road, at the bottom. Your father put on the brakes, but nothing happened. The brakes were gone! I thought our last moment had come." Luckily the hay wagon continued across the road, and we shot past it, missing it by at least a foot. "My heart was in my mouth," says my mother.

I didn't know until afterwards what had really happened. I was in the back seat, making bagpipe music, oblivious. The scenery was the same as it always was on car trips: my parents' heads, seen from behind, sticking up above the front seat. My father had his hat on, the one he wore to keep things from falling off the trees into his hair. My mother's hand was placed lightly on the back of his neck.

"You had such an acute sense of smell when you were younger," says my mother.

Now we are on more dangerous ground: my mother's childhood is one thing, my own quite another. This is the moment at which I start rattling the silverware, or ask for another cup of tea. "You used to march into houses that were strange to you, and you would say in a loud voice, 'What's that funny smell?'" If there are guests present, they shift a little away from me, conscious of their own emanations, trying not to look at my nose.

"I used to be so embarrassed," says my mother absentmindedly. Then she shifts gears. "You were such an easy child. You used to get up at six in the morning and play by yourself in the play room, singing away. . . ." There is a pause. A distant voice, mine, high and silvery, drifts over the space between us. "You used to talk a blue streak. Chatter, chatter, chatter, from morning to night." My mother sighs imperceptibly, as if wondering why I have become so silent, and gets up to poke the fire.

Hoping to change the subject, I ask whether or not the crocuses have come   55
up yet, but she is not to be diverted. "I never had to spank you," she says. "A harsh word, and you would be completely reduced." She looks at me sideways; she isn't sure what I have turned into, or how. "There were just one or two times. Once, when I had to go out and I left your father in charge." (This may be the real point of the story: the inability of men to second-guess small children.) "I came back along the street, and there were you and your brother, throwing mud balls at an old man out of the upstairs window."

We both know whose idea this was. For my mother, the proper construction to be put on this event is that my brother was a hell-raiser and I was his shadow, "easily influenced," as my mother puts it. "You were just putty in his hands."

"Of course, I had to punish both of you equally," she says. Of course. I smile a forgiving smile. The real truth is that I was sneakier than my brother, and got caught less often. No front-line charges into enemy machine-gun nests for me, if they could be at all avoided. My own solitary acts of wickedness were devious and well concealed; it was only in partnership with my brother that I would throw caution to the winds.

"He could wind you around his little finger," says my mother. "Your father made each of you a toy box, and the rule was—" (my mother is good at the devising of rules) "—the rule was that neither of you could take the toys out of the other one's toy box without permission. Otherwise he would have got all your toys away from you. But he got them anyway, mind you. He used to talk you into playing house, and he would pretend to be the baby. Then he would pretend to cry, and when you asked what he wanted, he'd demand whatever it was out of your toy box that he wanted to play with at the moment. You always gave it to him."

I don't remember this, though I do remember staging World War Two on the living-room floor, with armies of stuffed bears and rabbits; but surely some primal patterns were laid down. Have these early toy-box experiences—and "toy box" itself, as a concept, reeks with implications—have they made me suspicious of men who wish to be mothered, yet susceptible to them at the same time? Have I been conditioned to believe that if I am not solicitous, if I am not forthcoming, if I am not a never-ending cornucopia of entertaining delights, they will take their collections of milk-bottle tops and their mangy one-eared teddy bears and go away into the woods by themselves to play snipers? Probably. What my mother thinks was merely cute may have been lethal.

But this is not her only story about my suckiness and gullibility. She follows up with the *coup de grâce*, the tale of the bunny-rabbit cookies.   60

"It was in Ottawa. I was invited to a government tea," says my mother, and this fact alone should signal an element of horror: my mother hated official functions, to which however she was obliged to go because she was the wife of a civil servant. "I had to drag you kids along; we couldn't afford a lot of babysitters in those days." The hostess had made a whole plateful of decorated cookies for whatever children might be present, and my mother proceeds to describe these: wonderful cookies shaped like bunny rabbits, with faces and clothes of colored icing, little skirts for the little girl bunny rabbits, little pants for the little boy bunny rabbits.

"You chose one," says my mother. "You went off to a corner with it, by yourself. Mrs. X noticed you and went over. 'Aren't you going to eat your cookie?' she said. 'Oh, no,' you said. 'I'll just sit here and talk to it.' And there you sat, as happy as a clam. But someone had made the mistake of leaving the plate near your brother. When they looked again, there wasn't a single cookie left. He'd eaten every one. He was very sick that night, I can tell you."

Some of my mother's stories defy analysis. What is the moral of this one? That I was a simp is clear enough, but on the other hand it was my brother who got the stomach ache. Is it better to eat your food, in a straightforward materialistic way, and as much of it as possible, or go off into the corner and talk to it? This used to be a favorite of my mother's before I was married, when I would bring what my father referred to as "swains"° home for dinner. Along with the dessert, out would come the bunny-rabbit cookie story, and I would cringe and twiddle my spoon while my mother forged blithely on with it. What were the swains supposed to make of it? Were my kindliness and essential femininity being trotted out for their inspection? Were they being told in a roundabout way that I was harmless, that they could expect to be talked to by me, but not devoured? Or was she, in some way, warning them off? Because there is something faintly crazed about my behavior, some tinge of the kind of person who might be expected to leap up suddenly from the dinner table and shout, "Don't eat that! It's alive!"

There is, however, a difference between symbolism and anecdote. Listening to my mother, I sometimes remember this.

"In my next incarnation," my mother said once, "I'm going to be an ar-   65
chaeologist and go around digging things up." We were sitting on the bed that had once been my brother's, then mine, then my sister's; we were sorting out things from one of the trunks, deciding what could now be given away or thrown out. My mother believes that what you save from the past is mostly a matter of choice.

At that time something wasn't right in the family; someone wasn't happy. My mother was angry: her good cheer was not paying off.

This statement of hers startled me. It was the first time I'd ever heard my mother say that she might have wanted to be something other than what she was. I must have been thirty-five at the time, but it was still shocking and slightly offensive to me to learn that my mother might not have been totally contented fulfilling the role in which fate had cast her: that of being my mother. What thumbsuckers we all are, I thought, when it comes to mothers.

Shortly after this I became a mother myself, and this moment altered for me.

While she was combing my next-to-impossible hair, winding it around her long index finger, yanking out the snarls, my mother used to read me stories. Most of them are still in the house somewhere, but one has vanished. It may have been a library book. It was about a little girl who was so poor she had only one potato left for her supper, and while she was roasting it the potato got up and ran away. There was the usual chase, but I can't remember the ending: a significant lapse.

"That story was one of your favorites," says my mother. She is probably still   70
under the impression that I identified with the little girl, with her hunger and her sense of loss; whereas in reality I identified with the potato.

Early influences are important. It took that one a while to come out; probably until after I went to university and started wearing black stockings and pulling my hair back into a bun, and having pretentions. Gloom set in. Our next-door neighbor, who was interested in wardrobes, tackled my mother: "'If she would only *do* something about herself,'" my mother quotes, "'she could be *quite attractive.'"

"You always kept yourself busy," my mother says charitably, referring to this time. "You always had something cooking. Some project or other."

swains: Suitors.

It is part of my mother's mythology that I am as cheerful and productive as she is, though she admits that these qualities may be occasionally and temporarily concealed. I wasn't allowed much angst around the house. I had to indulge it in the cellar, where my mother wouldn't come upon me brooding and suggest I should go out for a walk, to improve my circulation. This was her answer to any sign, however slight, of creeping despondency. There wasn't a lot that a brisk sprint through dead leaves, howling winds, or sleet couldn't cure.

It was, I knew, the *zeitgeist* that was afflicting me, and against it such simple remedies were powerless. Like smog I wafted through her days, dankness spreading out from around me. I read modern poetry and histories of Nazi atrocities, and took to drinking coffee. Off in the distance, my mother vacuumed around my feet while I sat in chairs, studying, with car rugs tucked around me, for suddenly I was always cold.

My mother has few stories to tell about these times. What I remember from   75
them is the odd look I would sometimes catch in her eyes. It struck me, for the first time in my life, that my mother might be afraid of me. I could not even reassure her, because I was only dimly aware of the nature of her distress, but there must have been something going on in me that was beyond her: at any time I might open my mouth and out would come a language she had never heard before. I had become a visitant from outer space, a time-traveller come back from the future, bearing news of a great disaster.

Toni Cade Bambara   (b. 1939)

Toni Cade Bambara is widely known as a social activist. She has studied at universities in New York, Florence (Italy), and Paris, has performed as a dancer and mime, and currently works as a production consultant for television in Philadelphia. "The Lesson" comes from Gorilla, My Love *(1972), which was followed in 1977 by another collection of stories,* The Sea Birds Are Still Alive. *Her novel* The Salt Eaters *was published in 1980, and* If Blessing Comes *was published in 1987. "The Lesson" reveals a gift for language and an ear for the way people speak. In it Bambara captures the voices of bright black children on a makeshift field trip to the Mecca of toy worlds: F.A.O. Schwartz. However, these "babes in toyland" are different from anything conventional American wisdom would have expected. They are there not just to admire fancy toys, but to learn a lesson about why they must look but cannot touch. Another African-American writer, Lucille Clifton, reviewed* Gorilla My Love *and said, "She has captured it all, how we really talk, how we really are; and done it with both love and respect."*

THE LESSON   1972

Back in the days when everyone was old and stupid or young and foolish and me and Sugar were the only ones just right, this lady moved on our block with nappy hair and proper speech and no makeup. And quite naturally we laughed at her, laughed the way we did at the junk man who went about his business like he was some big-time president and his sorry-ass horse his secretary. And we kinda hated her too, hated the way we did the winos who cluttered up our parks and pissed on our handball walls and stank up our hallways and stairs so you couldn't halfway play hide-and-seek without a goddamn gas mask. Miss Moore was her name. The only woman on the block with no first name. And she was black as hell, cept for her feet, which were fish-white and spooky. And she was always planning these boring-ass things for us to do, us being my cousin, mostly, who lived on the block cause we all moved North the same time and to the same apartment then spread out gradual to breathe. And our parents would yank our heads into some kinda shape and crisp up our clothes so we'd be presentable for travel with Miss Moore, who always looked like she was going to church, though she never did. Which is just one of things the grown-ups talked about when they talked behind her back like a dog. But when she came calling with some sachet she'd sewed up or some gingerbread she'd made or some book, why then they'd all be too embarrassed to turn her down and we'd get handed over all spruced up. She'd been to college and said it was only right that she should take responsibility for the young ones' education, and she not even related by marriage or blood. So they'd go for it. Specially Aunt Gretchen. She was the main gofer in the family. You got some ole dumb shit foolishness you want somebody to go for, you send for Aunt Gretchen. She been screwed into the go-along for so long, it's a blood-deep natural thing with her. Which is how she got saddled with me and Sugar and Junior in the first place while our mothers were in a la-de-da apartment up the block having a good ole time.

So this one day Miss Moore rounds us all up at the mailbox and it's puredee hot and she's knockin herself out about arithmetic. And school suppose to let up in summer I heard, but she don't never let up. And the starch in my pinafore scratching the shit outta me and I'm really hating this nappy-head bitch and her goddamn college degree. I'd much rather go to the pool or to the show where it's cool. So me and Sugar leaning on the mailbox being surly, which is a Miss Moore word. And Flyboy checking out what everybody brought for lunch. And Fat Butt already wasting his peanut-butter-and-jelly sandwich like the pig he is. And Junebug punchin on Q.T.'s arm for potato chips. And Rosie Giraffe shifting from one hip to the other waiting for somebody to step on her foot or ask her if she from Georgia so she can kick ass, preferably Mercedes'. And Miss Moore asking us do we know what money is, like we a bunch of retards. I mean real money, she say, like it's only poker chips or monopoly papers we lay on the grocer. So right away I'm tired of this and say so. And would much rather snatch Sugar and go to the Sunset and terrorize the West Indian kids and take their hair ribbons and their money too. And Miss Moore files that remark away for next week's lesson on brotherhood, I can tell. And finally I say we oughta get to the subway cause it's cooler and besides we might meet some cute boys. Sugar done swiped her mama's lipstick, so we ready.

So we heading down the street and she's boring us silly about what things cost and what our parents make and how much goes for rent and how money ain't divided up right in this country. And then she gets to the part about we all poor and live in the slums, which I don't feature. And I'm ready to speak on that, but she steps out in the street and hails two cabs just like that. Then she hustles half the crew in with her and hands me a five-dollar bill and tells me to calculate 10 percent tip for the driver. And we're off. Me and Sugar and Junebug and Flyboy hangin out the window and hollering to everybody, putting lipstick on each other cause Flyboy a faggot anyway, and making farts with our sweaty armpits. But I'm mostly trying to figure how to spend this money. But they all fascinated with the meter ticking and Junebug starts laying bets as to how much it'll read when Flyboy can't hold his breath no more. Then Sugar lays bets as to how much it'll be when we get there. So I'm stuck. Don't nobody want to go for my plan, which is to jump out at the next light and run off to the first bar-b-que we can find. Then the driver tells us to get the hell out cause we there already. And the meter reads eighty-five cents. And I'm stalling to figure out the tip and Sugar say give him a dime. And I decide he don't need it bad as I do, so later for him. But then he tries to take off with Junebug foot still in the door so we talk about his mama something ferocious. Then we check out that we on Fifth Avenue and everybody dressed up in stockings. One lady in a fur coat, hot as it is. White folks crazy.

"This is the place," Miss Moore say, presenting it to us in the voice she uses at the museum. "Let's look in the windows before we go in."

"Can we steal?" Sugar asks very serious like she's getting the ground rules   5
squared away before she plays. "I beg your pardon," say Miss Moore, and we fall out. So she leads us around the windows of the toy store and me and Sugar screamin, "This is mine, that's mine, I gotta have that, that was made for me, I was born for that," till Big Butt drowns us out.

"Hey, I'm goin to buy that there."

"That there? You don't even know what it is, stupid."

"I do so," he say punchin on Rosie Giraffe. "It's a microscope."

"Whatcha gonna do with a microscope, fool?"

"Look at things."   10

"Like what, Ronald?" ask Miss Moore. And Big Butt ain't got the first notion. So here go Miss Moore gabbing about the thousands of bacteria in a drop of water and the somethinorother in a speck of blood and the million and one living things in the air around us is invisible to the naked eye. And what she say that for? Junebug go to town on that "naked" and we rolling. Then Miss Moore ask what it cost. So we all jam into the window smudgin it up and the price tag say $300. So then she ask how long'd take for Big Butt and Junebug to save up their allowances. "Too long," I say. "Yeh," adds Sugar, "outgrown it by that time." And Miss Moore say no, you never outgrow learning instruments. "Why, even medical students and interns and," blah, blah, blah. And we ready to choke Big Butt for bringing it up in the first damn place.

"This here costs four hundred eighty dollars," say Rosie Giraffe. So we pile up all over her to see what she pointin out. My eyes tell me it's a chunk of glass cracked with something heavy, and different-color inks dripped into the splits, then the whole thing put into a oven or something. But for $480 it don't make sense.

"That's a paperweight made of semi-precious stones fused together under tremendous pressure," she explains slowly, with her hands doing the mining and all the factory work.

"So what's a paperweight?" asks Rosie Giraffe.

"To weigh paper with, dumbbell," say Flyboy, the wise man from the East.   15

"Not exactly," say Miss Moore, which is what she say when you warm or way off too. "It's to weigh paper down so it won't scatter and make your desk untidy." So right away me and Sugar curtsy to each other and then to Mercedes who is more the tidy type.

"We don't keep paper on top of the desk in my class," say Junebug, figuring Miss Moore crazy or lyin one.

"At home, then," she say. "Don't you have a calendar and a pencil case and a blotter and a letter-opener on your desk at home where you do your homework?" And she know damn well what our homes look like cause she nosys around in them every chance she gets.

"I don't even have a desk," say Junebug. "Do we?"

"No. And I don't get no homework neither," say Big Butt.   20

"And I don't even have a home," say Flyboy like he do at school to keep the white folks off his back and sorry for him. Send this poor kid to camp posters, is his specialty.

"I do," says Mercedes. "I have a box of stationery on my desk and a picture of my cat. My godmother bought the stationery and the desk. There's a big rose on each sheet and the envelopes smell like roses."

"Who wants to know about your smelly-ass stationery," say Rosie Giraffe fore I can get my two cents in.

"It's important to have a work area all your own so that . . ."

"Will you look at this sailboat, please," say Flyboy, cuttin her off and pointin   25
to the thing like it was his. So once again we tumble all over each other to gaze at this magnificent thing in the toy store which is just big enough to maybe sail two kittens across the pond if you strap them to the posts tight. We all start reciting the price tag like we in assembly. "Handcrafted sailboat of fiberglass at one thousand one hundred ninety-five dollars."

"Unbelievable," I hear myself say and am really stunned. I read it again for myself just in case the group recitation put me in a trance. Same thing. For some reason this pisses me off. We look at Miss Moore and she lookin at us, waiting for I dunno what.

Who'd pay all that when you can buy a sailboat set for a quarter at Pop's, a tube of glue for a dime, and a ball of string for eight cents? "It must have a motor and a whole lot else besides," I say. "My sailboat cost me about fifty cents."

"But will it take water?" say Mercedes with her smart ass.

"Took mine to Alley Pond Park once," say Flyboy. "String broke, Lost it. Pity."

"Sailed mine in Central Park and it keeled over and sank. Had to ask my fa-   30
ther for another dollar."

"And you got the strap," laugh Big Butt. "The jerk didn't even have a string on it. My old man wailed on his behind."

Little Q.T. was staring hard at the sailboat and you could see he wanted it bad. But he too little and somebody'd just take it from him. So what the hell. "This boat for kids, Miss Moore?"

"Parents silly to buy something like that just to get all broke up," say Rosie Giraffe.

"That much money it should last forever," I figure.

"My father'd buy it for me if I wanted it."   35

"Your father, my ass," say Rosie Giraffe getting a chance to finally push Mercedes.

"Must be rich people shop here," say Q.T.

"You are a very bright boy," say Flyboy. "What was your first clue?" And he rap him on the head with the back of his knuckles, since Q.T. the only one he could get away with. Though Q.T. liable to come up behind you years later and get his licks in when you half expect it.

"What I want to know is," I says to Miss Moore though I never talk to her, I wouldn't give the bitch that satisfaction, "is how much a real boat costs? I figure a thousand'd get you a yacht any day."

"Why don't you check that out," she says, "and report back to the group?"   40
Which really pains my ass. If you gonna mess up a perfectly good swim day least you could do is have some answers. "Let's go in," she say like she got something up her sleeve. Only she don't lead the way. So me and Sugar turn the corner to where the entrance is, but when we get there I kinda hang back. Not that I'm scared, what's there to be afraid of, just a toy store. But I feel funny, shame. But what I got to be shamed about? Got as much right to go in as anybody. But somehow I can't seem to get hold of the door, so I step away for Sugar to lead. But she hangs back too. And I look at her and she looks at me and this is ridiculous. I mean, damn, I have never ever been shy about doing nothing or going nowhere. But then Mercedes steps up and then Rosie Giraffe and Big Butt crowd in behind and shove, and next thing we all stuffed into the doorway with only Mercedes squeezing past us, smoothing out her jumper and walking right down the aisle. Then the rest of us tumble in like a glued-together jigsaw done all wrong. And people lookin at us. And it's like the time me and Sugar crashed into the Catholic church on a dare. But once we got in there and everything so hushed and holy and the candles and the bow-in and the handkerchiefs on all the drooping heads, I just couldn't go through with the plan. Which was for me to run up to the altar and do a tap dance while Sugar played the nose flute and messed around in the holy water. And Sugar kept givin me the elbow. Then later teased me so bad I tied her up in the shower and turned it on and locked her in. And she'd be there till this day if Aunt Gretchen hadn't finally figured I was lyin about the boarder takin a shower.

Same thing in the store. We all walkin on tiptoe and hardly touchin the games and puzzles and things. And I watched Miss Moore who is steady watchin us like she waitin for a sign. Like Mama Drewery watches the sky and sniffs the air and takes note of just how much slant is in the bird formation. Then me and Sugar bump smack into each other, so busy gazing at the toys, 'specially the sailboat. But we don't laugh and go into our fat-lady bump-stomach routine. We just stare at that price tag. Then Sugar run a finger over the whole boat. And I'm jealous and want to hit her. Maybe not her, but I sure want to punch somebody in the mouth.

"Watcha bring us here for, Miss Moore?"

"You sound angry, Sylvia. Are you mad about something?" Givin me one of them grins like she tellin a grown-up joke that never turns out to be funny. And she's lookin very closely at me like maybe she plannin to do my portrait from memory. I'm mad, but I won't give her that satisfaction. So I slouch around the store bein very bored and say, "Let's go."

Me and Sugar at the back of the train watchin the tracks whizzin by large then small then gettin gobbled up in the dark. I'm thinkin about this tricky toy I saw in the store. A clown that somersaults on a bar then does chin-ups just cause you yank lightly at his leg. Cost $35. I could see me askin my mother for a $35 birthday clown. "You wanna who that costs what?" she'd say, cocking her head to the side to get a better view of the hole in my head. Thirty-five dollars could buy new bunk beds for Junior and Gretchen's boy. Thirty-five dollars and the whole household could go visit Granddaddy Nelson in the country. Thirty-five dollars would pay for the rent and the piano bill too. Who are these people that spend that much for performing clowns and $1,000 for toy sailboats? What kinda work they do and how they live and how come we ain't in on it? Where we are is who we are, Miss Moore always pointin out. But it don't necessarily have to be that way, she always adds then waits for somebody to say that poor people have to wake up and demand their share of the pie and don't none of us know what kind of pie she talkin about in the first damn place. But she ain't so smart cause I still got her four dollars from the taxi and she sure ain't gettin it. Messin up my day with this shift. Sugar nudges me in my pocket and winks.

Miss Moore lines us up in front of the mailbox where we started from, seem   45
like years ago, and I got a headache for thinkin so hard. And we lean all over each other so we can hold up under the draggy-ass lecture she always finishes us off with at the end before we thank her for borin us to tears. But she just looks at us like she readin tea leaves. Finally she say, "Well, what did you think of F.A.O. Schwartz?"

Rosie Giraffe mumbles, "White folks crazy."

"I'd like to go there again when I get my birthday money," says Mercedes, and we shove her out the pack so she has to lean on the mailbox by herself.

"I'd like a shower. Tiring day," say Flyboy.

Then Sugar surprises me by sayin, "You know, Miss Moore, I don't think all of us here put together eat in a year what that sailboat costs." And Miss Moore lights up like somebody goosed her. "And?" she say, urging Sugar on. Only I'm standin on her foot so she don't continue.

"Imagine for a minute what kind of society it is in which some people can   50
spend on a toy what it would cost to feed a family of six or seven. What do you think?"

"I think," say Sugar pushing me off her feet like she never done before, cause I whip her ass in a minute, "that this is not much of a democracy if you ask me. Equal chance to pursue happiness means an equal crack at the dough, don't it?" Miss Moore is besides herself and I am disgusted with Sugar's treachery. So I stand on her foot one more time to see if she'll shove me. She shuts up, and Miss Moore looks at me, sorrowfully I'm thinkin. And somethin weird is going on, I can feel it in my chest.

"Anybody else learn anything today?" lookin dead at me. I walk away and Sugar has to run to catch up and don't even seem to notice when I shrug her arm off my shoulder.

"Well, we got four dollars anyway," she says.

"Uh hunh."

"We could go to Hascombs and get half a chocolate layer and then go to   55
the Sunset and still have plenty money for potato chips and ice-cream sodas."

"Uh hunh."

"Race you to Hascombs," she say.

We start down the block and she gets ahead which is O.K. by me cause I'm goin to the West End and then over to the Drive to think this day through. She can run if she want to and even run faster. But ain't nobody gonna beat me at nuthin.

Ann Beattie   (b. 1947)

Ann Beattie writes about characters who often experience changes in "normal" social structures. "The Cinderella Waltz" explores a divorce in which one partner has gone off with his homosexual lover. Louise, the wise child of this marriage, seems adult in many ways, yet it is hard to tell how much she understands. Beattie's stories have appeared constantly since 1972, often in the New Yorker. Distortions, *a book of stories, and* Chilly Scenes of Winter, *a novel, were both published in 1976.* Secrets and Surprises *and* The Burning House, *from which this story comes, were published in 1982.* Picturing Will *(1989) concerns a woman making her living after a divorce by becoming a photographer.* What is Mine *(1991) is a collection of stories.*

THE CINDERELLA WALTZ   1982

Milo and Bradley are creatures of habit. For as long as I've known him, Milo has worn his moth-eaten blue scarf with the knot hanging so low on his chest that the scarf is useless. Bradley is addicted to coffee and carries a Thermos with him. Milo complains about the cold, and Bradley is always a little edgy. They come out from the city every Saturday—this is not habit but loyalty—to pick up Louise. Louise is even more unpredictable than most nine-year-olds; sometimes she waits for them on the front step, sometimes she hasn't even gotten out of bed when they arrive. One time she hid in a closet and wouldn't leave with them.

Today Louise has put together a shopping bag full of things she wants to take with her. She is taking my whisk and my blue pottery bowl, to make Sunday breakfast for Milo and Bradley; Beckett's *Happy Days*, which she has carried around for weeks, and which she looks through, smiling—but I'm not sure she's reading it; and a coleus growing out of a conch shell. Also, she has stuffed into one side of the bag the fancy Victorian-style nightgown her grandmother gave her for Christmas, and into the other she has tucked her octascope. Milo keeps a couple of dresses, a nightgown, a toothbrush, and extra sneakers and boots at his apartment for her. He got tired of rounding up her stuff to pack for her to take home, so he has brought some things for her that can be left. It annoys him that she still packs bags, because then he has to go around making sure that she has found everything before she goes home. She seems to know how to manipulate him, and after the weekend is over she calls tearfully to say that she has left this or that, which means that he must get his car out of the garage and drive all the way out to the house to bring it to her. One time, he refused to take the hour-long drive, because she had only left a copy of Tolkien's *The Two Towers*. The following weekend was the time she hid in the closet.

"I'll water your plant if you leave it here," I say now.

"I can take it," she says.

"I didn't say you couldn't take it. I just thought it might be easier to leave   5
it, because if the shell tips over the plant might get ruined."

"O.K.," she says. "Don't water it today, though. Water it Sunday afternoon."

I reach for the shopping bag.

"I'll put it back on my window sill," she says. She lifts the plant out and carries it as if it's made of Steuben glass. Bradley bought it for her last month, driving back to the city, when they stopped at a lawn sale. She and Bradley are both very choosy, and he likes that. He drinks French-roast coffee; she will debate with herself almost endlessly over whether to buy a coleus that is primarily pink or lavender or striped.

"Has Milo made any plans for this weekend?" I ask.

"He's having a couple of people over tonight, and I'm going to help them make crêpes for dinner. If they buy more bottles of that wine with the yellow flowers on the label, Bradley is going to soak the labels off for me."

"That's nice of him," I say. "He never minds taking a lot of time with things."

"He doesn't like to cook, though. Milo and I are going to cook. Bradley sets the table and fixes flowers in a bowl. He thinks it's frustrating to cook."

"Well," I say, "with cooking you have to have a good sense of timing. You have to coordinate everything. Bradley likes to work carefully and not be rushed."

I wonder how much she knows. Last week she told me about a conversation she'd had with her friend Sarah. Sarah was trying to persuade Louise to stay around on the weekends, but Louise said she always went to her father's. Then Sarah tried to get her to take her along, and Louise said that she couldn't. "You could take her if you wanted to," I said later. "Check with Milo and see if that isn't right. I don't think he'd mind having a friend of yours occasionally."

She shrugged. "Bradley doesn't like a lot of people around," she said.

"Bradley likes you, and if she's your friend I don't think he'd mind."

She looked at me with an expression I didn't recognize; perhaps she thought I was a little dumb, or perhaps she was just curious to see if I would go on. I didn't know how to go on. Like an adult, she gave a little shrug and changed the subject.

At ten o'clock Milo pulls into the driveway and honks his horn, which makes a noise like a bleating sheep. He knows the noise the horn makes is funny, and he means to amuse us. There was a time just after the divorce when he and Bradley would come here and get out of the car and stand around silently, waiting for her. She knew that she had to watch for them, because Milo wouldn't come to the door. We were both bitter then, but I got over it. I still don't think Milo would have come into the house again, though, if Bradley hadn't thought it was a good idea. The third time Milo came to pick her up after he'd left home, I went out to invite them in, but Milo said nothing. He was standing there with his arms at his sides like a wooden soldier, and his eyes were as dead to me as if they'd been painted on. It was Bradley whom I reasoned with. "Louise is over at Sarah's right now, and it'll make her feel more comfortable if we're all together when she comes in," I said to him, and Bradley turned to Milo and said, "Hey, that's right. Why don't we go in for a quick cup of coffee?" I looked into the back seat of the car and saw his red Thermos there; Louise had told me about it. Bradley meant that they should come in and sit down. He was giving me even more than I'd asked for.

It would be an understatement to say that I disliked Bradley at first. I was actually afraid of him, afraid even after I saw him, though he was slender, and more nervous than I, and spoke quietly. The second time I saw him, I persuaded myself that he was just a stereotype, but someone who certainly seemed harmless enough. By the third time, I had enough courage to suggest that they come into the house. It was embarrassing for all of us, sitting around the table—the same table where Milo and I had eaten our meals for the years we were married. Before he left, Milo had shouted at me that the house was a farce, that my playing the happy suburban housewife was a farce, that it was unconscionable of me to let things drag on, that I would probably kiss him and say, "How was your day, sweet-heart?" and that he should bring home flowers and the evening paper. "Maybe I would!" I screamed back. "Maybe it would be nice to do that, even if we were pretending, instead of you coming home drunk and not caring what had happened to me or to Louise all day." He was holding on to the edge of the kitchen table, the way you'd hold on to the horse's reins in a runaway carriage. "I care about Louise," he said finally. That was the most horrible moment. Until then, until he said it that way, I had thought that he was going through something horrible—certainly something was terribly wrong—but that, in his way, he loved me after all. "*You don't love me?*" I had whispered at once. It took us both aback. It was an innocent and pathetic question, and it made him come and put his arms around me in the last hug he ever gave me. "I'm sorry for you," he said, "and I'm sorry for marrying you and causing this, but you know who I love. I told you who I love." "But you were kidding," I said. "You didn't mean it. You were kidding."

When Bradley sat at the table that first day, I tried to be polite and not look at him much. I had gotten it through my head that Milo was crazy, and I guess I was expecting Bradley to be a horrible parody—Craig Russell doing Marilyn Monroe. Bradley did not spoon sugar into Milo's coffee. He did not even sit near him. In fact, he pulled his chair a little away from us, and in spite of his uneasiness he found more things to start conversations about than Milo and I did. He told me about the ad agency where he worked; he is a designer there. He asked if he could go out on the porch to see the brook—Milo had told him about the stream in the back of our place that was as thin as a pencil but still gave us our own watercress. He went out on the porch and stayed there for at least five minutes, giving us a chance to talk. We didn't say one word until he came back. Louise came home from Sarah's house just as Bradley sat down at the table again, and she gave him a hug as well as us. I could see that she really liked him. I was amazed that I liked him, too. Bradley had won and I had lost, but he was as gentle and low-key as if none of it mattered. Later in the week, I called him and asked him to tell me if any free-lance jobs opened in his advertising agency. (I do a little free-lance artwork, whenever I can arrange it.) The week after that, he called and told me about another agency, where they were looking for outside artists. Our calls to each other are always brief and for a purpose, but lately they're not just calls about business. Before Bradley left to scout some picture locations in Mexico, he called to say that Milo had told him that when the two of us were there years ago I had seen one of those big circular bronze Aztec calendars and I had always regretted not bringing it back. He wanted to know if I would like him to buy a calendar if he saw one like the one Milo had told him about.

Today, Milo is getting out of his car, his blue scarf flapping against his chest. Louise, looking out the window, asks the same thing I am wondering: "Where's Bradley?"

Milo comes in and shakes my hand, gives Louise a one-armed hug.

"Bradley thinks he's coming down with a cold," Milo says. "The dinner is still on, Louise. We'll do the dinner. We have to stop at Gristede's° when we get

20

Gristede's. A grocery store, part of an Eastern chain of upscale markets.

back to town, unless your mother happens to have a tin of anchovies and two sticks of unsalted butter."

"Let's go to Gristede's," Louise says. "I like to go there."

"Let me look in the kitchen," I say. The butter is salted, but Milo says that will do, and he takes three sticks instead of two. I have a brainstorm and cut the cellophane on a leftover Christmas present from my aunt—a wicker plate that holds nuts and foil-wrapped triangles of cheese—and, sure enough: one tin of anchovies.   25

"We can go to the museum instead," Milo says to Louise. "Wonderful."

But then, going out the door, carrying her bag, he changes his mind. "We can go to America Hurrah, and if we see something beautiful we can buy it," he says.

They go off in high spirits. Louise comes up to his waist, almost, and I notice again that they have the same walk. Both of them stride forward with great purpose. Last week, Bradley told me that Milo had bought a weathervane in the shape of a horse, made around 1800, at America Hurrah, and stood it in the bedroom, and then was enraged when Bradley draped his socks over it to dry. Bradley is still learning what a perfectionist Milo is, and how little sense of humor he has. When we were first married, I used one of our pottery casserole dishes to put my jewelry in, and he nagged me until I took it out and put the dish back in the kitchen cabinet. I remember his saying that the dish looked silly on my dresser because it was obvious what it was and people would think we left our dishes lying around. It was one of the things that Milo wouldn't tolerate, because it was improper.

When Milo brings Louise back on Sunday night they are not in a good mood. The dinner was all right, Milo says, and Griffin and Amy and Mark were amazed at what a good hostess Louise had been, but Bradley hadn't been able to eat.

"Is he still coming down with a cold?" I ask. I was still a little shy about asking questions about Bradley.   30

Milo shrugs. "Louise made him take megadoses of vitamin C all weekend."

Louise says, "Bradley said that taking too much vitamin C was bad for your kidneys, though."

"It's a rotten climate," Milo says, sitting on the living-room sofa, scarf and coat still on. "The combination of cold and air pollution . . ."

Louise and I look at each other, and then back at Milo. For weeks now, he has been talking about moving to San Francisco, if he can find work there. (Milo is an architect.) This talk bores me, and it makes Louise nervous. I've asked him not to talk to her about it unless he's actually going to move, but he doesn't seem to be able to stop himself.

"O.K.," Milo says, looking at us both. "I'm not going to say anything about San Francisco."   35

"*California* is polluted," I say. I am unable to stop myself, either.

Milo heaves himself up from the sofa, ready for the drive back to New York. It is the same way he used to get off the sofa that last year he lived here. He would get up, dress for work, and not even go into the kitchen for breakfast—just sit, sometimes in his coat as he was sitting just now, and at the last minute he would push himself up and go out to the driveway, usually without a goodbye, and get in the car and drive off either very fast or very slowly. I liked it better when he made the tires spin in the gravel when he took off.

He stops at the doorway now, and turns to face me. "Did I take all your butter?" he says.

"No," I say. "There's another stick." I point into the kitchen.

"I could have guessed that's where it would be," he says, and smiles at me.   40

When Milo comes the next weekend, Bradley is still not with him. The night
before, as I was putting Louise to bed, she said that she had a feeling he wouldn't
be coming.

"I had that feeling a couple of days ago," I said. "Usually Bradley calls once
during the week."

"He must still be sick," Louise said. She looked at me anxiously. "Do you
think he is?"

"A cold isn't going to kill him," I said. "If he has a cold, he'll be O.K."

Her expression changed; she thought I was talking down to her. She lay back   45
in bed. The last year Milo was with us, I used to tuck her in and tell her that everything was all right. What that meant was that there had not been a fight. Milo
had sat listening to music on the phonograph, with a book or the newspaper in
front of his face. He didn't pay very much attention to Louise, and he ignored
me entirely. Instead of saying a prayer with her, the way I usually did, I would say
to her that everything was all right. Then I would go downstairs and hope that
Milo would say the same thing to me. What he finally did say one night was "You
might as well find out from me as some other way."

"Hey, are you an old bag lady again this weekend?" Milo says now, stooping to kiss Louise's forehead.

"Because you take some things with you doesn't mean you're a bag lady,"
she says primly.

"Well," Milo says, "you start doing something innocently, and before you
know it it can take you over."

He looks angry, and acts as though it's difficult for him to make conversation, even when the conversation is full of sarcasm and double-entendres.

"What do you say we get going?" he says to Louise.   50

In the shopping bag she is taking is her doll, which she has not played with
for more than a year. I found it by accident when I went to tuck in a loaf of banana bread that I had baked. When I saw Baby Betsy, deep in the bag, I decided
against putting the bread in.

"O.K.," Louise says to Milo. "Where's Bradley?"

"Sick," he says.

"Is he too sick to have me visit?"

"Good heavens, no. He'll be happier to see you than to see me."   55

"I'm rooting some of my coleus to give him," she says. "Maybe I'll give it
to him like it is, in water, and he can plant it when it roots."

When she leaves the room, I go over to Milo. "Be nice to her," I say quietly.

"I'm nice to her," he says. "Why does everybody have to act like I'm going
to grow fangs every time I turn around?"

"You were quite cutting when you came in."

"I was being self-deprecating." He sighs. "I don't really know why I come   60
here and act this way," he says.

"What's the matter, Milo?"

But now he lets me know he's bored with the conversation. He walks over to the table and picks up a *Newsweek* and flips through it. Louise comes back with the coleus in a water glass.

"You know what you could do," I say. "Wet a napkin and put it around that cutting and then wrap it in foil, and put it in water when you get there. That way, you wouldn't have to hold a glass of water all the way to New York."

She shrugs. "This is O.K.," she says.

"Why don't you take your mother's suggestion," Milo says. "The water will slosh out of the glass."

"Not if you don't drive fast."

"It doesn't have anything to do with my driving fast. If we go over a bump in the road, you're going to get all wet."

"Then I can put on one of my dresses at your apartment."

"Am I being unreasonable?" Milo says to me.

"I started it," I say. "Let her take it in the glass."

"Would you, as a favor, do what your mother says?" he says to Louise.

Louise looks at the coleus, and at me.

"Hold the glass over the seat instead of over your lap, and you won't get wet," I say.

"Your first idea was the best," Milo says.

Louise gives him an exasperated look and puts the glass down on the floor, pulls on her poncho, picks up the glass again and says a sullen goodbye to me, and goes out the front door.

"Why is this my fault?" Milo says. "Have I done anything terrible? I—"

"Do something to cheer yourself up," I say, patting him on the back.

He looks as exasperated with me as Louise was with him. He nods his head yes, and goes out the door.

"Was everything all right this weekend?" I ask Louise.

"Milo was in a bad mood, and Bradley wasn't even there on Saturday," Louise says. "He came back today and took us to the Village for breakfast."

"What did you have?"

"I had sausage wrapped in little pancakes and fruit salad and a rum bun."

"Where was Bradley on Saturday?"

She shrugs. "I didn't ask him."

She almost always surprises me by being more grownup than I give her credit for. Does she suspect, as I do, that Bradley has found another lover?

"Milo was in a bad mood when you two left here Saturday," I say.

"I told him if he didn't want me to come next weekend, just to tell me." She looks perturbed, and I suddenly realize that she can sound exactly like Milo sometimes.

"You shouldn't have said that to him, Louise," I say. "You know he wants you. He's just worried about Bradley."

"So?" she says. "I'm probably going to flunk math."

"No, you're not, honey. You got a C-plus on the last assignment."

"It still doesn't make my grade average out to a C."

"You'll get a C. It's all right to get a C."

She doesn't believe me.

"Don't be a perfectionist, like Milo," I tell her. "Even if you got a D, you wouldn't fail."

Louise is brushing her hair—thin, shoulder-length, auburn hair. She is al- 95
ready so pretty and so smart in everything except math that I wonder what will
become of her. When I was her age, I was plain and serious and I wanted to be
a tree surgeon. I went with my father to the park and held a stethoscope—a real
one—to the trunks of trees, listening to their silence. Children seem older now.

"What do you think's the matter with Bradley?" Louise says. She sounds
worried.

"Maybe the two of them are unhappy with each other right now."

She misses my point. "Bradley's sad, and Milo's sad that he's unhappy."

I drop Louise off at Sarah's house for supper. Sarah's mother, Martine
Cooper, looks like Shelley Winters, and I have never seen her without a glass of
Galliano on ice in her hand. She has a strong candy smell. Her husband has left
her, and she professes not to care. She has emptied her living room of furniture
and put up ballet bars on the walls, and dances in a purple leotard to records by
Cher and Mac Davis. I prefer to have Sarah come to our house, but her mother
is adamant that everything must be, as she puts it, "fifty-fifty." When Sarah visited us a week ago and loved the chocolate pie I had made, I sent two pieces home
with her. Tonight, when I left Sarah's house, her mother gave me a bowl of Jell-
O fruit salad.

The phone is ringing when I come in the door. It is Bradley. 100

"Bradley," I say at once, "whatever's wrong, at least you don't have a neighbor who just gave you a bowl of maraschino cherries in green Jell-O with a Reddi-
Whip flower squirted on top."

"Jesus," he says. "You don't need me to depress you, do you?"

"What's wrong?" I say.

He sighs into the phone. "Guess what?" he says.

"What?" 105

"I've lost my job."

It wasn't at all what I was expecting to hear. I was ready to hear that he was
leaving Milo, and I had even thought that that would serve Milo right. Part of
me still wanted him punished for what he did. I was so out of my mind when
Milo left me that I used to go over and drink Galliano with Martine Cooper. I
even thought seriously about forming a ballet group with her. I would go to her
house in the afternoon, and she would hold a tambourine in the air and I would
hold my leg rigid and try to kick it.

"That's awful," I say to Bradley. "What happened?"

"They said it was nothing personal—they were laying off three people. Two
other people are going to get the ax at the agency within the next six months. I
was the first to go, and it was nothing personal. From twenty thousand bucks a
year to nothing, and nothing personal, either."

"But your work is so good. Won't you be able to find something again?" 110

"Could I ask you a favor?" he says. "I'm calling from a phone booth. I'm
not in the city. Could I come talk to you?"

"Sure," I say.

It seems perfectly logical that he should come alone to talk—perfectly logical until I actually see him coming up the walk. I can't entirely believe it. A year
after my husband has left me, I am sitting with his lover—a man, a person I like
quite well—and trying to cheer him up because he is out of work. ("Honey," my
father would say, "listen to Daddy's heart with the stethoscope, or you can turn

it toward you and listen to your own heart. You won't hear anything listening to a tree." Was my persistence willfulness, or belief in magic? Is it possible that I hugged Bradley at the door because I'm secretly glad he's down and out, the way I used to be? Or do I really want to make things better for him?)

He comes into the kitchen and thanks me for the coffee I am making, drapes his coat over the chair he always sits in.

"What am I going to do?" he asks. 115

"You shouldn't get so upset, Bradley," I say. "You know you're good. You won't have trouble finding another job."

"That's only half of it," he says. "Milo thinks I did this deliberately. He told me I was quitting on him. He's very angry at me. He fights with me, and then he gets mad that I don't enjoy eating dinner. My stomach's upset, and I can't eat anything."

"Maybe some juice would be better than coffee."

"If I didn't drink coffee, I'd collapse," he says.

I pour coffee into a mug for him, coffee into a mug for me. 120

"This is probably very awkward for you," he says. "That I come here and say all this about Milo."

"What does he mean about your quitting on him?"

"He said . . . he actually accused me of doing badly deliberately, so they'd fire me. I was so afraid to tell him the truth when I was fired that I pretended to be sick. Then I really *was* sick. He's never been angry at me this way. Is this always the way he acts? Does he get a notion in his head for no reason and then pick at a person because of it?"

I try to remember. "We didn't argue much," I say. "When he didn't want to live here, he made me look ridiculous for complaining when I knew something was wrong. He expects perfection, but what that means is that you do things his way."

"I *was*. I never wanted to sit around the apartment, the way he says I did. I 125 even brought work home with me. He made me feel so bad all week that I went to a friend's apartment for the day on Saturday. Then he said I had walked out on the problem. He's a little paranoid. I was listening to the radio, and Carole King was singing 'It's Too Late,' and he came into the study and looked very upset, as though I had planned for the song to come on. I couldn't believe it."

"Whew," I say, shaking my head. "I don't envy you. You have to stand up to him. I didn't do that. I pretended the problem would go away."

"And now the problem sits across from you drinking coffee, and you're being nice to him."

"I know it. I was just thinking we look like two characters in some soap opera my friend Martine Cooper would watch."

He pushes his coffee cup away from him with a grimace.

"But anyway, I like you now," I say. "And you're exceptionally nice to 130 Louise."

"I took her father," he says.

"Bradley—I hope you don't take offense, but it makes me nervous to talk about that."

"I don't take offense. But how can you be having coffee with me?"

"You invited yourself over so you could ask that?"

"Please," he says, holding up both hands. Then he runs his hands through 135 his hair. "Don't make me feel illogical. He does that to me, you know. He doesn't understand it when everything doesn't fall right into line. If I like fixing up the place, keeping some flowers around, therefore I can't like being a working person, too, therefore I deliberately sabotage myself in my job." Bradley sips his coffee.

"I wish I could do something for him," he says in a different voice.

This is not what I expected, either. We have sounded like two wise adults, and then suddenly he has changed and sounds very tender. I realize the situation is still the same. It is two of them on one side and me on the other, even though Bradley is in my kitchen.

"Come and pick up Louise with me, Bradley," I say. "When you see Martine Cooper, you'll cheer up about your situation."

He looks up from his coffee. "You're forgetting what I'd look like to Martine Cooper," he says.

Milo is going to California. He has been offered a job with a new San Francisco 140
architectural firm. I am not the first to know. His sister, Deanna, knows before I do, and mentions it when we're talking on the phone. "It's middle-age crisis," Deanna says sniffily. "Not that I need to tell you." Deanna would drop dead if she knew the way things are. She is scandalized every time a new display is put up in Bloomingdale's window. ("Those mannequins had eyes like an Egyptian princess, and *rags*. I swear to you, they had mops and brooms and ragged gauze dresses on, with whores' shoes—stiletto heels that prostitutes wear.")

I hang up from Deanna's call and tell Louise I'm going to drive to the gas station for cigarettes. I go there to call New York on their pay phone.

"Well, I only just knew," Milo says. "I found out for sure yesterday, and last night Deanna called and so I told her. It's not like I'm leaving tonight."

He sounds elated, in spite of being upset that I called. He's happy in the way he used to be on Christmas morning. I remember him once running into the living room in his underwear and tearing open the gifts we'd been sent by relatives. He was looking for the eight-slice toaster he was sure we'd get. We'd been given two-slice, four-slice, and six-slice toasters, but then we got no more. "Come out, my eight-slice beauty!" Milo crooned, and out came an electric clock, a blender, and an expensive electric pan.

"When are you leaving?" I ask him.

"I'm going out to look for a place to live next week." 145

"Are you going to tell Louise yourself this weekend?"

"Of course," he says.

"And what are you going to do about seeing Louise?"

"Why do you act as if I don't like Louise?" he says. "I will occasionally come back East, and I will arrange for her to fly to San Francisco on her vacations."

"It's going to break her heart." 150

"No it isn't. Why do you want to make me feel bad?"

"She's had so many things to adjust to. You don't have to go to San Francisco right now, Milo."

"It happens, if you care, that my own job here is in jeopardy. This is a real chance for me, with a young firm. They really want me. But anyway, all we need in this happy group is to have you bringing in a couple of hundred dollars a month with your graphic work and me destitute and Bradley so devastated by being fired that of course he can't even look for work."

"I'll bet he is looking for a job," I say.

"Yes. He read the want ads today and then fixed a crab quiche."   155

"Maybe that's the way you like things, Milo, and people respond to you. You forbade me to work when we had a baby. Do you say anything encouraging to him about finding a job, or do you just take it out on him that he was fired?"

There is a pause, and then he almost seems to lose his mind with impatience.

"I can hardly *believe*, when I am trying to find a logical solution to all our problems, that I am being subjected, by telephone, to an unflattering psychological analysis by my ex-wife." He says this all in a rush.

"All right, Milo. But don't you think that if you're leaving so soon you ought to call her, instead of waiting until Saturday?"

Milo sighs very deeply. "I have more sense than to have important conver-   160
sations on the telephone," he says.

Milo calls on Friday and asks Louise whether it wouldn't be nice if both of us came in and spent the night Saturday and if we all went to brunch together Sunday. Louise is excited. I never go into town with her.

Louise and I pack a suitcase and put it in the car Saturday morning. A cutting of ivy for Bradley has taken root, and she has put it in a little green plastic pot for him. It's heartbreaking, and I hope that Milo notices and has a tough time dealing with it. I am relieved I'm going to be there when he tells her, and sad that I have to hear it at all.

In the city, I give the car to the garage attendant, who does not remember me. Milo and I lived in the apartment when we were first married, and moved when Louise was two years old. When we moved, Milo kept the apartment and sublet it—a sign that things were not going well, if I had been one to heed such a warning. What he said was that if we were ever rich enough we could have the house in Connecticut *and* the apartment in New York. When Milo moved out of the house, he went right back to the apartment. This will be the first time I have visited there in years.

Louise strides in in front of me, throwing her coat over the brass coatrack in the entranceway—almost too casual about being there. She's the hostess at Milo's, the way I am at our house.

He has painted the walls white. There are floor-length white curtains in the   165
living room, where my silly flowered curtains used to hang. The walls are bare, the floor has been sanded, a stereo as huge as a computer stands against one wall of the living room, and there are four speakers.

"Look around," Milo says. "Show your mother around, Louise."

I am trying to remember if I have ever told Louise that I used to live in this apartment. I must have told her, at some point, but I can't remember it.

"Hello," Bradley says, coming out of the bedroom.

"Hi, Bradley," I say. "Have you got a drink?"

Bradley looks sad. "He's got champagne," he says, and looks nervously at   170
Milo.

"No one *has* to drink champagne," Milo says. "There's the usual assortment of liquor."

"Yes," Bradley says. "What would you like?"

"Some bourbon, please."

"Bourbon." Bradley turns to go into the kitchen. He looks different; his hair is different—more wavy—and he is dressed as though it were summer, in-straight-legged-white pants and black leather thongs.

"I want Perrier water with strawberry juice," Louise says, tagging along af-   175
ter Bradley. I have never heard her ask for such a thing before. At home, she drinks too many Cokes. I am always trying to get her to drink fruit juice.

Bradley comes back with two drinks and hands me one. "Did you want anything?" he says to Milo.

"I'm going to open the champagne in a moment," Milo says. "How have you been this week, sweetheart?"

"O.K.," Louise says. She is holding a pale-pink, bubbly drink. She sips it like a cocktail.

Bradley looks very bad. He has circles under his eyes, and he is ill at ease. A red light begins to blink on the phone-answering device next to where Bradley sits on the sofa, and Milo gets out of his chair to pick up the phone.

"Do you really want to talk on the phone right now?" Bradley asks Milo qui-   180
etly.

Milo looks at him. "No, not particularly," he says, sitting down again. After a moment, the red light goes out.

"I'm going to mist your bowl garden," Louise says to Bradley, and slides off the sofa and goes to the bedroom. "Hey, a little toadstool is growing in here!" she calls back. "Did you put it there, Bradley?"

"It grew from the soil mixture, I guess," Bradley calls back. "I don't know how it got there."

"Have you heard anything about a job?" I ask Bradley.

"I haven't been looking, really," he says. "You know."   185

Milo frowns at him. "Your choice, Bradley," he says. "I didn't ask you to follow me to California. You can stay here."

"No," Bradley says. "You've hardly made me feel welcome."

"Should we have some champagne—all four of us—and you can get back to your bourbons later?" Milo says cheerfully.

We don't answer him, but he gets up anyway and goes to the kitchen. "Where have you hidden the tulip-shaped glasses, Bradley?" he calls out after a while.

"They should be in the cabinet on the far left," Bradley says.   190

"You're going with him?" I say to Bradley. "To San Francisco?"

He shrugs, and won't look at me. "I'm not quite sure I'm wanted," he says quietly.

The cork pops in the kitchen. I look at Bradley, but he won't look up. His new hairdo makes him look older. I remember that when Milo left me I went to the hairdresser the same week and had bangs cut. The next week, I went to a therapist who told me it was no good trying to hide from myself. The week after that, I did dance exercises with Martine Cooper, and the week after that the therapist told me not to dance if I wasn't interested in dancing.

"I'm not going to act like this is a funeral," Milo says, coming in with the glasses. "Louise, come in here and have champagne! We have something to have a toast about."

Louise comes into the living room suspiciously. She is so used to being re-   195
fused even a sip of wine from my glass or her father's that she no longer even asks.
"How come I'm in on this?" she asks.

"We're going to drink a toast to me," Milo says.

Three of the four glasses are clustered on the table in front of the sofa. Milo's glass is raised. Louise looks at me, to see what I'm going to say. Milo raises his glass even higher. Bradley reaches for a glass. Louise picks up a glass. I lean forward and take the last one.

"This is a toast to me," Milo says, "because I am going to be going to San Francisco."

It was not a very good or informative toast. Bradley and I sip from our glasses. Louise puts her glass down hard and bursts into tears, knocking the glass over. The champagne spills onto the cover of a big art book about the Unicorn Tapestries. She runs into the bedroom and slams the door.

Milo looks furious. "Everybody lets me know just what my insufficiencies are, don't they?" he says. "Nobody minds expressing himself. We have it all right out in the open."

"He's criticizing me," Bradley murmurs, his head still bowed. "It's because I was offered a job here in the city and I didn't automatically refuse it."

I turn to Milo. "Go say something to Louise, Milo," I say. "Do you think that's what somebody who isn't brokenhearted sounds like?"

He glares at me and stomps into the bedroom, and I can hear him talking to Louise reassuringly. "It doesn't mean you'll *never* see me," he says. "You can fly there, I'll come here. It's not going to be that different."

"You lied!" Louise screams. "You said we were going to brunch."

"We are. We are. I can't very well take us to brunch before Sunday, can I?"

"You didn't say you were going to San Francisco. What *is* San Francisco, anyway?"

"I just said so. I bought us a bottle of champagne. You can come out as soon as I get settled. You're going to like it there."

Louise is sobbing. She has told him the truth and she knows it's futile to go on.

By the next morning, Louise acts the way I acted—as if everything were just the same. She looks calm, but her face is small and pale. She looks very young. We walk into the restaurant and sit at the table Milo has reserved. Bradley pulls out a chair for me, and Milo pulls out a chair for Louise, locking his finger with hers for a second, raising her arm above her head, as if she were about to take a twirl.

She looks very nice, really. She has a ribbon in her hair. It is cold, and she should have worn a hat, but she wanted to wear the ribbon. Milo has good taste: the dress she is wearing, which he bought for her, is a hazy purple plaid, and it sets off her hair.

"Come with me. Don't be sad," Milo suddenly says to Louise, pulling her by the hand. "Come with me for a minute. Come across the street to the park for just a second, and we'll have some space to dance, and your mother and Bradley can have a nice quiet drink."

She gets up from the table and, looking long-suffering, backs into her coat, which he is holding for her, and the two of them go out. The waitress comes to the table, and Bradley orders three Bloody Marys and a Coke, and eggs Benedict for everyone. He asks the waitress to wait awhile before she brings the food. I have hardly slept at all, and having a drink is not going to clear my head. I have to think of things to say to Louise later, on the ride home.

"He takes so many *chances*," I say. "He pushes things so far with people. I don't want her to turn against him."

"No," he says.

"Why are you going, Bradley? You've seen the way he acts. You know that 215 when you get out there he'll pull something on you. Take the job and stay here."

Bradley is fiddling with the edge of his napkin. I study him. I don't know who his friends are, how old he is, where he grew up, whether he believes in God, or what he usually drinks. I'm shocked that I know so little, and I reach out and touch him. He looks up.

"Don't go," I say quietly.

The waitress puts the glasses down quickly and leaves, embarrassed because she thinks she's interrupted a tender moment. Bradley pats my hand on his arm. Then he says the thing that has always been between us, the thing too painful for me to envision or think about.

"I love him," Bradley whispers.

We sit quietly until Milo and Louise come into the restaurant, swinging 220 hands. She is pretending to be a young child, almost a baby, and I wonder for an instant if Milo and Bradley and I haven't been playing house, too—pretending to be adults.

"Daddy's going to give me a first-class ticket," Louise says. "When I go to California we're going to ride in a glass elevator to the top of the Fairman Hotel."

"The Fairmont," Milo says, smiling at her.

Before Louise was born, Milo used to put his ear to my stomach and say that if the baby turned out to be a girl he would put her into glass slippers instead of bootees. Now he is the prince once again. I see them in a glass elevator, not long from now, going up and up, with the people below getting smaller and smaller, until they disappear.

Becky Birtha   (b. 1948)

Becky Birtha has two collections of short stories: For Nights Like This One: Stories of Loving Women *and* Lovers' Choice. *Her collection* The Forbidden Poems *appeared in 1991. Her work has appeared in feminist and other literary journals, and recently in Terry Macmillan's anthology* Breaking Ice *(1991), a collection of new black writing by young writers. Birtha currently lives in Philadelphia, where she is working on a novel.*

JOHNNIERUTH   1991

Summertime. Nighttime. Talk about steam heat. This whole city get like the bathroom when somebody in there taking a shower with the door shut. Nights like that, can't nobody sleep. Everybody be outside, sitting on they steps or else dragging half they furniture out on the sidewalk—kitchen chairs, card tables— even bringing TVs outside.

Womenfolks, mostly. All the grown women around my way look just the same. They all big—stout. They got big bosoms and big hips and fat legs, and they always wearing runover house shoes and them shapeless, flowered numbers with the buttons down the front. 'Cept on Sunday. Sunday morning they all turn into glamour girls, in them big hats and long gloves, with they skinny high heels and they skinny selves in them tight girdles—wouldn't nobody ever know what they look like the rest of the time.

When I was a little kid, I didn't wanna grow up, 'cause I never wanted to look like them ladies. I heard Miz Jenkins down the street one time say she don't mind being fat 'cause that way her husband don't get so jealous. She say it's more than one way to keep a man. Me, I don't have me no intentions of keeping no man. I never understood why they was in so much demand anyway, when it seem like all a woman can depend on 'em for is making sure she keep on having babies.

We got enough children in my neighborhood. In the summertime even the little kids allowed to stay up till eleven or twelve o'clock at night—playing in the street and hollering and carrying on—don't never seem to get tired. Don't nobody care, long as they don't fight.

Me—I don't hang around no front steps no more. Hot nights like that, I 5
get out my ten-speed and I be gone.

That's what I like to do more than anything else in the whole world. Feel that wind in my face keeping me cool as a air conditioner, shooting along like a snowball. My bike light as a kite. I can really get up some speed.

All the guys around my way got ten-speed bikes. Some of the girls got 'em, too, but they don't ride 'em at night. They pedal around during the day; but at nighttime they just hang around out front, watching babies and running they mouth. I didn't get my Peugeot° to be no conversation piece.

My mama don't like me to ride at night. I tried to point out to her that she ain't never said nothing to my brothers, and Vincent a year younger than me. (And Langston two years older, in case "old" is the problem.) She say, "That's different, Johnnieruth. You're a girl." Now I wanna know how is anybody gonna know that. I'm skinny as a knifeblade turned sideways, and all I ever wear is blue jeans and a Wrangler jacket. But if I bring that up, she liable to get started in on how come I can't be more of a young lady, and fourteen is old enough to start taking more pride in my appearance, and she gonna be ashamed to admit I'm her daughter.

I just tell her that my bike be moving so fast can't nobody hardly see me, and couldn't catch me if they did. Mama complain to her friends how I'm wild and she can't do nothing with me. She know I'm gonna do what I want no matter what she say. But she know I ain't getting in no trouble, neither.

Like some of the boys I know stole they bikes, but I didn't do nothing like 10
that. I'd been saving my money ever since I can remember, every time I could get a nickel or a dime outta anybody.

When I was a little kid, it was hard to get money. Seem like the only time they ever give you any was on Sunday morning, and then you had to put it in the offering. I used to hate to do that. In fact, I used to hate everything about Sunday morning. I had to wear all them ruffly dresses—that shiny slippery stuff in the wintertime that got to make a noise every time you move your ass a inch on them hard old benches. And that scratchy starchy stuff in the summertime with all them scratchy crinolines. Had to carry a pocketbook and wear them shiny shoes. And the church we went to was all the way over on Summit Avenue, so the whole

Peugeot: A French-made bicycle.

damn neighborhood could get a good look. At least all the other kids'd be dressed the same way. The boys think they slick 'cause they get to wear pants, but they still got to wear a white shirt and a tie; and them dumb hats they wear can't hide them baldheaded haircuts, 'cause they got to take the hats off in church.

There was one Sunday when I musta been around eight. I remember it was before my sister Corletta was born, 'cause right around then was when I put my foot down about that whole sanctimonious routine. Anyway, I was dragging my feet along Twenty-fifth Street in back of Mama and Vincent and them, when I spied this lady. I only seen her that one time, but I still remember just how she look. She don't look like nobody I ever seen before. I *know* she don't live around here. She real skinny. But she ain't no real young woman, neither. She could be old as my mama. She ain't nobody's mama—I'm sure. And she ain't wearing Sunday clothes. She got on blue jeans and a man's blue working shirt, with the tail hanging out. She got patches on her blue jeans, and she still got her chin stuck out like she some kinda African royalty. She ain't carrying no shiny pocketbook. It don't look like she care if she got any money or not, or who know it, if she don't. She ain't wearing no house shoes, or stockings or high heels neither.

Mama always speak to everybody, but when she pass by this lady she make like she ain't even seen her. But I get me a real good look, and the lady stare right back at me. She got a funny look on her face, almost like she think she know me from someplace. After she pass on by, I had to turn around to get another look, even though Mama say that ain't polite. And you know what? She was turning around, too, looking back at me. And she give me a great big smile.

I didn't know too much in them days, but that's when I first got to thinking about how it's got to be different ways to be, from the way people be around my way. It's got to be places where it don't matter to nobody if you all dressed up on Sunday morning or you ain't. That's how come I started saving money. So, when I got enough, I could go away to someplace like that.

Afterwhile I begun to see there wasn't no point in waiting around for hand-   15
outs, and I started thinking of ways to earn my own money. I used to be running errands all the time—mailing letters for old Grandma Whittaker and picking up cigarettes and newspapers up the corner for everybody. After I got bigger, I started washing cars in the summer, and shoveling people sidewalk in the wintertime. Now I got me a newspaper route. Ain't never been no girl around here with no paper route, but I guess everybody got it figured out by now that I ain't gonna be like nobody else.

The reason I got me my Peugeot was so I could start to explore. I figured I better start looking around right now, so when I'm grown, I'll know exactly where I wanna go. So I ride around every chance I get.

Last summer I used to ride with the boys a lot. Sometimes eight or ten of us'd just go cruising around the streets together. All of a sudden my mama decide she don't want me to do that no more. She say I'm too old to be spending so much time with boys. (That's what they tell you half the time, and the other half the time they worried 'cause you ain't interested in spending more time with boys. Don't make much sense.) She want me to have some girl friends, but I never seem to fit in with none of the things the girls doing. I used to think I fit in more with the boys.

But I seen how Mama might be right, for once. I didn't like the way the boys was starting to talk about girls sometimes. Talking about what some girl be like from the neck on down, and talking all up underneath somebody clothes and all. Even though I wasn't really friends with none of the girls, I still didn't like it. So now I mostly just ride around by myself. And Mama don't like that neither— you just can't please her.

This boy that live around the corner on North Street, Kenny Henderson, started asking me one time if I don't ever be lonely, 'cause he always see me by myself. He say don't I ever think I'd like to have me somebody special to go places with and stuff. Like I'd pick him if I did! Made me wanna laugh in his face. I do be lonely, a lotta times, but I don't tell nobody. And I ain't met nobody yet that I'd really rather be with than be by myself. But I will someday. When I find that special place where everybody different, I'm gonna find somebody there I can be friends with. And it ain't gonna be no dumb boy.

I found me one place already that I like to go to a whole lot. It ain't even   20 really that far away—by bike—but it's on the other side of the Avenue. So I don't tell Mama and them I go there, 'cause they like to think I'm right around the neighborhood someplace. But this neighborhood too dull for me. All the houses look just the same—no porches, no yards, no trees—not even no parks around here. Every block look so much like every other block it hurt your eyes to look at afterwhile. So I ride across Summit Avenue and go down that big steep hill there, and then make a sharp right at the bottom and cross the bridge over the train tracks. Then I head on out the boulevard—that's the nicest part, with all them big trees making a tunnel over the top, and lightning bugs shining in the bushes. At the end of the boulevard you get to this place call the Plaza.

It's something like a little park—the sidewalks is all bricks and they got flowers planted all over the place. The same kind my mama grow in that painted-up tire she got out front masquerading like a garden decoration—only seem like they smell sweeter here. It's a big high fountain right in the middle, and all the streetlights is the real old-fashion kind. That Plaza is about the prettiest place I ever been.

Sometimes something going on there. Like a orchestra playing music or some man or lady singing. One time they had a show with some girls doing some kinda foreign dances. They look like they were around my age. They all had on these fancy costumes, with different color ribbons all down they back. I wouldn't wear nothing like that, but it looked real pretty when they was dancing.

I got me a special bench in one corner where I like to sit, 'cause I can see just about everything, but wouldn't nobody know I was there. I like to sit still and think, and I like to watch people. A lotta people be coming there at night— to look at the shows and stuff, or just to hang out and cool off. All different kinda people.

This one night when I was sitting over in that corner where I always be at, there was this lady standing right near my bench. She mostly had her back turned to me and she didn't know I was there, but I could see her real good. She had on this shiny purple shirt and about a million silver bracelets. I kinda liked the way she look. Sorta exotic, like she maybe come from California or one of the islands. I mean she had class—standing there posing with her arms folded. She walk away a little bit. Then turn around and walk back again. Like she waiting for somebody.

Then I spotted this dude coming over. I spied him all the way 'cross the   25 Plaza. Looking real fine. Got on a three-piece suit. One of them little caps sitting on a angle. Look like leather. He coming straight over to this lady I'm watching and then she seen him, too, and she start to smile, but she don't move till he get right up next to her. And then I'm gonna look away, 'cause I can't stand to watch nobody hugging and kissing on each other, but all of a sudden I see it ain't no dude at all. It's another lady.

Now I can't stop looking. They smiling at each other like they ain't seen one another in ten years. Then the one in the purple shirt look around real quick— but she don't look just behind her—and sorta pull the other one right back into the corner where I'm sitting at, and then they put they arms around each other and kiss—for a whole long time. Now I really know I oughtta turn away, but I can't. And I know they gonna see me when they finally open they eyes. And they do.

They both kinda gasp and back up, like I'm the monster that just rose up outta the deep. And then I guess they can see I'm only a girl, and they look at one another—and start to laugh! Then they just turn around and start to walk away like it wasn't nothing at all. But right before they gone, they both look around again, and see I still ain't got my eye muscles and my jaw muscles working right again yet. And the one lady wink at me. And the other one say, "Catch you later."

I can't stop staring at they backs, all the way across the Plaza. And then, all of a sudden, I feel like I got to be doing something, got to be moving.

I wheel on outta the Plaza and I'm just concentrating on getting up my speed. 'Cause I can't figure out what to think. Them two women kissing and then, when they get caught, just laughing about it. And here I'm laughing, too, for no reason at all. I'm sailing down the boulevard laughing like a lunatic, and then I'm singing at the top of my lungs. And climbing that big old hill up to Summit Avenue is just as easy as being on a escalator.

Scott Bradfield   (b. 1955)

Scott Bradfield is a California writer whose first book of short stories, The Secret Life of Houses *(1988), was greeted with extraordinary critical interest. His work is imaginative, sometimes fantastic, and always deeply psychological, probing into the emotions of his characters' lives. His novel* The History of Luminous Motion *(1989) is about one of the strangest, most haunting childhoods imaginable, a childhood dominated by the unrealities of American television. Although he spends much of his time in London, Bradfield now teaches at the University of Connecticut.*

THE DREAM OF THE WOLF   1988

> *Without the dream one would have found no occasion for a division of the world.*
> —Nietzsche

"Last night I dreamed I was *Canis lupus tundarum*, the Alaskan tundra wolf," Larry Chambers said, confronted by hot Cream O' Wheat, one jelly donut, black coffee with sugar. "I was surrounded by a vast white plain and sparse gray patches of vegetation. I loped along at a brisk pace, quickening the hot pulse of my blood. I felt extraordinarily swift, hungry, powerful . . ." Larry gripped his donut; red jelly squirted across his knuckles. "My jaws were enormous, my paws heavy and calloused." He took a bite, chewed with his mouth open. "My pelt was thick and white and warm. The cold breeze carried aromas of fox, rabbit, caribou, rodent, fowl, mollusc . . ."

"Caroline!" Sherryl Chambers reached for the damp dish cloth. "Eat over the table, *please*. Just look at this. You've dripped cereal all over your new shoes."

Caroline gazed up intently at her father, her chin propped against the table edge. Her fist gripped a grainy spoon.

"I heard a noise behind me and I turned." Larry warmed his palms against the white coffee cup. "The mouse hesitated—just for a moment—and then quickly I pounced, pinned him beneath my paw. His eyes were wide with panic, his tiny heart fluttered wildly. His fear blossomed in the air like pollen—"

"What did you do, Daddy? What did you do to the mouse?"   5

Larry observed the clock radio. *KRQQ helicopter watch for a Monday, March twenty-third,* the radio said. *An overturned tanker truck has traffic backed up all the way to Civic Center . . .*

"I ate him," Larry said. The time was eight-fifteen.

"Caroline. Finish your cereal before it gets cold."

"But Daddy's a wolf again, Mommy. He caught a mouse and he *ate* it."

"I'm practically certain it was the *tundarum,*" Larry said, and pulled on his   10
sport coat.

"Please, Caroline. I won't ask you again."

"But I want the rest of Daddy's donut."

"Finish your cereal. *Then* we'll discuss Daddy's donut."

"I think I'll stop by the library again tonight." Larry got up from the table. His spoon remained gripped by the thickening cereal like a fossil in La Brea.°

"Sure, honey. And pick up some milk on the way home, will you? *Try* and   15
remember."

"I will," Larry said, "I'll try," recalling the brilliant white ice, the warm easy taste of the blood.

"And here—bend over." Sherryl moistened the tip of a napkin with her lips. "There's jelly all over your face."

"It's the blood, Daddy. It's the mouse's blood."

"Thanks," Larry said, and went into the living-room.

Caroline watched the kitchen door swing shut. After a few moments she   20
heard the front door open and close.

"Daddy forgot to kiss me goodbye," she said.

Sherryl spilled pots and pans into the sink. "Daddy's a little preoccupied this morning, dear."

Caroline thought for a moment. The bitten jelly donut sat in the middle of the table like a promise.

"Daddy ate a mouse," she said finally, and made a proud little flourish in the air with her spoon.

La Brea: A tar pit in Los Angeles in which fossil remains of saber tooth tigers have been found.

Canis lupus youngi, Canis lupus crassodon, Canis niger rufus, Larry thought,   25
and boarded the RTD at Beverly and Fairfax. The wolf, he thought. The wolf of
the dream, the wolf of the world. He showed the driver his pass. Wolves in Utah,
Northern Mexico, Baffin Island, even Hollywood. Wolves secretly everywhere,
Larry thought, and moved down the crowded aisle. Elderly women jostled fitfully in their seats like birds on a wire.

"Larry! Hey—Spaceman!"

Andrew Prytowsky waved his *Wall Street Journal.* "Sit here." He removed
his briefcase from the window seat and placed it in his lap. "Rest that frazzled
brain of yours. You may need it later."

"Thanks," Larry said, squeezed into the vacant seat and recalled an exotic
afternoon nap. *Canis lupus chanco,* Tibetan spring, crepuscular hour. His pack
downed a goat. Blood spattered the gray dust like droplets of quivering mercury.

"*That's* earnings, Larry. *That's* reliable income. *That's* retirement security, a
summer cottage, a sporty new car." Andrew shook the American Exchange Index
at him, as if reproving an unhousebroken puppy. "Fifteen points in two weeks,
just like I promised. Did you hear me? *Fifteen* points. Consolidated Plastics Ink.
Plastic bullets, the weapon of the future. Cheap, easy to manufacture, minimal
production overhead. You could have cut yourself a piece of that, Larry. I certainly gave you every opportunity. But then *my* word's not good enough for you,
is it? You've already got your savings account, your fixed interest, your automatic
teller, your free promotional albums. You've got yourself a coffin—*that's* what
you've got. Fixed interest is going to bury you. Listen to me, pal. I can help. Let's
talk tax-free municipal bonds for just one second—"

Larry sighed and gazed out the smudged window. Outside the Natural   30
History Museum sidewalk vendors sold hot dogs, lemonade and pretzels while
behind them ancient bones surfaced occasionally from the bubbling tar pit.

"—in the long run we're not just talking safety. We're talking variable income *and* easy liquidity." Prytowsky slapped Larry's chest with the rolled up newspaper. "Get *with* it, Spaceman. What are you, now? Late thirties, early forties?
You want to spend the rest of your life with your head in the clouds? Or do you
want to come back down to earth and enjoy a little of the *good* life? Your little
girl—Carol, Karen, whatever. She may be four or five now, pal, but college is *tomorrow. Tomorrow,* Spaceman. And you want your little girl to go to college,
don't you? Well, *don't* you? Of *course* you do! Of *course!*"

The traffic light turned green, the RTD's clutch connected with a sudden
sledgehammer sound. Oily gray smoke swirled outside the window.

"And what about that devilish little wife of yours? Take it from me, Spaceman.
A woman's eye is *always* looking out for those greener pastures. It's not their
fault, Spaceman—it's just their *nature* . . . Hey, *Larry.*" The rolled up newspaper jabbed Larry's side. "You even listening to me or what?"

"Sure," Larry said, and the bus entered Beverly Hills. Exorbitant hood ornaments flashed in the sun like grails. "Easy liquidity, interest variations. I'll think
about it. I really will. It's just I have a lot on my mind right now, that's all. I mean,
I'll get back to you on all this. I really will." *Canis lupus arabs, pallipes, baileyi,
nubilis, monstrabilis,* he thought. The wolves of the dream, the wolves of the
world.

"Still having those nutty dreams of yours, Spaceman? Your wife told my wife.   35
You dream you're a dog or something?"

"A wolf. *Canis lupus*. It's not even the same sub-species as a dog."

"Oh." Andrew discarded his newspaper under his seat. "Sure."

"Wolves are far more intelligent than any dog. They're fiercer hunters, loyaler mates. Their social organization alone—"

"Yeah—right, Spaceman. I stand corrected. I'll bet in your dreams you really raise hell with those stupid dogs—hey, Larry, old pal?" Andrew said, and disboarded with his briefcase at Westwood Boulevard.

As the bus approached 27th Avenue Larry moved back through the crowd   40
of passengers who stood and sat about with newspapers, magazines and detached
expressions as they vacantly chewed Certs, peanuts from a bag, impassive bubble
gum, like a herd of grazing buffalo while the wolf, the wolf of Larry's mind,
roamed casually among them, searching out the weak, the sickly, the injured, the
ones who always betrayed themselves with brief and anxious glances—the elderly
woman with the aluminum walker, the gawky adolescent with the bad complexion and crooked teeth. Wolves in Tibet, Montana, South America, Micronesia,
Larry thought, disembarked at 25th Avenue and entered Tower Tyre and Rubber
Company. He showed his pass to the security guard, then rode the humming elevator to the twelfth floor. When Larry stepped into the foyer the secretaries,
gathered around the receptionist's desk, exchanged quick significant glances like
secret memoranda. Larry heard them giggling as he disappeared into the maze of
high white partitions that organized office cubicles like discrete cells in an ant
farm.

Larry entered his office.

"Ready for Monday?" Marty Cabrillo asked.

Larry hung his coat on the rack, turned.

The Marketing Supervisor stood in front of Larry's aluminum bookshelf, gazing aimlessly at the spines of large gray Acco-Grip binders. "Frankly," Marty said, "I'd rather be in Shasta. How was your weekend?"

"Fine, just fine," Larry said, sat down at his desk and opened the top desk   45
drawer.

"I thought I'd drop by and see if the Orange County sales figures were in yet. Didn't mean to barge in, you know."

"Certainly. Help yourself." Larry gestured equivocally with his right hand, rummaged in the desk drawer with his left.

"Ed Conklin called from Costa Mesa and said he still hasn't received the Goodyear flyers. I told him no problem—you'd get right back to him. All right?"

"Right." Larry slammed shut one drawer and pulled open another. "No problem. Here we are . . ." He removed a large faded green hardcover book. One of the book's corners was bloated with dogeared pages. Larry wiped off dust and bits of paper against his trousers. *The Wolves of North America: Part 1, Classification of Wolves.*

Marty propped one hand casually in his pocket. "I hope you don't take this   50
the wrong way or anything, Larry . . . I mean, I'm not trying to pull rank on you
or anything. But maybe you could try being just a little bit more careful around
here the next few weeks or so. Think of it as a friendly warning, okay?"

Larry looked up from his book.

"It's not me, Larry." Marty placed his hand emphatically over his heart. "You know me, right? But district managers are starting to complain. Late orders, unitemized bills, stuff like that. *Harmless* stuff, really. Nothing I couldn't cover for you. But the guys upstairs aren't so patient—that's all I'm trying to say. I'm just trying to say it's my job, too. All right?"

Finally Larry located the *tundarum's* sub-species guide. *Type locality: Point Barrow, Alaska. Type Specimen: No. 16748, probably female, skull only, U.S. National Museum; collected by Lt. P. H. Ray* . . .

"But for God's sake don't take any of this personal or anything. It's not really serious. Everybody has their off-days—it's just the way things go. People get, well, *distracted*."

"I knew it." Larry pointed at the page. "Just what I thought. Look—*tun-*   55
darum is 'closely allied to *pambisileus*.' Exactly as I suspected. The dentition was a dead giveaway."

Marty fumbled for a cigarette from his shirt pocket, a Bic lighter from his slacks. "Well," he said, and took a long drag from his Kool. Then, after a moment, "You know, Larry, Beatrice and I have always been interested in this ecology stuff ourselves. You should visit our cabin in Shasta sometime. There's nothing like it—clean air, trees, privacy. We even joined the Sierra Club last year . . . But look, I could talk about this stuff all day, but we've *both* got to get back to work, right?" Marty paused outside the cubicle. "We'll get together and talk about it over lunch sometime, okay? And maybe you could drop the sales figures by my office later? Before noon, maybe?"

That night Larry returned home after the dinner dishes had been washed. He glanced into Caroline's room. She was asleep. Stuffed wolves, cubs, and an incongruous unicorn lay toppled around her on the bed like dominoes. He found Sherryl in the master-bedroom, applying Insta-Curls to her hair and balancing a black rectangular apparatus in her lap.

Larry sat on the edge of the bed, glimpsed himself in the vanity mirror. He had forgotten to shave that morning. His eyes were dark, sunken, feral. (The lone wolf lopes across an empty plain. Late afternoon, clear blue sky. The pale crescent moon appears on the horizon like a spectre. Other wolves howl in the distance.)

Larry turned to his wife. "I went all the way out to the UCLA Research Library, then found out the school's between quarters. The library closed at five."

"That's too bad, dear. Would you plug that in for me?"   60

Sherryl pulled a plastic cap over her head. Two coiled black wires attached the cap to the black rectangular box. Larry connected the plug to the wall-socket and the black box began to hum. Gradually the plastic cap inflated. "Larry, I wish I knew how to phrase this a bit more delicately, but it's been on my mind a lot lately." Sherryl turned the page of a K-Mart Sweepstakes Sale brochure. "You may not believe this, Larry, but there are actually people in this world who like to talk about some things besides *wolves* every once in a blue moon."

Larry turned again to his reflection. He had forgotten to finish Cabrillo's sales figures. Tomorrow, he assured himself. First thing.

"I remember when we had decent conversations. We went out occasionally. We went to movies, or even dancing. Do you remember the last time we went out together—I mean, just out of the *house*? It was that horrid PTA meeting last fall, with that dreadful woman—the hunchback with the butterfly glasses, you remember? Something about a rummage sale and new tether poles? Do you *know* how long ago that was? And frankly, Larry, I wouldn't call that much of a night *out.*"

Larry ran his hand lightly along the smooth edge of the humming black box. "Look, honey. I know I get a little out of hand sometimes . . . I *know* that. Especially lately." He placed his hand on his forehead. A soft pressure seemed to be increasing inside his skull, like an inflating plastic cap. "I've been forgetful . . . and I realize I must seem a little nutty at times . . ." The wolves, he thought, trying to strengthen himself. The call of the pack, the track of the moon, the hot quick pulse of the blood. But the wolves abruptly seemed very far away. "I know you don't understand. *I* don't really understand . . . But these aren't just dreams. When I'm a wolf, I'm *real*. The places I see, the feelings I feel—they're *real*. As real as I am now talking to you. As real as this bed." He grasped the king-size silk comforter. "I'm not making all this up . . . And I'll *try* to be a little more thoughtful. We'll go out to dinner this weekend, I promise. But try putting up with me a little longer. Give me a little credit, that's all . . ."

Sherryl glanced up. She took the humming black box from his hand.   65
"Did you say something, hon?" She patted the plastic cap. "Hold on and I'll be finished in a minute." She turned another page of the brochure. Then, with a heavy red felt marker, she circled the sale price of Handi-Wipes.

Larry walked into the bathroom and brushed his gleaming white teeth.

"Last night I dreamed of the Pleistocene."
"Where is that, Daddy?"
"It's not a place, honey. It's a time. A long time ago."   70
"You mean dinosaurs, Daddy? Did you dream you were a *dinosaur*?"
"No, darling. The dinosaurs were all gone by then. I was *Canis dirus*, I think. I'll check on it. The tundra was far colder and more desolate than before. The sky was filled with this weird, reddish glow I've never seen before, like the atmosphere of some alien planet. Ice was everywhere. Three of us remained in the pack. My mate had died the previous night beneath a shelf of ice while the rest of us huddled around to keep her warm. Dominant, I led the others across the white ice, my tail slightly erect. We were terribly cold, tired, hungry . . ."
"Weren't there any mice, Daddy? Or any snails?"
"No. We had travelled for days. We had discovered no spoor. Except one."
"Was it a deer, Daddy? Did you kill the deer and eat it?"   75
"No. It was Man's spoor. We were seeking an encampment of men." He turned. Sherryl was beating eggs into a bowl and watching David Hartman on the portable television. "Sherryl, that was the strangest part. I've read about it, anthropologists have suggested it—a prehistoric, communal bond between man and wolf. We weren't afraid. We sought shelter with them, food, companionship, allies in the hunt."

Larry watched his wife. After a moment she said, "That's nice, dear."

David Hartman said, "Later in this half-hour we'll be meeting Lorna Backus to discuss her new hit album, and then take an idyllic trip up the coast to scenic New Hampshire, the Garden State, as part of our 'States of the Union' series. Please stay with us."

"I've always wanted to live in New Hampshire," Sherryl said.

Every day on his way home from work Larry stopped at the Fairfax branch   80
library. Many of the books he needed he had to request through inter-library loan.
He read Lopez's *Of Wolves and Men*, Fox's *The Soul of the Wolf*, Mech's *The Wolf:
the Ecology and Behavior of an Endangered Species*, Pimlott's *The World of the Wolf*,
Mowat's *Never Cry Wolf*, Ewer's *The Carnivores*, and the pertinent articles and
symposiums published in *American Zoologist, American Scientist, Journal of
Zoology, Journal of Mammalogy*, and *The Canadian Field Naturalist*. Sherryl
pulled the blankets off the bed one day and three books came loose, thudding
onto the floor. "I'd really appreciate it, Larry, if you could start picking up after
yourself. It's bad enough with Caroline. And just look—this one's almost a month
overdue." Larry returned them to the library that night, checked out three more,
and xeroxed the "Canids" essay in *Grzimek's Animal Life Encyclopedia*.

On the way out the door he noticed a three-by-five file card tacked to the
Community Billboard. *Spiritual Counselling, Dream Analysis, Budget Rates, Free
Parking*. Her name was Anita Louise. She lived on the top floor of a faded Sunset
Boulevard brownstone, and claimed to be circuitously related to Tina Louise, the
former star of *Gilligan's Island*. Her living-room was furnished with tattered green
lawn-chairs and orange-crate bookshelves. She required a personal item; Larry
handed her his watch. She closed her eyes. "I can see the wolf now," she said.
Her fingers smudged the watch's crystal face, wound the stem, tested the flexible metal band. "While he leads you through the forest of life, he warns you of
the thorny paths. When the time comes, he will lead you into Paradise."

"The wolf doesn't guide me," Larry said. "I *am* the wolf. Sometimes *I* am
the guide, the leader of my pack."

"The ways of the spirit world are often baffling to those unlearned in its
ways," Anita told him. "I take Visa and Mastercard. I take personal checks, but I
need to see at least two pieces of I.D."

Before he left, Larry reminded her about his watch.

"I don't know, Evelyn. I really just don't know. I mean, I *love* Larry and all,   85
but you can't imagine how difficult life's been around here lately—especially the
last few months." Sherryl held the telephone receiver with her left hand, a cold
coffee cup with her right. She listened for a moment. "No, Evelyn, I don't think
you understand. This isn't a hobby. It's not as if Larry was collecting stamps, or
a *bowler* or something. I could understand that. *That* would be understandable.
But all Larry talks about anymore is wolves. Wolves this and wolves that. Wolves
at the dinner table, wolves in bed, wolves even when we're driving to the market.
Wolves are everywhere, he keeps saying. And honestly, Evelyn, sometimes I almost believe him. I start looking over my shoulder. I hear a dog bark and I make
sure the door's bolted . . . Well, *of course* I try to be understanding. I'm trying to
tell you that. But I have to worry about Caroline too, you know . . . Well, listen
for a minute and I'll tell you what happened yesterday. We're sitting at breakfast,
you see, and Larry starts telling Caroline—a four-year-old girl, remember—how
he's off in the woods somewhere, God only knows *where*, and he meets this female dog and, well, I can't go on . . . No, I simply can't. It's too embarrassing
. . . No, Evelyn. You've completely missed the point. It's mating season, get it?
And Larry starts going into explicit detail . . . Well, maybe. But that's not even
the worst part . . . Hold *on* for one second and I'll tell you. They, well, I don't
know how to phrase this delicately. They get *stuck* . . . *No*, Evelyn. Honestly,

sometimes I don't think you're even listening to me. They get stuck *together*. Can you believe that? What am I supposed to say? Caroline's not going to outgrow a trauma like this, though. I can promise you that." Sherryl heard the kitchen door opening behind her. "Hold on, Evelyn," she said, and turned.

Caroline blocked the door open with her foot. "What are you talking about?" Her hand gripped the plastic Pez dispenser. Wylie Coyote's head was propped back by her thumb, and a small pink lozenge extruded from his throat.

"It's Evelyn, dear. We're just talking."

Caroline's lips were flushed and purple; purple stains speckled her white dress. She thought for a moment, took the candy with her teeth and chewed. Finally she said, "I think somebody may have spilled grape-juice on one of Daddy's wolf books."

Larry read Guy Endore's *The Werewolf of Paris*, Hesse's *Steppenwolf*, Rowland's *Animals With Human Faces*, Pollard's *Wolves and Werewolves*, Lane's *The Wild Boy of Averyon*, Malson's *Wolf Children and the Problem of Human Nature*. Marty gave him the card of a Jungian° in Topanga Canyon who sat Larry in a plush chair, said "archetype" a few times, informed him that *everyone* is fascinated with evil, sadism, pain ("It's perfectly normal, perfectly *human*"), recommended Robert Eisler's *Man Into Wolf*, charged seventy-five dollars and offered him a valium prescription with refill. "But when I'm a wolf, I never know evil," Larry said as he was ushered out the door by a blonde receptionist. "When I'm a wolf, I know only peace."

"I don't know, Larry. It just gives me the creeps," Sherryl said that night after Caroline was in bed. "It's *weird*, that's what it is. Bullying defenseless little mice and deer that never hurt anybody. Talking about killing, and blood, and ice—and particularly at *breakfast*."

Larry was awake until two a.m. watching *The Wolf Man* on Channel Five. Claude Raines said, "There's good and evil in every man's soul. In this case, the evil takes the shape of a wolf." No, Larry thought, and read Freud's *The Case of the Wolf-Man*, the first chapter of Mack's *Nightmares and Human Conflict*. No. Then he went to bed and dreamed of the wolves.

"The wolf-spirit has always been considered very *wakan*,"° Hungry Bear said, his feet propped on his desk. He poked out his cigarette against the rim of the metal wastebasket, then prepared to light another. "Most tribes believe the wolf's howl portends bad things. The Lakota say, 'The man who dreams of the wolf is not really on his guard, but the man haughtily closes his eyes, for he is very much on his guard.' I don't know what that means, exactly, but I read it somewhere." Hungry Bear refilled his dixie-cup with vin rosé. His grimy teeshirt was taut against his large stomach; a band of pale skin bordered his belt. He wore a plaid Irish derby atop his braided hair. "I try to do a good deal of reading," he said, and fumbled in his diminished pack of Salems.

"So do I," Larry said. "Maybe you could recommend—"

Jungian: A psychiatrist and follower of psychologist Carl Jung (1875–1961), who believed that all humans share certain inherited ideas, or archetypes, that profoundly affect their behavior. *wakan*: Evil.

90

"I don't think the wolf was ever recognized as any sort of deity, but I could be wrong." Hungry Bear was watching the smoke unravel from his cigarette. "But still, you shouldn't be too worried. It's very common for animal spirits to possess a man. They use his body when he's asleep. When he awakes, he can't remember anything . . . oh, but wait. That's not quite right, is it? You said you *remember* your dreams? Well, again, I could be wrong. I guess you *could* remember. Sure, I don't see why not," Hungry Bear said, and poured more vin rosé.

"*I* inhabit the body of the *wolf*," Larry said, beginning to lose interest, and   95 glanced around the cluttered office. The venetian blinds were cracked and dusty, the floors littered with tattered men's magazines, empty wine bottles and crumpled cigarette packs. After a moment he added, "I don't even know what I should call you. *Mister* Bear?"

"No, of course not." Hungry Bear waved away the notion, dispersing smoke. "Call me Jim. That's my real name. Jim Prideux. I took Hungry Bear for business purposes. If you remember, Hungry Bear was the brand name of a terrific canned chili. It was discontinued after the war, though, I'm afraid." He checked his shirt pocket. "Do you see a pack of cigarettes over there? Seems I'm running short."

"You're not Indian?" Larry asked.

"Sure. Of course I'm Indian. One-eighth pure Shoshone. My great-grandmother was a Shoshone princess. Well, maybe not a princess, exactly. But *her* father was an authentic medicine man. I've inherited the gift." Jim Prideux rummaged through the papers on his desk. "Are you sure you don't see them? I'm sure I bought a pack less than an hour ago."

"This is very nice," Sherryl said, and swallowed her last bite of red snapper. She touched her lips delicately with the napkin. "It's *so* nice to get out of the house for a change. You wouldn't know how much."

"Sure I would, darling," Andrew Prytowsky said, and poured more Chenin   100 Blanc.

"No, I don't think you would, Andy. Your wife, Danielle, is *normal*. You wouldn't know what it's like living with someone as . . . well, as *unstable* as Larry's been acting lately."

"I'm sure it's been very difficult for you."

"Marty Cabrillo, Larry's boss at work, got Larry in touch with a doctor, a *good* doctor. Larry visits him *once* and then tells me he isn't going anymore. I say to Larry, don't you think he can help you? And Larry says no, he can't, he can't help him at all. He says the doctor is *stupid*. Can you believe that? I say to Larry, this man has a *Ph.D.* I don't think you can just call a man with a Ph.D. *stupid*. And so then Larry says *I* don't know what *I'm* talking about, either. Larry thinks he knows more than a man with a Ph.D. That's what Larry thinks."

"Here. Why don't you finish it?" Andrew put down the empty bottle and flagged the waiter with his upraised Mastercard.

"I'm sorry, Andy." Sherryl dabbed her eyes with the napkin. "It's just I'm   105 so shook up lately. All I ever asked for was a normal life. That's not too much, is it? A nice home, a normal husband. Someone who could give me a little help and support. Is that too much to ask? Is it?"

"Of course not." Andrew signed the check. After the waiter left he said, "I'm glad we could do this."

Sherryl folded her napkin and replaced it on the table. "I'm glad you called. This was very nice."

"We'll do it again."

"Yes," Sherryl said. "We should."

Two weeks later Larry returned home from work and found the letter on   110 the kitchen table.

Dear Larry,

I know you're going to take this the wrong way and I only hope you realize Caroline and I still care about you but I've thought about this a lot and even sought professional counselling on one occasion and I think it's the only solution right now at this moment in our lives. Especially Caroline who is at a very tender age. Please don't try calling because I told my mother not to tell you where we are for a while. Please realize I don't want to hurt you and this will probably be better for both of us in the long run, and I hope you make it through your difficulties and I'll think good thoughts for you often.

Sherryl

"You can't just keep moping around, Larry. Things'll get better, just you wait. I sense big improvements coming in your life. But first you've *got* to start being more careful around the office." Marty sat on the edge of Larry's desk. He pulled a string of magnetized paper clips in and out of a clear plastic dispenser. "Did I tell you Henderson asked about you yesterday? Asked about you *by name*. Now, I'm not trying to make you paranoid or anything, but if Henderson asked about you then you can bet your socks the *rest* of the guys in Management have been tossing your name around. And Henderson's not a bad guy, Larry. I'm not suggesting that. But there's been a sincere . . . a sincere *concern* about your performance around here lately. And don't think I don't understand. Really, Larry, I'm very sensitive to your position. Beatrice and I came close to breaking up a couple times ourselves—and I don't know *what* I'd do without Betty and the kids. But you've got to keep your chin up, buddy. Plow straight ahead. And re-member—I'm on *your* side."

At his desk, Larry made careful, persistent marks on a sheet of graph paper. The frequency of dreams had increased over the past few weeks: the line on the graph swooped upwards. Often three, even four times a night he started awake in bed, clicked on the reading lamp and reached for a pen and notepad from the end table, quickly jotting down terrain and sub-species characteristics while the aromas of forest, desert and tundra were displaced by the close stale odors of grimy bedsheets, leftover Swanson frozen dinner entrées, and Johnson's Chlorophyll-Scented Home Deodorizer.

"I'm really sincere about this, Larry. I can't keep covering for you. I need some assurances, I need to start seeing some real *effort* on your part. You're go-ing to start seeing Dave Boudreau on the third floor. He's our employee stress-counsellor—but that doesn't mean he's like a shrink or anything, Larry. I know how you feel about *them*. Dave Boudreau's just a regular guy like you and me who happens to have a lot of experience with these sorts of problems. You and Sherryl, I mean. All right, Larry? Does that sound fair to you?"

"Sure, Marty," Larry said, "I appreciate your help, I really do," and peeled another sheet from the Thrifty pad. Abscissa, he thought: real time. Ordinate: dream time.° At the top of the page he scribbled *Pleistocene.*

"I'm dreaming now more than ever," Larry told Dave Boudreau the fol- 115 lowing Thursday. "Sometimes half-a-dozen times each night. Look, I've kept a record—" Larry opened a large red loose-leaf binder, flipped through a sheaf of papers, and unclamped a sheet of graph paper. "There, that's last Friday. Six times." He held the sheet of paper over the desk, pointing at it. "And Sunday— *seven* times. And that's not even the significant part. I haven't even got to *that* part yet."

Dave Boudreau sat behind his desk and rocked slightly in a swivel chair. He glanced politely at the statistical chart. Then his abstract gaze returned to Tahitian surf in a framed travel poster. He heard the binder clamp click again.

Larry pulled up his chair until the armrests knocked the edge of the desk. "Increasingly I dream of the Pleistocene, the Ice Age. The Great Hunt, when man and wolf hunted together, bound by one pack, responsible to one commu- nity, seeking their common prey across the cold ice, beneath the cold sun. Is *that* something? Is that one hell of an archetype or what?"

Casually Boudreau opened the manilla folder on his desk.

CHAMBERS, LAWRENCE
SUPPLIES AND SERVICES DEPARTMENT
BORN: 3-6-45   EYES: BLUE

"And don't get me wrong. I'm just kidding about that archetype stuff. That's not even close, that's not even in the same ballpark. These aren't memories, for chrissakes. When I dream of the wolf, I *am* the wolf. I've been wolves in New York, Montana and Beirut. It's as if time and space, dream and reality, have just *opened up,* joined me with everything, everything *real.* I'm living the *one life,* un- derstand? The life of the hunter and the prey, the dream and the world, the blood and the spirit. It's really spectacular, don't you think? Have you ever heard any- thing like it?"

In the space reserved for Counsellor's Comments Boudreau scribbled "wolf 120 nut," and underlined it three times.

When Larry arrived at work the following Monday the security guard took his I.D. card and, after consulting his log, asked him to please wait one moment. The guard picked up his phone and asked the operator for Personnel Management. "This is station six. Mr. Lawrence Chambers has just arrived." The guard listened quietly to the voice at the other end. He snapped his pencil against the desk in four-four time.

Finally he put down the phone and said, "I'm sorry. I'll have to keep your card. Would you please follow me?"

They walked down the hall to Payroll. Larry was given his final paycheck and, in a separate envelope, another check for employee minimum compensation.

By the time Larry returned home it was still only ten a.m. He cleared the old newspapers from the stoop, unbound and opened the whitest, most recent one.

Abscissa . . . Ordinate: The horizontal and vertical axes of a geometric plane; here, probably sim- ply a reference to two "dimensions" of reality.

He read for a few minutes, then refolded the paper and placed it with the others beside the fireplace. He picked up Harrington and Paquet's *Wolves of the World* and put it down again. He got up and walked to the kitchen. Dishes piled high in the sink, four full bags of trash. The few remaining dishes in the dishwasher were swirled with white mineral deposits. In the refrigerator he found a garlic bulb with long green shoots, an empty bottle of Worcestershire Sauce, and an egg. He drank stale apple juice from the plastic green pitcher, then continued making his rounds. In the bathroom: toothpaste, toothbrush, comb, water glass, eyedrops, Mercurochrome, a stray bandage, Sherryl's Ph-balanced Spring Mountain Shampoo, his electric razor. All the clothes and toys were gone from Caroline's room. Over the bed the poster of a wolf gazed down at him, its eyes sharp, canny, primitively alert.

He tried to watch television. People won sailboats and trash-compacters on game shows, cheated one another and plotted financial coups on soap operas. After a while he got up again and returned to the bathroom, opened the medicine cabinet. Johnson's Baby Aspirin, an old stiffened toothbrush, mouthwash, a bobby-pin. High on the top shelf he found Sherryl's Seconal in a child-proof bottle. He took two. Then he got into bed. 125

Sometime after dawn he dreamed again of the wolves, but this time the dream was fragmentary and detached. He viewed the wolves from very far away. From atop a high bluff, perhaps, or hidden behind some bushes like Jane Goodall.° The wolves moved down into the gully and paused before a small stream, drinking. Two cubs splashed and chased one another through the puddles. The other wolves observed them dispassionately. The sun was going down. Larry woke up. It was just past six a.m.

He stayed indoors throughout the day. In the evening he might walk to the corner Liquor Mart to cash a check and purchase milk, scotch, Stouffer's frozen dinners. Sometimes, remembering Sherryl and Caroline, he turned the television up louder. It wasn't their physical presence he missed (he could hardly recall their faces anymore) but rather their noise: the clatter of dishes, the inconstant whir and jingle of mechanical toys. Soundless, the air seemed thinner, staler, more oppressive, as if he were sealed inside an air-tight crystal vault. The silence invested everything—the walls, the furniture, the diminishing vial of Seconal, the large empty bedrooms, even the mindless chatter of the Flintstones on television. He drank his beer beside the front window and watched the dust swirl soundlessly in the soundless shafts of light, recalling the wolves and the soundless expanse of white ice where not only the noise but even the aromas and textures of the landscape seemed to be leaking from the dreamlike atmosphere from the cracks in some domed underwater city. In the mornings, now, he hardly recalled his dreams at all anymore. Sporadic glimpses of wolf, prey, sky, moon, interspliced meaninglessly like the frames of some surrealist montage. He smoked three packs of cigarettes a day, just to give his hands something to do. The scotch and Seconal compelled him to take so many naps during the day that he couldn't sleep at night. Wolves, he thought. Wolves in Utah, Baffin Island, Tibet, even Hollywood. Wolves secretly everywhere . . . Eventually the dreams disappeared entirely. Sleep became a dark visionless place where nothing ever happened.

Jane Goodall: British naturalist who studies chimpanzees in natural habitats.

The Seconal, he thought one morning, and departed for the library. He squinted at the sunlight, staggered occasionally. People looked at him. A book entitled *Sleep* by Gay Gaer Luce and Julius Siegal confirmed his suspicions. Alcohol and barbiturates suppressed the dream stage of sleep. He returned home and poured the scotch down the sink, the remaining Seconal down the toilet. He lay in bed throughout the afternoon, night and following morning. He tossed and turned. He couldn't keep his eyes closed more than a minute. His heart palpitated disconcertingly. He tried to remember the wolf's image, and remembered only pictures in books. He tried to recall the prey's hot steaming blood, and tasted only yesterday's Chicken McNuggets. He wanted the map of the sky, and found only the close humid rectangle of the bedroom. He got up and went into the living-room. It was night again. In order to dream, he must sleep. In order to regain the real, he must dispel the illusion: newspapers, furniture, unswept carpets, Sherryl's letter, Caroline's toys, easy liquidity, magazines and books. He realized then that evil was not the wolf, but rather the wolf's disavowal. Violence wasn't something in nature, but rather something in nature's systematic repression. Madness isn't the dream, but rather the world deprived of the dream, he thought, selected a stale pretzel from the bowl, chewed, and gazed out the window at the dim, empty streets below where occasional streetlamps illuminated silent, unoccupied cars parked along the curbs. The moon made a faint impression against the high screen of fog. A distant siren wailed, a dog barked, and in their homes the population slept fitfully, often aided by Seconal and Dilantin, descending through soft penetrable stages of sleep, seeking that fugitive half-world in which they struggled to dream beneath the repressive shadows of the real.

A few weeks after signing Larry Chambers' termination notice, Marty Cabrillo took his wife to Shasta. "Two weeks alone," he promised her. "We'll leave the kids with your mother. Just the two of us, the trees, candlelight dinners again, just like I always said it would be." But Marty said nothing during the long drive. Beatrice put her arm around him and he shrugged at her. "Please," he said. "I can't get comfortable." At the cabin they sat out on the sundeck. Marty held paperbacks and turned the pages. Beatrice read *People Magazine*. After only a few days they returned home. "I'm sorry, honey," Marty said to her. "I'll make it up to you. I promise."

"What's the matter with you lately?" 130

"Nothing. Just things on my mind."

"Work?"

"Sort of."

After a while Beatrice said, "Larry," folded her arms, and gazed out the window at Ventura car-lots.

The following Sunday Marty drove to *Ralph's* in Fairfax, loaded four bags 135 of groceries into his Toyota station wagon, and drove to Larry's house on Clifton Boulevard. The front yard was brown and overgrown. Aluminum garbage cans, streaked with rust, lay overturned in the alley. Dormant snails studded the front of the house, their slick intricate trails glistening in the sunlight. Marty knocked, rang the bell a few times. The door was ajar and he pushed it open. A pyramid of bundled newspapers blocked the door, permitting him just to squeeze through. In the living-room, torn magazines and moldy dishes lay strewn across the sofa, chairs and floor. The telephone receiver was off the hook, wailing faintly like a distant, premonitory siren. At first the room seemed oddly disproportionate, as if the furniture had all been rearranged. Then he noticed Larry asleep on the middle of the floor, his head propped by a sofa cushion, his arm wrapped around a leg of the coffee table. "He must've lost eighty, ninety pounds," Marty told Beatrice later that night. "His clothes stank, he hadn't shaved or washed in I don't know how long. And all I could think looking at him there was it's all *my* fault. *I* was responsible. Me, Marty Cabrillo."

Marty followed the ambulance to St. John's, wishing they would run the siren. "Dehydration," the doctor told him, while Marty paid the deposit on a private room. Larry lay in a stiff, geometric white bed, a glucose bottle hanging beside him, a white tube connected to his arm by white adhesive tape. Every so often the glucose bubbled. "We'll bring him along slow, have him eating solid food in a couple days. I think he'll be all right," the doctor said, and handed Marty another form to sign.

"It's all my fault," Marty said when Larry regained consciousness the following morning. "Look, I brought you some books to read. And the flowers—they're from Sherryl. Beatrice got in touch with her last night and she's on her way here right now. The worst is over, pal. The worst is all behind you."

Later Sherryl told him, "We missed you. Caroline missed you. *I* missed you. Oh, Larry. You just look so *awful*." Sherryl laid her head in Larry's lap and cried, hugging him. Silently Larry stroked her long blonde hair. Sherryl had been staying with her sister in Burbank, working as a secretary at one of the studios. Her boss was a flushed, obese little man who put his hand on her knee while she took dictation, or snuck up behind her every once in a while and gave her a sharp pinch. "Loosen up, relax. Life's short," he told her. Caroline hated her new nursery school and cried nearly every day. Sherryl's sister had begun bringing the Classified Pages home, pointing out to her the best bets on her own apartment. Andy had promised to help out, but every time she called his office his secretary said he was still out of town on business. And then one of the Volvo's tires went flat, and in all the rush of moving she realized she had misplaced her triple-A card, and so she just started crying, right there on the side of the freeway, because it seemed as if nothing, nothing ever went right for her anymore.

"We need you, Larry," Sherryl said. "You need us. I'm sorry what happened, but I always loved you. It wasn't because I didn't love you. And Marty thinks he can get your old job back—"

Marty leaned forward, whispered something.   140

"He says he's certain. He's certain he can get it back. Did you hear, honey? Everything's going to be all right. We're all going to be happy again, just like before."

Sherryl brought Caroline home a month later.

"Is Daddy home?" Caroline asked.

"He's at work now, honey. But he'll be back soon. He's missed you."

Caroline waited to be unbuckled, climbed out of the car. The front yard was   145
green and delicate, the house repainted yellow. The place seemed only dimly familiar, like the photograph Mommy showed her of where she lived when she was born.

"All your toys are in your room, sweetheart. Be good and play for a while. Mommy'll fix dinner."

Caroline's room had been repainted, too. Over her bed hung a bright new Yosemite Sam poster. She opened the oak toy-chest. The toys were boxed and neatly arranged, just like on shelves at the store. She went into the bedroom and looked at Daddy's bookcase. The large picture books were gone, along with their photographs of wolves and deer and rabbits and forests and men with rifles and hairy, misshapen primitive men. Bent paperbacks had replaced them. The covers depicted beautiful men and women, Nazi insignia, secret dossiers, demonic children, cowboys on horses, murder weapons.

She heard the front door open. "Hi, honey. Sorry I'm late. I ran into Andy Prytowsky on the bus—remember him? I introduced you at a party last year. Anyway, I told him I'd drop by his office tomorrow. I figure it's time we started some sort of college fund for Caroline. I'm pretty excited about it. Andy says he can work us a nice little tax break, too. Oh, and look what else. I bought us some wine. For later."

Caroline walked halfway down the hall. Mommy and Daddy stood at the door, kissing.

"There she is. There's my little girl."   150

Daddy picked her up high in the air. His face seemed strange and unfamiliar, like the front of the house.

"So how have you been, sweetheart?" Daddy put her down.

"I'll finish dinner," Sherryl said.

"Come and sit down." Daddy led her to the sofa. "Tell me what you've been up to. Did you have fun at Aunt Judy's?"

Caroline picked at a scab on her knee. "I guess."   155

"What do you want to do? I thought we'd go to a movie later. Would you like that?"

Caroline clasped her hands in her lap. Here is the church, and here is the steeple. When you open the doors you see all the people.

"What should we do right now? Do you want to play a game? Do you want me to read you one of your Dr. Seuss books?"

Caroline thought for a while. Daddy's large rough hand ran through her hair, snagging it. Delicately, she pushed his hand away.

"I want to watch television," she said after a while.   160

Three nights each week Larry went to the YMCA with Marty. Sherryl began subscribing to *Sunset Magazine*, and over dinner they discussed a new home, or at least improvements on their present one. Finally Marty suggested they buy into his Shasta property. "Betty and I don't make it up there more than three or four times a year. The rest of the time it'd be all yours." Larry took out a second mortgage, paid Marty a lump sum, and began sharing the monthly payments. The first few months they drove up nearly every weekend. Then Larry received a promotion which required him to make weekly trips to the Bakersfield office. "I'm really bushed from all this driving," he told Sherryl. "We'll try and make Shasta *next* weekend." Caroline started grade school in the fall. Sherryl joined an ERA support group and was gone two nights a week. Occasionally Larry spent the night in Bakersfield, and drove from there directly to work the next morning.

"All I told Conklin was I've got a merchandise deficit from his store three months in a row. It wasn't like I called him a thief or anything. I just wanted an explanation. I'm entitled to that much, don't you think? It's my job, right?"

"I'm sure he didn't mean it, Larry. He was probably just upset." Sherryl sat on the sofa, smoking a cigarette.

"I'm sure he *was* upset. I'm sure he *was*." Larry sat at the dining-room table. The table was covered with inventories, company billing statements, and large gray Acco-Grip binders. His briefcase sat open on the chair beside him. "And now *I'm* a little upset, all right? Is that all right with you?"

"I'm sure you are, Larry. I was just saying maybe he didn't mean it, that's   165 all. That's all I said."

Larry put down his pencil. "No. I don't think that's all you said."

Sherryl looked at the *T.V. Guide* on the coffee table, considered picking it up. Then she thought she heard Caroline's bedroom door squeak open down the hall.

"What you said was I'm imagining things. Isn't *that* what you said?"

Sherryl crushed out her cigarette. "Larry, I really wish you'd stop snapping at *me* every time you're mad at somebody." She got up and went to the end of the hall. "Caroline? Aren't you supposed to be in bed?"

Caroline's door squeaked shut. Sherryl watched the parallelogram of light   170 on the hall floor diminish to a fine yellow line. "And turn off those lights, young lady. You heard me. Right now," Sherryl said. In high school Billy Mason had a crush on me, she thought, but I wouldn't give him the time of day. That morning she had seen Billy's picture on the cover of *Software World* at the supermarket.

"What I mean is, Larry, is that you're not the *only* person who's had a bad day sometimes—"

Sherryl was turning to face him when the telephone rang.

"Sometimes *my* day hasn't been that hot either," she said, and retreated to the telephone, picked up the receiver. "Hello?"

"Hi. Hello," the voice said. "I was hoping, well, I mean I didn't want to disturb anybody, but I wondered if Mr. Chambers was in. Mr. *Larry* Chambers, I think? Have I got that right?"

"This is his wife. Who's this?"   175

"Who is it?" Larry asked, picking up his pencil and jotting a number on his notepad.

Sherryl gazed expressionlessly over Larry's head at the dining-room window and, beyond, the 7-11 marquee. The voice on the phone filled her ears like radio static. "—I mean, I just had the article here a moment ago, let me see . . . Look, tell him Hungry Bear called, and by the time he calls back I'll find the article—wait, in fact here it is right here—no, sorry, *that's* not it. But still, tell him Jim called. Jim Prideux—" Sherryl looked around the kitchen. She had forgotten to clean up after dinner. The sink was filled with dirty dishes, the counter top littered with bread crumbs. Stray Cheerios from that morning's breakfast had attached themselves like barnacles to the formica table. She pulled up a chair and sat down, feeling suddenly tired. There was a television movie she had been looking forward to all week, and now, by the time she finished her cleaning, the show would practically be half over. She felt like saying to hell with it, to hell with all of it. She just wanted to go to bed. To hell with Larry, Caroline, the dishes, the vacuuming—every damn bit of it. The voice buzzed inconstantly in her ear like a mosquito, something about wolves, Navajo deities, sacred totems, irrepressible dreams of wolves, he wasn't exactly sure . . . Wolves wolves wolves, wolves everywhere, she thought, and strengthened her grip on the receiver. "Listen to me," she said. "Listen to me, Mr. Bear, or Mr. Prideux, or Mr. Whoever You Are. Listen to me for just one minute, and I'll say this as *nicely* as I can. Please don't call here anymore. Larry's not interested, *I'm* not interested. Frankly, Mr. Bear, I don't think *anybody's* interested. I don't think anybody's really interested at all."

In Sherryl's dream the men and wolves loped together across the white plain. Larry was there, and Caroline, and Andy and Evelyn and Marty and Beatrice. Sherryl recognized the mailman, the newspaper boy, supermarket employees, former boyfriends and lovers. Even her parents were there, keeping pace with wolves under the cold moonlight. Everybody was dressed as usual: the men wore slacks, ties, cufflinks and starched shirts, the women skirts, blouses, jewelry and high heels. Caroline carried one of her toys, Andy his briefcase, Marty his racquetball racquet, and Larry one of his largest gray Acco-Grip binders. Sherryl raised a greasy spatula in her right hand, a tarnished coffee pot in her left. We forgot to schedule Caroline's dental appointment, she told Larry. When I was a child you treated me as if I was stupid, she told her father, but I wasn't stupid. The sky is filled with stars, she told Davey Stewart, her high school sweetheart. The Milky Way: the Wolf's Trail. But nobody responded, nobody even seemed to notice her. The bright air was laced with the spoor of caribou. She felt a sudden elbow in her back, she turned and awoke in a dark room, a stiff bed. I forgot the shopping today, she thought. There isn't any milk in the house, or any coffee.

Beside her in bed, the man slowly moved.

Sherryl sat up, her pupils gradually dilating. Eventually she discerned the motel room's clean uncluttered angles. The thin and fragile dressing table, the water glasses wrapped in wax paper, the hot-plate, the aluminum hot cocoa packets. 180

"What's the matter, baby?" Andrew sat up beside her, his arm encircling her waist. "Nightmare? Tell me, sweetheart. You can tell lover." He kissed her neck, stroked her warm stomach.

"Please, Andy. Not now. Please." Sherryl climbed out of bed. Her clothes lay folded on a wooden chair.

"Sorry. Forget it." Andrew rolled over, adjusted his pillow, and listened to the rustle of Sherryl's clothing.

Sherryl stood at the window, gazing out through the blinds. Stars and moon were occluded by a high haze of lamplight. She heard the distant hishing of streetsweepers, and pulled on her blouse. Then she heard the rain begin, drumming hollowly against the cheap plywood door.

Andrew took his watch from the end table. The luminous dial said almost two a.m. "I'll call you," he said. 185

"No," she said. "I'll call you this time. I need a few days to think." She opened the door and stepped out into the rain. They always do that, she thought. *They* have to be the ones who call, *they* have to be the ones who say when you'll meet or where you'll go. She pulled her coat-collar up over her new perm, gripped the iron bannister, and descended one step at a time on darkling high heels. Puddles were already gathering on the warped cement stairs. "It's as if we don't have any brains of our own," she imagined herself telling Evelyn. "And I'm sure that's just what they think. That we haven't got the brains we were born with. That we have to be told *everything*." By the time she climbed into the Volvo the rain had ceased, as abruptly as if someone had just thrown a switch. Her coat was soaked through, and she laid it out on the back seat to dry.

At this hour, the streets were practically deserted. She drove past a succession of shops and restaurants: Bob's Big Boy, Li'l Pickle Sandwiches, Al's Exotic Birds, Ralph's Market. Inside Long's Drugs empty aisles of hair supplies, pet food, household appliances and vitamin supplements were illuminated by pale, watery fluorescents, like the inside of an aquarium. "It's not as if we couldn't do just as well without them," she would continue, awaiting Evelyn's quick nods of agreement. "I certainly didn't need to get married. I could have done just as well on my own. It's not as if it's some *man's* secret how to get by in this world. It's just a matter of keeping your feet on the ground, being objective about things, not fooling yourself. That's all there is to it. That's the big secret."

As she turned onto Beverly Glen her high-beams, sweeping through an alleyway, reflected off a pair of attentive red eyes. Being realistic, she thought, and heard the wolves emerge from alleyways, abandoned buildings, underground parking garages, their black calloused paws pattering like rain against the damp streets. They loped alongside her car for short distances, trailed off to gobble stray snails and mice, paused to bite and scratch their fleas. She refused to look, driving on through the deserted city. The alternating traffic lights cast shifting patterns and colors across the glimmering asphalt, like rotating spotlights on aluminum Christmas trees. Wolves, men, lovers, cars, streets, cities, worlds, stars. The real and the unreal, the true and the untrue. Unless you're careful it all starts looking like a dream, it all seems pretty strange and impossible, she thought, while all across the city the wolves began to howl.

Raymond Carver   (1938–1988)

Raymond Carver, a legendary hard-drinking writer, is sometimes regarded as a minimalist—one who achieves extraordinary effects with a minimum of language, detail, or fancy literary footwork. Zachary Leader described Carver's second collection of stories, What We Talk about When We Talk about Love *(1981), as "a spare, unsparing collection, grim, minimalist, 'postmodern' in its resistance to depth and the exaggerated blankness of its realism."[1] His first collection,* Will You Please Be Quiet, Please? *(1976), in which the following story appeared, was less "cut to the bone." His third collection,* Cathedral *(1983), returned to the "generosity" of the first collection and established his reputation as a writer of realistic fiction who introduces the reader to dispossessed Americans who are often down and out, wondering what their next move should be.*

NIGHT SCHOOL   1976

My marriage had just fallen apart. I couldn't find a job. I had another girl. But she wasn't in town. So I was at a bar having a glass of beer, and two women were sitting a few stools down, and one of them began to talk to me.

---

[1] From *The Times Literary Supplement* "A Chastened Gratitude" (Feb. 28, 1992): 16.

"You have a car?"

"I do, but it's not here," I said.

My wife had the car. I was staying at my parents' place. I used their car sometimes. But tonight I was walking.

The other woman looked at me. They were both about forty, maybe older.   5

"What'd you ask him?" the other woman said to the first woman.

"I said did he have a car."

"So do you have a car?" the second woman said to me.

"I was telling her. I have a car. But I don't have it with me," I said.

"That doesn't do us much good, does it?" she said.   10

The first woman laughed. "We had a brainstorm and we need a car to go through
with it. Too bad." She turned to the bartender and asked for two more beers.

I'd been nursing my beer along, and now I drank it off and thought they
might buy me a round. They didn't.

"What do you do?" the first woman asked me.

"Right now, nothing," I said. "Sometimes, when I can, I go to school."

"He goes to school," she said to the other woman. "He's a student. Where   15
do you go to school?"

"Around," I said.

"I told you," the woman said. "Doesn't he look like a student?"

"What are they teaching you?" the second woman said.

"Everything," I said.

"I mean," she said, "what do you plan to do? What's your big goal in life?   20
Everybody has a big goal in life."

I raised my empty glass to the bartender. He took it and drew me another
beer. I counted out some change, which left me with thirty cents from the two
dollars I'd started out with a couple of hours ago. She was waiting.

"Teach. Teach school," I said.

"He wants to be a teacher," she said.

I sipped my beer. Someone put a coin in the jukebox and a song that my
wife liked began to play. I looked around. Two men near the front were at the
shuffleboard. The door was open and it was dark outside.

"We're students too, you know," the first woman said. "We go to school."   25

"We take a night class," the other one said. "We take this reading class on
Monday nights."

The first woman said, "Why don't you move down here, teacher, so we don't
have to yell?"

I picked up my beer and my cigarets and moved down two stools.

"That's better," she said. "Now, did you say you were a student?"

"Sometimes, yes, but not now," I said.   30

"Where?"

"State College."

"That's right," she said. "I remember now." She looked at the other woman.
"You ever hear of a teacher over there name of Patterson? He teaches adult-ed-
ucation classes. He teaches this class we take on Monday nights. You remind me
a lot of Patterson."

They looked at each other and laughed.

"Don't bother about us," the first woman said. "It's a private joke. Shall we   35
tell him what we thought about doing, Edith? *Shall* we?"

Edith didn't answer. She took a drink of beer and she narrowed her eyes as she looked at herself, at the three of us, in the mirror behind the bar.

"We were thinking," the first woman went on, "if we had a car tonight we'd go over and see him. Patterson. Right, Edith?"

Edith laughed to herself. She finished her beer and asked for a round, one for me included. She paid for the beers with a five-dollar bill.

"Patterson likes to take a drink," Edith said.

"You can say that again," the other woman said. She turned to me. "We   40 talked about it in class one night. Patterson says he always has wine with his meals and a highball or two before dinner."

"What class is this?" I said.

"This reading class Patterson teaches. Patterson likes to talk about different things."

"We're learning to read," Edith said. "Can you believe it?"

"I'd like to read Hemingway and things like that," the other woman said. "But Patterson has us reading stories like in *Reader's Digest*."

"We take a test every Monday night," Edith said. "But Patterson's okay. He   45 wouldn't care if we came over for a highball. Wouldn't be much he could do, anyway. We have something on him. On Patterson," she said.

"We're on the loose tonight," the other woman said. "But Edith's car is in the garage."

"If you had a car now, we'd go over and see him," Edith said. She looked at me. "You could tell Patterson you wanted to be a teacher. You'd have something in common."

I finished my beer. I hadn't eaten anything all day except some peanuts. It was hard to keep listening and talking.

"Let's have three more, please, Jerry," the first woman said to the bartender.

"Thank you," I said.   50

"You'd get along with Patterson," Edith said.

"So call him," I said. I thought it was just talk.

"I wouldn't do that," she said. "He could make an excuse. We just show up on his porch, he'll have to let us in." She sipped her beer.

"So let's go!" the first woman said. "What're we waiting for? Where'd you say the car is?"

"There's a car a few blocks from here," I said. "But I don't know."   55

"Do you want to go or don't you?" Edith said.

"He said he does," the first woman said. "We'll get a six-pack to take with us."

"I only have thirty cents," I said.

"Who needs your goddamn money?" Edith said. "We need your goddamn car. Jerry, let's have three more. And a six-pack to go."

"Here's to Patterson," the first woman said when the beer came. "To   60 Patterson and his highballs."

"He'll drop his cookies," Edith said.

"Drink up," the first woman said.

On the sidewalk we headed south, away from town. I walked between the two women. It was about ten o'clock.

"I could drink one of those beers now," I said.

"Help yourself," Edith said.   65

She opened the sack and I reached in and tore a can loose.

"We think he's home," Edith said.

"Patterson," the other woman said. "We don't know for sure. But we think so."

"How much farther?" Edith said.

I stopped, raised the beer, and drained half the can. "The next block," I said. 70
"I'm staying with my parents. It's their place."

"I guess there's nothing wrong with it," Edith said. "But I'd say you're kind of old for that."

"That's not polite, Edith," the other woman said.

"Well, that's the way I am," Edith said. "He'll have to get used to it, that's all. That's the way I am."

"That's the way she is," the other woman said.

I finished the beer and tossed the can into some weeds. 75

"Now how far?" Edith said.

"This is it. Right here. I'll try and get the car key," I said.

"Well, hurry up," Edith said.

"We'll wait outside," the other woman said.

"Jesus!" Edith said. 80

I unlocked the door and went downstairs. My father was in his pajamas, watching television. It was warm in the apartment and I leaned against the jamb for a minute and ran a hand over my eyes.

"I had a couple of beers," I said. "What are you watching?"

"John Wayne," he said. "It's pretty good. Sit down and watch it. Your mother hasn't come in yet."

My mother worked the swing shift at Paul's, a *hofbrau*° restaurant. My father didn't have a job. He used to work in the woods, and then he got hurt. He'd had a settlement, but most of that was gone now. I asked him for a loan of two hundred dollars when my wife left me, but he refused. He had tears in his eyes when he said no and said he hoped I wouldn't hold it against him. I'd said it was all right, I wouldn't hold it against him.

I knew he was going to say no this time too. But I sat down on the other 85 end of the couch and said. "I met a couple of women who asked me if I'd give them a ride home."

"What'd you tell them?" he said.

"They're waiting for me upstairs," I said.

"Just let them wait," he said. "Somebody'll come along. You don't want to get mixed up with that." He shook his head. "You really didn't show them where we live, did you? They're not really upstairs?" He moved on the couch and looked again at the television. "Anyway, your mother took the keys with her." He nodded slowly, still looking at the television.

"That's okay," I said. "I don't need the car. I'm not going anywhere."

I got up and looked into the hallway, where I slept on a cot. There was an 90 ashtray, a Lux clock, and a few old paperbacks on a table beside the cot. I usually went to bed at midnight and read until the lines of print went fuzzy and I fell asleep with the light on and the book in my hands. In one of the paperbacks I

hofbrau: German-style.

was reading there was something I remembered telling my wife. It made a terrific impression on me. There's a man who has a nightmare and in the nightmare he dreams he's dreaming and wakes to see a man standing at his bedroom window. The dreamer is so terrified he can't move, can hardly breathe. The man at the window stares into the room and then begins to pry off the screen. The dreamer can't move. He'd like to scream, but he can't get his breath. But the moon appears from behind a cloud, and the dreamer in the nightmare recognizes the man outside. It is his best friend, the best friend of the dreamer but no one the man having the nightmare knows.

Telling it to my wife, I'd felt the blood come to my face and my scalp prickle. But she wasn't interested.

"That's only writing," she said. "Being betrayed by somebody in your own family, *there's* a real nightmare for you."

I could hear them shaking the outside door. I could hear footsteps on the sidewalk over my window.

"Goddamn that bastard!" I heard Edith say.

I went into the bathroom for a long time and then I went upstairs and let myself out. It was cooler, and I did up the zipper on my jacket. I started walking to Paul's. If I got there before my mother went off duty, I could have a turkey sandwich. After that I could go to Kirby's newsstand and look through the magazines. Then I could go to the apartment to bed and read the books until I read enough and I slept.

The women, they weren't there when I left, and they wouldn't be there when I got back.

95

WINDOW ON

Fiction and the Canon

Canon comes from a Greek word implying "measure," "rule," or "law," and its relatively recent application to literature derives from the fourth-century study of various books of the Bible. Since many ancient books competed for acceptance as "official" books of the New Testament, churchmen had to decide which books were truly part of the biblical canon. In other words, they had to decide which books "measured up" and which did not.

In modern literature a canon is a selection of authors and works that are considered important: the "classics." A short story becomes part of the canon by virtue of its excellence. But what constitutes excellence? This debate often centers around the large number of white male authors in the canon. Some argue that they are the best writers and must be recognized as such. Others maintain that they were chosen by white male critics in the past and that Asian, black, or female critics—if given a voice—would have chosen an entirely different canon. At the root of this debate is one question: Is excellence in the short story dependent on its artistry or its ideas? A New Critic would vote for artistic excellence; a political or cultural critic might vote for excellence in terms of ideas.

One way to judge excellence is to see how a work weathers through time. As John Guillory says, "For a work to be canonical must mean that over successive generations, preferably many generations, readers continue to affirm a judgment of greatness, almost as though each generation actually judged anew the quality of the work." In the cases of Boccaccio and Poe, such judgments have been made and continue to be made. Among modern short story writers in the canon of excellence are Seán O'Faoláin, John Cheever, Katherine Anne Porter, Anton Chekhov, Kate Chopin, Stephen Crane, Ralph Ellison, F. Scott Fitzgerald, Charlotte Perkins Gilman, Nathaniel Hawthorne, Mary Lavin, D. H. Lawrence, Ursula K. Le Guin, Doris Lessing, Katherine Mansfield, Gabriel García Márquez, Flannery O'Connor, John Updike, Virginia Woolf, James Joyce, Eudora Welty, and Joyce Carol Oates. Not all of these have weathered generations of judgment, but all have proven durable enough to survive a half-century and more of critical reading.

Many excellent writers are candidates for inclusion in the canon, and one purpose of this book is to introduce you to some of them. Suzanne Jacob, Ann Beattie, Charles Baxter, Bharati Mukherjee, Isabel Allende, Toni Cade Bambara, Becky Birtha, Scott Bradfield, Sandra Cisneros, Anita Desai, Louise Erdrich, Richard Ford, Jamaica Kincaid, Bobbie Ann Mason, Alice Munro, William Trevor, Alice Walker, and Fay Weldon are all living writers whose work merits inclusion in the canon.

The literary canon is not fixed and never was. As T. S. Eliot reminded us, it is altered every time a major writer appears. As you consider the question of the canon, read some of these stories in pairs: Crane's "The Open Boat" with Walker's "Everyday Use"; Hawthorne's "Rappaccini's Daughter" with Kincaid's "Lucy"; Chekhov's "Concerning Love" with Birtha's "Johnnieruth"; Gilman's "The Yellow Wallpaper" with Cisneros's "Never Marry a Mexican"; and Lawrence's "The Horse-Dealer's Daughter" with Erdrich's "Love Medicine." Ask yourself: What qualities of excellence do these stories share? Decide, after reading and interpreting them carefully, just which stories you feel should rightfully be part of the canon of short fiction. Establish, as well, your basis of judgment. Do you feel you judge the stories on their artistic merits, or do outside issues related to your personal social situation affect your judgment? Ask yourself: Is it ever possible to make objective judgments about the value of a short story?

Reading

Guillory, John. "Canon." In *Critical Terms for Literary Study*, edited by Frank Lentricchia and Thomas McLaughlin, 233–49. Chicago: University of Chicago Press, 1990.

von Hallberg, Robert, ed. *Canons.* Chicago: University of Chicago Press, 1985.

Harris, Wendell. "Canonicity." *PMLA* 106 (January 1991): 110–21.

Howe, Irving. "The Value of the Canon." *New Republic*, February 18, 1991, 40–47.

Levin, Harry. "Core, Canon, Curriculum." *College English* 43 (1981): 352–62.

Anton Chekhov   (1860–1904)

Anton Chekhov is revered as one of Russia's greatest modern dramatists. His four major dramas, The Seagull *(1887),* Uncle Vanya *(1897),* The Three Sisters *(1901), and* The Cherry Orchard *(1903), are all part of the world's repertory of most performed plays. However, he is also known as one of the most important modern short story writers. Since he had a large family to support, he wrote prodigiously, and his stories, most of which first appeared in newspapers, constitute a huge output. They are available today in the nine-volume complete works,* The Oxford Chekhov *(1964–80), but were originally published in individual volumes:* The Black Monk and Other Stories *(1903),* The Kiss and Other Stories *(1908),* The Lady with the Dog and Other Stories *(1917), and numerous others published after his death. Chekhov is notable for his careful detail, especially when describing his characters' psychology. In many ways he is the first genius of the modern short story.*

CONCERNING LOVE   1898

Translated by Ronald Hingley

For lunch next day delicious pasties, crayfish and mutton rissoles were served. During the meal Nikanor the cook came upstairs to ask what the guests wanted for dinner. He was a man of average height with a puffy face and small eyes—and so clean-shaven that his whiskers seemed to have been plucked out rather than cut off.

Alyokhin explained that the fair Pelageya was in love with this cook. He was a drunkard and a bit of a hooligan, so she didn't want to marry him, but she didn't mind "just living with him." He was very pious, though, and his religion forbade his just living with her. He insisted on marriage, didn't want her otherwise. He swore at her in his cups, and even beat her. She would hide upstairs, weeping, when he was drunk, while Alyokhin and his servants stayed at home to protect her if necessary.

The conversation turned to love.

"What makes people fall in love?" asked Alyokhin. "Why couldn't Pelageya love someone else more suited to her intellectually and physically? Why must she love this Nikanor—'Fat-face,' everyone calls him round here—seeing that personal happiness is an important factor in love? It's all very mysterious, there are any number of possible interpretations. So far we've only heard one incontrovertible truth about love: the biblical 'this is a great mystery.' Everything else written and spoken about love has offered no solution, but has just posed questions which have simply remained unanswered. What seems to explain one instance doesn't fit a dozen others. It's best to interpret each instance separately, in my view, without trying to generalize. We must isolate each individual case, as doctors say."

"Very true," agreed Burkin.   5

"Your ordinary decent Russian has a weakness for these unsolved problems. Where other peoples romanticize their love, garnishing it with roses and nightingales, we Russians bedizen ours with dubious profundities—and the most tedious available, at that. Back in my student days in Moscow I had a 'friend': a lovely lady who, when I held her in my arms, was always wondering what monthly allowance I would give her, and what was the price of a pound of beef. We're just the same. When we're in love we're for ever questioning ourselves. Are we being honorable or dishonorable? Wise or stupid? How will it end, this love? And so on. Whether this attitude is right or wrong I don't know, but that it is a nuisance, that it is unsatisfactory and frustrating—that I do know."

He seemed to have some story he wanted to tell. People who live alone always do have things on their minds that they are keen to talk about. Bachelors deliberately go to the public baths, and to restaurants in town, just to talk, and they sometimes tell bath attendants or waiters the most fascinating tales. In the country, though, it is their guests to whom they usually unbosom themselves. Grey sky and rain-soaked trees could be seen through the windows. There was nowhere to go in such weather—and nothing to do except swap yarns.

I've been living and farming in Sofyino for some time—since I took my degree (Alyokhin began). By upbringing I'm the armchair type, my leanings are academic. But this estate was badly in debt when I came here, and since it was partly through spending so much on my education that Father had run up those debts, I decided to stay on and work until I'd paid them off. I made my decision and started working here: not without a certain repugnance, frankly. The land isn't all that productive hereabouts, and if you don't want to farm at a loss you either have to use hired hands—slave labor, practically—or else you have to run the place peasant-fashion: do your own field work, that is, yourself and your family. There's no other way. But I hadn't gone into these subtleties at the time. Not one single plot of earth did I leave in peace, I corralled all the nearby villagers and their women, and I had us all working away like billy-o. I ploughed myself, I sowed and I reaped myself—bored stiff the while, and frowning fastidiously like a village cat eating gherkins in the vegetable patch because it's starving. My body ached, I was nearly dead on my feet. At first I thought I could easily combine this drudgery with the cultured life—all I had to do, thought I, was to observe a certain routine. I moved into the best rooms up here, I arranged for coffee and liqueurs to be served after lunch and dinner, and I read the *European Herald* in bed at night. But one day our priest, Father Ivan, turned up and scoffed my whole stock of liquor at a sitting. The priest also ran off with my *European Heralds*, or rather his daughters did, because I never managed to get as far as my bed in summer, especially during haymaking, but slept in the bar, in a sledge, or in some woodman's hut—hardly conducive to reading, that. I gradually moved downstairs, I began having my meals with the servants, and there's nothing left of my former gracious living but these same servants who once worked for my father, and whom I hadn't the heart to dismiss.

Quite early on I was elected an honorary justice of the peace, and had to go to town and then to take part in sessions and sit at the assizes, which I found entertaining. When you've been cooped up here for a couple of months, especially in winter, you end up yearning for a black frock-coat. Now, at the assizes you had your frock-coats, your uniforms, your tail-coats. They were all lawyers there, all educated men. They were the sort of people you could talk to. To sit in an armchair wearing clean underwear and light boots with your watch-chain on your chest . . . after sleeping in a sledge and eating with servants, that really was the height of luxury.

I was always welcome in town, and I liked meeting new people. Now, among   10
these new friendships the most serious—and, quite honestly, the most pleasant—was with Luganovich, the Deputy Chairman of Assize. You both know him: a most charming individual. This happened just after the famous arson case. The proceedings had lasted two days, we were worn out, and Luganovich looked in my direction.

"How about dinner at my place?"

I was surprised, barely knowing the man, and then only in an official capacity—I had never visited his home. After calling briefly at my hotel to change, I set off. This dinner led to my first meeting with Luganovich's wife, Anne. She was still very young, not more than twenty-two, and her first child had been born six months previously. It all happened so long ago that I'd be hard put to it, now, to define precisely what it was about her that so much attracted me. But at that dinner it was abundantly clear. I saw a woman—young, handsome, kind, intellectual and captivating—unlike any I had ever met before. I at once sensed that this creature was dear to me, I seemed to know her already—rather as if I'd once seen that face, those eager, intelligent eyes, when I was a little boy looking at the album on my mother's chest-of-drawers.

At the arson trial four Jews had been found guilty and it had been made a conspiracy charge: quite indefensibly in my view. I became rather agitated at dinner—most distressed, in fact—and I've forgotten what I said, now, except that Anne kept shaking her head and telling her husband that "I just can't believe it, Dmitry."

Luganovich is a good fellow, one of those simple-minded chaps who have got it into their heads that the man in the dock is always guilty, and that a sentence may be challenged only in writing, through the proper channels—most certainly not at a private dinner-table.

"You and I didn't start that fire," he said gently. "Which is why you and I   15
aren't being tried and sent to prison."

Husband and wife both pressed food and drink on me. From several details—the way they made coffee together, the way they understood each other almost without words—I concluded that they lived in peace and harmony, that they were pleased to be entertaining a guest. We played piano duets after dinner. Then it grew dark and I went to my lodgings.

This happened in early spring, after which I was stuck in Sofyino all summer. I didn't even think of town, I was so busy. But I was haunted all along by the memory of that slender, fair-haired woman. Not directly present in my consciousness, she seemed rather to cast a faint shadow over it.

In late autumn a charity performance was staged in town. I went into the Governor's box (having been invited in the interval), and there was Anne

Luganovich seated by the Governor's wife. Again I was struck by that same irre-
sistible vibrant beauty, by that charming, friendly expression in her eyes. And again
I sensed an intimacy shared.

We sat next to each other, we walked in the foyer, and she told me that I
had grown thinner. Had I been ill?

"Yes. I've had a bad shoulder, and I sleep poorly when it rains."   20

"You look worn out. When you came to dinner in the spring you seemed
younger, more sure of yourself. You were a bit carried away at the time, you talked
a lot, you were quite fascinating. I couldn't help being a bit taken with you, actually. I've often thought of you during the summer for some reason, and when
I was getting ready for the theatre tonight I felt sure I should see you."

She laughed. "But today you look worn out," she repeated. "It makes you
seem older."

I lunched at the Luganoviches' next day. Afterwards they drove out to their
holiday cottage to put it in shape for the winter. I went with them, I came back
to town with them, and at midnight I had tea with them in the peaceful setting
of their home: by a blazing fire, with the young mother going out from time to
time to see if her little girl was asleep. After that I always made a point of seeing
the Luganoviches when I was in town. We got to know each other, and I used
to call unannounced. I was just like one of the family.

"Who is that?" I would hear her ask from the back of the house in the slow
drawl which I found so attractive.

"It's Mr. Alyokhin," the maid or nanny would answer, and Anne would appear   25
looking worried. Why hadn't I been to see them sooner? Had anything happened?

Her gaze, the clasp of her fine, delicate hand, the clothes which she wore
about the house, the way she did her hair, her voice, her steps . . . they always
made me feel as if something new and out of the ordinary, something significant,
had happened to me. We enjoyed long conversations—and long silences, each
wrapt in his own thoughts. Or she would play the piano for me. When there was
no one at home I would wait, I'd talk to nanny, play with baby, or lie on the study
ottoman reading the newspaper. When Anne came in I would meet her in the
hall and take her shopping off her. I always carried that shopping so fondly and
triumphantly, somehow—just like a little boy.

It was a bit like the farmer's wife in the story, the one who had no troubles—
not, that is, until she went and bought herself a pig! The Luganoviches had no
troubles—so they went and chummed up with me! If I hadn't been to town recently, then I must be ill or something must have happened to me, and both
would be genuinely alarmed. What worried them was that I—an educated man
who knew foreign languages—didn't devote myself to learning or letters, but lived
in the country, going round and round the same old treadmill, that I worked so
much but was always hard up. I was bound to be unhappy, they felt, and if they
saw me talking, laughing or having a meal, I must be doing so merely to conceal
my anguish. Even when I was happy and relaxed I could feel them viewing me
with concern. They were particularly touching when I really was in a bit of a fix:
when some creditor was pressing me, when I couldn't meet some payment on
time. Husband and wife would then whisper together by the window, and he
would approach me looking very solemn.

"If you're a bit short, Paul, my wife and I would like to lend you something.
Please don't hesitate to ask." His ears would flush with embarrassment.

Or else he would come up with his red ears after one of those whispering sessions by the window, and say that he and his wife "do most urgently beg you to accept this gift." He would then present me with some studs, a cigarette-case or a lamp. In return I would send them something from the country: a bird for the table, butter, flowers. Both of them, incidentally, had money of their own. Now, I was always borrowing in the early days, and I wasn't particularly choosy about it—I took my loans where I could get them. But no power on earth would have induced me to borrow from the Luganoviches. Need I say more?

I was unhappy. At home, in my fields and in my barn my thoughts were of   30 her. I tried to plumb the mystery of a young, handsome, intelligent woman, the wife of an unattractive, almost elderly husband (the man was over forty) and the mother of his children. I also tried to plumb the mystery of this same unattractive husband, this good sort, this easy-going fellow with his boring, common-sensical views, who (when attending a party or dance) always cultivated the local fuddy-duddies, this listless misfit with his submissive air of being a spectator or a bale of goods put up for auction . . . of this man who still believed in his right to be happy and to have children by her. Why ever, I kept wondering, had she met him instead of me? To what purpose so drastic an error in our lives?

On my visits to town I could always tell from her eyes that she was expecting me, and she'd admit having had a special feeling all day—she'd guessed I'd be coming. We enjoyed our long conversations and silences, not declaring our love for each other but concealing it fearfully and jealously. We feared anything which might betray our secret to ourselves. Deep and tender though my love was, I tried to be sensible about it, speculating what the upshot might be if we should lack the strength to fight our passions. It seemed incredible that a love so quiet, so sad as mine could suddenly and crudely disrupt the happy tenor of her husband's and children's lives: disrupt an entire household where I was so loved and trusted. Was that the way for a decent man to behave? She would have gone away with me—but where to? Where could I take her? Things would have been different if my life had been romantic and enterprising: if I'd been fighting for my country's freedom, for instance, if I'd been a distinguished scholar, actor or artist. As it was I should be conveying her from one humdrum, colorless milieu into another equally humdrum, or even worse. How long would our happiness last? What would happen to her if I became ill or died? What if we just fell out of love?

Her reflections were evidently similar. She thought about her husband and children, thought about her mother who loved her husband like a son. If she yielded to her passions she would either have to lie or tell the truth, but both courses would be equally alarming and difficult to one in her situation. Would her love bring me happiness, she wondered agonizingly. Wouldn't it complicate my life: irksome enough anyway, and beset with all sorts of tribulations? She felt she was too old for me, that she lacked the drive and energy to start a new life. She often told her husband that I ought to marry some decent, intelligent girl who would be a good housewife and helpmeet—but she would add at once that such a paragon was unlikely to be found anywhere in town.

Meanwhile the years were passing. Anne now had two children. Whenever I visited the family the servants smiled their welcome, the children shouted that Uncle Paul had arrived and clung round my neck, and everyone rejoiced. Not understanding my innermost feelings, they thought I was rejoicing with them. They all saw me as the embodiment of integrity. Adults and children alike, they felt that integrity incarnate was walking about the room—which imparted a special charm to their relations with me, as if my presence made their lives purer and finer. Anne and I used to go to the theatre together, always on foot. We would sit beside each other in the stalls, our shoulders touching, and I'd silently take the opera glasses from her, sensing her nearness to me, sensing that she was mine, that we couldn't live without each other. But through some strange lack of *rapport* we always said good-bye when we left the theatre, and we parted like strangers. People were saying goodness knows what about us in town, but not one word of truth was there in all their gossip.

Anne had begun going away to her mother's and sister's more often in recent years. She had become subject to depressions: moods in which she was conscious that her life was unfulfilled and wasted. She didn't want to see her husband and children at such times. She was under treatment for a nervous condition.

And still we did not speak our minds. In company she would feel curiously   35
exasperated with me. She would disagree with everything I said, and if I became involved in an argument she would take my opponent's side. If I chanced to drop something she would coldly offer her "congratulations." If I forgot the opera glasses when we went to the theatre, she'd tell me she had "known very well I'd forget those."

Luckily or unluckily, there is nothing in our lives which doesn't end sooner or later. The time had now come for us to part: Luganovich had been appointed to a judgeship in the west country. They had to sell their furniture, horses and cottage. We drove out to the cottage, and as we turned back for one last look at the garden and green roof everyone was sad, and I knew that it was time for me to take my leave of rather more than a mere cottage. It had been decided that we should see Anne off to the Crimea (where her doctors had advised her to stay) at the end of August, and that Luganovich would take the children to the west a little later.

A large crowd of us went to see Anne off. She had already said good-bye to her husband and children, and the train was due to leave at any moment, when I dashed into her compartment to put a basket—which she had nearly left behind—on the luggage rack. It was my turn to say good-bye. Our eyes met there in the compartment, and we could hold back no longer. I put my arms around her, she pressed her face against my breast, and the tears flowed. Kissing her face, her shoulders, her tear-drenched hands—we were both so unhappy—I declared my love. With a burning pain in my heart, I saw how inessential, how trivial, how illusory it was . . . everything which had frustrated our love. I saw that, if you love, you must base your theory of love on something loftier and more significant than happiness or unhappiness, than sin or virtue as they are commonly understood. Better, otherwise, not to theorize at all.

I kissed her for the last time, I clasped her hand, and we parted—for ever. The train had already started. I sat down in the next compartment, which was empty . . . sat there, weeping, until the first stop. Then I walked home to Sofyino.

It had stopped raining while Alyokhin was telling his story, and the sun had peeped out. Burkin and Ivan Ivanovich went on to the balcony, which had a superb view of the garden, and of the river which now gleamed, mirror-like, in the sun. As they admired the view they felt sorry that this man with the kind, intelligent eyes—who had spoken with such sincere feeling—really was going round and round the same old treadmill, doing neither academic work nor anything else capable of making his life more pleasant. And they imagined how stricken that young woman must have looked when he had said good-bye to her in the train, kissing her head and shoulders. Both of them had met her in town. Burkin, indeed, had been a friend of hers and had thought her very good-looking.

Kate Chopin   (1850–1904)

Kate Chopin is a feminist writer who was not accepted in her own time. Born in St. Louis, where she enjoyed a prominent place in society, she went with her husband, Oscar Chopin, to live first in New Orleans and later in the bayou region of Louisiana. Her stories and novels reflect her own background as a French Creole descendant and her life among French Creoles in Louisiana. After her husband died, Chopin sold her holdings, returned to St. Louis, and, influenced by Guy de Maupassant and other French writers, decided to write. She began publishing with two collections of stories: Bayou Folk *(1894) and* A Night in Acadie *(1897). Some of her work was rejected for publication on the grounds that its feminist themes were too radical for the times. In 1899, after publication of* The Awakening, *the negative reaction was so great that publishers ignored her work and she died a literary outcast. It took some fifty years for Chopin to begin to get the recognition she deserved.*

THE STORY OF AN HOUR   1894

Knowing that Mrs. Mallard was afflicted with a heart trouble, great care was taken to break to her as gently as possible the news of her husband's death.

It was her sister Josephine who told her, in broken sentences, veiled hints that revealed in half concealing. Her husband's friend Richards was there, too, near her. It was he who had been in the newspaper office when intelligence of the railroad disaster was received, with Brently Mallard's name leading the list of "killed." He had only taken the time to assure himself of its truth by a second telegram, and had hastened to forestall any less careful, less tender friend in bearing the sad message.

She did not hear the story as many women have heard the same, with a paralyzed inability to accept its significance. She wept at once, with sudden, wild abandonment, in her sister's arms. When the storm of grief had spent itself she went away to her room alone. She would have no one follow her.

There stood, facing the open window, a comfortable, roomy armchair. Into this she sank, pressed down by a physical exhaustion that haunted her body and seemed to reach into her soul.

She could see in the open square before her house the tops of trees that were   5 all aquiver with the new spring life. The delicious breath of rain was in the air. In the street below a peddler was crying his wares. The notes of a distant song which someone was singing reached her faintly, and countless sparrows were twittering in the eaves.

There were patches of blue sky showing here and there through the clouds that had met and piled above the other in the west facing her window.

She sat with her head thrown back upon the cushion of the chair, quite motionless, except when a sob came up into her throat and shook her, as a child who has cried itself to sleep continues to sob in its dreams.

She was young, with a fair, calm face, whose lines bespoke repression and even a certain strength. But now there was a dull stare in her eyes, whose gaze was fixed away off yonder on one of those patches of blue sky. It was not a glance of reflection, but rather indicated a suspension of intelligent thought.

There was something coming to her and she was waiting for it, fearfully. What was it? She did not know; it was too subtle and elusive to name. But she felt it, creeping out of the sky, reaching toward her through the sounds, the scents, the color that filled the air.

Now her bosom rose and fell tumultuously. She was beginning to recognize   10
this thing that was approaching to possess her, and she was striving to beat it back with her will—as powerless as her two white slender hands would have been.

When she abandoned herself a little whispered word escaped her slightly parted lips. She said it over and over under her breath: "Free, free, free!" The vacant stare and the look of terror that had followed it went from her eyes. They stayed keen and bright. Her pulses beat fast, and the coursing blood warmed and relaxed every inch of her body.

She did not stop to ask if it were or were not a monstrous joy that held her. A clear and exalted perception enabled her to dismiss the suggestion as trivial.

She knew that she would weep again when she saw the kind, tender hands folded in death; the face that had never looked save with love upon her, fixed and gray and dead. But she saw beyond that bitter moment a long procession of years to come that would belong to her absolutely. And she opened and spread her arms out to them in welcome.

There would be no one to live for her during those coming years; she would live for herself. There would be no powerful will bending her in that blind persistence with which men and women believe they have a right to impose a private will upon a fellow-creature. A kind intention or a cruel intention made the act seem no less a crime as she looked upon it in that brief moment of illumination.

And yet she had loved him—sometimes. Often she had not. What did it mat-   15
ter! What could love, the unsolved mystery, count for in face of this possession of self-assertion which she suddenly recognized as the strongest impulse of her being!

"Free! Body and soul free!" she kept whispering.

Josephine was kneeling before the closed door with her lips to the keyhole, imploring for admission. "Louise, open the door! I beg; open the door—you will make yourself ill. What are you doing, Louise? For heaven's sake open the door."

"Go away. I am not making myself ill." No; she was drinking in a very elixir of life through that open window.

Her fancy was running riot along those days ahead of her. Spring days, and summer days, and all sorts of days that would be her own. She breathed a quick prayer that life might be long. It was only yesterday she had thought with a shudder that life might be long.

She arose at length and opened the door to her sister's importunities. There   20
was a feverish triumph in her eyes, and she carried herself unwittingly like a goddess of Victory. She clasped her sister's waist, and together they descended the stairs. Richards stood waiting for them at the bottom.

Someone was opening the front door with a latchkey. It was Brently Mallard who entered, a little travel-stained, composedly carrying his grip-sack and umbrella. He had been far from the scene of accident, and did not even know there had been one. He stood amazed at Josephine's piercing cry; at Richards' quick motion to screen him from the view of his wife.

But Richards was too late.

When the doctors came they said she had died of heart disease—of joy that kills.

Sandra Cisneros   (b. 1954)

One of the newest and most distinguished Chicana writers in America, Sandra Cisneros was born in Chicago and lives now in San Antonio, Texas. She graduated from the Iowa Writers' Workshop in 1978. Her early book of stories, The House on Mango Street *(1988), signaled her immediately as a writer of distinction with a fresh voice and a fresh vision. She has been a teacher of high school dropouts, a poet-in-the-schools, and a visiting writer in several colleges. She has also published a book of poems,* My Wicked Wicked Ways *(1990).* Woman Hollering Creek and Other Stories *(1991) won the PEN prize for best fiction in 1992. She is currently working on a novel,* Caramelo, *about "Mexican movies, Mexican songs, and Mexican love letters."*

NEVER MARRY A MEXICAN   1991

Never marry a Mexican, my ma said once and always. She said this because of my father. She said this though she was Mexican too. But she was born here in the U.S., and he was born there, and it's *not* the same, you know.

I'll *never* marry. Not any man. I've known men too intimately. I've witnessed their infidelities, and I've helped them to it. Unzipped and unhooked and agreed to clandestine maneuvers. I've been accomplice, committed premeditated crimes. I'm guilty of having caused deliberate pain to other women. I'm vindictive and cruel, and I'm capable of anything.

I admit, there was a time when all I wanted was to belong to a man. To wear that gold band on my left hand and be worn on his arm like an expensive jewel brilliant in the light of day. Not the sneaking around I did in different bars that all looked the same, red carpets with a black grillwork design, flocked wallpaper, wooden wagon-wheel light fixtures with hurricane lampshades a sick amber color like the drinking glasses you get for free at gas stations.

Dark bars, dark restaurants then. And if not—my apartment, with toothbrush firmly planted in the toothbrush holder like a flag on the North Pole. The bed so big because he never stayed the whole night. Of course not.

Borrowed. That's how I've had my men. Just the cream skimmed off the top. Just the sweetest part of the fruit, without the bitter skin that daily living with a spouse can rend. They've come to me when they wanted the sweet meat then.

So, no. I've never married and never will. Not because I couldn't, but because I'm too romantic for marriage. Marriage has failed me, you could say. Not a man exists who hasn't disappointed me, whom I could trust to love the way I've

5

loved. It's because I believe too much in marriage that I don't. Better to not marry than live a lie.

Mexican men, forget it. For a long time the men clearing off the tables or chopping meat behind the butcher counter or driving the bus I rode to school every day, those weren't men. Not men I considered as potential lovers. Mexican, Puerto Rican, Cuban, Chilean, Colombian, Panamanian, Salvadorean, Bolivian, Honduran, Argentine, Dominican, Venezuelan, Guatemalan, Ecuadorean, Nicaraguan, Peruvian, Costa Rican, Paraguayan, Uruguayan, I don't care. I never saw them. My mother did this to me.

I guess she did it to spare me and Ximena the pain she went through. Having married a Mexican man at seventeen. Having had to put up with all the grief a Mexican family can put on a girl because she was from *el otro lado*, the other side, and my father had married down by marrying her. If he had married a white woman from *el otro lado*, that would've been different. That would've been marrying up, even if the white girl was poor. But what could be more ridiculous than a Mexican girl who couldn't even speak Spanish, who didn't know enough to set a separate plate for each course at dinner, nor how to fold cloth napkins, nor how to set the silverware.

In my ma's house the plates were always stacked in the center of the table, the knives and forks and spoons standing in a jar, help yourself. All the dishes chipped or cracked and nothing matched. And no tablecloth, ever. And newspapers set on the table whenever my grandpa sliced watermelons, and how embarrassed she would be when her boyfriend, my father, would come over and there were newspapers all over the kitchen floor and table. And my grandpa, big hardworking Mexican man, saying Come, come and eat, and slicing a big wedge of those dark green watermelons, a big slice, he wasn't stingy with food. Never, even during the Depression. Come, come and eat, to whoever came knocking on the back door. Hobos sitting at the dinner table and the children staring and staring. Because my grandfather always made sure they never went without. Flour and rice, by the barrel and by the sack. Potatoes. Big bags of pinto beans. And watermelons, bought three or four at a time, rolled under his bed and brought out when you least expected. My grandpa had survived three wars, one Mexican, two American, and he knew what living without meant. He knew.

My father, on the other hand, did not. True, when he first came to this country he had worked shelling clams, washing dishes, planting hedges, sat on the back of the bus in Little Rock and had the bus driver shout. You—sit up here, and my father had shrugged sheepishly and said, No speak English. 10

But he was no economic refugee, no immigrant fleeing a war. My father ran away from home because he was afraid of facing his father after his first-year grades at the university proved he'd spent more time fooling around than studying. He left behind a house in Mexico City that was neither poor nor rich, but thought itself better than both. A boy who would get off a bus when he saw a girl he knew board if he didn't have the money to pay her fare. That was the world my father left behind.

I imagine my father in his *fanfarrón* clothes, because that's what he was, a *fanfarrón*. That's what my mother thought the moment she turned around to the voice that was asking her to dance. A big show-off, she'd say years later. Nothing but a big show-off. But she never said why she married him. My father in his shark-blue suits with the starched handkerchief in the breast pocket, his felt fedora, his tweed topcoat with the big shoulders, and heavy British wing tips with the pin-hole design on the heel and toe. Clothes that cost a lot. Expensive. That's what my father's things said. *Calidad.* Quality.

My father must've found the U.S. Mexicans very strange, so foreign from what he knew at home in Mexico City where the servant served watermelon on a plate with silverware and a cloth napkin, or mangos with their own special prongs. Not like this, eating with your legs wide open in the yard, or in the kitchen hunkered over newspapers. *Come, come and eat.* No, never like this.

How I make my living depends. Sometimes I work as a translator. Sometimes I get paid by the word and sometimes by the hour, depending on the job. I do this in the day, and at night I paint. I'd do anything in the day just so I can keep on painting.

I work as a substitute teacher, too, for the San Antonio Independent School   15
District. And that's worse than translating those travel brochures with their tiny print, believe me. I can't stand kids. Not any age. But it pays the rent.

Any way you look at it, what I do to make a living is a form of prostitution. People say, "A painter? How nice," and want to invite me to their parties, have me decorate the lawn like an exotic orchid for hire. But do they buy art?

I'm amphibious. I'm a person who doesn't belong to any class. The rich like to have me around because they envy my creativity; they know they can't buy *that.* The poor don't mind if I live in their neighborhood because they know I'm poor like they are, even if my education and the way I dress keeps us worlds apart. I don't belong to any class. Not to the poor, whose neighborhood I share. Not to the rich, who come to my exhibitions and buy my work. Not to the middle class from which my sister Ximena and I fled.

When I was young, when I first left home and rented that apartment with my sister and her kids right after her husband left, I thought it would be glamorous to be an artist. I wanted to be like Frida or Tina. I was ready to suffer with my camera and my paint brushes in that awful apartment we rented for $150 each because it had high ceilings and those wonderful glass skylights that convinced us we had to have it. Never mind there was no sink in the bathroom, and a tub that looked like a sarcophagus, and floorboards that didn't meet, and a hallway to scare away the dead. But fourteen-foot ceilings was enough for us to write a check for the deposit right then and there. We thought it all romantic. You know the place, the one on Zarzamora on top of the barber shop with the Casasola prints of the Mexican Revolution. Neon BIRRIA TEPATITLÁN sign round the corner, two goats knocking their heads together, and all those Mexican bakeries, Las Brisas for *huevos rancheros* and *carnitas* and *barbacoa* on Sundays, and fresh fruit milk shakes, and mango *paletas*, and more signs in Spanish than in English. We thought it was great, great. The barrio looked cute in the daytime, like Sesame Street. Kids hopscotching on the sidewalk, blessed little boogers. And hardware stores that still sold ostrich-feather dusters, and whole families marching out of Our Lady of Guadalupe Church on Sundays, girls in their swirly-whirly dresses and patent-leather shoes, boys in their dress Stacys and shiny shirts.

But nights, that was nothing like what we knew up on the north side. Pistols going off like the wild, wild West, and me and Ximena and the kids huddled in one bed with the lights off listening to it all, saying, Go to sleep, babies, it's just firecrackers. But we knew better. Ximena would say, Clemencia, maybe we should

go home. And I'd say, Shit! Because she knew as well as I did there was no home
to go home to. Not with our mother. Not with that man she married. After Daddy
died, it was like we didn't matter. Like Ma was so busy feeling sorry for herself,
I don't know. I'm not like Ximena. I still haven't worked it out after all this time,
even though our mother's dead now. My half brothers living in that house that
should've been ours, me and Ximena's. But that's—how do you say it?—water
under the damn? I can't ever get the sayings right even though I was born in this
country. We didn't say shit like that in our house.

Once Daddy was gone, it was like my ma didn't exist, like if she died, too.   20
I used to have a little finch, twisted one of its tiny red legs between the bars of
the cage once, who knows how. The leg just dried up and fell off. My bird lived
a long time without it, just a little red stump of a leg. He was fine, really. My
mother's memory is like that, like if something already dead dried up and fell off,
and I stopped missing where she used to be. Like if I never had a mother. And
I'm not ashamed to say it either. When she married that white man, and he and
his boys moved into my father's house, it was as if she stopped being my mother.
Like I never even had one.

Ma always sick and too busy worrying about her own life, she would've sold
us to the Devil if she could. "Because I married so young, *mi'ja,*"° she'd say.
"Because your father, he was so much older than me, and I never had a chance
to be young. Honey, try to understand . . ." Then I'd stop listening.

That man she met at work, Owen Lambert, the foreman at the photo-fin-
ishing plant, who she was seeing even while my father was sick. Even then. That's
what I can't forgive.

When my father was coughing up blood and phlegm in the hospital, half his
face frozen, and his tongue so fat he couldn't talk, he looked so small with all
those tubes and plastic sacks dangling around him. But what I remember most is
the smell, like death was already sitting on his chest. And I remember the doctor
scraping the phlegm out of my father's mouth with a white washcloth, and my
daddy gagging and I wanted to yell, Stop, you stop that, he's my daddy. Goddamn
you. Make him live. Daddy, don't. Not yet, not yet, not yet. And how I couldn't
hold myself up, I couldn't hold myself up. Like if they'd beaten me, or pulled my
insides out through my nostrils, like if they'd stuffed me with cinnamon and cloves,
and I just stood there dry-eyed next to Ximena and my mother, Ximena between
us because I wouldn't let her stand next to me. Everyone repeating over and over
the Ave Marías and Padre Nuestros. The priest sprinkling holy water, *mundo sin
fin, amén.*°

Drew, remember when you used to call me your Malinalli? It was a joke, a
private game between us, because you looked like a Cortez with that beard of
yours. My skin dark against yours. Beautiful, you said. You said I was beautiful,
and when you said it, Drew, I was.

My Malinalli, Malinche, my courtesan, you said, and yanked my head back   25
by the braid. Calling me that name in between little gulps of breath and the raw
kisses you gave, laughing from that black beard of yours.

---

mi'ja: Contraction of *mi hija,* "my daughter."   *mundo sin fin, amén:* "World without end,
amen."

Before daybreak, you'd be gone, same as always, before I even knew it. And it was as if I'd imagined you, only the teeth marks on my belly and nipples proving me wrong.

Your skin pale, but your hair blacker than a pirate's. Malinalli, you called me, remember? *Mi doradita.* I liked when you spoke to me in my language. I could love myself and think myself worth loving.

Your son. Does he know how much I had to do with his birth? I was the one who convinced you to let him be born. Did you tell him, while his mother lay on her back laboring his birth, I lay in his mother's bed making love to you.

You're nothing without me. I created you from spit and red dust. And I can snuff you between my finger and thumb if I want to. Blow you to kingdom come. You're just a smudge of paint I chose to birth on canvas. And when I made you over, you were no longer a part of her, you were all mine. The landscape of your body taut as a drum. The heart beneath that hide thrumming and thrumming. Not an inch did I give back.

I paint and repaint you the way I see fit, even now. After all these years. Did you know that? Little fool. You think I went hobbling along with my life, whimpering and whining like some twangy country-and-western when you went back to her. But I've been waiting. Making the world look at you from my eyes. And if that's not power, what is?

Nights I light all the candles in the house, the ones to La Virgen de Guadalupe, the ones to El Niño Fidencio, Don Pedrito Jaramillo, Santo Niño de Atocha, Nuestra Señora de San Juan de los Lagos, and especially, Santa Lucia, with her beautiful eyes on a plate.

Your eyes are beautiful, you said. You said they were the darkest eyes you'd ever seen and kissed each one as if they were capable of miracles. And after you left, I wanted to scoop them out with a spoon, place them on a plate under these blue blue skies, food for the blackbirds.

The boy, your son. The one with the face of that redheaded woman who is your wife. The boy red-freckled like fish food floating on the skin of water. That boy.

I've been waiting patient as a spider all these years, since I was nineteen and he was just an idea hovering in his mother's head, and I'm the one that gave him permission and made it happen, see.

Because your father wanted to leave your mother and live with me. Your mother whining for a child, at least *that*. And he kept saying, Later, we'll see, later. But all along it was me he wanted to be with, it was me, he said.

I want to tell you this evenings when you come to see me. When you're full of talk about what kind of clothes you're going to buy, and what you used to be like when you started high school and what you're like now that you're almost finished. And how everyone knows you as a rocker, and your band, and your new red guitar that you just got because your mother gave you a choice, a guitar or a car, but you don't need a car, do you, because I drive you everywhere. You could be my son if you weren't so light-skinned.

This happened. A long time ago. Before you were born. When you were a moth inside your mother's heart, I was your father's student, yes, just like you're mother's heart, I was your father's student, yes, just like you're mine now. And your father painted and painted me, because he said, I was his *doradita*, all golden and sun-baked, and that's the kind of woman he likes best, the ones brown as river sand, yes. And he took me under his wing and in his bed, this man, this teacher, your father. I was honored that he'd done me the favor. I was that young.

All I know is I was sleeping with your father the night you were born. In the same bed where you were conceived. I was sleeping with your father and didn't give a damn about that woman, your mother. If she was a brown woman like me, I might've had a harder time living with myself, but since she's not, I don't care. I was there first, always. I've always been there, in the mirror, under his skin, in the blood, before you were born. And he's been here in my heart before I even knew him. Understand? He's always been here. Always. Dissolving like a hibiscus flower, exploding like a rope into dust. I don't care what's right anymore. I don't care about his wife. She's not *my* sister.

And it's not the last time I've slept with a man the night his wife is birthing a baby. Why do I do that, I wonder? Sleep with a man when his wife is giving life, being suckled by a thing with its eyes still shut. Why do that? It's always given me a bit of crazy joy to be able to kill those women like that, without their knowing it. To know I've had their husbands when they were anchored in blue hospital rooms, their guts yanked inside out, the baby sucking their breasts while their husband sucked mine. All this while their ass stitches were still hurting.

Once, drunk on margaritas, I telephoned your father at four in the morn- 40 ing, woke the bitch up. Hello, she chirped. I want to talk to Drew. Just a moment, she said in her most polite drawing-room English. Just a moment. I laughed about that for weeks. What a stupid ass to pass the phone over to the lug asleep beside her. Excuse me, honey, it's for you. When Drew mumbled hello I was laughing so hard I could hardly talk. Drew? That dumb bitch of a wife of yours, I said, and that's all I could manage. That stupid stupid stupid. No Mexican woman would react like that. Excuse me, honey. It cracked me up.

He's got the same kind of skin, the boy. All the blue veins pale and clear just like his mama. Skin like roses in December. Pretty boy. Little clone. Little cells split into you and you and you. Tell me, baby, which part of you is your mother. I try to imagine her lips, her jaw, her long long legs that wrapped themselves around this father who took me to his bed.

This happened. I'm asleep. Or pretend to be. You're watching me, Drew. I feel your weight when you sit on the corner of the bed, dressed and ready to go, but now you're just watching me sleep. Nothing. Not a word. Not a kiss. Just sitting. You're taking me in under inspection. What do you think already?

I haven't stopped dreaming you. Did you know that? Do you think it's strange? I never tell, though. I keep it to myself like I do all the thoughts I think of you.

After all these years.

I don't want you looking at me. I don't want you taking me in while I'm 45 asleep. I'll open my eyes and frighten you away.

There. What did I tell you? *Drew? What is it?* Nothing. I'd knew you'd say that.

Let's not talk. We're no good at it. With you I'm useless with words. As if somehow I had to learn to speak all over again, as if the words I needed haven't been invented yet. We're cowards. Come back to bed. At least there I feel I have you for a little. For a moment. For a catch of the breath. You let go. You ache and tug. You rip my skin.

You're almost not a man without your clothes. How do I explain it? You're so much a child in my bed. Nothing but a big boy who needs to be held. I won't let anyone hurt you. My pirate. My slender boy of a man.

After all these years.

I didn't imagine it, did I? A Ganges, an eye of the storm. For a little. When   50
we forgot ourselves, you tugged me, I leapt inside you and split you like an apple. Opened for the other to look and not give back. Something wrenched itself loose. Your body doesn't lie. It's not silent like you.

You're nude as a pearl. You've lost your train of smoke. You're tender as rain. If I'd put you in my mouth you'd dissolve like snow.

You were ashamed to be so naked. Pulled back. But I saw you for what you are, when you opened yourself for me. When you were careless and let yourself through. I caught that catch of the breath. I'm not crazy.

When you slept, you tugged me toward you. You sought me in the dark. I didn't sleep. Every cell, every follicle, every nerve, alert. Watching you sigh and roll and turn and hug me closer to you. I didn't sleep. I was taking *you* in that time.

Your mother? Only once. Years after your father and I stopped seeing each other. At an art exhibition. A show on the photographs of Eugène Atget. Those images, I could look at them for hours. I'd taken a group of students with me.

It was your father I saw first. And in that instant I felt as if everyone in the   55
room, all the sepia-toned photographs, my students, the men in business suits, the high-heeled women, the security guards, everyone, could see me for what I was. I had to scurry out, lead my kids to another gallery, but some things destiny has cut out for you.

He caught up with us in the coat-check area, arm in arm with a redheaded Barbie doll in a fur coat. One of those scary Dallas types, hair yanked into a ponytail, big shiny face like the women behind the cosmetic counters at Neiman's. That's what I remember. She must've been with him all along, only I swear I never saw her until that second.

You could tell from a slight hesitancy, only slight because he's too suave to hesitate, that he was nervous. Then he's walking toward me, and I didn't know what to do, just stood there dazed like those animals crossing the road at night when the headlights stun them.

And I don't know why, but all of a sudden I looked at my shoes and felt ashamed at how old they looked. And he comes up to me, my love, your father, in that way of his with that grin that makes me want to beat him, makes me want to make love to him, and he says in the most sincere voice you ever heard, "Ah, Clemencia! *This* is Megan." No introduction could've been meaner. *This* is Megan. Just like that.

I grinned like an idiot and held out my paw—"Hello, Megan"—and smiled too much the way you do when you can't stand someone. Then I got the hell out of there, chattering like a monkey all the ride back with my kids. When I got home I had to lie down with a cold washcloth on my forehead and the TV on. All I could hear throbbing under the washcloth in that deep part behind my eyes: *This* is Megan.

And that's how I fell asleep, with the TV on and every light in the house   60
burning. When I woke up it was something like three in the morning. I shut the
lights and TV and went to get some aspirin, and the cats, who'd been asleep with
me on the couch, got up too and followed me into the bathroom as if they knew
what's what. And then they followed me into bed, where they aren't allowed, but
this time I just let them, fleas and all.

This happened, too. I swear I'm not making this up. It's all true. It was the
last time I was going to be with your father. We had agreed. All for the best. Surely
I could see that, couldn't I? My own good. A good sport. A young girl like me.
Hadn't I understood . . . responsibilities. Besides, he could *never* marry *me*. You
didn't think . . . ? *Never marry a Mexican. Never marry a Mexican* . . . No, of
course not. I see. I see.

We had the house to ourselves for a few days, who knows how. You and your
mother had gone somewhere. Was it Christmas? I don't remember.

I remember the leaded-glass lamp with the milk glass above the dining-room
table. I made a mental inventory of everything. The Egyptian lotus design on the
hinges of the doors. The narrow, dark hall where your father and I had made love
once. The four-clawed tub where he had washed my hair and rinsed it with a tin
bowl. This window. That counter. The bedroom with its light in the morning,
incredibly soft, like the light from a polished dime.

The house was immaculate, as always, not a stray hair anywhere, not a flake
of dandruff or a crumpled towel. Even the roses on the dining-room table held
their breath. A kind of airless cleanliness that always made me want to sneeze.

Why was I so curious about this woman he lived with? Every time I went to   65
the bathroom, I found myself opening the medicine cabinet, looking at all the
things that were hers. Her Estée Lauder lipsticks. Corals and pinks, of course. Her
nail polishes—mauve was as brave as she could wear. Her cotton balls and blond
hairpins. A pair of bone-colored sheepskin slippers, as clean as the day she'd bought
them. On the door hook—a white robe with a MADE IN ITALY label, and a silky
nightshirt with pearl buttons. I touched the fabrics. *Calidad*. Quality.

I don't know how to explain what I did next. While your father was busy in
the kitchen, I went over to where I'd left my backpack, and took out a bag of
gummy bears I'd bought. And while he was banging pots, I went around the
house and left a trail of them in places I was sure *she* would find them. One in her
lucite makeup organizer. One stuffed inside each bottle of nail polish. I untwisted
the expensive lipsticks to their full length and smushed a bear on the top before
recapping them. I even put a gummy bear in her diaphragm case in the very center of that luminescent rubber moon.

Why bother? Drew could take the blame. Or he could say it was the cleaning woman's Mexican voodoo. I knew that, too. It didn't matter. I got a strange
satisfaction wandering about the house leaving them in places only she would
look.

And just as Drew was shouting, "Dinner" I saw it on the desk. One of those
wooden babushka dolls Drew had brought her from his trip to Russia. I know.
He'd bought one just like it for me.

I just did what I did, uncapped the doll inside a doll inside a doll, until I got
to the very center, the tiniest baby inside all the others, and this I replaced with
a gummy bear. And then I put the dolls back, just like I'd found them, one in-

side the other, inside the other. Except for the baby, which I put inside my pocket. All through dinner I kept reaching in the pocket of my jean jacket. When I touched it, it made me feel good.

On the way home, on the bridge over the *arroyo* on Guadalupe Street, I   70 stopped the car, switched on the emergency blinkers, got out, and dropped the wooden toy into that muddy creek where winos piss and rats swim. The Barbie doll's toy stewing there in that muck. It gave me a feeling like nothing before and since.

Then I drove home and slept like the dead.

These mornings, I fix coffee for me, milk for the boy. I think of that woman, and I can't see a trace of my lover in this boy, as if she conceived him by immaculate conception.

I sleep with this boy, their son. To make the boy love me the way I love his father. To make him want me, hunger, twist in his sleep, as if he'd swallowed glass. I put him in my mouth. Here, little piece of my *corazón*. Boy with hard thighs and just a bit of down and a small hard downy ass like his father's, and that back like a valentine. Come here, *mi cariñito*. Come to *mamita*. Here's a bit of toast.

I can tell from the way he looks at me, I have him in my power. Come, sparrow. I have the patience of eternity. Come to *mamita*. My stupid little bird. I don't move. I don't startle him. I let him nibble. All, all for you. Rub his belly. Stroke him. Before I snap my teeth.

What is it inside me that makes me so crazy at 2 A.M.? I can't blame it on al-   75 cohol in my blood when there isn't any. It's something worse. Something that poisons the blood and tips me when the night swells and I feel as if the whole sky were leaning against my brain.

And if I killed someone on a night like this? And if it was *me* I killed instead. I'd be guilty of getting in the line of crossfire, innocent bystander, isn't it a shame. I'd be walking with my head full of images and my back to the guilty. Suicide? I couldn't say. I didn't see it.

Except it's not me who I want to kill. When the gravity of the planets is just right, it all tilts and upsets the visible balance. And that's when it wants to out from my eyes. That's when I get on the telephone, dangerous as a terrorist. There's nothing to do but let it come.

So. What do you think? Are you convinced now I'm as crazy as a tulip or a taxi? As vagrant as a cloud?

Sometimes the sky is so big and I feel so little at night. That's the problem with being cloud. The sky is so terribly big. Why is it worse at night, when I have such an urge to communicate and no language with which to form the words? Only colors. Pictures. And you know what I have to say isn't always pleasant.

Oh, love, there, I've gone and done it. What good is it? Good or bad, I've   80 done what I had to do and needed to. And you've answered the phone, and startled me away like a bird. And now you're probably swearing under your breath and going back to sleep, with that wife beside you, warm, radiating her own heat, alive under the flannel and down and smelling a bit like milk and hand cream, and that smell familiar and dear to you, oh.

Human beings pass me on the street, and I want to reach out and strum them as if they were guitars. Sometimes all humanity strikes me as lovely. I just want to reach out and stroke someone, and say There, there, it's all right, honey. There, there, there.

Stanley Elkin (1930–1995)

Stanley Elkin has been a force in American fiction for many years. His short stories were collected in Criers and Kibitzers, Kibitzers and Criers *(1965), and he won the National Book Critics Circle Award for fiction in 1983 for his novel* George Mills. *Among his numerous books is the comic novel* The Magic Kingdom *(1985), an allusion to Disney World. His most recent novel,* The MacGuffin *(1991), was a finalist for the National Book Award. Its title comes from Alfred Hitchcock's name for the concept or central gimmick around which he structured his films. A MacGuffin is a device such as Norman Bates impersonating his mother in* Psycho. *Elkin teaches at Washington University in St. Louis and is a member of the American Academy of Arts and Letters.*

A POETICS FOR BULLIES   1959

I'm Push the bully, and what I hate are new kids and sissies, dumb kids and smart, rich kids, poor kids, kids who wear glasses, talk funny, show off, patrol boys and wise guys and kids who pass pencils and water the plants—and cripples, *especially* cripples. I love nobody loved.

One time I was pushing this red-haired kid (I'm a pusher, no hitter, no belter; an aggressor of marginal violence, I hate *real* force) and his mother stuck her head out the window and shouted something I've never forgotten. "*Push,*" she yelled. "*You, Push.* You pick on him because you wish you had his red hair!" It's true; I *did* wish I had his red hair. I wish I were tall, or fat, or thin. I wish I had different eyes, different hands, a mother in the supermarket. I wish I were a man, a small boy, a girl in the choir. I'm a coveter, a Boston Blackie° of the heart, casing the world. Endlessly I covet and case. (Do you know what makes me cry? The Declaration of Independence. "All men are created equal." That's beautiful.)

If you're a bully like me, you use your head. Toughness isn't enough. You beat them up, they report you. Then where are you? I'm not even particularly strong. (I used to be strong. I used to do exercise, work out, but strength implicates you, and often isn't an advantage anyway—read the judo ads. Besides, your big bullies aren't bullies at all—they're *athletes.* With them, beating guys up is a sport.) But what I lose in size and strength I make up in courage. I'm very brave. That's a lie about bullies being cowards underneath. If you're a coward, get out of the business.

I'm best at torment.

A kid has a toy bow, toy arrows. "Let Push look," I tell him.

He's suspicious, he knows me. "Go way, Push," he says, this mama-warned Push doubter.

"Come on," I say, "come on."   5

Boston Blackie: Hard-boiled detective from the 1930s in film and on raido.

"No, Push. I can't. My mother said I can't."

I raise my arms, I spread them. I'm a bird—slow, powerful, easy, free. I move my head offering profile like something beaked. I'm the Thunderbird. "In the school where I go I have a teacher who teaches me magic," I say. "Arnold Salamancy, give Push your arrows. Give him one, he gives back two. Push is the God of the Neighborhood."

"Go way, Push," the kid says, uncertain. 10

"Right," Push says, himself again. "Right. I'll disappear. First the fingers." My fingers ball to fists. "My forearms next." They jackknife into my upper arms. "The arms." Quick as bird-blink they snap behind my back, fit between the shoulder blades like a small knapsack. (I am double-jointed, protean.) "My head," I say.

"No, Push," the kid says, terrified. I shudder and everything comes back, falls into place from the stem of self like a shaken puppet.

"The arrow, the arrow. Two where was one." He hands me an arrow.

"*Trouble, trouble, double rubble!*" I snap it and give back the pieces.

Well, sure. There *is* no magic. If there were I would learn it. I would find out the words, the slow turns and strange passes, drain the bloods and get the herbs, do the fires like a vestal. I would look for the main chants. *Then* I'd change things. *Push* would!

But there's only casuistical trick. Sleight-of-mouth, the bully's poetics. 15

You know the formulas:

"Did you ever see a match burn twice?" you ask. Strike. Extinguish. Jab his flesh with the hot stub.

"Play 'Gestapo'?"

"How do you play?"

"What's your name?" 20

"It's Morton."

I slap him. "You're lying."

"Adam and Eve and Pinch Me Hard went down to the lake for a swim. Adam and Eve fell in. Who was left?"

"Pinch Me Hard."

I do. 25

Physical puns, conundrums. Push the punisher, the conundrummer!

But there has to be more than tricks in a bag of tricks.

I don't know what it is. Sometimes I think *I'm* the only new kid. In a room, the school, the playground, the neighborhood, I get the feeling I've just moved in, no one knows me. You know what I like? To stand in crowds. To wait with them at the airport to meet a plane. Someone asks what time it is. I'm the first to answer. Or at the ball park when the vendor comes. He passes the hot dog down the long row. I want *my* hands on it, too. On the dollar going up, the change coming down.

I am ingenious, I am patient.

A kid is going downtown on the elevated train. He's got his little suit on, 30 his shoes are shined, he wears a cap. This is a kid going to the travel bureaus, the foreign tourist offices to get brochures, maps, pictures of the mountains for a unit at his school—a kid looking for extra credit. I follow him. He comes out of the Italian Tourist Information Center. His arms are full. I move from my place at the window. I follow for two blocks and bump into him as he steps from a curb.

It's a *collision*—The pamphlets fall from his arms. Pretending confusion, I walk on his paper Florence. I grind my heel in his Riviera. I climb Vesuvius and sack his Rome and dance on the Isle of Capri.

The Industrial Museum is a good place to find children. I cut somebody's five- or six-year-old kid brother out of the herd of eleven- and twelve-year-olds he's come with. "*Quick*," I say. I pull him along the corridors, up the stairs, through the halls, down to a mezzanine landing. Breathless, I pause for a minute. "I've got some gum. Do you want a stick?" He nods; I stick him. I rush him into an auditorium and abandon him. He'll be lost for hours.

I sidle up to a kid at the movies. "You smacked my brother," I tell him. "After the show—I'll be outside."

I break up games. I hold the ball above my head. "You want it? Take it."

I go into barber shops. There's a kid waiting. "I'm next," I tell him, "understand?"

One day Eugene Kraft rang my bell. Eugene is afraid of me, so he helps me. 35
He's fifteen and there's something wrong with his saliva glands and he drools. His chin is always chapped. I tell him he has to drink a lot because he loses so much water.

"Push? Push," he says. He's wiping his chin with his tissues. "Push, there's this kid—"

"Better get a glass of water, Eugene."

"No, Push, no fooling, there's this new kid—he just moved in. You've got to see this kid."

"Eugene, get some water, please. You're drying up. I've never seen you so bad. There are deserts in you, Eugene."

"All right, Push, but then you've got to see—" 40

"Swallow, Eugene. You better swallow."

He gulps hard.

"Push, this is a kid and a half. Wait, you'll see."

"I'm very concerned about you, Eugene. You're dying of thirst, Eugene. Come into the kitchen with me."

I push him through the door. He's very excited. I've never seen him so ex- 45
cited. He talks at me over his shoulder, his mouth flooding, his teeth like the lit-
tle stone pebbles at the bottom of a fishbowl. "He's got this sport coat, with a patch over the heart. Like a king, Push. No kidding."

"Be careful of the carpet, Eugene."

I turn on the taps in the sink. I mix in hot water. "Use your tissues, Eugene. Wipe your chin."

He wipes himself and puts the Kleenex in his pocket. All of Eugene's pockets bulge. He looks, with his bulging pockets, like a clumsy smuggler.

"Wipe, Eugene. Swallow, you're drowning."

"He's got this funny accent—you could die." Excited, he tamps at his mouth 50
like a diner, a tubercular.

"Drink some water, Eugene."

"No, Push. I'm not thirsty—really."

"Don't be foolish, kid. That's because your mouth's so wet. Inside where it counts you're drying up. It stands to reason. Drink some water."

"He has this crazy haircut."

"*Drink*," I command. I shake him. "*Drink!*" 55

"Push, I've got no glass. Give me a glass at least."

"I can't do that, Eugene. You've got a terrible sickness. How could I let you use our drinking glasses? Lean under the tap and open your mouth."

He knows he'll have to do it, that I won't listen to him until he does. He bends into the sink.

"Push, it's hot," he complains. The water splashes into his nose, it gets on his glasses and for a moment his eyes are magnified, enormous. He pulls away and scrapes his forehead on the faucet.

"Eugene, you touched it. Watch out, please. You're too close to the tap.   60
Lean your head deeper into the sink."

"It's *hot*, Push."

"Warm water evaporates better. With your affliction you've got to evaporate fluids before they get into your glands."

He feeds again from the tap.

"Do you think that's enough?" I ask after a while.

"I do, Push, I really do," he says. He is breathless.   65

"Eugene," I say seriously, "I think you'd better get yourself a canteen."

"A canteen, Push?"

"That's right. Then you'll always have water when you need it. Get one of those Boy Scout models. The two-quart kind with a canvas strap."

"But you hate the Boy Scouts, Push."

"They make very good canteens, Eugene. *And wear it*! I never want to see   70
you without it. Buy it today."

"All right, Push."

"Promise!"

"All right, Push."

"Say it out."

He made the formal promise that I like to hear.   75

"Well, then," I said, "let's go see this new kid of yours."

He took me to the schoolyard. "Wait," he said, "you'll see." He skipped ahead.

"Eugene," I said, calling him back. "Let's understand something. No matter what this new kid is like, nothing changes as far as you and I are concerned."

"Aw, Push," he said.

"Nothing, Eugene. I mean it. You don't get out from under me."   80

"Sure, Push, I know that."

There were some kids in the far corner of the yard, sitting on the ground, leaning up against the wire fence. Bats and gloves and balls lay scattered around them. (It was where they told dirty jokes. Sometimes I'd come by during the little kids' recess and tell them all about what their daddies do to their mommies.)

"There. See? Do you see him?" Eugene, despite himself, seemed hoarse.

"Be quiet," I said, checking him, freezing as a hunter might. I stared.

He was a *prince*, I tell you.   85

He was tall, tall, even sitting down. His long legs comfortable in expensive wool, the trousers of a boy who had been on ships, jets; who owned a horse, perhaps; who knew Latin—what *didn't* he know?—somebody made up, like a kid in a play with a beautiful mother and a handsome father; who took his breakfast from a sideboard, and picked, even at fourteen and fifteen and sixteen, his mail from a silver plate. He would have hobbies—stamps, stars, things lovely dead. He wore a sport coat, brown as wood, thick as heavy bark. The buttons were leather buds. His shoes seemed carved from horses' saddles, gunstocks. His clothes had once grown in nature. *What it must feel like inside those clothes*, I thought.

I looked at his face, his clear skin, and guessed at the bones, white as bleached wood. His eyes had skies in them. His yellow hair swirled on his head like a crayoned sun.

"Look, look at him," Eugene said. "The sissy. Get him, Push."

He was talking to them and I moved closer to hear his voice. It was clear, beautiful, but faintly foreign—like herb-seasoned meat.

When he saw me he paused, smiling. He waved. The others didn't look at   90
me.

"Hello there," he called. "Come over if you'd like. I've been telling the boys about tigers."

"Tigers," I said.

"Give him the 'match burn twice,' Push," Eugene whispered.

"Tigers, is it?" I said. "What do you know about tigers?" My voice was high.
"*The 'match burn twice,' Push.*"   95

"Not so much as a Master *Tugjah*. I was telling the boys. In India there are men of high caste—*Tugjahs*, they're called. I was apprenticed to one once in the Southern Plains and might perhaps have earned my mastership, but the Red Chinese attacked the northern frontier and . . . well, let's just say I had to leave. At any rate, these *Tugjahs* are as intimate with the tiger as you are with dogs. I don't mean they keep them as pets. The relationship goes deeper. Your dog is a service animal, as is your elephant."

"Did you ever see a match burn twice?" I asked suddenly.

"Why no, can you do that? Is it a special match you use?"

"No," Eugene said, "it's an ordinary match. He uses an ordinary match."

"Can you do it with one of mine, do you think?"   100

He took a matchbook from his pocket and handed it to me. The cover was exactly the material of his jacket, and in the center was a patch with a coat-of-arms identical to the one he wore over his heart.

I held the matchbook for a moment and then gave it back to him. "I don't feel like it," I said.

"Then some other time, perhaps," he said.

Eugene whispered to me. "His accent, Push, his funny *accent*."

"Some other time, perhaps," I said. I am a good mimic. I can duplicate a   105
particular kid's lisp, his stutter, a thickness in his throat. There were two or three here whom I had brought close to tears by holding up my mirror to their voices. I can parody their limps, their waddles, their girlish runs, their clumsy jumps. I can throw as they throw, catch as they catch. I looked around. "Some other time, perhaps," I said again. No one would look at me.

"I'm *so* sorry," the new one said, "we don't know each other's names. You are?"

"I'm so sorry," I said. "You are?"

He seemed puzzled. Then he looked sad, disappointed. No one said anything.

"It don't sound the same," Eugene whispered.

It was true. I sounded nothing like him. I could imitate only defects, only   110
flaws.

A kid giggled.

"Shh," the prince said. He put one finger to his lips.

"Look at that," Eugene said under his breath. "He's a sissy."

He had begun to talk to them again. I squatted, a few feet away. I ran gravel through my loose fists, one bowl in an hourglass feeding another.

He spoke of jungles, of deserts. He told of ancient trade routes traveled by strange beasts. He described lost cities and a lake deeper than the deepest level of the sea. There was a story about a boy who had been captured by bandits. A woman in the story—it wasn't clear whether she was the boy's mother—had been tortured. His eyes clouded for a moment when he came to this part and he had to pause before continuing. Then he told how the boy escaped—it was cleverly done—and found help, mountain tribesmen riding elephants. The elephants charged the cave in which the mo—the *woman*—was still a prisoner. It might have collapsed and killed her, but one old bull rushed in and, shielding her with his body, took the weight of the crashing rocks. Your elephant is a service animal.

I let a piece of gravel rest on my thumb and flicked it in a high arc above his head. Some of the others who had seen me stared, but the boy kept on talking. Gradually I reduced the range, allowing the chunks of gravel to come closer to his head.

"You see?" Eugene said quietly. "He's afraid. He pretends not to notice."

The arcs continued to diminish. The gravel went faster, straighter. No one was listening to him now, but he kept talking.

"—of magic," he said, "what occidentals call 'a witch doctor.' There are spices that induce these effects. The *Bogdovii* was actually able to stimulate the growth of rocks with the powder. The Dutch traders were ready to go to war for the formula. Well, you can see what it could mean for the Low Countries. Without accessible quarries they've never been able to construct a permanent system of dikes. But with the *Bogdovii's* powder"—he reached out and casually caught the speeding chip as if it had been a ping-pong ball—"they could turn a grain of sand into a pebble, use the pebbles to grow stones, the stones to grow rocks. This little piece of gravel, for example, could be changed into a mountain." He dipped his thumb into his palm as I had and balanced the gravel on his nail. He flicked it; it rose from his nail like a missile and climbed an impossible arc. It disappeared. "The *Bogdovii* never revealed how it was done."

I stood up. Eugene tried to follow me.

"Listen," he said, "you'll get him."

"Swallow," I told him. "Swallow, you pig!"

I have lived my life in pursuit of the vulnerable: Push the chink seeker, wheeler dealer in the flawed cement of the personality, a collapse maker. But what isn't vulnerable, *who* isn't? There is that which is unspeakable, so I speak it, that which is unthinkable, which I think. Me and the devil, we do God's dirty work, after all.

I went home after I left him. I turned once at the gate, and the boys were around him still. The useless Eugene had moved closer. *He* made room for him against the fence.

I ran into Frank the fat boy. He made a move to cross the street, but I had seen him and he went through a clumsy retractive motion. I could tell he thought I would get him for that, but I moved by, indifferent to a grossness in which I had once delighted. As I passed he seemed puzzled, a little hurt, a little—this was astonishing—guilty. *Sure* guilty. Why *not* guilty? The forgiven tire of their exemption. Nothing could ever be forgiven, and I forgave nothing. I held them to the mark. Who else cared about the fatties, about the dummies and slobs and clowns, about the gimps and squares and oafs and fools, the kids with a mouthful of mush, all those shut-ins of the mind and heart, all those losers? Frank the fat boy knew, and passed me shyly. His wide, fat body, stiffened, forced jokishly martial when he saw me, had already become flaccid as he moved by, had already made one more forgiven surrender. Who cared?

The streets were full of failure. Let them. Let them be. There was a paragon, a paragon loose. What could he be doing here, why had he come, what did he want? It was impossible that this hero from India and everywhere had made his home here; that he lived, as Frank the fat boy did, as Eugene did, as *I* did, in an apartment; that he shared our lives.

In the afternoon I looked for Eugene. He was in the park, in a tree. There was a book in his lap. He leaned against the thick trunk.

"Eugene," I called up to him.

"Push, they're closed. It's Sunday, Push. The stores are closed. I looked for the canteen. The stores are closed."

"Where is he?" 130

"Who, Push? What do you want, Push?"

"*Him*. Your pal. The prince. Where? Tell me, Eugene, or I'll shake you out of that tree. I'll burn you down. I swear it. Where is he?"

"No, Push. I was wrong about that guy. He's nice. He's really nice. Push, he told me about a doctor who could help me. Leave him alone, Push."

"Where, Eugene? *Where?* I count to three."

Eugene shrugged and came down the tree. 135

I found the name Eugene gave me—funny, foreign—over the bell in the outer hall. The buzzer sounded and I pushed open the door. I stood inside and looked up the carpeted stairs, the angled banisters.

"What is it?" She sounded old, worried.

"The new kid," I called, "the new kid."

"It's for you," I heard her say.

"Yes?" His voice, the one I couldn't mimic. I mounted the first stair. I leaned 140 back against the wall and looked up through the high, boxy banister poles. It was like standing inside a pipe organ.

"Yes?"

From where I stood at the bottom of the stairs I could see only a boot. He was wearing boots.

"Yes? What is it, please?"

"*You*," I roared. "Glass of fashion, mold of form, it's me! It's Push the bully!"

I heard his soft, rapid footsteps coming down the stairs—a springy, spongy 145 urgency. He jingled, the bastard. He had coins—I could see them: rough, golden, imperfectly round; raised, massively gowned goddesses, their heads fingered smooth, their arms gone—and keys to strange boxes, thick doors. I saw his boots. I backed away.

"I brought you down," I said.

"Be quiet, please. There's a woman who's ill. A boy who must study. There's a man with bad bones. An old man needs sleep."

"He'll get it," I said.

"We'll go outside," he said.

"No. Do you live here? What do you do? Will you be in our school? Were   150
you telling the truth?"

"Shh. Please. You're very excited."

"Tell me your name," I said. It could be my campaign, I thought. His *name*.
Scratched in new sidewalk, chalked onto walls, written on papers dropped in the
street. To leave it behind like so many clues, to give him a fame, to take it away, to
slash and cross out, to erase and to smear—my kid's witchcraft. "Tell me your name."

"It's John," he said softly.

"What?"

"It's John."   155

"John what? Come on now. I'm Push the bully."

"John Williams," he said.

"John Williams? John Williams? Only that? Only John Williams?"

He smiled.

"Who's that on the bell? The name on the box?"   160

"She needs me," he said.

"Cut it out."

"I help her," he said.

"You stop that."

"There's a man that's in pain. A woman who's old. A husband that's wor-   165
ried. A wife that despairs."

"You're the bully," I said. "Your John Williams is a service animal," I yelled
in the hall.

He turned and began to climb the stairs. His calves bloomed in their leather
sheathing.

"*Lover*," I whispered to him.

He turned to me at the landing. He shook his head sadly.

"We'll see," I said.   170

"We'll see what we'll see," he said.

That night I painted his name on the side of the gymnasium in enormous
letters. In the morning it was still there, but it wasn't what I meant. There was
nothing incantatory in the huge letters, no scream, no curse. I had never traveled
with a gang, there had been no togetherness in my tearing, but this thing on the
wall seemed the act of vandals, the low production of ruffians. When you looked
at it you were surprised they had gotten the spelling right.

Astonishingly, it was allowed to remain. And each day there was something
more celebrational in the giant name, something of increased hospitality, lavish
welcome. John Williams might have been a football hero, or someone back from
the kidnapers. Finally I had to take it off myself.

Something had changed.

Eugene was not wearing his canteen. Boys didn't break off their conversa-   175
tions when I came up to them. One afternoon a girl winked at me. (Push has
never picked on girls. *Their* submissiveness is part of their nature. They are ornamental. Don't get me wrong, please. There is a way in which they function as part
of the landscape, like flowers at a funeral. They have a strange cheerfulness. They
are the organizers of pep rallies and dances. They put out the Year Book. They
are *born* Gray Ladies. I can't bully them.)

John Williams was in the school, but except for brief glimpses in the hall I never saw him. Teachers would repeat the things he had said in their other classes. They read from his papers. In the gym the coach described plays he had made, set shots he had taken. Everyone talked about him, and girls made a reference to him a sort of love signal. If it was suggested that he had smiled at one of them, the girl referred to would blush or, what was worse, look aloofly mysterious. (*Then* I could have punished her, *then* I could.) Gradually his name began to appear on all their notebooks, in the margins of their texts. (It annoyed me to remember what *I* had done on the wall.) The big canvas books, with their careful, elaborate J's and W's, took on the appearance of ancient, illuminated fables. It was the un-conscious embroidery of love, hope's bright doodle. Even the administration was aware of him. In Assembly the principal announced that John Williams had bro-ken all existing records in the school's charity drives. She had never seen good citizenship like his before, she said.

It's one thing to live with a bully, another to live with a hero.

Everyone's hatred I understand, no one's love; everyone's grievance, no one's content.

I saw Mimmer. Mimmer should have graduated years ago. I saw Mimmer the dummy.

"Mimmer," I said, "you're in his class." 180

"He's very smart."

"Yes, but is it fair? You work harder. I've seen you study. You spend hours. Nothing comes. He was born knowing. You could have used just a little of what he's got so much of. It's not fair."

"He's very clever. It's wonderful," Mimmer says.

Slud is crippled. He wears a shoe with a built-up heel to balance himself.

"Ah, Slud," I say, "I've seen him run." 185

"He has beaten the horses in the park. It's very beautiful," Slud says.

"He's handsome, isn't he, Clob?" Clob looks contagious, radioactive. He has severe acne. He is ugly *under* his acne.

"He gets the girls." Clob says.

He gets *everything*, I think. But I'm alone in my envy, awash in my lust. It's as if I were a prophet to the deaf. Schnooks, schnooks, I want to scream, dopes and settlers. What good does his smile do you, of what use is his good heart?

The other day I did something stupid. I went to the cafeteria and shoved a 190 boy out of the way and took his place in line. It was foolish, but their fear is al-most all gone and I felt I had to show the flag. The boy only grinned and let me pass. Then someone called my name. It was *him*. I turned to face him. "Push," he said, "you forgot your silver." He handed it to a girl in front of him and she gave it to the boy in front of her and it came to me down the long line.

I plot, I scheme. Snares, I think; tricks and traps. I remember the old days when there were ways to snap fingers, crush toes, ways to pull noses, twist heads and punch arms—the old-timey Flinch Law I used to impose, the gone bully magic of deceit. But nothing works against him, I think. How does he know so much? He is bully-prepared, that one, not to be trusted.

It is worse and worse.

In the cafeteria he eats with Frank. "You don't want those potatoes," he tells him. "Not the ice cream, Frank. One sandwich, remember. You lost three pounds last week." The fat boy smiles his fat love at him. John Williams puts his arm around him. He seems to squeeze him thin.

He's helping Mimmer to study. He goes over his lessons and teaches him tricks, short cuts. "I want you up there with me on the Honor Roll, Mimmer."

I see him with Slud the cripple. They go to the gym. I watch from the bal- 195 cony. "Let's develop those arms, my friend." They work out with weights. Slud's muscles grow, they bloom from his bones.

I lean over the rail. I shout down, "He can bend iron bars. Can he peddle a bike? Can he walk on rough ground? Can he climb up a hill? Can he wait on a line? Can he dance with a girl? Can he go up a ladder or jump from a chair?"

Beneath me the rapt Slud sits on a bench and raises a weight. He holds it at arm's length, level with his chest. He moves it high, higher. It rises above his shoulders, his throat, his head. He bends back his neck to see what he's done. If the weight should fall now it would crush his throat. I stare down into his smile.

I see Eugene in the halls. I stop him. "Eugene, what's he done for you?" I ask. He smiles—he never did this—and I see his mouth's flood. "High tide," I say with satisfaction.

Williams has introduced Clob to a girl. They have double-dated.

A week ago John Williams came to my house to see me! I wouldn't let him in. 200

"Please open the door, Push. I'd like to chat with you. Will you open the door? Push? I think we ought to talk. I think I can help you to be happier."

I was furious. I didn't know what to say to him. "I don't want to be happier. Go way." It was what little kids used to say to me.

"*Please* let me help you."

"*Please* let me—" I begin to echo. "Please let me alone."

"We ought to be friends, Push." 205

"No deals." I am choking, I am close to tears. What can I do? *What?* I want to kill him.

I double-lock the door and retreat to my room. He is still out there. I have tried to live my life so that I could keep always the lamb from my door.

He has gone too far this time; and I think sadly, I will have to fight him, I will have to fight him. Push pushed. I think sadly of the pain. Push pushed. I will have to fight him. Not to preserve honor but its opposite. Each time I see him I will have to fight him. And then I think—*of course!* and *I* smile. He has done *me* a favor. I know it at once. If he fights me he fails. He fails if he fights me. *Push pushed pushes!* It's physics! Natural law! I know he'll beat me, but I won't prepare, I won't train, I won't use the tricks I know. It's strength against strength, and my strength is as the strength of ten because my jaw is glass! *He doesn't know everything, not everything he doesn't.* And I think, I could go out now, he's still there, I could hit him in the hall, but I think, No, I want them to see, I want *them* to see!

The next day I am very excited. I look for Williams. He's not in the halls. I miss him in the cafeteria. Afterward I look for him in the schoolyard where I first saw him. (He has them organized now. He teaches them games of Tibet, games of Japan; he gets them to play lost sports of the dead.) He does not disappoint me. He is there in the yard, a circle around him, a ring of the loyal.

I join the ring. I shove in between two kids I have known. They try to change 210 places; they murmur and fret.

Williams sees me and waves. His smile could grow flowers. "Boys," he says, "boys, make room for Push. Join hands, boys." They welcome me to the circle. One takes my hand, then another. I give to each calmly.

I wait. *He doesn't know everything.*

"Boys," he begins, "today we're going to learn a game that the knights of the lords and kings of old France used to play in another century. Now you may not realize it, boys, because today when we think of a knight we think, too, of his fine charger, but the fact is that a horse was a rare animal—not a domestic European animal at all, but Asian. In western Europe, for example, there was no such thing as a work horse until the eighth century. Your horse was just too expensive to be put to heavy labor in the fields. (This explains, incidentally, the prevalence of famine in western Europe, whereas famine is unrecorded in Asia until the ninth century, when Euro-Asian horse trading was at its height.) It wasn't only expensive to purchase a horse, it was expensive to keep one. A cheap fodder wasn't developed in Europe until the tenth century. Then, of course, when you consider the terrific risks that the warrior horse of a knight naturally had to run, you begin to appreciate how expensive it would have been for the lord—unless he was extremely rich—to provide all his knights with horses. He'd want to make pretty certain that the knights who got them knew how to handle a horse. (Only your knights errant—an elite, crack corps—ever had horses. We don't realize that most knights were *home* knights; *chevalier chez* they were called.)

"This game, then, was devised to let the lord, or king, see which of his knights had the skill and strength in his hands to control a horse. Without moving your feet, you must try to jerk the one next to you off balance. Each man has two opponents, so it's very difficult. If a man falls, or if his knee touches the ground, he's out. The circle is diminished but must close up again immediately. Now, once for practice only—"

"Just a minute," I interrupt.   215

"Yes, Push?"

I leave the circle and walk forward and hit him as hard as I can in the face.

He stumbles backward. The boys groan. He recovers. He rubs his jaw and smiles. I think he is going to let me hit him again. I am prepared for this. He knows what I'm up to and will use his passivity. Either way I win, but I am determined he shall hit me. I am ready to kick him, but as my foot comes up he grabs my ankle and turns it forcefully. I spin in the air. He lets go and I fall heavily on my back. I am surprised at how easy it was, but am content if they understand. I get up and am walking away, but there is an arm on my shoulder. He pulls me around roughly. He hits me.

"*Sic semper tyrannus,*" °he exults.

"Where's your other cheek?" °I ask, falling backward.

"One cheek for tyrants," he shouts. He pounces on me and raises his fist and   220
I cringe. His anger is terrific. I do not want to be hit again.

"You see? You see?" I scream at the kids, but I have lost the train of my former reasoning. I have in no way beaten him. I can't remember now what I had intended.

He lowers his fist and gets off my chest and they cheer. "Hurrah," they yell. "Hurrah, hurrah." The word seems funny to me.

---

†*Sic semper tyrannus:* Thus always for tyrants—implying that tyrants always fail.   *your other cheek*: A reference to Christ's command to be passive in the face of aggression: if hit on one cheek, turn the other to be hit.

He offers his hand when I try to rise. It is so difficult to know what to do. Oh God, it is so difficult to know which gesture is the right one. I don't even know this. He knows everything, and I don't even know this. I am a fool on the ground, one hand behind me pushing up, the other not yet extended but itching in the palm where the need is. It is better to give than receive, surely. It is best not to need at all.

Appalled, guessing what I miss, I rise alone.   225

"Friends?" he asks. He offers to shake.

"Take it, Push." It's Eugene's voice.

"Go ahead, Push." Slud limps forward.

"Push, hatred's so ugly," Clob says, his face shining.

"You'll feel better, Push," Frank, thinner, taller, urges softly.   230

"Push, don't be foolish," Mimmer says.

I shake my head. I may be wrong. I am probably wrong. All I know at last is what feels good. "Nothing doing," I growl. "No deals." I begin to talk, to spray my hatred at them. They are not an easy target even now. "Only your knights errant—your crack corps—ever have horses. Slud may dance and Clob may kiss but they'll never be good at it. *Push is no service animal.* No. *No.* Can you hear that, Williams? There isn't any magic, but your no is still stronger than your yes, and distrust is where I put my faith." I turn to the boys. "What have you settled for? Only your knights errant ever have horses. *What have you settled for?* Will Mimmer do sums in his head? How do you like your lousy hunger, thin boy? Slud, you can break me but you can't catch me. And Clob will never shave without pain, and ugly, let me tell you, is *still* in the eye of the beholder!"°

John Williams mourns for me. He grieves his gamy grief. No one has everything—not even John Williams. He doesn't have *me*. He'll never have me, I think. If my life were only to deny him that, it would almost be enough. I could do his voice now if I wanted. His corruption began when he lost me. "You," I shout, rubbing it in, "*indulger*, dispense me no dispensations. Push the bully hates your heart!"

"Shut him up, somebody," Eugene cries. His saliva spills from his mouth when he speaks.

"Swallow! *Pig, swallow!*"   235

He rushes toward me.

Suddenly I raise my arms and he stops. I feel a power in me. I am Push, Push the bully, God of the Neighborhood, its incarnation of envy and jealousy and need. I vie, strive, emulate, compete, a contender in every event there is. I didn't make myself. I probably can't save myself, but maybe that's the only need I don't have. I taste my lack and that's how I win—by having nothing to lose. It's not good enough! I want and I want and I will die wanting, but first I will have something. This time I will have something. I say it aloud. "This time I will have something." I step toward them. The power makes me dizzy. It is enormous. They feel it. They back away. They crouch in the shadow of my outstretched wings. It isn't deceit this time but the real magic at last, the genuine thing: the cabala of my hate, of my irreconcilableness.

Logic is nothing. Desire is stronger.

---

ugly . . . in the eye of the beholder. A play on "Beauty is in the eye of the beholder."

I move toward Eugene. "*I will have something,*" I roar. 240
"Stand back," he shrieks, "I'll spit in your eye."

"*I will have something.* I will have terror. I will have drought. I bring the dearth. Famine's contagious. Also is thirst. Privation, privation, barrenness, void. I dry up your glands, I poison your well."

He is choking, gasping, chewing furiously. He opens his mouth. It is dry. His throat is parched. There is sand on his tongue.

They moan. They are terrified, but they move up to see. We are thrown together. Slud, Frank, Clob, Mimmer, the others, John Williams, myself. I will not be reconciled, or halve my hate. *It's* what I have, all I can keep. My bully's sour solace. It's enough, I'll make do.

I can't stand them near me. I move against them. I shove them away. I force them off. I press them, thrust them aside. *I push through.*

WINDOW ON

Fiction and the Reader

In the 1920s a major corrective in literary criticism began to call into question the role of the reader's response to a work of literature. Critics began to assert that the excellence of a short story had nothing to do with the degree to which a reader felt uplifted, depressed, anxious, frightened, dubious, cheered, or joyful about it. Excellence was irrelevant to a reader's response. In the 1940s the term "affective fallacy" was coined to explain that it was inappropriate for readers to measure literature by the way it affected them.

Since the late 1970s critics have questioned this pronouncement. Today an entire school of literary criticism bases itself on the responses of readers. The danger of such criticism can be summed up quickly: The responses of emotionally immature readers can be easily manipulated to make them prefer derivative works with an obviously commercial appeal. To make reader response criticism work, readers must be as mature and well informed as possible if judgments of quality in literature are to be reliable. However, reader response critics are often less interested in judgments of quality than in studying the range of responses that a given work can produce.

Those who have read deeply in Faulkner will respond differently to "A Rose for Emily" from those who have never read Faulkner at all. Both responses are valid. However, if readers' responses are to decide the question of whether the story belongs in the canon of "classic" short stories then we would demand that the responses of the most well-informed readers take preference. It is a question of expert opinion. Literary experts have read widely and deeply. Their responses are expert responses. This means that one of the ways in which you learn about fiction is by examining your responses. The more you read, the greater the range of response you will have experienced, and thus the more expert you become.

Certain short stories are designed to produce certain responses. Horror stories, for example, depend on your response for their success. The same is true of comic or farcical stories. If a story aims at making you frightened, amused, or even perplexed, then it depends on your response for part of its success. The excellence of the story is often measured by its capacity to produce the effect it obviously aims for. Of course, most fine short stories do not have obvious effects. Instead, the response you give them will be unnameable, complex, and provocative. Such stories provoke both deep thought and deep emotional response. One consequence of accepting the view of the response critic is to see the reader as creating the meaning of the story. "This re-definition of what literature is," says Jane P. Tompkins, "i.e., not an object but an experience, obliterates the traditional separation between reader and text and makes the responses of the reader rather than the contents of the work the focus of critical attention."

For this critical method to work, your obligation as reader is to observe the text carefully so that you respond to it as richly as possible. The methods of examining a text for its details, as described in the introductory material on "Enjoying Short Fiction" and "Elements of Short Fiction," help make your responses useful. Maintaining a response journal outlining first and subsequent readings of the story provides you with a powerful instrument to inform you about the range and depth of your responses.

As a response critic you begin with your own responses, but they will change from first to last reading. You also find that your response will change as you read more and more stories. However, the greatest change in your pattern of response will come as a result of your own interpretations of literature. Interpretation, especially in written form, constitutes a form of self-creation in respect to literature. In other words, it is self-education.

As a response critic, you can learn a great deal about a story by observing your own responses over a period of time. You can also learn to read a story more sensitively by comparing your responses to those of others. The critic Stanley Fish explains that readers form interpretive communities: for instance, readers may form one community that responds similarly to a story, while others may form a completely different community with quite different responses. Examine a story such as Ralph Ellison's "Battle Royal." What distinct communities of interpretation can you identify in your own group of readers? What might account for differences in response?

Certain stories—like horror stories—seem to demand a powerful response. Examine Scott Bradfield's "The Dream of the Wolf" and Edgar Allan Poe's "The Masque of the Red Death." Do these evoke identifiable emotions from you or from others? How do these stories evoke those emotions? Do certain elements of fiction work more effectively than others to provoke your response? You might also ask whether your response at the end of the story is a beginning point for discussion or is it the final goal of the story? Nathaniel Hawthorne's "Rappaccini's Daughter" is a horror story of a kind. Does it evoke horror equally in the readers in your group? Is there a range of agreement concerning which emotions it evokes? Does the success of the story depend on the responses it demands of you?

Responding to literature involves moving through a narrative with specific expectations built on one's knowledge of genre. For example, those familiar with nineteenth-century writers, such as Nathaniel Hawthorne and Edgar Allan Poe, built in specific expectations regarding short stories. Such readers will expect a moral to develop from "Rappaccini's Daughter" and "The Masque of the Red Death." Experienced readers know that most mid-nineteenth-century stories relied on symbolism and emphasized certain aspects of plot, sometimes at the expense of developing character. The circumstance of Dr. Rappaccini's enclosing his daughter in a garden with poisonous herbs is more central to the story than the development of his daughter's response to her condition. In "The Masque of the Red Death," the symbolism carries throughout the story: the Red Death is mortality in any of its forms. Neither the Prince Prospero or any of his court can defy their fate. All the privileges of aristocracy are of no avail in the face of the inevitable. Meanwhile, the isolation of the courtiers implies an inhuman disregard for the majority of people who must face death without hope.

Readers used to traditional fiction, may find later stories, built on different attitudes toward moral principles, such as Anton Chekhov's or Scott Bradfield's to be confusing and unsatisfying. Until the reader becomes acclimated to the demands of minimalist writers such as Raymond Carver, Ann Beattie, or Richard Ford, who avoid making clear moral statements, their stories may seem incomplete.

Response criticism has also given rise to discussion of reader traps. Since fiction writers know your potential reaction to a given situation, sometimes they will trap you into giving a hasty response that you may later regret. Tim O'Brien's "Sweetheart of the Song Tra Bong" traps most readers in the beginning by presenting a heroine "fresh out of Cleveland Heights Senior High" in the middle of Vietnam. The "All-American girl," who wears cut-offs and a bathing suit top, invites social and gender prejudice. The ultimate development of seventeen-year-old Mary Anne Wells surprises everyone in the story, of course, but she especially surprises the reader, whose response can become a key to a carefully interpretation of the story.

Reading

David Bleich. *Subjective Criticism*. Baltimore: Johns Hopkins University Press, 1978.

Stanley Fish. *Is There a Text in This Class?* Cambridge: Harvard University Press, 1980.

Wolfgang Iser. *The Act of Reading*. Baltimore: Johns Hopkins University Press, 1980.

Susan Sulieman and Inge Crosman, eds. *The Reader in the Text*. Princeton University Press Princeton UP, 1980.

Jane Tompkins, ed. *Reader-Response Criticism*. Baltimore: Johns Hopkins University Press, 1980.

Ralph Ellison   (b. 1914)

Ralph Ellison is among the most celebrated and most influential writers in America. He was born in Oklahoma City and studied music for three years at Tuskegee Institute in Alabama. He joined the Federal Writers' Project in New York in the later 1930s. After serving in the Merchant Marine in World War II, he intended to write a war novel but found himself writing Invisible Man *(1952), one of the most widely read novels of mid-century. Its first chapter, the story appearing here, "Battle Royal," was originally published in* Horizon *under the title "Invisible Man." F. H. Langman has said of the novel that it "has suffered some fierce attacks, survived, and seems now to be taking its place as a classic." Ellison is also a distinguished essaysist, with the collection* Shadow and Act *(1964). Both his fiction and his essays concern the experience of African-Americans, depending often on his personal experiences.*

BATTLE ROYAL FROM *INVISIBLE MAN*   1947

It goes a long way back, some twenty years. All my life I had been looking for something, and everywhere I turned someone tried to tell me what it was. I accepted their answers too, though they were often in contradiction and even self-contradictory. I was naive. I was looking for myself and asking everyone except myself questions which I, and only I, could answer. It took me a long time and much painful boomeranging of my expectations to achieve a realization everyone else appears to have been born with: That I am nobody but myself. But first I had to discover that I am an invisible man!

And yet I am no freak of nature, nor of history. I was in the cards, other things having been equal (or unequal) eighty-five years ago. I am not ashamed of my grandparents for having been slaves. I am only ashamed of myself for having at one time been ashamed. About eighty-five years ago they were told that they were free, united with others of our country in everything pertaining to the common good, and, in everything social, separate like the fingers of the hand. And they believed it. They exulted in it. They stayed in their place, worked hard, and brought up my father to do the same. But my grandfather is the one. He was an odd old guy, my grandfather, and I am told I take after him. It was he who caused the trouble. On his deathbed he called my father to him and said, "Son, after I'm gone I want you to keep up the good fight. I never told you, but our life is a war and I have been a traitor all my born days, a spy in the enemy's country ever since I give up my gun back in the Reconstruction. Live with your head in the lion's mouth. I want you to overcome 'em with yeses, undermine 'em with grins, agree 'em to death and destruction, let 'em swoller you till they vomit or bust wide open." They thought the old man had gone out of his mind. He had been the meekest of men. The younger children were rushed from the room, the shades drawn and the flame of the lamp turned so low that it sputtered on the wick like the old man's breathing. "Learn it to the younguns," he whispered fiercely; then he died.

But my folks were more alarmed over his last words than over his dying. It was as though he had not died at all, his words caused so much anxiety. I was warned emphatically to forget what he had said and, indeed, this is the first time it has been mentioned outside the family circle. It had a tremendous effect upon me, however, I could never be sure of what he meant. Grandfather had been a quiet old man who never made any trouble, yet on his deathbed he had called himself a traitor and a spy, and he had spoken of his meekness as a dangerous activity. It became a constant puzzle which lay unanswered in the back of my mind. And whenever things went well for me I remembered my grandfather and felt guilty and uncomfortable. It was as though I was carrying out his advice in spite of myself. And to make it worse, everyone loved me for it. I was praised by the most lily-white men of the town. I was considered an example of desirable conduct—just as my grandfather had been. And what puzzled me was that the old man had defined it as *treachery*. When I was praised for my conduct I felt a guilt that in some way I was doing something that was really against the wishes of the white folks, that if they had understood they would have desired me to act just the opposite, that I should have been sulky and mean, and that that really would have been what they wanted, even though they were fooled and thought they wanted me to act as I did. It made me afraid that some day they would look upon me as a traitor and I would be lost. Still I was more afraid to act any other way because they didn't like that at all. The old man's words were like a curse. On my graduation day I delivered an oration in which I showed that humility was the secret, indeed, the very essence of progress. (Not that I believed this— how could I, remembering my grandfather?—I only believed that it worked.) It was a great success. Everyone praised me and I was invited to give the speech at a gathering of the town's leading white citizens. It was a triumph for our whole community.

It was in the main ballroom of the leading hotel. When I got there I discovered that it was on the occasion of a smoker, and I was told that since I was to be there anyway I might as well take part in the battle royal to be fought by some of my schoolmates as part of the entertainment. The battle royal came first.

All of the town's big shots were there in their tuxedoes, wolfing down the buffet foods, drinking beer and whiskey and smoking black cigars. It was a large room with a high ceiling. Chairs were arranged in neat rows around three sides of a portable boxing ring. The fourth side was clear, revealing a gleaming space of polished floor. I had some misgivings over the battle royal, by the way. Not from a distaste for fighting, but because I didn't care too much for the other fellows who were to take part. They were tough guys who seemed to have no grandfather's curse worrying their minds. No one could mistake their toughness. And besides, I suspected that fighting a battle royal might detract from the dignity of my speech. In those pre-invisible days I visualized myself as a potential Booker T. Washington.[1] But the other fellows didn't care too much for me either, and there were nine of them. I felt superior to them in my way, and I didn't like the manner in which we were all crowded together into the servants' elevator. Nor did they like my being there. In fact, as the warmly lighted floors flashed past the elevator we had words over the fact that I, by taking part in the fight, had knocked one of their friends out of a night's work.

We were led out of the elevator through a rococo hall into an anteroom and told to get into our fighting togs. Each of us was issued a pair of boxing gloves and ushered out into the big mirrored hall, which we entered looking cautiously about us and whispering, lest we might accidentally be heard above the noise of the room. It was foggy with cigar smoke. And already the whiskey was taking effect. I was shocked to see some of the most important men of the town quite tipsy. They were all there—bankers, lawyers, judges, doctors, fire chiefs, teachers, merchants. Even one of the more fashionable pastors. Something we could not see was going on up front. A clarinet was vibrating sensuously and the men were standing up and moving eagerly forward. We were a small tight group, clustered together, our bare upper bodies touching and shining with anticipatory sweat; while up front the big shots were becoming increasingly excited over something we still could not see. Suddenly I heard the school superintendent, who had told me to come, yell, "Bring up the shines, gentlemen! Bring up the little shines!"

We were rushed up to the front of the ballroom, where it smelled even more strongly of tobacco and whiskey. Then we were pushed into place. I almost wet my pants. A sea of faces, some hostile, some amused, ringed

5

---

[1]Negro educator (1856–1915), author of *Up from Slavery* (1901).

around us, and in the center, facing us, stood a magnificent blonde—stark naked. There was dead silence. I felt a blast of cold air chill me. I tried to back away, but they were behind me and around me. Some of the boys stood with lowered heads, trembling. I felt a wave of irrational guilt and fear. My teeth chattered, my skin turned to goose flesh, my knees knocked. Yet I was strongly attracted and looked in spite of myself. Had the price of looking been blindness, I would have looked. The hair was yellow like that of a circus kewpie doll, the face heavily powdered and rouged, as though to form an abstract mask, the eyes hollow and smeared a cool blue, the color of a baboon's butt. I felt a desire to spit upon her as my eyes brushed slowly over her body. Her breasts were firm and round as the domes of East Indian temples, and I stood so close as to see the fine skin texture and beads of pearly perspiration glistening like dew around the pink and erected buds of her nipples. I wanted at one and the same time to run from the room, to sink through the floor, or go to her and cover her from my eyes and the eyes of the others with my body; to feel the soft thighs, to caress her and destroy her, to love her and murder her, to hide from her, and yet to stroke where below the small American flag tattooed upon her belly her thighs formed a capital V. I had a notion that of all in the room she saw only me with her impersonal eyes.

And then she began to dance, a slow sensuous movement; the smoke of a hundred cigars clinging to her like the thinnest of veils. She seemed like a fair bird-girl girdled in veils calling to me from the angry surface of some gray and threatening sea. I was transported. Then I became aware of the clarinet playing and the bit shots yelling at us. Some threatened us if we looked and others if we did not. On my right I saw one boy faint. And now a man grabbed a silver pitcher from a table and stepped close as he dashed ice water upon him and stood him up and forced two of us to support him as his head hung and moans issued from his thick bluish lips. Another boy began to plead to go home. He was the largest of the group, wearing dark red fighting trunks much too small to conceal the erection which projected from him as though in answer to the insinuating low-registered moaning of the clarinet. He tried to hide himself with his boxing gloves.

And all the while the blonde continued dancing, smiling faintly at the big shots who watched her with fascination, and faintly smiling at our fear. I noticed a certain merchant who followed her hungrily, his lips loose and drooling. He was a large man who wore diamond studs in a shirtfront which swelled with the ample paunch underneath, and each time the blonde swayed her undulating hips he ran his hand through the thin hair of his bald head and, with his arms upheld, his posture clumsy like that of an intoxicated panda, wound his belly in a slow and obscene grind. This creature was completely hypnotized. The music had quickened. As the dancer flung herself about with a detached expression on her face, the men began reaching out to touch her. I could see their beefy fingers sink into the soft flesh. Some of the others tried to stop them and she began to move around the floor in graceful circles, as they gave chase, slipping and sliding over the polished floor. It was mad. Chairs went crashing, drinks were spilt, as they ran laughing and howling after her. They caught her just as she reached a door, raised her from the floor, and tossed her as college boys are tossed at a hazing, and above her red, fixed-smiling lips I saw the terror and disgust in her eyes, almost like my own terror and that which I saw in some of the other boys. As I watched, they tossed her twice and her soft breasts seemed to flatten against the air and her legs flung wildly as she spun. Some of the sober ones helped her to escape. And I started off the floor, heading for the anteroom with the rest of the boys.

Some were still crying and in hysteria. But as we tried to leave we were stopped and ordered to get into the ring. There was nothing to do but what we were told. All ten of us climbed under the ropes and allowed ourselves to be blindfolded with broad bands of white cloth. One of the men seemed to feel a bit sympathetic and tried to cheer us up as we stood with our backs against the ropes. Some of us tried to grin. "See that boy over there?" one of the men said. "I want you to run across at the bell and give it to him right in the belly. If you don't get him, I'm going to get you. I don't like his looks." Each of us was told the same. The blindfolds were put on. Yet even then I had been going over my speech. In my mind each word was as bright as flame. I felt the cloth pressed into place, and frowned so that it would be loosened when I relaxed.   10

But now I felt a sudden fit of blind terror. I was unused to darkness. It was as though I had suddenly found myself in a dark room filled with poisonous cottonmouths. I could hear the bleary voices yelling insistently for the battle royal to begin.

"Get going in there!"

"Let me at that big nigger!"

I strained to pick up the school superintendent's voice, as though to squeeze some security out of that slightly more familiar sound.

"Let me at those black sonsabitches!" someone yelled.   15

"No, Jackson, no!" another voice yelled. "Here, somebody, help me hold Jack."

"I want to get at that ginger-colored nigger. Tear him limb from limb," the first voice yelled.

I stood against the ropes trembling. For in those days I was what they called ginger-colored, and he sounded as though he might crunch me between his teeth like a crisp ginger cookie.

Quite a struggle was going on. Chairs were being kicked about and I could hear voices grunting as with a terrific effort. I wanted to see, to see more desperately than ever before. But the blindfold was tight as a thick skin-puckering scab and when I raised my gloved hands to push the layers of white aside a voice yelled, "Oh, no you don't, black bastard! Leave that alone!"

"Ring the bell before Jackson kills him a coon!" someone boomed in the   20 sudden silence. And I heard the bell clang and the sound of the feet scuffling forward.

A glove smacked against my head. I pivoted, striking out stiffly as someone went past, and felt the jar ripple along the length of my arm to my shoulder. Then it seemed as though all nine boys had turned upon me at once. Blows pounded me from all sides while I struck out as best I could. So many blows landed upon me that I wondered if I were not the only blindfolded fighter in the ring, or if the man called Jackson hadn't succeeded in getting me after all.

Blindfolded, I could no longer control my motions. I had no dignity. I stumbled about like a baby or a drunken man. The smoke had become thicker and with each new blow it seemed to sear and further restrict my lungs. My saliva became like hot bitter glue. A glove connected with my head, filling my mouth with warm blood. It was everywhere. I could not tell if the moisture I felt upon my body was sweat or blood. A blow landed hard against the nape of my neck. I felt myself going over, my head hitting the floor. Streaks of blue light filled the black world behind the blindfold. I lay prone, pretending that I was knocked out, but felt myself seized by hands and yanked to my feet. "Get going, black boy! Mix it up!" My arms were like lead, my head smarting from blows. I managed to feel my way to the ropes and held on, trying to catch my breath. A glove landed in my mid-section and I went over again, feeling as though the smoke had become a knife jabbed into my guts. Pushed this way and that by the legs milling around me, I finally pulled erect and discovered that I could see the black, sweat-washed forms weaving in the smoky-blue atmosphere like drunken dancers weaving to the rapid drum-like thuds of blows.

Everyone fought hysterically. It was complete anarchy. Everybody fought everybody else. No group fought together for long. Two, three, four, fought one, then turned to fight each other, were themselves attacked. Blows landed below the belt and in the kidney, with the gloves open as well as closed, and with my eye partly opened now there was not so much terror. I moved carefully, avoiding blows, although not too many to attract attention, fighting from group to group. The boys groped about like blind, cautious crabs crouching to protect their mid-sections, their heads pulled in short against their shoulders, their arms stretched nervously before them, with their fists testing the smoke-filled air like the knobbed feelers of hypersensitive snails. In one corner I glimpsed a boy violently punching the air and heard him scream in pain as he smashed his hand against a ring post. For a second I saw him bent over holding his hand, then going down as a blow caught his unprotected head. I played one group against the other, slipping in and throwing a punch then stepping out of range while pushing the others into the melee to take the blows blindly aimed at me. The smoke was agonizing and there were no rounds, no bells at three minute intervals to relieve our exhaustion. The room spun round me, a swirl of lights, smoke, sweating bodies sourrounded by tense white faces. I bled from both nose and mouth, the blood spattering upon my chest.

The men kept yelling, "Slug him, black boy! Knock his guts out!"
"Uppercut him! Kill him! Kill that big boy!"   25

Taking a fake fall, I saw a boy going down heavily beside me as though we were felled by a single blow, saw a sneaker-clad foot shot into his groin as the two who had knocked him down stumbled upon him. I rolled out of range, feeling a twinge of nausea.

The harder we fought the more threatening the men became. And yet, I had begun to worry about my speech again. How would it go? Would they recognize my ability? What would they give me?

I was fighting automatically when suddenly I noticed that one after another of the boys was leaving the ring. I was surprised, filled with panic, as though I had been left alone with an unknown danger. Then I understood. The boys had arranged it among themselves. It was the custom for the two men left in the ring to slug it out for the winner's prize. I discovered this too late. When the bell sounded two men in tuxedoes leaped into the ring and removed the blindfold. I found myself facing Tatlock, the biggest of the gang. I felt sick at my stomach. Hardly had the bell stopped ringing in my ears than it clanged again and I saw him moving swiftly toward me. Thinking of nothing else to do I hit him smash on the nose. He kept coming, bringing the rank sharp violence of stale sweat. His face was a black blank of a face, only his eyes alive—with hate of me and aglow with a feverish terror from what had happened to us all. I became anxious. I wanted to deliver my speech and he came at me as though he meant to beat it out of me. I smashed him again and again, taking his blows as they came. Then on a sudden impulse I struck him lightly and as we clinched, I whispered, "Fake like I knocked you out, you can have the prize."

"I'll break your behind," he whispered hoarsely.

"For *them*?"   30

"For *me*, sonofabitch!"

They were yelling for us to break it up and Tatlock spun me half around with a blow, and as a joggled camera sweeps in a reeling scene, I saw the howling red faces crouching tense beneath the cloud of blue-gray smoke. For a moment the world wavered, unraveled, flowed, then my head cleared and Tatlock bounced before me. The fluttering shadow before my eyes was his jabbing left hand. Then falling forward, my head against his damp shoulder, I whispered,

"I'll make it five dollars more."

"Go to hell!"

But his muscles relaxed a trifle beneath my pressure and I breathed,   35
"Seven?"

"Give it to your ma," he said, ripping me beneath the heart.

And while I still held him I butted him and moved away. I felt myself bombarded with punches. I fought back with hopeless desperation. I wanted to deliver my speech more than anything else in the world, because I felt that only these men could judge truly my ability, and now this stupid clown was ruining my chances. I began fighting carefully now, moving in to punch him and out again with my greater speed. A lucky blow to his chin and I had him going too—until I heard a loud voice yell, "I got my money on the big boy."

Hearing this, I almost dropped my guard. I was confused: Should I try to win against the voice out there? Would not this go against my speech, and was not this a moment for humility, for nonresistance? A blow to my head as I danced about sent my right eye popping like a jack-in-the-box and settled my dilemma. The room went red as I fell. It was a dream fall, my body languid and fastidious as to where to land, until the floor became impatient and smashed up to meet me. A moment later I came to. An hypnotic vice said FIVE emphatically. And I lay there, hazily watching a dark red spot of my own blood shaping itself into a butterfly, glistening and soaking into the soiled gray world of the canvas.

When the voice drawled TEN I was lifted up and dragged to a chair. I sat dazed. My eye pained and swelled with each throb of my pounding heart and I wondered if now I would be allowed to speak. I was wringing wet, my mouth still bleeding. We were grouped along the wall now. The other boys ignored me as they congratulated Tatlock and speculated as to how much they would be paid. One boy whimpered over his smashed hand. Looking up front, I saw attendants in white jackets rolling the portable ring away and placing a small square rug in the vacant space surrounded by chairs. Perhaps, I thought, I will stand on the rug to deliver my speech.

Then the M.C. called to us, "Come on up here boys and get your money." 40

We ran forward to where the men laughed and talked in their chairs, waiting. Everyone seemed friendly now.

"There it is on the rug," the man said. I saw the rug covered with coins of all dimensions and a few crumpled bills. But what excited me, scattered here and there, were the gold pieces.

"Boys, it's all yours," the man said. "You get all you grab."

"That's right, Sambo," a blond man said, winking at me confidentially.

I trembled with excitement, forgetting my pain. I would get the gold 45 and the bills, I thought. I would use both hands. I would throw my body against the boys nearest me to block them from the gold.

"Get down on the rug now," the man commanded, "and don't anyone touch it until I give the signal."

"This ought to be good," I heard.

As told, we got around the square rug on our knees. Slowly the man raised his freckled hand as we followed it upward with our eyes.

I heard, "These niggers look like they're about to pray!"

Then, "Ready," the man said, "Go!" 50

I lunged for a yellow coin lying on the blue design of the carpet, touching it and sending a surprised shriek to join those rising around me. I tried frantically to remove my hand but could not let go. A hot, violent force tore through my body, shaking me like a wet rage. The rug was electrified. The hair bristled up on my head as I shook myself free. My muscles jumped, my nerves jangled, writhed. But I saw that this was not stopping the other boys. Laughing in fear and embarrassment, some were holding back and scooping up the coins knocked off by the painful contortions of the others. The men roared above us as we struggled.

"Pick it up, goddamnit, pick it up!" someone called like a bass-voiced parrot. "Go on, get it!"

I crawled rapidly around the floor, picking up the coins, trying to avoid the coppers and to get greenbacks and the gold. Ignoring the shock by laughing, as I brushed the coins off quickly, I discovered that I could contain the electricity—a contradiction, but it works. Then the men began to push us onto the rug. Laughing embarrassedly, we struggled out of their hands and kept after the coins. We were all wet and slippery and hard to hold. Suddenly I saw a boy lifted into the air, glistening with sweat like a circus seal, and dropped, his wet back landing flush upon the charged rug, heard him yell and saw him literally dance upon his back, his elbows beating a frenzied tattoo upon the floor, his muscles twitching like the flesh of a horse stung by many flies. When he finally rolled off, his face was gray and no one stopped him when he ran from the floor amid booming laughter.

"Get the money," the M.C. called. "That's good hard American cash!"

And we snatched and grabbed, snatched and grabbed. I was careful not to come too close to the rug now, and when I felt the hot whiskey breath descend upon me like a cloud of foul air I reached out and grabbed the leg of a chair. It was occupied and I held on desperately. 55

"Leggo, nigger! Leggo!"

The huge face wavered down to mine as he tried to push me free. But my body was slippery and he was too drunk. It was Mr. Colcord, who owned a chain of movie houses and "entertainment palaces." Each time he grabbed me I slipped out of his hands. It became a real struggle. I feared the rug more than I did the drunk, so I held on, surprising myself for a moment by trying to topple *him* upon the rug. It was such an enormous idea that I found myself actually carrying it out. I tried not to be obvious, yet when I grabbed his leg, trying to tumble him out of the chair, he raised up roaring with laughter, and, looking at me with soberness dead in the eye, kicked me viciously in the chest. The chair leg flew out of my hand and I felt myself going and rolled. It was as though I had rolled through a bed of hot coals. It seemed a whole century would pass before I would roll free, a century in which I was seared through the deepest levels of my body to the fearful breath within me and the breath seared and heated to the point of explosion. It'll all be over in a flash, I thought as I rolled clear. It'll all be over in a flash.

But not yet, the men on the other side were waiting, red faces swollen as though from apoplexy as they bent forward in their chairs. Seeing their fingers coming toward me, I rolled away as a fumbled football rolls off the receiver's fingertips, back into the coals. That time I luckily sent the rug sliding out of place and heard the coins ringing against the floor and the boys scuffling to pick them up and the M.C. calling, "All right, boys that's all. Go get dressed and get your money."

I was limp as a dish rag. My back felt as though it had been beaten with wires.

When we had dressed the M.C. came in and gave us each five dollars,   60
except Tatlock, who got ten for being last in the ring. Then he told us to leave. I was not to get a chance to deliver my speech, I thought. I was going out into the dim alley in despair when I was stopped and told to go back. I returned to the ballroom, where the men were pushing back their chairs and gathering in groups to talk.

The M.C. knocked on a table for quiet. "Gentlemen," he said, "we almost forgot about an important part of the program. A most serious part, gentlemen. This boy was brought here to deliver a speech which he made at his graduation yesterday . . ."

"Bravo!"

"I'm told that he is the smartest boy we've got out there in Greenwood. I'm told that he knows more big words than a pocket-sized dictionary."

Much applause and laughter.

"So now, gentlemen, I want you to give him your attention."

There was still laughter as I faced them, my mouth dry, my eye throb-   65
bing. I began slowly, but evidently my throat was tense, because they began shouting, "Louder! Louder!"

"We of the younger generation extol the wisdom of that great leader and educator," I shouted, "who first spoke these flaming words of wisdom: 'A ship lost at sea for many days suddenly sighted a friendly vessel. From the mast of the unfortunate vessel was seen a signal: "Water, water; we die of thirst!" The answer from the friendly vessel came back: "Cast down your bucket where you are." The captain of the distressed vessel, at last heeding the injunction, cast down his bucket, and it came up fill of fresh sparkling water from the mouth of the Amazon River.' And like him I say, and in his words, 'To those of my race who depend upon bettering their condition in a foreign land, or who underestimate the importance of cultivating friendly relations with the Southern white man, who is his next-door neighbor, I would say: "Cast down your bucket where you are"—cast it down in making friends in every manly way of the people of all races by whom we are surrounded . . ."

I spoke automatically and with such fervor that I did not realize that the men were still talking and laughing until my dry mouth, filling up with blood from the cut, almost strangled me. I coughed, wanting to stop and go to one of the tall brass, sand-filled spittoons to relieve myself, but a few of the men, especially the superintendent, were listening and I was afraid. So I gulped it down, blood, saliva and all, and continued. (What powers of endurance I had during those days! What enthusiasm! What a belief in the rightness of things!) I spoke even louder in spite of the pain. But still they talked and still they laughed, as though deaf with cotton in dirty ears. So I spoke with greater emotional emphasis. I closed my ears and swallowed blood until I was nauseated. The speech seemed a hundred times as long as before, but I could not leave out a single word. All had to be said, each memorized nuance considered, rendered. Nor was that all. Whenever I uttered a word of three syllables a group of voices would yell for me to repeat it. I used the phrase "social responsibility" and they yelled:

"What's that word you say, boy?"

"Social responsibility," I said.

"What?" 70

"Social . . ."

"Louder."

". . . responsibility."

"More!"

"Respon—" 75

"Repeat!"

"—sibility."

The room filled with the uproar of laughter until, no doubt, distracted by having to gulp down my blood, I made a mistake and yelled a phrase I had often seen denounced in newspaper editorials, heard debated in private.

"Social . . ."

"What?" they yelled. 80

" . . . equality—"

The laughter hung smokelike in the sudden stillness. I opened my eyes, puzzled. Sounds of displeasure filled the room. The M.C. rushed forward. They shouted hostile phrases at me. But I did not understand.

A small dry mustached man in the front row blared out, "Say that slowly, son!"

"What, sir?"

"What you just said!" 85

"Social responsibility, sir," I said.

"You weren't being smart, were you, boy?" he said, not unkindly.

"No, sir!"

"You sure that about 'equality' was a mistake?"

"Oh, yes sir," I said. "I was swallowing blood." 90

"Well, you had better speak more slowly so we can understand. We mean to do right by you, but you've got to know your place at all times. All right, now, go on with your speech."

I was afraid. I wanted to leave but I wanted also to speak and I was afraid they'd snatch me down.

"Thank you, sir," I said, beginning where I had left off, and having them ignore me as before.

Yet when I finished there was a thunderous applause. I was surprised to see the superintendent come forth with a package wrapped in white tissue paper, and, gesturing for quiet, address the men.

"Gentlemen, you see that I did not overpraise this boy. He makes a 95 good speech and some day he'll lead his people in the proper paths. And I don't have to tell you that that is important in these days and times. This is a good, smart boy, and so to encourage him in the right direction, in the name of the Board of Education I wish to present him a prize in the form of this . . ."

He paused, removing the tissue paper and revealing a gleaming calfskin brief case.

" . . . in the form of this first-class article from Shad Whitmore's shop."

"Boy," he said, addressing me, "take this prize and keep it well. Consider it a badge of office. Prize it. Keep developing as you are and some day it will be filled with important papers that will help shape the destiny of your people."

I was so moved that I could hardly express my thanks. A rope of bloody saliva forming a shape like an undiscovered continent drooled upon the leather and I wiped it quickly away. I felt an importance that I had never dreamed.

"Open it and see what's inside," I was told. 100

My fingers a-tremble, I complied, smelling the fresh leather and finding an official-looking document inside. It was a scholarship to the state college for Negroes. My eyes filled with tears and I ran awkwardly off the floor.

I was overjoyed; I did not even mind when I discovered that the gold pieces I had scrambled for were brass pocket tokens advertising a certain make of automobile.

When I reached home everyone was excited. Next day the neighbors came to congratulate me. I even felt safe from grandfather, whose deathbed curse usually spoiled my triumphs. I stood beneath his photograph with my brief case in hand and smiled triumphantly into his stolid black peasant's face. It was a face that fascinated me. The eyes seemed to follow everywhere I went.

That night I dreamed I was at a circus with him and that he refused to laugh at the clowns no matter what they did. Then later he told me to open my brief case and read what was inside and I did, finding an official envelope stamped with the state seal; and inside the envelope, I found another and another, endlessly, and I thought I would fall of weariness. "Them's years," he said. "Now open that one." And I did and in it I found an engraved document containing a short message in letters of gold. "Read it," my grandfather said. "Out loud!"

"To Whom It May Concern," I intoned. "Keep This Nigger-Boy 105 Running."

I awoke with the old man's laughter ringing in my ears.

(It was a dream I was to remember and dream again for many years after. But at that time I had no insight into its meaning. First I had to attend college.)

Louise Erdrich   (b. 1954)

Because of her Chippewa background, Louise Erdrich speaks with authority about the experience of Native-Americans. Her poetry and fiction have marked her as one of the leading young American writers. She first published a book of poems, Jacklight *(1984), followed in the same year with* Love Medicine. *She won the National Book Critics Circle Award for this book, a series of fourteen connected stories of two families of the Turtle Mountain Chippewa group in the North Dakota and Minnesota area. The* Beet Queen *(1986) surveys the same region, but her characters are not from the reservation. Their struggles are powerful representations of those faced by masses of people in the region during and after the great Depression. Erdrich returned to the families in her first book of fiction for the characters in* Tracks *(1988). She currently lives in Hanover, NH, with her writer husband Michael Dorris, also Native-American, with whom she has collaborated.*

LOVE MEDICINE   1984

I never really done much with my life, I suppose. I never had a television. Grandma Kashpaw had one inside her apartment at the Senior Citizens, so I used to go there and watch my favorite shows. For a while she used to call me the biggest waste on the reservation and hark back to how she saved me from my own mother, who wanted to tie me in a potato sack and throw me in a slough. Sure, I was grateful to Grandma Kashpaw for saving me like that, for raising me, but gratitude gets old. After a while, stale. I had to stop thanking her. One day I told her I had paid her back in full by staying at her beck and call. I'd do anything for Grandma. She knew that. Besides, I took care of Grandpa like nobody else could, on account of what a handful he'd gotten to be.

But that was nothing. I know the tricks of mind and body inside out without ever having trained for it, because I got the touch. It's a thing you got to be born with. I got secrets in my hands that nobody ever knew to ask. Take Grandma Kashpaw with her tired veins all knotted up in her legs like clumps of blue snails. I take my fingers and I snap them on the knots. The medicine flows out of me. The touch. I run my fingers up the maps of those rivers of veins or I knock very gentle above their hearts or I make a circling motion on their stomachs, and it helps them. They feel much better. Some women pay me five dollars.

I couldn't do the touch for Grandpa, though. He was a hard nut. You know, some people fall right through the hole in their lives. It's invisible, but they come to it after time, never knowing where. There is this woman here, Lulu Lamartine, who always had a thing for Grandpa. She loved him since she was a girl and always said he was a genius. Now she says that his mind got so full it exploded.

How can I doubt that? I know the feeling when your mental power builds up too far. I always used to say that's why the Indians got drunk. Even statistically we're the smartest people on the earth. Anyhow with Grandpa I couldn't hardly believe it, because all my youth he stood out as a hero to me. When he started getting toward second childhood he went through different moods. He would stand in the woods and cry at the top of his shirt. It scared me, scared everyone, Grandma worst of all.

Yet he was so smart—do you believe it?—that he *knew* he was getting foolish.   5

He said so. He told me that December I failed school and come back on the train to Hoopdance. I didn't have nowhere else to go. He picked me up there and he said it straight out: "I'm getting into my second childhood." And then he said something else I still remember: "I been chosen for it. I couldn't say no." So I figure that a man so smart all his life—tribal chairman and the star of movies and even pictured in the statehouse and on cans of snuff—would know what he's doing by saying yes. I think he was called to second childhood like anybody else gets a call for the priesthood or the army or whatever. So I really did not listen too hard when the doctor said this was some kind of disease old people got eating too much sugar. You just can't tell me that a man who went to Washington and gave them bureaucrats what for could lose his mind from eating too much Milky Way. No, he put second childhood on himself.

Behind those songs he sings out in the middle of Mass, and back of those stories that everybody knows by heart, Grandpa is thinking hard about life. I know the feeling. Sometimes I'll throw up a smokescreen to think behind. I'll hitch up to Winnipeg and play the Space Invaders for six hours, but all the time there and back I will be thinking some fairly deep thoughts that surprise even me, and I'm used to it. As for him, if it was just the thoughts there wouldn't be no problem. Smokescreen is what irritates the social structure, see, and Grandpa has done things that just distract people to the point they want to throw him in the cookie jar where they keep the mentally insane. He's far from that, I know for sure, but even Grandma had trouble keeping her patience once he started sneaking off to Lamartine's place. He's not supposed to have his candy, and Lulu feeds it to him. That's *one* of the reasons why he goes.

Grandma tried to get me to put the touch on Grandpa soon after he began stepping out. I didn't want to, but before Grandma started telling me again what a bad state my bare behind was in when she first took me home, I thought I should at least pretend.

I put my hands on either side of Grandpa's head. You wouldn't look at him and say he was crazy. He's a fine figure of a man, as Lamartine would say, with all his hair and half his teeth, a beak like a hawk, and cheeks like the blades of a hatchet. They put his picture on all the tourist guides to North Dakota and even copied his face for artistic paintings. I guess you could call him a monument all of himself. He started grinning when I put my hands on his templates, and I knew right then he knew how come I touched him. I knew the smokescreen was going to fall.

And I was right just for a moment it fell.   10

"Let's pitch whoopee," he said across my shoulder to Grandma.

They don't use that expression much around here anymore, but for damn sure it must have meant something. It got her goat right quick.

She threw my hands off his head herself and stood in front of him, ever-matching him pound for pound, and taller too, for she had a growth spurt in middle age while he had shrunk, so now the length and breadth of her surpassed him. She glared up and spoke her piece into his face about how he was off at all hours tomcatting and chasing Lamartine again and making a damn old fool of himself.

"And you got no more whoopee to pitch anymore anyhow!" she yelled at last, surprising me so my jaw just dropped, for us kids all had pretended for so long that those rustling sounds we heard from their side of the room at night never happened. She sure had pretended it, up till now, anyway. I saw that tears were in her eyes. And that's when I saw how much grief and love she felt for him. And it gave me a real shock to the system. You see I thought love got easier over the years so it didn't hurt so bad when it hurt, or feel so good when it felt good. I thought it smoothed out and old people hardly noticed it. I thought it curled up and died, I guess. Now I saw it rear up like a whip and lash.

She loved him. She was jealous. She mourned him like the dead.   15

And he just smiled into the air, trapped in the seams of his mind.

So I didn't know what to do. I was in a laundry then. They was like parents to me, the way they had took me home and reared me. I could see her point for wanting to get him back the way he was so at least she could argue with him, sleep with him, not be shamed out by Lamartine. She'd always love him. That hit me like a ton of bricks. For one whole day I felt this odd feeling that cramped my hands. When you have the touch, that's where longing gets you. I never loved like that. It made me feel all inspired to see them fight, and I wanted to go out and find a woman who I would love until one of us died or went crazy. But I'm not like that really. From time to time I heal a person all up good inside, however when it comes to the long shot I doubt that I got staying power.

And you need that, staying power, going out to love somebody. I knew this quality was not going to jump on me with no effort. So I turned my thoughts back to Grandma and Grandpa. I felt her side of it with my hands and my tangled guts, and I felt his side of it within the stretch of my mentality. He had gone out to lunch one day and never came back. He was fishing in the middle of Lake Turcot. And there was big thoughts on his line, and he kept throwing them back for even bigger ones that would explain to him, say, the meaning of how we got here and why we have to leave so soon. All in all, I could not see myself treating Grandpa with the touch, bringing him back, when the real part of him had chose to be off thinking somewhere. It was only the rest of him that stayed around causing trouble, after all, and we could handle most of it without any problem.

Besides, it was hard to argue with his reasons for doing some things. Take Holy Mass. I used to go there just every so often, when I got frustrated mostly, because even though I know the Higher Power dwells everyplace, there's something very calming about the cool greenish inside of our mission. Or so I thought, anyway. Grandpa was the one who stripped off my delusions in this matter, for it was he who busted right through what Father Upsala calls the sacred serenity of the place.

We filed in that time. Me and Grandpa. We sat down in our pews. Then   20 the rosary got started up pre-Mass and that's when Grandpa filled up his chest and opened his mouth and belted out them words.

HAIL MARIE FULL OF GRACE.

He had a powerful set of lungs.

And he kept on like that. He did not let up. He hollered and he yelled them prayers, and I guess people was used to him by now, because they only muttered theirs and did not quit and gawk like I did. I was getting red-faced, I admit. I give him the elbow once or twice, but that wasn't nothing to him. He kept on. He shrieked to heaven and he pleaded like a movie actor and he pounded his chest like Tarzan in the Lord I Am Not Worthies. I thought he might hurt himself. Then after a while I guess I got used to it, and that's when I wondered: how come?

So afterwards I out and asked him. "How come? How come you yelled?"

"God don't hear me otherwise," said Grandpa Kashpaw.   25

I sweat. I broke right into a little cold sweat at my hairline because I knew this was perfectly right and for years not one damn other person had noticed it. God's been going deaf. Since the Old Testament, God's been deafening up on us. I read, see. Besides the dictionary, which I'm constantly in use of, I had this Bible once. I read it. I found there was discrepancies between then and now. It struck me. Here God used to raineth bread from clouds, smite the Phillipines, sling fire down on red-light districts where people got stabbed. He even appeared in person every once in a while. God used to pay attention, is what I'm saying.

Now there's your God in the Old Testament and there is Chippewa Gods as well. Indian Gods, good and bad, like tricky Nanabozho or the water monster, Missepeshu, who lives over in Lake Turcot. That water monster was the last God I ever heard to appear. It had a weakness for young girls and grabbed one of the Blues off her rowboat. She got to shore all right, but only after this monster had its way with her. She's an old lady now. Old Lady Blue. She still won't let her family fish that lake.

Our Gods aren't perfect, is what I'm saying, but at least they come around. They'll do a favor if you ask them right. You don't have to yell. But you do have to know, like I said, how to ask in the right way. That makes problems, because to ask proper was an art that was lost to the

Chippewas once the Catholics gained ground. Even now, I have to wonder if Higher Power turned it back, if we got to yell, or if we just don't speak its language.

I looked around me. How else could I explain what all I had seen in my short life—King smashing his fist in things, Gordie drinking himself down to the Bismarck hospitals, or Aunt June left by a white man to wander off in the snow. How else to explain the times my touch don't work, and farther back, to the oldtime Indians who was swept away in the outright germ warfare and dirty-dog killing of the whites. In those times, us Indians was so much kindlier than now.

We took them in.   30

Oh yes, I'm bitter as an old cutworm just thinking of how they done to us and doing still.

So Grandpa Kashpaw just opened my eyes a little there. Was there any sense relying on a God, whose ears was stopped? Just like the government? It says then, right off, maybe we got nothing but ourselves. And that's not much, just personally speaking. I know I don't got the cold hard potatoes it takes to understand everything. Still, there's things I'd like to do. For instance, I'd like to help some people like my Grandpa and Grandma Kashpaw get back some happiness within the tail ends of their lives.

I told you once before I couldn't see my way clear to putting the direct touch on Grandpa's mind, and I kept my moral there, but something soon happened to make me think a little bit of mental adjustment wouldn't do him and the rest of us no harm.

It was after we saw him one afternoon in the sunshine courtyard of the Senior Citizens with Lulu Lamartine. Grandpa used to like to dig there. He had his little dandelion fork out, and he was prying up them dandelions right and left while Lamartine watched him.

"He's scratching up the dirt, all right," said Grandma, watching   35
Lamartine watch Grandpa out the window.

Now Lamartine was about half the considerable size of Grandma, but you would never think of sizes anyway. They were different in an even more noticeable way. It was the difference between a house fixed up with paint and picky fence, and a house left to weather away into the soft earth, is what I'm saying. Lamartine was jacked up, latticed, shuttered, and vinyl sided, while Grandma sagged and bulged on her slipped foundations and let her hair go the silver gray of rain-dried lumber. Right now, she eyed the Lamartine's pert flowery dress with such a look it despaired me. I knew what this could lead to with Grandma. Alternating tongue storms and rock-hard silences was hard on a man, even one who didn't notice, like Grandpa. So I went fetching him.

But he was gone when I popped through the little screen door that led out on the courtyard. There was nobody out there either, to point which way they went. Just the dandelion fork quibbling upright in the ground. That gave me an idea. I snookered over to the Lamartine's door and I listened in first, then knocked. But nobody. So I went walking through the lounges and around the card tables. Still nobody. Finally it was my touch that led me to the laundry room. I cracked the door. I went in. There they were. And he was really loving her up good, boy, and she was going hell for leather. Sheets was flapping on the lines above, and washcloths, pillowcases, shirts was also flying through the air, for they was trying to clear out a place for themselves in a high-heaped but shallow laundry cart. The washers and dryers was all on, chock full of quarters, shaking and moaning. I couldn't hear what Grandpa and the Lamartine was billing and cooing and they couldn't hear me.

I didn't know what to do, so I went inside and shut the door.

The Lamartine wore a big curly light-brown wig. Looked like one of them squeaky little white-people dogs. Poodles they call them. Anyway, that wig is what saved us from the worse. For I could hardly shout and tell them I was in there, no more could I try and grab him. I was trapped where I was. There was nothing I could really do but hold the door shut. I was scared of somebody else upsetting in and really getting an eyeful. Turned out though, in the heat of the clinch, as I was trying to avert my eyes you see, the Lamartine's curly wig jumped off her head. And if you ever been in the midst of something and had a big change like that occur in the someone, you can't help know how it devastates your basic urges. Not only that, but her wig was almost with a life of its own Grandpa's eyes were bugging at the change already, and swear to God if the thing didn't rear up and pop him in the face like it was going to start something. He scrambled up, Grandpa did, and the Lamartine jumped up after him all addled looking. They just stared at each other, huffing and puffing, with quizzical expression. The surprise seemed to drive all sense completely out of Grandpa's mind.

"The letter was what started the fire," he said. "I never would have done   40
it."

"What letter?" said the Lamartine. She was stiff-necked now, and elegant even bald, like some alien queen. I gave her back the wig. The Lamartine replaced it on her head, and whenever I saw her after that, I couldn't help thinking of her bald, with special powers, as if from another planet.

"That was a close call," I said to Grandpa after she had left.

But I think he had already forgot the incident. He just stood there all quiet and thoughtful. You really wouldn't think he was crazy. He looked like he was just about to say something important, explaining himself. He said something all right, but it didn't have nothing to do with anything that made sense.

He wondered where the heck he put his dandelion fork. That's when I decided about the mental adjustment.

Now what was mostly our problem was not so much that he was not all   45
there, but that what was there of him often hankered after Lamartine. If we could put a stop to that, I thought, we might be getting someplace. But here,

see, my touch was of no use. For what could I snap my fingers at to make him faithful to Grandma? Like the quality of staying power, this faithfulness was invisible. I know it's something that you got to acquire, but I never known where from. Maybe there's no rhyme or reason to it, like my getting the touch, and then again maybe it's a kind of magic.

It was Grandma Kashpaw who thought of it in the end. She knows things. Although she will not admit she has a scrap of Indian blood in her, there's no doubt in my mind she's got some Chippewa. How else would you explain the way she'll be sitting there, in front of her TV story, rocking in her armchair and suddenly she turns on me, her brown eyes hard as lake-bed flint.

"Lipsha Morrisey," she'll say, "you went out last night and got drunk."

How did she know that? I'll hardly remember it myself. Then she'll say she just had a feeling or ache in the scar of her hand or a creak in her shoulder. She is constantly being told things by little aggravations in her joints or by her household appliances. One time she told Gordie never to ride with a crazy Lamartine boy. She had seen something in the polished-up tin of her bread toaster. She had seen something in the polished-up tin of her bread toaster. So he didn't. Sure enough, the time came we heard how Lyman and Henry went out of control in their car. ending up in the river. Lyman swam to the top, but Henry never made it.

Thanks to Grandma's toaster, Gordie was probably spared.

Someplace in the blood Grandma Kashpaw knows things. She also re-   50
members things, I found. She keeps things filed away. She's got a memory like them video games that don't forget your score. One reason she remembers so many details about the trouble I gave her in early life is so she can flash back her total when she needs to.

Like now. Take the love medicine. I don't know where she remembered that from. It came tumbling from her mind like an asteroid off the corner of the screen.

Of course she starts out by mentioning the time I had this accident in church and did she leave me there with wet overhalls? No she didn't. And ain't I glad? Yes I am. Now what you want now, Grandma?

But when she mentions them love medicines, I feel my back prickle at the danger. These love medicines is something of an old Chippewa specialty. No other tribe has got them down so well. But love medicines is not for the layman to handle. You don't just go out and get one without paying for it. Before you get one, even, you should go through one hell of a lot of mental condensation. You got to think it over. Choose the right one. You could really mess up your life grinding up the wrong little thing.

So anyhow, I said to Grandma I'd give this love medicine some thought. I knew the best thing was to go ask a specialist like Old Man Pillager, who lives up in a tangle of bush and never shows himself. But the truth is I was afraid of him, like everyone else. He was known for putting the twisted mouth on people, seizing up their hearts. Old Man Pillager was serious business, and I have always thought it best to steer clear of that whenever I could.

That's why I took the powers in my own hands. That's why I did what I could.

I put my whole mentality to it, nothing held back. After a while I started 55 to remember things I'd heard gossiped over.

I heard of this person once who carried a charm of seeds that looked like baby pearls. They was attracted to a metal knife, which made them powerful. But I didn't know where them seeds grew. Another love charm I heard about I couldn't go along with, because how was I suppose to catch frogs in the act, which it required. Them little creatures is slippery and fast. And then the powerfullest of all, the most extreme, involved nail clips and such. I wasn't anywhere near asking Grandma to provide me all the little body bits that this last love recipe called for. I went walking around for days just trying to think up something that would work.

Well I got it. If it hadn't been the early fall of the year, I never would have got it. But I was sitting underneath a tree one day down near the school just watching people's feet go by when something tells me, look up! Look up! So I look up, and I see two honkers, Canada geese, the kind with little masks on their faces, a bird what mates for life. I see them flying right over my head naturally preparing to land in some slough on the reservation, which they certainly won't get off of alive.

It hits me, anyway. Them geese, they mate for life. And I think to myself, just what if I went out and got a pair? And just what if I fed some part— say the goose heart—of the female to Grandma and Grandpa ate the other heart? Wouldn't that work? Maybe it's all invisible, and then maybe again it's magic. Love is a stony road. We know that for sure. If it's true that the higher feelings of devotion get lodged in the heart like people say, then we'd be home free. If not, eating goose heart couldn't harm nobody anyway. I thought it was worth my effort, and Grandma Kashpaw thought so, too. She had always known a good idea when she heard one. She borrowed me Grandpa's gun.

So I went out to this particular slough, maybe the exact same slough I never got thrown in by my mother, thanks to Grandma Kashpaw, and I hunched down in a good comfortable pile of rushes. I got my gun loaded up. I ate a few of these soft baloney sandwiches Grandma made me for lunch. And then I waited. The cattails blown back and forth above my head. Them stringy blue herons was spearing up their prey. The thing I know how to do best in this world, the thing I been training for all my life, is to wait. Sitting there and sitting there was no hardship on me. I got to thinking about some funny things that happened. There was this one time that Lulu Lamartine's little blue tweety bird, a paraclete, I guess you'd call it, flown up inside her dress and got lost within there. I recalled her running out into the hallway trying to yell something, shaking. She was doing a right good jig there, cutting the rug for sure, and the thing is it *never* flown out. To this day people speculate where it went. They fear she might perhaps of crushed it in her corsets. It sure hasn't ever yet been seen alive. I thought of funny things for a while, but then I used them up, and strange things that happened started weaseling their way into my mind.

I got to thinking quite naturally of the Lamartine's cousin named   60
Wristwatch. I never knew what his real name was. They called him Wristwatch because he got his father's broken wristwatch as a young boy when his father passed on. Never in his whole life did Wristwatch take his father's watch off. He didn't care if it worked, although after a while he got sensitive when people asked what time it was, teasing him. He often put it to his ear like he was listening to the tick. But it was broken for good and forever, people said so, at least that's what they thought.

Well I saw Wristwatch smoking in his pickup one afternoon and by nine that evening he was dead.

He died sitting at the Lamartine's table, too. As she told it, Wristwatch had just eaten himself a good-size dinner and she said would he take seconds on the hot dish when he fell over to the floor. They turnt him over. He was gone. But here's the strange thing: when the Senior Citizen's orderly took the pulse he noticed that the wristwatch Wristwatch wore was now working. The moment he died the wristwatch started keeping perfect time. They buried him with the watch still ticking on his arm.

I got to thinking. What if some gravediggers dug up Wristwatch's casket in two hundred years and that watch was still going? I thought what question they would ask and it was this. Whose hand wound it?

I started shaking like a piece of grass at just the thought.

Not to get off the subject or nothing. I was still hunkered in the slough. It   65
was passing late into the afternoon and still no honkers had touched down. Now I don't need to tell you that the waiting did not get to me, it was the chill. The rushes was very soft, but damp. I was getting cold and debating to leave, when they landed. Two geese swimming here and there as big as life, looking deep into each other's little pinhole eyes. Just the ones I was looking for. So I lifted Grandpa's gun to my shoulder and I aimed perfectly, and *blam*! *Blam*! I delivered two accurate shots. But the thing is, them shots missed. I couldn't hardly believe it. Whether it was that the stock had warped or the barrel got bent someways, I don't quite know, but anyway them geese flown off into the dim sky, and Lipsha Morrissey was left there in the rushes with evening fallen and his two cold hands empty. He had before him just the prospect of another day of bone-cracking chill in them rushes, and the thought of it got him depressed.

Now it isn't my style, in no way, to get depressed.

So I said to myself, Lipsha Morrissey, you're a happy S.O.B. who could be covered up with weeds by now down at the bottom of this slough, but instead you're alive to tell the tale. You might have problems in life, but you still got the touch. You got the power, Lipsha Morrissey. Can't argue that. So put your mind to it and figure out how not to be depressed.

I took my advice. I put my mind to it. But I never saw at the time how my thoughts led me astray toward a tragic outcome none could have known. I ignored all the danger, all the limits, for I was tired of sitting in the slough

and my feet were numb. My face was aching. I was chilled, so I played with
fire. I told myself love medicine was simple. I told myself the old superstitions
was just that—strange beliefs. I told myself to take the ten dollars Mary
MacDonald had paid me for putting the touch on her arthritis joint, and the
other five I hadn't spent yet from winning bingo last Thursday. I told myself
to go down to the Red Owl store.

And here is what I did that made the medicine backfire. I took an evil
shortcut. I looked at birds that was dead and froze.

All right. So now I guess you will say, "Slap a malpractice suit on Lipsha   70
Morrissey."

I heard of those suits. I used to think it was a color clothing quack doctors had to wear so you could tell them from the good ones. Now I know
better that it's law.

As I walked back from the Red Owl with the rock-hard, heavy turkeys,
I argued to myself about malpractice. I thought of faith. I thought to myself
that faith could be called belief against the odds and whether or not there's
any proof. How does that sound? I thought how we might have to yell to be
heard by High Power, but that's not saying it's not *there*. And that is faith for
you. It's belief even when the goods don't deliver. Higher Power makes
promises we all they they can't back up, but anybody ever go and slap an old
malpractice suit on God? Or the U.S. government? No they don't. Faith might
be stupid, but it gets us through. So what I'm heading at is this. I finally convinced myself that the real actual power to the love medicine was not the
goose heart itself but the faith in the cure.

I didn't believe it, I knew it was wrong, but by then I had waded so far
into my lie I was stuck there. And then I went one step further.

The next day, I cleaned the hearts away from the paper packages of
gizzards inside the turkeys. Then I wrapped them hearts with a clean hankie and brung them both to get blessed up at the mission. I wanted to get
official blessings from the priest, but when Father answered the door to
the rectory, wiping his hand on a little towel, I could tell he was a busy
man.

"Booshoo,[1] Father," I said. "I got a slight request to make of you this   75
afternoon."

"What is it?" he said.

"Would you bless this package?" I held out the hankie with the hearts
inside it.

He looked at the package, questioning it.

"It's turkey hearts," I honestly had to reply.

A look of annoyance crossed his face.   80

---

1. *bonjour*, French for "good day."

"Why don't you bring this matter over to Sister Martin," he said. "I have duties."

And so, although the blessing wouldn't be as powerful, I went over to the Sisters with the package.

I rung the bell, and they brought Sister Martin to the door. I had her as a music teacher, but I was always so shy then. I never talked out loud. Now, I had grown taller than Sister Martin. Looking down, I saw that she was not feeling up to snuff. Brown circles hung under her eyes.

"What's the matter?" she said, not noticing who I was.

"Remember me, Sister?"   85

She squinted up at me.

"Oh yes," she said after a moment. "I'm sorry, you're the youngest of the Kashpaws. Gordie's brother."

Her face warmed up.

"Lipsha," I said, "that's my name."

"Well, Lipsha," she said, smiling broad at me now, "what can I do for you?"   90

They always said she was the kindest-hearted of the Sisters up the hill, and she was. She brought me back into their own kitchen and made me take a big yellow wedge of cake and a glass of milk.

"Now tell me," she said, nodding at my package. "What have you got wrapped up so carefully in those handkerchiefs?"

Like before, I answered honestly.

"Ah," said Sister Martin. "Turkey hearts." She waited.

"I hoped you could bless them."   95

She waited some more, smiling with her eyes. Kindhearted though she was, I began to sweat. A person could not pull the wool down over Sister Martin. I stumbled through my mind for an explanation, quick, that wouldn't scare her off.

"They're a present," I said, "for Saint Kateri's statue."

"She's not a saint yet."

"I know," I stuttered on, "in the hopes they will crown her."

"Lipsha," she said, "I never heard of such a thing."   100

So I told her. "Well the truth is," I said, "it's a kind of medicine."

"For what?"

"Love."

"Oh Lipsha," she said after a moment, "you don't need any medicine. I'm sure any girl would like you exactly the way you are."

I just sat there. I felt miserable, caught in my pack of lies.   105

"Tell you what," she said, seeing how bad I felt, "my blessing won't make any difference anyway. But there is something you can do."

I looked up at her hopeless.

"Just be yourself."

I looked down at my plate. I knew I wasn't much to brag about right then, and I shortly became even less. For as I walked out the door I stuck my fingers in the cup of holy water that was sacred from their touches. I put my fingers in and blessed the hearts, quick, with my own hand.

I went back to Grandma and sat down in her little kitchen at the Senior 110 Citizens. I unwrapped them hearts on the table, and her hard agate eyes went soft. She said she wasn't even going to cook those hearts up but eat them raw so their power would go down strong as possible.

I couldn't hardly watch when she munched hers. Now that's true love. I was worried about how she would get Grandpa to eat his, but she told me she'd think of something and don't worry. So I did not. I was supposed to hide off in her bedroom while she put dinner on a plate for Grandpa and fixed up the heart so he'd eat it. I caught a glint of the plate she was making for him. She put that heart smack on a piece of lettuce like in a restaurant and then attached to it a little heap of boiled peas.

He sat down. I was listening in the next room.

She said, "Why don't you have some mash potato?" So he had some mash potato. Then she gave him a little piece of boiled meat. He ate that. Then she said, "Why you didn't never touch your salad yet. See that heart? I'm feeding you it because the doctor said your blood needs building up."

I couldn't help it, at that point I peeked through a crack in the door.

I saw Grandpa picking at that heart on his plate with a certain look. He 115 didn't look appetized at all, is what I'm saying. I doubted our plan was going to work. Grandma was getting worried, too. She told him one more time, loudly, that he had to eat that heart.

"Swallow it down," she said. "You'll hardly notice it."

He just looked at her straight on. The way he looked at her made me think I was going to see the smokescreen drop a second time, and sure enough it happened.

"What you want me to eat this for so bad?" he asked her uncannily.

Now Grandma knew the jig was up. She knew that he knew she was working medicine. He put his fork down. He rolled the heart around his saucer plate.

"I don't want to eat this," he said to Grandma. "It don't look good." 120

"Why it's fresh grade-A," she told him. "One hundred percent."

He didn't ask percent what, but his eyes took on an even more warier look.

"Just go on and try it," she said, taking the salt shaker up in her hand. She was getting annoyed. "Not tasty enough? You want me to salt it for you?" She waved the shaker over his plate.

"All right, skinny white girl!" She had got Grandpa mad. Oopsy-daisy, he popped the heart into his mouth. I was about to yawn loudly and come out of the bedroom I was about ready for this crash of wills to be over, when I saw he was still up to his old tricks. First he rolled it into one side of his cheek. "Mmmmm," he said. Then he rolled it into the other side of his cheek. "Mmmmmmm," again. Then he stuck his tongue out with the heart on it and put it back, and there was no time to react. He had pulled Grandma's leg once too far. Her goat was got. She was so mad she hopped up quick as a wink and slugged him between the shoulderblades to make him swallow.

Only thing is, he choked.   125

He choked real bad. A person can choke to death. You ever sit down at a restaurant table and up above you there is a list of instructions what to do if something slides down the wrong pipe? It sure makes you chew slow, that's for damn sure. When Grandpa fell off his chair better believe me that little graphic illustrated poster fled into my mind. I jumped out the bedroom. I done everything within my power that I could do to unlodge what was choking him. I squeezed underneath his ribcage. I socked him in the back. I was desperate. But here's the factor of decision: he wasn't choking on the heart alone. There was more to it than that. It was other things that choked him as well. It didn't seem like he wanted to struggle or fight. Death came and tapped his chest, so he went just like that. I'm sorry all through my body at what I done to him with that heart, and there's those who will say Lipsha Morrissey is just excusing himself off the hook by giving song and dance about how Grandpa gave up.

Maybe I can't admit what I did. My touch had gone worthless, that is true. But here is what I seen while he lay in my arms.

You hear a person's life will flash before their eyes when they're in danger. It was him in danger, not me, but it was *his* life come over me. I saw him dying, and it was like someone pulled the shade down in a room. His eyes clouded over and squeezed shut, but just before that I looked in. He was still fishing in the middle of Lake Turcot. Big thoughts was on his line and he had half a case of beer in the boat. He waved at me, grinned, and then the bobber went under.

Grandma had gone out of the room crying for help. I bunched my force up in my hands and I held him. I was so wound up I couldn't even breathe. All the moments he had spent with me, all the times he had hoisted me on his shoulders or pointed into the leaves was concentrated in that moment. Time was flashing back and forth like a pinball machine. Lights blinked and balls hopped and rubber bands chirped, until suddenly I realized the last ball had gone down the drain and there was nothing. I felt his force leaving him, flowing out of Grandpa never to return. I felt his mind weakening. The bobber going under in the lake. And I felt the touch retreat back into the darkness inside my body, from where it came.

One time, long ago, both of us were fishing together. We caught a big old   130
shapper what started towing us around like it was a motor. "This here fishline is pretty damn good", Grandpa said. "Let's keep this turtle on and see where he takes us." So we rode along behind that turtle, watching as from time to time it surfaced. The thing was just about the size of a washtub. It took us all around the lake twice, and as it was traveling. Grandpa said something as a joke. "Lipsha," he said, "we are glad your mother didn't want you because we was always looking for a boy like you who would tow us around the lake."

"I ain't no snapper. Snappers is so stupid they stay alive when their head's chopped off," I said.

"That ain't stupidity," said Grandpa. "Their brain's just in their heart, like yours is."

When I looked up, I knew the fuse had blown between my heart and my mind and that a terrible understanding was to be given.

Grandma got back into the room and I saw her stumble. And then she went down too. It was like a house you can't hardly believe has stood so long, through years of record weather, suddenly goes down in the worst yet. It makes sense, is what I'm saying, but you still can't hardly believe it. You think a person you know has got through death and illness and being broke and living on commodity rice will get through anything. Then they fold and you see how fragile were the stones that underpinned them. You see how instantly the ground can shift you thought was solid. You see the stop signs and the yellow dividing markers of roads you traveled and all the instructions you had played according to vanish. You see how all the everyday things you counted on was just a dream you had been having by which you run your whole life. She had been over me, like a sheer overhang of rock dividing Lipsha Morrissey from outer space. And now she went underneath. It was as though the banks gave way on the shores of Lake Turcot, and where Grandpa's passing was just the bobber swallowed under by his biggest thought, her fall was the house and the rock under it sliding after, sending half the lake splashing up to the clouds.

Where there was nothing.   135

You play them games never knowing what you see. When I fell into the dream alongside of both of them I saw that the dominions I had defended myself from anciently was but delusions of the screen. Blips of light. And I was scot-free now, whistling through space.

I don't know how I come back. I don't know from where. They was slapping my face when I arrived back at Senior Citizens and they was oxygenating her. I saw her chest move, almost unwilling. She sighed the way she would when some body bothered her in the middle of a row of beads she was counting. I think it irritated her to no end that they brought her back. I knew from the way she looked after they took the mask off, she was not going to forgive them disturbing her restful peace. Nor was she forgiving Lipsha Morrissey. She had been stepping out onto the road of death, she told the children later at the funeral. I asked was there any stop signs or dividing markers on that road, but she clamped her lips in a vise the way she always done when she was mad.

Which didn't bother me. I knew when things had cleared out she would-n't have no choice. I was not going to speculate where the blame was put for Grandpa's death. We was in it together. She had slugged him between the shoulders. My touch had failed him, never to return.

All the blood children and the took-in, like me, came home from Minneapolis and Chicago, where they had relocated years ago. They stayed with friends on the reservation or with Aurelia or slept on Grandma's floor. They were struck down with grief and bereavement to be sure, every one of them. At the funeral I sat down in the back of the church with Albertine. She had gotten all skinny and ragged haired from cramming all her years of study into two or three. She had decided that to be a nurse was not enough for her so she was going to be doctor. But the way she was straining her mind didn't look too hopeful. Her eyes were bloodshot from driving and crying. She took my hand. From the back we watched all the children and the mourners as they hunched over their prayers, their hands stuffed full of Kleenex. It was someplace in that long sad service that my vision shifted. I began to see things different, more clear. The family kneeling down turned to rocks in a field. It struck me how strong and reliable grief was, and death. Until the end of time, death would be our rock.

So I had perspective on it all, for death gives you that. All the Kashpaw's 140 children had done various things to me in their lives—shared their folks with me, loaned me cash, beat me up in secret—and I decided, because of death, then and there I'd call it quits. If I ever saw King again, I'd shake his hand. Forgiving somebody else made the whole thing easier to bear.

Everybody saw Grandpa off into the next world. And then the Kashpaws had to get back to their jobs, which was numerous and impressive. I had a few beers with them and I went back to Grandma, who had sort of got lost in the shuffle of everybody being sad about Grandpa and glad to see one another.

Zelda had sat beside her the whole time and was sitting with her now. I wanted to talk to Grandma, say how sorry I was, that it wasn't her fault, but only mine. I would have, but Zelda gave me one of her looks of strict warning as if to say, "I'll take care of Grandma. Don't horn in on the women."

If only Zelda knew, I thought, the sad realities would change her. But of course I couldn't tell the dark truth.

It was evening, late. Grandma's light was on underneath a crack in the door. About a week had passed since we buried Grandpa. I knocked first but there wasn't no answer, so I went right in. The door was unlocked. She was there but she didn't notice me at first. Her hands were tied up in her rosary, and her gaze was fully absorbed in the easy chair opposite her, the one that had always been Grandpa's favorite. I stood there, staring with her, at the little green nubs in the cloth and plastic armrest covers and the sad little hair-tonic stain he had made on the white dolly where he laid his head. For the life of me I couldn't figure what she was staring at. Thin space. Then she turned.

"He ain't gone yet," she said.   145

Remember that chill I luckily didn't get from waiting in the slough? I got it now. I felt it start from the very center of me, where fear hides, waiting to attack. It spiraled outward so that in minutes my fingers and teeth were shaking and clattering. I knew she told the truth. She seen Grandpa. Whether or not he had been there is not the point. She had *seen* him, and that meant anybody else could see him, too. Not only that but, as is usually the case with these here ghosts, he had a certain uneasy reason to come back. And of course Grandma Kashpaw had scanned it out.

I sat down. We sat together on the couch watching his chair out of the corner of our eyes. She had found him sitting in his chair when she walked in the door.

"It's the love medicine, my Lipsha," she said. "It was stronger than we thought. He came back even after death to claim me to his side."

I was afraid. "We shouldn't have tampered with it," I said. She agreed. For a while we sat still. I don't know what she thought, but my head felt screwed on backward. I couldn't accurately consider the situation, so I told Grandma to go to bed. I would sleep on the couch keeping my eye on Grandpa's chair. Maybe he would come back and maybe he wouldn't. I guess I feared the one as much as the other, but I got to thinking, see, as I lay there in darkness, that perhaps even through my terrible mistakes some good might come. If Grandpa did come back, I thought he'd return in his right mind. I could talk with him. I could tell him it was all my fault for playing with power I did not understand. Maybe he'd forgive me and rest in peace. I hoped this. I calmed myself and waited for him all night.

He fooled me though. He knew what I was waiting for, and it wasn't 150 what he was looking to hear. Come dawn I heard a blood-splitting cry from the bedroom and I rushed in there. Grandma turn the lights on. She was sitting on the edge of the bed and her face looked harsh, pinched-up, gray.

"He was here," she said. "He came and laid down next to me in bed. And he touched me."

Her heart broke down. She cried. His touch was so cold. She laid back in bed after a while, as it was morning, and I went to the couch. As I lay there, falling asleep, I suddenly felt Grandpa's presence and the barrier between us like a swollen river. I felt how I had wronged him. How awful was the place where I had sent him. Behind the wall of death, he'd watched the living eat and cry and get drunk. He was lonesome, but I understood he meant no harm.

"Go back," I said to the dark, afraid and yet full of pity. "You got to be with your own kind now," I said. I felt him retreating, like a sigh, growing less. I felt his spirit as it shrunk back through the walls, the blinds, the brick courtyard of Senior Citizens. "Look up Aunt June," I whispered as he left.

I slept late the next morning, a good hard sleep allowing the sun to rise and warm the earth. It was past noon when I awoke. There is nothing, to my mind, like a long sleep to make those hard decisions that you neglect under stress of wakefulness. Soon as I woke up that morning, I saw exactly what I'd say to Grandma. I had gotten humble in the past week, not just losing the touch but getting jolted into the understanding that would prey on me from here on out. Your life feels different on you, once you greet death and understand your heart's position. You wear your life like a garment from the mission bundle sale ever after—lightly because you realize you never paid nothing for it, cherishing because you know you won't ever come by such a bargain again. Also you have the feeling someone wore it before you and someone will after. I can't explain that, not yet, but I'm putting my mind to it.

"Grandma," I said, "I got to be honest about the love medicine." 155

She listened. I knew from then on she would be listening to me the way I had listened to her before. I told her about the turkey hearts and how I had them blessed. I told her what I used as love medicine was purely a fake, and then I said to her what my understanding brought me.

"Love medicine ain't what brings him back to you, Grandma. No, it's something else. He loved you over time and distance, but he went off so quick he never got the chance to tell you how he loves you, how he doesn't blame you, how he understands. It's true feeling, not no magic. No supermarket heart could have brung him back."

She looked at me. She was seeing the years and days I had no way of knowing, and she didn't believe me. I could tell this. Yet a look came on her face. It was like the look of mothers drinking sweetness from their children's eyes. It was tenderness.

"Lipsha," she said, "you was always my favorite."

She took the beads off the bedpost, where she kept them to say at night, 160 and she told me to put out my hand. When I did this, she shut the beads inside of my fist and held them there a long minute, tight, so my hand hurt. I almost cried when she did this. I don't really know why. Tears shot up behind my eyelids, and yet it was nothing. I didn't understand, except her hand was so strong, squeezing mine.

The earth was full of life and there were dandelions growing out the window, thick as thieves, already seeded, fat as big yellow plungers. She let my hand go. I got up. "I'll go out and dig a few dandelions," I told her.

Outside, the sun was hot and heavy as a hand on my back. I felt it flow down my arms, out my fingers, arrowing through the ends of the fork into the earth. With every root I prized up there was return, as if I was kin to its secret lesson. The touch got stronger as I worked through the grassy afternoon. Uncurling from me like a seed out of the blackness where I was lost, the touch spread. The spiked leaves full of bitter mother's milk. A buried root. A nuisance people dig up and throw in the sun to wither. A globe of frail seeds that's indestructible.

Fiction and Politics

When fiction and politics mix, there is always the risk of boredom. Political fiction ages badly because the concerns of our grandfathers are rarely our concerns. Imagine, for example, reading fiction championing Hitler's youth movement, Mao's Red Guard, or the bravery of Theodore Roosevelt wresting Cuba from Spain. Nowadays such stories would not wear well. However, the atmosphere of the 1990s, with concerns about freedom of speech and the political correctness expected of students and professors, reminds us that politics enters all corners of our life, including literature. Even stories that seem unconcerned with politics have political assumptions, such as the preservation of personal independence, the right to personal property, or the toleration of poverty.

The overriding concern of many critics of the short story centers on the conflict between aesthetics and politics in fiction. For example, the question of excellence in a short story is said by those who favor aesthetics to lie in the development of style. Most New Critics have emphasized the formal perfection of a short story such as William Faulkner's "A Rose for Emily," because its language, imagery, and symbolism are so carefully and satisfyingly crafted. However, that story also has interesting political implications that make it a favorite of critics who claim, as many do , that every piece of fiction is political in one way or another.

Those readers who favor excellence of style as a measure of lasting power in a short story fear that political critics will favor fiction that agrees with their personal political agenda. That is a serious issue and a genuine fear. They also fear that some stories will be favored for their political content despite their having a thoroughly defective style. Such things do happen. On the other hand, William Faulkner demonstrates that excellence of style can be merged with concerns for political issues, such as the way in which Jefferson's protection of Miss Emily permitted her to ignore post-Civil War political reality. The town of Jefferson metaphorically did the same. In some important ways, Faulkner's is a political story.

In this collection, Richard Ford's "Communist" may be considered a political story. One of its characters, Glen Baxter, is a former CIA man turned communist (according to the boy narrator) who, like the narrator's father, is a labor man. Glen Baxter's flirtation with communism may be more a ploy to shock his friends than a deep political commitment. Ford includes a few subtleties, such as having Glen Baxter arrive one day in a Nash Ambassador (an expensive car) and having the narrator remember a boxing match with an "Indian from Choteau." Tim O'Brien's "Sweetheart of the Song Tra Bong" may also be said to have a political theme.

However, the most interesting political concerns in fiction are usually not central themes. Often a writer will assume that a story's readers agree with the political presumptions of its characters. Presumptions are quiet, almost invisible, and in the stories in this book they are more common than overt political themes. For example, the most interesting political issues in Faulkner's "A Rose for Emily" lie in the presumptions of pre–Civil War Jefferson. Even though Homer Barron, as a postwar Yankee, represents a new era, his political presumptions are as prewar as those of Colonel Sartoris. That is evident in the way he treats the black workers whom he supervises. He gives them no more political independence than Miss Emily gives her nameless servant. Faulkner is clear on that political issue: Personal independence is for the white population of Jefferson.

Political criticism can take many forms. At the present time Marxist criticism is especially vital. Marxism as an ideology is not Russian, communist, or even anti-American. Rather, it is an intellectual system that begins with concerns about economic inequities. As James Kavanagh explains,

> For Marxist theory, every historical society is crucially defined by its class structure, a network of relations much wider and more fundamental than a "form of government." Every society, that is, embodies a specific relation between the dominant class, which owns and controls the major means of producing wealth (in our society, large industrial apparatuses), and the producing or working class, which depends for its survival on selling its labor power to the dominant class.[1]

Bharati Mukherjee's "Jasmine" is especially interesting to examine from this point of view. Jasmine is both cruelly used by and cruelly aware of class distinctions. Her India is a rigid class society with remnants of the untouchables. Therefore, she studies class distinctions in America. The Moffitts seem to her totally baffling because they do not fit into her sense of class. The Daboos would have belonged to a class far beneath her in India, but in the United States they control her life. She has trouble adjusting to this paradox. You could therefore profitably interpret "Jasmine" from the point of view of politics, including Jasmine's concerns with class and her bewilderment about the way in which color distinguishes class in the United States. Jasmine experiences several kinds of education in this story. One of them is a political education.

Of course, it is best to keep in mind that the Marxist approach is not always the most relevant. One of the realities of much good fiction is that not all writers are as concerned with political theories as are Marxist critics, who expend a great deal of energy examining the lack of concern for the class struggle, or the absence of awareness of "political realities," in many stories. For instance, a Marxist might criticize John Cheever's "The Swimmer" because it pays no attention to the fact that Neddy has no political conscience. He be-

---

[1]"Ideology," in *Critical Terms for Literary Study,* edited by Frank Lentricchia and Thomas McLaughlin, 308 (Chicago: University of Chicago Press, 1990).

longs to the class that controls wealth, and he swims his way through that class's emblem of wealth: their swimming pools. He also seems doomed to remove himself from that class by his drinking and fecklessness. But Cheever is less interested in political realities than in Neddy's personal loss of self. For Cheever the issue is moral and psychological: a question of character, not of politics.

With this qualification in mind, one can gain much from political criticism. Katherine Mansfield's "The Garden Party" and Gabriel García Márquez's "Eyes of a Blue Dog" contain rich political presumptions and embody complex political concerns. As you read, it is worth asking to what extent the emblems of social class are present in each story. To what extent do the stories treat those emblems critically? You might also want to ask whether these stories attempt to make an explicit or an implicit political statement.

Reading

Eagleton, Terry. *Literary Theory: An Introduction.* Oxford: Basil Blackwell, 1983.

———*Maxism and Literary Criticism.* Berkeley: University of California Press, 1976.

Hogan, Patrick. *The Politics of Interpretation.* New York: Oxford University Press, 1990.

Jameson, Frederic. *The Political Unconscious.* Ithaca: Cornell University Press, 1981.

Selden, Raman. *Criticism and Objectivity.* London: Allen & Unwin, 1984.

Williams, Raymond. *Marxism and Literature.* Oxford: Oxford University Press, 1977.

Richard Ford   (b. 1944)

Primarily a novelist, Richard Ford is often praised for his ability to produce a keen sense of place in his work. His unusual sensitivity to environment is clearly shown in his first novel, A Piece of My Heart *(1976), which is set in Mississippi, where he was born. But Ford also describes exotic environments, such as Oaxaca, Mexico, in* The Ultimate Good Luck *(1981), a high-tension story about a man trying to get his girlfriend's brother out of prison, where he is doing time for a drug deal. His third novel,* The Sportswriter *(1986), portrays a lost soul who has trouble making connections with his own family. As a southern writer, Ford has been inevitably compared with Faulkner, but his style is much more spare and his purposes— examining the surfaces of contemporary life—much different. He has connected himself with Raymond Carver, a friend and mentor.*

COMMUNIST   1987

My mother once had a boyfriend named Glen Baxter. This was in 1961. We—my mother and I—were living in the little house my father had left her up the Sun River, near Victory, Montana, west of Great Falls. My mother was thirty-two at the time. I was sixteen. Glen Baxter was somewhere in the middle, between us, though I cannot be exact about it.

We were living then off the proceeds of my father's life insurance policies, with my mother doing some part-time waitressing work up in Great Falls and going to the bars in the evenings, which I know is where she met Glen Baxter. Sometimes he would come back with her and stay in her room at night, or she would call up from town and explain that she was staying with him in his little place on Lewis Street by the GN yards. She gave me his number every time, but I never called it. I think she probably thought that what she was doing was terrible, but simply couldn't help herself. I thought it was all right, though. Regular life it seemed, and still does. She was young, and I knew that even then.

Glen Baxter was a Communist and liked hunting, which he talked about a lot. Pheasants. Ducks. Deer. He killed all of them, he said. He had been to Vietnam as far back as then, and when he was in our house he often talked about shooting the animals over there—monkeys and beautiful parrots—using military guns just for sport. We did not know what Vietnam was then, and Glen, when he talked about that, referred to it only as "the Far East." I think now he must've been in the CIA and been disillusioned by something he saw or found out about and been thrown out, but that kind of thing did not matter to us. He was a tall, dark-eyed man with short black hair, and was usually in a good humor. He had gone halfway through college in Peoria, Illinois, he said, where he grew up. But when he was around our life he worked wheat farms as a ditcher, and stayed out of work winters and in the bars drinking with women like my mother, who had work and some money. It is not an uncommon life to lead in Montana.

What I want to explain happened in November. We had not been seeing Glen Baxter for some time. Two months had gone by. My mother knew other men, but she came home most days from work and stayed inside watching television in her bedroom and drinking beers. I asked about Glen once, and she said only that she didn't know where he was, and I assumed they had had a fight and that he was gone off on a flyer back to Illinois or Massachusetts, where he said he had relatives. I'll admit that I liked him. He had something on his mind always. He was a labor man as well as a Communist, and liked to say that the country was poisoned by the rich, and strong men would need to bring it to life again, and I liked that because my father had been a labor man, which was why we had a house to live in and money coming through. It was also true that I'd had a few boxing bouts by then—just with town boys and one with an Indian from Choteau—and there were some girlfriends I knew from that. I did not like my mother being around the house so much at night, and I wished Glen Baxter would come back, or that another man would come along and entertain her somewhere else.

At two o'clock on a Saturday, Glen drove up into our yard in a car. He had had a big brown Harley-Davidson that he rode most of the year, in his black-and-red irrigators° and a baseball cap turned backwards. But this time he had a car, a blue Nash Ambassador.° My mother and I went out on the porch when he stopped inside the olive trees my father had planted as a shelter belt, and my mother had a look on her face of not much pleasure. It was starting to be cold in earnest by then. Snow was down already onto the Fairfield Bench, though on this day a chi-

5

---

irrigators. Galoshes.   *Nash Ambassador.* An expensive automobile nook was blowing, and it could as easily have been spring, though the sky above the Divide was turning over in silver and blue clouds of winter.

"We haven't seen you in a long time, I guess," my mother said coldly.

"My little retarded sister died," Glen said, standing at the door of his old car. He was wearing his orange VFW jacket and canvas shoes we called wino shoes, something I had never seen him wear before. He seemed to be in a good humor. "We buried her in Florida near the home."

"That's a good place," my mother said in a voice that meant she was a wronged party in something.

"I want to take this boy hunting today, Aileen," Glen said. "There're snow geese down now. But we have to go right away, or they'll be gone to Idaho by tomorrow."

"He doesn't care to go," my mother said.   10

"Yes I do," I said, and looked at her.

My mother frowned at me. "Why do you?"

"Why does he need a reason?" Glen Baxter said and grinned.

"I want him to have one, that's why." She looked at me oddly. "I think Glen's drunk, Les."

"No, I'm not drinking," Glen said, which was hardly ever true. He looked   15
at both of us, and my mother bit down on the side of her lower lip and stared at me in a way to make you think she thought something was being put over on her and she didn't like you for it. She was very pretty, though when she was mad her features were sharpened and less pretty by a long way. "All right, then I don't care," she said to no one in particular. "Hunt, kill, maim. Your father did that too." She turned to go back inside.

"Why don't you come with us, Aileen?" Glen was smiling still, pleased.

"To do what?" my mother said. She stopped and pulled a package of cigarettes out of her dress pocket and put one in her mouth.

"It's worth seeing."

"See dead animals?" my mother said.

"These geese are from Siberia, Aileen," Glen said. "They're not like a lot of   20
geese. Maybe I'll buy us dinner later. What do you say?"

"Buy what with?" my mother said. To tell the truth, I didn't know why she was so mad at him. I would've thought she'd be glad to see him. But she just suddenly seemed to hate everything about him.

"I've got some money," Glen said. "Let me spend it on a pretty girl tonight."

"Find one of those and you're lucky," my mother said, turning away toward the front door.

"I already found one," Glen Baxter said. But the door slammed behind her, and he looked at me then with a look I think now was helplessness, though I could not see a way to change anything.

My mother sat in the backseat of Glen's Nash and looked out the window   25
while we drove. My double gun was in the seat between us beside Glen's Belgian pump, which he kept loaded with five shells in case, he said, he saw something beside the road he wanted to shoot. I had hunted rabbits before, and had ground-sluiced pheasants and other birds, but I had never been on an actual hunt before, one where you drove out to some special place and did it formally. And I was ex-

cited. I had a feeling that something important was about to happen to me, and that this would be a day I would always remember.

My mother did not say anything for a long time, and neither did I. We drove up through Great Falls and out the other side toward Fort Benton, which was on the benchland where wheat was grown.

"Geese mate for life," my mother said, just out of the blue, as we were driving. "I hope you know that. They're special birds."

"I know that," Glen said in the front seat. "I have every respect for them."

"So where were you for three months?" she said. "I'm only curious."

"I was in the Big Hole for a while," Glen said, "and after that I went over to Douglas, Wyoming." 30

"What were you planning to do there?" my mother asked.

"I wanted to find a job, but it didn't work out."

"I'm going to college," she said suddenly, and this was something I had never heard about before. I turned to look at her, but she was staring out her window and wouldn't see me.

"I knew French once," Glen said. "*Rosé*'s pink. *Rouge*'s red." He glanced at me and smiled. "I think that's a wise idea, Aileen. When are you going to start?"

"I don't want Les to think he was raised by crazy people all his life," my mother said. 35

"Les ought to go himself," Glen said.

"After I go, he will."

"What do you say about that, Les?" Glen said, grinning.

"He says it's just fine," my mother said.

"It's just fine," I said. 40

Where Glen Baxter took us was out onto the high flat prairie that was disked for wheat and had high, high mountains out to the east, with lower heartbreak hills in between. It was, I remember, a day for blues in the sky, and down in the distance we could see the small town of Floweree, and the state highway running past it toward Fort Benton and the Hi-line. We drove out on top of the prairie on a muddy dirt road fenced on both sides, until we had gone about three miles, which is where Glen stopped.

"All right," he said, looking up in the rearview mirror at my mother. "You wouldn't think there was anything here, would you?"

"*We're* here," my mother said. "You brought us here."

"You'll be glad though," Glen said, and seemed confident to me. I had looked around myself but could not see anything. No water or trees, nothing that seemed like a good place to hunt anything. Just wasted land. "There's a big lake out there, Les," Glen said. "You can't see it now from here because it's low. But the geese are there. You'll see."

"It's like the moon out here, I recognize that," my mother said, "only it's worse." She was staring out at the flat wheatland as if she could actually see something in particular, and wanted to know more about it. "How'd you find this place?" 45

"I came once on the wheat push," Glen said.

"And I'm sure the owner told you just to come back and hunt anytime you like and bring anybody you wanted. Come one, come all. Is that it?"

"People shouldn't own land anyway," Glen said. "Anybody should be able to use it."

"Les, Glen's going to poach here," my mother said. "I just want you to know that, because that's a crime and the law will get you for it. If you're a man now, you're going to have to face the consequences."

"That's not true," Glen Baxter said, and looked gloomily out over the steer-   50
ing wheel down the muddy road toward the mountains. Though for myself I be-lieved it was true, and didn't care. I didn't care about anything at that moment except seeing geese fly over me and shooting them down.

"Well, I'm certainly not going out there," my mother said. "I like towns bet-ter, and I already have enough trouble."

"That's okay," Glen said. "When the geese lift up you'll get to see them. That's all I wanted. Les and me'll go shoot them, won't we, Les?"

"Yes," I said, and I put my hand on my shotgun, which had been my father's and was heavy as rocks.

"Then we should go on," Glen said, "or we'll waste our light."

We got out of the car with our guns. Glen took off his canvas shoes and put   55
on his pair of black irrigators out of the trunk. Then we crossed the barbed wire fence, and walked out into the high, tilled field toward nothing. I looked back at my mother when we were still not so far away, but I could only see the small, dark top of her head, low in the backseat of the Nash, staring out and thinking what I could not then begin to say.

On the walk toward the lake, Glen began talking to me. I had never been alone with him, and knew little about him except what my mother said—that he drank too much, or other times that he was the nicest man she had ever known in the world and that someday a woman would marry him, though she didn't think it would be her. Glen told me as we walked that he wished he had finished college, but that it was too late now, that his mind was too old. He said he had liked the Far East very much, and that people there knew how to treat each other, and that he would go back some day but couldn't go now. He said also that he would like to live in Russia for a while and mentioned the names of people who had gone there, names I didn't know. He said it would be hard at first, be-cause it was so different, but that pretty soon anyone would learn to like it and wouldn't want to live anywhere else, and that Russians treated Americans who came to live there like kings. There were Communists everywhere now, he said. You didn't know them, but they were there. Montana had a large number, and he was in touch with all of them. He said that Communists were always in dan-ger and that he had to protect himself all the time. And when he said that he pulled back his VFW jacket and showed me the butt of a pistol he had stuck un-der his shirt against his bare skin. "There are people who want to kill me right now," he said, "and I would kill a man myself if I thought I had to." And we kept walking. Though in a while he said, "I don't think I know much about you, Les. But I'd like to. What do you like to do?"

"I like to box," I said. "My father did it. It's a good thing to know."

"I suppose you have to protect yourself too," Glen said.

"I know how to," I said.

"Do you like to watch TV," Glen asked, and smiled.   60

"Not much."

"I love to," Glen said. "I could watch it instead of eating if I had one."

I looked out straight ahead over the green tops of sage that grew to the edge of the disked field, hoping to see the lake Glen said was there. There was an airishness and a sweet smell that I thought might be the place we were going, but I couldn't see it. "How will we hunt these geese?" I said.

"It won't be hard," Glen said. "Most hunting isn't even hunting. It's only shooting. And that's what this will be. In Illinois you would dig holes in the ground and hide and set out your decoys. Then the geese come to you, over and over again. But we don't have time for that here." He glanced at me. "You have to be sure the first time here."

"How do you know they're here now," I asked. And I looked toward the 65 Highwood Mountains twenty miles away, half in snow and half dark blue at the bottom. I could see the little town of Floweree then, looking shabby and dimly lighted in the distance. A red bar sign shone. A car moved slowly away from the scattered buildings.

"They always come November first," Glen said.

"Are we going to poach them?"

"Does it make any difference to you," Glen asked.

"No, it doesn't."

"Well then, we aren't," he said. 70

We walked then for a while without talking. I looked back once to see the Nash far and small in the flat distance. I couldn't see my mother, and I thought that she must've turned on the radio and gone to sleep, which she always did, letting it play all night in her bedroom. Behind the car the sun was nearing the rounded mountains southwest of us, and I knew that when the sun was gone it would be cold. I wished my mother had decided to come along with us, and I thought for a moment of how little I really knew her at all.

Glen walked with me another quarter-mile, crossed another barbed wire fence where sage was growing, then went a hundred yards through wheatgrass and spurge until the ground went up and formed a kind of long hillock bunker built by a farmer against the wind. And I realized the lake was just beyond us. I could hear the sound of a car horn blowing and a dog barking all the way down in the town, then the wind seemed to move and all I could hear then and after then were geese. So many geese, from the sound of them, though I still could not see even one. I stood and listened to the high-pitched shouting sound, a sound I had never heard so close, a sound with size to it—though it was not loud. A sound that meant great numbers and that made your chest rise and your shoulders tighten with expectancy. It was a sound to make you feel separate from it and everything else, as if you were of no importance in the grand scheme of things.

"Do you hear them singing," Glen asked. He held his hand up to make me stand still. And we both listened. "How many do you think, Les, just hearing?"

"A hundred," I said. "More than a hundred."

"Five thousand," Glen said. "More than you can believe when you see them. 75 Go see."

I put down my gun and on my hands and knees crawled up the earthwork through the wheatgrass and thistle, until I could see down to the lake and see the geese. And they were there, like a white bandage laid on the water, wide and long and continuous, a white expanse of snow geese, seventy yards from me, on the bank, but stretching far onto the lake, which was large itself—a half-mile across, with thick tules on the far side and wild plums farther and the blue mountain behind them.

"Do you see the big raft?" Glen said from below me, in a whisper.

"I see it," I said, still looking. It was such a thing to see, a view I had never seen and have not since.

"Are any on the land?" he said.

"Some are in the wheatgrass," I said, "but most are swimming."   80

"Good," Glen said. "They'll have to fly. But we can't wait for that now."

And I crawled backwards down the heel of land to where Glen was, and my gun. We were losing our light, and the air was purplish and cooling. I looked toward the car but couldn't see it, and I was no longer sure where it was below the lighted sky.

"Where do they fly to?" I said in a whisper, since I did not want anything to be ruined because of what I did or said. It was important to Glen to shoot the geese, and it was important to me.

"To the wheat," he said. "Or else they leave for good. I wish your mother had come, Les. Now she'll be sorry."

I could hear the geese quarreling and shouting on the lake surface. And I   85
wondered if they knew we were here now. "She might be," I said with my heart pounding, but I didn't think she would be much.

It was a simple plan he had. I would stay behind the bunker, and he would crawl on his belly with his gun through the wheatgrass as near to the geese as he could. Then he would simply stand up and shoot all the ones he could close up, both in the air and on the ground. And when all the others flew up, with luck some would turn toward me as they came into the wind, and then I could shoot them and turn them back to him, and he would shoot them again. He could kill ten, he said, if he was lucky, and I might kill four. It didn't seem hard.

"Don't show them your face," Glen said. "Wait till you think you can touch them, then stand up and shoot. To hesitate is lost in this."

"All right," I said. "I'll try it."

"Shoot one in the head, and then shoot another one," Glen said. "It won't be hard." He patted me on the arm and smiled. Then he took off his VFW jacket and put it on the ground, climbed up the side of the bunker, cradling his shotgun in his arms, and slid on his belly into the dry stalks of yellow grass out of my sight.

Then, for the first time in that entire day, I was alone. And I didn't mind it.   90
I sat squat down in the grass, loaded my double gun and took my other two shells out of my pocket to hold. I pushed the safety off and on to see that it was right. The wind rose a little, scuffed the grass and made me shiver. It was not the warm chinook now, but a wind out of the north, the one geese flew away from if they could.

Then I thought about my mother, in the car alone, and how much longer I would stay with her, and what it might mean to her for me to leave. And I wondered when Glen Baxter would die and if someone would kill him, or whether my mother would marry him and how I would feel about it. And though I didn't know why, it occurred to me that Glen Baxter and I would not be friends when all was said and done, since I didn't care if he ever married my mother or didn't.

Then I thought about boxing and what my father had taught me about it.

To tighten your fists hard. To strike out straight from the shoulder and never punch backing up. How to cut a punch by snapping your fist inwards, how to carry your chin low, and to step toward a man when he is falling so you can hit him again. And most important, to keep your eyes open when you are hitting in the face and causing damage, because you need to see what you're doing to encourage yourself, and because it is when you close your eyes that you stop hitting and get hurt badly. "Fly all over your man, Les," my father said. "When you see your chance, fly on him and hit him till he falls." That, I thought, would always be my attitude in things.

And then I heard the geese again, their voices in unison, louder and shouting, as if the wind had changed again and put all new sounds in the cold air. And then a *boom*. And I knew Glen was in among them and had stood up to shoot. The noise of geese rose and grew worse, and my fingers burned where I held my gun too tight to the metal, and I put it down and opened my fist to make the burning stop so I could feel the trigger when the moment came. *Boom*, Glen shot again, and I heard him shuck a shell, and all the sounds out beyond the bunker seemed to be rising—the geese, the shots, the air itself going up. *Boom*, Glen shot another time, and I knew he was taking his careful time to make his shots good. And I held my gun and started to crawl up the bunker so as not to be surprised when the geese came over me and I could shoot.

From the top I saw Glen Baxter alone in the wheatgrass field, shooting at a white goose with black tips of wings that was on the ground not far from him, but trying to run and pull into the air. He shot it once more, and it fell over dead with its wings flapping.

Glen looked back at me and his face was distorted and strange. The air around   95
him was full of white rising geese and he seemed to want them all. "Behind you, Les," he yelled at me and pointed. "They're all behind you now." I looked behind me, and there were geese in the air as far as I could see, more than I knew how many, moving so slowly, their wings wide out and working calmly and filling the air with noise, though their voices were not as loud or as shrill as I had thought they would be. And they were so close! Forty feet, some of them. The air around me vibrated and I could feel the wind from their wings and it seemed to me I could kill as many as the times I could shoot—a hundred or a thousand—and I raised my gun, put the muzzle on the head of a white goose, and fired. It shuddered in the air, its wide feet sank below its belly, its wings cradled out to hold back air, and it fell straight down and landed with an awful sound, a noise a human would make, a thick, soft, *hump* noise. I looked up again and shot another goose, could hear the pellets hit its chest, but it didn't fall or even break its pattern for flying. *Boom*, Glen shot again. And then again. "Hey," I heard him shout, "Hey, hey." And there were geese flying over me, flying in line after line. I broke my gun and reloaded, and thought to myself as I did: I need confidence here, I need to be sure with this. I pointed at another goose and shot it in the head, and it fell the way the first one had, wings out, its belly down, and with the same thick noise of hitting. Then I sat down in the grass on the bunker and let geese fly over me.

By now the whole raft was in the air, all of it moving in a slow swirl above me and the lake and everywhere, finding the wind and heading out south in long wavering lines that caught the last sun and turned to silver as they gained a distance. It was a thing to see, I will tell you now. Five thousand white geese all in the air around you, making a noise like you have never heard before. And I thought to myself then: this is something I will never see again. I will never forget this. And I was right.

Glen Baxter shot twice more. One he missed, but with the other he hit a goose flying away from him, and knocked it half falling and flying into the empty lake not far from shore, where it began to swim as though it was fine and make its noise.

Glen stood in the stubby grass, looking out at the goose, his gun lowered. "I didn't need to shoot that one, did I, Les?"

"I don't know," I said, sitting on the little knoll of land, looking at the goose swimming in the water.

"I don't know why I shoot 'em. They're so beautiful." He looked at me.   100
"I don't know either," I said.

"Maybe there's nothing else to do with them." Glen stared at the goose again and shook his head. "Maybe this is exactly what they're put on earth for."

I did not know what to say because I did not know what he could mean by that, though what I felt was embarrassment at the great numbers of geese there were, and a dulled feeling like a hunger because the shooting had stopped and it was over for me now.

Glen began to pick up his geese, and I walked down to my two that had fallen close together and were dead. One had hit with such an impact that its stomach had split and some of its inward parts were knocked out. Though the other looked unhurt, its soft white belly turned up like a pillow, its head and jagged bill-teeth, its tiny black eyes looking as they would if they were alive.

"What's happened to the hunters out here?" I heard a voice speak. It was   105
my mother, standing in her pink dress on the knoll above us, hugging her arms. She was smiling though she was cold. And I realized that I had lost all thought of her in the shooting. "Who did all this shooting? Is this your work, Les?"

"No," I said.

"Les is a hunter, though, Aileen," Glen said. "He takes his time." He was holding two white geese by their necks, one in each hand, and he was smiling. He and my mother seemed pleased.

"I see you didn't miss too many," my mother said and smiled. I could tell she admired Glen for his geese, and that she had done some thinking in the car alone. "It *was* wonderful, Glen," she said. "I've never seen anything like that. They were like snow."

"It's worth seeing once, isn't it?" Glen said. "I should've killed more, but I got excited."

My mother looked at me then. "Where's yours, Les?"   110
"Here," I said and pointed to my two geese on the ground beside me.

My mother nodded in a nice way, and I think she liked everything then and wanted the day to turn out right and for all of us to be happy. "Six, then. You've got six in all."

"One's still out there," I said, and motioned where the one goose was swimming in circles on the water.

"Okay," my mother said and put her hand over her eyes to look. "Where is it?"

Glen Baxter looked at me then with a strange smile, a smile that said he   115
wished I had never mentioned anything about the other goose. And I wished I

hadn't either. I looked up in the sky and could see the lines of geese by the thousands shining silver in the light, and I wished we could just leave and go home.

"That one's my mistake there," Glen Baxter said and grinned. "I shouldn't have shot that one, Aileen. I got too excited."

My mother looked out on the lake for a minute, then looked at Glen and back again. "Poor goose." She shook her head. "How will you get it, Glen?"

"I can't get that one now," Glen said.

My mother looked at him. "What do you mean?"

"I'm going to leave that one," Glen said.   120

"Well, no. You can't leave one," my mother said. "You shot it. You have to get it. Isn't that a rule?"

"No," Glen said.

And my mother looked from Glen to me. "Wade out and get it, Glen," she said in a sweet way, and my mother looked young then, like a young girl, in her flimsy short-sleeved waitress dress and her skinny, bare legs in the wheatgrass.

"No." Glen Baxter looked down at his gun and shook his head. And I didn't know why he wouldn't go, because it would've been easy. The lake was shallow. And you could tell that anyone could've walked out a long way before it got deep, and Glen had on his boots.

My mother looked at the white goose, which was not more than thirty yards   125 from the shore, its head up, moving in slow circles, its wings settled and relaxed so you could see the black tips. "Wade out and get it, Glenny, won't you, please?" she said. "They're special things."

"You don't understand the world, Aileen," Glen said. "This can happen. It doesn't matter."

"But that's so cruel, Glen," she said, and a sweet smile came on her lips.

"Raise up your own arms, 'Leeny," Glen said. "I can't see any angel's wings, can you, Les?" He looked at me, but I looked away.

"Then you go on and get it, Les," my mother said. "You weren't raised by crazy people." I started to go, but Glen Baxter suddenly grabbed me by my shoulder and pulled me back hard, so hard his fingers made bruises in my skin that I saw later.

"Nobody's going," he said. "This is over with now."   130

And my mother gave Glen a cold look then. "You don't have a heart, Glen," she said. "There's nothing to love in you. You're just a son of a bitch, that's all."

And Glen Baxter nodded at my mother, then, as if he understood something he had not understood before, but something that he was willing to know. "Fine," he said, "that's fine." And he took his big pistol out from against his belly, the big blue revolver I had only seen part of before and that he said protected him, and he pointed it out at the goose on the water, his arm straight away from him, and shot and missed. And then he shot and missed again. The goose made its noise once. And then he hit it dead, because there was no splash. And then he shot it three times more until the gun was empty and the goose's head was down and it was floating toward the middle of the lake where it was empty and dark blue. "Now who has a heart?" Glen said. But my mother was not there when he turned around. She had already started back to the car and was almost lost from sight in the darkness. And Glen smiled at me then and his face had a wild look on it. "Okay, Les?" he said.

"Okay," I said.

"There're limits to everything, right?"

"I guess so," I said.   135

"Your mother's a beautiful woman, but she's not the only beautiful woman in Montana." And I did not say anything. And Glen Baxter suddenly said, "Here," and he held the pistol out at me. "Don't you want this? Don't you want to shoot me? Nobody thinks they'll die. But I'm ready for it right now." And I did not know what to do then. Though it is true that what I wanted to do was to hit him, hit him as hard in the face as I could, and see him on the ground bleeding and crying and pleading for me to stop. Only at that moment he looked scared to me, and I had never seen a grown man scared before—though I have seen one since—and I felt sorry for him, as though he was already a dead man. And I did not end up hitting him at all.

A light can go out in the heart. All of this happened years ago, but I still can feel now how sad and remote the world was to me. Glen Baxter, I think now, was not a bad man, only a man scared of something he'd never seen before—something soft in himself—his life going a way he didn't like. A woman with a son. Who could blame him there? I don't know what makes people do what they do, or call themselves what they call themselves, only that you have to live someone's life to be the expert.

My mother had tried to see the good side of things, tried to be hopeful in the situation she was handed, tried to look out for us both, and it hadn't worked. It was a strange time in her life then and after that, a time when she had to adjust to being an adult just when she was on the thin edge of things. Too much awareness too early in life was her problem, I think.

And what I felt was only that I had somehow been pushed out into the world, into the real life then, the one I hadn't lived yet. In a year I was gone to hard-rock mining and no-paycheck jobs and not to college. And I have thought more than once about my mother saying that I had not been raised by crazy people, and I don't know what that could mean or what difference it could make, unless it means that love is a reliable commodity, and even that is not always true, as I have found out.

Late on the night that all this took place I was in bed when I heard my mother   140
say, "Come outside, Les. Come and hear this." And I went out onto the front porch barefoot and in my underwear, where it was warm like spring, and there was a spring mist in the air. I could see the lights of the Fairfield Coach in the distance, on its way up to Great Falls.

And I could hear geese, white birds in the sky, flying. They made their high-pitched sound like angry yells, and though I couldn't see them high up, it seemed to me they were everywhere. And my mother looked up and said, "Hear them?" I could smell her hair wet from the shower. "They leave with the moon," she said. "It's still half wild out here."

And I said, "I hear them," and I felt a chill come over my bare chest, and the hair stood up on my arms the way it does before a storm. And for a while we listened.

"When I first married your father, you know, we lived on a street called Bluebird Canyon, in California. And I thought that was the prettiest street and the prettiest name. I suppose no one brings you up like your first love. You don't mind if I say that, do you?" She looked at me hopefully.

"No," I said.

"We have to keep civilization alive somehow." And she pulled her little house- 145
coat together because there was a cold vein in the air, a part of the cold that would
be on us the next day. "I don't feel part of things tonight, I guess."

"It's all right," I said.

"Do you know where I'd like to go?"

"No," I said. And I suppose I knew she was angry then, angry with life, but
did not want to show me that.

"To the Straits of Juan de Fuca.° Wouldn't that be something? Would you
like that?"

"I'd like it," I said. And my mother looked off for a minute, as if she could 150
see the Straits of Juan de Fuca out against the line of mountains, see the lights of
things alive and a whole new world.

"I know you liked him," she said after a moment. "You and I both suffer
fools too well."

"I didn't like him too much," I said. "I didn't really care."

"He'll fall on his face. I'm sure of that," she said. And I didn't say anything
because I didn't care about Glen Baxter anymore, and was happy not to talk about
him. "Would you tell me something if I asked you? Would you tell me the truth?"

"Yes," I said.

And my mother did not look at me. "Just tell the truth," she said. 155

"All right," I said.

"Do you think I'm still very feminine? I'm thirty-two years old now. You
don't know what that means. But do you think I am?"

And I stood at the edge of the porch, with the olive trees before me, looking straight up into the mist where I could not see geese but could still hear them
flying, could almost feel the air move below their white wings. And I felt the way
you feel when you are on a trestle all alone and the train is coming, and you know
you have to decide. And I said, "Yes, I do." Because that was the truth. And I
tried to think of something else then and did not hear what my mother said after that.

And how old was I then? Sixteen. Sixteen is young, but it can also be a grown
man. I am forty-one years old now, and I think about that time without regret,
though my mother and I never talked in that way again, and I have not heard her
voice now in a long, long time.

Straits of Juan de Fuca: The long body of water between Canada and Washington State on the
West Coast.

WINDOW ON

Psychology: Freud and Fiction

Freud's impact on literature has been powerful since the first decades of the twentieth century. He alarmed the public by asserting that everyone, including infants, had a sexual life. He asserted that the mind consisted of several parts: the ego is the conscious mind; the id is a part of the unconscious mind that contains primitive urges; and the superego is the moral censor, also part of our unconscious. Guilt forces people unconsciously to repress unacceptable thoughts and desires arising from the id. The repressed desires must be sublimated, or expressed in a socially acceptable way, for the individual to maintain mental health. In their visible form, then, our desires are carefully masked.

This analysis can be applied both to the way writers write and the way critics read. According to this theory, when the unconscious communicates its primitive urges to the conscious mind, it does so in symbols, dreams, puns, and "Freudian slips" instead of in clear language. These symbols are rather basic, often connected with the sexual urge, and since they are from the unconscious, they must be interpreted. For example, Father Tim, in Seán O'Faoláin's "Falling Rocks, Narrowing Road, Cul-de-Sac, Stop," analyzes symbols in a Freudian manner. Not everyone believes that Freud's theories are reliable, but many find them useful in interpreting a character's true feelings.

Freud's *Interpretation of Dreams* described the significance of people's dreams. In later works he distinguished between two important issues: (1) the "story" of the dream and (2) its deeper significance. "What has been called the dream we shall describe as the text of the dream or the *manifest* dream, and what we are looking for, what we suspect, so to say, of lying behind the dream, we shall describe as the *latent* dream-thoughts. Having done this, we can express our two tasks as follows. We have to transform the manifest dream into the latent one, and to explain how, in the dreamer's mind, the latter has become the former."

This concept is significant for interpreters of literary texts, since you often find yourself looking beyond the "manifest" detail in a story to find a "latent" significance. You can do this with the emblem of the "fallen monument" in "A Rose for Emily," the hills in "Hills like White Elephants," and the "Lucinda stream" of connected swimming pools in "The Swimmer." Freudian analysis and literary analysis have this in common: They assume a deeper meaning than appears on the surface of the text. As François Meltzer says, "If things such as metaphors and other verbal or literary devices (puns, analogies, figures of speech, tropes in general) are ways in which the unconscious manifests itself for psychoanalysis, then it should not be surprising that many literary critics have called language in general, and literature in particular, the unconscious of psychoanalysis." If this is true, then studying literature can give us insight into otherwise invisible processes of human thought.

Freudian analysis can also be used to describe our responses. Norman Holland uses an *identity* theory of reading to account for the discrepancies in how people read. He assumes that readers respond to texts in specific ways because of their own psychological identity, and he uses four key terms—*defense, expectation, fantasy*, and *transformation* (DEFT)—to analyze reader responses. First, readers read *defensively*, allowing only certain meanings to come through. They also *expect* certain meanings. *Fantasies* are possibilities readers permit to come out from themselves and be expressed. Finally, *transformation* "endows the work [with] a meaning beyond time." For example, Holland observed that one reader of "A Rose for Emily" took Colonel Sartoris's description "He who fathered the edict that no Negro woman should appear on the streets without an apron" to be forceful but not threatening. Another reader, however, saw in it "an aristocratic sexualized master-slave relationship." A third saw it as much less forceful and cruel. These distinctions, Holland asserts, result from the way readers DEFT a text, the way their identity interacts with it. This then implies "a personal style (identity)" of reading for each of us.

You may apply some of these ideas to an interpretation of D. H. Lawrence's "The Horse-Dealer's Daughter." Examine the animal imagery and the connections Lawrence makes between horses, dogs, and people. Then, consider the relationship Mabel has had with her father and her especial irritation when he remarries at age fifty-four. Her love for her mother had been different, you are told, than her love for her father. Is it possible she has repressed unconscious incestuous desires? Is her relationship with Fergusson healthy, or is it the product of repression? Lawrence knew the work of Freud, and his stories sometimes reflect his responses to it.

Reading

Freud, Sigmund. *The Complete Psychological Works of Sigmund Freud*. Edited by James Strachey. London: Hogarth Press, 1964.

Holland, Norman N. *Five Readers Reading*. New Haven: Yale University Press, 1975.

———. "Reading and Identity: A Psychoanalytic Revolution." *Academy Forum* 23 (1979).

Meltzer, François. "Unconscious." In *Critical Terms for Literary Study*, edited by Frank Lentricchia and Thomas McLaughlin, 147–62. Chicago: University of Chicago Press, 1990.

Smith, Joseph H., ed. *The Literary Freud*. New Haven: Yale University Press, 1980.

Charlotte Perkins Gilman   (1860–1935)

Charlotte Perkins Gilman was born and raised in Hartford, Connecticut, in a circle of distinguished intellectuals. "The Yellow Wallpaper," for example, was written after her separation from her husband, Charles Walter Stetson, her cousin and an artist in Providence, where she had attended the Rhode Island School of Design. They had been married in 1884 and she suffered a mental breakdown after the birth of her daughter in 1885. After a period of separation from her husband, she realized that divorce would be her only salvation and hope for sanity. "The Yellow Wallpaper" was almost certainly a result of her reflection on the experiences during her breakdown. She then began a career as a writer and lecturer, distinguishing herself as an economist in her Women and Economics *(1898). Her autobiography,* The Living of Charlotte Perkins Gilman, *was published after her death in 1935. She is among the most important early American feminist writers.*

THE YELLOW WALLPAPER   1892

It is very seldom that mere ordinary people like John and myself secure ancestral halls for the summer.

A colonial mansion, a hereditary estate, I would say a haunted house and reach the height of romantic felicity—but that would be asking too much of fate!

Still I will proudly declare that there is something queer about it.

Else, why should it be let so cheaply? And why have stood so long untenanted?

John laughs at me, of course, but one expects that.   5

John is practical in the extreme. He has no patience with faith, an intense horror of superstition, and he scoffs openly at any talk of things not to be felt and seen and put down in figures.

John is a physician, and *perhaps*—(I would not say it to a living soul, of course, but this is dead paper and a great relief to my mind)—*perhaps* that is one reason I do not get well faster.

You see, he does not believe I am sick! And what can one do?

If a physician of high standing, and one's own husband, assures friends and relatives that there is really nothing the matter with one but temporary nervous depression—a slight hysterical tendency—what is one to do?

My brother is also a physician, and also of high standing, and he says the   10 same thing.

So I take phosphates or phosphites—whichever it is—and tonics, and air and exercise, and journeys, and am absolutely forbidden to "work" until I am well again.

Personally, I disagree with their ideas.

Personally, I believe that congenial work, with excitement and change, would do me good.

But what is one to do?

I did write for a while in spite of them; but it *does* exhaust me a good deal—   15 having to be so sly about it, or else meet with heavy opposition.

I sometimes fancy that in my condition, if I had less opposition and more society and stimulus—but John says the very worst thing I can do is to think about my condition, and I confess it always makes me feel bad.

So I will let it alone and talk about the house.

The most beautiful place! It is quite alone, standing well back from the road, quite three miles from the village. It makes me think of English places that you read about, for there are hedges and walls and gates that lock, and lots of separate little houses for the gardeners and people.

There is a *delicious* garden! I never saw such a garden—large and shady, full of box-bordered° paths, and lined with long grape-covered arbors with seats under them.

There were greenhouses, but they are all broken now.   20

There was some legal trouble, I believe, something about the heirs and coheirs; anyhow, the place has been empty for years.

That spoils my ghostliness, I am afraid, but I don't care—there is something strange about the house—I can feel it.

I even said so to John one moonlight evening, but he said what I felt was a draught, and shut the window.

I get unreasonably angry with John sometimes. I'm sure I never used to be so sensitive. I think it is due to this nervous condition.

But John says if I feel so I shall neglect proper self-control; so I take pains   25
to control myself—before him, at least, and that makes me very tired.

I don't like our room a bit. I wanted one downstairs that opened onto the piazza and had roses all over the window, and such pretty old-fashioned chintz hangings! But John would not hear of it.

He said there was only one window and not room for two beds, and no near room for him if he took another.

He is very careful and loving, and hardly lets me stir without special direction.

I have a schedule prescription for each hour in the day; he takes all care from me, and so I feel basely ungrateful not to value it more.

He said he came here solely on my account, that I was to have perfect rest   30
and all the air I could get. "Your exercise depends on your strength, my dear," said he, "and your food somewhat on your appetite; but air you can absorb all the time." So we took the nursery at the top of the house.

It is a big, airy room, the whole floor nearly, with windows that look all ways, and air and sunshine galore. It was nursery first, and then playroom and gymnasium, I should judge, for the windows are barred for little children, and there are rings and things in the walls.

The paint and paper look as if a boys' school had used it. It is stripped off—the paper—in great patches all around the head of my bed, about as far as I can reach, and in a great place on the other side of the room low down. I never saw a worse paper in my life. One of those sprawling, flamboyant patterns committing every artistic sin.

It is dull enough to confuse the eye in following, pronounced enough constantly to irritate and provoke study, and when you follow the lame uncertain curves for a little distance they suddenly commit suicide—plunge off at outrageous angles, destroy themselves in unheard-of contradictions.

The color is repellent, almost revolting: a smouldering unclean yellow,

---

box-bordered: Bordered with boxwood hedges.

strangely faded by the slow-turning sunlight. It is a dull yet lurid orange in some places, a sickly sulphur tint in others.

No wonder the children hated it! I should hate it myself if I had to live in this room long.   35

There comes John, and I must put this away—he hates to have me write a word.

We have been here two weeks, and I haven't felt like writing before, since that first day.

I am sitting by the window now, up in this atrocious nursery, and there is nothing to hinder my writing as much as I please, save lack of strength.

John is away all day, and even some nights when his cases are serious.

I am glad my case is not serious!   40

But these nervous troubles are dreadfully depressing.

John does not know how much I really suffer. He knows there is no reason to suffer, and that satisfies him.

Of course it is only nervousness. It does weigh on me so not to do my duty in any way!

I meant to be such a help to John, such a real rest and comfort, and here I am a comparative burden already!

Nobody would believe what an effort it is to do what little I am able—to   45
dress and entertain, and order things.

It is fortunate Mary is so good with the baby. Such a dear baby!

And yet I *cannot* be with him, it makes me so nervous.

I suppose John never was nervous in his life. He laughs at me so about this wallpaper!

At first he meant to repaper the room, but afterward he said that I was letting it get the better of me, and that nothing was worse for a nervous patient than to give way to such fancies.

He said that after the wallpaper was changed it would be the heavy bedstead,   50
and then the barred windows, and then that gate at the head of the stairs, and so on.

"You know the place is doing you good," he said, "and really, dear, I don't care to renovate the house just for a three months' rental."

"Then do let us go downstairs," I said. "There are such pretty rooms there."

Then he took me in his arms and called me a blessed little goose, and said he would go down cellar, if I wished, and have it whitewashed into the bargain.

But he is right enough about the beds and windows and things.

It is as airy and comfortable a room as anyone need wish, and, of course, I   55
would not be so silly as to make him uncomfortable just for a whim.

I'm really getting quite fond of the big room, all but that horrid paper.

Out of one window I can see the garden—those mysterious deep-shaded arbors, the riotous old-fashioned flowers, and bushes and gnarly trees.

Out of another I get a lovely view of the bay and a little private wharf belonging to the estate. There is a beautiful shaded lane that runs down there from the house. I always fancy I see people walking in these numerous paths and arbors, but John has cautioned me not to give way to fancy in the least. He says that with my imaginative power and habit of story-making, a nervous weakness like mine is sure to lead to all manner of excited fancies, and that I ought to use my will and good sense to check the tendency. So I try.

I think sometimes that if I were only well enough to write a little it would relieve the press of ideas and rest me.

But I find I get pretty tired when I try.

It is so discouraging not to have any advice and companionship about my work. When I get really well, John says we will ask Cousin Henry and Julia down for a long visit; but he says he would as soon put fireworks in my pillow-case as to let me have those stimulating people about now.

I wish I could get well faster.

But I must not think about that. This paper looks to me as if it *knew* what a vicious influence it had!

There is a recurrent spot where the pattern lolls like a broken neck and two bulbous eyes stare at you upside down.

I get positively angry with the impertinence of it and the everlastingness. Up and down and sideways they crawl, and those absurd unblinking eyes are everywhere. There is one place where two breadths didn't match, and the eyes go all up and down the line, one a little higher than the other.

I never saw so much expression in an inanimate thing before, and we all know how much expression they have! I used to lie awake as a child and get more entertainment and terror out of blank walls and plain furniture than most children could find in a toy-store.

I remember what a kindly wink the knobs of our big old bureau used to have, and there was one chair that always seemed like a strong friend.

I used to feel that if any of the other things looked too fierce I could always hop into that chair and be safe.

The furniture in this room is no worse than inharmonious, however, for we had to bring it all from downstairs. I suppose when this was used as a playroom they had to take the nursery things out, and no wonder! I never saw such ravages as the children have made here.

The wallpaper, as I said before, is torn off in spots, and it sticketh closer than a brother—they must have had perseverance as well as hatred.

Then the floor is scratched and gouged and splintered, the plaster itself is dug out here and there, and this great heavy bed, which is all we found in the room, looks as if it had been through the wars.

But I don't mind it a bit—only the paper.

There comes John's sister. Such a dear girl as she is, and so careful of me! I must not let her find me writing.

She is a perfect and enthusiastic housekeeper, and hopes for no better profession. I verily believe she thinks it is the writing which made me sick!

But I can write when she is out, and see her a long way off from these windows.

There is one that commands the road, a lovely shaded winding road, and one that just looks off over the country. A lovely country, too, full of great elms and velvet meadows.

This wallpaper has a kind of subpattern in a different shade, a particularly irritating one, for you can only see it in certain lights, and not clearly then.

But in the places where it isn't faded and where the sun is just so—I can see a strange, provoking, formless sort of figure that seems to skulk about behind that silly and conspicuous front design.

There's sister on the stairs!

Well, the Fourth of July is over! The people are all gone, and I am tired out.   80
John thought it might do me good to see a little company, so we just had Mother
and Nellie and the children down for a week.

Of course I didn't do a thing. Jennie sees to everything now.

But it tired me all the same.

John says if I don't pick up faster he shall send me to Weir Mitchell° in the
fall.

But I don't want to go there at all. I had a friend who was in his hands once,
and she says he is just like John and my brother, only more so!

Besides, it is such an undertaking to go so far.   85

I don't feel as if it was worthwhile to turn my hand over for anything, and
I'm getting dreadfully fretful and querulous.

I cry at nothing, and cry most of the time.

Of course I don't when John is here, or anybody else, but when I am alone.

And I am alone a good deal just now. John is kept in town very often by serious cases, and Jennie is good and lets me alone when I want her to.

So I walk a little in the garden or down that lovely lane, sit on the porch un-   90
der the roses, and lie down up here a good deal.

I'm getting really fond of the room in spite of the wallpaper. Perhaps *because*
of the wallpaper.

It dwells in my mind so!

I lie here on this great immovable bed—it is nailed down, I believe—and follow that pattern about by the hour. It is as good as gymnastics, I assure you. I
start, we'll say, at the bottom, down in the corner over there where it has not
been touched, and I determine for the thousandth time that I *will* follow that
pointless pattern to some sort of a conclusion.

I know a little of the principle of design, and I know this thing was not
arranged on any laws of radiation, or alternation, or repetition, or symmetry, or
anything else that I ever heard of.

It is repeated, of course, by the breadths, but not otherwise.   95

Looked at in one way, each breadth stands alone; the bloated curves and
flourishes—a kind of "debased Romanesque" with dilirium tremens go waddling
up and down in isolated columns of fatuity.

But, on the other hand, they connect diagonally, and the sprawling outlines
run off in great slanting waves of optic horror, like a lot of wallowing sea-weeds
in full chase.

The whole thing goes horizontally, too, at least it seems so, and I exhaust
myself trying to distinguish the order of its going in that direction.

They have used a horizontal breadth for a frieze, and that adds wonderfully
to the confusion.

There is one end of the room where it is almost intact, and there, when the   100
crosslights fade and the low sun shines directly upon it, I can almost fancy radiation after all—the interminable grotesque seems to form around a common center and rush off in headlong plunges of equal distraction.

It makes me tired to follow it. I will take a nap, I guess.

I don't know why I should write this.

Weir Mitchell: Dr. S. Weir Mitchell (1829–1914); a Philadelphia physician who developed the
"rest cure" for his women patients, including Gilman.

I don't want to.

I don't feel able.

And I know John would think it absurd. But I *must* say what I feel and think   105
in some way—it is such a relief!

But the effort is getting to be greater than the relief.

Half the time now I am awfully lazy, and lie down ever so much. John says
I mustn't lose my strength, and has me take cod liver oil and lots of tonics and
things, to say nothing of ale and wines and rare meat.

Dear John! He loves me very dearly, and hates to have me sick. I tried to
have a real earnest reasonable talk with him the other day, and tell him how I wish
he would let me go and make a visit to Cousin Henry and Julia.

But he said I wasn't able to go, nor able to stand it after I got there; and I
did not make out a very good case for myself, for I was crying before I had finished.

It is getting to be a great effort for me to think straight. Just this nervous   110
weakness, I suppose.

And dear John gathered me up in his arms, and just carried me upstairs and
laid me on the bed, and sat by me and read to me till it tired my head.

He said I was his darling and his comfort and all he had, and that I must take
care of myself for his sake, and keep well.

He says no one but myself can help me out of it, that I must use my will and
self-control and not let any silly fancies run away with me.

There's one comfort—the baby is well and happy, and does not have to occupy this nursery with the horrid wallpaper.

If we had not used it, that blessed child would have! What a fortunate es-   115
cape! Why, I wouldn't have a child of mine, an impressionable little thing, live in
such a room for worlds.

I never thought of it before, but it is lucky that John kept me here after all;
I can stand it so much easier than a baby, you see.

Of course I never mention it to them anymore—I am too wise—but I keep
watch for it all the same.

There are things in the wallpaper that nobody knows about but me, or ever
will.

Behind that outside pattern the dim shapes get clearer every day.

It is always the same shape, only very numerous.   120

And it is like a woman stooping down and creeping about behind that pattern. I don't like it a bit. I wonder—I begin to think—I wish John would take
me away from here!

It is so hard to talk with John about my case, because he is so wise, and because he loves me so.

But I tried it last night.

It was moonlight. The moon shines in all around just as the sun does.

I hate to see it sometimes, it creeps so slowly, and always comes in by one   125
window or another.

John was asleep and I hated to waken him, so I kept still and watched the
moonlight on that undulating wallpaper till I felt creepy.

The faint figure behind seemed to shake the pattern, just as if she wanted to
get out.

I got up softly and went to feel and see if the paper *did* move, and when I came back John was awake.

"What is it, little girl?" he said. "Don't go walking about like that—you'll get cold."

I thought it was a good time to talk, so I told him that I really was not gain-   130
ing here, and that I wished he would take me away.

"Why, darling!" said he. "Our lease will be up in three weeks, and I can't see how to leave before."

"The repairs are not done at home, and I cannot possibly leave town just now. Of course, if you were in any danger, I could and would, but you really are better, dear, whether you can see it or not. I am a doctor, dear, and I know. You are gaining flesh and color, your appetite is better, I feel really much easier about you."

"I don't weigh a bit more," said I, "nor as much; and my appetite may be better in the evening when you are here but it is worse in the morning when you are away!"

"Bless her little heart!" said he with a big hug. "She shall be as sick as she pleases! But now let's improve the shining hours by going to sleep, and talk about it in the morning!"

"And you won't go away?" I asked gloomily.   135

"Why, how can I, dear? It is only three weeks more and then we will take a nice little trip for a few days while Jennie is getting the house ready. Really, dear, you are better!"

"Better in body perhaps—" I began, and stopped short, for he sat up straight and looked at me with such a stern, reproachful look that I could not say another word.

"My darling," said he, "I beg you, for my sake and for our child's sake, as well as for your own, that you will never for one instant let that idea enter your mind! There is nothing so dangerous, so fascinating, to a temperament like yours. It is a false and foolish fancy. Can you trust me as a physician when I tell you so?"

So of course I said no more on that score, and we went to sleep before long. He thought I was asleep first, but I wasn't, and lay there for hours trying to de-cide whether that front pattern and the back pattern really did move together or separately.

On a pattern like this, by daylight, there is a lack of sequence, a defiance of   140
law, that is a constant irritant to a normal mind.

The color is hideous enough, and unreliable enough, and infuriating enough, but the pattern is torturing.

You think you have mastered it, but just as you get well under way in fol-lowing, it turns a back-somersault and there you are. It slaps you in the face, knocks you down, and tramples upon you. It is like a bad dream.

The outside pattern is a florid arabesque, reminding one of a fungus. If you can imagine a toadstool in joints, an interminable string of toadstools, budding and sprouting in endless convolutions—why, that is something like it.

That is, sometimes!

There is one marked peculiarity about this paper, a thing nobody seems to   145
notice but myself, and that is that it changes as the light changes.

When the sun shoots in through the east window—I always watch for that first long, straight ray—it changes so quickly that I never can quite believe it.

That is why I watch it always.

By moonlight—the moon shines in all night when there is a moon—I wouldn't know it was the same paper.

At night in any kind of light, in twilight, candlelight, lamplight, and worst of all by moonlight, it becomes bars! The outside pattern, I mean, and the woman behind it is as plain as can be.

I didn't realize for a long time what the thing was that showed behind, that 150 dim subpattern, but now I am quite sure it is a woman.

By daylight she is subdued, quiet. I fancy it is the pattern that keeps her so still. It is so puzzling. It keeps me quiet by the hour.

I lie down ever so much now. John says it is good for me, and to sleep all I can.

Indeed he started the habit by making me lie down for an hour after each meal.

It is a very bad habit, I am convinced, for you see, I don't sleep.

And that cultivates deceit, for I don't tell them I'm awake—oh, no! 155

The fact is I am getting a little afraid of John.

He seems very queer sometimes, and even Jennie has an inexplicable look.

It strikes me occasionally, just as a scientific hypothesis, that perhaps it is the paper!

I have watched John when he did not know I was looking, and come into the room suddenly on the most innocent excuses, and I've caught him several times *looking at the paper*! And Jennie too. I caught Jennie with her hand on it once.

She didn't know I was in the room, and when I asked her in a quiet, a very 160 quiet voice, with the most restrained manner possible, what she was doing with the paper, she turned around as if she had been caught stealing, and looked quite angry—asked me why I should frighten her so!

Then she said that the paper stained everything it touched, that she had found yellow smooches on all my clothes and John's and she wished we would be more careful!

Did not that sound innocent? But I know she was studying that pattern, and I am determined that nobody shall find it out but myself!

Life is very much more exciting now than it used to be. You see, I have something more to expect, to look forward to, to watch. I really do eat better, and am more quiet than I was.

John is so pleased to see me improve! He laughed a little the other day, and said I seemed to be flourishing in spite of my wallpaper.

I turned it off with a laugh. I had no intention of telling him it was *because* 165 of the wallpaper—he would make fun of me. He might even want to take me away.

I don't want to leave now until I have found it out. There is a week more, and I think that will be enough.

I'm feeling so much better!

I don't sleep much at night, for it is so interesting to watch developments; but I sleep a good deal during the daytime.

In the daytime it is tiresome and perplexing.

There are always new shoots on the fungus, and new shades of yellow all 170 over it. I cannot keep count of them, though I have tried conscientiously.

It is the strangest yellow, that wallpaper! It makes me think of all the yellow things I ever saw—not beautiful ones like buttercups, but old, foul, bad yellow things.

But there is something else about that paper—the smell! I noticed it the moment we came into the room, but with so much air and sun it was not bad. Now we have had a week of fog and rain, and whether the windows are open or not, the smell is here.

It creeps all over the house.

I find it hovering in the dining-room, skulking in the parlor, hiding in the hall, lying in wait for me on the stairs.

It gets into my hair. 175

Even when I go to ride, if I turn my head suddenly and surprise it—there is that smell!

Such a peculiar odor, too! I have spent hours in trying to analyze it, to find what it smelled like.

It is not bad—at first—and very gentle, but quite the subtlest, most enduring odor I ever met.

In this damp weather it is awful. I wake up in the night and find it hanging over me.

It used to disturb me at first. I thought seriously of burning the house—to 180 reach the smell.

But now I am used to it. The only thing I can think of that it is like is the *color* of the paper! A yellow smell.

There a very funny mark on this wall, low down, near the mopboard. A streak that runs round the room. It goes behind every piece of furniture, except the bed, a long, straight, even *smooch*, as if it had been rubbed over and over.

I wonder how it was done and who did it, and what they did it for. Round and round and round—round and round and round—it makes me dizzy!

I really have discovered something at last.

Through watching so much at night, when it changes so, I have finally found 185 out.

The front pattern *does* move—and no wonder! The woman behind shakes it!

Sometimes I think there are a great many women behind, and sometimes only one, and she crawls around fast, and her crawling shakes it all over.

Then in the very bright spots she keeps still, and in the very shady spots she just takes hold of the bars and shakes them hard.

And she is all the time trying to climb through. But nobody could climb through that pattern—it strangles so; I think that is why it has so many heads.

They get through and then the pattern strangles them off and turns them 190 upside down, and makes their eyes white!

If those heads were covered or taken off it would not be half so bad.

I think that woman gets out in the daytime!

And I'll tell you why—privately—I've seen her!

I can see her out of every one of my windows!

It is the same woman, I know, for she is always creeping, and most women 195 do not creep by daylight.

I see her in that long shaded lane, creeping up and down. I see her in those dark grape arbors, creeping all round the garden.

I see her on that long road under the trees, creeping along, and when a carriage comes she hides under the blackberry vines.

I don't blame her a bit. It must be very humiliating to be caught creeping by daylight!

I always lock the door when I creep by daylight. I can't do it at night, for I know John would suspect something at once.

And John is so queer now that I don't want to irritate him. I wish he would 200 take another room! Besides, I don't want anybody to get that woman out at night but myself.

I often wonder if I could see her out of all the windows at once.

But, turn as fast as I can, I can only see out of one at one time.

And though I always see her, she *may* be able to creep faster than I can turn! I have watched her sometimes away off in the open country, creeping as fast as a cloud shadow in a wind.

If only that top pattern could be gotten off from the under one! I mean to try it, little by little.

I have found out another funny thing, but I shan't tell it this time! It does 205 not do to trust people too much.

There are only two more days to get this paper off, and I believe John is beginning to notice. I don't like the look in his eyes.

And I heard him ask Jennie a lot of professional questions about me. She had a very good report to give.

She said I slept a good deal in the daytime.

John knows I don't sleep very well at night, for all I'm so quiet!

He asked me all sorts of questions too, and pretended to be very loving and 210 kind.

As if I couldn't see through him!

Still, I don't wonder he acts so, sleeping under this paper for three months.

It only interests me, but I feel sure John and Jennie are affected by it.

Hurrah! This is the last day, but it is enough. John is to stay in town over night, and won't be out until this evening.

Jennie wanted to sleep with me—the sly thing; but I told her I should un- 215 doubtedly rest better for a night all alone.

That was clever, for really I wasn't alone a bit! As soon as it was moonlight and that poor thing began to crawl and shake the pattern, I got up and ran to help her.

I pulled and she shook. I shook and she pulled, and before morning we had peeled off yards of that paper.

A strip about as high as my head and half around the room.

And then when the sun came and that awful pattern began to laugh at me, I declared I would finish it today!

We go away tomorrow, and they are moving all my furniture down again to 220 leave things as they were before.

Jennie looked at the wall in amazement, but I told her merrily that I did it out of pure spite at the vicious thing.

She laughed and said she wouldn't mind doing it herself, but I must not get tired.

How she betrayed herself that time!

But I am here, and no person touches this paper but Me—not *alive*!

She tried to get me out of the room—it was too patent! But I said it was so   225
quiet and empty and clean now that I believed I would lie down again and sleep
all I could, and not to wake me even for dinner—I would call when I woke.

So now she is gone, and the servants are gone, and the things are gone, and
there is nothing left but that great bedstead nailed down, with the canvas mattress we found on it.

We shall sleep downstairs tonight, and take the boat home tomorrow.

I quite enjoy the room, now it is bare again.

How those children did tear about here!

This bedstead is fairly gnawed!   230

But I must get to work.

I have locked the door and thrown the key down into the front path.

I don't want to go out, and I don't want to have anybody come in, till John
comes.

I want to astonish him.

I've got a rope up here that even Jennie did not find. If that woman does   235
get out, and tries to get away, I can tie her!

But I forgot I could not reach far without anything to stand on!

This bed will *not* move!

I tried to lift and push it until I was lame, and then I got so angry I bit off a
little piece at one corner—but it hurt my teeth.

Then I peeled off all the paper I could reach standing on the floor. It sticks
horribly and the pattern just enjoys it! All those strangled heads and bulbous eyes
and waddling fungus growths just shriek with derision!

I am getting angry enough to do something desperate. To jump out of the   240
window would be admirable exercise, but the bars are too strong even to try.

Besides I wouldn't do it. Of course not. I know well enough that a step like
that is improper and might be misconstrued.

I don't like to *look* out of the windows even—there are so many of those
creeping women, and they creep so fast.

I wonder if they all come out of that wallpaper as I did!

But I am securely fastened now by my well-hidden rope—you don't get *me*
out in the road there!

I suppose I shall have to get back behind the pattern when it comes night,   245
and that is hard!

It is so pleasant to be out in this great room and creep around as I please!

I don't want to go outside. I won't, even if Jennie asks me to.

For outside you have to creep on the ground, and everything is green instead of yellow.

But here I can creep smoothly on the floor, and my shoulder just fits in that
long smooch around the wall, so I cannot lose my way.

Why, there's John at the door!   250

It is no use, young man, you can't open it!

How he does call and pound!

Now he's crying to Jennie for an axe.

It would be a shame to break down that beautiful door!

"John, dear!" said I in the gentlest voice. "The key is down by the front   255
steps, under a plantain leaf!"

That silenced him for a few moments.

Then he said, very quietly indeed, "Open the door, my darling!"

"I can't," said I. "The key is down by the front door under a plantain leaf!"
And then I said it again, several times, very gently and slowly, and said it so often that he had to go and see, and he got it of course, and came in. He stopped
short by the door.

"What is the matter?" he cried. "For God's sake, what are you doing!"

I kept on creeping just the same, but I looked at him over my shoulder.   260

"I've got out at last," said I, "in spite of you and Jane. And I've pulled off
most of the paper, so you can't put me back!"

Now why should that man have fainted? But he did, and right across my path
by the wall, so that I had to creep over him every time!

Nathaniel Hawthorne   (1804–1864)

*Nathaniel Hawthorne was among the greatest nineteenth-century American
writers, dominating in both short fiction and the novel. His stories in* Twice-Told
Tales *(1837) and* Mosses on an Old Manse *(1846) helped establish the
independence of the American short story. They are dense, filled with atmosphere,
and in many ways mysterious. Hawthorne was himself haunted by associations
with his place of birth, Salem, Massachusetts, where his relatives presided at the
trials of witches who were found guilty and hanged. His novel* The Scarlet Letter
*(1850) explores the behavior of the Puritan community that Salem had once been,
and* The House of Seven Gables *(1851) examines the moral circumstances of the
age succeeding the one that hunted witches. His work is subtle and profound, and
his achievement established a tone of high seriousness for short fiction in America.*

RAPPACCINI'S DAUGHTER   1844

[From the Writings of Aubépine.]°

WE do not remember to have seen any translated specimens of the productions of M. de l'Aubépine—a fact the less to be wondered at, as his very name is
unknown to many of his own countrymen as well as to the student of foreign literature. As a writer, he seems to occupy an unfortunate position between the
Transcendentalists (who, under one name or another, have their share in all the
current literature of the world) and the great body of pen-and-ink men who address the intellect and sympathies of the multitude. If not too refined, at all events
too remote, too shadowy, and unsubstantial in his modes of development to suit

This introduction is Hawthorne writing about himself in a half-serious, half-playful manner. He
pretends he is a European, not American, writer (Aubépine means "hawthorne"), and proceeds
to mock himself and his writings, all the time, in subtle ways, making serious statements about
his work. Most of the titles refer to his works, such as *Twice Told Tales*, "The Celestial Railroad,"
"The New Adam and Eve," "Egotism; or, The Bosom Serpent," "Fire Worship," "Evenings in
a Garden of Spain," and "The Artist of the Beautiful," all short stories in the collection with
"Rappaccini's Daughter."

the taste of the latter class, and yet too popular to satisfy the spiritual or metaphysical requisitions of the former, he must necessarily find himself without an audience, except here and there an individual or possibly an isolated clique. His writings, to do them justice, are not altogether destitute of fancy and originality; they might have won him greater reputation but for an inveterate love of allegory, which is apt to invest his plots and characters with the aspect of scenery and people in the clouds, and to steal away the human warmth out of his conceptions. His fictions are sometimes historical, sometimes of the present day, and sometimes, so far as can be discovered, have little or no reference either to time or space. In any case, he generally contents himself with a very slight embroidery of outward manners,—the faintest possible counterfeit of real life,—and endeavors to create an interest by some less obvious peculiarity of the subject. Occasionally a breath of Nature, a raindrop of pathos and tenderness, or a gleam of humor, will find its way into the midst of his fantastic imagery, and make us feel as if, after all, we were yet within the limits of our native earth. We will only add to this very cursory notice that M. de l'Aubépine's productions, if the reader chance to take them in precisely the proper point of view, may amuse a leisure hour as well as those of a brighter man; if otherwise, they can hardly fail to look excessively like nonsense.

Our author is voluminous; he continues to write and publish with as much praiseworthy and indefatigable prolixity as if his efforts were crowned with the brilliant success that so justly attends those of Eugene Sue. His first appearance was by a collection of stories in a long series of volumes entitled "Contes deux fois racontées." The titles of some of his more recent works (we quote from memory) are as follows: "Le Voyage Céleste à Chemin de Fer," 3 tom., 1838; "Le nouveau Père Adam et la nouvelle Mère Eve," 2 tom., 1839; "Roderic; ou le Serpent à l'estomac," 2 tom., 1840; "Le Culte du Feu," a folio volume of ponderous research into the religion and ritual of the old Persian Ghebers, published in 1841; "La Soirée du Chateau en Espagne," 1 tom., 8vo, 1842; and "L'Artiste du Beau; ou le Papillon Mécanique," 5 tom., 4to, 1843. Our somewhat wearisome perusal of this startling catalogue of volumes has left behind it a certain personal affection and sympathy, though by no means admiration, for M. de l'Aubépine; and we would fain do the little in our power towards introducing him favorably to the American public. The ensuing tale is a translation of his "Beatrice; ou la Belle Empoisonneuse," recently published in "La Revue Anti-Aristocratique." This journal, edited by the Comte de Bearhaven, has for some years past led the defense of liberal principles and popular rights with a faithfulness and ability worthy of all praise.

A young man, named Giovanni Guasconti, came, very long ago, from the more southern region of Italy, to pursue his studies at the University of Padua. Giovanni, who had but a scanty supply of gold ducats in his pocket, took lodgings in a high and gloomy chamber of an old edifice which looked not unworthy to have been the palace of a Paduan noble, and which, in fact, exhibited over its entrance the armorial bearings of a family long since extinct. The young stranger, who was not unstudied in the great poem° of his country, recollected that one of the ancestors of this family, and perhaps an occupant of this very mansion, had been pictured by Dante as a partaker of the immortal agonies of his Inferno. These

---

great poem: Dante's *Inferno*, a poem about a journey through Hell.

reminiscences and associations, together with the tendency to heartbreak natural to a young man for the first time out of his native sphere, caused Giovanni to sigh heavily as he looked around the desolate and ill-furnished apartment.

"Holy Virgin, signor!" cried old Dame Lisabetta, who, won by the youth's remarkable beauty of person, was kindly endeavoring to give the chamber a habitable air, "what a sigh was that to come out of a young man's heart! Do you find this old mansion gloomy? For the love of Heaven, then, put your head out of the window, and you will see as bright sunshine as you have left in Naples."

Guasconti mechanically did as the old woman advised, but could not quite 5
agree with her that the Paduan sunshine was as cheerful as that of southern Italy. Such as it was, however, it fell upon a garden beneath the window and expended its fostering influences on a variety of plants, which seemed to have been cultivated with exceeding care.

"Does this garden belong to the house?" asked Giovanni.

"Heaven forbid, signor, unless it were fruitful of better pot herbs than any that grow there now," answered old Lisabetta. "No; that garden is cultivated by the own hands of Signor Giacomo Rappaccini, the famous doctor, who, I warrant him, has been heard of as far as Naples. It is said that he distils these plants into medicines that are as potent as a charm. Oftentimes you may see the signor doctor at work, and perchance the signora, his daughter, too, gathering the strange flowers that grow in the garden."

The old woman had now done what she could for the aspect of the chamber; and, commending the young man to the protection of the saints, took her departure.

Giovanni still found no better occupation than to look down into the garden beneath his window. From its appearance, he judged it to be one of those botanic gardens which were of earlier date in Padua than elsewhere in Italy or in the world. Or, not improbably, it might once have been the pleasure-place of an opulent family; for there was the ruin of a marble fountain in the center, sculptured with rare art, but so wofully shattered that it was impossible to trace the original design from the chaos of remaining fragments. The water, however, continued to gush and sparkle into the sunbeams as cheerfully as ever. A little gurgling sound ascended to the young man's window, and made him feel as if the fountain were an immortal spirit that sung its song unceasingly and without heeding the vicissitudes around it, while one century imbodied it in marble and another scattered the perishable garniture on the soil. All about the pool into which the water subsided grew various plants, that seemed to require a plentiful supply of moisture for the nourishment of gigantic leaves, and in some instances, flowers gorgeously magnificent. There was one shrub in particular, set in a marble vase in the midst of the pool, that bore a profusion of purple blossoms, each of which had the lustre and richness of a gem; and the whole together made a show so resplendent that it seemed enough to illuminate the garden, even had there been no sunshine. Every portion of the soil was peopled with plants and herbs, which, if less beautiful, still bore tokens of assiduous care, as if all had their individual virtues, known to the scientific mind that fostered them. Some were placed in urns, rich with old carving, and others in common garden pots; some crept serpent-like along the ground or climbed on high, using whatever means of ascent was offered them. One plant had wreathed itself round a statue of Vertumnus, which was thus quite veiled and shrouded in a drapery of hanging foliage, so happily arranged that it might have served a sculptor for a study.

While Giovanni stood at the window he heard a rustling behind a screen of   10
leaves, and became aware that a person was at work in the garden. His figure soon
emerged into view, and showed itself to be that of no common laborer, but a tall,
emaciated, sallow, and sickly-looking man, dressed in a scholar's garb of black.
He was beyond the middle term of life, with gray hair, a thin, gray beard, and a
face singularly marked with intellect and cultivation, but which could never, even
in his more youthful days, have expressed much warmth of heart.

Nothing could exceed the intentness with which this scientific gardener examined every shrub which grew in his path: it seemed as if he was looking into
their inmost nature, making observations in regard to their creative essence, and
discovering why one leaf grew in this shape and another in that, and wherefore
such and such flowers differed among themselves in hue and perfume.
Nevertheless, in spite of this deep intelligence on his part, there was no approach
to intimacy between himself and these vegetable existences. On the contrary, he
avoided their actual touch or the direct inhaling of their odors with a caution that
impressed Giovanni most disagreeably; for the man's demeanor was that of one
walking among malignant influences, such as savage beasts, or deadly snakes, or
evil spirits, which, should he allow them one moment of license, would wreak
upon him some terrible fatality. It was strangely frightful to the young man's imagination to see this air of insecurity in a person cultivating a garden, that most simple and innocent of human toils, and which had been alike the joy and labor of
the unfallen parents of the race. Was this garden, then, the Eden of the present
world? And this man, with such a perception of harm in what his own hands caused
to grow,—was he the Adam?

The distrustful gardener, while plucking away the dead leaves or pruning the
too luxuriant growth of the shrubs, defended his hands with a pair of thick gloves.
Nor were these his only armor. When, in his walk through the garden, he came
to the magnificent plant that hung its purple gems beside the marble fountain,
he placed a kind of mask over his mouth and nostrils, as if all this beauty did but
conceal a deadlier malice; but, finding his task still too dangerous, he drew back,
removed the mask, and called loudly, but in the infirm voice of a person affected
with inward disease,—

"Beatrice! Beatrice!"

"Here am I, my father. What would you?" cried a rich and youthful voice
from the window of the opposite house—a voice as rich as a tropical sunset, and
which made Giovanni, though he knew not why, think of deep hues of purple or
crimson and of perfumes heavily delectable. "Are you in the garden?"

"Yes, Beatrice," answered the gardener, "and I need your help."   15

Soon there emerged from under a sculptured portal the figure of a young
girl, arrayed with as much richness of taste as the most splendid of the flowers,
beautiful as the day, and with a bloom so deep and vivid that one shade more
would have been too much. She looked redundant with life, health, and energy;
all of which attributes were bound down and compressed, as it were, and girdled
tensely, in their luxuriance, by her virgin zone.° Yet Giovanni's fancy must have
grown morbid while he looked down into the garden; for the impression which

virgin zone: A belt worn by unmarried women.

the fair stranger made upon him was as if here were another flower, the human sister of those vegetable ones, as beautiful as they, more beautiful than the richest of them, but still to be touched only with a glove, nor to be approached without a mask. As Beatrice came down the garden path, it was observable that she handled and inhaled the odor of several of the plants which her father had most sedulously avoided.

"Here, Beatrice," said the latter, "see how many needful offices require to be done to our chief treasure. Yet, shattered as I am, my life might pay the penalty of approaching it so closely as circumstances demand. Henceforth, I fear, this plant must be consigned to your sole charge."

"And gladly will I undertake it," cried again the rich tones of the young lady, as she bent towards the magnificent plant and opened her arms as if to embrace it. "Yes, my sister, my splendor, it shall be Beatrice's task to nurse and serve thee; and thou shalt reward her with thy kisses and perfumed breath, which to her is as the breath of life."

Then, with all the tenderness in her manner that was so strikingly expressed in her words, she busied herself with such attentions as the plant seemed to require; and Giovanni, at his lofty window, rubbed his eyes and almost doubted whether it were a girl tending her favorite flower, or one sister performing the duties of affection to another. The scene soon terminated. Whether Dr. Rappaccini had finished his labors in the garden, or that his watchful eye had caught the stranger's face, he now took his daughter's arm and retired. Night was already closing in; oppressive exhalations seemed to proceed from the plants and steal upward past the open window; and Giovanni, closing the lattice, went to his couch and dreamed of a rich flower and beautiful girl. Flower and maiden were different, and yet the same, and fraught with some strange peril in either shape.

But there is an influence in the light of morning that tends to rectify whatever errors of fancy, or even of judgment, we may have incurred during the sun's decline, or among the shadows of the night, or in the less wholesome glow of moonshine. Giovanni's first movement, on starting from sleep, was to throw open the window and gaze down into the garden which his dreams had made so fertile of mysteries. He was surprised and a little ashamed to find how real and matter-of-fact an affair it proved to be, in the first rays of the sun which gilded the dew-drops that hung upon leaf and blossom, and, while giving a brighter beauty to each rare flower, brought everything within the limits of ordinary experience. The young man rejoiced that, in the heart of the barren city, he had the privilege of overlooking this spot of lovely and luxuriant vegetation. It would serve, he said to himself, as a symbolic language to keep him in communion with Nature. Neither the sickly and thoughtworn Dr. Giacomo Rappaccini, it is true, nor his brilliant daughter, were now visible; so that Giovanni could not determine how much of the singularity which he attributed to both was due to their own qualities and how much to his wonder-working fancy; but he was inclined to take a most rational view of the whole matter.

In the course of the day he paid his respects to Signor Pietro Baglioni, professor of medicine in the university, a physician of eminent repute to whom Giovanni had brought a letter of introduction. The professor was an elderly personage, apparently of genial nature, and habits that might almost be called jovial. He kept the young man to dinner, and made himself very agreeable by the freedom and liveliness of his conversation, especially when warmed by a flask or two

20-

of Tuscan wine. Giovanni, conceiving that men of science, inhabitants of the same city, must needs be on familiar terms with one another, took an opportunity to mention the name of Dr. Rappaccini. But the professor did not respond with so much cordiality as he had anticipated.

"Ill would it become a teacher of the divine art of medicine," said Professor Pietro Baglioni, in answer to a question of Giovanni, "to withhold due and well-considered praise of a physician so eminently skilled as Rappaccini; but, on the other hand, I should answer it but scantily to my conscience were I to permit a worthy youth like yourself, Signor Giovanni, the son of an ancient friend, to imbibe erroneous ideas respecting a man who might hereafter chance to hold your life and death in his hands. The truth is, our worshipful Dr. Rappaccini has as much science as any member of the faculty—with perhaps one single exception—in Padua, or all Italy; but there are certain grave objections to his professional character."

"And what are they?" asked the young man.

"Has my friend Giovanni any disease of body or heart, that he is so inquisitive about physicians?" said the professor, with a smile. "But as for Rappaccini, it is said of him—and I, who know the man well, can answer for its truth—that he cares infinitely more for science than for mankind. His patients are interesting to him only as subjects for some new experiment. He would sacrifice human life, his own among the rest, or whatever else was dearest to him, for the sake of adding so much as a grain of mustard seed to the great heap of his accumulated knowledge."

"Methinks he is an awful man indeed," remarked Guasconti, mentally recalling the cold and purely intellectual aspect of Rappaccini. "And yet, worshipful professor, is it not a noble spirit? Are there many men capable of so spiritual a love of science?" 25

"God forbid," answered the professor, somewhat testily; "at least, unless they take sounder views of the healing art than those adopted by Rappaccini. It is his theory that all medicinal virtues are comprised within those substances which we term vegetable poisons. These he cultivates with his own hands, and is said even to have produced new varieties of poison, more horribly deleterious than Nature, without the assistance of this learned person, would ever have plagued the world withal. That the signor doctor does less mischief than might be expected with such dangerous substances is undeniable. Now and then, it must be owned, he has effected, or seemed to effect, a marvellous cure; but, to tell you my private mind, Signor Giovanni, he should receive little credit for such instances of success,—they being probably the work of chance,—but should be held strictly accountable for his failures, which may justly be considered his own work."

The youth might have taken Baglioni's opinions with many grains of allowance had he known that there was a professional warfare of long continuance between him and Dr. Rappaccini, in which the latter was generally thought to have gained the advantage. If the reader be inclined to judge for himself, we refer him to certain black-letter tracts on both sides, preserved in the medical department of the University of Padua.

"I know not, most learned professor," returned Giovanni, after musing on what had been said of Rappaccini's exclusive zeal for science,—"I know not how dearly this physician may love his art; but surely there is one object more dear to him. He has a daughter."

"Aha!" cried the professor, with a laugh. "So now our friend Giovanni's secret is out. You have heard of this daughter, whom all the young men in Padua are wild about, though not half a dozen have ever had the good hap to see her face. I know little of the Signora Beatrice save that Rappaccini is said to have instructed her deeply in his science, and that, young and beautiful as fame reports her, she is already qualified to fill a professor's chair. Perchance her father destines her for mine! Other absurd rumors there be, not worth talking about or listening to. So now, Signor Giovanni, drink off your glass of lachryma."

Guasconti returned to his lodgings somewhat heated with the wine he had   30
quaffed, and which caused his brain to swim with strange fantasies in reference to Dr. Rappaccini and the beautiful Beatrice. On his way, happening to pass by a florist's, he bought a fresh bouquet of flowers.

Ascending to his chamber, he seated himself near the window, but within the shadow thrown by the depth of the wall, so that he could look down into the garden with little risk of being discovered. All beneath his eye was a solitude. The strange plants were basking in the sunshine, and now and then nodding gently to one another, as if in acknowledgment of sympathy and kindred. In the midst, by the shattered fountain, grew the magnificent shrub, with its purple gems clustering all over it; they glowed in the air, and gleamed back again out of the depths of the pool, which thus seemed to overflow with colored radiance from the rich reflection that was steeped in it. At first, as we have said, the garden was a solitude. Soon, however,—as Giovanni had half hoped, half feared, would be the case,—a figure appeared beneath the antique sculptured portal, and came down between the rows of plants, inhaling their various perfumes as if she were one of those beings of old classic fable that lived upon sweet odors. On again beholding Beatrice, the young man was even startled to perceive how much her beauty exceeded his recollection of it; so brilliant, so vivid, was its character, that she glowed amid the sunlight, and, as Giovanni whispered to himself, positively illuminated the more shadowy intervals of the garden path. Her face being now more revealed than on the former occasion, he was struck by its expression of simplicity and sweetness,—qualities that had not entered into his idea of her character, and which made him ask anew what manner of mortal she might be. Nor did he fail again to observe, or imagine, an analogy between the beautiful girl and the gorgeous shrub that hung its gemlike flowers over the fountain,—a resemblance which Beatrice seemed to have indulged a fantastic humor in heightening, both by the arrangement of her dress and the selection of its hues.

Approaching the shrub, she threw open her arms, as with a passionate ardor, and drew its branches into an intimate embrace—so intimate that her features were hidden in its leafy bosom and her glistening ringlets all intermingled with the flowers.

"Give me thy breath, my sister," exclaimed Beatrice; "for I am faint with common air. And give me this flower of thine, which I separate with gentlest fingers from the stem and place it close beside my heart."

With these words the beautiful daughter of Rappaccini plucked one of the richest blossoms of the shrub, and was about to fasten it in her bosom. But now, unless Giovanni's draughts of wine had bewildered his senses, a singular incident occurred. A small orange-colored reptile, of the lizard or chameleon species, chanced to be creeping along the path, just at the feet of Beatrice. It appeared to Giovanni,—but, at the distance from which he gazed, he could scarcely have seen

anything so minute,—it appeared to him, however, that a drop or two of moisture from the broken stem of the flower descended upon the lizard's head. For
an instant the reptile contorted itself violently, and then lay motionless in the sunshine. Beatrice observed this remarkable phenomenon, and crossed herself, sadly,
but without surprise; nor did she therefore hesitate to arrange the fatal flower in
her bosom. There it blushed, and almost glimmered with the dazzling effect of a
precious stone, adding to her dress and aspect the one appropriate charm which
nothing else in the world could have supplied. But Giovanni, out of the shadow
of his window, bent forward and shrank back, and murmured and trembled.

"Am I awake? Have I my senses?" said he to himself. "What is this being? 35
Beautiful shall I call her, or inexpressibly terrible?"

Beatrice now strayed carelessly through the garden, approaching closer beneath Giovanni's window, so that he was compelled to thrust his head quite out
of its concealment in order to gratify the intense and painful curiosity which she
excited. At this moment there came a beautiful insect over the garden wall; it had,
perhaps, wandered through the city, and found no flowers or verdure among those
antique haunts of men until the heavy perfumes of Dr. Rappaccini's shrubs had
lured it from afar. Without alighting on the flowers, this winged brightness seemed
to be attracted by Beatrice, and lingered in the air and fluttered about her head.
Now, here it could not be but that Giovanni Guasconti's eyes deceived him. Be
that as it might, he fancied that, while Beatrice was gazing at the insect with childish delight, it grew faint and fell at her feet; its bright wings shivered; it was dead—
from no cause that he could discern, unless it were the atmosphere of her breath.
Again Beatrice crossed herself and sighed heavily as she bent over the dead insect.

An impulsive movement of Giovanni drew her eyes to the window. There
she beheld the beautiful head of the young man—rather a Grecian than an Italian
head, with fair, regular features, and a glistening of gold among his ringlets—gazing down upon her like a being that hovered in mid air. Scarcely knowing what
he did, Giovanni threw down the bouquet which he had hitherto held in his hand.

"Signora," said he, "there are pure and healthful flowers. Wear them for the
sake of Giovanni Guasconti."

"Thanks, signor," replied Beatrice, with her rich voice, that came forth as it
were like a gush of music, and with a mirthful expression half childish and half
woman-like. "I accept your gift, and would fain recompense it with this precious
purple flower; but if I toss it into the air it will not reach you. So Signor Guasconti
must even content himself with my thanks."

She lifted the bouquet from the ground, and then, as if inwardly ashamed at 40
having stepped aside from her maidenly reserve to respond to a stranger's greeting, passed swiftly homeward through the garden. But few as the moments were,
it seemed to Giovanni, when she was on the point of vanishing beneath the sculptured portal, that his beautiful bouquet was already beginning to wither in her
grasp. It was an idle thought; there could be no possibility of distinguishing a
faded flower from a fresh one at so great a distance.

For many days after this incident the young man avoided the window that
looked into Dr. Rappaccini's garden, as if something ugly and monstrous would
have blasted his eyesight had he been betrayed into a glance. He felt conscious
of having put himself, to a certain extent, within the influence of an unintelligible power by the communication which he had opened with Beatrice. The wisest course would have been, if his heart were in any real danger, to quit his lodg-

ings and Padua itself at once; the next wiser, to have accustomed himself, as far as possible, to the familiar and daylight view of Beatrice—thus bringing her rigidly and systematically within the limits of ordinary experience. Least of all, while avoiding her sight, ought Giovanni to have remained so near this extraordinary being that the proximity and possibility even of intercourse should give a kind of substance and reality to the wild vagaries which his imagination ran riot continually in producing. Guasconti had not a deep heart—or, at all events, its depths were not sounded now; but he had a quick fancy, and an ardent southern temperament, which rose every instant to a higher fever pitch. Whether or no Beatrice possessed those terrible attributes, that fatal breath, the affinity with those so beautiful and deadly flowers which were indicated by what Giovanni had witnessed, she had at least instilled a fierce and subtle poison into his system. It was not love, although her rich beauty was a madness to him; nor horror, even while he fancied her spirit to be imbued with the same baneful essence that seemed to pervade her physical frame; but a wild offspring of both love and horror that had each parent in it, and burned like one and shivered like the other. Giovanni knew not what to dread; still less did he know what to hope; yet hope and dread kept a continual warfare in his breast, alternately vanquishing one another and starting up afresh to renew the contest. Blessed are all simple emotions, be they dark or bright! It is the lurid intermixture of the two that produces the illuminating blaze of the infernal regions.

Sometimes he endeavored to assuage the fever of his spirit by a rapid walk through the streets of Padua or beyond its gates: his footsteps kept time with the throbbings of his brain, so that the walk was apt to accelerate itself to a race. One day he found himself arrested; his arm was seized by a portly personage, who had turned back on recognizing the young man and expended much breath in overtaking him.

"Signor Giovanni! Stay, my young friend!" cried he. "Have you forgotten me? That might well be the case if I were as much altered as yourself."

It was Baglioni, whom Giovanni had avoided ever since their first meeting, from a doubt that the professor's sagacity would look too deeply into his secrets. Endeavoring to recover himself, he stared forth wildly from his inner world into the outer one and spoke like a man in a dream.

"Yes; I am Giovanni Guasconti. You are Professor Pietro Baglioni. Now let me pass!"

"Not yet, not yet, Signor Giovanni Guasconti," said the professor, smiling, but at the same time scrutinizing the youth with an earnest glance. "What! did I grow up side by side with your father? and shall his son pass me like a stranger in these old streets of Padua? Stand still, Signor Giovanni; for we must have a word or two before we part."

"Speedily, then, most worshipful professor, speedily," said Giovanni, with feverish impatience. "Does not your worship see that I am in haste?"

Now, while he was speaking there came a man in black along the street, stooping and moving feebly like a person in inferior health. His face was all overspread with a most sickly and sallow hue, but yet so pervaded with an expression of piercing and active intellect that an observer might easily have overlooked the merely physical attributes and have seen only this wonderful energy. As he passed, this person exchanged a cold and distant salutation with Baglioni, but fixed his eyes upon Giovanni with an intentness that seemed to bring out whatever was within him worthy of notice. Nevertheless, there was a peculiar quietness in the look, as if taking merely a speculative, not a human interest, in the young man.

"It is Dr. Rappaccini!" whispered the professor when the stranger had passed. "Has he ever seen your face before?"

"Not that I know," answered Giovanni, starting at the name. 50

"He *has* seen you! he must have seen you!" said Baglioni, hastily. "For some purpose or other, this man of science is making a study of you. I know that look of his! It is the same that coldly illuminates his face as he bends over a bird, a mouse, or a butterfly, which, in pursuance of some experiment, he has killed by the perfume of a flower; a look as deep as Nature itself, but without Nature's warmth of love. Signor Giovanni, I will stake my life upon it, you are the subject of one of Rappaccini's experiments!"

"Will you make a fool of me?" cried Giovanni, passionately. "*That*, signor professor, were an untoward experiment."

"Patience! patience!" replied the imperturbable professor. "I tell thee, my poor Giovanni, that Rappaccini has a scientific interest in thee. Thou hast fallen into fearful hands! And the Signora Beatrice,—what part does she act in this mystery?"

But Guasconti, finding Baglioni's pertinacity intolerable, here broke away, and was gone before the professor could again seize his arm. He looked after the young man intently and shook his head.

"This must not be," said Baglioni to himself. "The youth is the son of my 55 old friend, and shall not come to any harm from which the arcana of medical science can preserve him. Besides, it is too insufferable an impertinence in Rappaccini, thus to snatch the lad out of my own hands, as I may say, and make use of him for his infernal experiments. This daughter of his! It shall be looked to. Perchance, most learned Rappaccini, I may foil you where you little dream of it!"

Meanwhile Giovanni had pursued a circuitous route, and at length found himself at the door of his lodgings. As he crossed the threshold he was met by old Lisabetta, who smirked and smiled, and was evidently desirous to attract his attention; vainly, however, as the ebullition of his feelings had momentarily subsided into a cold and dull vacuity. He turned his eyes full upon the withered face that was puckering itself into a smile, but seemed to behold it not. The old dame, therefore, laid her grasp upon his cloak.

"Signor! signor!" whispered she, still with a smile over the whole breadth of her visage, so that it looked not unlike a grotesque carving in wood, darkened by centuries. "Listen, signor! There is a private entrance into the garden!"

"What do you say?" exclaimed Giovanni, turning quickly about, as if an inanimate thing should start into feverish life. "A private entrance into Dr. Rappaccini's garden?"

"Hush! hush! not so loud!" whispered Lisabetta, putting her hand over his mouth. "Yes; into the worshipful doctor's garden, where you may see all his fine shrubbery. Many a young man in Padua would give gold to be admitted among those flowers."

Giovanni put a piece of gold into her hand. 60

"Show me the way," said he.

A surmise, probably excited by his conversation with Baglioni, crossed his mind, that this interposition of old Lisabetta might perchance be connected with the intrigue, whatever were its nature, in which the professor seemed to suppose that Dr. Rappaccini was involving him. But such a suspicion, though it disturbed Giovanni, was inadequate to restrain him. The instant that he was aware of the possibility of approaching Beatrice, it seemed an absolute necessity of his existence to do so. It mattered not whether she were angel or demon; he was irrevocably within her sphere, and must obey the law that whirled him onward, in ever-lessening circles, towards a result which he did not attempt to foreshadow; and yet, strange to say, there came across him a sudden doubt whether this intense interest on his part were not delusory; whether it were really of so deep and positive a nature as to justify him in now thrusting himself into an incalculable position; whether it were not merely the fantasy of a young man's brain, only slightly or not at all connected with his heart.

He paused, hesitated, turned half about, but again went on. His withered guide led him along several obscure passages, and finally undid a door, through which, as it was opened, there came the sight and sound of rustling leaves, with the broken sunshine glimmering among them. Giovanni stepped forth, and, forcing himself through the entanglement of a shrub that wreathed its tendrils over the hidden entrance, stood beneath his own window in the open area of Dr. Rappaccini's garden.

How often is it the case that, when impossibilities have come to pass and dreams have condensed their misty substance into tangible realities, we find ourselves calm, and even coldly self-possessed, amid circumstances which it would have been a delirium of joy or agony to anticipate! Fate delights to thwart us thus. Passion will choose his own time to rush upon the scene, and lingers sluggishly behind when an appropriate adjustment of events would seem to summon his appearance. So was it now with Giovanni. Day after day his pulses had throbbed with feverish blood at the improbable idea of an interview with Beatrice, and of standing with her, face to face, in this very garden, basking in the Oriental sunshine of her beauty, and snatching from her full gaze the mystery which he deemed the riddle of his own existence. But now there was a singular and untimely equanimity within his breast. He threw a glance around the garden to discover if Beatrice or her father were present, and, perceiving that he was alone, began a critical observation of the plants.

The aspect of one and all of them dissatisfied him; their gorgeousness seemed fierce, passionate, and even unnatural. There was hardly an individual shrub which a wanderer, straying by himself through a forest, would not have been startled to find growing wild, as if an unearthly face had glared at him out of the thicket. Several also would have shocked a delicate instinct by an appearance of artificialness indicating that there had been such commixture, and, as it were, adultery, of various vegetable species, that the production was no longer of God's making, but the monstrous offspring of man's depraved fancy, glowing with only an evil mockery of beauty. They were probably the result of experiment, which in one or two cases had succeeded in mingling plants individually lovely into a compound possessing the questionable and ominous character that distinguished the whole growth of the garden. In fine, Giovanni recognized but two or three plants in the collection, and those of a kind that he well knew to be poisonous. While busy with these contemplations he heard the rustling of a silken garment, and, turning, beheld Beatrice emerging from beneath the sculptured portal.

Giovanni had not considered with himself what should be his deportment; whether he should apologize for his intrusion into the garden, or assume that he was there with the privity at least, if not by the desire, of Dr. Rappaccini or his daughter; but Beatrice's manner placed him at his ease, though leaving him still in doubt by what agency he had gained admittance. She came lightly along the path and met him near the broken fountain. There was surprise in her face, but brightened by a simple and kind expression of pleasure.

"You are a connoisseur in flowers, signor," said Beatrice, with a smile, alluding to the bouquet which he had flung her from the window. "It is no marvel, therefore, if the sight of my father's rare collection has tempted you to take a nearer view. If he were here, he could tell you many strange and interesting facts as to the nature and habits of these shrubs; for he has spent a lifetime in such studies, and this garden is his world."

"And yourself, lady," observed Giovanni, "if fame says true,—you likewise are deeply skilled in the virtues indicated by these rich blossoms and these spicy perfumes. Would you deign to be my instructress, I should prove an apter scholar than if taught by Signor Rappaccini himself."

"Are there such idle rumors?" asked Beatrice, with the music of a pleasant laugh. "Do people say that I am skilled in my father's science of plants? What a jest is there! No; though I have grown up among these flowers, I know no more of them than their hues and perfume; and sometimes methinks I would fain rid myself of even that small knowledge. There are many flowers here, and those not the least brilliant, that shock and offend me when they meet my eye. But pray, signor, do not believe these stories about my science. Believe nothing of me save what you see with your own eyes."

"And must I believe all that I have seen with my own eyes?" asked Giovanni, pointedly, while the recollection of former scenes made him shrink. "No, signora; you demand too little of me. Bid me believe nothing save what comes from your own lips." 70

It would appear that Beatrice understood him. There came a deep flush to her cheek; but she looked full into Giovanni's eyes, and responded to his gaze of uneasy suspicion with a queenlike haughtiness.

"I do so bid you, signor," she replied. "Forget whatever you may have fancied in regard to me. If true to the outward senses, still it may be false in its essence; but the words of Beatrice Rappaccini's lips are true from the depths of the heart outward. Those you may believe."

A fervor glowed in her whole aspect and beamed upon Giovanni's consciousness like the light of truth itself; but while she spoke there was a fragrance in the atmosphere around her, rich and delightful, though evanescent, yet which the young man, from an indefinable reluctance, scarcely dared to draw into his lungs. It might be the odor of the flowers. Could it be Beatrice's breath which thus embalmed her words with a strange richness, as if by steeping them in her heart? A faintness passed like a shadow over Giovanni and flitted away; he seemed to gaze through the beautiful girl's eyes into her transparent soul, and felt no more doubt or fear.

The tinge of passion that had colored Beatrice's manner vanished; she became gay, and appeared to derive a pure delight from her communion with the youth not unlike what the maiden of a lonely island might have felt conversing with a voyager from the civilized world. Evidently her experience of life had been confined within the limits of that garden. She talked now about matters as simple as the daylight or summer clouds, and now asked questions in reference to the city, or Giovanni's distant home, his friends, his mother, and his sisters—questions indicating such seclusion, and such lack of familiarity with modes and forms, that Giovanni responded as if to an infant. Her spirit gushed out before him like a fresh rill that was just catching its first glimpse of the sunlight and wondering at the reflections of earth and sky which were flung into its bosom. There came thoughts, too, from a deep source, and fantasies of a gemlike brilliancy, as if diamonds and rubies sparkled upward among the bubbles of the fountain. Ever and anon there gleamed across the young man's mind a sense of wonder that he should be walking side by side with the being who had so wrought upon his imagination, whom he had idealized in such hues of terror, in whom he had positively witnessed such manifestations of dreadful attributes,—that he should be conversing with Beatrice like a brother, and should find her so human and so maidenlike. But such reflections were only momentary; the effect of her character was too real not to make itself familiar at once.

In this free intercourse they had strayed through the garden, and now, after 75 many turns among its avenues, were come to the shattered fountain, beside which grew the magnificent shrub, with its treasury of glowing blossoms. A fragrance was diffused from it which Giovanni recognized as identical with that which he had attributed to Beatrice's breath, but incomparably more powerful. As her eyes fell upon it, Giovanni beheld her press her hand to her bosom as if her heart were throbbing suddenly and painfully.

"For the first time in my life," murmured she, addressing the shrub, "I had forgotten thee."

"I remember, signora," said Giovanni, "that you once promised to reward me with one of these living gems for the bouquet which I had the happy boldness to fling to your feet. Permit me now to pluck it as a memorial of this interview."

He made a step towards the shrub with extended hand; but Beatrice darted forward, uttering a shriek that went through his heart like a dagger. She caught his hand and drew it back with the whole force of her slender figure. Giovanni felt her touch thrilling through his fibres.

"Touch it not!" exclaimed she, in a voice of agony. "Not for thy life! It is fatal!"

Then, hiding her face, she fled from him and vanished beneath the sculp- 80 tured portal. As Giovanni followed her with his eyes, he beheld the emaciated figure and pale intelligence of Dr. Rappaccini, who had been watching the scene, he knew not how long, within the shadow of the entrance.

No sooner was Guasconti alone in his chamber than the image of Beatrice came back to his passionate musings, invested with all the witchery that had been gathering around it ever since his first glimpse of her, and now likewise imbued with a tender warmth of girlish womanhood. She was human; her nature was endowed with all gentle and feminine qualities; she was worthiest to be worshipped; she was capable, surely, on her part, of the height and heroism of love. Those tokens which he had hitherto considered as proofs of a frightful peculiarity in her physical and moral system were now either forgotten, or, by the subtle sophistry of passion transmitted into a golden crown of enchantment, rendering Beatrice the more admirable by so much as she was the more unique. Whatever had looked ugly was now beautiful; or, if incapable of such a change, it stole away and hid itself among those shapeless half ideas which throng the dim region beyond the daylight of our perfect consciousness. Thus did he spend the night, nor fell asleep until the dawn had begun to awake the slumbering flowers in Dr. Rappaccini's garden, whither Giovanni's dreams doubtless led him. Up rose the sun in his due season, and, flinging his beams upon the young man's eyelids, awoke him to a sense of pain. When thoroughly aroused, he became sensible of a burning and tingling agony in his hand—in his right hand—the very hand which Beatrice had grasped in her own when he was on the point of plucking one of the gemlike flowers. On the back of that hand there was now a purple print like that of four small fingers, and the likeness of a slender thumb upon his wrist.

Oh, how stubbornly does love,—or even that cunning semblance of love which flourishes in the imagination, but strikes no depth of root into the heart,—how stubbornly does it hold its faith until the moment comes when it is doomed to vanish into thin mist! Giovanni wrapped a handkerchief about his hand and wondered what evil thing had stung him, and soon forgot his pain in a reverie of Beatrice.

After the first interview, a second was in the inevitable course of what we call fate. A third; a fourth; and a meeting with Beatrice in the garden was no longer an incident in Giovanni's daily life, but the whole space in which he might be said to live; for the anticipation and memory of that ecstatic hour made up the remainder. Nor was it otherwise with the daughter of Rappaccini. She watched for the youth's appearance, and flew to his side with confidence as unreserved as if they had been playmates from early infancy—as if they were such playmates still. If, by any unwonted chance, he failed to come at the appointed moment, she stood beneath the window and sent up the rich sweetness of her tones to float around him in his chamber and echo and reverberate throughout his heart: "Giovanni! Giovanni! Why tarriest thou? Come down!" And down he hastened into that Eden of poisonous flowers.

But, with all this intimate familiarity, there was still a reserve in Beatrice's demeanor, so rigidly and invariably sustained that the idea of infringing it scarcely occurred to his imagination. By all appreciable signs, they loved; they had looked love with eyes that conveyed the holy secret from the depths of one soul into the depths of the other, as if it were too sacred to be whispered by the way; they had even spoken love in those gushes of passion when their spirits darted forth in articulated breath like tongues of long-hidden flame; and yet there had been no seal of lips, no clasp of hands, nor any slightest caress such as love claims and hallows. He had never touched one of the gleaming ringlets of her hair; her garment—so marked was the physical barrier between them—had never been waved against him by a breeze. On the few occasions when Giovanni had seemed tempted to overstep the limit, Beatrice grew so sad, so stern, and withal wore such a look of desolate separation, shuddering at itself, that not a spoken word was requisite to repel him. At such times he was startled at the horrible suspicions that rose, monster-like, out of the caverns of his heart and stared him in the face; his love grew thin and faint as the morning mist, his doubts alone had substance. But, when Beatrice's face brightened again after the momentary shadow, she was transformed at once from the mysterious, questionable being whom he had watched with so much awe and horror; she was now the beautiful and unsophisticated girl whom he felt that his spirit knew with a certainty beyond all other knowledge.

A considerable time had now passed since Giovanni's last meeting with Baglioni. One morning, however, he was disagreeably surprised by a visit from 85 the professor, whom he had scarcely thought of for whole weeks, and would willingly have forgotten still longer. Given up as he had long been to a pervading excitement, he could tolerate no companions except upon condition of their perfect sympathy with his present state of feeling. Such sympathy was not to be expected from Professor Baglioni.

The visitor chatted carelessly for a few moments about the gossip of the city and the university, and then took up another topic.

"I have been reading an old classic author lately," said he, "and met with a story that strangely interested me. Possibly you may remember it. It is of an Indian prince, who sent a beautiful woman as a present to Alexander the Great. She was as lovely as the dawn and gorgeous as the sunset; but what especially distinguished her was a certain rich perfume in her breath—richer than a garden of Persian roses. Alexander, as was natural to a youthful conqueror, fell in love at first sight with this magnificent stranger; but a certain sage physician, happening to be present, discovered a terrible secret in regard to her."

"And what was that?" asked Giovanni, turning his eyes downward to avoid those of the professor.

"That this lovely woman," continued Baglioni, with emphasis, "had been nourished with poisons from her birth upward, until her whole nature was so imbued with them that she herself had become the deadliest poison in existence. Poison was her element of life. With that rich perfume of her breath she blasted the very air. Her love would have been poison—her embrace death. Is not this a marvellous tale?"

"A childish fable," answered Giovanni, nervously starting from his chair. "I marvel how your worship finds time to read such nonsense among your graver studies." 90

"By the by," said the professor, looking uneasily about him, "what singular fragrance is this in your apartment? Is it the perfume of your gloves? It is faint, but delicious; and yet, after all, by no means agreeable. Were I to breathe it long, methinks it would make me ill. It is like the breath of a flower; but I see no flowers in the chamber."

"Nor are there any," replied Giovanni, who had turned pale as the professor spoke; "nor, I think, is there any fragrance except in your worship's imagination. Odors, being a sort of element combined of the sensual and the spiritual, are apt to deceive us in this manner. The recollection of a perfume, the bare idea of it, may easily be mistaken for a present reality."

"Ay; but my sober imagination does not often play such tricks," said Baglioni; "and, were I to fancy any kind of odor, it would be that of some vile apothecary drug, wherewith my fingers are likely enough to be imbued. Our worshipful friend Rappaccini, as I have heard, tinctures his medicaments with odors richer than those of Araby. Doubtless, likewise, the fair and learned Signora Beatrice would minister to her patients with draughts as sweet as a maiden's breath; but woe to him that sips them!"

Giovanni's face evinced many contending emotions. The tone in which the professor alluded to the pure and lovely daughter of Rappaccini was a torture to his soul; and yet the intimation of a view of her character, opposite to his own, gave instantaneous distinctness to a thousand dim suspicions, which now grinned at him like so many demons. But he strove hard to quell them and to respond to Baglioni with a true lover's perfect faith.

"Signor professor," said he, "you were my father's friend; perchance, too, it   95
is your purpose to act a friendly part towards his son. I would fain feel nothing
towards you save respect and deference; but I pray you to observe, signor, that
there is one subject on which we must not speak. You know not the Signora
Beatrice. You cannot, therefore, estimate the wrong—the blasphemy, I may even
say—that is offered to her character by a light or injurious word."

"Giovanni! my poor Giovanni!" answered the professor, with a calm expression of pity, "I know this wretched girl far better than yourself. You shall hear
the truth in respect to the poisoner Rappaccini and his poisonous daughter; yes,
poisonous as she is beautiful. Listen; for, even should you do violence to my gray
hairs, it shall not silence me. That old fable of the Indian woman has become a
truth by the deep and deadly science of Rappaccini and in the person of the lovely
Beatrice."

Giovanni groaned and hid his face.

"Her father," continued Baglioni, "was not restrained by natural affection
from offering up his child in this horrible manner as the victim of his insane zeal
for science; for, let us do him justice, he is as true a man of science as ever distilled his own heart in an alembic. What, then, will be your fate? Beyond a doubt
you are selected as the material of some new experiment. Perhaps the result is to
be death; perhaps a fate more awful still. Rappaccini, with what he calls the interest of science before his eyes, will hesitate at nothing."

"It is a dream," muttered Giovanni to himself; "surely it is a dream."

"But," resumed the professor, "be of good cheer, son of my friend. It is not   100
yet too late for the rescue. Possibly we may even succeed in bringing back this
miserable child within the limits of ordinary nature, from which her father's madness has estranged her. Behold this little silver vase! It was wrought by the hands
of the renowned Benvenuto Cellini,° and is well worthy to be a love gift to the
fairest dame in Italy. But its contents are invaluable. One little sip of this antidote
would have rendered the most virulent poisons of the Borgias° innocuous. Doubt
not that it will be as efficacious against those of Rappaccini. Bestow the vase, and
the precious liquid within it, on your Beatrice, and hopefully await the result."

Baglioni laid a small, exquisitely wrought silver vial on the table and withdrew, leaving what he had said to produce its effect upon the young man's mind.

"We will thwart Rappaccini yet," thought he, chuckling to himself, as he descended the stairs; "but, let us confess the truth of him, he is a wonderful man—
a wonderful man indeed; a vile empiric, however, in his practice, and therefore
not to be tolerated by those who respect the good old rules of the medical profession."

Throughout Giovanni's whole acquaintance with Beatrice, he had occasionally, as we have said, been haunted by dark surmises as to her character; yet
so thoroughly had she made herself felt by him as a simple, natural, most affectionate, and guileless creature, that the image now held up by Professor Baglioni
looked as strange and incredible as if it were not in accordance with his own original conception. True, there were ugly recollections connected with his first
glimpses of the beautiful girl; he could not quite forget the bouquet that withered in her grasp, and the insect that perished amid the sunny air, by no ostensi-
ble agency save the fragrance of her breath. These incidents, however, dissolving

Cellini: A famous goldsmith.   *Borgias*: An Italian family noted for its cruelty.

in the pure light of her character, had no longer the efficacy of facts, but were acknowledged as mistaken fantasies, by whatever testimony of the senses they might appear to be substantiated. There is something truer and more real than what we can see with the eyes and touch with the finger. On such better evidence had Giovanni founded his confidence in Beatrice, though rather by the necessary force of her high attributes than by any deep and generous faith on his part. But now his spirit was incapable of sustaining itself at the height to which the early enthusiasm of passion had exalted it; he fell down, grovelling among earthly doubts, and defiled therewith the pure whiteness of Beatrice's image. Not that he gave her up; he did but distrust. He resolved to institute some decisive test that should satisfy him, once for all, whether there were those dreadful peculiarities in her physical nature which could not be supposed to exist without some corresponding monstrosity of soul. His eyes, gazing down afar, might have deceived him as to the lizard, the insect, and the flowers; but if he could witness, at the distance of a few paces, the sudden blight of one fresh and healthful flower in Beatrice's hand, there would be room for no further question. With this idea he hastened to the florist's and purchased a bouquet that was still gemmed with the morning dew-drops.

It was now the customary hour of his daily interview with Beatrice. Before descending into the garden, Giovanni failed not to look at his figure in the mirror—a vanity to be expected in a beautiful young man, yet, as displaying itself at that troubled and feverish moment, the token of a certain shallowness of feeling and insincerity of character. He did gaze, however, and said to himself that his features had never before possessed so rich a grace, nor his eyes such vivacity, nor his cheeks so warm a hue of superabundant life.

"At least," thought he, "her poison has not yet insinuated itself into my sys-   105
tem. I am no flower to perish in her grasp."

With that thought he turned his eyes on the bouquet, which he had never once laid aside from his hand. A thrill of indefinable horror shot through his frame on perceiving that those dewy flowers were already beginning to droop; they wore the aspect of things that had been fresh and lovely yesterday. Giovanni grew white as marble, and stood motionless before the mirror, staring at his own reflection there as at the likeness of something frightful. He remembered Baglioni's remark about the fragrance that seemed to pervade the chamber. It must have been the poison in his breath! Then he shuddered—shuddered at himself. Recovering from his stupor, he began to watch with curious eye a spider that was busily at work hanging its web from the antique cornice of the apartment, crossing and recrossing the artful system of interwoven lines—as vigorous and active a spider as ever dangled from an old ceiling. Giovanni bent towards the insect, and emitted a deep, long breath. The spider suddenly ceased its toil; the web vibrated with a tremor originating in the body of the small artisan. Again Giovanni sent forth a breath, deeper, longer, and imbued with a venomous feeling out of his heart: he knew not whether he were wicked, or only desperate. The spider made a convulsive gripe with his limbs and hung dead across the window.

"Accursed! accursed!" muttered Giovanni, addressing himself. "Hast thou grown so poisonous that this deadly insect perishes by thy breath?"

At that moment a rich, sweet voice came floating up from the garden.

"Giovanni! Giovanni! It is past the hour! Why tarriest thou? Come down!"

"Yes," muttered Giovanni again. "She is the only being whom my breath   110
may not slay! Would that it might!"

He rushed down, and in an instant was standing before the bright and loving eyes of Beatrice. A moment ago his wrath and despair had been so fierce that he could have desired nothing so much as to wither her by a glance; but with her actual presence there came influences which had too real an existence to be at once shaken off: recollections of the delicate and benign power of her feminine nature, which had so often enveloped him in a religious calm; recollections of many a holy and passionate outgush of her heart, when the pure fountain had been unsealed from its depths and made visible in its transparency to his mental eye; recollections which, had Giovanni known how to estimate them, would have assured him that all this ugly mystery was but an earthly illusion, and that, whatever mist of evil might seem to have gathered over her, the real Beatrice was a heavenly angel. Incapable as he was of such high faith, still her presence had not utterly lost its magic. Giovanni's rage was quelled into an aspect of sullen insensibility. Beatrice, with a quick spiritual sense, immediately felt that there was a gulf of blackness between them which neither he nor she could pass. They walked on together, sad and silent, and came thus to the marble fountain and to its pool of water on the ground, in the midst of which grew the shrub that bore gem-like blossoms. Giovanni was affrighted at the eager enjoyment—the appetite, as it were—with which he found himself inhaling the fragrance of the flowers.

"Beatrice," asked he, abruptly, "whence came this shrub?"

"My father created it," answered she, with simplicity.

"Created it! created it!" repeated Giovanni. "What mean you, Beatrice?"

"He is a man fearfully acquainted with the secrets of Nature," replied Beatrice; 115 "and, at the hour when I first drew breath, this plant sprang from the soil, the offspring of his science, of his intellect, while I was but his earthly child. Approach it not!" continued she, observing with terror that Giovanni was drawing nearer to the shrub. "It has qualities that you little dream of. But I, dearest Giovanni,— I grew up and blossomed with the plant and was nourished with its breath. It was my sister, and I loved it with a human affection; for, alas!—hast thou not suspected it?—there was an awful doom."

Here Giovanni frowned so darkly upon her that Beatrice paused and trembled. But her faith in his tenderness reassured her, and made her blush that she had doubted for an instant.

"There was an awful doom," she continued, "the effect of my father's fatal love of science, which estranged me from all society of my kind. Until Heaven sent thee, dearest Giovanni, oh, how lonely was thy poor Beatrice!"

"Was it a hard doom?" asked Giovanni, fixing his eyes upon her.

"Only of late have I known how hard it was," answered she, tenderly. "Oh, yes; but my heart was torpid, and therefore quiet."

Giovanni's rage broke forth from his sullen gloom like a lightning flash out 120 of a dark cloud.

"Accursed one!" cried he, with venomous scorn and anger. "And, finding thy solitude wearisome, thou hast severed me likewise from all the warmth of life and enticed me into thy region of unspeakable horror!"

"Giovanni!" exclaimed Beatrice, turning her large bright eyes upon his face. The force of his words had not found its way into her mind; she was merely thunderstruck.

"Yes, poisonous thing!" repeated Giovanni, beside himself with passion. "Thou hast done it! Thou hast blasted me! Thou hast filled my veins with poison! Thou hast made me as hateful, as ugly, as loathsome and deadly a creature as thyself—a world's wonder of hideous monstrosity! Now, if our breath be happily as fatal to ourselves as to all others, let us join our lips in one kiss of unutterable hatred, and so die!"

"What has befallen me?" murmured Beatrice, with a low moan out of her heart. "Holy Virgin, pity me, a poor heart-broken child!"

"Thou,—dost thou pray?" cried Giovanni, still with the same fiendish scorn. 125 "Thy very prayers, as they come from thy lips, taint the atmosphere with death. Yes, yes; let us pray! Let us to church and dip our fingers in the holy water at the portal! They that come after us will perish as by a pestilence! Let us sign crosses in the air! It will be scattering curses abroad in the likeness of holy symbols!"

"Giovanni," said Beatrice, calmly, for her grief was beyond passion, "why dost thou join thyself with me thus in those terrible words? I, it is true, am the horrible thing thou namest me. But thou,—what hast thou to do, save with one other shudder at my hideous misery to go forth out of the garden and mingle with thy race, and forget there ever crawled on earth such a monster as poor Beatrice?"

"Dost thou pretend ignorance?" asked Giovanni, scowling upon her. "Behold! this power have I gained from the pure daughter of Rappaccini."

There was a swarm of summer insects flitting through the air in search of the food promised by the flower odors of the fatal garden. They circled round Giovanni's head, and were evidently attracted towards him by the same influence which had drawn them for an instant within the sphere of several of the shrubs. He sent forth a breath among them, and smiled bitterly at Beatrice as at least a score of the insects fell dead upon the ground.

"I see it! I see it!" shrieked Beatrice. "It is my father's fatal science! No, no, Giovanni; it was not I! Never! never! I dreamed only to love thee and be with thee a little time, and so to let thee pass away, leaving but thine image in mine heart; for, Giovanni, believe it, though my body be nourished with poison, my spirit is God's creature, and craves love as its daily food. But my father,—he has united us in this fearful sympathy. Yes; spurn me, tread upon me, kill me! Oh, what is death after such words as thine? But it was not I. Not for a world of bliss would I have done it."

Giovanni's passion had exhausted itself in its outburst from his lips. There 130 now came across him a sense, mournful, and not without tenderness, of the intimate and peculiar relationship between Beatrice and himself. They stood, as it were, in an utter solitude, which would be made none the less solitary by the densest throng of human life. Ought not, then, the desert of humanity around them to press this insulated pair closer together? If they should be cruel to one another, who was there to be kind to them? Besides, thought Giovanni, might there not still be a hope of his returning within the limits of ordinary nature, and leading Beatrice, the redeemed Beatrice, by the hand? O, weak, and selfish, and unworthy spirit, that could dream of an earthly union and earthly happiness as possible, after such deep love had been so bitterly wronged as was Beatrice's love by Giovanni's blighting words! No, no; there could be no such hope. She must pass heavily, with that broken heart, across the borders of Time—she must bathe her hurts in some font of paradise, and forget her grief in the light of immortality, and *there* be well.

But Giovanni did not know it.

"Dear Beatrice," said he, approaching her, while she shrank away as always at his approach, but now with a different impulse, "dearest Beatrice our fate is not yet so desperate. Behold! there is a medicine, potent, as a wise physician has assured me, and almost divine in its efficacy. It is composed of ingredients the most opposite to those by which thy awful father has brought this calamity upon thee and me. It is distilled of blessed herbs. Shall we not quaff it together, and thus be purified from evil?"

"Give it me!" said Beatrice, extending her hand to receive the little silver vial which Giovanni took from his bosom. She added, with a peculiar emphasis, "I will drink; but do thou await the result."

She put Baglioni's antidote to her lips; and, at the same moment, the figure of Rappaccini emerged from the portal and came slowly towards the marble fountain. As he drew near, the pale man of science seemed to gaze with a triumphant expression at the beautiful youth and maiden, as might an artist who should spend his life in achieving a picture or a group of statuary and finally be satisfied with his success. He paused; his bent form grew erect with conscious power; he spread out his hands over them in the attitude of a father imploring a blessing upon his children; but those were the same hands that had thrown poison into the stream of their lives. Giovanni trembled. Beatrice shuddered nervously, and pressed her hand upon her heart.

"My daughter," said Rappaccini, "thou art no longer lonely in the world. 135 Pluck one of those precious gems from thy sister shrub and bid thy bridegroom wear it in his bosom. It will not harm him now. My science and the sympathy between thee and him have so wrought within his system that he now stands apart from common men, as thou dost, daughter of my pride and triumph, from ordinary women. Pass on, then, through the world, most dear to one another and dreadful to all besides!"

"My father," said Beatrice, feebly,—and still as she spoke she kept her hand upon her heart,—"wherefore didst thou inflict this miserable doom upon thy child?"

"Miserable!" exclaimed Rappaccini. "What mean you, foolish girl? Dost thou deem it misery to be endowed with marvellous gifts against which no power nor strength could avail an enemy—misery, to be able to quell the mightiest with a breath—misery, to be as terrible as thou art beautiful? Wouldst thou, then, have preferred the condition of a weak woman, exposed to all evil and capable of none?"

"I would fain have been loved, not feared," murmured Beatrice, sinking down upon the ground. "But now it matters not. I am going, father, where the evil which thou hast striven to mingle with my being will pass away like a dream— like the fragrance of these poisonous flowers, which will no longer taint my breath among the flowers of Eden. Farewell, Giovanni! Thy words of hatred are like lead within my heart; but they, too, will fall away as I ascend. Oh, was there not, from the first, more poison in thy nature than in mine?"

To Beatrice,—so radically had her earthly part been wrought upon by Rappaccini's skill,—as poison had been life, so the powerful antidote was death; and thus the poor victim of man's ingenuity and of thwarted nature, and of the fatality that attends all such efforts of perverted wisdom, perished there, at the feet of her father and Giovanni. Just at that moment Professor Pietro Baglioni looked forth from the window, and called loudly, in a tone of triumph mixed with horror, to the thunderstricken man of science,—

"Rappaccini! Rappaccini! and is *this* the upshot of your experiment!" 140

Ernest Hemingway   (1899–1961)

Ernest Hemingway came to symbolize the "Lost Generation" of writers, those who, like Hemingway, spent much of their early productive lives in Europe between the world wars. He first arrived in Italy as a Red Cross ambulance driver and was wounded in 1918 while carrying a wounded Italian soldier to safety. His period of recovery in an Italian hospital was the basis of his novel A Farewell to Arms *(1929). Before that, he wrote several books that established his reputation as an innovative and significant writer. His story collections,* In Our Time *(1925) and* Men Without Women *(1927), signaled a powerful approach to language and subject matter.* The Sun Also Rises *(1926) made him famous. Hemingway spent the early 1920s in Paris, where he met Ezra Pound, Gertrude Stein, and James Joyce, the major modernist writers. His style is marked by an unusual economy of language: simple words, and few of them. He observed details closely and portrayed nuances of emotion with great clarity. His notebooks indicate the care with which he observed people, especially his friends. After the success of his novels, he published short stories in numerous magazines. "Hills Like White Elephants" appeared in 1938 in* The Fifth Column and the First Forty-nine Stories.

HILLS LIKE WHITE ELEPHANTS   1938

The hills across the valley of the Ebro were long and white. On this side there was no shade and no trees and the station was between two lines of rails in the sun. Close against the side of the station there was the warm shadow of the building and a curtain, made of strings of bamboo beads, hung across the open door into the bar, to keep out flies. The American and the girl with him sat at a table in the shade, outside the building. It was very hot and the express from Barcelona would come in forty minutes. It stopped at this junction for two minutes and went on to Madrid.

"What should we drink?" the girl asked. She had taken off her hat and put it on the table.

"It's pretty hot," the man said.

"Let's drink beer."

"*Dos cervezas,*"° the man said into the curtain.   5

"Big ones?" a woman asked from the doorway.

"Yes. Two big ones."

The woman brought two glasses of beer and two felt pads. She put the felt pads and the beer glasses on the table and looked at the man and the girl. The girl was looking off at the line of hills. They were white in the sun and the country was brown and dry.

"They look like white elephants," she said.

"I've never seen one," the man drank his beer.   10

"No, you wouldn't have."

"I might have," the man said. "Just because you say I wouldn't have doesn't prove anything."

Dos cervezas: "Two beers."

The girl looked at the bead curtain. "They've painted something on it," she said. "What does it say?"

"Anis del Toro. It's a drink."

"Could we try it?"   15

The man called "Listen" through the curtain. The woman came out from the bar.

"Four reales."

"We want two Anis del Toro."

"With water?"

"Do you want it with water?"   20

"I don't know," the girl said. "Is it good with water?"

"It's all right."

"You want them with water?" asked the woman.

"Yes, with water."

"It tastes like licorice," the girl said and put the glass down."   25

"That's the way with everything."

"Yes," said the girl. "Everything tastes of licorice. Especially all the things you've waited so long for, like absinthe."

"Oh, cut it out."

"You started it," the girl said. "I was being amused. I was having a fine time."

"Well, let's try and have a fine time."   30

"All right. I was trying. I said the mountains looked like white elephants. Wasn't that bright?"

"That was bright."

"I wanted to try this new drink: That's all we do, isn't it—look at things and try new drinks?"

"I guess so."

The girl looked across at the hills.   35

"They're lovely hills," she said. "They don't really look like white elephants. I just meant the coloring of their skin through the trees."

"Should we have another drink?"

"All right."

The warm wind blew the bead curtain against the table.

"The beer's nice and cool," the man said.   40

"It's lovely," the girl said.

"It's really an awfully simple operation, Jig," the man said. "It's not really an operation at all."

The girl looked at the ground the table legs rested on.

"I know you wouldn't mind it, Jig. It's really not anything. It's just to let the air in."

The girl did not say anything.   45

"I'll go with you and I'll stay with you all the time. They just let the air in and then it's all perfectly natural."

"Then what will we do afterward?"

"We'll be fine afterward. Just like we were before."

"What makes you think so?"

"That's the only thing that bothers us. It's the only thing that's made us un-   50
happy."

The girl looked at the bead curtain, put her hand out and took hold of two of the strings of beads.

"And you think then we'll be all right and be happy."

"I know we will. You don't have to be afraid. I've known lots of people that have done it."

"So have I," said the girl. "And afterward they were all so happy."

"Well," the man said, "if you don't want to you don't have to. I wouldn't   55
have you do it if you didn't want to. But I know it's perfectly simple."

"And you really want to?"

"I think it's the best thing to do. But I don't want you to do it if you don't really want to."

"And if I do it you'll be happy and things will be like they were and you'll love me?"

"I love you now. You know I love you."

"I know. But if I do it, then it will be nice again if I say things are like white   60
elephants, and you'll like it?"

"I'll love it. I love it now but I just can't think about it. You know how I get when I worry."

"If I do it you won't ever worry?"

"I won't worry about that because it's perfectly simple."

"Then I'll do it. Because I don't care about me."

"What do you mean?"   65

"I don't care about me."

"Well, I care about you."

"Oh, yes. But I don't care about me. And I'll do it and then everything will be fine."

"I don't want you to do it if you feel that way."

The girl stood up and walked to the end of the station. Across, on the other   70
side, were fields of grain and trees along the banks of the Ebro. Far away, beyond the river, were mountains. The shadow of a cloud moved across the field of grain and she saw the river through the trees.

"And we could have all this," she said. "And we could have everything and every day we make it more impossible."

"What did you say?"

"I said we could have everything."

"We can have everything."

"No, we can't."   75

"We can have the whole world."

"No, we can't."

"We can go everywhere."

"No, we can't. It isn't ours any more."

"It's ours."   80

"No, it isn't. And once they take it away, you never get it back."

"But they haven't taken it away."

"We'll wait and see."

"Come on back in the shade," he said. "You mustn't feel that way."

"I don't feel any way," the girl said. "I just know things."   85

"I don't want you to do anything that you don't want to do——"

"Nor that isn't good for me," she said. "I know. Could we have another beer?"

"All right. But you've got to realize——"

"I realize," the girl said. "Can't we maybe stop talking?"

They sat down at the table and the girl looked across at the hills on the dry   90
side of the valley and the man looked at her and at the table.

"You've got to realize," he said, "that I don't want you to do it if you don't want to. I'm perfectly willing to go through with it if it means anything to you."

"Doesn't it mean anything to you? We could get along."

"Of course it does. But I don't want anybody but you. I don't want anyone else. And I know it's perfectly simple."

"Yes, you know it's perfectly simple."

"It's all right for you to say that, but I do know it."   95

"Would you do something for me now?"

"I'd do anything for you."

"Would you please please please please please please please stop talking?"

He did not say anything but looked at the bags against the wall of the station. There were labels on them from all the hotels where they had spent nights.

"But I don't want you to," he said, "I don't care anything about it."   100

"I'll scream," the girl said.

The woman came out through the curtains with two glasses of beer and put them down on the damp felt pads. "The train comes in five minutes," she said.

"What did she say?" asked the girl.

"That the train is coming in five minutes."

The girl smiled brightly at the woman, to thank her.   105

"I'd better take the bags over to the other side of the station," the man said. She smiled at him.

"All right. Then come back and we'll finish the beer."

He picked up the two heavy bags and carried them around the station to the other tracks. He looked up the tracks but could not see the train. Coming back, he walked through the barroom, where people waiting for the train were drinking. He drank an Anis at the bar and looked at the people. They were all waiting reasonably for the train. He went out through the bead curtain. She was sitting at the table and smiled at him.

"Do you feel better?" he asked.

"I feel fine," she said. "There's nothing wrong with me. I feel fine."   110

James Joyce   (1882–1941)

Born in Dublin on February 2, 1882, James Joyce became the ranking English-language novelist of the twentieth century. His short stories appeared in a volume called Dubliners *in 1914, but the path to their publication was problematic. He began the stories in 1904, publishing the first of them in a new journal called* The Irish Homestead *and using the nom de plume Stephen Daedalus (later Dedalus) for the first three stories. The first printing of* Dubliners *in 1906 was destroyed because of fear of libel over Joyce's realistic technique of referring to actual businesses by their name.*

Joyce's method was to create in painstaking detail the realistic surfaces of experience in his stories. He is known for the use of stream of consciousness—the direct recording of his characters' thoughts. "Araby" perhaps reveals the main character's inner life most thoroughly. "Counterparts" is a violent story recording the effect of drink and humiliation on a father whose only outlet is to beat his son.

ARABY 1914

North Richmond Street, being blind,° was a quiet street except at the hour when the Christian Brothers' School set the boys free. An uninhabited house of two stories stood at the blind end, detached from its neighbors in a square ground. The other houses of the street, conscious of decent lives within them, gazed at one another with brown imperturbable faces.

The former tenant of our house, a priest, had died in the back drawing-room. Air, musty from having been long enclosed, hung in all the rooms, and the waste room behind the kitchen was littered with old useless papers. Among these I found a few paper-covered books, the pages of which were curled and damp: *The Abbot*,° by Walter Scott, *The Devout Communicant* and *The Memoirs of Vidocq*. I liked the last best because its leaves were yellow. The wild garden behind the house contained a central apple-tree and a few straggling bushes under one of which I found the late tenant's rusty bicycle-pump. He had been a very charitable priest; in his will he had left all his money to institutions and the furniture of his house to his sister.

When the short days of winter came dusk fell before we had well eaten our dinners. When we met in the street the houses had grown somber. The space of sky above us was the color of ever-changing violet and towards it the lamps of the street lifted their feeble lanterns. The cold air stung us and we played till our bodies glowed. Our shouts echoed in the silent street. The career of our play brought us through the dark muddy lanes behind the houses where we ran the gauntlet of the rough tribes from the cottages, to the back doors of the dark dripping gardens where odors arose from the ashpits, to the dark odorous stables where a coachman smoothed and combed the horse or shook music from the buckled harness. When we returned to the street light from the kitchen windows had filled the areas. If my uncle was seen turning the corner we hid in the shadow until we had seen him safely housed. Or if Mangan's sister came out on the doorstep to call her brother in to his tea we watched her from our shadow peer up and down the street. We waited to see whether she would remain or go in and, if she remained, we left our shadow and walked up to Mangan's steps resignedly. She was waiting for us, her figure defined by the light from the half-opened door. Her brother always teased her before he obeyed and I stood by the railings looking at her. Her dress swung as she moved her body and the soft rope of her hair tossed from side to side.

Every morning I lay on the floor in the front parlor watching her door. The blind was pulled down to within an inch of the sash so that I could not be seen. When she came out on the doorstep my heart leaped. I ran to the hall, seized my books and followed her. I kept her brown figure always in my eye and, when we

blind: A dead-end street. *The Abbot*: A popular historical romance by Sir Walter Scott (1771–1832). *The Devout Communicant*: A book of meditations. *The Memoirs of Vidocq*: A story based on the life of a Paris police detective.

came near the point at which our ways diverged, I quickened my pace and passed her. This happened morning after morning. I had never spoken to her, except for a few casual words, and yet her name was like a summons to all my foolish blood.

Her image accompanied me even in places the most hostile to romance. On   5
Saturday evenings when my aunt went marketing I had to go to carry some of the parcels. We walked through the flaring streets, jostled by drunken men and bargaining women, amid the curses of laborers, the shrill litanies of shop-boys who stood on guard by the barrels of pigs' cheeks, the nasal chanting of street-singers, who sang a *come-all-you* about O'Donovan Rossa,° or a ballad about the troubles in our native land. These noises converged in a single sensation of life for me: I imagined that I bore my chalice safely through a throng of foes. Her name sprang to my lips at moments in strange prayers and praises which I myself did not understand. My eyes were often full of tears (I could not tell why) and at times a flood from my heart seemed to pour itself out into my bosom. I thought little of the future. I did not know whether I would ever speak to her or not or, if I spoke to her, how I could tell her of my confused adoration. But my body was like a harp and her words and gestures were like fingers running upon the wires.

One evening I went into the back drawing-room in which the priest had died. It was a dark rainy evening and there was no sound in the house. Through one of the broken panes I heard the rain impinge upon the earth, the fine incessant needles of water playing in the sodden beds. Some distant lamp or lighted window gleamed below me. I was thankful that I could see so little. All my senses seemed to desire to veil themselves and, feeling that I was about to slip from them, I pressed the palms of my hands together until they trembled, murmuring: "*O love! O love!*" many times.

At last she spoke to me. When she addressed the first words to me I was so confused that I did not know what to answer. She asked me was I going to *Araby*.° I forgot whether I answered yes or no. It would be a splendid bazaar, she said; she would love to go.

"And why can't you?" I asked.

While she spoke she turned a silver bracelet round and round her wrist. She could not go, she said, because there would be a retreat that week in her convent. Her brother and two other boys were fighting for their caps and I was alone at the railings. She held one of the spikes, bowing her head towards me. The light from the lamp opposite our door caught the white curve of her neck, lit up her hair that rested there and, falling, lit up the hand upon the railing. It fell over one side of her dress and caught the white border of a petticoat, just visible as she stood at ease.

"It's well for you," she said.   10

"If I go," I said, "I will bring you something."

What innumerable follies laid waste my waking and sleeping thoughts after that evening! I wished to annihilate the tedious intervening days. I chafed against the work of school. At night in my bedroom and by day in the classroom her im-

---

O'Donovan Rossa: A leader of the Fenians, a secret revolutionary group formed in New York and Ireland to free Ireland from British rule.   *Araby*: A bazaar that was held in Dublin in May 1894. The attraction was its oriental (therefore exotic and romantic) theme.

age came between me and the page I strove to read. The syllables of the word *Araby* were called to me through the silence in which my soul luxuriated and cast an Eastern enchantment over me. I asked for leave to go to the bazaar on Saturday night. My aunt was surprised and hoped it was not some Freemason° affair. I answered few questions in class. I watched my master's face pass from amiability to sternness; he hoped I was not beginning to idle. I could not call my wandering thoughts together. I had hardly any patience with the serious work of life which, now that it stood between me and my desire, seemed to me child's play, ugly monotonous child's play.

On Saturday morning I reminded my uncle that I wished to go to the bazaar in the evening. He was fussing at the hallstand, looking for the hat-brush, and answered me curtly:

"Yes, boy, I know."

As he was in the hall I could not go into the front parlor and lie at the window. I felt the house in bad humor and walked slowly towards the school. The air was pitilessly raw and already my heart misgave me.

When I came home to dinner my uncle had not yet been home. Still it was early. I sat staring at the clock for some time and, when its ticking began to irritate me, I left the room. I mounted the staircase and gained the upper part of the house. The high cold empty gloomy rooms liberated me and I went from room to room singing. From the front window I saw my companions playing below in the street. Their cries reached me weakened and indistinct and, leaning my forehead against the cool glass, I looked over at the dark house where she lived. I may have stood there for an hour, seeing nothing but the brown-clad figure cast by my imagination, touched discreetly by the lamplight at the curved neck, at the hand upon the railings and at the border below the dress.

When I came downstairs again I found Mrs. Mercer sitting at the fire. She was an old garrulous woman, a pawnbroker's widow, who collected used stamps for some pious purpose. I had to endure the gossip of the tea-table. The meal was prolonged beyond an hour and still my uncle did not come. Mrs. Mercer stood up to go: she was sorry she couldn't wait any longer, but it was after eight o'clock and she did not like to be out late, as the night air was bad for her. When she had gone I began to walk up and down the room, clenching my fists. My aunt said:

"I'm afraid you may put off your bazaar for this night of Our Lord."

At nine o'clock I heard my uncle's latchkey in the halldoor. I heard him talking to himself and heard the hallstand rocking when it had received the weight of his overcoat. I could interpret these signs. When he was midway through his dinner I asked him to give me the money to go to the bazaar. He had forgotten.

"The people are in bed and after their first sleep now," he said.

I did not smile. My aunt said to him energetically:

"Can't you give him the money and let him go? You've kept him late enough as it is."

My uncle said he was very sorry he had forgotten. He said he believed in the old saying: "All work and no play makes Jack a dull boy." He asked me where I was going and, when I had told him a second time he asked me did I know *The*

15

20

Freemason: A secret international Protestant brotherhood emphasizing charity and mutual aid.

Arab's Farewell to his Steed. When I left the kitchen he was about to recite the opening lines of the piece to my aunt.

I held a florin tightly in my hand as I strode down Buckingham Street towards the station. The sight of the streets thronged with buyers and glaring with gas recalled to me the purpose of my journey. I took my seat in a third-class carriage of a deserted train. After an intolerable delay the train moved out of the station slowly. It crept onward among ruinous houses and over the twinkling river. At Westland Row Station a crowd of people pressed to the carriage doors; but the porters moved them back, saying that it was a special train for the bazaar. I remained alone in the bare carriage. In a few minutes the train drew up beside an improvised wooden platform. I passed out on to the road and saw by the lighted dial of a clock that it was ten minutes to ten. In front of me was a large building which displayed the magical name.

I could not find any sixpenny entrance and, fearing that the bazaar would   25
be closed, I passed in quickly through a turnstile, handing a shilling to a weary-looking man. I found myself in a big hall girdled at half its height by a gallery. Nearly all the stalls were closed and the greater part of the hall was in darkness. I recognized a silence like that which pervades a church after a service. I walked into the center of the bazaar timidly. A few people were gathered about the stalls which were still open. Before a curtain, over which the words *Café Chantant* were written in colored lamps, two men were counting money on a salver. I listened to the fall of the coins.

Remembering with difficulty why I had come I went over to one of the stalls and examined porcelain vases and flowered tea-sets. At the door of the stall a young lady was talking and laughing with two young gentlemen. I remarked their English accents and listened vaguely to their conversation.

"O, I never said such a thing!"

"O, but you did!"

"O, but I didn't!"

"Didn't she say that?"   30

"Yes. I heard her."

"O, there's a . . . fib!"

Observing me the young lady came over and asked me did I wish to buy anything. The tone of her voice was not encouraging; she seemed to have spoken to me out of a sense of duty. I looked humbly at the great jars that stood like eastern guards at either side of the dark entrance to the stall and murmured:

"No, thank you."

The young lady changed the position of one of the vases and went back to the two young men. They began to talk of the same subject. Once or twice the   35
young lady glanced at me over her shoulder.

I lingered before her stall, though I knew my stay was useless, to make my interest in her wares seem the more real. Then I turned away slowly and walked down the middle of the bazaar. I allowed the two pennies to fall against the sixpence in my pocket. I heard a voice call from one end of the gallery that the light was out. The upper part of the hall was now completely dark.

Gazing up into the darkness I saw myself as a creature driven and derided by vanity; and my eyes burned with anguish and anger.

COUNTERPARTS   1914

THE bell rang furiously and, when Miss Parker went to the tube,° a furious voice called out in a piercing North of Ireland accent:

"Send Farrington here!"

Miss Parker returned to her machine, saying to a man who was writing at a desk:

"Mr. Alleyne wants you upstairs."

The man muttered "*Blast* him!" under his breath and pushed back his chair   5 to stand up. When he stood up he was tall and of great bulk. He had a hanging face, dark wine-colored, with fair eyebrows and moustache: his eyes bulged forward slightly and the whites of them were dirty. He lifted up the counter and, passing by the clients, went out of the office with a heavy step.

He went heavily upstairs until he came to the second landing, where a door bore a brass plate with the inscription *Mr. Alleyne*. Here he halted, puffing with labor and vexation, and knocked. The shrill voice cried:

"Come in!"

The man entered Mr. Alleyne's room. Simultaneously Mr. Alleyne, a little man wearing gold-rimmed glasses on a clean-shaven face, shot his head up over a pile of documents. The head itself was so pink and hairless it seemed like a large egg reposing on the papers. Mr. Alleyne did not lose a moment:

"Farrington? What is the meaning of this? Why have I always to complain of you? May I ask you why you haven't made a copy of that contract between Bodley and Kirwan? I told you it must be ready by four o'clock."

"But Mr. Shelley said, sir——"   10

"*Mr. Shelley said, sir.* . . . Kindly attend to what I say and not to what *Mr. Shelley says, sir.* You have always some excuse or another for shirking work. Let me tell you that if the contract is not copied before this evening I'll lay the matter before Mr. Crosbie. . . . Do you hear me now?"

"Yes, sir."

"Do you hear me now? . . . Ay and another little matter! I might as well be talking to the wall as talking to you. Understand once for all that you get a half an hour for your lunch and not an hour and a half. How many courses do you want, I'd like to know. . . . Do you mind me now?"

"Yes, sir."

Mr. Alleyne bent his head again upon his pile of papers. The man stared   15 fixedly at the polished skull which directed the affairs of Crosbie & Alleyne, gauging its fragility. A spasm of rage gripped his throat for a few moments and then passed, leaving after it a sharp sensation of thirst. The man recognized the sensation and felt that he must have a good night's drinking. The middle of the month was passed and, if he could get the copy done in time, Mr. Alleyne might give him an order on the cashier.° He stood still, gazing fixedly at the head upon the pile of papers. Suddenly Mr. Alleyne began to upset all the papers, searching for something. Then, as if he had been unaware of the man's presence till that moment, he shot up his head again, saying:

tube: A voice-phone tube system for communicating between floors or offices.   *give him an order on the cashier*: Give him a voucher to get paid.

"Eh? Are you going to stand there all day? Upon my word, Farrington, you take things easy!"

"I was waiting to see . . ."

"Very good, you needn't wait to see. Go downstairs and do your work."

The man walked heavily towards the door and, as he went out of the room, he heard Mr. Alleyne cry after him that if the contract was not copied by evening Mr. Crosbie would hear of the matter.

He returned to his desk in the lower office and counted the sheets which re-   20
mained to be copied. He took up his pen and dipped it in the ink but he contin-ued to stare stupidly at the last words he had written: *In no case shall the said Bernard Bodley be* . . . The evening was falling and in a few minutes they would be lighting the gas: then he could write. He felt that he must slake the thirst in his throat. He stood up from his desk and, lifting the counter as before, passed out of the office. As he was passing out the chief clerk looked at him inquiringly.

"It's all right, Mr. Shelley," said the man, pointing with his finger to indi-cate the objective of his journey.

The chief clerk glanced at the hat-rack, but, seeing the row complete, of-fered no remark. As soon as he was on the landing the man pulled a shepherd's plaid cap out of his pocket, put it on his head and ran quickly down the rickety stairs. From the street door he walked on furtively on the inner side of the path towards the corner and all at once dived into a doorway. He was now safe in the dark snug of O'Neill's shop, and, filling up the little window that looked into the bar with his inflamed face, the color of dark wine or dark meat, he called out:

"Here, Pat, give us a g.p.,° like a good fellow."

The curate° brought him a glass of plain porter. The man drank it at a gulp and asked for a caraway seed. He put his penny on the counter and, leaving the curate to grope for it in the gloom, retreated out of the snug as furtively as he had entered it.

Darkness, accompanied by a thick fog, was gaining upon the dusk of February   25
and the lamps in Eustace Street had been lit. The man went up by the houses un-til he reached the door of the office, wondering whether he could finish his copy in time. On the stairs a moist pungent odor of perfumes saluted his nose: evi-dently Miss Delacour had come while he was out in O'Neill's. He crammed his cap back again into his pocket and re-entered the office, assuming an air of ab-sent-mindedness.

"Mr. Alleyne has been calling for you," said the chief clerk severely. "Where were you?"

The man glanced at the two clients who were standing at the counter as if to intimate that their presence prevented him from answering. As the clients were both male the chief clerk allowed himself a laugh.

"I know that game," he said. "Five times in one day is a little bit. . . . Well, you better look sharp and get a copy of our correspondence in the Delacour case for Mr. Alleyne."

This address in the presence of the public, his run upstairs and the porter he had gulped down so hastily confused the man and, as he sat down at his desk to get what was required, he realized how hopeless was the task of finishing his copy of the contract before half past five. The dark damp night was coming and he

---

g.p.: Glass of plain—dark beer.   *curate*: Ironic term for Irish bartenders.

longed to spend it in the bars, drinking with his friends amid the glare of gas and the clatter of glasses. He got out the Delacour correspondence and passed out of the office. He hoped Mr. Alleyne would not discover that the last two letters were missing.

The moist pungent perfume lay all the way up to Mr. Alleyne's room. Miss Delacour was a middle-aged woman of Jewish appearance. Mr. Alleyne was said to be sweet on her or on her money. She came to the office often and stayed a long time when she came. She was sitting beside his desk now in an aroma of perfumes, smoothing the handle of her umbrella and nodding the great black feather in her hat. Mr. Alleyne had swivelled his chair round to face her and thrown his right foot jauntily upon his left knee. The man put the correspondence on the desk and bowed respectfully but neither Mr. Alleyne nor Miss Delacour took any notice of his bow. Mr. Alleyne tapped a finger on the correspondence and then flicked it towards him as if to say: "*That's all right: you can go.*"

The man returned to the lower office and sat down again at his desk. He stared intently at the incomplete phrase: *In no case shall the said Bernard Bodley be . . .* and thought how strange it was that the last three words began with the same letter. The chief clerk began to hurry Miss Parker, saying she would never have the letters typed in time for post. The man listened to the clicking of the machine for a few minutes and then set to work to finish his copy. But his head was not clear and his mind wandered away to the glare and rattle of the public-house. It was a night for hot punches. He struggled on with his copy, but when the clock struck five he had still fourteen pages to write. Blast it! He couldn't finish it in time. He longed to execrate aloud, to bring his fist down on something violently. He was so enraged that he wrote *Bernard Bernard* instead of *Bernard Bodley* and had to begin again on a clean sheet.

He felt strong enough to clear out the whole office single-handed. His body ached to do something, to rush out and revel in violence. All the indignities of his life enraged him. . . . Could he ask the cashier privately for an advance? No, the cashier was no good, no damn good: he wouldn't give an advance. . . . He knew where he would meet the boys: Leonard and O'Halloran and Nosey Flynn. The barometer of his emotional nature was set for a spell of riot.

His imagination had so abstracted him that his name was called twice before he answered. Mr. Alleyne and Miss Delacour were standing outside the counter and all the clerks had turned round in anticipation of something. The man got up from his desk. Mr. Alleyne began a tirade of abuse, saying that two letters were missing. The man answered that he knew nothing about them, that he had made a faithful copy. The tirade continued: it was so bitter and violent that the man could hardly restrain his fist from descending upon the head of the manikin before him:

"I know nothing about any other two letters," he said stupidly.

"*You—know—nothing.* Of course you know nothing," said Mr. Alleyne. "Tell me," he added, glancing first for approval to the lady beside him, "do you take me for a fool? Do you think me an utter fool?"

The man glanced from the lady's face to the little egg-shaped head and back again; and, almost before he was aware of it, his tongue had found a felicitous moment:

"I don't think, sir," he said, "that that's a fair question to put to me."

There was a pause in the very breathing of the clerks. Everyone was astounded (the author of the witticism no less than his neighbors) and Miss Delacour, who was a stout amiable person, began to smile broadly. Mr. Alleyne flushed to the hue of a wild rose and his mouth twitched with a dwarf's passion. He shook his fist in the man's face till it seemed to vibrate like the knob of some electric machine:

"You impertinent ruffian! You impertinent ruffian! I'll make short work of you! Wait till you see! You'll apologize to me for your impertinence or you'll quit the office instanter!° You'll quit this, I'm telling you, or you'll apologize to me!"

He stood in a doorway opposite the office watching to see if the cashier   40
would come out alone. All the clerks passed out and finally the cashier came out with the chief clerk. It was no use trying to say a word to him when he was with the chief clerk. The man felt that his position was bad enough. He had been obliged to offer an abject apology to Mr. Alleyne for his impertinence but he knew what a hornet's nest the office would be for him. He could remember the way in which Mr. Alleyne had hounded little Peake out of the office in order to make room for his own nephew. He felt savage and thirsty and revengeful, annoyed with himself and with everyone else. Mr. Alleyne would never give him an hour's rest; his life would be a hell to him. He had made a proper fool of himself this time. Could he not keep his tongue in his cheek? But they had never pulled together from the first, he and Mr. Alleyne, ever since the day Mr. Alleyne had overheard him mimicking his North of Ireland accent to amuse Higgins and Miss Parker: that had been the beginning of it. He might have tried Higgins for the money, but sure Higgins never had anything for himself. A man with two establishments to keep up, of course he couldn't. . . .

He felt his great body again aching for the comfort of the public-house. The fog had begun to chill him and he wondered could he touch Pat in O'Neill's. He could not touch him for more than a bob°—and a bob was no use. Yet he must get money somewhere or other: he had spent his last penny for the g.p. and soon it would be too late for getting money anywhere. Suddenly, as he was fingering his watch-chain, he thought of Terry Kelly's pawn-office in Fleet Street. That was the dart! Why didn't he think of it sooner?

He went through the narrow alley of Temple Bar quickly, muttering to himself that they could all go to hell because he was going to have a good night of it. The clerk in Terry Kelly's said *A crown!*° but the consignor held out for six shillings; and in the end the six shillings was allowed him literally. He came out of the pawn-office joyfully, making a little cylinder of the coins between his thumb and fingers. In Westmoreland Street the footpaths were crowded with young men and women returning from business and ragged urchins ran here and there yelling out the names of the evening editions. The man passed through the crowd, looking on the spectacle generally with proud satisfaction and staring masterfully at the office-girls. His head was full of the noises of tram-gongs and swishing trolleys and his nose already sniffed the curling fumes of punch. As he walked on he preconsidered the terms in which he would narrate the incident to the boys:

---

instanter: Immediately, this instant.   *bob*: A shilling.   *crown*: Ten shilling coin. There were twenty shillings in a pound. Farrington's salary might have been three pounds ten shillings a week.

"So, I just looked at him—coolly, you know, and looked at her. Then I looked back at him again—taking my time, you know. 'I don't think that that's a fair question to put to me,' says I."

Nosey Flynn was sitting up in his usual corner of Davy Byrne's and, when he heard the story, he stood Farrington a half-one, saying it was as smart a thing as ever he heard. Farrington stood a drink in his turn. After a while O'Halloran and Paddy Leonard came in and the story was repeated to them. O'Halloran stood tailors of malt, hot, all round and told the story of the retort he had made to the chief clerk when he was in Callan's of Fownes's Street; but, as the retort was after the manner of the liberal shepherds in the eclogues,° he had to admit that it was not as clever as Farrington's retort. At this Farrington told the boys to polish off that and have another.

Just as they were naming their poisons who should come in but Higgins! Of   45
course he had to join in with the others. The men asked him to give his version of it, and he did so with great vivacity for the sight of five small hot whiskies was very exhilarating. Everyone roared laughing when he showed the way in which Mr. Alleyne shook his fist in Farrington's face. Then he imitated Farrington, saying, "*And here was my nabs,*° as cool as you please," while Farrington looked at the company out of his heavy dirty eyes, smiling and at times drawing forth stray drops of liquor from his moustache with the aid of his lower lip.

When that round was over there was a pause. O'Halloran had money but neither of the other two seemed to have any; so the whole party left the shop somewhat regretfully. At the corner of Duke Street Higgins and Nosey Flynn bevelled off to the left while the other three turned back towards the city. Rain was drizzling down on the cold streets and, when they reached the Ballast Office, Farrington suggested the Scotch House. The bar was full of men and loud with the noise of tongues and glasses. The three men pushed past the whining match-sellers at the door and formed a little party at the corner of the counter. They began to exchange stories. Leonard introduced them to a young fellow named Weathers who was performing at the Tivoli as an acrobat and knockabout *artiste.* Farrington stood a drink all round. Weathers said he would take a small Irish and Apollinaris. Farrington, who had definite notions of what was what, asked the boys would they have an Apollinaris too; but the boys told Tim to make theirs hot. The talk became theatrical. O'Halloran stood a round and then Farrington stood another round, Weathers protesting that the hospitality was too Irish. He promised to get them in behind the scenes and introduce them to some nice girls. O'Halloran said that he and Leonard would go, but that Farrington wouldn't go because he was a married man; and Farrington's heavy dirty eyes leered at the company in token that he understood he was being chaffed. Weathers made them all have just one little tincture at his expense and promised to meet them later on at Mulligan's in Poolbeg Street.

When the Scotch House closed they went round to Mulligan's. They went into the parlor at the back and O'Halloran ordered small hot specials all round. They were all beginning to feel mellow. Farrington was just standing another

---

liberal shepherds in the eclogues: Poet Edmund Spenser often commented wittily on contemporary politics in eclogues, which are pastoral poems featuring dialogues between shepherds.   *my nabs*: Slang for "my gentleman."

round when Weathers came back. Much to Farrington's relief he drank a glass of bitter this time. Funds were getting low but they had enough to keep them going. Presently two young women with big hats and a young man in a check suit came in and sat at a table close by. Weathers saluted them and told the company that they were out of the Tivoli. Farrington's eyes wandered at every moment in the direction of one of the young women. There was something striking in her appearance. An immense scarf of peacock-blue muslin was wound round her hat and knotted in a great bow under her chin; and she wore bright yellow gloves, reaching to the elbow. Farrington gazed admiringly at the plump arm which she moved very often and with much grace; and when, after a little time, she answered his gaze he admired still more her large dark brown eyes. The oblique staring expression in them fascinated him. She glanced at him once or twice and, when the party was leaving the room, she brushed against his chair and said "*O, pardon!*" in a London accent. He watched her leave the room in the hope that she would look back at him, but he was disappointed. He cursed his want of money and cursed all the rounds he had stood, particularly all the whiskies and Apollinaris which he had stood to Weathers. If there was one thing that he hated it was a sponge. He was so angry that he lost count of the conversation of his friends.

When Paddy Leonard called him he found that they were talking about feats of strength. Weathers was showing his biceps muscle to the company and boasting so much that the other two had called on Farrington to uphold the national honor. Farrington pulled up his sleeve accordingly and showed his biceps muscle to the company. The two arms were examined and compared and finally it was agreed to have a trial of strength. The table was cleared and the two men rested their elbows on it, clasping hands. When Paddy Leonard said "*Go!*" each was to try to bring down the other's hand on to the table. Farrington looked very serious and determined.

The trial began. After about thirty seconds Weathers brought his opponent's hand slowly down on to the table. Farrington's dark wine-colored face flushed darker still with anger and humiliation at having been defeated by such a stripling.

"You're not to put the weight of your body behind it. Play fair," he said.　50

"Who's not playing fair?" said the other.

"Come on again. The two best out of three."

The trial began again. The veins stood out on Farrington's forehead, and the pallor of Weathers' complexion changed to peony. Their hands and arms trembled under the stress. After a long struggle Weathers again brought his opponent's hand slowly on to the table. There was a murmur of applause from the spectators. The curate, who was standing beside the table, nodded his red head towards the victor and said with stupid familiarity:

"Ah! that's the knack!"

"What the hell do you know about it?" said Farrington fiercely, turning on　55 the man. "What do you put in your gab for?"

"Sh, sh!" said O'Halloran, observing the violent expression of Farrington's face. "Pony up, boys. We'll have just one little smahan more and then we'll be off."

A very sullen-faced man stood at the corner of O'Connell Bridge waiting for the little Sandymount tram to take him home. He was full of smoldering anger and revengefulness. He felt humiliated and discontented; he did not even feel drunk; and he had only twopence in his pocket. He cursed everything. He had done for himself in the office, pawned his watch, spent all his money; and he had not even got drunk. He began to feel thirsty again and he longed to be back again in the hot reeking public-house. He had lost his reputation as a strong man, having been defeated twice by a mere boy. His heart swelled with fury and, when he thought of the woman in the big hat who had brushed against him and said *Pardon*! his fury nearly choked him.

His tram let him down at Shelbourne Road and he steered his great body along in the shadow of the wall of the barracks. He loathed returning to his home. When he went in by the side-door he found the kitchen empty and the kitchen fire nearly out. He bawled upstairs:

"Ada! Ada!"

His wife was a little sharp-faced woman who bullied her husband when he   60
was sober and was bullied by him when he was drunk. They had five children. A little boy came running down the stairs.

"Who is that?" said the man, peering through the darkness.

"Me, pa."

"Who are you? Charlie?"

"No, pa. Tom."

"Where's your mother?"   65

"She's out at the chapel."

"That's right. . . . Did she think of leaving any dinner for me?"

"Yes, pa. I——"

"Light the lamp. What do you mean by having the place in darkness? Are the other children in bed?"

The man sat down heavily on one of the chairs while the little boy lit the   70
lamp. He began to mimic his son's flat accent, saying half to himself: "*At the chapel. At the chapel, if you please!*" When the lamp was lit he banged his fist on the table and shouted:

"What's for my dinner?"

"I'm going . . . to cook it, pa," said the little boy.

The man jumped up furiously and pointed to the fire.

"On that fire! You let the fire out! By God, I'll teach you to do that again!"

He took a step to the door and seized the walking-stick which was standing   75
behind it.

"I'll teach you to let the fire out!" he said, rolling up his sleeve in order to give his arm free play.

The little boy cried "*O, pa*!" and ran whimpering round the table, but the man followed him and caught him by the coat. The little boy looked about him wildly but, seeing no way of escape, fell upon his knees.

"Now, you'll let the fire out the next time!" said the man, striking at him vigorously with the stick. "Take that, you little whelp!"

The boy uttered a squeal of pain as the stick cut his thigh. He clasped his hands together in the air and his voice shook with fright.

"O, pa!" he cried. "Don't beat me, pa! And I'll . . . I'll say a *Hail Mary* for   80
you. . . . I'll say a *Hail Mary* for you, pa, if you don't beat me. . . . I'll say a *Hail Mary*. . . ."

Jamaica Kincaid   (b. 1949)

Jamaica Kincaid was born in St. John's, the capital of Antigua in the West Indies. Much of her work, like "Lucy," is either set in Antigua or recollects the atmosphere and experience of the island. The stories in At the Bottom of the River *(1983) and the connected stories of* Annie John *(1985) are set in Antigua and vibrate with the special qualities of its life and its language. In a review, Anne Tyler said of her first book of stories, "Jamaica Kincaid scrutinizes various particles of our world so closely and so solemnly that they begin to take on a nearly mystical importance." Her stories are deeply felt, close examinations of life. She says of America that it gave her "a place to be myself—but myself as I was formed somewhere else."*

LUCY   1990

It was January again; the world was thin and pale and cold again; I was making a new beginning again.

I had been a girl of whom certain things were expected, none of them too bad: a career as a nurse, for example; a sense of duty to my parents; obedience to the law and worship of convention. But in one year of being away from home, that girl had gone out of existence.

The person I had become I did not know very well. Oh, on the outside everything was familiar. My hair was the same, though now I wore it cut close to my head, and this made my face seem almost perfectly round, and so for the first time ever I entertained the idea that I might actually be beautiful. I knew that if I ever decided I was beautiful I would not make too big a thing of it. My eyes were the same. My ears were the same. The other important things about me were the same.

But the things I could not see about myself, the things I could not put my hands on—those things had changed, and I did not yet know them well. I understood that I was inventing myself, and that I was doing this more in the way of a painter than in the way of a scientist. I could not count on precision or calculation; I could only count on intuition. I did not have anything exactly in mind, but when the picture was complete I would know. I did not have position, I did not have money at my disposal. I had memory, I had anger, I had despair.

I was born on an island, a very small island, twelve miles long and eight miles   5
wide; yet when I left it at nineteen years of age I had never set foot on three-quarters of it. I had recently met someone who was born on the other side of the world from me but had visited this island on which my family had lived for generations; this person, a woman, had said to me, "What a beautiful place," and she named a village by the sea and then went on to describe a view that was unknown to me. At the time I was so ashamed I could hardly make a reply, for I had come to believe that people in my position in the world should know everything about the place they are from. I know this: it was discovered by Christopher Columbus in 1493; Columbus never set foot there but only named it in passing, after a church in Spain. He could not have known that he would have so many things to name, and I imagined how hard he had to rack his brain after he ran out of names honoring his benefactors, the saints he cherished, events important to him. A task like that would have killed a thoughtful person, but he went on to live a very long life.

I had realized that the origin of my presence on the island—my ancestral history—was the result of a foul deed; but that was not what made me, at fourteen or so, stand up in school choir practice and say that I did not wish to sing "Rule, Britannia! Britannia, rule the waves; Britons never, never shall be slaves," that I was not a Briton and that until not too long ago I would have been a slave. My action did not create a scandal; instead, my choir mistress only wondered if all their efforts to civilize me over the years would come to nothing in the end. At the time, my reasons were quite straightforward: I disliked the descendants of the Britons for being unbeautiful, for not cooking food well, for wearing ugly clothes, for not liking to really dance, and for not liking real music. If only we had been ruled by the French: they were prettier, much happier in appearance, so much more the kind of people I would have enjoyed being around. I once had a pen pal on a neighboring island, a French island, and even though I could see her island from mine, when we sent correspondence to each other it had to go to the ruler country, thousands of miles away, before reaching its destination. The stamps on her letter were always canceled with the French words for liberty, equality, and fraternity; on mine there were no such words, only the image of a stony-face, sour-mouth woman.° I understand the situation better now; I understand that, in spite of those words, my pen pal and I were in the same boat; but still I think those words have a better ring to them than the image of a stony-face, sour-mouth woman.

One day I was a child and then I was not. Everyone told me this: You are no longer a child. I had started to menstruate, I grew breasts, tufts of hair appeared under my arms and between my legs. I grew taller all of a sudden, and it was hard to manage so much new height all at once. One day I was living silently in a personal hell, without anyone to tell what I felt, without even knowing that the feelings I had were possible to have; and then one day I was not living like that at all. I had begun to see the past like this: there is a line; you can draw it yourself, or sometimes it gets drawn for you; either way, there it is, your past, a collection of people you used to be and things you used to do. Your past is the person you no longer are, the situations you are no longer in.

I used to be nineteen; I used to live in the household of Lewis and Mariah, and I used to be the girl who took care of their four children; I used to stand over the children, four girls, at the street corner, waiting for the stoplight to change color; I used to sit on a lakeshore with them; I used to sit in the kitchen, with the inevitable sun streaming through the window, with Mariah, drinking coffee she learned to make in France, and trying to explain to myself, by speaking to Mariah, how I got to feel the way I even now feel; I used to see Mariah with happiness an essential part of her daily existence, and then, when the perfect world she had known for so long vanished without warning, I saw sadness replace it; I used to lie naked in moonlight with a boy named Hugh; I used to not know who Lewis was, until one day he revealed himself to be just another man, an ordinary man, when I saw him in love with his wife's best friend; I used to be that person, and I used to be in those situations. That was how I had spent the year just past.

One day I was living in the large apartment of Lewis and Mariah (without Lewis, of course, for he had gone to live somewhere else all by himself, allowing

sour-mouth woman: Queen Elizabeth II.

a decent amount of time to pass before he gave Mariah the surprise of her life: he had fallen out of love with her because he had fallen in love with her best friend, Dinah), and the next day I was not.

My leaving began on the night I heard my father had died. When I had left 10 my parents, I had said to myself that I never wanted to see them again. These were words said in the way of a child; for a child might want someone dead, might even wish to do the deed herself, but would want the dead person to get up and carry on as before, only without the thing that made the child wish for the death in the first place. I had wished never to see my father again, and my wish had become true: I would never see my father again. I wondered how he looked in the coffin; I wondered who had made the coffin and if it was made of pine or mahogany; I wondered if he had been buried in his blue serge suit, the one he always saved for the special occasion that never seemed to come—perhaps my mother would have thought his burial was the special occasion. I had never imagined my father dying. I had never imagined my parents dying. When I told Mariah this, she said that no one ever thinks their parents will die, ever, and I had to suppress the annoyance I felt at her for once again telling me about everybody when I told her something about myself. Mariah said that I was feeling guilty. Guilty! I had always thought that was a judgment passed on you by others, and so it was new to me that it could be a judgment you pass on yourself. Guilty! But I did not feel like a murderer; I felt like Lucifer, doomed to build wrong upon wrong.

I had not been opening the letters my mother had been sending to me for months. In them she tried to give me a blow-by-blow description of how quickly the quality of her life had deteriorated since I had left her, but I only knew this afterward—after I had learned of my father's death, written to her and sent her money, and then opened the letter she sent in reply. For if I had seen those letters sooner, one way or another I would have died. I would have died if I did nothing; I would have died if I did something. I then made a last reply to her, though she did not know she might never hear from me again. I told her that I would come home soon, and how sorry I was for everything that had happened to her. I did not say that I loved her. I could not say that. I then told her that the family I was living with (Lewis and Mariah) were moving to another part of town; the address I gave her was one I made up off the top of my head. The moment I did that was the moment I knew I would soon make living with Lewis and Mariah the past.

After that, the days went by too slowly and too quickly: I could not wait to put this period of my life behind me, and each moment felt like a ball of lead; at the same time, I wanted to understand everything that was happening to me, and each day felt like a minute. It was gloomy inside the house, and gloomy outside, too. "The holidays are coming," Mariah said. "The holidays are coming." She should have been happy, but she said it as if she were expecting a funeral. The skies were hard and gray; it rained, and the rain felt like small, hard nails; the sun shone sometimes, but weakly, as if it held a grudge. I noticed how hard and cold and shut up tight the ground was. I noticed this because I used to wish it would just open up and take me in, I felt so bad. If I dropped dead from despair as I was crossing the street, I would just have to lie there in the cold. The ground would refuse me. To die in the cold was more than I could bear. I wanted to die in a hot place. The only hot place I knew was my home. I could not go home, and so I could not die yet.

When I told Mariah that I was leaving, she had said, "It's not a year yet. You are supposed to stay for at least a year." Her voice was full of anger, but I ignored it. It's always hard for the person who is left behind. And even as she said it she must have known how hollow it sounded, for it was only a matter of weeks before it would be a year since I had come to live with her. The reality of her situation was now clear to her: she was a woman whose husband had betrayed her. I wanted to say this to her: "Your situation is an everyday thing. Men behave in this way all the time. The ones who do not behave in this way are the exceptions to the rule." But I knew what her response would have been. She would have said, "What a cliché." She would have said, "What do you know about these things?" And she would have been right; it was a cliché, and I had no personal experience of a thing like that. But all the same, where I came from, every woman knew this cliché, and a man like Lewis would not have been a surprise; his behavior would not have cast a pall over any woman's life. It was expected. Everybody knew that men have no morals, that they do not know how to behave, that they do not know how to treat other people. It was why men like laws so much; it was why they had to invent such things—they need a guide. When they are not sure what to do, they consult this guide. If the guide gives them advice they don't like, they change the guide. This was something I knew; why didn't Mariah know it also? And if I were to tell it to her she would only show me a book she had somewhere which contradicted everything I said—a book most likely written by a woman who understood absolutely nothing.

The holidays came, and they did feel like a funeral because so many things had died. For the children's sake, she and Lewis put up a good front. He came and went, doing all the things he would have done if he were still living with them. He bought the fir tree, bought the children the presents they wanted, bought Mariah a coat made up from the skins of a small pesty animal who lived in the ground. She, of course, hated it, but for appearances' sake she kept her opinion to herself. He must have forgotten that she was not the sort of person who would wear the skin of another being if she could help it. Or perhaps in the rush of things he gave his old love his new love's present. Mariah gave me a necklace made up of pretty porcelain beads and small polished balls of wood. She said it was the handiwork of someone in Africa. It was the most beautiful thing anyone had ever given me.

The New Year came, and I was going somewhere new again. I gathered my things together; I had a lot more than when I first came. I had new clothes, all better suited to this new climate I now lived in. I had a camera and prints of the photographs I had taken, prints I had made myself. But mostly I had books—so many books, and they were mine; I would not have to part with them. It had always been a dream of mine to just own a lot of books, to never part with a book once I had read it. So there they were, resting nicely in small boxes—my own books, the books that I had read. Mariah spoke to me harshly all the time now, and she began to make up rules which she insisted that I follow; and I did, for after all, what else could she do? It was a last resort for her—insisting that I be the servant and she the master. She used to insist that we be friends, but that had apparently not worked out very well; now I was leaving. The master business did not become her at all, and it made me sad to see her that way. Still, it made me remember what my mother had said to me many times: for my whole life I should make sure the roof over my head was my own; such a thing was important, especially if you were a woman.

15

On the day I actually left, there was no sun; the sky had shut it out tightly. It was a Saturday. Lewis had taken the children to eat snails at a French restaurant. All four of them liked such things—and just as well, for that went with the life they were expected to lead eventually. Mariah helped me put my things in a taxi. It was a cold goodbye on her part. Her voice and her face were stony. She did not hug me. I did not take any of this personally; someday we would be friends again. I was numb, but it was from not knowing just what this new life would hold for me.

The next day I woke up in a new bed, and it was my own. I had bought it with my money. The roof over my head was my own—that is, as long as I could afford to pay the rent for it. The curtains at my windows had loud, showy flowers printed on them; I had chosen this pattern over a calico that the lady in the cloth store had recommended. It did look vulgar in this climate, but it would have been just right in the climate I came from. Through the curtains I could see that the day was just like the one before: gray, the sky shut up tight, the sun locked out. I knew then that even though I would always notice the absence or presence of the sun, even though I would always prefer a sunny day to a day without sun, I would get used to it; I wouldn't make an important decision based on the weather.

It was Peggy who had found the apartment. We were then still best friends. We had nothing in common except that we felt at ease in each other's company. From the moment we met we had recognized in each other the same restlessness, the same dissatisfaction with our surroundings, the same skin-doesn't-fit-ness. That was as far as it went. We had accepted each other's shortcomings and differences; then, just when we began to feel the yoke of each other's companionship, just when we began to feel the beginnings of what might eventually lead to lifelong loathing, we decided to move in together. It could have been worse. People marry at times like that; they then have ten children, live under the same roof for years and years, eventually die and arrange to be buried side by side. We only signed our names to a two-year lease.

It was a Sunday. I could hear church bells ringing. I had not been to church in over a year—not since leaving home. I supposed I still believed in God; after all, what else could I do? But no longer could I ask God what to do, since the answer, I was sure, would not suit me. I could do what suited me now, as long as I could pay for it. "As long as I could pay for it." That phrase soon became the tail that wagged my dog. If I had died then, it should have been my epitaph.

Peggy, who had been living with her parents all along, decided not to do so   20
anymore. She said that she was sick of them. She said it as if her parents were a style of dressing she had outgrown. I had never heard anyone speak of their parents in this way; I never even knew you could make them seem trivial, trinketlike, mere pests. I was not sure whether to admire her or feel sorry for her because she hadn't got parents whose personalities were on a larger scale, parents whose presence you are reminded of with each breath you take. Someone had told Peggy about this vacancy; it had two bedrooms, a sitting room, a kitchen, and a bathroom. I had spent my entire life not knowing the luxury of plumbing, hot and cold tap water, the privacy to be had by closing the door and taking off your clothes and stepping into a bathtub and staying there for as long as it pleased you. I could very well have gone through my entire life without knowledge of such

things, and on my list of unhappinesses this would not have made an appearance. But not so anymore. When I saw that the apartment had only one bathroom, I made note of it with disappointment. At Mariah and Lewis's house I had my own bathroom, and my smells were known only to me. Here the windows in the back had bars—not the decorative kind to keep children from falling out, but the criss-cross kind to keep people who meant us no good from coming in; the windows in the front allowed the sun, when it shone, to come in plenty. I used to lie in my bed at home, surrounded by all the things they say make for a contented life—a loving family, a safe full of food, harmonious surroundings—and not feel contented. I longed then to live in a place like this: bars on the windows to keep out people who might wish to do me harm, an unfriendly climate, uncertainty at every turn. History is full of great events; when the great events are said and done, there will always be someone, a little person, unhappy, dissatisfied, discontented, not at home in her own skin, ready to stir up a whole new set of great events again. I was not such a person, able to put in motion a set of great events, but I understood the phenomenon all the same.

There were many Sundays when I wished I could just lie in bed and not get up for anything, especially not for church. It was a Sunday, I was lying in bed, and I would get up only if I wished to. On the wall in front of me was a photograph I had taken with a camera borrowed from Hugh; it was of a body of water, the lake where I had spent the summer; there was nothing in the picture—there were no boats, no people, no signs of life—except the water, its surface of uniformly shaped ripplets, its depths dark, treacherous, and uninviting. It was the opposite of the water I was surrounded by on the island where I grew up. That water was three shades of blue, calm, inviting, warm; I had taken it for granted, so much so that it became one of the things I cursed.

Mariah had given me a small desk with many drawers. I had placed it near my bed, with a lamp on it. I reached into the top drawer and retrieved a small stack of official documents: my passport, my immigration card, my permission-to-work card, my birth certificate, and a copy of the lease to the apartment. These documents showed everything about me, and yet they showed nothing about me. They showed where I was born. They showed that I was born on the twenty-fifth of May 1949. They showed how tall I was. They showed that my skin and my eyes were the same color, brown, though they did not say if the shades were identical. These documents all said that my name was Lucy—Lucy Josephine Potter. I used to hate all three of those names. I was named Josephine after my mother's uncle Mr. Joseph, because he was rich, from money he had made in sugar in Cuba, and it was thought that he would remember the honor and leave something for me in his will. But when he died it was discovered that he had lost his fortune a while before and did not even have a roof over his head; he had been living in an old tomb in the Anglican churchyard. The Potter must have come from the Englishman who owned my ancestors when they were slaves; no one really knew, and I could hardly blame them for not caring to find out. The Lucy was the only part of my name that I would have cared to hold on to. When I had first begun to think of the significance of my three names, I disliked the name Lucy, because it seemed slight, without substance, not at all the person I thought I would like to be even then. In my own mind, I called myself other names: Emily, Charlotte, Jane. They were the names of the authoresses whose books I loved. I eventually settled on the name Enid, after the authoress Enid Blyton, because that name seemed the most unusual of all the names I thought of. One day when it was firm in my mind that the name Enid was the name I wanted to be known by, I told my mother. I said, "I do not like my name, Lucy. I want to change it to Enid. I like that name better." The moment I said this, she turned a dark color, the color of boiling blood. She turned toward me, and she was no longer my mother—she was a ball of fury, large, like a god. I wondered then, for the millionth time, how it came to be that of all the mothers in the world mine was not an ordinary human being but something from an ancient book. Not long after that I learned, through my usual habit of eavesdropping on conversations between my mother and her friends, that a woman with whom my father had had a child and who had tried to kill my mother and me through obeah was named Enid. I had never heard of that Enid before. When the mystery of my mother's behavior became clear to me, I felt ashamed of the mistake I had made. Even to hurt my mother I would not have wanted the same name as the woman who had tried to kill my mother and me.

Much later, when I no longer cared how I made her feel, I brought up the question of my name again. My mother was stooped over a bowl of fish, cleaning and seasoning them in preparation for our supper. She was pregnant with the last of her children. She did not want to be pregnant and three times had tried to throw away the child, but all her methods had failed and she remained pregnant. An old brown-and-white dog had become attached to her. We didn't know where the dog had come from—only that whenever my mother left our house it was always waiting outside and would follow only her. She did not like animals; where she came from, sometimes when someone wanted to harm someone else they sent the harm in the shape of an animal. When she saw the dog follow her around, she was sure it was something bad, and so she tried everything to get rid of it, but the dog would not go away. She stopped trying to get rid of the dog the day she realized that the dog was pregnant also. It was funny to see them walking down the street together—two female beings, a human and a dog, both of them pregnant. They went everywhere together, and they grew to look alike: thin, shriveled, undernourished (my mother had no appetite), unmaternal. They both became bad-tempered and would snarl at anyone who did anything they found offensive. As my mother was cleaning the fish, the dog was standing nearby, snapping at flies that were bothering her. They made such a picture: the dead fish, the flies, the pregnant woman, the pregnant dog.

It was this sight that was before me when I asked my mother why she had named me Lucy. The first time I asked, she made no reply, pretending that she had not heard me. I asked again, and this time under her breath she said, "I named you after Satan himself. Lucy, short for Lucifer. What a botheration from the moment you were conceived." I not only heard it quite clearly when she said it but I heard the words before they came out of her mouth. And yet I said, "What did you say?" But she wouldn't repeat it; she only said, "Why do you torment me so?" and wouldn't speak to me anymore. In the minute or so it took for all this to transpire, I went from feeling burdened and old and tired to feeling light, new, clean. I was transformed from failure to triumph. It was the moment I knew who I was. When I was quite young and just being taught to read, the books I was taught to read from were the Bible, *Paradise Lost,*° and some plays by William

---

Paradise Lost: An epic poem about man's fall from paradise, by John Milton (1608–1674).

Shakespeare. I knew well the Book of Genesis, and from time to time I had been made to memorize parts of *Paradise Lost*. The stories of the fallen were well known to me, but I had not known that my own situation could even distantly be related to them. Lucy, a girl's name for Lucifer. That my mother would have found me devil-like did not surprise me, for I often thought of her as god-like, and are not the children of gods devils? I did not grow to like the name Lucy—I would have much preferred to be called Lucifer outright—but whenever I saw my name I always reached out to give it a strong embrace.

I got out of bed and stood on an old rug Mariah had given me. I wanted to   25
stretch my arms up and out, but the room was cold, so I hugged myself. I walked through the apartment. Peggy was still asleep in her room; I could hear her snoring through her closed door. She had once gone to church every Sunday morning with her parents, and now said she would never do that again. In the bathroom I looked at my face in the mirror. I was twenty years old—not a long time to be alive—and yet there was not an ounce of innocence on my face. If I did not know everything yet, I would not be afraid to know *everything* as it came up. That life might be cold and hard would not surprise me.

I went to stare out the front window. When I looked down, I could see people, not as many as on a weekday, bustling about. I could see the roofs of other buildings far away. I could not see any trees. Everything I could see looked unreal to me; everything I could see made me feel I would never be part of it, never penetrate to the inside, never be taken in. A building across the way had a tower with a clock. I stared at the clock for a long time before I realized that it was broken, and it made me even more conscious of a feeling I had constantly now: my sense of time had changed, and I did not know if the day went by too quickly or too slowly.

Peggy came to look out the window, too. Was she seeing the same things as we looked out on the same view? Probably not. In the less than twenty-four hours we had been together under the same roof, our differences had been piling up. She preferred food that came in a tin, or already prepared, to food she had to cook herself. In general, she preferred having things done for her. She did not even know how to sew on a button. As she stood next to me at the window, she smelled of cigarettes and old food; she had not yet taken a bath or brushed her teeth. She rested her head on my shoulder and said, "Can you believe this? Can you believe we did it?" Her hair smelled of lemons—not real lemons, not lemons as I knew them to smell, not the sort of lemons that grew in my yard at home, but artificial lemons, made up in a laboratory. Peggy did not know what a real lemon smelled like. How am I going to get out of this?—the thought was welling up inside me, but I quickly placed a big rock on top of it. She lit a cigarette; I wished she had not done that. She wanted to make us cups of instant coffee, but I made us coffee with steaming-hot milk, the way Mariah had shown me. The afternoon passed. For a very long moment, I wondered what my mother was doing just then, and I saw her face; it was the face she used to have when she loved me without reservation.

Early that evening, Paul came by to see the apartment for the first time and to take us out to dinner. He brought us a large bouquet of small yellow roses, and he gave me a photograph he had taken of me standing over a boiling pot of food. In the picture I was naked from the waist up; a piece of cloth, wrapped around me, covered me from the waist down. That was the moment he got the idea he possessed me in a certain way, and that was the moment I grew tired of him. I had been singing a song out loud. The words were: "Your crazy, crazy love / Is what I am dreaming of." He thought I was in a certain state of mind, having to do only with him. But it was just a song I was singing; I meant nothing at all. He kissed me now in that possessive way, lingering over my mouth, pressing my whole body into his; and though I was not unmoved, it was not as special as he believed. I knew him better than he realized. He loved ruins; he loved the past but only if it had ended on a sad note, from a lofty beginning to a gradual, rotten decline; he loved things that came from far away and had a mysterious history. I could have told him that I had sized him up, but it was not as if he were going to matter to me for years and years to come. He took us to a restaurant where they served macaroni in many sizes and shapes and with all sorts of sauces, only it wasn't called macaroni but a name foreign to me, and so I felt false saying it that way. We went back to the apartment, and I realized when I crossed the threshold that I did not think of it as home, only as the place where I now lived. Paul stayed in my bed with me. I had never had a man stay with me in my own bed. If I had imagined that such a thing would be a desirable landmark, it meant not much to me now; I only made a note of it.

On that Monday I started a new job. When I told Mariah that I was leaving, I did not know what I would do. In fact, there was nothing I could really do. I had no experience, except being a student and a nursemaid. But I was not afraid. Somehow I was not afraid. Paul knew a man who took pictures of food and other things with no life any longer in them, and the photographs were sold to magazines. This man said he would pay me a salary for answering his telephone, taking messages, answering correspondence, and running errands. It was a small salary, but I was grateful all the same. Peggy had been preparing me for the world of employee-employer relationships. She had shown me how to behave when applying for a job, how to show the proper amount of respect, submission, eagerness to please, even though in my heart I would not mean any of those things; she said that as soon as I had the job and was safely in it, I could let my real personality come out. I was not opposed to deception, but I would have preferred not to start out that way.

That Monday morning was like many to come, as the rest of the day was like many to come also. Peggy and I silently made our arrangements for time in the bathroom, time in front of the full-length mirror in the passageway, time in the kitchen preparing our breakfasts. At the corner, she hugged me, kissed my cheek, and wished me good luck. Something in that moment, something buried underneath, made tears come to our eyes, but before they could spill out we turned and went our separate ways. I walked along the streets, trying to hold my head up and observe everything, wanting to remember how everything looked and felt, but I knew even then that later on the things that would stick in my mind were not the things my eyes were fixed on. I got to my job, I said good morning to everyone, I sat at my desk. I was now living a life I had always wanted to live. I was living apart from my family in a place where no one knew much about me; almost no one knew even my name, and I was free more or less to come and go as pleased me. The feeling of bliss, the feeling of happiness, the feeling of longing fulfilled that I had thought would come with this situation was nowhere to be found inside me.

The man I worked for was named Timothy Simon. I called him Mr. Simon, not Tim, or even Timothy, as he begged me to do; this made him not call me "honey," or "darling," the two endearments he used when addressing any woman. He was a friend of my friend, he said, and so he and I should be friends also. But I did not know men very well then; the things I did know about them were not so very good. Friendship is a simple thing, and yet complicated; friendship is on the surface, something natural, something taken for granted, and yet underneath one could find worlds. We did not become friends, but he interested me all the same. For he was the first person I had met who had deeply compromised himself. He did not want to be in a studio taking photographs of things with the life gone out of them; he had wanted to roam the world taking photographs of people who had suffered horribly and through no fault of their own. But the market for the work he really wanted to do was limited, he said, and this work that he did paid the bills. After he had said the word "bills" he pressed his lips together into one of those smiles that is not a smile at all but a way of warding off further inquiry.

Each morning I got up and had a breakfast that was becoming flimsier and flimsier until eventually it amounted to just a cup of tea. Peggy and I walked together as far as the corner and then parted, she heading north, I south. At the studio I performed my chores, some of them better than others; my typing skills, for instance, did not exist, but everyone agreed that I answered the phone better than it had ever been answered before. I took up the custom of drinking coffee all the time, though it tasted more like soiled water than the coffee I was used to. I ate lunches of cold moist food, sandwiches, or something that was a combination of gelatin and soured milk; I was sure none of it was good for me, and I liked that.

Mr. Simon allowed me to develop film in his darkroom when he was not using it. I did this in my own time. I had continued to take photographs, but I had no idea why. I even put aside a small amount of the money I earned so that I could take a course at night at a nearby university, but it was not with any ideas about my life in mind—it was only that I enjoyed doing this. Sometimes I would stay late at night, working in the darkroom, trying to get right a print of something I had made a snap of. I mostly liked to take pictures of people walking on the street. They were not pictures of individuals, just scenes of people walking about, hurrying to somewhere. I did not know them, and I did not care to. I would try and try to make a print that made more beautiful the thing I thought I had seen, that would reveal to me some of the things I had not seen, but I did not succeed.

I would walk home alone at night, the air a little thicker, a little warmer than when I had first started on this new phase of my life, for the winter had gone away. At home Peggy was already in her robe, her hair washed and smelling of that false lemon scent. She washed her hair every night and then slept with it wet to get an effect she wanted the next morning. It was after the first time I had come home and met her like this that she had told me she hoped to go to school to study hairdressing and beauty secrets. The way she put it, though, I found very touching, for she made it sound as if she were really going into public service. I knew then that I could never discuss with her my printmaking difficulties. Sometimes Paul would be there waiting for me; he waited for me in my bed, because Peggy felt his presence encroached on her privacy. I knew just what she meant. His presence in my bed was often not what I wanted at all, but unless a final goodbye came from him I had had enough of partings just now.

I was alone in the world. It was not a small accomplishment. I thought I   35
would die doing it. I was not happy, but that seemed too much to ask for. I had seen Mariah. She had asked me to come and have dinner with her. We were friends again; we said how much we missed each other's company. She looked even more thin than usual. She was alone, and she felt lonely. She lived with her four children, but children are not companions. She was going away, she said, far away, to live in a place of uncommon natural beauty. Everyone who lived in this place, she said, was filled with love and trust and greeted each other with the word "Peace." We sat on the floor and ate our food. Around us were some of the remains of her marriage: wine and water goblets made from crystal, china plates decorated with real gold around the edges, real silverware. She was giving all of this away, along with many other things from her married life. She told me to take anything I wanted, but I wanted nothing. I could not imagine living with any of it; everything she had reminded me, as it must have reminded her, too, of the weight of the world. As a present, she gave me a notebook she had bought in Italy a long time before. She found it while going through her old things. The cover was of leather, dyed blood red, and the pages were white and smooth like milk. Around the time I was leaving her for the life I now led, I had said to her that my life stretched out ahead of me like a book of blank pages. As she gave me the book, she reminded me of that; and in the way so typical of her, the way that I had come to love, she spoke of women, journals, and, of course, history. When we said goodbye, I did not know if I would ever see her again.

I was alone at home one night. Peggy was on an outing by herself. Paul was on an outing by himself. I had noticed that this happened more and more; the two of them were busy at something, and I suspected it was with each other. I only hoped they would not get angry and disrupt my life when they realized I did not care. I did all sorts of little things: I washed my underwear, scrubbed the stove, washed the bathroom floor, trimmed my nails, arranged my dresser, made sure I had enough sanitary napkins. When I got into bed, I lay there with the light on for a long time doing nothing. Then I saw the book Mariah had given me. It was on the night table next to my bed. Beside it lay my fountain pen full of beautiful blue ink. I picked up both, and I opened the book. At the top of the page I wrote my full name: Lucy Josephine Potter. At the sight of it, many thoughts rushed through me, but I could write down only this: "I wish I could love someone so much that I would die from it." And then as I looked at this sentence a great wave of shame came over me and I wept and wept so much that the tears fell on the page and caused all the words to become one great big blur.

Mary Lavin   (b. 1912)

Mary Lavin was born in Massachusetts, but she returned to Ireland with her parents at an early age and is thus an Irish short story writer. She has said that both of her novels, The House in Clewe Street *(1945) and* Mary O'Grady *(1950), might have been better as short stories. Among her numerous collections of stories are* Tales from Bective Bridge *(1942),* The Becker Wives and Other

Stories *(1946)*, The Great Wave and Other Stories *(1961)*, Happiness and
Other Stories *(1969), and several important collections published in the 1980s.
Lavin's work has a universal appeal, and its settings are not limited to Ireland.
She has a keen wit, a powerful gift of observation, and deep feeling for the
circumstances of her characters.*

HAPPINESS   1969

Mother had a lot to say. This does not mean she was always talking but that
we children felt the wells she drew upon were deep, deep, deep. Her theme was
happiness: what it was, what it was not; where we might find it, where not; and
how, if found, it must be guarded. Never must we confound it with pleasure. Nor
think sorrow its exact opposite.

"Take Father Hugh," Mother's eyes flashed as she looked at him. "According
to him, sorrow is an ingredient of happiness—a *necessary* ingredient, if you please!"
And when he tried to protest she put up her hand. "There may be a freakish truth
in the theory—for some people. But not for me. And not, I hope, for my children." She looked severely at us three girls. We laughed. None of us had had
much experience with sorrow. Bea and I were children and Linda only a year old
when our father died suddenly after a short illness that had not at first seemed serious. "I've known people to make sorrow a *substitute* for happiness," Mother
said.

Father Hugh protested again. "You're not putting me in that class, I hope?"

Father Hugh, ever since our father died, had been the closest of anyone to
us as a family, without being close to any one of us in particular—even to Mother.
He lived in a monastery near our farm in County Meath, and he had been one of
the celebrants at the Requiem High Mass our father's political importance had
demanded. He met us that day for the first time, but he took to dropping in to
see us, with the idea of filling the crater of loneliness left at our center. He did
not know that there was a cavity in his own life, much less that we would fill it.
He and Mother were both young in those days, and perhaps it gave scandal to
some that he was so often in our house, staying till late into the night and, indeed, thinking nothing of stopping all night if there was any special reason, such
as one of us being sick. He had even on occasion slept there if the night was too
wet for tramping home across the fields.

When we girls were young, we were so used to having Father Hugh around   5
that we never stood on ceremony with him but in his presence dried our hair and
pared our nails and never minded what garments were strewn about. As for
Mother—she thought nothing of running out of the bathroom in her slip, brushing her teeth or combing her hair, if she wanted to tell him something she might
otherwise forget. And she brooked no criticism of her behavior. "Celibacy was
never meant to take all the warmth and homeliness out of their lives," she said.

On this point, too, Bea was adamant. Bea, the middle sister, was our oracle.
"I'm so glad he *has* Mother," she said, "as well as her having him, because it must
be awful the way most women treat them—priests, I mean—as if they were pari-
ahs. Mother treats him like a human being—that's all!"

And when it came to Mother's ears that there had been gossip about her
making free with Father Hugh, she opened her eyes wide in astonishment. "But
he's only a priest!" she said.

Bea giggled. "It's a good job he didn't hear *that*," she said to me afterwards. "It would undo the good she's done him. You'd think he was a eunuch."

"Bea!" I said. "Do you think he's in love with her?"

"If so, he doesn't know it," Bea said firmly. "It's her soul he's after! Maybe he wants to make sure of her in the next world!"

But thoughts of the world to come never troubled Mother. "If anything ever happens to me, children," she said, "suddenly, I mean, or when you are not near me, or I cannot speak to you, I want you to promise you won't feel bad. There's no need! Just remember that I had a happy life—and that if I had to choose my kind of heaven I'd take it on this earth with you again, no matter how much you might annoy me!"

You see, annoyance and fatigue, according to Mother, and even illness and pain, could coexist with happiness. She had a habit of asking people if they were happy at times and in places that—to say the least of it—seemed to us inappropriate. "But are you happy?" she'd probe as one lay sick and bathed in sweat, or in the throes of a jumping toothache. And once in our presence she made the inquiry of an old friend as he lay upon his deathbed.

"Why not?" she said when we took her to task for it later. "Isn't it more important than ever to be happy when you're dying? Take my own father! You know what he said in his last moments? On his deathbed, he defied me to name a man who had enjoyed a better life. In spite of dreadful pain, his face *radiated* happiness!" Mother nodded her head comfortably. "Happiness drives out pain, as fire burns out fire."

Having no knowledge of our own to pit against hers, we thirstily drank in her rhetoric. Only Bea was sceptical. "Perhaps you *got* it from him, like spots, or fever," she said. "Or something that could at least be slipped from hand to hand."

"Do you think I'd have taken it if that were the case!" Mother cried. "Then, when he needed it most?"

"Not there and then!" Bea said stubbornly. "I meant as a sort of legacy."

"Don't you think in *that* case," Mother said, exasperated, "he would have felt obliged to leave it to your grandmother?"

Certainly we knew that in spite of his lavish heart our grandfather had failed to provide our grandmother with enduring happiness. He had passed that job on to Mother. And Mother had not made too good a fist of it, even when Father was living and she had him—and, later, us children—to help.

As for Father Hugh, he had given our grandmother up early in the game. "God Almighty couldn't make that woman happy," he said one day, seeing Mother's face, drawn and pale with fatigue, preparing for the nightly run over to her own mother's flat that would exhaust her utterly.

There were evenings after she came home from the library where she worked when we saw her stand with the car keys in her hand, trying to think which would be worse—to slog over there on foot, or take out the car again. And yet the distance was short. It was Mother's day that had been too long.

"Weren't you over to see her this morning?" Father Hugh demanded.

"No matter!" said Mother. She was no doubt thinking of the forlorn face our grandmother always put on when she was leaving. ("Don't say good night, Vera," Grandmother would plead. "It makes me feel too lonely. And you never can tell—you might slip over again before you go to bed!")

"Do you know the time?" Bea would say impatiently, if she happened to be

with Mother. Not indeed that the lateness of the hour counted for anything, because in all likelihood Mother *would* go back, if only to pass by under the window and see that the lights were out, or stand and listen and make sure that as
far as she could tell all was well.

"I wouldn't mind if she was happy," Mother said.

"And how do you know she's not?" we'd ask.

"When people are happy, I can feel it. Can't you?"

We were not sure. Most people thought our grandmother was a gay creature, a small birdy being who even at a great age laughed like a girl, and—more
remarkably—sang like one, as she went about her day. But beak and claw were of
steel. She'd think nothing of sending Mother back to a shop three times if her errands were not exactly right. "Not sugar like that—that's *too* fine; it's not castor
sugar I want. But *not* as coarse as *that*, either. I want an in-between kind."

Provoked one day, my youngest sister, Linda, turned and gave battle. "You're
mean!" she cried. "You love ordering people about!"

Grandmother preened, as if Linda had acclaimed an attribute. "I was always
hard to please," she said. "As a girl, I used to be called Miss Imperious."

And Miss Imperious she remained as long as she lived, even when she was a
great age. Her orders were then given a wry twist by the fact that as she advanced
in age she took to calling her daughter Mother, as we did.

There was one great phrase with which our grandmother opened every sentence: "if only." "If only," she'd say, when we came to visit her—"if only you'd
come earlier, before I was worn out expecting you!" Or if we were early, then if
only it was later, after she'd had a rest and could enjoy us, be *able* for us. And if
we brought her flowers, she'd sigh to think that if only we'd brought them the
previous day she'd have had a visitor to appreciate them, or say it was a pity the
stems weren't longer. If only we'd picked a few green leaves, or included some
buds, because, she said disparagingly, the poor flowers we'd brought were already
wilting. We might just as well not have brought them! As the years went on,
Grandmother had a new bead to add to her rosary: if only her friends were not
all dead! By their absence, they reduced to nil all *real* enjoyment in anything. Our
own father—her son-in-law—was the one person who had ever gone close to
pleasing her. But even here there had been a snag. "If only he was my real son!"
she used to say, with a sigh.

Mother's mother lived on through our childhood and into our early maturity (though she outlived the money our grandfather left her), and in our minds
she was a complicated mixture of valiance and defeat. Courageous and generous
within the limits of her own life, her simplest demand was yet enormous in the
larger frame of Mother's life, and so we never could see her with the same clarity
of vision with which we saw our grandfather, or our own father. Them we saw
only through Mother's eyes.

"Take your grandfather!" she'd cry, and instantly we'd see him, his eyes burning upon us—yes, upon *us*, although in his day only one of us had been born:
me. At another time, Mother would cry, "Take your own father!" and instantly
we'd see *him*—tall, handsome, young, and much more suited to marry one of us
than poor bedraggled Mother.

Most fascinating of all were the times Mother would say "Take me!" By
magic then, staring down the years, we'd see blazingly clear a small girl with black
hair and buttoned boots, who, though plain and pouting, burned bright, like a

25

30

star. "I was happy, you see," Mother said. And we'd strain hard to try and understand the mystery of the light that still radiated from her. "I used to lean along a tree that grew out over the river," she said, "and look down through the gray leaves at the water flowing past below, and I used to think it was not the stream that flowed but me, spread-eagled over it, who flew through the air! Like a bird! That I'd found the secret!" She made it seem there might *be* such a secret, just waiting to be found. Another time she'd dream that she'd be a great singer.

"We didn't know you sang, Mother!"   35

She had to laugh. "Like a crow," she said.

Sometimes she used to think she'd swim the Channel.

"Did you swim *that* well, Mother?"

"Oh, not really—just the breaststroke," she said. "And then only by the aid of two pig bladders blown up by my father and tied around my middle. But I used to throb—yes, throb—with happiness."

Behind Mother's back, Bea raised her eyebrows.   40

What was it, we used to ask ourselves—that quality that she, we felt sure, misnamed? Was it courage? Was it strength, health, or high spirits? Something you could not give or take—a conundrum? A game of catch-as-catch-can?

"I know," cried Bea. "A sham!"

Whatever it was, we knew that Mother would let no wind of violence from within or without tear it from her. Although, one evening when Father Hugh was with us, our astonished ears heard her proclaim that there might be a time when one had to slacken hold on it—let go—to catch at it again with a surer hand. In the way, we supposed, that the high-wire walker up among the painted stars of his canvas sky must wait to fling himself through the air until the bar he catches at has started to sway perversely from him. Oh no, no! That downward drag at our innards we could not bear, the belly swelling to the shape of a pear. Let happiness go by the board. "After all, lots of people seem to make out without it," Bea cried. It was too tricky a business. And might it not be that one had to be born with a flair for it?

"A flair would not be enough," Mother answered. "Take Father Hugh. He, if anyone, had a flair for it—a natural capacity! You've only to look at him when he's off guard, with you children, or helping me in the garden. But he rejects happiness! He casts it from him."

"That is simply not true, Vera," cried Father Hugh, overhearing her. "It's   45
just that I don't place an inordinate value on it like you. I don't think it's enough to carry one all the way. To the end, I mean—and after."

"Oh, don't talk about the end when we're only in the middle," cried Mother. And, indeed, at that moment her own face shone with such happiness it was hard to believe that her earth was not her heaven. Certainly it was her constant contention that of happiness she had had a lion's share. This, however, we, in private, doubted. Perhaps there were times when she had had a surplus of it—when she was young, say, with her redoubtable father, whose love blazed circles around her, making winter into summer and ice into fire. Perhaps she did have a brimming measure in her early married years. By straining hard, we could find traces left in our minds from those days of milk and honey. Our father, while he lived, had cast a magic over everything, for us as well as for her. He held his love up over us like an umbrella and kept off the troubles that afterwards came down on us, pouring cats and dogs!

But if she did have more than the common lot of happiness in those early days, what use was that when we could remember so clearly how our father's death had ravaged her? And how could we forget the distress it brought on us when, afraid to let her out of our sight, Bea and I stumbled after her everywhere, through the woods and along the bank of the river, where, in the weeks that followed, she tried vainly to find peace.

The summer after Father died, we were invited to France to stay with friends, and when she went walking on the cliffs at Fécamp our fears for her grew frenzied, so that we hung on to her arm and dragged at her skirt, hoping that like leaded weights we'd pin her down if she went too near to the edge. But at night we had to abandon our watch, being forced to follow the conventions of a family still whole—a home still intact—and go to bed at the same time as the other children. It was at that hour, when the coast guard was gone from his rowing boat offshore and the sand was as cold and gray as the sea, that Mother liked to swim. And when she had washed, kissed, and left us, our hearts almost died inside us and we'd creep out of bed again to stand in our bare feet at the mansard and watch as she ran down the shingle, striking out when she reached the water where, far out, wave and sky and mist were one, and the grayness closed over her. If we took our eyes off her for an instant, it was impossible to find her again.

"Oh, make her turn back, God, please!" I prayed out loud one night.

Startled, Bea turned away from the window. "She'll *have* to turn back some- 50 time, won't she? Unless. . . ?"

Locking our damp hands together, we stared out again. "She wouldn't!" I whispered. "It would be a sin!"

Secure in the deterring power of sin, we let out our breath. Then Bea's breath caught again. "What if she went out so far she used up all her strength? She couldn't swim back! It wouldn't be a sin then!"

"It's the intention that counts," I whispered.

A second later, we could see an arm lift heavily up and wearily cleave down, and at last Mother was in the shallows, wading back to shore.

"Don't let her see us!" cried Bea. As if our chattering teeth would not give 55 us away when she looked in at us before she went to her own room on the other side of the corridor, where, later in the night, sometimes the sound of crying would reach us.

What was it worth—a happiness bought that dearly.

Mother had never questioned it. And once she told us, "On a wintry day, I brought my own mother a snowdrop. It was the first one of the year—a bleak bud that had come up stunted before its time—and I meant it for a sign. But do you know what your grandmother said? 'What good are snowdrops to me now?' Such a thing to say! What good is a snowdrop at all if it doesn't hold its value always, and never lose it! Isn't that the whole point of a snowdrop? And that is the whole point of happiness, too! What good would it be if it could be erased without out trace? Take me and those daffodils!" Stooping, she buried her face in a bunch that lay on the table waiting to be put in vases. "If they didn't hold their beauty absolute and inviolable, do you think I could bear the sight of them after what happened when your father was in hospital?"

It was a fair question. When Father went to hospital, Mother went with him and stayed in a small hotel across the street so she could be with him all day from early to late. "Because it was so awful for him—being in Dublin!" she said. "You have no idea how he hated it."

That he was dying neither of them realized. How could they know, as it rushed through the sky, that their star was a falling star! But one evening when she'd left him asleep Mother came home for a few hours to see how we were faring, and it broke her heart to see the daffodils out all over the place—in the woods, under the trees, and along the sides of the avenue. There had never been so many, and she thought how awful it was that Father was missing them. "You sent up little bunches to him, you poor dears!" she said. "Sweet little bunches, too— squeezed tight as posies by your little fists! But stuffed into vases they couldn't really make up to him for not being able to see them growing!"

So on the way back to the hospital she stopped her car and pulled a great   60 bunch—the full of her arms. "They took up the whole back seat," she said, "and I was so excited at the thought of walking into his room and dumping them on his bed—you know—just plomping them down so he could smell them, and feel them, and look and look! I didn't mean them to be put in vases, or anything ridiculous like that—it would have taken a rainwater barrel to hold them. Why, I could hardly see over them as I came up the steps; I kept tripping. But when I came into the hall, that nun—I told you about her—that nun came up to me, sprang out of nowhere it seemed, although I know now that she was waiting for me, knowing that somebody had to bring me to my senses. But the way she did it! Reached out and grabbed the flowers, letting lots of them fall—I remember them getting stood on. "Where are you going with those foolish flowers, you foolish woman?" she said. "Don't you know your husband is dying? Your prayers are all you can give him now!"

"She was right. I *was* foolish. But I wasn't cured. Afterwards, it was nothing but foolishness the way I dragged you children after me all over Europe. As if any one place was going to be different from another, any better, any less desolate. But there was great satisfaction in bringing you places your father and I had planned to bring you—although in fairness to him I must say that he would not perhaps have brought you so young. And he would not have had an ulterior motive. But above all, he would not have attempted those trips in such a dilapidated car."

Oh, that car! It was a battered and dilapidated red sports car, so depleted of accessories that when, eventually, we got a new car Mother still stuck out her hand on bends, and in wet weather jumped out to wipe the windscreen with her sleeve. And if fussed, she'd let down the window and shout at people, forgetting she now had a horn. How we had ever fitted into it with all our luggage was a miracle.

"You were never lumpish—any of you!" Mother said proudly. "But you were very healthy and very strong." She turned to me. "Think of how you got that car up the hill in Switzerland!"

"The Alps are not hills, Mother!" I pointed out coldly, as I had done at the time, when, as actually happened, the car failed to make it on one of the inclines. Mother let it run back until it wedged against the rock face, and I had to get out and push till she got going again in first gear. But when it got started it couldn't be stopped to pick me up until it got to the top, where they had to wait for me, and for a very long time.

"Ah, well," she said, sighing wistfully at the thought of those trips. "You got   65 something out of them, I hope. All that traveling must have helped you with your geography and your history."

We looked at each other and smiled, and then Mother herself laughed. "Remember the time," she said, "when we were in Italy, and it was Easter, and all the shops were chock-full of food? The butchers' shops had poultry and game hanging up outside the doors, fully feathered, and with their poor heads dripping blood, and in the windows they had poor little lambs and suckling pigs and young goats, all skinned and hanging by their hind feet." Mother shuddered. "They think so much about food. I found it revolting. I had to hurry past. But Linda, who must have been only four then, dragged at me and stared and stared. You know how children are at that age; they have a morbid fascination for what is cruel and bloody. Her face was flushed and her eyes were wide. I hurried her back to the hotel. But next morning she crept into my room. She crept up to me and pressed against me. 'Can't we go back, just once, and look again at that shop?' she whispered. 'The shop where they have the little children hanging up for Easter!' It was the young goats, of course, but I'd said 'kids,' I suppose. How we laughed." But her face was grave. "You were *so* good on those trips, all of you," she said. "You were really very good children in general. Otherwise I would never have put so much effort into rearing you, because I wasn't a bit maternal. You brought out the best in me! I put an unnatural effort into you, of course, because I was taking my standards from your father, forgetting that his might not have remained so inflexible if he had lived to middle age and was beset by life, like other parents."

"Well, the job is nearly over now, Vera," said Father Hugh. "And you didn't do so badly."

"That's right, Hugh," said Mother, and she straightened up, and put her hand to her back the way she sometimes did in the garden when she got up from her knees after weeding. "I didn't go over to the enemy anyway! We survived!" Then a flash of defiance came into her eyes. "And we were happy. That's the main thing!"

Father Hugh frowned. "There you go again!" he said.

Mother turned on him. "I don't think you realize the onslaughts that were ⁷⁰ made upon our happiness! The minute Robert died, they came down on me— cohorts of relatives, friends, even strangers, all draped in black, opening their arms like bats to let me pass into their company. 'Life is a vale of tears,' they said. 'You are privileged to find it out so young!' Ugh! After I staggered onto my feet and began to take hold of life once more, they fell back defeated. And the first day I gave a laugh—pouff, they were blown out like candles. They weren't living in a real world at all; they belonged to a ghostly world where life was easy: all one had to do was sit and weep. It takes effort to push back the stone from the mouth of the tomb and walk out."

Effort. Effort. Ah, but that strange-sounding word could invoke little sympathy from those who had not learned yet what it meant. Life must have been hardest for Mother in those years when we older ones were at college—no longer children, and still dependent on her. Indeed, we made more demands on her than ever then, having moved into new areas of activity and emotion. And our friends! Our friends came and went as freely as we did ourselves, so that the house was often like a café—and one where pets were not prohibited but took their places on our chairs and beds, as regardless as the people. And anyway it was hard to have sympathy for someone who got things into such a state as Mother. All over the house there was clutter. Her study was like the returned-letter department of a post office, with stacks of paper everywhere, bills paid and unpaid, letters answered and unanswered, tax returns, pamphlets, leaflets. If by mistake we left the door open on a windy day, we came back to find papers flapping through the air like frightened birds. Efficient only in that she managed eventually to conclude every task she began, it never seemed possible to outsiders that by Mother's methods anything whatever could be accomplished. In an attempt to keep order elsewhere, she made her own room the clearinghouse into which the rest of us put everything: things to be given away, things to be mended, things to be stored, things to be treasured, things to be returned—even things to be thrown out! By the end of the year, the room resembled an obsolescence dump. And no one could help her; the chaos of her life was as personal as an act of creation—one might as well try to finish another person's poem.

As the years passed, Mother rushed around more hectically. And although Bea and I had married and were not at home anymore, except at holiday time and for occasional weekends, Linda was noisier than the two of us put together had been, and for every follower we had brought home she brought twenty. The house was never still. Now that we were reduced to being visitors, we watched Mother's tension mount to vertigo, knowing that, like a spinning top, she could not rest till she fell. But now at the smallest pretext Father Hugh would call in the doctor and Mother would be put on the mail boat and dispatched for London. For it was essential that she get far enough away to make phoning home every night prohibitively costly.

Unfortunately, the thought of departure often drove a spur into her and she redoubled her effort to achieve order in her affairs. She would be up until the early hours ransacking her desk. To her, as always, the shortest parting entailed a preparation as for death. And as if it were her end that was at hand, we would all be summoned, although she had no time to speak a word to us, because five minutes before departure she would still be attempting to reply to letters that were the acquisition of weeks and would have taken whole days to dispatch.

"Don't you know the taxi is at the door, Vera?" Father Hugh would say, running his hand through his gray hair and looking very disheveled himself. She had him at times as distracted as herself. "You can't do any more. You'll have to leave the rest till you come back."

"I can't, I can't!" Mother would cry. "I'll have to cancel my plans." 75

One day, Father Hugh opened the lid of her case, which was strapped up in the hall, and with a swipe of his arm he cleared all the papers on the top of the desk pell-mell into the suitcase. "You can sort them on the boat," he said, "or the train to London!"

Thereafter, Mother's luggage always included an empty case to hold the unfinished papers on her desk. And years afterwards a steward on the Irish Mail told us she was a familiar figure, working away at letters and bills nearly all the way from Holyhead to Euston. "She gave it up about Rugby or Crewe," he said. "She'd get talking to someone in the compartment." He smiled. "There was one time coming down the train I was just in time to see her close up the window with a guilty look. I didn't say anything, but I think she'd emptied those papers of hers out the window!"

Quite likely. When we were children, even a few hours away from us gave her composure. And in two weeks or less, when she'd come home, the well of her spirit would be freshened. We'd hardly know her—her step so light, her eye so bright, and her love and patience once more freely flowing. But in no time at all the house would fill up once more with the noise and confusion of too many people and too many animals, and again we'd be fighting our corner with cats and dogs, bats, mice, bees, and even wasps. "Don't kill it!" Mother would cry if we raised a hand to an angry wasp. "Just catch it, dear, and put it outside. Open the window and let it fly away!" But even this treatment could at times be deemed too harsh. "Wait a minute. Close the window!" she'd cry. "It's too cold outside. It will die. That's why it came in, I suppose! Oh dear, what will we do?" Life would be going full blast again.

There was only one place Mother found rest. When she was at breaking point and fit to fall, she'd go out into the garden—not to sit or stroll around but to dig, to drag up weeds, to move great clumps of corms or rhizomes, or indeed quite frequently to haul huge rocks from one place to another. She was always laying down a path, building a dry wall, or making compost heaps as high as hills. However jaded she might be going out, when dark forced her in at last her step had the spring of a daisy. So if she did not succeed in defining happiness to our understanding, we could see that whatever it was, she possessed it to the full when she was in her garden.

One of us said as much one Sunday when Bea and I had dropped round for the afternoon. Father Hugh was with us again. "It's an unthinking happiness, though," he caviled. We were standing at the drawing-room window, looking out to where in the fading light we could see Mother on her knees weeding, in the long border that stretched from the house right down to the woods. "I wonder how she'd take it if she were stricken down and had to give up that heavy work!" he said. Was he perhaps a little jealous of how she could stoop and bend? He himself had begun to use a stick. I was often a little jealous of her myself, because although I was married and had children of my own, I had married young and felt the weight of living as heavy as a weight of years. "She doesn't take enough care of herself," Father Hugh said sadly. "Look at her out there with nothing under her knees to protect her from the damp ground." It was almost too dim for us to see her, but even in the drawing room it was chilly. "She should not be let stay out there after the sun goes down."

"Just you try to get her in then!" said Linda, who had come into the room in time to hear him. "Don't you know by now anyway that what would kill another person only seems to make Mother thrive?"

Father Hugh shook his head again. "You seem to forget it's not younger she's getting!" He fidgeted and fussed, and several times went to the window to stare out apprehensively. He was really getting quite elderly.

"Come and sit down, Father Hugh," Bea said, and to take his mind off Mother she turned on the light and blotted out the garden. Instead of seeing through the window, we saw into it as into a mirror, and there between the flower-laden tables and the lamps it was ourselves we saw moving vaguely. Like Father Hugh, we, too, were waiting for her to come in before we called an end to the day.

"Oh, this is ridiculous!" Father Hugh cried at last. "She'll have to listen to reason." And going back to the window he threw it open. "Vera!" he called. "Vera!"—sternly, so sternly that, more intimate than an endearment, his tone shocked us. "She didn't hear me," he said, turning back blinking at us in the lighted room. "I'm going out to get her." And in a minute he was gone from the room. As he ran down the garden path, we stared at each other, astonished; his step, like his voice, was the step of a lover. "I'm coming, Vera!" he cried.

Although she was never stubborn except in things that mattered, Mother   85
had not moved. In the wholehearted way she did everything, she was bent down close to the ground. It wasn't the light only that was dimming; her eyesight also was failing, I thought, as instinctively I followed Father Hugh.

But halfway down the path I stopped. I had seen something he had not: Mother's hand that appeared to support itself in a forked branch of an old tree peony she had planted as a bride was not in fact gripping it but impaled upon it. And the hand that appeared to be grubbing in the clay in fact was sunk into the soft mold. "Mother!" I screamed, and I ran forward, but when I reached her I covered my face with my hands. "Oh Father Hugh!" I cried. "Is she dead?"

It was Bea who answered, hysterical. "She is! She is!" she cried, and she began to pound Father Hugh on the back with her fists, as if his pessimistic words had made this happen.

But Mother was not dead. And at first the doctor even offered hope of her pulling through. But from the moment Father Hugh lifted her up to carry her into the house we ourselves had no hope, seeing how effortlessly he, who was not strong, could carry her. When he put her down on her bed, her head hardly creased the pillow. Mother lived for four more hours.

Like the days of her life, those four hours that Mother lived were packed tight with concern and anxiety. Partly conscious, partly delirious, she seemed to think the counterpane was her desk, and she scrabbled her fingers upon it as if trying to sort out a muddle of bills and correspondence. No longer indifferent now, we listened, anguished, to the distracted cries that had for all our lifetime been so familiar to us. "Oh, where is it? Where is it? I had it a minute ago! Where on earth did I put it?"

"Vera, Vera, stop worrying," Father Hugh pleaded, but she waved him away   90
and went on sifting through the sheets as if they were sheets of paper. "Oh, Vera!" he begged. "Listen to me. Do you not know—"

Bea pushed between them. "You're not to tell her!" she commanded. "Why frighten her?"

"But it ought not to frighten her," said Father Hugh. "This is what I was always afraid would happen—that she'd be frightened when it came to the end."

At that moment, as if to vindicate him, Mother's hands fell idle on the coverlet, palm upward and empty. And turning her head she stared at each of us in turn, beseechingly. "I cannot face it," she whispered. "I can't! I can't! I can't!"

"Oh, my God!" Bea said, and she started to cry.

"Vera. For God's sake listen to me," Father Hugh cried, and pressing his   95
face to hers, as close as a kiss, he kept whispering to her, trying to cast into the dark tunnel before her the light of his own faith.

But it seemed to us that Mother must already be looking into God's exigent eyes. "I can't!" she cried. "I can't!"

Then her mind came back from the stark world of the spirit to the world where her body was still detained, but even that world was now a whirling kaleidoscope of things which only she could see. Suddenly her eyes focused, and, catching at Father Hugh, she pulled herself up a little and pointed to something we could not see. "What will be done with them?" Her voice was anxious. "They ought to be put in water anyway," she said, and, leaning over the edge of the bed, she pointed to the floor. "Don't step on that one!" she said sharply. Then, more sharply still, she addressed us all. "Have them sent to the public ward," she said peremptorily. "Don't let that nun take them; she'll only put them on the altar. And God doesn't want them! He made them for *us*—not for Himself!"

It was the familiar rhetoric that all her life had characterized her utterances. For a moment we were mystified. Then Bea gasped. "The daffodils!" she cried. "The day Father died!" And over her face came the light that had so often blazed over Mother's. Leaning across the bed, she pushed Father Hugh aside. And, putting out her hands, she held Mother's face between her palms as tenderly as if it were the face of a child. "It's all right, Mother. You don't *have* to face it! It's over!" Then she who had so fiercely forbade Father Hugh to do so blurted out the truth. "You've finished with this world, Mother," she said, and, confident that her tidings were joyous, her voice was strong.

Mother made the last effort of her life and grasped at Bea's meaning. She let out a sigh, and, closing her eyes, she sank back, and this time her head sank so deep into the pillow that it would have been dented had it been a pillow of stone.

D. H. Lawrence   (1885–1930)

One of the giants of twentieth-century literature, D. H. Lawrence was born in Eastwood, Nottinghamshire, England, and knew the coal miner's life well. He avoided that fate by going to Nottingham University College. His early fiction, influenced by Freudianism and the psychoanalytic movement, rejected rationalism and celebrated dark, fiery spirits associated with the libido—the sex drive. After marriage to Frieda von Richtofen, he traveled widely in Europe, Australia, Mexico, and the American southwest. His major novels are the autobiographical Sons and Lovers *(1913),* The Rainbow *(1915), and* Women in Love *(1920).* Lady Chatterly's Lover *(1928) became famous because it was banned for its sexual frankness. His short stories, collected after his death, establish him as an important innovator. Critic Frank Amon has said of his stories, that they "all depend, as stories, upon subtle psychological changes of character."*

THE HORSE-DEALER'S DAUGHTER   1922

"Well, Mabel, and what are you going to do with yourself?" asked Joe, with foolish flippancy. He felt quite safe himself. Without listening for an answer, he turned aside, worked a grain of tobacco to the tip of his tongue, and spat it out. He did not care about anything, since he felt safe himself.

The three brothers and the sister sat round the desolate breakfast-table, attempting some sort of desultory consultation. The morning's post had given the final tap to the family fortunes, and all was over. The dreary dining-room itself, with its heavy mahogany furniture, looked as if it were waiting to be done away with.

But the consultation amounted to nothing. There was a strange air of ineffectuality about the three men, as they sprawled at table, smoking and reflecting vaguely on their own condition. The girl was alone, a rather short, sullen-looking young woman of twenty-seven. She did not share the same life as her brothers. She would have been good-looking, save for the impassive fixity of her face, "bull-dog," as her brothers called it.

There was a confused tramping of horses' feet outside. The three men all sprawled round in their chairs, to watch. Beyond the dark holly-bushes that separated the strip of lawn from the high road, they could see a cavalcade of shire horses swinging out of their own yard, being taken for exercise. This was the last time. These were the last horses that would go through their hands. The young men watched with critical, callous look. They were all frightened at the collapse of their lives, and the sense of disaster in which they were involved left them no inner freedom.

Yet they were three fine, well-set fellows enough. Joe, the eldest, was a man   5
of thirty-three, broad and handsome in a hot, flushed way. His face was red, he twisted his black moustache over a thick finger, his eyes were shallow and restless. He had a sensual way of uncovering his teeth when he laughed, and his bearing was stupid. Now he watched the horses with a glazed look of helplessness in his eyes, a certain stupor of downfall.

The great draft-horses° swung past. They were tied head to tail, four of them, and they heaved along to where a lane branched off from the high road, planting their great hoofs floutingly in the fine black mud, swinging their great rounded haunches sumptuously, and trotting a few sudden steps as they were led into the lane, round the corner. Every movement showed a massive, slumbrous strength, and a stupidity which held them in subjection. The groom at the head looked back, jerking the leading rope. And the cavalcade moved out of sight up the lane, the tail of the last horse, bobbed up tight and stiff, held out taut from the swinging great haunches as they rocked behind the hedges in a motion like sleep.

Joe watched with glazed, hopeless eyes. The horses were almost like his own body to him. He felt he was done for now. Luckily he was engaged to a woman as old as himself, and therefore her father, who was steward of a neighboring estate, would provide him with a job. He would marry and go into harness. His life was over, he would be a subject animal now.

He turned uneasily aside, the retreating steps of the horses echoing in his ears. Then, with foolish restlessness, he reached for the scraps of bacon-rind from the plates, and, making a faint whistling sound, flung them to the terrier that lay against the fender. He watched the dog swallow them, and waited till the creature looked into his eyes. Then a faint grin came on his face, and in a high, foolish voice he said:

"You won't get much more bacon, shall you, you little b———?"

The dog faintly and dismally wagged its tail, then lowered its haunches, cir-   10
cled round, and lay down again.

There was another helpless silence at the table. Joe sprawled uneasily in his seat, not willing to go till the family conclave was dissolved. Fred Henry, the second brother, was erect, clean-limbed, alert. He had watched the passing of the horses with more *sang-froid*. If he was an animal, like Joe, he was an animal which controls, not one which is controlled. He was master of any horse, and he carried himself with a well-tempered air of mastery. But he was not master of the situations of life. He pushed his coarse brown moustache upwards, off his lip, and glanced irritably at his sister, who sat impassive and inscrutable.

---

draft-horses. Large work horses.

"You'll go and stop with Lucy for a bit, shan't you?" he asked. The girl did not answer.

"I don't see what else you can do," persisted Fred Henry.

"Go as a skivvy,"° Joe interpolated laconically.

The girl did not move a muscle.   15

"If I was her, I should go in for training for a nurse," said Malcolm, the youngest of them all. He was the baby of the family, a young man of twenty-two, with a fresh, jaunty *museau*.°

But Mabel did not take any notice of him. They had talked at her and round her for so many years, that she hardly heard them at all.

The marble clock on the mantelpiece softly chimed the half-hour, the dog rose uneasily from the hearthrug and looked at the party at the breakfast-table. But still they sat on in ineffectual conclave.

"Oh all right," said Joe suddenly, *à propos* of nothing. "I'll get a move on."

He pushed back his chair, straddled his knees with a downward jerk, to get   20
them free, in horsey fashion, and went to the fire. Still he did not go out of the room, he was curious to know what the others would do or say. He began to charge his pipe, looking down at the dog and saying, in a high, affected voice:

"Going wi' me? Going wi' me are ter? Tha'rt goin' further than tha counts on just now, dost hear?"

The dog faintly wagged its tail, the man stuck out his jaw and covered his pipe with his hands, and puffed intently, losing himself in the tobacco, looking down all the while at the dog, with an absent brown eye. The dog looked up at him in mournful distrust. Joe stood with his knees stuck out, in real horsey fashion.

"Have you had a letter from Lucy?" Fred Henry asked of his sister.

"Last week," came the neutral reply.

"And what does she say?"   25

There was no answer.

"Does she *ask* you to go and stop there?" persisted Fred Henry.

"She says I can if I like."

"Well, then, you'd better. Tell her you'll come on Monday."

This was received in silence.   30

"That's what you'll do then, is it?" said Fred Henry, in some exasperation.

But she made no answer. There was a silence of futility and irritation in the room. Malcolm grinned fatuously.

"You'll have to make up your mind between now and next Wednesday," said Joe loudly, "or else find yourself lodgings on the curbstone."

The face of the young woman darkened, but she sat on immutable.

"Here's Jack Fergusson!" exclaimed Malcolm, who was looking aimlessly   35
out of the window.

"Where?" exclaimed Joe loudly.

"Just gone past."

"Coming in?"

Malcolm craned his neck to see the gate.

"Yes," he said.   40

There was a silence. Mabel sat on like one condemned, at the head of the

---

skivvy. A contemptuous term for housemaid.   *museau*: French for nose; used as slang for face.

table. Then a whistle was heard from the kitchen. The dog got up and barked sharply. Joe opened the door and shouted:

"Come on."

After a moment, a young man entered. He was muffled up in overcoat and a purple woollen scarf, and his tweed cap, which he did not remove, was pulled down on his head. He was of medium height, his face was rather long and pale, his eyes looked tired.

"Hallo, Jack! Well, Jack!" exclaimed Malcolm and Joe. Fred Henry merely said "Jack!"

"What's doing?" asked the newcomer, evidently addressing Fred Henry.   45

"Same. We've got to be out by Wednesday.—Got a cold?"

"I have—got it bad, too."

"Why don't you stop in?"

"*Me* stop in? When I can't stand on my legs, perhaps I shall have a chance." The young man spoke huskily. He had a slight Scotch accent.

"It's a knock-out, isn't it," said Joe boisterously, "if a doctor goes round   50 croaking with a cold. Looks bad for the patients, doesn't it?"

The young doctor looked at him slowly.

"Anything the matter with *you*, then?" he asked sarcastically.

"Not as I know of. Damn your eyes, I hope not. Why?"

"I thought you were very concerned about the patients, wondered if you might be one yourself."

"Damn it, no, I've never been patient to no flaming doctor, and hope I never   55 shall be," returned Joe.

At this point Mabel rose from the table, and they all seemed to become aware of her existence. She began putting the dishes together. The young doctor looked at her, but did not address her. He had not greeted her. She went out of the room with the tray, her face impassive and unchanged.

"When are you off then, all of you?" asked the doctor.

"I'm catching the eleven-forty," replied Malcolm. "Are you goin' down wi' th' trap,° Joe?"

"Yes, you young b——, I've told you I'm going down wi' th' trap, haven't I?"

"We'd better be getting her in then.—So long, Jack, if I don't see you be-   60 fore I go," said Malcolm, shaking hands.

He went out, followed by Joe, who seemed to have his tail between his legs.

"Well, this is the devil's own," exclaimed the doctor when he was left alone with Fred Henry. "Going before Wednesday, are you?"

"That's the orders," replied the other.

Where, to Northampton?"

"That's it."   65

"The devil!" exclaimed Fergusson with quiet chagrin.

And there was silence between the two.

"All settled up, are you?" asked Fergusson.

"About."

There was another pause.   70

"Well, I shall miss yer, Freddy boy," said the young doctor.

trap: A light, two-wheeled carriage.

"And I shall miss thee, Jack," returned the other.

"Miss you like Hell," mused the doctor.

Fred Henry turned aside. There was nothing to say. Mabel came in again, to finish clearing the table.

"What are *you* going to do then, Miss Pervin?" asked Fergusson. "Going to your sister's, are you?" 75

Mabel looked at him with her steady, dangerous eyes, that always made him uncomfortable, unsettling his superficial ease.

"No," she said.

"Well, what in the name of fortune *are* you going to do? Say what you *mean* to do," cried Fred Henry with futile intensity.

But she only averted her head and continued her work. She folded the white tablecloth, and put on the chenille cloth.

"The sulkiest bitch that ever trod!" muttered her brother. 80

But she finished her task with perfectly impassive face, the young doctor watching her interestedly all the while. Then she went out.

Fred Henry stared after her, clenching his lips, his blue eyes fixing in sharp antagonism, as he made a grimace of sour exasperation.

"You could bray her into bits, and that's all you'd get out of her," he said in a small, narrowed tone.

The doctor smiled faintly.

"What's she *going* to do then?" he asked. 85

"Strike me if *I* know!" returned the other.

There was a pause. Then the doctor stirred.

"I'll be seeing you to-night, shall I?" he said to his friend.

"Ay—where's it to be? Are we going over to Jessdale?"

"I don't know. I've got such a cold on me. I'll come round to the Moon and Stars,° anyway." 90

"Let Lizzie and May miss their night for once, eh?"

"That's it—if I feel as I do now."

"All's one——"

The two young men went through the passage and down to the back door together. The house was large, but it was servantless now, and desolate. At the back was a small bricked house-yard, and beyond that a big square, gravelled fine and red, and having stables on two sides. Sloping, dank, winter-dark fields stretched away on the open sides.

But the stables were empty. Joseph Pervin, the father of the family, had been 95 a man of no education, who had become a fairly large horse-dealer. The stables had been full of horses, there was a great turmoil and come-and-go of horses and of dealers and grooms. Then the kitchen was full of servants. But of late things had declined. The old man had married a second time, to retrieve his fortunes. Now he was dead and everything was gone to the dogs, there was nothing but debt and threatening.

For months Mabel had been servantless in the big house, keeping the home together in penury for her ineffectual brothers. She had kept house for ten years. But previously it was with unstinted means. Then, however brutal and coarse everything was, the sense of money had kept her proud, confident. The men might

Moon and Stars: A local tavern.

be foul-mouthed, the women in the kitchen might have bad reputations, her brothers might have illegitimate children. But so long as there was money, the girl felt herself established, and brutally proud, reserved.

No company came to the house, save dealers and coarse men. Mabel had no associates of her own sex, after her sister went away. But she did not mind. She went regularly to church, she attended to her father. And she lived in the memory of her mother, who had died when she was fourteen, and whom she had loved. She had loved her father too, in a different way, depending upon him, and feeling secure in him, until at the age of fifty-four he married again. And then she had set hard against him. Now he had died and left them all hopelessly in debt.

She had suffered badly during the period of poverty. Nothing, however, could shake the curious sullen, animal pride that dominated each member of the family. Now, for Mabel, the end had come. Still she would not cast about her. She would follow her own way just the same. She would always hold the keys of her own situation. Mindless and persistent, she endured from day to day. Why should she think? Why should she answer anybody? It was enough that this was the end, and there was no way out. She need not pass anymore darkly along the main street of the small town, avoiding every eye. She need not demean herself anymore, going into the shops and buying the cheapest food. This was at an end. She thought of nobody, not even of herself. Mindless and persistent, she seemed in a sort of ecstasy to be coming nearer to her fulfilment, her own glorification, approaching her dead mother, who was glorified.

In the afternoon she took a little bag, with shears and sponge and a small scrubbing brush, and went out. It was a grey, wintry day, with saddened, dark-green fields and an atmosphere blackened by the smoke of foundries not far off. She went quickly, darkly along the causeway, heeding nobody, through the town to the churchyard.

There she always felt secure, as if no one could see her, although as a mat-   100
ter of fact she was exposed to the stare of everyone who passed along under the churchyard wall. Nevertheless, once under the shadow of the great looming church, among the graves, she felt immune from the world, reserved within the thick churchyard wall as in another country.

Carefully she clipped the grass from the grave, and arranged the pinky-white, small chrysanthemums in the tin cross. When this was done, she took an empty jar from a neighboring grave, brought water, and carefully, most scrupulously sponged the marble head-stone and the coping-stone.°

It gave her sincere satisfaction to do this. She felt in immediate contact with the world of her mother. She took minute pains, went through the work in a state bordering on pure happiness, as if in performing this task she came into a subtle, intimate connection with her mother. For the life she followed here in the world was far less real than the world of death she inherited from her mother.

The doctor's house was just by the church. Fergusson, being a mere hired assistant, was slave to the countryside. As he hurried now to attend to the out-patients in the surgery, glancing across the graveyard with his quick eye he saw the girl at her task at the grave. She seemed so intent and remote, it was like looking into another world. Some mystical element was touched in him. He slowed down as he walked, watching her as if spellbound.

---

coping-stone: Uppermost layer of stones under the headstone.

She lifted her eyes, feeling him looking. Their eyes met. And each looked away again at once, each feeling in some way found out by the other. He lifted his cap and passed on down the road. There remained distinct in his consciousness, like a vision, the memory of her face, lifted from the tombstone in the churchyard, and looking at him with slow, large, portentous eyes. It *was* portentous, her face. It seemed to mesmerize him. There was a heavy power in her eyes which laid hold of his whole being, as if he had drunk some powerful drug. He had been feeling weak and done before. Now the life came back into him, he felt delivered from his own fretted, daily self.

He finished his duties at the surgery as quickly as might be, hastily filling up   105
the bottles of the waiting people with cheap drugs. Then, in perpetual haste, he set off again to visit several cases in another part of his round before tea-time. At all times he preferred to walk, if he could, but particularly when he was not well. He fancied the motion restored him.

The afternoon was falling. It was grey, deadened, and wintry, with a slow, moist, heavy coldness sinking in and deadening all the faculties. But why should he think or notice? He hastily climbed the hill and turned across the dark-green fields, following the black cinder-track. In the distance, across a shallow dip in the country, the small town was clustered like smoldering ash, a tower, a spire, a heap of low, raw, extinct houses. And on the nearest fringe of the town, sloping into the dip, was Oldmeadow, the Pervins' house. He could see the stables and the outbuildings distinctly, as they lay towards him on the slope. Well, he would not go there many more times! Another resource would be lost to him, another place gone: the only company he cared for in the alien, ugly little town, he was losing. Nothing but work, drudgery, constant hastening from dwelling to dwelling among the colliers and the iron-workers. It wore him out, but at the same time he had a craving for it. It was a stimulant to him to be in the homes of the working people, moving, as it were, through the innermost body of their life. His nerves were excited and gratified. He could come so near, into the very lives of the rough, inarticulate, powerfully emotional men and women. He grumbled, he said he hated the hellish hole. But as a matter of fact it excited him, the contact with the rough, strongly-feeling people was a stimulant applied direct to his nerves.

Below Oldmeadow, in the green, shallow, soddened hollows of fields, lay a square deep pond. Roving across the landscape, the doctor's quick eye detected a figure in black passing through the gates of the field, down towards the pond. He looked again. It would be Mabel Pervin. His mind suddenly became alive and attentive.

Why was she going down there? He pulled up on the path on the slope above, and stood staring. He could just make sure of the small black figure moving in the hollow of the failing day. He seemed to see her in the midst of such obscurity, that he was like a clairvoyant, seeing rather with the mind's eye than with ordinary sight. Yet he could see her positively enough, whilst he kept his eye attentive. He felt, if he looked away from her, in the thick, ugly, falling dusk, he would lose her altogether.

He followed her minutely as she moved, direct and intent, like something transmitted rather than stirring in voluntary activity, straight down the field towards the pond. There she stood on the bank for a moment. She never raised her head. Then she waded slowly into the water.

He stood motionless as the small black figure walked slowly and deliberately   110 towards the center of the pond, very slowly, gradually moving deeper into the motionless water, and still moving forward as the water got up to her breast. Then he could see her no more in the dusk of the dead afternoon.

"There!" he exclaimed. "Would you believe it?"

And he hastened straight down, running over the wet, soddened fields, pushing through the hedges, down into the depression of callous wintry obscurity. It took him several minutes to come to the pond. He stood on the bank, breathing heavily. He could see nothing. His eyes seemed to penetrate the dead water. Yes, perhaps that was the dark shadow of her black clothing beneath the surface of the water.

He slowly ventured into the pond. The bottom was deep, soft clay; he sank in, and the water clasped dead cold round his legs. As he stirred he could smell the cold, rotten clay that fouled up into the water. It was objectionable in his lungs. Still, repelled and yet not heeding, he moved deeper into the pond. The cold water rose over his thighs, over his loins, upon his abdomen. The lower part of his body was all sunk in the hideous cold element. And the bottom was so deeply soft and uncertain, he was afraid of pitching with his mouth underneath. He could not swim, and was afraid.

He crouched a little, spreading his hands under the water and moving them round, trying to feel for her. The dead cold pond swayed upon his chest. He moved again, a little deeper, and again, with his hands underneath, he felt all around under the water. And he touched her clothing. But it evaded his fingers. He made a desperate effort to grasp it.

And so doing he lost his balance and went under, horribly, suffocating in the   115
foul, earthy water, struggling madly for a few moments. At last, after what seemed an eternity, he got his footing, rose again into the air and looked around. He gasped, and knew he was in the world. Then he looked at the water. She had risen near him. He grasped her clothing, and, drawing her nearer, turned to take his way to land again.

He went very slowly, carefully, absorbed in the slow progress. He rose higher, climbing out of the pond. The water was now only about his legs; he was thankful, full of relief to be out of the clutches of the pond. He lifted her and staggered on to the bank, out of the horror of wet grey clay.

He laid her down on the bank. She was quite unconscious and running with water. He made the water come from her mouth, he worked to restore her. He did not have to work very long before he could feel the breathing begin again in her, she was breathing naturally. He worked a little longer. He could feel her live beneath his hands, she was coming back. He wiped her face, wrapped her in his overcoat, looked round into the dim, dark-grey world, then lifted her and staggered down the bank and across the fields.

It seemed an unthinkably long way, and his burden so heavy he felt he would never get to the house. But at last he was in the stable-yard, and then in the house-yard. He opened the door and went into the house. In the kitchen he laid her down on the hearthrug, and called. The house was empty. But the fire was burning in the grate.

Then again he kneeled to attend to her. She was breathing regularly, her eyes were wide open and as if conscious, but there seemed something missing in her look. She was conscious in herself, but unconscious of her surroundings.

He ran upstairs, took blankets from a bed, and put them before the fire to   120 warm. Then he removed her saturated, earthy-smelling clothing, rubbed her dry with a towel, and wrapped her naked in the blankets. Then he went into the dining-room to look for spirits. There was a little whisky. He drank a gulp himself, and put some into her mouth.

The effect was instantaneous. She looked full into his face, as if she had been seeing him for some time, and yet had only just become conscious of him.

"Dr. Fergusson?" she said.

"What?" he answered.

He was divesting himself of his coat, intending to find some dry clothing upstairs. He could not bear the smell of the dead, clayey water, and he was mortally afraid for his own health.

"What did I do?" she asked.   125

"Walked into the pond," he replied. He had begun to shudder like one sick, and could hardly attend to her. Her eyes remained full on him; he seemed to be going dark in his mind, looking back at her helplessly. The shuddering became quieter in him, his life came back in him, dark and unknowing, but strong again.

"Was I out of my mind?" she asked, while her eyes were fixed on him all the time.

"Maybe, for the moment," he replied. He felt quiet, because his strength had come back. The strange fretful strain had left him.

"Am I out of my mind now?" she asked.

"Are you?" he reflected a moment. "No," he answered truthfully, "I don't   130
see that you are." He turned his face aside. He was afraid, now, because he felt dazed, and felt dimly that her power was stronger than his, in this issue. And she continued to look at him fixedly all the time. "Can you tell me where I shall find some dry things to put on?" he asked.

"Did you dive into the pond for me?" she asked.

"No," he answered. "I walked in. But I went in overhead as well."

There was silence for a moment. He hesitated. He very much wanted to go upstairs to get into dry clothing. But there was another desire in him. And she seemed to hold him. His will seemed to have gone to sleep, and left him, standing there slack before her. But he felt warm inside himself. He did not shudder at all, though his clothes were sodden on him.

"Why did you?" she asked.

"Because I didn't want you to do such a foolish thing," he said.   135

"It wasn't foolish," she said, still gazing at him as she lay on the floor, with a sofa cushion under her head. "It was the right thing to do. _I_ knew best, then."

"I'll go and shift these wet things," he said. But still he had not the power to move out of her presence, until she sent him. It was as if she had the life of his body in her hands, and he could not extricate himself. Or perhaps he did not want to.

Suddenly she sat up. Then she became aware of her own immediate condition. She felt the blankets about her, she knew her own limbs. For a moment it seemed as if her reason were going. She looked round, with wild eye, as if seeking something. He stood still with fear. She saw her clothing lying scattered.

"Who undressed me?" she asked, her eyes resting full and inevitable on his face.

"I did," he replied, "to bring you round."   140

For some moments she sat and gazed at him awfully, her lips parted.

"Do you love me then?" she asked.

He only stood and stared at her fascinated. His soul seemed to melt.

She shuffled forward on her knees, and put her arms round him, round his legs, as he stood there, pressing her breasts against his knees and thighs, clutching him with strange, convulsive certainty, pressing his thighs against her, drawing him to her face, her throat, as she looked up at him with flaring, humble eyes of transfiguration, triumphant in first possession.

"You love me," she murmured, in strange transport, yearning and triumphant   145
and confident. "You love me. I know you love me, I know."

And she was passionately kissing his knees through the wet clothing, passionately and indiscriminately kissing his knees, his legs, as if unaware of everything.

He looked down at the tangled wet hair, the wild, bare, animal shoulders. He was amazed, bewildered, and afraid. He had never thought of loving her. He had never wanted to love her. When he rescued her and restored her, he was a doctor and she was a patient. He had had no single personal thought of her. Nay, this introduction of the personal element was very distasteful to him, a violation of his professional honor. It was horrible to have her there embracing his knees. It was horrible. He revolted from it violently. And yet—and yet—he had not the power to break away.

She looked at him again, with the same supplication of powerful love, and that same transcendent, frightening light of triumph. In view of the delicate flame which seemed to come from her face like a light, he was powerless. And yet he had never intended to love her. He had never intended. And something stubborn in him could not give way.

"You love me," she repeated, in a murmur of deep, rhapsodic assurance. "You love me."

Her hands were drawing him, drawing him down to her. He was afraid, even   150
a little horrified. For he had really no intention of loving her. Yet her hands were drawing him towards her. He put out his hand quickly to steady himself, and grasped her bare shoulder. A flame seemed to burn the hand that grasped her soft shoulder. He had no intention of loving her: his whole will was against his yielding. It was horrible—— And yet wonderful was the touch of her shoulder, beautiful the shining of her face. Was she perhaps mad? He had a horror of yielding to her. Yet something in him ached also.

He had been staring away at the door, away from her. But his hand remained on her shoulder. She had gone suddenly very still. He looked down at her. Her eyes were now wide with fear, with doubt, the light was dying from her face, a shadow of terrible greyness was returning. He could not bear the touch of her eyes' question upon him, and the look of death behind the question.

With an inward groan he gave way, and let his heart yield towards her. A sudden gentle smile came on his face. And her eyes, which never left his face, slowly, slowly filled with tears. He watched the strange water rise in her eyes, like some slow fountain coming up. And his heart seemed to burn and melt in his breast.

He could not bear to look at her anymore. He dropped on his knees and caught her head with his arm and pressed her face against his throat. She was very still. His heart, which seemed to have broken, was burning with a kind of agony in his breast. And he felt her slow, hot tears wetting his throat. But he could not move.

He felt the hot tears wet his neck and the hollows of his neck, and he remained motionless, suspended through one of man's eternities. Only now it had become indispensable to him to have her face pressed close to him, he could never let her go again. He could never let her head go away from the close clutch of his arm. He wanted to remain like that for ever, with his heart hurting him in a pain that was also life to him. Without knowing, he was looking down on her damp, soft brown hair.

Then, as it were suddenly, he smelt the horrid stagnant smell of that water. 155
And at the same moment she drew away from him and looked at him. Her eyes were wistful and unfathomable. He was afraid of them, and he fell to kissing her, not knowing what he was doing. He wanted her eyes not to have that terrible wistful, unfathomable look.

When she turned her face to him again, a faint delicate flush was glowing, and there was again dawning that terrible shining of joy in her eyes, which really terrified him, and yet which he now wanted to see, because he feared the look of doubt still more.

"You love me?" she said, rather faltering.

"Yes." The word cost him a painful effort. Not because it wasn't true. But because it was too newly true, the *saying* seemed to tear open again his newly-torn heart. And he hardly wanted it to be true, even now.

She lifted her face to him, and he bent forward and kissed her on the mouth, gently, with the one kiss that is an eternal pledge. And as he kissed her his heart strained again in his breast. He never intended to love her. But now it was over. He had crossed over the gulf to her, and all that he had left behind had shrivelled and become void.

After the kiss, her eyes again slowly filled with tears. She sat still, away from 160
him, with her face dropped aside, and her hands folded in her lap. The tears fell very slowly. There was complete silence. He too sat there motionless and silent on the hearthrug. The strange pain of his heart that was broken seemed to consume him. That he should love her! That this was love! That he should be ripped open in this way!—him, a doctor!—How they would all jeer if they knew!—It was agony to him to think they might know.

In the curious naked pain of the thought he looked again to her. She was sitting there drooped into a muse. He saw a tear fall, and his heart flared hot. He saw for the first time that one of her shoulders was quite uncovered, one arm bare, he could see one of her small breasts; dimly, because it had become almost dark in the room.

"Why are you crying?" he asked in an altered voice.

She looked up at him, and behind her tears the consciousness of her situation for the first time brought a dark look of shame to her eyes.

"I'm not crying, really," she said, watching him half frightened.

He reached his hand, and softly closed it on her bare arm. 165

"I love you! I love you!" he said in a soft, low, vibrating voice, unlike himself.

She shrank, and dropped her head. The soft, penetrating grip of his hand on her arm distressed her. She looked up at him.

"I want to go," she said, "I want to go and get you some dry things."

"Why?" he said. "I'm all right."

"But I want to go," she said. "And I want you to change your things." 170

He released her arm, and she wrapped herself in the blanket, looking at him rather frightened. And still she did not rise.

"Kiss me," she said wistfully.

He kissed her, but briefly, half in anger.

Then, after a second, she rose nervously, all mixed up in the blanket. He watched her in her confusion, as she tried to extricate herself and wrap herself up so that she could walk. He watched her relentlessly, as she knew. And as she went, the blanket trailing, and as he saw a glimpse of her feet and her white leg, he tried to remember her as she was when he had wrapped her in the blanket. But he didn't want to remember, because she had been nothing to him then, and his nature revolted from remembering what she was when she was nothing to him.

A tumbling, muffled noise from within the dark house startled him. Then 175 he heard her voice:—"There are clothes." He rose and went to the foot of the stairs, and gathered up the garments she had thrown down. Then he came back to the fire, to rub himself down and dress. He grinned at his own appearance when he had finished.

The fire was sinking, so he put on coal. The house was now quite dark, save for the light of a street-lamp that shone in faintly from beyond the holly trees. He lit the gas with matches he found on the mantelpiece. Then he emptied the pockets of his own clothes, and threw all his wet things in a heap into the scullery. After which he gathered up her sodden clothes, gently, and put them in a separate heap on the copper-top in the scullery.

It was six o'clock on the clock. His own watch had stopped. He ought to go back to the surgery. He waited, and still she did not come down. So he went to the foot of the stairs and called:

"I shall have to go."

Almost immediately he heard her coming down. She had on her best dress of black voile, and her hair was tidy, but still damp. She looked at him—and, in spite of herself, smiled.

"I don't like you in those clothes," she said. 180

"Do I look a sight?" he answered.

They were shy of one another.

"I'll make you some tea," she said.

"No, I must go."

"Must you?" And she looked at him again with the wide, strained, doubtful 185 eyes. And again, from the pain of his breast, he knew how he loved her. He went and bent to kiss her, gently, passionately, with his heart's painful kiss.

"And my hair smells so horrible," she murmured in distraction. "And I'm so awful, I'm so awful! Oh, no, I'm too awful," and she broke into bitter, heartbroken sobbing. "You can't want to love me, I'm horrible."

"Don't be silly, don't be silly," he said, trying to comfort her, kissing her, holding her in his arms. "I want you, I want to marry you; we're going to be married, quickly, quickly—tomorrow if I can."

But she only sobbed terribly, and cried:

"I feel awful. I feel awful. I feel I'm horrible to you."

"No, I want you, I want you," was all he answered, blindly, with that terri- 190 ble intonation which frightened her almost more than her horror lest he should *not* want her.

WINDOW ON

Feminist Fiction

Feminist approaches to literature have achieved two important successes in recent decades. The first is the recovery of women whose work was not part of the teaching canon in the first three quarters of the twentieth century. Kate Chopin and Charlotte Perkins Gilman were not only recovered but have been granted significance as important short story writers. The second achievement is the development of a feminist criticism that examines literature from a stylistic as well as thematic perspective.

One early feminist development was the "images of women" school. Feminist critics charged that many male writers portrayed women as incomplete, stereotypical beings: They were "other," marginally human, sexual objects designed to satisfy males or beings who could not shape their own destiny because of their various shortcomings, moral or otherwise. "Feminist criticism," Josephine Donovan says, "is moral because it sees that one of the central problems of Western literature is that in much of it women are not human beings. . . . They are objects . . . used to facilitate, explain away, or redeem the projects of men." Another criticism is that women are stereotyped as either virgins or whores. Literature that portrays women as either of these extremes—with no intermediate portrayal—is aesthetically as well as morally unsatisfactory because it is too simplistic.

Another aspect of feminist criticism concerns critical method. Elaine Showalter describes Marxist, structuralist, and other critical schools dominated by men as "not intuitive, expressive, and feminine, but strenuous, rigorous, impersonal and virile." She sees in them the absence of a concern for women's experience. Moreover, she declares that feminist criticism needs to assert itself in a language that departs from the masculine logical, objective, and dominating traditions. In other words, she and other feminists expect to make language work in a distinctly feminine way. One implication is that women will respond positively to short stories written by women that men might dislike. This view is controversial and currently under debate. Virginia Woolf, for one, seems to have considered the existence of male and female sentences (she is not the only modern writer to do so). If this is true, one could then have a masculine and feminine style in fiction.

Women's presence in literature is dependent to some extent on genre. As a rule, one can say that the older the genre the less evident the presence of women. For example, in poetry and drama, which are ancient genres, women do not appear as significant writers until relatively recently. The novel, however, is quite new, generally a product of the eighteenth century, and women took an important role in novel writing within a few decades of its development. The short story, despite the existence of Boccaccio and a few others, is usually thought of as blooming in the nineteenth century. Here too, women have a dominant position. For that reason, the short story is a good laboratory for the examination of feminist concerns of image and style.

For example, you can profitably examine the portraits of women in stories by men to see to what extent they fall into stereotypes or depend upon the image of woman who is somehow incomplete without a man. Faulkner's "A Rose for Emily" and Hemingway's "Hills Like White Elephants" take on interesting significance when interpreted from this perspective. It would be especially profitable to examine Virginia Woolf's "The New Dress," Fay Weldon's "Weekend," or Margaret Atwood's "Significant Moments in the Life of My Mother" to see if they share approaches to writing that might constitute a feminine style. Think about special techniques of characterization, special choices of images or metaphors, or unusual points of view. Do you see evidence of "female sentences"?

Finally, like Marxist and related critical studies, feminist criticism has been condemned for being political. Formalist critics have been especially harsh in condemning any critical practice that seems more political than artistic in aim. However, feminists and others have pointed out that there can be no neutral literature or criticism; all literature and all criticism are political, even if the practitioners are unaware of that fact. Whether we talk about the political struggles between nations, between individuals in corporations, between men and women, between people of different races, or between characters with different needs, all literature has a political component. As Toril Moi says, "The principal objective of feminist criticism has always been political: it seeks to expose, not to perpetuate, patriarchal practices."

Reading

de Lauretis, Theresa, ed. *Feminist Studies, Critical Studies.* Bloomington: Indiana University Press, 1986.
Donovan, Josephine. *Feminist Literary Criticism: Explorations in Theory.* Lexington: University of Kentucky Press, 1975.
Eagleton, Mary. *Feminist Literary Theory: A Reader.* Oxford: Blackwell, 1986.
Moi, Toril. *Sexual/Textual Politics: Feminist Literary Theory.* London: Methuen, 1985.
Showalter, Elaine, ed. *The New Feminist Criticism: Essays on Women, Literature and Theory.* New York: Pantheon, 1985.

Ursula K. Le Guin   (b. 1929)

Ursula K. Le Guin was born in Berkeley, California, and was educated at Radcliffe College and Columbia University. She has taught writing and has written and edited a large number of books of fantasy and science fiction, for which she has long been acclaimed. One critic has said, "When one enters the world of her fiction, one encounters a distinctive universe of discourse." However, Le

Guin herself has said, "I write science fiction because that is what publishers call my books. Left to myself, I should call them novels." Some of her works are interconnected, such as the Hainish cycle—Rocannon (1966), Planet of Exile (1966), City of Illusions (1968), The Left Hand of Darkness (1969), The Dispossessed (1974), and The Word for World Is Forest (1976)—and the Earthsea trilogy, which includes A Wizard of Earthsea (1968), The Tombs of Atuan (1971), and The Farthest Shore (1972). Among her volumes of short stories are The Wind's Twelve Quarters (1975), also connected with the Hainish cycle; Orsinian Tales (1976); and The Compass Rose (1982). Her background in the sciences and her interest in history are clearly evident in all her stories.

SUR° 1982

A Summary Report of the Yelcho Expedition to the Antarctic, 1909–10

Although I have no intention of publishing this report, I think it would be nice if a grandchild of mine, or somebody's grandchild, happened to find it some day; so I shall keep it in the leather trunk in the attic, along with Rosita's christening dress and Juanito's silver rattle and my wedding shoes and finneskos.°

The first requisite for mounting an expedition—money—is normally the hardest to come by. I grieve that even in a report destined for a trunk in the attic of a house in a very quiet suburb of Lima I dare not write the name of the generous benefactor, the great soul without whose unstinting liberality the Yelcho Expedition would never have been more than the idlest excursion into daydream. That our equipment was the best and most modern—that our provisions were plentiful and fine—that a ship of the Chilean government, with her brave officers and gallant crew, was twice sent halfway round the world for our convenience: all this is due to that benefactor whose name, alas!, I must not say, but whose happiest debtor I shall be till death.

When I was little more than a child, my imagination was caught by a newspaper account of the voyage of the *Belgica*, which, sailing south from Tierra del Fuego, was beset by ice in the Bellingshausen Sea and drifted a whole year with the floe, the men aboard her suffering a great deal from want of food and from the terror of the unending winter darkness. I read and reread that account, and later followed with excitement the reports of the rescue of Dr. Nordenskjöld from the South Shetland Islands by the dashing Captain Irizar of the *Uruguay*, and the adventures of the *Scotia* in the Weddell Sea. But all these exploits were to me but forerunners of the British National Antarctic Expedition of 1901–04, in the *Discovery*, and the wonderful account of that expedition by Captain Scott.° This book, which I ordered from London and reread a thousand times, filled me with longing to see with my own eyes that strange continent, last Thule of the South, which lies on our maps and globes like a white cloud, a void, fringed here and there with scraps of coastline, dubious capes, supposititious islands, headlands that may or may not be there: Antarctica. And the desire was as pure as the polar snows: to go, to see—no more, no less. I deeply respect the scientific accom-

---

Sur: South. *finneskos*: Accessories.   *Scott*: Robert Falcon Scott (1868–1912), British Antarctic explorer.

plishments of Captain Scott's expedition, and have read with passionate interest the findings of physicists, meteorologists, biologists, etc.; but having had no train- ing in any science, nor any opportunity for such training, my ignorance obliged me to forgo any thought of adding to the body of scientific knowledge concern- ing Antarctica, and the same is true for all the members of my expedition. It seems a pity; but there was nothing we could do about it. Our goal was limited to ob- servation and exploration. We hoped to go a little farther, perhaps, and see a lit- tle more; if not, simply to go and to see. A simple ambition, I think, and essen- tially a modest one.

Yet it would have remained less than an ambition, no more than a longing, but for the support and encouragement of my dear cousin and friend Juana————. (I use no surnames, lest this report fall into strangers' hands at last, and embarrass- ment or unpleasant notoriety thus be brought upon unsuspecting husbands, sons, etc.) I had lent Juana my copy of *The Voyage of the "Discovery,"* and it was she who, as we strolled beneath our parasols across the Plaza de Armas after Mass one Sunday in 1908, said, "Well, if Captain Scott can do it, why can't we?"

It was Juana who proposed that we write Carlota————in Valparaíso. 5 Through Carlota we met our benefactor, and so obtained our money, our ship, and even the plausible pretext of going on retreat in a Bolivian convent, which some of us were forced to employ (while the rest of us said we were going to Paris for the winter season). And it was my Juana who in the darkest moments remained resolute, unshaken in her determination to achieve our goal.

And there were dark moments, especially in the spring of 1909—times when I did not see how the Expedition would ever become more than a quarter ton of pemmican gone to waste and a lifelong regret. It was so very hard to gather our expeditionary force together! So few of those we asked even knew what we were talking about—so many thought we were mad, or wicked, or both! And of those few who shared our folly, still fewer were able, when it came to the point, to leave their daily duties and commit themselves to a voyage of at least six months, at- tended with not inconsiderable uncertainty and danger. An ailing parent; an anx- ious husband beset by business cares; a child at home with only ignorant or in- competent servants to look after it: these are not responsibilities lightly to be set aside. And those who wished to evade such claims were not the companions we wanted in hard work, risk, and privation.

But since success crowned our efforts, why dwell on the setbacks and delays, or the wretched contrivances and downright lies that we all had to employ? I look back with regret only to those friends who wished to come with us but could not, by any contrivance, get free—those we had to leave behind to a life without dan- ger, without uncertainty, without hope.

On the seventeenth of August, 1909, in Punta Arenas, Chile, all the mem- bers of the Expedition met for the first time: Juana and I, the two Peruvians; from Argentina, Zoe, Berta, and Teresa; and our Chileans, Carlota and her friends Eva, Pepita, and Dolores. At the last moment I had received word that María's hus- band, in Quito, was ill and she must stay to nurse him, so we were nine, not ten. Indeed, we had resigned ourselves to being but eight when, just as night fell, the indomitable Zoe arrived in a tiny pirogue manned by Indians, her yacht having sprung a leak just as it entered the Straits of Magellan.

That night before we sailed we began to get to know one another, and we agreed, as we enjoyed our abominable supper in the abominable seaport inn of

Punta Arenas, that if a situation arose of such urgent danger that one voice must be obeyed without present question, the unenviable honor of speaking with that voice should fall first upon myself; if I were incapacitated, upon Carlota; if she, then upon Berta. We three were then toasted as "Supreme Inca," "La Araucana," and "The Third Mate," amid a lot of laughter and cheering. As it came out, to my very great pleasure and relief, my qualities as a "leader" were never tested; the nine of us worked things out amongst us from beginning to end without any orders being given by anybody, and only two or three times with recourse to a vote by voice or show of hands. To be sure, we argued a good deal. But then, we had time to argue. And one way or another the arguments always ended up in a decision, upon which action could be taken. Usually at least one person grumbled about the decision, sometimes bitterly. But what is life without grumbling and the occasional opportunity to say "I told you so"? How could one bear housework, or looking after babies, let alone the rigors of sledge-hauling in Antarctica, without grumbling? Officers—as we came to understand aboard the *Yelcho*—are forbidden to grumble; but we nine were, and are, by birth and upbringing, unequivocally and irrevocably, all crew.

Though our shortest course to the southern continent, and that originally   10 urged upon us by the captain of our good ship, was to the South Shetlands and the Bellingshausen Sea, or else by the South Orkneys into the Weddell Sea, we planned to sail west to the Ross Sea, which Captain Scott had explored and described, and from which the brave Ernest Shackleton° had returned only the previous autumn. More was known about this region than any other portion of the coast of Antarctica, and though that more was not much, yet it served as some insurance of the safety of the ship, which we felt we had no right to imperil. Captain Pardo had fully agreed with us after studying the charts and our planned itinerary; and so it was westward that we took our course out of the Straits next morning.

Our journey half round the globe was attended by fortune. The little *Yelcho* steamed cheerily along through gale and gleam, climbing up and down those seas of the Southern Ocean that run unbroken round the world. Juana, who had fought bulls and the far more dangerous cows on her family's *estancia*,° called the ship *la vaca valiente*,° because she always returned to the charge. Once we got over being seasick, we all enjoyed the sea voyage, though oppressed at times by the kindly but officious protectiveness of the captain and his officers, who felt that we were only "safe" when huddled up in the three tiny cabins that they had chivalrously vacated for our use.

We saw our first iceberg much farther south than we had looked for it, and saluted it with Veuve Clicquot° at dinner. The next day we entered the ice pack, the belt of floes and bergs broken loose from the land ice and winter-frozen seas of Antarctica which drifts northward in the spring. Fortune still smiled on us: our little steamer, incapable, with her unreinforced metal hull, of forcing a way into the ice, picked her way from lane to lane without hesitation, and on the third day we were through the pack, in which ships have sometimes struggled for weeks and been obliged to turn back at last. Ahead of us now lay the dark-gray waters

Shackleton: Sir Ernest Henry Shackleton (1874–1922), Irish-born British Antarctic explorer. *estancia*: Small farm.   *la vaca valiente*: The valiant cow.   *Veuve Clicquot*: Expensive champagne.

of the Ross Sea, and beyond that, on the horizon, the remote glimmer, the cloud-reflected whiteness of the Great Ice Barrier.°

Entering the Ross Sea a little east of Longitude West 160°, we came in sight of the Barrier at the place where Captain Scott's party, finding a bight in the vast wall of ice, had gone ashore and sent up their hydrogen-gas balloon for reconnaissance and photography. The towering face of the Barrier, its sheer cliffs and azure and violet waterworn caves, all were as described, but the location had changed: instead of a narrow bight, there was a considerable bay, full of the beautiful and terrific orca whales playing and spouting in the sunshine of that brilliant southern spring.

Evidently masses of ice many acres in extent had broken away from the Barrier (which—at least for most of its vast extent—does not rest on land but floats on water) since the *Discovery's* passage in 1902. This put our plan to set up camp on the Barrier itself in a new light; and while we were discussing alternatives, we asked Captain Pardo to take the ship west along the Barrier face toward Ross Island and McMurdo Sound. As the sea was clear of ice and quite calm, he was happy to do so and, when we sighted the smoke plume of Mt. Erebus, to share in our celebration—another half case of Veuve Clicquot.

The *Yelcho* anchored in Arrival Bay, and we went ashore in the ship's boat.   15 I cannot describe my emotions when I set foot on the earth, on that earth, the barren, cold gravel at the foot of the long volcanic slope. I felt elation, impatience, gratitude, awe, familiarity. I felt that I was home at last. Eight Adélie penguins immediately came to greet us with many exclamations of interest not unmixed with disapproval. "Where on earth have you been? What took you so long? The Hut is around this way. Please come this way. Mind the rocks!" They insisted on our going to visit Hut Point, where the large structure built by Captain Scott's party stood, looking just as in the photographs and drawings that illustrate his book. The area about it, however, was disgusting—a kind of graveyard of seal skins, seal bones, penguin bones, and rubbish, presided over by the mad, screaming skua gulls. Our escorts waddled past the slaughterhouse in all tranquillity, and one showed me personally to the door, though it would not go in.

The interior of the hut was less offensive but very dreary. Boxes of supplies had been stacked up into a kind of room within the room; it did not look as I had imagined it when the *Discovery* party put on their melodramas and minstrel shows in the long winter night. (Much later, we learned that Sir Ernest had rearranged it a good deal when he was there just a year before us.) It was dirty, and had about it a mean disorder. A pound tin of tea was standing open. Empty meat tins lay about; biscuits were spilled on the floor; a lot of dog turds were underfoot—frozen, of course, but not a great deal improved by that. No doubt the last occupants had had to leave in a hurry, perhaps even in a blizzard. All the same, they could have closed the tea tin. But housekeeping, the art of the infinite, is no game for amateurs.

Teresa proposed that we use the hut as our camp. Zoe counterproposed that we set fire to it. We finally shut the door and left it as we had found it. The penguins appeared to approve, and cheered us all the way to the boat.

Great Ice Barrier. The Ross Ice Shelf that closes the bay.

McMurdo Sound was free of ice, and Captain Pardo now proposed to take us off Ross Island and across to Victoria Land, where we might camp at the foot of the Western Mountains, on dry and solid earth. But those mountains, with their storm-darkened peaks and hanging cirques and glaciers, looked as awful as Captain Scott had found them on his western journey, and none of us felt much inclined to seek shelter among them.

Aboard the ship that night we decided to go back and set up our base as we had originally planned, on the Barrier itself. For all available reports indicated that the clear way south was across the level Barrier surface until one could ascend one of the confluent glaciers to the high plateau that appears to form the whole interior of the continent. Captain Pardo argued strongly against this plan, asking what would become of us if the Barrier "calved"—if our particular acre of ice broke away and started to drift northward. "Well," said Zoe, "then you won't have to come so far to meet us." But he was so persuasive on this theme that he persuaded himself into leaving one of the *Yelcho*'s boats with us when we camped, as a means of escape. We found it useful for fishing, later on.

My first steps on Antarctic soil, my only visit to Ross Island, had not been 20
pleasure unalloyed. I thought of the words of the English poet,

Though every prospect pleases,
And only Man is vile.

But then, the backside of heroism is often rather sad; women and servants know that. They know also that the heroism may be no less real for that. But achievement is smaller than men think. What is large is the sky, the earth, the sea, the soul. I looked back as the ship sailed east again that evening. We were well into September now, with eight hours or more of daylight. The spring sunset lingered on the twelve-thousand-foot peak of Erebus and shone rosy-gold on her long plume of steam. The steam from our own small funnel faded blue on the twilit water as we crept along under the towering pale wall of ice.

On our return to "Orca Bay"—Sir Ernest, we learned years later, had named it the Bay of Whales—we found a sheltered nook where the Barrier edge was low enough to provide fairly easy access from the ship. The *Yelcho* put out her ice anchor, and the next long, hard days were spent in unloading our supplies and setting up our camp on the ice, a half kilometre in from the edge: a task in which the *Yelcho*'s crew lent us invaluable aid and interminable advice. We took all the aid gratefully, and most of the advice with salt.

The weather so far had been extraordinarily mild for spring in this latitude; the temperature had not yet gone below –20°F, and there was only one blizzard while we were setting up camp. But Captain Scott had spoken feelingly of the bitter south winds on the Barrier, and we had planned accordingly. Exposed as our camp was to every wind, we built no rigid structures above-ground. We set up tents to shelter in while we dug out a series of cubicles in the ice itself, lined them with hay insulation and pine boarding, and roofed them with canvas over bamboo poles, covered with snow for weight and insulation. The big central room was instantly named Buenos Aires by our Argentineans, to whom the center, wherever one is, is always Buenos Aires. The heating and cooking stove was in Buenos Aires. The storage tunnels and the privy (called Punta Arenas) got some back heat from the stove. The sleeping cubicles opened off Buenos Aires, and were very small, mere tubes into which one crawled feet first; they were lined deeply with hay and soon warmed by one's body warmth. The sailors called them coffins and worm holes, and looked with horror on our burrows in the ice. But our little warren or prairie-dog village served us well, permitting us as much warmth and privacy as one could reasonably expect under the circumstances. If the *Yelcho* was unable to get through the ice in February and we had to spend the winter in Antarctica, we certainly could do so, though on very limited rations. For this coming summer, our base—Sudamérica del Sur, South South America, but we generally called it the Base—was intended merely as a place to sleep, to store our provisions, and to give shelter from blizzards.

To Berta and Eva, however, it was more than that. They were its chief architect-designers, its most ingenious builder-excavators, and its most diligent and contented occupants, forever inventing an improvement in ventilation, or learning how to make skylights, or revealing to us a new addition to our suite of rooms, dug in the living ice. It was thanks to them that our stores were stowed so handily, that our stove drew and heated so efficiently, and that Buenos Aires, where nine people cooked, ate, worked, conversed, argued, grumbled, painted, played the guitar and banjo, and kept the Expedition's library of books and maps, was a marvel of comfort and convenience. We lived there in real amity; and if you simply had to be alone for a while, you crawled into your sleeping hole head first.

Berta went a little farther. When she had done all she could to make South South America livable, she dug out one more cell just under the ice surface, leaving a nearly transparent sheet of ice like a greenhouse roof; and there, alone, she worked at sculptures. They were beautiful forms, some like a blending of the reclining human figure with the subtle curves and volumes of the Weddell seal, others like the fantastic shapes of ice cornices and ice caves. Perhaps they are there still, under the snow, in the bubble in the Great Barrier. There where she made them, they might last as long as stone. But she could not bring them north. That is the penalty for carving in water.

Captain Pardo was reluctant to leave us, but his orders did not permit him   25
to hang about the Ross Sea indefinitely, and so at last, with many earnest injunctions to us to stay put—make no journeys—take no risks—beware of frostbite—don't use edge tools—look out for cracks in the ice—and a heartfelt promise to return to Orca Bay on February 20th, or as near that date as wind and ice would permit, the good man bade us farewell, and his crew shouted us a great goodbye cheer as they weighed anchor. That evening, in the long orange twilight of October, we saw the topmast of the *Yelcho* go down the north horizon, over the edge of the world, leaving us to ice, and silence, and the Pole.

That night we began to plan the Southern Journey.

The ensuing month passed in short practice trips and depot-laying. The life we had led at home, though in its own way strenuous, had not fitted any of us for the kind of strain met with in sledge-hauling at ten or twenty degrees below freezing. We all needed as much working out as possible before we dared undertake a long haul.

My longest exploratory trip, made with Dolores and Carlota, was southwest toward Mt. Markham, and it was a nightmare—blizzards and pressure ice° all the way out, crevasses and no view of the mountains when we got there, and white weather and sastrugi all the way back. The trip was useful, however, in that we could begin to estimate our capacities; and also in that we had started out with a very heavy load of provisions, which we depoted at a hundred and a hundred and thirty miles south-southwest of Base. Thereafter other parties pushed on farther, till we had a line of snow cairns and depots right down to Latitude 80° 43′, where Juana and Zoe, on an exploring trip, had found a kind of stone gateway opening on a great glacier leading south. We established these depots to avoid, if possible, the hunger that had bedevilled Captain Scott's Southern Party, and the consequent misery and weakness. And we also established to our own satisfaction— intense satisfaction—that we were sledge-haulers at least as good as Captain Scott's husky dogs. Of course we could not have expected to pull as much or as fast as his men. That we did so was because we were favored by much better weather than Captain Scott's party ever met on the Barrier; and also the quantity and quality of our food made a very considerable difference. I am sure that the fifteen percent of dried fruits in our pemmican helped prevent scurvy; and the potatoes, frozen and dried according to an ancient Andean Indian method, were very nourishing yet very light and compact—perfect sledding rations. In any case, it was with considerable confidence in our capacities that we made ready at last for the Southern Journey.

The Southern Party consisted of two sledge teams: Juana, Dolores, and myself; Carlota, Pepita, and Zoe. The support team of Berta, Eva, and Teresa set out before us with a heavy load of supplies, going right up onto the glacier to prospect routes and leave depots of supplies for our return journey. We followed five days behind them, and met them returning between Depot Ercilla and Depot Miranda. That "night"—of course, there was no real darkness—we were all nine together in the heart of the level plain of ice. It was November 15th, Dolores's birthday. We celebrated by putting eight ounces of pisco in the hot chocolate, and became very merry. We sang. It is strange now to remember how thin our voices sounded in that great silence. It was overcast, white weather, without shadows and without visible horizon or any feature to break the level; there was nothing to see at all. We had come to that white place on the map, that void, and there we flew and sang like sparrows.

After sleep and a good breakfast the Base Party continued north and the Southern Party sledged on. The sky cleared presently. High up, thin clouds passed over very rapidly from southwest to northeast, but down on the Barrier it was calm and just cold enough, five or ten degrees below freezing, to give a firm surface for hauling.

On the level ice we never pulled less than eleven miles (seventeen kilometres) a day, and generally fifteen or sixteen miles (twenty-five kilometres). (Our instruments, being British-made, were calibrated in feet, miles, degrees Fahrenheit, etc., but we often converted miles to kilometres, because the larger numbers sounded more encouraging.) At the time we left South America, we knew only that Mr. Ernest Shackleton had mounted another expedition to the

30

pressure ice: Loud-sounding ice cracking under pressure.

Antarctic in 1907, had tried to attain the Pole but failed, and had returned to England in June of the current year, 1909. No coherent report of his explorations had yet reached South America when we left; we did not know what route he had gone, or how far he had got. But we were not altogether taken by surprise when, far across the featureless white plain, tiny beneath the mountain peaks and the strange silent flight of the rainbow-fringed cloud wisps, we saw a fluttering dot of black. We turned west from our course to visit it: a snow heap nearly buried by the winter's storms—a flag on a bamboo pole, a mere shred of threadbare cloth, an empty oil-can—and a few footprints standing some inches above the ice. In some conditions of weather the snow compressed under one's weight remains when the surrounding soft snow melts or is scoured away by the wind; and so these reversed footprints had been left standing all these months, like rows of cobbler's lasts—a queer sight.

We met no other such traces on our way. In general I believe our course was somewhat east of Mr. Shackleton's. Juana, our surveyor, had trained herself well and was faithful and methodical in her sightings and readings, but our equipment was minimal—a theodolite on tripod legs, a sextant with artificial horizon, two compasses, and chronometers. We had only the wheel meter on the sledge to give distance actually travelled.

In any case, it was the day after passing Mr. Shackleton's waymark that I first saw clearly the great glacier among the mountains to the southwest, which was to give us a pathway from the sea level of the Barrier up to the altiplano, ten thousand feet above. The approach was magnificent: a gateway formed by immense vertical domes and pillars of rock. Zoe and Juana had called the vast ice river that flowed through that gateway the Florence Nightingale Glacier, wishing to honor the British, who had been the inspiration and guide of our Expedition; that very brave and very peculiar lady seemed to represent so much that is best, and strangest, in the island race. On maps, of course, this glacier bears the name Mr. Shackleton gave it: the Beardmore.

The ascent of the Nightingale was not easy. The way was open at first, and well marked by our support party, but after some days we came among terrible crevasses, a maze of hidden cracks, from a foot to thirty feet wide and from thirty to a thousand feet deep. Step by step we went, and step by step, and the way always upward now. We were fifteen days on the glacier. At first the weather was hot—up to 20°F—and the hot nights without darkness were wretchedly uncomfortable in our small tents. And all of us suffered more or less from snow blindness just at the time when we wanted clear eyesight to pick our way among the ridges and crevasses of the tortured ice, and to see the wonders about and before us. For at every day's advance more great, nameless peaks came into view in the west and southwest, summit beyond summit, range beyond range, stark rock and snow in the unending noon.

We gave names to these peaks, not very seriously, since we did not expect 35 our discoveries to come to the attention of geographers. Zoe had a gift for naming, and it is thanks to her that certain sketch maps in various suburban South American attics bear such curious features as "Bolívar's Big Nose," "I Am General Rosas," "The Cloudmaker," "Whose Toe?," and "Throne of Our Lady of the Southern Cross." And when at last we got up onto the altiplano, the great interior plateau, it was Zoe who called it the pampa, and maintained that we walked there among vast herds of invisible cattle, transparent cattle pastured on the spindrift snow, their gauchos the restless, merciless winds. We were by then all a little crazy with exhaustion and the great altitude—twelve thousand feet—and the cold and the wind blowing and the luminous circles and crosses surrounding the suns, for often there were three or four suns in the sky, up there.

That is not a place where people have any business to be. We should have turned back; but since we had worked so hard to get there, it seemed that we should go on, at least for a while.

A blizzard came, with very low temperatures, so we had to stay in the tents, in our sleeping bags, for thirty hours—a rest we all needed, though it was warmth we needed most, and there was no warmth on that terrible plain anywhere at all but in our veins. We huddled close together all that time. The ice we lay on is two miles thick.

It cleared suddenly and became, for the plateau, good weather: twelve below zero and the wind not very strong. We three crawled out of our tent and met the others crawling out of theirs. Carlota told us then that her group wished to turn back. Pepita had been feeling very ill; even after the rest during the blizzard, her temperature would not rise above 94°. Carlota was having trouble breathing. Zoe was perfectly fit, but much preferred staying with her friends and lending them a hand in difficulties to pushing on toward the Pole. So we put the four ounces of pisco that we had been keeping for Christmas into the breakfast cocoa, and dug out our tents, and loaded our sledges, and parted there in the white daylight on the bitter plain.

Our sledge was fairly light by now. We pulled on to the south. Juana calculated our position daily. On the twenty-second of December, 1909, we reached the South Pole. The weather was, as always, very cruel. Nothing of any kind marked the dreary whiteness. We discussed leaving some kind of mark or monument, a snow cairn, a tent pole and flag; but there seemed no particular reason to do so. Anything we could do, anything we were, was insignificant, in that awful place. We put up the tent for shelter for an hour and made a cup of tea, and then struck "90° Camp."

Dolores, standing patient as ever in her sledging harness, looked at the snow;   40
it was so hard frozen that it showed no trace of our footprints coming, and she said, "Which way?"

"North," said Juana.

It was a joke, because at that particular place there is no other direction. But we did not laugh. Our lips were cracked with frostbite and hurt too much to let us laugh. So we started back, and the wind at our backs pushed us along, and dulled the knife edges of the waves of frozen snow.

All that week the blizzard wind pursued us like a pack of mad dogs. I cannot describe it. I wished we had not gone to the Pole. I think I wish it even now. But I was glad even then that we had left no sign there, for some man longing to be first might come some day, and find it, and know then what a fool he had been, and break his heart.

We talked, when we could talk, of catching up to Carlota's party, since they might be going slower than we. In fact they used their tent as a sail to catch the following wind and had got far ahead of us. But in many places they had built snow cairns or left some sign for us; once, Zoe had written on the lee side of a ten-foot sastruga, just as children write on the sand of the beach at Miraflores, "This Way Out!" The wind blowing over the frozen ridge had left the words perfectly distinct.

In the very hour that we began to descend the glacier, the weather turned   45
warmer, and the mad dogs were left to howl forever tethered to the Pole. The
distance that had taken us fifteen days going up we covered in only eight days going down. But the good weather that had aided us descending the Nightingale
became a curse down on the Barrier ice, where we had looked forward to a kind
of royal progress from depot to depot, eating our fill and taking our time for the
last three hundred-odd miles. In a tight place on the glacier I lost my goggles—
I was swinging from my harness at the time in a crevasse—and then Juana broke
hers when we had to do some rock-climbing coming down to the Gateway. After
two days in bright sunlight with only one pair of snow goggles to pass amongst
us, we were all suffering badly from snow blindness. It became acutely painful to
keep lookout for landmarks or depot flags, to take sightings, even to study the
compass, which had to be laid down on the snow to steady the needle. At
Concolorcorvo Depot, where there was a particularly good supply of food and
fuel, we gave up, crawled into our sleeping bags with bandaged eyes, and slowly
boiled alive like lobsters in the tent exposed to the relentless sun. The voices of
Berta and Zoe were the sweetest sound I ever heard. A little concerned about us,
they had skied south to meet us. They led us home to Base.

We recovered quite swiftly, but the altiplano left its mark. When she was very
little, Rosita asked if a dog "had bitted Mama's toes." I told her yes—a great,
white, mad dog named Blizzard! My Rosita and my Juanito heard many stories
when they were little, about that fearful dog and how it howled, and the transparent cattle of the invisible gauchos, and a river of ice eight thousand feet high
called Nightingale, and how Cousin Juana drank a cup of tea standing on the bottom of the world under seven suns, and other fairy tales.

We were in for one severe shock when we reached Base at last. Teresa was
pregnant. I must admit that my first response to the poor girl's big belly and
sheepish look was anger—rage—fury. That one of us should have concealed anything, and such a thing, from the others! But Teresa had done nothing of the
sort. Only those who had concealed from her what she most needed to know were
to blame. Brought up by servants, with four years' schooling in a convent, and
married at sixteen, the poor girl was still so ignorant at twenty years of age that
she had thought it was "the cold weather" that made her miss her periods. Even
this was not entirely stupid, for all of us on the Southern Journey had seen our
periods change or stop altogether as we experienced increasing cold, hunger, and
fatigue. Teresa's appetite had begun to draw general attention; and then she had
begun, as she said pathetically, "to get fat." The others were worried at the thought
of all the sledge-hauling she had done, but she flourished, and the only problem
was her positively insatiable appetite. As well as could be determined from her shy
references to her last night on the hacienda with her husband, the baby was due
at just about the same time as the *Yelcho*, February 20th. But we had not been
back from the Southern Journey two weeks when, on February 14th, she went
into labor.

Several of us had borne children and had helped with deliveries, and anyhow
most of what needs to be done is fairly self-evident; but a first labor can be long
and trying, and we were all anxious, while Teresa was frightened out of her wits.
She kept calling for her José till she was as hoarse as a skua. Zoe lost all patience
at last and said, "By God, Teresa, if you say 'José!' once more, I hope you have

a penguin!" But what she had, after twenty long hours, was a pretty little red-faced girl.

Many were the suggestions for that child's name from her eight proud midwife aunts: Polita, Penguina, McMurdo, Victoria . . . But Teresa announced, after she had had a good sleep and a large serving of pemmican, "I shall name her Rosa—Rosa del Sur," Rose of the South. That night we drank the last two bottles of Veuve Clicquot (having finished the pisco at 88° 60′ South) in toasts to our little Rose.

On the nineteenth of February, a day early, my Juana came down into Buenos   50
Aires in a hurry. "The ship," she said, "the ship has come," and she burst into tears—she who had never wept in all our weeks of pain and weariness on the long haul.

Of the return voyage there is nothing to tell. We came back safe.

In 1912 all the world learned that the brave Norwegian Amundsen° had reached the South Pole; and then, much later, we heard the accounts of how Captain Scott and his men had come there after him but did not come home again.

Just this year, Juana and I wrote to the captain of the *Yelcho*, for the newspapers have been full of the story of his gallant dash to rescue Sir Ernest Shackleton's men from Elephant Island, and we wished to congratulate him, and once more to thank him. Never one word has he breathed of our secret. He is a man of honor, Luis Pardo.

I add this last note in 1929. Over the years we have lost touch with one another. It is very difficult for women to meet, when they live as far apart as we do. Since Juana died, I have seen none of my old sledgemates, though sometimes we write. Our little Rosa del Sur died of the scarlet fever when she was five years old. Teresa had many other children. Carlota took the veil in Santiago ten years ago. We are old women now, with old husbands, and grown children, and grandchildren who might some day like to read about the Expedition. Even if they are rather ashamed of having such a crazy grandmother, they may enjoy sharing in the secret. But they must not let Mr. Amundsen know! He would be terribly embarrassed and disappointed. There is no need for him or anyone else outside the family to know. We left no footprints, even.

Amundsen: Roald Amundsen (1872–1928) was the first man to reach the South Pole (1911).

Doris Lessing   (b. 1919)

Although Doris Lessing has lived in London since 1949, her work has been conditioned by her experiences in Africa. She was born in Iran but was raised in Zimbabwe, the setting for much of her writing. She has said, "Writers brought up in Africa have many advantages—being at the center of a modern battlefield; part of a society in rapid, dramatic change. But in a long run it can also be a handicap: to wake up every working day with one's eyes on a fresh evidence of inhumanity . . . can be limiting." African Stories (1981) is a gathering from earlier collections dealing with Africa, many of which examine racial injustice. Her novel The Golden Notebook (1962) examines another kind of injustice, the sexual attitudes held by men and women. Among her works are The Grass Is

Singing *(1950) and* Martha Quest *(1952), whose title is also the name of the heroine of the* Children of Violence *series, which includes* A Proper Marriage *(1954),* A Ripple from the Storm *(1958),* Landlocked *(1966), and* The Four-Gated City *(1967). Lessing's writing has often been described as autobiographical, with Martha Quest growing up on an African farm and following in some of Lessing's footsteps.*

TO ROOM 19   1963

This is a story, I suppose, about a failure in intelligence: the Rawlings' marriage was grounded in intelligence.

They were older when they married than most of their married friends: in their well-seasoned late twenties. Both had had a number of affairs, sweet rather than bitter; and when they fell in love—for they did fall in love—had known each other for some time. They joked that they had saved each other "for the real thing." That they had waited so long (but not too long) for this real thing was to them a proof of their sensible discrimination. A good many of their friends had married young, and now (they felt) probably regretted lost opportunities; while others, still unmarried, seemed to them arid, self-doubting, and likely to make desperate or romantic marriages.

Not only they, but others, felt they were well-matched: their friends' delight was an additional proof of their happiness. They had played the same roles, male and female, in this group or set, if such a wide, loosely connected, constantly changing constellation of people could be called a set. They had both become, by virtue of their moderation, their humor, and their abstinence from painful experience, people to whom others came for advice. They could be, and were, relied on. It was one of those cases of a man and a woman linking themselves whom no one else had ever thought of linking, probably because of their similarities. But then everyone exclaimed: Of course! How right! How was it we never thought of it before!

And so they married amid general rejoicing, and because of their foresight and their sense for what was probable, nothing was a surprise to them.

Both had well-paid jobs. Matthew was a subeditor on a large London newspaper, and Susan worked in an advertising firm. He was not the stuff of which editors or publicized journalists are made, but he was much more than "a subeditor," being one of the essential background people who in fact steady, inspire, and make possible the people in the limelight. He was content with this position. Susan had a talent for commercial drawing. She was humorous about the advertisements she was responsible for, but she did not feel strongly about them one way or the other.

Both, before they married, had had pleasant flats, but they felt it unwise to base a marriage on either flat, because it might seem like a submission of personality on the part of the one whose flat it was not. They moved into a new flat in South Kensington on the clear understanding that when their marriage had settled down (a process they knew would not take long, and was in fact more a humorous concession to popular wisdom than what was due to themselves) they would buy a house and start a family.

And this is what happened. They lived in their charming flat for two years, giving parties and going to them, being a popular young married couple, and then

5

Susan became pregnant, she gave up her job, and they bought a house in Richmond. It was typical of this couple that they had a son first, then a daughter, then twins, son and daughter. Everything right, appropriate, and what everyone would wish for, if they could choose. But people did feel these two had chosen; this balanced and sensible family was no more than what was due to them because of their infallible sense for *choosing* right.

And so they lived with their four children in their gardened house in Richmond and were happy. They had everything they had wanted and had planned for.

And yet . . .

Well, even this was expected, that there must be a certain flatness. . . .   10

Yes, yes, of course, it was natural they sometimes felt like this. Like what?

Their life seemed to be like a snake biting its tail. Matthew's job for the sake of Susan, children, house, and garden—which caravanserai needed a well-paid job to maintain it. And Susan's practical intelligence for the sake of Matthew, the children, the house, and the garden—which unit would have collapsed in a week without her.

But there was no point about which either could say: "For the sake of *this* is all the rest." Children? But children can't be a center of life and a reason for being. They can be a thousand things that are delightful, interesting, satisfying, but they can't be a wellspring to live from. Or they shouldn't be. Susan and Matthew knew that well enough.

Matthew's job? Ridiculous. It was an interesting job, but scarcely a reason for living. Matthew took pride in doing it well, but he could hardly be expected to be proud of the newspaper; the newspaper he read, *his* newspaper, was not the one he worked for.

Their love for each other? Well, that was nearest it. If this wasn't a center,   15 what was? Yes, it was around this point, their love, that the whole extraordinary structure revolved. For extraordinary it certainly was. Both Susan and Matthew had moments of thinking so, of looking in secret disbelief at this thing they had created: marriage, four children, big house, garden, charwomen, friends, cars . . . and this *thing*, this entity, all of it had come into existence, been blown into being out of nowhere, because Susan loved Matthew and Matthew loved Susan. Extraordinary. So that was the central point, the wellspring.

And if one felt that it simply was not strong enough, important enough, to support it all, well whose fault was that? Certainly neither Susan's nor Matthew's. It was in the nature of things. And they sensibly blamed neither themselves nor each other.

On the contrary, they used their intelligence to preserve what they had created from a painful and explosive world: they looked around them, and took lessons. All around them, marriages collapsing, or breaking, or rubbing along (even worse, they felt). They must not make the same mistakes, they must not.

They had avoided the pitfall so many of their friends had fallen into—of buying a house in the country *for the sake of the children*, so that the husband became a weekend husband, a weekend father, and the wife always careful not to ask what went on in the town flat which they called (in joke) a bachelor flat. No, Matthew was a full-time husband, a full-time father, and at night, in the big married bed in the big married bedroom (which had an attractive view of the river), they lay beside each other talking and he told her about his day, and what he had done, and whom he had met; and she told him about her day (not as interesting, but that was not her fault), for both knew of the hidden resentments and deprivations of the woman who has lived her own life—and above all, has earned her own living—and is now dependent on a husband for outside interests and money.

Nor did Susan make the mistake of taking a job for the sake of her independence, which she might very well have done, since her old firm, missing her qualities of humor, balance, and sense, invited her often to go back. Children needed their mother to a certain age, that both parents knew and agreed on; and when these four healthy, wisely brought up children were of the right age, Susan would work again, because she knew, and so did he, what happened to women of fifty at the height of their energy and ability, with grown-up children who no longer needed their full devotion.

So here was this couple, testing their marriage, looking after it, treating it   20
like a small boat full of helpless people in a very stormy sea. Well, of course, so it was. . . . The storms of the world were bad, but not too close—which is not to say they were selfishly felt: Susan and Matthew were both well-informed and responsible people. And the inner storms and quicksands were understood and charted. So everything was all right. Everything was in order. Yes, things were under control.

So what did it matter if they felt dry, flat? People like themselves, fed on a hundred books (psychological, anthropological, sociological), could scarcely be unprepared for the dry, controlled wistfulness which is the distinguishing mark of the intelligent marriage. Two people, endowed with education, with discrimination, with judgment, linked together voluntarily from their will to be happy together and to be of use to others—one sees them everywhere, one knows them, one even is that thing oneself: sadness because so much is after all so little. These two, unsurprised, turned towards each other with even more courtesy and gentle love: this was life, that two people, no matter how carefully chosen, could not be everything to each other. In fact, even to say so, to think in such a way, was banal; they were ashamed to do it.

It was banal, too, when one night Matthew came home late and confessed he had been to a party, taken a girl home and slept with her. Susan forgave him, of course. Except that forgiveness is hardly the word. Understanding, yes. But if you understand something, you don't forgive it, you are the thing itself: forgiveness is for what you *don't* understand. Nor had he *confessed*—what sort of word is that?

The whole thing was not important. After all, years ago they had joked: Of course I'm not going to be faithful to you, no one can be faithful to one other person for a whole lifetime. (And there was the word "faithful"—stupid, all these words, stupid, belonging to a savage old world.) But the incident left both of them irritable. Strange, but they were both bad-tempered, annoyed. There was something unassimilable about it.

Making love splendidly after he had come home that night, both had felt that the idea that Myra Jenkins, a pretty girl met at a party, could be even relevant was ridiculous. They had loved each other for over a decade, would love each other for years more. Who, then, was Myra Jenkins?

Except, thought Susan, unaccountably bad-tempered, she was (is?) the first.   25
In ten years. So either the ten years' fidelity was not important, or she isn't. (No, no, there is something wrong with this way of thinking, there must be.) But if

she isn't important, presumably it wasn't important either when Matthew and I first went to bed with each other that afternoon whose delight even now (like a very long shadow at sundown) lays a long, wandlike finger over us. (Why did I say sundown?) Well, if what we felt that afternoon was not important, nothing is important, because if it hadn't been for what we felt, we wouldn't be Mr. and Mrs. Rawlings with four children, et cetera, et cetera. The whole thing is *absurd*— for him to have come home and told me was absurd. For him not to have told me was absurd. For me to care or, for that matter, not to care, is absurd . . . and who is Myra Jenkins? Why, no one at all.

There was only one thing to do, and of course these sensible people did it; they put the thing behind them, and consciously, knowing what they were do-ing, moved forward into a different phase of their marriage, giving thanks for past good fortune as they did so.

For it was inevitable that the handsome, blond, attractive, manly man, Matthew Rawlings, should be at times tempted (oh, what a word!) by the at-tractive girls at parties she could not attend because of the four children; and that sometimes he would succumb (a word even more repulsive, if possible) and that she, a good-looking woman in the big well-tended garden at Richmond, would sometimes be pierced as by an arrow from the sky with bitterness. Except that bitterness was not in order, it was out of court. Did the casual girls touch the mar-riage? They did not. Rather it was they who knew defeat because of the hand-some Matthew Rawlings' marriage body and soul to Susan Rawlings.

In that case why did Susan feel (though luckily not for longer than a few sec-onds at a time) as if life had become a desert, and that nothing mattered, and that her children were not her own?

Meanwhile her intelligence continued to assert that all was well. What if her Matthew did have an occasional sweet afternoon, the odd affair? For she knew quite well, except in her moments of aridity, that they were very happy, that the affairs were not important.

Perhaps that was the trouble? It was in the nature of things that the adven-tures and delights could no longer be hers, because of the four children and the big house that needed so much attention. But perhaps she was secretly wishing, and even knowing that she did, that the wildness and the beauty could be his. But he was married to her. She was married to him. They were married inextri-cably. And therefore the gods could not strike him with the real magic, not really. Well, was it Susan's fault that after he came home from an adventure he looked harassed rather than fulfilled? (In fact, that was how she knew he had been *unfaithful*, because of his sullen air, and his glances at her, similar to hers at him: What is it that I share with this person that shields all delight from me?) But none of it by anybody's fault. (But what did they feel ought to be somebody's fault?) Nobody's fault, nothing to be at fault, no one to blame, no one to offer or to take it . . . and nothing wrong, either, except that Matthew never was really struck, as he wanted to be, by joy; and that Susan was more and more often threatened by emptiness. (It was usually in the garden that she was invaded by this feeling: she was coming to avoid the garden, unless the children or Matthew were with her.) There was no need to use the dramatic words "unfaithful," "forgive," and the rest: intelligence forbade them. Intelligence barred, too, quarreling, sulking, anger, silences of withdrawal, accusations and tears. Above all, intelligence for-bids tears.

30

A high price has to be paid for the happy marriage with the four healthy children in the large white gardened house.

And they were paying it, willingly, knowing what they were doing. When they lay side by side or breast to breast in the big civilized bedroom overlooking the wild sullied river, they laughed, often, for no particular reason; but they knew it was really because of these two small people, Susan and Matthew, supporting such an edifice on their intelligent love. The laugh comforted them; it saved them both, though from what, they did not know.

They were now both fortyish. The older children, boy and girl, were ten and eight, at school. The twins, six, were still at home. Susan did not have nurses or girls to help her: childhood is short; and she did not regret the hard work. Often enough she was bored, since small children can be boring; she was often very tired; but she regretted nothing. In another decade, she would turn herself back into being a woman with a life of her own.

Soon the twins would go to school, and they would be away from home from nine until four. These hours, so Susan saw it, would be the preparation for her own slow emancipation away from the role of hub-of-the-family into woman-with-her-own-life. She was already planning for the hours of freedom when all the children would be "off her hands." That was the phrase used by Matthew and by Susan and by their friends, for the moment when the youngest child went off to school. "They'll be off your hands, darling Susan, and you'll have time to yourself." So said Matthew, the intelligent husband, who had often enough commended and consoled Susan, standing by her in spirit during the years when her soul was not her own, as she said, but her children's.

What it amounted to was that Susan saw herself as she had been at twenty-eight, unmarried; and then again somewhere about fifty, blossoming from the root of what she had been twenty years before. As if the essential Susan were in abeyance, as if she were in cold storage. Matthew said something like this to Susan one night: and she agreed that it was true—she did feel something like that. What, then, was this essential Susan? She did not know. Put like that it sounded ridiculous, and she did not really feel it. Anyway, they had a long discussion about the whole thing before going off to sleep in each other's arms.   35

So the twins went off to their school, two bright affectionate children who had no problems about it, since their older brother and sister had trodden this path so successfully before them. And now Susan was going to be alone in the big house, every day of the school term, except for the daily woman who came in to clean.

It was now, for the first time in this marriage, that something happened which neither of them had foreseen.

This is what happened. She returned, at nine-thirty, from taking the twins to the school by car, looking forward to seven blissful hours of freedom. On the first morning she was simply restless, worrying about the twins "naturally enough" since this was their first day away at school. She was hardly able to contain herself until they came back. Which they did happily, excited by the world of school, looking forward to the next day. And the next day Susan took them, dropped them, came back, and found herself reluctant to enter her big and beautiful home because it was as if something was waiting for her there that she did not wish to confront. Sensibly, however, she parked the car in the garage, entered the house, spoke to Mrs. Parkes, the daily woman, about her duties, and went up to her bedroom. She was possessed by a fever which drove her out again, downstairs, into the kitchen, where Mrs. Parkes was making cake and did not need her, and into the garden. There she sat on a bench and tried to calm herself looking at trees, at a brown glimpse of the river. But she was filled with tension, like a panic: as if an enemy was in the garden with her. She spoke to herself severely, thus: All this is quite natural. First, I spent twelve years of my adult life working, *living my own life*. Then I married, and from the moment I became pregnant for the first time I signed myself over, so to speak, to other people. To the children. Not for one moment in twelve years have I been alone, had time to myself. So now I have to learn to be myself again. That's all.

And she went indoors to help Mrs. Parkes cook and clean, and found some sewing to do for the children. She kept herself occupied every day. At the end of the first term she understood she felt two contrary emotions. First: secret astonishment and dismay that during those weeks when the house was empty of children she had in fact been more occupied (had been careful to keep herself occupied) than ever she had been when the children were around her needing her continual attention. Second: that now she knew the house would be full of them, and for five weeks, she resented the fact she would never be alone. She was already looking back at those hours of sewing, cooking (but by herself) as at a lost freedom which would not be hers for five long weeks. And the two months of term which would succeed the five weeks stretched alluringly open to her—freedom. But what freedom—when in fact she had been so careful *not* to be free of small duties during the last weeks? She looked at herself, Susan Rawlings, sitting in a big chair by the window in the bedroom, sewing shirts or dresses, which she might just as well have bought. She saw herself making cakes for hours at a time in the big family kitchen: yet usually she bought cakes. What she saw was a woman alone, that was true, but she had not felt alone. For instance, Mrs. Parkes was always somewhere in the house. And she did not like being in the garden at all, because of the closeness there of the enemy—irritation, restlessness, emptiness, whatever it was—which keeping her hands occupied made less dangerous for some reason.

Susan did not tell Matthew of these thoughts. They were not sensible. She did not recognize herself in them. What should she say to her dear friend and husband, Matthew? "When I go into the garden, that is, if the children are not there, I feel as if there is an enemy there waiting to invade me." "What enemy, Susan darling?" "Well I don't know, really . . ." "Perhaps you should see a doctor?"

No, clearly this conversation should not take place. The holidays began and Susan welcomed them. Four children, lively, energetic, intelligent, demanding: she was never, not for a moment of her day, alone. If she was in a room, they would be in the next room, or waiting for her to do something for them; or it would soon be time for lunch or tea, or to take one of them to the dentist. Something to do: five weeks of it, thank goodness.

On the fourth day of these so welcome holidays, she found she was storming with anger at the twins: two shrinking beautiful children who (and this is what checked her) stood hand in hand looking at her with sheer dismayed disbelief. This was their calm mother, shouting at them. And for what? They had come to her with some game, some bit of nonsense. They looked at each other, moved closer for support, and went off hand in hand, leaving Susan holding on to the windowsill of the living room, breathing deep, feeling sick. She went to lie down, telling the older children she had a headache. She heard the boy Harry telling the little ones: "It's all right, Mother's got a headache." She heard that *It's all right* with pain.

That night she said to her husband: "Today I shouted at the twins, quite unfairly." She sounded miserable, and he said gently: "Well, what of it?"

"It's more of an adjustment than I thought, their going to school."

"But Susie, Susie darling . . ." For she was crouched weeping on the bed.   45
He comforted her: "Susan, what is all this about? You shouted at them? What of it? If you shouted at them fifty times a day it wouldn't be more than the little devils deserve." But she wouldn't laugh. She wept. Soon he comforted her with his body. She became calm. Calm, she wondered what was wrong with her, and why she should mind so much that she might, just once, have behaved unjustly with the children. What did it matter? They had forgotten it all long ago: Mother had a headache and everything was all right.

It was a long time later that Susan understood that that night, when she had wept and Matthew had driven the misery out of her with his big solid body, was the last time, ever in their married life, that they had been—to use their mutual language—with each other. And even that was a lie, because she had not told him of her real fears at all.

The five weeks passed, and Susan was in control of herself, and good and kind, and she looked forward to the holidays with a mixture of fear and longing. She did not know what to expect. She took the twins off to school (the elder children took themselves to school) and she returned to the house determined to face the enemy wherever he was, in the house, or the garden or—where?

She was again restless, she was possessed by restlessness. She cooked and sewed and worked as before, day after day, while Mrs. Parkes remonstrated: "Mrs. Rawlings, what's the need for it? I can do that, it's what you pay me for."

And it was so irrational that she checked herself. She would put the car into the garage, go up to her bedroom, and sit, hands in her lap, forcing herself to be quiet. She listened to Mrs. Parkes moving around the house. She looked out into the garden and saw the branches shake the trees. She sat defeating the enemy, restlessness. Emptiness. She ought to be thinking about her life, about herself. But she did not. Or perhaps she could not. As soon as she forced her mind to think about Susan (for what else did she want to be alone for?), it skipped off to thoughts of butter or school clothes. Or it thought of Mrs. Parkes. She realized that she sat listening for the movements of the cleaning woman, following her every turn, bend, thought. She followed her in her mind from kitchen to bathroom, from table to oven, and it was as if the duster, the cleaning cloth, the saucepan, were in her own hand. She would hear herself saying: No, not like that, don't put that there. . . . Yet she did not give a damn what Mrs. Parkes did, or if she did it at all. Yet she could not prevent herself from being conscious of her, every minute. Yes, this was what was wrong with her: she needed, when she was alone, to be really alone, with no one near. She could not endure the knowledge that in ten minutes or in half an hour Mrs. Parkes would call up the stairs: "Mrs. Rawlings, there's no silver polish. Madam, we're out of flour."

So she left the house and went to sit in the garden where she was screened   50
from the house by trees. She waited for the demon to appear and claim her, but he did not.

She was keeping him off, because she had not, after all, come to an end of arranging herself.

She was planning how to be somewhere where Mrs. Parkes would not come after her with a cup of tea, or a demand to be allowed to telephone (always irritating, since Susan did not care who she telephoned or how often), or just a nice talk about something. Yes, she needed a place, or a state of affairs, where it would not be necessary to keep reminding herself: In ten minutes I must telephone Matthew about . . . and at half past three I must leave early for the children because the car needs cleaning. And at ten o'clock tomorrow I must remember. . . . She was possessed with resentment that the seven hours of freedom in every day (during weekdays in the school term) were not free, that never, not for one second, ever, was she free from the pressure of time, from having to remember this or that. She could never forget herself; never really let herself go into forgetfulness.

Resentment. It was poisoning her. (She looked at this emotion and thought it was absurd. Yet she felt it.) She was a prisoner. (She looked at this thought too, and it was no good telling herself it was a ridiculous one.) She must tell Matthew— but what? She was filled with emotions that were utterly ridiculous, that she despised, yet that nevertheless she was feeling so strongly she could not shake them off.

The school holidays came round, and this time they were for nearly two months, and she behaved with a conscious controlled decency that nearly drove her crazy. She would lock herself in the bathroom, and sit on the edge of the bath, breathing deep, trying to let go into some kind of calm. Or she went up into the spare room, usually empty, where no one would expect her to be. She heard the children calling "Mother, Mother," and kept silent, feeling guilty. Or she went to the very end of the garden, by herself, and looked at the slow-moving brown river; she looked at the river and closed her eyes and breathed slow and deep, taking it into her being, into her veins.

Then she returned to the family, wife and mother, smiling and responsible, feeling as if the pressure of these people—four lively children and her husband— were a painful pressure on the surface of her skin, a hand pressing on her brain. She did not once break down into irritation during these holidays, but it was like living out a prison sentence, and when the children went back to school, she sat on a white stone near the flowing river, and she thought: It is not even a year since the twins went to school, since *they were off my hands* (What on earth did I think I meant when I used that stupid phrase?), and yet I'm a different person. I'm simply not myself. I don't understand it.

Yet she had to understand it. For she knew that this structure—big white house, on which the mortgage still cost four hundred a year, a husband, so good and kind and insightful; four children, all doing so nicely; and the garden where she sat; and Mrs. Parkes, the cleaning woman—all this depended on her, and yet she could not understand why, or even what it was she contributed to it.

She said to Matthew in their bedroom: "I think there must be something wrong with me."

And he said: "Surely not, Susan? You look marvelous—you're as lovely as ever."

She looked at the handsome blond man, with his clear, intelligent, blue-eyed face, and thought: Why is it I can't tell him? Why not? And she said: "I need to be alone more than I am."

55

At which he swung his slow blue gaze at her, and she saw what she had been   60
dreading: Incredulity. Disbelief. And fear. An incredulous blue stare from a
stranger who was her husband, as close to her as her own breath.

He said: "But the children are at school and off your hands."

She said to herself: I've got to force myself to say: Yes, but do you realize
that I never feel free? There's never a moment I can say to myself: There's nothing I have to remind myself about, nothing I have to do in half an hour, or an
hour, or two hours. . . .

But she said: "I don't feel well."

He said: "Perhaps you need a holiday."

She said, appalled: "But not without you, surely?" For she could not imag-   65
ine herself going off without him. Yet that was what he meant. Seeing her face,
he laughed, and opened his arms, and she went into them, thinking: Yes, yes, but
why can't I say it? And what is it I have to say?

She tried to tell him, about never being free. And he listened and said: "But
Susan, what sort of freedom can you possibly want—short of being dead! Am I
ever free? I go to the office, and I have to be there at ten—all right, half past ten,
sometimes. And I have to do this or that, don't I? Then I've got to come home
at a certain time—I don't mean it, you know I don't—but if I'm not going to be
back home at six I telephone you. When can I ever say to myself: I have nothing
to be responsible for in the next six hours?"

Susan, hearing this, was remorseful. Because it was true. The good marriage,
the house, the children, depended just as much on his voluntary bondage as it
did on hers. But why did he not feel bound? Why didn't he chafe and become
restless? No, there was something really wrong with her and this proved it.

And that word "bondage"—why had she used it? She had never felt marriage, or the children, as bondage. Neither had he, or surely they wouldn't be together lying in each other's arms content after twelve years of marriage.

No, her state (whatever it was) was irrelevant, nothing to do with her real
good life with her family. She had to accept the fact that, after all, she was an irrational person and to live with it. Some people had to live with crippled arms, or
stammers, or being deaf. She would have to live knowing she was subject to a
state of mind she could not own.

Nevertheless, as a result of this conversation with her husband, there was a   70
new regime next holidays.

The spare room at the top of the house now had a cardboard sign saying:
PRIVATE! DO NOT DISTURB! on it. (This sign had been drawn in colored chalks
by the children, after a discussion between the parents in which it was decided
this was psychologically the right thing.) The family and Mrs. Parkes knew this
was "Mother's Room" and that she was entitled to her privacy. Many serious conversations took place between Matthew and the children about not taking Mother
for granted. Susan overheard the first, between father and Harry, the older boy,
and was surprised at her irritation over it. Surely she could have a room somewhere in that big house and retire into it without such a fuss being made? Without
it being so solemnly discussed? Why couldn't she simply have announced: "I'm
going to fit out the little top room for myself, and when I'm in it I'm not to be
disturbed for anything short of fire"? Just that, and finished; instead of long earnest
discussions. When she heard Harry and Matthew explaining it to the twins with
Mrs. Parkes coming in—"Yes, well, a family sometimes gets on top of a woman"—

she had to go right away to the bottom of the garden until the devils of exasperation had finished their dance in her blood.

But now there was a room, and she could go there when she liked, she used
it seldom: she felt even more caged there than in her bedroom. One day she had
gone up there after a lunch for ten children she had cooked and served because
Mrs. Parkes was not there, and had sat alone for a while looking into the garden.
She saw the children stream out from the kitchen and stand looking up at the
window where she sat behind the curtains. They were all—her children and their
friends—discussing Mother's Room. A few minutes later, the chase of children in
some game came pounding up the stairs, but ended as abruptly as if they had
fallen over a ravine, so sudden was the silence. They had remembered she was
there, and had gone silent in a great gale of "Hush! Shhhhhh! Quiet, you'll disturb her. . . ." And they went tiptoeing downstairs like criminal conspirators.
When she came down to make tea for them, they all apologized. The twins put
their arms around her, from front and back, making a human cage of loving limbs,
and promised it would never occur again. "We forgot, Mummy, we forgot all
about it!"

What it amounted to was that Mother's Room, and her need for privacy,
had become a valuable lesson in respect for other people's rights. Quite soon
Susan was going up to the room only because it was a lesson it was a pity to drop.
Then she took sewing up there, and the children and Mrs. Parkes came in and
out: it had become another family room.

She sighed, and smiled, and resigned herself—she made jokes at her own expense with Matthew over the room. That is, she did from the self she liked, she
respected. But at the same time, something inside her howled with impatience,
with rage. . . . And she was frightened. One day she found herself kneeling by her
bed and praying: "Dear God, keep it away from me, keep him away from me."
She meant the devil, for she now thought of it, not caring if she was irrational, as
some sort of demon. She imagined him, or it, as a youngish man, or perhaps a
middle-aged man pretending to be young. Or a man young-looking from im-
maturity? At any rate, she saw the young-looking face which, when she drew closer,
had dry lines about mouth and eyes. He was thinnish, meager in build. And he
had a reddish complexion, and ginger hair. That was he—a gingery, energetic
man, and he wore a reddish hairy jacket, unpleasant to the touch.

Well, one day she saw him. She was standing at the bottom of the garden,   75
watching the river ebb past, when she raised her eyes and saw this person, or being, sitting on the white stone bench. He was looking at her, and grinning. In his
hand was a long crooked stick, which he had picked off the ground, or broken
off the tree above him. He was absentmindedly, out of an absentminded or freakish impulse of spite, using the stick to stir around in the coils of a blindworm or
a grass snake (or some kind of snakelike creature: it was whitish and unhealthy to
look at, unpleasant). The snake was twisting about, flinging its coils from side to
side in a kind of dance of protest against the teasing prodding stick.

Susan looked at him, thinking: Who is the stranger? What is he doing in our
garden? Then she recognized the man around whom her terrors had crystallized.
As she did so, he vanished. She made herself walk over to the bench. A shadow
from a branch lay across thin emerald grass, moving jerkily over its roughness,
and she could see why she had taken it for a snake, lashing and twisting. She went
back to the house thinking: Right, then, so I've seen him with my own eyes, so

I'm not crazy after all—there *is* a danger because I've seen him. He is lurking in the garden and sometimes even in the house, and he wants to *get into me and to take me over.*

She dreamed of having a room or a place, anywhere, where she could go and sit, by herself, no one knowing where she was.

Once, near Victoria, she found herself outside a news agent that had Rooms to Let advertised. She decided to rent a room, telling no one. Sometimes she could take the train in to Richmond and sit alone in it for an hour or two. Yet how could she? A room would cost three or four pounds a week, and she earned no money, and how could she explain to Matthew that she needed such a sum? What for? It did not occur to her that she was taking it for granted she wasn't going to tell him about the room.

Well, it was out of the question, having a room; yet she knew she must.

One day, when a school term was well established, and none of the children had measles or other ailments, and everything seemed in order, she did the shopping early, explained to Mrs. Parkes she was meeting an old school friend, took the train to Victoria, searched until she found a small quiet hotel, and asked for a room for the day. They did not let rooms by the day, the manageress said, looking doubtful, since Susan so obviously was not the kind of woman who needed a room for unrespectable reasons. Susan made a long explanation about not being well, being unable to shop without frequent rests for lying down. At last she was allowed to rent the room provided she paid a full night's price for it. She was taken up by the manageress and a maid, both concerned over the state of her health . . . which must be pretty bad if, living at Richmond (she had signed her name and address in the register), she needed a shelter at Victoria.

The room was ordinary and anonymous, and was just what Susan needed. She put a shilling in the gas fire, and sat, eyes shut, in a dingy armchair with her back to a dingy window. She was alone. She was alone. She was alone. She could feel pressures lifting off her. First the sounds of traffic came very loud; then they seemed to vanish; she might even have slept a little. A knock on the door: it was Miss Townsend, the manageress, bringing her a cup of tea with her own hands, so concerned was she over Susan's long silence and possible illness.

Miss Townsend was a lonely woman of fifty, running this hotel with all the rectitude expected of her, and she sensed in Susan the possibility of understanding companionship. She stayed to talk. Susan found herself in the middle of a fantastic story about her illness, which got more and more impossible as she tried to make it tally with the large house at Richmond, well-off husband, and four children. Suppose she said instead: Miss Townsend, I'm here in your hotel because I need to be alone for a few hours, above all *alone and with no one knowing where I am.* She said it mentally, and saw, mentally, the look that would inevitably come on Miss Townsend's elderly maiden's face. "Miss Townsend, my four children and my husband are driving me insane, do you understand that? Yes, I can see from the gleam of hysteria in your eyes that comes from loneliness controlled but only just contained that I've got everything in the world you've ever longed for. Well, Miss Townsend, I don't want any of it. You can have it, Miss Townsend. I wish I was absolutely alone in the world, like you. Miss Townsend, I'm besieged by seven devils, Miss Townsend, Miss Townsend, let me stay here in your hotel where the devils can't get me. . . ." Instead of saying all this, she described her anemia, agreed to try Miss Townsend's remedy for it, which was raw liver, minced,

80

between whole-meal bread, and said yes, perhaps it would be better if she stayed at home and let a friend do shopping for her. She paid her bill and left the hotel, defeated.

At home Mrs. Parkes said she didn't really like it, no, not really, when Mrs. Rawlings was away from nine in the morning until five. The teacher had telephoned from school to say Joan's teeth were paining her, and she hadn't known what to say; and what was she to make for the children's tea, Mrs. Rawlings hadn't said.

All this was nonsense, of course. Mrs. Parkes's complaint was that Susan had withdrawn herself spiritually, leaving the burden of the big house on her.

Susan looked back at her day of "freedom" which had resulted in her becoming a friend of the lonely Miss Townsend, and in Mrs. Parkes's remonstrances. Yet she remembered the short blissful hour of being alone, really alone. She was determined to arrange her life, no matter what it cost, so that she could have that solitude more often. An absolute solitude, where no one knew her or cared about her.

But how? She thought of saying to her old employer: I want you to back me up in a story with Matthew that I am doing part-time work for you. The truth is that . . . But she would have to tell him a lie, too, and which lie? She could not say: I want to sit by myself three or four times a week in a rented room. And besides, he knew Matthew, and she could not really ask him to tell lies on her behalf, apart from being bound to think it meant a lover.

Suppose she really took a part-time job, which she could get through fast and efficiently, leaving time for herself. What job? Addressing envelopes? Canvassing?

And there was Mrs. Parkes, working widow, who knew exactly what she was prepared to give to the house, who knew by instinct when her mistress withdrew in spirit from her responsibilities. Mrs. Parkes was one of the servers of this world, but she needed someone to serve. She had to have Mrs. Rawlings, her madam, at the top of the house or in the garden, so that she could come and get support from her: "Yes, the bread's not what it was when I was a girl. . . . Yes, Harry's got a wonderful appetite, I wonder where he puts it all. . . . Yes, it's lucky the twins are so much of a size, they can wear each other's shoes, that's a saving in these hard times. . . . Yes, the cherry jam from Switzerland is not a patch on the jam from Poland, and three times the price. . . ." And so on. That sort of talk Mrs. Parkes must have, every day, or she would leave, not knowing herself why she left.

Susan Rawlings, thinking these thoughts, found that she was prowling through the great thicketed garden like a wild cat: she was walking up the stairs, down the stairs, through the rooms into the garden, along the brown running river, back, up through the house, down again. . . . It was a wonder Mrs. Parkes did not think it strange. But, on the contrary, Mrs. Rawlings could do what she liked, she could stand on her head if she wanted, provided she was *there*. Susan Rawlings prowled and muttered through her house, hating Mrs. Parkes, hating poor Miss Townsend, dreaming of her hour of solitude in the dingy respectability of Miss Townsend's hotel bedroom, and she knew quite well she was mad. Yes, she was mad.

She said to Matthew that she must have a holiday. Matthew agreed with her. This was not as things had been once—how they had talked in each other's arms

85

90

in the marriage bed. He had, she knew, diagnosed her finally as *unreasonable.* She had become someone outside himself that he had to manage. They were living side by side in this house like two tolerably friendly strangers.

Having told Mrs. Parkes—or rather, asked for her permission—she went off on a walking holiday in Wales. She chose the remotest place she knew of. Every morning the children telephoned her before they went off to school, to encourage and support her, just as they had over Mother's Room. Every evening she telephoned them, spoke to each child in turn, and then to Matthew. Mrs. Parkes, given permission to telephone for instructions or advice, did so every day at lunchtime. When, as happened three times, Mrs. Rawlings was out on the mountainside, Mrs. Parkes asked that she should ring back at such-and-such a time, for she would not be happy in what she was doing without Mrs. Rawlings' blessing.

Susan prowled over wild country with the telephone wire holding her to her duty like a leash. The next time she must telephone, or wait to be telephoned, nailed her to her cross. The mountains themselves seemed trammeled by her unfreedom. Everywhere on the mountains, where she met no one at all, from breakfast time to dusk, excepting sheep, or a shepherd, she came face-to-face with her own craziness, which might attack her in the broadest valleys, so that they seemed too small, or on a mountaintop from which she could see a hundred other mountains and valleys, so that they seemed too low, too small, with the sky pressing down too close. She would stand gazing at a hillside brilliant with ferns and bracken, jeweled with running water, and see nothing but her devil, who lifted inhuman eyes at her from where he leaned negligently on a rock, switching at his ugly yellow boots with a leafy twig.

She returned to her home and family, with the Welsh emptiness at the back of her mind like a promise of freedom.

She told her husband she wanted to have an *au pair* girl.°

They were in their bedroom, it was late at night, the children slept. He sat, shirted and slippered, in a chair by the window, looking out. She sat brushing her hair and watching him in the mirror. A time-hallowed scene in the connubial bedroom. He said nothing, while she heard the arguments coming into his mind, only to be rejected because every one was *reasonable.*

"It seems strange to get one now; after all, the children are in school most of the day. Surely the time for you to have help was when you were stuck with them day and night. Why don't you ask Mrs. Parkes to cook for you? She's even offered to—I can understand if you are tired of cooking for six people. But you know that an *au pair* girl means all kinds of problems; it's not like having an ordinary char° in during the day. . . ."

Finally he said carefully: "Are you thinking of going back to work?"

"No," she said, "no, not really." She made herself sound vague, rather stupid. She went on brushing her black hair and peering at herself so as to be oblivious of the short uneasy glances her Matthew kept giving her. "Do you think we can't afford it?" she went on vaguely, not at all the old efficient Susan who knew exactly what they could afford.

"It's not that," he said, looking out of the window at dark trees, so as not to look at her. Meanwhile she examined a round, candid, pleasant face with clear dark brows and clear grey eyes. A sensible face. She brushed thick healthy black

95

---

au pair *girl*: Live-in baby sitter and family helper. *char*: Cleaning person.

hair and thought: Yet that's the reflection of a madwoman. How very strange! Much more to the point if what looked back at me was the gingery green-eyed demon with his dry meager smile. . . . Why wasn't Matthew agreeing? After all, what else could he do? She was breaking her part of the bargain and there was no way of forcing her to keep it: that her spirit, her soul, should live in this house, so that the people in it could grow like plants in water, and Mrs. Parkes remain content in their service. In return for this, he would be a good loving husband, and responsible towards the children. Well, nothing like this had been true of either of them for a long time. He did his duty, perfunctorily; she did not even pretend to do hers. And he had become like other husbands, with his real life in his work and the people he met there, and very likely a serious affair. All this was her fault.

At last he drew heavy curtains, blotting out the trees, and turned to force   100 her attention: "Susan, are you really sure we need a girl?" But she would not meet his appeal at all. She was running the brush over her hair again and again, lifting fine black clouds in a small hiss of electricity. She was peering in and smiling as if she were amused at the clinging hissing hair that followed the brush.

"Yes, I think it would be a good idea, on the whole," she said, with the cunning of a madwoman evading the real point.

In the mirror she could see her Matthew lying on his back, his hands behind his head, staring upwards, his face sad and hard. She felt her heart (the old heart of Susan Rawlings) soften and call out to him. But she set it to be indifferent.

He said: "Susan, the children?" It was an appeal that *almost* reached her. He opened his arms, lifting them palms up, empty. She had only to run across and fling herself into them, onto his hard, warm chest, and melt into herself, into Susan. But she could not. She would not see his lifted arms. She said vaguely: "Well, surely it'll be even better for them? We'll get a French or a German girl and they'll learn the language."

In the dark she lay beside him, feeling frozen, a stranger. She felt as if Susan had been spirited away. She disliked very much this woman who lay here, cold and indifferent beside a suffering man, but she could not change her.

Next morning she set about getting a girl, and very soon came Sophie Traub   105 from Hamburg, a girl of twenty, laughing, healthy, blue-eyed, intending to learn English. Indeed, she already spoke a good deal. In return for a room—"Mother's Room"—and her food, she undertook to do some light cooking, and to be with the children when Mrs. Rawlings asked. She was an intelligent girl and understood perfectly what was needed. Susan said: "I go off sometimes, for the morning or for the day—well, sometimes the children run home from school, or they ring up, or a teacher rings up. I should be here, really. And there's the daily woman. . . ." And Sophie laughed her deep fruity fräulein's laugh, showed her fine white teeth and her dimples, and said: "You want some person to play mistress of the house sometimes, not so?"

"Yes, that is just so," said Susan, a bit dry, despite herself, thinking in secret fear how easy it was, how much nearer to the end she was than she thought. Healthy Fräulein Traub's instant understanding of their position proved this to be true.

The *au pair* girl, because of her own common sense, or (as Susan said to herself, with her new inward shudder) because she had been *chosen* so well by Susan, was a success with everyone, the children liking her, Mrs. Parkes forgetting almost at once that she was German, and Matthew finding her "nice to have around the house." For he was now taking things as they came, from the surface of life, withdrawn both as a husband and a father from the household.

One day Susan saw how Sophie and Mrs. Parkes were talking and laughing in the kitchen, and she announced that she would be away until teatime. She knew exactly where to go and what she must look for. She took the District Line to South Kensington, changed to the Circle, got off at Paddington, and walked around looking at the smaller hotels until she was satisfied with one which had FRED'S HOTEL painted on window-panes that needed cleaning. The façade was a faded shiny yellow, like unhealthy skin. A door at the end of a passage said she must knock; she did, and Fred appeared. He was not at all attractive, not in any way, being fattish, and run-down, and wearing a tasteless striped suit. He had small sharp eyes in a white creased face, and was quite prepared to let Mrs. Jones (she chose the farcical name deliberately, staring him out) have a room three days a week from ten until six. Provided of course that she paid in advance each time she came? Susan produced fifteen shillings (no price had been set by him) and held it out, still fixing him with a bold unblinking challenge she had not known until then she could use at will. Looking at her still, he took up a ten-shilling note from her palm between thumb and forefinger, fingered it; then shuffled up two half-crowns, held out his own palm with these bits of money displayed thereon, and let his gaze lower broodingly at them. They were standing in the passage, a red-shaded light above, bare boards beneath, and a strong smell of floor polish rising about them. He shot his gaze up at her over the still-extended palm, and smiled as if to say: What do you take me for? "I shan't," said Susan, "be using this room for the purposes of making money." He still waited. She added another five shillings, at which he nodded and said: "You pay, and I ask no questions." "Good," said Susan. He now went past her to the stairs, and there waited a moment: the light from the street door being in her eyes, she lost sight of him momentarily. Then she saw a sober-suited, white-faced, white-balding little man trotting up the stairs like a waiter, and she went after him. They proceeded in utter silence up the stairs of this house where no questions were asked—Fred's Hotel, which could afford the freedom for its visitors that poor Miss Townsend's hotel could not. The room was hideous. It had a single window, with thin green brocade curtains, a three-quarter bed that had a cheap green satin bedspread on it, a fireplace with a gas fire and a shilling meter by it, a chest of drawers, and a green wicker armchair.

"Thank you," said Susan, knowing that Fred (if this was Fred, and not George, or Herbert or Charlie) was looking at her, not so much with curiosity, an emotion he would not own to, for professional reasons, but with a philosophical sense of what was appropriate. Having taken her money and shown her up and agreed to everything, he was clearly disapproving of her for coming here. She did not belong here at all, so his look said. (But she knew, already, how very much she did belong: the room had been waiting for her to join it.) "Would you have me called at five o'clock, please?" and he nodded and went downstairs.

It was twelve in the morning. She was free. She sat in the armchair, she simply sat, she closed her eyes and sat and let herself be alone. She was alone and no one knew where she was. When a knock came on the door she was annoyed, and prepared to show it: but it was Fred himself; it was five o'clock and he was calling her as ordered. He flicked his sharp little eyes over the room—bed, first. It

110

was undisturbed. She might never have been in the room at all. She thanked him, said she would be returning the day after tomorrow, and left. She was back home in time to cook supper, to put the children to bed, to cook a second supper for her husband and herself later. And to welcome Sophie back from the pictures where she had gone with a friend. All these things she did cheerfully, willingly. But she was thinking all the time of the hotel room; she was longing for it with her whole being.

Three times a week. She arrived promptly at ten, looked Fred in the eyes, gave him twenty shillings, followed him up the stairs, went into the room, and shut the door on him with gentle firmness. For Fred, disapproving of her being here at all, was quite ready to let friendship, or at least acquaintanceship, follow his disapproval, if only she would let him. But he was content to go off on her dismissing nod, with the twenty shillings in his hand.

She sat in the armchair and shut her eyes.

What did she *do* in the room? Why, nothing at all. From the chair, when it had rested her, she went to the window, stretching her arms, smiling, treasuring her anonymity, to look out. She was no longer Susan Rawlings, mother of four, wife of Matthew, employer of Mrs. Parkes and of Sophie Traub, with these and those relations with friends, schoolteachers, tradesmen. She no longer was mistress of the big white house and garden, owning clothes suitable for this and that activity or occasion. She was Mrs. Jones, and she was alone, and she had no past and no future. Here I am, she thought, after all these years of being married and having children and playing those roles of responsibility—and I'm just the same. Yet there have been times I thought that nothing existed of me except the roles that went with being Mrs. Matthew Rawlings. Yes, here I am, and if I never saw any of my family again, here I would still be . . . how very strange that is! And she leaned on the sill, and looked into the street, loving the men and women who passed, because she did not know them. She looked at the downtrodden buildings over the street, and at the sky, wet and dingy, or sometimes blue, and she felt she had never seen buildings or sky before. And then she went back to the chair, empty, her mind a blank. Sometimes she talked aloud, saying nothing—an exclamation, meaningless, followed by a comment about the floral pattern on the thin rug, or a stain on the green satin coverlet. For the most part, she wool-gathered—what word is there for it?—brooded, wandered, simply went dark, feeling emptiness run deliciously through her veins like the movement of her blood.

This room had become more her own than the house she lived in. One morning she found Fred taking her a flight higher than usual. She stopped, refusing to go up, and demanded her usual room, Number 19. "Well, you'll have to wait half an hour, then," he said. Willingly she descended to the dark disinfectant-smelling hall, and sat waiting until the two, man and woman, came down the stairs, giving her swift indifferent glances before they hurried out into the street, separating at the door. She went up to the room, *her* room, which they had just vacated. It was no less hers, though the windows were set wide open, and a maid was straightening the bed as she came in.

After these days of solitude, it was both easy to play her part as mother and wife, and difficult—because it was so easy: she felt an impostor. She felt as if her shell moved here, with her family, answering to Mummy, Mother, Susan, Mrs. Rawlings. She was surprised no one saw through her, that she wasn't turned out of doors, as a fake. On the contrary, it seemed the children loved her more; 115

Matthew and she "got on" pleasantly, and Mrs. Parkes was happy in her work under (for the most part, it must be confessed) Sophie-Traub. At night she lay beside her husband, and they made love again, apparently just as they used to, when they were really married. But she, Susan, or the being who answered so readily and improbably to the name of Susan, was not there: she was in Fred's Hotel, in Paddington, waiting for the easing hours of solitude to begin.

Soon she made a new arrangement with Fred and with Sophie. It was for five days a week. As for the money, five pounds, she simply asked Matthew for it. She saw that she was not even frightened he might ask what for: he would give it to her, she knew that, and yet it was terrifying it could be so, for this close couple, these partners, had once known the destination of every shilling they must spend. He agreed to give her five pounds a week. She asked for just so much, not a penny more. He sounded indifferent about it. It was as if he were paying her, she thought: *paying her off*—yes, that was it. Terror came back for a moment when she understood this, but she stilled it: things had gone too far for that. Now, every week, on Sunday nights, he gave her five pounds, turning away from her before their eyes could meet on the transaction. As for Sophie Traub, she was to be somewhere in or near the house until six at night, after which she was free. She was not to cook, or to clean; she was simply to be there. So she gardened or sewed, and asked friends in, being a person who was bound to have a lot of friends. If the children were sick, she nursed them. If teachers telephoned, she answered them sensibly. For the five daytimes in the school week, she was altogether the mistress of the house.

One night in the bedroom, Matthew asked: "Susan, I don't want to interfere—don't think that, please—but are you sure you are well?"

She was brushing her hair at the mirror. She made two more strokes on either side of her head, before she replied: "Yes, dear, I am sure I am well."

He was again lying on his back, his blond head on his hands, his elbows angled up and part-concealing his face. He said: "Then Susan, I have to ask you this question, though you must understand, I'm not putting any sort of pressure on you." (Susan heard the word "pressure" with dismay, because this was inevitable; of course she could not go on like this.) "Are things going to go on like this?"

"Well," she said, going vague and bright and idiotic again, so as to escape: 120 "Well, I don't see why not."

He was jerking his elbows up and down, in annoyance or in pain, and, looking at him, she saw he had got thin, even gaunt; and restless angry movements were not what she remembered of him. He said: "Do you want a divorce, is that it?"

At this, Susan only with the greatest difficulty stopped herself from laughing: she could hear the bright bubbling laughter she *would* have emitted, had she let herself. He could only mean one thing: she had a lover, and that was why she spent her days in London, as lost to him as if she had vanished to another continent.

Then the small panic set in again: she understood that he hoped she did have a lover, he was begging her to say so, because otherwise it would be too terrifying.

She thought this out as she brushed her hair, watching the fine black stuff fly up to make its little clouds of electricity, hiss, hiss, hiss. Behind her head, across the room, was a blue wall. She realized she was absorbed in watching the black hair making shapes against the blue. She should be answering him. "Do *you* want a divorce, Matthew?"

He said: "That surely isn't the point, is it?"   125

"You brought it up, I didn't," she said, brightly, suppressing meaningless tinkling laughter.

Next day she asked Fred: "Have inquiries been made for me?"

He hesitated, and she said: "I've been coming here a year now. I've made no trouble, and you've been paid every day. I have a right to be told."

"As a matter of fact, Mrs. Jones, a man did come asking."

"A man from a detective agency?"   130

"Well, he could have been, couldn't he?"

"I was asking you.. . . . Well, what did you tell him?"

"I told him a Mrs. Jones came every weekday from ten until five or six and stayed in Number 19 by herself."

"Describing me?"

"Well, Mrs. Jones, I had no alternative. Put yourself in my place."   135

"By rights I should deduct what that man gave you for the information."

He raised shocked eyes: she was not the sort of person to make jokes like this! Then he chose to laugh: a pinkish wet slit appeared across his white crinkled face; his eyes positively begged her to laugh, otherwise he might lose some money. She remained grave, looking at him.

He stopped laughing and said: "You want to go up now?"—returning to the familiarity, the comradeship, of the country where no questions are asked, on which (and he knew it) she depended completely.

She went up to sit in her wicker chair. But it was not the same. Her husband had searched her out. (The world had searched her out.) The pressures were on her. She was here with his connivance. He might walk in at any moment, here, into Room 19. She imagined the report from the detective agency: "A woman calling herself Mrs. Jones, fitting the description of your wife (et cetera, et cetera, et cetera), stays alone all day in Room No. 19. She insists on this room, waits for it if it is engaged. As far as the proprietor knows, she receives no visitors there, male or female." A report something on these lines Matthew must have received.

Well, of course he was right: things couldn't go on like this. He had put an   140
end to it all simply by sending the detective after her.

She tried to shrink herself back into the shelter of the room, a snail pecked out of its shell and trying to squirm back. But the peace of the room had gone. She was trying consciously to revive it, trying to let go into the dark creative trance (or whatever it was) that she had found there. It was no use, yet she craved it, she was as ill as a suddenly deprived addict.

Several times she returned to the room, to look for herself there, but instead she found the unnamed spirit of restlessness, a pricking fevered hunger for movement, an irritable self-consciousness that made her brain feel as if it had colored lights going on and off inside it. Instead of the soft dark that had been the room's air, were now waiting for her demons that made her dash blindly about, muttering words of hate; she was impelling herself from point to point like a moth dashing itself against a windowpane, sliding to the bottom, fluttering off on broken wings, then crashing into the invisible barrier again. And again and again. Soon she was exhausted, and she told Fred that for a while she would not be needing the room, she was going on holiday. Home she went, to the big white house by the river. The middle of a weekday, and she felt guilty at returning to her own home when not expected. She stood unseen, looking in at the kitchen window. Mrs. Parkes, wearing a discarded floral overall of Susan's, was stooping to slide something into the oven. Sophie, arms folded, was leaning her back against a cupboard and laughing at some joke made by a girl not seen before by Susan—a dark foreign girl, Sophie's visitor. In an armchair Molly, one of the twins, lay curled, sucking her thumb and watching the grown-ups. She must have some sickness, to be kept from school. The child's listless face, the dark circles under her eyes, hurt Susan: Molly was looking at the three grown-ups working and talking in exactly the same way Susan looked at the four through the kitchen window: she was remote, shut off from them.

But then, just as Susan imagined herself going in, picking up the little girl, and sitting in an armchair with her, stroking her probably heated forehead, Sophie did just that: she had been standing on one leg, the other knee flexed, its foot set against the wall. Now she let her foot in its ribbon-tied red shoe slide down the wall, stood solid on two feet, clapping her hands before and behind her, and sang a couple of lines in German, so that the child lifted her heavy eyes at her and began to smile. Then she walked, or rather skipped, over to the child, swung her up, and let her fall into her lap at the same moment she sat herself. She said "Hopla! Hopla! Molly . . ." and began stroking the dark untidy young head that Molly laid on her shoulder for comfort.

Well. . . . Susan blinked the tears of farewell out of her eyes, and went quietly up through the house to her bedroom. There she sat looking at the river through the trees. She felt at peace, but in a way that was new to her. She had no desire to move, to talk, to do anything at all. The devils that had haunted the house, the garden, were not there; but she knew it was because her soul was in Room 19 in Fred's Hotel; she was not really here at all. It was a sensation that should have been frightening: to sit at her own bedroom window, listening to Sophie's rich young voice sing German nursery songs to her child, listening to Mrs. Parkes clatter and move below, and to know that all this had nothing to do with her: she was already out of it.

Later, she made herself go down and say she was home: it was unfair to be here unannounced. She took lunch with Mrs. Parkes, Sophie, Sophie's Italian friend Maria, and her daughter Molly, and felt like a visitor. 145

A few days later, at bedtime, Matthew said: "Here's your five pounds," and pushed them over at her. Yet he must have known she had not been leaving the house at all.

She shook her head, gave it back to him, and said, in explanation, not in accusation: "As soon as you knew where I was, there was no point."

He nodded, not looking at her. He was turned away from her: thinking, she knew, how best to handle this wife who terrified him.

He said: "I wasn't trying to . . . It's just that I was worried."

"Yes, I know." 150

"I must confess that I was beginning to wonder . . ."

"You thought I had a lover?"

"Yes, I am afraid I did."

She knew that he wished she had. She sat wondering how to say: "For a year now I've been spending all my days in a very sordid hotel room. It's the place where I'm happy. In fact, without it I don't exist." She heard herself saying this, and understood how terrified he was that she might. So instead she said: "Well, perhaps you're not far wrong."

Probably Matthew would think the hotel proprietor lied: he would want to   155 think so.

"Well," he said, and she could hear his voice spring up, so to speak, with relief, "in that case I must confess I've got a bit of an affair on myself."

She said, detached and interested: "Really? Who is she?" and saw Matthew's startled look because of this reaction.

"It's Phil. Phil Hunt."

She had known Phil Hunt well in the old unmarried days. She was thinking: No, she won't do, she's too neurotic and difficult. She's never been happy yet. Sophie's much better. Well, Matthew will see that himself, as sensible as he is.

This line of thought went on in silence, while she said aloud: "It's no point   160 telling you about mine, because you don't know him."

Quick, quick, invent, she thought. Remember how you invented all that nonsense for Miss Townsend.

She began slowly, careful not to contradict herself: "His name is Michael" (*Michael What?*)—"Michael Plant." (What a silly name!) "He's rather like you—in looks, I mean." And indeed, she could imagine herself being touched by no one but Matthew himself. "He's a publisher." (Really? Why?) "He's got a wife already and two children."

She brought out this fantasy, proud of herself.

Matthew said: "Are you two thinking of marrying?"

She said, before she could stop herself: "Good, God, *no!*"   165

She realized, if Matthew wanted to marry Phil Hunt, that this was too emphatic, but apparently it was all right, for his voice sounded relieved as he said: "It is a bit impossible to imagine oneself married to anyone else, isn't it?" With which he pulled her to him, so that her head lay on his shoulder. She turned her face into the dark of his flesh, and listened to the blood pounding through her ears saying: I am alone, I am alone, I am alone.

In the morning Susan lay in bed while he dressed.

He had been thinking things out in the night, because now he said: "Susan, why don't we make a foursome?"

Of course, she said to herself, of course he would be bound to say that. If one is sensible, if one is reasonable, if one never allows oneself a base thought or an envious emotion, naturally one says: Let's make a foursome!

"Why not?" she said.   170

"We could all meet for lunch. I mean, it's ridiculous, you sneaking off to filthy hotels, and me staying late at the office, and all the lies everyone has to tell."

What on earth did I say his name was?—she panicked, then said: "I think it's a good idea, but Michael is away at the moment. When he comes back, though—and I'm sure you two would like each other."

"He's away, is he? So that's why you've been . . ." Her husband put his hand to the knot of his tie in a gesture of male coquetry she would not before have associated with him; and he bent to kiss her cheek with the expression that goes with the words: Oh you naughty little puss! And she felt its answering look, naughty and coy, come onto her face.

Inside she was dissolving in horror at them both, at how far they had both sunk from honesty of emotion.

So now she was saddled with a lover, and he had a mistress! How ordinary, 175
how reassuring, how jolly! And now they would make a foursome of it, and go
about to theatres and restaurants. After all, the Rawlings could well afford that
sort of thing, and presumably the publisher Michael Plant could afford to do himself and his mistress quite well. No, there was nothing to stop the four of them
developing the most intricate relationship of civilized tolerance, all enveloped in
a charming afterglow of autumnal passion. Perhaps they would all go off on holidays together? She had known people who did. Or perhaps Matthew would draw
the line there? Why should he, though, if he was capable of talking about "four-
somes" at all?

She lay in the empty bedroom, listening to the car drive off with Matthew
in it, off to work. Then she heard the children clattering off to school to the accompaniment of Sophie's cheerfully ringing voice. She slid down into the hollow
of the bed, for shelter against her own irrelevance. And she stretched out her hand
to the hollow where her husband's body had lain, but found no comfort there:
he was not her husband. She curled herself up in a small tight ball under the
clothes: she could stay here all day, all week, indeed, all her life.

But in a few days she must produce Michael Plant, and—but how? She must
presumably find some agreeable man prepared to impersonate a publisher called
Michael Plant. And in return for which she would—what? Well, for one thing
they would make love. The idea made her want to cry with sheer exhaustion. Oh,
no, she had finished with all that—the proof of it was that the words "make love,"
or even imagining it, trying hard to revive no more than the pleasures of sensu-
ality, let alone affection, or love, made her want to run away and hide from the
sheer effort of the thing. . . . Good Lord, why make love at all? Why make love
with anyone? Or if you are going to make love, what does it matter who with?
Why shouldn't she simply walk into the street, pick up a man, and have a roaring
sexual affair with him? Why not? Or even with Fred? What difference did it make?

But she had let herself in for it—an interminable stretch of time with a lover,
called Michael, as part of a gallant civilized foursome. Well, she could not, and
she would not.

She got up, dressed, went down to find Mrs. Parkes, and asked her for the
loan of a pound, since Matthew, she said, had forgotten to leave her money. She
exchanged with Mrs. Parkes variations on the theme that husbands are all the
same, they don't think, and without saying a word to Sophie, whose voice could
be heard upstairs from the telephone, walked to the underground, traveled to
South Kensington, changed to the Inner Circle, got out at Paddington, and walked
to Fred's Hotel. There she told Fred that she wasn't going on holiday after all,
she needed the room. She would have to wait an hour, Fred said. She went to a
busy tearoom-cum-restaurant around the corner, and sat watching the people
flow in and out the door that kept swinging open and shut, watched them mingle and merge, and separate, felt her being flow into them, into their movement.
When the hour was up, she left a half-crown for her pot of tea, and left the place
without looking back at it, just as she had left her house, the big, beautiful white
house, without another look, but silently dedicating it to Sophie. She returned
to Fred, received the key of Number 19, now free, and ascended the grimy stairs
slowly, letting floor after floor fall away below her, keeping her eyes lifted, so that
floor after floor descended jerkily to her level of vision, and fell away out of sight.

Number 19 was the same. She saw everything with an acute, narrow, check- 180 ing glance: the cheap shine of the satin spread, which had been replaced carelessly after the two bodies had finished their convulsions under it; a trace of powder on the glass that topped the chest of drawers; an intense green shade in a fold of the curtain. She stood at the window, looking down, watching people pass and pass and pass until her mind went dark from the constant movement. Then she sat in the wicker chair, letting herself go slack. But she had to be careful, because she did not want, today, to be surprised by Fred's knock at five o'clock.

The demons were not here. They had gone forever, because she was buying her freedom from them. She was slipping already into the dark fructifying dream that seemed to caress her inwardly, like the movement of her blood . . . but she had to think about Matthew first. Should she write a letter for the coroner? But what should she say? She would like to leave him with the look on his face she had seen this morning—banal, admittedly, but at least confidently healthy. Well, that was impossible, one did not look like that with a wife dead from suicide. But how to leave him believing she was dying because of a man—because of the fascinating publisher Michael Plant? Oh, how ridiculous! How absurd! How humiliating! But she decided not to trouble about it, simply not to think about the living. If he wanted to believe she had a lover, he would believe it. And he *did* want to believe it. Even when he had found out that there was no publisher in London called Michael Plant, he would think: Oh poor Susan, she was afraid to give me his real name.

And what did it matter whether he married Phil Hunt or Sophie? Though it ought to be Sophie, who was already the mother of those children . . . and what hypocrisy to sit here worrying about the children, when she was going to leave them because she had not got the energy to stay.

She had about four hours. She spent them delightfully, darkly, sweetly, letting herself slide gently, gently, to the edge of the river. Then, with hardly a break in her consciousness, she got up, pushed the thin rug against the door, made sure the windows were tight shut, put two shillings in the meter, and turned on the gas. For the first time since she had been in the room she lay on the hard bed that smelled stale, that smelled of sweat and sex.

She lay on her back on the green satin cover, but her legs were chilly. She got up, found a blanket folded in the bottom of the chest of drawers, and carefully covered her legs with it. She was quite content lying there, listening to the faint soft hiss of the gas that poured into the room, into her lungs, into her brain, as she drifted off into the dark river.

Katherine Mansfield   (1888–1923)

Katherine Mansfield changed her name from Kathleen Beauchamp when she began writing. She was born in Wellington, New Zealand, and was educated at school in England, where she eventually decided to remain. Her first collection of stories, In a German Pension *(1911), developed mostly in response to a short period spent in Bavaria. Determined to be a writer, Mansfield produced short stories and reviews on a regular basis and eventually married the critic John Middleton Murry in 1918. Her New Zealand background is apparent in her collections* Bliss and Other Stories *(1920) and* The Garden-Party and Other Stories *(1922). Mansfield's writing career was short. She contracted tuberculosis, and after a sickness of several years—during which she worked continuously—she died at the age of thirty-four. Much of her work was published after her death, including stories, letters, criticism, and poems.* Collected Stories *was published in 1945. She has been praised for having given the short story a modern direction away from concentration on plot and more toward development of character through the use of stream of consciousness.*

THE GARDEN-PARTY   1922

And after all the weather was ideal. They could not have had a more perfect day for a garden-party if they had ordered it. Windless, warm, the sky without a cloud. Only the blue was veiled with a haze of light gold, as it is sometimes in early summer. The gardener had been up since dawn, mowing the lawns and sweeping them, until the grass and the dark flat rosettes where the daisy plants had been seemed to shine. As for the roses, you could not help feeling they understood that roses are the only flowers that impress people at garden-parties; the only flowers that everybody is certain of knowing. Hundreds, yes, literally hundreds, had come out in a single night; the green bushes bowed down as though they had been visited by archangels.

Breakfast was not yet over before the men came to put up the marquee.

"Where do you want the marquee put, mother?"

"My dear child, it's no use asking me. I'm determined to leave everything to you children this year. Forget I am your mother. Treat me as an honored guest."

But Meg could not possibly go and supervise the men. She had washed her   5
hair before breakfast, and she sat drinking her coffee in a green turban, with a dark wet curl stamped on each cheek. Jose, the butterfly, always came down in a silk petticoat and a kimono jacket.

"You'll have to go, Laura; you're the artistic one."

Away Laura flew, still holding her piece of bread-and-butter. It's so delicious to have an excuse for eating out of doors, and besides, she loved having to arrange things; she always felt she could do it so much better than anybody else.

Four men in their shirt-sleeves stood grouped together on the garden path. They carried staves covered with rolls of canvas, and they had big tool-bags slung on their backs. They looked impressive. Laura wished now that she had not got the bread-and-butter, but there was nowhere to put it, and she couldn't possibly throw it away. She blushed and tried to look severe and even a little bit short-sighted as she came up to them.

"Good morning," she said, copying her mother's voice. But that sounded so fearfully affected that she was ashamed, and stammered like a little girl, "Oh—er—have you come—is it about the marquee?"

"That's right, miss," said the tallest of the men, a lanky, freckled fellow, and   10
he shifted his tool-bag, knocked back his straw hat and smiled down at her. "That's about it."

His smile was so easy, so friendly that Laura recovered. What nice eyes he had, small, but such a dark blue! And now she looked at the others, they were smiling too. "Cheer up, we won't bite," their smile seemed to say. How very nice workmen were! And what a beautiful morning! She mustn't mention the morning; she must be businesslike. The marquee.

"Well, what about the lily-lawn? Would that do?"

And she pointed to the lily-lawn with the hand that didn't hold the bread-and-butter. They turned, they stared in the direction. A little fat chap thrust out his under-lip, and the tall fellow frowned.

"I don't fancy it," said he. "Not conspicuous enough. You see, with a thing like a marquee," and he turned to Laura in his easy way, "you want to put it somewhere where it'll give you a bang slap in the eye, if you follow me."

Laura's upbringing made her wonder for a moment whether it was quite re- 15
spectful of a workman to talk to her of bangs slap in the eye. But she did quite follow him.

"A corner of the tennis-court," she suggested. "But the band's going to be in one corner."

"H'm, going to have a band, are you?" said another of the workmen. He was pale. He had a haggard look as his dark eyes scanned the tennis court. What was he thinking?

"Only a very small band," said Laura gently. Perhaps he wouldn't mind so much if the band was quite small. But the tall fellow interrupted.

"Look here, miss, that's the place. Against those trees. Over there. That'll do fine."

Against the karakas.° Then the karaka-trees would be hidden. And they were 20
so lovely, with their broad, gleaming leaves, and their clusters of yellow fruit. They were like trees you imagined growing on a desert island, proud, solitary, lifting their leaves and fruits to the sun in a kind of silent splendor. Must they be hidden by a marquee?

They must. Already the men had shouldered their staves and were making for the place. Only the tall fellow was left. He bent down, pinched a sprig of lavender, put his thumb and forefinger to his nose and snuffed up the smell. When Laura saw that gesture she forgot all about the karakas in her wonder at him caring for things like that—caring for the smell of lavender. How many men that she knew would have done such a thing? Oh, how extraordinarily nice workmen were, she thought. Why couldn't she have workmen for friends rather than the silly boys she danced with and who came to Sunday night supper? She would get on much better with men like these.

It's all the fault, she decided, as the tall fellow drew something on the back of an envelope, something that was to be looped up or left to hang, of these absurd class distinctions. Well, for her part, she didn't feel them. Not a bit, not an atom. . . . And now there came the chock-chock of wooden hammers. Someone whistled, someone sang out, "Are you right there, matey?" "Matey!" The friendliness of it, the—the——Just to prove how happy she was, just to show the tall fellow how at home she felt, and how she despised stupid conventions, Laura took a big bite of her bread-and-butter as she stared at the little drawing. She felt just like a work-girl.

"Laura, Laura, where are you? Telephone, Laura!" a voice cried from the house.

"Coming!" Away she skimmed, over the lawn, up the path, up the steps, across the veranda, and into the porch. In the hall her father and Laurie were brushing their hats ready to go to the office.

---

karakas: New Zealand trees somewhat resembling laurels.

"I say, Laura," said Laurie very fast, "you might just give a squiz at my coat   25
before this afternoon. See if it wants pressing."

"I will," said she. Suddenly she couldn't stop herself. She ran at Laurie and
gave him a small, quick squeeze. "Oh, I do love parties, don't you?" gasped Laura.

"Ra-ther," said Laurie's warm, boyish voice, and he squeezed his sister too,
and gave her a gentle push. "Dash off to the telephone, old girl."

The telephone. "Yes, yes; oh yes. Kitty? Good morning, dear. Come to lunch?
Do, dear. Delighted of course. It will only be a very scratch meal—just the sandwich crusts and broken meringue-shells and what's left over. Yes, isn't it a perfect
morning? Your white? Oh, I certainly should. One moment—hold the line.
Mother's calling." And Laura sat back. "What, mother? Can't hear."

Mrs. Sheridan's voice floated down the stairs. "Tell her to wear that sweet
hat she had on last Sunday."

"Mother says you're to wear that *sweet* hat you had on last Sunday. Good.   30
One o'clock. Bye-bye."

Laura put back the receiver, flung her arms over her head, took a deep breath,
stretched and let them fall. "Huh," she sighed, and the moment after the sigh she
sat up quickly. She was still, listening. All the doors in the house seemed to be open.
The house was alive with soft, quick steps and running voices. The green baize door
that led to the kitchen regions swung open and shut with a muffled thud. And now
there came a long, chuckling absurd sound. It was the heavy piano being moved
on its stiff castors. But the air! If you stopped to notice, was the air always like this?
Little faint winds were playing chase, in at the tops of the windows, out at the doors.
And there were two tiny spots of sun, one on the inkpot, one on a silver photograph frame, playing too. Darling little spots. Especially the one on the inkpot lid.
It was quite warm. A warm little silver star. She could have kissed it.

The front door bell pealed, and there sounded the rustle of Sadie's print skirt
on the stairs. A man's voice murmured; Sadie answered, careless, "I'm sure I don't
know. Wait. I'll ask Mrs. Sheridan."

"What is it, Sadie?" Laura came into the hall.

"It's the florist, Miss Laura."

It was, indeed. There, just inside the door, stood a wide, shallow tray full of   35
pots of pink lilies. No other kind. Nothing but lilies—canna lilies, big pink flowers, wide open, radiant, almost frighteningly alive on bright crimson stems.

"O-oh, Sadie!" said Laura, and the sound was like a little moan. She crouched
down as if to warm herself at that blaze of lilies; she felt they were in her fingers,
on her lips, growing in her breast.

"It's some mistake," she said faintly. "Nobody ever ordered so many. Sadie,
go and find mother."

But at that moment Mrs. Sheridan joined them.

"It's quite right," she said calmly. "Yes, I ordered them. Aren't they lovely?"
She pressed Laura's arm. "I was passing the shop yesterday, and I saw them in
the window. And I suddenly thought for once in my life I shall have enough canna
lilies. The garden-party will be a good excuse."

"But I thought you said you didn't mean to interfere," said Laura. Sadie had   40
gone. The florist's man was still outside at his van. She put her arm round her
mother's neck and gently, very gently, she bit her mother's ear.

"My darling child, you wouldn't like a logical mother, would you? Don't do
that. Here's the man."

He carried more lilies still, another whole tray.

"Bank them up, just inside the door, on both sides of the porch, please," said Mrs. Sheridan. "Don't you agree, Laura?"

"Oh, I *do*, mother."

In the drawing-room Meg, Jose and good little Hans had at last succeeded   45
in moving the piano.

"Now, if we put this chesterfield against the wall and move everything out of the room except the chairs, don't you think?"

"Quite."

"Hans, move these tables into the smoking-room, and bring a sweeper to take these marks off the carpet and—one moment, Hans———" Jose loved giving orders to the servants, and they loved obeying her. She always made them feel they were taking part in some drama. "Tell mother and Miss Laura to come here at once."

"Very good, Miss Jose."

She turned to Meg. "I want to hear what the piano sounds like, just in case   50
I'm asked to sing this afternoon. Let's try over 'This life is Weary.'"

Pom! Ta-ta-ta *Tee*-ta! The piano burst out so passionately that Jose's face changed. She clasped her hands. She looked mournfully and enigmatically at her mother and Laura as they came in.

> This Life is *Wee*-ary,
> A Tear—a Sigh,
> A Love that *Chan*-ges,
>   This Life is *Wee*-ary,
> A Tear—a Sigh.
> A Love that *Chan*-ges,
> And then . . . Good-bye!

But at the word "Good-bye," and although the piano sounded more desperate than ever, her face broke into a brilliant, dreadfully unsympathetic smile.

"Aren't I in good voice, mummy?" she beamed.

> This Life is *Wee*-ary,
> Hope comes to Die.
> A Dream—a *Wa*-kening.

But now Sadie interrupted them. "What is it, Sadie?"

"If you please, m'm, cook says have you got the flags for the sandwiches?"   55

"The flags for the sandwiches, Sadie?" echoed Mrs. Sheridan dreamily. And the children knew by her face that she hadn't got them. "Let me see." And she said to Sadie firmly, "Tell cook I'll let her have them in ten minutes."

Sadie went.

"Now, Laura," said her mother quickly. "Come with me into the smoking-room. I've got the names somewhere on the back of an envelope. You'll have to write them out for me. Meg, go upstairs this minute and take that wet thing off your head. Jose, run and finish dressing this instant. Do you hear me, children, or shall I have to tell your father when he comes home to-night? And—and, Jose, pacify cook if you do go into the kitchen, will you? I'm terrified of her this morning."

The envelope was found at last behind the dining-room clock, though how it had got there Mrs. Sheridan could not imagine.

"One of you children must have stolen it out of my bag, because I remem- 60 ber vividly——cream cheese and lemon-curd. Have you done that?"

"Yes."

"Egg and——" Mrs. Sheridan held the envelope away from her. "It looks like mice. It can't be mice, can it?"

"Olive, pet," said Laura, looking over her shoulder.

"Yes, of course, olive. What a horrible combination it sounds. Egg and olive."

They were finished at last, and Laura took them off to the kitchen. She found 65 Jose there pacifying the cook, who did not look at all terrifying.

"I have never seen such exquisite sandwiches," said Jose's rapturous voice. "How many kinds did you say there were, cook? Fifteen?"

"Fifteen, Miss Jose."

"Well, cook, I congratulate you."

Cook swept up crusts with the long sandwich knife, and smiled broadly.

"Godber's has come," announced Sadie, issuing out of the pantry. She had 70 seen the man pass the window.

That meant the cream puffs had come. Godber's were famous for their cream puffs. Nobody ever thought of making them at home.

"Bring them in and put them on the table, my girl," ordered cook.

Sadie brought them in and went back to the door. Of course Laura and Jose were far too grown-up to really care about such things. All the same, they could- n't help agreeing that the puffs looked very attractive. Very. Cook began arranging them, shaking off the extra icing sugar.

"Don't they carry one back to all one's parties?" said Laura.

"I suppose they do," said practical Jose, who never liked to be carried back. 75 "They look beautifully light and feathery, I must say."

"Have one each, my dears," said cook in her comfortable voice. "Yer ma won't know."

Oh, impossible. Fancy cream puffs so soon after breakfast. The very idea made one shudder. All the same, two minutes later Jose and Laura were licking their fingers with that absorbed inward look that only comes from whipped cream.

"Let's go into the garden, out by the back way," suggested Laura. "I want to see how the men are getting on with the marquee. They're such awfully nice men."

But the back door was blocked by cook, Sadie, Godber's man and Hans. Something had happened. 80

"Tuk-tuk-tuk," clucked cook like an agitated hen. Sadie had her hand clapped to her cheek as though she had toothache. Hans's face was screwed up in the ef- fort to understand. Only Godber's man seemed to be enjoying himself; it was his story.

"What's the matter? What's happened?"

"There's been a horrible accident," said cook. "A man killed."

"A man killed! Where? How? When?"

But Godber's man wasn't going to have his story snatched from under his 85 very nose.

"Know those little cottages just below here, miss?" Know them? Of course, she knew them. "Well, there's a young chap living there, name of Scott, a carter.

His horse shied at a traction-engine, corner of Hawke Street this morning, and he was thrown out on the back of his head. Killed."

"Dead!" Laura stared at Godber's man.

"Dead when they picked him up," said Godber's man with relish. "They were taking the body home as I come up here." And he said to the cook, "He's left a wife and five little ones."

"Jose, come here." Laura caught hold of her sister's sleeve and dragged her through the kitchen to the other side of the green baize door. There she paused and leaned against it. "Jose!" she said, horrified, "however are we going to stop everything?"

"Stop everything, Laura!" cried Jose in astonishment. "What do you mean?"   90

"Stop the garden-party, of course." Why did Jose pretend?

But Jose was still more amazed. "Stop the garden-party? My dear Laura, don't be so absurd. Of course we can't do anything of the kind. Nobody expects us to. Don't be so extravagant."

"But we can't possibly have a garden-party with a man dead just outside the front gate."

That really was extravagant, for the little cottages were in a lane to themselves at the very bottom of a steep rise that led up to the house. A broad road ran between. True, they were far too near. They were the greatest possible eyesore, and they had no right to be in that neighborhood at all. They were little mean dwellings painted a chocolate brown. In the garden patches there was nothing but cabbage stalks, sick hens and tomato cans. The very smoke coming out of their chimneys was poverty-stricken. Little rags and shreds of smoke, so unlike the great silvery plumes that uncurled from the Sheridans' chimneys. Washerwomen lived in the lane and sweeps° and a cobbler, and a man whose house-front was studded all over with minute bird-cages. Children swarmed. When the Sheridans were little they were forbidden to set foot there because of the revolting language and of what they might catch. But since they were grown up, Laura and Laurie on their prowls sometimes walked through. It was disgusting and sordid. They came out with a shudder. But still one must go everywhere; one must see everything. So through they went.

"And just think of what the band would sound like to that poor woman,"   95 said Laura.

"Oh, Laura!" Jose began to be seriously annoyed. "If you're going to stop a band playing every time some one has an accident, you'll lead a very strenuous life. I'm every bit as sorry about it as you. I feel just as sympathetic." Her eyes hardened. She looked at her sister just as she used to when they were little and fighting together. "You won't bring a drunken workman back to life by being sentimental," she said softly.

"Drunk! Who said he was drunk?" Laura turned furiously on Jose. She said, just as they had used to say on those occasions, "I'm going straight up to tell mother."

"Do, dear," cooed Jose.

"Mother, can I come into your room?" Laura turned the big glass doorknob.

---

sweeps: Chimney sweeps.

"Of course, child. Why, what's the matter? What's given you such a color?" 100
And Mrs. Sheridan turned round from her dressing-table. She was trying on a
new hat.

"Mother, a man's been killed," began Laura.

"*Not* in the garden?" interrupted her mother.

"No, no!"

"Oh, what a fright you gave me!" Mrs. Sheridan sighed with relief, and took
off the big hat and held it on her knees.

"But listen, mother," said Laura. Breathless, half-choking, she told the dread- 105
ful story. "Of course, we can't have our party, can we?" she pleaded. "The band
and everybody arriving. They'd hear us, mother; they're nearly neighbors!"

To Laura's astonishment her mother behaved just like Jose; it was harder to
bear because she seemed amused. She refused to take Laura seriously.

"But, my dear child, use your common sense. It's only by accident we've
heard of it. If someone had died there normally—and I can't understand how
they keep alive in those poky little holes—we should still be having our party,
shouldn't we?"

Laura had to say "yes" to that, but she felt it was all wrong. She sat down
on her mother's sofa and pinched the cushion frill.

"Mother, isn't it really terribly heartless of us?" she asked.

"Darling!" Mrs. Sheridan got up and came over to her, carrying the hat. 110
Before Laura could stop her she had popped it on. "My child!" said her mother,
"the hat is yours. It's made for you. It's much too young for me. I have never seen
you look such a picture. Look at yourself!" And she held up her hand-mirror.

"But, mother," Laura began again. She couldn't look at herself; she turned
aside.

This time Mrs. Sheridan lost patience just as Jose had done.

"You are being very absurd, Laura," she said coldly. "People like that don't
expect sacrifices from us. And it's not very sympathetic to spoil everybody's enjoyment as you're doing now."

"I don't understand," said Laura, and she walked quickly out of the room
into her own bedroom. There, quite by chance, the first thing she saw was this
charming girl in the mirror, in her black hat trimmed with gold daisies, and a long
black velvet ribbon. Never had she imagined she could look like that. Is mother
right? she thought. And now she hoped her mother was right. Am I being extravagant? Perhaps it was extravagant. Just for a moment she had another glimpse
of that poor woman and those little children, and the body being carried into the
house. But it all seemed blurred, unreal, like a picture in the newspaper. I'll remember it again after the party's over, she decided. And somehow that seemed
quite the best plan. . . .

Lunch was over by half-past one. By half-past two they were all ready for the 115
fray. The green-coated band had arrived and was established in a corner of the
tennis-court.

"My dear!" trilled Kitty Maitland, "aren't they too like frogs for words? You
ought to have arranged them round the pond with the conductor in the middle
on a leaf."

Laurie arrived and hailed them on his way to dress. At the sight of him Laura
remembered the accident again. She wanted to tell him. If Laurie agreed with the
others, then it was bound to be all right. And she followed him into the hall.

"Laurie!"

"Hallo!" He was half-way upstairs, but when he turned round and saw Laura he suddenly puffed out his cheeks and goggled his eyes at her. "My word, Laura! You do look stunning," said Laurie. "What an absolutely topping hat!"

Laura said faintly "Is it?" and smiled up at Laurie, and didn't tell him after all.   120

Soon after that people began coming in streams. The band struck up; the hired waiters ran from the house to the marquee. Wherever you looked there were couples strolling, bending to the flowers, greeting, moving on over the lawn. They were like bright birds that had alighted in the Sheridans' garden for this one afternoon, on their way to—where? Ah, what happiness it is to be with people who all are happy, to press hands, press cheeks, smile into eyes.

"Darling Laura, how well you look!"

"What a becoming hat, child!"

"Laura, you look quite Spanish. I've never seen you look so striking."

And Laura, glowing, answered softly, "Have you had tea? Won't you have   125 an ice? The passion-fruit ices really are rather special." She ran to her father and begged him. "Daddy darling, can't the band have something to drink?"

And the perfect afternoon slowly ripened, slowly faded, slowly its petals closed.

"Never a more delightful garden-party . . ." "The greatest success . . ." "Quite the most . . ."

Laura helped her mother with the good-byes. They stood side by side in the porch till it was all over.

"All over, all over, thank heaven," said Mrs. Sheridan. "Round up the others, Laura. Let's go and have some fresh coffee. I'm exhausted. Yes, it's been very successful. But oh, these parties, these parties! Why will you children insist on giving parties!" And they all of them sat down in the deserted marquee.

"Have a sandwich, daddy dear. I wrote the flag."   130

"Thanks." Mr. Sheridan took a bite and the sandwich was gone. He took another. "I suppose you didn't hear of a beastly accident that happened today?" he said.

"My dear," said Mrs. Sheridan, holding up her hand, "we did. It nearly ruined the party. Laura insisted we should put it off."

"Oh, mother!" Laura didn't want to be teased about it.

"It was a horrible affair all the same," said Mr. Sheridan. "The chap was married too. Lived just below in the lane, and leaves a wife and half a dozen kiddies, so they say."

An awkward little silence fell. Mrs. Sheridan fidgeted with her cup. Really,   135 it was very tactless of father. . .

Suddenly she looked up. There on the table were all those sandwiches, cakes, puffs, all uneaten, all going to be wasted. She had one of her brilliant ideas.

"I know," she said. "Let's make up a basket. Let's send that poor creature some of this perfectly good food. At any rate, it will be the greatest treat for the children. Don't you agree? And she's sure to have neighbors calling in and so on. What a point to have it all ready prepared. Laura!" She jumped up. "Get me the big basket out of the stairs cupboard."

"But, mother, do you really think it's a good idea?" said Laura.

Again, how curious, she seemed to be different from them all. To take scraps from their party. Would the poor woman really like that?

"Of course! What's the matter with you today? An hour or two ago you were   140
insisting on us being sympathetic, and now——"

Oh, well! Laura ran for the basket. It was filled, it was heaped by her mother.

"Take it yourself, darling," said she. "Run down just as you are. No, wait,
take the arum lilies too. People of that class are so impressed by arum lilies."

"The stems will ruin her lace frock," said practical Jose.

So they would. Just in time. "Only the basket, then. And, Laura!"—her
mother followed her out of the marquee—"don't on any account——"

"What, mother?"   145

No, better not put such ideas into the child's head! "Nothing! Run along."

It was just growing dusky as Laura shut their garden gates. A big dog ran by
like a shadow. The road gleamed white, and down below in the hollow the little
cottages were in deep shade. How quiet it seemed after the afternoon. Here she
was going down the hill to somewhere where a man lay dead, and she couldn't
realize it. Why couldn't she? She stopped a minute. And it seemed to her that
kisses, voices, tinkling spoons, laughter, the smell of crushed grass were somehow
inside her. She had no room for anything else. How strange! She looked up at
the pale sky, and all she thought was, "Yes, it was the most successful party."

Now the broad road was crossed. The lane began, smoky and dark. Women
in shawls and men's tweed caps hurried by. Men hung over the palings; the children played in the doorways. A low hum came from the mean little cottages. In
some of them there was a flicker of light, and a shadow, crab-like, moved across
the window. Laura bent her head and hurried on. She wished now she had put
on a coat. How her frock shone! And the big hat with the velvet streamer—if only
it was another hat! Were the people looking at her? They must be. It was a mistake to have come; she knew all along it was a mistake. Should she go back even
now?

No, too late. This was the house. It must be. A dark knot of people stood
outside. Beside the gate an old, old woman with a crutch sat in a chair, watching.
She had her feet on a newspaper. The voices stopped as Laura drew near. The
group parted. It was as though she was expected, as though they had known she
was coming here.

Laura was terribly nervous. Tossing the velvet ribbon over her shoulder, she   150
said to a woman standing by, "Is this Mrs. Scott's house?" and the woman, smiling queerly, said, "It is, my lass."

Oh, to be away from this! She actually said, "Help me, God," as she walked
up the tiny path and knocked. To be away from those staring eyes, or to be covered up in anything, one of those women's shawls even. I'll just leave the basket
and go, she decided. I shan't even wait for it to be emptied.

Then the door opened. A little woman in black showed in the gloom.

Laura said, "Are you Mrs. Scott?" But to her horror the woman answered,
"Walk in please, miss," and she was shut in the passage.

"No," said Laura, "I don't want to come in. I only want to leave this basket. Mother sent——"

The little woman in the gloomy passage seemed not to have heard her. "Step   155
this way, please, miss," she said in an oily voice, and Laura followed her.

She found herself in a wretched little low kitchen, lighted by a smoky lamp.
There was a woman sitting before the fire.

"Em," said the little creature who had let her in. "Em! It's a young lady." She turned to Laura. She said meaningly, "I'm 'er sister, Miss. You'll excuse 'er, won't you?"

"Oh, but of course!" said Laura. "Please, please don't disturb her. I—I only want to leave——"

But at that moment the woman at the fire turned round. Her face, puffed up, red, with swollen eyes and swollen lips, looked terrible. She seemed as though she couldn't understand why Laura was there. What did it mean? Why was this stranger standing in the kitchen with a basket? What was it all about? And the poor face puckered up again.

"All right, my dear," said the other. "I'll thenk the young lady."   160

And again she began, "You'll excuse her, miss, I'm sure," and her face, swollen too, tried an oily smile.

Laura only wanted to get out, to get away. She was back in the passage. The door opened. She walked straight through into the bedroom, where the dead man was lying.

"You'd like a look at 'im, wouldn't you?" said Em's sister, and she brushed past Laura over to the bed. "Don't be afraid, my lass,—" and now her voice sounded fond and sly, and fondly she drew down the sheet—" 'e looks a picture. There's nothing to show. Come along, my dear."

Laura came.

There lay a young man, fast asleep—sleeping so soundly, so deeply, that he   165 was far, far away from them both. Oh, so remote, so peaceful. He was dreaming. Never wake him up again. His head was sunk in the pillow, his eyes were closed; they were blind under the closed eyelids. He was given up to his dream. What did garden-parties and baskets and lace frocks matter to him? He was far from all those things. He was wonderful, beautiful. While they were laughing and while the band was playing, this marvel had come to the lane. Happy . . . happy. . . . All is well, said that sleeping face. This is just as it should be. I am content.

But all the same you had to cry, and she couldn't go out of the room without saying something to him. Laura gave a loud childish sob.

"Forgive my hat," she said.

And this time she didn't wait for Em's sister. She found her way out of the door, down the path, past all those dark people. At the corner of the lane she met Laurie.

He stepped out of the shadow. "Is that you, Laura?"

"Yes."   170

"Mother was getting anxious. Was it all right?"

"Yes, quite. Oh, Laurie!" She took his arm, she pressed up against him.

"I say, you're not crying, are you?" asked her brother.

Laura shook her head. She was.

Laurie put his arm round her shoulder. "Don't cry," he said in his warm,   175 loving voice. "Was it awful?"

"No," sobbed Laura. "It was simply marvellous. But, Laurie——" She stopped, she looked at her brother. "Isn't life," she stammered, "isn't life——" But what life was she couldn't explain. No matter. He quite understood.

"*Isn't* it, darling?" said Laurie.

WINDOW ON

Fiction and Culture

When John Cheever published "The Swimmer" (1964) and James Thurber published "The Secret Life of Walter Mitty" (1942) in the *New Yorker*, they anticipated a sophisticated readership whose social profile reflected the suburban New York worlds of their fiction. Today the *New Yorker* publishes a wider range of fiction reflecting the cultures of Antigua in the work of Jamaica Kincaid, Ireland in William Trevor's fiction, and many more besides. This change is reflected in new collections and in journals that publish short fiction throughout the country.

In the early part of the twentieth century, most fiction in English reflected the British or American paradigms of white, middle-class culture. Ernest Hemingway, F. Scott Fitzgerald, Katherine Anne Porter, and Virginia Woolf wrote for people who shared their perceptions of the world—the values and mores of their middle-class culture. Although Hemingway observed Spain and Cuba with care, just as Fitzgerald meditated on the superrich, their focus was on white, middle-class society.

The stories in this collection reflect a greater diversity. Stories such as Bharata Mukherjee's "Jasmine" examine cultural collision on a number of levels, both within the Indian community and in the Canadian community. Stories such as Gabriel García Márquez's "Eyes of a Blue Dog," and Isabel Allende's "Walimai" thrust average North American readers into worlds that demand new ways of thinking and ask us to respond to ideas that are not only foreign, but in some ways unreasonable. They force us to evaluate our own cultural presumptions.

Another kind of cultural awareness is given by the work of James Joyce, which presumes a special knowledge of Irish culture at the turn of the century. Writing about *Dubliners*, from which all the stories in this collection come, he explained that he was portraying a culture of moral paralysis. Dublin, he felt, was a middle-class culture dominated by materialism and self-satisfaction, lacking in vision and self-awareness. The cultural values of drink, good fellowship, male chauvinism, and egotism—accepted by Dubliners as the norm—are presented to us under a microscope for examination.

However, many of these stories are not foreign in any national sense, but are by native writers who attempt to close cultural gaps that have been long neglected in fiction. For example, one of the most powerful stories in this collection is Louise Erdrich's "Love Medicine," which portrays certain ancient customs and non-European medical practices. Erdrich, who is both German-American and Chippewa, describes life on the reservation in *Love Medicine*, a volume of interrelated stories that focus on characters such as Lipsha Morrissey. The reservation shares many of the problems of everyday life—poverty, violence, love, religious fervor, and joy—but "Love Medicine" focuses on Indian ways that are culturally distinct from those of mainline urban life in North America.

Several other voices are also included here. The Mexican-American experience is central to the work of Sandra Cisneros, whose "Never Marry a Mexican" examines the world of a Chicana, a woman who sees more than one culture at a time and whose creativity permits her to say, "I belong to no class." The African-American experience has produced its own distinct cultural interests, some of which are reflected in the work of important African-American writers such as Ralph Ellison and Alice Walker. Their writing has spanned several generations and has aimed at helping white America recognize the cultural diversity of the larger community. More contemporary writers have dealt with more subtle emotional displacement: Jamaica Kincaid's "Lucy" studies the self-image of a young girl in a strange land; Becky Birtha's "Johnnieruth" includes a portrait of lesbian romance; and Toni Cade Bambara's "The Lesson" is a cultural lesson on buying power.

Finally, the culture of the South is described by several writers. Stories like "The Worn Path," by Eudora Welty, draw some of their power from the disjunction between the cultural expectations of white and black Mississippi. For those in the story, such a distinction might be invisible; for us, it is unmistakable. "Livvie" and "Lily Daw and the Three Ladies" do not depend on racial themes, but they do describe the distinctive culture of the American South in the 1930s and 1940s. The same is true of Flannery O'Connor's "A Good Man Is Hard to Find." All these stories give profound insights into cultural realities.

Reading

Barth, Frederik. *Ethnic Groups and Boundaries.* Boston: Little, Brown, 1969.

Gates, Henry Louis, ed. *"Race," Writing and Difference.* Chicago: University of Chicago Press, 1983.

Gayle, Addison. *The Black Aesthetic.* Garden City: Doubleday, 1972.

Graff, Gerald. *Literature against Itself.* Chicago: University of Chicago Press, 1979.

Kohn, Hans. *The Idea of Nationalism.* New York: Collier Books, 1967.

Gabriel García Márquez   (b. 1928)

Born in Colombia, Gabriel García Márquez won the Nobel Prize for fiction in 1982. Like other great Latin American writers, he creates a unique blend of realism and fantasy in his stories, many of which take place in the fictional town Macondo, based on his native Aracataca. Among his novels are One Hundred Years of Solitude *(1967),* The Autumn of the Patriarch *(1976), and* Love in the Time of Cholera *(1988), all impressive successes. When* One Hundred Years of Solitude *was published, his usual print run for a book was seven hundred copies, but the publisher had so much faith in it that he printed eight thousand. To date, this book has sold over ten million copies in thirty languages.* Garcia Márquez's collections of stories include No One Writes to the Colonel and Other Stories *(1968),* Leaf Storm and Other Stories *(1972), and* Innocent Erendira and Other Stories *(1978). His early years were spent as a journalist, and he has said, "I'm fascinated by the relationship between literature and* journalism. *I began my career as a journalist in Colombia, and a reporter is something I have never stopped being."*

EYES OF A BLUE DOG   1968

Then she looked at me. I thought that she was looking at me for the first time. But then, when she turned around behind the lamp and I kept feeling her slippery and oily look in back of me, over my shoulder, I understood that it was I who was looking at her for the first time. I lit a cigarette. I took a drag on the harsh, strong smoke, before spinning in the chair, balancing on one of the rear legs. After that I saw her there, as if she'd been standing beside the lamp looking at me every night. For a few brief minutes that's all we did: look at each other. I looked from the chair, balancing on one of the rear legs. She stood, with a long and quiet hand on the lamp, looking at me. I saw her eyelids lighted up as on every night. It was then that I remembered the usual thing, when I said to her: "Eyes of a blue dog." Without taking her hand off the lamp she said to me: "That. We'll never forget that." She left the orbit, sighing: "Eyes of a blue dog. I've written it everywhere."

I saw her walk over to the dressing table. I watched her appear in the circular glass of the mirror looking at me now at the end of a back and forth of mathematical light. I watched her keep on looking at me with her great hot-coal eyes: looking at me while she opened the little box covered with pink mother of pearl. I saw her powder her nose. When she finished, she closed the box, stood up again, and walked over to the lamp once more, saying: "I'm afraid that someone is dreaming about this room and revealing my secrets." And over the flame she held the same long and tremulous hand that she had been warming before sitting down at the mirror. And she said: "You don't feel the cold." And I said to her: "Sometimes." And she said to me: "You must feel it now." And then I understood why I couldn't have been alone in the seat. It was the cold that had been giving me the certainty of my solitude. "Now I feel it," I said. "And it's strange because the night is quiet. Maybe the sheet fell off." She didn't answer. Again she began to move toward the mirror and I turned again in the chair, keeping my back to her. Without seeing her, I knew what she was doing. I knew that she was sitting in front of the mirror again, seeing my back, which had had time to reach the depths of the mirror and be caught by her look, which had also had just enough time to reach the depths and return—before the hand had time to start the second turn—until her lips were anointed now with crimson, from the first turn of her hand in front of the mirror. I saw, opposite me, the smooth wall, which was like another blind mirror in which I couldn't see her—sitting behind me—but could imagine her where she probably was as if a mirror had been hung in place of the wall. "I see you," I told her. And on the wall I saw what was as if she had raised her eyes and had seen me with my back turned toward her from the chair, in the depths of the mirror, my face turned toward the wall. Then I saw her lower her eyes again and remain with her eyes always on her brassiere, not talking. And I said to her again: "I see you." And she raised her eyes from her brassiere again. "That's impossible," she said. I asked her why. And she, with her eyes quiet and on her brassiere again: "Because your face is turned toward the wall." Then I spun the chair around. I had the cigarette clenched in my mouth. When I stayed facing the mirror she was back by the lamp. Now she had her hands open over the flame, like the two wings of a hen, toasting herself, and with her face shaded by her own fingers. "I think I'm going to catch cold," she said. "This must be a city of ice." She turned her face to profile and her skin, from copper to red, suddenly became sad. "Do something about it," she said. And she began to get undressed, item by item, starting at the top with the brassiere. I told her: "I'm going to turn back to the wall." She said: "No. In any case, you'll see me the way you did when your back was turned." And no sooner had she said it than she was almost completely undressed, with the flame licking her long copper skin. "I've always wanted to see you like that, with the skin of your belly full of deep pits, as if you'd been beaten." And before I realized that my words had become clumsy at the sight of her nakedness, she became motionless, warming herself on the globe of the lamp, and she said: "Sometimes I think I'm made of metal." She was silent for an instant. The position of her hands over the flame varied slightly. I said: "Sometimes, in other dreams, I've thought you were only a little bronze statue in the corner of some museum. Maybe that's why you're cold." And she said: "Sometimes, when I sleep on my heart, I can feel my body growing hollow and my skin is like plate. Then, when the blood beats inside me, it's as if someone were calling by knocking on my stomach and I can feel my own copper sound in the bed. It's like—what do you call it—laminated metal." She drew closer to the lamp. "I would have liked to hear you," I said. And she said: "If we find each other sometime, put your ear to my ribs when I sleep on the left side and you'll hear me echoing. I've always wanted you to do it sometime." I heard her breathe heavily as she talked. And she said that for years she'd done nothing different. Her life had been dedicated to finding me in reality, through that identifying phrase: "Eyes of a blue dog." And she went along the street saying it aloud, as a way of telling the only person who could have understood her:

"I'm the one who comes into your dreams every night and tells you: 'Eyes of a blue dog.' " And she said that she went into restaurants and before ordering said to the waiters: "Eyes of a blue dog." But the waiters bowed reverently, without remembering ever having said that in their dreams. Then she would write on the napkins and scratch on the varnish of the tables with a knife: "Eyes of a blue dog." And on the steamed-up windows of hotels, stations, all public buildings, she would write with her forefinger: "Eyes of a blue dog." She said that once she went into a drugstore and noticed the same smell that she had smelled in her room one night after having dreamed about me. "He must be near," she thought, seeing the clean, new tiles of the drugstore. Then she went over to the clerk and said to him: "I always dream about a man who says to me: 'Eyes of a blue dog.' " And she said the clerk had looked at her eyes and told her: "As a matter of fact, miss, you do have eyes like that." And she said to him: "I have to find the man who told me those very words in my dreams." And the clerk started to laugh and moved to the other end of the counter. She kept on seeing the clean tile and smelling the odor. And she opened her purse and on the tiles, with her crimson lipstick, she wrote in red letters: "Eyes of a blue dog." The clerk came back from where he had been. He told her: "Madam, you have dirtied the tiles." He gave her a damp cloth, saying: "Clean it up." And she said, still by the lamp, that she had spent the whole afternoon on all fours, washing the tiles and saying: "Eyes of a blue dog," until people gathered at the door and said she was crazy.

Now, when she finished speaking, I remained in the corner, sitting, rocking in the chair. "Every day I try to remember the phrase with which I am to find you," I said. "Now I don't think I'll forget it tomorrow. Still, I've always said the same thing and when I wake up I've always forgotten what the words I can find you with are." And she said: "You invented them yourself on the first day." And I said to her: "I invented them because I saw your eyes of ash. But I never remember the next morning." And she, with clenched fists, beside the lamp, breathed deeply: "If you could at least remember now what city I've been writing it in."

Her tightened teeth gleamed over the flame. "I'd like to touch you now," 5 I said. She raised the face that had been looking at the light; she raised her look, burning, roasting, too, just like her, like her hands, and I felt that she saw me, in the corner where I was sitting, rocking in the chair. "You'd never told me that," she said. "I tell you now and it's the truth," I said. From the other side of the lamp she asked for a cigarette. The butt had disappeared between my fingers. I'd forgotten that I was smoking. She said: "I don't know why I can't remember where I wrote it." And I said to her: "For the same reason that tomorrow I won't be able to remember the words." And she said sadly: "No. It's just that sometimes I think that I've dreamed that too." I stood up and walked toward the lamp. She was a little beyond, and I kept on walking with the cigarettes and matches in my hand, which would not go beyond the lamp. I held the cigarette out to her. She squeezed it between her lips and leaned over to reach the flame before I had time to light the match. "In some city in the world, on all the walls, those words have to appear in writing: 'Eyes of a blue dog,' " I said. "If I remembered them tomorrow I could find you." She raised her head again and now the lighted coal was between her lips. "Eyes of a blue dog," she sighed, remembered, with the cigarette drooping over her chin and one eye half closed. Then she sucked in the smoke with the cigarette between her fingers and exclaimed: "This is something else now. I'm warming up." And she said it with her voice a little lukewarm and fleeting, as if she hadn't really said it, but as if she had written it on a piece of paper and had brought the paper close to the flame while I read: "I'm warming," and she had continued with the paper between her thumb and forefinger, turning it around as it was being consumed and I had just read " . . . up," before the paper was completely consumed and dropped all wrinkled to the floor, diminished, converted into light ash dust. "That's better," I said. "Sometimes it frightens me to see you that way. Trembling beside a lamp."

We had been seeing each other for several years. Sometimes, when we were already together, somebody would drop a spoon outside and we would wake up. Little by little we'd been coming to understand that our friendship was subordinated to things, to the simplest of happenings. Our meetings always ended that way, with the fall of a spoon early in the morning.

Now, next to the lamp, she was looking at me. I remembered that she had also looked at me in that way in the past, from that remote dream where I made the chair spin on its back legs and remained facing a strange woman with ashen eyes. It was in that dream that I asked her for the first time: "Who are you?" And she said to me: "I don't remember." I said to her: "But I think we've seen each other before." And she said, indifferently: "I think I dreamed about you once, about this same room." And I told her: "That's it. I'm beginning to remember now." And she said: "How strange. It's certain that we've met in other dreams."

She took two drags on the cigarette. I was still standing, facing the lamp, when suddenly I kept looking at her. I looked her up and down and she was still copper; no longer hard and cold metal, but yellow, soft, malleable copper. "I'd like to touch you," I said again. And she said: "You'll ruin everything." I said: "It doesn't matter now. All we have to do is turn the pillow over in order to meet again." And I held my hand out over the lamp. She didn't move. "You'll ruin everything," she said again before I could touch her. "Maybe, if you come around behind the lamp, we'd wake up frightened in who knows what part of the world." But I insisted: "It doesn't matter." And she said: "If we turned over the pillow, we'd meet again. But when you wake up you'll have forgotten." I began to move toward the corner. She stayed behind, warming her hands over the flame. And I still wasn't beside the chair when I heard her say behind me: "When I wake up at midnight, I keep turning in bed, with the fringe of the pillow burning my knee, and repeating until dawn: 'Eyes of a blue dog.' "

Then I remained with my face toward the wall. "It's already dawning," I said without looking at her. "When it struck two I was awake and that was a long time back." I went to the door. When I had the knob in my hand, I heard her voice again, the same, invariable. "Don't open that door," she said. "The hallway is full of difficult dreams." And I asked her: "How do you know?" And she told me: "Because I was there a moment ago and I had to come back when I discovered I was sleeping on my heart." I had the door half opened. I moved it a little and a cold, thin breeze brought me the fresh smell of vegetable earth, damp fields. She spoke again. I gave the turn, still moving the door, mounted on silent hinges, and I told her: "I don't think there's any hallway outside here. I'm getting the smell of country." And she, a little distant, told me: "I know that better than you. What's happening is that there's a woman outside dreaming about the country." She crossed her arms over the flame. She continued speaking: "It's that woman who always wanted to have a house in the country and was never able to leave the city." I remembered having seen the woman in some previous dream, but I knew, with the door ajar now, that within half an hour I would have to go down for breakfast. And I said: "In any case, I have to leave here in order to wake up."

Outside the wind fluttered for an instant, then remained quiet, and the breathing of someone sleeping who had just turned over in bed could be heard. The wind from the fields had ceased. There were no more smells. "Tomorrow I'll recognize you from that," I said. "I'll recognize you when on the street I see a woman writing 'Eyes of a blue dog' on the walls." And she, with a sad smile— which was already a smile of surrender to the impossible, the unreachable—said: "Yet you won't remember anything during the day." And she put her hands back over the lamp, her features darkened by a bitter cloud. "You're the only man who doesn't remember anything of what he's dreamed after he wakes up."

10

Alice Munro (b. 1931)

Alice Munro, born and raised in Canada, still lives in southwestern Ontario. Although her stories usually reflect the circumstances of life in Canada, their subject matter is contemporary and universal in appeal. Her work in fiction has been almost entirely in the short story, and she describes her novel Lives of Girls and Women *(1971) as a series of connected stories. Among her collections are* Dance of the Happy Shades *(1968),* Who Do You Think You Are? *(1978),* The Moons of Jupiter *(1983), and* The Progress of Love *(1986). Joyce Carol Oates has said that Munro "writes stories that have the density—moral, emotional, sometimes historical—of other writers' novels," and Munro herself has said, "I want to write the story that will zero in and give you intense, but not connected, moments of experience. I guess that's the way I see life."*

THE MOONS OF JUPITER   1983

I found my father in the heart wing, on the eighth floor of Toronto General Hospital. He was in a semi-private room. The other bed was empty. He said that his hospital insurance covered only a bed in the ward, and he was worried that he might be charged extra.

"I never asked for a semi-private," he said.

I said the wards were probably full.

"No. I saw some empty beds when they were wheeling me by."

"Then it was because you had to be hooked up to that thing," I said. "Don't   5
worry. If they're going to charge you extra, they tell you about it."

"That's likely it," he said. "They wouldn't want those doohickeys set up in the wards. I guess I'm covered for that kind of thing."

I said I was sure he was.

He had wires taped to his chest. A small screen hung over his head. On the screen a bright jagged line was continually being written. The writing was accompanied by a nervous electronic beeping. The behavior of his heart was on display. I tried to ignore it. It seemed to me that paying such close attention—in fact, dramatizing what ought to be a most secret activity—was asking for trouble. Anything exposed that way was apt to flare up and go crazy.

My father did not seem to mind. He said they had him on tranquillizers. You know, he said, the happy pills. He did seem calm and optimistic.

It had been a different story the night before. When I brought him into the   10
hospital, to the emergency room, he had been pale and closemouthed. He had opened the car door and stood up and said quietly, "Maybe you better get me one of those wheelchairs." He used the voice he always used in a crisis. Once, our chimney caught on fire; it was on a Sunday afternoon and I was in the dining room pinning together a dress I was making. He came in and said in that same matter-of-fact, warning voice, "Janet. Do you know where there's some baking powder?" He wanted it to throw on the fire. Afterwards he said, "I guess it was your fault—sewing on Sunday."

I had to wait for over an hour in the emergency waiting room. They summoned a heart specialist who was in the hospital, a young man. He called me out into the hall and explained to me that one of the valves of my father's heart had deteriorated so badly that there ought to be an immediate operation.

I asked him what would happen otherwise.

"He'd have to stay in bed," the doctor said.

"How long?"

"Maybe three months."   15

"I meant, how long would he live?"

"That's what I meant, too," the doctor said.

I went to see my father. He was sitting up in bed in a curtained-off corner. "It's bad, isn't it?" he said. "Did he tell you above the valve?"

"It's not as bad as it could be," I said. Then I repeated, even exaggerated, anything hopeful the doctor had said. "You're not in any immediate danger. Your physical condition is good, otherwise."

"Otherwise," said my father, gloomily.   20

I was tired from the drive—all the way up to Dalgleish, to get him, and back to Toronto since noon—and worried about getting the rented car back on time, and irritated by an article I had been reading in a magazine in the waiting room. It was about another writer, a woman younger, better-looking, probably more talented than I am. I had been in England for two months and so I had not seen this article before, but it crossed my mind while I was reading that my father would have. I could hear him saying, Well, I didn't see anything about you in *Maclean's*.° And if he had read something about me he would say, Well, I didn't think too much of that writeup. His tone would be humorous and indulgent but would produce in me a familiar dreariness of spirit. The message I got from him was simple: Fame must be striven for, then apologized for. Getting or not getting it, you will be to blame.

I was not surprised by the doctor's news. I was prepared to hear something of the sort and was pleased with myself for taking it calmly, just as I would be pleased with myself for dressing a wound or looking down from the frail balcony of a high building. I thought, Yes, it's time; there has to be something, here it is. I did not feel any of the protest I would have felt twenty, even ten, years before. When I saw from my father's face that he felt it—that refusal leapt up in him as readily as if he had been thirty or forty years younger—my heart hardened, and I spoke with a kind of badgering cheerfulness. "Otherwise is plenty," I said.

The next day he was himself again.

That was how I would have put it. He said it appeared to him now that the young fellow, the doctor, might have been a bit too eager to operate. "A bit knife-happy," he said. He was both mocking and showing off the hospital slang. He said that another doctor had examined him, an older man, and had given it as his opinion that rest and medication might do the trick.

I didn't ask what trick.   25

"He says I've got a defective valve, all right. There's certainly some damage. They wanted to know if I had rheumatic fever when I was a kid. I said I didn't think so. But half the time then you weren't diagnosed what you had. My father was not one for getting the doctor."

The thought of my father's childhood, which I always pictured as bleak and dangerous—the poor farm, the scared sisters, the harsh father—made me less resigned to his dying. I thought of him running away to work on the lake boats,

Maclean's: Popular magazine.

running along the railway tracks, toward Goderich, in the evening light. He used
to tell about that trip. Somewhere along the track he found a quince tree. Quince
trees are rare in our part of the country; in fact, I have never seen one. Not even
the one my father found, though he once took us on an expedition to look for
it. He thought he knew the crossroad it was near, but we could not find it. He
had not been able to eat the fruit, of course, but he had been impressed by its existence. It made him think he had got into a new part of the world.

The escaped child, the survivor, an old man trapped here by his leaky heart.
I didn't pursue these thoughts. I didn't care to think of his younger selves. Even
his bare torso, thick and white—he had the body of a workingman of his generation, seldom exposed to the sun—was a danger to me; it looked so strong and
young. The wrinkled neck, the age-freckled hands and arms, the narrow, courteous head, with its thin gray hair and mustache, were more what I was used to.

"Now, why would I want to get myself operated on?" said my father reasonably. "Think of the risk at my age, and what for? A few years at the outside. I
think the best thing for me to do is go home and take it easy. Give in gracefully.
That's all you can do, at my age. Your attitude changes, you know. You go through
some mental changes. It seems more natural."

"What does?" I said.   30

"Well, death does. You can't get more natural than that. No, what I mean,
specifically, is not having the operation."

"That seems more natural?"

"Yes."

"It's up to you," I said, but I did approve. This was what I would have expected of him. Whenever I told people about my father I stressed his independence, his self-sufficiency, his forbearance. He worked in a factory, he worked in
his garden, he read history books. He could tell you about the Roman emperors
or the Balkan wars. He never made a fuss.

Judith, my younger daughter, had come to meet me at Toronto Airport two   35
days before. She had brought the boy she was living with, whose name was Don.
They were driving to Mexico in the morning, and while I was in Toronto I was
to stay in their apartment. For the time being, I live in Vancouver. I sometimes
say I have my headquarters in Vancouver.

"Where's Nichola?" I said, thinking at once of an accident or an overdose.
Nichola is my older daughter. She used to be a student at the Conservatory, then
she became a cocktail waitress, then she was out of work. If she had been at the
airport, I would probably have said something wrong. I would have asked her
what her plans were, and she would have gracefully brushed back her hair and
said, "Plans?"—as if that was a word I had invented.

"I knew the first thing you'd say would be about Nichola," Judith said.

"It wasn't. I said hello and I—"

"We'll get your bag," Don said neutrally.

"Is she all right?"   40

"I'm sure she is," said Judith, with a fabricated air of amusement. "You
wouldn't look like that if I was the one who wasn't here."

"Of course I would."

"You wouldn't. Nichola is the baby of the family. You know, she's four years
older than I am."

"I ought to know."

Judith said she did not know where Nichola was exactly. She said Nichola   45
had moved out of her apartment (that dump!) and had actually telephoned (which
is quite a deal, you might say, Nichola phoning) to say she wanted to be incommunicado for a while but she was fine.

"I told her you would worry," said Judith more kindly on the way to their
van. Don walked ahead carrying my suitcase. "But don't. She's all right, believe
me."

Don's presence made me uncomfortable. I did not like him to hear these
things. I thought of the conversations they must have had, Don and Judith. Or
Don and Judith and Nichola, for Nichola and Judith were sometimes on good
terms. Or Don and Judith and Nichola and others whose names I did not even
know. They would have talked about me. Judith and Nichola comparing notes,
relating anecdotes; analyzing, regretting, blaming, forgiving. I wished I'd had a
boy and a girl. Or two boys. They wouldn't have done that. Boys couldn't possibly know so much about you.

I did the same thing at that age. When I was the age Judith is now I talked
with my friends in the college cafeteria or, late at night, over coffee in our cheap
rooms. When I was the age Nichola is now I had Nichola herself in a carry-cot or
squirming in my lap, and I was drinking coffee again all the rainy Vancouver afternoons with my one neighborhood friend, Ruth Boudreau, who read a lot and
was bewildered by her situation, as I was. We talked about our parents, our childhoods, though for some time we kept clear of our marriages. How thoroughly
we dealt with our fathers and mothers, deplored their marriages, their mistaken
ambitions or fear of ambition, how competently we filed them away, defined them
beyond any possibility of change. What presumption.

I looked at Don walking ahead. A tall ascetic-looking boy, with a St. Francis
cap of black hair, a precise fringe of beard. What right did he have to hear about
me, to know things I myself had probably forgotten? I decided that his beard and
hairstyle were affected.

Once, when my children were little, my father said to me, "You know those   50
years you were growing up—well, that's all just a kind of a blur to me. I can't sort
out one year from another." I was offended. I remembered each separate year
with pain and clarity. I could have told how old I was when I went to look at the
evening dresses in the window of Benbow's Ladies' Wear. Every week through
the winter a new dress, spotlit—the sequins and tulle, the rose and lilac, sapphire,
daffodil—and me a cold worshipper on the slushy sidewalk. I could have told how
old I was when I forged my mother's signature on a bad report card, when I had
measles, when we papered the front room. But the years when Judith and Nichola
were little, when I lived with their father—yes, blur is the word for it. I remember hanging out diapers, bringing in and folding diapers; I can recall the kitchen
counters of two houses and where the clothesbasket sat. I remember the television programs—*Popeye the Sailor*, *The Three Stooges*, *Funorama*. When *Funorama*
came on it was time to turn on the lights and cook supper. But I couldn't tell the
years apart. We lived outside Vancouver in a dormitory suburb: Dormir, Dormer,
Dormouse—something like that. I was sleepy all the time then; pregnancy made
me sleepy, and the night feedings, and the West Coast rain falling. Dark dripping
cedars, shiny dripping laurel; wives yawning, napping, visiting, drinking coffee,
and folding diapers; husbands coming home at night from the city across the wa-

ter. Every night I kissed my homecoming husband in his wet Burberry° and hoped he might wake me up; I served up meat and potatoes and one of the four vegetables he permitted. He ate with a violent appetite, then fell asleep on the living-room sofa. We had become a cartoon couple, more middle-aged in our twenties than we would be in middle age.

Those bumbling years are the years our children will remember all their lives. Corners of the yards I never visited will stay in their heads.

"Did Nichola not want to see me?" I said to Judith.

"She doesn't want to see anybody, half the time," she said. Judith moved ahead and touched Don's arm. I knew that touch—an apology, an anxious reassurance. You touch a man that way to remind him that you are grateful, that you realize he is doing for your sake something that bores him or slightly endangers his dignity. It made me feel older than grandchildren would to see my daughter touch a man—a boy—this way. I felt her sad jitters, could predict her supple attentions. My blunt and stocky, blonde and candid child. Why should I think she wouldn't be susceptible, that she would always be straightforward, heavy-footed, self-reliant? Just as I go around saying that Nichola is sly and solitary, cold, seductive. Many people must know things that would contradict what I say.

In the morning Don and Judith left for Mexico. I decided I wanted to see somebody who wasn't related to me, and who didn't expect anything in particular from me. I called an old lover of mine, but his phone was answered by a machine: "This is Tom Shepherd speaking. I will be out of town for the month of September. Please record your message, name, and phone number."

Tom's voice sounded so pleasant and familiar that I opened my mouth to   55
ask him the meaning of this foolishness. Then I hung up. I felt as if he had deliberately let me down, as if we had planned to meet in a public place and then he hadn't shown up. Once, he had done that, I remembered.

I got myself a glass of vermouth, though it was not yet noon, and I phoned my father.

"Well, of all things," he said. "Fifteen more minutes and you would have missed me."

"Were you going downtown?"

"Downtown Toronto."

He explained that he was going to the hospital. His doctor in Dalgleish   60
wanted the doctors in Toronto to take a look at him, and had given him a letter to show them in the emergency room.

"Emergency room?" I said.

"It's not an emergency. He just seems to think this is the best way to handle it. He knows the name of a fellow there. If he was to make me an appointment, it might take weeks."

"Does your doctor know you're driving to Toronto?" I said.

"Well, he didn't say I couldn't."

The upshot of this was that I rented a car, drove to Dalgleish, brought my   65
father back to Toronto, and had him in the emergency room by seven o'clock that evening.

Before Judith left I said to her, "You're sure Nichola knows I'm staying here?"

Burberry: Raincoat.

"Well, I told her," she said.

Sometimes the phone rang, but it was always a friend of Judith's.

"Well, it looks like I'm going to have it," my father said. This was on the fourth day. He had done a complete turnaround overnight. "It looks like I might as well."

I didn't know what he wanted me to say. I thought perhaps he looked to   70
me for a protest, an attempt to dissuade him.

"When will they do it?" I said.

"Day after tomorrow."

I said I was going to the washroom. I went to the nurses' station and found a woman there who I thought was the head nurse. At any rate, she was gray-haired, kind, and serious-looking.

"My father's having an operation the day after tomorrow?" I said.

"Oh, yes."   75

"I just wanted to talk to somebody about it. I thought there'd been a sort of decision reached that he'd be better not to. I thought because of his age."

"Well, it's his decision and the doctor's." She smiled at me without condescension. "It's hard to make these decisions."

"How were his tests?"

"Well, I haven't seen them all."

I was sure she had. After a moment she said, "We have to be realistic. But   80
the doctors here are very good."

When I went back into the room my father said, in a surprised voice, "*Shoreless seas.*"

"What?" I said. I wondered if he had found out how much, or how little, time he could hope for. I wondered if the pills had brought on an untrustworthy euphoria. Or if he had wanted to gamble. Once, when he was talking to me about his life, he said, "The trouble was I was always afraid to take chances."

I used to tell people that he never spoke regretfully about his life, but that was not true. It was just that I didn't listen to it. He said that he should have gone into the Army as a tradesman—he would have been better off. He said he should have gone on his own, as a carpenter, after the war. He should have got out of Dalgleish. Once, he said, "A wasted life, eh?" But he was making fun of himself, saying that, because it was such a dramatic thing to say. When he quoted poetry, too, he always had a scoffing note in his voice, to excuse the showing-off and the pleasure.

"Shoreless seas," he said again. " 'Behind him lay the gray Azores, / Behind the Gates of Hercules; / Before him not the ghost of shores, / Before him only shoreless seas.' That's what was going through my head last night. But do you think I could remember what kind of seas? I could not. Lonely seas? Empty seas? I was on the right track but I couldn't get it. But there now when you came into the room and I wasn't thinking about it at all, the word popped into my head. That's always the way, isn't it? It's not all that surprising. I ask my mind a question. The answer's there, but I can't see all the connections my mind's making to get it. Like a computer. Nothing out of the way. You know, in my situation the thing is, if there's anything you can't explain right away, there's a great temptation to—well, to make a mystery out of it. There's a great temptation to believe in—You know."

"The soul?" I said, speaking lightly, feeling an appalling rush of love and　85
recognition.

"Oh, I guess you could call it that. You know, when I first came into this
room there was a pile of papers here by the bed. Somebody had left them here—
one of those tabloid sort of things I never looked at. I started reading them. I'll
read anything handy. There was a series running in them on personal experiences
of people who had died, medically speaking—heart arrest, mostly—and had been
brought back to life. It was what they remembered of the time when they were
dead. Their experiences."

"Pleasant or un-?" I said.

"Oh, pleasant. Oh yes. They'd float up to the ceiling and look down on
themselves and see the doctors working on them, on their bodies. Then float on
further and recognize some people they knew who had died before them. Not
see them exactly but sort of sense them. Sometimes there would be a humming
and sometimes a sort of—what's that light that there is or color around a person?"

"Aura?"

"Yes. But without the person. That's about all they'd get time for; then they　90
found themselves back in the body and feeling all the mortal pain and so on—
brought back to life."

"Did it seem—convincing?"

"Oh, I don't know. It's all in whether you want to believe that kind of thing
or not. And if you are going to believe it, take it seriously, I figure you've got to
take everything else seriously that they print in those papers."

"What else do they?"

"Rubbish—cancer cures, baldness cures, bellyaching about the younger generation and the welfare bums. Tripe about movie stars."

"Oh, yes. I know."　95

"In my situation you have to keep a watch," he said, "or you'll start playing
tricks on yourself." Then he said, "There's a few practical details we ought to get
straight on," and he told me about his will, the house, the cemetery plot.
Everything was simple.

"Do you want me to phone Peggy?" I said. Peggy is my sister. She is married to an astronomer and lives in Victoria.

He thought about it. "I guess we ought to tell them," he said finally. "But
tell them not to get alarmed."

"All right."

"No, wait a minute. Sam is supposed to be going to a conference the end of　100
this week, and Peggy was planning to go along with him. I don't want them wondering about changing their plans."

"Where is the conference?"

"Amsterdam," he said proudly. He did take pride in Sam, and kept track of
his books and articles. He would pick one up and say, "Look at that, will you?
And I can't understand a word of it!" in a marvelling voice that managed nevertheless to have a trace of ridicule.

"Professor Sam," he would say. "And the three little Sams." This is what he
called his grandsons, who did resemble their father in braininess and in an almost
endearing pushness—an innocent energetic showing-off. They went to a private
school that favored old-fashioned discipline and started calculus in Grade Five.

"And the dogs," he might enumerate further, "who have been to obedience school. And Peggy . . ."

But if I said, "Do you suppose she has been to obedience school, too?" he would play the game no further. I imagine that when he was with Sam and Peggy he spoke of me in the same way—hinted at my flightiness just as he hinted at their stodginess, made mild jokes at my expense, did not quite conceal his amazement (or pretended not to conceal his amazement) that people paid money for things I had written. He had to do this so that he might never seem to brag, but he would put up the gates when the joking got too rough. And of course I found later, in the house, things of mine he had kept—a few magazines, clippings, things I had never bothered about.

Now his thoughts travelled from Peggy's family to mine. "Have you heard from Judith?" he said.   105

"Not yet."

"Well, it's pretty soon. Were they going to sleep in the van?"

"Yes."

"I guess it's safe enough, if they stop in the right places."

I knew he would have to say something more and I knew it would come as a joke.   110

"I guess they put a board down the middle, like the pioneers?"

I smiled but did not answer.

"I take it you have no objections?"

"No," I said.

"Well, I always believed that, too. Keep out of your children's business. I tried not to say anything. I never said anything when you left Richard."   115

"What do you mean, 'said anything'? Criticize?"

"It wasn't any of my business."

"No."

"But that doesn't mean I was pleased."

I was surprised—not just at what he said but at his feeling that he had any right, even now, to say it. I had to look out the window and down at the traffic to control myself.   120

"I just wanted you to know," he added.

A long time ago, he said to me in his mild way, "It's funny. Richard when I first saw him reminded me of what my father used to say. He'd say if that fellow was half as smart as he thinks he is, he'd be twice as smart as he really is."

I turned to remind him of this, but found myself looking at the line his heart was writing. Not that there seemed to be anything wrong, any difference in the beeps and points. But it was there.

He saw where I was looking. "Unfair advantage," he said.

"It is," I said. "I'm going to have to get hooked up, too."   125

We laughed, we kissed formally; I left. At least he hadn't asked me about Nichola, I thought.

The next afternoon I didn't go to the hospital, because my father was having some more tests done, to prepare for the operation. I was to see him in the evening instead. I found myself wandering through the Bloor Street dress shops, trying on clothes. A preoccupation with fashion and my own appearance had descended on me like a raging headache. I looked at the women in the street, at the clothes in the shops, trying to discover how a transformation might be made, what I would have to buy. I recognized this obsession for what it was but had trouble shaking it. I've had people tell me that waiting for life-or-death news they've stood in front of an open refrigerator eating anything in sight—cold boiled potatoes, chili sauce, bowls of whipped cream. Or have been unable to stop doing cross-word puzzles. Attention narrows in on something—some distraction—grabs on, becomes fanatically serious. I shuffled clothes on the racks, pulled them on in hot little changing rooms in front of cruel mirrors. I was sweating; once or twice I thought I might faint. Out on the street again, I thought I must remove myself from Bloor Street, and decided to go to the museum.

I remembered another time, in Vancouver. It was when Nichola was going to Kindergarten and Judith was a baby. Nichola had been to the doctor about a cold, or maybe for a routine examination, and the blood test revealed something about her white blood cells—either that there were too many of them or that they were enlarged. The doctor ordered further tests, and I took Nichola to the hospital for them. Nobody mentioned leukemia but I knew, of course, what they were looking for. When I took Nichola home I asked the babysitter who had been with Judith to stay for the afternoon and I went shopping. I bought the most daring dress I ever owned, a black silk sheath with some laced-up arrangement in front. I remembered that bright spring afternoon, the spike-heeled shoes in the department store, the underwear printed with leopard spots.

I also remembered going home from St. Paul's Hospital over the Lions Gate Bridge on the crowded bus and holding Nichola on my knee. She suddenly re-called her baby name for bridge and whispered to me, "Whee—over the whee." I did not avoid touching my child—Nichola was slender and graceful even then, with a pretty back and fine dark hair—but realized I was touching her with a dif-ference, though I did not think it could ever be detected. There was a care—not a withdrawal exactly but a care—not to feel anything much. I saw how the forms of love might be maintained with a condemned person but with the love in fact measured and disciplined, because you have to survive. It could be done so dis-creetly that the object of such care would not suspect, any more than she would suspect the sentence of death itself. Nichola did not know, would not know. Toys and kisses and jokes would come tumbling over her; she would never know, though I worried that she would feel the wind between the cracks of the manufactured holidays, the manufactured normal days. But all was well. Nichola did not have leukemia. She grew up—was still alive, and possibly happy. Incommunicado.

I could not think of anything in the museum I really wanted to see, so I 130 walked past it to the planetarium. I had never been to a planetarium. The show was due to start in ten minutes. I went inside, bought a ticket, got in line. There was a whole class of schoolchildren, maybe a couple of classes, with teachers and volunteer mothers riding herd on them. I looked around to see if there were any other unattached adults. Only one—a man with a red face and puffy eyes, who looked as if he might be here to keep himself from going to a bar.

Inside, we sat on wonderfully comfortable seats that were tilted back so that you lay in a sort of hammock, attention directed to the bowl of the ceiling, which soon turned dark blue, with a faint rim of light all around the edge. There was some splendid, commanding music. The adults all around were shushing the chil-dren, trying to make them stop crackling their potato-chip bags. Then a man's voice, an eloquent professional voice, began to speak slowly, out of the walls. The voice reminded me a little of the way radio announcers used to introduce a piece of classical music or describe the progress of the Royal Family to Westminster Abbey on one of their royal occasions. There was a faint echo-chamber effect.

The dark ceiling was filling with stars. They came out not all at once but one after another, the way the stars really do come out at night, though more quickly. The Milky Way appeared, was moving closer; stars swam into brilliance and kept on going, disappearing beyond the edges of the sky-screen or behind my head. While the flow of light continued, the voice presented the stunning facts. A few light-years away, it announced, the sun appears as a bright star, and the planets are not visible. A few dozen light-years away, the sun is not visible, either, to the naked eye. And that distance—a few dozen light-years—is only about a thousandth part of the distance from the sun to the center of our galaxy, one galaxy, which itself contains about two hundred billion suns. And is, in turn, one of millions, perhaps billions, of galaxies. Innumerable repetitions, innumerable variations. All this rolled past my head, too, like balls of lightning.

Now realism was abandoned, for familiar artifice. A model of the solar system was spinning away in its elegant style. A bright bug took off from the earth, heading for Jupiter. I set my dodging and shrinking mind sternly to recording facts. The mass of Jupiter two and a half times that of all the other planets put together. The Great Red Spot. The thirteen moons. Past Jupiter, a glance at the eccentric orbit of Pluto, the icy rings of Saturn. Back to Earth and moving in to hot and dazzling Venus. Atmospheric pressure ninety times ours. Moonless Mercury rotating three times while circling the sun twice; an odd arrangement, not as satisfying as what they used to tell us—that it rotated once as it circled the sun. No perpetual darkness after all. Why did they give out such confident information, only to announce later that it was quite wrong? Finally, the picture already familiar from magazines: the red soil of Mars, the blooming pink sky.

When the show was over I sat in my seat while the children clambered across me, making no comments on anything they had just seen or heard. They were pestering their keepers for eatables and further entertainments. An effort had been made to get their attention, to take it away from canned pop and potato chips and fix it on various knowns and unknowns and horrible immensities, and it seemed to have failed. A good thing, too, I thought. Children have a natural immunity, most of them, and it shouldn't be tampered with. As for the adults who would deplore it, the ones who promoted this show, weren't they immune themselves to the extent that they could put in the echo-chamber effects, the music, the churchlike solemnity, simulating the awe that they supposed they ought to feel? Awe—what was that supposed to be? A fit of the shivers when you looked out the window? Once you knew what it was, you wouldn't be courting it.

Two men came with brooms to sweep up the debris the audience had left 135 behind. They told me that the next show would start in forty minutes. In the meantime, I had to get out.

"I went to the show at the planetarium," I said to my father. "It was very exciting—about the solar system." I thought what a silly word I had used: "exciting." "It's like a slightly phony temple," I added.

He was already talking. "I remember when they found Pluto. Right where they thought it had to be. Mercury, Venus, Earth, Mars," he recited. "Jupiter, Saturn, Nept—no, Uranus, Neptune, Pluto. Is that right?"

"Yes," I said. I was just as glad he hadn't heard what I said about the phony temple. I had meant that to be truthful, but it sounded slick and superior. "Tell me the moons of Jupiter."

"Well, I don't know the new ones. There's a bunch of new ones, isn't there?"

"Two. But they're not new."   140

"New to us," said my father. "You've turned pretty cheeky now I'm going under the knife."

" 'Under the knife.' What an expression."

He was not in bed tonight, his last night. He had been detached from his apparatus, and was sitting in a chair by the window. He was bare-legged, wearing a hospital dressing gown, but he did not look self-conscious or out of place. He looked thoughtful but good-humored, an affable host.

"You haven't even named the old ones," I said.

" Give me time. Galileo named them. Io."   145

"That's a start."

"The moons of Jupiter were the first heavenly bodies discovered with the telescope." He said this gravely, as if he could see the sentence in an old book. "It wasn't Galileo named them, either; it was some German. Io, Europa, Ganymede, Callisto. There you are."

"Yes."

"Io and Europa, they were girlfriends of Jupiter's, weren't they? Ganymede was a boy. A shepherd? I don't know who Callisto was."

"I think she was a girlfriend, too," I said. "Jupiter's wife—Jove's wife—   150 changed her into a bear and stuck her up in the sky. Great Bear and Little Bear. Little Bear was her baby."

The loudspeaker said that it was time for visitors to go.

"I'll see you when you come out of the anesthetic," I said.

"Yes."

When I was at the door, he called to me, "Ganymede wasn't any shepherd. He was Jove's cupbearer."

When I left the planetarium that afternoon, I had walked through the mu-   155 seum to the Chinese garden. I saw the stone camels again, the warriors, the tomb. I sat on a bench looking toward Bloor Street. Through the evergreen bushes and the high grilled iron fence I watched people going by in the late-afternoon sunlight. The planetarium show had done what I wanted it to after all—calmed me down, drained me. I saw a girl who reminded me of Nichola. She wore a trenchcoat and carried a bag of groceries. She was shorter than Nichola—not really much like her at all—but I thought that I might see Nichola. She would be walking along some street maybe not far from here—burdened, preoccupied, alone. She was one of the grownup people in the world now, one of the shoppers going home.

If I did see her, I might just sit and watch, I decided. I felt like one of those people who have floated up to the ceiling, enjoying a brief death. A relief, while it lasts. My father had chosen and Nichola had chosen. Someday, probably soon, I would hear from her, but it came to the same thing.

I meant to get up and go over to the tomb, to look at the relief carvings, the stone pictures, that go all the way around it. I always mean to look at them and I never do. Not this time, either. It was getting cold out, so I went inside to have coffee and something to eat before I went back to the hospital.

Joyce Carol Oates   (b. 1938)

Joyce Carol Oates is one of the most prolific of modern American writers. Born in Lockport, New York, she went to Syracuse University where she graduated first in her class. Like the poet Sylvia Plath, she won a Mademoiselle *award when she was in college, and began publishing short fiction very early, with her first book of stories* By the North Gate *(1963) in print by the time she was twenty-five. She has averaged almost two books a year ever since. In 1970 she won the National Book Award for them, a novel about people caught in the cycle of inner city violence and poverty. She has published more than sixteen collections of short stories, among them* The Wheel of Love and Other Stories *(1970),* Marriages and Infidelities *(1972),* Where Are You Going, Where Have You Been? *: Stories of Young America (1974),* A Sentimental Education *(1981), and* Raven's Wing: Stories *(1986). Her output of more than twenty novels has attracted a wide and delighted readership as well as the praise of critics. Her stories are engaging, sometimes suspenseful, and always entertaining. Her concerns are usually serious, and her social awareness shows deep in the grain of her work. She is a member of the American Academy of Arts and Letters and has been professor and writer in residence at Princeton since 1978.*

WHERE ARE YOU GOING, WHERE HAVE YOU BEEN?   1970

For Bob Dylan

Her name was Connie. She was fifteen and she had a quick, nervous giggling habit of craning her neck to glance into mirrors or checking other people's faces to make sure her own was all right. Her mother, who noticed everything and knew everything and who hadn't much reason any longer to look at her own face, always scolded Connie about it. "Stop gawking at yourself. Who are you? You think you're so pretty?" she would say. Connie would raise her eyebrows at these familiar old complaints and look right through her mother, into a shadowy vision of herself as she was right at that moment: she knew she was pretty and that was everything. Her mother had been pretty once too, if you could believe those old snapshots in the album, but now her looks were gone and that was why she was always after Connie.

"Why don't you keep your room clean like your sister? How've you got your hair fixed—what the hell stinks? Hair spray? You don't see your sister using that junk."

Her sister June was twenty-four and still lived at home. She was a secretary in the high school Connie attended, and if that wasn't bad enough—with her in the same building—she was so plain and chunky and steady that Connie had to hear her praised all the time by her mother and her mother's sisters. June did this, June did that, she saved money and helped clean the house and cooked and Connie couldn't do a thing, her mind was all filled with trashy daydreams. Their father was away at work most of the time and when he came home he wanted supper and he read the newspaper at supper and after supper he went to bed. He didn't bother talking much to them, but around his bent head Connie's mother kept picking at her until Connie wished her mother was dead and she herself was dead and it was all over. "She makes me want to throw up sometimes," she complained to her friends. She had a high, breathless, amused voice that made everything she said sound a little forced, whether it was sincere or not.

There was one good thing: June went places with girl friends of hers, girls who were just as plain and steady as she, and so when Connie wanted to do that her mother had no objections. The father of Connie's best girl friend drove the girls the three miles to town and left them at a shopping plaza so they could walk through the stores or go to a movie, and when he came to pick them up again at eleven he never bothered to ask what they had done.

They must have been familiar sights, walking around the shopping plaza in their shorts and flat ballerina slippers that always scuffed the sidewalk, with charm bracelets jingling on their thin wrists; they would lean together to whisper and laugh secretly if someone passed who amused or interested them. Connie had long dark blond hair that drew anyone's eye to it, and she wore part of it pulled up on her head and puffed out and the rest of it she let fall down her back. She wore a pull-over jersey blouse that looked one way when she was at home and another way when she was away from home. Everything about her had two sides to it, one for home and one for anywhere that was not home: her walk, which could be childlike and bobbing, or languid enough to make anyone think she was hearing music in her head; her mouth, which was pale and smirking most of the time, but bright and pink on these evenings out; her laugh, which was cynical and drawling at home—"Ha, ha, very funny,"—but high-pitched and nervous anywhere else, like the jingling of the charms on her bracelet.

Sometimes they did go shopping or to a movie, but sometimes they went across the highway, ducking fast across the busy road, to a drive-in restaurant where older kids hung out. The restaurant was shaped like a big bottle, though squatter than a real bottle, and on its cap was a revolving figure of a grinning boy holding a hamburger aloft. One night in midsummer they ran across, breathless with daring, and right away someone leaned out a car window and invited them over, but it was just a boy from high school they didn't like. It made them feel good to be able to ignore him. They went up through the maze of parked and cruising cars to the bright-lit, fly-infested restaurant, their faces pleased and expectant as if they were entering a sacred building that loomed up out of the night to give them what haven and blessing they yearned for. They sat at the counter and crossed their legs at the ankles, their thin shoulders rigid with excitement, and listened to the music that made everything so good: the music was always in the background, like music at a church service; it was something to depend upon.

A boy named Eddie came in to talk with them. He sat backwards on his stool, turning himself jerkily around in semicircles and then stopping and turning back again, and after a while he asked Connie if she would like something to eat. She said she would and so she tapped her friend's arm on her way out—her friend pulled her face up into a brave, droll look—and Connie said she would meet her at eleven, across the way. "I just hate to leave her like that," Connie said earnestly, but the boy said that she wouldn't be alone for long. So they went out to his car, and on the way Connie couldn't help but let her eyes wander over the windshields and faces all around her, her face gleaming with a joy that had nothing to do with Eddie or even this place; it might have been the music. She drew her shoulders up and sucked in her breath with the pure pleasure of being alive, and just at that moment she happened to glance at a face just a few feet from hers. It was a boy with shaggy black hair, in a convertible jalopy painted gold. He stared at her and

5

then his lips widened into a grin. Connie slit her eyes at him and turned away, but she couldn't help glancing back and there he was, still watching her. He wagged a finger and laughed and said, "Gonna get you, baby," and Connie turned away again without Eddie noticing anything.

She spent three hours with him, at the restaurant where they ate hamburg-ers and drank Cokes in wax cups that were always sweating, and then down an alley a mile or so away, and when he left her off at five to eleven only the movie house was still open at the plaza. Her girl friend was there, talking with a boy. When Connie came up, the two girls smiled at each other and Connie said, "How was the movie?" and the girl said, "*You* should know." They rode off with the girl's father, sleepy and pleased, and Connie couldn't help but look back at the darkened shopping plaza with its big empty parking lot and its signs that were faded and ghostly now, and over at the drive-in restaurant where cars were still circling tirelessly. She couldn't hear the music at this distance.

Next morning June asked her how the movie was and Connie said, "So-so."

She and that girl and occasionally another girl went out several times a week,   10 and the rest of the time Connie spent around the house—it was summer vaca-tion—getting in her mother's way and thinking, dreaming about the boys she met. But all the boys fell back and dissolved into a single face that was not even a face but an idea, a feeling, mixed up with the urgent insistent pounding of the music and the humid night air of July. Connie's mother kept dragging her back to the daylight by finding things for her to do or saying suddenly, "What's this about the Pettinger girl?"

And Connie would say nervously, "Oh, her. That dope." She always drew thick clear lines between herself and such girls, and her mother was simple and kind enough to believe it. Her mother was so simple, Connie thought, that it was maybe cruel to fool her so much. Her mother went scuffling around the house in old bedroom slippers and complained over the telephone to one sister about the other, then the other called up and the two of them complained about the third one. If June's name was mentioned her mother's tone was approving, and if Connie's name was mentioned it was disapproving. This did not really mean she disliked Connie, and actually Connie thought that her mother preferred her to June just because she was prettier, but the two of them kept up a pretense of exasperation, a sense that they were tugging and struggling over something of lit-tle value to either of them. Sometimes, over coffee, they were almost friends, but something would come up—some vexation that was like a fly buzzing suddenly around their heads—and their faces went hard with contempt.

One Sunday Connie got up at eleven—none of them bothered with church—and washed her hair so that it could dry all day long in the sun. Her parents and sister were going to a barbecue at an aunt's house and Connie said no, she wasn't interested, rolling her eyes to let her mother know just what she thought of it. "Stay home alone then," her mother said sharply. Connie sat out back in a lawn chair and watched them drive away, her father quiet and bald, hunched around so that he could back the car out, her mother with a look that was still angry and not at all softened through the windshield, and in the back seat poor old June, all dressed up as if she didn't know what a barbecue was, with all the running yelling kids and the flies. Connie sat with her eyes closed in the sun, dreaming and dazed with the warmth about her as if this were a kind of love, the caresses of love, and her mind slipped over onto thoughts of the boy she had been with the night before and how nice he had been, how sweet it always was, not the way someone like June would suppose but sweet, gentle, the way it was in movies and promised in songs; and when she opened her eyes she hardly knew where she was, the back yard ran off into weeds and a fence-like line of trees and behind it the sky was perfectly blue and still. The asbestos "ranch house" that was now three years old startled her—it looked small. She shook her head as if to get awake.

It was too hot. She went inside the house and turned on the radio to drown out the quiet. She sat on the edge of her bed, barefoot, and listened for an hour and a half to a program called XYZ Sunday Jamboree, record after record of hard, fast, shrieking songs she sang along with, interspersed by exclamations from "Bobby King": "An' look here, you girls at Napoleon's—Son and Charley want you to pay real close attention to this song coming up!"

And Connie paid close attention herself, bathed in a glow of slow-pulsed joy that seemed to rise mysteriously out of the music itself and lay languidly about the airless little room, breathed in and breathed out with each gentle rise and fall of her chest.

After a while she heard a car coming up the drive. She sat up at once, star- 15
tled, because it couldn't be her father so soon. The gravel kept crunching all the way in from the road—the driveway was long—and Connie ran to the window. It was a car she didn't know. It was an open jalopy, painted a bright gold that caught the sunlight opaquely. Her heart began to pound and her fingers snatched at her hair, checking it, and she whispered, "Christ. Christ," wondering how bad she looked. The car came to a stop at the side door and the horn sounded four short taps, as if this were a signal Connie knew.

She went into the kitchen and approached the door slowly, then hung out the screen door, her bare toes curling down off the step. There were two boys in the car and now she recognized the driver: he had shaggy, shabby black hair that looked crazy as a wig and he was grinning at her.

"I ain't late, am I?" he said.

"Who the hell do you think you are?" Connie said.

"Toldja I'd be out, didn't I?"

"I don't even know who you are." 20

She spoke sullenly, careful to show no interest or pleasure, and he spoke in a fast, bright monotone. Connie looked past him to the other boy, taking her time. He had fair brown hair, with a lock that fell onto his forehead. His side-burns gave him a fierce, embarrassed look, but so far he hadn't even bothered to glance at her. Both boys wore sunglasses. The driver's glasses were metallic and mirrored everything in miniature.

"You wanta come for a ride?" he said.

Connie smirked and let her hair fall loose over one shoulder.

"Don'tcha like my car? New paint job," he said. "Hey."

"What?" 25

"You're cute."

She pretended to fidget, chasing flies away from the door.

"Don'tcha believe me, or what?" he said.

"Look, I don't even know who you are," Connie said in disgust.

"Hey, Ellie's got a radio, see. Mine broke down." He lifted his friend's arm 30
and showed her the little transistor radio the boy was holding, and now Connie

began to hear the music. It was the same program that was playing inside the house.

"Bobby King?" she said.

"I listen to him all the time. I think he's great."

"He's kind of great," Connie said reluctantly.

"Listen, that guy's *great*. He knows where the action is."

Connie blushed a little, because the glasses made it impossible for her to see   35
just what this boy was looking at. She couldn't decide if she liked him or if he was just a jerk, and so she dawdled in the doorway and wouldn't come down or go back inside. She said, "What's all that stuff painted on your car?"

"Can'tcha read it?" He opened the door very carefully, as if he were afraid it might fall off. He slid out just as carefully, planting his feet firmly on the ground, the tiny metallic world in his glasses slowing down like gelatine hardening, and in the midst of it Connie's bright green blouse. "This here is my name, to begin with," he said. ARNOLD FRIEND was written in tarlike black letters on the side, with a drawing of a round, grinning face that reminded Connie of a pumpkin, except it wore sunglasses. "I wanta introduce myself, I'm Arnold Friend and that's my real name and I'm gonna be your friend, honey, and inside the car's Ellie Oscar, he's kinda shy." Ellie brought his transistor radio up to his shoulder and balanced it there. "Now, these numbers are a secret code, honey," Arnold Friend explained. He read off the numbers 33, 19, 17 and raised his eyebrows at her to see what she thought of that, but she didn't think much of it. The left rear fender had been smashed and around it was written, on the gleaming gold background: DONE BY CRAZY WOMAN DRIVER. Connie had to laugh at that. Arnold Friend was pleased at her laughter and looked up at her. "Around the other side's a lot more—you wanta come and see them?"

"No."

"Why not?"

"Why should I?"

"Don'tcha wanta see what's on the car? Don'tcha wanta go for a ride?"   40

"I don't know."

"Why not?"

"I got things to do."

"Like what?"

"Things."   45

He laughed as if she had said something funny. He slapped his thighs. He was standing in a strange way, leaning back against the car as if he were balancing himself. He wasn't tall, only an inch or so taller than she would be if she came down to him. Connie liked the way he was dressed, which was the way all of them dressed: tight faded jeans stuffed into black, scuffed boots, a belt that pulled his waist in and showed how lean he was, and a white pull-over shirt that was a little soiled and showed the hard small muscles of his arms and shoulders. He looked as if he probably did hard work, lifting and carrying things. Even his neck looked muscular. And his face was a familiar face, somehow: the jaw and chin and cheeks slightly darkened because he hadn't shaved for a day or two, and the nose long and hawklike, sniffing as if she were a treat he was going to gobble up and it was all a joke.

"Connie, you ain't telling the truth. This is your day set aside for a ride with me and you know it," he said, still laughing. The way he straightened and recovered from his fit of laughing showed that it had been all fake.

"How do you know what my name is?" she said suspiciously.

"It's Connie."

"Maybe and maybe not."   50

"I know my Connie," he said, wagging his finger. Now she remembered him even better, back at the restaurant, and her cheeks warmed at the thought of how she had sucked in her breath just at the moment she passed him—how she must have looked to him. And he had remembered her. "Ellie and I come out here especially for you," he said. "Ellie can sit in back. How about it?"

"Where?"

"Where what?"

"Where're we going?"

He looked at her. He took off the sunglasses and she saw how pale the skin   55
around his eyes was, like holes that were not in shadow but instead in light. His eyes were like chips of broken glass that catch the light in an amiable way. He smiled. It was as if the idea of going for a ride somewhere, to someplace, was a new idea to him.

"Just for a ride, Connie sweetheart."

"I never said my name was Connie," she said.

"But I know what it is. I know your name and all about you, lots of things," Arnold Friend said. He had not moved yet but stood still leaning back against the side of his jalopy. "I took a special interest in you, such a pretty girl, and found out all about you—like I know your parents and sister are gone somewheres and I know where and how long they're going to be gone, and I know who you were with last night, and your best girl friend's name is Betty. Right?"

He spoke in a simple lilting voice, exactly as if he were reciting the words to a song. His smile assured her that everything was fine. In the car Ellie turned up the volume on his radio and did not bother to look around at them.

"Ellie can sit in the back seat," Arnold Friend said. He indicated his friend   60
with a casual jerk of his chin, as if Ellie did not count and she should not bother with him.

"How'd you find out all that stuff?" Connie said.

"Listen: Betty Schultz and Tony Fitch and Jimmy Pettinger and Nancy Pettinger," he said in a chant. "Raymond Stanley and Bob Hutter—"

"Do you know all those kids?"

"I know everybody."

"Look, you're kidding. You're not from around here."   65

"Sure."

"But—how come we never saw you before?"

"Sure you saw me before," he said. He looked down at his boots, as if he were a little offended. "You just don't remember."

"I guess I'd remember you," Connie said.

"Yeah?" He looked up at this, beaming. He was pleased. He began to mark   70
time with the music from Ellie's radio, tapping his fists lightly together. Connie looked away from his smile to the car, which was painted so bright it almost hurt her eyes to look at it. She looked at that name, ARNOLD FRIEND. And up at the front fender was an expression that was familiar—MAN THE FLYING SAUCERS. It was an expression kids had used the year before but didn't use this year. She looked at it for a while as if the words meant something to her that she did not yet know.

"What're you thinking about? Huh?" Arnold Friend demanded. "Not worried about your hair blowing around in the car, are you?"

"No."

"Think I maybe can't drive good?"

"How do I know?"

"You're a hard girl to handle. How come?" he said. "Don't you know I'm   75
your friend? Didn't you see me put my sign in the air when you walked by?"

"What sign?"

"My sign." And he drew an X in the air, leaning out toward her. They were maybe ten feet apart. After his hand fell back to his side the X was still in the air, almost visible. Connie let the screen door close and stood perfectly still inside it, listening to the music from her radio and the boy's blend together. She stared at Arnold Friend. He stood there so stiffly relaxed, pretending to be relaxed, with one hand idly on the door handle as if he were keeping himself up that way and had no intention of ever moving again. She recognized most things about him, the tight jeans that showed his thighs and buttocks and the greasy leather boots and the tight shirt, and even that slippery friendly smile of his, that sleepy dreamy smile that all the boys used to get across ideas they didn't want to put into words. She recognized all this and also the singsong way he talked, slightly mocking, kidding, but serious and a little melancholy, and she recognized the way he tapped one fist against the other in homage to the perpetual music behind him. But all these things did not come together.

She said suddenly, "Hey, how old are you?"

His smiled faded. She could see then that he wasn't a kid, he was much older—thirty, maybe more. At this knowledge her heart began to pound faster.

"That's a crazy thing to ask. Can'tcha see I'm your own age?"   80

"Like hell you are."

"Or maybe a coupla years older. I'm eighteen."

"Eighteen?" she said doubtfully.

He grinned to reassure her and lines appeared at the corners of his mouth. His teeth were big and white. He grinned so broadly his eyes became slits and she saw how thick the lashes were, thick and black as if painted with a black tar-like material. Then, abruptly, he seemed to become embarrassed and looked over his shoulder at Ellie. "*Him*, he's crazy," he said. "Ain't he a riot? He's a nut, a real character." Ellie was still listening to the music. His sunglasses told nothing about what he was thinking. He wore a bright orange shirt unbuttoned halfway to show his chest, which was a pale, bluish chest and not muscular like Arnold Friend's. His shirt collar was turned up all around and the very tips of the collar pointed out past his chin as if they were protecting him. He was pressing the transistor radio up against his ear and sat there in a kind of daze, right in the sun.

"He's kinda strange," Connie said.   85

"Hey, she says you're kinda strange! Kinda strange!" Arnold Friend cried. He pounded on the car to get Ellie's attention. Ellie turned for the first time and Connie saw with shock that he wasn't a kid either—he had a fair, hairless face, cheeks reddened slightly as if the veins grew too close to the surface of his skin, the face of a forty-year-old baby. Connie felt a wave of dizziness rise in her at this sight and she stared at him as if waiting for something to change the shock of the moment, make it all right again. Ellie's lips kept shaping words, mumbling along with the words blasting in his ear.

"Maybe you two better go away," Connie said faintly.

"What? How come?" Arnold Friend cried. "We come out here to take you for a ride. It's Sunday." He had the voice of the man on the radio now. It was the same voice, Connie thought. "Don'tcha know it's Sunday all day? And honey, no matter who you were with last night, today you're with Arnold Friend and don't you forget it! Maybe you better step out here," he said, and this last was in a different voice. It was a little flatter, as if the heat was finally getting to him.

"No. I got things to do."

"Hey."   90

"You two better leave."

"We ain't leaving until you come with us."

"Like hell I am—"

"Connie, don't fool around with me. I mean—I mean, don't fool *around*," he said, shaking his head. He laughed incredulously. He placed his sunglasses on top of his head, carefully, as if he were indeed wearing a wig, and brought the stems down behind his ears. Connie stared at him, another wave of dizziness and fear rising in her so that for a moment he wasn't even in focus but was just a blur standing there against his gold car, and she had the idea that he had driven up the driveway all right but had come from nowhere before that and belonged nowhere and that everything about him and even about the music that was so familiar to her was only half real.

"If my father comes and sees you—"   95

"He ain't coming. He's at a barbecue."

"How do you know that?"

"Aunt Tillie's. Right now they're—uh—they're drinking. Sitting around," he said vaguely, squinting as if he were staring all the way to town and over to Aunt Tillie's back yard. Then the vision seemed to get clear and he nodded energetically. "Yeah. Sitting around. There's your sister in a blue dress, huh? And high heels, the poor sad bitch—nothing like you, sweetheart! And your mother's helping some fat woman with the corn, they're cleaning the corn—husking the corn—"

"What fat woman?" Connie cried.

"How do I know what fat woman, I don't know every goddamn fat woman   100 in the world!" Arnold Friend laughed.

"Oh, that's Mrs. Hornsby. . . . Who invited her?" Connie said. She felt a little lightheaded. Her breath was coming quickly.

"She's too fat. I don't like them fat. I like them the way you are, honey," he said, smiling sleepily at her. They stared at each other for a while through the screen door. He said softly, "Now, what you're going to do is this: you're going to come out that door. You're going to sit up front with me and Ellie's going to sit in the back, the hell with Ellie, right? This isn't Ellie's date. You're my date. I'm your lover, honey."

"What? You're crazy—"

"Yes, I'm your lover. You don't know what that is but you will," he said. "I know that too. I know all about you. But look: it's real nice and you couldn't ask for nobody better than me, or more polite. I always keep my word. I'll tell you how it is, I'm always nice at first, the first time. I'll hold you so tight you won't think you have to try to get away or pretend anything because you'll know you can't. And I'll come inside you where it's all secret and you'll give in to me and you'll love me—"

"Shut up! You're crazy!" Connie said. She backed away from the door. She   105
put her hands up against her ears as if she'd heard something terrible, something
not meant for her. "People don't talk like that, you're crazy," she muttered. Her
heart was almost too big now for her chest and its pumping made sweat break
out all over her. She looked out to see Arnold Friend pause and then take a step
toward the porch, lurching. He almost fell. But, like a clever drunken man, he
managed to catch his balance. He wobbled in his high boots and grabbed hold
of one of the porch posts.

"Honey?" he said. "You still listening?"

"Get the hell out of here!"

"Be nice, honey. Listen."

"I'm going to call the police—"

He wobbled again and out of the side of his mouth came a fast spat curse,   110
an aside not meant for her to hear. But even this "Christ!" sounded forced. Then
he began to smile again. She watched this smile come, awkward as if he were smiling from inside a mask. His whole face was a mask, she thought wildly, tanned
down to his throat but then running out as if he had plastered make-up on his
face but had forgotten about his throat.

"Honey—? Listen, here's how it is. I always tell the truth and I promise you
this: I ain't coming in that house after you."

"You better not! I'm going to call the police if you—if you don't—"

"Honey," he said, talking right through her voice, "honey, I'm not coming
in there but you are coming out here. You know why?"

She was panting. The kitchen looked like a place she had never seen before,
some room she had run inside but that wasn't good enough, wasn't going to help
her. The kitchen window had never had a curtain, after three years, and there were
dishes in the sink for her to do—probably—and if you ran your hand across the
table you'd probably feel something sticky there.

"You listening, honey? Hey?"   115

"—going to call the police—"

"Soon as you touch the phone I don't need to keep my promise and can
come inside. You won't want that."

She rushed forward and tried to lock the door. Her fingers were shaking. "But
why lock it," Arnold Friend said gently, talking right into her face. "It's just a screen
door. It's just nothing." One of his boots was at a strange angle, as if his foot wasn't
in it. It pointed out to the left, bent at the ankle. "I mean, anybody can break through
a screen door and glass and wood and iron or anything else if he needs to, anybody
at all, and specially Arnold Friend. If the place got lit up with a fire, honey, you'd
come runnin' out into my arms, right into my arms an' safe at home—like you knew
I was your lover and'd stopped fooling around. I don't mind a nice shy girl but I
don't like no fooling around." Part of those words were spoken with a slight rhythmic lilt, and Connie somehow recognized them—the echo of a song from last year,
about a girl rushing into her boy friend's arms and coming home again—

Connie stood barefoot on the linoleum floor, staring at him. "What do you
want?" she whispered.

"I want you," he said.   120

"What?"

"Seen you that night and thought, that's the one, yes sir. I never needed to
look anymore."

"But my father's coming back. He's coming to get me. I had to wash my hair first—" She spoke in a dry, rapid voice, hardly raising it for him to hear.

"No, your daddy is not coming and yes, you had to wash your hair and you washed it for me. It's nice and shining and all for me. I thank you sweetheart," he said with a mock bow, but again he almost lost his balance. He had to bend and adjust his boots. Evidently his feet did not go all the way down; the boots must have been stuffed with something so that he would seem taller. Connie stared out at him and behind him at Ellie in the car, who seemed to be looking off toward Connie's right, into nothing. This Ellie said, pulling the words out of the air one after another as if he were just discovering them, "You want me to pull out the phone?"

"Shut your mouth and keep it shut," Arnold Friend said, his face red from   125
bending over or maybe from embarrassment because Connie had seen his boots. "This ain't none of your business."

"What—what are you doing? What do you want?" Connie said. "If I call the police they'll get you, they'll arrest you—"

"Promise was not to come in unless you touch that phone, and I'll keep that promise," he said. He resumed his erect position and tried to force his shoulders back. He sounded like a hero in a movie, declaring something important. But he spoke too loudly and it was as if he were speaking to someone behind Connie. "I ain't made plans for coming in that house where I don't belong but just for you to come out to me, the way you should. Don't you know who I am?"

"You're crazy," she whispered. She backed away from the door but did not want to go into another part of the house, as if this would give him permission to come through the door. "What do you . . . you're crazy, you. . . ."

"Huh? What're you saying, honey?"

Her eyes darted everywhere in the kitchen. She could not remember what it   130
was, this room.

"This is how it is, honey: you come out and we'll drive away, have a nice ride. But if you don't come out we're gonna wait till your people come home and then they're all going to get it."

"You want that telephone pulled out?" Ellie said. He held the radio away from his ear and grimaced, as if without the radio the air was too much for him.

"I toldja shut up, Ellie," Arnold Friend said, "you're deaf, get a hearing aid, right? Fix yourself up. This little girl's no trouble and's gonna be nice to me, so Ellie keep to yourself, this ain't your date—right? Don't hem in on me, don't hog, don't crush, don't bird dog, don't trail me," he said in a rapid, meaningless voice, as if he were running through all the expressions he'd learned but was no longer sure which of them was in style, then rushing on to new ones, making them up with his eyes closed. "Don't crawl under my fence, don't squeeze in my chipmunk hole, don't sniff my glue, suck my popsicle, keep your own greasy fingers on yourself!" He shaded his eyes and peered in at Connie, who was backed against the kitchen table. "Don't mind him, honey, he's just a creep. He's a dope. Right? I'm the boy for you and like I said, you come out here nice like a lady and give me your hand, and nobody else gets hurt, I mean, your nice old bald-headed daddy and your mummy and your sister in her high heels. Because listen: why bring them in this?"

"Leave me alone," Connie whispered.

"Hey, you know that old woman down the road, the one with the chickens   135
and stuff—you know her?"

"She's dead!"

"Dead? What? You know her?" Arnold Friend said.

"She's dead—"

"Don't you like her?"

"She's dead—she's—she isn't here anymore—"   140

"But don't you like her, I mean, you got something against her? Some grudge or something?" Then his voice dipped as if he were conscious of a rudeness. He touched the sunglasses perched up on top of his head as if to make sure they were still there. "Now, you be a good girl."

"What are you going to do?"

"Just two things, or maybe three," Arnold Friend said. "But I promise it won't last long and you'll like me the way you get to like people you're close to. You will. It's all over for you here, so come on out. You don't want your people in any trouble, do you?"

She turned and bumped against a chair or something, hurting her leg, but she ran into the back room and picked up the telephone. Something roared in her ear, a tiny roaring, and she was so sick with fear that she could do nothing but listen to it—the telephone was clammy and very heavy and her fingers groped down to the dial but were too weak to touch it. She began to scream into the phone, into the roaring. She cried out, she cried for her mother, she felt her breath start jerking back and forth in her lungs as if it were something Arnold Friend was stabbing her with again and again with no tenderness. A noisy sorrowful wailing rose all about her and she was locked inside it the way she was locked inside this house.

After a while she could hear again. She was sitting on the floor with her wet 145
back against the wall.

Arnold Friend was saying from the door, "That's a good girl. Put the phone back."

She kicked the phone away from her.

"No, honey. Pick it up. Put it back right."

She picked it up and put it back. The dial tone stopped.

"That's a good girl. Now, you come outside."   150

She was hollow with what had been fear but what was now just an emptiness. All that screaming had blasted it out of her. She sat, one leg cramped under her, and deep inside her brain was something like a pinpoint of light that kept going and would not let her relax. She thought, I'm not going to see my mother again. She thought, I'm not going to sleep in my bed again. Her bright green blouse was all wet.

Arnold Friend said, in a gentle-loud voice that was like a stage voice, "The place where you came from ain't there anymore, and where you had in mind to go is cancelled out. This place you are now—inside your daddy's house—is nothing but a cardboard box I can knock down any time. You know that and always did know it. You hear me?"

She thought, I have got to think. I have got to know what to do.

"We'll go out to a nice field, out in the country here where it smells so nice and it's sunny," Arnold Friend said. "I'll have my arms tight around you so you won't need to try to get away and I'll show you what love is like, what it does. The hell with this house! It looks solid all right," he said. He ran a fingernail down the screen and the noise did not make Connie shiver, as it would have the day before. "Now, put your hand on your heart, honey. Feel that? That feels solid too but we know better. Be nice to me, be sweet like you can because what else is there for a girl like you but to be sweet and pretty and give in?—and get away before her people come back?"

She felt her pounding heart. Her hand seemed to enclose it. She thought for   155
the first time in her life that it was nothing that was hers, that belonged to her, but just a pounding, living thing inside this body that wasn't really hers either.

"You don't want them to get hurt," Arnold Friend went on. "Now, get up, honey. Get up all by yourself."

She stood.

"Now, turn this way. That's right. Come over here to me.—Ellie, put that away, didn't I tell you? You dope. You miserable creepy dope," Arnold Friend said. His words were not angry but only part of an incantation. The incantation was kindly. "Now, come out through the kitchen to me, honey, and let's see a smile, try it, you're a brave, sweet little girl and now they're eating corn and hot dogs cooked to bursting over an outdoor fire, and they don't know one thing about you and never did and honey, you're better than them because not a one of them would have done this for you."

Connie felt the linoleum under her feet; it was cool. She brushed her hair back out of her eyes. Arnold Friend let go of the post tentatively and opened his arms for her, his elbows pointing in toward each other and his wrists limp, to show that this was an embarrassed embrace and a little mocking, he didn't want to make her self-conscious.

She put out her hand against the screen. She watched herself push the door   160
slowly open as if she were safe back somewhere in the other doorway, watching this body and this head of long hair moving out into the sunlight where Arnold Friend waited.

"My sweet little blue-eyed girl," he said, in a half-sung sigh that had nothing to do with her brown eyes but was taken up just the same by the vast sunlit reaches of the land behind him and on all sides of him, so much land that Connie had never seen before and did not recognize except to know that she was going to it.

WINDOW ON

History and Fiction

There are many ways to talk about history and fiction. One is to discuss the historical development of plot or characterization and make useful comparisons between older and more modern stories. For example, one could compare the medieval writers Boccaccio and Geoffrey Chaucer (who wrote narrative poems) with Edgar Allan Poe and Nathanial Hawthorne, and then with Anton Chekhov and James Joyce.

Another form of literary history recaptures the historical circumstances of a given story. Dr. Rappaccini in "Rappaccini's Daughter" depends on the power of the herbs growing in his garden. In order to understand the importance of this detail, we need to know that in Hawthorne's age medicines were developed from herbs, not chemicals; in fact, only since the early twentieth century has our pharmacopeia been chemical. Since our age has lost sight of the power associated with rare herbs, we need some history to appreciate the story.

Some writers deliberately play with our sense of history, as Ursula K. Le Guin does in "Sur: A Summary Report of the Yelcho Expedition to the Antarctic, 1909–10." With a straight face she writes a "report" that imitates documents of several expeditions to remote places. But Le Guin's explorers are women, and in 1909 it was impossible for women to get backing and support for such an expedition. To fully feel this irony, one might begin by reading authentic historical reports of the time. Many parties had tried to reach the South Pole but had failed. R.F. Scott, however, did reach it on December 14, 1911, with four men and fifty-two dogs. E.H. Shackleton's *Scott's Last Expedition* (1913) and *South* (1922) would help you appreciate the success of Le Guin's parody of male expeditions and the range of her irony.

Of course, you need not read Shackleton to enjoy Le Guin's story: she provides enough material to enjoy it on its own. But a New Historian would say that reading original historical documents relevant to the story will alter your interpretation. Perhaps you will observe the stylistic achievement of Le Guin in a new way because you have a comparison. Perhaps you will detect ironies that Le Guin has built into the story by making direct—if covert—allusions to Scott's historic trek. Indeed, when you read history in relation to fiction, you cannot be sure how your interpretation will change. But if the New Historians are correct, you can definitely count on a change occurring.

In Faulkner's "A Rose for Emily," the historical setting definitely affects your interpretation. Information on Jefferson's place in the Civil War, its reverence of Confederate tradition, and its attitude not only toward women and Miss Emily but also toward the Grierson family in general permits you to see the story in a richer light than if you had ignored history entirely. The same would be true if you examined the history of slavery in Mississippi. At the same time, however, you must ask: Are these historical issues intrinsic in "A Rose for Emily," or are they extrinsic? Do I locate the historical issues within the story as I read it, or do I bring them to the story after I read it? The answer to that question will help you decide whether a historical approach to these works is legitimate.

One experiment in literary history would be to compare the depth of characterization in Kate Chopin's "The Story of an Hour" with that in Mary Lavin's "Happiness." Chopin did not have the advantage of modern psychology; Lavin did. Another experiment would be to read about the legal rights of wives in the period of Charlotte Perkins Gilman's "The Yellow Wallpaper." Gilman's own book, *Women and Economics: A Study of the Economic Relation between Men and Women as a Factor in Social Evolution* (1898), provides historical material on this subject.

Reading

Greenblatt, Stephen. *Renaissance Self-Fashioning.* Chicago: University of Chicago Press, 1980.

Huizinga, Jonathan. "The Task of Cultural History." In *Men and Ideas,* translated by James S. Holms and Hans van Marle. New York: Meridian, 1959.

Newton, Judith. "History as Usual? Feminism and the 'New Historicism.' " *Cultural Critique* 9 (1988).

Simpson, David. "Literary Criticism and the Return to 'History.' " *Critical Inquiry* 14 (1988).

Tim O'Brien   (b. 1946)

Tim O'Brien has made the Vietnam War a major subject. He grew up in Minnesota, went to Macalaster College and Harvard University and was drafted into the army. He went to Vietnam where he became a sergeant and was eventually wounded and awarded the Purple Heart. Among his books are If I Die in a Combat Zone, Box Me Up and Ship Me Home *(1973), an autobiographical account of some of his experiences in the war, and* Northern Lights *(1974), a novel. He became a widely celebrated writer after the publication of* Going after Cacciato *(1978), a surrealist novel of men searching for one of their unit heading AWOL from Vietnam. It won him the National Book Award in 1979. His stories have appeared in* Esquire *and other national magazines. "Sweetheart of the Song Tra Bong" first appeared in* Esquire *and is collected in* The Things They Carried *(1990). The dedication page of that book reads: "This book is lovingly dedicated to the men of Alpha Company, and in particular to Jimmy Cross, Norman Bowker, Rat Kiley, Mitchell Sanders, Henry Dobbins, and Kiowa."*

SWEETHEART OF THE SONG TRA BONG   1987

Vietnam was full of strange stories, some improbable, some well beyond that, but the stories that will last forever are those that swirl back and forth across the border between trivia and bedlam, the mad and the mundane. This one keeps returning to me. I heard it from Rat Kiley, who swore up and down to its truth, although in the end, I'll admit, that doesn't amount to much of a warranty. Among the men in Alpha Company, Rat had a reputation for exaggeration and overstatement, a compulsion to rev up the facts, and for most of us it was normal procedure to discount sixty or seventy percent of anything he had to say. If Rat told you, for example, that he'd slept with four girls one night, you could figure it was about a girl and a half. It wasn't a question of deceit. Just the opposite: he wanted to heat up the truth, to make it burn so hot that you would feel exactly what he felt. For Rat Kiley, I think, facts were formed by sensation, not the other way around, and when you listened to one of his stories, you'd find yourself performing rapid calculations in your head, subtracting superlatives, figuring the square root of an absolute and then multiplying by maybe.

Still, with this particular story, Rat never backed down. He claimed to have witnessed the incident with his own eyes, and I remember how upset he became one morning when Mitchell Sanders challenged him on its basic premise.

"It can't happen," Sanders said. "Nobody ships his honey over to Nam. It don't ring true. I mean, you just can't import your own personal poontang."

Rat shook his head. "I *saw* it, man. I was right there. This guy did it."

"His girlfriend?"   5

"Straight on. It's a fact." Rat's voice squeaked a little. He paused and looked at his hands. "Listen, the guy sends her the money. Flies her over. This cute blonde—just a kid, just barely out of high school—she shows up with a suitcase and one of those plastic cosmetic bags. Comes right out to the boonies. I swear to God, man, she's got on culottes. White culottes and this sexy pink sweater. There she *is*."

I remember Mitchell Sanders folding his arms. He looked over at me for a second, not quite grinning, not saying a word, but I could read the amusement in his eyes.

Rat saw it, too.

"No lie," he muttered. "Culottes."

When he first arrived in-country, before joining Alpha Company, Rat had   10
been assigned to a small medical detachment up in the mountains west of Chu Lai, near the village of Tra Bong, where along with eight other enlisted men he ran an aid station that provided basic emergency and trauma care. Casualties were flown in by helicopter, stabilized, then shipped out to hospitals in Chu Lai or Danang. It was gory work, Rat said, but predictable. Amputations, mostly—legs and feet. The area was heavily mined, thick with Bouncing Betties° and home-made booby traps. For a medic, though, it was ideal duty, and Rat counted himself lucky. There was plenty of cold beer, three hot meals a day, a tin roof over his head. No humping at all. No officers, either. You could let your hair grow, he said, and you didn't have to polish your boots or snap off salutes or put up with the usual rear-echelon nonsense. The highest ranking NCO was an E-6 named Eddie Diamond, whose pleasures ran from dope to Darvon, and except for a rare field inspection there was no such thing as military discipline.

As Rat described it, the compound was situated at the top of a flat-crested hill along the northern outskirts of Tra Bong. At one end was a small dirt heli-pad; at the other end, in a rough semicircle, the mess hall and medical hootches overlooked a river called the Song Tra Bong. Surrounding the place were tangled rolls of concertina wire, with bunkers and reinforced firing positions at staggered intervals, and base security was provided by a mixed unit of RFs, PFs, and ARVN° infantry. Which is to say virtually no security at all. As soldiers, the ARVNs were useless; the Ruff-and-Puffs were outright dangerous. And yet even with decent troops the place was clearly indefensible. To the north and west the country rose up in thick walls of wilderness, triple-canopied jungle, mountains unfolding into higher mountains, ravines and gorges and fast-moving rivers and waterfalls and exotic butterflies and steep cliffs and smoky little hamlets and great valleys of bam-boo and elephant grass. Originally, in the early 1960s, the place had been set up as a Special Forces outpost, and when Rat Kiley arrived nearly a decade later, a

Bouncing Betties: Land mines.   *ARVN*: South Vietnamese Regular Troops.

squad of six Green Berets still used the compound as a base of operations. The Greenies were not social animals. Animals, Rat said, but far from social. They had their own hootch at the edge of the perimeter, fortified with sandbags and a metal fence, and except for the bare essentials they avoided contact with the medical detachment. Secretive and suspicious, loners by nature, the six Greenies would sometimes vanish for days at a time, or even weeks, then late in the night they would just as magically reappear, moving like shadows through the moonlight, filing in silently from the dense rain forest off to the west. Among the medics there were jokes about this, but no one asked questions.

While the outpost was isolated and vulnerable, Rat said, he always felt a curious sense of safety there. Nothing much ever happened. The place was never mortared, never taken under fire, and the war seemed to be somewhere far away. On occasion, when casualties came in, there were quick spurts of activity, but otherwise the days flowed by without incident, a smooth and peaceful time. Most mornings were spent on the volleyball court. In the heat of midday the men would head for the shade, lazing away the long afternoons, and after sundown there were movies and card games and sometimes all-night drinking sessions.

It was during one of those late nights that Eddie Diamond first brought up the tantalizing possibility. It was an offhand comment. A joke, really. What they should do, Eddie said, was pool some bucks and bring in a few mama-sans° from Saigon, spice things up, and after a moment one of the men laughed and said, "Our own little EM club," and somebody else said, "Hey, yeah, we pay our fuckin' dues, don't we?" It was nothing serious. Just passing time, playing with the possibilities, and so for a while they tossed the idea around, how you could actually get away with it, no officers or anything, nobody to clamp down, then they dropped the subject and moved on to cars and baseball.

Later in the night, though, a young medic named Mark Fossie kept coming back to the subject.

"Look, if you think about it," he said, "it's not that crazy. You could actu-   15
ally do it."

"Do what?" Rat said.

"You know. Bring in a girl. I mean, what's the problem?"

Rat shrugged. "Nothing. A war."

"Well, see, that's the thing," Mark Fossie said. "No war *here*. You could really do it. A pair of solid brass balls, that's all you'd need."

There was some laughter, and Eddie Diamond told him he'd best strap down   20
his dick, but Fossie just frowned and looked at the ceiling for a while and then went off to write a letter.

Six weeks later his girlfriend showed up.

The way Rat told it, she came in by helicopter along with the daily resupply shipment out of Chu Lai. A tall, big-boned blonde. At best, Rat said, she was seventeen years old, fresh out of Cleveland Heights Senior High. She had long white legs and blue eyes and a complexion like strawberry ice cream. Very friendly, too.

At the helipad that morning, Mark Fossie grinned and put his arm around her and said, "Guys, this is Mary Anne."

The girl seemed tired and somewhat lost, but she smiled.

There was a heavy silence. Eddie Diamond, the ranking NCO, made a small   25

mama-sans: Women.

motion with his hand, and some of the others murmured a word or two, then they watched Mark Fossie pick up her suitcase and lead her by the arm down to the hootches. For a long while the men were quiet.

"That fucker," somebody finally said.

At evening chow Mark Fossie explained how he'd set it up. It was expensive, he admitted, and the logistics were complicated, but it wasn't like going to the moon. Cleveland to Los Angeles, LA to Bangkok, Bangkok to Saigon. She'd hopped a C-130 up to Chu Lai and stayed overnight at the USO and the next morning hooked a ride west with the resupply chopper.

"A cinch," Fossie said, and gazed down at his pretty girlfriend. "Thing is, you just got to *want* it enough."

Mary Anne Bell and Mark Fossie had been sweethearts since grammar school. From the sixth grade on they had known for a fact that someday they would be married, and live in a fine gingerbread house near Lake Erie, and have three healthy yellow-haired children, and grow old together, and no doubt die in each other's arms and be buried in the same walnut casket. That was the plan. They were very much in love, full of dreams, and in the ordinary flow of their lives the whole scenario might well have come true.

On the first night they set up house in one of the bunkers along the perimeter, near the Special Forces hootch, and over the next two weeks they stuck together like a pair of high school steadies. It was almost disgusting, Rat said, the way they mooned over each other. Always holding hands, always laughing over some private joke. All they needed, he said, were a couple of matching sweaters. But among the medics there was some envy. It was Vietnam, after all, and Mary Anne Bell was an attractive girl. Too wide in the shoulders, maybe, but she had terrific legs, a bubbly personality, a happy smile. The men genuinely liked her. Out on the volleyball court she wore cut-off blue jeans and a black swimsuit top, which the guys appreciated, and in the evenings she liked to dance to music from Rat's portable tape deck. There was a novelty to it; she was good for morale. At times she gave off a kind of come-get-me energy, coy and flirtatious, but apparently it never bothered Mark Fossie. In fact he seemed to enjoy it, just grinning at her, because he was so much in love, and because it was the sort of show that a girl will sometimes put on for her boyfriend's entertainment and education.

Though she was young, Rat said, Mary Anne Bell was no timid child. She was curious about things. During her first days in-country she liked to roam around the compound asking questions: What exactly was a trip flare? How did a Claymore° work? What was behind those scary green mountains to the west? Then she'd squint and listen quietly while somebody filled her in. She had a good quick mind. She paid attention. Often, especially during the hot afternoons, she would spend time with the ARVNs out along the perimeter, picking up little phrases of Vietnamese, learning how to cook rice over a can of Sterno, how to eat with her hands. The guys sometimes liked to kid her about it—our own little native, they'd say—but Mary Anne would just smile and stick out her tongue. "I'm here," she'd say, "I might as well learn something."

The war intrigued her. The land, too, and the mystery. At the beginning of her second week she began pestering Mark Fossie to take her down to the village at the foot of the hill. In a quiet voice, very patiently, he tried to tell her that it

Claymore: U.S. personnel mine.

30

was a bad idea, way too dangerous, but Mary Anne kept after him. She wanted to get a feel for how people lived, what the smells and customs were. It did not impress her that the VC owned the place.

"Listen, it can't be that bad," she said. "They're human beings, aren't they? Like everybody else?"

Fossie nodded. He loved her.

And so in the morning Rat Kiley and two other medics tagged along as se-   35
curity while Mark and Mary Anne strolled through the ville like a pair of tourists. If the girl was nervous, she didn't show it. She seemed comfortable and entirely at home; the hostile atmosphere did not seem to register. All morning Mary Anne chattered away about how quaint the place was, how she loved the thatched roofs and naked children, the wonderful simplicity of village life. A strange thing to watch, Rat said. This seventeen-year-old doll in her goddamn culottes, perky and fresh-faced, like a cheerleader visiting the opposing team's locker room. Her pretty blue eyes seemed to glow. She couldn't get enough of it. On their way back up to the compound she stopped for a swim in the Song Tra Bong, stripping down to her underwear, showing off her legs while Fossie tried to explain to her about things like ambushes and snipers and the stopping power of an AK-47.

The guys, though, were impressed.

"A real tiger," said Eddie Diamond. "D-cup guts, trainer-bra brains."

"She'll learn," somebody said.

Eddie Diamond gave a solemn nod. "There's the scary part. I promise you, this girl will most definitely learn."

In parts, at least, it was a funny story, and yet to hear Rat Kiley tell it you'd   40
almost think it was intended as straight tragedy. He never smiled. Not even at the crazy stuff. There was always a dark, far-off look in his eyes, a kind of sadness, as if he were troubled by something sliding beneath the story's surface. Whenever we laughed, I remember, he'd sigh and wait it out, but the one thing he could not tolerate was disbelief. He'd get edgy if someone questioned one of the details. "She *wasn't* dumb," he'd snap. "I never said that. Young, that's all I said. Like you and me. A *girl*, that's the only difference, and I'll tell you something: it didn't amount to jack. I mean, when we first got here—all of us—we were real young and innocent, full of romantic bullshit, but we learned pretty damn quick. And so did Mary Anne."

Rat would peer down at his hands, silent and thoughtful. After a moment his voice would flatten out.

"You don't believe it?" he'd say. "Fine with me. But you don't know human nature. You don't know Nam."

Then he'd tell us to listen up.

A good sharp mind, Rat said. True, she could be silly sometimes, but she picked up on things fast. At the end of the second week, when four casualties came in, Mary Anne wasn't afraid to get her hands bloody. At times, in fact, she seemed fascinated by it. Not the gore so much, but the adrenaline buzz that went with the job, that quick hot rush in your veins when the choppers settled down and you had to do things fast and right. No time for sorting through options, no thinking at all; you just stuck your hands in and started plugging up holes. She was quiet and steady. She didn't back off from the ugly cases. Over the next day or two, as more casualties trickled in, she learned how to clip an artery and pump up a plastic splint and shoot in morphine. In times of action her face took on a sudden new composure, almost serene, the fuzzy blue eyes narrowing into a tight, intelligent focus. Mark Fossie would grin at this. He was proud, yes, but also amazed. A different person, it seemed, and he wasn't sure what to make of it.

Other things, too. The way she quickly fell into the habits of the bush. No cosmetics, no fingernail filing. She stopped wearing jewelry, cut her hair short and wrapped it in a dark green bandana. Hygiene became a matter of small consequence. In her second week Eddie Diamond taught her how to disassemble an M-16, how the various parts worked, and from there it was a natural progression to learning how to use the weapon. For hours at a time she plunked away at C-ration cans, a bit unsure of herself, but as it turned out she had a real knack for it. There was a new confidence in her voice, a new authority in the way she carried herself. In many ways she remained naive and immature, still a kid, but Cleveland Heights now seemed very far away.

Once or twice, gently, Mark Fossie suggested that it might be time to think about heading home, but Mary Anne laughed and told him to forget it. "Everything I want," she said, "is right here."

She stroked his arm, and then kissed him.

On one level things remained the same between them. They slept together. They held hands and made plans for after the war. But now there was a new imprecision in the way Mary Anne expressed her thoughts on certain subjects. Not necessarily three kids, she'd say. Not necessarily a house on Lake Erie. "Naturally we'll still get married," she'd tell him, "but it doesn't have to be right away. Maybe travel first. Maybe live together. Just test it out, you know?"

Mark Fossie would nod at this, even smile and agree, but it made him uncomfortable. He couldn't pin it down. Her body seemed foreign somehow—too stiff in places, too firm where the softness used to be. The bubbliness was gone. The nervous giggling, too. When she laughed now, which was rare, it was only when something struck her as truly funny. Her voice seemed to reorganize itself at a lower pitch. In the evenings, while the men played cards, she would sometimes fall into long elastic silences, her eyes fixed on the dark, her arms folded, her foot tapping out a coded message against the floor. When Fossie asked about it one evening, Mary Anne looked at him for a long moment and then shrugged. "It's nothing," she said. "Really nothing. To tell the truth, I've never been happier in my whole life. Never."

Twice, though, she came in late at night. Very late. And then finally she did not come in at all.

Rat Kiley heard about it from Fossie himself. Before dawn one morning, the kid shook him awake. He was in bad shape. His voice seemed hollow and stuffed up, nasal-sounding, as if he had a bad cold. He held a flashlight in his hand, clicking it on and off.

"Mary Anne," he whispered, "I can't *find* her."

Rat sat up and rubbed his face. Even in the dim light it was clear that the boy was in trouble. There were dark smudges under his eyes, the frayed edges of somebody who hadn't slept in a while.

"Gone," Fossie said. "Rat, listen, she's sleeping with somebody. Last night, she didn't even . . . I don't know what to *do*."

Abruptly then, Fossie seemed to collapse. He squatted down, rocking on his heels, still clutching the flashlight. Just a boy—eighteen years old. Tall and blond. A gifted athlete. A nice kid, too, polite and good-hearted, although for the moment none of it seemed to be serving him well.

He kept clicking the flashlight on and off.

"All right, start at the start," Rat said. "Nice and slow. Sleeping with who?"

"I don't know who. Eddie Diamond."

"Eddie?"

"Has to be. The guy's always there, always hanging on her."   60

Rat shook his head. "Man, I don't know. Can't say it strikes a right note, not with Eddie."

"Yes, but he's—"

"Easy does it," Rat said. He reached out and tapped the boy's shoulder. "Why not just check some bunks? We got nine guys. You and me, that's two, so there's seven possibles. Do a quick body count."

Fossie hesitated. "But I can't . . . If she's there, I mean, if she's with somebody—"

"Oh, Christ."   65

Rat pushed himself up. He took the flashlight, muttered something, and moved down to the far end of the hootch. For privacy, the men had rigged up curtained walls around their cots, small makeshift bedrooms, and in the dark Rat went quickly from room to room, using the flashlight to pluck out the faces. Eddie Diamond slept a hard deep sleep—the others, too. To be sure, though, Rat checked once more, very carefully, then he reported back to Fossie.

"All accounted for. No extras."

"Eddie?"

"Darvon dreams." Rat switched off the flashlight and tried to think it out. "Maybe she just—I don't know—maybe she camped out tonight. Under the stars or something. You search the compound?"

"Sure I did."   70

"Well, come on," Rat said. "One more time."

Outside, a soft violet light was spreading out across the eastern hillsides. Two or three ARVN soldiers had built their breakfast fires, but the place was mostly quiet and unmoving. They tried the helipad first, then the mess hall and supply hootches, then they walked the entire six hundred meters of perimeter.

"Okay," Rat finally said. "We got a problem."

When he first told the story, Rat stopped there and looked at Mitchell Sanders for a time.

"So what's your vote? Where was she?"   75

"The Greenies," Sanders said.

"Yeah?"

Sanders smiled. "No other option. That stuff about the Special Forces—how they used the place as a base of operations, how they'd glide in and out—all that had to be there for a *reason*. That's how stories work, man."

Rat thought about it, then shrugged.

"All right, sure, the Greenies. But it's not what Fossie thought. She wasn't   80
sleeping with any of them. At least not exactly. I mean, in a way she was sleeping with *all* of them, more or less, except it wasn't sex or anything. They was just lying together, so to speak, Mary Anne and these six grungy weirded-out Green Berets."

"Lying down?" Sanders said.

"You got it."

"Lying down how?"

Rat smiled. "Ambush. All night long, man, Mary Anne's out on fuckin' *ambush*."

Just after sunrise, Rat said, she came trooping in through the wire, tired-looking but cheerful as she dropped her gear and gave Mark Fossie a brisk hug. The six Green Berets did not speak. One of them nodded at her, and the others gave Fossie a long stare, then they filed off to their hootch at the edge of the compound. 85

"Please," she said. "Not a word."

Fossie took a half step forward and hesitated. It was as though he had trouble recognizing her. She wore a bush hat and filthy green fatigues; she carried the standard M-16 automatic assault rifle; her face was black with charcoal.

Mary Anne handed him the weapon. "I'm exhausted," she said. "We'll talk later."

She glanced over at the Special Forces area, then turned and walked quickly across the compound toward her own bunker. Fossie stood still for a few seconds. A little dazed, it seemed. After a moment, though, he set his jaw and whispered something and went after her with a hard, fast stride.

"Not later!" he yelled. "Now!" 90

What happened between them, Rat said, nobody ever knew for sure. But in the mess hall that evening it was clear that an accommodation had been reached. Or more likely, he said, it was a case of setting down some new rules. Mary Anne's hair was freshly shampooed. She wore a white blouse, a navy blue skirt, a pair of plain black flats. Over dinner she kept her eyes down, poking at her food, subdued to the point of silence. Eddie Diamond and some of the others tried to nudge her into talking about the ambush—What was the feeling out there? What exactly did she see and hear?—but the questions seemed to give her trouble. Nervously, she'd look across the table at Fossie. She'd wait a moment, as if to receive some sort of clearance, then she'd bow her head and mumble out a vague word or two. There were no real answers.

Mark Fossie, too, had little to say.

"Nobody's business," he told Rat that night. Then he offered a brief smile. "One thing for sure, though, there won't be any more ambushes. No more late nights."

"You laid down the law?"

"Compromise," Fossie said. "I'll put it this way—we're officially engaged." 95

Rat nodded cautiously.

"Well hey, she'll make a sweet bride," he said. "Combat ready."

Over the next several days there was a strained, tightly wound quality to the way they treated each other, a rigid correctness that was enforced by repetitive acts of willpower. To look at them from a distance, Rat said, you would think they were the happiest two people on the planet. They spent the long afternoons sunbathing together, stretched out side by side on top of their bunker, or playing backgammon in the shade of a giant palm tree, or just sitting quietly. A model of togetherness, it seemed. And yet at close range their faces showed the tension.

Too polite, too thoughtful. Mark Fossie tried hard to keep up a self-assured pose, as if nothing had ever come between them, or ever could, but there was a fragility to it, something tentative and false. If Mary Anne happened to move a few steps away from him, even briefly, he'd tighten up and force himself not to watch her. But then a moment later he'd be watching.

In the presence of others, at least, they kept on their masks. Over meals they talked about plans for a huge wedding in Cleveland Heights—a two-day bash, lots of flowers. And yet even then their smiles seemed too intense. They were too quick with their banter; they held hands as if afraid to let go.

It had to end, and eventually it did.   100

Near the end of the third week Fossie began making arrangements to send her home. At first, Rat said, Mary Anne seemed to accept it, but then after a day or two she fell into a restless gloom, sitting off by herself at the edge of the perimeter. She would not speak. Shoulders hunched, her blue eyes opaque, she seemed to disappear inside herself. A couple of times Fossie approached her and tried to talk it out, but Mary Anne just stared out at the dark green mountains to the west. The wilderness seemed to draw her in. A haunted look, Rat said—partly terror, partly rapture. It was as if she had come up on the edge of something, as if she were caught in that no-man's-land between Cleveland Heights and deep jungle. Seventeen years old. Just a child, blond and innocent, but then weren't they all?

The next morning she was gone. The six Greenies were gone, too.

In a way, Rat said, poor Fossie expected it, or something like it, but that did not help much with the pain. The kid couldn't function. The grief took him by the throat and squeezed and would not let go.

"Lost," he kept whispering.

It was nearly three weeks before she returned. But in a sense she never re-   105
turned. Not entirely, not all of her.

By chance, Rat said, he was awake to see it. A damp misty night, he couldn't sleep, so he'd gone outside for a quick smoke. He was just standing there, he said, watching the moon, and then off to the west a column of silhouettes appeared as if by magic at the edge of the jungle. At first he didn't recognize her—a small, soft shadow among six other shadows. There was no sound. No real substance either. The seven silhouettes seemed to float across the surface of the earth, like spirits, vaporous and unreal. As he watched, Rat said, it made him think of some weird opium dream. The silhouettes moved without moving. Silently, one by one, they came up the hill, passed through the wire, and drifted in a loose file across the compound. It was then, Rat said, that he picked out Mary Anne's face. Her eyes seemed to shine in the dark—not blue, though, but a bright glowing jungle green. She did not pause at Fossie's bunker. She cradled her weapon and moved swiftly to the Special Forces hootch and followed the others inside.

Briefly, a light came on, and someone laughed, then the place went dark again.

Whenever he told the story, Rat had a tendency to stop now and then, interrupting the flow, inserting little clarifications or bits of analysis and personal opinion. It was a bad habit, Mitchell Sanders said, because all that matters is the raw material, the stuff itself, and you can't clutter it up with your own half-baked commentary. That just breaks the spell. It destroys the magic. What you have to do, Sanders said, is trust your own story. Get the hell out of the way and let it tell itself.

But Rat Kiley couldn't help it. He wanted to bracket the full range of meaning.

"I know it sounds far-out," he'd tell us, "but it's not like *impossible* or any-   110
thing. We all heard plenty of wackier stories. Some guy comes back from the bush, tells you he saw the Virgin Mary out there, she was riding a goddamn goose or something. Everybody buys it. Everybody smiles and asks how fast was they going, did she have spurs on. Well, it's not like that. This Mary Anne wasn't no virgin but at least she was real. I saw it. When she came in through the wire that night, I was right there, I saw those eyes of hers, I saw how she wasn't even the same person no more. What's so impossible about that? She was a girl, that's all. I mean, if it was a guy, everybody'd say, Hey, no big deal, he got caught up in the Nam shit, he got seduced by the Greenies. See what I mean? You got these blinders on about women. How gentle and peaceful they are. All that crap about how if we had a pussy for president there wouldn't be no more wars. Pure garbage. You got to get rid of that sexist attitude."

Rat would go on like that until Mitchell Sanders couldn't tolerate it any longer. It offended his inner ear.

"The story," Sanders would say. "The whole tone, man, you're wrecking it."

"Tone?"

"The *sound*. You need to get a consistent sound, like slow or fast, funny or sad. All these digressions, they just screw up your story's *sound*. Stick to what happened."

Frowning, Rat would close his eyes.   115

"Tone?" he'd say. "I didn't know it was all that complicated. The girl joined the zoo. One more animal—end of story."

"Yeah, fine. But tell it right."

At daybreak the next morning, when Mark Fossie heard she was back, he stationed himself outside the fenced-off Special Forces area. All morning he waited for her, and all afternoon. Around dusk Rat brought him something to eat.

"She has to come out," Fossie said. "Sooner or later, she has to."

"Or else what?" Rat said.   120

"I go get her. I bring her out."

Rat shook his head. "Your decision. I was you, though, no way I'd mess around with any Greenie types, not for nothing."

"It's Mary Anne in there."

"Sure, I know that. All the same, I'd knock real extra super polite."

Even with the cooling night air Fossie's face was slick with sweat. He looked   125
sick. His eyes were bloodshot; his skin had a whitish, almost colorless cast. For a few minutes Rat waited with him, quietly watching the hootch, then he patted the kid's shoulder and left him alone.

It was after midnight when Rat and Eddie Diamond went out to check on him. The night had gone cold and steamy, a low fog sliding down from the mountains, and somewhere out in the dark they heard music playing. Not loud but not soft either. It had a chaotic, almost unmusical sound, without rhythm or form or progression, like the noise of nature. A synthesizer, it seemed, or maybe an electric organ. In the background, just audible, a woman's voice was half singing, half chanting, but the lyrics seemed to be in a foreign tongue.

They found Fossie squatting near the gate in front of the Special Forces area. Head bowed, he was swaying to the music, his face wet and shiny. As Eddie bent down beside him, the kid looked up with dull eyes, ashen and powdery, not quite in register.

"Hear that?" he whispered. "You *hear*? It's Mary Anne."

Eddie Diamond took his arm. "Let's get you inside. Somebody's radio, that's all it is. Move it now."

"Mary Anne. Just listen."   130

"Sure, but—"

"Listen!"

Fossie suddenly pulled away, twisting sideways, and fell back against the gate. He lay there with his eyes closed. The music—the noise, whatever it was—came from the hootch beyond the fence. The place was dark except for a small glowing window, which stood partly open, the panes dancing in bright reds and yellows as though the glass were on fire. The chanting seemed louder now. Fiercer, too, and higher pitched.

Fossie pushed himself up. He wavered for a moment then forced the gate open.

"That voice," he said. "Mary Anne."   135

Rat took a step forward, reaching out for him, but Fossie was already moving fast toward the hootch. He stumbled once, caught himself, and hit the door hard with both arms. There was a noise—a short screeching sound, like a cat—and the door swung in and Fossie was framed there for an instant, his arms stretched out, then he slipped inside. After a moment Rat and Eddie followed quietly. Just inside the door they found Fossie bent down on one knee. He wasn't moving.

Across the room a dozen candles were burning on the floor near the open window. The place seemed to echo with a weird deep-wilderness sound—tribal music—bamboo flutes and drums and chimes. But what hit you first, Rat said, was the smell. Two kinds of smells. There was a topmost scent of joss sticks and incense, like the fumes of some exotic smokehouse, but beneath the smoke lay a deeper and much more powerful stench. Impossible to describe, Rat said. It paralyzed your lungs. Thick and numbing, like an animal's den, a mix of blood and scorched hair and excrement and the sweet-sour odor of moldering flesh—the stink of the kill. But that wasn't all. On a post at the rear of the hootch was the decayed head of a large black leopard; strips of yellow-brown skin dangled from the overhead rafters. And bones. Stacks of bones—all kinds. To one side, propped up against a wall, stood a poster in neat black lettering: ASSEMBLE YOUR OWN GOOK!! FREE SAMPLE KIT!! The images came in a swirl, Rat said, and there was no way you could process it all. Off in the gloom a few dim figures lounged in hammocks, or on cots, but none of them moved or spoke. The background music came from a tape deck near the circle of candles, but the high voice was Mary Anne's.

After a second Mark Fossie made a soft moaning sound. He started to get up but then stiffened.

"Mary Anne?" he said.

Quietly then, she stepped out of the shadows. At least for a moment she   140 seemed to be the same pretty young girl who had arrived a few weeks earlier. She was barefoot. She wore her pink sweater and a white blouse and a simple cotton skirt.

For a long while the girl gazed down at Fossie, almost blankly, and in the candlelight her face had the composure of someone perfectly at peace with herself. It took a few seconds, Rat said, to appreciate the full change. In part it was her eyes: utterly flat and indifferent. There was no emotion in her stare, no sense of the person behind it. But the grotesque part, he said, was her jewelry. At the girl's throat was a necklace of human tongues. Elongated and narrow, like pieces of blackened leather, the tongues were threaded along a length of copper wire, one overlapping the next, the tips curled upward as if caught in a final shrill syllable.

Briefly, it seemed, the girl smiled at Mark Fossie.

"There's no sense talking," she said. "I know what you think, but it's not . . . it's not *bad.*"

"Bad?" Fossie murmured.

"It's not."   145

In the shadows there was laughter.

One of the Greenies sat up and lighted a cigar. The others lay silent.

"You're in a place," Mary Anne said softly, "where you don't belong."

She moved her hand in a gesture that encompassed not just the hootch but everything around it, the entire war, the mountains, the mean little villages, the trails and trees and rivers and deep misted-over valleys.

"You just don't *know*," she said. "You hide in this little fortress, behind wire 150 and sandbags, and you don't know what it's all about. Sometimes I want to *eat* this place. Vietnam. I want to swallow the whole country—the dirt, the death— I just want to eat it and have it there inside me. That's how I feel. It's like . . . this appetite. I get scared sometimes—lots of times—but it's not *bad*. You know? I feel close to myself. When I'm out there at night, I feel close to my own body, I can feel my blood moving, my skin and my fingernails, everything, it's like I'm full of electricity and I'm glowing in the dark—I'm on fire almost—I'm burning away into nothing—but it doesn't matter because I know exactly who I am. You can't feel like that anywhere else."

All this was said softly, as if to herself, her voice slow and impassive. She was not trying to persuade. For a few moments she looked at Mark Fossie, who seemed to shrink away, then she turned and moved back into the gloom.

There was nothing to be done.

Rat took Fossie's arm, helped him up, and led him outside. In the darkness there was that weird tribal music, which seemed to come from the earth itself, from the deep rain forest, and a woman's voice rising up in a language beyond translation.

Mark Fossie stood rigid.

"Do something," he whispered. "I can't just let her go like that."   155

Rat listened for a time, then shook his head.

"Man, you must be deaf. She's already gone."

Rat Kiley stopped there, almost in midsentence, which drove Mitchell Sanders crazy.

"What next?" he said.

"Next?"   160

"The girl. What happened to her?"

Rat made a small, tired motion with his shoulders. "Hard to tell for sure.

Maybe three, four days later I got orders to report here to Alpha Company. Jumped the first chopper out, that's the last I ever seen of the place. Mary Anne, too."

Mitchell Sanders stared at him.

"You can't do that."

"Do what?"   165

"Jesus Christ, it's against the *rules*," Sanders said. "Against human *nature*. This elaborate story, you can't say, Hey, by the way, I don't know the *ending*. I mean, you got certain obligations."

Rat gave a quick smile. "Patience, man. Up to now, everything I told you is from personal experience, the exact truth, but there's a few other things I heard secondhand. Thirdhand, actually. From here on it gets to be . . . I don't know what the word is."

"Speculation."

"Yeah, right." Rat looked off to the west, scanning the mountains, as if expecting something to appear on one of the high ridgelines. After a second he shrugged. "Anyhow, maybe two months later I ran into Eddie Diamond over in Bangkok—I was on R&R, just this fluke thing—and he told me some stuff I can't vouch for with my own eyes. Even Eddie didn't really see it. He heard it from one of the Greenies, so you got to take this with a whole shakerful of salt."

Once more, Rat searched the mountains, then he sat back and closed his   170
eyes.

"You know," he said abruptly, "I loved her."

"Say again?"

"A lot. We all did, I guess. The way she looked, Mary Anne made you think about those girls back home, how clean and innocent they all are, how they'll never understand any of this, not in a billion years. Try to tell them about it, they'll just stare at you with those big round candy eyes. They won't understand zip. It's like trying to tell somebody what chocolate tastes like."

Mitchell Sanders nodded. "Or shit."

"There it is, you got to taste it, and that's the thing with Mary Anne. She   175
was *there*. She was up to her eyeballs in it. After the war, man, I promise you, you won't find nobody like her."

Suddenly, Rat pushed up to his feet, moved a few steps away from us, then stopped and stood with his back turned. He was an emotional guy.

"Got hooked, I guess," he said. "I loved her. So when I heard from Eddie about what happened, it almost made me . . . Like you say, it's pure speculation."

"Go on," Mitchell Sanders said. "Finish up."

What happened to her, Rat said, was what happened to all of them. You come over clean and you get dirty and then afterward it's never the same. A question of degree. Some make it intact, some don't make it at all. For Mary Anne Bell, it seemed, Vietnam had the effect of a powerful drug: that mix of unnamed terror and unnamed pleasure that comes as the needle slips in and you know you're risking something. The endorphins start to flow, and the adrenaline, and you hold your breath and creep quietly through the moonlit nightscapes; you become intimate with danger; you're in touch with the far side of yourself, as though it's another hemisphere, and you want to string it out and go wherever the trip takes you and be host to all the possibilities inside yourself. Not *bad*, she'd said. Vietnam made her glow in the dark. She wanted more, she wanted to penetrate deeper

into the mystery of herself, and after a time the wanting became needing, which
turned then to craving.

According to Eddie Diamond, who heard it from one of the Greenies, she   180
took a greedy pleasure in night patrols. She was good at it; she had the moves.
All camouflaged up, her face smooth and vacant, she seemed to flow like water
through the dark, like oil, without sound or center. She went barefoot. She stopped
carrying a weapon. There were times, apparently, when she took crazy, death-
wish chances—things that even the Greenies balked at. It was as if she were taunting some wild creature out in the bush, or in her head, inviting it to show itself,
a curious game of hide-and-go-seek that was played out in the dense terrain of a
nightmare. She was lost inside herself. On occasion, when they were taken under
fire, Mary Anne would stand quietly and watch the tracer rounds snap by, a little
smile at her lips, intent on some private transaction with the war. Other times she
would simply vanish altogether—for hours, for days.

And then one morning, all alone, Mary Anne walked off into the mountains
and did not come back.

No body was ever found. No equipment, no clothing. For all he knew, Rat
said, the girl was still alive. Maybe up in one of the high mountain villes, maybe
with the Montagnard tribes. But that was guesswork.

There was an inquiry, of course, and a week-long air search, and for a time
the Tra Bong compound went crazy with MP and CID° types. In the end, however, nothing came of it. It was a war and the war went on. Mark Fossie was busted
to PFC, shipped back to a hospital in the States, and two months later received a
medical discharge. Mary Anne Bell joined the missing.

But the story did not end there. If you believed the Greenies, Rat said, Mary
Anne was still somewhere out there in the dark. Odd movements, odd shapes.
Late at night, when the Greenies were out on ambush, the whole rain forest
seemed to stare in at them—a watched feeling—and a couple of times they almost saw her sliding through the shadows. Not quite, but almost. She had crossed
to the other side. She was part of the land. She was wearing her culottes, her pink
sweater, and a necklace of human tongues. She was dangerous. She was ready for
the kill.

MP and CID: Military Police and Criminal Investigation Department.

Flannery O'Connor   (1925–1964)

*Flannery O'Connor was born in Savannah, Georgia, and lived most of her life in
Milledgeville, Georgia. She took her undergraduate degree from Georgia Women's
College in 1945 and an M.F.A. from the State University of Iowa in 1947. She
won numerous awards for her writing, including the National Book Award for*
The Complete Short Stories, *won posthumously in 1972. Unfortunately, her life
was cut short by lupus at the age of thirty-nine. Not only is O'Connor a decidedly
southern writer, in the sense that her settings and characters are from the south, as
in the case of Eudora Welty, but also in the sense that her stories focus on moral
issues with a gothic flavor associated with the violent and grotesque. She was a
lifelong Roman Catholic and called attention to her faith in statements such as, "I
see from the standpoint of Christian orthodoxy. This means that for me the*

meaning of life is centered in our Redemption by Christ and that what I see in the world I see in relation to that." Among her important works are Wise Blood *(1952) and* The Violent Bear It Away *(1964), novels, and* A Good Man Is Hard to Find *(1955) and* Everything That Rises Must Converge *(1965), collections of short stories. Her reputation has grown since her death, and some critics have pronounced her as perhaps the best short story writer of our time.*

A GOOD MAN IS HARD TO FIND   1955

The dragon is by the side of the road, watching those who pass. Beware lest he devour you. We go to the Father of Souls, but it is necessary to pass by the dragon.

—St. Cyril of Jerusalem

The grandmother didn't want to go to Florida. She wanted to visit some of her connections in east Tennessee and she was seizing at every chance to change Bailey's mind. Bailey was the son she lived with, her only boy. He was sitting on the edge of his chair at the table, bent over the orange sports section of the *Journal.* "Now look here, Bailey," she said, "see here, read this," and she stood with one hand on her thin hip and the other rattling the newspaper at his bald head. "Here this fellow that calls himself The Misfit is aloose from the Federal Pen and headed toward Florida and you read here what it says he did to these people. Just you read it. I wouldn't take my children in any direction with a criminal like that aloose in it. I couldn't answer to my conscience if I did."

Bailey didn't look up from his reading so she wheeled around then and faced the children's mother, a young woman in slacks, whose face was as broad and in- nocent as a cabbage and was tied around with a green head-kerchief that had two points on the top like a rabbit's ears. She was sitting on the sofa, feeding the baby his apricots out of a jar. "The children have been to Florida before," the old lady said. "You all ought to take them somewhere else for a change so they would see different parts of the world and be broad. They never have been to east Tennessee."

The children's mother didn't seem to hear her but the eight-year-old boy, John Wesley, a stocky child with glasses, said, "If you don't want to go to Florida, why dontcha stay at home?" He and the little girl, June Star, were reading the funny papers on the floor.

"She wouldn't stay at home to be queen for a day," June Star said without raising her yellow head.

"Yes and what would you do if this fellow, The Misfit, caught you?" the   5
grandmother asked.

"I'd smack his face," John Wesley said.

"She wouldn't stay at home for a million bucks," June Star said. "Afraid she'd miss something. She has to go everywhere we go."

"All right, Miss," the grandmother said. "Just remember that the next time you want me to curl your hair."

June Star said her hair was naturally curly.

The next morning the grandmother was the first one in the car, ready to go.   10
She had her big black valise that looked like the head of a hippopotamus in one corner, and underneath it she was hiding a basket with Pitty Sing, the cat, in it. She didn't intend for the cat to be left alone in the house for three days because

he would miss her too much and she was afraid he might brush against one of the gas burners and accidentally asphyxiate himself. Her son, Bailey, didn't like to arrive at a motel with a cat.

She sat in the middle of the back seat with John Wesley and June Star on either side of her. Bailey and the children's mother and the baby sat in front and they left Atlanta at eight forty-five with the mileage on the car at 55890. The grandmother wrote this down because she thought it would be interesting to say how many miles they had been when they got back. It took them twenty minutes to reach the outskirts of the city.

The old lady settled herself comfortably, removing her white cotton gloves and putting them up with her purse on the shelf in front of the back window. The children's mother still had on slacks and still had her head tied up in a green kerchief, but the grandmother had on a navy blue straw sailor hat with a bunch of white violets on the brim and a navy blue dress with a small white dot in the print. Her collars and cuffs were white organdy trimmed with lace and at her neckline she had pinned a purple spray of cloth violets containing a sachet. In case of an accident, anyone seeing her dead on the highway would know at once that she was a lady.

She said she thought it was going to be a good day for driving, neither too hot nor too cold, and she cautioned Bailey that the speed limit was fifty-five miles an hour and that the patrolmen hid themselves behind billboards and small clumps of trees and sped out after you before you had a chance to slow down. She pointed out interesting details of the scenery: Stone Mountain; the blue granite that in some places came up to both sides of the highway; the brilliant red clay banks slightly streaked with purple; and the various crops that made rows of green lacework on the ground. The trees were full of silver-white sunlight and the meanest of them sparkled. The children were reading comic magazines and their mother had gone back to sleep.

"Let's go through Georgia fast so we won't have to look at it much," John Wesley said.

"If I were a little boy," said the grandmother, "I wouldn't talk about my native state that way. Tennessee has the mountains and Georgia has the hills."   15

"Tennessee is just a hillbilly dumping ground," John Wesley said, "and Georgia is a lousy state too."

"You said it," June Star said.

"In my time," said the grandmother, folding her thin veined fingers, "children were more respectful of their native states and their parents and everything else. People did right then. Oh look at the cute little pickaninny!" she said and pointed to a Negro child standing in the door of a shack. "Wouldn't that make a picture, now?" she asked and they all turned and looked at the little Negro out of the back window. He waved.

"He didn't have any britches on," June Star said.

"He probably didn't have any," the grandmother explained. "Little niggers   20
in the country don't have things like we do. If I could paint, I'd paint that picture," she said.

The children exchanged comic books.

The grandmother offered to hold the baby and the children's mother passed him over the front seat to her. She set him on her knee and bounced him and told him about the things they were passing. She rolled her eyes and screwed up her mouth and stuck her leathery thin face into his smooth bland one. Occasionally he gave her a faraway smile. They passed a large cotton field with five or six graves fenced in the middle of it, like a small island.

"Look at the graveyard!" the grandmother said, pointing it out. "That was the old family burying ground. That belonged to the plantation."

"Where's the plantation?" John Wesley asked.

"Gone With the Wind," said the grandmother. "Ha. Ha." 25

When the children finished all the comic books they had brought, they opened the lunch and ate it. The grandmother ate a peanut butter sandwich and an olive and would not let the children throw the box and the paper napkins out the window. When there was nothing else to do they played a game by choosing a cloud and making the other two guess what shape it suggested. John Wesley took one the shape of a cow and June Star guessed a cow and John Wesley said, no, an automobile, and June Star said he didn't play fair, and they began to slap each other over the grandmother.

The grandmother said she would tell them a story if they would keep quiet. When she told a story, she rolled her eyes and waved her head and was very dramatic. She said once when she was a maiden lady she had been courted by a Mr. Edgar Atkins Teagarden from Jasper, Georgia. She said he was a very good-looking man and a gentleman and that he brought her a watermelon every Saturday afternoon with his initials cut in it, E. A. T. Well, one Saturday, she said, Mr. Teagarden brought the watermelon and there was nobody at home and he left it on the front porch and returned in his buggy to Jasper, but she never got the watermelon, she said, because a nigger boy ate it when he saw the initials, E. A. T.! This story tickled John Wesley's funny bone and he giggled and giggled but June Star didn't think it was any good. She said she wouldn't marry a man that just brought her a watermelon on Saturday. The grandmother said she would have done well to marry Mr. Teagarden because he was a gentleman and had bought Coca-Cola stock when it first came out and that he had died only a few years ago, a very wealthy man.

They stopped at The Tower for barbecued sandwiches. The Tower was a part stucco and part wood filling station and dance hall set in a clearing outside of Timothy. A fat man named Red Sammy Butts ran it and there were signs stuck here and there on the building and for miles up and down the highway saying, TRY RED SAMMY'S FAMOUS BARBECUE. NONE LIKE FAMOUS RED SAMMY'S! RED SAM! THE FAT BOY WITH THE HAPPY LAUGH! A VETERAN! RED SAMMY'S YOUR MAN!

Red Sammy was lying on the bare ground outside The Tower with his head under a truck while a gray monkey about a foot high, chained to a small chinaberry tree, chattered nearby. The monkey sprang back into the tree and got on the highest limb as soon as he saw the children jump out of the car and run toward him.

Inside, The Tower was a long dark room with a counter at one end and ta- 30
bles at the other and dancing space in the middle. They all sat down at a board table next to the nickelodeon and Red Sam's wife, a tall burnt-brown woman with hair and eyes lighter than her skin, came and took their order. The children's mother put a dime in the machine and played "The Tennessee Waltz," and the grandmother said that tune always made her want to dance. She asked Bailey if he would like to dance but he only glared at her. He didn't have a naturally sunny

disposition like she did and trips made him nervous. The grandmother's brown eyes were very bright. She swayed her head from side to side and pretended she was dancing in her chair. June Star said play something she could tap to so the children's mother put in another dime and played a fast number and June Star stepped out onto the dance floor and did her tap routine.

"Ain't she cute?" Red Sam's wife said, leaning over the counter. "Would you like to come be my little girl?"

"No I certainly wouldn't," June Star said. "I wouldn't live in a broken-down place like this for a million bucks!" and she ran back to the table.

"Ain't she cute?" the woman repeated, stretching her mouth politely.

"Aren't you ashamed?" hissed the grandmother.

Red Sam came in and told his wife to quit lounging on the counter and hurry   35
up with these people's order. His khaki trousers reached just to his hip bones and his stomach hung over them like a sack of meal swaying under his shirt. He came over and sat down at a table nearby and let out a combination sigh and yodel. "You can't win," he said. "You can't win," and he wiped his sweating red face off with a gray handkerchief. "These days you don't know who to trust," he said. "Ain't that the truth?"

"People are certainly not nice like they used to be," said the grandmother.

"Two fellers come in here last week," Red Sammy said, "driving a Chrysler. It was a old beat-up car but it was a good one and these boys looked all right to me. Said they worked at the mill and you know I let them fellers charge the gas they bought? Now why did I do that?"

"Because you're a good man!" the grandmother said at once.

"Yes'm, I suppose so," Red Sam said as if he were struck with this answer.

His wife brought the orders, carrying the five plates all at once without a   40
tray, two in each hand and one balanced on her arm. "It isn't a soul in this green world of God's that you can trust," she said. "And I don't count nobody out of that, not nobody," she repeated, looking at Red Sammy.

"Did you read about that criminal, The Misfit, that's escaped?" asked the grandmother.

"I wouldn't be a bit surprised if he didn't attact this place right here," said the woman. "If he hears about it being here, I wouldn't be none surprised to see him. If he hears it's two cent in the cash register, I wouldn't be a tall surprised if he . . ."

"That'll do," Red Sam said. "Go bring these people their Co'-Colas," and the woman went off to get the rest of the order.

"A good man is hard to find," Red Sammy said. "Everything is getting terrible. I remember the day you could go off and leave your screen door unlatched. Not no more."

He and the grandmother discussed better times. The old lady said that in   45
her opinion Europe was entirely to blame for the way things were now. She said the way Europe acted you would think we were made of money and Red Sam said it was no use talking about it, she was exactly right. The children ran outside into the white sunlight and looked at the monkey in the lacy chinaberry tree. He was busy catching fleas on himself and biting each one carefully between his teeth as if it were a delicacy.

They drove off again into the hot afternoon. The grandmother took cat naps and woke up every few minutes with her own snoring. Outside of Toombsboro she woke up and recalled an old plantation that she had visited in this neighborhood once when she was a young lady. She said the house had six white columns across the front and that there was an avenue of oaks leading up to it and two little wooden trellis arbors on either side in front where you sat down with your suitor after a stroll in the garden. She recalled exactly which road to turn off to get to it. She knew that Bailey would not be willing to lose any time looking at an old house, but the more she talked about it, the more she wanted to see it once again and find out if the little twin arbors were still standing. "There was a secret panel in this house," she said craftily, not telling the truth but wishing that she were, "and the story went that all the family silver was hidden in it when Sherman° came through but it was never found . . ."

"Hey!" John Wesley said. "Let's go see it! We'll find it! We'll poke all the woodwork and find it! Who lives there? Where do you turn off at? Hey Pop, can't we turn off there?"

"We never have seen a house with a secret panel!" June Star shrieked. "Let's go to the house with the secret panel! Hey Pop, can't we go see the house with the secret panel!"

"It's not far from here, I know," the grandmother said. "It wouldn't take over twenty minutes."

Bailey was looking straight ahead. His jaw was as rigid as a horseshoe. "No,"   50
he said.

The children began to yell and scream that they wanted to see the house with the secret panel. John Wesley kicked the back of the front seat and June Star hung over her mother's shoulder and whined desperately into her ear that they never had any fun even on their vacation, that they could never do what THEY wanted to do. The baby began to scream and John Wesley kicked the back of the seat so hard that his father could feel the blows in his kidney.

"All right!" he shouted and drew the car to a stop at the side of the road. "Will you all shut up? Will you all just shut up for one second? If you don't shut up, we won't go anywhere."

"It would be very educational for them," the grandmother murmured.

"All right," Bailey said, "but get this: this is the only time we're going to stop for anything like this. This is the one and only time."

"The dirt road that you have to turn down is about a mile back," the grand-   55
mother directed. "I marked it when we passed."

"A dirt road," Bailey groaned.

After they had turned around and were headed toward the dirt road, the grandmother recalled other points about the house, the beautiful glass over the front doorway and the candle-lamp in the hall. John Wesley said that the secret panel was probably in the fireplace.

"You can't go inside this house," Bailey said. "You don't know who lives there."

"While you all talk to the people in front, I'll run around behind and get in a window," John Wesley suggested.

"We'll all stay in the car," his mother said.   60

Sherman: William Tecumseh Sherman (1820–1891), Union Army general famous for his devastating marches through the South during the Civil War.

They turned onto the dirt road and the car raced roughly along in a swirl of pink dust. The grandmother recalled the times when there were no paved roads and thirty miles was a day's journey. The dirt road was hilly and there were sudden washes in it and sharp curves on dangerous embankments. All at once they would be on a hill, looking down over the blue tops of trees for miles around, then the next minute, they would be in a red depression with the dust-coated trees looking down on them.

"This place had better turn up in a minute," Bailey said, "or I'm going to turn around."

The road looked as if no one had traveled on it in months.

"It's not much farther," the grandmother said and just as she said it, a horrible thought came to her. The thought was so embarrassing that she turned red in the face and her eyes dilated and her feet jumped up, upsetting her valise in the corner. The instant the valise moved, the newspaper top she had over the basket under it rose with a snarl and Pitty Sing, the cat, sprang onto Bailey's shoulder.

The children were thrown to the floor and their mother, clutching the baby, 65 was thrown out the door onto the ground; the old lady was thrown into the front seat. The car turned over once and landed right-side-up in a gulch off the side of the road. Bailey remained in the driver's seat with the cat—gray-striped with a broad white face and an orange nose—clinging to his neck like a caterpillar.

As soon as the children saw they could move their arms and legs, they scrambled out of the car, shouting, "We've had an ACCIDENT!" The grandmother was curled up under the dashboard, hoping she was injured so that Bailey's wrath would not come down on her all at once. The horrible thought she had had before the accident was that the house she had remembered so vividly was not in Georgia but in Tennessee.

Bailey removed the cat from his neck with both hands and flung it out the window against the side of a pine tree. Then he got out of the car and started looking for the children's mother. She was sitting against the side of the red gutted ditch, holding the screaming baby, but she only had a cut down her face and a broken shoulder. "We've had an ACCIDENT!" the children screamed in a frenzy of delight.

"But nobody's killed," June Star said with disappointment as the grandmother limped out of the car, her hat still pinned to her head but the broken front brim standing up at a jaunty angle and the violet spray hanging off the side. They all sat down in the ditch, except the children, to recover from the shock. They were all shaking.

"Maybe a car will come along," said the children's mother hoarsely.

"I believe I have injured an organ," said the grandmother, pressing her side, 70 but no one answered her. Bailey's teeth were clattering. He had on a yellow sport shirt with bright blue parrots designed in it and his face was as yellow as the shirt. The grandmother decided that she would not mention that the house was in Tennessee.

The road was about ten feet above and they could see only the tops of the trees on the other side of it. Behind the ditch they were sitting in there were more woods, tall and dark and deep. In a few minutes they saw a car some distance away on top of a hill, coming slowly as if the occupants were watching them. The grandmother stood up and waved both arms dramatically to attract their attention. The car continued to come on slowly, disappeared around a bend and appeared again, moving even slower, on top of the hill they had gone over. It was a big black battered hearselike automobile. There were three men in it.

It came to a stop just over them and for some minutes, the driver looked down with a steady expressionless gaze to where they were sitting, and didn't speak. Then he turned his head and muttered something to the other two and they got out. One was a fat boy in black trousers and a red sweat shirt with a silver stallion embossed on the front of it. He moved around on the right side of them and stood staring, his mouth partly open in a kind of loose grin. The other had on khaki pants and a blue striped coat and a gray hat pulled down very low, hiding most of his face. He came around slowly on the left side. Neither spoke.

The driver got out of the car and stood by the side of it, looking down at them. He was an older man than the other two. His hair was just beginning to gray and he wore silver-rimmed spectacles that gave him a scholarly look. He had a long creased face and didn't have on any shirt or undershirt. He had on blue jeans that were too tight for him and was holding a black hat and a gun. The two boys also had guns.

"We've had an ACCIDENT!" the children screamed.

The grandmother had the peculiar feeling that the bespectacled man was   75
someone she knew. His face was as familiar to her as if she had known him all her life but she could not recall who he was. He moved away from the car and began to come down the embankment, placing his feet carefully so that he wouldn't slip. He had on tan and white shoes and no socks, and his ankles were red and thin. "Good afternoon," he said. "I see you all had you a little spill."

"We turned over twice!" said the grandmother.

"Oncet," he corrected. "We seen it happen. Try their car and see will it run, Hiram," he said quietly to the boy with the gray hat.

"What you got that gun for?" John Wesley asked. "Whatcha gonna do with that gun?"

"Lady," the man said to the children's mother, "would you mind calling them children to sit down by you? Children make me nervous. I want all you all to sit down right together there where you're at."

"What are you telling US what to do for?" June Star asked.   80

Behind them the line of woods gaped like a dark open mouth. "Come here," said their mother.

"Look here now," Bailey began suddenly, "we're in a predicament! We're in . . ."

The grandmother shrieked. She scrambled to her feet and stood staring. "You're The Misfit!" she said. "I recognized you at once!"

"Yes'm," the man said, smiling slightly as if he were pleased in spite of himself to be known, "but it would have been better for all of you, lady, if you hadn't of reckernized me."

Bailey turned his head sharply and said something to his mother that shocked   85
even the children. The old lady began to cry and The Misfit reddened.

"Lady," he said, "don't you get upset. Sometimes a man says things he don't mean. I don't reckon he meant to talk to you thataway."

"You wouldn't shoot a lady, would you?" the grandmother said and removed a clean handkerchief from her cuff and began to slap at her eyes with it.

The Misfit pointed the toe of his shoe into the ground and made a little hole and then covered it up again. "I would hate to have to," he said.

"Listen," the grandmother almost screamed, "I know you're a good man. You don't look a bit like you have common blood. I know you must come from nice people!"

"Yes mam," he said, "finest people in the world." When he smiled he showed 90 a row of strong white teeth. "God never made a finer woman than my mother and my daddy's heart was pure gold," he said. The boy with the red sweat shirt had come around behind them and was standing with his gun at his hip. The Misfit squatted down on the ground. "Watch them children, Bobby Lee," he said. "You know they make me nervous." He looked at the six of them huddled together in front of him and he seemed to be embarrassed as if he couldn't think of anything to say. "Ain't a cloud in the sky," he remarked, looking up at it. "Don't see no sun but don't see no cloud neither."

"Yes, it's a beautiful day," said the grandmother. "Listen," she said, "you shouldn't call yourself The Misfit because I know you're a good man at heart. I can just look at you and tell."

"Hush!" Bailey yelled. "Hush! Everybody shut up and let me handle this!" He was squatting in the position of a runner about to sprint forward but he didn't move.

"I pre-chate that, lady," The Misfit said and drew a little circle in the ground with the butt of his gun.

"It'll take a half a hour to fix this here car," Hiram called, looking over the raised hood of it.

"Well, first you and Bobby Lee get him and that little boy to step over yon- 95 der with you," The Misfit said, pointing to Bailey and John Wesley. "The boys want to ast you something," he said to Bailey. "Would you mind stepping back in them woods there with them?"

"Listen," Bailey began, "we're in a terrible predicament! Nobody realizes what this is," and his voice cracked. His eyes were as blue and intense as the parrots in his shirt and he remained perfectly still.

The grandmother reached up to adjust her hat brim as if she were going to the woods with him but it came off in her hand. She stood staring at it and after a second she let it fall on the ground. Hiram pulled Bailey up by the arm as if he were assisting an old man. John Wesley caught hold of his father's hand and Bobby Lee followed. They went off toward the woods and just as they reached the dark edge, Bailey turned and supporting himself against a gray naked pine trunk, he shouted, "I'll be back in a minute, Mamma, wait on me!"

"Come back this instant!" his mother shrilled but they all disappeared into the woods.

"Bailey Boy!" the grandmother called in a tragic voice but she found she was looking at The Misfit squatting on the ground in front of her. "I just know you're a good man," she said desperately. "You're not a bit common!"

"Nome, I ain't a good man," The Misfit said after a second as if he had con- 100 sidered her statement carefully, "but I ain't the worst in the world neither. My daddy said I was a different breed of dog from my brothers and sisters. 'You know,' Daddy said, 'it's some that can live their whole life out without asking about it and it's others has to know why it is, and this boy is one of the latters. He's going to be into everything!'" He put on his black hat and looked up suddenly and then away deep into the woods as if he were embarrassed again. "I'm sorry I don't have on a shirt before you ladies," he said, hunching his shoulders slightly. "We buried our clothes that we had on when we escaped and we're just making do until we can get better. We borrowed these from some folks we met," he explained.

"That's perfectly all right," the grandmother said. "Maybe Bailey has an extra shirt in his suitcase."

"I'll look and see terrectly," The Misfit said.

"Where are they taking him?" the children's mother screamed.

"Daddy was a card himself," The Misfit said. "You couldn't put anything over on him. He never got in trouble with the Authorities though. Just had the knack of handling them."

"You could be honest too if you'd only try," said the grandmother. "Think 105 how wonderful it would be to settle down and live a comfortable life and not have to think about somebody chasing you all the time."

The Misfit kept scratching in the ground with the butt of his gun as if he were thinking about it. "Yes'm, somebody is always after you," he murmured.

The grandmother noticed how thin his shoulder blades were just behind his hat because she was standing up looking down on him. "Do you ever pray?" she asked.

He shook his head. All she saw was the black hat wiggle between his shoulder blades. "Nome," he said.

There was a pistol shot from the woods, followed closely by another. Then silence. The old lady's head jerked around. She could hear the wind move through the tree tops like a long satisfied insuck of breath. "Bailey Boy!" she called.

"I was a gospel singer for a while," The Misfit said. "I been most everything. 110 Been in the arm service, both land and sea, at home and abroad, been twict married, been an undertaker, been with the railroads, plowed Mother Earth, been in a tornado, seen a man burnt alive oncet," and looked up at the children's mother and the little girl who were sitting close together, their faces white and their eyes glassy; "I even seen a woman flogged," he said.

"Pray, pray," the grandmother began, "pray, pray . . ."

"I never was a bad boy that I remember of," The Misfit said in an almost dreamy voice, "but somewheres along the line I done something wrong and got sent to the penitentiary. I was buried alive," and he looked up and held her attention to him by a steady stare.

"That's when you should have started to pray," she said. "What did you do to get sent to the penitentiary that first time?"

"Turn to the right, it was a wall," The Misfit said, looking up again at the cloudless sky. "Turn to the left, it was a wall. Look up it was a ceiling, look down it was a floor. I forget what I done, lady. I set there and set there, trying to remember what it was I done and I ain't recalled it to this day. Oncet in a while, I would think it was coming to me, but it never come."

"Maybe they put you in by mistake," the old lady said vaguely. 115

"Nome," he said. "It wasn't no mistake. They had the papers on me."

"You must have stolen something," she said.

The Misfit sneered slightly. "Nobody had nothing I wanted," he said. "It was a head-doctor at the penitentiary said what I had done was kill my daddy but I known that for a lie. My daddy died in nineteen ought nineteen of the epidemic flu and I never had a thing to do with it. He was buried in the Mount Hopewell Baptist churchyard and you can go there and see for yourself."

"If you would pray," the old lady said, "Jesus would help you."

"That's right," The Misfit said.   120

"Well then, why don't you pray?" she asked trembling with delight suddenly.

"I don't want no hep," he said. "I'm doing all right by myself."

Bobby Lee and Hiram came ambling back from the woods. Bobby Lee was dragging a yellow shirt with bright blue parrots in it.

"Throw me that shirt, Bobby Lee," The Misfit said. The shirt came flying at him and landed on his shoulder and he put it on. The grandmother couldn't name what the shirt reminded her of. "No, lady," The Misfit said while he was buttoning it up, "I found out the crime don't matter. You can do one thing or you can do another, kill a man or take a tire off his car, because sooner or later you're going to forget what it was you done and just be punished for it."

The children's mother had begun to make heaving noises as if she couldn't   125 get her breath. "Lady," he asked, "would you and that little girl like to step off yonder with Bobby Lee and Hiram and join your husband?"

"Yes, thank you," the mother said faintly. Her left arm dangled helplessly and she was holding the baby, who had gone to sleep, in the other. "Hep that lady up, Hiram," The Misfit said as she struggled to climb out of the ditch, "and Bobby Lee, you hold onto that little girl's hand."

"I don't want to hold hands with him," June Star said. "He reminds me of a pig."

The fat boy blushed and laughed and caught her by the arm and pulled her off into the woods after Hiram and her mother.

Alone with The Misfit, the grandmother found that she had lost her voice. There was not a cloud in the sky nor any sun. There was nothing around her but woods. She wanted to tell him that he must pray. She opened and closed her mouth several times before anything came out. Finally she found herself saying, "Jesus, Jesus," meaning, Jesus will help you, but the way she was saying it, it sounded as if she might be cursing.

"Yes'm," The Misfit said as if he agreed. "Jesus thown everything off bal- 130 ance. It was the same case with Him as with me except He hadn't committed any crime and they could prove I had committed one because they had the papers on me. Of course," he said, "they never shown me my papers. That's why I sign myself now. I said long ago, you get you a signature and sign everything you do and keep a copy of it. Then you'll know what you done and you can hold up the crime to the punishment and see do they match and in the end you'll have something to prove you ain't been treated right. I call myself The Misfit," he said, "because I can't make what all I done wrong fit what all I gone through in punishment."

There was a piercing scream from the woods, followed closely by a pistol report. "Does it seem right to you, lady, that one is punished a heap and another ain't punished at all?"

"Jesus!" the old lady cried. "You've got good blood! I know you wouldn't shoot a lady! I know you come from nice people! Pray! Jesus, you ought not to shoot a lady. I'll give you all the money I've got!"

"Lady," The Misfit said, looking beyond her far into the woods, "there never was a body that give the undertaker a tip."

There were two more pistol reports and the grandmother raised her head like a parched old turkey hen crying for water and called, "Bailey Boy, Bailey Boy!" as if her heart would break.

"Jesus was the only One that ever raised the dead." The Misfit continued, 135
"and He shouldn't have done it. He thrown everything off balance. If He did
what He said, then it's nothing for you to do throw away everything and follow
Him, and if He didn't, then it's nothing for you to do but enjoy the few minutes
you got left the best way you can—by killing somebody or burning down his
house or doing some other meanness to him. No pleasure but meanness," he said
and his voice had become almost a snarl.

"Maybe He didn't raise the dead," the old lady mumbled, not knowing what
she was saying and feeling so dizzy that she sank down in the ditch with her legs
twisted under her.

"I wasn't there so I can't say He didn't," The Misfit said. "I wisht I had of
been there," he said, hitting the ground with his fist. "It ain't right I wasn't there
because if I had of been there I would of known. Listen lady," he said in a high
voice, "if I had of been there I would of known and I wouldn't be like I am now."
His voice seemed about to crack and the grandmother's head cleared for an instant. She saw the man's face twisted close to her own as if he were going to cry
and she murmured, "Why you're one of my babies. You're one of my own children!" She reached out and touched him on the shoulder. The Misfit sprang back
as if a snake had bitten him and shot her three times through the chest. Then he
put his gun down on the ground and took off his glasses and began to clean them.

Hiram and Bobby Lee returned from the woods and stood over the ditch,
looking down at the grandmother who half sat and half lay in a puddle of blood
with her legs crossed under her like a child's and her face smiling up at the cloudless sky.

Without his glasses, The Misfit's eyes were red-rimmed and pale and de-
fenseless-looking. "Take her off and throw her where you thrown the others," he
said, picking up the cat that was rubbing itself against his leg.

"She was a talker, wasn't she?" Bobby Lee said, sliding down the ditch with 140
a yodel.

"She would of been a good woman," The Misfit said, "if it had been somebody there to shoot her every minute of her life."

"Some fun!" Bobby Lee said.

"Shut up, Bobby Lee," The Misfit said. "It's no real pleasure in life."

William Trevor   (b. 1928)

*William Trevor was born in County Cork, Ireland, with the name William
Trevor Cox, which he eventually shortened as a way of insulating his family from
his success (or possible failure) as a writer. He took his undergraduate degree from
Trinity College, Dublin, in 1950 and became a history teacher first in Northern
Ireland and then in England. In 1960 he went into advertising copywriting and
since 1965 has made his living by writing. His settings are frequently Irish and
though he lives now in rural Devon, England, he is considered among the best
living Irish short story writers. His individual collections of short stories include*
The Day We Got Drunk on Cake, and Other Stories *(1967),* The Ballroom of
Romance and Other Stories *(1972),* Angels at the Ritz and Other Stories
(1975), and Beyond the Pale *(1981). He has published two volumes of collected
stories since 1983. He has written several novels,* The Old Boys *(1964), which he*

adapted as a play, Lovers of Their Time *(1979), and* Other People's Worlds *(1980). Trevor's stories are impressive for the evocation of their setting and for the sensitive way he reveals the characters of often inarticulate people. Although his people are often in strange and painful bonds, his writing encourages our sympathy and respect.*

THE BALLROOM OF ROMANCE   1971

On Sundays, or on Mondays if he couldn't make it and often he couldn't, Sunday being his busy day, Canon O'Connell arrived at the farm in order to hold a private service with Bridie's father, who couldn't get about anymore, having had a leg amputated after gangrene had set in. They'd had a pony and cart then and Bridie's mother had been alive: it hadn't been difficult for the two of them to help her father onto the cart in order to make the journey to Mass. But two years later the pony had gone lame and eventually had to be destroyed; not long after that her mother had died. "Don't worry about it at all," Canon O'Connell had said, referring to the difficulty of transporting her father to Mass. "I'll slip up by the week, Bridie."

The milk lorry called daily for the single churn of milk, Mr. Driscoll delivered groceries and meal in his van, and took away the eggs that Bridie had collected during the week. Since Canon O'Connell had made his offer, in 1953, Bridie's father hadn't left the farm.

As well as Mass on Sundays and her weekly visits to a wayside dance hall Bridie went shopping once every month, cycling to the town early on a Friday afternoon. She bought things for herself, material for a dress, knitting wool, stockings, a newspaper, and paper-backed Wild West novels for her father. She talked in the shops to some of the girls she'd been at school with, girls who had married shop assistants or shopkeepers, or had become assistants themselves. Most of them had families of their own by now. "You're lucky to be peaceful in the hills," they said to Bridie, "instead of stuck in a hole like this." They had a tired look, most of them, from pregnancies and their efforts to organize and control their large families.

As she cycled back to the hills on a Friday Bridie often felt that they truly envied her her life, and she found it surprising that they should do so. If it hadn't been for her father she'd have wanted to work in the town also, in the tinned meat factory maybe, or in a shop. The town had a cinema called the Electric, and a fish-and-chip shop where people met at night, eating chips out of newspaper on the pavement outside. In the evenings, sitting in the farmhouse with her father, she often thought about the town, imagining the shop windows lit up to display their goods and the sweetshops still open so that people could purchase chocolates or fruit to take with them to the Electric cinema. But the town was eleven miles away, which was too far to cycle, there and back, for an evening's entertainment.

"It's a terrible thing for you, girl," her father used to say, genuinely troubled, "tied up to a one-legged man." He would sigh heavily, hobbling back from the fields, where he managed as best he could. "If your mother hadn't died," he'd say, not finishing the sentence.

If her mother hadn't died her mother could have looked after him and the scant acres he owned, her mother could somehow have lifted the milk churn onto

5

the collection platform and attended to the few hens and the cows. "I'd be dead without the girl to assist me," she'd heard her father saying to Canon O'Connell, and Canon O'Connell replied that he was certainly lucky to have her.

"Amn't I as happy here as anywhere?" she'd say herself, but her father knew she was pretending and was saddened because the weight of circumstances had so harshly interfered with her life.

Although her father still called her a girl, Bridie was thirty-six. She was tall and strong: the skin of her fingers and her palms were stained, and harsh to touch. The labor they'd experienced had found its way into them, as though juices had come out of vegetation and pigment out of soil: since childhood she'd torn away the rough scotch grass that grew each spring among her father's mangolds and sugar beet; since childhood she'd harvested potatoes in August, her hands daily rooting in the ground she loosened and turned. Wind had toughened the flesh of her face, sun had browned it; her neck and nose were lean, her lips touched with early wrinkles.

But on Saturday nights Bridie forgot the scotch grass and the soil. In different dresses she cycled to the dance hall, encouraged to make the journey by her father. "Doesn't it do you good, girl?" he'd say, as though he imagined she begrudged herself the pleasure. "Why wouldn't you enjoy yourself?" She'd cook him his tea and then he'd settle down with the wireless, or maybe a Wild West novel. In time, while still she danced, he'd stoke the fire up and hobble his way upstairs to bed.

The dance hall, owned by Mr. Justin Dwyer, was miles from anywhere, a lone building by the roadside with treeless boglands all around and a gravel expanse in front of it. On pink pebbled cement its title was painted in an azure blue that matched the depth of the background shade yet stood out well, unfussily proclaiming *The Ballroom of Romance*. Above these letters four colored bulbs— in red, green, orange, and mauve—were lit at appropriate times, an indication that the evening rendezvous was open for business. Only the façade of the building was pink, the other walls being a more ordinary gray. And inside, except for pink swing doors, everything was blue.

On Saturday nights Mr. Justin Dwyer, a small, thin man, unlocked the metal grid that protected his property and drew it back, creating an open mouth from which music would later pour. He helped his wife to carry crates of lemonade and packets of biscuits from their car, and then took up a position in the tiny vestibule between the drawn-back grid and the pink swing doors. He sat at a card table, with money and tickets spread out before him. He'd made a fortune, people said: he owned other ballrooms also.

People came on bicycles or in old motorcars, country people like Bridie from remote hill farms and villages. People who did not often see other people met there, girls and boys, men and women. They paid Mr. Dwyer and passed into his dance hall, where shadows were cast on pale blue walls and light from a crystal bowl was dim. The band, known as the Romantic Jazz Band, was composed of clarinet, drums, and piano. The drummer sometimes sang.

Bridie had been going to the dance hall since first she left the Presentation Nuns, before her mother's death. She didn't mind the journey, which was seven miles there and seven miles back: she'd traveled as far every day to the Presentation Nuns on the same bicycle, which had once been the property of her mother, an old Rudge purchased originally in 1936. On Sundays she cycled six miles to Mass, but she never minded either: she'd grown quite used to all that.

10

"How're you, Bridie?" inquired Mr. Justin Dwyer when she arrived in a new scarlet dress one autumn evening in 1971. She said she was all right and in reply to Mr. Dwyer's second query she said that her father was all right also. "I'll go up one of these days," promised Mr. Dwyer, which was a promise he'd been making for twenty years.

She paid the entrance fee and passed through the pink swing doors. The   15
Romantic Jazz Band was playing a familiar melody of the past, "The Destiny Waltz." In spite of the band's title, jazz was not ever played in the ballroom: Mr. Dwyer did not personally care for that kind of music, nor had he cared for various dance movements that had come and gone over the years. Jiving, rock and roll, twisting, and other such variations had all been resisted by Mr. Dwyer, who believed that a ballroom should be, as much as possible, a dignified place. The Romantic Jazz Band consisted of Mr. Maloney, Mr. Swanton, and Dano Ryan on drums. They were three middle-aged men who drove out from the town in Mr. Maloney's car, amateur performers who were employed otherwise by the tinned-meat factory, the Electricity Supply Board, and the County Council.

"How're you, Bridie?" inquired Dano Ryan as she passed him on her way to the cloakroom. He was idle for a moment with his drums, "The Destiny Waltz" not calling for much attention from him.

"I'm all right, Dano," she said. "Are you fit yourself? Are the eyes better?" The week before he'd told her that he'd developed a watering of the eyes that must have been some kind of cold or other. He'd woken up with it in the morning and it had persisted until the afternoon: it was a new experience, he'd told her, adding that he'd never had a day's illness or discomfort in his life.

"I think I need glasses," he said now, and as she passed into the cloakroom she imagined him in glasses, repairing the roads, as he was employed to do by the County Council. You hardly ever saw a road mender with glasses, she reflected, and she wondered if all the dust that was inherent in his work had perhaps affected his eyes.

"How're you, Bridie?" a girl called Eenie Mackie said in the cloakroom, a girl who'd left the Presentation Nuns only a year ago.

"That's a lovely dress, Eenie," Bridie said. "Is it nylon, that?"   20

"Tricel actually. Drip-dry."

Bridie took off her coat and hung it on a hook. There was a small washbasin in the cloakroom above which hung a discolored oval mirror. Used tissues and pieces of cotton wool, cigarette butts, and matches covered the concrete floor. Lengths of green-painted timber partitioned off a lavatory in a corner.

"Jeez, you're looking great, Bridie," Madge Dowding remarked, waiting for her turn at the mirror. She moved towards it as she spoke, taking off a pair of spectacles before endeavoring to apply makeup to the lashes of her eye. She stared myopically into the oval mirror, humming while the other girls became restive.

"Will you hurry up, for God's sake!" shouted Eenie Mackie. "We're standing here all night, Madge."

Madge Dowding was the only one who was older than Bridie. She was thirty-   25
nine, although often she said she was younger. The girls sniggered about that, saying that Madge Dowding should accept her condition—her age and her squint and her poor complexion—and not make herself ridiculous going out after men. What man would be bothered with the like of her anyway? Madge Dowding would do better to give herself over to do Saturday night work for the Legion of Mary: wasn't Canon O'Connell always looking for aid?

"Is that fellow there?" she asked now, moving away from the mirror. "The guy with the long arms. Did anyone see him outside?"

"He's dancing with Cat Bolger," one of the girls replied. "She has herself glued to him."

"Lover boy," remarked Patty Byrne, and everyone laughed because the person referred to was hardly a boy anymore, being over fifty it was said, a bachelor who came only occasionally to the dance hall.

Madge Dowding left the cloakroom rapidly, not bothering to pretend she was not anxious about the conjunction of Cat Bolger and the man with the long arms. Two sharp spots of red had come into her cheeks, and when she stumbled in her haste the girls in the cloakroom laughed. A younger girl would have pretended to be casual.

Bridie chatted, waiting for the mirror. Some girls, not wishing to be delayed, 30 used the mirrors of their compacts. Then in twos and threes, occasionally singly, they left the cloakroom and took their places on upright wooden chairs at one end of the dance hall, waiting to be asked to dance. Mr. Maloney, Mr. Swanton, and Dano Ryan played "Harvest Moon" and "I Wonder Who's Kissing Her Now" and "I'll Be Around."

Bridie danced. Her father would be falling asleep by the fire; the wireless, tuned in to Radio Eireann, would be murmuring in the background. Already he'd have listened to *Faith and Order* and *Spot the Talent*. His Wild West novel, *Three Rode Fast* by Jake Matall, would have dropped from his single knee on to the flagged floor. He would wake with a jerk as he did every night and, forgetting what night it was, might be surprised not to see her, for usually she was sitting there at the table, mending clothes or washing eggs. "Is it time for the news?" he'd automatically say.

Dust and cigarette smoke formed a haze beneath the crystal bowl, feet thudded, girls shrieked and laughed, some of them dancing together for want of a male partner. The music was loud, the musicians had taken off their jackets. Vigorously they played a number of tunes from *State Fair* and then, more romantically, "Just One of Those Things." The tempo increased for a Paul Jones, after which Bridie found herself with a youth who told her he was saving up to emigrate, the nation in his opinion being finished. "I'm up in the hills with the uncle," he said, "laboring fourteen hours a day. Is it any life for a young fellow?" She knew his uncle, a hill farmer whose stony acres were separated from her father's by one other farm only. "He has me gutted with work," the youth told her. "Is there sense in it at all, Bridie?"

At ten o'clock there was a stir, occasioned by the arrival of three middle-aged bachelors who'd cycled over from Carey's public house. They shouted and whistled, greeting other people across the dancing area. They smelt of stout and sweat and whiskey.

Every Saturday at just this time they arrived, and, having sold them their tickets, Mr. Dwyer folded up his card table and locked the tin box that held the evening's takings: his ballroom was complete.

"How're you, Bridie?" one of the bachelors, known as Bowser Egan, in- 35 quired. Another one, Tim Daly, asked Patty Byrne how she was. "Will we take the floor?" Eyes Horgan suggested to Madge Dowding, already pressing the front of his navy blue suit against the net of her dress. Bridie danced with Bowser Egan, who said she was looking great.

The bachelors would never marry, the girls of the dance hall considered: they were wedded already, to stout and whiskey and laziness, to three old mothers somewhere up in the hills. The man with the long arms didn't drink but he was the same in all other ways: he had the same look of a bachelor, a quality in his face.

"Great," Bowser Egan said, feather-stepping in an inaccurate and inebriated manner. "You're a great little dancer, Bridie."

"Will you lay off that!" cried Madge Dowding, her voice shrill above the sound of the music. Eyes Horgan had slipped two fingers into the back of her dress and was now pretending they'd got there by accident. He smiled blearily, his huge red face streaming with perspiration, the eyes which gave him his nickname protuberant and bloodshot.

"Watch your step with that one," Bowser Egan called out, laughing so that spittle sprayed on to Bridie's face. Eenie Mackie, who was also dancing near the incident, laughed also and winked at Bridie. Dano Ryan left his drums and sang. "Oh, how I miss your gentle kiss," he crooned, "and long to hold you tight."

Nobody knew the name of the man with the long arms. The only words he'd 40 ever been known to speak in the Ballroom of Romance were the words that formed his invitation to dance. He was a shy man who stood alone when he wasn't performing on the dance floor. He rode away on his bicycle afterwards, not saying good night to anyone.

"Cat has your man leppin' tonight," Tim Daly remarked to Patty Byrne, for the liveliness that Cat Bolger had introduced into foxtrot and waltz was noticeable.

"I think of you only," sang Dano Ryan. "Only wishing, wishing you were by my side."

Dano Ryan would have done, Bridie often thought, because he was a different kind of bachelor: he had a lonely look about him, as if he'd become tired of being on his own. Every week she thought he would have done, and during the week her mind regularly returned to that thought. Dano Ryan would have done because she felt he wouldn't mind coming to live in the farmhouse while her one-legged father was still about the place. Three could live as cheaply as two where Dano Ryan was concerned because giving up the wages he earned as a road worker would be balanced by the saving made on what he paid for lodgings. Once, at the end of an evening, she'd pretended that there was a puncture in the back wheel of her bicycle and he'd concerned himself with it while Mr. Maloney and Mr. Swanton waited for him in Mr. Maloney's car. He'd blown the tire up with the car pump and had said he thought it would hold.

It was well known in the dance hall that she fancied her chances with Dano Ryan. But it was well known also that Dano Ryan had got into a set way of life and had remained in it for quite some years. He lodged with a widow called Mrs. Griffin and Mrs. Griffin's mentally affected son, in a cottage on the outskirts of the town. He was said to be good to the affected child, buying him sweets and taking him out for rides on the crossbar of his bicycle. He gave an hour or two of his time every week to the Church of Our Lady Queen of Heaven, and he was loyal to Mr. Dwyer. He performed in the two other rural dance halls that Mr. Dwyer owned, rejecting advances from the town's more sophisticated dance hall, even though it was more conveniently situated for him and the fee was more substantial than that paid by Mr. Dwyer. But Mr. Dwyer had discovered Dano Ryan and Dano had not forgotten it, just as Mr. Maloney and Mr. Swanton had not forgotten their discovery by Mr. Dwyer either.

"Would we take a lemonade?" Bowser Egan suggested. "And a packet of   45
biscuits, Bridie?"

No alcoholic liquor was ever served in the Ballroom of Romance, the premises not being licensed for this added stimulant. Mr. Dwyer in fact had never sought a license for any of his premises, knowing that romance and alcohol were difficult commodities to mix, especially in a dignified ballroom. Behind where the girls sat on the wooden chairs Mr. Dwyer's wife, a small stout woman, served the bottles of lemonade, with straws, and the biscuits and the crisps. She talked busily while doing so, mainly about the turkeys she kept. She'd once told Bridie that she thought of them as children.

"Thanks," Bridie said, and Bowser Egan led her to the trestle table. Soon it would be the intermission: soon the three members of the band would cross the floor also for refreshment. She thought up questions to ask Dano Ryan.

When first she'd danced in the Ballroom of Romance, when she was just sixteen, Dano Ryan had been there also, four years older than she was, playing the drums for Mr. Maloney as he played them now. She'd hardly noticed him then because of his not being one of the dancers: he was part of the ballroom's scenery, like the trestle table and the lemonade bottles, and Mrs. Dwyer and Mr. Dwyer. The youths who'd danced with her then in their Saturday-night blue suits had later disappeared into the town, or to Dublin or Britain, leaving behind them those who became the middle-aged bachelors of the hills. There'd been a boy called Patrick Grady whom she had loved in those days. Week after week she'd ridden away from the Ballroom of Romance with the image of his face in her mind, a thin face, pale beneath black hair. It had been different, dancing with Patrick Grady, and she'd felt that he found it different dancing with her, although he'd never said so. At night she'd dreamed of him and in the daytime too, while she helped her mother in the kitchen or her father with the cows. Week by week she'd returned to the ballroom, smiling on its pink façade and dancing then in the arms of Patrick Grady. Often they'd stood together drinking lemonade, not saying anything, not knowing what to say. She knew he loved her, and she believed then that he would lead her one day from the dim, romantic ballroom, from its blueness and its pinkness and its crystal bowl of light and its music. She believed he would lead her into sunshine, to the town and the Church of Our Lady Queen of Heaven; to marriage and smiling faces. But someone else had got Patrick Grady, a girl from the town who'd never danced in the wayside ballroom. She'd scooped up Patrick Grady when he didn't have a chance.

Bridie had wept, hearing that. By night she'd lain in her bed in the farmhouse, quietly crying, the tears rolling into her hair and making the pillow damp. When she woke in the early morning the thought was still naggingly with her and it remained with her by day, replacing her daytime dreams of happiness. Someone told her later on that he'd crossed to Britain, to Wolverhampton, with the girl he'd married, and she imagined him there, in a place she wasn't able properly to visualize, laboring in a factory, his children being born and acquiring the accent of the area. The Ballroom of Romance wasn't the same without him, and when no one else stood out for her particularly over the years and when no one offered her marriage, she found herself wondering about Dano Ryan. If you couldn't have love, the next best thing was surely a decent man.

Bowser Egan hardly fell into that category, nor did Tim Daly. And it was 50
plain to everyone that Cat Bolger and Madge Dowding were wasting their time
over the man with the long arms. Madge Dowding was already a figure of fun in
the ballroom, the way she ran after the bachelors; Cat Bolger would end up the
same if she wasn't careful. One way or another it wasn't difficult to be a figure of
fun in the ballroom, and you didn't have to be as old as Madge Dowding: a girl
who'd just left the Presentation Nuns had once asked Eyes Horgan what he had
in his trouser pocket and he told her it was a penknife. She'd repeated this afterwards in the cloakroom, how she'd requested Eyes Horgan not to dance so close
to her because his penknife was sticking into her. "Jeez, aren't you the right baby!"
Patty Byrne had shouted delightedly: everyone had laughed, knowing that Eyes
Horgan only came to the ballroom for stuff like that. He was no use to any girl.

"Two lemonades, Mrs. Dwyer," Bowser Egan said, "and two packets of Kerry
Creams. Is Kerry Creams all right, Bridie?"

She nodded, smiling. Kerry Creams would be fine, she said.

"Well, Bridie, isn't that the great outfit you have!" Mrs. Dwyer remarked.
"Doesn't the red suit her, Bowser?"

By the swing doors stood Mr. Dwyer, smoking a cigarette that he held cupped
in his left hand. His small eyes noted all developments. He had been aware of
Madge Dowding's anxiety when Eyes Horgan had inserted two fingers into the
back opening of her dress. He had looked away, not caring for the incident, but
had it developed further he would have spoken to Eyes Horgan, as he had on
other occasions. Some of the younger lads didn't know any better and would
dance very close to their partners, who generally were too embarrassed to do anything about it, being young themselves. But that, in Mr. Dwyer's opinion, was a
different kettle of fish altogether because they were decent young lads who'd in
no time at all be doing a steady line with a girl and would end up as he had himself with Mrs. Dwyer, in the same house with her, sleeping in a bed with her,
firmly married. It was the middle-aged bachelors who required the watching: they
came down from the hills like mountain goats, released from their mammies and
from the smell of animals and soil. Mr. Dwyer continued to watch Eyes Horgan,
wondering how drunk he was.

Dano Ryan's song came to an end, Mr. Swanton laid down his clarinet, Mr. 55
Maloney rose from the piano. Dano Ryan wiped sweat from his face and the three
men slowly moved towards Mrs. Dwyer's trestle table.

"Jeez, you have powerful legs," Eyes Horgan whispered to Madge Dowding,
but Madge Dowding's attention was on the man with the long arms, who had
left Cat Bolger's side and was proceeding in the direction of the men's lavatory.
He never took refreshments. She moved, herself, towards the men's lavatory, to
take up a position outside it, but Eyes Horgan followed her. "Would you take a
lemonade, Madge?" he asked. He had a small bottle of whiskey on him: if they
went into a corner they could add a drop of it to the lemonade. She didn't drink
spirits, she reminded him, and he went away.

"Excuse me a minute," Bowser Egan said, putting down his bottle of lemonade. He crossed the floor to the lavatory. He too, Bridie knew, would have a small
bottle of whiskey on him. She watched while Dano Ryan, listening to a story Mr.
Maloney was telling, paused in the center of the ballroom, his head bent to hear
what was being said. He was a big man, heavily made, with black hair that was
slightly touched with grey, and big hands. He laughed when Mr. Maloney came

to the end of his story and then bent his head again, in order to listen to a story told by Mr. Swanton.

"Are you on your own, Bridie?" Cat Bolger asked, and Bridie said she was waiting for Bowser Egan. "I think I'll have a lemonade," Cat Bolger said.

Younger boys and girls stood with their arms still around one another, queueing up for refreshments. Boys who hadn't danced at all, being nervous because they didn't know any steps, stood in groups, smoking and making jokes. Girls who hadn't been danced with yet talked to one another, their eyes wandering. Some of them sucked at straws in lemonade bottles.

Bridie, still watching Dano Ryan, imagined him wearing the glasses he'd re-   60
ferred to, sitting in the farmhouse kitchen, reading one of her father's Wild West novels. She imagined the three of them eating a meal she'd prepared, fried eggs and rashers and fried potato cakes and tea and bread and butter and jam, brown bread and soda and shop bread. She imagined Dano Ryan leaving the kitchen in the morning to go out to the fields in order to weed the mangolds, and her father hobbling off behind him, and the two men working together. She saw hay being cut, Dano Ryan with the scythe that she'd learned to use herself, her father using a rake as best he could. She saw herself, because of the extra help, being able to attend to things in the farmhouse, things she'd never had time for because of the cows and the hens and the fields. There were bedroom curtains that needed repairing where the net had ripped, and wallpaper that had become loose and needed to be stuck up with flour paste. The scullery required whitewashing.

The night he'd blown up the tire of her bicycle she'd thought he was going to kiss her. He'd crouched on the ground in the darkness with his ear to the tire, listening for escaping air. When he could hear none he'd straightened up and said he thought she'd be all right on the bicycle. His face had been quite close to hers and she'd smiled at him. At that moment, unfortunately, Mr. Maloney had blown an impatient blast on the horn of his motorcar.

Often she'd been kissed by Bowser Egan, on the nights when he insisted on riding part of the way home with her. They had to dismount in order to push their bicycles up a hill and the first time he'd accompanied her he'd contrived to fall against her, steadying himself by putting a hand on her shoulder. The next thing she was aware of was the moist quality of his lips and the sound of his bicycle as it clattered noisily on the road. He'd suggested then, regaining his breath, that they should go into a field.

That was nine years ago. In the intervening passage of time she'd been kissed as well, in similar circumstances, by Eyes Horgan and Tim Daly. She'd gone into fields with them and permitted them to put their arms about her while heavily they breathed. At one time or another she had imagined marriage with one or other of them, seeing them in the farmhouse with her father, even though the fantasies were unlikely.

Bridie stood with Cat Bolger, knowing that it would be some time before Bowser Egan came out of the lavatory. Mr. Maloney, Mr. Swanton, and Dano Ryan approached, Mr. Maloney insisting that he would fetch three bottles of lemonade from the trestle table.

"You sang the last one beautifully," Bridie said to Dano Ryan. "Isn't it a   65
beautiful song?"

Mr. Swanton said it was the finest song ever written, and Cat Bolger said she preferred "Danny Boy," which in her opinion was the finest song ever written.

"Take a suck of that," said Mr. Maloney, handing Dano Ryan and Mr. Swanton bottles of lemonade. "How's Bridie tonight? Is your father well, Bridie?" Her father was all right, she said.

"I hear they're starting a cement factory," said Mr. Maloney. "Did anyone hear talk of that? They're after striking some commodity in the earth that makes good cement. Ten feet down, over at Kilmalough."

"It'll bring employment," said Mr. Swanton. "It's employment that's nec- 70 essary in this area."

"Canon O'Connell was on about it," Mr. Maloney said. "There's Yankee money involved."

"Will the Yanks come over?" inquired Cat Bolger. "Will they run it them- selves, Mr. Maloney?"

Mr. Maloney, intent on his lemonade, didn't hear the questions and Cat Bolger didn't repeat them.

"There's stuff called Optrex," Bridie said quietly to Dano Ryan, "that my father took the time he had a cold in his eyes. Maybe Optrex would settle the wa- tering, Dano."

"Ah sure, it doesn't worry me that much—" 75

"It's terrible, anything wrong with the eyes. You wouldn't want to take a chance. You'd get Optrex in a chemist, Dano, and a little bowl with it so that you can bathe the eyes."

Her father's eyes had become red-rimmed and unsightly to look at. She'd gone into Riordan's Medical Hall in the town and had explained what the trou- ble was, and Mr. Riordan had recommended Optrex. She told this to Dano Ryan, adding that her father had had no trouble with his eyes since. Dano Ryan nod- ded.

"Did you hear that, Mrs. Dwyer?" Mr. Maloney called out. "A cement fac- tory for Kilmalough."

Mrs. Dwyer wagged her head, placing empty bottles in a crate. She'd heard references to the cement factory, she said: it was the best news for a long time.

"Kilmalough'll never know itself," her husband commented, joining her in 80 her task with the empty lemonade bottles.

"'Twill bring prosperity certainly," said Mr. Swanton. "I was saying just there, Justin, that employment's what's necessary."

"Sure, won't the Yanks—"began Cat Bolger, but Mr. Maloney interrupted her.

"The Yanks'll be in at the top, Cat, or maybe not here at all—maybe only inserting money into it. It'll be local labor entirely."

"You'll not marry a Yank, Cat," said Mr. Swanton, loudly laughing. "You can't catch those fellows."

"Haven't you plenty of homemade bachelors?" suggested Mr. Maloney. He 85 laughed also, throwing away the straw he was sucking through and tipping the bottle into his mouth. Cat Bolger told him to get on with himself. She moved towards the men's lavatory and took up a position outside it, not speaking to Madge Dowding, who was still standing there.

"Keep a watch on Eyes Horgan," Mrs. Dwyer warned her husband, which was advice she gave him at this time every Saturday night, knowing that Eyes Horgan was drinking in the lavatory. When he was drunk Eyes Horgan was the most difficult of the bachelors.

"I have a drop of it left, Dano," Bridie said quietly. "I could bring it over on Saturday. The eye stuff."

"Ah, don't worry yourself, Bridie—"

"No trouble at all. Honestly now—"

"Mrs. Griffin has me fixed up for a test with Dr. Cready. The old eyes are   90
no worry, only when I'm reading the paper or at the pictures. Mrs. Griffin says I'm only straining them due to lack of glasses."

He looked away while he said that, and she knew at once that Mrs. Griffin was arranging to marry him. She felt it instinctively: Mrs. Griffin was going to marry him because she was afraid that if he moved away from her cottage, to get married to someone else, she'd find it hard to replace him with another lodger who'd be good to her affected son. He'd become a father to Mrs. Griffin's affected son, to whom already he was kind. It was a natural outcome, for Mrs. Griffin had all the chances, seeing him every night and morning and not having to make do with weekly encounters in a ballroom.

She thought of Patrick Grady, seeing in her mind his pale, thin face. She might be the mother of four of his children now, or seven or eight maybe. She might be living in Wolverhampton, going out to the pictures in the evenings, instead of looking after a one-legged man. If the weight of circumstances hadn't intervened she wouldn't be standing in a wayside ballroom, mourning the marriage of a road mender she didn't love. For a moment she thought she might cry, standing there thinking of Patrick Grady in Wolverhampton. In her life, on the farm and in the house, there was no place for tears. Tears were a luxury, like flowers would be in the fields where the mangolds grew, or fresh whitewash in the scullery. It would-n't have been fair ever to have wept in the kitchen while her father sat listening to *Spot the Talent*: her father had more right to weep, having lost a leg. He suffered in a greater way, yet he remained kind and concerned for her.

In the Ballroom of Romance she felt behind her eyes the tears that it would have been improper to release in the presence of her father. She wanted to let them go, to feel them streaming on her cheeks, to receive the sympathy of Dano Ryan and of everyone else. She wanted them all to listen to her while she told them about Patrick Grady who was now in Wolverhampton and about the death of her mother and her own life since. She wanted Dano Ryan to put his arm around her so that she could lean her head against it. She wanted him to look at her in his decent way and to stroke with his road mender's fingers the backs of her hands. She might wake in a bed with him and imagine for a moment that he was Patrick Grady. She might bathe his eyes and pretend.

"Back to business," said Mr. Maloney, leading his band across the floor to their instruments.

"Tell your father I was asking for him," Dano Ryan said. She smiled and she   95
promised, as though nothing had happened, that she would tell her father that.

She danced with Tim Daly and then again with the youth who'd said he in-tended to emigrate. She saw Madge Dowding moving swiftly towards the man with the long arms as he came out of the lavatory, moving faster than Cat Bolger. Eyes Horgan approached Cat Bolger. Dancing with her, he spoke earnestly, at-tempting to persuade her to permit him to ride part of the way home with her. He was unaware of the jealousy that was coming from her as she watched Madge Dowding holding close to her the man with the long arms while they performed a quickstep. Cat Bolger was in her thirties too.

"Get away out of that," said Bowser Egan, cutting in on the youth who was dancing with Bridie. "Go home to your mammy, boy." He took her into his arms, saying again that she was looking great tonight. "Did you hear about the cement factory?" he said. "Isn't it great for Kilmalough?"

She agreed. She said what Mr. Swanton and Mr. Maloney had said: that the cement factory would bring employment to the neighborhood.

"Will I ride home with you a bit, Bridie?" Bowser Egan suggested, and she pretended not to hear him. "Aren't you my girl, Bridie, and always have been?" he said, a statement that made no sense at all.

His voice went on whispering at her, saying he would marry her tomorrow only his mother wouldn't permit another woman in the house. She knew what it was like herself, he reminded her, having a parent to look after: you couldn't leave them to rot, you had to honor your father and your mother. 100

She danced to "The Bells Are Ringing," moving her legs in time with Bowser Egan's while over his shoulder she watched Dano Ryan softly striking one of his smaller drums. Mrs. Griffin had got him even though she was nearly fifty, with no looks at all, a lumpish woman with lumpish legs and arms. Mrs. Griffin had got him just as the girl had got Patrick Grady.

The music ceased, Bowser Egan held her hard against him, trying to touch her face with his. Around them, people whistled and clapped: the evening had come to an end. She walked away from Bowser Egan, knowing that not ever again would she dance in the Ballroom of Romance. She'd been a figure of fun, trying to promote a relationship with a middle-aged County Council laborer, as ridiculous as Madge Dowding dancing on beyond her time.

"I'm waiting outside for you, Cat," Eyes Horgan called out, lighting a cigarette as he made for the swing doors.

Already the man with the long arms—made long, so they said, from carrying rocks off his land—had left the ballroom. Others were moving briskly. Mr. Dwyer was tidying the chairs.

In the cloakroom the girls put on their coats and said they'd see one another at Mass the next day. Madge Dowding hurried. "Are you O.K., Bridie?" Patty Byrne asked and Bridie said she was. She smiled at little Patty Byrne, wondering if a day would come for the younger girl also, if one day she'd decide that she was a figure of fun in a wayside ballroom. 105

"Good night so," Bridie said, leaving the cloakroom, and the girls who were still chatting there wished her good night. Outside the cloakroom she paused for a moment. Mr. Dwyer was still tidying the chairs, picking up empty lemonade bottles from the floor, setting the chairs in a neat row. His wife was sweeping the floor. "Good night, Bridie," Mr. Dwyer said. "Good night, Bridie," his wife said.

Extra lights had been switched on so that the Dwyers could see what they were doing. In the glare the blue walls of the ballroom seemed tatty, marked with hair oil where men had leaned against them, inscribed with names and initials and hearts with arrows through them. The crystal bowl gave out a light that was ineffective in the glare; the bowl was broken here and there, which wasn't noticeable when the other lights weren't on.

"Good night so," Bridie said to the Dwyers. She passed through the swing doors and descended the three concrete steps on the gravel expanse in front of the ballroom. People were gathered on the gravel, talking in groups, standing with their bicycles. She saw Madge Dowding going off with Tim Daly. A youth rode away with a girl on the crossbar of his bicycle. The engines of motorcars started.

"Good night, Bridie," Dano Ryan said.

"Good night, Dano," she said.   110

She walked across the gravel towards her bicycle, hearing Mr. Maloney, somewhere behind her, repeating that no matter how you looked at it the cement factory would be a great thing for Kilmalough. She heard the bang of a car door and knew it was Mr. Swanton banging the door of Mr. Maloney's car because he always gave it the same loud bang. Two other doors banged as she reached her bicycle and then the engine started up and the headlights went on. She touched the two tires of the bicycle to make certain she hadn't a puncture. The wheels of Mr. Maloney's car traversed the gravel and were silent when they reached the road.

"Good night, Bridie," someone called, and she replied, pushing her bicycle towards the road.

"Will I ride a little way with you?" Bowser Egan asked.

They rode together and when they arrived at the hill for which it was necessary to dismount she looked back and saw in the distance the four colored bulbs that decorated the façade of the Ballroom of Romance. As she watched the lights went out, and she imagined Mr. Dwyer pulling the metal grid across the front of his property and locking the two padlocks that secured it. His wife would be waiting with the evening's takings, sitting in the front of their car.

"D'you know what it is, Bridie," said Bowser Egan, "you were never look- 115
ing better than tonight." He took from a pocket of his suit the small bottle of whiskey he had. He uncorked it and drank some and then handed it to her. She took it and drank. "Sure, why wouldn't you?" he said, surprised to see her drinking because she never had in his company before. It was an unpleasant taste, she considered, a taste she'd experienced only twice before, when she'd taken whiskey as a remedy for toothache. "What harm would it do you?" Bowser Egan said as she raised the bottle again to her lips. He reached out a hand for it, though, suddenly concerned lest she should consume a greater share than he wished her to.

She watched him drinking more expertly than she had. He would always be drinking, she thought. He'd be lazy and useless, sitting in the kitchen with the *Irish Press.* He'd waste money buying a secondhand motorcar in order to drive into the town to go to the public houses on fair days.

"She's shook these days," he said, referring to his mother. "She'll hardly last two years, I'm thinking." He threw the empty whiskey bottle into the ditch and lit a cigarette. They pushed their bicycles. He said:

"When she goes, Bridie, I'll sell the bloody place up. I'll sell the pigs and the whole damn one and twopence worth." He paused in order to raise the cigarette to his lips. He drew in smoke and exhaled it. "With the cash that I'll get I could improve some place else, Bridie."

They reached a gate on the left-hand side of the road and automatically they pushed their bicycles towards it and leaned them against it. He climbed over the gate into the field and she climbed after him. "Will we sit down here, Bridie?" he said, offering the suggestion as one that had just occurred to him, as though they'd entered the field for some other purpose.

"We could improve a place like your own one," he said, putting his right 120
arm around her shoulders. "Have you a kiss in you, Bridie?" He kissed her, exerting pressure with his teeth. When his mother died he would sell his farm and

spend the money in the town. After that he would think of getting married because he'd have nowhere to go, because he'd want a fire to sit at and a woman to cook food for him. He kissed her again, his lips hot, the sweat on his cheeks sticking to her. "God, you're great at kissing," he said.

She rose, saying it was time to go, and they climbed over the gate again. "There's nothing like a Saturday," he said. "Good night to you so, Bridie."

He mounted his bicycle and rode down the hill, and she pushed hers to the top and then mounted it also. She rode through the night as on Saturday nights for years she had ridden and never would ride again because she'd reached a certain age. She would wait now and in time Bowser Egan would seek her out because his mother would have died. Her father would probably have died also by then. She would marry Bowser Egan because it would be lonesome being by herself in the farmhouse.

Alice Walker   (b. 1944)

Alice Walker, born to sharecropper parents in Georgia, found her way, through the support of teachers and parents, to Spelman College in Atlanta, a college for black women, and then to Sarah Lawrence College in Bronxville, New York. From Sarah Lawrence, she published her first book of poems, Once *(1968). In 1979 she published* The Temple of My Familiar, *a novel, and then in 1982 her most famous novel,* The Color Purple. *Her story collections include* Love and Trouble: Stories of Black Women *(1973) and* You Can't Keep a Good Woman Down *(1981). Her stories and novels, most of which explore the worlds of African-American women, were inspired to a large extent by her mother, whose life she has chronicled in her essays. She has said, "The black woman is one of America's greatest heroes. . . . Not enough credit has been given to the black woman who has been oppressed beyond recognition." Walker has won innumerable awards and honors for her writing, including the Pulitzer Prize and the National Book Award.*

EVERYDAY USE   1973

for your grandmama

I will wait for her in the yard that Maggie and I made so clean and wavy yesterday afternoon. A yard like this is more comfortable than most people know. It is not just a yard. It is like an extended living room. When the hard clay is swept clean as a floor and the fine sand around the edges lined with tiny, irregular grooves, anyone can come and sit and look up into the elm tree and wait for the breezes that never come inside the house.

Maggie will be nervous until after her sister goes: she will stand hopelessly in corners, homely and ashamed of the burn scars down her arms and legs, eying her sister with a mixture of envy and awe. She thinks her sister has held life always in the palm of one hand, that "no" is a word the world never learned to say to her.

You've no doubt seen those TV shows where the child who has "made it" is confronted, as a surprise, by her own mother and father, tottering in weakly from backstage. (A pleasant surprise, of course: What would they do if parent and child came on the show only to curse out and insult each other?) On TV mother and child embrace and smile into each other's faces. Sometimes the mother and father weep, the child wraps them in her arms and leans across the table to tell how she would not have made it without their help. I have seen these programs.

Sometimes I dream a dream in which Dee and I are suddenly brought together on a TV program of this sort. Out of a dark and soft-seated limousine I am ushered into a bright room filled with many people. There I meet a smiling, gray, sporty man like Johnny Carson who shakes my hand and tells me what a fine girl I have. Then we are on the stage and Dee is embracing me with tears in her eyes. She pins on my dress a large orchid, even though she has told me once that she thinks orchids are tacky flowers.

In real life I am a large, big-boned woman with rough, man-working hands.   5 In the winter I wear flannel nightgowns to bed and overalls during the day. I can kill and clean a hog as mercilessly as a man. My fat keeps me hot in zero weather. I can work outside all day, breaking ice to get water for washing; I can eat pork liver cooked over the open fire minutes after it comes steaming from the hog. One winter I knocked a bull calf straight in the brain between the eyes with a sledge hammer and had the meat hung up to chill before nightfall. But of course all this does not show on television. I am the way my daughter would want me to be: a hundred pounds lighter, my skin like an uncooked barley pancake. My hair glistens in the hot bright lights. Johnny Carson has much to do to keep up with my quick and witty tongue.

But that is a mistake. I know even before I wake up. Who ever knew a Johnson with a quick tongue? Who can even imagine me looking a strange white man in the eye? It seems to me I have talked to them always with one foot raised in flight, with my head turned in whichever way is farthest from them. Dee, though. She would always look anyone in the eye. Hesitation was no part of her nature.

"How do I look, Mama?" Maggie says, showing just enough of her thin body enveloped in pink skirt and red blouse for me to know she's there, almost hidden by the door.

"Come out into the yard," I say.

Have you ever seen a lame animal, perhaps a dog run over by some careless person rich enough to own a car, sidle up to someone who is ignorant enough to be kind to him? That is the way my Maggie walks. She has been like this, chin on chest, eyes on ground, feet in shuffle, ever since the fire that burned the other house to the ground.

Dee is lighter than Maggie, with nicer hair and a fuller figure. She's a woman   10 now, though sometimes I forget. How long ago was it that the other house burned? Ten, twelve years? Sometimes I can still hear the flames and feel Maggie's arms sticking to me, her hair smoking and her dress falling off her in little black papery flakes. Her eyes seemed stretched open, blazed open by the flames reflected in them. And Dee. I see her standing off under the sweet gum tree she used to dig gum out of; a look of concentration on her face as she watched the last dingy gray board of the house fall in toward the red-hot brick chimney. Why don't you do a dance around the ashes? I'd wanted to ask her. She had hated the house that much.

I used to think she hated Maggie, too. But that was before we raised the money, the church and me, to send her to Augusta to school. She used to read to us without pity; forcing words, lies, other folks' habits, whole lives upon us two, sitting trapped and ignorant underneath her voice. She washed us in a river of make-believe, burned us with a lot of knowledge we didn't necessarily need to know. Pressed us to her with the serious way she read, to shove us away at just the moment, like dimwits, we seemed about to understand.

Dee wanted nice things. A yellow organdy dress to wear to her graduation from high school; black pumps to match a green suit she'd made from an old suit somebody gave me. She was determined to stare down any disaster in her efforts. Her eyelids would not flicker for minutes at a time. Often I fought off the temptation to shake her. At sixteen she had a style of her own: and knew what style was.

I never had an education myself. After second grade the school was closed down. Don't ask me why: in 1927 colored asked fewer questions than they do now. Sometimes Maggie reads to me. She stumbles along good-naturedly but can't see well. She knows she is not bright. Like good looks and money, quickness passed her by. She will marry John Thomas (who has mossy teeth in an earnest face) and then I'll be free to sit here and I guess just sing church songs to myself. Although I never was a good singer. Never could carry a tune. I was always better at a man's job. I used to love to milk till I was hooked in the side in '49. Cows are soothing and slow and don't bother you, unless you try to milk them the wrong way.

I have deliberately turned my back on the house. It is three rooms, just like the one that burned, except the roof is tin; they don't make shingle roofs any more. There are no real windows, just some holes cut in the sides, like the portholes in a ship, but not round and not square, with rawhide holding the shutters up on the outside. This house is in a pasture, too, like the other one. No doubt when Dee sees it she will want to tear it down. She wrote me once that no matter where we "choose" to live, she will manage to come see us. But she will never bring her friends. Maggie and I thought about this and Maggie asked me, "Mama, when did Dee ever *have* any friends?"

She had a few. Furtive boys in pink shirts hanging about on washday after   15
school. Nervous girls who never laughed. Impressed with her they worshiped the well-turned phrase, the cute shape, the scalding humor that erupted like bubbles in lye. She read to them.

When she was courting Jimmy T she didn't have much time to pay to us, but turned all her faultfinding power on him. He *flew* to marry a cheap city girl from a family of ignorant flashy people. She hardly had time to recompose herself.

When she comes I will meet—but there they are!

Maggie attempts to make a dash for the house, in her shuffling way, but I stay her with my hand. "Come back here," I say. And she stops and tries to dig a well in the sand with her toe.

It is hard to see them clearly through the strong sun. But even the first glimpse of leg out of the car tells me it is Dee. Her feet were always neat-looking, as if God himself had shaped them with a certain style. From the other side of the car comes a short, stocky man. Hair is all over his head a foot long and hanging from his chin like a kinky mule tail. I hear Maggie suck in her breath. "Uhnnnh," is what it sounds like. Like when you see the wriggling end of a snake just in front of your foot on the road. "Uhnnnh."

Dee next. A dress down to the ground, in this hot weather. A dress so loud 20
it hurts my eyes. There are yellows and oranges enough to throw back the light of the sun. I feel my whole face warming from the heat waves it throws out. Earrings gold, too, and hanging down to her shoulders. Bracelets dangling and making noises when she moves her arm up to shake the folds of the dress out of her armpits. The dress is loose and flows, and as she walks closer, I like it. I hear Maggie go "Uhnnnh" again. It is her sister's hair. It stands straight up like the wool on a sheep. It is black as night and around the edges are two long pigtails that rope about like small lizards disappearing behind her ears.

"Wa-su-zo-Tean-o!"° she says, coming on in that gliding way the dress makes her move. The short stocky fellow with the hair to his navel is all grinning and he follows up with "Asalamalakim,° my mother and sister!" He moves to hug Maggie but she falls back, right up against the back of my chair. I feel her trembling there and when I look up I see the perspiration falling off her chin.

"Don't get up," says Dee. Since I am stout it takes something of a push. You can see me trying to move a second or two before I make it. She turns, showing white heels through her sandals, and goes back to the car. Out she peeks next with a Polaroid. She stoops down quickly and lines up picture after picture of me sitting there in front of the house with Maggie cowering behind me. She never takes a shot without making sure the house is included. When a cow comes nibbling around the edge of the yard she snaps it and me and Maggie *and* the house. Then she puts the Polaroid in the back seat of the car, and comes up and kisses me on the forehead.

Meanwhile Asalamalakim is going through motions with Maggie's hand. Maggie's hand is as limp as a fish, and probably as cold, despite the sweat, and she keeps trying to pull it back. It looks like Asalamalakim wants to shake hands but wants to do it fancy. Or maybe he don't know how people shake hands. Anyhow, he soon gives up on Maggie.

"Well," I say. "Dee."

"No, Mama," she says. "Not 'Dee,' Wangero Leewanika Kemanjo!" 25

"What happened to 'Dee'?" I wanted to know.

"She's dead," Wangero said. "I couldn't bear it any longer, being named after the people who oppress me."

"You know as well as me you was named after your aunt Dicie," I said. Dicie is my sister. She named Dee. We called her "Big Dee" after Dee was born.

"But who was *she* named after?" asked Wangero.

"I guess after Grandma Dee," I said. 30

"And who was she named after?" asked Wangero.

"Her mother," I said, and saw Wangero was getting tired. "That's about as far back as I can trace it," I said. Though, in fact, I probably could have carried it back beyond the Civil War through the branches.

"Well," said Asalamalakim, "there you are."

"Uhnnnh," I heard Maggie say.

Wa-su-zo-Tean-o!: Swahili hello.   *Asalamalakim*: Arabic hello.

"There I was not," I said, "before 'Dicie' cropped up in our family, so why   35
should I try to trace it that far back?"

He just stood there grinning, looking down on me like somebody inspecting a Model A car. Every once in a while he and Wangero sent eye signals over
my head.

"How do you pronounce this name?" I asked.

"You don't have to call me by it if you don't want to," said Wangero.

"Why shouldn't I?" I asked. "If that's what you want us to call you, we'll
call you."

"I know it might sound awkward at first," said Wangero.   40

"I'll get used to it," I said. "Ream it out again."

Well, soon we got the name out of the way. Asalamalakim had a name twice
as long and three times as hard. After I tripped over it two or three times he told
me to just call him Hakim-a-barber. I wanted to ask him was he a barber, but I
didn't really think he was, so I didn't ask.

"You must belong to those beef-cattle peoples down the road," I said. They
said "Asalamalakim" when they met you, too, but they didn't shake hands. Always
too busy: feeding the cattle, fixing the fences, putting up salt-lick shelters, throwing down hay. When the white folks poisoned some of the herd the men stayed
up all night with rifles in their hands. I walked a mile and a half just to see the
sight.

Hakim-a-barber said, "I accept some of their doctrines, but farming and raising cattle is not my style." (They didn't tell me, and I didn't ask, whether Wangero
(Dee) had really gone and married him.)

We sat down to eat and right away he said he didn't eat collards and pork   45
was unclean. Wangero, though, went on through the chitlins and corn bread, the
greens and everything else. She talked a blue streak over the sweet potatoes.
Everything delighted her. Even the fact that we still used the benches her daddy
made for the table when we couldn't afford to buy chairs.

"Oh, Mama!" she cried. Then turned to Hakim-a-barber. "I never knew
how lovely these benches are. You can feel the rump prints," she said, running
her hands underneath her and along the bench. Then she gave a sigh and her
hand closed over Grandma Dee's butter dish. "That's it!" she said. "I knew there
was something I wanted to ask you if I could have." She jumped up from the
table and went over in the corner where the churn stood, the milk in it clabber
by now. She looked at the churn and looked at it.

"This churn top is what I need," she said. "Didn't Uncle Buddy whittle it
out of a tree you all used to have?"

"Yes," I said.

"Uh huh," she said happily. "And I want the dasher, too."

"Uncle Buddy whittle that, too?" asked the barber.   50

Dee (Wangero) looked up at me.

"Aunt Dee's first husband whittled the dash," said Maggie so low you almost couldn't hear her. "His name was Henry, but they called him Stash."

"Maggie's brain is like an elephant's," Wangero said, laughing. "I can use
the churn top as a centerpiece for the alcove table," she said, sliding a plate over
the churn, "and I'll think of something artistic to do with the dasher."

When she finished wrapping the dasher the handle stuck out. I took it for a
moment in my hands. You didn't even have to look close to see where hands

pushing the dasher up and down to make butter had left a kind of sink in the wood. In fact, there were a lot of small sinks; you could see where thumbs and fingers had sunk into the wood. It was beautiful light yellow wood, from a tree that grew in the yard where Big Dee and Stash had lived.

After dinner Dee (Wangero) went to the trunk at the foot of my bed and   55
started rifling through it. Maggie hung back in the kitchen over the dishpan. Out came Wangero with two quilts. They had been pieced by Grandma Dee and then Big Dee and me had hung them on the quilt frames on the front porch and quilted them. One was in the Lone Star pattern. The other was Walk Around the Mountain. In both of them were scraps of dresses Grandma Dee had worn fifty and more years ago. Bits and pieces of Grandpa Jarrell's Paisley shirts. And one teeny faded blue piece, about the size of a penny matchbox, that was from Great Grandpa Ezra's uniform that he wore in the Civil War.

"Mama," Wangero said sweet as a bird. "Can I have these old quilts?"

I heard something fall in the kitchen, and a minute later the kitchen door slammed.

"Why don't you take one or two of the others?" I asked. "These old things was just done by me and Big Dee from some tops your grandma pieced before she died."

"No," said Wangero. "I don't want those. They are stitched around the borders by machine."

"That'll make them last better," I said.   60

"That's not the point," said Wangero. "These are all pieces of dresses Grandma used to wear. She did all this stitching by hand. Imagine!" She held the quilts securely in her arms, stroking them.

"Some of the pieces, like those lavender ones, come from old clothes her mother handed down to her," I said, moving up to touch the quilts. Dee (Wangero) moved back just enough so that I couldn't reach the quilts. They already belonged to her.

"Imagine!" she breathed again, clutching them closely to her bosom.

"The truth is," I said, "I promised to give them quilts to Maggie, for when she marries John Thomas."

She gasped like a bee had stung her.   65

"Maggie can't appreciate these quilts!" she said. "She'd probably be backward enough to put them to everyday use."

"I reckon she would," I said. "God knows I been saving 'em for long enough with nobody using 'em. I hope she will!" I didn't want to bring up how I had offered Dee (Wangero) a quilt when she went away to college. Then she had told me they were old-fashioned, out of style.

"But they're *priceless*!" she was saying now, furiously; for she has a temper. "Maggie would put them on the bed and in five years they'd be in rags. Less than that!"

"She can always make some more," I said. "Maggie knows how to quilt."

Dee (Wangero) looked at me with hatred. "You just will not understand.   70
The point is these quilts, *these* quilts!"

"Well," I said, stumped. "What would *you* do with them?"

"Hang them," she said. As if that was the only thing you *could* do with quilts.

Maggie by now was standing in the door. I could almost hear the sound her feet made as they scraped over each other.

"She can have them, Mama," she said, like somebody used to never winning anything, or having anything reserved for her. "I can 'member Grandma Dee without the quilts."

I looked at her hard. She had filled her bottom lip with checkerberry snuff   75 and it gave her face a kind of dopey, hangdog look. It was Grandma Dee and Big Dee who taught her how to quilt herself. She stood there with her scarred hands hidden in the folds of her skirt. She looked at her sister with something like fear but she wasn't mad at her. This was Maggie's portion. This was the way she knew God to work.

When I looked at her like that something hit me in the top of my head and ran down to the soles of my feet. Just like when I'm in church and the spirit of God touches me and I get happy and shout. I did something I never had done before: hugged Maggie to me, then dragged her on into the room, snatched the quilts out of Miss Wangero's hands and dumped them into Maggie's lap. Maggie just sat there on my bed with her mouth open.

"Take one or two of the others," I said to Dee.

But she turned without a word and went out to Hakim-a-barber.

"You just don't understand," she said, as Maggie and I came out to the car.

"What don't I understand?" I wanted to know.   80

"Your heritage," she said. And then she turned to Maggie, kissed her, and said, "You ought to try to make something of yourself, too, Maggie. It's really a new day for us. But from the way you and Mama still live you'd never know it."

She put on some sunglasses that hid everything above the tip of her nose and her chin.

Maggie smiled; maybe at the sunglasses. But a real smile, not scared. After we watched the car dust settle I asked Maggie to bring me a dip of snuff. And then the two of us sat there just enjoying, until it was time to go in the house and go to bed.

Fay Weldon   (b. 1933)

Born in England, Fay Weldon now lives in Somerset and London. After a stint in advertising and television, she has had a prolific career writing novels, television scripts, and short stories. Her early work established her as a feminist writer who portrays the lives of women oppressed and manipulated by unworthy men. Novels such as The Fat Woman's Joke *(1967),* Down among the Women *(1971), and* Female Friends *(1975) introduce us to men who want to have everything their own way and who give very little to the women in their lives.* Life and Loves of a She-Devil *(1984), one of her best-known works, details the revenge of a spurned wife on her husband and his mistress. One critic describes some of her male characters as candidates "for sarcastic entombment." Her collections of short stories include* Watching Me, Watching You *(1981),* Polaris and Other Stories *(1985), and* Moon over Minneapolis *(1992). Critic Carol Sternhell has said that Weldon "has been preserving women's lives in brittle, ironic prose; like a feminist Jane Austen, she has a sharp eye and tongue for the least romantic side of human relationships." Fay Weldon herself is as witty as her characters and appears much more tolerant of male foibles.*

WEEKEND   1978

By seven-thirty they were ready to go. Martha had everything packed into the car and the three children appropriately dressed and in the back seat, complete with educational games and wholewheat biscuits. When everything was ready in the car Martin would switch off the television, come downstairs, lock up the house, front and back, and take the wheel.

Weekend! Only two hours' drive down to the cottage on Friday evenings: three hours' drive back on Sunday nights. The pleasures of greenery and guests in between. They reckoned themselves fortunate, how fortunate!

On Fridays Martha would get home on the bus at six-twelve and prepare tea and sandwiches for the family: then she would strip four beds and put the sheets and quilt covers in the washing machine for Monday: take the country bedding from the airing basket, plus the books and the games, plus the weekend food—acquired at intervals throughout the week, to lessen the load—plus her own folder of work from the office, plus Martin's drawing materials (she was a market researcher in an advertising agency, he a freelance designer) plus hairbrushes, jeans, spare T-shirts, Jolyon's antibiotics (he suffered from sore throats), Jenny's recorder, Jasper's cassette player, and so on—ah, the so on!—and would pack them all, skilfully and quickly, into the boot. Very little could be left in the cottage during the week. ("An open invitation to burglars": Martin) Then Martha would run round the house tidying and wiping, doing this and that, finding the cat at one neighbor's and delivering it to another, while the others ate their tea; and would usually, proudly, have everything finished by the time they had eaten their fill. Martin would just catch the BBC 2 news, while Martha cleared away the tea table, and the children tossed up for the best positions in the car. "Martha," said Martin, tonight, "you ought to get Mrs. Hodder to do more. She takes advantage of you."

Mrs. Hodder came in twice a week to clean. She was over seventy. She charged two pounds an hour. Martha paid her out of her own wages: well, the running of the house was Martha's concern. If Martha chose to go out to work—as was her perfect right, Martin allowed, even though it wasn't the best thing for the children, but that must be Martha's moral responsibility—Martha must surely pay her domestic stand-in. An evident truth, heard loud and clear and frequent in Martin's mouth and Martha's heart.

"I expect you're right," said Martha. She did not want to argue. Martin had   5
had a long hard week, and now had to drive. Martha couldn't. Martha's license had been suspended four months back for drunken driving. Everyone agreed that the suspension was unfair: Martha seldom drank to excess: she was for one thing usually too busy pouring drinks for other people or washing other people's glasses to get much inside herself. But Martin had taken her out to dinner on her birthday, as was his custom, and exhaustion and excitement mixed had made her imprudent, and before she knew where she was, why there she was, in the dock, with a distorted lamppost to pay for and a new bonnet for the car and six months' suspension.

So now Martin had to drive her car down to the cottage, and he was always tired on Fridays, and hot and sleepy on Sundays, and every rattle and clank and bump in the engine she felt to be somehow her fault.

Martin had a little sports car for London and work: it could nip in and out of the traffic nicely: Martha's was an old estate car,° with room for the children, picnic baskets, bedding, food, games, plants, drink, portable television, and all the things required by the middle classes for weekends in the country. It lumbered rather than zipped and made Martin angry. He seldom spoke a harsh word, but Martha, after the fashion of wives, could detect his mood from what he did not say rather than what he did, and from the tilt of his head, and the way his crinkly, merry eyes seemed crinklier and merrier still—and of course from the way he addressed Martha's car.

"Come along, you old banger you! Can't you do better than that? You're too old, that's your trouble. Stop complaining. Always complaining, it's only a hill. You're too wide about the hips. You'll never get through there."

Martha worried about her age, her tendency to complain, and the width of her hips. She took the remarks personally. Was she right to do so? The children noticed nothing: it was just funny lively laughing Daddy being witty about Mummy's car. Mummy, done for drunken driving. Mummy, with the roots of melancholy somewhere deep beneath the bustling, busy, everyday self. Busy: ah so busy!

Martin would only laugh if she said anything about the way he spoke to her car and warn her against paranoia. "Don't get like your mother, darling." Martha's mother had, towards the end, thought that people were plotting against her. Martha's mother had led a secluded, suspicious life, and made Martha's childhood a chilly and a lonely time. Life now, by comparison, was wonderful for Martha. People, children, houses, conversations, food, drink, theatres—even, now, a career. Martin standing between her and the hostility of the world—popular, easy, funny Martin, beckoning the rest of the world into earshot.

Ah, she was grateful: little earnest Martha, with her shy ways and her penchant for passing boring exams—how her life had blossomed out! Three children too—Jasper, Jenny, and Jolyon—all with Martin's broad brow and open looks, and the confidence born of her love and care, and the work she had put into them since the dawning of their days.

Martin drives. Martha, for once, drowses.

The right food, the right words, the right play. Doctors for the tonsils: dentists for the molars. Confiscate guns: censor television: encourage creativity. Paints and paper to hand: books on the shelves: meetings with teachers. Music teachers. Dancing lessons. Parties. Friends to tea. School plays. Open days. Junior orchestra.

Martha is jolted awake. Traffic lights. Martin doesn't like Martha to sleep while he drives.

Clothes. Oh, clothes Can't wear this: must wear that. Dress shops. Piles of clothes in corners: duly washed, but waiting to be ironed, waiting to be put away.

Get the piles off the floor, into the laundry baskets. Martin doesn't like a mess.

Creativity arises out of order, not chaos. Five years off work while the children were small: back to work with seniority lost. What, did you think something was for nothing? If you have children, mother, that is your reward. It lies not in the world.

Have you taken enough food? Always hard to judge.

---

estate car: Station wagon.

Food. Oh, food! Shop in the lunch-hour. Lug it all home. Cook for the freezer on Wednesday evenings while Martin is at his car-maintenance evening class, and isn't there to notice you being unrestful. Martin likes you to sit down in the evenings. Fruit, meat, vegetables, flour for home-made bread. Well, shop bread is full of pollutants. Frozen food, even your own, loses flavor. Martin often remarks on it. Condiments. Everyone loves mango chutney. But the expense!

London Airport to the left. Look, look, children! Concorde? No, idiot, of   20
course it isn't Concorde.

Ah, to be all things to all people: children, husband, employer, friends! It can be done: yes, it can: super woman.

Drink. Home-made wine. Why not? Elderberries grown thick and rich in London: and at least you know what's in it. Store it in high cupboards: lots of room: up and down the step-ladder. Careful! Don't slip. Don't break anything.

No such think as an accident. Accidents are Freudian slips: they are wilful, bad-tempered things.

Martin can't bear bad temper. Martin likes slim ladies. Diet. Martin rather likes his secretary. Diet. Martin admires slim legs and big bosoms. How to achieve them both? Impossible. But try, oh try, to be what you ought to be, not what you are. Inside and out.

Martin brings back flowers and chocolates: whisks Martha off for holiday   25
weekends. Wonderful! The best husband in the world: look into his crinkly, merry, gentle eyes; see it there. So the mouth slopes away into something of a pout. Never mind. Gaze into the eyes. Love. It must be love. You married him. *You.* Surely *you* deserve true love?

Salisbury Plain. Stonehenge. Look, children, look! Mother, we've seen Stonehenge a hundred times. Go back to sleep.

Cook! Ah cook. People love to come to Martin and Martha's dinners. Work it out in your head in the lunch-hour. If you get in at six-twelve, you can seal the meat while you beat the egg white while you feed the cat while you lay the table while you string the beans while you set out the cheese, goat's cheese, Martin loves goat's cheese, Martha tries to like goat's cheese—oh, bed, sleep, peace, quiet.

Sex! Ah sex. Orgasm, please. Martin requires it. Well, so do you. And you don't want his secretary providing a passion you neglected to develop. Do you? Quick, quick, the cosmic bond. Love. Married loved.

Secretary! Probably a vulgar suspicion: nothing more. Probably a fit of paranoics, à la mother, now dead and gone.

At peace.   30

R.I.P.°

Chilly, lonely mother, following her suspicions where they led.

Nearly there, children. Nearly in paradise, nearly at the cottage. Have another biscuit.

Real roses round the door.

Roses. Prune, weed, spray, feed, pick. Avoid thorns. One of Martin's few   35
harsh words.

"Martha, you can't not want roses! What kind of person am I married to? An anti-rose personality?"

R.I.P.: Rest in peace.

Green grass. Oh, God, grass. Grass must be mown. Restful lawns, daisies bobbing, buttercups glowing. Roses and grass and books. Books.

Please, Martin, do we have to have the two hundred books, mostly twenties' first editions, bought at Christie's book sale on one of your afternoons off? Books need dusting.

Roars of laughter from Martin, Jasper, Jenny, and Jolyon. Mummy says we shouldn't have the books: books need dusting!

Roses, green grass, books, and peace.   40

Martha woke up with a start when they got to the cottage, and gave a little shriek which made them all laugh. Mummy's waking shriek, they called it.

Then there was the car to unpack and the beds to make up, and the electricity to connect, and the supper to make, and the cobwebs to remove, while Martin made the fire. Then supper—pork chops in sweet and sour sauce ("Pork is such a *dull* meat if you don't cook it properly": Martin), green salad from the garden, or such green salad as the rabbits had left. ("Martha, did you really net them properly? Be honest, now!": Martin) and sauté potatoes. Mash is so stodgy and ordinary, and instant mash unthinkable. The children studied the night sky with the aid of their star map. Wonderful, rewarding children!

Then clear up the supper: set the dough to prove for the bread: Martin already in bed: exhausted by the drive and lighting the fire. ("Martha, we really ought to get the logs stacked properly. Get the children to do it, will you?": Martin) Sweep and tidy: get the TV aerial right. Turn up Jasper's jeans where he has trodden the hem undone. ("He can't go around like *that*, Martha. Not even Jasper": Martin)

Midnight. Good night. Weekend guests arriving in the morning. Seven for lunch and dinner on Saturday. Seven for Sunday breakfast, nine for Sunday lunch. ("Don't fuss, darling. You always make such a fuss": Martin) Oh, God, forgotten the garlic squeezer. That means ten minutes with the back of a spoon and salt. Well, who wants *lumps* of garlic? No one. Not Martin's guests. Martin said so. Sleep.

Colin and Katie. Colin is Martin's oldest friend. Katie is his new young wife.   45
Janet, Colin's other, earlier wife, was Martha's friend. Janet was rather like Martha, quieter and duller than her husband. A nag and a drag, Martin rather thought, and said, and of course she'd let herself go, everyone agreed. No one exactly excused Colin for walking out, but you could see the temptation.

Katie versus Janet.

Katie was languid, beautiful, and elegant. She drawled when she spoke. Her hands were expressive: her feet were little and female. She had no children.

Janet plodded round on very flat, rather large feet. There was something wrong with them. They turned out slightly when she walked. She had two children. She was, frankly, boring. But Martha liked her: when Janet came down to the cottage she would wash up. Not in the way that most guests washed up—washing dutifully and setting everything out on the draining board, but actually drying and putting away too. And Janet would wash the bath and get the children all sat down, with chairs for everyone, even the littlest, and keep them quiet and satisfied so the grown-ups—well, the men—could get on with their conversation and their jokes and their love of country weekends, while Janet stared into space, as if grateful for the rest, quite happy.

Janet would garden, too. Weed the strawberries, while the men went for their walk; her great feet standing firm and square and sometimes crushing a plant or so, but never mind, oh never mind. Lovely Janet; who understood.

Now Janet was gone and here was Katie. 50

Katie talked with the men and went for walks with the men, and moved her ashtray rather impatiently when Martha tried to clear the drinks round it.

Dishes were boring, Katie implied by her manner, and domesticity was boring, and anyone who bothered with that kind of thing was a fool. Like Martha. Ash should be allowed to stay where it was, even if it was in the butter, and conversations should never be interrupted.

Knock, knock. Katie and Colin arrived at one-fifteen on Saturday morning, just after Martha had got to bed. "You don't mind? It was the moonlight. We couldn't resist it. You should have seen Stonehenge! We didn't disturb you? Such early birds!"

Martha rustled up a quick meal of omelettes. Saturday nights' eggs. ("Martha makes a lovely omelette": Martin) ("Honey, make one of your mushroom omelettes: cook the mushrooms separately, remember, with lemon. Otherwise the water from the mushrooms gets into the egg, and spoils everything.") Sunday supper mushrooms. But ungracious to say anything.

Martin had revived wonderfully at the sight of Colin and Katie. He brought 55 out the whisky bottle. Glasses. Ice. Jug for water. Wait. Wash up another sinkful, when they're finished. 2 A.M.

"Don't do it tonight, darling."

"It'll only take a sec." Bright smile, not a hint of self-pity. Self-pity can spoil everyone's weekend.

Martha knows that if breakfast for seven is to be manageable the sink must be cleared of dishes. A tricky meal, breakfast. Especially if bacon, eggs, and tomatoes must all be cooked in separate pans. ("Separate pans means separate flavors!": Martin)

She is running around in her nightie. Now if that had been Katie—but there's something so *practical* about Martha. Reassuring, mind; but the skimpy nightie and the broad rump and the thirty-eight years are all rather embarrassing. Martha can see it in Colin and Katie's eyes. Martin's too. Martha wishes she did not see so much in other people's eyes. Her mother did, too. Dear, dead mother. Did I misjudge you?

This was the second weekend Katie had been down with Colin but without 60 Janet. Colin was a photographer: Katie had been his accessorizer. First Colin and Janet: then Colin, Janet, and Katie: now Colin and Katie!

Katie weeded with rubber gloves on and pulled out pansies in mistake for weeds and laughed and laughed along with everyone when her mistake was pointed out to her, but the pansies died. Well, Colin had become with the years fairly rich and fairly famous, and what does a fairly rich and famous man want with a wife like Janet when Katie is at hand?

On the first of the Colin/Janet/Katie weekends Katie had appeared out of the bathroom. "I say," said Katie, holding out a damp towel with evident distaste, "I can only find this. No hope of a dry one?" And Martha had run to fetch a dry towel and amazingly found one, and handed it to Katie who flashed her a brilliant smile and said, "I can't bear damp towels. Anything in the world but damp towels," as if speaking to a servant in a time of shortage of staff, and took all the water so there was none left for Martha to wash up.

The trouble, of course, was drying anything at all in the cottage. There were no facilities for doing so, and Martin had a horror of clothes lines which might spoil the view. He toiled and moiled all week in the city simply to get a country view at the weekend. Ridiculous to spoil it by draping it with wet towels! But now Martha had bought more towels, so perhaps everyone could be satisfied. She would take nine damp towels back on Sunday evenings in a plastic bag and see to them in London.

On this Saturday morning, straight after breakfast, Katie went out to the car—she and Colin had a new Lamborghini; hard to imagine Katie in anything duller—and came back waving a new Yves St. Laurent towel. "See! I brought my own, darlings."

They'd brought nothing else. No fruit, no meat, no vegetables, not even 65
bread, certainly not a box of chocolates. They'd gone off to bed with alacrity, the night before, and the spare room rocked and heaved: well, who'd want to do washing-up when you could do that, but what about the children? Would they get confused? First Colin and Janet, now Colin and Katie?

Martha murmured something of her thoughts to Martin, who looked quite shocked. "Colin's my best friend. I don't expect him to bring anything," and Martha felt mean. "And good heavens, you can't protect the kids from sex for ever, don't be so prudish," so that Martha felt stupid as well. Mean, complaining, and stupid.

Janet had rung Martha during the week. The house had been sold over her head, and she and the children had been moved into a small flat. Katie was trying to persuade Colin to cut down on her allowance, Janet said.

"It does one no good to be materialistic," Katie confided. "I have nothing. No home, no family, no ties, no possessions. Look at me! Only me and a suitcase of clothes." But Katie seemed highly satisfied with the me, and the clothes were stupendous. Katie drank a great deal and became funny. Everyone laughed, including Martha. Katie had been married twice. Martha marvelled at how someone could arrive in their mid-thirties with nothing at all to their name, neither husband, nor children, nor property and not mind.

Mind you, Martha could see the power of such helplessness. If Colin was all Katie had in the world, how could Colin abandon her? And to what? Where would she go? How would she live? Oh, clever Katie.

"My teacup's dirty," said Katie, and Martha ran to clean it, apologizing, and 70
Martin raised his eyebrows, at Martha, not Katie.

"I wish *you'd* wear scent," said Martin to Martha, reproachfully. Katie wore lots. Martha never seemed to have time to put any on, though Martin bought her bottle after bottle. Martha leapt out of bed each morning to meet some emergency—miaowing cat, coughing child, faulty alarm clock, postman's knock—when was Martha to put on scent? It annoyed Martin all the same. She ought to do more to charm him.

Colin looked handsome and harrowed and younger than Martin, though they were much the same age. "Youth's catching," said Martin in bed that night. "It's nice he found Katie." Found, like some treasure. Discovered; something exciting and wonderful, in the dreary world of established spouses.

On Saturday morning Jasper trod on a piece of wood ("Martha, why isn't he wearing shoes? It's too bad": Martin) and Martha took him into the hospital to have a nasty splinter removed. She left the cottage at ten and arrived back at one, and they were still sitting in the sun, drinking, empty bottles glinting in the long grass. The grass hadn't been cut. Don't forget the bottles. Broken glass means more mornings at the hospital. Oh, don't fuss. Enjoy yourself. Like other people. Try.

But no potatoes peeled, no breakfast cleared, nothing. Cigarette ends still amongst old toast, bacon rind, and marmalade. "You could have done the potatoes," Martha burst out. Oh, bad temper! Prime sin. They looked at her in amazement and dislike. Martin too.

"Goodness," said Katie. "Are we doing the whole Sunday lunch bit on 75 Saturday? Potatoes! Ages since I've eaten potatoes. Wonderful!"

"The children expect it," said Martha.

So they did. Saturday and Sunday lunch shone like reassuring beacons in their lives. Saturday lunch: family lunch: fish and chips. ("So much better cooked at home than bought": Martin) Sunday. Usually roast beef, potatoes, peas, apple pie. Oh, of course. Yorkshire pudding. Always a problem with oven temperatures. When the beef's going slowly, the Yorkshire should be going fast. How to achieve that? Like big bosom and little hips.

"Just relax," said Martin. "I'll cook dinner, all in good time. Splinters always work their own way out: no need to have taken him to hospital. Let life drift over you, my love. Flow with the waves, that's the way."

And Martin flashed Martha a distant, spiritual smile. His hand lay on Katie's slim brown arm, with its many gold bands.

"Anyway, you do too much for the children," said Martin. "It isn't good for 80 them. Have a drink."

So Martha perched uneasily on the step and had a glass of cider, and wondered how, if lunch was going to be late, she would get cleared up and the meat out of the marinade for the rather formal dinner that would be expected that evening. The marinaded lamb ought to cook for at least four hours in a low oven; and the cottage oven was very small, and you couldn't use that and the grill at the same time and Martin liked his fish grilled, not fried. Less cholesterol.

She didn't say as much. Domestic details like this were very boring, and any mild complaint was registered by Martin as a scene. And to make a scene was so ungrateful.

This was the life. Well, wasn't it? Smart friends in large cars and country living and drinks before lunch and roses and bird song—"Don't drink *too* much," said Martin, and told them about Martha's suspended driving licence.

The children were hungry so Martha opened them a can of beans and sausages and heated that up. ("Martha, do they have to eat that crap? Can't they wait?": Martin)

Katie was hungry: she said so, to keep the children in face. She was lovely 85 with children—most children. She did not particularly like Colin and Janet's children. She said so, and he accepted it. He only saw them once a month now, not once a week.

"Let me make lunch," Katie said to Martha. "You do so much, poor thing!"

And she pulled out of the fridge all the things Martha had put away for the next day's picnic lunch party—Camembert cheese and salad and salami and made a wonderful tomato salad in two minutes and opened the white wine—"Not very cold, darling. Shouldn't it be chilling?"—and had it all on the table in five amazing competent minutes. "That's all we need, darling," said Martin. "You are funny with your fish-and-chip Saturdays! What could be nicer than this? Or simpler?"

Nothing, except there was Sunday's buffet lunch for nine gone, in place of Saturday's fish for six, and would the fish stretch? No. Katie had had quite a lot to drink. She pecked Martha on the forehead. "Funny little Martha," she said. "She reminds me of Janet. I really do like Janet." Colin did not want to be reminded of Janet, and said so. "Darling, Janet's a fact of life," said Katie. "If you'd only think about her more, you might manage to pay her less." And she yawned and stretched her lean, childless body and smiled at Colin with her inviting, naughty little girl eyes, and Martin watched her in admiration.

Martha got up and left them and took a paint pot and put a coat of white gloss on the bathroom wall. The white surface pleased her. She was good at painting. She produced a smooth, even surface. Her legs throbbed. She feared she might be getting varicose veins.

Outside in the garden the children played badminton. They were bad-tempered, but relieved to be able to look up and see their mother working, as usual: making their lives forever better and nicer: organizing, planning, thinking ahead, side-stepping disaster, making preparations, like a mother hen, fussing and irritating: part of the natural boring scenery of the world. | 90

On Saturday night Katie went to bed early: she rose from her chair and stretched and yawned and poked her head into the kitchen where Martha was washing saucepans. Colin had cleared the table and Katie had folded the napkins into pretty creases, while Martin blew at the fire, to make it bright. "Good night," said Katie.

Katie appeared three minutes later, reproachfully holding out her Yves St. Laurent towel, sopping wet. "Oh dear," cried Martha. "Jenny must have washed her hair!" And Martha was obliged to rout Jenny out of bed to rebuke her, publicly, if only to demonstrate that she knew what was right and proper. That meant Jenny would sulk all weekend, and that meant a treat or an outing mid-week, or else by the following week she'd be having an asthma attack. "You fuss the children too much," said Martin. "That's why Jenny has asthma." Jenny was pleasant enough to look at, but not stunning. Perhaps she was a disappointment to her father? Martin would never say so, but Martha feared he thought so.

An egg and an orange each child, each day. Then nothing too bad would go wrong. And it hadn't. The asthma was very mild. A calm, tranquil environment, the doctor said. Ah, smile, Martha smile. Domestic happiness depends on you. 21×52 oranges a year. Each one to be purchased, carried, peeled, and washed up after. And what about potatoes. 12×52 pounds a year? Martin liked his potatoes carefully peeled. He couldn't bear to find little cores of black in the mouthful. ("Well, it isn't very nice, is it?": Martin)

Martha dreamt she was eating coal, by handfuls, and liking it.

Saturday night. Martin made love to Martha three times. Three times? How | 95
virile he was, and clearly turned on by the sounds from the spare room. Martin said he loved her. Martin always did. He was a courteous lover; he knew the importance of foreplay. So did Martha. Three times.

Ah, sleep. Jolyon had a nightmare. Jenny was woken by a moth. Martin slept through everything. Martha pottered about the house in the night. There was a moon. She sat at the window and stared out into the summer night for five minutes, and was at peace, and then went back to bed because she ought to be fresh for the morning.

But she wasn't. She slept late. The others went out for a walk. They'd left a note, a considerate note: "Didn't wake you. You looked tired. Had a cold breakfast so as not to make too much mess. Leave everything 'til we get back." But it was ten o'clock, and guests were coming at noon, so she cleared away the bread, the butter, the crumbs, the smears, the jam, the spoons, the spilt sugar, the cereal, the milk (sour by now) and the dirty plates, and swept the floors, and tidied up quickly, and grabbed a cup of coffee, and prepared to make a rice and fish dish, and a chocolate mousse and sat down in the middle to eat a lot of bread and jam herself. Broad hips. She remembered the office work in her file and knew she wouldn't be able to do it. Martin anyway thought it was ridiculous for her to bring work back at the weekends. "It's your holiday," he'd say. "Why should they impose?" Martha loved her work. She didn't have to smile at it. She just did it.

Katie came back upset and crying. She sat in the kitchen while Martha worked and drank glass after glass of gin and bitter lemon. Katie liked ice and lemon in gin. Martha paid for all the drink out of her wages. It was part of the deal between her and Martin—the contract by which she went out to work. All things to cheer the spirit, otherwise depressed by working wife and mother, were to be paid for by Martha. Drink, holidays, petrol, outings, puddings, electricity, heating: it was quite a joke between them. It didn't really make any difference: it was their joint money, after all. Amazing how Martha's wages were creeping up, almost to the level of Martin's. One day they would overtake. Then what?

Work, honestly, was a piece of cake.

Anyway, poor Katie was crying. Colin, she'd discovered, kept a photograph 100 of Janet and the children in his wallet. "He's not free of her. He pretends he is, but he isn't. She has him by a stranglehold. It's the kids. His bloody kids. Moaning Mary and that little creep Joanna. It's all he thinks about. I'm nobody."

But Katie didn't believe it. She knew she was somebody all right. Colin came in, in a fury. He took out the photograph and set fire to it, bitterly, with a match. Up in smoke they went. Mary and Joanna and Janet. The ashes fell on the floor. (Martha swept them up when Colin and Katie had gone. It hardly seemed polite to do so when they were still there.) "Go back to her," Katie said. "Go back to her. I don't care. Honestly, I'd rather be on my own. You're a nice old fashioned thing. Run along then. Do your thing, I'll do mine. Who cares?"

"Christ, Katie, the fuss! She only just happens to be in the photograph. She's not there on purpose to annoy. And I do feel bad about her. She's been having a hard time."

"And haven't you, Colin? She twists a pretty knife, I can tell you. Don't you have rights too? Not to mention me. Is a little loyalty too much to expect?"

They were reconciled before lunch, up in the spare room. Harry and Beryl Elder arrived at twelve-thirty. Harry didn't like to hurry on Sundays; Beryl was flustered with apologies for their lateness. They'd brought artichokes from their garden. "Wonderful," cried Martin. "Fruits of the earth? Let's have a wonderful soup! Don't fret, Martha. I'd do it."

"Don't fret." Martha clearly hadn't been smiling enough. She was in dan- 105 ger, Martin implied, of ruining everyone's weekend. There was an emergency in the garden very shortly—an elm tree which had probably got Dutch elm disease— and Martha finished the artichokes. The lid flew off the blender and there was artichoke purée everywhere. "Let's have lunch outside," said Colin. "Less work for Martha."

Martin frowned at Martha: he thought the appearance of martyrdom in the face of guests to be an unforgivable offense.

Everyone happily joined in taking the furniture out, but it was Martha's experience that nobody ever helped to bring it in again. Jolyon was stung by a wasp. Jasper sneezed and sneezed from hay fever and couldn't find the tissues and he wouldn't use loo paper. ("Surely you remembered the tissues, darling?": Martin)

Beryl Elder was nice. "Wonderful to eat out," she said, fetching the cream for her pudding, while Martha fished a fly from the liquefying Brie ("You shouldn't have bought it so ripe, Martha": Martin)—"except it's just some other woman has to do it. But at least it isn't *me*." Beryl worked too, as a secretary, to send the boys to boarding school, where she'd rather they weren't. But her husband was from a rather grand family, and she'd been only a typist when he married her, so her life was a mass of amends, one way or another. Harry had lately opted out of the stockbroking rat race and become an artist, choosing integrity rather than money, but that choice was his alone and couldn't of course be inflicted on the boys.

Katie found the fish and rice dish rather strange, toyed at it with her fork, and talked about Italian restaurants she knew. Martin lay back soaking in the sun: crying, "Oh, this is the life." He made coffee, nobly, and the lid flew off the grinder and there were coffee beans all over the kitchen especially in amongst the row of cookery books which Martin gave Martha Christmas by Christmas. At least they didn't have to be brought back every weekend. ("The burglars won't have the sense to steal those": Martin)

Beryl fell asleep and Katie watched her, quizzically. Beryl's mouth was open 110 and she had a lot of fillings, and her ankles were thick and her waist was going, and she didn't look after herself. "I love women," sighed Katie. "They look so wonderful asleep. I wish I could be an earth mother."

Beryl woke with a start and nagged her husband into going home, which he clearly didn't want to do, so didn't. Beryl thought she had to get back because his mother was coming round later. Nonsense! Then Beryl tried to stop Harry drinking more home-made wine and was laughed at by everyone. He was driving. Beryl couldn't, and he did have a nasty scar on his temple from a previous road accident. Never mind.

"She does come on strong, poor soul," laughed Katie when they'd finally gone. "I'm never going to get married,"—and Colin looked at her yearningly because he wanted to marry her more than anything in the world, and Martha cleared the coffee cups.

"Oh don't *do* that," said Katie, " do just sit *down*, Martha, you make us all feel bad," and Martin glared at Martha who sat down and Jenny called out for her and Martha went upstairs and Jenny had started her first period and Martha cried and cried and knew she must stop because this must be a joyous occasion for Jenny or her whole future would be blighted, but for once, Martha couldn't.

Her daughter Jenny: wife, mother, friend.

Eudora Welty in Depth

Eudora Welty (b. 1909) has lived most of her life in her birthplace, Jackson, Mississippi, and has set most of her works—including those presented here—in the American South. She is part of a generation of writers who have given the South a distinctive literary voice. Welty has said that she has been careful to include nothing, including names, that would not be normal and expected in the environment of her stories. Among her novels are Delta Wedding *(1946),* Ponder Heart *(1954), and* Optimist's Daughter *(1972). Her collections of stories include* Curtain of Green and Other Stories *(1941),* The Wide Net *(1943), and* The Bride of Inishfallen and Other Stories *(1955). She has also written essays on writing.*

Cleanth Brooks has said of Eudora Welty that she "is the author of works that make use of the resources of our language at its highest level. The interior life, the world of fantasy and imagination, is the subject matter of much of her fiction." Some critics have also insisted that Welty is not naturally a novelist, but a short story writer at heart. Her novels, they suggest, are merely extended stories, and her true achievement is as a short story writer. Welty's skill in this literary form is certainly considerable. Most of her famous stories were written in her earliest collections, when, as she explains, writing came easily and naturally. They are realistic, apparently simple, and uncluttered; Once examined, however, they open up and reveal inner depths. As critic Jonathan Yardley put it, "Reading her best work, one peels off layer after layer of mood and meaning, each more subtle and more difficult to find than its predecessor."

A WORN PATH   1941

It was December—a bright frozen day in the early morning. Far out in the country there was an old Negro woman with her head tied in a red rag, coming along a path through the pinewoods. Her name was Phoenix Jackson. She was very old and small and she walked slowly in the dark pine shadows, moving a little from side to side in her steps, with the balanced heaviness and lightness of a pendulum in a grandfather clock. She carried a thin, small cane made from an umbrella, and with this she kept tapping the frozen earth in front of her. This made a grave and persistent noise in the still air, that seemed meditative like the chirping of a solitary little bird.

She wore a dark striped dress reaching down to her shoe tops, and an equally long apron of bleached sugar sacks, with a full pocket: all neat and tidy, but every time she took a step she might have fallen over her shoelaces, which dragged from her unlaced shoes. She looked straight ahead. Her eyes were blue with age. Her skin had a pattern all its own of numberless branching wrinkles and as though a whole little tree stood in the middle of her forehead, but a golden color ran underneath, and the two knobs of her cheeks were illumined by a yellow burning under the dark. Under the red rag her hair came down on her neck in the frailest of ringlets, still black, and with an odor like copper.

Now and then there was a quivering in the thicket. Old Phoenix said, "Out of my way, all you foxes, owls, beetles, jack rabbits, coons and wild animals! . . . Keep out from under these feet, little bob-whites. Keep the big wild hogs out of my path. Don't let none of those come running my direction. I got a long way." Under her small black-freckled hand her cane, limber as a buggy whip, would switch at the brush as if to rouse up any hiding things.

On she went. The woods were deep and still. The sun made the pine needles almost too bright to look at, up where the wind rocked. The cones dropped as light as feathers. Down in the hollow was the mourning dove—it was not too late for him.

The path ran up a hill. "Seem like there is chains about my feet, time I   5 get this far," she said, in the voice of argument old people keep to use with themselves. "Something always take a hold of me on this hill—pleads I should stay."

After she got to the top she turned and gave a full, severe look behind her where she had come. "Up through pines," she said at length. "Now down through oaks."

Her eyes opened their widest, and she started down gently. But before she got to the bottom of the hill a bush caught her dress.

Her fingers were busy and intent, but her skirts were full and long, so that before she could pull them free in one place they were caught in another. It was not possible to allow the dress to tear. "I in the thorny bush," she said. "Thorns, you doing your appointed work. Never want to let folks pass, no sir. Old eyes thought you was a pretty little *green* bush."

Finally, trembling all over, she stood free, and after a moment dared to stoop for her cane.

"Sun so high!" she cried, leaning back and looking, while the thick tears   10 went over her eyes. "The time getting all gone here."

At the foot of this hill was a place where a log was laid across the creek.

"Now comes the trial," said Phoenix.

Putting her right foot out, she mounted the log and shut her eyes. Lifting her skirt, leveling her cane fiercely before her, like a festival figure in some parade, she began to march across. Then she opened her eyes and she was safe on the other side.

"I wasn't as old as I thought," she said.

But she sat down to rest. She spread her skirts on the bank around her and folded her hands over her knees. Up above her was a tree in a pearly cloud of mistletoe. She did not dare to close her eyes, and when a little boy brought her a plate with a slice of marble-cake on it she spoke to him. "That would be acceptable," she said. But when she went to take it there was just her own hand in the air. 15

So she left that tree, and had to go through a barbed-wire fence. There she had to creep and crawl, spreading her knees and stretching her fingers like a baby trying to climb the steps. But she talked loudly to herself: she could not let her dress be torn now, so late in the day, and she could not pay for having her arm or her leg sawed off if she got caught fast where she was.

At last she was safe through the fence and risen up out in the clearing. Big dead trees, like black men with one arm, were standing in the purple stalks of the withered cotton field. There sat a buzzard.

"Who you watching?"

In the furrow she made her way along.

"Glad this not the season for bulls," she said, looking sideways, "and the good Lord made his snakes to curl up and sleep in the winter. A pleasure I don't see no two-headed snake coming around that tree, where it come once. It took a while to get by him, back in the summer." 20

She passed through the old cotton and went into a field of dead corn. It whispered and shook and was taller than her head. "Through the maze now," she said, for there was no path.

Then there was something tall, black, and skinny there, moving before her.

At first she took it for a man. It could have been a man dancing in the field. But she stood still and listened, and it did not make a sound. It was as silent as a ghost.

"Ghost," she said sharply, "who be you the ghost of? For I have heard of nary death close by."

But there was no answer—only the ragged dancing in the wind. 25

She shut her eyes, reached out her hand, and touched a sleeve. She found a coat and inside that an emptiness, cold as ice.

"You scarecrow," she said. Her face lighted. "I ought to be shut up for good," she said with laughter. "My senses is gone. I too old. I the oldest people I ever know. Dance, old scarecrow," she said, "while I dancing with you."

She kicked her foot over the furrow, and with mouth drawn down, shook her head once or twice in a little strutting way. Some husks blew down and whirled in streamers about her skirts.

Then she went on, parting her way from side to side with the cane, through the whispering field. At last she came to the end, to a wagon track where the silver grass blew between the red ruts. The quail were walking around like pullets, seeming all dainty and unseen.

"Walk pretty," she said. "This the easy place. This the easy going." 30

She followed the track, swaying through the quiet bare fields, through the little strings of trees silver in their dead leaves, past cabins silver from weather, with the doors and windows boarded shut, all like old women under a spell sitting there. "I walking in their sleep," she said, nodding her head vigorously.

In a ravine she went where a spring was silently flowing through a hollow log. Old Phoenix bent and drank. "Sweet-gum makes the water sweet," she said, and drank more. "Nobody know who made this well, for it was here when I was born."

The track crossed a swampy part where the moss hung as white as lace from every limb. "Sleep on, alligators, and blow your bubbles." Then the track went into the road.

Deep, deep the road went down between the high green-colored banks. Overhead the live-oaks met, and it was as dark as a cave.

A black dog with a lolling tongue came up out of the weeds by the ditch. 35 She was meditating, and not ready, and when he came at her she only hit him a little with her cane. Over she went in the ditch, like a little puff of milkweed.

Down there, her senses drifted away. A dream visited her, and she reached her hand up, but nothing reached down and gave her a pull. So she lay there and presently went to talking. "Old woman," she said to herself, "that black dog come up out of the weeds to stall you off, and now there he sitting on his fine tail, smiling at you."

A white man finally came along and found her—a hunter, a young man, with his dog on a chain.

"Well, Granny!" he laughed. "What are you doing there?"

"Lying on my back like a June-bug waiting to be turned over, mister," she said, reaching up her hand.

He lifted her up, gave her a swing in the air, and set her down. "Anything 40 broken, Granny?"

"No sir, them old dead weeds is springy enough," said Phoenix, when she had got her breath. "I thank you for your trouble."

"Where do you live, Granny?" he asked, while the two dogs were growling at each other.

"Away back yonder, sir, behind the ridge. You can't even see it from here."

"On your way home?"

"No sir, I going to town." 45

"Why, that's too far! That's as far as I walk when I come out myself, and I get something for my trouble." He patted the stuffed bag he carried, and there hung down a little closed claw. It was one of the bob-whites, with its beak hooked bitterly to show it was dead. "Now you go on home, Granny!"

"I bound to go to town, mister," said Phoenix. "The time come around."

He gave another laugh, filling the whole landscape. "I know you old colored people! Wouldn't miss going to town to see Santa Claus!"

But something held old Phoenix very still. The deep lines in her face went into a fierce and different radiation. Without warning, she had seen with her own eyes a flashing nickel fall out of the man's pocket onto the ground.

"How old are you, Granny?" he was saying. 50

"There is no telling, mister," she said, "no telling."

Then she gave a little cry and clapped her hands and said, "Git on away from here, dog! Look! Look at that dog!" She laughed as if in admiration. "He ain't scared of nobody. He a big black dog." She whispered, "Sic him!"

"Watch me get rid of that cur," said the man. "Sic him, Pete! Sic him!"

Phoenix heard the dogs fighting, and heard the man running and throwing sticks. She even heard a gunshot. But she was slowly bending forward by that time, further and further forward, the lids stretched down over her eyes, as if she were doing this in her sleep. Her chin was lowered almost to her knees. The yellow palm of her hand came out from the fold of her apron. Her fingers slid down and along the ground under the piece of money with the grace and care they would have in lifting an egg from under a setting hen. Then she slowly straightened up, she stood erect, and the nickel was in her apron pocket. A bird flew by. Her lips moved. "God watching me the whole time. I come to stealing."

The man came back, and his own dog panted about them. "Well, I scared him off that time," he said, and then he laughed and lifted his gun and pointed it at Phoenix.

She stood straight and faced him.

"Doesn't the gun scare you?" he said, still pointing it.

"No, sir, I seen plenty go off closer by, in my day, and for less than what I done," she said, holding utterly still.

He smiled, and shouldered the gun. "Well, Granny," he said, "you must be a hundred years old, and scared of nothing. I'd give you a dime if I had any money with me. But you take my advice and stay home, and nothing will happen to you."

"I bound to go on my way, mister," said Phoenix. She inclined her head in the red rag. Then they went in different directions, but she could hear the gun shooting again and again over the hill.

She walked on. The shadows hung from the oak trees to the road like curtains. Then she smelled wood-smoke, and smelled the river, and she saw a steeple and the cabins on their steep steps. Dozens of little black children whirled around her. There ahead was Natchez shining. Bells were ringing. She walked on.

In the paved city it was Christmas time. There were red and green electric lights strung and crisscrossed everywhere, and all turned on in the daytime. Old Phoenix would have been lost if she had not distrusted her eyesight and depended on her feet to know where to take her.

She paused quietly on the sidewalk where people were passing by. A lady came along in the crowd, carrying an armful of red-, green- and silver-wrapped presents; she gave off perfume like the red roses in hot summer, and Phoenix stopped her.

"Please, missy, will you lace up my shoe?" She held up her foot.

"What do you want, Grandma?"

"See my shoe," said Phoenix. "Do all right for out in the country, but wouldn't look right to go in a big building."

"Stand still then, Grandma," said the lady. She put her packages down on the sidewalk beside her and laced and tied both shoes tightly.

"Can't lace 'em with a cane," said Phoenix. "Thank you, missy. I doesn't mind asking a nice lady to tie up my shoe, when I gets out on the street."

Moving slowly and from side to side, she went into the big building, and into a tower of steps, where she walked up and around and around until her feet knew to stop.

She entered a door, and there she saw nailed up on the wall the document that had been stamped with the gold seal and framed in the gold frame, which matched the dream that was hung up in her head.

"Here I be," she said. There was a fixed and ceremonial stiffness over her body.

55

60

65

70

"A charity case, I suppose," said an attendant who sat at the desk before her.

But Phoenix only looked above her head. There was sweat on her face, the wrinkles in her skin shone like a bright net.

"Speak up, Grandma," the woman said. "What's your name? We must have your history, you know. Have you been here before? What seems to be the trouble with you?"

Old Phoenix only gave a twitch to her face as if a fly were bothering her.   75

"Are you deaf?" cried the attendant.

But then the nurse came in.

"Oh, that's just old Aunt Phoenix," she said. "She doesn't come for herself—she has a little grandson. She makes these trips just as regular as clockwork. She lives away back off the Old Natchez Trace." She bent down. "Well, Aunt Phoenix, why don't you just take a seat? We won't keep you standing after your long trip." She pointed.

The old woman sat down, bolt upright in the chair.

"Now, how is the boy?" asked the nurse.   80

Old Phoenix did not speak.

"I said, how is the boy?"

But Phoenix only waited and stared straight ahead, her face very solemn and withdrawn into rigidity.

"Is his throat any better?" asked the nurse. "Aunt Phoenix, don't you hear me? Is your grandson's throat any better since the last time you came for the medicine?"

With her hands on her knees, the old woman waited, silent, erect and mo-   85
tionless, just as if she were in armor.

"You mustn't take up on our time this way, Aunt Phoenix," the nurse said. "Tell us quickly about your grandson, and get it over. He isn't dead, is he?"

At last there came a flicker and then a flame of comprehension across her face, and she spoke.

"My grandson. It was my memory had left me. There I sat and forgot why I made my long trip."

"Forgot?" The nurse frowned. "After you came so far?"

Then Phoenix was like an old woman begging a dignified forgiveness for   90
waking up frightened in the night. "I never did go to school, I was too old at the Surrender," she said in a soft voice. "I'm an old woman without an education. It was my memory fail me. My little grandson, he is just the same, and I forgot it in the coming."

"Throat never heals, does it?" said the nurse, speaking in a loud, sure voice to old Phoenix. By now she had a card with something written on it, a little list. "Yes. Swallowed lye. When was it?—January—two-three years ago—"

Phoenix spoke unasked now. "No, missy, he not dead, he just the same. Every little while his throat begin to close up again, and he not able to swallow. He not get his breath. He not able to help himself. So the time come around, and I go on another trip for the soothing medicine."

"All right. The doctor said as long as you came to get it, you could have it," said the nurse. "But it's an obstinate case."

"My little grandson, he sit up there in the house all wrapped up, waiting by himself," Phoenix went on. "We is the only two left in the world. He suffer and it don't seem to put him back at all. He got a sweet look. He going to last. He wear a little patch quilt and peep out holding his mouth open like a little bird. I remembers so plain now. I not going to forget him again, no, the whole enduring time. I could tell him from all the others in creation."

"All right." The nurse was trying to hush her now. She brought her a bottle of medicine. "Charity," she said, making a check mark in a book.   95

Old Phoenix held the bottle close to her eyes, and then carefully put it into her pocket.

"I thank you," she said.

"It's Christmas time, Grandma," said the attendant. "Could I give you a few pennies out of my purse?"

"Five pennies is a nickel," said Phoenix stiffly.

"Here's a nickel," said the attendant.   100

Phoenix rose carefully and held out her hand. She received the nickel and then fished the other nickel out of her pocket and laid it beside the new one. She stared at her palm closely, with her head on one side.

Then she gave a tap with her cane on the floor.

"This is what come to me to do," she said. "I going to the store and buy my child a little windmill they sells, made out of paper. He going to find it hard to believe there such a thing in the world. I'll march myself back where he waiting, holding it straight up in this hand."

She lifted her free hand, gave a little nod, turned around, and walked out of the doctor's office. Then her slow step began on the stairs, going down.

LIVVIE   1942

Solomon carried Livvie twenty-one miles away from her home when he married her. He carried her away up on the Old Natchez Trace into the deep country to live in his house. She was sixteen—an only girl, then. Once people said he thought nobody would ever come along there. He told her himself that it had been a long time, and a day she did not know about, since that road was a traveled road with *people* coming and going. He was good to her, but he kept her in the house. She had not thought that she could not get back. Where she came from, people said an old man did not want anybody in the world to ever find his wife, for fear they would steal her back from him. Solomon asked her before he took her, "Would she be happy?"—very dignified, for he was a colored man that owned his land and had it written down in the courthouse; and she said, "Yes, sir," since he was an old man and she was young and just listened and answered. He asked her, if she was choosing winter, would she pine for spring, and she said, "No indeed." Whatever she said, always, was because he was an old man . . . while nine years went by. All the time, he got old, and he got so old he gave out. At last he slept the whole day in bed, and she was young still.

It was a nice house, inside and outside both. In the first place, it had three rooms. The front room was papered in holly paper, with green palmettos from the swamp spaced at careful intervals over the walls. There was fresh newspaper cut with fancy borders on the mantel-shelf, on which were propped photographs of old or very young men printed in faint yellow—Solomon's people. Solomon had a houseful of furniture. There was a double settee, a tall scrolled rocker and an organ in the front room, all around a three-legged table with a pink marble top, on which was set a lamp with three gold feet, besides a jelly glass with pretty hen feathers in it. Behind the front room, the other room had the bright iron bed with the polished knobs like a throne, in which Solomon slept all day. There were snow-white curtains of wiry lace at the window, and a lace bed-spread belonged on the bed. But what old Solomon slept so sound under was a big feather-stitched piece-quilt in the pattern "Trip Around the World," which had twenty-one different colors, four hundred and forty pieces, and a thousand yards of thread, and that was what Solomon's mother made in her life and old age. There was a table holding the Bible, and a trunk with a key. On the wall were two calendars, and a diploma from somewhere in Solomon's family, and under that Livvie's one possession was nailed, a picture of the little white baby of the family she worked for, back in Natchez before she was married. Going through that room and on to the kitchen, there was a big wood stove and a big round table always with a wet top and with the knives and forks in one jelly glass and the spoons in another, and a cut-glass vinegar bottle between, and going out from those, many shallow dishes of pickled peaches, fig preserves, watermelon pickles and blackberry jam always sitting there. The churn sat in the sun, the doors of the safe were always both shut, and there were four baited mouse-traps in the kitchen, one in every corner.

The outside of Solomon's house looked nice. It was not painted, but across the porch was an even balance. On each side there was one easy chair with high springs, looking out, and a fern basket hanging over it from the ceiling, and a dishpan of zinnia seedlings growing at its foot on the floor. By the door was a plow-wheel, just a pretty iron circle, nailed up on one wall and a square mirror on the other, a turquoise-blue comb stuck up in the frame, with the wash stand beneath it. On the door was a wooden knob with a pearl in the end, and Solomon's black hat hung on that, if he was in the house.

Out front was a clean dirt yard with every vestige of grass patiently uprooted and the ground scarred in deep whorls from the strike of Livvie's broom. Rose bushes with tiny blood-red roses blooming every month grew in threes on either side of the steps. On one side was a peach tree, on the other a pomegranate. Then coming around up the path from the deep cut of the Natchez Trace below was a line of bare crape-myrtle trees with every branch of them ending in a colored bottle, green or blue. There was no word that fell from Solomon's lips to say what they were for, but Livvie knew that there could be a spell put in trees, and she was familiar from the time she was born with the way bottle trees kept evil spirits from coming into the house—by luring them inside the colored bottles, where they cannot get out again. Solomon had made the bottle trees with his own hands over the nine years, in labor amounting to about a tree a year, and without a sign that he had any uneasiness in his heart, for he took as much pride in his precautions against spirits coming in the house as he took in the house, and sometimes in the sun the bottle trees looked prettier than the house did.

It was a nice house. It was in a place where the days would go by and surprise anyone that they were over. The lamplight and the firelight would shine out the door after dark, over the still and breathing country, lighting the roses and the bottle trees, and all was quiet there.

But there was nobody, nobody at all, not even a white person. And if there had been anybody, Solomon would not have let Livvie look at them, just as he would not let her look at a field hand, or a field hand look at her. There was no house near, except for the cabins of the tenants that were forbidden to her, and there was no house as far as she had been, stealing away down the still, deep Trace. She felt as if she waded a river when she went, for the dead leaves on the ground reached as high as her knees, and when she was all scratched and bleeding she said it was not like a road that went anywhere. One day, climbing up the high bank, she had found a graveyard without a church, with ribbon-grass growing about the foot of an angel (she had climbed up because she thought she saw angel wings), and in the sun, trees shining like burning flames through the great caterpillar nets which enclosed them. Scarey thistles stood looking like the prophets in the Bible in Solomon's house. Indian paint brushes° grew over her head, and the mourning dove made the only sound in the world. Oh for a stirring of the leaves, and a breaking of the nets! But not by a ghost, prayed Livvie, jumping down the bank. After Solomon took to his bed, she never went out, except one more time.

Livvie knew she made a nice girl to wait on anybody. She fixed things to eat on a tray like a surprise. She could keep from singing when she ironed, and to sit by a bed and fan away the flies, she could be so still she could not hear herself breathe. She could clean up the house and never drop a thing, and wash the dishes without a sound, and she would step outside to churn, for churning sounded too sad to her, like sobbing, and if it made her home-sick and not Solomon, she did not think of that.

But Solomon scarcely opened his eyes to see her, and scarcely tasted his food. He was not sick or paralyzed or in any pain that he mentioned, but he was surely wearing out in the body, and no matter what nice hot thing Livvie would bring him to taste, he would only look at it now, as if he were past seeing how he could add anything more to himself. Before she could beg him, he would go fast asleep. She could not surprise him anymore, if he would not taste, and she was afraid that he was never in the world going to taste another thing she brought him—and so how could he last?

But one morning it was breakfast time and she cooked his eggs and grits, carried them in on a tray, and called his name. He was sound asleep. He lay in a dignified way with his watch beside him, on his back in the middle of the bed. One hand drew the quilt up high, though it was the first day of spring. Through the white lace curtains a little puffy wind was blowing as if it came from round cheeks. All night the frogs had sung out in the swamp, like a commotion in the room, and he had not stirred, though she lay wide awake and saying "Shh, frogs!" for fear he would mind them.

He looked as if he would like to sleep a little longer, and so she put back the tray and waited a little. When she tiptoed and stayed so quiet, she surrounded herself with a little reverie, and sometimes it seemed to her when she was so stealthy that the quiet she kept was for a sleeping baby, and that she had a baby and was its mother. When she stood at Solomon's bed and looked down at him, she would be thinking, "He sleeps so well," and she would hate to wake him up. And in some other way, too, she was afraid to wake him up because even in his sleep he seemed to be such a strict man.

Of course, nailed to the wall over the bed—only she would forget who it was—there was a picture of him when he was young. Then he had a fan of hair over his forehead like a king's crown. Now his hair lay down on his head, the spring had gone out of it. Solomon had a lightish face, with eyebrows scattered

10

Indian paint brushes. A type of flaming red flower.

but rugged, the way privet grows, strong eyes, with second sight, a strict mouth, and a little gold smile. This was the way he looked in his clothes, but in bed in the daytime he looked like a different and smaller man, even when he was wide awake, and holding the Bible. He looked like somebody kin to himself. And then sometimes when he lay in sleep and she stood fanning the flies away, and the light came in, his face was like new, so smooth and clear that it was like a glass of jelly held to the window, and she could almost look through his forehead and see what he thought.

She fanned him and at length he opened his eyes and spoke her name, but he would not taste the nice eggs she had kept warm under a pan.

Back in the kitchen she ate heartily, his breakfast and hers, and looked out the open door at what went on. The whole day, and the whole night before, she had felt the stir of spring close to her. It was as present in the house as a young man would be. The moon was in the last quarter and outside they were turning the sod and planting peas and beans. Up and down the red fields, over which smoke from the brush-burning hung showing like a little skirt of sky, a white horse and a white mule pulled the plow. At intervals hoarse shouts came through the air and roused her as if she dozed neglectfully in the shade, and they were telling her, "Jump up!" She could see how over each ribbon of field were moving men and girls, on foot and mounted on mules, with hats set on their heads and bright with tall hoes and forks as if they carried streamers on them and were going to some place on a journey—and how as if at a signal now and then they would all start at once shouting, hollering, cajoling, calling and answering back, running, being leaped on and breaking away, flinging to earth with a shout and lying motionless in the trance of twelve o'clock. The old women came out of the cabins and brought them the food they had ready for them, and then all worked together, spread evenly out. The little children came too, like a bouncing stream overflowing the fields, and set upon the men, the women, the dogs, the rushing birds, and the wave-like rows of earth, their little voices almost too high to be heard. In the middle distance like some white and gold towers were the haystacks, with black cows coming around to eat their edges. High above everything, the wheel of fields, house, and cabins, and the deep road surrounding like a moat to keep them in, was the turning sky, blue with long, far-flung white mare's-tail clouds, serene and still as high flames. And sound asleep while all this went around him that was his, Solomon was like a little still spot in the middle.

Even in the house the earth was sweet to breathe. Solomon had never let Livvie go any farther than the chicken house and the well. But what if she would walk now into the heart of the fields and take a hoe and work until she fell stretched out and drenched with her efforts, like other girls, and laid her cheek against the laid-open earth, and shamed the old man with her humbleness and delight? To shame him! A cruel wish could come in uninvited and so fast while she looked out the back door. She washed the dishes and scrubbed the table. She could hear the cries of the little lambs. Her mother, that she had not seen since her wedding day, had said one time, "I rather a man be anything, than a woman be mean."

So all morning she kept tasting the chicken broth on the stove, and when it was right she poured off a nice cup-ful. She carried it in to Solomon, and there he lay having a dream. Now what did he dream about? For she saw him sigh gently as if not to disturb some whole thing he held round in his mind, like a fresh egg. So even an old man dreamed about something pretty. Did he dream of her, 15 while his eyes were shut and sunken, and his small hand with the wedding ring curled close in sleep around the quilt? He might be dreaming of what time it was, for even through his sleep he kept track of it like a clock, and knew how much of it went by, and waked up knowing where the hands were even before he consulted the silver watch that he never let go. He would sleep with the watch in his palm, and even holding it to his cheek like a child that loves a plaything. Or he might dream of journeys and travels on a steamboat to Natchez. Yet she thought he dreamed of her; but even while she scrutinized him, the rods of the foot of the bed seemed to rise up like a rail fence between them, and she could see that people never could be sure of anything as long as one of them was asleep and the other awake. To look at him dreaming of her when he might be going to die frightened her a little, as if he might carry her with him that way, and she wanted to run out of the room. She took hold of the bed and held on, and Solomon opened his eyes and called her name, but he did not want anything. He would not taste the good broth.

Just a little after that, as she was taking up the ashes in the front room for the last time in the year, she heard a sound. It was somebody coming. She pulled the curtains together and looked through the slit.

Coming up the path under the bottle trees was a white lady. At first she looked young, but then she looked old. Marvelous to see, a little car stood steaming like a kettle out in the field-track—it had come without a road.

Livvie stood listening to the long, repeated knockings at the door, and after a while she opened it just a little. The lady came in through the crack, though she was more than middle-sized and wore a big hat.

"My name is Miss Baby Marie," she said.

Livvie gazed respectfully at the lady and at the little suitcase she was hold- 20
ing close to her by the handle until the proper moment. The lady's eyes were running over the room, from palmetto to palmetto, but she was saying, "I live at home . . . out from Natchez . . . and get out and show these pretty cosmetic things to the white people and the colored people both . . . all around . . . years and years. . . . Both shades of powder and rouge. . . . It's the kind of work a girl can do and not go clear 'way from home . . ." And the harder she looked, the more she talked. Suddenly she turned up her nose and said, "It is not Christian or sanitary to put feathers in a vase," and then she took a gold key out of the front of her dress and began unlocking the locks on her suitcase. Her face drew the light, the way it was covered with intense white and red, with a little patty-cake of white between the wrinkles by her upper lip. Little red tassels of hair bobbed under the rusty wires of her picture-hat, as with an air of triumph and secrecy she now drew open her little suitcase and brought out bottle after bottle and jar after jar, which she put down on the table, the mantel-piece, the settee, and the organ.

"Did you ever see so many cosmetics in your life?" cried Miss Baby Marie.

"No'm," Livvie tried to say, but the cat had her tongue.

"Have you ever applied cosmetics?" asked Miss Baby Marie next.

"No'm," Livvie tried to say.

"Then look!" she said, and pulling out the last thing of all, "Try this!" she 25
said. And in her hand was unclenched a golden lipstick which popped open like magic. A fragrance came out of it like incense, and Livvie cried out suddenly, "Chinaberry flowers!"

Her hand took the lipstick, and in an instant she was carried away in the air through the spring, and looking down with a half-drowsy smile from a purple cloud she saw from above a chinaberry tree, dark and smooth and neatly leaved, neat as a guinea hen in the dooryard, and there was her home that she had left. On one side of the tree was her mama holding up her heavy apron, and she could see it was loaded with ripe figs, and on the other side was her papa holding a fish-pole over the pond, and she could see it transparently, the little clear fishes swimming up to the brim.

"Oh no, not chinaberry flowers—secret ingredients," said Miss Baby Marie. "My cosmetics have secret ingredients—not chinaberry flowers."

"It's purple," Livvie breathed, and Miss Baby Marie said, "Use it freely. Rub it on."

Livvie tiptoed out to the wash stand on the front porch and before the mirror put the paint on her mouth. In the wavery surface her face danced before her like a flame. Miss Baby Marie followed her out, took a look at what she had done, and said, "That's it."

Livvie tried to say "Thank you" without moving her parted lips where the   30 paint lay so new.

By now Miss Baby Marie stood behind Livvie and looked in the mirror over her shoulder, twisting up the tassels of her hair. "The lipstick I can let you have for only two dollars," she said, close to her neck.

"Lady, but I don't have no money, never did have," said Livvie.

"Oh, but you don't pay the first time. I make another trip, that's the way I do. I come back again—later."

"Oh," said Livvie, pretending she understood everything so as to please the lady.

"But if you don't take it now, this may be the last time I'll call at your house,"   35 said Miss Baby Marie sharply. "It's far away from anywhere, I'll tell you that. You don't live close to anywhere."

"Yes'm. My husband, he keep the *money*," said Livvie, trembling. "He is strict as he can be. He don't know *you* walk in here—Miss Baby Marie!"

"Where is he?"

"Right now, he in yonder sound asleep, an old man. I wouldn't ever ask him for anything."

Miss Baby Marie took back the lipstick and packed it up. She gathered up the jars for both black and white and got them all inside the suitcase, with the same little fuss of triumph with which she had brought them out. She started away.

"Goodbye," she said, making herself look grand from the back, but at the   40 last minute she turned around in the door. Her old hat wobbled as she whispered, "Let me see your husband."

Livvie obediently went on tiptoe and opened the door to the other room. Miss Baby Marie came behind her and rose on her toes and looked in.

"My, what a little tiny old, old man!" she whispered, clasping her hands and shaking her head over them. "What a beautiful quilt! What a tiny old, old man!"

"He can sleep like that all day," whispered Livvie proudly.

They looked at him awhile so fast asleep, and then all at once they looked at each other. Somehow that was as if they had a secret, for he had never stirred. Livvie then politely, but all at once, closed the door.

"Well! I'd certainly like to leave you with a lipstick!" said Miss Baby Marie 45
vivaciously. She smiled in the door.

"Lady, but I told you I don't have no money, and never did have."

"And never will?" In the air and all around, like a bright halo around the
white lady's nodding head, it was a true spring day.

"Would you take eggs, lady?" asked Livvie softly.

"No, I have plenty of eggs—plenty," said Miss Baby Marie.

"I still don't have no money," said Livvie, and Miss Baby Marie took her 50
suitcase and went on somewhere else.

Livvie stood watching her go, and all the time she felt her heart beating in
her left side. She touched the place with her hand. It seemed as if her heart beat
and her whole face flamed from the pulsing color of her lips. She went to sit by
Solomon and when he opened his eyes he could not see a change in her. "He's
fixin' to die," she said inside. That was the secret. That was when she went out
of the house for a little breath of air.

She went down the path and down the Natchez Trace a way, and she did
not know how far she had gone, but it was not far, when she saw a sight. It was
a man, looking like a vision—she standing on one side of the Old Natchez Trace
and he standing on the other.

As soon as this man caught sight of her, he began to look himself over.
Starting at the bottom with his pointed shoes, he began to look up, lifting his
peg-top pants the higher to see fully his bright socks. His coat long and wide and
leaf-green he opened like doors to see his high-up tawny pants and his pants he
smoothed downward from the points of his collar, and he wore a luminous baby-
pink satin shirt. At the end, he reached gently above his wide platter-shaped round
hat, the color of a plum, and one finger touched at the feather, emerald green,
blowing in the spring winds.

No matter how she looked, she could never look so fine as he did, and she
was not sorry for that, she was pleased.

He took three jumps, one down and two up, and was by her side. 55

"My name is Cash," he said.

He had a guinea pig in his pocket. They began to walk along. She stared on
and on at him, as if he were doing some daring spectacular thing, instead of just
walking beside her. It was not simply the city way he was dressed that made her
look at him and see hope in its insolence looking back. It was not only the way
he moved along kicking the flowers as if he could break through everything in
the way and destroy anything in the world, that made her eyes grow bright. It
might be, if he had not appeared the way he did appear that day she would never
have looked so closely at him, but the time people come makes a difference.

They walked through the still leaves of the Natchez Trace, the light and the
shade falling through trees about them, the white irises shining like candles on
the banks and the new ferns shining like green stars up in the oak branches. They
came out at Solomon's house, bottle trees and all. Livvie stopped and hung her
head.

Cash began whistling a little tune. She did not know what it was, but she
had heard it before from a distance, and she had a revelation. Cash was a field
hand. He was a transformed field hand. Cash belonged to Solomon. But he had
stepped out of his overalls into this. There in front of Solomon's house he laughed.
He had a round head, a round face, all of him was young, and he flung his head

up, rolled it against the mare's-tail sky in his round hat, and he could laugh just to see Solomon's house sitting there. Livvie looked at it, and there was Solomon's black hat hanging on the peg on the front door, the blackest thing in the world.

"I been to Natchez," Cash said, wagging his head around against the sky. "*I* taken a trip, *I* ready for Easter!" 60

How was it possible to look so fine before the harvest? Cash must have stolen the money, stolen it from Solomon. He stood in the path and lifted his spread hand high and brought it down again and again in his laughter. He kicked up his heels. A little chill went through her. It was as if Cash was bringing that strong hand down to beat a drum or to rain blows upon a man, such an abandon and menace were in his laugh. Frowning, she went closer to him and his swinging arm drew her in at once and the fright was crushed from her body, as a little match-flame might be smothered out by what it lighted. She gathered the folds of his coat behind him and fastened her red lips to his mouth, and she was dazzled by herself then, the way he had been dazzled at himself to begin with.

In that instant she felt something that could not be told—that Solomon's death was at hand, that he was the same to her as if he were dead now. She cried out, and uttering little cries turned and ran for the house.

At once Cash was coming, following after, he was running behind her. He came close, and halfway up the path he laughed and passed her. He even picked up a stone and sailed it into the bottle trees. She put her hands over her head, and sounds clattered through the bottle trees like cries of outrage. Cash stamped and plunged zigzag up the front steps and in at the door.

When she got there, he had stuck his hands in his pockets and was turning slowly about in the front room. The little guinea pig peeped out. Around Cash, the pinned-up palmettos looked as if a lazy green monkey had walked up and down and around the walls leaving green prints of his hands and feet.

She got through the room and his hands were still in his pockets, and she 65 fell upon the closed door to the other room and pushed it open. She ran to Solomon's bed, calling "Solomon! Solomon!" The little shape of the old man never moved at all, wrapped under the quilt as if it were winter still.

"Solomon!" She pulled the quilt away, but there was another one under that, and she fell on her knees beside him. He made no sound except a sigh, and then she could hear in the silence the light springy steps of Cash walking and walking in the front room, and the ticking of Solomon's silver watch, which came from the bed. Old Solomon was far away in his sleep, his face looked small, relentless, and devout, as if he were walking somewhere where she could imagine the snow falling.

Then there was a noise like a hoof pawing the floor, and the door gave a creak, and Cash appeared beside her. When she looked up, Cash's face was so black it was bright, and so bright and bare of pity that it looked sweet to her. She stood up and held up her head. Cash was so powerful that his presence gave her strength even when she did not need any.

Under their eyes Solomon slept. People's faces tell of things and places not known to the one who looks at them while they sleep, and while Solomon slept under the eyes of Livvie and Cash his face told them like a mythical story that all his life he had built, little scrap by little scrap, respect. A beetle could not have been more laborious or more ingenious in the task of its destiny. When Solomon was young, as he was in his picture overhead, it was the infinite thing with him, and he could see no end to the respect he would contrive and keep in a house. He had built a lonely house, the way he would make a cage, but it grew to be the same with him as a great monumental pyramid and sometimes in his absorption of getting it erected he was like the builder-slaves of Egypt who forgot or never knew the origin and meaning of the thing to which they gave all the strength of their bodies and used up all their days. Livvie and Cash could see that as a man might rest from a life-labor he lay in his bed, and they could hear how, wrapped in his quilt, he sighed to himself comfortably in sleep, while in his dreams he might have been an ant, a beetle, a bird, an Egyptian, assembling and carrying on his back and building with his hands, or he might have been an old man of India or a swaddled baby, about to smile and brush all away.

Then without warning old Solomon's eyes flew wide open under the hedge-like brows. He was wide awake.

And instantly Cash raised his quick arm. A radiant sweat stood on his temples. But he did not bring his arm down—it stayed in the air, as if something might have taken hold.   70

It was not Livvie—she did not move. As if something said "Wait," she stood waiting. Even while her eyes burned under motionless lids, her lips parted in a stiff grimace, and with her arms stiff at her sides she stood above the prone old man and the panting young one, erect and apart.

Movement when it came came in Solomon's face. It was an old and strict face, a frail face, but behind it, like a covered light, came an animation that could play hide and seek, that would dart and escape, had always escaped. The mystery flickered in him, and invited from his eyes. It was that very mystery that Cash with his quick arm would have to strike, and that Livvie could not weep for. But Cash only stood holding his arm in the air, when the gentlest flick of his great strength, almost a puff of his breath, would have been enough, if he had known how to give it, to send the old man over the obstruction that kept him away from death.

If it could not be that the tiny illumination in the fragile and ancient face caused a crisis, a mystery in the room that would not permit a blow to fall, at least it was certain that Cash, throbbing in his Easter clothes, felt a pang of shame that the vigor of a man would come to such an end that he could not be struck without warning. He took down his hand and stepped back behind Livvie, like a round-eyed schoolboy on whose unsuspecting head the dunce cap has been set.

"Young ones can't wait," said Solomon.

Livvie shuddered violently, and then in a gush of tears she stooped for a glass   75
of water and handed it to him, but he did not see her.

"So here come the young man Livvie wait for. Was no prevention. No prevention. Now I lay eyes on young man and it come to be somebody I know all the time, and been knowing since he were born in a cotton patch, and watched grow up year to year, Cash McCord, growed to size, growed up to come in my house in the end—ragged and barefoot."

Solomon gave a cough of distaste. Then he shut his eyes vigorously, and his lips began to move like a chanter's.

"When Livvie married, her husband were already somebody. He had paid great cost for his land. He spread sycamore leaves over the ground from wagon to door, day he brought her home, so her foot would not have to touch ground.

He carried her through his door. Then he growed old and could not lift her, and she were still young."

Livvie's sobs followed his words like a soft melody repeating each thing as he stated it. His lips moved for a little without sound, or she cried too fervently, and unheard he might have been telling his whole life, and then he said, "God forgive Solomon for sins great and small. God forgive Solomon for carrying away too young girl for wife and keeping her away from her people and from all the young people would clamor for her back."

Then he lifted up his right hand toward Livvie where she stood by the bed   80 and offered her his silver watch. He dangled it before her eyes, and she hushed crying; her tears stopped. For a moment the watch could be heard ticking as it always did, precisely in his proud hand. She lifted it away. Then he took hold of the quilt; then he was dead.

Livvie left Solomon dead and went out of the room. Stealthily, nearly without noise, Cash went beside her. He was like a shadow, but his shiny shoes moved over the floor in spangles, and the green downy feather shone like a light in his hat. As they reached the front room, he seized her deftly as a long black cat and dragged her hanging by the waist round and round him, while he turned in a circle, his face bent down to hers. The first moment, she kept one arm and its hand stiff and still, the one that held Solomon's watch. Then the fingers softly let go, all of her was limp, and the watch fell somewhere on the floor. It ticked away in the still room, and all at once there began outside the full song of a bird.

They moved around and around the room and into the brightness of the open door, then he stopped and shook her once. She rested in silence in his trembling arms, unprotesting as a bird on a nest. Outside the redbirds were flying and crisscrossing, the sun was in all the bottles on the prisoned trees, and the young peach was shining in the middle of them with the bursting light of spring.

LILY DAW AND THE THREE LADIES   1941

Mrs. Watts and Mrs. Carson were both in the post office in Victory when the letter came from the Ellisville Institute for the Feeble-Minded of Mississippi. Aimee Slocum, with her hand still full of mail, ran out in front and handed it straight to Mrs. Watts, and they all three read it together. Mrs. Watts held it taut between her pink hands, and Mrs. Carson underscored each line slowly with her thimbled finger. Everybody else in the post office wondered what was up now.

"What will Lily say," beamed Mrs. Carson at last, "when we tell her we're sending her to Ellisville!"

"She'll be tickled to death," said Mrs. Watts, and added in a guttural voice to a deaf lady, "Lily Daw's getting in at Ellisville!"

"Don't you all dare go off and tell Lily without me!" called Aimee Slocum, trotting back to finish putting up the mail.

"Do you suppose they'll look after her down there?" Mrs. Carson began to   5 carry on a conversation with a group of Baptist ladies waiting in the post office. She was the Baptist preacher's wife.

"I've always heard it was lovely down there, but crowded," said one.

"Lily lets people walk over her so," said another.

"Last night at the tent show—" said another, and then popped her hand over her mouth.

"Don't mind me, I know there are such things in the world," said Mrs. Carson, looking down and fingering the tape measure which hung over her bosom.

"Oh, Mrs. Carson. Well, anyway, last night at the tent show, why, the man was just before making Lily buy a ticket to get in." 10

"A ticket!"

"Till my husband went up and explained she wasn't bright, and so did everybody else."

The ladies all clucked their tongues.

"Oh, it was a very nice show," said the lady who had gone. "And Lily acted so nice. She was a perfect lady—just set in her seat and stared."

"Oh, she can be a lady—she can be," said Mrs. Carson, shaking her head 15 and turning her eyes up. "That's just what breaks your heart."

"Yes'm, she kept her eyes on—what's that thing makes all the commotion?— the xylophone," said the lady. "Didn't turn her head to the right or to the left the whole time. Set in front of me."

"The point is, what did she do after the show?" asked Mrs. Watts practically. "Lily has gotten so she is very mature for her age."

"Oh, Etta!" protested Mrs. Carson, looking at her wildly for a moment.

"And that's how come we are sending her to Ellisville," finished Mrs. Watts.

"I'm ready, you all," said Aimee Slocum, running out with white powder all 20 over her face. "Mail's up. I don't know how good it's up."

"Well, of course, I do hope it's for the best," said several of the other ladies. They did not go at once to take their mail out of their boxes; they felt a little left out.

The three women stood at the foot of the water tank.

"To find Lily is a different thing," said Aimee Slocum.

"Where in the wide world do you suppose she'd be?" It was Mrs. Watts who was carrying the letter.

"I don't see a sign of her either on this side of the street or on the other 25 side," Mrs. Carson declared as they walked along.

Ed Newton was stringing Redbird school tablets on the wire across the store.

"If you're after Lily, she come in here while ago and tole me she was fixin' to git married," he said.

"Ed Newton!" cried the ladies all together, clutching one another. Mrs. Watts began to fan herself at once with the letter from Ellisville. She wore widow's black, and the least thing made her hot.

"Why she is not. She's going to Ellisville, Ed," said Mrs. Carson gently. "Mrs. Watts and I and Aimee Slocum are paying her way out of our own pockets. Besides, the boys of Victory are on their honor. Lily's not going to get married, that's just an idea she's got in her head."

"More power to you, ladies," said Ed Newton, spanking himself with a tablet. 30

When they came to the bridge over the railroad tracks, there was Estelle Mabers, sitting on a rail. She was slowly drinking an orange Ne-Hi.

"Have you seen Lily?" they asked her.

"I'm supposed to be out here watching for her now," said the Mabers girl, as though she weren't there yet. "But for Jewel—Jewel says Lily come in the store while ago and picked out a two-ninety-eight hat and wore it off. Jewel wants to swap her something else for it."

"Oh, Estelle, Lily says she's going to get married!" cried Aimee Slocum.

"Well, I declare," said Estelle; she never understood anything.   35

Loralee Adkins came riding by in her Willys-Knight, tooting the horn to find out what they were talking about.

Aimee threw up her hands and ran out into the street. "Loralee, Loralee, you got to ride us up to Lily Daws'. She's up yonder fixing to get married!"

"Hop in, my land!"

"Well, that just goes to show you right now," said Mrs. Watts, groaning as she was helped into the back seat. "What we've got to do is persuade Lily it will be nicer to go to Ellisville."

"Just to think!"   40

While they rode around the corner Mrs. Carson was going on in her sad voice, sad as the soft noises in the hen house at twilight. "We buried Lily's poor defenseless mother. We gave Lily all her food and kindling and every stitch she had on. Sent her to Sunday school to learn the Lord's teachings, had her baptized a Baptist. And when her old father commenced beating her and tried to cut her head off with the butcher knife, why, we went and took her away from him and gave her a place to stay."

The paintless frame house with all the weather vanes was three stories high in places and had yellow and violet stained-glass windows in front and gingerbread around the porch. It leaned steeply to one side, toward the railroad, and the front steps were gone. The car full of ladies drew up under the cedar tree.

"Now Lily's almost grown up," Mrs. Carson continued. "In fact, she's grown," she concluded, getting out.

"Talking about getting married," said Mrs. Watts disgustedly. "Thanks, Loralee, you run on home."

They climbed over the dusty zinnias onto the porch and walked through the   45
open door without knocking.

"There certainly is always a funny smell in this house. I say it every time I come," said Aimee Slocum.

Lily was there, in the dark of the hall, kneeling on the floor by a small open trunk.

When she saw them she put a zinnia in her mouth, and held still.

"Hello, Lily," said Mrs. Carson reproachfully.

"Hello," said Lily. In a minute she gave a suck on the zinnia stem that sounded   50
exactly like a jay bird. There she sat, wearing a petticoat for a dress, one of the things Mrs. Carson kept after her about. Her milky-yellow hair streamed freely down from under a new hat. You could see the wavy scar on her throat if you knew it was there.

Mrs. Carson and Mrs. Watts, the two fattest, sat in the double rocker. Aimee Slocum sat on the wire chair donated from the drugstore that burned.

"Well, what are you doing, Lily?" asked Mrs. Watts, who led the rocking.

Lily smiled.

The trunk was old and lined with yellow and brown paper, with an asterisk pattern showing in darker circles and rings. Mutely the ladies indicated to each other that they did not know where in the world it had come from. It was empty except for two bars of soap and a green washcloth, which Lily was now trying to arrange in the bottom.

"Go on and tell us what you're doing, Lily," said Aimee Slocum.   5

"Packing, silly," said Lily.

"Where are you going?"

"Going to get married, and I bet you wish you was me now," said Lily. But shyness overcame her suddenly, and she popped the zinnia back into her mouth.

"Talk to me, dear," said Mrs. Carson. "Tell old Mrs. Carson why you want to get married."

"No," said Lily, after a moment's hesitation.   60

"Well, we've thought of something that will be so much nicer," said Mrs. Carson. "Why don't you go to Ellisville!"

"Won't that be lovely?" said Mrs. Watts. "Goodness, yes."

"It's a lovely place," said Aimee Slocum uncertainly.

"You've got bumps on your face," said Lily.

"Aimee, dear, you stay out of this, if you don't mind," said Mrs. Carson anx-   65
iously. "I don't know what it is comes over Lily when you come around her."

Lily stared at Aimee Slocum meditatively.

"There! Wouldn't you like to go to Ellisville now?" asked Mrs. Carson.

"No'm," said Lily.

"Why not?" All the ladies leaned down toward her in impressive astonishment.

"'Cause I'm goin' to get married," said Lily.   70

"Well, and who are you going to marry, dear?" asked Mrs. Watts. She knew how to pin people down and make them deny what they'd already said.

Lily bit her lip and began to smile. She reached into the trunk and held up both cakes of soap and wagged them.

"Tell us," challenged Mrs. Watts. "Who you're going to marry, now."

"A man last night."

There was a gasp from each lady. The possible reality of a lover descended   75
suddenly like a summer hail over their heads. Mrs. Watts stood up and balanced herself.

"One of those show fellows! A musician!" she cried.

Lily looked up in admiration.

"Did he—did he do anything to you?" In the long run, it was still only Mrs. Watts who could take charge.

"Oh, yes'm," said Lily. She patted the cakes of soap fastidiously with the tips of her small fingers and tucked them in with the washcloth.

"What?" demanded Aimee Slocum, rising up and tottering before her scream.   80
"What?" she called out in the hall.

"Don't ask her what," said Mrs. Carson, coming up behind. "Tell me, Lily— just yes or no—are you the same as you were?"

"He had a red coat," said Lily graciously. "He took little sticks and went *ping-pong! ding-dong!*"

"Oh, I think I'm going to faint," said Aimee Slocum, but they said, "No, you're not."

"The xylophone!" cried Mrs. Watts. "The xylophone player! Why, the coward, he ought to be run out of town on a rail!"

"Out of town? He is out of town, by now," cried Aimee. "Can't you read?—   85
the sign in the café—Victory on the ninth, Como on the tenth? He's in Como.
Como!"

"All right! We'll bring him back!" cried Mrs. Watts. "He can't get away from
me!"

"Hush," said Mrs. Carson. "I don't think it's any use following that line of
reasoning at all. It's better in the long run for him to be gone out of our lives for
good and all. That kind of a man. He was after Lily's body alone and he wouldn't
ever in this world make the poor little thing happy, even if we went out and forced
him to marry her like he ought—at the point of a gun."

"Still—" began Aimee, her eyes widening.

"Shut up," said Mrs. Watts. "Mrs. Carson, you're right, I expect."

"This is my hope chest—see?" said Lily politely in the pause that followed.   90
"You haven't even looked at it. I've already got soap and a washrag. And I have
my hat—on. What are you all going to give me?"

"Lily," said Mrs. Watts, starting over, "we'll give you lots of gorgeous things
if you'll only go to Ellisville instead of getting married."

"What will you give me?" asked Lily.

"I'll give you a pair of hemstitched pillowcases," said Mrs. Carson.

"I'll give you a big caramel cake," said Mrs. Watts.

"I'll give you a souvenir from Jackson—a little toy bank," said Aimee Slocum.   95
"Now will you go?"

"No," said Lily.

"I'll give you a pretty little Bible with your name on it in real gold," said
Mrs. Carson.

"What if I was to give you a pink crêpe de Chine brassière with adjustable
shoulder straps?" asked Mrs. Watts grimly.

"Oh, Etta."

"Well, she needs it," said Mrs. Watts. "What would they think if she ran all   100
over Ellisville in a petticoat looking like a Fiji?"

"I wish *I* could go to Ellisville," said Aimee Slocum luringly.

"What will they have for me down there?" asked Lily softly.

"Oh! lots of things. You'll have baskets to weave, I expect. . . ." Mrs. Carson
looked vaguely at the others.

"Oh, yes indeed, they will let you make all sorts of baskets," said Mrs. Watts;
then her voice too trailed off.

"No'm, I'd rather get married," said Lily.   105

"Lily Daw! Now that's just plain stubbornness!" cried Mrs. Watts. "You almost said you'd go and then you took it back!"

"We've all asked God, Lily," said Mrs. Carson finally, "and God seemed to
tell us—Mr. Carson, too—that the place where you ought to be, so as to be happy,
was Ellisville."

Lily looked reverent, but still stubborn.

"We've really just got to get her there—now!" screamed Aimee Slocum all
at once. "Suppose—! She can't stay here!"

"Oh, no, no, no," said Mrs. Carson hurriedly. "We mustn't think that."   110
They sat sunken in despair.

"Could I take my hope chest—to go to Ellisville?" asked Lily shyly, looking
at them sidewise.

"Why, yes," said Mrs. Carson blankly.

Silently they rose once more to their feet.

"Oh, if I could just take my hope chest!"   115

"All the time it was just her hope chest," Aimee whispered.

Mrs. Watts struck her palms together. "It's settled!"

"Praise the fathers," murmured Mrs. Carson.

Lily looked up at them, and her eyes gleamed. She cocked her head and spoke out in a proud imitation of someone—someone utterly unknown.

"O.K.—Toots!"   120

The ladies had been nodding and smiling and backing away toward the door.

"I think I'd better stay," said Mrs. Carson, stopping in her tracks. "Where—where could she have learned that terrible expression?"

"Pack up," said Mrs. Watts. "Lily Daw is leaving for Ellisville on Number One."

In the station the train was puffing. Nearly everyone in Victory was hanging around waiting for it to leave. The Victory Civic Band had assembled without any orders and was scattered through the crowd. Ed Newton gave false signals to start on his bass horn. A crate full of baby chickens got loose on the platform. Everybody wanted to see Lily all dressed up, but Mrs. Carson and Mrs. Watts had sneaked her into the train from the other side of the tracks.

The two ladies were going to travel as far as Jackson to help Lily change 125 trains and be sure she went in the right direction.

Lily sat between them on the plush seat with her hair combed and pinned up into a knot under a small blue hat which was Jewel's exchange for the pretty one. She wore a traveling dress made out of part of Mrs. Watts's last summer's mourning. Pink straps glowed through. She had a purse and a Bible and a warm cake in a box, all in her lap.

Aimee Slocum had been getting the outgoing mail stamped and bundled. She stood in the aisle of the coach now, tears shaking from her eyes.

"Good-bye, Lily," she said. She was the one who felt things.

"Good-bye, silly," said Lily.

"Oh, dear, I hope they get our telegram to meet her in Ellisville!" Aimee 130 cried sorrowfully, as she thought how far away it was. "And it was so hard to get it all in ten words, too."

"Get off, Aimee, before the train starts and you break your neck," said Mrs. Watts, all settled and waving her dressy fan gaily. "I declare, it's so hot, as soon as we get a few miles out of town I'm going to slip my corset down."

"Oh, Lily, don't cry down there. Just be good, and do what they tell you—it's all because they love you." Aimee drew her mouth down. She was backing away, down the aisle.

Lily laughed. She pointed across Mrs. Carson's bosom out the window toward a man. He had stepped off the train and just stood there, by himself. He was a stranger and wore a cap.

"Look," she said, laughing softly through her fingers.

"Don't—look," said Mrs. Carson very distinctly, as if, out of all she had ever 135 spoken, she would impress these two solemn words upon Lily's soft little brain. She added, "Don't look at anything till you get to Ellisville."

Outside, Aimee Slocum was crying so hard she almost ran into the stranger. He wore a cap and was short and seemed to have on perfume, if such a thing could be.

"Could you tell me, madam," he said, "where a little lady lives in this burg name of Miss Lily Daw?" He lifted his cap—and he had red hair.

"What do you want to know for?" Aimee asked before she knew it.

"Talk louder," said the stranger. He almost whispered, himself.

"She's gone away—she's gone to Ellisville!"   140

"Gone?"

"Gone to Ellisville!"

"Well, I like that!" The man stuck out his bottom lip and puffed till his hair jumped.

"What business did you have with Lily?" cried Aimee suddenly.

"We was only going to get married, that's all," said the man.   145

Aimee Slocum started to scream in front of all those people. She almost pointed to the long black box she saw lying on the ground at the man's feet. Then she jumped back in fright.

"The xylophone! The xylophone!" she cried, looking back and forth from the man to the hissing train. Which was more terrible? The bell began to ring hollowly, and the man was talking.

"Did you say Ellisville? That in the state of Mississippi?" Like lightning he had pulled out a red notebook entitled, "Permanent Facts & Data." He wrote down something. "I don't hear well."

Aimee nodded her head up and down, and circled around him.

Under "Ellis-Ville Miss" he was drawing a line; now he was flicking it with 150
two little marks. "Maybe she didn't say she would. Maybe she said she wouldn't." He suddenly laughed very loudly, after the way he had whispered. Aimee jumped back. "Women!—Well, if we play anywheres near Ellisville, Miss., in the future I may look her up and I may not," he said.

The bass horn sounded the true signal for the band to begin. White steam rushed out of the engine. Usually the train stopped for only a minute in Victory, but the engineer knew Lily from waving at her, and he knew this was her big day.

"Wait!" Aimee Slocum did scream. "Wait, mister! I can get her for you. Wait, Mister Engineer! Don't go!"

Then there she was back on the train, screaming in Mrs. Carson's and Mrs. Watts's faces.

"The xylophone player! The xylophone player to marry her! Yonder he is!"

"Nonsense," murmured Mrs. Watts, peering over the others to look where 155
Aimee pointed. "If he's there I don't see him. Where is he? You're looking at One-Eye Beasley."

"The little man with the cap—no, with the red hair! Hurry!"

"Is that really him?" Mrs. Carson asked Mrs. Watts in wonder. "Mercy! He's small, isn't he?"

"Never saw him before in my life!" cried Mrs. Watts. But suddenly she shut up her fan.

"Come on! This is a train we're on!" cried Aimee Slocum. Her nerves were all unstrung.

"All right, don't have a conniption fit, girl," said Mrs. Watts. "Come on," 160
she said thickly to Mrs. Carson.

"Where are we going now?" asked Lily as they struggled down the aisle.

"We're taking you to get married," said Mrs. Watts. "Mrs. Carson, you'd
better phone up your husband right there in the station."

"But I don't want to git married," said Lily, beginning to whimper. "I'm
going to Ellisville."

"Hush, and we'll all have some ice-cream cones later," whispered Mrs.
Carson.

Just as they climbed down the steps at the back end of the train, the band 165
went into "Independence March."

The xylophone player was still there, patting his foot. He came up and said,
"Hello, Toots. What's up—tricks?" and kissed Lily with a smack, after which she
hung her head.

"So you're the young man we've heard so much about," said Mrs. Watts.
Her smile was brilliant. "Here's your little Lily."

"What say?" asked the xylophone player.

"My husband happens to be the Baptist preacher of Victory," said Mrs.
Carson in a loud, clear voice. "Isn't that lucky? I can get him here in five minutes: I know exactly where he is."

They were in a circle around the xylophone player, all going into the white 170
waiting room.

"Oh, I feel just like crying, at a time like this," said Aimee Slocum. She looked
back and saw the train moving slowly away, going under the bridge at Main Street.
Then it disappeared around the curve.

"Oh, the hope chest!" Aimee cried in a stricken voice.

"And whom have we the pleasure of addressing?" Mrs. Watts was shouting,
while Mrs. Carson was ringing up the telephone.

The band went on playing. Some of the people thought Lily was on the train,
and some swore she wasn't. Everybody cheered, though, and a straw hat was
thrown into the telephone wires.

Research Materials on Eudora Welty

Eudora Welty

*Eudora Welty recollects, in this brief excerpt, some of the moments of childhood that
led her toward writing as a career. Most important was her intense curiosity,
which made her listen for stories.*

ONE WRITER'S BEGINNINGS   1984

This was a day when ladies' and children's clothes were very often made at
home. My mother cut out all the dresses and her little boys' rompers, and a sewing
woman would come and spend the day upstairs in the sewing room fitting and
stitching them all. This was Fannie. This old black sewing woman, along with her
speed and dexterity, brought along a great provision of up-to-the-minute news.
She spent her life going from family to family in town and worked right in its bosom, and nothing could stop her. My mother would try, while I stood being

pinned up. "Fannie, I'd rather Eudora didn't hear that." "That" would be just what I was longing to hear, whatever it was. "I don't want her exposed to gossip"—as if gossip were measles and I could catch it. I did catch some of it but not enough. "Mrs. O'Neil's oldest daughter she had her wedding dress *tried on*, and all her fine underclothes featherstitched and ribbon run in and then—" "I think that will do, Fannie," said my mother. It was tantalizing never to be exposed long enough to hear the end.

Fannie was the worldliest old woman to be imagined. She could do whatever her hands were doing without having to stop talking; and she could speak in a wonderfully derogatory way with any number of pins stuck in her mouth. Her hands steadied me like claws as she stumped on her knees around me, tacking me together. The gist of her tale would be lost on me, but Fannie didn't bother about the ear she was telling it to; she just liked telling. She was like an author. In fact, for a good deal of what she said, I daresay she *was* the author.

Long before I wrote stories, I listened for stories. Listening *for* them is something more acute than listening *to* them. I suppose it's an early form of participation in what goes on. Listening children know stories are *there*. When their elders sit and begin, children are just waiting and hoping for one to come out, like a mouse from its hole.

It was taken entirely for granted that there wasn't any lying in our family, and I was advanced in adolescence before I realized that in plenty of homes where I played with schoolmates and went to their parties, children lied to their parents and parents lied to their children and to each other. It took me a long time to realize that these very same everyday lies, and the strategems and jokes and tricks and dares that went with them, were in fact the basis of the *scenes* I so well loved to hear about and hoped for and treasured in the conversation of adults.

My instinct—the dramatic instinct—was to lead me, eventually, on the right track for a storyteller: the *scene* was full of hints, pointers, suggestions, and promises of things to find out and know about human beings. I had to grow up and learn to listen for the unspoken as well as the spoken—and to know a truth, I also had to recognize a lie.

From One Writer's Beginnings

Eudora Welty

This essay by Eudora Welty was designed to answer questions that came so frequently from readers of "A Worn Path" that she realized a public statement was necessary. In it Welty gives us a rare glimpse of how she decides on a problem of meaning in her work.

"IS PHOENIX JACKSON'S GRANDSON REALLY DEAD?" 1974

A story writer is more than happy to be read by students; the fact that these serious readers think and feel something in response to his work he finds life-giving. At the same time he may not always be able to reply to their specific questions in kind. I wondered if it might clarify something, for both the questioners and myself, if I set down a general reply to the question that comes to me most often in the mail, from both students and their teachers, after some classroom discussion. The unrivaled favorite is this: "Is Phoenix Jackson's grandson really *dead?*"

It refers to a short story I wrote years ago called "A Worn Path," which tells of a day's journey an old woman makes on foot from deep in the country into town and into a doctor's office on behalf of her little grandson; he is at home, periodically ill, and periodically she comes for his medicine; they give it to her as usual, she receives it and starts the journey back.

I had not meant to mystify readers by withholding any fact; it is not a writer's business to tease. The story is told through Phoenix's mind as she undertakes her errand. As the author at one with the character as I tell it, I must assume that the boy is alive. As the reader, you are free to think as you like, of course: the story invites you to believe that no matter what happens, Phoenix for as long as she is able to walk and can hold to her purpose will make her journey. The *possibility* that she would keep on even if he were dead is there in her devotion and its single-minded, single-track errand. Certainly the *artistic* truth, which should be good enough for the fact, lies in Phoenix's own answer to that question. When the nurse asks, "He isn't dead, is he?" she speaks for herself: "He still the same. He going to last."

The grandchild is the incentive. But it is the journey, the going of the errand, that is the story, and the question is not whether the grandchild is in reality alive or dead. It doesn't affect the outcome of the story or its meaning from start to finish. But it is not the question itself that has struck me as much as the idea, almost without exception implied in the asking, that for Phoenix's grandson to be dead would somehow make the story "better."

It's *all right*, I want to say to the students who write to me, for things to be   5
what they appear to be, and for words to mean what they say. It's all right, too, for words and appearances to mean more than one thing—ambiguity is a fact of life. A fiction writer's responsibility covers not only what he presents as the facts of a given story but what he chooses to stir up as their implications; in the end, these implications, too, become facts, in the larger, fictional sense. But it is not all right, not in good faith, for things *not* to mean what they say.

The grandson's plight was real and it made the truth of the story, which is the story of an errand of love carried out. If the child no longer lived, the truth would persist in the "wornness" of the path. But his being dead can't increase the truth of the story, can't affect it one way or the other. I think I signal this, because the end of the story has been reached before old Phoenix gets home again: she simply starts back. To the question "Is the grandson really dead?" I could reply that it doesn't make any difference. I could also say that I did not make him up in order to let him play a trick on Phoenix. But my best answer would be: "*Phoenix* is alive."

The origin of a story is sometimes a trustworthy clue to the author—or can provide him with the clue—to its key image; maybe in this case it will do the same for the reader. One day I saw a solitary old woman like Phoenix. She was walking; I saw her, at middle distance, in a winter country landscape, and watched her slowly make her way across my line of vision. That sight of her made me write the story. I invented an errand for her, but that only seemed a living part of the figure she was herself: what errand other than for someone else could be making her go? And her going was the first thing, her persisting in her landscape was the real thing, and the first and the real were what I wanted and worked to keep. I brought her up close enough, by imagination, to describe her face, make her present to the eyes, but the full-length figure moving across the winter fields was the indelible one and the image to keep, and the perspective extending into the vanishing distance the true one to hold in mind.

I invented for my character, as I wrote, some passing adventures—some dreams and harassments and a small triumph or two, some jolts to her pride, some flights of fancy to console her, one or two encounters to scare her, a moment that gave her cause to feel ashamed, a moment to dance and preen—for it had to be a *journey*, and all these things belonged to that, parts of life's uncertainty.

A narrative line is in its deeper sense, of course, the tracing out of a meaning, and the real continuity of a story lies in this probing forward. The real dramatic force of a story depends on the strength of the emotion that has set it going. The emotional value is the measure of the reach of the story. What gives any such content to "A Worn Path" is not its circumstances but its *subject*: the deep-grained habit of love.

What I hoped would come clear was that in the whole surround of this story,   10
the world it threads through, the only certain thing at all is the worn path. The habit of love cuts through confusion and stumbles or contrives its way out of difficulty, it remembers the way even when it forgets, for a dumbfounded moment, its reason for being. The path is the thing that matters.

Her victory—old Phoenix's—is when she sees the diploma in the doctor's office, when she finds "nailed up on the wall the document that had been stamped with the gold seal and framed in the gold frame, which matched the dream that was hung up in her head." The return with the medicine is just a matter of retracing her own footsteps. It is the part of the journey, and of the story, that can now go without saying.

In the matter of function, old Phoenix's way might even do as a sort of parallel to your way of work if you are a writer of stories. The way to get there is the all-important, all-absorbing problem, and this problem is your reason for undertaking the story. Your only guide, too, is your sureness about your subject, about what this subject is. Like Phoenix, you work all your life to find your way, through all the obstructions and the false appearances and the upsets you may have brought on yourself, to reach a meaning—using inventions of your imagination, perhaps helped out by your dreams and bits of good luck. And finally too, like Phoenix, you have to assume that what you are working in aid of is life, not death.

But you would make the trip anyway—wouldn't you?—just on hope.

From *The Eye of the Story: Selected Essays and Reviews*

Ruth M. Vande Kieft

Ruth M. Vande Kieft is one of the best-known critics of Eudora Welty. Her discussion of "Livvie" gives us insight into the potential meanings of details and names in the story, especially those that connect us to the Bible.

TECHNIQUE IN "LIVVIE"   1987

. . . In the story "Livvie," however, we find the reverse: a narrative method disarmingly simple and clear, but a thematic structure far more complex and subtly adjusted to the ambiguities of human experience. The beautiful balance of the opposing values, their easy, natural embodiment in character and situation, the purity of the language, and the sympathy and detachment of the vision, give this story a deservedly high place among Eudora Welty's works.

Livvie's return to life (the original title of the story was "Livvie Is Back") through the death of her old husband, Solomon, and her surrender to Cash, the field hand who comes to claim her, is an obvious but not a complete and clear gain; for there is a corresponding loss and destruction of certain positive values.

As his name implies, Solomon stands for order, control, wisdom, security. His house is "nice"—neat and orderly. Patterns are delightfully worked out in groups of twos, threes, and fours. On each side of the porch, in perfect balance, is an easy chair with overhanging fern and a dishpan of seedlings growing at its foot; a plow-wheel hanging on one side of the door is balanced by a square mirror on the other side. In the house are three rooms; in the living room is a three-legged table with a pink marble top, and on it is a lamp with three gold feet; on the kitchen table are three objects: two jelly glasses holding spoons, knives, and forks, with a cut-glass vinegar bottle between them; even the tiny blood-red roses that bloom on the bushes outside grow in threes on either side of the steps. And there are four baited mouse-traps in the kitchen, one in every corner. Each pictured detail of the house, inside and out, speaks of the balance and symmetry that characterize a dignified, well-disciplined, quiet and peaceful mode of existence.

Safety and security are suggested by the two safedoors that are always kept shut and by the bottled branches of the crape-myrtle trees, a precaution taken, as Livvie knows, to keep "evil spirits from coming into the house—by luring them inside the colored bottles, where they cannot get out again." Solomon's life is moral and pious—he seems to Livvie "such a strict man"; he has his Bible on the bedside table (and uses it); he keeps track of time like a clock, sleeping with his silver watch in his palm "and even holding it to his cheek like a child that loves a plaything."

As mistress of Solomon's golden palace, Livvie passes her days in serenity and comfort; in a sense she shares in Solomon's kingly opulence, though she serves her now-ancient, fragile master by waiting on him in his illness. But since the "nice house" has also been her gilded cage for nine years, she is vaguely restless and discontent, unconsciously oppressed by the wintry atmosphere, by her barren and lonely existence. Once she had ventured forth through the dead leaves in the deep Trace, and there, over a bank in a graveyard, she had had a vision both of her bondage and her possible release. She had seen "in the sun, trees shining like burning flames through the great caterpillar nets which enclosed them," even though "scary thistles stood looking like the prophets in the Bible in Solomon's house." And she had thought, "Oh for a stirring of the leaves, and a breaking of the nets!"

Her release comes on the first day of spring, which brings a "little puffy wind," and on it the sounds of the distant shouts of men and girls plowing in the red fields and of the small piping cries of children playing. The harbinger of Livvie's release is Miss Baby-Marie, an amusingly vulgar, red-haired woman who travels around selling cosmetics to "white and colored" and is herself covered with "intense white and red" makeup. Livvie is tempted to apply some lipstick, and when she looks in the mirror, her face "dance[s] before her like a flame." The outside world has impinged on her secure, withdrawn world in a form crassly commercial, but its effect is romantically exciting. Pulsating with her new self-consciousness, Livvie is stirred to a further insight which she shares, unspoken, with Miss Baby-Marie as the two of them look at Solomon sleeping: he is about to die. Livvie rushes out for air.

Then Cash comes in his fine Easter clothes, and Livvie is purely dazzled. Cash is, as Robert Penn Warren has suggested, a black buck, a kind of field god; but that identification overlooks the fact that his gaudy clothes have been purchased with money stolen from Solomon, the fact that his luminous baby-pink shirt is the color of Miss Baby-Marie's lipstick. He is a commercially transformed field god, dressed in "the city way"; and if he destroys the nets that are binding Livvie, he is also destroying a certain decency and reserve, even a certain moral order. As she walks beside him, Livvie senses this threat in "the way he move[s] along kicking the flowers as if he could break through everything in the way and destroy anything in the world." Her eyes grow bright at that; she sees "hope in its insolence looking back"; but a little chill goes through her when he lifts his spread hand and laughingly brings it down, "as if Cash was bringing that strong hand down to beat a drum or to rain blows upon a man, such an abandon and menace were in his laugh." Soon afterwards when Cash sends a stone sailing through the bottle trees, the sounds of broken glass clatter "like cries of outrage"—the outrage perpetrated against Solomon's prevention and protection. Surely, by implication, a few more evil spirits have been released to wander freely and work their mischief in the world.

When Livvie rushes in to Solomon's bedside, she hears his watch ticking and sees him withdrawn in sleep, his old face looking "small, relentless, and devout, as if he were walking somewhere where she could imagine the snow falling." She feels the strength of his austerity, his pure dedication; and that is why the sight of Cash's bright, pitiless black face is "sweet" to her: she would have to be cruel to break with Solomon. Now as Solomon sleeps under the eyes of Cash and Livvie, his face tells them "like a mythical story that all his life he had built, little scrap by little scrap, respect." The images used to describe his purpose and method— that of an ant or beetle collecting, or an Egyptian builder-slave industriously working on the pyramid, so absorbed in his pursuit that he forgets the origins and meaning of his work—imply a curious blend of sympathy and criticism. Respectability, as Robert Penn Warren states, is "the dream, the idea, which has withered"; but nonetheless a simple wisdom and nobility characterize the process of this old man's life, the achievement of which is not entirely vitiated by the dubious value of its goal.

When Solomon wakes up, Cash raises his arm to strike; but the arm is fixed in mid-air as if held. A mysterious illumination flickers across Solomon's face: "It was that very mystery that Cash with his quick arm would have to strike, and that Livvie could not weep for." Though Cash is an impatiently pawing buck, he is momentarily stayed—if not by the sense of Solomon's mystery, at least because he feels "a pang of shame that the vigor of a man would come to such an end that he could not be struck without warning." Cash is sufficiently human to realize human vulnerability, if not dignity: he could not, without ceasing to be human, do violence to Solomon—push him over the trembling edge of life—in this moment of the old man's greatest strength and helplessness. Solomon must be permitted to surrender his ghost, and he does so with beautiful candor and dignity. Gently he reviews his own purpose for Livvie; without rebellion he faces the disagreeable fact of his failure (since there was "no prevention"), and the irony of its being Cash who has come to claim Livvie: "somebody I know all the time, and been knowing since he was born in a cotton patch, . . . Cash McCord, growed to size, growed up to come in my house in the end." With humility he confesses his fault: "God forgive Solomon for carrying away too young girl for wife and keeping her away from . . . all the young people would clamor for her back." Finally he offers to Livvie his most valued possession, the symbol of his very life, his dignified, orderly existence; and the moment she receives the silver watch from his hand, Solomon dies.

The denouement is swift and joyful. Back in the front room, Cash seizes Livvie and drags her round him and out toward the door in a whirling embrace. As a final fleeting gesture of loyalty, Livvie keeps stiff and still the arm and hand holding Solomon's watch; then her fingers relax, the watch falls somewhere on the floor, all at once "the full song of a bird" is heard, and outside "the sun was in all the bottles on the prisoned trees, and the young peach was shining in the middle of them with the bursting light of spring."

The triumph of life, youth, passion would appear to be complete. But Eudora Welty has shown us that just as Solomon's death is a necessary prelude to Livvie's new life with Cash, so all of Solomon's values and achievements must suffer a death. The new freedom and joy are not the uncomplicated pagan sort embodied in Don McInnis; they are, in part, a "cash" purchase, and their characteristic hue is a gaudy pink.

From Eudora Welty, Revised Edition

Ruth D. Weston

In the following brief discussion, Ruth D. Weston points to folk tale elements in "Lily Daw and the Three Ladies." She emphasizes the imagery of restraint common to folk tales. The folk tale repetition—three times for everything—has a ritual significance that deepens the significance of the story. The charm is designed to help Lily Daw escape from the bondage of the three ladies, whose power is akin to that of witches.

LILY DAW AND THE THREE LADIES   1989

Mrs. Carson carries a tape measure on her bosom. Mrs. Watts knows how to "pin people down." Aimee Slocum makes her living stamping and bundling mail, and she even observes the ten-word limit in her telegram to Ellisville. Mrs. Watts is confined in a tight corset from which she plans to free herself as soon as the train pulls out, while she attempts to restrict even Lily's view from the train. Lily's stranger is limited too and confesses that he doesn't hear well. And in the crowd of representatively limited folk are those described as small, as one-eyed, and finally as cheering without knowing why.

More serious implications of limitation result from the grotesque comparisons of humans with animals and inanimate objects. Aimee wonders which is more terrible, "the man [or] the hissing train"; and the narrator implies a connection as "the bell began to ring hollowly, and the man was talking." The ladies cluck their tongues and make noises "sad as the soft noises in the henhouse at twilight"; people and chicks run wild on the station platform; and Lily, named for a jackdaw and sucking on a zinnia between her teeth, makes a sound "exactly like a jaybird." Pictures of redbirds on a school tablet adorn wires inside the store, while Estelle perches outside on a rail fence. The story reads like the script for an absurdist comedy in which the silent and controlled pantomime of modern dance alternates with the apparent randomness of what was called in the 1960s a theatrical happening.

In "Lily Daw," Welty has utilized the rhetorical patterning of a folk or fairy tale, in which things often happen in threes. She combines mnemonic qualities of the oral folk tradition with the rhythms and shapes of the drama and of the plastic and painterly folk and fine arts. Her story depicts a lyric and individual impulse toward freedom in Lily's carefree bestowal of favor and unconventional behavior. And it portrays the culture's limitation of such freedom because of its threat to safe conventions and its attempt to hide the other than normal (that which cannot be neatly stamped and bundled) behind institutional walls. And, not least, it reveals the ironic situation of women who, blessed and limited by fertility, must therefore be controlled when they are "mature for [their] age." It portrays a community tangle of women who close in around a little innocent wild life to see it safely entrusted to one institution or another—to the asylum or to marriage. The flat (unrealistic), yet hauntingly real, characters are effective metaphors for the flat, unreal roles that Ruth Vande Kieft has noted are not only assumed by men but that are often forced by men on women in Welty's South; but in "Lily Daw," as in other Welty stories, these stereotypical roles are forced on women by other women who have become so rigid in their assigned roles that they do not realize they are performing. In their own way, like Fay in *The Optimist's Daughter*, Welty's three ladies are "making a scene."

While such human concerns are important in the story, the piece itself is less a social treatise than an abstract design that evokes a sense of grotesque human limitation. Its treatment in spatial, more than temporal, terms underscores its metaphoric confining lines and spaces. Even the language itself functions as a metaphor for limitation. For, as Welty has said, "We start from scratch, and words don't," her own critical vocabulary suggesting a linguistic dimension of the concept of limitation. Language is loaded with accumulated meanings; it is a grotesquely limited and delimiting automatism that Welty extends by creating the illusion of spatiality. "Lily Daw and the Three Ladies" is Welty's earliest portrait of the virtual confinement of women in society by their inscription in its linguistic and cultural codes. Lily herself symbolizes the victim of such limitation as well as the hope of escape; and the circling, threatening, talking ladies reveal woman's own complicity in what Michel Foucault has called a "carceral society," one that not only supervises criminal incarceration but also incorporates a series of enclosing devices, a network of forces, including "walls, space, institution, rules, discourse," all intended to normalize human beings in accord with the prevailing cultural mythos. The few props in the setting for "Lily Daw" contribute to the sense of a "bare stage" on which Lily is cruelly exposed to the elements in her world that threaten her freedom, investing her small figure, however deflated, with dramatic monumentality.

At the story's end, Lily understandably hangs her head, for her hope chest is gone on the train to Ellisville, while she herself is as trapped as the hat thrown into the electric wires. Welty leaves us with an image as graphic and functional as the fused sword and plow that she admires in Cather's *My Ántonia*. For, in the final scene, those electric lines, like the lines of perspective in a painting, now draw our attention past Lily to the focal point that represents her: the hat itself, an object caught.

From "American Folk Art, Fine Art and Eudora Welty" in
Eudora Welty: Eve of the Storyteller, edited by Dawn Trouard

Peter Schmidt

Peter Schmidt raises some feminist issues in "Lily Daw and the Three Ladies," showing us the ways in which life is circumscribed for women in the environment of Victory, Mississippi. Schmidt's approach introduces some of the psychological elements that drive the action.

LILY DAW AND THE THREE LADIES   1991

Of all the stories in *A Curtain of Green*, "Lily Daw and the Three Ladies" represents most clearly the choice open to white southern women in Welty's early stories. (Perhaps it is for this reason that Welty chose it to open her first collection.) That choice is suggested by the story's title: a woman may be either a married and respectable lady, like Mrs. Carter and her friend Mrs. Watts, or she may be eccentric like the retarded girl Lily Daw, continually threatened by scandal, madness, and confinement.

Lily grew up as a ward of the ladies of Victory, Mississippi, but now, in her teens, she has suddenly begun acting independently, talking back to her elders, sneaking away to circuses, and showing an interest in the opposite sex. The town's matriarchs first decide that confinement in an asylum can be the only remedy, but then, in a comic reversal caused partly by Lily's boyfriend's faithfulness and partly by the rebellion of one of their own members, Aimee Slocum, they decide that Lily's marrying her boyfriend must be accepted after all. By juxtaposing marriage and madness in such an exaggerated way, Welty's story comically subverts the ladies' authority. Their ideal of marriage comes to seem a kind of confining madness, whereas Lily's unconscious defiance of the community's standards becomes a liberating sanity, an escape and transformation. Yet even this twist is not the last the story has in store for us. Our euphoria over Lily's apparent victory over the ladies fades slightly when the story is reread: even as she is united with her lover we can see the ladies extending their control over her again. The story's acerbity and exuberance hardly suggest anxiety on Welty's part, yet its pointed linking of rebelliousness and madness provides an appropriate entry into the other, darker stories in *A Curtain of Green* about the potentially disastrous consequences of nonconformity.

Lily Daw's defection from the ladies' rule comes very suddenly; they hear that she went to a traveling circus the night before and became entranced with the red-headed boy playing the xylophone.

> "Oh, it was a very nice show," said the lady who had gone. "And Lily acted so nice. She was a perfect lady—just set in her seat and stared."

"Oh, she can be a lady—she can be," said Mrs. Carson, shaking her head and turning her eyes up. "That's just what breaks your heart."

"Yes'm, she kept her eyes on—what's that thing makes all the commotion?—the xylophone," said the lady. "Didn't turn her head to the right or to the left the whole time. Set in front of me."

"The point is, what did she do after the show?" asked Mrs. Watts practically.

"Lily has gotten so she is very mature for her age."

"Oh, Etta!" protested Mrs. Carson, looking at her wildly for a moment.

"And that's how come we are sending her to Ellisville," finished Mrs. Watts.

Here, acting the part of a "perfect lady" means a careful suppression of what Mrs. Watts delicately calls "maturity." Mrs. Carson and her cohorts recognize that Lily's retardedness means that she will never learn to play the part of a lady well; she is too susceptible to "commotion"—to the excitement of music, the xylophone player's red hair and racy slang. When Mrs. Carson, Mrs. Watts, and Aimee Slocum hear about what happened at the circus, they realize that they have arranged just in time to entomb her permanently within propriety at the Institute for the Feeble-Minded at Ellisville: "Lily Daw's getting in at Ellisville," they whisper to the other women in the post office, as if she had graduated from high school and been accepted at the prestigious college of her choice.

Welty's portrayal of the three ladies in the story's opening scene shows how they have carefully repressed the sensual, "natural" Lily within themselves in order to construct their status as "ladies." Mrs. Carson is a prim, self-righteous Baptist minister's wife. Other women in the town are embarrassed even to mention the circus in her presence, but when they do, she unctuously replies, " 'Don't mind me, I know there are such things in the world,' . . . looking down and fingering the tape measure which hung over her bosom." Mrs. Watts, the most authoritative of the three, wears "widow's black, and the least thing made her hot." The third woman in the group, a spinster named Aimee Slocum, has distinctly less success in turning herself into a lady. Not only is she addressed by her first name, as Lily is, but she works in the post office and is bumbling and ugly—even Lily can see that. She is the only one of the three ladies whom Lily dares to insult.

Welty deftly demonstrates the stature that these three women hold in the town by setting the first scene in the town's post office while the day's mail is being put up in everyone's boxes. The post office is a major gathering place in any small southern town (hence Sister's proud retreat to it in "Why I Live at the P.O."), and the hour that the mail is put up is naturally a social highlight of the day. During this time, Mrs. Carson and Mrs. Watts reign supreme. The ladies' power, however, is hardly absolute. It is dependent upon the institution of marriage; they could not achieve their eminence in society without it. This is why Mrs. Carson murmurs "praise the fathers" when Lily finally consents to give up her plans to marry and go to Ellisville: she sees herself as defending the standards of God the Father and the male representatives of His authority on earth, including her husband. Thus the near absence of males in the story does not mean that the town is run by women, but rather that the women's power would be impossible unless sanctioned by the "fathers." The story is thus not a satire of women with too much power but of women self-righteously acting on behalf of the "fathers"—the patriarchal authority that defines "proper" roles for both men and women to play.

Throughout the narrative, the third-person narrator appears to side with the ladies' point of view towards the events, imitating their language and adopting their reasoning. The narrator takes their opinions and presents them as objective fact, as when it is said of one of the women in the town, "she never understood anything." As the story develops and the women's tyrannization over Lily becomes more obvious, however, a reader cannot help but notice ironic parallels between their ideas of marriage and confinement in a madhouse. Lily's retardation means that the women can bribe her into going to Ellisville by offering to give her presents for her bridal "hope chest" and threatening to refuse to give her anything if she goes through with her plan to marry the xylophonist, but the fact that Lily and her lady's hope chest will be sent to Ellisville suggests an ironic link between getting married and getting institutionalized in an insane asylum. How different, in fact, is Mrs. Carson's and Mrs. Watts's position? After all, they are dependent on an institution for their status, possessions, power, and even their names. Welty's story raises this question, but her readers are the only ones who hear it asked; Mrs. Carson and Mrs. Watts certainly do not, nor do the townspeople. They greet the train that will carry Lily to Ellisville and even arrange for a band to play a comically inappropriate piece called the "Independence March" to honor Lily's departure.

The story of Lily Daw of course turns out differently from what the three ladies expect: the xylophonist shows up in the crowd at the last minute, just as the train is about to pull out of the station, and Aimee Slocum defects and decides to rescue Lily, eventually persuading her to give up her "gift" of the train ride to Ellisville. Lily's seeming passivity and shyness during this final scene should not mislead us: Lily's own earlier acts of rebellion in the story have apparently awakened Aimee's own dormant sense of independence, and she arranges a reunion that seems to force the ladies of Victory to accept Lily's marrying the man she loves as the "right" and "proper" ending. Even Mrs. Watts must smile and greet the musician cordially.

Yet Welty's story leaves several issues unresolved, repressed for the sake of the comic ending and the narrative's gentle mockery of the three ladies. The first is the fact of Lily's anger. It surfaces only once in the story, when Lily lashes out at Aimee Slocum's ugliness, but it is ever-present and powerful, just as male power is. We feel it in Lily's flight from the ladies and in her frenzied efforts to gather her belongings together when they finally catch up with her at her house and entrap her. We also sense it in Welty's description of Lily's house, the first of many Gothic portraits of decrepit and rambling houses of women in *A Curtain of Green*. The house lacks front steps, as if it, like Lily, will not easily accommodate visitors from the town, and it "leaned steeply to one side, toward the railroad," as if desiring to flee. (This latter detail was added when Welty revised the story, thus drawing its hidden undercurrents closer to the surface.)

The second issue that the comic ending of the story does not confront is the question of why Mrs. Carson and Mrs. Watts suddenly capitulate to Aimee Slocum's demands and let Lily marry. They seem startled by the musician's presence and Aimee's unprecedented resoluteness, but why should they not simply override Aimee, as they often have before? One answer that suggests itself is that they are afraid that they may be sending a pregnant woman to Ellisville; once the musician appears they realize that marrying Lily off may very well be the safer course. Another is that they realize that their power over Lily once she is married may very well increase rather than diminish. Mrs. Carson's first comment when she sees Lily's future husband in the crowd, before they have agreed to let Lily get off the train ("Mercy! He's small, isn't he?"), implies a victory for the ladies of Victory: Lily may yet be forced to conform to the standards of the "fathers" for being a lady. Despite her sometimes unconventional behavior and instinctive distrust of the three ladies, Lily has fully absorbed her society's standards for what a proper lady is: her treasured hope chest contains two bars of soap and a washcloth, and she is delighted when the ladies promise her other items associated with proper femininity, such as a Bible, hemstitched pillowcases, and a brassiere. The most revealing gift the women have bestowed on Lily is associated with mourning, not marriage: throughout the story Mrs. Watts wears "widow's black," and the dress she gives Lily to cover up the petticoat Lily prefers wearing in public is "made out of part of Mrs. Watts's last summer's mourning." Lily thus wears second-hand mourning to her wedding. There is something funereal about everything the three ladies do, in spite of their frantic energy, and the rite of marriage as they conceive it is more an act of entombment than of metamorphosis.

The complexities of the story's comic ending parallel the complexities of the story's narrative voice. Standard critical labels that may be used to define the narrative voice, such as "third-person" and "omniscient," are misleading. Recently the work of M. M. Bakhtin has advanced beyond Wayne Booth's classic *The Rhetoric of Fiction*, teaching us new ways of conceiving of the ironic play of meanings possible within a "third-person" voice. We must learn to notice the irony and the unspoken in Welty's narrative voices in *A Curtain of Green* and her later fiction; in Bakhtin's sense, these narrative voices are always dialogical, ironically quoting the language of social authority so that it can be questioned, can be engaged in dialogue rather than treated as a monologue. Apparent praise of the "fathers" (or of the ladies) is thus not necessarily praise. Just as importantly, we must learn to see how "omniscient" narrators in Welty always have blind spots and that the alleged unity of her "third-person" narrators is in practice fractured and multivocal. Indeed, Welty's third-person narrators are really no more unified than the "three ladies" in "Lily Daw": they may appear to speak in a single voice, but actually they are in perpetual contention with themselves and with opposing voices such as Lily's that they can so vividly imagine.

From The Heart of The Story, Eudora Welty's Short Fiction

Poetry

6

Enjoying Poetry

Poetry defies definition and mocks those who attempt to pin it down. To some extent it is mysterious, linked as it is in prehistory with religious chants and mystic prayers. Since ancient times, poets have talked about being inspired by the muse, a power of divine origin greater than themselves. When poets have written poems much better than they knew they could, their only explanation was that they were inspired. Some poets write only when they can induce in themselves a feeling of being moved to write—which is to say, the psychological condition of being inspired.

Although Robert Frost said that poetry was what was lost in the translation, good translators have given us versions of poems from other languages that preserve their poetic nature. But Frost's point is that poetry is a condition of language. If painting represents a way of seeing, then poetry represents a way of saying. All poetry has language at its heart.

Fortunately, as with many things that cannot be defined, poetry is almost instantly recognizable. Some of its qualities are special uses of language and rhythm: rhyme, imagery, metaphor, symbol, onomatopoiea, meter, and repetition. Some are special visual tips on the printed page: stanzas, and forms such as couplets, quatrains, sonnets, capitalized first lines, and short lines. Others are compression of language, tension, tone, seriousness of ideas, or utter playfulness. The poems in this collection illustrate all of these qualities and more. Some poems masquerade as prose, or advertisements, or even shapes, increasing the pleasures of poetry by increasing its possibilities.

POETRY AND PERFORMANCE

Rap poets make their living by performing their work. They excite audiences not just because they say something interesting, but because they say it with a beat, a lilting rhyme, and the illusion that they are talking spontaneously, making it up as they go along. Some rappers do improvise, but most are like other poets: they work out the details in advance, write them down, then memorize them. Rappers are also like song writers in that their work is much more interesting in performance than in reading.

Many poets, such as T. S. Eliot, Langston Hughes, Robert Frost, Dylan Thomas, Adrienne Rich, and Marge Piercy, have recorded their poems. Their performances vary because some of them are better readers than others. But they have a special authority: they wrote the poetry they read. On the other hand, many recordings feature actors such as Richard Burton and Siobhan McKenna. Listening to them also helps us develop an ear for poetry.

Poetry is always amenable to performance even without the original poets or actors. Reciting them yourself is one of the best ways to perform poems. All the poems in this collection need recitation, which may range from memorization and dramatic interpretation—through modulation of voice or gesture—to the simple act of saying them out loud. The following anonymous poem is a somewhat waggish rhyme that seems to demand to be said aloud:

> It isn't the cough
> That carries you off.
> It's the coffin
> They carry you off in.

The poem's gallows humor is intensified by some lovely tricks of rhyme and language. The connection between cough and coffin was always there, of course, but never perceived so fully as after one recites this poem. Even the different senses of the expression "carry you off" resonate in the air after a recitation. One of the most amusing aspects of the poem may be its portability: it is brief, compressed, complete.

Built into the act of recitation is another aspect of performance: rereading. Poetry is a language artifact intended to be reread. That is not true of all literature; mystery stories are usually of no interest after the first reading. Poetry needs rereading because its compression of language, its fireworks of metaphor and imagery, and its tension and play of rhythm and meter all work simultaneously, making it almost impossible to interpret everything at first reading. A poem is like a brilliant high-action sequence in a film that moves so fast you want to rewind and see it again.

HOW POEMS PLEASE US

Poems, like all kinds of play, amuse us when we get caught up in the action. Like double-Dutch jump-rope, they also show us something difficult made to look easy. Clever rhymes, surprising conjunctions of words and sounds, and tricky rhythms are complex constructions, and we admire the poet for meeting the challenge. "Jabberwocky" by Lewis Carroll (1832–1898) is a dazzling example. It is familiar to readers of *Through the Looking Glass*, the story of Alice in Wonderland, and has been entertaining us for more than a century.

Lewis Carroll (1832–1898)

JABBERWOCKY 1871

'Twas brillig, and the slithy toves
  Did gyre and gimble in the wabe:
All mimsy were the borogoves,
    And the mome raths outgrabe.

"Beware the Jabberwock, my son!   5
  The jaws that bite, the claws that catch!
Beware the Jubjub bird, and shun
    The frumious Bandersnatch!"

He took his vorpal sword in hand:
  Long time the manxome foe he sought—   10
So rested he by the Tumtum tree,
    And stood awhile in thought.

And, as in uffish thought he stood,
  The Jabberwock, with eyes of flame,
Came whiffling through the tulgey wood,   15
    And burbled as it came!

One, two! One, two! And through and through
  The vorpal blade went snicker-snack!
He left it dead, and with its head
    He went galumphing back.   20

"And hast thou slain the Jabberwock?
  Come to my arms, my beamish boy!
O frabjous day! Callooh! Callay!"
    He chortled in his joy.

'Twas brillig, and the slithy toves   25
  Did gyre and gimble in the wabe:
All mimsy were the borogoves,
    And the mome raths outgrabe.

Humpty Dumpty tells Alice, "I can explain all the poems that ever were invented—and a good many that haven't been invented yet." After she recites the first verse, Humpty "explains" it:

> "That's enough to begin with," Humpty Dumpty interrupted: "there are plenty of hard words there. '*Brillig*' means four o'clock in the afternoon—the time when you begin *broiling* things for dinner."
>
> "That'll do very well," said Alice "and '*slithy*'?"
>
> "Well, '*slithy*' means 'lithe and slimy.' 'Lithe' is the same as 'active.' You see it's like a portmanteau—there are two meanings packed up into one word."
>
> "I see it now," Alice remarked thoughtfully: "and what are '*toves*'?"
>
> "Well, '*toves*' are something like badgers—they're something like lizards—and they're something like corkscrews."
>
> "They must be very curious-looking creatures."
>
> "They are that," said Humpty Dumpty; "also they make their nests under sun-dials—also they live on cheese."
>
> "And what's to '*gyre*' and to '*gimble*'?"
>
> "To '*gyre*' is to go round and round like a gyroscope. To '*gimble*' is to make holes like a gimlet."
>
> "And '*the wabe*' is the grass-plot round a sun-dial, I suppose?" said Alice, surprised at her own ingenuity.
>
> "Of course, it is. It's called '*wabe*' you know, because it goes a long way before it, and a long way behind it—"
>
> "And a long way beyond it on each side," Alice added.
>
> "Exactly so. Well, then, '*mimsy*' is 'flimsy and miserable' (there's another portmanteau for you). And a '*borogove*' is a thin shabby-looking bird with its feathers sticking out all round—something like a live mop."
>
> "And then '*mome raths*'?" said Alice. "I'm afraid I'm giving you a great deal of trouble."
>
> "Well, a '*rath*' is a sort of green pig: but '*mome*' I'm not certain about. I think it's short for 'from home'—meaning that they'd lost their way, you know."
>
> "And what does '*outgrabe*' mean?"
>
> "Well, '*outgribing*' is something between bellowing and whistling, with a kind of sneeze in the middle; however, you'll hear it done, maybe—down in the wood yonder—and, when you've once heard it, you'll be *quite* content. Who's been repeating all that hard stuff to you?"
>
> "I read it in a book," said Alice.

Lewis Carroll delights us by treating nonsense as if it were a serious subject. Humpty Dumpty's "interpretation" is as much fun as the poem itself because it, too, of course, is nonsense. The general narrative of the poem is classic: a young man goes out to fight the Jabberwock, equivalent to the dragon of old. With his vorpal blade he kills the beast, to the delight of the narrator, who calls him "my beamish boy!" More than this about the "plot" we really need not know. The poem has a classic narrative, a happy ending, and plenty of linguistic amusement along the way.

WORDS AND SOUNDS

Most poetry enjoys playing with sound. In the nineteenth century, when Edgar Allan Poe wrote "The Bells," the air of most cities and towns was filled with bells. Church steeple bells rang on the hour and half-hour. They also rang to announce weddings and funerals, and they rang for fires. Bicycles, carriages, sleighs, and sledges announced themselves with bells. Thus bells spoke a language of urgency, but they were also various, musical, and interesting in themselves. Poe's poem exploits all the associations of bells while also using language to resemble the sound of bells.

Edgar Allan Poe   (1809–1849)
  THE BELLS   1849

I

>   Hear the sledges with the bells—
>   Silver bells!
> *What* a world of merriment their melody foretells!
>   How they tinkle, tinkle, tinkle,
>   In the icy air of night!   5
>   While the stars that oversprinkle
>   All the Heavens, seem to twinkle
>   With a crystalline delight;
>   Keeping time, time, time,
>   In a sort of Runic rhyme,   10
> To the tintinabulation that so musically wells
>   From the bells, bells, bells, bells,
>   Bells, bells, bells—
>   From the jingling and the tinkling of the bells.

II

>   Hear the mellow wedding bells—   15
>   Golden bells!
> *What* a world of happiness their harmony foretells!
>   Through the balmy air of night
>   How they ring out their delight!—
>   From the molten-golden notes   20
>   And all in tune,
>   What a liquid ditty floats

> To the turtle-dove that listens while she gloats
>> On the moon!
>> Oh, from out the sounding cells 25
> *What* a gush of euphony voluminously wells!
>>> How it swells!
>>> How it dwells
>>> On the Future!—how it tells
>>> Of the rapture that impels 30
>> To the swinging and the ringing
>> Of the bells, bells, bells!—
> Of the bells, bells, bells, bells,
>>> Bells, bells, bells—
> To the rhyming and the chiming of the bells! 35

III

>> Hear the loud alarum bells—
>>> Brazen bells!
> *What* tale of terror, now, their turbulency tells!
>> In the startled ear of Night
>> How they scream out their affright! 40
>>> Too much horrified to speak,
>>> They can only shriek, shriek,
>>> Out of tune,
> In a clamorous appealing to the mercy of the fire—
> In a mad expostulation with the deaf and frantic fire, 45
>>> Leaping higher, higher, higher,
>>> With a desperate desire
>> And a resolute endeavor
>> Now—now to sit, or never,
> By the side of the pale-faced moon. 50
>>> Oh, the bells, bells, bells!
>>> What a tale their terror tells
>>> Of despair!
>> How they clang and clash and roar!
>> What a horror they outpour 55
> In the bosom of the palpitating air!
>>> Yet the ear, it fully knows,
>>>> By the twanging
>>>> And the clanging,
>>> How the danger ebbs and flows:— 60
>> Yes, the ear distinctly tells,
>>>> In the jangling
>>>> And the wrangling,
>>> How the danger sinks and swells,
> By the sinking or the swelling in the anger of the bells— 65

                Of the bells—
        Of the bells, bells, bells, bells,
            Bells, bells, bells—
        In the clamor and the clangor of the bells.

IV

            Hear the tolling of the bells—   70
                Iron bells!
    What a world of solemn thought their monody compels!
            In the silence of the night
            How we shiver with affright
    At the melancholy meaning of the tone!   75
            For every sound that floats
            From the rust within their throats
                Is a groan.
                And the people—ah, the people
                They that dwell up in the steeple   80
                    All alone,
            And who, tolling, tolling, tolling,
                In that muffled monotone,
            Feel a glory in so rolling
                On the human heart a stone—   85
        They are neither man nor woman—
        They are neither brute nor human,
                They are Ghouls:—
        And their king it is who tolls:—
        And he rolls, rolls, rolls, rolls   90
                A Paean from the bells!
            And his merry bosom swells
                With the Paean of the bells!
            And he dances and he yells;
        Keeping time, time, time,   95
        In a sort of Runic rhyme,
                To the Paean of the bells—
                Of the bells:—
        Keeping time, time, time,
        In a sort of Runic rhyme,   100
                To the throbbing of the bells—
        Of the bells, bells, bells—
                To the sobbing of the bells:—
        Keeping time, time, time,
                As he knells, knells, knells,   105
        In a happy Runic rhyme,
                To the rolling of the bells—

> Of the bells, bells, bells:—
> To the tolling of the bells—
> Of the bells, bells, bells, bells,   110
>   Bells, bells, bells—
> To the moaning and the groaning of the bells.

Poe explores a wide range of sounds, emotional associations, and suggestions in the various kinds of bells he describes. The sledge bells suggest the merriment of a hayride. The wedding bells suggest happiness and harmony; the alarum bells suggest terror. The iron bells suggest an otherworldly "affright," since they toll for death. These are the bells of which the poet John Donne said: "Ask not for whom the bell tolls. It tolls for thee." Poe has explored a wide range of human feeling and significance in the tolling of bells while at the same time making his poem imitate the sounds themselves. The word *bells* is repeated so often, especially in a rhyming position, that it begins to take on the sound of a bell. Poe also plays with rhythms of language, interspersing one or two long lines in stanzas made up essentially of short lines. He does the same with careful word choices. Most of his words are one syllable, like *bells*, but occasionally he uses multisyllable words for rhythmic effect, words like *merriment* and *melody* in line 3 and the remarkable, six-syllable word *tintinabulation* in line 11, which is followed by *musically*.

Because the effects Poe wants are explicitly musical, any interpretation of the poem will center on questions of form or on audience response, especially since Poe calls our attention to the emotional range excited by bells. Examination of any stanza will show that the use of language for rhythmic effect contributes considerably to our response and enjoyment of the poem. Even a single-syllable word like *Ghouls* in stanza 4 has a special effect because it comes as a surprise in a poem that is otherwise upbeat. When Poe introduces the iron bells with their rust and groans, he becomes mordant and gothic in his imagery, suddenly plunging us into a cemetery mood haunted by ghouls and threatening spirits. Some commentators have called the emotion associated with this imagery the "metaphysical shudder" because it is strongly associated with the graveyard beside the church (next to the bell-steeple).

Though Poe's poem ends on this solemn note, there is no mistaking its main purpose: to explore and enjoy sound. The following two poems are further reminders that at the core of all poetry is the element of play and enjoyment. The first is by Edward Lear, who is famous for writing "The Owl and the Pussycat" as well as other nonsense verse. In this poem, he manages, with detailed images and lighthearted rhymes, to poke fun at himself. In "Nephelidia," which means "little clouds," Algernon Swinburne affects a tone of exceptionally high seriousness to mock those who think they are writing poetry just because they are being "serious." As part of his jest, Swinburne pushes the technique of alliteration—repeating a sound at the beginning of successive words—so far that it becomes ridiculous. He also relies upon an unusual metrical foot, the anapest, in which the first two syllables are unaccented and the third is accented: ˘ ˘ ´. "Nephelidia" is often given to actors in training to help them improve their diction. Although Swinburne is certainly mocking the pretentiousness of some highfalutin poets, he is also having fun in doing so. In other words, he is still writing poetry.

Edward Lear   (1812–1888)

HOW PLEASANT TO KNOW MR. LEAR   1871

"How pleasant to know Mr. Lear!"
  Who has written such volumes of stuff!
Some think him ill-tempered and queer,
  But a few think him pleasant enough.

His mind is concrete and fastidious,   5
  His nose is remarkably big;
His visage is more or less hideous,
  His beard it resembles a wig.

He has ears, and two eyes, and ten fingers,
  Leastways if you reckon two thumbs;   10
Long ago he was one of the singers,
  But now he is one of the dumbs.

He sits in a beautiful parlor,
  With hundreds of books on the wall;
He drinks a great deal of Marsala,   15
  But never gets tipsy at all.

He has many friends, lay men and clerical,
  Old Foss is the name of his cat;
His body is perfectly spherical,
  He weareth a runcible° hat.   20

When he walks in waterproof white,
  The children run after him so!
Calling out, "He's come out in his night-
  Gown, that crazy old Englishman, oh!"

He weeps by the side of the ocean,   25
  He weeps on the top of the hill;
He purchases pancakes and lotion,
  And chocolate shrimps from the mill.

---

20 *runcible*: Coined by Lear in *The Owl and the Pussycat* for "runcible spoon." He uses it to mean wide.

He reads, but he cannot speak, Spanish,
   He cannot abide ginger beer: 30
Ere the days of his pilgrimage vanish,
   How pleasant to know Mr. Lear!

Algernon Charles Swinburne   (1837–1909)
NEPHELIDIA   1880

From the depth of the dreamy decline of the dawn through a notable
   nimbus of nebulous noonshine,
   Pallid and pink as the palm of the flag-flower that flickers with fear
     of the flies as they float,
Are they looks of our lovers that lustrously lean from a marvel of
   mystic miraculous moonshine,
   These that we feel in the blood of our blushes that thicken and
     threaten with throbs through the throat?
Thicken and thrill as a theatre thronged at appeal of an actor's appalled   5
   agitation,
   Fainter with fear of the fires of the future than pale with the promise
     of pride in the past;
Flushed with the famishing fullness of fever that reddens with radiance
   of rathe recreation,
   Gaunt as the ghastliest of glimpses that gleam through the gloom of
     the gloaming when ghosts go aghast?
Nay, for the nick of the tick of the time is a tremulous touch on the
   temples of terror,
   Strained as the sinews yet strenuous with strife of the dead who is   10
     dumb as the dust-heaps of death:
Surely no soul is it, sweet as the spasm of erotic emotional exquisite
   error,
   Bathed in the balms of beatified bliss, beatific itself by beatitude's
     breath.
Surely no spirit or sense of a soul that was soft to the spirit and soul of
   our senses
   Sweetens the stress of suspiring suspicion that sobs in the semblance
     and sound of a sigh;
Only this oracle opens Olympian,° in mystical moods and triangular   15
   tenses—
   "Life is the lust of a lamp for the light that is dark till the dawn of
     the day when we die."

---

15 *Olympian:* Olympus was the mountain on which the Greek classical gods dwelt.

Mild is the mirk and monotonous music of memory, melodiously
    mute as it may be,
  While the hope in the heart of a hero is bruised by the breach of
    men's rapiers, resigned to the rod;
Made meek as a mother whose bosom-beats bound with the bliss-
    bringing bulk of a balm-breathing baby.
  As they grope through the grave-yard of creeds, under skies growing   20
    green at a groan for the grimness of God.
Blank is the book of his bounty beholden of old, and its binding is
    blacker than bluer:
  Out of blue into black is the scheme of the skies, and their dews are
    the wine of the bloodshed of things;
Till the darkling desire of delight shall be free as a fawn that is freed
    from the fangs that pursue her,
  Till the heart-beats of hell shall be hushed by a hymn from the hunt
    that has harried the kennel of kings.

7

Elements of Poetry

Most poets do not think about their poem's separate elements (although some do); they are too busy orchestrating feelings, ideas, and whatever else they feel will work. Because of this, examining elements separately is an artificial critical exercise. Nevertheless, it is useful, especially if you remember to put the poem back together again. A good close reading of a poem will depend on observing specific elements as they serve the purpose of the poet. Likewise, all interpretive strategies depend on the ability to be specific, to note special uses of language and special effects.

We can talk about two general kinds of poems: the **lyric** and the **narrative**. The lyric originates from ancient poems sung to a lyre, and the narrative was probably chanted with the accompaniment of a similar stringed instrument. Lyrics are short, such as Aphra Behn's "Song" (p. 586). Narratives are longer, such as Frost's "Home Burial" (p. 762). Included under the general class of lyrics are special forms such as sonnets, odes, and villanelles, discussed in this chapter. Poems such as *Paradise Lost*—much too long to be included here—are epics and therefore narrative poems. However, some of the longer poems in the album are clearly narratives, such as Robert Hayden's "Middle Passage" (p. 805) about the transportation of Africans to the new world. The line between lyric and narrative often blurs in longer forms such as ballads, but both kinds of poems rely upon the same elements.

We will focus on eight elements and their effects.

Language   Poets often become poets because they love language and are able to use it creatively and imaginatively. Poe's "tintinabulation" of the bells is a good example: he found a wonderful multisyllable word to contrast with *bells* and gave us a fresh look at a word that many of us will forever associate with bells and poetry. Some poems, such as "Letter to the Local Police" by

June Jordan (p. 806), are more *discursive* than imagistic; that is, they depend on the language of discourse—*telling* us something—more than on the use of imagery, which *shows* us something. Poetic language can be formal or informal, and it often plays on the connotations of words. The poet usually controls language not only through meaning but also through sound. **Euphony** is the term for words that sound good together. It is present in virtually any line of Poe's "The Bells" and in the first line of John Masefield's "Cargoes": "Quinquireme of Nineveh from distant Ophir." One hardly cares what the words mean (we will discuss this poem later) because they sound so musical. **Cacophony** refers to sounds that grate, annoy, or create a sense of distaste. John Milton, in *Paradise Lost*, uses cacophony to intensify the transformation of the devils into serpents in hell:

> dreadful was the din
> Of hissing through the Hall, thick swarming now
> With complicated monsters, head and tail,
> Scorpion and Asp, and *Amphisbaena* dire,
> *Cerastes* horn'd, *Hydrus*, and *Ellops* drear,
> And *Dipsas* (not so thick swarm'd once the Soil
> Bedropt with blood of *Gorgon*, or the Isle
> *Ophiusa*)
>
> > (X. 521–28)

Onomatopoeia imitates the sound it refers to James Thurber (p. 136) uses "ta-pocketa, ta-pocketa" to refer to the sound of imaginary machinery over which Walter Mitty presides in one of his daydreams. And Poe depends on onomatopoeia in "The Bells":

> To the tintinabulation that so musically wells
> > From the bells, bells, bells, bells,
> > > Bells, bells, bells—
> > From the jingling and the tinkling of the bells.

Imagery   Images appeal directly to one of the senses: touch, sight, hearing, smell, or taste. Imagist poets (see discussion on p. 747) make every effort to excite our responses through images rather than through discursive language. They want us to react to images in poetry the way we do in life. When we see a flower in nature, we respond directly to it, and when poets describe a flower as if it were in front of us, they expect us to recreate the image in our imagination and respond as directly as possible. When an image, such as Ezra Pound's "petals on a wet, black bough," appeals to two or more senses at the same time, it is said to possess **synaesthesia**.

Tone   Tone may be thought of as arising from the voice the poet projects. Poems can adopt any of the tones of voice that we use in conversation. They can be ironic, conversational, angry, satirical, or judgmental. The varieties of tone are virtually unlimited, and every poem must be examined on its own terms.

Rhythm and Rhyme   For many poets and readers the core of a poem is its **rhythm**, and some want all poems to have a regular beat. For other readers a poem is not a poem until it **rhymes**. We often refer to rhymed and metrical poetry as **verse** in order to make a cautious distinction between poetry in general and poems that have regular rhythms and rhymes. Although this term is used derisively by some important poets and critics, be aware that contemporary poetry often depends upon rhyme for its power and prose poetry depends on rhythm to signal that it is poetry.

Metaphor and Figurative Language   For many people **metaphor**, the implied comparison of two unlike things, instantly evokes the idea of poetry, since poetry achieves so many of its effects metaphorically. We often use metaphor in conversation: "You're chicken!" implies a comparison between "you" and the spineless chicken. Other devices related to metaphor are the simile, allegory, and symbol, discussed in this chapter. All of these function by means of comparisons that depend on the careful selection of certain qualities. For example, "You're chicken!" ignores the laying of eggs, the roosterly crowing in the morning, and all other qualities except the quality of cowardice. The chicken's scurrying away in haste is an emblem of fear, the quality we metaphorize. Metaphor is a kind of **figurative language**, which also includes such wordplays as puns and **oxymorons** (a contradiction such as "black light," or "hot ice"), as well as other devices.

Symbol and Allegory   **Symbols** are special forms of metaphor. A symbol may be universal in its nature, as when we say that "sailing westward" usually symbolizes preparation for death. But a symbol can also be more private, as in Robert Frost's "The Road Not Taken" (p. 766). For Frost, the symbol of the road may represent a professional path he might have chosen, but did not. For the reader, it may suggest something similar, but not exactly the same thing. Symbols, unlike **allegories**, are not fixed. Gerald Manley Hopkins uses allegory in "The Windhover," (p. 820) in which the Falcon is an allegory for Christ. They tend to respond to the context in which they are found, and consequently they are not always easy to identify. However, everyone uses symbols in language much of the time. Recognizing their use in poetry will help you see them in daily language, either spoken or written.

Form   All poems have form, but some forms are more specific than others. **Sonnets** have fourteen lines and usually rhyme according to one of several patterns. In some rare instances, a sonnet will have thirteen, or even sixteen lines, and will rhyme or not rhyme. **Quatrains** are groups of four rhyming lines, and although they do not usually function as whole poems, they are important forms within a poem. Some specialized forms, such as the **sestina** and the **villanelle**, depend on repeated lines, words, phrases, or rhymes to satisfy their formal requirements. Some forms are very tight and demanding, such as **haiku** (seventeen syllables in three lines of five, seven, and five syllables) and **terza rima** (three-line stanzas rhyming *aba, bcb, cdc,* and so on); others are relatively loose, such as the **epigram** (a short, pithy poem) and the **ode** (a long, irregular poem). Some poets feel they work best when the form is tight; others feel that tight forms limit creativity. Most of these forms are discussed on page 612.

Ideas Most poems contain ideas; very few do not. When we interpret a poem, we usually attempt to establish the nature of its ideas and their significance. Aristotle used the term *thought* and some critics use the term *theme* to describe the ideas the poet works with. **Theme** may be reductive because it implies that the poem has one idea, whereas most poems concerned with ideas have many. Although poems usually have a focus, sometimes even a "message," sometimes they ruminate on an idea, looking at it from several perspectives.

The most important point to remember is that poets use all these elements in most of their poems, and looking at only one of them represents a kind of distortion. Our efforts will be to attain a balance that will permit us to examine specific elements of a poem without losing sight of how they interact. The achievement of a poem results from the subtle cooperation of all of its elements.

LANGUAGE

Language is the stuff of poetry, and the love of words is probably as basic to the poet as love of color or form is to a painter. Poets love the way words sound, the way they surprise a reader with their shape or their many syllables, and the way words build up meanings through modern associations and an understanding of ancient roots. Some poets like uncommon words, like *vetch* or *gorse,* names for undergrowth and grasses. Some like words that have many possible meanings, such as *score,* which can mean something related to a sports event, a sexual event, or a manufacturing event, depending on its context.

In some poems the language is quite **formal**; in others it is very **informal**. The difference is in tone. Edward Hirsch's "Fast Break" (p. 642) begins informally with a description: "A hook shot kisses the rim and / Hangs there helplessly, but doesn't drop." It continues as if it were telling us about any special play in a basketball game. By contrast, William Wordsworth (1770–1850) is much more formal when he addresses the dead poet whom he most admired: "Milton! thou shouldst be living at this hour: / England hath need of thee: she is a fen / Of stagnant waters." The formality sets a tone of respect and admiration, whereas in Edward Hirsch's poem the tone is somewhat the opposite. Hirsch relies on the informal language of basketball and the easy tone of the sports buff.

Individual words can excite humorous or sad responses. Poe uses words in "The Bells" to excite emotions as diverse as the hopefulness of marriage and the despair of death. Sometimes a poet uses a word with a special emotional association, like "Balaclava," the site of a battle, or "Aghadoe," a place in Ireland that had meaning for the Irish poet John Todhunter (1839–1916). The first stanza of "Aghadoe" is as follows:

> There's a glade in Aghadoe, Aghadoe, Aghadoe,
> There's a green and silent glade in Aghadoe,
> Where we met, my love and I, Lover's fair planet in the sky,
> O'er that sweet and silent glade in Aghadoe.

Every stanza thereafter repeats *Aghadoe* at least four times while the lover tells the story of hiding her sweetheart from the British redcoats only to have him betrayed by her own brother. Through this repetition, the word *Aghadoe* builds up a melancholy power.

Repetition is also important in the following poem by T. S. Eliot, who wrote *Old Possum's Book of Practical Cats*, the basis of the long-running musical *Cats*. This poem repeats the name of its hero, Macavity, for comical effect.

T. S. Eliot (1888–1965)

MACAVITY: THE MYSTERY CAT   1939

> Macavity's a Mystery Cat: he's called the Hidden Paw—
> For he's the master criminal who can defy the Law.
> He's the bafflement of Scotland Yard, the Flying Squad's despair:
> For when they reach the scene of crime—*Macavity's not there!*
>
> Macavity, Macavity, there's no one like Macavity,   5
> He's broken every human law, he breaks the law of gravity.
> His powers of levitation would make a fakir stare,
> And when you reach the scene of crime—*Macavity's not there!*
> You may seek him in the basement, you may look up in the air—
> But I tell you once and once again, *Macavity's not there!*   10
>
> Macavity's a ginger cat, he's very tall and thin;
> You would know him if you saw him, for his eyes are sunken in.
> His brow is deeply lined with thought, his head is highly domed;
> His coat is dusty from neglect, his whiskers are uncombed.
> He sways his head from side to side, with movements like a snake;   15
> And when you think he's half asleep, he's always wide awake.

Macavity, Macavity, there's no one like Macavity,
For he's a fiend in feline shape, a monster of depravity.
You may meet him in a by-street, you may see him in the square—
But when a crime's discovered, then *Macavity's not there!*   20

He's outwardly respectable. (They say he cheats at cards.)
And his footprints are not found in any file of Scotland Yard's.
And when the larder's looted, or the jewel-case is rifled,
Or when the milk is missing, or another Peke's° been stifled,
Or the greenhouse glass is broken, and the trellis past repair—   25
Ay, there's the wonder of the thing! *Macavity's not there!*

And when the Foreign Office find a Treaty's gone astray,
Or the Admiralty lose some plans and drawings by the way,
There may be a scrap of paper in the hall or on the stair—
But it's useless to investigate—*Macavity's not there!*   30
And when the loss has been disclosed, the Secret Service say:
"It *must* have been Macavity!"—but he's a mile away.
You'll be sure to find him resting, or a-licking of his thumbs,
Or engaged in doing complicated long division sums.

Macavity, Macavity, there's no one like Macavity,   35
There never was a Cat of such deceitfulness and suavity.
He always has an alibi, and one or two to spare:
At whatever time the deed took place—MACAVITY WASN'T
     THERE!
And they say that all the Cats whose wicked deeds are widely known
(I might mention Mungojerrie, I might mention Griddlebone)   40
Are nothing more than agents for the Cat who all the time
Just controls their operations: the Napoleon of Crime!

24 *Peke*: Pekinese dog.

The refrain "Macavity, Macavity, there's no one like Macavity" runs throughout the poem. *Gravity* rhymes humorously with *Macavity*, since the two words are inappropriate together, except for their sound. *Depravity* may seem more appropriate, given Macavity's predilection for crime, and *suavity* fits in with his jewel-thief activities. In addition, excursions into the informal language of the criminal world—"Hidden Paw," "bafflement of Scotland Yard," "when the larder's looted," and the final touch, "the Napoleon of Crime!"—tend to inflate the situation to the point of absurdity. Eliot pushes Macavity's crimes from the trivial breaking of the "greenhouse glass" to the cosmic importance of the Admiralty's treaty; having gone astray, it is also, in a sense, broken.

The following poem also uses a mixture of formal and informal language to link high seriousness with the preposterous. The poem is about hell—

Beelzebub is the "Lord of the Flies," another name for Satan—but instead of being fearful, the author is sometimes silly.

Edith Sitwell (1887–1964)

SIR BEELZEBUB 1922

When
Sir
Beelzebub called for his syllabub in the hotel in Hell
      Where Proserpine first fell,
Blue as the gendarmerie were the waves of the sea   5

      (Rocking and shocking the bar-maid).

Nobody comes to give him his rum but the
Rim of the sky hippopotamus-glum
Enhances the chances to bless with a benison
Alfred Lord Tennyson crossing the bar laid   10
With cold vegetation from pale deputations
Of temperance workers (all signed In Memoriam)
Hoping with glory to trip up the Laureate's feet

      (Moving in classical metres) . . .

Like Balaclava, the lava came down from the   15
Roof, and the sea's blue wooden gendarmerie
Took them in charge while Beelzebub roared for his rum.

      . . . None of them come!

The slow opening lines, each consisting of one word, prepare us for seriousness, but then the third line moves embarrassingly fast, with an internal rhyme in *Beelzebub* and *syllabub* and a reference to a "hotel in Hell," another internal rhyme. These are here for fun. A syllabub is a frothy dessert made of wine and cream and not likely to hold up to the rigors of Hell's weather. What is it doing here? It's rhyming. That is its entire function, and we enjoy it on that level. Even the comparison of the "gendarmerie"—the French police, who wear dark blue uniforms—with the sea is silly. The "bar-maid" seems out of place, too, but it reveals another function of language: **allusion** (reference to another work of literature). Not every reader will know Alfred Lord Tennyson (1809–1892), the poet laureate of England, but those who do may recognize the allusion to his poems "Crossing the Bar" (1889) (thus getting in the "bar-maid") and "In Memoriam" (1850), about the death of a friend. Because they are about death, Tennyson's poems credit the underworld with power (Proserpine is the classical goddess of the underworld, Hades). But Sitwell refers to them after complaining that Beelzebub sits "hippopotamus-glum" because no one brings him his rum. Then, what does "Like Balaclava, the lava" really mean? Balaclava is another allusion to Tennyson, this time through the site of the cavalry madness memorialized in Tennyson's "Charge of the Light Brigade" (1854), but it has little to do with lava, except for the rhyme. Thus Sitwell manages to be funny and serious at the same time.

A final distinction of language is that of connotation and denotation. A word's **denotation** is what it means on the dictionary level: a *rat* is a rodent. **Connotation** is what it means on an emotional level: a *rat* is a person you don't trust. Poems often exploit the double meanings of connotation and denotation.

In the following poem, note how snatches of common phrases are juxtaposed for satirical effect. While you first read it, examine the unusual uses of conversational tone and voice as well as the background voice which interrupts from time to time. Moreover, the reliance on juxtaposing informal with formal language as well as playing with denotation and connotation make this poem both challenging and amusing to read.

E. E. Cummings   (1894–1962)

POEM,OR BEAUTY HURTS MR.VINAL   1926

take it from me kiddo
believe me
my country,'tis of

you, land of the Cluett
Shirt Boston Garter and Spearmint   5
Girl With The Wrigley Eyes(of you
land of the Arrow Ide
and Earl &
Wilson
Collars)of you i   10
sing: land of Abraham Lincoln and Lydia E. Pinkham,°
land above all of Just Add Hot Water And Serve—
from every B.V.D.

let freedom ring

amen. i do however protest,anent the un   15
-spontaneous and otherwise scented merde which
greets one(Everywhere Why)as divine poesy per
that and this radically defunct periodical. i would

suggest that certain ideas gestures
rhymes,like Gillette Razor Blades   20

---

11 *Lydia E. Pinkham*: Inventor of a woman's patent medicine for anemia.

having been used and reused
to the mystical moment of dullness emphatically are
Not To Be Resharpened. (Case in point

if we are to believe these gently O sweetly
melancholy trillers amid the thrillers   25
these crepuscular violinists among my and your
skyscrapers—Helen & Cleopatra were Just Too Lovely,
The Snail's On The Thorn° enter Morn and God's
In His andsoforth

do you get me?)according   30
to such supposedly indigenous
throstles° Art is O World O Life
a formula:example,Turn Your Shirttails Into
Drawers and If It Isn't An Eastman It Isn't A
Kodak therefore my friends let   35
us now sing each and all fortissimo A-
mer
i

ca,I
love,   40
You. And there're a
hun-dred-mil-lion-oth-ers,like
all of you successfully if
delicately gelded(or spaded)
gentlemen(and ladies)—pretty   45

littleliverpill-
hearted-Nujolneeding°-There's-A-Reason
americans(who tensetendoned and with
upward vacant eyes,painfully
perpetually crouched,quivering,upon the   50
sternly allotted sandpile
—how silently
emit a tiny violetflavoured nuisance:Odor?

ono.
comes out like a ribbon lies flat on the brush   55

28 *Snail's . . . Thorn*: Parody of second-rate poetry.   32 *throstles*: thrush, or songbird.
47 *Nujolneeding*: Patent medicine, a tonic.

Questions for Close Reading

1. Find the echoes of "My Country, 'Tis of Thee," which begin in the third
   line and which continue to break through every so often. Does Cummings
   make it difficult for you to "hear" the echoes in this poem?

2. Identify the different kinds of language Cummings uses. Which lines are conversational and colloquial, like the first? Which lines suggest the language of advertising, like the last?

3. Some lines suggest an artificiality, a kind of hoity-toity tone, such as "Art is O World O Life." Find other examples of that tone. What is the point of using such language?

4. Cummings uses the obsolete word *anent*, meaning "regarding." In the next line he uses a French word for shit: *merde*. What effect does he get by using these words?

5. Advertising is basic to the poem. What product names can you find? Which ones are still being advertised? Why does Cummings emphasize advertising to such an extent?

Bessie Smith is known throughout the world as a blues singer. The blues, which is related to jazz, was extremely popular in the United States during the depression of the 1930s. At that time it was thought to be a basically disreputable kind of music and was therefore inappropriate for "polite" society. Bessie Smith usually sang with a very small group, piano, drums, and guitar, and she wrote many of her own tunes. "Empty Bed Blues" is typical of her songs. Its language is informal, virtually conversational, sometimes casual speech. The use of connotation—"coffee grinder" and "brand new grind" rely on double-meaning for effect—is a chief linguistic element of the poem.

Bessie Smith   (1894–1937)
EMPTY BED BLUES   1928

> I woke up this mornin'
> With an awful achin' head,
> I woke up this mornin'
> With an awful achin' head,
> My new man had left me,   5
> Just a room and an empty bed.
>
> Bought me a coffee grinder,
> The best one I could find.
> Bought me a coffee grinder,
> The best one I could find.   10
> Oh, he could grind my coffee,
> 'Cause he had a brand-new grind.
>
> He's deep, deep diver,
> With a stroke that can't go wrong.
> He's deep, deep diver,   15
> With a stroke that can't go wrong.

Oh, he can touch the bottom,
And his wind holds out so long.

He knows how to thrill me,
And he thrills me night and day.   20
He knows how to thrill me,
And he thrills me night and day.
He's got a new way of lovin',
Almost takes my breath away.

Lord, he's got that sweet somethin',   25
And I told my gal-friend Lu.
He's got that sweet somethin',
And I told my gal-friend Lu.
For the way she's ravin',
She must have gone and tried it too.   30

When my bed is empty,
Makes me feel awful mean and blue.
When my bed is empty,
Makes me feel awful mean and blue.
My springs are getting rusty,   35
Living single like I do.

Bought him a blanket,
Pillow for his head at night.
Bought him a blanket,
Pillow for his head at night.   40
Then I bought him a mattress,
So he could lay just right.

He came home one ev'nin',
With his spirit way up high.
He came home one ev'nin',   45
With his spirit way up high.
What he had to give me
Made we wring my hands and cry.

He gave me a lesson
That I never had before.   50
He gave me a lesson
That I never had before.
When he got through teachin',
From my elbows down was sore.

He boiled first my cabbage,   55
And he made it awful hot.
He boiled first my cabbage,

And he made it awful hot.
When he put in the bacon,
It overflowed the pot.   60

When you get good lovin',
Never go and spread the news.
When you get good lovin',
Never go and spread the news.
Else he'll double-cross you   65
And leave you with them empty bed blues.

Questions for Close Reading

1. Which language in the poem is especially formal or informal? What qualities establish it one way or the other?
2. Because this is a song, each stanza is sung to the same melody. What special uses of language help you identify the poem as appropriate for singing? Would you find it possible to "invent" a tune and sing it just from looking at the words?
3. The blues and jazz music always contained sexual overtones. The title of this poem directly introduces a sexual theme. However, most of the poem depends on double entendre—or the difference between denotation and connotation—for its effect. Go through the poem stanza by stanza. Does every stanza make use of the difference between denotation and connotation? Which stanzas do so most effectively?
4. To some readers, this poem might be immoral. Why? What is the "moral" in the last stanza of the poem?

IMAGERY

Some poems depend upon **images** for their effect: they impress us with a visual, aural, or tactile description much like a painting or melody. Images are said to be "concrete" because they cause us to imagine a sensation on the basis of our personal experience. Poets who use images rely on their knowledge of the reader's experience, but they also try to control the reader's responses. Thus when Carol Rumens mentions "cellophaned flowers," she does not tell us what kind they are, but we imagine floral colors showing through a crinkly, shiny cellophane.

The imagist poets of the early twentieth century (discussed on p. 747) felt that no poem was truly poetic unless it expressed itself entirely through images. They discounted discursive poetry because it argued with the reader, discoursed on philosophy, or told instead of showed what something meant. In other words, discursive poetry depended on abstract language, language that is not rooted in a sensory experience. To say, "my heart is sad and weary" is to use abstract language, since no one can perceive a heart being sad and weary. One of the most famous of the imagist poems is by the American Ezra Pound. Its title refers to a subway platform in Paris, where the subway is called the Metro.

Ezra Pound   (1885–1972)

IN A STATION OF THE METRO   1916

The apparition of these faces in the crowd;
Petals on a wet, black bough.

By reading Chinese poets, Pound found a way of compressing his language, focusing his vision, and suggesting his emotional state through images. Each line offers a visual image. The first is straightforward: faces in a crowd, something we would expect in a subway station. However, by using the word *apparition*, Pound gives the image a special quality, suggesting the ghostlike passing of faces. The second line, in using the word *wet*, appeals to our sense of touch as well as sight. We can imagine the petals of a recently flowered tree on wet, springtime branches. They resemble the faces in the crowd, but Pound does not tell us that they are "like" the faces. Instead, he provides two separate images that we can relate in our own mind. The poem says what it has to say in terms of imagery. We are not told what to think about the images, nor how to link them.

Ordinarily, images do not constitute an entire poem but rather appear within it. In Carol Rumens's "An Easter Garland," images such as flowers are focal points. The reader recreates the flowers in the imagination and then explores their implications.

Carol Rumens   (b. 1944)

AN EASTER GARLAND   1983

I

The flowers did not seem to unfurl from slow bulbs.
They were suddenly there,
shivering swimmers on the edge of a gala
—nude whites and yellows shocking the raw air.
They'd switched themselves on like streetlamps   5
waking at dawn, feeling wrong,
to blaze nervously all day at the chalky sky.
Are they masks, the frills on bruised babies?
I can't believe in them,
as I can't believe in the spruces and lawns and bricks   10
they publicize, the misted light of front lounges
twinned all the way down the road,

twinned like their occupants, little weather-house people
who hide inside and do not show their tears
—the moisture that drives one sadly to a doorway.   15

II

My father explained the workings of the weather-house
as if he seriously loved such things,
told me why Grandpa kept a blackening tress
of seaweed in the hall.
He was an expert on atmosphere,   20
having known a weight of dampness
—the fog in a sick brother's lungs
where he lost his childhood; later, the soft squalls
of marriage and the wordier silences.
In the atmosphere of the fire   25
that took him back to bone
and beyond bone, he smiled.
The cellophaned flowers outside
went a slower way, their sweat
dappling the linings of their glassy hoods.   30

III

My orphaned grass
is standing on tiptoe to look for you.
Your last gift to a work-shy daughter
was to play out and regather
the slow thread of your breath   35
behind the rattling blades,
crossing always to darker green,
till the lawn was a well-washed quilt
drying, the palest on the line,
and you rested over the handlebars   40
like a schoolboy, freewheeling
through your decades of green-scented, blue,
suburban English twilights.

IV

In the lonely garden of the page,
something has happened to your silence.   45
The stone cloud has rolled off.
You make yourself known,
as innocently abrupt
as the flared wings of the almond,
cherry, magnolia;   50
and I, though stupid with regret,

would not be far wrong
if I took you for the gardener.

The title of the poem reveals that the season is spring, and the flowers, because they come from bulbs, are daffodils and/or tulips. The image of the bulb is carried over into the image of the streetlamps, and the flowers "switched themselves on," suggesting an electric image. Rumens explores the possibilities of her imagery in surprising and refreshing ways. The sky is not just overcast but "chalky," a term that gives us a concrete impression. She sees the flowers as swimmers in the air: "nude whites and yellows." A tactile image is invoked with "the raw air." The flowers "blaze" all day, like confused streetlamps. They "publicize" "spruces and lawns and bricks."

The appeal to the senses continues throughout the poem. In line 13, Rumens invokes a new image, that of "weather-house people," figures in a mechanical house that come out to indicate a change: a figure in a raincoat for rain, a figure in a sun suit for sunny days. The second stanza focuses on weather, making the abstract quality of "dampness" concrete by giving it "weight" (line 21). Dampness is a "fog" in a "brother's lungs." All these are perceptible images. Even the arguments of marriage, the "soft squalls," are expressed in weather imagery. The third stanza invokes memories of the speaker's father, who mowed the lawn until it looked like a "well-washed quilt." The final stanza refers to "the page"—presumably the page on which she writes—as being a kind of garden similar to the garden her father tended for decades. The image of the "stone cloud" can refer to the stony-colored overcast sky or to the stone that may be the father's headstone. The father makes himself "known," much as the flowers of the first stanza: abruptly, without warning, coming up of a sudden—but here in the imagination of the speaker. She associates him with the "almond, cherry, magnolia" trees blossoming in this Easter scene. When she thinks of him as "the gardener," she implies that she, too, has been tended by his hand.

The following poem uses unusual images.

Henri Coulette   (1927–1988)

CORRESPONDENCE   1990

The letter lies unanswered, thus free of lies.
The light all day has travelled the crowded pages,
Shifting the shadows, changing the hue of ink.
The truths, if truths there are, are stationary.

Now night comes on, from your time zone to mine.   5
The moon is tentative, not wholly herself,
And the owl bells, and the owl's mate bells back,
A dialogue of sorts, question and answer,

The answer being but the question asked.
East of your sleep, deep in the zodiac,   10
Tomorrow is already chronicled.
Oh, I shall write you what you want to hear.

Questions for Close Reading

1. What images are suggested by the second line? Are they purely visual, or do they suggest other sensory experience?
2. If the word *stationary* is a pun on *stationery*, would it then be an image?
3. What imagery do you recreate in line 6: "The moon is tentative, not wholly herself"? What is suggested by making the moon's gender female? Is that an image?
4. Are there any images in the third stanza?

Many poems refer to paintings or visual artists, and sometimes they attempt to interpret a painting or work of art. The following poem is about the impressionist painter Paul Gauguin (1848–1903), who spent part of his life as a painter in France.

Andrew Hudgins   (b. 1951)
GAUGUIN: THE YELLOW CHRIST   1990

After the last harvest, when the fields
are stripped of grain and trees blaze orange,
three peasant women walk
out of their blue-roofed houses, trudge

through barren fields and kneel, heads bowed,   5
before the yellow Christ. Gauguin has chosen
a dying meadow near their village
to paint his last cross, spread his arms

and nail himself to its
enormous dark-brown reaching. Gauguin: 10
there's no mistaking that thin beard,
that face, that tilt of head. But even

the artist knows it isn't he
the women walk so far to worship.
He is no longer Paul Gauguin.   15
Bright yellow tinged with green—just like

the autumn fields stretched out behind him—
he's Christ. He's harvested: cut, bundled,

and, like a last shock of late wheat,
left in the field past gathering.   20

And this Christ knows he's dying. He yearns
to return—budding, green—to blossom,
seed, wither, die, and come again.
The women gathered at his feet

pray they will live the winter through,   25
pray they will eat, keep warm, and prosper.
But Christ, who was once Paul Gauguin,
sags on his cross. The yellow hills,

the yellow valleys and the gleaned,
dry yellow hills—all dying—call,   30
O Son of Man, we're coming back.
Put down your soul and follow us.

Questions for Close Reading

1. Which images are most dependent on colors? Which colors are mentioned,
   and how do you feel they would work in a painting?
2. Gauguin is described in stanza 3. How effective is that imagery? How "concrete" is it?
3. The poem is filled with imagery associated with harvest and autumn. Which
   of those images strikes you as most powerful?
4. Identify the religious images. Which ones work best for you? Why might
   some readers think the line "But Christ, who was once Paul Gauguin"
   would be in bad taste? What does Hudgins mean by it? Is that line an example of imagery?

The author of the following poem was a pilot in the U. S. Air Force from
1957 to 1971, through the Vietnam War. "The Food Pickers of Saigon,"
which contrasts many images, is set on the edges of Tan Son Nhut, the largest
airfield in South Vietnam and the center of most U.S. air activity during the
war.

Walter McDonald   (b. 1934)

THE FOOD PICKERS OF SAIGON   1987

Rubbish like compost heaps burned every hour
of my days and nights at Tan Son Nhut.
Ragpickers scoured the edges of our junk,

risking the flames, bent over,
searching for food. A ton of tin cans   5

piled up each month, sharp-edged, unlabeled.
Those tiny anonymous people could stick
their hands inside and claw out whatever
remained, scooping it into jars, into their
mouths. No one went hungry. At a distance,   10

the dump was like a coal mine fire burning
out of control, or Moses' holy bush
which was not consumed. Watching them labor
in the field north of my barracks, trying
to think of something good to write my wife,   15

I often thought of bears in Yellowstone
our first good summer in a tent. I wrote
about the bears, helping us both focus
on how they waddled to the road and begged,
and came some nights into the campground   20

so long ago and took all food they found.
We sat helplessly naive outside our tent
and watched them, and one night rolled
inside laughing when one great bear
turned and shoulder-swayed his way toward us.   25

Through the zipped mosquito netting
we watched him watching us. Slack-jawed,
he seemed to grin, to thank us for all
he was about to receive from our table.
We thought how lovely, how much fun   30

to be this close to danger. No campers
had died in that Disneyland national park
for years. Now, when my children
eat their meat and bread and leave
good broccoli or green beans   35

on their plates, I call them back
and growl, I can't help it. It's like hearing
my father's voice again. I never tell them
why they have to eat it. I never say
they're like two beautiful children   40

I found staring at me one night
through the screen of my window,
at Tan Son Nhut, bone-faced. Or that
when I crawled out of my stifling monsoon
dream to feed them, they were gone.   45

Questions for Close Reading

1. Some stanzas concentrate on a powerful image. Which words in the first stanza produce images for you? Is the imagery purely descriptive, or does it suggest comparisons like the *bulb-streetlamps* comparisons in Carol Rumens's poem?
2. What imagery does the verb *claw* produce for you in stanza 2?
3. In stanza 3, McDonald thinks of a religious image, the burning bush in Genesis that flamed but was not burned up. Is a religious image appropriate? What is its effect?
4. What effect is gained by the bear imagery in stanzas 4, 5, and 6? This imagery introduces a comic element. Is that appropriate for this poem? Disneyland calls up many images. How does it work in stanza 7?
5. Two contrasting images of children dominate the last three stanzas. Why does McDonald present them to us? To what extent do images haunt him?

TONE

The manner in which something is said—its **tone**—controls much of what we perceive in a poem. Some poems are ironic, in that they seem to speak of their subject approvingly only to reveal at the last minute that they do not approve at all. Laments, usually questioning the death of a loved one, can be sad, angry, resigned, or distressed. Conversational poems imitate various tones we hear in people's voices: joy, irritation, despair, agony, and grief. Other poems are explicitly satirical. They may satirize a person, an office, an institution, or society by being scornful or by ridiculing its faults.

Irish poets have been so famous for their satirical wit that kings were careful of their behavior when in the company of a satirist to avoid being attacked in a poem that might outlast them for generations. No one wanted to be the butt of an Irish satirist. The following is an adaptation from a seventeenth-century Irish poet named David O'Bruadair from Limerick. Stephens reshaped the poem so as to attack a bar maid who "cut him off" from his drink. In Stephens' hands, satire becomes a weapon.

James Stephens   (1880–1950)

A GLASS OF BEER   1918

> The lanky hank of a she in the inn over there
> Nearly killed me for asking the loan of a glass of beer;
> May the devil grip the whey-faced slut by the hair,
> And beat bad manners out of her skin for a year.
>
> That parboiled ape, with the toughest jaw you will see   5
> On virtue's path, and a voice that would rasp the dead,

Came roaring and raging the minute she looked at me,
And threw me out of the house on the back of my head!

If I asked her master he'd give me a cask a day;
But she, with the beer at hand, not a gill would arrange!   10
May she marry a ghost and bear him a kitten, and may
The High King of Glory permit her to get the mange.

Part of the vehemence of the poem comes from Stephens's ability to cast a curse on "the whey-faced slut" who refused him a glass of beer. He insults her in every way he can. This phrase casts doubt on her morals; her apelike jaw is emblematic of her toughness; and her voice would raise the dead. Her physical size is implied by the fact that she threw him out of the inn on his head. The last two lines are typical of the terrible curses the Irish poets could cast on their victims. The voice of the poet railing against the barmaid is so loud that it nearly masks the regularity of the lines and the rhyme scheme. Of course, this version and O'Bruadair's both conveniently omit any discussion of what their behavior might have been in the inn and why the barmaid responded so fiercely.

The tone of the following poem is totally different: it is whimsical, filled with anticipation, joy, and the enthusiastic use of ritual cries.

Judith Rodriguez   (b. 1936)

ESKIMO OCCASION   1976

I am in my Eskimo-hunting-song mood,
Aha!
The lawn is tundra   the car will not start
the sunlight is an avalanche   we are avalanche-struck at our
                                                      breakfast   5
struck with sunlight through glass   me and my spoon-fed
                                               daughters
out of this world in our kitchen.

I will sing the song of my daughter-hunting,
Oho!   10
The waves lay down   the ice grew strong
I sang the song   of dark water under ice
the song of winter fishing   the magic for seal rising
among the ancestor-masks.

I waited by water to dream new spirits,   15
Hoo!
The water spoke   the ice shouted
the sea opened   the sun made young shadows

they breathed my breathing   I took them from deep water
I brought them fur-warmed home.   20

I am dancing the years of the two great hunts,
Ya-hay!
It was I who waited   cold in the wind-break
I stamp like the bear   I call like the wind of the thaw
I leap like the sea spring-running.   My sunstruck daughters   25
                                                    splutter
and chuckle and bang their spoons:

Mummy is singing at breakfast and dancing!
So big!

The Australian Judith Rodriguez is a poet of many moods, and as she
says in this poem, "I am in my Eskimo-hunting-song mood." The tone depends on certain devices. The interjection of the dance cries, "Aha!", "Oho!",
"Hoo!", "Ya-hay!", and the final cry, "So big!", are amusing and light spirited. They also remind those who have seen Inuit dances of the joy of the
"tundra." The lines are broken into **hemistichs**; that is, each line is separated
in the middle by a pause. Much of the tone seems formal, perhaps because
the Eskimo culture is foreign to most readers. Rodriguez adopts an Eskimo
persona because she is in the right "mood" and can adopt any persona she
wishes. Now that we have her model we can do so ourselves.

A. E. Housman, the author of the next poem, was a classics professor at
University College, London, and later at Cambridge. The title of his poem,
"Terence, This Is Stupid Stuff," seems at first to allude to the Roman playwright Terence, but in fact it refers to the persona Housman invented for his
volume of poems, *A Shropshire Lad*, which was going to be called *The Poems
of Terence Hearsay*. In other words, Housman is satirizing himself, as well as
other things along the way. The poem's most famous lines are "Malt does
more than Milton can / To justify God's ways to man," which indirectly, of
course, satirizes John Milton, who wrote the great epic *Paradise Lost* to justify the ways of God to man.

A. E. Housman   (1859–1936)

TERENCE, THIS IS STUPID STUFF   1896

  "Terence, this is stupid stuff:
You eat your victuals fast enough;
There can't be much amiss, 'tis clear,
To see the rate you drink your beer.
But oh, good Lord, the verse you make,   5
It gives a chap the belly-ache.
The cow, the old cow, she is dead;

It sleeps well, the horned head:
We poor lads, 'tis our turn now
To hear such tunes as killed the cow. 10
Pretty friendship 'tis to rhyme
Your friends to death before their time
Moping melancholy mad:
Come, pipe a tune to dance to, lad."

   Why, if 'tis dancing you would be, 15
There's brisker pipes than poetry.
Say, for what were hop-yards meant,
Or why was Burton built on Trent?°
Oh many a peer of England brews
Livelier liquor than the Muse, 20
And malt does more than Milton can
To justify God's ways to man.
Ale, man, ale's the stuff to drink
For fellows whom it hurts to think:
Look into the pewter pot 25
To see the world as the world's not.
And faith, 'tis pleasant till 'tis past:
The mischief is that 'twill not last.
Oh I have been to Ludlow fair
And left my necktie God knows where, 30
And carried half-way home, or near,
Pints and quarts of Ludlow beer:
Then the world seemed none so bad,
And I myself a sterling lad;
And down in lovely muck I've lain, 35
Happy till I woke again.
Then I saw the morning sky:
Heigho, the tale was all a lie;
The world, it was the old world yet,
I was I, my things were wet, 40
And nothing now remained to do
But begin the game anew.

   Therefore, since the world has still
Much good, but much less good than ill,
And while the sun and moon endure 45
Luck's a chance, but trouble's sure,
I'd face it as a wise man would,
And train for ill and not for good.
'Tis true, the stuff I bring for sale
Is not so brisk a brew as ale: 50

18 *Burton . . . Trent*: Burton-on-Trent was famous for its breweries.

Out of a stem that scored the hand°
I wrung it in a weary land.
But take it: if the smack is sour,
The better for the embittered hour;
It should do good to heart and head   55
When your soul is in my soul's stead;
And I will friend you, if I may,
In the dark and cloudy day.

There was a king reigned in the East:
There, when kings will sit to feast,   60
They get their fill before they think
With poisoned meat and poisoned drink.
He gathered all that springs to birth
From the many-venomed earth;
First a little, thence to more,   65
He sampled all her killing store;
And easy, smiling, seasoned sound,
Sate the king when healths went round.
They put arsenic in his meat
And stared aghast to watch him eat;   70
They poured strychnine in his cup
And shook to see him drink it up:
They shook, they stared as white's their shirt:
Them it was their poison hurt.
—I tell the tale that I heard told.   75
Mithridates,° he died old.

51 *stem . . . hand*: Housman implies the pen that scores the hand.   75 *Mithridates*: Mithridates
VI (c. 132–63 B.C.) was king of Pontus, an ancient kingdom in Asia Minor.

Questions for Close Reading

1. The first stanza, which addresses Terence, assesses Terence's poetry. What
   is that assessment? What apparently is the effect of his poetry on others?
   Why does the speaker establish in lines 1 and 2 that Terence is eating well?
2. The second stanza, which begins Terence's reply, talks about the effects
   of beer and ale on Terence, who is well experienced with them both. What
   are those effects, and in what tone does Terence inform us of them?
3. The tone alters in stanza 3. Is this stanza more or less serious than the first
   two? Is it more or less optimistic about the world?
4. Stanza 4 tells of Mithridates VI, who made himself immune to poison by
   taking it in small quantities. What is the relationship between Mithridates
   and Terence? What is the relationship between the speaker of the first
   stanza and "Them" in "Them it was their poison hurt"?

5. Compare the tone of the first stanza with the tone of the last stanza. Would you conclude that the overall tone of the poem is one of seriousness? Satire? Light humor?

The next poem has yet another tone. Ben Jonson, the first English poet laureate, made a living with his pen and knew Shakespeare. Venerated as "rare Ben," he lived a life of robust adventure in and out of the social world of king and court. He killed a man in a duel, got into trouble for political innuendoes in his dramatic work, and wrote gala entertainments in the royal courts of Queen Elizabeth and King James. "On My First Son," however, was written for a private occasion.

Ben Jonson   (1572–1637)

ON MY FIRST SON   1616 (1603?)

Farewell, thou child of my right hand, and joy;
My sin was too much hope of thee, loved boy,
Seven years thou wert lent to me, and I thee pay,
Exacted by thy fate, on the just day.°
O, could I lose all father,° now. For why   5
Will man lament the state he should envy?
To have so soon 'scaped world's, and flesh's rage,
And, if no other misery, yet age!
Rest in soft peace, and, asked, say here doth lie
Ben Jonson his best piece of poetry.   10
For whose sake, henceforth, all his vows be such,
As what he loves may never like too much.

4 *Exacted . . . day*: His son is a "loan" he must repay God. His son died on his seventh birthday.   5 *could . . . father*: Now he could renounce fatherhood entirely.

Questions for Close Reading

1. The poem addresses Jonson's dead son. What tone of voice does Jonson seem to be using? Is there an unusual tone of frankness to his mode of address? Is he sad, resigned, content, dissatisfied? Can you tell from the tone of the poem how he feels?
2. Jonson's child was named Benjamin, meaning "child of my right hand." But the expression "to sit at my right hand" also implies offering someone a favorite spot, and therefore recognizes the child's importance. How would you describe the tone of the first line? Does it evoke a response in you?
3. This poem is a lament. However, in lines 5–6 the poet questions his reasons for lamenting his son's death. How does this questioning affect the tone?

4. Why does Jonson call his son "his best piece of poetry"? What is his resolution now that he has lost his son? Is his resolution offered in a different tone?

Of course, tone also suggests a certain actual tone of voice, and the poet has great power to suggest how a poem should be read aloud, just as dramatists can control the tone of their dialogues. **Dramatic monologues** present one side of a conversation, one voice that the reader "hears." There are several examples of this convention in this book. Sometimes it narrates an event, as in Robert Frost's "Mending Wall" (p. 607) and "Birches" (p. 659). But it may also be a conversation with oneself, as in Housman's "Terence, This Is Stupid Stuff" (p. 580), which appears to be a lighthearted tongue-lashing of the poet by himself: "There can't be much amiss, 'tis clear, / To see the rate you drink your beer." E. E. Cummings's "Poem, or Beauty Hurts Mr. Vinal" (p. 567), is another monologue, one side of an imaginary conversation: "take it from me kiddo / believe me." One of the most famous examples of the dramatic monologue is Robert Browning's "My Last Duchess" (p. 703). In this poem, a man shows a guest a painting of his late wife, all the while explaining his attitudes toward her in a way that reveals his own shortcomings and limitations. An **internal dramatic monologue**—a stream-of-consciousness version of the dramatic monologue—is used in T.S. Eliot's "The Love Song of J. Alfred Prufrock" (p. 752). Finally, Allen Ginsburg's "Howl" (p. 776) may represent a special form of dramatic monologue in the form of an angry poet ranting against the culture that oppresses him. The varieties of tone possible in dramatic monologue are unlimited.

RHYTHM AND RHYME

The spelling of *rhythm* and *rhyme* indicate their close relationship and imply their importance to the poet. **Rhythm** is the pacing, from slow to fast, and the pauses, stops, and starts that we perceive as we speak or read the words and lines of a poem. When read aloud, some lines demand a slow, stately, even tempo. Other lines lurch and jostle, hip and hop, or bounce and lope. Some poems demand a slow beginning, a fast middle, and a slower ending.

End-stopped lines have a pause at the end of the line, usually indicated by punctuation. **Run-on lines** force you to read beyond their end into the beginning of the next line; the use of these lines is called **enjambment**. When Andrew Marvell (1621–1678) wrote the following lines, he had survived the English Civil War and was looking back on prewar England as a peaceful, paradisal garden. However, his recollections of soldiers and sentinels still produced a marchlike movement:

> See how the flowers, as at parade,   *a*
> Under their colors stand displayed;   *a*

Each regiment in order grows,   *b*
That of the tulip, pink, and rose.   *b*

All these lines are end-stopped, some more completely than others. The lines that end with a comma are pauses; those that end with a semicolon or period are full stops. Breaks within the lines are called **caesuras**. The first line has a caesura after the comma, just as the commas in the last lines provide more pauses. Sometimes a caesura brings you to a complete halt, but more often it simply indicates a pause, as in these lines. In Marvell's time, end-stopped lines were the norm for English poetry.

These four lines also illustrate **rhyme**, or regular sound patterns. The two couplets rhyme in the pattern *aa, bb*. Marvell uses masculine rhyme (see below), in which only the last syllable of the first line echoes the last syllable of the next line: *-ade, -played* and *grows, rose*.

Types of Rhyme

Masculine Rhyme   One syllable rhymes: *still, fill*.

Feminine Rhyme   Two syllables rhyme: *Balaclava, lava*.

Slant Rhyme   Sounds almost echo each other: *mousse, clues*.

Assonantal Rhyme   Vowels echo each other: *tube, mood*.

Consonantal Rhyme   Consonants echo each other: *klutz, blitz*.

Internal Rhyme   End word rhymes with a word in the middle of the same line or another nearby line: *turned the air, a prayer*.

Eye Rhyme   Words look alike but do not sound alike: *blood, food*.

All but the first two of these are **off-rhymes**, not quite true rhymes. Specialized versions of these off-rhymes exist, such as rhyming only the first or last consonant in rhyme words. Many poets want to avoid the closure or end-stopping of Marvell's rhymes but still maintain the discipline of rhyme by using slant, assonantal, or consonantal rhyme techniques.

Aphra Behn, the first professional woman playwright in England, led an adventurous life and is rumored to have been a spy in Europe. She visited South America with her husband and wrote a novel about her adventures called *Oroonoko* (c. 1688). Her "Song" is typical of the late seventeenth century in its rhythm and its rhyme. The lines maintain a regular **meter**: they measure their syllables into units or **metrical feet**. The usual metrical foot in English is **iambic**: an unaccented syllable followed by an accented syllable: ˘ ´. The word *begin* follows that pattern: its first syllable is unaccented and its second syllable is accented. Sometimes it is difficult to know which syllable receives an accent, but one reliable guide is the dictionary, which usually breaks words into their syllables: *be-gin´*. Since poets shift accents from their normal place usually only for humorous effect, it is safe to assume that competent poets will rely on normal pronunciation.

Aphra Behn   (1640–1689)

   SONG   1665

Love in fantastic triumph sat	*a*	
Whilst bleeding hearts around him flowed,	*b*	
For whom fresh pains he did create	*a*	
And strange tyrranic power he showed:	*b*	
From thy bright eyes he took his fires,	*c*	5
Which round about in sport he hurled;	*d*	
But 'twas from mine he took desires	*c*	
Enough t'undo the amorous world.	*d*	
From me he took his sighs and tears,	*e*	
From thee his pride and cruelty;	*f*	10
From me his languishments and fears,	*e*	
And every killing dart from thee.	*f*	
Thus thou and I the god° have armed	*g*	
And set him up a deity;	*h*	
But my poor heart alone is harmed,	*g*	15
Whilst thine the victor is, and free!	*h*	

13 *god*: Cupid.

In order to **scan** a poem, or determine its meter, the best procedure is to sound out one of the middle lines of the first verse. In this case, the third line will do:

$$\breve{\ } \acute{\ } \quad \breve{\ } \acute{\ } \quad \breve{\ } \acute{\ } \quad \breve{\ } \acute{\ }$$

For whom | fresh pains | he did | cre ate

The bars separate each metrical foot in this **scansion**. This line has four metrical feet. Each foot is iambic; therefore, this line is *iambic tetrameter*.

Number of Metrical Feet in a Line

   one foot per line: monometer

   two feet per line: dimeter

three feet per line: trimeter

four feet per line: tetrameter

five feet per line: pentameter

six feet per line: hexameter

seven feet per line: septameter

eight feet per line: octameter

Aphra Behn's poem is written entirely in four-foot lines, and most of its metrical feet are iambic; therefore, we say the poem is written in iambic tetrameter, one of the most common metrical patterns in English poetry.

However, not all Behn's metrical feet are iambs. Before we examine her differences, consider this table of the normal metrical feet you will encounter in this book. Those with two syllables are called **duple meter**, and those with three syllables are **triple meter**.

Metrical Foot	Pattern	Example
iambic (iamb)	˘ ´	in-sist´
trochaic (trochee)	´ ˘	pen-´cil
anapestic (anapest)	˘ ˘ ´	in a fix´
dactylic (dactyl)	´ ˘ ˘	im-´pli-cate
spondaic (spondee)	´ ´	top´ gun´
pyrrhic (pyrrhic)	˘ ˘	of a
amphribrachic (amphibrach)	˘ ´ ˘	in-ter-´nal
cretic (cretic)	´ ˘ ´	med-´i-tate´

The iamb and anapest are usually called **rising rhythms** because they begin with an unstressed syllable and proceed to a final stress. The trochee and dactyl, referred to as **falling rhythms**, begin with a stressed syllable and end on an unstressed syllable.

The opening lines of poems are usually the most difficult to scan because in those lines the poet aims at diversity and attention-getting rhythms. Here is one way of scanning the opening lines of Behn's poem:

Love in | fantas | tic tri | umph sat

   Whilst bleed | ing hearts | around | him flowed,

The device Behn uses in the first two feet, a trochee followed by an iamb, is common in the first lines of poems. The rhythm of this combination moves the reader rapidly into the line. The succeeding iambs establish the poem as highly regular iambic tetrameter. Scan the rest of the poem, and you will find its meter identical with the second and third lines. The only substitute foot is the opening trochee. Poems with such regularity risk dullness, but Behn expects this poem to be sung aloud. The music thrives on the regularity of meter and stress and provides another layer to the poem.

Like the meter, the ideas of the poem are also familiar and expected. Behn tells how the behavior of lovers establishes the god of love as their deity. Their own experiences, her "languishments and fears," her lover's "pride and cruelty," have "armed" the deity, or given it its powers. In this case, the cost is borne by the woman: "my poor heart alone is harmed." Behn strongly implies that this is the usual outcome.

Some poets poke fun at the demands of meter and rhyme. Algernon Swinburne's "Nephelidia," which we encountered in Chapter 6, does this. In this poem Swinburne uses triple meter, or three syllables for each foot, and depends on **alliteration**, the repetition of consonant sounds at the beginning of words, to intensify the beat of the accents. He does this partly to show off and partly to ridicule those who put too much emphasis on metrical virtuosity. Here is a scansion of the first two lines.

From the depth ǀ of the dream ǀ y decline ǀ of the dawn
   through a no ǀ table nim ǀ bus of neb ǀ ulous noonshine,
Pallid ǀ and pink ǀ as the palm ǀ of the flag ǀ -flower that
   flick ǀ ers with fear ǀ of the flies ǀ as they float,

Each line has eight mostly anapestic feet; therefore, the meter of the poem is anapestic octameter. The first half of line 1 alliterates *d-*, and the last half *n-*, the last consonant of *dawn*. The second line alliterates *p-* for the first half, employing *f-*, the consonant in *of*, to finish the alliteration of the line. This method is followed throughout.

The following poem shows the effectiveness of simple rhyme and rhythm. Such simplicity is a memory aid.

A. E. Housman   (1859–1936)

WITH RUE MY HEART IS LADEN   1922

With rue my heart is laden
   For golden friends I had,
For many a rose-lipped maiden
   And many a lightfoot lad.

By brooks too broad for leaping   5
   The lightfoot boys are laid;
The rose-lipped girls are sleeping
   In fields where roses fade.

Questions for Close Reading

1. Both stanzas use both feminine and masculine rhyme. Which is which?
2. What is the primary metrical foot of this verse? How many metrical feet are in each line? What, then, do we call the meter of this verse?
3. Scan the entire poem after you have spoken it out loud to identify the accented syllables. Do the accents fall on the most important words in the poem or on the least important words? How do the accents help bring the point of the poem home?
4. The verse is simple, light, and direct. What is the relationship of your metrical description to the ideas in the poem? What is Housman saying about his friends?

The next poem mixes several different kinds of rhyme, and although the lines look metrical and regular to the eyes, they are free verse: irregular and not metrical. Some lines seem conversational and unmetrical, and others seem as regularly iambic as Aphra Behn's. Cummings mixes the lines liberally and repeats certain basic lines with variations: "spring summer autumn winter" and "sun moon stars rain." It would be difficult to see either of those lines as metrical and regular, despite their accented and unaccented syllables.

E. E. Cummings   (1894–1962)
ANYONE LIVED IN A PRETTY HOW TOWN   1940

anyone lived in a pretty how town
(with up so floating many bells down)
spring summer autumn winter
he sang his didn't he danced his did.

Women and men(both little and small)   5
cared for anyone not at all
they sowed their isn't they reaped their same
sun moon stars rain

children guessed(but only a few
and down they forgot as up they grew   10
autumn winter spring summer)
that noone loved him more by more

when by now and tree by leaf
she laughed his joy she cried his grief
bird by snow and stir by still   15
anyone's any was all to her

someones married their everyones
laughed their cryings and did their dance

(sleep wake hope and then)they
said their nevers they slept their dream   20

stars rain sun moon
(and only the snow can begin to explain
how children are apt to forget to remember
with up so floating many bells down)

one day anyone died i guess   25
(and noone stooped to kiss his face)
busy folk buried them side by side
little by little and was by was

all by all and deep by deep
and more by more they dream their sleep   30
noone and anyone earth by april
wish by spirit and if by yes.

Women and men(both dong and ding)
summer autumn winter spring
reaped their sowing and went their came   35
sun moon stars rain

Questions for Close Reading

1. Scan the fourth line of the first stanza: "he sang his didn't he danced his did." Is this a metrically regular line? Does this line indicate the general metrical character of the poem?
2. The first thing a reader may notice is that the poem seems to verge on nonsense. The expression "pretty how town" has no denotative meaning, although it may suggest many connotations to you. Making "anyone" a character who "sang his didn't" and "danced his did" is also unusual. Does the rhythm of the poem help you interpret these expressions as significant? In other words, does it contribute to the poem's meaning?
3. Compare this poem with Lewis Carroll's "Jabberwocky" (p. 551). What do these poems have in common rhythmically? How would you summarize the general structure of Cummings's narrative? How does it compare with the narrative in "Jabberwocky"? Does Cummings express emotion over the deaths of anyone and noone?
4. The rhyme patterns vary throughout the poem. In stanza 1 the first two lines are full rhyme: *town* and *down*. Lines 3 and 4 are assonantal rhyme: *winter* and *did*. The same is true for the second stanza. In the third stanza the *m*'s are consonantal rhymes in the third and fourth lines: *summer* and *more*. What are the rhyming techniques of the rest of the stanzas? Look for slant rhyme, assonantal rhyme, consonantal rhyme, and internal rhyme.

The following poem gives a portrait of a seventh-grade teacher, "Miss Arbuckle," who taught about the Romantic poets. The rhyme scheme uses many off-rhyming techniques and then ends purposely and surprisingly with a very clichéd full rhyme: *June, moon.*

Peter Meinke   (b. 1932)

MISS ARBUCKLE   1981

Miss Arbuckle taught seventh grade.
She hid her lips against her teeth:
her bottom like the ace of spades
was guarded by the virgin queen.

Miss Arbuckle wore thick-soled shoes,   5
blue dresses with white polka dots.
She followed and enforced the rules:
what she was paid to teach, she taught.

She said that Wordsworth liked the woods,
that Blake had never seen a tiger,   10
that Byron was not always good
but died in Greece, a freedom-fighter.

She gave her students rigid tests
and when the school let out in June,
she painted rings around her breasts   15
and danced by the light of the moon.

Questions for Close Reading

1. Scan the second line of the poem. What is the basic metrical foot, and how many are there? Scan the third line. What would you say the basic meter of the poem is?
2. Scan the first line of the poem. The name *Miss Arbuckle* will give you trouble. Meinke knows this, so what is his point? How well does "*Miss Arbuckle*" fit into this poem?
3. Examine the rhymes in stanza 1. What kind of rhymes are *grade, spades* and *teeth, queen*? Examine stanzas 2 and 3. They rhyme *abab,* as do all the stanzas. What kinds of rhymes does Meinke prefer? Can you see the reasons for his preference?
4. Identify the end-stopped lines by putting a mark at the end of each. Identify the run-on lines by connecting the end of one line with the beginning of the next. What rhythmic effects do you find interesting in the first three stanzas?

5. The last stanza surprises us with full rhyme: *tests, breasts* and *June, moon.*
   What else is surprising? Does the rhyme or the meter help reinforce what
   Meinke tells us of Miss Arbuckle?

The next short poem also uses rhyme and meter to reinforce its ideas.

Howard Nemerov   (b. 1920)

BECAUSE YOU ASKED ABOUT THE LINE BETWEEN PROSE AND POETRY   1980

Sparrows were feeding in a freezing drizzle
That while you watched turned into pieces of snow
Riding a gradient invisible
From silver aslant to random, white, and slow.

There came a moment that you couldn't tell.   5
And then they clearly flew instead of fell.

Questions for Close Reading

1. What kinds of rhymes does Nemerov use?
2. What kind of change is taking place in the weather Nemerov describes?
   What changes take place in the rhyming and metrical qualities of the lines
   from the first stanza to the second?
3. Is the mix of run-on and end-stopped lines effective in light of what
   Nemerov talks about?
4. When do you become aware that this poem is becoming a poem?

Nemerov seems to be talking about the distinction between ordinary
workaday prose, such as what we see in magazines and newspapers, and poetry. However, some poems, such as Carolyn Forché's "The Colonel" (p.
761), are not set up in a recognizable system of individual lines. These are
known as **prose poems**. Although they do not appear to be poems, they still
"fly" because of their fusion of language, imagery, and idea, as well as, quite
often, their rhythm.

The following poem shows some unique uses of rhyme and meter.
("Dustbins" are what the British call garbage cans.)

Stevie Smith   (1902–1971)

MOTHER, AMONG THE DUSTBINS   1976

Mother, among the dustbins and the manure
I feel the measure of my humanity, an allure
As of the presence of God. I am sure

In the dustbins, in the manure, in the cat at play,
Is the presence of God, in a sure way   5
He moves there. Mother, what do you say?

I too have felt the presence of God in the broom
I hold, in the cobwebs in the room,
But most of all in the silence of the tomb.

Ah! but that thought that informs the hope of our kind   10
Is but an empty thing, what lies behind?—
Naught but the vanity of a protesting mind

That would not die. This is the thought that bounces
Within a conceited head and trounces
Inquiry. Man is most frivolous when he pronounces.   15

Well Mother, I shall continue to think as I do,
And I think you would be wise to do so too,
Can you question the folly of man in the creation of God?
   Who are you?

Questions for Close Reading

1. Scan lines 2 and 3 of stanza 1. Do you have a clear sense of the metrical
   character of the poem?
2. Examine the rhyme scheme. The poem rhymes *aaa, bbb, ccc, ddd, eee, fff.*
   Triple rhyme is unusual in English. What is Smith's reason for using it?
   When do you become aware of her reason?
3. Examine the meter of the last line, scanning it syllable by syllable. How
   does it connect with the rhyme scheme?

The word *prosody* is used to define particular systems of rhyme and meter, as well as the *study* of how rhyme and meter function in a poem. We have
only begun such a study, and there are many more metrical feet and details
of rhythm and meter than those given here. Nonetheless, these definitions
should help you make good sense of most of the poems in this volume and
most that you are likely to read. In an effective poem the prosody contributes
to the overall purpose: it does not function as a separate layer. Thus Peter
Meinke uses interesting variations in rhyme and meter to point up the problems that Miss Arbuckle presented to him as a young poet. Aphra Behn makes
a light song out of a very serious issue partly to ensure that her poem will be
received by people in her own time. Its innocent and ordinary prosody is like
camouflage; only after reading and thinking about the poem would her audience begin to see the nature of her critical position. E. E. Cummings uses
the most ordinary of rhythms to tell a story that we realize we already have
within us. Like the "plot" of "Jabberwocky," the narrative of anyone meeting noone and getting married and living happily ever after is already built

into our expectations. Cummings uses the most comfortable rhythms and is able to make a moving poem out of very common details. Whenever you find the rhythms of a poem exciting and interesting, examine them for their relationship to the overall effect of the poem.

METAPHOR AND SIMILE

Metaphor is one of the greatest resources of poetic language. A **metaphor** invokes a comparison between two things: one is usually the subject at hand, and the other is something associated with it. The comparison is not stated directly but implied. The purpose of the association is to use some qualities of the distant "something" to illuminate an unsuspected quality of the subject at hand. There are several varieties of metaphor.

Noun Metaphor "Love is a sickness full of woes." You are not told love is *like* a sickness; you are told it *is* one. Thus we have a metaphor comparing the subject *love* with the noun *sickness*. "Come, Sleep; O Sleep! the certain knot of peace." The comparison is with *Sleep*, the subject at hand, and the noun *knot*. Sleep is a knot that unites the speaker with peace.

Verb Metaphor "Love guards the roses of thy lips." *Guards* is a verb comparing *Love* with a sentinel; *roses* is a noun metaphor compared with *lips*.

Implied Metaphor When the metaphor is not stated directly, it may be implied. Instead of saying "This is the autumn of my life," which would be a clear metaphor, Shakespeare implies the same idea when he begins Sonnet 73 with the following:

That time of year thou mayst in me behold
When yellow leaves, or none, or few, do hang
Upon those boughs which shake against the cold,
Bare, ruined choirs, where late the sweet birds sang.

Implied metaphors are often so subtle that they are not recognized right away. This is also an example of **extended metaphor**, in which the same metaphor is continued over several lines.

Prepositional Metaphor "The winter of our discontent." The comparison is the prepositional phrase *of our discontent* with the *year*, which has seasons. This metaphor implies that *discontent* could have a summer or other season, although *winter* fits perfectly with discontent. "She was the apple of my eye." *Apple* is a metaphor of something important in relation to the *eye*, which is also a metaphor for admiration or desire. The prepositional phrase is *of my eye*.

A **simile** is like a metaphor except that it makes the comparison explicit by using *like, as,* or *as if.* In the line "My love is like a red red rose," the simile is open-ended. Love is said to share some of the qualities of the rose—beauty, perishability, and rarity—but you can also add your own qualities to the list. In "Beauty, sweet Love, is like the morning dew," beauty shares the qualities of freshness and perishability with dew. This comes from an **extended simile**, in which the comparison is stretched over several lines:

> Beauty, sweet Love, is like the morning dew,
> Whose short refresh upon the tender green
> Cheers for a time, but till the sun doth show,
> And straight 'tis gone as it had never been.

Metaphor and simile are subtle in their effect, penetrating the subconscious and operating there "out of sight." Often one's most powerful response to poetry depends upon the power of metaphor because the comparisons are open-ended and resonant. You may read a metaphoric poem one day and respond to one set of felt comparisons, and then later you may perceive an entirely new set. Metaphors are filled with surprises and constitute one of the richest resources of poetry. Shakespeare's sonnets, for example, use powerful metaphoric language, as in this poem.

William Shakespeare   (1564–1616)

SONNET 73: THAT TIME OF YEAR THOU MAYST IN ME BEHOLD   1609

> That time of year thou mayst in me behold
> When yellow leaves, or none, or few, do hang
> Upon those boughs which shake against the cold,
> Bare, ruined choirs, where late the sweet birds sang.
> In me thou seest the twilight of such day   5
> As after sunset fadeth in the west,
> Which by and by black night doth take away,
> Death's second self, that seals up all in rest.
> In me thou seest the glowing of such fire
> That on the ashes of his youth doth lie,   10
> As the death-bed whereon it must expire,
> Consumed with that which it was nourished by.
>   This thou perceiv'st, which makes thy love more strong,
>   To love that well, which thou must leave ere long.

The poet talks about himself to another person, someone for whom he cares. This is a sonnet (discussed shortly), which has several distinct units:

three quatrains and a couplet. The first four lines are a unit (quatrain) end-ing with a period. The same is true of the next four lines and the next four. The last two lines (couplet) end with a period. In each of these units Shakespeare develops metaphors. The first quatrain begins with a metaphor of the season: the "time of year" we "behold" in him must be autumn, im-plied by the "yellow leaves." But the emphasis shifts to the boughs, high in the air (the choir is high in a church and these boughs shake against "Bare, ruined choirs"). Shakespeare invites a comparison of his head and hair—pre-sumably growing thin in his autumn years—with boughs in which birds sang. He as a poet sang, as well. The second quatrain suggests another noun metaphor, but the comparison moves from a season to a single day: "the twi-light of such day." In this quatrain Shakespeare invokes "black night," "Death's second self," thus introducing a menacing idea. The day ends with sleep, as life ends with death. The third quatrain invokes a new metaphor: a fire, but one that is fed with "the ashes of his youth." This prepositional metaphor likens youth to a timber that is in limited supply and can be con-sumed. Life is like a fire that burns itself. These three quatrains, dominated by three extended metaphors, constitute a powerful argument to "prove" the message of the couplet: love that well which you must leave soon. In other words, love life; it does not last. The power of metaphor in this poem is largely subliminal. The images of a person's autumn or twilight years and of being consumed by flames of time are very compelling. We do not have to think hard to grasp and feel these comparisons.

The next four-stanza song uses metaphors in every stanza. (A *canción* is a song.)

Denise Levertov   (b. 1923)

CANCIÓN   1975

When I am the sky
a glittering bird
slashes at me with the knives of song.

When I am the sea
fiery clouds plunge into my mirrors,   5
fracture my smooth breath with crimson sobbing.

When I am the earth
I feel my flesh of rock wearing down:
pebbles, grit, finest dust, nothing.

When I am a woman—O, when I am   10
a woman,
my wells of salt brim and brim,
poems force the lock of my throat.

These metaphors are often violent and tortured, such as the opening comparison of song with knives. The description is clear enough: birds do "slash" the sky and seem knifelike if seen from one point of view. This violent metaphor contrasts with the calmness of "When I am the sky," also a metaphor. Some of the metaphors in the second stanza are surrealistic: "fiery clouds plunge into my mirrors / fracture my smooth breath with crimson sobbing." The clouds metaphorically "plunge," "fracture," and sob. In the third stanza, when the speaker is the earth, she feels "the flesh of rock wearing down." Finally, in the last stanza, when "I" is a woman, the "wells of salt brim and brim," a metaphor for her eyes producing salt tears. She expresses herself by forcing "the lock of [her] throat." The underlying violence of all these metaphors makes this poem function like a volcano. The pressure builds and builds until we become aware that the poem has realized its message: it has forced the locks and expressed itself. Levertov invokes all four elements—air, earth, fire, and water—to encompass the entire universe of experience.

The next poem is an example of an extended and implied metaphor; note also how rhythm contributes to its meaning.

E. E. Cummings   (1894–1962)
SHE BEING BRAND / -NEW   1926

she being Brand

-new; and you
know consequently a
little stiff i was
careful of her and(having   5

thoroughly oiled the universal
joint tested my gas felt of
her radiator made sure her springs were O.

K.)i went right to it flooded-the-carburetor cranked her

up, slipped the   10
clutch(and then somehow got into reverse she
kicked what
the hell)next
minute i was back in neutral tried and

again slo-wly;bare,ly nudg.   ing(my   15

lev-er Right-
oh and her gears being in
A 1 shape passed
from low through

second-in-to-high like   20
greasedlightning)just as we turned the corner of Divinity

avenue i touched the accelerator and give

her the juice,good

                    (it
was the first ride and believe i we was   25
happy to see how nice she acted right up to
the last minute coming back down by the Public
Gardens i slammed on
the

internalexpanding   30
&
externalcontracting
brakes Bothatonce and

brought allofher tremB
-ling   35
to a:dead.

stand-
;Still)

Questions for Close Reading

1. Read the poem silently and mark those passages that need to be read quickly
   and those that should be read slowly or haltingly. Then read the poem
   aloud. The poem is not metrical, but it does have rhythm. How would
   you describe the rhythm? How does the movement of the lines operate
   metaphorically to suggest the movement of an automobile?
2. The extended metaphor works in terms of the distinction between denotative and connotative language. Are there any noun, verb, or prepositional metaphors in the text of the poem? What connotations do you perceive in the language of the poem? What metaphorically could the
   automobile be compared with?
3. Some readers may not "get" this comparison right away. This raises the
   question, To what extent does the double meaning depend on the reader?
   Who is responsible for the interpretation of a metaphoric comparison?

The author of the next poem was in the air force in World War II, so its
imagery and details have a special authenticity. The power of the controlling
metaphor has made this brief poem one of the most memorable to come from
that war.

Randall Jarrell   (1914–1965)

THE DEATH OF THE BALL TURRET° GUNNER   1945

From my mother's sleep I fell into the State,
And I hunched in its belly till my wet fur froze,
Six miles from earth, loosed from its dream of life,
I woke to black flak° and the nightmare fighters.
When I died they washed me out of the turret with a hose.   5

Ball Turret: The transparent capsule under a bomber where the machine gunner sat, sometimes
upside down.   5 *flak*: Antiaircraft fire: explosions in the air.

Questions for Close Reading

1. What metaphor is implied in the first line of the poem? Why is *State* capitalized?
2. In the second line the gunner says he "hunched in its belly." What metaphor
   is implied in that expression? Why is it effective?
3. The third line refers to "its dream of life." Is "dream of life" a prepositional metaphor? What is being compared to a dream? Who is the "its" in
   this line?
4. Is the last line metaphoric? The entire poem is an extended metaphor, but
   of what?

   The following poem employs an extended simile. We are like the great
princes of old, who, after a day's work in the field hunting stags or other noble beasts, came back to the palace to live a life that was appropriate for royalty. Honig's simile is a commentary on the way we live now.

Edwin Honig   (b. 1919)

AS A GREAT PRINCE   1955

As a great prince after the hunt comes
Stomping through the antlered spear-hung hall
Of his overnourished leisure, flopping his weight
   Of rich self-certitude to dream in thick
   Bearskin the teasing horror of a beast   5
Outstaring axe blows, questioning the onslaught,
In immortal posture gazing and uncaught,

   So we inhabit a drowsy movie dark,
Amid love's trophies deliberating self-content,
Moist anticipants of the overplayed crescendo   10

Clutching the smoking guns of pleasure,
Till suddenly blond beast removes a robe
And pulsing reel relaxes to a still
Of smiling passion frozen in our death of will.

Questions for Close Reading

1. The metaphors of lines 3 and 4 point to physical qualities of the "great prince." What are they? Why is metaphor an effective means of making us aware of the physicality of the prince?
2. The second half of the poem invites a metaphoric comparison: for us the prince's great hall has become a darkened "movie." How, then, does this metaphor compare us with the prince?
3. What are the "smoking guns of pleasure"?
4. What metaphors do you see at work in the final line?

OTHER FIGURATIVE LANGUAGE

Poetry has many special kinds of figurative language besides metaphoric techniques. You will encounter some of them in the poetry in this section, but you will have already seen some of them in other kinds of literature. Here is a list of the most important techniques.

Irony   Irony is saying one thing but meaning another, or giving an apparently innocent comparison that reveals the shortcoming of the subject. For example, Edwin Honig's "As a Great Prince" compares today's householder with a great prince of old, only to make us aware of how puny the contemporary householder is in relation to the nobility of the prince.

   Verbal irony is commonly used in conversation, as when someone claims to be bad, intending the listener to know that exactly the opposite is meant. Advertisers recognize the value of such irony when they recommend "killer" systems for audio, video, or computer equipment. Verbal irony does not always connote the opposite of what it says, but it always connotes something different from the literal meaning of the words used.

   Dramatic irony is not limited to words but spills over into actions. It is not only found in plays. In poetic or other narratives, dramatic irony heightens suspense and the reader's anticipation. When a character wishes for something desirable, gets it, then discovers it to be the source of ruin or damnation, the poet has used dramatic irony. In *Oedipus Rex* Oedipus constantly vows to avenge the murder of Laius, no matter who the murderer is. In that play, Oedipus's quest is not just dramatic irony, but **tragic irony** because the result is the tragic end of a great hero.

Irony is a subtle resource for the poet because it has many links with life, which is filled with ironies. In literature such ironies are controlled to produce maximum psychological effect. One of the pleasures of irony is that the audience usually understands the ironic circumstances when the characters do not. For example, in *Hamlet* Claudio kneels to pray only to realize his conscience is not clear. Hamlet hesitates in killing him because he thinks his prayer is genuine and that Claudio would be dispatched to heaven instead of hell if he were to be killed then. The audience knows otherwise.

Edgar Arlington Robinson's "Richard Cory" (p. 918) may be an example of **cosmic irony**, in that the man admired by all who knew him turns out to be so miserable as to commit suicide. Cosmic irony shows fate reaching from the heavens to make an otherwise admirable person—Richard Cory, the man who has everything—so unhappy as to cause his death. In every case irony functions in terms of a reversal of appearances. Usually the reader is aware of the irony before the characters, and so is in a special relation to the action.

Paradox   A **paradox** is an apparently impossible circumstance, situation, or condition. The line in Denise Levertov's poem, "I feel my flesh of rock," is paradoxical. It cannot be explained rationally.

Personification   **Personification** is giving a nonbeing the characteristics of a person, as when Jarrell suggests that the "State" has a "belly" or Honig tells us that a "reel relaxes." The entire effect of "she being Brand / –new" is achieved by personifying an automobile as a woman.

Pun   A **pun** is a play on words that usually depends on a word having several meanings or sounding like another word with a different meaning. The reference to "death-bed" in Shakespeare's Sonnet 73 (p. 595) is a pun on the bed of ashes (as in "bed of coals").

Metonymy   When you use one thing in place of something closely related to it, you use **metonymy**. Calling an athlete a "jock"; referring to a casino as "the house"; calling the police "the heat" are examples of metonymy.

Synecdoche   **Synecdoche**, closely related to metonymy, uses a part for the whole, as when one uses *wheels* to mean an automobile, *wings* to mean an airplane, *rifles* to mean a regiment of soldiers, or *hands* to mean sailors in "all hands on deck."

Hyperbole   **Hyperbole** is **overstatement** for effect. "I fell into the State" is a form of hyperbole which Jarrell depends upon for part of the power of his poem. The last line, "When I died they washed me out of the turret with a hose," may seem to be hyperbole, but unfortunately it may be a literal description, given the nature of World War II bombing missions.

Litotes   The opposite of overstatement, **litotes**, is **understatement** (a word we sometimes use instead of *litotes*): it downplays for effect. When one refers to World War II as a "pretty little squabble," one uses litotes. Litotes often relies on a negative structure, as in "it was not unpopular" when one means it was wildly popular, or as in "it did not go unappreciated" for something that may have won general appreciation and high regard.

Some of these figures may be seen at work in William Wordsworth's sonnet, "London, 1802." The poem invokes the memory of Wordsworth's greatest influence, John Milton (1608–1672), the revolutionary poet who supported the defeat and beheading of Charles I during the English Civil War. When Wordsworth wrote, France had undergone the most important revolution of modern times, and Wordsworth was excited by the rise of democracy and Europe's potential for overthrowing kings, princes, and all backward systems of government. He saw Milton as the spiritual leader in the fight for republicanism.

William Wordsworth   (1770–1850)
LONDON, 1802   1807 (1802?)

> Milton! thou should'st be living at this hour:
> England hath need of thee: she is a fen
> Of stagnant waters: altar, sword, and pen,
> Fireside, the heroic wealth of hall and bower,
> Have forfeited their ancient English dower   5
> Of inward happiness. We are selfish men;
> Oh! raise us up, return to us again;
> And give us manners, virtue, freedom, power.
> Thy soul was like a star, and dwelt apart:
> Thou hadst a voice whose sound was like the sea: 10
> Pure as the naked heavens, majestic, free,
> So didst thou travel on life's common way,
> In cheerful godliness; and yet thy heart
> The lowliest duties on herself did lay.

Wordsworth uses paradox in addressing Milton in the first place, since Milton had been long dead. He uses hyperbole in lines 2 and 3 in claiming that England is a fen of stagnant waters. In "altar, sword, and pen" he uses metonymy to allude to religious leaders, military leaders, and writers (politicians). "Hall and bower" are synecdoches for the English manor house, from which traditional stability and government had come. In light of England's problems, the half-line "We are selfish men" may be thought of as an instance of litotes. Wordsworth's praise of Milton in the latter part of the poem—"Thy soul was like a star," "Thou hadst a voice . . . like the sea"—is hyperbole. "Heart" in line 13 is metonymy, just as "soul" in line 9 may be metonymic for Milton's spiritual nature. Even in a relatively brief poem, such figurative devices operate quite forcefully. They contribute an emotional density to the poem, especially as they synchronize with its imagery and metaphors.

The following poem derives its entire effect from the use of figurative language.

Gerald Costanzo   (b. 1945)

AT IRONY'S PICNIC   1974

> Silence is sight-reading
> Swahili. Sin lumbers by on
>
> stilts. Where did he get
> that Hawaiian shirt? those
>
> rose-colored glasses? Down   5
> by the lake Desire is fondling
>
> Regret's mother. Jealousy
> and Happiness dance the mazurka.
>
> Justice, wearing the same
> old swimsuit, is cutting the   10
>
> ballyhoo. Irony himself
> isn't even here.

Questions for Close Reading

1. What is the primary irony in this poem?
2. Which pun is most effective?
3. How many examples of personification does Costanzo use?
4. Why is personification so important to Costanzo?
5. Which personification does Costanzo most extensively develop? Do the attributes Costanzo links with that figure give us a better understanding, or do they contribute to confusion?
6. Are the "rose-colored glasses" an example of imagery, metaphor, metonymy, synecdoche, or a combination of these figures? What do rose-colored glasses signify?

Poets do not always know which figures they will use in a poem, and when you begin examining a poem for its use of figures you may not know what you will find. In a poem titled "Irony's Picnic," one would expect to find irony, and Costanzo does not disappoint us (or does he?). Is Irony's absence at the picnic ironic? Or if it is ironic, does that mean irony is present in the poem? Costanzo is not just having fun; he is making a point about poetry, language, and life. All figurative language contributes to the subtle effect of a poem, no matter what its significance or purpose may be.

SYMBOL AND ALLEGORY

A **symbol** is a specialized use of metaphor. It begins with a comparison, but the reader is not always immediately aware that the comparison is important. Without saying so, the poet makes one thing—the thing he or she specifically talks about—stand for another—something not specifically talked about. The poet does not substitute the subject for the symbol but instead speaks about both simultaneously. The reader gradually becomes aware that the subject of the poem is taking on larger meanings, larger associations, and suggestions of meaning than was first apparent. For example, the scarlet letter *A*, which stands for adultery in Nathaniel Hawthorne's novel *The Scarlet Letter*, is supposed to identify Hester Prynne's shame among her Puritan citizens. However, it soon begins to symbolize the shame of the community that has treated her as outcast.

Certain conventional symbols abound in literature. The sun symbolizes masculinity; the moon symbolizes femininity. Fire symbolizes passion; air symbolizes the spirit; water symbolizes rejuvenation; earth symbolizes the mother. Some points of the compass are symbols: north symbolizes the devil; west, death; east, beginnings. These are age-old symbols and are by no means rigid or fixed. Water, for example, can symbolize life, but in too great abundance it can also mean death. Poets use symbols in a variety of ways, sometimes relying on tradition and sometimes breaking with it.

William Blake's poem "The Tiger" demonstrates how a symbol slowly gathers meaning. In its original published form, the poem was accompanied by Blake's drawing of a tiger, and the reader would have expected the poem to concern a tiger, and not necessarily something beyond that.

William Blake (1757–1827)
THE TIGER 1794

Tiger, tiger, burning bright
In the forests of the night,
What immortal hand or eye
Could frame thy fearful symmetry?

In what distant deeps or skies 5
Burnt the fire of thine eyes?

On what wings dare he aspire?
What the hand dare seize the fire?

And what shoulder and what art
Could twist the sinews of thy heart? 10
And when thy heart began to beat,
What dread hand? And what dread feet?

What the hammer? What the chain?
In what furnace was thy brain?
What the anvil? What dread grasp 15
Dare its deadly terrors clasp?

When the stars threw down their spears
And watered Heaven with their tears,
Did he smile his work to see?
Did he who made the Lamb make thee? 20

Tiger, tiger, burning bright
In the forests of the night,
What immortal hand or eye
Dare frame thy fearful symmetry?

That this is no ordinary tiger seems clear in the opening stanza, in which Blake tells us that it burns and that its fire illumines the forests of the night. Modern psychologists would see "forests of the night" as symbolic of the unconscious world of dreams. The dream world is forested because it is uncleared, dark, and threatening. The tiger becomes part of that unconscious because it stands for an elemental violence and predatory behavior that may be in every person as a result of evolutionary forces. Blake meditates on the creation of the tiger in the second stanza, imagining a creator in some "distant deeps" seizing the fire of the tiger's eyes, the spark of its creation. Building on this idea in the third and fourth stanzas, Blake imagines a creator in the guise of a blacksmith forging the shape of this terrifying predator. We see at the end of stanza 4 that whoever created the tiger must somehow be greater even than that beast: "What dread grasp / Dare its deadly terrors clasp?" But then, in stanza 5, Blake wonders if the tiger pleased the creator. He further wonders if the same creator made both the ferocious tiger and the peaceful, defenseless lamb. He capitalizes "Lamb," which many commentators assume is a symbolic reference to Jesus.

Symbols imply a range of significance, not a single significance. Therefore, the tiger of this poem can be seen to symbolize the terrors of nature as present in predators and violent death. The lamb can be seen to symbolize innocence, mildness, and the gentleness of nature, as well as the gentleness and innocence associated with God and godliness. But then the tiger can symbolize the wrath of God and the terror associated with an angry God.

The fact that both the tiger and the lamb exist in the same universe, whether physical or spiritual, is the central, and possibly paradoxical, idea in this poem.

Blake works with elemental ideas and elemental forces, but he does not pin them down. By contrast, when you make a symbol stand for only one thing, you have created an **allegory**. Allegory is related to metaphor because it implies a comparison, but the emphasis is usually on the hidden meaning, not both parts. Allegory is a form of "other-speak," in which the language on the surface must be translated according to a kind of key to get the true meaning. In George Orwell's novel *Animal Farm*, certain animals allegorically represented certain governments. The French, for example, were allegorized as roosters, the English as bulls (John Bull), and the Russians as bears. These are age-old allegories that Orwell appropriated. The Jabberwocky (p. 551) is an allegory for all the dragons and dangerous beasts who lie in the way of the virtuous young hero. In Stevie Smith's poem "Mother, among the Dustbins" (p. 592), the dustbins may be an allegory for the dust we all become at death. E. E. Cummings expects us to see the allegorical relationship between a new car and a young virgin in "she being Brand / -new." Once one gets the key to this poem, one basically forgets about the car and concentrates on the woman and all the details that precisely fit that meaning. Allegory is highly useful in situations in which free and open speech is not possible, and so was useful for Cummings in 1926.

E. E. Cummings plays with both symbol and allegory in the following poem.

E. E. Cummings   (1894–1962)

l(a   1958

l(a

le

af

fa

ll   5

s)

one

l

iness

Questions for Close Reading

1. What does the shape of the poem resemble?
2. The poem consists of two parts: one is an image. What is the image?
3. The second part of the poem is a single, long, word. What is that word?
4. Why does one part of the poem interrupt the other?
5. What symbolism do you see at work here?

Cummings seems to have had a good time exploring the resources of shape in this poem. If you were to take a pencil and follow the curved and vertical lines of the typography, you would have a diagram of something like a leaf falling. Note the way the parentheses imply a swirling motion and the way the *af, fa* lines resemble a twist in a falling spiral (pencil a line through the *a*'s and another through the *f*'s. The last line is like the recumbent leaf. Then look at the repetition of the concept of "one." First, the opening *l* on the typewriter is the same as the number 1 (this poem is also number 1 in its original collection). The first letter after the parenthesis is *a*, the first letter of the alphabet. In French, *le* means premier, or first. The two *l*'s in line 5 emphasize the oneness; then *one* (line 7) is reinforced by *l* in the next line; and finally, *iness* may be taken as *oneness* or *I-ness*, which are closely related.

The primary image of the poem is in parentheses, broken into spiraling parts, and it reads: "a leaf falls." This image interrupts—and in so doing illustrates—a single word: *loneliness*. But Cummings explores that single word by breaking it into several parts, all of which reinforce the basic idea of oneness. That leaf, when it was in the tree, was part of a vast community. However, when it died, when it fell from the tree, it did so alone, and every swirl, every downward move, reinforced its oneness. If the leaf is symbolic, then we can see it reinforcing our sense of community with other people but reminding us of our individuality, which for better or worse will assert itself when we die. The falling leaf is an allegory for loneliness; but it is a symbol for humanity.

Robert Frost often worked with materials from New England farming country, finding in them significances that we may think of as symbolic. When he speaks of apple-picking or of a road not taken, we begin with what seem to be straightforward descriptions of experience that gain meaning as we examine them. The following poem is typical of Frost's method.

Robert Frost   (1874–1963)
MENDING WALL   1914

Something there is that doesn't love a wall,
That sends the frozen-ground-swell under it
And spills the upper boulders in the sun,
And makes gaps even two can pass abreast.
The work of hunters is another thing: 5
I have come after them and made repair

Where they have left not one stone on a stone,
But they would have the rabbit out of hiding,
To please the yelping dogs. The gaps I mean,
No one has seen them made or heard them made,   10
But at spring mending-time we find them there.
I let my neighbor know beyond the hill;
And on a day we meet to walk the line
And set the wall between us once again.
We keep the wall between us as we go.   15
To each the boulders that have fallen to each.
And some are loaves and some so nearly balls
We have to use a spell to make them balance:
"Stay where you are until our backs are turned!"
We wear our fingers rough with handling them.   20
Oh, just another kind of outdoor game,
One on a side. It comes to little more:
There where it is we do not need the wall:
He is all pine and I am apple orchard.
My apple trees will never get across   25
And eat the cones under his pines, I tell him.
He only says, "Good fences make good neighbors."
Spring is the mischief in me, and I wonder
If I could put a notion in his head:
"*Why* do they make good neighbors? Isn't it   30
Where there are cows? But here there are no cows.
Before I built a wall I'd ask to know
What I was walling in or walling out,
And to whom I was like to give offense.
Something there is that doesn't love a wall,   35
That wants it down." I could say "Elves" to him,
But it's not elves exactly, and I'd rather
He said it for himself. I see him there,
Bringing a stone grasped firmly by the top
In each hand, like an old-stone savage armed.   40
He moves in darkness as it seems to me,
Not of woods only and the shade of trees.
He will not go behind his father's saying,
And he likes having thought of it so well
He says again, "Good fences make good neighbors."   45

Questions for Close Reading

1. When do you become aware that the wall is more than a specific pile of
   stones? Is there a line that begins to suggest a symbolic significance? What
   clues do you get to suggest such a significance?

2. What does Frost seem to mean by saying he and his neighbor "set the wall between us once again"?
3. Are the words *loaves* and *balls* in line 17 symbolic? Are they images? Are they metaphors?
4. Is line 27 meant to be symbolic? What does the neighbor seem to mean by it? How does the speaker of the poem seem to interpret it?
5. The speaker of the poem repeats the first line in line 35. Why? What has happened in the poem to make him reconsider the possibility that "Something there is that doesn't love a wall"?
6. What does Frost gain by the way he says line 35? Would it be better to say, "There is something that doesn't like a wall"? Is it really different?
7. In line 40, the speaker sees his neighbor as "like an old-stone savage armed." Why? What is the meaning of such a simile?
8. What does the neighbor's repetition of "Good fences make good neighbors" achieve at the end of the poem? What thoughts are you left with? What do you think walls symbolize?

Patrick Kavanagh, the author of the next poem, grew up in Ireland in a farming county. His father was a cobbler and for a time he took up the trade, but he soon abandoned it for the literary life. Some of his early poetry resembles Frost's in that its imagery is drawn from the land and its surfaces often suggest a deeper meaning. The horse-drawn machine referred to in this poem is designed to break up the ground to prepare it for seeding. The harrow is also associated with Jesus Christ, who after his crucifixion was said to have gone into hell and harrowed it, bringing out the souls who had been waiting for his coming and who deserved to be in heaven. Thus some of the imagery of the poem depends on a familiarity with the Bible as well as with farming.

Patrick Kavanagh (1905–1967)
TO THE MAN AFTER THE HARROW 1936

Now leave the check-reins slack,
The seed is flying far to-day—
The seed like stars against the black
Eternity of April clay.

This seed is potent as the seed   5
Of knowledge in the Hebrew Book,
So drive your horses in the creed
Of God the Father as a stook.°

---

8 *stook*: A bundle of sheaves of straw.

Forget the men on Brady's° hill.
Forget what Brady's boy may say.   10
For destiny will not fulfill
Unless you let the harrow play.

Forget the worm's opinion too
Of hooves and pointed harrow-pins,
For you are driving your horses through   15
The mist where Genesis begins.

9 *Brady's:* His neighbor's hill.

Questions for Close Reading

1. April is a possible allegory for both spring and Easter, an agricultural and religious time. How does Kavanagh make you aware of their relationship in stanza 1?
2. The seed is "like stars," but it is set "against the black / Eternity of April clay." What effect do this simile and this metaphor have? How might they prepare you to read the poem symbolically?
3. The seed that the farmer sows is compared to "the seed / Of knowledge" in the Bible. How can Kavanagh make that comparison? What does the farmer share with God the Father? Is their relationship symbolic, metaphoric, or both?
4. How does Kavanagh elevate the farmer's importance in stanza 3? What does "destiny" imply? Whose destiny is the subject of this stanza?
5. What does the worm symbolize in the last stanza? Is it appropriate in this poem?
6. Mists are vague. "The mist where Genesis begins" is also vague in that one cannot pin it down, but it is rich in associations. What are they? What is mist meant to symbolize for the farmer driving the harrow? How does it enrich the significance of the poem?

The next poem creates a symbol of modern life. At first it is difficult to interpret the tone, but eventually the reader wonders just how serious the author is in describing an action that we are pretty sure he did not commit. However, the fact that we are not 100 percent sure tells us something. If we were Freudian psychologists, we might interpret this poem as a wish fulfillment dream.

William Carpenter   (b. 1940)
FIRE   1987

This morning, on the opposite shore of the river,
I watch a man burning his own house.
It is a cold day, and the man wears thick gloves
and a fur hat that gives him a Russian look.

I envy his energy, since I'm still on the sunporch   5
in my robe, with morning coffee, my day not
even begun, while my neighbor has already piled
spruce boughs against his house and poured
flammable liquids over them to send a ribbon
of black smoke into the air, a column surrounded   10
by herring gulls, who think he's having a barbecue
or has founded a new dump. I hadn't known what labor
it took to burn something. Now the man's working
at such speed, he's like the criminal in a silent
movie, as if he had a deadline, as if he had   15
to get his house burned by a certain time, or it
would be all over. I see his kids helping, bringing
him matches and kindling, and I'd like to help out
myself, I'd like to bring him coffee and a bagel,
but the Penobscot River separates us, icebergs   20
the size of small ships drifting down the tide.
Moreover, why should I help him when I have a house
myself, which needs burning as much as anyone's?
It has begun to leak. I think it has carpenter ants.
I hear them making sounds at night like writing, only   25
they aren't writing, they are building small tubular
cities inside the walls. I start burning in the study,
working from within so it will go faster, so I can
catch up, and soon there's a smoke column on either
side, like a couple of Algonquins having a dialogue   30
on how much harder it is to destroy than to create.
I shovel books and poems into the growing fire. If
I burn everything, I can start over, with a future
like a white rectangle of paper. Then I notice
my neighbor has a hose, that he's spraying his house   35
with water, the coward, he has bailed out, but I
keep throwing things into the fire: my stamps,
my Berlioz collection, my photos of nude people,
my correspondence dating back to grade school.
Over there, the fire engines are reaching his home.   40
His wife is crying with relief, his fire's extinguished.
He has walked down to the shore to see the ruins
of the house across the river, the open cellar,
the charred timbers, the man laughing and singing
in the snow, who has been finally freed from his   45
possessions, who has no clothes, no library, who has
gone back to the beginning, when we lived in nature:
no refuge from the elements, no fixed address.

Questions for Close Reading

1. The speaker of the poem talks about the "labor / it took to burn something" as if it were a challenge. What has Carpenter done to prepare you to accept this point of view? Do you find yourself receptive to it?
2. When the speaker says he has a house "which needs burning as much as anyone's," what does he seem to mean? Has he begun to speak symbolically at this point of the poem, or is he still being literal?
3. What does the speaker think about the condition of his home when he begins to burn it too? Why does he compare himself and his neighbor to two Algonquin Indians having a dialogue with smoke signals?
4. The speaker explicitly mentions shoveling "books and poems into the growing fire." Why are these items mentioned?
5. What do you make of all the special "collectibles" that he piles onto his fire? Do they give you a clue to his character?
6. Why did his neighbor put out the fire? Why didn't the speaker put out his?
7. Symbolically, what has the speaker achieved? What has the fire done for him? Is he a happy man at the end of the poem?

FORM

One of the fascinating qualities of poetry is that it thrives amid constraints. The constraint to rhyme, for example, has produced many surprising and magical moments. The constraint to maintain a metrical pattern is so powerful that for most readers it identifies what poetry is. Free verse, which uses neither rhyme nor meter, is for many people simply not poetry. That is an extreme position, but the point is that one of the great resources of poetry comes from its capacity not just to resist constraints but to overcome them brilliantly.

The form of some poems is even more constraining than most rhyme and meter because it is established before the poet begins. A couplet is two rhyming lines, a tercet is three rhyming lines, a quatrain is four rhyming lines, and so on. The metrical pattern is also usually decided on in advance. The poet's job is to use these beforehand decisions to best advantage. However, these small forms are relatively simple to work with. Much more elaborate forms have interested poets, and their success has inspired poets throughout history.

Verse refers to any poem that is metrical in character, as well as a line or a stanza of such poetry. In common use, it also refers to a stanza of a song, as in the first or second verse of "Old Man River." Although modern poets do not regard verse as highly as did the poets of earlier centuries, the general public normally expects a poem to be a form of verse: with established rhyme and meter. A. E. Housman's poems (see p. 588) are good examples of what is commonly called verse.

Blank verse is unrhymed iambic pentameter (five iambic feet) and takes on special importance because it is the line that Shakespeare used for most of his plays and that Milton used for *Paradise Lost, Paradise Regained*, and *Samson Agonistes*. It is a highly flexible line especially suited for dramatic narrative.

Free verse avoids preestablished rhyme, stanza pattern, or meter. You have seen several examples in earlier discussions, such as Ezra Pound's "In a Station of the Metro" (p. 572), Judith Rodriguez's "Eskimo Occasion" (p. 579), Denise Levertov's "Canción" (p. 596), E. E. Cummings's "she being Brand/-new" (p. 597), and Gerald Costanzo's "At Irony's Picnic" (p. 603). Modern poets have been fond of free verse since the time of Walt Whitman in the 1850s, but many poets in the 1990s have rediscovered the virtues of poetry that uses fixed forms.

Most **fixed forms** depend upon a predetermined **rhyme scheme**, a pattern of sounds at the ends of lines of verse that sound alike, look alike, or sound very close to one another. In describing a rhyme scheme we assign a letter to the end sound of each line, using the same letter when that sound repeats:

The explosive sound above the hill	*a*
Made me stop with climber's skill;	*a*
Holding on where goats once walked	*b*
I listened as if God had talked.	*b*

The first *a* refers to *hill*, the second to its rhyme word, *skill*. The first *b* refers to *walked*, the second to its rhyme word, *talked*. As discussed earlier, often the rhyme will not be the entire end word but only its last syllable (see p. 585). Sometimes it will be more than one syllable. The predetermined form for the rhyme in this example is the **couplet**: each line rhymes with the next line. When lines fall into units of four, we call them **quatrains**, which might rhyme *abab* or *abba*. **Tercets** are units of three lines, which might rhyme *aaa*, *aba*, or *abc* (in the last case, the next tercet will also be *abc*). As you will see, the sonnet is normally composed of groupings of quatrains, tercets, and/or couplets. Fixed forms sometimes establish patterns of rhyme, stanza length, and repetition of lines, as in the villanelle, discussed below. The most common forms begin with the sonnet, which has flourished since the Renaissance.

The Sonnet

Sonnets have fourteen lines of iambic pentameter: ˘ ´ | ˘ ´ | ˘ ´ | ˘ ´ | ˘ ´. These lines are not always regular, and substitute feet normally occur. Sonnets also follow certain patterns of structure and rhyme, each of which has its own name.

Petrarchan, or Italian   The **Petrarchan**, or **Italian, sonnet** (named after the fourteenth-century poet Petrarch) is divided into an eight-line segment called an **octave** rhyming **abbaabba**, followed by a six-line segment called a **sestet** rhyming *cdecde, cdcdcd, cdcdee,* or *cdedce.* The normal pattern is to state the main idea in the first four lines of the octave and then elaborate that idea in the next four lines. Between the octave and the sestet is a "turn": a change of tone, action, or concept. The first part of the sestet sometimes has an example or complication of the idea developed in the octave, and the last three lines conclude the poem. The lines of both octave and sestet are usually end-stopped, with very strong stops after most rhymes. The end-stopped lines reinforce the individual treatment of ideas in each segment of the sonnet.

Shakespearian, or English   The **Shakespearian**, or **English, sonnet** establishes three quatrains rhyming *abab, cdcd, efef* and ends with a couplet: *gg.* It spends the first twelve lines elaborating on an idea or a problem with details and examples. The last two lines of the poem resolve the issues raised by the first three quatrains. The couplet usually sounds like a tag or resolution, and sometimes adopts the form of a moral, as with Shakespeare's Sonnet 73: "This thou perceiv'st, which makes thy love more strong, / To love that well, which thou must leave ere long."

Sir Philip Sidney was among the most accomplished of English sonneteers. His sonnet cycle, *Astrophel and Stella* (1591), is the first of several important Elizabethan collections of sonnets that narrate a complex story. The title means "starlover and star," a reference to his (the starlover's) devotion to Penelope Devereaux Rich, the "star" whom he admired. Many of the poems reflect on the skies, the stars, or, like the following, the moon. This is a type of Petrarchan sonnet popular in his day.

Sir Philip Sidney   (1554–1586)

SONNET 31: WITH HOW SAD STEPS OH MOON, THOU CLIMB'ST THE SKIES!   1591 (1582?)

With how sad steps Oh Moon, thou climb'st the skies!	*a*	
How silently, and with how wan a face!	*b*	
What, may it be that even in heavenly place	*b*	
That busy archer° his sharp arrows tries?	*a*	
Sure,° if that long-with-love-acquainted eyes	*a*	5
Can judge of love, thou feel'st a lover's case,	*b*	
I read it in thy looks; thy languished grace,	*b*	
To me, that feel the like, thy state descries.°	*a*	
Then, even of fellowship, Oh Moon, tell me,	*c*	

4 *archer*: Cupid.   5 *Sure*: Surely.   8 *descries*: Makes known.

Is constant love deemed there but want of wit?	*d*	10
Are beauties there as proud as here they be?	*c*	
Do they above love to be loved, and yet	*d*	
Those lovers scorn whom that love doth possess?	*e*	
Do they call virtue there ungratefulness?	*e*	

The octave compares the speaker to the moon. The moon has a wan face, as he does; it languishes, as he does; it seems to be love-struck, as he is. Having established that, the sestet turns, and, making a friend of the moon, asks questions: Is there love in the heavens? Does being faithful to one's lover in heaven win contempt (as he has presumably done)? Do the proud beauties of heaven scorn those who love them? Is ungratefulness a virtue in heaven, as it seems to be in his world? The tone of the sestet is ironic, especially in the last line, when virtue and gratefulness, contradictions, are equated.

Sidney's reliance on rhetorical questions (which expect no answer), along with the relative absence of imagery, establishes the poem as discursive. The Petrarchan sonnet frequently complained about the pangs of love in an argumentative fashion. The sonnet argues that Sidney had been stung by inconstancy (implied in the moon's changeableness) and ingratitude (implied in the moon's cool light). He asks, reasonably, Is this the way things are done in heaven? Is that why the moon looks so glum? The moon is the most complex image in the poem, and its qualities are employed in whatever way Sidney needs them.

William Shakespeare's Sonnet 29 is also from an extensive cycle, one of whose themes is love. Though this sonnet follows the Shakespearian structure, the turn of thought occurs at the end of the octave, as in the Petrarchan sonnet.

William Shakespeare   (1564–1616)

SONNET 29: WHEN IN DISGRACE WITH FORTUNE AND MEN'S EYES   1609

When in disgrace with Fortune and men's eyes	*a*	
I all alone beweep my outcast state,	*b*	
And trouble deaf heaven with my bootless° cries,	*a*	
And look upon myself and curse my fate,	*b*	
Wishing me like to one more rich in hope,	*c*	5
Featured like him, like him with friends possessed	*d*	
Desiring this man's art, and that man's scope,	*c*	
With what I most enjoy contented least;	*d*	
Yet in these thoughts myself almost despising,	*e*	

---

3 *bootless*: Useless.

Haply I think on thee, and then my state   *f*   10
(Like to the lark at break of day arising   *e*
From sullen° earth) sings hymns at heaven's gate,   *f*
   For thy sweet love remembered such wealth brings,   *g*
   That then I scorn to change my state with kings.   *g*

12 *sullen*: Dull, heavy.

The octave tells us how the speaker feels when he is emotionally down. He describes moments when he feels outcast and envies all others' successes. Even the things he most likes displease him. The turn comes, however, at the darkest moment ("myself almost despising"); he shifts his attention to his beloved and realizes in the sestet how much he has to be grateful for. The images of the sestet—the lark rising, and singing "hymns at heaven's gate"—have been extremely memorable and uplifting to many readers. This poem begins on an emotional downslide, a virtual avalanche, only to turn again upward, rising to a sublimity resembling the status of the monarch. Thus in fourteen lines, an overwhelming transformation has taken place.

John Donne wrote a relatively brief series of holy sonnets which do not constitute a cycle, although they are on religious subjects. The most famous of those follows.

John Donne   (1573–1631)

HOLY SONNET 10: DEATH, BE NOT PROUD   1633

Death, be not proud, though some have calléd thee
Mighty and dreadful, for thou art not so;
For those whom thou think'st thou dost overthrow
Die not, poor Death, nor yet canst thou kill me.
From rest and sleep, which but thy pictures be,   5
Much pleasure; then from thee much more must flow,
And soonest our best men with thee do go,
Rest of their bones, and soul's delivery.
Thou art slave to fate, chance, kings, and desperate men,
And dost with poison, war, and sickness dwell,   10
And poppy° or charms can make us sleep as well
And better than thy stroke; why swell'st° thou then?
One short sleep past, we wake eternally
And death shall be no more; Death, thou shalt die.

11 *poppy*: Opium.   12 *swell'st*: Puff out your chest with pride (a reference to the first line of the poem).

Questions for Close Reading

1. The first quatrain establishes Donne's argument about Death. What, essentially, does he say?
2. The second quatrain compares Death with rest and sleep. What is the point of these comparisons?
3. The third quatrain clinches the argument against Death. What is its basis? To what extent is this quatrain derived from the first two?
4. The final couplet establishes the point of the poem. How does well does it fit with the first twelve lines?
5. Examine the lines for their rhythm. Mark the end-stopped lines with a pencil. Which lines have a break, or caesura, in the middle? What is the effect of the caesura? Examine the lines for the relative strength of the breaks or end-stops. Are some more powerful than others? Is there any relation between them and death (another form of end-stopping)?

Miltonic   The **Miltonic sonnet**, named for John Milton (1608–1672), uses the same rhyme pattern as the Petrarchan for the octave but varies the rhyme scheme of the sestet and places the turn, or change of development, after the ninth, tenth, or eleventh lines of the poem, if it occurs at all. The result is that the Miltonic sonnet feels less segmented and develops its main idea straight through with a special intensity. William Wordsworth's "London, 1802" (p. 602) is an example of the Miltonic sonnet, with its sestet rhyming *cddece*. Like Milton, Wordsworth uses some end-stopped lines, but he depends on enjambed, or run-on lines, especially in the last part of the sestet. If there is a turn, it comes between the octave and the sestet, but there may be no turn at all, since the poem moves intensely forward, developing a single idea.

Many of Milton's sonnets treated personal matters, such as his blindness, his memory of his dead wife, and his anxiety about his own talent. Other sonnets examine public matters, such as his concern for the behavior of parliament, his admiration of friends, and his anger at atrocities against innocent citizens. The sonnet below concerns the murder of a Protestant religious group called the Waldensians who lived peacefully in Italian Piedmont until 1655, when Catholic Piedmontese troops with the church's approval attacked them. Milton, working for the Protestant government of England at the time, was outraged.

John Milton   (1608–1672)

ON THE LATE MASSACRE IN PIEDMONT   1655

> Avenge, O Lord, thy slaughtered Saints, whose bones
>> Lie scattered on the Alpine mountains cold,
>> Ev'n them who kept thy truth so pure of old
>> When all our Fathers worshipped Stocks and Stones,

Forget not: in thy book record their groans 5
 Who were thy Sheep and in their ancient Fold
 Slain by the bloody *Piemontese* that rolled
 Mother with Infant down the Rocks. Their moans
The Vales redoubled to the Hills, and they
 To Heav'n. Their martyred blood and ashes sow 10
 O'er all th' Italian fields where still doth sway
The triple Tyrant:° that from these may grow
 A hundredfold, who having learnt thy way
 Early may fly the Babylonian woe.°

12 *triple Tyrant*: A reference to the triple tiara of the Pope. 14 *Babylonian woe*: The Roman Catholic church.

Questions for Close Reading

1. Are the breaks in rhythm primarily made with end-stopped lines or with caesuras? How many can you identify?
2. The quatrains and tercets are clearly marked by indentation. Are they also units of thought in the poem? What is the function of the indentation?
3. To whom is the poem addressed? Why?
4. How does the rhythmic movement of the lines help intensify Milton's emotional expression?
5. To what extent do you see the form of a sonnet as compressing and intensifying emotion?

 Many modern poets have also used the sonnet. The following poem combines an analysis of the resources of the sonnet with the sonnet itself.

Peter Meinke (b. 1932)

THE POET, TRYING TO SURPRISE GOD 1981

The poet, trying to surprise his God
composed new forms from secret harmonies,
tore from his fiery vision galaxies
of unrelated shapes, both even & odd.
But God just smiled, and gave His know-all nod 5
saying, "There's no surprising One who sees
the acorn, root, and branch of centuries;
I swallow all things up, like Aaron's rod.°

So hold this thought beneath your poet-bonnet:
no matter how free-seeming flows your sample 10

8 *Aaron's rod*: Aaron was Moses's older brother. His rod, a symbol of authority, alone among the rods of other priests, bloomed.

God is by definition the Unsurprised."
"Then I'll return," the poet sighed, "to sonnets
of which this is a rather pale example."

"Is that right?" said God. "I hadn't realized. . . ."

Questions for Close Reading

1. What does Meinke mean in line 2 by "secret harmonies"? What is secret about them?
2. What makes this poem different from the ones discussed earlier?
3. Is this an Italian or an English sonnet?
4. Is this sonnet a "pale example"?
5. What is surprising about it?

The Ballad

The general widespread use of the term *ballad* implies a song, usually sung slowly and lyrically. In poetry a **ballad** is a form sometimes sung or recited to a guitar or lute. Traditionally, the ballad told a story, often one filled with love, promises, war, and disappointment. Ballads often depend on the repetition of key lines for their effect. Some examples in the album include Robert Creeley's "Ballad of the Despairing Husband" (p. 720) which depends on couplet rhyme: "Oh wife, oh wife—I tell you true, / I never loved no one but you." It also uses colloquial language and careful repetition, as in the repeated phrases, "Oh lovely lady" and "Oh loveliest of ladies." Langston Hughes's "Ballad of the Landlord" tells a story familiar to some who live in the city:

> Landlord, landlord
> My roof has sprung a leak.
> Don't you 'member I told you about it
> Way last week?

Hughes wrote many ballads concerning the lives of African-Americans in the 1930s and 1940s. His sensitivity to music and his ear for local dialect and conversational language make his ballads among the most touching of modern examples.

The Ode

The **ode**, a long irregular poem, was originally meant to be a form of sublime poetic utterance inspired by the gods: lyric in nature and exalted in tone. The text of *Oedipus Rex* shows that the ode in ancient Greek drama depended on strophe, antistrophe, and epode. The **strophe** was chanted walking to the right, the **antistrophe** while walking to the left, and the **epode** while standing still in the center. Similarly, odes are usually predicated on oppositions;

the subject of one stanza (the antistrophe) may sometimes reevaluate the subject of the previous stanza (the strophe). The end of the ode (epode) usually attempts to resolve the tensions raised by the body of the poem.

The ode exists in two basic forms. The first, the **Horatian ode**, is usually composed of two or more long stanzas of the same or similar form; its rhyme pattern and meter vary, although most in English rely on rhyming couplets. It tends to be meditative and philosophical. The second, the **Pindaric ode**, is somewhat more flamboyant in that its stanza patterns are highly imaginative and singular. Pindaric odes use rhyme but rarely rely on couplets, and they often mix very short and very long lines in the same stanza.

Some of these forms are also maintained in modern odes. The following modern ode is Horatian (John Keats's "Ode to a Nightingale" [p. 844] is Pindaric). The author does a kind of literary history emphasizing the figures she feels shaped English and American literary modernism.

Anne Stevenson   (b. 1933)

THE FICTION-MAKERS   1982

We were the wrecked elect,
the ruined few. Youth,
youth, the Café Iruña
and the bullfight set,
looped on Lepanto brandy   5
but talking "truth"—
Hem,° the 4 A.M. wisecrack,
the hard way in,
that story we were all at the end of
and couldn't begin—   10
we thought we were living now,
but we were living then.

Sanctified Pound,° a knot
of nerves in his fist,
squeezing the Goddamn iamb   15
out of our verse,
making it new in his
archaeological plot—
to maintain "the sublime"
in the factive?° Couldn't be done.   20
Something went wrong
with "new" in the Pisan pen.

---

7 *Hem*: Ernest Hemingway (1899–1961), American novelist of the "Lost Generation"; the Café Iruña was one of his literary hangouts.   13 *Pound*: Ezra Pound (1885–1972), American poet: the "Pisan Cantos" were written while he was in an American military prison after World War II.   20 *factive*: Concerned with making.

He thought he was making now,
but he was making then.

Virginia, Vanessa,°   25
a teapot, a Fitzroy° fuss,
"Semen?" asks Lytton,
eyeing a smudge on a dress.
How to educate England
and keep a correct address   30
on the path to the river through
Auschwitz? Belsen?
Auden and Isherwood°
stalking glad boys in Berlin—
they thought they were suffering now,   35
but they were suffering then.

Out of pink-cheeked Cwmdonkin,
Dylan° with his Soho grin.
Planted in the fiercest of flames,
gold ash on a stem.   40
When Henry jumped out of his joke,
Mr. Bones sat in.°
Even you, with your breakable heart
in your ruined skin,
those poems all written   45
that have to be you, dear friend,
you guessed you were dying now,
but you were dying then.

Here is a table with glasses,
ribbed cages tipped back,   50
or turned on a hinge to each other
to talk, to talk,
mouths that are drinking or smiling
or quoting some book,
or laughing out laughter as candletongues   55
lick at the dark—
so bright in this fiction
forever becoming its end,
we think we are laughing now,
but we are laughing then.   60

25 *Virginia, Vanessa*: Virginia Woolf (1882–1941), English novelist; Vanessa Bell, English painter; and Lytton Strachey (1880–1932), English historian (see line 27); all were members of the Bloomsbury Group, which flourished in London in the 1930s.   26 *Fitzroy*: Reference to controversial "Fitzroy St. Nude," painting by Sir Matthew Smith (1879–1959).   33 *Auden, Isherwood*: W. H. Auden (1907–1973), poet, and Christopher Isherwood (1904–1980), novelist, were homosexual modernists.   38 *Dylan*: Dylan Thomas (1914–1953), Welsh poet from Cwmdonkin, drank regularly in Soho's White Horse Tavern.

Stevenson's modern interpretation of the ode is elevated, meditative, and lyric. Each stanza treats an aspect of her theme: the modern fiction-makers who dominated her literary world. The poem does not rhyme, but every stanza ends with variations on the same refrain: "we think we are laughing now, / but we are laughing then." The poem does not maintain an exact meter, but individual lines can be scanned and are metrical. The stanzas all have twelve lines, some short, some long. Each stanza treats an aspect of modernist literature, meditating on its scope and success.

The Villanelle

The **villanelle** is not a common fixed form, but it is one of the most surprising. Originally French, a language rich in rhymes, the villanelle is extremely difficult in English. The following poem, however, appears to be effortless.

Dylan Thomas (1914–1953)

DO NOT GO GENTLE INTO THAT
GOOD NIGHT (1951, 1952)

Do not go gentle into that good night,
Old age should burn and rave at close of day;
Rage, rage against the dying of the light.

Though wise men at their end know dark is right,
Because their words had forked no lightning they   5
Do not go gentle into that good night.

Good men, the last wave by, crying how bright
Their frail deeds might have danced in a green bay,
Rage, rage against the dying of the light.

Wild men who caught and sang the sun in flight,   10
And learn, too late, they grieved it on its way,
Do not go gentle into that good night.

Grave men, near death, who see with blinding sight
Blind eyes could blaze like meteors and be gay,
Rage, rage against the dying of the light.   15

And you, my father, there on the sad height,
Curse, bless, me now with your fierce tears, I pray.
Do not go gentle into that good night.
Rage, rage against the dying of the light.

Villanelles have six stanzas of iambic pentameter: five with three lines, and the last with four lines. There are only two rhymes, in this case, *night* and *day*. Thomas chose those purposely for their opposition. The first line and the third line of the first stanza repeat throughout the poem: stanza 2 ends with line 1; stanza 3 ends with line 3; stanza 4 ends with line 1; stanza 5 ends with line 3; stanza 6 ends with lines 1 and 3.

Any villanelle is a major achievement, but a poem such as Dylan Thomas's is especially remarkable. Because it is so moving, many readers are totally unaware that it is so tightly patterned. Its emotional qualities and sincerity seem evident in every line, demonstrating Thomas's outstanding technical abilities. He often chose extremely demanding forms because they helped him in his composition.

Part of our delight in poetry is being surprised. Peter Meinke reminds us that form can be surprising. Dylan Thomas reminds us that tight formal demands do not rob a poem of its importance or significance. To some extent, we admire the poet who can employ a dazzling technique: after all, poetry, like other literature, demands technique or else it fails. But we are also suspicious of writers whose only virtue is a flashy technique. What we admire most is the combination of serious motives and competent formal technique. The poems we have studied offer insight into that combination.

IDEAS

Poems are about something. When a poet such as E. E. Cummings composes a complex structure like "l(a" (p. 606), he shows us that a poem can focus on a single idea, loneliness, and come close to "performing" the idea. When we interpret a poem, we usually focus on its ideas. The other elements of poetry are marshaled in the service of the ideas, and by seeing how they work, we confront the ideas. In some poems, the ideas are very basic; in others, they are diffuse, complex, ambiguous, sometimes paradoxical, and sometimes even contradictory.

Ideas in poetry are not necessarily as straightforward as other elements, such as meter or rhyme. Meter and rhyme may be slippery, but a consensus can usually be reached well enough for you to describe a poem as, say, a sonnet, in terms of its pattern of rhyme and meter. But ideas are apparent only when you have begun the process of interpretation, which usually coordinates with your first reading. Close reading permits you to examine the ideas in detail and to see that poems can suggest one kind of idea when approached from one point of view and quite a different kind when approached from another. However, even when readers agree on the presence of an idea in a poem, they may disagree totally on what to make of it.

When we examine poems here for their ideas—in the sense that their ideas are an element of the poem—we try not to be judgmental. For example, the main idea of Cummings's poem "1(a" is definitely loneliness. In that sense the idea is an element of the poem. But whether the poem implies that loneliness is good, bad, inevitable, avoidable, or even neutral is a question of interpretation. Some poems naturally demand more interpretation than others, but all poems can stand up under close scrutiny. Readers may evaluate ideas in the same fashion they evaluate metaphors, rhyme patterns, imagery, or any other element of a poem.

The following poem is from a tradition called *carpe diem*, which means "seize the day." Carpe diem poems remind us that we are not going to live forever, and they exhort us to live now because tomorrow we may die. Such poems have been with us from the most ancient times.

Robert Herrick   (1591–1674)

TO THE VIRGINS, TO MAKE MUCH OF TIME   1648

Gather ye rosebuds while ye may,
   Old time is still a flying;
And this same flower that smiles today
   Tomorrow will be dying.

The glorious lamp of heaven, the sun,   5
   The higher he's a getting;
The sooner will his race be run,
   And nearer he's to setting.

That age is best which is the first,
   When youth and blood are warmer;   10
But being spent, the worse and worst
   Times still succeed the former.

Then be not coy, but use your time;
   And while ye may, go marry:
For, having lost but once your prime,   15
   You may for ever tarry.

Like a sonnet, this poem is segmented: each stanza treats an issue relative to the overall idea of seizing the day, and all these stanzas have a cumulative effect. The main idea is that we are like flowers who bloom in our youth for only a short time, then fade quickly; therefore, we should make the most of our youth and get married. The first stanza uses flowers in two ways. First, they are the rewards our youth can bring us—"Gather ye rosebuds." Second, the smiling, dying flower is metaphorically ourselves. The second stanza tells us that the sun rises and sets, and like Shakespeare in his Sonnet 73 (p. 595), Herrick uses the day as a metaphor for our entire life. Each stanza presents us with evidence that we can examine from nature around us, and we conclude that we, like all natural things, will age and die. The third stanza argues that old age is not much good, whereas youth is not only first, but "best." The last stanza urges the reader not to hold back ("be not coy") but "go marry." If you miss your chance, "You may for ever tarry."

The historical circumstances of the poem need to be taken into account primarily because the life expectancy in the seventeenth century was not comparable to ours. And, since medical science was primitive and based on erroneous theories, old age would have been painful and tormented by a wide variety of sicknesses and agonies. Consequently, it is not difficult to see why Herrick would have urged the young to take advantage of their youth, even to the point of rushing things. The idea that one should seize the day is clearly expressed in the form of an argument, and one that has been convincing enough to make this poem famous. Andrew Marvell and many others have used the same idea, and its appeal is not likely to diminish. Of course, any poem that presents its ideas in the form of an argument is susceptible to counterargument, as when Sir Walter Raleigh's "The Nymph's Reply to the Shepherd" (p. 906) contradicts Christopher Marlowe's "The Passionate Shepherd to His Love" (p. 878).

Parody is a mimic of another poem implying a reinterpretation of one poet's work by another poet. Thus all parodies use the same form as the poem they parody, with perhaps some variations. Often the purpose is to have fun; sometimes it is to mock; sometimes it is to show respect. Parodies critique both a poem's form and its ideas. Several parodies follow in the album of poems. Marilyn Waniek shows respect both to Emily Dickinson and E. E. Cummings in her "Emily Dickinson's Defunct" (p. 974), which parodies Cummings's "Buffalo Bill's Defunct" (p. 725). The reader must decide what purposes are served by Louis Simpson's witty "New Lines for Cuscuscaraway and Mirza Murad Ali Beg" (p. 942), which parodies T. S. Eliot's "Lines for Cuscuscaraway and Mirza Murad Ali Beg" (p. 751). It has often been said that only good poems can be successfully parodied, so in a way a parody is a form of praise.

The next poem, written in 1867, explores quite different ideas, which modern readers have seen as prophetic of the coming wars on the European continent in 1914 and 1939. Arnold believed that the modern world abandoned important values of religious faith and that the results would be terrifying.

Matthew Arnold   (1822–1888)
DOVER BEACH   1867

The sea is calm to-night.
The tide is full, the moon lies fair
Upon the straits;—on the French coast the light

Gleams and is gone; the cliffs of England stand,
Glimmering and vast, out in the tranquil bay.   5
Come to the window, sweet is the night-air!

Only, from the long line of spray
Where the sea meets the moon-blanch'd land,
Listen! you hear the grating roar
Of pebbles which the waves draw back, and fling,   10
At their return, up the high strand,
Begin, and cease, and then again begin,
With tremulous cadence slow, and bring
The eternal note of sadness in.

Sophocles long ago   15
Heard it on the Aegean, and it brought
Into his mind the turbid ebb and flow
Of human misery; we
Find also in the sound a thought,
Hearing it by this distant northern sea.   20

The Sea of Faith
Was once, too, at the full, and round earth's shore
Lay like the folds of a bright girdle furl'd.
But now I only hear
Its melancholy, long, withdrawing roar,   25
Retreating, to the breath
Of the night-wind, down the vast edges drear
And naked shingles° of the world.

Ah, love, let us be true
To one another! for the world, which seems   30
To lie before us like a land of dreams,
So various, so beautiful, so new,
Hath really neither joy, nor love, nor light,
Nor certitude, nor peace, nor help for pain;
And we are here as on a darkling plain   35
Swept with confused alarms of struggle and flight,
Where ignorant armies clash by night.

28 *Shingles.* Pebbly beaches.

The reader becomes slowly aware that the narrator of the poem is speaking to his beloved while looking out from Dover, where the English channel, only twenty miles wide, is close enough to see lights in French towns. The narrator hears the sounds of the waves drawing the pebbles back along the beach, and the steadiness of the sea reminds him of the normal rhythms of change, the ebb and flow of history, as Sophocles knew it in his play *Antigone,* when its memory "brought / Into his mind the turbid ebb and flow / Of human misery." The rhythm of ebb and flow pertains to "The Sea of Faith" as well, and Arnold's point is that faith is ebbing: "now I only hear / Its melancholy, long, withdrawing roar." He sees the new age as having "neither joy, nor love, nor light, / Nor certitude, nor peace, nor help for pain." In consequence, he implores himself and his beloved to "be true / To one another!" It is their only assurance in a world in which armies struggle relentlessly for command of the world. These armies are metaphors for forces that command individuals' belief in political, economic, or religious systems. The image of Arnold and his beloved on a "darkling plain" has had special power in part because so many decisive battles of history, since ancient times, have been fought on plains.

The following poem by Anne Sexton is about her father. It is filled with ideas, and it may be fair to say no single idea stands out, as it does, for example, in Herrick's poem. If you feel that the main idea is Sexton's forgiveness of her father, as stated in her last line, then you will also have to admit that she takes a long time to get to it. Yet all the ideas in the poem are linked to her feelings and thoughts about her father now that he is dead.

Anne Sexton   (1928–1974)

ALL MY PRETTY ONES   1962

All my pretty ones?
Did you say all? O hell-kite! All?
What! all my pretty chickens and their dam
At one fell swoop? . . .
I cannot but remember such things were,
That were most precious to me.°

—Macbeth

Father, this year's jinx° rides us apart
where you followed our mother to her cold slumber,
a second shock boiling its stone to your heart,
leaving me here to shuffle and disencumber
you from the residence you could not afford: 5
a gold key, your half of a woollen mill,
twenty suits from Dunne's, an English Ford,
the love and legal verbiage of another will,
boxes of pictures of people I do not know.
I touch their cardboard faces. They must go.   10

But the eyes, as thick as wood in this album,
hold me. I stop here, where a small boy
waits in a ruffled dress for someone to come . . .

All . . . me: In these lines Macduff realizes that his wife and children have been killed by Macbeth.
1 *jinx:* Sexton's mother died in March and her father in June of 1959.

for this soldier who holds his bugle like a toy
or for this velvet lady who cannot smile.   15
Is this your father's father, this commodore
in a mailman suit? My father, time meanwhile
has made it unimportant who you are looking for.
I'll never know what these faces are all about.
I lock them into their book and throw them out.   20

This is the yellow scrapbook that you began
the year I was born; as crackling now and wrinkly
as tobacco leaves: clippings where Hoover outran
the Democrats, wiggling his dry finger at me
and Prohibition; news where the Hindenburg went   25
down and recent years where you went flush
on war. This year, solvent but sick, you meant
to marry that pretty widow in a one-month rush.
But before you had that second chance, I cried
on your fat shoulder. Three days later you died.   30

These are the snapshots of marriage, stopped in places.
Side by side at the rail toward Nassau° now;
here, with the winner's cup at the speedboat races,
here, in tails at the Cotillion, you take a bow,
here, by our kennel of dogs with their pink eyes,   35
running like show-bred pigs in their chain-link pen;
here, at the horseshow where my sister wins a prize;
and here, standing like a duke among groups of men.
Now I fold you down, my drunkard, my navigator,
my first lost keeper, to love or look at later.   40

I hold a five-year diary that my mother kept
for three years, telling all she does not say
of your alcoholic tendency. You overslept,
she writes. My God, father, each Christmas Day
with your blood, will I drink down your glass   45
of wine? The diary of your hurly-burly years
goes to my shelf to wait for my age to pass.
Only in this hoarded span will love persevere.
Whether you are pretty or not, I outlive you,
bend down my strange face to yours and forgive you.   50

32 *Nassau*: There are snapshots from her parents' honeymoon trip to the Bahamas.

Questions for Close Reading

1. Can you establish Sexton's feelings toward her father from the tone of the
   first stanza?

2. What can you tell about her father's way of living from the first stanza?
3. In the second stanza Sexton sees her father as a child standing like a soldier with a bugle. As in the first stanza, she decides to throw out all the photographs. Has she made the right decision?
4. How does she react to the scrapbook her father started when she was born? Why keep clippings of historical events in her scrapbook? Are her father's feelings revealed in that detail?
5. What style of life do the snapshots in stanza 5 reveal? How does the tone change in the last two lines of that stanza?
6. How does your reading of the last stanza change in light of the knowledge that Sexton was worried about her own alcoholic tendencies? Why can't she read the diary of her father's "hurly-burly years"?
7. How does the next to last line connect with the epigraph from *Macbeth*? How effective is the irony of her lamenting her father in contrast with Macduff's lamenting his children?
8. What does Sexton have to forgive her father for? Should she forgive him?

The author of the following poem, Derek Walcott, is winner of the Nobel Prize for literature and the best-known poet of the West Indies. He was born in St. Lucia and educated in Jamaica. His plays have been seen in Europe and the Americas. This poem's title is a pun, since "A Far Cry" can be taken in several ways. In a sense, it is connected with the main ideas of the poem.

Derek Walcott   (b. 1930)

A FAR CRY FROM AFRICA   1962

A wind is ruffling the tawny pelt
Of Africa. Kikuyu,° quick as flies,
Batten upon the bloodstreams of the veldt.
Corpses are scattered through a paradise.
Only the worm, colonel of carrion, cries: 5
"Waste no compassion on these separate dead!"
Statistics justify and scholars seize
The salients of colonial policy.
What is that to the white child hacked in bed?
To savages, expendable as Jews?   10

Threshed out by beaters, the long rushes break
In a white dust of ibises whose cries
Have wheeled since civilization's dawn
From the parched river or beast-teeming plain.
The violence of beast on beast is read   15
As natural law, but upright man

2 *Kikuyu*: A tribal group in Kenya.

Seeks his divinity by inflicting pain.
Delirious as these worried beasts, his wars
Dance to the tightened carcass of a drum,
While he calls courage still that native dread   20
Of the white peace contracted by the dead.

Again brutish necessity wipes its hands
Upon the napkin of a dirty cause, again
A waste of our compassion, as with Spain,°
The gorilla wrestles with the superman.   25

I who am poisoned with the blood of both,
Where shall I turn, divided to the vein?
I who have cursed
The drunken officer of British rule, how choose
Between this Africa and the English tongue I love?   30
Betray them both, or give back what they give?
How can I face such slaughter and be cool?
How can I turn from Africa and live?

24 *Spain*: A reference to the Spanish Civil War in the late 1930s.

Questions for Close Reading

1. The Kikuyu were the Mau-Mau terrorists killing British settlers in Kenya during the 1960s. Whose corpses are "scattered through a paradise"? What seem to be the "salients of colonial policy"?
2. Stanza 2 treats an important idea of modern life: nature is savage but humans are expected to be humane. How does this idea relate to Africa?
3. How do "native dread" and "white peace" relate to each other in stanza 2?
4. What is the "napkin of a dirty cause"? What idea is expressed in stanza 3?
5. What does Walcott mean by "I who am poisoned with the blood of both"? What is his predicament? How does the last stanza make his situation felt?
6. English is Walcott's language. Why is it a problem for him?

Ishmael Reed, an African-American poet, sometimes writes polemical, idea-laden poems and often finds surprising connections between popular culture and the most serious concerns of civilization. The main idea behind the poem that follows is a theory of literary criticism: that the reader and the poem are not totally separate.

Ishmael Reed   (b. 1938)

BEWARE : DO NOT READ THIS POEM   1968

tonite, thriller was
abt an ol woman, so vain she

surrounded herself w/
    many mirrors

it got so bad that finally she   5
locked herself indoors & her
whole life became the
    mirrors

one day the villagers broke
into her house , but she was too   10
swift for them . she disappeared
    into a mirror
each tenant who bought the house
after that , lost a loved one to
    the ol woman in the mirror   :   15
      first a little girl
      then a young woman
      then   the   young   woman/s   husband

the hunger of this poem is legendary
it has taken in many victims   20
back off from this poem
it has drawn in yr feet
back off from this poem
it has drawn in yr legs

back off from this poem   25
it is a greedy mirror
you are into this poem   .   from
    the waist down
nobody can hear you can they ?
this poem has had you up to here   30
    belch
this poem aint got no manners
you cant call out frm this poem
relax now & go w/ this poem

move & roll on to this poem   35
do not resist this poem
this poem has yr eyes
this poem has his head
this poem has his arms
this poem has his fingers   40
this poem has his fingertips

this poem is the reader & the
reader this poem

> statistic : the us bureau of missing persons re-
> ports that in 1968 over 100,000 people   45
> disappeared leaving no solid clues
>   nor trace   only
>   a space   in the lives of their friends

Questions for Close Reading

1. What unusual stylistic techniques do you see in the poem? What conventions of spelling, writing, and expression is Reed experimenting with? Are his experiments effective?
2. Judging from what Reed says, what do poems do?
3. Why do you continue reading when the poem plainly says, "back off from this poem"?
4. When Reed says, "do not resist this poem," do you find yourself resisting it or not?
5. Why does the pronoun shift near the end from "yr" to "his" in "this poem has yr eyes / this poem has his head"?
6. Is it true that "this poem is the reader & the / reader this poem"?

THE ELEMENTS WORKING TOGETHER

Close reading means seeing many elements of poetry at work in combination to produce a total effect. We learn about language, imagery, tone, rhythms and rhymes, metaphor and figurative language, symbol, form, and ideas so we can recognize them at work, but they work together. When you read a poem, any one of these elements may strike you first as very important, but only if you know what the elements of a poem are in the first place. Otherwise, your impression of a poem may be vague and imprecise: you may have the sense that you like or dislike a poem but have no concrete idea why, or even what it is that you like or dislike. Understanding what the components of a poem are helps you clarify your impressions and solidify your understanding.

Before beginning to work on the following poem, read it through and develop an overall impression; then consider the commentary that follows.

Patricia Goedicke   (b. 1931)

WISE OWL   1968

An old black bird on a strand of silk,
Sidewise my father walks the white ice
Between two fields of snow.
It is night. The air is like thin milk,

Icicles click in the wind like dice,   5
His steps are crabbed and slow,

But dapper as a magpie with a game leg
The old brave gambler bets his hide
Against the glittering street,
Though the moon is a bright metallic egg,   10
The cold snaps at his twisted side,
And the snow flusters his feet.

Beside him the languorous featherbed fields
Dovecall comfort to the old crow:
If he would stop he would stay,   15
Lose and find himself softly concealed,
Sunk in the mothering mounded snow,
Nested the easiest way

But no. Not for this wise owl. The road
May dwindle away to an icy thread   20
But the dream of a new design
Mumbles and broods in his hunched head
Better luck next time, the gambler's goad
That keeps him along the lifeline.

So like a sparrow on a telephone wire   25
He balances down the tightrope track,
The road that must narrow as the night
Must finally constrict the flow of fire,
Harden, pinch the heart, and crack:
Ahead is the home light.   30

Before discussing the poem in detail, we will take a brief look at some of its most obvious elements.

Language The language is conversational, easy. Goedicke speaks to a friend (or to herself) with little or no artificiality. The key words all connect with key images: "crabbed," "dapper," "languorous."

Imagery The setting of the poem is a snowy pathway at night, so much of the description is relevant to snow, ice, the moon, and darkness.

Tone The tone of the poem is not easy to discern, since there seems to be at once a reverence toward the subject, "my father," and at the same time a critical attitude, implied in all the references to him as a gambler who "bets his hide."

Rhythm and Rhyme   The rhythm of the poem is not unusual: the lines are often end-stopped and sometimes run-on. They rarely break in the middle, except in line 4. The rhyme pattern is consistent: *abcabc*, and so on. However, the lines are not metrically regular; the accents fall freely and the lines vary in length.

An old | black bird | on a strand | of silk,

Sidewise | my fa | ther walks | the white ice

Metaphor and Figurative Language   The poem makes many references to birds that seem to be metaphoric. Even the title is an important metaphor. The use of dice and the reference to gambling may be metaphoric.

Symbol   The "wise owl" seems to be a symbolic reference to the poet's father. The track down which the father travels seems to be symbolic of the path of life, especially since it "must narrow as the night."

Form   The poem is strophic; its six-line stanzas are all alike in form. These stanzas have no special name; however, poems which use such strophic stanzas are often odes, as this one seems to be.

Ideas   The main idea seems to be connected with the risk taking involved in pursuing the path of life. Survival is a key issue in the poem.

Working with these elements together helps us get a full grasp of the poem. The regularity of the repeated stanza structure reassures us, since we know we can rely upon the repetition and completion of the pattern. The structure of the ode implies that the poem will meditate on a serious subject, one that can be reflected upon from two points of view. The poet's father is a "wise owl"—a phrase that most people would have amended to say, "wise old owl." The owl is a symbol of wisdom, so the title reinforces itself and also makes us aware of its relevance as a descriptor of the father. The father, cautious as he gets older, walks sidewise ("crabbed and slow"), along the ice. He is like "An old black bird" (it is night) and the "Icicles click in the wind like dice" because the old father takes his chances. When he is called the "old brave gambler," the tone becomes one of respect and admiration because the father continues taking his chances in life even though the snow "flusters his feet."

The imagery associated with the path implies that the father has to struggle. Things are not easy for him, not even walking. The season has placed impediments before him, and some of them are dangerous. The poet's admiration continues in her descriptive imagery of him as "dapper as a magpie," implying that he is trim, self-aware (maybe even a bit vain), and roguish (the magpie is often characterized as thieving). In stanza 3 a new idea enters in the metaphoric comparison of the snow field: "featherbed fields / Dovecall comfort to the old crow." We remember that it is winter, and as in Shakespeare's sonnet, winter symbolizes the end of life. Here the poet points out that the end of life implies rest. Were her father to stop on his path, he could rest in the "mothering mounded snow." He could find peace and comfort. When we encounter this image, we realize the meaning of the first rhyme in the poem: *silk* with *milk*. Both imply softness, perhaps mothering, perhaps comfort. By the time we have read through the third stanza, we can see that the other early rhymes—*ice, dice* and *snow, slow*—reinforce the main ideas of the poem.

Once it is plain, in stanza 5, that the father will not stop, will not rest, we realize that the power of the rhythms of line 19 reinforce the entire poem: "But no. Not for this wise owl. The road / May dwindle" contains two caesuras with strong periods breaking the line twice. When the line continues, it runs on powerfully into the next line. Every successive line is a run-on line, implying the need to continue moving, to keep on the "road" that has become a "lifeline." The stanza enacts the idea of continuous motion.

The last stanza recognizes, however, that the journey must someday be over. "The road . . . must narrow as the night," but when it does, what is "Ahead is the home light." The poet thus prepares for the inevitable death of her father, but only after seeing him as persisting in his struggle, taking his chances, refusing to give up. The bird of the last stanza is a sparrow, perhaps alluding to Hamlet's "There is special providence in the fall of a sparrow" (V.II.223–24), by which he means that God takes notice even of the slightest of his creatures when they die. Like Hamlet, Goedicke's narrator is prepared for death because she has observed life so closely. By watching her father, she has become a wise owl herself.

This close reading of the text relies on a formalist critical approach. It would be possible to develop a fuller formalist interpretation of the poem, but its basis would be in the close reading done here. Moreover, this reading will also support a variety of other interpretive strategies. Consider a psychoanalytic approach, for example, with the complications of the poet/daughter learning to accept the weakening and eventual death of the father. The use of the bird imagery is also very complex and suggestive from a psychoanalytic point of view, especially since there is no consideration of a mother (apart from the suggestion of the "bright metallic egg" of the moon). The feminist would also examine the tone of the poem to examine the relationship between father and daughter. Other interpretive strategies can be brought to bear on the poem, but all will benefit from a close reading of the text.

John Keats, famous for his great odes, used a poetic strategy that may have inspired Patricia Goedicke. His "Ode on a Grecian Urn" also has five strophic stanzas. His rhyme scheme is: *ababcdedce,* and his lines follow a regular meter: iambic pentameter. Like Goedicke, Keats focuses entirely on something outside himself. Goedicke focuses on her father making his way through difficult snowy paths; Keats focuses on a genuine Grecian urn that still exists in the British Museum. When he addresses the urn (Goedicke never addresses her father), he points to the scenes that are on its surface with the understanding that they represent a life that is long gone, the life of ancient Greece. The scenes are equivalent to a language; they function in the same way that a letter from ancient times would function. Keats turns the urn about and regards its different scenes, calling the urn a "sylvan historian" because it tells the history of rural (sylvan) life.

John Keats   (1795–1821)

ODE ON A GRECIAN URN   1819

I

 Thou° still unravished bride of quietness,
  Thou foster-child of silence and slow time,
 Sylvan historian, who canst thus express
  A flowery tale more sweetly than our rhyme:
 What leaf-fringed legend haunts about thy shape   5
  Of deities or mortals, or of both,
   In Tempe or the dales of Arcady?
 What men or gods are these? What maidens loth?
 What mad pursuit? What struggle to escape?
   What pipes and timbrels? What wild ecstasy?   10

II

 Heard melodies are sweet, but those unheard
  Are sweeter;° therefore, ye soft pipes, play on;
 Not to the sensual ear, but, more endeared,
  Pipe to the spirit ditties of no tone:
 Fair youth, beneath the trees, thou canst not leave   15
  Thy song, nor ever can those trees be bare;
   Bold lover, never, never canst thou kiss,
 Though winning near the goal—yet, do not grieve;
   She cannot fade, though thou hast not thy bliss,
  Forever wilt thou love, and she be fair!   20

III

 Ah, happy, happy boughs! that cannot shed
  Your leaves, nor ever bid the spring adieu;
 And, happy melodist, unwearied,
  Forever piping songs forever new;

---

1 *Thou*: The urn itself.   11–12 *Heard . . . sweeter*: Platonic theory held that the inaudible "music of the spheres" was the most beautiful sound in the universe.

More happy love! more happy, happy love!   25
  Forever warm and still to be enjoyed,
    Forever panting, and forever young;
All breathing human passion far above,
  That leaves a heart high-sorrowful and cloyed,
    A burning forehead, and a parching tongue.   30

IV

Who are these coming to the sacrifice?
  To what green altar, O mysterious priest,
Lead'st thou that heifer lowing at the skies,
  And all her silken flanks with garlands drest?
What little town by river or sea shore,   35
  Or mountain-built with peaceful citadel,
    Is emptied of this folk, this pious morn?
And, little town, thy streets forevermore
  Will silent be; and not a soul to tell
    Why thou art desolate, can e'er return.   40

V

O Attic° shape! Fair attitude! with brede°
  Of marble men and maidens overwrought,
With forest branches and the trodden weed;
  Thou, silent form, dost tease us out of thought
As doth eternity: Cold Pastoral!   45
  When old age shall this generation waste,
    Thou shalt remain, in midst of other woe
Than ours, a friend to man, to whom thou say'st,
  "Beauty is truth, truth beauty,"—that is all
    Ye know on earth, and all ye need to know.°   50

41 *Attic*: Referring to Athens. *brede*: Woven pattern. 49–50 *"Beauty . . . know*: An early edition closed the quotation after "know," thus making the urn's message the last two lines.

Again, it will help to perform a simple listing of the poem's elements.

Language Keats uses a number of interesting word combinations for effect: *foster-child, leaf-fringed,* and *high-sorrowful* to raise the emotional pitch of the poem. He also repeats key words, as in the six repetitions of *happy* in stanza 3. Another key use of language is the rhetorical question (a question which expects no answer), as in the end of stanza 1 and the beginning of stanza 4. The entire poem is a direct address to the urn itself.

Imagery Several kinds of imagery are at work in the poem. First, there is the imagery associated with the urn as an urn, as when it is called a "still unravished bride" or "sylvan historian." Then there is the imagery of the scenes pictured on the urn, in the classical "dales of Arcady," the Greek paradise. In stanza 2 there is some aural imagery ("soft pipes").

Tone   The tone is established in the reverence of the poet's questions and the solemnity of Keats's address in the opening two lines. If one may be said to hold an object in awe, Keats seems to do so in this poem.

Rhythm and Rhyme   The lines are metrical:

Thou still | unrav | ished bride | of qui | etness,

with each line essentially iambic pentameter: five feet (ten syllables). Most of the lines are end-stopped, with often the first and second lines of a stanza running on to keep the rhythm intense and swift.

Metaphor and Figurative Language   The most important metaphor may be the urn itself as "sylvan historian." It tells a tale from ancient days, revealing the continuity of life.

Symbol   The urn may be a symbol of perfection or of beauty. For Keats, who was dying of tuberculosis, it was a symbol of the endurance of art.

Form   The ode has five strophic stanzas of exactly the same form, with each stanza meditating on an aspect of the urn.

Ideas   Implied throughout the poem is a contrast of the "Cold Pastoral" of the scenes around the urn with "A burning forehead, and a parching tongue" of the feverish, tubercular world in which Keats lived. The idea of the endurance of art possesses Keats's imagination. Finally, the message that the urn speaks to us: "Beauty is truth, truth beauty," is a key idea in the poem. The question of whether or not it "is all / Ye know on earth, and all ye need to know" is central to all discussions of the poem.

Any interpretation of the poem would need to take into account an expansion of these issues. In addition, each of the scenes on the urn needs to be examined for its imagery, its contribution to the poem. Keats says that the urn tells a "tale more sweetly than our rhyme," and it is important for us to examine each of its scenes of shepherds and priests of ancient Greece ("deities or mortals"). The word *legend* has two meanings: one refers to what is written on the object before us (Keats's first meaning), and the other to mythic story, Keats's important secondary meaning.

Implied in the poem is a contrast of the present with the ancient Greek world. Keats and other Romantic poets were deeply touched by the struggle of the Greeks to free their homeland, and many English poets visited Greece. One, Lord Byron, died there hoping to fight for Greek independence. Keats offers us a Romantic view of Greece by centering only on the imagery of the dancers and musicians in stanza 1, the shepherd boy with his shepherd's pipes and the lovers about to kiss in stanza 2, and the priests bringing the heifer to the altar of their gods in stanza 4, thus creating an ideal world.

Keats also concentrates on the mystery of the urn by reminding us that it cannot speak, and that we divine its meaning from its scenes. Its shape is an ideal form of beauty as Keats understands it. Upon it are "overwrought" "marble men and maidens" representing people who once lived and loved and prayed. They remind him that "old age shall this generation waste," so the urn becomes not just a thing of beauty but a *memento mori*—a reminder of death. Since Keats knew he was dying as he wrote the poem, the urn had a special meaning.

A full interpretation should take into account the fact that there are two versions of the poem. The other version has the urn speaking both last lines, thus telling us that its message is all we know on earth or need to know. No one has successfully unriddled this confusion, although theories are numerous. An interpretation might consider that mystery; it also should ask why Keats tells us in the beginning that the urn is silent and then goes on to make it talk.

Perhaps the question of why Keats demands that the urn speak would be answered by analysis from a psychoanalytic perspective, regarding the urn as a parent in the artistic sense. Some of these comments refer to Keats's dying of tuberculosis, and an interpretation of the poem in light of his illness would depend on research. A detailed historical interpretation would also involve research into the influence of Greek culture in the world of the educated English citizen of the early 1800s. Keats wrote after Napoleon's defeat at Waterloo (1814) and after the huge military campaigns that introduced northeastern Europe to the then exotic worlds of Egypt, Greece, and the Middle East. A critical view that took economics into account might quarrel with Keats's idealizing the scenes on the urn, venerating the perfection of its shape, and then focusing on a limited aesthetic message assigning truth to beauty and nothing else. The political critic would find the treatment of power in this poem unsatisfying. How, for example, do the priests wield their power, and who gives it to them? However complex any of these interpretations may be, they will depend on a close reading of the text. Since this has been a favorite of formalist critics, one may profitably reflect on the possibility that Keats is himself a formalist critic in dealing with the form of the urn itself and interpreting its implied narrative.

The next poem is in the tradition of John Donne's *Holy Sonnets*. Like Donne, Hopkins was a priest. He was part of a religious revival among British intellectuals in the second half of the nineteenth century, and he taught in University College Dublin. In some ways his poem is antiurban and what we might call today "environmentalist." But Hopkins' environment is spiritual, not just physical.

Gerard Manley Hopkins   (1844–1889)

GOD'S GRANDEUR   1877

The world is charged wíth the grándeur of God.
   It will flame out, like shining from shook foil;
   It gathers tó a greatness, like the ooze of oil
Crushed. Why do men then now not reck his rod?
Génerátions have trod, have trod, have trod;   5
   And all is seared with trade; bleared, smeared, with toil;
   And wears man's smudge and shares man's smell: the soil
Is bare now, nor can foot feel, being shod.

Ánd, for all this, náture is never spent;
   There lives the dearest freshness deep down things;   10
And though the last lights off the black West went
   Oh, morning, at the brown brink eastward, springs—
Because the Holy Ghost óver the bent
   World broods with warm breast and with ah! bright wings.

Language   Hopkins uses language in special ways: repetition in lines 5 and
6, alliteration in *ooze of oil, reck his rod, foot feel,* and especially the *w*
sounds in the last line.

Imagery   The images appeal to many senses: the sense of sight—"shining
from shook foil"; touch—"ooze of oil," "nor can foot feel"; and smell—
"shares man's smell." Flame imagery, associated with God, is also associated in "seared" with trade and industry. The final image of the Holy
Ghost as a bird brooding over the world, as if it were an egg, is quite
powerful.

Tone   At first the tone is magisterial, proclaiming that "The world is charged
with the grandeur of God." But it becomes almost chastening when it
asks why people do "not reck his rod," that is, pay attention and behave
themselves. The octave ends with the sense that we have ruined planet
earth; the sestet returns with the hopeful message that it will renew itself, and the tone becomes reverent and filled with hope in describing
the Holy Ghost.

Rhythm and Rhyme   The lines are metrical:

The world I is charged I with the I grandeur I of God.

Each line is essentially iambic pentameter: five feet (ten syllables), as in
all traditional sonnets. Most of the lines are end-stopped, with the last
four lines of the poem run-on so as to exploit the emotional intensity

of the final imagery. Certain syllables are accented to help the reader find the stresses Hopkins intended, and the arcs over words in line 3 indicate rapid movement, so *gathers* and *to a* must be spoken as if they were one-syllable words. Hopkins had his own system of scansion, sometimes referred to as "sprung rhythm," reminiscent of school rhymes. The marks over words in this poem help us see his method. The rhymes are very interesting: *God* and *rod* suggest that God can punish as well as love. *Foil, oil, toil, soil* are very unusual rhymes, but all relate to one another. Hopkins also depends on internal rhyme, such as *seared, bleared, smeared* in line 6.

Metaphor and Figurative Language   The metaphor of the world being charged as if it were a battery (or explosive) is dominant in the octave, and the metaphor of nature as something that can be spent, either as in one's energy or one's money, is dominant in the sestet.

Symbol   One might ask if nature is a symbol for God, but answering such a question poses interesting difficulties.

Form   This is a Petrarchan sonnet rhyming *abbaabba*, then *cdcdcd*. Relying on so few rhymes increases the challenge. The octave establishes what man has done to the world in modern times. The sestet explains why, even in the darkest night, the sunrise spells hope and a new beginning.

Ideas   It may be that the first line contains the primary ideas of the poem, in which case it is a statement of faith in the power of nature and God. Hopkins tells us that nature is never spent, but he predicates this view on a highly spiritual belief. His God is the conventional God of his time and religion, and he expects us to treat this as a religious poem. One can also see this as an environmental plea to save the earth, but one would have to keep God in the picture to be true to the poem.

Questions for Close Reading

1. Which elements work best together in reinforcing the idea that the "world is charged with the grandeur of God"?
2. How do the limits of iambic pentameter and only four rhymes contribute to the idea expressed in line 9 that "nature is never spent"?
3. Do the elements function well in this poem in light of its demand that it be considered a religious poem? What does it mean for a poem to be religious? Do you feel it is religious?
4. How do the elements of the poem reinforce its main ideas?

The author of the following poem, Edward Hirsch, is an American poet whose poem uses the American game of basketball as its basis. Just as Patricia

Goedicke focuses on her father as a wise owl, John Keats focuses on the Grecian urn, and Gerard Manley Hopkins focuses on the "grandeur of God," Hirsch focuses on a fast break to meditate on an important aspect of life.

Edward Hirsch   (b. 1950)

FAST BREAK   1985

In memory of Dennis Turner, 1946–1984

A hook shot kisses the rim and
hangs there, helplessly, but doesn't drop,

and for once our gangly starting center
boxes out his man and times his jump

perfectly, gathering the orange leather   5
from the air like a cherished possession

and spinning around to throw a strike
to the outlet who is already shoveling

an underhand pass toward the other guard
scissoring past a flat-footed defender   10

who looks stunned and nailed to the floor
in the wrong direction, trying to catch sight

of a high, gliding dribble and a man
letting the play develop in front of him

in slow motion, almost exactly   15
like a coach's drawing on the blackboard,

both forwards racing down the court
the way that forwards should, fanning out

and filling the lanes in tandem, moving
together as brothers passing the ball   20

between them without a dribble, without
a single bounce hitting the hardwood

until the guard finally lunges out
and commits to the wrong man

while the power-forward explodes past them   25
in a fury, taking the ball into the air

by himself now and laying it gently
against the glass for a lay-up,

but losing his balance in the process,
inexplicably falling, hitting the floor   30

with a wild, headlong motion
for the game he loved like a country

and swiveling back to see an orange blur
floating perfectly through the net.

Questions for Close Reading

1. Examine the form of the poem, especially the end-stopped and run-on
   lines, and the rhythmic qualities. Are they especially appropriate to the
   game of basketball?
2. Do two-line stanzas contribute to the overall power of the poem?
3. The language of the poem depends on a knowledge of basketball. If you
   are unfamiliar with it, ask a knowledgeable friend to explain terms like *fast
   break, outlet, power-forward, boxes out his man,* and *dribble.*
4. The poem is dedicated to "Dennis Turner, 1946–1984." What ideas are
   thus implied? Why would Hirsch dedicate a poem about basketball to a
   dead friend?
5. How do the elements of the poem give the fast break larger significance?
   How do they impart importance to this fast break?
6. Do the elements work together to give the fast break a symbolic importance?

   This entire section on the elements of poetry should serve to help you
develop close readings basic to any interpretation of a poem. Not all the elements will be of great importance all the time, but whatever elements the poet
chooses to rely upon will work—and work together—to produce whatever
power the poem has.

8

Interpreting Poetry

CLOSE READING

CLOSE READING

Close reading does not necessarily ignore issues that lie outside a text. When Wordsworth talks about London in his sonnet (p. 602) or Milton refers to the slaughter of the Waldensians by the Piedmontese in 1655 (p. 617), they expect you to understand their references. Judith Rodriguez expects you to know what an Eskimo is in "Eskimo Occasion" (p. 579). When A. E. Housman refers to "rue," "brooks," and "roses" (p. 588), he expects you to have referents drawn from outside the poem to make sense of the words he uses. Even nonsense poems like "Jabberwocky" (p. 551) and "anyone lived in a pretty how town" (p. 589) point outside themselves to general experience. Most poems demand a wide repertory of experience from us, and the richer our experience, the richer our interpretation.

Close reading of the poetic text involves a careful examination of details and the way the elements of the poem function. As much as possible, it begins from a holistic reading of the poem. Your first impression, derived from a careful reading, guides your early responses. Rereading helps you evaluate the qualities within the poem that help produce your initial impression. If your first reading produces no distinct response, then you must rely upon rereading with an eye toward examining specific elements, such as imagery, ideas, and use of language.

Once you have read a poem closely, larger interpretive issues begin to take over and direct your understanding. The relationship of part to whole—the image to the overall form, for example—may play an extensive role in a formalist interpretation of a poem examining the ways the poem achieves unity. Social issues expressed, implied, or altogether omitted may take clues from certain elements, such as the poem's ideas or its language. Likewise, the language, tone, imagery, or rhythms in the poem may point toward possible feminist, political, economic, or cultural interpretations. But all will begin with a close reading of the poem.

John Masefield was the poet laureate of Great Britain for much of his life, and his poems were read by schoolchildren and their parents for decades. One of his most celebrated short poems is "Cargoes," a strophic poem whose separate stanzas treat separate moments in history in terms of the cargoes that were carried in trade from one part of the world to another.

John Masefield   (1878–1967)

CARGOES   1902

Quinquireme° of Nineveh from distant Ophir,°
Rowing home to haven in sunny Palestine,
With a cargo of ivory,
And apes and peacocks,
Sandalwood, cedarwood, and sweet white wine.   5

Stately Spanish galleon coming from the Isthmus,
Dipping through the Tropics by the palm-green shores,
With a cargo of diamonds,
Emeralds, amethysts,
Topazes, and cinnamon, and gold moidores.°   10

Dirty British coaster with a salt-caked smoke stack,
Butting through the Channel in the mad March days,
With a cargo of Tyne° coal,
Road-rails, pig-lead,
Firewood, iron-ware, and cheap tin trays.   15

1 *Quinquireme*: A large ancient ship, with five men at each rowing station.   *Ophir*: Probably a city in Africa, mentioned as having gold in the Bible.   10 *moidores*: Renaissance coins used in coastal trade in Africa and China.   13 *Tyne*: Newcastle-upon-Tyne was a coal-producing center in England.

This poem has long been a favorite because it reads magnificently. Masefield had a sense of both language and sound. The way one must assume a stately tone when saying "Quinquireme of Nineveh from distant Ophir" charmed most readers. The rhythms of each first line are insistent:

Quinqui|reme of | Nine|veh from | distant | Ophir,

Stately | Spanish | galleon | coming | from the | Isthmus,

Dirty | British | coaster | with a | salt-caked | smoke stack,

The hammering trochaic hexameter of these lines reinforces the sense of labor involved in the activities described. But even more interesting is the shift in language from stanza to stanza. Masefield maintains a high, sonorous tone in the first stanza that is dependent on repetition of *n* and half-open vowel sounds (*-eh, O*), then moves to a smooth-sounding language relying on soft, sibilant *s* alliteration, and finally comes to the brutal plosives of *D-, Bri-, co-*, and the one-syllable combinations of *s—k* sounds.

Any interpretation of this poem that examines only its formal elements has to praise it as a tour de force. The first stanza conjures up ancient riches in terms of marvelous imagery appealing to the sense of touch ("ivory"), sight ("peacocks"), smell ("sandalwood"), and taste ("sweet white wine"). The riches of the second stanza conjure up images of jewels and treasure. But the last stanza, of contemporary times, is couched in terms of unpleasant images of "coal," "pig-lead," and "cheap tin trays." The dominant idea of the poem is that the modern age has not lived up to the glories of the past. Modern British trade is ghastly in comparison with the greatness of the Assyrians of Nineveh in the seventh century B.C. or the Spaniards of the Golden Age of the sixteenth and seventeenth centuries A.D. The sounds and the imagery of this poem argue for the grandness of the past and the tawdriness of the present, as seen through the emblems of its worldwide trade.

All this works very well in this poem unless the reader brings to bear some knowledge of the historical circumstances that Masefield does not want to discuss. A politically sensitive interpretation would point out the following important facts.

- The quinquiremes were huge five-level ships that were rowed by slaves won in battle. Each level had ten to forty slaves rowing on each side of the ship. The slaves rarely lasted more than a few months chained to their seats. When they died they were cast overboard like garbage. The Assyrian government in Nineveh was harsh, violent, tyrannical, and absolute. Those receiving the treasures on this quinquireme were absolute and terrible rulers.

- The stately Spanish galleon was sailing from the New World with the treasures it had essentially stolen. The crew of the galleon was largely impounded from foreign ports, and the death rate on board was high. The diamonds, topazes, and amethysts were destined for royalty and the church hierarchy. Again, the government was aristocratic and antidemocratic, and held human life as cheap.

- The dirty British coaster of the late nineteenth century brought goods for a more democratic society. It was not a classless society; Masefield's attitude tells us that much, since he looks down on the ordinary people who need the wares the coaster carries ("cheap tin trays"). However, none of the hands on board this coaster were slaves.

This historical information comes from outside the poem, but it is all implied inside it. Masefield seems to have intended that we ignore the negative values connected with the quinquireme and the galleon, but not the coaster. For years readers did so, but contemporary critics have observed that Masefield ends up praising obnoxious social systems on questionable grounds.

Feminist critics might point out that women will eventually be given some of the products being shipped in these boats, but if so they will be given them by men. Women have no role in the governments indirectly praised by Masefield and become little more than ornaments of the society. Moreover, feminists critique the masculine quest for domination over people, nature, and social systems and would see this poem as representative of the point of view that maintains dominance over women as well. Masefield's worldview is also backward-looking, a "retro-spect," which feminists have condemned.

These antagonistic interpretations of the poem rely on ideas implied in the poem but obviously pressed into the background by the poet. Some readers will feel this view does the poem injustice because it focuses on issues that the poem expressly ignores. It seems to contradict the author's intentions. On the other hand, feminist and political interpreters remind us that their methods are effective with poems that disguise the truth or ignore the crucial issues in the poem. In light of their interpretation, one might think twice before praising the grandeur of ancient Assyria and Renaissance Spain in contrast with more modern Great Britain.

Elements such as rhythm, meter, imagery, rhyme, and metaphor work so effectively in "Cargoes" that most of its original readers ignored Masefield's distortions. On the other hand, many poems do not handle the elements in a virtuoso fashion. Sometimes readers trained in responding to elements of poetry tend to overlook or undervalue poems that do not give imagery, rhyme, metaphor, or other elements a prominent position. Yet every poem can respond to an analysis through its elements; after all, all poems use language and have ideas, and most employ imagery. However, a poem whose elements are subtly developed can be momentarily puzzling. In terms of interpretation, one might feel there is little or nothing to do or say. Consider the interpretive approaches possible in reading W. S. Merwin's "Fly."

W. S. Merwin   (b. 1929)

FLY   1974

I have been cruel to a fat pigeon
Because he would not fly
All he wanted was to live like a friendly old man

He had let himself become a wreck filthy and confiding
Wild for his food beating the cat off the garbage   5
Ignoring his mate perpetually snotty at the beak

Smelling waddling having to be
Carried up the ladder at night content

Fly I said throwing him into the air
But he would drop and run back expecting to be fed   10
I said it again and again throwing him up
As he got worse
He let himself be picked up every time
Until I found him in the dovecote dead
Of the needless efforts   15

So that is what I am

Pondering his eye that could not
Conceive that I was a creature to run from

I who have always believed too much in words

Questions for Close Reading

1. When you first read the title of the poem, what did you think it meant? If you thought the title was the name of an insect, what were your expectations?
2. What constitutes the poet's "cruelty" to the pigeon? Can you tell what the poet's emotional state is in response to the events of the poem?
3. What does the poet expect of pigeons in a dovecote?
4. How would you characterize the desires of the pigeon? How do they contrast with those of the poet?
5. In the relationship between the poet and the pigeon, who has the power? What is the power? Is the power expressed as an important element in the poem?
6. What poetic elements are important in the poem?
7. How is the pigeon described? Why is the description unflattering and negatively critical?
8. Why did the pigeon die?
9. What does the poet mean by "So that is what I am"?
10. Why does the poet say he "always believed too much in words"?

Interpretations of this poem can lead in many directions. First, one may begin with the question of emotional response. The poem describes the poet's demanding that the pigeon "fly" rather than "waddling" around after food "like a friendly old man." The poet tosses the bird in the air and the bird drops to the ground. After enough of this, the bird dies, apparently of the trauma of being thrown. The poet then feels guilt for his cruelty and blames himself for demanding something of the bird that the bird could not give. He feels he believed in words too much because to him the concept of "fly" was an essential quality of pigeons.

The second stanza is not pleasant description. The poet "stacks the deck" against the pigeon by describing it in negative terms. It has become a "wreck," "beating the cat off the garbage," "perpetually snotty," "smelling," and needing to be "Carried up the ladder at night." The poet makes all these qualities seem undesirable, offensive, and ugly. Because they produce in him a sense of revulsion, he wants to force the pigeon to fly. As you interpret this poem, you might ask whether the description causes you to feel revulsion as well. Or do you feel sympathy for the pigeon? The poet has described things to make us feel that the pigeon would be much better off if it lost some weight and flew back into its cage on its own and paid some attention to its mate. To respond any other way takes immense effort on our part.

The negative description of the pigeon gives way in the third stanza. The poet simply tells us what he did and what its results were, and in the process builds up some sympathy for the pigeon, who patiently dropped and ran "back expecting to be fed." After the pigeon's death, the word *needless* takes on special force. The word is the poet's admission that his efforts were wrong, and in the last lines of the poem, that the pigeon's trust was misplaced. The pigeon would have been better off if it had stayed away from the poet, if it had never trusted him. When the poet says, "So that is what I am," he is saying many things: that he is cruel and untrustworthy. He realizes that he makes demands based not on what the pigeon's needs are but on what he has presumed the pigeon's nature is. Instead of paying attention to the pigeon, he has paid attention to his ideal of the pigeon. It is a false ideal, but the pigeon must die before the poet realizes he is wrong.

In the process of offering a close reading of the poem, we have also begun an interpretation. The two are often inseparable because close readings depend on interpretation of details. However, a close reading is preparatory to a higher-level interpretation. For example, nothing has been said in this commentary about the significance of the action the poet has described or the lesson, if any, that the poet has learned. Further, nothing has been said about the meaning that a careful reader might take away from the poem. Here are two ways in which a reading may be developed and the significance of the poem established.

INTERPRETIVE STRATEGIES

Cultural

One way of looking at this poem is to think of how individuals establish expectations of others, whether the others are pigeons, people, institutions, or nations. The poem focuses on a very special relationship between a nominally wild animal, a pigeon, and a poet who is a keeper of that animal. The act of keeping it in a "dovecote" alters the nature of the animal and erases part of its wildness, but not all of it (the pigeon can still be wild in relation to the cat). But the poet is unable to see until it is vastly too late, that the relationship he has established has altered the nature of the pigeon dramatically. The word *Fly* is italicized because it is in the imperative mood: it is a command. The command is followed by physical abuse: tossing an overweight old pigeon up in the air until it dies. The poet simply does not get the message until it is too late, and only then will he understand that he paid more attention to his presumptions than to the realities of a situation that he himself created and for which he himself is responsible.

It should not be difficult to move from the example of this pigeon to other examples of relationships in which a dependence is established and then blindly ignored. When parents rob children of independence by overparenting, they sometimes expect the children to grow up instantly and "fly" on their own. When they do not, the results can be painful. Extending this model to social programs involving any minority group in relation to the majority can produce a similar situation. When a society permits one group to become dependent on another, the results may follow the model established in "Fly."

Reader Response

Readers will respond variously to the poem, possibly depending on their experience with a trusting pet. Anyone who has had the responsibility of a pet will realize the depth to which pets will trust even a brutalizing master. The very word *master*, used in this way, will cause a painful response, since it is clear that the unpleasant associations that come with the word can be operative in the poem. The narrator attempts to master the pigeon, to master its nature and direct its behavior no matter what the cost. However, even those who have had no pet will sense an injustice in the poem. The claim that the master has been "cruel" is partly based on his having been unjust. Why not let the pigeon be? Why not respect its wishes? True, the pigeon is slothful, lazy, fat, and filthy, but why worry? Who is responsible for its current condition if not the "master"?

A reader-based reading of this poem involves much more than an examination of possible emotional responses to its narrative. For one thing, the pigeon might be a symbol for something else (as well as being a pigeon). Even thinking in terms of one's pet, a reader begins to think symbolically. But moving to a larger symbolic issue, such as any situation in which the pigeon might represent dependent social groups like people on welfare, people in prison, or native Americans on a reservation, demands an act of will on the part of the reader. Where in the poem, for example, is the evidence that such a symbolic reading is reasonable? Does the poem invite this interpretation? Is there specific evidence to support such a reading? Many poems have much more specific symbolism than this one. Herrick's symbolism, for example, has many details to back it up (p. 624). However, Merwin's poem is more bare-bones. There is no rhyme, no meter, no predictable stanzas, no regular line length. The poem does without most of the elements of poetry.

Nevertheless, its last line implies that it has important ideas and that the poet has learned a lesson.

One clue to a larger meaning is the fact that few readers keep pigeons in a dovecote: so the poem must mean more than this. However, the poet leaves it to the reader to decide just what the meaning might be. Is it possible we believe too much in words? If so, what do we learn from this pigeon? The poem pushes us toward a symbolic interpretation by taking this narrative so seriously that it becomes a story with a moral. In a sense, then, it is like a fable from *Aesop's Fables*, whose barnyard anecdotes become moral fables demanding a symbolic interpretation. The fable of the rooster discovering a precious gem is not really about roosters. Ultimately, the decision that a fable is symbolic or possesses greater significance is the responsibility of the reader who can "read between the lines." "Fly's" seriousness invites such a reading.

A STUDENT INTERPRETATION

Robert Frost's "Birches" is in the deceptively simple style that helped make him America's first poet laureate. Frost (1874–1963) portrays himself as a New Englander with experiences tied to the land and to the world of farmers: simple people, hard living, and a reverent regard for life. The actual facts tend to contradict this portrait and reveal a pattern of self-constructed identity that has fascinated Frost's biographers. For example, Frost was not born a New England farmer. He was born in San Francisco, where his father was a journalist on the *San Francisco Bulletin*, and he lived there until he was eleven. His father died in 1885, and his family moved to Lawrence, Massachusetts, where his father wanted to be buried. They did not live on a farm, but in an industrial mill town. His father had been born in New Hampshire, so there was a legitimate family connection with the state that Frost enjoyed and with which he associated himself. Frost shaped himself carefully as a poet, coming to know the most important English-language poets of his time: Amy Lowell, W. B. Yeats, Ezra Pound, and T. S. Eliot. His work contrasted with theirs, and his image as a poet has survived as a grand old philosopher of the land.

Robert Frost   (1874–1963)

BIRCHES   1916

> When I see birches bend to left and right
> Across the lines of straighter darker trees,
> I like to think some boy's been swinging them.
> But swinging doesn't bend them down to stay
> As ice storms do. Often you must have seen them   5

Loaded with ice a sunny winter morning
After a rain. They click upon themselves
As the breeze rises, and turn many-colored
As the stir cracks and crazes their enamel.
Soon the sun's warmth makes them shed crystal shells   10
Shattering and avalanching on the snow crust—
Such heaps of broken glass to sweep away
You'd think the inner dome of heaven had fallen.
They are dragged to the withered bracken by the load,
And they seem not to break; though once they are bowed   15
So low for long, they never right themselves:
You may see their trunks arching in the woods
Years afterwards, trailing their leaves on the ground
Like girls on hands and knees that throw their hair
Before them over their heads to dry in the sun.   20
But I was going to say when Truth broke in
With all her matter of fact about the ice storm,
I should prefer to have some boy bend them
As he went out and in to fetch the cows—
Some boy too far from town to learn baseball,   25
Whose only play was what he found himself,
Summer or winter, and could play alone.
One by one he subdued his father's trees
By riding them down over and over again
Until he took the stiffness out of them,   30
And not one but hung limp, not one was left
For him to conquer. He learned all there was
To learn about not launching out too soon
And so not carrying the tree away
Clear to the ground. He always kept his poise   35
To the top branches, climbing carefully
With the same pains you use to fill a cup
Up to the brim, and even above the brim.
Then he flung outward, feet first, with a swish,
Kicking his way down through the air to the ground.   40
So was I once myself a swinger of birches.
And so I dream of going back to be.
It's when I'm weary of considerations,
And life is too much like a pathless wood
Where your face burns and tickles with the cobwebs   45
Broken across it, and one eye is weeping
From a twig's having lashed across it open.
I'd like to get away from earth awhile
And then come back to it and begin over.
May no fate willfully misunderstand me   50

And half grant what I wish and snatch me away
Not to return. Earth's the right place for love:
I don't know where it's likely to go better.
I'd like to go by climbing a birch tree,
And climb black branches up a snow-white trunk   55
Toward heaven, till the tree could bear no more,
But dipped its top and set me down again.
That would be good both going and coming back.
One could do worse than be a swinger of birches.

Beginning with Close Reading

Many of our examples of close reading have begun with a series of questions.
However, a response journal can also help begin the close-reading process.
The following is a freewriting passage recording first impressions of the poem.

```
The poem seems to be about the birch trees. I've never been in
New England, so I have to take Frost's word for what happens in a
storm when they get iced up. They get bent over and don't
straighten up. Ice storms do a lot of damage. Frost says he'd
rather see a boy do the damage than the ice storm. I get the
feeling he was a boy who liked to ride the birches. There's a lot
here about how the boy learned not to ruin the trees entirely, so
he's probably thinking about his own experience. You know that for
sure when he tells us that he was once a swinger of birches. The
end of the poem turns philosophical and even makes you think that
the poet is worried about dying. Riding up the birches is like
reaching for heaven, and maybe Frost has that on his mind in this
poem. Generally, it's the kind of poem that you can read and pretty
much understand, but you also know that it's got something going on
beneath the surface that will take a little getting into to figure
out.
```

Just as close reading concentrated on the details of the short story, it always helps to examine the poem and take note of its important details. The
following is one person's listing of details.

```
In the first five lines the narrator tells us he likes to
imagine that birches that sway "left and right" were bent by boys
having fun riding them. There are "darker trees" in the background
```

that are not as flexible as the birches--and I guess not as much fun for boys. They don't bend.

There's a choice: boys can bend them, or ice storms can do it, but ice storms make them bend so "they never right themselves."

The imagery in lines 6 to 16 is strong. Frost uses sound: "click"; vision: "many-colored," "crazes their enamel." He also uses metaphor when he calls the fallen ice "heaps of broken glass." The same happens when he talks about "the inner dome of heaven" in line 13. That's when you know he's talking about more than kids and trees.

The simile of the trees "Like girls on hands and knees that throw their hair / Before them" is nice, but is it supposed to mean that the poem is about something sexual? Boys and girls, not just trees?

"Truth" has a capital T, so something is happening in line 21. Maybe he means that dreaming about boys bending the trees is fantasy because the truth is that the trees were bent by nature.

The description of the boy beginning on line 25 is pretty clearly a description of the narrator, or so it seems. Frost makes a special point of telling us that the boy learned how to climb trees without hurting them. It's a skill like filling the cup "Up to the brim" as he says in line 38. But it's also basic to growing up, and when "not one was left / For him to conquer" maybe he was already grown up.

In line 41 the poem shifts. He says he was once a swinger of birches "And so I dream of going back to be." That's a key line in the poem, I think. I need to figure out what that is supposed to mean.

He talks about getting tired of things in line 44 and maybe reaching up off the earth. But then he's worried that "fate" will "misunderstand me" and "snatch me away." He doesn't want that. He wants to climb up on the tree, "<u>Toward</u> heaven," but he wants to come back to earth because "That would be good both going and coming back."

The last line makes you realize that what he did as a boy is still good to do now that he's a man.

Much of the work of brainstorming has been done by the notes above. One of the realities of writing about poetry is that since a poem is much

shorter than a story, play, or essay, a close reading that accounts for details
will sometimes get you in a position to think about writing. You can devote
some of your freewriting to examining the important elements that the poet
uses.

Analyzing the Elements

It is not always necessary to take each element of poetry by itself, but it helps
to note how the most important elements function in the poem. Certainly
the language, imagery, metaphor, and symbolism are important enough to
warrant special notice.

There are no unusual terms and no complicated language. Frost
talks the way most people do--or at least the way an older New
Englander might.

The poem is not sarcastic or ironic. The narrator speaks so
honestly that you get the feeling it is Frost himself talking.
Maybe it is.

Frost doesn't rhyme the poem, so it has an easy-going style.
But the lines are metrical, or seem so. They seem to have ten
syllables and most of the feet I've scanned are iambic, so the poem
is probably iambic pentameter. That helps give a sense of shape and
form to it, although it doesn't allow for any sudden shift in
meaning or emotion. Maybe it doesn't need it.

Metaphor is pretty well developed here. The birches have to be
a metaphor for something; maybe they are symbolic. They're natural,
so they must stand for something good: maybe reaching for
something, like ambition or something. Climbing without breaking
them is a challenge, so the boy learns a skill. The man must be
much too big to climb a birch tree, but since he wants to do it
again it must stand for something important.

One simile that's odd is the trees bent like girls after the
ice storm has broken them: "Years afterwards, trailing their leaves
on the ground." I'm not so sure there's anything sexual about that.
It might actually be sexist.

The ideas are interesting, and I'm not sure I've got them
fully under control. The birches represent a challenge and the
chance to become skilled. That's something a man can benefit from
throughout life. So the narrator says he'd like to be able to
climb birches now just so long as he doesn't die trying. So he

must think of swinging on birches as being risky, challenging, and dangerous.

Freewriting

One of the best ways to begin an interpretation is to take some important details discussed above and freewrite to develop a thesis. Several important ideas have already been raised in the notes above, so it makes sense to examine them. The writer took several of those details and wrote without self-censorship for three minutes on each one, hoping to develop material that could be used in an interpretation.

> One thing that gets me is that Frost really talks about little boys and not little girls. The idea of jumping up on the birches and swinging them down is a real challenge to him as a boy, and the grown-up narrator tells you that it's important. It is not a bad thing to be a swinger of birches. The idea that you "conquer" the birches is probably the most important detail there. Boys like to conquer things. It's part of the masculine mystique, I guess. But they also want to be sure they can take chances and not necessarily get wiped out. I think that's what Frost means when he says at the end that he'd like to be able to swing on birches again but not necessarily risk "fate," which might think he is reaching for the heavens because he wants to die. That's the trick: take the risk, but succeed.

The writer took the question of conquering the trees, mentioned in line 32, and developed it in connection with the description of boys growing up. Below, the writer takes another approach to freewriting. Instead of focusing on a detail and working up ideas about it, the writer has chosen to answer one basic question. He spent three minutes without censorship trying to answer it.

> What do the birches symbolize?
> The birches could symbolize any challenge, anything that is difficult and worthwhile doing. But they also symbolize challenges that help build skill in men. The birches have to be climbed, so that means the boy has to reach beyond "mother earth" and reach for the heavens. But Frost makes it clear that he hopes to try to do

something challenging like reaching for the heavens, but he doesn't
want to get to heaven--not yet. He wants to end up back on earth
because that's where "love" goes best. Maybe the birches symbolize
something like the challenge of writing poetry or being imaginative
or creative. I say that because little children are more naturally
creative than adults. It takes an effort for a man to take the
risks that children accept as normal.

Dealing with the symbolism of the birches offers an interesting way into the poem, since the writer has sensed that much more is implied in the imagery of the birches than just trees. Even the boy swinging on birches seems to be doing more than just having fun in the woods.

Sample Essay: A Formalist/Feminist Interpretation

Going over annotation, notes, and freewriting, the writer began to see that it was possible to talk about feminist issues in the poem while also taking into account some of the formal elements implied in the oppositions that seemed important to Frost. On the basis of the writing above, the writer created these potential statements, hoping to use one for a thesis.

Although the narrator in the poem seems to be talking only
about birches, he is actually talking about the opportunities boys
have in childhood to learn how to be men.
The "birches" in this poem represent the challenges life
offers for boys to grow up as conquerors, as men who use power
carefully.
"Birches" talks about two kinds of power. One is the terrible
power of nature's ice storms, which permanently damage trees so
they resemble girls. The other is the power of boys who learn to be
skilled enough to subdue nature but not permanently damage it.

The writer decided to try to work with the third of these statements, keeping the other two in reserve as supporting statements in later paragraphs. The job was to write a three-page interpretation without using outside references, so the writer set about to construct a working outline, knowing that it would change as the writing progressed. The basic outline, after some false starts and revision, came out this way.

"Boys, Birches, and Power"

I. Boys and birches

  A. Birches bend

    1. Boys bend them through swinging

    2. Or, ice storms permanently bend them

  B. The poet prefers boys to swing the birches

    1. The poet constructs a fantasy of boys swinging

    2. Truth, with a capital T, breaks in on the fantasy

II. Ice storms and birches

  A. Ice storms are beautiful

    1. Beautiful visual images

    2. Beautiful sounds

  B. Ice storms are destructive

    1. They are the power of nature

    2. Their effect is permanent

    3. Damaged birches look like bent-over girls

III. The portrait of the lonely boy

  A. Poet imagines the boy as a dairy farmer

    1. He manages cows--a symbol for the female

    2. Not a city boy, doesn't play team sports

    3. Learns to play alone

  B. The boy is "privileged"

    1. The trees are his "father's"

    2. The boy will inherit them when he is grown

IV. Conquering trees is a skill for boys

  A. By learning the proper skill, the boy conquers the trees

    1. Conquering controls but does not destroy

    2. Ice storms conquer, but destroy

    1. Life now is "too much like a pathless wood"

      a. He feels too many "considerations," presumably for others

      b. Swinging birches is solitary and something he would like to do again

    2. "Earth's the right place for love"

      a. As a grown man he would like to swing up toward heaven alone

      b. But he wants to be sure to come back to earth

    3. Being a swinger of birches is a fantasy wish

      a. Recalls childhood independence

      b. It's not a bad thing

The actual paper, based on this outline, came out like this.

Marcus Hemphill
Prof. Jacobus
English 109-03

Boys, Birches, and Power

Two kinds of power exist in the poem, the power of man
symbolized by the growing boy, and the power of nature symbolized
by the ice storm. Of the two kinds of trees in the poem, one is the
white birch and the other is the "straighter darker" tree,
mysterious and not good for climbing. Ice storms do not bother
them, either. But birches bend, and you can either see them bent by
boys who are trying out their skills as conquerors, or see them
bent to the ground by ice storms. Boys do not ruin the trees, but
the ice storms do.

The narrator begins by imagining a fantasy about boys swinging
birches. The darker reality of nature permanently bending the
birches--the narrator calls it "Truth" "With all her matter of
fact"--"broke in" on his fantasy. The ice storm is beautiful but
destructive, just as Truth is bothersome to the imagery of boys
swinging birches. Frost uses beautiful imagery and description for
birches in the ice storm: "They click upon themselves," "turn many-
colored," and have "crystal shells." This beauty is destructive and
leaves the birches useless, "Like girls." The image of the bent-
over birches suggests that girls are not as strong or adventurous
as boys, and the fact that Truth is a "her" suggests that the
narrator might be annoyed with females. He never says so, but the
imagery makes you wonder.

The narrator paints a portrait of an ideal boy who manages
cows, another female symbol, and who lives in the country. He's
lonely and doesn't play games with other kids. He plays alone, so
swinging birches is ideal. The birches the boy swings belong to his
father and will someday probably belong to him. So in a way you
could say that the swinging he does on the trees gets him ready to
take over the farm and his father's role. The boy the narrator
describes in lines 23 to 41 begins as an imaginary boy, but pretty
soon you realize the narrator is describing himself. "He learned

all there was / To learn about not launching out too soon," and "He
always kept his poise."

In line 32 the narrator tells us the trees were there for "him
to conquer," and from that you get the impression that the whole
thing about growing up the way the boy does is to learn how to
conquer things without ruining them. If you leave things bent over
"Like girls" that is not good. It is interesting that girls do not
swing on birches. Only boys. It's as if the narrator was saying
that this conquering game is appropriate only for boys and helps
them become men.

Now that he is a man looking back on himself ("So was I once
myself a swinger of birches"), he no longer swings birches. He
would like to try because now,

> life is too much like a pathless wood
> Where your face burns and tickles with the cobwebs
> Broken across it, and one eye is weeping
> From a twig's having lashed across it open. (44-47)

He wants to "climb black branches up a snow-white trunk /
Toward heaven" again, but he does not want to get to heaven just
yet. He wants to come back because "Earth's the right place for
love: / I don't know where it's likely to go better" (52-53). Then
he says, "I'd like to go by climbing a birch tree," but it is not
clear what he means by "go" in this sentence. Does he mean die? Or
does he meaning something related to the previous line in "go
better"? It is hard to tell.

Another thing that is hard to tell is what kind of love he
means in line 52. The way he seems to idealize the independence of
his boyhood and his negative imagery about women makes you wonder
if the problems of being "weary of considerations" (43) might have
something to do with adjusting to living with a woman. It is easy
to be a conqueror when a boy is swinging birches, but a man cannot
behave the way a boy does. In the end, I think the nostalgia the
narrator feels for the simplicity of his childhood has to do with
the fact that he mastered the skills he needed then, and now looks
back at that time as one when he had a great deal of power. Now as
a man there are too many "considerations" and he has to learn to
live with them and accept their pain. Maybe he also has to accept
the fact that he has less power.

Further Strategies for Interpretation

Feminist   The imagery of ice-damaged trees resembling girls on their hands and knees and the constant reference to boys and their development suggests an approach to the poem through a potentially feminist reading. Such a reading would consider Frost's emphasis on boys and their efforts to develop skill, while essentially ignoring girls and their growing up. However, a balanced reading would take into account the fact that Frost is a male and has a right to discuss growing up from the point of view of a man. An important question is whether the imagery of the damaged trees is a demeaning reference to femaleness. Frost in his later years carefully presented himself as a white-haired patriarch of poetry. A feminist reading of this poem might ask whether his true posture was patriarchic in the negative sense of dominating and conquering the environment.

Formalist   A formalist approach to the poem might concentrate on the regularity of the meter of the lines, pointing out that iambic pentameter is one of the most historically durable lines in English. Shakespeare's plays, Milton's *Paradise Lost*, and almost every sonnet use that line. The poem is built on obvious oppositions: boy and man; boys and ice storms; rural and urban; heaven and earth; boys and girls; conquering and not conquering. The formalist reading would attempt to clarify these oppositions and the meaning of birches for the narrator. It assumes that the reader's job is to study the formal qualities along with the poem's explicit language to see how the form clarifies, reinforces, and creates meaning.

Political-Economic   One could suggest a political-economic interpretation by studying the childhood relationship to the land and seeing that it has now become uncertain for the adult narrator. If he was a dairy farmer's son once, he seems not to have grown to be a dairy farmer himself, and so he is not as connected to the earth as he had been. He is obviously wistful for earlier times. An economic discussion would question the kind of skill that the boy learned in riding the birches and what the man grew up to conquer. The description of being "weary of considerations" and of his present life being like a "pathless wood" (line 44) and painful suggests that he is no longer in the immediate relationship to the earth's economy as he once was.

Reader Response   A reader response approach might examine how the style is designed to put the reader at ease and to make the experience of reading the poem especially nonthreatening. We all know that some poets need unusual complexity of language to sustain their thinking or depend on allusion to other literature to establish a special audience for their poetry. In contrast, the style of this poem suggests that one can get right in and understand everything without much effort. But we know that is not the case. Frost puts the reader at ease, but he also gives the reader more than the reader expects: the language, though simple, hides complex meanings. The poem sucks the reader in almost like quicksand. Analyzing how Frost answers a reader's expectations and then frustrates them could produce a fascinating interpretation. Another approach—and a good way to begin discussing the poem—would be to use one's personal experience with birches, the country, and even childhood. What experiences does Frost expect the reader to bring to the poem? The narrator is clearly aware of the audience when he says, "Often you have seen them / Loaded with ice a sunny winter morning." Well, not everyone has seen ice-covered birches, but those who have not will probably be able to imagine them without difficulty. The reader is led carefully in this poem, and Frost never loses sight of the reader's potential response to the imagery, the narrative, or the narrator's personality.

When deciding what kind of strategy to use to interpret "Birches," one must think about the poem and its overall effect. For some readers a feminist or political-economic reading might appear to distort the poem. This is not to rule out such readings, only to suggest they might treat issues peripheral to the poem. Some readers may feel the same way about a reader response or even a formalist reading. You will have to decide how to approach any poem on the basis of your reading and rereading and your impression of the poem's overall purposes. Your job will be to decide what approach is most reasonable for you, most responsible to the poem itself, and most capable of producing an insightful reading.

Diane Ackerman   (b. 1948)

PATRICK EWING° TAKES A FOUL SHOT   1983

Ewing sweating,
molding the ball
with spidery hands,
packing it, packing it,
into a snowball's   5
chance of a goal,
rolling his shoulders
through a silent earthquake,
rocking from one foot
to the other, sweating,   10
bouncing it, oh, sweet
honey, molding it,
packing it tight,
he fires:

floats it up on one palm   15
as if surfacing
from the clear green Caribbean
with a shell
whose roar wraps around him,
whose surf breaks   20
deep into his arena
where light and time

Patrick Ewing: Center for the National Basketball Association's New York Knickerbockers.

and pupils jump
because he jumps

Diane Ackerman   (b. 1948)

ON LOOKING INTO SYLVIA PLATH'S°
COPY OF GOETHE'S FAUST°   1991

You underlined the "jugglery of flame"
with ink sinewy and black as an ocelot.
Pensive about ash, you ran to detail,
you ran the mad sweetshop of the soul,
keen for Faust's appetite, not Helen's° beauty.   5
No stranger to scalpel or garden,
you collected bees, knew how to cook,
dressed simply, and undressed the flesh
in word mirrors. Armed and dangerous
with the nightstick of desire,   10
you became the doll of insight we knew
to whom nearly all lady poets write,
a morbid Santa Claus who could die on cue.
You had the gift of rage, and a savage wistfulness.
You wanted life to derange you,   15
to sample its real muscle, you wanted
to be a word on the lips of the abyss.
You wanted to unlock the weather system
in your cells, and one day you did.

I never loved the pain you wore as a shroud,   20
but your keen naturalist's eye,
avid and roaming, your nomad curiosity,
and the cautionless ease with which your mind
slid into the soft flesh of an idea.
I thought you found serenity in the plunge   25
of a hot image into cool words.
I thought you took the pledge
that sunlight makes to living things,
could be startled to joy
by the green epaulets of a lily.   30
But you were your own demonology,
balancing terror's knife on one finger,
until you numbed, and the edge fell free.

Sylvia Plath: A major poet who committed suicide when very young. See section on Plath, p.1005.
Faust: Johann Wolfgang von Goethe (1749–1832) wrote the dramatic Poem *Faust* in two parts
(1808; 1832). It is a Romantic portrait of a man who defied God. 5 *Helen:* Helen of Troy,
whom Faust conjured from the dead.

Diane Ackerman   (b. 1948)
LETTER TO WALLACE STEVENS°   1991

Heartless in a Hartford long dissolved,
  you were the axis
    of my revolving world

when, at nineteen, I desired your gift
  and Dylan Thomas's: 5
    his voluptousness of mind,
      your sensuous rigor.

I didn't know then that Art
  is the best one rises to,
    a momentary privilege.   10

I didn't know that bad men
  could write good poems,
    be spiteful to all,

cruel to their children,
  but wholly compassionate   15
    to ideal compassion.

Rude, icy, alert to advantage,
  rapt but condescending,
    terrified to be cornered
      into a friendship,   20

you knew the dollar each lily concealed
  and fantasized a Paris
    laminated by distance,

whose essence you took
  in strong, cunning draughts.   25
    Few speak well of you,
      the glacial man in the baggy suit.

The new biography makes me a fortuneteller
  in reverse. I watch you weaken
    in your garden robust with peonies   30

where you ushered in the world
  and escaped your wife (whose face, on the liberty dime,°
    sat in your pants pocket all day).

Wallace Stevens. An important modern poet, in this collection; see p. 957. Stevens lived in
Hartford, Connecticut.   **32** *dime:* Elsie Moll modeled for the face of Liberty.

But your poems, what madrigals,
    canny and luscious, in which the Sinbads   35
        of thought wear twirling knives,

and you steer by the polestar
    of your own invention. Your nomadic eye
       roamed the seven seas
        of the seven senses.   40

By heart, and by law,
    you could toss a bucketful of light
       onto any dim object, make ideas fluoresce,

and stain the willows with a glance.
    You named the chaos.   45
       You could dry out the sun.

I wish you'd reveled in the deserts—
    Egypt, Africa, the Southwest—
       but it wasn't your fault

that world is ampler than you knew.   50
    Anyway, a coral key can be played
       to the absolute,

and desert bluffs arrive by ship in New England,
    where tide can be touched
       and night is a leopard.   55

Diane Ackerman (b. 1948)
ANNE DONNE° TO HER HUSBAND   1978

    Come to bed, Jack, the candle's shed
to its waxy skirt, and I can read
    your straying wits by the moon.
A brain-fly must be buzzing your head!
    What is it now, that new ice, sheeting   5
the pond like a scald on hot milk? The swoon
    of dam-water, like a silent diphthong?
Lucky pond, to hold your gaze so long.

Anne Donne: Wife of Poet John Donne, in this collection. This poem parodies the love poems
Donne wrote to his wife, which often expressed an impatient desire to get on with physical lovemaking, as in "The Flea," p. 745.

My eiderdown is greener than a glade;
you gave it me yourself, high   10
    when you dubbed me your *new found land,*
and swore, my continents your quest, you'd trade
    along the shores of my dark timbered eyes,
where unwooed lusheries of life meander,
    and time drops sail like a ketch in a lagoon.   15
Well, then, what keeps you?

    Come away from the window!
You get ideas like other men catch cold.
    Mid-morning, a trifle waylaid you again,
and now your eyes, like twin hyenas,   20
    pick dinner in the silvery light
from the moon. Enough of your lyric flight!
    Enough peeking under the night's black shirt!
All day, you've been sickening with a verse.

    For God's sake, quit gaming   25
with love, in poems abstruse, or as physical
    as if you were a physical
man. Maybe this one you'll title "Love's Dynasty,"
    and begin with a sunset, lying
on the horizon like an eel   30
    twitching its thick brown hide,
then hint at things matrimonial.

    And who'll guess that tonight, upright as an easel,
you've earth on the brain, not me.
    Though I'd tie you in lawless knots   35
if I could, my heart knows
    no rhetoric but your name,
Jack, that, like a doomed colonial,
    sails out with a seed-chest full of hope,
and raises so little crop.   40

    How can I compete with a vision?
What holy logic could my wiles defy?
    Your muse that's fat and sassy
as a cow, could I stint her even one
    of her piquancies? Her powwows? Her sprees?   45
What would it cost, in hard daily coin,
    if I shook you loose from this reverie?
I am not love's barrister (wish I were),

    but an offput woman on a night growing bleaker,
and night was never longer, or woman weaker.   50

Bella Akhmadulina   (b. 1937)
VOLCANOES   1963

Translated from Russian by W. H. Auden

Extinct volcanoes are silent:
Ash chokes craters and vent.
There giants hide from the sun
After the evil they have done.

Realms ever denser and colder   5
Weigh on each brutal shoulder,
But the old wicked visions keep
Visiting them in their sleep.

They behold a city, sure
Here summer will endure,   10
Though columns carved from congealed
Lava frame garden and field.

It is long ago: in sunlit hours
Girls gather armfuls of flowers
And Bacchantes° give a meaning sign   15
To men as they sip their wine.

A feast is in progress: louder
The diners grow, more heated and lewder . . .
O my Pompei in your cindery grave,
Child of a princess and a slave!   20

What future did you assume,
What were you thinking of and whom
When you leaned your elbow thus
Thoughtlessly on Vesuvius?

Were you carried away by his stories?   25
Did you gaze with astonished eyes?
Didn't you guess—were you *that* innocent?—
Passion can be violent?

And then, when that day ended,
Did he lay a knowing forehead   30
At your dead feet? Did he, didn't he,
Bellow: "Forgive me!"?

15 *Bacchantes:* Priestesses of Bacchus, God of Wine.

Anna Akhmatova   (1889–1966)
LOT'S WIFE°   1969

Translated from Russian by Richard Wilbur

The just man followed then his angel guide
Where he strode on the black highway, hulking and bright;
But a wild grief in his wife's bosom cried,
Look back, it is not too late for a last sight

Of the red towers of your native Sodom, the square   5
Where once you sang, the gardens you shall mourn,
And the tall house with empty windows where
You loved your husband and your babes were born.

She turned, and looking on the bitter view
Her eyes were welded shut by mortal pain;   10
Into transparent salt her body grew,
And her quick feet were rooted in the plain.

Who would waste tears upon her? Is she not
The least of our losses, this unhappy wife?
Yet in my heart she will not be forgot   15
Who, for a single glance, gave up her life.

Lot's wife: See Gen. 19:1–26. Lot, a "just man" in the evil city of Sodom, was warned by God's angels to leave the city before it was destroyed by fire and to not look back. Lot's wife disobeyed, looked back, and was changed into a pillar of salt.

Agha Shahid Ali   (b. 1949)
HOMAGE TO FAIZ AHMED FAIZ°   1987

(d. 20 November 1984)

"You are welcome to make your adaptations of my poems."

I

You wrote this from Beirut, two years before
the Sabra-Shatila massacres.° That city's
refugee air was open, torn
by jets and the voices of reporters.
As always, you were witness to "rains of stones,"   5

Faiz Ahmed Faiz: 1911–1984; well-known Pakistani political activist and poet (see "Before You Came," p. 760) who spent time in solitary confinement for his views.   2 *Sabra-Shatila massacres*: 1982 massacre of refugees in Beirut by Christian phalangists.

though you were away from Pakistan, from
the laws of home which said: the hands
of thieves will be surgically
amputated. But the subcontinent always spoke
to you: in Ghalib's Urdu,° and sometimes through   10

the old masters who sang of twilight
but didn't live, like Ghalib, to see the wind
rip the collars of the dawn: the summer
of 1857,° the trees of Delhi
became scaffolds: 30,000 men   15

were hanged. Wherever you were, Faiz, that
language spoke to you; and when you heard it,
you were alone—in Tunis, Beirut,
London, or Moscow. Those poets' laments
concealed, as yours revealed, the sorrows   20

of a broken time. You knew Ghalib was right:
blood must not merely follow routine, must not
just flow as the veins' uninterrupted
river. Sometimes it must flood the eyes,
surprise them by being clear as water.   25

II

I didn't listen when my father
recited your poems to us
by heart. What could it mean to a boy

that you had redefined the cruel
beloved, that figure who already   30
was Friend, Woman, God? In your hands

she was Revolution. You gave
her silver hands, her lips were red.
Impoverished lovers waited all

night every night, but she remained   35
only a glimpse behind
light. When I learned of her,

---

10 *Ghalib's Urdu*: Ghalib: Mirzā Asadullāh Khān Naushāh (d. 1869), most influential of Delhi
poets wrote mostly in Persian, but his Urdu—the primary language of Pakistan—was widely
praised.   14 *1857*: In this year Indian regulars rose against their British superiors and were
brutally crushed. The event marked the beginning of British national rule over India.

I was no longer a boy, and Urdu
a silhouette traced
by the voices of singers,   40

by Begum Akhtar,° who wove your couplets
into ragas: both language and music
were sharpened. I listened:

and you became, like memory,
necessary. *Dast-e-Saba,*°   45
I said to myself. And quietly

the wind opened its palms: I read
there of the night: the secrets
of lovers, the secrets of prisons.

III

When you permitted my hands to turn to stone,   50
as must happen to a translator's hands,

I thought of you writing *Zindan-Nama*°
on prison walls, on cigarette packages,

on torn envelopes. Your lines were measured
so carefully to become in our veins   55

the blood of prisoners. In the free verse
of another language I imprisoned

each line—but I touched my own exile.
This hush, while your ghazals° lay in my palms,

was accurate, as is this hush that falls   60
at news of your death over Pakistan

and India and over all of us no
longer there to whom you spoke in Urdu.

Twenty days before your death you finally
wrote, this time from Lahore, that after the sack   65

of Beirut you had no address . . . I
had gone from poem to poem, and found

you once, terribly alone, speaking
to yourself: "Bolt your doors, Sad heart! Put out

---

41 *Begum Akhtar:* Famous Indian singer. Ali memorialized her in another poem.   45 *Dast-e-Saba:* Present thoughts.   52 *Zindan-Nama:* Faiz's book, *Hands of the Morning Breeze.*
59 *ghazals:* A form of rhyming lyric poetry.

the candles, break all cups of wine. No one,   70
now no one will ever return." But you

still waited, Faiz, for that God, that Woman,
that Friend, that Revolution, to come
at last. And because you waited,
I listen as you pass with some song,   75

a memory of musk, the rebel face of hope.

WINDOW ON

Backgrounds: Chicano Poetry

The term *Chicano* was originally a pejorative for Mexicans "de classe inferior," as Tino Villanueva put it. But that is no longer true: today the term,
along with *Chicana*, refers to all Mexican-Americans. Chicano poets often refer to their country as Aztlán, which takes on many different emotional meanings but which refers geographically to the American Southwest and northern Mexico, the site from which their ancestors come.

Chicano poetry experiments with language, especially variant spellings,
in an effort to express the way people actually speak. Another hallmark of
this poetry is the use of English and Spanish as if the two languages were
interchangeable. The Chicano poet expects the reader to be familiar with
both languages and rarely translates from one into the other, as poets who
use a foreign expression sometimes do. Neither language, of course, is foreign to the Chicano reader. Like most American poetry of the second half
of the century, modern Chicano poetry is also free and experimental in
form, its rhythms having been influenced by popular culture, music, and
urban life.

Felipe de Ortego y Gasca reminds us that "Chicano poetry communicates whatever any other poetry communicates. Like poetry everywhere and
in all times, Chicano poetry sifts experience, preserves the continuity of a people, probes the past and ponders the future, consecrates the word in acts of
language (English, Spanish, or both) to expose truths of life." José Antonio
Burciaga's poems on the American bicentennial, in 1976, asked Americans
to avoid hypocrisy by recalling the nation's ignoble deeds, especially in relation to slavery and the genocide of native Americans. His "Berta Crocker's
Bicentennial Recipe" is part of his series, and for many readers, this recipe will
have a bitter taste.

One of the principal ingredients of modern Chicano poetry, Ortego also
points out, is "the identification of Chicanos with their Indian past." An ex-

ample would be Bernice Zamora's (b. 1938) "Restless Serpents," which refers to the Aztec and Mayan serpent gods, emblems common in much Chicano poetry. Zamora focuses on the serpent's restlessness and the caution that the master must take in providing the "lyrics" that soothe it.

Alurista, the pen name of Alberto Baltazar Urista (b. 1947), who lives in San Diego, also uses the past in his poetry. In his early poems he is disenchanted with the United States and looks back toward his ancient Indian roots. One critic, Gary D. Keller, sees in Alurista's work the theme of recuperation: "a process of delving into, elucidating, and disabusing facets of self which were there all along, but which like certain Palenques and Uxmales [ancient Mayan ruins] required the efforts of the visionary archaeologist to unearth." Throughout his work, Alurista experiments with language, not just by mixing Spanish and English, but also by using dialect and nonstandard forms. In a revolutionary mode, for example, he says, "tronó where i gonna go when the volcano blow / mon u better wach your feet / ¡lava burn mon, lava hot!" In "Who Are We? . . . Somos Aztlán: A Letter to 'El Jefe Corky,'" Alurista analyzes the question of identity that plagues Chicanos, those who say "Somos Aztlán"—"We are Aztlán." His poem explores open forms, open language, and open criticism. but the criticism is not unfocused: he wants to change "northamerikkka, yankeeland" with "our weapon justicia." In the end Alurista's complaints are universal. For example, "Urban Prison" describes conditions in our cities that the nation has had to face, both the riots and the presidential commissions that usually follow them.

For critic Joseph Summers, Chicano poetry is not merely ethnic poetry. Rather, it concerns itself with the problem of ethnic fusion, a conjunction of cultures and cultural values made all the more explicit by the conjunction of languages. In working with several languages, the Chicano poet has an unusual opportunity to develop a unique fusion of thought, feeling, and expression. Thus the poet both looks back to the archaeology of "an Indian past" and also looks forward to a transformation of culture that is already under way.

Reading

Bruce-Novoa. *Chicano Poetry*. Austin: University of Texas Press, 1982.

de Dwyer, Carlota Cárdenas. *Chicano Voices*. Boston: Houghton Mifflin, 1975.

Ortego, Philip D. *We Are Chicanos*. New York: Washington Square Press, 1973.

Summers, Joseph, and Tomás Ybarra-Frausto, eds. *Modern Chicano Writers*. Englewood Cliffs: Prentice-Hall, 1979.

Villanueva, Tino. *Chicanos: Antologia histórica y literaria*. Mexico City: Fondo de Cultura Económica, 1980. In Spanish.

Alurista° (b. 1947)

FIRE AND EARTH 1982

tronó° where i gonna go when the volcano blow
mon u better wach your feet
¡lava burn mon, lava hot!
better love me now before volcano blow!
din't wanna land in the city . . .   5
the dump . . . the junkyard . . . don't wanna land
nowhere where u is not
wanna land in your forests, your peaks
your sighs and moans, your thighs and thoughts
tronó where i gonna go when the volcano blow   10
mon u better wach your feet
¡lava burn mon, lava hot!

Alurista: Alberto Baltazar Urista.   1 *tronó*: Patrón, a term for landlords and people in power.

Alurista

WITH 1982

with out u darling, ling, sling
                    shot to thee heart
locked up in blues, ling sling
                    shot centered
                    on the toes of a   5
                    twirling turn
                    yeah! yeah!
                    for u, oh girl
                    do it, duet one more
                    time cain't git   10
                        e, nough
                        ee, nough
                        i, nough
        o'
        u   15
        babe
        gulp culp
        writ hulk
            pulk
            e,   20

       i k
           corazón
heart i
  still dia, dia
    logue, logo   25
      with u, xé°

26 xé: Sound "che" for Xicano.

Alurista

WHO ARE WE? . . . SOMOS AZTLÁN:°
A LETTER TO "EL JEFE CORKY"°   1982

a dog walks waggling
    its tail, proud
its chest out
    and its head high
another comes   5
    and fights him under the moon
tear all possible skin
    off each other
the first
    wins   10
and walks away in darkness
    having established power
through violent struggle, the other runs
    a month later
the dog no longer walks waggling   15
    its tail
another dog tears him
    ragged and fearful, the night before
with its tail between
    its legs, defeated, runs himself in darkness again   20
defeated by the people's
first natural enemy:
    fear
the fear that all
    of us once face   25
before our christian ignorance
we see unknown evils/the devil or communism

Somos Aztlán: "We are Aztlán" (of the American Southwest, the country of the Chicanos).   "*El Jefe Corky*": The chief, Corky.

unknown feelings/the body or violence
unknown thoughts/the mind or guilt
unknown threats/death or god   30
unknown pictures/dreams or nightmares
and we run, we run
we run, when we could walk, and see clearly;
without violence,
       we could walk   35
the path we all must walk:
      the path of peace, the path of peace
for those who want the power
      to impart life, knowledge, nourishment, and health.
weed out the paths of war   40
of those who exploit the power
      to bring death
and genocide
against one's self, the human race, suicide
      through governments   45
built with firepower
      and violent
military dictatorships.
in this country
      the united states   50
of (i beg your pardon)
         northamerikkka, yankeeland
general george washington
      became its first
commander general of the armed forces   55
      and its first
military dictator, president
      today, thursday
september ten
      san diego a.m.   60
before dawn break
      two thirds of every
u.s. federal tax dollar
      is spent
      on the military/for defense   65
we do not believe in suicide,
      or homicide,
      or genocide, or biocide
we do not wish to walk the deadly path
      of fear while living   70
we shall walk the path of courage
      and disciplined,

defeat the people's enemy, fear, with nonviolently
rooted power, our weapon justicia
to: establish peace,   75
restore the earth,
and respect the sun;
peace, earth and sun: peace, earth and sun
can bring our
liberation from   80
ignorance, war, hunger, disease,
and military dictatorships
be they white
or black,
their violence must end   85
with our culture, our heart, and our peace.

Alurista

URBAN PRISON   1982

la gorda de aluminum foil°
arroz with corn and chícharos°
on top
presidio hill
where the honchos   5
on top
rule
the time has come for all
good men to come to the
aid of their nation   10
and the ones
on the bottom in aztlán°
struggle to breathe freedom
only to find
the bondage of the slave   15
in the skies covered
with clotting blood clouds
of smog bars and
dark chains of
factories smoking death   20
and coughing life in spasms

---

1 *la gorda . . . foil*: Foil cooking bag.   2 *arroz . . . chícharos*: Rice with corn and chickpeas.
12 *aztlán*: Of the American Southwest, or, the country of the Chicanos.

Maya Angelou (b. 1928)

THESE YET TO BE UNITED STATES   1990

Tremors of your network
cause kings to disappear.
Your open mouth in anger
makes nations bow in fear.
Your bombs can change the seasons,   5
obliterate the spring.
What more do you long for?
Why are you suffering?

You control the human lives
in Rome and Timbuktu.   10
Lonely nomads wandering
owe Telstar to you.
Seas shift at your bidding,
your mushrooms fill the sky.
Why are you unhappy?   15
Why do your children cry?

They kneel alone in terror
with dread in every glance.
Their nights are threatened daily
by a grim inheritance.   20
You dwell in whitened castles
with deep and poisoned moats
and cannot hear the curses
which fill your children's throats.

Anonymous

SUMER IS ICUMEN IN   MEDIEVAL

Sumer is icumen in,°
Lhude° sing, cuccu!°
Groweth sed° and bloweth° med°
And springth the wude° nu.°
Sing, cuccu!   5

Awe° bleteth after lomb,
Lhouth° after calve° cu,°

1 *Sumer is icumen in*: Summer has come in.   2 *Lhude*: Loudly.   *cuccu*: Cuckoo.   3 *sed*:
Seed.   *bloweth*: Blooms.   *med*: Meadow.   4 *wude*: Wood.   *nu*: Now.   6 *Awe*: Ewe.
7 *Lhouth*: Lows.   *calve*: Calf.   *cu*: Cow.

Bulluc sterteth,° bucke ferteth.°
Murie° sing, cuccu!
Cuccu, cuccu,   10

Wel singes thu, cuccu.
Ne swik° thu naver° nu!

Sing cuccu nu, sing cuccu!
Sing cuccu, sing cuccu nu!

---

8 *sterteth*: Leaps up. *ferteth*: Farts.   9 *Murie*: Merrily.   12 *swik*: Cease. *naver*: Never.

W. H. Auden   (1907–1973)
MUSÉE DES BEAUX ARTS°   1938

About suffering they were never wrong,
The Old Masters: how well they understood
Its human position; how it takes place
While someone else is eating or opening a window or just walking
      dully along;
How, when the aged are reverently, passionately waiting   5
For the miraculous birth,° there always must be
Children who did not specially want it to happen, skating
On a pond at the edge of the wood:
They never forgot
That even the dreadful martyrdom must run its course   10
Anyhow in a corner, some untidy spot
Where the dogs go on with their doggy life and the torturer's horse
Scratches its innocent behind on a tree.

In Breughel's *Icarus*,° for instance: how everything turns away
Quite leisurely from the disaster; the ploughman may   15
Have heard the splash, the forsaken cry,
But for him it was not an important failure; the sun shone
As it had to on the white legs disappearing into the green
Water; and the expensive delicate ship that must have seen
Something amazing, a boy falling out of the sky,   20
Had somewhere to get to and sailed calmly on.

Musée des Beaux Arts: Museum of Fine Arts.   6 *miraculous birth*: The Nativity, a painting by
Breughel.   14 *Breughel's* Icarus: A painting entitled *Landscape with the Fall of Icarus*, by Pieter
Breughel the Elder (c. 1525–1569). In the legend, when Icarus flew too close to the sun his
wings melted and he fell into the sea.

W. H. Auden   (1907–1973)

IN MEMORY OF W. B. YEATS   1940

d. Jan. 1939

I

He disappeared in the dead of winter:
The brooks were frozen, the airports almost deserted,
And snow disfigured the public statues;
The mercury sank in the mouth of the dying day.
What instruments we have agree   5
The day of his death was a dark cold day.

Far from his illness
The wolves ran on through the evergreen forests,
The peasant river was untempted by the fashionable quays;
By mourning tongues   10
The death of the poet was kept from his poems.

But for him it was his last afternoon as himself,
An afternoon of nurses and rumors;
The provinces of his body revolted,
The squares of his mind were empty,   15
Silence invaded the suburbs,
The current of his feeling failed; he became his admirers.

Now he is scattered among a hundred cities
And wholly given over to unfamiliar affections;
To find his happiness in another kind of wood   20
And be punished under a foreign code of conscience.
The words of a dead man
Are modified in the guts of the living.

But in the importance and noise of tomorrow
When the brokers are roaring like beasts on the floor of the Bourse,°   25
And the poor have the sufferings to which they are fairly accustomed,
And each in the cell of himself is almost convinced of his freedom,
A few thousand will think of this day
As one thinks of a day when one did something slightly unusual.

25 *Bourse*: The Paris Stock Exchange.

What instruments we have agree   30
The day of his death was a dark cold day.

II

You were silly like us; your gift survived it all;
The parish of rich women, physical decay,
Yourself: mad Ireland hurt you into poetry.
Now Ireland has her madness and her weather still,   35
For poetry makes nothing happen: it survives
In the valley of its saying where executives
Would never want to tamper; it flows south
From ranches of isolation and the busy griefs,
Raw towns that we believe and die in; it survives,   40
A way of happening, a mouth.

III

Earth, receive an honored guest:
William Yeats is laid to rest.
Let the Irish vessel lie
Emptied of its poetry.   45

In the nightmare of the dark
All the dogs of Europe bark,
And the living nations wait,
Each sequestered in its hate;

Intellectual disgrace   50
Stares from every human face,
And the seas of pity lie
Locked and frozen in each eye.

Follow, poet, follow right
To the bottom of the night,   55
With your unconstraining voice
Still persuade us to rejoice;

With the farming of a verse
Make a vineyard of the curse,
Sing of human unsuccess   60
In a rapture of distress;

In the deserts of the heart
Let the healing fountain start,
In the prison of his days
Teach the free man how to praise.   65

Imamu Amiri Baraka   (b. 1934)
IN MEMORY OF RADIO   1961

Who has ever stopped to think of the divinity of Lamont Cranston?°
(Only Jack Kerouac,° that I know of: & me.
The rest of you probably had on WCBS and Kate Smith,°
Or something equally unattractive.)

What can I say?   5
It is better to have loved and lost
Than to put linoleum in your living rooms?

Am I a sage or something?
Mandrake's hypnotic gesture of the week?°
(Remember, I do not have the healing powers of Oral Roberts . . .   10
I cannot, like F. J. Sheen,° tell you how to get saved *& rich*!
I cannot even order you to gaschamber satori like Hitler or
      Goody Knight°

& Love is an evil word.
Turn it backwards/see, see what I mean?   15
An evol word. & besides
who understands it?
I certainly wouldn't like to go out on that kind of limb.

Saturday mornings we listened to *Red Lantern*° & his undersea folk.
At 11, *Let's Pretend*°/& we did/&I, the poet, still do, Thank God!   20

What was it he° used to say (after the transformation, when he was safe
& invisible & the unbelievers couldn't throw stones?) "Heh, heh, heh,
Who knows what evil lurks in the hearts of men? The Shadow knows."

O, yes he does
O, yes he does.   25
An evil word it is,
This Love.

1 *Lamont Cranston*: Fictional radio character who became The Shadow.   2 *Jack Kerouac*: Writer
(1922–1969), one of The Beats, known for *On The Road*.   3 *Kate Smith*: Popular American
singer.   9 *Mandrake's . . . week*: Mandrake the Magician, a weekly comic feature.   11 *F. J.
Sheen*: Fulton J. Sheen, popular radio evangelist.   13 *Goody Knight*: Unknown reference.   19
Red Lantern: Comic book hero.   20 *Let's Pretend*: Radio program.   21 *he*: The Shadow.

Grace Bauer

EVE RECOLLECTING THE GARDEN   1990

Was it your nakedness
or the knack you had

for naming I learned
to love? *Crow*, you whispered

and wings flapped black   5
as satin in the sky

Bee, and sweetness thickened
on my tongue, *Lion*

and something roared beneath
the ribs you claimed   10

you sacrificed. Our first quarrel
arose about the beast

I thought deserved a nobler tag
than *Dog*. And *Orchid*—

a sound more delicate. Admit it!   15
Dolphin, Starling, Antelope

were syllables you stole
from me, and you

were the one who swore
we'd have to taste those blood   20

red globes of fruit
before we'd find the right word

for that god-forsaken tree.

Patricia Beer   (b. 1924)
JANE AUSTEN° AT THE WINDOW   1970

When she was young and dancing,
Pregnant women sometimes took
The floor, shamelessly bouncing,
Treating it as a good joke.

In her middle age they loomed   5
Always larger and larger.
She pitied them. They were doomed
To lose looks, health and figure.

Poor sex objects, animals,
Slack and worn out at thirty.   10
She pitied with failing pulse.
They lived on to be eighty.

Jane Austen: 1775–1817; English novelist who recorded the changing social customs of England
in the early nineteenth century in novels such as *Pride and Prejudice.*

In her last illness she sat
At the window in a caul,
Watching them lurch down the street   15
Heavy with a funeral.

Marvin Bell   (b. 1937)
ICARUS THOUGHT   1990

The nature of a circle prevents it
from ever being a human hand.
And the essence of a rectangle
prevents it from ever being a skull.
Yet important people who can see   5
for themselves can't get this straight.
So others have to give them a picture
of the moon burning inside a mouth
and worms nesting within a cloud
and an empty sleeve that screams.   10

One who knows the hollows of a skull
will have felt the remorse of a knife.
And one who truly sees the moon
will know the sadness of the twilight.
But that fool we were in wax,   15
he will be lifted always by emptiness
and made to embrace the music,
first of the sun and then of the moon,
and learn the ambivalence of doorways
and a dawn that looks like evening.   20

Elizabeth Bishop   (1911–1979)
POEM   1976

About the size of an old-style dollar bill,
American or Canadian,
mostly the same whites, gray greens, and steel grays
—this little painting (a sketch for a larger one?)
has never earned any money in its life.   5
Useless and free, it has spent seventy years
as a minor family relic
handed along collaterally to owners
who looked at it sometimes, or didn't bother to.

It must be Nova Scotia; only there   10
does one see gabled wooden houses
painted that awful shade of brown.
The other houses, the bits that show, are white.
Elm trees, low hills, a thin church steeple
—that gray-blue wisp—or is it? In the foreground   15
a water meadow with some tiny cows,
two brushstrokes each, but confidently cows;
two minuscule white geese in the blue water,
back-to-back, feeding, and a slanting stick.
Up closer, a wild iris, white and yellow,   20
fresh-squiggled from the tube.
The air is fresh and cold; cold early spring
clear as gray glass; a half inch of blue sky
below the steel-gray storm clouds.
(They were the artist's specialty.)   25
A specklike bird is flying to the left.
Or is it a flyspeck looking like a bird?

Heavens, I recognize the place, I know it!
It's behind—I can almost remember the farmer's name.
His barn backed on that meadow. There it is,   30
titanium white, one dab. The hint of steeple,
filaments of brush-hairs, barely there,
must be the Presbyterian church.
Would that be Miss Gillespie's house?
Those particular geese and cows   35
are naturally before my time.

A sketch done in an hour, "in one breath,"
once taken from a trunk and handed over.
*Would you like this? I'll probably never
have room to hang these things again.*   40
*Your Uncle George, no, mine, my Uncle George,
he'd be your great-uncle, left them all with Mother
when he went back to England.
You know, he was quite famous, an R.A.°*

I never knew him. We both knew this place,   45
apparently, this literal small backwater,
looked at it long enough to memorize it,
our years apart. How strange. And it's still loved,
or its memory is (it must have changed a lot).

---

44 *R.A.:* Member of the Royal Academy, therefore an important recognized painter.

Our visions coincided—"visions" is   50
too serious a word—our looks, two looks:
art "copying from life" and life itself,
life and the memory of it so compressed
they've turned into each other. Which is which?
Life and the memory of it cramped,   55
dim, on a piece of Bristol board,
dim, but how live, how touching in detail
—the little that we get for free,
the little of our earthly trust. Not much.
About the size of our abidance   60
along with theirs: the munching cows,
the iris, crisp and shivering, the water
still standing from spring freshets,
the yet-to-be-dismantled elms, the geese.

Elizabeth Bishop   (1911–1979)
SEASCAPE   1946

This celestial seascape, with white herons got up as angels,
flying as high as they want and as far as they want sidewise
in tiers and tiers of immaculate reflections;
the whole region, from the highest heron
down to the weightless mangrove island   5
with bright green leaves edged neatly with bird-droppings
like illumination in silver,
and down to the suggestively Gothic arches of the mangrove
                                                                   roots
and the beautiful pea-green back-pasture   10
where occasionally a fish jumps, like a wild-flower
in an ornamental spray of spray;
this cartoon by Raphael for a tapestry for a Pope:
it does look like heaven.
But a skeletal lighthouse standing there   15
in black and white clerical dress,
who lives on his nerves, thinks he knows better.
He thinks that hell rages below his iron feet,
that that is why the shallow water is so warm,
and he knows that heaven is not like this.   20
Heaven is not like flying or swimming,
but has something to do with blackness and a strong glare
and when it gets dark he will remember something
strongly worded to say on the subject.

Elizabeth Bishop   (1911–1979)

THE FISH   1946

I caught a tremendous fish
and held him beside the boat
half out of water, with my hook
fast in a corner of his mouth.
He didn't fight.   5
He hadn't fought at all.
He hung a grunting weight,
battered and venerable
and homely. Here and there
his brown skin hung in strips   10
like ancient wallpaper,
and its pattern of darker brown
was like wallpaper:
shapes like full-blown roses
stained and lost through age.   15
He was speckled with barnacles,
fine rosettes of lime,
and infested
with tiny white sea-lice,
and underneath two or three   20
rags of green weed hung down.
While his gills were breathing in
the terrible oxygen
—the frightening gills,
fresh and crisp with blood,   25
that can cut so badly—
I thought of the coarse white flesh
packed in like feathers,
the big bones and the little bones,
the dramatic reds and blacks   30
of his shiny entrails,
and the pink swim-bladder
like a big peony.
I looked into his eyes
which were far larger than mine   35
but shallower, and yellowed,
the irises backed and packed
with tarnished tinfoil
seen through the lenses
of old scratched isinglass.   40
They shifted a little, but not
to return my stare.

—It was more like the tipping
of an object toward the light.
I admired his sullen face,   45
the mechanism of his jaw,
and then I saw
that from his lower lip
—if you could call it a lip—
grim, wet, and weaponlike,   50
hung five old pieces of fish-line,
or four and a wire leader
with the swivel still attached,
with all their five big hooks
grown firmly in his mouth.   55
A green line, frayed at the end
where he broke it, two heavier lines,
and a fine black thread
still crimped from the strain and snap
when it broke and he got away.   60
Like medals with their ribbons
frayed and wavering,
a five-haired beard of wisdom
trailing from his aching jaw.
I stared and stared   65
and victory filled up
the little rented boat,
from the pool of bilge
where oil had spread a rainbow
around the rusted engine   70
to the bailer rusted orange,
the sun-cracked thwarts,
the oarlocks on their strings,
the gunnels—until everything
was rainbow, rainbow, rainbow!   75
And I let the fish go.

William Blake   (1757–1827)
INTRODUCTION   1789

From *Songs of Innocence°*

Piping down the valleys wild,
Piping songs of pleasant glee,

Songs of Innocence: These poems were published both separately and with *Songs of Experience.*
Together they were intended to show "the two contrary states of the human soul."

On a cloud I saw a child.
And he laughing said to me,

Pipe a song about a Lamb;   5
So I piped with merry cheer.
Piper pipe that song again—
So I piped; he wept to hear.

Drop thy pipe, thy happy pipe;
Sing thy songs of happy cheer.   10
So I sung the same again
While he wept with joy to hear.

Piper sit thee down and write
In a book that all may read—
So he vanished from my sight.   15
And I plucked a hollow reed.

And I made a rural pen,
And I stained the water clear,
And I wrote my happy songs
Every child may joy to hear.   20

William Blake   (1757–1827)

THE CHIMNEY SWEEPER   1789

From *Songs of Innocence*°

When my mother died I was very young,
And my father sold me° while yet my tongue,
Could scarcely cry 'weep 'weep 'weep 'weep.°
So your chimneys I sweep and in soot I sleep.

There's little Tom Dacre, who cried when his head   5
That curled like a lamb's back, was shaved, so I said,
Hush, Tom, never mind it, for when your head's bare,
You know that the soot cannot spoil your white hair.

And so he was quiet, and that very night,
As Tom was a-sleeping he had such a sight,   10
That thousands of sweepers, Dick, Joe, Ned, and Jack,
Were all of them locked up in coffins of black.

And by came an Angel who had a bright key,
And he opened the coffins and set them all free.

Songs of Innocence: See note to "Introduction."   2 *sold me*: A reference to the church's use of child labor under the guise of charity.   3 *weep*: The child is trying to say "sweep."

Then down a green plain leaping, laughing, they run   15
And wash in a river and shine in the Sun.

Then naked and white, all their bags left behind,
They rise upon clouds, and sport in the wind.
And the Angel told Tom, if he'd be a good boy,
He'd have God for his father and never want joy.   20

And so Tom awoke and we rose in the dark
And got with our bags and our brushes to work.
Though the morning was cold, Tom was happy and warm;
So if all do their duty, they need not fear harm.

William Blake   (1757–1827)

THE LITTLE BOY LOST   1789

From *Songs of Innocence*

Father, father, where are you going?
O, do not walk so fast.
Speak, father, speak to your little boy,
Or else I shall be lost.

The night was dark, no father was there,   5
The child was wet with dew.
The mire was deep, and the child did weep,
And away the vapor flew.

William Blake   (1757–1827)

THE LITTLE BOY FOUND   1789

From *Songs of Innocence*

The little boy lost in the lonely fen,
Led by the wand'ring light,
Began to cry, but God ever nigh,
Appeared like his father in white.

He kissed the child and by the hand led   5
And to his mother brought,
Who in sorrow pale, through the lonely dale
Her little boy weeping sought.

William Blake (1757–1827)
THE CLOD AND THE PEBBLE 1794

From *Songs of Experience*

Love seeketh not Itself to please,
Nor for itself hath any care;
But for another gives its ease,
And builds a Heaven in Hell's despair.

So sang a little Clod of Clay,   5
Trodden with the cattles' feet:
But a Pebble of the brook,
Warbled out these meters meet:°

Love seeketh only Self to please,
To bind another to its delight;   10
Joys in another's loss of ease,
And builds a Hell in Heaven's despite.°

8 *meet*: Fitting, suitable.   12 *despite:* Scorn, anger, defiance.

William Blake (1757–1827)
THE CHIMNEY SWEEPER 1794

From *Songs of Experience*

A little black thing among the snow:
Crying "'weep, weep" in notes of woe!
"Where are thy father and mother? say?"
"They are both gone up to the church to pray."

"Because I was happy upon the heath,"   5
And smiled among the winter's snow:
They clothed me in the clothes of death,
And taught me to sing the notes of woe.

"And because I am happy, and dance and sing,
They think they have done me no injury: 10
And are gone to praise God and his Priest and King,
Who make up a heaven of our misery."

The Chimney Sweeper: See all notes to "The Chimney Sweeper," p. 689.

William Blake   (1757–1827)
THE GARDEN OF LOVE   1794

From *Songs of Experience*

I went to the Garden of Love,
And saw what I never had seen:
A Chapel° was built in the midst,
Where I used to play on the green.

And the gates of this Chapel were shut,   5
And "Thou shalt not" writ over the door;
So I turned to the Garden of Love,
That so many sweet flowers bore;

And I saw it was filled with graves,
And tomb-stones where flowers should be: 10
And Priests in black gowns were walking their rounds,
And binding with briars my joys and desires.

3 *Chapel*: See notes to "The Chimney Sweeper," p. 689.

William Blake   (1757–1827)
LONDON   1794

From *Songs of Experience*

I wander through each chartered° street,
Near where the chartered Thames does flow,
And mark in every face I meet
Marks of weakness, marks of woe.

In every cry of every Man,   5
In every Infant's cry of fear,
In every voice, in every ban,
The mind-forged manacles I hear—

How the Chimney-sweeper's cry
Every black'ning Church° appalls,   10
And the hapless Soldier's sigh
Runs in blood down Palace walls.

1 *chartered*: Defined or licensed by written law. This meaning becomes ironic when used with a river in the next line because a river is free-flowing and cannot be chartered.   10 *Church*: See notes to "The Chimney Sweeper," p. 689.

But most through midnight streets I hear
How the youthful Harlot's curse
Blasts the new-born Infant's tear   15
And blights with plagues the Marriage hearse.

Peter Blue Cloud   (b. 1935)

WOLF   1974

burrowing deep into earth until the grave is complete,
hiding in daytime shadows, panting,
                         sweat,
    dry matted blood
    and stump of a leg,   5
wolf, his growls into whimpers of pain unending.

she-wolf keening the stiffened, frozen cubs,
licking the frosted muzzles cyanide tracings,
                        sweet
    the steaming meat   10
    she gently places
as an offering, though she knows they are dead.

run down to earth and snow with bursting heart,
down to the bright red hammering pulse, and further
                            down   15
    one by one
    the rifle shot
echo resounding a terrible, alien blood lust.

protruding blackened tongues, no more the night chant,
blanket of sound, the earth her moaning,   20
                    futile,
    her emptied womb,
    and the seed
dried and rustling among forgotten leaves.

a wind of running leaves across the prairie,   25
a scent of pine in frozen north the muskeg
    lakes
              lent footprints
      cast in sandstone
grains rubbing time the desert's constant edge.   30

softly contoured voices moaning night,
the wolves in circle council the moon
    shadows

        bent starlight
     of fingered sleet   35
rattles the gourd of earth down feathered roots.

beyond beginnings the earth her many tribes
and clans their life songs merge into one
     chant
          welcome dance   40
    to the unborn
awaiting birth in the sun-fingered dawn.

and to each creation the heartline trail
is etched in delicate memory pattern
     webs   45
        so intricate
    in a unity
of day into night the seasons follow.

the moaning low of wolves to ears of men
first wisdom gained by another's quiet   50
     song
       of meditation
     circle of council
bound together by their basic power.

and the quiet way of learning was the food   55
and spark the hearth of compassion warm
     enfolding
          all others
    born of earth
in the harmony of mutual need.   60

in thanks the minds of curious men
sought further wisdom from the brother
     wolf
       his clan
     a social order   65
of strength through lasting kinship.

and recognized the she-wolf's place
in balance with that of the male leader
     heads
       of family   70
    to be obeyed
because their first law was survival.

and studied the pattern of the hunt
where each had a particular role
       defined   75
          by need
    and acted upon
without the slightest hesitation.

and moaning low the wolf song
head bent the drummer and voice to sky   80
    singer
           in thanks
    to brother wolf,
now your song we will sing in our voices.

again the rifle shot and snapping jaws   85
of steel traps and poisoned bait,
the bounty hunter and fur trapper
    predators
    of greed
whose minds create vast lies.   90

and moaning low in death chant
the one remaining wolf staggers
    and falls
    to death
as winds carry his voice into tomorrow.   95

and the voice is an accusation howling
within the brain heart pulling sinews
    harshly,
    you, too,
I hang my death about your neck in circle.   100

mourn the buffalo and the beaver,
keen the fox and mountain cat,
    shout
    the grizzly
antelope elk moose caribou and many   105

more gone into death the prime breeders
to fashion garments of vanity,
    Indian,
    brother,
cleanse the blood lust from your naked spirit   110

and fast and pray your spirit's new growth
and be reborn into childhood innocence
       purity
       our maker
awaits your ancient promise.   115

the wolf in dream has petitioned
for his voice to be heard in council
       now
       in this place
let us open our minds.   120

scattered and lost the people fall,
orphaned, the child feels hunger,
       where is tomorrow,
       where does it hide?
there are four voices coming   125
from four directions
       the center is harmony,
       the center is beginning.
scouts and messengers called back,
the council is the mind   130
       it is merging thought
       the nation's birth.
now, when warriors feast,
they eat of embers
       the fire's heat   135
       stored energy.
the warrior society
is the wolf society
       is the clan family
       heart of tribe.   140
anger seeking wisdom,
council after meditation
       there is a vision
       held in sacred trust.

I dance upon my three remaining legs,   145
                look,
the memory of the fourth keeps my balance,
                    see,
my wispy white and cyanide fog-breath,
                hah!   150
taut sinews vibrate the sky's held thunder,

                                        huh!
steel traps I weave a necklace of your making,
                                hah!
puffs of dust I quick-stomp with paw feet,   160
                        huh!
I am becoming you dancing for them,
                        hah!
I jump upon your back a heavy robe,
                                huh!   165
my shadow will nip your pumping ankle,
                                huh!
you will think you me in the full moon night,
                                huh!
I crush your long bones sucking marrow,   170
nose your severed head before me the trail,
tear strips of flesh the ribbons weave a net,
chew hair and fingernails into mash
I slap upon my festered stump your human glue,
                                hah!   175
now you are dancing,
                brother,
                        now you are dancing.

Louise Bogan   (1897–1970)
MEDUSA°   1923

I had come to the house, in a cave of trees,
Facing a sheer sky.
Everything moved,—a bell hung ready to strike,
Sun and reflection wheeled by.

When the bare eyes were before me   5
And the hissing hair,
Held up at a window, seen through a door.
The stiff bald eyes, the serpents on the forehead
Formed in the air.

This is a dead scene forever now.   10
Nothing will ever stir.
The end will never brighten it more than this,
Nor the rain blur.

Medusa: In classical literature a gorgon, a female with snakes for hair. Any man who looked on her was turned to stone.

Louise Bogan   (1897–1970)
WOMEN   1923

Women have no wilderness in them,
They are provident instead,
Content in the tight hot cell of their hearts
To eat dusty bread.

They do not see cattle cropping red winter grass,   5
They do not hear
Snow water going down under culverts
Shallow and clear.

They wait, when they should turn to journeys,
They stiffen, when they should bend.   10
They use against themselves that benevolence
To which no man is friend.

They cannot think of so many crops to a field
Or of clean wood cleft by an axe.
Their love is an eager meaninglessness   15
Too tense, or too lax.

They hear in every whisper that speaks to them
A shout and a cry.
As like as not, when they take life over their door-sills
They should let it go by.   20

Arna Bontemps   (1902–1973)
A BLACK MAN TALKS OF REAPING   1940

I have sown beside all waters in my day.
I planted deep, within my heart the fear
That wind or fowl would take the grain away.
I planted safe against this stark, lean year.

I scattered seed enough to plant the land   5
In rows from Canada to Mexico,
But for my reaping only what the hand
Can hold at once is all that I can show.

Yet what I sowed and what the orchard yields
My brother's sons are gathering stalk and root,   10
Small wonder then my children glean in fields
They have not sown, and feed on bitter fruit.

Anne Bradstreet   (1612–1672)

TO MY DEAR AND LOVING HUSBAND   1678

If ever two were one, then surely we.
If ever man were loved by wife, then thee;
If ever wife was happy in a man,
Compare with me ye women if you can.
I prize thy love more than whole Mines of gold,   5
Or all the riches that the East doth hold.
My love is such that Rivers cannot quench,
Nor ought° but love from thee, give recompense.
Thy love is such I can no way repay;
The heavens reward thee manifold, I pray.   10
Then while we live, in love let's so persevere,
That when we live no more, we may live ever.

8 *ought*: Aught; anything whatever.

Anne Bradstreet   (1612–1672)

THE AUTHOR TO HER BOOK   1678

Thou ill-formed offspring of my feeble brain,
Who after birth did'st by my side remain,
Till snatched from thence by friends, less wise than true,
Who thee abroad, exposed to public view,
Made thee in rags, halting to the press to trudge,   5
Where errors were not lessened (all may judge).
At thy return my blushing was not small,
My rambling brat (in print) should mother call,
I cast thee by as one unfit for light,
Thy visage was so irksome in my sight;   10
Yet being mine own, at length affection would
Thy blemishes amend, if so I could:
I washed thy face, but more defects I saw,
And rubbing off a spot still made a flaw.
I stretched thy joints to make thee even feet,°   15
Yet still thou run'st more hobbling than is meet;°
In better dress to trim thee was my mind,
But nought save° homespun cloth in the house I find.
In this array 'mongst vulgars may'st thou roam.
In critic's hands beware thou dost not come,   20

15 *feet*: Metaphorically she "stretched" the book's hinges in order to make its "feet"—meter—
more regular and even.   16 *meet*: Fitting, suitable.   18 *nought save*: Nothing but.

And take thy way where yet thou art not known.
If for thy father asked, say thou hadst none;
And for thy mother, she alas is poor,
Which caused her thus to send thee out of door.

Anne Bradstreet   (1612–1672)

IN MEMORY OF MY DEAR GRANDCHILD ANNE BRADSTREET

WHO DECEASED JUNE 20, 1669,

BEING THREE YEARS AND SEVEN MONTHS OLD   1678

With troubled heart and trembling hand I write,
The heavens have changed to sorrow my delight.
How oft with disappointment have I met,
When I on fading things my hopes have set?
Experience might 'fore this have made me wise,   5
To value things according to their price.
Was ever stable joy yet found below?
Or perfect bliss without mixture of woe?
I knew she was but as a withering flower,
That's here today, perhaps gone in an hour;   10
Like as a bubble, or the brittle glass,
Or like a shadow turning as it was.
More fool then I to look on that was lent
As if mine own, when thus impermanent.
Farewell dear child, thou ne'er shall come to me,   15
But yet a while, and I shall go to thee;
Mean time my throbbing heart's cheered up with this:
Thou with thy Savior art in endless bliss.

Gwendolyn Brooks   (b. 1917)

THE MOTHER   1953

Abortions will not let you forget.
You remember the children you got that you did not get,
The damp small pulps with a little or with no hair,
The singers and workers that never handled the air.
You will never neglect or beat   5
Them, or silence or buy with a sweet.
You will never wind up the sucking-thumb
Or scuttle off ghosts that come.

You will never leave them, controlling your luscious sigh,
Return for a snack of them, with gobbling mother-eye.   10

I have heard in the voices of the wind the voices of my dim killed
    children.
I have contracted. I have eased
My dim dears at the breasts they could never suck.
I have said, Sweets, if I sinned, if I seized
Your luck   15
And your lives from your unfinished reach,
If I stole your births and your names,
Your straight baby tears and your games,
Your stilted or lovely loves, your tumults, your marriages, aches, and
    your deaths,
If I poisoned the beginnings of your breaths,   20
Believe that even in my deliberateness I was not deliberate.
Though why should I whine,
Whine that the crime was other than mine?—
Since anyhow you are dead.
Or rather, or instead,   25
You were never made.

But that too, I am afraid,
Is faulty: oh, what shall I say, how is the truth to be said?
You were born, you had body, you died.
It is just that you never giggled or planned or cried.   30

Believe me, I loved you all.
Believe me, I knew you, though faintly, and I loved, I loved you
All.

Gwendolyn Brooks   **(b. 1917)**
WE REAL COOL   1959

The Pool Players.
Seven at the Golden Shovel.

We real cool. We
Left school. We

Lurk late. We
Strike straight. We

Sing sin. We   5
Thin gin. We

Jazz June. We
Die soon.

Elizabeth Barrett Browning   (1806–1861)
TO GEORGE SAND°   1844

A Desire

Thou large-brained woman and large-hearted man,
Self-called George Sand! whose soul, amid the lions
Of thy tumultuous senses, moans defiance
And answers roar for roar, as spirits can:
I would some mild miraculous thunder ran   5
Above the applauded circus, in appliance
Of thine own nobler nature's strength and science,
Drawing two pinions, white as wings of swan,
From thy strong shoulders, to amaze the place
With holier light! that thou to woman's claim   10
And man's, mightst join beside the angel's grace
Of a pure genius sanctified from blame,
Till child and maiden pressed to thine embrace
To kiss upon thy lips a stainless fame.

George Sand: Pen name of Amandine Aurore Lucie Dupin, Baroness Dudevant (1804–1876).
Sand was a French novelist who scandalized society by living and loving as she pleased. She
ordinarily dressed like a man so as to move and behave more freely.

Elizabeth Barrett Browning   (1806–1861)
TO GEORGE SAND   1844

A Recognition

True genius, but true woman! dost deny
The woman's nature with a manly scorn,
And break away the gauds and armlets worn
By weaker women in captivity?
Ah, vain denial! that revolted cry   5
Is sobbed in by a woman's voice forlorn,—
Thy woman's hair, my sister, all unshorn
Floats back dishevelled strength in agony,
Disproving thy man's name: and while before
The world thou burnest in a poet-fire,   10
We see thy woman-heart beat evermore
Through the large flame. Beat purer, heart, and higher,
Till God unsex thee on the heavenly shore
Where unincarnate spirits purely aspire!

Robert Browning   (1812–1889)
MY LAST DUCHESS   1842

Ferrara°

That's my last Duchess painted on the wall,
Looking as if she were alive. I call
That piece a wonder, now: Frà Pandolf's° hands
Worked busily a day, and there she stands.
Will't please you sit and look at her? I said   5
"Frà Pandolf" by design, for never read
Strangers like you that pictured countenance,
The depth and passion of its earnest glance,
But to myself they turned (since none puts by
The curtain I have drawn for you, but I)   10
And seemed as they would ask me, if they durst,
How such a glance came there; so, not the first
Are you to turn and ask thus. Sir, 'twas not
Her husband's presence only, called that spot
Of joy into the Duchess' cheek; perhaps   15
Frà Pandolf chanced to say "Her mantle laps
Over my lady's wrist too much," or "Paint
Must never hope to reproduce the faint
Half-flush that dies along her throat": such stuff
Was courtesy, she thought, and cause enough   20
For calling up that spot of joy. She had
A heart—how shall I say?—too soon made glad,
Too easily impressed; she liked whate'er
She looked on, and her looks went everywhere.
Sir, 'twas all one! My favor at her breast,   25
The dropping of the daylight in the West,
The bough of cherries some officious fool
Broke in the orchard for her, the white mule
She rode with round the terrace—all and each
Would draw from her alike the approving speech,   30
Or blush, at least. She thanked men,—good! but thanked
Somehow—I know not how—as if she ranked
My gift of a nine-hundred-years-old name
With anybody's gift. Who'd stoop to blame
This sort of trifling? Even had you skill   35
In speech—(which I have not)—to make your will
Quite clear to such an one, and say, "Just this

Ferrara: This poem may be based on the life of an Italian nobleman, the Duke of Ferrara, whose
first wife is believed to have been poisoned.   3 *Frà Pandolf*: A fictitious painter.

Or that in you disgusts me; here you miss,
Or there exceed the mark"—and if she let
Herself be lessoned so, nor plainly set   40
Her wits to yours, forsooth, and made excuse,
—E'en then would be some stooping; and I choose
Never to stoop. Oh sir, she smiled, no doubt,
Whene'er I passed her; but who passed without
Much the same smile? This grew; I gave commands;   45
Then all smiles stopped together. There she stands
As if alive. Will't please you rise? We'll meet
The company below, then. I repeat,
The Count your master's known munificence
Is ample warrant that no just pretence   50
Of mine for dowry will be disallowed;
Though his fair daughter's self, as I avowed
At starting, is my object. Nay, we'll go
Together down, sir. Notice Neptune, though,
Taming a sea-horse, thought a rarity,   55
Which Claus of Innsbruck° cast in bronze for me!

56 *Claus of Innsbruck*: A fictitious sculptor.

Christopher Buckley   (b. 1948)
SERENADE IN BLUE   1993

Where is the sea, that once solved the whole loneliness Of the Midwest?
                                                        —*James Wright*

Because my father knew that loneliness, that tedium in a breeze
slip-streaming behind his Oldsmobile as it bent back sleepy heads
of blackeyed susans along the interstate while he moved around
all those years—station to radio station, remote broadcast to
        broadcast—
he brought me to the Pacific where the sea's blue notes scaled the cliffs   5
and salt air, where the white gulls lolled day-long on the spindrift light
as wind pulled apart the surf and offered it up—foam-flowers and song
as signs of grace, as means and end—into my arms . . .
                                                But I should begin
with silence and with 1942, the sky over the Atlantic at dusk, two
        swaths
of blue—deep water and diming air—banded like an Ohio Blue Tip
        match,   10
one that he keeps in his shirt pocket and flicks to light his Lucky
        Strikes,

which is appropriate, for he is from Ohio, steaming east at 4 knots tops
on the John C. Calhoun, a *Liberty Ship*, meaning some sorry freighter
over-loaded with men and supplies. He knows they're sitting ducks
for U-boats though they zig-zag 48 days to Takerati and the African
    Gold   15
Coast—but feels almost fortunate, knowing they carry lumber below
    and
above deck, figuring they might float if hit. Sitting out on deck as
    night
comes down, lights out, no smoking allowed, he sees clear to the
    curved
horizon where ships are going up like the flare of matches struck
    against
the dark. He's not thinking of the life behind, of his father wearing
    down   20
in a shoe factory in Washington Court House, or those boys gone off
to college and football in Columbus, gone to Pensacola for Air Cadets;
he doesn't even give a thought to that neighbor girl with a solid
    backhand
and her own tennis court, the balmy aroma of grass splashed and
    hover-
ing on the air as his first serve *thwacks* in . . . He's not even envisioning   25
wings—the wings on the Sphinx° because they are headed for Cairo,
    wings
on human-headed bulls° at the Assyrian gate because the beard he will
    grow
in the desert will have him looking like an Assyrian, and because the
    bulls
are said to bring good luck.   No, he's humming one of Glenn Miller's   30
sweetest orchestrations, remembering where the vocalist comes in,
    thinking
of bands he sang with in Miami and Chilicothe. He's got it in his head
for the whole war, even while he and Howard, his one home-town
    friend,
swim untouched amid schools of barracuda in Takerati Bay, bounce
    their DC3,
landing *with* the wind, or navigate to Ascension Island so they can
    refuel   35
on the round trip to South America—a rock in the South Atlantic
    others
knew they'd missed when that big bass beat in their engines died and
    they

---

26 *Sphinx:* Reference to the monolithic sculpture of the sphinx outside Cairo.   27 *bulls:*
Another reference to ancient statues of half-human, half-animal creatures.

headed for the soundless center of the sea.

He'd never heard of Clarinda,
Iowa before Miller's plane sank into the blue between London and
Paris.   40
He was state side, in time for Christmas, calling home with a telegram
that said Howard was killed on a last instruction flight, a day before
discharge;
and his mother, who had never heard of such things, had gone to
answer
the doorbell, and there was Howard in his astral body, floating in an
azure
light, and so she said she knew.   45

He began then to think about the future,
a family, decided to study radio and give up singing. Yet I see him, the
way
I think he will always see himself, after that last time he sang with a
band—
stepping up to the standing michrophone, his right hand cupped over
his ear
as he picked up the trombone's fading cue to croon, *When I hear that*   50
Serenade in Blue, I'm somewhere in another world, alone, with you . . .

José Antonio Burciaga   (b. 1940)
BERTA CROCKER'S BICENTENNIAL RECIPE   1976

Con tu filero°
. . . . cut along the dotted line . . . .
Don't wait for the light to change to brown.
Adentro°
You will find   5
Tres paquetes:

One Red
One White
One Blue

Mézclalos°.   10

Pero con huevos.°

Stick it in the oven for 200 years
And let it rise and propagate

And you will have a beautiful brown cake.

---

1 *Con tu filero*: For your file.   4 *Adentro*: First.   10 *Mézclalos*: Mix.   11 *Pero con huevos*:
But with eggs.

José Antonio Burciaga   (b. 1940)
WORLD PREMIERE   1976

To the sergeant who told me,
    "At least you admit it."

To a neighbor down the street who told me,
    "You don't even belong here.
    Go back where you came from."   5

To the honky tonk from Mineral Wells, Texas, who said,
    "We caint help it.
    We was raised to hate Meskins."

To the Redwood City California Chief of Police
Who told his flunky,   10
    "Stay here till the last DOG leaves."

To the flunky who answered,
    "Yes Chief, till the laaaaaast DOG leaves."

To Herbert Hoover who warned the nation,
    "Mexicans are bad shots but watch out if they have a knife."   15

To the U.S. Senator from California
Whose name I forgot, but said,
    "Mexicans were built low to the ground for picking."

To Frito Lay
    Who made a mascot of a people   20
    And millions from their staple.

To the Dallas policeman
    Who shot a defenceless,
          handcuffed,
          12 year old,   25
          Santos Rodrigues.

To Officer Michael Cogley of the Oakland Police Farce,
    Who shot José Barlow Benavides with a shotgun,
    When José was spread eagled against a squad car.

Kathryn Stripling Byer   (b. 1944)
CHESTNUT FLAT MINE   1992

They say the fringe of her shawl clung
like lichen to creek rock
and under the laurel her sash looked
for all the sad world like a garter snake.

Farther on something so sheer   5
it was almost invisible floated away
on the Toe River. Red
said the woman who watched it go by,

baby-blue said her little girl stoning
the water with acorns. (Did he stroke   10
her silken leg after he'd unlaced
her tiny black shoe? Did he say Little

Darling, you're mine and what good
are your fancy ways now?) God Almighty,
the way they heard screams floating   15
downhill like what I imagine a town woman

wears underneath all her finery,
but when they came to the old mine by late
afternoon, they found only her gloves
thrown aside in the larkspur. Her dress   20

was laid out like a corpse with a rose
in its lap, on its lily-white bosom
a bird's nest of wrinkles as if a man's
head had lain ever so gently there.

Juanita Casey   (b. 1925)
PEGASUS°   1964

Do you sometimes hear
A sound
Of great wings overhead?
Many people who see nothing
Tell me they do.   5

And have you seen,
Even if you are no horseman,
This horse
Which paces from the valley
On the chalk road to the uplands,   10
Watching you as he climbs,
First with one eye,
Then the other,
As horses will.
It will be   15
One of those special moments

Pegasus. In Greek mythology, Pegasus is the winged horse symbolizing poetic inspiration.

When it is like the first morning.
The mist lingering
Like threads laid by night
For her return at cockcrow.   20
Can you hold
The bold onyx eye
Of the horse approaching,
Unafraid
If unaccustomed to horses,   25
Without sense of inferiority,
Or if a horseman,
Without flinching
From so redoubtable a stallion,
Who, breasting the proud light,   30
Challenges the sun
As rival to his own blood.
You are aware this is Horse.
Everything is,
The bay-brown river,   35
Piebald and roan mountains,
Branded hills moving against the sky
Like Oncus' mares.
And unknowingly, you know
That this astonishing animal   40
Is coming quite unbidden
To your hand.

When it happened to me,
He greeted me,
Because although I am a woman   45
And no poet,
He knew I had my kingdom amongst his nation.
I told him
Women cannot be poets.
If they try   50
They become masculine apologies,
Or apologies for women.
They must be content
To be spiritual and physical bran tubs
For real poets,   55
Who by a lucky delve may now and then
Find a pearl
Amongst all the bran.

When he came to me,
There was in his eye   60

A look which some earth-bound horses show.
But they are rare these days,
The singing blood is deadened,
And should honor be sought
Amongst the conditioned?   65
They stand
Like falcons chained° to an ignoble hand.
And they stand,
Shining out of the dark
Like Blake's tiger.°   70
While the warnings rustle like rats in straw,
A rogue. He killed a man.° Beware.
Waiting for one
To step out of the centuries
And greet him,   75
Ho, my good horse.
And they search great horizons
Past our heads,
Back over Babylon,
Tigris and Thessaly,   80
They look for those Twins
Or for him who carried Wisdom's bridle
To the spring that day.
How sweetly
They would step under that hand,   85
Guided by the traditional
Silken thread
Between mind, not metal.
Good Horse,
Do you too search for someone worthy of your blood,   90
Who would not slide off ignominiously
At the first clap of wings
As though you'd crowed as well!
Or taking the harshest curb
Bend you to impossible propriety   95
In classes designed
To exhibit the exhibitor.
And no one would wish these days to drink with you
From Hippocrene.°
There would be mention   100

---

67 *falcons chained*: Trained falcons are usually kept on a leash tied to the wrist.   70 *Blake's tiger*: A reference to the poem "The Tyger" by William Blake; which begins, "Tiger, Tiger, burning bright / In the forests of the night."   72 *man*: Ben Jonson (1572?–1637), the poet's poet.   99 *Hippocrene*: Fountain of the Muses, thus the inspiration of the poet—it rose from a spot struck by the hoof of Pegasus.

Of worms, bacteria, hygiene.
(Hygeia, girl, blush for them)
Perhaps he knows I could ride him,
But will not.
It would be an insult.   105
I'm surprised at those who did.
Perseus°—
Though due to possible artistic misinterpretation—
Coal-bucket on head as though
All set for a celestial scramble,   110
And nothing to do with horses,
Cretinous shield in hand,
And all smirk and sandals.
Or Bellerophon.°
Whose appalling horsemanship   115
Ended in degradation
And an arseful of brambles.

Now he is up with me, what a horse this is.
How are you bred,
Horse?   120
Sired by the Mind
Out of Light,
Or a cloud covering the night?
A Horse
From a handful of Libyan wind?   125
Or from Poseidon's° line of sea-thrown winners,
By the stallion Ocean,
Put him to the mare Demeter,°
She is a black,
A wild one, snake-headed and uncertain.   130
But she could go the distance
In Time's stakes.
She'd scorch the last lap of Eternity
Though her heart burst . . .
However you're bred, Horse,   135
No matter.
Pedigree unknown, they might write.
But there is no disguising that in form
And spirit
You were tempered   140
By that old Damascene, Truth.

---

107 *Perseus:* Hero who slayed Medusa, from whose trunk sprang Pegasus.   114 *Bellerophon:*
Hero who killed the Chimera with the help of Pegasus.   126 *Poseidon:* The horse was sacred
to Poseidon, god of the sea.   128 *Demeter:* Goddess of architecture and fertility.

I am glad he came,
Just this once.
That for a moment
I scratched that place under the mane   145
Which entrances all horses,
And made the immortal lip bunch and twitch.
I saw his teeth unringed
And ageless,
Time cannot bishop him.   150
I told him
Go back,
Back to his lusher centuries,
Away from
This close cropped age.   155
Back
Good horse,
Here you will be a freak, and it is better
To return
Even though you graze Time bare.   160

Marilyn Chin   (b. 1955)

HOW I GOT THAT NAME   1990

An essay on assimilation—
or: Deng Xiao Ping,° are we not your children?

I am Marilyn Mei Ling Chin.
Oh, how I love the resoluteness
of that first person singular
followed by that stalwart indicative
of "be," without the uncertain i-n-g   5
of "becoming." Of course,
the name had been changed
somewhere between Angel Island and the sea,
when my father the paperson
in the late 1950s   10
obsessed with some bombshell blonde
transliterated "Mei Ling" to "Marilyn."
And nobody dared question
his initial impulse—for we all know
lust drove men to greatness,   15

Deng Xiao Ping: 1904–; Chinese Communist leader, resigned 1987.

not goodness, not decency.
And there I was, a wayward pink baby,
named after some tragic
white woman, swollen with gin and Nembutal.°
My mother couldn't pronounce the "r."   20
She dubbed me "Numba one female offshoot"
for brevity: henceforth, she will live and die
in sublime ignorance, flanked
by loving children and the "kitchen deity."
While my father dithers,   25
a tomcat in Hong Kong trash—
a gambler, a petty thug,
who bought a chain of chopsuey joints
in Piss River, Oregon
with bootlegged Gucci cash.   30
Nobody dared question his integrity given
his nice, devout daughters
and his bright industrious sons.
As if filial piety were the standard
with which all earthly men were measured.   35

Oh, how trustworthy our daughters,
how thrifty our sons!
How we've managed to fool the experts
in education, statistics and demography—
We're not very creative but not adverse to rote-learning.   40
Indeed, you can *use* us.
But the "Model Minority" is a tease.
We know you are watching now,
so we refuse to give you any!
Oh, bamboo shoots, bamboo shoots!   45
The further west we go, we'll hit east;
The deeper down we dig, we'll find China.
History has turned its stomach
on a black, polluted beach—
where life doesn't hinge   50
on that red, red wheelbarrow,°
but on whether or not our new lover
in the final episode of "Santa Barbara"°
will lean over a scented candle
and call us a "bitch."   55

19 *gin and Nembutal*: A reference to Marilyn Monroe's supposed dependency on drugs and alcohol.   51   *red wheelbarrow*: See "The Red Wheelbarrow," p. 985.   53   "*Santa Barbara*":
TV series about trendy Californians.

Oh god, where have we gone wrong?
We have no inner resources!

Then, one redolent spring morning
the Great Patriarch Chin
peered down from his kiosk in heaven   60
and saw that his descendants were ugly.
One had a squarish head and a nose without a bridge.
Another's profile—long and knobbed as a gourd.
A third, the sad, brutish one
may never, never marry.   65
And I, his least favorite—
"not quite boiled, not quite cooked,"
a plump pomfret simmering in my juices—
too listless to fight for my people's destiny.
"To kill without resistance is not slaughter"   70
says the proverb. So, I wait for imminent death.
The fact that this death is also metaphorical
is testament to my lethargy.

So, here lies Marilyn Mei Ling Chin,
married once, twice to so-and-so, a Lee and a Wong,   75
granddaughter of Jack "the patriarch" Chin
and the brooding Suilin Fong,
daughter of the virtuous Yuet Kuen Wong
and G. G. Chin the infamous,
sister of a dozen, cousin of a billion,   80
survived by everybody and forgotten by all.
She was neither black nor white,
neither cherished nor vanquished,
just another squatter in her own bamboo grove
minding her poetry—   85
when one day heaven was unmerciful,
And a chasm opened where she then stood.
Like the jowls of a mighty white whale,
or the daws of a metaphysical Godzilla,
it swallowed her whole.   90
She did not flinch nor writhe,
nor fret about the afterlife,
but stayed! Solid as wood, happily
a little gnawed, tattered, mesmerized
by all that was lavished upon her   95
and all that was taken away!

for Gwendolyn Brooks

Lady Mary Chudleigh   (1656–1710)
TO THE LADIES   1703

Wife and servant are the same,
But only differ in the name:
For when that fatal knot is tied,
Which nothing, nothing can divide:
When she the word *obey* has said,   5
And man by law supreme has made,
Then all that's kind is laid aside,
And nothing left but state° and pride:
Fierce as an Eastern prince he grows,
And all his innate rigor shows: 10
Then but to look, to laugh, or speak,
Will the nuptual contract break.
Like mutes she signs alone must make,
And never any freedom take:
But still be governed by a nod,   15
And fear her husband as her God:
Him still must serve, him still obey,
And nothing act, and nothing say,
But what her haughty lord thinks fit,
Who with the power, has all the wit.   20
Then shun, oh! shun that wretched state,
And all the fawning flatterers hate:
Value your selves, and men despise,
You must be proud, if you'll be wise.

8 *state*: Stateliness; ceremony.

Amy Clampitt   (1920–1994)
BEACH GLASS   1983

While you walk the water's edge,
turning over concepts
I can't envision, the honking buoy
serves notice that at any time
the wind may change,   5
the reef-bell clatters
its treble monotone, deaf as Cassandra°
to any note but warning. The ocean,

cumbered by no business more urgent
than keeping open old accounts   10
that never balanced,
goes on shuffling its millenniums
of quartz, granite, basalt.
                    It behaves
toward the permutations of novelty—   15
driftwood and shipwreck, last night's
beer cans, spilt oil, the coughed-up
residue of plastic—with random
impartiality, playing catch or tag
or touch-last like a terrier,   20
turning the same thing over and over,
over and over. For the ocean, nothing
is beneath consideration.

                    The houses
of so many mussels and periwinkles   25
have been abandoned here, it's hopeless
to know which to salvage. Instead
I keep a lookout for beach glass—
amber of Budweiser, chrysoprase
of Almadén and Gallo, lapis   30
by way of (no getting around it,
I'm afraid) Phillips'
Milk of Magnesia, with now and then a rare
translucent turquoise or blurred amethyst
of no known origin.   35
                    The process
goes on forever: they came from sand,
they go back to gravel,
along with the treasuries
of Murano,° the buttressed   40
astonishments of Chartres,°
which even now are readying
for being turned over and over as gravely
and gradually as an intellect
engaged in the hazardous   45
redefinition of structures
no one has yet looked at.

---

7 Cassandra: Prophetess in Aeschylus' *Agamemnon.*   40 *Murano:* Island near Venice renowned for its glassware.   41 *Chartres:* Reference to the cathedral in Chartres (France), which has flying buttresses.

Samuel Taylor Coleridge   (1772–1834)

KUBLA KHAN°   1816

In Xanadu did Kubla Khan
A stately pleasure-dome decree:
Where Alph,° the sacred river, ran
Through caverns measureless to man
    Down to a sunless sea.   5
So twice five miles of fertile ground
With walls and towers were girdled round:
And there were gardens bright with sinuous rills,
Where blossomed many an incense-bearing tree;
And here were forests ancient as the hills,   10
Enfolding sunny spots of greenery.

But oh! that deep romantic chasm which slanted
Down the green hill athwart a cedarn cover!°
A savage place! as holy and enchanted
As e'er beneath a waning moon was haunted   15
By woman wailing for her demon-lover!
And from this chasm, with ceaseless turmoil seething,
As if this earth in fast thick pants were breathing,
A mighty fountain momently was forced:
Amid whose swift half-intermitted burst   20
Huge fragments vaulted like rebounding hail,
Or chaffy grain beneath the thresher's flail:
And 'mid these dancing rocks at once and ever
It flung up momently the sacred river.
Five miles meandering with a mazy motion   25
Through wood and dale the sacred river ran,
Then reached the caverns measureless to man,
And sank in tumult to a lifeless ocean:
And 'mid this tumult Kubla heard from far
Ancestral voices prophesying war!   30

    The shadow of the dome of pleasure
    Floated midway on the waves;
    Where was heard the mingled measure
    From the fountain and the caves.

Kubla Khan: Coleridge relates that he was reading about the palace and gardens of Kublai Khan (1216–1294), the founder of the Mongol dynasty in China, when he fell asleep under the influence of some opium and dreamed the following dream. When he awoke he began writing quickly but lost his concentration when he was interrupted by a visitor. The poem therefore is unfinished, a "fragment."   3 *Alph*: This is Alpheus, the river in John Milton's *Lycidas* and in Greek myth. 13 *athwart . . . cover*: Across a forest of cedars.

It was a miracle of rare device,   35
A sunny pleasure-dome with caves of ice!

   A damsel with a dulcimer
   In a vision once I saw:
   It was an Abyssinian maid,
   And on her dulcimer she played,   40
   Singing of Mount Abora.
   Could I revive within me
   Her symphony and song,
   To such a deep delight 'twould win me,
That with music loud and long,   45
I would build that dome in air,
That sunny dome! those caves of ice!
And all who heard should see them there,
And all should cry, Beware! Beware!
His flashing eyes, his floating hair!   50
Weave a circle round him thrice,
And close your eyes with holy dread,
For he on honey-dew hath fed,
And drunk the milk of Paradise.

John Cotton   (b. 1925)
REPORT BACK   1971

"O dark dark dark. They all go into the dark,
The vacant interstellar spaces"
       —T.S. Eliot: *East Coker*

Galactic probe seven-thousand and four
Reports an uneventful journey, free
From any serious meteoric collisions.
Geological and radiation
Surveys are now being prepared, though our first   5
Instrumentation suggests little, if
Any, difficulty in setting up
The usual research apparatus.

        And looking into the void
        From the far edge of our empire   10
        We see the next galaxy
        A rapidly receding
        Thumb-smudge of light in a mid-

Night violet sky pierced by the
Dead-lights of a handful of planets,   15
Red-tinged and steady like the
Eyes of disappointed lovers,
And our perspective's gone.

Gravity repulsion is now reduced
To a minimum, while preliminary   20
Spectrascopic analysis suggests
Possible vegetation, though we seem,
At present, on what is clearly a desert.

Pock-marked with small craters
To the edge of a ragged   25
Horizon, and long-shadowed
In what passes for a moon
On the galactic periphery,
Here is an austere beauty,
Barren, uncompromising,   30
Like that which must have been
Experienced by men
On the ice-caps and deserts
As they once existed on earth
Before their urbanization.   35
Harsh and unambiguous
It throws, as it were, a man
Into himself. Is this what
The early poets wrote about?

Our first extra-craft exploration has   40
Returned with specimens, one of which may
Be a new mineral. We are working
On the uranium breakdown now.
We have found, also, what appear to be
Pebbles, which suggest the action of seas,   45
Suggesting life, if not now, at some time.
With the spectrascopic analysis
This could prove most interesting. We will
Begin work radio-gravitation
Project immediate first light. Meanwhile,   50
We are now occupied with lab. work as
It is eighty hours until the next "dawn."
The darkness, as expected, is intense.

O the dark, the deep hard dark
Of these galactic nights!   55
Even the planets have set

> *Leaving it slab and impenetrable,*
> *As dark and directionless*
> *As those long nights of the soul*
> *The ancient mystics spoke of.* 60
> *Beyond there is nothing,*
> *Nothing we have known or experienced.*
> *It is such a dark*
> *To be lost in which a man*
> *Might, perhaps, find himself.* 65

Excessive hyperwarp has set up
A fault in our auxiliary booster,
Could you contact the depot-ship asking
To send a supply-cruiser with a spare?
And, while they are at it, some playing-cards 70
Or a set of Galaxtopoly with
A few of the latest girlie magazines.
Anything to kill the time.

> *If a man could stare out*
> *Such a darkness and endure,* 75
> *In such a darkness a man*
> *Might, perhaps, find himself,*
> *Scoured to the quick*
> *In the timeless sands of the void.*

Anything, as I said, to kill the time. 80

Robert Creeley (b. 1926)

BALLAD OF THE DESPAIRING HUSBAND 1982

My wife and I lived all alone,
contention was our only bone.
I fought with her, she fought with me,
and things went on right merrily.

But now I live here by myself 5
with hardly a damn thing on the shelf,
and pass my days with little cheer
since I have parted from my dear.

Oh come home soon, I write to her.
Go fuck yourself, is her answer. 10
Now what is that, for Christian word?
I hope she feeds on dried goose turd.

But still I love her, yes I do.
I love her and the children too.
I only think it fit that she   15
should quickly come right back to me.

Ah no, she says, and she is tough,
and smacks me down with her rebuff.
Ah no, she says, I will not come
after the bloody things you've done.   20

Oh wife, oh wife—I tell you true,
I never loved no one but you.
I never will, it cannot be
another woman is for me.

That may be right, she will say then,   25
but as for me, there's other men.
And I will tell you I propose
to catch them firmly by the nose.

And I will wear what dresses I choose!
And I will dance, and what's to lose!   30
I'm free of you, you little prick,
and I'm the one can make it stick.

Was this the darling I did love?
Was this that mercy from above
did open violets in the spring—   35
and made my own worn self to sing?

She was. I know. And she is still,
and if I love her? then so I will.
And I will tell her, and tell her right . . .

Oh lovely lady, morning or evening or afternoon.   40
Oh lovely lady, eating with or without a spoon.
Oh most lovely lady, whether dressed or undressed or partly.
Oh most lovely lady, getting up or going to bed or sitting only.

Oh loveliest of ladies, than whom none is more fair, more gracious,
  more beautiful.
Oh loveliest of ladies, whether you are just or unjust, merciful,
  indifferent, or cruel.   45
Oh most loveliest of ladies, doing whatever, seeing whatever, being
  whatever.
Oh most loveliest of ladies, in rain, in shine, in any weather.

Oh lady, grant me time,
please, to finish my rhyme.

Countee Cullen   (1913–1946)
  HERITAGE°   1925

(For Harold Jackman)

What is Africa to me:
Copper sun or scarlet sea,
Jungle star or jungle track,
Strong bronzed men, or regal black
Women from whose loins I sprang   5
When the birds of Eden sang?
One three centuries removed
From the scenes his fathers loved,
Spicy grove, cinnamon tree,
What is Africa to me?   10

So I lie, who all day long
Want no sound except the song
Sung by wild barbaric birds
Goading massive jungle herds,
Juggernauts of flesh that pass   15
Trampling tall defiant grass
Where young forest lovers lie,
Plighting troth beneath the sky.
So I lie, who always hear,
Though I cram against my ear   20
Both my thumbs, and keep them there,
Great drums throbbing through the air.
So I lie, whose fount of pride,
Dear distress, and joy allied,
Is my somber flesh and skin,   25
With the dark blood dammed within
Like great pulsing tides of wine
That, I fear, must burst the fine
Channels of the chafing net
Where they surge and foam and fret.   30

Africa? A book one thumbs
Listlessly, till slumber comes.
Unremembered are her bats
Circling through the night, her cats
Crouching in the river reeds,   35
Stalking gentle flesh that feeds
By the river brink; no more
Does the bugle-throated roar

Heritage: See window on p. 875, Poetic School: The Harlem Renaissance.

Cry that monarch claws have leapt
From the scabbards where they slept.   40
Silver snakes that once a year
Doff the lovely coats you wear,
Seek no covert in your fear
Lest a mortal eye should see;
What's your nakedness to me?   45
Here no leprous flowers rear
Fierce corollas in the air;
Here no bodies sleek and wet,
Dripping mingled rain and sweat,
Tread the savage measures of   50
Jungle boys and girls in love.
What is last year's snow to me,
Last year's anything? The tree
Budding yearly must forget
How its past arose or set—   55
Bough and blossom, flower, fruit,
Even what shy bird with mute
Wonder at her travail there,
Meekly labored in its hair.
One three centuries removed   60
From the scenes his fathers loved,
Spicy grove, cinnamon tree,
What is Africa to me?

So I lie, who find no peace
Night or day, no slight release   65
From the unremittent beat
Made by cruel padded feet
Walking through my body's street.
Up and down they go, and back,
Treading out a jungle track.   70
So I lie, who never quite
Safely sleep from rain at night—
I can never rest at all
When the rain begins to fall;
Like a soul gone mad with pain   75
I must match its weird refrain;
Ever must I twist and squirm,
Writhing like a baited worm,
While its primal measures drip
Through my body, crying, "Strip!   80
Doff this new exuberance.
Come and dance the Lover's Dance!"
In an old remembered way
Rain works on me night and day.

Quaint, outlandish heathen gods   85
Black men fashion out of rods,
Clay, and brittle bits of stone,
In a likeness like their own,
My conversion came high-priced;
I belong to Jesus Christ,   90
Preacher of humility;
Heathen gods are naught to me.

Father, Son, and Holy Ghost,
So I make an idle boast;
Jesus of the twice-turned cheek,   95
Lamb of God, although I speak
With my mouth thus, in my heart
Do I play a double part.
Ever at Thy glowing altar
Must my heart grow sick and falter,   100
Wishing He I served were black,
Thinking then it would not lack
Precedent of pain to guide it,
Let who would or might deride it;
Surely then this flesh would know   105
Yours had borne a kindred woe.
Lord, I fashion dark gods, too,
Daring even to give You
Dark despairing features where,
Crowned with dark rebellious hair,   110
Patience wavers just so much as
Mortal grief compels, while touches
Quick and hot, of anger, rise
To smitten cheek and weary eyes.
Lord, forgive me if my need   115
Sometimes shapes a human creed.

All day long and all night through,
One thing only must I do:
Quench my pride and cool my blood,
Lest I perish in the flood.   120
Lest a hidden ember set
Timber that I thought was wet
Burning like the dryest flax,
Melting like the merest wax,
Lest the grave restore its dead.   125
Not yet has my heart or head
In the least way realized
They and I are civilized.

E.E. Cummings   (1894–1962)
BUFFALO BILL'S DEFUNCT   1923

Buffalo Bill's
defunct
      who used to
      ride a watersmooth-silver
                          stallion   5
and break onetwothreefourfive pigeonsjustlikethat
                                 Jesus
he was a handsome man
                    and what i want to know is
how do you like your blueeyed boy   10
Mister Death

E.E. Cummings   (1894–1962)
MY SWEET OLD ETCETERA   1926

my sweet old etcetera
aunt lucy during the recent

war could and what
is more did tell you just
what everybody was fighting   5

for,
my sister

isabel created hundreds
(and
hundreds)of socks not to   10
mention shirts fleaproof earwarmers

etcetera wristers etcetera, my
mother hoped that

i would die etcetera
bravely of course my father used   15
to become hoarse talking about how it was
a privilege and if only he
could meanwhile my

self etcetera lay quietly
in the deep mud et   20

cetera
(dreaming,

et
  cetera, of
Your smile   25
eyes knees and of your Etcetera)

Philip Dacey   (b. 1939)

JACK, AFTERWARDS°   1977

It's difficult to say what it all meant.
The whole experience, in memory,
Seems like a story someone might invent
Who was both mad and congenitally cheery.
I have to remind myself, it happened to me.   5
The stalk's gone now, and Alma, the old cow;
And I fear only the dream with the shadow.

My mother had a lot to do with it.
In fact, you might say it was her beanstalk—
She scattered the seeds, I didn't, when she hit   10
My full hand and said all I was good for was talk.
She haunted me in those days: I couldn't walk
Anywhere without seeing her face,
Even on the crone in the giant's palace.

Throughout this whole time, my father was dead.   15
I think I must have felt his not-being-there
More than I would have his being-there. Instead
Of his snoring, his absence was everywhere.
So the old man with the beans, poor and threadbare
As he was, became the more important   20
To my boyish needs. Not to mention the giant.

Oddly enough, the beanstalk itself, which some
Might think the most wonderful part of all this,
Pales in time's perspective. Though my true home
Between the earth and sky, and though no less   25
Than magic, that stalk, in the last analysis,
Was but a means to an end. Yet, I must say,
I still recall the beanflowers' sweet bouquet.

Then there's the giant. What can be said? Nothing
And everything. Or this: if the truth be known   30
About someone so great, it was surprising
How vulnerable he seemed, and how alone.
Not that I wasn't frightened. I was, to the bone—

Jack, Afterwards: Reference to Jack in "Jack and the Beanstalk."

But it was his weakness, joined to such power,
I feared most, and fear now, any late hour.   35

The fruits of it all were gold, a hen, and a harp.
I wish I could say I miss my poverty,
When my appetite, if not my wit, was sharp,
But I don't. A little fat hasn't hurt me
Much. Still it's that strange harp's melody,   40
Beauty willing itself, not golden eggs,
Whose loss would leave me, I hope, one who begs.

Of everything, the strangest was to see
Alma the cow come back home at the end,
Her two horns wreathed in wild briony   45
And traveler's joy. Did the old man send
Her as a gift? She seemed, somehow, lightened.
I'd like to think I traded her away
To get her back, sea-changed, in such array.

So I sit here, my dying, blind mother   50
To tend to, and wonder how it was
I escaped, smiling, from such an adventure.
If events in those days conformed to laws,
I'd like to know—not least, nor only, because
What happened then still makes me ask, Why me?   55
Not even my mother knew, when she could see.

Philip Dacey   (b. 1939)
JILL, AFTERWARDS°   1977

He had this idea about the hill,
How at the top there would be water
Sweeter than any in any pail
Lugged previously, and to come down
Would be the easiest part of all.   5
I told him it was a kids' story.

Before I had knockers that story
Was making the rounds in my gang. Hell,
We laughed at it even then. We all
Knew better than to think sweet water   10
Could be had for the price of a pail
And a little leg-work up and down

Jill Afterwards. Reference to Jill in "Jack and Jill went up the hill" nursery rhyme.

A hill that had been standing there, dawn
To dreary dawn, our whole life's story
Long. Not to mention the probabil-   15
ity such a thing as sweet water,
Hill or no hill, didn't exist. I'll
Give him credit for this, though: a wall

Couldn't have been more stubborn. He'd call
Me late at night even, to break down   20
My resistance. Okay, I said, I'll
Go. The truth is, he was cute. Starry-
eyed, but cute. And I wondered whether
He had anything in his pants. Pale

Dawn found us taking turns with the pail   25
As we rose above the town. Not all
The money down there beats the water
We'll find, he said. Now I was poor, down
To a few bucks. It's no mystery
Money talks. Loud. But I climbed the hill.   30

To the top. And there was this big hole.
And deep. I got dizzy to look down
It. He had rope and let the pail fall
Yards and yards. "Got something," he yelled, pull-
ing the catch in. Later, the story   35
He told, back in town, was the water

Spilled out. But the fact of the matter
Is I saw what he had. Nothing. Damn
If he didn't claim different, though. Al-
ways. Damn, too, if his pants weren't full.   40
I've got these kids to prove that story.
When they whine, I tell them: climb a hill.

WINDOW ON

Poetry in Translation: African Poets

The study of poetry, and especially the close reading necessary to sustain a thorough interpretation, depends on language, since the poet, more than any other
writer, makes language work in surprising, exciting, and unique ways. Thus

the familiar phrase "It was lost in translation" pertains especially to the study of poetry. With every translation, something from the original is inevitably lost.

However much this is true, though, readers can still derive much pleasure from an expert translation. Shakespeare, for example, is known throughout the world through translations in every major language, some of which have a special beauty of their own. Likewise, Russian poets such as Bella Akhmadulina and Anna Akhmatova, both celebrated in their country, are widely translated and widely available. If one does not read Russian, then one must rely on translation or else have no experience of these writers at all. The same is true for those whose language is not English: if they wish to experience Shakespeare, they must hope the translation is artful and expressive.

Translations accommodate more than just the literal meaning of the words. Imagine, for example, translating E. E. Cummings's "l(a," into an Eskimo language for a reader who has never seen a tree lose its leaves. That poem may well be untranslatable. Cultural emblems and images that have great emotional power in a given environment can be translated, but they cannot be responded to by the reader from another culture and in another language except approximately.

A number of interesting poems included in this collection come from francophone Africa and are by African poets writing in French. Bernard Dadié's (b. 1916) "In Memoriam," from a longer poem called *Africa Arise*! memorializes an ordinary man—"And he was a man like you / a man like me / a man like them"—in such a way as to make the African experience universal. His language is conversational, direct, and moving. "I Thank You, Lord" is essentially a prayer of thanksgiving, a conversation between the speaker and his god. Dadié was born and educated in the Ivory Coast, has lived in Senegal, and has been a powerful voice in his country's development both as a writer and as a politician.

Birago Diop (b. 1906), Senegalese, has made a career of retelling Senegalese folk tales, many of which are included in his volume *Tales of Amadou Koumba* (1966). They are translated from French into English, but they were originally told to Diop by griots (storytellers) who spoke Wolof, one of the primary languages of Senegal. The title of his poem "Viaticum" is a Latin word meaning a preparation for a journey, sometimes the journey into death. Diop's poem refers to a journey in life, but a journey that relies on the ancestral "Spirits of the Elders" for protection. Thus his poem requires a knowledge of numerous languages and cultures.

Léopold Sédar Senghor (b. 1906) has not only been president of Senegal but has been one of the most vocal and influential of the world's black intellectuals, championing the cultural influence of Africans the world over. Educated in Paris, he became a teacher of Latin, Greek, and French. After World War II he returned to Africa to take a leadership role in Senegal's independence and to produce a large body of poetry. In "Night of Sine," the description of a night by the river Sine, he listens to the inner spirit, "the deep pulse beat of Africa in the mist of lost villages." Like Diop's, this meditative poem reminds us of the presence of the dead, the ancestors who live among the villages and participate with life.

Fily-Dabo Sissoko (1900–1964) was born in Mali, educated in Dakar, and may have been killed while being held as a political prisoner in Mali in a time of government crisis. He writes somewhat like a painter, creating visual images of the world of Africa as he knew it. In "Brush Fire" his images are vital, his language vibrant: "the blazing circle climbs straight ahead, flooding the sky with globules of fire, dancing a saraband to dazzled eyes." This is a poem for which an understanding of the original language would make a great difference, but even in translation we can sense the power of the original.

The elements that survive translation will depend on the gifts of the translator, and although it is preferable to read translations written by poets, the most important thing to keep in mind is that the poem has a life of its own in another language. One must be satisfied to enjoy that new life and new shape on its own terms.

Reading

Fanon, Frantz. *Black Skin, White Masks.* New York: Grove, 1969.

Kennedy, Ellen Conroy. *The Negritude Poets.* New York: Thunder's Mouth Press, 1989.

Kesteloot, Lilyan. *Black Writers in French: A Literary History of Negritude.* Philadelphia: Temple University Press, 1974.

Moore, Gerald, ed. *African Literature and the Universities.* Ibadan: Ibadan University Press, 1965.

Bernard Dadié   (b. 1916)
IN MEMORIAM   1975

From Africa Arise!
Tr. Ellen Conroy Kennedy

"Starved to death,"
He died of hunger,
but it won't be written on his tomb
for they put him in an unmarked grave,
it won't be written there in stone   5
for the government rejects the truth.

He had gone to all the offices,
the factories, the farms:
no jobs . . .

And thread by thread, his clothing turned to rags.   10
This, with a thousand bales of surplus cloth nearby . . .
He slept beneath the stars.

And he was a man like you
a man like me,
a man like them,   15
and he lay beneath the stars,
this man, on the bare ground
before the palaces,
while on the docks mountains of cement were growing hard.
It won't be written there on stone   20
that he died
beside a palace
with hunger in his belly,
cold gnawing at his bones,
his flesh grown colorless and limp, his ribs collapsing, 25
the sockets of his bones rebelling.

It won't be written on his tomb
that he died of hunger, slowly,
slowly, while flour mildewed in the stores,
while behind the counters with the iron grills,   30
behind warehouses filled with goods
they were pulling in the profits . . .
A man is dying.
A man like you,
a man like me,   35
a man like them.
A man is dying of hunger,
starving, in the midst of plenty.

"Starved to Death"
won't be written on his tomb.   40
Dishonor on the government
that degrades mankind and brings him low.
It won't be written on his grave
"Dead, of Hunger."

But you, remember   45
that he starved to death,
slowly
died of hunger,

a man like them
a man like you   50
slowly
died of hunger
bit by bit
in the midst of plenty
staring at deaf heaven.   55

This was a man
like you,
like them,
a man . . .
Remember!   60

Bernard Dadié   (b. 1916)
I THANK YOU, LORD   1975

Tr. Ellen Conroy Kennedy   1975

I thank you, Lord, for having made me Black,
for having made me
the sum of all griefs,
for having put upon my head
the World.   5
I wear the livery of the Centaur°
and I have carried the World since the first morning.

White is the color of the great occasions.
Black the color of everyday.
And I have carried the World since the first evening.   10

I am content
with the shape of my head
made to carry the World.
Satisfied
with the shape of my nose   15
made to inhale the four winds of the World.
Pleased
with the shape of my legs
ready to run to the end of the Earth.

I thank you, Lord, for having made me Black,   20
for having made me
the sum of all pain.
A thousand swords have pierced my heart.
A thousand brands have burned me.
And my blood has reddened the snow of all the calvaries,   25
and my blood, at each dawn, has reddened all horizons.

Yet I am content
to carry the World.

---

6 *Centaur:* In Greek mythology, half-man, half-horse, one who bridges nature and humanity.

Happy with my short arms
   with my long arms   30
      with my thick lips.

I thank you, Lord, for having made me Black.
I have carried the World since the dawn of time
and in the night my laughter at the World
   creates the day.   35

Carl Dennis   (b. 1939)

OEDIPUS THE KING   1990

Hard to forgive Freud,° the exposer of fictions,
When he borrows the name of a great mythical king
To cover our common wish not to share mom
With anyone, not even with dad.

Oedipus, solver of riddles too hard for us,   5
Freud's inspiration and mentor,
Teacher and pupil of one mind with the sphinx
That man is the mystery,
Three people at least in one.
But even Freud, with all his interpreting,   10
Didn't manage to save a city, as Oedipus did.
Vienna could have done without him,
He knew, and would go on as before,
Winning and wasting.

We never imagine Oedipus one of us   15
Except for a moment, just after the plague arrives,
When he vows to rid the city of its pollution,
To root the murderer out, no matter where.
We too could have made a mistake like that.
But when the question changes slowly   20
To who exactly his parents are
We would have stopped, as the prophet advises,
While the King, suspecting the worst, presses on.

Freud may have taken the facts, however painful,
As evidence he was only human,   25
Alive and desiring.
But Oedipus chooses to be guilty,

---

1 *Freud*: Sigmund Freud (1856–1939), founder of psychoanalysis, who believed the story of
Oedipus (see Sophocles, *Oedipus the King*, in this volume) illustrated every man's desire to sleep
with his mother. See also "Freud, Oedipus, and Drama," p. 1434.

To blind himself, to banish himself
And go the gods one better, the father gods
Who didn't love him as a father should.   30

As for his mother, if he has one then,
It's the earth, who feels him tapping
Her breast with his cane
As he hobbles along outside the walls.
"Where are you going, dear Son?" she calls.   35
"For you the door to my dark house stands open.
No other house will take you in."

James Dickey   (b. 1923)

ON THE HILL BELOW THE LIGHTHOUSE   1967

Now I can be sure of my sleep;
I have lost the blue sea in my eyelids.
From a place in the mind too deep
For thought, a light like a wind is beginning.
    Now I can be sure of my sleep.   5

When the moon is held strongly within it,
The eye of the mind opens gladly.
Day changes to dark, and is bright,
And miracles trust to the body,
    When the moon is held strongly within it.   10

A woman comes true when I think her.
Her eyes on the window are closing.
She has dressed the stark wood of a chair.
Her form and my body are facing.
    A woman comes true when I think her.   15

Shade swings, and she lies against me.
The lighthouse has opened its brain.
A browed light travels the sea.
Her clothes on the chair spread their wings.
    Shade swings, and she lies against me.   20

Let us lie in returning light,
As a bright arm sweeps through the moon.
The sun is dead, thinking of night
Swung round like a thing on a chain.
    Let us lie in returning light.   25

Let us lie where your angel is walking
In shadow, from wall onto wall,

Cast forth from your off-cast clothing
To pace the dim room where we fell.
   Let us lie where your angel is walking,   30

Coming back, coming back, going over.
An arm turns the light world around
The dark. Again we are waiting to hover
In a blaze in the mind like a wind
   Coming back, coming back, going over.   35

   Now I can be sure of my sleep;
   The moon is held strongly within it.
   A woman comes true when I think her.
   Shade swings, and she lies against me.
   Let us lie in returning light;   40
   Let us lie where your angel is walking,
   Coming back, coming back, going over.

WINDOW ON

Biography and Poetry: Emily Dickinson

The question of the relationship between a poet's life and his or her poetry has shifted over the years. Once central to any discussion of poetry, the narrator of most poems, unless a fictional character, was treated as the voice of the author. The New Criticism issued in the new view that biography was tangential, distracting, and unessential to an understanding of the poem, which stood, like a vase or sculpture, as a thing in itself apart from its creator or historical situation. However, even New Critics wrote critical biographies of poets and their work. In general, then, the problems involved in discussing biography and poetry center around the temptation to explain away complex poetry by pointing to possible biographical "explanations." Although biography can supply referents that the poet has whittled away in refining the poem, every interpreter of a poem needs to be cautious about relying on speculative biographical connections.

    Emily Dickinson (1830–1886), one of the most mysterious of poets, was educated at Amherst Academy and spent a year at Mount Holyoke, seven miles from home. She left in less than a year as a result of homesickness and spent the rest of her life unmarried in her home in Amherst, Massachusetts, with a small circle of friends. She rarely greeted vistors, and often sat behind her bedroom door while she talked with them. She traveled very little and not at all in mid and later life. She dressed in white as a sign of her celibacy and in her twenties sometimes took part in local agricultural fairs. No one knows why she remained at home in seclusion, although she refers in 1860 to an event, "a terror," about which she could speak to no one. Most biographers have speculated that she had an unhappy romance.

Emily's father was a strict Calvinist, virtually a Puritan in his beliefs. He was treasurer of Amherst College and a man of commanding physical and psychological presence. In some ways, he dominated her life. For a time, she shared his religious beliefs, but she ceased attending church early in life. When her father died in 1874, she did not attend the funeral, which was downstairs in her home. Biographers do not regard her action as a form of denial or rejection because she listened to the funeral upstairs through her bedroom door. At that point in her life, she saw very few people.

Emily devoted most of her adult life to writing poems. We have almost eighteen hundred, some of which were included in letters to friends. Yet she published only eight in her lifetime and was not truly discovered as an important poet until the twentieth century. Therefore, this highly original, distinctive imagination could not have affected the poetry of her own time. She has been regarded, along with her older contemporary, Walt Whitman, as one of the founders of modern American poetry. Her work follows no pattern. Most of her poems are short lyrics, usually punctuated with dashes (she punctuated her recipes this way, too), sometimes fully rhymed, sometimes slant rhymed, and sometimes unrhymed. Her images are striking, rooted in everyday experience, and intensely memorable.

Emily Dickinson may not have lived an adventurous life, but she lived a thoroughly examined life. As she says, "Inebriate of Air—am I— / And Debauchee of Dew—." Little things such as air (if these are little) were of profound importance to her and stirred rich emotions. In "I felt a Funeral, in my Brain," she describes a common occurrence in her time, a funeral. This one may have been real or imagined—the poem is dated close to 1861, when she was thirty-one,—but it was deeply felt. She also speaks with extraordinary authority in "After great pain, a formal feeling comes—," or so we imagine from what little we know of her life. This, too, is a poem from her early thirties, and in her imagination of death—"This is the Hour of Lead—"—she brings considerable imaginative conviction.

In one of her few published poems, "A narrow Fellow in the Grass," Dickinson writes from a point of view that baffles biography, since the narrator is clearly "a Boy, and Barefoot." Thus what we have in Emily Dickinson is a mystery that invites readers to imagine solutions. Why did she write so many poems when she knew they would not be published? Why did she stay by herself and avoid the normal social pleasures of a bustling Amherst, filled with interesting people? What was the "terror" or disappointment in her life? We may never know the answers to these questions. However, those who pursue them have the poetry for clues, and it is very tempting to leave the poem behind in an effort to solve the problems of biography. The same is true for many poets. Emily Dickinson is one of the most fascinating because her work is so powerful, so personal, so modern in sensibility, that we think of her more as one of us than as a reclusive nineteenth-century spinster.

Reading

Dickinson, Emily. *Letters.* 3 vols. Cambridge: Harvard University Press, 1958.
———. *Life & Letters.* Edited by Martha Bianchi. Boston: Houghton Mifflin, 1924.
Hall, Donald. *Remembering Poets and More Poets.* New York: Ticknor and Fields, 1992.
Johnson, Thomas H. *Emily Dickinson: An Interpretive Biography.* Cambridge: Harvard University Press, 1955.
Leyda, Jay, ed. *The Years and Hours of Emily Dickinson.* 2 vols. New Haven: Yale University Press, 1960.

Emily Dickinson   (1830–1886)
SUCCESS IS COUNTED SWEETEST   1878 (c. 1859)

(67)

Success is counted sweetest
By those who ne'er succeed.
To comprehend a nectar
Requires sorest need.

Not one of all the purple Host   5
Who took the Flag today
Can tell the definition
So clear of Victory

As he defeated—dying—
On whose forbidden ear   10
The distant strains of triumph
Burst agonized and clear!

Emily Dickinson   (1830–1886)
I TASTE A LIQUOR NEVER BREWED—   1861 (c. 1860)

(214)

I taste a liquor never brewed—
From Tankards scooped in Pearl—

Not all the Vats upon the Rhine
Yield such an Alcohol!

Inebriate of Air—am I—   5
And Debauchee of Dew—
Reeling—thro endless summer days—
From inns of Molten Blue—

When "Landlords" turn the drunken Bee
Out of the Foxglove's door—   10
When Butterflies—renounce their "drams"—
I shall but drink the more!

Till Seraphs swing their snowy Hats—
And Saints—to windows run—
To see the little Tippler   15
Leaning against the—Sun—

Emily Dickinson   (1830–1886)
I FELT A FUNERAL, IN MY BRAIN,   1896 (c. 1861)

(280)

I felt a Funeral, in my Brain,
And Mourners to and fro
Kept treading—treading—till it seemed
That Sense was breaking through—

And when they all were seated,   5
A Service, like a Drum—
Kept beating—beating—till I thought
My Mind was going numb—

And then I heard them lift a Box
And creak across my Soul   10
With those same Boots of Lead, again,
Then Space—began to toll,

As all the Heavens were a Bell,
And Being, but an Ear,
And I, and Silence, some strange Race   15
Wrecked, solitary, here—

And then a Plank in Reason, broke,
And I dropped down, and down—
And hit a World, at every plunge,
And Finished knowing—then—   20

Emily Dickinson   (1830–1886)
AFTER GREAT PAIN, A FORMAL FEELING COMES—
1929 (c. 1862)

(341)

After great pain, a formal feeling comes—
The Nerves sit ceremonious, like Tombs—
The stiff Heart questions was it He, that bore,
And Yesterday, or Centuries before?

The Feet, mechanical, go round—   5
Of Ground, or Air, or Ought—
A Wooden way
Regardless grown,
A Quartz contentment, like a stone—

This is the Hour of Lead—   10
Remembered, if outlived,
As Freezing persons, recollect the Snow—
First—Chill—then Stupor—then the letting go—

Emily Dickinson   (1830–1886)
I HEARD A FLY BUZZ—WHEN I DIED—   1896 (c. 1862)

(465)

I heard a Fly buzz—when I died—
The Stillness in the Room
Was like the Stillness in the Air—
Between the Heaves of Storm—

The Eyes around—had wrung them dry—   5
And Breaths were gathering firm
For that last Onset—when the King
Be witnessed—in the Room—

I willed my Keepsakes—Signed away
What portion of me be   10
Assignable—and then it was
There interposed a Fly—

With Blue—uncertain stumbling Buzz—
Between the light—and me—
And then the Windows failed—and then   15
I could not see to see—

Emily Dickinson   (1830–1886)
BECAUSE I COULD NOT STOP FOR DEATH—
1890 (c. 1863)

(712)

Because I could not stop for Death—
He kindly stopped for me—
The Carriage held but just Ourselves—
And Immortality.

We slowly drove—He knew no haste   5
And I had put away
My labor and my leisure too,
For His Civility—

We passed the School, where Children strove
At Recess—in the Ring—   10
We passed the Fields of Gazing Grain—
We passed the Setting Sun—

Or rather—He passed Us—
The Dews drew quivering and chill—
For only Gossamer, my Gown—   15
My Tippet—only Tulle—

We paused before a House that seemed
A Swelling of the Ground—
The Roof was scarcely visible—
The Cornice—in the Ground—   20

Since then—'tis Centuries—and yet
Feels shorter than the Day
I first surmised the Horses' Heads
Were toward Eternity—

Emily Dickinson   (1830–1886)
A NARROW FELLOW IN THE GRASS   1866 (c. 1865)

(986)

A narrow Fellow in the Grass
Occasionally rides—
You may have met Him—did you not
His notice sudden is—

The Grass divides as with a Comb—   5
A spotted shaft is seen—

And then it closes at your feet
And opens further on—

He likes a Boggy Acre
A Floor too cool for Corn—   10
Yet when a Boy, and Barefoot—
I more than once at Noon

Have passed, I thought, a Whip lash
Unbraiding in the Sun
When stooping to secure it   15
It wrinkled, and was gone—

Several of Nature's People
I know, and they know me—
I feel for them a transport
Of cordiality—   20

But never met this Fellow
Attended, or alone
Without a tighter breathing
And Zero at the Bone—

Emily Dickinson   (1830–1886)

TELL ALL THE TRUTH BUT TELL IT SLANT—

1945 (c. 1868)

(1129)

Tell all the Truth but tell it slant—
Success in Circuit lies
Too bright for our infirm Delight
The Truth's superb surprise
As Lightning to the Children eased   5
With explanation kind
The Truth must dazzle gradually
Or every man be blind—

Sheila Dietz   (b. 1949)

THE BABY IN THE BASKET   1992

Is this a picture of you as a baby? No,
I was the baby in the basket, but the picture
was of someone else. My mother's brother

died in a car crash and we had to fly back
to the States right away. *What did the baby*   5
see the mother do? Hurry, get a passport,
a picture, a basket. Pick out a suit. *Something*
bothers me about this mother. But isn't it wonderful
about her father's railroad car meeting the plane
in Florida? *What else does the baby in the basket know?*   10
In those days, Argentina and Florida were farther
apart than they are now. *No, I mean about the mother.*
I have a map of the abandoned field. *What else*
did she tell you? The crash landing. The white hotel.
Verandas. A bar, but no money! Just this silly   15
quarter. Call Daddy. No more money. A drink?
A nice man. Milk for the baby, and a martini for Mommy.
What else did she tell you? Well, what is she
supposed to do with this baby? Another martini
for Mommy, I keep crying.   20

Sheila Dietz   (b. 1949)

NOT REMEMBERING MORE   1992

That Christmas Eve, the train derailed between St. Louis
        grandparents and my mother's parents in Springfield,
Illinois. In the dark, Mom and Dad hauled luggage

through swirling snow, had us kids hold hands stepping
        over iced tracks. Sliding doors hissed back so Dad   5
could lift each child into the white haired conductor's

navy blue arms. This train promised we'd be there
        by Christmas, and, sure enough, hours later,
squeezed onto jump seats in Grandfather's black

"Checker," I counted Christmas trees flickering   10
        from houses we passed in the still dark hours
of Christmas morning. So many it would have

been easier to count the few dark homes. Back
        then I counted colored lights as joy. But later,
at Grandma's Christmas party, he pulled me—It was   15

Uncle Ed, not a real uncle, who lifted me onto his
        lap, scared. Then his wet mouth on mine, too long,
but gone before my parents turned around. Smoothing

his hair he said "Let's go to the playhouse." Mother's

big playhouse in the backyard. No. It's too cold. I   20
don't want to. Didn't anyone hear me? Or did someone

say, "Sheila, why don't you go?" Out the door, crunching
    across snow. I used to pretend I was waiting for someone
to come home. I'd push little red curtains aside, look

out the window. No—not here yet. Time to make dinner.   25
    Is anybody coming? Open the cabinet doors wide,
use the best china dishes decorated with blue flowers.

Set the table. The fork goes here, the knife, put it
    down there. Close the curtains. No one's coming. Him
over my shoulder. The wooden floor? Then the party,   30

and scraps of a dream. Bluberry children from Grandma's
    Scandinavian storybooks. Big red and black candy, red
for cinnamon, black licorice, and deep in the woods,

a candy house. Hansel and Gretel. After Christmas, riding
    to the train station in the same Checker, back down   35
the same streets. Back, past one dark house after another.

Birago Diop   (b. 1906)
VIATICUM°

Tr. Ellen Conroy Kennedy   1967 (tr. 1977)

Into one of three pots,
three pots to which on certain evenings
souls serene and satisfied return—
the breathing of ancestors,
ancestors who were men,   5
forefathers who were sages—
Mother dipped three fingers,
three fingers of her left hand:
the thumb, the first and middle fingers.

With her three fingers red with blood   10
with dog's blood,
with bull's blood,
with goat's blood,
three times Mother touched me.
With her thumb she touched my brow,   15

Viaticum: Latin for preparation for a journey. See discussion on p. 729.

with her index my left breast,
and my navel with her third.

I, I held my fingers red with blood
with dog's blood,
with bull's blood,   20
with goat's blood,
I held these three fingers to the winds,
to the North winds, to the winds of the rising sun,
to the South winds, to the winds of the setting sun;
and I raised my three fingers toward the moon,   25
the full moon, the full and naked moon,
reflected in the bottom of the biggest pot.

Then I put these three fingers in the sand,
into the sand that had grown cold,
and Mother said: "Go, go into the World!   30
They will follow in your steps for life."

Since then I go my way
along the pathways,
the pathways and the roads,
across the sea and farther, farther still   35
beyond the sea and farther than beyond.
And when evil ones draw near,
men with black hearts,
when I approach the envious,
men with black hearts   40
before me move the Spirits of the Elders.

Thomas M. Disch   (b. 1940)

THE RAPIST'S VILLANELLE   1981

She spent her money with such perfect style
The clerks would gasp at each new thing she'd choose.
I couldn't help myself—I had to smile

Or burst. Her slender purse was crocodile,
Her blouse was from Bendel's, as were her shoes.   5
She spent her money with such perfect style!

I loved her so! She shopped—and all the while
My soul that bustling image would perfuse.
I couldn't help myself: I had to smile

At her hand-knitted sweater from the Isle   10
Of Skye,° at après-skis° of bold chartreuse.
She spent her money with such perfect style.

Enchanted by her, mile on weary mile
I tracked my darling down the avenues.
I couldn't help myself. I had to smile   15

At how she never once surmised my guile.
My heart was hers—I'd nothing else to lose.
She spent her money with such perfect style
I couldn't help myself. I had to smile.

10–11 *Isle of Skye*: Island in Scotland where warm sweaters are needed.   11 *après-skis*: In the
lodge after skiing.

John Donne   (1572–1631)
THE FLEA   1633

Mark but° this flea, and mark in this,
How little that which thou deniest me is;
Me it sucked first, and now sucks thee,
And in this flea our two bloods mingled be;
Thou know'st that this cannot be said   5
A sin, or shame, or loss of maidenhead,
 Yet this enjoys before it woo,
 And pampered swells with one blood made of two,
 And this, alas, is more than we would do.

Oh stay, three lives in one flea spare,   10
Where we almost, nay more than married, are.
This flea is you and I, and this
Our marriage bed and marriage temple is;
Though parents grudge, and you, we are met,
And cloistered in these living walls of jet,   15
 Though use° make you apt to kill me
 Let not to that, self-murder added be,
 And sacrilege, three sins in killing three.

Cruel and sudden, hast thou since
Purpled thy nail, in blood of innocence?   20
Wherein could this flea guilty be,
Except in that drop which it sucked from thee?
 Yet thou triumph'st, and say'st that thou

1 *Mark but*: Note only.   16 *use*: Habit.

Find'st not thy self nor me the weaker now;
   'Tis true, then learn how false tears be;   25
Just so much honor, when thou yield'st to me,
   Will waste, as this flea's death took life from thee.

John Donne (1572–1631)

A VALEDICTION: FORBIDDING MOURNING 1633

As virtuous men pass mildly away,
   And whisper to their souls to go,
Whilst some of their sad friends do say
   The breath goes now, and some say, No;

So let us melt, and make no noise,   5
   No tear-floods, nor sigh-tempests move,
'Twere profanation of our joys
   To tell the laity our love.

Moving of th' earth° brings harms and fears,
   Men reckon what it did and meant;   10
But trepidation of the spheres,
   Though greater far, is innocent.°

Dull sublunary° lovers' love
   (Whose soul is sense) cannot admit
Absence, because it doth remove   15
   Those things which elemented° it.

But we by a love so much refined
   That our selves know not what it is,
Inter-assuréd of the mind,
   Care less, eyes, lips, and hands to miss.   20

Our two souls therefore, which are one,
   Though I must go, endure not yet
A breach, but an expansion,
   Like gold to airy thinness beat.

If they be two, they are two so   25
   As stiff twin compasses are two;
Thy soul, the fixed foot, makes no show
   To move, but doth, if th' other do.

---

9 *Moving of th' earth:* Earthquakes.   11–12 *trepidation of the spheres . . . innocent:* According to Ptolemaic astronomy, the planets rocked, but this motion was not felt on earth.   13 *sublunary:* Below the moon, that is, on earth.   16 *elemented:* Composed.

And though it in the center sit,
   Yet when the other far doth roam,   30
It leans and hearkens after it,
   And grows erect, as that comes home.

Such wilt thou be to me, who must
   Like th' other foot, obliquely run;
Thy firmness makes my circle just,   35
   And makes me end where I begun.

John Donne   (1572–1631)

HOLY SONNET 14   1633

Batter my heart, three-personed God; for you
As yet but knock, breathe, shine, and seek to mend;
That I may rise, and stand, o'erthrow me, and bend
Your force, to break, blow, burn, and make me new.
I, like an usurped town, to another due,   5
Labor to admit you, but oh, to no end,
Reason, your viceroy in me, me should defend,
But is captived, and proves weak or untrue.
Yet dearly I love you, and would be loved fain,
But am betrothed unto your enemy: 10
Divorce me, untie, or break that knot again,
Take me to you, imprison me, for I,
Except you enthral me, never shall be free,
Nor ever chaste, except you ravish me.

WINDOW ON

Poetic School: Imagists

Poetic schools develop around the particular talent and interests of poets who share similar values. Often such schools are "created" by the press, such as the Beat school of the 1950s, most of whose members denied they were part of the school. However, the imagists were a self-promoting group whose work cohered in important ways and whose members knew what other members were doing. They felt poetry should meet specific demands, and many poets on the edges of the school joined in with their own versions of imagism.

    Imagism was most active from 1904 to the end of World War I, in 1918, but its influence was felt for many years after. Ezra Pound (1885–1972),

H. D. (Hilda Doolittle) (1886–1961), and Amy Lowell (1874–1925) were among its most important proponents, but T. S. Eliot was sympathetic, and much of his early work, up through "The Waste Land," reveals the mark of imagism. The earliest forms of imagism held to a few important doctrines:

- The poem should be brief, intense, and concentrated.
- Its primary vocabulary should be visual and auditory imagery.
- Discursive language should be avoided: the poem must show what it means, not spell it out.
- All clichés and sentimentality should be avoided.
- The poem should use the language of general conversational speech, but with precision.

The imagists produced a poetry of suggestion and impression, and often of surprising vitality. They held that a poet can express thoughts in terms of images with much greater emotional power than by language that argues or preaches. Above all, they expected the reader to respond at a deep emotional level—through the subconscious—rather than intellectually.

One of the most memorable imagist poems is Ezra Pound's "In a Station of the Metro," discussed above. In many ways it epitomizes the ambition of the imagists. H. D.'s "Helen" directs our attention to Helen of Troy, whose image, as Homer and others have told us, brought on a catastrophic war, resulting in the total destruction of Troy and the enslavement of the Trojans. H. D. focuses on her face and complexion, her expressions, and her figure, but reminds us that the Greeks hated her. The only image of her that they would have admired is the image of her ashes in a funeral urn, which offers an interesting contrast to H. D.'s imagery. "Heat" attempts to make us feel heat through distinct visual and tactile images.

Another imagist poem, Amy Lowell's "Venus Transiens," alludes to the painting by Botticelli showing Venus coming to shore in a half scallop shell, the wind slightly rippling her hair. The painting has been used in countless advertisements, has been made into countless posters, and was a cultural icon in Lowell's time as well as ours. Lowell asks Ada Russell, her companion, to whom the poem is addressed, to compare herself with that image of perfection. Like Helen of Troy, Venus is the emblem of desire and desirability, the image of romantic perfection. The language of the poem, although not entirely conversational, is matter-of-fact and unsentimental, but the images clothe deep feelings.

Ezra Pound's inspiration for "The River-Merchant's Wife: A Letter" is the original poem in Chinese by Rihaku (Li T'ai Po). Pound's translation tries to emulate in English the power of the Chinese characters, which are themselves images. The result is strong images of people, landscape, and seasons. The poem does not argue a point, express opinions, or attempt to move the reader to take action. Instead, it is, like a Chinese landscape painting, a collection of pictures that have their own vitality and power. Pound's effort was to make the poem as complete as a visual artifact. Unlike Alexander Pope's "Essay on Man," it does not present a philosophy, and it cannot be argued with. It can simply be contemplated.

The legacy of imagism is still with us in that many poets try to make their images do the emotional work of their poetry. W. B. Yeats was close with Pound in the period before 1917, and Pound tried to convince him to use the techniques of imagism. In poems such as "The Lake Isle of Innisfree," Yeats seems to have paid attention. Robert Frost, too, was influenced by Pound in the early years of the century, and many of his poems absorbed the teachings of the imagists. William Carlos Williams (1883–1963) continued the practice of imagism into the second half of the century.

What the imagists did was to remind poets that discursive poetry that argued philosophical cases might be interesting and quotable, but it did not move readers emotionally. They attempted to make the reader feel deeply. If they could not do that, they felt they had failed.

Reading

Coffman, Stanley, Jr. *Imagism: A Chapter for the History of Modern Poetry.* Norman: University of Oklahoma Press, 1951.

Gage, John T. *In the Arresting Eye: The Rhetoric of Imagism.* Baton Rouge: Louisiana State University Press, 1981.

Jones, Peter. *Imagist Poetry.* Harmondsworth: Penguin, 1973.

Pratt, W. C. *The Imagist Poem.* New York: Dutton, 1963.

H.D. (Hilda Doolittle)   (1886–1961)
HEAT   1916

O wind, rend open the heat,
cut apart the heat,
rend it to tatters.

Fruit cannot drop
through this thick air—   5
fruit cannot fall into heat
that presses up and blunts
the points of pears
and rounds the grapes.

Cut the heat—   10
plough through it,
turning it on either side
of your path.

H.D. (Hilda Doolittle)   (1886–1961)
HELEN°   1925

All Greece hates
the still eyes in the white face,
the lustre as of olives
where she stands,
and the white hands.   5

All Greece reviles
the wan face when she smiles,
hating it deeper still
when it grows wan and white,
remembering past enchantments   10
and past ills.

Greece sees unmoved,
God's daughter, born of love,
the beauty of cool feet
and slenderest knees,   15
could love indeed the maid,
only if she were laid,
white ash amid funereal cypresses.

Helen: See discussion of this poem on p. 748.

Rita Dove   (b. 1952)
USED   c. 1989

The conspiracy's to make us thin. Size three's
all the rage, and skirts ballooning above twinkling knees
are every man-child's preadolescent dream.
Tabula rasa. No slate's *that* clean—

we've earned the navels sunk in grief   5
when the last child emptied us of their brief
interior light. Our muscles say *We have been used.*

Have you ever tried silk sheets? I did,
persuaded by postnatal dread
and a Macy's clerk to bargain for more zip.   10
We couldn't hang on, slipped
to the floor and by morning the quilts
had slid off, too. Enough of guilt—
It's hard work staying cool.

James Doyle   (b. 1937)

THE VILLAGE   1990

The mountain breaks us into tiny stick
figures. It takes away the very air
we breathe. It shrouds our windows
and plays black dice with our children.

We live in a cage of nagging trees.   5
The food we eat only comes in scraps.
Fruit rinds harden beneath our feet.
The beds we sleep in are rusted leaves.

The sun is too hard for planting.
It cuts our fields and skin to tatters.   10
Our goats are like walking bones.
We survive on the edge of gristle.

When we make love, we say only
that the sky wears a faded eye patch
over its light. When we dream,   15
we smother in heat our leaking skins.

Our smallest building is the church.
It is large enough to hold our god.
If he lives here, he can give us
nothing we ever need but endings.   20

T. S. Eliot   (1888–1965)

LINES FOR CUSCUSCARAWAY AND MIRZA MURAD ALI
BEG°   1933

How unpleasant to meet Mr. Eliot!
With his features of clerical cut,
And his brow so grim
And his mouth so prim
And his conversation, so nicely   5
Restricted to What Precisely
And If and Perhaps and But.
How unpleasant to meet Mr. Eliot!
With a bobtail cur
In a coat of fur   10
And a porpentine cat

Lines . . . Beg: The title is meant as a joke, but see Louis Simpson's "reply."

And a wopsical hat:
How unpleasant to meet Mr. Eliot!
    (Whether his mouth be open or shut).

T. S. Eliot (1888–1965)

THE LOVE SONG OF J. ALFRED PRUFROCK   1915

S'io credessi che mia risposta fosse
a persona che mai tornasse al mondo,
questa fiamma staria senza più scosse.
Ma per ciò che giammai di questo fondo
non tornò vivo alcun, s'i' odo il vero,
senza tema d'infamia ti rispondo.°

Let us go then, you° and I,
When the evening is spread out against the sky
Like a patient etherized upon a table;
Let us go, through certain half-deserted streets,
The muttering retreats   5
Of restless nights in one-night cheap hotels
And sawdust restaurants with oyster-shells:
Streets that follow like a tedious argument
Of insidious intent
To lead you to an overwhelming question . . .   10
Oh, do not ask, "What is it?"
Let us go and make our visit.

In the room the women come and go
Talking of Michelangelo.

The yellow fog that rubs its back upon the window-panes,   15
The yellow smoke that rubs its muzzle on the window-panes,
Licked its tongue into the corners of the evening,
Lingered upon the pools that stand in drains,
Let fall upon its back the soot that falls from chimneys,
Slipped by the terrace, made a sudden leap,   20
And seeing that it was a soft October night,
Curled once about the house, and fell asleep.

S'io . . . rispondo: In Dante's *Inferno,* canto 27, Dante asks one of hell's sufferers to identify himself. The sufferer, who speaks through a flame, replies: "If I thought that I was speaking to someone who would return to the world, this flame would shake no more. But since no one has ever returned alive from this place, if what I hear is true, I answer you without fear of infamy." 1 *you:* According to Eliot, the speaker's male companion. See comments regarding this poem in window: The Long Poem on p. 804.

And indeed there will be time
For the yellow smoke that slides along the street
Rubbing its back upon the window-panes;   25
There will be time, there will be time
To prepare a face to meet the faces that you meet;
There will be time to murder and create,
And time for all the works and days° of hands
That lift and drop a question on your plate;   30
Time for you and time for me,
And time yet for a hundred indecisions,
And for a hundred visions and revisions,
Before the taking of a toast and tea.

In the room the women come and go   35
Talking of Michelangelo.

And indeed there will be time
To wonder, "Do I dare?" and, "Do I dare?"
Time to turn back and descend the stair,
With a bald spot in the middle of my hair—   40
(They will say: "How his hair is growing thin!")
My morning coat, my collar mounting firmly to the chin,
My necktie rich and modest, but asserted by a simple pin—
(They will say: "But how his arms and legs are thin!")
Do I dare   45
Disturb the universe?
In a minute there is time
For decisions and revisions which a minute will reverse.

For I have known them all already, known them all—
Have known the evenings, mornings, afternoons,   50
I have measured out my life with coffee spoons;
I know the voices dying with a dying fall
Beneath the music from a farther room.
    So how should I presume?

And I have known the eyes already, known them all—   55
The eyes that fix you in a formulated phrase,
And when I am formulated, sprawling on a pin,
When I am pinned and wriggling on the wall,
Then how should I begin
To spit out all the butt-ends of my days and ways?   60
    And how should I presume?

___

29 *works and days:* An allusion to a poem by Hesiod (8th century B.C.).

And I have known the arms already, known them all—
Arms that are braceleted and white and bare
(But in the lamplight, downed with light brown hair!)
Is it perfume from a dress   65
That makes me so digress?
Arms that lie along a table, or wrap about a shawl.
    And should I then presume?
    And how should I begin?

    · · · · ·

Shall I say, I have gone at dusk through narrow streets   70
And watched the smoke that rises from the pipes
Of lonely men in shirt-sleeves, leaning out of windows? . . .

I should have been a pair of ragged claws
Scuttling across the floors of silent seas.

    · · · · ·

And the afternoon, the evening, sleeps so peacefully!   75
Smoothed by long fingers,
Asleep . . . tired . . . or it malingers,
Stretched on the floor, here beside you and me.
Should I, after tea and cakes and ices,
Have the strength to force the moment to its crisis?   80
But though I have wept and fasted, wept and prayed,
Though I have seen my head (grown slightly bald) brought in upon a
    platter,°
I am no prophet—and here's no great matter;
I have seen the moment of my greatness flicker,
And I have seen the eternal Footman° hold my coat, and snicker,   85
And in short, I was afraid.

And would it have been worth it, after all,
After the cups, the marmalade, the tea,
Among the porcelain, among some talk of you and me,
Would it have been worth while,   90
To have bitten off the matter with a smile,
To have squeezed the universe into a ball°
To roll it towards some overwhelming question,
To say: "I am Lazarus,° come from the dead,
Come back to tell you all, I shall tell you all"—   95
If one, settling a pillow by her head,

---

82 *head . . . platter*: See Matt. 14:3–11; Mark 6:17–29. Herod's wife had John the Baptist beheaded and his head brought to her on a platter. Christ said of John that there was no one greater
"born of women."   85 *eternal Footman*: Death (?).   92 *squeezed the universe into a ball*:
See Andrew Marvell, "To His Coy Mistress," p. 879, lines 41–42.   94 *Lazarus*: See John
11:1–44. Lazarus was raised by Christ from the dead. See also Luke 16:19–31.

Should say: "That is not what I meant at all.
That is not it, at all."

And would it have been worth it, after all,
Would it have been worth while,   100
After the sunsets and the dooryards and the sprinkled streets,
After the novels, after the teacups, after the skirts that trail along the
    floor—
And this, and so much more?—
It is impossible to say just what I mean!
But as if a magic lantern threw the nerves in patterns on a screen: 105
Would it have been worth while
If one, settling a pillow or throwing off a shawl,
And turning toward the window, should say:
    "That is not it at all,
    That is not what I meant, at all."   110

    . . . . .

No! I am not Prince Hamlet, nor was meant to be;
Am an attendant lord,° one that will do
To swell a progress,° start a scene or two,
Advise the prince; no doubt, an easy tool,
Deferential, glad to be of use,   115
Politic, cautious, and meticulous;
Full of high sentence, but a bit obtuse;
At times, indeed, almost ridiculous—°
Almost, at times, the Fool.

I grow old . . . I grow old . . .   120
I shall wear the bottoms of my trousers rolled.°

Shall I part my hair behind?° Do I dare to eat a peach?
I shall wear white flannel trousers, and walk upon the beach.
I have heard the mermaids singing,° each to each.

I do not think that they will sing to me.   125

I have seen them riding seaward on the waves
Combing the white hair of the waves blown back
When the wind blows the water white and black.

We have lingered in the chambers of the sea
By sea-girls wreathed with seaweed red and brown   130
Till human voices wake us, and we drown.

112 *attendant lord*: As in a Shakespeare play, a minor character.   113 *swell a progress*: Help
make up a royal procession.   118 See the character Polonius in *Hamlet*.   121 *trousers rolled*:
The latest fashion.   122 *part my hair behind*: A daring new fashion.   124 *mermaids singing*:
An image used by older poets to express the impossible.

T.S. Eliot   (1888–1965)

THE HOLLOW MEN   1925

Mistah Kurtz—he dead.°
A penny for the Old Guy°

I

We are the hollow men
We are the stuffed men
Leaning together
Headpiece filled with straw. Alas!
Our dried voices, when   5
We whisper together
Are quiet and meaningless
As wind in dry grass
Or rats' feet over broken glass
In our dry cellar   10

Shape without form, shade without color,
Paralyzed force, gesture without motion;

Those who have crossed
With direct eyes, to death's other Kingdom°
Remember us—if at all—not as lost   15
Violent souls, but only
As the hollow men
The stuffed men.

II

Eyes I dare not meet in dreams
In death's dream kingdom   20
These do not appear:
There, the eyes are
Sunlight on a broken column
There, is a tree swinging
And voices are   25
In the wind's singing
More distant and more solemn
Than a fading star.

Mistah Kurtz—he dead: In the novel *Heart of Darkness* by Joseph Conrad (1857–1924), the character Kurtz penetrates deep into the jungle alone and there becomes morally depraved. His dying words are "the horror!" *A penny for the Old Guy*: Guy Fawkes was a conspirator who threatened to blow up Parliament. English children celebrate his execution day by burning straw effigies of him and begging for money for fireworks.   14 *death's other Kingdom*: Where saved souls go, not hollow men. In this kingdom, people can look at each other directly (see lines 19–38). An image from Dante.

Let me be no nearer
In death's dream kingdom   30
Let me also wear
Such deliberate disguises
Rat's coat, crowskin, crossed staves
In a field
Behaving as the wind behaves   35
No nearer—

Not that final meeting
In the twilight kingdom

III

This is the dead land
This is cactus land   40
Here the stone images
Are raised, here they receive
The supplication of a dead man's hand
Under the twinkle of a fading star.

Is it like this   45
In death's other kingdom
Waking alone
At the hour when we are
Trembling with tenderness
Lips that would kiss   50
Form prayers to broken stone.

IV

The eyes are not here
There are no eyes here
In this valley of dying stars
In this hollow valley   55
This broken jaw of our lost kingdoms

In this last of meeting places
We grope together
And avoid speech

Gathered on this beach of the tumid river°   60

Sightless, unless
The eyes reappear
As the perpetual star

---

60 *tumid river.* In Dante, the river that encircles hell.

Multifoliate rose°
Of death's twilight kingdom   65
The hope only
Of empty men.

V

Here we go round the prickly pear°
Prickly pear prickly pear
Here we go round the prickly pear   70
At five o'clock in the morning.

Between the idea
And the reality
Between the motion
And the act   75
Falls the Shadow

                                    For Thine is the Kingdom

Between the conception
And the creation
Between the emotion   80
And the response
Falls the Shadow

                                            Life is very long

Between the desire
And the spasm   85
Between the potency
And the existence
Between the essence
And the descent
Falls the Shadow   90

                                    For Thine is the Kingdom

For Thine is
Life is
For Thine is the

This is the way the world ends   95
This is the way the world ends
This is the way the world ends
Not with a bang but a whimper.

---

64 *Multifoliate rose*: A reference to the image of heaven in Dante's *Paradiso* (28.30), where souls surround God like petals of a rose.   68 *Prickly pear*: Cactus; used instead of Mulberry bush because "This is cactus land" (40).

Gretel Ehrlich   (b. 1946)

THE ORCHARD   c. 1981

We go into it at night.
In Wyoming an orchard is the
only city around—so many blossoms going up
into trees like lights
and windfall apples like lives   5
coming down.

In the pickup, heads on the tailgate,
we lie on last year's hay and wait
for the orchard to bloom.

A great horned owl sweeps between   10
trees as if to cropdust the rising
sap with white for the flowers.

"The first blossom to come," you say,
"I'll give the apple that grows there to you."

Another owl lands   15
on a bare branch and drops
a plug of micebones to the roots.
Under him, the tree does not think of
the sap's struggle.
I listen to your heart. Divided by   20
beats and rests, it says yes, then no, then yes.

Above us the Milky Way seams the sky and is
stirred by a hand too big to see.
We watch the stars.

Tonight so many of them fall.   25

Lynn Emanuel   (b. 1949)

THE SLEEPING   c. 1984

I have imagined all this:
In 1940 my parents were in love
And living in the loft on West 10th
Above Mark Rothko who painted cabbage roses
On their bedroom walls the night they got married.   5

I can guess why he did it.
My mother's hair was the color of yellow apples
And she wore a black velvet hat with her pajamas.

I was not born yet. I was remote as starlight.
It is hard for me to imagine that   10
My parents made love in a roomful of roses
And I wasn't there.

But now I am. My mother is blushing.
This is the wonderful thing about art.
It can bring back the dead. It can wake the sleeping   15
As it might have late that night
When my father and mother made love above Rothko
Who lay in the dark thinking *Roses, Roses, Roses.*

Faiz Ahmed Faiz°   (1914–1984)

BEFORE YOU CAME   1988

Translated by Agha Shahid Ali

Before you came,
things were as they should be:
the sky was the dead-end of sight,
the road was just a road, wine merely wine—

Now everything is like my heart,   5
a color at the edge of blood:
the grey of your absence, the color of poison, of thorns,
the gold when we meet, the season ablaze,
the yellow of autumn, the red of flowers, of flames,
and the black when you cover the earth   10
with the coal of dead fires.

And the sky, the road, the glass of wine?
The sky is a shirt wet with tears,
the road a vein about to break,
and the glass of wine a mirror in which   15
the sky, the road, the world keep changing.

Don't leave now that you're here—
the world will become like itself again:
the sky will be the sky,
the road a road,   20
and the glass of wine not a mirror, just a glass of wine.

Faiz Ahmed Faiz: See notes to "Homage to Faiz Ahmed Faiz," p. 669.

Anne Finch   (1661–1720)
A LETTER TO DAPHNIS,° APRIL 2, 1685   1864; 1903

This to the crown and blessing of my life,
The much loved husband of a happy wife,
To him whose constant passion found the art
To win a stubborn and ungrateful heart;
And to the world by tenderest proof discovers   5
They err, who say that husbands can't be lovers.
With such return of passion, as is due,
Daphnis I love, Daphnis my thoughts pursue,
Daphnis, my hopes, my joys, are bounded all in you:
Even I, for Daphnis, and my promise sake,   10
What I in women censure,° undertake.
But this from love, not vanity, proceeds;
You know who writes; and I who 'tis that reads.
Judge not my passion by my want of skill,
Many love well, though they express it ill;   15
And I your censure could with pleasure bear,
Would you but soon return, and speak it here.

Daphnis: Poetic name for Finch's husband, Heneage Finch.   11 *censure:* Disapprove.

Carolyn Forché   (b. 1950)
THE COLONEL   1978

What you have heard is true. I was in his house. His wife carried
a tray of coffee and sugar. His daughter filed her nails, his son went
out for the night. There were daily papers, pet dogs, a pistol on the
cushion beside him. The moon swung bare on its black cord over
the house. On the television was a cop show. It was in English.   5
Broken bottles were embedded in the walls around the house to
scoop the kneecaps from a man's legs or cut his hands to lace. On
the windows there were gratings like those in liquor stores. We had
dinner, rack of lamb, good wine, a gold bell was on the table for
calling the maid. The maid brought green mangoes, salt, a type of   10
bread. I was asked how I enjoyed the country. There was a brief
commercial in Spanish. His wife took everything away. There was
some talk then of how difficult it had become to govern. The parrot
said hello on the terrace. The colonel told it to shut up, and pushed
himself from the table. My friend said to me with his eyes: say   15
nothing. The colonel returned with a sack used to bring groceries
home. He spilled many human ears on the table. They were like

dried peach halves. There is no other way to say this. He took one
of them in his hands, shook it in our faces, dropped it into a water
glass. It came alive there. I am tired of fooling around he said. As   20
for the rights of anyone, tell your people they can go fuck themselves. He swept the ears to the floor with his arm and held the last
of his wine in the air. Something for your poetry, no? he said. Some
of the ears on the floor caught this scrap of his voice. Some of the
ears on the floor were pressed to the ground.   25

Robert Frost   (1874–1963)

HOME BURIAL   1914

He saw her from the bottom of the stairs
Before she saw him. She was starting down,
Looking back over her shoulder at some fear.
She took a doubtful step and then undid it
To raise herself and look again. He spoke   5
Advancing toward her: "What is it you see
From up there always?—for I want to know."
She turned and sank upon her skirts at that,
And her face changed from terrified to dull.
He said to gain time: "What is it you see?"   10
Mounting until she cowered under him.
"I will find out now—you must tell me, dear."
She, in her place, refused him any help,
With the least stiffening of her neck and silence.
She let him look, sure that he wouldn't see,   15
Blind creature; and awhile he didn't see.
But at last he murmured, "Oh," and again, "Oh."

"What is it—what?" she said.
                              "Just that I see."

"You don't," she challenged. "Tell me what it is."   20

"The wonder is I didn't see at once.
I never noticed it from here before.
I must be wonted to it—that's the reason.
The little graveyard where my people are!
So small the window frames the whole of it.   25
Not so much larger than a bedroom, is it?
There are three stones of slate and one of marble,
Broad-shouldered little slabs there in the sunlight
On the sidehill. We haven't to mind *those*.
But I understand: it is not the stones,   30

But the child's mound——"
     "Don't, don't, don't, don't," she cried.

She withdrew, shrinking from beneath his arm
That rested on the banister, and slid downstairs;
And turned on him with such a daunting look,   35
He said twice over before he knew himself:
"Can't a man speak of his own child he's lost?"

"Not you!—Oh, where's my hat? Oh, I don't need it!
I must get out of here. I must get air.—
I don't know rightly whether any man can."   40

"Amy! Don't go to someone else this time.
Listen to me. I won't come down the stairs."
He sat and fixed his chin between his fists.
"There's something I should like to ask you, dear."

"You don't know how to ask it."   45
     "Help me, then."

Her fingers moved the latch for all reply.

"My words are nearly always an offense.
I don't know how to speak of anything
So as to please you. But I might be taught,   50
I should suppose. I can't say I see how.
A man must partly give up being a man
With womenfolk. We could have some arrangement
By which I'd bind myself to keep hands off
Anything special you're a-mind to name.   55
Though I don't like such things 'twixt those that love.
Two that don't love can't live together without them.
But two that do can't live together with them."
She moved the latch a little. "Don't—don't go.
Don't carry it to someone else this time.   60
Tell me about it if it's something human.
Let me into your grief. I'm not so much
Unlike other folks as your standing there
Apart would make me out. Give me my chance.
I do think, though, you overdo it a little.   65
What was it brought you up to think it the thing
To take your mother-loss of a first child
So inconsolably—in the face of love.
You'd think his memory might be satisfied——"

"There you go sneering now!"   70
     "I'm not, I'm not!
You make me angry. I'll come down to you.

God, what a woman! And it's come to this,
A man can't speak of his own child that's dead."

"You can't because you don't know how to speak.   75
If you had any feelings, you that dug
With your own hand—how could you?—his little grave;
I saw you from that very window there,
Making the gravel leap and leap in air,
Leap up, like that, like that, and land so lightly   80
And roll back down the mound beside the hole.
I thought, Who is that man? I didn't know you.
And I crept down the stairs and up the stairs
To look again, and still your spade kept lifting.
Then you came in. I heard your rumbling voice   85
Out in the kitchen, and I don't know why,
But I went near to see with my own eyes.
You could sit there with the stains on your shoes
Of the fresh earth from your own baby's grave
And talk about your everyday concerns.   90
You had stood the spade up against the wall
Outside there in the entry, for I saw it."

"I shall laugh the worst laugh I ever laughed.
I'm cursed. God, if I don't believe I'm cursed."

"I can repeat the very words you were saying: 95
'Three foggy mornings and one rainy day
Will rot the best birch fence a man can build.'
Think of it, talk like that at such a time!
What had how long it takes a birch to rot
To do with what was in the darkened parlor?   100
You *couldn't* care! The nearest friends can go
With anyone to death, comes so far short
They might as well not try to go at all.
No, from the time when one is sick to death,
One is alone, and he dies more alone.   105
Friends make pretense of following to the grave,
But before one is in it, their minds are turned
And making the best of their way back to life
And living people, and things they understand.
But the world's evil. I won't have grief so   110
If I can change it. Oh, I won't, I won't!"

"There, you have said it all and you feel better.
You won't go now. You're crying. Close the door.
The heart's gone out of it: why keep it up?
Amy! There's someone coming down the road!"   115

"*You*—oh, you think the talk is all. I must go—
Somewhere out of this house. How can I make you——"

"If—you—do!" She was opening the door wider.
"Where do you mean to go? First tell me that.
I'll follow and bring you back by force. I *will!*—"   120

Robert Frost   (1874–1963)

AFTER APPLE-PICKING   1914

My long two-pointed ladder's sticking through a tree
Toward heaven still,
And there's a barrel that I didn't fill
Beside it, and there may be two or three
Apples I didn't pick upon some bough.   5
But I am done with apple-picking now.
Essence of winter sleep is on the night,
The scent of apples: I am drowsing off.
I cannot rub the strangeness from my sight
I got from looking through a pane of glass   10
I skimmed this morning from the drinking trough
And held against the world of hoary grass.
It melted, and I let it fall and break.
But I was well
Upon my way to sleep before it fell,   15
And I could tell
What form my dreaming was about to take.
Magnified apples appear and disappear,
Stem end and blossom end,
And every fleck of russet showing clear.   20
My instep arch not only keeps the ache,
It keeps the pressure of a ladder-round.
I feel the ladder sway as the boughs bend.
And I keep hearing from the cellar bin
The rumbling sound   25
Of load on load of apples coming in.
For I have had too much
Of apple-picking: I am overtired
Of the great harvest I myself desired.
There were ten thousand thousand fruit to touch,   30
Cherish in hand, lift down, and not let fall.
For all
That struck the earth,
No matter if not bruised or spiked with stubble,

Went surely to the cider-apple heap   35
As of no worth.
One can see what will trouble
This sleep of mine, whatever sleep it is.
Were he not gone,
The woodchuck could say whether it's like his   40
Long sleep, as I describe its coming on,
Or just some human sleep.

Robert Frost   (1874–1963)

THE ROAD NOT TAKEN   1916

Two roads diverged in a yellow wood,
And sorry I could not travel both
And be one traveler, long I stood
And looked down one as far as I could
To where it bent in the undergrowth;   5

Then took the other, as just as fair,
And having perhaps the better claim,
Because it was grassy and wanted wear;
Though as for that, the passing there
Had worn them really about the same,   10

And both that morning equally lay
In leaves no step had trodden black.
Oh, I kept the first for another day!
Yet knowing how way leads on to way,
I doubted if I should ever come back.   15

I shall be telling this with a sigh
Somewhere ages and ages hence:
Two roads diverged in a wood, and I—
I took the one less traveled by,
And that has made all the difference.   20

Robert Frost   (1874–1963)

THE OVEN BIRD   1916

There is a singer everyone has heard,
Loud, a mid-summer and a mid-wood bird,
Who makes the solid tree trunks sound again.
He says that leaves are old and that for flowers
Mid-summer is to spring as one to ten.   5

He says the early petal-fall is past,
When pear and cherry bloom went down in showers
On sunny days a moment overcast;
And comes that other fall we name the fall.
He says the highway dust is over all. 10
The bird would cease and be as other birds
But that he knows in singing not to sing.
The question that he frames in all but words
Is what to make of a diminished thing.

Robert Frost   (1874–1963)
"OUT, OUT—"   1916

The buzz saw snarled and rattled in the yard
And made dust and dropped stove-length sticks of wood,
Sweet-scented stuff when the breeze drew across it.
And from there those that lifted eyes could count
Five mountain ranges one behind the other 5
Under the sunset far into Vermont.
And the saw snarled and rattled, snarled and rattled,
As it ran light, or had to bear a load.
And nothing happened: day was all but done.
Call it a day, I wish they might have said 10
To please the boy by giving him the half hour
That a boy counts so much when saved from work.
His sister stood beside them in her apron
To tell them "Supper." At the word, the saw,
As if to prove saws knew what supper meant, 15
Leaped out at the boy's hand, or seemed to leap—
He must have given the hand. However it was,
Neither refused the meeting. But the hand!
The boy's first outcry was a rueful laugh,
As he swung toward them holding up the hand, 20
Half in appeal, but half as if to keep
The life from spilling. Then the boy saw all—
Since he was old enough to know, big boy
Doing a man's work, though a child at heart—
He saw all spoiled. "Don't let him cut my hand off— 25
The doctor, when he comes. Don't let him, sister!"
So. But the hand was gone already.
The doctor put him in the dark of ether.
He lay and puffed his lips out with his breath.
And then—the watcher at his pulse took fright. 30
No one believed. They listened at his heart.

Little—less—nothing!—and that ended it.
No more to build on there. And they, since they
Were not the one dead, turned to their affairs.

Robert Frost   (1874–1963)

STOPPING BY WOODS ON A SNOWY EVENING   1923

Whose woods these are I think I know.
His house is in the village, though;
He will not see me stopping here
To watch his woods fill up with snow.

My little horse must think it queer   5
To stop without a farmhouse near
Between the woods and frozen lake
The darkest evening of the year.

He gives his harness bells a shake
To ask if there is some mistake.   10
The only other sound's the sweep
Of easy wind and downy flake.

The woods are lovely, dark, and deep,
But I have promises to keep,
And miles to go before I sleep,   15
And miles to go before I sleep.

Robert Frost   (1874–1963)

ACQUAINTED WITH THE NIGHT   1928

I have been one acquainted with the night.
I have walked out in rain—and back in rain.
I have outwalked the furthest city light.

I have looked down the saddest city lane.
I have passed by the watchman on his beat   5
And dropped my eyes, unwilling to explain.

I have stood still and stopped the sound of feet
When far away an interrupted cry
Came over houses from another street,

But not to call me back or say good-by;   10
And further still at an unearthly height
One luminary clock against the sky

Proclaimed the time was neither wrong nor right.
I have been one acquainted with the night.

Robert Frost   (1874–1963)

WEST-RUNNING BROOK   1928

"Fred, where is north?" "North?

North is there, my love.
The brook runs west."

"West-Running Brook then call it."
(West-Running Brook men call it to this day.)   5
"What does it think it's doing running west
When all the other country brooks flow east
To reach the ocean? It must be the brook
Can trust itself to go by contraries
The way I can with you—and you with me—   10
Because we're—we're—I don't know what we are.
What are we?"

"Young or new?"

"We must be something
We've said we two. Let's change that to we three.   15
As you and I are married to each other,
We'll both be married to the brook. We'll build
Our bridge across it, and the bridge shall be
Our arm thrown over it asleep beside it.
Look, look, it's waving to us with a wave   20
To let us know it hears me."

"Why, my dear,
That wave's been standing off this jut of shore—"
(The black stream, catching on a sunken rock,
Flung backward on itself in one white wave,   25
And the white water rode the black forever,
Not gaining but not losing, like a bird
White feathers from the struggle of whose breast
Flecked the dark stream and flecked the darker pool
Below the point, and were at last driven wrinkled   30
In a white scarf against the far-shore alders.)
"That wave's been standing off this jut of shore
Ever since rivers, I was going to say,
Were made in heaven. It wasn't waved to us."

"It wasn't, yet it was. If not to you,   35
It was to me—in an annunciation."

"Oh, if you take it off to lady-land,
As't were the country of the Amazons
We men must see you to the confines of
And leave you there, ourselves forbid to enter—   40
It is your brook! I have no more to say."

"Yes, you have, too. Go on. You thought of something."

"Speaking of contraries, see how the brook
In that white wave runs counter to itself.
It is from that in water we were from   45
Long, long before we were from any creature.
Here we, in our impatience of the steps,
Get back to the beginning of beginnings,
The stream of everything that runs away.
Some say existence like a Pirouot   50
And Pirouette, forever in one place,
Stands still and dances, but it runs away;
It seriously, sadly, runs away
To fill the abyss's void with emptiness.
It flows beside us in this water brook,   55
But it flows over us. It flows between us
To separate us for a panic moment.
It flows between us, over us, and *with* us.
And it is time, strength, tone, light, life, and love—
And even substance lapsing unsubstantial;   60
The universal cataract of death
That spends to nothingness—and unresisted,
Save by some strange resistance in itself,
Not just a swerving, but a throwing back,
As if regret were in it and were sacred.   65
It has this throwing backward on itself
So that the fall of most of it is always
Raising a little, sending up a little.
Our life runs down in sending up the clock.
The brook runs down in sending up our life.   70
The sun runs down in sending up the brook.
And there is something sending up the sun.
It is this backward motion toward the source,
Against the stream, that most we see ourselves in,
The tribute of the current to the source.   75
It is from this in nature we are from.
It is most us."

                    "Today will be the day

You said so."

"No, today will be the day
You said the brook was called West-Running Brook."

"Today will be the day of what we both said."

Robert Frost   (1874–1963)
NEITHER OUT FAR NOR IN DEEP   1936

The people along the sand
All turn and look one way.
They turn their back on the land.
They look at the sea all day.

As long as it takes to pass   5
A ship keeps raising its hull;
The wetter ground like glass
Reflects a standing gull.

The land may vary more;
But wherever the truth may be—   10
The water comes ashore,
And the people look at the sea.

They cannot look out far.
They cannot look in deep.
But when was that ever a bar   15
To any watch they keep?

Robert Frost   (1874–1963)
PROVIDE, PROVIDE   1936

The witch that came (the withered hag)
To wash the steps with pail and rag
Was once the beauty Abishag,

The picture pride of Hollywood.
Too many fall from great and good   5
For you to doubt the likelihood.

Die early and avoid the fate.
Or if predestined to die late,
Make up your mind to die in state.

Make the whole stock exchange your own!   10
If need be occupy a throne,
Where nobody can call *you* crone.

Some have relied on what they knew,
Others on being simply true.
What worked for them might work for you.   15

No memory of having starred
Atones for later disregard
Or keeps the end from being hard.

Better to go down dignified
With boughten friendship at your side   20
Than none at all. Provide, provide!

Robert Frost   (1874–1963)
AUSPEX   1960

Once in a California Sierra
I was swooped down upon when I was small,
And measured, but not taken after all,
By a great eagle bird in all its terror.

Such auspices are very hard to read.   5
My parents when I ran to them averred
I was rejected by the royal bird
As one who would not make a Ganymede.°

Not find a barkeep unto Jove in me?
I have remained resentful to this day   10
When any but myself presumed to say
That there was anything I couldn't be.

8 *Ganymede:* Cupbearer to Jove, chief of Roman gods.

Margaret Gibson   (b. 1944)
OUT IN THE OPEN   1989

In memory of R. H. B. M.

I.

The first signs of your illness I misread.
A change in character, I thought, annoyed
at the stubborn frequency of your needs.
Like a dog, you snapped at strangers.
Like a child, you had me up at night.   5
You'd want to go outside at any hour,

and you'd go, you'd stare at the moon
or the hard shell of snow left in the yard.
Sudden things far away seemed near.
You'd fix on them, stare off. Too fond,   10
you'd follow me about, insist some part
of your body towards mine, just touch.
Then the sheer fact of distance wore
you out. The tree in the open field
we'd walk to—too far. No memory   15
moved you from the quiet you slid into.
But when your skin seemed to loosen
and slur, when it slipped like an ill-
fitting cap down towards your eyes,
I called the doctors. They tested,   20
I bargained, made promises, pressed
down on hope as if hope were a seal
of eventual success. I held you, talked
nonsense, and sense, tried to tempt
you with food. I force-fed you, a tube   25
in the side of your slack jaw. Then
the shots, the intervals, the hours.
I'd go off to calm myself, come back
to find you'd managed to pull yourself
slowly over to the wall, find the corner,   30
a blind meeting, and stand there without
any sign of what it was you wanted,
as if you were pulled to an invisible
threshold, as of course you were.

II.

Before any of this, months before, an echo   35
of the unforeseen spun out of the blind spot
in my eye and made itself visible. I made
note of it, logged it in a journal of dreams,
more taken frankly by other things—a new
word, *piezoelectric,*° and the fact that the bow   40
of a violin drawn deftly across the edge of
a metal plate shows the pattern of that note
in white powder on the surface of the metal.
That I magnified, forgetting the sand
that blew across the path of my dream, the dust   45

---

40 *piezoelectric:* Electricity created by pressure—usually on crystals. Here, connected to the pressure of the violin on metal shifting patterns of powder, it is an emblem of mysterious cause and effect like a form of life.

that insisted itself into all the open crevices
of my clothes and into my watch; forgetting
how I called you to me, hoarse, wanting
you to stay, at the same time distracted
by a replica of bird, long-legged and blue,   50
by shells and other artful surfaces that took
my fancy, ignoring the point of steep descent,
the black hole we stood at the edge of—
a dense space where night felt like justice,
and more—the sense that the bird of the dream   55
had that emptiness for its nest.

III.

Today, putting to rights your things,
fully aware of the elsewhere that sinks
through the edges of everything I touch,
I recall that dream, in the mood for echoes.   60
The doorbell rings, and I open to a kid
up the street who loved you, too. Unsteady
on his roller skates, he's brought down
an envelope sealed tight. He touches
the threshold for balance, letting air out   65
shy between the spaces of his teeth.
The note says everything simply and right,
if transformed by the code of his spelling.
You he's drawn underneath the tree in the open
field, beneath a squat yellow sun and a deft   70
V of birds drawn into a distant vanishing
point beyond paper. He watches me read
and laugh through tears and praise his art—
but neither of us, I think, can think to see
the dark blue silhouette of bird he's put   75
in the branches of the tree, long-legged,
for what it is. We hug, he skates off
on the shifting winter sand of the road,
and for one brief moment, watching him go,
I see everything out in the open—not knowing   80
which to bless more—your life, life itself,
or the patterns, blind in time, we learn to see.

Margaret Gibson   (b. 1944)

UNBORN CHILD ELEGY   1982

Tell me a story
                        whispers my always unborn child
and I pause, listening. Whenever a word

shapes itself outward in speech
there's a hush.   5
                    In the beginning, I tell her, nothing—
if you can imagine nothing. Just so, and patiently, the ancient
stories begin.
                    Once, lying down in the backseat of my parents'
car—their heads dark on the windshield, telephone poles   10
outside and the heads of trees blown back against the stars—
I tried to imagine nothing. Warm air rushed on my eyes
erasing the car, the trees, the stars. I inched across
a bridge of thread called emptiness, cold.

Then I knew you were there inside,   15
asleep in one of the body's seedbeds.
I could hold my breath and find
you, small as a syllable,
a grain like pearled barley in the hourglass of my brain,
a stitch in my side.   20

We made a pact. I'd bring the world inside,
the moon your heart,
a dark plum your eyesight.
You'd bring me so close to the unspoken I'd shake,
some of the mystery spilling like salt.   25

Today snow sparks the air like mica—the sun's
just so, cocked right angles to the wind.
I bring you the snow and it isn't enough.
You whisper you want to be born.

I study your whisper, I study my fear.   30
You're bound, my mother said, to pain.
Each child pries you open.

No one will believe
how alive and present to me you are if I refuse
you a body. But I believe in nothing, a transparent   35
breath from which all form and color rise
in a passion of wings and leaves.

In the ancient stories, the world begins by surprise
when zero speaks, from mere words
weaving sun and moon, the fire   40
the flash of snow.

Be the zero who speaks for me.
Be birth and death, the emptiness
only a child, and never a child, can fill.

Allen Ginsberg   (b. 1926)
HOWL   1956

San Francisco 1955–1956
For Carl Solomon°

I

I saw the best minds of my generation destroyed by madness, starving
    hysterical naked,
dragging themselves through the negro streets at dawn looking for an
    angry fix,
angelheaded hipsters burning for the ancient heavenly connection to
    the starry dynamo in the machinery of night,
who poverty and tatters and hollow-eyed and high sat up smoking in
    the supernatural darkness of cold-water flats floating across the
    tops of cities contemplating jazz,
who bared their brains to Heaven under the El° and saw
    Mohammedan angels staggering on tenement roofs illuminated,   5
who passed through universities with radiant cool eyes hallucinating
    Arkansas° and Blake-light tragedy among the scholars of war,
who were expelled from the academies for crazy & publishing obscene
    odes on the windows of the skull,
who cowered in unshaven rooms in underwear, burning their money
    in wastebaskets and listening to the Terror through the wall,
who got busted in their pubic beards returning through Laredo with a
    belt of marijuana for New York,
who ate fire in paint hotels or drank turpentine in Paradise Alley,°
    death, or purgatoried their torsos night after night   10
with dreams, with drugs, with waking nightmares, alcohol and cock
    and endless balls,
incomparable blind streets of shuddering cloud and lightning in the
    mind leaping toward poles of Canada & Paterson,° illuminating
    all the motionless world of Time between,
Peyote solidities of halls, backyard green tree cemetery dawns, wine
    drunkenness over the rooftops, storefront boroughs of teahead
    joyride neon blinking traffic light, sun and moon and tree
    vibrations in the roaring winter dusks of Brooklyn, ashcan
    rantings and kind king light of mind,
who chained themselves to subways for the endless ride from Battery
    to holy Bronx on benzedrine until the noise of wheels and

Carl Solomon: (b. 1928) Ginsberg met Solomon while they were patients in Columbia Psychiatric
Institute in 1949.   5 *El:* The elevated railway.   6 *Arkansas:* Reference to various drug-in-
duced hallucinations, including the voice of poet William Blake.   10 *Paradise Alley:* In the
Lower East Side of New York, setting for one of beat writer Jack Kerouac's novels.   12 *Canada
& Paterson:* Ginsberg's birthplace in New Jersey.

children brought them down shuddering mouth-wracked and
    battered bleak of brain all drained of brilliance in the drear light
    of Zoo,°
who sank all night in submarine light of Bickford's° floated out and sat
    through the stale beer afternoon in desolate Fugazzi's,°
    listening to the crack of doom on the hydrogen jukebox,   15
who talked continuously seventy hours from park to pad to bar to
    Bellevue° to museum to the Brooklyn Bridge,
a lost battalion of platonic conversationalists jumping down the stoops
    off fire escapes off windowsills off Empire State out of the
    moon,
yacketayakking screaming vomiting whispering facts and memories and
    anecdotes and eyeball kicks and shocks of hospitals and jails and
    wars,
whole intellects disgorged in total recall for seven days and nights with
    brilliant eyes, meat for the Synagogue cast on the pavement,
who vanished into nowhere Zen° New Jersey leaving a trail of
    ambiguous picture postcards of Atlantic City Hall,   20
suffering Eastern sweats and Tangerian bone-grindings and migraines
    of China under junk-withdrawal in Newark's bleak furnished
    room,
who wandered around and around at midnight in the railroad yard
    wondering where to go, and went, leaving no broken hearts,
who lit cigarettes in boxcars boxcars boxcars racketing through snow
    toward lonesome farms in grandfather night,
who studied Plotinus Poe St. John of the Cross telepathy and bop
    kabbalah° because the cosmos instinctively vibrated at their feet
    in Kansas,
who loned it through the streets of Idaho seeking visionary indian
    angels who were visionary indian angels,   25
who thought they were only mad when Baltimore gleamed in
    supernatural ecstasy,
who jumped in limousines with the Chinaman of Oklahoma on the
    impulse of winter midnight streetlight smalltown rain,
who lounged hungry and lonesome through Houston seeking jazz or
    sex or soup, and followed the brilliant Spaniard to converse
    about America and Eternity, a hopeless task, and so took ship
    to Africa,
who disappeared into the volcanoes of Mexico leaving behind nothing
    but the shadow of dungarees and the lava and ash of poetry
    scattered in fireplace Chicago,

---

14 *Zoo*: The Bronx Zoo in New York City.   15 *Bickford's*: A cafeteria where Ginsberg once
worked. *Fugazzi's*: A Greenwich Village bar.   16 *Bellevue*: A hospital often associated with
care for the insane.   20 *Zen*: Zen Buddhism, important to Beat generation in 1950s.
24 *Plotinus . . . Kabbalah*: All these people and texts are associated with mysticism and visionary religious experience.

who reappeared on the West Coast investigating the FBI in beards and
    shorts with big pacifist eyes sexy in their dark skin passing out
    incomprehensible leaflets,   30

who burned cigarette holes in their arms protesting the narcotic
    tobacco haze of Capitalism,

who distributed Supercommunist pamphlets in Union Square weeping
    and undressing while the sirens of Los Alamos wailed them
    down, and wailed down Wall, and the Staten Island ferry also
    wailed,

who broke down crying in white gymnasiums naked and trembling
    before the machinery of other skeletons,

who bit detectives in the neck and shrieked with delight in policecars
    for committing no crime but their own wild cooking pederasty
    and intoxication,

who howled on their knees in the subway and were dragged off the
    roof waving genitals and manuscripts,   35

who let themselves be fucked in the ass by saintly motorcyclists, and
    screamed with joy,

who blew and were blown by those human seraphim, the sailors,
    caresses of Atlantic and Caribbean love,

who balled in the morning in the evenings in rosegardens and the
    grass of public parks and cemeteries scattering their semen
    freely to whomever come who may,

who hiccuped endlessly trying to giggle but wound up with a sob
    behind a partition in a Turkish Bath when the blond & naked
    angel° came to pierce them with a sword,

who lost their loveboys to the three old shrews of fate the one eyed
    shrew of the heterosexual dollar the one eyed shrew that winks
    out of the womb and the one eyed shrew that does nothing but
    sit on her ass and snip the intellectual golden threads of the
    craftsman's loom,   40

who copulated ecstatic and insatiate with a bottle of beer a sweetheart
    a package of cigarettes a candle and fell off the bed, and
    continued along the floor and down the hall and ended fainting
    on the wall with a vision of ultimate cunt and come eluding the
    last gyzym° of consciousness,

who sweetened the snatches of a million girls trembling in the sunset,
    and were red eyed in the morning but prepared to sweeten the
    snatch of the sunrise, flashing buttocks under barns and naked
    in the lake,

who went out whoring through Colorado in myriad stolen night-cars,
    N.C.,° secret hero of these poems, cocksman and Adonis of

---

39 *angel*: Possible reference to the ecstasy of St. Theresa, who was pierced by an angel.
41 *gyzym*: Slang for sperm.   43 *N.C.*: Neal Cassady (1926–1968), who traveled with Jack
Kerouac (as Dean Moriarty) and was memorialized in *On The Road* (1957).

Denver—joy to the memory of his innumerable lays of girls in
empty lots & diner backyards, moviehouses' rickety rows, on
mountaintops in caves or with gaunt waitresses in familiar
roadside lonely petticoat upliftings & especially secret gas-
station solipsisms of johns, & hometown alleys too,

who faded out in vast sordid movies, were shifted in dreams, woke on
a sudden Manhattan, and picked themselves up out of
basements hungover with heartless Tokay and horrors of Third
Avenue iron dreams & stumbled to unemployment offices,

who walked all night with their shoes full of blood on the snowbank
docks waiting for a door in the East River to open to a room
full of steamheat and opium,   45

who created great suicidal dramas on the apartment cliff-banks of the
Hudson under the wartime blue floodlight of the moon & their
heads shall be crowned with laurel in oblivion,

who ate the lamb stew of the imagination or digested the crab at the
muddy bottom of the rivers of Bowery,°

who wept at the romance of the streets with their pushcarts full of
onions and bad music,

who sat in boxes breathing in the darkness under the bridge, and rose
up to build harpsichords in their lofts,

who coughed on the sixth floor of Harlem crowned with flame under
the tubercular sky surrounded by orange crates of theology,   50

who scribbled all night rocking and rolling over lofty incantations
which in the yellow morning were stanzas of gibberish,

who cooked rotten animals lung heart feet tail borsht & tortillas
dreaming of the pure vegetable kingdom,

who plunged themselves under meat trucks looking for an egg,

who threw their watches off the roof to cast their ballot for Eternity
outside of Time, & alarm clocks fell on their heads every day
for the next decade,

who cut their wrists three times successively unsuccessfully, gave up
and were forced to open antique stores where they thought
they were growing old and cried,   55

who were burned alive in their innocent flannel suits on Madison
Avenue amid blasts of leaden verse & the tanked-up clatter of
the iron regiments of fashion & the nitroglycerine shrieks of the
fairies of advertising & the mustard gas of sinister intelligent
editors, or were run down by the drunken taxicabs of Absolute
Reality,

who jumped off the Brooklyn Bridge this actually happened and
walked away unknown and forgotten into the ghostly daze of
Chinatown soup alleyways & firetrucks, not even one free beer,

---

47 *Bowery:* Famous in New York for its alcoholics and down-and-outers.

who sang out of their windows in despair, fell out of the subway
    window, jumped in the filthy Passaic,° leaped on negroes, cried
    all over the street, danced on broken wineglasses barefoot
    smashed phonograph records of nostalgic European 1930s
    German jazz finished the whiskey and threw up groaning into
    the bloody toilet, moans in their ears and the blast of colossal
    steamwhistles,
who barreled down the highways of the past journeying to each
    other's hotrod-Golgotha jail-solitude watch or Birmingham
    jazz incarnation,
who drove crosscountry seventytwo hours to find out if I had a vision
    or you had a vision or he had a vision to find out Eternity,   60
who journeyed to Denver, who died in Denver, who came back to
    Denver & waited in vain, who watched over Denver & brooded
    & loned in Denver and finally went away to find out the Time,
    & now Denver is lonesome for her heroes,
who fell on their knees in hopeless cathedrals praying for each other's
    salvation and light and breasts, until the soul illuminated its hair
    for a second,
who crashed through their minds in jail waiting for impossible
    criminals with golden heads and the charm of reality in their
    hearts who sang sweet blues to Alcatraz,
who retired to Mexico to cultivate a habit, or Rocky Mount to tender
    Buddha or Tangiers to boys or Southern Pacific to the black
    locomotive or Harvard to Narcissus to Woodlawn° to the
    daisychain or grave,
who demanded sanity trials accusing the radio of hypnotism & were
    left with their insanity & their hands & a hung jury,   65
who threw potato salad at CCNY lecturers on Dadaism° and
    subsequently presented themselves on the granite steps of the
    madhouse with shaven heads and harlequin speech of suicide,
    demanding instantaneous lobotomy,
and who were given instead the concrete void of insulin Metrazol°
    electricity hydrotherapy psychotherapy occupational therapy
    pingpong & amnesia,
who in humorless protest overturned only one symbolic pingpong
    table, resting briefly in catatonia,
returning years later truly bald except for a wig of blood, and tears
    and fingers, to the visible madman doom of the wards of the
    madtowns of the East,
Pilgrim State's Rockland's and Greystone's° foetid halls, bickering
    with the echoes of the soul, rocking and rolling in the midnight

---

58 *Passaic*: A river in New Jersey.   64 *Narcissus to Woodlawn*: Ginsberg refers to quests by beats
John Burroughs (b. 1914), Kerouac, and himself for drugs, sex, and even death: Woodlawn is a
cemetery.   66 *Dadaism*: Absurdist avant garde art movement following World War I.
67 *Metrazol*: Shock therapy induced chemically.   70 *Pilgrim . . . Greystone's*: Mental hospitals.

solitude-bench dolmen-realms of love, dream of life a
    nightmare, bodies turned to stone as heavy as the moon,   70
with mother finally ******°, and the last fantastic book flung out of
    the tenement window, and the last door closed at 4 A.M. and the
    last telephone slammed at the wall in reply and the last furnished
    room emptied down to the last piece of mental furniture, a
    yellow paper rose twisted on a wire hanger in the closet, and even
    that imaginary nothing but a hopeful little bit of hallucination—
ah, Carl, while you are not safe I am not safe, and now you're really in
    the total animal soup of time—
and who therefore ran through the icy streets obsessed with a sudden
    flash of the alchemy of the use of the ellipse the catalog the
    meter & the vibrating plane,
who dreamt and made incarnate gaps in Time & Space through
    images juxtaposed, and trapped the archangel of the soul
    between 2 visual images and joined the elemental verbs and set
    the noun and dash of consciousness together jumping with
    sensation of Pater Omnipotens Aeterna Deus°
to recreate the syntax and measure of poor human prose and stand
    before you speechless and intelligent and shaking with shame,
    rejected yet confessing out the soul to conform to the rhythm
    of thought in his naked and endless head,   75
the madman bum and angel beat in Time, unknown, yet putting down
    here what might be left to say in time come after death,
and rose reincarnate in the ghostly clothes of jazz in the goldhorn
    shadow of the band and blew the suffering of America's naked
    mind for love into an eli eli lamma lamma sabacthani°
    saxophone cry that shivered the cities down to the last radio
with the absolute heart of the poem of life butchered out of their own
    bodies good to eat a thousand years.

II

What sphinx of cement and aluminum bashed open their skulls and ate
    up their brains and imagination?
Moloch!° Solitude! Filth! Ugliness! Ashcans and unobtainable dollars!
    Children screaming under the stairways! Boys sobbing in
    armies! Old men weeping in the parks!   80
Moloch! Moloch! Nightmare of Moloch! Moloch the loveless! Mental
    Moloch! Moloch the heavy judger of men!
Moloch the incomprehensible prison! Moloch the crossbone soulless
    jailhouse and Congress of sorrows! Moloch whose buildings are

---

71 ******: Ginsberg's mother Naomi was hospitalized for paranoia and died in 1956.
74 *Pater Omnipoteus Aeterna Deus:* "Father omnipotent, eternal God." From a letter by the
painter Paul Cézanne (1839–1906).   77 *eli eli lamma . . . sabacthani:* "My God, my God,
why have you forsaken me?"—Christ's words on the cross.   80 *Moloch:* An ancient god worshiped with human sacrifices.

judgment! Moloch the vast stone of war! Moloch the stunned
governments!

Moloch whose mind is pure machinery! Moloch whose blood is
running money! Moloch whose fingers are ten armies! Moloch
whose breast is a cannibal dynamo! Moloch whose ear is a
smoking tomb!

Moloch whose eyes are a thousand blind windows! Moloch whose
skyscrapers stand in the long streets like endless Jehovahs!
Moloch whose factories dream and croak in the fog! Moloch
whose smokestacks and antennae crown the cities!

Moloch whose love is endless oil and stone! Moloch whose soul is
electricity and banks! Moloch whose poverty is the specter of
genius! Moloch whose fate is a cloud of sexless hydrogen!
Moloch whose name is the Mind!   85

Moloch in whom I sit lonely! Moloch in whom I dream Angels! Crazy
in Moloch! Cocksucker in Moloch! Lacklove and manless in
Moloch!

Moloch who entered my soul early! Moloch in whom I am a
consciousness without a body! Moloch who frightened me out
of my natural ecstasy! Moloch whom I abandon! Wake up in
Moloch! Light streaming out of the sky!

Moloch! Moloch! Robot apartments! invisible suburbs! skeleton
treasuries! blind capitals! demonic industries! spectral nations!
invincible madhouses! granite cocks! monstrous bombs!

They broke their backs lifting Moloch to Heaven! Pavements, trees,
radios, tons! lifting the city to Heaven which exists and is
everywhere about us!

Visions! omens! hallucinations! miracles! ecstasies! gone down the
American river!   90

Dreams! adorations! illuminations! religions! the whole boatload of
sensitive bullshit!

Breakthroughs! over the river! flips and crucifixions! gone down the
flood! Highs! Epiphanies! Despairs! Ten years' animal screams
and suicides! Minds! New loves! Mad generation! down on the
rocks of Time!

Real holy laughter in the river! They saw it all! the wild eyes! the holy
yells! They bade farewell! They jumped off the roof! to
solitude! waving! carrying flowers! Down to the river! into the
street!

III

Carl Solomon! I'm with you in Rockland°
where you're madder than I am

---

95 *Rockland*: New York psychiatric hospital.

I'm with you in Rockland
> where you must feel very strange   95
I'm with you in Rockland
> where you imitate the shade of my mother
I'm with you in Rockland
> where you've murdered your twelve secretaries
I'm with you in Rockland
> where you laugh at this invisible humor
I'm with you in Rockland
> where we are great writers on the same dreadful typewriter
I'm with you in Rockland
> where your condition has become serious and is reported on
> the radio   100
I'm with you in Rockland
> where the faculties of the skull no longer admit the worms of
> the senses
I'm with you in Rockland
> where you drink the tea of the breasts of the spinters of Utica°
I'm with you in Rockland
> where you pun on the bodies of your nurses the harpies of the
> Bronx
I'm with you in Rockland
> where you scream in a straightjacket that you're losing the
> game of the actual pingpong of the abyss
I'm with you in Rockland
> where you bang on the catatonic piano the soul is innocent and
> immortal it should never die ungodly in an armed madhouse   105
I'm with you in Rockland
> where fifty more shocks will never return your soul to its body
> again from its pilgrimage to a cross in the void
I'm with you in Rockland
> where you accuse your doctors of insanity and plot the Hebrew
> socialist revolution against the fascist national Golgotha
I'm with you in Rockland
> where you will split the heavens of Long Island and resurrect
> your living human Jesus from the superhuman tomb
I'm with you in Rockland
> where there are twentyfive thousand mad comrades all together
> singing the final stanzas of the Internationale°
I'm with you in Rockland
> where we hug and kiss the United States under our bedsheets
> the United States that coughs all night and won't let us sleep   110

---

102 *spinsters of Utica*: Reference to Solomon's birthplace (?).   109 *Internationale*:
Communist anthem.

I'm with you in Rockland
> where we wake up electrified out of the coma by our own souls'
> airplanes roaring over the roof they've come to drop angelic
> bombs the hospital illuminates itself imaginary walls collapse   O
> skinny legions run outside   O starry-spangled shock of mercy the
> eternal war is here   O victory forget your underwear we're free

I'm with you in Rockland
> in my dreams you walk dripping from a sea-journey on the
> highway across America in tears to the door of my cottage in
> the Western night

Louise Glück   (b. 1943)

BROWN CIRCLE   c. 1990

My mother wants to know
why, if I hate
family so much,
I went ahead and
had one. I don't   5
answer my mother.
What I hated
was being a child,
having no choice about
what people I loved.   10

I don't love my son
the way I meant to love him.
I thought I'd be
the lover of orchids who finds
red trillium growing   15
in the pine shade, and doesn't
touch it, doesn't need
to possess it. What I am
is the scientist,
who comes to that flower   20
with a magnifying glass
and doesn't leave, though
the sun burns a brown
circle of grass around
the flower. Which is   25
more or less the way
my mother loved me.

I must learn
to forgive my mother,
now that I'm helpless   30
to spare my son.

Louise Glück   (b. 1943)
PALAIS DES ARTS°   c. 1980

Love long dormant showing itself:
the large expected gods
caged really, the columns
sitting on the lawn, as though perfection
were not timeless but stationary—that   5
is the comedy, she thinks,
that they are paralyzed. Or like the matching swans,
insular, circling the pond: restraint so passionate
implies possession. They hardly speak.
On the other bank, a small boy throws bits of bread   10
into the water. The reflected monument
is stirred, briefly, stricken with light—
She can't touch his arm in innocence again.
They have to give that up and begin
as male and female, thrust and ache.   15

Palais des Arts. Arts palace: a museum.

Louise Glück   (b. 1943)
THE MIRROR   c. 1980

Watching you in the mirror I wonder
what it is like to be so beautiful
and why you do not love
but cut yourself, shaving
like a blind man. I think you let me stare   5
so you can turn against yourself
with greater violence,
needing to show me how you scrape the flesh away
scornfully and without hesitation
until I see you correctly,   10
as a man bleeding, not
the reflection I desire.

Louise Glück   (b. 1943)
BROODING LIKENESS   c. 1981

I was born in the month of the bull,°
the month of heaviness,
or of the lowered, the destructive head,

1 *month of the bull*: April 21–May 21: Taurus.

or of purposeful blindness. So I know, beyond the shadowed
patch of grass, the stubborn one, the one who doesn't look up,   5
still senses the rejected world. It is
a stadium, a well of dust. And you who watch him
looking down in the face of death, what do you know
of commitment? If the bull lives
one controlled act of revenge, be satisfied   10
that in the sky, like you, he is always moving,
not of his own accord but through the black field
like grit caught on a wheel, like shining freight.

Louise Glück   (b. 1943)
MATINS°   1992

Forgive me if I say I love you: the powerful
are always lied to since the weak are always
driven by panic. I cannot love
what I can't conceive, and you disclose
virtually nothing: are you like the hawthorn tree,   5
always the same thing in the same place,
or are you more the foxglove, inconsistent, first springing up
a pink spike on the slope behind the daisies,
and the next year, purple in the rose garden? You must see
it is useless to us, this silence that promotes belief   10
you must be all things, the foxglove and the hawthorn tree,
the vulnerable rose and tough daisy—we are left to think
you couldn't possibly exist. Is this
what you mean us to think, does this explain
the silence of the morning,   15
the crickets not yet rubbing their wings, the cats
not fighting in the yard?

MATINS: Early morning prayer usually recited aloud at daybreak. The poem is addressed to God.

Louise Glück   (b. 1943)
VESPERS°   1992

Even as you appeared to Moses, because
I need you, you appear to me, not
often, however. I live essentially
in darkness. You are perhaps training me to be

VESPERS: Late afternoon prayer recited or sung aloud.

responsive to the slightest brightening. Or, like the poets,   5
are you stimulated by despair, does grief
move you to reveal your nature? This afternoon,
in the physical world to which you commonly
contribute your silence, I climbed
the small hill above the wild blueberries, metaphysically   10
descending, as on all my walks: did I go deep enough
for you to pity me, as you have sometimes pitied
others who suffer, favoring those
with theological gifts? As you anticipated,
I did not look up. So you came down to me: 15
at my feet, not the wax
leaves of the wild blueberry but your fiery self, a whole
pasture of fire, and beyond, the red sun neither falling nor rising—
I was not a child; I could take advantage of illusions.

Lorna Goodison   (b. 1947)
MY LAST POEM   1980

I once wrote poems
that emerged so fine
with a rough edge for honing
a soft cloth for polishing
and a houseproud eye   5
I'd pride myself in making them shine.
But in this false winter
with the real cold to come
no, this season's shift
there are no winters here,   10
well call it what you will but the cold time is here
with its memorial crosses to mark
my father's dying
and me wondering where next year will find me
in whose vineyard toiling.   15
I gave my son
to a kind woman to keep
and walked down through the valley
on my scarred feet,
across the river   20
and into the guilty town
in search of bread
but they had closed the bakery down.
So I returned and said child
there was no bread   25
I'll write you my last poem instead.

My last poem is not my best
all things weaken towards the end.
O but it should be laid out
and chronicled, crazy like my life   30
with a place for all my several lives
daughter, sister, mistress, friend, warrior
wife
and a high holy ending for the blessed
one   35
me as mother to a man.
There should be a place for
messages and replies
you are too tightly bound, too whole
he said   40
I loosened my hair and I bled
now you send conflicting signals they said
divided I turned both ways and fled.
There should be a place for all this
but I'm almost at the end of my last poem   45
and I'm almost a full woman.
I warm my son's clothes
in this cold time
in the deep of my bosom
and I'm not afraid of love.   50
In fact, should it be
that these are false signals I'm receiving
and not a real unqualified ending
I'm going to keep the word love
and use it in my next poem.   55
I know it's just the wordsmith's failing
to forge a new metal to ring like its rhyme
but I'll keep its fool's gold
for you see it's always bought me time.
And if I write another poem   60
I'm going to use it
for it has always used me
and if I ever write another poem
I'm going to return that courtesy.

Lorna Goodison   (b. 1947)

JAMAICA 1980   1980

It trails always behind me
a webbed seine with a catch of fantasy
a penance I pay for being me

who took the order of poetry.
Always there with the gaping holes   5
and the mended ones, and the stand-in words.
But this time my Jamaica
my green-clad muse
this time your callings are of no use
I am spied on by your mountains   10
wire-tapped by your secret streams
your trees dripping blood-leaves
and jasmine selling tourist-dreams.

For over all this edenism
hangs the smell of necromancy   15
and each man eats his brother's flesh
Lord, so much of the cannibal left
in the jungle on my people's tongues.

We've sacrificed babies
and burnt our mothers   20
as payment to some viridian-eyed God dread
who works in cocaine under hungry men's heads.

And mine the task of writing it down
as I ride in shame round this blood-stained town.
And when the poem refuses to believe   25
and slimes to aloes in my hands
mine is the task of burying the dead
I the late madonna of barren lands.

Lorna Goodison   (b. 1947)

MY LAST POEM (AGAIN)   1987

I'm approaching the end of my penance of poems.
I can tell because the rosary beads are colder
and it's becoming harder to hold them.

So then, let them go! I'll be glad to see the last of them
once born they sometimes evoked (like most babies)   5
wonderment. But the delivery of them!
Good-bye poems, you bled me shiny bottles of red feelings.
Poems, you were blood leeches attaching yourself to me
in my should-have-been-brighter moments.
You put to flight lovers who could not compete   10
you forced yourself into my birthing bed
so I delivered one son and a poem.
When the King of Swords° gutted me
and left me for dead, in my insides were found

clots of poems, proving that poets are made of poems   15
and poems are truth demanding punctuation of light
and your all, and that makes my head vie with night all day.
I don't want to live this way anymore.
Somewhere there is a clean kind man
with a deep and wide understanding   20
of the mercy and the peace and the infinity.
And we will, if we are lucky, live by the sea
and serve and heal eating of life's salt and bread
and at night lie close to each other and read poems
for which somebody else besides me bled . . .   25
and that will make me want to write poems.

13 *King of Swords*: A card in the Tarot deck implying danger.

George Gordon, Lord Byron   (1788–1824)

SONG   1810

Ζώη μοῦ, σάς ἀγαπῶ°
Athens, 1810

I.

> Maid of Athens, ere we part,
> Give, oh, give me back my heart!
> Or, since that has left my breast,
> Keep it now, and take the rest!
> Hear my vow before I go,   5
> Ζώη μοῦ, σάς ἀγαπῶ.

II.

> By those tresses unconfined,
> Wooed by each Aegean wind;
> By those lids whose jetty fringe
> Kiss thy soft cheeks' blooming tinge;   10
> By those wild eyes like the roe,
> Ζώη μοῦ, σάς ἀγαπῶ.

III.

> By that lip I long to taste;
> By that zone° encircled waist;
> By all the token-flowers that tell   15
> What words can never speak so well;
> By Love's alternate joy and woe,
> Ζώη μοῦ, σάς ἀγαπῶ.

Ζώη μοῦ, σάς ἀγαπῶ: (Pronounced "zoe mon tas agapo") "My Life, I Love You." Also
used as the refrain.   14 *Zone*: A belt worn by virgins.

IV.

> Maid of Athens! I am gone:
> Think of me, sweet! when alone.   20
> Though I fly to Istambul,
> Athens holds my heart and soul:
> Can I cease to love thee? No!
> Ζώη μοῦ, σάς ἀγαπῶ.

George Gordon, Lord Byron   (1788–1824)
SHE WALKS IN BEAUTY   1814

I.

> She walks in beauty, like the night
>   Of cloudless climes and starry skies;
> And all that's best of dark and bright
>   Meet in her aspect and her eyes:
> Thus mellowed to that tender light   5
>   Which heaven to gaudy day denies.

II.

> One shade the more, one ray the less,
>   Had half impaired the nameless grace
> Which waves in every raven tress,
>   Or softly lightens o'er her face;   10
> Where thoughts serenely sweet express
>   How pure, how dear their dwelling place.

III.

> And on that cheek, and o'er that brow,
>   So soft, so calm, yet eloquent,
> The smiles that win, the tints that glow,   15
>   But tell of days in goodness spent,
> A mind at peace with all below,
>   A heart whose love is innocent!

Jorie Graham   (b. 1951)
THE HIDING PLACE   1991

> The last time I saw it was 1968.
> Paris, France. The time of the *disturbances*.
> We had claims. Schools shut down.
> Three million *workers* and *students* on strike.°

---

4 *strike*: Graham was educated at the Sorbonne in Paris during a period of great political unrest in France and the United States. Some of the protest was against the war in Vietnam.

Marches, sit-ins, helicopters, gas.   5
They stopped you at gunpoint asking for papers.

    I spent eleven nights sleeping in the halls. Arguments.
Negotiations.
Hurrying in the dawn looking for a certain leader,
    I found his face above an open street fire.   10
No, he said, tell them *no concessions.*
    His voice above the fire as if there were no fire—

language floating everywhere above the sleeping bodies;
    and crates of fruit donated in secret;
and torn sheets (for tear gas) tossed down from shuttered windows; 15
    and bread; and blankets, stolen from the firehouse.
The CRS (the government police) would swarm in around dawn
    in small blue vans and round us up.
Once I watched the searchbeams play on some flames.
    The flames push up into the corridor of light.   20

In the cell we were so crowded no one could sit or lean.
    People peed on each other. I felt a girl
vomiting gently onto my back.
    I found two Americans rounded up by chance,
their charter left that morning, they screamed, what were they
    going to do?   25

    Later a man in a uniform came in with a stick.
He started beating here and there, found the girl in her eighth
    month.
He beat her frantically over and over.
He pummelled her belly. Screaming aren't you ashamed?

    I remember the cell vividly,   30
but is it from a photograph? I think the shadows as I
    see them still—the slatted brilliant bits
against the wall—I think they're true—but are they from a
    photograph?
    Do I see it from inside now—his hands, her face—or

is it from the news account?   35
    The strangest part of getting out again was *streets.*
The light running down them.
    Everything spilling whenever the wall breaks.
And the air—thick with dwellings—the air filled—doubled—
    as if the open   40

had been made to render—
    the open squeezed for space until the hollows spill out,

story upon story of them
    starting to light up as I walked out.
How thick was the empty meant to be?   45
    What were we finding in the air?

What were we meant to find?
I went home slowly, sat in my rented room.
    Sat for a long time the window open,

    watched the white gauze curtain sluff this way then that a bit—   50
    watched the air suck it out, push it back in. Lung
of the room with street cries in it. Watched until the lights
    outside made it gold, pumping gently.
Was I meant to get up again? I was inside. The century clicked by.
    The woman below called down *not to forget the*   55

    loaf. Crackle of helicopters. Voice on a loudspeaker issuing
    warnings.
    They made agreements, we all returned to work.
The government fell but then it was all right again.
    The man above the fire, listening to my question,   60

the red wool shirt he wore: where is it? who has it?
    He looked straight back into the century: no concessions.
I took the message back.
    The look in his eyes—shoving out—into the open—
    expressionless with thought: 65
no—tell them *no*—

Jorie Graham   (b. 1951)

HISTORY   1983

Into whose ear the deeds are spoken. The only
listener. So I believed
he would remember everything, the murmuring trees,
the sunshine's zealotry, its deep
unevenness. For history   5
is the opposite
of the eye
for whom, for instance, six million bodies in portions
of hundreds and
the flowerpots broken by a sudden wind stand as   10
equivalent. What more
is there
than fact? *I'll give ten thousand dollars to the man*
who proves the holocaust really

occurred said the exhausted solitude   15
in San Francisco
in 1980. Far in the woods
in a faded photograph
in 1942 the man with his own
genitalia in his mouth and hundreds of   20
slow holes
a pitchfork has opened
over his face
grows beautiful. The ferns and deepwood
lilies catch   25
the eye. Three men in ragged uniforms
with guns keep laughing
nervously. They share the day
with him. A bluebird
sings. The feathers of the shade touch every inch   30
of skin—the hand holding down the delicate gun,
the hands holding down the delicate
hips. And the sky
is visible between the men, between
the trees, a blue spirit   35
enveloping
anything. Late in the story, in Northern Italy,
a man cuts down some trees for winter
fuel. We read this in the evening
news. Watching the fire burn late   40
one night, watching it change and change, a hand grenade,
lodged in the pulp the young tree
grew around, explodes, blinding the man, killing
his wife. Now who
will tell the children   45
fairytales? The ones where simple
crumbs over the forest
floor endure
to help us home?

Thomas Gray   (1716–1771)

ELEGY WRITTEN IN A COUNTRY CHURCHYARD   1753

The Curfew tolls the knell of parting day,
The lowing herd wind slowly o'er the lea,
The plowman homeward plods his weary way,
And leaves the world to darkness and to me.

Now fades the glimmering landscape on the sight,   5
And all the air a solemn stillness holds,
Save where the beetle wheels his droning flight,
And drowsy tinklings lull the distant folds;

Save° that from yonder ivy-mantled tower
The moping owl does to the moon complain   10
Of such, as wandering near her secret bower,
Molest her ancient solitary reign.

Beneath those rugged elms, that yew-tree's shade,
Where heaves the turf in many a moldering heap,
Each in his narrow cell forever laid,   15
The rude Forefathers of the hamlet sleep.

The breezy call of incense-breathing Morn,
The swallow twittering from the straw-built shed,
The cock's shrill clarion, or the echoing horn,
No more shall rouse them from their lowly bed.   20

For them no more the blazing hearth shall burn,
Or busy housewife ply her evening care:
No children run to lisp their sire's return,
Or climb his knees the envied kiss to share.

Oft did the harvest to their sickle yield,   25
Their furrow oft the stubborn glebe has broke;
How jocund did they drive their team afield!
How bowed the woods beneath their sturdy stroke!

Let not Ambition mock their useful toil,
Their homely joys, and destiny obscure;   30
Nor Grandeur hear with a disdainful smile,
The short and simple annals of the poor.

The boast of heraldry, the pomp of power,
And all that beauty, all that wealth e'er gave,
Awaits alike the inevitable hour.   35
The paths of glory lead but to the grave.

Nor you, ye Proud, impute to These the fault,
If Memory o'er their Tomb no Trophies raise,
Where through the long-drawn isle and fretted vault
The pealing anthem swells the note of praise.   40

Can storied urn or animated bust
Back to its mansion call the fleeting breath?

---

9 *Save*: Except.

Can Honor's voice provoke the silent dust,
Or Flattery sooth the dull cold ear of Death?

Perhaps in this neglected spot is laid   45
Some heart once pregnant with celestial fire,
Hands, that the rod of empire might have swayed,
Or waked to ecstasy the living lyre.

But Knowledge to their eyes her ample page
Rich with the spoils of time did ne'er unroll;   50
Chill Penury repressed their noble rage,
And froze the genial current of the soul.

Full many a gem of purest ray serene,
The dark unfathomed caves of ocean bear:
Full many a flower is born to blush unseen,   55
And waste its sweetness on the desert air.

Some village-Hampden,° that with dauntless breast
The little Tyrant of his fields withstood;
Some mute inglorious Milton° here may rest,
Some Cromwell° guiltless of his country's blood.   60

The applause of listening senates to command,
The threats of pain and ruin to despise,
To scatter plenty o'er a smiling land,
And read their history in a nation's eyes

Their lot forbade: nor circumscribed alone°   65
Their growing virtues, but their crimes confined;
Forbade to wade through slaughter to a throne,
And shut the gates of mercy on mankind,

The struggling pangs of conscious truth to hide,
To quench the blushes of ingenuous shame,   70
Or heap the shrine of Luxury and Pride
With incense kindled at the Muse's flame.

Far from the madding crowd's ignoble strife,
Their sober wishes never learned to stray;
Along the cool sequestered vale of life   75
They kept the noiseless tenor of their way.

Yet even these bones from insult to protect
Some frail memorial still erected nigh,

---

57 *Hampden*: John Hampden (1594–1643), English parliamentarian who protested King Charles I's method of taxation.   59 John Milton, in this volume.   60 *Cromwell*: Oliver Cromwell (1599–1658), English revolutionary leader.   65 *nor . . . alone*: Not . . . only.

With uncouth rhymes and shapeless sculpture decked,
Implores the passing tribute of a sigh.   80

Their name, their years, spelt by the unlettered muse,
The place of fame and elegy supply:
And many a holy text around she strews,
That teach the rustic moralist to die.

For who, to dumb Forgetfulness a prey,   85
This pleasing anxious being e'er resigned,
Left the warm precincts of the cheerful day,
Nor cast one longing lingering look behind?

On some fond breast the parting soul relies,
Some pious drops the closing eye requires;   90
Even from the tomb the voice of Nature cries,
Even in our Ashes live their wonted Fires.

For thee,° who mindful of the unhonored Dead
Dost in these lines their artless tale relate;
If chance, by lonely contemplation led,   95
Some kindred Spirit shall inquire thy fate,

Haply some hoary-headed Swain may say,
"Oft have we seen him at the peep of dawn
Brushing with hasty steps the dews away
To meet the sun upon the upland lawn.   100

"There at the foot of yonder nodding beech
That wreathes its old fantastic roots so high,
His listless length at noontide would he stretch,
And pore upon the brook that babbles by.

"Hard by yon wood, now smiling as in scorn,   105
Muttering his wayward fancies he would rove,
Now drooping, woeful wan, like one forlorn,
Or crazed with care, or crossed in hopeless love.

"One morn I missed him on the customed° hill,
Along the heath and near his favorite tree;   110
Another came; nor yet beside the rill,
Nor up the lawn, nor at the wood was he,

"The next with dirges due in sad array
Slow through the church-way path we saw him borne.
Approach and read (for thou canst read) the lay,   115
Graved on the stone beneath yon agèd thorn."

---

93 *thee*: The poet, who is writing these lines.   109 *customed*: Accustomed, usual.

THE EPITAPH

Here rests his head upon the lap of Earth
A Youth to Fortune and to Fame unknown,
Fair Science° frowned not on his humble birth,
And Melancholy marked him for her own.   120

Large was his bounty, and his soul sincere,
Heaven did a recompense as largely send:
He gave to Misery all he had, a tear,
He gained from Heaven ('twas all he wished) a friend.

No farther seek his merits to disclose,   125
Or draw his frailties from their dread abode,
(There they alike in trembling hope repose)
The bosom of his Father and his God.

119 *Science*: Learning, education. In other words, he was uneducated.

Linda Gregg   (b. 1942)
WHOLE AND WITHOUT BLESSING   c. 1981

What is beautiful alters, has undertow.
Otherwise I have no tactics to begin with.
Femininity is a sickness. I open my eyes
out of this fever and see the meaning
of my life clearly. A thing like a hill.   5
I proclaim myself whole and without blessing,
or need to be blessed. A fish of my own
spirit. I belong to no one. I do not move.
Am not required to move. I lie naked on a sheet
and the indifferent sun warms me.   10
I was bred for slaughter, like the other
animals. To suffer exactly at the center,
where there are no clues except pleasure.

Marilyn Hacker   (b. 1942)
ELEKTRA° ON THIRD AVENUE   c. 1974

FOR LINK

At six, when April chills our hands and feet
walking downtown, we stop at Clancy's Bar
or Bickford's, where the part-time hustlers are,

Elektra: Daughter of Agamemnon. Elektra supported Orestes in killing their mother, Clytemnestra, who, with her lover, had murdered Agamemnon.

scoffing between the mailroom and the street.
Old pensioners appraise them while they eat,   5
and so do we, debating half in jest
which piece of hasty pudding we'd like best.
I know you know I think your mouth is sweet
as anything exhibited for sale,
fresh coffee cake or boys fresh out of jail,   10
which tender hint of incest brings me near
to ordering more coffee or more beer.
The homebound crowd provides more youth to cruise.
We nurse our cups, nudge knees, and pick and choose.

Marilyn Hacker   (b. 1942)
LE MANUSCRIT°   c. 1986

Four women in a restaurant for gay men,
feasting, after Marthe and I had seen
a play, while Iva watched Jax' miniscreen:
Iva, mouth full: "Mom, Ray is *seventeen*
years younger than you are?" I snort, the others   5
snicker. It was "birthdays" brought it on.
"Marie is how much older?"
                                   "Twenty-one
years. No problems."
                         "Yeah, but you're *friends*, not lovers."   10
I could say to you both, my casuists,°
that we've not yet been tempered by the fire
scorching our skivvies, and that makes us—what?
Two thousand years of Western literature:
potions and swords, the quests, the songs, the trysts,   15
call us what Iva, if she knew, would not.

Le Manuscrit: Manuscript—in this sense, the script lovers follow.   11 *casuists*: Logicians, those who reason closely and sometimes falsely.

Marilyn Hacker   (b. 1942)
DID YOU LOVE WELL WHAT VERY SOON YOU LEFT?°   c. 1986

Did you love well what very soon you left?
Come home and take me in your arms and take
away this stomach ache, headache, heartache.

Did you love . . . left?: A play on Shakespeare's Sonnet 73, which ends, "To love that well which thou must leave ere long."

Never so full, I never was bereft
so utterly. The winter evenings drift   5
dark to the window. Not one word will make
you, where you are, turn in your day, or wake
from your night toward me. The only gift
I got to keep or give is what I've cried,
floodgates let down to mourning for the dead   10
chances, for the end of being young,
for everyone I loved who really died.
I drank our one year out in brine instead
of honey from the seasons of your tongue.

Marilyn Hacker   (b. 1942)

SONNET ENDING WITH A FILM SUBTITLE°   1980

For Judith Landry°

Life has its nauseating ironies:
The good die young, as often has been shown;
Chaste spouses catch Venereal Disease;
And feminists sit by the telephone.
Last night was rather bleak, tonight is starker.   5
I may stare at the wall till half-past-one.
My friends are all convinced Dorothy Parker
Lives, but is not well, in Marylebone.°
I wish that I could imitate my betters
And fortify my rhetoric with guns.   10
Some day we women all will break our fetters
And raise our daughters to be Lesbians.
(I wonder if the bastard kept my letters?)
Here follow untranslatable French puns.

Film Subtitle: The translation projected in foreign films.   7–8 *Dorothy Parker . . . Marylebone*:
Parker, poet and writer in this collection. Marylebone is a London suburb.

Joy Harjo   (b. 1951)

SANTA FE   1990

The wind blows lilacs out of the east. And it isn't lilac season. And I am
walking the street in front of St. Francis Cathedral in Santa Fe. Oh, and
it's a few years earlier and more. That's how you tell real time. It is here,

it is there. The lilacs have taken over everything: the sky, the narrow streets, my shoulders, my lips. I talk lilac. And there is nothing else until a woman the size of a fox breaks through the bushes, breaks the purple web. She is tall and black and gorgeous. She is the size of a fox on the arm of a white man who looks and tastes like cocaine. She lies for cocaine, dangles on the arm of cocaine. And lies to me now from a room in the DeVargas Hotel, where she has eaten her lover, white powder on her lips. That is true now; it is not true anymore. Eventually space curves, walks over and taps me on the shoulder. On the sidewalk I stand near St. Francis; he has been bronzed, a perpetual tan, with birds on his hand, his shoulder, deer at his feet. I am Indian and in this town I will never be a saint. I am seventeen and shy and wild. I have been up until three at a party, but there is no woman in the DeVargas Hotel, for that story hasn't yet been invented. A man whose face I will never remember, and never did, drives up on a Harley-Davidson. There are lilacs on his arm; they spill out from the spokes of his wheels. He wants me on his arm, on the back of his lilac bike touring the flower kingdom of San Francisco. And for a piece of time the size of a nickel, I think, maybe. But maybe is vapor, has no anchor here in the sun beneath St. Francis Cathedral. And space is as solid as the bronze statue of St. Francis, the fox breaking through the lilacs, my invention of this story, the wind blowing.

Joy Harjo   (b. 1951)
CROSSING WATER   1990

I return like a detective to the dance floor in New York, or was it someplace else invented to look like October? I turn back to a music the d.j. never played because the room was too blue for falling angels. Nothing by Aretha, nothing by chance. A woman chased by spirits kept asking you to dance, made a gift of her hands. I add her to the evidence: we were there. She was a witness but I don't have her name. Or yours or mine, or was the shift in axis an event in the imagination? I should be writing poems to change the world. They would appear as a sacrifice of deer for the starving. Or poems of difficulty to place my name in the Book of Poets. I should get on with it. Instead I walk back through the dark in my shoes the color of hearts to find us embraced in a ring of smoke. Hey, I wanted you in your jeans and casual sweater with your caramel lips. The next time I looked we were laughing and drunk, kissing in the car before crossing water. The Brooklyn Bridge tilted to heaven. I want you eternally ever, but this is the puzzle. There is no dance floor on Nineteenth Street. The woman with spirits left no forwarding address. There is no getaway car, no Brooklyn Bridge. The evidence floats by like rings over sweet water. Like rings over sweet water.

Joy Harjo   (b. 1951)
NINE LIVES   1990

A storm tangles in the east and will disappear in a paradise of midnight. The moon is a stripped lizard half here and half visible by the eye on the other side of the world. Someone up the alley is singing Happy Birthday to a packed house. I am downwind of the beer foam, the laughter. Death with its coat of tender wings is close to my shoulder, while the neighbor's cat fights for one of its nine lives. In the morning the winner will be grinning at the door of my sleep. I know you can understand the structure of the spiraled world in an ordinary moment, or by falling through the crack of a perfumed nightmare. Cicadas climb out of the carcasses their voices make, into their wings of fragile promises to glide over the wet grass. We are all spun within a crescendo of abalone light, unseen beneath the wild storm. What spins us now, in this neighborhood chrysalis at exactly midnight? Don't tell me unless it will turn me into something as perfect as a perfect monarch butterfly.

Michael Harper   (b. 1938)
LAST AFFAIR: BESSIE'S° BLUES SONG   1972

Disarticulated
arm torn out,
large veins cross
her shoulder intact,
her tourniquet   5
her blood in all-white big bands:

Can't you see
what love and heartache's done to me
I'm not the same as I used to be
this is my last affair   10

Mail truck or parked car
in the fast lane,
afloat at forty-three
on a Mississippi road,
Two-hundred-pound muscle on her ham bone,   15
'nother nigger dead 'fore noon:

Can't you see
what love and heartache's done to me
I'm not the same as I used to be
this is my last affair   20

Bessie: Bessie Smith, blues singer in this collection. The refrain is similar to those she sang.

Fifty-dollar record
cut the vein in her neck,
fool about her money
toll her black train wreck,
white press missed her fun'ral   25
in the same stacked deck:

Can't you see
what love and heartache's done to me
I'm not the same as I used to be
this is my last affair   30

Loved a little blackbird
heard she could sing,
Martha in her vineyard
pestle in her spring,
Bessie had a bad mouth   35
made my chimes ring:

Can't you see
what love and heartache's done to me
I'm not the same as I used to be
this is my last affair   40

WINDOW ON

The Long Poem

Most modern poems are relatively short, a page or even less. Some have a suspiciously "narrow body," as if they were designed for newspaper column
width. Long poems, however, have a distinguished tradition. Poets have been
recognized to possess, as Shakespeare said, a "fine frenzy" that permits them
to see deeply into events and to interpret experience. Traditionally they aim
to shape the culture by revealing truths produced through inspiration, elevated imagination, and insight.

In ancient times the book-length epic was the highest achievement of
the poet, serving several important functions. Aeneas in Virgil's *Aeneid*, for
example, fled Troy to found Rome, thus furnishing an explanation for the
origins of the Roman empire. Like many epics, it also provided a rationale for
the imperial ambitions of the nation and in the process glorified war, the instrument of those ambitions. Homer, the earliest-known epic poet, was blind
but nevertheless a seer: possessing insight into the human soul. The *Iliad* narrates the Greek siege of Troy, and the *Odyssey* tells of one man's struggles

coming home from Troy. The best-known English epic is John Milton's *Paradise Lost*, which moves from praising worldly empire to praising the empire of the individual soul.

Walt Whitman's (1819–1892) "Song of Myself" is a huge, sprawling poem celebrating Whitman's discovery of himself and his exploration of his soul. He describes in detail American culture of the mid-1800s by casting his vision through all walks of life.

The lines are long, unrhymed, and not metrical, their rhythms being determined by what is said. Whitman "celebrates" himself in his poem, but he also tells some interesting stories, as in his direct and simple recollection of helping a runaway slave: "The runaway slave came to my house and stopped outside, / I heard his motions crackling the twigs of the woodpile, / Through the swung half-door of the kitchen I saw him limpsy and weak, / And went where he sat on a log and led him in and assured him" (lines 189–92). "Song of Myself" is epic in scope and spirit, and in its expansiveness gives us a positive image of both Whitman and ourselves.

T. S. Eliot's (1888–1965) "The Love Song of J. Alfred Prufrock" and "The Hollow Men" react to to social circumstances of Europe late in World War I, 1915–1917, then in the unsettled period after the war, 1925, which was marked by a dramatic rise in materialism throughout Europe and the industrialized world. Eliot was known as a religious poet who protested the widespread materialism of his time. The hollowness of the hollow men resulted from their inability to develop a spiritual core. The fact that J. Alfred Prufrock was indecisive, ineffective, and unable to respond to love was due in large measure to his failure to commit to spiritual values. Eliot's poetry aimed squarely at these issues throughout his life. He became a sharp critic of the upper classes—of which he was a member—and the other social classes that had become unsettled in their beliefs as a result of the turmoil and changes of World War I.

Denise Levertov's "Matins" (p. 862) focuses on spiritual content, since its title refers to morning prayers and its structure seems tuned to theirs. Her quest is stated in the opening line: "The authentic!" Her search is for the authentic in life, which she finds in the small moments of existence. Galway Kinnell's extensive meditation on his life echoes to the refrain which is its title as well as the opening and closing line of every stanza: "when one has lived a long time alone" (p. 852). Both these poems move in a direction different from the long philosophical poem in that they do not tackle the huge questions. Instead, they approach life's mysteries through everyday details. Richard Jackson's "Benediction" (p. 833), while also personal, deals with cosmic issues, moving from the angels of Milton to the teachings of Blaise Pascal. He refers to Roman and modern history and ranges from architecture and sculpture to the beggars of India. He attempts to embrace a world of experience as he meditates on the death of a friend.

Robert Hayden's "Middle Passage" details the journey that brought Africans to the new world to serve as slaves. The refrain in one form or another of "Jesus Savior Pilot Me" is ironic in face of the pleas that might have been made from the cargo, if the cargo were given a voice. The middle passage was cruel, dangerous, and resulted in the death of many or most of the Africans. During the period before emancipation, when it was prohibited to bring more slaves to the United States, the slavers would sometimes throw their human cargo overboard to their death in order to escape inspection by United States cutters.

Hayden's poem is fascinating for its use of multiple voices and its effort to respect the fashion in which those on board ship had to keep a careful log during their watch. Hayden records events that were almost common on the terrifying journey from Africa to New Orleans. In Part III, Hayden recounts part of the story of the Amistad, a ship seized by its African passengers. Most of the officers and crew were killed and two—one the narrator—were preserved to operate the ship with the intent of returning to Africa. However, the sailors brought the ship to New Haven. A subsequent trial freed the Africans. The narrator, from whose point of view the story is clearly told, is displeased with that decision. He is a slaver.

The long poem has many challenges, but it is a key to the age's analysis of itself. It performs one of the most important functions of poetry: the examination of the culture. Some other important long poems in this collection are Allen Ginsberg, "Howl"; Thomas Gray, "Elegy in a Country Churchyard"; Robert Hayden, "Middle Passage"; John Keats, "The Eve of St. Agnes"; and Anne Sexton, "Red Riding Hood."

There is no agreement about how long a "long" poem has to be. Some people rightly feel that it is not the number of lines but the fullness of the discourse—the weight of what is said—that determines a long poem. You are at liberty to make that judgment on the basis of your reading.

Reading

Bowra, C. M. *Heroic Poetry.* London: Macmillan, 1952.

Friedman, Susan Stanford. "When a Long Poem Is a 'Big' Poem." *Lit: Literature Interpretation Theory* 2–1 (1990): 9–25.

Li, Victor P. H. "The Vanity of Length." *Genre* 19 (Spring 1986): 3–20.

Robert Hayden   (1913–1980)

MIDDLE PASSAGE°   1962

I

> *Jesús, Estrella, Esperanza, Mercy:*°
> Sails flashing to the wind like weapons,
> sharks following the moans the fever and the dying;
> horror the corposant and compass rose.

Middle Passage: The sea passage between Africa and the West Indies, the principal route for slave ships.   1 *Jesús . . . Mercy:* Names of slave ships. *Esperanza* is Spanish for hope.

Middle Passage: 5
    voyage through death
        to life upon these shores.

   "10 April 1800—
   Blacks rebellious. Crew uneasy. Our linguist says
   their moaning is a prayer for death,   10
   ours and their own. Some try to starve themselves.
   Lost three this morning leaped with crazy laughter
   to the waiting sharks, sang as they went under."

Desire, Adventure, Tartar, Ann:°
   Standing to America, bringing home   15
   black gold, black ivory, black seed.

     Deep in the festering hold thy father lies,
     of his bones New England pews are made,
     those are altar lights that were his eyes.°

Jesus Savior Pilot Me   20
Over Life's Tempestuous Sea°

We pray that Thou wilt grant, O Lord,
safe passage to our vessels bringing
heathen souls unto Thy chastening.

Jesus Savior   25

   "8 bells. I cannot sleep, for I am sick
   with fear, but writing eases fear a little
   since still my eyes can see these words take shape
   upon the page & so I write, as one
   would turn to exorcism. 4 days scudding,   30
   but now the sea is calm again. Misfortune
   follows in our wake like sharks (our grinning
   tutelary gods). Which one of us
   has killed an albatross°? A plague among
   our blacks—Ophthalmia: blindness—& we   35
   have jettisoned the blind to no avail.
   It spreads, the terrifying sickness spreads.
   Its claws have scratched sight from the Capt.'s eyes
   & there is blindness in the fo'c'sle
   & we must sail 3 weeks before we come   40
   to port."

---

14 *Tartar, Ann:* More ships names.   17–19 *Deep . . . eyes:* A grim play on the beautiful image from Shakespeare's *The Tempest* (1.2.397–99): "Full fathom five thy father lies; / Of his bones are coral made; / Those are pearls that were his eyes." See also lines 108–110, p. 808.
20–21 *Jesus . . . Sea:* A Protestant hymn.   34 *killed an albatross:* Considered a crime that brings on bad luck.

What port awaits us, Davy Jones'
or home? I've heard of slavers drifting, drifting,
playthings of wind and storm and chance, their crews
gone blind, the jungle hatred   45
crawling up on deck.

Thou Who Walked On Galilee

"Deponent further sayeth *The Bella J*
left the Guinea Coast
with cargo of five hundred blacks and odd   50
for the barracoons of Florida:

"That there was hardly room 'tween-decks for half
the sweltering cattle stowed spoon-fashion there;
that some went mad of thirst and tore their flesh
and sucked the blood: 55

"That Crew and Captain lusted with the comeliest
of the savage girls kept naked in the cabins;
that there was one they called The Guinea Rose
and they cast lots and fought to lie with her:

"That when the Bo's'n piped all hands, the flames   60
spreading from starboard already were beyond
control, the negroes howling and their chains
entangled with the flames:

"That the burning blacks could not be reached,
that the Crew abandoned ship,   65
leaving their shrieking negresses behind,
that the Captain perished drunken with the wenches:

"Further Deponent sayeth not."

Pilot Oh Pilot Me

II

Aye, lad, and I have seen those factories,   70
Gambia, Rio Pongo, Calabar;°
have watched the artful mongos° baiting traps
of war wherein the victor and the vanquished

Were caught as prizes for our barracoons.
Have seen the nigger kings whose vanity   75
and greed turned wild black hides of Fellatah,
Mandingo, Ibo, Kru° to gold for us.

71 *Gambia, Rio Pongo, Calabar:* African rivers, cities.   72 *mongos:* Negroes.   76–77 *Fellatah,*
Mandingo, Ibo, Kru: African tribes.

And there was one—King Anthracite we named him—
fetish face beneath French parasols
of brass and orange velvet, impudent mouth   80
whose cups were carven skulls of enemies:

He'd honor us with drum and feast and conjo°
and palm-oil-glistening wenches deft in love,
and for tin crowns that shone with paste,
red calico and German-silver trinkets   85

Would have the drums talk war and send
his warriors to burn the sleeping villages
and kill the sick and old and lead the young
in coffles to our factories.

Twenty years a trader, twenty years,   90
for there was wealth aplenty to be harvested
from those black fields, and I'd be trading still
but for the fevers melting down my bones.

III

Shuttles in the rocking loom of history,
the dark ships move, the dark ships move,   95
their bright ironical names
like jests of kindness on a murderer's mouth;
plough through thrashing glister toward
fata morgana's° lucent melting shore,
weave toward New World littorals that are   100
mirage and myth and actual shore.

Voyage through death,
                    voyage whose chartings are unlove.

A charnel stench, effluvium of living death
spreads outward from the hold,   105
where the living and the dead, the horribly dying,
lie interlocked, lie foul with blood and excrement.

> *Deep in the festering hold thy father lies,*
> *the corpse of mercy rots with him,*
> *rats eat love's rotten gelid eyes.*   110

> *But, oh, the living look at you*
> *with human eyes whose suffering accuses you,*
> *whose hatred reaches through the swill of dark*
> *to strike you like a leper's claw.*

---

82 *conjo*: Dance.   99 *fata morgana*: A mirage sometimes seen at sea.

You cannot stare that hatred down   115
or chain the fear that stalks the watches
and breathes on you its fetid scorching breath;
cannot kill the deep immortal human wish,
the timeless will.

"But for the storm that flung up barriers   120
of wind and wave, *The Amistad,*° senõres,
would have reached the port of Príncipe in two,
three days at most; but for the storm we should
have been prepared for what befell.
Swift as the puma's leap it came. There was   125
that interval of moonless calm filled only
with the water's and the rigging's usual sounds,
then sudden movement, blows and snarling cries
and they had fallen on us with machete
and marlinspike. It was as though the very   130
air, the night itself were striking us.
Exhausted by the rigors of the storm,
we were no match for them. Our men went down
before the murderous Africans. Our loyal
Celestino ran from below with gun   135
and lantern and I saw, before the cane-
knife's wounding flash, Cinquez,
that surly brute who calls himself a prince,
directing, urging on the ghastly work.
He hacked the poor mulatto down, and then   140
he turned on me. The decks were slippery
when daylight finally came. It sickens me
to think of what I saw, of how these apes
threw overboard the butchered bodies of
our men, true Christians all, like so much jetsam.   145
Enough, enough. The rest is quickly told:
Cinquez was forced to spare the two of us
you see to steer the ship to Africa,
and we like phantoms doomed to rove the sea
voyaged east by day and west by night,   150
deceiving them, hoping for rescue,
prisoners on our own vessel, till
at length we drifted to the shores of this
your land, America, where we were freed
from our unspeakable misery. Now we   155
demand, good sirs, the extradition of

121 Name of a Spanish ship; means friendship.

Cinquez and his accomplices to La
Havana. And it distresses us to know
there are so many here who seem inclined
to justify the mutiny of these blacks.   160
We find it paradoxical indeed
that you whose wealth, whose tree of liberty
are rooted in the labor of your slaves
should suffer the august John Quincy Adams
to speak with so much passion of the right   165
of chattel slaves to kill their lawful masters
and with his Roman rhetoric weave a hero's
garland for Cinquez. I tell you that
we are determined to return to Cuba
with our slaves and there see justice done. Cinquez—   170
or let us say 'the Prince'—Cinquez shall die."

The deep immortal human wish,
the timeless will:

Cinquez its deathless primaveral image,
life that transfigures many lives.   175

Voyage through death
                    to life upon these shores.

Seamus Heaney   (b. 1939)
DIGGING   1964

Between my finger and my thumb
The squat pen rests; snug as a gun.

Under my window, a clean rasping sound
When the spade sinks into gravelly ground:
My father, digging. I look down   5

Till his straining rump among the flowerbeds
Bends low, comes up twenty years away
Stooping in rhythm through potato drills
Where he was digging.

The coarse boot nestled on the lug, the shaft   10
Against the inside knee was levered firmly.
He rooted out tall tops, buried the bright edge deep
To scatter new potatoes that we picked
Loving their cool hardness in our hands.

By God, the old man could handle a spade.   15
Just like his old man.

My grandfather cut more turf in a day
Than any other man on Toner's bog.
Once I carried him milk in a bottle
Corked sloppily with paper. He straightened up   20
To drink it, then fell to right away

Nicking and slicing neatly, heaving sods
Over his shoulder, going down and down
For the good turf. Digging.

The cold smell of potato mould, the squelch and slap   25
Of soggy peat, the curt cuts of an edge
Through living roots awaken in my head.
But I've no spade to follow men like them.

Between my finger and my thumb
The squat pen rests.   30
I'll dig with it.

Seamus Heaney   (b. 1939)

THE GRAUBALLE MAN°   1975

As if he had been poured
in tar, he lies
on a pillow of turf
and seems to weep

the black river of himself.   5
The grain of his wrists
is like bog oak,
the ball of his heel

like a basalt egg.
His instep has shrunk   10
cold as a swan's foot
or a wet swamp root.

His hips are the ridge
and purse of a mussel,
his spine an eel arrested   15
under a glisten of mud.

The head lifts,
the chin is a visor

Grauballe Man: A well-preserved corpse taken from a bog in Denmark. Many early corpses have
been discovered there and in Ireland's bogs.

raised above the vent
of his slashed throat   20

that has tanned and toughened.
The cured wound
opens inwards to a dark
elderberry place.

Who will say "corpse"   25
to his vivid cast?
Who will say "body"
to his opaque repose?

And his rusted hair,
a mat unlikely   30
as a foetus's.
I first saw his twisted face

in a photograph,
a head and shoulder
out of the peat,   35
bruised like a forceps baby,

but now he lies
perfected in my memory,
down to the red horn
of his nails,   40

hung in the scales
with beauty and atrocity:
with the Dying Gaul°
too strictly compassed

on his shield,   45
with the actual weight
of each hooded victim,
slashed and dumped.

43 *Dying Gaul*: Roman statue commemorating the bravery of Celts who fought against the
Roman Legion.

Seamus Heaney   (b. 1939)
PUNISHMENT°   1975

I can feel the tug
of the halter at the nape
of her neck, the wind
on her naked front.

Punishment: Heaney refers to a female corpse from the bogs, imagining her as having been punished for a crime.

It blows her nipples
to amber beads,
it shakes the frail rigging
of her ribs.

I can see her drowned
body in the bog,
the weighing stone,
the floating rods and boughs.

Under which at first
she was a barked sapling
that is dug up
oak-bone, brain-firkin:

her shaved head
like a stubble of black corn,
her blindfold a soiled bandage,
her noose a ring

to store
the memories of love.
Little adulteress,
before they punished you

you were flaxen-haired,
undernourished, and your
tar-black face was beautiful.
My poor scapegoat,

I almost love you
but would have cast, I know,
the stones of silence.
I am the artful voyeur

of your brain's exposed
and darkened combs,
your muscles' webbing
and all your numbered bones:

I who have stood dumb
when your betraying sisters,
cauled in tar,
wept by the railings,

who would connive
in civilized outrage
yet understand the exact
and tribal, intimate revenge.

5

10

15

20

25

30

35

40

Seamus Heaney   (b. 1939)
THE TOLLUND MAN°   1972

I

> Some day I will go to Aarhus°
> To see his peat-brown head,
> The mild pods of his eye-lids,
> His pointed skin cap.
>
> In the flat country nearby   5
> Where they dug him out,
> His last gruel of winter seeds
> Caked in his stomach,
>
> Naked except for
> The cap, noose and girdle,   10
> I will stand a long time.
> Bridegroom to the goddess,
>
> She tightened her torc° on him
> And opened her fen,
> Those dark juices working   15
> Him to a saint's kept body,°
>
> Trove of the turfcutters'
> Honeycombed workings.
> Now his stained face
> Reposes at Aarhus.   20

II

> I could risk blasphemy,
> Consecrate the cauldron bog
> Our holy ground and pray
> Him to make germinate
>
> The scattered, ambushed   25
> Flesh of laborers,
> Stockinged corpses
> Laid out in the farmyards,
>
> Tell-tale skin and teeth
> Flecking the sleepers   30

Tollund Man: A body preserved in a peat bog in Denmark.   1 *Aarhus*: Town in Denmark.
13 *torc*: Necklace, choker.   16 *saint's kept body*: Saints' bodies are said not to decay.

Of four young brothers, trailed
For miles along the lines.

III

Something of his sad freedom
As he rode the tumbril°
Should come to me, driving,   35
Saying the names

Tollund, Grauballe, Nebelgard,°
Watching the pointing hands
Of country people,
Not knowing their tongue.   40

Out there in Jutland
In the old man-killing parishes
I will feel lost,
Unhappy and at home.

---

34 *tumbril*: Cart transporting him to death.   37 *Grauballe, Nebelgard*: Other places where
such bodies have been found.

George Herbert   (1593–1633)
THE ALTAR°   1633

A broken A L T A R, Lord, thy servant rears,
Made of a heart, and cemented with tears:
  Whose parts are as thy hand did frame;
  No workman's tool hath touched the same.
       A H E A R T alone   5
       Is   such   a   stone,
       As   nothing   but
       Thy power doth cut.
       Wherefore each part
       Of my hard heart   10
       Meets in this frame,
       To praise thy name.
  That if I chance to hold my peace,
  These stones to praise thee may not cease.
O let thy blessèd S A C R I F I C E be mine,   15
And sanctify this A L T A R to be thine.

The Altar: The shape of this poem resembles an altar.

George Herbert   (1593–1633)
EASTER WINGS   1633

Lord, who createdst man in wealth and store,
    Though foolishly he lost the same,
        Decaying more and more,
           Till   he   became
             Most   poor: 5
             With   thee
           O   let   me   rise
        As   larks,   harmoniously,
    And sing this day thy victories:
Then shall the fall further the flight° in me   10

My tender age in sorrow did begin:
    And still with sicknesses and shame
        Thou didst so punish sin,
           That   I   became
             Most   thin.
             With   thee   15
           Let   me   combine,
    And feel this day thy victory:
    For, if I imp° my wing on thine,
Affliction shall advance the flight in me.   20

10 *fall ... flight*: The fall into sin and weakness allows for his redemption by Christ (flight).
19 *imp*: Graft.

Geoffrey Hill   (b. 1932)

SEPTEMBER SONG   1986

born 19.6.32—deported 24.9.42

Undesirable you may have been, untouchable
you were not. Not forgotten
or passed over at the proper time.

As estimated, you died. Things marched,
sufficient, to that end.   5
Just so much Zyklon° and leather, patented
terror, so many routine cries.

6 *Zyklon*: Poison gas Nazis used to kill Jews in Auschwitz and other camps.

(I have made
an elegy for myself it
is true)   10

September fattens on vines. Roses
flake from the wall. The smoke
of harmless fires drifts to my eyes.

This is plenty. This is more than enough.

Christine Holbo
GOMORRAH°   1992

Also, in Gomorrah, there were plays,
a life of the mind;
there were the schools
and the quiet temples; Sodom
and "the new theatre"   5
were conveniently located,
just an hour's ride away. There
the wife of Lot held her
gatherings, "my *petites
soirées*," for the priests   10
and the politicians
and the intellectual élite.

> *And in the hills the wild dogs cried
> And the sand shifted on the desert stones.*

But Gomorrah was mostly as you will have heard: 15
litigious, polyglot, city of worlds; a scene
from a favorite story frequently told.
There was the traffic, the market banter—
merchants crying catalogues of marvels: uncut
rubies, silver mirrors, porcelain,   20
parrots, olives at discount, clocks and
sea salt, carbuncles, pearls—the streets
full of crowds, the dirty gypsies,
the quick brown-ankled girls,
the old men smoking on the temple   25
stoop, the smells of hashish and tanneries,
the bellowing herds.

Gomorrah: See Gen. 19:1–26. God warned Lot and his family to flee Sodom and Gomorrah before he destroyed them by fire for their wickedness. Lot's wife looked back as she fled and was turned into a pillar of salt.

And in the hills the wild dogs cried
And the desert gods shifted sand across the stones.

The wife of Lot   30
was not *so* young anymore.
She didn't laugh like
the brown-ankled girls;
the wife of Lot wore a veil in public,
and held her tongue.   35
And she kept the books
in the family establishment,
was quick with an abacus
or a bon mot or advice about money;
knew how to cook   40
wild duck with rice, how to
pack a camel—and the best caterers
in town "just like old friends,"
and most of the city councilmen.
The wife of Lot   45
did what she thought
fitting and appropriate
for the wife of a public figure
and a pillar of the community.

       And the gods ran along the desert   50
       And a voice echoed across the stones.

Also, the forenamed woman kept
the books from "my schoolgirl days"
at the Temple. She remembered
learning how to pray,   55
and the philosophers, taught
by an old and frightening priest
at the gilded knees of an idol.
"Someday I'll get back to
them," she would say.   60

The wife of Lot
had two pretty daughters,
"the very image of their mother";
they were sent, like the mother,
to the Temple school, the very best,   65
and were taught French
and the philosophers, and could
quite intelligently discuss
"the name of God" or, alternatively,

"the common good."   70
                    They were only young girls,
of course; they liked best to laugh
and they were beautifully dressed
and were like all girls silly.
                    She asked, "Who am I   75
thus to be blessed?"

And a spirit cried, "Atone, atone,"
And the wind ran along the desert stone.

Once in a generation or so,
a war or an epiphany occurs,   80
or a transformation, or a revolution,
or a waiting God stirs; a name
comes into a city, a word
is passed down—an Idea seeks
ten righteous men to save,   85
the rest, the evidently lost, to reap;
to separate those who have kept
her faith from the too far gone,
and from those who have lost
what they'd sought to keep.   90
Once in a generation
a warning is heard—

Flee, flee to the hills, flee to the valleys,
The cities. Abandon. Atone.

Lot consulted his in-laws,   95
And the two daughters wept,
And the wife of Lot packed, asking
herself, "How much should we keep?
How much can be kept?"
                    They made   100
the abandoning leap—
but you know the rest: how
Lot and his daughters fled
from that place, how they passed
the test. And how   105
a moment's recollection,
a sudden grief, a backward
glance revealed what she
had quietly foreseen: a pocky
and astringent silent thing.   110

Gerard Manley Hopkins   (1844–1889)
THE WINDHOVER:° 1918

To Christ our Lord

I caught this morning morning's minion,° king-
   dom of daylight's dauphin,° dapple-dawn-drawn Falcon, in his
   riding
Of the rolling level underneath him steady air, and striding
High there, how he rung upon the rein° of a wimpling wing
In his ecstasy! then off, off forth on swing,   5
   As a skate's heel sweeps smooth on a bow-bend: the hurl and
   gliding
Rebuffed the big wind. My heart in hiding
Stirred for a bird,—the achieve of, the mastery of the thing!

Brute beauty and valor and act, oh, air, pride, plume here
Buckle!° and the fire that breaks from thee then, a billion   10
Times told lovelier, more dangerous, O my chevalier!

No wonder of it: shéer plód makes plough down sillion°
Shine, and blue-bleak embers, ah my dear,
   Fall, gall themselves, and gash gold-vermilion.

Windhover: Sparrow-hawk, or kestrel, so named because it can hover motionless in the face of a wind.   1 *minion*: Darling, beloved.   2 *dauphin*: Prince.   4 *rung upon the rein*: An image from horse training: to hold steady at the end of a rein.   10 *Buckle*: Various possible meanings: to prepare for battle, to make a dive.   12 *sillion*: Ridge or strip between two furrows often glinting with mica.

Gerard Manley Hopkins   (1844–1889)
PIED BEAUTY 1918

Glory be to God for dappled things—
   For skies of couple-color as a brinded° cow;
     For rose-moles all in stipple upon trout that swim;
Fresh-firecoal chestnut-falls,° finches' wings;
   Landscape plotted and pieced—fold, fallow, and plough;   5
     And áll trádes, their gear and tackle and trim.

All things counter, original, spare, strange;
   Whatever is fickle, freckled (who knows how?)
     With swift, slow; sweet, sour; adazzle, dim;
He fathers-forth whose beauty is past change: 10
        Praise him.

2 *brinded*: Streaked.   4 *chestnut-falls*: Roasted chestnuts stripped of their husks.

Langston Hughes   (1902–1967)
HARLEM   1951

What happens to a dream deferred?

> Does it dry up
> like a raisin in the sun?
> Or fester like a sore—
> And then run?   5
> Does it stink like rotten meat?
> Or crust and sugar over—
> like a syrupy sweet?
>
> Maybe it just sags
> like a heavy load.   10
>
> *Or does it explode?*

Langston Hughes   (1902–1967)
THE NEGRO SPEAKS OF RIVERS   1926

I've known rivers:
I've known rivers ancient as the world and older than the flow of
   human blood in human veins.

My soul has grown deep like the rivers.

I bathed in the Euphrates when dawns were young.
I built my hut near the Congo and it lulled me to sleep.   5
I looked upon the Nile and raised the pyramids above it.
I heard the singing of the Mississippi when Abe Lincoln went down to
   New Orleans, and I've seen its muddy bosom turn all golden in
   the sunset.

I've known rivers:
Ancient, dusky rivers.

My soul has grown deep like the rivers.   10

Langston Hughes   (1902–1967)
THE WEARY BLUES   1926

Droning a drowsy syncopated tune,
Rocking back and forth to a mellow croon,
   I heard a Negro play.
Down on Lenox Avenue the other night

By the pale dull pallor of an old gas light   5
    He did a lazy sway. . . .
    He did a lazy sway. . . .
To the tune o' those Weary Blues.
With his ebony hands on each ivory key
He made that poor piano moan with melody.   10
    O Blues!
Swaying to and fro on his rickety stool
He played that sad raggy tune like a musical fool.
    Sweet Blues!
Coming from a black man's soul.   15
    O Blues!
In a deep song voice with a melancholy tone
I heard that Negro sing, that old piano moan—
    "Ain't got nobody in all this world,
    Ain't got nobody but ma self.   20
    I's gwine to quit ma frownin'
    And put ma troubles on the shelf."
Thump, thump, thump, went his foot on the floor.
He played a few chords then he sang some more—
    "I got the Weary Blues   25
    And I can't be satisfied.
    Got the Weary Blues
    And can't be satisfied—
    I ain't happy no mo'
    And I wish that I had died."   30
And far into the night he crooned that tune.
The stars went out and so did the moon.
The singer stopped playing and went to bed
While the Weary Blues echoed through his head.
He slept like a rock or a man that's dead.   35

Langston Hughes   (1902–1967)

MADAM AND THE RENT MAN   1949

The rent man knocked.
He said, Howdy-do?
I said, What
Can I do for you?
He said, You know   5
Your rent is due.

I said, Listen,
Before I'd pay

I'd go to Hades
And rot away!   10

The sink is broke,
The water don't run,
And you ain't done a thing
You promised to've done.

Back window's cracked,   15
Kitchen floor squeaks,
There's rats in the cellar,
And the attic leaks.

He said, Madam,
It's not up to me.   20
I'm just the agent,
Don't you see?

I said, Naturally,
You pass the buck.
If it's money you want   25
You're out of luck.

He said, Madam,
I ain't pleased!
I said, Neither am I.

So we agrees!   30

Langston Hughes   (1902–1967)
BALLAD OF THE LANDLORD   1951

Landlord, landlord,
My roof has sprung a leak.
Don't you 'member I told you about it
Way last week?

Landlord, landlord,   5
These steps is broken down.
When you come up yourself
It's a wonder you don't fall down.

Ten Bucks you say I owe you?
Ten Bucks you say is due?   10
Well, that's Ten Bucks more'n I'll pay you
Till you fix this house up new.

What? You gonna get eviction orders?
You gonna cut off my heat?

You gonna take my furniture and   15
Throw it in the street?

Um-huh! You talking high and mighty.
Talk on—till you get through.
You ain't gonna be able to say a word
If I land my fist on you.   20

Police! Police!
Come and get this man!
He's trying to ruin the government
And overturn the land!

Copper's whistle!   25
Patrol bell!
Arrest.

Precinct Station.
Iron cell.
Headlines in press: 30

MAN THREATENS LANDLORD

∴

TENANT HELD NO BAIL

∴

JUDGE GIVES NEGRO **90** DAYS IN COUNTY JAIL

Langston Hughes   (1902–1967)
THEME FOR ENGLISH B   1959

The instructor said,

> *Go home and write*
> *a page tonight.*
> *And let that page come out of you—*
> *Then, it will be true.*   5

I wonder if it's that simple?
I am twenty-two, colored, born in Winston-Salem.
I went to school there, then Durham, then here
to this college on the hill above Harlem.
I am the only colored student in my class.   10
The steps from the hill lead down into Harlem,
through a park, then I cross St. Nicholas,
Eighth Avenue, Seventh, and I come to the Y,

the Harlem Branch Y, where I take the elevator
up to my room, sit down, and write this page: 15

It's not easy to know what is true for you or me
at twenty-two, my age. But I guess I'm what
I feel and see and hear, Harlem, I hear you:
hear you, hear me—we two—you, me, talk on this page.
(I hear New York, too.) Me—who?   20

Well, I like to eat, sleep, drink, and be in love.
I like to work, read, learn, and understand life.
I like a pipe for a Christmas present,
or records—Bessie, bop, or Bach.
I guess being colored doesn't make me *not* like   25
the same things other folks like who are other races.
So will my page be colored that I write?
Being me, it will not be white.
But it will be
a part of you, instructor.   30
You are white—
yet a part of me, as I am a part of you.
That's American.
Sometimes perhaps you don't want to be a part of me.
Nor do I often want to be a part of you.   35
But we are, that's true!
As I learn from you,
I guess you learn from me—
although you're older—and white—
and somewhat more free.   40

This is my page for English B.

Ted Hughes   (b. 1930)
SKYLARKS   1967

I

The lark begins to go up
Like a warning
As if the globe were uneasy—

Barrel-chested for heights,
Like an Indian of the high Andes,   5

A whippet head, barbed like a hunting arrow,

But leaden
With muscle

For the struggle
Against
Earth's center.

And leaden
For ballast
In the rocketing storms of the breath.

Leaden
Like a bullet
To supplant
Life from its center.

II

Crueler than owl or eagle
A towered bird, shot through the crested head
With the command, Not die
But climb

Climb

Sing

Obedient as to death a dead thing.

III

I suppose you just gape and let your gaspings
Rip in and out through your voicebox
                          O lark

And sing inwards as well as outwards
Like a breaker of ocean milling the shingle
                          O lark

O song, incomprehensibly both ways—
Joy! Help! Joy! Help!
                          O lark

IV

You stop to rest, far up, you teeter
Over the drop

But not stopping singing

Resting only a second

Dropping just a little

Then up and up and up

Like a mouse with drowning fur

Bobbing and bobbing at the well-wall

Lamenting, mounting a little—

But the sun will not take notice
And the earth's center smiles.   45

V

My idleness curdles
Seeing the lark labor near its cloud
Scrambling
In a nightmare difficulty
Up through the nothing   50

Its feathers thrash, its heart must be drumming like a motor,
As if it were too late, too late

Dithering in ether
Its song whirls faster and faster
And the sun whirls   55

The lark is evaporating
Till my eye's gossamer snaps,
                    and my hearing floats back widely to earth.

After which the sky lies blank open
Without wings, and the earth is a folded clod.   60

Only the sun goes silently and endlessly on with the lark's song.

VI

All the dreary Sunday morning
Heaven is a madhouse
With the voices and frenzies of the larks,

Squealing and gibbering and cursing   65

Heads flung back, as I see them,
Wings almost torn off backward—far up

Like sacrifices set floating
The cruel earth's offerings

The mad earth's missionaries.   70

VII

Like those flailing flames
The lift from the fling of a bonfire
Claws dangling full of what they feed on

The larks carry their tongues to the last atom

Battering and battering their last sparks out at the limit—   75
So it's a relief, a cool breeze
When they've had enough, when they're burned out
And the sun's sucked them empty
And the earth gives them the O.K.

And they relax, drifting with changed notes   80

Dip and float, not quite sure if they may
Then they are sure and they stoop
And maybe the whole agony was for this
The plummeting dead drop

With long cutting screams buckling like razors   85

But just before they plunge into the earth

They flare and glide off low over grass, then up
To land on a wall-top, crest up,

Weightless,
Paid-up,   90
Alert,

Conscience perfect.

VIII

Manacled with blood,
Cuchulain° listened bowed,
Strapped to his pillar (not to die prone)   95
Hearing the far crow
Guiding the near lark nearer
With its blind song

"That some sorry little wight more feeble and misguided than thyself
Take thy head   100
Thine ear
And thy life's career from thee."

94 *Cuchulain*: Ancient Irish hero of the *Tain Bo Cuailgne*, epic poem. He strapped himself to
a pillar stone near the end of a great battle so he would die on his feet fighting. Cuchulain's arch-
enemy was the supernatural Morrigan, who took the shape of the crow.

Ted Hughes   (b. 1930)

PIKE   1960

Pike, three inches long, perfect
Pike in all parts, green tigering the gold.
Killers from the egg: the malevolent aged grin.
They dance on the surface among the flies.

Or move, stunned by their own grandeur,   5
Over a bed of emerald, silhouette
Of submarine delicacy and horror.
A hundred feet long in their world.

In ponds, under the heat-struck lily pads—
Gloom of their stillness: 10
Logged on last year's black leaves, watching upwards.
Or hung in an amber cavern of weeds

The jaws' hooked clamp and fangs
Not to be changed at this date;
A life subdued to its instrument;   15
The gills kneading quietly, and the pectorals.

Three we kept behind glass,
Jungled in weed: three inches, four,
And four and a half: fed fry to them—
Suddenly there were two. Finally one.   20

With a sag belly and the grin it was born with.
And indeed they spare nobody.
Two, six pounds each, over two feet long,
High and dry and dead in the willow-herb—

One jammed past its gills down the other's gullet: 25
The outside eye stared: as a vice locks—
The same iron in this eye
Though its film shrank in death.

A pond I fished, fifty yards across,
Whose lilies and muscular tench   30
Had outlasted every visible stone
Of the monastery that planted them—

Stilled legendary depth:
It was as deep as England. It held
Pike too immense to stir, so immense and old   35
That past nightfall I dared not cast

But silently cast and fished
With the hair frozen on my head
For what might move, for what eye might move.
The still splashes on the dark pond,   40

Owls hushing the floating woods
Frail on my ear against the dream
Darkness beneath night's darkness had freed,
That rose slowly toward me, watching.

Ted Hughes   (b. 1930)

EXAMINATION AT THE WOMB-DOOR   1970

Who owns these scrawny little feet?   *Death.*
Who owns this bristly scorched-looking face?   *Death.*
Who owns these still-working lungs?   *Death.*
Who owns this utility coat of muscles?   *Death.*
Who owns these unspeakable guts?   *Death.*   5
Who owns these questionable brains?   *Death.*
All this messy blood?   *Death.*
These minimum-efficiency eyes?   *Death.*
This wicked little tongue?   *Death.*
This occasional wakefulness?   *Death.*   10

Given, stolen, or held pending trial? *Held.*

Who owns the whole rainy, stony earth?   *Death.*
Who owns all of space?   *Death.*

Who is stronger than hope?   *Death.*   15
Who is stronger than the will?   *Death.*
Stronger than love?   *Death.*
Stronger than life?   *Death.*

But who is stronger than death?
                              Me, evidently.   20

Pass, Crow.°

21 *Crow*: A frequent figure in Hughes' poetry. *Crow* (1971) explores nature with Crow as a main character.

Ted Hughes   (b. 1930)

CROW'S FIRST LESSON   1970

God tried to teach Crow° how to talk.
"Love," said God. "Say, Love."
Crow gaped, and the white shark crashed into the sea
And went rolling downwards, discovering its own depth.

"No, no," said God, "Say Love. Now try it. LOVE."   5
Crow gaped, and a bluefly, a tsetse, a mosquito
Zoomed out and down
To their sundry flesh-pots.

1 *Crow*: See note to "Examination at the Womb-Door."

"A final try," said God. "Now, LOVE."
Crow convulsed, gaped, retched and   10
Man's bodiless prodigious head
Bulbed out onto the earth, with swiveling eyes,
Jabbering protest—

And Crow retched again, before God could stop him.
And woman's vulva dropped over man's neck and tightened.   15
The two struggled together on the grass.
God struggled to part them, cursed, wept—

Crow flew guiltily off.

Lynda Hull   (1954–1994)
MIDNIGHT REPORTS   1991

That's how billboards give up their promises—
they look right into your window, then whisper
sex, success. The Salem girl's smoke plume
marries the gulf between the high-rise projects,
the usual knife's edge ballet enacted nightly there   5
for the benefit of no one. It's just that
around midnight every love I've known flicks open
like a switchblade and I have to start talking,
talking to drown out the man in the radio
who instructs me I'm on the edge of a new day   10
in this city of Newark which is not a city

of roses, just one big hockshop. I can't tell you
how it labors with its grilled storefronts, air
rushing over the facts of diamonds, appliances,
the trick carnations. But you already know that.   15
The M-16 Vinnie sent—piece by piece—from Vietnam
is right where you left it the day you skipped town
with the usherette of the Paradise Triple-X Theater.
You liked the way she played her flashlight down
those rows of men, plaster angels flanked around   20
that screen. Sometimes you'd go fire rounds over
the landfill, said it felt better than crystal meth,°
a hit that leaves a trail of neon, ether.

I keep it clean, oiled, and some nights it seems
like a good idea to simply pick up that rifle   25
and hold it, because nothing's safe. You know

---

22 *meth*: Methamphetamin, a drug.

how it is: one minute you're dancing, the next you're flying
through plate glass and the whole damn town is burning
again with riots and looters, the bogus politicians.
We'd graduated that year, called the city ours,   30
a real bed of Garden State roses. I've drawn x's
over our eyes in the snapshot Vinnie took commencement
night, a line of x's over our linked hands. The quartet
onstage behind us sang a cappella°—four brothers
from Springfield Ave. spinning in sequined tuxedos,   35

palms outstretched to the crowd, the Latin girls
from Ironbound shimmering in the brief conflagration
of their beauty, before the kids, before
the welfare motels, corridors of cries and exhalations.
I wore the heels you called my blue suede shoes,   40
and you'd given yourself a new tattoo, my name across
your bicep, in honor of finishing, in honor of the future
we were arrogant enough to think would turn out right.
I was laughing in that picture, laughing when the rain
caught us later and washed the blue dye from my shoes—   45
blue, the color of bruises, of minor regrets.

34 *a cappella*: Without instrumental accompaniment.

T.R. Hummer   (b. 1950)

THE RURAL CARRIER DISCOVERS THAT LOVE IS EVERYWHERE   1982

A registered letter for the Jensens. I walk down their drive
Through the gate of their thick-hedged yard, and by God there they
    are,
On a blanket in the grass, asleep, buck-naked, honeymooners
Not married a month. I smile, turn to leave,
But can't help looking back. Lord, they're a pretty sight,   5
Both of them, tangled up in each other, easy in their skin—
It's their own front yard, after all, perfectly closed in
By privet hedge and country. Maybe they were here all night.

I want to believe they'd do that, not thinking of me
Or anyone but themselves, alone in the world   10
Of the yard with its clipped grass and fresh-picked fruit trees.
Whatever this letter says can wait. To hell with the mail.
I slip through the gate, silent as I came, and leave them
Alone. There's no one they need to hear from.

T.R. Hummer (b. 1950)

THE RURAL CARRIER STOPS TO KILL A NINE-FOOT COTTONMOUTH 1982

Lord God, I saw the son-of-a-bitch uncoil
In the road ahead of me, uncoil and squirm
For the ditch, squirm a hell of a long time.
Missed him with the car. When I got back to him, he was all
But gone, nothing left on the road but the tip-end   5
Of his tail, and that disappearing into Johnson grass.
I leaned over the ditch and saw him, balled up now, hiss.
I aimed for the mouth and shot him. And shot him again.

Then I got a good strong stick and dragged him out.
He was long and evil, thick as the top of my arm.   10
There are things in this world a man can't look at without
Wanting to kill. Don't ask me why. I was calm
Enough, I thought. But I felt my spine
Squirm suddenly. I admit it. It was mine.

Richard Jackson (b. 1946)

BENEDICTION 1990

Every Angel is terrifying.
          —Rilke

I'd even given you part in my shared fear:
This personal responsibility
For a whole world's disease that is our nightmare.
          —Sidney Keyes

It is not easy to live on this earth as an angel,
to live as Pascal lamented, between two worlds, one
too large to walk out of, the second too small to enter.°
My subject is terror. The place is Split, Yugoslavia,
where I'm sitting between two ages in the outdoor café   5
beside Diocletian's° Palace. The rocky light of evening
catches the top of Marjan peninsula near the Meštrović°

2–3 *to live . . . to enter:* Blaise Pascal (1623–1662), French philosopher and mathematician. *Diocletian:* (245–313 A.D.) Roman emperor born in Dalmatia, Yugoslavia. He helped revive the old religion and persecuted Christians. He assumed the role of a god and revived ancient ceremonies and rituals.   7 *Meštrović:* Ivan Meštrović (1883–1962), Yugoslav sculptor. He became a U.S. citizen in 1952.

gallery where the sculptor's figures endure whatever
terrifying visions seem to have filled the empty space
around them. I am watching the young men strut for   10
girls along the Totova Obala centuries after the emperor
but only a few years after Meštrović escaped the Nazis
who still haunt these ruins. I'm thinking of his *Angel
With Flute,* a small wooden figure with no hips at all,
no halo, just tilting his head as if the tune were too   15
lamentable to play facing us directly, as if he were
blessing whatever trouble we know, the right leg
crossed over the left, a wing folding down as if it were
part of his hair, standing exposed, the pure shape
of a reed. This is not one of Milton's angels, afraid of sex,°   20
hovering around the peach orchards on the way to Trogir,°
hesitant to taste. The young men strutting are not the angels
I am thinking of either.

                    Tonight I am looking at what must be
one of earth's best angels peering out from the tabloid
someone left in a chair, the frog boy born in Peru and kept   25
alive by authorities like a tadpole. I am thinking of how
the soldiers massacred the little town of Segovia near him.
I want to bless his eyes, bulging from his forehead,
his webbed hands reaching as if he were pushing aside
a curtain. I want to bless the way he has to fight for love   30
in that small village, how he wonders what the trucks
trailing dust into the next valley must mean, how he has
to fight for attention on the front page with the snake boy
and the incredible human stump° from India supporting
his family by performing for tourists—it does not matter   35
if it is a lie—pouring his own tea, writing brief notes. I am
thinking of the small skeleton° I saw once in the Last Chance
Saloon, Tombstone, Arizona, the lizard creature with its glued
head, almost human, tilted up from under the glass as if
it did not know which world it had come from or which   40
it should enter. Here, where the darkness begins
like ground fog, rising up from the water, Diocletian tried
to make himself a god, rising with the darkness. I am
thinking of the way he spent his last years here, afraid
of disease and assassins, afraid for his daughter's future,   45
afraid his wife would become a Christian, walking

20–21 *Milton's angels. . . . Trogir:* Reference to the Archangel Raphael who in Book V of *Paradise Lost* blushed when Adam asked if the angels enjoyed sexual intercourse (they did).   34 *human stump:* Beggars in India often parade their own and their children's deformities to get money.
37 *small skeleton:* Of a lizard, but because it is amphibious it spans two worlds.

this street dreaming, like one of these young men, perhaps,
afraid to return to Rome, afraid to die here alone.°

I pull my jacket around me, entering the lives I imagine.
In the morning I will go to the market he might have,   50
I will buy a little cheese and wine, a little fruit and bread,
I will kick a soccer ball with a few children again and they
will want their favorite stories, Beatrix Potter,° though I will not
tell them how she spent thirty years locked in a room,
how she had supper sent up by her parents, how she lived   55
as lonely as this emperor, capturing small animals to draw
or reinvent before they died. What is terror but a way
of remembering what we lose? I can imagine Diocletian
touching one of these walls, knowing that beyond them
a bird flies across a farmer's path changing the course of   60
a whole day he will never know, a wife will weep for
her legionnaire or sailor, someone else will buy figs
or oranges, or a vessel filled with wine and spices will
dock carrying a disease no one will suspect for days.

I am beginning to suspect there is no limit to the terror we endure. 65
For a while now I have been thinking of Mary, the circus
elephant who crushed a man to death and so was hanged
in Erwin, Tennessee, Sept. 13, 1916. In one picture, hanging
from a derrick and chain, she looks out like the frog boy,
and I want to bless her, bless her trust as they lowered   70
the chains, bless her swaying gently just before they raised
her, bless the way she tilts her head like Meštrović's angel.

I am tilting my own head now, catching the last few
grains of light approaching with the harbor white caps.
I am tilting my head the way Keyes° described the drowned   75
sailors, the lucky ones who washed into the harbor at Bordeaux
or Marseilles, who faced the moon or lovers they abandoned.
I am worrying with Keyes *what important life of the world*
goes on under water, how we stand between it and the sky
like a dead flower in a book, and I am remembering   80
Mike Connally, our left fielder, who washed up on the shore of
the Tennessee river he chose as his death, and Andy Harris,
our right fielder, who, terrified by some secret demon,
locked the door and knifed himself to death a few weeks ago
in Houston, Texas. These were the angels of the outfield,   85

---

48 *alone*: Pascal said, "We all die alone."   53 *Beatrix Potter*: 1866–1943; English writer and
illustrator of children's books dealing with small creatures like mice and rabbits who behave an-
thropomorphically.   75 *Keyes*: Sidney Keyes, (1922–1943), English poet.

tilting their heads toward the sky, these were the angels
who caught the fly balls, who made the long throws home while
I watched from center field, while I watch now—Oh angel
of death—wondering if I'm next. I am thinking of Keyes,
how he wrote the day he died, not yet 21, that he wanted   90
to make an art of love, I am wondering what happened
to his last poems, to whatever dreams he left that night
to face the German advance in a desert with a few friends.
Here, in Split, the Germans left only a few scattered dreams,
you can see them still, sitting on a park bench, these dreams,   95
with no bodies left, only souls, looking over a chessboard
and through themselves as Milton's bodiless angels might do,
they are so thin. Some nights Keyes would hum an aria
from Rimski-Korsakov's *The Snow Maiden*,° imagining
his dear Renee in her place, imagining her heart, too,   100
might melt, consumed by the flames of a lost love,
imagining himself to be the young composer, mourned
by lovers he'd forgotten or abandoned. I am tilting my head
to the memory of Keyes, to the memory of the Snow Maiden,
trying to understand why Andy Harris would lock himself in,   105
why Beatrix Potter was content with her prison, why
even the great Diocletian made his own prison with the rocky
light of this shore.
                      I am tilting my head to look out
across the harbor, half expecting to see Byron° on his way   110
to Greece, *between two worlds life hovers like a star*,
he wrote, as his own life vanished the way the fishermen's
lights do, clearing the point, knowing, near the end,
what a terrible truth his life had become. What can we do
to not lose the world we have? We leave a few rearguard   115
dreams to protect ourselves against whatever terror betrays us,
what the frog boy must do—dear child, trying to reach
his way out of that picture—what Diocletian could not do,
frightened once by a bird trapped in the great hall,
a Roman legend that meant death, the descendants of   120
those same birds nesting in the ivy above me—what I hear
now, calling them all back, these angels, dear Mike, dear Andy,
blessed angels of memory—calling them across the dark water,
tilting my head for their terrible truth, for loss and for love,

---

99 *The Snow Maiden*: Reference to fairy image that lures people into a world of frozen time.
Nikolai Rimsky-Korsakov (1844–1908) produced his opera *The Snow Maiden* in 1880.
110 *Byron*: George Gordon, Lord Byron (in this volume), who exiled himself to Greece once
his incestuous affair with his sister became public. Byron died on his way to fight for Greek independence.

tilting my head toward that dark world between worlds   125
that no snow maiden with a heart of ice, no dream, no terror,
no angel of earth, could ever abandon or betray.

Elizabeth Jennings   (b. 1926)

FRAGMENT FOR THE DARK   1977

Let it not come near me, let it not
Fold round or over me. One weak hand
Clutches a foot of air, asks the brisk buds
To suffer grey winds, spear through
Fog I feel in me. Give me the magic   5
To see grounded starlings, their polish
As this threat of all-day night. Mind, mind
In me, make thoughts candles to light me
Out of the furthest reach of possible nights.
Lantern me, stars, if I look up through wet hands,   10
Show assurance in blurred shining. I have
Put every light in the house on.
May their filaments last till true morning.

Elizabeth Jennings   (b. 1926)

THE CHILD'S STORY   1985

When I was small and they talked about love I laughed
But I ran away and I hid in a tall tree
Or I lay in asparagus beds
But I still listened.
The blue dome sang with the wildest birds   5
And the new sun sang in the idle noon
But then I heard love, love, rung from the steeples, each belfry,
And I was afraid and I watched the cypress trees
Join the deciduous chestnuts and oaks in a crowd of shadows
And then I shivered and ran and ran to the tall   10
White house with the green shutters and dark red door
And I cried "Let me in even if you must love me"
And they came and lifted me up and told me the name
Of the near and the far stars,
And so my first love was.   15

Elizabeth Jennings   (b. 1926)
WONDER   1975

(Homage to Wallace Stevens)°

> Wonder exerts itself now as the sky
> Holds back a crescent moon, contains the stars.
> So we are painters of a yesterday
> Cold and decisive. We are feverish
> With meditations of a Winter Law   5
> Though Spring was brandished at us for a day.
>
> Citizens of climate we depend
> Not on the comfortable clock, the warm
> Cry of a morning song, but on the shape
> Of hope, the heralding imagination,   10
> The sanguine making and the lonely rites
> We exercise in space we leave alone.
>
> Prophets may preside and they will choose
> Clouds for a throne. The background to their speech
> Will be those fiery peaks a painter gives   15
> As a composer shares an interval,
> As poet pauses, holding sound away
> From wood, as worshippers draw back from gods.

Wallace Stevens: Included in this collection; see p. 987. Stevens was one of the most respected modernist poets.

June Jordan   (b. 1936)
LETTER TO THE LOCAL POLICE   1977–1980

Dear Sirs:

I have been enjoying the law and order of our
community throughout the past three months since
my wife and I, our two cats, and miscellaneous
photographs of the six grandchildren belonging to   5
our previous neighbors (with whom we were very
close) arrived in Saratoga Springs which is clearly
prospering under your custody

Indeed, until yesterday afternoon and despite my
vigilant casting about, I have been unable to discover   10

a single instance of reasons for public-spirited concern,
much less complaint

You may easily appreciate, then, how it is that
I write to your office, at this date, with utmost
regret for the lamentable circumstances that force   15
my hand

Speaking directly to the issue of moment:

I have encountered a regular profusion of certain
unidentified roses, growing to no discernible purpose,
and according to no perceptible control, approximately   20
one quarter mile west of the Northway, on the southern
side

To be specific, there are practically thousands of
the aforementioned abiding in perpetual near riot
of wild behavior, indiscriminate coloring, and only   25
the Good Lord Himself can say what diverse soliciting
of promiscuous cross-fertilization

As I say, these roses, no matter what the apparent
background, training, tropistic tendencies, age,
or color, do not demonstrate the least inclination   30
toward categorization, specified allegiance, resolute
preference, consideration of the needs of others, nor
any other minimal traits of decency

May I point out that I did not assiduously seek out
this colony, as it were, and that these certain   35
unidentified roses remain open to viewing even by
children, with or without suitable supervision

(My wife asks me to append a note as regards the
seasonal but nevertheless seriously licentious
phenomenon of honeysuckle under the moon that one may   40
apprehend at the corner of Nelson and Main

However, I have recommended that she undertake direct
correspondence with you, as regards this: yet
another civic disturbance in our midst)

I am confident that you will devise and pursue   45
appropriate legal response to the roses in question
If I may aid your efforts in this respect, please
do not hesitate to call me into consultation

                              Respectfully yours,

June Jordan   (b. 1936)

A RIGHT-TO-LIFER IN GRAND FORKS, NORTH DAKOTA   1977–1980

For Sandy Donaldson

We stayed.
Through finger drifts and drifts to bury trees.
Men frozen on the road home from town.
Babies dead because the doctor could not see
the house for the snow.   5
Women dead from death.
Children trained to trust the first door the nearest
hand.
River flood.
Mud.   10
Wind down from Canada.
Blizzards from hell.
Winter long as life.
We stayed.
After the Buffalo.   15
After the Indians.
After the westward hustling types.
After the sunrise.
We stayed.
On land big and empty as the entire sky.   20
We stayed.
Sugar beets.
Barley.
Sunflowers.
Wheat.   25
Potatoes.
Sure:
We stayed.
Right to life?
Hell, yeah!   30
What you suppose this trouble's been
all about?

Jenny Joseph   (b. 1932)

WARNING   1974

When I am an old woman I shall wear purple
With a red hat which doesn't go, and doesn't suit me.
And I shall spend my pension on brandy and summer gloves

And satin sandals, and say we've no money for butter.
I shall sit down on the pavement when I'm tired   5
And gobble up samples in shops and press alarm bells
And run my stick along the public railings
And make up for the sobriety of my youth.
I shall go out in my slippers in the rain
And pick the flowers in other people's gardens   10
And learn to spit.

You can wear terrible shirts and grow more fat
And eat three pounds of sausages at a go
Or only bread and pickle for a week
And hoard pens and pencils and beermats and things in boxes.   15

But now we must have clothes that keep us dry
And pay our rent and not swear in the street
And set a good example for the children.
We must have friends to dinner and read the papers.

But maybe I ought to practise a little now?   20
So people who know me are not too shocked and surprised
When suddenly I am old, and start to wear purple.

Donald Justice   (b. 1925)

A MAP OF LOVE   1959

Your face more than others' faces
Maps the half-remembered places
I have come to while I slept—
Continents a dream had kept
Secret from all waking folk   5
Till to your face I awoke,
And remembered then the shore,
And the dark interior.

WINDOW ON

Romantic Poetry

The Romantic Movement affected all poetry written in English and European languages from the beginning of the French Revolution in 1789 to 1832, the date of the first great liberal reform bill in England's parliament. It has been characterized as a political and artistic development rooted in the development of democracy, the liberalization of penal laws and work laws, and the expansion of economies in North America, South America, and Europe. There is no one brand of Romantic poetry, but you can connect it with experimentation in language and form, an interest in dramatic situations, and a new attitude toward the individual in society. The most famous English Romantics are William Blake, Samuel Taylor Coleridge, William Wordsworth, John Keats, Percy Bysshe Shelley, and George Gordon, Lord Byron, all represented in this collection. Walt Whitman is the most celebrated American Romantic poet.

Not all Romantic poets wrote alike; however, they generally exalted inspiration, deep emotional response, and poetic feeling. The previous age, now called neoclassical because of its love of Greek and Roman art, had put great value in reason, planning, and emotionless detachment. The Romantics believed passion was more important, and they sometimes lived—as did Byron— as if they were heroes in their own poetry. Byron died in the Mediterranean while preparing to fight for Greek independence against the Turks. Blake, a religious enthusiast, saw visions throughout his life and combined visual art with his poetry. Shelley abandoned his wife, who later committed suicide, and married Mary Wollstonecraft Godwin, the author of *Frankenstein*. Herself a Romantic, Mary died in childbirth. Keats died of tuberculosis at twenty-six. All these figures are models for the Romantic poet, who drank life deeply, expressed deep emotions, and wrote rapturous lyrics and brooding narratives.

Romanticism implies the following views and practices:

- An effort to make poetic language resemble everyday speech
- A move away from rhymed couplets to more inventive stanzas, often rhymed but imaginatively organic
- The inclusion of myth, personal biography, and folklore
- Praise of nature as a guide to human behavior
- An emphasis on individualism
- An interest in the supernatural
- Emotional expressiveness in an effort to transcend the ordinary

Not all Romantic poets were concerned with political movements, but Wordsworth and Shelley were deeply stirred by the French Revolution and saw the coming democracy as welcome and necessary.

A look at the list above tells us that the Romantics left a legacy, since most modern poets tend to follow their path. For that reason, many critics still see contemporary literature as fundamentally Romantic. Such a view is reasonable: Asian, African, and virtually all modern poets have been affected by the Romantics' work and follow their practices to some extent.

William Wordsworth's "Lines Composed a Few Miles above Tintern Abbey" is a long poem that is in many ways an epitome of English Romanticism. It is rooted in a deep personal response to a familiar landscape, whose waters, cliffs, and trees stir Wordsworth's emotional depths as well as his imagination when he describes a hermit's cave in the landscape. He contrasts the vision of the countryside with the "din / Of towns and cities," and feels that in a moment of repose "We see into the life of things." In the fourth stanza he meditates on the young person he was five years before. His connection with nature then was more as a young animal, and now things have changed:

> I have learned
> To look on nature, not as in the hour
> Of thoughtless youth, but hearing oftentimes
> The still, sad music of humanity,
> Nor harsh nor grating, though of ample power
> To chasten and subdue. And I have felt
> A presence that disturbs me with the joy
> Of elevated thoughts; a sense sublime
> Of something far more deeply interfused,
> Whose dwelling is the light of setting suns.
>   (lines 88–97)

For some readers these lines imply a pantheism, but they may express Wordsworth's sense that humanity and nature are connected in a godlike harmony, an insight that is more likely to come from a meditation in the countryside than in the heart of the city. This kind of celebration of spiritual joy is often seen as the heart of the Romantic Movement.

Reading

Abrams, M. H. *The Mirror and the Lamp*. New York: Oxford University Press, 1953.

Cooke, Michael. *The Romantic Will*. New Haven: Yale University Press, 1976.

Frye, Northrop. *A Study of English Romanticism*. New York: Random House, 1968.

Kermode, Frank. *The Romantic Image*. London: Routledge and Kegan Paul, 1957.

John Keats (1795–1821)

ODE TO A NIGHTINGALE 1820

I

My heart aches, and a drowsy numbness pains
  My sense, as though of hemlock I had drunk,
Or emptied some dull opiate to the drains
    One minute past, and Lethe-wards° had sunk:
'Tis not through envy of thy happy lot,   5
  But being too happy in thine happiness,—
    That thou, light-wingèd Dryad of the trees,
      In some melodious plot
Of beechen green, and shadows numberless,
    Singest of summer in full-throated ease.   10

II

O, for a draught of vintage! that hath been
Cooled a long age in the deep-delvèd earth,
Tasting of Flora° and the country green,
  Dance, and Provençal song, and sunburnt mirth!
O for a beaker full of the warm South,   15
  Full of the true, the blushful Hippocrene,
    With beaded bubbles winking at the brim,
      And purple-stainèd mouth;
That I might drink, and leave the world unseen,
    And with thee fade away into the forest dim: 20

III

Fade far away, dissolve, and quite forget
  What thou among the leaves hast never known,
The weariness, the fever, and the fret
  Here, where men sit and hear each other groan;
Where palsy shakes a few, sad, last gray hairs,   25
  Where youth grows pale, and specter-thin, and dies;
    Where but to think is to be full of sorrow
      And leaden-eyed despairs,
Where Beauty cannot keep her lustrous eyes,
    Or new Love pine at them beyond tomorrow.   30

---

4 *Lethe-wards*: Toward Lethe, in Greek mythology the river of forgetfulness, oblivion.
13 *Flora*: Roman goddess of flowers.

IV

Away! away! for I will fly to thee,
   Not charioted by Bacchus and his pards,°
But on the viewless wings of Poesy,
   Though the dull brain perplexes and retards:
Already with thee! tender is the night,   35
   And haply the Queen-Moon is on her throne,
      Clustered around by all her starry Fays;
         But here there is no light,
   Save what from heaven is with the breezes blown
      Through verdurous glooms and winding mossy ways.   40

V

I cannot see what flowers are at my feet,
   Nor what soft incense hangs upon the boughs,
But, in embalmèd darkness, guess each sweet
   Wherewith the seasonable month endows
The grass, the thicket, and the fruit-tree wild;   45
   White hawthorn, and the pastoral eglantine;
      Fast fading violets covered up in leaves;
         And mid-May's eldest child,
   The coming musk-rose, full of dewy wine,
      The murmurous haunt of flies on summer eves.   50

VI

Darkling I listen; and, for many a time
   I have been half in love with easeful Death,
Called him soft names in many a musèd rhyme,
   To take into the air my quiet breath;
Now more than ever seems it rich to die,   55
   To cease upon the midnight with no pain,
      While thou art pouring forth thy soul abroad
         In such an ecstasy!
   Still wouldst thou sing, and I have ears in vain—
      To thy high requiem become a sod.   60

VII

Thou wast not born for death, immortal Bird!
   No hungry generations tread thee down;
The voice I hear this passing night was heard
   In ancient days by emperor and clown:
Perhaps the self-same song that found a path   65

---

32 *Bacchus and his pards.* The Greek god of wine and his leopards (which pulled his chariot).

Through the sad heart of Ruth,° when, sick for home,
    She stood in tears amid the alien corn;
        The same that oft-times hath
Charmed magic casements, opening on the foam
    Of perilous seas, in faery lands forlorn.   70

VIII

Forlorn! the very word is like a bell
    To toll me back from thee to my sole self!
Adieu! the fancy cannot cheat so well
    As she is famed to do, deceiving elf.
Adieu! adieu! thy plaintive anthem fades   75
    Past the near meadows, over the still stream,
        Up the hill-side; and now 'tis buried deep
            In the next valley-glades:
    Was it a vision, or a waking dream?
        Fled is that music:—Do I wake or sleep?   80

---

66 *Ruth*: In the biblical Book of Ruth, the heroine leaves her home to work in a strange land.

John Keats   (1795–1821)
LA BELLE DAME SANS MERCI°   1820

A Ballad

I

O what can ail thee, knight at arms,
    Alone and palely loitering?
The sedge has withered from the lake,
    And no birds sing.

II

O what can ail thee, knight at arms,   5
    So haggard and so woe-begone?
The squirrel's granary is full,
    And the harvest's done.

III

I see a lily on thy brow
    With anguish moist and fever dew,   10
And on thy cheeks a fading rose
    Fast withereth too.

La Belle Dame sans Merci: "The Beautiful Lady without Pity."

IV

    I met a lady in the meads,
        Full beautiful, a fairy's child;
    Her hair was long, her foot was light,   15
        And her eyes were wild.

V

    I made a garland for her head,
        And bracelets too, and fragrant zone;°
    She looked at me as she did love,
        And made sweet moan.   20

VI

    I set her on my pacing steed,
        And nothing else saw all day long,
    For sidelong would she bend, and sing
        A fairy's song.

VII

    She found me roots of relish sweet,   25
        And honey wild, and manna dew,
    And sure in language strange she said—
        "I love thee true."

VIII

    She took me to her elfin grot,
        And there she wept, and sighed full sore,   30
    And there I shut her wild wild eyes
        With kisses four.

IX

    And there she lullèd me asleep,
        And there I dreamed—Ah! woe betide!
    The latest dream I ever dreamed   35
        On the cold hill's side.

X

    I saw pale kings, and princes too,
        Pale warriors, death pale were they all;
    They cried—"La belle dame sans merci
        Hath thee in thrall!"   40

18 *zone*: Belt, girdle.

XI

I saw their starved lips in the gloam
  With horrid warning gapèd wide,
And I awoke and found me here
    On the cold hill's side.

XII

And this is why I sojourn here,   45
  Alone and palely loitering,
Though the sedge is withered from the lake,
  And no birds sing.

John Keats (1795–1821)

WHEN I HAVE FEARS THAT I MAY CEASE TO BE (1818; 1848)

When I have fears that I may cease to be
  Before my pen has gleaned my teeming brain,
Before high piled books, in charactery,
  Hold like rich garners the full ripened grain;
When I behold, upon the night's starred face,   5
  Huge cloudy symbols of a high romance,
And think that I may never live to trace
  Their shadows, with the magic hand of chance;
And when I feel, fair creature of an hour,
  That I shall never look upon thee more,   10
Never have relish in the fairy power
  Of unreflecting love;—then on the shore
Of the wide world I stand alone, and think
Till love and fame to nothingness do sink.

John Keats (1795–1821)

ON FIRST LOOKING INTO CHAPMAN'S HOMER° 1816

Much have I traveled in the realms of gold,
  And many goodly states and kingdoms seen;
  Round many western islands have I been
Which bards in fealty to Apollo hold.
Oft of one wide expanse had I been told   5

Chapman's Homer: Keats had never read the Greek epic poet Homer until he read Chapman's translations.

That deep-browed Homer ruled as his demesne;
    Yet did I never breathe its pure serene°
Till I heard Chapman speak out loud and bold:
Then felt I like some watcher of the skies
    When a new planet swims into his ken;   10
Or like stout Cortez° when with eagle eyes
    He stared at the Pacific—and all his men
Looked at each other with a wild surmise—
    Silent, upon a peak in Darien.°

7 *serene*: Often interpreted to mean air; could also mean serenity, clarity, grandeur.
11 *Cortez*: A famous error; the Pacific was discovered by Balboa.   14 *Darien*: The old name
for the Isthmus of Panama.

Brigit Pegeen Kelly   (b. 1951)
YOUNG WIFE'S LAMENT   c. 1988

The mule that lived on the road
where I was married
would bray to wake the morning,
but could not wake me.
How many summers I slept   5
lost in my hair. How many
mules on how many hills singing.
Back of a deep ravine
he lived, above a small river
on a beaten patch of land.   10
I walked up in the day and walked down,
having been given nothing
else to do. The road grew no longer,
I grew no wiser, my husband
was away selling things to people who buy.   15
He went up the road, too, but
the road was full of doors for him,
the road was his belt and,
one notch at a time, he loosened it
on his way. I would sit   20
on the hill of stones and look down
on the trees, on the lake
far away with its boats and those
who ride in boats
and I could not pray. Some of us   25
have mule minds,
are foolish as sails whipping

in the wind, senseless
as sheets rolling through the fields,
some of us are not given   30
even a wheel of the tinker's cart
upon which to pray.
When I came back I pumped water
in the yard under the trees
by the fence where the cows came up,   35
but water is not wisdom
and change is not made by wishes.
Else I would have ridden something,
even a mule, over
those hills and away.   40

Dolores Kendrick   (b. 1927)

LEAH: IN FREEDOM   1989

I run away
          I keep runnin' away
                    they won't let me alone
                              they won't let me bear
my misery to the river   5
                    and out
                              over the sky
                                        or even
                                                  under the trees
in moles' holes   10
                    and wolves' caves
                              and blackberry patches
                                        with my feet
skiddin' and bleedin'
                    on the thorns   15
                              and then it rains
                                        on my run
as quick as my momma's voice
                    on the slippery road
                              to freedom.   20
They catch me
                    all the time they catch me
                              and bring me back
and whip me
                    till I'm blind and deaf   25
                              and dumb,
          and put me in the cabin
                    where the blood soak my back

like scaldin' water
                    and take me out to the fields   30
and whip me some more.

                    Oh! the sky is so big!
                    Ain't it?

                    The trees are so tall!
                    Ain't they?   35

                    The river's so wide!
                    Ain't it?

                    Don't you hear?
                    Cain't you hear

                    all that callin', Leah?   40
                    Leah's gotta go!

And I run again
          all twenty-three years of me
                              all white and black of me
all the angels in me   45
                    and the wings
                              growing out of my armpits
flapping against my thighs
                    makin' me move
                              when I can't,   50
when I don't want to,
                    when my back is so sore
                              and painful
that every flight
          makes my wings stick to my side sometimes   55
                              and keep me slow
and earthbound;
          all my momma in me.
                    So soon they catch me again
and beat me again.   60
                    That was the last time for that.
                              I lay here
on the hard floor on my back
          only place that's soft:
                    guess it's the flesh,   65
the wounds that do it,
                    guess it's the salt, too.
                              So much pain
it don't pain no more,
          only the want of freedom pains,   70

only the fear
of dyin' before I'm free.
Yesterday they took out
one of my front teeth
to identify me   75
in case I 'scape again
and now when I ain't doin'
the housework
they put me in an iron collar.
Three days they gives me   80
three days I got for my wings
to heal
but they's bent and dirty
and tattered, need washin'
they's not the same   85
don't round themselves right
somehow.
I can see the roots of trees now,
don't see the tops no more.
The mole and me   90
we's on our own.
These days I go
to my mistress' room
sew her clothes and cloaks
though the wounds be still breakin' through my shawl   95
and I be sore.
She got lots of holes
under her armpits
of her dresses: 100
that makes me shiver,
think of my momma.
Mistress say, "good mawnin', Leah"
(won't look at me)
and tell me about faith   105
and Jesus.

Galway Kinnell   (b. 1927)

WHEN ONE HAS LIVED A LONG TIME ALONE   1990

I

When one has lived a long time alone,
one refrains from swatting the fly
and lets him go, and one hesitates to strike

the mosquito, though more than willing to slap
the flesh under her, and one lifts the toad   5
from the pit too deep for him to hop out of
and carries him to the grass, without minding
the toxic urine he slicks his body with,
and one envelops, in a towel, the swift
who fell down the chimney and knocks herself   10
against the window glass and releases her outside
and watches her fly free, a life line flung at reality,
when one has lived a long time alone.

II

When one has lived a long time alone,
one grabs the snake behind the head   15
and holds him until he stops trying to stick
the orange tongue, which splits at the end
into two black filaments and jumps out
like a fire-eater's belches and has little
in common with the pimpled pink lump that shapes   20
sounds and sleeps inside the human mouth,
into one's flesh, and clamps it between his jaws,
letting the gaudy tips show, as children do
when concentrating, and as very likely
one does oneself, without knowing it,   25
when one has lived a long time alone.

III

When one has lived a long time alone,
among regrets so immense the past occupies
nearly all the room there is in consciousness,
one notices in the snake's eyes, which look back   30
without paying less attention to the future,
the first coating of the opaque milky-blue
leucoma snakes get when about to throw
their skins and become new—meanwhile continuing,
of course, to grow old—the exact *bleu passé*   35
that discolors the corneas of the blue-eyed
when they lie back at last and look for heaven,
a blurring one can see means they will never find it,
when one has lived a long time alone.

IV

When one has lived a long time alone,   40
one holds the snake near a loudspeaker disgorging

gorgeous sound and watches him crook
his forepart into four right angles
as though trying to slow down the music
flowing through him, in order to absorb it   45
like milk of paradise into the flesh,
and now a glimmering appears at his mouth,
such a drop of intense fluid as, among humans,
could form after long exciting at the tip
of the penis, and as he straightens himself out   50
he has the pathos one finds in the penis,
when one has lived a long time alone.

V

When one has lived a long time alone,
one can fall to poring upon a creature,
contrasting its eternity's-face to one's own   55
full of hours, taking note of each difference,
exaggerating it, making it everything,
until the other is utterly other, and then,
with hard effort, possibly with tongue sticking out,
going back over each one once again   60
and cancelling it, seeing nothing now
but likeness, until . . . half an hour later
one starts awake, taken aback at how eagerly
one swoons into the happiness of kinship,
when one has lived a long time alone.   65

VI

When one has lived a long time alone
and listens at morning to mourning doves
sound their *kyrie eleison,* or the small thing
spiritualizing onto one's shoulder cry "pewit-phoebe!"
or peabody-sparrows at midday send schoolboys'   70
whistlings across the field, or at dusk, undamped,
unforgiving clinks, as from stonemasons' chisels,
or on trees' backs tree frogs scratch the thighs'
needfire awake, or from the frog pond pond frogs
raise their *ave verum corpus*°—listens to those   75
who hop or fly call down upon us the mercy
of other tongues—one hears them as inner voices,
when one has lived a long time alone.

---

75 *ave verum corpus.* The priest at communion says This—"Hail the true body [of Christ]."
Kyrie eleison means *Lord have mercy on us.*

VII

When one has lived a long time alone,
one knows only consciousness consummates,   80
and as the conscious one among these others
uttering compulsory cries of being here—
the least flycatcher witching up "che-bec,"
or redheaded woodpecker clanging out his
music from a metal drainpipe, or ruffed grouse   85
drumming "thrump thrump thrump thrump-thrump-
thrump-thrump-rup-rup-rup-rup-rup-r-r-r-r-r"
through the trees, all of them in time's
unfolding trying to cry themselves into self-knowing—
one knows one is here to hear them into shining,   90
when one has lived a long time alone.

VIII

When one has lived a long time alone,
one likes alike the pig, who brooks no deferment
of gratification, and the porcupine, or thorned pig,
who enters the cellar but not the house itself   95
because of eating down the cellar stairs on the way up,
and one likes the worm, who by bunching herself together
and expanding rubs her way through the ground,
no less than the butterfly, who totters full of worry
among the day-lilies, as they darken,   100
and more and more one finds one likes
any other species better than one's own,
which has gone amok, making one self-estranged,
when one has lived a long time alone.

IX

When one has lived a long time alone,   105
sour, misanthropic, one fits to one's defiance
the satanic boast—*It is better to reign
in hell than to submit on earth*—°
and forgets one's kind, as does the snake,
who has stopped trying to escape and moves   110
at ease across one's body, slumping into its contours,
adopting its temperature, and abandons hope
of the sweetness of friendship or love
—before long can barely remember what they are—

108 *on earth*: A variant on Milton's Satan in *Paradise Lost*, who says it is better to reign in Hell than to serve in Heaven.

and covets the stillness in inorganic matter,   115
in a self-dissolution one may not know how to halt,
when one has lived a long time alone.

X

When one has lived a long time alone,
and the hermit thrush calls and there is an answer,
and the bullfrog, head half out of water, remembers   120
the exact sexual cantillations of his first spring,
and the snake slides over the threshold and disappears
among the stones, one sees they all live
to mate with their kind, and one knows,
after a long time of solitude, after the many steps taken   125
away from one's kind, toward the kingdom of strangers,
the hard prayer inside one's own singing
is to come back, if one can, to one's own,
a world almost lost, in the exile that deepens,
when one has lived a long time alone.   130

XI

When one has lived a long time alone,
one wants to live again among men and women,
to return to that place where one's ties with the human
broke, where the disquiet of death and now
also of history glimmers its firelight on faces,   135
where the gaze of the new baby looks past the gaze
of the great-granny, and where lovers speak,
on lips blowsy from kissing, that language
the same in each mouth, and like birds at daybreak
blether the song that is both earth's and heaven's,   140
until the sun has risen, and they stand
in a halo of being united: kingdom come,
when one has lived a long time alone.

Rachel Korn   (1898–1987)
KEEP HIDDEN FROM ME   1967

Translated from Yiddish by Carolyn Kizer

Keep from me all that I might comprehend!
O God, I ripen toward you in my unknowing.

The barely burgeoning leaf on the roadside tree
Limns innocence: here endeth the first lesson.

Keep from me, God, all forms of certainty: 5
The steady tread that paces off the self

And forms it, seamless, ignorant of doubt
Or failure, hell-bent for fulfilment.

To know myself: is not that the supreme disaster?
To know Thee, one must sink on trembling knees.   10

To hear Thee, only the terrified heart may truly listen;
To see Thee, only the gaze half-blind with dread.

Though the day darken, preserve my memory
From Your bright oblivion. Erase not my faulty traces.

If I aspire again to make four poor walls my house,   15
Let me pillow myself on the book of my peregrinations.

God, grant me strength to give over false happiness,
And the sense that suffering has earned us Your regard.

Elohim! Though sorrow fill me to the brim,
Let me carefully bear the cup of myself to Thee.   20

Mazisi Kunene   (b. 1930)

FROM THE RAVAGES OF LIFE WE CREATE   1970

And the suns are torn from the cord of the skies
And fall to the ground humiliated by the cluster of leaves.
The eternal feet travel on on their journey.
The bars of iron pierce through, feeding on their blood.
The wedding party walks proudly   5
And catches a glimpse of the moon disintegrating.
Beyond this aberration in the land of the hostile winds,
The tall woman is seized by madness.
She covers her face with a black cloth
Imitating the dance of the ecstatic children.   10
Then the ruined man of time fondles her
Until she gives birth, and gives birth to the infants of stone.
We are their kin whose ribs are wide with their power,
We are one with those who wander everywhere.
A man enters and marks down our generation   15
And tells us how suddenly summer has come
And makes us sing though our hearts are bleeding

Knowing how because of us,
We who are the locusts with broken wings,
Our shadows shelter the earth from the sun.   20

Mazisi Kunene   (b. 1930)
PLACE OF DREAMS   1970

There is a place
Where the dream is dreaming us,
We who are the shepherds of the stars.
It stands towering as tall as the mountains
Spreading its fire over the sun   5
Until when we take one great stride
We speed with the eagle on our journey.
It is the eagle that plays its wings on our paths,
Wakening another blind dream.
Together with other generations hereafter   10
They shall dream them like us.
When they wake on their journeys they will say:
Someone, somewhere, is dreaming us, in the ruins.

Mazisi Kunene   (b. 1930)
THE POLITICAL PRISONER   1970

I desired to talk
And talk with words as numerous as sands,
The other side of the wire,
The other side of the fortress of stone.

I found a widow travelling   5
Passing the prisoners with firewood.
It is this woman who forbade me to sleep
Who filled me with dreams.

The dream is always the same.
It turns on an anchor   10
Until it finds a place to rest:
It builds its cobwebs from the hours.

One day someone arrives and opens the gate.
The sun explodes its fire
Spreading its flames over the earth,   15
Touching the spring of mankind.

Behind us there are mountains
Where the widow is abandoned.
She remains there unable to give birth
Priding herself only in the shadows of yesterdays.   20

Philip Larkin   (1922–1992)

FAITH HEALING   1979

Slowly the women file to where he stands
Upright in rimless glasses, silver hair,
Dark suit, white collar. Stewards tirelessly
Persuade them onwards to his voice and hands,
Within whose warm spring rain of loving care   5
Each dwells some twenty seconds. *Now, dear child,*
What's wrong, the deep American voice demands,
And, scarcely pausing, goes into a prayer
Directing God about this eye, that knee.
Their heads are clasped abruptly; then, exiled   10

Like losing thoughts, they go in silence; some
Sheepishly stray, not back into their lives
Just yet; but some stay stiff, twitching and loud
With deep hoarse tears, as if a kind of dumb
And idiot child within them still survives   15
To re-awake at kindness, thinking a voice
At last calls them alone, that hands have come
To lift and lighten; and such joy arrives
Their thick tongues blort, their eyes squeeze grief, a crowd
Of huge unheard answers jam and rejoice—   20

What's wrong! Moustached in flowered frocks they shake:
By now, all's wrong. In everyone there sleeps
A sense of life lived according to love.
To some it means the difference they could make
By loving others, but across most it sweeps   25
As all they might have done had they been loved.
That nothing cures. An immense slackening ache,
As when, thawing, the rigid landscape weeps,
Spreads slowly through them—that, and the voice above
Saying *Dear child*, and all time has disproved.   30

Philip Larkin   (1922–1992)

CHURCH GOING   1955

Once I am sure there's nothing going on
I step inside, letting the door thud shut.
Another church: matting, seats, and stone,
And little books; sprawlings of flowers, cut
For Sunday, brownish now; some brass and stuff   5

Up at the holy end; the small neat organ;
And a tense, musty, unignorable silence,
Brewed God knows how long. Hatless, I take off
My cycle-clips in awkward reverence,

Move forward, run my hand around the font.   10
From where I stand, the roof looks almost new—
Cleaned, or restored? Someone would know: I don't.
Mounting the lectern, I peruse a few
Hectoring large-scale verses, and pronounce
"Here endeth" much more loudly than I'd meant.   15
The echoes snigger briefly. Back at the door
I sign the book, donate an Irish sixpence,
Reflect the place was not worth stopping for.

Yet stop I did: in fact I often do,
And always end much at a loss like this,   20
Wondering what to look for; wondering, too,
When churches fall completely out of use
What we shall turn them into, if we shall keep
A few cathedrals chronically on show,
Their parchment, plate and pyx° in locked cases,   25
And let the rest rent-free to rain and sheep.
Shall we avoid them as unlucky places?

Or, after dark, will dubious women come
To make their children touch a particular stone;
Pick simples° for a cancer; or on some   30
Advised night see walking a dead one?
Power of some sort or other will go on
In games, in riddles, seemingly at random;
But superstition, like belief, must die,
And what remains when disbelief has gone?   35
Grass, weedy pavement, brambles, buttress, sky,

A shape less recognizable each week,
A purpose more obscure. I wonder who
Will be the last, the very last, to seek
This place for what it was; one of the crew   40
That tap and jot and know what rood-lofts° were?
Some ruin-bibber, randy for antique,°
Or Christmas-addict, counting on a whiff
Of gown-and-bands and organ-pipes and myrrh?
Or will he be my representative,   45

---

25 *pyx:* Box for communion wafers.   30 *simples:* Herbs for medicine.   41 *rood-lofts:* Where
the crucifix is erected in a church.   42 *Some ruin-bibber, randy for antique:* Someone who
"drinks in" ruins, lusts for antiques.

Bored, uninformed, knowing the ghostly silt
Dispersed, yet tending to this cross of ground
Through suburb scrub because it held unspilt
So long and equably what since is found
Only in separation—marriage, and birth,   50
And death, and thoughts of these—for whom was built
This special shell? For, though I've no idea
What this accoutred frowsty barn is worth,
It pleases me to stand in silence here;

A serious house on serious earth it is,   55
In whose blent air all our compulsions meet,
Are recognized, and robed as destinies.
And that much never can be obsolete,
Since someone will forever be surprising
A hunger in himself to be more serious,   60
And gravitating with it to this ground,
Which, he once heard, was proper to grow wise in,
If only that so many dead lie round.

Denise Levertov   (b. 1923)

O TASTE AND SEE   1964

The world is
not with us enough.°
O taste and see

the subway Bible poster said,
meaning *The Lord,* meaning   5
if anything all that lives
to the imagination's tongue,

grief, mercy, language,
tangerine, weather, to
breathe them, bite,   10
savor, chew, swallow, transform

into our flesh our
deaths, crossing the street, plum, quince,
living in the orchard and being
hungry, and plucking   15
the fruit.

1–2 *The world . . . enough:* A play on Wordsworth's poem "The World Is Too Much with Us,"
p. 987.

Denise Levertov   (b. 1923)
MATINS   1961

I

The authentic! Shadows of it
sweep past in dreams, one could say imprecisely,
evoking the almost-silent
ripping apart of giant
sheets of cellophane. No.   5
It thrusts up close. Exactly in dreams
it has you off-guard, you
recognize it before you have time.
For a second before waking
the alarm bell is a red conical hat, it   10
takes form.

II

The authentic! I said
rising from the toilet seat.
The radiator in rhythmic knockings
spoke of the rising steam.   15
The authentic, I said
breaking the handle of my hairbrush as I
brushed my hair in
rhythmic strokes: That's it,
that's joy, it's always   20
a recognition, the known
appearing fully itself, and
more itself than one knew.

III

The new day rises
as heat rises,   25
knocking in the pipes
with rhythms it seizes for its own
to speak of its invention—
the real, the new-laid
egg whose speckled shell   30
the poet fondles and must break
if he will be nourished.

IV

A shadow painted where
yes, a shadow must fall.

The cow's breath   35
not forgotten in the mist, in the
words. Yes,
verisimilitude draws up
heat in us, zest
to follow through,   40
follow through,
follow
transformations of day
in its turning, in its becoming.

V

Stir the holy grains, set   45
the bowls on the table and
call the child to eat.

While we eat we think,
as we think an undercurrent
of dream runs through us   50
faster than thought
towards recognition.

Call the child to eat,
send him off, his mouth
tasting of toothpaste, to go down   55
into the ground, into a roaring train
and to school.

His cheeks are pink
his black eyes hold his dreams, he has left
forgetting his glasses.   60

Follow down the stairs at a clatter
to give them to him and save
his clear sight.

Cold air
comes in at the street door.   65

VI

The authentic! It rolls
just out of reach, beyond
running feet and
stretching fingers, down
the green slope and into   70
the black waves of the sea.
Speak to me, little horse, beloved,

tell me
how to follow the iron ball,
how to follow through to the country   75
beneath the waves
to the place where I must kill you and you step out
of your bones and flystrewn meat
tall, smiling, renewed,
formed in your own likeness   80

VII

Marvelous Truth, confront us
at every turn,
in every guise, iron ball,
egg, dark horse, shadow,
cloud   85
of breath on the air,

dwell
in our crowded hearts
our steaming bathrooms, kitchens full of
things to be done, the   90
ordinary streets.

Thrust close your smile
that we know you, terrible joy.

Jan Heller Levi   (b. 1954)

SEX IS NOT IMPORTANT   1990

I

Sex is not important. That's why
we have conversation. In the dark,
the unforgivable dark, it's hope
that's important, and hope
is something I do alone.   5

II

So here comes the unfortunate part.
Sisters, forgive me:
what we always love about the other
man is that he doesn't
care;   10
he's got an itch he's going to scratch;

he's going to lick you like a puppy
hungry for salt;
he's going to cry out and he's going to fall,
sweating and flushed and finished,   15
beside your trembling.
He's going to keep his eyes open and his mouth shut.
And he's going to leave you, not knowing what he's left.

III

It's not your body, is it,
that glows in the night,   20
and it's not me,
that woman in that hotel room,
doing all that wanting?

It can't be. I'm too smart
for all this;   25
too smart to disturb
those hospital corners
with all this unaccountable thrashing.

It must be my mind.
It's oozing.   30
It's evaluated the situation
and suggested
that my back should arch,
arch, arch. Oh!,

you're so interesting.   35
When we're ourselves
again, we really should
talk about this.
Have you ever seen
those teenagers clenched   40

on street corners
and repetitively touching lips?
I think it's because
they have nothing to say.

But you and I   45
have so much in common,
as I seem to recall.

IV

Sex is not important. That's why
we have everything else: friends,

husband, work, books, politics,   50
postcards, art, and poetry.
That's why, when the telephone rings,
we answer. That's why
we wake up in the morning,
sick to our stomach with dreams,   55
and ready to live.

V

That's why I have my circle game:
no one here but me and my abstract fame.

Everything unspoken
an endearment.   60

A woman's nipple—mine—
finds a finger.

Amy Lowell   (1874–1925)
VENUS TRANSIENS°   1919

Tell me,
Was Venus more beautiful
Than you are,
When she topped
The crinkled waves,   5
Drifting shoreward
On her plaited shell?
Was Botticelli's vision
Fairer than mine;
And were the painted rosebuds   10
He tossed his lady,
Of better worth
Than the words I blow about you
To cover your too great loveliness
As with a gauze   15
Of misted silver?
For me,
You stand poised
In the blue and buoyant air,
Cinctured by bright winds,   20
Treading the sunlight.

Venus Transiens: See discussion of this poem on p. 716.

And the waves which precede you
Ripple and stir
The sands at my feet.

Robert Lowell   (1917–1977)
SKUNK HOUR°   1959

(For Elizabeth Bishop)°

Nautilus Island's hermit
heiress still lives through winter in her Spartan cottage;
her sheep still graze above the sea.
Her son's a bishop. Her farmer
is first selectman in our village;   5
she's in her dotage.

Thirsting for
the hierarchic privacy
of Queen Victoria's century,
she buys up all   10
the eyesores facing her shore,
and lets them fall.

The season's ill—
we've lost our summer millionaire,
who seemed to leap from an L. L. Bean°   15
catalogue. His nine-knot yawl
was auctioned off to lobstermen.
A red fox stain covers Blue Hill.°

And now our fairy
decorator brightens his shop for fall;   20
his fishnet's filled with orange cork,
orange, his cobbler's bench and awl;
there is no money in his work,
he'd rather marry.

One dark night,°   25
my Tudor Ford climbed the hill's skull;
I watched for love-cars. Lights turned down,
they lay together, hull to hull,

Skunk Hour: The setting is Lowell's summer house in Maine. *Bishop*: This poem is modeled on
Bishop's "The Armadillo."   15 *L.L. Bean*: A sporting mail-order store in Maine.   18 *Blue
Hill*: Lowell said that Blue Hill had a "rusty reddish color" in the fall.   25 *One dark night*: A
reference to a spiritual crisis in his life.

where the graveyard shelves on the town. . . .
My mind's not right.   30

A car radio bleats,
"Love, O careless Love. . . ."° I hear
my ill-spirit sob in each blood cell,
as if my hand were at its throat. . . .
I myself am hell;°   35
nobody's here—

only skunks, that search
in the moonlight for a bite to eat.
They march on their soles up Main Street;
white stripes, moonstruck eyes' red fire   40
under the chalk-dry and spar spire
of the Trinitarian Church.

I stand on top
of our back steps and breathe the rich air—
a mother skunk with her column of kittens swills the garbage pail.   45
She jabs her wedge-head in a cup
of sour cream, drops her ostrich tail,
and will not scare.

32 *"Love . . . Love"*: A blues/jazz tune.   35 *I . . . hell*: An allusion to Satan's claim in Milton's
Paradise Lost (IV.75).

Robert Lowell   (1917–1977)
ROBERT FROST   1969

Robert Frost at midnight, the audience gone
to vapor, the great act laid on the shelf in mothballs,
his voice musical, raw and raw—he writes in the flyleaf:
"Robert Lowell from Robert Frost, his friend in the art."
"Sometimes I feel too full of myself," I say.   5
And he, misunderstanding, "When I am low,
I stray away. My son° wasn't your kind. The night
we told him Merrill Moore° would come to treat him,
he said, 'I'll kill him first.' One of my daughters thought things,
knew every male she met was out to make her;   10
the way she dresses, she couldn't make a whorehouse."
And I, "Sometimes I'm so happy I can't stand myself."
And he, "When I am too full of joy, I think
how little good my health did anyone near me."

7 *Son*: Frost's son committed suicide.   8 *Moore*: A psychoanalyst.

Wing Tek Lum   (b. 1946)
AT A CHINAMAN'S GRAVE   1987

*"Kingston, too, looked critically at it ['Chinaman'] as not being meaningful for her
. . . She said she even tried 'Chinaperson' and 'Chinawoman' and found they didn't
work either, the first sounding 'terrible' and the second being inaccurate."*

—The Honolulu Advertiser, *July 22, 1978*

My grandmother's
brother here
died all alone, wife
and children back
in the village. He   5
answered to
"Chinaman" like all
the others
of our race back then.
The Demons hired   10
only lonely
men, not their
sweethearts,
tai pos, baby
daughters. They laid   15
ties, cut cane, but
could not
proliferate. They took
on woman's
work, by default,   20
washing shirts,
frying eggs and sausages.
Granduncle cooked.
From what he earned
he sent   25
money home,
gambled perhaps, maybe hid
some away—all for
one purpose. Those old men:
they lived   30
their whole
lives with souls
somewhere else, their hearts
burdened of
hopes, waiting to   35

be reunited.
Some succeeded
and we
are the fruits of those
reunions. Some   40
did not,
and they are
now forgotten, but for
these tombstones,
by the rest.   45

Wing Tek Lum   (b. 1946)
MINORITY POEM   1987

Why
we're just as American
as apple pie—
that is, if you count
the leftover peelings   5
lying on the kitchen counter
which the cook has forgotten about
or doesn't know
quite what to do with
except hope that the maid   10
when she cleans off the chopping block
will chuck them away
into a garbage can she'll take out
on leaving for the night.

George Ella Lyon   (b. 1949)
SALVATION   (1982)

"What does the Lord want with Virgil's heart?
And what is Virgil going to do without one?"

O Lord, spare him the Call.
You're looking for bass
in a pond stocked with catfish.
Pass him by.
You got our best.   5
You took Mammy and the truck and the second hay.
What do you want with Virgil's heart?

Virgil, he comes in of a night
so wore out he can hardly chew
blacked with dust   10
that don't come off at the bathhouse.
He washes again
eats onions and beans with the rest of us
then gives the least one a shoulder ride to bed
slow and singing   15

      Down in some lone valley
      in some lonesome place
      where the wild birds do whistle . . .

After that, he sags like a full feed sack
on a couch alongside the TV   20
and watches whatever news Your waves are giving.
His soul sifts out
like feed from a slit in that sack
and he's gone—
wore out and give out and plumb used up, Lord.   25
What do You want with his heart?

George Ella Lyon   (b. 1949)
PROGRESS   1984

I reckon it was in the early Fifties
when they finally got the electric up at Smith.
I was hired to go behind the linemen
selling stoves, washers, frigidaires.

Anyway, there was this one woman   5
I saw as I came around a bend
with her washtub set up by a poplar
singing like a bird at first light.

She seemed awful glad to see me—
took my hand in her soapy hand—   10
but it wasn't any washer that she wanted.
No sir, she wanted a hi-fi.

Paid cash, a hundred and some dollars,
set the cabinet on the dirt floor.
Full blast, Nashville filled the holler   15
and saved her all the drudgery of song.

Mekeel McBride   (b. 1950)

IF I'D BEEN BORN IN TENNESSEE   1988

I'd have long ago married somebody
named Sweet Pea Russell. Sour mash, shoot,
I guess. And my name'd be Rita Louise.
I'd find me a Chinaberry to sit up in
with old blind Henry's monkey and maybe   5
I'd play the banjo and maybe I'd just talk
monkey talk and wait for Sweet Pea to come looking.

There'd be no trouble telling how God's
got hold of the mockingbird's throat
making it tell its kinda repeat truth   10
just in a way you can't quite get hold of.
Or how the Lord's slinked his way
up the spine of the sunflower that leans over
eavesdropping on everything.

Reading aloud would be easier, too; vowels,   15
those old wheels going no place special
spinning their worn-outness on the red cart
those idiot twins drive around in,
their over-alls so dusty you ain't never
gonna tell what color they was to begin with.   20
There's rules. There's always rules.

But then there's what's got to be done.
And if I went out into the honeysuckle-
soaked night with someone I ain't naming.
And if we laid down on Double Wedding Ring   25
quilts and never slept the whole time and
never made much mind of if we got caught.
Well, I guess that's my own business.
I could give up

reading altogether and look for Jesus   30
in the garden with his gold scissors
cutting June-bugs and poke brush, black
snakes outta my way. I could say
God damn, just like that and be old,
the oldest woman ever was, without getting tired   35
of discoursing with whatever passes by—

three legged mongrel, hunter's moon,
or the reverend who wears the eye patch,

although the Lord ain't taken no sight
out of that eye. Holy past all telling, he talks   40
with no patience for the primrose path
which I do believe I have walked
all my life. Sour mash, shoot, I guess.

J. D. McClatchy   (b. 1945)
THE WINDOW   1990

after Pavese

Even during the war, I used to get up at noon. The weariness—a damp,
musky, still warm mold of myself—stayed in bed while I made coffee. If   5
an idea disturbed this first surface of the day—like one of those tiny
whirlpools that form the closer you come to the falls—it was easily ignored.
I'd stand at the window in my underwear and blow on my cup and watch
them drink in the café across the square. Afternoons, I'd sit in the back of
the cinema, smoking, as sad and useless as a god. Long, crumpled nylons   10
of cigarette smoke would drift up toward the projectionist's opening, then
wrap around that single beam of romance from which, in those days, everything that counted came—the orphan on the train, the machine guns and
lipstick, the water ballet, the ambush in the hotel corridor. When did it
start? The moment you raised your arm to wave to someone across the   15
street? The day you didn't answer the telephone and showed up later with
your hair mussed? It wasn't until the war ended and the men came home
that they too realized what had happened. By then they had lived so long
in the hills and cellars and hardened themselves against regret that they
hadn't the energy to retrieve any delicacy of feeling. Some bought that   20
cheap religion, love, until they had no more belief to spend. Others tried
the commonplaces left out of their dreams: they made their beds in the
morning and washed with plenty of soap, or stood round after round of
drinks at the café, or counted on their children like the new government.
Myself, I had my old habits, the letters to write to M., my diary, the dog.   25
My train back—was it as long as a year ago now?—followed the shoreline
by night. I could see little fires in the distance, and the moon laid like a
compress on what beach the tide was giving up. By dawn the steam was
settling on the fields. The tree-curtains parted to show a house on the crest
of the hill, a lemon grove metallic against the blue sky, and then, closer,   30
bullet-pocked, the red brick wall of a farm stable. The woman beside me
had awakened by then, and asked me to help her with the window. It is
easy to be good when you're not in love. You do someone a favor, and
how soon you come to hate her grateful, radiant face.

Walter McDonald   (b. 1934)
FATHER'S STRAIGHT RAZOR   1990

This old razor loves a beard, the subtle
scrape of flesh all it asks for.
It glides the moist, soaped stubble
like a water spider, sharp enough
to puncture flesh, balanced on the stretched   5
surface tension of skin.

I remember its touch along my jaw,
the cold Toledo steel slicing me
squeegee clean, before I grew a beard.
Unfolded, sharpened back and forth   10
on my father's stiff, black leather strop,
it smoothed my honeymoon face twice daily,

leaving no shadow to burn my bride.
I remember my father's face when I flew home
after his attack, the nights in CCU,   15
the first wave of his hand, his last request,
to shave him before he saw Mother.
I remember his eyes barely wavering,

his scalp buried in the pillow
exposing the slack stretch of his face,   20
when I touched him, the soft prickle of a week's
white growth under my nervous thumb
and fingers, the willing tilt of his chin,
the short, slick flicks of the blade

on his throat and jaw, floating   25
over his blue-veined skin and bone, his face
coming clean and true through the lather,
my own eyes barely wavering, like nothing
I'd ever get to do again, nothing
I wouldn't have done to save him.   30

WINDOW ON

Poetic School: The Harlem Renaissance

After World War I, a migration of African-Americans from southern states to northern cities began a major population shift that continued until well after World War II. During the early 1920s a group of African-American writers settled in Harlem and made it their cultural capital on the model of Paris, then an artistic capital. Like the imagists, they knew one another and self-consciously crafted their work in light of each other's accomplishments. At this time, Harlem was the center of American jazz, with the great bands of Jimmy Lunceford, Count Basie, and especially Duke Ellington dominating the clubs. Other arts, such as painting and photography, also thrived in a stimulating environment only hinted at in some of the interesting documentary films of the period.

The major forces in poetry during the Harlem Renaissance were Langston Hughes (1902–1967), Claude McKay (1890–1948), Jean Toomer (1894–1967), Arna Bontemps (1902–1973), and Countee Cullen (1903–1946), all about the same age, and all with artistic visions formed in part by the African-American experience. Jean Toomer is the only writer not represented in this collection. After publishing his one influential book, *Cane* (1923), he ceased writing as abruptly as he had begun and devoted himself to spiritual self-development.

Some of the best work of the Renaissance contemplated the condition of the African-American in the New World, as Arna Bontemps does in "A Black Man Talks of Reaping." His poem, three quatrains that rhyme *abab*, belies its serene surface, ending with a muffled bitterness: "and feed on bitter fruit." The disjunction of the poem's form with its ideas is intentional, controlled, and the source of its power.

Countee Cullen was born in New York and educated at New York University, then at Harvard, where he received an M.A. in English. His poetic roots were deep in Romanticism, and he looked to Keats and the early imagists for inspiration. He spent most of his life as a teacher in New York City schools, and his writings include poetry, a novel, and a play. "Heritage" uses rhymed couplets to explore Cullen's relationship to Africa. Here he meditates on his distance in time and lost memories from the "Eden" of his origin. The questions asked in this poem are similar to those that motivated Alex Haley's *Roots*, but Cullen broaches them in complex ways. He is not interested in his personal antecedents, his family; instead, he is in search of a culture. When he meditates on his religion, he realizes, "My conversion came high-priced; / I belong to Jesus Christ." He knows that "Quaint, outlandish heathen gods / Black men fashion out of rods," and they have little to do with him: "Heathen gods are naught to me." Yet while acknowledging his new culture, he also knows there is something within him that alerts him to his past, that began in Africa "three centuries removed."

The poem is almost a dialogue. On one hand, he says, "What is Africa to me?" as if it were not important; on the other hand, he knows that his image of Africa has power over him.

Claude McKay, the oldest member of the Renaissance, was born and raised in Jamaica, where he began writing poetry. After winning a prize that permitted him to come to the United States, he studied at Tuskegee Institute and Kansas State, and then moved to Harlem in 1914. His work is heavily influenced by traditional Romantic poets, and many of his best poems are, like "The Harlem Dancer," carefully crafted sonnets from his book *Harlem Shadows* (1922). His sonnet "America" (not in this collection), begins:

> Although she feeds me bread of bitterness,
> And sinks into my throat her tiger's tooth,
> Stealing my breath of life, I will confess
> I love this cultured hell that tests my youth!

This ambivalence of feeling is almost a trademark of the poetry of the Harlem Renaissance.

Langston Hughes is the best known of all the writers of the Renaissance, but in many ways the least like the rest. His work is not influenced as much by traditional poetic forms as that of Cullen or McKay, and he was not in Harlem during the twenties. Instead, he went to college, dropped out, and then shipped out to Africa and France, working for a year in Paris. He later went to Washington, D. C., began writing poems seriously, and finally went to Lincoln University for his degree in 1929. Hughes wrote prose as well as poetry. Some of his most interesting work is autobiography. His poetry is marked by an affection for the blues, which, as he pointed out, sounds grim when you read it, but makes people laugh when you sing it.

Reading

Bontemps, Arna, ed. *The Harlem Renaissance Remembered.* New York: Dodd, Mead, 1972.

Huggins, Nathan Irving. *Harlem Renaissance.* New York: Oxford University Press, 1971.

Perry, Margaret. *The Harlem Renaissance.* New York: Garland, 1982.

Wagner, Jean. *Black Poets of the United States.* Urbana: University of Illinois Press, 1963.

Claude McKay   (1890–1948)

THE HARLEM DANCER   1922

> Applauding youths laughed with young prostitutes
> And watched her perfect, half-clothed body sway;
> Her voice was like the sound of blended flutes

Blown by black players upon a picnic day.
She sang and danced on gracefully and calm,   5
The light gauze hanging loose about her form;
To me she seemed a proudly-swaying palm
Grown lovelier for passing through a storm.
Upon her swarthy neck black shiny curls
Luxuriant fell; and tossing coins in praise,   10
The wine-flushed, bold-eyed boys, and even the girls,
Devoured her shape with eager, passionate gaze;
But looking at her falsely-smiling face,
I knew her self was not in that strange place.

Naomi Long Madgett   (b. 1923)
MIDWAY   1959

I've come this far to freedom and I won't turn back.
I'm climbing to the highway from my old dirt track.
    I'm coming and I'm going
    And I'm stretching and I'm growing
And I'll reap what I've been sowing or my skin's not black.   5

I've prayed and slaved and waited and I've sung my song.
You've bled me and you've starved me but I've still grown strong.
    You've lashed me and you've treed me
    And you've everything but freed me
But in time you'll know you need me and it won't be long.   10

I've seen the daylight breaking high above the bough.
I've found my destination and I've made my vow;
    So whether you abhor me
    Or deride me or ignore me,
Mighty mountains loom before me and I won't stop now.   15

Naomi Long Madgett   (b. 1923)
THE RACE QUESTION   1963

(For one whose fame depends on keeping The Problem a problem)

Would it please you if I strung my tears
In pearls for you to wear?
Would you like a gift of my hands' endless beating
Against old bars?

This time I can forget my Otherness,   5
Silence my drums of discontent awhile
And listen to the stars.

Wait in the shadows if you choose.
Stand alert to catch
The thunder and first sprinkle of unrest   10
Your insufficiency demands.
But you will find no comfort.
I will not feed your hunger with my blood
Nor crown your nakedness
With jewels of my elegant pain.   15

Christopher Marlowe   (1564–1593)
THE PASSIONATE SHEPHERD TO HIS LOVE   1599

[Six-stanza version from Englands Helicon*]*

Come live with me, and be my love,
And we will all the pleasures prove,
That Valleys, groves, hills, and fields,
Woods, or steepy mountain yields.

And we will sit upon the Rocks,   5
Seeing the Shepherds feed their flocks,
By shallow Rivers, to whose falls,
Melodious birds sing Madrigals.

And I will make thee beds of Roses,
And a thousand fragrant posies,   10
A cap of flowers, and a kirtle,
Imbroidered all with leaves of Myrtle.

A gown made of the finest wool,
Which from our pretty Lambs we pull,
Fair lined slippers for the cold: 15
With buckles of the purest gold.

A belt of straw, and Ivy buds,
With Coral clasps and Amber studs,
And if these pleasures may thee move,
Come live with me, and be my love.   20

The Shepherds' Swains shall dance and sing,
For thy delight each May-morning.
If these delights thy mind may move;
Then live with me, and be my love.

Andrew Marvell   (1621–1678)

TO HIS COY MISTRESS   1681

Had we but world enough, and time,
This coyness, Lady, were no crime.
We would sit down, and think which way
To walk, and pass our long love's day.
Thou by the Indian Ganges' side   5
Shouldst rubies find: I by the tide
Of Humber would complain. I would
Love you ten years before the flood:
And you should, if you please, refuse
Till the conversion of the Jews.   10
My vegetable love should grow
Vaster than empires, and more slow.
An hundred years should go to praise
Thine eyes, and on thy forehead gaze.
Two hundred to adore each breast: 15
But thirty thousand to the rest.
An age at least to every part,
And the last age should show your heart:
For, Lady, you deserve this state;
Nor would I love at lower rate.   20
    But at my back I always hear
Time's wingèd chariot hurrying near:
And yonder all before us lie
Deserts of vast eternity.
Thy beauty shall no more be found;   25
Nor, in thy marble vault, shall sound
My echoing song: then worms shall try
That long-preserved virginity:
And your quaint honor turn to dust;
And into ashes all my lust.   30
The grave's a fine and private place,
But none, I think, do there embrace.
    Now, therefore, while the youthful glue
Sits on thy skin like morning dew,
And while thy willing soul transpires   35
At every pore with instant fires,
Now let us sport us while we may;
And now, like amorous birds of prey,
Rather at once our time devour,
Than languish in his slow-chapped° power.   40

40 *Chapped*: Jawed.

Let us roll all our strength, and all
Our sweetness, up into one ball:
And tear our pleasures with rough strife,
Thorough° the iron gates of life.
Thus, though we cannot make our sun   45
Stand still, yet we will make him run.

44 *Thorough*: Through.

W.S. Merwin   (b. 1927)

FOR A COMING EXTINCTION   1974

Gray whale
Now that we are sending you to The End
That great god
Tell him
That we who follow you invented forgiveness   5
And forgive nothing

I write as though you could understand
And I could say it
One must always pretend something
Among the dying   10
When you have left the seas nodding on their stalks
Empty of you
Tell him that we were made
On another day

The bewilderment will diminish like an echo   15
Winding along your inner mountains
Unheard by us
And find its way out
Leaving behind it the future
Dead   20
And ours

When you will not see again
The whale calves trying the light
Consider what you will find in the black garden
And its court   25
The sea cows the Great Auks the gorillas
The irreplaceable hosts ranged countless
And fore-ordaining as stars
Our sacrifices
Join your word to theirs   30
Tell him
That it is we who are important

Edna St. Vincent Millay   (1892–1950)

CHILDHOOD IS THE KINGDOM WHERE NOBODY
DIES   1934

Childhood is not from birth to a certain age and at a certain age
The child is grown, and puts away childish things.
Childhood is the kingdom where nobody dies.

Nobody that matters, that is. Distant relatives of course
Die, whom one never has seen or has seen for an hour,   5
And they gave one candy in a pink-and-green stripéd bag, or a jack-
    knife,
And went away, and cannot really be said to have lived at all.

And cats die. They lie on the floor and lash their tails,
And their reticent fur is suddenly all in motion
With fleas that one never knew were there,   10
Polished and brown, knowing all there is to know,
Trekking off into the living world.
You fetch a shoe-box, but it's much too small, because she won't curl
    up now:
So you find a bigger box, and bury her in the yard, and weep.

But you do not wake up a month from then, two months,   15
A year from then, two years, in the middle of the night
And weep, with your knuckles in your mouth, and say Oh, God! Oh,
    God!
Childhood is the kingdom where nobody dies that matters,—mothers
    and fathers don't die.

And if you have said, "For heaven's sake, must you always be kissing a
    person?"
Or, "I do wish to gracious you'd stop tapping on the window with
    your thimble!"   20
Tomorrow, or even the day after tomorrow if you're busy having fun,
Is plenty of time to say, "I'm sorry, mother."

To be grown up is to sit at the table with people who have died, who
    neither listen nor speak;
Who do not drink their tea, though they always said
Tea was such a comfort.   25

Run down into the cellar and bring up the last jar of raspberries; they
    are not tempted.
Flatter them, ask them what was it they said exactly
That time, to the bishop, or to the overseer, or to Mrs. Mason;

They are not taken in.
Shout at them, get red in the face, rise,   30
Drag them up out of their chairs by their stiff shoulders and shake
    them and yell at them;
They are not startled, they are not even embarrassed; they slide back
    into their chairs.

Your tea is cold now.
You drink it standing up,
And leave the house.   35

Edna St. Vincent Millay   (1892–1950)
APOSTROPHE TO MAN   1934

(on reflecting that the world is ready to go to war again)

Detestable race, continue to expunge yourself, die out.
Breed faster, crowd, encroach, sing hymns, build bombing airplanes;
Make speeches, unveil statues, issue bonds, parade;
Convert again into explosives the bewildered ammonia and the
    distracted cellulose;
Convert again into putrescent matter drawing flies   5
The hopeful bodies of the young; exhort,
Pray, pull long faces, be earnest, be all but overcome, be
    photographed;
Confer, perfect your formulae, commercialize
Bacteria harmful to human tissue,
Put death on the market;   10
Breed, crowd, encroach, expand, expunge yourself, die out,
Homo called *sapiens.*

John Milton   (1608–1674)
HOW SOON HATH TIME, THE SUBTLE THIEF OF
YOUTH   1632

How soon hath Time, the subtle thief of youth,
    Stolen on his wing my three and twentieth year!
    My hasting days fly on with full career,
    But my late spring no bud or blossom showeth.°
Perhaps my semblance might deceive the truth   5
    That I to manhood am arrived so near,
    And inward ripeness doth much less appear,

4 *my late . . . showeth:* I haven't accomplished much yet.

That some more timely-happy spirits endueth.°
Yet be it less or more, or soon or slow,
    It shall be still° in strictest measure even°   10
    To that same lot, however mean or high,
Toward which Time leads me, and the will of Heaven;
    All is, if I have grace to use it so,
    As ever in my great task-master's eye.

7–8 *And inward . . . endueth*: His spiritual (inward) ripeness is much less apparent than physical maturity in others.   10 *still*: Always. *even*: Equivalent, regular.

John Milton   (1608–1674)

WHEN I CONSIDER HOW MY LIGHT IS SPENT   1655

When I consider how my light is spent,°
    Ere half my days in this dark world and wide,
    And that one Talent which is death to hide
    Lodged with me useless, though my Soul more bent
To serve therewith my Maker, and present   5
    My true account, lest he returning chide,°
    "Doth God exact day labor, light denied?"°
    I fondly° ask. But patience, to prevent
That murmur, soon replies, "God doth not need
    Either man's work or his own gifts. Who best   10
    Bear his mild yoke,° they serve him best. His State
Is Kingly. Thousands at his bidding speed
    And post o'er Land and Ocean without rest:
    They also serve who only stand and wait."

1 *how my light is spent*: Milton was completely blind by 1651.   3–6 *And that one Talent . . . returning chide*: See the parable in Matt. 25:14–30, in which the "slothful" servant, out of fear, hides his one talent (unit of money) rather than investing it, for which he is rebuked and punished. 7 *Doth . . . denied*: See John 9:4–5 and 12:35.   8 *fondly*: Foolishly.   11 *yoke*: See Matt. 11:28–30, especially "For my yoke is easy."

John Milton   (1608–1674)

SONNET 23   1658

Methought I saw my late espousèd Saint°
    Brought to me like Alcestis from the grave,
    Whom Jove's great Son to her glad Husband gave,
    Rescued from death by force though pale and faint.
Mine, as whom washed from spot of childbed taint,   5

1 *late espousèd Saint*: Spirit of his dead wife.

Purification in the old Law did save,°
And such, as yet once more I trust to have
Full sight of her° in Heaven without restraint,
Came vested all in white, pure as her mind:
    Her face was veiled, yet to my fancied sight,   10
    Love, sweetness, goodness, in her person shined
So clear, as in no face with more delight.
    But O, as to embrace me she inclined,
    I waked, she fled, and day brought back my night.

5–6 *Mine, as whom washed . . . Law did save*: In the Old Testament, women are considered unclean after childbirth and must be purified. Milton's first wife, Mary, died in childbirth; his second
wife, Katherine, died after the feast of the Purification of the Virgin. Reference could be to either
one.   8 *full sight of her*: If Milton is speaking of Katherine, he was blind when he married her.

Cheng Min   (b. 1924)

STUDENT 1972

Translated from Chinese by Kenneth Rexroth and Ling Chung

I go one step forward,
Then stumble one step back.
I join the march
And then slip away to the sidelines.
I look at the posters on the left wall,   5
And the people gathered around them.
I look at the posters on the right wall,
And the people gathered around them.
They are like soldiers in two bunkers,
Shooting at one another   10
With arrows that fly away over my head.
O Socrates of the streets,
Where are you?
I heard that you can bring the young to face the truth
Like a shepherd who herds his sheep   15
Onto the right path,
Like a kind passerby
Who returns a lost child to its mother.
But why have you forgotten
This country more baffled than any other country,   20
This time more doubtful
Than any other time?
Here yes and no are indistinguishable
Like East and West at the Poles.

Here truth is a puppet 25
That doubles in two roles.
One self says, "Whatever is mine must be truth."
The other says, "When your 'whatever'
Becomes my 'whatever', then it is truth."
Truth becomes a tasty bait 30
To lure fish obsessed with books.
In their short-sighted, round eyes
They cannot see the many hooks of fraud.
Socrates, if you cannot reappear
In the network of streets 35
Of the Twentieth Century,
Why cannot truth become simply a baby
That laughs when it is happy,
And cries when it is hurt,
As if to tell me which is itself? 40

N. Scott Momaday (b. 1934)
COMPARATIVES 1976

Sunlit sea,
the drift of fronds,
and banners
of bobbing boats—
the seaside 5
of any day—
except: this
cold, bright body
of the fish
upon the planks, 10
the coil and
crescent of flesh
extending
just into death.

Even so, 15
in the distant,
inland sea,
a shadow runs,
radiant,
rude in the rock: 20
fossil fish,
fissure of bone
forever.

It is perhaps
the same thing,   25
an agony
twice perceived.

It is most like
wind on waves—
mere commotion,   30
mute and mean,
perceptible—
that is all.

Marianne Moore   (1887–1972)
POETRY   1924

I, too, dislike it.
    Reading it, however, with a perfect contempt for it, one dis-
                                                        covers in
    it, after all, a place for the genuine.

Larry Neal   (1938–1981)
GHOST POEM # 1   1989

You would never shoot smack°
or lay in one of these Harlem
doorways pissing on yourself
that is not your way   not the
way of Alabama boys groomed slick   5
for these wicked cities momma
warned us of

You were always swifter than that:
the fast money was the Murphy game°
or the main supply before the cutting—   10
so now you lean with the shadows
(at the dark end of Turk's bar)
aware that the hitman is on your ass

You know that there is something inevitable
about it   15
You know that he will come   as sure as shit
snorting blow° for courage
and he will burn° you at the peak of your peacocking
glory

1 *smack*: Heroin.   9 *Murphy game*: Being a dealer or merchant in drugs   17 *blow*: Cocaine.
18 *burn*: Shoot.

And when momma gets the news   20
she will shudder over the evening meal
and moan: "Is that my Junie Boy runnin
with that fast crowd?"

Sharon Olds   (b. 1942)
THE DEATH OF MARILYN MONROE   c. 1983

The ambulance men touched her cold
body, lifted it, heavy as iron,
onto the stretcher, tried to close the
mouth, closed the eyes, tied the
arms to the sides, moved a caught   5
strand of hair, as if it mattered,
saw the shape of her breasts, flattened by
gravity, under the sheet,
carried her, as if it were she,
down the steps.   10

These men were never the same. They went out
afterwards, as they always did,
for a drink or two, but they could not meet
each other's eyes.
                    Their lives took   15
a turn—one had nightmares, strange
pains, impotence, depression. One did not
like his work, his wife looked
different, his kids. Even death
seemed different to him—a place where she   20
would be waiting,

and one found himself standing at night
in the doorway to a room of sleep, listening to a
woman breathing, just an ordinary
woman   25
breathing.

Sharon Olds   (b. 1942)
THINGS THAT ARE WORSE THAN DEATH   1982

For Margaret Randall

You are speaking of Chile,
of the woman who was arrested

with her husband and their five-year-old son.
You tell how the guards tortured the woman, the man, the child,
in front of each other,   5
"as they like to do."
Things that are worse than death.
I can see myself taking my son's ash-blond hair in my fingers,
tilting back his head before he knows what is happening,
slitting his throat, slitting my own throat   10
to save us that. Things that are worse than death:
this new idea enters my life.
The guard enters my life, the sewage of his body,
"as they like to do." The eyes of the five-year-old boy, Dago,
watching them with his mother. The eyes of his mother   15
watching them with Dago. And in my living room as a child,
the word, Dago. And nothing I experienced was worse than death,
life was beautiful as our blood on the stone floor
to save us that—my son's eyes on me,
my eyes on my son—the ram-boar on our bodies   20
making us look at our old enemy and bow in welcome,
gracious and eternal death
who permits departure.

Sharon Olds   (b. 1942)

THE ONE GIRL AT THE BOYS PARTY   c. 1983

When I take my girl to the swimming party
I set her down among the boys. They tower and
bristle, she stands there smooth and sleek,
her math scores unfolding in the air around her.
They will strip to their suits, her body hard and   5
indivisible as a prime number,
they'll plunge in the deep end, she'll subtract
her height from ten feet, divide it into
hundreds of gallons of water, the numbers
bouncing in her mind like molecules of chlorine   10
in the bright blue pool. When they climb out,
her ponytail will hang its pencil lead
down her back, her narrow silk suit
with hamburgers and french fries printed on it
will glisten in the brilliant air, and they will   15
see her sweet face, solemn and
sealed, a factor of one, and she will
see their eyes, two each,
their legs, two each, and the curves of their sexes,

one each, and in her head she'll be doing her   20
wild multiplying, as the drops
sparkle and fall to the power of a thousand from her body.

Mary Oliver   (b. 1935)
MARENGO°   1992

Out of the sump rise the marigolds.
From the rim of the marsh, muslin with mosquitoes,
rises the egret, in his cloud-cloth.
Through the soft rain, like mist, and mica,
the withered acres of moss begin again.   5

When I have to die, I would like to die
on a day of rain—
long rain, slow rain, the kind you think will never end.

And I would like to have whatever little ceremony there might be
take place while the rain is shoveled and shoveled out of the sky,   10

and anyone who comes must travel, slowly and with thought,
as around the edges of the great swamp.

Marengo: Site of a major victory by Napoleon (1800) in Austria.

Mary Oliver   (b. 1935)

SOME QUESTIONS YOU MIGHT ASK   1990

Is the soul solid, like iron?
Or is it tender and breakable, like
the wings of a moth in the beak of the owl?
Who has it, and who doesn't?
I keep looking around me.   5
The face of the moose is as sad
as the face of Jesus.
The swan opens her white wings slowly.
In the fall, the black bear carries leaves into the darkness.
One question leads to another.   10
Does it have a shape? Like an iceberg?
Like the eye of a hummingbird?
Does it have one lung, like the snake and the scallop?
Why should I have it, and not the anteater
who loves her children?   15
Why should I have it, and not the camel?

Come to think of it, what about the maple trees?
What about the blue iris?
What about all the little stones, sitting alone in the moonlight?
What about roses, and lemons, and their shining leaves?   20
What about the grass?

Mary Oliver   (b. 1935)

THE SUMMER DAY   1990

Who made the world?
Who made the swan, and the black bear?
Who made the grasshopper?
This grasshopper, I mean—
the one who has flung herself out of the grass,   5
the one who is eating sugar out of my hand,
who is moving her jaws back and forth instead of up and down—
who is gazing around with her enormous and complicated eyes.
Now she lifts her pale forearms and thoroughly washes her face.
Now she snaps her wings open, and floats away.   10
I don't know exactly what a prayer is.
I do know how to pay attention, how to fall down
into the grass, how to kneel down in the grass,
how to be idle and blessed, how to stroll through the fields,
which is what I have been doing all day.   15
Tell me, what else should I have done?
Doesn't everything die at last, and too soon?
Tell me, what is it you plan to do
with your one wild and precious life?

Simon Ortiz   (b. 1941)

JUANITA, WIFE OF MANUELITO   c. 1976

after seeing a photograph of her in Dine Baa-Hani

I can see by your eyes
the gray in them like by Sonsela Butte,
the long ache
that comes about when I think
about where the road climbs   5
up onto the Roof Butte.

I can see
the whole sky

when it is ready to rain
over Whiskey Creek,   10
and a small girl
driving her sheep
and she looks so pretty
her hair tied up
with a length of yarn.   15

I can see
by the way you stare
out of a photograph
that you are a stern woman
informed by the history   20
of a long walk
and how it must have felt
to leave the canyons
and the mountains of your own land.

I can see, Navajo woman,   25
that it is possible for dreams
to occur, the prayers full of the mystery
of children, laughter, the dances,
my own humanity, so it can last unto forever.

That is what I want to teach my son.   30

Wilfred Owen   (1893–1918)

DULCE ET DECORUM EST°   1917

Bent double, like old beggars under sacks,
Knock-kneed, coughing like hags, we cursed through sludge,
Till on the haunting flares we turned our backs
And towards our distant rest began to trudge.
Men marched asleep. Many had lost their boots   5
But limped on, blood-shod. All went lame; all blind;
Drunk with fatigue; deaf even to the hoots
Of tired, outstripped Five-Nines° that dropped behind.

Gas! GAS! Quick, boys!—An ecstasy of fumbling,
Fitting the clumsy helmets just in time;   10
But someone still was yelling out and stumbling,
And flound'ring like a man in fire or lime . . .

Dulce et decorum est: A phrase from Horace's line *Dulce et decorum est pro patria mori*—"It is
sweet and fitting to die for one's country." Owen died fighting in World War I.   8 *Five-Nines*:
Shells containing poison gas.

Dim, through the misty panes and thick green light,
As under a green sea, I saw him drowning.

In all my dreams, before my helpless sight,   15
He plunges at me, guttering, choking, drowning.

If in some smothering dreams you too could pace
Behind the wagon that we flung him in,
And watch the white eyes writhing in his face,
His hanging face, like a devil's sick of sin;   20
If you could hear, at every jolt, the blood
Come gargling from the froth-corrupted lungs,
Obscene as cancer, bitter as the cud
Of vile, incurable sores on innocent tongues,—
My friend, you would not tell with such high zest   25
To children ardent for some desperate glory,
The old Lie: Dulce et decorum est
Pro patria mori.

Wilfred Owen   (1893–1918)
ARMS AND THE BOY°   1917

Let the boy try along this bayonet-blade
How cold steel is, and keen with hunger of blood;
Blue with all malice, like a madman's flash;
And thinly drawn with famishing for flesh.

Lend him to stroke these blind, blunt bullet-leads,   5
Which long to nuzzle in the hearts of lads,
Or give him cartridges whose fine zinc teeth
Are sharp with sharpness of grief and death.

For his teeth seem for laughing round an apple.
There lurk no claws behind his fingers supple;   10
And God will grow no talons at his heels,
Nor antlers through the thickness of his curls.

Arms and the Boy. A play on a line from Virgil's heroic war poem the *Aeneid*: "Of arms and the
man I sing."

Wilfred Owen   (1893–1918)
SPRING OFFENSIVE   1917

Halted against the shade of a last hill
They fed, and eased of pack-loads, were at ease;
And leaning on the nearest chest or knees

Carelessly slept.
         But many there stood still   5
To face the stark blank sky beyond the ridge,
Knowing their feet had come to the end of the world.
Marvelling they stood, and watched the long grass swirled
By the May breeze, murmurous with wasp and midge;
And though the summer oozed into their veins   10
Like an injected drug for their bodies' pains,
Sharp on their souls hung the imminent ridge of grass,
Fearfully flashed the sky's mysterious glass.

Hour after hour they ponder the warm field
And the far valley behind, where buttercups   15
Had blessed with gold their slow boots coming up;
When even the little brambles would not yield
But clutched and clung to them like sorrowing arms.
They breathe like trees unstirred.

Till like a cold gust thrills the little word   20
At which each body and its soul begird
And tighten them for battle. No alarms
Of bugles, no high flags, no clamorous haste,—
Only a lift and flare of eyes that faced
The sun, like a friend with whom their love is done.   25
O larger shone that smile against the sun,—
Mightier than his whose bounty these have spurned.

So, soon they topped the hill, and raced together
Over an open stretch of herb and heather
Exposed. And instantly the whole sky burned   30
With fury against them; earth set sudden cups
In thousands for their blood; and the green slope
Chasmed and deepened sheer to infinite space.

Of them who running on that last high place
Breasted the surf of bullets, or went up   35
On the hot blast and fury of hell's upsurge,
Or plunged and fell away past this world's verge,
Some say God caught them even before they fell.

But what say such as from existence' brink
Ventured but drave° too swift to sink,   40
The few who rushed in the body to enter hell,
And there out-fiending all its fiends and flames
With superhuman inhumanities,
Long-famous glories, immemorial shames—

40 *drave*: Drove.

And crawling slowly back, have by degrees   45
Regained cool peaceful air in wonder—
Why speak not they of comrades that went under?

Dorothy Parker   (1893–1967)

GENERAL REVIEW OF THE SEX SITUATION   1926

Woman wants monogamy;
Man delights in novelty.
Love is woman's moon and sun;
Man has other forms of fun.
Woman lives but in her lord;   5
Count to ten, and man is bored.
With this the gist and sum of it,
What earthly good can come of it?

Dorothy Parker   (1893–1967)

INCURABLE   1928

And if my heart be scarred and burned,
The safer, I, for all I learned;
The calmer, I, to see it true
That ways of love are never new—
The love that sets you daft and dazed   5
Is every love that ever blazed;
The happier, I, to fathom this:
A kiss is every other kiss.
The reckless vow, the lovely name,
When Helen° walked, were spoke the same;   10
The weighted breast, the grinding woe,
When Phaon° fled, were ever so.
Oh, it is sure as it is sad
That any lad is every lad,
And what's a girl, to dare implore   15
Her dear be hers forevermore?
Though he be tried and he be bold,
And swearing death should he be cold,
He'll run the path the others went. . . .
But you, my sweet, are different.   20

---

10 *Helen*: Helen of Troy, whose beauty started the Trojan War.   12 *Phaon*: Supposedly a romantic interest of the poet Sappho.

Dorothy Parker   (1893–1967)
MEN   1926

They hail you as their morning star
Because you are the way you are.
If you return the sentiment,
They'll try to make you different;
And once they have you, safe and sound,   5
They want to change you all around.
Your moods and ways they put a curse on;
They'd make of you another person.
They cannot let you go your gait;
They influence and educate.   10
They'd alter all that they admired.
They make me sick, they make me tired.

Dorothy Parker   (1893–1967)
NOW AT LIBERTY   1926

Little white love, your way you've taken;
   Now I am left alone, alone.
Little white love, my heart's forsaken.
   (Whom shall I get by telephone?)
Well do I know there's no returning;   5
   Once you go out, it's done, it's done.
All of my days are gray with yearning.
   (Nevertheless, a girl needs fun.)

Little white love, perplexed and weary,
   Sadly your banner fluttered down.   10
Sullen the days, and dreary, dreary.
   (Which of the boys is still in town?)
Radiant and sure, you came a-flying;
   Puzzled, you left on lagging feet.
Slow in my breast, my heart is dying.   15
   (Nevertheless, a girl must eat.)

Little white love, I hailed you gladly;
   Now I must wave you out of sight.
Ah, but you used me badly, badly.
   (Who'd like to take me out tonight?)   20
All of the blundering words I've spoken,
   Little white love, forgive, forgive.
Once you went out, my heart fell, broken.
   (Nevertheless, a girl must live.)

Dorothy Parker   (1893–1967)

OBSERVATION   1926

If I don't drive around the park,
I'm pretty sure to make my mark.
If I'm in bed each night by ten,
I may get back my looks again.
If I abstain from fun and such,   5
I'll probably amount to much;
But I shall stay the way I am,
Because I do not give a damn.

Dorothy Parker   (1893–1967)

SYMPTOM RECITAL   1926

I do not like my state of mind;
I'm bitter, querulous, unkind.
I hate my legs, I hate my hands,
I do not yearn for lovelier lands.
I dread the dawn's recurrent light;   5
I hate to go to bed at night.
I snoot at simple, earnest folk.
I cannot take the gentlest joke.
I find no peace in paint or type.
My world is but a lot of tripe.   10
I'm disillusioned, empty-breasted.
For what I think, I'd be arrested.
I am not sick, I am not well.
My quondam dreams are shot to hell.
My soul is crushed, my spirit sore;   15
I do not like me any more.
I cavil, quarrel, grumble, grouse.
I ponder on the narrow house.
I shudder at the thought of men. . . .
I'm due to fall in love again.   20

Marge Piercy   (b. 1936)

THE SECRETARY CHANT   1971

My hips are a desk.
From my ears hang
chains of paper clips.

Rubber bands form my hair.
My breasts are wells of mimeograph ink.   5
My feet bear casters.
Buzz. Click.
My head
is a badly organized file.
My head is a switchboard   10
where crossed lines crackle.
My head is a wastebasket
of worn ideas.
Press my fingers
and in my eyes appear   15
credit and debit.
Zing. Tinkle.
My naval is a reject button.
From my mouth issue canceled reams.
Swollen, heavy, rectangular   20
I am about to be delivered
of a baby
xerox machine.
File me under W
because I wonce   25
was
a woman.

Donald Platt   (b. 1957)

ARIA FOR THIS LISTENING AREA   1990

       Turn the dial,
voices spill
       like mercury,
fill and brim
       the empty ear's   5
semi-circular
       cisterns: scattered
showers, the best
       in used cars,
grand opera, pop,   10
       and punk rock,
talk shows
       on UFO's,
crank calls,
       "Unless you die   15
and are born again

you shall not enter
my kingdom,"
Local Wheat-Growers
Mutual Hail   20
and Life Insurance,
low premiums,
another love song,
aluminum siding
all scrambled in   25
one listening area.

What poetry!
This radio
whose dial you spin
until you find   30
a frequency
on which the soul
sings a cappella°
or plays calypso
with wooden mallets   35
on marimbas
and steel drums.
Are poets only
deadbeat DJ's
doing time   40
on the night shift,
those virtuosos
of ventriloquism,
their programs mostly
pre-recorded?   45
Impromptu talkers
stalk
the wavelengths
for invisible
listeners.   50
What aria
for an area
with insomnia?

I love any
area   55
that "listens."

---

33 *a cappella*: Without instrumental accompaniment.

How many
pairs of ears
            per square mile
in North Dakota?   60
                Who else tunes
into this station
                and hears
Heartbreak Hotel
                go out   65
to Mary Lee
            from Stormin' Norman
at 4 A.M.?

                Language, not
geography,   70
                is where we live.
Tennessee's
            a way of talking.
I listen for
            the idioms   75
that mean I'm home,
                    a neighbor
saying "He's not
                wrapped tight,"
or "She's   80
            a couple
of sandwiches
                short of a picnic,"
or "You're whining
                like a dog   85
shitting
            persimmon seeds."

Can we map
            a dialect
the way we can   90
                the Appalachians,
this landslide
            of syllables
which never ends,
                or is speech more   95
a river that loves
                switching beds
in a flash flood?

           In my split-
level duplex,   100
           the man who lives
above me keeps
           his blinds down
and TV tuned
           to game shows,   105
soaps, reruns
           of Guiding Light,
Di-Gel, mouthwash,
           the evening news
"Mass murderer loose   110
           in Arkansas
celebrates Christmas,
           kills his wife
and seven children,"
           then sitcoms, Wheel   115
of Fortune, weather,
           whatever plays
the air waves
           at five hundred-sixty
megacycles   120
           near the end
of our broadcast day.
           Because my neighbor's
hard of hearing
           and his floor is my ceiling,   125
what seeps down,
           in the small hours
when I can not sleep,
           is the restless world's
raw nerves,   130
           an insomniac's static,
the monotone
           of loneliness.

Katha Pollitt   (b. 1949)

THE OLD NEIGHBORS   1990

The weather's turned, and the old neighbors creep out
from their crammed rooms to blink in the sun, as if
surprised to find they've lived through another winter.
Though steam heat's left them pale and shrunken
like old root vegetables,   5
Mr. and Mrs. Tozzi are already

hard at work on their front-yard mini-Sicily:
a Virgin-Mary birdbath, a thicket of roses,
and the only outdoor aloes in Manhattan.
It's the old immigrant story,   10
the beautiful babies
grown up into foreigners. Nothing's
turned out the way they planned
as sweethearts in the sinks of Palermo. Still,
each waves a dirt-caked hand   15
in geriatric fellowship with Stanley,
the former tattoo king of the Merchant Marine,
turning the corner with his shaggy collie,
who's hardly three but trots
arthritically in sympathy. It's only   20
the young who ask if life's worth living, not
Mrs. Sansanowitz, who for the last hour
has been inching her way down the sidewalk, lifting and placing
her new aluminum walker as carefully
as a spider testing its web. On days like these,   25
I stand for a long time
under the wild gnarled root of the ancient wisteria,
dry twigs that in a week
will manage a feeble shower of purple blossom,
and I believe it: this is all there is,   30
all history's brought us here to our only life
to find, if anywhere,
our hanging gardens° and our street of gold:
cracked stoops, geraniums, fire escapes, these old
stragglers basking in their bit of sun.   35

33 *hanging gardens.* A reference to biblical gardens of Babylon.

Katha Politt   (b. 1949)
IN MEMORY   c. 1982–1985

"But can we not sometimes speak of a darkening (for example) of our memory-image?"
                                                              —*Wittgenstein*

Over the years, they've darkened, like old paintings
or wainscotting in a damp house in the country,
until now the streets where you roller-skated brim with twilight,
your mother drinks morning coffee from a cup of shadows,
and out in the garden, the hardest August noon   5
is washed with a tender, retrospective blue—

like woodsmoke, or the shade of an unseen lilac.
Upstairs, you can hardly make yourself out, a child
peering out the window, speechless with happiness,
reciting your future in an endless summer dusk.   10

At first, this maddened you. You wanted to see
your life as a rope of diamonds: permanent, flashing.
Strange, then, how lately this darkening of memory moves you,
as though what it claimed it also made more true,
the way discoloring varnish on a portrait   15
little by little engulfs the ornate background—
the overstuffed sofa, the velvet-and-gold festoons
framing an elegant vista—but only deepens
the calm and serious face. The speaking eyes.

Alexander Pope   (1688–1744)
ODE ON SOLITUDE°   ca. 1700–1709

Happy the man, whose wish and care
A few paternal acres bound,
Content to breathe his native air,
              In his own ground.

Whose herds with milk, whose fields with bread,   5
Whose flocks supply him with attire,
Whose trees in summer yield him shade,
              In winter fire.

Blest! who can unconcern'dly find
Hours, days, and years slide soft away,   10
In health of body, peace of mind,
              Quiet by day,

Sound sleep by night; study and ease
Together mixed; sweet recreation,
And innocence, which most does please,   15
              With meditation.

Thus let me live, unseen, unknown;
Thus unlamented let me die;
Steal from the world, and not a stone
              Tell where I lie.   20

Ode on Solitude: Pope said he wrote this when he was twelve (1700) but the manuscript dates to 1709.

Ezra Pound (1885–1972)

ANCIENT MUSIC 1909 (?)

Winter is icummen in,°
Lhude sing Goddamm,
Raineth drop and staineth slop,
And how the wind doth ramm!
    Sing: Goddamm.   5
Skiddeth bus and sloppeth us,
An ague hath my ham.
Freezeth river, turneth liver,
    Damn you, sing: Goddamm.
Goddamm, Goddamm, 'tis why I am, Goddamm,   10
    So 'gainst the winter's balm.
Sing goddamm, damm, sing Goddamm.
Sing goddamm, sing goddamm, DAMM.

This is not folk music, but Dr. Ker writes that the tune is to be found under the Latin words of a very ancient canon. [Pound's note] 1 *Winter is icummen in*: See "Sumer is icumen in," p. 678.

Ezra Pound (1885–1972)

THE RETURN 1912

See, they return; ah, see the tentative
Movements, and the slow feet,
The trouble in the pace and the uncertain
Wavering!

See, they return, one, and by one,   5
With fear, as half-awakened;
As if the snow should hesitate
And murmur in the wind,
    and half turn back;
These were the "Wing'd-with-Awe,"   10
    Inviolable,

Gods of the wingèd shoe!
With them the silver hounds,
    sniffing the trace of air!

Haie! Haie!   15
    These were the swift to harry;
These the keen-scented;
These were the souls of blood.

Slow on the leash,
                    pallid the leash-men!   20

Ezra Pound   (1885–1972)
THE RIVER-MERCHANT'S WIFE: A LETTER°   1915

By Rihaku (Li T`ai Po)

While my hair was still cut straight across my forehead
Played I about the front gate, pulling flowers.
You came by on bamboo stilts, playing horse,
You walked about my seat, playing with blue plums.
And we went on living in the village of Chōkan: 5
Two small people, without dislike or suspicion.

At fourteen I married My Lord you.
I never laughed, being bashful.
Lowering my head, I looked at the wall.
Called to, a thousand times, I never looked back.   10

At fifteen I stopped scowling,
I desired my dust to be mingled with yours
Forever and forever and forever.
Why should I climb the look out?

At sixteen you departed,   15
You went into far Ku-tō-en, by the river of swirling eddies,
And you have been gone five months.
The monkeys make sorrowful noise overhead.

You dragged your feet when you went out.
By the gate now, the moss is grown, the different mosses,   20
Too deep to clear them away!
The leaves fall early this autumn, in wind.
The paired butterflies are already yellow with August
Over the grass in the West garden;
They hurt me. I grow older.   25
If you are coming down through the narrows of the river Kiang,
Please let me know beforehand,
And I will come out to meet you
                    As far as Chō-fū-Sa.

The River-Merchant's Wife: A Letter. See discussion of this poem on p. 748.

Parody: Poems Responding to Poems

Poets have always read the works of other poets, and sometimes have responded to them. One form of response is known as allusion, which is an indirect way of referring to another poet or poem. For example, W. H. Auden's "In Memory of W. B. Yeats" ends with a stanza beginning: "Earth receive an honored guest," imitating the meter of one of Yates's great last poems as a way to further pay homage to him. Carl Dennis does much the same in his "Oedipus the King," alluding to Sophocles. When Wilfred Owen titled his war poem "Arms and the Boy," he alluded to the first line of Virgil's *Aeneid*, which would have been studied by all advanced Latin schoolboys when Owen was attending school. Virgil began his poem with "Of arms and the man I sing." By changing "man" to "boy," Owen used an allusion to make an important statement.

Response poems are yet another way to express awareness of the work of other writers. When Christopher Marlowe wrote the *carpe diem* poem "The Passionate Shepherd to His Love," Sir Walter Raleigh playfully responded with "The Nymph's Reply to the Shepherd." The first poem argues for seduction, and the second against it. Each poem can stand on its own, but the two poems obviously complement each other.

Parody is a special response which adds a dimension of humor to poetry. Sometimes parodists intend to make fun of other writers, and sometimes they wish only to tap into the special energy associated with well-known or very successful poems. For example, when Marilyn Waniek wrote "Emily Dickinson's Defunct," she also had E. E. Cummings's poem "Buffalo Bill's Defunct," in mind, and the result is a homage to both poets. Waniek imitates Cummings's way of expressing himself ("believe me") and certain rhythms, and she ends by alluding to Dickinson's "I heard a Fly buzz—When I died—." Another example is Louis Simpson's "New Lines for Cuscuscaraway and Mirza Murad Ali Beg," which parodies T. S. Eliot's poem "Lines for Cuscuscaraway and Mirza Murad Ali Beg," which parodies Edward Lear's "How Pleasant to Know Mr. Lear" (p. 577). There are numerous parodies in this collection.

Marilyn Hacker's sonnet "Did You Love Well What Very Soon You Left?" (p. 799) parodies Shakespeare's Sonnet 73, (p. 595), whose ending line warns his readers to "love that well which thou must leave ere long." His poem reminds us that life is short. Hacker's poem brings us the point of view of the lover left behind, the one "bereft/so utterly." Her tone is respectful of Shakespeare's poem, which she uses as a basis, a platform from which to move. Her tone is mournful; she is a mourner in pain. And more than that, she admits regret, saying, "I drank our one year out of brine instead / of honey from the seasons of your tongue." She, like Shakespeare concerns herself with loss of youth, "for the end of being young." In her poem, death is the end punctuation mark of youth—but it is the death of a lover who leaves her to grieve.

Tone also tells us whether the poet admires the poem being parodied. One of the classic canonical poems of the Romantic era is John Keats's "On First Looking into Chapman's Homer," about his recollection of first reading Homer's *Iliad* in the English translation of George Chapman, an Elizabethan writer. George Starbuck's "On First Looking in on Blodgett's Keats's 'Chapman's Homer' " is completely irreverent: it begins with sexual discovery and ends with the narrator's girlfriend tossing a book of Keats's poems into the ocean. In this way Starbuck gives his own version of how it feels to be a student, and of what is truly exciting in this world.

Reading

The Antic Muse. New York: Meridian, 1957.
The Oxford Book of Parodies. London: Oxford University Press, 1990.

Sir Walter Raleigh   (1552–1618)
THE NYMPH'S REPLY TO THE SHEPHERD°   1600

If all the world and love were young,
And truth in every shepherd's tongue,
These pretty pleasures might me move,
To live with thee and be thy love.

Time drives the flocks from field to fold,   5
When rivers rage, and rocks grow cold,
And Philomel° becometh dumb,
The rest complains of cares to come.

The flowers do fade, and wanton fields,
To wayward winter reckoning yields,   10
A honey tongue, a heart of gall,
Is fancy's spring, but sorrow's fall.

Thy gowns, thy shoes, thy beds of roses,
Thy cap, thy kirtle, and thy posies,
Soon break, soon wither, soon forgotten,   15
In folly ripe, in reason rotten.

The Nymph's Reply to the Shepherd: See Christopher Marlowe, "The Passionate Shepherd to His Love," p. 878.   7 *Philomel*: In Greek mythology, the princess whom the gods changed into a nightingale after her brother-in-law raped her and cut out her tongue.

The belt of straw and ivy buds,
Thy coral clasps and amber studs,
All these in me no means can move,
To come to thee, and be thy love.   20

But could youth last, and love still breed,
Had joys no date, nor age no need,
Then these delights my mind might move,
To live with thee, and be thy love.

Henry Reed   (b. 1914)

NAMING OF PARTS   1946

Today we have naming of parts. Yesterday,
We had daily cleaning. And tomorrow morning,
We shall have what to do after firing. But today,
Today we have naming of parts. Japonica
Glistens like coral in all of the neighboring gardens,   5
     And today we have naming of parts.

This is the lower sling swivel. And this
Is the upper sling swivel, whose use you will see,
When you are given your slings. And this is the piling swivel,
Which in your case you have not got. The branches   10
Hold in the gardens their silent, eloquent gestures,
     Which in our case we have not got.

This is the safety-catch, which is always released
With an easy flick of the thumb. And please do not let me
See anyone using his finger. You can do it quite easy   15
If you have any strength in your thumb. The blossoms
Are fragile and motionless, never letting anyone see
     Any of them using their finger.

And this you can see is the bolt. The purpose of this
Is to open the breech, as you see. We can slide it   20
Rapidly backwards and forwards: we call this
Easing the spring. And rapidly backwards and forwards
The early bees are assaulting and fumbling the flowers:
     They call it easing the Spring.

They call it easing the Spring: it is perfectly easy   25
If you have any strength in your thumb: like the bolt,
And the breech, and the cocking-piece, and the point of balance,
Which in our case we have not got; and the almond-blossom
Silent in all of the gardens and the bees going backwards and forwards,
     For today we have naming of parts.   30

Carter Revard   (b. 1931)
WHAT THE EAGLE FAN SAYS°   1992

*(For Bob and Evelyne Voelker, Dale and Arlene Besse, and the St. Louis Gourd
Dancers.)*

I strung dazzling thrones	of thunder beings	
on a spiraling thread	of spinning flight,	
beading dawn's blood	and blue of noon	
to the gold and dark	of day's leaving,	
circling with Sun	the soaring heaven	5
over turquoise eyes	of Earth below,	
her silver veins,	her sable fur,	
heard human relatives	hunting beneath	
calling me down,	crying their need	
that I bring them closer	to Wakonda's° ways,	10
and I turned from heaven	to help them then.	
When the bullet came	it caught my heart,	
the hunter's hands	gave earth its blood,	
loosened light beings	and let us float	
toward the sacred center	of song in the drum,	15
but fixed us first	firm in tree-heart	
that green light-dancers	gave to men's knives,	
ash-heart in hiding where	a deer's heart had beat,	
and a one-eyed serpent	with silver-straight head	
strung tiny rattles	around white softness	20
in beaded harmonies	of blue and red—	
now I move lightly	in a man's left hand,	
above dancing feet	follow the sun	
around old songs	soaring toward heaven	
on human breath,	and I help them rise.	25

What the Eagle Fan Says. This poem offers thanks for the honor of being given eagle feathers,
which were then set into a beaded fan. It tells how the eagle in flight pierces clouds just as a bead-
worker's needle goes through beads and buckskin, spiraling round sky and fan-handle; and how
the eagle flies from dawn to sunset, linking day and night colors as they are linked on a Gourd
Dancer's blanket (half crimson, half blue), and just as they are beaded onto the handle of this
eagle fan. In such "riddles" ordinary things receive mysterious names: tree leaves are green *light-
dancers,* wood is *tree-heart* or *ash-heart,* clouds are *thrones of thunder beings.* Readers will deci-
pher for themselves the *one-eyed serpent.* [Revard's note]   10 *Wakonda:* A spirit god.

Poetry and Feminism

Gender issues in poetry have sparked a great deal of controversy in recent years. Numerous women poets have insisted that they are simply poets and that gender distinctions are both unnecessary and destructive. Amy Lowell felt this way, and her presence in the imagist school was as powerful as that of Ezra Pound and H. D. Helen Vendler, one of the most influential critics of contemporary poetry, has complained of "the current particularism that insists on defining each of us by race, class, and gender" insisting that these "contextualisms" (reading poets mainly in the context of their gender) are limiting and destructive. Vendler is certainly correct if such contextualisms are used to "explain everything" about poetry or to limit its power.

The feminist critics who have made claims for a distinctive style in women's poetry seem primarily interested in making audiences aware that certain assumptions drawn from traditional masculine poetic practice may not be universally valid. The emphasis on objectivity, control of emotions, and logical discourse is seen as masculine, and perhaps not always appropriate to the materials of a feminist poetic discourse.

The question of whether there is a feminist poetic discourse is yet to be decided. Some critics, such as Elaine Showalter, suggest that there is; Helen Vendler does not. Some of the early feminist theorists began discussing poetry hoping to demonstrate that there was no difference between the poetry of men and women. Amy Lowell and Emily Dickinson may well have subscribed to such a view. But as feminist critics examined how women write and read poetry, "the promised land in which gender would lose its power," as Elaine Showalter put it, began to disappear. Instead, as Showalter continues, "we realize that the land promised to us is not the serenely undifferentiated universality of texts but the tumultuous and intriguing wilderness of difference itself."

According to the most theoretical critics, these differences are not just biological but also linguistic, psychological, and cultural. If such differences are detectable, then a feminist criticism is not only possible but essential to a full understanding of poetry. Aspects of such a criticism would take into account the emotions portrayed in women's poetry, the projection of ego or sense of self, and the issues surrounding cultural deprivation. Christiane Rochefort calls women's poetry a literature of "the colonized," implying that women have been controlled by a masculine society. Therefore, interpretations of women's poetry must take into account the price of powerlessness, however that may be expressed. Adrienne Rich's "Trying to Talk with a Man" is a useful example.

Many of the poets in this collection are feminists in their politics as well as in their poetry. By looking at their work, you can begin to develop a sense of the issues on which a feminist interpretation of poetry might focus. Marilyn Hacker's (b. 1942) "Sonnet Ending with a Film Subtitle" is direct and aggressive to the point of almost violent anger as a result of life's "nauseating ironies." She threatens to "fortify . . . rhetoric with guns" and promises that "Some day we women all will break our fetters / And raise our daughters to be Lesbians." A feminist interpretation of this poem would examine it for the source of Hacker's anger. She mentions Dorothy Parker, who wrote a short story about a woman waiting for a man to call on the telephone. The man, conspicuous by his absence in Hacker's sonnet, is guilty of not living up to Parker's expectation. The question is whether he deserves her wrath.

Dorothy Parker (1893–1967) is not a modern feminist; she was a humorist, part of a circle of witty New York columnists and writers. However, her best work examines the relationship of men and women, and in light of contemporary feminism it looks especially timely. In "Symptom Recital," for example, the narrator runs through all the physical and mental qualities that she abhors about herself and then ends with an amusing irony: She's on the verge of falling in love. When you read "Observation," ask yourself if you would have thought this poem to be written by a man. If you say no, then why not? You might ask that of any of Parker's poems, and see whether there is a difference, as Showalter suggests.

Adrienne Rich (b. 1929) has clearly expressed a feminist agenda, and her work is deeply concerned with the roles women play and the problems women face. The feminist critic Mary Jacobus has said that psychological realities are the forces that create the differences Showalter feels have surfaced through the feminist interpretation of women's poetry. Rich's "Diving into the Wreck" would be a case in point: it is a metaphoric journey into the psyche, which she discovers is bisexual. "Grandmothers" expresses another feminist theme, that the heritage of women writers derives from earlier women writers. As Rich says in "Snapshots of a Daughter-in-Law," "A thinking woman sleeps with monsters," and much of her work seems set on rooting them out.

Reading

Ellmann, Mary. *Thinking about Women*. New York: Harcourt, 1978.

Jacobus, Mary. *Reading Woman*. New York: Columbia University Press, 1986.

Juhasz, Susan. *Naked and Fiery Forms: Modern American Poetry by Women*. New York: Harper and Row, 1976.

Showalter, Elaine. *The New Feminist Criticism*. New York: Pantheon, 1985.

Adrienne Rich   (b. 1929)

TRYING TO TALK WITH A MAN   1971

Out in this desert we are testing bombs,

that's why we came here.

Sometimes I feel an underground river
forcing its way between deformed cliffs
an acute angle of understanding   5
moving itself like a locus of the sun
into this condemned scenery.

What we've had to give up to get here—
whole LP collections, films we starred in
playing in the neighborhoods, bakery windows   10
full of dry, chocolate-filled Jewish cookies,
the language of love-letters, of suicide notes,
afternoons on the riverbank
pretending to be children

Coming out to this desert   15
we meant to change the face of
driving among dull green succulents
walking at noon in the ghost town
surrounded by a silence

that sounds like the silence of the place   20
except that it came with us
and is familiar
and everything we were saying until now
was an effort to blot it out—
coming out here we are up against it   25

Out here I feel more helpless
with you than without you
You mention the danger
and list the equipment
we talk of people caring for each other   30
in emergencies—laceration, thirst—
but you look at me like an emergency

Your dry heat feels like power
your eyes are stars of a different magnitude
they reflect lights that spell out: EXIT   35
when you get up and pace the floor

talking of the danger
as if it were not ourselves
as if we were testing anything else.

Adrienne Rich   (b. 1929)

DIVING INTO THE WRECK°   (1973)

First having read the book of myths,
and loaded the camera,
and checked the edge of the knife-blade,
I put on
the body-armor of black rubber   5
the absurd flippers
the grave and awkward mask.
I am having to do this
not like Cousteau with his
assiduous team   10
aboard the sun-flooded schooner
but here alone.

There is a ladder.
The ladder is always there
hanging innocently   15
close to the side of the schooner.
We know what it is for,
we who have used it.
Otherwise
it's a piece of maritime floss   20
some sundry equipment.

I go down.
Rung after rung and still
the oxygen immerses me
the blue light   25
the clear atoms
of our human air.
I go down.
My flippers cripple me,
I crawl like an insect down the ladder   30
and there is no one
to tell me when the ocean
will begin.

First the air is blue and then
it is bluer and then green and then   35
black I am blacking out and yet
my mask is powerful
it pumps my blood with power
the sea is another story

Diving into the Wreck: See discussion of this poem on p. 910.

the sea is not a question of power   40
I have to learn alone
to turn my body without force
in the deep element.

And now: it is easy to forget
what I came for   45
among so many who have always
lived here
swaying their crenellated fans
between the reefs
and besides   50
you breathe differently down here.

I came to explore the wreck.
The words are purposes.
The words are maps.
I came to see the damage that was done   55
and the treasures that prevail.
I stroke the beam of my lamp
slowly along the flank
of something more permanent
than fish or weed   60

the thing I came for:
the wreck and not the story of the wreck
the thing itself and not the myth
the drowned face always staring
toward the sun   65
the evidence of damage
worn by salt and sway into this threadbare beauty
the ribs of the disaster
curving their assertion
among the tentative haunters.   70

This is the place.
And I am here, the mermaid whose dark hair
streams black, the merman in his armored body
We circle silently
about the wreck   75
we dive into the hold.
I am she: I am he

whose drowned face sleeps with open eyes
whose breasts still bear the stress
whose silver, copper, vermeil cargo lies   80
obscurely inside barrels
half-wedged and left to rot

we are the half-destroyed instruments
that once held to a course
the water-eaten log   85
the fouled compass

We are, I am, you are
by cowardice or courage
the one who find our way
back to this scene   90
carrying a knife, a camera
a book of myths
in which
our names do not appear.

Adrienne Rich   (b. 1929)
SONG

You're wondering if I'm lonely:
OK then, yes, I'm lonely
as a plane rides lonely and level
on its radio beam, aiming
across the Rockies   5
for the blue-strung aisles
of an airfield on the ocean

You want to ask, am I lonely?
Well, of course, lonely
as a woman driving across country   10
day after day, leaving behind
mile after mile
little towns she might have stopped
and lived and died in, lonely

If I'm lonely   15
it must be the loneliness
of waking first, of breathing
dawn's first cold breath on the city
of being the one awake
in a house wrapped in sleep   20

If I'm lonely
it's with the rowboat ice-fast on the shore
in the last red light of the year
that knows what it is, that knows it's neither
ice nor mud nor winter light   25
but wood, with a gift for burning

Adrienne Rich (b. 1929)

SNAPSHOTS OF A DAUGHTER-IN-LAW   1958–1960

I

You, once a belle in Shreveport,
with henna-colored hair, skin like a peachbud,
still have your dresses copied from that time,
and play a Chopin prelude
called by Cortot:° "*Delicious recollections*   5
float like perfume through the memory."

Your mind now, moldering like wedding-cake,
heavy with useless experience, rich
with suspicion, rumor, fantasy,
crumbling to pieces under the knife-edge   10
of mere fact. In the prime of your life.

Nervy, glowering, your daughter
wipes the teaspoons, grows another way.

II

Banging the coffee-pot into the sink
she hears the angels chiding, and looks out   15
past the raked gardens to the sloppy sky.
Only a week since They said: *Have no patience.*

The next time it was: *Be insatiable.*
Then: *Save yourself; others you cannot save.*
Sometimes she's let the tapstream scald her arm,   20
a match burn to her thumbnail,

or held her hand above the kettle's snout
right in the woolly steam. They are probably angels,
since nothing hurts her any more, except
each morning's grit blowing into her eyes.   25

III

A thinking woman sleeps with monsters.
The beak that grips her, she becomes. And Nature,
that sprung-lidded, still commodious
steamer-trunk of *tempora* and *mores*
gets stuffed with it all: the mildewed orange-flowers,   30
the female pills, the terrible breasts
of Boadicea beneath flat foxes' heads and orchids.

---

5 *Cortot*: Alfred Cortot (1877–1962), French pianist.

Two handsome women, gripped in argument,
each proud, acute, subtle, I hear scream
across the cut glass and majolica   35
like Furies cornered from their prey:
The argument *ad feminam,*° all the old knives
that have rusted in my back, I drive in yours,
ma semblable, ma soeur!°

IV

Knowing themselves too well in one another: 40
their gifts no pure fruition, but a thorn,
the prick filed sharp against a hint of scorn . . .
Reading while waiting
for the iron to heat,
writing, *My Life had stood—a Loaded Gun—*   45

in that Amherst pantry while the jellies boil and scum,
or, more often,
iron-eyed and beaked and purposed as a bird,
dusting everything on the whatnot every day of life.

V

Dulce ridens, dulce loquens°   50
she shaves her legs until they gleam
like petrified mammoth-tusk.

VI

When to her lute Corinna sings°
neither words nor music are her own;
only the long hair dipping   55
over her cheek, only the song
of silk against her knees
and these
adjusted in reflections of an eye.

Poised, trembling and unsatisfied, before   60
an unlocked door, that cage of cages,
tell us, you bird, you tragical machine—
is this *fertilisante douleur?*° Pinned down
by love, for you the only natural action,
are you edged more keen   65
to prise the secrets of the vault? has Nature shown

---

37 *ad feminam*: A play on *ad hominum*—arguing to the man—now to the woman—instead of
to the point.   39 *ma semblable, ma soeur*: A play on Rimbaud, meaning, my resemblance, my
sister.   50 *Dulce ridens, dulce loquens*: Sweet laughter, sweet talk.   53 *When . . . sings*: The
first line of a poem by Thomas Campion (1567–1620) praising the power of his lady to stir his
emotions with her music.   63 *fertilisante douleur*: Fertilizing sadness.

her household books to you, daughter-in-law,
that her sons never saw?

VII

"*To have in this uncertain world some stay
which cannot be undermined, is*   70
of the utmost consequence."
                    Thus wrote
a woman, partly brave and partly good,
who fought with what she partly understood.
Few men about her would or could do more,
hence she was labeled harpy, shrew and whore.   75

VIII

"You all die at fifteen," said Diderot,°
and turn part legend, part convention.
Still, eyes inaccurately dream
behind closed windows blankening with steam.
Deliciously, all that we might have been,   80
all that we were—fire, tears,
wit, taste, martyred ambition—
stirs like the memory of refused adultery
the drained and flagging bosom of our middle years.

IX

Not that it is done well, but   85
that it is done at all.° Yes, think
of the odds! or shrug them off forever.
This luxury of the precocious child,
Time's precious chronic invalid,—
would we, darlings, resign it if we could?   90
Our blight has been our sinecure:
mere talent was enough for us—
glitter in fragments and rough drafts.

Sigh no more, ladies.
                Time is male
and in his cups drink to the fair.   95
Bemused by gallantry, we hear
our mediocrities over-praised,
indolence read as abnegation,
slattern thought styled intuition,
every lapse forgiven, our crime   100

---

76 *Diderot*: Denis Diderot (1713–1784), French philosopher.   85–86 *Not . . . all*: Reference
to Samuel Johnson's observation on women preachers.

only to cast too bold a shadow
or smash the mold straight off.

For that, solitary confinement,
tear gas, attrition shelling.
Few applicants for that honor.

X

        Well,
she's long about her coming, who must be   105
more merciless to herself than history.
Her mind full to the wind, I see her plunge
breasted and glancing through the currents,
taking the light upon her   110
at least as beautiful as any boy
or helicopter,
      poised, still coming,
her fine blades making the air wince

but her cargo
no promise then: 115
delivered
palpable
ours.

Edward Arlington Robinson (1869–1935)
RICHARD CORY 1897

Whenever Richard Cory went down town,
We people on the pavement looked at him:
He was a gentleman from sole to crown,
Clean favored, and imperially slim.

And he was always quietly arrayed,   5
And he was always human when he talked;
But still he fluttered pulses when he said,
"Good-morning," and he glittered when he walked.

And he was rich—yes, richer than a king—
And admirably schooled in every grace: 10
In fine, we thought that he was everything
To make us wish that we were in his place.

So on we worked, and waited for the light,
And went without the meat, and cursed the bread;

And Richard Cory, one calm summer night,   15
Went home and put a bullet through his head.

Theodore Roethke   (1907–1963)
ELEGY FOR JANE   1953

My Student, Thrown by a Horse

I remember the neckcurls, limp and damp as tendrils;
And her quick look, a sidelong pickerel smile;
And how, once startled into talk, the light syllables leaped for her,
And she balanced in the delight of her thought,
A wren, happy, tail into the wind,   5
Her song trembling the twigs and small branches.
The shade sang with her;
The leaves, their whispers turned to kissing;
And the mold sang in the bleached valleys under the rose.

Oh, when she was sad, she cast herself down into such a pure depth, 10
Even a father could not find her:
Scraping her cheek against straw;
Stirring the clearest water.

My sparrow, you are not here,
Waiting like a fern, making a spiny shadow.   15
The sides of wet stones cannot console me,
Nor the moss, wound with the last light.

If only I could nudge you from this sleep,
My maimed darling, my skittery pigeon.
Over this damp grave I speak the words of my love: 20
I, with no rights in this matter,
Neither father nor lover.

Theodore Roethke   (1907–1963)
MY PAPA'S WALTZ   1948

The whiskey on your breath
Could make a small boy dizzy;
But I hung on like death:
Such waltzing was not easy.

We romped until the pans   5
Slid from the kitchen shelf;

My mother's countenance
Could not unfrown itself.

The hand that held my wrist
Was battered on one knuckle;   10
At every step you missed
My right ear scraped a buckle.

You beat time on my head
With a palm caked hard by dirt,
Then waltzed me off to bed   15
Still clinging to your shirt.

Theodore Roethke   (1907–1963)
DOLOR   1943

I have known the inexorable sadness of pencils,
Neat in their boxes, dolor of pad and paper-weight,
All the misery of manilla folders and mucilage,
Desolation in immaculate public places,
Lonely reception room, lavatory, switchboard,   5
The unalterable pathos of basin and pitcher,
Ritual of multigraph, paper-clip, comma,
Endless duplication of lives and objects.
And I have seen dust from the walls of institutions,
Finer than flour, alive, more dangerous than silica,   10
Sift, almost invisible, through long afternoons of tedium,
Dropping a fine film on nails and delicate eyebrows,
Glazing the pale hair, the duplicate grey standard faces.

Christina Rossetti   (1830–1894)
SONG   1848

When I am dead, my dearest,
    Sing no sad songs for me;
Plant thou no roses at my head,
    Nor shady cypress tree:
Be the green grass above me   5
    With showers and dewdrops wet:
And if thou wilt, remember,
    And if thou wilt, forget.

I shall not see the shadows,
    I shall not feel the rain;   10

I shall not hear the nightingale
   Sing on as if in pain:
And dreaming through the twilight
   That doth not rise nor set,
Haply I may remember,   15
   And haply may forget.

Christina Rossetti   (1830–1894)
REMEMBER   1849

Remember me when I am gone away,

   Gone far away into the silent land;
   When you can no more hold me by the hand,
Nor I half turn to go yet turning stay.
Remember me when no more day by day   5
   You tell me of our future that you planned:
   Only remember me: you understand
It will be late to counsel then or pray.
Yet if you should forget me for a while
   And afterwards remember, do not grieve: 10
   For if the darkness and corruption leave
A vestige of the thoughts that once I had,
Better by far you should forget and smile
   Than that you should remember and be sad.

Christina Rossetti   (1830–1894)
ECHO   1854

Come to me in the silence of the night;
   Come in the sleeping silence of a dream;
Come with soft rounded cheeks and eyes as bright
   As sunlight on a stream;
      Come back in tears,   5
O memory, hope, love of finished years.

O dream how sweet, too sweet, too bitter sweet,
   Whose wakening should have been in Paradise,
Where souls brimfull of love abide and meet,
   Where thirsting longful eyes   10
      Watch the slow door
That opening, letting in, lets out no more.

Yet come to me in dreams, that I may live

My very life again though cold in death:
Come back to me in dreams, that I may give   15
Pulse for pulse, breath for breath:
    Speak low, lean low,
As long ago, my love, how long ago.

Christina Rossetti (1830–1894)

IN AN ARTIST'S STUDIO 1856

One face looks out from all his canvases,
    One selfsame figure sits or walks or leans:
    We found her hidden just behind those screens,
That mirror gave back all her loveliness.
A queen in opal or in ruby dress,   5
    A nameless girl in freshest summer-greens,
    A saint, an angel—every canvas means
The same one meaning, neither more nor less.
He feeds upon her face by day and night,
    And she with true kind eyes looks back on him,   10
Fair as the moon and joyful as the light:
    Not wan with waiting, not with sorrow dim;
Not as she is, but was when hope shone bright;
    Not as she is, but as she fills his dream.

Muriel Rukeyser (1913–1980)

***FROM* LETTER TO THE FRONT** 1944

To be a Jew in the twentieth century
Is to be offered a gift. If you refuse,
Wishing to be invisible, you choose
Death of the spirit, the stone insanity.
Accepting, take full life. Full agonies: 5
Your evening deep in labyrinthine blood
Of those who resist, fail, and resist; and God
Reduced to a hostage among hostages.

The gift is torment. Not alone the still
Torture, isolation; or torture of the flesh.   10
That may come also. But the accepting wish,
The whole and fertile spirit as guarantee
For every human freedom, suffering to be free,
Daring to live for the impossible.

Muriel Rukeyser   (1913–1980)
MYTH   1973

Long afterward, Oedipus,° old and blinded, walked the
roads.   He smelled a familiar smell.   It was
the Sphinx.   Oedipus said, "I want to ask one question.
Why didn't I recognize my mother?"   "You gave the
wrong answer," said the Sphinx.   "But that was what   5
made everything possible," said Oedipus.   "No," she said.
"When I asked, What walks on four legs in the morning,
two at noon, and three in the evening, you answered,
Man.   You didn't say anything about woman."
"When you say Man," said Oedipus, "you include women   10
too. Everyone knows that."   She said, "That's what
you think."

1 *Oedipus.* See Sophocles' *Oedipus Rex* in the section on drama. By solving the riddle of the
Sphinx Oedipus moved closer to his fate; which was to marry his own mother.

Léopold Sédar Senghor   (b. 1906)
NIGHT OF SINE°   1975

Tr. Ellen Conroy Kennedy

Woman, rest your balsam hands upon my brow, softer your hands are
      than fur.
Above, the swaying palms rustle faintly in the evening breeze.
Not quite a lullaby.
May the rhythmic silence cradle us.
Let us listen to its song, listen to our dark blood beat,   5
Let us listen to it beat, the deep pulse beat of Africa in the mist of lost
      villages.

Lazily the moon inclines into her slack sea bed.
Laughter dies away, and even storytellers
Begin to nod their heads like sleepy children dozing on their mothers'
      backs.
The dancers' feet grow heavy now, as the alternating choirs cease.   10

It's star time, and dreamily the Night leans her elbows on this cloudy
      hill, draped in her long, milky robe.
Tenderly the rooftops gleam. What are they confiding to the stars?
Within, the fire burns low in the privacy of odors sharp and sweet.

Sine: A river; also the province where Senghor was born.

Woman, light the limpid butter lamp, so around it ancestors can come
    to chat like parents when their children are in bed.
Let us listen to the ancients of Elissa.° Exiled, like us.   15
They did not wish to die, or lose their fertile torrent in the sands.
Let me listen in the smoky hut where friendly souls have come to visit,
My head upon your breast, warm as couscous newly steaming from the
    fire.
Let me breathe the odor of our Dead, let me gather and repeat their
    living voices, let me learn
To live before I sink, deeper than a diver, into the lofty depths of
    sleep.   20

15 *Elissa*: The home of Senghor's ancestors.

Anne Sexton   (1928–1974)
HER KIND   1960

I have gone out, a possessed witch,
haunting the black air, braver at night;
dreaming evil, I have done my hitch
over the plain houses, light by light:
lonely thing, twelve-fingered, out of mind.   5
A woman like that is not a woman, quite.
I have been her kind.

I have found the warm caves in the woods,
filled them with skillets, carvings, shelves,
closets, silks, innumerable goods;   10
fixed the suppers for the worms and the elves:
whining, rearranging the disaligned.
A woman like that is misunderstood.
I have been her kind.

I have ridden in your cart, driver,   15
waved my nude arms at villages going by,
learning the last bright routes, survivor
where your flames still bite my thigh
and my ribs crack where your wheels wind.
A woman like that is not ashamed to die.   20
I have been her kind.

Anne Sexton   (1928–1974)
RINGING THE BELLS   1960

And this is the way they ring
the bells in Bedlam
and this is the bell-lady

who comes each Tuesday morning
to give us a music lesson   5
and because the attendants make you go
and because we mind by instinct,
like bees caught in the wrong hive,
we are the circle of the crazy ladies
who sit in the lounge of the mental house   10
and smile at the smiling woman
who passes us each a bell,
who points at my hand
that holds my bell, E flat,
and this is the gray dress next to me   15
who grumbles as if it were special
to be old, to be old,
and this is the small hunched squirrel girl
on the other side of me
who picks at the hairs over her lip,   20
who picks at the hairs over her lip all day,
and this is how the bells really sound,
as untroubled and clean
as a workable kitchen,
and this is always my bell responding   25
to my hand that responds to the lady
who points at me, E flat;
and although we are no better for it,
they tell you to go. And you do.

Anne Sexton   (1928–1974)

FOR MY LOVER, RETURNING TO HIS WIFE   1969

She is all there.
She was melted carefully down for you
and cast up from your childhood,
cast up from your one hundred favorite aggies.
She has always been there, my darling.   5
She is, in fact, exquisite.
Fireworks in the dull middle of February
and as real as a cast-iron pot.

Let's face it, I have been momentary.
A luxury. A bright red sloop in the harbor.   10
My hair rising like smoke from the car window.
Littleneck clams out of season.

She is more than that. She is your have to have,
has grown you your practical your tropical growth.
This is not an experiment. She is all harmony.   15
She sees to oars and oarlocks for the dinghy,

has placed wild flowers at the window at breakfast,
sat by the potter's wheel at midday,
set forth three children under the moon,
three cherubs drawn by Michelangelo,   20

done this with her legs spread out
in the terrible months in the chapel.
If you glance up, the children are there
like delicate balloons resting on the ceiling.

She has also carried each one down the hall   25
after supper, their heads privately bent,
two legs protesting, person to person,
her face flushed with a song and their little sleep.

I give you back your heart.
I give you permission—   30

for the fuse inside her, throbbing
angrily in the dirt, for the bitch in her
and the burying of her wound—
for the burying of her small red wound alive—

for the pale flickering flare under her ribs,   35
for the drunken sailor who waits in her left pulse,
for the mother's knee, for the stockings,
for the garter belt, for the call—

the curious call
when you will burrow in arms and breasts   40
and tug at the orange ribbon in her hair
and answer the call, the curious call.

She is so naked and singular.
She is the sum of yourself and your dream.
Climb her like a monument, step after step.   45
She is solid.

As for me, I am a watercolor.
I wash off.

Anne Sexton   (1928–1974)

RED RIDING HOOD   1971

Many are the deceivers:

The suburban matron,
proper in the supermarket,
list in hand so she won't suddenly fly,
buying her Duz and Chuck Wagon dog food,   5
meanwhile ascending from earth,
letting her stomach fill up with helium,
letting her arms go loose as kite tails,
getting ready to meet her lover
a mile down Apple Crest Road   10
in the Congregational Church parking lot.

Two seemingly respectable women
come up to an old Jenny
and show her an envelope
full of money   15
and promise to share the booty
if she'll give them ten thou
as an act of faith.
Her life savings are under the mattress
covered with rust stains   20
and counting.
They are as wrinkled as prunes
but negotiable.
The two women take the money and disappear.
Where is the moral?   25
Not all knives are for
stabbing the exposed belly.
Rock climbs on rock
and it only makes a seashore.
Old Jenny has lost her belief in mattresses   30
and now she has no wastebasket in which
to keep her youth.

The standup comic
on the "Tonight" show
who imitates the Vice President   35
and cracks up Johnny Carson
and delays sleep for millions
of bedfellows watching between their feet,
slits his wrist the next morning
in the Algonquin's° old-fashioned bathroom,   40

40 *Algonquin*: A hotel in New York's theatre district.

the razor in his hand like a toothbrush,
wall as anonymous as a urinal,
the shower curtain his slack rubberman audience,
and then the slash
as simple as opening a letter   45
and the warm blood breaking out like a rose
upon the bathtub with its claw and ball feet.

And I. I too.
Quite collected at cocktail parties,
meanwhile in my head   50
I'm undergoing open-heart surgery.
The heart, poor fellow,
pounding on his little tin drum
with a faint death beat.
The heart, that eyeless beetle,   55
enormous that Kafka beetle,°
running panicked through his maze,
never stopping one foot after the other
one hour after the other
until he gags on an apple   60
and it's all over.

And I. I too again.
I built a summer house on Cape Ann.
A simple A-frame and this too was
a deception—nothing haunts a new house.   65
When I moved in with a bathing suit and tea bags
the ocean rumbled like a train backing up
and at each window secrets came in
like gas. My mother, that departed soul,
sat in my Eames chair° and reproached me   70
for losing her keys to the old cottage.
Even in the electric kitchen there was
the smell of a journey. The ocean
was seeping through its frontiers
and laying me out on its wet rails.   75
The bed was stale with my childhood
and I could not move to another city
where the worthy make a new life.

Long ago
there was a strange deception: 80
a wolf dressed in frills,

---

56 *Kafka beetle*: Franz Kafka's *Metamophosis* begins with a character who wakes up as a cockroach.   70 *Eames chair*: Expensive metal and leather designer chair by Charles Eames.

a kind of transvestite.
But I get ahead of my story.
In the beginning
there was just little Red Riding Hood,   85
so called because her grandmother
made her a red cape and she was never without it.
It was her Linus blanket, besides
it was red, as red as the Swiss flag,
yes it was red, as red as chicken blood.   90
But more than she loved her riding hood
she loved her grandmother who lived
far from the city in the big wood.

This one day her mother gave her
a basket of wine and cake   95
to take to her grandmother
because she was ill.
Wine and cake?
Where's the aspirin? The penicillin?
Where's the fruit juice?   100
Peter Rabbit got camomile tea.
But wine and cake it was.

On her way in the big wood
Red Riding Hood met the wolf.
Good day, Mr. Wolf, she said,   105
thinking him no more dangerous
than a streetcar or a panhandler.
He asked where she was going
and she obligingly told him.
There among the roots and trunks   110
with the mushrooms pulsing inside the moss
he planned how to eat them both,
the grandmother an old carrot
and the child a shy budkin
in a red red hood.   115
He bade her to look at the bloodroot,
the small bunchberry and the dogtooth
and pick some for her grandmother.
And this she did.
Meanwhile he scampered off   120
to Grandmother's house and ate her up
as quick as a slap.
Then he put on her nightdress and cap
and snuggled down into the bed.
A deceptive fellow.   125

Red Riding Hood
knocked on the door and entered
with her flowers, her cake, her wine.
Grandmother looked strange,
a dark and hairy disease it seemed.   130
Oh Grandmother, what big ears you have,
ears, eyes, hands and then the teeth.
The better to eat you with, my dear.
So the wolf gobbled Red Riding Hood down
like a gumdrop. Now he was fat.   135
He appeared to be in his ninth month
and Red Riding Hood and her grandmother
rode like two Jonahs up and down with
his every breath. One pigeon. One partridge.

He was fast asleep,   140
dreaming in his cap and gown
wolfless.
Along came a huntsman who heard
the loud contented snores
and knew that was no grandmother.   145
He opened the door and said,
So it's you, old sinner.
He raised his gun to shoot him
when it occurred to him that maybe
the wolf had eaten up the old lady.   150
So he took a knife and began cutting open
the sleeping wolf, a kind of caesarian section.

It was a carnal knife that let
Red Riding Hood out like a poppy,
quite alive from the kingdom of the belly.   155
And grandmother too
still waiting for cakes and wine.
The wolf, they decided, was too mean
to be simply shot so they filled his belly
with large stones and sewed him up.   160
He was as heavy as a cemetery
and when he woke up and tried to run off
he fell over dead. Killed by his own weight.
Many a deception ends on such a note.

The huntsman and the grandmother and Red Riding Hood   165
sat down by his corpse and had a meal of wine and cake.
Those two remembering
nothing naked and brutal

from that little death,
that little birth, 170
from their going down
and their lifting up.

Anne Sexton   (1928–1974)

SNOW WHITE AND THE SEVEN DWARFS   1971

No matter what life you lead
the virgin is a lovely number:
cheeks as fragile as cigarette paper,
arms and legs made of Limoges,°
lips like Vin Du Rhône,° 5
rolling her china-blue doll eyes
open and shut.
Open to say,
Good Day Mama,
and shut for the thrust 10
of the unicorn.
She is unsoiled.
She is as white as a bonefish.

Once there was a lovely virgin
called Snow White. 15
Say she was thirteen.
Her stepmother,
a beauty in her own right,
though eaten, of course, by age,
would hear of no beauty surpassing her own. 20
Beauty is a simple passion,
but, oh my friends, in the end
you will dance the fire dance in iron shoes.
The stepmother had a mirror to which she referred—
something like the weather forecast— 25
a mirror that proclaimed
the one beauty of the land.
She would ask,
Looking glass upon the wall,
who is fairest of us all? 30
And the mirror would reply,
You are fairest of us all.
Pride pumped in her like poison.

4 *Limoges*: A kind of fine French China.   5 *Vin Du Rhône*: Red wine from the Rhône district of France.

Suddenly one day the mirror replied,
Queen, you are full fair, 'tis true,   35
but Snow White is fairer than you.
Until that moment Snow White
had been no more important
than a dust mouse under the bed.
But now the queen saw brown spots on her hand   40
and four whiskers over her lip
so she condemned Snow White
to be hacked to death.
Bring me her heart, she said to the hunter,
and I will salt it and eat it.   45
The hunter, however, let his prisoner go
and brought a boar's heart back to the castle.
The queen chewed it up like a cube steak.
Now I am fairest, she said,
lapping her slim white fingers.   50

Snow White walked in the wildwood
for weeks and weeks.
At each turn there were twenty doorways
and at each stood a hungry wolf,
his tongue lolling out like a worm.   55
The birds called out lewdly,
talking like pink parrots,
and the snakes hung down in loops,
each a noose for her sweet white neck.
On the seventh week   60
she came to the seventh mountain
and there she found the dwarf house.
It was as droll as a honeymoon cottage
and completely equipped with
seven beds, seven chairs, seven forks   65
and seven chamber pots.
Snow White ate seven chicken livers
and lay down, at last, to sleep.

The dwarfs, those little hot dogs,
walked three times around Snow White,   70
the sleeping virgin. They were wise
and wattled like small czars.
Yes. It's a good omen,
they said, and will bring us luck.
They stood on tiptoes to watch   75
Snow White wake up. She told them
about the mirror and the killer-queen

and they asked her to stay and keep house.
Beware of your stepmother,
they said.   80
Soon she will know you are here.
While we are away in the mines
during the day, you must not
open the door.

Looking glass upon the wall . . .   85
The mirror told
and so the queen dressed herself in rags
and went out like a peddler to trap Snow White.
She went across seven mountains.
She came to the dwarf house   90
and Snow White opened the door
and bought a bit of lacing.
The queen fastened it tightly
around her bodice,
as tight as an Ace bandage,   95
so tight that Snow White swooned.
She lay on the floor, a plucked daisy.
When the dwarfs came home they undid the lace
and she revived miraculously.
She was as full of life as soda pop.   100
Beware of your stepmother,
they said.
She will try once more.

Looking glass upon the wall . . .
Once more the mirror told   105
and once more the queen dressed in rags
and once more Snow White opened the door.
This time she bought a poison comb,
a curved eight-inch scorpion,
and put it in her hair and swooned again.   110
The dwarfs returned and took out the comb
and she revived miraculously.
She opened her eyes as wide as Orphan Annie.
Beware, beware, they said,
but the mirror told,   115
the queen came,
Snow White, the dumb bunny,
opened the door
and she bit into a poison apple
and fell down for the final time.   120
When the dwarfs returned

they undid her bodice,
they looked for a comb,
but it did no good.
Though they washed her with wine   125
and rubbed her with butter
it was to no avail.
She lay as still as a gold piece.

The seven dwarfs could not bring themselves
to bury her in the black ground   130
so they made a glass coffin
and set it upon the seventh mountain
so that all who passed by
could peek in upon her beauty.
A prince came one June day   135
and would not budge.
He stayed so long his hair turned green
and still he would not leave.
The dwarfs took pity upon him
and gave him the glass Snow White—   140
its doll's eyes shut forever—
to keep in his far-off castle.
As the prince's men carried the coffin
they stumbled and dropped it
and the chunk of apple flew out   145
of her throat and she woke up miraculously.

And thus Snow White became the prince's bride.
The wicked queen was invited to the wedding feast
and when she arrived there were
red-hot iron shoes,   150
in the manner of red-hot roller skates,
clamped upon her feet.
First your toes will smoke
and then your heels will turn black
and you will fry upward like a frog,   155
she was told.
And so she danced until she was dead,
a subterranean figure,
her tongue flicking in and out
like a gas jet.   160
Meanwhile Snow White held court,
rolling her china-blue doll eyes open and shut
and sometimes referring to her mirror
as women do.

WINDOW ON

Poetry and the Canon

For critic Richard Ohmann the canon is "a shared understanding of what work is worth preserving." In other words, it is the poetry that we (whoever "we" may be) think is of lasting value. William Shakespeare, John Donne, John Milton, John Keats, William Wordsworth, William Blake, Walt Whitman, Emily Dickinson, Robert Frost, T. S. Eliot, Dylan Thomas, Anne Sexton, Langston Hughes, and Sylvia Plath have all been recognized by readers, critics, teachers, and anthologists as canonical. Each of these poets is represented in this book by a number of well-known poems. Influential anthologies, such as Palgrave's *Golden Treasury* and the various editions of the *Oxford Anthology of English Poetry* and *Oxford Anthology of American Poetry*, have helped establish who is canonical and which works are worth reading. Every anthology, including this one, contributes toward establishing a canon.

The controversy regarding the literary canon concerns the fact that any selection of important poetry will be shaped by the critical views of those doing the selecting. The historical critic will select writers such as Shakespeare and Milton, who respond to historical influences. The Marxist critic might choose William Blake and Allen Ginsberg. The New Critic will move toward John Keats, Elizabeth Bishop, Wallace Stevens, and William Butler Yeats. The feminist critic will emphasize Anne Sexton, Denise Levertov, Anna Akhmatova, and Sylvia Plath. Ethnic critics may emphasize Langston Hughes, June Jordan, Imamu Amiri Baraka, Ishmael Reed, Peter Blue Cloud, N. Scott Momaday, Ray A. Young Bear, Carter Revard, or Leslie Marmon Silko. This is not to say that any of these critics would choose such poets exclusively, but only that their sense of what is good and what is canonically important will be shaped by their critical premises. That principle is fundamental to the way canons are formed.

Those who wish to expand the canon to include writers traditionally excluded expect anthologies to reflect current attitudes toward what makes a poem important and lasting. Today criticism is no longer dominated entirely by one model, such as historicism or the formalist New Criticism, which informed most anthologies of poetry composed up to 1980. With the rise of feminist, ethnic, and political criticism, poets who might have been excluded have found their way into new collections.

One of the ways in which you can participate in the philosophical issues regarding canon formation is to make a series of choices of your own. Read one poem from each of the following ten poets: Marvin Bell, Peter Blue Cloud, William Blake, Marilyn Chin, E. E. Cummings, Bernard Dadié, Robert Frost,

June Jordan, Adrienne Rich, and Stevie Smith. Then choose three poems you want your friends to read. Then justify your choices. You can learn even more about canon formation if you perform this experiment with a group of people all working from the same poems. If a canon is formed by consensus, on what is the consensus based?

The canon of English-language poetry has been formed in part by tradition handed down in schools. The poems in school change from generation to generation, but not as much as one might suspect. Examining old schoolbooks will show that "tried and true" poets such as Shakespeare, Milton, Keats, Wordsworth, Arnold, and Frost appear again and again. But since control over the poems being taught is in the hands of the teacher choosing them, the teacher's critical principles will prevail. Therefore, another experiment would be to find five poems that are not in this anthology but that you think belong in it by virtue of their importance or their achievement. Submit those poems to the consensus of your group and if possible photocopy the one poem that your group feels is best from each individual's choice of five and make an anthology for your own consideration. In this way you will contribute to canon formation in a concrete way, seeing some of the practical as well as theoretical problems involved in the process.

Finally, if we assume that the canon should include lasting poems of new writers as well as those who are already "household names," you can conduct yet another experiment by reading some new poets whose work is not yet part of the canon. Which of the following poets do you feel belongs in the canon: Agha Shahid Ali, Sheila Dietz, James Doyle, Christine Holbo, Jenny Joseph, or Richard Jackson? Choose only one and if possible compare your choice with that of others, perhaps also comparing your poet with poets you feel are certainly regarded as canonical now.

Reading

Fiedler, Leslie, and Houston A. Baker, Jr., eds. *English Literature: Opening Up the Canon*. Baltimore: Johns Hopkins University Press, 1981.

Gates, Henry Louis. "Whose Canon Is It, Anyway?" *New York Times Book Review*, 26 February 1989, p. 1.

Gorak, Jan. *The Making of the Modern Canon: Genesis and Crisis of a Literary Idea*. London: Athlone, 1991.

Guillory, John. "Canonical and Non-Canonical: A Critique of the Current Debate." *English Literary History* 54 (1987): 483–527.

———. *Cultural Capital: The Problem of Literary Canon Formation*. Chicago: Chicago University Press, 1993.

Said, Edward. *The World, the Text, and the Critic*. London: Faber and Faber, 1984.

William Shakespeare   (1564–1616)

SONNET 18: SHALL I COMPARE THEE TO A SUMMER'S DAY?   1609

Shall I compare thee to a summer's day?
Thou art more lovely and more temperate:
Rough winds do shake the darling buds of May,
And summer's lease hath all too short a date;
Sometime too hot the eye of heaven shines,   5
And often is his gold complexion dimmed,
And every fair from fair° sometime declines,
By chance or nature's changing course untrimmed:
But thy eternal summer shall not fade,
Nor lose possession of that fair thou ow'st,°   10
Nor shall Death brag thou wand'rest in his shade,
When in eternal lines to time thou grow'st.
   So long as men can breathe or eyes can see,
   So long lives this, and this gives life to thee.

---

7 *fair . . . fair:* Every beautiful thing ceases to be beautiful.   10 *ow'st:* Ownest.

William Shakespeare   (1564–1616)

SONNET 30: WHEN TO THE SESSIONS OF SWEET SILENT THOUGHT   1609

When to the sessions° of sweet silent thought
I summon up remembrance of things past,
I sigh the lack of many a thing I sought,
And with old woes new wail my dear time's waste;
Then can I drown an eye (unused to flow)   5
For precious friends hid in death's dateless° night,
And weep afresh love's long since cancelled° woe,
And moan the expense° of many a vanished sight;
Then can I grieve at grievances foregone,
And heavily° from woe to woe tell o'er   10
The sad account of fore-bemoanèd moan,
Which I new pay as if not paid before:
   But if the while I think on thee, dear friend,
   All losses are restored, and sorrows end.

---

1 *sessions:* Sessions of a law court.   6 *dateless:* Timeless.   7 *cancelled:* Paid for.   8 *expense:* Loss.   10 *heavily:* Sadly.

William Shakespeare   (1564–1616)

SONNET 106: WHEN IN THE CHRONICLE OF WASTED TIME   1609

When in the chronicle of wasted time
I see descriptions of the fairest wights,
And beauty making beautiful old rhyme
In praise of ladies dead and lovely knights,
Then in the blazon of sweet beauty's best,   5
Of hand, of foot, of lip, of eye, of brow,
I see their antique pen would have expressed
Even such a beauty as you master now.
So all their praises are but prophecies
Of this our time, all you prefiguring,   10
And for° they looked but with divining° eyes,
They had not still enough your worth to sing:
 For we which now behold these present days
 Have eyes to wonder, but lack tongues to praise.

11 *for*: Because. *divining*: Guessing.

William Shakespeare   (1564–1616)

SONNET 116: LET ME NOT TO THE MARRIAGE OF TRUE MINDS   1609

Let me not to the marriage of true minds
Admit impediments; love is not love
Which alters when it alteration finds,
Or bends with the remover to remove.
O no, it is an ever-fixèd mark   5
That looks on tempests and is never shaken;
It is the star to every wandering bark,
Whose worth's unknown, although his height be taken.
Love's not Time's fool, though rosy lips and cheeks
Within his bending sickle's compass come;   10
Love alters not with his brief hours and weeks,
But bears it out even to the edge of doom.
 If this be error and upon me proved,
 I never writ, nor no man ever loved.

William Shakespeare   (1564–1616)

SONNET 129: THE EXPENSE OF SPIRIT IN A WASTE OF SHAME   1609

The expense of spirit° in a waste of shame
Is lust in action, and till action,° lust
Is perjured, murderous, bloody, full of blame,
Savage, extreme, rude, cruel, not to trust,
Enjoyed no sooner but despisèd straight,°   5
Past reason° hunted, and no sooner had,
Past reason hated as a swallowed bait
On purpose laid to make the taker mad:
Mad in pursuit and in possession so,
Had, having, and in quest to have, extreme,   10
A bliss in proof,° and proved, a very woe,
Before, a joy proposed; behind, a dream.
    All this the world well knows, yet none knows well
    To shun the heaven that leads men to this hell.

1 *expense of spirit*: Ejaculation of semen, or any waste of vitality.   2 *till action*: Until consummation.   5 *straight*: Immediately.   6 *past reason*: Madly.   11 *in proof*: While being
experienced, tested.

William Shakespeare   (1564–1616)

SONNET 135: WHOEVER HATH HER WISH, THOU HAST THY WILL,   1609

Whoever hath her wish, thou hast thy Will,°
And Will to boot,° and Will in overplus;
More than enough am I that vex thee still,
To thy sweet will making addition thus.°
Wilt thou, whose will is large and spacious,   5
Not once vouchsafe to hide my will in thine?
Shall will in others seem right gracious,
And in my will no fair acceptance shine?
The sea, all water, yet receives rain still,
And in abundance addeth to his store,   10
So thou being rich in Will add to thy Will
One will of mine to make thy large Will more.
    Let no unkind, no fair beseechers kill;
    Think all but one, and me in that one Will.

1 *Will*: Shakespeare puns on his name, on will as lustful desire.   2 *to boot*: In addition.   4 *mak-*
ing addition thus: That is, by adding him.

William Shakespeare (1564–1616)
SONNET 144: TWO LOVES I HAVE OF COMFORT AND DESPAIR, 1609

Two loves I have of comfort and despair,
Which like two spirits do suggest me still:°
The better angel is a man right fair,
The worser spirit a woman colored ill.°
To win me soon to hell, my female evil   5
Tempteth my better angel from my side,
And would corrupt my saint to be a devil,
Wooing his purity with her foul pride.°
And whether that my angel be turned fiend
Suspect I may, yet not directly tell,   10
But being both from me, both to each friend,°
I guess one angel in another's hell.
    Yet this shall I ne'er know, but live in doubt,
    Till my bad angel fire my good one out.°

2 *suggest me still*: Always tempt me. 4 *colored ill*: A brunette. 8 *pride*: Sexual desire.
11 *both to each friend*: Friends to one another. 14 *fire . . . out*: Reject, or give venereal disease to (which would prove they slept together).

Leslie Marmon Silko (b. 1948)
FOUR MOUNTAIN WOLVES 1973

(Chinle, late winter, 1973, when the wolves came)

I

Gray mist wolf
        from mountain frozen lake
traveling southwest
           over deep snow crust   singing
               Ah ouoo   5
               Ah ouoo
        the fog hangs belly high
        and the deer have all gone.
        Ah ouoo
        Ah ouoo   10
Lonely for deer gone down to the valley
Lonely for wild turkey all flown away.
        Ah ouoo
        Ah ouoo

Gray mist wolf 15
    following the edge of the Sun.

II

Swirling snow wolf
  spill the yellow-eyed wind
                    on blue lake stars
                        Orion 20
                              Saturn.

Swirling snow wolf
      tear the heart from the silence
      rip the tongue from the darkness.
      Shake the earth with your breathing 25
      and explode gray ice dreams of eternity.

III

Mountain white mist wolf
    frozen crystals on silver hair
    icy whiskers
            steaming silver mist from his mouth. 30

Gray fog wolf
      silent
  swift and wet
        howling along cliffs of midnight sky,
you have traveled the years 35
        on your way to Black Mountain.

Call to the centuries as you pass
      howling wolf wind
            their fear is your triumph
            they huddle in the distances 40
                        weak.

Lean wolf running
      where miles become faded in time,
      the urge   the desire   is always with me
      the dream of green eyes wolf 45
      as she reaches the swollen belly elk
        softly
      her pale lavender outline
      startled into eternity.

Louis Simpson   (b. 1923)

NEW LINES FOR CUSCUSCARAWAY AND MIRZA MURAD ALI BEG° 1988

. . . the particular verse we are going to get will be cheerful, dry and sophisticated.

—*T. E. HULME*

O amiable prospect!
O kingdom of heaven on earth!
I saw Mr. Eliot leaning over a fence
Like a cheerful embalmer,
And two little Indians with black umbrellas   5
Seeking admission,
And I was rapt in a song
Of so*phis*tication.
O City of God!
Let us be thoroughly dry.   10
Let us sing a new song unto the Lord,
A song of exclusion.
For it is not so much a matter of being chosen
As of not being excluded.
I will sing unto the Lord   15
In a voice that is cheerfully dry.

New Lines . . . Ali Beg. See T.S. Eliot, "Lines for Cuscuscaraway and Mirza Murad Ali Beg," p. 741.

Fily-Dabo Sissoko   (1900–1964)

BRUSH FIRE   1964

Tr. Ellen Conroy Kennedy

At the onset of its sprint, the blazing circle climbs straight ahead, flooding the sky with globules of fire, dancing a saraband to dazzled eyes.

Beaten down in the last strong gusts, grasses carpet the underbrush in yellow. Shivering beneath, one feels the teeming life of animals and serpents, wild and small.

Come hunter or honey-seeker, the brush fire lights.

From crackling to crackling, closer and closer it tongues its way. Green grasshoppers, dizzy butterflies take flight. The wind rises, the trees howl death. Sheets of flame, suddenly tall, spring in gusts to storm the summits.

Nothing will stop the brush fire's furious race. Jumping over the thin
curtain of greenery that runs along the riverbanks, it crosses streams,
frightening does and palm-squirrels, pythons and panthers, cobras
and elk.   5

Up to the naked foot of cliffs it creeps, to do final battle there with some
fallen veteran whose ashes, dragged afar, will whiten the burnt earth.

Then, at night, here and there along the length of the horizon, one sees
upon the slopes great spots of flame flickering in the debris.

For long days, brush fire has overcome the steppe.

Charlotte Smith   (1749–1806)

Pressed by the moon, mute arbitress of tides   1786

Written in the churchyard at Middleton in Sussex

Pressed by the moon, mute arbitress of tides,
   While the loud equinox° its power combines,
   The sea no more its swelling surge confines,
But o'er the shrinking land sublimely rides.
The wild blast, rising from the western cave,   5
   Drives the huge billows from their heaving bed,
   Tears from their grassy tombs the village dead,
And breaks the silent sabbath° of the grave!
With shells and seaweed mingled, on the shore
   Lo! their bones whiten in the frequent wave;   10
   But vain to them the winds and waters rave;
They hear the warring elements no more:
While I am doomed—by life's long storm oppressed,
To gaze with envy on their gloomy rest.

2 *equinox*: March 21 or September 21, when days and nights are equal. The March equinox is
often marked by strong winds in England.   8 *sabbath*: Peace, rest.

Dave Smith   (b. 1942)

ON A FIELD TRIP AT FREDERICKSBURG°   1975

The big steel tourist shield says maybe
fifteen thousand got it here. No word
of either Whitman° or one uncle

Fredericksburg: A bloody Civil War battlefield.   3 *Whitman*: Walt Whitman was a Civil War nurse.

I barely remember in the smoke
that filled his tiny mountain house.   5

If each finger were a thousand of them
I could clap my hands and be dead
up to my wrists. It was quick
though not so fast as we can do it
now, one bomb, atomic or worse,   10
one silly pod slung on wing-tip,
high up, an egg cradled
by some rapacious mockingbird.

Hiroshima canned nine times their number
in a flash. Few had the time   15
to moan or feel the feeling
ooze back in the groin.

In a ditch I stand
above Marye's Heights,° the book-
boned faces of Brady's° fifteen-year-old   20
drummers, before battle, rigid°
as August's dandelions
all the way to the Potomac
rolling in my skull.

If Audubon came here, the names   25
of birds would gush, the marvel
single feathers make
evoke a cloud, a nation,
a gray blur preserved
on a blue horizon, but   30
there is only a wandering child,
one dark stalk snapped off
in her hand, held out to me.
Taking it, I try to help her
hold its obscure syllables   35
one instant in her mouth,
like a drift of wind
at the forehead, the front door,
the black, numb fingernails.

---

19 *Marye's Heights:* The stone wall that Union troops tried to take; over 12,000 Union soldiers died in the attempt.   20 *Brady:* Matthew Brady (c. 1823–1896), famous for his photographs of the Civil War.   21 *rigid:* People in old photographs had to stand a long time
for the photographer.

Stevie Smith   (1902–1971)

THE GALLOPING CAT   1966

Oh I am a cat that likes to
Gallop about doing good
So
One day when I was
Galloping about doing good, I saw   5
A Figure in the path; I said:
Get off! (Be-
cause
I am a cat that likes to
Gallop about doing good)   10
But he did not move, instead
He raised his hand as if
To land me a cuff
So I made to dodge so as to
Prevent him bringing it orf,   15
Un-for-tune-ately I slid
On a banana skin
Some Ass had left instead
Of putting in the bin. So
His hand caught me on the cheek   20
I tried
To lay his arm open from wrist to elbow
With my sharp teeth
Because I am
A cat that likes to gallop about doing good.   25
Would you believe it?
He wasn't there
My teeth met nothing but air,
But a Voice said: Poor cat,
(Meaning me) and a soft stroke   30
Came on me head
Since when
I have been bald.
I regard myself as
A martyr to doing good.   35
Also I heard a swoosh
As of wings, and saw
A halo shining at the height of
Mrs Gubbins's backyard fence,
So I thought: What's the good   40
Of galloping about doing good

When angels stand in the path
And do not do as they should
Such as having an arm to be bitten off
All the same I   45
Intend to go on being
A cat that likes to
Gallop about doing good
So
Now with my bald head I go,   50
Chopping the untidy flowers down, to and fro,
An' scooping up the grass to show
Underneath
The cinder path of wrath
Ha ha ha ha, ho,   55
Angels aren't the only ones who do not know
What's what and that
Galloping about doing good
Is a full-time job
That needs   60
An experienced eye of earthly
Sharpness, worth I dare say
(If you'll forgive a personal note)
A good deal more
Than all that skyey stuff   65
Of angels that make so bold as
To pity a cat like me that
Gallops about doing good.

Stevie Smith (1902–1971)

SCORPION 1971

"This night shall thy soul be required of thee"
My soul is never required of *me*
It always has to be somebody else of course
Will my soul be required of me tonight perhaps?

(I often wonder what it will be like   5
To have one's soul required of one
But all I can think of is the Out-Patients' Department—
"Are you Mrs. Briggs, dear?"
No, I am Scorpion.)

I should like my soul to be required of me, so as   10
To waft over grass till it comes to the blue sea

I am very fond of grass, I always have been, but there must
Be no cow, person or house to be seen.

Sea and *grass* must be quite empty
Other souls can find somewhere *else*.   15

O Lord God please come
And require the soul of thy Scorpion

Scorpion so wishes to be gone.

Stevie Smith   (1902–1971)
AWAY, MELANCHOLY   1957

Away, melancholy,
Away with it, let it go.

Are not the trees green,
The earth as green?
Does not the wind blow,   5
Fire leap and the rivers flow?
Away melancholy.

The ant is busy
He carrieth his meat,
All things hurry   10
To be eaten or eat.
Away, melancholy.

Man, too, hurries,
Eats, couples, buries,
He is an animal also   15
With a hey ho melancholy,
Away with it, let it go.

Man of all creatures
Is superlative
(Away melancholy)   20
He of all creatures alone
Raiseth a stone
(Away melancholy)
Into the stone, the god,
Pours what he knows of good   25
Calling good, God.
Away melancholy, let it go.

Speak not to me of tears,
Tyranny, pox, wars,

Saying, Can God   30
Stone of man's thought, be good?

Say rather it is enough
That the stuffed
Stone of man's good, growing,
By man's called God.   35
Away, melancholy, let it go.

Man aspires
To good,
To love
Sighs;   40

Beaten, corrupted, dying
In his own blood lying
Yet heaves up an eye above
Cries, Love, love.
It is his virtue needs explaining,   45
Not his failing.

Away, melancholy,
Away with it, let it go.

Gary Snyder   (b. 1930)
RIPRAP   1965

Lay down these words
Before your mind like rocks.
   placed solid, by hands
In choice of place, set
Before the body of the mind   5
   in space and time:
Solidity of bark, leaf, or wall
   riprap of things:
Cobble of milky way,
   straying planets,   10
These poems, people,
   lost ponies with
Dragging saddles
   and rocky sure-foot trails.
The worlds like an endless   15
   four-dimensional
Game of *Go*.
   ants and pebbles

In the thin loam, each rock a word
        a creek-washed stone   20
Granite: ingrained
        with torment of fire and weight
Crystal and sediment linked hot
        all change, in thoughts,
As well as things.   25

Cathy Song   (b. 1955)

THE YOUNGEST DAUGHTER   c. 1983

The sky has been dark
for many years.
My skin has become as damp
and pale as rice paper
and feels the way   5
mother's used to before the drying sun
parched it out there in the fields.

        Lately, when I touch my eyelids,
my hands react as if
I had just touched something   10
hot enough to burn.
My skin, aspirin colored,
tingles with migraine. Mother
has been massaging the left side of my face
especially in the evenings   15
when the pain flares up.

This morning
her breathing was graveled,
her voice gruff with affection
when I wheeled her into the bath.   20
She was in a good humor,
making jokes about her great breasts,
floating in the milky water
like two walruses,
flaccid and whiskered around the nipples.   25
I scrubbed them with a sour taste
in my mouth, thinking:
six children and an old man
have sucked from these brown nipples.

I was almost tender   30
when I came to the blue bruises

that freckle her body,
places where she has been injecting insulin
for thirty years. I soaped her slowly,
she sighed deeply, her eyes closed.   35
It seems it has always
been like this: the two of us
in this sunless room,
the splashing of the bathwater.

In the afternoons   40
when she has rested,
she prepares our ritual of tea and rice,
garnished with a shred of gingered fish,
a slice of pickled turnip,
a token for my white body.   45
We eat in the familiar silence.
She knows I am not to be trusted,
even now planning my escape.
As I toast to her health
with the tea she has poured,   50
a thousand cranes curtain the window,
fly up in a sudden breeze.

Marcia Southwick   (b. 1949)

OWNING A DEAD MAN   c. 1980

The geese fly off, but sometimes they don't take
their voices with them. Stretched out like this,
I think my future is simple, like a cornfield
filling with light. I'm happy,
because of the way the geese have left their shadows   5
drying on the lawn around me, and the way
the long docks lean out into the water,
letting the unpainted boats knock against them.
Once, my mother told me, a woman came to this place
with an urn that held her dead husband's ashes.   10
The woman's pale hands tossed bits of gray-white
bone and soot onto the marsh, where the quail hid.
My mother was angry that the bones had trespassed
her land. *In a way*, she said, *I own a dead man*.

Now as I lie here, I think of the coming winter,   15
of his bones, mixed with the bones of the mouse
and the gull, cleansed and shining in the new snow,

but if I try to think too deeply, it's as if a bird
were pulling straws from a dried out nest!
So I wonder if I have ever witnessed the middle   20
of winter: the birch trees' inability to lose
anything more, or if I have ever seen myself
as more irrelevant than in December—
In that cold and stillness, my blood
and my muscles contracting as I tramp through the snow   25
couldn't possibly mean anything. And there *are* days
when a landscape feels nothing for its real trees,
only for what lies still in the snow,
or only for what has been.

Marcia Southwick   (b. 1949)
DUSK   c. 1980

I cannot worry
about what lies beneath the surface,
so I walk into the fragile dusk,
breaking the backs of field mice
still asleep under the snow.   5
The sunlight that does not reach me
illuminates the distance
between this world and God's,
where winter is simply the white
of perfect concentration.   10
I would like to believe in God,
just as I would like to believe there is an angel
weeping beneath the Chinese elms,
but He is an abstraction, like forgetfulness
or mathematics. In the mind of God,   15
winter can be summarized as one dark tree!
And yet, as I walk out over the frozen pond,
the pure white of this winter
enters my mind, and I become more open,
like a clearing in the woods   20
where light accentuates the dead underbrush
without emphasizing its ugliness.
And so I can live with my faults.
I can be touched
and not feel like a passing shadow.   25

Maura Stanton (b. 1946)
CHILDHOOD 1984

I used to lie on my back, imagining
A reverse house on the ceiling of my house
Where I could walk around in empty rooms
All by myself. There was no furniture
Up there, only a glass globe in the floor,   5
And knee-high barriers at every door.
The low silled windows opened on blue air.
Nothing hung in the closet; even the kitchen
Seemed immaculate, a place for thought.
I liked to walk across the swirling plaster   10
Into the parts of the house I couldn't see.
The hum from the other house, now my ceiling,
Reached me only faintly. I'd look up
To find my brothers watching old cartoons,
Or my mother vacuuming the ugly carpet.   15
I'd stare amazed at unmade beds, the clutter,
Shoes, half-dressed dolls, the telephone,
Then return dizzily to my perfect floorplan
Where I never spoke or listened to anyone.

I must have turned down the wrong hall,   20
Or opened a door that locked shut behind me,
For I live on the ceiling now, not the floor.
This is my house, room after empty room.
How do I ever get back to the real house
Where my sisters spill milk, my father calls,   25
And I am at the table, eating cereal?
I fill my white rooms with furniture,
Hang curtains over the piercing blue outside.
I lie on my back. I strive to look down.
This ceiling is higher than it used to be,   30
The floor so far away I can't determine
Which room I'm in, which year, which life.

Maura Stanton (b. 1946)
BIOGRAPHY C. 1984

Perhaps biography is the flat map
Abstracted from the globe of someone's life:
We are interested in the routes and detours.

So I found myself last summer in a storm
Driving down the Main Street of Red Cloud   5
Looking for Willa Cather's° house, which was closed.
Then I drove to the Geographic Center
Of the United States, where she may have once walked
When the red grasses covered the prairie.
I tried to see for a moment through her eyes.   10
I looked at cows; I turned my head away
From the abandoned motel and two roadside tables—
But it was those forlorn shapes I remembered
Back in my own life, out on the highway.

6 *Willa Cather*: Novelist (1873–1947) who wrote about the Midwest.

George Starbuck   (b. 1931)

ON FIRST LOOKING IN ON BLODGETT'S KEATS'S
"CHAPMAN'S HOMER"°   1960

(Sum. ¹/₂C. M9–II)°

Mellifluous as bees,° these brittle men
droning of Honeyed Homer give me hives.
I scratch, yawn like a bear, my arm arrives
at yours—oh, Honey, and we're back again,
me the Balboa, you the Darien,   5
lording the loud Pacific sands, our lives
as hazarded as when a petrel dives
to yank the dull sea's coverlet, or when,

breaking from me across the sand that's rink
and record of our weekend boning up   10
on *The Romantic Agony,*° you sink
John Keats a good surf-fisher's cast out—plump
in the sun's wake—and the parched pages drink
that great whales' blanket party hump and hump.

On First . . . "Chapman's Homer": See discussion of this poem on p. 906. *Blodgett* is an edition of Keats.   (*Sum. ¹/₂C. M9–II*): A comic reference to the source of the poem.
1 *Mellifluous as bees*: Buzzing like busy bees.   11 *The Romantic Agony*: A critical study of
the Romantics by Mario Praz.

WINDOW ON

Modernism

The modernist movement in twentieth-century poetry was a response to the horrors of the Boer War in South Africa, World War I, the Great Depression of the 1930s, and World War II. Experts disagree on when the movement began and ended, but it generally refers to the fifty years from 1914 to 1965. James Joyce, T. S. Eliot, Ezra Pound, and W. H. Auden were its primary proponents; other modernists include H. D. (Hilda Doolittle), Elizabeth Sitwell, E. E. Cummings, Dylan Thomas, Gertrude Stein, Wallace Stevens, and William Carlos Williams. These were joined by many other poets of their time.

The wide variety of modernist approaches to poetry makes a definition of modernism difficult. One branch of modernism concentrated on developing imagism. Wallace Stevens, Gertrude Stein, and especially William Carlos Williams, for whom the image did virtually all the work (as in "The Red Wheelbarrow"), wrote much of their poetry in the imagist tradition. They broke so completely with the traditions of conventional verse—as expressed, say, by Shakespeare's sonnets or Keats's odes—that for most modern readers they still seem experimental and surprising. Along with this change came experiments in free verse, which has been the norm since the 1920s. Indeed, only now in the 1990s is there a movement to return to formal poetry.

Among the qualities modernist poets usually shared was a willingness to break with the great tradition of poetry that they had inherited up to the early twentieth century. That meant breaking from the tradition of optimism, sentimentalism, cheerful religious enthusiasm, and confidence in the progress of the human race. The modernists were like warriors with bludgeons, demanding that the audience listen instead to shrill complaints, pained reevaluations, and their personal angst. Ezra Pound, in one of his first published poems, refers to the American reading public as "a mass of dolts." Pound led one wing of the modernist movement in that he forced his readers to acquire some learning in order to read him. Eliot, Yeats, Wallace Stevens, and others did the same in their own way. Modernist poetry was determined to be difficult as a way of demonstrating that modernists would not cater to popular taste. It hoped to create a new kind of reading public, as separate from the masses as the poets themselves.

Part of the modernist movement emphasized discontinuity. T. S. Eliot's modernist landmark, "The Hollow Men" enacts discontinuity in its form, which Eliot describes as "fragments." Moreover, the discontinuity of history—the sense that we are detached from the history of the previous century—is everywhere in their poetry. Some modernists seemed to attempt to reattach themselves to a historical continuity, much as W. H. Auden connected himself to the achievement of W. B. Yeats in his funeral elegy, written at the beginning of World War II. But most saw themselves as hopelessly apart.

Many modernists also expressed a sense of alienation from the community, feeling that the world's rulers were separate, indifferent, and insensitive, leaving the poets to suffer and express the emotional agonies of their culture. Modernist poets criticized the social order that produced horrendous, endless slaughter in war, and then the plague of the Great Depression, which left the average person hopeless and in a state of abject despair for a large part of a generation. So-called traditional values—as defined by Joyce in *A Portrait of the Artist as a Young Man* (1914): nation, church, and family—were thought to be hindrances to the development of the artist. Thus modernism accentuated and institutionalized the detachment and alienation of the artist from society, a process that had begun in Lord Byron's time.

There have been many schools of poetry in Europe, the United States, Puerto Rico, the Caribbean, Russia, Africa, and China in the twentieth century, but in English-language poetry none has had a more profound influence on modern literature, art, and culture than modernism.

Reading

Faulkner, Peter. *Modernism*. New York: Methuen, 1977.

Spears, Monroe K. *Dionysus and the City: Modernism in Twentieth-Century Poetry*. New York: Oxford University Press, 1970.

Symons, Julian. *Makers of the New: The Revolution in Literature 1912–1939*. New York: Random House, 1987.

Wallace Stevens   (1879–1955)

THE EMPEROR OF ICE-CREAM   1923

Call the roller of big cigars,
The muscular one, and bid him whip
In kitchen cups concupiscent curds.
Let the wenches dawdle in such dress
As they are used to wear, and let the boys   5
Bring flowers in last month's newspapers.
Let be be finale of seem.
The only emperor is the emperor of ice-cream.

Take from the dresser of deal,°
Lacking the three glass knobs, that sheet   10
On which she embroidered fantails once

9 *deal*: Fir or pine wood.

And spread it so as to cover her face.
If her horny feet protrude, they come
To show how cold she is, and dumb.
Let the lamp affix its beam.   15
The only emperor is the emperor of ice-cream.

Wallace Stevens   (1879–1955)

THIRTEEN WAYS OF LOOKING AT A BLACKBIRD   1923

I

Among twenty snowy mountains,
The only moving thing
Was the eye of the blackbird.

II

I was of three minds,
Like a tree   5
In which there are three blackbirds.

III

The blackbird whirled in the autumn winds.
It was a small part of the pantomime.

IV

A man and a woman
Are one.   10
A man and a woman and a blackbird
Are one.

V

I do not know which to prefer,
The beauty of inflections
Or the beauty of innuendoes,   15
The blackbird whistling
Or just after.

VI

Icicles filled the long window
With barbaric glass.
The shadow of the blackbird   20
Crossed it, to and fro.
The mood
Traced in the shadow
An indecipherable cause.

VII

    O thin men of Haddam,°   25
    Why do you imagine golden birds?
    Do you not see how the blackbird
    Walks around the feet
    Of the women about you?

VIII

    I know noble accents   30
    And lucid, inescapable rhythms;
    But I know, too,
    That the blackbird is involved
    In what I know.

IX

    When the blackbird flew out of sight,   35
    It marked the edge
    Of one of many circles.

X

    At the sight of blackbirds
    Flying in a green light,
    Even the bawds of euphony   40
    Would cry out sharply.

XI

    He rode over Connecticut
    In a glass coach.
    Once a fear pierced him,
    In that he mistook   45
    The shadow of his equipage
    For blackbirds.

XII

    The river is moving.
    The blackbird must be flying.

XIII

    It was evening all afternoon.   50
    It was snowing
    And it was going to snow.
    The blackbird sat
    In the cedar-limbs.

25 *thin men of Haddam*: Reference to town of Haddam on the Connecticut River. Stevens said he just liked the name and used it.

Wallace Stevens   (1879–1955)

THE IDEA OF ORDER AT KEY WEST   1935

She sang beyond the genius of the sea.
The water never formed to mind or voice,
Like a body wholly body, fluttering
Its empty sleeves; and yet its mimic motion
Made constant cry, caused constantly a cry,   5
That was not ours although we understood,
Inhuman, of the veritable ocean.

The sea was not a mask. No more was she.
The song and water were not medleyed sound
Even if what she sang was what she heard,   10
Since what she sang was uttered word by word.
It may be that in all her phrases stirred
The grinding water and the gasping wind;
But it was she and not the sea we heard.

For she was the maker of the song she sang.   15
The ever-hooded, tragic-gestured sea
Was merely a place by which she walked to sing.
Whose spirit is this? we said, because we knew
It was the spirit that we sought and knew
That we should ask this often as she sang.   20

If it was only the dark voice of the sea
That rose, or even colored by many waves;
If it was only the outer voice of sky
And cloud, of the sunken coral water-walled,
However clear, it would have been deep air,   25
The heaving speech of air, a summer sound
Repeated in a summer without end
And sound alone. But it was more than that,
More even than her voice, and ours, among
The meaningless plungings of water and the wind,   30
Theatrical distances, bronze shadows heaped
On high horizons, mountainous atmospheres
Of sky and sea.
                        It was her voice that made
The sky acutest at its vanishing.
She measured to the hour its solitude.   35
She was the single artificer of the world
In which she sang. And when she sang, the sea,
Whatever self it had, became the self
That was her song, for she was the maker. Then we,

As we beheld her striding there alone,   40
Knew that there never was a world for her
Except the one she sang and, singing, made.

Ramon Fernandez, tell me, if you know,
Why, when the singing ended and we turned
Toward the town, tell why the glassy lights,   45
The lights in the fishing boats at anchor there,
As the night descended, tilting in the air,
Mastered the night and portioned out the sea,
Fixing emblazoned zones and fiery poles,
Arranging, deepening, enchanting night.   50

Oh! Blessed rage for order, pale Ramon,
The maker's rage to order words of the sea,
Words of the fragrant portals, dimly-starred,
And of ourselves and of our origins,
In ghostlier demarcations, keener sounds.   55

Anne Stevenson   (b. 1933)
CAIN°   1977

Lord have mercy upon the angry.
The anguished can take care of each other.
The angels will take care of themselves.
But the angry have no daughters or mothers;
only brute brothers, themselves.   5
Hearing that faint "Abel, Abel" they stop their ears.
Watching that approved flame snake to the sky
they beat stubby blades out of ploughshares,°
cut the sun out of the air,
Stamp on small fires they might have seen by.   10

Cain: In Genesis 4, Cain, the oldest son of Adam and Eve, murdered his brother Abel because the "approved flame" (line 7) of Abel's sacrifice to God was accepted and Cain's was not.
8 *blades out of ploughshares:* A reversal of the biblical phrase *to turn swords into ploughshares,* that is, instruments of war into instruments of peace.

Anne Stevenson   (b. 1933)
BY THE BOAT HOUSE, OXFORD   1977

They belong here in their own quenched country.
I had forgotten nice women could be so nice,
smiling beside large sons on the makeshift quay,
frail, behind pale faces and hurt eyes.

Their husbands are plainly superior, with them, without them.   5
Their boys wear privilege like a clear inheritance, easily.
(Now a swan's neck couples with its own reflection,
making in the simple water a perfect 3.)

The punts° seem resigned to an unexciting mooring.
But the women? It's hard to tell. Do their fine grey hairs   10
and filament lips approve or disdain the loving
that living alone, or else lonely in pairs, impairs?

9 *punts.* Flat-bottomed boats.

Ruth Stone   (b. 1915)
WHERE I CAME FROM   c. 1987

My father put me in my mother
but he didn't pick me out.
I am my own quick woman.
What drew him to my mother?
Beating his drumsticks   5
he thought—why not?
And he gave her an umbrella.
Their marriage was like that.
She hid ironically in her apron.
Sometimes she cried into the biscuit dough.   10
When she wanted to make a point
she would sing a hymn or an old song.
He was loose-footed. He couldn't be counted on
until his pockets were empty.
When he was home the kettle drums,   15
the snare drum, the celeste,
the triangle throbbed.
While he changed their heads,
the drum skins soaked in the bathtub.
Collapsed and wrinkled, they floated   20
like huge used condoms.

Mark Strand   (b. 1934)
WHERE ARE THE WATERS OF CHILDHOOD?   1978

See where the windows are boarded up,
where the gray siding shines in the sun and salt air
and the asphalt shingles on the roof have peeled or fallen off,

where tiers of oxeye daisies float on a sea of grass?
That's the place to begin.   5

Enter the kingdom of rot,
smell the damp plaster, step over the shattered glass,
the pockets of dust, the rags, the soiled remains of a mattress,
look at the rusted stove and sink, at the rectangular stain
on the wall where Winslow Homer's *Gulf Stream* hung.   10

Go to the room where your father and mother
would let themselves go in the drift and pitch of love,
and hear, if you can, the creak of their bed,
then go to the place where you hid.

Go to your room, to all the rooms whose cold, damp air you
     breathed,   15
to all the unwanted places where summer, fall, winter, spring,
seem the same unwanted season, where the trees you knew have died
and other trees have risen. Visit that other place
you barely recall, that other house half hidden.

See the two dogs burst into sight. When you leave,   20
they will cease, snuffed out in the glare of an earlier light.
Visit the neighbors down the block; he waters his lawn,
she sits on her porch, but not for long.
When you look again they are gone.

Keep going back, back to the field, flat and sealed in mist.   25
On the other side, a man and a woman are waiting;
they have come back, your mother before she was gray,
your father before he was white.

Now look at the North West Arm, how it glows a deep cerulean
     blue.
See the light on the grass, the one leaf burning, the cloud   30
that flares. You're almost there, in a moment your parents
will disappear, leaving you under the light of a vanished star,
under the dark of a star newly born. Now is the time.

Now you invent the boat of your flesh and set it upon the waters
and drift in the gradual swell, in the laboring salt.   35
Now you look down. The waters of childhood are there.

Jonathan Swift   (1667–1745)

THE PROGRESS OF BEAUTY   1719–1720

    When first Diana° leaves her Bed,
Vapors and Steams her Looks disgrace;

---

1 *Diana*: The moon.

A frowzy dirty-colored red
Sits on her cloudy wrinkled Face.

But by degrees when mounted high   5
Her artificial Face appears,
Down from her Window in the Sky,
Her Spots are gone, her Visage clears.

'Twixt earthly Females and the Moon
All Parallels exactly run;   10
If Celia° should appear too soon,
Alas, the Nymph would be undone.

To see her from her Pillow rise
All reeking in a cloudy Steam,
Cracked Lips, foul Teeth, and gummy Eyes,   15
Poor Strephon, how would he blaspheme!

The Soot or Powder which was wont
To make her Hair look black as Jet,
Falls from her Tresses on her Front,
A mingled Mass of Dirt and Sweat.   20

Three Colors, Black, and Red, and White,
So graceful in their proper Place,
Remove them to a different Light—
They form a frightful hideous Face,

For instance: when the Lily slips   25
Into the Precincts of the Rose,
And takes Possession of the Lips,
Leaving the Purple to the Nose.

So Celia went entire to bed,
All her Complexions safe and sound,   30
But when she rose, the black and red,
Though still in Sight, had changed their Ground.

The Black, which would not be confined,
A more inferior Station seeks,
Leaving the fiery red behind,   35
And mingles in her muddy Cheeks.

The Paint by Perspiration cracks,
And falls in Rivulets of Sweat;
On either Side you see the Tracks,
While at her Chin the Confluents met.   40

___

11 *Celia*: A lady of fashion.

A Skillful Housewife thus her Thumb
With Spittle while she spins, anoints,
And thus the brown Meanders come
In trickling Streams betwixt her Joints.

But Celia can with ease reduce   45
By help of Pencil, Paint and Brush
Each Color to its Place and Use,
And teach her Cheeks again to blush.

She knows her Early self no more,
But filled with Admiration, stands,   50
As Other Painters oft adore
The Workmanship of their own Hands.

Thus after four important Hours
Celia's the Wonder of her Sex;
Say, which among the Heavenly Powers   55
Could cause such wonderful Effects.

Venus, indulgent to her Kind,
Gave Women all their Hearts could wish
When first she taught them where to find
White Lead, and Lusitanian Dish.°   60

Love with White lead cements his Wings,
White lead was sent us to repair
Two brightest, brittlest, earthly Things:
A Lady's Face, and China ware.

She ventures now to lift the Sash;   65
The Window is her proper Sphere;
Ah, Lovely Nymph, be not too rash,
Nor let the Beaux approach too near.

Take Pattern by your Sister Star:
Delude at once and Bless our Sight;   70
When you are seen, be seen from far,
And chiefly choose to shine by Night.

In the Pellmell when passing by,
Keep up the Glasses of your Chair;°
Then each transported Fop will cry,   75
G—d d—m me, Jack, she's wondrous fair.

But, Art no longer can prevail
When the Materials all are gone;
The best Mechanic Hand must fail
Where Nothing's left to work upon.   80

---

60 *Lusitanian Dish*: Portuguese dish holding her makeup.   74 *Glasses of your Chair*:
Windows on the chair she's carried in.

Matter, as wise Logicians say,
Cannot without a Form subsist,
And Form, say I, as well as They,
Must fail if Matter brings no Grist.

And this is fair Diana's Case,   85
For, all Astrologers maintain
Each Night a Bit drops off her Face
When Mortals say she's in her Wane.

While Partridge wisely shows the Cause
Efficient of the Moon's Decay,   90
That Cancer with his poisonous Claws
Attacks her in the milky Way:

But Gadbury in Art profound
From her pale Cheeks pretends to show
That Swain Endymion is not sound,   95
Or else, that Mercury's her Foe.

But, let the Cause be what it will,
In half a Month she looks so thin
That Flamstead° can with all his Skill
See but her Forehead and her Chin.   100

Yet as she wastes, she grows discreet,
Till Midnight never shows her Head;
So rotting Celia strolls the Street
When sober Folks are all abed.

For sure if this be Luna's° Fate,   105
Poor Celia, but of mortal Race,
In vain expects a longer Date
To the Materials of Her Face.

When Mercury her Tresses mows,
To think of Oil and Soot is vain;   110
No Painting can restore a Nose,
Nor will her Teeth return again.

Two Balls of Glass may serve for Eyes;
White Lead can plaster up a Cleft,
But these, alas, are poor Supplies   115
If neither Cheeks nor Lips be left.

Ye Powers who over Love preside,
Since mortal Beauties drop so soon,
If you would have us well supplied,
Send us new Nymphs with each new Moon.   120

---

99 *Flamstead*: John Flamstead (1646–1719), an astronomer.   105 *Luna*: The moon.

Alfred, Lord Tennyson   (1809–1892)
ULYSSES°   1833

It little profits that an idle king,
By this still hearth, among these barren crags,
Matched with an agèd wife, I mete and dole
Unequal laws unto a savage race,
That hoard, and sleep, and feed, and know not me.   5

I cannot rest from travel: I will drink
Life to the lees: all times I have enjoyed
Greatly, have suffered greatly, both with those
That loved me, and alone; on shore, and when
Through scudding drifts the rainy Hyades°   10
Vexed the dim sea: I am become a name;
For always roaming with a hungry heart
Much have I seen and known; cities of men
And manners, climates, councils, governments,
Myself not least, but honored of them all;   15
And drunk delight of battle with my peers,
Far on the ringing plains of windy Troy.
I am a part of all that I have met;
Yet all experience is an arch wherethrough
Gleams that untravelled world, whose margin fades   20
For ever and for ever when I move.
How dull it is to pause, to make an end,
To rust unburnished, not to shine in use!
As though to breathe were life. Life piled on life
Were all too little, and of one° to me   25
Little remains: but every hour is saved
From that eternal silence, something more,
A bringer of new things; and vile it were
For some three suns to store and hoard myself,
And this gray spirit yearning in desire   30
To follow knowledge like a sinking star,
Beyond the utmost bound of human thought.

　　This is my son, mine own Telemachus,
To whom I leave the scepter and the isle—
Well-loved of me, discerning to fulfil   35
This labor, by slow prudence to make mild
A rugged people, and through soft degrees

Ulysses: The hero whose sea adventures form Homer's *Odyssey*. Tennyson here pictures Ulysses back home and bored.   **10** *Hyades:* A cluster of stars supposed to signal coming storms. **25** *of one:* Of time. Ulysses is old.

Subdue them to the useful and the good.
Most blameless is he, centered in the sphere,
Of common duties, decent not to fail   40
In offices of tenderness, and pay
Meet adoration to my household gods,
When I am gone. He works his work, I mine.

    There lies the port; the vessel puffs her sail:
There gloom the dark broad seas. My mariners,   45
Souls that have toiled, and wrought, and thought with me—
That ever with a frolic welcome took
The thunder and the sunshine, and opposed
Free hearts, free foreheads—you and I are old;
Old age hath yet his honor and his toil;   50
Death closes all: but something ere the end,
Some work of noble note, may yet be done,
Not unbecoming men that strove with Gods.
The lights begin to twinkle from the rocks:
The long day wanes: the slow moon climbs: the deep   55
Moans round with many voices. Come, my friends,
'Tis not too late to seek a newer world.
Push off, and sitting well in order smite
The sounding furrows; for my purpose holds
To sail beyond the sunset, and the baths   60
Of all the western stars, until I die.
It may be that the gulfs will wash us down:
It may be we shall touch the Happy Isles,°
And see the great Achilles, whom we knew.
Though much is taken, much abides; and though   65
We are not now that strength which in old days
Moved earth and heaven; that which we are, we are;
One equal temper of heroic hearts,
Made weak by time and fate, but strong in will
To strive, to seek, to find, and not to yield.   70

63 *Happy Isles:* The paradise for heroes after death.

Dylan Thomas   (1914–1953)
FERN HILL   1946

Now as I was young and easy under the apple boughs
About the lilting house and happy as the grass was green,
    The night above the dingle starry,

Time let me hail and climb
Golden in the heydays of his eyes,   5
And honored among wagons I was prince of the apple towns
And once below a time I lordly had the trees and leaves
Trail with daisies and barley
Down the rivers of the windfall light.

And as I was green and carefree, famous among the barns   10
About the happy yard and singing as the farm was home,
In the sun that is young once only,
Time let me play and be
Golden in the mercy of his means,
And green and golden I was huntsman and herdsman, the calves   15
Sang to my horn, the foxes on the hills barked clear and cold,
And the sabbath rang slowly
In the pebbles of the holy streams.

All the sun long it was running, it was lovely, the hay
Fields high as the house, the tunes from the chimneys, it was air   20
And playing, lovely and watery
And fire green as grass.
And nightly under the simple stars
As I rode to sleep the owls were bearing the farm away,
All the moon long I heard, blessed among stables, the nightjars   25
Flying with the ricks, and the horses
Flashing into the dark.

And then to awake, and the farm, like a wanderer white
With the dew, come back, the cock on his shoulder: it was all
Shining, it was Adam and maiden,   30
The sky gathered again
And the sun grew round that very day.
So it must have been after the birth of the simple light
In the first, spinning place, the spellbound horses walking warm
Out of the whinnying green stable   35
On to the fields of praise.

And honored among foxes and pheasants by the gay house
Under the new made clouds and happy as the heart was long,
In the sun born over and over,
I ran my heedless ways,   40
My wishes raced through the house high hay
And nothing I cared, at my sky blue trades, that time allows
In all his tuneful turning so few and such morning songs
Before the children green and golden
Follow him out of grace,   45

Nothing I cared, in the lamb white days, that time would take me
Up to the swallow thronged loft by the shadow of my hand,
   In the moon that is always rising,
     Nor that riding to sleep
I should hear him fly with the high fields   50
And wake to the farm forever fled from the childless land.
Oh as I was young and easy in the mercy of his means,
     Time held me green and dying
     Though I sang in my chains like the sea.

Dylan Thomas   (1914–1953)

POEM IN OCTOBER 1944

    It was my thirtieth year to heaven
Woke to my hearing from harbor and neighbor wood
    And the mussel pooled and the heron
       Priested shore
      The morning beckon   5
With water praying and call of seagull and rook
And the knock of sailing boats on the net webbed wall
      Myself to set foot
       That second
    In the still sleeping town and set forth.   10

    My birthday began with the water-
Birds and the birds of the winged trees flying my name
    Above the farms and the white horses
       And I rose
      In rainy autumn   15
And walked abroad in a shower of all my days.
High tide and the heron dived when I took the road
      Over the border
      And the gates
    Of the town closed as the town awoke.   20

    A springful of larks in a rolling
Cloud and the roadside bushes brimming with whistling
    Blackbirds and the sun of October
       Summery
      On the hill's shoulder,   25
Here were fond climates and sweet singers suddenly
Come in the morning where I wandered and listened
      To the rain wringing

Wind blow cold
In the wood faraway under me.   30

Pale rain over the dwindling harbor
And over the sea wet church the size of a snail
With its horns through mist and the castle
Brown as owls
But all the gardens   35
Of spring and summer were blooming in the tall tales
Beyond the border and under the lark full cloud.
There could I marvel
My birthday
Away but the weather turned around.   40

It turned away from the blithe country
And down the other air and the blue altered sky
Streamed again a wonder of summer
With apples
Pears and red currants   45
And I saw in the turning so clearly a child's
Forgotten mornings when he walked with his mother
Through the parables
Of sun light
And the legends of the green chapels   50

And the twice told fields of infancy
That his tears burned my cheeks and his heart moved in mine.
These were the woods the river and sea
Where a boy
In the listening   55
Summertime of the dead whispered the truth of his joy
To the trees and the stones and the fish in the tide.
And the mystery
Sang alive
Still in the water and singingbirds.   60

And there could I marvel my birthday
Away but the weather turned around. And the true
Joy of the long dead child sang burning
In the sun.
It was my thirtieth   65
Year to heaven stood there then in the summer noon
Though the town below lay leaved with October blood.
O may my heart's truth
Still be sung
On this high hill in a year's turning.   70

David Wagoner   (b. 1926)

THE SHOOTING OF JOHN DILLINGER°
OUTSIDE THE BIOGRAPH THEATER,
JULY 22, 1934   1969

Chicago ran a fever of a hundred and one that groggy Sunday.
A reporter fried an egg on a sidewalk; the air looked shaky.
And a hundred thousand people were in the lake like shirts in a
    laundry.
Why was Johnny lonely?
Not because two dozen solid citizens, heat-struck, had keeled over
    backward.   5
Not because those lawful souls had fallen out of their sockets and
    melted.
But because the sun went down like a lump in a furnace or a bull in
    the Stockyards.
Where was Johnny headed?
Under the Biograph Theater sign that said, "Our Air is Refrigerated."
Past seventeen FBI men and four policemen who stood in doorways
    and sweated.   10
Johnny sat down in a cold seat to watch Clark Gable get
    electrocuted.
Had Johnny been mistreated?
Yes, but Gable told the D. A. he'd rather fry than be shut up forever.
Two women sat by Johnny. One looked sweet, one looked like J.
    Edgar Hoover.
Polly Hamilton made him feel hot, but Anna Sage made him shiver. 15
Was Johnny a good lover?
Yes, but he passed out his share of squeezes and pokes like a jittery
    masher.
While Agent Purvis sneaked up and down the aisle like an extra
    usher,
Trying to make sure they wouldn't slip out till the show was over.
Was Johnny a fourflusher?   20
No, not if he knew the game. He got it up or got it back.
But he liked to take snapshots of policemen with his own Kodak,
And once in a while he liked to take them with an automatic.
Why was Johnny frantic?
Because he couldn't take a walk or sit down in a movie   25
Without being afraid he'd run smack into somebody
Who'd point at his rearranged face and holler, "Johnny!"
Was Johnny ugly?

John Dillinger: 1902–1934; notorious American bank robber.

Yes, because Dr. Wilhelm Loeser had given him a new profile
With a baggy jawline and squint eyes and an erased dimple,   30
With kangaroo-tendon cheekbones and a gigolo's mustache that
    should've been illegal.
Did Johnny love a girl?
Yes, a good-looking, hard-headed Indian named Billie Frechette.
He wanted to marry her and lie down and try to get over it,
But she was locked in jail for giving him first-aid and comfort.   35
Did Johnny feel hurt?
He felt like breaking a bank or jumping over a railing
Into some panicky teller's cage to shout, "Reach for the ceiling!"
Or like kicking some vice president in the bum checks and smiling.
What was he really doing?   40
Going up the aisle with the crowd and into the lobby
With Polly saying, "Would *you* do what Clark done?" And Johnny
    saying, "Maybe."
And Anna saying, "If he'd been smart, he'd of acted like Bing
    Crosby."
Did Johnny look flashy?
Yes, his white-on-white shirt and tie were luminous.   45
His trousers were creased like knives to the tops of his shoes,
And his yellow straw hat came down to his dark glasses.
Was Johnny suspicious?
Yes, and when Agent Purvis signalled with a trembling cigar,
Johnny ducked left and ran out of the theater,   50
And innocent Polly and squealing Anna were left nowhere.
Was Johnny a fast runner?
No, but he crouched and scurried past a friendly liquor store
Under the coupled arms of double-daters, under awnings, under
    stars,
To the curb at the mouth of an alley. He hunched there.   55
Was Johnny a thinker?
No, but he was thinking more or less of Billie Frechette
Who was lost in prison for longer than he could possibly wait,
And then it was suddenly too hard to think around a bullet.
Did anyone shoot straight?   60
Yes, but Mrs. Etta Natalsky fell out from under her picture hat.
Theresa Paulus sprawled on the sidewalk, clutching her left foot.
And both of them groaned loud and long under the streetlight.
Did Johnny like that?
No, but he lay down with those strange women, his face in the
    alley,   65
One shoe off, cinders in his mouth, his eyelids heavy.
When they shouted questions at him, he talked back to nobody.
Did Johnny lie easy?

Yes, holding his gun and holding his breath as a last trick,
He waited, but when the Agents came close, his breath wouldn't
    work.   70
Clark Gable walked his last mile; Johnny ran half a block.
Did he run out of luck?
Yes, before he was cool, they had him spread out on dished-in marble
In the Cook County Morgue, surrounded by babbling people
With a crime reporter presiding over the head of the table.   75
Did Johnny have a soul?
Yes, and it was climbing his slippery wind-pipe like a trapped burglar.
It was beating the inside of his ribcage, hollering, "Let me out of
    here!"
Maybe it got out, and maybe it just stayed there.
Was Johnny a money-maker?   80
Yes, and thousands paid 25¢ to see him, mostly women,
And one said, "I wouldn't have come, except he's a moral lesson,"
And another, "I'm disappointed. He feels like a dead man."
Did Johnny have a brain?
Yes, and it always worked best through the worst of dangers,   85
Through flat-footed hammerlocks, through guarded doors, around
    corners,
But it got taken out in the morgue and sold to some doctors.
Could Johnny take orders?
No, but he stayed in the wicker basket carried by six men
Through the bulging crowd to the hearse and let himself be locked
    in,   90
And he stayed put as it went driving south in a driving rain.
And he didn't get stolen?
No, not even after his old hard-nosed dad refused to sell
The quick-drawing corpse for $10,000 to somebody in a carnival.
He figured he'd let *Johnny* decide how to get to Hell.   95
Did anyone wish him well?
Yes, half of Indiana camped in the family pasture,
And the minister said, "With luck, he could have been a minister."
And up the sleeve of his oversized gray suit, Johnny twitched a
    finger.
Does anyone remember?   100
Everyone still alive. And some dead ones. It was a new kind of
    holiday
With hot and cold drinks and hot and cold tears. They planted
    him in a cemetery
With three unknown vice presidents, Benjamin Harrison, and
    James Whitcomb Riley,
Who never held up anybody.

Diane Wakoski   (b. 1937)

SESTINA TO THE COMMON GLASS OF BEER: I DO NOT
DRINK BEER   1976

What calendar do you consult for an explosion of the sun?
And how does it affect our poor histories?
The event might be no different to our distant perspective
than a whole hillside of daffodils,
flashing   5
their own trumpet faces; or a cup of coffee, a glass of beer.

A familiar thing to common people: a beer,
when it is hot, and the sun
flashing
into your eyes. Makes you forget history's   10
only meaningful in retrospect. While flowers, like daffodils,
only have their meaning in the fleshy present. Perspective

cannot explain sexual feelings, though. Perspectively,
viewing a glass of beer,
we compare the color to daffodils   15
and perhaps a simple morning view of the sun.
The appetite is history's
fact. Common. Dull. Repetitious. Not flashing.

Suddenly, without explanation. The routine of bowels and lips.
    Flashing
past like a train, they come. No previews or perspective.   20
Sexual feelings are unexplained, as unexpected beauty. History's
no good at telling us about love either. Over beer
in a cafe, you might stay up till sun-
rise, but even that's routine for some, as every spring the returning
    daffodils,

waxy, yellow as caged canaries, spring daffodils   25
make me want to touch them. Is this the flashing
disappearing feeling of love and sex the sun
also brings to my body? With no object, no other body's perspective,
only the satisfaction of self wanting completion? I wdn't order beer,
I'd order a cognac or wine, instead. History's   30

full of exceptions, and I think I'm one. Yet, what history's
really about is how common, recurring, we all are. The daffodils,
once planted, really do come back each spring. And drinking beer
is a habit most ordinary men have. The flashing
gold liquid recurs in war, in factories and farms. The sun   35

has explosions that we do not know, record, or ever keep in
    perspective.

Thus, the sun embodies more of the unknown than most human
    histories.
We get little perspective outside ourselves. Daffodils
lift me above (to the sun), the faces flashing
each springtime when my friends, not I,   40
sit in some bar or outdoor cafe,
drinking beer.

Marilyn Nelson Waniek   (b. 1946)
EMILY DICKINSON'S DEFUNCT   1978

She used to
pack poems
in her hip pocket.
Under all the
gray old lady   5
clothes she was
dressed for action.
She had hair,
imagine,
in certain places, and   10
believe me
she smelled human
on a hot summer day.
Stalking snakes
or counting   15
the thousand motes
in sunlight
she walked just
like an Indian.
She was New England's   20
favorite daughter,
she could pray
like the devil.
She was a
two-fisted woman,   25
this babe.
All the flies
just stood around

and buzzed
when she died.   30

Belle Waring   (b. 1951)
WHAT HURTS   1990

is waking up flung cold across
the bed, right where I left myself, these eyes
spooked, like my father's after a binge.
Just what the hell is he doing in my face?
I don't booze. I'm not like him.   5
But that scared and blowsy stare
I recognize after this stark dream of looking
for Max, my hopeless ex, world without end.
Some nights my father spent stripped in a cell
to sober up. I learned to sleep in my clothes.   10
Sentry. Night watch. Mother by a sickbed.
Doctor on call. No surprise. Ready for
a shit storm. Praying for a cool sunrise.

Belle Waring   (b. 1951)
CHILDREN MUST HAVE MANNERS   1990

Not morals. Manners. Grist for the guests.
They suck up the Scotch. Daddy
rattles my school report under their snouts.
See. I'm his prize piggie.
But soon as they exit,   5
he slaps my fat face
'cause I dropped a whole fifth.
Twelve years old.
The praise must have gone
to my head, Daddy says.   10

"Pig," he spits.
But when company's here,
pig's to smile till it splits.
One jangled day I'll forget
this face. Show up for breakfast   15
pig scraped to the bone.
Nights, alone with my face,
I peel it away, wring out the grin,

rinse it in pilfered rosewater.
While I sleep, let it work its roots.   20

Candace Warne   (b. 1945)

BLACKBIRD SESTINA

Below me on the road, the blackbirds
have awaited my descent; the town
is darkened by them, starting like a wind
up the hill to meet me, shaking trees
like dry bones to conjure a new snow.   5
My road will be trackless, going down.

No one will have seen me going down;
there is only myself, and blackbirds
are the only movement except the snow
falling, like white hair, past to the town.   10
Coming up through the rattling trees,
I hear the quick ascension of a wind.

Some vague expectation of this wind
has veiled my hesitation to go down,
or perhaps it is the hope these trees   15
will hide me from the crying of blackbirds.
They have left the unfamiliar town
to look for me in their whirling snow.

There is an indifference in this snow;
it moves only in accord with wind,   20
confusing my footsteps toward town,
closing in behind as I move down,
showing my movements to the blackbirds
that are coming closer through the trees.

I have lost sight of all but the trees   25
nearest me; all else is hid by snow.
Still, I hear the approach of blackbirds
and their confusing talk in the wind
sounds practically human, blowing down
toward me. I can not find the town.   30

It is too dark to look for the town.
Dark sleep falls from the gathering trees.
Cold has numbed to warmth; my falling down
cannot be undone; the weight of snow

blankets me from the rasping of wind,   35
muffling the sound of the blackbirds.

The lost town is singing in the snow;
The trees run away in the mad wind.
The stars fall down to become blackbirds.

John Weiners   (b. 1934)
THE EAGLE BAR   1986

A lamp lit in the corner
the Chinese girl talks to her lover
At bar, saxophone blares—

blue music, while boy in white turtleneck sweater
seduces the polka player from Poland   5
left over from Union party.

Janet sits beside me,
Barbra Streisand sings on Juke box
James tends bar

It's the same old scene   10
in Buffalo or Boston
yen goes on, continues in the glare

of night, searching for its lover
oh will we go
where will we search   15

between potato chips and boys,
for impeccable one—
that impossible lover

who does not come in,
with fresh air and sea   20
off Lake Erie

but stays home, hidden in the sheets
with his wife and child, alone
ah, the awful ache

as cash register rings   25
and James the bartender sweeps
bottles off the bar.

Walt Whitman   (1819–1892)
FROM **SONG OF MYSELF°**   1855–1891

I

I celebrate myself, and sing myself,
And what I assume you shall assume,
For every atom belonging to me as good belongs to you.

I loaf and invite my soul,
I lean and loaf at my ease observing a spear of summer grass.   5

My tongue, every atom of my blood, formed from this soil, this air,
Born here of parents born here from parents the same, and their
        parents the same,
I, now thirty-seven years old in perfect health begin,
Hoping to cease not till death.

Creeds and schools in abeyance,   10
Retiring back a while sufficed at what they are, but never forgotten,
I harbor for good or bad, I permit to speak at every hazard,
Nature without check with original energy.

II

Houses and rooms are full of perfumes, the shelves are crowded with
        perfumes,
I breathe the fragrance myself and know it and like it,   15
The distillation would intoxicate me also, but I shall not let it.
The atmosphere is not a perfume, it has no taste of distillation, it is
        odorless,
It is for my mouth forever, I am in love with it,
I will go to the bank by the wood and become undisguised and
        naked,
I am mad for it to be in contact with me.   20

The smoke of my own breath,
Echoes, ripples, buzzed whispers, love-root, silk-thread, crotch and
        vine,
My respiration and inspiration, the beating of my heart, the passing
        of blood and air through my lungs,
The sniff of green leaves and dry leaves, and of the shore and dark-
        colored sea-rocks, and of hay in the barn,
The sound of the belched words of my voice loosed to the eddies of
        the wind,   25
A few light kisses, a few embraces, a reaching around of arms,

Song of Myself: See discussion of this poem on p. 804.

The play of shine and shade on the trees as the supple boughs wag,
The delight alone or in the rush of the streets, or along the fields
  and hillsides,
The feeling of health, the full-noon trill, the song of me rising from
  bed and meeting the sun.

Have you reckoned a thousand acres much? Have you reckoned the
  earth much?   30
Have you practiced so long to learn to read?
Have you felt so proud to get at the meaning of poems?

Stop this day and night with me and you shall possess the origin of
  all poems,
You shall possess the good of the earth and sun (there are millions
  of suns left),
You shall no longer take things at second or third hand, nor look
  through the eyes of the dead, nor feed on the specters in
  books,   35
You shall not look through my eyes either, nor take things from me,
You shall listen to all sides and filter them from your self.

III

I have heard what the talkers were talking, the talk of the beginning
  and the end,
But I do not talk of the beginning or the end.

There was never any more inception than there is now,   40
Nor any more youth or age than there is now,
And will never be any more perfection than there is now,
Nor any more heaven or hell than there is now.

Urge and urge and urge,
Always the procreant urge of the world.   45
Out of the dimness opposite equals advance, always substance and
  increase, always sex,
Always a knit of identity, always distinction, always a breed of life.

To elaborate is no avail, learned and unlearned feel that it is so.

Sure as the most certain sure, plumb in the uprights, well
  entretied,° braced in the beams,
Stout as a horse, affectionate, haughty, electrical,   50
I and this mystery here we stand.

Clear and sweet is my soul, and clear and sweet is all that is not my
  soul.

---

49 *entretied*: Plastered.

Lack one lacks both, and the unseen is proved by the seen,
Till that becomes unseen and receives proof in its turn.

Showing the best and dividing it from the worst age vexes age, 55
Knowing the perfect fitness and equanimity of things, while they
    discuss I am silent, and go bathe and admire myself.

Welcome is every organ and attribute of me, and of any man hearty
    and clean,
Not an inch nor a particle of an inch is vile, and none shall be less
    familiar than the rest.

I am satisfied—I see, dance, laugh, sing;
As the hugging and loving bedfellow sleeps at my side through the
    night, and withdraws at the peep of the day with stealthy
    tread, 60
Leaving me baskets covered with white towels swelling the house
    with their plenty,
Shall I postpone my acceptation and realization and scream at my
    eyes,
That they turn from gazing after and down the road,
And forthwith cipher and show me to a cent,
Exactly the value of one and exactly the value of two, and which is
    ahead? 65

IV

Trippers and askers surround me,
People I meet, the effect upon me of my early life or the ward and
    city I live in, or the nation,
The latest dates, discoveries, inventions, societies, authors old and
    new,
My dinner, dress, associates, looks, compliments, dues,
The real or fancied indifference of some man or woman I love, 70
The sickness of one of my folks or of myself, or ill-doing or loss or
    lack of money, or depressions or exaltations,
Battles, the horrors of fratricidal war, the fever of doubtful news, the
    fitful events;
These come to me days and nights and go from me again,
But they are not the Me myself.

Apart from the pulling and hauling stands what I am, 75
Stands amused, complacent, compassionating, idle, unitary,
Looks down, is erect, or bends an arm on an impalpable certain rest,
Looking with side-curved head curious what will come next,
Both in and out of the game and watching and wondering at it.

Backward I see in my own days where I sweated through fog with
    linguists and contenders,   80
I have no mockings or arguments, I witness and wait.

V

I believe in you my soul, the other I am must not abase itself to you,
And you must not be abased to the other.

Loaf with me on the grass, loose the stop from your throat,
Not words, not music or rhyme I want, not custom or lecture, not
    even the best,   85
Only the lull I like, the hum of your valvèd voice.

I mind how once we lay such a transparent summer morning,
How you settled your head athwart my hips and gently turned over
    upon me,
And parted the shirt from my bosom-bone, and plunged your
    tongue to my bare-stripped heart,
And reached till you felt my beard, and reached till you held my
    feet.   90

Swiftly arose and spread around me the peace and knowledge that
    pass all the argument of the earth,
And I know that the hand of God is the promise of my own,
And I know that the spirit of God is the brother of my own,
And that all the men ever born are also my brothers, and the women
    my sisters and lovers,
And that a kelson of the creation is love,   95
And limitless are leaves stiff or drooping in the fields,
And brown ants in the little wells beneath them,
And mossy scabs of the worm fence, heaped stones, elder, mullein
    and poke-weed.

VI

A child said *What is the grass?* fetching it to me with full hands;
How could I answer the child? I do not know what it is any more
    than he.   100

I guess it must be the flag of my disposition, out of hopeful green
    stuff woven.

Or I guess it is the handkerchief of the Lord,
A scented gift and remembrancer designedly dropped,
Bearing the owner's name someway in the corners, that we may see
    and remark, and say *Whose?*

Or I guess the grass is itself a child, the produced babe of the
  vegetation.   105

Or I guess it is a uniform hieroglyphic,
And it means, Sprouting alike in broad zones and narrow zones,
Growing among black folks as among white,
Kanuck, Tuckahoe, Congressman, Cuff, I give them the same, I
  receive them the same.

And now it seems to me the beautiful uncut hair of graves.   110

Tenderly will I use you curling grass,
It may be you transpire from the breasts of young men,
It may be if I had known them I would have loved them,
It may be you are from old people, or from offspring taken soon
  out of their mothers' laps,
And here you are the mothers' laps.   115

This grass is very dark to be from the white heads of old mothers,
Darker than the colorless beards of old men,
Dark to come from under the faint red roofs of mouths.

O I perceive after all so many uttering tongues,
And I perceive they do not come from the roofs of mouths for
  nothing.   120

I wish I could translate the hints about the dead young men and
  women,
And the hints about old men and mothers, and the offspring taken
  soon out of their laps.

What do you think has become of the young and old men?
And what do you think has become of the women and children?

They are alive and well somewhere,   125
The smallest sprout shows there is really no death,
And if ever there was it led forward life, and does not wait at the
  end to arrest it,
And ceased the moment life appeared.

All goes onward and outward, nothing collapses,
And to die is different from what any one supposed, and luckier.   130

VII

Has any one supposed it lucky to be born?
I hasten to inform him or her it is just as lucky to die, and I know
  it.

I pass death with the dying and birth with the new-washed babe,
  and am not contained between my hat and boots,

And peruse manifold objects, no two alike and every one good,
The earth good and the stars good, and their adjuncts all good.   135

I am not an earth nor an adjunct of an earth,
I am the mate and companion of people, all just as immortal and
    fathomless as myself
(They do not know how immortal, but I know).

Every kind for itself and its own, for me mine male and female,
For me those that have been boys and that love women,   140
For me the man that is proud and feels how it stings to be
    slighted,
For me the sweetheart and the old maid, for me mothers and the
    mothers of mothers,
For me lips that have smiled, eyes that have shed tears,
For me children and the begetters of children.

Undrape! you are not guilty to me, nor stale nor discarded,   145
I see through the broadcloth and gingham whether or no,
And am around, tenacious, acquisitive, tireless, and cannot be
    shaken away.

VIII

The little one sleeps in its cradle,
I lift the gauze and look a long time, and silently brush away flies
    with my hand.

The youngster and the red-faced girl turn aside up the bushy hill,   150
I peeringly view them from the top.

The suicide sprawls on the bloody floor of the bedroom,
I witness the corpse with its dabbled hair, I note where the pistol
    has fallen.

The blab of the pave,° tires of carts, sluff of boot-soles, talk of the
    promenaders,
The heavy omnibus, the driver with his interrogating thumb, the
    clank of the shod horses on the granite floor,   155
The snow-sleighs, clinking, shouted jokes, pelts of snowballs,
The hurrahs for popular favorites, the fury of roused mobs,
The flap of the curtained litter, a sick man inside borne to the
    hospital,
The meeting of enemies, the sudden oath, the blows and fall,
The excited crowd, the policeman with his star quickly working his
    passage to the center of the crowd,   160
The impassive stones that receive and return so many echoes,

---

154 *blab of the pave*: The sound of the pavement, the streets.

What groans of over-fed or half-starved who fall sunstruck or in fits,
What exclamations of women taken suddenly who hurry home and
    give birth to babes,
What living and buried speech is always vibrating here, what howls
    restrained by decorum,
Arrests of criminals, slights, adulterous offers made, acceptances,
    rejections with convex lips,   165
I mind them or the show or resonance of them—I come and I
    depart.

IX

The big doors of the country barn stand open and ready,
The dried grass of the harvest-time loads the slow-drawn wagon,
The clear light plays on the brown gray and green intertinged,
The armfuls are packed to the sagging mow.   170

I am there, I help, I came stretched atop of the load,
I felt its soft jolts, one leg reclined on the other,
I jump from the crossbeams and seize the clover and timothy,
And roll head over heels and tangle my hair full of wisps.

X

Alone far in the wilds and mountains I hunt,   175
Wandering amazed at my own lightness and glee,
In the late afternoon choosing a safe spot to pass the night,
Kindling a fire and broiling the fresh-killed game,
Falling asleep on the gathered leaves with my dog and gun by my
    side.

The Yankee clipper is under her sky-sails, she cuts the sparkle and
    scud,   180
My eyes settle the land, I bend at her prow or shout joyously from
    the deck.

The boatmen and clam-diggers arose early and stopped for me,
I tucked my trowser-ends in my boots and went and had a good
    time;
You should have been with us that day round the chowder-kettle.

I saw the marriage of the trapper in the open air in the far west,
    the bride was a red girl,   185
Her father and his friends sat near cross-legged and dumbly
    smoking, they had moccasins to their feet and large thick
    blankets hanging from their shoulders,
On a bank lounged the trapper, he was dressed mostly in skins,
    his luxuriant beard and curls protected his neck, he held his
    bride by the hand,

She had long eyelashes, her head was bare, her coarse straight locks
    descended upon her voluptuous limbs and reached to her feet.

The runaway slave came to my house and stopped outside,
I heard his motions crackling the twigs of the woodpile,   190
Through the swung half-door of the kitchen I saw him limpsy and
    weak,
And went where he sat on a log and led him in and assured him,
And brought water and filled a tub for his sweated body and
    bruised feet,
And gave him a room that entered from my own, and gave him
    some coarse clean clothes,
And remember perfectly well his revolving eyes and his
    awkwardness,   195
And remember putting plasters on the galls of his neck and ankles;
He stayed with me a week before he was recuperated and passed
    north,
I had him sit next me at table, my fire-lock leaned in the corner.

William Carlos Williams   (1883–1963)
THE RED WHEELBARROW   1923

so much depends
upon

a red wheel
barrow

glazed with rain   5
water

beside the white
chickens.

William Carlos Williams   (1883–1963)
DANSE RUSSE   1944

If when my wife is sleeping
and the baby and Kathleen
are sleeping
and the sun is a flame-white disc
in silken mists   5
above shining trees,—
if I in my north room

dance naked, grotesquely
before my mirror
waving my shirt round my head   10
and singing softly to myself:
"I am lonely, lonely.
I was born to be lonely,
I am best so!"
If I admire my arms, my face,   15
my shoulders, flanks, buttocks
against the yellow drawn shades,—

Who shall say I am not
the happy genius of my household?

Terence Winch   (b. 1945)

THE MEANEST GANG IN THE BRONX   1985

once when I was in the fifth grade
I heard a rumor that the Fordham Baldies
were going to invade my school during the lunch hour
I was terrified   everybody knew the Baldies
were the meanest gang in the Bronx   5
who not only killed people but were known
to carve tic tac toe with their knives
on the bellies of their girl victims
since my father was custodian of the school
I tried to warn him about the attack   10
so that he could shut the school down
but he didn't pay me any mind
and the Fordham Baldies never showed up
once they did come into our neighborhood
looking for the Elsmere Tims   our local gang   15
but the brave Tims were no where to be found

Terence Winch   (b. 1945)

SIX FAMILIES OF PUERTO RICANS   1985

I guess it was the summer of nineteen
fifty five   I just got back from Rockaway°
the first thing I heard when I got back
was the news that

2 *Rockaway.* A town in Long Island.

six families of Puerto Ricans had moved   5
into nineteen fifteen Daly Avenue   the Mitchells'
building   as time went on
more and more pee ars moved into
the neighborhood   there was great hostility
on both sides   once on the fourth of July   10
Martin Conlon threw some cherry bombs
and ash cans through the windows of the Puerto
Ricans   they were just spics to us
I remember a Puerto Rican shooting
at me and some friends with a bee bee gun   15
from his roof   you could hear the bee bees
bouncing off the cars   bodegas opened
on Tremont Avenue   Spanish kids dropped
water balloons on Irish kids   there was
a Sunday mass in Spanish in the church basement   20
this was worse than a potato famine
and the Irish started moving out
Mr. Zayas moved in next door to us
where the Gormans had lived   Mr. Zayas
had a son named Efrain who married   25
a beautiful girl named Carmen   Puerto Rican men
played dominoes on the sidewalk
when me and my father left the block
in the fall of nineteen sixty eight
we were among a handful of Irish still   30
in the neighborhood   things were so bad
by then that even the respectable Puerto Ricans
like Mr. Zayas were long gone
we used to think Puerto Ricans
weren't too far from being animals   35
even if they were Catholics

William Wordsworth   (1770–1850)

THE WORLD IS TOO MUCH WITH US   1807

The world is too much with us; late and soon,
Getting and spending, we lay waste our powers:
Little we see in nature that is ours;
We have given our hearts away, a sordid boon!
This Sea that bares her bosom to the moon;   5
The Winds that will be howling at all hours
And are upgathered now like sleeping flowers;
For this, for everything, we are out of tune;

It moves us not—Great God! I'd rather be
A Pagan suckled in a creed outworn;   10
So might I, standing on this pleasant lea,
Have glimpses that would make me less forlorn;
Have sight of Proteus coming from the sea;
Or hear old Triton blow his wreathèd horn.

William Wordsworth   (1770–1850)

LINES COMPOSED A FEW MILES ABOVE TINTERN ABBEY° 1798

On Revisiting The Banks Of The Wye During A Tour, July 13, 1798

Five years have passed; five summers, with the length
Of five long winters! and again I hear
These waters, rolling from their mountain-springs
With a sweet inland murmur.—Once again
Do I behold these steep and lofty cliffs,   5
Which on a wild secluded scene impress
Thoughts of more deep seclusion; and connect
The landscape with the quiet of the sky.
The day is come when I again repose
Here, under this dark sycamore, and view   10
These plots of cottage-ground, these orchard-tufts,
Which, at this season, with their unripe fruits,
Among the woods and copses lose themselves,
Nor, with their green and simple hue, disturb
The wild green landscape. Once again I see   15
These hedge-rows, hardly hedge-rows, little lines
Of sportive wood run wild; these pastoral farms
Green to the very door; and wreaths of smoke
Sent up, in silence, from among the trees,
With some uncertain notice, as might seem,   20
Of vagrant dwellers in the houseless woods,
Or of some hermit's cave, where by his fire
The hermit sits alone.

                 Though absent long,
These forms of beauty have not been to me,
As is a landscape to a blind man's eye: 25

Lines . . . Tintern Abbey. See discussion of this poem on p. 833.

But oft, in lonely rooms, and mid the din
Of towns and cities, I have owed to them,
In hours of weariness, sensations sweet,
Felt in the blood, and felt along the heart,
And passing even into my purer mind   30
With tranquil restoration:—feelings too
Of unremembered pleasure; such, perhaps,
As may have had no trivial influence
On that best portion of a good man's life;
His little, nameless, unremembered acts   35
Of kindness and of love. Nor less, I trust,
To them I may have owed another gift,
Of aspect more sublime; that blessed mood,
In which the burden of the mystery,
In which the heavy and the weary weight   40
Of all this unintelligible world
Is lightened:—that serene and blessed mood,
In which the affections gently lead us on,
Until, the breath of this corporeal frame,
And even the motion of our human blood   45
Almost suspended, we are laid asleep
In body, and become a living soul:
While with an eye made quiet by the power
Of harmony, and the deep power of joy,
We see into the life of things.

                If this   50
Be but a vain belief, yet, oh! how oft,
In darkness, and amid the many shapes
Of joyless daylight; when the fretful stir
Unprofitable, and the fever of the world,
Have hung upon the beatings of my heart,   55
How oft, in spirit, have I turned to thee
O sylvan Wye! Thou wanderer through the woods,
How often has my spirit turned to thee!

And now, with gleams of half-extinguished thought,
With many recognitions dim and faint,   60
And somewhat of a sad perplexity,
The picture of the mind revives again:
While here I stand, not only with the sense
Of present pleasure, but with pleasing thoughts
That in this moment there is life and food   65
For future years. And so I dare to hope
Though changed, no doubt, from what I was, when first

I came among these hills; when like a roe
I bounded o'er the mountains, by the sides
Of the deep rivers, and the lonely streams,   70
Wherever nature led; more like a man
Flying from something that he dreads, than one
Who sought the thing he loved. For nature then
(The coarser pleasures of my boyish days,
And their glad animal movements all gone by)   75
To me was all in all.—I cannot paint
What then I was. The sounding cataract
Haunted me like a passion: the tall rock,
The mountain, and the deep and gloomy wood,
Their colors and their forms, were then to me   80
An appetite: a feeling and a love,
That had no need of a remoter charm,
By thought supplied, or any interest
Unborrowed from the eye.—That time is past,
And all its aching joys are now no more,   85
And all its dizzy raptures. Not for this
Faint I, nor mourn nor murmur: other gifts
Have followed, for such loss, I would believe,
Abundant recompence. For I have learned
To look on nature, not as in the hour   90
Of thoughtless youth, but hearing oftentimes
The still, sad music of humanity,
Not harsh nor grating, though of ample power
To chasten and subdue. And I have felt
A presence that disturbs me with the joy   95
Of elevated thoughts; a sense sublime
Of something far more deeply interfused,
Whose dwelling is the light of setting suns,
And the round ocean, and the living air,
And the blue sky, and in the mind of man,   100
A motion and a spirit, that impels
All thinking things, all objects of all thought,
And rolls through all things. Therefore am I still
A lover of the meadows and the woods,
And mountains; and of all that we behold   105
From this green earth; of all the mighty world
Of eye and ear, both what they half-create,
And what perceive; well pleased to recognize
In nature and the language of the sense,
The anchor of my purest thoughts, the nurse,   110
The guide, the guardian of my heart, and soul
Of all my moral being.

                                        Nor, perchance,
If I were not thus taught, should I the more
Suffer my genial spirits to decay:
For thou art with me, here, upon the banks   115
Of this fair river; thou, my dearest Friend,
My dear, dear Friend, and in thy voice I catch
The language of my former heart, and read
My former pleasures in the shooting lights
Of thy wild eyes. Oh! yet a little while   120
May I behold in thee what I was once,
My dear, dear Sister! And this prayer I make,
Knowing that Nature never did betray
The heart that loved her; 'tis her privilege,
Through all the years of this our life, to lead   125
From joy to joy: for she can so inform
The mind that is within us, so impress
With quietness and beauty, and so feed
With lofty thoughts, that neither evil tongues,
Rash judgments, nor the sneers of selfish men,   130
Nor greetings where no kindness is, nor all
The dreary intercourse of daily life,
Shall e'er prevail against us, or disturb
Our chearful faith that all which we behold
Is full of blessings. Therefore let the moon   135
Shine on thee in thy solitary walk;
And let the misty mountain winds be free
To blow against thee: and in after years,
When these wild ecstasies shall be matured
Into a sober pleasure, when thy mind   140
Shall be a mansion for all lovely forms,
Thy memory be as a dwelling-place
For all sweet sounds and harmonies; Oh! then,
If solitude, or fear, or pain, or grief,
Should be thy portion, with what healing thoughts   145
Of tender joy wilt thou remember me,
And these my exhortations! Nor, perchance,
If I should be, where I no more can hear
Thy voice, nor catch from thy wild eyes these gleams
Of past existence, wilt thou then forget   150
That on the banks of this delightful stream
We stood together; and that I, so long
A worshipper of Nature, hither came,
Unwearied in that service: rather say
With warmer love, oh! with far deeper zeal   155
Of holier love. Nor wilt thou then forget,

That after many wanderings, many years
Of absence, these steep woods and lofty cliffs,
And this green pastoral landscape, were to me
More dear, both for themselves, and for thy sake.   160

James Wright   (1927–1980)
AT THE EXECUTED MURDERER'S GRAVE   1971

(for J.L.D.)

Why should we do this? What good is it to us? Above all, how can we do such a thing? How can it possibly be done?

—Freud

I

My name is James A. Wright, and I was born
Twenty-five miles from this infected grave,
In Martins Ferry, Ohio, where one slave
To Hazel-Atlas Glass became my father.
He tried to teach me kindness. I return   5
Only in memory now, aloof, unhurried,
To dead Ohio, where I might lie buried,
Had I not run away before my time.
Ohio caught George Doty. Clean as lime,
His skull rots empty here. Dying's the best   10
Of all the arts men learn in a dead place.
I walked here once. I made my loud display,
Leaning for language on a dead man's voice.
Now sick of lies, I turn to face the past.
I add my easy grievance to the rest: 15

II

Doty, if I confess I do not love you,
Will you let me alone? I burn for my own lies.
The nights electrocute my fugitive,
My mind. I run like the bewildered mad
At St. Clair Sanitarium, who lurk,   20
Arch and cunning, under the maple trees,
Pleased to be playing guilty after dark.
Staring to bed, they croon self-lullabies.
Doty, you make me sick. I am not dead.
I croon my tears at fifty cents per line.   25

III

Idiot, he demanded love from girls,
And murdered one. Also, he was a thief.

He left two women, and a ghost with child.
The hair, foul as a dog's upon his head,
Made such revolting Ohio animals   30
Fitter for vomit than a kind man's grief.
I waste no pity on the dead that stink,
And no love's lost between me and the crying
Drunks of Belaire, Ohio, where police
Kick at their kidneys till they die of drink.   35
Christ may restore them whole, for all of me.
Alive and dead, those giggling muckers who
Saddled my nightmares thirty years ago
Can do without my widely printed sighing
Over their pains with paid sincerity.   40
I do not pity the dead, I pity the dying.

IV

    I pity myself, because a man is dead.
If Belmont County killed him, what of me?
His victims never loved him. Why should we?
And yet, nobody had to kill him either.   45
It does no good to woo the grass, to veil
The quicklime hole of a man's defeat and shame.
Nature-lovers are gone. To hell with them.
I kick the clods away, and speak my name.

V

    This grave's gash festers. Maybe it will heal,   50
When all are caught with what they had to do
In fear of love, when every man stands still
By the last sea,
And the princes of the sea come down
To lay away their robes, to judge the earth   55
And its dead, and we dead stand undefended everywhere,
And my bodies—father and child and unskilled criminal—
Ridiculously kneel to bare my scars,
My sneaking crimes, to God's unpitying stars.

VI

    Staring politely, they will not mark my face   60
From any murderer's, buried in this place.
Why should they? We are nothing but a man.

VII

    Doty, the rapist and the murderer,
Sleeps in a ditch of fire, and cannot hear;
And where, in earth or hell's unholy peace,   65

Men's suicides will stop, God knows, not I.
Angels and pebbles mock me under trees.
Earth is a door I cannot even face.
Order be damned, I do not want to die,
Even to keep Belaire, Ohio, safe.   70
The hackles on my neck are fear, not grief.
(Open, dungeon! Open, roof of the ground!)
I hear the last sea in the Ohio grass,
Heaving a tide of gray disastrousness.
Wrinkles of winter ditch the rotted face   75
Of Doty, killer, imbecile, and thief:
Dirt of my flesh, defeated, underground.

WINDOW ON

Background: Yeats and Byzantium

William Butler Yeats (1865–1939), one of the most commanding presences in modern English poetry, was Irish, fervently nationalistic, and hopeful that a revival of Irish culture would bring with it an antidote to what he saw as the encroachment of materialism in the modern world. Yeats had an aversion to business and money and spent his life examining ancient Irish myth, Indian religion, and other spiritual sources for their relevance to life in the twentieth century. He belonged to the Theosophical Society, a group that reviewed spiritual research and spiritual practices. He also spent many years in contact with spirits that he was certain were transmitting to him some of the most important secrets of the universe. His book, *A Vision*, records the information he gathered and describes a system of growth and change in history based on the analogy of the changing faces of the moon. His views are interesting from modern psychological perspectives, since much of what he portrays corresponds to Freud's breakdown of the human mind into the ego, id, libido, and superego. One of his first literary achievements was editing the poetry of William Blake, whose own approach to spiritualism included visions and contacts with the spirit world.

"Sailing to Byzantium" and "Byzantium," written late in Yeats's life, express views that coincide with his despair over modern crassness and materialism. Byzantium is the name of a city now called Istanbul, in Turkey, which, in A.D. 1000, was the center of medieval Christianity. It lives in the modern imagination in the great vivid mosaics of religious subjects in Hagia Sophia (Holy Wisdom), the great mosque in Istanbul. Byzantium was a center of great religious scholarship and learning. Yeats's reading about Byzantine culture gave him an image of a perfect society that, for a brief time, somehow balanced materialism with spiritual values to permit the flourishing of a spiritual art and a culture of devotion.

In "Sailing to Byzantium," Yeats imagines himself on a journey that is not geographical but through time. His first line, "That is no country for old men," is spoken over his shoulder, looking back on his own time, the year 1927, when the poem was written, and presumably looking back at England. By 1927, Yeats was sixty-two and feeling his age. The world was much younger, indifferent to the beauties that he felt redeemed the stark materialism created by the rise of bourgeois culture.

Stanza 1 tells us that the great art of the past is neglected by the present: "Caught in that sensual music all neglect / Monuments of unageing intellect." In his second stanza, he invokes memorable and powerful images: "An aged man is but a paltry thing, / A tattered coat upon a stick, unless / Soul clap its hands and sing." When he says, "Nor is there singing school but studying / Monuments of its own magnificence," he refers to the study of great art such as the gold mosaics of stanza 3. In stanzas 3 and 4 Yeats hopes somehow to be immortalized in art, imagining his poetic self as a bird "of hammered gold and gold enamelling," "set upon a golden bough." Poetry, he sees, has the power of prophecy and revelation.

"Byzantium" is less regular in form. It rhymes, and its stanzas are essentially symmetrical, but the strictness of feeling associated with the first poem is gone. "Byzantium" functions differently because it does not address the reader in the same tone. The narrator speaks almost to himself: "Before me floats an image, man or shade, / Shade more than man, more image than a shade." It is as if Yeats were attempting to describe an out-of-body experience of the kind that he expects to find in Byzantium. The imagery seems almost medieval—"The Emperor's drunken soldiery are abed"—and the strange, otherworldly images of "Flames that no faggot feeds," and "An agony of flame that cannot singe a sleeve" imply a transcendence of the world that Yeats looks at over his shoulder in "Sailing to Byzantium."

Yet "Byzantium" also looks back on the world of the living, of nature, and in doing so concentrates on the physical—"Those images that yet / Fresh images beget"—rather than on the spiritual life. No one can fully interpret the final line, "That dolphin-torn, that gong-tormented sea," but we can feel its significance as a weightiness of physicality and perceive it as a kind of antithesis of the spiritual. Yet the dolphin has traditionally been a symbol of Christ, and the gong implies the ringing of a bell that may signal the end or the beginning of something. Therefore, this line may imply a hope, a new beginning, a spiritual potential even to the life he has left behind.

Reading

Ellmann, Richard. *The Identity of Yeats.* 2nd ed. New York: Oxford University Press, 1970.

———. *Yeats, the Man and the Masks.* New York: Macmillan, 1948.

Jeffares, A. Norman. *W. B. Yeats: A New Biography*. London: Hutchinson, 1989.

O'Donnell, James P. *Sailing to Byzantium*. New York: Octagon, 1971.

Unterecker, John. *A Reader's Guide to W. B. Yeats*. New York: Noonday, 1959.

William Butler Yeats   (1865–1939)

SAILING TO BYZANTIUM°   1927

I

That is no country for old men. The young
In one another's arms, birds in the trees
—Those dying generations—at their song,
The salmon-falls, the mackerel-crowded seas,
Fish, flesh, or fowl, commend all summer long   5
Whatever is begotten, born, and dies.
Caught in that sensual music all neglect
Monuments of unageing intellect.

II

An aged man is but a paltry thing,
A tattered coat upon a stick, unless   10
Soul clap its hands and sing, and louder sing
For every tatter in its mortal dress,
Nor is there singing school but studying
Monuments of its own magnificence;
And therefore I have sailed the seas and come   15
To the holy city of Byzantium.

III

O sages standing in God's holy fire
As in the gold mosaic of a wall,
Come from the holy fire, perne in a gyre,°
And be the singing-masters of my soul.   20
Consume my heart away; sick with desire
And fastened to a dying animal
It knows not what it is; and gather me
Into the artifice of eternity.

Sailing to Byzantium: See discussion of this poem on p. 994.   19 *perne in a gyre*: Spin in a whirling vortex; a perne is a spool on which yarn is wound.

IV

Once out of nature I shall never take   25
My bodily form from any natural thing,
But such a form as Grecian goldsmiths make
Of hammered gold and gold enamelling
To keep a drowsy Emperor awake;
Or set upon a golden bough to sing   30
To lords and ladies of Byzantium
Of what is past, or passing, or to come.

William Butler Yeats   (1865–1939)

BYZANTIUM°   1930

THE unpurged images of day recede;
The Emperor's drunken soldiery are abed;
Night resonance recedes, night-walkers'° song
After great cathedral gong;
A starlit or a moonlit dome disdains   5
All that man is,
All mere complexities,
The fury and the mire of human veins.

Before me floats an image, man or shade,
Shade more than man, more image than a shade;   10
For Hades' bobbin bound in mummy-cloth
May unwind the winding path;°
A mouth that has no moisture and no breath
Breathless mouths may summon;
I hail the superhuman;   15
I call it death-in-life and life-in-death.

Miracle, bird or golden handiwork,
More miracle than bird or handiwork,
Planted on the star-lit golden bough,
Can like the cocks of Hades crow,   20
Or, by the moon embittered, scorn aloud
In glory of changeless metal
Common bird or petal
And all complexities of mire or blood.

At midnight on the Emperor's pavement flit   25
Flames that no faggot feeds, nor steel has lit,

Byzantium: See discussion of this poem on p.994.   **3** *night-walkers*: Prostitutes.   **11–12** *Hades'*
bobbin . . . path: The dead man is unwinding his life as a spinning bobbin unwinds its threads.

Nor storm disturbs, flames begotten of flame,
Where blood-begotten spirits come
And all complexities of fury leave,
Dying into a dance,   30
An agony of trance,
An agony of flame that cannot singe a sleeve.

Astraddle on the dolphin's mire and blood,
Spirit after spirit! The smithies break the flood,
The golden smithies of the Emperor!   35
Marbles of the dancing floor
Break bitter furies of complexity,
Those images that yet
Fresh images beget,
That dolphin-torn, that gong-tormented sea.   40

William Butler Yeats (1865–1939)
THE LAKE ISLE OF INNISFREE 1892

I will arise and go now, and go to Innisfree,
And a small cabin build there, of clay and wattles made:
Nine bean-rows will I have there, a hive for the honeybee,
And live alone in the bee-loud glade.

And I shall have some peace there, for peace comes dropping slow,   5
Dropping from the veils of the morning to where the cricket sings;
There midnight's all a glimmer, and noon a purple glow,
And evening full of the linnet's wings.

I will arise and go now, for always night and day
I hear lake water lapping with low sounds by the shore;   10
While I stand on the roadway, or on the pavements grey,
I hear it in the deep heart's core.

William Butler Yeats (1865–1939)
AMONG SCHOOL CHILDREN 1927

I

I walk through the long schoolroom questioning;
A kind old nun in a white hood replies;
The children learn to cipher and to sing,
To study reading-books and history,
To cut and sew, be neat in everything   5

In the best modern way—the children's eyes
In momentary wonder stare upon
A sixty-year-old smiling public man.

II

I dream of a Ledaean° body, bent
Above a sinking fire, a tale that she   10
Told of a harsh reproof, or trivial event
That changed some childish day to tragedy—
Told, and it seemed that our two natures blent
Into a sphere from youthful sympathy,
Or else, to alter Plato's parable,°   15
Into the yolk and white of the one shell.

III

And thinking of that fit of grief or rage
I look upon one child or t'other there
And wonder if she stood so at that age—
For even daughters of the swan can share   20
Something of every paddler's heritage—
And had that color upon cheek or hair,
And thereupon my heart is driven wild:
She stands before me as a living child.

IV

Her present image floats into the mind—   25
Did Quattrocento° finger fashion it
Hollow of cheek as though it drank the wind
And took a mess of shadows for its meat?
And I though never of Ledaean kind
Had pretty plumage once—enough of that,   30
Better to smile on all that smile, and show
There is a comfortable kind of old scarecrow.

V

What youthful mother, a shape upon her lap
Honey of generation had betrayed,
And that must sleep, shriek, struggle to escape   35
As recollection or the drug decide,°
Would think her son, did she but see that shape

---

9 *Ledaean*: Like Helen, the daughter of Leda in Greek mythology. Yeats is dreaming of the revolutionary Maud Gonne, whom he loved for most of his life.   15 *Plato's parable*: Plato's idea
that we are always seeking our "other half" from which we have been separated.
26 *Quattrocento*: Italian 15th-century painter.

With sixty or more winters on its head,
A compensation for the pang of his birth,
Or the uncertainty of his setting forth?   40

VI

Plato thought nature but a spume that plays
Upon a ghostly paradigm of things;°
Solider Aristotle played the taws
Upon the bottom of a king of kings;°
World-famous golden-thighed Pythagoras   45
Fingered upon a fiddle-stick or strings
What a star sang and careless Muses heard:°
Old clothes upon old sticks to scare a bird.°

VII

Both nuns and mothers worship images,°
But those the candles light are not as those   50
That animate a mother's reveries,
But keep a marble or a bronze repose.
And yet they too break hearts—O Presences
That passion, piety or affection knows,
And that all heavenly glory symbolize—   55
O self-born mockers of man's enterprise;

VIII

Labor is blossoming or dancing where
The body is not bruised to pleasure soul,
Nor beauty born out of its own despair,
Nor blear-eyed wisdom out of midnight oil.   60
O chestnut-tree, great-rooted blossomer,
Are you the leaf, the blossom or the bole?
O body swayed to music, O brightening glance,
How can we know the dancer from the dance?

34–36 *Honey of generation . . . drug decide:* An image from Porphyry (3rd century B.C.): souls are tempted by a kind of drug to come down to earth and be born; if the drug works well, they do not know what has happened to them.   41–42 *Plato . . . things:* Plato considered what we see to be a veil ("spume") covering an underlying reality ("ghostly paradigm").   43–44 *Solider . . . Kings:* Aristotle, a more pragmatic ("solider") philosopher, was Alexander the Great's tutor, here pictured as spanking the young King ("played the taws").   45–47 *World-famous . . . heard:* Pythagoras (6th–5th century B.C.) worked out the notes of the scale and from this the "music of the universe"; he was said to have had a golden thigh.   48 *Old . . . bird:* All these great thinkers are still just old men, scarecrows.   49 *images:* The images are ideals constructed in part by the imagination; one kind is religious, the other the idealizing of a mother.

Ray A. Young Bear   (b. 1950)
THE WAY THE BIRD SAT   1975

even for the wind there was no room.
the wind kept the cool to itself
and it seemed that his skin
also grew more selfish to feelings
for he was like a window   5
jealous of the light going through
denied his shadow the sun's warmth
when being alone brought him
the cool.

the way the bird sat   10
dividing the weather through songs
cleaning the snow and rain
from the underside of its wings
was evidence.
in its singing the bird counted   15
and acknowledged the changes
in the coolness of the wind.
he somehow held the bird responsible
as it flew about taking in puffs
of air.   20

often the image of blue hearts
in the form of deer crossed his mind
outdoing all magic and distortion
of the hummingbird who had previously
been the source of his dreams.   25
the bird who had tunneled
through the daylight
creating lines in the air
for the people in his dreams to follow.

now his thoughts took him out   30
into a cornfield where he felt himself
bundled up concerned about the deer
and their hearts.
the hummingbird who had been dodging
the all-day rain stopped   35
and hovered beside him
before it flew off
licking the rain from the trees.

having killed and eaten so many deer
it was wrong to blame his weakness 40
on the sun and wind.
to accuse anyone nearby he thought
was as foolish as the consideration
to once save his morning's spit
with the intention of showing it 45
to people as proof that his blood
and time were almost out.
he even wanted to ask
if it was possible to leave it behind
for worship but all this faded away 50
like the flutter of wings
he always heard shooting past
the shadow of his foot before it
touched the ground.

once his nose bled all day 55
and he saved the blood
testing to see if his notions were true.
he allowed the blood to run into a cup
until the cup collected.
toward evening he emptied 60
the cup in the yard
and just before the sun left
the standing forms of blood glistened.
when he woke he found
his blood missing. 65
his dog looked content with blood
along the rim of his mouth.
there was nothing but dark spots
on the grass:

the daylight was full and the birds 70
walked through his yard
speaking to each other
and sometimes gathering
around the area where he had set
his blood. 75

it was strange as he watched.
each time they walked away
from the area it was smooth
and directed.
in his mind it reminded him 80
of a ceremony and he left lines

on where each bird had stepped
where each had circled
what words it might have said
even the prayers it might have sung   85
and when the birds had sticks
in their mouths he saw singers
with their notched sticks.
their beaks moved up and down
the sticks making a rasping noise   90
and when they hummed
it was a song he knew very well.
he danced to the rhythm
as he watched from the window.
the birds had faces of people   95
he had met and lost
but there was one he could not recognize
its face was of a deer.
he felt puzzled licking the rain
from the trees.   100

Bernice Zamora   (b. 1938)
PUEBLO, 1950   1976

I remember you, Fred Montoya.
You were the first *vato* to ever kiss me.
I was twelve years old.
My mother said shame on you,
my teacher said shame on you, and   5
I said shame on me, and nobody
          said a word to you

Bernice Zamora   (b. 1938)
RESTLESS SERPENTS°   1976

*The duty of a cobra's master
is fraught with fettered chores.*

Spite strikes the
humbling stroke of
neglect—coiling,
recoiling, pricking

Restless Serpents. See discussion of this poem on p. 673.

the master's veins
of lapse, draining
a bounded resurrection
to numb the drumming
pain. Lyrics,
lyrics alone soothe
restless serpents.

From all corners
precision humming
and rhythmic sounds
fill the mindful
master who laps
about the droppings
of disregard. Lyrics,
lyrics alone soothe
restless serpents, strokes
more devastating than
devastation arrived.

Sylvia Plath in Depth

When Sylvia Plath (1932–1963) committed suicide, she had published only one book of poetry, The Collosus (1962). Her most famous book of poems, Ariel (1965), was published posthumously. Her autobiographical novel The Bell Jar (1967), written originally under a pseudonym, details much of her life at Smith College, where she was an outstanding student, Phi Beta Kappa, graduating summa cum laude. Even in 1963 Plath was known among poets and writers for the power of her work. Among her early successes was a prize story for Mademoiselle magazine, with a $500 check, as much as she would earn that summer waiting on tables in a resort hotel on Cape Cod. Perhaps her most pleasant honor was having been selected as an editor for Mademoiselle's annual college edition, which necessitated a summer working in New York.

Plath's early death made her in some ways a cult figure. She had a reputation for being supersensitive, a careful and sometimes mysterious writer, always striving for excellence and recognition. She has left behind a remarkable collection of almost seven hundred letters to her mother Aurelia, much of them discussing her work and her ambitions as a writer. Her husband, the British poet Ted Hughes, lived for a year early in their marriage in Northampton, Massachusetts, while she taught at Smith. Her letters to her mother in this period describe anxieties about domestic life and her role in relation to a husband.

Teaching took too much of her writing time, and Hughes and Plath first moved to Boston, where Plath took odd jobs and also attended a poetry class run by Robert Lowell at Boston University. Lowell's poetry, especially his "Skunk Hour," had an important influence on her at this time. When she became pregnant, she and Hughes moved to England, where they eventually had two children, Frieda and Nicholas. They lived at first in London during a period in which Ted Hughes began to publish and receive important recognition through prizes and offers of readings. Plath was an energetic supporter of Hughes's work, acting as his typist, secretary, and agent. Biographers have pointed out that she accepted the same kind *of role in relation to her husband as her mother had done with her father. Both her parents were German in background, and they accepted the traditional roles of husband and wife. Plath, knowing full well the risks she ran, did the same. Eventually, she and Ted bought a thatched-roof house in Devon in the English countryside, where they felt they would have space in which to write and a place to raise their children.*

Her marriage began to fail in 1962, when Ted began seeing another woman. Hughes left and she busied herself with the children and with learning to ride her horse Ariel. But after a period of extraordinary productivity in her writing, Sylvia began to feel depressed in the countryside and in need of the stimulation of literary London. She moved back into London without her husband. Those who knew only her work were shocked to find that she committed suicide on February 11, 1963, barely thirty years old. However, her letters, some poems, recollections of close friends, an earlier breakdown and suicide attempt, and her novel The Bell Jar *all provide signs that might have been better understood by those who could have helped.*

Unfortunately, no adequate biography exists, nor is it likely to for many years. The emphasis critics have placed on her personal life in some ways distracts from the work, which is demanding and complex. Yet her poems sometimes point directly at her own life, as does "Daddy," which describes a recollection of her father, Otto Plath, a German-speaking immigrant from Poland who taught German at Boston University and who published a book on bumblebees in 1934. He died in 1940, so Sylvia's memories stem from early childhood, and the poem reflects the influence of the general anxiety of the United States in the early 1940s regarding the Nazis and Hitler's threat to world security. The violence of the language and imagery of the poem is totally unexpected given everything we know about Plath's early experiences with her father.

Sylvia Plath's work is rich, inventive, and filled with the ambition of one who wished to be recognized as an important writer. Critics attracted to Plath regard her from numerous angles. The biographical-historicist approach is certainly common; because of the existence of a detailed journal, extensive letters, and many personal recollections of friends, information about Sylvia Plath's personal life is widely available, even if it is not always complete. Plath's work also demands close attention to the formalist elements of image, rhythm, the narrator or persona of the poem, and the many shocking disjunctions that bring a reader up short. Feminist approaches have also been used. Whatever their angle, critics agree that her poems are engaging and deeply moving.

DADDY   1963

You do not do, you do not do
Any more, black shoe
In which I have lived like a foot
For thirty years, poor and white,
Barely daring to breathe or Achoo.   5

Daddy, I have had to kill you.
You died before I had time——
Marble-heavy, a bag full of God,
Ghastly statue with one grey toe
Big as a Frisco seal   10

And a head in the freakish Atlantic
Where it pours bean green over blue
In the waters off beautiful Nauset.°
I used to pray to recover you.
Ach, du.°   15

In the German tongue, in the Polish town°
Scraped flat by the roller
Of wars, wars, wars.
But the name of the town is common.
My Polack friend   20

Says there are a dozen or two.
So I never could tell where you
Put your foot, your root,
I never could talk to you.
The tongue stuck in my jaw.   25

It stuck in a barb wire snare.
Ich, ich, ich, ich,°
I could hardly speak.
I thought every German was you.
And the language obscene   30

An engine, an engine
Chuffing me off like a Jew.
A Jew to Dachau, Auschwitz, Belsen.
I began to talk like a Jew.
I think I may well be a Jew.   35

The snows of the Tyrol, the clear beer of Vienna
Are not very pure or true.
With my gypsy ancestress and my weird luck
And my Taroc pack and my Taroc pack
I may be a bit of a Jew.   40

I have always been scared of *you,*
With your Luftwaffe, your gobbledygoo.

---

13 *Nauset:* An inlet on Cape Cod.   15 *Ach du:* Oh, you.   16 *Polish town:* Where he was
born.   27 *Ich:* I.

And your neat moustache
And your Aryan eye, bright blue.
Panzer-man, panzer-man, O You——   45

Not God but a swastika
So black no sky could squeak through.
Every woman adores a Fascist,
The boot in the face, the brute
Brute heart of a brute like you.   50

You stand at the blackboard, daddy,
In the picture I have of you,
A cleft in your chin instead of your foot
But no less a devil for that, no not
Any less the black man who   55

Bit my pretty red heart in two.
I was ten when they buried you.
At twenty I tried to die
And get back, back, back to you.
I thought even the bones would do   60

But they pulled me out of the sack,
And they stuck me together with glue.
And then I knew what to do.
I made a model of you,
A man in black with a Meinkampf° look   65

And a love of the rack and the screw.
And I said I do, I do.
So daddy, I'm finally through.
The black telephone's off at the root,
The voices just can't worm through.   70

If I've killed one man, I've killed two——
The vampire who said he was you
And drank my blood for a year,
Seven years,° if you want to know.
Daddy, you can lie back now.   75

There's a stake in your fat black heart
And the villagers never liked you.
They are dancing and stamping on you.
They always *knew* it was you.
Daddy, daddy, you bastard, I'm through.   80

---

65 *Meinkampf:* An allusion to Hitler's autobiography *Mein Kampf* (*My Struggle*).   74 *Seven years:* Plath was married to Ted Hughes for seven years.

ARIEL° 1963

Stasis in darkness.
Then the substanceless blue
Pour of tor and distances.

God's lioness,
How one we grow,   5
Pivot of heels and knees!—The furrow

Splits and passes, sister to
The brown arc
Of the neck I cannot catch,

Nigger-eye   10
Berries cast dark
Hooks——

Black sweet blood mouthfuls,
Shadows.
Something else   15

Hauls me through air——
Thighs, hair;
Flakes from my heels.

White
Godiva, I unpeel——   20
Dead hands, dead stringencies.

And now I
Foam to wheat, a glitter of seas.
The child's cry

Melts in the wall.   25
And I
Am the arrow,

The dew that flies
Suicidal, at one with the drive
Into the red   30

Eye, the cauldron of morning.

Ariel: The name of Plath's horse. It comes from the attendant spirit in Shakespeare's *The Tempest*.
Ariel is a spirit with supernatural powers.

ELM   1965

For Ruth Fainlight

I know the bottom, she says. I know it with my great tap root:
It is what you fear.
I do not fear it: I have been there.

Is it the sea you hear in me,
Its dissatisfactions?   5
Or the voice of nothing, that was your madness?

Love is a shadow.
How you lie and cry after it.
Listen: these are its hooves: it has gone off, like a horse.

All night I shall gallop thus, impetuously,   10
Till your head is a stone, your pillow a little turf,
Echoing, echoing.

Or shall I bring you the sound of poisons?
This is rain now, this big hush.
And this is the fruit of it: tin-white, like arsenic.   15

I have suffered the atrocity of sunsets.
Scorched to the root
My red filaments burn and stand, a hand of wires.

Now I break up in pieces that fly about like clubs.
A wind of such violence   20
Will tolerate no bystanding: I must shriek.

The moon, also, is merciless: she would drag me
Cruelly, being barren.
Her radiance scathes me. Or perhaps I have caught her.

I let her go. I let her go   25
Diminished and flat, as after radical surgery.
How your bad dreams possess and endow me.

I am inhabited by a cry.
Nightly it flaps out
Looking, with its hooks, for something to love.   30

I am terrified by this dark thing
That sleeps in me;
All day I feel its soft, feathery turnings, its malignity.

Clouds pass and disperse.
Are those the faces of love, those pale irretrievables?   35
Is it for such I agitate my heart?

I am incapable of more knowledge.
What is this, this face
So murderous in its strangle of branches?

Its snaky acids kiss.   40
It petrifies the will. These are the isolate, slow faults
That kill, that kill, that kill.

METAPHORS   1960

I'm a riddle in nine syllables,
An elephant, a ponderous house,
A melon strolling on two tendrils.
O red fruit, ivory, fine timbers!
This loaf's big with its yeasty rising.   5
Money's new-minted in this fat purse.
I'm a means, a stage, a cow in calf.
I've eaten a bag of green apples,
Boarded the train there's no getting off.

MIRROR   1963

I am silver and exact. I have no preconceptions.
Whatever I see I swallow immediately
Just as it is, unmisted by love or dislike.
I am not cruel, only truthful—
The eye of a little god, four-cornered.   5
Most of the time I meditate on the opposite wall.
It is pink, with speckles. I have looked at it so long
I think it is a part of my heart. But it flickers.
Faces and darkness separate us over and over.

Now I am a lake. A woman bends over me,   10
Searching my reaches for what she really is.
Then she turns to those liars, the candles or the moon.
I see her back, and reflect it faithfully.
She rewards me with tears and an agitation of hands.
I am important to her. She comes and goes.   15
Each morning it is her face that replaces the darkness.
In me she has drowned a young girl, and in me an old woman
Rises toward her day after day, like a terrible fish.

MORNING SONG   1965

Love set you going like a fat gold watch.
The midwife slapped your footsoles, and your bald cry
Took its place among the elements.

Our voices echo, magnifying your arrival. New statue.
In a drafty museum, your nakedness   5
Shadows our safety. We stand round blankly as walls.

I'm no more your mother
Than the cloud that distils a mirror to reflect its own slow
Effacement at the wind's hand.

All night your moth-breath   10
Flickers among the flat pink roses. I wake to listen:
A far sea moves in my ear.

One cry, and I stumble from bed, cow-heavy and floral
In my Victorian nightgown.
Your mouth opens clean as a cat's. The window square   15

Whitens and swallows its dull stars. And now you try
Your handful of notes;
The clear vowels rise like balloons.

TULIPS   1962

The tulips are too excitable, it is winter here.
Look how white everything is, how quiet, how snowed-in.
I am learning peacefulness, lying by myself quietly
As the light lies on these white walls, this bed, these hands.
I am nobody; I have nothing to do with explosions.   5
I have given my name and my day-clothes up to the nurses
And my history to the anaesthetist and my body to surgeons.

They have propped my head between the pillow and the sheet-cuff
Like an eye between two white lids that will not shut.
Stupid pupil, it has to take everything in.   10
The nurses pass and pass, they are no trouble,
They pass the way gulls pass inland in their white caps,
Doing things with their hands, one just the same as another,
So it is impossible to tell how many there are.

My body is a pebble to them, they tend it as water   15
Tends to the pebbles it must run over, smoothing them gently.
They bring me numbness in their bright needles, they bring me sleep.

Now I have lost myself I am sick of baggage
My patent leather overnight case like a black pillbox,
My husband and child smiling out of the family photo;   20
Their smiles catch onto my skin, little smiling hooks.

I have let things slip, a thirty-year-old cargo boat
Stubbornly hanging on to my name and address.
They have swabbed me clear of my loving associations.
Scared and bare on the green plastic-pillowed trolley   25
I watched my tea-set, my bureaus of linen, my books
Sink out of sight, and the water went over my head.
I am a nun now, I have never been so pure.

I didn't want any flowers, I only wanted
To lie with my hands turned up and be utterly empty.   30
How free it is, you have no idea how free——
The peacefulness is so big it dazes you,
And it asks nothing, a name tag, a few trinkets.
It is what the dead close on, finally; I imagine them
Shutting their mouths on it, like a Communion tablet.   35

The tulips are too red in the first place, they hurt me.
Even through the gift paper I could hear them breathe
Lightly, through their white swaddlings, like an awful baby.
Their redness talks to my wound, it corresponds.
They are subtle: they seem to float, though they weigh me down,   40
Upsetting me with their sudden tongues and their color,
A dozen red lead sinkers round my neck.

Nobody watched me before, now I am watched.
The tulips turn to me, and the window behind me
Where once a day the light slowly widens and slowly thins,   45
And I see myself, flat, ridiculous, a cut-paper shadow
Between the eye of the sun and the eyes of the tulips,
And I have no face, I have wanted to efface myself.
The vivid tulips eat my oxygen.

Before they came the air was calm enough,   50
Coming and going, breath by breath, without any fuss.
Then the tulips filled it up like a loud noise.
Now the air snags and eddies round them the way a river
Snags and eddies round a sunken rust-red engine.
They concentrate my attention, that was happy   55
Playing and resting without committing itself.

The walls, also, seem to be warming themselves.
The tulips should be behind bars like dangerous animals;
They are opening like the mouth of some great African cat,

And I am aware of my heart: it opens and closes   60
Its bowl of red blooms out of sheer love of me.
The water I taste is warm and salt, like the sea,
And comes from a country far away as health.

THE COLOSSUS   1960

I shall never get you put together entirely,
Pieced, glued, and properly jointed.
Mule-bray, pig-grunt and bawdy cackles
Proceed from your great lips.
It's worse than a barnyard.   5

Perhaps you consider yourself an oracle,
Mouthpiece of the dead, or of some god or other.
Thirty years now I have labored
To dredge the silt from your throat.
I am none the wiser.   10

Scaling little ladders with gluepots and pails of lysol
I crawl like an ant in mourning
Over the weedy acres of your brow
To mend the immense skull plates and clear
The bald, white tumuli of your eyes.   15

A blue sky out of the Oresteia°
Arches above us. O father, all by yourself
You are pithy and historical as the Roman Forum.
I open my lunch on a hill of black cypress.
Your fluted bones and acanthine hair are littered   20

In their old anarchy to the horizon-line.
It would take more than a lightning-stroke
To create such a ruin.
Nights, I squat in the cornucopia
Of your left ear, out of the wind,   25

Counting the red stars and those of plum-color.
The sun rises under the pillar of your tongue.
My hours are married to shadow.
No longer do I listen for the scrape of a keel
On the blank stones of the landing.   30

16 *Oresteia:* Three tragedies by Aeschylus (525?–456 B.C.)—*Agamemnon, The Libation Bearers, The Eumenides*—all concerning the murder of Agamemnon and the revenge of his son Orestes on his mother Clytemnestra.

THE MOON AND THE YEW TREE   1963

This is the light of the mind, cold and planetary.
The trees of the mind are black. The light is blue.
The grasses unload their griefs on my feet as if I were God,
Prickling my ankles and murmuring of their humility.
Fumy, spiritous mists inhabit this place   5
Separated from my house by a row of headstones.
I simply cannot see where there is to get to.

The moon is no door. It is a face in its own right,
White as a knuckle and terribly upset.
It drags the sea after it like a dark crime; it is quiet   10
With the O-gape of complete despair.° I live here.
Twice on Sunday, the bells startle the sky——
Eight great tongues affirming the Resurrection.
At the end, they soberly bong out their names.

The yew tree points up. It has a Gothic shape.   15
The eyes lift after it and find the moon.
The moon is my mother. She is not sweet like Mary.
Her blue garments unloose small bats and owls.
How I would like to believe in tenderness——
The face of the effigy, gentled by candles,   20
Bending, on me in particular, its mild eyes.

I have fallen a long way. Clouds are flowering
Blue and mystical over the face of the stars.
Inside the church, the saints will be all blue,
Floating on their delicate feet over the cold pews,   25
Their hands and faces stiff with holiness.
The moon sees nothing of this. She is bald and wild.
And the message of the yew tree is blackness—blackness and silence.

11 *despair:* The gape of despair is from Queen Niobe's mourning her murdered children as Keats
describes her in one of his poems.

LADY LAZARUS   1963

I have done it again.
One year in every ten
I manage it——

A sort of walking miracle, my skin
Bright as a Nazi lampshade,   5
My right foot

A paperweight,
My face a featureless, fine
Jew linen.

Peel off the napkin   10
O my enemy.
Do I terrify?——

The nose, the eye pits, the full set of teeth?
The sour breath
Will vanish in a day.   15

Soon, soon the flesh
The grave cave ate will be
At home on me

And I a smiling woman.
I am only thirty.   20
And like the cat I have nine times to die.

This is Number Three.
What a trash
To annihilate each decade.

What a million filaments.   25
The peanut-crunching crowd
Shoves in to see

Them unwrap me hand and foot——
The big strip tease.
Gentleman, ladies,   30

These are my hands,
My knees.
I may be skin and bone,

Nevertheless, I am the same, identical woman.
The first time it happened I was ten.   35
It was an accident.

The second time I meant
To last it out and not come back at all.
I rocked shut

As a seashell.   40
They had to call and call
And pick the worms off me like sticky pearls.

Dying
Is an art, like everything else.
I do it exceptionally well.   45

I do it so it feels like hell.
I do it so it feels real.
I guess you could say I've a call.

It's easy enough to do it in a cell.
It's easy enough to do it and stay put.   50
It's the theatrical

Comeback in broad day
To the same place, the same face, the same brute
Amused shout:

"A miracle!"   55
That knocks me out.
There is a charge

For the eyeing of my scars, there is a charge
For the hearing of my heart——
It really goes.   60

And there is a charge, a very large charge,
For a word or a touch
Or a bit of blood

Or a piece of my hair or my clothes.
So, so, Herr Doktor.   65
So, Herr Enemy.

I am your opus,
I am your valuable,
The pure gold baby

That melts to a shriek.   70
I turn and burn.
Do not think I underestimate your great concern.

Ash, ash——
You poke and stir.
Flesh, bone, there is nothing there——   75

A cake of soap,
A wedding ring,
A gold filling.

Herr God, Herr Lucifer,
Beware   80
Beware.

Out of the ash
I rise with my red hair
And I eat men like air.

PARALYTIC   1965

It happens. Will it go on?——
My mind a rock,
No fingers to grip, no tongue,
My god the iron lung

That loves me, pumps   5
My two
Dust bags in and out,
Will not

Let me relapse
While the day outside glides by like ticker tape.   10
The night brings violets,
Tapestries of eyes,

Lights,
The soft anonymous
Talkers: "You all right?"   15
The starched, inaccessible breast.

Dead egg, I lie
Whole
On a whole world I cannot touch,
At the white, tight   20

Drum of my sleeping couch
Photographs visit me——
My wife, dead and flat, in 1920 furs,
Mouth full of pearls,

Two girls   25
As flat as she, who whisper "We're your daughters."
The still waters
Wrap my lips,

Eyes, nose and ears,
A clear   30
Cellophane I cannot crack.
On my bare back

I smile, a buddha, all
Wants, desire
Falling from me like rings   35
Hugging their lights.

The claw
Of the magnolia,

Drunk on its own scents,
Asks nothing of life.   40

MARY'S SONG   1963

The Sunday lamb cracks in its fat.
The fat
Sacrifices its opacity. . . .

A window, holy gold.
The fire makes it precious,   5
The same fire

Melting the tallow heretics,
Ousting the Jews.
Their thick palls float

Over the cicatrix of Poland, burnt-out   10
Germany.
They do not die.

Grey birds obsess my heart,
Mouth-ash, ash of eye.
They settle. On the high   15

Precipice
That emptied one man into space
The ovens glowed like heavens, incandescent.

It is a heart,
This holocaust I walk in,   20
O golden child the world will kill and eat.

Research Materials

Sylvia Plath

A COMPARISON   1962

*In this essay, Plath talks about the novelist in relation to the poet. Her
language is metaphoric and rich in images, but her meaning is clear: The poet does
her work in minutes, but the novelist can take years. In quoting Ezra Pound's "In
a Station of the Metro," Plath reveals some of her leanings toward imagist poems.
Her comments on "The Moon and the Yew Tree" offer a special insight into her
way of thinking about poetry.*

How I envy the novelist!

I imagine him—better say her, for it is the women I look to for a parallel—I imagine her, then, pruning a rosebush with a large pair of shears, adjusting her spectacles, shuffling about among the teacups, humming, arranging ashtrays or babies, absorbing a slant of light, a fresh edge to the weather, and piercing, with a kind of modest, beautiful X-ray vision, the psychic interiors of her neighbors—her neighbors on trains, in the dentist's waiting room, in the corner teashop. To her, this fortunate one, what is there that *isn't* relevant! Old shoes can be used, doorknobs, air letters, flannel nightgowns, cathedrals, nail varnish, jet planes, rose arbors and budgerigars; little mannerisms—the sucking at a tooth, the tugging at a hemline—any weird or warty or fine or despicable thing. Not to mention emotions, motivations—those rumbling, thunderous shapes. Her business is Time, the way it shoots forward, shunts back, blooms, decays and double-exposes itself. Her business is people in Time. And she, it seems to me, has all the time in the world. She can take a century if she likes, a generation, a whole summer.

I can take about a minute.

I'm not talking about epic poems. We all know how long *they* can take. I'm talking about the smallish, unofficial garden-variety poem. How shall I describe it?—a door opens, a door shuts. In between you have had a glimpse: a garden, a person, a rainstorm, a dragonfly, a heart, a city. I think of those round glass Victorian paperweights which I remember, yet can never find—a far cry from the plastic mass-productions which stud the toy counters in Woolworth's. This sort of paperweight is a clear globe, self-complete, very pure, with a forest or village or family group within it. You turn it upside down, then back. It snows. Everything is changed in a minute. It will never be the same in there—not the fir trees, nor the gables, nor the faces.

So a poem takes place.

And there is really so little room! So little time! The poet becomes an expert packer of suitcases:

> The apparition of these faces in the crowd;
> Petals on a wet black bough.

There it is: the beginning and the end in one breath. How would the novelist manage that? In a paragraph? In a page? Mixing it, perhaps, like paint, with a little water, thinning it, spreading it out.

Now I am being smug, I am finding advantages.

If a poem is concentrated, a closed fist, then a novel is relaxed and expansive, an open hand: it has roads, detours, destinations; a heart line, a head line; morals and money come into it. Where the fist excludes and stuns, the open hand can touch and encompass a great deal in its travels.

I have never put a toothbrush in a poem.

I do not like to think of all the things, familiar, useful and worthy things, I have never put into a poem. I did, once, put a yew tree in. And that yew tree began, with astounding egotism, to manage and order the whole affair. It was not a yew tree by a church on a road past a house in a town where a certain woman lived . . . and so on, as it might have been in a novel. Oh, no. It stood squarely in the middle of my poem, manipulating its dark shades, the voices in the churchyard, the clouds, the birds, the tender melancholy with which I contemplated it—everything! I couldn't subdue it. And, in the end, my poem was a poem about a yew tree. That yew tree was just too proud to be a passing black mark in a novel.

Perhaps I shall anger some poets by implying that the *poem* is proud. The poem, too, can include everything, they will tell me. And with far more precision and power than those baggy, disheveled and undiscriminate creatures we call novels. Well, I concede these poets their steamshovels and old trousers. I really *don't* think poems should be all that chaste. I would, I think, even concede a toothbrush, if the poem was a real one. But these apparitions, these poetical toothbrushes, are rare. And when they do arrive, they are inclined, like my obstreperous yew tree, to think themselves singled out and rather special.

Not so in novels.

There the toothbrush returns to its rack with beautiful promptitude and is forgot. Time flows, eddies, meanders, and people have leisure to grow and alter before our eyes. The rich junk of life bobs all about us: bureaus, thimbles, cats, the whole much-loved, well-thumbed catalog of the miscellaneous which the novelist wishes us to share. I do not mean that there is no pattern, no discernment, no rigorous ordering here.

I am only suggesting that perhaps the pattern does not insist so much.

The door of the novel, like the door of the poem, also shuts.

But not so fast, nor with such manic, unanswerable finality.

From *Johnny Panic and the Bible of Dreams*

Sylvia Plath

FROM HER JOURNAL: ON SUICIDE

Plath's suicide contributed to making her a cult figure in poetry, much the way John Keats's early death in the previous century did the same for him. Her journal, kept at Smith College in the early 1950s, offers insight into her psychological state as she grew up. This passage reveals her capacity to explore her emotions, then to pull back, examine her circumstances as a beginning writer, then respond and move on.

NORTHAMPTON

November 3. God, if ever I have come close to wanting to commit suicide, it is now, with the groggy sleepless blood dragging through my veins, and the air thick and gray with rain and the damn little men across the street pounding on the roof with picks and axes and chisels, and the acrid hellish stench of tar. I fell into bed again this morning, begging for sleep, withdrawing into the dark, warm, fetid escape from action, from responsibility. No good. The mail bell rang and I jerked myself up to answer it. A letter from Dick.° Sick with envy, I read it, thinking of him lying up there, rested, fed, taken care of, free to explore books and

---

1 *Dick*: Dick Norton, who was recuperating from tuberculosis.

thoughts at any whim. I thought of the myriad of physical duties I had to perform: write Prouty°; *Life* back to Cal; write-up Press Board; call Marcia. The list mounted obstacle after fiendish obstacle; they jarred, they leered, they fell apart in chaos, and the revulsion, the desire to end the pointless round of objects, of things, of actions, rose higher. To annihilate the world by annihilation of one's self is the deluded height of desperate egoism. The simple way out of all the little brick dead ends we scratch our nails against. Irony it is to see Dick raised, lifted to the pinnacles of irresponsibility to anything but care of his body—to feel his mind soaring, reaching, and mine caged, crying, impotent, self-reviling, and imposter. How to justify myself, my bold, brave humanitarian faith? My world falls apart, crumbles, "the centre cannot hold." There is no integrating force, only the naked fear, the urge of self-preservation.

I am afraid. I am not solid, but hollow. I feel behind my eyes a numb, paralyzed cavern, a pit of hell, a mimicking nothingness. I never thought. I never wrote, I never suffered. I want to kill myself, to escape from responsibility, to crawl back abjectly into the womb. I do not know who I am, where I am going— and I am the one who has to decide the answers to these hideous questions. I long for a noble escape from freedom—I am weak, tired, in revolt from the strong constructive humanitarian faith which presupposes a healthy, active intellect and will. There is nowhere to go—not home, where I would blubber and cry, a grotesque fool, into my mother's skirts—not to men, where I want more than ever now their stern, final, paternal directive—not to church, which is liberal, free—no, I turn wearily to the totalitarian dictatorship where I am absolved of all personal responsibility and can sacrifice myself in a "splurge of altruism" on the altar of the Cause with a capital "C."

Now I sit here, crying almost, afraid, seeing the finger writing my hollow futility on the wall, damning me—God, where is the integrating force going to come from? My life up till now seems messy, inconclusive, disorganized: I arranged my courses wrong, played my strategy without unifying rules—got excited at my own potentialities, yet amputated some to serve others. I am drowning in negativism, self-hate, doubt, madness—and even I am not strong enough to deny the routine, the rote, to simplify. No, I go plodding on, afraid that the blank hell in back of my eyes will break through, spewing forth like a dark pestilence, afraid that the disease which eats away the pith of my body with merciless impersonality will break forth in obvious sores and warts, screaming "Traitor, sinner, imposter."

I can begin to see the compulsion for admitting original sin, for adoring Hitler, for taking opium. I have long wanted to read and explore the theories of philosophy, psychology, national, religious, and primitive consciousness, but it seems now too late for anything—I am a conglomerate garbage heap of loose ends—selfish, scared, contemplating devoting the rest of my life to a cause—going naked to send clothes to the needy, escaping to a convent, into hypochondria, into religious mysticism, into the waves—anywhere, anywhere, where the burden, the terrifying hellish weight of self-responsibility and ultimate self-judgment, is lifted. I can see ahead only into dark, sordid alleys, where the dregs, the sludge, the filth of my life lies, unglorified, unchanged—transfigured by nothing: no nobility, not even the illusion of a dream.

Reality is what I make it. That is what I have said I believed. Then I look at   5

Prouty. Olive Higgins Prouty, a novelist and friend. She sponsored Plath's scholarship at Smith College.

the hell I am wallowing in, nerves paralyzed, action nullified—fear, envy, hate: all the corrosive emotions of insecurity biting away at my sensitive guts. Time, experience: the colossal wave, sweeping tidal over me, drowning, drowning. How can I ever find that permanence, that continuity with past and future, that communication with other human beings that I crave? Can I ever honestly accept an artificial imposed solution? How can I justify, how can I rationalize the rest of my life away?

The most terrifying realization is that so many millions in the world would like to be in my place: I am not ugly, not an imbecile, not poor, not crippled—I am, in fact, living in the free, spoiled, pampered country of America and going for hardly any money at all to one of the best colleges. I have earned $1000 in the last three years by writing. Hundreds of dreaming ambitious girls would like to be in my place. They write me letters, asking if they may correspond with me. Five years ago, if I could have seen myself now: at Smith (instead of Wellesley) with seven acceptances from *Seventeen* and one from *Mlle*, with a few lovely clothes, and one intelligent, handsome boy—I would have said: that is all I could ever ask!

And there is the fallacy of existence: the idea that one would be happy forever and age with a given situation or series of accomplishments. Why did Virginia Woolf commit suicide? Or Sara Teasdale or the other brilliant women? Neurotic? Was their writing sublimation (oh, horrible word) of deep, basic desires? If only I knew. If only I knew how high I could set my goals, my requirements for my life! I am in the position of a blind girl playing with a slide rule of values. I am now at the nadir of my calculating powers.

The future? God—will it get worse and worse? Will I never travel, never integrate my life, never have purpose, meaning? Never have time—long stretches, to investigate ideas, philosophy—to articulate the vague seething desires in me? Will I be a secretary—a self-rationalizing, uninspired housewife, secretly jealous of my husband's ability to grow intellectually and professionally while I am impeded? Will I submerge my embarrassing desires and aspirations, refuse to face myself, and go either mad or become neurotic?

Whom can I talk to? Get advice from? No one. A psychiatrist is the god of our age. But they cost money. And I won't take advice, even if I want it. I'll kill myself. I am beyond help. No one here has time to probe, to aid me in understanding myself . . . so many others are worse off than I. How can I selfishly demand help, solace, guidance? No, it is my own mess, and even if now I have lost my sense of perspective, thereby my creative sense of humor, I will not let myself get sick, go mad, or retreat like a child into blubbering on someone else's shoulder. Masks are the order of the day—and the least I can do is cultivate the illusion that I am gay, serene, not hollow and afraid. Someday, god knows when, I will stop this absurd, self-pitying, idle, futile despair. I will begin to think again, and to act according to the way I think. Attitude is a pitifully relative and capricious quality to base a faith on. Like the proverbial sand, it slides, founders, sucks me down to hell.

At present, the last thing I can do is be objective, self-critical, diagnostic—but I *do* know that my philosophy is too subjective, relative and personal to be strong and creative in all circumstances. It is fine in fair weather, but it dissolves when the forty-day rains come. I must submerge it before a larger, transcending goal or craft; what that is I cannot now imagine.

From *The Journals of Sylvia Plath*, edited by Ted Hughes

Sylvia Plath

FROM LETTERS TO HER MOTHER: ON THE
MADEMOISELLE PRIZE   1952

Sylvia Plath wrote hundreds of letters to her mother while she was in college. Most of them talk about her personal psychology, her wishes, anxieties, and dreams. Many of them talk about her ambitions as a writer. When Plath won $500 in a prize for young writers in Mademoiselle *magazine, she was ecstatic. Several of her letters, signed "Sivvy," give a very clear sense of her response and her hopes for the future.*

THE BELMONT HOTEL, CAPE COD
JUNE 11, 1952

Your amazing telegram [*telegram announcing $500* Mademoiselle *prize for "Sunday at the Mintons'," which I forwarded*] came just as I was scrubbing tables in the shady interior of The Belmont dining room. I was so excited that I screamed and actually threw my arms around the head waitress who no doubt thinks I am rather insane! Anyhow, psychologically, the moment couldn't have been better. I felt tired—first night's sleep in new places never *are* peaceful—and I didn't get much! To top it off, I was the only girl waitress here, and had been scrubbing furniture, washing dishes and silver, lifting tables, etc. since 8 a.m. Also, I just learned since I am completely inexperienced, I am not going to be working in the main dining room, but in the "side hall" where the managers and top hotel brass eat. So, tips will no doubt net much less during the summer and the company be less interesting. So I was beginning to worry about money when your telegram came. God! To think "Sunday at the Mintons'" is *one* of *two* prize stories to be put in a big national slick!!! Frankly, I can't believe it!

The first thing I thought of was: Mother can keep her intersession money and buy some pretty clothes and a special trip or something! At least I get a winter coat and extra special suit out of the Mintons. I *think* the prize is $500!!!!!!!!!
ME! Of all people! . . .

So it's really looking up around here, now that I don't have to be scared stiff about money . . . Oh, I say, even if my feet kill me after this first week, and I drop 20 trays, I will have the beach, boys to bring me beer, sun, and young gay companions. What a life.

Love, your crazy old daughter. (Or as Eddie said: "One hell of a sexy dame"!)   5
x x x Sivvy

JUNE 12, 1952

No doubt after I catch up on sleep, and learn to balance trays high on my left hand, I'll feel much happier. As it is now, I feel stuck in the midst of a lot of loud, brassy Irish Catholics, and the only way I can jolly myself is to say, "Oh, well, it's only for a summer, and I can maybe write about them all." At least I've got a new name for my next protagonist—Marley, a gabby girl who knows her way around but good. The ratio of boys to girls has gotten less and less, so I'll be lucky if I get tagged by the youngest kid here. Lots of the girls are really wise, drinking flirts. As for me, being the conservative, quiet, gracious type, I don't stand much chance of dating some of the cutest ones . . . If I can only get "in" as a pal with these girls, and never for a minute let them know I'm the gentle intellectual type, it'll be O.K.

As for the *Mlle* news, I don't think it's really sunk in yet. I felt sure they made a mistake, or that you'd made it up to cheer me. The big advantage will be that I won't have to worry about earning barely $300 this summer. I would really have been sick otherwise. I can't wait till August when I can go casually down to the drug store and pick up a slick copy of *Mlle*, flip to the index, and see ME, one of two college girls in the U.S.!

Really, when I think of how I started it over spring vacation, polished it at school, and sat up till midnight in the Haven House kitchen typing it amidst noise and chatter, I can't get over how the story soared to where it did. One thing about *Mlle* college fiction—although that great one last year by the Radcliffe girl was tremendous and realistic—I remembered the first issue I read where there were two queer part-fantasies, one about the hotel the woman kept for queer people, and the other about an elderly married couple. So I guess the swing of the pendulum dictated something like good old Henry and Elizabeth Minton. Elizabeth has been floating around in my head in her lavender dress, giggling very happily about her burst into the world of print. She always wanted to show Henry she could be famous if she ever worked at it!

One thing I am partly scared and partly curious about is Dick's° reaction when he reads the story in print. I'm glad Dick hasn't read it yet, but Henry started out by being him and Elizabeth me (and they grew old and related in the process). But nevertheless I wonder if Dick will recognize his dismembered self! It's funny how one always, somewhere, has the germ of reality in a story, no matter how fantastic . . .

I get great pleasure out of sharing it [*her feeling about the story*] with *you*,   10 who really understand how terribly much it means as a tangible testimony that I *have* got a germ of writing ability even if *Seventeen* has forgotten about it. The only thing, I probably won't have a chance to win *Mlle* again, so I'll try for a guest editorship maybe next year or my senior year, and set my sights for the *Atlantic*. God, I'm glad I can talk about it with you—probably you're the only outlet that I'll have that won't get tired of my talking about writing . . .

Speaking again of Henry and Liz, it was a step for me to a story where the protagonist isn't always ME, and proved that I am beginning to use imagination to transform the actual incident. I was scared that would never happen, but I think it's an indication that my perspective is broadening.

Sometimes I think—heck, I don't know why I didn't stay home all summer, writing, doing physical science, and having a small part-time job. I could "afford" to now, but it doesn't do much good to yearn about that, I guess. Although it would have been nice. Oh well, I'll cheer up. I love you.

Your own Sivvy

JUNE 15, 1952

9 *Dick:* Dick Norton, a close friend.

Dear Mother,

     . . . Do write me letters, Mommy, because I am in a very dangerous state of feeling sorry for myself . . . Just at present, life is awful. *Mademoiselle* seems quite unreal, and I am exhausted, scared, incompetent, unenergetic and generally low in spirits . . . Working in side hall puts me apart, and I feel completely uprooted and clumsy. The more I see the main hall girls expertly getting special dishes, fixing shaved ice and fruit, etc., the more I get an inferiority complex and feel that each day in side hall leaves me further behind . . . But as tempted as I am to be a coward and escape by crawling back home, I have resolved to give it a good month's trial—till July 10 . . . Don't worry about me, but do send me little pellets of advice now and then.

From Letters Home

Helen Vendler
AN INTRACTABLE METAL   1985

A distinguished critic of poetry, Helen Vendler reviews the critical approaches through psychoanalytic and political strategies. In this piece she moves from feminist approaches to Plath to look closely at Plath's life. After that she focuses on the language and the techniques, showing the extraordinary resources of Plath as poet.

     The Collected Poems of Sylvia Plath finally appeared in 1982, almost twenty years after Plath's suicide, on February 11, 1963. Nothing in the introduction, written by her former husband, the British poet Ted Hughes, quite explains the long delay in the publication of this collection. Before Plath died, she had prepared the volume called *Ariel* for the press, but the "*Ariel* eventually published in 1965 was a somewhat different volume from the one she had planned," Hughes tells us; it incorporated poems she had planned to keep for a subsequent book, and "omitted some of the more personally aggressive poems from 1962"—those concerning her husband's infidelity, which led to the dissolution of the marriage and to Plath's move from Devon to London. Her daughter, Frieda, was two at the time of the move; her son, Nicholas, not yet a year old. Less than a month after his first birthday, Plath was dead. She had managed to live and to write after previous attempts at suicide, but, like Cesare Pavese (to cite a comparable case), she continually needed to find reasons *not* to kill herself, rather than a reason to do so.

     Until recently, most of the writing about Plath has been psychologically or politically motivated. The time of her fame coincided with a widespread acceptance of the Freudian myths of selfhood (which she also embraced) and with the rise of women's liberation. Plath's life seemed a textbook illustration of the "Electra complex"° (as she herself called it, schooled by her therapists and her college reading in psychology), and she also seemed an instance of the damage done to gifted

---

Electra complex: Opposite of Oedipus Complex, in which a daughter wishes to kill the mother and marry the father.

women by social convention. Plath's language—a heady cross of *Kinder, Küche,* *Freud,* and *Frazer°*—found an audience that already knew and shared its world of reference. An electric current jumped between *Ariel* and a large (mostly female) set of readers; and from then on, the poetry of Plath became a part of the feminist canon. *Crossing the Water* and *Winter Trees* were published in 1971; they, together with *The Colossus* (the only volume published in Plath's lifetime, in 1960) and *Ariel,* made up the Plath poetic canon until *The Collected Poems.*

Plath scholars know most of the work published therein. Ted Hughes and his sister Olwyn have been publishing, bit by bit, small groups of the poems in limited editions in England (all royalties are assigned to the two children). The poems not previously published in any form were mostly very early; the few later ones in this category were undistinguished. For the general reader, however, *The Collected Poems* conveyed for the first time the whole of Plath's work, arranged chronologically by date of composition. Fifty very early poems are printed in an appendix; the chronological arrangement begins with the year 1956, when Plath, who was born in 1932, was twenty-three. But the memorable poems do not begin until she turns twenty-four—after her marriage, in June 1956. She had six years of mature writing before she died, at thirty. Those years included her second year as a Fulbright fellow at Newnham College, Cambridge; a year of teaching at Smith, where she had been an undergraduate; a year in Boston, where she audited Robert Lowell's writing class at Boston University; and her return to England. In London, after she and Hughes had decided to give up teaching and to live as writers, she had, in succession, a child, a three-month miscarriage, and an appendectomy. There she also wrote her autobiographical novel, *The Bell Jar* (published in England under the pseudonym Victoria Lucas). In 1961, she and Ted Hughes moved from London to Devon, and she had their second child. Then came the separation from Hughes which produced a remarkable spate of writing: in the thirty-one days of October 1962, Plath finished twenty-five poems (while in the entire year of 1960—which included the last three months of her first pregnancy, the birth of her daughter, and her first months of motherhood—she wrote only twelve).

The events of Plath's life during these years—though some, like the transatlantic move, are slightly unusual—are on the whole those that many women have lived through, not excepting marital disappointments, the discovery of infidelity, and finding oneself a single mother. These events, banal to everyone except the one experiencing them, have been the occasion in the twentieth century of any number of banal poems. As subjects, they are as well-worn as the subject of parents (Plath's other topic). What is striking, and satisfying, about reading Plath's poems is how well she holds her own, and how firmly she transforms the topics she masters—how her best poems maintain themselves in passion without lacking a strict, informing intelligence. In some of the poems (notably the early ones), intelligence averts its eyes from feeling or overcontrols feeling; later, the balance sometimes tips in the other direction, and Plath becomes merely vituperative or spiteful, angrily refusing the acuteness of reflection present in her best work. Her piercing strength when intelligence and feeling cooperate is not easily forgotten.

Plath seems very young now to any older reader, and her career seems cru-

---

Kinder, Küche, Freud, and Frazer: Children, home, Freud, and mythographer James Frazer. Reference is to the homelike language informed by Freudian Psychology and myth studies.

elly self-aborted. Remembering ourselves at thirty, we wish she could have had
the years of living that would inevitably have provided her with new views of her
past and, in consequence, new views of herself. Her suicide, for all her attempt to
dress it in Greek necessity, seems an unhappy accident—a failure of social resource,
a failure of medicine (a hospital bed could not be found for her), and even a failure of weather (she hated the cold, and died in London's coldest winter in years).
We are more conscious now of the physiological causes of (and remedies for) depression, thanks to poets like Lowell who have expressed considerable irony about
the sedulous efforts of therapists to ascribe to environmental causes what turns
out to be a lack of lithium.

By the time she died, Plath had written at least two scenarios of her life. In
the first scenario, her father, Otto (an entomologist who died, when she was eight,
of willfully uncared-for diabetes), is a doting parent, a hero, and a god, and she
is his mourning daughter; her mother, Aurelia, is a heroine who keeps Plath and
her brother alive by working as a teacher of secretarial skills. (Plath's devotion to
her mother and Aurelia Plath's to her daughter appear in the incessant letters they
exchanged; some of Sylvia's were collected in *Letters Home*, published in 1975.)
In the second scenario, Otto Plath becomes an incestuously seductive father, a
Nazi, and a vampire; and Sylvia is his victim, a Jew in his concentration camp.
Aurelia Plath in this scenario is a tentacular mother, a barnacle obsessively clinging to her daughter, a "blubbery Mary." Plath's scenarios about Ted Hughes un-
derwent comparable changes, as he metamorphosed from fertility god into monster; and Plath's fictions about herself changed, too—from the fruitful bride of
the sun, "quick with seed," bearing a king as she crouches in the grass, she turns
into Lady Lazarus, who eats men like air. Eventually, if Plath had managed to stay
alive, all the scenarios would probably have revised themselves; she would have
seen her parents in yet another guise, and perhaps her husband, too. Certainly
she would have seen both herself and her children differently. As she writes about
them, her children are infants, pure and poignant, untroubled by their mother's
anxieties:

> Your clear eye is the one absolutely beautiful thing.
> I want to fill it with color and ducks,
> the zoo of the new
>
> Whose names you meditate . . .
>
> ("Child")

When, in the future, they became contrary and baffling adolescents, Plath
would have needed to find another fiction for them, and for herself.

The one thing that recommends Plath to us most strongly now is her ability to change her mind when she saw a new truth. She was on the lookout for
new truths; never one to receive the world passively, she hunted for accuracy and
excoriated herself for her failures. She changed her mind, when it was necessary,
in a violent way, repudiating her previous position with all the force of her daunting energy. She had no Keatsian capacity for maintaining two contrary truths at
once. But it is not impossible that in middle age she might have come to entertain her scenarios as plural truths, to find some of the equilibrium granted, late,
to Lowell, who ended by seeing his parents less harshly. Sylvia Plath, when she

died, had at last begun to recognize a monstrousness in herself. If her father was
a vampire, so was she. She had also begun to realize that "there is no terminus,"
no point at which the world is arranged for good, with all its truths established:

> There is no terminus, only suitcases
> Out of which the same self unfolds like a suit
> Bald and shiny, with pockets of wishes,
> Notions and tickets, short circuits and folding mirrors.

This realization could be the chief principle of interest in life—more wishes,
more notions, more tickets—but to Plath, in her tiredness, it seemed a nightmare.

What is regrettable in Plath's work is not the domestic narrowness of her
subject matter (Emily Dickinson and George Herbert made faultless poetry out
of matter as putatively "narrow") but the narrowness of tone. She has wit and sar-
donic irony; she has blank despair; and she has neutral judgment and observation,
and even, at the end, tenderness. But she veers from zero to one hundred like a
dangerously swinging needle; she has none of the ravishing variety of tone that
colors Herbert's colloquies with God. Plath has another narrowness, too—her
scrupulous refusal to generalize, in her best poems, beyond her own case. She will
not speak about the human condition, in the way Emily Dickinson emboldened
herself to. Dickinson had an acute, generalizing mind as well as an eye for minute
particulars; in Plath we miss the sudden, illuminating widening of perspective that
Dickinson learned from Emerson. Plath was stubbornly truthful, and she may
have felt herself the exception rather than the rule. But her sense of herself as ex-
ceptional prevented her from seeing herself as one of many.

There are two hundred and twenty-four mature poems in *The Collected Poems*,
and those after *The Colossus* are better (as most critics have said) than those composed for that volume. Plath assiduously worked and worked on poetry, as she
had worked on academic subjects; no poet has worked harder. Either marriage
and childbearing alone or the encouragement and help of Ted Hughes—or, more
probably, both—changed her style. She discovered ways to make lines seem inevitable, not only in sound but also (her most interesting discovery) in looks. She
had worked hard at imitating Dylan Thomas, and had early mastered certain coarse
sound effects. But in a late line like "The shadows of ringdoves chanting, but easing nothing," she has given up on a bald imitation of Thomas and has found her
own voice. Some of the binding devices in such a line are familiar—the parallel
of "chanting" and "easing," the repetition of words of two syllables. But what is
more unusual is the matching of "nothing," though it is syntactically not parallel, with "chanting" and "easing." Such ear-rhymes are a true binding and a false
binding at once, setting the words aslant. The last half of the word "shadows"—
"dows"—almost matches the "doves" of "ringdoves" in the same witty way.
Plath's later style is full of such cunning; her eye-rhymes (often without any aural equivalent like that in "doves" and "dows") continue vigorously to the end of
her career, and replace her earlier, self-conscious overwriting for the ear. We require of a poem that the words spring toward each other in magnetic attraction,
but we are offended when the trick is done obviously. Plath's later rapproche-
ments seem almost casual by contrast with her obtrusive early rhymes and rhythms,
but they are far more premeditated. She began keeping drafts, Hughes tells us.
Eventually, they may be published, and testify to the angle of revision she favored.

The later poems, at their best, bear witness to Plath's painstaking work to make their parts fall into place and lock.

When Plath began to be able to find adequate language for her feelings, she redid a great number of her earlier themes. Here is early (pre-1956) Plath writing about the moon, always for her the presider:

> The choice between the mica mystery
> of moonlight or the pockmarked face we see
>   through the scrupulous telescope
> is always to be made: innocence
> is a fairy-tale; intelligence
>   hangs itself on its own rope.
>   ("Metamorphoses of the Moon")

"Intelligence hangs itself on its own rope" is a formulation better than what turns up in most college verse, but the language of this poem is Audenesque, prematurely "disillusioned," and arch. (Auden must have been the recommended intellectual model at college in those days; he is equally present in early Rich.) Only the end sounds particularly vigorous; "the mica mystery of moonlight" (in a poem alliteratively named "Metamorphoses of the Moon") shows off Plath's easy alliteration, which in fact does *not* draw the words together but pushes them apart, by calling attention to its own flashiness.

This is from "The Moon and the Yew Tree," written in 1961, just before Plath's twenty-ninth birthday:

> The moon is no door. It is a face in its own right,
> White as a knuckle and terribly upset.
> It drags the sea after it like a dark crime; it is quiet
> With the O-gape of complete despair. . . .

The complacency of the earlier poem is replaced by a distraught but tenacious appropriation of both the world and earlier poetry. (The "gape" is from the gape of Niobe mourning her children in Keats's "Endymion.") This appropriation comes as much from the poet's staring at the moon and staring at a particular line of Keats as from her staring at herself. In any case, the merely fashionable is cast aside, and Plath now seeks out her own affinities—helped, it seems clear, by Hughes.

Plath's phrasemaking went from strength to strength in her last two years, and it is a steady instruction to see her exact eye (with "no preconceptions," as she said of a mirror) attempt to take in reality afresh. An owl cries "from its cold indigo," and the chill lies in the matching c-o-d-i-d-i-g-o, where the "c" and the "g" are only variants of one sound. Under Plath's clinical gaze, her lungs are "two gray, papery bags"; at a funeral, as the open grave yawns, "for a minute the sky pours into the hole like plasma"; the buzz of bees in a bee box is a "furious Latin"; the glittering snow is "marshaling its brilliant cutlery" (a theft from Emily Dickinson); the darkness of a storeroom is "the black bunched in there like a bat," and the compression of "bunched" hides a beast waiting to spring; the flesh of a cut thumb is, as a detached eye takes a cool look, "red plush"; glistening worms are "sticky pearls" (with the shock coming from the sudden endowing of the inorganic word "pearls" with gluey life); a calla lily displays "cold folds of ego" (the "cold indigo" trick again, but with the added surprise of a pairing like "sticky pearls"); and on the farm in winter Plath sees "the barbarous holly with its viridian/Scallops, pure iron," matching the holly leaf's shape with scallops, viridian with iron, and erecting a stiff, bristling fence of "r"s—"barbarous," "viridian," "pure," "iron." These are all virtuoso phrases, and no poetry could be made up of such things exclusively, but they reassure us that in her most violent moments Plath's eye and ear could remain undisturbedly, and even laboriously, accurate.

Plath used to berate herself for not remembering everything in detail—a room she had seen, or what a person had been wearing—and in her journal she noted things down with meticulous exactness. She apparently deceived all of Cambridge into seeing her as a gushing, if intelligent, American coed, but it is to her credit that she could not deceive herself. "That is the latent terror, a symptom: it is suddenly either all or nothing; either you break the surface shell into the whistling void or you don't," she wrote in the journal in 1956. The terse, diagnostic language authorizes the experience even to those of us who may not have had it: "The horror is the sudden folding up and away of the phenomenal world, leaving nothing. Just rags. Human rooks which say: Fraud."

The poems of Plath's last years find a way of giving illustration to that folding up of the phenomenal world. For her, the poems also filled the void: "If I sit still and don't do anything, the world goes on beating like a slack drum, without meaning," she says in the journal. The best of her poems illustrate both the fullness and the emptiness of the universe: how it is filled with complicated, rich, obdurate, and significant forms—yew trees, gothic letters, blackberries—and how these forms are shadowed by others, diaphanous, elusive, obscuring, and blank, whether moonlight, fog, cloud, or ocean. This dialectic of forms is brought at times to an almost supernatural beauty. For example, under the threatening veils of "a sky/Palely and flamily/Igniting its carbon monoxides" there open the poppies in October:

> O my God, what am I
> that these late mouths should cry open
> In a forest of frost, in a dawn of cornflowers.
>   ("Poppies in October")

That is from a poem written on her thirtieth birthday, the same day as "Ariel," with its equally riveting balance of "substanceless blue" and "the red/Eye, the cauldron of morning."

A bleaker version of form appears in "Blackberrying," where the organic is both beautiful and disgusting:

> I come to one bush of berries so ripe it
>   is a bush of flies,
> Hanging their bluegreen bellies and their
>   wing panes in a Chinese screen.

A "last hook" in the downward path through the blackberry brambles takes Plath from the overdetermined berry/fly bushes to the obscure emptiness of the sea:

> A last hook brings me
> to the hills' northern face, and the face is orange rock
> that looks out on nothing, nothing but a great space
> of white and pewter lights, and a din like silversmiths
> beating and beating at an intractable metal.

The resistance of experience to meaning, expressed here in the word "intractable," appears in comparable words all through Plath's poetry: I note, at random, "indefatigable," "irrefutable," "irreplaceable," "irretrievable," "inaccessible," "invisible," "untouchable," "inexorable," "unbreakable," "impossible," "indeterminate," "unintelligible," "indigestible," "unidentifiable," "incapable," and "ineradicable"—a family of barriers to soul, mind, and body. Against those glassy barriers Plath heroically went about her business of constructing meaning, both psychic and literary. She knew enough to choose "The Colossus," a poem about this wearing struggle, as the title poem of her first book. The poem resembles the anxiety dreams Plath had as a child, about tasks too large ever to be done adequately. She addresses, in the poem, the broken statue of her father:

> I shall never get you put together entirely,
> pieced, glued, and properly jointed.
> . . . .
> Thirty years now I have labored
> to dredge the silt from your throat.
> I am none the wiser.
>
> Scaling little ladders with gluepots and pails of Lysol
> I crawl like an ant in mourning
> over the weedy acres of your brow
> To mend the immense skull-plates and clear
> the bald, white tumuli of your eyes.

The many poems about Plath's father, including the famous bee poems (Otto Plath had written a book called *Bumblebees and Their Ways*), take up many myths of explanation, including Freudian diagrams, folk myths, fairy tales, and religious analogies. While we may all need such myths to approach the mystery of family relations, Plath not only, with new insights, replaced one myth with another but also changed her style to fit the myth. The sacrificial victim of the bee poems speaks in a style of obedient, paralyzed sentences, in a dead-toned drama. Occasionally, it modulates to melodrama ("I have a self to recover, a queen"), but in style that melodrama is never satisfactorily voiced in the bee sequence. It awaits its cold and controlled derangement in "Lady Lazarus" and in "Daddy," where style turns to slashing caricature of Freudian self-knowledge:

> Every woman adores a Fascist,
> the boot in the face, the brute
> Brute heart of a brute like you.
> ("Daddy")

Gone are the elegant vicissitudes of rhyme, slant rhyme, and syllabics, and all the genteel college writing-class conventions:

But they pulled me out of the sack,
and they stuck me together with glue.
And then I knew what to do.
I made a model of you,
A man in black with a Meinkampf look

And a love of the rack and the screw.
And I said I do, I do.

("Daddy")

This "Threepenny Opera" style is an effect usable only once; the violence
done to the self here (provoked by the violence Plath suffered under the shock of
Hughes's desertion) is the substance of the jeering style. Plath lashes out at her
former idolatry of her father and at her subsequent idolatry of her husband, but
she also demolishes the noble myths of her own earlier poems, turning the
Freudian-Hellenic colossus into a "Ghastly statue with one gray toe/Big as a
Frisco seal . . ."

"Lady Lazarus," written in the same feverish thirtieth-birthday month that
produced "Daddy" and "Ariel," is a mélange of incompatible styles, as though in
a meaningless world every style could have its day: bravado ("I have done it again"),
slang ("A sort of walking miracle"), perverse fashion commentary ("my
skin/Bright as a Nazi lampshade"), melodrama ("Do I terrify?"), wit ("like the
cat I have nine times to die"), boast ("This is Number Three"), self-disgust ("What
a trash/To annihilate each decade"). The poem moves on through reductive dismissal ("The big strip tease") to public announcement, with a blasphemous swipe
at the *ecce homo* ("Gentlemen, ladies/These are my hands/My knees"), and comes
to its single lyric moment, recalling Plath's suicide attempt in the summer before
her senior year at Smith:

I rocked shut

As a seashell.
They had to call and call
And pick the worms off me like sticky pearls.

Almost every stanza of "Lady Lazarus" picks up a new possibility for this theatrical voice, from mock movie talk ("So, so, Herr Doktor./So, Herr Enemy")
to bureaucratic politeness ("Do not think I underestimate your great concern")
to witch warnings ("I rise with my red hair/And I eat men like air"). When an
author makes a sort of headcheese of style in this way—a piece of gristle, a piece
of meat, a piece of gelatin, a piece of rind—the disbelief in style is countered by
a competitive faith in it. Style (as something consistent) is meaningless, but styles
(as dizzying provisional skepticism) are all.

Poems like "Daddy" and "Lady Lazarus" are in one sense demonically intelligent, in their wanton play with concepts, myths, and language, and in another, and more important, sense not intelligent at all, in that they willfully refuse,
for the sake of a cacophony of styles (a tantrum of style), the steady, centripetal
effect of thought. Instead, they display a wild dispersal, a centrifugal spin to further and further reaches of outrage. They are written in a loud version of what
Plath elsewhere calls "the zoo yowl, the mad soft/Mirror talk you love to catch

me at." And that zoo yowl has a feral slyness about it, which rises to a heated ha-tred in the poems about Hughes and about Plath's rivals (as she saw them)—her mother, Hughes's sister Olwyn, and Hughes's mistress. The distress of these poems unbalanced them aesthetically. When Plath turns her loathing back on her-self, she instantly resumes control of structure, and the newly stoic poems recover shape and power: "The heart shuts,/The sea slides back/The mirrors are sheeted."

Plath's cold verdict on her own choices admits the irreconcilables in her psy-chic constitution: "Perfection is terrible, it cannot have children." Her drive to-ward perfection (of which she had such a clear and distinct idea, and toward which she slaved) was incompatible—or so it seemed to her in her depleted state—with the act that had, along with poetry, brought her real happiness: the bearing of children. The verdict of the poems is against perfection and for children. This conviction enlarged and deepened her last poems, in which she alternated, pitiably, between a deathly resignation and a despair that envied the narcissistically appet-itive flowers:

> The claw
> of the magnolia,
> drunk on its own scents,
> asks nothing of life.
> ("Paralytic")

There is more outrage and satire and hysteria in some of the last poems than there is steady thought, especially steady thought evinced in style. Plath, for what-ever reason, could not rise to the large concerns of tragedy in a Keatsian way. Her unevenness recalls Hart Crane, but she did not have Crane's open generosity of vision. She did possess—and it gives her a claim on us—a genius for the tran-scription in words of those wild states of feeling which in the rest of us remain so inchoate that we quail under them, speechless.

From *Ariel Ascending: Writings about Sylvia Plath* by Paul Alexander

Jacqueline Rose (b. 1949)
PLATH'S "DADDY"   1991

Jacqueline Rose offers a contemporary critical reading of "Daddy," looking at the poem from a psychological and biographical point of view and taking into account the historical circumstances surrounding the poem. She also discusses some of the controversy regarding its reception by critics.

"Daddy" is a much more difficult poem [than "Little Fugue"] to write about. It is of course the poem of the murder of the father which at the very least raises the psychic stakes. It is, quite simply, the more aggressive poem. Hence, no doubt, its founding status in the mythology of Sylvia Plath. Reviewing the American pub-lication of *Ariel* in 1966, *Time* magazine wrote:

> Within a week of her death, intellectual London was hunched over copies of a
> strange and terrible poem she had written during her last sick slide toward

suicide. "Daddy" was its title; its subject was her morbid love-hatred of her father; its style was as brutal as a truncheon. What is more, "Daddy" was merely the first jet of flame from a literary dragon who in the last months of her life breathed a burning river of bale across the literary landscape.

Writing on the Holocaust, Jean-François Lyotard suggests that two motifs tend to operate in tension, or to the mutual exclusion of each other—the preservation of memory against forgetfulness and the accomplishment of vengeance. Do "Little Fugue" and "Daddy" take up the two motifs one after the other, or do they present something of their mutual relation, the psychic economy that ties them even as it forces them apart? There is a much clearer narrative in "Daddy"—from victimization to revenge. In this case it is the form of that sequence which has allowed the poem to be read purely personally as Plath's vindictive assault on Otto Plath and Ted Hughes (the transition from the first to the second mirroring the biographical pattern of her life). Once again, however, it is only that preliminary privileging of the personal which allows the reproach for her evocation of history—more strongly this time, because this is the poem in which Plath identifies with the Jew.

The first thing to notice is the trouble in the time sequence of this poem in relation to the father, the technically impossible temporality which lies at the center of the story it tells, which echoes that earlier impossibility of language in "Little Fugue":

DADDY

You do not do, you do not do
Any more, black shoe
In which I have lived like a foot
For thirty years, poor and white,
Barely daring to breathe, or Achoo.

Daddy, I have had to kill you.
You died before I had time–
Marble-heavy, a bag full of God,
Ghastly statue, with one gray toe
big as a Frisco seal

And a head in the freakish Atlantic
Where it pours bean green over blue
In the waters off beautiful Nauset.
I used to pray to recover you.
Ach, du.

What is the time sequence of these verses? On the one hand, a time of unequivocal resolution, the end of the line, a story that once and for all will be brought to a close: "You do not do, you do not do / Any more." This story is legendary. It is the great emancipatory narrative of liberation which brings, some would argue, all history to an end. In this case, it assimilates, combines into one entity, more than one form of oppression—daughter and father, poor and rich—licensing a reading which makes of the first the meta-narrative of all forms of inequality (patriarchy the cause of all other types of oppression, which it then subordinates to itself). The poem thus presents itself as protest and emancipation from a condition which reduces the one oppressed to the barest minimum of human, but inarticulate, life: "Barely daring to breathe or Achoo" (it is hard not to read here a reference to Plath's sinusitis). Blocked, hardly daring to breathe or to sneeze, this body suffers because the father has for too long oppressed.

If the poem stopped here then it could fairly be read, as it has often been read, in triumphalist terms—instead of which it suggests that such an ending is only a beginning, or repetition, which immediately finds itself up against a wholly other order of time: "Daddy, I have had to kill you. / You died before I had time." In Freudian terms, this is the time of "*Nachtraglichkeit*" or after-effect: a murder which has taken place, but after the fact, because the father who is killed is already dead; a father who was once mourned ("I used to pray to recover you") but whose recovery has already been signaled, by what precedes it in the poem, as the precondition for his death to be repeated. Narrative as repetition—it is a familiar drama in which the father must be killed in so far as he is already dead. This at the very least suggests that, if this is the personal father, it is also what psychoanalysis terms the father of individual prehistory, the father who establishes the very possibility (or impossibility) of history as such. It is through this father that the subject discovers—or fails to discover—her own history, as at once personal and part of a wider symbolic place. The time of historical emancipation immediately finds itself up against the problem of a no less historical, but less certain, psychic time.

This is the father as godhead, as origin of the nation and the word—graphically figured in the image of the paternal body in bits and pieces spreading across the American nation state: bag full of God, head in the Atlantic, big as a Frisco seal. Julia Kristeva terms this father "*Père imaginaire*," which she then abbreviates "PI." Say those initials out loud in French and what you get is "pays" (country or nation)—the concept of the exile. Much has been made of Plath as an exile, as she goes back and forth between England and the United States. But there is another history of migration, another prehistory, which this one overlays—of her father, born in Grabow, the Polish Corridor, and her mother's Austrian descent: "you are talking to me as a general American. In particular, my background is, may I say, German and Austrian."

If this poem is in some sense about the death of the father, a death both willed and premature, it is no less about the death of language. Returning to the roots of language, it discovers a personal and political history (the one as indistinguishable from the other) which once again fails to enter into words:

> In the German tongue, in the Polish town
> Scraped flat by the roller
> Of wars, wars, wars.
> But the name of the town is common.
> My Polack friend
>
> Says there are a dozen or two.
> So I never could tell where you
> Put your foot, your root,
> I never could talk to you.
> The tongue stuck in my jaw.

It stuck in a barb wire snare.
Ich, ich, ich, ich,
I could hardly speak.
I thought every German was you.
And the language obscene

Twice over, the origins of the father, physically and in language, are lost—
through the wars which scrape flat German tongue and Polish town, and then
through the name of the town itself, which is so common that it fails in its
function to identify, fails in fact to name. Compare Claude Lanzmann, the
film-maker of *Shoah*, on the Holocaust as "a crime to forget the name," or
Lyotard: "the destruction of whole worlds of names." Wars wipe out names,
the father cannot be spoken to, and the child cannot talk, except to repeat
endlessly, in a destroyed obscene language, the most basic or minimal unit of
self-identity in speech: "ich, ich, ich, ich" (the first draft has "incestuous" for
"obscene"). The notorious difficulty of the first-person pronoun in relation
to identity—its status as shifter, the division or splitting of the subject which
it both carries and denies—is merely compounded by its repetition here. In
a passage taken out of her journals, Plath comments on this "I":

> I wouldn't be I. But I am I now; and so many other millions are so
> irretrievably their own special variety of "I" that I can hardly bear to think of
> it. I: how firm a letter; how reassuring the three strokes: one vertical, proud
> and assertive, and then the two short horizontal lines in quick, smug,
> succession. The pen scratches on the paper I . . . I . . . I . . . I . . . I . . . I.

The effect, of course, if you read it aloud, is not one of assertion but, as with
"ich, ich, ich, ich," of the word sticking in the throat. Pass from that trauma
of the "I" back to the father as a "bag full of God," and "Daddy" becomes
strikingly resonant of the case of a woman patient described at Hamburg, suspended between two utterances: "I am God's daughter" and "I do not know
what I am" (she was the daughter of a member of Himmler's SS).

In the poem, the "I" moves backwards and forwards between German and
English, as does the "you" ("Ach, du"). The dispersal of identity in language follows the lines of a division or confusion between nations and tongues. In fact language in this part of the poem moves in two directions at once. It appears in the
form of translation, and as a series of repetitions and overlappings—"ich," "Ach,"
"Achoo"—which dissolve the pronoun back into infantile patterns of sound. Note
too how the rhyming pattern of the poem sends us back to the first line. "You do
not do, you do not do," and allows us to read it as both English and German:
"You du not du," "You you not you"—"you" as "not you" because "you" do
not exist inside a space where linguistic address would be possible.

I am not suggesting, however, that we apply to Plath's poem the idea of poetry as *écriture* (women's writing as essentially multiple, the other side of normal
discourse, fragmented by the passage of the unconscious and the body into words).
Instead the poem seems to be outlining the conditions under which that celebrated loss of the symbolic function takes place. Identity and language lose them-

selves in the place of the father whose absence gives him unlimited powers. Far from presenting this as a form of liberation—language into pure body and play— Plath's poem lays out the high price, at the level of fantasy, that such a psychic process entails. Irruption of the semiotic (Kristeva's term for that other side of normal language), which immediately transposes itself into an alien, paternal tongue.

Plath's passionate desire to learn German and her constant failure to do so, is one of the refrains of both her journals and her letters home: "Wickedly didn't do German for the last two days, in a spell of perversity and paralysis" . . . "do German (that I *can* do)" . . . "German and French would give me self-respect, why don't I act on this?" . . . "Am very painstakingly studying German two hours a day" . . . "At least I have begun my German. Painful, as if 'part were cut out of my brain' " . . . "Worked on German for two days, then let up" . . . "Take hold. Study German today." In *The Bell Jar*, Esther Greenwood says: "every time I picked up a German dictionary or a German book, the very sight of those dense, black, barbed wire letters made my mind shut like a clam."

If we go back to the poem, then I think it becomes clear that it is this crisis of representation in the place of the father which is presented by Plath as engendering—forcing, even—her identification with the Jew. Looking for the father, failing to find him anywhere, the speaker finds him everywhere instead. Above all, she finds him everywhere in the language which she can neither address to him nor barely speak. It is this hallucinatory transference which turns every German into the image of the father, makes for the obscenity of the German tongue, and leads directly to the first reference to the Holocaust:

> And the language obscene
>
> An engine, an engine
> Chuffing me off like a Jew.
> A Jew to Dachau, Auschwitz, Belsen.
> I began to talk like a Jew.
> I think I may well be a Jew.
>
> The snows of the Tyrol, the clear beer of Vienna
> Are not very pure or true.
> With my gypsy ancestress and my weird luck
> And my Taroc pack and my Taroc pack
> I may be a bit of a Jew.

From *The Haunting of Sylvia Plath*

Robert Phillips   (b. 1938)

A READING OF "THE MOON AND THE YEW TREE" AND "DADDY"   1973

Phillip's commentary on Plath's poems focuses on the psychological imagery and the "growth and development of Plath's psychic life." Phillips also provides useful information on the background to Plath's "Daddy," a poem that moves rapidly away from the actual details of her own father's life.

The drive toward God is explored in "The Moon and the Yew Tree," in which Plath identifies with the moon and longs for religious belief. The moon identification is simple to comprehend, with its connotations of the imagination and the maternal, its mysterious connection between the lunar cycle and the menstrual cycle. Like woman, the moon is the celestial body which suffers painful changes in shape (as did Plath in pregnancy). There is also a parallel between Plath's being subject to changes as is the moon, with both hiding their dark sides. The moon is a female symbol because it is the passive sphere, only reflecting the glory of the male sun, a state of being similar to Plath's view of the conventional roles assigned wife and husband.

The poem's other central symbol, the yew tree, is also a conventional one, traditionally implying inexhaustible life and immortality. The ancient tree also seems to me to function here as a representative of the growth and development of Plath's psychic life as distinct from the instinctual life symbolized by animals such as the rabbit and the horse Ariel. That it is an important symbol to her is implicit in the fact that the yew appears in other poems, "Little Fugue" and "The Munich Mannequins" as well. In "The Moon and the Yew Tree" the tree's "Gothic shape" reinforces the implication that Plath aspired toward Christian belief and the Church, a quest which was to end only in coldness and blackness. There is no comfort to be found in institutional Christianity. Yet she repeats her desire to see, and therefore to enter the temple of God, in "A Birthday Present," the poem which follows. But ultimately religion fails her, and only through hallucination does she achieve Paradise, as in "Fever 103°," of which Plath herself wrote, "This poem is about two kinds of fire—the fires of hell, which merely agonize, and the fires of heaven, which purify. During the poem, the first sort of fire suffers itself into the second."

The only way Plath was to achieve relief, to become an independent self, was to kill her father's memory, which in "Daddy" she does by a metaphorical murder of the father figure. Making her father a Nazi and herself a Jew, she dramatizes the war in her soul. It is a terrible poem, full of blackness, one of the most nakedly confessional poems ever written. From its opening image onward, that of the father as a "black shoe" in which the daughter has lived for thirty years—an explicitly phallic image, according to Freud—the sexual pull and tug is manifest, as is the degree of Plath's mental suffering, supported by references to Dachau, Auschwitz, and Belsen. (Elsewhere in Plath the references to hanged men also are emblems of suffering while swinging. In Jungian psychology the swinging motion would be symbolic of her ambivalent state and her unfulfilled longing as well.) Plath then confesses that, after failing to escape her predicament through suicide, she married a surrogate father, "A man in black with a Meinkampf look" who obligingly was just as much a vampire of her spirit—one who "drank my blood for a year, / Seven years, if you want to know." (Sylvia Plath was married to the poet Ted Hughes for seven years.) When Plath drives the stake through her father's heart, she not only is exorcising the demon of her father's memory, but metaphorically is killing her husband and all men as well.

It is a poem of total rejection. And when she writes that "The black telephone's off at the root," she is turning her back on the modern world as well. Such rejection of family and society leads to that final rejection, that of the self. Plath's suicide is predicted everywhere in the book, in poems of symbolic annihilation such as "Totem" and statements of human fascination with death, such as "Edge"—in which to be dead is to be perfected. Plath's earlier terror at death becomes a romance with it, and her poems themselves are what M. L. Rosenthal called "yearnings toward that condition." Freud believed the aim of all life is death, and for Plath life was poetry. By extension, then, poetry for Plath became death, both conditions inseparable. She herself as much as said so: "The blood jet is poetry, / There is no stopping it." In the act of committing her confession to paper, she was committing her life to death. The source of her creative energy was her self-destructiveness. She did not have Sexton's or Roethke's humor to save her. (Instead of committing suicide, Roethke continually became a child again.)

And what burden of her life led Plath to cancel it? Many, surely. But none so overpowering as the psychological necessity to link herself with her father, spiritually and physically. Suicide then became a sexual act, the deathbed the marriage bed. This obsession is nowhere more apparent than in the four bee poems which, as an informal group, are the glory of the concluding pages of *Ariel*. Plath's fascination with bees, of course, is yet another attempt to reconstruct her father's life. Not only that Otto Plath was the author of a book on bumblebees, as I have noted; but also bees themselves, with the monarchic organization, are a potent symbol for order and obedience. To be a bee is to report to an authority figure.

"The Bee Meeting" opens with a vivid imaging of Plath's vulnerability before the hive. In the poem all the villagers but her are protected from the bees, and she equates this partial nudity with her condition of being unloved. In the symbolic marriage ceremony which follows, a rector, a midwife, and Plath herself—a bride clad in black—appear. Plath seems always to remember that even the arrows which Eros used to shoot into the ground to create new life were poisoned darts. And just as her search for a Divine Father was tempered by her fear there was none, so too her search for consolation from her earthly father created an intensity of consciousness in which she no longer had any guarantee of security. Eros was for her ever accompanied by the imminence of death. We are reminded here of the frequent word play in Italian literature between amore, love, and morte, death. Certainly every mythology relates the sex act to the act of dying, most clearly perhaps in the tale of Tristan and Iseult. And in nature the connection is even more explicit. Sylvia Plath's personal mythology of the hive anticipates this: the male bee always dies after inseminating the queen. When the central figure of authority, the queen, is her father, the daughter/worker must die after the incestuous act, as she does at the conclusion of "The Bee Meeting." The long white box in the grove is in fact her own coffin; only in this light can she answer her own questions, "what have they accomplished, why am I cold?"

In the second bee poem, "The Arrival of the Bee Box," the coffin analogy is made again, and Plath confesses she "can't keep away from it." The unintelligible syllables of the bees are the mystery of the unknown, the cipher of her life and her father's. In "Stings" she herself becomes the queen, the self that needs recovering captured in a wax house, a mausoleum. The queen is the father and the daughter united, for by assuming his body she effectively kills him (just as Freud assured us the joining of the bodies in sexual congress results in a kind of death, speaking of the "likeness of the condition of that following complete sexual satisfaction to dying, and for the fact that death coincides with the act of copulation in lower animals. These creatures die in the act of reproduction because, after Eros has been eliminated through the process of satisfaction, the death instinct has a free hand for accomplishing its purpose"). Such a symbolic death of her father provided for Plath enormous psychic and physical release, and the occasion for one final invective against men ("Wintering"):

> The bees are all women,
> Maids and the long royal lady.
> They have got rid of the men,
>
> The blunt, clumsy stumblers, the boors.

Sylvia Plath ended her life in the early morning of February 11, 1963. At the time she was living separately from her husband.

From *The Dark Funnel: A Reading of Sylvia Plath*

A. Alvarez   (b. 1929)
PLATH'S "ARIEL"   1970

A. Alvarez is a British critic and writer who has struggled against depression and suicide, ultimately making it the subject of one of his books. He was also a friend of both Ted Hughes and Sylvia Plath when they lived in Devon. Consequently, his study of "Ariel" uncovers material that would not be observable to most readers, such as the fact that the title is also the name of Sylvia's horse. The horse, too, is Pegasus, the emblem of poetry.

. . . This, I think, is the key to the later poems; the more vivid and imaginative the details are, the more resolutely she turns them inwards. The more objective they seem, the more subjective they, in fact, become. Take, for example, a poem about her favorite horse, "Ariel":

> Stasis in darkness.
> Then the substanceless blue
> Pour of tor and distances.
>
> God's lioness,
> How one we grow,
> Pivot of heels and knees!—The furrow
>
> Splits and passes, sister to
> The brown arc
> Of the neck I cannot catch,
>
> Nigger-eye
> Berries cast dark
> Hooks—

Black sweet blood mouthfuls,
Shadows.
Something else

Hauls me through air—
Thighs, hair;
Flakes from my heels.

White
Godiva, I unpeel——
Dead hands, dead stringencies.

And now I
Foam to wheat, a glitter of seas.
The child's cry

Melts in the wall.
And I
Am the arrow,

The dew that flies
Suicidal, at one with the drive
Into the red

Eye, the cauldron of morning.

The difficulty with this poem lies in separating one element from another. Yet that is also its theme; the rider is one with the horse, the horse is one with the furrowed earth, and the dew on the furrow is one with the rider. The movement of the imagery, like that of the perceptions, is circular. There is also another peculiarity: although the poem is nominally about riding a horse, it is curiously "substanceless"—to use her own word. You are made to *feel* the horse's physical presence, but not to see it. The detail is all inward. It is as though the horse itself were an emotional state. So finally the poem is not just about the stallion "Ariel"; it is about what happens when the "stasis in darkness" ceases to be static, when the potential violence of the animal is unleashed. And also the violence of the rider.

In a way, most of her later poems are about just that: about the unleashing of power, about tapping the roots of her own inner violence. There is, of course, nothing so very extraordinary about that. I think that this, in general, is the direction all the best contemporary poetry is taking. She, certainly, did not claim to be original in the kind of writing she was doing:

I've been very excited by what I feel is the new breakthrough that came with, say, Robert Lowell's *Life Studies*. This intense breakthrough into very serious, very personal emotional experience, which I feel has been partly taboo. Robert Lowell's poems about his experiences in a mental hospital, for example, interest me very much. These peculiar private and taboo subjects I feel have been explored in recent American poetry—I think particularly of the poetess Anne Sexton, who writes also about her experiences as a mother; as a mother who's had a nervous breakdown, as an extremely emotional and feeling young

woman. And her poems are wonderfully craftsmanlike poems, and yet they
have a kind of emotional and psychological depth which I think is something
perhaps quite new and exciting.[1]

From *Beyond All This Fiddle*

Lynda K. Bundtzen   (b. 1947)
"LADY LAZARUS": PLATH'S REBORN WOMAN   1983

*Bundtzen's critical approach to Plath through feminism uses imagery from a
number of sources, especially the Christian religion. However, she also emphasizes
references to the Nazi persecution of Jews. Plath grew up thoroughly aware of the
horrors of World War II, which were later expressed in her poetry.*

. . . Plath does create a reborn woman: Lady Lazarus. Her appearance, however, is, as we have seen, commonly read as a negative phenomenon. Here is the
"bitch goddess," the "ugly and hairy" monster woman, celebrating her escape
and vengeance on men. This poem is where the Lady who "knows the worst"
claims, "Dying is an art," a phrase repeated many times in critical commentary as
evidence for Plath's sickness and suicidal tendencies. As a partial test of these cen-
sorious pronouncements about Plath's overall significance and her development
of a "madwoman" persona, let us take a look at that line in context. It comes
from the middle of "Lady Lazarus."

I do it so it feels like hell.
I do it so it feels real.
I guess you could say I've a call.

It's easy enough to do it in a cell.
It's easy enough to do it and stay put.
It's the theatrical

Comeback in broad day
To the same place, the same face, the same brute
Amused shout:

"A miracle!"
That knocks me out.
There is a charge

For the eyeing of my scars, there is a charge
For the hearing of my heart—
It really goes.

---

[1]From an interview and reading of poems made by her for the British Council.

And there is a charge, a very large charge
For a word or a touch
Or a bit of blood

Or a piece of my hair or my clothes.

These are boasting lines. Lady Lazarus tells us twice that the easy part is dying. It's the "comeback" before a "peanut-crunching crowd" that demands special skills—that really knocks her out.

Throughout the poem, Christian symbolism is yoked with three other actions: the sideshow striptease; the suffering inflicted by the Nazis on the Jews; and the personal acts of self-destruction compulsively repeated each decade. Plath stresses the public nature of the spectacle, so that her suicide attempts are no more private or personal than the Oberammergau Passion Play and its ritualized repetition of Christ's crucifixion and resurrection every ten years. Lady Lazarus's suffering is also a religious calling, a vocation. Her comeback is a "miracle" like Christ's resurrection of Lazarus, and the purpose is apparently the same: to provide visible proof of God's power over life and death to a skeptical audience. Once the brutish spectacle is over, the clothes strewn in Lady Lazarus's striptease, like the shroud left in the tomb by Christ's risen body, will be sold as religious relics with special healing and restorative powers.

Howe regards this use of Christian myth and the Jewish holocaust as illegitimate—bold but offensive devices for drawing attention to the poet's personal suffering. But Plath is not concerned primarily with personal afflictions, except as they represent a wider feminine condition. As she puts it in "Daddy," "Every woman adores a fascist"; and Lady Lazarus, no less than the daughter in "Daddy," has a masochistic relationship to the male god who raises her from the dead. While Christian myth magnifies the significance of the relationship between Lady Lazarus and her persecutor Herr God, Lady Lazarus's irony simultaneously undercuts her Passion.

The story of Lazarus, ordinarily regarded, I suppose, as one of the happier moments of divine intervention in human affairs, is continually mocked by Lady Lazarus's name-calling. The deity is a Nazi and addressed as Herr Doktor, Herr God, Herr Lucifer, and "my Enemy," all of which deride the malignity of his purpose. His most important attribute is his power over her. Initially he appears as Herr Doktor, a physician in a Nazi concentration camp, and Lady Lazarus makes her entrance as one of Frankenstein's monsters—an experiment by Herr Doktor. As such, she is a bizarre amalgam of inanimate objects, barely patched together into a living being—a true monster-woman.

A sort of walking miracle, my skin
Bright as a Nazi lampshade,
My right foot a paperweight,

My face a featureless, fine Jew linen.

There is little art to Herr Doktor's manufacture of paperweights and lampshades. Only the Lady's sense of death and rebirth as an art of self-creation instills these lifeless objects with any power to fascinate a peanut-crunching crowd.

The circus setting, too, diminishes Herr God, providing him with less than divine identities which alter our perception of his control over her. Various lines suggest that he is a wild animal trainer, a ringmaster, or a sideshow barker who displays Lady Lazarus like a carnival freak. Her special trick is suffering, dying, and reviving for the amusement of an audience like that in the Roman Coliseum. In this version of the Biblical miracle, everyone is a collaborator: God is a flim-flam man interested in drumming up money-paying suckers; Lady Lazarus enjoys baring her body and soul; and the audience won't avert its gaze until the show is over and they have seen it all. The more grotesque the spectacle, the better the effect and the bigger the "charge" for everyone.

Lady Lazarus's shifting relationship to Herr God and to her audience raises the question of complicity in her own suffering. Like her Biblical counterpart, she sometimes seems to be the passive medium for her creator's powers: "I am your opus, I am your valuable." As the Jewess, she is an innocent scapegoat—"the pure gold baby that melts to a shriek." But as a stripteaser in a sideshow, she partici-pates in her degradation, a masochist who cultivates pain for the thrill of exhibi-tion. Lady Lazarus's attitude toward the audience is equally unsteady. At times, she sounds flip and bored with the whole act: "What a trash/To annihilate each decade." At others, she has a gift for the sarcastic understatement: "I turn and burn,/Do not think I underestimate your great concern." And at one moment, an introduction to the audience turns into a painful supplication.

> Gentlemen, ladies,
>
> These are my hands,
> My knees.

These shifts in tone are not inconsistencies in character so much as a waver-ing between unflinching pride and self-disgust. There is a perpetual antagonism between Lady Lazarus and her spectators, as though she wants and needs their sympathy, but will laugh in their faces if they dare to pity her. And so she both appeals to them and insults them with her casual attitude toward atrocity, as if to say, "Oh well, if you'd been to hell and back as I have, you'd look a fright, too."

> Do I terrify?
>
> The nose, the eyepits, the full set of teeth?
> The sour breath
> Will vanish in a day
>
> And I a smiling woman.

These multiple, contradictory relationships between Lady Lazarus and both her audience and her creator are resolved in the last four stanzas of the poem. Still another Lady Lazarus emerges from the Nazi ovens, very different from the per-sonalities we have seen so far.

> Ash, ash—
> You poke and stir,
> Flesh, bone, there is nothing there.

> A cake of soap,
> A wedding ring,
> A gold filling.
>
> Herr God, Herr Lucifer,
> Beware
> Beware,
>
> Out of the ash
> I rise with my red hair
> And I eat men like air.

In the final invocation to Herr God, Herr Lucifer, there is no self-mockery. She is in deadly earnest. The warning "Beware" sounds as though a dangerous circus animal has escaped and refuses to perform anymore. The lioness turns on trainer and audience alike, baring her claws instead of her wounds, and revealing her untamed powers for the first time. She gives everyone a bigger "charge" than they wanted or expected.

With this shift in tone, there is a reversal on all levels of the action. Lady Lazarus is resurrected twice, first as the "opus," the "valuable" of Herr Doktor, the clumsy artist of paperweights and lampshades. Again he melts her down to the accumulated trash of her life—"A cake of soap, / A wedding ring, / A gold filling"—and pokes and stirs, thinking he might create something from the ashes. But "there is nothing there." He misses the flamelike exhalation from the oven and the incarnation of Lady Lazarus as a body of fire, a man-eating phoenix woman. The Jewess turns on her Nazi oppressor. The stripteaser who pleases men transforms herself into a man-eater. The scapegoat becomes a predator. And most important, the creator-creature relationship that supersedes all others in this poem is inverted. The creature takes over the task of resurrection and is her own miracle. It is as if Lazarus were to say, "I'd rather do it myself."

From this perspective, "Lady Lazarus" is an allegory about the woman artist's struggle for autonomy. The female creature of a male artist-god is asserting independent creative powers. Next to Lady Lazarus's miraculous rise at the end, the male god's art is an inept engineering feat. Where at the beginning of the poem the Lady merely manifests his potency—indeed, prostituting her imagination by playing the role of female exhibitionist—by the end of the poem she is a creator in her own right.

Given the shifting and complex set of relationships that Plath sets up in "Lady Lazarus," it seems a waste to dwell overlong on the poem's confessional aspects, to worry about whether this or that stanza refers to some incident in Plath's life, or to belabor the fact that Herr God may be a representation of her father or her husband. Whatever his origins in the circumstances of Plath's life, in this poem he is the usurper of Lady Lazaru's artistic powers, and he is defeated on those grounds.

It is important to note as well that Lady Lazarus is not simply an escape artist. She directly confronts and challenges Herr God at the end of the poem with her own self-resurrection, and this new self is surely less monstrous than Herr God's swaddled cadaver. As a poem about overcoming the woman writer's anxiety of authorship, "Lady Lazarus" provides a new reading of the monster-woman. She is neither mad nor "ugly and hairy," but a phoenix, a flame of released bodily energy. The insanity was her complicity in Herr God's sleazy sideshow, not in the choice of self-incarnation. Just as the male author allays his anxieties by calling their source bad names—witch, bitch, fiend, monster—so Plath allays her anxieties by identifying the father-god with Nazi brutality, calling him Herr Doktor, Herr Enemy, Herr Lucifer, or, in "Daddy," "a man in black with a Meinkampf look." Plath also goes beyond simple name-calling; she manages to demonstrate his dependence on female passivity. His creative power is not his own, but derived from the woman's body and its capacity for rebirth. In this revision of mythology, both the male authorial will and "the angel in the house" are deconstructed. The angel is renamed a masochistic Jewess and she, rather than the madwoman, is the enemy within, the saboteur of woman's independence.

From Plath's Incarnations

$\mathcal{D}$rama

9

Enjoying Drama

The critic Martin Esslin has said that drama is the "most social of the art forms," reminding us that **drama** is storytelling by actors performing before our eyes, speaking words, and enacting moments in imaginary lives. Today audiences respond to the physical presence of actors such as James Dean, Meryl Streep, and James Earl Jones. Before theaters had artificial lighting, audiences could also see each other and interact. Sometimes players were prompted by audience members when they forgot their lines, and often they played to the audience, depending on their relationship with it, which was usually based on their reputation. In most plays, then and now, the audience reacts together, laughing, crying, in suspense or awe.

Because of its social character, most people find drama impossible to resist. One of the basic functions of human socialization is the capacity to empathize with others. In drama, that capacity is the most important element used by the playwright. Witnessing the suffering or joy of others causes us to share those feelings, and sharing helps educate our emotional life. Indeed, this may be one of the chief functions of literature. However, in drama it is more immediate simply because audiences see another human being experiencing something that they can "relate to" with ease.

Itself a genre of literature, drama can also be divided into two main genres: **tragedy** and **comedy**. These two genres, along with the satyr play, a quasi-pornographic **farce**, constituted the forms of drama known to the Greeks. Successive ages have added the genre **tragicomedy**, a mixed form. For instance, the Elizabethan stage added **histories** and **romances**, which sometimes combined tragedy and comedy. Later ages have relied on these distinctions, with modern plays such as Henrik Ibsen's *A Doll House*, Anton Chekhov's *The Cherry Orchard*, Tennessee Williams's *The Glass Menagerie*, and Athol Fugard's *"Master Harold" . . . and the boys* continuing the development of tragicomedy.

TRAGEDY

Like most interesting concepts in literature, **tragedy** is difficult to define. Perhaps it will help to list some of its most important traditional qualities.

- Tragedy tells of the fall of a worthwhile, usually noble, character. Greek and Elizabethan tragedies relied on a **protagonist**—the hero, or primary character—who was of high station, but modern tragedies also use protagonists of low or middle station as a means of exploring their worthiness.

- Traditionally, tragic heroes or heroines faced an unexpected fate. Fate, or destiny, dominates tragedy, and the plot reveals the protagonist resisting fate before finally yielding to it. Fate in classical tragedy was determined by the will of the gods; in modern tragedy it is sometimes determined by inherent characteristics of the heroes, by the force of the environment, or by both.

- Tragic heroes and heroines face their fate with determination, courage, and bravery. Thus, they are worthy of our respect.

- Tragedy hinges on **hamartia**, the wrong action that leads to the tragic fall. This is sometimes referred to as the character's **tragic flaw**, but it is not always a flaw of character.

- The **peripeteia** is the tragic hero's **reversal** of fortune. Before the peripeteia the protagonist seems to make favorable progress, but as he or she seeks knowledge—**recognition** or **anagnorisis**—the peripeteia or reversal ironically pushes the protagonist to his or her fate.

- The ancient Greek philosopher Aristotle recommended that tragedy have a single plot that follows the actions of a single character or set of characters without the distraction of a secondary plot (especially avoiding a comic subplot).

As we have come to use the term, *tragedy* is, above all, serious in tone and importance. It focuses on a hero or heroine whose potential is great but whose efforts to realize that potential are thwarted by fate: circumstances beyond his or her control. Traditionally, the tragic hero has been of royal blood, like Oedipus. Thus the fall from such a height can be terrifying. Sophocles' *Oedipus Rex* (in this collection) was, for Aristotle, the model of what a tragedy should be. It is the quintessential tragedy and has established the tragic genre in the minds of most successive playwrights.

Because the classical tragedy insisted on a protagonist of high station, usually a king or queen, some critics have felt that in our modern age of relatively democratic institutions there can be no true tragedy. However, modern plays such as John Millington Synge's *Riders to the Sea* and Arthur Miller's *Death of a Salesman* find enough greatness in a peasant or average person to justify calling them tragedies. Despite the fact that the Shakespearean critic

Sigurd Burckhardt said, "A tragedy—to define it very simply—is a *killing poem*," the hero or heroine need not die. Oedipus does not die in *Oedipus Rex*, and Maurya does not die in *Riders to the Sea*. On the other hand, Antigone, King Lear, Hamlet, and Macbeth all die at the end of their plays.

The Emotions of Pity and Terror

The earliest efforts to examine tragedy defined the kinds of emotions that were or should be evoked in the audience. In essence, Aristotle focused on a form of reader response criticism. If the tragic hero or heroine was well drawn, sympathetic, and touching, then the audience felt the emotion of pity. Such an emotion stems from the audience's capacity to emphathize with the tragic hero. The emotion of terror, watching the hero's fall, also stems from empathy, since the audience can imagine being in the same situation.

Aristotle claimed that tragic drama not only produced such emotions in the audience but also purged the audience of them. It is not clear what he meant. However, he may have referred to the anxiety audiences felt about their own security and their own fate. If one thinks of the anxiety Elizabethan Calvinists felt when they were told God had decided beforehand whether they were saved or not, then one can imagine how Greeks may have felt knowing their fate was ordained. Their anxiety might have made them neurotic or dysfunctional. Examining their emotions—just releasing them—would help them immensely. Even today audiences respond powerfully to the tragic ironies deep in the heart of *Oedipus Rex*.

Tragedies produce anticipation because the audience knows that the main character will fall. In Synge's *Riders to the Sea* the characters will ride to the sea—the title tells us so. But when the audience learns that Maurya has lost her husband and all of her sons but one to the sea, the audience senses that she will lose Bartley, her last son, and the suspense, even in this brief play, becomes intense. Maurya is old; she will suffer her pain and pass on. But the daughters must somehow live on without a man to supply the food they will need to survive.

Very often, in tragedies, the emotions of terror and dread are reinforced by a supernatural element. Hamlet sees ghosts and Maurya sees a vision of a ghost horse and horseman. Willy Loman in *Death of a Salesman* hears voices. Thus even in some modern plays the "other world"—the world we do not understand, whether it comes from without or within—often seems to reach into the ordinariness of the characters' lives, calling attention to their fear and giving it good reason.

A Modern Tragedy

Riders to the Sea (1904) is an example of a short modern tragedy that differs from Greek or Elizabethan tragedies most obviously in that its protagonist is not of royal blood. However, John Millington Synge (pronounced "sing") (1871–1909) is careful to make us feel a sense of nobility about his characters. Synge visited the Aran Islands, the setting of *Riders to the Sea*, in 1900 and began writing plays in 1901. Many of his plays, such as *In the Shadow of the Glen* (1903), *The Well of the Saints* (1905), and *The Tinker's Wedding* (1907), portray poor people in the west of Ireland. His most famous play, *The Playboy of the Western World* (1907), caused riots in the Abbey Theatre in Ireland when it was first produced. The middle class audience reacted negatively to what they felt was an improper portrait of the Irish. However, the play has endured and has become part of the repertory of modern Irish drama. His last play, *Deirdre of the Sorrows* (1910), was not quite finished when he died.

Synge's dialogue is poetic and beautiful. In his inn in Ireland's Aran Islands, he had overheard women cleaning up in the kitchen. Since he was a student of music and language, his ear was tuned to catch the special way in which people in the west of Ireland speak. Thus Synge gives Maurya a way of speaking that distances her from us. She accepts her fate without flinching, and she sees that no convenient platitudes—such as those of the young, inexperienced priest—can console her. Her consolation is that she has done her best.

The supporting characters in this play are carefully distinguished. The younger daughter, Nora, speaks with innocence and eagerness: "And it's destroyed [Bartley will] be going till dark night, and he after eating nothing since the sun went up." But Cathleen, who is older and more skeptical, knows that it is the nature of young men to risk their lives on the sea, no matter how dependent their family may be on them. She says, "It's the life of a young man to be going on the sea, and who would listen to an old woman with one thing and she saying it over?"

John Millington Synge (1871–1909)
RIDERS TO THE SEA 1904

Characters

    Maurya, an old woman   *Nora,* a younger daughter
    Bartley, her son   *Men and Women*
    Cathleen, her daughter

(Scene: An Island off the West of Ireland.)
(Cottage kitchen, with nets, oilskins, spinning wheel, some new boards standing by the wall, etc. Cathleen, a girl of about twenty, finishes kneading cake, and puts it down in the pot-oven by the fire; then wipes her hands, and begins to spin at the wheel. Nora, a young girl, puts her head in at the door.)

Nora (in a low voice): Where is she?
Cathleen: She's lying down, God help her, and may be sleeping, if she's able.

(Nora comes in softly and takes a bundle from under her shawl.)

Cathleen *(spinning the wheel rapidly)*:   What is it you have?

Nora: The young priest is after bringing them. It's a shirt and a plain stocking were got off a drowned man in Donegal.

(Cathleen stops her wheel with a sudden movement, and leans out to listen.)

Nora: We're to find out if it's Michael's they are, some time herself will be down looking by the sea.

Cathleen: How would they be Michael's, Nora. How would he go the length of that way to the far north?

Nora: The young priest says he's known the like of it. "If it's Michael's they are," says he, "you can tell herself he's got a clean burial by the grace of God, and if they're not his, let no one say a word about them, for she'll be getting her death," says he, "with crying and lamenting."

(The door which Nora half closed is blown open by a gust of wind.)

Cathleen *(looking out anxiously)*:   Did you ask him would he stop Bartley going this day with the horses to the Galway fair?

Nora: "I won't stop him," says he, "but let you not be afraid. Herself does be saying prayers half through the night, and the Almighty God won't leave her destitute," says he, "with no son living."

Cathleen: Is the sea bad by the white rocks, Nora?

Nora: Middling bad, God help us. There's a great roaring in the west, and it's worse it'll be getting when the tide's turned to the wind. *(She goes over to the table with the bundle.)* Shall I open it now?

Cathleen: Maybe she'd wake up on us, and come in before we'd done. *(Coming to the table.)* It's a long time we'll be, and the two of us crying.

Nora *(goes to the inner door and listens)*:   She's moving about on the bed. She'll be coming in a minute.

Cathleen: Give me the ladder, and I'll put them up in the turf-loft, the way she won't know of them at all, and maybe when the tide turns she'll be going down to see would he be floating from the east.

(They put the ladder against the gable of the chimney; Cathleen goes up a few steps and hides the bundle in the turf-loft. Maurya comes from the inner room.)

Maurya *(looking up at Cathleen and speaking querulously)*:   Isn't it turf enough you have for this day and evening?

Cathleen: There's a cake baking at the fire for a short space *(throwing down the turf)* and Bartley will want it when the tide turns if he goes to Connemara.

(Nora picks up the turf and puts it round the pot-oven.)

Maurya *(sitting down on a stool at the fire)*:   He won't go this day with the wind rising from the south and west. He won't go this day, for the young priest will stop him surely.

Nora: He'll not stop him, mother, and I heard Eamon Simon and Stephen Pheety and Colum Shawn saying he would go.

Maurya: Where is he itself?

Nora: He went down to see would there be another boat sailing in the week, and I'm thinking it won't be long till he's here now, for the tide's turning at the green head,° and the hooker's° tacking from the east.

Cathleen: I hear some one passing the big stones.

Nora (looking out):   He's coming now, and he in a hurry.

Bartley (comes in and looks round the room. Speaking sadly and quietly): Where is the bit of new rope, Cathleen, was bought in Connemara?

Cathleen (coming down):   Give it to him. Nora; it's on a nail by the white boards. I hung it up this morning, for the pig with the black feet was eating it.

Nora (giving him a rope):   Is that it, Bartley?

Maurya: You'd do right to leave that rope, Bartley, hanging by the boards. (*Bartley takes the rope.*) It will be wanting in this place, I'm telling you, if Michael is washed up tomorrow morning, or the next morning, or any morning in the week, for it's a deep grave we'll make him by the grace of God.

Bartley (beginning to work with the rope):   I've no halter the way I can ride down on the mare, and I must go now quickly. This is the one boat going for two weeks or beyond it, and the fair will be a good fair for horses I heard them saying below.

Maurya: It's a hard thing they'll be saying below if the body is washed up and there's no man in it to make the coffin, and I after giving a big price for the finest white boards you'd find in Connemara.

    (*She looks round at the boards.*)

Bartley: How would it be washed up, and we after looking each day for nine days, and a strong wind blowing a while back from the west and south?

Maurya: If it wasn't found itself, that wind is raising the sea, and there was a star up against the moon, and it rising in the night. If it was a hundred horses, or a thousand horses you had itself, what is the price of a thousand horses against a son where there is one son only?

Bartley (working at the halter, to Cathleen):   Let you go down each day, and see the sheep aren't jumping in on the rye, and if the jobber comes you can sell the pig with the black feet if there is a good price going.

Maurya: How would the like of her get a good price for a pig?

---

green head: An outcropping of land.   *hooker:* A fishing boat under sail.

Bartley (to Cathleen):   If the west wind holds with the last bit of the moon let you and Nora get up weed enough for another cock for the kelp.°
It's hard set we'll be from this day with no one in it but one man to work.

Maurya: It's hard set we'll be surely the day you're drownd'd with the rest. What way will I live and the girls with me, and I an old woman looking for the grave?

(Bartley lays down the halter, takes off his old coat, and puts on a newer one of the same flannel.)

Bartley (to Nora):   Is she coming to the pier?

Nora (looking out):   She's passing the green head and letting fall her sails.

Bartley (getting his purse and tobacco):   I'll have half an hour to go down, and you'll see me coming again in two days, or in three days, or maybe in four days if the wind is bad.

Maurya (turning round to the fire, and putting her shawl over her head):   Isn't it a hard and cruel man won't hear a word from an old woman, and she holding him from the sea?

Cathleen: It's the life of a young man to be going on the sea, and who would listen to an old woman with one thing and she saying it over?

Bartley (taking the halter):   I must go now quickly. I'll ride down on the red mare, and the gray pony'll run behind me. . . . The blessing of God on you.

(He goes out.)

Maurya (crying out as he is in the door):   He's gone now, God spare us, and we'll not see him again. He's gone now, and when the black night is falling I'll have no son left me in the world.

Cathleen: Why wouldn't you give him your blessing and he looking round in the door? Isn't it sorrow enough is on every one in this house without your sending him out with an unlucky word behind him, and a hard word in his ear?

(Maurya takes up the tongs and begins raking the fire aimlessly without looking round.)

Nora (turning toward her):   You're taking away the turf from the cake.

Cathleen (crying out):   The Son of God forgive us, Nora, we're after forgetting his bit of bread.

(She comes over to the fire.)

Nora: And it's destroyed he'll be going till dark night, and he after eating nothing since the sun went up.

Cathleen (turning the cake out of the oven):   It's destroyed he'll be, surely. There's no sense left on any person in a house where an old woman will be talking forever.

---

cock for the kelp: Kelp is a seaweed used for fertilizer.

(Maurya sways herself on her stool.)

Cathleen (*cutting off some of the bread and rolling it in a cloth; to Maurya*):
Let you go down now to the spring well and give him this and he
passing. You'll see him then and the dark word will be broken, and
you can say "God speed you," the way he'll be easy in his mind.

Maurya (*taking the bread*): Will I be in it as soon as himself?

Cathleen: If you go now quickly.

Maurya (*standing up unsteadily*): It's hard set I am to walk.

Cathleen (*looking at her anxiously*): Give her the stick, Nora, or maybe
she'll slip on the big stones.

Nora: What stick?

Cathleen: The stick Michael brought from Connemara.

Maurya (*taking a stick Nora gives her*): In the big world the old people
do be leaving things after them for their sons and children, but in this
place it is the young men do be leaving things behind for them that do
be old.

(She goes out slowly. Nora goes over to the ladder.)

Cathleen: Wait, Nora, maybe she'd turn back quickly. She's that sorry,
God help her, you wouldn't know the thing she'd do.

Nora: Is she gone round by the bush?

Cathleen (*looking out*): She's gone now. Throw it down quickly, for the
Lord knows when she'll be out of it again.

Nora (*getting the bundle from the loft*): The young priest said he'd be
passing tomorrow, and we might go down and speak to him below if
it's Michael's they are surely.

Cathleen (*taking the bundle*): Did he say what way they were found?

Nora (*coming down*): "There were two men," says he, "and they rowing
round with poteen° before the cocks crowed, and the oar of one of
them caught the body, and they passing the black cliffs of the north."

Cathleen (*trying to open the bundle*): Give me a knife, Nora, the string's
perished with the salt water, and there's a black knot on it you
wouldn't loosen in a week.

Nora (*giving her a knife*): I've heard tell it was a long way to Donegal.

Cathleen (*cutting the string*): It is surely. There was a man in here a while
ago—the man sold us that knife—and he said if you set off walking
from the rocks beyond, it would be seven days you'd be in Donegal.

Nora: And what time would a man take, and he floating?

*(Cathleen opens the bundle and takes out a bit of a stocking. They look at
them eagerly.)*

Cathleen (*in a low voice*): The Lord spare us, Nora! isn't it a queer hard
thing to say if it's his they are surely?

Nora: I'll get his shirt off the hook the way we can put the one flannel on

poteen: Homemade whiskey.

the other. (*She looks through some clothes hanging in the corner.*) It's not with them, Cathleen, and where will it be?

Cathleen: I'm thinking Bartley put it on him in the morning, for his own shirt was heavy with the salt in it (*pointing to the corner*). There's a bit of a sleeve was of the same stuff. Give me that and it will do.

(*Nora brings it to her and they compare the flannel.*)

Cathleen: It's the same stuff, Nora; but if it is itself aren't there great rolls of it in the shops of Galway, and isn't it many another man may have a shirt of it as well as Michael himself?

Nora (*who has taken up the stocking and counted the stitches, crying out*):
It's Michael, Cathleen, it's Michael; God spare his soul, and what will herself say when she hears this story, and Bartley on the sea?

Cathleen (*taking the stocking*):   It's a plain stocking.

Nora: It's the second one of the third pair I knitted, and I put up three score stitches, and I dropped four of them.

Cathleen (*counts the stitches*):   It's that number is in it. (*Crying out.*) Ah, Nora, isn't it a bitter thing to think of him floating that way to the far north, and no one to keen him but the black hags that do be flying on the sea?

Nora (*swinging herself round, and throwing out her arms on the clothes*):
And isn't it a pitiful thing when there is nothing left of a man who was a great rower and fisher, but a bit of an old shirt and a plain stocking?

Cathleen (*after an instant*):   Tell me is herself coming, Nora? I hear a little sound on the path.

Nora (*looking out*):   She is, Cathleen. She's coming up to the door.

Cathleen: Put these things away before she'll come in. Maybe it's easier she'll be after giving her blessing to Bartley, and we won't let on we've heard anything the time he's on the sea.

Nora (*helping Cathleen to close the bundle*):   We'll put them here in the corner.

(*They put them into a hole in the chimney corner. Cathleen goes back to the spinning wheel.*)

Nora: Will she see it was crying I was?

Cathleen: Keep your back to the door the way the light'll not be on you.

(*Nora sits down at the chimney corner, with her back to the door. Maurya comes in very slowly, without looking at the girls, and goes over to her stool at the other side of the fire. The cloth with the bread is still in her hand. The girls look at each other, and Nora points to the bundle of bread.*)

Cathleen (*after spinning for a moment*):   You didn't give him his bit of bread?

(*Maurya begins to keen° softly, without turning round.*)

---

keen: Wail in mourning.

Cathleen: Did you see him riding down?

(Maurya goes on keening.)

Cathleen (a little impatiently):   God forgive you; isn't it a better thing to raise your voice and tell what you seen, than to be making lamentation for a thing that's done? Did you see Bartley, I'm saying to you.

Maurya (with a weak voice):   My heart's broken from this day.

Cathleen (as before):   Did you see Bartley?

Maurya: I seen the fearfulest thing.

Cathleen (leaves her wheel and looks out):   God forgive you; he's riding the mare now over the green head, and the gray pony behind him.

Maurya (starts, so that her shawl falls back from her head and shows her white tossed hair. With a frightened voice):   The gray pony behind him.

Cathleen (coming to the fire):   What is it ails you, at all?

Maurya (speaking very slowly):   I've seen the fearfulest thing any person has seen, since the day Bride Dara seen the dead man with the child in his arms.

Cathleen and Nora: Uah.

(They crouch down in front of the old woman at the fire.)

Nora: Tell us what it is you seen.

Maurya: I went down to the spring well, and I stood there saying a prayer to myself. Then Bartley came along, and he riding on the red mare with the gray pony behind him. *(She puts up her hands, as if to hide something from her eyes.)* The Son of God spare us, Nora!

Cathleen: What is it you seen.

Maurya: I seen Michael himself.

Cathleen (speaking softly):   You did not, mother; It wasn't Michael you seen, for his body is after being found in the far north, and he's got a clean burial by the grace of God.

Maurya (a little defiantly):   I'm after seeing him this day, and he riding and galloping. Bartley came first on the red mare; and I tried to say "God speed you," but something choked the words in my throat. He went by quickly; and "the blessing of God on you," says he, and I could say nothing. I looked up then, and I crying, at the gray pony, and there was Michael upon it—with fine clothes on him, and new shoes on his feet.

Cathleen (begins to keen):   It's destroyed we are from this day. It's destroyed, surely.

Nora: Didn't the young priest say the Almighty God wouldn't leave her destitute with no son living?

Maurya (in a low voice, but clearly):   It's little the like of him knows of the sea. . . . Bartley will be lost now, and let you call in Eamon and make me a good coffin out of the white boards, for I won't live after them. I've had a husband, and a husband's father, and six sons in this house—six fine men, though it was a hard birth I had with every one of them and they coming to the world—and some of them were found and some of them were not found, but they're gone now the lot of them. . . . There were Stephen, and Shawn, were lost in the great wind, and found after in the Bay of Gregory of the Golden Mouth, and carried up the two of them on the one plank, and in by that door.

(She pauses for a moment, the girls start as if they heard something through the door that is half open behind them.)

Nora (in a whisper): Did you hear that, Cathleen? Did you hear a noise in the northeast?

Cathleen (in a whisper): There's some one after crying out by the seashore.

Maurya (continues without hearing anything): There was Sheamus and his father, and his own father again, were lost in a dark night, and not a stick or sign was seen of them when the sun went up. There was Patch after was drowned out of a curagh° that turned over. I was sitting here with Bartley, and he a baby, lying on my two knees, and I seen two women, and three women, and four women coming in, and they crossing themselves, and not saying a word. I looked out then, and there were men coming after them, and they holding a thing in the half of a red sail, and water dripping out of it—it was a dry day, Nora—and leaving a track to the door.

(She pauses again with her hand stretched out toward the door. It opens softly and old women begin to come in, crossing themselves on the threshold, and kneeling down in front of the stage with red petticoats over their heads.)

Maurya (half in a dream, to Cathleen): Is it Patch, or Michael, or what is it at all?

Cathleen: Michael is after being found in the far north, and when he is found there how could he be here in this place?

Maurya: There does be a power of young men floating round in the sea, and what way would they know if it was Michael they had, or another man like him, for when a man is nine days in the sea, and the wind blowing, it's hard set his own mother would be to say what man was it.

Cathleen: It's Michael, God spare him, for they're after sending us a bit of his clothes from the far north.

(She reaches out and hands Maurya the clothes that belonged to Michael. Maurya stands up slowly and takes them in her hands. Nora looks out.)

Nora: They're carrying a thing among them and there's water dripping out of it and leaving a track by the big stones.

Cathleen (in a whisper to the women who have come in): Is it Bartley it is?

One of the Women: It is surely, God rest his soul.

---

curagh: A canoe like boat made of laths and tarred canvas.

(Two younger women come in and pull out the table. Then men carry in the body of Bartley, laid on a plank, with a bit of a sail over it, and lay it on the table.)

Cathleen (to the women, as they are doing so): What way was he drowned?

One of the Women: The gray pony knocked him into the sea, and he was washed out where there is a great surf on the white rocks.

(Maurya has gone over and knelt down at the head of the table. The women are keening softly and swaying themselves with a slow movement. Cathleen and Nora kneel at the other end of the table. The men kneel near the door.)

Maurya (raising her head and speaking as if she did not see the people around her): They're all gone now, and there isn't anything more the sea can do to me. . . . I'll have no call now to be up crying and praying when the wind breaks from the south, and you can hear the surf is in the east, and the surf is in the west, making a great stir with the two noises, and they hitting one on the other. I'll have no call now to be going down and getting Holy Water in the dark nights after Samhain,° and I won't care what way the sea is when the other women will be keening. *(To Nora.)* Give me the Holy Water, Nora, there's a small sup still on the dresser.

(Nora gives it to her.)

Maurya (drops Michael's clothes across Bartley's feet, and sprinkles the Holy Water over him): It isn't that I haven't prayed for you, Bartley, to the Almighty God. It isn't that I haven't said prayers in the dark night till you wouldn't know what I'ld be saying; but it's a great rest I'll have now, and it's time surely. It's a great rest I'll have now, and great sleeping in the long nights after Samhain, if it's only a bit of wet flour we do have to eat, and maybe a fish that would be stinking.

(She kneels down again, crossing herself, and saying prayers under her breath.)

Cathleen (to an old man): Maybe yourself and Eamon would make a coffin when the sun rises. We have fine white boards herself bought, God help her, thinking Michael would be found, and I have a new cake you can eat while you'll be working.

The Old Man (looking at the boards): Are there nails with them?

Cathleen: There are not, Colum; we didn't think of the nails.

Another Man: It's great wonder she wouldn't think of the nails, and all the coffins she's seen made already.

Cathleen: It's getting old she is, and broken.

(Maurya stands up again very slowly and spreads out the pieces of Michael's clothes beside the body, sprinkling them with the last of the Holy Water.)

Nora (in a whisper to Cathleen): She's quiet now and easy; but the day

---

Samhain: Feast of All Saints, November 1. Pronounced Sow-an.

Michael was drowned you could hear her crying out from this to the spring well. It's fonder she was of Michael, and would anyone have thought that?

Cathleen (*slowly and clearly*):   An old woman will be soon tired with anything she will do, and isn't it nine days herself is after crying and keening, and making great sorrow in the house?

Maurya (*puts the empty cup mouth downward on the table, and lays her hands together on Bartley's feet*):   They're all together this time, and the end is come. May the Almighty God have mercy on Bartley's soul, and on Michael's soul, and on the souls of Sheamus and Patch, and Stephen and Shawn (*bending her head*); and may He have mercy on my soul, Nora, and on the soul of every one is left living in the world.

(*She pauses, and the keen rises a little more loudly from the women, then sinks away.*)

Maurya (*continuing*):   Michael has a clean burial in the far north, by the grace of the Almighty God. Bartley will have a fine coffin out of the white boards, and a deep grave surely. What more can we want than that? No man at all can be living forever, and we must be satisfied.

(*She kneels down again and the curtain falls slowly.*)

Questions for close reading

1. Is Maurya the protagonist of the play? What convinces you?
2. What is the protagonist's hamartia (wrong move or flaw)? When does the peripeteia take place?
3. Describe the environment of the play.
4. The only male character in the play is Bartley. Describe his character.
5. What are Bartley's motivations for wanting to go to the "fair for horses"?
6. What part does weather play in the thoughts of the characters?
7. Do Maurya, Cathleen, and Nora sense that they are fated?
8. Does fate seem connected with the will of God in this play? What role does the young priest play in defining or clarifying the will of God?

Questions for interpretation

1. The tragic heroine always seems larger than life, one who can bear the sufferings of the drama in a heroic way. Is Maurya's character substantial enough in your mind to sustain the role of the tragic heroine? Do others in the play see her as special? Do they regard her as heroic?
2. These characters live in a harsh environment. Is that the message of the play? Are these characters victims of their environment? Would they achieve tragic greatness if they lived in a city and did not have to face making a living from a relentless sea?
3. The primary characters in the play are women who depend on men for their food and their living. Is this a feminist play? Do the men appear to

victimize or disregard the women? Are the women victims of a social situation that is beyond their control and that treats them unequally because of their gender?

4. Many of the images in the play are religious. The supernatural world seems very "real" to everyone in the play. In what sense can this play be said to be a religious drama with a religious significance? If it is a religious drama, can it then also be a tragedy? Is there a religious consolation at the end of the play? Is there any consolation at all?

5. There is a serious question about whether this play is a tragedy. If possible, compare it to *Oedipus Rex.* In both plays, is there a period of uncertainty in which the main character searches for the truth and slowly discovers what he or she does not want to know? Is there a point of reversal in both plays? Are the main characters noble in our eyes? Are the emotions of pity and terror evident in both plays? Comment on how each play demands an emotional response.

COMEDY

Comedy is a less serious kind of drama than tragedy. It is not always funny, nor do things always end absolutely happily, but the resolution is brighter than in tragedies. Comedies are also more amusing and do not excite the emotions of pity and terror. Again, some of the qualities of comedy can be listed.

- A comedy generally presents characters of middle station, rather than noble or serious characters. For the Greeks, who originated the genre, comedy was defined in part by its reliance on ordinary citizens for its characters.
- Comedy often relies on complications that center on mistaken identity, conflicts between generations, and numerous misunderstandings.
- Comedy usually relies on wit and humor for its effect.
- Comedy frequently ends in marriage or marriages.
- The subject of comedy is often the weakness of human ambition or the pretenses of characters who think they are better than others.
- Comedy often relies on the dynamics of multiple plots, often contrasting the actions of characters in high station with those in low station.

Among the many subgenres of comedy several are well known. **Burlesque** is a form of exaggerated ridicule in which people, usually of high station, are made to look asinine. **Parody** is a form of comedy in which a playwright pokes fun at a specific play or specific action. **Travesty** makes fun of an entire kind of drama; for example, Woody Allen's *Death Knocks* travesties most tragedies.

Satire is ridicule with a moral purpose; thus it is not always comic, since it usually intends to improve the manners or habits of its audience. Susan Glaspell's *Suppressed Desires*, a good example of comic satire, makes fun of the extreme interpretations of Freudian psychology then prevalent in popular publications and in literary society. Tina Howe's *Teeth* satirizes our visits to the dentist while adding a note of seriousness regarding life's impermanence. **Farce** is a form of comedy built on a joke or a gag, such as the joke of Death climbing a drainpipe to get to Nat Ackerman in *Death Knocks*. The very title of that play—implying that Death would be polite and never come unannounced—is farcical.

High comedy is a term applied to comedies with serious themes such as Marsha Norman's *Getting Out* and possibly *The Cherry Orchard*. **Low comedy** is a term reserved for farce and burlesque, such as *Death Knocks*. Low comedy uses many **sight gags**: visual tricks such as mugging (making weird faces), pratfalls, and mimicking of other characters on stage. The Three Stooges were masters of such gags. Early films, such as those by Charlie Chaplin and the Keystone Kops, gave rise to the term **slapstick comedy**, which looked for every conceivable opportunity to include a sight gag, pratfall, or preposterous piece of **stage business**—extra action that is not in the script. Some of the devices associated with low comedy can be used in productions of plays such as *Death Knocks*. They are up to the discretion of the director. However, unless the playwright has included stage directions in the play itself, the reader will miss such additions.

Types of Comedy

The plot of a **romantic comedy** pits the young lovers struggling against artificial difficulties created by parents. Often the difficulties are resolved by the discovery of the "true" identity of one of the lovers; for example, an unworthy suitor may turn out to be worthy after all. This dramatic formula still works, despite our modern age's relative indifference to the social status of young people about to marry. The parents in such comedies are **blocking characters**. Despite many changes in culture and style, parents have tried to block marriages or liaisons between children for the last twenty-five hundred years and more. But there are also many other kinds of blocking characters: misers, tyrants, bosses, fools, and do-gooders. The pleasure of comedy often derives from watching these characters get their comeuppance.

The oldest comedy—the **comedy of situation**—seems to have depended on ridiculous situations for its energy. Men forced to dress up as women, a poor man mistaken for a millionaire, women forcing peace by withholding sex from their warrior husbands—all have been popular. Such plays, originating with the Greeks, have come to be known as **Old Comedy**. They verge on slapstick and farce and survive today in sitcoms (situation comedies) on commercial television. Television classics such as *The Honeymooners*, *I Love Lucy*, *The Carol Burnett Show*, and many more reveal the continuing power of comedies of situation.

The **comedy of manners** expanded situation comedy by aiming at a critique of the way people lived. It then became an instrument of social criticism, often poking fun at people who are hypocrites, stuffed-shirts, or intellectually pretentious. In many ways John Guare's *Six Degrees of Separation* examines the manners and assumptions of sophisticated New Yorkers. Its concerns are serious but it critiques the social mores of people much like those who sit in the audience.

The **comedy of intrigue** involves the manipulation of characters by another character or characters, usually for ends that are less than noble. In *Six Degrees of Separation*, one watches as Paul cons Ouisa and Flan into thinking he needs help because he has been mugged. By the end of the play the audience realizes that the question of who manipulates whom is more complicated than it at first appears. Susan Glaspell's *Suppressed Desires* is partly a comedy of intrigue, since the husband, Stephen Brewster, intrigues to trick his wife, Henrietta, back into what he thinks is common-sense behavior. He tricks her by using her own method of interpreting everything according to Freudian symbols—but this time to her disadvantage. Comedies of intrigue have a durability not because they suggest social reform or because they show the preposterousness of the situations people get into, but because they amuse us with the ingenuity of the ways in which characters manipulate each other.

Comedies have turned out to be extremely effective instruments in helping societies see themselves as they really are. It is easier to accept criticism if one can laugh at the same time. Of course, serious plays often include social commentary. Most of the plays in the album combine social commentary with dramatic action.

A MODERN COMEDY

Woody Allen (b. 1935) has made a living out of playing and writing about the schlemiel, the hapless nerd whom everyone abuses. Somehow he makes his audiences feel sympathy for this character, despite the fact that we usually treat such characters as being ridiculous. The schlemiel is the opposite of the tragic hero. Whereas the tragic hero is brave, the schlemiel is cowardly, and inverts all the virtues of the tragic hero. For that reason, he becomes a perfect comic hero. In the hands of Woody Allen, the schlemiel has become neurotic, paranoid, and frightened: a candidate for the psychiatrist's couch. In other words, he has become up to date.

Death Knocks (1971) depends on a ridiculous situation. The very thought that Death would knock in mock politeness seems absurd. Further, Death makes a bizarre comic entrance by climbing a drainpipe and popping in through Nat Ackerman's window—all to make a dramatic appearance. Nat Ackerman is a victim of bad timing. He has just merged his company with Modiste Originals, expecting great things from his business future. Death, on the other hand, turns out to be something of a schlemiel himself; after all, he is Nat Ackerman's death. That is the comic premise of the play.

Allen interprets comedy as contrasting with tragedy. He alludes to a film that had influenced him greatly: Ingmar Bergman's *The Seventh Seal.* In that film a knight—definitely not a schlemiel, but a brave and self-sacrificing hero— plays chess with Death to win time to save the lives of a peasant family. In the process he sacrifices himself to achieve his goal. Allen reduces that gesture to comic absurdity by having Nat Ackerman suggest a game of gin rummy as a way of winning more time. Ackerman is anything but self-sacrificing. He is like most of us: looking for a way out of his dilemma.

Woody Allen   (b. 1935)
DEATH KNOCKS   1971

Characters
   Nat
   Death

(The play takes place in the bedroom of the Nat Ackermans' two-story house, somewhere in Kew Gardens. The carpeting is wall-to-wall. There is a big double bed and a large vanity. The room is elaborately furnished and cur- tained, and on the walls there are several paintings and a not really at- tractive barometer. Soft theme music as the curtain rises. Nat Ackerman, a bald, paunchy fifty-seven-year-old dress manufacturer, is lying on the bed finishing off tomorrow's Daily News. *He wears a bathrobe and slippers, and reads by a bed light clipped to the white headboard of the bed. The time is near midnight. Suddenly we hear a noise, and Nat sits up and looks at the window.)*

Nat: What the hell is that?

(Climbing awkwardly through the window is a sombre, caped figure. The intruder wears a black hood and skintight black clothes. The hood covers his head but not his face, which is middle-aged and stark white. He is some- thing like Nat in appearance. He huffs audibly and then trips over the win- dowsill and falls into the room.)

Death (for it is no one else):   Jesus Christ. I nearly broke my neck.
Nat (watching with bewilderment):   Who are you?
Death: Death.
Nat: Who?
Death: Death. Listen—can I sit down? I nearly broke my neck. I'm shaking like a leaf.
Nat: Who *are* you?
Death: *Death.* You got a glass of water?
Nat: Death? What do you mean, Death?
Death: What is wrong with you? You see the black costume and the whitened face?

Nat: Yeah.

Death: Is it Halloween?

Nat: No.

Death: Then I'm Death. Now can I get a glass of water—or a Fresca?

Nat: If this is some joke—

Death: What kind of joke? You're fifty-seven? Nat Ackerman? One eighteen Pacific Street? Unless I blew it—where's that call sheet? (*He fumbles through pocket, finally producing a card with an address on it. It seems to check.*)

Nat: What do you want with me?

Death: What do I want? What do you think I want?

Nat: You must be kidding. I'm in perfect health.

Death (unimpressed): Uh-huh. (*Looking around.*) This is a nice place. You do it yourself?

Nat: We had a decorator, but we worked with her.

Death (looking at picture on the wall): I love those kids with the big eyes.

Nat: I don't want to go yet.

Death: *You* don't want to go? Please don't start in. As it is, I'm nauseous from the climb.

Nat: What climb?

Death: I climbed up the drainpipe. I was trying to make a dramatic entrance. I see the big windows and you're awake reading. I figure it's worth a shot. I'll climb up and enter with a little—you know . . . (*Snaps fingers.*) Meanwhile, I get my heel caught on some vines, the drainpipe breaks, and I'm hanging by a thread. Then my cape begins to tear. Look, let's just go. It's been a rough night.

Nat: You broke my drainpipe?

Death: Broke. It didn't break. It's a little bent. Didn't you hear anything? I slammed into the ground.

Nat: I was reading.

Death: You must have really been engrossed. (*Lifting newspaper Nat was reading.*) "NAB COEDS IN POT ORGY." Can I borrow this?

Nat: I'm not finished.

Death: Er—I don't know how to put this to you, pal. . . .

Nat: Why didn't you just ring downstairs?

Death: I'm telling you, I could have, but how does it look? This way I get a little drama going. Something. Did you read "Faust"?

Nat: What?

Death: And what if you had company? You're sitting there with important people. I'm Death—I should ring the bell and traipse right in the front? Where's your thinking?

Nat: Listen, Mister, it's very late.

Death: Yeah. Well, you want to go?

Nat: Go where?

Death: Death. It. The Thing. The Happy Hunting Grounds. (*Looking at *his own knee.*) Y'know, that's a pretty bad cut. My first job, I'm liable to get gangrene yet.

Nat: Now, wait a minute. I need time. I'm not ready to go.

Death: I'm sorry. I can't help you. I'd like to, but it's the moment.

Nat: How can it be the moment? I just merged with Modiste Originals.

Death: What's the difference, a couple of bucks more or less.

Nat: Sure, what do you care? You guys probably have all your expenses paid.

Death: You want to come along now?

Nat (studying him): I'm sorry, but I cannot believe you're Death.

Death: Why? What'd you expect—Rock Hudson?

Nat: No, it's not that.

Death: I'm sorry if I disappointed you.

Nat: Don't get upset. I don't know, I always thought you'd be . . . uh . . . taller.

Death: I'm five seven. It's average for my weight.

Nat: You look a little like me.

Death: Who should I look like? I'm your death.

Nat: Give me some time. Another day.

Death: I can't. What do you want me to say?

Nat: One more day. Twenty-four hours.

Death: What do you need it for? The radio said rain tomorrow.

Nat: Can't we work out something?

Death: Like what?

Nat: You play chess?

Death: No, I don't.

Nat: I once saw a picture of you playing chess.

Death: Couldn't be me, because I don't play chess. Gin rummy, maybe.

Nat: You play gin rummy?

Death: Do I play gin rummy? Is Paris a city?

Nat: You're good, huh?

Death: Very good.

Nat: I'll tell you what I'll do—

Death: Don't make any deals with me.

Nat: I'll play you gin rummy. If you win, I'll go immediately. If I win, give me some more time. A little bit—one more day.

Death: Who's got time to play gin rummy?

Nat: Come on. If you're so good.

Death: Although I feel like a game . . .

Nat: Come on. Be a sport. We'll shoot for a half hour.

Death: I really shouldn't.

Nat: I got the cards right here. Don't make a production.

Death: All right, come on. We'll play a little. It'll relax me.

Nat (getting cards, pad, and pencil): You won't regret this.

Death: Don't give me a sales talk. Get the cards and give me a Fresca and put out something. For God's sake, a stranger drops in, you don't have potato chips or pretzels.

Nat: There's M&M's downstairs in a dish.

Death: M&M's. What if the President came? He'd get M&M's, too?

Nat: You're not the President.

Death: Deal.

    (Nat deals, turns up a five.)

Nat: You want to play a tenth of a cent a point to make it interesting?

Death: It's not interesting enough for you?

Nat: I play better when money's at stake.

Death: Whatever you say, Newt.

Nat: Nat. Nat Ackerman. You don't know my name?

Death: Newt, Nat—I got such a headache.

Nat: You want that five?

Death: No.

Nat: So pick.

Death (surveying his hand as he picks):   Jesus, I got nothing here.

Nat: What's it like?

Death: What's what like?

    (Throughout the following, they pick and discard.)

Nat: Death.

Death: What should it be like? You lay there.

Nat: Is there anything after?

Death: Aha, you're saving twos.

Nat: I'm asking. Is there anything after?

Death (absently):   You'll see.

Nat: Oh, then I will actually see something?

Death: Well, maybe I shouldn't have put it that way. Throw.

Nat: To get an answer from you is a big deal.

Death: I'm playing cards.

Nat: All right, play, play.

Death: Meanwhile, I'm giving you one card after another.

Nat: Don't look through the discards.

Death: I'm not looking. I'm straightening them up. What was the knock card?

Nat: Four. You ready to knock already?

Death: Who said I'm ready to knock. All I asked was what was the knock card.

Nat: And all I asked was is there anything for me to look forward to.

Death: Play.

Nat: Can't you tell me anything? Where do we go?

Death: We? To tell you the truth, *you* fall in a crumpled heap on the floor.

Nat: Oh, I can't wait for that! Is it going to hurt?

Death: Be over in a second.

Nat: Terrific. (*Sighs.*) I needed this. A man merges with Modiste Originals . . .

Death: How's four points?

Nat: You're knocking?

Death: Four points is good?

Nat: No, I got two.

Death: You're kidding.

Nat: No, you lose.

Death: Holy Christ, and I thought you were saving sixes.

Nat: No. Your deal. Twenty points and two boxes. Shoot. (*Death deals.*) I must fall on the floor, eh? I can't be standing over the sofa when it happens?

Death: No. Play.

Nat: Why not?

Death: Because you fall on the floor! Leave me alone. I'm trying to concentrate.

Nat: Why must it be on the floor? That's all I'm saying! Why can't the whole thing happen and I'll stand next to the sofa?

Death: I'll try my best. Now can we play?

Nat: That's all I'm saying. You remind me of Moe Lefkowitz. He's also stubborn.

Death: I remind him of Moe Lefkowitz. I'm one of the most terrifying figures you could possibly imagine, and him I remind of Moe Lefkowitz. What is he, a furrier?

Nat: You should be such a furrier. He's good for eighty thousand a year. Passementeries. He's got his own factory. Two points.

Death: What?

Nat: Two points. I'm knocking. What have you got?

Death: My hand is like a basketball score.

Nat: And it's spades.

Death: If you didn't talk so much.

(*They redeal and play on.*)

Nat: What'd you mean before when you said this was your first job?

Death: What does it sound like?

Nat: What are you telling me—that nobody ever went before?

Death: Sure they went. But I didn't take them.

Nat: So who did?

Death: Others.

Nat: There's others?

Death: Sure. Each one has his own personal way of going.

Nat: I never knew that.

Death: Why should you know? Who are you?

Nat: What do you mean who am I? Why—I'm nothing?

Death: Not nothing. You're a dress manufacturer. Where do you come to knowledge of the eternal mysteries?

Nat: What are you talking about? I make a beautiful dollar. I sent two kids through college. One is in advertising, the other's married. I got my own home. I drive a Chrysler. My wife has whatever she wants. Maids, mink coat, vacations. Right now she's at the Eden Roc. Fifty dollars a day because she wants to be near her sister. I'm supposed to join her next week, so what do you think I am—some guy off the street?

Death: All right. Don't be so touchy.

Nat: Who's touchy?

Death: How would you like it if I got insulted quickly?

Nat: Did I insult you?

Death: You didn't say you were disappointed in me?

Nat: What do you expect? You want me to throw you a block party?

Death: I'm not talking about that. I mean me personally. I'm too short, I'm this, I'm that.

Nat: I said you looked like me. It's like a reflection.

Death: All right, deal, deal.

> *(They continue to play as music steals in and the lights dim until all is in total darkness. The lights slowly come up again, and now it is later and their game is over. Nat tallies.)*

Nat: Sixty-eight . . . one-fifty . . . Well, you lose.

Death (dejectedly looking through the deck):   I knew I shouldn't have thrown that nine. Damn it.

Nat: So I'll see you tomorrow.

Death: What do you mean you'll see me tomorrow?

Nat: I won the extra day. Leave me alone.

Death: You were serious?

Nat: We made a deal.

Death: Yeah, but—

Nat: Don't "but" me. I won twenty-four hours. Come back tomorrow.

Death: I didn't know we were actually playing for time.

Nat: That's too bad about you. You should pay attention.

Death: Where am I going to go for twenty-four hours?

Nat: What's the difference? The main thing is I won an extra day.

Death: What do you want me to do—walk the streets?

Nat: Check into a hotel and go to a movie. Take a *schvitz.*° Don't make a federal case.

Death: Add the score again.

Nat: Plus you owe me twenty-eight dollars.

Death: *What?*

Nat: That's right, Buster. Here it is—read it.

Death (going through pockets):   I have a few singles—not twenty-eight dollars.

schvitz: Turkish bath or sauna.

Nat: I'll take a check.

Death: From what account?

Nat: Look who I'm dealing with.

Death: Sue me. Where do I keep my checking account?

Nat: All right, gimme what you got and we'll call it square.

Death: Listen, I need that money.

Nat: Why should you need money?

Death: What are you talking about? You're going to the Beyond.

Nat: So?

Death: So—you know how far that is?

Nat: So?

Death: So where's gas? Where's tolls?

Nat: We're going by car!

Death: You'll find out. (*Agitatedly.*) Look—I'll be back tomorrow, and you'll give me a chance to win the money back. Otherwise I'm in definite trouble.

Nat: Anything you want. Double or nothing we'll play. I'm liable to win an extra week or a month. The way you play, maybe years.

Death: Meantime I'm stranded.

Nat: See you tomorrow.

Death (*being edged to the doorway*): Where's a good hotel? What am I talking about hotel, I got no money. I'll go sit in Bickford's. (*He picks up the* News.)

Nat: Out. Out. That's my paper. (*He takes it back.*)

Death (*exiting*): I couldn't just take him and go. I had to get involved in rummy.

Nat (*calling after him*): And be careful going downstairs. On one of the steps the rug is loose.

> (*And, on cue, we hear a terrific crash. Nat sighs, then crosses to the bedside table and makes a phone call.*)

Nat: Hello, Moe? Me. Listen, I don't know if somebody's playing a joke, or what, but Death was just here. We played a little gin, . . . No, Death. In person. Or somebody who claims to be Death. But, Moe, he's such a *schlep!*°

schlep: Jerk.

Questions for close reading

1. In what ways does Death resemble Nat Ackerman?
2. How does Allen upset your expectations of Death? How do you respond to Death?
3. Why does Death consult a "call sheet"?
4. What do you learn about the decoration of Ackerman's apartment?
5. What do you learn about time from Nat Ackerman's appeals to Death?

6. Why is Ackerman disappointed in Death? What did he expect?
7. Why does Death like to play gin rummy? What makes him agree to play?
8. Why does Death ignore Nat's questions about the afterlife?
9. Nat has many worldly achievements of which he is proud. How does Death react to them?
10. What does Nat Ackerman win when he wins the gin rummy game?

Questions for interpretation

1. Part of the pleasure of this play comes from noticing the mirroring of Death and Nat Ackerman—and by extension, of death and life. What are the most important reflections you see of Death in Nat and of Nat in Death? What do you make of those reflections? What significance do they have for the play?
2. Part of the point of the play is that each person has a personal, tailor-made death. Choose a fictional or real character and establish the kind of death that will come for that character.
3. Is Nat Ackerman any less of a schlemiel at the end of the play than at the beginning? Do you feel more sympathy for him or for Death at the end of the play? Is Death an even greater schlemiel?
4. Can this play be interpreted from an economic or political point of view? For example, to what end is all the emphasis on the material wealth and achievement of Nat Ackerman? He talks about making a "beautiful dollar." At the end of the play Death has no money and is going to have to spend the night in the park: Death is homeless. Is this a social-political point? Is there a class struggle between Death and Ackerman? If Death is a reflection of Ackerman, why is he so poor?
5. What will happen when Death returns? What has winning the gin rummy game done to Death's declaration that this is Nat's "moment" to die? Is this comedy basically funny or basically serious?

TRAGICOMEDY

Tragedy usually ends with exile, death, or a similar resolution. Comedy usually ends with a new beginning: a marriage or another chance of some sort. But **tragicomedy** often ends with no clear resolution: the circumstances are so complex that the audience may feel perplexed at the ending. For example, in "*Master Harold*" . . . *and the boys* the ending does not clearly point to a bright future. Although characters and relationships have been permanently changed, it is not absolutely clear that the results implied by this change are entirely hopeful.

Tragicomedy cannot be described in terms of nameable emotions such as pity and fear or ridicule and contempt. Every tragicomedy explores a range of emotions that may include all these and more. Thus the audience response to tragicomedy is usually complex and unsettling. Drama reflects not only the values but also the presumptions and beliefs of the time. Tragicomedy today reflects the modern sense that experience is shaped by forces beyond our control, such as fate, and that life has no convenient or meaningful resolutions.

Some of the qualities of tragicomedy are as follows.

- Tragicomedy mixes aspects of tragedy with aspects of comedy.
- Tragicomedy usually begins in seriousness and seems to veer toward the tragic, but is relieved by actions that permit the play to end on a happy or neutral note.
- Clear resolutions are often not possible in tragicomedy. The complexity of circumstances are such that the audience is left in a form of suspension, often hopeful, but sometimes uncertain of the long-term future of the characters.
- Some tragicomedies begin comically, almost farcically, and slowly move toward a greater and greater seriousness.
- Most tragicomedies rely on a single plot.

Modern dramatists whose work seems most concerned with respecting the complexity of modern experience—such as Henrik Ibsen, Marsha Norman, John Guare, David Mamet, Manuel Puig, and August Wilson, all of whom appear in this book—avoid convenient and reassuring resolutions. Their plays are tragicomedies and continue to help define the genre.

A Modern Tragicomedy

Fugard is one of Africa's most important playwrights. His plays include *Boesman and Lena* (1969), *Sizwe Banzi is Dead* (1972), *A Lesson from Aloes* (1978), and *The Road to Mecca* (1984). In the 1950s and 1960s he worked with interracial theater groups in Johannesburg, South Africa, when such activities were illegal, and there he established a close theatrical relationship with Zakes Mokae, who played Sam in *"Master Harold"... and the boys* (1982). Fugard, himself an actor in films and on stage, played opposite Mokae when Fugard's *The Blood Knot* (1961) premiered in Johannesburg. This play concerns two brothers, one black and one white, who meet and discuss their separate conditions. It created a powerful stir in South Africa and toured throughout the world.

Fugard's concern for racial justice is a constant in his work, and his notebooks reveal that Hally in *Master Harold* could have been modeled on his own personal experience. His parents owned a hotel where a waiter named Sam became, says Fugard, "the most significant—the only—friend of my boyhood years." Yet, for reasons that he cannot unravel, Fugard once spat in Sam's face. The shame that overwhelmed him as a result of that willful act of disdain lived with Fugard and may have been the seed from which *Master*

Harold grew. Fugard remains committed to undoing the damage apartheid has caused the entire society of South Africa.

"Master Harold" . . . *and the boys* is a tragicomedy that begins on a comic note and ends on a tragic note. It is not clear how the characters will be able to continue after Hally's racist outburst. In many ways, the circumstances of the play reflect those of modern South Africa.

Athol Fugard   (b. 1932)

"MASTER HAROLD" . . . AND THE BOYS   1982

Characters
> *Willy*
> *Sam*
> *Hally*

> (*Scene: The St. George's Park Tea Room on a wet and windy Port Elizabeth afternoon.*)

> (*Tables and chairs have been cleared and are stacked on one side except for one which stands apart with a single chair. On this table a knife, fork, spoon and side plate in anticipation of a simple meal, together with a pile of comic books.*)

> (*Other elements: a serving counter with a few stale cakes under glass and a not very impressive display of sweets, cigarettes and cool drinks, etc.; a few cardboard advertising handouts—Cadbury's Chocolate, Coca-Cola—and a blackboard on which an untrained hand has chalked up the prices of Tea, Coffee, Scones, Milkshakes—all flavors—and Cool Drinks; a few sad ferns in pots; a telephone; an old-style jukebox.*)

> (*There is an entrance on one side and an exit into a kitchen on the other.*)

> (*Leaning on the solitary table, his head cupped in one hand as he pages through one of the comic books, is Sam. A black man in his mid-forties. He wears the white coat of a waiter. Behind him on his knees, mopping down the floor with a bucket of water and a rag, is Willie. Also black and about the same age as Sam. He has his sleeves and trousers rolled up.*)

> (*The year: 1950.*)

Willie (*singing as he works*):   "She was scandalizin' my name, she took my money, she called me honey but she was scandalizin' my name. Called it love but was playin' a game. . . ."

> (*He gets up and moves the bucket. Stands thinking for a moment, then, raising his arms to hold an imaginary partner, he launches into an intricate ballroom dance step. Although a mildly comic figure, he reveals a reasonable degree of accomplishment.*)

Hey, Sam.

(*Sam, absorbed in the comic book, does not respond.*)

Hey, Boet° Sam!

(*Sam looks up.*)

I'm getting it. The quickstep. Look now and tell me. (*He repeats the step.*)
Well?

Sam (*encouragingly*):   Show me again.
Willie: Okay, count for me.
Sam: Ready?
Willie: Ready.
Sam: Five, six, seven, eight. . . . (*Willie starts to dance.*) A-n-d one two
  three four . . . and one two three four. . . . (*Ad libbing as Willie
  dances.*) Your shoulders, Willie . . . your shoulders! Don't look down!
  Look happy, Willie! Relax, Willie!

Willie (*desperate but still dancing*):   I am relax.

Sam: No, you're not.

Willie (*he falters*):   Ag no man, Sam! Mustn't talk. You make me make
  mistakes.

Sam: But you're stiff.
Willie: Yesterday I'm not straight . . . today I'm too stiff!
Sam: Well, you are. You asked me and I'm telling you.
Willie: Where?
Sam: Everywhere. Try to glide through it.
Willie: Glide?
Sam: Ja, make it smooth. And give it more style. It must look like you're
  enjoying yourself.
Willie (*emphatically*):   I wasn't.
Sam: Exactly.
Willie: How can I enjoy myself? Not straight, too stiff and now it's also
  glide, give it more style, make it smooth. . . . Haai! Is hard to
  remember all those things, Boet Sam.
Sam: That's your trouble. You're trying too hard.
Willie: I try hard because it *is* hard.
Sam: But don't let me see it. The secret is to make it look easy. Ballroom
  must look happy, Willie, not like hard work. It must. . . . Ja! . . . it
  must look like romance.
Willie: Now another one! What's romance?
Sam: Love story with happy ending. A handsome man in tails, and in his
  arms, smiling at him, a beautiful lady in evening dress!

Boet: Brother.

Willie: Fred Astaire, Ginger Rogers.

Sam: You got it. Tapdance or ballroom, it's the same. Romance. In two weeks' time when the judges look at you and Hilda, they must see a man and a woman who are dancing their way to a happy ending. What I saw was you holding her like you were frightened she was going to run away.

Willie: Ja! Because that is what she wants to do! I got no romance left for Hilda anymore, Boet Sam.

Sam: Then pretend. When you put your arms around Hilda, imagine she is Ginger Rogers.

Willie: With no teeth? You try.

Sam: Well, just remember, there's only two weeks left.

Willie: I know, I know! (*To the jukebox.*) I do it better with music. You got sixpence for Sarah Vaughan?

Sam: That's a slow foxtrot. You're practicing the quickstep.

Willie: I'll practice slow foxtrot.

Sam (*shaking his head*):   It's your turn to put money in the jukebox.

Willie: I only got bus fare to go home. (*He returns disconsolately to his work.*) Love story and happy ending! She's doing it all right, Boet Sam, but is not me she's giving happy endings. Fuckin' whore! Three nights now she doesn't come practice. I wind up gramophone, I get record ready and I sit and wait. What happens? Nothing. Ten o'clock I start dancing with my pillow. You try and practice romance by yourself, Boet Sam. Struesgod, she doesn't come tonight I take back my dress and ballroom shoes and I find me new partner. Size twenty-six. Shoes size seven. And now she's also making trouble for me with the baby again. Reports me to Child Wellfed, that I'm not giving her money. She lies! Every week I am giving her money for milk. And how do I know is my baby? Only his hair looks like me. She's fucking around all the time I turn my back. Hilda Samuels is a bitch! (*Pause.*) Hey, Sam!

Sam: Ja.

Willie: You listening?

Sam: Ja.

Willie: So what you say?

Sam: About Hilda?

Willie: Ja.

Sam: When did you last give her a hiding?

Willie (*reluctantly*):   Sunday night.

Sam: And today is Thursday.

Willie (*he knows what's coming*):   Okay.

Sam: Hiding on Sunday night, then Monday, Tuesday, and Wednesday she doesn't come to practice . . . and you are asking me why?

Willie: I said okay, Boet Sam!

Sam: You hit her too much. One day she's going to leave you for good.

Willie: So? She makes me the hell-in too much.

Sam (*emphasizing his point*):   *Too* much and *too* hard. You had the same trouble with Eunice.

Willie: Because she also make the hell-in, Boet Sam. She never got the steps right. Even the waltz.

Sam: Beating her up every time she makes a mistake in the waltz? (*Shaking his head.*) No, Willie! That takes the pleasure out of ballroom dancing.

Willie: Hilda is not too bad with the waltz, Boet Sam. Is the quickstep where the trouble starts.

Sam (*teasing him gently*):   How's your pillow with the quickstep?

Willie (*ignoring the tease*):   Good! And why? Because it got no legs. That's her trouble. She can't move them quick enough, Boet Sam. I start the record and before halfway Count Basie is already winning. Only time we catch up with him is when gramophone runs down. (*Sam laughs.*) Haaikona, Boet Sam, is not funny.

Sam (*snapping his fingers*):   I got it! Give her a handicap.

Willie: What's that?

Sam: Give her a ten-second start and then let Count Basie go. Then I put my money on her. Hot favorite in the Ballroom Stakes: Hilda Samuels ridden by Willie Malopo.

Willie (*turning away*):   I'm not talking to you no more.

Sam (*relenting*):   Sorry, Willie. . . .

Willie: It's finish between us.

Sam: Okay, okay . . . I'll stop.

Willie: You can also fuck off.

Sam: Willie, listen! I want to help you!

Willie: No more jokes?

Sam: I promise.

Willie: Okay. Help me.

Sam (*his turn to hold an imaginary partner*):   Look and learn. Feet together. Back straight. Body relaxed. Right hand placed gently in the small of her back and wait for the music. Don't start worrying about making mistakes or the judges or the other competitors. It's just you, Hilda and the music, and you're going to have a good time. What Count Basie do you play?

Willie: "You the cream in my coffee, you the salt in my stew."

Sam: Right. Give it to me in strict tempo.

Willie: Ready?

Sam: Ready.

Willie: A-n-d . . . (*Singing.*) "You the cream in my coffee. You the salt in my stew. You will always be my necessity. I'd be lost without you. . . ." (*etc.*)

(*Sam launches into the quickstep. He is obviously a much more accomplished dancer than Willie. Hally enters. A seventeen-year-old white boy. Wet raincoat and school case. He stops and watches Sam. The demonstration comes to an end with a flourish. Applause from Hally and Willie.*)

Hally: Bravo! No question about it. First place goes to Mr. Sam Semela.

Willie (in total agreement):   You was gliding with style, Boet Sam.

Hally (cheerfully):   How's it, chaps?

Sam: Okay, Hally.

Willie (springing to attention like a soldier and saluting):   At your service, Master Harold!

Hally: Not long to the big event, hey!

Sam: Two weeks.

Hally: You nervous?

Sam: No.

Hally: Think you stand a chance?

Sam: Let's just say I'm ready to go out there and dance.

Hally: It looked like it. What about you, Willie?

> (*Willie groans.*)

What's the matter?

Sam: He's got leg trouble.

Hally (innocently):   Oh, sorry to hear that, Willie.

Willie: Boet Sam! You promised. (*Willie returns to his work.*)

> (*Hally deposits his school case and takes off his raincoat. His clothes are a little neglected and untidy: black blazer with school badge, gray flannel trousers in need of an ironing, khaki shirt and tie, black shoes. Sam has fetched a towel for Hally to dry his hair.*)

Hally: God, what a lousy bloody day. It's coming down cats and dogs out there. Bad for business, chaps. . . . (*Conspiratorial whisper.*) . . . but it also means we're in for a nice quiet afternoon.

Sam: You can speak loud. Your Mom's not here.

Hally: Out shopping?

Sam: No. The hospital.

Hally: But it's Thursday. There's no visiting on Thursday afternoons. Is my Dad okay?

Sam: Sounds like it. In fact, I think he's going home.

Hally (stopped short by Sam's remark):   What do you mean?

Sam: The hospital phoned.

Hally: To say what?

Sam: I don't know. I just heard your Mom talking.

Hally: So what makes you say he's going home?

Sam: It sounded as if they were telling her to come and fetch him.

> (*Hally thinks about what Sam has said for a few seconds.*)

Hally: When did she leave?

Sam: About an hour ago. She said she would phone you. Want to eat?

> (*Hally doesn't respond.*)

Hally, want your lunch?

Hally: I suppose so. (*His mood has changed.*) What's on the menu? . . . as if I don't know.

Sam: Soup, followed by meat pie and gravy.

Hally: Today's?

Sam: No.

Hally: And the soup?

Sam: Nourishing pea soup.

Hally: Just the soup. (*The pile of comic books on the table.*) And these?

Sam: For your Dad. Mr. Kempston brought them.

Hally: You haven't been reading them, have you?

Sam: Just looking.

Hally (*examining the comics*): *Jungle Jim . . . Batman and Robin . . . Tarzan . . .* God, what rubbish! Mental pollution. Take them away.

(*Sam exits waltzing into the kitchen. Hally turns to Willie.*)

Hally: Did you hear my Mom talking on the telephone, Willie?

Willie: No, Master Hally. I was at the back.

Hally: And she didn't say anything to you before she left?

Willie: She said I must clean the floors.

Hally: I mean about my Dad.

Willie: She didn't say nothing to me about him, Master Hally.

Hally (*with conviction*): No! It can't be. They said he needed at least another three weeks of treatment. Sam's definitely made a mistake. (*Rummages through his school case, finds a book and settles down at the table to read.*) So, Willie!

Willie: Yes, Master Hally! Schooling okay today?

Hally: Yes, okay . . . . (*He thinks about it.*) . . . No, not really. Ag, what's the difference? I don't care. And Sam says you've got problems.

Willie: Big problems.

Hally: Which leg is sore?

(*Willie groans.*)

Both legs.

Willie: There is nothing wrong with my legs. Sam is just making jokes.

Hally: So then you *will* be in the competition.

Willie: Only if I can find a partner.

Hally: But what about Hilda?

Sam (*returning with a bowl of soup*): She's the one who's got trouble with her legs.

Hally: What sort of trouble, Willie?

Sam: From the way he describes it, I think the lady has gone a bit lame.

Hally: Good God! Have you taken her to see a doctor?

Sam: I think a vet would be better.

Hally: What do you mean?

Sam: What do you call it again when a racehorse goes very fast?

Hally: Gallop?

Sam: That's it!

Willie: Boet Sam!

Hally: "A gallop down the homestretch to the winning post." But what's that got to do with Hilda?

Sam: Count Basie always gets there first.

(*Willie lets fly with his slop rag. It misses Sam and hits Hally.*)

Hally (*furious*): For Christ's sake, Willie! What the hell do you think you're doing?

Willie: Sorry, Master Hally, but it's him. . . .

Hally: Act your bloody age! (*Hurls the rag back at Willie.*) Cut out the nonsense now and get on with your work. And you too, Sam. Stop fooling around.

(*Sam moves away.*)

No. Hang on. I haven't finished! Tell me exactly what my Mom said.

Sam: I have. "When Hally comes, tell him I've gone to the hospital and I'll phone him."

Hally: She didn't say anything about taking my Dad home?

Sam: No. It's just that when she was talking on the phone. . . .

Hally (*interrupting him*): No, Sam. They can't be discharging him. She would have said so if they were. In any case, we saw him last night and he wasn't in good shape at all. Staff nurse even said there was talk about taking more X-rays. And now suddenly today he's better? If anything, it sounds more like a bad turn to me . . . which I sincerely hope it isn't. Hang on . . . how long ago did you say she left?

Sam: Just before two . . . (*his wrist watch*) . . . hour and a half.

Hally: I know how to settle it. (*Behind the counter to the telephone. Talking as he dials.*) Let's give her ten minutes to get to the hospital, ten minutes to load him up, another ten, at the most, to get home, and another ten to get him inside. Forty minutes. They should have been home for at least half an hour already. (*Pause—he waits with the receiver to his ear.*) No reply, chaps. And you know why? Because she's at his bedside in hospital helping him pull through a bad turn. You definitely heard wrong.

Sam: Okay.

(*As far as Hally is concerned, the matter is settled. He returns to his table, sits down, and divides his attention between the book and his soup. Sam is at his school case and picks up a textbook.*)

Modern Graded Mathematics for Standards Nine and Ten. (*Opens it at random and laughs at something he sees.*) Who is this supposed to be?

Hally: Old fart-face Prentice.

Sam: Teacher?

Hally: Thinks he is. And believe me, that is not a bad likeness.

Sam: Has he seen it?

Hally: Yes.

Sam: What did he say?

Hally: Tried to be clever, as usual. Said I was no Leonardo da Vinci and that bad art had to be punished. So, six of the best, and his are bloody good.

Sam: On your bum?

Hally: Where else? The days when I got them on my hands are gone forever, Sam.

Sam: With your trousers down!

Hally: No. He's not quite that barbaric.

Sam: That's the way they do it in jail.

Hally (flicker of morbid interest): Really?

Sam: Ja. When the magistrate sentences you to "strokes with a light cane."

Hally: Go on.

Sam: They make you lie down on a bench. One policeman pulls down your trousers and holds your ankles, another one pulls your shirt over your head and holds your arms. . . .

Hally: Thank you! That's enough.

Sam: . . . and the one that gives you the strokes talks to you gently and for a long time between each one. (*He laughs.*)

Hally: I've heard enough, Sam! Jesus! It's a bloody awful world when you come to think of it. People can be real bastards.

Sam: That's the way it is, Hally.

Hally: It doesn't *have* to be that way. There is something called progress, you know. We don't exactly burn people at the stake anymore.

Sam: Like Joan of Arc.

Hally: Correct. If she was captured today, she'd be given a fair trial.

Sam: And then the death sentence.

Hally (a world-weary sigh): I know, I know! I oscillate between hope and despair for this world as well, Sam. But things will change, you wait and see. One day somebody is going to get up and give history a kick up the backside and get it going again.

Sam: Like who?

Hally (after thought): They're called social reformers. Every age, Sam, has got its social reformer. My history book is full of them.

Sam: So where's ours?

Hally: Good question. And I hate to say it, but the answer is: I don't know. Maybe he hasn't even been born yet. Or is still only a babe in arms at his mother's breast. God, what a thought.

Sam: So we just go on waiting.

Hally: Ja, looks like it. (*Back to his soup and the book.*)

Sam (reading from the textbook): "Introduction: In some mathematical problems only the magnitude. . . ." (*He mispronounces the word "magnitude."*)

Hally (*correcting him without looking up*):   Magnitude.

Sam: What's it mean?

Hally: How big it is. The size of the thing.

Sam (*reading*):   ". . . magnitude of the quantities is of importance. In other problems we need to know whether these quantities are negative or positive. For example, whether there is a debit or credit bank balance . . ."

Hally: Whether you're broke or not.

Sam: ". . . whether the temperature is above or below Zero. . . ."

Hally: Naught degrees. Cheerful state of affairs! No cash and you're freezing to death. Mathematics won't get you out of that one.

Sam: "All these quantities are called . . ." (*spelling the word*) . . . s-c-a-l. . . .

Hally: Scalars.

Sam: Scalars! (*Shaking his head with a laugh.*) You understand all that?

Hally (*turning a page*):   No. And I don't intend to try.

Sam: So what happens when the exams come?

Hally: Failing a maths exam isn't the end of the world, Sam. How many times have I told you that examination results don't measure intelligence?

Sam: I would say about as many times as you've failed one of them.

Hally (*mirthlessly*):   Ha, ha, ha.

Sam (*simultaneously*):   Ha, ha, ha.

Hally: Just remember Winston Churchill didn't do particularly well at school.

Sam: You've also told me that one many times.

Hally: Well, it just so happens to be the truth.

Sam (*enjoying the word*):   Magnitude! Magnitude! Show me how to use it.

Hally (*after thought*):   An intrepid social reformer will not be daunted by the magnitude of the task he has undertaken.

Sam (*impressed*):   Couple of jaw-breakers in there!

Hally: I gave you three for the price of one. Intrepid, daunted, and magnitude. I did that once in an exam. Put five of the words I had to explain in one sentence. It was half a page long.

Sam: Well, I'll put my money on you in the English exam.

Hally: Piece of cake. Eighty percent without even trying.

Sam (*another textbook from Hally's case*):   And history?

Hally: So-so. I'll scrape through. In the fifties if I'm lucky.

Sam: You didn't do too badly last year.

Hally: Because we had World War One. That at least has some action. You try to find that in the South African Parliamentary system.

Sam (*reading from the history textbook*):   "Napoleon and the principle of equality." Hey! This sounds interesting. "After concluding peace with Britain in 1802, Napoleon used a brief period of calm to in-sti-tute . . ."

Hally: Introduce.

Sam: ". . . many reforms. Napoleon regarded all people as equal before the law and wanted them to have equal opportunities for advancement. All ves-ti-ges of the feu-dal sys-tem with its oppression of the poor were abol-ished." Vestiges, feudal system, and abolished. I'm all right on oppression.

Hally: I'm thinking. He swept away . . . abolished . . . the last remains . . . vestiges . . . of the bad old days . . . feudal system.

Sam: Ha! There's the social reformer we're waiting for. He sounds like a man of some magnitude.

Hally: I'm not so sure about that. It's a damn good title for a book, though. A man of magnitude!

Sam: He sounds pretty big to me, Hally.

Hally: Don't confuse historical significance with greatness. But maybe I'm being a bit prejudiced. Have a look in there and you'll see he's two chapters long. And hell! . . . has he only got dates, Sam, all of which you've got to remember! This campaign and that campaign, and then, because of all the fighting, the next thing is we get Peace Treaties all over the place. And what's the end of the story? Battle of Waterloo, which he loses. Wasn't worth it. No, I don't know about him as a man of magnitude.

Sam: Then who would you say was?

Hally: To answer that, we need a definition of greatness, and I suppose that would be somebody who . . . somebody who benefited all mankind.

Sam: Right. But like who?

Hally: (*he speaks with total conviction*): Charles Darwin. Remember him? That big book from the library. *The Origin of the Species.*

Sam: Him?

Hally: Yes. For his Theory of Evolution.

Sam: You didn't finish it.

Hally: I ran out of time. I didn't finish it because my two weeks was up. But I'm going to take it out again after I've digested what I read. It's safe. I've hidden it away in the Theology section. Nobody ever goes in there. And anyway who are you to talk? You hardly even looked at it.

Sam: I tried. I looked at the chapters in the beginning and I saw one called "The Struggle for an Existence." Ah ha, I thought. At last! But what did I get? Something called the mistiltoe which needs the apple tree and there's too many seeds and all are going to die except one . . . ! No, Hally.

Hally (*intellectually outraged*): What do you mean, No! The poor man had to start somewhere. For God's sake, Sam, he revolutionized science. Now we know.

Sam: What?

Hally: Where we come from and what it all means.

Sam: And that's a benefit to mankind? Anyway, I still don't believe it.

Hally: God, you're impossible. I showed it to you in black and white.

Sam: Doesn't mean I got to believe it.

Hally: It's the likes of you that kept the Inquisition in business. It's called bigotry. Anyway, that's my man of magnitude. Charles Darwin! Who's yours?

Sam (without hesitation):   Abraham Lincoln.

Hally: I might have guessed as much. Don't get sentimental, Sam. You've never been a slave, you know. And anyway we freed your ancestors here in South Africa long before the Americans. But if you want to thank somebody on their behalf, do it to Mr. William Wilberforce.° Come on. Try again. I want a real genius.

(*Now enjoying himself, and so is Sam. Hally goes behind the counter and helps himself to a chocolate.*)

Sam: William Shakespeare.

Hally (no enthusiasm):   Oh. So you're also one of them, are you? You're basing that opinion on only one play, you know. You've only read my *Julius Caesar* and even I don't understand half of what they're talking about. They should do what they did with the old Bible: bring the language up to date.

Sam: That's all you've got. It's also the only one *you've* read.

Hally: I know. I admit it. That's why I suggest we reserve our judgment until we've checked up on a few others. I've got a feeling, though, that by the end of this year one is going to be enough for me, and I can give you the names of twenty-nine other chaps in the Standard Nine class of the Port Elizabeth Technical College who feel the same. But if you want him, you can have him. My turn now. (*Pacing.*) This is a damned good exercise, you know! It started off looking like a simple question and here it's got us really probing into the intellectual heritage of our civilization.

Sam: So who is it going to be?

Hally: My next man . . . and he gets the title on two scores: social reform and literary genius . . . is Leo Nikolaevich Tolstoy.

Sam: That Russian.

Hally: Correct. Remember the picture of him I showed you?

Sam: With the long beard.

Hally (Trying to look like Tolstoy):   And those burning, visionary eyes. My God, the face of a social prophet if ever I saw one! And remember my words when I showed it to you? Here's a *man*, Sam!

Sam: Those were words, Hally.

Hally: Not many intellectuals are prepared to shovel manure with the peasants and then go home and write a "little book" called *War and Peace*. Incidentally, Sam, he was somebody else who, to quote, ". . . did not distinguish himself scholastically."

Sam: Meaning?

Mr. William Wilberforce: (1759–1833), British statesman who supported a bill outlawing the slave trade and suppressing slavery in the British Empire.

Hally: He was also no good at school.

Sam: Like you and Winston Churchill.

Hally (*mirthlessly*): Ha, ha, ha.

Sam (*simultaneously*): Ha, ha, ha.

Hally: Don't get clever, Sam. That man freed his serfs of his own free will.

Sam: No argument. He was a somebody, all right. I accept him.

Hally: I'm sure Count Tolstoy will be very pleased to hear that. Your turn. Shoot. (*Another chocolate from behind the counter.*) I'm waiting, Sam.

Sam: I've got him.

Hally: Good. Submit your candidate for examination.

Sam: Jesus.

Hally (*stopped dead in his tracks*): Who?

Sam: Jesus Christ.

Hally: Oh, come on, Sam!

Sam: The Messiah.

Hally: Ja, but still . . . No, Sam. Don't let's get started on religion. We'll just spend the whole afternoon arguing again. Suppose I turn around and say Mohammed?

Sam: All right.

Hally: All right.

Hally: You can't have them both on the same list!

Sam: Why not? You like Mohammed, I like Jesus.

Hally: I *don't* like Mohammed. I never have. I was merely being hypothetical. As far as I'm concerned, the Koran is as bad as the Bible. No. Religion is out! I'm not going to waste my time again arguing with you about the existence of God. You know perfectly well I'm an atheist . . . and I've got homework to do.

Sam: Okay, I take him back.

Hally: You've got time for one more name.

Sam (*after thought*): I've got one I know we'll agree on. A simple straightforward great Man of Magnitude . . . and no arguments. And *he* really *did* benefit all mankind.

Hally: I wonder. After your last contribution I'm beginning to doubt whether anything in the way of an intellectual agreement is possible between the two of us. Who is he?

Sam: Guess.

Hally: Socrates? Alexandre Dumas? Karl Marx, Dostoevsky? Nietzsche?

(*Sam shakes his head after each name.*)

Give me a clue.

Sam: The letter *P* is important. . . .

Hally: Plato!

Sam: . . . and his name begins with an *F.*

Hally: I've got it. Freud and Psychology.

Sam: No. I didn't understand him.

Hally: That makes two of us.

Sam: Think of moldy apricot jam.

Hally (*after a delighted laugh*):   Penicillin and Sir Alexander Fleming! And the title of the book: *The Microbe Hunters.* (*Delighted.*) Splendid, Sam! Splendid. For once we are in total agreement. The major breakthrough in medical science in the Twentieth Century. If it wasn't for him, we might have lost the Second World War. It's deeply gratifying, Sam, to know that I haven't been wasting my time in talking to you. (*Strutting around proudly.*) Tolstoy may have educated his peasants, but I've educated you.

Sam: Standard Four to Standard Nine.

Hally: Have we been at it as long as that?

Sam: Yep. And my first lesson was geography.

Hally (*intrigued*):   Really? I don't remember.

Sam: My room there at the back of the old Jubilee Boarding House. I had just started working for your Mom. Little boy in short trousers walks in one afternoon and asks me seriously: "Sam, do you want to see South Africa?" Hey man! Sure I wanted to see South Africa!

Hally: Was that me?

Sam: . . . So the next thing I'm looking at a map you had just done for homework. It was your first one and you were very proud of yourself.

Hally: Go on.

Sam: Then came my first lesson. "Repeat after me, Sam: Gold in the Transvaal, mealies° in the Free State, sugar in Natal, and grapes in the Cape." I still know it!

Hally: Well, I'll be buggered. So that's how it all started.

Sam: And your next map was one with all the rivers and the mountains they came from. The Orange, the Vaal, the Limpopo, the Zambezi. . . .

Hally: You've got a phenomenal memory!

Sam: You should be grateful. That is why you started passing your exams. You tried to be better than me.

(*They laugh together. Willie is attracted by the laughter and joins them.*)

Hally: The old Jubilee Boarding House. Sixteen rooms with board and lodging, rent in advance and one week's notice. I haven't thought about it for donkey's years . . . and I don't think that's an accident. God, was I glad when we sold it and moved out. Those years are not remembered as the happiest ones of an unhappy childhood.

Willie (*knocking on the table and trying to imitate a woman's voice*):   "Hally, are you there?"

Hally: Who's that supposed to be?

Willie: "What you doing in there, Hally? Come out at once!"

°*mealies:* Corn.

Hally (*to Sam*):   What's he talking about?

Sam: Don't you remember?

Willie: "Sam, Willie . . . is he in there with you boys?"

Sam: Hiding away in our room when your mother was looking for you.

Hally (*another good laugh*):   Of course! I used to crawl and hide under your bed! But finish the story, Willie. Then what used to happen? You chaps would give the game away by telling her I was in there with you. So much for friendship.

Sam: We couldn't lie to her. She knew.

Hally: Which meant I got another rowing for hanging around the "servants' quarters." I think I spent more time in there with you chaps than anywhere else in that dump. And do you blame me? Nothing but bloody misery wherever you went. Somebody was always complaining about the food, or my mother was having a fight with Micky Nash because she'd caught her with a petty officer in her room. Maud Meiring was another one. Remember those two? They were prostitutes, you know. Soldiers and sailors from the troopships. Bottom fell out of the business when the war ended. God, the flotsam and jetsam that life washed up on our shores! No joking, if it wasn't for your room, I would have been the first certified ten-year-old in medical history. Ja, the memories are coming back now. Walking home from school and thinking: "What can I do this afternoon?" Try out a few ideas, but sooner or later I'd end up in there with you fellows. I bet you I could still find my way to your room with my eyes closed. (*He does exactly that.*) Down the corridor . . . telephone on the right, which my Mom keeps locked because somebody is using it on the sly and not paying . . . past the kitchen and unappetizing cooking smells . . . around the corner into the backyard, hold my breath again because there are more smells coming when I pass your lavatory, then into that little passageway, first door on the right and into your room. How's that?

Sam: Good. But, as usual, you forgot to knock.

Hally: Like that time I barged in and caught you and Cynthia . . . at it. Remember? God, was I embarrassed! I didn't know what was going on at first.

Sam: Ja, that taught you a lesson.

Hally: And about a lot more than knocking on doors, I'll have you know, and I don't mean geography either. Hell, Sam, couldn't you have waited until it was dark?

Sam: No.

Hally: Was it that urgent?

Sam: Yes, and if you don't believe me, wait until your time comes.

Hally: No, thank you. I am not interested in girls. (*Back to his memories. . . . Using a few chairs he re-creates the room as he lists the items.*) A gray little room with a cold cement floor. Your bed against

that wall . . . and I now know why the mattress sags so much! . . .
Willie's bed . . . it's propped up on bricks because one leg is broken
. . . that wobbly little table with the washbasin and jug of water . . .
Yes! . . . stuck to the wall above it are some pin-up pictures from
magazines. Joe Louis. . . .

Willie: Brown Bomber. World Title. (*Boxing pose.*) Three rounds and
knockout.

Hally: Against who?

Sam: Max Schmeling.

Hally: Correct. I can also remember Fred Astaire and Ginger Rogers, and
Rita Hayworth in a bathing costume which always made me hot and
bothered when I looked at it. Under Willie's bed is an old suitcase
with all his clothes in a mess, which is why I never hide there. Your
things are neat and tidy in a trunk next to your bed, and on it there is
a picture of you and Cynthia in your ballroom clothes, your first silver
cup for third place in a competition and an old radio which doesn't
work anymore. Have I left out anything?

Sam: No.

Hally: Right, so much for the stage directions. Now the characters. (*Sam
and Willie move to their appropriate positions in the bedroom.*) Willie is
in bed, under his blankets with his clothes on, complaining nonstop
about something, but we can't make out a word of what he's saying
because he's got his head under the blankets as well. You're on your
bed trimming your toenails with a knife—not a very edifying sight—
and as for me. . . . What am I doing?

Sam: You're sitting on the floor giving Willie a lecture about being a
good loser while you get the checkerboard and pieces ready for a
game. Then you go to Willie's bed, pull off the blankets and make him
play with you first because you know you're going to win, and that
gives you the second game with me.

Hally: And you certainly were a bad loser, Willie!

Willie: Haai!

Hally: Wasn't he, Sam? And so slow! A game with you almost took the
whole afternoon. Thank God I gave up trying to teach you how to
play chess.

Willie: You and Sam cheated.

Hally: I never saw Sam cheat, and mine were mostly the mistakes of youth.

Willie: Then how is it you two was always winning?

Hally: Have you ever considered the possibility, Willie, that it was
because we were better than you?

Willie: Every time better?

Hally: Not every time. There were occasions when we deliberately let you
win a game so that you would stop sulking and go on playing with us.
Sam used to wink at me when you weren't looking to show me it was
time to let you win.

Willie: So then you two didn't play fair.

Hally: It was for your benefit, Mr. Malopo, which is more than being fair. It was an act of self-sacrifice. (*To Sam.*) But you know what my best memory is, don't you?

Sam: No.

Hally: Come on, guess. If your memory is so good, you must remember it as well.

Sam: We got up to a lot of tricks in there, Hally.

Hally: This one was special, Sam.

Sam: I'm listening.

Hally: It started off looking like another of those useless nothing-to-do afternoons. I'd already been down to Main Street looking for adventure, but nothing had happened. I didn't feel like climbing trees in the Donkin Park or pretending I was a private eye and following a stranger . . . so as usual: See what's cooking in Sam's room. This time it was you on the floor. You had two thin pieces of wood and you were smoothing them down with a knife. It didn't look particularly interesting, but when I asked you what you were doing, you just said, "Wait and see, Hally. Wait . . . and see" . . . in that secret sort of way of yours, so I knew there was a surprise coming. You teased me, you bugger, by being deliberately slow and not answering my questions!

(*Sam laughs.*)

And whistling while you worked away! God, it was infuriating! I could have brained you! It was only when you tied them together in a cross and put that down on the brown paper that I realized what you were doing. "Sam is making a kite?" And when I asked you and you said "Yes" . . . ! (*Shaking his head with disbelief.*) The sheer audacity of it took my breath away. I mean, seriously, what the hell does a black man know about flying a kite? I'll be honest with you, Sam, I had no hopes for it. If you think I was excited and happy, you got another guess coming. In fact, I was shit-scared that we were going to make fools of ourselves. When we left the boarding house to go up onto the hill, I was praying quietly that there wouldn't be any other kids around to laugh at us.

Sam (*enjoying the memory as much as Hally*): Ja, I could see that.

Hally: I made it obvious, did I?

Sam: Ja. You refused to carry it.

Hally: Do you blame me? Can you remember what the poor thing looked like? Tomato-box wood and brown paper! Flour and water for glue! Two of my mother's old stockings for a tail, and then all those bits and pieces of string you made me tie together so that we could fly it! Hell, no, that was now only asking for a miracle to happen.

Sam: Then the big argument when I told you to hold the string and run with it when I let go.

Hally: I was prepared to run, all right, but straight back to the boarding house.

Sam (knowing what's coming): So what happened?

Hally: Come on, Sam, you remember as well as I do.

Sam: I want to hear it from you.

(*Hally pauses. He wants to be as accurate as possible.*)

Hally: You went a little distance from me down the hill, you held it up ready to let it go. . . . "This is it," I thought. "Like everything else in my life, here comes another fiasco." Then you shouted, "Go, Hally!" and I started to run. (*Another pause.*) I don't know how to describe it, Sam. Ja! The miracle happened! I was running, waiting for it to crash to the ground, but instead suddenly there was something alive behind me at the end of the string, tugging at it as if it wanted to be free. I looked back . . . (*Shakes his head.*) . . . I still can't believe my eyes. It was flying! Looping around and trying to climb even higher into the sky. You shouted to me to let it have more string. I did, until there was none left and I was just holding that piece of wood we had tied it to. You came up and joined me. You were laughing.

Sam: So were you. And shouting, "It works, Sam! We've done it!"

Hally: And we had! I was so proud of us! It was the most splendid thing I had ever seen. I wished there were hundreds of kids around to watch us. The part that scared me, though, was when you showed me how to make it dive down to the ground and then just when it was on the point of crashing, swoop up again!

Sam: You didn't want to try yourself.

Hally: Of course not! I would have been suicidal if anything had happened to it. Watching you do it made me nervous enough. I was quite happy just to see it up there with its tail fluttering behind it. You left me after that, didn't you? You explained how to get it down, we tied it to the bench so that I could sit and watch it, and you went away. I wanted you to stay, you know. I was a little scared of having to look after it by myself.

Sam (quietly): I had work to do, Hally.

Hally: It was sort of sad bringing it down, Sam. And it looked sad again when it was lying there on the ground. Like something that had lost its soul. Just tomato-box wood, brown paper and two of my mother's old stockings! But, hell, I'll never forget that first moment when I saw it up there. I had a stiff neck the next day from looking up so much.

(*Sam laughs. Hally turns to him with a question he never thought of asking before.*)

Why did you make that kite, Sam?

Sam (evenly): I can't remember.

Hally: Truly?

Sam: Too long ago, Hally.

Hally: Ja, I suppose it was. It's time for another one, you know.

Sam: Why do you say that?

Hally: Because it feels like that. Wouldn't be a good day to fly it, though.

Sam: No. You can't fly kites on rainy days.

Hally (*he studies Sam. Their memories have made him conscious of the man's presence in his life*): How old are you, Sam?

Sam: Two score and five.

Hally: Strange, isn't it?

Sam: What?

Hally: Me and you.

Sam: What's strange about it?

Hally: Little white boy in short trousers and a black man old enough to be his father flying a kite. It's not every day you see that.

Sam: But why strange? Because the one is white and the other black?

Hally: I don't know. Would have been just as strange, I suppose, if it had been me and my Dad . . . cripple man and a little boy! Nope! There's no chance of me flying a kite without it being strange. (*Simple statement of fact—no self-pity.*) There's a nice little short story there. "The Kite-Flyers." But we'd have to find a twist in the ending.

Sam: Twist?

Hally: Yes. Something unexpected. The way it ended with us was too straightforward . . . me on the bench and you going back to work. There's no drama in that.

Willie: And me?

Hally: You?

Willie: Yes me.

Hally: You want to get into the story as well, do you? I got it! Change the title: "Afternoons in Sam's Room" . . . expand it and tell all the stories. It's on its way to being a novel. Our days in the old Jubilee. Sad in a way that they're over. I almost wish we were still in that little room.

Sam: We're still together.

Hally: That's true. It's just that life felt the right size in there . . . not too big and not too small. Wasn't so hard to work up a bit of courage. It's got so bloody complicated since then.

(*The telephone rings. Sam answers it.*)

Sam: St. George's Park Tea Room . . . Hello, Madam. . . Yes, Madam, he's here. . . . Hally, it's your mother.

Hally: Where is she phoning from?

Sam: Sounds like the hospital. It's a public telephone.

Hally (*relieved*): You see! I told you. (*The telephone.*) Hello, Mom . . . Yes . . . Yes no fine. Everything's under control here. How's things with poor old Dad? . . . Has he had a bad turn? . . . What? . . . Oh, God! . . . Yes, Sam told me, but I was sure he'd made a mistake. But what's this all about, Mom? He didn't look at all good last night. How can he get better so quickly? . . . Then very obviously you must say no. Be firm with him. You're the boss. . . . You know what it's going to be like if he comes home. . . . Well then, don't blame me when I fail my exams at the end of the year. . . . Yes! How am I expected to be fresh for school when I spend half the night massaging his gammy leg? . . . So am I! . . . So tell him a white lie. Say Dr. Colley wants more X-rays of his stump. Or bribe him. We'll sneak in double tots of brandy in future. . . . What? . . . Order him to get back into bed at once! If he's going to behave like a child, treat him like one. . . . All right, Mom! I was just trying to . . . I'm sorry. . . . I said I'm sorry. . . . Quick, give me your number. I'll phone you back. (*He hangs up and waits a few seconds.*) Here we go again! (*He dials.*) I'm sorry, Mom. . . . Okay. . . . But now listen to me carefully. All it needs is for you to put your foot down. Don't take no for an answer. . . . Did you hear me? And whatever you do, don't discuss it with him. . . . Because I'm frightened you'll give in to him. . . . Yes, Sam gave me lunch. . . . I ate all of it! . . . No, Mom not a soul. It's still raining here. . . . Right, I'll tell them. I'll just do some homework and then lock up. . . . But remember now, Mom. Don't listen to anything he says. And phone me back and let me know what happens. . . . Okay. Bye, Mom. (*He hangs up. The men are staring at him.*) My Mom says that when you're finished with the floors you must do the windows. (*Pause.*) Don't misunderstand me, chaps. All I want is for him to get better. And if he was, I'd be the first person to say: "Bring him home." But he's not, and we can't give him the medical care and attention he needs at home. That's what hospitals are there for. (*Brusquely.*) So don't just stand there! Get on with it!

(*Sam clears Hally's table.*)

You heard right. My Dad wants to go home.

Sam: Is he better?

Hally (*sharply*): No! How the hell can he be better when last night he was groaning with pain? This is not an age of miracles!

Sam: Then he should stay in hospital.

Hally (*seething with irritation and frustration*): Tell me something I don't know, Sam. What the hell do you think I was saying to my Mom? All I can say is fuck-it-all.

Sam: I'm sure he'll listen to your Mom.

Hally: You don't know what she's up against. He's already packed his shaving kit and pajamas and is sitting on his bed with his crutches, dressed and ready to go. I know him when he gets in that mood. If she tries to reason with him, we've had it. She's no match for him when it comes to a battle of words. He'll tie her up in knots. (*Trying to hide his true feelings.*)

Sam: I suppose it gets lonely for him in there.

Hally: With all the patients and nurses around? Regular visits from the Salvation Army? Balls! It's ten times worse for him at home. I'm at school and my mother is here in the business all day.

Sam: He's at least got you at night.

Hally (before he can stop himself): And we've got him! Please! I don't want to talk about it anymore. (*Unpacks his school case, slamming down books on the table.*) Life is just a plain bloody mess, that's all. And people are fools.

Sam: Come on, Hally.

Hally: Yes, they are! They bloody well deserve what they get.

Sam: Then don't complain.

Hally: Don't try to be clever, Sam. It doesn't suit you. Anybody who thinks there's nothing wrong with this world needs to have his head examined. Just when things are going along all right, without fail someone or something will come along and spoil everything. Somebody should write that down as a fundamental law of the Universe. The principle of perpetual disappointment. If there is a God who created this world, he should scrap it and try again.

Sam: All right, Hally, all right. What you got for homework?

Hally: Bullshit, as usual. (*Opens an exercise book and reads.*) "Write five hundred words describing an annual event of cultural or historical significance."

Sam: That should be easy enough for you.

Hally: And also plain bloody boring. You know what he wants, don't you? One of their useless old ceremonies. The commemoration of the landing of the 1820 Settlers, or if it's going to be culture, Carols by Candlelight every Christmas.

Sam: It's an impressive sight. Make a good description, Hally. All those candles glowing in the dark and the people singing hymns.

Hally: And it's called religious hysteria. (*Intense irritation.*) Please, Sam! Just leave me alone and let me get on with it. I'm not in the mood for games this afternoon. And remember my Mom's orders . . . you're to help Willie with the windows. Come on now, I don't want any more nonsense in here.

Sam: Okay, Hally, okay.

(*Hally settles down to his homework; determined preparations . . . pen, ruler, exercise book, dictionary, another cake . . . all of which will lead to nothing.*)

(*Sam waltzes over to Willie and starts to replace tables and chairs. He practices a ballroom step while doing so. Willie watches. When Sam is finished, Willie tries.*)

Good! But just a little bit quicker on the turn and only move in to her after she's crossed over. What about this one?

(*Another step. When Sam is finished, Willie again has a go.*)

Much better. See what happens when you just relax and enjoy
yourself? Remember that in two weeks' time and you'll be all right.

Willie: But I haven't got partner, Boet Sam.

Sam: Maybe Hilda will turn up tonight.

Willie: No, Boet Sam. (*Reluctantly.*) I gave her a good hiding.

Sam: You mean a bad one.

Willie: Good bad one.

Sam: Then you mustn't complain either. Now you pay the price for
losing your temper.

Willie: I also pay two pounds ten shilling entrance fee.

Sam: They'll refund you if you withdraw now.

Willie (*appalled*):   You mean, don't dance?

Sam: Yes.

Willie: No! I wait too long and I practice too hard. If I find me a new
partner, you think I can be ready in two weeks? I ask Madam for my
leave now and we practice every day.

Sam: Quickstep nonstop for two weeks. World record, Willie, but you'll
be mad at the end.

Willie: No jokes, Boet Sam.

Sam: I'm not joking.

Willie: So then what?

Sam: Find Hilda. Say you're sorry and promise you won't beat her
again.

Willie: No.

Sam: Then withdraw. Try again next year.

Willie: No.

Sam: Then I give up.

Willie: Haaikona, Boet Sam, you can't.

Sam: What do you mean, I can't? I'm telling you: I give up.

Willie (*adamant*):   No! (*Accusingly.*) It was you who start me ballroom
dancing.

Sam: So?

Willie: Before that I use to be happy. And is you and Miriam who bring
me to Hilda and say here's partner for you.

Sam: What are you saying, Willie?

Willie: You!

Sam: But me what? To blame?

Willie: Yes.

Sam: Willie . . . ? (*Bursts into laughter.*)

Willie: And now all you do is make jokes at me. You wait. When Miriam
leaves you is my turn to laugh. Ha! Ha! Ha!

Sam (*he can't take Willie seriously any longer*):   She can leave me tonight! I
know what to do. (*Bowing before an imaginary partner.*) May I have
the pleasure? (*He dances and sings.*)

"Just a fellow with his pillow . . .

Dancin' like a willow . . .

In an autumn breeze. . . ."

Willie: There you go again!

(*Sam goes on dancing and singing.*)

Boet Sam!

Sam: There's the answer to your problem! Judges' announcement in two weeks' time: "Ladies and gentlemen, the winner in the open section . . . Mr. Willie Malopo and his pillow!"

(*This is too much for a now really angry Willie. He goes for Sam, but the latter is too quick for him and puts Hally's table between the two of them.*)

Hally (*exploding*): For Christ's sake, you two!

Willie (*still trying to get at Sam*): I donner you, Sam! Struesgod!

Sam (*still laughing*): Sorry, Willie . . . Sorry. . . .

Hally: Sam! Willie! (*Grabs his ruler and gives Willie a vicious whack on the bum.*) How the hell am I supposed to concentrate with the two of you behaving like bloody children!

Willie: Hit him too!

Hally: Shut up, Willie.

Willie: He started jokes again.

Hally: Get back to your work. You too, Sam. (*His ruler.*) Do you want another one, Willie?

(*Sam and Willie return to their work. Hally uses the opportunity to escape from his unsuccessful attempt at homework. He struts around like a little despot, ruler in hand, giving vent to his anger and frustration.*)

Suppose a customer had walked in then? Or the Park Superintendent. And seen the two of you behaving like a pair of hooligans. That would have been the end of my mother's license, you know. And your jobs? Well, this is the end of it. From now on there will be no more of your ballroom nonsense in here. This is a business establishment, not a bloody New Brighton dancing school. I've been far too lenient with the two of you. (*Behind the counter for a green cool drink and a dollop of ice cream. He keeps up his tirade as he prepares it.*) But what really makes me bitter is that I allow you chaps a little freedom in here when business is bad and what do you do with it? The foxtrot! Specially you, Sam. There's more to life than trotting around a dance floor and I thought at least you knew it.

Sam: It's a harmless pleasure, Hally. It doesn't hurt anybody.

Hally: It's also a rather simple one, you know.

Sam: You reckon so? Have you ever tried?

Hally: Of course not.

Sam: Why don't you? Now.

Hally: What do you mean? Me dance?

Sam: Yes. I'll show you a simple step—the waltz—then you try it.

Hally: What will that prove?

Sam: That it might not be as easy as you think.

Hally: I didn't say it was easy. I said it was simple—like in simple-minded, meaning mentally retarded. You can't exactly say it challenges the intellect.

Sam: It does other things.

Hally: Such as?

Sam: Make people happy.

Hally: (*the glass in his hand*):   So do American cream sodas with ice cream. For God's sake, Sam, you're not asking me to take ballroom dancing serious, are you?

Sam: Yes.

Hally: (*sigh of defeat*):   Oh, well, so much for trying to give you a decent education. I've obviously achieved nothing.

Sam: You still haven't told me what's wrong with admiring something that's beautiful and then trying to do it yourself.

Hally: Nothing. But we happen to be talking about a foxtrot, not a thing of beauty.

Sam: But that is just what I'm saying. If you were to see two champions doing, two masters of the art . . . !

Hally: Oh God, I give up. So now it's also art!

Sam: Ja.

Hally: There's a limit, Sam. Don't confuse art and entertainment.

Sam: So then what is art?

Hally: You want a definition?

Sam: Ja.

Hally (*he realizes he has got to be careful. He gives the matter a lot of thought before answering*):   Philosophers have been trying to do that for centuries. What is Art? What is Life? But basically I suppose it's . . . the giving of meaning to matter.

Sam: Nothing to do with beautiful?

Hally: It goes beyond that. It's the giving of form to the formless.

Sam: Ja, well, maybe it's not art, then. But I still say it's beautiful.

Hally: I'm sure the word you mean to use is entertaining.

Sam (*adamant*):   No. Beautiful. And if you want proof come along to the Centenary Hall in New Brighton in two weeks' time.

(*The mention of the Centenary Hall draws Willie over to them.*)

Hally: What for? I've seen the two of you prancing around in here often enough.

Sam (*he laughs*):   This isn't the real thing, Hally. We're just playing around in here.

Hally: So? I can use my imagination.

Sam: And what do you get?

Hally: A lot of people dancing around and having a so-called good time.

Sam: That all?

Hally: Well, basically it is that, surely.

Sam: No, it isn't. Your imagination hasn't helped you at all. There's a lot more to it than that. We're getting ready for the championships, Hally, not just another dance. There's going to be a lot of people, all right, and they're going to have a good time, but they'll only be spectators, sitting around and watching. It's just the competitors out there on the dance floor. Party decorations and fancy lights all around the walls! The ladies in beautiful evening dresses!

Hally: My mother's got one of those, Sam, and, quite frankly, it's an embarrassment every time she wears it.

Sam (undeterred):   Your imagination left out the excitement.

(*Hally scoffs.*)

Oh, yes. The finalists are not going to be out there just to have a good time. One of those couples will be the 1950 Eastern Province Champions. And your imagination left out the music.

Willie: Mr. Elijah Gladman Guzana and his Orchestral Jazzonions.

Sam: The sound of the big band, Hally. Trombone, trumpet, tenor and alto sax. And then, finally, your imagination also left out the climax of the evening when the dancing is finished, the judges have stopped whispering among themselves and the Master of Ceremonies collects their scorecards and goes up onto the stage to announce the winners.

Hally: All right. So you make it sound like a bit of a do. It's an occasion. Satisfied?

Sam (victory):   So you admit that!

Hally: Emotionally yes, intellectually no.

Sam: Well, I don't know what you mean by that, all I'm telling you is that it is going to be *the* event of the year in New Brighton. It's been sold out for two weeks already. There's only standing room left. We've got competitors coming from Kingwilliamstown, East London, Port Alfred.

(*Hally starts pacing thoughtfully.*)

Hally: Tell me a bit more.

Sam: I thought you weren't interested . . . intellectually.

Hally (mysteriously):   I've got my reasons.

Sam: What do you want to know?

Hally: It takes place every year?

Sam: Yes. But only every third year in New Brighton. It's East London's turn to have the championships next year.

Hally: Which, I suppose, makes it an even more significant event.

Sam: Ah ha! We're getting somewhere. Our "occasion" is now a "significant event."

Hally: I wonder.

Sam: What?

Hally: I wonder if I would get away with it.

Sam: But what?

Hally (*to the table and his exercise book*):   "Write five hundred words describing an annual event of cultural or historical significance." Would I be stretching poetic license a little too far if I called your ballroom championships a cultural event?

Sam: You mean . . . ?

Hally: You think we could get five hundred words out of it, Sam?

Sam: Victor Sylvester has written a whole book on ballroom dancing.

Willie: You going to write about it, Master Hally?

Hally: Yes, gentlemen, that is precisely what I am considering doing. Old Doc Bromely—he's my English teacher—is going to argue with me, of course. He doesn't like natives. But I'll point out to him that in strict anthropological terms the culture of a primitive black society includes its dancing and singing. To put my thesis in a nutshell: The war-dance has been replaced by the waltz. But it still amounts to the same thing: the release of primitive emotions through movement. Shall we give it a go?

Sam: I'm ready.

Willie: Me also.

Hally: Ha! This will teach the old bugger a lesson. (*Decision taken.*) Right. Let's get ourselves organized. (*This means another cake on the table. He sits.*) I think you've given me enough general atmosphere, Sam, but to build the tension and suspense I need facts. (*Pencil poised.*)

Willie: Give him facts, Boet Sam.

Hally: What you called the climax . . . how many finalists?

Sam: Six couples.

Hally (*making notes*):   Go on. Give me the picture.

Sam: Spectators seated right around the hall. (*Willie becomes a spectator.*)

Hally: . . . and it's a full house.

Sam: At one end, on the stage, Gladman and his Orchestral Jazzonions. At the other end is a long table with the three judges. The six finalists go onto the dance floor and take up their positions. When they are ready and the spectators have settled down, the Master of Ceremonies goes to the microphone. To start with, he makes some jokes to get people laughing. . . .

Hally: Good touch. (*As he writes.*) ". . . creating a relaxed atmosphere which will change to one of tension and drama as the climax is approached."

Sam (*onto a chair to act out the M.C.*):   "Ladies and gentlemen, we come now to the great moment you have all been waiting for this evening. . . . The finals of the 1950 Eastern Province Open Ballroom Dancing Championships. But first let me introduce the finalists! Mr. and Mrs. Welcome Tchabalala from Kingwilliamstown . . ."

Willie (*he applauds after every name*): Is when the people clap their hands and whistle and make a lot of noise, Master Hally.

Sam: "Mr. Mulligan Njikelane and Miss Nomhle Nkonyeni of Grahamstown; Mr. and Mrs. Norman Nchinga from Port Alfred; Mr. Fats Bokolane and Miss Dina Plaatjies from East London; Mr. Sipho Dugu and Mrs. Mable Magada from Peddie; and from New Brighton our very own Mr. Willie Malopo and Miss Hilda Samuels."

(*Willie can't believe his ears. He abandons his role as spectator and scrambles into position as a finalist.*)

Willie: Relaxed and ready to romance!

Sam: The applause dies down. When everybody is silent, Gladman lifts up his sax, nods at the Orchestral Jazzonions. . . .

Willie: Play the jukebox please, Boet Sam!

Sam: I also only got bus fare, Willie.

Hally: Hold it, everybody. (*Heads for the cash register behind the counter.*) How much is in the till, Sam?

Sam: Three shillings. Hally . . . Your Mom counted it before she left.

(*Hally hesitates.*)

Hally: Sorry, Willie. You know how she carried on the last time I did it. We'll just have to pool our combined imaginations and hope for the best. (*Returns to the table.*) Back to work. How are the points scored, Sam?

Sam: Maximum of ten points each for individual style, deportment, rhythm, and general appearance.

Willie: Must I start?

Hally: Hold it for a second, Willie. And penalties?

Sam: For what?

Hally: For doing something wrong. Say you stumble or bump into somebody . . . do they take off any points?

Sam (*aghast*): Hally . . . !

Hally: When you're dancing. If you and your partner collide into another couple.

(*Hally can get no further. Sam has collapsed with laughter. He explains to Willie.*)

Sam: If me and Miriam bump into you and Hilda. . . .

(*Willie joins him in another good laugh.*)

Hally, Hally . . . !

Hally (*perplexed*): Why? What did I say?

Sam: There's no collisions out there, Hally. Nobody trips or stumbles or bumps into anybody else. That's what that moment is all about. To be one of those finalists on that dance floor is like . . . like being in a dream about a world in which accidents don't happen.

Hally (*genuinely moved by Sam's image*):   Jesus, Sam! That's beautiful!

Willie (*can endure waiting no longer*):   I'm starting!

(*Willie dances while Sam talks.*)

Sam: Of course it is. That's what I've been trying to say to you all afternoon. And it's beautiful because that is what we want life to be like. But instead, like you said, Hally, we're bumping into each other all the time. Look at the three of us this afternoon: I've bumped into Willie, the two of us have bumped into you, you've bumped into your mother, she bumping into your Dad. . . . None of us knows the steps and there's no music playing. And it doesn't stop with us. The whole world is doing it all the time. Open a newspaper and what do you read? America has bumped into Russia, England is bumping into India, rich man bumps into poor man. Those are big collisions, Hally. They make for a lot of bruises. People get hurt in all that bumping, and we're sick and tired of it now. It's been going on for too long. Are we never going to get it right? . . . Learn to dance life like champions instead of always being just a bunch of beginners at it?

Hally (*deep and sincere admiration of the man*):   You've got a vision, Sam!

Sam: Not just me. What I'm saying to you is that everybody's got it. That's why there's only standing room left for the Centenary Hall in two weeks' time. For as long as the music lasts, we are going to see six couples get it right, the way we want life to be.

Hally: But is that the best we can do, Sam . . . watch six finalists dreaming about the way it should be?

Sam: I don't know. But it starts with that. Without the dream we won't know what we're going for. And anyway I reckon there are a few people who have got past just dreaming about it and are trying for something real. Remember that thing we read once in the paper about the Mahatma Gandhi? Going without food to stop those riots in India?

Hally: You're right. He certainly was trying to teach people to get the steps right.

Sam: And the Pope.

Hally: Yes, he's another one. Our old General Smuts° as well, you know. He's also out there dancing. You know, Sam, when you come to think of it, that's what the United Nations boils down to . . . a dancing school for politicians!

Sam: And let's hope they learn.

Hally (*a little surge of hope*):   You're right. We mustn't despair. Maybe there's some hope for mankind after all. Keep it up, Willie. (*Back to his table with determination.*) This is a lot bigger than I thought. So what have we got? Yes, our title: "A World Without Collisions."

General Smuts: (1870-1950), South African statesman who fought the British in the Boer War in 1899, was instrumental in forming the Union of South Africa in 1910, and was active in the creation of the United Nations.

Sam: That sounds good! "A World Without Collisions."

Hally: Subtitle: "Global Politics on the Dance Floor." No. A bit too heavy, hey? What about "Ballroom Dancing as a Political Vision"?

(*The telephone rings. Sam answers it.*)

Sam: St. George's Park Tea Room . . . Yes, Madam . . . Hally, it's your Mom.

Hally (back to reality):   Oh, God, yes! I'd forgotten all about that. Shit! Remember my words, Sam! Just when you're enjoying yourself, someone or something will come along and wreck everything.

Sam: You haven't heard what she's got to say yet.

Hally: Public telephone?

Sam: No.

Hally: Does she sound happy or unhappy?

Sam: I couldn't tell. (*Pause.*) She's waiting, Hally.

Hally (to the telephone):   Hello, Mom . . . No, everything is okay here. Just doing my homework. . . . What's your news? . . . You've what? . . . (*Pause. He takes the receiver away from his ear for a few seconds. In the course of Hally's telephone conversation, Sam and Willie discreetly position the stacked tables and chairs. Hally places the receiver back to his ear.*) Yes, I'm still here. Oh, well, I give up now. Why did you do it, Mom? . . . Well, I just hope you know what you've let us in for. . . . (*Loudly.*) I said I hope you know what you've let us in for! It's the end of the peace and quiet we've been having. (*Softly.*) Where is he? (*Normal voice.*) He can't hear us from in there. But for God's sake, Mom, what happened? I told you to be firm with him. . . . Then you and the nurses should have held him down, taken his crutches away. . . . I know only too well he's my father! . . . I'm not being disrespectful, but I'm sick and tired of emptying stinking chamber pots full of phlegm and piss. . . . Yes, I do! When you're not there, he asks *me* to do it. . . . If you really want to know the truth, that's why I've got no appetite for my food. . . . Yes! There's a lot of things you don't know about. For your information, I still haven't got that science textbook I need. And you know why? He borrowed the money you gave me for it. . . . Because I didn't want to start another fight between you two. . . . He says that every time. . . . All right, Mom! (*Viciously.*) Then just remember to start hiding your bag away again, because he'll be at your purse before long for money for booze. And when he's well enough to come down here, you better keep an eye on the till as well, because that is also going to develop a leak. . . . Then don't complain to me when he starts his old tricks. . . . Yes, you do. I get it from you on one side and from him on the other, and it makes life hell for me. I'm not going to be the peacemaker anymore. I'm warning you now: when the two of you start fighting again, I'm leaving home. . . . Mom, if you start crying, I'm going to put down the receiver. . . . Okay. . . . (*Lowering his voice to a vicious whisper.*) Okay, Mom, I heard you. (*Desperate.*) No. . . . Because I don't want to. I'll see him when I get home! Mom! . . . (*Pause. When he speaks again, his tone changes completely. It is not simply pretense. We sense a genuine emotional conflict.*) Welcome home, chum! . . . What's that? . . . Don't be silly, Dad. You being home is just about the best news in the world. . . . I bet you are. Bloody depressing there with everybody going on about their ailments, hey! . . . How you feeling? . . . Good. . . . Here as well, pal. Coming down cats and dogs. . . . That's right. Just the day for a kip° and a toss in your old Uncle Ned. . . . Everything's just hunky-dory on my side, Dad. . . . Well, to start with, there's a nice pile of comics for you on the counter. . . . Yes, old Kemple brought them in. *Batman and Robin, Submariner* . . . just your cup of tea. . . . I will. . . . Yes, we'll spin a few yarns tonight. . . . Okay, chum, see you in a little while. . . . No, I promise. I'll come straight home. . . . (*Pause—his mother comes back on the phone.*) Mom? Okay. I'll lock up now. . . . What? . . . Oh, the brandy . . . Yes, I'll remember! . . . I'll put it in my suitcase now, for God's sake. I know well enough what will happen if he doesn't get it. . . . (*Places a bottle of brandy on the counter.*) I was kind to him, Mom. I didn't say anything nasty! . . . All right. Bye. (*End of telephone conversation. A desolate Hally doesn't move. A strained silence.*)

Sam (*quietly*): That sounded like a bad bump, Hally.

Hally (*having a hard time controlling his emotions. He speaks carefully*): Mind your own business, Sam.

Sam: Sorry. I wasn't trying to interfere. Shall we carry on? Hally? (*He indicates the exercise book. No response from Hally.*)

Willie (*also trying*): Tell him about when they give out the cups, Boet Sam.

Sam: Ja! That's another big moment. The presentation of the cups after the winners have been announced. You've got to put that in.

(*Still no response from Hally.*)

Willie: A big silver one, Master Hally, called floating trophy for the champions.

Sam: We always invite some big-shot personality to hand them over. Guest of honor this year is going to be His Holiness Bishop Jabulani of the All African Free Zionist Church.

(*Hally gets up abruptly, goes to his table, and tears up the page he was writing on.*)

Hally: So much for a bloody world without collisions.

Sam: Too bad. It was on its way to being a good composition.

Hally: Let's stop bullshitting ourselves, Sam.

kip: Nap.

Sam: Have we been doing that?

Hally: Yes! That's what all our talk about a decent world has been . . . just so much bullshit.

Sam: We did say it was still only a dream.

Hally: And a bloody useless one at that. Life's a fuckup and it's never going to change.

Sam: Ja, maybe that's true.

Hally: There's no maybe about it. It's a blunt and brutal fact. All we've done this afternoon is waste our time.

Sam: Not if we'd got your homework done.

Hally: I don't give a shit about my homework, so, for Christ's sake, just shut up about it. (*Slamming books viciously into his school case.*) Hurry up now and finish your work. I want to lock up and get out of here. (*Pause.*) And then go where? Home-sweet-fucking-home. Jesus, I hate that word.

(*Hally goes to the counter to put the brandy bottle and comics in his school case. After a moment's hesitation, he smashes the bottle of brandy. He abandons all further attempts to hide his feelings. Sam and Willie work away as unobtrusively as possible.*)

Do you want to know what is really wrong with your lovely little dream, Sam? It's not just that we are all bad dancers. That does happen to be perfectly true, but there's more to it than just that. You left out the cripples.

Sam: Hally!

Hally (*now totally reckless*):   Ja! Can't leave them out, Sam. That's why we always end up on our backsides on the dance floor. They're also out there dancing . . . like a bunch of broken spiders trying to do the quickstep! (*An ugly attempt at laughter.*) When you come to think of it, it's a bloody comical sight. I mean, it's bad enough on two legs . . . but one and a pair of crutches! Hell, no, Sam. That's guaranteed to turn that dance floor into a shambles. Why you shaking your head? Picture it, man. For once this afternoon let's use our imaginations sensibly.

Sam: Be careful, Hally.

Hally: Of what? The truth? I seem to be the only one around here who is prepared to face it. We've had the pretty dream, it's time now to wake up and have a good long look at the way things really are. Nobody knows the steps, there's no music, the cripples are also out there tripping up everybody and trying to get into the act, and it's all called the All-Comers-How-to-Make-a-Fuckup-of-Life Championships. (*Another ugly laugh.*) Hang on, Sam! The best bit is still coming. Do you know what the winner's trophy is? A beautiful big chamber pot with roses on the side, and it's full to the brim with piss. And guess who I think is going to be this year's winner.

Sam (*almost shouting*):   Stop now!
Hally (*suddenly appalled by how far he has gone*):   Why?
Sam: Hally? It's your father you're talking about.
Hally: So?
Sam: Do you know what you've been saying?

> (*Hally can't answer. He is rigid with shame. Sam speaks to him sternly.*)

No, Hally, you mustn't do it. Take back those words and ask for forgiveness! It's a terrible sin for a son to mock his father with jokes like that. You'll be punished if you carry on. Your father is your father, even if he is a . . . cripple man.

Willie: Yes, Master Hally. Is true what Sam say.
Sam: I understand how you are feeling, Hally, but even so. . . .
Hally: No, you don't!
Sam: I think I do.
Hally: And I'm telling you you don't. Nobody does. (*Speaking carefully as his shame turns to rage at Sam.*) It's your turn to be careful, Sam. Very careful! You're treading on dangerous ground. Leave me and my father alone.
Sam: I'm not the one who's been saying things about him.
Hally: What goes on between me and my Dad is none of your business!
Sam: Then don't tell me about it. If that's all you've got to say about him, I don't want to hear.

> (*For a moment Hally is at loss for a response.*)

Hally: Just get on with your bloody work and shut up.
Sam: Swearing at me won't help you.
Hally: Yes, it does! Mind your own fucking business and shut up!
Sam: Okay. If that's the way you want it, I'll stop trying.

> (*He turns away. This infuriates Hally even more.*)

Hally: Good. Because what you've been trying to do is meddle in something you know nothing about. All that concerns you in here, Sam, is to try and do what you get paid for—keep the place clean and serve the customers. In plain words, just get on with your job. My mother is right. She's always warning me about allowing you to get too familiar. Well, this time you've gone too far. It's going to stop right now.

> (*No response from Sam.*)

You're only a servant in here, and don't forget it.

> (*Still no response. Hally is trying hard to get one.*)

And as far as my father is concerned, all you need to remember is that he is your boss.

Sam (*needled at last*):   No, he isn't. I get paid by your mother.

Hally: Don't argue with me, Sam!

Sam: Then don't say he's my boss.

Hally: He's a white man and that's good enough for you.

Sam: I'll try to forget you said that.

Hally: Don't! Because you won't be doing me a favor if you do. I'm telling you to remember it.

(*A pause. Sam pulls himself together and makes one last effort.*)

Sam: Hally, Hally . . . ! Come on now. Let's stop before it's too late. You're right. We *are* on dangerous ground. If we're not careful, somebody is going to get hurt.

Hally: It won't be me.

Sam: Don't be so sure.

Hally: I don't know what you're talking about, Sam.

Sam: Yes, you do.

Hally (furious): Jesus, I wish you would stop trying to tell me what I do and what I don't know.

(*Sam gives up. He turns to Willie.*)

Sam: Let's finish up.

Hally: Don't turn your back on me! I haven't finished talking.

(*He grabs Sam by the arm and tries to make him turn around. Sam reacts with a flash of anger.*)

Sam: Don't do that, Hally! (*Facing the boy.*) All right, I'm listening. Well? What do you want to say to me?

Hally (pause as Hally looks for something to say): To begin with, why don't you also start calling me Master Harold, like Willie.

Sam: Do you mean that?

Hally: Why the hell do you think I said it?

Sam: And if I don't?

Hally: You might just lose your job.

Sam (quietly and very carefully): If you make me say it once, I'll never call you anything else again.

Hally: So? (*The boy confronts the man.*) Is that meant to be a threat?

Sam: Just telling you what will happen if you make me do that. You must decide what it means to you.

Hally: Well, I have. It's good news. Because that is exactly what Master Harold wants from now on. Think of it as a little lesson in respect, Sam, that's long overdue, and I hope you remember it as well as you do your geography. I can tell you now that somebody who will be glad to hear I've finally given it to you will be my Dad. Yes! He agrees with my Mom. He's always going on about it as well. "You must teach the boys to show you more respect, my son."

Sam: So now you can stop complaining about going home. Everybody is going to be happy tonight.

Hally: That's perfectly correct. You see, you mustn't get the wrong idea about me and my Dad, Sam. We also have our good times together. Some bloody good laughs. He's got a marvelous sense of humor. Want to know what our favorite joke is? He gives out a big groan, you see, and says: "It's not fair, is it, Hally?" Then I have to ask: "What, chum?" And then he says: "A nigger's arse" . . . and we both have a good laugh.

(*The men stare at him with disbelief.*)

What's the matter, Willie? Don't you catch the joke? You always were a bit slow on the uptake. It's what is called a pun. You see, fair means both light in color and to be just and decent. (*He turns to Sam.*) I thought *you* would catch it, Sam.

Sam: Oh ja, I catch it all right.

Hally: But it doesn't appeal to your sense of humor.

Sam: Do you really laugh?

Hally: Of course.

Sam: To please him? Make him feel good?

Hally: No, for heavens sake! I laugh because I think it's a bloody good joke.

Sam: You're really trying hard to be ugly, aren't you? And why drag poor old Willie into it? He's done nothing to you except show you the respect you want so badly. That's also not being fair, you know . . . and *I* mean just or decent.

Willie: It's all right, Sam. Leave it now.

Sam: It's me you're after. You should just have said "Sam's arse" . . . because that's the one you're trying to kick. Anyway, how do you know it's not fair? You've never seen it. Do you want to? (*He drops his trousers and underpants and presents his backside for Hally's inspection.*) Have a good look. A real Basuto arse . . . which is about as nigger as they can come. Satisfied? (*Trousers up.*) Now you can make your Dad even happier when you go home tonight. Tell him I showed you my arse and he is quite right. It's not fair. And if it will give him an even better laugh next time, I'll also let *him* have a look. Come, Willie, let's finish up and go.

(*Sam and Willie start to tidy up the tea room. Hally doesn't move. He waits for a moment when Sam passes him.*)

Hally (*quietly*): Sam . . .

(*Sam stops and looks expectantly at the boy. Hally spits in his face. A long and heartfelt groan from Willie. For a few seconds Sam doesn't move.*)

Sam (*taking out a handkerchief and wiping his face*): It's all right, Willie.

(*To Hally.*)

Ja, well, you've done it . . . Master Harold. Yes, I'll start calling you that from now on. It won't be difficult anymore. You've hurt yourself,

Master Harold. I saw it coming. I warned you, but you wouldn't listen. You've just hurt yourself *bad*. And you're a coward, Master Harold. The face you should be spitting in is your father's . . . but you used mine, because you think you're safe inside your fair skin . . . and this time I don't mean just or decent. (*Pause, then moving violently toward Hally.*) Should I hit him, Willie?

Willie (*stopping Sam*):   No, Boet Sam.

Sam (*violently*):   Why not?

Willie: It won't help, Boet Sam.

Sam: I don't want to help! I want to hurt him.

Willie: You also hurt yourself.

Sam: And if he had done it to you, Willie?

Willie: Me? Spit at me like I was a dog? (*A thought that had not occurred to him before. He looks at Hally.*) Ja. Then I want to hit him. I want to hit him hard!

(*A dangerous few seconds as the men stand staring at the boy. Willie turns away, shaking his head.*)

But maybe all I do is go cry at the back. He's little boy, Boet Sam. Little *white* boy. Long trousers now, but he's still little boy.

Sam (*his violence ebbing away into defeat as quickly as it flooded*):   You're right. So go on, then: groan again, Willie. You do it better than me. (*To Hally.*) You don't know all of what you've just done . . . Master Harold. It's not just that you've made me feel dirtier than I've ever been in my life . . . I mean, how do I wash off yours and your father's filth? . . . I've also failed. A long time ago I promised myself I was going to try and do something, but you've just shown me . . . Master Harold . . . that I've failed. (*Pause.*) I've also got a memory of a little white boy when he was still wearing short trousers and a black man, but they're not flying a kite. It was the old Jubilee days, after dinner one night. I was in my room. You came in and just stood against the wall, looking down at the ground, and only after I'd asked you what you wanted, what was wrong, I don't know how many times, did you speak and even then so softly I almost didn't hear you. "Sam, please help me to go and fetch my Dad." Remember? He was dead drunk on the floor of the Central Hotel Bar. They'd phoned for your Mom, but you were the only one at home. And do you remember how we did it? You went in first by yourself to ask permission for me to go into the bar. Then I loaded him onto my back like a baby and carried him back to the boarding house with you following behind carrying his crutches. (*Shaking his head as he remembers.*) A crowded Main Street with all the people watching a little white boy following his drunk father on a nigger's back! I felt for that little boy . . . Master Harold. I felt for him. After that we still had to clean him up, remember? He'd messed in his trousers, so we had to clean him up and get him into bed.

Hally (great pain):   I love him, Sam.

Sam: I know you do. That's why I tried to stop you from saying these things about him. It would have been so simple if you could have just despised him for being a weak man. But he's your father. You love him and you're ashamed of him. You're ashamed of so much! . . . And now that's going to include yourself. That was the promise I made to myself: to try and stop that happening. (*Pause.*) After we got him to bed you came back with me to my room and sat in a corner and carried on just looking down at the ground. And for days after that! You hadn't done anything wrong, but you went around as if you owed the world an apology for being alive. I didn't like seeing that! That's not the way a boy grows up to be a man! . . . But the one person who should have been teaching you what that means was the cause of your shame. If you really want to know, that's why I made you that kite. I wanted you to look up, be proud of something, of yourself . . . (*bitter smile at the memory*) . . . and you certainly were that when I left you with it up there on the hill. Oh, ja . . . something else! . . . If you ever do write it as a short story, there *was* a twist in our ending. I couldn't sit down there and stay with you. It was a "Whites Only" bench. You were too young, too excited to notice then. But not anymore. If you're not careful . . . Master Harold . . . you're going to be sitting up there by yourself for a long time to come, and there won't be a kite in the sky. (*Sam has got nothing more to say. He exits into the kitchen, taking off his waiter's jacket.*)

Willie: Is bad. Is all bad in here now.

Hally (books into his school case, raincoat on):   Willie . . . (*It is difficult to speak.*) Will you lock up for me and look after the keys?

Willie: Okay.

(*Sam returns. Hally goes behind the counter and collects the few coins in the cash register. As he starts to leave . . . .*)

Sam: Don't forget the comic books.

(*Hally returns to the counter and puts them in his case. He starts to leave again.*)

Sam (to the retreating back of the boy):   Stop . . . Hally. . . .

(*Hally stops, but doesn't turn to face him.*)

Hally . . . I've got no right to tell you what being a man means if I don't behave like one myself, and I'm not doing so well at that this afternoon. Should we try again, Hally?

Hally: Try what?

Sam: Fly another kite, I suppose. It worked once, and this time I need it as much as you do.

Hally: It's still raining, Sam. You can't fly kites on rainy days, remember.

Sam: So what do we do? Hope for better weather tomorrow?

Hally (*helpless gesture*):   I don't know. I don't know anything anymore.

Sam: You sure of that, Hally? Because it would be pretty hopeless if that
was true. It would mean nothing has been learnt in here this
afternoon, and there was a hell of a lot of teaching going on . . . one
way or the other. But anyway, I don't believe you. I reckon there's
one thing you know. You don't *have* to sit up there by yourself. You
know what that bench means now, and you can leave it any time you
choose. All you've got to do is stand up and walk away from it.

(*Hally leaves. Willie goes up quietly to Sam.*)

Wilie: Is okay, Boet Sam. You see. Is . . . (*he can't find any better words*)
. . . is going to be okay tomorrow. (*Changing his tone.*) Hey, Boet
Sam! (*He is trying hard.*) You right. I think about it and you right.
Tonight I find Hilda and say sorry. And make promise I won't beat
her no more. You hear me, Boet Sam?

Sam: I hear you, Willie.

Willie: And when we practice I relax and romance with her from
beginning to end. Nonstop! You watch! Two weeks' time: "First
prize for promising newcomers: Mr. Willie Malopo and Miss Hilda
Samuels." (*Sudden impulse.*) To hell with it! I walk home. (*He goes to
the jukebox, puts in a coin and selects a record. The machine comes to life
in the gray twilight, blushing its way through a spectrum of soft, romantic
colors.*) How did you say it, Boet Sam? Let's dream. (*Willie sways with
the music and gestures for Sam to dance.*)

(*Sarah Vaughan sings.*)

"Little man you're crying,
I know why you're blue,
Someone took your kiddy car away;
Better go to sleep now,
Little man you've had a busy day." (*etc., etc.*) You lead. I follow.

(*The men dance together.*)

"Johnny won your marbles,
Tell you what we'll do;
Dad will get you new ones right away; Better go to sleep now,
Little man you've had a busy day."

Questions for close reading

1. Describe the setting, "St. George's Park Tea Room." Who was St.
   George?
2. What do we learn about Sam and Willie early in the play?
3. What kind of dances does Willie rehearse? Why?
4. What is the difference between Willie's attitude toward Hilda Samuels at
   the beginning of the play and his attitude at the end?

5. What differences between Willie and Sam and Hally seem most important?
6. How does Hally treat his father? What do we know about his father?
7. What is Sam reading from the history book?
8. What is Hally learning in school? Did Willie and Sam learn the same things?
9. What was Hally doing hiding in Willie's room when he was little?
10. What games do Hally and Willie play? Why don't they play chess?
11. When does Hally become most irritated at Sam?
12. What is the difference between Sam's and Willie's reaction to Hally's insults?
13. What are Hally's insults? What does he say that hurts Sam? How do his insults alter their relationship?
14. Why does Sam want to fly a kite at the end of the play?

Questions for interpretation

1. Hally's attitudes toward his mother and father are quite different. Is the difference significant? Given the nature of the play, what importance should we place on the fact that women are talked about but not present in the action?
2. Why does Willie place so much importance on the upcoming dance which he is rehearsing for? What significance could dancing have for the overall drama? Is dancing symbolic of another kind of activity?
3. Sam taught Hally how to fly a kite properly. Why does Hally describe the action in such detail in the middle of the play? Is flying a kite a symbol of a larger action? The entire issue is raised again at the end of the play. Why?
4. What is the significance of Hally's always beating Willie at games? They explore the reasons for his winning; why does Fugard emphasize the issue?
5. Compare the three characters for evidence of selfishness in any of them. Who seems most selfish in the play? What does selfishness have to do with the main action of the drama?
6. To what extent is Hally's attitude toward his father similar to his attitude toward Willie and Sam? Are Willie and Sam portrayed as substitute fathers? What has been their relation to Hally since Hally's childhood?
7. Hally's anger at Sam and Willie erupts when Sam tries to tell Hally that he should be more respectful of his father. Why does Hally become so angry? Why does he challenge Sam by telling him to remember he is only a servant? A profound change takes place when Hally says, "You're only a servant in here, and don't forget it." What are the implications of Hally's demanding to be called Master Harold? Is his behavior racist? Is his behavior marked by a class distinction?
8. Should Sam have hit Hally at the end of the play? Why does Willie hold him back? Would it have been just to hit Hally?
9. How do you interpret the ending of the play? To what extent is the future hopeful? To what extent is it hopeless?

10

Elements of Drama

Some elements of drama, such as plot, characterization, setting, dialogue, and theme, overlap those of short fiction. Others, such as stage directions, are specific to drama. In certain kinds of plays specific elements may dominate. In plays such as Woody Allen's *Death Knocks*, the plot is more important than character, but in tragedies such as *Hamlet*, character shares importance with plot. In some plays scenery dominates, although such plays are rarely significant enough to study. In most good plays the elements balance one another. We will focus on seven elements of drama.

PLOT

The **plot** of a play is the pattern of the characters' actions. Tragedies and tragicomedies usually have a single plot with a beginning, middle, and end. Not all plays follow this pattern, but most tragedies begin by introducing the characters with an **exposition** of previous action that reveals their current circumstances. The **rising action** introduces the **conflict**: the problems that must be solved or the trials that must be faced. The rising action in *Hamlet* begins with the appearance of the ghost, and the **exciting force** is the ghost's revelation that he has been murdered and that Hamlet must avenge him. The middle of the drama includes the conflicts facing the hero. Among them in *Hamlet* are Hamlet's mixed feelings regarding his mother, Claudius's attempt to get Hamlet to stop mourning his father, the plot to spy on Hamlet, and Hamlet's own efforts to discover the truth about his father's death. All of these constitute the rising action, the period in which the hero is in ascendancy.

The **falling action** includes the elements of the plot in which the hero moves steadily toward the inevitable conclusion. The **climax** occurs when the forces of the hero and the antagonist meet head-on. In some plays it occurs simultaneously with the **crisis**, the moment in which the rising action changes to the falling action. In *Hamlet* the climax occurs when Hamlet forces Claudius's hand during the play-within-a-play scene and Claudius rises in guilt at watching an enactment of the murder of Gonzago. The crisis, or falling action, begins when Hamlet erroneously kills Polonius. He was within reach of achieving his end of avenging his father, but after the death of Polonius and the entrance of Rosencrantz and Guildenstern, he suffers a **reversal** (**peripeteia**), when his fortunes change. The coincidence of climax, crisis, and reversal all within a short space of time builds great dramatic tension into the middle of the play.

The **conclusion** includes the remaining falling action. In *Hamlet*, Hamlet returns to face Laertes, Polonius's son bent on revenge for his own father's death. Eventually he faces Laertes in a rigged duel, kills both Laertes and Claudius, watches his mother die from poison, and then dies himself. This section of the play is called the **denouement**, which means an untying or unraveling. One description of a dramatic plot is the tying of a knot: the beginning and middle of the play tie things into knots; the denouement unties the knot or unravels the plot. In a tragedy, the denouement is often called the **catastrophe**.

In comedy, many of the same plot details apply. For example, the concept of a plot as a knot tied and then untied is common in comedy. The rising action often accompanies a misunderstanding or a mix-up in identities. One common pattern, especially in romantic comedies, is that of young, worthy lovers frustrated in their desire for marriage by **blocking characters**, usually parents, stepparents, or guardians. The action thwarts the blocking characters by revealing their weaknesses or by revealing the true identities of the prospective lovers. The denouement usually includes a marriage or several marriages.

Many of these plot elements are at work in tragicomedies as well, as in Marsha Norman's *Getting Out*. In this play, a simple dramatic device establishes the most important exposition: the warden's voice in a blackout (the stage totally lightless) announces the release of Arlene Holsclaw and reveals her crime to the audience. She has murdered a cab driver eight or more years earlier, so we know she has been in the Pine Ridge prison ever since. We are told that she has been "rehabilitated," so there has been a significant change in her: She is no longer "Arlie"—the person Arlene was when she was young: "Arlie girl landed herself in prison. Arlene is out, O.K.?" Some exposition is also handled by this character Arlie, who tells the story of how she got a little boy's collection of frogs and threw them one by one at passing cars. Her amusement at this carnage tells us a great deal about her character. It also establishes the necessary suspense to make you wonder what will happen in the rest of the drama. Thus the beginning establishes that the conflict is between Arlie, the outlaw she was, and Arlene, the woman she now is.

The middle of the play produces the rising action, the movement toward a moment of great dramatic tension. When the tension reaches its greatest point the drama reaches its climax, when, in a sense, there is a showdown, usually between the protagonist—in this case Arlene—and the antagonist—Arlie. The climax occurs when Arlene realizes she should not do what the chaplain at the prison told her: kill Arlie, her "hateful self." After a hysterical moment, she realizes she must learn to accept and control Arlie, not kill her. Once she reaches this point in the drama, the falling action begins, leading to its final resolution.

CHARACTERIZATION

Characterization is the creation of the persons of the drama, such as Hamlet in *Hamlet* or Willy Loman in *Death of a Salesman*. Characterization is achieved through several methods. In some plays the exposition establishes character through dialogue—speech between two or more characters that describes one of them or an absent character. Often several minor players perform this function, such as the daughters speaking about Maurya in *Riders to the Sea*. Another way is through a soliloquy, a speech by a character alone on stage that describes himself or herself. The unseen voice in the beginning of Marsha Norman's *Getting Out* is yet another approach. But character can also be revealed gradually through dialogue and action. This is the method chosen by Henrik Ibsen in *A Doll House* and *Hedda Gabler*. Nora Helmer and Hedda Gabler are characterized largely by the way they conduct themselves and interact with others.

Getting Out provides interesting problems of characterization. The most important is the split of Arlie and Arlene. If you do not read the note Marsha Norman appends to the play explaining that Arlie is Arlene's younger self, you will take some time to figure it out. Theater audiences do figure it out relatively quickly, but in the meantime the confusion is productive because it demands intense involvement with the characters. Thus Marsha Norman has created a powerful dramatic innovation in placing both Arlie and Arlene on stage at the same time and even permitting the two to interact and speak with each other.

As in fiction, drama depends on **flat characters**—those who are only developed minimally and who behave predictably—and **round characters**—those who are fleshed out and fully developed. In *Getting Out* Arlie and Arlene are both round characters. They are complex, many-sided, and not totally predictable. Carl, on the other hand, is relatively flat and obvious in his attitudes and his needs. **Type characters** (also called **stock characters**), such as the Doctor, the Warden, and even Arlene's Mother, behave true to their type, or what we expect of them. See "Types, Stereotypes, and Archetypes" (p. 1678) for more on such methods of characterization.

SETTING

The **setting** of the play includes the scenery, the time of the action, and the props. Some settings are very simple, such as the living room of Nat Ackerman in *Death Knocks* or the simple cottage room of Maurya and her daughters in *Riders to the Sea*. In *Getting Out* the setting is complicated (see Figure 10–1). Downstage right (the audience's left) is an area set up as a cell, with a cot. Downstage center is an area that is Arlene's bedroom. Upstage rear is a kitchen, with stove, refrigerator, closet, and chair. Stage left is reserved for an institution door and hall and an institution table with two chairs. The props include the kitchen appliances, the beds, the chairs, and many other details that would be expected in the environments established by the setting. The setting of *Getting Out* works as well as it does primarily because the lighting can be controlled to illuminate various areas independently. In plays produced before the late nineteenth century, such effects were impossible. However, Shakespeare overcame the problems of lighting—and sometimes the absence of props and elaborate furniture—by having the audience use its imagination. Shakespeare's dialogue would reveal the setting if it had not been otherwise established. However, modern editors of Shakespeare, lacking the visual clues supplied to Shakespeare's audience by costumes, gestures, and instruments such as burning torches (indicating it is night), cannot always be sure where certain scenes take place. Shakespeare's stage directions are few and rudimentary.

DIALOGUE

Dialogue is the conversation or speech of two or more characters. Since a drama is a story told in dialogue, the playwright's choices for dialogue are critical to the success of the drama. Dialogue has several tasks in a play: (1) to advance the action of the drama in a natural way, (2) to embody the ideas or theme of the play without sending a blatant "message" to the audience, (3) to reveal the personality of each character, (4) to vary with each character so as to preserve the character's individuality, and (5) to resemble normal speech between persons so as to preserve the illusion of reality.

Some dialogue consists of rapid exchanges, such as those between Bennie and Arlene in *Getting Out*. But some dialogue can be extensive, such as Arlie's description of childhood in the beginning of the play and Arlene's reflections at the end, when she tells of stabbing herself with a fork in order to kill the Arlie in her. In some plays the dialogue resembles everyday speech, as in *Getting Out* and *Death Knocks*, but in many poetic dramas, such as *Oedipus Rex* and *Hamlet*, the dialogue avoids the conversational and aims at a more formal effect. Long passages of dialogue sometimes contain the philosophical parts of the play, as in the ending speeches of Maurya in *Riders to the Sea*.

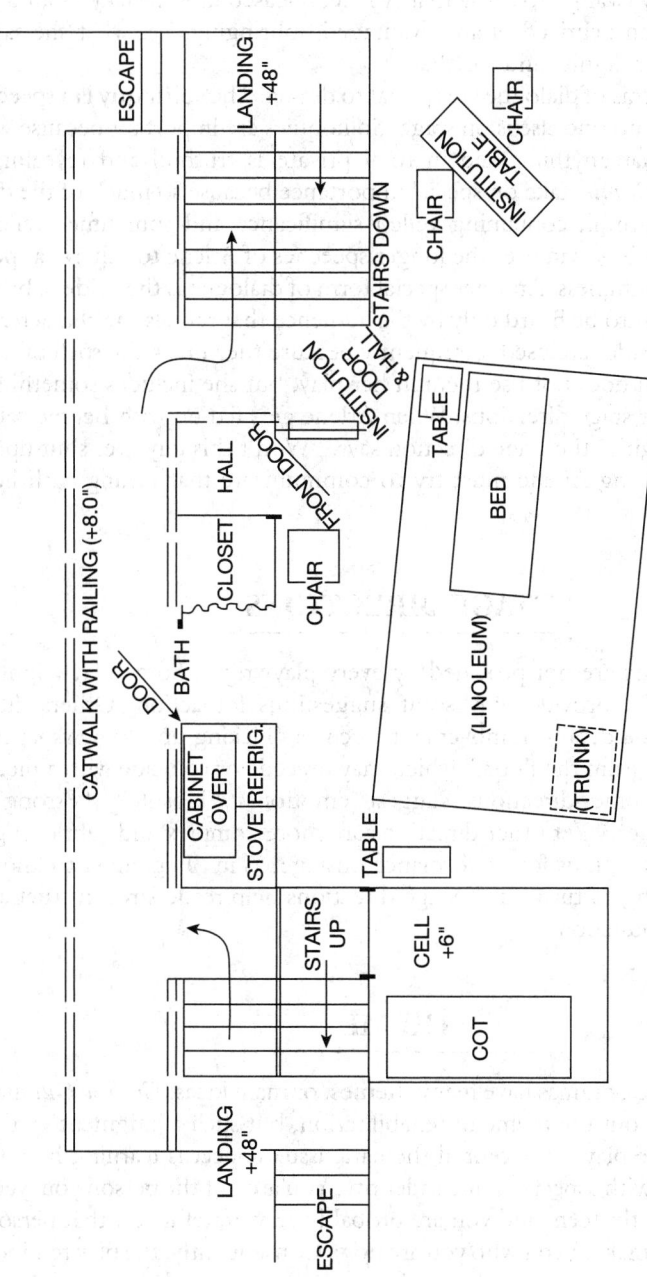

Figure 10-1   Scene Design for *Getting Out*

Dialogue reveals character. In *Getting Out* it is supposed to be delivered with "a country twang" to show that Arlene, released in Kentucky, is an uneducated woman deprived of an advantaged upbringing. Yet what she says also projects her dignity and worth.

Certain forms of dialogue are special to drama. The **soliloquy** is a speech delivered while no one else is on stage. Soliloquies are important because we may assume that anything said in total private is truthful and revealing. Soliloquies in *Hamlet* take on special importance because so much of the dialogue is untruthful, containing veiled significance and sometimes veiled threats. Marsha Norman uses the longer speeches of Arlene to achieve a special level of truthfulness. Another special form of dialogue is the **aside**, a brief comment meant to be heard only by the audience that reveals the character's true feelings. Asides are used infrequently because they break the spell of the drama. Norman does not use them in her play, but she includes something like them in her stage directions. When Arlene gets fed up with Bennie calling her "Arlie girl," the stage direction says, "Won't this guy ever shut up?" The actress playing Arlene must try to communicate that feeling with her gesture.

STAGE DIRECTIONS

Stage directions are not provided by every playwright. Some playwrights, like Shakespeare, provide only scant suggestions for action. Others, like Norman, provide details of movement, such as "Picking up old newspapers and other trash from the floor," which may precede or coincide with a piece of dialogue. Some directions suggest emotions: "Hostile"; "Strong"; "Increasing anger." Yet other directions are more complex and subtle, suggesting difficult actions for performance onstage, as in "Beginning to know how this is going to turn out." Stage directions help readers reconstruct an imaginative production.

THEME

Like short stories, dramas have many **themes**, or main ideas. *Getting Out* may be said to be about the theme of rehabilitation, but such a judgment would oversimplify the play. One central thematic issue concerns learning how to come to terms with aspects of one's identity. You are not the person you were when you were thirteen, and you are probably very grateful. Yet that person contributed to making you who you are now. Consequently, the play reminds us of the problems everyone has with integrating the elements of personality. Arlene's efforts to kill her former self were misdirected. When the play ends, we feel she is on the right road to making herself whole. Perhaps it is also fair to say that one theme of the play concerns the fragmentation of personality over moral issues, such as crime. Some people report a darker self, a criminal self lurking below the surface. *Getting Out* describes one way of exorcising that dark self.

STYLE

Dramas can use numerous **styles**, ways of presenting their material. Aristotle said that drama was mimetic, by which he meant that it mirrored life and gave us insight into who we are. Realistic approaches to mimesis depend on answering the expectations of probability: people are expected to behave as they do in life, with all the limitations we assume are normal. Characters are human, not immortal; they do not become invisible or defy gravity; they often work for a living; they often live in environments much like our own and conduct their lives as the audience does. What the characters do in John Guare's *Six Degrees of Separation* is quite recognizable as "normal," despite the action's improbability. Indeed, the play is based on a story that actually happened in a manner similar to the way it happens in the play. But the style of presentation—with characters stepping into lighted areas to "speak" on the phone—moves toward fantasy and temporarily breaks the realistic tone. Expressionist plays take liberties with the limitations of realism and play against it, as Woody Allen does in *Death Knocks* by presenting Death as a character, and as Marsha Norman does in *Getting Out* by presenting the same character simultaneously as a mature woman and a young girl. In some ways Manuel Puig's *Kiss of the Spider Woman* combines both realism and expressionism.

Realism

The primary style of modern drama is probably best described as **realism**: the action is kept faithful to events that are probable. The details of everyday activity in *Getting Out* are extremely probable and realistic, so much so that they are also "naturalistic." The term **naturalism**, applied to some of Strindberg's plays, was meant to suggest a realism that included sordid details of life that plays such as *Hedda Gabler*, *The Cherry Orchard*, or *Death of a Salesman* would leave out. The coarse language Arlene and Arlie use, for example, is a detail of naturalism. People do, indeed, speak with such expletives, especially if they have been in prison.

Expressionism

Expressionism depends on nonrealistic details, settings, or situations to express an emotional value or to intensify an emotional effect. When Norman places Arlie and Arlene onstage simultaneously, she is being expressionistic. Such a situation cannot exist in a normal environment—it is unrealistic. In

Hamlet, the ghost of Hamlet's father actually appears onstage and eventually speaks to Hamlet. Witches appear in *Macbeth*, and the dead return in *Richard III*. Such events were outside the bounds of realism even in 1600. To be sure, some audiences in the seventeenth century believed in ghosts—some people still do—but in general this detail is expressionistic: it breaks the bounds of naturalism for effect. When Maurya returns from the well explaining that she saw Michael and Bartley, and Michael with new shoes on him, she reports seeing not just one, but two ghosts. That detail, however, happens offstage, so its expressionistic value is much limited.

Getting Out is useful to examine in relation to style because it encompasses realism and expressionism simultaneously. We witness a detailed psychological study of Arlene's efforts to return to society and not be sidetracked by Carl, who would have her go back to a life of crime, or be compromised by Arlie, the self she was before she went to prison and whom she has now grown out of. But the play also switches back and forth in time, something impossible in life. It is also impossible in life to have two aspects of one character speak to each other. Yet, the details and actions of the scenes are extremely realistic, even naturalistic in that the seamy side of prison life is clearly portrayed.

Style: A Realistic and Expressionistic Play

Marsha Norman (b. 1947), a Pulitzer Prize winner, is among the most successful of contemporary American playwrights. She grew up in Kentucky and eventually worked in Kentucky schools and in a hospital in Atlanta. In a program for gifted students in Kentucky, she began to develop some insight into her own loneliness as a gifted child in a regular school program in Kentucky. She began working in media and the arts and eventually became involved in the Actors Theatre of Louisville, Kentucky. In 1977 her first play, *Getting Out*, produced originally at the Actors Theatre, was brought to New York, where it played for almost two hundred fifty performances. It was called "one of the prides of off-Broadway." Since that time Marsha Norman has produced some one-act plays, including *The Laundromat*, and three full-length plays, and she won the Pulitzer Prize for *'night, Mother* (1983). She has also written for television and screen and has published a novel, *The Fortune Teller* (1987).

Marsha Norman   (b. 1947)
    GETTING OUT   1977

Characters
    Arlene, a thin, drawn woman in her late twenties, who has just served
    an eight-year prison term for murder

Arlie, Arlene at various times earlier in her life
Bennie, an Alabama prison guard in his fifties
Evans, a prison guard
Doctor, a psychiatrist in a juvenile institution
Caldwell, a prison guard
Mother, Arlene's mother
School Principal
Ronnie, a teenager in a juvenile institution
Carl, Arlene's former pimp and partner in various crimes, in his late twenties
Warden, Superintendent of Pine Ridge Correctional Institute for Women
Ruby, Arlene's upstairs neighbor, a cook in a diner, also an ex-con, in her late thirties

(*Scene: Both acts are set in a dingy one-room apartment in a run-down section of downtown Louisville, Kentucky. There is a twin bed and one chair. There is a sink, an apartment-size combination stove and refrigerator, and a counter with cabinets above. Dirty curtains conceal the bars on the outside of the single window. There is one closet and a door to the bathroom. The door to the apartment opens into a hall.*)
(*A catwalk stretches above the apartment and a prison cell, Stage Right, connects to it by stairways. An apron Downstage and Stage Left completes the enclosure of the apartment in playing areas for the past. The apartment must seem imprisoned.*)

NOTES

Arlie is the violent kid Arlene was until her last stretch in prison. She may walk through the apartment quite freely, but no one there will acknowledge her presence. Most of her scenes take place in the prison areas.

Arlie, in a sense, is Arlene's memory of herself, called up by fears, needs and even simple word cues. The memory haunts, attacks and warns. But mainly, the memory will not go away.

Arlie's life should be as vivid as Arlene's, if not as continuous. There must be hints in both physical type and gesture that Arlie and Arlene are the same person, though seen at different times in her life. They both speak with a country twang, but Arlene is suspicious and guarded, withdrawal is always a possibility. Arlie is unpredictable and incorrigible. The change seen in Arlie during the second act represents a movement toward the adult Arlene, but the transition should never be complete. Only in the final scene are they enjoyably aware of each other.

The life in the prison "surround" needs to convince without distracting. The guards do not belong to any specific institution, but rather, to all the places where Arlene has done time.

MARSHA NORMAN

OVER LOUDSPEAKER—BEFORE ACT I CURTAIN

(These announcements will be broadcast beginning 5 minutes before the house lights come down for Act I. A woman's voice is preferred; a droning loudspeaker tone is essential.)

Kitchen workers, all kitchen workers report immediately to the kitchen. Kitchen workers to the kitchen. The library will not be open today. Those scheduled for book check-out should remain in morning work assignments. Kitchen workers to the kitchen. No library hours today. Library hours resume tomorrow as usual. All kitchen workers to the kitchen.

Frances Mills, you have a visitor at the front gate. All residents and staff, all residents and staff . . . Do not, repeat, Do not, walk on the front lawn today or use the picnic tables on the front lawn during your break after lunch or dinner.

Your attention please. The exercise class for Dorm A residents has been cancelled. Mrs. Fischer should be back at work in another month. She thanks you for your cards and wants all her girls to know she had an 8 pound baby girl.

Doris Creech, see Mrs. Adams at the library before lunch. Frances Mills, you have a visitor at the front gate. The Women's Associates' picnic for the beauty school class has been postponed until Friday. As picnic lunches have already been prepared, any beauty school member who so wishes, may pick up a picnic lunch and eat it at her assigned lunch table during the regular lunch period.

Frances Mills, you have a visitor at the front gate. Doris Creech to see Mrs. Adams at the library before lunch. I'm sorry, that's Frankie Hill, you have a visitor at the front gate. Repeat, Frankie Hill, not Frances Mills, you have a visitor at the front gate.

ACT I

(The warden's voice on tape is heard in the blackout.)

Warden's Voice: The Alabama State Parole Board hereby grants parole to Holsclaw, Arlene, subject having served eight years at Pine Ridge Correctional Institute for the second degree murder of a cab driver in conjunction with a filling station robbery involving attempted kidnapping of attendant. Crime occurred during escape from Lakewood State Prison where subject Holsclaw was serving three years for forgery and prostitution. Extensive juvenile records from the state of Kentucky appended hereto. (*As Warden continues, light comes up on Arlene, walking around the cell, waiting to be picked up for the ride home. Arlie is visible, bust just barely,* D.C.° *Warden's voice, continuing.*) Subject now considered completely rehabilitated is returned to Kentucky under interstate parole agreement in consideration of family residence and appropriate support personnel in

---

D.C.: Downstage center. *D.R.* is downstage right, and so on.

the area. Subject will remain under the supervision of Kentucky parole officers for a period of five years. Prospects for successful integration into community rated good. Psychological evaluation, institutional history and health records attached in Appendix C, this document.

Bennie's Voice: Arlie! (*Arlene leaves the cell, light comes up on Arlie, seated D.C. She tells this story rather simply. She enjoys it, but its horror is not lost on her. She may be doing some semi-absorbing activity such as painting her toenails.*)

Arlie: So, there was this little kid, see, this creepy little fucker next door. Had glasses an somethin wrong with his foot. I don't know, seven, maybe. Anyhow, ever time his daddy went fishin, he'd bring this kid back some frogs. They built this little fence around em in the back yard like they was pets or somethin. An we'd try to go over an see em but he'd start screamin to his mother to come out an git rid of us. Real snotty like. So we got sick of him bein such a goody-goody an one night me an June snuck over there an put all his dumb of frogs in this sack. You never heared such a fuss. (*Makes croaking sounds.*) Slimy bastards, frogs. We was plannin to let em go all over the place, but when they started jumpin an all, we just figured they was askin for it. So, we taken em out front to the porch an we throwed em, one at a time, into the street. (*Laughs.*) Some of em hit cars goin by but most of em jus got squashed, you know, runned over? It was great, seein how far we could throw em, over back of our backs an under our legs an God, it was really fun watchin em fly through the air then SPLAT (*claps hands*) all over somebody's car window or somethin. Then the next day, we was waitin and this little kid comes out in his back yard lookin for his stupid frogs and he don't see any an he gets so crazy, cryin and everything. So me an June goes over an tells him we seen this big mess out in the street, an he goes out an sees all them frogs legs and bodies an shit all over the everwhere, an, man, it was so funny. We bout killed ourselves laughin. Then his mother come out and she wouldn't let him go out an pick up all the pieces, so he jus had to stand there watchin all the cars go by smush his little babies right into the street. I's gonna run out an git him a frog's head, but June yellin at me "Arlie, git over here fore some car slips on them frog guts an crashes into you." (*Pause.*) I never had so much fun in one day in my whole life. (*Arlie will remain seated as Arlene enters the apartment. It is late evening. Two sets of footsteps are heard coming up the stairs. Arlene opens the door and walks into the room. She stands still, surveying the littered apartment. Bennie is heard dragging a heavy trunk up the stairs. Bennie is wearing his guard uniform. He is a heavy man, but obviously used to physical work.*)

Bennie (from outside):   Arlie?

Arlene: Arlene.

Bennie: Arlene? (*Bringing the trunk just inside the door.*)

Arlene: Leave it. I'll git it later.

Bennie: Oh, now, let me bring it in for you. You ain't as strong as you was.

Arlene: I ain't as mean as I was. I'm strong as ever. You go on now. (*Beginning to walk around the room.*)

Arlie (irritated, as though someone is calling her): Lay off! (*Gets up and walks past Bennie.*)

Bennie (scoots the trunk into the room a little further): Go on where, Arlie?

Arlene: I don't know where. How'd I know where you'd be goin?

Bennie: I can't go til I know you're gonna do all right.

Arlene: Look, I'm gonna do all right. I done all right before Pine Ridge, an I done all right at Pine Ridge. An I'm gonna do all right here.

Bennie: But you don't know nobody. I mean, nobody nice.

Arlene: Lay off.

Bennie: Nobody to take care of you.

Arlene (picking up old newspapers and other trash from the floor): I kin take care of myself. I been doin it long enough.

Bennie: Sure you have, an you landed yourself in prison doin it, Arlie girl.

Arlene (wheels around, won't this guy ever shut up?): Arlie girl landed herself in prison. Arlene is out, O.K.?

Bennie: Hey, now, I know we said we wasn't gonna say nuthin about that, but I been lookin after you for a long time. I been watchin you eat your dinner for eight years now. I got used to it, you know?

Arlene: Well, you kin jus' git unused to it.

Bennie: Then why'd you ask me to drive you all the way up here?

Arlene: I didn't, now. That was all your big ideal.

Bennie: And what were you gonna do? Ride the bus, pick up some soldier, git yourself in another mess of trouble?

Arlie (struts back into the apartment from the closet door, going over as if to a soldier sitting at a bar): O.K., who's gonna buy me a beer?

Arlene: You oughta go by Fort Knox on your way home.

Arlie: Fuckin soldiers, don't care where they get theirself drunk. (*Stops.*)

Arlene: You'd like it.

Arlie: Well, Arlie girl, take your pick.

Arlene: They got tanks right out on the grass to look at.

Arlie (now appears to lean on a bar rail): You git that haircut today, honey?

Bennie: I just didn't want you given your 20 dollars the warden gave you to the first pusher you come across. (*Arlie laughs.*)

Arlene: That's what you think I been waitin for? (*A guard appears and motions for Arlie to follow him.*)

Arlie: Yeah! I heard ya. (*The guard "escorts" Arlie to the cell and slams the door.*)

Bennie: But God Almighty, I hate to think what you'd done to the first ol bugger tried to make you in that bus station. You got grit, Arlie girl. I gotta credit you for that.

Arlie (from the cell, as she dumps a plate of food on the floor): Officer!

Bennie: The screamin you'd do. Wake the dead.

Arlene: Uh-huh.

Bennie: An there ain't nobody can beat you for throwin plates. (*Proudly.*)

Arlie: Are you gonna clean up this shit or do I have to sit here and look at it til I vomit? (*As the guard comes in to clean it up.*)

Bennie: Listen, ever prison in Alabama's usin' plastic forks now on account of what you done.

Arlene: You can quit talkin' just any time now.

Arlie: Some life you got, fatso. Bringin me my dinner then wipin it off the walls. (*Laughs.*)

Bennie: Some of them officers was pretty leery of you. Even the chaplain.

Arlene: No he wasn't either.

Bennie: Not me, though. You was just wild, that's all.

Arlene: Animals is wild, not people. That's what he said.

Arlie (mocking): Good behavior, good behavior. Shit.

Bennie: Now what could that four-eyes chaplain know about wild? (*Arlene looks up sharply.*) O.K. Not wild, then . . .

Arlie: I kin git outta here anytime I want. (*Leaves the cell.*)

Bennie: But you got grit, Arlie.

Arlene: I have said for you to call me Arlene.

Bennie: O.K. O.K.

Arlene: Huh?

Bennie: Don't git riled. You want me to call you Arlene, then Arlene it is. Yes Ma'am. Now, (*slapping the trunk*) where do you want this? (*No response.*) Arlene, I said, where do you want this trunk?

Arlene: I don't care. (*Bennie starts to put it at the foot of the bed. Arlene sees him.*) No! (*Then calmer.*) I seen it there too long. (*Bennie is understandably irritated.*) Maybe over here. (*Points to a spot near the window.*) I could put a cloth on it and sit an look out the . . . (*She pulls the curtains apart, sees the bars on the window.*) What's these bars doin here?

Bennie (stops moving the trunk): I think they're to keep out burglars, you know. (*Sits on the trunk.*)

Arlene: Yeah, I know.

Arlie (appearing on the catwalk, as if stopped during a break-in): We ain't breakin in, cop, we're just admirin this beautiful window.

Arlene: I don't want them there. Pull them out.

Bennie: You can't go tearin up the place, Arlene. Landlord wouldn't like it.

Arlie (to the unseen policeman): Maybe I got a brick in my hand and maybe I don't.

Bennie: Not one bit.

Arlie: An I'm standin on this garbage can because I like to, all right?

Arlene: I ain't gonna let no landlord tell me what to do. (*Fairly strong, walking back toward him.*)

Bennie: The landlord owns the building. You gotta do what he says or he'll throw you out right on your pretty little *behind*. (*Gives her a familiar pat.*)

Arlene (slaps his hand away):   You watch your mouth. I won't have no dirty talk.

Arlie: Just shut the fuck up, cop! Go bust a wino or somethin. (*Returns to the cell.*)

Arlene: Here, put the trunk over here. (*Points* D.R.)

Bennie: What you got in here, anyhow? Rocks? Rocks from the rock pile? (*Carrying the trunk over to the spot she has picked.*)

Arlene: That ain't funny.

Bennie: Oh sweetie, I didn't mean nuthin by that.

Arlene: And I ain't your sweetie.

Bennie: We really did have us a rock pile, you know, at the old Men's Prison, yes we did. And those boys, time they did nine or ten years carryin' rocks around, they was pret-ty mean, I'm here to tell you. And strong? God.

Arlene: Well, what did you expect? (*Beginning to unpack the trunk.*)

Bennie: You're tellin' me. It was dumb, I kept tellin the warden that. They coulda killed us all, easy, any time, that outfit. Except, we did have the guns.

Arlene: Uh-huh.

Bennie: One old bastard sailed a throwin-rock at me one day, woulda took my eye out if I hadn't turned around just then. Still got the scar, see? (*Reaches up to the back of his head.*)

Arlene: You shoot him?

Bennie: Nope. Somebody else did. I forget who. Hey! (*Walking over to the window.*) These bars won't be so bad. Maybe you could get you some plants so's you don't even see them. Yeah, plants'd do it up just fine. Just fine.

Arlene (pulls a cheaply framed picture of Jesus out of the trunk):   Chaplain give me this.

Bennie: He got it for free, I bet.

Arlene: Now, look here. That chaplain was good to me, so you can shut up about him.

Bennie: Fine. Fine. (*Backing down.*)

Arlene: Here. (*Handing him the picture.*) You might as well be useful 'fore you go.

Bennie: Where you want it?

Arlene: Don't matter.

Bennie: Course it matters. Wouldn't want me puttin it inside the closet, would you? You gotta make decisions now, Arlene. Gotta decide things.

Arlene: I don't care.

Bennie (insisting):   Arlene.

Arlene: There. (*Pointing to a prominent position on the apartment wall,* c.)

Bennie: Yeah. Good place. See it first thing when you get up. (*Arlene lights a cigarette, as Arlie retrieves a hidden lighter from the toilet in the cell.*)

Arlie: There's ways . . . gettin outta bars . . . (*Appears to light a fire in the cell, catching her blouse on fire too.*)

Bennie (as Arlie is lighting the fire): This ol nail's pretty loose. I'll find something better to hang it with . . . somewhere or other . . .

Arlie (screams and the Doctor runs toward her, getting the attention of Evans, a guard who has been goofing off on the catwalk): Let me outta here! There's a fuckin fire in here! (*Doctor arrives at the cell, pats his pockets as if looking for the keys.*) Officer!

Doctor: Guard! (*Guard begins his run to the cell.*)

Arlie: It's burnin me!

Doctor: Hurry!

Guard-Evans: I'm comin! I'm comin!

Doctor: What the hell were you . . .

Guard-Evans: Come on, come on. (*Fumbling for the right key.*)

Doctor: For Chrissake! (*Urgent. Guard gets the door open, they rush in. Doctor, wrestling Arlie to the ground, opens his bag.*) Lay still, dammit. (*Arlie collapses, Doctor may appear to give an injection.*) Ow! (*Grabbing his hand.*)

Guard-Evans (lifting Arlie up to the bed): Get bit, Doc?

Doctor: You going to let her burn this place down before you start payin attention up there?

Guard-Evans: (*walks to the toilet, feels under the rim*): Uh-huh.

Bennie: There, that what you had in mind?

Arlene: Yeah, thanks.

Guard-Evans: She musta had them matches hid right here.

Bennie (who has hung the picture and is now staring at it): How you think he kept his beard trimmed all nice?

Arlene (preoccupied with unloading the trunk): Who?

Bennie (pointing to the picture): Jesus.

Doctor (quite stern): I'll have to report you for this.

Arlene: I don't know.

Doctor: That injection should hold her. I'll check back later. (*Leaves.*)

Guard-Evans (walking over to the bed): Report me, my ass. We got cells don't have potties, Holsclaw. (*Begins to search her and the bed, handling her very roughly.*) So where is it now? Got it up your pookie, I bet. Oh, that'd be good. Doc comin back an me with my fingers up your . . . roll over . . . don't weigh hardly nuthin, do you, dollie?

Bennie: Never seen him without a moustache either.

Arlene: Huh?

Bennie: The picture.

Guard-Evans: Aw now . . . (*Finding the lighter under the mattress.*) That wasn't hard at all. Don't you know bout hide an seek, Arlie, girl?

Gonna hide somethin, hide it where it's fun to find it. (*Standing up, going to the door.*) Crazy fuckin someday-we-ain't-gonna-come-save-you bitch!

Bennie: Well, Arlie girl, (*Guard slams cell door and leaves*) that ol trunk's bout as empty as my belly.

Arlene: You have been talkin bout your belly ever since we left this mornin.

Bennie: You hungry? Them hotdogs we had give out around Nashville.

Arlene: No. Not really.

Bennie: You gotta eat, Arlene.

Arlene: Says who?

Bennie (laughs; this is a familiar response):   How bout I pick us up some chicken, give you time to clean yourself up. We'll have a nice little dinner, just the two of us.

Arlene: I git sick if I eat this late. Besides, I'm tired.

Bennie: You'll feel better soon's you git somethin on your stomach. Like I always said, "Can't plow less'n you feed the mule."

Arlene: I ain't never heard you say that.

Bennie: There's lots you don't know about me, Arlene. You been seein me ever day, but you ain't been payin attention. You'll get to like me now we're out.

Arlene: You . . . was always out.

Bennie: Yes sir, I'm gonna like bein retired. I kin tell already. An I can take care of you, like I been, only now . . .

Arlene (interrupting):   You tol me you was jus takin a vacation.

Bennie: I was gonna tell you.

Arlene: You had some time off an nothin to do . . .

Bennie: Figured you knew already.

Arlene: You said you ain't never seen Kentucky like you always wanted to. Now you tell me you done quit at the prison? (*Increasingly angry.*)

Bennie: They wouldn't let me drive you up here if I was still on the payroll, you know. Rules, against the rules. Coulda got me in big trouble doin that.

Arlene: You ain't goin back to Pine Ridge?

Bennie: Nope.

Arlene: An you drove me all the way up here plannin to stay here?

Bennie: I was thinkin on it.

Arlene: Well what are you gonna do?

Bennie (not positive, just a possibility):   Hardware.

Arlene: Sell guns?

Bennie (laughs and shakes his head "no"):   Nails. Always wanted to. Some little store with bins and barrels full of nails and screws. Count em out. Put em in little sacks.

Arlene: I don't need nobody hangin around remindin me where I been.

Bennie: We had us a good time drivin up here, didn't we? You throwin that tomato outta the car . . . hit that No Litterin sign square in the middle. (*Grabs her arm as if to feel the muscle.*) Good arm you got.

Arlene (pulling away sharply): Don't you go grabbin me.

Bennie: Listen, you take off them clothes and have yourself a nice hot bath. (*Heading for the bathroom.*) See, I'll start the water. And me, I'll go get us some chicken. (*Coming out of the bathroom.*) You like slaw or potato salad?

Arlene: Don't matter.

Bennie (asking her to decide): Arlene . . .

Arlene: Slaw.

Bennie: One big bucket of slaw comin right up. An extra rolls. You have a nice bath, now, you hear? I'll take my time so's you don't have to hurry fixin yourself up.

Arlene: I ain't gonna do no fixin.

Bennie (a knowing smile): I know how you gals are when you get in the tub. You got any bubbles?

Arlene: What?

Bennie: Bubbles. You know, stuff to make bubbles with . . . bubble bath.

Arlene: I thought you was goin.

Bennie: Right. Right. Goin right now. (*Bennie leaves, locking the door behind him. He has left his hat on the bed. Arlene checks the stove and refrigerator, then goes into the bathroom when noted.*)

Guard-Caldwell (opening the cell door, carrying a plastic dinner carton): Got your grub, girlie.

Arlie: Get out!

Guard-Caldwell: Can't. Doc says you gotta take the sun today.

Arlie: You take it! I ain't hungry. (*Guard and Arlie begin walk to the D. table area.*)

Guard-Caldwell: You gotta eat, Arlie.

Arlie: Says who?

Guard-Caldwell: Says me. Says the Warden. Says the Department of Corrections. Brung you two rolls.

Arlie: And you know what you can do with your . . .

Guard-Caldwell: Stuff em in your bra, why don't you?

Arlie: Ain't you got somebody to go beat up somewhere?

Guard-Caldwell: Gotta see you get fattened up.

Arlie: What do you care? (*Arlene goes into the bathroom.*)

Guard-Caldwell: Oh, we care all right. (*Setting the food down on the table.*) Got us a two-way mirror in the shower room. (*She looks up, hostile.*) And you don't know which one it is, do you? (*He forces her onto the seat.*) Yes Ma'am. Eat. (*Pointing to the food.*) We sure do care if you go gittin too skinny. (*Walks away, folding his arms and standing watching her, her anger building, despite her hunger.*) Yes Mam. We care a hog lickin lot.

Arlie: Sons-a bitches! (*Throws the whole carton at him. Mother's knock is heard on the apartment door.*)

Mother: Arlie? Arlie girl you in there? (*Arlene walks out of the bathroom, stands still, looking at the door. Arlie hears the knock at the same time and slips into the apartment and over to the bed, putting the pillow between her legs and holding the yellow teddy bear Arlene has unpacked. Knocking louder.*) Arlie?

Arlie (*pulling herself up weakly on one elbow, speaking with the voice of a very young child*): Mama? Mama? (*Arlene walks slowly toward the door.*)

Mother (*now pulling the doorknob from the outside, angry that the door is locked*): Arlie? I know you're in there.

Arlie: I can't git up, Mama. (*Hands between her legs.*) My legs is hurt.

Mother: What's takin you so long?

Arlene (*smoothing out her dress*): Yeah, I'm comin. (*Puts Bennie's hat out of sight under the bed.*) Hold on.

Mother: I brung you some stuff but I ain't gonna stand here all night. (*Arlene opens the door and stands back. Mother looks strong but badly worn. She is wearing her cab driver's uniform and is carrying a plastic laundry basket stuffed with cleaning fluids, towels, bug spray, etc.*)

Arlene: I didn't know if you'd come.

Mother: Ain't I always?

Arlene: How are you? (*Moves as if to hug her. Mother stands still, Arlene backs off.*)

Mother: Bout the same. (*Walking into the room.*)

Arlene: I'm glad to see you.

Mother (*not looking at Arlene*): You look tired.

Arlene: It was a long drive.

Mother (*putting the laundry basket on the trunk*): Didn't fatten you up none, I see. (*Walks around the room, looking the place over.*) You always was too skinny. (*Arlene straightens her clothes again.*) Shoulda beat you like your daddy said. Make you eat.

Arlie: Nobody done this to me, Mama. (*Protesting, in pain.*) No! No!

Mother: He weren't a mean man, though, your daddy.

Arlie: Was . . . (*Quickly.*) my bike. My bike hurt me. The seat bumped me.

Mother: You remember that black chewing gum he got you when you was sick?

Arlene: I remember he beat up on you.

Mother: Yeah, (*proudly*) and he was real sorry a coupla times. (*Looking in the closet.*) Filthy dirty. Hey! (*Slamming the closet door, Arlene jumps at the noise.*) I brung you all kinda stuff. Just like Candy not leavin you nuthin. (*Walking back to the basket.*) Some kids I got.

Arlie (*curling up into a ball*): No, Mama, don't touch it. It'll git well. It git well before.

Arlene: Where is Candy?

Mother: You got her place so what do you care? I got her outta my house so whatta I care? This'll be a good place for you.

Arlene (going to the window):   Wish there was a yard, here.

Mother (beginning to empty the basket):   Nice things, see? Bet you ain't had no colored towels where you been.

Arlene: No.

Mother (putting some things away in cabinets):   No place like home. Got that up on the kitchen wall now.

Arlie: I don't want no tea, Mama.

Arlene: Yeah?

Mother (repeating Arlene's answers):   No . . . yeah? . . . You forgit how to talk? I ain't gonna be here all that long. Least you can talk to me while I'm here.

Arlene: You ever git that swing you wanted?

Mother: Dish towels, an see here? June sent along this teapot. You drink tea, Arlie?

Arlene: No.

Mother: June's havin another baby. Don't know when to quit, that girl. Course, I ain't one to talk. (*Starting to pick up trash on the floors, etc.*)

Arlene: Have you seen Joey?

Arlie: I'm tellin you the truth.

Mother: An Ray . . .

Arlie (pleading):   Daddy didn't do nuthin to me.

Mother: Ray ain't had a day of luck in his life.

Arlie: Ask him. He saw me fall on my bike.

Mother: Least bein locked up now, he'll keep off June til the baby gits here.

Arlene: Have you seen Joey?

Mother: Your daddy ain't doin' too good right now. Man's been dyin for ten years, to hear him tell it. You'd think he'd git tired of it an jus go ahead . . . pass on.

Arlene: Mother . . . (*Wanting an answer.*)

Mother: Yeah, I seen 'im. Bout two years ago. Got your stringy hair.

Arlene: You got a picture?

Mother: You was right to give him up. Foster homes is good for some kids.

Arlie: Where's my Joey-bear? Yellow Joey-bear? Mama?

Arlene: How'd you see him?

Mother: I was down at Detention Center pickin up Pete. (*Beginning her serious cleaning now.*)

Arlene: How is he? (*Less than interested.*)

Mother: I could be workin at the Detention Center I been there so much. All I gotta do's have somethin big goin on an I git a call to come after one of you. Can't jus have kids, no, gotta be pickin em up all over town.

Arlene: You was just tellin me . . .

Mother: Pete is taller, that's all.

Arlene: You was just tellin me how you saw Joey.

Mother: I'm comin back in the cab an I seen him waitin for the bus.

Arlene: What'd he say?

Mother: Oh, I didn't stop. (*Arlene looks up quickly, hurt and angry.*) If the kid don't even know you, Arlie, he sure ain't gonna know who I am.

Arlene: How come he couldn't stay at Shirley's?

Mother: Cause Shirley never was crazy about washin more diapers. She's the only smart kid I got. Anyway, social worker only put him there til she could find him a foster home.

Arlene: But I coulda seen him.

Mother: Thatta been trouble, him bein in the family. Kid wouldn't have known who to listen to, Shirley or you.

Arlene: But I'm his mother.

Mother (interrupting):   See, now you don't have to be worryin about him. No kids, no worryin.

Arlene: He just had his birthday, you know.

Arlie: Don't let daddy come in here, Mama. Just you an me. Mama?

Arlene: When I git workin, I'll git a nice rug for this place. He could come live here with me.

Mother: Fat chance.

Arlene: I done my time.

Mother: You never really got attached to him anyway.

Arlene: How do you know that? (*Furious.*)

Mother: Now don't you go gettin het up. I'm tellin you . . .

Arlene: But . . .

Mother: Kids need rules to go by an he'll get em over there.

Arlie: No Daddy! I didn't tell her nuthin. I didn't! I didn't! (*Screaming, gets up from the bed, terrified.*)

Mother: Here, help me with these sheets. (*Hands Arlene the sheets from the laundry basket.*) Even got you a spread. Kinda goes with them curtains. (*Arlene is silent.*) You ain't thanked me, Arlie girl.

Arlene (going to the other side of the bed):   They don't call me Arlie no more. It's Arlene now. (*Arlene and Mother make up the bed. Arlie jumps up, looks around and goes over to Mother's purse. She looks through it hurriedly and pulls out the wallet. She takes some money and runs* D.L. *where she is caught by a School Principal.*)

Principal: Arlie? You're in an awfully big hurry for such a little girl. (*Brushes at Arlie's hair.*) That is you under all that hair, isn't it? (*Arlie resists this gesture.*) Now, you can watch where you're going.

Arlie: Gotta git home.

Principal: But school isn't over for another three hours. And there's peanut butter and chili today. (*As if this mattered.*)

Arlie: Ain't hungry. (*Struggling free.*)

Principal (now sees Arlie's hands clenched behind her back):   What do we have in our hands, Arlie? (*Sticky sweet over suspicion.*)

Arlie: Nuthin.

Principal: Let me see your hands, Arlie. Open up your hands. (*Expecting the worse.*)

Arlie (bringing hands around in front, opening them, showing crumpled dollars):   It's my money. I earned it.

Principal (taking the money):   And how did we earn this money?

Arlie: Doin things.

Principal: What kind of things?

Arlie: For my daddy.

Principal: Well, we'll see about that. You'll have to come with me.

Arlie: No. (*Resisting as Principal pulls her.*)

Principal: Your mother was right after all. She said put you in a special school. (*Quickly.*) No, what she said was put you away somewhere and I said, No, she's too young, well I was wrong. I have four hundred other children to take care of here and what have I been doing? Breaking up your fights, talking to your truant officer and washing your writing off the bathroom wall. Well, I've had enough. You've made your choice. You *want* out of regular school and you're going to *get* out of regular school.

Arlie (becoming more violent):   You can't make me go nowhere, bitch!

Principal (backing off in cold anger):   I'm not making you go. You've earned it. You've worked hard for this, well, they're used to your type over there. They'll know exactly what to do with you. (*Principal stalks off, leaving Arlie alone.*)

Mother (smoothing out the spread):   Spread ain't new, but it don't look so bad. Think we got it right after we got you. No, I remember now. I was pregnant with you an been real sick the whole time. (*Arlene lights a cigarette, Mother takes one, Arlene retrieves the pack quickly.*) Your daddy brung me home this big bowl of chili an some jelly doughnuts. Some fare from the airport give him a big tip. Anyway, I'd been eatin peanut brittle all day, only thing that tasted any good. Then in he come with this chili an no sooner'n I got in bed I thrown up all over everwhere. Lucky I didn't throw you up, Arlie girl. Anyhow, that's how come us to get a new spread. This one here. (*Sits on the bed.*)

Arlene: You drivin the cab any?

Mother: Any? Your daddy ain't drove it at all a long time now. Six years, seven maybe.

Arlene: You meet anybody nice?

Mother: Not anymore. Mostly drivin old ladies to get their shoes. Guess it got around the nursin homes I was reliable. (*Sounds funny to her.*) You remember that time I took you drivin with me that night after you been in a fight an that soldier bought us a beer? Shitty place, hole in the wall?

Arlene: You made me wait in the car.

Mother (standing up):   Think I'd take a child of mine into a dump like that?

Arlene: You went in.

Mother: Weren't no harm in it. (*Walking over for the bug spray.*) I didn't always look so bad, you know.

Arlene: You was pretty.

Mother (beginning to spray the floors): You could look better'n you do. Do somethin with your hair. I always thought if you'd looked better you wouldn't have got in so much trouble.

Arlene (pleased and curious): Joey got my hair?

Mother: And skinny.

Arlene: I took some beauty school at Pine Ridge.

Mother: Yeah, a beautician?

Arlene: I don't guess so.

Mother: Said you was gonna work.

Arlene: They got a law here. Ex-cons can't get no license.

Mother: Shoulda stayed in Alabama, then. Worked there.

Arlene: They got a law there, too.

Mother: Then why'd they give you the trainin?

Arlene: I don't know.

Mother: Maybe they thought it'd straighten you out.

Arlene: Yeah.

Mother: But you are gonna work, right? (*Doesn't want another burden.*)

Arlene: Yeah. Cookin maybe. Somethin that pays good.

Mother: You? Cook? (*Laughs.*)

Arlene: I could learn it.

Mother: Your daddy ain't never forgive you for that bologna sandwich. (*Arlene laughs a little, finally enjoying a memory.*) Oh, I wish I'd seen you spreadin' that Colgate on that bread. He'd have smelled that toothpaste if he hadn't been so sloshed. Little snotty-nosed kid tryin to kill her daddy with a bologna sandwich. An him bein so pleased when you brung it to him . . . (*Laughing.*)

Arlene (no longer enjoying the memory): He beat me good.

Mother: Well, now, Arlie, you gotta admit you had it comin to you. (*Wiping tears from laughing.*)

Arlene: I guess.

Mother: You got a broom?

Arlene: No.

Mother: Well, I got one in the cab I brung just in case. I can't leave it here, but I'll sweep up fore I go. (*Walking toward the door.*) You jus rest til I git back. Won't find no work lookin the way you do. (*Mother leaves. Arlene finds some lipstick and a mirror in her purse. She makes an attempt to look better while Mother is gone.*)

Arlie (jumps up, as if talking to another kid): She is not skinny!

Arlene (looking at herself in the mirror): I guess I could . . .

Arlie: And she don't have to git them stinky permanents. Her hair just comes outta her head curly.

Arlene: Some lipstick.

Arlie (serious):   She drives the cab to buy us stuff, cause we don't take no charity from nobody, cause we got money cause she earned it.

Arlene (closing the mirror, dejected, afraid Mother might be right):   But you're too skinny and you got stringy hair. (*Sitting on the floor.*)

Arlie (more angry):   She drives at night cause people needs rides at night. People goin to see their friends that are sick, or people's cars broken down an they gotta get to work at the . . . nobody calls my Mama a whore!

Mother (coming back in with the broom):   If I'd known you were gonna sweep up with your butt, I wouldn't have got this broom. Get up! (*Sweeps at Arlene to get her to move.*)

Arlie: You're gonna take that back or I'm gonna rip out all your ugly hair and stuff it down your ugly throat.

Arlene (tugging at her own hair):   You still cut hair?

Mother (noticing some spot on the floor):   Gonna take a razor blade to get out this paint.

Arlene: Nail polish.

Arlie: Wanna know what I know about your Mama? She's dyin. Somethin's eatin up her insides piece by piece, only she don't want you to know it.

Mother (continuing to sweep):   So, you're callin' yourself Arlene, now?

Arlene: Yes.

Mother: Don't want your girlie name no more?

Arlene: Somethin like that.

Mother: They call you Arlene in prison?

Arlene: Not at first when I was bein hateful. Just my number then.

Mother: You always been hateful.

Arlene: There was this chaplain, he called me Arlene from the first day he come to talk to me. Here, let me help you. (*Arlene reaches for the broom.*)

Mother: I'll do it.

Arlene: You kin rest.

Mother: Since when? (*Arlene backs off, Mother sweeping harder now.*) I ain't hateful, how come I got so many hateful kids? Poor dumb as hell Pat, stealin them wigs, Candy screwin since day one, Pete cuttin up ol Mac down at the grocery, June sellin dope like it was Girl Scout cookies, and you . . . thank God I can't remember it all.

Arlene (a very serious request):   Maybe I could come out on Sunday for . . . you still make that pot roast?

Mother (now sweeping over by the picture of Jesus):   That your picture?

Arlene: That chaplain give it to me.

Mother: The one give you your "new name."

Arlene: Yes.

Mother: It's crooked. (*Doesn't straighten it.*)

Arlene: I liked those potatoes with no skins. An that ketchup squirter we had, jus like in a real restaurant.

Mother: People that run them institutions now, they jus don't know how to teach kids right. Let em run around an get in more trouble. They should get you up at the crack of dawn an set you to scrubbin the floor. That's what kids need. Trainin. Hard work.

Arlene (a clear request):   I'll probably git my Sundays off.

Mother: Sunday . . . is my day to clean house now. (*Arlene gets the message, finally walks over to straighten the picture. Mother now feels a little bad about this rejection, stops sweeping for a moment.*) I woulda wrote you but I didn't have nuthin to say. An no money to send, so what's the use?

Arlene: I made out.

Mother: They pay you for workin?

Arlene: Bout three dollars a month.

Mother: How'd you make it on three dollars a month? (*Answers her own question.*) You do some favors?

Arlene (sitting down in the chair under the picture, a somewhat smug look):   You jus can't make it by yourself.

Mother (pauses, suspicious, then contemptuous):   You play, Arlie?

Arlene: You don't know nuthin about that.

Mother: I hear things. Girls callin each other "mommy" an bringin things back from the canteen for their "husbands." Makes me sick. You got family, Arlie, what you want with that playin? Don't want nobody like that in my house.

Arlene: You don't know what you're talkin about.

Mother: I still got two kids at home. Don't want no bad example. (*Not finishing the sweeping. Has all the dirt in one place, but doesn't get it up off the floor yet.*)

Arlene: I could tell them some things.

Mother: Like about that cab driver. (*Vicious.*)

Arlene: Look, that was a long time ago. I wanna work, now, make somethin of myself. I learned to knit. People'll buy nice sweaters. Make some extra money.

Mother: We sure could use it.

Arlene: An then if I have money, maybe they'd let me take Joey to the fair, buy him hotdogs an talk to him. Make sure he ain't foolin around.

Mother: What makes you think he'd listen to you? Alice, across the street? Her sister took care her kids while she was at Lexington. You think they pay any attention to her now? Ashamed, that's what. One of em told me his mother done died. Gone to see a friend and died there.

Arlene: Be different with me and Joey.

Mother: He don't even know who you are, Arlie.

Arlene: Arlene. (*She can't respond; this is all she can say.*)

Mother: You forgot already what you was like as a kid. At Waverly, tellin them lies about that campin trip we took, sayin your Daddy made you watch while he an me . . . you know. I'd have killed you then if them social workers hadn't been watchin.

Arlene: Yeah.

Mother: Didn't want them thinkin I weren't fit. Well, what do they know? Each time you'd get out of one of them places, you'd be actin worse than ever. Go right back to that junkie, pimp, Carl, sellin the stuff he steals, savin his ass from the police. He follow you home this time, too?

Arlene: He's got four more years at Bricktown.

Mother: Glad to hear it. Here . . . (*Handing her a bucket.*) Water. (*Arlene fills up the bucket and Mother washes several dirty spots on the walls, floor and furniture. Arlene knows better than to try to help. The Doctor walks*
D. *to find Arlie for their counseling session.*)

Doctor: So you refuse to go to camp?

Arlie: Now why'd I want to go to your fuckin camp? Camp's for babies. You can go shit in the woods if you want to, but I ain't goin.

Doctor: Oh, you're goin.

Arlie: Wanna bet?

Mother: Arlie, I'm waitin. (*For the water.*)

Arlie: 'Sides, I'm waitin.

Doctor: Waiting for what?

Arlie: For Carl to come git me.

Doctor: And who is Carl?

Arlie: Jus some guy. We're goin to Alabama.

Doctor: You don't go till we say you can go.

Arlie: Carl's got a car.

Doctor: Does he have a driver's license to go with it?

Arlie (enraged, impatient): I'm goin now. (*She stalks away, then backs up toward him again. He has information she wants.*)

Doctor: Hey!

Arlene: June picked out a name for the baby?

Mother: Clara . . . or Clarence. Got it from this fancy shampoo she bought.

Arlie: I don't feel good. I'm pregnant, you know.

Doctor: The test was negative.

Arlie: Well, I should know, shouldn't I?

Doctor: No. You want to be pregnant, is that it?

Arlie: I wouldn't mind. Kids need somebody to bring em up right.

Doctor: Raising children is a big responsibility, you know.

Arlie: Yeah, I know it. I ain't dumb. Everybody always thinks I'm so dumb.

Doctor: You could learn if you wanted to. That's what the teachers are here for.

Arlie: Shit.

Doctor: Or so they say.

Arlie: All they teach us is about geography. Why'd I need to know about Africa. Jungles and shit.

Doctor: They want you to know about other parts of the world.

Arlie: Well, I ain't goin there so whatta I care?

Doctor: What's this about Cindy?

Arlie (hostile):   She told Mr. Dawson some lies about me.

Doctor: I bet.

Arlie: She said I fuck my Daddy for money.

Doctor: And what did you do when she said that?

Arlie: What do you think I did? I beat the shit out of her.

Doctor: And that's a good way to work out your problem?

Arlie: She ain't done it since. (*Proud.*)

Doctor: She's been in traction, since.

Arlie: So, whatta I care? She say it again, I'll do it again. Bitch!

Arlene (looking down at the dirt Mother is gathering on the floor):   I ain't got a can. Just leave it.

Mother: And have you sweep it under the bed after I go? (*Wraps the dirt in a piece of newspaper and puts it in her laundry basket.*)

Doctor (looking at his clipboard):   You're on unit clean-up this week.

Arlie: I done it last week!

Doctor: Then you should remember what to do. The session is over. (*Getting up, walking away.*) And stand up straight! And take off that hat! (*Doctor and Arlie go offstage as Mother finds Bennie's hat.*)

Mother: This your hat?

Arlene: No.

Mother: Guess Candy left it here.

Arlene: Candy didn't leave nuthin. (*Then realizes this was a mistake.*)

Mother: Then whose is it? (*Arlene doesn't answer.*) Do you know whose hat this is? (*Arlene turns away.*) I'm askin you a question and I want an answer. (*Arlene turns her back to Mother.*) Whose hat is this? You tell me right now, whose hat is this?

Arlene: It's Bennie's.

Mother: And who's Bennie?

Arlene: Guy drove me home from Pine Ridge. A guard.

Mother (upset):   I knew it. You been screwin a goddamn guard. (*Throws the hat on the bed.*)

Arlene: He jus drove me up here, that's all.

Mother: Sure.

Arlene: I git sick on the bus.

Mother: You expect me to believe that?

Arlene: I'm tellin you, he jus . . .

Mother: No man alive gonna drive a girl 500 miles for nuthin.

Arlene: He ain't never seen Kentucky.

Mother: It ain't Kentucky he wants to see.

Arlene: He ain't gettin nuthin from me.

Mother: That's what you think.

Arlene: He done some nice things for me at Pine Ridge. Gum, funny stories.

Mother: He'd be tellin stories all right, tellin his buddies where to find you.

Arlene: He's gettin us some dinner right now.

Mother: And how're you gonna pay him? Huh? Tell me that.

Arlene: I ain't like that no more.

Mother: Oh you ain't. I'm your mother. I know what you'll do.

Arlene: I tell you I ain't.

Mother: I knew it. Well, when you got another bastard in you, don't come cryin to me, cause I done told you.

Arlene: Don't worry.

Mother: An I'm gettin myself outta here fore your boyfriend comes back.

Arlene: He ain't my boyfriend. (*Increasing anger.*)

Mother: I been a lotta things, but I ain't dumb, Arlene. (*"Arlene" is mocking.*)

Arlene: I didn't say you was. (*Beginning to know how this is going to turn out.*)

Mother: Oh no? You lied to me!

Arlene: How?

Mother: You took my spread without even sayin thank you. (*Not an answer. Just going on with the fury.*) You're hintin at comin to my house for pot roast just like nuthin ever happened, an all the time you're hidin a goddamn guard under your bed. (*Furious.*) Uh-huh.

Arlene: Mama? (*Quietly.*)

Mother: What? (*Cold, fierce.*)

Arlene: What kind of meat makes a pot roast?

Mother: A roast makes a pot roast. Buy a roast. Shoulder, chuck . . .

Arlene: Are you comin back?

Mother: You ain't got no need for me.

Arlene: I gotta ask you to come see me?

Mother: I come tonight, didn't I, an nobody asked me?

Arlene: Just forget it.

Mother (getting her things together now, ready to go): An if I hadn't told them about this apartment, you wouldn't be out at all, how bout that!

Arlene: Forget it! (*Stronger.*)

Mother: Don't you go talkin to me that way. You remember who I am. I'm the one took you back after all you done all them years. I brung you that teapot. I scrubbed your place. You remember that when you talk to me.

Arlene: Sure.

Mother: Uh-huh. (*Now goes to the bed, rips off the spread and stuffs it in her basket.*) I knowed I shouldn't have come. You ain't changed a bit.

Arlene: Same hateful brat, right? (*Back to Mother.*)

Mother: Same hateful brat. Right. (*Arms full, heading for the door.*)

Arlene (rushing toward her): Mama . . .

Mother: Don't you touch me. (*Mother leaves. Arlene stares out the door, stunned and hurt; finally, she slams the door and turns back into the room.*)

Arlene: No! Don't you touch Mama, Arlie.

Ronnie (a fellow juvenile offender, runs across the catwalk, waving a necklace and being chased by Arlie):   Arlie got a boyfriend, Arlie got a boyfriend. (*Throws the necklace* D.) Whoo!

Arlie (chasing him):   Ronnie, you ugly mother, I'll smash your fuckin . . .

Arlene: You might steal all . . . (*Getting more angry.*)

Ronnie (running down the stairs):   Arlie got a boyfriend . . .

Arlie: Gimme that necklace or I'll . . .

Arlene: . . . or eat all Mama's precious pot roast . . .

Ronnie (as they wrestle on the D. *apron):*   You'll tell the Doctor on me? And get your private room back? (*Laughing.*)

Arlene (cold and hostile):   No, don't touch Mama, Arlie. Cause you might slit Mama's throat. (*Goes into the bathroom.*)

Arlie: You wanna swallow all them dirty teeth?

Ronnie: Tell me who give it to you.

Arlie: No, you tell me where it's at.

Ronnie (breaks away, pushing Arlie in the opposite direction, runs for the necklace):   It's right here. (*Drops it down his pants.*) Come an git it.

Arlie: Oh now, that was really ignorant, you stupid pig.

Ronnie (backing away, daring her):   Jus reach right in. First come, first served.

Arlie: Now, how you gonna pee after I throw your weenie over the fence?

Ronnie: You ain't gonna do that, girl. You gonna fall in love. (*She turns vicious, pins him down, attacking. This is no longer play. He screams. Doctor appears on the catwalk.*)

Doctor: Arlie! (*Heads down the stairs to stop this.*)

Carl (from outside the apartment door):   Arlie!

Doctor: Arlie!

Arlie: Stupid, ugly . . .

Ronnie: Help! (*Arlie runs off, hides* D.L.)

Doctor: That's three more weeks of isolation, Arlie. (*Bending down to Ronnie.*) You all right? Can you walk?

Ronnie (looking back to Arlie as he gets up in great pain):   She was tryin to kill me.

Doctor: Yeah. Easy now. You shouldn've known, Ronnie.

Arlie (yelling at Ronnie):   You'll get yours, crybaby.

Carl: Arlie . . .

Arlie: Yeah, I'm comin!

Carl: Bad-lookin dude says move your ass an open up this here door, girl. (*Arlene does not come out of the bathroom. Carl twists the door knob violently, then kicks in the door and walks in. Carl is thin and cheaply*

dressed. Carl's walk and manner are imitative of black pimps, but he
can't quite carry it off.) Where you at, Mama?

Arlene: Carl?

Carl: Who else? You 'spectin' Leroy Brown?

Arlene: I'm takin a bath!

Carl (walking toward the bathroom):   I like my ladies clean. Matter of
professional pride.

Arlene: Don't come in here.

Carl (mocking her tone):   Don't come in here. I seen it all before, girl.

Arlene: I'm gittin out. Sit down or somethin.

Carl (talking loud enough for her to hear him through the door):   Ain't got
the time. (*Opens her purse, then searches the trunk.*) Jus come by to tell
you it's tomorrow. We be takin our feet to the New York street. (*As
though she will be pleased.*) No more fuckin around with these jiveass
southern turkeys. We're goin to the big city, baby. Get you some red
shades and some red shorts an the john's be linin' up fore we hit town.
Four tricks a night. How's that sound? No use wearin out that cute ass
you got. Way I hear it, only way to git busted up there's be stupid, an
I ain't lived this long bein stupid.

Arlene (coming out of the bathroom wearing a towel):   That's exactly how
you lived your whole life—bein stupid.

Carl: Arlie . . . (*Moving in on her.*) be sweet, sugar.

Arlene: Still got your curls.

Carl (trying to hug her):   You're lookin O.K. yourself.

Arlene: Oh, Carl. (*Noticing the damage to the door, breaking away from
any closeness he might try to force.*)

Carl (amused):   Bent up your door, some.

Arlene: How come you're out?

Carl: Sweetheart, you done broke out once, been nabbed and sent to
Pine Ridge and got yourself paroled since I been in. I got a right to a
little free time too, ain't that right?

Arlene: You escape?

Carl: Am I standin here or am I standin here? They been fuckin with you,
I can tell.

Arlene: They gonna catch you.

Carl (going to the window):   Not where we're going. Not a chance.

Arlene: Where you goin they won't git you?

Carl: Remember that green hat you picked out for me down in
Birmingham? Well, I ain't ever wore it yet, but I kin wear it in New
York cause New York's where you wear whatever you feel like. One
guy tol me he saw this dude wearin a whole ring of feathers roun his
leg, right here (*grabs his leg above the knee*) an he weren't in no circus
nor no Indian neither.

Arlene: I ain't seen you since Birmingham. How come you think I wanna
see you now?

Arlie (appearing suddenly, confronts Carl): Carl, I ain't goin with that dude, he's weird. (*Pointing as if there is a trick waiting.*)

Carl: Cause we gotta go collect the johns' money, that's "how come."

Arlie: I don't need you pimpin for me.

Arlene (very strong): I'm gonna work.

Carl: Work?

Arlene: Yeah.

Carl: What's this "work"?

Arlie: You always sendin me to them ol' droolers . . .

Carl: You kin do two things, girl . . .

Arlie: They slobberin all over me . . .

Carl: Breakin out an hookin.

Arlie: They tyin me to the bed!

Arlene: I mean real work.

Arlie (now screaming, gets further away from him): I could git killed working for you. Some sicko, some crazy drunk . . . (*Goes offstage, guard puts her in the cell sometime before Bennie's entrance.*)

Carl: You forget, we seen it all on TV in the dayroom, you bustin outta Lakewood like that. Fakin that palsy fit, then beatin that guard half to death with his own key ring. Whoo-ee! Then that spree you went on . . . stoppin at that fillin station for some cash, then kidnappin the old dude pumpin the gas.

Arlene: Yeah.

Carl: Then that cab driver comes outta the bathroom an tries to mess with you and you shoots him with his own piece. (*Fires an imaginary pistol.*) That there's nice work, Mama. (*Going over to her, putting his arms around her.*)

Arlene: That gun . . . it went off, Carl.

Carl (getting more determined with his affection): That's what guns do, doll. They go off.

Bennie's Voice (from outside): Arlene? Arlene?

Carl: Arlene? (*Jumping up.*) Well, la de da. (*Bennie opens the door, carrying the chicken dinners. He is confused seeing Arlene wearing a towel and talking to Carl.*)

Arlene: Bennie, this here's Carl.

Carl: You're interruptin, Jack. Me an Arlie got business.

Bennie: She's callin herself Arlene.

Carl: I call my ladies what I feel like, chicken man, an you call yourself "gone."

Bennie: I don't take orders from you.

Carl: Well, you been takin orders from somebody, or did you git that outfit at the army surplus store?

Arlene: Bennie brung me home from Pine Ridge.

Carl (walking toward him): Oh, it's a guard now, is it? That chicken break out or what? (*Grabs the chicken.*)

Bennie: I don't know what you're doin here, but . . .

Carl: What you gonna do about it, huh? Lock me up in the toilet? You an who else, Batman?

Bennie (taking the chicken back, walking calmly to the counter): Watch your mouth, punk. (*Condescending. Doesn't want a fight, for Arlene's sake, but doesn't want to appear threatened either.*)

Carl (kicks a chair toward Bennie): Punk!

Arlene (trying to stop this): I'm hungry.

Bennie: You heard her, she's hungry.

Carl (vicious): Shut up! (*Mocking.*) Ossifer.

Bennie: Arlene, tell this guy if he knows what's good for him . . .

Carl (walking to the counter where Bennie has left the chicken): Why don't you write me a parkin ticket? (*Shoves the chicken on the floor.*) Don't fuck with me, Dad. It ain't healthy.

Bennie (pauses, a real standoff. Finally, bends down and picks up the chicken): You ain't worth dirtyin' my hands. (*Carl walks by him, laughing.*)

Carl: Hey, Arlie. I got some dude to see. (*For Bennie's benefit as he struts to the door.*) What I need with another beat up guard? All that blood, jus ugly up my threads. (*Very sarcastic.*) Bye y'all.

Arlene: Bye, Carl.

Carl (turns back quickly at the door, stopping Bennie who was following him): You really oughta shine them shoes, man. (*Vindictive laugh, slams the door in Bennie's face.*)

Bennie (relieved, trying to change the atmosphere): Well, how bout if we eat? You'll catch your death dressed like that.

Arlene: Turn around then. (*Arlene gets a shabby housecoat from the closet. She puts it on over her towel, buttons it up, then pulls the towel out from under it. This has the look of a prison ritual.*)

Bennie (as she is dressing): Your parole officer's gonna tell you to keep away from guys like that . . . for your own good, you know. Those types, just like the suckers on my tomatoes back home. Take everything right outta you. Gotta pull em off, Arlie, uh, Arlene.

Arlene: Now, I'm decent now.

Bennie: You hear what I said?

Arlene: I told him that. That's exactly what I did tell him. (*Going to the bathroom for her hairbrush.*)

Bennie: Who was that anyhow? (*Sits down on the bed, opens up the chicken.*)

Arlene (from the bathroom): Long time ago, me an Carl took a trip together.

Bennie: When you was a kid, you mean?

Arlene: I was at this place for kids.

Bennie: And Carl was there?

Arlene: No, he picked me up an we went to Alabama. There was this wreck an all. I ended up at Lakewood for forgery. It was him that done it. Got me pregnant too.

Bennie: That was Joey's father?

Arlene: Yeah, but he don't know that. (*Sits down.*)

Bennie: Just as well. Guy like that, don't know what they'd do.

Arlene: Mother was here while ago. Says she's seen Joey. (*Taking a napkin from Bennie.*)

Bennie: Wish I had a kid. Life ain't, well, complete, without no kids to play ball with an take fishin. Dorrie, though, she had them backaches an that neuralgia, day I married her to the day she died. Good woman though. No drinkin, no card playin, real sweet voice . . . what was that song she used to sing? . . . Oh, yeah . . .

Arlene: She says Joey's a real good-lookin kid.

Bennie: Well, his Mom ain't bad.

Arlene: At Lakewood, they tried to git me to have an abortion.

Bennie: They was just thinkin of you, Arlene.

Arlene: I told em I'd kill myself if they done that. I would have too. (*Matter-of-fact, no self-pity.*)

Bennie: But they took him away after he was born.

Arlene: Yeah. (*Bennie waits, knowing she is about to say more.*) An I guess I went crazy after that. Thought if I could jus git out an find him . . .

Bennie: I don't remember any of that on the TV.

Arlene: No.

Bennie: Just remember you smilin at the cameras, yellin how you tol that cab driver not to touch you.

Arlene: I never seen his cab. (*Now forces herself to begin to eat.*)

Arlie (in the cell, holding a pillow and singing):   Rock-a-bye baby, on the tree top, when the wind blows, the cradle will . . . (*Not remembering.*) cradle will . . . (*now talking*) what you gonna be when you grow up, pretty boy baby? You gonna be a doctor? You gonna give people medicine an take out they . . . no, don't be no doctor . . . be . . . be a preacher . . . sayin Our Father who is in Heaven . . . Heaven, that's where people go when they dies, when doctors can't save em or somebody kills em fore they even git a chance to . . . no, don't be no preacher neither . . . be . . . go to school an learn good (*tone begins to change*) so you kin . . . make everbody else feel so stupid all the time. Best thing you to be is stay a baby cause nobody beats up on babies or puts them . . . (*much more quiet*) that ain't true, baby. People is mean to babies, so you stay right here with me so nobody kin git you an make you cry an they lay one finger on you (*hostile*) an I'll beat the screamin shit right out of em. They even blow on you an I'll kill em. (*Bennie and Arlene have finished their dinner. Bennie puts one carton of slaw in the refrigerator, then picks up all the paper, making a garbage bag out of one of the sacks.*)

Bennie: Ain't got a can, I guess. Jus use this ol sack for now.

Arlene: I ain't never emptyin another garbage can.

Bennie: Yeah, I reckon you know how by now. (*Yawns.*) You bout ready for bed?

Arlene (stands up):   I spose.

Bennie (stretches):   Little tired myself.

Arlene: Thanks for the chicken. (*Dusting the crumbs off the bed.*)

Bennie: You're right welcome. You look beat. How bout I rub your back. (*Grabs her shoulders.*)

Arlene (pulling away):   No. (*Walking to the sink.*) You go on now.

Bennie: Oh come on. (*Wiping his hands on his pants.*) I ain't all that tired.

Arlene: *I'm* tired.

Bennie: Well, see then, a back rub is just what the doctor ordered.

Arlene: No. I don't . . . (*Pulling away.*)

Bennie (grabs her shoulders and turns her around, sits her down hard on the trunk, starts rubbing her back and neck):   Muscles git real tight like, right in here.

Arlene: You hurtin me.

Bennie: Has to hurt a little or it won't do no good.

Arlene (jumps; he has hurt her):   Oh, stop it! (*Slips away from him and out into the room. She is frightened.*)

Bennie (smiling, coming after her, toward the bed):   Be lot nicer if you was layin down. Wouldn't hurt as much.

Arlene: Now, I ain't gonna start yellin. I'm jus tellin you to go.

Bennie (straightens up as though he's going to cooperate):   O.K. then. I'll jus git my hat. (*He reaches for the hat, then turns quickly, grabs her and throws her down on the bed. He starts rubbing again.*) Now, you just relax. Don't you go bein scared of me.

Arlene: You ain't gettin nuthin from me.

Bennie: I don't want nuthin, honey. Jus tryin to help you sleep.

Arlene (struggling):   Don't you call me honey.

Bennie (stops rubbing, but keeps one hand on her back. Rubs her hair with his free hand):   See? Don't that feel better?

Arlene: Let me up.

Bennie: Why, I ain't holdin you down. (*So innocent.*)

Arlene: Then let me up.

Bennie (takes hands off):   O.K. Git up.

Arlene (turns over slowly, begins to lift herself up on her elbows. Bennie puts one hand on her leg):   Move your hand.

Bennie (Arlene gets up, moves across the room):   I'd be happy to stay here with you tonight. Make sure you'll be all right. You ain't spent a night by yourself for a long time.

Arlene: I remember how.

Bennie: Well how you gonna git up? You got a alarm?

Arlene: It ain't all that hard.

Bennie (puts one hand in his pocket, leers a little):   Oh yeah it is. (*Walks toward her again.*) Gimme a kiss. Then I'll go.

Arlene: You stay away from me. (*Edging along the counter, seeing she's trapped.*)

Bennie (reaches for her, clamping her hands behind her, pressing up against her): Now what's it going to hurt you to give me a little ol kiss?

Arlene: Git out! I said git out! (*Struggling.*)

Bennie: You don't want me to go. You're jus beginning to git interested. Your ol girlie temper's flarin up. I like that in a woman.

Arlene: Yeah, you'd love it if I'd swat you one. (*Gettin away from him.*)

Bennie: I been hit by you before. I kin take anything you got.

Arlene: I could mess you up good.

Bennie: Now, Arlie. You ain't had a man in a long time. And the ones you had been no count.

Arlene: Git out! (*Slaps him. He returns the slap.*)

Bennie (moving in): Ain't natural goin without it too long. Young thing like you. Git all shriveled up.

Arlene (Arlie turning on, now): All right, you sunuvabitch, you asked for it! (*Goes into a violent rage, hitting and kicking him.*)

Bennie (overpowering her capably, prison guard style): Little outta practice, ain't you? (*Amused.*)

Arlene (screaming): I'll kill you, you creep!

Bennie (struggle continues, Bennie pinning her arms under his legs as he kneels over her on the bed. Arlene is terrified and in pain): You will? You'll kill ol Bennie . . . kill ol Bennie like you done that cab driver? (*A cruel reminder he employs to stun and mock her. Arlene looks as though she has been hit. Bennie is still fired up; he unzips his pants.*)

Arlene (passive, cold and bitter): This how you got your Dorrie, rapin?

Bennie (unbuttoning his shirt): That what you think this is, rape?

Arlene: I oughta know.

Bennie: Uh-huh.

Arlene: First they unzip their pants. (*Bennie pulls his shirt out.*) Sometimes they take off their shirt.

Bennie: They do huh?

Arlene: But mostly, they just pull it out and stick it in. (*Bennie stops, one hand goes to his fly, finally hearing what she has been saying. He straightens up, obviously shocked. He puts his arms back in his shirt.*)

Bennie: Don't you call me no rapist. (*Pause, then insistent.*) No, I ain't no rapist, Arlie. (*Gets up, begins to tuck his shirt back in and zip up his pants.*)

Arlene: And I ain't Arlie.

Bennie (Arlene remains on the bed as he continues dressing): No, I guess you ain't.

Arlene (quietly and painfully): Arlie coulda killed you.

OVER LOUDSPEAKER—BEFORE ACT II CURTAIN

(These announcements will be heard during the last 5 minutes of the intermission.)

Garden workers will, repeat, will, report for work this afternoon. Bring a hat and raincoat and wear boots. All raincoats will be checked at the front gate at the end of work period and returned to you after supper.

Your attention please. A checkerboard was not returned to the recreation area after dinner last night. Anyone with information regarding the black and red checkerboard missing from the recreation area will please contact Mrs. Duvall after lunch. No checkerboards or checkers will be distributed until this board is returned.

Betty Rickey and Mary Alice Wolf report to the laundry. Doris Creech and Arlie Holsclaw report immediately to the superintendent's office. The movie this evening will be "Dirty Harry" starring Clint Eastwood. Doris Creech and Arlie Holsclaw report to the superintendent's office immediately.

The bus from St. Mary's this Sunday will arrive at 1:00 P.M. as usual. Those residents expecting visitors on that bus will gather on the front steps promptly at 1:20 and proceed with the duty officer to the visiting area after it has been confirmed that you have a visitor on the bus.

Attention all residents. Attention all residents. (*Pause.*) Mrs. Helen Carson has taught needlework classes here at Pine Ridge for thirty years. She will be retiring at the end of this month and moving to Florida where her husband has bought a trailer park. The resident council and the Superintendent's staff has decided on a suitable retirement present. We want every resident to participate in this project—which is—a quilt, made from scraps of material collected from the residents and sewn together by residents and staff alike. The procedure will be as follows. A quilting room has been set up in an empty storage area just off the infirmary. Scraps of fabric will be collected as officers do evening count. Those residents who would enjoy cutting up old uniforms and bedding no longer in use should sign up for this detail with your dorm officer. If you would like to sign your name or send Mrs. Carson some special message on your square of fabric, the officers will have tubes of embroidery paint for that purpose. The backing for the quilt has been donated by the Women's Associates as well as the refreshments for the retirement party to be held after lunch on the 30th. Thank you very much for your attention and participation in this worthwhile tribute to someone we are all very fond of here. You may resume work at this time. Doris Creech and Arlie Holsclaw report to the superintendent's office immediately.

ACT II

(The next morning. Arlene is asleep on the bed. Arlie is locked in a maximum security cell. We do not see the officer to whom she speaks.)

Arlie: No, I don't have to shut up, neither. You already got me in seg-re-ga-tion, what else you gonna do? I got all day to sleep, while everbody else is out bustin ass in the laundry. (*Laughs.*) Hey! I know . . . you ain't gotta go do no dorm count, I'll just tell you an you jus sit. Huh? You preciate that? Ease them corns you been moanin about . . . yeah . . . O.K. Write this down. (*Pride, mixed with alternating contempt and amusement.*) Startin down by the john on the back side, we got Mary Alice. Sleeps with her pillow stuffed in her mouth. Says her Mom says it'd keep her from grindin down her teeth or somethin. She be suckin that pillow like she gettin paid for it. (*Laughs.*) Next, it's Betty the Frog. Got her legs all opened out like some fuckin . . . (*Makes croaking noises.*) Then it's Doris eatin pork rinds. Thinks somebody gonna grab em outta her mouth if she eats em during the day. Doris ain't dumb. She fat, but she ain't dumb. Hey! You notice how many girls is fat here? Then it be Rhonda, snorin, Marvene, wheezin and Suzanne, coughin. Then Clara an Ellie be still whisperin. Family shit, who's gettin outta line, which girls is gittin a new work 'signment, an who kin git extra desserts an for how much. Them's the two really run this place. My bed right next to Ellie, for sure it's got some of her shit hid in it by now. Crackers or some crap gonna leak out all over my sheets. Last time I found a fuckin grilled cheese in my pillow. Even had two of them little warty pickles. Christ! O.K. Linda and Lucille. They be real quiet, but they ain't sleepin. Prayin, that's them. Linda be sayin them Hell Mary's till you kin just about scream. An Lucille, she tol me once she didn't believe in no God, jus some stupid spirits whooshin aroun everwhere makin people do stuff. Weird. Now, I'm goin back down the other side, there's . . . (*Screams.*) I'd like to see you try it! I been listenin at you for the last three hours. Your husband's gettin laid off an your lettuce is gettin eat by rabbits. Crap City. *You* shut up! Whadda I care if I wake everybody up? I want the nurse . . . I'm gittin sick in here . . . an there's bugs in here! (*The light comes up in the apartment. Faint morning traffic sounds are heard. Arlene does not wake up. The Warden walks across the catwalk. The Guard-Evans catches up with him near Arlie's cell. Bennie is stationed at the far end of the walk.*)

Loudspeaker: Dorm A may now eat lunch.

Guard-Evans: Warden, I thought 456 . . . (*nodding in Arlie's direction*) was leavin here.

Warden: Is there some problem?

Guard-Evans: Oh, we can take care of her all right. We're just tired of takin her shit, if you'll pardon the expression.

Arlie (interrupting): You ain't seen nuthin yet, you mother.

Warden: Washington will decide on her transfer. Til then, you do your job.

Guard-Evans: She don't belong here. Rest of . . .

Loudspeaker (interrupts him): Betty Rickey and Mary Alice Wolf report to the laundry.

Guard-Evans: Most of these girls are mostly nice people, go along with things. She needs a cage.

Arlie (vicious):   I need a knife.

Warden: Had it occurred to you that we could send the rest of them home and just keep her? (*Very curt. Walks away.*)

Loudspeaker: Dorm A may now eat lunch. A Dorm to lunch.

Guard-Evans (turning around, muttering to himself):   Oh, that's a swell idea. Let everybody out except bitches like Holsclaw. (*She makes an obscene gesture at him; he turns back toward the catwalk.*) Smartass Warden, thinks he's runnin a hotel.

Bennie (having overheard this last interchange):   Give you some trouble, did she?

Guard-Evans: I can wait.

Bennie: For what?

Guard-Evans: For the day she tries gettin out an I'm here by myself. I'll show that screachin slut a thing or . . .

Bennie: That ain't the way, Evans.

Guard-Evans: The hell it ain't. Beat the livin . . .

Bennie: Outta a little thing like her? Gotta do her like all the rest. You got your shorts washed by givin Betty Rickey *Milky Ways*. You git your chairs fixed givin Frankie Hill extra time in the shower with Lucille Smith. An you git ol Arlie girl to behave herself with a stick of gum. Gotta have her brand, though.

Guard-Evans: You screwin that wildcat?

Bennie (starts walk to Arlie's cell):   Watch. (*Arlie is silent as he approaches, but is watching intently.*) Now, (*to nobody in particular*) where was that piece of Juicy Fruit I had in this pocket. Gotta be here somewhere. (*Takes a piece of gum out of his pocket and drops it within Arlie's reach.*) Well, (*feigning disappointment*) I guess I already chewed it. (*Arlie reaches for the gum and gets it.*) Oh, (*looking down at her now*) how's it goin, kid?

Arlie: O.K. (*Arlie says nothing, but unwraps the gum and chews it. Bennie leaves the cell area, motioning to the other guard as if to say, "See, that's how it's done." A loud siren goes by in the street below the apartment. Arlene bolts up out of bed, then turns back to it quickly, making it up in a frenzied, ritual manner. As she tucks the spread up under the pillow, the siren stops and so does she. For the first time, now, she looks around the room, realizing where she is and the habit she has just played out. A jackhammer noise gets louder. She walks over to the window and looks out. There is a wolf-whistle from a worker below. She shuts the window in a fury, then grabs the bars. She starts to shake them, but then her hand goes limp. She looks around the room, as if trying to remember what she is doing there. She looks at her watch, now aware that it is late and that she has slept in her clothes.*)

Arlene: People don't sleep in their clothes, Arlene. An people git up fore noon. (*Arlene makes a still disoriented attempt to pull herself together, changing shoes, combing her hair, washing her face, etc., as guards and other prison life continues on the catwalk.*)

Warden (walking up to Arlie, remaining some distance from her, but talking directly to her, as he appears to check files or papers.):   Good afternoon, Arlie.

Arlie: Fuck you. (*Warden walks away.*) Wait! I wanna talk to you.

Warden: I'm listening.

Arlie: When am I gittin outta here?

Warden: That's up to you.

Arlie: The hell it is.

Warden: When you can show that you can be with the other girls, you can get out.

Arlie: How'm I supposed to prove that bein in here?

Warden: And then you can have mail again and visitors.

Arlie: You're just fuckin with me. You ain't ever gonna let me out. I been in this ad-just-ment room four months, I think.

Warden: Arlie, you see the other girls on the dorm walking around, free to do whatever they want? If we felt the way you seem to think we do, everyone would be in lockup. When you get out of segregation, you can go to the records office and have your time explained to you.

Arlie: It won't make no sense.

Warden: They'll go through it all very slowly . . . when you're eligible for parole, how many days of good time you have, how many industrial days you've earned, what constitutes meritorious good time . . . and how many days you're set back for your write-ups and all your time in segregation.

Arlie: I don't even remember what I done to git this lockup.

Warden: Well, I do. And if you ever do it again, or anything like it again, you'll be right back in lockup where you will stay until you forget *how* to do it.

Arlie: What was it?

Warden: You just remember what I said.

Arlene: Now, then . . . (*Sounds as if she has something in mind to do. Looks as though she doesn't.*)

Arlie: What was it?

Warden: Oh, and Arlie, the prison chaplain will be coming by to visit you today.

Arlie: I don't want to see no chaplain!

Warden: Did I ask you if you wanted to see the chaplain? No, I did not. I said, the chaplain will be coming by to visit you today. Mrs. Roberts, why hasn't this light bulb been replaced? (*To an unseen guard. Walks away.*)

Arlie (screaming):   Get out of my hall! (*Warden walks away. Arlene walks to the refrigerator and opens it. She picks out a carton of slaw Bennie put there last night. She walks away from the door, then turns around, remembering to close it. She looks at the slaw, as guard comes up to Arlie's cell with a plate.*)

Arlene: I ain't never eatin no more scrambled eggs.

Guard-Caldwell: Chow time, cutie pie.

Arlie: These eggs ain't scrambled, they's throwed up! And I want a fork! (*Arlene realizes she has no fork, then fishes one out of the garbage sack from last night. She returns to the bed, takes a bite of slaw and gets her wallet out of her purse. She lays the bills out on the bed one at a time.*)

Arlene: That's for coffee . . . and that's for milk and bread . . . an that's cookies . . . an cheese an crackers . . . an shampoo an soap . . . an bacon an livercheese. No, pickle loaf . . . an ketchup and some onions . . . an peanut butter an jelly . . . an shoe polish. Well, ain't no need gettin everything all at once. Coffee, milk, ketchup, cookies, cheese, onions, jelly. Coffee, milk . . . oh, shampoo . . .

Ruby (off° *banging on the door, yelling*):   Candy, I gotta have my five dollars back.

Arlene (*quickly stuffing her money back in her wallet*):   Candy ain't here!

Ruby: It's Ruby, upstairs. She's got five dollars I loaned her . . . Arlie? That Arlie? Candy told me her sister be . . . (*Arlene opens the door hesitantly.*) It is Arlie, right?

Arlene: It's Arlene. (*Does not extend her hand.*)

Ruby: See, I got these shoes in layaway . . . (*Puts her hand back in her pockets.*) she said you been . . . you just got . . . you seen my money?

Arlene: No.

Ruby: I don't get em out today they go back on the shelf.

Arlene (*doesn't understand*):   They sell your shoes?

Ruby: Yeah. Welcome back.

Arlene: Thank you. (*Embarrassed, but relieved.*)

Ruby: She coulda put it in my mailbox. (*Ruby starts to leave, Arlene is closing the door behind her, when Ruby turns around.*) Uh . . . listen . . . if you need a phone, I got one most of the time.

Arlene: I do have to make this call.

Ruby: Ain't got a book though . . . well, I got one but it's holdin up my bed. (*Laughs.*)

Arlene: I got the number.

Ruby: Well, then . . . (*Awkward.*)

Arlene: Would you . . . wanna come in?

Ruby: You sure I'm not interruptin anything?

Arlene: I'm sposed to call my parole officer.

Ruby: Good girl. Most of them can't talk but you call em anyway. (*Arlene does not laugh.*) Candy go back to that creep?

Arlene: I guess.

Ruby: I's afraid of that. (*Looking around.*) Maybe an envelope with my name on it? Really cleaned out the place, didn't she?

Arlene: Yeah. Took everything. (*They laugh a little.*)

Ruby: Didn't have much. Didn't do nuthin here 'cept . . . sleep.

off: Offstage.

Arlene: Least the rent's paid til the end of the month. I'll be workin by then.

Ruby: You ain't seen Candy in a while.

Arlene: No. Think she was in the 7th grade when . . .

Ruby: She's growed up now, you know.

Arlene: Yeah. I was thinkin she might come by.

Ruby: Honey, she won't be comin by. He keeps all his . . . (*starting over*) his place is pretty far from here. But . . . (*Stops, trying to decide what to say.*)

Arlene: But what?

Ruby: But she had a lot of friends, you know. *They* might be comin by.

Arlene: Men, you mean.

Ruby: Yeah. (*Quietly, waiting for Arlene's reaction.*)

Arlene (realizing the truth): Mother said he was her boyfriend.

Ruby: I shouldn't have said nuthin. I jus didn't want you to be surprised if some john showed up, his tongue hangin out an all. (*Sits down on the bed.*)

Arlene: It's O.K. I shoulda known anyway. (*Now suddenly angry.*) No, it ain't O.K. Guys got their dirty fingernails all over her. Some pimp's out buyin green pants while she . . . Goddamn her.

Ruby: Hey now, that ain't your problem. (*Moves toward her. Arlene backs away.*)

Arlie (pointing): You stick your hand in here again Doris an I'll bite it off.

Ruby: She'll figure it out soon enough.

Arlie (pointing to another person): An you, you ain't my Mama, so you can cut the Mama crap.

Arlene: I wasn't gonna cuss no more.

Ruby: Nuthin in the parole rules says you can't git pissed. My first day outta Gilbertsville I done the damn craziest . . . (*Arlene looks around, surprised to hear Ruby has done time.*) Oh yeah, a long time ago, but . . . hell, I heaved a whole gallon of milk right out the window my first day.

Arlene (somewhat cheered): It hit anybody?

Ruby: It bounced! Make me feel a helluva lot better. I said, "Ruby, if a gallon of milk can bounce back, so kin you."

Arlene: That's really what you thought?

Ruby: Well, not exactly. I had to keep sayin it for bout a year fore I finally believed it. I's moppin this lady's floor once an she come in an heard me sayin "gallon-a'-milk, gallon-a'-milk," fired me. She did. Thought I was too crazy to mop her floors. (*Laughs, but is still bitter. Arlene wasn't listening. Ruby wants to change the subject now.*) Hey! You have a good trip? Candy said you was in Arkansas.

Arlene: Alabama. It was O.K. This guard, well he used to be a guard, he just quit. He ain't never seen Kentucky, so he drove me. (*Watching for Ruby's response.*)

Ruby: Pine Ridge?

Arlene: Yeah.

Ruby: It's co-ed now, ain't it?

Arlene: Yeah. That's dumb, you know. They put you with men so's they can git you if you're seen with em.

Ruby: Sposed to be more natural, I guess.

Arlene: I guess.

Ruby: Well, I say it sucks. Still a prison. No matter how many pictures they stick up on the walls or how many dirty movies they show, you still gotta be counted 5 times a day. (*Now beginning to worry about Arlene's silence.*) You don't seem like Candy said.

Arlene: She tell you I was a killer?

Ruby: More like the meanest bitch that ever walked. I seen lots worse than you.

Arlene: I been lots worse.

Ruby: Got to you, didn't it? (*Arlene doesn't respond, but Ruby knows she's right.*) Well, you jus gotta git over it. Bein out, you gotta . . .

Arlene: Don't you start in on me.

Ruby (realizing her tone): Right, sorry.

Arlene: It's O.K.

Ruby: Ex-cons is the worst. I'm sorry.

Arlene: It's O.K.

Ruby: Done that about a year ago. New waitress we had. Gave my little goin straight speech, "No booze, no men, no buyin on credit," shit like that, she quit that very night. Stole my fuckin raincoat on her way out. Some speech, huh? (*Laughs, no longer resenting this theft.*)

Arlene: You a waitress?

Ruby: I am the Queen of Grease. Make the finest french fries you ever did see.

Arlene: You make a lot of money?

Ruby: I sure know how to. But I ain't about to go back inside for doin it. Cookin out's better'n eatin in, I say.

Arlene: You think up all these things you say?

Ruby: Know what I hate? Makin salads—cuttin up all that stuff 'n floppin it in a bowl. Some day . . . some day . . . I'm gonna hear "tossed salad" an I'm gonna do jus that. Toss out a tomato, toss out a head a' lettuce, toss out a big ol carrot. (*Miming the throwing act and enjoying herself immensely.*)

Arlene (laughing): Be funny seein all that stuff flyin outta the kitchen.

Ruby: Hey Arlene! (*Gives her a friendly pat.*) You had your lunch yet?

Arlene (pulling away immediately): I ain't hungry.

Ruby (carefully): I got raisin toast.

Arlene: No. (*Goes over to the sink, twists knobs as if to stop a leak.*)

Arlie: Whaddaya mean, what did she do to me? You got eyes or is they broke? You only seein what you feel like seein. I git ready to protect myself from a bunch of weirdos an then you look.

Arlene: Sink's stopped up. (*Begins to work on it.*)

Arlie: You ain't seein when they's leavin packs of cigarettes on my bed an then thinking I owe em or somethin.

Ruby: Stopped up, huh? (*Squashing a bug on the floor.*)

Arlie: You ain't lookin when them kitchen workers lets up their mommies in line nights they know they only baked half enough brownies.

Ruby: Let me try.

Arlie: You ain't seen all the letters comin in an goin out with visitors. I'll tell you somethin. One of them workmen buries dope for Betty Rickey in little plastic bottles under them sticker bushes at the water tower. You see that? No, you only seein me. Well, you don't see shit.

Ruby (a quiet attempt):   Gotta git you some Drano if you're gonna stay here.

Arlie: I'll tell you what she done. Doris brung me some rollers from the beauty school class. Three fuckin pink rollers. Them plastic ones with the little holes. I didn't ask her. She jus done it.

Ruby: Let me give her a try.

Arlene: I can fix my own sink.

Arlie: I's stupid. I's thinkin maybe she were different from all them others. Then that night everybody disappears from the john and she's wantin to brush my hair. Sure, brush my hair. How'd I know she was gonna crack her head open on the sink? I jus barely even touched her.

Ruby (walking to the bed now, digging through her purse):   Want a Chiclet?

Arlie: You ain't asked what she was gonna do to me. Huh? When you gonna ask that? You don't give a shit about that cause Doris such a good girl.

Arlene: Don't work. (*Giving up.*)

Ruby: We got a dishwasher quittin this week if you're interested.

Arlene: I need somethin that pays good.

Ruby: You type?

Arlene: No.

Ruby: Do any clerk work?

Arlene: No.

Ruby: Any key punch?

Arlene: No.

Ruby: Well, then I hate to tell you, but all us old-timers already got all the good cookin and cleanin jobs. (*Smashes another bug, goes to the cabinet to look for the bug spray.*) She even took the can of Raid! Just as well, empty anyway. (*Arlene doesn't respond.*) She hit the bugs with it. (*Still no response.*) Now, there's that phone call you was talkin about.

Arlene: Yeah.

Ruby (walking toward the door):   An I'll git you that number for the dishwashin job, just in case. (*Arlene backs off.*) How bout cards? You play any cards? Course you do. I get sick of beatin myself all the time at solitaire. Damn borin bein so good at it.

Arlene (goes for her purse):   Maybe I'll jus walk to the corner an make my call from there.

Ruby: It's always broke.

Arlene: What?

Ruby: The phone . . . at the corner. Only it ain't at the corner. It's inside the A & P.

Arlene: Maybe it'll be fixed.

Ruby: Look, I ain't gonna force you to play cards with me. It's time for my programs anyway.

Arlene: I gotta git some pickle loaf an . . . things.

Ruby: Suit yourself. I'll be there if you change your mind.

Arlene: I have some things I gotta do here first.

Ruby (trying to leave on a friendly basis):   Look, I'll charge you a dime if it'll make you feel better.

Arlene (takes her seriously):   O.K.

Ruby (laughs, then realizes Arlene is serious):   Mine's the one with the little picture of Johnny Cash on the door. (*Walks to the door and leaves. Bennie's singing begins almost immediately, as Arlene walks toward the closet. She is delaying going to the store, but is determined to go. She checks little things in the room, remembers to get a scarf, change shoes, checks her wallet, finally, as she is walking out, she stops and looks at the picture of Jesus, then moves closer, having noticed a dirty spot. She goes back into the bathroom for a tissue, wets it in her mouth, then dabs at the offending spot. She puts the tissue in her purse then leaves the room when noted.*)

Bennie (to the tune of "I'll Toe The Line," walks across the catwalk carrying a tray with cups and a pitcher of water):   I keep my pants up with a piece of twine. I keep my eyes wide open all the time, Da da da da-da da da da da da. (*Doesn't know this line.*) If you'll be mine, please pull the twine.

Arlie: You can't sing for shit.

Bennie (starts down the stairs toward Arlie's cell):   You know what elephants got between their toes?

Arlie: I don't care.

Bennie: Slow natives. (*Laughs.*)

Arlie: That ain't funny.

Guard-Evans (as Bennie opens Arlie's door):   Hey, Davis.

Bennie: Conversation is rehabilitatin, Evans. Want some water?

Arlie: O.K.

Bennie: How bout some Kool-Aid to go in it? (*Gives her a glass of water.*)

Arlie: When does the chaplain come?

Bennie: Want some gum?

Arlie: Is it today?

Bennie: Kool-Aid's gone up, you know. 15¢ and tax. You get out, you'll learn all about that.

Arlie: Does the chaplain come today?

Bennie (going back up the catwalk):   Income tax, sales tax, property tax, gas and electric, water, rent . . .

Arlie: Hey!

Bennie: Yeah, he's comin, so don't mess up.

Arlie: I ain't.

Bennie: What's he tell you anyway, get you so starry-eyed?

Arlie: He jus talks to me.

Bennie: I talk to you.

Arlie: Where's Frankie Hill?

Bennie: Gone.

Arlie: Out?

Bennie: Pretty soon.

Arlie: When.

Bennie: Miss her don't you? Ain't got nobody to bullshit with. Stories you gals tell . . . whoo-ee!

Arlie: Get to cut that grass now, Frankie, honey.

Bennie: Huh?

Arlie: Stupidest thing she said. (*Gently.*) Said first thing she was gonna do when she got out . . . (*Arlene leaves the apartment.*)

Bennie: Get laid.

Arlie: Shut up. First thing was gonna be going to the garage. Said it always smelled like car grease an turpur . . . somethin.

Bennie: Turpentine.

Arlie: Yeah, an gasoline, wet. An she'll bend down an squirt oil in the lawnmower, red can with a long pointy spout. Then cut the grass in the back yard, up an back, up an back. They got this grass catcher on it. Says she likes scoopin up that cut grass an spreadin it out under the trees. Says it makes her real hungry for some lunch. (*A quiet curiosity about all this.*)

Bennie: I got a power mower, myself.

Arlie: They done somethin to her. Took out her nerves or somethin. She . . .

Bennie: She jus got better, that's all.

Arlie: Hah, Know what else? They give her a fork to eat with last week. A fork. A fuckin fork. Now how long's it been since I had a fork to eat with?

Bennie (getting ready to leave the cell):   Wish I could help you with that, honey.

Arlie (loud):   Don't call me honey.

Bennie (locks the door behind him):   That's my girl.

Arlie: I ain't your girl.

Bennie (on his way back up the stairs):   Screechin wildcat.

Arlie: What time is it? (*Very quiet. Arlene walks back into the apartment. She is out of breath and has some trouble getting the door open. She is carrying a big sack of groceries. As she sets the bag on the counter, it breaks open, spilling cans and packages all over the floor. She just stands and looks at the mess. She takes off her scarf and sets down her purse, still looking at the spilled groceries. Finally, she bends down and picks up the package of pickle loaf. She starts to put it on the counter, then turns suddenly and throws it at the door. She stares at it as it falls.*)

Arlene: Bounce? (*In disgust.*) Shit. (*Arlene sinks to the floor. She tears open the package of pickle loaf and eats a piece of it, tearing off the bites in her mouth. She is still angry, but is completely unable to do anything about her anger.*)

Arlie: Who's out there? Is anybody out there? (*Reading.*) Depart from evil and do good. (*Yelling.*) Now, you pay attention out there cause this is right out of the Lord's mouth. (*Reading.*) And dwell, that means live, dwell for-ever-more. (*Speaking.*) That's like for longer than I've been in here or longer than . . . this Bible the chaplain give me's got my name right in the front of it. Hey! Somebody's sposed to be out there watchin me. Wanna hear some more? (*Reading.*) For the Lord for . . . (*The word is "forsaketh".*) I can't read in here, you turn on my light, you hear me? Or let me out and I'll go read it in the TV room. Please let me out. I won't scream or nuthin. I'll just go right to sleep, O.K.? Somebody! I'll go right to sleep. O.K.? You won't even know I'm there. Hey! Goddammit, somebody let me out of here, I can't stand it in here anymore. Somebody! (*Her spirit finally broken.*)

Arlene (*she draws her knees up, wraps her arms around them and rests her head on her arms*):   Jus gotta git a job an make some money an everything will be all right. You hear me, Arlene? You git yourself up an go find a job. (*Continues to sit.*) An you kin start by cleanin up this mess you made cause food don't belong on the floor. (*Still sitting. Carl appears in the doorway of the apartment. When he sees Arlene on the floor, he goes into a fit of vicious, sadistic laughter.*)

Carl: What's happenin, Mama? You havin lunch with the bugs?

Arlene (*quietly*):   Fuck off.

Carl (*threatening*):   What'd you say?

Arlene (*reconsidering*):   Go away.

Carl: You watch your mouth or I'll close it up for you.

Arlene (*stands up now. Carl goes to the window and looks out, as if checking for someone*):   They after you, ain't they? (*Carl sniffs, scratches at his arm.*)

Carl (*finding a plastic bag near the bed, stuffed with brightly colored knitted things. He pulls out baby sweaters, booties and caps*):   What the fuck is this?

Arlene: You leave them be.

Carl: You got a baby hid here somewhere? I foun its little shoes. (*Laughs, dangling them in front of him.*)

Arlene: Them's mine. (*Chasing him.*)

Carl: Aw sugar, I ain't botherin nuthin. Just lookin. (*Pulls more out of the sack, dropping one or two on the floor, kicking them away with his feet.*)

Arlene (picking up what he's dropped): I ain't tellin you again. Give me them.

Carl (turns around quickly, walking away with a few of the sweaters): How much these go for?

Arlene: I don't know yet.

Carl: I'll jus take care of em for you—a few coin for the trip. You *are* gonna have to pay your share, you know.

Arlene: You give me them. I ain't goin with you. (*She walks toward him.*)

Carl: You ain't? (*Mocking, Arlene walks up close to him now, taking the bag in her hands. He knocks her away and onto the bed.*) Straighten up, girlie. (*Now kneels over her.*) You done forgot how to behave yourself. (*Moves as if to threaten her, but kisses her on the forehead, then moves out into the room.*)

Arlene (sitting up): I worked hard on them things. They's nice, too, for babies and little kids.

Carl: I bet you fooled them officers good, doin this shit. (*Throws the bag in the sink.*)

Arlene: I weren't . . .

Carl (interrupting): I kin see that scene. They sayin . . . (*puts on a high Southern voice*) "I'd jus love one a' them nice yella sweaters."

Arlene: They liked them.

Carl: Those turkeys, sure they did. Where else you gonna git your free sweaters an free washin an free step-right-up-git-your-convict-special-shoe-shine. No, don't give me no money, officer. I's jus doin this cause I likes you. (*Uncle Tom talk.*)

Arlene: They give em for Christmas presents.

Carl (checks the window again, then peers into the grocery sack): What you got sweet, Mama? (*Pulls out a box of cookies and begins to eat them.*)

Arlie: I'm sweepin, Doris, cause it's like a pigpen in here. So you might like it, but I don't, so if you get some mops, I'll take one of them, too.

Arlene: You caught another habit, didn't you?

Carl: You turned into a narc or what?

Arlene: You scratchin an sniffin like crazy.

Carl: I see a man eatin cookies an that's what you see too.

Arlene: An you was laughin at me sittin on the floor! You got cops lookin for you an you ain't scored yet this morning. You better git yourself back to prison where you can git all you need.

Carl: Since when Carl couldn't find it if he really wanted it?

Arlene: An I bought them cookies for me.

Carl: An I wouldn't come no closer if I's you.

Arlene (stops, then walks to the door): Then take the cookies an git out.

Carl (imitating Bennie): Oh, please, Miss Arlene, come go with Carl to the big city. We'll jus have us the best time.

Arlene: I'm gonna stay here an git a job an save up money so's I kin git Joey. (*Opening the door.*) Now, I ain't sposed to see no ex-cons.

Carl (big laugh): You don't know nobody else. Huh, Arlie? Who you
 know ain't a "con-vict"?

Arlene: I'll meet em.

Carl: And what if they don't wanna meet you? You ain't exactly a nice
 girl, you know. An you gotta be jivin about that job shit. (*Throws the
 sack of cookies on the floor.*)

Arlene: I kin work. (*Retrieving the cookies.*)

Carl: Doin what?

Arlene: I don't know. Cookin, cleanin, somethin that pays good.

Carl: You got your choice, honey. You can do cookin an cleanin OR you
 can do somethin that pays good. You ain't gonna git rich working on
 your knees. You come with me an you'll have money. You stay here,
 you won't have shit.

Arlene: Ruby works an she does O.K.

Carl: You got any Kool-Aid? (*Looking in the cabinets, moving Arlene out
 of his way.*) Ruby who?

Arlene: Upstairs. She cooks. Works nights an has all day to do just what
 she wants.

Carl: And what, exactly, do she do? See flicks take rides in cabs to pick up
 see-through shoes?

Arlene: She watches TV, plays cards, you know.

Carl: Yeah, I know. Sounds just like the dayroom in the fuckin joint.

Arlene: She likes it.

Carl (exasperated): All right. Say you stay here an *finally* find yourself
 some job. (*Grabs the picture of Jesus off the wall.*) This your boyfriend?

Arlene: The chaplain give it to me.

Carl: Say it's dishwashin, O.K.? (*Arlene doesn't answer.*) O.K.?

Arlene: O.K. (*Takes the picture, hangs it back up.*)

Carl: An you git maybe 75 a week. 75 for standin over a sink full of
 greasy gray water, fishin out blobs of bread an lettuce. People puttin
 pieces of chewed up meat in their napkins and you gotta pick it out. 8
 hours a day, 6 days a week, to make 75 lousy pictures of Big Daddy
 George. Now, how long it'll take you to make 75 workin for me?

Arlene: A night. (*Sits on the bed, Carl pacing in front of her.*)

Carl: Less than a night. Two hours maybe. Now, it's the same fuckin 75
 bills. You can either work all week for it or make it in 2 hours. You
 work two hours a night for me an how much you got in a week?
 (*Arlene looks puzzled by the multiplication required. Carl sits down
 beside her, even more disgusted.*) Two 75's is 150. Three 150's is 450.
 You stay here you git 75-a week. You come with me an you git 450 a
 week. Now, 450, Arlie, is *more* than 75. You stay here you gotta work
 eight hours a day and your hands git wrinkled and your feet swell up.
 (*Suddenly distracted.*) There was this guy at Bricktown had webby toes
 like a duck. (*Back now.*) You come home with me you work two hours
 a night an you kin sleep all mornin an spend the day buyin eyelashes

an tryin out perfume. Come home, have some guy openin the door for you sayin, "Good Evenin, Miss Holsclaw, nice night now ain't it? (*Puts his arm around her.*)

Arlene: It's Joey I'm thinkin about.

Carl: If you was a kid, would you want your Mom to git so dragged out washin dishes she don't have no time for you an no money to spend on you? You come with me, you kin send him big orange bears an Sting-Ray bikes with his name wrote on the fenders. He'll like that. Holsclaw. (*Amused.*) Kinda sounds like coleslaw, don't it? Joey be tellin all his friends bout his Mom livin up in New York City an bein so rich an sendin him stuff all the time.

Arlene: I want to be with him.

Carl (now stretches out on the bed, his head in her lap):   So, fly him up to see you. Take him on that boat they got goes roun the island. Take him up to the Empire State Building, let him play King Kong. (*Rubs her hair, unstudied tenderness.*) He be talkin bout that trip his whole life.

Arlene (smoothing his hair):   I don't want to go back to prison, Carl.

Carl (jumps up, moves toward the refrigerator):   There any chocolate milk? (*Distracted again.*) You know they got this motel down in Mexico named after me? Carlsbad Cabins. (*Proudly.*) Who said anything about goin back to prison? (*Slams the refrigerator door, really hostile.*) What do you think I'm gonna be doin? Keepin you out, that's what!

Arlene (stands up):   Like last time? Like you gettin drunk? Like you lookin for kid junkies to beat up?

Carl: God, ain't it hot in this dump. You gonna come or not? You wanna wash dishes, I could give a shit. (*Now yelling.*) But you comin with me, you say it right now, lady! (*Grabs her by the arm.*) Huh?

Ruby (knocks on the door):   Arlene?

Carl: She ain't here! (*Yelling.*)

Ruby (alarmed):   Arlene! You all right?

Arlene: That's Ruby I was tellin you about.

Carl (catches her arm again, very rough):   We ain't through!

Ruby (opening the door):   Hey! (*Seeing the rough treatment.*) Goin to the store. (*Very firm.*) Thought maybe you forgot somethin.

Carl (turns Arlene loose):   You this cook I been hearin about?

Ruby: I cook. So what?

Carl: Buys you nice shoes, don't it, cookin? Why don't you hock your watch an have somethin done to your hair? If you got a watch.

Ruby: Why don't you drop by the coffee shop. I'll spit in your eggs.

Carl: They let you bring home the half-eat chili dogs?

Ruby: You . . . you got half-eat chili dogs for brains. (*To Arlene.*) I'll stop by later. (*Contemptuous look for Carl.*)

Arlene: No. Stay. (*Carl gets the message.*)

Carl (goes over to the sink to get a drink of water out of the faucet, then looks down at his watch):   Piece a' shit. (*Thumps it with his finger.*) Shoulda took the dude's hat, jack. Guy preachin about the end of the world ain't gonna own a watch that works.

Arlene (walks over to the sink, bends over Carl):   You don't need me. I'm gittin too old for it, anyway.

Carl: I don't discuss my business with strangers in the room. (*Heads for the door.*)

Arlene: When you leavin?

Carl: Six. You wanna come, meet me at this bar. (*Gives her a brightly colored matchbook.*) I'm havin my wheels delivered. (*With faintly uncertain pride.*)

Arlene: You stealin a car?

Carl: Take a cab. (*Gives her a dollar.*) You don't come . . . well, I already laid it out for you. I ain't never lied to you, have I girl?

Arlene: No.

Carl: Then you be there. That's all the words I got. (*Makes an unconscious move toward her.*) I don't beg nobody. (*Backs off.*) Be there. (*Turns abruptly and leaves. Arlene watches him go, folding up the money in the matchbook. The door remains open.*)

Arlie (reading, or trying to, from a small testament):   For the Lord forsaketh not his Saints, but the seed of the wicked shall be cut off.

Ruby (walks over to the counter, starts to pick up some of the groceries lying on the floor, then stops):   I 'magine you'll want to be puttin these up yourself. (*Arlene continues to stare out the door.*) He do this?

Arlene: No.

Ruby: Can't trust these sacks. I seen bag boys punchin holes in em at the store.

Arlene: Can't trust anybody. (*Finally turning around.*)

Ruby: Well, you don't want to trust him, that's for sure.

Arlene: We spent a lot of time together, me an Carl.

Ruby: He live here?

Arlene: No, he jus broke outta Bricktown near where I was. I got word there sayin he'd meet me. I didn't believe it then, but he don't lie, Carl don't.

Ruby: You thinkin of goin with him?

Arlene: They'll catch him. I told him but he don't listen.

Ruby: Funny ain't it, the number a' men come without ears.

Arlene: How much that dishwashin job pay?

Ruby: I don't know. Maybe 75.

Arlene: That's what he said.

Ruby: He tell you you was gonna wear out your hands and knees grubbin for nuthin, git old an be broke an never have a nice dress to wear? (*Sitting down.*)

Arlene: Yeah.

Ruby: He tell you nobody's gonna wanna be with you cause you done time?

Arlene: Yeah.

Ruby: He tell you your kid gonna be ashamed of you an nobody's gonna believe you if you tell em you changed?

Arlene: Yeah.

Ruby: Then he was right. (*Pauses.*) But when you make your two nickels, you can keep both of em.

Arlene (shattered by these words):   Well, I can't do that.

Ruby: Can't do what?

Arlene: Live like that. Be like bein dead.

Ruby: You kin always call in sick . . . stay home, send out for pizza an watch your Johnny Carson on TV . . . or git a bus way out Preston Street an go bowlin . . .

Arlene (anger building):   What am I gonna do? I can't git no work that will pay good cause I can't do nuthin. It'll be years fore I have a nice rug for this place. I'll never even have some ol Ford to drive around, I'll never take Joey to no fair. I won't be invited home for pot roast and I'll have to wear this fuckin dress for the rest of my life. What kind of life is that?

Ruby: It's outside.

Arlene: Outside? Honey I'll either be *inside* this apartment or *inside* some kitchen sweatin over the sink. Outside's where you get to do what you want, not where you gotta do some shit job jus so's you can eat worse than you did in prison. That ain't why I quit bein so hateful, so I could come back and rot in some slum.

Ruby (word "slum" hits hard):   Well, you can wash dishes to pay the rent on your "slum," or you can spread your legs for any shit that's got the ten dollars. (*With obvious contempt.*)

Arlene (not hostile):   An I don't need you agitatin me.

Ruby: An I don't live in no slum.

Arlene (sensing Ruby's hurt):   Well, I'm sorry . . . it's just . . . I thought . . . (*Increasingly upset.*)

Ruby (finishing her sentence to her):   . . . it was gonna be different. Well, it ain't. And the sooner you believe it, the better off you'll be. (*A guard enters Arlie's cell.*)

Arlie: Where's the chaplain? I got somethin to tell him.

Arlene: They said I's . . .

Guard-Caldwell: He ain't comin.

Arlene: . . . he tol me if . . . I thought once Arlie . . .

Arlie: It's Tuesday. He comes to see me on Tuesday.

Guard-Caldwell: Chaplain's been transferred, dollie. Gone. Bye-bye. You know.

Arlene: He said the meek, meek, them that's quiet and good . . . the meek . . . as soon as Arlie . . .

Ruby: What, Arlene? Who said what?

Arlie: He's not comin back?

Arlene: At Pine Ridge there was . . .

Arlie: He woulda told me if he couldn't come back.

Arlene: I was . . .

Guard-Caldwell: He left this for you.

Arlene: I was . . .

Guard-Caldwell: Picture of Jesus, looks like.

Arlene: . . . this chaplain . . .

Ruby: Arlene . . . (*Trying to call her back from this hysteria.*)

Arlie (hysterical):   I need to talk to him.

Arlene: This chaplain . . .

Arlie: You tell him to come back and see me.

Arlene: I was in lockup . . .

Arlie (a final, anguished plea):   I want the chaplain!

Arlene: I don't know . . . years . . .

Ruby: And . . .

Arlene: This chaplain said I had . . . said Arlie was my hateful self and she
    was hurtin me and God would find some way to take her away . . . and
    it was God's will so I could be the meek . . . the meek, them that's
    quiet and good an git whatever they want . . . I forgit that word . . .
    they git the Earth.

Ruby: Inherit.

Arlene: Yeah. And that's why I done it.

Ruby: Done what?

Arlene: What I done. Cause the chaplain he said . . . I'd sit up nights
    waitin for him to come talk to me.

Ruby: Arlene, what did you do? What are you talkin about?

Arlene: They tol me . . . after I's out an it was all over . . . they said after
    the chaplain got transferred . . . I didn't know why he didn't come no
    more til after . . . they said it was three whole nights at first, me
    screamin to God to come git Arlie an kill her. They give me this
    medicine an thought I's better . . . then that night it happened, the
    officer was in the dorm doin count . . . an they didn't hear nuthin but
    they come back out where I was an I'm standin there tellin em to
    come see, real quiet I'm tellin em, but there's all this blood all over my
    shirt an I got this fork I'm holdin real tight in my hand . . . (*clenches
    one hand now, the other hand fumbling with the buttons as if she's going
    to show Ruby*) this fork, they said Doris stole it from the kitchen an
    give it to me so I'd kill myself and shut up botherin her . . . an there's
    all these holes all over me where I been stabbin myself an I'm sayin
    Arlie is dead for what she done to me, Arlie is dead an it's God's will
    . . . I didn't scream it, I was jus sayin it over and over . . . Arlie is dead,
    Arlie is dead . . . they couldn't git that fork outta my hand til . . . I
    woke up in the infirmary an they said I almost died. They said they's

glad I didn't. (*Smiling.*) They said did I feel better now an they was real nice, bringing me chocolate puddin . . .

Ruby: I'm sorry, Arlene. (*Reaches out for her, but Arlene pulls away sharply.*)

Arlene: I'd be eatin or jus lookin at the ceiling an git a tear in my eye, but it'd jus dry up, you know, it didn't run out or nuthin. An then pretty soon, I's well, an officers was sayin they's seein such a change in me an givin me yarn to knit sweaters an how'd I like to have a new skirt to wear an sometimes lettin me chew gum. They said things ain't never been as clean as when I's doin the housekeepin at the dorm. (*So proud.*) An then I got in the honor cottage an nobody was foolin with me no more or nuthin. An I didn't git mad like before or nuthin. I jus done my work an knit . . . an I don't think about it what happened, cept . . . (*now losing control*) people here keep callin me Arlie an . . . (*has trouble saying "Arlie"*) I didn't mean to do it, what I done . . .

Ruby: Oh, honey . . . (*Trying to help.*)

Arlene: I did . . . (*This is very difficult.*) I mean, Arlie was a pretty mean kid, but I did . . . (*Very quickly.*) I didn't know what I . . . (*Breaks down completely, screaming, crying, falling over into Ruby's lap.*) Arlie! (*Grieving for this lost self.*)

Ruby (rubs her back, her hair, waiting for the calm she knows will come. Finally, but very quietly): You can still . . . (*now obviously referring to some personal loss of her own*) . . . you can still love people that's gone. (*Ruby continues to hold her tenderly, rocking as with a baby. A terrible crash is heard on the steps outside the apartment.*)

Bennie's Voice: Well, chicken pluckin, hog kickin shit!

Ruby: Don't you move now, it's just somebody out in the hall.

Arlene: That's . . .

Ruby: It's O.K., Arlene. Everything's gonna be just fine. Nice and quiet now.

Arlene: That's Bennie that guard I told you about.

Ruby: I'll get it. You stay still now. (*She walks to the door, and looks out into the hall, hands on hips.*) Why you dumpin them flowers on the stairs like that? Won't git no sun at all! (*Turns back to Arlene.*) Arlene, there's a man plantin a garden out in the hall. You think we should call the police or get him a waterin' can?

Bennie (appearing in the doorway, carrying a box of dead looking plants): I didn't try to fall, you know.

Ruby: Well, when you git ready to *try,* I wanna watch! (*Blocking the door.*)

Arlene: I thought you's gone.

Ruby (to Bennie): You got a visitin pass?

Bennie (coming into the room): Arlie . . . (*Quickly.*) Arlene. I brung you some plants. You know, plants for your window. Like we talked about, so's you don't see them bars.

Ruby (picking up one of the plants): They sure is scraggly lookin things. Next time, git plastic.

Bennie: I'm sorry I dropped em, Arlene. We kin get em back together an they'll do real good. (*Setting them down on the trunk.*) These ones don't take the sun. I asked just to make sure. Arlene?

Ruby: You up for seein this petunia killer?

Arlene: It's O.K. Bennie, this is Ruby, upstairs.

Bennie (bringing one flower over to show Arlene, stuffing it back into its pot): See? It ain't dead.

Ruby: Poor little plant. It comes from a broken home.

Bennie (walks over to the window, getting the box and holding it up to the window): That's gonna look real pretty. Cheerful-like.

Ruby: Arlene ain't gettin the picture yet. (*Walking to the window and holding her plant up, too, posing.*) Now. (*Arlene looks, but is not amused.*)

Bennie (putting the plants back down): I jus thought, after what I done last night . . . I jus wanted to do somethin nice.

Arlene (calmer now): They is nice. Thanks.

Ruby: Arlene says you're a guard.

Bennie: I was. I quit. Retired.

Arlene: Bennie's goin back to Alabama.

Bennie: Well, I ain't leavin right away. There's this guy at the motel says the bass is hittin pretty good right now. Thought I might fish some first.

Arlene: Then he's goin back.

Bennie (to Ruby as he washes his hands): I'm real fond of this little girl. I ain't goin til I'm sure she's gonna do O.K. Thought I might help some.

Ruby: Arlene's had about all the help she can stand.

Bennie: I got a car, Arlene. An money. An . . . (*reaching into his pocket*) I brung you some gum.

Arlene: That's real nice, too. An I 'preciate what you done, bringin me here an all, but . . .

Bennie: Well, look. Least you can take my number at the motel an give me a ring if you need somethin. (*Gives her a piece of paper.*) Here, I wrote it down for you. (*Arlene takes the paper.*) Oh, an somethin else, these towel things . . . (*reaching into his pocket, pulling out the packaged towelettes*) they was in the chicken last night. I thought I might be needin em, but they give us new towels every day at that motel.

Arlene: O.K. then. I got your number.

Bennie (backing up toward the door): Right. Right. Any ol thing, now. Jus any ol thing. You even run outta gum an you call.

Ruby: Careful goin down.

Arlene: Bye Bennie.

Bennie: Right. The number now. Don't lose it. You know, in case you need somethin.

Arlene: No. (*Bennie leaves, Arlene gets up and picks up the matchbook Carl gave her and holds it with Bennie's piece of paper.*)

Ruby (watches a moment, sees Arlene trying to make this decision, knowing that what she says now is very important):   We had this waitress put her phone number in matchbooks, give em to guys left her nice tips. Anyway, one night this little ol guy calls her and comes over and says he works at this museum an he don't have any money but he's got this hat belonged to Queen Victoria. An she felt real sorry for him so she screwed him for this little ol lacy hat. Then she takes the hat back the next day to the museum thinkin she'll git a reward or somethin an you know what they done? (*Pause.*) Give her a free membership. Tellin her thanks so much an we're so grateful an wouldn't she like to see this mummy they got downstairs . . . an all the time jus stallin . . . waiting cause they called the police.

Arlene: You do any time for that?

Ruby (admitting the story was about her):   County jail.

Arlene (quietly, looking at the matchbook):   County jail. (*Arlene tears up the matchbook and drops it in the sack of trash.*) You got any Old Maids?

Ruby: Huh?

Arlene: You know.

Ruby: Cards? (*Surprised and pleased.*)

Arlene (laughs a little):   It's the only one I know.

Ruby: Old Maid, huh? (*Not her favorite game.*)

Arlene: I gotta put my food up first.

Ruby: Bout an hour?

Arlene: I'll come up.

Ruby: Great. (*Stopping by the plants on her way to the door.*) These plants is real ugly. (*Fondly. Exits. Arlene watches her, then turns back to the groceries still on the floor. Slowly, but with great determination, she picks up the items one at a time and puts them away in the cabinet above the counter. Arlie appears on the catwalk, one light on each of them.*)

Arlie: Hey! You member that time we was playin policeman an June locked me up in Mama's closet an then took off swimmin? An I stood around with them dresses itchin my ears an crashin into that door tryin to git outta there? It was dark in there. So, finally, (*very proud*) I went around an peed in all Mama's shoes. But then she come home an tried to git in the closet only June taken the key so she said, "Who's in there?" an I said, "It's me!" and she said, "What you doin in there?" an I started gigglin an she started pullin on the door an yellin, "Arlie, what you doin in there?" (*Big laugh.*)

Arlie and Arlene (Arlene has begun to smile during the story, now they say together, both standing as Mama did, one hand on her hip):   Arlie, what you doin in there?

Arlene (still smiling and remembering, stage dark except for one light on her face):   Aw shoot. (*Light dims on her fond smile as Arlie laughs once more.*)

Questions for close reading

1. What differences in attitude, language, and behavior contrast Arlie and Arlene at the beginning of the play?
2. Does Bennie reveal his motives in helping Arlene set up her apartment?
3. Arlie carries the weight of exposition in her scenes. What kind of life did she have when she was young?
4. Describe Arlene's relationship with her mother. What was her relationship with her father? What are Arlene's sisters and brother like?
5. Why does the chaplain give Arlie her new name? Why does she accept it?
6. What does Carl offer Arlene? What are his motives?
7. What is the significance of the conflict between Bennie and Carl?
8. Why does Act II begin with a replication of prison life?
9. How important is Ruby to helping Arlene maintain her sense of self?
10. Arlie's character changes slightly in Act II. What are the marks of that change?
11. What are the differences between the kind of life Carl offers Arlene and the life that Arlene envisions for herself? Are the choices realistic?
12. Is Bennie's decision to back off and leave Arlene alone realistic?

Questions for interpretation

1. Although the chaplain does not appear in the play, he is responsible for bringing Arlie to the point of becoming Arlene. The play quotes the Bible frequently, especially that passage concerning the meek inheriting the earth. Can the play be interpreted as describing a religious conversion? How religious are the various characters in the play? What role does religion have in the drama?
2. Examine the characters for their motivations and eventual behaviors. Does Arlie seem well enough motivated to become Arlene? Does Arlene seem strong enough to resist Bennie and Carl? Is Carl's behavior reasonable given that he has traveled so far to find Arlene?
3. Regarding this play as a tragicomedy, is it possible that environment and upbringing could take on the role of fate in Arlie's life? Review the circumstances of Arlene's history as told by her mother. Is Arlene a victim of circumstances? If so, how is she able to overcome them? Does fate enter into the action of the play?
4. What is the relationship of men and women in this play? Can the play be interpreted as a feminist or antifeminist drama?
5. Can the drama be interpreted psychologically? Is it psychologically significant that Arlie murdered a cab driver and that her father was a cab driver? Does Arlie seem to have been abused psychologically?
6. Describe the plot of the drama. How does the action that is reported to us from the past relate to the action that takes place on stage? Is the plot a more important element than characterization?

11

Interpreting Drama

Like all literature, drama invites interpretation. However, unlike other forms of literature, drama is live action, so there are many things beyond the text to interpret. For example, vocal inflection or physical movement can suggest meanings invisible in the text. Despite these problems, you can still interpret dramatic texts without having seen full-scale productions if you take the time to recreate them as you read.

A good reading of a play provides the basis of a good interpretation. It includes paying close attention to stage directions and trying to translate those directions into an imaginative structure. Reading the key lines aloud can also help. In plays, you cannot always rely on description and authorial comment for a clue to character. Instead, you need to rely on your powers of observation. For example, Strindberg is careful not to tell you whether Jean or Miss Julie is more sexually aggressive. Which of them seduced the other? In order to decide, you need to interpret the dialogue and the stage directions very carefully. The evidence of the text does not include a commentary.

CLOSE READING

A close reading examines the text for its use of the elements of drama, such as plot, characterization, style, and setting. The stage directions usually provide enough clues to imagine the actors in motion. For some plays that require more theatricality than others, of course, a close reading of the text alone might yield less than an analysis of a performance. However, close reading is always essential to an interpretation.

Because drama is performed for an audience, it is much more likely to be concerned with audience response than other kinds of literature. For that reason, close reading usually aims at uncovering the elements that most clearly affect the audience. It raises questions about the portrayal of character, the believability of a dramatic situation, the genre of the play (tragedy, comedy, tragicomedy), the use of dramatic irony, thematic questions (especially if it is a "message" play), and style. In certain plays close reading needs to account for imagery, symbolism, and patterns of repetition. Since every play is unique, every play requires a certain kind of attention. For example, in *Riders to the Sea* the language, because it attempts to recreate the way people in the west of Ireland spoke, has a special hypnotic effect on the audience, something like the effect of music. If you are to understand the power of this play, then, you need to hear this music as you read.

The first question in a drama is: What happens? Thus the first thing to examine is the plot. In *Riders to the Sea* the action concerns a mother and her daughters losing the last man in the family to the sea. Bartley literally rides to the sea on a horse, but there is also a mythic element in the play that converts all the men in Maurya's family into riders to the sea. It is not the Greek myth of Poseidon, but instead an Irish myth of the "Steeds of Mananaan," the horses of those who live "under the sea." Most Irish would have learned this myth in school, and they would have understood that Synge tapped into the power of the myth by showing that the horsemen of "under-the-sea" were once mortals, now converted into mythic characters.

Among the themes of the play is naturally the theme of loss. But loss is connected to the harsh ways in which the characters must live. All Maurya has are some white deal boards to use for making her coffin, and now they must go to Bartley's coffin. She is so old and worn she has forgotten the nails. Life has taken its toll, and her willingness to continue despite the suffering she feels could be considered a powerful theme of the play.

INTERPRETIVE STRATEGIES

As with fiction, drama can sustain interpretation from many viewpoints: formalist New Criticism, psychological criticism, feminist criticism, political-economic criticism, cultural criticism, or historical criticism. Naturally, not every play responds equally well to every kind of interpretive strategy. For example, you might find it somewhat daunting to interpret *Riders to the Sea* from a psychological or political-economic perspective. What, for example, is the class struggle in the play? If there is one, how important is it in relation to other ideas in the play? What is the psychological theme? On the other hand, you might find feminist criticism a very useful approach. For example, the women are the ultimate victims of the play because they must live in poverty with the men dead. The men die—so they are victims, too—but they do not always die needfully. Bartley, for example, rides off to the fair, not like his father going to sea to earn the bread for the table. Bartley is reckless. Why? Because he is a man, and he does what men do in this society: leave women to suffer without help.

Similarly, the psychological issues in Woody Allen's *Death Knocks* are worth interpreting in detail, whereas the feminist issues are hardly evident. Nat Ackerman is reflected in his Death. We do not think of Death as a realistic character any more than we think of the play as a realistic play. It is absurd, but absurd in a way that permits us to gain insight into the issues of the drama. Nat Ackerman's Death has many of his weaknesses, especially a weakness for gin rummy. The point is that our personality—a product of psychological forces, among other things—in a very complex way "chooses" our Death. This is comic partly because it is absurd, but also partly because it is the opposite of tragedy, in which the fates choose our death. By referring to the question of tragedy and comedy, you raise formalist issues. The extent to which Allen clarifies the comic form is central to formalist interpretive strategy. The same is true for *Riders to the Sea*.

Political issues and related feminist issues are dominant in Strindberg's *Miss Julie*. Any interpretive strategy that totally ignored the differences in social class between Jean and Julie might be interesting, but it could not be complete. *Miss Julie* admits of many different interpretive strategies. First, the constant stress between the main characters engendered by the difference in their social rank is so great that it dominates the play. Jean talks about it all the time. Kristin alludes to it. The presence of the Count—offstage, but as powerful as the abstract idea of society—is foreboding and threatening. Julie tries to pretend it does not matter. Yet, she reminds us of her mother's questionable past and implies that Julie may have been compromised genetically.

Yet, beyond the political issues central to the play are also the issues of gender. Miss Julie wishes to dominate Jean. Jean, because he is a man, cannot abide the thought of that. He sees his role as a traditional dominating seducer, and yet he is undermined because of his servile position in the play. As he says, he always has something of the lackey in him. It compromises him. There would be no play if Jean were the Count's son and Julie were a serving-maid. Ironically, the situation would be too common. But with the gender roles reversed, the play contains complexities that have made it one of the most-produced of Scandinavian drama.

A psychological approach might be very telling with this drama, since the Count, as Julie's father, takes on the role of a dark shadow, a threatening presence whom Julie fears, but loves at the same time. Jean's relation with the Count is much the same. The sexual energy in the play seems to awaken Freudian possibilities in the interpretation. Now that her same-sex parent is "dead" she is free to complete the Oedipal wish and "have" her father. But since her father will not have her, the closest she can get to him is to seduce his valet, the man who is as devoted to him as a son. From this perspective, the play becomes rich and complex, adding to its political dimension.

A STUDENT INTERPRETATION

The following sections describe the development of an interpretation of Susan Glaspell's brief comedy *Suppressed Desires*. Susan Glaspell (1876–1948) founded the most important theater movement in twentieth-century American drama: the Provincetown Playhouse. After graduating from Drake University, she began a career in journalism. Soon she published her first novel, *The Glory of the Conquered* (1909), which was followed with a collection of stories, *Lifted Masks* (1912), and a second novel, *Fidelity* (1915). She went to Paris on the earnings of her first novel and returned to meet and marry the novelist George Cram Cook. Cook, known as Jig, kidded Glaspell about her serious interest in Freudian psychology, and their joking produced so many good lines of dialogue that they suddenly realized they might have an amusing play. In this way *Suppressed Desires* was formed. Jig Cook helped develop the idea, and Susan Glaspell finished the dialogue. The Provincetown Playhouse began in Susan Glaspell's living room, where the play was first read. Eventually a stage was found in Provincetown for full productions, and soon it moved to New York.

Susan Glaspell wrote a letter to the Editor of *The New York Times* (February 15, 1920) in response to a review of *Suppressed Desires* in which she explains her purposes in writing.

> It seems to me that in calling *Suppressed Desires* a jeering travesty on psychoanalysis you are forgetting what the play is leveled at. It is having fun with the people who went off their heads about psychoanalysis—went "bugs"—when this subject reached the first circle in New York to know of it—some years in advance of reaching other circles. If you had known some of those people as we knew them you would certainly have felt them legitimate game for some form of comic treatment. The psychoanalysts knew them, and writers on psychoanalysis and practicing analysts have been among the play's best friends. Surely there is a real distinction here. You are not making fun of a thing when you make fun of people who are absurdly uncritical about that thing.
>
> Mr. Cook and I have been students of psychoanalysis for a number of years and we feel it a bit unfair to put us in the light of people unaware of its significance.

Glaspell wrote several more plays and won the Pulitzer Prize for playwriting in 1930 for *Alison's House*, a play about Emily Dickinson.

Susan Glaspell   (1876–1948)
SUPPRESSED DESIRES   1914

with the collaboration of George Cram Cook

Characters
   Henrietta Brewster
   Stephen Brewster
   Mabel

(Place: A New York apartment. Time: today.)
(A period of two weeks is supposed to elapse between the first and second scenes.)

SCENE I

(The stage represents a studio, used as living and dining room in an upper story, Washington Square South. Through an immense north window in the back wall appear tree tops and the upper part of the Washington Arch. Beyond it you look up Fifth Avenue. There are rugs, bookcases, a divan. Near the window is a big table, loaded at one end with serious-looking books and austere scientific periodicals. At the other end are architects drawings, blueprints, dividing compasses, square, ruler, etc. There is a door in each side wall. Near the one to the spectator's right stands a costumer with hats and coats masculine and feminine. There is a breakfast table set for three but only two seated at it—namely Henrietta and Stephen Brewster. As the curtains withdraw Steve pushes back his coffee cup and sits dejected.)

Henrietta: It isn't the coffee, Steve dear. There's nothing the matter with the coffee. There's something the matter with *you.*

Steve (doggedly):   There may be something the matter with my stomach.

Henrietta (scornfully):   Your stomach! The trouble is not with your stomach but in your subconscious mind.

Steve: Subconscious piffle! (*Takes morning paper and tries to read.*)

Henrietta: Steve, you never used to be so disagreeable. You certainly have got some sort of a complex. You're all inhibited. You're no longer open to new ideas. You won't listen to a word about psychoanalysis.

Steve: A word! I've listened to volumes!

Henrietta: You've ceased to be creative in architecture—your work isn't going well. You're not sleeping well——

Steve: How can I sleep, Henrietta, when you're always waking me up in the night to find out what I'm dreaming?

Henrietta: But dreams are so important, Steve.

Steve: There's nothing wrong with me.

Henrietta: You don't even talk as well as you used to.

Steve: Talk? I can't say a thing without you looking at me in that dark fashion you have when you're on the trail of a complex.

Henrietta: This very irritability indicates that you're suffering from some suppressed desire.

Steve: I'm suffering from a suppressed desire for a little peace.

Henrietta: Dr. Russell is doing simply wonderful things with nervous cases. Won't you go to him, Steve?

Steve (slamming down his newspaper):   No, Henrietta, I won't!

Henrietta: But, Stephen—!

Steve: Tst! I hear Mabel coming. Let's not be at each other's throats the first day of her visit. (*He takes out cigarettes. Enter Mabel from door left, the side opposite Steve, so that he is facing her. She is wearing a rather fussy negligee and breakfast cap in contrast to Henrietta, who wears "radical" clothes. Mabel is what is called plump.*)

Mabel: Good morning.

Henrietta: Oh, here you are, little sister.

Steve: Good morning, Mabel. (*Mabel nods to him and turns, her face lighting up, to Henrietta.*)

Henrietta (giving Mabel a hug as she leans against her): It's so good to have you here.

Mabel: It's so good to be here—with you.

Henrietta: I was going to let you sleep, thinking you'd be tired after the long trip. Sit down. There'll be fresh toast in a few minutes and (*rising from her chair*) will you have——

Mabel: Oh, I ought to have told you, Henrietta. Don't get anything for me. I'm not eating any breakfast.

Henrietta (at first in mere surprise): Not eating breakfast? (*She sits down, then leans toward Mabel and scrutinizes her.*)

Steve (half to himself): The psychoanalytical look!

Henrietta: Mabel, why are you not eating any breakfast?

Mabel (a little startled): Why, no particular reason. I just don't care much for breakfast, and they say it keeps down—that is, it's a good thing to go without it.

Henrietta: Don't you sleep well? Did you sleep well last night?

Mabel: Oh, yes, I slept all right. Yes, I slept fine last night, only (*laughing*) I did have the funniest dream!

Steve: S—h! S—t!

Henrietta (moving closer): And what did you dream, Mabel?

Steve: Look-a-here, Mabel, I feel it's my duty to put you on. Don't tell Henrietta your dreams. If you do she'll find out that you have an underground desire to kill your father and marry your mother.

Henrietta: Don't be absurd, Stephen Brewster. (*Sweetly to Mabel.*) What was your dream, dear?

Mabel (laughing): Well, I dreamed I was a hen.

Henrietta: A hen?

Steve (solemnly): A hen.

Mabel: Yes; and I was pushing along through a crowd as fast as I could, but being a hen I couldn't walk very fast—it was like having a tight skirt, you know; and there was some sort of creature in a blue cap—you know how mixed up dreams are—and it kept shouting after me and saying, "Step, Hen! Step, Hen!" until I got all excited and just couldn't move at all.

Henrietta (resting chin in palm and peering): You say you became much excited?

Mabel (laughing): Oh, yes; I was in a terrible state.

Henrietta (leaning back, murmurs):   This is significant.

Steve: She dreams she's a hen. She is told to step lively. She becomes violently agitated. What can it mean?

Henrietta (turning impatiently from him):   Mabel, do you know anything about psychoanalysis?

Mabel (feebly):   Oh—not much. No—I—(*Brightening.*) It's something about the war, isn't it?

Steve: Not that kind of war.

Mabel (abashed):   I thought it might be the name of a new explosive.

Steve: It *is*.

Mabel (apologetically to Henrietta, who is frowning):   You see, Henrietta, I—we do not live in touch with intellectual things, as you do. Bob being a dentist—somehow—our friends—

Steve (softly):   Oh, to be a dentist! (*Goes to window and stands looking out.*)

Henrietta: Don't you ever see anything more of that editorial writer— what was his name?

Mabel: Lyman Eggleston?

Henrietta: Yes, Eggleston. He was in touch with things. Don't you see him?

Mabel: Yes, I see him once in a while. Bob doesn't like him very well.

Henrietta: Your husband does not like Lyman Eggleston? (*Mysteriously.*) Mabel, are you perfectly happy with your husband?

Steve (sharply):   Oh, come now, Henrietta—that's going a little strong!

Henrietta: Are you perfectly happy with him, Mabel? (*Steve goes to worktable.*)

Mabel: Why—yes—I guess so. Why—of course I am!

Henrietta: Are you happy? Or do you only think *you* are? Or do you only think you *ought* to be?

Mabel: Why, Henrietta, I don't know what you mean!

Steve (seizes stack of books and magazines and dumps them on the breakfast table):   This is what she means, Mabel. Psychoanalysis. My worktable groans with it. Books by Freud, the new Messiah; books by Jung, the new St. Paul; the *Psychoanalytical Review*—back numbers two-fifty per.

Mabel: But what is it all about?

Steve: All about your sub, un, nonconscious mind and desires you know not of. They may be doing you a great deal of harm. You may go crazy with them. Oh, yes! People are doing it right and left. Your dreaming you're a hen—— (*Shakes his head darkly.*)

Mabel (hastily, to avert a quarrel):   But what do you say it is, Henrietta?

Steve (looking at his watch):   Oh, if Henrietta's going to start that! (*He goes to his worktable, and during Henrietta's next speech settles himself and sharpens a lead pencil.*)

Henrietta: It's like this, Mabel. You want something. You think you can't have it. You think it's wrong. So you try to think you don't want it.

Your mind protects you—avoids pain—by refusing to think the forbidden thing. But it's there just the same. It stays there shut up in your unconscious mind, and it festers.

Steve: Sort of an ingrowing mental toenail.

Henrietta: Precisely. The forbidden impulse is there full of energy which has simply got to do something. It breaks into your consciousness in disguise, masks itself in dreams, makes all sorts of trouble. In extreme cases it drives you insane.

Mabel (with a gesture of horror): Oh!

Henrietta (reassuring): But psychoanalysis has found out how to save us from that. It removes the obstruction, brings into consciousness the suppressed desire that was making all the trouble. In a word psychoanalysis is simply the latest scientific method of preventing and curing insanity.

Steve (from his table): It is also the latest scientific method of separating families.

Henrietta (mildly): Families that ought to be separated.

Steve: The Dwights, for instance. You must have met them, Mabel, when you were here before. Helen was living, apparently, in peace and happiness with good old Joe. Well—she went to this psychoanalyzer she was "psyched," and biff!—bang!—Home she comes with an unsuppressed desire to leave her husband. (*He starts work, drawing lines on a drawing board with a T-square.*)

Mabel: How terrible! Yes, I remember Helen Dwight. But—but did she have such a desire?

Steve: First she'd known of it.

Mabel: And she *left* him?

Henrietta (coolly): Yes, she did.

Mabel: Wasn't he good to her?

Henrietta: Why yes, good enough.

Mabel: Wasn't he kind to her?

Henrietta: Oh, yes—kind to her.

Mabel: And she left her good, kind husband—!

Henrietta: Oh, Mabel! "Left her good, kind husband!" How naive— forgive me, dear, but how bourgeois you are! She came to know herself. And she had the courage!!

Mabel: I may be very naive and—bourgeois—but I don't see the good of a new science that breaks up homes. (*Steve claps hands, applauding.*)

Steve: In enlightening Mabel, we mustn't neglect to mention the case of Art Holden's private secretary, Mary Snow, who has just been informed of her suppressed desire for her employer.

Mabel: Why, I think it is terrible, Henrietta! It would be better if we didn't know such things about ourselves.

Henrietta: No, Mabel, that is the old way.

Mabel: But—but her employer? Is he married?

Steve (grunts): Wife and four children.

Mabel: Well, then, what good does it do the girl to be told she has a desire for him? There's nothing that can be done about it.

Henrietta: Old institutions will have to be reshaped so that something can be done in such cases. It happens, Mabel, that this suppressed desire was on the point of landing Mary Snow in the insane asylum. Are you so tight-minded that you'd rather have her in the insane asylum than break the conventions?

Mabel: But—but have people always had these awful suppressed desires?

Henrietta: Always.

Steve: But they've just been discovered.

Henrietta: The harm they do has just been discovered. And free, sane people must face the fact that they have to be dealt with.

Mabel (stoutly): I don't believe they have them in Chicago.

Henrietta (business of giving Mabel up): People "have them" wherever the living Libido—the center of the soul's energy—is in conflict with petrified moral codes. That means everywhere in civilization. Psychoanalysis—

Steve: Good God! I've got the roof in the cellar! (*Holds plan at arm's length.*)

Henrietta: The roof in the cellar! That's what psychoanalysis could undo. (*To Mabel.*) Is it any wonder I'm concerned about Steve? He dreamed the other night that the walls of his room melted away and he found himself alone in a forest. Don't you see how significant it is for an architect to have *walls* slip away from him like that? It symbolizes his loss of grip in his work. There's some suppressed desire——

Steve: (*hurling his ruined plan viciously to the floor*): Suppressed hell!

Henrietta: You speak more truly than you know. It is through suppressions that hells are formed in us.

Mabel (looking at Steve, who is tearing his hair): Don't you think it would be a good thing, Henrietta, if we went somewhere else? (*They rise and begin to pick up the dishes. Mabel drops a plate which breaks. Henrietta draws up short and looks at her—the psychoanalytic look.*) I'm sorry, Henrietta. One of the Spode plates, too. (*Surprised and resentful as Henrietta continues to peer at her.*) Don't take it so to heart, Henrietta.

Henrietta: I can't help taking it to heart.

Mabel: I'll get you another. (*Pause. More sharply as Henrietta does not answer.*) I said I'll get you another plate, Henrietta.

Henrietta: It's not the plate.

Mabel: For heaven's sake, what is it then?

Henrietta: It's the significant little false movement once in a while.

Mabel: Well, I suppose everyone makes a false movement once in a while.

Henrietta: Yes, Mabel, but these false movements all mean something.

Mabel (about to cry): I don't think that's very nice! It was just because I happened to think of Mabel Snow you were talking about——

Henrietta: *Mabel Snow*!

Mabel: Snow—Snow—Well, what was her name, then?

Henrietta: Her name is Mary.

Mabel: Well, *Mary* Snow, then; *Mary* Snow. I never heard her name but once. I don't see anything to make such a fuss about.

Henrietta (gently):   Mabel dear—mistakes like that in names——

Mabel (desperately):   They don't mean something, too, do they?

Henrietta (gently):   I am sorry, but they do.

Mabel: But I am always doing that!

Henrietta (after a start of horror):   My poor little sister, tell me all about it.

Mabel: About what?

Henrietta: About your not being happy. About your yearnings for another sort of life.

Mabel: But I *don't.*

Henrietta: Ah, I understand these things, dear. You feel Bob is limiting you to a life which you do not feel free——

Mabel: Henrietta! When did I ever say such a thing?

Henrietta: You said you are not in touch with things intellectual. You showed your feelings that it is Bob's profession—that has engendered a resentment which has colored your whole life with him.

Mabel: Why—Henrietta!

Henrietta: Don't be afraid, little sister. There's nothing can shock me or turn me from you. I am not like that. I wanted you to come for this visit because I had a feeling that you needed more from life than you were getting. No one of these things I have seen would excite my suspicion. It's the combination. You don't eat breakfast; you make false moves; you substitute your own name for the name of another *whose love is misdirected.* You're nervous; you look queer; in your eyes there's a frightened look that is most unlike you. And this dream. A *hen*—Come with me this afternoon to Dr. Russell! Your whole life may be at stake, Mabel.

Mabel (gasping):   Henrietta, I—you—you always were the smartest in the family, and all that, but—this is terrible! I don't think we *ought* to think such things, and—(*Brightening.*) Why, I'll tell you why I dreamed I was a hen. It was because last night, telling about that time in Chicago, you said I was as mad as a wet hen.

Henrietta (superior):   Did you dream you were a *wet* hen?

Mabel (forced to admit it):   No.

Henrietta: No. You dreamed you were a *dry* hen. And why, being a hen, were you urged to step?

Mabel: Maybe it's because when I am getting on a street-car it always irritates me to have them call "Step lively."

Henrietta: No, Mabel, that is only a child's view of it—if you will forgive me. You see merely the elements used in the dream. You do not see into the dream; you do not see its meaning. This dream of the hen——

Steve: Hen—hen—wet hen—dry hen—mad hen! (*Jumps up in a rage.*) Let me out of this!

Henrietta (hastily picking up dishes, speaks soothingly): Just a minute, dear, and we'll have things so you can work in quiet. Mabel and I are going to sit in my room. (*She goes out with both hands full of dishes.*)

Steve (seizing hat and coat from the costumer): I'm going to be psychoanalyzed. I'm going now! I'm going straight to that infallible doctor of hers—that priest of this new religion. If he's got honesty enough to tell Henrietta there's nothing the matter with my unconscious mind, perhaps I can be let alone about it, and then I *will* be all right. (*From the door in a low voice.*) Don't tell Henrietta I'm going. It might take weeks, and I couldn't stand all the talk. (*Exit desperately.*)

(*Enter Henrietta.*)

Henrietta: Where's Steve? Gone? (*With hopeless gesture.*) You see how impatient he is!—how unlike himself! I tell you, Mabel, I am nearly distracted about Steve.

Mabel: I think he's a little distracted, too.

Henrietta: Well, if he's gone—you might as well stay in this room. I have a committee meeting at the bookshop, and will have to leave you to yourself for an hour or two. (*As she puts her hat on, her eye, lighting up almost carnivorously, falls on an enormous volume on the floor beside the worktable. The book has been half hidden from the audience by the wastebasket. She picks it up and carries it around the table toward Mabel.*) Here, dear, this is one of the simplest statements of psychoanalysis. You read it and then we can talk more intelligently. (*Mabel takes volume and staggers back under its weight to chair rear center; Henrietta goes to outer door, stops and asks abruptly.*) How old is Lyman Eggleston?

Mabel (promptly): He isn't forty yet. Why, what made you ask that, Henrietta? (*As she turns her head to look at Henrietta her hands move toward the upper corners of the book balanced on her knees.*)

Henrietta: Oh, nothing. Au revoir. (*Exit.*)

(*Mabel stares at the ceiling. The book slides to the floor. She starts; looks at the book, then at the broken plate on the table.*) The plate! The book! (*She lifts her eyes, leans forward elbow on knee, chin on knuckles and plaintively queries:*) Am I unhappy?

SCENE II

(*The stage is set as in Scene I except that the breakfast table has been removed and set back against the wall. During the first few minutes the dusk of a winter afternoon deepens. Out of the darkness spring rows of double street-lights almost meeting in the distance. Henrietta is disclosed at the psychoanalytical end of Steve's worktable. Surrounded by open books and periodicals, she is writing. Steve enters briskly.*)

Steve: What are you doing, my dear?

Henrietta: My paper for the Liberal Club.

Steve: Your paper on——?

Henrietta: On a subject which does not have your sympathy.

Steve: Oh, I'm not sure I'm wholly out of sympathy with psychoanalysis, Henrietta. You worked it so hard. I couldn't even take a bath without it's meaning something.

Henrietta (loftily): I talked it because I knew you needed it.

Steve: You haven't said much about it these last two weeks. Uh—your faith in it hasn't weakened any?

Henrietta: Weakened? It's grown stronger with each new thing I've come to know. And Mabel. She is with Dr. Russell now. Dr. Russell is wonderful. From what Mabel tells me I believe he is going to prove that I was right. Today I discovered a remarkable confirmation of my theory in the hen-dream.

Steve: What is your theory?

Henrietta: Well, you know about Lyman Eggleston. I've wondered about him from the first. I've never seen him, but I know he's less bourgeois than Mabel's other friends—more intellectual—and (*significantly*) she doesn't see much of him because Bob doesn't like him.

Steve: But what's the confirmation?

Henrietta: Today I noticed the first syllable of his name.

Steve: Ly?

Henrietta: No—egg.

Steve: Egg?

Henrietta (patiently): Mabel dreamed she was a *hen*. (*Steve laughs.*) You wouldn't laugh if you knew how important names are in interpreting dreams. Freud is full of just such cases in which a whole hidden complex is revealed by a single significant syllable—like this egg.

Steve: Doesn't the traditional relation of hen and egg suggest rather a maternal feeling?

Henrietta: There is something maternal in Mabel—love, of course, but that's only one element.

Steve: Well, suppose Mabel hasn't a suppressed desire to be this gentleman's mother, but his beloved. What's to be done about it? What about Bob? Don't you think it's going to be a little rough on him?

Henrietta: That can't be helped. Bob, like everyone else, must face the facts of life. If Dr. Russell should arrive independently at this same interpretation I shall not hesitate to tell Mabel to leave her present husband.

Steve: Um—um! (*The lights go up on Fifth Avenue. Steve goes to the window and looks out.*) How long is it we've lived here, Henrietta?

Henrietta: Why, this is the third year, Steve.

Steve: I—we—one would miss this view if one went away, wouldn't one?

Henrietta: How strangely you speak! Oh, Stephen, I *wish* you'd go to Dr. Russell. Don't think my fears have abated because I have been able to restrain myself. I felt I must on account of Mabel. It wouldn't do for her to hear you discrediting it while she was being analyzed. But now, dear—won't you go?

Steve: I—(*He breaks off, turns on the light, then comes and sits beside Henrietta.*) How long have we been married, Henrietta?

Henrietta: Stephen, I don't understand you! You must go to Dr. Russell.

Steve: I *have* gone.

Henrietta: You—what?

Steve (jauntily): Yes, Henrietta, I've been psyched.

Henrietta: You went to Dr. Russell?

Steve: The same.

Henrietta: And what did he say?

Steve: He said—I—I was a little surprised by what he said, Henrietta.

Henrietta (breathlessly): Of course—one can so seldom anticipate. But tell me—your dream, Stephen? It means——?

Steve: It means—I was considerably surprised by what it means.

Henrietta: *Don't* be so exasperating!

Steve: It means—you really want to know, Henrietta?

Henrietta: Stephen, you'll drive me mad!

Steve: He said—Of course he may be wrong in what he said.

Henrietta: He *isn't* wrong. *Tell* me!

Steve: He said my dream of the walls receding and leaving me alone in a forest indicates a suppressed desire—

Henrietta: Yes—yes!

Steve: To be freed from——

Henrietta: Yes—freed from——?

Steve: Marriage.

Henrietta (crumples. Stares): Marriage!

Steve: He—he may be mistaken, you know.

Henrietta: *May* be mistaken!

Steve: I—well, of course, I haven't taken any stock in it myself. It was only your great confidence——

Henrietta: Stephen, are you telling me that Dr. Russell—Dr. A. R. Russell—told you this? (*Steve nods.*) Told you you have a suppressed desire to separate from me?

Steve: That's what he said.

Henrietta: Did he know who you were?

Steve: Yes.

Henrietta: That you were married to me?

Steve: Yes, he knew that.

Henrietta (rising): And he told you to leave me?

Steve: It seems he must be wrong, Henrietta.

Henrietta: And I've sent him more patients—! (*Catches herself and resumes coldly.*) What reason did he give for this analysis?

Steve: He says the confining walls are a symbol of my feeling about marriage and that their fading away is a wish-fulfillment.

Henrietta (gulping): Well, is it? Do you want our marriage to end?

Steve: Well, it was a surprise to me that I did, Henrietta—a great surprise. You see I hadn't known what was in my unconscious mind.

Henrietta (flaming): What did you tell Dr. Russell about me? What did you tell him to make him think you were not happy?

Steve: I never told him a thing, Henrietta. He got it all from his confound-clever inferences. I—I tried to refute them, but he said that was only part of my self-protective lying.

Henrietta: And that's why you were so—happy—when you came in just now!

Steve: Why, Henrietta, how can you say such a thing? I was *sad*. Didn't I speak sadly of—of the view? Didn't I ask you how long we had been married?

Henrietta (rising): Stephen Brewster, have you no sense of the seriousness of this? Dr. Russell doesn't know what our marriage has been. You do. You should have laughed him down! Confined—in life with me? Why didn't you tell him that I believed in freedom?

Steve: I very emphatically told him that his results were a great surprise to me.

Henrietta: But you accepted them.

Steve: Oh, not at all. I merely couldn't refute his arguments. I'm not a psychologist. I came home to talk it over with you. You being a disciple of psychoanalysis——

Henrietta (whirling): If you are going, I wish you would go tonight!

Steve: Oh, my dear! I—surely couldn't do that! Think of my feelings. And my laundry hasn't come home yet.

Henrietta: I ask you to go tonight. Some women would falter at this, Steve, but I am not such a woman. I leave you free. I do not repudiate psychoanalysis, I say again that it has done great things. It has also made mistakes, of course. But since you accept this analysis—(*She sits down and pretends to begin work.*) I have to finish this paper. I wish you would leave me.

Steve (scratches his head, goes to the inner door): I'm sorry, Henrietta, about my unconscious mind. (*Exit.*) (*Henrietta's face betrays her outraged state of mind—disconcerted, resentful, trying to pull herself together. She attains an air of bravely bearing an outrageous thing. Mabel enters in great excitement.*)

Mabel (breathless): Henrietta, I'm so glad you're here. And alone? (*Looks toward the inner door.*) Are you alone, Henrietta?

Henrietta (with reproving dignity): Very much so.

Mabel (rushing to her): Henrietta, he's found it!

Henrietta (aloof):   Who has found what?

Mabel: Who has found what? Dr. Russell has found my suppressed desire.

Henrietta: That is interesting.

Mabel: He finished with me today—he got hold of my complex—in the most amazing way! But, oh, Henrietta—it is so terrible!

Henrietta: Do calm yourself, Mabel. Surely there's no occasion for all this agitation.

Mabel: But there is! And when you think of the lives that are affected—the readjustments that must be made in order to bring the suppressed hell out of me and save me from the insane asylum——!

Henrietta: The insane asylum!

Mabel: You said that's where these complexes brought people?

Henrietta: What did the doctor tell you, Mabel?

Mabel: Oh, I don't know how I can tell you—it is so awful—so unbelievable. Henrietta, who would ever have thought it? How can it be true? But the doctor is perfectly certain that I have a suppressed desire for——(*Looks at Henrietta, unable to go on.*)

Henrietta: Oh, go on, Mabel. I'm not unprepared for what you have to say.

Mabel: Not unprepared? You mean you have suspected it?

Henrietta: From the first. It's been my theory all along.

Mabel: But, Henrietta, I didn't know myself that I had this secret desire for Stephen.

Henrietta (jumps up):   Stephen!

Mabel: My brother-in-law! My own sister's husband!

Henrietta: *You* have a suppressed desire for *Stephen*!

Mabel: Oh, Henrietta, aren't these unconscious selves terrible? They seem so unlike us!

Henrietta: What insane things are you driving at?

Mabel (blubbering):   Henrietta, don't you use that word to me. I don't *want* to go to the insane asylum.

Henrietta (stonily):   What did Dr. Russell say?

Mabel: Well, you see—oh, it's the strangest thing! But you know the voice in my dream that called "Step, Hen!" Dr. Russell found out today that when I was a little girl I had a story-book in words of one syllable and I read the name Stephen wrong. I used to read it S-t-e-p, step, h-e-n, hen. (*Dramatically.*) Step Hen is Stephen. (*Enter Stephen, his head bent over a time-table.*) Stephen is Step Hen!

Steve: I? Step Hen!

Mabel (triumphantly):   S-t-e-p, step, H-e-n, hen, Stephen!

Henrietta (exploding):   Well, what if Stephen is Step Hen? (*Scornfully.*) Step Hen! Step Hen! For that ridiculous coincidence——

Mabel: Coincidence! But it's so childish to look at the mere elements of a dream. You have to look into it—you have to see what it means!

Henrietta: And do you mean to say that on account of that trivial,

meaningless play on syllables—on that flimsy basis—you are ready—
(*Wails.*) O-h!

Steve: What on earth's the matter? What has happened? Suppose I *am*
Step Hen? What about it? What does it mean?

Mabel (crying): It means—that I—have a suppressed desire for *you*!

Steve: For me! The deuce you have? (*Feebly.*) What—er—makes you think
so?

Mabel: Dr. Russell has worked it out scientifically.

Henrietta: Yes. Through the amazing discovery that Step Hen equals
Stephen!

Mabel (tearfully): Oh, that isn't all—that isn't near all. Henrietta won't
give me a chance to tell it. She'd rather I'd go to the insane asylum
than be unconventional.

Henrietta: We'll all go there if you can't control yourself. We are still
waiting for some rational report.

Mabel (drying her eyes): Oh, there's such a lot about names. (*With some
pride.*) I don't see how I ever did it. It all works in together. I
dreamed I was a hen because that's the first syllable of *Hen*-rietta's
name, and when I dreamed I was a hen, I was putting myself in
Henrietta's place.

Henrietta: With Stephen?

Mabel: With Stephen.

Henrietta (outraged): Oh! (*Turns in rage upon Stephen, who is fanning
himself with the time-table.*) What are you doing with that time-table?

Steve: Why—I thought—you were so keen to have me go tonight—I
thought I'd just take a run up to Canada, and join Billy—a little
shooting—but——

Mabel: But there's more about the names.

Henrietta: Mabel, have you thought of Bob—dear old Bob—your good,
kind husband?

Mabel: Oh, Henrietta, "my good kind husband"!

Henrietta: Just think of him out there in Chicago, working his head off,
fixing people's teeth—for you!

Mabel: Yes, but think of the living Libido—in conflict with petrified
moral codes! And think of the perfectly wonderful way the names all
prove it. Dr. Russell said he's never seen anything more convincing.
Just look at Stephen's last name—Brewster. I dream I'm a hen, and
the name Brewster—you have to say its first letter by itself—and then
the hen, that's me, she says to him: "Stephen, Be Rooster!"

(*Henrietta and Stephen both collapse on chair and divan.*)

Mabel: I think it's perfectly wonderful! Why, if it wasn't for
psychoanalysis you'd never find out how wonderful your own mind is!

Steve (begins to chuckle): Be Rooster, Stephen, Be Rooster!

Henrietta: You think it's funny, do you?

Steve: Well, what's to be done about it? Does Mabel have to go away with me?

Henrietta: Do you *want* Mabel to go away with you?

Steve: Well, but Mabel herself—her complex—her suppressed desire—!

Henrietta: Mabel, are you going to insist on going away with Stephen?

Mabel: I'd rather go with Stephen than go to the insane asylum!

Henrietta: For Heaven's Sake, Mabel, drop that insane asylum! If you *did* have a suppressed desire for Stephen hidden away in you—God knows it isn't hidden *now*. Dr. Russell has brought it into consciousness— with a vengeance. That's all that's necessary to break up a complex. Psychoanalysis doesn't say you have to *gratify* every suppressed desire.

Steve (softly):   Unless it's for Lyman Eggleston.

Henrietta (turning on him):   Well, if it comes to that, Stephen Brewster, I'd like to know why that interpretation of mine isn't as good as this one? Step, Hen!

Steve: But Be Rooster! (*He pauses, chuckling to himself.*) Step-Hen B-rooster *and* Henrietta. Pshaw, my dear, Doc Russell's got you beat a mile! (*He turns away and chuckles.*) Be rooster!

Mabel: What has Lyman Eggleston got to do with it?

Steve: According to Henrietta's interpretation, you, the hen, have a suppressed desire for Lyman *Egg*leston, the egg.

Mabel: Henrietta, I think that's indecent of you! He is bald as an egg and little and fat—the idea of you thinking such a thing of me!

Henrietta: Well, Bob isn't little and bald and fat! Why don't you stick to your own husband? (*Turns on Stephen.*) What if Dr. Russell's interpretation has got mine "beat a mile"? (*Resentful look at him.*) It would only mean that Mabel doesn't want Eggleston and does want you. Does that mean she is to have you?

Mabel: But you said Mabel Snow——

Henrietta: *Mary* Snow!! You're not as much like her as you think— substituting your name for hers! The cases are entirely different. Oh, I wouldn't have believed this of you, Mabel. I brought you here for a pleasant visit—thought you needed brightening up—wanted to be nice to you—and now you—my husband—you insist—(*Begins to cry. Makes a movement which brushes to the floor some sheets from the psychoanalytical table.*)

Steve (with solicitude):   Careful, dear. Your paper on psychoanalysis! (*Gathers up sheets and offers them to her.*)

Henrietta (crying):   I don't want my paper on psychoanalysis! I'm sick of psychoanalysis!

Steve (eagerly):   Do you mean that, Henrietta?

Henrietta: Why shouldn't I mean it? Look at all I've done for psychoanalysis—and—what has psychoanalysis done for me?

Steve: Do you mean, Henrietta, that you're going to stop taking psychoanalysis?

Henrietta: Why shouldn't I stop taking it? Haven't I seen what it does to people? Mabel has gone crazy about psychoanalysis! (*At the word "crazy" Mabel sinks with a moan into the armchair and buries her face in her hands.*) I'm done with it!

Steve (solemnly): Do you swear never to wake me up in the night to find out what I'm dreaming?

Henrietta: Dream what you please—I don't care what you're dreaming.

Steve: Will you clear off my worktable so that the *Journal of Morbid Psychology* doesn't stare me in the face when I'm trying to plan a house?

Henrietta (pushing a stack of periodicals off the table): I'll *burn* the *Journal of Morbid Psychology!*

Steve: My dear Henrietta, if you're going to separate from psychoanalysis, there's no reason why I should separate from you. (*They embrace ardently. Mabel lifts her head and looks at them woefully.*)

Mabel (jumping up and going toward them): But what about me? What am I to do with my suppressed desire?

Steve (with one arm still around Henrietta, gives Mabel a brotherly hug): Mabel, you just keep right on suppressing it.

Beginning with Close Reading

One of the first steps in close reading is to keep track of some of the play's most important details. Here is one person's list.

```
The play opens with Henrietta "henpecking" Steve about
    psychoanalysis.
Steve is an architect.
Henrietta tells Steve his dreams are important.
She interprets his irritability as rooted in a suppressed desire.
Mabel is Henrietta's sister; she enters in a "fussy negligee."
Henrietta assumes there is a "reason" that Mabel does not eat
    breakfast.
She discovers that Mabel had a dream.
The dream involves a hen and a shout: "Step, hen!"
Henrietta assumes the dream means something important.
She finds out Mabel's husband does not like Lyman Eggleston.
Henrietta asks if Mabel is happy or only thinks she is.
Henrietta explains psychoanalysis as the modern way of preventing
    insanity.
Henrietta mentions several examples of women acting on suppressed
    desires and leaving their husbands.
```

Henrietta says "old institutions will have to be reshaped."

When Steve dreams about walls, "walls" suddenly have important
    meaning, a suppressed desire.

Henrietta sees significance in "little false movements" and in
    mistakes of names—these are Freudian slips.

Henrietta was "always the smartest in the family."

Steve decides to go to the doctor to get psychoanalyzed.

Henrietta gives Mabel a huge book on psychoanalysis.

Mabel ends Scene I wondering if she is happy.

Scene II opens with Henrietta preparing a paper on psychoanalysis.

She interprets Mabel's dream to suggest she is in love with Lyman
    Eggleston.

The reversal takes place when Steve explains he has been "psyched"
    and has a suppressed desire to be freed from marriage.

Henrietta tries to conceal her shock.

The doctor's analysis was based on "confounded-clever inferences."

Steve did not accept the doctor's arguments; he "merely couldn't
    refute them."

Henrietta suggests he leave immediately; she does not "repudiate
    psychoanalysis."

Stage directions indicate that she is more upset than she reveals.

Mabel enters and tells her that Dr. Russell has uncovered her
    suppressed desire: it is for Stephen.

Henrietta tries to remind her of her "good, kind husband" Bob.

Mabel sees great meaning in names, as in "Be Rooster" for Brewster.

Henrietta finally says that the important thing is not to "*gratify*
    every suppressed desire"—bringing it up in the consciousness
    is all that is needed to "break up a complex."

Henrietta interprets Mabel's dream differently than Dr. Russell.

Finally she breaks down and repudiates psychoanalysis, casting her
    paper to the floor.

She accuses Mabel of "going crazy over psychoanalysis."

Steve gets Henrietta to give up psychoanalysis and then tells Mabel
    to keep on suppressing her desires.

    Different readers will produce different lists of details or may want to add
to this one. You may find it useful to discuss *Suppressed Desires* with other
readers to see which details impress them.

Keeping a Response Journal

The following entries from a response journal concentrate on an overview of the play.

Feb. 26. I thought the play was funny. It is a comedy, not a tragicomedy because everything works out all right and nobody suffers for anything. Henrietta is a dominating kind of person and Steve seems to be easygoing and a little overwhelmed. Not much actually happens on stage--people basically sit or stand and talk, and the "action" occurs in the ideas that they talk about. There is a conflict. The conflict is between Henrietta and everyone else. She assumes that dreams, mistakes, and other slips of language all have meaning and the meaning reveals the deep desires people have. Suppressed desires. All the ones in this play seem to be involved in sexual freedom. Obviously that makes you wonder if Susan Glaspell doesn't have some of the same desires. Apparently Glaspell's husband decided to live in Delphi, Greece, on a hillside like a Greek peasant. He died there in the late 1920s and she was with him most of the time. Maybe she had a suppressed desire of her own.

Feb. 27. A thought occurred to me. Steve says he's going to go to the doctor to get "psyched" but I wonder if he really went at all. He says he's going, but that could be a smokescreen. I wonder. Henrietta is all in favor of other women acting on their suppressed desires, but not Mabel. When Mabel says the doctor told her she had a desire for Stephen, Henrietta reacts. At first she is a "disciple" of psychoanalysis--as long as it doesn't affect her. But when it backfires, she gets rid of it. This is the reversal in the play, and I suppose you could say it is the source of its comedy. Or one source, anyway.

Feb. 28. One thing seems to be that the play is about interpreting things. Dreams are like stories, and Henrietta interprets them. There's that line near the end about Dr. Russell's interpretation being better than Henrietta's. That's a lot like interpreting a text. The dream is a text. The way it's interpreted is what counts.

Freewriting

The writer has found a number of interesting points. One is that the source of the comedy is in the reversal of Henrietta's beliefs in psychoanalysis when the interpretations of dreams begin to affect her negatively. Another point is

that interpretation is one theme of the play, and may be a useful beginning
for discussing the play. However, before going further, the writer sat down
and did some freewriting, hoping to make a discovery or two that would be
useful later.

Lots of things going on in the play. Glaspell was a feminist and
she has Henrietta say a lot of things that feminists might say. For
example, she says that there are worn-out moral principles that
keep women from fulfilling themselves--or something to that effect.
She must mean marriages that don't work. In the beginning of the
play she says right away that people have to act on their
suppressed desires or else go insane, and she has some examples--
Helen Dwight and Mary Snow. They both acted on their desires and
got out of a bad situation. In the beginning of the play
psychoanalysis is like a religion. She's a disciple. Freud is the
Messiah and Jung the St. Paul, so it's a religion. That must mean
it should reveal the truth even about what you can't see. Like
Moses tells us what God said, but we can't see God. The
subconscious is not "seeable" either and psychoanalysis is the only
way we can get in touch with it. Henrietta believes it all as long
as only other people are affected by it. Even Steve says he feels
sorry for Helen Dwight's decent husband. She never feels anything
for him. Then when things are reversed, she loses it.

By now the reader was ready to try out some paragraphs for the essay.
One fact was clear: *Suppressed Desires* could be approached in several ways.
For example, the strong feminist concern in the play could be one focus, and
psychoanalysis could be another. However, psychoanalysis could also be considered a formal element because it is the theme. One could also examine this
play as a comedy, and perhaps study its use of dramatic irony. Political, ethnic, cultural, and historical approaches are always possible, but in a sense they
would be long shots. The most obvious and relevant strategies are the first
three: feminism, psychoanalysis, and formalism. The writer began to develop
some paragraphs in an effort to find the best interpretive strategy.

Henrietta is an idealist. By that I mean she is committed to
ideas that she thinks should tell people how to live. For example,
she believes in being up to date and not suppressing desires even
when that involves breaking up with a "good, kind husband," as
Helen Dwight did. She believes that "old institutions have to be

reshaped" so as to avoid insanity, one of the results of
suppressing strong desires.

Her husband, Steve, is a practical type. He has heard a lot
about psychoanalysis, but he does not have any faith in it. The
reason is that he thinks Helen Dwight was wrong in running off from
her husband. He also agrees with Mabel, who thinks Mary Snow should
have suppressed her desire for her employer because her employer had
a wife and four children. Steve is also a good, kind husband. But it
is also clear that he is just tolerating Henrietta's commitment to
psychoanalysis in the hopes that it will go away. He does not believe
in it in Scene I. But Henrietta spends a great deal of time in
amateur psychology trying to find the significance of Mabel's dream.

Amateur psychology is basically nothing more than
interpretation. The play gets most interesting when the
interpretations of individuals conflict. For example, when
Henrietta interprets Mabel's dream as indicating a symbolic
yearning for Lyman Eggleston, she relies on the syllable "Egg" in
his name. When Dr. Russell interprets it, the object of her desire
suddenly becomes Steve because "Step hen" is his name. Henrietta's
name could also be involved, and so could Mabel's idea that being
called "a wet hen" might have triggered the dream. I think the
point of the play is that you can't go around choosing one set of
evidence just because it is convenient. You can see the results of
that when things go against Henrietta in Scene II. Suddenly she is
an idealist who doesn't like the ideas she has to deal with.

The writer went over this material and saw that there was enough to begin an interpretation. Several important points emerged from the prewriting process, and either separately or together, they could be used as the basis of a good interpretation.

1.   The play is about interpreting behavior so as to reveal
hidden meanings. But Henrietta, who believes in psychoanalysis, is
happy only when she is in control of the interpretation.

2.   Henrietta's feminism is as important to her as her
belief in psychoanalysis. However, in both cases she is happy only
when the ideas work to her advantage.

3.   *Suppressed Desires* shows us how difficult it is to
believe in ideas that are worthwhile but which can sometimes work

against us. To be an idealist is very difficult if the idealist
does not have some practicality.

The writer decided to work with the first point and compose an opening paragraph. The strategy combines a feminist and formalist approach. The other two points would serve later for developing the overall essay. Here is the opening paragraph.

Suppressed Desires is a study of how new ideas affect people.
Henrietta is a "disciple" of psychoanalysis, and her husband Steve
has been hearing so much about it that he is getting tired. He
compares it to a religion. But he does not mean that it is good.
When Henrietta tells him he is suffering from some kind of
suppressed desire, a bad sign in psychoanalysis, he says, "a
suppressed desire for a little peace." He wants some peace because
Henrietta has found a new idea that gives her power over other
people. She sees that everything they dream and every mistake they
make, especially a mistake in a name, has a hidden meaning. But she
is the only one who can interpret that meaning. That gives her
power.

Developing an Outline

At this point the writer decided to try to use this as an opening and prepare an outline for the rest of the interpretation. This assignment was for writing a three-page essay without using outside sources or help. Class discussion had provided some background biographical information on Susan Glaspell, but apart from general comments, no special critical studies.

> Outline: "Interpretation as Power in Suppressed Desires"
>
> I.   Introduction: Interpretation is power
>
>   A.   Henrietta controls the new idea: psychoanalysis
>
>   B.   Steve is subservient
>
> II.   Henrietta dominates Mabel
>
>   A.   Mabel's dream
>
>   B.   Mabel's interpretation
>
>   C.   Harriet's interpretation
>
> III.   Henrietta explains psychoanalysis
>
>   A.   Her examples: Helen and Mary
>
>   B.   Feminism and suppressed desires

The writer moved on from here to do a draft of the essay, using the first paragraph above and referring to earlier notes. After a waiting period, the writer went back to the first draft, revised it, and produced the essay that follows.

SAMPLE ESSAY: A FORMALIST INTERPRETATION

Tina Muriello

English 109-08

Paper Four

Prof. Jacobus

Interpretation as Power in *Suppressed Desires*

Susan Glaspell shows that the person who can interpret the meaning of things has power over others. She also shows that there can be conflicts between interpreters, and when that happens the loser sometimes gives up the new ideas that made the interpretation possible to begin with. The first conflict in the play is between Henrietta and her husband Steve. She is a "disciple" of psychoanalysis, and Steve, an architect, has been hearing so much about it he is getting worn out. He compares it to a religion, "with books by Freud, the new Messiah." But he does not mean this positively. He is fed up with Henrietta and psychoanalysis. When she tells him he is suffering from a suppressed desire, he tells her it is "a suppressed desire for a little peace." He's tired because Henrietta uses psychoanalysis as a weapon to get power over people. She tells them what their dreams mean, what their mistakes in language mean, and what their hidden desires are. Someone like this could be very annoying. One reason Henrietta has so much power is that she's an expert in psychoanalysis. But another reason is that Steve is henpecked and gives in to her.

Henrietta even dominates her sister Mabel, who is visiting from Chicago, where her husband is a dentist. When she begins to tell people her "funniest" dream, Steve tries to shush her up. He tells her that Henrietta will uncover an Oedipus complex: "she'll find out that you have an underground desire to kill your father and marry your mother." Mabel interprets her dream of "being a hen" told by a creature in a "blue cap" to "step, hen" as about being on a street car and being told to step lively. She says the dream was suggested by Henrietta calling her a "wet hen" earlier in the evening. Henrietta ridicules that interpretation by calling it "only a child's view."

Henrietta interprets the dream as concealing a suppressed desire for an old boyfriend, Lyman Eggleston. Her interpretation depends on the first syllable of his last name. Henrietta explains how Helen Dwight and Mary Snow both had suppressed desires that were driving them insane. Psychoanalysis, she tells them, "is simply the latest scientific method of preventing and curing insanity." Henrietta's examples both involve breaking up a marriage in order to express the suppressed desires. She approves both women's behavior on feminist grounds. The "old institutions will have to be reshaped" if women are to be free.

The conflict grows when Steve and Mabel go to Dr. Russell. He "psyches" them and interprets their suppressed desires. Steve supposedly wants to be free from Henrietta, and Mabel supposedly wants Steve. Henrietta is "alarmed" at this interpretation. But she already said, "If Dr. Russell should arrive independently at this same interpretation I shall not hesitate to advise Mabel to leave her present husband." But when she is told what Dr. Russell says, she can hardly believe it. The stage directions, "*Catches herself and resumes coldly*" and "*gulping*," show that she is not able to accept what he says, but she puts on a good front.

The reversal puts Henrietta in an ironic position. If she keeps her faith in psychoanalysis her marriage is gone. If she keeps her faith in feminism Mabel gets her husband. She says, "What if Dr. Russell's interpretation has got mine 'beat a mile'?" She doesn't care. She realizes that the interpretation does not matter when it goes against her. What matters is that she should keep her husband and that Mabel should go back to hers. Finally, Henrietta rejects psychoanalysis by pushing over a stack of journals. She and Steve *"embrace ardently."* Henrietta gives up her power in order to save her family.

Henrietta shows how interpretation can make life uncomfortable sometimes. In psychoanalysis, if you have the power to control the interpretation (because you have more knowledge), things are fine. Otherwise you become a potential victim, like Henrietta. I wondered if Steve and Mabel might not have made up the story of going to Dr. Russell and just made up their interpretations to spite Henrietta. The play does not say so, but I think it would be even more ironic if they did.

Further Strategies for Interpretation

This interpretation focuses on one element of the play, the theme of domination, which provides the material for analysis. The writer was interested in seeing how Henrietta's commitment to ideals worked as long as they were to her advantage. What the writer uncovered was an all too human tendency to hold on to ideals as long as they are useful, then to abandon them when they get threatening. The writer might have said so more directly and clearly, but the implication is present in the essay. There are, however, some other strategies that could also work well in interpreting the play.

Formalist.   As always, many formalist approaches could be developed to interpret the play. For example, one could emphasize the basic irony that the very ideas Henrietta holds most dear come back to torment her. The irony is not that she thinks psychoanalysis is powerful or true, but that she thinks anyone can practice it after reading a few books about it. One marvelous irony would be the verification of the writer's suspicion above: that Steve and Mabel "invented" the story about going to Dr. Russell. If you could, from a study of the play, establish that Steve and Mabel made up their stories to "cure" Henrietta, that would add a powerful ironic twist by giving them the same kind of power over Henrietta that she had over them. Small ironic details would also figure into a reading of the play. For example, the book Henrietta gives Mabel is supposed to be a small treatise on psychoanalysis, but it is so heavy it almost knocks Mabel down. Ironically, it is much too heavy for anyone in the play.

Feminist.   Feminist issues in this play are problematic. Henrietta seems to be a feminist and seems to believe strongly that women should be free to express themselves. She appears to be willing to accept the fact that marriages may have to be shattered for feminists to realize themselves. However, her beliefs are shaken when she becomes the victim of one woman, her sister, who threatens to take Steve away from her. Either this means that Henrietta is not as strong a feminist as she says she is or that Susan Glaspell's own beliefs in feminism are limited. An essay on this subject would have to account for the essential reversal at the end of the play: Henrietta's dominance by Steve and his "striking a deal" with her about psychoanalysis. Because the play was written in 1914, you might be able to argue that early feminists risked exactly what Henrietta could not face. She may be a model for all early feminists. But it may also be argued that the conventional American theatergoers of 1914 were not yet ready for the full force of feminism. Consequently the play had to be rendered conventional and acceptable by having Steve, the husband, end up victorious.

Reader Response.   Responses to the play will be quite individual. However, one response may be impatience with how both Steve and Mabel tolerate Henrietta's dominance over them. The fact that the audience is probably uniformly pleased when Henrietta gets her comeuppance may also annoy those who are feminists or people who feel that Freudian psychology has provided the world with important insights. Why, such viewers might ask, should we feel pleased to see the defeat of a character holding such views? Perhaps Glaspell knew well in advance that her audience would not tolerate approving such a character. Therefore, to get the audience to listen to *any* feminist or psychoanalytic theories, she had to reward them with the response they wanted and maybe the only response they could tolerate: delight at seeing someone whose theories they disagreed with get "shot down." This interpretation would then propose the theory that Susan Glaspell was not selling out feminism or Freudian psychology, both positions that she personally championed. Instead, she was being realistic and taking the ideas as far as they would go, but no further. If Henrietta's dominance had gone unchallenged, the audience would have rejected the entire play. Given the way Glaspell handled the play, the audience had a great deal to think about after having had the superficial pleasure of rejecting Henrietta and her ideas.

These suggestions represent only a few possibilities. By using combinations and variations on patterns of interpretation, you can develop a highly personal approach. The point is to develop the interpretive strategy that you think works best.

History of Drama

One historicist approach to drama concentrates on the historical circumstances of a given play. The great age of Greek drama extended from about 534 to 406 B.C., during a period of great political development of Athens and other Greek city-states. Sophocles' *Oedipus Rex* (c. 430–427 B.C.) was played in the afternoon on a circular area about sixty feet across, called an **orchestra**, behind which stood the **skene**, a low building one hundred fifty feet long, with ramps at either end, that represented a palace as a backdrop to the action. Stage machinery was very popular, especially one that lowered the **deus ex machina** (god out of the machine), a divine figure who intervened in the action to set things straight. The audience was present in huge numbers, with as many as twelve or fourteen thousand seated on three sides of the action. The plays were part of the *dionysia*, a series of religious festivals occurring at different times of the year that often coincided with the harvesting of grapes, associated with the god Dionysus. Greek drama centered on the actions of fate and the lives of noble leaders; though we can still become powerfully involved in these plays, some meanings are no doubt lost to us.

The Elizabethan theater (1558–1603) was circular or hexagonal and tall, with several levels of seating. The center was open to the air and light, and the audiences of as many as three thousand people would have paid a penny (perhaps ten dollars in today's money) for admission and another penny for a good seat. The Elizabethan audience enjoyed historical plays, moral tragedies, moral comedies, and sometimes gory tragicomedies. *Hamlet* is related to a genre of bloody revenge tragedies that had special significance for Elizabethans. The Elizabethan playwright worked with a stage approximately twenty-five by forty feet that projected into the open space from one wall. Audience members, called groundlings, stood on all sides of the **apron** of the stage. There was seating in front, the several sides, and above in upper galleries. Part of the theater was roofed over in order to contain machinery that lowered actors in special devices, like the deus ex machina. Trapdoors permitted special entrances and exits, such as may have been used by Hamlet's ghost. The audience was there for entertainment and did not associate the drama with special religious or other festivals.

The seventeenth-century drama played indoors with artificial light and sometimes elaborate **sets**. Painted backdrops, unknown in Greek or Elizabethan theaters (except for the royal **masques**, musical dance entertainments for nobility), were sometimes changed to represent changes in location of the action. Elaborate costumes were developed for actors in this period. Since plays could be performed at night, the theaters sometimes attracted gay blades and risqué audiences, thus getting an uncertain reputation.

The nineteenth century saw the rise of **realism**, a style that treated important social concerns, such as feminist issues, class tensions, and philosophical conflicts. Because the artificial light—first gaslight, then electricity—was bright and efficient, the scenery had to be very realistic and detailed to help the overall effect of realism. Henrik Ibsen's *A Doll House* (1879) and *Hedda Gabler* (1890) are good examples of realist drama of the period. The characters have problems that are not smoothed over by sentimental resolutions or artificial solutions. Instead, we can believe that they suffer. Chekhov's *The Cherry Orchard* (1903) is in the same tradition, concentrating on contemporary issues, such as the dissolution of the moneyed upper classes and their replacement by hardworking serfs. Strindberg's *Miss Julie* (1888) is a **symbolist** play, less concerned with the realism of Julie and Jean's situation than in the symbolic issues concerned with a romance that crosses class boundaries and is dominated by a mythic figure—Julie's father—who never appears on stage.

The modern stage has benefited from great technical advances, such as computerized lighting, movable stages, and multiple levels of action—put to considerable use in, for instance, John Guare's *Six Degrees of Separation* (1990).

Certain contemporary plays concentrate on issues that are particular to modern times, such as the problem of AIDS in Paula Vogel's *The Baltimore Waltz* (1991) and the problems of political imprisonment and homophobia, joined in Manuel Puig's *The Kiss of the Spider Woman* (1986). David Mamet's *Oleanna* (1992), treats the power relationships involved in the militant feminist interpretation of sexual harassment in the universities.

The audiences in major cities are asked to pay high prices for seats, but in the latter part of the twentieth century the provincial theaters in most industrialized nations have provided high-level, relatively inexpensive productions of major plays, including all of those named above. August Wilson's *Fences* (1985) has toured around the world after debuting in New Haven and going on to Broadway to win the New York Drama Critics' Circle Award for best play of the year. College and university players have produced almost all the plays in this book in often highly credible productions. Despite complaints of high prices and high costs of production, live drama is probably more available to more people than ever before.

Reading

Bieber, Margaret. *The History of the Greek and Roman Theater.* 2nd ed. Princeton: Princeton University Press, 1961.

Chambers, E. K. *The Elizabethan Stage.* 4 vols. Oxford: Oxford University Press, 1923.

Nicoll, Allardyce. *A History of Restoration Drama, 1600–1700.* New York: Cambridge University Press, 1923.

Wellworth, George E. *The Theater of Protest and Paradox.* New York: New York University Press, 1971.

Whitaker, Thomas R. *Fields of Play in Modern Drama.* Princeton: Princeton University Press, 1977.

Anton Chekhov   (1860–1904)

Anton Chekhov seems to have been inspired to write plays by having seen a production of Uncle Tom's Cabin *in 1877, shortly before he went to medical school. During his early years of practice, he gained fame as a writer by publishing many short stories in Russian newspapers. In the mid-1880s his plays began to attract attention. After some failures, he produced* The Seagull *(1896), which was followed by* Uncle Vanya *(1897).* Three Sisters *(1901) and* The Cherry Orchard *(1903), usually regarded as his best plays, came at the end of his life.*

The Moscow Art Theatre, led by Konstantin Stanislavsky (the director/actor whose writings inspired method acting, a style in which the actor uses personal psychological experience for inspiration), produced Chekhov's plays but sometimes disagreed on whether they were comedies or tragedies. The Cherry Orchard *is a case in point. Chekhov saw the play as a comedy, but Stanislavsky thought the destruction of the cherry orchard implied that it was a tragedy. This disagreement results from the value placed upon the beauty of the orchard in contrast with the value of the social rise of Lopahin, the merchant who buys and develops the property. The question of interpretation remains with us, especially in light of the general success of twentieth-century real estate developers.*

Chekhov derives his power from personal observation. The surfaces of his plays are detailed and realistic, whereas the deep structure is tragic.

THE CHERRY ORCHARD   1903

Translated by Constance Garnett

Characters

Madame Ranevsky	*Semyonov-Pishtchik*, a landower
(Lyubov Andreyevna), the	*Charlotta Ivanovna,*
owner of the Cherry Orchard	a governess

Anya, her daughter,
   age seventeen
Varya, her adopted daughter,
   age twenty four
Gaev (Leonid Andreyevitch),
   brother of Madame Ranevsky
Lopahin (Yermolay Alexeyevitch),
   a merchant
Trofimov (Pyotr Sergeyevitch),
   a student

Epihodov (Semyon
   Pantaleyevitch), a clerk
Dunyasha, a maid
Firs, an old valet,
   age eighty-seven
Yasha, a young valet
A Wayfarer
The Stationmaster
A Post-Office Clerk
Visitors, Servants

The action takes place on the estate of Madame Ranevsky.

ACT I

(*Scene: A room, which has always been called the nursery. One of the doors leads into Anya's room. Dawn, sun rises during the scene. May, the cherry trees in flower, but it is cold in the garden with the frost of early morning. Windows closed.*
    Enter Dunyasha with a candle and Lopahin with a book in his hand.)

Lopahin: The train's in, thank God. What time is it?

Dunyasha: Nearly two o'clock. (*Puts out the candle.*) It's daylight already.

Lopahin: The train's late! Two hours, at least. (*Yawns and stretches.*) I'm a pretty one; what a fool I've been. Came here on purpose to meet them at the station and dropped asleep. . . . Dozed off as I sat in the chair. It's annoying. . . . You might have waked me.

Dunyasha: I thought you had gone. (*Listens.*) There, I do believe they're coming!

Lopahin (listens):   No, what with the luggage and one thing and another. (*A pause.*) Lyubov Andreyevna has been abroad five years; I don't know what she is like now. . . . She's a splendid woman. A good-natured, kind-hearted woman. I remember when I was a lad of fifteen, my poor father—he used to keep a little shop here in the village in those days—gave me a punch in the face with his fist and made my nose bleed. We were in the yard here, I forget what we'd come about—he had had a drop. Lyubov Andreyevna—I can see her now—she was a slim young girl then—took me to wash my face, and then brought me into this very room, into the nursery. "Don't cry, little peasant," says she, "it will be well in time for your wedding day." . . . (*A pause.*) Little peasant. . . . My father was a peasant, it's true, but here am I in a white waistcoat and brown shoes, like a pig in a bun shop. Yes, I'm a rich man, but for all my money, come to think, a peasant I was, and a peasant I am. (*Turns over the pages of the book.*) I've been reading this book and I can't make head or tail of it. I fell asleep over it.

(*A pause.*)

Dunyasha: The dogs have been awake all night, they feel that the mistress is coming.

Lopahin: Why, what's the matter with you, Dunyasha?

Dunyasha: My hands are all of a tremble. I feel as though I should faint.

Lopahin: You're a spoilt soft creature, Dunyasha. And dressed like a lady too, and your hair done up. That's not the thing. One must know one's place.

(*Enter Epihodov with a nosegay; he wears a pea jacket and highly polished creaking top boots; he drops the nosegay as he comes in.*)

Epihodov (picking up the nosegay):   Here! the gardener's sent this, says you're to put it in the dining room. (*Gives Dunyasha the nosegay.*)

Lopahin: And bring me some kvass.

Dunyasha: I will. (*Goes out.*)

Epihodov: It's chilly this morning, three degrees of frost, though the cherries are all in flower. I can't say much for our climate. (*Sighs.*) I can't. Our climate is not often propitious to the occasion. Yermolay Alexeyevitch, permit me to call your attention to the fact that I purchased myself a pair of boots the day before yesterday, and they creak, I venture to assure you, so that there's no tolerating them. What ought I to grease them with?

Lopahin: Oh, shut up! Don't bother me.

Epihodov: Every day some misfortune befalls me. I don't complain, I'm used to it, and I wear a smiling face. (*Dunyasha comes in, hands Lopahin the kvass.*) I am going. (*Stumbles against a chair, which falls over.*) There! (*As though triumphant.*) There you see now, excuse the expression, an accident like that among others. . . . It's positively remarkable. (*Goes out.*)

Dunyasha: Do you know, Yermolay Alexeyevitch, I must confess, Epihodov has made me a proposal.

Lopahin: Ah!

Dunyasha: I'm sure I don't know. . . . He's a harmless fellow, but sometimes when he begins talking, there's no making anything of it. It's all very fine and expressive, only there's no understanding it. I've a sort of liking for him too. He loves me to distraction. He's an unfortunate man; every day there's something. They tease him about it—two and twenty misfortunes they call him.

Lopahin (listening):   There! I do believe they're coming.

Dunyasha: They are coming! What's the matter with me? . . . I'm cold all over.

Lopahin: They really are coming. Let's go and meet them. Will she know me? It's five years since I saw her.

Dunyasha (in a flutter):   I shall drop this very minute. . . . Ah, I shall drop.

(There is a sound of two carriages driving up to the house. Lopahin and Dunyasha go out quickly. The stage is left empty. A noise is heard in the adjoining rooms. Firs, who has driven to meet Madame Ranevsky, crosses the stage hurriedly leaning on a stick. He is wearing old-fashioned livery and a high hat. He says something to himself, but not a word can be distinguished. The noise behind the scenes goes on increasing. A voice: "Come, let's go in here." Enter Lyubov Andreyevna, Anya, and Charlotta Ivanovna with a pet dog on a chain, all in traveling dresses. Varya in an outdoor coat with a kerchief over her head, Gaev, Semyonov-Pishtchik, Lopahin, Dunyasha with bag and parasol, servants with other articles. All walk across the room.)

Anya: Let's come in here. Do you remember what room this is, mamma?

Lyubov (joyfully, through her tears):   The nursery!

Varya: How cold it is, my hands are numb. (*To Lyubov Andreyevna.*) Your rooms, the white room and the lavender one, are just the same as ever, mamma.

Lyubov: My nursery, dear delightful room. . . . I used to sleep here when I was little. . . . (*Cries.*) And here I am, like a little child. . . . (*Kisses her brother and Varya, and then her brother again.*) Varya's just the same as ever, like a nun. And I knew Dunyasha. (*Kisses Dunyasha.*)

Gaev: The train was two hours late. What do you think of that? Is that the way to do things?

Charlotta (to Pishtchik):   My dog eats nuts, too.

Pishtchik (wonderingly):   Fancy that!

(They all go out except Anya and Dunyasha.)

Dunyasha: We've been expecting you so long. (*Takes Anya's hat and coat.*)

Anya: I haven't slept for four nights on the journey. I feel dreadfully cold.

Dunyasha: You set out in Lent, there was snow and frost, and now? My darling! (*Laughs and kisses her.*) I *have* missed you, my precious, my joy. I must tell you . . . I can't put it off a minute. . . .

Anya (wearily):   What now?

Dunyasha: Epihodov, the clerk, made me a proposal just after Easter.

Anya: It's always the same thing with you. . . . (*Straightening her hair.*) I've lost all my hairpins. (*She is staggering from exhaustion.*)

Dunyasha: I don't know what to think, really. He does love me, he does love me so!

Anya (looking toward her door, tenderly):   My own room, my windows just as though I had never gone away. I'm home! Tomorrow morning I shall get up and run into the garden. . . . Oh, if I could get to sleep! I haven't slept all the journey, I was so anxious and worried.

Dunyasha: Pyotr Sergeyevitch came the day before yesterday.

Anya (joyfully): Petya!

Dunyasha: He's asleep in the bath house, he has settled in there. I'm afraid of being in their way, says he. (*Glancing at her watch.*) I was to have waked him, but Varvara Mihalovna told me not to. Don't you wake him, says she.

(*Enter Varya with a bunch of keys at her waist.*)

Varya: Dunyasha, coffee and make haste . . . Mamma's asking for coffee.

Dunyasha: This very minute. (*Goes out.*)

Varya: Well, thank God, you've come. You're home again. (*Petting her.*) My little darling has come back! My precious beauty has come back again!

Anya: I have had a time of it!

Varya: I can fancy.

Anya: We set off in Holy Week—it was so cold then, and all the way Charlotta would talk and show off her tricks. What did you want to burden me with Charlotta for?

Varya: You couldn't have traveled all alone, darling. At seventeen!

Anya: We got to Paris at last, it was cold there—snow. I speak French shockingly. Mamma lives on the fifth floor, I went up to her and there were a lot of French people, ladies, an old priest with a book. The place smelt of tobacco and so comfortless. I felt sorry, oh! so sorry for mamma all at once, I put my arms round her neck, and hugged her and wouldn't let her go. Mamma was as kind as she could be, and she cried. . . .

Varya (through her tears): Don't speak of it, don't speak of it!

Anya: She had sold her villa at Mentone, she had nothing left, nothing. I hadn't a farthing left either, we only just had enough to get here. And mamma doesn't understand! When we had dinner at the stations, she always ordered the most expensive things and gave the waiters a whole ruble. Charlotta's just the same. Yasha too must have the same as we do; it's simply awful. You know Yasha is mamma's valet now, we brought him here with us.

Varya: Yes, I've seen the young rascal.

Anya: Well, tell me—have you paid the arrears on the mortgage?

Varya: How could we get the money?

Anya: Oh, dear! Oh, dear!

Varya: In August the place will be sold.

Anya: My goodness!

Lopahin (peeps in at the door and moos like a cow): Moo! (*Disappears.*)

Varya (weeping): There, that's what I could do to him. (*Shakes her fist.*)

Anya (embracing Varya, softly): Varya, has he made you an offer? (*Varya shakes her head.*) Why, but he loves you. Why is it you don't come to an understanding? What are you waiting for?

Varya: I believe that there never will be anything between us. He has a lot to do, he has no time for me . . . and takes no notice of me. Bless the man, it makes me miserable to see him. . . . Everyone's talking of our being married, everyone's congratulating me, and all the while there's really nothing in it; it's all like a dream. (*In another tone.*) You have a new brooch like a bee.

Anya (*mournfully*):   Mamma bought it. (*Goes into her own room and talks in a lighthearted childish tone.*) And you know, in Paris I went up in a balloon!

Varya: My darling's home again! My pretty is home again!

(*Dunyasha returns with the coffeepot and is making the coffee.*)

Varya (*standing at the door*):   All day long, darling, as I go about looking after the house, I keep dreaming all the time. If only we could marry you to a rich man, then I should feel more at rest. Then I would go off by myself on a pilgrimage to Kiev, to Moscow . . . and so I would spend my life going from one holy place to another. . . . I would go on and on. . . . What bliss!

Anya: The birds are singing in the garden. What time is it?

Varya: It must be nearly three. It's time you were asleep, darling. (*Going into Anya's room.*) What bliss!

(*Yasha enters with a rug and a traveling bag.*)

Yasha (*crosses the stage, mincingly*):   May one come in here, pray?

Dunyasha: I shouldn't have known you, Yasha. How you have changed abroad.

Yasha: H'm! . . . And who are you?

Dunyasha: When you went away, I was that high. (*Shows distance from floor.*) Dunyasha, Fyodor's daughter. . . . You don't remember me!

Yasha: H'm! . . . You're a peach! (*Looks round and embraces her: she shrieks and drops a saucer. Yasha goes out hastily.*)

Varya (*in the doorway, in a tone of vexation*):   What now?

Dunyasha (*through her tears*):   I have broken a saucer.

Varya: Well, that brings good luck.

Anya (*coming out of her room*):   We ought to prepare mamma: Petya is here.

Varya: I told them not to wake him.

Anya (*dreamily*):   It's six years since father died. Then only a month later little brother Grisha was drowned in the river, such a pretty boy he was, only seven. It was more than mamma could bear, so she went away, went away without looking back. (*Shuddering.*) . . . How well I understand her, if only she knew! (*A pause.*) And Petya Trofimov was Grisha's tutor, he may remind her.

(*Enter Firs; he is wearing a pea jacket and a white waistcoat.*)

Firs (*goes up to the coffeepot, anxiously*):   The mistress will be served here. (*Puts on white gloves.*) Is the coffee ready? (*Sternly to Dunyasha.*) Girl! Where's the cream?

Dunyasha: Ah, mercy on us! (*Goes out quickly.*)

Firs (fussing round the coffeepot): Ech! you good-for-nothing! (*Muttering to himself.*) Come back from Paris. And the old master used to go to Paris too . . . horses all the way. (*Laughs.*)

Lyubov: Can it really be me sitting here? (*Laughs.*) I want to dance about and clap my hands. (*Covers her face with her hands.*) And I could drop asleep in a moment! God knows I love my country, I love it tenderly; I couldn't look out of the window in the train, I kept crying so. (*Through her tears.*) But I must drink my coffee, though. Thank you, Firs, thanks, dear old man. I'm so glad to find you still alive.

Firs: The day before yesterday.

Gaev: He's rather deaf.

Lopahin: I have, to set off for Harkov directly, at five o'clock. . . . It is annoying! I wanted to have a look at you, and a little talk. . . . You are just as splendid as ever.

Pishtchik (breathing heavily): Handsomer, indeed. . . . Dressed in Parisian style . . . completely bowled me over.

Lopahin: Your brother, Leonid Andreyevitch here, is always saying that I'm a low-born knave, that I'm a money-grubber, but I don't care one straw for that. Let him talk. Only I do want you to believe in me as you used to. I do want your wonderful tender eyes to look at me as they used to in the old days. Merciful God! My father was a serf of your father and of your grandfather, but you—you—did so much for me once, that I've forgotten all that; I love you as though you were my kin . . . more than my kin.

Lyubov: I can't sit still, I simply can't. . . . (*Jumps up and walks about in violent agitation.*) This happiness is too much for me. . . . You may laugh at me, I know I'm silly. . . . My own bookcase. (*Kisses the bookcase.*) My little table.

Gaev: Nurse died while you were away.

Lyubov (sits down and drinks coffee): Yes, the Kingdom of Heaven be hers! You wrote me of her death.

Gaev: And Anastasy is dead. Squinting Petruchka has left me and is in service now with the police captain in the town. (*Takes a box of caramels out of his pocket and sucks one.*)

Pishtchik: My daughter, Dashenka, wishes to be remembered to you.

Lopahin: I want to tell you something very pleasant and cheering. (*Glancing at his watch.*) I'm going directly . . . there's no time to say much . . . well, I can say it in a couple of words. I needn't tell you your cherry orchard is to be sold to pay your debts; the 22nd of August is the date fixed for the sale; but don't you worry, dearest lady, you may sleep in peace, there is a way of saving it. . . . This is what I propose. I beg your attention! Your estate is not twenty miles from the town, the railway runs close by it, and if the cherry orchard and the land along the river bank were cut up into building plots and then let on lease for summer villas, you would make an income of at least 25,000 rubles a year out of it.

Gaev: That's all rot, if you'll excuse me.

Lyubov: I don't quite understand you, Yermolay Alexeyevitch.

Lopahin: You will get a rent of at least twenty-five rubles a year for a three-acre plot from summer visitors, and if you say the word now, I'll bet you what you like there won't be one square foot of ground vacant by the autumn, all the plots will be taken up. I congratulate you; in fact, you are saved. It's a perfect situation with that deep river. Only, of course, it must be cleared—all the old buildings, for example, must be removed, this house too, which is really good for nothing, and the old cherry orchard must be cut down.

Lyubov: Cut down? My dear fellow, forgive me, but you don't know what you are talking about. If there is one thing interesting—remarkable indeed—in the whole province, it's just our cherry orchard.

Lopahin: The only thing remarkable about the orchard is that it's a very large one. There's a crop of cherries every alternate year, and then there's nothing to be done with them, no one buys them.

Gaev: This orchard is mentioned in the *Encyclopedia*.

Lopahin (glancing at his watch):   If we don't decide on something and don't take some steps, on the 22nd of August the cherry orchard and the whole estate too will be sold at auction. Make up your minds! There is no other way of saving it, I'll take my oath on that. No, No!

Firs: In old days, forty or fifty years ago, they used to dry the cherries, soak them, pickle them, make jam too, and they used—

Gaev: Be quiet, Firs.

Firs: And they used to send the preserved cherries to Moscow and to Markov by the wagonload. That brought the money in! And the preserved cherries in those days were soft and juicy, sweet and fragrant. . . . They knew the way to do them then. . . .

Lyubov: And where is the recipe now?

Firs: It's forgotten. Nobody remembers it.

Pishtchik (to Lyubov Andreyevna):   What's it like in Paris? Did you eat frogs there?

Lyubov: Oh, I ate crocodiles.

Pishtchik: Fancy that now!

Lopahin: There used to be only the gentlefolks and the peasants in the country, but now there are these summer visitors. All the towns, even the small ones, are surrounded, nowadays by these summer villas. And one may say for sure, that in another twenty years there'll be many more of these people and that they'll be everywhere. At present the summer visitor only drinks tea in his veranda, but maybe he'll take to working his bit of land too, and then your cherry orchard would become happy, rich and prosperous. . . .

Gaev (indignant):   What rot!

(*Enter Varya and Yasha.*)

Varya: There are two telegrams for you, mamma. (*Takes out keys and opens an old-fashioned bookcase with a loud crack.*) Here they are.

Lyubov: From Paris. (*Tears the telegrams, without reading them.*) I have done with Paris.

Gaev: Do you know, Lyuba, how old that bookcase is? Last week I pulled out the bottom drawer and there I found the date branded on it. The bookcase was made just a hundred years ago. What do you say to that? We might have celebrated its jubilee. Though it's an inanimate object, still it is a *book*case.

Pishtchik (amazed):   A hundred years! Fancy that now.

Gaev: Yes. . . . It is a thing. . . . (*Feeling the bookcase.*) Dear, honored, bookcase! Hail to thee who for more than a hundred years hast served the pure ideals of good and justice; thy silent call to fruitful labor has never flagged in those hundred years, maintaining (*in tears*) in the generations of man, courage and faith in a brighter future and fostering in us ideals of good and social consciousness.

(*A pause.*)

Lopahin: Yes . . .

Lyubov: You are just the same as ever, Leonid.

Gaev (a little embarrassed):   Cannon off the right into the pocket!°

Lopahin (looking at his watch):   Well, it's time I was off.

Yasha (handing Lyubov Andreyevna medicine):   Perhaps you will take your pills now.

Pishtchik: You shouldn't take medicines, my dear madam . . . they do no harm and no good. Give them here . . . honored lady. (*Takes the pillbox, pours the pills into the hollow of his hand, blows on them, puts them in his mouth and drinks off some kvass.*) There!

Lyubov (in alarm):   Why, you must be out of your mind!

Pishtchik: I have taken all the pills.

Lopahin: What a glutton!

(*All laugh.*)

Firs: His honor stayed with us in Easter week, ate a gallon and a half of cucumbers. . . . (*Mutters.*)

Lyubov: What is he saying?

Varya: He has taken to muttering like that for the last three years. We are used to it.

Yasha: His declining years!

(*Charlotta Ivanovna, a very thin, lanky figure in a white dress with a lorgnette in her belt, walks across the stage.*)

Cannon . . . pocket: Throughout the play Gaev interjects phrases from billiards.

Lopahin: I beg your pardon, Charlotta Ivanovna, I have not had time to greet you. (*Tries to kiss her hand.*)

Charlotta (pulling away her hand): If I let you kiss my hand, you'll be wanting to kiss my elbow, and then my shoulder.

Lopahin: I've no luck today! (*All laugh.*) Charlotta Ivanovna, show us some tricks!

Lyubov: Charlotta, do show us some tricks!

Charlotta: I don't want to. I'm sleepy. (*Goes out.*)

Lopahin: In three weeks' time we shall meet again. (*Kisses Lyubov Andreyevna's hand.*) Good-by till then—I must go. (*To Gaev.*) Good-by. (*Kisses Pishtchik.*) Good-by. (*Gives his hand to Varya, then to Firs and Yasha.*) I don't want to go. (*To Lyubov Andreyevna.*) If you think over my plan for the villas and make up your mind, then let me know; I will lend you 50,000 rubles. Think of it seriously.

Varya (angrily): Well, do go, for goodness' sake.

Lopahin: I'm going, I'm going. (*Goes out.*)

Gaev: Low-born knave! I beg pardon, though . . . Varya is going to marry him, he's Varya's fiancé.

Varya: Don't talk nonsense, uncle.

Lyubov: Well, Varya, I shall be delighted. He's a good man.

Pishtchik: He is, one must acknowledge, a most worthy man. And my Dashenka . . . says too that . . . she says . . . various things. (*Snores, but at once wakes up.*) But all the same, honored lady, could you oblige me . . . with a loan of 240 rubles . . . to pay the interest on my mortgage tomorrow?

Varya (dismayed): No, no.

Lyubov: I really haven't any money.

Pishtchik: It will turn up. (*Laughs.*) I never lose hope. I thought everything was over, I was a ruined man, and lo and behold—the railway passed through my land and . . . they paid me for it. And something else will turn up again, if not today, then tomorrow . . . Dashenka'll win two hundred thousand . . . she's got a lottery ticket.

Lyubov: Well, we've finished our coffee, we can go to bed.

Firs (brushes Gaev, reprovingly): You have got on the wrong trousers again! What am I to do with you?

Varya (softly): Anya's asleep. (*Softly opens the window.*) Now the sun's risen, it's not a bit cold. Look, mamma, what exquisite trees! My goodness! And the air! The starlings are singing!

Gaev (opens another window): The orchard is all white. You've not forgotten it, Lyuba? That long avenue that runs straight, straight as an arrow, how it shines on a moonlight night. You remember? You've not forgotten?

Lyubov (looking out of the window into the garden): Oh, my childhood, my innocence! It was in this nursery I used to sleep, from here I looked out into the orchard, happiness waked with me every morning and in those days the orchard was just the same, nothing has changed. (*Laughs with delight.*) All, all white! Oh, my orchard! After the dark gloomy autumn, and the cold winter; you are young again and full of happiness, the heavenly angels have never left you. . . . If I could cast off the burden that weighs on my heart, if I could forget the past!

Gaev: H'm! and the orchard will be sold to pay our debts; it seems strange. . . .

Lyubov: See, our mother walking . . . all in white, down the avenue! (*Laughs with delight.*) It is she!

Gaev: Where?

Varya: Oh, don't, mamma!

Lyubov: There is no one. It was my fancy. On the right there, by the path to the arbor, there is a white tree bending like a woman. . . . (*Enter Trofimov wearing a shabby student's uniform and spectacles.*) What a ravishing orchard! White masses of blossom, blue sky. . . .

Trofimov: Lyubov Andreyevna! (*She looks round at him.*) I will just pay my respects to you and then leave you at once. (*Kisses her hand warmly.*) I was told to wait until morning, but I hadn't the patience to wait any longer. . . .

(*Lyubov Andreyevna looks at him in perplexity.*)

Varya (through her tears):   This is Petya Trofimov.

Trofimov: Petya Trofimov, who was your Grisha's tutor. . . . Can I have changed so much?

(*Lyubov Andreyevna embraces him and weeps quietly.*)

Gaev (in confusion):   There, there, Lyuba.

Varya (crying):   I told you, Petya, to wait till tomorrow.

Lyubov: My Grisha . . . my boy . . . Grisha . . . my son!

Varya: We can't help it, mamma, it is God's will.

Trofimov (softly through his tears):   There . . . there.

Lyubov (weeping quietly):   My boy was lost . . . drowned. Why? Oh, why, dear Petya? (*More quietly.*) Anya is asleep in there, and I'm talking loudly . . . making this noise. . . . But, Petya? Why have you grown so ugly? Why do you look so old?

Trofimov: A peasant-woman in the train called me a mangy-looking gentleman.

Lyubov: You were quite a boy then, a pretty little student, and now your hair's thin—and spectacles. Are you really a student still? (*Goes toward the door.*)

Trofimov: I seem likely to be a perpetual student.

Lyubov (kisses her brother, then Varya):   Well, go to bed. . . . You are older too, Leonid.

Pishtchik (follows her):   I suppose it's time we were asleep. . . . Ugh! my gout. I'm staying the night! Lyubov Andreyevna, my dear soul, if you could . . . tomorrow morning . . . 240 rubles.

Gaev: That's always his story.

Pishtchik: 240 rubles . . . to pay the interest on my mortgage.

Lyubov: My dear man, I have no money.

Pishtchik: I'll pay it back, my dear . . . a trifling sum.

Lyubov: Oh, well, Leonid will give it you . . . . You give him the money, Leonid.

Gaev: Me give it him! Let him wait till he gets it!

Lyubov: It can't be helped, give it him. He needs it. He'll pay it back.

> *(Lyubov Andreyevna, Trofimov, Pishtchik, and Firs go out. Gaev, Varya, and Yasha remain.)*

Gaev: Sister hasn't got out of the habit of flinging away her money. (*To Yasha.*) Get away, my good fellow, you smell of the henhouse.

Yasha (with a grin):   And you, Leonid Andreyevitch, are just the same as ever.

Gaev: What's that? (*To Varya.*) What did he say?

Varya (to Yasha):   Your mother has come from the village; she has been sitting in the servants' room since yesterday, waiting to see you.

Yasha: Oh, bother her!

Varya: For shame!

Yasha: What's the hurry? She might just as well have come tomorrow. (*Goes out.*)

Varya: Mamma's just the same as ever, she hasn't changed a bit. If she had her own way, she'd give away everything.

Gaev: Yes. (*A pause.*) If a great many remedies are suggested for some disease, it means that the disease is incurable. I keep thinking and racking my brains; I have many schemes, a great many, and that really means none. If we could only come in for a legacy from somebody, or marry our Anya to a very rich man, or we might go to Yaroslavl and try our luck with our old aunt, the Countess. She's very, very rich, you know.

Varya (weeps):   If God would help us.

Gaev: Don't blubber. Aunt's very rich, but she doesn't like us. First, sister married a lawyer instead of a nobleman. . . . (*Anya appears in the doorway.*) And then her conduct, one can't call it virtuous. She is good, and kind, and nice, and I love her, but, however one allows for extenuating circumstances, there's no denying that she's an immoral woman. One feels it in her slightest gesture.

Varya (in a whisper):   Anya's in the doorway.

Gaev: What do you say? (*A pause.*) It's queer, there seems to be something wrong with my right eye. I don't see as well as I did. And on Thursday when I was in the district Court . . .

> *(Enter Anya.)*

Varya: Why aren't you asleep, Anya?

Anya: I can't get to sleep.

Gaev: My pet. (*Kisses Anya's face and hands.*) My child. (*Weeps.*) You are not my niece, you are my angel, you are everything to me. Believe me, believe. . . .

Anya: I believe you, uncle. Everyone loves you and respects you . . . but, uncle dear, you must be silent . . . simply be silent. What were you saying just now about my mother, about your own sister? What made you say that?

Gaev: Yes, yes. . . . (*Puts his hand over his face.*) Really, that was awful! My God, save me! And today I made a speech to the bookcase . . . so stupid! And only when I had finished, I saw how stupid it was.

Varya: It's true, uncle, you ought to keep quiet. Don't talk, that's all.

Anya: If you could keep from talking, it would make things easier for you, too.

Gaev: I won't speak. (*Kisses Anya's and Varya's hands.*) I'll be silent. Only this is about business. On Thursday I was in the district Court; well, there was a large party of us there and we began talking of one thing and another, and this and that, and do you know, I believe that it will be possible to raise a loan on an I.O.U. to pay the arrears on the mortgage.

Varya: If the Lord would help us!

Gaev: I'm going on Tuesday; I'll talk of it again. (*To Varya.*) Don't blubber. (*To Anya.*) Your mamma will talk to Lopahin; of course, he won't refuse her. And as soon as you're rested you shall go to Yaroslavl to the Countess, your great-aunt. So we shall all set to work in three directions at once, and the business is done. We shall pay off arrears. I'm convinced of it. (*Puts a caramel in his mouth.*) I swear on my honor, I swear by anything you like, the estate shan't be sold. (*Excitedly.*) By my own happiness, I swear it! Here's my hand on it, call me the basest, vilest of men, if I let it come to an auction! Upon my soul I swear it!

Anya (her equanimity has returned, she is quite happy): How good you are, uncle, and how clever! (*Embraces her uncle.*) I'm at peace now! Quite at peace! I'm happy!

(*Enter Firs.*)

Firs (reproachfully): Leonid Andreyevitch, have you no fear of God? When are you going to bed?

Gaev: Directly, directly. You can go, Firs. I'll . . . yes, I will undress myself. Come, children, by-by. We'll go into details tomorrow, but now go to bed. (*Kisses Anya and Varya.*) I'm a man of the eighties. They run down that period, but still I can say I have had to suffer not a little for my convictions in my life, it's not for nothing that the peasant loves me. One must know the peasant! One must know how. . . .

Anya: At it again, uncle!

Varya: Uncle dear, you'd better be quiet!

Firs (angrily):   Leonid Andreyevitch!

Gaev: I'm coming. I'm coming. Go to bed. Potted the shot—there's a shot for you! A beauty! (*Goes out, Firs hobbling after him.*)

Anya: My mind's at rest now. I don't want to go to Yaroslavl, I don't like my great-aunt, but still my mind's at rest. Thanks to uncle. (*Sits down.*)

Varya: We must go to bed. I'm going. Something unpleasant happened while you were away. In the old servants' quarters there are only the old servants, as you know—Efimyushka, Polya and Yevstigney—and Karp too. They began letting stray people in to spend the night—I said nothing. But all at once I heard they had been spreading a report that I gave them nothing but pease pudding to eat. Out of stinginess, you know. . . And it was all Yevstigney's doing. . . Very well, I said to myself. . . If that's how it is, I thought, wait a bit. I sent for Yevstigney. . . (*Yawns.*) He comes. . . "How's this, Yevstigney," I said, "you could be such a fool as to? . . ." (*Looking at Anya.*) Anitchka! (*A pause.*) She's asleep. (*Puts her arm around Anya.*) Come to bed . . . come along! (*Leads her.*) My darling has fallen asleep! Come . . . (*They go. Far away beyond the orchard a shepherd plays on a pipe. Trofimov crosses the stage and, seeing Varya and Anya, stands still.*) Sh! asleep, asleep. Come, my own.

Anya (softly, half asleep):   I'm so tired. Still those bells. Uncle . . . dear . . . mamma and uncle. . . .

Varya: Come, my own, come along.

(*They go into Anya's room.*)

Trofimov (*tenderly*):   My sunshine! My spring.

ACT II

(*Scene: The open country. An old shrine, long abandoned and fallen out of the perpendicular; near it a well, large stones that have apparently once been tombstones, and an old garden seat. The road to Gaev's house is seen. On one side rise dark poplars; and there the cherry orchard begins. In the distance a row of telegraph poles and far, far away on the horizon there is faintly outlined a great town, only visible in very fine clear weather. It is near sunset. Charlotta, Yasha, and Dunyasha are sitting on the seat. Epihodov is standing near, playing something mournful on a guitar. All sit plunged in thought. Charlotta wears an old forage cap; she has taken a gun from her shoulder and is tightening the buckle on the strap.*)

Charlotta (musingly):   I haven't a real passport of my own, and I don't know how old I am, and I always feel that I'm a young thing. When I was a little girl, my father and mother used to travel about to fairs and give performances—very good ones. And I used to do *salto mortale*°

---

salto mortale: A standing somersault.

and all sorts of things. And when papa and mamma died, a German lady took me and had me educated. And so I grew up and became a governess. But where I came from, and who I am, I don't know. . . . Who my parents were, very likely they weren't married. . . . I don't know. (*Takes a cucumber out of her pocket and eats.*) I know nothing at all. (*A pause.*) One wants to talk and has no one to talk to. . . . I have nobody.

Epihodov (plays on the guitar and sings): "What care I for the noisy world! What care I for friends or foes!" How agreeable it is to play on the mandolin!

Dunyasha: That's a guitar, not a mandolin. (*Looks in a hand-mirror and powders herself.*)

Epihodov: To a man mad with love, it's a mandolin. (*Sings.*) "Were her heart but aglow with love's mutual flame."

(*Yasha joins in.*)

Charlotta: How shockingly these people sing! Foo! Like jackals!

Dunyasha (to Yasha): What happiness, though, to visit foreign lands.

Yasha: Ah, yes! I rather agree with you there. (*Yawns, then lights a cigar.*)

Epihodov: That's comprehensible. In foreign lands everything has long since reached full complexion.

Yasha: That's so, of course.

Epihodov: I'm a cultivated man, I read remarkable books of all sorts, but I can never make out the tendency I am myself precisely inclined for, whether to live or to shoot myself, speaking precisely, but nevertheless I always carry a revolver. Here it is. . . . (*Shows revolver.*)

Charlotta: I've had enough, and now I'm going. (*Puts on the gun.*) Epihodov, you're a very clever fellow, and a very terrible one too, all the women must be wild about you. Br-r-r! (*Goes.*) These clever fellows are all so stupid; there's not a creature for me to speak to. . . . Always alone, alone, nobody belonging to me . . . and who I am, and why I'm on earth, I don't know. (*Walks away slowly.*)

Epihodov: Speaking precisely, not touching upon other subjects, I'm bound to admit about myself, that destiny behaves mercilessly to me, as a storm to a little boat. If, let us suppose, I am mistaken, then why did I wake up this morning, to quote an example, and look round, and there on my chest was a spider of fearful magnitude . . . like this. (*Shows with both hands.*) And then I take up a jug of kvass, to quench my thirst, and in it there is something in the highest degree unseemly of the nature of a cockroach. (*A pause.*) Have you read Buckle?° (*A pause.*) I am desirous of troubling you, Dunyasha, with a couple of words.

Dunyasha: Well, speak.

Epihodov: I should be desirous to speak with you alone. (*Sighs.*)

Buckle: Thomas Henry Buckle (1821–1862), a historian with radical theories about climate, agriculture, population, and wealth.

Dunyasha (embarrassed):   Well—only bring me my mantle first. It's by the cupboard. It's rather damp here.

Epihodov: Certainly. I will fetch it. Now I know what I must do with my revolver. (*Takes guitar and goes off playing on it.*)

Yasha: Two and twenty misfortunes! Between ourselves, he's a fool. (*Yawns.*)

Dunyasha: God grant he doesn't shoot himself! (*A pause.*) I am so nervous, I'm always in a flutter. I was a little girl when I was taken into our lady's house, and now I have quite grown out of peasant ways, and my hands are white, as white as a lady's. I'm such a delicate, sensitive creature, I'm afraid of everything. I'm so frightened. And if you deceive me, Yasha, I don't know what will become of my nerves.

Yasha (kisses her):   You're a peach! Of course a girl must never forget herself; what I dislike more than anything is a girl being flighty in her behavior.

Dunyasha: I'm passionately in love with you, Yasha; you are a man of culture—you can give your opinion about anything.

(*A pause.*)

Yasha (yawns):   Yes, that's so. My opinion is this: if a girl loves anyone, that means that she has no principles. (*A pause.*) It's pleasant smoking a cigar in the open air. (*Listens.*) Someone's coming this way . . . it's the gentlefolk. (*Dunyasha embraces him impulsively.*) Go home, as though you had been to the river to bathe; go by that path, or else they'll meet you and suppose I have made an appointment with you here. That I can't endure.

Dunyasha (coughing softly):   The cigar has made my head ache. . . .

(*Goes off. Yasha remains sitting near the shrine. Enter Lyubov Andreyevna, Gaev, and Lopahin.*)

Lopahin: You must make up your mind once for all—there's no time to lose. It's quite a simple question, you know. Will you consent to letting the land for building or not? One word in answer: Yes or no? Only one word!

Lyubov: Who is smoking such horrible cigars here? (*Sits down.*)

Gaev: Now the railway line has been brought near, it's made things very convenient. (*Sits down.*) Here we have been over and lunched in town. Cannon off the white! I should like to go home and have a game.

Lyubov: You have plenty of time.

Lopahin: Only one word! (*Beseechingly.*) Give me an answer!

Gaev (yawning):   What do you say?

Lyubov (looks in her purse):   I had quite a lot of money here yesterday, and there's scarcely any left today. My poor Varya feeds us all on milk soup for the sake of economy; the old folks in the kitchen get nothing but pease pudding, while I waste my money in a senseless way. (*Drops purse, scattering gold pieces.*) There, they have all fallen out! (*Annoyed.*)

Yasha: Allow me. I'll soon pick them up. (*Collects the coins.*)

Lyubov: Pray do, Yasha. And what did I go off to the town to lunch for? Your restaurant's a wretched place with its music and the tablecloth smelling of soap. . . . Why drink so much, Leonid? And eat so much? And talk so much? Today you talked a great deal again in the restaurant, and all so inappropriately. About the era of the seventies, about the decadents. And to whom? Talking to waiters about decadents!

Lopahin: Yes.

Gaev (waving his hand):   I'm incorrigible; that's evident. (*Irritably to Yasha.*) Why is it you keep fidgeting about in front of us!

Yasha (laughs):   I can't help laughing when I hear your voice.

Gaev (to his sister):   Either I or he. . . .

Lyubov: Get along! Go away, Yasha.

Yasha (gives Lyubov Andreyevna her purse):   Directly. (*Hardly able to suppress his laughter.*) This minute. . . . (*Goes off.*)

Lopahin: Deriganov, the millionaire, means to buy your estate. They say he is coming to the sale himself.

Lyubov: Where did you hear that?

Lopahin: That's what they say in town.

Gaev: Our aunt in Yaroslavl has promised to send help; but when, and how much she will send, we don't know.

Lopahin: How much will she send? A hundred thousand? Two hundred?

Lyubov: Oh, well! . . . Ten or fifteen thousand, and we must be thankful to get that.

Lopahin: Forgive me, but such reckless people as you are—such queer, unbusinesslike people—I never met in my life. One tells you in plain Russian your estate is going to be sold, and you seem not to understand it.

Lyubov: What are we to do? Tell us what to do.

Lopahin: I do tell you every day. Every day I say the same thing. You absolutely must let the cherry orchard and the land on building leases; and do it at once, as quick as may be—the auction's close upon us! Do understand! Once make up your mind to build villas, and you can raise as much money as you like, and then you are saved.

Lyubov: Villas and summer visitors—forgive me saying so—it's so vulgar.

Gaev: There I perfectly agree with you.

Lopahin: I shall sob, or scream, or fall into a fit. I can't stand it! You drive me mad! (*To* Gaev.) You're an old woman!

Gaev: What do you say?

Lopahin: An old woman! (*Gets up to go.*)

Lyubov (in dismay):   No, don't go! Do stay, my dear friend! Perhaps we shall think of something.

Lopahin: What is there to think of?

Lyubov: Don't go, I entreat you! With you here it's more cheerful, anyway. (*A pause.*) I keep expecting something, as though the house were going to fall about our ears.

Gaev (in profound dejection): Potted the white! It fails—a kiss.

Lyubov: We have been great sinners. . . .

Lopahin: You have no sins to repent of.

Gaev (puts a caramel in his mouth): They say I've eaten up my property in caramels. (*Laughs.*)

Lyubov: Oh, my sins! I've always thrown my money away recklessly like a lunatic. I married a man who made nothing but debts. My husband died of champagne—he drank dreadfully. To my misery I loved another man, and immediately—it was my first punishment—the blow fell upon me, here, in the river . . . my boy was drowned and I went abroad—went away forever, never to return, not to see that river again . . . I shut my eyes, and fled, distracted, and *he* after me . . . pitilessly, brutally. I bought a villa at Mentone, for *he* fell ill there, and for three years I had no rest day or night. His illness wore me out, my soul was dried up. And last year, when my villa was sold to pay my debts, I went to Paris and there he robbed me of everything and abandoned me for another woman; and I tried to poison myself. . . . So stupid, so shameful! . . . And suddenly I felt a yearning for Russia, for my country, for my little girl. . . . (*Dries her tears.*) Lord, Lord, be merciful! Forgive my sins! Do not chastise me more! (*Takes a telegram out of her pocket.*) I got this today from Paris. He implores forgiveness, entreats me to return. (*Tears up the telegram.*) I fancy there is music somewhere. (*Listens*).

Gaev: That's our famous Jewish orchestra. You remember, four violins, a flute and a double bass.

Lyubov: That still in existence? We ought to send for them one evening, and give a dance.

Lopahin (listens): I can't hear. . . . (*Hums softly.*) "For money the Germans will turn a Russian into a Frenchman." (*Laughs.*) I did see such a piece at the theater yesterday! It was funny!

Lyubov: And most likely there was nothing funny in it. You shouldn't look at plays, you should look at yourselves a little oftener. How gray your lives are! How much nonsense you talk.

Lopahin: That's true. One may say honestly, we live a fool's life. (*Pause.*) My father was a peasant, an idiot; he knew nothing and taught me nothing, only beat me when he was drunk, and always with his stick. In reality I am just such another blockhead and idiot. I've learned nothing properly. I write a wretched hand. I write so that I feel ashamed before folks, like a pig.

Lyubov: You ought to get married, my dear fellow.

Lopahin: Yes . . . that's true.

Lyubov: You should marry our Varya, she's a good girl.

Lopahin: Yes.

Lyubov: She's a good-natured girl, she's busy all day long, and what's more, she loves you. And you have liked her for ever so long.

Lopahin: Well? I'm not against it. . . . She's a good girl.

(Pause.)

Gaev: I've been offered a place in the bank: 6,000 rubles a year. Did you know?

Lyubov: You would never do for that! You must stay as you are.

(Enter Firs with overcoat.)

Firs: Put it on, sir, it's damp.

Gaev (putting it on): You bother me, old fellow.

Firs: You can't go on like this. You went away in the morning without leaving word. (*Looks him over.*)

Lyubov: You look older, Firs!

Firs: What is your pleasure?

Lopahin: You look older, she said.

Firs: I've had a long life. They were arranging my wedding before your papa was born. . . . (*Laughs.*) I was the head footman before the emancipation came. I wouldn't consent to be set free then; I stayed on with the old master. . . . (*A pause.*) I remember what rejoicings they made and didn't know themselves what they were rejoicing over.

Lopahin: Those were fine old times. There was flogging anyway.

Firs (not hearing): To be sure! The peasants knew their place, and the masters knew theirs; but now they're all at sixes and sevens, there's no making it out.

Gaev: Hold your tongue, Firs. I must go to town tomorrow. I have been promised an introduction to a general, who might let us have a loan.

Lopahin: You won't bring that off. And you won't pay your arrears, you may rest assured of that.

Lyubov: That's all his nonsense. There is no such general.

(Enter Trofimov, Anya, and Varya.)

Gaev: Here come our girls.

Anya: There's mamma on the seat.

Lyubov (tenderly): Come here, come along. My darlings! (*Embraces Anya and Varya.*) If you only knew how I love you both. Sit beside me, there, like that. (*All sit down.*)

Lopahin: Our perpetual student is always with the young ladies.

Trofimov: That's not your business.

Lopahin: He'll soon be fifty, and he's still a student.

Trofimov: Drop your idiotic jokes.

Lopahin: Why are you so cross, you queer fish?

Trofimov: Oh, don't persist!

Lopahin (laughs): Allow me to ask you what's your idea of me?

Trofimov: I'll tell you my idea of you. Yermolay Alexeyevitch; you are a rich man, you'll soon be a millionaire. Well, just as in the economy of nature a wild beast is of use, who devours everything that comes in his way, so you too have your use.

(All laugh.)

Varya: Better tell us something about the planets, Petya.

Lyubov: No, let us go on with the conversation we had yesterday.

Trofimov: What was it about?

Gaev: About pride.

Trofimov: We had a long conversation yesterday, but we came to no conclusion. In pride, in your sense of it, there is something mystical. Perhaps you are right from your point of view; but if one looks at it simply, without subtlety, what sort of pride can there be, what sense is there in it, if man in his physiological formation is very imperfect, if in the immense majority of cases he is coarse, dull-witted, profoundly unhappy? One must give up glorification of self. One should work, and nothing else.

Gaev: One must die in any case.

Trofimov: Who knows? And what does it mean—dying? Perhaps man has a hundred senses, and only the five we know are lost at death, while the other ninety-five remain alive.

Lyubov: How clever you are, Petya!

Lopahin (ironically):   Fearfully clever!

Trofimov: Humanity progresses, perfecting its powers. Everything that is beyond its ken now will one day become familiar and comprehensible; only we must work, we must with all our powers aid the seeker after truth. Here among us in Russia the workers are few in number as yet. The vast majority of the intellectual people I know, seek nothing, do nothing, are not fit as yet for work of any kind. They call themselves intellectual, but they treat their servants as inferiors, behave to the peasants as though they were animals, learn little, read nothing seriously, do practically nothing, only talk about science and know very little about art. They are all serious people, they all have severe faces, they all talk of weighty matters and air their theories, and yet the vast majority of us—ninety-nine per cent—live like savages, at the least thing fly to blows and abuse, eat piggishly, sleep in filth and stuffiness, bugs everywhere, stench and damp and moral impurity. And it's clear all our fine talk is only to divert our attention and other people's. Show me where to find the *crèches*° there's so much talk about, and the reading-rooms? They only exist in novels: in real life there are none of them. There is nothing but filth and vulgarity and Asiatic apathy.° I fear and dislike very serious faces. I'm afraid of serious conversation. We should do better to be silent.

---

crèches: Day nurseries.   *Asiatic apathy:* The common prejudice was that Asians were apathetic.

Lopahin: You know, I get up at five o'clock in the morning, and I work from morning to night; and I've money, my own and other people's, always passing through my hands, and I see what people are made of all round me. One has only to begin to do anything to see how few honest decent people there are. Sometimes when I lie awake at night, I think: "Oh! Lord, thou hast given us immense forests, boundless plains, the widest horizons, and living here we ourselves ought really to be giants."

Lyubov: You ask for giants! They are no good except in storybooks; in real life they frighten us.

(Epihodov advances in the background, playing on the guitar.)

Lyubov (dreamily):   There goes Epihodov.

Anya (dreamily):   There goes Epihodov.

Gaev: The sun has set, my friends.

Trofimov: Yes.

Gaev (not loudly, but, as it were, declaiming):   O nature, divine nature, thou art bright with eternal luster, beautiful and indifferent! Thou, whom we call mother, thou dost unite within thee life and death! Thou dost give life and dost destroy!

Varya (in a tone of supplication):   Uncle!

Anya: Uncle, you are at it again!

Trofimov: You'd much better be cannoning off the red!

Gaev: I'll hold my tongue, I will.

(All sit plunged in thought. Perfect stillness. The only thing audible is the muttering of Firs. Suddenly there is a sound in the distance, as it were from the sky—the sound of a breaking harp-string, mournfully dying away.)

Lyubov: What is that?

Lopahin: I don't know. Somewhere far away a bucket fallen and broken in the pits. But somewhere very far away.

Gaev: It might be a bird of some sort—such as a heron.

Trofimov: Or an owl.

Lyubov (shudders):   I don't know why, but it's horrid.

(A pause.)

Firs: It was the same before the calamity—the owl hooted and the samovar hissed all the time.

Gaev: Before what calamity?

Firs: Before the emancipation.

(A pause.)

Lyubov: Come, my friends, let us be going; evening is falling. (*To Anya.*) There are tears in your eyes. What is it, darling? (*Embraces her.*)

Anya: Nothing, mamma; it's nothing.

Trofimov: There is somebody coming.

(The Wayfarer appears in a shabby white forage cap and an overcoat; he is slightly drunk.)

Wayfarer: Allow me to inquire, can I get to the station this way?

Gaev: Yes. Go along that road.

Wayfarer: I thank you most feelingly. (*Coughing.*) The weather is superb. (*Declaims.*) My brother, my suffering brother! . . . Come out to the Volga! Whose groan do you hear? . . . (*To Varya.*) Mademoiselle, vouchsafe a hungry Russian thirty kopecks.

(Varya utters a shriek of alarm.)

Lopahin (angrily):   There's a right and a wrong way of doing everything!

Lyubov (hurriedly):   Here, take this. (*Looks in her purse.*) I've no silver. No matter—here's gold for you.

Wayfarer: I thank you most feelingly! (*Goes off.*)

(Laughter.)

Varya (frightened):   I'm going home—I'm going. . . . Oh, mamma, the servants have nothing to eat, and you gave him gold!

Lyubov: There's no doing anything with me. I'm so silly! When we get home, I'll give you all I possess, Yermolay Alexeyevitch, you will lend me some more! . . .

Lopahin: I will.

Lyubov: Come, friends, it's time to be going. And Varya, we have made a match of it for you. I congratulate you.

Varya (through her tears):   Mamma, that's not a joking matter.

Lopahin: "Ophelia, get thee to a nunnery!"°

Gaev: My hands are trembling; it's a long while since I had a game of billiards.

Lopahin: "Ophelia! Nymph, in thy orisons be all my sins remember'd."

Lyubov: Come, it will soon be supper-time.

Varya: How he frightened me! My heart's simply throbbing.

Lopahin: Let me remind you, ladies and gentlemen: on the 22nd of August the cherry orchard will be sold. Think about that! Think about it!

(All go off, except Trofimov and Anya.)

Anya (laughing):   I'm grateful to the wayfarer! He frightened Varya and we are left alone.

Trofimov: Varya's afraid we shall fall in love with each other, and for days together she won't leave us. With her narrow brain she can't grasp that we are above love. To eliminate the petty and transitory which hinder us from being free and happy—that is the aim and meaning of our life. Forward! We go forward irresistibly toward the bright star that shines yonder in the distance. Forward! Do not lag behind, friends.

Anya (claps her hands):   How well you speak! (*A pause.*) It is divine here today.

"Ophelia . . . nunnery":   Lopahin starts quoting from *Hamlet.*

Trofimov: Yes, it's glorious weather.

Anya: Somehow, Petya, you've made me so that I don't love the cherry orchard as I used to. I used to love it so dearly. I used to think that there was no spot on earth like our garden.

Trofimov: All Russia is our garden. The earth is great and beautiful—there are many beautiful places in it. (*A pause.*) Think only, Anya, your grandfather, and great-grandfather, and all your ancestors were slave-owners—the owners of living souls—and from every cherry in the orchard, from every leaf, from every trunk there are human creatures looking at you. Cannot you hear their voices? Oh, it is awful! Your orchard is a fearful thing, and when in the evening or at night one walks about the orchard, the old bark on the trees glimmers dimly in the dusk, and the old cherry trees seem to be dreaming of centuries gone by and tortured by fearful visions. Yes! We are at least two hundred years behind, we have really gained nothing yet, we have no definite attitude to the past, we do nothing but theorize or complain of depression or drink vodka. It is clear that to begin to live in the present, we must first expiate our past; we must break with it; and we can expiate it only by suffering, by extraordinary unceasing labor. Understand that, Anya.

Anya: The house we live in has long ceased to be our own, and I shall leave it, I give you my word.

Trofimov: If you have the house keys, fling them into the well and go away. Be free as the wind.

Anya (in ecstasy):   How beautifully you said that!

Trofimov: Believe me, Anya, believe me! I am not thirty yet. I am young. I am still a student, but I have gone through so much already! As soon as winter comes I am hungry, sick, careworn, poor as a beggar, and what ups and downs of fortune have I not known! And my soul was always, every minute, day and night, full of inexplicable forebodings. I have a foreboding of happiness, Anya. I see glimpses of it already.

Anya (pensively):   The moon is rising.

(*Epihodov is heard playing still the same mournful song on the guitar. The moon rises. Somewhere near the poplars Varya is looking for Anya and calling "Anya! where are you?"*)

Trofimov: Yes, the moon is rising. (*A pause.*) Here is happiness—here it comes! It is coming nearer and nearer; already I can hear its footsteps. And if we never see it—if we may never know it—what does it matter? Others will see it after us.

Varya's voice: Anya! Where are you?

Trofimov: That Varya again! (*Angrily.*) It's revolting!

Anya: Well, let's go down to the river. It's lovely there.

Trofimov: Yes, let's go.

(*They go.*)

Varya's voice: Anya! Anya!

ACT III

(Scene: A drawing room divided by an arch from a larger drawing room. A chandelier burning. The Jewish orchestra, the same that was mentioned in Act II, is heard playing in the anteroom. It is evening. In the larger drawing room they are dancing the grand chain. The voice of Semyonov-Pishtchik: "Promenade à une paire!"° They enter the drawing room in couples, first Pishtchik and Charlotta Ivanovna, then Trofimov and Lyubov Andreyevna, thirdly Anya with the Post-office Clerk, fourthly Varya with the stationmaster, and other guests. Varya is quietly weeping and wiping away her tears as she dances. In the last couple is Dunyasha. They move across the drawing room. Pishtchik shouts: "Grand rond, balancez!" and "Les Cavaliers à genou et remerciez vos dames."°)

(Firs in a swallowtail coat brings in seltzer water on a tray. Pishtchik and Trofimov enter the drawing room.)

Pishtchik: I am a full-blooded man; I have already had two strokes. Dancing's hard work for me, but as they say, if you're in the pack, you must bark with the rest. I'm as strong, I may say, as a horse. My parent, who would have his joke—may the Kingdom of Heaven be his!—used to say about our origin that the ancient stock of the Semyonov-Pishtchiks was derived from the very horse that Caligula° made a member of the senate. (Sits down.) But I've no money, that's where the mischief is. A hungry dog believes in nothing but meat. (Snores, but at once wakes up.) That's like me . . . I can think of nothing but money.

Trofimov: There really is something horsy about your appearance.

Pishtchik: Well . . . a horse is a fine beast . . . a horse can be sold.

(There is the sound of billiards being played in an adjoining room. Varya appears in the arch leading to the larger drawing room.)

Trofimov (teasing): Madame Lopahin! Madame Lopahin!

Varya (angrily): Mangy-looking gentleman!

Trofimov: Yes, I am a mangy-looking gentleman, and I'm proud of it!

Varya (pondering bitterly): Here we have hired musicians and nothing to pay them! (Goes out.)

Trofimov (to Pishtchik): If the energy you have wasted during your lifetime in trying to find the money to pay your interest had gone to something else, you might in the end have turned the world upside down.

Pishtchik: Nietzsche, the philosopher, a very great and celebrated man . . .

"Promenade à une paire!": "Walk in pairs" (French).   "Grand rond . . . vos dames": "Form a large circle" and "Gentlemen kneel and thank your ladies."   Caligula: Roman emperor (A.D. 37–41) who reputedly put a horse in the Senate.

of enormous intellect . . . says in his works, that one can make forged banknotes.

Trofimov: Why, have you read Nietzsche?

Pishtchik: What next . . . Dashenka told me. . . . And now I am in such a position, I might just as well forge banknotes. The day after tomorrow I must pay 310 rubles—130 I have procured. (*Feels in his pockets, in alarm.*) The money's gone! I have lost my money! (*Through his tears.*) Where's the money? (*Gleefully.*) Why, here it is behind the lining. . . . It has made me hot all over.

(*Enter Lyubov Andreyevna and Charlotta Ivanovna.*)

Lyubov (hums the Lezginka°):   Why is Leonid so long? What can he be doing in town? (*To Dunyasha.*) Offer the musicians some tea.

Trofimov: The sale hasn't taken place, most likely.

Lyubov: It's the wrong time to have the orchestra, and the wrong time to give a dance. Well, never mind. (*Sits down and hums softly.*)

Charlotta (gives Pishtchik a pack of cards):   Here's a pack of cards. Think of any card you like.

Pishtchik: I've thought of one.

Charlotta: Shuffle the pack now. That's right. Give it here, my dear Mr. Pishtchik. *Ein, zwei, drei°*—now look, it's in your breast pocket.

Pishtchik (taking a card out of his breast pocket):   The eight of spades! Perfectly right! (*Wonderingly.*) Fancy that now!

Charlotta (holding pack of cards in her hands, to Trofimov):   Tell me quickly which is the top card.

Trofimov: Well, the queen of spades.

Charlotta: It is! (*To Pishtchik.*) Well, which card is uppermost?

Pishtchik: The ace of hearts.

Charlotta: It is! (*Claps her hands, pack of cards disappears.*) Ah! what lovely weather it is today! (*A mysterious feminine voice which seems coming out of the floor answers her.* "Oh, yes, it's magnificent weather, madam.")! You are my perfect ideal.

Voice: And I greatly admire you too, madam.

Stationmaster (applauding):   The lady ventriloquist—bravo!

Pishtchik (wonderingly):   Fancy that now! Most enchanting, Charlotta Ivanovna. I'm simply in love with you.

Charlotta: In love? (*Shrugging shoulders.*) What do you know of love, *guter Mensch, aber schlechter Musikant.°*

Trofimov (pats Pishtchik on the shoulder):   You dear old horse. . . .

Charlotta: Attention, please! Another trick! (*Takes a traveling rug from a chair.*) Here's a very good rug; I want to sell it. (*Shaking it out.*) Doesn't anyone want to buy it?

Lezginka: A Russian dance tune.   *Ein, zwei, drei:* One, two, three.   *guter Mensch, aber schlechter Musikant:* Good person but terrible musician (German).

Pishtchik (wonderingly):   Fancy that!

Charlotta: *Ein, zwei, drei!*

> *(Quickly picks up rug she has dropped; behind the rug stands Anya; she makes a curtsey, runs to her mother, embraces her and runs back into the larger drawing room amidst general enthusiasm.)*

Lyubov (applauds):   Bravo! Bravo!

Charlotta: Now again; *Ein, zwei, drei!*

> *(Lifts up the rug; behind the rug stands Varya, bowing.)*

Pishtchik (wonderingly):   Fancy that now!

Charlotta: That's the end. (*Throws the rug at Pishtchik, makes a curtsey, runs into the larger drawing room.*)

Pishtchik (hurries after her):   Mischievous creature! Fancy! (*Goes out.*)

Lyubov: And still Leonid doesn't come. I can't understand what he's doing in the town so long! Why, everything must be over by now. The estate is sold, or the sale has not taken place. Why keep us so long in suspense?

Varya (trying to console her):   Uncle's bought it. I feel sure of that.

Trofimov (ironically):   Oh, yes!

Varya: Great-aunt sent him an authorization to buy it in her name, and transfer the debt. She's doing it for Anya's sake, and I'm sure God will be merciful. Uncle will buy it.

Lyubov: My aunt in Yaroslavl sent fifteen thousand to buy the estate in her name, she doesn't trust us—but that's not enough even to pay the arrears. (*Hides her face in her hands.*) My fate is being sealed today, my fate. . . .

Trofimov (teasing Varya):   Madame Lopahin.

Varya (angrily):   Perpetual student! Twice already you've been sent down from the University.

Lyubov: Why are you angry, Varya? He's teasing you about Lopahin. Well, what of that? Marry Lopahin if you like, he's a good man, and interesting; if you don't want to, don't! Nobody compels you, darling.

Varya: I must tell you plainly, mamma, I look at the matter seriously; he's a good man, I like him.

Lyubov: Well, marry him. I can't see what you're waiting for.

Varya: Mamma. I can't make him an offer myself. For the last two years, everyone's been talking to me about him. Everyone talks; but he says nothing or else makes a joke. I see what it means. He's growing rich, he's absorbed in business, he has no thoughts for me. If I had money, were it ever so little, if I had only a hundred rubles, I'd throw everything up and go far away. I would go into a nunnery.

Trofimov: What bliss!

Varya (to Trofimov):   A student ought to have sense! (*In a soft tone with tears.*) How ugly you've grown, Petya! How old you look! (*To Lyubov Andreyevna, no longer crying.*) But I can't do without work, mamma; I must have something to do every minute.

(*Enter Yasha.*)

Yasha (*hardly restraining his laughter*):   Epihodov has broken a billiard cue! (*Goes out.*)

Varya: What is Epihodov doing here? Who gave him leave to play billiards? I can't make these people out. (*Goes out.*)

Lyubov: Don't tease her, Petya. You see she has grief enough without that.

Trofimov: She is so very officious, meddling in what's not her business. All the summer she's given Anya and me no peace. She's afraid of a love affair between us. What's it to do with her? Besides, I have given no grounds for it. Such triviality is not in my line. We are above love!

Lyubov: And I suppose I am beneath love. (*Very uneasily.*) Why is it Leonid's not here? If only I could know whether the estate is sold or not! It seems such an incredible calamity that I really don't know what to think. I am distracted. . . . I shall scream in a minute . . . I shall do something stupid. Save me, Petya, tell me something, talk to me!

Trofimov: What does it matter whether the estate is sold today or not? That's all done with long ago. There's no turning back, the path is overgrown. Don't worry yourself, dear Lyubov Andreyevna. You mustn't deceive yourself; for once in your life you must face the truth!

Lyubov: What truth? You see where the truth lies, but I seem to have lost my sight, I see nothing. You settle every great problem so boldly, but tell me, my dear boy, isn't it because you're young—because you haven't yet understood one of your problems through suffering? You look forward boldly, and isn't it that you don't see and don't expect anything dreadful because life is still hidden from your young eyes? You're bolder, more honest, deeper than we are, but think, be just a little magnanimous, have pity on me. I was born here, you know, my father and mother lived here, my grandfather lived here, I love this house. I can't conceive of life without the cherry orchard, and if it really must be sold, then sell me with the orchard. (*Embraces Trofimov, kisses him on the forehead.*) My boy was drowned here. (*Weeps.*) Pity me, my dear kind fellow.

Trofimov: You know I feel for you with all my heart.

Lyubov: But that should have been said differently, so differently. (*Takes out her handkerchief, telegram falls on the floor.*) My heart is so heavy today. It's so noisy here, my soul is quivering at every sound, I'm shuddering all over, but I can't go away; I'm afraid to be quiet and alone. Don't be hard on me, Petya . . . I love you as though you were one of ourselves. I would gladly let you marry Anya—I swear I would—only, my dear boy, you must take your degree, you do nothing—you're simply tossed by fate from place to place. That's so strange. It is, isn't it? And you must do something with your beard to make it grow somehow. (*Laughs.*) You look so funny!

Trofimov (picks up the telegram): I've no wish to be a beauty.

Lyubov: That's a telegram from Paris. I get one every day. One yesterday and one today. That savage creature is ill again, he's in trouble again. He begs forgiveness, beseeches me to go, and really I ought to go to Paris to see him. You look shocked, Petya. What am I to do, my dear boy, what am I to do? He is ill, he is alone and unhappy, and who'll look after him, who'll keep him from doing the wrong thing, who'll give him his medicine at the right time? And why hide it or be silent? I love him, that's clear. I love him! I love him! He's a millstone about my neck, I'm going to the bottom with him, but I love that stone and can't live without it. (*Presses Trofimov's hand.*) Don't think ill of me, Petya, don't tell me anything, don't tell me. . . .

Trofimov (through his tears): For God's sake forgive my frankness: why, he robbed you!

Lyubov: No! No! No! You mustn't speak like that. (*Covers her ears.*)

Trofimov: He is a wretch! You're the only person that doesn't know it! He's a worthless creature! A despicable wretch!

Lyubov (getting angry, but speaking with restraint): You're twenty-six or twenty-seven years old, but you're still a schoolboy.

Trofimov: Possibly.

Lyubov: You should be a man at your age! You should understand what love means! And you ought to be in love yourself. You ought to fall in love! (*Angrily.*) Yes, yes, and it's not purity in you, you're simply a prude, a comic fool, a freak.

Trofimov (in horror): The things she's saying!

Lyubov: I am above love! You're not above love, but simply as our Firs here says, "You are a good-for-nothing." At your age not to have a mistress!

Trofimov (in horror): This is awful! The things she is saying! (*Goes rapidly into the larger drawing room clutching his head.*) This is awful! I can't stand it! I'm going. (*Goes off, but at once returns.*) All is over between us! (*Goes off into the anteroom.*)

Lyubov (shouts after him): Petya! Wait a minute! You funny creature! I was joking! Petya! (*There is a sound of somebody running quickly downstairs and suddenly falling with a crash, Anya and Varya scream, but there is a sound of laughter at once.*) What has happened?

(*Anya runs in.*)

Anya (laughing): Petya's fallen downstairs! (*Runs out.*)

Lyubov: What a queer fellow that Petya is! (*The stationmaster stands in the middle of the larger room and reads* The Magdalene, *by Alexey Tolstoy.° They listen to him, but before he has recited many lines strains of a waltz are heard from the anteroom and the reading is broken off. All dance.*)

Alexey Tolstoy: 1817–1875; Russian novelist, dramatist, and poet.

Trofimov, Anya, Varya, and Lyubov Andreyevna come in from the anteroom.) Come, Petya—come, pure heart! I beg your pardon. Let's have a dance!

(*Dances with Petya. Anya and Varya dance. Firs comes in, puts his stick down near the side door. Yasha also comes into the drawing room and looks on at the dancing.*)

Yasha: What is it, old man?

Firs: I don't feel well. In old days we used to have generals, barons and admirals dancing at our balls, and now we send for the post-office clerk and the stationmaster and even they're not overanxious to come. I am getting feeble. The old master, the grandfather, used to give sealing-wax for all complaints. I have been taking sealing-wax for twenty years or more. Perhaps that's what's kept me alive.

Yasha: You bore me, old man! (*Yawns.*) It's time you were done with.

Firs: Ach, you're a good-for-nothing! (*Mutters.*)

(*Trofimov and Lyubov Andreyevna dance in larger room and then on to the stage.*)

Lyubov: Merci. I'll sit down a little. (*Sits down.*) I'm tired.

(*Enter Anya.*)

Anya (excitedly):   There's a man in the kitchen has been saying that the cherry orchard's been sold today.

Lyubov: Sold to whom?

Anya: He didn't say to whom. He's gone away.

(*She dances with Trofimov, and they go off into the larger room.*)

Yasha: There was an old man gossiping there, a stranger.

Firs: Leonid Andreyevitch isn't here yet, he hasn't come back. He has his light overcoat on, *demi-saison,*° he'll catch cold for sure. *Ach!* Foolish young things!

Lyubov: I feel as though I should die. Go, Yasha, find out to whom it has been sold.

Yasha: But he went away long ago, the old chap. (*Laughs.*)

Lyubov (with slight vexation):   What are you laughing at? What are you pleased at?

Yasha: Epihodov is so funny. He's a silly fellow, two and twenty misfortunes.

Lyubov: Firs, if the estate is sold, where will you go?

Firs: Where you bid me, there I'll go.

Lyubov: Why do you look like that? Are you ill? You ought to be in bed.

Firs: Yes. (*Ironically.*) Me go to bed and who's to wait here? Who's to see to things without me? I'm the only one in all the house.

---

demi-saison: Between seasons.

Yasha (to Lyubov Andreyevna):   Lyubov Andreyevna, permit me to make a request of you; if you go back to Paris again, be so kind as to take me with you. It's positively impossible for me to stay here. (*Looking about him; in an undertone.*) There's no need to say it, you see for yourself— an uncivilized country, the people have no morals, and then the dullness! The food in the kitchen's abominable, and then Firs runs after one muttering all sorts of unsuitable words. Take me with you, please do!

(*Enter Pishtchik.*)

Pishtchik: Allow me to ask you for a waltz, my dear lady. (*Lyubov Andreyevna goes with him.*) Enchanting lady, I really must borrow of you just 180 rubles, (*dances*) only 180 rubles.

(*They pass into the larger room. In the larger drawing room, a figure in a gray top hat and in checked trousers is gesticulating and jumping about. Shouts of* "Bravo, Charlotta Ivanovna.")

Dunyasha (she has stopped to powder herself):   My young lady tells me to dance. There are plenty of gentlemen, and too few ladies, but dancing makes me giddy and makes my heart beat. Firs, the post-office clerk said something to me just now that quite took my breath away.

(*Music becomes more subdued.*)

Firs: What did he say to you?
Dunyasha: He said I was like a flower.
Yasha (yawns):   What ignorance! (*Goes out.*)
Dunyasha: Like a flower. I am a girl of such delicate feelings, I am awfully fond of soft speeches.
Firs: Your head's being turned.

(*Enter Epihodov.*)

Epihodov: You have no desire to see me, Dunyasha. I might be an insect. (*Sighs.*) Ah! life!
Dunyasha: What is it you want?
Epihodov: Undoubtedly you may be right. (*Sighs.*) But, of course, if one looks at it from that point of view, if I may so express myself, you have, excuse my plain speaking, reduced me to a complete state of mind. I know my destiny. Every day some misfortune befalls me and I have long ago grown accustomed to it, so that I look upon my fate with a smile. You gave me your word, and though I—
Dunyasha: Let us have a talk later, I entreat you, but now leave me in peace, for I am lost in reverie. (*Plays with her fan.*)
Epihodov: I have a misfortune every day, and if I may venture to express myself, I merely smile at it, I even laugh.

(*Varya enters from the larger drawing room.*)

Varya: You still have not gone, Epihodov. What a disrespectful creature you are, really! (*To Dunyasha.*) Go along, Dunyasha! (*To Epihodov.*) First you play billiards and break the cue, then you go wandering about the drawing room like a visitor!

Epihodov: You really cannot, if I may so express myself, call me to account like this.

Varya: I'm not calling you to account, I'm speaking to you. You do nothing but wander from place to place and don't do your work. We keep you as a counting-house clerk, but what use you are I can't say.

Epihodov (offended):   Whether I work or whether I walk, whether I eat or whether I play billiards, is a matter to be judged by persons of understanding and my elders.

Varya: You dare to tell me that! (*Firing up.*) You dare! You mean to say I've no understanding. Begone from here! This minute!

Epihodov (intimidated):   I beg you to express yourself with delicacy.

Varya (beside herself with anger):   This moment! get out! away! (*He goes toward the door, she following him.*) Two and twenty misfortunes! Take yourself off! Don't let me set eyes on you! (*Epihodov has gone out, behind the door his voice,* "I shall lodge a complaint against you.") What! You're coming back? (*Snatches up the stick Firs has put down near the door.*) Come! Come! Come! I'll show you! What! you're coming? Then take that! (*She swings the stick, at the very moment that Lopahin comes in.*)

Lopahin: Very much obliged to you!

Varya (angrily and ironically):   I beg your pardon!

Lopahin: Not at all! I humbly thank you for your kind reception!

Varya: No need of thanks for it. (*Moves away, then looks round and asks softly.*) I haven't hurt you?

Lopahin: Oh, no! Not at all! There's an immense bump coming up, though!

Voices from Larger Room: Lopahin has come! Yermolay Alexeyevitch!

Pishtchik: What do I see and hear? (*Kisses Lopahin.*) There's a whiff of cognac about you, my dear soul, and we're making merry here too!

(*Enter Lyubov Andreyevna.*)

Lyubov: Is it you, Yermolay Alexeyevitch? Why have you been so long? Where's Leonid?

Lopahin: Leonid Andreyevitch arrived with me. He is coming.

Lyubov (in agitation):   Well! Well! Was there a sale? Speak!

Lopahin (embarrassed, afraid of betraying his joy):   The sale was over at four o'clock. We missed our train—had to wait till half-past nine. (*Sighing heavily.*) Ugh! I feel a little giddy.

(*Enter Gaev. In his right hand he has purchases, with his left hand he is wiping away his tears.*)

Lyubov: Well, Leonid? What news? (*Impatiently, with tears.*) Make haste, for God's sake!

Gaev (makes her no answer, simply waves his hand. To Firs, weeping): Here, take them; there's anchovies, Kertch herrings. I have eaten nothing all day. What I have been through! (*Door into the billiard room is open. There is heard a knocking of balls and the voice of Yasha saying "Eighty-seven." Gaev's expression changes, he leaves off weeping.*) I am fearfully tired. Firs, come and help me change my things. (*Goes to his own room across the larger drawing room.*)

Pishtchik: How about the sale? Tell us, do!

Lyubov: Is the cherry orchard sold?

Lopahin: It is sold.

Lyubov: Who has bought it?

Lopahin: I have bought it. (*A pause. Lyubov is crushed; she would fall down if she were not standing near a chair and table. Varya takes keys from her waistband, flings them on the floor in middle of drawing room and goes out.*) I have bought it! Wait a bit, ladies and gentlemen, pray. My head's a bit muddled, I can't speak. (*Laughs.*) We came to the auction. Deriganov was there already. Leonid Andreyevitch only had 15,000 and Deriganov bid 30,000, besides the arrears, straight off. I saw how the land lay. I bid against him. I bid 40,000, he bid 45,000, I said 55, and so he went on, adding 5 thousands and I adding 10. Well . . . So it ended. I bid 90, and it was knocked down to me. Now the cherry orchard's mine! Mine! (*Chuckles.*) My God, the cherry orchard's mine! Tell me that I'm drunk, that I'm out of my mind, that it's all a dream. (*Stamps with his feet.*) Don't laugh at me! If my father and my grandfather could rise from their graves and see all that has happened! How their Yermolay, ignorant, beaten Yermolay, who used to run about barefoot in winter, how that very Yermolay has bought the finest estate in the world! I have bought the estate where my father and grandfather were slaves, where they weren't even admitted into the kitchen. I am asleep, I am dreaming! It is all fancy, it is the work of your imagination plunged in the darkness of ignorance. (*Picks up keys, smiling fondly.*) She threw away the keys; she means to show she's not the housewife now. (*Jingles the keys.*) Well, no matter. (*The orchestra is heard tuning up.*) Hey, musicians! Play! I want to hear you. Come, all of you, and look how Yermolay Lopahin will take the ax to the cherry orchard, how the trees will fall to the ground! We will build houses on it and our grandsons and great-grandsons will see a new life springing up there. Music! Play up!

(*Music begins to play. Lyubov Andreyevna has sunk into a chair and is weeping bitterly.*)

Lopahin (reproachfully): Why, why didn't you listen to me? My poor friend! Dear lady, there's no turning back now. (*With tears.*) Oh, if all this could be over, oh, if our miserable disjointed life could somehow soon be changed!

Pishtchik (takes him by the arm, in an undertone):   She's weeping, let us go and leave her alone. Come. (*Takes him by the arm and leads him into the larger drawing room.*)

Lopahin: What's that? Musicians, play up! All must be as I wish it. (*With irony.*) Here comes the new master, the owner of the cherry orchard! (*Accidentally tips over a little table, almost upsetting the candelabra.*) I can pay for everything!

(*Goes out with Pishtchik. No one remains on the stage or in the larger drawing room except Lyubov, who sits huddled up, weeping bitterly. The music plays softly. Anya and Trofimov come in quickly. Anya goes up to her mother and falls on her knees before her. Trofimov stands at the entrance to the larger drawing room.*)

Anya: Mamma! Mamma, you're crying, dear, kind, good mamma! My precious! I love you! I bless you! The cherry orchard is sold, it is gone, that's true, that's true! But don't weep, mamma! Life is still before you, you have still your good, pure heart! Let us go, let us go, darling, away from here! We will make a new garden, more splendid than this one; you will see it, you will understand. And joy, quiet, deep joy, will sink into your soul like the sun at evening! And you will smile, mamma! Come, darling, let us go!

ACT IV

(*Scene: Same as in Act I. There are neither curtains on the windows nor pictures on the walls: only a little furniture remains piled up in a corner as if for sale. There is a sense of desolation; near the outer door and in the background of the scene are packed trunks, traveling bags, etc. On the left the door is open, and from here the voices of Varya and Anya are audible. Lopahin is standing waiting. Yasha is holding a tray with glasses full of champagne. In front of the stage Epihodov is tying up a box. In the background behind the scene a hum of talk from the peasants who have come to say good-by. The voice of Gaev: "Thanks, brothers, thanks!"*)

Yasha: The peasants have come to say good-by. In my opinion, Yermolay Alexeyevitch, the peasants are good-natured, but they don't know much about things.

(*The hum of talk dies away. Enter across front of stage. Lyubov Andreyevna and Gaev. She is not weeping, but is pale; her face is quivering—she cannot speak.*)

Gaev: You gave them your purse, Lyuba. That won't do—that won't do!

Lyubov: I couldn't help it! I couldn't help it!

(Both go out.)

Lopahin (in the doorway, calls after them):   You will take a glass at parting? Please do. I didn't think to bring any from the town, and at the station I could only get one bottle. Please take a glass. (*A pause.*) What? You don't care for any? (*Comes away from the door.*) If I'd known, I wouldn't have bought it. Well, and I'm not going to drink it. (*Yasha carefully sets the tray down on a chair.*) You have a glass, Yasha, anyway.

Yasha: Good luck to the travelers, and luck to those that stay behind! (*Drinks.*) This champagne isn't the real thing, I can assure you.

Lopahin: It cost eight rubles the bottle. (*A pause.*) It's devilish cold here.

Yasha: They haven't heated the stove today—it's all the same since we're going. (*Laughs.*)

Lopahin: What are you laughing for?

Yasha: For pleasure.

Lopahin: Though it's October, it's as still and sunny as though it were summer. It's just right for building! (*Looks at his watch; says in doorway.*) Take note, ladies and gentlemen, the train goes in forty-seven minutes; so you ought to start for the station in twenty minutes. You must hurry up!

(Trofimov comes in from out of doors wearing a great-coat.)

Trofimov: I think it must be time to start, the horses are ready. The devil only knows what's become of my galoshes; they're lost. (*In the doorway.*) Anya! My galoshes aren't here. I can't find them.

Lopahin: And I'm getting off to Harkov. I am going in the same train with you. I'm spending all the winter at Harkov. I've been wasting all my time gossiping with you and fretting with no work to do. I can't get on without work. I don't know what to do with my hands, they flap about so queerly, as if they didn't belong to me.

Trofimov: Well, we're just going away, and you will take up your profitable labors again.

Lopahin: Do take a glass.

Trofimov: No, thanks.

Lopahin: Then you're going to Moscow now?

Trofimov: Yes. I shall see them as far as the town, and tomorrow I shall go on to Moscow.

Lopahin: Yes, I dare say, the professors aren't giving any lectures, they're waiting for your arrival.

Trofimov: That's not your business.

Lopahin: How many years have you been at the University?

Trofimov: Do think of something newer than that—that's stale and flat. (*Hunts for galoshes.*) You know we shall most likely never see each other again, so let me give you one piece of advice at parting: don't wave your arms about—get out of the habit. And another thing, building villas, reckoning up that the summer visitors will in time become independent farmers—reckoning like that, that's not the thing to do either. After all, I am fond of you: you have fine delicate fingers like an artist, you've a fine delicate soul.

Lopahin (embraces him):   Good-by, my dear fellow. Thanks for everything. Let me give you money for the journey, if you need it.

Trofimov: What for? I don't need it.

Lopahin: Why, you haven't got a half-penny.

Trofimov: Yes, I have, thank you. I got some money for a translation. Here it is in my pocket, (*anxiously*) but where can my galoshes be!

Varya (from the next room):   Take the nasty things! (*Flings a pair of galoshes onto the stage.*)

Trofimov: Why are you so cross, Varya? h'm! . . . but those aren't my galoshes.

Lopahin: I sowed three thousand acres with poppies in the spring, and now I have cleared forty thousand profit. And when my poppies were in flower, wasn't it a picture! So here, as I say, I made forty thousand, and I'm offering you a loan because I can afford to. Why turn up your nose? I am a peasant—I speak bluntly.

Trofimov: Your father was a peasant, mine was a chemist—and that proves absolutely nothing whatever. (*Lopahin takes out his pocketbook.*) Stop that—stop that. If you were to offer me two hundred thousand I wouldn't take it. I am an independent man, and everything that all of you, rich and poor alike, prize so highly and hold so dear, hasn't the slightest power over me—it's like so much fluff fluttering in the air. I can get on without you. I can pass by you. I am strong and proud. Humanity is advancing toward the highest truth, the highest happiness which is possible on earth, and I am in the front ranks.

Lopahin: Will you get there?

Trofimov: I shall get there. (*A pause.*) I shall get there, or I shall show others the way to get there.

(In the distance is heard the strike of an ax on a tree.)

Lopahin: Good-by, my dear fellow; it's time to be off. We turn up our noses at one another, but life is passing all the while. When I am working hard without resting, then my mind is more at ease, and it seems to me as though I too know what I exist for; but how many people are in Russia, my dear boy, who exist, one doesn't know what for. Well, it doesn't matter. That's not what keeps things spinning. They tell me Leonid Andreyevitch has taken a situation. He is going to be a clerk at the bank—6,000 rubles a year. Only, of course, he won't stick to it—he's too lazy.

Anya (in the doorway):   Mamma begs you not to let them chop down the orchard until she's gone.

Trofimov: Yes, really, you might have the tact. (*Walks out across the front of the stage.*)

Lopahin: I'll see to it! I'll see to it! Stupid fellows! (*Goes out after him.*)

Anya: Has Firs been taken to the hospital?

Yasha: I told them this morning. No doubt they have taken him.

Anya (to Epihodov, who passes across the drawing room): Semyon Pantaleyevitch, inquire, please, if Firs has been taken to the hospital.

Yasha (in a tone of offense): I told Yegor this morning—why ask a dozen times?

Epihodov: Firs is advanced in years. It's my conclusive opinion no treatment would do him good; it's time he was gathered to his fathers. And I can only envy him. (*Puts a trunk down on a cardboard hatbox and crushes it.*) There, now, of course—I knew it would be so.

Yasha (jeeringly): Two and twenty misfortunes!

Varya (through the door): Has Firs been taken to the hospital?

Anya: Yes.

Varya: Why wasn't the note for the doctor taken too?

Anya: Oh, then, we must send it after them. (*Goes out.*)

Varya (from the adjoining room): Where's Yasha? Tell him his mother's come to say good-by to him.

Yasha (waves his hand): They put me out of all patience!

> (*Dunyasha has all this time been busy about the luggage. Now, when Yasha is left alone, she goes up to him.*)

Dunyasha: You might just give me one look, Yasha. You're going away. You're leaving me. (*Weeps and throws herself on his neck.*)

Yasha: What are you crying for? (*Drinks the champagne.*) In six days I shall be in Paris again. Tomorrow we shall get into the express train and roll away in a flash. I can scarcely believe it! *Vive la France!* It doesn't suit me here—it's not the life for me; there's no doing anything. I have seen enough of the ignorance here. I have had enough of it. (*Drinks champagne.*) What are you crying for? Behave yourself properly, and then you won't cry.

Dunyasha (powders her face, looking in a pocket-mirror): Do send me a letter from Paris. You know how I loved you, Yasha—how I loved you! I am a tender creature, Yasha.

Yasha: Here, they are coming!

> (*Busies himself about the trunks, humming softly. Enter Lyubov Andreyevna, Gaev, Anya and Charlotta Ivanovna.*)

Gaev: We ought to be off. There's not much time now. (*Looking at Yasha.*) What a smell of herrings!

Lyubov: In ten minutes we must get into the carriage. (*Casts a look about the room.*) Farewell, dear house, dear old home of our fathers! Winter will pass and spring will come, and then you will be no more; they will tear you down! How much those walls have seen! (*Kisses her daughter passionately.*) My treasure, how bright you look! Your eyes are sparkling like diamonds! Are you glad? Very glad?

Anya: Very glad! A new life is beginning, mamma.

Gaev: Yes, really, everything is all right now. Before the cherry orchard was sold, we were all worried and wretched, but afterward, when once the question was settled conclusively, irrevocably, we all felt calm and even cheerful. I am a bank clerk now—I am a financier—cannon off the red. And you, Lyuba, after all, you are looking better; there's no question of that.

Lyubov: Yes. My nerves are better, that's true. (*Her hat and coat are handed to her.*) I'm sleeping well. Carry out my things, Yasha. It's time. (*To Anya.*) My darling, we shall soon see each other again. I am going to Paris. I can live there on the money your Yaroslavl auntie sent us to buy the estate with—hurrah for auntie!—but that money won't last long.

Anya: You'll come back soon, mamma, won't you? I'll be working up for my examination in the high school, and when I have passed that, I shall set to work and be a help to you. We will read all sorts of things together, mamma, won't we? (*Kisses her mother's hands.*) We will read in the autumn evenings. We'll read lots of books, and a new wonderful world will open out before us. (*Dreamily.*) Mamma, come soon.

Lyubov: I shall come, my precious treasure.

(*Embraces her. Enter Lopahin. Charlotta softly hums a song.*)

Gaev: Charlotta's happy; she's singing!

Charlotta (picks up a bundle like a swaddled baby):   By, by, my baby. (*A baby is heard crying:* "Ooah! ooah!") Hush, hush, my pretty boy! ("Ooah! ooah!") Poor little thing! (*Throws the bundle back.*) You must please find me a situation. I can't go on like this.

Lopahin: We'll find you one, Charlotta Ivanovna. Don't worry yourself.

Gaev: Everyone's leaving us. Varya's going away. We have become of no use all at once.

Charlotta: There's nowhere for me to be in the town. I must go away. (*Hums.*) What care I . . .

(*Enter Pishtchik.*)

Lopahin: The freak of nature.

Pishtchik (gasping):   Oh . . . Let me get my breath. . . . I'm worn out . . . my most honored . . . Give me some water.

Gaev: Want some money, I suppose? Your humble servant! I'll go out of the way of temptation. (*Goes out.*)

Pishtchik: It's a long while since I have been to see you . . . dearest lady. (*To Lopahin.*) You are here . . . glad to see you . . . a man of immense intellect . . . take . . . here. (*Gives to Lopahin.*) 400 rubles. That leaves me owing 840.

Lopahin: (*shrugging his shoulders in amazement*):   It's like a dream. Where did you get it?

Pishtchik: Wait a bit . . . I'm hot . . . a most extraordinary occurrence!

Some Englishmen came along and found in my land some sort of white clay. (*To Lyubov Andreyevna.*) And 400 for you . . . most lovely . . . wonderful. (*Gives money.*) The rest later. (*Sips water.*) A young man in the train was telling me just now that a great philosopher advises jumping off a house-top. "Jump!" says he; "the whole gist of the problem lies in that." (*Wonderingly.*) Fancy that, now! Water, please!

Lopahin: What Englishmen?

Pishtchik: I have made over to them the rights to dig the clay for twenty-four years . . . and now, excuse me . . . I can't stay . . . I must be trotting on. I'm going to Znoikovo . . . to Kardamanovo. . . . I'm in debt all round. (*Sips.*) . . . To your very good health! . . . I'll come in on Thursday.

Lyubov: We are just off to the town, and tomorrow I start for abroad.

Pishtchik: What! (*In agitation.*) Why to the town? Oh, I see the furniture . . . the boxes. No matter . . . (*Through his tears.*) . . . no matter . . . men of enormous intellect . . . these Englishmen. . . . Never mind . . . be happy. God will succor you . . . no matter . . . everything in this world must have an end. (*Kisses Lyubov Andreyevna's hand.*) If the rumor reaches you that my end has come, think of this . . . old horse, and say: "There once was such a man in the world . . . Semyonov-Pishtchik . . . the Kingdom of Heaven be his!" . . . most extraordinary weather . . . yes. (*Goes out in violent agitation, but at once returns and says in the doorway.*) Dashenka wishes to be remembered to you. (*Goes out.*)

Lyubov: Now we can start. I leave with two cares in my heart. The first is leaving Firs ill. (*Looking at her watch.*) We have still five minutes.

Anya: Mamma, Firs has been taken to the hospital. Yasha sent him off this morning.

Lyubov: My other anxiety is Varya. She is used to getting up early and working; and now, without work, she's like a fish out of water. She is thin and pale, and she's crying, poor dear! (*A pause.*) You are well aware, Yermolay Alexeyevitch, I dreamed of marrying her to you, and everything seemed to show that you would get married. (*Whispers to Anya and motions to Charlotta and both go out.*) She loves you—she suits you. And I don't know—I don't know why it is you seem, as it were, to avoid each other. I can't understand it!

Lopahin: I don't understand it myself, I confess. It's queer somehow, altogether. If there's still time, I'm ready now at once. Let's settle it straight off, and go ahead; but without you, I feel I shan't make her an offer.

Lyubov: That's excellent. Why, a single moment's all that's necessary. I'll call her at once.

Lopahin: And there's champagne all ready too. (*Looking into the glasses.*) Empty! Someone's emptied them already. (*Yasha coughs.*) I call that greedy.

Lyubov (eagerly):   Capital! We will go out. Yasha, *allez!*° I'll call her in. (*At the door.*) Varya, leave all that; come here. Come along! (*Goes out with Yasha.*)

Lopahin (looking at his watch):   Yes.

(*A pause. Behind the door, smothered laughter and whispering, and, at last, enter Varya.*)

Varya (looking a long while over the things):   It is strange, I can't find it anywhere.

Lopahin: What are you looking for?

Varya: I packed it myself, and I can't remember.

(*A pause.*)

Lopahin: Where are you going now, Varvara Mihailova?

Varya: I? To the Ragulins. I have arranged to go to them to look after the house—as a housekeeper.

Lopahin: That's in Yashnovo? It'll be seventy miles away. (*A pause.*) So this is the end of life in this house!

Varya (looking among the things):   Where is it? Perhaps I put it in the trunk. Yes, life in this house is over—there will be no more of it.

Lopahin: And I'm just off to Harkov—by this next train. I've a lot of business there. I'm leaving Epihodov here, and I've taken him on.

Varya: Really!

Lopahin: This time last year we had snow already, if you remember; but now it's so fine and sunny. Though it's cold, to be sure—three degrees of frost.

Varya: I haven't looked. (*A pause.*) And besides, our thermometer's broken.

(*A pause. Voice at the door from the yard:*   "Yermolay Alexeyevitch!")

Lopahin (as though he had long been expecting this summons):   This minute!

(*Lopahin goes out quickly. Varya sitting on the floor and laying her head on a bag full of clothes, sobs quietly. The door opens, Lyubov Andreyevna comes in cautiously.*)

Lyubov: Well? (*A pause.*) We must be going.

Varya (has wiped her eyes and is no longer crying):   Yes, mamma, it's time to start. I shall have time to get to the Ragulins today, if only you're not late for the train.

Lyubov (in the doorway):   Anya, put your things on. (*Enter Anya, then Gaev and Charlotta Ivanovna. Gaev has on a warm coat with a hood. Servants and cabmen come in. Epihodov bustles about the luggage.*) Now we can start on our travels.

---

allez!: Go (French).

Anya (joyfully):   On our travels!

Gaev: My friends—my dear, my precious friends! Leaving this house forever, can I be silent? Can I refrain from giving utterance at leave-taking to those emotions which now flood all my being?

Anya (supplicatingly):   Uncle!

Varya: Uncle, you mustn't!

Gaev (dejectedly):   Cannon and into the pocket . . . I'll be quiet . . .

(*Enter Trofimov and afterward Lopahin.*)

Trofimov: Well, ladies and gentlemen, we must start.

Lopahin: Epihodov, my coat!

Lyubov: I'll stay just one minute. It seems as though I have never seen before what the walls, what the ceilings in this house were like, and now I look at them with greediness, with such tender love.

Gaev: I remember when I was six years old sitting in that window on Trinity Day watching my father going to church.

Lyubov: Have all the things been taken?

Lopahin: I think all. (*Putting on overcoat, to Epihodov.*) You, Epihodov, mind you see everything is right.

Epihodov (in a husky voice):   Don't you trouble, Yermolay Alexeyevitch.

Lopahin: Why, what's wrong with your voice?

Epihodov: I've just had a drink of water, and I choked over something.

Yasha (contemptuously):   The ignorance!

Lyubov: We are going—and not a soul will be left here.

Lopahin: Not till the spring.

Varya (pulls a parasol out of a bundle, as though about to hit someone with it. Lopahin makes a gesture as though alarmed):   What is it? I didn't mean anything.

Trofimov: Ladies and gentlemen, let us get into the carriage. It's time. The train will be in directly.

Varya: Petya, here they are, your galoshes, by that box. (*With tears.*) And what dirty old things they are!

Trofimov (putting on his galoshes):   Let us go, friends!

Gaev (greatly agitated, afraid of weeping):   The train—the station! Double balk, ah!

Lyubov: Let us go!

Lopahin: Are we all here? (*Locks the side door on left.*) The things are all here. We must lock up. Let us go!

Anya: Good-by, home! Good-by to the old life!

Trofimov: Welcome to the new life!

(*Trofimov goes out with Anya. Varya looks round the room and goes out slowly. Yasha and Charlotta Ivanovna, with her dog, go out.*)

Lopahin: Till the spring, then! Come, friends, till we meet! (*Goes out.*)

(Lyubov Andreyevna and Gaev remain alone. As though they had been waiting for this, they throw themselves on each other's necks, and break into subdued smothered sobbing, afraid of being overheard.)

Gaev *(in despair):*   Sister, my sister!

Lyubov: Oh, my orchard!—my sweet, beautiful orchard! My life, my youth, my happiness, good-by! good-by!

Voice of Anya *(calling gaily):*   Mamma!

Voice of Trofimov *(gaily, excitedly):*   Aa—oo!

Lyubov: One last look at the walls, at the windows. My dear mother loved to walk about this room.

Gaev: Sister, sister!

Voice of Anya: Mamma!

Voice of Trofimov: Aa—oo!

Lyubov: We are coming.

(They go out. The stage is empty. There is the sound of the doors being locked up, then of the carriages driving away. There is silence. In the stillness there is the dull stroke of an ax in a tree, clanging with a mournful lonely sound. Footsteps are heard. Firs appears in the doorway on the right. He is dressed as always—in a pea jacket and white waistcoat, with slippers on his feet. He is ill.)

Firs *(goes up to the doors, and tries the handles):*   Locked! They have gone . . . (*Sits down on sofa.*) They have forgotten me. . . . Never mind . . . I'll sit here a bit. . . . I'll be bound Leonid Andreyevitch hasn't put his fur coat on and has gone off in his thin overcoat. (*Sighs anxiously.*) I didn't see after him. . . . These young people . . . (*Mutters something that can't be distinguished.*) Life has slipped by as though I hadn't lived. (*Lies down.*) I'll lie down a bit. . . . There's no strength in you, nothing left you—all gone! Ech! I'm good for nothing.

(Lies motionless. A sound is heard that seems to come from the sky, like a breaking harp-string, dying away mournfully. All is still again, and there is heard nothing but the strokes of the ax far away in the orchard.)

John Guare   (b. 1938)

John Guare was educated at Georgetown University and then took his M.F.A. at Yale Drama School, where he studied play writing with John Gassner and set design with Richard Oenslager. He credits Oenslager with having taught him more about writing plays than anyone else. His earliest success was Muzeeka *(1967), a critique of American society (especially the dulling effects of Muzak) that grew from Guare's own Vietnam War protest. The main character, Jack Argue, stabs himself rather than return from war to a job that symbolizes the pollution of America. Guare won an Obie for the play and was recognized as the year's most promising new playwright. He has played upon this description—using it, for example, in* Rich and Famous *(1976). Guare's early plays often relied on farce and humor for their effects, but they also aimed at revealing the pain and difficulties inherent in "normal" family relationships.*

Guare's most important early play is The House of Blue Leaves *(1971), which won an Obie and the New York Critics Circle Award for the best American play. It condemns the fantasies encouraged by Catholicism and the popular media, and much of it draws upon Guare's observation of his parents' difficult relationship and his own sense of independence from his family. The writing of this play was marked by many difficulties. The first act was presented in a staged reading in 1966, but the rest of the play evolved through many drafts and many years of effort and reflection.*

Other recent plays include Bosoms and Neglect *(1979), about a mother whose self-neglect ends in breast cancer—a black comedy that relies on painful subjects, suffering, and anger for its content. Guare's taste for the grotesque is notably developed in this play.* Six Degrees of Separation *(1990) is more realistic and less in the absurdist tradition than some of his earlier work. However, it is a powerful critique of social expectations. The original story was drawn from the* New York Times *and is based on a true experience of a young man posing as Sidney Poitier's son who then conned several wealthy families into befriending him. The original conman, whose character is Paul, later sued Guare and the producers for a share of the ticket sales of the play, and lost. But Guare's subject goes beyond the question of who is conning whom and into the circumstances that make the con possible. As in most of his work, Guare also reveals the tensions that exist between parents and children regarding expectations and understanding.*

SIX DEGREES OF SEPARATION 1990

Characters

Ouisa	*Woody*
Flan	*Ben*
Geoffrey	*Dr. Fine*
Paul	*Doug*
Hustler	*Policeman/Doorman*
Kitty	*Trent*
Larkin	*Rick*
Detective	*Elizabeth*
Tess	

Kandinsky: Wassili Kandinsky (1866–1944), Russian painter in Germany and France. His paintings are abstract and extremely expensive.

(A painting revolves slowly high over the stage. The painting is by Kandinsky.° He has painted on either side of the canvas in two different styles. One side is geometric and somber. The other side is wild and vivid. The painting stops its revolve and opts for the geometric side.)

    (A couple runs on stage, in nightdress, very agitated. Flanders Kittredge is forty-four. Louisa Kittredge is forty-three. They are very attractive. They speak to us.)

Ouisa: Tell them!

Flan: I am shaking.

Ouisa: You have to do *something*!

Flan: It's awful.

Ouisa: Is anything gone?

Flan: How can I look? I'm shaking.

Ouisa (to us):   Did he take anything?

Flan: Would you concentrate on yourself?

Ouisa: I want to know if anything's gone?

Flan (to us):   We came in the room.

Ouisa: I went in first. You didn't see what I saw.

Flan: Calm down.

Ouisa: We could have been killed.

Flan: The silver Victorian inkwell.

Ouisa: How can you think of *things*? We could have been murdered.

(An actor appears for a moment holding up an ornate Victorian inkwell capped by a silver beaver.)

Flan: There's the inkwell. Silver beaver. Why?

Ouisa: Slashed—our throats slashed.

(Another actor appears for a moment holding up a framed portrait of a dog, say, a pug.)

Flan: And there's the watercolor. Our dog.

Ouisa: Go to bed at night happy and then murdered. Would we have woken up?

Flan: Now I lay me down to sleep—the most terrifying words—just think of it—

Ouisa: I pray the Lord my soul to keep—

Flan: The nightmare part—If I should die before I wake—

Ouisa: If I should die—I pray the Lord my soul to take—

Flan and Ouisa: Oh.

Ouisa: It's awful.

Flan: We're alive. *(Flan stops, frightened suddenly, listening.)* Hello? *(He holds her.)* Hello!

Ouisa (whispers):   You don't call out Hello unless—

Flan: I think we'd tell if someone else were here.

Ouisa: We didn't all night. Oh, it was awful awful awful awful.

(They pull off their robes and are smartly dressed for dinner.)

Flan (to us): We were having a wonderful evening last night.
Ouisa (to us): A friend we hadn't seen for many years came by for dinner.
Flan (portentously): A friend from South Africa—
Ouisa: Don't say it so portentously.
Flan (bright): A friend from South Africa.
Ouisa: Don't be ga-ga.
Flan (to us): I'm an art dealer. Private sales. Purchases.
Ouisa (to us): We knew our friend from South Africa
Flan: through our children when they all lived in New York.
Ouisa: They had gone back to South Africa.
Flan: He was here in New York briefly on business and asked us to ask
      him for dinner.
Ouisa: He's King Midas rich. Literally. Gold mines.
Flan: Seventy thousand workers in just one gold mine.
Ouisa: But he is always short of cash because his government won't let its
      people—
Flan: its white people—
Ouisa:—its white people take out any money. So it's like taking in a War
      Baby.
Flan: When he called it was like a bolt from the blue as I had a deal
      coming up and was short by
Ouisa: two million.
Flan: The figure is superfluous.
Ouisa: I hate when you use the word "superfluous." I mean, he needed
      two million and we hadn't seen Geoffrey in a long time and while
      Geoffrey might not have the price of a dinner he easily might have two
      million dollars.
Flan: The currents last night were very churny.
Ouisa: We weren't sucking up. We like Geoffrey.
Flan: It's that awful thing of having truly rich folk for friends.
Ouisa: Face it. The money does get in the—
Flan: Only if you let it. The fact of the money shouldn't get in—
Ouisa: Having a rich friend is like drowning and your friend makes life
      boats. But the friend gets very touchy if you say one word: life boat.
      Well, that's two words. We were afraid our South African friend might
      say "You only love me for my life boats?" But we *like* Geoffrey.
Flan: It wasn't a life-threatening evening.
Ouisa: Rich people can do something for you even if you're not sure
      what it is you want them to do.
Flan: Hardly a life boat evening—
Ouisa (sing-song): Portentous.

Flan: But when he called and asked us to take him for dinner, he made a sudden pattern in life's little tea leaves because who wants to go to banks? Geoffrey called and our tempests settled into showers and life was manageable. What more can you want?

(*Geoffrey is there, an elegant, impeccably British South African, slightly older than Ouisa and Flan. Flan passes drinks.*)

Geoffrey: Listen. *(They do.)* It always amazes me when New York is so quiet.

Ouisa: With the kids away, we get used to a lower noise quotient.

Flan: Geoffrey, you have to move out of South Africa. You'll be killed. Why do you stay in South Africa?

Geoffrey: One has to stay there to educate the black workers and we'll know we've been successful when they kill us.

Flan: Planning the revolution that will destroy you.

Ouisa: Putting your life on the line.

Geoffrey: You don't think of it like that. I wish you'd come visit.

Ouisa: But we'd visit you and sit in your gorgeous house planning trips into the townships demanding to see the poorest of the poor. "Are you sure they're the worst off? I mean, we've come all this way. We don't want to see people just mildly victimized by apartheid. We demand shock." It doesn't seem right sitting on the East Side talking about revolution.

Flan: Only small murky cafes for Pepe le Moko° here.

Ouisa: No. La Pasionaria. I will come to South Africa and build barricades and lean against them, singing.

Flan: And the people would follow.

Ouisa: "Follow Follow Follow." What's that song?

Flan: The way Gorbachev cheered on the striking coal miners in the Ukraine—yes, you must strike—it is your role in history to dismantle this system. Russia and Poland—you can't believe the developments in the world—*The Fantasticks,* "Follow Follow Follow."

Ouisa: China.

Flan and Ouisa (despair):   Oh.

Geoffrey: Oy vay China. As my grandmother would say. *(They all laugh.)* Our role in history. And we offer ourselves up to it.

Flan: That is your role in history. Not our role.

Ouisa: A role in history. To say that so easily.

Flan (to Geoffrey):   Do you want another drink before we go out?

Ouisa: The phrase—striking coal miners—I see all these very striking coal miners modelling the fall fashions—

Geoffrey: Where should we?

Pepe le Moko: A romantic criminal in exile from French cinema.

Flan: There's good Szechuan. And Hunan.

Ouisa The sign painter screwed up the sign. Instead of The Hunan Wok, he painted The Human Wok.

Geoffrey: God! The restaurants! New York has become the Florence of the sixteenth century. Genius on every corner.

Ouisa: I don't think genius has kissed the Human Wok.

Geoffrey: The new Italian looked cheery.

Flan and Ouisa: Good.

Flan: We made reservations.

Ouisa: They wrap ravioli up like salt water taffy.

Flan: Six on a plate for a few hundred dollars.

Geoffrey: You have to come to South Africa so I can pay you back. I'll take you on my plane into the Okavango Swamps—

Ouisa: Did you hear—to take back to Johannesburg. Out in East Hampton

Flan: last weekend

Ouisa: a guy goes into one of the better food stores—

Flan: Dean and DeLuca—

Ouisa: one of the Dean and DeLuca look alikes. Gets a pack of cigarettes and an ice cream bar. Goes up front. Sees there's a line at the register. Slaps down two twenty dollar bills and goes out.

Flan: We sent it to the *Times.*

Ouisa: They have the joke page of things around New York.

Flan: They send you a bottle of champagne.

   (They all laugh brightly.)

Ouisa (to us):   We weren't auditioning but I kept thinking Two million dollars two million dollars.

Flan (to us):   It's like when people say "Don't think about elephants" and all you can think about is elephants.

Ouisa (to us):   Two million dollars two million dollars.

(They laugh brightly. The doorbell rings) To Flan. Whatever you do, don't think about elephants. *(Ouisa goes.)*

Geoffrey: Elephants?

Flan: Louisa is a Dada manifesto.°

Geoffrey: Tell me about the Cézanne?

Flan: Mid-period. Landscape of a dark green forest. In the far distance you see the sunlight. One of his first uses of a pale color being forced to carry the weight of the picture. The experiment that would pay off in the apples. A burst of color asked to carry so much. The Japanese don't like anything about it except it's a Cézanne—

   (A young black man—Paul—enters, supported by the doorman. Paul is in his early twenties, very handsome, very preppy. He has been beaten

---

Dada manifesto: Reference to a radical post-World War I art movement that emphasized the absurd in art.

badly. Blood seeps through his white Brooks Brothers shirt. Ouisa follows at a loss. The doorman helps Paul to the sofa and stands at the door warily.)

Paul: I'm so sorry to bother you, but I've been hurt and I've lost everything and I didn't know where to go. Your children—I'm a friend of—

Ouisa (to us):   And he mentioned our daughter's name.

Flan (to us):   And the school where they went.

Ouisa (to Flan):   Harvard. You can say Harvard.

Flan (to us):   We don't want to get into libel.

Paul: I was mugged. Out there. In Central Park. By the statue of that Alaskan husky. I was standing there trying to figure out why there is a statue of a dog who saved lives in the Yukon in Central Park and I was standing there trying to puzzle it out when—

Ouisa: Are you okay?

Paul: They took my money and my briefcase. I said my thesis is in there—

Flan: His shirt's bleeding.

Ouisa: His shirt is not bleeding. He's bleeding.

Paul (a wave of nausea):   I get this way around blood.

Flan: Not on the rug.

Paul: I don't mind the money. But in this age of mechanical reproduction they managed to get the only copy of my thesis.

Flan: Eddie, get the doctor—

Paul: No! I'll survive.

Flan: You'll be fine.

(Flan helps Paul out of the room. The Doorman goes.)

Ouisa (to us):   We bathed him. We did First Aid.

Geoffrey (leaving):   It's been wonderful seeing you—

Ouisa (very cheery):   No no no! Stay!—*(To us.)* Two million dollars two million dollars—

Geoffrey: My time is so short—before I leave America, I really should see—

Flan (calling from the hall):   Where are the bandages!?—

Ouisa: The Red Cross advises: Press edges of the wound firmly together, wash area with water—

Geoffrey: May I use your phone?

Ouisa: You darling old poop—just sit back—this'll only take a mo— *(Calling.)* Flan, go into Woody's room and get him a clean shirt. Geoffrey, have you seen the new book on Cézanne? *(To us.)* I ran down the hall to get the book on Cézanne, got the gauze from my bathroom, gave the Cézanne to Flan who wanted the gauze, gave the gauze to Geoffrey who wanted Cézanne. Two million dollars two million dollars—

(Flan comes back in the room.)

Flan: He's going to be fine.

Ouisa (to us): And peace was restored.

> *(Paul enters, slightly recovered, wearing a clean pink shirt. He winces as he pulls on his blazer.)*

Paul: Your children said you were kind. All the kids were sitting around the dorm one night dishing the shit out of their parents. But your kids were silent and said, No, not our parents. Not Flan and Ouisa. Not the Kittredges. The Kittredges are kind. So after the muggers left, I looked up and saw these Fifth Avenue apartments. Mrs. Onassis lives there. I know the Babcocks live over there. The Auchinclosses live there. But you lived here. I came here.

Ouisa: Can you believe what the kids said?

Flan (to us): We mentioned our kids' names.

Ouisa: We can mention our kids' names. Our children are not going to sue us for using their names.

Paul: But your kids—I love them. Talbot and Woody mean the world to me.

Flan: He lets you call him Woody? Nobody's called him Woody in years.

Paul: They described this apartment in detail. The Kandinsky!—that's a double. One painted on either side.

Flan: We flip it around for variety.

Paul: It's wonderful.

Flan (to us): Wassily Kandinsky. Born 1866 Moscow. Blue Rider Exhibition 1914. He said "It is clear that the choice of object that is one of the elements in the harmony of form must be decided only by a corresponding vibration in the human soul." Died 1944 France.

Paul: It's the way they said it would be.

Ouisa (to us): Geoffrey had been silent up to now.

Geoffrey: Did you bitch your parents?

Paul: As a matter of fact. No. Your kids and I . . . we both liked our parents . . . loved our—look, am I getting in the way? I burst in here, hysterical. Blood. I didn't mean to—

Flan and Ouisa: No!

Ouisa: Tell us about our children.

Flan (to us): Three. Two at Harvard. Another girl at Groton.

Ouisa: How is Harvard?

Paul: Well, fine. It's just there. Everyone's in a constant state of luxurious despair and constant discovery and paralysis.

Ouisa (to us): We asked him where home was.

Flan (to us): Out West, he said.

Paul: Although I've lived all over. My folks are divorced. He's remarried. He's doing a movie.

Ouisa: He's in the movies?

Paul: He's directing this one but he does act.

Flan: What's he directing?

Paul: Cats.°

Ouisa: Someone is directing a film of *Cats*?

Flan: Don't be snooty.

Paul: You've seen it? T.S. Eliot—

Flan: Well, yes. Years ago.

Ouisa: A benefit for some disease or school—

Flan: Surely they can't make the movie of *Cats*.

Ouisa: Of course they can.

Paul: They're going to try. My father'll be here auditioning—

Ouisa: Cats?

Paul: He's going to use people.

Ouisa: What a courageous stand!

Paul: They thought of lots of ways to go. Animation.

Flan: Animation would be nice.

Paul: But he found a better way. As a matter of fact, he turned it down at first. He went to tell the producers—as a courtesy—all the reasons why you couldn't make a movie of *Cats* and in going through all the reasons why you couldn't make a movie of *Cats*, he suddenly saw how you could make a movie of *Cats*—

Ouisa: Eureka in the bathtub. How wonderful.

Flan: May we ask who—

Ouisa (to us):   And it was here we pulled up—ever so slightly—pulled up closer—

Flan (to us):   And he told us.

Ouisa (to us):   He named the greatest black star in movies. Sidney—

Flan: Don't say it. We're trying to keep this abstract. Plus libel laws.

Ouisa: Sidney Poitier! There. I don't care. We have to have truth. *(To us.)* He started out as a lawyer and is terrified of libel. I'm not.

(Paul steps forward cheerily.)

Paul (to us):   Sidney Poitier, the future Jackie Robinson of films, was born the twenty-fourth of February 1927 in Miami during a visit his parents made to Florida—legally?—to sell tomatoes they had grown on their farm in the Bahamas. He grew up on Cat Island, "so poor they didn't even own dirt" he has said. Neglected by his family, my father would sit on the shore, and, as he told me many times, "conjure up the kind of worlds that were on the other side and what I'd do in them." He arrived in New York City from the Bahamas in the winter of 1943 at age fifteen and a half and lived in the pay toilet of the bus station across from the old Madison Square Garden at Fiftieth and Eighth Avenue. He moved to the roof of the Brill Building, commonly known

---

Cats: Broadway musical based on T.S. Eliot's *Old Possum's Book of Practical Cats.* See his poem, "McCavity: The Mystery Cat."

as Tin Pan Alley, and washed dishes at the Turf Restaurant for $4.11 a night. He taught himself to read by reading the newspaper. In the black newspaper, the theater page was opposite the want ad page. Among his 42 films are *No Way Out*, 1950; *Cry the Beloved Country*, 1952; *Blackboard Jungle*, 1955; *The Defiant Ones*, 1958; *Raisin in the Sun*, 1961; *Lilies of the Field*, 1963; *In the Heat of the Night*, 1967; *To Sir With Love*, 1967; *Shoot to Kill*, 1988; and, of course, *Guess Who's Coming to Dinner*. He won the Oscar for *Lilies of the Field* and was twice named top male box-office star in the country. My father made no films from 1977 to 1987 but worked as director and author. Dad said to me once, "I still don't fully understand how all that came about in the sequence it came about." (*Paul returns to the sofa.*) Dad's not in till tomorrow at the Sherry. I came down from Cambridge. Thought I'd stay at some fleabag for adventure. Orwell. Down and Out.° I really don't know New York. I know Rome and Paris and Los Angeles a lot better.

Ouisa: We're going out to dinner. You'll come.

Paul: Out to dinner?

Flan: Out to dinner.

Paul: But why go out to dinner?

Ouisa: Because we have reservations and oh my god what time is it? Have we lost the reservations and we don't have a damn thing in the house and it's sixteenth-century Florence and there's genius on every block.

Geoffrey: Don't mock.

(She kisses Geoffrey.)

Paul: You must have something in the fridge.

Flan: A frozen steak from the Ice Age.

Paul: Why spend a hundred dollars on a bowl of rice? Let me into the kitchen. Cooking calms me. What I'd like to do is calm down, pay back your kids—

Ouisa (to us):   He mentioned our kids' names—

Flan (to us):   Two. Two at Harvard. A daughter at Groton.

Paul: who've been wonderful to me.

Ouisa: They've never mentioned you.

Flan: What are they supposed to say? We've become friends with the son of Sidney Poitier, barrier breaker of the fifties and sixties?

Geoffrey: Your father means a great deal in South Africa.

Ouisa (to us):   Even Geoffrey was touched.

Paul: I'm glad of that. Dad and I went to Russia once to a film festival and he was truly amazed how much his presence meant—

Orwell. Down and Out: A reference to George Orwell's book *Down and Out in Paris and London*.

Ouisa: Oh no! Tell us stories of movie stars tying up their children and being cruel.

Paul: I wish.

Geoffrey: You wish?

Paul: If I wanted to write a book about him, I really couldn't. No one would want to read it. He's decent. I admire him.

Ouisa: He's married to an actress who was in one of—she's white? Am I right?

Paul: That is not my mother. That is his second wife. He met Joanna making *The Lost Man*. He left my mother, who had stuck by him in the lean years. I had just been born. *The Lost Man* is the only film of my father's I can't bring myself to see.

Ouisa: Oh, I'm sorry. We didn't mean to—

Paul (bright):   No! We're all good friends now. His kids from that marriage. Us—the old kids. I'd love to get in that kitchen.

Flan (to Ouisa):   What should we do?

Ouisa (to us):   It's Geoffrey's only night in New York.

Geoffrey: I vote stay in.

Ouisa, Flan and Paul: Good!

(*Paul goes off to the kitchen.*)

Ouisa (to us):   We moved into the kitchen.

Flan (to us):   We watched him cook.

Ouisa (to us):   We watched him cook and chop.

Flan (to us):   He sort of did wizardry—

Ouisa (to us):   An old jar of sun-dried tomatoes—

Flan (to us):   Leftovers—tuna fish—olives—onions—

(*Paul returns with three dishes heaped with food.*)

Paul: Here's dinner. All ready.

Ouisa: Shall we move into the dining room?

Paul: No, let's stay in here. It's nice in here.

(*Ouisa, Flan, and Geoffrey take plates skeptically.*)

Ouisa: Have you declared your major yet?

Paul: You're like all parents. What's your major?

Flan: Geoffrey, Harvard has all those great titles the students give courses.

Ouisa: The Holocaust and Ethics—

Flan: Krauts and Doubts.

(*They eat. Surprise. It's delicious.*)

Geoffrey: This is the best pasta I've ever—

Paul: My father insisted we learn to cook.

Flan: Isn't he from Jamaica? There's a taste of—

Geoffrey: The islands.

Paul: Yes. Before he made it, he ran four restaurants in Harlem. You have good buds!

Geoffrey: See? Good buds. I've never been complimented on my buds—

Paul (to Geoffrey): You're from—

Geoffrey: Johannesburg.

(Pause.)

Paul: My dad took me to a movie shot in South Africa. The camera moved from this vile rioting in the streets to a villa where people picked at lunch on a terrace, the only riot the flowers and the birds— gorgeous plumage and petals. And I didn't understand. And Dad said to me, "You meet these young blacks who are having a terrible time. They've had a totally inadequate education and yet in '76—the year of the Soweto riots—they took on a tremendous political responsibility. It just makes you wonder at the maturity that is in them. It makes you realize that the 'crummy childhood' theory, that everything can be blamed in a Freudian fashion on the fact that you've had a bad upbringing, just doesn't hold water." Is everything okay?

(Flan, Ouisa, and Geoffrey are mesmerized, and then resume eating.)

Flan, Ouisa, and Geoffrey (while eating): Mmmmmm . . . yes.

Geoffrey: What about being black in America?

Paul: My problem is I've never felt American. I grew up in Switzerland. Boarding school. Villa Rosey.

Ouisa: There is a boarding school in Switzerland that takes you at age eighteen months.

Paul: That's not me. I've never felt people liked me for my connections. Movie star kid problems. None of those. May I?

Flan: Oh, please.

(Paul pours a brandy.)

Paul: But I never knew I was black in that racist way till I was sixteen and came back here. Very protected. White servants. After the divorce we moved to Switzerland, my mother, brother and I. I don't feel American. I don't even feel black. I suppose that's very lucky for me even though Freud says there's no such thing as luck. Just what you make.

Ouisa: Does Freud say that? I think we're lucky having this dinner. Isn't this the finest time? A toast to you.

Geoffrey: To *Cats!*

Flan: Blunt question. What's he like?

Ouisa: Let's not be star fuckers.

Flan: I'm not a star fucker.

Paul: My father, being an actor, has no real identity. You say to him, Pop, what's new? And he says, "I got an interesting script today. I was asked to play a lumberjack up in the Yukon. Now, I've been trained as a preacher, but my church fell apart. My wife says we have to get money to get through this winter. And I sign up as part of this team where all my beliefs are challenged. But I hold firm. In spite of prejudice. Because I want to get back to you. Out of this forest, back to the church . . ." And my father is in tears and I say Pop, this is not a real event, this is some script that was sent to you. And my father says "I'm trying it out to see how it fits on me." But he has no life—he has no memory—only the scripts producers send him in the mail through his agents. That's his past.

Ouisa (to us):   I just loved the kid so much. I wanted to reach out to him.

Flan (to us):   And then we asked him what his thesis was on.

Geoffrey: The one that was stolen. Please?

Paul: Well . . . A substitute teacher out on Long Island was dropped from his job for fighting with a student. A few weeks later, the teacher returned to the classroom, shot the student unsuccessfully, held the class hostage and then shot himself. Successfully. This fact caught my eye: last sentence. *Times.* A neighbor described him as a nice boy. Always reading *Catcher in the Rye.*°

The nitwit—Chapman—who shot John Lennon said he did it because he wanted to draw the attention of the world to *The Catcher in the Rye* and the reading of that book would be his defense.

And young Hinckley, the whiz kid who shot Reagan and his press secretary, said if you want my defense all you have to do is read *Catcher in the Rye.* It seemed to be time to read it again.

Flan: I haven't read it in years.

(Ouisa shushes Flan.)

Paul: I borrowed a copy from a young friend of mine because I wanted to see what she had underlined and I read this book to find out why this touching, beautiful, sensitive story published in July 1951 had turned into this manifesto of hate.

I started reading. It's exactly as I remembered. Everybody's a phoney. Page two: "My brother's in Hollywood being a prostitute." Page three: "What a phony slob his father was." Page nine: "People never notice anything."

Then on page twenty-two my hair stood up. Remember Holden Caulfield—the definitive sensitive youth—wearing his red hunter's cap. "A deer hunter hat? Like hell it is. I sort of closed one eye like I was taking aim at it. This is a people-shooting hat. I shoot people in this hat."

Hmmm, I said. This book is preparing people for bigger moments in their lives than I ever dreamed of. Then on page eighty-nine: "I'd rather push a guy out the window or chop his head off with

---

Catcher in the Rye: The novel by J. D. Salinger.

an ax than sock him in the jaw. I hate fist fights . . . what scares me
most is the other guy's face . . ."

I finished the book. It's a touching story, comic because the boy
wants to do so much and can't do anything. Hates all phoniness and
only lies to others. Wants everyone to like him, is only hateful, and is
completely self-involved. In other words, a pretty accurate picture of a
male adolescent.

And what alarms me about the book—not the book so much as
the aura about it—is this: The book is primarily about paralysis. The
boy can't function. And at the end, before he can run away and start a
new life, it starts to rain and he folds.

Now there's nothing wrong in writing about emotional and
intellectual paralysis. It may indeed, thanks to Chekhov and Samuel
Beckett, be the great modern theme.

The extraordinary last lines of *Waiting for Godot*°—"Let's go."
"Yes, let's go." Stage directions: They do not move.

But the aura around this book of Salinger's—which perhaps
should be read by everyone *but* young men—is this: It mirrors like a
fun house mirror and amplifies like a distorted speaker one of the great
tragedies of our times—the death of the imagination.

Because what else is paralysis?

The imagination has been so debased that imagination—being
imaginative—rather than being the lynchpin of our existence now
stands as a synonym for something outside ourselves like science
fiction or some new use for tangerine slices on raw pork chops—what
an imaginative summer recipe—and *Star Wars*! So imaginative! And
Star Trek—so imaginative! And *Lord of the Rings*—all those dwarves—
so imaginative—The imagination has moved out of the realm of being
our link, our most personal link, with our inner lives and the world
outside that world—this world we share. What is schizophrenia but a
horrifying state where what's in here doesn't match up with what's out
there?

Why has imagination become a synonym for style?

I believe that the imagination is the passport we create to take us
into the real world.

I believe the imagination is another phrase for what is most
uniquely *us*.

Jung says the greatest sin is to be unconscious.

Our boy Holden says "what scares me most is the other guy's
face—it wouldn't be so bad if you could both be blindfolded—most of
the time the faces we face are not the other guys' but our own faces.
And it's the worst kind of yellowness to be so scared of yourself you
put blindfolds on rather than deal with yourself . . ."

Waiting for Godot: An absurdist play (1954) by Irish playwright Samuel Beckett (1906–1989).

> To face ourselves.
> That's the hard thing.
> The imagination.
> That's God's gift to make the act of self-examination bearable.

(Pause.)

Ouisa: Well, indeed.

(Pause.)

Flan: I hope your muggers read every word.

Ouisa: Darling.

Geoffrey: I'm going to buy a copy of *Catcher in the Rye* at the airport and read it.

Ouisa: Cover to cover.

Paul: I'll test you. I should be going.

Flan: Where will you stay?

Ouisa: Not some flea bag.

Paul: I get into the Sherry tomorrow morning. It's not so far off. I can walk around. I don't think they'll mug me twice in one evening.

Ouisa: You'll stay here tonight.

Paul: No! I have to be there at seven.

Ouisa: We'll get you up.

Paul: I have to be at the hotel at seven sharp or Dad will have a fit.

Ouisa: Up at six-fifteen, which is any moment now, and we have that wedding in Roxbury—

Flan: There's an alarm in that room.

Paul: If it's any problem—

Flan: It's only a problem if you leave.

Paul: Six-fifteen? I'll tiptoe out.

Flan: And we want to be in *Cats*.

Ouisa: Flan!

Paul: It's done.

Geoffrey: I'll fly back. With my wife.

Ouisa: Pushy. Both of you.

Paul: He's not. Dad said I could be in charge of the extras. You'd just be extras. That's all I can promise.

Flan: In cat suits?

Paul: No. You can be humans.

Flan: That's very important. It has to be in our contracts. We are humans.

Geoffrey: We haven't got any business done tonight.

Flan: Forget it. It was only an evening at home.

Ouisa: Whatever you do, don't think about elephants.

Paul: Did I intrude?

Flan and Ouisa: No!

Paul: I'm sorry—oh Christ—

Geoffrey (to Flan):   There's all ways of doing business. Flanders, walk me
to the elevator.

Ouisa: Love to Diana. *(To us.)* We embraced. And Flan and Geoffrey
left—

*(Flan and Geoffrey go. Pause. Paul and Ouisa look at each other. Is it
uncomfortable? Then:)*

Paul: Let me clean up—

Ouisa: No! Leave it for—

Paul: Nobody comes in on Sunday.

Ouisa: Yvonne will be in on Tuesday.

Paul: You'll have every bug in Christendom—

(They both reach for the dishes.)

Ouisa: Let me—

(Paul takes the dishes.)

Paul: No. You watch. It gives me a thrill to be looked at.

(Pause. Paul goes off.)

Ouisa: *(to us, amazed):*   He washed up.

(Flan returns, amazed.)

Flan: He's in.

Ouisa: He's in?

Flan: He's in for two million.

Ouisa: Two million!

Flan: He says the Cézanne is a great investment. We should get it for six
million and sell it to the Tokyo bunch for ten.

Ouisa: Happy days! Oh god!

(Paul returns.)

Paul: Two million dollars?

Ouisa: Figure it out. He doesn't have the price of a dinner but he can
cough up two million dollars and the Japs will go ten! Break all those
dishes! Two million! Go to ten! And we put up nothing?

Flan: He sold that Hockney° print I know he bought for a hundred
bucks fifteen years ago for thirty-four thousand dollars. Sotheby took
their cut, sure, but still—Two million! Wildest dreams. Paul, I should
give you a commission.

Paul: Your kids said you were an art dealer. But you don't have a gallery.
I don't understand—

Flan: People want to sell privately. Not go through a gallery.

Ouisa: A divorce. Taxes. Publicity.

Flan: People come to me looking for a certain school of painting.

Hockney: David Hockney, contemporary British Painter. Sotheby is an international auctioneer
of art.

Ouisa: A modern. Impressionist. Renaissance.

Flan: But don't want museums to know where it is.

Ouisa: Japanese.

Flan: I've got Japanese looking for a Cézanne. I have a syndicate that will buy the painting. There is a great second-level Cézanne coming up for sale in a very messy divorce.

Ouisa: Wife doesn't want hubby to know she owns a Cézanne.

Flan: I needed an extra two million. Geoffrey called. Invited him here for dinner.

Ouisa: Tonight was a very nervous very casual very big thing.

Paul: I couldn't tell—

Ouisa: All the better.

Paul: I'm glad I helped—

Ouisa: You were wonderful!

Paul: I'm so pleased I was wonderful. All this *and* a pink shirt.

Ouisa: Keep it. Look at the time.

Paul: It's going to be time for me to get up.

Flan: Then we'll say our good-nights now.

Paul: Oh Christ. Regretfully. I'll tiptoe.

(Flan takes out his wallet.)

Flan: Take fifty dollars.

Ouisa: Give him fifty dollars.

Paul: Don't need it.

Ouisa: Suppose your father's plane is late?

Flan: A strike. Air controllers.

Ouisa: Walking-around money. I wouldn't want my kids to be stuck in the street without a nickel.

Flan: And you saved us a fortune. Do you know what our bill would've been at that little Eye-tie store front?

Ouisa: And we picked up two million dollars. One billionth of a percent commission is—

Flan: Fifty dollars.

(Flan hands him the money. Paul hesitates, then takes it.)

Paul: But I'll get it back to you tomorrow. I want my father to meet you.

Ouisa: We'd love to. Bring him up for dinner.

Paul: Could I?

Flan: You see how easy it is.

Ouisa: Sure. If Paul does the cooking. *(They all laugh.)*

Flan, Ouisa, and Paul: Good night.

(Flan points Paul to his room.)

Flan: Second door on the right. *(Paul goes. Flan and Ouisa get ready for bed, pulling on their robes.)* I want to get on my knees and thank God—money—

Ouisa: Who said when artists dream they dream of money? I must be such an artist. Bravo. Bravo.

Flan: I don't want to lose our life here. I don't want all the debt to pile up and crush us.

Ouisa: It won't. We're safe.

Flan: For a while. We almost lost it. If I didn't get this money, Ouisa, I would've lost the Cézanne. It would've gone. I had nowhere to get it.

Ouisa: Why don't you tell me how much these things mean? You wait till the last minute—

Flan: I don't want to worry you.

Ouisa: Not worry me? I'm your partner.

(They embrace.)

Flan: There is a God.

Ouisa: And his name is—

Flan: Geoffrey?

Ouisa: Sidney. *(Flan goes. Ouisa curls up on the sofa. To us.)* I dreamt of Sidney Poitier and his rise to acclaim. I dreamt that Sidney Poitier sat at the edge of my bed and I asked him what troubled him. Sidney? What troubles you? Is it right to make a movie of *Cats?*

(Paul appears as Sidney Poitier in dinner clothes.)

Paul/Sidney: I'll tell you why I have to make a movie of *Cats.* I know what *Cats* is, Louisa. May I call you Louisa? I have no illusions about the merits of *Cats.* But the world has been too heavy with all the right-to-lifers. Protect the lives of the unborn. Constitutional amendments. Marches! When does life begin? Or the converse. The end of life. The right to die. Why is life at this point in the twentieth century so focused on the very beginning of life and the very end of life? What about the eighty years we have to live between those two inexorable bookends?

Ouisa: And you can get all that into *Cats?*

Paul/Sidney: I'm going to try.

Ouisa: Thank you. Thank you. You shall.

(Darkness. Then Flan appears.)

Flan (to us): This is what I dreamt. I didn't dream so much as realize this. I felt so close to the paintings. I wasn't just selling them like pieces of meat. I remembered why I loved paintings in the first place—what had got me into this—and I thought—dreamed—remembered—how easy it is for a painter to *lose* a painting. He can paint and paint—work on a canvas for months and one day he loses it—just loses the structure—loses the sense of it—you lose the painting.

When the kids were little, we went to a parents' meeting at their school and I asked the teacher why all her students were geniuses in the second grade? Look at the first grade. Blotches of green and black.

Look at the third grade. Camouflage. But the second grade—your grade. Matisses everyone. You've made my child a Matisse. Let me study with you. Let me into second grade! What is your secret? And this is what she said: "Secret? I don't have any secret. I just know when to take their drawings away from them."

I dreamt of color. I dreamt of our son's pink shirt. I dreamt of pinks and yellows and the new van Gogh that MOMA got and the "Irises" that sold for 53.9 million and, wishing a van Gogh was mine, I looked at my English hand-lasted shoes and thought of van Gogh's tragic shoes. I remembered me as I was. A painter losing a painting. But a South African awaiting revolution came to dinner. We were safe.

(Darkness. Ouisa appears.)

Ouisa (to us):   And it was six A.M. and I woke up so happy looking at my clean kitchen, all the more memorable because the previous evening had left no traces, and the paper was at the front door and I sat in the kitchen happily doing the crossword puzzle in ink. Everybody does it in ink. I never met one person who didn't say they did it in ink. And I'm doing the puzzle and I see the time and it's nearly seven and Paul had to meet his father and I didn't want him to be late and was he healthy after his stabbing?

I went down the hall to the room where we had put him. The hall is eighteen feet long. I stopped in front of the door. Paul? *(She calls into the darkness.)*

Paul's Voice (moaning):   Yes Yes

Ouisa: Paul??

Paul's voice (moaning):   Yes Yes

Ouisa: Are you all right? *(to us.)* I opened the door and turned on the light. *(Screams.)* Flan!!!

(The stage is blindingly bright. Paul, startled, sits up in bed. A naked guy stands up on the bed.)

Hustler: What the fuck is going on here? Who the fuck are you?!

Ouisa: Flan!

Flan: What is it?

(Flan appears from the dark, tying his robe around him. The Hustler, naked but for white socks, comes into the room.)

Hustler: Hey! How ya doin'?

Flan: Oh my God!

Ouisa (a scream):   Ahhh!

(The Hustler stretches out on the sofa.)

Hustler: I gotta get some sleep—

(Paul runs into the room pulling on his clothes.)

Paul: I can explain.

(Paul tosses The Hustler's clothes onto the sofa.)

Ouisa: You went out after we went to sleep and picked up this thing?
Paul: I am so sorry.
Flan: You brought this thing into our house! Thing! Thing! Get out! Get out of my house!

(Flan tips the sofa, hurling The Hustler onto the floor. The Hustler leaps at Flan threateningly.)

Ouisa: Stop it! He might have a gun!
Hustler: I might have a gun. I might have a knife.
Ouisa: He has a gun! He has a knife!

(The Hustler chases Ouisa around the room.)

Paul: I can explain!
Flan: Give me my fifty dollars.
Paul: I spent it.
Ouisa: Get out!
Flan: Take your clothes. Go back to sleep in the gutter.

(He flings The Hustler's clothes into the hall. The Hustler viciously grabs Flan by the lapels of his robe.)

Hustler: Fuck you!

(The Hustler throws Flan back, picks up his clothes and leaves. Flan catches his breath. Ouisa is terrified.)

Paul: Please. Don't tell my father. I don't want him to know. I haven't told him. He doesn't know. I got so lonely. I got so afraid. My dad coming. I had the money. I went out after we went to sleep and I brought him back. I couldn't be alone. You had so much. I couldn't be alone. I was so afraid.
Ouisa: Just go.
Paul: I'm so sorry.

(Paul goes. Flan and Ouisa, at a loss, straighten out the pillows on the sofa. They are exhausted.)

Ouisa (to us):   And that's that.
Flan: I am shaking.
Ouisa: You have to do *something*!
Flan: It's awful.
Ouisa: Is anything gone?
Flan: How can I look? I'm shaking.
Ouisa: Did he take anything?
Flan: Would you concentrate on yourself?
Ouisa: I want to know if anything's gone?
Flan: Calm down.
Ouisa: We could have been killed.
Flan: The silver Victorian inkwell.

Ouisa: How can you think of *things?* We could have been murdered.

(An actor appears for a moment holding up an ornate Victorian inkwell capped by a silver beaver.)

Flan: There's the inkwell. Silver beaver. Why?

Ouisa: Slashed—our throats slashed.

(Another actor appears for a moment holding up a framed portrait of a dog, say, a pug.)

Flan: And there's the watercolor. Our dog.

Ouisa: Go to bed at night happy and then murdered. Would we have woken up?

Flan: We're alive.

Ouisa: We called our kids.

Flan: No answer.

(The phone rings. They clutch each other.)

Ouisa: It's him! *(Flan goes to the phone.)* Don't pick it up!

(Flan does. Geoffrey appears.)

Geoffrey: Flanders, I'm at the airport. Look, I've been thinking. Those Japs really want the Cézanne. They'll pay. You can depend on me for an additional overcall of two-fifty.

Flan: Two hundred and fifty thousand?

Geoffrey: And I was thinking for South Africa. What about a Black American Film Festival? With this Spike Lee you have now and of course get Poitier down to be the president of the jury and I know Cosby and I love this Eddie Murphy and my wife went fishing in Norway with Diana Ross and her new Norwegian husband. And also they must have some *new* blacks—

Flan: Yes. It sounds a wonderful idea.

Geoffrey: I'll call him at the Sherry—

Flan: No! We'll call!

Geoffrey: They're calling my plane—And again last night—

Flan: No need to thank. See you shortly.

Geoffrey: The banks.

Flan: My lawyer.

Geoffrey: Exactly.

Flan: Safe trip.

(Geoffrey goes. Another couple in their forties, Kitty and Larkin, appear. Ouisa and Flan take off their robes and are dressed for day.)

Ouisa: Do we have a story to tell you!

Kitty: Do we have a story to tell *you!*

Ouisa (to us):   Our two and their son are at Harvard together.

(Kitty and Larkin are pleased about this.)

Flan: Let me tell you our story.

Larkin: When did your story happen?

Flan: Last night. We are still zonked.

Kitty: We win. Our story happened Friday night. So we go first.

Larkin: We're going to be in the movies.

Kitty: We are going to be in the movie of *Cats*.

   (Ouisa and Flan look at each other.)

Ouisa: You tell your story first.

Larkin: Friday night we were home, the doorbell rang—

Kitty: I am not impressed but it was the son of—

Ouisa and Flan (to us):   You got it.

Kitty: The kid was mugged. We had to go out. We left him. He was so charming. His father was taking the red eye. He couldn't get into the hotel till seven A.M. He stayed with us.

   (She is very pleased.)

Larkin: In the middle of the night, we heard somebody screaming Burglar! Burglar! We came out in the hall. Paul is chasing this naked blonde thief down the corridor. The blond thief runs out, the alarm goes off. The kid saved our lives.

Flan: That was no burglar.

Ouisa: You had another house guest.

   (Kitty and Larkin laugh.)

Larkin: We feel so guilty. Paul could've been killed by that intruder. He was very understanding—

Ouisa: Was anything missing from your house?

Larkin: Nothing.

Flan: Did you give him money?

Kitty: Twenty-five dollars until his father arrived.

Flan (to us):   We told them our story.

Kitty and Larkin: Oh.

Ouisa: Have you talked to your kids?

Kitty: Can't get through.

   (Ouisa makes a phone call.)

Ouisa: Sherry Netherlands. I'd like—

Larkin (to us):   She gave the name.

Kitty: Sidney Poitier must be registered.

   (The doorbell rings. Flan goes.)

Ouisa: No! I'm not a fan. This is not a fan call. We know he's there. His son is a friend of—

   (Click. The Sherry's hung up.)

Larkin: He must be there under another name.

(Another phone call.)

Ouisa: Hi. Celebrity Service? I'm not sure how you work.

Kitty: Greta Garbo used the name Harriet Brown.

Ouisa: You track down celebrities? Am I right?

Larkin: Everybody must have known she was Greta Garbo.

Ouisa: I'm trying to find out how one would get in touch with—No, I'm
not a press agent—No, I'm not with anyone—My husband. Flanders
Kittredge. *(Click.)* Celebrity Service doesn't give out information over
the phone.

Larkin: Try the public library.

Kitty: Try *Who's Who.*

*(Flan returns carrying an elaborate arrangement of flowers. Flan reads
the card.)*

Flan: "To thank you for a wonderful time. Paul Poitier." *(Flan reaches
into the bouquet. He takes out a pot of jam.)* A pot of jam?

Larkin: A pot of jam.

(They back off as if it might explode.)

Kitty: I think we should call the police.

(A Detective appears.)

Detective: What are the charges?

Ouisa: He came into our house.

Flan: He cooked us dinner.

Ouisa: He told us the story of *Catcher in the Rye.*

Flan: He said he was the son of Sidney Poitier.

Detective: Was he?

Ouisa: We don't know.

Flan: We gave him fifty dollars.

Kitty: We gave him twenty-five.

Larkin: Shhhh!

Ouisa: He picked up a hustler.

Flan: He left.

Kitty: He chased the burglar out of our house.

Ouisa: He didn't steal anything.

Larkin: We looked and looked.

Kitty: Top to bottom. Nothing gone.

(The Detective closes his notebook.)

Ouisa: Granted this does not seem major now.

Detective: Look. We're very busy.

Flan: You can't chuck us out.

Detective: Come up with charges. Then I'll do something.

(The Detective goes.)

Ouisa (to us):   Our kids came down from Harvard.

(Their children, Woody and Tess, and Kitty and Larkin's boy, Ben, enter, groaning.)

Flan:—the details he knew—how would he know about the painting? Although I think it's a very fine Kandinsky.

Ouisa: And none of you know this fellow? He has this wild quality—yet a real elegance and a real concern and a real consideration—

Tess: Well, Mom, you should have let him stay. You should have divorced all your children and just let this dreamboat stay. Plus he sent you flowers.

Flan: And jam.

The Kids: Oooooo.

Ouisa: I wish I knew how to get hold of his father. Just to see if there is any truth in it.

Larkin: Who knows Sidney Poitier so we could just call him up and ask him?

Kitty (eager):   I have a friend who does theatrical law. I bet he—

Larkin: What friend?

Kitty: Oh, it's nobody.

Larkin: I want to know.

Kitty (screams):   Nobody!

Larkin: Whatever's going on anywhere, I do not want to know. I don't want to know. I don't want to know . . .

Kitty (overlapping):   Nobody. Nobody. Nobody . . .

Ben: Dad. Mom. Please. For once. Please?

(Ben, Kitty, Larkin go in anguish.)

Flan: Tess, when you see your little sister, don't tell her that he and the, uh, hustler, used her bed.

Tess: You put him in that bed. I'm not going to get involved with any conspiracy.

Flan: It's not a conspiracy. It's a *family.*

(Tess and Flan growl at each other. Darkness. Ouisa, alone, stretches out on the sofa. Paul appears wearing the pink shirt.)

Paul: The imagination. That's our out. Our imagination teaches us our limits and then how to grow beyond those limits. The imagination says Listen to me. I am your darkest voice. I am your 4 A.M. voice. I am the voice that wakes you up and says this is what I'm afraid of. Do not listen to me at your peril. The imagination is the noon voice that sees clearly and says yes, this is what I want for my life. It's there to sort out your nightmare, to show you the exit from the maze of your nightmare, to transform the nightmare into dreams that become your bedrock. If we don't listen to that voice, it dies. It shrivels. It vanishes.

(Paul takes out a switchblade and opens it.)

The imagination is not our escape. On the contrary, the imagination is the place we are all trying to get to.

(Paul lifts his shirt and stabs himself. Ouisa sits up and screams. Paul is gone. The phone rings. It's The Detective.)

Detective: I got a call that might interest you.

(Dr. Fine appears, a very earnest professional man in his fifties.)

Dr. Fine *(to us):*   I was seeing a patient. I'm an obstetrician at New York Hospital. The nurse opened my office door and said there's a friend of your son's here . . . *(Paul appears.)* I treated the kid. He was more scared than hurt. A knife wound, a few bruises.

Paul: I don't know how to thank you, sir. My father is coming here.

(The four parents appear.)

Flan and Ouisa and Kitty and Larkin: He's making a film of *Cats.*

Dr. Fine: And he told me the name of a matinee idol of my youth. Somebody who had really forged ahead and made new paths for blacks just by the strength of his own talent. Strangely, I had identified with him before I started medical school. I mean, I'm a Jew. My grandparents were killed in the war. I had this sense of self-hatred, of fear. And this kid's father—the bravery of his films—had given me a direction, a confidence. Simple as that. We're always paying off debts.

   Then my beeper went off. A patient in her tenth month of labor. Her water finally broke. I gave him the keys.

(Paul catches the keys.)

Paul: Doug told me all about your brownstone. How you got it at a great price because there had been a murder in it and for a while people thought it had a curse but you were a scientific man and were courageous!

Dr. Fine: Well, yes! Courageous! I ran off to the delivery room. Twins! Two boys. I thought of my son. I dialed my boy at Dartmouth. Amazingly, he was in his room. Doing *what* I hate to ask. *(Doug, twenty, appears.)* So you accuse me of having no interest in your life, not doing for friends, being a rotten father. Well, you should be very happy.

Doug: The son of who? Dad, I never heard of him. Dad, as usual, you are a real cretin. You gave him the keys? You gave a complete stranger who happens to mention my name the keys to our house? Dad, sometimes it is so obvious to me why Mom left. I am so embarrassed to know you. You gave the keys to a stranger who shows up at your office? Mother told me you beat her! Mom told me you were a rotten lover and drank so much your body smelled of cheap white wine. Mom said sleeping with you was like sleeping with a salad made of bad dressing. Why you had to bring me into the world!

Dr. Fine: There are two sides to every story—
Doug: You're an idiot! You're an idiot!

(*Doug goes into the dark, screaming.*)

Dr. Fine: I went home—courageously—with a policeman.

(*A Policeman accompanies Dr. Fine. Paul appears wearing a silk robe, carrying a snifter of brandy.*) Arrest him!

Paul: Pardon?
Dr. Fine: Breaking and entering.
Paul: Breaking and entering?
Dr. Fine: You're an imposter.
Paul: Officer, your honor, your eminence, Dr. Fine *gave* me the keys to his brownstone. Isn't that so?
Dr. Fine: My son doesn't know you.
Paul: This man gave me the keys to the house. Isn't that so?
Policeman (screams): Did you give him the key to the house?
Dr. Fine: Yes! But under false pretenses. This fucking black kid crack addict came into my office lying—
Paul: I have taken this much brandy but can pour the rest back into the bottle. And I've used electricity listening to the music, but I think you'll find that nothing's taken from the house.

(*Paul goes.*)

Dr. Fine: I want you to arrest this fraud.

(*The Policeman walks away. Doug returns.*)

Doug: A cretin. A creep! No wonder mother left you!

(*Doug goes. Pause.*)

Dr. Fine: Two sides. Every story.

(*Ouisa holds up a book.*)

Ouisa: I went down to the Strand. I got Sidney Poitier's autobiography. (*Reads.*) "Back in New York with Juanita and the children, I began to become aware that our marriage, while working on some levels, was falling apart in other fundamental areas."
Flan: There's a picture of him and his four—daughters. No sons. Four daughters. The book's called *This Life.*
Dr. Fine: Published by Knopf.
Kitty: 1980.
Larkin: Out of print.
Kitty: Oh dear.
Ouisa: This kid bulldozing his way into our lives.
Larkin: We let him in our lives. I run a foundation. You're a dealer. You're a doctor. You'd think we'd be satisfied with our achievements.
Flan: Agatha Christie would ask, what do we all have in common?

Ouisa: It seems the common thread linking us all is an overwhelming need to be in the movie of *Cats*.

Kitty: Our kids. Struggling through their lives.

Larkin: I don't want to know anything about the spillover of their lives.

Ouisa: All we have in common is our children went to boarding school together.

Flan (to Dr. Fine):   How come we never met?

Dr. Fine: His mother had custody. I lived out West. After he graduated from high school, she moved West. I moved East.

Larkin: I think we should drop it right here.

Kitty: Are you afraid Ben is mixed up in this fraud?

Larkin: I don't want to know too much about my kid.

Kitty: You think Ben is hiding things from us? I tell you, I'm getting to the bottom of this. My son has no involvements with any black frauds. Doctor, you said something about crack?

Larkin: I don't want to know.

Dr. Fine: It just leaped out of my mouth. No proof. Oh dear god, no proof.

Flan: We'll take a vote. Do we pursue this to the end no matter what we find out about our kids?

Ouisa: I vote yes.

Dr. Fine: I trust Doug. Yes.

Larkin: No.

Kitty: Yes.

Flan: Yes.

(*Kitty looks through the Poitier autobiography.*)

Kitty: Listen to the last page. ". . . making it better for our children. Protecting them. From what? The truth is what we were protecting those little people from . . . there is a lot to worry about and I'd better start telling the little bastards—start worrying!" The end.

(*Kitty closes the book in dismay. All the children, Tess, Woody, Ben, Doug, enter, groaning.*)

Flan: It's obvious. It's somebody you went to high school with, since you each go to different colleges.

Ouisa: He knows the details about our lives.

Flan: Who in your high school, part of your gang, has become homosexual or is deep into drugs?

Tess: That's like, about fifteen people.

Larkin: I don't want to know.

Tess: I find it really insulting that you would assume that it has to be a guy. This movie star's son could have had a relationship with a girl in high school—

Ben: That's your problem in a nutshell. You're so limited.

Tess: That's why I'm going to Afghanistan. To climb mountains.

Ouisa: You are not climbing mountains.

Flan: We have not invested all this money in you to scale the face of K-2.

Tess: Is that all I am? An investment?

Ouisa: All right. Track down everybody in your high school class. Male. Female. Whatever. Not just homosexuals. Drug addicts. The kid might be a drug dealer.

Doug: Why do you look at me when you say that? Do you think I'm an addict? A drug pusher? I really resent the accusations.

Dr. Fine: No one is accusing you of anything.

Larkin: I don't want to know. I don't want to know. I don't want to know.

Flan: Nobody is accusing anyone of anything. I'm asking you to go on a detective search and find out from your high school class if anyone has met a black kid pretending to be a movie star's son.

Ben: He promised you parts in *Cats*?

Ouisa: It wasn't just that. It was fun.

Tess: You went to *Cats.* You said it was an all-time low in a lifetime of theater-going.

Ouisa: Film is a different medium.

Tess: You said Aeschylus did not invent theater to have it end up a bunch of chorus kids wondering which of them will go to Kitty Kat Heaven.

Ouisa: I don't remember saying that.

Flan: No, I think that was *Starlight Express*—

Tess: Well, maybe he'll make a movie of *Starlight Express* and you can all be on roller skates—

Doug: This is so humiliating.

Ben: This is so pathetic.

Tess: This is so racist.

Ouisa: This is *not* racist!

Doug: How can I get in touch with anybody in high school? I've outgrown them.

Kitty: How can you outgrow them? You graduated a year ago!

Ouisa: Here is a copy of your yearbook. I want you to get the phone numbers of everybody in your class. You all went to the same boarding school. You can phone from here.

Dr. Fine: You can charge it to my phone.

Ouisa: Call everyone in your class and ask them if they know—

Doug: Never!

Tess: This is the KGB.

Dr. Fine: You're on the phone all the time. Now I ask you to make calls all over the country and you become reticent.

Tess: This is the entire McCarthy period.

Woody: I just want to get one thing straight.

Flan: Finally, we hear from the peanut gallery.

Woody: You gave him my pink shirt? You gave a complete stranger my pink shirt? That pink shirt was a Christmas present from *you*. I treasured that shirt. I loved that shirt. My collar size has grown a full size from weight lifting. And you saw my arms had grown, you saw my neck had grown. And you bought me that shirt for my new body. I loved that shirt. The first shirt for my new body. And you gave that shirt away. I can't believe it. I hate it here. I hate this house. I hate you.

Doug: You never do anything for me.

Tess: You've never done anything but tried to block me.

Ben: I'm only this pathetic extension of your eighth-rate personality.

Doug: Social Darwinism pushed beyond all limits.

Woody: You gave away my pink shirt?

Tess: You want me to be everything you weren't.

Doug: You said drugs and looked at me.

(*The parents leave, speechless, defeated. The kids look through their high school yearbook. Tess spots a face.*)

Tess: Trent Conway.

All The Kids: Trent Conway.

(*Trent Conway appears.*)

Tess: Trent Conway. Look at those beady eyes staring out at me. Trent Conway. He's at MIT. (*To us.*) So I went to MIT. He was there in his computer room and I just pressed him and pressed him and pressed him. I had a tape recorder strapped to me.

(*Darkness.*)

Trent's Voice Taped: Yes, I knew Paul.

Tess's Voice Taped: But what happened between you?

Trent's Voice Taped: It was . . . It was . . .

(*The lights come up slowly. Paul and Trent appear. Rain. Distant thunder. Jazz playing somewhere off. Paul is dressed in jeans and a tank top, high-top sneakers.*)

Trent: This is the way you must speak. Hear my accent. Hear my voice. Never say you're going horse-back riding. You say you're going riding. And don't say couch. Say sofa. And you say *bodd*-ill. It's bottle. Say bottle of beer.

Paul: Bodd-ill a bee-ya.

Trent: Bottle of beer.

(*Paul sits on the sofa. He pulls out a thick address book from under him.*)

Paul: What's this?

Trent: My address book.

Paul: All these names. Addresses. Tell me about these people.

(*Trent sits beside him.*)

Trent: I want you to come to bed with me.
Paul (fierce):   Tell me about these people, man!
Trent: I just want to look at you. Sorry.

   (Paul is hypnotized by the address book.)

Paul: Are these all rich people?
Trent: No. Hand to mouth on a higher plateau.
Paul: I think it must be very hard to be with rich people. You have to have money. You have to give them presents.
Trent: Not at all. Rich people do something nice for you, you give them a pot of jam.
Paul: That's what pots of jam are for?
Trent: Orange. Grapefruit. Strawberry. But fancy. They have entire stores filled with fancy pots of jam wrapped in cloth. English. Or French.
Paul: I'll tell you what I'll do. I pick a name. You tell me about them. Where they live. Secrets. And for each name you get a piece of clothing.
Trent: All right.
Paul: Kittredge. Talbot and Woodrow.
Trent: Talbot, called Tess, was anorexic and was in a hospital for a while.

   (Paul takes off a shoe and kicks it to Trent.)

Paul: Their parents.
Trent: Ouisa and Flan, for Flanders, Kittredge. Rhode Island, I believe. Newport, but not along the ocean. The street behind the ocean. He's an art dealer. They have a Kandinsky.
Paul: A Kan—what—ski?
Trent: Kandinsky. A double-sided Kandinsky. *(Paul kicks off his other shoe. Trent catches it joyously.)* I feel like Scheherazade! *(He embraces Paul with fierce tenderness.)* I don't want you to leave me, Paul. I'll go through my address book and tell you about family after family. You'll never not fit in again. We'll give you a new identity. I'll make you the most eagerly sought-after young man in the East. And then I'll come into one of these homes one day—and you'll be there and I'll be presented to you. And I'll pretend to meet you for the first time and our friendship will be witnessed by my friends, our parents' friends. If it all happens under their noses, they can't judge me. They can't disparage you. I'll make you a guest in their houses. Ask me another name. I'd like to try for the shirt.

   (Paul kisses Trent.)

Paul: That's enough for today.

   (Paul takes his shoes and the address book and goes. Trent turns to Tess.)

Trent: Paul stayed with me for three months. We went through the address book letter by letter. Paul vanished by the L's. He took the

address book with him. Well, he's already been in all your houses.
Maybe I will meet him again. I sure would like to.

Tess: His past? His real name?

Trent: I don't know anything about him. It was a rainy night in Boston.
He was in a doorway. That's all.

Tess: He took stuff from you?

Trent: Besides the address book? He took my stereo and sport jacket and
my word processor and my laser printer. And my skis. And my TV.

Tess: Will you press charges?

Trent: No.

Tess: It's a felony.

Trent: Why do they want to find him?

Tess: They say to help him. If there's a crime, the cops will get involved.

Trent: Look, we must keep in touch. We were friends for a brief bit in
school. I mean we were really good friends.

Tess: Won't you press charges?

Trent: Please.

(*They go. Ouisa appears.*)

Ouisa (to us):   Tess played me the tapes.

Tess's Voice Taped: Won't you press charges?

Trent's Voice Taped: Please.

Ouisa (to us):   Can you believe it? Paul learned all that in three months.
Three months! Who would have thought it? Trent Conway, the Henry
Higgins of our time. Paul looked at those names and said I am
Columbus. I am Magellan. I will sail into this new world.

I read somewhere that everybody on this planet is separated by
only six other people. Six degrees of separation. Between us and
everybody else on this planet. The president of the United States. A
gondolier in Venice. Fill in the names. I find that (A) tremendously
comforting that we're so close and (B) like Chinese water torture that
we're so close. Because you have to find the right six people to make
the connection. It's not just big names. It's *anyone*. A native in a rain
forest. A Tierra del Fuegan. An Eskimo. I am bound to everyone on
this planet by a trail of six people. It's a profound thought. How Paul
found us. How to find the man whose son he pretends to be. Or
perhaps *is* his son, although I doubt it. How every person is a new
door, opening up into other worlds. Six degrees of separation
between me and everyone else on this planet. But to find the right six
people.

(*Flan appears.*)

Flan (to us):   We didn't hear for a while. We went about our lives.

(*The Doorman appears.*)

Ouisa (to us): And then one day our doorman, whom we tip very well at Christmas and any time he does something nice for us—our doorman spit at my husband, J. Flanders Kittredge. I mean, spit at him.

(The Doorman spits at Flan.)

Doorman: Your son! I know all about your son.

Flan: What about my son?

Doorman: Not the little shit who lives here. The other son. The secret son. The Negro son you deny.

(The Doorman spits at Flan again.)

Flan: The Negro son?

Doorman: The black son you make live in Central Park.

Ouisa (to us): The next chapter. Rick and Elizabeth and Paul sit on the grass in Central Park.

(Rick, Elizabeth, and Paul run on laughing in Central Park. Rick, a nice young guy in his mid-twenties, plays the guitar energetically. He and Paul and Elizabeth, a beautiful girl in her mid-twenties, are having a great time singing a cheery song, say James Taylor's "Shower The People," until Rick hits the wrong chord. They try to break down the harmony. Rick can't for the life of him find the right chord. The three of them laugh. Paul is wearing the pink shirt.)

Paul: Tell me about yourselves.

Rick: We're here from Utah.

Paul: Do they have any black people in Utah?

Rick: Maybe two. Yes, the Mormons brought in two.

Elizabeth: We came to be actors.

Rick: She won the all-state competition for comedy and drama.

Paul: My gosh!

Elizabeth: "The quality of mercy is not strained. It droppeth like the gentle rain from heaven."

Rick: And we study and we wait tables.

Elizabeth: Because you have to have technique.

Paul: Like the painters. Cézanne looked for the rules behind the spontaneity of Impressionism.

Rick: Céz—That's a painter?

Elizabeth: We don't know anything about painting.

Paul: My dad loves painting. He has a Kandinsky but he loves Cézanne the most. He lives up there.

Rick: What?

Paul: He lives up there. Count six windows over. John Flanders Kittredge. His chums call him Flan. I was the child of Flan's hippie days. His radical days. He went down South as a freedom marcher, to register black voters—his friends were killed. Met my mother. Registered her and married her in a fit of sentimental righteousness and knocked her

up with me and came back here and abandoned her. Went to Harvard.
He's now a fancy art dealer. Lives up there. Count six windows over.
Won't see me. The new wife—the white wife—The Louisa Kittredge
Call Me Ouisa Wife—the mother of the new children wife—

Rick: Your brothers and sisters?

Paul (bitter):   They go to Andover and Exeter and Harvard and Yale. The
awful thing is my father started out good. My mother says there is a
good man inside J. Flanders Kittredge.

Elizabeth: He'll see you if he was that good. He can't forget you entirely.

Paul: I call him. He hangs up.

Rick: Go to his office—

Paul: He doesn't have an office. He works out of there. They won't even
let me in the elevator.

Rick: Dress up as a messenger.

Elizabeth: Say you have a masterpiece for him. "I got the Mona Lisa
waitin' out in the truck."

Paul: I don't want to embarrass him. Look, this is so fucking tacky.
   (*Pause.*) You love each other?

Elizabeth: A lot.

   (*Rick and Elizabeth touch each other's hands.*)

Paul: I hope we can meet again.

   (*Paul turns to go.*)

Rick: Where do you live?

Paul: Live? I'm home.

Elizabeth: You're not out on the streets?

Paul: You're such assholes. Where would I live?

Rick: Stay with us.

Elizabeth: We just have a railroad flat in a tenement—

Rick: It's over a roller disco. The last of the roller discos but it's quiet by
five A.M. and a great narrow space—

Elizabeth: A railroad loft and we could give you a corner. The tub's in the
kitchen but there's light in the morning—

Rick (to us):   And he did!

   (*The light changes to the loft.*)

Paul: This is the way you must speak. Hear my accent. Hear my voice.
Never say you're going horse-back riding. You say you're going riding.
And don't say couch. Say sofa. And you say bodd-ill. It's bottle. Say
bottle of beer.

Rick: Bodd-ill a bee-ya.

Paul: Bottle of beer. And never be afraid of rich people. You know what
they love? A fancy pot of jam. That's all. Get yourself a patron. That's
what you need. You shouldn't be waiting tables. You're going to wake
up one day and the temporary job you picked up to stay alive is going

to be your full-time life. (*Elizabeth embraces Paul gratefully.*) You've given me courage. I'm going to try and see him right now.

(*Paul goes. Rick and Elizabeth lie on their backs and dream.*)

Rick: I'll tell you all the parts I want to do. Vanya in *Uncle Vanya.*

Elizabeth: Masha in *Three Sisters.* No, Irina first. The young one who yearns for love. Then Masha who loves. Then the oldest one, Olga, who never knows love.

Rick: I'd like a shot at Laertes. I think it's a much better part.

(*Elizabeth gazes in a mirror.*)

Elizabeth: Do you think it'll hurt me?

Rick: What'll hurt you?

Elizabeth: My resemblance to Liv Ullmann.

(*Paul runs in.*)

Paul: HE WROTE ME! I WROTE HIM AND HE WROTE ME BACK!!! He's going to give me a thousand dollars! And that's just for starters! He sold a Cézanne to the Japanese and made millions and he can give me money without her knowing it.

Elizabeth: I knew it!

Paul: I'm moving out of here!

Elizabeth: You can't!

Rick: No!

Paul: But I am going to give you the money to put on a showcase of any play you want and you'll be in it and agents will come see you and you'll be seen and you'll be started. And when you win your Oscars— both of you—you'll look in the camera and thank me—

Elizabeth: I want to thank Paul Kittredge.

Rick: Thanks, Paul!

Paul: One hitch. I'm going to meet him in Maine. He's up there visiting his parents in Dark Harbor. My grandparents whom I've never met. He's finally going to tell my grandparents about me. He's going to make up for lost time. He's going to give me money. I can go back home. Get my momma that beauty parlor she's wanted all her life. One problem. How am I going to get to Maine? The wife checks all the bills. He has to account for the money. She handles the purse strings. Where the hell am I going to get two hundred and fifty dollars to get to Maine?

Elizabeth: How long would you need it for?

Paul: I'll be gone a week. But I could wire it back to you.

Ric (quiet):   We could lend it to him for a week.

Elizabeth (quiet):   We can't. If something happens—

Rick (quiet):   You're like his stepmother. These women holding on to all the purse strings.

Elizabeth: No. We worked too hard to save that. I'm sorry. I'll meet you both after work. If your father loves you, he'll get you the ticket up there.

(She goes.)

Rick (to us): We stopped by the bank. I withdrew the money. He took it.
Paul: Let's celebrate!

(Elizabeth appears.)

Elizabeth (to us): I went to a money machine to get twenty dollars and I couldn't get anything. The machine devoured my card. I called up the emergency number and the voice said my account was closed. They had withdrawn all the money and closed the account. I went to that apartment on Fifth Avenue. I told the doorman: I want my money. I work tables. I work hard. I saved. I'm here trying to get to meet people. I am stranded. Who do I know to go to? "The quality of mercy is not strained?" Fuck you, quality of mercy.

(She goes. Rick appears.)

Rick (to us): He told me he had some of his own money and he wanted to treat me. We went to a store that rented tuxedos and we dressed to the nines. We went to the Rainbow Room. We danced. High over New York City. I swear. He stood up and held out my chair and we danced and there was a stir. Nothing like this ever happened in Utah. And we danced. And I'll tell you nothing like that must have ever happened at the Rainbow Room because we were asked to leave. I tell you. It was so funny.

And we walked out and walked home and I knew Elizabeth was waiting for me and I would have to explain about the money and calm her down because we'll get it back but I forgot because we took a carriage ride in the park and he asked me if he could fuck me and I had never done anything like that and he did and it was fantastic. It was the greatest night I ever had and before we got home he kissed me on the mouth and he vanished.

Later I realized he had no money of his own. He had spent my money—our money—on that night at the Rainbow Room.

How am I going to face Elizabeth? What have I done? What did I let him do to me? I wanted experience. I came here to have experience. But I didn't come here to do this or lose that or be this or do this to Elizabeth. I didn't come here to be *this*. My father said I was a fool and I can't have him be right. What have I done?

(He goes into the dark. Larkin and Kitty appear.)

Larkin: Kitty and I were at a roller disco two clients opened.
Kitty: And it was Valentine's Day
Larkin: and we came out and we saw a body on the street.
Kitty: My legs were still shaky from the roller skating which I have not

done in I hate to tell you how many years and we knew the body had just landed there in that clump

Larkin: because the blood seeping out had not reached the gutter yet.

Kitty: You could see the blood just oozing out slowly towards the curb.

Larkin: The boy had jumped from above.

Kitty: The next day we walked through the park by Gracie Mansion

Larkin: and it was cold and we saw police putting a jacket on a man sitting on a bench.

Kitty: Only we got closer and it wasn't a sweater.

Larkin: It was a body bag. A homeless person had frozen during the night.

Kitty: Was it that cold?

Larkin: Sometimes there are periods where you see death everywhere.

(Darkness. Ouisa and Flan appear in their robes with the Detective and Elizabeth.)

Detective: This young girl came forward with the story. She told me the black kid was your son, lived here. It all seemed to come into place. What I'm saying is she'll press charges.

Elizabeth: I want him dead. He took all our money. He took my life. Rick's dead! You bet your life I'll press charges.

Ouisa: We haven't seen him since that night.

Detective: Find him. We have a case.

Flan: I'll release it to the papers. I have friends. I can call the *Times.*

Ouisa (to us):   Which is what happened.

Flan (to us):   The paper of note—the *Times*—ran a story on so-called smart, sophisticated, tough New Yorkers being boondoggled by a confidence man now wanted by the police. Who says New Yorkers don't have a heart? They promised it would either run in the Living section or the Home section.

Kitty (to us):   The story ran.

Dr. Fine (to us):   In the B section front page.

Detective (to us):   Smart New Yorkers.

Larkin (to us):   We never heard from Sidney Poitier.

Ouisa (to us):   Six degrees. Six degrees. (*They all go except for Ouisa and Flan, who pull off their robes; they are dressing for the evening.*) We are bidding tonight on an Henri Matisse.

Flan (to us):   We will go as high as—

Ouisa: Don't tell all the family secrets—

Flan (to us):   Well over twenty-five million.

Ouisa (to us):   Out of which he will keep—

Flan (to us):   I'll have to give most of it away, but the good part is it gives me a credibility in this new market. I mean, a David fucking Hockney print sold for a hundred bucks fifteen years ago went for thirty-four thousand dollars! A print! A flower. You know Geoffrey. Our South African—

Ouisa (to us):—it's a black-tie auction—Sotheby's—

Flan: I know we'll get it.

Ouisa (noting the time):   Flan—

Flan: I know the Matisse will be mine—for a few hours. Then off to Tokyo. Or Saudi.

(Flan leaves as Ouisa phones Tess.)

Ouisa (to Tess):   I'm totally dolled up. The black. Have you seen it? I have to tell you the sign I saw today. Cruelty-free cosmetics. A store was selling cruelty-free cosmetics.

Tess: Mother, that is such a beautiful thing. Do you realize the agony cosmetic companies put rabbits through to test eye shadow?

Ouisa: Dearest, I know that. I'm only talking about the phrase. Cruelty-free cosmetics should take away all evidence of time and cellulite and—

Tess: Mother, I'm getting married.

Ouisa: I thought you were going to Afghanistan.

Tess: I am going to get married and then go to Afghanistan.

Ouisa: One country at a time. You are not getting married.

Tess: Immediately so deeply negative—

Ouisa: I know everyone you know and you are not marrying any of them.

Tess: The arrogance that you would assume you know everyone I know. The way you say it: I know everyone you know—

Ouisa: Unless you met them in the last two days—you can't hold a secret. *(The other line rings.)* Wait—I'm putting you on hold—

Tess: No one ever calls on that number.

Ouisa: Wait. Hold on.

Tess: Mother!

Ouisa: Hello?

(Paul appears, frightened.)

Paul: Hello.

Ouisa: Paul?

Paul: I saw the story in the paper. I didn't know the boy killed himself. He gave me the money.

Ouisa: Let me put you on hold. I'm talking to my child—

Paul: If you put me on hold, I'll be gone and you'll never hear from me again.

(Ouisa pauses. Tess fades into black.)

Ouisa: You have to turn yourself in. The boy committed suicide. You stole the money. The girl is pressing charges. They're going to get you. Why not turn yourself in and you can get off easier. You can strike a bargain. Learn when you're trapped. You're so brilliant. You have such promise. You need help.

Paul: Would you help me?

Ouisa: What would you want me to do?

Paul: Stay with you.

Ouisa: That's impossible.

Paul: Why?

Ouisa: My husband feels you betrayed him.

Paul: Do you?

Ouisa: You were lunatic! And picking that drek off the street. Are you suicidal? Do you have AIDS? Are you infected?

Paul: I do not have it. It's a miracle. But I don't. Do you feel I betrayed you? If you do, I'll hang up and never bother you again—

Ouisa: Where have you been?

Paul: Travelling.

Ouisa: You're not in trouble? I mean, more trouble?

Paul: No, I only visited you. I didn't like the first people so much. They went out and just left me alone. I didn't like the doctor. He was too eager to please. And he left me alone. But you. You and your husband. We all stayed together.

Ouisa: What did you want from us?

Paul: Everlasting friendship.

Ouisa: Nobody has that.

Paul: You do.

Ouisa: What do you think we are?

Paul: You're going to tell me secrets? You're not what you appear to be? You have no secrets. Trent Conway told me what your kids have told him over the years.

Ouisa: What have the kids told him about us?

Paul: I don't tell that. I save that for blackmail.

Ouisa: Then perhaps I'd better hang up.

Paul (panic): No! I went to a museum! I liked Toulouse-Lautrec!

Ouisa: As well you should.

Paul: I read *The Andy Warhol Diaries*.

Ouisa: Ahh, you've become an aesthete.

Paul: Are you laughing at me?

Ouisa: No. I read them too.

Paul: I read *The Agony and the Ecstasy*, by Irving Stone, about Michelangelo painting the Sistine Chapel.

Ouisa: You're ahead of me there.

Paul: Have you seen the Sistine Chapel?

Ouisa: Oh yes. Even gone to the top of it in a rickety elevator to watch the men clean it.

Paul: You've been to the top of the Sistine Chapel?

Ouisa: Absolutely. Stood right under the hand of God touching the hand of man. The workman said "Hit it. Hit it. It's only a fresco." I did. I slapped God's hand.

Paul: You did?

Ouisa: And you know what they clean it with? All this technology. Q-tips and water.

Paul: No!

Ouisa: Clean away the years of grime and soot and paint-overs. Q-tips and water changing the history of Western Art. Vivid colors.

Paul: Take me to see it?

Ouisa: Take you to see it? Paul, they think you might have murdered someone! You stole money!

(Flan appears, needing help with his studs.)

Flan: Honey, could you give me a hand with—

Ouisa (mouths to Flan):   It's Paul.

(Flan goes to the other phone.)

Flan: I'll call that detective.

(The other line rings. Tess appears.)

Tess: Dad! We were cut off. I'm getting marr—

Flan: Darling, could you call back—

Tess: I'm getting married and going to Afghanistan—

Flan: We cannot talk about this now—

Tess: I'm going to ruin my life and get married and throw away everything you want me to be because it's the only way to hurt you!

(Tess goes. The Detective appears.)

Flan: I've got that kid on the line.

Detective: Find out where he is.

(The Detective goes.)

Flan (mouths to Ouisa):   Find out where he is???

Paul: Who's there?

Ouisa: Look, why don't you come here. Where are you?

Paul: I come there and you'll have the cops waiting.

Ouisa: You have to trust us.

Paul: Why?

Ouisa: Because—we like you.

Flan (mouths):   Where is he?

Paul: Who's there?

Ouisa: It's—

Flan: I'm not here.

Ouisa: It's Flan.

Paul: Are you in tonight? I could come and make a feast for you.

Ouisa: We're going out now. But you could be here when we come back.

Flan: Are you nuts! Tell a crook we're going out. The house is empty.

Paul: Where are you going?

Ouisa: To Sotheby's.

   (*Flan grabs the phone.*)

Flan: The key's under the mat!
Paul: Hi! Can I come to Sotheby's?

   (*Flan hands the phone back to Ouisa.*)

Ouisa: Hi.
Paul: I said hi to Flan.
Ouisa: Paul says hi.
Flan: Hi.
Ouisa: Sotheby's.
Paul: That's wonderful! I'll come!
Ouisa: You can't.
Paul: Why? I was helpful last time—
Flan: Thank him—he was very help—(*Ouisa hands Flan the phone.*) Paul?
   You were helpful getting me this contract—
Paul: Really! I was thinking maybe that's what I should do is what you
   do—in art but making money out of art and meeting people and not
   working in an office—
Flan: You only see the glam side of it. There's a whole grotty side that—
Paul: I could learn the grotty—
Flan: You have to have art history. You have to have language. You have
   to have economics—
Paul: I'm fast. I could do it. Do your kids want to—
Flan: No, it's not really a profession you hand down from generation to
   gen—what the hell am I talking career counselling to you! You
   embarrassed me in my building! You stole money. There is a warrant
   out for your arrest!

   (*Ouisa wrests the phone away.*)

Ouisa: Don't hang up! *Paul?* Are you there? *Paul?* (*To Flan.*) You made
   him hang up—
Paul: I'm here.
Ouisa: You are! Who are you? What's your real name?
Paul: If you let me stay with you, I'll tell you. That night was the
   happiest night I ever had.
Ouisa (to Flan):   It was the happiest night he ever had.
Flan: Oh please. I am not a bullshitter but never bullshit a bullshitter.

   (*Flan goes.*)

Ouisa: Why?
Paul: You let me use all the parts of myself that night—
Ouisa: It was magical. That Salinger stuff—
Paul: Graduation speech at Groton two years ago.
Ouisa: Your cooking—

Paul: Other people's recipes. Did you see Donald Barthelme's° obituary? He said collage was the art form of the twentieth century.

Ouisa: Everything is somebody else's.

Paul: Not your children. Not your life.

Ouisa: Yes. You got me there. That is mine. It is no one else's.

Paul: You don't sound happy.

Ouisa: There's so much you don't know. You are so smart and so stupid—

Paul (furious): Never say I'm stupid—

Ouisa: Have some flexibility. You're stupid not to recognize what you could be.

Paul: What could I be?

Ouisa: So much.

Paul: With you behind me?

Ouisa: Perhaps. You liked that night? I've thought since that you spent all your time laughing at us.

Paul: No.

Ouisa: That you had brought that awful hustling thing back to show us your contempt—

Paul: I was so happy. I wanted to add sex to it. Don't you do that?

   (Pause.)

Ouisa: No.

Paul: I'll tell you my name.

Ouisa: Please?

Paul: It's Paul Poitier-Kittredge. It's a hyphenated name.

   (Pause.)

Ouisa: Paul, you need help. Go to the police. Turn yourself in. You'll be over it all the sooner. You can start.

Paul: Start what?

Ouisa: Your life.

Paul: Will you help me?

   (Ouisa pauses, and makes a decision.)

Ouisa: I will help you. But you have to go to the police and go to jail and—

Paul: Will you send me books and polaroids of you and cassettes? And letters?

Ouisa: Yes.

Paul: Will you visit me?

Ouisa: I will visit you.

Paul: And when you do, you'll wear your best clothes and knock em dead?

Barthelme: Donald Barthelme (1931–1989), a short story writer often featured in *The New Yorker.*

Ouisa: I'll knock em dead. But you've got to be careful in prison. You have to use condoms.

Paul: I won't have sex in prison. I only have sex when I'm happy.

Ouisa: Go to the police.

Paul: Will you take me?

Ouisa: I'll give you the name of the detective to see—

Paul: I'll be treated with care if you take me to the police. If they don't know you're special, they kill you.

Ouisa: I don't think they kill you.

Paul: Mrs. Louisa Kittredge, I am black.

Ouisa: I will deliver you to them with kindness and affection.

Paul: And I'll plead guilty and go to prison and serve a few months.

Ouisa: A few months tops.

Paul: Then I'll come out and work for you and learn—

Ouisa: We'll work that out.

Paul: I want to know now.

Ouisa: Yes. You'll work for us.

Paul: Learn all the trade. Not just the grotty part.

Ouisa: Top to bottom.

Paul: And live with you.

Ouisa: No.

Paul: Your kids are away.

Ouisa: You should have your own place.

Paul: You'll help me find a place?

Ouisa: We'll help you find a place.

Paul: I have no furniture.

Ouisa: We'll help you out.

Paul: I made a list of things I liked in the museum. Philadelphia Chippendale.

Ouisa (bursts out laughing): Believe it or not, we have two Philadelphia Chippendale chairs—

Paul: I'd rather have one nice piece than a room full of junk.

Ouisa: Quality. Always. You'll have all that. Philadelphia Chippendale.

Paul: All I have to do is go to the police.

Ouisa: Make it all history. Put it behind you.

Paul: Tonight.

Ouisa: It can't be tonight. I will take you tomorrow. We have an auction tonight at Sotheby's—

Paul: Bring me?

Ouisa: I can't. It's black tie.

Paul: I have black tie from a time I went to the Rainbow Room. Have you ever been to the Rainbow Room?

Ouisa: Yes.

Paul: What time do you have to be there?

Ouisa: Eight o'clock.

Paul: It's five-thirty now. You could come get me now and take me to the police tonight and then go to Sotheby's—

Ouisa: We're going to drinks before at the Pierre.

Paul: Japanese?

Ouisa: Germans.

Paul: You're just like my father.

Ouisa: Which father?

Paul: Sidney!

  (Pause.)

Ouisa: Paul. He's not your father. And Flanders is not your father.

  (Flan comes in, dressed.)

Flan: Oh fuck. We have drinks with the Japanese at six-fifteen—Get off that fucking phone. Is it that kid? Get him out of our life! Get off that phone or I'll rip it out of the wall!

  (Ouisa looks at Flan.)

Ouisa (to Paul): Paul, I made a mistake. It is not the Germans. We will come right now and get you. Where are you? Tell me? I'll take you to the police. They will treat you with dignity.

Paul: I'm in the lobby of the Waverly movie theater on Sixth Avenue and Third Street.

Ouisa: We'll be there in half an hour.

Paul: I'll give you fifteen minutes grace time.

Ouisa: We'll be there. Paul. We love you.

Paul: Ouisa. I love you. Ouisa Kittredge. Hey? Bring a pink shirt.

Ouisa: We'll have a wonderful life. *(She hangs up. Paul goes into the dark.)* We can skip the shmoozing. Pick the boy up, take him to the police and be at Sotheby's before eight.

  (The Detective appears.)

Flan: He's at the Waverly Theater. Sixth Avenue and Third Street. The lobby.

Ouisa: We promised we would bring him to you. He's special. Remember that he's special. Honor our promise. *(The Detective nods and goes. To us):* We go. Traffic on the FDR.

Flan (to us): We get there. I run into the theater. No one.

Ouisa: A young man. Black. Have you seen him?

Flan (to us): The girl in the box office said the police were there, had arrested a young man. Dragged him kicking, screaming into a squad car. He was a kid waiting for his family. We could never get through or find out.

Ouisa (to us): We weren't family.

Flan (to us): That detective was transferred.

Ouisa (to us): And we didn't know Paul's name.

We called the precinct. Another precinct had made the arrest. Why? Were there other charges? We couldn't find out.

We weren't family. We didn't know Paul's name.

We called the district attorney's office. We weren't family. We didn't know Paul's name.

I called the Criminal Courts. I wasn't family. I didn't know Paul's name.

Flan: Why does it mean so much to you?

Ouisa: He wanted to be us. Everything we are in the world, this paltry thing—our life—he wanted it. He stabbed himself to get in here. He envied us. We're not enough to be envied.

Flan: Like the papers said. We have hearts.

Ouisa: Having a heart is not the point. We were hardly taken in. We believed him—for a few hours. He did more for us in a few hours than our children ever did. He wanted to be your child. Don't let that go. He sat out in that park and said that man is my father. He's in trouble and we don't know how to help him.

Flan: Help him? He could've killed me. And you.

Ouisa: You were attracted to him—

Flan: Cut me out of that pathology! You are on your own—

Ouisa: Attracted by youth and his talent and the embarrassing prospect of being in the movie version of *Cats.* Did you put that in your *Times* piece? And we turn him into an anecdote to dine out on. Or dine in on. But it was an experience. I will not turn him into an anecdote. How do we fit what happened to us into life without turning it into an anecdote with no teeth and a punch line you'll mouth over and over for years to come. "Tell the story about the imposter who came into our lives—" "That reminds me of the time this boy,—." And we become these human juke boxes spilling out these anecdotes. But it was an experience. How do we *keep* the experience?

Flan (to us):   That's why I love paintings. Cézanne. The problems he brought up are the problems painters are still dealing with. Color. Structure. Those are problems.

Ouisa: There is color in my life, but I'm not aware of any structure.

Flan (to us):   Cézanne would leave blank spaces in his canvasses if he couldn't account for the brush stroke, give a reason for the color.

Ouisa: Then I am a collage of unaccounted-for brush strokes. I am all random. God, Flan, how much of your life can you account for?

Flan: Are you drunk? The Cézanne sale went through. We are rich. Geoffrey's rich. Tonight there's a Matisse we'll get and next month there's a Bonnard and after that—

(*She considers him.*)

Ouisa: These are the times I would take a knife and dig out your heart. Answer me? How much of your—

Flan:—life can I account for! *All*! I am a gambler!

(Pause.)

Ouisa: We're a terrible match. (*To us.*) Time passes. I read today that a
young man committed suicide in Riker's Island. Tied a shirt around
his neck and hanged himself. Was it the pink shirt? This burst of color?
The pink shirt. Was it Paul? Who are you? We never found out who
you are?

Flan: I'm sure it's not him. He'll be back. We haven't heard the last of
him. The imagination. He'll find a way. (*To us.*) We have to go. An
auction. I'll get the elevator.

(Flan goes.)

Ouisa (to us):   But if it was the pink shirt. Pink. A burst of pink. The
Sistine Chapel. They've cleaned it and it's all these colors.

Flan's Voice: Darling—

(Ouisa starts to go. She looks up. Paul is there, wearing the pink shirt.)

Paul: The Kandinsky. It's painted on two sides.

*(He glows for a moment and is gone. She considers. She smiles. The
Kandinsky begins it slow revolve.)*

Tina Howe   (b. 1937)

Tina Howe won the 1983 Obie Award for distinguished playwriting for Painting
Churches *(1983), her best-known play. The play centers on Mags, a woman who
returns home to paint a portrait of her parents, the Churches. The Churches, a
formidable pair, intellectual, accomplished, and self-possessed, are skeptical of their
daughter's artistic abilities—as is Mags herself—and most of the play explores her
and her parents' efforts at self-discovery. Among Howe's other works are* The Nest
(1969), Birth and Afterbirth *(1973),* Museum *(1976),* Coastal Disturbances
(1986), and Approaching Zanzibar *(1987), all of which have been well received.*
Teeth *(1990) follows a pattern typical of Howe's plays. In an interview she said, "I
take a familiar reality and lift it about six feet off the ground." She feels her plays
veer away from realism because they distort experience for dramatic purposes.*
Teeth, *for example, plays with the idea of permanence and solidity—especially
against the background music of Bach's "A Mighty Fortress Is Our God." Going to
the dentist is a common, if unsettling, experience, but in the hands of Tina Howe
it takes on metaphysical proportions that help us begin to question the solidity of
even the most obviously permanent aspects of our existence.*

TEETH   1990

*(Scene: A modest one-man dentist's office in midtown Manhattan. An FM
radio is tuned to a classical music station. It's March 21, Johann
Sebastian Bach's birthday, and Glenn Gould° is playing the rollicking*

Glenn Gould: Virtuoso Canadian pianist (1932–1982).

Presto from his Toccata in C minor. The whine of a high-powered dentist's drill slowly asserts itself. In blackout . . .)

Dr. Rose: Still with me . . . ?

Amy (garbled because his hands are in her mouth): Aaargh . . .

Dr. Rose (hums along as the drilling gets louder): You've heard his Goldberg reissue, haven't you?

Amy: Aaargh . . .

Dr. Rose (groans with pleasure): Unbelievable!

(The drilling gets ferocious.)

Amy: Ow . . . ow!

Dr. Rose: Woops, sorry about that. Okay, you can rinse. (*Lights up on Amy lying prone in a dentist's chair with a bib around her neck. She rises up, takes a swig of water, sloshes it around in her mouth, and spits it emphatically into the little bowl next to her. She flops back down, wiping her mouth. She's in her forties. Dr. Rose is several years older and on the disheveled side.)* Glenn Gould. Glenn Gould is the penultimate Bach keyboard artist of this century, period! Open, please. (*He resumes drilling.)* No one else can touch him!

Amy: Aarg . . .

Dr. Rose: Wanda Landowska, Roselyn Turek, Trevor Pinnock . . . forget it!

Amy: Aarg. . . .

Dr. Rose (Drilling with rising intensity): Andras Schiff, Igor Kipness, Anthony Newman . . . no contest!

Amy: Aarg . . .

Dr. Rose: Listen to the man . . . ! The elegance of his phrasing, the clarity of his touch . . . The joy! The Joy! (*He roars.)*

Amy (practically jumping out of her seat): Ooooowwwwwww!

Dr. Rose: Sorry, sorry, afraid I slipped. (*His drilling returns to normal.)* Hear how he hums along in a different key? The man can't contain himself . . . (*He roars again, then calms down for a spate of drilling. He idly starts humming along with Gould.)* You know, you're my third patient . . . no, make that fourth . . . that's pulled out a filling with candy this week. What was the culprit again?

Amy (garbled): Bit O'Honey.

Dr. Rose: Almond Roca . . . ?

Amy (garbled): Bit O'Honey.

Dr. Rose: Jujubes?

Amy (less garbled): Bit O'Honey, Bit O'Honey!

Dr. Rose: Yup, saltwater taffy will do it every time! Okay, Amy, the worst is over. You can rinse. (*He hangs up the drill. Amy rinses and spits with even more fury.)* Hey, hey, hey don't break my bowl on me! (*Fussing with his tools.)* Now, where did I put that probe . . . ? I can't seem to hold on to anything these days . . . (*Amy flops back down with a sigh.*

In a little singsong.) Where are you? . . . Where are you . . .? Ahhhhh,
here it is! Okay . . . let's just take one more last look before we fill you
up. Open. (*He disappears into her mouth with the probe.*) Amy, Amy,
you're still grinding your teeth at night, aren't you!

Amy (anguished):   Aaaaarrrrrrrhhh!

Dr. Rose: You've got to wear that rubber guard I gave you!

Amy (completely garbled):   But I can't breathe when it's on!

Amy (incomprehensible):   I feel like
I'm choking! I've tried to wear
it, I really have, I just always
wake up gasping for air. See, I
can't breathe through my nose.
If I could breathe through my
nose, it wouldn't be a
problem. . . .

Dr. Rose: I know they take getting
used to, but you're doing
irreparable damage to your
supporting bone layer, and
once that goes . . . (*He whistles
her fate.*)

(A radio announcer has come on in the background during this.)

Radio Announcer: That was Glenn Gould playing Bach's Toccata in C
minor, BWV listing 911. And to continue with our birthday tribute to
J. S. Bach, we now turn to his Cantata BWV 80, "Ein Feste Burg," as
performed by the English Chamber Orchestra under the direction of
Raymond Leppard. (*It begins.*)

Dr. Rose (comes out of her mouth):   Well, let's whip up a temporary filling
and get you out of here. (*He rummages through his tray of tools.*)

Amy: Dr. Rose, could I ask you something?

Dr. Rose: Of course, today's March twenty-first, Bach's birthday! (*Some
instruments fall; he quickly recovers them.*) Woops . . .

Amy: I keep having this recurring nightmare.

Dr. Rose: Oh, I love this piece. I used to sing it in college. Mind if I turn
it up?

Amy: I just wonder if you've heard it before.

*Dr. Rose (turns up the volume, singing along. He returns to his tray and
starts sorting out his things, which keep dropping. He quickly retrieves
them, never stopping his singing):*
"*Ein feste Burg ist unser Gott,*
Ein gute Wehr und Waffen. . . . woops.
Er hilft uns frei aus aller, Not,
Die uns itzt hat . . . woops . . . *betroffen.*"

Amy: I have it at least three times a week now.

Dr. Rose: I came this close to being a music major. *This* close!

Amy: I wake up exhausted with my whole jaw throbbing. Waa . . . waa
. . . waa!

Dr. Rose: Okay, let's just open this little bottle of cement here. (*He starts
struggling with the lid.*)

Amy: You know, the old . . . *teeth-granulating-on-you dream!* (*She stifles a sob.*) You're at a party flashing a perfect smile when suddenly you hear this splintering sound like someone smashing teacups in the next room. . . . ping . . . tock . . . crackkkkkkkkkk . . . tinkle, tinkle. "Well, someone's having a good time!" you say to yourself, expecting to see some maniac swinging a sledgehammer. . . .

(Having a worse and worse time with the bottle, Dr. Rose moves behind her chair so she can't see him.)

Dr. Rose: Ugh . . . ugh . . . ugh . . . ugh . . . ugh!

Amy: So you casually look around, and of course there *is* no maniac . . . ! Then you feel these prickly shards clinging to your lips. . . . You try and brush them away, but suddenly your mouth is filled with them. You can't spit them out fast enough! (*She tries.*)

Dr. Rose: Goddamnit! (*He goes through a series of silent contortions trying to open it—behind his back, up over his head, down between his legs, etc. etc.*)

Amy (still spitting and wiping): People are starting to stare. . . . You try to save face. (*To the imagined partygoers.*) "Well, what do you know. . . . I seem to have taken a bite out of my coffee cup! Silly me!" (*She laughs, frantically wiping.*)

Dr. Rose: Goddamn son of a bitch, what's going on here?

Amy: That's just what *I* want to know!

Dr. Rose: Is this some kind of conspiracy or what?

Amy: Why me? What did I do?

Dr. Rose: They must weld these tops on.

Amy: Then I catch a glimpse of myself in the mirror . . .

Dr. Rose (starting to cackle): Think you can outsmart me . . . ? (*He starts whacking a heavy tool down on the lid.*)

Amy: You got it! My teeth are spilling out of my mouth in little pieces. I frantically try and moosh them back in, but there's nothing to hold on to. Then they start granulating on me . . . fsssssssssssssssss. . . . It's like trying to build a sand castle inside an hourglass! (*Dr. Rose is having a worse and worse time. He finally just sits on the floor and bangs the bottle down as hard as he can, again and again.*) My mouth is a blaze of gums. We are talking pink for *miles* . . . ! Magellan staring out over the Pacific Ocean during a sunset in 1520—(*As Magellan.*) "Pink . . . pink . . . pink . . . pink!" (*Dr. Rose starts to whimper as he pounds.*) What does it *mean*, is what I'd like to know! I mean, teeth are supposed to last forever, right? They hold up through floods, fires, earthquakes, and wars . . . the one part of us that endures.

Dr. Rose: Open, damnit. Open, damnit. Open, damnit. . . .

Amy: So if they granulate on you, where does that leave you? *Nowhere!*

Dr. Rose (curls into the fetal position and focuses on smaller moves in a tiny voice): Come on . . . come on . . . Please? Pretty please? Pretty, lovely, ravishing please?

Amy: You could have been rain or wind, for all anybody knows. That's
pretty scary . . . (*Starting to get weepy.*) One minute you're laughing at
a party and the next you've evaporated into thin air. . . . (*Putting on a
voice.*) "Remember Amy? Gee, I wonder whatever happened to her?"
(*In another voice.*) "Gosh, it's suddenly gotten awfully chilly in here.
Where's that *wind* coming from?" (*Teary again.*) I mean, we're not
around for that long as it is, so then to suddenly . . . I'm sorry, I'm
sorry. It's just I have this um . . . long-standing . . . Oh, God, here we
go . . . (*Starting to break down.*) Control yourself! Control . . .
control! (*Dr. Rose is now rolled up in a ball beyond speech. He clutches
the bottle, whimpering and emitting strange little sobs.*) See, I have this
long-standing um . . . fear of death? It's something you're born with. I
used to sob in my father's arms when I was only . . . Oh, boy! See,
once you start thinking about it, I mean . . . *really* thinking about it
. . . You know, time going on for ever and ever and ever and ever and
you're not there. . . . It can get pretty scary . . . ! We're not talking
missing out on a few measly centuries here, but all . . . time! You
know, dinosaurs, camel trains, cities, holy wars, boom! and back to
dinosaurs again? (*More and more weepy.*) Eternity! . . . Camel trains,
cities, holy wars, boom! Dinosaurs, camel trains, cities, holy wars,
boom! . . . Dinosaurs, camel trains, cities, holy wars. . . . Stop it
Amy. . . . just . . . *stop it*!
Dr. Rose (broken):   I can't open this bottle.
Amy (wiping away her tears):   Dr. Rose! What are you doing down there?
Dr. Rose: I've tried everything.
Amy: What's wrong?
Dr. Rose (reaching the bottle up to her):   I can't open it.
Amy (taking it):   Oh, here, let me try.
Dr. Rose: I'm afraid I'm having a breakdown.
Amy: I'm good at this kind of thing.
Dr. Rose: I don't know, for some time now I just haven't . . .
*Amy (puts the bottle in her mouth, clamps down on it with her back teeth, and
unscrews the lid with one turn. She hands it back to him):*   Here you go.
Dr. Rose (rises and advances toward her menacingly):   You should never
. . . *Never do that!*
Amy (drawing back):   What?
Dr. Rose: Open a bottle with your teeth.
Amy: I do it all the time.
Dr. Rose: Teeth are very fragile. They're not meant to be used as tools!
Amy: Sorry, sorry.
Dr. Rose: I just don't believe the way people mistreat them. We're only
given one set of permanent teeth in a lifetime. *One set and that's it!*
Amy: I won't do it again. I promise.
Dr. Rose: Species flourish and disappear, only our teeth remain. Open,
please. (*He puts cotton wadding in her mouth.*) You must respect them,

take care of them. . . . Oh, why even bother talking about it; no one ever listens to me, anyway. Wider, please. (*He puts in more cotton and a bubbling saliva drain.*) Okay, let's fill this baby and get you on your way. (*He dabs in bits of compound.*) So, how's work these days?

Amy: Aarg . . .

Dr. Rose: Same old rat race, huh?

Amy: Aarg . . . (*During this, the final chorus, "Das Wort sie sollen lassen stahn" has started to play. Slightly garbled.*) What is that tune? It's so familiar.

Dr. Rose: "A Mighty Fortress Is Our God."

Amy: Right, right! I used to sing it in Sunday school a hundred years ago.

Dr. Rose: Actually, Bach stole the melody from Martin Luther.

Amy (bursts into song, garbled, the saliva drain bubbling): "A Mighty Fortress Is Our God . . ."

Amy: . . . a bulwark never failing . . .
Our helper he amid the flood
of mortal ills prevailing.
For still our ancient foe,
Doth seek to work us woe . . .

Dr. Rose (joining her): . . . Und
kein' Dank dazu haben,
Er ist bei uns wehl auf dem Plan
Mit seinem Geist und Gaben.
Nehmen sie uns den Leib,
Gut, Ehr, Kind und Weib. . . .

(*Their voices swell louder and louder.*)

75

80

Window On

Feminist Drama

Feminist drama takes a special interest in the psychosocial circumstances of women. Historically, women have been deprived of property rights, choice of husbands, education, careers, and the vote. Yet they have figured largely in drama from the time of the Greeks to the present. When women became playwrights—the first professional in England was Aphra Behn in the late 1660s—they did not immediately become feminists. Their themes were often similar to their male counterparts. However, in the nineteenth century feminist themes emerged in fiction, poetry, and drama.

Intellectual circles in Scandinavia were especially receptive to feminist ideas in the latter part of the century. The popular press, newspapers, and the stage all examined issues of considerable importance to women. The most important related to a woman's right to direct her own life as she chose. The traditional view had always been that a woman must defer to her husband or father in all matters of importance. Such views were questioned by those in a position to think independently.

Strindberg, although he developed into a misogynist, explored important aspects of feminist thought in *Miss Julie*. Julie is a willful woman who wishes to dominate the man in her life. The breaking-off of her planned marriage is described in enough detail to make us think that her husband-to-be could not accept her authority. The shadow of her father, the Count, affects not only Jean the servant, but Julie, the daughter. The tragic ending of the play suggests the dimension of the problem of any woman who wished to be independent of male authority in Strindberg's Sweden.

Henrik Ibsen, also a Scandinavian, took part in feminist debates. *Hedda Gabler* and *A Doll House* are among the foremost feminist plays of the century, but they also reach beyond their own century. Both plays are still produced today throughout the world. Hedda Gabler is dominated by the image of a powerful father. His emblems are military and his authority absolute. In many ways Hedda has shaped herself in his image, and the result is that the men in her life are weaklings in comparison with her. Nora in *A Doll House* shocked the middle-class nineteenth-century audience by slamming the door on her prim, protected, unbearable life and taking her chances in the real world. In Ingmar Bergman's 1991 production, Nora does not slam the door on the stage set but strides offstage into the audience and slams the door of the theater itself. The message is clear: even today, more than a hundred years after its original production, Nora's problems beset women sitting in modern audiences watching her agony.

Feminist issues, which usually center on the restrictions on the freedom of women to choose their own paths in life, are not restricted to women writers. Women playwrights do not automatically qualify as feminists, as we can see from reading Susan Glaspell's *Suppressed Desires*. In that play her primary interests are elsewhere. However, even when a playwright focuses on other issues, the feminist critic may see matters of importance. For example, feminist critics have found the portrayal of women in Tennessee William's plays, including *The Glass Menagerie*, as especially pertinent. The question of Laura Wingfield's acceptance of her mother's values is particularly telling in the play. Amanda Wingfield has chosen to define herself in terms of a husband, even though she has no husband at the time of the action. Laura, therefore, must do the same, although she is completely different from her mother and is not likely to attract a beau. The pain involved in the play is connected directly to that issue, which is, among other things, a feminist issue.

Reading

Betsko, Kathleen, and Rachel Koenig. *Interviews with Contemporary Women Playwrights*. New York: Beech Tree, 1987.

Hardwick, Elizabeth. *Seduction and Betrayal*. New York: Random, 1974.

Moore, Honor. *The New Women's Theatre.* New York: Random, 1977.
Styan, J. L. *Modern Drama in Theory and Practice.* 3 vols. New York: Cambridge University Press, 1980.
Sullivan, Victoria, and James Hatch. *Plays by and about Women.* New York: Random, 1973.
Wandor, Marlene. *Plays by Women.* 8 vols. London: Methuen, 1990.

David Mamet   (b. 1947)

One of the most prolific and fascinating of contemporary American playwrights, Mamet has established himself as a powerful voice in international theater. He has also written several film scripts which have made his work known to many who have not seen his stage plays. Among the most important of his plays are Sexual Perversity in Chicago *(1976),* Duck Variations *(1976),* A Life in the Theatre *(1978),* Sketches of War *(1988), and* Where Were You When It Went Down *(1991). His screenplays include* House of Games *(1987), which he also directed. His plays are a searing analysis of contemporary life, from the seamy world of petty criminals in* American Buffalo *(1975) to the pretentious backbiting of Hollywood in* Speed the Plow *(1988) and the dishonest delusions of real estate schemes in* Glen Garry Glen Ross *(1983).* Oleanna *(1992) is an excursion not only into the relations of professor and student in a university but also into the entire issue of male and female power and the various ways in which the expectations of each gender can be frustrated. It also explores the ways in which power can shift suddenly, depending on motive and opportunity. Mamet's examination of these issues is designed to arouse the ire of those who support either side of the equation. "Oleanna" is the name of a Norwegian folk tune popular with college glee clubs in the 1950s.*

OLEANNA   1992

The want of fresh air does not seem much to affect the happiness of children in a London alley: the greater part of them sing and play as though they were on a moor in Scotland. So the absence of a genial mental atmosphere is not commonly recognized by children who have never known it. Young people have a marvelous faculty of either dying or adapting themselves to circumstances. Even if they are unhappy—very unhappy—it is astonishing how easily they can be prevented from finding it out, or at any rate from attributing it to any other cause than their own sinfulness.

> *The Way of All Flesh*
> Samuel Butler

"Oh, to be in *Oleanna,*
That's where I would rather be.
Than be bound in Norway
And drag the chains of slavery."

—folk song

Characters

    Carol, A woman of twenty   *John,* A man in his forties

    (The play takes place in John's office.)

ONE

    (John is talking on the phone. Carol is seated across the desk from him.)

John *(on phone):* And what about the land. (*Pause.*) The land. And what about the land? (*Pause.*) What about it? (*Pause.*) No. I don't understand. Well, yes, I'm I'm . . . no, I'm *sure* it's signif . . . I'm sure it's significant. (*Pause.*) Because it's significant to mmmmmm . . . did you call Jerry? (*Pause.*) Because . . . no, no, no, no, no. What did they say . . . ? Did you speak to the *real* estate . . . where *is* she . . . ? Well, well, all right. Where are her notes? Where are the notes we took with her. (*Pause.*) I thought you were? No. No, I'm sorry, I didn't mean that, I just thought that I saw you, when we were there . . . what . . . ? I thought I saw you with a *pencil.* WHY NOW? is what I'm say . . . well, that's why I say "call Jerry." Well, I can't right now, be . . . no, I *didn't* schedule any . . . Grace: I *didn't* . . . I'm well aware . . . Look: Look. Did you call Jerry? Will you call Jerry . . . ? Because I can't now. I'll be there, I'm sure I'll be there in fifteen, in twenty. I intend to. No, we aren't *going* to lose the, we aren't *going* to lose the house. Look: Look, I'm not minimizing it. The "easement." Did she say "easement"? (*Pause.*) What did she *say; is* it a "term of art," are we *bound* by it . . . I'm sorry . . . (*pause*) are: we: yes. *Bound* by . . . Look: (*he checks his watch*) before the other side *goes home,* all right? "a term of art." Because: that's right. (*Pause.*) The yard for the boy. Well, that's the whole . . . Look: I'm going to meet you there . . . (*He checks his watch.*) Is the realtor there? All right, tell her to show you the basement again. Look at the *this* because . . . Bec . . . I'm leaving in, I'm leaving in ten or fifteen . . . Yes. No, no, I'll meet you at the new . . . That's a good. If he thinks it's necc . . . you tell Jerry to meet . . . All right? We *aren't* going to lose the deposit. All right? I'm sure it's going to be . . . (*Pause.*) I hope so. (*Pause.*) I love you, too. (*Pause.*) I love you, too. As soon as . . . I will. (*He hangs up. He bends over the desk and makes a note. He looks up. To Carol.*) I'm sorry . . .

Carol *(pause):* What is a "term of art"?

John *(pause):* I'm sorry . . . ?

Carol *(pause):* What is a "term of art"?

John: Is that what you want to talk about?

Carol: . . . to talk about . . . ?

John: Let's take the mysticism out of it, shall we? Carol? (*Pause.*) Don't you think? I'll tell you: when you have some "thing." Which must be broached. (*Pause.*) Don't you think . . . ? (*Pause.*)

Carol: . . . don't I think . . . ?

John: Mmm?

Carol: . . . did I . . . ?

John: . . . what?

Carol: Did . . . did I . . . did I say something wr . . .

John (pause): No. I'm sorry. No. You're right. I'm very sorry. I'm somewhat rushed. As you see. I'm sorry. You're right. (*Pause.*) What is a "term of art"? It seems to mean a *term*, which has come, through its use, to mean something *more specific* than the words would, to someone *not acquainted* with them . . . indicate. That, I believe, is what a "term of art," would mean. (*Pause.*)

Carol: You don't know what it means . . . ?

John: I'm not sure that I know what it means. It's one of those things, perhaps you've had them, that, you look them up, or have someone explain them to you, and you say "aha," and, you immediately *forget* what . . .

Carol: You don't do that.

John: . . . I . . . ?

Carol: You don't do . . .

John: . . . I don't, what . . . ?

Carol: . . . for . . .

John: . . . I don't for . . .

Carol: . . . no . . .

John: . . . forget things? Everybody does that.

Carol: No, they don't.

John: They don't . . .

Carol: No.

John (pause): No. Everybody does that.

Carol: Why would they do that . . . ?

John: Because. I don't know. Because it doesn't interest them.

Carol: No.

John: I think so, though. (*Pause.*) I'm sorry that I was distracted.

Carol: You don't have to say that to me.

John: You paid me the compliment, or the "obeisance"—all right—of coming in here . . . All right. *Carol.* I find that I am at a *standstill.* I find that I . . .

Carol: . . . what . . .

John: . . . one moment. In regard to your . . . to your . . .

Carol: Oh, oh. You're buying a new house!

John: No, let's get on with it.

Carol: "get on"? (*Pause.*)

John: I know how . . . *believe* me. I know how . . . potentially *humiliating* these . . . I have no desire to . . . I have no desire other than to help you. But: (*He picks up some papers on his desk.*) I won't even say "but." I'll say that as I go back over the . . .

Carol: I'm just, I'm just trying to . . .

John: . . . no, it will not do.

Carol: . . . what? What will . . . ?

John: No. I see, I see what you, it . . . (*he gestures to the papers*) but your work . . .

Carol: I'm just: I sit in class I . . . (*She holds up her notebook.*) I take notes . . .

John (simultaneously with "notes"):   Yes. I understand. What I am trying to *tell* you is that some, some basic . . .

Carol: . . . I . . .

John: . . . one moment: some basic missed communi . . .

Carol: I'm doing what I'm told. I bought your book, I read your . . .

John: No, I'm sure you . . .

Carol: No, no, no. I'm doing what I'm told. It's *difficult* for me. It's *difficult* . . .

John: . . . but . . .

Carol: I don't . . . lots of the *language* . . .

John: . . . please . . .

Carol: The *language*, the "things" that you say . . .

John: I'm sorry. No. I don't think that that's true.

Carol: It *is* true. I . . .

John: I think . . .

Carol: It *is* true.

John: . . . I . . .

Carol: Why would I . . . ?

John: I'll tell you why: you're an incredibly bright girl.

Carol: . . . I . . .

John: You're an incredibly . . . you have no problem with the . . . Who's kidding who?

Carol: . . . I . . .

John: No. No. I'll tell you why. I'll tell. . . . I think you're *angry*, I . . .

Carol: . . . why would I . . .

John: . . . wait one moment. I . . .

Carol: It *is* true. I have *problems* . . .

John: . . . every . . .

Carol: . . . I come from a different *social* . . .

John: . . . ev . . .

Carol: a different economic . . .

John: . . . Look:

Carol: No. I: when I *came* to this school:

John: Yes. Quite . . . (*Pause.*)

Carol: . . . does that mean nothing . . . ?

John: . . . but look: look . . .

Carol: . . . I . . .

John (picks up paper):   Here: Please: Sit down. (*Pause.*) Sit down. (*Reads from her paper.*) "I think that the ideas contained in this work express

the author's feelings in a way that he intended, based on his results."
What can that mean? Do you see? What . . .

Carol: I, the best that I . . .

John: I'm saying, that perhaps this course . . .

Carol: No, no, no, you can't, you can't . . . I have to . . .

John: . . . how . . .

Carol: . . . I have to pass it . . .

John: Carol, I:

Carol: I *have* to pass this course, I . . .

John: Well.

Carol: . . . don't you . . .

John: Either the . . .

Carol: . . . I . . .

John: . . . either the, I . . . either the *criteria* for judging progress in the class are . . .

Carol: No, no, no, no, I have to pass it.

John: Now, look: I'm a human being, I . . .

Carol: I did what you told me. I did, I did everything that, I read your *book*, you told me to buy your book and read it. Everything you *say* I . . . (*She gestures to her notebook. The phone rings.*) I do. . . . Ev . . .

John: . . . look:

Carol: . . . everything I'm told . . .

John: Look. Look. I'm not your *father*. (*Pause.*)

Carol: What?

John: I'm.

Carol: Did I say you were my father?

John: . . . no . . .

Carol: Why did you say that . . . ?

John: I . . .

Carol: . . . why . . . ?

John: . . . in class I . . . (*He picks up the phone. Into phone.*) Hello. I can't talk now. Jerry? Yes? I underst . . . I can't talk now. I know . . . I know . . . Jerry. I can't *talk* now. Yes, I. Call me back in . . . Thank you. (*He hangs up. To Carol.*) What do you want me to do? We are two people, all right? Both of whom have subscribed to . . .

Carol: No, no . . .

John: . . . certain arbitrary . . .

Carol: No. You have to help me.

John: Certain institutional . . . you tell me what you want me to do. . . . You tell me what you want me to . . .

Carol: How can I go back and tell them the *grades* that I . . .

John: . . . what can I do . . . ?

Carol: *Teach* me. *Teach* me.

John: . . . I'm trying to teach you.

Carol: I read your book. I read it. I don't under . . .

John: . . . you don't understand it.

Carol: No.

John: Well, perhaps it's not well *written* . . .

Carol (*simultaneously with* "written"):   No. No. No. I want to *understand* it.

John: What don't you understand? (*Pause.*)

Carol: *Any* of it. What you're trying to say. When you talk about . . .

John: . . . yes . . . ? (*She consults her notes.*)

Carol: "Virtual warehousing of the young" . . .

John: "Virtual warehousing of the young." If we artificially prolong adolescence . . .

Carol: . . . and about "The Curse of Modern Education."

John: . . . well . . .

Carol: I don't . . .

John: Look. It's just a *course*, it's just a *book*, it's just a . . .

Carol: No. No. There are *people* out there. People who came *here*. To know something they didn't *know*. Who *came* here. To be *helped*. To be *helped*. So someone would *help* them. To *do* something. To *know* something. To get, what do they say? "To get on in the world." How can I do that if I don't, if I fail? But I don't *understand*. I don't *understand*. I don't understand what anything means . . . and I walk around. From morning 'til night: with this one thought in my head. I'm *stupid*.

John: No one thinks you're stupid.

Carol: No? What am I . . . ?

John: I . . .

Carol: . . . what am I, then?

John: I think you're angry. Many people are. I have a *telephone* call that I have to make. And an *appointment*, which is rather *pressing*; though I sympathize with your concerns, and though I wish I had the time, this was not a previously scheduled meeting and I . . .

Carol: . . . you think I'm nothing . . .

John: . . . have an appointment with a *realtor*, and with my wife and . . .

Carol: You think that I'm stupid.

John: No. I certainly don't.

Carol: You said it.

John: No. I did not.

Carol: You did.

John: When?

Carol: . . . you . . .

John: No. I never did, or never would say that to a student, and . . .

Carol: You said, "What can that mean?" (*Pause.*) "What can that mean?" . . . (*Pause.*)

John: . . . and what did that mean to you . . . ?

Carol: That meant I'm stupid. And I'll never learn. That's what that meant. And you're right.

John: . . . I . . .

Carol: But then. But then, what am I doing here . . . ?

John: . . . if you thought that I . . .

Carol: . . . when nobody wants me, and . . .

John: . . . if you interpreted . . .

Carol: Nobody *tells* me anything. And I *sit* there . . . in the *corner*. In the *back*. And everybody's talking about "this" all the time. And "concepts," and "precepts" and, and, and, and, and, WHAT IN THE WORLD ARE YOU *TALKING* ABOUT? And I read your book. And they said, "Fine, go in that class." Because you talked about responsibility to the young. I DON'T KNOW WHAT IT MEANS AND I'M *FAILING* . . .

John: May . . .

Carol: No, you're right. "Oh, hell." I failed. Flunk me out of it. It's garbage. Everything I do. "The ideas contained in this work express the author's feelings." That's right. That's right. I know I'm stupid. I know what I am. (*Pause.*) I know what I am, Professor. You don't have to tell me. (*Pause.*) It's pathetic. Isn't it?

John: . . . Aha . . . (*Pause.*) Sit down. Sit down. Please. (*Pause.*) Please sit down.

Carol: Why?

John: I want to talk to you.

Carol: Why?

John: Just sit down. (*Pause.*) Please. Sit down. Will you, please . . . ? (*Pause. She does so.*) Thank you.

Carol: What?

John: I want to tell you something.

Carol (pause):   What?

John: Well, I know what you're talking about.

Carol: No. You don't.

John: I think I do. (*Pause.*)

Carol: How can you?

John: I'll tell you a story about myself. (*Pause.*) Do you mind? (*Pause.*) I was raised to think myself stupid. That's what I want to tell you. (*Pause.*)

Carol: What do you mean?

John: Just what I said. I was brought up, and my earliest, and most persistent memories are of being told that I was stupid. "You have such *intelligence*. Why must you behave so *stupidly*?" Or, "Can't you *understand*? Can't you *understand*?" And I could *not* understand. I could *not* understand.

Carol: What?

John: The simplest problem. Was beyond me. It was a mystery.

Carol: What was a mystery?

John: How people learn. How *I* could learn. Which is what I've been speaking of in class. And of *course* you can't hear it. Carol. Of *course* you can't. (*Pause.*) I used to speak of "real people," and wonder what the *real* people did. The *real* people. Who were they? *They* were the people other than myself. The *good* people. The *capable* people. The people who could do the things, *I* could not do: learn, study, retain . . . all that *garbage*—which is what I have been talking of in class, and that's *exactly* what I have been talking of—If you are told. . . . Listen to this. If the young child is told he cannot understand. Then he takes it as a *description* of himself. What am I? I am *that which cannot understand.* And I saw you out there, when we were speaking of the concepts of . . .

Carol: I can't understand any of them.

John: Well, then, that's *my* fault. That's not your fault. And that is not verbiage. That's what I firmly hold to be the truth. And I am sorry, and I owe you an apology.

Carol: Why?

John: And I suppose that I have had some *things* on my mind. . . . We're buying a *house,* and . . .

Carol: People said that you were stupid . . . ?

John: Yes.

Carol: When?

John: I'll tell you when. Through my life. In my childhood; and, perhaps, they stopped. But I heard them continue.

Carol: And what did they say?

John: They said I was incompetent. Do you see? And when I'm tested the, the, the *feelings* of my youth about the *very subject of learning* come up. And I . . . I become, I feel "unworthy," and "unprepared." . . .

Carol: . . . yes.

John: . . . eh?

Carol: . . . yes.

John: And I feel that I must fail. (*Pause.*)

Carol: . . . but then you *do* fail. (*Pause.*) You have to. (*Pause.*) Don't you?

John: A *pilot.* Flying a plane. The pilot is flying the plane. He thinks: Oh, my *God,* my mind's been drifting! Oh, my God! What kind of a cursed imbecile am I, that I, with this so precious cargo of *Life* in my charge, would allow my attention to wander. Why was I born? How deluded are those who put their trust in me, . . . et cetera, so on, and he crashes the plane.

Carol (pause): He could just . . .

John: That's right.

Carol: He could say:

John: My attention *wandered* for a moment . . .

Carol: . . . uh huh . . .

John: I had a *thought* I did not like . . . but now:

Carol: . . . but now it's . . .

John: That's what I'm telling you. It's time to put my attention . . . see: it is not: this is what I learned. It is Not Magic. Yes. Yes. *You.* You are going to be frightened. When faced with what may or may not be but which you are going to perceive as a test. You will become frightened. And you will say: "I am incapable of . . ." and everything *in* you will think these two things. "I must. But I can't." And you will think: Why was I born to be the laughingstock of a world in which everyone is better than I? In which I am entitled to nothing. Where I cannot learn.

(Pause.)

Carol: Is that . . . (*Pause.*) Is that what I have . . . ?

John: Well. I don't know if I'd put it that way. Listen: I'm talking to you as I'd talk to my son. Because that's what I'd like him to have that I never had. I'm talking to you the way I wish that someone had talked to me. I don't know how to do it, other than to be *personal*, . . . but . . .

Carol: Why would you want to be personal with me?

John: Well, you see? That's what I'm saying. We can only interpret the behavior of others through the screen we . . . (*The phone rings.*) Through . . . (*To phone.*) Hello . . . ? (*To Carol.*) Through the screen we create. (*To phone.*) Hello. (*To Carol.*) Excuse me a moment. (*To phone.*) Hello? No, I can't talk nnn . . . I know I did. In a few . . . I'm . . . is he coming to the . . . yes. I talked to him. We'll meet you at the No, because I'm with a *student*. It's going to be fff . . . This is important, too. I'm with a *student*, Jerry's going to . . . Listen: the sooner I get off, the sooner I'll be down, all right. I love you. Listen, listen, I said "I love you," it's going to work *out* with the, because I feel that it is, I'll be right down. All right? Well, then it's going to take as long as it takes. (*He hangs up. To Carol.*) I'm sorry.

Carol: What was that?

John: There are some problems, as there usually are, about the final agreements for the new house.

Carol: You're buying a new house.

John: That's right.

Carol: Because of your promotion.

John: Well, I suppose that that's right.

Carol: Why did you stay here with me?

John: Stay here.

Carol: Yes. When you should have gone.

John: Because I like you.

Carol: You like me.

John: Yes.

Carol: Why?

John: Why? Well? Perhaps we're similar. (*Pause.*) Yes. (*Pause.*)

Carol: You said "everyone has problems."

John: Everyone has problems.

Carol: Do they?

John: Certainly.

Carol: You do?

John: Yes.

Carol: What are they?

John: Well. (*Pause.*) Well, you're perfectly right. (*Pause.*) If we're going to take off the Artificial *Stricture*, of "Teacher," and "Student," why should *my* problems be any more a mystery than your own? Of *course* I have problems. As you saw.

Carol: . . . with what?

John: With my *wife* . . . with *work* . . .

Carol: With work?

John: Yes. And, and, perhaps my problems are, do you see? *Similar* to yours.

Carol: Would you tell me?

John: All right. (*Pause.*) I came *late* to teaching. And I found it Artificial. The notion of "I know and you do not"; and I saw an *exploitation* in the education process. I told you. I hated school, I hated teachers. I hated everyone who was in the position of a "boss" because I *knew*—I didn't *think*, mind you, I *knew* I was going to fail. Because I was a fuckup. I was just no goddamned good. When I . . . late in life . . . (*Pause.*) When I *got out from under* . . . when I worked my way out of the need to fail. When I . . .

Carol: How do you do that? (*Pause.*)

John: You have to look at what you are, and what you feel, and how you act. And, finally, you have to look at how you act. And say: If that's what I *did*, that must be how I think of myself.

Carol: I don't understand.

John: If I fail all the time, it must be that I think of myself as a failure. If I do not want to think of myself as a failure, perhaps I should begin by *succeeding* now and again. Look. The tests, you see, which you encounter, in school, in college, in life, were designed, in the most part, for idiots. *By* idiots. There is no need to fail at them. They are not a test of your worth. They are a test of your ability to retain and spout back misinformation. Of *course* you fail them. They're *nonsense*. And I . . .

Carol: . . . no . . .

John: Yes. They're *garbage*. They're a *joke*. Look at me. Look at me. The Tenure Committee. The Tenure Committee. Come to judge me. The Bad Tenure Committee.
    The "Test." Do you see? They put me to the test. Why, they had people voting on me I wouldn't employ to wax my car. And yet, I go before the Great Tenure Committee, and I have an urge, to *vomit*, to,

to, to puke my *badness* on the table, to show them: "I'm no good. Why would you pick *me*?"

Carol: They granted you tenure.

John: Oh no, they announced it, but they haven't *signed*. Do you see? "At any moment . . ."

Carol: . . . mmm . . .

John: "They might not *sign*" . . . I might not . . . the *house* might not go through . . . Eh? Eh? They'll find out my "dark secret." (*Pause.*)

Carol: . . . what is it . . . ?

John: There *isn't* one. But *they* will find an index of my badness . . .

Carol: Index?

John: A ". . . pointer." A "Pointer." You see? Do you see? I *understand* you. I. Know. That. Feeling. Am I entitled to my job, and my nice *home*, and my *wife*, and my *family*, and so on. This is what I'm saying: That theory of education which, that *theory*:

Carol: I . . . I . . . (*Pause.*)

John: What?

Carol: I . . .

John: What?

Carol: I want to know about my grade. (*Long pause.*)

John: Of course you do.

Carol: Is that bad?

John: No.

Carol: Is it bad that I asked you that?

John: No.

Carol: Did I upset you?

John: No. And I apologize. Of *course* you want to know about your grade. And, of course, you can't concentrate on anyth . . . (*The telephone starts to ring.*) Wait a moment.

Carol: I should go.

John: I'll make you a deal.

Carol: No, you have to . . .

John: Let it ring. I'll make you a deal. You stay here. We'll start the whole course over. I'm going to say it was not you, it was I who was not paying attention. We'll start the whole course over. Your grade is an "A." Your final grade is an "A." (*The phone stops ringing.*)

Carol: But the class is only half over . . .

John (*simultaneously with* "over"):   Your grade for the whole term is an "A." If you will come back and meet with me. A few more times. Your grade's an "A." Forget about the paper. You didn't like it, you didn't like writing it. It's not important. What's important is that I awake your interest, if I can, and that I answer your questions. Let's start over. (*Pause.*)

Carol: Over. With what?

John: Say this is the beginning.

Carol: The beginning.

John: Yes.

Carol: Of what?

John: Of the class.

Carol: But we can't start over.

John: I say we can. (*Pause.*) I say we can.

Carol: But I don't believe it.

John: Yes, I know that. But it's true. What is The Class but you and me? (*Pause.*)

Carol: There are rules.

John: Well. We'll break them.

Carol: How can we?

John: We won't tell anybody.

Carol: Is that all right?

John: I say that it's fine.

Carol: Why would you do this for me?

John: I like you. Is that so difficult for you to . . .

Carol: Um . . .

John: There's no one here but you and me. (*Pause.*)

Carol: All right. I did not understand. When you referred . . .

John: All right, yes?

Carol: When you referred to hazing.

John: Hazing.

Carol: You wrote, in your book. About the comparative . . . the comparative . . . (*She checks her notes.*)

John: Are you checking your notes . . . ?

Carol: Yes.

John: Tell me in your own . . .

Carol: I want to make sure that I have it right.

John: No. Of course. You want to be exact.

Carol: I want to know everything that went on.

John: . . . that's good.

Carol: . . . so I . . .

John: That's very good. But I was suggesting, many times, that that which we wish to retain is retained oftentimes, I think, *better* with less expenditure of effort.

Carol (of notes):   Here it is: you wrote of *hazing*.

John: . . . that's correct. Now: I said "hazing." It means ritualized annoyance. We shove this book at you, we say read it. Now, you say you've read it? I think that you're *lying*. I'll *grill* you, and when I find you've lied, you'll be disgraced, and your life will be ruined. It's a sick game. Why do we do it? Does it educate? In no sense. Well, then, what is higher education? It is something-other-than-useful.

Carol: What is "something-other-than-useful?"

John: It has become a ritual, it has become an article of faith. That all must be subjected to, or to put it differently, that all are entitled to Higher Education. And my point . . .

Carol: You disagree with that?

John: Well, let's address that. What do you think?

Carol: I don't know.

John: What do you think, though? (*Pause.*)

Carol: I don't know.

John: I spoke of it in class. Do you remember my example?

Carol: Justice.

John: Yes. Can you repeat it to me? (*She looks down at her notebook.*) Without your notes? I ask you as a favor to me, so that I can see if my idea was interesting.

Carol: You said "justice" . . .

John: Yes?

Carol: . . . that all are entitled . . . (*Pause.*) I . . . I . . . I . . .

John: Yes. To a speedy trial. To a fair trial. But they needn't be given a trial *at all* unless they stand accused. Eh? Justice is their right, should they choose to avail themselves of it, they should have a fair trial. It does not follow, of necessity, a person's life is incomplete without a trial in it. Do you see?

My point is a confusion between equity and *utility* arose. So we confound the *usefulness* of higher education with our, granted, right to equal access to the same. We, in effect, create a *prejudice* toward it, completely independent of . . .

Carol: . . . that it is prejudice that we should go to school?

John: Exactly. (*Pause.*)

Carol: How can you say that? How . . .

John: Good. Good. *Good.* That's right! Speak up! What is a prejudice? An unreasoned belief. We are all subject to it. None of us is not. When it is threatened, or opposed, we feel anger, and feel, do we not? As you do now. Do you not? Good.

Carol: . . . but how can you . . .

John: . . . let us examine. Good.

Carol: How . . .

John: Good. Good. When . . .

Carol: I'M SPEAKING . . . (*Pause.*)

John: I'm sorry.

Carol: How can you . . .

John: . . . I beg your pardon.

Carol: That's all right.

John: I beg your pardon.

Carol: That's all right.

John: I'm sorry I interrupted you.

Carol: That's all right.

John: You were saying?

Carol: I was saying . . . I was saying . . . (*She checks her notes.*) How can you say in a class. Say in a college class, that college education is prejudice?

John: I said that our predilection for it . . .

Carol: Predilection . . .

John: . . . you know what that means.

Carol: Does it mean "liking"?

John: Yes.

Carol: But how can you say that? That College . . .

John: . . . that's my *job*, don't you know.

Carol: What is?

John: To provoke you.

Carol: No.

John: Oh. Yes, though.

Carol: To provoke me?

John: That's right.

Carol: To make me mad?

John: That's right. To force you . . .

Carol: . . . to make me mad is your job?

John: To force you to . . . listen: (*Pause.*) Ah. (*Pause.*) When I was young somebody told me, are you ready, the rich copulate less often than the poor. But when they do, they take more of their clothes off. Years. Years, mind you, I would compare experiences of my own to this dictum, saying, aha, this fits the norm, or ah, this is a variation from it. What did it mean? Nothing. It was some jerk thing, some school kid told me that took up room inside my head. (*Pause.*)

   Somebody told *you*, and you hold it as an article of faith, that higher education is an unassailable good. This notion is so dear to you that when I question it you become angry. Good. Good, I say. Are not those the very things which we should question? I say college education, since the war, has become so a matter of course, and such a fashionable necessity, for those either of or aspiring *to* to the new vast middle class, that we *espouse* it, as a matter of right, and have ceased to ask, "What is it good for?" (*Pause.*)

   What might be some reasons for pursuit of higher education?

   One: A love of learning.

   Two: The wish for mastery of a skill.

   Three: For economic betterment.

   (*Stops. Makes a note.*)

Carol: I'm keeping you.

John: One moment. I have to make a note . . .

Carol: It's something that I said?

John: No, we're buying a house.

Carol: You're buying the new house.

John: To go with the tenure. That's right. Nice *house*, close to the *private school* . . . (*He continues making his note.*) . . . We were talking of economic *betterment* (*Carol writes in her notebook.*) . . . I was thinking of the School Tax. (*He continues writing. To himself.*) . . . *where is it written* that I have to send my child to public school. . . . Is it a law that I have to improve the City Schools at the expense of my own interest? And, is this not simply *The White Man's Burden*? Good. And (*looks up to Carol*) . . . does this interest you?

Carol: No. I'm taking notes . . .

John: You don't have to take notes, you know, you can just listen.

Carol: I want to make sure I remember it. (*Pause.*)

John: I'm not lecturing you, I'm just trying to tell you some things I think.

Carol: What do you think?

John: Should all kids go to college? *Why* . . .

Carol (pause): To learn.

John: But if he does not learn.

Carol: If the child does not learn?

John: Then why is he in college? Because he was told it was his "right"?

Carol: Some might find college instructive.

John: I would hope so.

Carol: But how do they feel? Being told they are wasting their time?

John: I don't think I'm telling them that.

Carol: You said that education was "prolonged and systematic hazing."

John: Yes. It can be so.

Carol: . . . if education is so *bad*, why do you do it?

John: I do it because I love it. (*Pause.*) Let's. . . . I suggest you look at the demographics, wage-earning capacity, college- and non-college-educated men and women, 1855 to 1980, and let's see if we can wring some worth from the statistics. Eh? And . . .

Carol: No.

John: What?

Carol: I can't understand them.

John: . . . you . . . ?

Carol: . . . the "charts." The *Concepts*, the . . .

John: "Charts" are simply . . .

Carol: When I leave here . . .

John: Charts, do you see . . .

Carol: No, I can't . . .

John: You can, though.

Carol: NO, NO—I DON'T UNDERSTAND. DO YOU SEE?‽ I DON'T *UNDERSTAND* . . .

John: What?

Carol: *Any* of it. *Any* of it. I'm *smiling* in class, I'm *smiling*, the whole time. What are you *talking* about? What is everyone *talking* about? I don't *understand*. I don't know what it *means*. I don't know what it

means to *be* here . . . you tell me I'm intelligent, and then you tell me
I should not be *here*, what do you *want* with me? What does it *mean*?
Who should I *listen* to . . . I . . . (*He goes over to her and puts his arm
around her shoulder.*) NO! (*She walks away from him.*)

John: Sshhhh.

Carol: No, I don't under . . .

John: Sshhhhh.

Carol: I don't know what you're *saying* . . .

John: Sshhhhh. It's all right.

Carol: . . . I have no . . .

John: Sshhhhh. Sshhhhh. Let it go a moment. (*Pause.*) Sshhhhh . . . let it
go. (*Pause.*) Just let it go. (*Pause.*) Just let it go. It's all right. (*Pause.*)
Sshhhhh. (*Pause.*) I understand . . . (*Pause.*) What do you feel?

Carol: I feel bad.

John: I know. It's all right.

Carol: I . . . (*Pause.*)

John: What?

Carol: I . . .

John: What? Tell me.

Carol: I don't understand you.

John: I know. It's all right.

Carol: I . . .

John: What? (*Pause.*) What? *Tell* me.

Carol: I can't tell you.

John: No, you must.

Carol: I can't.

John: No. Tell me. (*Pause.*)

Carol: I'm bad. (*Pause.*) Oh, God. (*Pause.*)

John: It's all right.

Carol: I'm . . .

John: It's all right.

Carol: I can't talk about this.

John: It's all right. Tell me.

Carol: Why do you want to know this?

John: I don't want to know. I want to know whatever you . . .

Carol: I always . . .

John: . . . good . . .

Carol: I always . . . all my life . . . I have never told anyone this . . .

John: Yes. Go on. (*Pause.*) Go on.

Carol: All of my life . . . (*The phone rings. Pause. John goes to the phone and
picks it up.*)

John (into phone):   I can't talk now. (*Pause.*) What? (*Pause.*) Hmm.
(*Pause.*) All right, I . . . I. Can't. Talk. Now. No, no, no, I *Know* I
did, but. . . . What? Hello. What? She *what*? She *can't*, she said the
agreement is void? How, how is the agreement *void*? *That's Our House.*

I have the *paper*, when we come down, next week, with the payment, and the paper, that house is . . . wait, wait, wait, wait, wait, wait, wait: Did Jerry . . . is Jerry there? (*Pause.*) Is *she* there . . . ? Does she have a *lawyer* . . . ? How the *hell*, how the *Hell*. That is . . . it's a question, you said, of the *easement*. I don't underst . . . it's not the *whole agreement.* It's just the *easement,* why would she? Put, put, put, *Jerry* on. (*Pause.*) Jer, *Jerry:* What the *Hell* . . . that's my *house.* That's . . . Well, I'm, no, no, no, I'm *not* coming ddd . . . List, *Listen, screw* her. You *tell* her. You, listen: I want you to take *Grace,* you take Grace, and get out of that house. You *leave* her there. Her and her lawyer, and you *tell* them, we'll see them in court next . . . no. No. Leave her there, leave her to *stew* in it: You tell her, we're *getting* that house, and we are going to . . . No. I'm *not* coming down. I'll be damned if I'll sit in the same rrr . . . the next, you tell her the next time I *see* her is in court . . . I . . . (*Pause.*) What? (*Pause.*) What? I don't understand. (*Pause.*) Well, what about the house? (*Pause.*) There isn't any problem with the hhh . . . (*Pause.*) No, no, no, that's all right. All ri . . . All right . . . (*Pause.*) Of course. Tha . . . Thank you. No, I will. Right away. (*He hangs up. Pause.*)

Carol: What is it? (*Pause.*)

John: It's a surprise party.

Carol: It is.

John: Yes.

Carol: A party for you.

John: Yes.

Carol: Is it your birthday?

John: No.

Carol: What is it?

John: The tenure announcement.

Carol: The tenure announcement.

John: They're throwing a party for us in our new house.

Carol: Your new house.

John: The house that we're buying.

Carol: You have to go.

John: It seems that I do.

Carol (pause):   They're proud of you.

John: Well, there are those who would say it's a form of aggression.

Carol: What is?

John: A surprise.

TWO

(*John and Carol seated across the desk from each other.*)

John: You see, (*pause*) I love to teach. And flatter myself I am *skilled* at it. And I love the, the aspect of *performance.* I think I must confess that.

When I found I loved to teach I swore that I would not become that cold, rigid automaton of an instructor which I had encountered as a child.

Now, I was not unconscious that it was given me to err upon the other side. And, so, I asked and *ask* myself if I engaged in heterodoxy, I will not say "gratuitously" for I do not care to posit orthodoxy as a given good—but, "to the detriment of, of my students." (*Pause.*)

As I said. When the possibility of tenure opened, and, of course, I'd long pursued it, I was, of course *happy*, and *covetous* of it.

I asked myself if I was wrong to covet it. And thought about it long, and, I hope, truthfully, and saw in myself several things in, I think, no particular order. (*Pause.*)

That I *would* pursue it. That I *desired* it, that I was not pure of longing for security, and that that, perhaps, was not reprehensible in me. That I had duties *beyond* the school, and that my duty to my home, for instance, was, or should be, if it were not, of an equal weight. That tenure, and security, and yes, and *comfort*, were not, of themselves, to be scorned; and were even worthy of honorable pursuit. And that it was given me. Here, in this place, which I enjoy, and in which I find comfort, to assure myself of—as far as it rests in The Material—a continuation of that joy and comfort. In exchange for what? Teaching. Which I love.

What was the price of this security? To obtain *tenure*. Which tenure the committee is in the process of granting me. And on the basis of which I contracted to purchase a house. Now, as you don't have your own family, at this point, you may not know what that means. But to me it is important. A home. A Good Home. To raise my family. Now: The Tenure Committee will meet. This is the process, and a *good* process. Under which the school has functioned for quite a long time. They will meet, and hear your complaint—which you have the right to make; and they will dismiss it. They will *dismiss* your complaint; and, in the intervening period, I will lose my house. I will not be able to close on my house. I will lose my *deposit*, and the home I'd picked out for my wife and son will go by the boards. Now: I see I have angered you. I understand your anger at teachers. I was angry with mine. I felt hurt and humiliated by them. Which is one of the reasons that I went into education.

Carol: What do you want of me?

John (pause): I was hurt. When I received the report. Of the tenure committee. I was shocked. And I was hurt. No, I don't mean to subject you to my weak sensibilities. All right. Finally, I didn't understand. Then I thought: is it not always at those points at which

we reckon ourselves unassailable that we are most vulnerable and . . .
(*Pause.*) Yes. All right. You find me pedantic. Yes. I am. By nature, by
birth, by profession, I don't know . . . I'm always looking for a
paradigm for . . .

Carol: I don't know what a paradigm is.

John: It's a model.

Carol: Then why can't you use that word? (*Pause.*)

John: If it is important to you. Yes, all right. I was looking for a model.
To continue: I feel that one point . . .

Carol: I . . .

John: One second . . . upon which I am unassailable is my unflinching
concern for my students' dignity. I asked you here to . . . in the spirit
of *investigation*, to ask you . . . to ask . . . (*Pause.*) What have I done
to you? (*Pause.*) And, and, I suppose, how I can make amends. Can
we not settle this now? It's pointless, really, and I want to know.

Carol: What you can do to force me to retract?

John: That is not what I meant at all.

Carol: To bribe me, to convince me . . .

John: . . . No.

Carol: To retract . . .

John: That is not what I meant at all. I think that you know it is not.

Carol: That is not what I know. I *wish* I . . .

John: I do not want to . . . you wish what?

Carol: No, you said what amends can you make. To force me to retract.

John: That is not what I said.

Carol: I have my notes.

John: Look. Look. The Stoics say . . .

Carol: The Stoics?

John: The Stoical Philosophers say if you remove the phrase "I have been
injured," you have removed the injury. Now: Think: I know that
you're upset. Just tell me. Literally. Literally: what wrong have I done
you?

Carol: Whatever you have done to me—to the extent that you've done it
to *me*, do you know, rather than to me as a *student*, and, so, to the
student body, is contained in my report. To the tenure committee.

John: Well, all right. (*Pause.*) Let's see. (*He reads.*) I find that I am sexist.
That I am *elitist*. I'm not sure I know what that means, other than it's
a derogatory word, meaning "bad." That I . . . That I insist on wasting
time, in nonprescribed, in self-aggrandizing and theatrical *diversions*
from the prescribed *text* . . . that these have taken both sexist and
pornographic forms . . . here we find listed . . . (*Pause.*) Here we find
listed . . . instances ". . . closeted with a student" . . . "Told a
rambling, sexually explicit story, in which the frequency and attitudes
of fornication of the poor and rich are, it would seem, the central

point . . . moved to *embrace* said student and . . . all part of a pattern
. . ." (*Pause.*)

(*He reads.*) That I used the phrase "The White Man's Burden"
. . . that I told you how I'd asked you to my room because I quote like
you. (*Pause.*)

(*He reads.*) "He said he 'liked' me. That he 'liked being with
me.' He'd let me write my examination paper over, if I could come
back oftener to see him in his office." (*Pause. To Carol.*) It's *ludicrous.*
Don't you know that? It's not *necessary.* It's going to *humiliate* you,
and it's going to cost me my *house,* and . . .

Carol: It's "*ludicrous . . .*"?

(*John picks up the report and reads again.*)

John: "He told me he had problems with his wife; and that he wanted to
take off the artificial stricture of Teacher and Student. He put his arm
around me . . ."

Carol: Do you deny it? Can you deny it . . .? Do you see? (*Pause.*) Don't
you see? You don't see, do you?

John: I don't see . . .

Carol: You think, you think you can deny that these things happened; or,
if they *did,* if they *did,* that they meant what you *said* they meant.
Don't you see? You drag me in here, you drag us, to listen to you "go
on"; and "go on" about this, or that, or we don't "express" ourselves
very well. We don't say what we mean. Don't we? Don't we? We *do*
say what we mean. And you say that "I don't understand you . . .":
Then *you* . . . (*Points.*)

John: "Consult the Report"?

Carol: . . . that's right.

John: You see. You see. Can't you. . . . You see what I'm saying? Can't
you tell me in your own words?

Carol: Those are my own words. (*Pause.*)

John (*he reads*): "He told me that if I would stay alone with him in his
office, he would change my grade to an A." (*To Carol.*) What have I
done to you? Oh. My God, are you so hurt?

Carol: What I "feel" is irrelevant. (*Pause.*)

John: Do you know that I tried to help you?

Carol: What I know I have reported.

John: I would like to help you now. I would. Before this escalates.

Carol (*simultaneously with* "escalates"): You see. I don't think that I need
your help. I don't think I need anything you have.

John: I feel . . .

Carol: I don't *care* what you feel. Do you see? DO YOU SEE? You can't
do that anymore. You. Do. Not. Have. The. Power. Did you misuse it?
Someone did. Are you part of that group? *Yes. Yes.* You. Are. You've

done these things. And to say, and to say, "Oh. Let me help you with
your problem . . ."

John: Yes. I understand. I understand. You're *hurt*. You're *angry*. Yes. I
think your *anger* is *betraying* you. Down a path which helps no one.

Carol: I don't *care* what you think.

John: You don't? (*Pause.*) But you talk of *rights*. Don't you see? *I* have
rights too. Do you see? I have a *house* . . . part of the *real* world; and
The Tenure Committee, Good Men and True . . .

Carol: . . . Professor . . .

John: . . . Please: *Also* part of that world: you understand? This is my *life*.
I'm not a *bogeyman*. I don't "stand" for something, I . . .

Carol: . . . Professor . . .

John: . . . I . . .

Carol: Professor. I came here as a *favor*. At your personal request.
Perhaps I should not have done so. But I did. On my behalf, and on
behalf of my group. And you speak of the tenure committee, one of
whose members is a woman, as you know. And though you might call
it Good Fun, or An Historical Phrase, or An Oversight, or, All of the
Above, to refer to the committee as Good Men and True, it is a
demeaning remark. It is a sexist remark, and to overlook it is to
countenance continuation of that method of thought. It's a remark
. . .

John: OH COME ON. Come on. . . . Sufficient to deprive a family of . . .

Carol: Sufficient? Sufficient? Sufficient? Yes. It is a *fact* . . . and that story,
which I quote, is *vile* and *classist*, and *manipulative* and *pornographic*.
It . . .

John: . . . it's pornographic . . . ?

Carol: What gives you the *right*. Yes. To speak to a *woman* in your private
. . . Yes. Yes. I'm sorry. I'm sorry. You feel yourself empowered . . .
you say so yourself. To *strut*. To *posture*. To "perform." To "Call me
in here . . ." Eh? You say that higher education is a joke. And treat it as
such, you *treat* it as such. And *confess* to a taste to play the *Patriarch* in
your class. To grant *this*. To deny *that*. To embrace your students.

John: How can you assert. How can you stand there and . . .

Carol: How can you *deny* it. You did it to me. *Here*. You *did*. . . . You
confess. You love the Power. To *deviate*. To *invent*, to transgress . . . to
transgress whatever norms have been established for us. And you think
it's charming to "question" in yourself this taste to mock and destroy.
But you should question it. Professor. And you pick those things
which you feel *advance* you: publication, *tenure*, and the steps to get
them you call "harmless rituals." And you perform those steps.
Although you say it is hypocrisy. But to the aspirations of your
students. Of *hardworking students*, who come here, who *slave* to come
here—you have no idea what it cost me to come to this school—you
mock us. You call education "hazing," and from your so-protected, so-

elitist seat you hold our confusion as a *joke*, and our hopes and efforts with it. Then you sit there and say "what have I done?" And ask me to understand that *you* have aspirations too. But I tell you. I tell you. That you are vile. And that you are exploitative. And if you possess one ounce of that inner honesty you describe in your book, you can look in yourself and see those things that I see. And you can find revulsion equal to my own. Good day. (*She prepares to leave the room.*)

John: Wait a second, will you, just one moment. (*Pause.*) Nice day today.

Carol: What?

John: You said "Good day." I think that it is a nice day today.

Carol: *Is* it?

John: Yes, I think it is.

Carol: And why is that important?

John: Because it is the essence of all human communication. I say something conventional, you respond, and the information we exchange is not about the "weather," but that we both agree to converse. In effect, we agree that we are both human. (*Pause.*) I'm not a . . . "exploiter," and you're not a . . . "deranged," what? *Revolutionary* . . . that we may, that we may have . . . positions, and that we may have . . . desires, which are in *conflict*, but that we're just human. (*Pause.*) That means that sometimes we're *imperfect*. (*Pause.*) Often we're in conflict . . . (*Pause.*) *Much* of what we do, you're right, in the name of "principles" is *self-serving* . . . much of what we do is *conventional*. (*Pause.*) You're right. (*Pause.*) You said you came in the class because you wanted to learn about *education*. I don't know that I can teach you about education. But I know that I can tell you what I *think* about education, and then *you* decide. And you don't have to fight with me. *I'm* not the subject. (*Pause.*) And where I'm *wrong* . . . perhaps it's not your job to "fix" me. I don't want to fix *you*. I would like to tell you what I *think*, because that *is* my job, conventional as it is, and flawed as I may be. And then, if you can show me some better *form*, then we can proceed from there. But, just like "nice day, isn't it . . . ?" I don't think we can proceed until we accept that each of us is human. (*Pause.*) And we still can have difficulties. We *will* have them . . . that's all right too. (*Pause.*) Now:

Carol: . . . wait . . .

John: Yes. I want to hear it.

Carol: . . . the . . .

John: Yes. Tell me frankly.

Carol: . . . my position . . .

John: I want to hear it. In your own words. What you want. And what you feel.

Carol: . . . I . . .

John: . . . yes . . .

Carol: My Group.

John: Your "Group" . . . ? (*Pause.*)

Carol: The people I've been talking to . . .

John: There's no shame in that. Everybody needs advisers. Everyone needs to expose themselves. To various points of view. It's not wrong. It's essential. Good. Good. Now: You and I . . . (*The phone rings.*) You and I . . . (*He hesitates for a moment, and then picks it up. Into phone.*) Hello. (*Pause.*) Um . . . no, I know they do. (*Pause.*) I know she does. Tell her that I . . . can I call you back? . . . Then tell her that I think it's going to be fine. (*Pause.*) Tell her just, just hold on, I'll . . . can I get back to you? . . . Well . . . no, no, no, we're *taking* the house . . . we're . . . no, no, nn . . . no, she will nnn, it's not a *question* of refunding the dep . . . no . . . it's not a *question* of the deposit . . . will you call Jerry? Babe, baby, will you just call Jerry? Tell him, nnn . . . tell him they, well, they're to keep the deposit, because the deal, be . . . because the deal is going to go *through* . . . because I know . . . be . . . will you please? Just *trust* me. Be . . . well, I'm dealing with the complaint. Yes. Right *Now.* Which is why I . . . yes, no, no, it's really, I can't *talk* about it now. Call Jerry, and I can't talk now. Ff . . . fine. Gg . . . good-bye. (*Hangs up. Pause.*) I'm sorry we were interrupted.

Carol: No . . .

John: I . . . I was saying:

Carol: You said that we should agree to talk about my complaint.

John: That's correct.

Carol: But we *are* talking about it.

John: Well, that's correct too. You see? This is the *gist* of education.

Carol: No, no. I mean, we're talking about it at the Tenure Committee Hearing. (*Pause.*)

John: Yes, but I'm saying: we can talk about it *now*, as easily as . . .

Carol: No. I think that we should stick to the process . . .

John: . . . wait a . . .

Carol: . . . the "conventional" process. As you said. (*She gets up.*) And you're right, I'm sorry if I was, um, if I was "discourteous" to you. You're right.

John: Wait, wait a . . .

Carol: I really should go.

John: Now, look, granted. I have an interest. In the status quo. All right? Everyone does. But what I'm saying is that the *committee* . . .

Carol: Professor, you're right. Just don't impinge on me. We'll take our differences, and . . .

John: You're going to make a . . . look, look, look, you're going to . . .

Carol: I shouldn't have come here. They told me . . .

John: One moment. No. No. There are *norms*, here, and there's no reason. Look: I'm trying to *save* you . . .

Carol: No one *asked* you to . . . you're trying to save *me*? Do me the courtesy to . . .

John: I *am* doing you the courtesy. I'm talking *straight* to you. We can settle this *now*. And I want you to sit *down* and . . .

Carol: You must excuse me . . . (*She starts to leave the room.*)

John: Sit down, it seems we each have a. . . . Wait one moment. Wait one moment . . . just do me the courtesy to . . . (*He restrains her from leaving.*)

Carol: LET ME GO.

John: I have no desire to *hold* you, I just want to *talk* to you . . .

Carol: LET ME GO. LET ME GO. WOULD SOMEBODY *HELP* ME? WOULD SOMEBODY *HELP* ME PLEASE . . . ?

THREE

(*At rise, Carol and John are seated.*)

John: I have asked you here. (*Pause.*) I have asked you here against, against my . . .

Carol: I was most surprised you asked me.

John: . . . against my better *judgment*, against . . .

Carol: I was most surprised . . .

John: . . . against the . . . yes. I'm sure.

Carol: . . . If you would like me to leave, I'll leave. I'll go right now . . . (*She rises.*)

John: Let us begin *correctly*, may we? I feel . . .

Carol: That is what I wished to do. That's why I came here, but now . . .

John: . . . I feel . . .

Carol: But now perhaps you'd like me to leave . . .

John: I don't want you to leave. I asked you to come . . .

Carol: I didn't have to come here.

John: No. (*Pause.*) Thank you.

Carol: All right. (*Pause. She sits down.*)

John: Although I feel that it *profits*, it would *profit* you something, to . . .

Carol: . . . what I . . .

John: If you would hear me out, if you would hear me out.

Carol: I came here to, the court officers told me not to come.

John: . . . the "court" officers . . . ?

Carol: I was shocked that you asked.

John: . . . wait . . .

Carol: Yes. But I did *not* come here to hear what it "profits" me.

John: The "court" officers . . .

Carol: . . . no, no, perhaps I should leave . . . (*She gets up.*)

John: Wait.

Carol: No. I shouldn't have . . .

John: . . . wait. Wait. Wait a moment.

Carol: Yes? What is it you want? (*Pause.*) What is it you want?

John: I'd like you to stay.

Carol: You want me to stay.

John: Yes.

Carol: You do.

John: Yes. (*Pause.*) Yes. I would like to have you hear me out. If you would. (*Pause.*) Would you please? If you would do that I would be in your debt. (*Pause. She sits.*) Thank You. (*Pause.*)

Carol: What is it you wish to tell me?

John: All right. I cannot . . . (*Pause.*) I cannot help but feel you are owed an apology. (*Pause. Of papers in his hands.*) I have read. (*Pause.*) And reread these accusations.

Carol: What "accusations"?

John: The, the tenure comm . . . what other accusations . . . ?

Carol: The tenure committee . . . ?

John: Yes.

Carol: Excuse me, but those are not accusations. They have been *proved.* They are facts.

John: . . . I . . .

Carol: No. Those are not "accusations."

John: . . . those?

Carol: . . . the committee (*The phone starts to ring.*) the committee has . . .

John: . . . All right . . .

Carol: . . . those are not accusations. The Tenure Committee.

John: ALL RIGHT. ALL RIGHT. ALL RIGHT. (*He picks up the phone.*) Hello. Yes. No. I'm here. Tell Mister . . . No, I can't talk to him now . . . I'm sure he has, but I'm fff . . . I know . . . No, I have no time t . . . tell Mister . . . tell Mist . . . tell Jerry that I'm *fine* and that I'll call him right aw . . . (*Pause.*) My wife . . . Yes. I'm sure she has. Yes, thank you. Yes, I'll call her too. I cannot talk to you now. (*He hangs up. Pause.*) All right. It was good of you to come. Thank you. I have studied. I have spent some time studying the indictment.

Carol: You will have to explain that word to me.

John: An "indictment" . . .

Carol: Yes.

John: Is a "bill of particulars." A . . .

Carol: All right. Yes.

John: In which is alleged . . .

Carol: No. I cannot allow that. I cannot allow that. Nothing is alleged. Everything is proved . . .

John: Please, wait a sec . . .

Carol: I cannot *come* to allow . . .

John: If I may . . . If I may, from whatever you feel is "established," by . . .

Carol: The issue here is not what I "feel." It is not my "feelings," but the feelings of women. And men. Your superiors, who've been "polled," do you see? To whom *evidence* has been presented, who have *ruled*, do you see? Who have weighed the testimony and the evidence, and have *ruled*, do you see? That you are *negligent*. That you are *guilty*, that you are found *wanting*, and in *error*; and are *not*, for the reasons so-told, to be given tenure. That you are to be disciplined. For facts. For *facts*. Not "alleged," what is the word? But *proved*. Do you see? *By your own actions*.

That is what the tenure committee has said. That is what my lawyer said. For what you did in class. For what you did *in this office*.

John: They're going to discharge me.

Carol: As full well they should. You don't understand? You're angry? What has *led* you to this place? Not your sex. Not your race. Not your class. YOUR OWN ACTIONS. And you're *angry*. You *ask* me here. What *do* you want? You want to "charm" me. You want to "convince" me. You want me to recant. I will *not* recant. Why should I . . . ? What I say is right. You tell me, you are going to tell me that you have a wife and child. You are going to say that you have a career and that you've worked for twenty years for this. Do you know what you've *worked* for? *Power*. For *power*. Do you understand? And you sit there, and you tell me *stories*. About your *house*, about all the private *schools*, and about *privilege*, and how you are entitled. To *buy*, to *spend*, to *mock*, to *summon*. All your stories. All your silly weak *guilt*, it's all about *privilege*; and you won't know it. Don't you see? You worked twenty years for the right to *insult* me. And you feel entitled to be *paid* for it. Your Home. Your Wife . . . Your sweet "deposit" on your house . . .

John: Don't you have feelings?

Carol: That's my point. You see? Don't you have feelings? Your final argument. What is it that has no feelings. *Animals*. I don't take your side, you question if I'm Human.

John: Don't you have feelings?

Carol: I have a responsibility. I . . .

John: . . . to . . . ?

Carol: To? This institution. To the *students*. To my *group*.

John: . . . your "group." . . .

Carol: Because I speak, yes, not for myself. But for the group; for those who suffer what I suffer. On behalf of whom, even if I, were, inclined, to what, forgive? Forget? What? Overlook your . . .

John: . . . my behavior?

Carol: . . . it would be wrong.

John: Even if you were inclined to "forgive" me.

Carol: It would be wrong.

John: And what would transpire.

Carol: Transpire?

John: Yes.

Carol: "Happen?"

John: Yes.

Carol: Then *say* it. For Christ's sake. Who the *hell* do you think that you are? You want a post. You want unlimited power. To do and to say what you want. As it pleases you—Testing, Questioning, Flirting . . .

John: I never . . .

Carol: Excuse me, one moment, will you? (*She reads from her notes.*) The twelfth: "Have a good day, dear." The fifteenth: "Now, don't *you* look fetching . . ." April seventeenth: "If you girls would come over here . . ." I saw you. I saw you, Professor. For two semesters sit there, stand there and exploit our, as you thought, "paternal prerogative," and what is that but rape; I swear to God. You asked me in here to explain something to me, as a child, that I did not understand. But I came to explain something to you. You Are Not God. You ask me why I came? I came here to instruct you. (*She produces his book.*) And your book? You think you're going to show me some "light"? You "*maverick.*" Outside of tradition. No, no, (*she reads from the book's liner notes*) "*of* that fine tradition of *inquiry*. Of Polite *skepticism*" . . . and you say you believe in free intellectual discourse. YOU BELIEVE IN NOTHING. YOU BELIEVE IN NOTHING AT ALL.

John: I believe in freedom of thought.

Carol: Isn't that fine. *Do* you?

John: Yes. I do.

Carol: Then why do you question, for one moment, the committee's decision refusing your tenure? Why do you question your suspension? You believe in what *you call* freedom of thought. Then, fine. *You* believe in freedom-of-thought *and* a home, and, *and* prerogatives for your kid, *and* tenure. And I'm going to tell you. You believe *not* in "freedom of thought," but in an elitist, in, in a protected hierarchy which rewards you. And for whom you are the clown. And you mock and exploit the system which pays your rent. You're wrong. I'm not wrong. You're wrong. You think that I'm full of hatred. I know what you think I am.

John: Do you?

Carol: You think I'm a, of course I do. You think I am a frightened, repressed, confused, I don't know, abandoned young thing of some doubtful sexuality, who wants, power and revenge. (*Pause.*) *Don't* you? (*Pause.*)

John: Yes. I do. (*Pause.*)

Carol: Isn't that better? And I feel that that is the first moment which you've treated me with respect. For you told me the truth. (*Pause.*) I did not come here, as you are assured, to gloat. Why would I want to gloat? I've profited nothing from your, your, as you say, your "misfortune." I came here, as you did me the honor to *ask* me here, I came here to *tell* you something.

(*Pause.*) That I think . . . that I think you've been wrong. That I think you've been terribly wrong. Do you hate me now? (*Pause.*)

John: Yes.

Carol: Why do you hate me? Because you think me wrong? No. Because I have, you think, *power* over you. Listen to me. Listen to me, Professor. (*Pause.*) It is the power that you hate. So deeply that, that any atmosphere of free discussion is impossible. It's not "unlikely." It's *impossible.* Isn't it?

John: Yes.

Carol: *Isn't* it . . . ?

John: Yes. I suppose.

Carol: Now. The thing which you find so cruel is the selfsame process of selection I, and my group, go through *every day of our lives.* In admittance to school. In our tests, in our class rankings. . . . Is it unfair? I can't tell you. But, if it is fair. Or even if it is "unfortunate but necessary" for us, then, by God, so must it be for you. (*Pause.*) You write of your "responsibility to the young." Treat us with respect, and that will *show* you your responsibility. You write that education is just hazing. (*Pause.*) But we worked to get to this school. (*Pause.*) And some of us. (*Pause.*) Overcame prejudices. Economic, sexual, you cannot begin to imagine. And endured humiliations I *pray* that you and those you love never will encounter. (*Pause.*) To gain admittance here. To pursue that same dream of security *you* pursue. We, who, who are, at any moment, in danger of being deprived of it. By . . .

John: . . . by . . . ?

Carol: By the administration. By the teachers. By *you.* By, say, one low grade, that keeps us out of graduate school; by one, say, one capricious or inventive answer on our parts, which, perhaps you don't find amusing. Now you *know,* do you see? What it is to be subject to that power. (*Pause.*)

John: I don't understand. (*Pause.*)

Carol: My charges are not trivial. You see that in the haste, I think, with which they were accepted. A *joke* you have told, with a sexist tinge. The language you use, a verbal or physical caress, yes, yes, I know, you say that it is meaningless. I understand. I differ from you. To lay a hand on someone's shoulder.

John: It was devoid of sexual content.

Carol: I say it was not. I SAY IT WAS NOT. Don't you begin to *see* . . . ? Don't you begin to understand? IT'S NOT FOR YOU TO SAY.

John: I take your point, and I see there is much good in what you refer to.

Carol: . . . do you think so . . . ?

John: . . . but, and this is not to say that I cannot change, in those things in which I am deficient . . . But, the . . .

Carol: Do you hold yourself harmless from the charge of sexual exploitativeness . . . ? (*Pause.*)

John: Well, I . . . I . . . I . . . You know I, as I said. I . . . think I am not too old to *learn*, and I *can* learn, I . . .

Carol: Do you hold yourself innocent of the charge of . . .

John: . . . wait, wait, wait . . . All right, let's go back to . . .

Carol: YOU FOOL. Who do you think I am? To come here and be taken in by a *smile*. You little yapping fool. You think I want "revenge." I don't want revenge. I WANT UNDERSTANDING.

John: . . . *do* you?

Carol: I do. (*Pause.*)

John: What's the use. It's over.

Carol: Is it? What is?

John: My job.

Carol: Oh. Your job. That's what you want to talk about. (*Pause. She starts to leave the room. She steps and turns back to him.*) All right. (*Pause.*) What if it were possible that my Group withdraws its complaint. (*Pause.*)

John: What?

Carol: That's right. (*Pause.*)

John: Why.

Carol: Well, let's say as an act of friendship.

John: An act of friendship.

Carol: Yes. (*Pause.*)

John: In exchange for what.

Carol: Yes. But I don't think, "exchange." Not "in exchange." For what do we derive from it? (*Pause.*)

John: "Derive."

Carol: Yes.

John (pause):   Nothing. (*Pause.*)

Carol: That's right. We derive nothing. (*Pause.*) Do you see that?

John: Yes.

Carol: That is a little word, Professor. "Yes." "I see that." But you will.

John: And you might speak to the committee . . . ?

Carol: To the committee?

John: Yes.

Carol: Well. Of course. That's on your mind. We might.

John: "If" what?

Carol: "Given" what. Perhaps. I think that that is more friendly.

John: GIVEN WHAT?

Carol: And, believe me, I understand your rage. It is not that I don't feel it. But I do not see that it is deserved, so I do not resent it. . . . All right. I have a list.

John: . . . a list.

Carol: Here is a list of books, which we . . .

John: . . . a list of books . . . ?

Carol: That's right. Which we find questionable.

John: What?

Carol: Is this so bizarre . . . ?

John: I can't believe . . .

Carol: It's not necessary you believe it.

John: Academic freedom . . .

Carol: Someone chooses the books. If you can choose them, others can. What are you, "God"?

John: . . . no, no, the "dangerous." . . .

Carol: You have an agenda, we have an agenda. I am not interested in your feelings or your motivation, but your actions. If you would like me to speak to the Tenure Committee, here is my list. You are a Free Person, you decide. (*Pause.*)

John: Give me the list. (*She does so. He reads.*)

Carol: I think you'll find . . .

John: I'm capable of reading it. Thank you.

Carol: We have a number of *texts* we need re . . .

John: I see that.

Carol: We're amenable to . . .

John: Aha. Well, let me look over the . . . (*He reads.*)

Carol: I think that . . .

John: LOOK. I'm reading your demands. All right?! (*He reads. Pause.*) You want to ban my book?

Carol: We do not . . .

John (of list):   It says here . . .

Carol: . . . We want it removed from inclusion as a representative example of the university.

John: Get out of here.

Carol: If you put aside the issues of personalities.

John: Get the fuck out of my office.

Carol: No, I think I would reconsider.

John: . . . you think you can.

Carol: We can and we *will.* Do you want our support? That is the only quest . . .

John: . . . to ban my *book* . . . ?

Carol: . . . that is correct . . .

John: . . . this . . . this is a *university* . . . we . . .

Carol: . . . and we have a statement . . . which we need you to . . . (*She hands him a sheet of paper.*)

John: No, no. It's out of the question. I'm sorry. I don't know what I was thinking of. I want to tell you something. I'm a teacher. I am a teacher. Eh? It's my *name* on the door, and *I* teach the class, and that's what I do. I've got a book with my name on it. And my son will *see* that *book* someday. And I have a respon . . . No, I'm sorry I have a *responsibility* . . . to *myself*, to my *son*, to my *profession*. . . . I haven't been *home* for two days, do you know that? Thinking this out.

Carol: . . . you haven't?

John: I've been, no. If it's of interest to you. I've been in a *hotel*. *Thinking.* (*The phone starts ringing.*) *Thinking* . . .

Carol: . . . you haven't been home?

John: . . . *thinking*, do you see.

Carol: Oh.

John: And, and, I owe you a debt, I see that now. (*Pause.*) You're *dangerous*, you're *wrong* and it's my *job* . . . to say no to you. That's my job. You are absolutely right. You want to ban my book? Go to *hell*, and they can do whatever they want to me.

Carol: . . . you haven't been home in two days . . .

John: I think I told you that.

Carol: . . . you'd better get that phone. (*Pause.*) I think that you should pick up the phone. (*Pause.*)

(*John picks up the phone.*)

John (on phone): Yes. (*Pause.*) Yes. Wh . . . I. I. I had to be away. All ri . . . did they wor . . . did they worry ab . . . No. I'm all right, now, Jerry. I'm f . . . I got a little turned *around*, but I'm *sitting* here and . . . I've got it figured out. I'm fine. I'm fine don't worry about me. I got a little bit mixed up. But I am not sure that it's not a blessing. It cost me my job? Fine. Then the job was not worth having. Tell Grace that I'm coming home and everything is fff . . . (*Pause.*) What? (*Pause.*) *What?* (*Pause.*) What do you *mean?* WHAT? Jerry . . . Jerry. They . . . Who, who, what can they do . . . ? (*Pause.*) NO. (*Pause.*) NO. They can't do th . . . What do you mean? (*Pause.*) But how . . . (*Pause.*) She's, she's, she's *here* with me. To . . . Jerry. I don't underst . . . (*Pause. He hangs up. To Carol.*) What does this mean?

Carol: I thought you knew.

John: What. (*Pause.*) What does it mean. (*Pause.*)

Carol: You tried to rape me. (*Pause.*) According to the law. (*Pause.*)

John: . . . what . . . ?

Carol: You tried to rape me. I was leaving this office, you "pressed" yourself into me. You "pressed" your body into me.

John: . . . I . . .

Carol: My Group has told your lawyer that we may pursue criminal charges.

John: . . . no . . .

Carol: . . . under the statute. I am told. It was battery.

John: . . . no . . .

Carol: Yes. And attempted rape. That's right. (*Pause.*)

John: I think that you should go.

Carol: Of course. I thought you knew.

John: I have to talk to my lawyer.

Carol: Yes. Perhaps you should. (*The phone rings again. Pause.*)

John (picks up phone. Into phone):   Hello? I . . . Hello . . . ? I . . . Yes, he just called. No . . . I. I can't talk to you now, Baby. (*To Carol.*) Get out.

Carol: . . . your wife . . . ?

John: . . . who it is is no concern of yours. Get out. (*To phone.*) No, no, it's going to be all right. I. I can't talk now, Baby. (*To Carol.*) Get out of here.

Carol: I'm going.

John: Good.

Carol (exiting):   . . . and don't call your wife "baby."

John: What?

Carol: Don't call your wife baby. You heard what I said.

(*Carol starts to leave the room. John grabs her and begins to beat her.*)

John: You vicious little bitch. You think you can come in here with your political correctness and destroy my life?

(*He knocks her to the floor.*)

After how I treated you . . . ? You should be . . . *Rape you* . . . ? Are you kidding me . . . ?

(*He picks up a chair, raises it above his head, and advances on her.*)

I wouldn't touch you with a ten-foot pole. You little *cunt* . . .

(*She cowers on the floor below him. Pause. He looks down at her. He lowers the chair. He moves to his desk, and arranges the papers on it. Pause. He looks over at her.*)

. . . well . . .

(*Pause. She looks at him.*)

Carol: Yes. That's right. (*She looks away from him, and lowers her head. To herself.*) . . . yes. That's right.

Arthur Miller   (b. 1915)

By the time his first major play, Death of a Salesman *(1949), established him as one of the great American playwrights, Arthur Miller had already been writing radio plays, screenplays, articles, and fiction for ten years. Political issues, especially anti-Semitism and the red-scare blacklisting and paranoia surrounding communism, became some of his central themes. All My Sons (1947) ran on Broadway for almost a year. It concerns a manager of a defense plant who knew that flaws in the parts he built for warplanes would cause some of the fliers to crash. The Crucible (1953), about witch hunts in the seventeenth century, invited comparison with the communist witch hunts of the 1950s.* A View from the Bridge *(1955) treats immigrants and their hopes in America. Miller's personal life became tabloid material when he married Marilyn Monroe; and* The Misfits *(1960), from his script, remains one of her most interesting films. Once his marriage ended he wrote* After the Fall *(1964), about a divorced writer getting his thinking together while considering a third marriage.* Incident at Vichy *(1964) and* The Price *(1967) were both successful. Miller's later plays have been well received in England, including a musical,* The American Clock *(1980). His newest play,* Broken Glass *(1994), is about a crisis in the life of a Jewish immigrant couple in Brooklyn in 1938. His work continues to explore issues of significance and to set a standard for American drama.*

DEATH OF A SALESMAN   1949

Characters

Willy Loman	*Charley*
Linda	*Uncle Ben*
Biff	*Howard Wagner*
Happy	*Jenny*
Bernard	*Stanley*
The Woman	*Miss Forsythe*

(*Scene: The action takes place in Willy Loman's house and yard and in various places he visits in the New York and Boston of today.*)

(*Throughout the play, in the stage directions, left and right mean stage left and stage right.*)

ACT I

(*A melody is heard, played upon a flute. It is small and fine, telling of grass and trees and the horizon. The curtain rises.*)

(*Before us is the Salesman's house. We are aware of towering, angular shapes behind it, surrounding it on all sides. Only the blue light of the sky falls upon the house and forestage; the surrounding area shows an angry glow of orange. As more light appears, we see a solid vault of apartment houses around the small, fragile-seeming home. An air of the dream clings to the place, a dream rising out of reality. The kitchen at center seems actual enough, for there is a kitchen table with three chairs, and a refrigerator. But no other fixtures are seen. At the back of the kitchen there is a draped entrance, which leads to the living room. To the right of the kitchen, on a level raised two feet, is a bedroom furnished only with a brass bedstead and a straight chair. On a shelf over the bed a silver athletic trophy stands. A window opens onto the apartment house at the side.*)

(*Behind the kitchen, on a level raised six and a half feet, is the boys' bedroom, at present barely visible. Two beds are dimly seen, and at the*) *back of the room a dormer window. [This bedroom is above the unseen living room.] At the left a stairway curves up to it from the kitchen.)*

(The entire setting is wholly or, in some places, partially transparent. The roofline of the house is one-dimensional; under and over it we see the apartment buildings. Before the house lies an apron, curving beyond the forestage into the orchestra. This forward area serves as the back yard as well as the locale of all Willy's imaginings and of his city scenes. Whenever the action is in the present the actors observe the imaginary wall-lines, entering the house only through its door at the left. But in the scenes of the past these boundaries are broken, and characters enter or leave a room by stepping "through" a wall onto the forestage.)

(From the right, Willy Loman, the Salesman, enters, carrying two large sample cases. The flute plays on. He hears but is not aware of it. He is past sixty years of age, dressed quietly. Even as he crosses the stage to the doorway of the house, his exhaustion is apparent. He unlocks the door, comes into the kitchen, and thankfully lets his burden down, feeling the soreness of his palms. A word-sigh escapes his lips—it might be "Oh, boy, oh, boy." He closes the door, then carries his cases out into the living room, through the draped kitchen doorway.)

(Linda, his wife, has stirred in her bed at the right. She gets out and puts on a robe, listening. Most often jovial, she has developed an iron repression of her exceptions to Willy's behavior—she more than loves him, she admires him, as though his mercurial nature, his temper, his massive dreams and little cruelties, served her only as sharp reminders of the turbulent longings within him, longings which she shares but lacks the temperament to utter and follow to their end.)

Linda (hearing Willy outside the bedroom, calls with some trepidation): Willy!

Willy: It's all right. I came back.

Linda: Why? What happened? (*Slight pause.*) Did something happen, Willy?

Willy: No, nothing happened.

Linda: You didn't smash the car, did you?

Willy (with casual irritation):   I said nothing happened. Didn't you hear me?

Linda: Don't you feel well?

Willy: I'm tired to the death. (*The flute has faded away. He sits on the bed beside her, a little numb.*) I couldn't make it. I just couldn't make it, Linda.

Linda (very carefully, delicately):   Where were you all day? You look terrible.

Willy: I got as far as a little above Yonkers. I stopped for a cup of coffee. Maybe it was the coffee.

Linda: What?

Willy (after a pause): I suddenly couldn't drive anymore. The car kept going off onto the shoulder, y'know?

Linda (helpfully): Oh. Maybe it was the steering again. I don't think Angelo knows the Studebaker.

Willy: No, it's me, it's me. Suddenly I realize I'm goin' sixty miles an hour and I don't remember the last five minutes. I'm—I can't seem to—keep my mind to it.

Linda: Maybe it's your glasses. You never went for your new glasses.

Willy: No, I see everything. I came back ten miles an hour. It took me nearly four hours from Yonkers.

Linda (resigned): Well, you'll just have to take a rest, Willy, you can't continue this way.

Willy: I just got back from Florida.

Linda: But you didn't rest your mind. Your mind is overactive, and the mind is what counts, dear.

Willy: I'll start out in the morning. Maybe I'll feel better in the morning. (*She is taking off his shoes.*) These goddam arch supports are killing me.

Linda: Take an aspirin. Should I get you an aspirin? It'll soothe you.

Willy (with wonder): I was driving along, you understand? And I was fine. I was even observing the scenery. You can imagine, me looking at scenery, on the road every week of my life. But it's so beautiful up there, Linda, the trees are so thick, and the sun is warm. I opened the windshield and just let the warm air bathe over me. And then all of a sudden I'm goin' off the road! I'm tellin' ya, I absolutely forgot I was driving. If I'd've gone the other way over the white line I might've killed somebody. So I went on again—and five minutes later I'm dreamin' again, and I nearly—(*He presses two fingers against his eyes.*) I have such thoughts, I have such strange thoughts.

Linda: Willy, dear. Talk to them again. There's no reason why you can't work in New York.

Willy: They don't need me in New York. I'm the New England man. I'm vital in New England.

Linda: But you're sixty years old. They can't expect you to keep traveling every week.

Willy: I'll have to send a wire to Portland. I'm supposed to see Brown and Morrison tomorrow morning at ten o'clock to show the line. Goddammit, I could sell them! (*He starts putting on his jacket.*)

Linda (taking the jacket from him): Why don't you go down to the place tomorrow and tell Howard you've simply got to work in New York? You're too accommodating, dear.

Willy: If old man Wagner was alive I'd a been in charge of New York now! That man was a prince, he was a masterful man. But that boy of his, that Howard, he don't appreciate. When I went north the first time, the Wagner Company didn't know where New England was!

Linda: Why don't you tell those things to Howard, dear?

Willy (encouraged):   I will, I definitely will. Is there any cheese?

Linda: I'll make you a sandwich.

Willy: No, go to sleep. I'll take some milk. I'll be up right away. The boys in?

Linda: They're sleeping. Happy took Biff on a date tonight.

Willy (interested):   That so?

Linda: It was so nice to see them shaving together, one behind the other, in the bathroom. And going out together. You notice? The whole house smells of shaving lotion.

Willy: Figure it out. Work a lifetime to pay off a house. You finally own it, and there's nobody to live in it.

Linda: Well, dear, life is a casting off. It's always that way.

Willy: No, no, some people—some people accomplish something. Did Biff say anything after I went this morning?

Linda: You shouldn't have criticized him, Willy, especially after he just got off the train. You mustn't lose your temper with him.

Willy: When the hell did I lose my temper? I simply asked him if he was making any money. Is that a criticism?

Linda: But, dear, how could he make any money?

Willy (worried and angered):   There's such an undercurrent in him. He became a moody man. Did he apologize when I left this morning?

Linda: He was crestfallen, Willy. You know how he admires you. I think if he finds himself, then you'll both be happier and not fight anymore.

Willy: How can he find himself on a farm? Is that a life? A farmhand? In the beginning, when he was young, I thought, well, a young man, it's good for him to tramp around, take a lot of different jobs. But it's more than ten years now and he has yet to make thirty-five dollars a week!

Linda: He's finding himself, Willy.

Willy: Not finding yourself at the age of thirty-four is a disgrace!

Linda: Shh!

Willy: The trouble is he's lazy, goddammit!

Linda: Willy, please!

Willy: Biff is a lazy bum!

Linda: They're sleeping. Get something to eat. Go on down.

Willy: Why did he come home? I would like to know what brought him home.

Linda: I don't know. I think he's still lost, Willy. I think he's very lost.

Willy: Biff Loman is lost. In the greatest country in the world a young man with such—personal attractiveness, gets lost. And such a hard worker. There's one thing about Biff—he's not lazy.

Linda: Never.

Willy (with pity and resolve):   I'll see him in the morning; I'll have a nice talk with him. I'll get him a job selling. He could be big in no time.

My God! Remember how they used to follow him around in high school? When he smiled at one of them their faces lit up. When he walked down the street . . . (*He loses himself in reminiscences.*)

Linda (trying to bring him out of it): Willy, dear, I got a new kind of American-type cheese today. It's whipped.

Willy: Why do you get American when I like Swiss?

Linda: I just thought you'd like a change—

Willy: I don't want a change! I want Swiss cheese. Why am I always being contradicted?

Linda (with a covering laugh): I thought it would be a surprise.

Willy: Why don't you open a window in here, for God's sake?

Linda (with infinite patience): They're all open, dear.

Willy: The way they boxed us in here. Bricks and windows, windows and bricks.

Linda: We should've bought the land next door.

Willy: The street is lined with cars. There's not a breath of fresh air in the neighborhood. The grass don't grow anymore, you can't raise a carrot in the back yard. They should've had a law against apartment houses. Remember those two beautiful elm trees out there? When I and Biff hung the swing between them?

Linda: Yeah, like being a million miles from the city.

Willy: They should've arrested the builder for cutting those down. They massacred the neighborhood. (*Lost.*) More and more I think of those days, Linda. This time of year it was lilac and wisteria. And then the peonies would come out, and the daffodils. What fragrance in this room!

Linda: Well, after all, people had to move somewhere.

Willy: No, there's more people now.

Linda: I don't think there's more people. I think—

Willy: There's more people! That's what's ruining this country! Population is getting out of control. The competition is maddening! Smell the stink from that apartment house! And another one on the other side . . . How can they whip cheese?

(*On Willy's last line, Biff and Happy raise themselves up in their beds, listening.*)

Linda: Go down, try it. And be quiet.

Willy (turning to Linda, guiltily): You're not worried about me, are you, sweetheart?

Biff: What's the matter?

Happy: Listen!

Linda: You've got too much on the ball to worry about.

Willy: You're my foundation and my support, Linda.

Linda: Just try to relax, dear. You make mountains out of molehills.

Willy: I won't fight with him anymore. If he wants to go back to Texas, let him go.

Linda: He'll find his way.

Willy: Sure. Certain men just don't get started till later in life. Like Thomas Edison, I think. Or B. F. Goodrich. One of them was deaf. (*He starts for the bedroom doorway.*) I'll put my money on Biff.

Linda: And Willy—if it's warm Sunday we'll drive in the country. And we'll open the windshield, and take lunch.

Willy: No, the windshields don't open on the new cars.

Linda: But you opened it today.

Willy: Me? I didn't. (*He stops.*) Now isn't that peculiar! Isn't that a remarkable—(*He breaks off in amazement and fright as the flute is heard distantly.*)

Linda: What, darling?

Willy: That is the most remarkable thing.

Linda: What, dear?

Willy: I was thinking of the Chevvy. (*Slight pause.*) Nineteen twenty-eight . . . when I had that red Chevvy—(*Breaks off.*) That funny? I coulda sworn I was driving that Chevvy today.

Linda: Well, that's nothing. Something must've reminded you.

Willy: Remarkable. Ts. Remember those days? The way Biff used to simonize that car? The dealer refused to believe there was eighty thousand miles on it. (*He shakes his head.*) Heh! (*To Linda.*) Close your eyes, I'll be right up. (*He walks out of the bedroom.*)

Happy (to Biff):   Jesus, maybe he smashed up the car again!

Linda (calling after Willy):   Be careful on the stairs, dear! The cheese is on the middle shelf! (*She turns, goes over to the bed, takes his jacket, and goes out of the bedroom.*)

(*Light has risen on the boys' room. Unseen, Willy is heard talking to himself, "Eighty thousand miles," and a little laugh. Biff gets out of bed, comes downstage a bit, and stands attentively. Biff is two years older than his brother Happy, well built, but in these days bears a worn air and seems less self-assured. He has succeeded less, and his dreams are stronger and less acceptable than Happy's. Happy is tall, powerfully made. Sexuality is like a visible color on him, or a scent that many women have discovered. He, like his brother, is lost, but in a different way, for he has never allowed himself to turn his face toward defeat and is thus more confused and hard-skinned, although seemingly more content.*)

Happy (getting out of bed):   He's going to get his license taken away if he keeps that up. I'm getting nervous about him, y'know, Biff?

Biff: His eyes are going.

Happy: No, I've driven with him. He sees all right. He just doesn't keep his mind on it. I drove into the city with him last week. He stops at a green light and then it turns red and he goes. (*He laughs.*)

Biff: Maybe he's color-blind.

Happy: Pop? Why he's got the finest eye for color in the business. You know that.

Biff (sitting down on his bed): I'm going to sleep.

Happy: You're not still sour on Dad, are you, Biff?

Biff: He's all right, I guess.

Willy (underneath them, in the living room): Yes, sir, eighty thousand miles—eighty-two thousand!

Biff: You smoking?

Happy (holding out a pack of cigarettes): Want one?

Biff (taking a cigarette): I can never sleep when I smell it.

Willy: What a simonizing job, heh!

Happy (with deep sentiment): Funny, Biff, y'know? Us sleeping in here again? The old beds. (*He pats his bed affectionately.*) All the talk that went across those two beds, huh? Our whole lives.

Biff: Yeah. Lotta dreams and plans.

Happy (with a deep and masculine laugh): About five hundred women would like to know what was said in this room.

(*They share a soft laugh.*)

Biff: Remember that big Betsy something—what the hell was her name— over on Bushwick Avenue?

Happy (combing his hair): With the collie dog!

Biff: That's the one. I got you in there, remember?

Happy: Yeah, that was my first time—I think. Boy, there was a pig. (*They laugh, almost crudely.*) You taught me everything I know about women. Don't forget that.

Biff: I bet you forgot how bashful you used to be. Especially with girls.

Happy: Oh, I still am, Biff.

Biff: Oh, go on.

Happy: I just control it, that's all. I think I got less bashful and you got more so. What happened, Biff? Where's the old humor, the old confidence? (*He shakes Biff's knee. Biff gets up and moves restlessly about the room.*) What's the matter?

Biff: Why does Dad mock me all the time?

Happy: He's not mocking you, he—

Biff: Everything I say there's a twist of mockery on his face. I can't get near him.

Happy: He just wants you to make good, that's all. I wanted to talk to you about Dad for a long time, Biff. Something's—happening to him. He—talks to himself.

Biff: I noticed that this morning. But he always mumbled.

Happy: But not so noticeable. It got so embarrassing I sent him to Florida. And you know something? Most of the time he's talking to you.

Biff: What's he say about me?

Happy: I can't make it out.

Biff: What's he say about me?

Happy: I think the fact that you're not settled, that you're still kind of up in the air . . .

Biff: There's one or two other things depressing him, Happy.

Happy: What do you mean?

Biff: Never mind. Just don't lay it all to me.

Happy: But I think if you just got started—I mean—is there any future for you out there?

Biff: I tell ya, Hap, I don't know what the future is. I don't know—what I'm supposed to want.

Happy: What do you mean?

Biff: Well, I spent six or seven years after high school trying to work myself up. Shipping clerk, salesman, business of one kind or another. And it's a measly manner of existence. To get on that subway on the hot mornings in summer. To devote your whole life to keeping stock, or making phone calls, or selling or buying. To suffer fifty weeks of the year for the sake of a two-week vacation, when all you really desire is to be outdoors, with your shirt off. And always to have to get ahead of the next fella. And still—that's how you build a future.

Happy: Well, you really enjoy it on a farm? Are you content out there?

Biff (with rising agitation):   Hap, I've had twenty or thirty different kinds of jobs since I left home before the war, and it always turns out the same. I just realized it lately. In Nebraska when I herded cattle, and the Dakotas, and Arizona, and now in Texas. It's why I came home now, I guess, because I realized it. This farm I work on, it's spring there now, see? And they've got about fifteen new colts. There's nothing more inspiring or—beautiful than the sight of a mare and a new colt. And it's cool there now, see? Texas is cool now, and it's spring. And whenever spring comes to where I am, I suddenly get the feeling, my God, I'm not gettin' anywhere! What the hell am I doing, playing around with horses, twenty-eight dollars a week! I'm thirty-four years old, I oughta be makin' my future. That's when I come running home. And now, I get here, and I don't know what to do with myself. (*After a pause.*) I've always made a point of not wasting my life, and every time I come back here I know that all I've done is to waste my life.

Happy: You're a poet, you know that, Biff? You're a—you're an idealist!

Biff: No, I'm mixed up very bad. Maybe I oughta get married. Maybe I oughta get stuck into something. Maybe that's my trouble. I'm like a boy. I'm not married, I'm not in business, I just—I'm like a boy. Are you content, Hap? You're a success, aren't you? Are you content?

Happy: Hell, no!

Biff: Why? You're making money, aren't you?

Happy: (*moving about with energy, expressiveness*): All I can do now is wait

for the merchandise manager to die. And suppose I get to be
merchandise manager? He's a good friend of mine, and he just built a
terrific estate on Long Island. And he lived there about two months
and sold it, and now he's building another one. He can't enjoy it once
it's finished. And I know that's just what I would do. I don't know
what the hell I'm workin' for. Sometimes I sit in my apartment—all
alone. And I think of the rent I'm paying. And it's crazy. But then, it's
what I always wanted. My own apartment, a car, and plenty of women.
And still, goddammit, I'm lonely.

Biff (with enthusiasm):   Listen, why don't you come out West with me?

Happy: You and I, heh?

Biff: Sure, maybe we could buy a ranch. Raise cattle, use our muscles.
Men built like we are should be working out in the open.

Happy (avidly):   The Loman Brothers, heh?

Biff (with vast affection):   Sure, we'd be known all over the counties!

Happy (enthralled):   That's what I dream about, Biff. Sometimes I want
to just rip my clothes off in the middle of the store and outbox that
goddam merchandise manager. I mean I can outbox, outrun, and
outlift anybody in that store, and I have to take orders from those
common, petty sons-of-bitches till I can't stand it anymore.

Biff: I'm tellin' you, kid, if you were with me I'd be happy out there.

Happy (enthused):   See, Biff, everybody around me is so false that I'm
constantly lowering my ideals . . .

Biff: Baby, together we'd stand up for one another, we'd have someone
to trust.

Happy: If I were around you—

Biff: Hap, the trouble is we weren't brought up to grub for money. I
don't know how to do it.

Happy: Neither can I!

Biff: Then let's go!

Happy: The only thing is—what can you make out there?

Biff: But look at your friend. Builds an estate and then hasn't the peace of
mind to live in it.

Happy: Yeah, but when he walks into the store the waves part in front of
him. That's fifty-two thousand dollars a year coming through the
revolving door, and I got more in my pinky finger than he's got in his
head.

Biff: Yeah, but you just said—

Happy: I gotta show some of those pompous, self-important executives
over there that Hap Loman can make the grade. I want to walk into
the store the way he walks in. Then I'll go with you, Biff. We'll be
together yet, I swear. But take those two we had tonight. Now
weren't they gorgeous creatures?

Biff: Yeah, yeah, most gorgeous I've had in years.

Happy: I get that any time I want, Biff. Whenever I feel disgusted. The

only trouble is, it gets like bowling or something. I just keep knockin'
them over and it doesn't mean anything. You still run around a lot?

Biff: Naa. I'd like to find a girl—steady, somebody with substance.

Happy: That's what I long for.

Biff: Go on! You'd never come home.

Happy: I would! Somebody with character, with resistance! Like Mom,
y'know? You're gonna call me a bastard when I tell you this. That girl
Charlotte I was with tonight is engaged to be married in five weeks.
(*He tries on his new hat.*)

Biff: No kiddin'!

Happy: Sure, the guy's in line for the vice-presidency of the store. I don't
know what gets into me, maybe I just have an overdeveloped sense of
competition or something, but I went and ruined her, and
furthermore I can't get rid of her. And he's the third executive I've
done that to. Isn't that a crummy characteristic? And to top it all, I go
to their weddings! (*Indignantly, but laughing.*) Like I'm not supposed
to take bribes. Manufacturers offer me a hundred-dollar bill now and
then to throw an order their way. You know how honest I am, but it's
like this girl, see. I hate myself for it. Because I don't want the girl,
and, still, I take it and—I love it!

Biff: Let's go to sleep.

Happy: I guess we didn't settle anything, heh?

Biff: I just got one idea that I think I'm going to try.

Happy: What's that?

Biff: Remember Bill Oliver?

Happy: Sure, Oliver is very big now. You want to work for him again?

Biff: No, but when I quit he said something to me. He put his arm on
my shoulder, and he said, "Biff, if you ever need anything, come to
me."

Happy: I remember that. That sounds good.

Biff: I think I'll go to see him. If I could get ten thousand or even seven
or eight thousand dollars I could buy a beautiful ranch.

Happy: I bet he'd back you. 'Cause he thought highly of you, Biff. I
mean, they all do. You're well liked, Biff. That's why I say to come
back here, and we both have the apartment. And I'm tellin' you, Biff,
any babe you want . . .

Biff: No, with a ranch I could do the work I like and still be something. I
just wonder though. I wonder if Oliver still thinks I stole that carton
of basketballs.

Happy: Oh, he probably forgot that long ago. It's almost ten years.
You're too sensitive. Anyway, he didn't really fire you.

Biff: Well, I think he was going to. I think that's why I quit. I was never
sure whether he knew or not. I know he thought the world of me,
though. I was the only one he'd let lock up the place.

Willy (*below*): You gonna wash the engine, Biff?

Happy: Shh!

(Biff looks at Happy, who is gazing down, listening. Willy is mumbling in the parlor.)

Happy: You hear that?

(They listen. Willy laughs warmly.)

Biff (growing angry):   Doesn't he know Mom can hear that?

Willy: Don't get your sweater dirty, Biff!

(A look of pain crosses Biff's face.)

Happy: Isn't that terrible? Don't leave again, will you? You'll find a job here. You gotta stick around. I don't know what to do about him, it's getting embarrassing.

Willy: What a simonizing job!

Biff: Mom's hearing that!

Willy: No kiddin', Biff, you got a date? Wonderful!

Happy: Go on to sleep. But talk to him in the morning, will you?

Biff (reluctantly getting into bed):   With her in the house. Brother!

Happy (getting into bed):   I wish you'd have a good talk with him.

(The light on their room begins to fade.)

Biff (to himself in bed):   That selfish, stupid . . .

Happy: Sh . . . Sleep, Biff.

(Their light is out. Well before they have finished speaking, Willy's form is dimly seen below in the darkened kitchen. He opens the refrigerator, searches in there, and takes out a bottle of milk. The apartment houses are fading out, and the entire house and surroundings become covered with leaves. Music insinuates itself as the leaves appear.)

Willy: Just wanna be careful with those girls, Biff, that's all. Don't make any promises. No promises of any kind. Because a girl, y'know, they always believe what you tell 'em, and you're very young, Biff, you're too young to be talking seriously to girls. (*Light rises on the kitchen. Willy, talking, shuts the refrigerator door and comes downstage to the kitchen table. He pours milk into a glass. He is totally immersed in himself, smiling faintly.*) Too young entirely, Biff. You want to watch your schooling first. Then when you're all set, there'll be plenty of girls for a boy like you. (*He smiles broadly at a kitchen chair.*) That so? The girls pay for you? (*He laughs.*) Boy, you must really be makin' a hit. (*Willy is gradually addressing—physically—a point offstage, speaking through the wall of the kitchen, and his voice has been rising in volume to that of a normal conversation.*) I been wondering why you polish the car so careful. Ha! Don't leave the hubcaps, boys. Get the chamois to the hubcaps. Happy, use newspaper on the windows, it's the easiest thing. Show him how to do it, Biff! You see, Happy? Pad it up, use it like a pad. That's it, that's it, good work. You're doin' all right, Hap.

(*He pauses, then nods in approbation for a few seconds, then looks upward.*) Biff, first thing we gotta do when we get time is clip that big branch over the house. Afraid it's gonna fall in a storm and hit the roof. Tell you what. We get a rope and sling her around, and then we climb up there with a couple of saws and take her down. Soon as you finish the car, boys, I wanna see ya. I got a surprise for you, boys.

Biff (offstage):   Whatta ya got, Dad?

Willy: No, you finish first. Never leave a job till you're finished— remember that. (*Looking toward the "big trees."*) Biff, up in Albany I saw a beautiful hammock. I think I'll buy it next trip, and we'll hang it right between those two elms. Wouldn't that be something? Just swingin' there under those branches. Boy, that would be . . .

(*Young Biff and Young Happy appear from the direction Willy was addressing. Happy carries rags and a pail of water. Biff, wearing a sweater with a block "S," carries a football.*)

Biff (pointing in the direction of the car offstage):   How's that, Pop, professional?

Willy: Terrific. Terrific job, boys. Good work, Biff.

Happy: Where's the surprise, Pop?

Willy: In the back seat of the car.

Happy: Boy! (*He runs off.*)

Biff: What is it, Dad? Tell me, what'd you buy?

Willy (laughing, cuffs him):   Never mind, something I want you to have.

Biff (turns and starts off):   What is it, Hap?

Happy (offstage):   It's a punching bag!

Biff: Oh, Pop!

Willy: It's got Gene Tunney's signature on it!

(*Happy runs onstage with a punching bag.*)

Biff: Gee, how'd you know we wanted a punching bag?

Willy: Well, it's the finest thing for the timing.

Happy (lies down on his back and pedals with his feet):   I'm losing weight, you notice, Pop?

Willy (to Happy):   Jumping rope is good too.

Biff: Did you see the new football I got?

Willy (examining the ball):   Where'd you get a new ball?

Biff: The coach told me to practice my passing.

Willy: That so? And he gave you the ball, heh?

Biff: Well, I borrowed it from the locker room. (*He laughs confidentially.*)

Willy (laughing with him at the theft):   I want you to return that.

Happy: I told you he wouldn't like it!

Biff (angrily):   Well, I'm bringing it back!

Willy (stopping the incipient argument, to Happy):   Sure, he's gotta

practice with a regulation ball, doesn't he? (*To Biff.*) Coach'll probably
congratulate you on your initiative!

Biff: Oh, he keeps congratulating my initiative all the time, Pop.

Willy: That's because he likes you. If somebody else took that ball there'd
be an uproar. So what's the report, boys, what's the report?

Biff: Where'd you go this time, Dad? Gee we were lonesome for you.

*Willy (pleased, puts an arm around each boy and they come down to the
apron):* Lonesome, heh?

Biff: Missed you every minute.

Willy: Don't say? Tell you a secret, boys. Don't breathe it to a soul.
Someday I'll have my own business, and I'll never have to leave home
anymore.

Happy: Like Uncle Charley, heh?

Willy: Bigger than Uncle Charley! Because Charley is not—liked. He's
liked, but he's not—well liked.

Biff: Where'd you go this time, Dad?

Willy: Well, I got on the road, and I went north to Providence. Met the
Mayor.

Biff: The Mayor of Providence!

Willy: He was sitting in the hotel lobby.

Biff: What'd he say?

Willy: He said, "Morning!" And I said, "You got a fine city here,
Mayor." And then he had coffee with me. And then I went to
Waterbury. Waterbury is a fine city. Big clock city, the famous
Waterbury clock. Sold a nice bill there. And then Boston—Boston is
the cradle of the Revolution. A fine city. And a couple of other towns
in Mass., and on to Portland and Bangor and straight home!

Biff: Gee, I'd love to go with you sometime, Dad.

Willy: Soon as summer comes.

Happy: Promise?

Willy: You and Hap and I, and I'll show you all the towns. America is full
of beautiful towns and fine, upstanding people. And they know me,
boys, they know me up and down New England. The finest people.
And when I bring you fellas up, there'll be open sesame for all of us,
'cause one thing, boys: I have friends. I can park my car in any street in
New England, and the cops protect it like their own. This summer,
heh?

Biff and Happy (together): Yeah! You bet!

Willy: We'll take our bathing suits.

Happy: We'll carry your bags, Pop!

Willy: Oh, won't that be something! Me comin' into the Boston stores
with you boys carryin' my bags. What a sensation! (*Biff is prancing
around, practicing passing the ball.*) You nervous, Biff, about the
game?

Biff: Not if you're gonna be there.

Willy: What do they say about you in school, now that they made you
 captain?

Happy: There's a crowd of girls behind him every time the classes change.

Biff (taking Willy's hand):   This Saturday, Pop, this Saturday—just for
 you, I'm going to break through for a touchdown.

Happy: You're supposed to pass.

Biff: I'm takin' one play for Pop. You watch me, Pop, and when I take off
 my helmet, that means I'm breakin' out. Then you watch me crash
 through that line!

Willy (kisses Biff):   Oh, wait'll I tell this in Boston!

(*Bernard enters in knickers. He is younger than Biff, earnest and loyal, a
 worried boy.*)

Bernard: Biff, where are you? You're supposed to study with me today.

Willy: Hey, looka Bernard. What're you lookin' so anemic about,
 Bernard?

Bernard: He's gotta study, Uncle Willy. He's got Regents next week.

Happy (tauntingly, spinning Bernard around):   Let's box, Bernard!

Bernard: Biff! (*He gets away from Happy.*) Listen, Biff, I heard Mr.
 Birnbaum say that if you don't start studyin' math he's gonna flunk
 you, and you won't graduate. I heard him!

Willy: You better study with him, Biff. Go ahead now.

Bernard: I heard him!

Biff: Oh, Pop, you didn't see my sneakers! (*He holds up a foot for Willy to
 look at.*)

Willy: Hey, that's a beautiful job of printing!

Bernard (wiping his glasses):   Just because he printed University of Virginia
 on his sneakers doesn't mean they've got to graduate him, Uncle
 Willy!

Willy (angrily):   What're you talking about? With scholarships to three
 universities they're gonna flunk him?

Bernard: But I heard Mr. Birnbaum say—

Willy: Don't be a pest, Bernard! (*To his boys.*) What an anemic!

Bernard: Okay, I'm waiting for you in my house, Biff.

(*Bernard goes off. The Lomans laugh.*)

Willy: Bernard is not well liked, is he?

Biff: He's liked, but he's not well liked.

Happy: That's right, Pop.

Willy: That's just what I mean. Bernard can get the best marks in school,
 y'understand, but when he gets out in the business world,
 y'understand, you are going to be five times ahead of him. That's why
 I thank Almighty God you're both built like Adonises. Because the
 man who makes an appearance in the business world, the man who
 creates personal interest, is the man who gets ahead. Be liked and you

will never want. You take me, for instance. I never have to wait in line to see a buyer. "Willy Loman is here!" That's all they have to know, and I go right through.

Biff: Did you knock them dead, Pop?

Willy: Knocked 'em cold in Providence, slaughtered 'em in Boston.

Happy (on his back, pedaling again):   I'm losing weight, you notice, Pop?

(*Linda enters as of old, a ribbon in her hair, carrying a basket of washing.*)

Linda (with youthful energy):   Hello, dear!

Willy: Sweetheart!

Linda: How'd the Chevvy run?

Willy: Chevrolet, Linda, is the greatest car ever built. (*To the boys.*) Since when do you let your mother carry wash up the stairs?

Biff: Grab hold there, boy!

Happy: Where to, Mom?

Linda: Hang them up on the line. And you better go down to your friends, Biff. The cellar is full of boys. They don't know what to do with themselves.

Biff: Ah, when Pop comes home they can wait!

Willy (laughs appreciatively):   You better go down and tell them what to do, Biff.

Biff: I think I'll have them sweep out the furnace room.

Willy: Good work, Biff.

Biff (goes through wall-line of kitchen to doorway at back and calls down):   Fellas! Everybody sweep out the furnace room! I'll be right down!

Voices: All right! Okay, Biff.

Biff: George and Sam and Frank, come out back! We're hangin' up the wash! Come on, Hap, on the double! (*He and Happy carry out the basket.*)

Linda: The way they obey him!

Willy: Well, that's training, the training. I'm tellin' you, I was sellin' thousands and thousands, but I had to come home.

Linda: Oh, the whole block'll be at that game. Did you sell anything?

Willy: I did five hundred gross in Providence and seven hundred gross in Boston.

Linda: No! Wait a minute, I've got a pencil. (*She pulls pencil and paper out of her apron pocket.*) That makes your commission . . . Two hundred—my God! Two hundred and twelve dollars!

Willy: Well, I didn't figure it yet, but . . .

Linda: How much did you do?

Willy: Well, I—I did—about a hundred and eighty gross in Providence. Well, no—it came to—roughly two hundred gross on the whole trip.

Linda (without hesitation):   Two hundred gross. That's . . . (*She figures.*)

Willy: The trouble was that three of the stores were half-closed for
inventory in Boston. Otherwise I woulda broke records.

Linda: Well, it makes seventy dollars and some pennies. That's very good.

Willy: What do we owe?

Linda: Well, on the first there's sixteen dollars on the refrigerator—

Willy: Why sixteen?

Linda: Well, the fan belt broke, so it was a dollar eighty.

Willy: But it's brand new.

Linda: Well, the man said that's the way it is. Till they work themselves
in, y'know.

(They move through the wall-line into the kitchen.)

Willy: I hope we didn't get stuck on that machine.

Linda: They got the biggest ads of any of them!

Willy: I know, it's a fine machine. What else?

Linda: Well, there's nine-sixty for the washing machine. And for the
vacuum cleaner there's three and a half due on the fifteenth. Then the
roof, you got twenty-one dollars remaining.

Willy: It don't leak, does it?

Linda: No, they did a wonderful job. Then you owe Frank for the
carburetor.

Willy: I'm not going to pay that man! That goddam Chevrolet, they
ought to prohibit the manufacture of that car!

Linda: Well, you owe him three and a half. And odds and ends, comes to
around a hundred and twenty dollars by the fifteenth.

Willy: A hundred and twenty dollars! My God, if business don't pick up I
don't know what I'm gonna do!

Linda: Well, next week you'll do better.

Willy: Oh, I'll knock 'em dead next week. I'll go to Hartford. I'm very
well liked in Hartford. You know, the trouble is, Linda, people don't
seem to take to me.

(They move onto the forestage.)

Linda: Oh, don't be foolish.

Willy: I know it when I walk in. They seem to laugh at me.

Linda: Why? Why would they laugh at you? Don't talk that way, Willy.

*(Willy moves to the edge of the stage. Linda goes into the kitchen and
starts to darn stockings.)*

Willy: I don't know the reason for it, but they just pass me by. I'm not
noticed.

Linda: But you're doing wonderful, dear. You're making seventy to a
hundred dollars a week.

Willy: But I gotta be at it ten, twelve hours a day. Other men—I don't
know—they do it easier. I don't know why—I can't stop myself—I

talk too much. A man oughta come in with a few words. One thing about Charley. He's a man of few words, and they respect him.

Linda: You don't talk too much, you're just lively.

Willy (smiling): Well, I figure, what the hell, life is short, a couple of jokes. (*To himself.*) I joke too much! (*The smile goes.*)

Linda: Why? You're—

Willy: I'm fat. I'm very—foolish to look at, Linda. I didn't tell you, but Christmas time I happened to be calling on F. H. Stewarts, and a salesman I know, as I was going in to see the buyer I heard him say something about—walrus. And I—I cracked him right across the face. I won't take that. I simply will not take that. But they do laugh at me. I know that.

Linda: Darling . . .

Willy: I gotta overcome it. I know I gotta overcome it. I'm not dressing to advantage, maybe.

Linda: Willy, darling, you're the handsomest man in the world—

Willy: Oh, no, Linda.

Linda: To me you are. (*Slight pause.*) The handsomest. (*From the darkness is heard the laughter of a woman. Willy doesn't turn to it, but it continues through Linda's lines.*) And the boys, Willy. Few men are idolized by their children the way you are.

(*Music is heard as behind a scrim, to the left of the house, The Woman, dimly seen, is dressing.*)

Willy (with great feeling): You're the best there is, Linda, you're a pal, you know that? On the road—on the road I want to grab you sometimes and just kiss the life outa you. (*The laughter is loud now, and he moves into a brightening area at the left, where The Woman has come from behind the scrim and is standing, putting on her hat, looking into a "mirror" and laughing.*) 'Cause I get so lonely—especially when business is bad and there's nobody to talk to. I get the feeling that I'll never sell anything again, that I won't make a living for you, or a business, a business for the boys. (*He talks through The Woman's subsiding laughter; The Woman primps at the "mirror."*) There's so much I want to make for—

The Woman: Me? You didn't make me, Willy. I picked you.

Willy (pleased): You picked me?

The Woman (who is quite proper-looking, Willy's age): I did. I've been sitting at that desk watching all the salesmen go by, day in, day out. But you've got such a sense of humor, and we do have such a good time together, don't we?

Willy: Sure, sure. (*He takes her in his arms.*) Why do you have to go now?

The Woman: It's two o'clock . . .

Willy: No, come on in! (*He pulls her.*)

The Woman: . . . my sisters'll be scandalized. When'll you be back?

Willy: Oh, two weeks about. Will you come up again?

The Woman: Sure thing. You do make me laugh. It's good for me. (*She squeezes his arm, kisses him.*) And I think you're a wonderful man.

Willy: You picked me, heh?

The Woman: Sure. Because you're so sweet. And such a kidder.

Willy: Well, I'll see you next time I'm in Boston.

The Woman: I'll put you right through to the buyers.

Willy (slapping her bottom): Right. Well, bottoms up!

The Woman (slaps him gently and laughs): You just kill me, Willy. (*He suddenly grabs her and kisses her roughly.*) You kill me. And thanks for the stockings. I love a lot of stockings. Well, good night.

Willy: Good night. And keep your pores open!

The Woman: Oh, Willy!

> (*The Woman bursts out laughing, and Linda's laughter blends in. The Woman disappears into the dark. Now the area at the kitchen table brightens. Linda is sitting where she was at the kitchen table, but now is mending a pair of her silk stockings.*)

Linda: You are, Willy. The handsomest man. You've got no reason to feel that—

Willy (coming out of The Woman's dimming area and going over to Linda): I'll make it all up to you, Linda, I'll—

Linda: There's nothing to make up, dear. You're doing fine, better than—

Willy (noticing her mending): What's that?

Linda: Just mending my stockings. They're so expensive—

Willy (angrily, taking them from her): I won't have you mending stockings in this house! Now throw them out!

> (*Linda puts the stockings in her pocket.*)

Bernard (entering on the run): Where is he? If he doesn't study!

Willy (moving to the forestage, with great agitation): You'll give him the answers!

Bernard: I do, but I can't on a Regents! That's a state exam! They're liable to arrest me!

Willy: Where is he? I'll whip him, I'll whip him!

Linda: And he'd better give back that football, Willy, it's not nice.

Willy: Biff! Where is he? Why is he taking everything?

Linda: He's too rough with the girls, Willy. All the mothers are afraid of him!

Willy: I'll whip him!

Bernard: He's driving the car without a license!

> (*The Woman's laugh is heard.*)

Willy: Shut up!

Linda: All the mothers—

Willy: Shut up!

Bernard (backing quietly away and out):   Mr. Birnbaum says he's stuck up.

Willy: Get outa here!

Bernard: If he doesn't buckle down he'll flunk math! (*He goes off.*)

Linda: He's right, Willy, you've gotta—

Willy (exploding at her):   There's nothing the matter with him! You want him to be a worm like Bernard? He's got spirit, personality . . . (*As he speaks, Linda, almost in tears, exits into the living room. Willy is alone in the kitchen, wilting and staring. The leaves are gone. It is night again, and the apartment houses look down from behind.*) Loaded with it. Loaded! What is he stealing? He's giving it back, isn't he? Why is he stealing? What did I tell him? I never in my life told him anything but decent things.

(*Happy in pajamas has come down the stairs; Willy suddenly becomes aware of Happy's presence.*)

Happy: Let's go now, come on.

Willy (sitting down at the kitchen table):   Huh! Why did she have to wax the floors herself? Everytime she waxes the floors she keels over. She knows that!

Happy: Shh! Take it easy. What brought you back tonight?

Willy: I got an awful scare. Nearly hit a kid in Yonkers. God! Why didn't I go to Alaska with my brother Ben that time! Ben! That man was a genius, that man was success incarnate! What a mistake! He begged me to go.

Happy: Well, there's no use in—

Willy: You guys! There was a man started with the clothes on his back and ended up with diamond mines!

Happy: Boy, someday I'd like to know how he did it.

Willy: What's the mystery? The man knew what he wanted and went out and got it! Walked into a jungle, and comes out, the age of twenty-one, and he's rich! The world is an oyster, but you don't crack it open on a mattress!

Happy: Pop, I told you I'm gonna retire you for life.

Willy: You'll retire me for life on seventy goddam dollars a week? And your women and your car and your apartment, and you'll retire me for life! Christ's sake, I couldn't get past Yonkers today! Where are you guys, where are you? The woods are burning! I can't drive a car!

(*Charley has appeared in the doorway. He is a large man, slow of speech, laconic, immovable. In all he says, despite what he says, there is pity, and, now, trepidation. He has a robe over pajamas, slippers on his feet. He enters the kitchen.*)

Charley: Everything all right?

Happy: Yeah, Charley, everything's . . .

Willy: What's the matter?

Charley: I heard some noise. I thought something happened. Can't we do something about the walls? You sneeze in here, and in my house hats blow off.

Happy: Let's go to bed, Dad. Come on.

(Charley signals to Happy to go.)

Willy: You go ahead, I'm not tired at the moment.

Happy (to Willy):   Take it easy, huh? (*He exits.*)

Willy: What're you doin' up?

Charley (sitting down at the kitchen table opposite Willy):   Couldn't sleep good. I had a heartburn.

Willy: Well, you don't know how to eat.

Charley: I eat with my mouth.

Willy: No, you're ignorant. You gotta know about vitamins and things like that.

Charley: Come on, let's shoot. Tire you out a little.

Willy (hesitantly):   All right. You got cards?

Charley (taking a deck from his pocket):   Yeah, I got them. Someplace. What is it with those vitamins?

Willy (dealing):   They build up your bones. Chemistry.

Charley: Yeah, but there's no bones in a heartburn.

Willy: What are you talkin' about? Do you know the first thing about it?

Charley: Don't get insulted.

Willy: Don't talk about something you don't know anything about.

(They are playing. Pause.)

Charley: What're you doin' home?

Willy: A little trouble with the car.

Charley: Oh. (*Pause.*) I'd like to take a trip to California.

Willy: Don't say.

Charley: You want a job?

Willy: I got a job. I told you that. (*After a slight pause.*) What the hell are you offering me a job for?

Charley: Don't get insulted.

Willy: Don't insult me.

Charley: I don't see no sense in it. You don't have to go on this way.

Willy: I got a good job. (*Slight pause.*) What do you keep comin' in here for?

Charley: You want me to go?

Willy (after a pause, withering):   I can't understand it. He's going back to Texas again. What the hell is that?

Charley: Let him go.

Willy: I got nothin' to give him, Charley, I'm clean, I'm clean.

Charley: He won't starve. None a them starve. Forget about him.

Willy: Then what have I got to remember?

Charley: You take it too hard. To hell with it. When a deposit bottle is broken you don't get your nickel back.

Willy: That's easy enough for you to say.

Charley: That ain't easy for me to say.

Willy: Did you see the ceiling I put up in the living room?

Charley: Yeah, that's a piece of work. To put up a ceiling is a mystery to me. How do you do it?

Willy: What's the difference?

Charley: Well, talk about it.

Willy: You gonna put up a ceiling?

Charley: How could I put up a ceiling?

Willy: Then what the hell are you bothering me for?

Charley: You're insulted again.

Willy: A man who can't handle tools is not a man. You're disgusting.

Charley: Don't call me disgusting, Willy.

(Uncle Ben, carrying a valise and an umbrella, enters the forestage from around the right corner of the house. He is a stolid man, in his sixties, with a mustache and an authoritative air. He is utterly certain of his destiny, and there is an aura of far places about him. He enters exactly as Willy speaks.)

Willy: I'm getting awfully tired, Ben.

(Ben's music is heard. Ben looks around at everything.)

Charley: Good, keep playing; you'll sleep better. Did you call me Ben?

(Ben looks at his watch.)

Willy: That's funny. For a second there you reminded me of my brother Ben.

Ben: I only have a few minutes. *(He strolls, inspecting the place. Willy and Charley continue playing.)*

Charley: You never heard from him again, heh? Since that time?

Willy: Didn't Linda tell you? Couple of weeks ago we got a letter from his wife in Africa. He died.

Charley: That so.

Ben (chuckling):   So this is Brooklyn, eh?

Charley: Maybe you're in for some of his money.

Willy: Naa, he had seven sons. There's just one opportunity I had with that man . . .

Ben: I must make a train, William. There are several properties I'm looking at in Alaska.

Willy: Sure, sure! If I'd gone with him to Alaska that time, everything would've been totally different.

Charley: Go on, you'd froze to death up there.

Willy: What're you talking about?

Ben: Opportunity is tremendous in Alaska, William. Surprised you're not up there.

Willy: Sure, tremendous.

Charley: Heh?

Willy: There was the only man I ever met who knew the answers.

Charley: Who?

Ben: How are you all?

Willy (taking a pot, smiling): Fine, fine.

Charley: Pretty sharp tonight.

Ben: Is Mother living with you?

Willy: No, she died a long time ago.

Charley: Who?

Ben: That's too bad. Fine specimen of a lady, Mother.

Willy (to Charley): Heh?

Ben: I'd hoped to see the old girl.

Charley: Who died?

Ben: Heard anything from Father, have you?

Willy (unnerved): What do you mean, who died?

Charley (taking a pot): What're you talkin' about?

Ben (looking at his watch): William, it's half-past eight!

Willy (as though to dispel his confusion he angrily stops Charley's hand):
  That's my build!

Charley: I put the ace—

Willy: If you don't know how to play the game I'm not gonna throw my
  money away on you!

Charley (rising): It was my ace, for God's sake!

Willy: I'm through, I'm through!

Ben: When did Mother die?

Willy: Long ago. Since the beginning you never knew how to play
  cards.

Charley (picks up the cards and goes to the door): All right! Next time I'll
  bring a deck with five aces.

Willy: I don't play that kind of game!

Charley (turning to him): You ought to be ashamed of yourself!

Willy: Yeah?

Charley: Yeah! (*He goes out.*)

Willy (slamming the door after him): Ignoramus!

Ben (as Willy comes toward him through the wall-line of the kitchen): So
  you're William.

Willy (shaking Ben's hand): Ben! I've been waiting for you so long!
  What's the answer? How did you do it?

Ben: Oh, there's a story in that.

  (*Linda enters the forestage, as of old, carrying the wash basket.*)

Linda: Is this Ben?

Ben (gallantly): How do you do, my dear.

Linda: Where've you been all these years? Willy's always wondered why
  you—

Willy (pulling Ben away from her impatiently):   Where is Dad? Didn't you follow him? How did you get started?

Ben: Well, I don't know how much you remember.

Willy: Well, I was just a baby, of course, only three or four years old—

Ben: Three years and eleven months.

Willy: What a memory, Ben!

Ben: I have many enterprises, William, and I have never kept books.

Willy: I remember I was sitting under the wagon in—was it Nebraska?

Ben: It was South Dakota, and I gave you a bunch of wild flowers.

Willy: I remember you walking away down some open road.

Ben (laughing):   I was going to find Father in Alaska.

Willy: Where is he?

Ben: At that age I had a very faulty view of geography, William. I discovered after a few days that I was heading due south, so instead of Alaska, I ended up in Africa.

Linda: Africa!

Willy: The Gold Coast!

Ben: Principally diamond mines.

Linda: Diamond mines!

Ben: Yes, my dear. But I've only a few minutes—

Willy: No! Boys! Boys! (*Young Biff and Happy appear.*) Listen to this. This is your Uncle Ben, a great man! Tell my boys, Ben!

Ben: Why, boys, when I was seventeen I walked into the jungle, and when I was twenty-one I walked out. (*He laughs.*) And by God I was rich.

Willy (to the boys):   You see what I been talking about? The greatest things can happen!

Ben (glancing at his watch):   I have an appointment in Ketchikan Tuesday week.

Willy: No, Ben! Please tell about Dad. I want my boys to hear. I want them to know the kind of stock they spring from. All I remember is a man with a big beard, and I was in Mamma's lap, sitting around a fire, and some kind of high music.

Ben: His flute. He played the flute.

Willy: Sure, the flute, that's right!

(*New music is heard, a high, rollicking tune.*)

Ben: Father was a very great and a very wild-hearted man. We would start in Boston, and he'd toss the whole family into the wagon, and then he'd drive the team right across the country; through Ohio, and Indiana, Michigan, Illinois, and all the Western states. And we'd stop in the towns and sell the flutes that he'd made on the way. Great inventor, Father. With one gadget he made more in a week than a man like you could make in a lifetime.

Willy: That's just the way I'm bringing them up, Ben—rugged, well liked, all-around.

Ben: Yeah? (*To Biff.*) Hit that, boy—hard as you can. (*He pounds his stomach.*)

Biff: Oh, no, sir!

Ben (taking boxing stance):   Come on, get to me! (*He laughs.*)

Willy: Go to it, Biff! Go ahead, show him!

Biff: Okay! (*He cocks his fists and starts in.*)

Linda (to Willy):   Why must he fight, dear?

Ben (sparring with Biff):   Good boy! Good boy!

Willy: How's that, Ben, heh?

Happy: Give him the left, Biff!

Linda: Why are you fighting?

Ben: Good boy! (*Suddenly comes in, trips Biff, and stands over him, the point of his umbrella poised over Biff's eye.*)

Linda: Look out, Biff!

Biff: Gee!

Ben (patting Biff's knee):   Never fight fair with a stranger, boy. You'll never get out of the jungle that way. (*Taking Linda's hand and bowing.*) It was an honor and a pleasure to meet you, Linda.

Linda (withdrawing her hand coldly, frightened):   Have a nice—trip.

Ben (to Willy):   And good luck with your—what do you do?

Willy: Selling.

Ben: Yes. Well . . . (*He raises his hand in farewell to all.*)

Willy: No, Ben, I don't want you to think . . . (*He takes Ben's arm to show him.*) It's Brooklyn, I know, but we hunt too.

Ben: Really, now.

Willy: Oh, sure, there's snakes and rabbits and—that's why I moved out here. Why, Biff can fell any one of these trees in no time! Boys! Go right over to where they're building the apartment house and get some sand. We're gonna rebuild the entire front stoop right now! Watch this, Ben!

Biff: Yes, sir! On the double, Hap!

Happy (as he and Biff run off):   I lost weight, Pop, you notice?

   (*Charley enters in knickers, even before the boys are gone.*)

Charley: Listen, if they steal anymore from that building the watchman'll put the cops on them!

Linda (to Willy):   Don't let Biff . . .

   (*Ben laughs lustily.*)

Willy: You shoulda seen the lumber they brought home last week. At least a dozen six-by-tens worth all kinds a money.

Charley: Listen, if that watchman—

Willy: I gave them hell, understand. But I got a couple of fearless characters there.

Charley: Willy, the jails are full of fearless characters.

Ben (clapping Willy on the back, with a laugh at Charley):   And the stock exchange, friend!

Willy (joining in Ben's laughter):   Where are the rest of your pants?

Charley: My wife bought them.

Willy: Now all you need is a golf club and you can go upstairs and go to sleep. (*To Ben.*) Great athlete! Between him and his son Bernard they can't hammer a nail!

Bernard (rushing in):   The watchman's chasing Biff!

Willy (angrily):   Shut up! He's not stealing anything!

Linda (alarmed, hurrying off left):   Where is he? Biff, dear! (*She exits.*)

Willy (moving toward the left, away from Ben):   There's nothing wrong. What's the matter with you?

Ben: Nervy boy. Good!

Willy (laughing):   Oh, nerves of iron, that Biff!

Charley: Don't know what it is. My New England man comes back and he's bleedin', they murdered him up there.

Willy: It's contacts, Charley, I got important contacts!

Charley (sarcastically):   Glad to hear it, Willy. Come in later, we'll shoot a little casino. I'll take some of your Portland money. (*He laughs at Willy and exits.*)

Willy (turning to Ben):   Business is bad, it's murderous. But not for me, of course.

Ben: I'll stop by on my way back to Africa.

Willy (longingly):   Can't you stay a few days? You're just what I need, Ben, because I—I have a fine position here, but I—well, Dad left when I was such a baby and I never had a chance to talk to him and I still feel—kind of temporary about myself.

Ben: I'll be late for my train.

(*They are at opposite ends of the stage.*)

Willy: Ben, my boys—can't we talk? They'd go into the jaws of hell for me, see, but I —

Ben: William, you're being first-rate with your boys. Outstanding, manly chaps!

Willy (hanging on to his words):   Oh, Ben, that's good to hear! Because sometimes I'm afraid that I'm not teaching them the right kind of— Ben, how should I teach them?

Ben (giving great weight to each word, and with a certain vicious audacity): William, when I walked into the jungle, I was seventeen. When I walked out I was twenty-one. And, by God, I was rich! (*He goes off into darkness around the right corner of the house.*)

Willy: . . . was rich! That's just the spirit I want to imbue them with! To walk into a jungle! I was right! I was right! I was right!

(*Ben is gone, but Willy is still speaking to him as Linda, in nightgown and robe, enters the kitchen, glances around for Willy, then goes to the door of the house, looks out and sees him. Comes down to his left. He looks at her.*)

Linda: Willy, dear? Willy?

Willy: I was right!

Linda: Did you have some cheese? (*He can't answer.*) It's very late, darling. Come to bed, heh?

Willy (looking straight up):   Gotta break your neck to see a star in this yard.

Linda: You coming in?

Willy: Whatever happened to that diamond watch fob? Remember? When Ben came from Africa that time? Didn't he give me a watch fob with a diamond in it?

Linda: You pawned it, dear. Twelve, thirteen years ago. For Biff's radio correspondence course.

Willy: Gee, that was a beautiful thing. I'll take a walk.

Linda: But you're in your slippers.

Willy (starting to go around the house at the left):   I was right! I was! (*Half to Linda, as he goes, shaking his head.*) What a man! There was a man worth talking to. I was right!

Linda (calling after Willy):   But in your slippers, Willy!

(*Willy is almost gone when Biff, in his pajamas, comes down the stairs and enters the kitchen.*)

Biff: What is he doing out there?

Linda: Sh!

Biff: God Almighty, Mom, how long has he been doing this?

Linda: Don't, he'll hear you.

Biff: What the hell is the matter with him?

Linda: It'll pass by morning.

Biff: Shouldn't we do anything?

Linda: Oh, my dear, you should do a lot of things, but there's nothing to do, so go to sleep.

(*Happy comes down the stair and sits on the steps.*)

Happy: I never heard him so loud, Mom.

Linda: Well, come around more often; you'll hear him. (*She sits down at the table and mends the lining of Willy's jacket.*)

Biff: Why didn't you ever write me about this, Mom?

Linda: How would I write to you? For over three months you had no address.

Biff: I was on the move. But you know I thought of you all the time. You know that, don't you, pal?

Linda: I know, dear, I know. But he likes to have a letter. Just to know that there's still a possibility for better things.

Biff: He's not like this all the time, is he?

Linda: It's when you come home he's always the worst.

Biff: When I come home?

Linda: When you write you're coming, he's all smiles, and talks about the future, and—he's just wonderful. And then the closer you seem to come, the more shaky he gets, and then, by the time you get here, he's arguing, and he seems angry at you. I think it's just that maybe he can't bring himself to—to open up to you. Why are you so hateful to each other? Why is that?

Biff (evasively): I'm not hateful, Mom.

Linda: But you no sooner come in the door than you're fighting!

Biff: I don't know why. I mean to change. I'm tryin', Mom, you understand?

Linda: Are you home to stay now?

Biff: I don't know. I want to look around, see what's doin'.

Linda: Biff, you can't look around all your life, can you?

Biff: I just can't take hold, Mom. I can't take hold of some kind of a life.

Linda: Biff, a man is not a bird, to come and go with the springtime.

Biff: Your hair . . . (*He touches her hair.*) Your hair got so gray.

Linda: Oh, it's been gray since you were in high school. I just stopped dyeing it, that's all.

Biff: Dye it again, will ya? I don't want my pal looking old. (*He smiles.*)

Linda: You're such a boy! You think you can go away for a year and . . . You've got to get it into your head now that one day you'll knock on this door and there'll be strange people here—

Biff: What are you talking about? You're not even sixty, Mom.

Linda: But what about your father?

Biff (lamely): Well, I meant him too.

Happy: He admires Pop.

Linda: Biff, dear, if you don't have any feeling for him, then you can't have any feeling for me.

Biff: Sure I can, Mom.

Linda: No. You can't just come to see me, because I love him. (*With a threat, but only a threat, of tears.*) He's the dearest man in the world to me, and I won't have anyone making him feel unwanted and low and blue. You've got to make up your mind now, darling, there's no leeway anymore. Either he's your father and you pay him that respect, or else you're not to come here. I know he's not easy to get along with—nobody knows that better than me—but . . .

Willy (from the left, with a laugh): Hey, hey, Biffo!

Biff (starting to go out after Willy): What the hell is the matter with him? (*Happy stops him.*)

Linda: Don't—don't go near him!

Biff: Stop making excuses for him! He always, always wiped the floor with you. Never had an ounce of respect for you.

Happy: He's always had respect for—

Biff: What the hell do you know about it?

Happy (surlily): Just don't call him crazy!

Biff: He's got no character—Charley wouldn't do this. Not in his own house—spewing out that vomit from his mind.

Happy: Charley never had to cope with what he's got to.

Biff: People are worse off than Willy Loman. Believe me, I've seen them!

Linda: Then make Charley your father, Biff. You can't do that, can you? I don't say he's a great man. Willy Loman never made a lot of money. His name was never in the paper. He's not the finest character that ever lived. But he's a human being, and a terrible thing is happening to him. So attention must be paid. He's not to be allowed to fall into his grave like an old dog. Attention, attention must be finally paid to such a person. You called him crazy—

Biff: I didn't mean—

Linda: No, a lot of people think he's lost his—balance. But you don't have to be very smart to know what his trouble is. The man is exhausted.

Happy: Sure!

Linda: A small man can be just as exhausted as a great man. He works for a company thirty-six years this March, opens up unheard-of territories to their trademark, and now in his old age they take his salary away.

Happy (indignantly): I didn't know that, Mom.

Linda: You never asked, my dear! Now that you get your spending money someplace else you don't trouble your mind with him.

Happy: But I gave you money last—

Linda: Christmas time, fifty dollars! To fix the hot water it cost ninety-seven fifty! For five weeks he's been on straight commission, like a beginner, an unknown!

Biff: Those ungrateful bastards!

Linda: Are they any worse than his sons? When he brought them business, when he was young, they were glad to see him. But now his old friends, the old buyers that loved him so and always found some order to hand him in a pinch—they're all dead, retired. He used to be able to make six, seven calls a day in Boston. Now he takes his valises out of the car and puts them back and takes them out again and he's exhausted. Instead of walking he talks now. He drives seven hundred miles, and when he gets there no one knows him anymore, no one welcomes him. And what goes through a man's mind, driving seven hundred miles home without having earned a cent? Why shouldn't he talk to himself? Why? When he has to go to Charley and borrow fifty dollars a week and pretend to me that it's his pay? How long can that go on? How long? You see what I'm sitting here and waiting for? And you tell me he has no character? The man who never worked a day but for your benefit? When does he get the medal for that? Is this his reward—to turn around at the age of sixty-three and find his sons, who he loved better than his life, one a philandering bum—

Happy: Mom!

Linda: That's all you are, my baby! (*To Biff.*) And you! What happened to the love you had for him? You were such pals! How you used to talk to him on the phone every night! How lonely he was till he could come home to you!

Biff: All right, Mom. I'll live here in my room, and I'll get a job. I'll keep away from him, that's all.

Linda: No, Biff. You can't stay here and fight all the time.

Biff: He threw me out of this house, remember that.

Linda: Why did he do that? I never knew why.

Biff: Because I know he's a fake and he doesn't like anybody around who knows!

Linda: Why a fake? In what way? What do you mean?

Biff: Just don't lay it all at my feet. It's between me and him—that's all I have to say. I'll chip in from now on. He'll settle for half my pay check. He'll be all right. I'm going to bed. (*He starts for the stairs.*)

Linda: He won't be all right.

Biff (turning on the stairs, furiously): I hate this city and I'll stay here. Now what do you want?

Linda: He's dying, Biff.

(*Happy turns quickly to her, shocked.*)

Biff (after a pause): Why is he dying?

Linda: He's been trying to kill himself.

Biff (with great horror): How?

Linda: I live from day to day.

Biff: What're you talking about?

Linda: Remember I wrote you that he smashed up the car again? In February?

Biff: Well?

Linda: The insurance inspector came. He said that they have evidence. That all these accidents in the last year—weren't—weren't—accidents.

Happy: How can they tell that? That's a lie.

Linda: It seems there's a woman . . . (*She takes a breath as*)

Biff (sharply but contained): ⎱ What woman?
Linda (simultaneously): ⎰ . . . and this woman . . .

Linda: What?

Biff: Nothing. Go ahead.

Linda: What did you say?

Biff: Nothing. I just said what woman?

Happy: What about her?

Linda: Well, it seems she was walking down the road and saw his car. She says that he wasn't driving fast at all, and that he didn't skid. She says he came to that little bridge, and then deliberately smashed into the railing, and it was only the shallowness of the water that saved him.

Biff: Oh, no, he probably just fell asleep again.

Linda: I don't think he fell asleep.

Biff: Why not?

Linda: Last month . . . (*With great difficulty.*) Oh, boys, it's so hard to say a thing like this! He's just a big stupid man to you, but I tell you there's more good in him than in many other people. (*She chokes, wipes her eyes.*) I was looking for a fuse. The lights blew out, and I went down the cellar. And behind the fuse box—it happened to fall out— was a length of rubber pipe—just short.

Happy: No kidding!

Linda: There's a little attachment on the end of it. I knew right away. And sure enough, on the bottom of the water heater there's a new little nipple on the gas pipe.

Happy (angrily):   That—jerk.

Biff: Did you have it taken off?

Linda: I'm—I'm ashamed to. How can I mention it to him? Every day I go down and take away that little rubber pipe. But, when he comes home, I put it back where it was. How can I insult him that way? I don't know what to do. I live from day to day, boys. I tell you, I know every thought in his mind. It sounds so old-fashioned and silly, but I tell you he put his whole life into you and you've turned your backs on him. (*She is bent over in the chair, weeping, her face in her hands.*) Biff, I swear to God! Biff, his life is in your hands!

Happy (to Biff):   How do you like that damned fool!

Biff (kissing her):   All right, pal, all right. It's all settled now. I've been remiss. I know that, Mom. But now I'll stay, and I swear to you, I'll apply myself. (*Kneeling in front of her, in a fever of self-reproach.*) It's just—you see, Mom, I don't fit in business. Not that I won't try. I'll try, and I'll make good.

Happy: Sure you will. The trouble with you in business was you never tried to please people.

Biff: I know, I—

Happy: Like when you worked for Harrison's. Bob Harrison said you were tops, and then you go and do some damn fool thing like whistling whole songs in the elevator like a comedian.

Biff (against Happy):   So what? I like to whistle sometimes.

Happy: You don't raise a guy to a responsible job who whistles in the elevator!

Linda: Well, don't argue about it now.

Happy: Like when you'd go off and swim in the middle of the day instead of taking the line around.

Biff (his resentment rising):   Well, don't you run off? You take off sometimes, don't you? On a nice summer day?

Happy: Yeah, but I cover myself!

Linda: Boys!

Happy: If I'm going to take a fade the boss can call any number where

I'm supposed to be and they'll swear to him that I just left. I'll tell you something that I hate to say, Biff, but in the business world some of them think you're crazy.

Biff (angered): Screw the business world!

Happy: All right, screw it! Great, but cover yourself!

Linda: Hap, Hap!

Biff: I don't care what they think! They've laughed at Dad for years, and you know why? Because we don't belong in this nuthouse of a city! We should be mixing cement on some open plain, or—or carpenters. A carpenter is allowed to whistle!

(Willy walks in from the entrance of the house, at left.)

Willy: Even your grandfather was better than a carpenter. (*Pause. They watch him.*) You never grew up. Bernard does not whistle in the elevator, I assure you.

Biff (as though to laugh Willy out of it): Yeah, but you do, Pop.

Willy: I never in my life whistled in an elevator! And who in the business world thinks I'm crazy?

Biff: I didn't mean it like that, Pop. Now don't make a whole thing out of it, will ya?

Willy: Go back to the West! Be a carpenter, a cowboy, enjoy yourself!

Linda: Willy, he was just saying—

Willy: I heard what he said!

Happy (trying to quiet Willy): Hey, Pop, come on now . . .

Willy (continuing over Happy's line): They laugh at me, heh? Go to Filene's, go to the Hub, go to Slattery's, Boston. Call out the name Willy Loman and see what happens! Big shot!

Biff: All right, Pop.

Willy: Big!

Biff: All right!

Willy: Why do you always insult me?

Biff: I didn't say a word. (*To Linda.*) Did I say a word?

Linda: He didn't say anything, Willy.

Willy (going to the doorway of the living room): All right, good night, good night.

Linda: Willy, dear, he just decided . . .

Willy (to Biff): If you get tired hanging around tomorrow, paint the ceiling I put up in the living room.

Biff: I'm leaving early tomorrow.

Happy: He's going to see Bill Oliver, Pop.

Willy (interestedly): Oliver? For what?

Biff (with reserve, but trying, trying): He always said he'd stake me. I'd like to go into business, so maybe I can take him up on it.

Linda: Isn't that wonderful?

Willy: Don't interrupt. What's wonderful about it? There's fifty men

in the City of New York who'd stake him. (*To Biff.*) Sporting
  goods?

Biff: I guess so. I know something about it and—

Willy: He knows something about it! You know sporting goods better
  than Spalding, for God's sake! How much is he giving you?

Biff: I don't know, I didn't even see him yet, but—

Willy: Then what're you talkin' about?

Biff (getting angry):   Well, all I said was I'm gonna see him, that's all!

Willy (turning away):   Ah, you're counting your chickens again.

Biff (starting left for the stairs):   Oh, Jesus, I'm going to sleep!

Willy (calling after him):   Don't curse in this house!

Biff (turning):   Since when did you get so clean?

Happy (trying to stop them):   Wait a . . .

Willy: Don't use that language to me! I won't have it!

Happy (grabbing Biff, shouts):   Wait a minute! I got an idea. I got a
  feasible idea. Come here, Biff, let's talk this over now, let's talk some
  sense here. When I was down in Florida last time, I thought of a great
  idea to sell sporting goods. It just came back to me. You and I, Biff—
  we have a line, the Loman Line. We train a couple of weeks, and put
  on a couple of exhibitions, see?

Willy: That's an idea!

Happy: Wait! We form two basketball teams, see? Two water polo teams.
  We play each other. It's a million dollars' worth of publicity. Two
  brothers, see? The Loman Brothers. Displays in the Royal Palms—all
  the hotels. And banners over the ring and the basketball court:
  "Loman Brothers." Baby, we could sell sporting goods!

Willy: That is a one-million-dollar idea!

Linda: Marvelous!

Biff: I'm in great shape as far as that's concerned.

Happy: And the beauty of it is, Biff, it wouldn't be like a business. We'd
  be out playin' ball again . . .

Biff (enthused):   Yeah, that's . . .

Willy: Million-dollar . . .

Happy: And you wouldn't get fed up with it, Biff. It'd be the family
  again. There'd be the old honor, and comradeship, and if you wanted
  to go off for a swim or somethin'—well, you'd do it! Without some
  smart cooky gettin' up ahead of you!

Willy: Lick the world! You guys together could absolutely lick the
  civilized world.

Biff: I'll see Oliver tomorrow. Hap, if we could work that out . . .

Linda: Maybe things are beginning to—

Willy (wildly enthused, to Linda):   Stop interrupting! (*To Biff.*) But don't
  wear sport jacket and slacks when you see Oliver.

Biff: No, I'll—

Willy: A business suit, and talk as little as possible, and don't crack any jokes.

Biff: He did like me. Always liked me.

Linda: He loved you!

Willy (to Linda): Will you stop! (*To Biff.*) Walk in very serious. You are not applying for a boy's job. Money is to pass. Be quiet, fine, and serious. Everybody likes a kidder, but nobody lends him money.

Happy: I'll try to get some myself, Biff. I'm sure I can.

Willy: I see great things for you kids, I think your troubles are over. But remember, start big and you'll end big. Ask for fifteen. How much you gonna ask for?

Biff: Gee, I don't know—

Willy: And don't say "Gee." "Gee" is a boy's word. A man walking in for fifteen thousand dollars does not say "Gee!"

Biff: Ten, I think, would be top though.

Willy: Don't be so modest. You always started too low. Walk in with a big laugh. Don't look worried. Start off with a couple of your good stories to lighten things up. It's not what you say, it's how you say it— because personality always wins the day.

Linda: Oliver always thought the highest of him—

Willy: Will you let me talk?

Biff: Don't yell at her, Pop, will ya?

Willy (angrily): I was talking, wasn't I?

Biff: I don't like you yelling at her all the time, and I'm tellin' you, that's all.

Willy: What're you, takin' over this house?

Linda: Willy—

Willy (turning to her): Don't take his side all the time, goddammit!

Biff (furiously): Stop yelling at her!

Willy (suddenly pulling on his cheek, beaten down, guilt ridden): Give my best to Bill Oliver—he may remember me. (*He exits through the living room doorway.*)

Linda (her voice subdued): What'd you have to start that for? (*Biff turns away.*) You see how sweet he was as soon as you talked hopefully? (*She goes over to Biff.*) Come up and say good night to him. Don't let him go to bed that way.

Happy: Come on, Biff, let's buck him up.

Linda: Please, dear. Just say good night. It takes so little to make him happy. Come. (*She goes through the living room doorway, calling upstairs from within the living room.*) Your pajamas are hanging in the bathroom, Willy!

Happy (looking toward where Linda went out): What a woman! They broke the mold when they made her. You know that, Biff?

Biff: He's off salary. My God, working on commission!

Happy: Well, let's face it: he's no hot-shot selling man. Except that sometimes, you have to admit, he's a sweet personality.

Biff (deciding): Lend me ten bucks, will ya? I want to buy some new ties.

Happy: I'll take you to a place I know. Beautiful stuff. Wear one of my striped shirts tomorrow.

Biff: She got gray. Mom got awful old. Gee, I'm gonna go in to Oliver tomorrow and knock him for a—

Happy: Come on up. Tell that to Dad. Let's give him a whirl. Come on.

Biff (steamed up):   You know, with ten thousand bucks, boy!

Happy (as they go into the living room):   That's the talk, Biff, that's the first time I've heard the old confidence out of you! (*From within the living room, fading off.*) You're gonna live with me, kid, and any babe you want just say the word . . . (*The last lines are hardly heard. They are mounting the stairs to their parents' bedroom.*)

Linda (entering her bedroom and addressing Willy, who is in the bathroom. She is straightening the bed for him):   Can you do anything about the shower? It drips.

Willy (from the bathroom):   All of a sudden everything falls to pieces. Goddam plumbing, oughta be sued, those people. I hardly finished putting it in and the thing . . . (*His words rumble off.*)

Linda: I'm just wondering if Oliver will remember him. You think he might?

Willy (coming out of the bathroom in his pajamas):   Remember him? What's the matter with you, you crazy? If he'd've stayed with Oliver he'd be on top by now! Wait'll Oliver gets a look at him. You don't know the average caliber anymore. The average young man today—(*he is getting into bed*)—is got a caliber of zero. Greatest thing in the world for him was to bum around.

(*Biff and Happy enter the bedroom. Slight pause.*)

Willy (stops short, looking at Biff):   Glad to hear it, boy.

Happy: He wanted to say good night to you, sport.

Willy (to Biff):   Yeah. Knock him dead, boy. What'd you want to tell me?

Biff: Just take it easy, Pop. Good night. (*He turns to go.*)

Willy (unable to resist):   And if anything falls off the desk while you're talking to him—like a package or something—don't you pick it up. They have office boys for that.

Linda: I'll make a big breakfast—

Willy: Will you let me finish? (*To Biff.*) Tell him you were in the business in the West. Not farm work.

Biff: All right, Dad.

Linda: I think everything—

Willy (going right through her speech):   And don't undersell yourself. No less than fifteen thousand dollars.

Biff (unable to bear him):   Okay. Good night, Mom. (*He starts moving.*)

Willy: Because you got a greatness in you, Biff, remember that. You got all kinds of greatness . . . (*He lies back, exhausted. Biff walks out.*)

Linda (calling after Biff):   Sleep well, darling!

Happy: I'm gonna get married, Mom. I wanted to tell you.

Linda: Go to sleep, dear.

Happy (going):   I just wanted to tell you.

Willy: Keep up the good work. (*Happy exits.*) God . . . remember that Ebbets Field game? The championship of the city?

Linda: Just rest. Should I sing to you?

Willy: Yeah. Sing to me. (*Linda hums a soft lullaby.*) When that team came out—he was the tallest, remember?

Linda: Oh, yes. And in gold.

> (*Biff enters the darkened kitchen, takes a cigarette, and leaves the house. He comes downstage into a golden pool of light. He smokes, staring at the night.*)

Willy: Like a young god. Hercules—something like that. And the sun, the sun all around him. Remember how he waved to me? Right up from the field, with the representatives of three colleges standing by? And the buyers I brought, and the cheers when he came out—Loman, Loman, Loman! God Almighty, he'll be great yet. A star like that, magnificent, can never really fade away!

> (*The light on Willy is fading. The gas heater begins to glow through the kitchen wall, near the stairs, a blue flame beneath red coils.*)

Linda (timidly):   Willy dear, what has he got against you?

Willy: I'm so tired. Don't talk anymore.

> (*Biff slowly returns to the kitchen. He stops, stares toward the heater.*)

Linda: Will you ask Howard to let you work in New York?

Willy: First thing in the morning. Everything'll be all right. (*Biff reaches behind the heater and draws out a length of rubber tubing. He is horrified and turns his head toward Willy's room, still dimly lit, from which the strains of Linda's desperate but monotonous humming rise. Staring through the window into the moonlight*): Gee, look at the moon moving between the buildings!

> (*Biff wraps the tubing around his hand and quickly goes up the stairs.*)

ACT II

> (*Music is heard, gay and bright. The curtain rises as the music fades away. Willy, in shirt sleeves, is sitting at the kitchen table, sipping coffee, his hat in his lap. Linda is filling his cup when she can.*)

Willy: Wonderful coffee. Meal in itself.

Linda: Can I make you some eggs?

Willy: No. Take a breath.

Linda: You look so rested, dear.

Willy: I slept like a dead one. First time in months. Imagine, sleeping till ten on a Tuesday morning. Boys left nice and early, heh?

Linda: They were out of here by eight o'clock.

Willy: Good work!

Linda: It was so thrilling to see them leaving together. I can't get over the shaving lotion in this house!

Willy (smiling):   Mmm—

Linda: Biff was very changed this morning. His whole attitude seemed to be hopeful. He couldn't wait to get downtown to see Oliver.

Willy: He's heading for a change. There's no question, there simply are certain men that take longer to get—solidified. How did he dress?

Linda: His blue suit. He's so handsome in that suit. He could be a—anything in that suit!

(Willy gets up from the table. Linda holds his jacket for him.)

Willy: There's no question, no question at all. Gee, on the way home tonight I'd like to buy some seeds.

Linda (laughing):   That'd be wonderful. But not enough sun gets back there. Nothing'll grow anymore.

Willy: You wait, kid, before it's all over we're gonna get a little place out in the country, and I'll raise some vegetables, a couple of chickens . . .

Linda: You'll do it yet, dear.

(Willy walks out of his jacket. Linda follows him.)

Willy: And they'll get married, and come for a weekend. I'd build a little guest house. 'Cause I got so many fine tools, all I'd need would be a little lumber and some peace of mind.

Linda (joyfully):   I sewed the lining . . .

Willy: I could build two guest houses, so they'd both come. Did he decide how much he's going to ask Oliver for?

Linda (getting him into the jacket):   He didn't mention it, but I imagine ten or fifteen thousand. You going to talk to Howard today?

Willy: Yeah. I'll put it to him straight and simple. He'll just have to take me off the road.

Linda: And Willy, don't forget to ask for a little advance, because we've got the insurance premium. It's the grace period now.

Willy: That's a hundred . . . ?

Linda: A hundred and eight, sixty-eight. Because we're a little short again.

Willy: Why are we short?

Linda: Well, you had the motor job on the car . . .

Willy: That goddam Studebaker!

Linda: And you got one more payment on the refrigerator . . .

Willy: But it just broke again!

Linda: Well, it's old, dear.

Willy: I told you we should've bought a well-advertised machine. Charley bought a General Electric and it's twenty years old and it's still good, that son-of-a-bitch.

Linda: But, Willy—

Willy: Whoever heard of a Hastings refrigerator? Once in my life I would like to own something outright before it's broken! I'm always in a race with the junkyard! I just finished paying for the car and it's on its last legs. The refrigerator consumes belts like a goddamn maniac. They time those things. They time them so when you finally paid for them, they're used up.

Linda (buttoning up his jacket as he unbuttons it): All told, about two hundred dollars would carry us, dear. But that includes the last payment on the mortgage. After this payment, Willy, the house belongs to us.

Willy: It's twenty-five years!

Linda: Biff was nine years old when we bought it.

Willy: Well, that's a great thing. To weather a twenty-five year mortgage is—

Linda: It's an accomplishment.

Willy: All the cement, the lumber, the reconstruction I put in this house! There ain't a crack to be found in it anymore.

Linda: Well, it served its purpose.

Willy: What purpose? Some stranger'll come along, move in, and that's that. If only Biff would take this house, and raise a family . . . (*He starts to go.*) Good-by, I'm late.

Linda (suddenly remembering): Oh, I forgot! You're supposed to meet them for dinner.

Willy: Me?

Linda: At Frank's Chop House on Forty-eighth near Sixth Avenue.

Willy: Is that so! How about you?

Linda: No, just the three of you. They're gonna blow you to a big meal!

Willy: Don't say! Who thought of that?

Linda: Biff came to me this morning, Willy, and he said, "Tell Dad, we want to blow him to a big meal." Be there six o'clock. You and your two boys are going to have dinner.

Willy: Gee whiz! That's really somethin'. I'm gonna knock Howard for a loop, kid. I'll get an advance, and I'll come home with a New York job. God-dammit, now I'm gonna do it!

Linda: Oh, that's the spirit, Willy!

Willy: I will never get behind a wheel the rest of my life!

Linda: It's changing, Willy, I can feel it changing!

Willy: Beyond a question. G'by, I'm late. (*He starts to go again.*)

Linda (calling after him as she runs to the kitchen table for a handkerchief): You got your glasses?

Willy (feels for them, then comes back in): Yeah, yeah, got my glasses.

Linda (giving him the handkerchief): And a handkerchief.

Willy: Yeah, handkerchief.
Linda: And your saccharine?
Willy: Yeah, my saccharine.
Linda: Be careful on the subway stairs.

(*She kisses him, and a silk stocking is seen hanging from her hand. Willy notices it.*)

Willy: Will you stop mending stockings? At least while I'm in the house. It gets me nervous. I can't tell you. Please.

(*Linda hides the stocking in her hand as she follows Willy across the forestage in front of the house.*)

Linda: Remember, Frank's Chop House.
Willy (passing the apron):   Maybe beets would grow out there.
Linda (laughing):   But you tried so many times.
Willy: Yeah. Well, don't work hard today. (*He disappears around the right corner of the house.*)
Linda: Be careful! (*As Willy vanishes, Linda waves to him. Suddenly the phone rings. She runs across the stage and into the kitchen and lifts it.*) Hello? Oh, Biff! I'm so glad you called, I just . . . Yes, sure, I just told him. Yes, he'll be there for dinner at six o'clock, I didn't forget. Listen, I was just dying to tell you. You know that little rubber pipe I told you about? That he connected to the gas heater? I finally decided to go down the cellar this morning and take it away and destroy it. But it's gone! Imagine? He took it away himself, it isn't there! (*She listens.*) When? Oh, then you took it. Oh—nothing, it's just that I'd hoped he'd taken it away himself. Oh, I'm not worried, darling, because this morning he left in such high spirits, it was like the old days! I'm not afraid anymore. Did Mr. Oliver see you? . . . Well, you wait there then. And make a nice impression on him, darling. Just don't perspire too much before you see him. And have a nice time with Dad. He may have big news too! . . . That's right, a New York job. And be sweet to him tonight, dear. Be loving to him. Because he's only a little boat looking for a harbor. (*She is trembling with sorrow and joy.*) Oh, that's wonderful, Biff, you'll save his life. Thanks, darling. Just put your arm around him when he comes into the restaurant. Give him a smile. That's the boy . . . Good-by, dear. . . . You got your comb? . . . That's fine. Good-by, Biff dear.

(*In the middle of her speech, Howard Wagner, thirty-six, wheels in a small typewriter table on which is a wire-recording machine and proceeds to plug it in. This is on the left forestage. Light slowly fades on Linda as it rises on Howard. Howard is intent on threading the machine and only glances over his shoulder as Willy appears.*)

Willy: Pst! Pst!
Howard: Hello, Willy, come in.

Willy: Like to have a little talk with you, Howard.

Howard: Sorry to keep you waiting. I'll be with you in a minute.

Willy: What's that, Howard?

Howard: Didn't you ever see one of these? Wire recorder.

Willy: Oh. Can we talk a minute?

Howard: Records things. Just got delivery yesterday. Been driving me crazy, the most terrific machine I ever saw in my life. I was up all night with it.

Willy: What do you do with it?

Howard: I bought it for dictation, but you can do anything with it. Listen to this. I had it home last night. Listen to what I picked up. The first one is my daughter. Get this. (*He flicks the switch and "Roll out the Barrel" is heard being whistled.*) Listen to that kid whistle.

Willy: That is lifelike, isn't it?

Howard: Seven years old. Get that tone.

Willy: Ts, ts. Like to ask a little favor if you . . .

(*The whistling breaks off, and the voice of Howard's daughter is heard.*)

His Daughter: "Now you, Daddy."

Howard: She's crazy for me! (*Again the same song is whistled.*) That's me! Ha! (*He winks.*)

Willy: You're very good!

(*The whistling breaks off again. The machine runs silent for a moment.*)

Howard: Sh! Get this now, this is my son.

His Son: "The capital of Alabama is Montgomery; the capital of Arizona is Phoenix; the capital of Arkansas is Little Rock; the capital of California is Sacramento . . ." (*and on, and on*)

Howard (holding up five fingers):   Five years old, Willy!

Willy: He'll make an announcer someday!

His Son (continuing):   "The capital . . ."

Howard: Get that—alphabetical order! (*The machine breaks off suddenly.*) Wait a minute. The maid kicked the plug out.

Willy: It certainly is a—

Howard: Sh, for God's sake!

His Son: "It's nine o'clock, Bulova watch time. So I have to go to sleep."

Willy: That really is—

Howard: Wait a minute! The next is my wife.

(*They wait.*)

Howard's Voice: "Go on, say something." (*Pause.*) "Well, you gonna talk?"

His Wife: "I can't think of anything."

Howard's Voice: "Well, talk—it's turning."

His Wife (shyly, beaten):   "Hello." (*Silence.*) "Oh, Howard, I can't talk into this . . ."

Howard (snapping the machine off):   That was my wife.

Willy: That is a wonderful machine. Can we—

Howard: I tell you, Willy, I'm gonna take my camera, and my bandsaw, and all my hobbies, and out they go. This is the most fascinating relaxation I ever found.

Willy: I think I'll get one myself.

Howard: Sure, they're only a hundred and a half. You can't do without it. Supposing you wanna hear Jack Benny, see? But you can't be at home at that hour. So you tell the maid to turn the radio on when Jack Benny comes on, and this automatically goes on with the radio . . .

Willy: And when you come home you . . .

Howard: You can come home twelve o'clock, one o'clock, any time you like, and you get yourself a Coke and sit yourself down, throw the switch, and there's Jack Benny's program in the middle of the night!

Willy: I'm definitely going to get one. Because lots of times I'm on the road, and I think to myself, what I must be missing on the radio!

Howard: Don't you have a radio in the car?

Willy: Well, yeah, but who ever thinks of turning it on?

Howard: Say, aren't you supposed to be in Boston?

Willy: That's what I want to talk to you about, Howard. You got a minute? (*He draws a chair in from the wing.*)

Howard: What happened? What're you doing here?

Willy: Well . . .

Howard: You didn't crack up again, did you?

Willy: Oh, no. No . . .

Howard: Geez, you had me worried there for a minute. What's the trouble?

Willy: Well, tell you the truth, Howard. I've come to the decision that I'd rather not travel anymore.

Howard: Not travel! Well, what'll you do?

Willy: Remember, Christmas time, when you had the party here? You said you'd try to think of some spot for me here in town.

Howard: With us?

Willy: Well, sure.

Howard: Oh, yeah, yeah. I remember. Well, I couldn't think of anything for you, Willy.

Willy: I tell ya, Howard. The kids are all grown up, y'know. I don't need much anymore. If I could take home—well, sixty-five dollars a week, I could swing it.

Howard: Yeah, but Willy, see I—

Willy: I tell ya why, Howard. Speaking frankly and between the two of us, y'know—I'm just a little tired.

Howard: Oh, I could understand that, Willy. But you're a road man, Willy, and we do a road business. We've only got a half-dozen salesmen on the floor here.

Willy: God knows, Howard, I never asked a favor of any man. But I was with the firm when your father used to carry you in here in his arms.

Howard: I know that, Willy, but—

Willy: Your father came to me the day you were born and asked me what I thought of the name Howard, may he rest in peace.

Howard: I appreciate that, Willy, but there just is no spot here for you. If I had a spot I'd slam you right in, but I just don't have a single solitary spot.

(He looks for his lighter. Willy has picked it up and gives it to him. Pause.)

Willy (with increasing anger): Howard, all I need to set my table is fifty dollars a week.

Howard: But where am I going to put you, kid?

Willy: Look, it isn't a question of whether I can sell merchandise, is it?

Howard: No, but it's business, kid, and everybody's gotta pull his own weight.

Willy (desperately): Just let me tell you a story, Howard—

Howard: 'Cause you gotta admit, business is business.

Willy (angrily): Business is definitely business, but just listen for a minute. You don't understand this. When I was a boy—eighteen, nineteen—I was already on the road. And there was a question in my mind as to whether selling had a future for me. Because in those days I had a yearning to go to Alaska. See, there were three gold strikes in one month in Alaska, and I felt like going out. Just for the ride, you might say.

Howard (barely interested): Don't say.

Willy: Oh, yeah, my father lived many years in Alaska. He was an adventurous man. We've got quite a little streak of self-reliance in our family. I thought I'd go out with my older brother and try to locate him, and maybe settle in the North with the old man. And I was almost decided to go, when I met a salesman in the Parker House. His name was Dave Singleman. And he was eighty-four years old, and he'd drummed merchandise in thirty-one states. And old Dave, he'd go up to his room, y'understand, put on his green velvet slippers—I'll never forget—and pick up his phone and call the buyers, and without ever leaving his room, at the age of eighty-four, he made his living. And when I saw that, I realized that selling was the greatest career a man could want. 'Cause what could be more satisfying than to be able to go, at the age of eighty-four, into twenty or thirty different cities, and pick up a phone, and be remembered and loved and helped by so many different people? Do you know? When he died—and by the way he died the death of a salesman, in his green velvet slippers in the smoker of the New York, New Haven and Hartford, going into Boston—when he died, hundreds of salesmen and buyers were at his funeral. Things were sad on a lotta trains for months after that. (*He stands up. Howard has not looked at him.*) In those days there was personality in it, Howard. There was respect, and comradeship, and gratitude in it. Today, it's all cut and dried, and there's no chance for bringing friendship to bear—or personality. You see what I mean? They don't know me anymore.

Howard (moving away, to the right):   That's just the thing, Willy.

Willy: If I had forty dollars a week—that's all I'd need. Forty dollars, Howard.

Howard: Kid, I can't take blood from a stone, I—

Willy (desperation is on him now):   Howard, the year Al Smith was nominated, your father came to me and—

Howard (starting to go off):   I've got to see some people, kid.

Willy (stopping him):   I'm talking about your father! There were promises made across this desk! You mustn't tell me you've got people to see—I put thirty-four years into this firm, Howard, and now I can't pay my insurance! You can't eat the orange and throw the peel away—a man is not a piece of fruit! (*After a pause.*) Now pay attention. Your father— in 1928 I had a big year. I averaged a hundred and seventy dollars a week in commissions.

Howard (impatiently):   Now, Willy, you never averaged—

Willy (banging his hand on the desk):   I averaged a hundred and seventy dollars a week in the year of 1928! And your father came to me—or rather, I was in the office here—it was right over this desk—and he put his hand on my shoulder—

Howard (getting up):   You'll have to excuse me, Willy, I gotta see some people. Pull yourself together. (*Going out.*) I'll be back in a little while.

(*On Howard's exit, the light on his chair grows very bright and strange.*)

Willy: Pull myself together! What the hell did I say to him? My God, I was yelling at him! How could I? (*Willy breaks off, staring at the light, which occupies the chair, animating it. He approaches this chair, standing across the desk from it.*) Frank, Frank, don't you remember what you told me that time? How you put your hand on my shoulder, and Frank . . . (*He leans on the desk and as he speaks the dead man's name he accidentally switches on the recorder, and instantly:*)

Howard's Son: ". . . of New York is Albany. The capital of Ohio is Cincinnati, the capital of Rhode Island is . . ." (*The recitation continues.*)

Willy (leaping away with fright, shouting):   Ha! Howard! Howard! Howard!

Howard (rushing in):   What happened?

Willy (pointing at the machine, which continues nasally, childishly, with the capital cities):   Shut it off! Shut it off!

Howard (pulling the plug out):   Look, Willy . . .

Willy (pressing his hands to his eyes):   I gotta get myself some coffee. I'll get some coffee . . .

(Willy starts to walk out. Howard stops him.)

Howard (rolling up the cord):   Willy, look . . .

Willy: I'll go to Boston.

Howard: Willy, you can't go to Boston for us.

Willy: Why can't I go?

Howard: I don't want you to represent us. I've been meaning to tell you for a long time now.

Willy: Howard, are you firing me?

Howard: I think you need a good long rest, Willy.

Willy: Howard—

Howard: And when you feel better, come back, and we'll see if we can work something out.

Willy: But I gotta earn money, Howard. I'm in no position to—

Howard: Where are your sons? Why don't your sons give you a hand?

Willy: They're working on a very big deal.

Howard: This is no time for false pride, Willy. You go to your sons and you tell them that you're tired. You've got two great boys, haven't you?

Willy: Oh, no question, no question, but in the meantime . . .

Howard: Then that's that, heh?

Willy: All right, I'll go to Boston tomorrow.

Howard: No, no.

Willy: I can't throw myself on my sons. I'm not a cripple!

Howard: Look, kid, I'm busy this morning.

Willy (grasping Howard's arm):   Howard, you've got to let me go to Boston!

Howard (hard, keeping himself under control):   I've got a line of people to see this morning. Sit down, take five minutes, and pull yourself together, and then go home, will ya? I need the office, Willy. (*He starts to go, turns, remembering the recorder, starts to push off the table holding the recorder.*) Oh, yeah. Whenever you can this week, stop by and drop off the samples. You'll feel better, Willy, and then come back and we'll talk. Pull yourself together, kid, there's people outside.

(Howard exits, pushing the table off left. Willy stares into space, exhausted. Now the music is heard—Ben's music—first distantly, then closer, closer. As Willy speaks, Ben enters from the right. He carries valise and umbrella.)

Willy: Oh, Ben, how did you do it? What is the answer? Did you wind up the Alaska deal already?

Ben: Doesn't take much time if you know what you're doing. Just a short business trip. Boarding ship in an hour. Wanted to say good-by.

Willy: Ben, I've got to talk to you.

Ben (glancing at his watch):   Haven't the time, William.

Willy (crossing the apron to Ben):   Ben, nothing's working out. I don't know what to do.

Ben: Now, look here, William. I've bought timberland in Alaska and I need a man to look after things for me.

Willy: God, timberland! Me and my boys in those grand outdoors!

Ben: You've a new continent at your doorstep, William. Get out of these cities, they're full of talk and time payments and courts of law. Screw on your fists and you can fight for a fortune up there.

Willy: Yes, yes! Linda, Linda!

(Linda enters as of old, with the wash.)

Linda: Oh, you're back?

Ben: I haven't much time.

Willy: No, wait! Linda, he's got a proposition for me in Alaska.

Linda: But you've got—(*To Ben.*) He's got a beautiful job here.

Willy: But in Alaska, kid, I could—

Linda: You're doing well enough, Willy!

Ben (to Linda):   Enough for what, my dear?

Linda (frightened of Ben and angry at him):   Don't say those things to him! Enough to be happy right here, right now. (*To Willy, while Ben laughs.*) Why must everybody conquer the world? You're well liked, and the boys love you, and someday—(*to Ben*)—why, old man Wagner told him just the other day that if he keeps it up he'll be a member of the firm, didn't he, Willy?

Willy: Sure, sure. I am building something with this firm, Ben, and if a man is building something he must be on the right track, mustn't he?

Ben: What are you building? Lay your hand on it. Where is it?

Willy (hesitantly):   That's true, Linda, there's nothing.

Linda: Why? (*To Ben.*) There's a man eighty-four years old—

Willy: That's right, Ben, that's right. When I look at that man I say, what is there to worry about?

Ben: Bah!

Willy: It's true, Ben. All he has to do is go into any city, pick up the phone, and he's making his living and you know why?

Ben (picking up his valise):   I've got to go.

Willy (holding Ben back):   Look at this boy! (*Biff, in his high school sweater, enters carrying suitcase. Happy carries Biff's shoulder guards, gold helmet, and football pants.*) Without a penny to his name, three great universities are begging for him, and from there the sky's the limit, because it's not what you do, Ben. It's who you know and the smile on your face! It's contacts, Ben, contacts! The whole wealth of Alaska passes over the lunch table at the Commodore Hotel, and that's the wonder, the wonder of this country, that a man can end with diamonds here on the basis of being liked! (*He turns to Biff.*) And that's why when you get out on that field today it's important. Because thousands of people will be rooting for you and loving you. (*To Ben, who has again begun to leave.*) And Ben! when he walks into a business office his name will sound out like a bell and all the doors will open to him! I've seen it, Ben, I've seen it a thousand times! You can't feel it with your hand like timber, but it's there!

Ben: Good-by, William.

Willy: Ben, am I right? Don't you think I'm right? I value your advice.

Ben: There's a new continent at your doorstep, William. You could walk out rich. Rich! (*He is gone.*)

Willy: We'll do it here, Ben! You hear me? We're gonna do it here!

(*Young Bernard rushes in. The gay music of the Boys is heard.*)

Bernard: Oh, gee, I was afraid you left already!

Willy: Why? What time is it?

Bernard: It's half-past one!

Willy: Well, come on, everybody! Ebbets Field next stop! Where's the pennants? (*He rushes through the wall-line of the kitchen and out into the living room.*)

Linda (to Biff):   Did you pack fresh underwear?

Biff (who has been limbering up):   I want to go!

Bernard: Biff, I'm carrying your helmet, ain't I?

Happy: No, I'm carrying the helmet.

Bernard: Oh, Biff, you promised me.

Happy: I'm carrying the helmet.

Bernard: How am I going to get in the locker room?

Linda: Let him carry the shoulder guards. (*She puts her coat and hat on in the kitchen.*)

Bernard: Can I, Biff? 'Cause I told everybody I'm going to be in the locker room.

Happy: In Ebbets Field it's the clubhouse.

Bernard: I meant the clubhouse. Biff!

Happy: Biff!

Biff (grandly, after a slight pause):   Let him carry the shoulder guards.

Happy (as he gives Bernard the shoulder guards):   Stay close to us now.

(*Willy rushes in with the pennants.*)

Willy (handing them out):   Everybody wave when Biff comes out on the field. (*Happy and Bernard run off.*) You set now, boy?

(*The music has died away.*)

Biff: Ready to go, Pop. Every muscle is ready.

Willy (at the edge of the apron):   You realize what this means?

Biff: That's right, Pop.

Willy (feeling Biff's muscles):   You're comin' home this afternoon captain of the All-Scholastic Championship Team of the City of New York.

Biff: I got it, Pop. And remember, pal, when I take off my helmet, that touchdown is for you.

Willy: Let's go! (*He is starting out, with his arm around Biff, when Charley enters, as of old, in knickers.*) I got no room for you, Charley.

Charley: Room? For what?

Willy: In the car.

Charley: You goin' for a ride? I wanted to shoot some casino.

Willy: (*furiously*):   Casino! (*Incredulously.*) Don't you realize what today is?

Linda: Oh, he knows, Willy. He's just kidding you.

Willy: That's nothing to kid about!

Charley: No, Linda, what's goin' on?

Linda: He's playing in Ebbets Field.

Charley: Baseball in this weather?

Willy: Don't talk to him. Come on, come on! (*He is pushing them out.*)

Charley: Wait a minute, didn't you hear the news?

Willy: What?

Charley: Don't you listen to the radio? Ebbets Field just blew up.

Willy: You go to hell! (*Charley laughs. Pushing them out.*) Come on, come on! We're late.

Charley (as they go):   Knock a homer, Biff, knock a homer!

Willy (the last to leave, turning to Charley):   I don't think that was funny, Charley. This is the greatest day of his life.

Charley: Willy, when are you going to grow up?

Willy: Yeah, heh? When this game is over, Charley, you'll be laughing out of the other side of your face. They'll be calling him another Red Grange. Twenty-five thousand a year.

Charley (kidding):   Is that so?

Willy: Yeah, that's so.

Charley: Well, then, I'm sorry, Willy. But tell me something.

Willy: What?

Charley: Who is Red Grange?

Willy: Put up your hands. Goddam you, put up your hands! (*Charley, chuckling, shakes his head and walks away, around the left corner of the stage. Willy follows him. The music rises to a mocking frenzy.*) Who the hell do you think you are, better than everybody else? You don't know everything, you big, ignorant, stupid . . . Put up your hands!

(*Light rises, on the right side of the forestage, on a small table in the reception room of Charley's office. Traffic sounds are heard. Bernard, now mature, sits whistling to himself. A pair of tennis rackets and an overnight bag are on the floor beside him.*)

Willy (offstage):   What are you walking away for? Don't walk away! If you're going to say something say it to my face! I know you laugh at me behind my back. You'll laugh out of the other side of your goddam face after this game. Touchdown! Touchdown! Eighty thousand people! Touchdown! Right between the goal posts.

(Bernard is a quiet, earnest, but self-assured young man. Willy's voice is coming from right upstage now. Bernard lowers his feet off the table and listens. Jenny, his father's secretary, enters.)

Jenny (distressed):   Say, Bernard, will you go out in the hall?

Bernard: What is that noise? Who is it?

Jenny: Mr. Loman. He just got off the elevator.

Bernard (getting up):   Who's he arguing with?

Jenny: Nobody. There's nobody with him. I can't deal with him anymore, and your father gets all upset everytime he comes. I've got a lot of typing to do, and your father's waiting to sign it. Will you see him?

Willy (entering):   Touchdown! Touch—(*He sees Jenny.*) Jenny, Jenny, good to see you. How're ya? Workin'? Or still honest?

Jenny: Fine. How've you been feeling?

Willy: Not much anymore, Jenny. Ha, ha! (*He is surprised to see the rackets.*)

Bernard: Hello, Uncle Willy.

Willy (almost shocked):   Bernard! Well, look who's here! (*He comes quickly, guiltily, to Bernard and warmly shakes his hand.*)

Bernard: How are you? Good to see you.

Willy: What are you doing here?

Bernard: Oh, just stopped by to see Pop. Get off my feet till my train leaves. I'm going to Washington in a few minutes.

Willy: Is he in?

Bernard: Yes, he's in his office with the accountant. Sit down.

Willy (sitting down):   What're you going to do in Washington?

Bernard: Oh, just a case I've got there, Willy.

Willy: That so? (*Indicating the rackets.*) You going to play tennis there?

Bernard: I'm staying with a friend who's got a court.

Willy: Don't say. His own tennis court. Must be fine people, I bet.

Bernard: They are, very nice. Dad tells me Biff's in town.

Willy (with a big smile):   Yeah, Biff's in. Working on a very big deal, Bernard.

Bernard: What's Biff doing?

Willy: Well, he's been doing very big things in the West. But he decided to establish himself here. Very big. We're having dinner. Did I hear your wife had a boy?

Bernard: That's right. Our second.

Willy: Two boys! What do you know!

Bernard: What kind of a deal has Biff got?

Willy: Well, Bill Oliver—very big sporting-goods man—he wants Biff very badly. Called him in from the West. Long distance, carte blanche, special deliveries. Your friends have their own private tennis court?

Bernard: You still with the old firm, Willy?

Willy (after a pause):   I'm—I'm overjoyed to see how you made the grade, Bernard, overjoyed. It's an encouraging thing to see a young man really—really—Looks very good for Biff—very—(*He breaks off, then.*) Bernard—(*He is so full of emotion, he breaks off again.*)

Bernard: What is it, Willy?

Willy (small and alone):   What—what's the secret?

Bernard: What secret?

Willy: How—how did you? Why didn't he ever catch on?

Bernard: I wouldn't know that, Willy.

Willy (confidentially, desperately):   You were his friend, his boyhood friend. There's something I don't understand about it. His life ended after that Ebbets Field game. From the age of seventeen nothing good ever happened to him.

Bernard: He never trained himself for anything.

Willy: But he did, he did. After high school he took so many correspondence courses. Radio mechanics; television; God knows what, and never made the slightest mark.

Bernard (taking off his glasses):   Willy, do you want to talk candidly?

Willy (rising, faces Bernard):   I regard you as a very brilliant man, Bernard. I value your advice.

Bernard: Oh, the hell with the advice, Willy. I couldn't advise you. There's just one thing I've always wanted to ask you. When he was supposed to graduate, and the math teacher flunked him—

Willy: Oh, that son-of-a-bitch ruined his life.

Bernard: Yeah, but, Willy, all he had to do was go to summer school and make up that subject.

Willy: That's right, that's right.

Bernard: Did you tell him not to go to summer school?

Willy: Me? I begged him to go. I ordered him to go!

Bernard: Then why wouldn't he go?

Willy: Why? Why! Bernard, that question has been trailing me like a ghost for the last fifteen years. He flunked the subject, and laid down and died like a hammer hit him!

Bernard: Take it easy, kid.

Willy: Let me talk to you—I got nobody to talk to. Bernard, Bernard, was it my fault? Y'see? It keeps going around in my mind, maybe I did something to him. I got nothing to give him.

Bernard: Don't take it so hard.

Willy: Why did he lay down? What is the story there? You were his friend!

Bernard: Willy, I remember, it was June, and our grades came out. And he'd flunked math.

Willy: That son-of-a-bitch!

Bernard: No, it wasn't right then. Biff just got very angry, I remember, and he was ready to enroll in summer school.

Willy (surprised):   He was?

Bernard: He wasn't beaten by it at all. But then, Willy, he disappeared from the block for almost a month. And I got the idea that he'd gone up to New England to see you. Did he have a talk with you then? (*Willy stares in silence.*) Willy?

Willy (with a strong edge of resentment in his voice):   Yeah, he came to Boston. What about it?

Bernard: Well, just that when he came back—I'll never forget this, it always mystifies me. Because I'd thought so well of Biff, even though he'd always taken advantage of me. I loved him, Willy, y'know? And he came back after that month and took his sneakers—remember those sneakers with "University of Virginia" printed on them? He was so proud of those, wore them every day. And he took them down in the cellar, and burned them up in the furnace. We had a fist fight. It lasted at least half an hour. Just the two of us, punching each other down the cellar, and crying right through it. I've often thought of how strange it was that I knew he'd given up his life. What happened in Boston, Willy? (*Willy looks at him as at an intruder.*) I just bring it up because you asked me.

Willy (angrily):   Nothing. What do you mean, "What happened?" What's that got to do with anything?

Bernard: Well, don't get sore.

Willy: What are you trying to do, blame it on me? If a boy lays down is that my fault?

Bernard: Now, Willy, don't get—

Willy: Well, don't—don't talk to me that way! What does that mean, "What happened?"

(*Charley enters. He is in his vest, and he carries a bottle of bourbon.*)

Charley: Hey, you're going to miss that train. (*He waves the bottle.*)

Bernard: Yeah, I'm going. (*He takes the bottle.*)Thanks, Pop. (*He picks up his rackets and bag.*) Good-by, Willy, and don't worry about it. You know, "If at first you don't succeed . . ."

Willy: Yes, I believe in that.

Bernard: But sometimes, Willy, it's better for a man just to walk away.

Willy: Walk away?

Bernard: That's right.

Willy: But if you can't walk away?

Bernard (after a slight pause):   I guess that's when it's tough. (*Extending his hand.*) Good-by, Willy.

Willy (shaking Bernard's hand):   Good-by, boy.

Charley (an arm on Bernard's shoulder):   How do you like this kid? Gonna argue a case in front of the Supreme Court.

Bernard (protesting):   Pop!

Willy (genuinely shocked, pained, and happy):   No! The Supreme Court!

Bernard: I gotta run. 'By, Dad!
Charley: Knock 'em dead, Bernard!

(*Bernard goes off.*)

Willy (as Charley takes out his wallet):   The Supreme Court! And he didn't even mention it!

Charley (counting out money on the desk):   He don't have to—he's gonna do it.

Willy: And you never told him what to do, did you? You never took any interest in him.

Charley: My salvation is that I never took any interest in anything. There's some money—fifty dollars. I got an accountant inside.

Willy: Charley, look . . . (*With difficulty.*) I got my insurance to pay. If you can manage it—I need a hundred and ten dollars. (*Charley doesn't reply for a moment; merely stops moving.*) I'd draw it from my bank but Linda would know, and I . . .

Charley: Sit down, Willy.

Willy (moving toward the chair):   I'm keeping an account of everything, remember. I'll pay every penny back. (*He sits.*)

Charley: Now listen to me, Willy.

Willy: I want you to know I appreciate . . .

Charley (sitting down on the table):   Willy, what're you doin'? What the hell is goin' on in your head?

Willy: Why? I'm simply . . .

Charley: I offered you a job. You make fifty dollars a week. And I won't send you on the road.

Willy: I've got a job.

Charley: Without pay? What kind of a job is a job without pay? (*He rises.*) Now, look, kid, enough is enough. I'm no genius but I know when I'm being insulted.

Willy: Insulted!

Charley: Why don't you want to work for me?

Willy: What's the matter with you? I've got a job.

Charley: Then what're you walkin' in here every week for?

Willy (getting up):   Well, if you don't want me to walk in here—

Charley: I'm offering you a job.

Willy: I don't want your goddam job!

Charley: When the hell are you going to grow up?

Willy (furiously):   You big ignoramus, if you say that to me again I'll rap you one! I don't care how big you are! (*He's ready to fight.*)

(*Pause.*)

Charley (kindly, going to him):   How much do you need, Willy?

Willy: Charley, I'm strapped. I'm strapped. I don't know what to do. I was just fired.

Charley: Howard fired you?

Willy: That snotnose. Imagine that? I named him. I named him Howard.

Charley: Willy, when're you gonna realize that them things don't mean anything? You named him Howard, but you can't sell that. The only thing you got in this world is what you can sell. And the funny thing is that you're a salesman, and you don't know that.

Willy: I've always tried to think otherwise, I guess. I always felt that if a man was impressive, and well liked, that nothing—

Charley: Why must everybody like you? Who liked J. P. Morgan?° Was he impressive? In a Turkish bath he'd look like a butcher. But with his pockets on he was very well liked. Now listen, Willy, I know you don't like me, and nobody can say I'm in love with you, but I'll give you a job because—just for the hell of it, put it that way. Now what do you say?

Willy: I—I just can't work for you, Charley.

Charley: What're you, jealous of me?

Willy: I can't work for you, that's all, don't ask me why.

Charley (angered, takes out more bills):   You been jealous of me all your life, you dammed fool! Here, pay your insurance. (*He puts the money in Willy's hand.*)

Willy: I'm keeping strict accounts.

Charley: I've got some work to do. Take care of yourself. And pay your insurance.

Willy (moving to the right):   Funny, y'know? After all the highways, and the trains, and the appointments, and the years, you end up worth more dead than alive.

Charley: Willy, nobody's worth nothin' dead. (*After a slight pause.*) Did you hear what I said? (*Willy stands still, dreaming.*) Willy!

Willy: Apologize to Bernard for me when you see him. I didn't mean to argue with him. He's a fine boy. They're all fine boys, and they'll end up big—all of them. Someday they'll all play tennis together. Wish me luck, Charley. He saw Bill Oliver today.

Charley: Good luck.

Willy (on the verge of tears):   Charley, you're the only friend I got. Isn't that a remarkable thing? (He goes out.)

Charley: Jesus!

(*Charley stares after him a moment and follows. All light blacks out. Suddenly raucous music is heard, and a red glow rises behind the screen at right. Stanley, a young waiter, appears, carrying a table, followed by Happy, who is carrying two chairs.*)

Stanley (putting the table down):   That's all right, Mr. Loman, I can handle it myself. (*He turns and takes the chairs from Happy and places them at the table.*)

J. P. Morgan: (1837–1913), wealthy financier and art collector whose money was made chiefly in banking, railroads, and steel.

Happy (glancing around):   Oh, this is better.

Stanley: Sure, in the front there you're in the middle of all kinds of noise. Whenever you got a party, Mr. Loman, you just tell me and I'll put you back here. Y'know, there's a lotta people they don't like it private, because when they go out they like to see a lotta action around them because they're sick and tired to stay in the house by theirself. But I know you, you ain't from Hackensack. You know what I mean?

Happy (sitting down):   So how's it coming, Stanley?

Stanley: Ah, it's a dog life. I only wish during the war they'd a took me in the Army. I coulda been dead by now.

Happy: My brother's back, Stanley.

Stanley: Oh, he come back, heh? From the Far West.

Happy: Yeah, big cattle man, my brother, so treat him right. And my father's coming too.

Stanley: Oh, your father too!

Happy: You got a couple of nice lobsters?

Stanley: Hundred percent, big.

Happy: I want them with the claws.

Stanley: Don't worry, I don't give you no mice. (*Happy laughs.*) How about some wine? It'll put a head on the meal.

Happy: No. You remember, Stanley, that recipe I brought you from overseas? With the champagne in it?

Stanley: Oh, yeah, sure. I still got it tacked up yet in the kitchen. But that'll have to cost a buck apiece anyways.

Happy: That's all right.

Stanley: What'd you, hit a number or somethin'?

Happy: No, it's a little celebration. My brother is—I think he pulled off a big deal today. I think we're going into business together.

Stanley: Great! That's the best for you. Because a family business, you know what I mean?—that's the best.

Happy: That's what I think.

Stanley: 'Cause what's the difference? Somebody steals? It's in the family. Know what I mean? (*Sotto voce.°*) Like this bartender here. The boss is goin' crazy what kinda leak he's got in the cash register. You put it in but it don't come out.

Happy (raising his head):   Sh!

Stanley: What?

Happy: You notice I wasn't lookin' right or left, was I?

Stanley: No.

Happy: And my eyes are closed.

Stanley: So what's the—?

Happy: Strudel's comin'.

Stanley (catching on, looks around):   Ah, no, there's no—(*He breaks off as a*

Sotto voce: In a soft voice or stage whisper.

furred, lavishly dressed girl enters and sits at the next table. Both follow her with their eyes.) Geez, how'd ya know?

Happy: I got radar or something. (*Staring directly at her profile.*) Oooooooo . . . Stanley.

Stanley: I think that's for you, Mr. Loman.

Happy: Look at that mouth. Oh, God. And the binoculars.

Stanley: Geez, you got a life, Mr. Loman.

Happy: Wait on her.

Stanley (going to the Girl's table):   Would you like a menu, ma'am?

Girl: I'm expecting someone, but I'd like a—

Happy: Why don't you bring her—excuse me, miss, do you mind? I sell champagne, and I'd like you to try my brand. Bring her a champagne, Stanley.

Girl: That's awfully nice of you.

Happy: Don't mention it. It's all company money. (*He laughs.*)

Girl: That's a charming product to be selling, isn't it?

Happy: Oh, gets to be like everything else. Selling is selling, y'know.

Girl: I suppose.

Happy: You don't happen to sell, do you?

Girl: No, I don't sell.

Happy: Would you object to a compliment from a stranger? You ought to be on a magazine cover.

Girl (looking at him a little archly):   I have been.

(*Stanley comes in with a glass of champagne.*)

Happy: What'd I say before, Stanley? You see? She's a cover girl.

Stanley: Oh, I could see, I could see.

Happy (to the Girl):   What magazine?

Girl: Oh, a lot of them. (*She takes the drink.*) Thank you.

Happy: You know what they say in France, don't you? "Champagne is the drink of the complexion"—Hya, Biff!

(*Biff has entered and sits with Happy.*)

Biff: Hello, kid. Sorry I'm late.

Happy: I just got here. Uh, Miss—?

Girl: Forsythe.

Happy: Miss Forsythe, this is my brother.

Biff: Is Dad here?

Happy: His name is Biff. You might've heard of him. Great football player.

Girl: Really? What team?

Happy: Are you familiar with football?

Girl: No, I'm afraid I'm not.

Happy: Biff is quarterback with the New York Giants.

Girl: Well, that is nice, isn't it? (*She drinks.*)

Happy: Good health.

Girl: I'm happy to meet you.

Happy: That's my name. Hap. It's really Harold, but at West Point they called me Happy.

Girl (now really impressed):   Oh, I see. How do you do? (*She turns her profile.*)

Biff: Isn't Dad coming?

Happy: You want her?

Biff: Oh, I could never make that.

Happy: I remember the time that idea would never come into your head. Where's the old confidence, Biff?

Biff: I just saw Oliver—

Happy: Wait a minute. I've got to see that old confidence again. Do you want her? She's on call.

Biff: Oh, no. (*He turns to look at the Girl.*)

Happy: I'm telling you. Watch this. (*Turning to the Girl*):   Honey? (*She turns to him.*) Are you busy?

Girl: Well, I am . . . but I could make a phone call.

Happy: Do that, will you, honey? And see if you can get a friend. We'll be here for a while. Biff is one of the greatest football players in the country.

Girl (standing up):   Well, I'm certainly happy to meet you.

Happy: Come back soon.

Girl: I'll try.

Happy: Don't try, honey, try hard. (*The Girl exits. Stanley follows, shaking his head in bewildered admiration.*) Isn't that a shame now? A beautiful girl like that? That's why I can't get married. There's not a good woman in a thousand. New York is loaded with them, kid!

Biff: Hap, look—

Happy: I told you she was on call!

Biff (strangely unnerved):   Cut it out, will ya? I want to say something to you.

Happy: Did you see Oliver?

Biff: I saw him all right. Now look, I want to tell Dad a couple of things and I want you to help me.

Happy: What? Is he going to back you?

Biff: Are you crazy? You're out of your goddam head, you know that?

Happy: Why? What happened?

Biff (breathlessly):   I did a terrible thing today, Hap. It's been the strangest day I ever went through. I'm all numb, I swear.

Happy: You mean he wouldn't see you?

Biff: Well, I waited six hours for him, see? All day. Kept sending my name in. Even tried to date his secretary so she'd get me to him, but no soap.

Happy: Because you're not showin' the old confidence, Biff. He remembered you, didn't he?

Biff (stopping Happy with a gesture):   Finally, about five o'clock, he comes out. Didn't remember who I was or anything. I felt like such an idiot, Hap.

Happy: Did you tell him my Florida idea?

Biff: He walked away. I saw him for one minute. I got so mad I could've torn the walls down! How the hell did I ever get the idea I was a salesman there? I even believed myself that I'd been a salesman for him! And then he gave me one look and—I realized what a ridiculous lie my whole life has been! We've been talking in a dream for fifteen years. I was a shipping clerk.

Happy: What'd you do?

Biff (with great tension and wonder): Well, he left, see. And the secretary went out. I was all alone in the waiting room. I don't know what came over me, Hap. The next thing I know I'm in his office—paneled walls, everything. I can't explain it. I—Hap, I took his fountain pen.

Happy: Geez, did he catch you?

Biff: I ran out. I ran down all eleven flights. I ran and ran and ran.

Happy: That was an awful dumb—what'd you do that for?

Biff (agonized): I don't know, I just—wanted to take something, I don't know. You gotta help me, Hap. I'm gonna tell Pop.

Happy: You crazy? What for?

Biff: Hap, he's got to understand that I'm not the man somebody lends that kind of money to. He thinks I've been spiting him all these years and it's eating him up.

Happy: That's just it. You tell him something nice.

Biff: I can't.

Happy: Say you got a lunch date with Oliver tomorrow.

Biff: So what do I do tomorrow.

Happy: You leave the house tomorrow and come back at night and say Oliver is thinking it over. And he thinks it over for a couple of weeks, and gradually it fades away and nobody's the worse.

Biff: But it'll go on forever!

Happy: Dad is never so happy as when he's looking forward to something! (*Willy enters.*) Hello, scout!

Willy: Gee, I haven't been here in years!

(*Stanley has followed Willy in and sets a chair for him. Stanley starts off but Happy stops him.*)

Happy: Stanley!

(*Stanley stands by, waiting for an order.*)

Biff (going to Willy with guilt, as to an invalid): Sit down, Pop. You want a drink?

Willy: Sure, I don't mind.

Biff: Let's get a load on.

Willy: You look worried.

Biff: N-no. (*To Stanley.*) Scotch all around. Make it doubles.

Stanley: Doubles, right. (*He goes.*)

Willy: You had a couple already, didn't you?

Biff: Just a couple, yeah.

Willy: Well, what happened, boy? (*Nodding affirmatively, with a smile.*) Everything go all right?

Biff (takes a breath, then reaches out and grasps Willy's hand):   Pal . . . (*He is smiling bravely, and Willy is smiling too.*) I had an experience today.

Happy: Terrific, Pop.

Willy: That so? What happened?

Biff (high, slightly alcoholic, above the earth):   I'm going to tell you everything from first to last. It's been a strange day. (*Silence. He looks around, composes himself as best he can, but his breath keeps breaking the rhythm of his voice.*) I had to wait quite a while for him, and—

Willy: Oliver?

Biff: Yeah, Oliver. All day, as a matter of cold fact. And a lot of—instances—facts, Pop, facts about my life came back to me. Who was it, Pop? Who ever said I was a salesman with Oliver?

Willy: Well, you were.

Biff: No, Dad, I was a shipping clerk.

Willy: But you were practically—

Biff (with determination):   Dad, I don't know who said it first, but I was never a salesman for Bill Oliver.

Willy: What're you talking about?

Biff: Let's hold on to the facts tonight, Pop. We're not going to get anywhere bullin' around. I was a shipping clerk.

Willy (angrily):   All right, now listen to me—

Biff: Why don't you let me finish?

Willy: I'm not interested in stories about the past or any crap of that kind because the woods are burning, boys, you understand? There's a big blaze going on all around. I was fired today.

Biff (shocked):   How could you be?

Willy: I was fired, and I'm looking for a little good news to tell your mother, because the woman has waited and the woman has suffered. The gist of it is that I haven't got a story left in my head, Biff. So don't give me a lecture about facts and aspects. I am not interested. Now what've you got to say to me? (*Stanley enters with three drinks. They wait until he leaves.*) Did you see Oliver?

Biff: Jesus, Dad!

Willy: You mean you didn't go up there?

Happy: Sure he went up there.

Biff: I did. I—saw him. How could they fire you?

Willy (on the edge of his chair):   What kind of a welcome did he give you?

Biff: He won't even let you work on commission?

Willy: I'm out! (*Driving.*) So tell me, he gave you a warm welcome?

Happy: Sure, Pop, sure!

Biff (driven):   Well, it was kind of—
Willy: I was wondering if he'd remember you. (*To Happy.*) Imagine, man doesn't see him for ten, twelve years and gives him that kind of a welcome!
Happy: Damn right!
Biff (trying to return to the offensive):   Pop, look—
Willy: You know why he remembered you, don't you? Because you impressed him in those days.
Biff: Let's talk quietly and get this down to the facts, huh?
Willy (as though Biff had been interrupting):   Well, what happened? It's great news, Biff. Did he take you into his office or'd you talk in the waiting room?
Biff: Well, he came in, see, and—
Willy (with a big smile):   What'd he say? Betcha he threw his arm around you.
Biff: Well, he kinda—
Willy: He's a fine man. (*To Happy.*) Very hard man to see, y'know.
Happy (agreeing):   Oh, I know.
Willy (to Biff):   Is that where you had the drinks?
Biff: Yeah, he gave me a couple of—no, no!
Happy (cutting in):   He told him my Florida idea.
Willy: Don't interrupt. (*To Biff.*) How'd he react to the Florida idea?
Biff: Dad, will you give me a minute to explain?
Willy: I've been waiting for you to explain since I sat down here! What happened? He took you into his office and what?
Biff: Well—I talked. And—and he listened, see.
Willy: Famous for the way he listens, y'know. What was his answer?
Biff: His answer was—(*He breaks off, suddenly angry.*) Dad, you're not letting me tell you what I want to tell you!
Willy (accusing, angered):   You didn't see him, did you?
Biff: I did see him!
Willy: What'd you insult him or something? You insulted him, didn't you?
Biff: Listen, will you let me out of it, will you just let me out of it!
Happy: What the hell!
Willy: Tell me what happened!
Biff (to Happy):   I can't talk to him!

(*A single trumpet note jars the ear. The light of green leaves stains the house, which holds the air of night and a dream. Young Bernard enters and knocks on the door of the house.*)

Young Bernard (frantically):   Mrs. Loman, Mrs. Loman!
Happy: Tell him what happened!
Biff (to Happy):   Shut up and leave me alone!
Willy: No, no! You had to go and flunk math!

Biff: What math? What're you talking about?

Young Bernard: Mrs. Loman, Mrs. Loman!

   (Linda appears in the house, as of old.)

Willy (wildly):   Math, math, math!

Biff: Take it easy, Pop!

Young Bernard: Mrs. Loman!

Willy (furiously):   If you hadn't flunked you'd've been set by now!

Biff: Now, look, I'm gonna tell you what happened, and you're going to listen to me.

Young Bernard: Mrs. Loman!

Biff: I waited six hours—

Happy: What the hell are you saying?

Biff: I kept sending in my name but he wouldn't see me. So finally he . . .

   (He continues unheard as light fades low on the restaurant.)

Young Bernard: Biff flunked math!

Linda: No!

Young Bernard: Birnbaum flunked him! They won't graduate him!

Linda: But they have to. He's gotta go to the university. Where is he? Biff! Biff!

Young Bernard: No, he left. He went to Grand Central.

Linda: Grand—You mean he went to Boston!

Young Bernard: Is Uncle Willy in Boston?

Linda: Oh, maybe Willy can talk to the teacher. Oh, the poor, poor boy!

   (Light on house area snaps out.)

Biff (at the table, now audible, holding up a gold fountain pen):   . . . so I'm washed up with Oliver, you understand? Are you listening to me?

Willy (at a loss):   Yeah, sure. If you hadn't flunked—

Biff: Flunked what? What're you talking about?

Willy: Don't blame everything on me! I didn't flunk math—you did! What pen?

Happy: That was awful dumb, Biff, a pen like that is worth—

Willy (seeing the pen for the first time):   You took Oliver's pen?

Biff (weakening):   Dad, I just explained it to you.

Willy: You stole Bill Oliver's fountain pen!

Biff: I didn't exactly steal it! That's just what I've been explaining to you!

Happy: He had it in his hand and just then Oliver walked in, so he got nervous and stuck it in his pocket!

Willy: My God, Biff!

Biff: I never intended to do it, Dad!

Operator's Voice: Standish Arms, good evening!

Willy (shouting):   I'm not in my room!

Biff (frightened):   Dad, what's the matter? *(He and Happy stand up.)*

Operator: Ringing Mr. Loman for you!

Willy: I'm not there, stop it!

Biff (horrified, gets down on one knee before Willy):   Dad, I'll make good,
   I'll make good. (*Willy tries to get to his feet. Biff holds him down.*) Sit
   down now.

Willy: No, you're no good, you're no good for anything.

Biff: I am, Dad, I'll find something else, you understand? Now
   don't worry about anything. (*He holds up Willy's face.*) Talk to me,
   Dad.

Operator: Mr. Loman does not answer. Shall I page him?

Willy (attempting to stand, as though to rush and silence the Operator):   No,
   no, no!

Happy: He'll strike something, Pop.

Willy: No, no . . .

Biff (desperately, standing over Willy):   Pop, listen! Listen to me! I'm
   telling you something good. Oliver talked to his partner about the
   Florida idea. You listening? He—he talked to his partner, and he came
   to me . . . I'm going to be all right, you hear? Dad, listen to me, he
   said it was just a question of the amount!

Willy: Then you . . . got it?

Happy: He's gonna be terrific, Pop!

Willy (trying to stand):   Then you got it, haven't you? You got it! You got
   it!

Biff (agonized, holds Willy down):   No, no. Look, Pop. I'm supposed to
   have lunch with them tomorrow. I'm just telling you this so you'll
   know that I can still make an impression, Pop. And I'll make good
   somewhere, but I can't go tomorrow, see?

Willy: Why not? You simply—

Biff: But the pen, Pop!

Willy: You give it to him and tell him it was an oversight!

Happy: Sure, have lunch tomorrow!

Biff: I can't say that—

Willy: You were doing a crossword puzzle and accidentally used his pen!

Biff: Listen, kid, I took those balls years ago, now I walk in with his
   fountain pen? That clinches it, don't you see? I can't face him like that!
   I'll try elsewhere.

Page's Voice: Paging Mr. Loman!

Willy: Don't you want to be anything?

Biff: Pop, how can I go back?

Willy: You don't want to be anything, is that what's behind it?

Biff (now angry at Willy for not crediting his sympathy):   Don't take it that
   way! You think it was easy walking into that office after what I'd done
   to him? A team of horses couldn't have dragged me back to Bill
   Oliver!

Willy: Then why'd you go?

Biff: Why did I go? Why did I go! Look at you! Look at what's become
   of you!

(Off left, The Woman laughs.)

Willy: Biff, you're going to go to that lunch tomorrow, or—

Biff: I can't go. I've got no appointment!

Happy: Biff, for . . . !

Willy: Are you spiting me?

Biff: Don't take it that way! Goddammit!

Willy (strikes Biff and falters away from the table):   You rotten little louse! Are you spiting me?

The Woman: Someone's at the door, Willy!

Biff: I'm no good, can't you see what I am?

Happy (separating them):   Hey, you're in a restaurant! Now cut it out, both of you! (*The girls enter.*) Hello, girls, sit down.

(The Woman laughs, off left.)

Miss Forsythe: I guess we might as well. This is Letta.

The Woman: Willy, are you going to wake up?

Biff (ignoring Willy):   How're ya, miss, sit down. What do you drink?

Miss Forsythe: Letta might not be able to stay long.

Letta: I gotta get up very early tomorrow. I got jury duty. I'm so excited! Were you fellows ever on a jury?

Biff: No, but I been in front of them! (*The girls laugh.*) This is my father.

Letta: Isn't he cute? Sit down with us, Pop.

Happy: Sit him down, Biff!

Biff (going to him):   Come on, slugger, drink us under the table. To hell with it! Come on, sit down, pal.

(On Biff's last insistence, Willy is about to sit.)

The Woman (now urgently):   Willy, are you going to answer the door!

(The Woman's call pulls Willy back. He starts right, befuddled.)

Biff: Hey, where are you going?

Willy: Open the door.

Biff: The door?

Willy: The washroom . . . the door . . . where's the door?

Biff (leading Willy to the left):   Just go straight down.

(Willy moves left.)

The Woman: Willy, Willy, are you going to get up, get up, get up, get up?

(Willy exits left.)

Letta: I think it's sweet you bring your daddy along.

Miss Forsythe: Oh, he isn't really your father!

Biff (at left, turning to her resentfully):   Miss Forsythe, you've just seen a prince walk by. A fine, troubled prince. A hard-working, unappreciated prince. A pal, you understand? A good companion. Always for his boys.

Letta: That's so sweet.

Happy: Well, girls, what's the program? We're wasting time. Come on, Biff. Gather round. Where would you like to go?

Biff: Why don't you do something for him?

Happy: Me!

Biff: Don't you give a damn for him, Hap?

Happy: What're you talking about? I'm the one who—

Biff: I sense it, you don't give a good goddam about him. (*He takes the rolled-up hose from his pocket and puts it on the table in front of Happy.*) Look what I found in the cellar, for Christ's sake. How can you bear to let it go on?

Happy: Me? Who goes away? Who runs off and—

Biff: Yeah, but he doesn't mean anything to you. You could help him—I can't! Don't you understand what I'm talking about? He's going to kill himself, don't you know that?

Happy: Don't I know it! Me!

Biff: Hap, help him! Jesus . . . help him . . . Help me, help me, I can't bear to look at his face! (*Ready to weep, he hurries out, up right.*)

Happy (starting after him): Where are you going?

Miss Forsythe: What's he so mad about?

Happy: Come on, girls, we'll catch up with him.

Miss Forsythe (as Happy pushes her out): Say, I don't like that temper of his!

Happy: He's just a little overstrung, he'll be all right!

Willy (off left, as The Woman laughs): Don't answer! Don't answer!

Letta: Don't you want to tell your father—

Happy: No, that's not my father. He's just a guy. Come on, we'll catch Biff, and, honey, we're going to paint this town! Stanley, where's the check! Hey, Stanley!

(*They exit. Stanley looks toward left.*)

Stanley (calling to Happy indignantly): Mr. Loman! Mr. Loman!

(*Stanley picks up a chair and follows them off. Knocking is heard off left. The Woman enters, laughing. Willy follows her. She is in a black slip; he is buttoning his shirt. Raw, sensuous music accompanies their speech.*)

Willy: Will you stop laughing? Will you stop?

The Woman: Aren't you going to answer the door? He'll wake the whole hotel.

Willy: I'm not expecting anybody.

The Woman: Whyn't you have another drink, honey, and stop being so damn self-centered?

Willy: I'm so lonely.

The Woman: You know you ruined me, Willy? From now on, whenever you come to the office, I'll see that you go right through to the buyers. No waiting at my desk anymore, Willy. You ruined me.

Willy: That's nice of you to say that.

The Woman: Gee, you are self-centered! Why so sad? You are the saddest, self-centeredest soul I ever did see-saw. (*She laughs, He kisses her.*) Come on inside, drummer boy. It's silly to be dressing in the middle of the night. (*As knocking is heard.*) Aren't you going to answer the door?

Willy: They're knocking on the wrong door.

The Woman: But I felt the knocking. And he heard us talking in here. Maybe the hotel's on fire!

Willy (his terror rising): It's a mistake.

The Woman: Then tell him to go away!

Willy: There's nobody there.

The Woman: It's getting on my nerves, Willy. There's somebody standing out there and it's getting on my nerves!

Willy (pushing her away from him): All right, stay in the bathroom here, and don't come out. I think there's a law in Massachusetts about it, so don't come out. It may be that new room clerk. He looked very mean. So don't come out. It's a mistake, there's no fire.

(*The knocking is heard again. He takes a few steps away from her, and she vanishes into the wing. The light follows him, and now he is facing Young Biff, who carries a suitcase. Biff steps toward him. The music is gone.*)

Biff: Why didn't you answer?

Willy: Biff! What are you doing in Boston?

Biff: Why didn't you answer? I've been knocking for five minutes, I called you on the phone—

Willy: I just heard you. I was in the bathroom and had the door shut. Did anything happen home?

Biff: Dad—I let you down.

Willy: What do you mean?

Biff: Dad . . .

Willy: Biffo, what's this about? (*Putting his arm around Biff.*) Come on, let's go downstairs and get you a malted.

Biff: Dad, I flunked math.

Willy: Not for the term?

Biff: The term. I haven't got enough credits to graduate.

Willy: You mean to say Bernard wouldn't give you the answers?

Biff: He did, he tried, but I only got a sixty-one.

Willy: And they wouldn't give you four points?

Biff: Birnbaum refused absolutely. I begged him, Pop, but he won't give me those points. You gotta talk to him before they close the school. Because if he saw the kind of man you are, and you just talked to him in your way, I'm sure he'd come through for me. The class came right before practice, see, and I didn't go enough. Would you talk to him?

He'd like you, Pop. You know the way you could talk.

Willy: You're on. We'll drive right back.

Biff: Oh, Dad, good work! I'm sure he'll change it for you!

Willy: Go downstairs and tell the clerk I'm checkin' out. Go right down.

Biff: Yes, sir! See, the reason he hates me, Pop—one day he was late for class so I got up at the blackboard and imitated him. I crossed my eyes and talked with a lithp.

Willy (laughing): You did? The kids like it?

Biff: They nearly died laughing!

Willy: Yeah? What'd you do?

Biff: The thquare root of thixthy twee is . . . (*Willy bursts out laughing; Biff joins.*) And in the middle of it he walked in!

(*Willy laughs and The Woman joins in offstage.*)

Willy (without hesitation): Hurry downstairs and—

Biff: Somebody in there?

Willy: No, that was next door.

(*The Woman laughs offstage.*)

Biff: Somebody got in your bathroom!

Willy: No, it's the next room, there's a party—

The Woman (enters, laughing. She lisps this): Can I come in? There's something in the bathtub, Willy, and it's moving!

(*Willy looks at Biff, who is staring open-mouthed and horrified at The Woman.*)

Willy: Ah—you better go back to your room. They must be finished painting by now. They're painting her room so I let her take a shower here. Go back, go back . . . (*He pushes her.*)

The Woman (resisting): But I've got to get dressed, Willy, I can't—

Willy: Get out of here! Go back, go back . . . (*Suddenly striving for the ordinary.*) This is Miss Francis, Biff, she's a buyer. They're painting her room. Go back, Miss Francis, go back . . .

The Woman: But my clothes, I can't go out naked in the hall!

Willy (pushing her offstage): Get outa here! Go back, go back!

(*Biff slowly sits down on his suitcase as the argument continues offstage.*)

The Woman: Where's my stockings? You promised me stockings, Willy!

Willy: I have no stockings here!

The Woman: You had two boxes of size nine sheers for me, and I want them!

Willy: Here, for God's sake, will you get outa here!

The Woman (enters holding a box of stockings): I just hope there's nobody in the hall. That's all I hope. (*To Biff.*) Are you football or baseball?

Biff: Football.

The Woman (angry, humiliated): That's me too. G'night. (*She snatches her clothes from Willy, and walks out.*)

Willy (after a pause): Well, better get going. I want to get to the school first thing in the morning. Get my suits out of the closet. I'll get my valise. (*Biff doesn't move.*) What's the matter! (*Biff remains motionless, tears falling.*) She's a buyer. Buys for J. H. Simmons. She lives down the hall—they're painting. You don't imagine—(*He breaks off. After a pause.*) Now listen, pal, she's just a buyer. She sees merchandise in her room and they have to keep it looking just so . . . (*Pause. Assuming command.*) All right, get my suits. (*Biff doesn't move.*) Now stop crying and do as I say. I gave you an order. Biff, I gave you an order! Is that what you do when I give you an order? How dare you cry! (*Putting his arm around Biff.*) Now look, Biff, when you grow up you'll understand about these things. You mustn't—you mustn't overemphasize a thing like this. I'll see Birnbaum first thing in the morning.

Biff: Never mind.

Willy (getting down beside Biff): Never mind! He's going to give you those points. I'll see to it.

Biff: He wouldn't listen to you.

Willy: He certainly will listen to me. You need those points for the U. of Virginia.

Biff: I'm not going there.

Willy: Heh? If I can't get him to change that mark you'll make it up in summer school. You've got all summer to—

Biff (his weeping breaking from him): Dad . . .

Willy (infected by it): Oh, my boy . . .

Biff: Dad . . .

Willy: She's nothing to me, Biff. I was lonely, I was terribly lonely.

Biff: You—you gave her Mama's stockings! (*His tears break through and he rises to go.*)

Willy (grabbing for Biff): I gave you an order!

Biff: Don't touch me, you—liar!

Willy: Apologize for that!

Biff: You fake! You phony little fake! You fake! (*Overcome, he turns quickly and weeping fully goes out with his suitcase. Willy is left on the floor on his knees.*)

Willy: I gave you an order! Biff, come back here or I'll beat you! Come back here! I'll whip you! (*Stanley comes quickly in from the right and stands in front of Willy.*) (*shouts at Stanley*): I gave you an order . . .

Stanley: Hey, let's pick it up, pick it up, Mr. Loman. (*He helps Willy to his feet.*) Your boys left with the chippies. They said they'll see you home.

(*A second waiter watches some distance away.*)

Willy: But we were supposed to have dinner together.

(*Music is heard, Willy's theme.*)

Stanley: Can you make it?

Willy: I'll—sure, I can make it. (*Suddenly concerned about his clothes.*) Do
I—I look all right?

Stanley: Sure, you look all right. (*He flicks a speck off Willy's lapel.*)

Willy: Here—here's a dollar.

Stanley: Oh, your son paid me. It's all right.

Willy (putting it in Stanley's hand): No, take it. You're a good boy.

Stanley: Oh, no, you don't have to . . .

Willy: Here—here's some more, I don't need it anymore. (*After a slight
pause.*) Tell me—is there a seed store in the neighborhood?

Stanley: Seeds? You mean like to plant?

(*As Willy turns, Stanley slips the money back into his jacket pocket.*)

Willy: Yes. Carrots, peas . . .

Stanley: Well, there's hardware stores on Sixth Avenue, but it may be too
late now.

Willy (anxiously): Oh, I'd better hurry. I've got to get some seeds. (*He
starts off to the right.*) I've got to get some seeds, right away. Nothing's
planted. I don't have a thing in the ground.

(*Willy hurries out as the light goes down. Stanley moves over to the right
after him, watches him off. The other waiter has been staring at Willy.*)

Stanley (to the waiter): Well, whatta you looking at?

(*The waiter picks up the chairs and moves off right. Stanley takes the table
and follows him. The light fades on this area. There is a long pause, the
sound of the flute coming over. The light gradually rises on the kitchen,
which is empty. Happy appears at the door of the house, followed by Biff.
Happy is carrying a large bunch of long-stemmed roses. He enters the
kitchen, looks around for Linda. Not seeing her, he turns to Biff, who is
just outside the house door, and makes a gesture with his hands,
indicating "Not here, I guess." He looks into the living room and freezes.
Inside, Linda, unseen, is seated, Willy's coat on her lap. She rises
ominously and quietly and moves toward Happy, who backs up into the
kitchen, afraid.*)

Happy: Hey, what're you doing up? (*Linda says nothing but moves toward
him implacably.*) Where's Pop? (*He keeps backing to the right, and now
Linda is in full view in the doorway to the living room.*) Is he sleeping?

Linda: Where were you?

Happy (trying to laugh it off): We met two girls, Mom, very fine types.
Here, we brought you some flowers. (*Offering them to her.*) Put them
in your room, Ma. (*She knocks them to the floor at Biff's feet. He has now
come inside and closed the door behind him. She stares at Biff, silent.*)

Now what'd you do that for? Mom, I want you to have some
flowers—

Linda (cutting Happy off, violently to Biff):   Don't you care whether he
lives or dies?

Happy (going to the stairs):   Come upstairs, Biff.

Biff (with a flare of disgust, to Happy):   Go away from me! (*To Linda.*)
What do you mean, lives or dies? Nobody's dying around here, pal.

Linda: Get out of my sight! Get out of here!

Biff: I wanna see the boss.

Linda: You're not going near him!

Biff: Where is he? (*He moves into the living room and Linda follows.*)

Linda (shouting after Biff):   You invite him for dinner. He looks forward
to it all day—(*Biff appears in his parents' bedroom, looks around, and
exits*)—and then you desert him there. There's no stranger you'd do
that to!

Happy: Why? He had a swell time with us. Listen, when I—(*Linda comes
back into the kitchen*)—desert him I hope I don't outlive the day!

Linda: Get out of here!

Happy: Now look, Mom . . .

Linda: Did you have to go to women tonight? You and your lousy rotten
whores!

(*Biff reenters the kitchen.*)

Happy: Mom, all we did was follow Biff around trying to cheer him up!
(*To Biff.*) Boy, what a night you gave me!

Linda: Get out of here, both of you, and don't come back! I don't
want you tormenting him anymore. Go on now, get your things
together! (*To Biff.*) You can sleep in his apartment. (*She starts to
pick up the flowers and stops herself.*) Pick up this stuff, I'm not your
maid anymore. Pick it up, you bum, you! (*Happy turns his back to
her in refusal. Biff slowly moves over and gets down on his knees,
picking up the flowers.*) You're a pair of animals! Not one, not
another living soul would have had the cruelty to walk out on that
man in a restaurant!

Biff (not looking at her):   Is that what he said?

Linda: He didn't have to say anything. He was so humiliated he nearly
limped when he came in.

Happy: But, Mom, he had a great time with us—

Biff (cutting him off violently):   Shut up!

(*Without another word, Happy goes upstairs.*)

Linda: You! You didn't even go in to see if he was all right!

*Biff (still on the floor in front of Linda, the flowers in his hand; with self-
loathing):*   No. Didn't. Didn't do a damned thing. How do you like
that, heh? Left him babbling in a toilet.

Linda: You louse, You . . .

Biff: Now you hit it on the nose! (*He gets up, throws the flowers in the wastebasket.*) The scum of the earth, and you're looking at him!

Linda: Get out of here!

Biff: I gotta talk to the boss, Mom. Where is he?

Linda: You're not going near him. Get out of this house!

Biff (with absolute assurance, determination):   No. We're gonna have an abrupt conversation, him and me.

Linda: You're not talking to him.

> (*Hammering is heard from outside the house, off right. Biff turns toward the noise.*)

Linda (suddenly pleading):   Will you please leave him alone?

Biff: What's he doing out there?

Linda: He's planting the garden!

Biff (quietly):   Now? Oh, my God!

> (*Biff moves outside, Linda following. The light dies down on them and comes up on the center of the apron as Willy walks into it. He is carrying a flashlight, a hoe, and a handful of seed packets. He raps the top of the hoe sharply to fix it firmly, and then moves to the left, measuring off the distance with his foot. He holds the flashlight to look at the seed packets, reading off the instructions. He is in the blue of night.*)

Willy: Carrots . . . quarter-inch apart. Rows . . . one-foot rows. (*He measures it off.*) One foot. (*He puts down a package and measures off.*) Beets. (*He puts down another package and measures again.*) Lettuce. (*He reads the package, puts it down.*) One foot—(*He breaks off as Ben appears at the right and moves slowly down to him.*) What a proposition, ts, ts. Terrific, terrific. 'Cause she's suffered, Ben, the woman has suffered. You understand me? A man can't go out the way he came in, Ben, a man has got to add up to something. You can't, you can't— (*Ben moves toward him as though to interrupt.*) You gotta consider, now. Don't answer so quick. Remember, it's a guaranteed twenty-thousand-dollar proposition. Now look, Ben, I want you to go through the ins and outs of this thing with me. I've got nobody to talk to, Ben, and the woman has suffered, you hear me?

Ben (standing still, considering):   What's the proposition?

Willy: It's twenty thousand dollars on the barrelhead. Guaranteed, gilt-edged, you understand?

Ben: You don't want to make a fool of yourself. They might not honor the policy.

Willy: How can they dare refuse? Didn't I work like a coolie to meet every premium on the nose? And now they don't pay off? Impossible!

Ben: It's called a cowardly thing, William.

Willy: Why? Does it take more guts to stand here the rest of my life ringing up a zero?

Ben (yielding):   That's a point, William. (*He moves, thinking, turns.*) And twenty thousand—that *is* something one can feel with the hand, it is there.

Willy (now assured, with rising power): Oh, Ben, that's the whole beauty of it! I see it like a diamond, shining in the dark, hard and rough, that I can pick up and touch in my hand. Not like—like an appointment! This would not be another damned-fool appointment, Ben, and it changes all the aspects. Because he thinks I'm nothing, see, and so he spites me. But the funeral—(*Straightening up.*) Ben, that funeral will be massive! They'll come from Maine, Massachusetts, Vermont, New Hampshire! All the old-timers with the strange license plates—that boy will be thunderstruck, Ben, because he never realized—I am known! Rhode Island, New York, New Jersey—I am known, Ben, and he'll see it with his eyes once and for all. He'll see what I am, Ben! He's in for a shock, that boy!

Ben (coming down to the edge of the garden): He'll call you a coward.

Willy (suddenly fearful): No, that would be terrible.

Ben: Yes. And a damned fool.

Willy: No, no, he mustn't, I won't have that! (*He is broken and desperate.*)

Ben: He'll hate you, William.

(*The gay music of the Boys is heard.*)

Willy: Oh, Ben, how do we get back to all the great times? Used to be so full of light, and comradeship, the sleigh-riding in winter, and the ruddiness on his cheeks. And always some kind of good news coming up, always something nice coming up ahead. And never even let me carry the valises in the house, and simonizing, simonizing that little red car! Why, why can't I give him something and not have him hate me?

Ben: Let me think about it. (*He glances at his watch.*) I still have a little time. Remarkable proposition, but you've got to be sure you're not making a fool of yourself.

(*Ben drifts off upstage and goes out of sight. Biff comes down from the left.*)

Willy (suddenly conscious of Biff, turns and looks up at him, then begins picking up the packages of seeds in confusion): Where the hell is that seed? (*Indignantly.*) You can't see nothing out here! They boxed in the whole goddam neighborhood!

Biff: There are people all around here. Don't you realize that?

Willy: I'm busy. Don't bother me.

Biff (taking the hoe from Willy): I'm saying good-by to you, Pop. (*Willy looks at him, silent, unable to move.*) I'm not coming back anymore.

Willy: You're not going to see Oliver tomorrow?

Biff: I've got no appointment, Dad.

Willy: He put his arm around you, and you've got no appointment?

Biff: Pop, get this now, will you? Everytime I've left it's been a fight that sent me out of here. Today I realized something about myself and I tried to explain it to you and I—I think I'm just not smart enough to make any sense out of it for you. To hell with whose fault it is or anything like that. (*He takes Willy's arm.*) Let's just wrap it up, heh? Come on in, we'll tell Mom. (*He gently tries to pull Willy to left.*)

Willy (frozen, immobile, with guilt in his voice):   No, I don't want to see her.

Biff: Come on! (*He pulls again, and Willy tries to pull away.*)

Willy (highly nervous):   No, no, I don't want to see her.

Biff (tries to look into Willy's face, as if to find the answer there):   Why don't you want to see her?

Willy (more harshly now):   Don't bother me, will you?

Biff: What do you mean, you don't want to see her? You don't want them calling you yellow, do you? This isn't your fault; it's me, I'm a bum. Now come inside! (*Willy strains to get away.*) Did you hear what I said to you?

(*Willy pulls away and quickly goes by himself into the house. Biff follows.*)

Linda (to Willy):   Did you plant, dear?

Biff (at the door, to Linda):   All right, we had it out. I'm going and I'm not writing anymore.

Linda (going to Willy in the kitchen):   I think that's the best way, dear. 'Cause there's no use drawing it out, you'll just never get along.

(*Willy doesn't respond.*)

Biff: People ask where I am and what I'm doing, you don't know, and you don't care. That way it'll be off your mind and you can start brightening up again. All right? That clears it, doesn't it? (*Willy is silent, and Biff goes to him.*) You gonna wish me luck, scout? (*He extends his hand.*) What do you say?

Linda: Shake his hand, Willy.

Willy (turning to her, seething with hurt):   There's no necessity to mention the pen at all, y'know.

Biff (gently):   I've got no appointment, Dad.

Willy (erupting fiercely):   He put his arm around . . . ?

Biff: Dad, you're never going to see what I am, so what's the use of arguing? If I strike oil I'll send you a check. Meantime forget I'm alive.

Willy (to Linda):   Spite, see?

Biff: Shake hands, Dad.

Willy: Not my hand.

Biff: I was hoping not to go this way.

Willy: Well, this is the way you're going. Good-by.

(*Biff looks at him a moment, then turns sharply and goes to the stairs.*)

Willy (stops him with):   May you rot in hell if you leave this house!

Biff (turning):   Exactly what is it that you want from me?

Willy: I want you to know, on the train, in the mountains, in the valleys, wherever you go, that you cut down your life for spite!

Biff: No, no.

Willy: Spite, spite, is the word of your undoing! And when you're down and out, remember what did it. When you're rotting somewhere beside the railroad tracks, remember, and don't you dare blame it on me!

Biff: I'm not blaming it on you!

Willy: I won't take the rap for this, you hear?

(*Happy comes down the stairs and stands on the bottom step, watching.*)

Biff: That's just what I'm telling you!

Willy (sinking into a chair at a table, with full accusation):   You're trying to put a knife in me—don't think I don't know what you're doing!

Biff: All right, phony! Then let's lay it on the line. (*He whips the rubber tube out of his pocket and puts it on the table.*)

Happy: You crazy . . .

Linda: Biff! (*She moves to grab the hose, but Biff holds it down with his hand.*)

Biff: Leave it there! Don't move it!

Willy (not looking at it):   What is that?

Biff: You know goddam well what that is.

Willy (caged, wanting to escape):   I never saw that.

Biff: You saw it. The mice didn't bring it into the cellar! What is this supposed to do, make a hero out of you? This supposed to make me sorry for you?

Willy: Never heard of it.

Biff: There'll be no pity for you, you hear it? No pity!

Willy (to Linda):   You hear the spite!

Biff: No, you're going to hear the truth—what you are and what I am!

Linda: Stop it!

Willy: Spite!

Happy (coming down toward Biff):   You cut it now!

Biff (to Happy):   The man don't know who we are! The man is gonna know! (*To Willy.*) We never told the truth for ten minutes in this house!

Happy: We always told the truth!

Biff (turning on him):   You big blow, are you the assistant buyer? You're one of the two assistants to the assistant, aren't you?

Happy: Well, I'm practically . . .

Biff: You're practically full of it! We all are! and I'm through with it. (*To Willy.*) Now hear this, Willy, this is me.

Willy: I know you!

Biff: You know why I had no address for three months? I stole a suit in Kansas City and I was in jail. (*To Linda, who is sobbing.*) Stop crying. I'm through with it.

(Linda turns away from them, her hands covering her face.)

Willy: I suppose that's my fault!

Biff: I stole myself out of every good job since high school!

Willy: And whose fault is that?

Biff: And I never got anywhere because you blew me so full of hot air I could never stand taking orders from anybody! That's whose fault it is!

Willy: I hear that!

Linda: Don't, Biff!

Biff: It's goddam time you heard that! I had to be boss big shot in two weeks, and I'm through with it!

Willy: Then hang yourself! For spite, hang yourself!

Biff: No! Nobody's hanging himself, Willy! I ran down eleven flights with a pen in my hand today. And suddenly I stopped, you hear me? And in the middle of that office building, do you hear this? I stopped in the middle of that building and I saw—the sky. I saw the things that I love in this world. The work and the food and time to sit and smoke. And I looked at the pen and said to myself, what the hell am I grabbing this for? Why am I trying to become what I don't want to be? What am I doing in an office, making a contemptuous, begging fool of myself, when all I want is out there, waiting for me the minute I say I know who I am! Why can't I say that, Willy? *(He tries to make Willy face him, but Willy pulls away and moves to the left.)*

Willy (with hatred, threateningly): The door of your life is wide open!

Biff: Pop! I'm a dime a dozen, and so are you!

Willy (turning on him now in an uncontrolled outburst): I am not a dime a dozen! I am Willy Loman, and you are Biff Loman!

(Biff starts for Willy, but is blocked by Happy. In his fury, Biff seems on the verge of attacking his father.)

Biff: I am not a leader of men, Willy, and neither are you. You were never anything but a hard-working drummer who landed in the ash can like all the rest of them! I'm one dollar an hour, Willy! I tried seven states and couldn't raise it. A buck an hour! Do you gather my meaning? I'm not bringing home any prizes anymore, and you're going to stop waiting for me to bring them home!

Willy (directly to Biff): You vengeful, spiteful mutt!

(Biff breaks from Happy. Willy, in fright, starts up the stairs. Biff grabs him.)

Biff (at the peak of his fury): Pop, I'm nothing! I'm nothing, Pop. Can't you understand that? There's no spite in it anymore. I'm just what I am, that's all.

(Biff's fury has spent itself and he breaks down, sobbing, holding on to Willy, who dumbly fumbles for Biff's face.)

Willy (astonished): What're you doing? What're you doing? (*To Linda.*) Why is he crying?

Biff (crying, broken): Will you let me go, for Christ's sake? Will you take that phony dream and burn it before something happens? (*Struggling to contain himself he pulls away and moves to the stairs.*) I'll go in the morning. Put him—put him to bed. (*Exhausted, Biff moves up the stairs to his room.*)

Willy (after a long pause, astonished, elevated): Isn't that—isn't that remarkable? Biff—he likes me!

Linda: He loves you, Willy!

Happy (deeply moved): Always did, Pop.

Willy: Oh, Biff! (*Staring wildly.*) He cried! Cried to me. (*He is choking with his love, and now cries out his promise.*) That boy—that boy is going to be magnificent!

(*Ben appears in the light just outside the kitchen.*)

Ben: Yes, outstanding, with twenty thousand behind him.

Linda (sensing the racing of his mind, fearfully, carefully): Now come to bed, Willy. It's all settled now.

Willy (finding it difficult not to rush out of the house): Yes, we'll sleep. Come on. Go to sleep, Hap.

Ben: And it does take a great kind of a man to crack the jungle.

(*In accents of dread, Ben's idyllic music starts up.*)

Happy (his arm around Linda): I'm getting married, Pop, don't forget it. I'm changing everything. I'm gonna run that department before the year is up. You'll see, Mom. (*He kisses her.*)

Ben: The jungle is dark but full of diamonds, Willy.

(*Willy turns, moves, listening to Ben.*)

Linda: Be good. You're both good boys, just act that way, that's all.

Happy: 'Night, Pop. (*He goes upstairs.*)

Linda (to Willy): Come, dear.

Ben (with greater force): One must go in to fetch a diamond out.

Willy (to Linda, as he moves slowly along the edge of kitchen, toward the door): I just want to get settled down, Linda. Let me sit alone for a little.

Linda (almost uttering her fear): I want you upstairs.

Willy (taking her in his arms): In a few minutes, Linda. I couldn't sleep right now. Go on, you look awful tired. (*He kisses her.*)

Ben: Not like an appointment at all. A diamond is rough and hard to the touch.

Willy: Go on now. I'll be right up.

Linda: I think this is the only way, Willy.

Willy: Sure, it's the best thing.

Ben: Best thing!

Willy: The only way. Everything is gonna be—go on, kid, get to bed. You look so tired.

Linda: Come right up.

Willy: Two minutes. (*Linda goes into the living room, then reappears in her bedroom. Willy moves just outside the kitchen door.*) Loves me. (*Wonderingly.*) Always loved me. Isn't that a remarkable thing? Ben, he'll worship me for it!

Ben (with promise):   It's dark there, but full of diamonds.

Willy: Can you imagine that magnificence with twenty thousand dollars in his pocket?

Linda (calling from her room):   Willy! Come up!

Willy (calling into the kitchen):   Yes! yes. Coming! It's very smart, you realize that, don't you, sweetheart? Even Ben sees it. I gotta go, baby. 'By! 'By! (*Going over to Ben, almost dancing.*) Imagine? When the mail comes he'll be ahead of Bernard again!

Ben: A perfect proposition all around.

Willy: Did you see how he cried to me? Oh, if I could kiss him, Ben!

Ben: Time, William, time!

Willy: Oh, Ben, I always knew one way or another we were gonna make it, Biff and I!

Ben (looking at his watch):   The boat. We'll be late. (*He moves slowly off into the darkness.*)

Willy (elegiacally, turning to the house):   Now when you kick off, boy, I want a seventy-yard boot, and get right down the field under the ball, and when you hit, hit low and hit hard, because it's important, boy. (*He swings around and faces the audience.*) There's all kinds of important people in the stands, and the first thing you know . . . (*Suddenly realizing he is alone.*) Ben! Ben, where do I . . . ? (*He makes a sudden movement of search.*) Ben, how do I . . . ?

Linda (calling):   Willy, you coming up?

Willy (uttering a gasp of fear, whirling about as if to quiet her):   Sh! (*He turns around as if to find his way; sounds, faces, voices, seem to be swarming in upon him and he flicks at them, crying, Sh! Sh! Suddenly music, faint and high, stops him. It rises in intensity, almost to an unbearable scream. He goes up and down on his toes, and rushes off around the house.*) Shhh!

Linda: Willy?

(*There is no answer. Linda waits. Biff gets up off his bed. He is still in his clothes. Happy sits up. Biff stands listening.*)

Linda (with real fear):   Willy, answer me! Willy! (*There is the sound of a car starting and moving away at full speed.*) No!

Biff (rushing down the stairs):   Pop!

(*As the car speeds off, the music crashes down in a frenzy of sound, which becomes the soft pulsation of a single cello string. Biff slowly returns to his bedroom. He and Happy gravely don their jackets. Linda slowly walks out of her room. The music has developed into a dead march. The leaves of day are appearing over everything. Charley and Bernard, somberly dressed,*) *appear and knock on the kitchen door. Biff and Happy slowly descend the stairs to the kitchen as Charley and Bernard enter. All stop a moment when Linda, in clothes of mourning, bearing a little bunch of roses, comes through the draped doorway into the kitchen. She goes to Charley and takes his arm. Now all move toward the audience, through the wall-line of the kitchen. At the limit of the apron, Linda lays down the flowers, kneels, and sits back on her heels. All stare down at the grave.)*

REQUIEM

Charley: It's getting dark, Linda.

(Linda doesn't react. She stares at the grave.)

Biff: How about it, Mom? Better get some rest, heh? They'll be closing the gate soon.

(Linda makes no move. Pause.)

Happy (deeply angered):   He had no right to do that. There was no necessity for it. We would've helped him.

Charley (grunting):   Hmmm.

Biff: Come along, Mom.

Linda: Why didn't anybody come?

Charley: It was a very nice funeral.

Linda: But where are all the people he knew? Maybe they blame him.

Charley: Naa. It's a rough world, Linda. They wouldn't blame him.

Linda: I can't understand it. At this time especially. First time in thirty-five years we were just about free and clear. He only needed a little salary. He was even finished with the dentist.

Charley: No man only needs a little salary.

Linda: I can't understand it.

Biff: There were a lot of nice days. When he'd come home from a trip; or on Sundays, making the stoop; finishing the cellar; putting on the new porch; when he built the extra bathroom; and put up the garage. You know something, Charley, there's more of him in that front stoop than in all the sales he ever made.

Charley: Yeah. He was a happy man with a batch of cement.

Linda: He was so wonderful with his hands.

Biff: He had the wrong dreams. All, all, wrong.

Happy (almost ready to fight Biff):   Don't say that!

Biff: He never knew who he was.

Charley (stopping Happy's movement and reply. To Biff):   Nobody dast blame this man. You don't understand: Willy was a salesman. And for a salesman, there is no rock bottom to the life. He don't put a bolt to a nut, he don't tell you the law or give you medicine. He's a man way out there in the blue, riding on a smile and a shoeshine. And when they start not smiling back—that's an earthquake. And then you get yourself a couple of spots on your hat, and you're finished. Nobody dast blame this man. A salesman is got to dream, boy. It comes with the territory.

Biff: Charley, the man didn't know who he was.

Happy (infuriated):   Don't say that!

Biff: Why don't you come with me, Happy?

Happy: I'm not licked that easily. I'm staying right in this city, and I'm gonna beat this racket! (*He looks at Biff, his chin set.*) The Loman Brothers!

Biff: I know who I am, kid.

Happy: All right, boy. I'm gonna show you and everybody else that Willy Loman did not die in vain. He had a good dream. It's the only dream you can have—to come out number-one man. He fought it out here, and this is where I'm gonna win it for him.

Biff (with a hopeless glance at Happy, bends toward his mother):   Let's go, Mom.

Linda: I'll be with you in a minute. Go on, Charley. (*He hesitates.*) I want to, just for a minute. I never had a chance to say good-by. (*Charley moves away, followed by Happy. Biff remains a slight distance up and left of Linda. She sits there, summoning herself. The flute begins, not far away, playing behind her speech.*) Forgive me, dear. I can't cry. I don't know what it is, but I can't cry. I don't understand it. Why did you ever do that? Help me, Willy, I can't cry. It seems to me that you're just on another trip. I keep expecting you. Willy, dear, I can't cry. Why did you do it? I search and search and I search, and I can't understand it, Willy. I made the last payment on the house today. Today, dear. And there'll be nobody home. (*A sob rises in her throat.*) We're free and clear. (*Sobbing more fully, released.*) We're free. (*Biff comes slowly toward her.*) We're free . . . We're free . . .

(*Biff lifts her to her feet and moves out up right with her in his arms. Linda sobs quietly. Bernard and Charley come together and follow them, followed by Happy. Only the music of the flute is left on the darkening stage as over the house the hard towers of the apartment buildings rise into sharp focus, and the curtain falls.*)

WINDOW ON

Politics, Ethnicity, and Drama

Drama has often dealt with political and ethnic questions, and some critics insist that it has always done so. Greek drama, especially comedies, commented broadly and sometimes ferociously on political issues and individuals with well-known political views. Whether these comedies changed anything is another question, but drama has frequently voiced political and social concerns. In countries run by tyrants or monolithic governments, criticism is often disguised, but in countries such as England, the United States, Ireland, postwar Germany and prewar Italy drama has been openly critical of existing and past systems.

Political concerns surface in Strindberg's *Miss Julie*, especially in Jean's fear of the Count and Julie's certainty that she is socially superior. In *The Kiss of the Spider Woman*, however, the political issues are much more evident. Valentin is a political prisoner in a South American jail. In the latter part of the twentieth century, such a sentence conjures scenes of torture and death. Certain Latin American governments have been harsh, absolute, and in many basic ways inhuman in their treatment of opponents. Valentin is an idealist. When Molina mocks him by asking him if he thinks he can change the world, he says, "Yes, and I don't care that you laugh. It makes people laugh to hear this, but what I have to do before anything is to change the world." But in the Villa Devoto prison, the most they can hope for is to change themselves. That, too, is a political act.

Political issues underlie the action of David Mamet's *Oleanna*. The relationship of professor to student is marked by unequal power, itself a fundamental political concern. Further, when the professor is male and the student female, the political stakes are raised markedly. For the audience, the relationship between John and Carol is not entirely clear from the first. Things said innocently come back to haunt John. Carol tries to make him aware of the extent to which he assumes his own power is to be taken for granted, how much he unconsciously patronizes Carol. In the second act we learn that Carol represents a group and is thereby part of what can be regarded as a political front with a political agenda. The question of agendas becomes a major issue in the drama, which reveals that an apparently ordinary circumstance is fraught with political issues.

Both *Kiss of the Spider Woman* and *Oleanna* also focus on gender politics, with homosexuality and homophobia present in Puig's play, and feminism and potential misogyny in Mamet's. These are especially powerful issues since audience members are ordinarily aligned on one or another side of issues concerning gay rights and feminism. These plays face up to the political significance of each of these themes by establishing their power and the potential shifts in power that circumstance and opportunity can create.

Although Paula Vogel's play is not explicitly about AIDS, it has been widely accepted as an AIDS play. The mysterious disease that cripples Carl is AIDS-like, and the introductory material from Paula Vogel's brother, who died of AIDS, makes it clear what her sources of inspiration are. Productions of the play drive home the political realities by virtue of the many characters played by The Third Man, who ranges from Doctor to The Little Dutch Boy. Each of the characters has a power over Carl and Anna, sometimes a sinister power. And no matter where they go, they cannot escape the fate of the disease.

Ethnic issues naturally concern a question of power, and minorities have always been aware of inequities in opportunity even in nations that guarantee equality. August Wilson is embarked on a project to write a number of plays on the experiences of blacks in America. *Fences* is one of them. On one level the play is about the relationship of a dominating father and a son discovering his own power. On another level, it is about a black family's fight for survival and the price it extracts from them. The father's rejection by the establishment of whites-only baseball was fatal, and it soured his entire life. That pain is visited, in the manner of the Bible, on the son, who must somehow deal with it. Wilson is the son of a white father and a black mother, and his ethnic sensibilities are as finely tuned as those of any American dramatist, past or present.

John Guare's *Six Degrees of Separation* centers around a genuine incident in which a young black student represented himself as the son of the famous actor Sidney Poitier and found himself accepted by wealthy white families in New York's Upper East Side. The liberal political attitudes of these families made them easy to manipulate, but Guare is interested in the range of responses Paul elicits from parents and their children. In the process the relationship of parents and children reveals a painful contempt that may imply a concern for the politics of the family itself. Dr. Fine's son scolds him for accepting Paul on face value and credits Dr. Fine's wife for having had the wisdom to divorce him. It is a bitter moment in a play that explores bitterness in many forms.

These are not the only plays in the collection that approach ethnic themes and their political consequences. Anglo, Italian, Irish, and other European ethnicities are often central to plays that seem to have no special interest in ethnicity at all, such as *Death of a Salesman*. Those plays may be read ethnically if one realizes that in drama the absence of ethnicity may be an illusion resulting from a special kind of cultural blindness.

Reading

Hill, Errol, ed. *The Theatre of Black Americans.* 2 vols. Englewood Cliffs: Prentice-Hall, 1980.

Osborn, M. Elizabeth, ed. *On New Ground: Contemporary Hispanic-American Plays.* New York: Theatre Communications, 1987.

Piscator, Erwin. *The Political Theatre: A History, 1914–1929.* Tr. Hugh Rorrison. London: Eyre Methuen, 1980.
Wellworth, George E. *The Theatre of Protest and Paradox.* New York: New York University Press, 1971.

Manuel Puig   (1923–1990)

Puig was an Argentinian novelist, dramatist, and filmmaker. The Kiss of the Spider Woman *(1981) began as a novel, although soon after its publication Puig wrote the stage play. The film (1985) starred William Hurt as Molina and Raoul Julia as Valentin. Its popularity and success caught the interest of theater people as well as the general public, resulting in recent productions of the play in regional and major urban theaters across the United States and in Europe and South America. Among Puig's other plays are* Mystery of the Rose Bouquet *(1981) and* Under the Mantle of Stars *(1982).*

Like some of his other works, The Kiss of the Spider Woman *is set in an enclosed world populated by only two people. The setting, an Argentinian prison, is frightening, especially in the 1980s during the period of the "Disappeareds," those thousands of people who were summarily whisked away by police never to be seen or heard from again. The background of the play is that of official terror maintained by the government. One of the subversive themes is revolution: Valentin is a macho Marxist fighting against a fascist regime. Another theme is homosexual love. Molina is a gay window dresser imprisoned for molesting a fifteen-year-old. Ironically, they "escape" the prison by reliving old B-movies, which were themselves somewhat fascist in origin and content. They also learn to love each other. Theirs is a relationship filled with surprises.*

THE KISS OF THE SPIDER WOMAN   1981

Translated by Allan J. Baker
A Play by Manuel Puig Based on his Novel of the Same Title

ACT ONE

Scene I

(Scene: A small cell in the Villa Devoto prison in Buenos Aires. The stage is in total darkness. Suddenly two overhead white spots light up the heads of the two men. They are sitting down, looking in opposite directions.)

Molina: You can see there's something special about her, that she's not any ordinary woman. Quite young . . . and her face more round than oval, with a little pointy chin like a cat's.

Valentin: And her eyes?

Molina: Most probably green. She looks up at the model, the black panther lying down in its cage in the zoo. But she scratches her pencil against the sketch pad and the panther sees her.

Valentin: How come it didn't smell her before?

Molina (deliberately not answering):   But, who's that behind her? Someone trying to light a cigarette, but the wind blows out the match.

Valentin: Who is it?

Molina: Hold on. She flusters. He's no matinée idol but he's nice-looking, in a hat with a low brim. He touches the brim like he's saluting and says the drawing is terrific. She fiddles with the curls of her fringe.

Valentin: Go on.

Molina: He can tell she's a foreigner by her accent. She tells him that she came to New York when the war broke out. He asks her if she's homesick. And then it's like a cloud passes across her eyes and she tells him she comes from the mountains, someplace not far from Transylvania.

Valentin: Where Dracula comes from.

Molina: The next day he's in his office with some colleagues—he's an architect—and this girl, another architect he works with—and when the clock strikes three he just wants to drop everything and go to the zoo. It's right across the street. And the architect girl asks him why he's so happy. Deep down, she's really in love with him, no use her pretending otherwise.

Valentin: Is she a dog?

Molina: No, nothing out of this world: chestnut hair, but pleasant enough. But the other one, the one at the zoo, Irene—no, Irina—has disappeared. As time goes by he just can't get her out of his mind until one day he's walking down this fashionable avenue and he notices something in the window of an art gallery. They're pictures by an artist who only paints . . . panthers. The guy goes in and there's Irina being congratulated by all the guests. And I don't remember what comes next.

Valentin: Try to remember . . .

Molina: Hold on a sec . . . Okay, . . . then the architect goes up and congratulates her too. She drops the critics and walks off with him. He tells her that he just happened to be passing by, really he was on his way to buy a present.

Valentin: For the girl architect.

Molina: Now he's wondering if he's got enough money with him to buy two presents. And he stops outside a shop and she gets a funny feeling when she sees what kind of shop it is. There are all different kinds of birds in little cages sipping fresh water from their bowls.

Valentin: Excuse me . . . is there any water in the bottle?

Molina: Yes, I filled it up when they let us out to the toilet.

(The white light which up till now has lit just their heads widens to fully light both actors: we see the cell for the first time.)

Valentin: That's okay then.

Molina: Do you want some? It's nice and cool.

Valentin: No or we won't have enough for tea in the morning. Go on.

Molina: Don't exaggerate. We've got enough to last all day.

Valentin: Don't spoil me. I forgot to fetch some when they let us out to shower. If it wasn't for you we wouldn't have any.

Molina: Look, there's plenty . . . Anyway, when they go inside that shop it's like—I don't know what—it's like the devil just came in. The birds, blind with fear, fly into the wire mesh and hurt their wings. She grabs his hand and drags him outside. Straight away the birds calm down. She asks him to let her go home. When he comes back into the shop the birds are chirruping and singing just like normal and he buys one for the other girl's birthday. And then . . . it's no good, I can't remember what happens next, I'm pooped.

Valentin: Just a little more.

Molina: When I'm sleepy my memory goes. I'll carry on with the morning tea.

Valentin: No, it's better at night. During the day I don't want to bother with this trivia. There are more important things . . . (*Molina shrugs.*) If I'm not reading and I'm keeping quiet it's because I'm thinking. But don't take it wrong.

Molina (upset by Valentin's remark. With almost concealed irony):   I shan't bother you. You can count on that!

Valentin: I see you understand. See you in the morning. (*He settles down to sleep.*)

Molina: Till tomorrow. Pleasant dreams of Irina. (*Molina settles down too, but he is troubled by something.*)

Valentin: I prefer the architect girl.

Molina: I'd already guessed that.

Scene II

(Scene: Molina and Valentin are sitting in different positions. They do not look at one another. Only their heads are lit: seconds later the night light comes on.)

Molina: So they go on seeing each other and they fall in love. She pampers him, cuddles up in his arms, but when he wants to hold her tight and kiss her she slips away from him. She asks him not to kiss her but to let her kiss him with her full lips, but she keeps her mouth shut tight. (*Valentin is about to interrupt but Molina forges ahead.*) So, on their next date they go to this quaint restaurant. He tells her she's prettier than ever in her shimmering black blouse. But she's lost her appetite, she can't manage a thing, and they leave. It's snowing gently.

The noise of the city is muffled but far away you can just hear the growling of wild animals. The zoo's close, that's why. Barely in a whisper she says she's afraid to return to her house and spend the night alone. He hails a taxi and they go to his house. It's a huge place, all *fin de siècle*; it used to be his mother's.

Valentin: And what does he do?

Molina: Nothing. He lights up his pipe and looks over at her. You always guessed he had a kind heart.

Valentin: I'd like to ask you something: how do you picture his mother?

Molina: So you can make fun of her?

Valentin: I swear I won't.

Molina: I don't know . . . someone really charming. She made her husband happy and her children too. She's always well groomed.

Valentin: And do you picture her scrubbing floors?

Molina: No, she's always impeccable. The high-necked dress hides the wrinkles round her throat.

Valentin: Always impeccable. With servants. People with no other choice than to fetch and carry for her. And, of course, she was happy with her husband who also exploited her in his turn, kept her locked up in the house like a slave, waiting for him . . .

Molina: . . . Listen . . .

Valentin: . . . waiting for him to come home every night from his chambers or his surgery. And she condoned the system, fed all this crap to her son and now he trips over the panther woman. Serves him right.

Molina (irritated): Why did you have to bring up all that? . . . I'd forgotten all about this dump while I was telling you the movie.

Valentin: I'd forgotten about it too.

Molina: Well, then . . . Why d'you have to go and break the spell?

Valentin: Let me explain. . . .

Molina: Fine, but not now, tomorrow. . . . Why did I get lumbered with you and not the panther woman's boyfriend?

Valentin: That's another story and one that doesn't interest me.

Molina: Are you frightened to talk about it?

Valentin: It bores me. I know all about it—even though you've never said a word.

Molina: Fine. I told you I got done for corruption of minors. There's nothing else to add. So don't come the psychologist with me.

Valentin (shielding himself behind humor): Admit that you like him because he smokes a pipe.

Molina: No, it's not that. It's because he's gentle and understanding.

Valentin: His mother castrated him, that's all.

Molina: I like him and that's that. And you like the architect girl—what's so Bolshy about her?

Valentin: I prefer her to the panther woman, that's for sure. But the guy with the pipe won't suit you.

Molina: Why not?

Valentin: Your intentions aren't exactly chaste, are they?

Molina: Of course not.

Valentin: Exactly. He likes Irina because she's frigid and he doesn't have to pounce on her and that's why he takes her to the house where his mother is still present even if she is dead.

Molina (getting angrier and angrier): Continue.

Valentin: If he's still kept all his mother's things it's because he wants to remain a child. He doesn't bring home a woman but a child to play with.

Molina: That's all in your head. I don't even know if the place is his mother's—I said that because I liked the place and since I saw antiques there I told you it belonged to his mother. For all I know he rents it furnished.

Valentin: So you're making up half the movie?

Molina: I'm not, I swear. But—you know—there are some things I add to fill it out for you. The house, for example. And, in any case, don't forget I'm a window dresser and that's almost like being an interior designer. . . . Well, she begins to tell him her story but I don't remember all the details. . . . I remember that in her village, a long time ago, there used to be panther-women. And these tales frightened her a lot when she was a little girl.

Valentin: And the birds? . . . Why were they afraid of her?

Molina: That's what the architect asks her. And what does she say? She doesn't say anything! And the scene ends with him in pyjamas and a dressing gown, good quality, no pattern, something serviceable—and he looks at her sleeping on the sofa from his bedroom door and he lights up his pipe and stands there . . . thoughtful.

Valentin: Do you know what I like about it? That it's like an allegory of women's fear of submitting to the male, because when it comes to sex, the animal part takes over. You see?

Molina (he doesn't approve of Valentin's comments): Irina wakes up, it's morning already.

Valentin: She wakes up because of the cold, like us.

Molina (irritated): I knew you were going to say that. . . . She's woken up by the canary, singing in its cage. At first she's afraid to go near it, but the little bird is chirpy so she dares to move a little closer. She heaves a big sigh of relief because the bird isn't frightened of her. And then she makes breakfast . . . toast and cereals and pancakes . . .

Valentin: Don't mention food.

Molina: . . . and pancakes . . .

Valentin: I'm serious. Neither food nor women.

Molina: She wakes him up and he's all happy to see her settling in and so he asks her to stay there forever and marry him. And she says, yes, from the bottom of her heart and she looks around and the curtains look so beautiful to her, they're made of thick dark velvet.

(*Aggressively.*) And now you can fully appreciate the *fin de siècle* decor. Then Irina asks him if he truly wants her to be his wife to give her just a little more time, just long enough for her to get over her fears.

Valentin: You can see what's going on with her, can't you?

Molina: Hold on. He agrees and they get married. And on their wedding night she sleeps in the bed and he sleeps on the couch.

Valentin: Looking at his mother's ornaments. Admit it, it's your ideal home, isn't it?

Molina: Of course it is! Now I've got to put up with you telling me the same thing they all say.

Valentin: What d'you mean? What do they all say?

Molina: They're all the same, they all tell me the same thing.

Valentin: What?

Molina: That I was fussed over as a kid and that's why I'm like I am now, that I was clinging to my mother's skirts, but it's never too late to straighten out and all I need is a good woman because there's nothing better than a good woman.

Valentin: And that's what they all tell you?

Molina: And this is what I tell them. . . . You're dead right! . . . and since there's nothing better than a woman . . . I want to be one! So spare me the advice please, because I know what I feel like and it's all as clear as day to me.

Valentin: I don't see it as clear—at least, not the way you've just put it.

Molina: I don't need you telling me what's what—if you want I'll go on with the picture, if not, ciao. . . . I'll just whisper it to myself, and *arrivederci*, Sparafucile!

Valentin: Who's Sparafucile?

Molina: You don't have a clue about opera. He's the hatchet man in *Rigoletto*. . . . Where were we?

Valentin: The wedding night. He hasn't laid a finger on her.

Molina: And I forgot to tell you that they'd agreed she'd go and see a psychoanalyst.

Valentin: Excuse me again . . . don't get upset.

Molina: What is it?

Valentin (less communicative than ever, somber): I can't keep my mind on the story.

Molina: Is it boring you?

Valentin: No, it's not that. It's . . . My head is in a state. (*He talks more to himself than to Molina.*) I just want to be quiet for a while. I don't know if this has ever happened to you, that you're just about to understand something, you've got the end of the thread and if you don't yank it now . . . you'll lose it.

Molina: Why do you like the architect girl?

Valentin: It has to come out some way or other. . . . (*Self-contemptuous.*) Weakness, I mean . . .

Molina: Ttt . . . it's not weakness.

Valentin: *(bitter, impersonally):*   Funny how you just can't avoid getting attached to something. It's . . . it's as if the mind just oozed sentiment constantly.

Molina: Is that what you believe?

Valentin: Like a leaky tap. Drips falling over anything.

Molina: Anything?

Valentin: You can't stop the drips.

Molina: And you don't want to be reminded of your girlfriend, is that it?

Valentin (mistrustful):   How do you know whether I have a girlfriend?

Molina: It's only natural.

Valentin: I can't help it. . . . I get attached to anything that reminds me of her. Anyway, I'd do better to get my mind on what I ought to, right?

Molina: Yank the thread.

Valentin: Exactly.

Molina: And if you get it all in a tangle, Missy Valentina, you'll flunk needlework.

Valentin: Don't worry on my account.

Molina: Okay, I won't say another word.

Valentin: And don't call me Valentina. I'm not a woman.

Molina: How should I know?

Valentin: I'm sorry, Molina, but I don't give demonstrations.

Molina: I wasn't asking for one.

Scene III

(Scene: Night. The prison light is on. Molina and Valentin are sitting on the floor, eating.)

Valentin (speaking as soon as he finishes his last mouthful):   You're a good cook.

Molina: Thank you, Valentin.

Valentin: It could cause problems later on. I'm getting spoiled.

Molina: You're crazy. Live for today!

Valentin: I don't believe in that live for today crap. We haven't earned that paradise yet.

Molina: Do you believe in Heaven and Hell?

Valentin: Hold on a minute. If we're going to have a discussion then we need a framework. Otherwise you'll just ramble on.

Molina: I'm not going to ramble.

Valentin: Okay. I'll state an opening proposition. Let me put it to you like this.

Molina: Put it any way you like.

Valentin: I can't live just for today. All I do is determined by the ongoing political struggle. D'you get me? Everything that I endure here, which is bad enough . . . is nothing if you compare it to torture . . . but you don't know what that's like.

Molina: I can imagine.

Valentin: No, Molina, you can't imagine what it's like. . . . Well, anyway, I can put up with all this because there's a blueprint. The essential thing is the social revolution and the pleasures of the senses come second. The greatest pleasure, well, it's knowing that I'm part of the most noble cause . . . my ideas, for instance . . . (*The prison lights go out. The BLUE nighttime light stays on.*) It's eight . . .

Molina: What do you mean "your ideas"?

Valentin: My ideals. Marxism. And that good feeling is one I can experience anywhere, even here in this cell, and even in torture. And that's my strength.

Molina: And what about your girlfriend?

Valentin: That has to be second too. And I'm second for her. Because she also knows what's most important. (*Molina remains silent.*) You don't look convinced.

Molina: Don't mind me. I'm going to turn in soon.

Valentin: You're mad! What about the panther-woman?

Molina: Tomorrow.

Valentin: What's up?

Molina: Look, Valentin, that's me. I get hurt easy. I cooked that food for you, with my supplies, and worse still I give you half my avocado—which is my favorite and could have eaten tomorrow . . . Result? You throw it in my face that I'm spoiling you. . . .

Valentin: Don't be so soft! It's just like a . . .

Molina: Say it!

Valentin: Say what?

Molina: I know what you were going to say, Valentin.

Valentin: Cut it out.

Molina: "It's just like a woman." That's what you were going to say.

Valentin: Yes.

Molina: And what's wrong with being soft like a woman? Why can't a man—or whatever—a dog, or a fairy—why can't he be sensitive if he feels like it?

Valentin: In excess, it can get in a man's way.

Molina: In the way of what? Of torturing someone?

Valentin: No, of getting rid of the torturers.

Molina: But if all men were like women then there'd be no torturers.

Valentin: And what would you do without men?

Molina: You're right. They're brutes, but I need them.

Valentin: Molina . . . you just said that if all men were like women there'd be no torturers. You've got a point there; kind of weird, but a point at least.

Molina: The way you say things. (*Imitating Valentin.*) "A point at least."

Valentin: I'm sorry I upset you.

Molina: I'm not upset.

Valentin: Well, cheer up, don't reproach me.

Molina: Do you want me to go on with the picture?

Valentin: Yeah, man, of course.

Molina: Man? What man? Tell me so he won't get away.

Valentin (trying to hide that he finds this funny):   Start.

Molina: Irina goes along to the psychoanalyst who's a ladykiller, real handsome.

Valentin: Tell me what you mean by real handsome. I'd like to know.

Molina: Well, let's get this straight, he isn't my type at all.

Valentin: Who's the actor?

Molina: I don't remember. Too skinny for my taste. With a pencil moustache. But there's something about him, so full of himself, he just puts you off. And he puts off Irina. She skips the next appointment, she lies to her husband and instead of going to the doctor's she puts on that black fleecy coat and goes to the zoo, to look at the panther. The keeper comes along, opens the cage, throws in the meat and closes the door again. But he's absent-minded and leaves the key in the lock. Irina sneaks up to the door and puts her hand on the key. And she just stands there, musing, rapt in her thoughts.

Valentin: What does she do then?

Molina: That's all for tonight. I'll continue tomorrow.

Valentin: At least, let me ask you something.

Molina: What?

Valentin: Who do you identify with? Irina or the architect girl?

Molina: With Irina—who do you think? *Moi*—always with the leading lady.

Valentin: Continue.

Molina: What about you? I guess you're stuck because the guy is such a wimp.

Valentin: Don't laugh—with the psychoanalyst. But I didn't say anything about your choice, so don't mock mine. . . . You know something? I'm finding it hard to keep my mind on it.

Molina: What's the problem?

Valentin: Nothing.

Molina: Come on, open up a little.

Valentin: When you said the girl was there in front of the cage, I imagined it was my girl who was in danger.

Molina: I understand.

Valentin: I shouldn't be telling you this, Molina. But I guess you've figured it all out for yourself anyhow. My girl is in the organization too.

Molina: So what.

Valentin: It's only that I don't want to burden you with information it's better you don't know.

Molina: With me, it's not a woman, a girlfriend I mean. It's my mother. She's got blood pressure and a weak heart.

Valentin: People can live for years with that.

Molina: Sure, but they don't need more aggravation, Valentin. Imagine the shame of having a son inside—and why.

Valentin: Look, the worst has already happened, hasn't it?

Molina: Yes, but the risk is ever-present inside her. It's that dodgy heart.

Valentin: She's waiting for you. Eight years'll fly by, what with remission and all that. . . .

Molina (a little contrived): Tell me about your girlfriend if you like. . . .

Valentin: I'd give anything to hold her in my arms right now.

Molina: It won't be long. You're not in for life.

Valentin: Something might happen to her.

Molina: Write to her, tell her not to take chances, that you need her.

Valentin: Never. Impossible. If you think like that you'll never change anything in the world.

Molina (not realizing he's mocking Valentin): And you think you're going to change the world?

Valentin: Yes, and I don't care that you laugh. It makes people laugh to hear this, but what I have to do before anything is to change the world.

Molina: Sure, but you can't do it just like that, *and* on your own.

Valentin: But I'm not on my own—that's it! I'm with her and all those other people who think like we do. That's the end of the thread that slips through my fingers. . . I'm not apart from my comrades—I'm with them, right now! . . . It doesn't matter whether I can see them or not.

Molina (with a slight drawl, skeptically): If that makes you feel good, terrific!

Valentin: Christ, what a moron!

Molina: Sticks and stones . . .

Valentin: Don't provoke me then. I'm not some loudmouth who just spouts off about politics in a bar. The proof is that I'm in here.

Molina: I'm sorry.

Valentin: It's okay . . .

Molina (pretending not to pry): You were going to tell me something . . . about your girlfriend.

Valentin: We'd better drop that.

Molina: As you like . . .

Valentin: Why it gets me so upset, I can't fathom.

Molina: Better not, then, if it upsets you . . .

Valentin: The one thing I shouldn't tell you is her name.

Molina: What sort of girl is she?

Valentin: She's twenty-four, two years younger than me.

Molina: Thirteen years younger than me. . . . No, I tell a lie, sixteen.

Valentin: She was always politically conscious. First it was . . . well, I needn't be shy with you, at first it was because of the sexual revolution.

Molina (bracing himself for some saucy tidbit): That I wouldn't miss.

Valentin: She comes from a bourgeois family, not really wealthy, but comfortably off. But as a kid and all through her adolescence she had to watch her parents destroy each other. Her father was cheating her mother, you know what I mean?

Molina: No, I don't.

Valentin: Cheating her by not telling her he needed other relationships. I don't hold with monogamy.

Molina: But it's beautiful when a couple love each other for ever and ever.

Valentin: Is that what you'd like?

Molina: It's my dream.

Valentin: Why do you like men then?

Molina: What's that got to do with it? I want to marry a man—to love and to cherish, for ever and ever.

Valentin: So, basically, you're just a bourgeois man?

Molina: A bourgeois lady, please.

Valentin: If you were a woman you'd think otherwise.

Molina: The only thing I want is to live forever with a wonderful man.

Valentin: And that's impossible because . . . well, if he's a man, he wants a woman . . . you'll always be living in a fool's paradise.

Molina: Go on about your girlfriend. I don't want to talk about me.

Valentin: She was brought up to be the lady of the house. Piano lessons, French, drawing. . . . I'll tell you the rest tomorrow, Molina . . . I want to think about something I was studying today.

Molina: Now you're getting your own back.

Valentin: No, silly. I'm tired, too.

Molina: I'm not sleepy at all.

Scene IV

(Scene: Night. The prison lights are on. Valentin is engrossed in a book. Molina, restless, is flicking through a magazine he already knows backwards.)

Valentin (lifting his head from the book):   Why are they late with dinner? Next door had it ages ago.

Molina (ironic):   Is *that* all you're studying tonight? I'm not hungry, thank goodness.

Valentin: That's unusual. Don't you feel well?

Molina: No, just nerves.

Valentin: Listen . . . I think they're coming.

Molina: Hide the magazines or they'll pinch them.

Valentin: I'm famished.

Molina: Please Valentin, don't make a scene with the guards.

Valentin: No.

(Through the grille in the door come two plates of porridge—one visibly more loaded than the other. Molina looks at Valentin.)

Valentin: Porridge.

Molina: Yes. (*Molina looks at the two plates which Valentin has collected from the hatch. Exchanging an enigmatic glance with the invisible guard):* Thank you.

Valentin (to guard): What about this one? Why's it got less? (*To Molina.*) I didn't say anything for your sake. Otherwise I'd have thrown it in his face, this bloody glue.

Molina: What's the use of complaining?

Valentin: One plate's only got half as much as the other. That bastard guard, he's out of his fucking mind.

Molina: It's okay, Valentin, I'll take the small portion.

Valentin (serving Molina the large one): No, you like porridge, you always lap it up.

Molina: Skip the chivalry. You have it.

Valentin: I told you no.

Molina: Why should I have the big one?

Valentin: Because I know you like porridge.

Molina: But I'm not hungry.

Valentin: Eat it, it'll do you good. (*Valentin starts eating from the small plate.*)

Molina: No.

Valentin: It's not too bad today.

Molina: I don't want it.

Valentin: Afraid of putting on weight?

Molina: No.

Valentin: Get stuck in then. This porridge à la glue isn't so bad today. This small plate is plenty for me.

Molina (starts eating, overcoming his resistance: his voice nostalgic now): Thursday. Ladies day. The cinema in my neighborhood used to show a romantic triple feature on Thursdays. Years ago now.

Valentin: Is that where you saw the panther-woman?

Molina: No, that was in a smart little cinema in that German neighborhood where all those posh houses with gardens are. My house was near there, but in the rundown part. Every Monday they'd show a German-language feature. Even during the war. They still do.

Valentin: Nazi propaganda films.

Molina: But the musical numbers were fabulous!

Valentin: You're touched. (*He finishes his dinner.*) They'll be turning off the lights soon, that's it for studying today. (*Unconsciously authoritarian.*) You can go on with the film now—Irina's hand was on the key in the lock.

Molina (picking at his porridge): She takes the key out of the lock and gives it back to the keeper. The old fellow thanks her and she goes back home to wait for her husband. She's all out to kiss him, on the mouth this time.

Valentin (absorbed): Mmmm . . .

Molina: Irina calls him up at his office, it's getting late, and the girl architect answers. Irina hangs up. She's eaten up with jealousy. She paces up and down the apartment like a caged beast, and when she walks by the bird cage she notices that the bird's wings are flapping frenetically. She can't control herself and she opens the little door and puts her hand right inside the cage. The little bird drops stone dead before she even touches it. Irina panics and flees from the house looking for her husband, but, of course, she has to go past the bar on the corner and she sees them both inside. And she just wants to tear the other woman to shreds. Irina only wears black clothes but she's never again worn that blouse he liked so much, the one in the restaurant scene, with all the rhinestones.

Valentin: What are they?

Molina (shocked): Rhinestones! I don't believe this! You don't know . . . ?

Valentin: I haven't the faintest.

Molina: They're like diamonds only worthless; little pieces of glass that shine.

(At this moment the cell light goes out.)

Valentin: I'm going to turn in early tonight. I've had enough of all this drivel.

Molina (overreacting, but deeply hurt): Thank goodness there's no light so I don't have to see your face. Don't ever speak another word to me!

(Note: The production must establish that when the blue light is on—meaning nighttime—THEY CANNOT SEE EACH OTHER, and so are free to express themselves as they like in gestures and body language.)

Valentin: I'm sorry . . . (*Molina stays silent.*) Really, I'm sorry, I didn't think you'd get so upset.

Molina: You upset me because it's one of my favorite movies, you can't know . . . (*He starts to cry.*) . . . you didn't see it.

Valentin: Are you crazy? It's nothing to cry about.

Molina: I'll . . . I'll cry if I feel like it.

Valentin: Suit yourself. . . . I'm very sorry.

Molina: And don't get the idea you've made me cry. It's because today's my mother's birthday and I'm dying to be with her. . . . And not with you. (*Pause.*) Ay! . . . Ay! . . . I don't feel well.

Valentin: What's wrong?

Molina: Ay! . . . Ay!

Valentin: What is it? What's the matter?

Molina: The girl's fucked!

Valentin: Which girl?

Molina: Me, dummy. It's my stomach.

Valentin: Do you want to throw up?

Molina: The pain's lower down. It's in my guts.

Valentin: I'll call the guard, okay?

Molina: No, it'll pass, Valentin.

Valentin: The food didn't do anything to me.

Molina: I bet it's my nerves. I've been on edge all day. I think it's letting up now.

Valentin: Try to relax. Relax your arms and legs, let them go loose.

Molina: Yes, that's better. I think it's going.

Valentin: Do you want to go to sleep?

Molina: I don't know . . . Ugh! it's awful . . .

Valentin: Maybe it'd be better if you talk, it'll take your mind off the pain.

Molina: You mean the movie?

Valentin: Where had we got to?

Molina: Afraid I'm going to croak before we get to the end?

Valentin: This is for your benefit. We broke off when they were in the bar on the corner.

Molina: Okay . . . the two of them get up together to leave and Irina takes cover behind a tree. The architect girl decides to take the shortcut home through the park. He told her everything while they were in the bar, that Irina doesn't make love to him, that she has nightmares about panther-women and all. The other girl, who'd just got used to the idea that she'd lost him, now begins to think maybe she has a chance again. So she's walking along and then you hear heels clicking behind her. She turns round and sees the silhouette of a woman. And then the clicking gets faster and now, right, the girl begins to get frightened, because you know what it's like when you've been talking about scary things. . . . But she's right in the middle of the park and if she starts to run she'll be in even worse trouble . . . and, then, suddenly, you can't hear the human footsteps anymore. . . . Ay! . . . Ay! . . . it's still hurting me.

Scene V

(Scene: Day. Valentin is lying down, doubled up with stomach pains. Molina stands looking on at him.)

Valentin: You can't imagine how much it hurts. Like a stabbing pain.

Molina: Just what I had two days ago.

Valentin: And each time it gets worse, Molina.

Molina: You should go to the clinic.

Valentin: Don't be thick, I already told you I don't want to go.

Molina: They'll only give you a little seconol. It can't harm you.

Valentin: Of course it can; you can get hooked on it. You don't have a clue.

Molina: About what?

Valentin: Nothing.

Molina: Go on, tell me. Don't be like that.

Valentin: It happened to one of my comrades once. They got him hooked, his willpower just went. A political prisoner can't afford to end up in a prison hospital. You follow me? Never. Once you're in there they come along and interrogate you and you have no resistance. . . . Ay! . . . Ay! . . . It feels like my guts are splitting open. Aaargh!

Molina: I told you not to gobble down your food like that.

Valentin (raising himself with difficulty): You were right. I'm ready to burst.

Molina: Stretch out a little.

Valentin: No, I don't want to sleep, I had nightmares all last night and this morning.

Molina (relenting, like a middle-class housewife): I swore I wouldn't tell you another film. I'll probably go to hell for breaking my word.

Valentin: Ay! . . . Oh, fucking hell. . . . (*Molina hesitates.*) You carry on. Pay no attention if I groan.

Molina: I'll tell you another movie, one for tummy ache. Now, you seemed keen on those German movies, am I right?

Valentin: In their propaganda machine . . . but, listen, go on with the panther-woman. We left off where the architect girl stopped hearing the human footsteps behind her in the park.

Molina: Well . . . she's shaking with fear, she won't dare turn around in case she sees the panther. She stops for a second to see if she still can't hear the woman's footsteps, but there's nothing, absolute silence, and then suddenly she begins to notice this rustling noise coming from the bushes being stirred by the wind . . . or maybe by something else. . . . (*Molina imitates the actions he describes.*) And she turns round with a start.

Valentin: I think I want to go to the toilet again.

Molina: Shall I call them to open up?

Valentin: They'll catch on that I'm ill.

Molina: They're not going to whip you into hospital for a dose of the runs.

Valentin: It'll go away, carry on with the story.

Molina: Okay . . . (*Repeating the same actions.*) . . . she turns around with a start . . .

Valentin: Ay! . . . ay! the pain . . .

Molina (suddenly): Tell me something: you never told me why your mother doesn't bring you any food.

Valentin: She's a . . . a difficult woman. That's why I don't talk about her. She could never stand my ideas—she believes she's entitled to everything she's got, her family's got a certain position to keep up.

Molina: The family name.

Valentin: Only second league, but a name all the same.

Molina: Let her know that she can bring you a week's supplies at a time. You're only spiting yourself.

Valentin: If I'm in here it's because I brought it on myself, it's got nothing to do with her.

Molina: My mother didn't visit lately 'cos she's ill, did I tell you?

Valentin: You never mentioned it.

Molina: She thinks she's going to recover from one minute to the next. She won't let anyone but her bring me food, so I'm in a pickle.

Valentin: If you could get out of this hole she'd improve, right?

Molina: You're a mind reader. . . . Okay, let's get on with it. (*Repeating the same action as before.*) She turns round with a start.

Valentin: Ay! . . . Ay! . . . What have I gone and done? I'm sorry.

Molina: No, no . . . hold still, don't clean yourself with the sheet, wait a second.

Valentin: No, not your shirt . . .

Molina: Here, take it, wipe yourself with it. You'll need the sheet to keep warm.

Valentin: No, you haven't got a change of shirt.

Molina: Wait . . . get up, that way it won't go through . . . like this . . . mind it doesn't soil the sheet.

Valentin: Did it go through?

Molina: Your underpants held it in. Here, take them off . . .

Valentin: I'm embarrassed . . .

Molina: Didn't you say you have to be a man . . . ? So what's all this about being embarrassed?

Valentin: Wrap my underpants up well, Molina, so they don't smell.

Molina: I know how to handle this. You see . . . all wrapped up in the shirt. It'll be easier to wash than the sheet. Take the toilet paper.

Valentin: No, not yours. You'll have none left.

Molina: You never had any. So cut it out.

Valentin: Thank you. (*He takes the tissue and wipes himself and hands the roll back to Molina.*)

Molina: You're welcome. Relax a little, you're shaking.

Valentin: It's with rage. I could cry . . . I'm furious for letting myself get caught.

Molina: Calm down. Pull yourself together. (*Valentin watches Molina wrap the shirt and soiled tissue in a newspaper.*)

Valentin: Good idea . . . so it won't smell, eh?

Molina: Clever, isn't it?

Valentin: I'm freezing.

Molina (*Meanwhile lighting the stove and putting water on to boil*):   I'm just making some tea. We're down to the last little bag. It's camomile, good for the nerves.

Valentin: No, leave it, it'll go away now.

Molina: Don't be silly.

Valentin: You're crazy—you're using up all your supplies.

Molina: I'll be getting more soon.

Valentin: But your mother's sick and can't come.

Molina: I'll continue. (*With irony. Repeating the same gestures as before but without the same élan.*) She turns round with a start. The rustling

noise gets nearer and she lets rip with a desperate scream, when . . .
whack! the door of the bus opens in front of her. The driver saw her
standing there and stopped for her. . . . The tea's almost ready.
(*Molina pours the hot water.*)

Valentin: Thanks. I mean that sincerely. And I want to apologize. . . .
sometimes I get too rough and hurt people without thinking.

Molina: Don't talk nonsense.

Valentin: Instead of a film, I want to tell you something real. About me.
I lied when I told you about my girlfriend. I was talking about another
one, someone I loved very much. I didn't tell you the truth about my
real girlfriend, you'd like her a lot, she's just a sweet and simple kid,
but really courageous.

Molina: Please don't tell me anything about her. I don't want to know
anything about your political business.

Valentin: Don't be dumb. Who's going to question you about me?

Molina: They might interrogate me.

Valentin (finishing his tea; much improved):   You trust me, don't you?

Molina: Yes . . .

Valentin: Well, then . . . Inside here it's got to be share and share alike.

Molina: It's not that . . .

Valentin (he lies down on the pillow, relaxing):   There's nothing worse than
feeling bad about having hurt someone. And I hurt her, I forced her
to join the organization when she wasn't ready for it, she's very . . .
unsophisticated.

Molina: But don't tell me anymore now. I'm doing the telling for the
moment. Where were we? Where did we stop? . . . (*Hearing no
response, Molina looks at Valentin who has fallen asleep.*) How did it
continue? What comes next? (*Molina feels proud of having helped his
fellow cellmate.*)

Scene VI

(*Scene: Daylight. Both Molina and Valentin are stretched out on their
beds, lost in a private sorrow. In the distance we hear a bolero tune.*)

Molina (singing softly):   "My love, I write to you again
  The night brings an urge to inquire
  If you, too, dear, recall the tender pain
  And the sad dreams our love would inspire."

Valentin: What's that you're singing?

Molina: A bolero. "My letter."

Valentin: Only you would go for that stuff.

Molina: What's wrong with it?

Valentin: It's romantic eyewash, that's what. You're daft.

Molina: I'm sorry. I think I've put my foot in it.

Valentin: In what?

Molina: Well, after you got that letter you were really down in the dumps
and here I am singing about sad love letters.

Valentin: It was some bad news. You can read it if you like.

Molina: Better not.

Valentin: Don't start all that again; no one's going to ask you anything. Besides, they read it through before I did. (*He unfolds the letter and reads it as he talks.*)

Molina: The handwriting's like hen's tracks.

Valentin: She didn't have much education. . . . One of the comrades was killed, and now she's leader of the group. It's all written in CODE.

Molina: Ah . . .

Valentin: And she writes that she's having relations with another of the lads, just like I told her.

Molina: What relations?

Valentin: She was missing me too much. In the organization we take an oath not to get too involved with someone because it can paralyze you when you go into action.

Molina: Into action?

Valentin: Direct action. Risking your life. . . . We can't afford to worry about someone who wants us to go on living because it makes you scared of dying. Well, maybe not scared exactly, but you hate the suffering it'll cause others. And that's why she's having a relationship with another comrade.

Molina: You said that your girlfriend wasn't really the one you told me about.

Valentin: Damn, staring at this letter has made me dizzy again.

Molina: You're still weak.

Valentin: I'm shivering and I feel queasy. (*He covers himself with the sheet.*)

Molina: I told you not to start taking food again.

Valentin: But I was famished. (*Molina helps Valentin wrap up well.*)

Molina: You were getting better yesterday and then you went and ate and got sick again. And today it's the same story. Promise me you won't touch a thing tomorrow.

Valentin: The girl I told you about, the bourgeois one, she joined the organization with me but she dropped out and tried to persuade me to split with her.

Molina: Why?

Valentin: She loved life too much and she was happy just to be with me, that's all she wanted. So we had to break up.

Molina: Because you loved each other too much.

Valentin: You make it sound like one of your boleros.

Molina: The truth is you mock those songs because they're too close to home. You laugh to keep from crying. As a tango says.

Valentin: I was lying low for a while in that guy's flat, the one they killed. With his wife and kid. I even used to change the kid's nappies. . . . And do you want to know what the worst of it is? I can't write to a single one of them without blowing them to the police.

Molina: Not even to your girlfriend?

Valentin (struggling to hold back his tears): Oh, God! . . . what a mess! . . . it's all so sad!

Molina: There's nothing you can do.

Valentin: Help me . . . get my arm from under . . . the blanket.

Molina: What for?

Valentin: Give me your hand, Molina. Squeeze hard . . .

Molina: Hold it tight.

Valentin: There's something else. It's wrecking me. It's shameful, awful . . .

Molina: Tell me, get it off your chest.

Valentin: It's . . . the girl I want to hear from, the one I want to have next to me right now and hug and kiss . . . it's not the one in the movement, but the other one . . . Marta, that's her name . . .

Molina: If that's what you feel deep down . . . Oh, I forgot, if your stomach feels real empty, there's a few digestives I'd forgotten all about. (*Without taking his hand from Valentin's he reaches for the packet of digestives.*)

Valentin: For all I shoot my mouth off about progress . . . when it comes to women, what I really like is a woman with class and I'm just like all the reactionary sons-of-bitches that killed my comrade. . . . The same, exactly the same . . .

Molina: That's not true . . .

Valentin: And sometimes I think maybe I don't even love Marta because of who she is but because she's got . . . class . . . I'm just like all the other class-conscious sons-of-bitches . . . in the world.

Guard's Voice: Luis Alberto Molina! To the visiting room!

(*Valentin and Molina let go of each other's hand as if caught in a shameful act. The cell door opens and Molina exits, but not before he's managed to slip the biscuits under Valentin's blanket. Hereafter, the dialogue is on prerecorded tape. Meanwhile, Valentin remains on stage and takes the biscuits from under his covers, manages to find just three at the bottom of the large packet and begins to eat them, one at a time, savoring each one.*)

Warden's Voice: Stop shaking, man, no one's going to do anything to you.

Molina's Voice: I had a bad stomach ache before, sir, but I'm fine now.

Warden's Voice: You've got nothing to be afraid of. We've made it look like you've had a visitor. The other one won't suspect a thing.

Molina's Voice: No, he won't suspect anything.

Warden's Voice: At home last night I had dinner with your protector and he had some good news for you. Your mother is on the road to recovery . . . it seems the chance of your pardon is doing her good . . .

Molina's Voice: Are you sure?

Warden's Voice: What's the matter with you? Why are you trembling? . . . You should be jubilant. . . . Well, have you got any news for me yet? Has he told you anything? Is he opening up to you?

Molina's Voice: No, sir, not so far. You have to take these things a step at a time.

Warden's Voice: Didn't it help at all when we weakened him physically?

Molina's Voice: I had to eat the first plate of fixed food myself.

Warden's Voice: You shouldn't have done that.

Molina's Voice: The truth is he doesn't like porridge and since one portion was bigger than the other . . . he insisted I eat it. If I'd refused he might have got suspicious. You told me, sir, that the doctored food would be on the newest plate but they made a mistake piling it high like that.

Warden's Voice: Ah, well, in that case, I'm obliged to you, Molina. I'm sorry about the mistake.

Molina's Voice: Now you should let him get some of his strength back.

Warden's Voice (irritated):   That's for us to decide. We know what we're doing. And when you get back to your cell say you had a visit from your mother. That'll explain why you're so excited.

Molina's Voice: No, I couldn't say that, she always brings me a food parcel.

Warden's Voice: Okay, we'll send out for some groceries. Think of it as a reward for the trouble with the porridge. Poor Molina!

Molina's Voice: Thank you, Warden.

Warden's Voice: Reel off a list of what she usually brings. (*Pause.*) Now!

Molina's Voice: To you?

Warden's Voice: Yes, and be quick about it, I've got work to catch up with.

Molina's Voice (as the curtain falls):   A tin of treacle, a can of peaches . . . two roast chickens . . . a big bag of sugar . . . two packs of tea, one breakfast, one camomile . . . powdered milk, a bar of soap, bathsize . . . oh, let me think a second, my mind's a complete blank . . .

ACT II

Scene VII

(*Scene: Lighting as in previous scene. The cell door opens and Molina enters with a shopping bag.*)

Molina: Look what I've got!!!

Valentin: No! Your mother?

Molina: Yes!!

Valentin: So she's better now?

Molina: A little better. . . . And look what she brought me. Ooops! Sorry, brought us!

Valentin (secretly flattered):   No, it's for you. Cut the nonsense.

Molina: Shut it, you're the invalid. The chickens are for you, they'll get you back on your feet.

Valentin: No, I won't let you do this.

Molina: It's no sacrifice. I can go without the chicken if it means I don't have to put up with your pong . . . No, listen, I'm being serious now, you've got to stop eating this pig swill they serve in here. At least for a day or two.

Valentin: You think so?

Molina: And then when you're better . . . Close your eyes. (*Valentin closes his eyes and Molina places a large tin in one of his hands.*) Three guesses . . .

Valentin: Ahem . . . er . . . er . . . (*Enjoying the game. Molina places an identical one in Valentin's other hand.*)

Molina: The weight ought to help you . . .

Valentin: Heavy all right . . . I give up.

Molina: Open your eyes.

Valentin: Treacle!

Molina: But you can't have it yet, not until you're better. And this is for both of us.

Valentin: Marvellous.

Molina: First . . . we'll have a cup of camomile tea because my nerves are shot and you can have a drumstick, no, better not, it's only five. . . . Anyway, we can have tea and some biscuits, they're even lighter than those digestives.

Valentin: Please, can't I have one right away?

Molina: Why not! But no treacle on it—just marmalade! . . . Luckily, everything she brought is easy to get down so it won't give you any trouble. Except the treacle for the time being.

Valentin: Oh, Molina, I'm wilting with hunger. Why won't you let me have that chicken leg now?

Molina (he hesitates a moment):   Here . . .

Valentin (wolfing down the chicken):   Honest, I really was beginning to feel bad. . . . (*He devours the chicken.*) Thanks . . .

Molina: You're welcome.

Valentin (his mouth full):   But there's just one thing missing to round off the picnic.

Molina: Tut, and I thought I was supposed to be the pervert here.

Valentin: Stop fooling around! What we need is a movie . . .

Molina: Ah! . . . Well, now there's a scene where Irina has a completely new hairstyle.

Valentin: Oh, I'm sorry, I don't feel too good, it's that dizziness again.

Molina: Are you positive?

Valentin: Yes, it's been threatening all night.

Molina: But it can't be the chicken. Maybe you're imagining it.

Valentin: I felt full up all of a sudden.

Molina: That's because you wolfed it down without even chewing.

Valentin: And this itching is driving me wild. I don't know when I last had a bath.

Molina: Don't even think about that. That freezing water in your present state! (*Pause.*) Anyway, she looks stunning here, you can see her reflection in a windowpane, it's drizzling and all the drops are running down the glass. She's got raven black hair and it's all scooped up in a bun. Let me describe it to you. . . .

Valentin: It's all scooped up, okay, never mind the silly details. . . .

Molina: Silly, my foot! And she's got a rhinestone flower in her hair.

Valentin (very agitated now because of his itch):   I know what rhinestones are so you can save your breath!

Molina: My, you are touchy today!

Valentin: Do you mind if I say something?

Molina: Go ahead.

Valentin: I feel all screwed up—and confused. If it's not too much trouble I'd like to dictate a letter to her. Would you mind taking it down? . . . I get dizzy if I try to focus my eyes too hard.

Molina: Let me get a pencil.

Valentin: You're very kind to me.

Molina: We'll do a rough draft first on a bit of paper.

Valentin: Here, take my pen-case.

Molina: Wait till I sharpen this pencil.

Valentin (short-tempered):   I told you! Use one of mine!

Molina: Okay, don't blow your top!

Valentin: I'm sorry, it's just that everything is going black.

Molina: Okay, ready, shoot . . .

Valentin (very sad):   Dear Marta . . . you don't expect this letter. . . . In your case, it won't endanger you. . . . I'm feeling . . . lonely, I need you, I want to be . . . near you . . . I want you to give me . . . a word of encouragement.

Molina: . . . "of encouragement" . . .

Valentin: . . . in this moment I couldn't face my comrades, I'd be ashamed of being so weak. . . . I have sores all over inside, I need somebody to pour some honey . . . over my wounds. . . . And only you could understand . . . because you too were brought up in a nice clean house to enjoy life to the full, . . . I can't accept becoming a martyr, it makes me angry to be one . . . or, it isn't that, I see it clearer now . . . I'm afraid because I'm sick, horribly afraid of dying . . . that it may just end here, that my life has amounted to nothing more than this, I never exploited anyone . . . and ever since I had any sense I've been struggling against the exploitation of my fellow man . . .

Molina: Go on.

Valentin: Where was I?

Molina: "My fellow man" . . .

Valentin: . . . because I want to go out into the street one day and not die. And sometimes I get this idea that never ever again will I be able to touch a woman, and I can't accept it, and when I think of women I only see you, and what a relief it would be to believe that right until I finish writing this letter you'll be thinking of me . . . and that you'll be running your hands over your body I so well remember . . .

Molina: Hold on, don't go so fast.

Valentin: over your body I so well remember, and you'll be thinking that it's my hand . . . it would be as if I were touching you, darling . . . because there's still something of me inside you, isn't that so? Just as your own scent has stayed in my nose . . . beneath my fingertips lies a sort of memory of your skin, do you understand me? Although it's not a matter of understanding . . . it's a matter of believing, and sometimes I'm convinced that I took something of you with me . . . and that I haven't lost it, and then sometimes not, I feel there's just me all alone in this cell . . . (*Pause.*)

Molina: Yes, "all alone in this cell" . . . Go on.

Valentin: . . . because nothing leaves any trace, and my luck in having had such happiness with you, of spending those nights and afternoons and mornings of sheer enjoyment, none of this is any use now, just the opposite, it all turns against me, because I miss you madly, and all I can feel is the torture of my loneliness, and in my nose there is only the stench of this cell, and of myself . . . and I can't have a wash because I'm ill, really weak, and the cold water would give me pneumonia and beneath my fingertips what I feel is the chill of my fear of death, I can feel it in my joints . . . what a terrible thing to lose hope and that's what's happened to me . . .

Molina: I'm sorry for butting in . . .

Valentin: What is it?

Molina: When you finish dictating the letter there's something I want to say.

Valentin (wound up):   What?

Molina: Because if you take one of those freezing showers it'll kill you.

Valentin (almost hysterical):   And? . . . So what? Tell me, for Christ's sake.

Molina: I could help you to get cleaned up. You see, we've got the hot water we were going to use to boil the potatoes and we've got two towels, so we lather one of them and you do your front and I'll do the back and then you can dry yourself with the other towel.

Valentin: And then I'd stop itching?

Molina: Sure. And we'd clean a bit at a time so you won't catch cold.

Valentin: And you'll help me?

Molina: Of course I will.

Valentin: When?

Molina: Now, if you like. The water's boiling, we can mix it with a little cold water. (*Molina starts to do this.*)

Valentin (who can't believe in such happiness):   And I'd be able to get to sleep without scratching?

Molina: Take your shirt off. I'll put some more water on. (*He mixes the hot and cold water.*)

Valentin: But you're using up all your parafin.
Molina: I don't mind.
Valentin: Give me the letter, Molina.
Molina: What for?
Valentin: Just hand it over.
Molina: Here. (*Valentin tears it up.*) What are you doing???
Valentin: This. (*He tears it into quarters.*) Let's not mention it again.
Molina: As you like . . .
Valentin: It's wrong to get carried away like that by despair.
Molina: But it's good to get it into the open. You said so yourself.
Valentin: But it's bad for me. I have to learn to restrain myself. (*Pause.*)
    Listen, I mean it, one day I'll thank you properly for all this. (*Molina*
    puts more water on the stove.) Are you going to waste all that water?
Molina: Yes . . . and don't be daft, there's no need to thank me. (*Molina*
    signals to Valentin to turn around.)
Valentin: Tell me, how does the movie end, just the last scene.
Molina (scrubbing Valentin's back):   It's either all or nothing.
Valentin: Why?
Molina: Because of the details. Her hairdo is important, it's the style that
    women wear, or used to wear, when they wanted to show that this was
    a crucial moment in their lives, because the hair all scooped up in a
    bun which left the neck bare, gave the woman's face a certain nobility.
    (*Valentin, despite the tensions and turmoil of this difficult day, changes*
    his expression and smiles.) Why have you got that mocking little grin on
    your face? I don't see anything to laugh at.
Valentin: Because my back doesn't itch anymore!

Scene VIII

(*Scene: Day. Molina is tidying up his belongings with extreme care so as*
not to wake Valentin. Valentin, nevertheless, wakes up. Both of them are
charged with renewed energy and the dialogue begins at its normal pace
but accelerates rapidly into tenseness.)

Valentin: Good morning.
Molina: Good morning.
Valentin: What's the time?
Molina: Ten past ten. I call my mother "ten past ten," the poor dear,
    because of the way her feet stick out when she walks.
Valentin: It's late.
Molina: When they brought the tea round you just turned over and
    carried on sleeping.
Valentin: What were you saying about your old lady?
Molina: Look who's still sleeping. Nothing. Sleep well?
Valentin: I feel a lot better.
Molina: You don't feel dizzy?

Valentin: Lying in bed, no.

Molina: Great—why don't you try to walk a little?

Valentin: No—you'll laugh.

Molina: At what?

Valentin: Something that happens to a normal healthy man when he wakes up in the morning with too much energy.

Molina: You've got a hard-on? Well, God bless . . .

Valentin: But look away, please. I get embarrassed . . . (*He gets up to wash his face with water from the jug.*)

Molina (he puts his hand over his eyes and looks away):   My eyes are shut tight.

Valentin: It's all thanks to your food. My legs are a bit shaky still, but I don't feel queasy. You can look now. (*He gets back into bed.*) I'll lie down a bit more.

Molina (overprotective and smothering):   I'll put the water on for tea.

Valentin: No, just reheat the crap they brought us this morning.

Molina: I threw it out when I went to the loo. You must look after yourself properly if you want to get better.

Valentin: It embarrasses me to use up your things. I'm better now.

Molina: Button it.

Valentin: No, listen . . .

Molina: Listen nothing. My mother's bringing stuff again.

Valentin: Okay, thanks, but just for today. (*He collects his books together.*)

Molina: And no reading. Rest! . . . I'll start another film while I'm making the tea.

Valentin: I'd better try and study, if I can, now that I'm on form. (*He starts to read.*)

Molina: Won't it be too tiring?

Valentin: I'll give it a go.

Molina: You're a real fanatic.

Valentin (throwing the book to the ground as his tenseness increases):   I can't . . . the words are jumping around.

Molina: I told you so. Are you feeling dizzy?

Valentin: Only when I try to read.

Molina: You know what it is? It's probably just a temporary weakness—if you have a ham sandwich you'll be right as rain.

Valentin: Do you think so?

Molina: Sure, and then later, after you've had lunch and another little snooze you'll feel up to studying again.

Valentin: I feel lazy as hell. I'll just lie down.

Molina (schoolmistressy):   No, lying in bed only weakens the constitution, you'd be better standing or at least sitting up. (*Molina hands him the tea.*)

Valentin: This is the last day I'm taking any more of this.

Molina (mistress of the situation):   Ha! Ha! I already told the guard not to bring you any more tea in the morning.

Valentin: Listen, you decide what you want for yourself, but I want them to bring me the tea even if it is horse's piss.

Molina: You don't know the first thing about a healthy diet.

Valentin (trying to control himself):   I'm not joking Molina, I don't like other people controlling my life.

Molina (counting on his fingers):   Today is Wednesday . . . everything will hang on what happens on Monday. That's what my lawyer says. I don't believe in appeals and all that but if there's someone who can pull a few strings, maybe there's a chance.

Valentin: I hope so.

Molina (with concealed cunning, as he makes more tea):   If they let me out. . . . who knows who you'll get as a cellmate.

Valentin: Haven't you had breakfast yet?

Molina: I didn't want to disturb you. You were sleeping. (*He takes Valentin's cup to refill it.*) Will you join me in another cup?

Valentin: No, thanks.

Molina (opening a new packet, not letting Valentin see):   Tell me, what are you going to study later on?

Valentin: What are you doing?

Molina: A surprise. Tell me what you're reading.

Valentin: Nothing . . .

Molina: Cat got your tongue? . . . And now . . . we untie the mystery parcel . . . which I had hidden about my person . . . and, what have we got here? . . . Something that goes a treat with tea . . . a cherry madeira!

Valentin: No, thanks.

Molina: What d'you mean "no"? . . . the kettle's on . . . Oh, I know why not—you want to go to the loo. Ask them to open up and then fly back here.

Valentin: For Christ's sake, don't tell me what to do!

Molina (he squeezes Valentin's chin):   Oh, come on, let me pamper you a little.

Valentin: That's enough . . . you prick!

Molina: Are you crazy? . . . What's the matter with you?

Valentin (he hurls the teacup and the cake against the wall):   Shut your fucking trap!

Molina: The cake . . . (*Valentin is silent.*) Look what you've done . . . if the stove's broke, we're done for. . . . (*Pause.*) . . . and the saucer . . . (*Pause.*) . . . and the tea . . .

Valentin: I'm sorry . . . (*Molina is silent now.*) I lost control . . . I'm really sorry. (*Molina remains silent.*) The stove is okay; but the paraffin spilled. (*Molina still doesn't answer.*) . . . I'm sorry I got carried away, forgive me. . . .

Molina (deeply wounded):   There's nothing to forgive.

Valentin: There is. A lot.

Molina: Forget it. Nothing happened.

Valentin: It did, I'm dying with shame. (*Molina says nothing.*) . . . I
   behaved like an animal. . . . Look, I'll call the guard and fill up the
   bottle while I'm at it. We're almost out of water. . . . Molina, please,
   look at me. Raise your head. (*Molina remains silent.*)
Guard's Voice: Luis Alberto Molina. To the visiting room!

(*The door opens and Molina exits. The recorded dialogue begins as soon as
Molina moves toward the door. Molina returns with the provisions to find
Valentin picking up the things he has just thrown on the floor. Molina
starts to unpack the shopping bag. The recorded dialogue is heard while
the action takes place on stage.*)

Warden's Voice: Today's Monday, Molina, what have you got for me?
Molina'S Voice: Nothing, I'm afraid, sir.
Warden's Voice: Indeed.
Molina's Voice: But he's taking me more into his confidence.
Warden's Voice: The problem is they're putting pressure on me, Molina.
   From the top: from the President's private office. You understand
   what I'm saying to you, Molina? They want to try interrogation again.
   Less carrot, more stick.
Molina's Voice: Not that sir. It'd be even worse if you lost him in
   interrogation.
Warden's Voice: That's what I tell them, but they won't listen.
Molina's Voice: Just one more week, sir. Please. I have an idea . . .
Warden's Voice: What?
Molina's Voice: He's a hard nut but he has an emotional side.
Warden's Voice: So?
Molina's Voice: Well, if the guard were to come and say they're moving
   me to another block in a week's time because of the appeal, that might
   really soften him up.
Warden's Voice: What are you driving at?
Molina's Voice: Nothing, I swear. It's just a hunch. If he thinks I'm
   leaving soon he'll feel like opening up even more with me. Prisoners
   are like that, sir . . . when one of their pals is leaving they feel more
   defenseless than ever.

(*At this moment Molina is back in the cell and he takes out the food as the
Warden's Voice mentions each item. Valentin looks at Molina.*)

Warden's Voice: Guard, take this down: two roast chickens, four baked
   apples, one carton of coleslaw, one pound of bacon, one pound of
   cooked ham, four French loaves, four pieces of crystallized fruit (*the
   recorded voice begins to fade out*) . . . a carton of orange juice, two
   cherry madeiras . . .
Molina (very calm and very sad; still upset by Valentin's remarks):   This is
   the bacon and this one's the ham. I'm going to make a sandwich while
   the bread's fresh. You fix yourself whatever you want.

Valentin (deeply ashamed): Thank you.

Molina (reserved, calm): I'm going to cut this roll in half and spread it with butter and have a ham sandwich. And a baked apple.

Valentin: Sounds delicious.

Molina: If you'd like some of the chicken while it's still warm, go ahead. Feel free.

Valentin: Thank you, Molina.

Molina: We'll each fend for ourselves. Then I won't get on your nerves.

Valentin: If that's what you prefer.

Molina: There's some crystallized fruit, too. All I ask is you leave me the pumpkin. Otherwise, take what you want.

Valentin (finding it hard to apologize): I'm still embarrassed . . . because of that tantrum.

Molina: Don't be silly.

Valentin: If I got annoyed with you . . . it was because you were kind to me . . . and I didn't want . . . to treat you the same way.

Molina: Look, I've been thinking too and I remembered something you once said, right? . . . that when you're involved in a struggle like that, well, it's not too convenient to get fond of someone. Well, fond is maybe going too far. . . . Or, why not? Fond as a friend.

Valentin: That's a very noble way of looking at it.

Molina: You see, sometimes I do understand what you tell me.

Valentin: But are we so fettered by the world outside that we can't act like human beings just for a minute . . . ? Is the enemy out there that powerful?

Molina: I don't follow.

Valentin: Our persecutors are on the outside, not inside this cell. . . . The problem is I'm so brainwashed that it freaks me out when someone is nice to me without asking anything in return.

Molina: I don't know about that . . .

Valentin: About what?

Molina: Don't get me wrong, but if I'm nice to you, well, it's because I want you to be my friend . . . and why not admit it? . . . I want your affection. Just like I treat my mother well because she's a good person and I want her to love me. And you're a good person too, and unselfish because you're risking your life for an ideal . . . that I don't understand but, all the same, it's not just for yourself. . . . Don't look away like that, are you embarrassed?

Valentin: A bit. (*He looks Molina in the face.*)

Molina: And that's why I respect you and have warm feelings toward you . . . and why I want you to like me . . . because, you see, my mother's love is the only good thing I've felt in my life, because she likes me . . . just the way I am.

Valentin (pointing to the loaf Molina put aside): Can I cut the loaf for you?

Molina: Of course . . .

Valentin (cutting the loaf): And did you never have good friends that
   meant a lot to you?

Molina: My friends were all . . . screaming queens, like me, we never
   really count on each other because . . . how can I express it?—because
   we know we're so easily frightened off. We're always looking, you
   know, for friendship, or whatever, with somebody more serious, with a
   man, you see? And that just doesn't happen, right? because what a
   man wants is a woman.

Valentin (taking a slice of ham for Molina's sandwich): And are all
   homosexuals like that?

Molina: Oh no, there are some who fall in love with each other. But me
   and my friends we're women. One hundred percent. We don't go in
   for those little games. We're normal women; *we* only go to bed with
   men.

Valentin (too absorbed to see the funny side of this): Butter?

Molina: Yes, thanks. There's something I have to tell you.

Valentin: Of course, the movie . . .

Molina (with cunning, but nervous all the same): My lawyer said things
   were looking up.

Valentin: What a creep I am! I didn't ask you.

Molina: And when there's an appeal pending, the prisoner gets moved to
   another block in the prison. They'll probably shift me within a week or
   so.

Valentin (upset by this but dissimulating): That's terrific . . . you ought to
   be pleased.

Molina: I don't want to dwell on it too much, build my hopes. . . . Have
   some coleslaw.

Valentin: Should I?

Molina: It's very good.

Valentin: Your news made me lose my appetite. (*He gets up.*)

Molina: Pretend I didn't say anything, nothing's settled yet.

Valentin: No, it all looks good for you, we should be happy.

Molina: Have some salad.

Valentin: I don't know what's wrong, but all of a sudden I don't feel too
   good.

Molina: Is your stomach hurting?

Valentin: No . . . it's my head. I'm all confused.

Molina: About what?

Valentin: Let me rest for a while.

   (*Valentin sits down again, resting his head in his palms. The light
   changes to indicate a shift to a different time—the two characters stay
   where they are: there is a special tension, a hypersensitivity in the air.*)

Molina: The guy is all muddled up, he doesn't know how to handle this
   freaky wife of his. She comes in, sees that he's dead serious and goes to

the bathroom to put away her shoes, all dirty with mud. He says he went to the doctor's to look for her and found out that she didn't go anymore. Then she breaks into tears and tells him that she's just what she always feared, a mad woman with hallucinations or even worse, a panther-woman. Then he gives in and takes her in his arms and you were right, she's really just a little girl for him, because when he sees her so defenseless and lost, he feels again he loves her with all his heart and tells her that everything will sort itself out. . . . (*Molina sighs deeply.*) Ahhh. . . !

Valentin: What a sigh!

Molina: Life is so difficult. . . .

Valentin: What's the matter?

Molina: I don't know, I'm afraid of building up my hopes of getting out of here . . . and that I'll get put in some other cell and spend my life there with God knows what sort of creep.

Valentin: Don't lose sight of this. Your mother's health is the most precious thing to you, right?

Molina: Yes . . .

Valentin: Think about her recovery. Period!

Molina (he laughs involuntarily in his distress): I don't want to think about it.

Valentin: What's wrong?

Molina: Nothing!

Valentin: Don't bury your head in the pillow. . . . Are you keeping something from me?

Molina: It's . . .

Valentin: It's what? . . . Look, when you get out of here you're going to be a free man. You can join a political organization if you like.

Molina: You're crazy! They won't trust a fag.

Valentin: But I can tell you who to speak to. . . .

Molina (suddenly forceful, raising his head from the pillow): Promise me on whatever you hold most dear, never, never, you understand, never tell me anything about your comrades.

Valentin: But who would ever think you're seeing them?

Molina: They could interrogate me, whatever, but if I know nothing, I say nothing.

Valentin: In any case, there are all kinds of groups, of political action; there are even some who just sit and talk. When you get out things'll be different.

Molina: Things *won't* be different. That's the worst of it.

Valentin: How many times have I seen you cry? Come on, you annoy me with your sniveling.

Molina: It's just that I can't take any more. . . . I've had nothing but bad luck . . . always. (*The prison light goes out.*)

Valentin: Lights out already? . . . In the first place you must join a group, avoid being alone.

Molina: I don't understand any of that . . . (*Suddenly grave.*) . . . and I don't believe in it much either.

Valentin (tough):   Then like it or lump it.

Molina (still crying a little):   Let's . . . skip it.

Valentin (conciliatory):   Come on, don't be like that. . . . (*He pats Molina on the back affectionately.*)

Molina: I'm asking you . . . please don't touch me.

Valentin: Can't a friend pat you on the back?

Molina: It makes it worse. . . .

Valentin: Why? . . . Tell me what's troubling you. . . .

Molina (with deep, deep feeling):   I'm so tired, Valentin. . . . I'm tired of suffering. I hurt all over inside.

Valentin: Where does it hurt you?

Molina: Inside my chest and my throat. . . . Why does sadness always get you there? It's choking me, like a knot. . . .

Valentin: It's true, that's where people always feel it. (*Molina is quiet.*) Is it hurting you a lot, this knot?

Molina: Yes.

Valentin: Is it here?

Molina: Yes.

Valentin: Want me to stroke it . . . here?

Molina: Yes.

Valentin (after a short pause):   This is relaxing. . . .

Molina: Why relaxing, Valentin?

Valentin: Not to think about myself for a while. Thinking about you, that you need me, and I can be of some use to you.

Molina: You're always looking for explanations. . . . You're crazy.

Valentin: I don't want events to get the better of me. I want to know why they happen.

Molina: Can I touch you?

Valentin: Yes . . .

Molina: I want to touch that mole—the little round one over your eye. (*Pause. Molina touches the mole.*) You're very kind.

Valentin: No, you're the one who's kind.

Molina: If you like you can do what you want with me . . . because I want it too. . . . If it won't disgust you . . .

Valentin: Don't say that—let's not say anything. (*Valentin goes under Molina's top sheet.*) Shift a bit closer to the wall. . . . (*Pause.*) You can't see a thing it's so dark.

Molina: Gently . . . (*Pause.*) No, it hurts too much like that. (*Pause.*) Slowly please . . . (*Pause.*) That's it . . . (*Pause.*) . . . thanks . . .

Valentin: Thank you, too. Are you feeling better?

Molina: Yes. And what about you, Valentin?

Valentin: Don't ask me. . . . I don't know anything anymore. . . .

Molina: Oh, . . . it's beautiful . . .

Valentin: Don't say anything . . . not for now . . .

Molina: It's just that I feel . . . such strange things. . . . Without thinking, I just lifted my hand to my eye, looking for that mole.

Valentin: What mole? . . . *I'm* the one with the mole, not you.

Molina: I know, but I just lifted up my hand . . . to touch the mole . . . I don't have.

Valentin: Ssh, try and keep quiet for a while. . . .

Molina: And do you know what else I felt, but only for a minute, no longer . . .

Valentin: Tell me, but keep still, like that. . . .

Molina: For just a minute, it felt like I wasn't here . . . not in here, nor anywhere else . . . (*Pause.*) It felt like I wasn't here, there was just you. . . . Or that I wasn't me anymore. As if I was . . . you.

Scene IX

(*Scene: Day. Molina and Valentin are in their beds.*)

Valentin: Good morning. (*He is reinvigorated, happy.*)

Molina (also highly charged):   Good morning, Valentin.

Valentin: Did you sleep well?

Molina: Yes. (*Calmly, not insisting.*) Would you like tea or coffee?

Valentin: Coffee. To wake me up well—and study. Try to get back into the swing of things. . . . What about you? Is the gloom over? Or not?

Molina: Yes it is, but I feel groggy. I can't think . . . my mind's a blank.

Valentin: I don't want to think about anything either, so I'm going to read. That'll keep my mind off things.

Molina: Off what? Feeling guilty about what happened?

Valentin: I'm more and more convinced that sex is innocence itself.

Molina: Can I ask you a favor? . . . Let's not discuss anything, just for today.

Valentin: Whatever you like.

Molina: I feel . . . fine and I don't want anything to rob me of that feeling. I haven't felt so good since I was a kid. Since my mother bought me some toy.

Valentin: Do you remember what toy you liked most?

Molina: A doll.

Valentin: Ay!! (*He starts to laugh.*)

Molina: What's funny about that?

Valentin: As a psychologist I would starve.

Molina: Why?

Valentin: Nothing . . . I was just wondering if there was any link between your favorite toy and . . . me.

Molina (playing along):   It was your own fault for asking.

Valentin: Are you sure it wasn't a boy doll?

Molina: Absolutely. She had blond braids and a little Tyrolese folk dress. (*They laugh together, unselfconsciously.*)

Valentin: One question. . . . Physically, you're as much a man as I am.

Molina: Ummm . . .

Valentin: Why then don't you behave like a man. . . . I don't mean with women if you're not attracted to them, but with another man?

Molina: It's not me. I only enjoy myself like that.

Valentin: Well, if you like being a woman . . . you shouldn't feel diminished because of that. (*Molina doesn't answer.*) I mean you shouldn't feel you owe anyone, or feel obliged to them because that's what you happen to like. . . . You shouldn't yield . . .

Molina: But if a man is . . . my husband, he has to be boss to feel good. That's only natural.

Valentin: No, the man and the woman should be equal partners inside the home. Otherwise, it's exploitation. Don't you see?

Molina: But there's no thrill in that.

Valentin: What?

Molina: Since you want to know about it. . . . The thrill is that when a man embraces you, you're a bit afraid.

Valentin: Who put that idea into your head? That's all crap.

Molina: But it's what I feel.

Valentin: It's not what you feel—it's what you were taught to feel. Being a woman doesn't make you . . . how should I say? . . . a martyr. And if I didn't think it would hurt like hell I'd ask you to do it to me, to show you that all this business about being macho doesn't give anyone rights over another person.

Molina (now disturbed): This is getting us nowhere.

Valentin: On the contrary, I want to talk about it.

Molina: Well, I don't, so that's it. I'm begging you, no more please.

Guard's Voice: Prisoner Luis Alberto Molina! To the visiting room!

(*The door opens and Molina exits. Valentin, contented, sorts through his books, lays out his pencil and paper and begins to read. Meanwhile, we hear the Warden's Voice.*)

Warden's Voice: Put me through to your boss, please. . . . How's it going? Nothing this end. Yes, that's why I called. He's on his way here now. . . . Yes, they need the information, I'm aware of that. . . . And if Molina still hasn't found out anything, what should I do with him? . . . Are you sure? . . . Let him out today? . . . But why today? . . . Yes, of course, there's no time to lose. Quite, and if the other one gives him a message Molina will lead us straight to the group. . . . I've got it, yes, we'll give him just enough time for the other to pass on the message. . . . The tricky thing will be if Molina catches on that he's under surveillance. . . . It's hard to anticipate the reactions of someone like Molina: a pervert after all.

(*The cell door opens and Molina comes back in, totally deflated.*)

Molina: Poor Valentin, you're looking at my hands.

Valentin: I didn't mean to.

Molina: Your eyes give you away, poor love. . . .

Valentin: Such language . . .

Molina: I didn't get a parcel. You'll have to forgive me. . . . Ay! Valentin
. . .

Valentin: What's wrong?

Molina: Ay, you can't imagine . . .

Valentin: What's up? Tell me!

Molina: I'm going.

Valentin: To another cell. . . . What a nuisance!

Molina: No, they're releasing me.

Valentin: No.

Molina: I'm out on parole.

Valentin (exploding with unexpected happiness):   But that's incredible!

Molina (confused by the way Valentin's taking this):   You're very kind to be
so pleased for me.

Valentin: I'm happy for you too, of course . . . but, it's terrific! And I
guarantee there's not the slightest risk.

Molina: What are you saying?

Valentin: Listen, . . . I had to get urgent information out to my people
and I was dying with frustration because I couldn't do anything about
it. I was racking my brains trying to find a way. . . . And you come and
serve it to me on a plate.

Molina (as if he'd just had an electric shock):   I can't do that, you're out of
your head.

Valentin: You'll memorize it in a minute. That's how easy it is. All you
have to do is tell them that Number Three Command has been
knocked out and they have to go to Corrientes for new orders.

Molina: No, I'm on parole, they can lock me up again for anything.

Valentin: I give you my word there's no risk.

Molina: I'm pleading with you. I don't want to hear another word. Not
who they are or where they are. Nothing.

Valentin: Don't you want me to get out one day too?

Molina: Of here?

Valentin: Yes, to be free.

Molina: There's nothing I want more. But listen to me, I'm telling you
this for your own good. . . . I'm not good at this sort of thing, if they
catch me, I'll spill everything.

Valentin: I'll answer for my comrades. You just have to wait a few days
and then call from a public telephone, and make an appointment with
someone in some bogus place.

Molina: What do you mean "a bogus place"?

Valentin: You just give them name in code, let's say the Ritz cinema, and
that means a certain bench in a particular square.

Molina: I'm frightened.

Valentin: You won't be when I explain the procedure to you.

Molina: But if the phone's tapped I'll get in trouble.

Valentin: Not from a public callbox and if you disguise your voice. It's the easiest thing in the world, I'll show you how to do it. There are millions of ways—a sweet in your mouth, or a toothpick under your tongue . . .

Molina: No.

Valentin: We'll discuss it later.

Molina: No!!!

Valentin: Whatever you say. (*Molina flops on the bed, all done in, and buries his face in the pillow.*) Look at me please.

Molina (*not looking at Valentin*):   I made a promise, I don't know who to, maybe God, even though I don't much believe in that.

Valentin: Yes . . .

Molina: I swore that I'd sacrifice anything if I could only get out of here and look after my mother. And my wish has come true.

Valentin: It was very generous of you to put someone else first.

Molina: But where's the justice in it? I always get left with nothing. . . .

Valentin: You have your mother and she needs you. You have to assume that responsibility.

Molina: Listen, my mother's already had her life, she's lived, been married, had a child . . . she's old now, and her life is almost finished. . . .

Valentin: But she's still alive. . . .

Molina: And so am I . . . But when is my life going to begin? . . . When is it my turn for something good to happen? To have something for myself?

Valentin: You can start a new life outside. . . .

Molina: All I want is to stay with you. . . . (*Valentin doesn't say anything.*) Does that embarrass you?

Valentin: No, . . . er, well, yes . . .

Molina: Yes what?

Valentin: That . . . it makes me a little embarrassed.

Molina: If I can relay the information will you get out sooner?

Valentin: It's a way of helping the cause.

Molina: But you won't get out quickly? You just think it'll bring the revolution a bit closer.

Valentin: Yes, Molinita. . . . Don't dwell on it, we'll discuss it later.

Molina: There's no time left to discuss.

Valentin: Besides, we have to finish the panther movie.

Molina: It's a sad ending.

Valentin: How?

Molina: She's a flawed woman. (*With his usual irony.*) All of us flawed women come to a sad ending.

Valentin (*laughing*):   And the psychoanalyst? Does he get her in the end?

Molina: She gets him! And good! No, it's not so terrible, she just tears him to pieces.

Valentin: Does she kill him?

Molina: In the movie, yes. In real life, no.

Valentin: Tell me.

Molina: Let's see. Irina goes from bad to worse, she's insanely jealous of the other girl and tries to kill her. But the other one's lucky like hell and she gets away. Then one day the husband, who's at his wits' end now, arranges to meet the psychoanalyst at their house while she's out. But things get all muddled up and when the psychoanalyst arrives she's there on her own. He tries to take advantage of the situation and throws himself at her and kisses her. And right there she turns into a panther. By the time the husband he gets home the guy's bled to death. Meanwhile, Irina has made it to the zoo and she sidles up to the panther's cage. She's all alone, in the night. That afternoon she got the key when the keeper left it in the lock. It's like Irina's in another world. The husband is on his way with the cops at top speed. Irina opens the panther's cage and it pounces on her and mortally wounds her with the first blow. The animal is scared away by the police siren, it dashes out into the street, a car runs over it and kills it.

Valentin: I'm going to miss you, Molinita.

Molina: The movies, at least.

Valentin: At least.

Molina: I want to ask you for a going-away present. Something that we never did, although we got up to worse.

Valentin: What?

Molina: A kiss.

Valentin: It's true. We never did.

Molina: But right at the end, just as I'm leaving.

Valentin: Okay.

Molina: I'm curious. . . . Did the idea of kissing me disgust you?

Valentin: Ummm . . . Maybe I was afraid you'd turn into a panther.

Molina: I'm not the panther-woman.

Valentin: I know.

Molina: It's not fun to be a panther-woman, no one can kiss you. Or anything else.

Valentin: You're the spider-woman who traps men in her web.

Molina (flattered):   How sweet! I like that!

Valentin: And now it's your turn to promise me something: that you'll make people respect you, that you won't let anybody take advantage of you. . . . Promise me you won't let anybody degrade you.

Guard's Voice: Prisoner Luis Alberto Molina, be ready with your belongings!

Molina: Valentin . . .

Valentin: What?

Molina: Nothing, it doesn't matter. . . . (*Pause.*) Valentin . . .

Valentin: What is it?

Molina: Rubbish, skip it.

Valentin: Do you want . . . ?

Molina: What?

Valentin: The kiss.

Molina: No, it was something else.

Valentin: Don't you want your kiss now?

Molina: Yes, if it won't disgust you.

Valentin: Don't get me mad. (*He walks over to Molina and timidly gives him a kiss on the mouth.*)

Molina: Thank you.

Valentin: Thank you.

Molina (after a long pause):   And now give me the number of your comrades.

Valentin: If you want.

Molina: I'll get the message to them.

Valentin: Okay . . . Is that what you wanted to ask?

Molina: Yes.

Valentin (he kisses Molina one more time):   You don't know how happy you've made me. It's 323-1025.

> (*Bolero music starts playing: it chokes Valentin's voice as he gives his instructions. Molina and Valentin separate slowly. Molina puts all his belongings into a duffel bag. They are now openly brokenhearted; Molina can hardly keep his mind on what he's doing. Valentin looks at him in total helplessness. Thier taped voices are heard as all this action takes place on stage.*)

Molina's Voice: What happened to me, Valentin, when I got out of here?

Valentin's Voice: The police kept you under constant surveillance, listened in on your phone, everything. The first call you got was from an uncle, your godfather: he told you not to dally with minors again. You told him what he deserved, that he should go to hell, because in jail you'd learned what dignity was. Your friends telephoned and you called each other Greta and Marlene and Marilyn and the police thought maybe it was a secret code. You got a job as a window dresser and then finally one day you called my comrades. You took your mother to the movies and bought her some fashion magazines. And one day you went to meet my friends but the police were shadowing you and they arrested you. My friends opened fire and killed you from their getaway car as you'd asked them to if the police caught you. And that was all. . . . And what about me, Molina, what happened to me?

Molina's Voice: They tortured you a lot . . . and then your wounds turned septic. A nurse took pity on you and secretly he gave you some morphine and you had a dream.

Valentin's Voice: About what?

Molina's Voice: You dreamed that inside you, in your chest, you were carrying Marta and that you'd never ever be apart from one another.

And she asked you if you regretted what had happened to me, my death, which she said was your fault.

Valentin's Voice: And what did I answer her?

Molina's Voice: You replied that I had died for a noble and selfless ideal. And she said that wasn't true, she said that I had sacrificed myself just so I could die like the heroine in a movie. And you said that only I knew the answer. And you dreamed you were very hungry when you escaped from prison and that you ended up on a savage island and in the middle of the jungle you met a spider woman who gave you food to eat. And she was so lonely there in the jungle but you had to carry on with your struggle and go back to join your comrades, and your strength was restored by the food the spider woman gave you.

Valentin's Voice: And, at the end, did I get away from the police or did they catch up with me?

Molina's Voice: No, at the end you left the island, you were glad to be reunited with your comrades in the struggle, because it was a short dream, but a pleasant one. . . .

(The door opens: Molina and Valentin embrace one another with infinite sadness. Molina exits. The door closes behind him. Curtain.)

WINDOW ON

Freud, Oedipus, and Drama

Sigmund Freud asserted in the *Interpretation of Dreams* that one component of neurosis was usually expressed in what he called the Oedipus complex, which begins in childhood. "Being in love with one parent and hating the other are among the essential constituents of the stock of psychical impulses which is formed at that time and which is of such importance in determining the symptoms of the later neurosis." Freud asserted that the truth of his observation of neurotics was embedded in the legend of Oedipus, already both ancient and well known when Sophocles wrote his tragedy. Freud went so far as to say it was "a legend whose profound and universal power to move can only be understood if the hypothesis I have put forward in regard to the psychology of children has an equally universal validity."

Greek plays, especially tragedies, were usually on subjects that everyone knew and considered important. The legends on which they are based may or may not have historical validity, but they certainly have psychological validity. Even if Freud's hypothesis is proved wrong, the psychological dimension of Greek tragedy is so powerful that theatergoers come away with considerable insight into the human condition. Freud's great insight for literature is simply that Greek tragedy explores the human psyche in a complex and detailed fashion.

In his discussion of *Oedipus Rex* Freud points out that the entire play resembles the process of psychoanalysis because it focuses on revealing the hidden truth. On the surface, the play resembles a modern thriller: Thebes is under a cloud because of mysterious causes linked to an unsolved murder. When Oedipus as king of Thebes declares he will find the causes no matter what it takes, he ironically begins a process of exposing his own actions and establishing himself—quite unknown to himself—as the murderer. In the end, he is forced to face the realities about his own nature in a way that he never expected.

Even if Freud's psychological theories are superseded, his insights into *Oedipus Rex* will remain sound. For one thing, he showed us clearly that the play, like many tragedies, is a constant search for the truth. Once the search is begun, nothing can stop it. Even Oedipus's disbelief will not change the truth. He resorts to witnesses and hard evidence, and in the end accepts the unbelievable.

Freud's theory of the unconscious insists that individuals act without awareness of what is in the unconscious mind. In other words, the neurotic who subconsciously loves one parent and wishes the other dead never knows consciously that such feelings exist. Indeed, like Oedipus, such a claim may be totally unbelievable. Only by analyzing the deep meaning of the conscious gestures can the unconscious be revealed. Freud's theories cast a new light on the ancient Greek concept of fate. They suggest that we bear our fate within us, in our unconscious mind. For the Greeks, fate was a force that lay outside the individual and operated despite every effort of the individual to subvert it. The nobility of a tragic hero was measured by the degree of greatness he or she achieved in the process of struggling against an unwelcome fate.

According to Francis Fergusson, tragedies such as *Oedipus Rex* follow a pattern called a "tragic rhythm." The tragic hero passes through three stages: *poiema* (purpose), *pathema* (passion), and *mathema* (perception). In the first stage, the hero expresses a purpose, such as Oedipus's purpose in finding the causes of the plague that ravages Thebes. In the second stage, the hero suffers deeply as a result of pursuing that purposeful goal, usually wrestling with powerfully conflicting feelings and disbelief. In the final stage, the hero perceives the unpleasant truth and then faces it squarely, either to die or to suffer rejection, as does Oedipus.

We have long felt that the great Greek and Elizabethan tragedies have a magnificent psychological power. The psychological dimension of *Hamlet*, for example, was a mark of wonder for centuries before psychology became an accepted science. It may be no surprise to know that Ernest Jones, a psychoanalyst and follower of Freud, wrote a book on *Hamlet* establishing that Hamlet also was victim of the Oedipus complex. When you reflect on Hamlet's passionate rejection of his mother's new husband and his behavior toward his mother in her bedroom chamber, you may begin to think Jones has an argument.

Reading

Faas, Ekbert. *Tragedy and After.* Kingston, Canada: McGill-Queens University Press, 1984.

Fergusson, Francis. *The Idea of a Theatre.* Garden City, N.Y.:   Doubleday, 1953.

Freud, Sigmund. *The Complete Psychological Works of Sigmund Freud,* ed. James Strachey. London: Hogarth Press, 1964.

Jones, Ernest. *Hamlet and Oedipus.* Garden City, N.Y.:   Doubleday, 1955.

Smith, Joseph H., ed. *The Literary Freud.* New Haven: Yale University Press, 1980.

William Shakespeare   (1564–1616)

Shakespeare was born into a middle-class family in Stratford-upon-Avon, England, and seems to have come up to London already a writer of distinction. His early years are clouded with mystery, although recent scholarship suggests he may have spent time with a wandering theater group performing in central England. In London, after failing to attract a wealthy patron to support his writing, he turned to the popular stage, producing a succession of brilliant history plays, comedies, tragedies, and, in the latter part of his career, romances. His success as a playwright matched his success as a businessman, since he ended his career as a part owner of the theater in which his works were performed.

Shakespeare's plays were performed in large open theaters that accommodated as many as two or three thousand spectators. His works were a popular as well as literary success, with large approving audiences for his three Henry VI *plays (in the 1580s) and his very popular* King Richard III *(1592–1593).* The Taming of the Shrew *(1593–1594),* Romeo and Juliet *(1595–1596),* A Midsummer Night's Dream *(1594–1595),* Julius Caesar *(1599),* Othello *(1602),* King Lear *(1605),* Macbeth *(1606), and* The Tempest *(1611) alone rank him as the greatest dramatist in the English language.*

No records connect Shakespeare with a grammar school or university, yet his range of learning and mastery of languages mark him as a deeply educated man. He has been claimed as a professional in medicine, law, and theology on the basis of his writings, and his expertise in literatures in many languages establishes him as a scholar of rare depth. His plays have been interpreted for their political and economic interests as well as their formal excellence. Feminists have explored the plays in depth; psychoanalytic critics have found fertile ground in his work; response critics have found no end of exploration; and, as many literary successors have pointed out, Shakespeare has something for everyone. His work is rich and inexhaustible.

HAMLET

Hamlet is a scholar returned from Wittenberg, where he presumably studies theology, the main curriculum available to one his age. Everything he does has a moral impact, and the evidence of his father's ghostly return from the grave makes him aware that his own actions may also be fatal. He learns that he risks not only his life, but his soul as well.

The form of this play follows convention, but also moves beyond tradition. It is a revenge tragedy, which usually requires the revenge of a relative—especially a father avenged by a son, the appearance of a ghost, hesitation on the part of the hero, real or pretended insanity, suicide, political intrigue, a spy, soliloquies, especially philosophic in content, and sensational horror and gore. In addition to following convention, Shakespeare manages to give his major characters a lively psychological dimension.

Hamlet has been described as one of the most psychologically complex of all literary characters. His self-analysis, expressed in extensive soliloquies, implies total honesty, and reveals a mind whose vision is almost limitless. Unlike Greek characters, inexorably drawn to their fate, Hamlet seems to wander toward it. He surveys his options until he takes action.

In contrast to Hamlet, certain characters are flat and almost undeveloped. Polonius is the stereotypical pompous old fool. Laertes is his eager-to-please son. Then, characters such as Gertrude and Ophelia, who might have become a stereotypical mother and girlfriend, become astonishingly complex by virtue of their struggle to understand Hamlet. Gertrude is torn between her loyalty to her husband and her love for her son. Part of the tension of the drama is Hamlet's effort to warn her of Claudius and to make her see that his father was a better man than the brother who married her. The institution of marriage in Elizabethan times was such that even a queen owed absolute loyalty to her husband, so Gertrude's struggle between two loyalties is profound. Ophelia owes her allegiance to her father, but she loves Hamlet. Given the way she is used, it is hardly a wonder that she becomes insane.

The circumstances of Hamlet's return to court are so dangerous that he sees quickly that something is wrong. The ghost begins to confirm his suspicions, and the "mousetrap," the play he puts on to expose the king, reveals the truth to him at last. As the audience, we can sense his fears, his danger, and the threats that make him cautious.

William Shakespeare   (1564–1616)
HAMLET, PRINCE OF DENMARK   c. 1600

[*Dramatis Personae*

Claudius, king of Denmark	*Francisco,* a soldier
Hamlet, son to the late King Hamlet, and nephew to the present king	*Reynaldo,* servant to Polonius
	Players
	Two Clowns, grave-diggers

Polonius, Lord Chamberlain
Horatio, friend to Hamlet
Laertes, son to Polonius
Voltimand,
Cornelius,
Rosencrantz, ⎫
Guildenstern, ⎬ courtiers
Osric,
Gentleman,
Priest, or *Doctor of Divinity*
Marcellus, ⎫
Bernardo, ⎬ officers

Fortinbras, Prince of Norway
Captain
English Ambassadors

Gertrude, Queen of Denmark,
    mother to Hamlet
Ophelia, daughter to Polonius

Lords, Ladies, Officers, Soldiers,
    Sailors, Messengers, and other
    Attendants
Ghost of Hamlet's father

Scene: Denmark.]

[ACT I

Scene I]°

(*Enter Bernardo and Francisco, two sentinels, [meeting].*)

Bernardo: Who's there?
Francisco: Nay, answer me.° Stand and unfold yourself.
Bernardo: Long live the King!
Francisco: Bernardo?   5
Bernardo: He.
Francisco: You come most carefully upon your hour.
Bernardo: 'Tis now struck twelve. Get thee to bed, Francisco.
Francisco: For this relief much thanks. 'Tis bitter cold,
    And I am sick at heart.   10
Bernardo: Have you had quiet guard?
Francisco: Not a mouse stirring.
Bernardo: Well, good night.
    If you do meet Horatio and Marcellus,
    The rivals° of my watch, bid them make haste.   15

(*Enter Horatio and Marcellus.*)

Francisco: I think I hear them. Stand, ho! Who is there?
Horatio: Friends to this ground.
Marcellus: And liegemen to the Dane.°
Francisco: Give you° good night.   20

NOTE: The text of Hamlet has come down to us in different versions—such as the first quarto, the second quarto, and the first Folio. The copy of the text used here is largely drawn from the second quarto. Passages enclosed in square brackets are taken from one of the other versions, in most cases the first Folio.   I. I. LOCATION: Elsinore castle. A guard platform.   3 *me:* Francisco emphasizes that *he* is the sentry currently on watch.   15 *rivals:* Partners.   19 *liegemen to the Dane:* Men sworn to serve the Danish king.   20 *Give you:* God give you.

Marcellus: O, farewell, honest soldier.
　　Who hath relieved you?
Francisco: Bernardo hath my place.
　　Give you good night.   *(Exit Francisco.)*
Marcellus: Holla, Bernardo!   25
Bernardo: Say,
　　What, is Horatio there?
Horatio: A piece of him.
Bernardo: Welcome, Horatio. Welcome, good Marcellus.   30
Horatio: What, has this thing appear'd again tonight?
Bernardo: I have seen nothing.
Marcellus: Horatio says 'tis but our fantasy,
　　And will not let belief take hold of him
　　Touching this dreaded sight, twice, seen of us.   35
　　Therefore I have entreated him along
　　With us to watch the minutes of this night,
　　That if again this apparition come
　　He may approve° our eyes and speak to it.
Horatio: Tush, tush, 'twill not appear.   40
Bernardo: Sit down awhile,
　　And let us once again assail your ears,
　　That are so fortified against our story,
　　What we have two nights seen.
Horatio: Well, sit we down,   45
　　And let us hear Bernardo speak of this.
Bernardo: Last night of all,
　　When yond same star that's westward from the pole°
　　Had made his° course t'illume that part of heaven
　　Where now it burns, Marcellus and myself,   50
　　The bell then beating one—

(Enter Ghost.)

Marcellus: Peace, break thee off! Look where it comes again!
Bernardo: In the same figure, like the King that's dead.
Marcellus: Thou art a scholar.° Speak to it, Horatio.   55
Bernardo: Looks 'a° not like the King? Mark it, Horatio.
Horatio: Most like. It harrows me with fear and wonder.
Bernardo: It would be spoke to.°
Marcellus: Speak to it, Horatio.
Horatio: What art thou that usurp'st this time of night,   60
　　Together with that fair and warlike form
　　In which the majesty of buried Denmark°
　　Did sometimes° march? By heaven I charge thee speak!

39 *approve:* Corroborate.   48 *pole:* Polestar.   49 *his:* Its.   55 *scholar:* One learned in Latin and able to address spirits.   56 *'a:* He.   58 *It . . . to:* A ghost could not speak until spoken to.   62 *buried Denmark:* The buried king of Denmark.   63 *sometimes:* Formerly.

Marcellus: It is offended.
Bernardo: See, it stalks away.   65
Horatio: Stay! Speak, speak. I charge thee, speak.

(Exit Ghost.)

Marcellus: 'Tis gone, and will not answer.
Bernardo: How now, Horatio? You tremble and look pale.
    Is not this something more than fantasy?   70
    What think you on 't?
Horatio: Before my God, I might not this believe
    Without the sensible° and true avouch
    Of mine own eyes.
Marcellus: Is it not like the King?   75
Horatio: As thou art to thyself.
    Such was the very armor he had on
    When he the ambitious Norway° combated.
    So frown'd he once when, in an angry parle,°
    He smote the sledded° Polacks° on the ice.   80
    'Tis strange.
Marcellus: Thus twice before, and jump° at this dead hour,
    With martial stalk hath he gone by our watch.
Horatio: In what particular thought to work I know not,
    But, in the gross and scope° of mine opinion,   85
    This bodes some strange eruption to our state.
Marcellus: Good now,° sit down, and tell me, he that knows,
    Why this same strict and most observant watch
    So nightly toils° the subject° of the land,
    And why such daily cast° of brazen cannon,   90
    And foreign mart° for implements of war,
    Why such impress° of shipwrights, whose sore task
    Does not divide the Sunday from the week.
    What might be toward,° that this sweaty haste
    Doth make the night joint-laborer with the day?   95
    Who is 't that can inform me?
Horatio: That can I,
    At least, the whisper goes so. Our last king,
    Whose image even but now appear'd to us,
    Was, as you know, by Fortinbras of Norway,   100
    Thereto prick'd on° by a most emulate° pride,
    Dar'd to the combat; in which our valiant Hamlet—

73 *sensible:* Confirmed by the senses.   78 *Norway:* King of Norway.   79 *parle:* Parley.   80
sledded: Traveling on sleds.   *Polacks:* Poles.   82 *jump:* Exactly.   85 *gross and scope:* General
view.   87 *Good now:* An expression denoting entreaty or expostulation.   89 *toils:* Causes to
toil.   *subject:* Subjects.   90 *cast:* Casting.   91 *mart:* Buying and selling.   92 *impress:*
Impressment, conscription.   94 *toward:* In preparation.   101 *prick'd on:* Incited.   *emulate:* Ambitious.

For so this side of our known world esteem'd him—
Did slay this Fortinbras; who, by a seal'd compact,
Well ratified by law and heraldry,   105
Did forfeit, with his life, all those his lands
Which he stood seiz'd° of, to the conqueror;
Against the° which a moi'ty competent°
Was gaged° by our king, which had return'd
To the inheritance of Fortinbras   110
Had he been vanquisher, as, by the same comart°
And carriage° of the article design'd,
His fell to Hamlet. Now, sir, young Fortinbras,
Of unimproved° mettle hot and full,
Hath in the skirts° of Norway here and there   115
Shark'd up° a list of lawless resolutes°
For food and diet° to some enterprise
That hath a stomach° in 't, which is no other—
As it doth well appear unto our state—
But to recover of us, by strong hand   120
And terms compulsatory, those foresaid lands
So by his father lost. And this, I take it,
Is the main motive of our preparations,
The source of this our watch, and the chief head°
Of this post-haste and romage° in the land.   125
Bernardo: I think it be no other but e'en so.
Well may it sort° that this portentous figure
Comes armed through our watch so like the King
That was and is the question of these wars.
Horatio: A mote° it is to trouble the mind's eye.   130
In the most high and palmy° state of Rome,
A little ere the mightiest Julius fell,
The graves stood tenantless and the sheeted° dead
Did squeak and gibber in the Roman streets;
As° stars with trains of fire and dews of blood,   135
Disasters° in the sun; and the moist star°
Upon whose influence Neptune's° empire stands°
Was sick almost to doomsday° with eclipse.

---

107 *seiz'd:* Possessed.   108 *Against the:* In return for.   *moi'ty competent:* Sufficient portion.
109 *gaged:* Engaged, pledged.   111 *comart:* Joint Bargain (?).   112 *carriage:* Import, bearing.   114 *unimproved:* Not turned to account (?) or untested (?).   115 *skirts:* Outlying regions, outskirts.   116 *Shark'd up:* Got together in haphazard fashion.   *resolutes:*
Desperadoes.   117 *food and diet:* No pay but their keep.   118 *stomach:* Relish of danger.
124 *head:* Source.   125 *romage:* Bustle, commotion.   127 *sort:* Suit.   130 *mote:* Speck
of dust.   131 *palmy:* Flourishing.   133 *sheeted:* Shrouded.   135 *As:* This abrupt transition suggests that matter is possibly omitted between lines 134 and 135.   136 *Disasters:*
Unfavorable signs of aspects.   *moist star:* Moon, governing tides.   137 *Neptune:* God of the
sea.   *stands:* Depends.   138 *sick . . . doomsday:* See Matt. 24:29 and Rev. 6:12.

And even the like precurse° of fear'd events,
As harbingers° preceding still° the fates   140
And prologue to the omen° coming on,
Have heaven and earth together demonstrated
Unto our climatures° and countrymen.

(Enter Ghost.)

But soft, behold! Lo where it comes again!   145
I'll cross° it, though it blast me. Stay, illusion!
If thou hast any sound, or use of voice,
Speak to me!   *(It spreads his arms.)*
If there be any good thing to be done
That may to thee do ease and grace to me,   150
Speak to me!
If thou art privy to thy country's fate,
Which, happily,° foreknowing may avoid,
O, speak!
Or if thou hast uphoarded in thy life   155
Extorted treasure in the womb of earth,
For which, they say, you spirits oft walk in death,

                                    (The cock crows.)

Speak of it. Stay, and speak! Stop it, Marcellus.
Marcellus: Shall I strike at it with my partisan?°   160
Horatio: Do, if it will not stand. [*They strike at it.*]
Bernardo: 'Tis here!
Horatio: 'Tis here!
Marcellus: 'Tis gone.   [*Exit Ghost.*]
We do it wrong, being so majestical,   165
To offer it the show of violence;
For it is, as the air, invulnerable,
And our vain blows malicious mockery.
Bernardo: It was about to speak when the cock crew.
Horatio: And then it started like a guilty thing   170
Upon a fearful summons. I have heard,
The cock, that is the trumpet to the morn,
Doth with his lofty and shrill-sounding throat
Awake the god of day, and, at his warning,
Whether in sea or fire, in earth or air,   175
Th' extravagant and erring° spirit hies
To his confine; and of the truth herein
This present object made probation.°

---

139 *precurse:* Heralding, foreshadowing.   140 *harbingers:* Forerunners.   *still:* Continually.
141 *omen:* Calamitous event.   143 *climatures:* Regions.   146 *cross:* Meet, face directly.
153 *happily:* Haply, perchance.   160 *partisan:* Long-handled spear.   176 *extravagant and erring:* Wandering. (The words have similar meaning.)   178 *probation:* Proof.

Marcellus: It faded on the crowing of the cock.
  Some say that ever 'gainst° that season comes   180
  Wherein our Savior's birth is celebrated,
  The bird of dawning singeth all night long,
  And then, they say, no spirit dare stir abroad;
  The nights are wholesome, then no planets strike,°
  No fairy takes,° nor witch hath power to charm,   185
  So hallowed and so gracious° is that time.
Horatio: So have I heard and do in part believe it.
  But, look, the morn, in russet mantle clad,
  Walks o'er the dew of yon high eastward hill.
  Break we our watch up, and by my advice   190
  Let us impart what we have seen tonight
  Unto young Hamlet; for, upon my life,
  This spirit, dumb to us, will speak to him.
  Do you consent we shall acquaint him with it,
  As needful in our loves, fitting our duty?   195
Marcellus: Let's do 't, I pray, and I this morning know
  Where we shall find him most conveniently.

  (Exeunt.)°

180 *'gainst:* Just before. 184 *strike:* Exert evil influence. 185 *takes:* Bewitches. 186 *gracious:* Full of goodness. 198 *Exeunt:* Latin for "they go out."

[Scene II]°

(Flourish. Enter Claudius, King of Denmark, Gertrude the Queen, Councilors, Polonius and his son Laertes, Hamlet, cum aliis° [including Voltimand and Cornelius].)

King: Though yet of Hamlet our dear brother's death
  The memory be green, and that it us befitted   5
  To bear our hearts in grief and our whole kingdom
  To be contracted in one brow of woe,
  Yet so far hath discretion fought with nature
  That we with wisest sorrow think on him,
  Together with remembrance of ourselves.   10
  Therefore our sometime sister, now our queen,
  Th' imperial jointress° to this warlike state,
  Have we, as 'twere with a defeated joy—
  With an auspicious and a dropping eye,
  With mirth in funeral and with dirge in marriage,   15
  In equal scale weighing delight and dole—

I. II. LOCATION: The castle. 2 *cum aliis:* With others. 12 *jointress:* Woman possessed of a joint tenancy of an estate.

Taken to wife. Nor have we herein barr'd
Your better wisdoms, which have freely gone
With this affair along. For all, our thanks.
Now follows that you know° young Fortinbras,   20
Holding a weak supposal° of our worth,
Or thinking by our late dear brother's death
Our state to be disjoint and out of frame,
Colleagued with° this dream of his advantage,°
He hath not fail'd to pester us with message   25
Importing° the surrender of those lands
Lost by his father, with all bands° of law,
To our most valiant brother. So much for him.
Now for ourself and for this time of meeting.
Thus much the business is: we have here writ   30
To Norway, uncle of young Fortinbras—
Who, impotent and bed-rid, scarcely hears
Of this his nephew's purpose—to suppress
His° further gait° herein, in that the levies,
The lists, and full proportions are all made   35
Out of his Subject;° and we here dispatch
You, good Cornelius, and you, Voltimand,
For bearers of this greeting to old Norway,
Giving to you no further personal power
To business with the King, more than the Scope   40
Of these delated° articles allow.   *[Gives a paper.]*
Farewell, and let your haste commend your duty.
Cornelius, Voltimand: In that, and all things, will we show our duty.
King: We doubt it nothing. Heartily farewell.

                                  [Exit Voltimand and Cornelius.]   45

And now, Laertes, what's the news with you?
You told us of some suit; what is 't, Laertes?
You cannot speak of reason to the Dane°
And lose your voice.° What wouldst thou beg, Laertes,
That shall not be my offer, not thy asking?   50
The head is not more native° to the heart,
The hand more instrumental° to the mouth,
Than is the throne of Denmark to thy father.
What wouldst thou have, Laertes?

---

20 *know:* Be informed (that).   21 *weak supposal:* Low estimate.   24 *Colleagued with:* Joined to, allied with.   *dream . . . advantage:* Illusory hope of success.   26 *Importing:* Pertaining to.   27 *bands:* Contracts.   34 *His:* Fortinbras's.   *gait:* Proceeding.   34–36 *in that . . . subject:* Since the levying of troops and supplies is drawn entirely from the King of Norway's own subject.   41 *delated:* Detailed. (Variant of *dilated.*)   48 *the Dane:* The Danish king.   49 *lose your voice:* Waste your speech.   51 *native:* Closely connected, related.   52 *instrumental:* Serviceable.

Laertes: My dread lord,
    Your leave and favor to return to France,   55
    From whence though willingly I came to Denmark
    To show my duty in your coronation,
    Yet now I must confess, that duty done,
    My thoughts and wishes bend again toward France
    And bow them to your gracious leave and pardon.°   60
King: Have you your father's leave? What says Polonius?
Polonius: H'ath,° my lord, wrung from me my slow leave
    By laborsome petition, and at last
    Upon his will I seal'd my hard° consent.
    I do beseech you, give him leave to go.   65
King: Take thy fair hour, Laertes. Time be thine,
    And thy best graces spend it at thy will!
    But now, my cousin° Hamlet, and my son—
Hamlet: A little more than kin, and less than kind.°
King: How is it that the clouds still hang on you?   70
Hamlet: Not so, my lord. I am too much in the sun.°
Queen: Good Hamlet, cast thy nighted color off,
    And let thine eye look like a friend on Denmark.
    Do not forever with thy vailed° lids
    Seek for thy noble father in the dust.   75
    Thou know'st 'tis common,° all that lives must die,
    Passing through nature to eternity.
Hamlet: Ay, madam, it is common.
Queen: If it be,
    Why seems it so particular with thee?   80
Hamlet: Seems, madam! Nay, it is. I know not "seems."
    'Tis not alone my inky cloak, good mother,
    Nor customary suits of solemn black,
    Nor windy suspiration of forc'd breath,
    No, nor the fruitful° river in the eye,   85
    Nor the dejected havior° of the visage,
    Together with all forms, moods, shapes of grief,
    That can denote me truly. These indeed seem,
    For they are actions that a man might play.
    But I have that within which passes show;   90
    These but the trappings and the suits of woe.

---

60 *leave and pardon:* Permission to depart.   62 *H'ath:* He hath (has).   64 *hard:* Reluctant.
68 *cousin:* Any kin not of the immediate family.   69 *A little . . . kind:* Closer than an ordinary
nephew (since I am stepson), and yet more separated in natural feeling (with pun on *kind,* meaning *affectionate* and *natural, lawful.* This line is often read as an aside, but it need not be.)   71
sun: The sunshine of the King's royal favor (with pun on *son*).   74 *vailed:* Downcast.   76
common: Of universal occurrence. (But Hamlet plays on the sense of *vulgar* in line 76.)   85
fruitful: Abundant.   86 *havior:* appearance.

King: 'Tis sweet and commendable in your nature, Hamlet,
　　　To give these mourning duties to your father.
　　　But you must know your father lost a father,
　　　That father lost, lost his, and the survivor bound　　　　　95
　　　In filial obligation for some term
　　　To do obsequious° sorrow. But to persever°
　　　In obstinate condolement° is a course
　　　Of impious stubbornness. 'Tis unmanly grief.
　　　It shows a will most incorrect to heaven,　　　　　100
　　　A heart unfortified, a mind impatient,
　　　An understanding simple and unschool'd.
　　　For what we know must be and is as common
　　　As any the most vulgar thing to sense,°
　　　Why should we in our peevish opposition　　　　　105
　　　Take it to heart? Fie, 'tis a fault to heaven,
　　　A fault against the dead, a fault to nature,
　　　To reason most absurd, whose common theme
　　　Is death of fathers, and who still hath cried,
　　　From the first corse° till he that died today,　　　　　110
　　　"This must be so." We pray you, throw to earth
　　　This unprevailing° woe, and think of us
　　　As of a father; for let the world take note,
　　　You are the most immediate° to our throne,
　　　And with no less nobility of love　　　　　115
　　　Than that which dearest father bears his son
　　　Do I impart toward you. For your intent
　　　In going back to school in Wittenberg,°
　　　It is most retrograde° to our desire,
　　　And we beseech you, bend you° to remain　　　　　120
　　　Here in the cheer and comfort of our eye,
　　　Our chiefest courtier, cousin, and our son.
Queen: Let not thy mother lose her prayers, Hamlet.
　　　I pray thee stay with us, go not to Wittenberg.
Hamlet: I shall in all my best obey you, madam.　　　　　125
King: Why, 'tis a loving and a fair reply.
　　　Be as ourself in Denmark. Madam, come.
　　　This gentle and unforc'd accord of Hamlet
　　　Sits smiling to my heart, in grace whereof
　　　No jocund° health that Denmark drinks today　　　　　130
　　　But the great cannon to the clouds shall tell,

---

97 *obsequious:* Suited to obsequies or funerals.　*persever:* Persevere.　98 *condolement:*
Sorrowing.　104 *As . . . sense:* As the most ordinary experience.　110 *corse:* Corpse.　112
unprevailing: Unavailing.　114 *most immediate:* Next in succession.　118 *Wittenberg:*
Famous German university founded in 1502.　119 *retrograde:* Contrary.　120 *bend you:*
Incline yourself.　130 *jocund:* Merry.

And the King's rouse° the heaven shall bruit again,°
Respeaking earthly thunder.° Come away.

(Flourish. Exeunt all but Hamlet.)

Hamlet: O, that this too too sullied° flesh would melt,   135
Thaw, and resolve itself into a dew!
Or that the Everlasting had not fix'd
His canon° 'gainst self-slaughter! O God, God,
How weary, stale, flat, and unprofitable
Seem to me all the uses of this world!   140
Fie on 't, ah, fie! 'Tis an unweeded garden
That grows to seed. Things rank and gross in nature
Possess it merely.° That it should come to this!
But two months dead—nay, not so much, not two.
So excellent a king, that was to° this   145
Hyperion° to a satyr; so loving to my mother
That he might not beteem° the winds of heaven
Visit her face too roughly. Heaven and earth,
Must I remember? Why, she would hang on him
As if increase of appetite had grown   150
By what it fed on, and yet, within a month—
Let me not think on 't. Frailty, thy name is woman!—
A little month, or ere those shoes were old
With which she followed my poor father's body,
Like Niobe,° all tears, why she, even she—   155
O God, a beast, that wants discourse of reason,°
Would have mourn'd longer—married with my uncle,
My father's brother, but no more like my father
Than I to Hercules. Within a month,
Ere yet the salt of most unrighteous tears   160
Had left the flushing in her galled° eyes,
She married. O, most wicked speed, to post
With such dexterity to incestuous° sheets!
It is not nor it cannot come to good.
But break, my heart, for I must hold my tongue.   165

(Enter Horatio, Marcellus, and Bernardo.)

132 *rouse:* Draft of liquor.   *bruit again:* Loudly echo.   133 *thunder:* Of trumpet and kettledrum, sounded when the King drinks; see I. IV. 12–16.   135 *sullied:* Defiled. (The early
quartos read *sallied,* the Folio *solid.*)   138 *canon:* Law.   143 *merely:* Completely.   145 *to:*
In comparison to.   146 *Hyperion:* Titan sun-god, father of Helios.   147 *beteem:* Allow.
155 *Niobe:* Tantalus's daughter, Queen of Thebes, who boasted that she had more sons and
daughters than Leto; for this, Apollo and Artemis, children of Leto, slew her fourteen children.
She was turned by Zeus into a stone which continually dropped tears.   156 *wants . . . reason:*
Lacks the faculty of reason.   161 *galled:* Irritated, inflamed.   163 *incestuous:* In
Shakespeare's day, the marriage of a man like Claudius to his deceased brother's wife was considered incestuous.

Horatio: Hail to your lordship!
Hamlet: I am glad to see you well.
          Horatio!—or I do forget myself.
Horatio: The same, my lord, and your poor servant ever.   170
Hamlet: Sir, my good friend; I'll change° that name with you.
          And what make° you from Wittenberg, Horatio?
          Marcellus?
Marcellus: My good lord.
Hamlet: I am very glad to see you.   *[To Bernardo.]*   175
          Good even, sir.—
          But what, in faith, make you from Wittenberg?
Horatio: A truant disposition, good my lord.
Hamlet: I would not hear your enemy say so,
          Nor shall you do my ear that violence   180
          To make it truster of your own report
          Against yourself. I know you are no truant.
          But what is your affair in Elsinore?
          We'll teach you to drink deep ere you depart.
Horatio: My lord, I came to see your father's funeral.   185
Hamlet: I prithee do not mock me, fellow student;
          I think it was to see my mother's wedding.
Horatio: Indeed, my lord, it followed hard° upon.
Hamlet: Thrift, thrift, Horatio! The funeral bak'd meats
          Did coldly furnish forth the marriage tables.   190
          Would I had met my dearest° foe in heaven
          Or° ever I had seen that day, Horatio!
          My father!—Methinks I see my father.
Horatio: Where, my lord?
Hamlet: In my mind's eye, Horatio.   195
Horatio: I saw him once. 'A° was a goodly king.
Hamlet: 'A was a man, take him for all in all,
          I shall not look upon his like again.
Horatio: My lord, I think I saw him yesternight.
Hamlet: Saw? Who?   200
Horatio: My lord, the King your father.
Hamlet: The King my father?
Horatio: Season your admiration° for a while
          With an attent° ear, till I may deliver,
          Upon the witness of these gentlemen,   205
          This marvel to you.
Hamlet: For God's love, let me hear!
Horatio: Two nights together had these gentlemen,

---

171 *change:* Exchange (i.e., the name of friend).   172 *make:* Do.   188 *hard:* Close.   191
dearest: Direst.   192 *or:* Ere, before.   196 *'A:* He.   203 *Season your admiration:* Restrain
your astonishment.   204 *attent:* Attentive.

Marcellus and Bernardo, on their watch,
In the dead waste and middle of the night,   210
Been thus encount'red. A figure like your father,
Armed at point° exactly, cap-a-pe,°
Appears before them, and with solemn march
Goes slow and stately by them. Thrice he walk'd
By their oppress'd and fear-surprised eyes   215
Within his truncheon's° length, whilst they, distill'd
Almost to jelly with the act° of fear,
Stand dumb and speak not to him. This to me
In dreadful secrecy impart they did,
And I with them the third night kept the watch,   220
Where, as they had delivered, both in time,
Form of the thing, each word made true and
Good, the apparition comes. I knew your father;
These hands are not more like.
Hamlet: But where was this?   225
Marcellus: My lord, upon the platform where we watch.
Hamlet: Did you not speak to it?
Horatio: My lord, I did.
But answer made it none. Yet once methought
It lifted up it° head and did address   230
Itself to motion, like as it would speak;
But even then the morning cock crew loud,
And at the sound it shrunk in haste away,
And vanish'd from our sight.
Hamlet: 'Tis very strange,   235
Horatio: As I do live, my honor'd lord, 'tis true,
And we did think it writ down in our duty
To let you know of it.
Hamlet: Indeed, indeed, sirs. But this troubles me.
Hold you the watch tonight?   240
All: We do, my lord.
Hamlet: Arm'd, say you?
All: Arm'd, my lord.
Hamlet: From top to toe?
All: My lord, from head to foot.   245
Hamlet: Then saw you not his face?
Horatio: O, yes, my lord. He wore his beaver° up.
Hamlet: What, looked he frowningly?
Horatio: A countenance more
In sorrow than in anger.   250
Hamlet: Pale or red?

212 *at point:* Completely.   *cap-a-pe:* From head to foot.   216 *truncheon:* Officer's staff.
217 *act:* Action, operation.   230 *it:* Its.   247 *beaver:* Visor on the helmet.

Horatio: Nay, very pale.
Hamlet: And fix'd his eyes upon you?
Horatio: Most constantly.
Hamlet: I would I had been there.   255
Horatio: It would have much amaz'd you.
Hamlet: Very like, very like. Stay'd it long?
Horatio: While one with moderate haste might tell° a hundred.
Marcellus, Bernardo: Longer, longer.
Horatio: Not when I saw't.   260
Hamlet: His beard was grizzl'd,—no?
Horatio: It was, as I have seen it in his life,
     A sable silver'd.°
Hamlet: I will watch tonight.
     Perchance 'twill walk again.   265
Horatio: I warr'nt it will.
Hamlet: If it assume my noble father's person,
     I'll speak to it, though hell itself should gape
     And bid me hold my peace. I pray you all,
     If you have hitherto conceal'd this sight,   270
     Let it be tenable° in your silence still,
     And whatsomever else shall hap tonight,
     Give it an understanding, but no tongue.
     I will requite your loves. So, fare you well.
     Upon the platform, 'twixt eleven and twelve,   275
     I'll visit you.
All: Our duty to your honor.
Hamlet: Your loves, as mine to you. Farewell.

                              (Exeunt [all but Hamlet].)

     My father's spirit in arms! All is not well.   280
     I doubt° some foul play. Would the night were come!
     Till then sit still, my soul. Foul deeds will rise,
     Though all the earth o'erwhelm them, to men's eyes.

                                        (Exit.)   285

---

258 *tell:* Count.   263 *sable silver'd:* Black mixed with white.   271 *tenable:* Held tightly.
281 *doubt:* Suspect.

[Scene III]°

(Enter Laertes and Ophelia, his sister.)

Laertes: My necessaries are embark'd. Farewell.
     And, sister, as the winds give benefit
     And convoy is assistant,° do not sleep
     But let me hear from you.   5

I. III. LOCATION: Polonius's chambers.   4 *convoy is assistant:* Means of conveyance are available.
able.

Ophelia: Do you doubt that?
Laertes: For Hamlet, and the trifling of his favor,
   Hold it a fashion and a toy in blood,°
   A violet in the youth of primy° nature,
   Forward,° not permanent, sweet, not lasting,   10
   The perfume and suppliance° of a minute—
   No more.
Ophelia: No more but so?
Laertes: Think it no more.
   For nature crescent° does not grow alone   15
   In thews° and bulk, but, as this temple° waxes,
   The inward service of the mind and soul
   Grows wide withal.° Perhaps he loves you now,
   And now no soil° nor cautel° doth besmirch
   The virtue of his will;° but you must fear,   20
   His greatness weigh'd,° his will is not his own.
   [For he himself is subject to his birth.]
   He may not, as unvalued persons do,
   Carve° for himself; for on his choice depends
   The safety and health of this whole state,   25
   And therefore must his choice be circumscrib'd
   Unto the voice and yielding° of that body
   Whereof he is the head. Then if he says he loves you,
   It fits your wisdom so far to believe it
   As he in his particular act and place   30
   May give his saying deed,° which is no further
   Than the main voice of Denmark goes withal.
   Then weigh what loss your honor may sustain
   If with too credent° ear you list° his songs,
   Or lose your heart, or your chaste treasure open   35
   To his unmaster'd importunity.
   Fear it, Ophelia, fear it, my dear sister,
   And keep you in the rear of your affection,
   Out of the shot° and danger of desire.
   The chariest° maid is prodigal enough   40
   If she unmask her beauty to the moon.
   Virtue itself scapes not calumnious strokes.
   The canker galls° the infants of the spring

---

8 *toy in blood:* Passing amorous fancy.   9 *primy:* In its prime, springtime.   10 *Forward:* Precocious.   11 *suppliance:* Supply, filler.   15 *crescent:* Growing, waxing.   16 *thews:* Bodily strength.   *temple:* Body.   18 *Grows wide withal:* Grows along with it.   19 *soil:* Blemish.   *cautel:* Deceit.   20 *will:* Desire.   21 *greatness weigh'd:* High position considered.   24 *Carve:* Choose pleasure.   27 *Voice and yielding:* Assent, approval.   31 *deed:* Effect.   34 *credent:* Credulous.   *list:* Listen to.   39 *shot:* Range.   40 *chariest:* Most scrupulously modest.   43 *canker galls:* Cankerworm destroys.

Too oft before their buttons° be disclos'd,°
And in the morn and liquid dew° of youth   45
Contagious blastments° are most imminent.
Be wary then; best safety lies in fear.
Youth to itself rebels, though none else near.
Ophelia: I shall the effect of this good lesson keep
As watchman to my heart. But, good my brother,   50
Do not, as some ungracious pastors do,
Show me the steep and thorny way to heaven,
Whiles, like a puff'd° and reckless libertine,
Himself the primrose path of dalliance treads,
And recks° not his own rede.°   55

(Enter Polonius.)

Laertes: O, fear me not.
I stay too long. But here my father comes.
A double blessing is a double° grace;
Occasion° smiles upon a second leave.   60
Polonius: Yet here, Laertes? Aboard, aboard, for shame!
The wind sits in the shoulder of your sail,
And you are stay'd for.° There—my blessing with thee!
And these few precepts in thy memory
Look thou character.° Give thy thoughts no tongue,   65
Nor any unproportion'd thought his° act.
Be thou familiar,° but by no means vulgar.°
Those friends thou hast, and their adoption tried,°
Grapple them to thy soul with hoops of steel,
But do not dull thy palm with entertainment   70
Of each new-hatch'd, unfledg'd courage.° Beware
Of entrance to a quarrel, but, being in,
Bear't that° th' opposed may beware of thee.
Give every man thy ear, but few thy voice;
Take each man's censure,° but reserve thy judgment.   75
Costly thy habit as thy purse can buy,
But not express'd in fancy; rich, not gaudy,
For the apparel oft proclaims the man,
And they in France of the best rank and station
Are of a most select and generous chief° in that.   80
Neither a borrower nor a lender be,
For loan oft loses both itself and friend,

44 *buttons:* Buds. *disclos'd:* Opened.   45 *liquid dew:* Time when dew is fresh.   46 *blastments:* Blights.   53 *puff'd:* Bloated.   55 *recks:* Heeds.   *rede:* Counsel.   59 *double:* I.e., Laertes has already bidden his father good-by.   60 *Occasion:* Opportunity.   63 *stay'd for:* Waited for.   65 *character:* Inscribe.   66 *his:* Its.   67 *familiar:* Sociable.   *vulgar:* Common.   68 *tried:* Tested.   71 *courage:* Young man of spirit.   73 *Bear't that:* Manage it so that.   75 *censure:* Opinion, judgment.   80 *generous chief:* Noble eminence (?).

And borrowing dulleth edge of husbandry.°
This above all: to thine own self be true,
And it must follow, as the night the day,   85
Thou canst not then be false to any man.
Farewell. My blessing season° this in thee!
Laertes: Most humbly do I take my leave, my lord.
Polonius: The time invests° you. Go, your servants tend.°
Laertes: Farewell, Ophelia, and remember well.   90
    What I have said to you.
Ophelia: 'Tis in my memory lock'd
    And you yourself shall keep the key of it.
Laertes: Farewell.   *(Exit Laertes.)*
Polonius: What is 't, Ophelia, he hath said to you?   95
Ophelia: So please you, something touching the Lord Hamlet.
Polonius: Marry,° well bethought.
    'Tis told me he hath very oft of late
    Given private time to you, and you yourself
    Have of your audience been most free and bounteous.   100
    If it be so—as so 'tis put on° me,
    And that in way of caution—I must tell you
    You do not understand yourself so clearly
    As it behooves my daughter and your honor.
    What is between you? Give me up the truth.   105
Ophelia: He hath, my lord, of late made many tenders°
    Of his affection to me.
Polonius: Affection? Pooh! You speak like a green girl,
    Unsifted° in such perilous circumstance.
    Do you believe his tenders, as you call them?   110
Ophelia: I do not know, my lord, what I should think.
Polonius: Marry, I will teach you. Think yourself a baby
    That you have ta'en these tenders° for true pay,
    Which are not sterling.° Tender° yourself more dearly,
    Or—not to crack the wind° of the poor phrase,   115
    Running it thus—you'll tender me a fool.°
Ophelia: My lord, he hath importun'd me with love
    In honorable fashion.
Polonius: Ay, fashion° you may call it. Go to, go to.
Ophelia: And hath given countenance° to his speech, my lord,   120
    With almost all the holy vows of heaven.

---

83 *husbandry:* Thrift.   87 *season:* Mature.   89 *invests:* Besieges.   *tend:* Attend, wait.
97 *Marry:* By the Virgin Mary (a mild oath).   101 *put on:* Impressed on, told to.   106 *tenders:* Offers.   109 *Unsifted:* Untried.   113 *tenders:* With added meaning here of *promises to pay.*   114 *sterling:* Legal currency.   *Tender:* Hold.   115 *crack the wind:* Run it until it is broken, winded.   116 *tender me a fool:* (1) Show yourself to me as a fool; (2) show me up as a fool; (3) present me with a grandchild (*fool* was a term of endearment for a child).   119 *fashion:* Mere form, pretense.   120 *countenance:* Credit, support.

Polonius: Ay, springes° to catch woodcocks.° I do know,
When the blood burns, how prodigal the soul
Lends the tongue vows. These blazes, daughter,
Giving more light than heat, extinct in both   125
Even in their promise, as it is a-making,
You must not take for fire. From this time
Be something scanter of your maiden presence.
Set your entreatments° at a higher rate
Than a command to parle.° For Lord Hamlet,   130
Believe so much in him° that he is young,
And with a larger tether may he walk
Than may be given you. In few,° Ophelia,
Do not believe his vows, for they are brokers,°
Not of that dye° which their investments° show,   135
But mere implorators° of unholy suits,
Breathing° like sanctified and pious bawds,
The better to beguile. This is for all:
I would not, in plain terms, from this time forth
Have you so slander° any moment leisure   140
As to give words or talk with the Lord Hamlet.
Look to 't, I charge you. Come your ways.
Ophelia: I shall obey, my lord.   *(Exeunt.)*

122 *springes:* Snares.   *woodcocks:* Birds easily caught; here used to connote gullibility.
129 *entreatments:* Negotiations for surrender (a military term).   130 *parle:* Discuss terms with
the enemy. (Polonius urges his daughter, in the metaphor of military language, not to meet with
Hamlet and consider giving in to him merely because he requests an interview.)   131 *so . . .
him:* This much concerning him.   133 *In few:* Briefly.   134 *brokers:* Go-betweens, procur-
ers.   135 *dye:* Color or sort.   *investments:* Clothes (i.e., they are not what they seem).
136 *mere implorators:* Out and out solicitors.   137 *Breathing:* Speaking.   140 *slander:*
Bring disgrace or reproach upon.

[Scene IV]°

(Enter Hamlet, Horatio, and Marcellus.)

Hamlet: The air bites shrewdly; it is very cold.
Horatio: It is a nipping and an eager air.
Hamlet: What hour now?
Horatio: I think it lacks of twelve.   5
Marcellus: No, it is struck.
Horatio: Indeed? I heard it not.
It then draws near the season
wherein the spirit held his wont to walk.

                *(A flourish of trumpets, and two pieces° go off
                                              [within].)*   10

What does this mean, my lord?

I. IV. LOCATION: The guard platform.   9 *pieces:* I.e., of ordnance, cannon.

Hamlet: The King doth wake° tonight and takes his rouse,°
         Keeps wassail,° and the swagg'ring up-spring° reels;
         And as he drains his draughts of Rhenish° down,
         The kettle-drum and trumpet thus bray out   15
         The triumph of his pledge.°
Horatio: Is it a custom?
Hamlet: Ay, marry, is 't,
         But to my mind, though I am native here
         And to the manner° born, it is a custom   20
         More honor'd in the breach than the observance.°
         This heavy-headed revel east and west°
         Makes us traduc'd and tax'd of° other nations.
         They clepe° us drunkards, and with swinish phrase°
         Soil our addition;° and indeed it takes   25
         From our achievements, though perform'd at height,°
         The pith and marrow of our attribute.
         So, oft it chances in particular men,
         That for some vicious mole of nature° in them,
         As in their birth—wherein they are not guilty,   30
         Since nature cannot choose his° origin—
         By the o'ergrowth of some complexion,°
         Oft breaking down the pales° and forts of reason,
         Or by some habit that too much o'er-leavens°
         The form of plausive° manners, that these men,   35
         Carrying, I say, the stamp of one defect,
         Being nature's livery,° or fortune's star,°
         Their virtues else, be they as pure as grace,
         As infinite as man may undergo,
         Shall in the general censure take corruption   40
         From that particular fault. The dram of eale°
         Doth all the noble substance of a doubt°
         To his own scandal.°

         (Enter Ghost.)

---

12 *wake:* Stay awake and hold revel.   *rouse:* Carouse, drinking bout.   13 *wassail:* Carousal.
up-spring: Wild German dance.   14 *Rhenish:* Rhine wine.   16 *triumph . . . pledge:* His feat
in draining the wine in a single draught.   20 *manner:* Custom (of drinking).   21 *More . . .
observance:* Better neglected than followed.   22 *east and west:* I.e., everywhere.   23 *tax'd of:*
Censured by.   24 *clepe:* Call.   *with swinish phrase:* By calling us swine.   25 *addition:*
Reputation.   26 *at height:* Outstandingly.   29 *mole of nature:* Natural blemish in one's constitution.   31 *his:* Its.   32 *complexion:* Humor (i.e., one of the four humors or fluids thought
to determine temperament).   33 *pales:* Palings, fences (as of a fortification).   34 *o'er-leav-
ens:* Induces a change throughout (as yeast works in dough).   35 *plausive:* Pleasing.   37 *nature's livery:* Endowment from nature.   *fortune's star:* Mark placed by fortune.   41 *dram of
eale:* Small amount of evil (?).   42 *of a doubt:* A famous crux, sometimes emended to *oft about*
or *often dout,* i.e., "often erase" or "do out," or to *antidote,* counteract.   43 *To . . . scandal:*
To the disgrace of the whole enterprise.

Horatio: Look, my lord, it comes!   45
Hamlet: Angels and ministers of grace defend us!
    Be thou a spirit of health° or goblin damn'd,
    Bring with thee airs from heaven or blasts from hell,
    Be thy intents wicked or charitable,
    Thou com'st in such a questionable° shape   50
    That I will speak to thee. I'll call thee Hamlet,
    King, father, royal Dane. O, answer me!
    Let me not burst in ignorance; but tell
    Why thy canoniz'd° bones, hearsed° in death,
    Have burst their cerements;° why the sepulcher   55
    Wherein we saw thee quietly interr'd
    Hath op'd his ponderous and marble jaws
    To cast thee up again. What may this mean,
    That thou, dead corse, again in complete steel
    Revisits thus the glimpses of the moon,°   60
    Making night hideous, and we fools of nature°
    So horridly to shake our disposition
    With thoughts beyond the reaches of our souls?
    Say, why is this? Wherefore? What should we do?

                            ([Ghost] beckons [Hamlet].)   65

Horatio: It beckons you to go away with it,
    As if it some impartment° did desire
    To you alone.
Marcellus: Look with what courteous action
    It waves you to a more removed ground.   70
    But do not go with it.
Horatio: No, by no means.
Hamlet: It will not speak. Then I will follow it.
Horatio: Do not, my lord.
Hamlet: Why, what should be the fear?   75
    I do not set my life at a pin's fee,°
    And for my soul, what can it do to that,
    Being a thing immortal as itself?
    It waves me forth again. I'll follow it.
Horatio: What if it tempt you toward the flood, my lord,   80
    Or to the dreadful summit of the cliff
    That beetles o'er° his° base into the sea,
    And there assume some other horrible form

---

47 *of health:* Of spiritual good.   50 *questionable:* Inviting question or conversation.
54 *canoniz'd:* Buried according to the canons of the church.   *hearsed:* Coffined.   55 *cerements:* Grave-clothes.   60 *glimpses of the moon:* Earth by night.   61 *fools of nature:* Mere men, limited to natural knowledge.   67 *impartment:* Communication.   76 *fee:* Value.   82 *beetles o'er:* Overhangs threateningly.   *his:* Its.

Which might deprive your sovereignty of reason,°
And draw you into madness? Think of it. 85
The very place puts toys of desperation,°
Without more motive, into every brain
That looks so many fathoms to the sea
And hears it roar beneath.
Hamlet: It waves me still. 90
  Go on, I'll follow thee.
Marcellus: You shall not go, my lord.

[They try to stop him.]

Hamlet: Hold off your hands! 95
Horatio: Be rul'd, you shall not go.
Hamlet: My fate cries out,
  And makes each petty artery° in this body
  As hardy as the Nemean lion's° nerve.°
  Still am I call'd. Unhand me, gentlemen. 100
  By heaven, I'll make a ghost of him that lets° me!
  I say, away! Go on. I'll follow thee.

(Exeunt Ghost and Hamlet.)

Horatio: He waxes desperate with imagination.
Marcellus: Let's follow. 'Tis not fit thus to obey him. 105
Horatio: Have after. To what issue° will this come?
Marcellus: Something is rotten in the state of Denmark.
Horatio: Heaven will direct it.°
Marcellus: Nay, let's follow him.   *(Exeunt.)*

---

  84 *deprive . . . reason:* Take away the rule of reason over your mind.   86 *toys of desperation:*
Fancies of desperate acts, i.e., suicide.   98 *artery:* Sinew.   99 *Nemean lion:* One of the mon-
sters slain by Hercules in his twelve labors.   *nerve:* Sinew.   101 *lets:* Hinders.   106 *issue:*
Outcome.   108 *it:* The outcome.

[Scene V]°

(Enter Ghost and Hamlet.)

Hamlet: Whither wilt thou lead me? Speak. I'll go no further.
Ghost: Mark me.
Hamlet: I will.
Ghost: My hour is almost come, 5
  When I to sulph'rous and tormenting flames
  Must render up myself.
Hamlet: Alas, poor ghost!
Ghost: Pity me not, but lend thy serious hearing
  To what I shall unfold. 10

I. v. LOCATION: The battlements of the castle.

Hamlet: Speak. I am bound to hear.
Ghost: So art thou to revenge, when thou shalt hear.
Hamlet: What?
Ghost: I am thy father's spirit,
 Doom'd for a certain term to walk the night,   15
 And for the day confin'd to fast° in fires,
 Till the foul crimes° done in my days of nature
 Are burnt and purg'd away. But that° I am forbid
 To tell the secrets of my prison-house,
 I could a tale unfold whose lightest word   20
 Would harrow up thy soul, freeze thy young blood,
 Make thy two eyes, like stars, start from their spheres,°
 Thy knotted and combined locks° to part,
 And each particular hair to stand an end,°
 Like quills upon the fearful porpentine.°   25
 But this eternal blazon° must not be
 To ears of flesh and blood. List, list, O, list!
 If thou didst ever thy dear father love—
Hamlet: O God!
Ghost: Revenge his foul and most unnatural murder.   30
Hamlet: Murder?
Ghost: Murder most foul, as in the best it is,
 But this most foul, strange, and unnatural.
Hamlet: Haste me to know't, that I, with wings as swift
 As meditation or the thoughts of love,   35
 May sweep to my revenge.
Ghost: I find thee apt;
 And duller shouldst thou be than the fat weed
 That roots itself in ease on Lethe° wharf,°
 Wouldst thou not stir in this. Now, Hamlet, hear.   40
 'Tis given out that, sleeping in my orchard,
 A serpent stung me. So the whole ear of Denmark
 Is by a forged process° of my death
 Rankly abus'd.° But know, thou noble youth,
 The serpent that did sting thy father's life   45
 Now wears his crown.
Hamlet: O my prophetic soul!
 My uncle!
Ghost: Ay, that incestuous, that adulterate° beast,

16 *fast:* Do penance. 17 *crimes:* Sins. 18 *But that:* Were it not that. 22 *spheres:* Eye sockets, here compared to the orbits or transparent revolving spheres in which, according to Ptolemaic astronomy, the heavenly bodies were fixed. 23 *knotted . . . locks:* Hair neatly arranged and confined. 24 *an end:* On end. 25 *fearful porpentine:* Frightened porcupine. 26 *eternal blazon:* Revelation of the secrets of eternity. 39 *Lethe:* The river of forgetfulness in Hades. *wharf:* Bank. 43 *forged process:* Falsified account. 44 *abus'd:* Deceived. 49 *adulterate:* Adulterous.

With witchcraft of his wits, with traitorous gifts—   50
O wicked wit and gifts, that have the power
So to seduce!—won to his shameful lust
The will of my most seeming-virtuous queen.
O Hamlet, what a falling-off was there!
From me, whose love was of that dignity   55
That it went hand in hand even with the vow
I made to her in marriage, and to decline
Upon a wretch whose natural gifts were poor
To those of mine!
But virtue, as it never will be moved,   60
Though lewdness court it in a shape of heaven,°
So lust, though to a radiant angel link'd,
Will sate itself in a celestial bed,
And prey on garbage.
But, soft, methinks I scent the morning air.   65
Brief let me be. Sleeping within my orchard,
My custom always of the afternoon,
Upon my secure° hour thy uncle stole,
With juice of cursed hebona° in a vial,
And in the porches of my ears did pour   70
The leprous° distillment, whose effect
Holds such an enmity with blood of man
That swift as quicksilver it courses through
The natural gates and alleys of the body,
And with a sudden vigor it doth posset°   75
And curd, like eager° droppings into milk,
The thin and wholesome blood. So did it mine,
And a most instant tetter° bark'd° about,
Most lazar-like,° with vile and loathsome crust,
All my smooth body.   80
Thus was I, sleeping, by a brother's hand
Of life, of crown, of queen, at once dispatch'd,°
Cut off even in the blossoms of my sin,
Unhous'led,° disappointed,° unanel'd,°
No reck'ning made, but sent to my account   85
With all my imperfections on my head.
O, horrible! O, horrible, most horrible!

---

61 *shape of heaven:* Heavenly form.   68 *secure:* Confident, unsuspicious.   69 *hebona:* Poison. (The word seems to be a form of *ebony*, though it is perhaps thought to be related to *henbane*, a poison, or to *ebenus*, yew.)   71 *leprous:* Causing leprosy-like disfigurement. 75 *posset:* Coagulate, curdle.   76 *eager:* Sour, acid.   78 *tetter:* Eruption of scabs.   *bark'd:* Covered with a rough covering, like bark on a tree.   79 *lazar-like:* Leper-like.   82 *dispatch'd:* Suddenly deprived.   84 *Unhous'led:* Without having received the sacrament (of Holy Communion).   *disappointed:* Unready (spiritually) for the last journey.   *unanel'd:* Without having received extreme unction.

If thou hast nature° in thee, bear it not.
Let not the royal bed of Denmark be
A couch for luxury° and damned incest.   90
But, howsomever thou pursues this act,
Taint not thy mind, nor let thy soul contrive
Against thy mother aught. Leave her to heaven
And to those thorns that in her bosom lodge,
To prick and sting her. Fare thee well at once.   95
The glow-worm shows the matin° to be near,
And 'gins to pale his uneffectual fire.°
Adieu, adieu, adieu! Remember me.   *[Exit.]*
Hamlet: O all you host of heaven! O earth! What else?
And shall I couple° hell? O fie! Hold, hold, my heart,   100
And you, my sinews, grow not instant old,
But bear me stiffly up. Remember thee!
Ay, thou poor ghost, whiles memory holds a seat
In this distracted globe.° Remember thee!
Yea, from the table° of my memory   105
I'll wipe away all trivial fond° records,
All saws° of books, all forms,° all pressures° past
That youth and observation copied there,
And thy commandment all alone shall live
Within the book and volume of my brain,   110
Unmix'd with baser matter. Yes, by heaven!
O most pernicious woman!
O villain, villain, smiling, damned villain!
My tables—meet it is I set it down,
That one may smile, and smile, and be a villain.   115
At least I am sure it may be so in Denmark.

                                              [Writing.]

So, uncle, there you are. Now to my word;
it is "Adieu, adieu! Remember me."
I have sworn 't.   120

(Enter Horatio and Marcellus.)

Horatio: My lord, my lord!
Marcellus: Lord Hamlet!
Horatio: Heavens secure him!
Hamlet: So be it!   125
Marcellus: Illo, ho, ho, my lord!
Hamlet: Hillo, ho, ho,° boy! Come, bird, come.

---

88 *nature:* The promptings of a son.   90 *luxury:* Lechery.   96 *matin:* Morning.   97 *uneffectual fire:* Cold light.   100 *couple:* Add.   104 *globe:* Head.   105 *table:* Writing tablet.
106 *fond:* Foolish.   107 *saws:* Wise sayings.   *forms:* Images.   *pressures:* Impressions
stamped.   127 *Hillo, ho, ho:* A falconer's call to a hawk in air. Hamlet is playing upon Marcellus's
Illo, i.e., *halloo.*

Marcellus: How is 't, my noble lord?
Horatio: What news, my lord?
Hamlet: O, wonderful!   130
Horatio: Good my lord, tell it.
Hamlet: No, you will reveal it.
Horatio: Not I, my lord, by heaven.
Marcellus: Nor I, my lord.
Hamlet: How say you, then, would heart of man once think it?   135
But you'll be secret?
Horatio, Marcellus: Ay, by heaven, my lord.
Hamlet: There's never a villain dwelling in all Denmark.
But he's an arrant° knave.
Horatio: There needs no ghost, my lord, come from the grave   140
To tell us this.
Hamlet: Why, right, you are in the right.
And so, without more circumstances° at all,
I hold it fit that we shake hands and part,
You, as your business and desire shall point you—   145
For every man hath business and desire,
Such as it is—and for my own poor part,
Look you, I'll go pray.
Horatio: These are but wild and whirling words, my lord.
Hamlet: I am sorry they offend you, heartily;   150
Yes, faith, heartily.
Horatio: There's no offense, my lord.
Hamlet: Yes, by Saint Patrick,° but there is, Horatio,
And much offense too. Touching this vision here,
It is an honest° ghost, that let me tell you.   155
For your desire to know what is between us,
O'ermaster 't as you may. And now, good friends,
As you are friends, scholars, and soldiers,
Give me one poor request.
Horatio: What is 't, my lord? We will.   160
Hamlet: Never make known what you have seen tonight.
Horatio, Marcellus: My lord, we will not.
Hamlet: Nay, but swear 't.
Horatio: In faith,
My lord, not I.   165
Marcellus: Nor I, my lord, in faith.
Hamlet: Upon my sword.°   *[Holds out his sword.]*
Marcellus: We have sworn, my lord, already.

139 *arrant:* Thoroughgoing.   143 *circumstance:* Ceremony.   153 *Saint Patrick:* The
keeper of purgatory and patron saint of all blunders and confusion.   155 *honest:* I.e., a real
ghost and not an evil spirit.   167 *sword:* The hilt in the form of a cross.

Hamlet: Indeed, upon my sword, indeed.

(Ghost cries under the stage.)   170

Ghost: Swear.
Hamlet: Ha, ha, boy, say'st thou so? Art thou there, truepenny?°
Come on, you hear this fellow in the cellarage.
Consent to swear.
Horatio: Propose the oath, my Lord.   175
Hamlet: Never to speak of this that you have seen,
Swear by my sword.
Ghost [beneath]:   Swear.
Hamlet: Hic et ubique?° Then we'll shift our ground.

[He moves to another spot.]   180

Come hither, gentlemen,
And lay your hands again upon my sword.
Swear by my sword
Never to speak of this that you have heard.
Ghost [beneath]:   Swear by his sword.   185
Hamlet: Well said, old mole! Canst work i' th' earth so fast?
A worthy pioner!° Once more remove, good friends.

[Moves again.]

Horatio: O day and night, but this is wondrous strange!
Hamlet: And therefore as a stranger give it welcome.   190
There are more things in heaven and earth, Horatio,
Than are dreamt of in your philosophy.°
But come;
Here, as before, never, so help you mercy,
How strange or odd soe'er I bear myself—   195
As I perchance hereafter shall think meet
To put an antic° disposition on—
That you, at such times seeing me, never shall,
With arms encumb'red° thus, or this headshake,
Or by pronouncing of some doubtful phrase,   200
As "Well, well, we know," or "We could, an if° we would,"
Or "If we list° to speak," or "There be, an if they might,"
Or such ambiguous giving out,° to note°
That you know aught of me—this do swear,
So grace and mercy at your most need help you.   205
Ghost [beneath]:   Swear.   *[They swear.]*

172 *truepenny:* Honest old fellow.   179 *Hic et ubique:* Here and everywhere (Latin).
187 *pioner:* Pioneer, digger, miner.   192 *your philosophy:* This subject called "natural philosophy" or "science" that people talk about.   197 *antic:* Fantastic.   199 *encumb'red:* Folded
or entwined.   201 *an if:* If.   202 *list:* Were inclined.   203 *giving out:* Profession of knowledge.   *note:* Give a sign, indicate.

Hamlet: Rest, rest, perturbed spirit! So, gentlemen,
   With all my love I do commend me to you;
   And what so poor a man as Hamlet is
   May do, t' express his love and friending to you,   210
   God willing, shall not lack. Let us go in together,
   And still° your fingers on your lips, I pray.
   The time is out of joint. O cursed spite,
   That ever I was born to set it right!

                    [They wait for him to leave first.]   215
   Nay, come, let's go together.   *(Exeunt.)*

212 *still:* Always.

[ACT II

Scene I]°

(Enter old Polonius, with his man [Reynaldo].)

Polonius: Give him this money and these notes, Reynaldo.
Reynaldo: I will, my lord.
Polonius: You shall do marvel's° wisely, good Reynaldo,
   Before you visit him, to make inquire   5
   Of his behavior.
Reynaldo: My lord, I did intend it.
Polonius: Marry, well said, very well said. Look you, sir,
   Inquire me first what Danskers° are in Paris,
   And how, and who, what means,° and where they keep,°   10
   What company, at what expense; and finding
   By this encompassment° and drift° of question
   That they do know my son, come you more nearer
   Than your particular demands will touch it.°
   Take° you, as 'twere, some distant knowledge of him,   15
   As thus, "I know his father and his friends,
   And in part him." Do you mark this, Reynaldo?
Reynaldo: Ay, very well, my lord.
Polonius: "And in part him, but," you may say, "not well.
   But, if 't be he I mean, he's very wild,   20
   Addicted so and so," and there put on° him
   What forgeries° you please—marry, none so rank
   As may dishonor, him take heed of that,

II. i. LOCATION: Polonius's chambers.   4 *marvel's:* Marvelous(ly).   9 *Danskers:* Danes.
10 *what means:* What wealth (they have).   *keep:* Dwell.   12 *encompassment:* Roundabout
talking.   *drift:* Gradual approach or course.   13–14 *come . . . it:* You will find out more this
way than by asking pointed questions (*particular demands*).   15 *Take:* Assume, pretend.
21 *put on:* Impute to.   22 *forgeries:* Invented tales.

But, sir, such wanton,° wild, and usual slips,
As are companions noted and most known   25
  To youth and liberty.
Reynaldo: As gaming, my lord.
Polonius: Ay, or drinking, fencing, swearing,
  Quarreling, drabbing°—you may go so far.
Reynaldo: My lord, that would dishonor him.   30
Polonius: Faith, no, as you may season° it in the charge.
  You must not put another scandal on him
  That he is open to incontinency;°
  That's not my meaning. But breathe his faults so quaintly°
  That they may seem the taints of liberty,°   35
  The flash and outbreak of a fiery mind,
  A savageness in unreclaimed° blood,
  Of general assault.°
Reynaldo: But, my good lord—
Polonius: Wherefore should you do this?   40
Reynaldo: Ay, my lord,
  I would know that.
Polonius: Marry, sir, here's my drift,
  And, I believe, it is a fetch of wit.°
  You laying these slight sullies on my son,   45
  As 'twere a thing a little soil'd i' th' working,°
  Mark you,
  Your party in converse,° him you would sound,°
  Having ever° seen in the prenominate crimes°
  The youth you breathe° of guilty, be assur'd   50
  He closes with you in this consequence:°
  "Good sir," or so, or "friend," or "gentleman,"
  According to the phrase or the addition°
  Of man and country.
Reynaldo: Very good, my lord.   55
Polonius: And then, sir, does 'a this—'a does—what was I about to say?
  By the mass, I was about to say something.
  Where did I leave?
Reynaldo: At "closes in the consequence."
Polonius: At "closes in the consequence," ay, marry.   60
  He closes thus: "I know the gentleman;
  I saw him yesterday, or th' other day,

24 *wanton:* Sportive, unrestrained.   29 *drabbing:* Whoring.   31 *season:* Temper, soften.
33 *incontinency:* Habitual loose behavior.   34 *quaintly:* Delicately, ingeniously.   35 *taints
of liberty:* Faults resulting from freedom.   37 *unreclaimed:* Untamed.   38 *general assault:*
Tendency that assails all unrestrained youth.   44 *fetch of wit:* Clever trick.   46 *soil'd i' th'
working:* Shopworn.   48 *converse:* Conversation.   *sound:* Sound out.   49 *Having ever:* If
he has ever.   *prenominate crimes:* Before-mentioned offenses.   50 *breathe:* Speak.
51 *closes . . . consequence:* Follows your lead in some fashion as follows.   53 *addition:* Title.

Or then, or then, with such, or such, and, as you say,
There was 'a gaming, there o'ertook in 's rouse,°
There falling out° at tennis," or perchance,   65
"I saw him enter such a house of sale,"
Videlicet,° a brothel, or so forth. See you now,
Your bait of falsehood takes this carp° of truth;
And thus do we of wisdom and of reach,°
With windlasses° and with assays of bias,°   70
By indirections find directions° out.
So by my former lecture and advice
Shall you my son. You have me, have you not?
Reynaldo: My lord, I have.
Polonius: God buy ye; fare ye well.   75
Reynaldo: Good my lord.
Polonius: Observe his inclination in yourself.°
Reynaldo: I shall, my lord.
Polonius: And let him ply° his music.
Reynaldo: Well, my lord.   80
Polonius: Farewell.   *(Exit Reynaldo.)*

                        (Enter Ophelia.)

        How now, Ophelia, what's the matter?
Ophelia: O, my lord, my lord, I have been so affrighted!
Polonius: With what, i' th' name of God?   85
Ophelia: My lord, as I was sewing in my closet,°
Lord Hamlet, with his doublet° all unbrac'd,°
No hat upon his head, his stockings fouled,
Ungart'red, and down-gyved to his ankle,°
Pale as his shirt, his knees knocking each other,   90
And with a look so piteous in purport
As if he had been loosed out of hell
To speak of horrors—he comes before me.
Polonius: Mad for thy love?
Ophelia: My lord, I do not know,   95
But truly I do fear it.
Polonius: What said he?
Ophelia: He took me by the wrist and held me hard.
Then goes he to the length of all his arm,

---

64 *o'ertook in's rouse:* Overcome by drink.   65 *falling out:* Quarreling.   67 *Videlicet:* Namely.   68 *carp:* A fish.   69 *reach:* Capacity, ability.   70 *windlasses:* Circuitous paths (literally, circuits made to head off the game in hunting).   *assays of bias:* Attempts through indirection (like the curving path of the bowling ball which is biased or weighted to one side). 71 *directions:* The way things really are.   77 *in yourself:* In your own person (as well as by asking questions).   79 *let him ply:* See that he continues to study.   86 *closet:* Private chamber. 87 *doublet:* Close-fitting jacket.   *unbrac'd:* Unfastened.   89 *down-gyved to his ankle:* Fallen to the ankles (like gyves or fetters).

And, with his other hand thus o'er his brow,   100
He falls to such perusal of my face
As 'a would draw it. Long stay'd he so.
At last, a little shaking of mine arm
And thrice his head thus waving up and down,
He rais'd a sigh so piteous and profound   105
As it did seem to shatter all his bulk°
And end his being. That done, he lets me go,
And, with his head over his shoulder turn'd,
He seem'd to find his way without his eyes,
For out o' doors he went without their helps,   110
And, to the last, bended their light on me.
Polonius: Come, go with me. I will go seek the King.
This is the very ecstasy° of love,
Whose violent property° fordoes° itself
And leads the will to desperate undertakings   115
As oft as any passion under heaven
That does afflict our natures. I am sorry.
What, have you given him any hard words of late?
Ophelia: No, my good lord, but, as you did command,
I did repel his letters and denied   120
His access to me.
Polonius: That hath made him mad.
I am sorry that with better heed and judgment
I had not quoted° him. I fear'd he did but trifle
And meant to wrack thee; but, beshrew my jealousy!°   125
By heaven, it is as proper to our age°
To cast beyond° ourselves in our opinions
As it is common for the younger sort
To lack discretion. Come, go we to the King.
This must be known, which, being kept close,° might move   130
More grief to hide than hate to utter love.°
Come.   *(Exeunt.)*

106 *bulk:* Body.   113 *ecstasy:* Madness.   114 *property:* Nature.   *fordoes:* Destroys.
124 *quoted:* Observed.   125 *beshrew my jealousy:* A plague upon my suspicious nature.
126 *proper . . . age:* Characteristic of us (old) men.   127 *cast beyond:* Overshoot, miscalculate.
130 *close:* Secret.   130–131 *might . . . move:* Might cause more grief (to others) by hiding the
knowledge of Hamlet's strange behavior to Ophelia than hatred by telling it.

[Scene II]°

*(Flourish. Enter King and Queen, Rosencrantz, and Guildenstern
[with others].)*

King: Welcome, dear Rosencrantz and Guildenstern.
Moreover that° we much did long to see you,

I. II. LOCATION: The castle.   4 *Moreover that:* Besides the fact that.

The need we have to use you did provoke   5
Our hasty sending. Something have you heard
Of Hamlet's transformation—so call it,
Sith° nor th' exterior nor° the inward man
Resembles that° it was. What it should be,
More than his father's death, that thus hath put him   10
So much from th' understanding of himself,
I cannot dream of. I entreat you both
That, being of so young days° brought up with him,
And sith so neighbor'd to his youth and havior,
That you vouchsafe your rest° here in our court   15
Some little time, so by your companies
To draw him on to pleasures, and to gather
So much as from occasion you may glean,
Whether aught to us unknown afflicts him thus,
That, open'd,° lies within our remedy.   20
Queen: Good gentlemen, he hath much talk'd of you,
And sure I am two men there is not living
To whom he more adheres. If it will please you
To show us so much gentry° and good will
As to expend your time with us awhile   25
For the supply and profit° of our hope,
Your visitation shall receive such thanks
As fits a king's remembrance.
Rosencrantz: Both your Majesties
Might, by the sovereign power you have of us,   30
Put your dread pleasures more into command
Than to entreaty.
Guildenstern: But we both obey,
And here give up ourselves in the full bent°
To lay our service freely at your feet,   35
To be commanded.
King: Thanks, Rosencrantz and gentle Guildenstern.
Queen: Thanks, Guildenstern and gentle Rosencrantz.
And I beseech you instantly to visit
My too much changed son. Go, some of you,   40
And bring these gentlemen where Hamlet is.
Guildenstern: Heavens make our presence and our practices
Pleasant and helpful to him!
Queen: Ay, amen!

---

8 *Sith:* Since.   *nor . . . nor:* Neither . . . nor.   9 *that:* What.   13 *of . . . days:* From such early
youth.   15 *vouchsafe your rest:* Please to stay.   20 *open'd:* Revealed.   24 *gentry:* Courtesy.
26 *supply and profit:* Aid and successful outcome.   34 *in . . . bent:* To the utmost degree of
our capacity.

    (Exeunt Rosencrantz and Guildenstern [with some Attendants].)   45

    (Enter Polonius.)

Polonius: Th' ambassadors from Norway, my good lord,
    Are joyfully return'd.
King: Thou still° hast been the father of good news.
Polonius: Have I, my lord? I assure my good liege   50
    I hold my duty, as I hold my soul,
    Both to my God and to my gracious king;
    And I do think, or else this brain of mine
    Hunts not the trail of policy so sure
    As it hath us'd to do, that I have found   55
    The very cause of Hamlet's lunacy.
King: O, speak of that! That do I long to hear.
Polonius: Give first admittance to th' ambassadors.
    My news shall be the fruit° to that great feast.
King: Thyself do grace to them, and bring them in.   60

                              (Exit Polonius.)

    He tells me, my dear Gertrude, he hath found
    The head and source of all your son's distemper.
Queen: I doubt° it is no other but the main,°
    His father's death, and our o'erhasty marriage.   65

    (Enter Ambassadors [Voltimand and Cornelius, with Polonius].)

King: Well, we shall sift him.—Welcome, my good friends!
    Say, Voltimand, what from our brother Norway?
Voltimand: Most fair return of greetings and desires.
    Upon our first,° he sent out to suppress   70
    His nephew's levies, which to him appear'd
    To be a preparation 'gainst the Polack,
    But, better look'd into, he truly found
    It was against your Highness. Whereat griev'd
    That so his sickness, age, and impotence   75
    Was falsely borne in hand,° sends out arrests
    On Fortinbras, which he, in brief, obeys,
    Receives rebuke from Norway, and in fine°
    Makes vow before his uncle never more
    To give th' assay° of arms against your Majesty.   80
    Whereon old Norway, overcome with joy,
    Gives him three score thousand crowns in annual fee,
    And his commission to employ those soldiers,
    So levied as before, against the Polack,

---

49 *still:* Always.   59 *fruit:* Dessert.   64 *doubt:* Fear, suspect.   *main:* Chief point, principal concern.   70 *Upon our first:* At our first words on the business.   76 *borne in hand:* Deluded, taken advantage of.   78 *in fine:* In the end.   80 *assay:* Trial.

With an entreaty, herein further shown,   85

                          [Giving a paper.]

That it might please you to give quiet pass
Through your dominions for this enterprise,
On such regards of safety and allowance°
As therein are set down.   90
King: It likes° us well;
And at our more consider'd° time we'll read,
Answer, and think upon this business.
Meantime we thank you for your well-took labor.
Go to your rest; at night we'll feast together.   95
Most welcome home!   *(Exeunt Ambassadors.)*
Polonius: This business is well ended.
My liege, and madam, to expostulate°
What majesty should be, what duty is,
Why day is day, night night, and time is time,   100
Were nothing but to waste night, day, and time.
Therefore, since brevity is the soul of wit,°
And tediousness the limbs and outward flourishes,
I will be brief. Your noble son is mad.
Mad call I it, for, to define true madness,   105
What is 't but to be nothing else but mad?
But let that go.
Queen: More matter, with less art.
Polonius: Madam, I swear I use no art at all.
That he is mad, 'tis true; 'tis true 'tis pity,   110
And pity 'tis 'tis true—a foolish figure,°
But farewell it, for I will use no art.
Mad let us grant him, then, and now remains
That we find out the cause of this effect,
Or rather say, the cause of this defect,   115
For this effect defective comes by cause.°
Thus it remains, and the remainder thus.
Perpend.°
I have a daughter—have while she is mine—
Who, in her duty and obedience, mark,   120
Hath given me this. Now gather, and surmise.
[*Reads the letter.*] "To the celestial and my soul's idol,
The most beautified Ophelia"—
That's an ill phrase, a vile phrase; "beautified" is a vile

---

89 *On . . . allowance:* With such pledges of safety and provisos.   91 *likes:* Pleases.   92 *consider'd:* Suitable for deliberation.   98 *expostulate:* Expound.   102 *wit:* Sound sense or judgment.   111 *figure:* Figure of speech.   116 *For . . . cause:* I.e., for this defective behavior, this madness has a cause.   118 *Perpend:* Consider.

Phrase. But you shall hear. Thus: *[Reads.]* 125
"In her excellent white bosom, these, etc."
Queen: Came this from Hamlet to her?
Polonius: Good madam, stay awhile; I will be faithful.

                                      [Reads.]

"Doubt° thou the stars are fire, 130
    Doubt that the sun doth move,
Doubt truth to be a liar,
    But never doubt I love.
O dear Ophelia, I am ill at these numbers.° I have
not art to reckon° my groans. But that I love thee 135
best, O most best, believe it. Adieu.
    Thine evermore, most dear lady, whilst this machine° is to him,
      Hamlet."
This in obedience hath my daughter shown me,
And, more above,° hath his solicitings, 140
As they fell out° by time, by means, and place,
All given to mine ear.
King: But how hath she
Receiv'd his love?
Polonius: What do you think of me? 145
King: As of a man faithful and honorable.
Polonius: I would fain prove so. But what might you think,
When I had seen this hot love on the wing—
As I perceiv'd it, I must tell you that,
Before my daughter told me—what might you, 150
Or my dear Majesty your Queen here, think,
If I had play'd the desk or table-book,°
Or given my heart a winking,° mute and dumb,
Or look'd upon this love with idle sight?°
What might you think? No, I went round° to work, 155
And my young mistress thus I did bespeak:°
"Lord Hamlet is a prince, out of thy star;°
This must not be." And then I prescripts gave her,
That she should lock herself from his resort,
Admit no messengers, receive no tokens. 160
Which done, she took the fruits of my advice;
And he, repelled—a short tale to make—
Fell into a sadness, then into a fast,

---

130 *Doubt:* Suspect, question.   134 *ill ... numbers:* Unskilled at writing verses.
135 *reckon:* (1) Count, (2) number metrically, scan.   138 *machine:* Body.   140 *more above:*
Moreover.   141 *fell out:* Occurred.   152 *play'd ... table-book:* Remained shut up, concealing the information.   153 *winking:* Closing of the eyes.   154 *with idle sight:* Complacently
or incomprehendingly.   155 *round:* Roundly, plainly.   156 *bespeak:* Address.   157 *out of
thy star:* Above your sphere, position.

Thence to a watch,° thence into a weakness,
Thence to a lightness,° and, by this declension,°   165
Into the madness wherein now he raves,
And all we mourn for.
King: Do you think this?
Queen: It may be, very like.
Polonius: Hath there been such a time—I would fain know that—   170
That I have positively said "'Tis so,"
When it prov'd otherwise?
King: Not that I know.
Polonius [pointing to his head and shoulder]:   Take this from this, if this
be otherwise.   175
If circumstances lead me, I will find
Where truth is hid, though it were hid indeed
Within the center.°
King: How may we try it further?
Polonius: You know, sometimes he walks four hours together   180
Here in the lobby.
Queen: So he does indeed.
Polonius: At such a time I'll loose my daughter to him.
Be you and I behind an arras° then.
Mark the encounter. If he love her not   185
And be not from his reason fall'n thereon,°
Let me be no assistant for a state,
But keep a farm and carters.
King: We will try it.

(*Enter Hamlet [reading on a book].*)   190

Queen: But look where sadly the poor wretch comes reading.
Polonius: Away, I do beseech you both, away.
I'll board° him presently.

(*Exeunt King and Queen [with Attendants].*)

                          O, give me leave.   195
How does my good Lord Hamlet?
Hamlet: Well, God-a-mercy.°
Polonius: Do you know me, my lord?
Hamlet: Excellent well. You are a fishmonger.°
Polonius: Not I, my Lord.   200
Hamlet: Then I would you were so honest a man.
Polonius: Honest, my lord?

164 *watch:* State of sleeplessness.   165 *lightness:* Lightheadedness.   *declension:* Decline, de-
terioration.   178 *center:* Middle point of the earth (which is also the center of the Ptolemaic
universe).   184 *arras:* Hanging, tapestry.   186 *thereon:* On that account.   193 *board:*
Accost.   197 *God-a-mercy:* Thank you.   199 *fishmonger:* Fish merchant (with connotation
of *bawd, procurer?*).

Hamlet: Ay, sir. To be honest, as this world goes, is to be one man pick'd out of ten thousand.

Polonius: That's very true, my lord.   205

Hamlet: For if the sun breed maggots in a dead dog, being a good kissing carrion°—Have you a daughter?

Polonius: I have, my lord.

Hamlet: Let her not walk i' th' sun.° Conception° is a blessing, but as your daughter may conceive, friend, look to 't.   210

Polonius [aside]: How say you by that? Still harping on my daughter. Yet he knew me not at first; 'a said I was a fishmonger. 'A is far gone. And truly in my youth I suff'red much extremity for love, very near this. I'll speak to him again.—What do you read, my lord?

Hamlet: Words, words, words.   215

Polonius: What is the matter,° my lord?

Hamlet: Between who?

Polonius: I mean, the matter that you read, my lord.

Hamlet: Slanders, sir; for the satirical rogue says here that old men have gray beards, that their faces are wrinkled, their eyes purging°   220
thick amber and plum-tree gum, and that they have a plentiful lack of wit, together with most weak hams. All which, sir, though I most powerfully and potently believe, yet I hold it not honesty° to have it thus set down, for you yourself, sir, shall grow old as I am, if like a crab you could go backward.   225

Polonius [aside]: Though this be madness, yet there is method in 't.— Will you walk out of the air, my lord?

Hamlet: Into my grave.

Polonius: Indeed, that's out of the air. [*Aside.*] How pregnant° sometimes his replies are! A happiness° that often madness hits on,   230
which reason and sanity could not so prosperously° be deliver'd of. I will leave him, [and suddenly contrive the means of meeting between him] and my daughter.—My honorable lord, I will most humbly take my leave of you.

Hamlet: You cannot, sir, take from me any thing that I will more   235
willingly part withal—except my life, except my life, except my life.

(*Enter Guildenstern and Rosencrantz.*)

Polonius: Fare you well, my lord.

Hamlet: These tedious old fools!°

Polonius: You go to seek the Lord Hamlet; there he is.   240

206–07 *good kissing carrion:* A good piece of flesh for kissing, or for the sun to kiss.   209 *i'*
th' sun: With additional implication of the sunshine of princely favors. *Conception:* (1)
Understanding, (2) Pregnancy.   216 *matter:* Substance (but Hamlet plays on the sense of *ba-sis for a dispute*).   220 *purging:* Discharging.   223 *honesty:* Decency.   229 *pregnant:* Full
of meaning.   *happiness:* Felicity of expression.   231 *prosperously:* Successfully.   239 *old*
fools: I.e., old men like Polonius.

Rosencrantz [to Polonius]:   God save you, sir!

[Exit Polonius.]

Guildenstern: My honor'd lord!

Rosencrantz: My most dear lord!

Hamlet: My excellent good friends! How dost thou, Guildenstern?   245
Ah, Rosencrantz! Good lads, how do you both?

Rosencrantz: As the indifferent° children of the earth.

Guildenstern: Happy in that we are not over-happy. On Fortune's cap
we are not the very button.

Hamlet: Nor the soles of her shoe?   250

Rosencrantz: Neither, my lord.

Hamlet: Then you live about her waist, or in the middle of her favors?

Guildenstern: Faith, her privates° we.

Hamlet: In the secret parts of Fortune? O, most true; she is a strumpet.°
What news?   255

Rosencrantz: None, my lord, but the world's grown honest.

Hamlet: Then is doomsday near. But your news is not true. [Let me
question more in particular. What have you, my good friends, de-
serv'd at the hands of Fortune that she sends you to prison hither?

Guildenstern: Prison, my lord?   260

Hamlet: Denmark's a prison.

Rosencrantz: Then is the world one.

Hamlet: A goodly one, in which there are many confines,° wards,°
and dungeons, Denmark being one o' th' worst.

Rosencrantz: We think not so, my lord.   265

Hamlet: Why then 'tis none to you, for there is nothing either good
or bad but thinking makes it so. To me it is a prison.

Rosencrantz: Why then, your ambition makes it one. 'Tis too narrow
for your mind.

Hamlet: O God, I could be bounded in a nutshell and count myself   270
a king of infinite space, were it not that I have bad dreams.

Guildenstern: Which dreams indeed are ambition, for the very substance of the ambitious° is merely the shadow of a dream.

Hamlet: A dream itself is but a shadow.

Rosencrantz: Truly, and I hold ambition of so airy and light a quality   275
that it is but a shadow's shadow.

Hamlet: Then are our beggars bodies,° and our monarchs and outstretch'd° heroes the beggars' shadows. Shall we to th' court? For,
by my fay,° I cannot reason.

247 *indifferent:* Ordinary.   253 *privates:* Close acquaintances (with sexual pun on *private
parts*).   254 *strumpet:* Prostitute (a common epithet for indiscriminate Fortune; see line 478).
263 *confines:* Places of confinement.   *wards:* Cells.   272–73 *the very . . . ambitious:* That
seemingly very substantial thing which the ambitious pursue.   277 *bodies:* Solid substances
rather than shadows (since beggars are not ambitious).   278 *outstretch'd:* (1) Far-reaching in
their ambition, (2) elongated as shadows.   279 *fay:* Faith.

Rosencrantz, Guildenstern: We'll wait upon° you.   280

Hamlet: No such matter. I will not sort° you with the rest of my servants, for, to speak to you like an honest man, I am most
dreadfully attended.°] But, in the beaten way° of friendship, what
make° you at Elsinore?

Rosencrantz: To visit you, my lord, no other occasion.   285

Hamlet: Beggar that I am, I am even poor in thanks; but I thank you,
and sure, dear friends, my thanks are too dear a halfpenny.° Were
you not sent for? Is it your own inclining? Is it a free visitation?
Come, come, deal justly with me. Come, come; nay, speak.

Guildenstern: What should we say, my lord?   290

Hamlet: Why, anything, but to th' purpose. You were sent for; and
there is a kind of confession in your looks which your modesties
have not craft enough to color. I know the good King and Queen
have sent for you.

Rosencrantz: To what end, my lord?   295

Hamlet: That you must teach me. But let me conjure° you, by the
rights of our fellowship, by the consonancy of our youth,° by the
obligation of our ever-preserv'd love, and by what more dear a
better proposer° could charge° you withal, be even° and direct
with me, whether you were sent for, or no?   300

Rosencrantz [aside to Guildenstern]:   What say you?

Hamlet [aside]:   Nay then, I have an eye of° you.—If you love me,
hold not off.

Guildenstern: My lord, we were sent for.

Hamlet: I will tell you why; so shall my anticipation prevent your   305
discovery,° and your secrecy to the King and Queen molt no
feather.° I have of late—but wherefore I know not—lost all my
mirth, forgone all custom of exercises; and indeed it goes so heavily with my disposition that this goodly frame, the earth, seems to
me a sterile promontory; this most excellent canopy, the air, look   310
you, this brave° o'erhanging firmament, this majestical roof
fretted° with golden fire, why, it appeareth nothing to me but a
foul and pestilent congregation of vapors. What a piece of work is
a man! How noble in reason, how infinite in faculties, in form and
moving how express° and admirable, in action how like an angel,   315

---

280 *wait upon:* Accompany, attend.   281 *sort:* Class, associate.   283 *dreadfully attended:*
Waited upon in slovenly fashion.   *beaten way:* Familiar path.   284 *make:* Do.   287 *dear*
a halfpenny: Expensive at the price of a halfpenny, i.e., of little worth.   296 *conjure:* Adjure,
entreat.   297 *consonancy of our youth:* The fact that we are of the same age.   299 *better pro-*
poser: More skillful propounder.   *charge:* Urge.   *even:* Straight, honest.   302 *of:* On.
305–06 *prevent your discovery:* Forestall your disclosure.   306–07 *molt no feather:* Not diminish in the least.   311 *brave:* Splendid.   312 *fretted:* Adorned (with fretwork, as in a
vaulted ceiling).   315 *express:* Well-framed (?), exact (?).

in apprehension how like a god! The beauty of the world, the
paragon of anmals! And yet, to me, what is this quintessence° of
dust? Man delights not me—no, nor woman neither, though by
your smiling you seem to say so.

Rosencrantz: My lord, there was no such stuff in my thoughts.   320

Hamlet: Why did you laugh then, when I said "man delights not me"?

Rosencrantz: To think, my lord, if you delight not in man, what lenten
entertainment° the players shall receive from you. We coted° them
on the way, and hither are they coming, to offer you service.

Hamlet: He that plays the king shall be welcome; his Majesty shall have   325
tribute of me. The adventurous knight shall use his foil and target,°
the lover shall not sigh gratis, the humorous man° shall end his part
in peace, [the clown shall make those laugh whose lungs are tickle
o' th' sere°], and the lady shall say her mind freely, or the blank verse
shall halt° for 't. What players are they?   330

Rosencrantz: Even those you were wont to take such delight in, the
tragedians of the city.

Hamlet: How chances it they travel? Their residence,° both in reputation and profit, was better both ways.

Rosencrantz: I think their inhibition° comes by the means of the in-   335
novation.°

Hamlet: Do they hold the same estimation they did when I was in the
city? Are they so follow'd?

Rosencrantz: No, indeed, are they not.

Hamlet: How comes it? Do they grow rusty?   340

Rosencrantz: Nay, their endeavor keeps in the wonted° pace. But there
is, sir, an aery° of children, little eyases,° that cry out on the top of
question,° and are most tyrannically° clapp'd for 't. These are now
the fashion, and so berattle° the common stages°—so they call
them—that many wearing rapiers° are afraid of goose-quills° and   345
dare scarce come thither.

---

317 *quintessence:* The fifth essence of ancient philosophy, beyond earth, water, air, and fire, supposed to be the substance of the heavenly bodies and to be latent in all things.   323 *lenten entertainment:* Meager reception (appropriate to Lent).   *coted:* Overtook and passed beyond.
326 *foil and target:* Sword and shield.   327 *humorous man:* Eccentric character, dominated
by one trait or "humor."   328–29 *tickle o' th' sere:* Easy on the trigger, ready to laugh easily.
(*Sere* is part of a gunlock.)   330 *halt:* Limp.   333 *residence:* Remaining in one place, i.e., in
the city.   335 *inhibition:* Formal prohibition (from acting plays in the city).   336 *innovation:* I.e., the new fashion in satirical plays performed by boy actors in the "private" theaters; or
possibly a political uprising; or the strict limitations set on the theater in London in 1600.
341 *wonted:* Usual.   342 *aery:* Nest.   *eyases:* Young hawks.   342–43 *cry ... question:*
Speak shrilly, dominating the controversy (in decrying the public theaters).   *tyrannically:*
Outrageously.   344 *berattle:* Berate.   *common stages:* Public theaters.   345 *many wearing
rapiers:* Many men of fashion, who were afraid to patronize the common players for fear of being satirized by the poets who wrote for the children.   *goose-quills:* Pens of satirists.

Hamlet: What, are they children? Who maintains 'em? How are they
    escoted?° Will they pursue the quality° no longer than they can   350
    sing?° Will they not say afterwards, if they should grow themselves
    to common° players—as it is most like, if their means are no
    better—their writers do them wrong, to make them exclaim against
    their own succession?°

Rosencrantz: Faith, there has been much to do° on both sides; and   355
    the nation holds it no sin to tarre° them to controversy. There was,
    for a while, no money bid for argument° unless the poet and the
    player went to cuffs in the question.°

Hamlet: Is 't possible?

Guildenstern: O, there has been much throwing about of brains.   360

Hamlet: Do the boys carry it away?°

Rosencrantz: Ay, that they do, my lord—Hercules and his load° too.°

Hamlet: It is not very strange; for my uncle is King of Denmark, and
    those that would make mouths° at him while my father liv'd, give
    twenty, forty, fifty, a hundred ducats° apiece for his picture in   365
    little.° 'Sblood,° there is something in this more than natural, if
    philosophy could find it out.

                             (A flourish [of trumpets within].)

Guildenstern: There are the players.

Hamlet: Gentlemen, you are welcome to Elsinore. Your hands, come   370
    then. Th' appurtenance of welcome is fashion and ceremony. Let
    me comply° with you in this garb,° lest my extent° to the players,
    which, I tell you, must show fairly outwards,° should more appear
    like entertainment° than yours. You are welcome. But my uncle-
    father and aunt-mother are deceiv'd.   375

Guildenstern: In what, my dear lord?

Hamlet: I am but mad north-north-west.° When the wind is southerly
    I know a hawk from a handsaw.°

    (Enter Polonius.)

Polonius: Well be with you, gentlemen!   380

---

350 *escoted:* Maintained.   *quality:* (Acting) profession.   350–51 *no longer . . . sing:* Only until
their voices change.   352 *common:* Regular, adult.   354 *succession:* Future careers.   355 *to
do:* Ado.   356 *tarre:* Set on (as dogs).   357 *argument:* Plot for a play.   358 *went . . . question:* Came to blows in the play itself.   361 *carry it away:* Win the day.   362 *Hercules . . . load:*
Thought to be an allusion to the sign of the Globe Theatre, which was Hercules bearing the world
on his shoulder.   342–362 *How . . . load too:* The passage omitted from the early quartos, alludes
to the so-called War of the Theatres, 1599–1602, the rivalry between the children companies and
the adult actors.   364 *mouths:* Faces.   365 *ducats:* Gold coins.   365–66 *in little:* In miniature.   366 *'Sblood:* By His (God's, Christ's) blood.   372 *comply:* Observe the formalities of
courtesy.   *garb:* Manner.   *my extent:* The extent of my showing courtesy.   373 *show fairly outwards:* Look cordial to outward appearances.   374 *entertainment:* A (warm) reception.
377 *north-north-west:* Only partly, at times.   378 *hawk, handsaw:* Mattock (or *hack*) and a carpenter's cutting tool, respectively; also birds, with a play on *hernshaw* or heron.

Hamlet: Hark you, Guildenstern, and you too; at each ear a hearer.
That great baby you see there is not yet out of his swaddling-clouts.°
Rosencrantz: Happily° he is the second time come to them; for they
say an old man is twice a child.
Hamlet: I will prophesy he comes to tell me of the players; mark it.—   385
You say right, sir, o' Monday morning, 'twas then indeed.
Polonius: My lord, I have news to tell you.
Hamlet: My lord, I have news to tell you. When Roscius° was an
actor in Rome—
Polonius: The actors are come hither, my lord.   390
Hamlet: Buzz,° buzz!
Polonius: Upon my honor—
Hamlet: Then came each actor on his ass—
Polonius: The best actors in the world, either for tragedy, comedy, his-
tory,   pastoral,   pastoral-comical,   historical-pastoral,   tragical-   395
historical, tragical-comical-historical-pastoral, scene individable,°
or poem unlimited.° Seneca° cannot be too heavy, nor Plautus° too
light. For the law of writ and the liberty,° these are the only men.
Hamlet: O Jephthah, judge of Israel,° what a treasure hadst thou!
Polonius: What a treasure had he, my lord?   400
Hamlet: Why,
        "One fair daughter, and no more,
            The which he loved passing° well."
Polonius [aside]:   Still on my daughter.
Hamlet: Am I not i' th' right, old Jephthah?   405
Polonius: If you call me Jephthah, my lord, I have a daughter that I
love passing well.
Hamlet: Nay, that follows not.
Polonius: What follows, then, my lord?
Hamlet: Why,   410
        "As by lot, God wot,"°
and then, you know,
        "It came to pass, as most like° it was."
The first row° of the pious chanson° will show you more, for look
where my abridgement° comes.   415

---

382 *swaddling-clouts:* Cloths in which to wrap a newborn baby.   383 *Happily:* Haply, perhaps.   388 *Roscius:* A famous Roman actor who died in 62 B.C.   391 *Buzz:* An interjection
used to denote stale news.   396 *scene individable:* A play observing the unity of place.
397 *poem unlimited:* A play disregarding the unities of time and place.   *Seneca:* Writer of Latin
tragedies.   *Plautus:* Writer of Latin comedy.   398 *law . . . liberty:* Dramatic composition both
according to rules and without rules, i.e., "classical" and "romantic" dramas.   399 *Jephthah
. . . Israel:* Jephthah had to sacrifice his daughter; see Judges 11. Hamlet goes on to quote from
a ballad on the theme.   403 *passing:* Surpassingly.   411 *wot:* Knows.   413 *like:* Likely,
probable.   414 *row:* Stanza.   *chanson:* Ballad, song.   415 *my abridgement:* Something
that cuts short my conversation; also, a diversion.

(Enter the Players.)

You are welcome, masters; welcome, all. I am glad to see thee well.
Welcome, good friends. O, old friend! Why, thy face is valanc'd°
since I saw thee last. Com'st thou to beard° me in Denmark? What,
my young lady° and mistress? By 'r lady, your ladyship is nearer to   420
heaven than when I saw you last, by the altitude of a chopine.°
Pray God your voice, like a piece of uncurrent° gold, be not
crack'd within the ring.° Masters, you are all welcome. We'll e'en
to 't like French falconers, fly at anything we see. We'll have a
speech straight.° Come, give us a taste of your quality; come, a   425
passionate speech.

First Player: What speech, my good lord?

Hamlet: I heard thee speak me a speech once, but it was never acted,
   or, if it was, not above once, for the play, I remember, pleas'd
   not the million; 'twas caviary to the general.° But it was—as I re-   430
   ceiv'd it, and others, whose judgments in such matters cried in
   the top of° mine—an excellent play, well digested in the scenes,
   set down with as much modesty as cunning.° I remember one
   said there were no sallets° in the lines to make the matter savory,
   nor no matter in the phrase that might indict° the author of af-   435
   fectation, but call'd it an honest method, as wholesome as sweet,
   and by very much more handsome than fine.° One speech in 't
   I chiefly lov'd: 'twas Aeneas' tale to Dido, and thereabout of it
   especially when he speaks of Priam's slaughter.° If it live in your
   memory, begin at this line: let me see, let me see—   440
   "The rugged Pyrrhus,° like th' Hyrcanian beast"°—
   'Tis not so. It begins with Pyrrhus:
   "The rugged Pyrrhus, he whose sable° arms,
   Black as his purpose, did the night resemble
   When he lay couched in the ominous horse,°   445
   Hath now this dread and black complexion smear'd
   With heraldry more dismal.° Head to foot

418 *valanc'd:* Fringed (with a beard).   419 *beard:* Confront (with obvious pun).
420 *young lady:* Boy playing women's parts.   421 *chopine:* Thick-soled shoe of Italian fashion.   422 *uncurrent:* Not passable as lawful coinage.   423 *crack'd . . . ring:* Changed from
adolescent to male voice, no longer suitable for women's roles. (Coins featured rings enclosing
the sovereign's head; if the coin was cracked within this ring, it was unfit for currency.)
425 *straight:* At once.   430 *caviary to the general:* Caviar to the multitude, i.e., a choice dish
too elegant for coarse tastes.   431–32 *cried in the top of:* Spoke with greater authority than.
433 *cunning:* Skill.   434 *sallets:* Salad, i.e., spicy improprieties.   435 *indict:* Convict.
437 *fine:* Elaborately ornamented, showy.   439 *Priam's slaughter:* The slaying of the rule of
Troy, when the Greeks finally took the city.   441 *Pyrrhus:* A Greek hero in the Trojan War,
also known as Neoptolemus, son of Achilles.   *Hyrcanian beast:* I.e., the tiger. (See Virgil,
Aeneid IV. 266; compare the whole speech with Marlowe's *Dido Queen of Carthage* II. I. 214
ff.)   443 *sable:* Black (for reasons of camouflage during the episode of the Trojan horse).
445 *ominous horse:* Trojan horse, by which the Greeks gained access to Troy.   447 *dismal:* Ill-
omened.

Now is he total gules,° horridly trick'd°
With blood of fathers, mothers, daughters, sons,
Bak'd and impasted° with the parching streets,°   450
That lend a tyrannous and a damned light
To their lord's° murder. Roasted in wrath and fire,
And thus o'er-sized° with coagulate, gore,
With eyes like carbuncles, the hellish Pyrrhus
Old grandsire Priam seeks."   455
So proceed you.

Polonius: 'Fore God, my lord, well spoken, with good accent and
good discretion.

First Player: "Anon he finds him
Striking too short at Greeks. His antique sword,   460
Rebellious to his arm, lies where it falls,
Repugnant° to command. Unequal match'd,
Pyrrhus at Priam drives, in rage strikes wide,
But with the whiff and wind of his fell° sword
Th' unnerved father falls. [Then senseless Ilium,°]   465
Seeming to feel this blow, with flaming top
Stoops to his° base, and with a hideous crash
Takes prisoner Pyrrhus' ear. For, lo! His sword,
Which was declining on the milky head
Of reverend Priam, seem'd i' th' air to stick.   470
So as a painted° tyrant Pyrrhus stood,
And, like a neutral to his will and matter,°
Did nothing.
But, as we often see, against° some storm,
A silence in the heavens, the rack° stand still,   475
The bold winds speechless, and the orb below
As hush as death, anon the dreadful thunder
Doth rend the region,° so, after Pyrrhus' pause,
Aroused vengeance sets him new a-work,
And never did the Cyclops'° hammers fall   480
On Mars's armor forg'd for proof eterne°
With less remorse than Pyrrhus' bleeding sword
Now falls on Priam.
Out, out, thou strumpet Fortune! All you gods,
In general synod,° take away her power!   485

---

448 *gules:* Red (a heraldic term).   *trick'd:* Adorned, decorated.   450 *impasted:* Crusted, like a thick paste.   *with . . . streets:* By the parching heat of the streets (because of the fires everywhere).   452 *their lord's:* Priam's.   453 *o'er-sized:* Covered as with size or glue. 462 *Repugnant:* Disobedient, resistant.   464 *fell:* Cruel.   465 *senseless Ilium:* Insensate Troy.   467 *his:* Its.   471 *painted:* Painted in a picture.   472 *like . . . matter:* As though poised indecisively between his intention and its fulfillment.   474 *against:* Just before. 475 *rack:* Mass of clouds.   478 *region:* Sky.   480 *Cyclops:* Giant armor-makers in the smithy of Vulcan.   481 *proof eterne:* Eternal resistance to assault.   485 *synod:* Assembly.

Break all the spokes and fellies° from her wheel,
And bowl the round nave° down the hill of heaven,
As low as to the fiends!"

Polonius: This is too long.

Hamlet: It shall to the barber's with your beard.—   490
Prithee say on. He's for a jig° or a tale of bawdry,
Or he sleeps. Say on; come to Hecuba.°

First Player: "But who, ah woe! had seen the mobled° queen"—

Hamlet: "The mobled queen?"

Polonius: That's good. "Mobled queen" is good.   495

First Player: "Run barefoot up and down, threat'ning the flames
With bisson rheum,° a clout° upon that head
Where late the diadem stood, and for a robe,
About her lank and all o'er-teemed° loins,
A blanket, in the alarm of fear caught up—   500
Who this had seen, with tongue in venom steep'd,
'Gainst Fortune's state° would treason have pronounc'd.°
But if the gods themselves did see her then
When she saw Pyrrhus make malicious sport
In mincing with his sword her husband's limbs,   505
The instant burst of clamor that she made,
Unless things mortal move them not at all,
Would have made milch° the burning eyes of heaven,
And passion in the gods."

Polonius: Look whe'er° he has not turn'd his color and has tears in 's   510
eyes. Prithee, no more.

Hamlet: 'Tis well; I'll have thee speak out the rest of this soon. Good
my lord, will you see the players well bestow'd?° Do you hear, let
them be well us'd, for they are the abstract° and brief chronicles
of the time. After your death you were better have a bad epitaph   515
than their ill report while you live.

Polonius: My lord, I will use them according to their desert.

Hamlet: God's bodkin,° man, much better! Use every man after his
desert, and who shall scape whipping? Use them after your own
honor and dignity. The less they deserve, the more merit is in your   520
bounty. Take them in.

Polonius: Come, sirs.

Hamlet: Follow him, friends. We'll hear a play tomorrow. [*As they
start to leave, Hamlet detains the First Player.*] Dost thou hear me,
old friend? Can you play the Murder of Gonzago?   525

---

486 *fellies:* Pieces of wood forming the rim of a wheel.   487 *nave:* Hub.   491 *jig:* Comic song
and dance often given at the end of a play.   492 *Hecuba:* Wife of Priam.   493 *mobled:* Muffled.
497 *bisson rheum:* Blinding tears.   *clout:* Cloth.   499 *o'er-teemed:* Worn out with bearing children.   502 *state:* Rule, managing.   *pronounc'd:* Proclaimed.   508 *milch:* Milky, moist with
tears.   510 *whe'er:* Whether.   513 *bestow'd:* Lodged.   514 *abstract:* Summary account.
518 *God's bodkin:* By God's (Christ's) little body, *bodykin* (not to be confused with *bodkin*, dagger).

First Player: Ay, my lord.

Hamlet: We'll ha 't tomorrow night. You could, for need, study a
speech of some dozen or sixteen lines, which I would set down
and insert in 't, could you not?

First Player: Ay, my lord.   530

Hamlet: Very well, Follow that lord, and look you mock him not.—
My good friends, I'll leave you till night. You are welcome to
Elsinore.

(Exeunt Polonius and Players.)

Rosencrantz: Good my lord!   535

(Exeunt [Rosencrantz and Guildenstern].)

Hamlet: Ay, so, God buy you.—Now I am alone.
O, what a rogue and peasant slave am I!
Is it not monstrous that this player here,
But in a fiction, in a dream of passion,   540
Could force his soul so to his own conceit°
That from her working all his visage wann'd,°
Tears in his eyes, distraction in his aspect,
A broken voice, and his whole function suiting
With forms to his conceit?° And all for nothing!   545
For Hecuba!
What's Hecuba to him, or he to Hecuba,
That he should weep for her? What would he do,
Had he the motive and the cue for passion
That I have? He would drown the stage with tears   550
And cleave the general ear with horrid speech,
Make mad the guilty and appall the free,°
Confound the ignorant, and amaze indeed
The very faculties of eyes and ears. Yet I,
A dull and muddy-mettled° rascal, peak,°   555
Like John-a-dreams,° unpregnant of° my cause,
And can say nothing—no, not for a king
Upon whose property° and most dear life
A damn'd defeat was made. Am I a coward?
Who calls me villain? Breaks my pate across?   560
Plucks off my beard, and blows it in my face?
Tweaks me by the nose? Gives me the lie° i' th' throat,
As deep as to the lungs? Who does me this?
Ha, 'swounds, I should take it; for it cannot be

---

541 *conceit:* Conception.   542 *wann'd:* Grew pale.   544–45 *his whole . . . conceit:* His whole
being responded with actions to suit his thought.   552 *free:* Innocent.   555 *muddy-met-
tled:* Dull-spirited.   *peak:* Mope, pine.   556 *John-a-dreams:* Sleepy dreaming idler.   *unpregnant of:* Not quickened by.   558 *property:* The crown; perhaps also character, quality.
562 *Gives me the lie:* Calls me a liar.

But I am pigeon-liver'd,° and lack gall   565
To make oppression bitter, or ere this
I should have fatted all the region kites°
With this slave's offal. Bloody, bawdy villain!
Remorseless, treacherous, lecherous, kindless° villain!
[O, vengeance!]   570
Why, what an ass am I! This is most brave,
That I, the son of a dear father murder'd,
Prompted to my revenge by heaven and hell,
Must, like a whore, unpack my heart with words,
And fall a-cursing, like a very drab,°   575
A stallion!° Fie upon 't, foh! About,° my brains!
Hum, I have heard
That guilty creatures sitting at a play
Have by the very cunning of the scene
Been struck so to the soul that presently°   580
They have proclaim'd their malefactions;
For murder, though it have no tongue, will speak
With most miraculous organ. I'll have these players
Play something like the murder of my father
Before mine uncle. I'll observe his looks;   585
I'll tent° him to the quick. If 'a do blench,°
I know my course. The spirit that I have seen
May be the devil, and the devil hath power
T' assume a pleasing shape; yea, and perhaps
Out of my weakness and my melancholy,   590
As he is very potent with such spirits,°
Abuses° me to damn me. I'll have grounds
More relative° than this. The play's the thing
Wherein I'll catch the conscience of the King.

                                                               (*Exit.*)   595

565 *pigeon-liver'd:* The pigeon or dove was popularly supposed to be mild because it secreted
no gall.   567 *region kites:* Kites (birds of prey) of the air, from the vicinity.   569 *kindless:*
Unnatural.   575 *drab:* Prostitute.   576 *stallion:* Prostitute (male or female). (Many editors
follow the Folio reading of *scullion.*)   *About:* About it, to work.   580 *presently:* At once.
586 *tent:* Probe.   *blench:* Quail, flinch.   591 *spirits:* Humors (of melancholy).   592 *Abuses:*
Deludes.   593 *relative:* Closely related, pertinent.

[ACT III

Scene I]°

(*Enter King, Queen, Polonius, Ophelia, Rosencrantz,
Guildenstern, Lords.*)

King: And can you, by no drift of conference,°
         Get from him why he puts on this confusion,

III. I. Location: The castle.   3 *drift of conference:* Direction of conversation.

Grating so harshly all his days of quiet   5
With turbulent and dangerous lunacy?

Rosencrantz: He does confess he feels himself distracted,
But from what cause 'a will by no means speak.

Guildenstern: Nor do we find him forward° to be sounded,°
But with a crafty madness keeps aloof   10
When we would bring him on to some confession
Of his true state.

Queen: Did he receive you well?

Rosencrantz: Most like a gentleman.

Guildenstern: But with much forcing of his disposition.°   15

Rosencrantz: Niggard of question,° but of our demands
Most free in his reply.

Queen: Did you assay° him
To any pastime?

Rosencrantz: Madam, it so fell out that certain players   20
We o'er-raught° on the way. Of these we told him,
And there did seem in him a kind of joy
To hear of it. They are here about the court,
And, as I think, they have already order
This night to play before him.   25

Polonius: 'Tis most true,
And he beseech'd me to entreat your Majesties
To hear and see the matter.

King: With all my heart, and it doth much content me
To hear him so inclin'd.   30
Good gentlemen, give him a further edge,°
And drive his purpose into these delights.

Rosencrantz: We shall, my lord.

(*Exeunt Rosencrantz and Guildenstern.*)

King: Sweet Gertrude, leave us too,   35
For we have closely° sent for Hamlet hither,
That he, as 'twere by accident, may here
Affront° Ophelia.
Her father and myself, [lawful espials,°]
Will so bestow ourselves that seeing, unseen,   40
We may of their encounter frankly judge,
And gather by him, as he is behav'd,
If 't be th' affliction of his love or no
That thus he suffers for.

Queen: I shall obey you.   45
And for your part, Ophelia, I do wish

9 *forward:* Willing.   *sounded:* Tested deeply.   15 *disposition:* Inclination.   16 *question:*
Conversation.   18 *assay:* Try to win.   21 *o'er-raught:* Overtook and passed.   31 *edge:*
Incitement.   36 *closely:* Privately.   38 *Affront:* Confront, meet.   39 *espials:* Spies.

That your good beauties be the happy cause
Of Hamlet's wildness. So shall I hope your virtues
Will bring him to his wonted way again,
To both your honors.   50
Ophelia: Madam, I wish it may.

[Exit Queen.]

Polonius: Ophelia, walk you here.—Gracious,° so please you,
We will bestow ourselves. [*To Ophelia.*] Read on this book,

[Gives her a book.]   55

That show of such an exercise° may color°
Your loneliness. We are oft to blame in this—
'Tis too much prov'd°—that with devotion's visage
And pious action we do sugar o'er
The devil himself.   60
King [aside]:   O, 'tis too true!
How smart a lash that speech doth give my conscience!
The harlot's cheek, beautied with plast'ring art,
Is not more ugly to° the thing° that helps it
Than is my deed to my most painted word.   65
O heavy burden!
Polonius: I hear him coming. Let's withdraw, my lord.

[King and Polonius withdraw.°]

(Enter Hamlet. [Ophelia pretends to read a book.])

Hamlet: To be, or not to be, that is the question: 70
Whether 'tis nobler in the mind to suffer
The slings and arrows of outrageous fortune,
Or to take arms against a sea of troubles,
And by opposing end them. To die, to sleep—
No more—and by a sleep to say we end   75
The heart-ache and the thousand natural shocks
That flesh is heir to. 'Tis a consummation
Devoutly to be wish'd. To die, to sleep;
To sleep, perchance to dream. Ay, there's the rub,°
For in that sleep of death what dreams may come   80
When we have shuffled° off this mortal coil,°
Must give us pause. There's the respect°

---

53 *Gracious:* Your Grace (i.e., the King).   56 *exercise:* Act of devotion. (The book she reads
is one of devotion.)   *color:* Give a plausible appearance to.   58 *too much prov'd:* Too often
shown to be true, too often practiced.   64 *to:* Compared to.   *thing:* I.e., the cosmetic.
68 *withdraw:* (The King and Polonius may retire behind an arras. The stage directions specify
that they "enter" again near the end of the scene.)   79 *rub:* Literally, an obstacle in the game
of bowls.   81 *shuffled:* Sloughed, cast.   *coil:* Turmoil.   82 *respect:* Consideration.

That makes calamity of so long life.°
For who would bear the whips and scorns of time,
Th' oppressor's wrong, the proud man's contumely,°   85
The pangs of despis'd° love, the law's delay,
The insolence of office,° and the spurns°
That patient merit of th' unworthy takes,
When he himself might his quietus° make
With a bare bodkin?° Who would fardels° bear,   90
To grunt and sweat under a weary life,
But that the dread of something after death,
The undiscover'd country from whose bourn°
No traveler returns, puzzles the will,
And makes us rather bear those ills we have   95
Than fly to others that we know not of?
Thus conscience does make cowards of us all
And thus the native hue° of resolution
Is sicklied o'er with the pale cast° of thought,
And enterprises of great pitch° and moment°   100
With this regard° their currents° turn awry,
And lose the name of action.—Soft you now,
The fair Ophelia. Nymph, in thy orisons°
Be all my sins rememb'red.
Ophelia: Good my lord,   105
How does your honor for this many a day?
Hamlet: I humbly thank you; well, well, well.
Ophelia: My lord, I have remembrances of yours,
That I have longed long to re-deliver.
I pray you, now receive them.   *[Offers tokens.]* 110
Hamlet: No, not I, I never gave you aught.
Ophelia: My honor'd lord, you know right well you did,
And with them words of so sweet breath compos'd
As made these things more rich. Their perfume lost,
Take these again, for to the noble mind   115
Rich gifts wax poor when givers prove unkind.
There, my lord.   *[Gives tokens.]*
Hamlet: Ha, ha! Are you honest?°
Ophelia: My lord?
Hamlet: Are you fair?°   120
Ophelia: What means your lordship?

83 *of. . .life:* So long-lived.   85 *contumely:* Insolent abuse.   86 *despis'd:* Rejected.   87 *office:* Officialdom.   *spurns:* Insults.   89 *quietus:* Acquittance; here, death.   90 *bodkin:* Dagger.   *fardels:* Burdens.   93 *bourn:* Boundary.   98 *native hue:* Natural color, complexion.   99 *cast:* Shade of color.   100 *pitch:* Height (as of a falcon's flight).   *moment:* Importance.   101 *regard:* Respect, consideration.   *currents:* Courses.   103 *orisons:* Prayers.   118 *honest:* (1) Truthful, (2) chaste.   120 *fair:* (1) Beautiful, (2) just, honorable.

Hamlet: That if you be honest and fair, your honesty° should admit
no discourse° to your beauty.

Ophelia: Could beauty, my lord, have better commerce° than with
honesty?   125

Hamlet: Ay, truly; for the power of beauty will sooner transform
honesty from what it is to a bawd than the force of honesty can
translate beauty into his likeness. This was sometime° a paradox,°
but now the time° gives it proof. I did love you once.

Ophelia: Indeed, my lord, you made me believe so.   130

Hamlet: You should not have believ'd me, for virtue cannot so
inoculate° our old stock but we shall relish of it.° I lov'd you not.

Ophelia: I was the more deceiv'd.

Hamlet: Get thee to a nunn'ry.° Why wouldst thou be a breeder of
sinners? I am myself indifferent honest;° but yet I could accuse me   135
of such things that it were better my mother had not borne me:
I am very proud, revengeful, ambitious, with more offenses at my
beck° than I have thoughts to put them in, imagination to give
them shape, or time to act them in. What should such fellows as
I do crawling between earth and heaven? We are arrant knaves, all;   140
believe none of us. Go thy ways to a nunn'ry. Where's your father?

Ophelia: At home, my lord.

Hamlet: Let the doors be shut upon him, that he may play the fool
nowhere but in 's own house. Farewell.

Ophelia: O, help him, you sweet heavens!   145

Hamlet: If thou dost marry, I'll give thee this plague for thy dowry:
be thou as chaste as ice, as pure as snow, thou shalt not escape
calumny. Get thee to a nunn'ry, farewell. Or, if thou wilt needs
marry, marry a fool, for wise men know well enough what
monsters° you° make of them. To a nunn'ry, go, and quickly too.   150
Farewell.

Ophelia: Heavenly powers, restore him!

Hamlet: I have heard of your paintings too, well enough. God hath
given you one face, and you make yourselves another. You jig,°
and amble, and you lisp, you nickname God's creatures, and make   155
your wantonness your ignorance.° Go to, I'll no more on 't; it hath
made me mad. I say, we will have no moe° marriage. Those that
are married already—all but one—shall live. The rest shall keep as
they are. To a nunn'ry, go.   *(Exit.)*

---

122 *your honesty:* Your chastity.   123 *discourse:* Familiar dealings.   124 *commerce:* Dealings.
128 *sometime:* Formerly.   *paradox:* A view opposite to commonly held opinion.   129 *the
time:* The present age.   132 *inoculate:* Graft, be engrafted to.   *but ... it:* That we do not
still have about us a taste of the old stock; i.e., retain our sinfulness.   134 *nunn'ry:* (1) Convent,
(2) brothel.   135 *indifferent honest:* Reasonably virtuous.   138 *beck:* Command.
150 *monsters:* An allusion to the horns of a cuckold.   *you:* You women.   154 *jig:* Dance and
sing affectedly and wantonly.   155–56 *make ... ignorance:* Excuse your affection on the
grounds of your ignorance.   157 *moe:* More.

Ophelia: O, what a noble mind is here o'erthrown!   160
    The courtier's, soldier's, scholar's, eye, tongue, sword,
    Th' expectancy and rose of the fair state,°
    The glass of fashion and the mold of form,°
    Th' observ'd of all observers,° quite, quite down!
    And I, of ladies most deject and wretched,   165
    That suck'd the honey of his music vows,
    Now see that noble and most sovereign reason,
    Like sweet bells jangled, out of time and harsh,
    That unmatch'd form and feature of blown°
    Youth blasted with ecstacy.° O, woe is me,   170
    T' have seen what I have seen, see what I see!

(Enter King and Polonius.)

King: Love? His affections do not that way tend;
    Nor what he spake, though it lack'd form a little,
    Was not like madness. There's something in his soul,   175
    O'er which his melancholy sits on brood,
    And I do doubt° the hatch and the disclose°
    Will be some danger; which for to prevent,
    I have in quick determination
    Thus set it down: he shall with speed to England,   180
    For the demand of° our neglected tribute.
    Haply the seas and countries different
    With variable° objects shall expel
    This something-settled° matter in his heart,
    Whereon his brains still beating puts him thus   185
    From fashion of himself.° What think you on 't?
Polonius: It shall do well. But yet do I believe
    The origin and commencement of his grief
    Sprung from neglected love.—How now, Ophelia?
    You need not tell us what Lord Hamlet said;   190
    We heard it all.—My lord, do as you please,
    But, if you hold it fit, after the play
    Let his queen mother all alone entreat him
    To show his grief. Let her be round° with him;
    And I'll be plac'd, so please you, in the ear of all their conference.   195
    If she find him not, to England send him,
    Or confine him where your wisdom best shall think.

---

162 *Th' expectancy . . . state:* The hope and ornament of the kingdom made fair (by him).
163 *The glass . . . form:* The mirror of fashion and the pattern of courtly behavior.   164 *ob-
serv'd . . . observers:* The center of attention and honor in the court.   169 *blown:* Booming.
170 *ecstasy:* Madness.   177 *doubt:* Fear.   *disclose:* Disclosure.   181 *For . . . of:* To demand.
183 *variable:* Various.   184 *something-settled:* Somewhat settled.   186 *From . . . himself:*
Out of his natural manner   194 *round:* Blunt.

King: It shall be so.
Madness in great ones must not unwatch'd go.

                                        (*Exeunt.*)

[Scene II]°

(*Enter Hamlet and three of the Players.*)

Hamlet: Speak the speech, I pray you, as I pronounc'd it to you,
trippingly on the tongue. But if you mouth it, as many of our
players° do, I had as lief the town-crier spoke my lines. Nor do not
saw the air too much with your hand, thus, but use all gently; for   5
in the very torrent, tempest, and, as I may say, whirlwind of your
passion, you must acquire and beget a temperance that may give
it smoothness. O, it offends me to the soul to hear a robustious°
periwig-pated° fellow tear a passion to tatters, to very rags, to split
the ears of the groundlings,° who for the most part are capable of°   10
nothing but inexplicable dumb-shows and noise. I would have
such a fellow whipp'd for o'er-doing Termagant.° It out-herods
Herod.° Pray you, avoid it.
First Player: I warrant your honor.
Hamlet: Be not too tame neither, but let your own discretion be your   15
tutor. Suit the action to the word, the word to the action, with
this special observance, that you o'erstep not the modesty of
nature. For anything so o'erdone is from° the purpose of playing,
whose end, both at the first and now, was and is, to hold, as
't were, the mirror up to nature, to show virtue her feature, scorn   20
her own image, and the very age and body of the time his° form
and pressure.° Now this overdone, or come tardy off,° though it
makes the unskillful laugh, cannot but make the judicious grieve,
the censure of which one° must in your allowance o'erweigh a
whole theater of others. O, there be players that I have seen play,   25
and heard others praise, and that highly, not to speak it profanely,
that, neither having th' accent of Christians nor the gait of
Christian, pagan, nor man, have so strutted and bellow'd that I
have thought some of nature's journeymen° had made men and
not made them well, they imitated humanity so abominably.   30

III. II. LOCATION: The castle.   3–4 *our players:* Indefinite use; i.e., *players nowadays.*   8 *robustious:* Violent, boisterous.   9 *periwig-pated:* Wearing a wig.   10 *groundlings:* Spectators who paid least and stood in the yard of the theater.   *capable of:* Susceptible of being influenced by.   12 *Termagant:* A god of the Saracens; a character in the St. Nicholas play, where one of his worshipers, leaving him in charge of goods, returns to find them stolen; whereupon he beats the god or idol, which howls vociferously.   13 *Herod:* Herod of Jewry (a character in *The Slaughter of the Innocents* and other cycle plays; the part was played with great noise and fury).   18 *from:* Contrary to.   21 *his:* Its.   22 *pressure:* Stamp, impressed character.   *come tardy off:* Inadequately done.   24 *the censure . . . one:* The judgment of even one of whom.   29 *journeymen:* Laborers not yet masters in their trade.

First Player: I hope we have reform'd that indifferently° with us, sir.
Hamlet: O, reform it altogether. And let those that play your clowns
speak no more than is set down for them; for there be of them°
that will themselves laugh, to set on some quantity of barren°
spectators to laugh too, though in the mean time some necessary   35
question of the play be then to be consider'd. That's villainous,
and shows a most pitiful ambition in the fool that uses it. Go, make
you ready.

[Exeunt Players.]

(Enter Polonius, Guildenstern, and Rosencrantz.)   40

How now, my lord? Will the King hear this piece of work?
Polonius: And the Queen too, and that presently.°
Hamlet: Bid the players make haste.

[Exit Polonius.]

Will you two help to hasten them?   45
Rosencrantz: Ay, my lord.

(Exeunt they two.)

Hamlet: What ho, Horatio!

(Enter Horatio.)

Horatio: Here, sweet lord, at your service.   50
Hamlet: Horatio, thou art e'en as just a man as e'er my conversation
cop'd withal.°
Horatio: O, my dear lord—
Hamlet: Nay, do not think I flatter;
For what advancement may I hope from thee   55
That no revenue hast but thy good spirits,
To feed and clothe thee? Why should the poor be flatter'd?
No, let the candied° tongue lick absurd pomp,
And crook the pregnant° hinges of the knee
Where thrift° may follow fawning. Dost thou hear?   60
Since my dear soul was mistress of her choice
And could of men distinguish her election,
Sh'hath seal'd thee for herself, for thou hast been
As one, in suff'ring all, that suffers nothing,
A man that Fortune's buffets and rewards   65
Hast ta'en with equal thanks; and blest are those
Whose blood° and judgment are so well commeddled°
That they are not a pipe for Fortune's finger

---

31 *indifferently:* Tolerably.   33 *of them:* Some among them.   34 *barren:* I.e., of wit.
42 *presently:* At once.   51–52 *my . . . withal:* My contact with people provided opportunity
for   encounter   with.   58 *candied:* Sugared,   flattering.   59 *pregnant:* Compliant.
60 *thrift:* Profit.   67 *blood:* Passion.   *commeddled:* Commingled.

To sound what stop° she please. Give me that man
That is not passion's slave, and I will wear him   70
In my heart's core, ay, in my heart of heart,
As I do thee.—Something too much of this.—
There is a play tonight before the King.
One scene of it comes near the circumstance
Which I have told thee of my father's death.   75
I prithee, when thou seest that act afoot,
Even with the very comment of thy soul°
Observe my uncle. If his occulted° guilt
Do not itself unkennel in one speech,
It is a damned° ghost that we have seen,   80
And my imaginations are as foul
As Vulcan's stithy.° Give him heedful note,
For I mine eyes will rivet to his face,
And after we will both our judgments join
In censure of his seeming.°   85
Horatio: Well, my lord.
If 'a steal aught the whilst this play is playing,
and scape detecting, I will pay the theft.

*([Flourish.] Enter trumpets and kettledrums, King, Queen,
Polonius, Ophelia, [Rosencrantz, Guildenstern, and other Lords,*   90
with Guards carrying torches].)

Hamlet: They are coming to the play. I must be idle. Get you a place.

[The King, Queen, and courtiers sit.]

King: How fares our cousin Hamlet?
Hamlet: Excellent, i' faith, of the chameleon's dish:° I eat the air,   95
promise-cramm'd. You cannot feed capons so.
King: I have nothing with° this answer, Hamlet. These words are not
mine.°
Hamlet: No, nor mine now. [*To Polonius.*] My lord, you played once
i' th' university, you say?   100
Polonius: That did I, my lord; and was accounted a good actor.
Hamlet: What did you enact?
Polonius: I did enact Julius Caesar. I was killed i' th' Capitol; Brutus
kill'd me.

---

69 *stop:* Hole in a wind instrument for controlling the sound.   77 *very . . . soul:* Inward and
sagacious criticism.   78 *occulted:* Hidden.   80 *damned:* In league with Satan.   82 *stithy:*
Smithy, place of stiths (anvils).   85 *censure of his seeming:* Judgment of his appearance or behavior.   95 *chameleon's dish:* Chameleons were supposed to feed on air. Hamlet deliberately
misinterprets the King's *fares* as *feeds.* By his phrase *eat the air* he also plays on the idea of feeding himself with the promise of succession, of being the *heir.*   97 *have . . . with:* Make nothing of.   97–98 *are not mine:* Do not respond to what I asked.

Hamlet: It was a brute part of him to kill so capital a calf there. Be   105
the players ready?

Rosencrantz: Ay, my lord; they stay upon your patience.

Queen: Come hither, my dear Hamlet, sit by me.

Hamlet: No, good mother, here's metal more attractive.

Polonius [to the King]:   O, ho, do you mark that?   110

Hamlet: Lady, shall I lie in your lap?

> *[Lying down at Ophelia's feet.]*

Ophelia: No, my lord.

[*Hamlet:*   I mean, my head upon your lap?

Ophelia: Ay, my lord.]   115

Hamlet: Do you think I meant country° matters?

Ophelia: I think nothing, my lord.

Hamlet: That's a fair thought to lie between maids' legs.

Ophelia: What is, my lord?

Hamlet: Nothing.   120

Ophelia: You are merry, my lord.

Hamlet: Who, I?

Ophelia: Ay, my lord.

Hamlet: O God, your only jig-maker.° What should a man do but be
merry? For look you how cheerfully my mother looks, and my   125
father died within 's° two hours.

Ophelia: Nay, 'tis twice two months, my lord.

Hamlet: So long? Nay then, let the devil wear black, for I'll have a
suit of sables.° O heavens! Die two months ago, and not
forgotten yet? Then there's hope a great man's memory may   130
outlive his life half a year. But, by 'r lady, 'a must build churches,
then, or else shall 'a suffer not thinking on,° with the hobby-horse,
whose epitaph is "For, O, for, O, the hobby-horse is forgot."°

(The trumpets sound. Dumb show follows.)

(Enter a King and a Queen [very lovingly]; the Queen embracing   135
him, and he her. [She kneels, and makes show of protestation unto
him.] He takes her up, and declines his head upon her neck. He lies
him down upon a bank of flowers. She, seeing him asleep, leaves him.
Anon comes in another man, takes off his crown, kisses it, pours
poison in the sleeper's ears, and leaves him. The Queen returns; finds   140
the King dead, makes passionate action. The Poisoner, with some

---

116 *country:* With a bawdy pun.   124 *only jig-maker:* Very best composer of jigs (song and
dance).   126 *within 's:* Within this.   129 *suit of sables:* Garments trimmed with the fur of
the sable and hence suited for a wealthy person, not a mourner (with a pun on *sable* black).
132 *suffer . . . on:* Undergo oblivion.   133 *"For . . . forgot":* Verse of a song occurring also in
Love's Labor's Lost III. I. 30. The hobby-horse was a character made up to resemble a horse, appearing in the Morris Dance and such May-game sports. This song laments the disappearance of
such customs under pressure from the Puritans.

*three or four, come in again, seem to condole with her. The dead
body is carried away. The Poisoner woos the Queen with gifts; she
seems harsh awhile, but in the end accepts love.)*

[Exeunt.]   145

Ophelia: What means this, my lord?

Hamlet: Marry, this' miching mallecho;° it means mischief.

Ophelia: Belike° this show imports the argument° of the play.

(Enter Prologue.)

Hamlet: We shall know by this fellow. The players cannot keep   150
counsel;° they'll tell all.

Ophelia: Will 'a tell us what this show meant?

Hamlet: Ay, or any show that you will show him. Be not you°
asham'd to show, he'll not shame to tell you what it means.

Ophelia: You are naught, you are naught.° I'll mark the play.   155

Prologue: For us, and for our tragedy, here stooping° to your
clemency, we beg your hearing patiently.

[Exit.]

Hamlet: Is this a prologue, or the posy of a ring?°

Ophelia: 'Tis brief, my lord.   160

Hamlet: As woman's love.

(Enter [two Players as] King and Queen.)

Player King: Full thirty times hath Phoebus' cart° gone round
Neptune's salt wash° and Tellus'° orbed ground,
And thirty dozen moons with borrowed° sheen   165
About the world have times twelve thirties been,
Since love our hearts and Hymen° did our hands
Unite commutual° in most sacred bands.

Player Queen: So many journeys may the sun and moon
Make us again count o'er ere love be done!   170
But, woe is me, you are so sick of late,
So far from cheer and from your former state,
That I distrust you. Yet, though I distrust,°
Discomfort you, my lord, it nothing° must.
For women's fear and love hold quantity;°   175
In neither aught, or in extremity.
Now, what my love is, proof° hath made you know,

---

147 *this' miching mallecho:* This is sneaking mischief.   148 *Belike:* Probably.   *argument:*
Plot.   151 *counsel:* Secret.   153 *Be not you:* If you are not.   155 *naught:* Indecent.
156 *stooping:* Bowing.   159 *posy . . . ring:* Brief motto in verse inscribed in a ring.
163 *Phoebus' cart:* The sun god's chariot.   164 *salt wash:* The sea.   *Tellus:* Goddess of the
earth, of the *orbed ground.*   165 *borrowed:* Reflected.   167 *Hymen:* God of matrimony.
168 *commutual:* Mutually.   173 *distrust:* Am anxious about.   174 *nothing:* Not at all.
175 *hold quantity:* Keep proportion with one another.   177 *proof:* Experience.

And as my love is siz'd, my fear is so.
Where love is great, the littlest doubts are fear;
Where little fears grow great, great love grows there.   180
Player King: Faith, I must leave thee, love, and shortly too;
My operant° powers their functions leave to do.°
And thou shalt live in this fair world behind,
Honor'd, belov'd; and haply one as kind
For husband shalt thou—   185
Player Queen: O, confound the rest!
Such love must needs be treason in my breast.
In second husband let me be accurst!
None wed the second but who kill'd the first.
Hamlet: Wormwood, wormwood.   190
Player Queen: The instances° that second marriage move°
Are base respects of thrift,° but none of love.
A second time I kill my husband dead,
When second husband kisses me in bed.
Player King: I do believe you think what now you speak,   195
But what we do determine oft we break.
Purpose is but the slave to memory,°
Of violent birth, but poor validity,°
Which now, like fruit unripe, sticks on the tree,
But fall unshaken when they mellow be.   200
Most necessary 'tis that we forget
To pay ourselves what to ourselves in debt.°
What to ourselves in passion we propose,
The passion ending, doth the purpose lose.
The violence of either grief or joy   205
Their own enactures° with themselves destroy.
Where joy most revels, grief doth most lament;
Grief joys, joy grieves, on slender accident.
This world is not for aye,° nor 'tis not strange
That even our loves should with our fortunes change;   210
For 'tis a question left us yet to prove,
Whether love lead fortune, or else fortune love.
The great man down, you mark his favorite flies;
The poor advanc'd makes friends of enemies.
And hitherto doth love on fortune tend;   215
For who not needs° shall never lack a friend,

---

182 *operant:* Active.   *leave to do:* Cease to perform.   191 *instances:* Motives.   *move:*
Motivate.   192 *base . . . thrift:* Ignoble considerations of material prosperity.   197 *Purpose
. . . memory:* Our good intentions are subject to forgetfulness.   198 *validity:* Strength, durability.   201–202 *Most . . . debt:* It's inevitable that in time we forget the obligations we have
imposed on ourselves.   206 *enactures:* Fulfillments.   209 *aye:* Ever.   216 *who not needs:*
He who is not in need (of wealth).

And who in want° a hollow friend doth try,°
Directly seasons him° his enemy.
But, orderly to end where I begun,
Our wills and fates do so contrary run   220
That our devices still° are overthrown;
Our thoughts are ours, their ends° none of our own.
So think thou wilt no second husband wed,
But die thy thoughts when thy first lord is dead.

Player Queen: Nor earth to me give food, nor heaven light,   225
Sport and repose lock from me day and night,
To desperation turn my trust and hope,
An anchor's cheer° in prison be my scope!°
Each opposite° that blanks° the face of joy
Meet what I would have well and it destroy!   230
Both here and hence° pursue me lasting strife,
If, once a widow, ever I be wife!

Hamlet: If she should break it now!

Player King: 'Tis deeply sworn. Sweet, leave me here awhile;
My spirits grow dull, and fain I would beguile   235
The tedious day with sleep.   *[Sleeps.]*

Player Queen: Sleep rock thy brain,
And never come mischance between us twain!

                                                                    [Exit.]

Hamlet: Madam, how like you this play?   240

Queen: The lady doth protest too much, methinks.

Hamlet: O, but she'll keep her word.

King: Have you heard the argument?° Is there no offense in 't?

Hamlet: No, no, they do but jest, poison in jest; no offense i' th'
    world.   245

King: What do you call the play?

Hamlet: "The Mouse-trap." Marry, how? Tropically.° This play is the
    image of a murder done in Vienna. Gonzago is the Duke's name;
    his wife, Baptista. You shall see anon. 'Tis a knavish piece of work,
    but what of that? Your Majesty, and we that have free° souls, it   250
    touches us not. Let the gall'd jade° winch,° our withers° are
    unwrung.°

---

217 *who in want:* He who is in need.   *try:* Test (his generosity).   218 *seasons him:* Ripens
him into.   221 *devices still:* Intentions continually.   222 *ends:* Results.   228 *anchor's
cheer:* Anchorite's or hermit's fare.   *my scope:* The extent of my happiness.   229 *opposite:*
Adverse thing.   *blanks:* Causes to blanch or grow pale.   231 *hence:* In the life hereafter.
243 *argument:* Plot.   247 *Tropically:* Figuratively. (The first quarto reading, *trapically,* suggests a pun on *trap* in *Mouse-trap.*)   250 *free:* Guiltless.   251 *gall'd jade:* Horse whose hide
is rubbed by saddle or harness.   *Winch:* Wince.   *withers:* The part between the horse's shoulder blades.   252 *unwrung:* Not rubbed sore.

(Enter Lucianus.)

This is one Lucianus, nephew to the King.

Ophelia: You are as good as a chorus,° my lord.   255

Hamlet: I could interpret between you and your love, if I could see
the puppets dallying.°

Ophelia: You are keen, my lord, you are keen.

Hamlet: It would cost you a groaning to take off mine edge.

Ophelia: Still better, and worse.°   260

Hamlet: So° you mistake° your husbands. Begin, murderer; leave thy
damnable faces, and begin. Come, the croaking raven doth
bellow for revenge.

Lucianus: Thoughts black, hands apt, drugs fit, and time agreeing,
Confederate season,° else no creature seeing,   265
Thou mixture rank, of midnight weeds collected,
With Hecate's ban° thrice blasted, thrice infected,
Thy natural magic and dire property
On wholesome life usurp immediately.

[Pours the poison into the sleeper's ears.]   270

Hamlet: 'A poisons him i' th' garden for his estate. His name's
Gonzago. The story is extant, and written in very choice Italian. You
shall see anon how the murderer gets the love of Gonzago's wife.

[Claudius raises.]

Ophelia: The King rises.   275

[*Hamlet:*   What, frighted with false fire?°]

Queen: How fares my lord?

Polonius: Give o'er the play.

King: Give me some light. Away!

Polonius: Lights, lights, lights!   280

(Exeunt all but Hamlet and Horatio.)

Hamlet: "Why, let the strucken deer go weep,
The hart ungalled° play.
For some must watch,° while some must sleep;
Thus runs the world away."°   285

---

255 *chorus:* In many Elizabethan plays the forthcoming action was explained by an actor known as the "chorus"; at a puppet show the actor who spoke the dialogue was known as an "interpreter," as indicated by the lines following.   257 *dallying:* With sexual suggestion, continued in *keen,* i.e., sexually aroused, *groaning,* i.e., moaning in pregnancy, and *edge,* i.e., sexual desire or impetuosity.   260 *Still . . . worse:* More keen-witted and less decorous.   261 *So:* Even thus (in marriage).   *mistake:* Mis-take, take erringly, falseheartedly.   265 *Confederate season:* The time and occasion conspiring (to assist the murderer).   267 *Hecate's ban:* The curse of Hecate, the goddess of witchcraft.   276 *false fire:* The blank discharge of a gun loaded with powder but not shot.   283 *ungalled:* Unafflicted.   284 *watch:* Remain awake. 282–285 *Why . . . away:* Probably from an old ballad, with allusion to the popular belief that a wounded deer retires to weep and die; cf. *As You Like It* II.i.66.

Would not this,° sir, and a forest of feathers°—
If the rest of my fortunes turn Turk with° me—
With two Provincial roses° on my raz'd° shoes, get
Me a fellowship in a cry of players?°
Horatio: Half a share.   290
Hamlet: A whole one, I.
   "For thou dost know, O Damon dear,
      This realm dismantled° was
   Of Jove himself, and now reigns here
      A very, very—pajock."°   295
Horatio: You might have rhym'd.
Hamlet: O good Horatio, I'll take the ghost's word for a thousand
   pound. Didst perceive?
Horatio: Very well, my lord.
Hamlet: Upon the talk of pois'ning?   300
Horatio: I did very well note him.
Hamlet: Ah, ha! Come, some music! Come, the recorders!° "For if
   the King like not the comedy, Why then, belike, he likes it not,
   perdy"° Come, some music!

(Enter Rosencrantz and Guildenstern.)   305

Guildenstern: Good my lord, vouchsafe me a word with you.
Hamlet: Sir, a whole history.
Guildenstern: The King, sir—
Hamlet: Ay, sir, what of him?
Guildenstern: Is in his retirement marvelous distemp'red.   310
Hamlet: With drink, sir?
Guildenstern: No, my lord, with choler.°
Hamlet: Your wisdom should show itself more richer to signify this
   to the doctor, for for me to put him to his purgation would
   perhaps plunge him into more choler.   315
Guildenstern: Good my lord, put your discourse into some frame°
   and start not so wildly from my affair.
Hamlet: I am tame, sir. Pronounce.
Guildenstern: The Queen, your mother, in most great affliction of
   spirit, hath sent me to you.   320
Hamlet: You are welcome.
Guildenstern: Nay, good my lord, this courtesy is not of the right

---

286 *this:* The play.   *feathers:* Allusion to the plumes which Elizabethan actors were fond of
wearing.   287 *turn Turk with:* Turn renegade against, go back on.   288 *provincial roses:*
Rosettes of ribbon like the roses of a part of France.   *raz'd:* With ornamental slashing.
289 *fellowship...players:* Partnership in a theatrical company.   293 *dismantled:* Stripped, di-
vested.   295 *pajock:* Peacock, a bird with a bad reputation (here substituted for the obvious
rhyme-word *ass*).   302 *recorders:* Wind instruments of the flute kind.   304 *perdy:* A corruption of the French *par dieu,* "by God."   312 *choler:* Anger. (But Hamlet takes the word
in its more basic humors sense of *bilious disorder.*)   316 *frame:* Order.

breed. If it shall please you to make me a wholesome answer, I will do your mother's commandment; if not, your pardon° and my return shall be the end of my business. 325

Hamlet: Sir, I cannot.

Rosencrantz: What, my lord?

Hamlet: Make you a wholesome answer; my wit's diseas'd. But, sir, such answer as I can make, you shall command, or rather, as you say, my mother. Therefore no more, but to the matter. My mother, 330 you say—

Rosencrantz: Then thus she says: your behavior hath struck her into amazement and admiration.°

Hamlet: O wonderful son, that can so stonish a mother! But is there no sequel at the heels of this mother's admiration? Impart. 335

Rosencrantz: She desires to speak with you in her closet,° ere you go to bed.

Hamlet: We shall obey, were she ten times our mother. Have you any further trade with us?

Rosencrantz: My lord, you once did love me. 340

Hamlet: And do still, by these pickers and stealers.°

Rosencrantz: Good my lord, what is your cause of distemper? You do surely bar the door upon your own liberty, if you deny your griefs to your friend.

Hamlet: Sir, I lack advancement. 345

Rosencrantz: How can that be, when you have the voice of the King himself for your succession in Denmark?

Hamlet: Ay, sir, but "While the grass grows"°—the proverb is something° musty.

(Enter the Players with recorders.) 350

O, the recorders! Let me see one. [*He takes a recorder.*] To withdraw° with you: why do you go about to recover the wind° of me, as if you would drive me into a toil?°

Guildenstern: O, my lord, if my duty be too bold, my love is too unmannerly.° 355

Hamlet: I do not well understand that. Will you play upon this pipe?

Guildenstern: My lord, I cannot.

Hamlet: I pray you.

Guildenstern: Believe me, I cannot.

Hamlet: I do beseech you. 360

---

324 *pardon:* Permission to depart. 333 *admiration:* Wonder. 336 *closet:* Private chamber. 341 *pickers and stealers:* Hands (so called from the catechism, "to keep my hands from picking and stealing"). 348 *"While . . . grows":* The rest of the proverb is "the silly horse starves"; Hamlet may not live long enough to succeed to the kingdom. 349 *something:* Somewhat. 352 *withdraw:* Speak privately. *recover the wind:* Get the windward side. 353 *toil:* Snare. 354–55 *if . . . unmannerly:* If I am using an unmannerly boldness, it is my love which occasions it.

Guildenstern: I know no touch of it, my lord.

Hamlet: It is as easy as lying. Govern these ventages° with your fingers and thumb, give it breath with your mouth, and it will discourse most eloquent music. Look you, these are the stops.

Guildenstern: But these cannot I command to any utt'rance of   365 harmony; I have not the skill.

Hamlet: Why, look you now, how unworthy a thing you make of me! You would play upon me, you would seem to know my stops, you would pluck out the heart of my mystery, you would sound me from my lowest note to the top of my compass,° and there is much   370 music, excellent voice, in this little organ,° yet cannot you make it speak. 'Sblood, do you think I am easier to be play'd on than a pipe? Call me what instrument you will, though you can fret° me, you cannot play upon me.

(Enter Polonius.)   375

God bless you, sir!

Polonius: My lord, the Queen would speak with you, and presently.°

Hamlet: Do you see yonder cloud that's almost in shape of a camel?

Polonius: By th' mass, and 'tis like a camel, indeed.

Hamlet: Methinks it is like a weasel.   380

Polonius: It is back'd like a weasel.

Hamlet: Or like a whale?

Polonius: Very like a whale.

Hamlet: Then I will come to my mother by and by.° [*Aside.*] They fool me° to the top of my bent.°—I will come by and by.   385

Polonius: I will say so.

                                     [*Exit.*]

Hamlet: "By and by" is easily said. Leave me, friends.

                          [*Exeunt all but Hamlet.*]

'Tis now the very witching time° of night,   390
When churchyards yawn and hell itself breathes out
Contagion to this world. Now could I drink hot blood,
And do such bitter business as the day
Would quake to look on. Soft, now to my mother.
O heart, lose not thy nature! Let not ever   395
The soul of Nero° enter this firm bosom. Let me be cruel,
not unnatural; I will speak daggers to her, but use none.
My tongue and soul in this be hypocrites:

---

362 *ventages:* Stops of the recorder.   370 *compass:* Range (of voice).   371 *organ:* Musical instrument.   373 *fret:* Irritate (with a quibble on *fret* meaning the piece of wood, gut, or metal which regulates the fingering on an instrument).   377 *presently:* At once.   384 *by and by:* Immediately.   385 *fool me:* Make me play the fool.   *top of my bent:* Limit of my ability or endurance (literally, the extent to which a bow may be bent).   390 *witching time:* Time when spells are cast and evil is abroad.   396 *Nero:* Murderer of his mother, Agrippina.

How in my words somever° she be shent,°
To give them seals° never, my soul, consent!   400

(Exit.)

399 *How . . . somever:* However much by my words.   *shent:* Rebuked.   400 *give them seals:*
Confirm them with deeds.

[Scene III]°

(Enter King, Rosencrantz, and Guildenstern.)

King: I like him not, nor stands it safe with us
   To let his madness range. Therefore prepare you.
   I your commission will forthwith dispatch,°
   And he to England shall along with you.   5
   The terms° of our estate° may not endure
   Hazard so near 's as doth hourly grow
   Out of his brows.°
Guildenstern: We will ourselves provide.
   Most holy and religious fear it is   10
   To keep those many many bodies safe
   That live and feed upon your Majesty.
Rosencrantz: The single and peculiar° life is bound
   With all the strength and armor of the mind
   To keep itself from noyance,° but much more   15
   That spirit upon whose weal depends and rests
   The lives of many. The cess° of majesty
   Dies not alone, but like a gulf° doth draw
   What's near it with it; or it is a massy wheel
   Fix'd on the summit of the highest mount,   20
   To whose huge spokes ten thousand lesser things
   Are mortis'd and adjoin'd, which, when it falls,
   Each small annexment, petty consequence,
   Attends° the boist'rous ruin. Never alone
   Did the King sigh, but with a General groan.   25
King: Arm° you, I pray you, to this speedy voyage,
   For we will fetters put about this fear,
   Which now goes too free-footed.
Rosencrantz: We will haste us.

(Exeunt Gentlemen [Rosencrantz and Guildenstern].)   30

(Enter Polonius.)

III. III. LOCATION: The castle.   4 *dispatch:* Prepare, cause to be drawn up.   6 *terms:*
Condition, circumstances.   *our estate:* My royal position.   8 *brows:* Effronteries, threatening
frowns (?), brain (?).   13 *single and peculiar:* Individual and private.   15 *noyance:* Harm.
17 *cess:* Decease.   18 *gulf:* Whirlpool.   24 *Attends:* Participates in.   26 *Arm:* Prepare.

Polonius: My lord, he's going to his mother's closet.
Behind the arras° I'll convey myself
To hear the process.° I'll warrant she'll tax him home,°
And, as you said, and wisely was it said,   35
'Tis meet that some more audience than a mother,
Since nature makes them partial, should o'erhear
The speech, of vantage.° Fare you well, my liege.
I'll call upon you ere you go to bed,
And tell you what I know. Thanks, dear my lord.   40

(Exit [Polonius].)

King: O, my offense is rank, it smells to heaven;
It hath the primal eldest curse° upon 't,
A brother's murder. Pray can I not,
Though inclination be as sharp as will.°   45
My stronger guilt defeats my strong intent,
And, like a man to double business bound,
I stand in pause where I shall first begin,
And both neglect. What if this cursed hand
Were thicker than itself with brother's blood,   50
Is there not rain enough in the sweet heavens
To wash it white as snow? Whereto serves mercy
But to confront the visage of offense?°
And what's in prayer but this twofold force,
To be forestalled° ere we come to fall,   55
Or pardon'd being down? Then I'll look up;
My fault is past. But, O, what form of prayer
Can serve my turn? "Forgive me my foul murder"?
That cannot be, since I am still possess'd
Of those effects for which I did the murder,   60
My crown, mine own ambition, and my queen.
May one be pardon'd and retain th' offense?
In the corrupted currents° of this world
Offense's gilded hand° may shove by justice,
And oft 'tis seen the wicked prize° itself   65
Buys out the law. But 'tis not so above.
There is no shuffling,° there the action lies°

---

33 *arras:* Screen of tapestry placed around the walls of household apartments. (On the Elizabethan stage, the arras was presumably over a door or discovery space in the tiring house facade.)   34 *process:* Proceedings.   *tax him home:* Reprove him severely.   38 *of vantage:* From an advantageous place.   43 *primal eldest curse:* The curse of Cain, the first murderer; he killed his brother Abel.   45 *Though . . . will:* Though my desire is as strong as my determination.   52–53 *Whereto . . . offense:* For what function does mercy serve other than to undo the effects of sin?   55 *forestalled:* Prevented (from sinning).   63 *currents:* Courses.   64 *gilded hand:* Hand offering gold as a bribe.   65 *wicked prize:* Prize won by wickedness.   67 *shuffling:* Escape by trickery.   *the action lies:* The accusation is made manifest, comes up for consideration (a legal metaphor).

In his° true nature, and we ourselves compell'd,
Even to the teeth and forehead° of our faults,
To give in evidence. What then? What rests?°   70
Try what repentance can. What can it not?
Yet what can it, when one cannot repent?
O wretched state! O bosom black as death!
O limed° soul, that, struggling to be free,
Art more engag'd!° Help, angels! Make assay.°   75
Bow, stubborn knees, and heart with strings of steel,
Be soft as sinews of the new-born babe!
All may be well.

                                    [He kneels.]

(Enter Hamlet [with sword drawn].)   80

Hamlet: Now might I do it pat,° now 'a is apraying;
And now I'll do 't. And so 'a goes to heaven;
And so am I reveng'd. That would be scann'd:°
A villain kills my father, and for that,
I, his sole son, do this same villain send   85
To heaven.
Why, this is hire and salary, not revenge.
'A took my father grossly,° full of bread,°
With all his crimes broad blown,° as flush° as May;
And how his audit° stands who knows save heaven?   90
But in our circumstance and course° of thought,
'Tis heavy with him. And am I then reveng'd,
To take him in the purging of his soul,
When he is fit and season'd for his passage?
No!   95
Up, sword, and know thou a more horrid hent.°

                             [Puts up his sword.]

When he is drunk asleep, or in his rage,
Or in th' incestuous pleasure of his bed,
At game a-swearing, or about some act   100
That has no relish of salvation in 't—
Then trip him, that his heels may kick at heaven,
And that his soul may be as damn'd and black
As hell, whereto it goes. My mother stays.

---

68 *his:* Its.   69 *teeth and forehead:* Face to face, concealing nothing.   70 *rests:* Remains.
74 *limed:* Caught as with birdlime, a sticky substance used to ensnare birds.   75 *engag'd:*
Embedded.   *assay:* Trial.   81 *pat:* Opportunely.   83 *would be scann'd:* Needs to be
looked into.   88 *grossly:* Not spiritually prepared.   *full of bread:* Enjoying his wordly pleasures. (See Ezek. 16:49.)   89 *crimes broad blown:* Sins in full bloom.   *flush:* Lusty.
90 *audit:* Account.   91 *in . . . course:* As we see it in our mortal situation.   96 *know . . .
hent:* Await to be grasped by me on a more horrid occasion.

This physic° but prolongs thy sickly days.   105

(Exit.)

King: My words fly up, my thoughts remain below.
Words without thoughts never to heaven go.

(Exit.)

105 *physic:* Purging (by prayer).

[Scene IV]°

(*Enter [Queen] Gertrude and Polonius.*)

Polonius: 'A will come straight. Look you lay° home to him.
Tell him his pranks have been too broad° to bear with,
And that your Grace hath screen'd and stood between
Much heat° and him. I'll sconce° me even here.
Pray you, be round° [with him.   5
Hamlet (within):   Mother, mother, mother!]
Queen: I'll warrant you, fear me not. Withdraw,
I hear him coming.

[Polonius hides behind the arras.]

(*Enter Hamlet.*)   10

Hamlet: Now, mother, what's the matter?
Queen: Hamlet, thou hast thy father° much offended.
Hamlet: Mother, you have my father much offended.
Queen: Come, come, you answer with an idle° tongue.
Hamlet: Go, go, you question with a wicked tongue.   15
Queen: Why, how now, Hamlet?
Hamlet: What's the matter now?
Queen: Have you forgot me?
Hamlet: No, by the rood,° not so:
You are the Queen, your husband's brother's wife,   20
And—would it were not so!—you are my mother.
Queen: Nay, then, I'll set those to you that can speak.
Hamlet: Come, come, and sit you down; you shall not budge.
You go not till I set you up a glass
Where you may see the inmost part of you.   25
Queen: What wilt thou do? Thou wilt not murder me? Help, ho!
Polonius [behind]:   What, ho! Help!
Hamlet [drawing]:   How now? A rat? Dead, for a ducat, dead!

[Makes a pass through the arras.]

III. IV. LOCATION: The Queen's private chamber.   1 *lay:* Thrust (i.e., reprove him soundly).
2 *broad:* Unrestrained.   4 *Much heat:* The King's anger.   *sconce:* Ensconce, hide.   5 *round:*
Blunt.   12 *thy father:* Your stepfather, Claudius.   14 *idle:* Foolish.   19 *rood:* Cross.

Polonius [behind]:   O, I am slain!   *[Falls and dies.]*   30
Queen: O me, what hast thou done?
Hamlet: Nay, I know not. Is it the King?
Queen: O, what a rash and bloody deed is this!
Hamlet: A bloody deed—almost as bad, good mother,
    As kill a king, and marry with his brother.   35
Queen: As kill a king!

                   [Parts the arras and discovers Polonius.]

Hamlet: Ay, lady, it was my word.
    Thou wretched, rash, intruding fool, farewell!
    I took thee for thy better. Take thy fortune.   40
    Thou find'st to be too busy is some danger.—
    Leave wringing of your hands. Peace, sit you down,
    And let me wring your heart, for so I shall,
    If it be made of penetrable stuff,
    If damnèd custom° have not braz'd° it so   45
    That it be proof° and bulwark against sense.°
Queen: What have I done, that thou dar'st wag thy tongue
    In noise so rude against me?
Hamlet: Such an art
    That blurs the grace and blush of modesty,   50
    Calls virtue hypocrite, takes off the rose
    From the fair forehead of an innocent love
    And sets a blister° there, makes marriage-vows
    As false as dicers' oaths. O, such a deed
    As from the body of contraction° plucks   55
    The very soul, and sweet religion° makes
    A rhapsody° of words. Heaven's face does glow
    O'er this solidity and compound mass
    With heated visage, as against the doom,
    Is thought-sick at the act.°   60
Queen: Ay me, what act,
    That roars so loud and thunders in the index?°
Hamlet: Look here, upon this picture, and on this, the counterfeit
    presentment° of two brothers.

                         [Shows her two likenesses.]   65

    See, what a grace was seated on this brow:

45 *damned custom:* Habitual wickedness.   *braz'd:* Brazened, hardened.   46 *proof:* Armor.
sense: Feeling.   53 *sets a blister:* Brands as a harlot.   55 *contraction:* The marriage contract.
56 *religion:* Religious vows.   57 *rhapsody:* Senseless string.   57–60 *Heaven's . . . act:*
Heaven's face flushes with anger to look down upon this solid world, this compound mass, with
hot face as though the day of doom were near, and is thought-sick at the deed (i.e., Gertrude's
marriage).   62 *index:* Table of contents, prelude, or preface.   63–64 *counterfeit present-*
ment: Portrayed representation.

Hyperion's° curls, the front° of Jove himself,
An eye like Mars, to threaten and command,
A station° like the herald Mercury
New-lighted on a heaven-kissing hill—   70
A combination and a form indeed,
Where every god did seem to set his seal,
To give the world assurance of a man.
This was your husband. Look you now, what follows:
Here is your husband, like a mildew'd ear,°   75
Blasting his wholesome brother. Have you eyes?
Could you on this fair mountain leave to feed,
And batten° on this moor?° Ha, have you eyes?
You cannot call it love, for at your age
The heyday° in the blood is tame, it's humble,   80
And waits upon the judgment, and what judgment
Would step from this to this? Sense,° sure, you have,
Else could you not have motion, but sure that sense
Is apoplex'd,° for madness would not err,
Nor sense to ecstasy was ne'er so thrall'd   85
But it reserv'd some quantity of choice
To serve in such a difference. What devil was 't
That thus hath cozen'd° you at hoodman-blind?°
Eyes without feeling, feeling without sight,
Ears without hands or eyes, smelling sans° all,   90
Or but a sickly part of one true sense
Could not so mope.°
O shame, where is thy blush? Rebellious hell,
If thou canst mutine° in a matron's bones,
To flaming youth let virtue be as wax,   95
And melt in her own fire. Proclaim no shame
When the compulsive ardor gives the charge,
Since frost itself as actively doth burn,
And reason panders will.°
Queen: O Hamlet, speak no more!   100
        Thou turn'st mine eyes into my very soul,

---

67 *Hyperion:* The sun god.   *front:* Brow.   69 *station:* Manner of standing.   75 *ear:* I.e.,
of grain.   78 *batten:* Gorge.   *moor:* Barren upland.   80 *heyday:* State of excitement.
82 *Sense:* Perception through the five senses (the functions of the middle or sensible soul).
84 *apoplex'd:* Paralyzed. (Hamlet goes on to explain that without such a paralysis of will, mere
madness would not so err, nor would the five senses so enthrall themselves to *ecstasy* or lunacy;
even such deranged states of mind would be able to make the obvious choice between Hamlet
Senior and Claudius.)   88 *cozen'd:* Cheated.   *hoodman-blind:* Blindman's buff.   90 *sans:*
Without.   92 *mope:* Be dazed, act aimlessly.   94 *mutine:* Mutiny.   96–99 *Proclaim
. . . will:* Call it no shameful business when the compelling ardor of youth delivers the attack, i.e.,
commits lechery, since the frost of advanced age burns with as active a fire of lust and reason per-
verts itself by fomenting lust rather than restraining it.

And there I see such black and grained° spots
As will not leave their tinct.°
Hamlet: Nay, but to live
In the rank sweat of an enseamed° bed,   105
Stew'd in corruption, honeying and making love
Over the nasty sty—
Queen: O, speak to me no more.
These words, like daggers, enter in my ears.
No more, sweet Hamlet!   110
Hamlet: A murderer and a villain,
A slave that is not twentieth part the tithe°
Of your precedent° lord, a vice° of kings,
A cutpurse of the empire and the rule,
That from a shelf the precious diadem stole,   115
And put it in his pocket!
Queen: No more!

   (*Enter Ghost [in his nightgown].*)

Hamlet: A king of shreds and patches°—
Save me, and hover o'er me with your wings,   120
You heavenly guards! What would your gracious figure?
Queen: Alas, he's mad!
Hamlet: Do you not come your tardy son to chide,
That, laps'd in time and passion,° lets go by
Th' important° acting of your dread command? O, say!   125
Ghost: Do not forget. This visitation
Is but to whet thy almost blunted purpose.
But, look, amazement° on thy mother sits.
O, step between her and her fighting soul!
Conceit° in weakest bodies strongest works.   130
Speak to her, Hamlet.
Hamlet: How is it with you, lady?
Queen: Alas, how is 't with you,
That you do bend your eye on vacancy,
And with th' incorporal° air do hold discourse?   135
Forth at your eyes your spirits wildly peep,
And, as the sleeping soldiers in th' alarm,
Your bedded° hair, like life in excrements,°
Start up and stand an° end. O gentle son,

---

102 *grained:* Dyed in grain, indelible.   103 *tinct:* Color.   105 *enseamed:* Laden with
grease.   112 *tithe:* Tenth part.   113 *precedent:* Former (i.e., the elder Hamlet).   *vice:*
Buffoon (a reference to the vice of the morality plays).   119 *shreds and patches:* Motley, the
traditional costume of the clown or fool.   124 *laps'd . . . passion:* Having allowed time to lapse
and passion to cool.   125 *important:* Importunate, urgent.   128 *amazement:* Distraction.
130 *Conceit:* Imagination.   135 *incorporal:* Immaterial.   138 *bedded:* Laid in smooth
layers.   *excrements:* Outgrowths.   139 *an:* On.

Upon the heat and flame of thy distemper   140
Sprinkle cool patience. Whereon do you look?
Hamlet: On him, on him! Look you how pale he glares!
His form and cause conjoin'd,° preaching to stones,
Would make them capable.°—Do not look upon me,
Lest with this piteous action you convert   145
My stern effects.° Then what I have to do
Will want true color°—tears perchance for blood.
Queen: To whom do you speak this?
Hamlet: Do you see nothing there?
Queen: Nothing at all; yet all that is I see.   150
Hamlet: Nor did you nothing hear?
Queen: No, nothing but ourselves.
Hamlet: Why, look you there, look how it steals away!
My father, in his habit° as he lived!
Look, where he goes, even now, out at the portal!   155

(Exit Ghost.)

Queen: This is the very coinage of your brain.
This bodiless creation ecstasy°
Is very cunning in.
Hamlet: Ecstasy?   160
My pulse, as yours, doth temperately keep time,
And makes as healthful music. It is not madness
That I have utter'd. Bring me to the test,
And I the matter will reword, which madness
Would gambol° from. Mother, for love of grace,   165
Lay not that flattering unction° to your soul
That not your trespass but my madness speaks.
It will but skin and film the ulcerous place,
Whiles rank corruption, mining° all within,
Infects unseen. Confess yourself to heaven,   170
Repent what's past, avoid what is to come,
And do not spread the compost° on the weeds
To make them ranker. Forgive me this my virtue;°
For in the fatness° of these pursy° times
Virtue itself of vice must pardon beg,   175
Yea, curb° and woo for leave° to do him good.
Queen: O Hamlet, thou hast cleft my heart in twain.
Hamlet: O, throw away the worser part of it,

---

143 *His...conjoin'd:* His appearance joined to his cause for speaking.   144 *capable:* Receptive.
145–46 *convert...effects:* Divert me from my stern duty.   147 *want true color:* Lack plausi-
bility so that (with a play on the normal sense of *color*) I shall shed tears instead of blood.   154
habit: Dress.   158 *ecstasy:* Madness.   165 *gambol:* Skip away.   166 *unction:* Ointment.
169 *mining:* Working under the surface.   172 *compost:* Manure.   173 *this my virtue:* My
virtuous talk in reproving you.   174 *fatness:* Grossness.   *pursy:* Short-winded, corpulent.
176 *curb:* Bow, bend the knee.   *leave:* Permission.

And live the purer with the other half.
Good night. But go not to my uncle's bed; 180
Assume a virtue, if you have it not.
That monster, custom, who all sense doth eat,°
Of habits devil,° is angel yet in this,
That to the use of actions fair and good
He likewise gives a frock or livery° 185
That aptly is put on. Refrain tonight,
And that shall lend a kind of easiness
To the next abstinence; the next more easy;
For use° almost can change the stamp of nature,
And either° . . . the devil, or throw him out 190
With wondrous potency. Once more, good night;
And when you are desirous to be bless'd,°
I'll blessing beg of you, For this same lord,

                              [Pointing to Polonius.]

I do repent; but heaven hath pleas'd it so 195
To punish me with this, and this with me,
That I must be their scourge and minister.°
I will bestow° him, and will answer well
The death I gave him. So, again, good night.
I must be cruel only to be kind. 200
Thus bad begins and worse remains behind.°
One word more, good lady.
Queen: What shall I do?
Hamlet: Not this, by no means, that I bid you do:
Let the bloat° king tempt you again to bed, 205
Pinch wanton on your cheek, call you his mouse,
And let him, for a pair of reechy° kisses,
Or paddling in your neck with his damn'd fingers,
Make you to ravel all this matter out,
That I essentially am not in madness, 210
But mad in craft. 'Twere good° you let him know,
For who that's but a queen, fair, sober, wise,
Would from a paddock,° from a bat, a gib,°
Such dear concernings° hide? Who would do so?

---

182 *who . . . eat:* Who consumes all proper or natural feeling.   183 *Of habits devil:* Devil-like in prompting evil habits.   185 *livery:* An outer appearance, a customary garb (and hence a predisposition easily assumed in time of stress).   189 *use:* Habit.   190 *And either:* A defective line usually emended by inserting the word *master* after *either,* following the fourth quarto and early editors.   192 *be bless'd:* Become blessed, i.e., repentant.   197 *their scourge and minister:* Agent of heavenly retribution. (By *scourge,* Hamlet also suggests that he himself will eventually suffer punishment in the process of fulfilling heaven's will.)   198 *bestow:* Stow, dispose of.   201 *behind:* To come.   205 *bloat:* Bloated.   207 *reechy:* Dirty, filthy.   211 *good:* Said ironically; also the following 8 lines.   213 *paddock:* Toad.   *gib:* Tomcat.   214 *dear concernings:* Important affairs.

No, in despite of sense and secrecy,   215
Unpeg the basket° on the house's top,
Let the birds fly, and, like the famous ape,°
To try conclusions,° in the basket creep
And break your own neck down.

Queen: Be thou assur'd, if words be made of breath,   220
And breath of life, I have no life to breathe
What thou hast said to me.

Hamlet: I must to England; you know that?

Queen: Alack, I had forgot. 'Tis so concluded on.

Hamlet: There's letters seal'd, and my two school-fellows,   225
Whom I will trust as I will adders fang'd,
They bear the mandate; they must sweep my way,°
And marshal me to knavery. Let it work.
For 'tis the sport to have the enginer°
Hoist with° his own petar,° and 't shall go hard   230
But I will delve one yard below their mines,°
And blow them at the moon. O, 'tis most sweet,
When in one line two crafts° directly meet.
This man shall set me packing,°
I'll lug the guts into the neighbor room.   235
Mother, good night indeed. This counselor
Is now most still, most secret, and most grave,
Who was in life a foolish prating knave.
Come, sir, to draw toward an end° with you.
Good night, mother.   240

(Exeunt [severally, Hamlet dragging in Polonius].)

216 *Unpeg the basket:* Open the cage, i.e., let out the secret.   217 *famous ape:* In a story now lost.   218 *conclusions:* Experiments (in which the ape apparently enters a cage from which birds have been released and then tries to fly out of the cage as they have done, falling to his death).   227 *sweep my way:* Go before me.   229 *enginer:* Constructor of military contrivances.   230 *Hoist with:* Blown up by.   *petar:* Petard, an explosive used to blow in a door or make a breach.   231 *mines:* Tunnels used in warfare to undermine the enemy's emplacements; Hamlet will countermine by going under their mines.   233 *crafts:* Acts of guile, plots. 234 *set me packing:* Set me to making schemes, and set me to lugging (him) and, also, send me off in a hurry.   239 *draw . . . end:* Finish up (with a pun on *draw*, pull).

[*ACT IV*

Scene I]°

(Enter King and Queen, with Rosencrantz and Guildenstern.)

King: There's matter in these sighs, these profound heaves
You must translate; 'tis fit we understand them.
Where is your son?

IV. I. LOCATION: The castle.

Queen: Bestow this place on us a little while.

[Exeunt Rosencrantz and Guildenstern.]   5

Ah, mine own lord, what have I seen tonight!
King: What, Gertrude? How does Hamlet?
Queen: Mad as the sea and wind when both contend
Which is the mightier. In his lawless fit,
Behind the arras hearing something stir,   10
Whips out his rapier, cries, "A rat, a rat!"
And, in this brainish apprehension,° kills
The unseen good old man.
King: O heavy deed!
It had been so with us, had we been there.   15
His liberty is full of threats to all—
To you yourself, to us, to everyone.
Alas, how shall this bloody deed be answer'd?
It will be laid to us, whose providence°
Should have kept short,° restrain'd, and out of haunt°   20
This mad young man. But so much was our love
We would not understand what was most fit,
But, like the owner of a foul disease,
To keep it from divulging,° let it feed
Even on the pith of life. Where is he gone?   25
Queen: To draw apart the body he hath kill'd,
O'er whom his very madness, like some ore°
Among a mineral° of metals base,
Shows itself pure: 'a weeps for what is done.
King: O Gertrude, come away!   30
The sun no sooner shall the mountains touch
But we will ship him hence; and this vile deed
We must, with all our majesty and skill,
Both countenance and excuse. Ho, Guildenstern!

(Enter Rosencrantz and Guildenstern.)   35

Friends both, go join you with some further aid.
Hamlet in madness hath Polonius slain,
And from his mother's closet hath he dragg'd him.
Go seek him out; speak fair, and bring the body
Into the chapel. I pray you, haste in this.   40

[Exeunt Rosencrantz and Guildenstern.]

Come, Gertrude, we'll call up our wisest friends
And let them know both what we mean to do

---

12 *brainish apprehension:* Headstrong conception.   19 *providence:* Foresight.   20 *short:* On
a short tether.   *out of haunt:* Secluded.   24 *divulging:* Becoming evident.   27 *ore:* Vein of
gold.   28 *mineral:* Mine.

And what's untimely done°. . . . .
Whose whisper o'er the world's diameter,°   45
As level° as the cannon to his blank,°
Transports his pois'ned shot, may miss our name,
And hit the woundless° air. O, come away!
My soul is full of discord and dismay.   *(Exeunt.)*

44 *And . . . done:* A defective line; conjectures as to the missing words include *so, haply, slander* (Capell and others); *for, haply, slander* (Theobald and others).   45 *diameter:* Extent from side to side.   46 *As level:* With as direct aim.   *blank:* White spot in the center of a target. 48 *woundless:* Invulnerable.

[Scene II]°

(Enter Hamlet.)

Hamlet: Safely stow'd.
[Rosencrantz, Guildenstern (within): Hamlet! Lord Hamlet!]
Hamlet: But soft, what noise? Who calls on Hamlet? O, here they come.

(Enter Rosencrantz and Guildenstern.)   5

Rosencrantz: What have you done, my lord, with the dead body?
Hamlet: Compounded it with dust, whereto 'tis kin.
Rosencrantz: Tell us where 'tis, that we may take it thence and bear it to the chapel.
Hamlet: Do not believe it.   10
Rosencrantz: Believe what?
Hamlet: That I can keep your counsel and not mine own. Besides, to be demanded of° a sponge, what replication° should be made by the son of a king?
Rosencrantz: Take you me for a sponge, my lord?   15
Hamlet: Ay, sir, that soaks up the King's countenance,° his rewards, his authorities. But such officers do the King best service in the end. He keeps them, like an ape an apple, in the corner of his jaw, first mouth'd, to be last swallow'd. When he needs what you have glean'd, it is but squeezing you, and, sponge, you shall   20
be dry again.
Rosencrantz: I understand you not, my lord.
Hamlet: I am glad of it. A knavish speech sleeps in° a foolish ear.
Rosencrantz: My lord, you must tell us where the body is, and go with us to the King.   25
Hamlet: The body is with the King, but the King is not with the body.° The King is a thing—

IV. II. LOCATION: The castle.   13 *demanded of:* Questioned by.   *replication:* Reply. 16 *countenance:* Favor.   23 *sleeps in:* Has no meaning to.   26–27 *The . . . body:* Perhaps alludes to the legal commonplace of "the king's two bodies," which drew a distinction between the sacred office of kingship and the particular mortal who possessed it at any given time.

Guildenstern: A thing, my lord?

Hamlet: Of nothing.° Bring me to him. [Hide fox, and all after.°]

                                                (Exeunt.)   30

29 *Of nothing:* Of no account.   *Hide . . . after:* An old signal cry in the game of hide-and-seek, suggesting that Hamlet now runs away from them.

[Scene III]°

(Enter King, and two or three.)

King: I have sent to seek him, and to find the body.
How dangerous is it that this man goes loose!
Yet must not we put the strong law on him.
He's lov'd of the distracted° multitude,
Who like not in their judgment, but their eyes,   5
And where 'tis so, th' offender's scourge° is weigh'd,°
But never the offense. To bear° all smooth and even,
This sudden sending him away must seem
Deliberate pause.° Diseases desperate grown
By desperate appliance are reliev'd,   10
Or not at all.

(Enter Rosencrantz, [Guildenstern,] and all the rest.)

                    How now? What hath befall'n?

Rosencrantz: Where the dead body is bestow'd, my lord,
We cannot get from him.   15

King: But where is he?

Rosencrantz: Without, my lord; guarded, to know your pleasure.

King: Bring him before us.

Rosencrantz: Ho! Bring in the lord.

(They enter [with Hamlet].)   20

King: Now, Hamlet, where's Polonius?

Hamlet: At supper.

King: At supper? Where?

Hamlet: Not where he eats, but where 'a is eaten. A certain
convocation of politic worms° are e'en at him. Your worm is your   25
only emperor for diet.° We fat all creatures else to fat us, and we
fat ourselves for maggots. Your fat king and your lean beggar is
but variable service,° two dishes, but to one table—that's the end.

King: Alas, alas!

IV. III. LOCATION: The castle.   4 *distracted:* Fickle, unstable.   6 *scourge:* Punishment. *weigh'd:* Taken into consideration.   7 *bear:* Manage   9 *Deliberate pause:* Carefully considered action.   25 *politic worms:* Crafty worms (suited to a master spy like Polonius).   26 *diet:* Food, eating (with perhaps a punning reference to the Diet of Worms, a famous *convocation* held in 1521).   28 *variable service:* Different courses of a single meal.

Hamlet: A man may fish with the worm that hath eat° of a king, and   30
eat of the fish that hath fed of that worm.

King: What dost thou mean by this?

Hamlet: Nothing but to show you how a king may go a progress°
through the guts of a beggar.

King: Where is Polonius?   35

Hamlet: In heaven. Send thither to see. If your messenger find him
not there, seek him i' th' other place yourself. But if indeed you
find him not within this month, you shall nose him as you go up
the stairs into the lobby.

King [to some Attendants]:   Go seek him there.   40

Hamlet: 'A will stay till you come.

                                          [Exit Attendants.]

King: Hamlet, this deed, for thine especial safety.—
Which we do tender,° as we dearly° grieve
For that which thou hast done—must send thee hence   45
[With fiery quickness.] Therefore prepare thyself.
The bark° is ready, and the wind at help,
Th' associates tend,° and everything is bent°
For England.

Hamlet: For England!   50

King: Ay, Hamlet.

Hamlet: Good.

King: So is it, if thou knew'st our purposes.

Hamlet: I see a cherub° that sees them. But, come, for England!
Farewell, dear mother.   55

King: Thy loving father, Hamlet.

Hamlet: My mother. Father and mother is man and wife, man and
wife is one flesh, and so, my mother. Come, for England!

                                          (Exit.)

King: Follow him at foot;° tempt him with speed aboard.   60
Delay it not; I'll have him hence tonight.
Away! For everything is seal'd and done
That else leans on° th' affair. Pray you, make haste.

                                          [Exeunt all but the King.]

And, England,° if my love thou hold'st at aught—   65
As my great power thereof may give thee sense,
Since yet thy cicatrice° looks raw and red

---

30 *eat:* Eaten (pronounced *et*).   **33** *progress:* Royal journey of state.   **44** *tender:* Regard,
hold dear.   *dearly:* Intensely.   **47** *bark:* Sailing vessel.   **48** *tend:* Wait.   *bent:* In readiness.   **54** *cherub:* Cherubim are angels of knowledge.   **60** *at foot:* Close behind, at heel.
63 *leans on:* Bears upon, is related to.   **65** *England:* King of England.   **67** *cicatrice:* Scar.

After the Danish sword, and thy free awe°
Pays homage to us—thou mayst not coldly set°
Our sovereign process,° which imports at full,   70
By letters congruing° to that effect,
The present° death of Hamlet. Do it, England,
For like the hectic° in my blood he rages,
And thou must cure me. Till I know 'tis done,
Howe'er my haps,° my joys were ne'er begun.   75

                                    (Exit.)

68 *free awe:* Voluntary show of respect.   69 *set:* Esteem.   70 *process:* Command.
71 *congruing:* Agreeing.   72 *present:* Immediate.   73 *hectic:* Persistent fever.   75 *haps:*
Fortunes.

[Scene IV]°

(Enter Fortinbras with his Army over the stage.)

Fortinbras: Go, captain, from me greet the Danish king.
    Tell him that, by his license,° Fortinbras
    Craves the conveyance° of a promis'd march
    Over his kingdom. You know the rendezvous.
    If that his Majesty would aught with us,   5
    We shall express our duty in his eye;°
    And let him know so.
Captain: I will do 't, my lord.
Fortinbras: Go softly° on.

                         [Exeunt all but the Captain.]   10

(Enter Hamlet, Rosencrantz, [Guildenstern,] etc.)

Hamlet: Good sir, whose powers° are these?
Captain: They are of Norway, sir.
Hamlet: How purposed, sir, I pray you?
Captain: Against some part of Poland.   15
Hamlet: Who commands them, sir?
Captain: The nephew to old Norway, Fortinbras.
Hamlet: Goes it against the main° of Poland, sir,
    Or for some frontier?
Captain: Truly to speak, and with no addition,°   20
    We go to gain a little patch of ground
    That hath in it no profit but the name.
    To pay° five ducats, five, I would not farm it;°

IV. IV. LOCATION: The coast of Denmark.   2 *license:* Permission.   3 *conveyance:* Escort, convoy.   6 *eye:* Presence.   9 *softly:* Slowly.   12 *powers:* Forces.   18 *main:* Main part.
20 *addition:* Exaggeration.   23 *To pay:* I.e., for a yearly rental of.   *farm it:* Take a lease of it.

Nor will it yield to Norway or the Pole
A ranker° rate, should it be sold in fee.°   25
Hamlet: Why, then the Polack never will defend it.
Captain: Yes, it is already garrison'd.
Hamlet: Two thousand souls and twenty thousand ducats
    Will not debate the question of this straw.°
    This is th' imposthume° of much wealth and peace,   30
    That inward breaks, and shows no cause without
    Why the man dies. I humbly thank you, sir.
Captain: God buy you, sir.   *[Exit.]*
Rosencrantz: Will 't please you go, my lord?
Hamlet: I'll be with you straight. Go a little before.   35

                              [Exit all except Hamlet.]

    How all occasions do inform against° me,
    And spur my dull revenge! What is a man,
    If his chief good and market of° his time
    Be but to sleep and feed? A beast, no more.   40
    Sure he that made us with such large discourse,°
    Looking before and after, gave us not
    That capability and god-like reason
    To fust° in us unus'd. Now, whether it be
    Bestial oblivion,° or some craven scruple   45
    Of thinking too precisely on th' event°—
    A thought which, quarter'd, hath but one part wisdom
    And ever three parts coward—I do not know
    Why yet I live to say "This thing's to do,"
    Sith° I have cause and will and strength and means   50
    To do 't. Examples gross° as earth exhort me:
    Witness this army of such mass and charge°
    Led by a delicate and tender prince,
    Whose spirit, with divine ambition puff'd
    Makes mouths° at the invisible event,   55
    Exposing what is mortal and unsure
    To all that fortune, death, and danger dare,
    Even for an egg-shell. Rightly to be great
    Is not to stir without great argument,
    But greatly to find quarrel in a straw   60
    When honor's at the stake. How stand I then,
    That have a father kill'd, a mother stain'd,

---

25 *ranker:* Higher. *in fee:* Fee simple, outright.   29 *debate . . . straw:* Settle this trifling matter.   30 *imposthume:* Abscess.   37 *inform against:* Denounce, betray; take shape against.   39 *market of:* Profit of, compensation for.   41 *discourse:* Power of reasoning.   44 *fust:* Grow moldy.   45 *oblivion:* Forgetfulness.   46 *event:* Outcome.   50 *Sith:* Since.   51 *gross:* Obvious.   52 *charge:* Expense.   55 *Makes mouths:* Makes scornful faces.

Excitements of° my reason and my blood,
And let all sleep, while, to my shame, I see
The imminent death of twenty thousand men,   65
That, for a fantasy° and trick° of fame,
Go to their graves like beds, fight for a plot°
Whereon the numbers cannot try the cause,°
Which is not tomb enough and continent°
To hide the slain? O, from this time forth,   70
My thoughts be bloody, or be nothing worth!

(Exit.)

63 *Excitements of:* Promptings by.   66 *fantasy:* Fanciful caprice.   *trick:* Trifle.   67 *plot:*
I.e., of ground.   68 *Whereon . . . cause:* On which there is insufficient room for the soldiers
needed to engage in a military contest.   69 *continent:* Receptacle, container.

[Scene V]°

(Enter Horatio, [Queen] Gertrude, and a Gentleman.)

Queen: I will not speak with her.
Gentleman: She is importunate, indeed distract.
   Her mood will needs be pitied.
Queen: What would she have?
Gentleman: She speaks much of her father, says she hears   5
   There's tricks° i' th' world, and hems, and beats her heart,°
   Spurns enviously at straws,° speaks things in doubt°
   That carry but half sense. Her speech is nothing,
   Yet the unshaped use° of it doth move
   The hearers to collection;° they yawn° at it,   10
   And botch° the words up fit to their own thoughts,
   Which, as her winks and nods and gestures yield° them,
   Indeed would make one think there might be thought,°
   Though nothing sure, yet much unhappily.
Horatio: 'Twere good she were spoken with, for she may strew   15
   Dangerous conjectures in ill-breeding° minds.
Queen: Let her come in.

                                   [Exit Gentlemen.]

   [*Aside.*] To my sick soul, as sin's true nature is,
   Each toy° seems prologue to some great amiss.°   20
   So full of artless jealousy is guilt,
   It spills itself in fearing to be spilt.°

IV. V. LOCATION: The castle.   6 *tricks:* Deceptions.   *heart:* Breast.   7 *Spurns . . . straws:*
Kicks spitefully, takes offense at trifles.   *in doubt:* Obscurely.   9 *unshaped use:* Distracted
manner.   10 *collection:* Inference, a guess at some sort of meaning.   *yawn:* Wonder, grasp.
11 *botch:* Patch.   12 *yield:* Deliver, bring forth (her words).   13 *thought:* Conjectured.
16 *ill-breeding:* Prone to suspect the worst.   20 *toy:* Trifle.   *amiss:* Calamity.   21–22 *So
. . . spilt:* Guilt is so full of suspicion that it unskillfully betrays itself in fearing betrayal.

(Enter Ophelia [distracted].)

Ophelia: Where is the beauteous majesty of Denmark?
Queen: How now, Ophelia?   25
Ophelia (she sings): "How should I your true love know
>   From another one?
>   By his cockle hat° and staff,
>   And his sandal shoon."°
Queen: Alas, sweet lady, what imports this song?   30
Ophelia: Say you? Nay, pray you, mark.
>   "He is dead and gone, lady,   *(Song.)*
>   He is dead and gone;
>   At his head a grass-green turf,
>   At his heels a stone."   35
>   O, ho!
Queen: Nay, but Ophelia—
Ophelia: Pray you mark.
> [*Sings.*] "White his shroud as the mountain snow"—

(Enter King.)   40

Queen: Alas, look here, my lord.
Ophelia: "Larded° all with flowers   *(Song.)*
>   Which bewept to the ground did not go
>   With true-love showers."
King: How do you, pretty lady?   45
Ophelia: Well, God 'ild° you! They say the owl° was a baker's
daughter. Lord, we know what we are, but know not what
we may be. God be at your table!
King: Conceit° upon her father.
Ophelia: Pray let's have no words of this; but when they ask you   50
what it means, say you this:
>   "Tomorrow is Saint Valentine's° day.   *(Song.)*
>   All in the morning betime,
>   And I a maid at your window,
>   To be your Valentine.   55
>   Then up he rose, and donn'd his clo'es,
>   And dupp'd° the chamber-door,
>   Let in the maid, that out a maid
>   Never departed more."
King: Pretty Ophelia!   60

---

28 *cockle hat:* Hat with cockleshell stuck in it as a sign that the wearer had been a pilgrim to the shrine of St. James of Compostella in Spain.   29 *shoon:* Shoes.   41 *Larded:* Decorated.
45 *God 'ild:* God yield or reward.   *owl:* Refers to a legend about a baker's daughter who was turned into an owl for refusing Jesus bread.   49 *Conceit:* Brooding.   52 *Valentine's:* This song alludes to the belief that the first girl seen by a man on the morning of this day was his valentine or true love.   57 *dupp'd:* Opened.

Ophelia: Indeed, la, without an oath, I'll make an end on 't:
  [*Sings.*] "By Gis° and by Saint Charity,
    Alack, and fie for shame!
  Young men will do 't, if they come to 't;
    By Cock,° they are to blame.   65
  Quoth she, 'Before you tumbled me,
    You promised me to wed.' "
  He answers:
  " 'So would I ha' done, by yonder sun,
    An thou hadst not come to my bed.' " '   70
King: How long hath she been thus?
Ophelia: I hope all will be well. We must be patient, but I cannot
  choose but weep, to think they would lay him i' th' cold ground.
  My brother shall know of it; and so I thank you for your good
  counsel. Come, my coach! Good night, ladies; good night, sweet   75
  ladies; good night, good night.

                                              [*Exit.*]

King: Follow her close; give her good watch, I pray you.

                                  [*Exit Horatio.*]

  O, this is the poison of deep grief; it springs   80
  All from her father's death—and now behold!
  O Gertrude, Gertrude,
  When sorrows come, they come not single spies,°
  But in battalions. First, her father slain;
  Next, your son gone, and he most violent author   85
  Of his own just remove; the people muddied,°
  Thick and unwholesome in their thoughts and whispers,
  For good Polonius' death; and we have done but greenly,°
  In hugger-mugger° to inter him; poor Ophelia
  Divided from herself and her fair judgment,   90
  Without the which we are pictures, or mere beasts;
  Last, and as much containing as all these,
  Her brother is in secret come from France,
  Feeds on his wonder, keeps himself in clouds,°
  And wants° not buzzers° to infect his ear   95
  With pestilent speeches of his father's death,
  Wherein necessity, of matter beggar'd,°
  Will nothing stick our person to arraign
  In ear and ear.° O my dear Gertrude, this,

---

62 *Gis:* Jesus.   65 *Cock:* A perversion of *God* in oaths.   83 *spies:* Scouts sent in advance of
the main force.   86 *muddied:* Stirred up, confused.   88 *greenly:* Imprudently, foolishly.
89 *hugger-mugger:* Secret haste.   94 *in clouds:* I.e., of suspicion and rumor.   95 *wants:*
Lacks.   *buzzers:* Gossipers, informers.   97 *of matter beggar'd:* Unprovided with facts.
98–99 *Will . . . ear:* Will not hesitate to accuse my (royal) person in everybody's ears.

Like to a murd'ring-piece,° in many places   100
Gives me superfluous death.   *(A noise within.)*
[*Queen:* Alack, what noise is this?]
King: Attend!
Where are my Switzers?° Let them guard the door.

(Enter a Messenger.)
                                                                              105
What is the matter?
Messenger: Save yourself, my lord!
The ocean, overpeering of his list,°
Eats not the flats° with more impiteous° haste
Than young Laertes, in a riotous head,°   110
O'erbears your officers. The rabble call him lord,
And, as° the world were now but to begin,
Antiquity forgot, custom not known,
The ratifiers and props° of every word,°
They cry, "Choose we! Laertes shall be king!"   115
Caps, hands, and tongues applaud it to the clouds,
"Laertes shall be king, Laertes king!"

                                              (A noise within.)

Queen: How cheerfully on the false trail they cry!
O, this is counter,° you false Danish dogs!   120

(Enter Laertes with others.)

King: The doors are broke.
Laertes: Where is this King? Sirs, stand you all without.
All: No, let's come in.
Laertes: I pray you, give me leave.   125
All: We will, we will.

                                    [They retire without the door.]

Laertes: I thank you. Keep the door. O thou vile king,
Give me my father!
Queen: Calmly, good Laertes.   130

                                    [She tries to hold him back.]

Laertes: That drop of blood that's calm proclaims me bastard,
Cries cuckold to my father, brands the harlot
Even here, between the chaste unsmirched brow
Of my true mother.   135
King: What is the cause, Laertes,

---

100 *murd'ring-piece:* Cannon loaded so as to scatter its shot.   104 *Switzers:* Swiss guards, mercenaries.   108 *overpeering of his list:* Overflowing its shore.   109 *flats:* Flatlands near shore. *impiteous:* Pitiless.   110 *head:* Armed force.   112 *as:* As if.   114 *ratifiers and props:* Refer to *antiquity* and *custom.*   *word:* Promise.   120 *counter:* A hunting term meaning to follow the trail in a direction opposite to that which the game has taken.

That thy rebellion looks so giant-like?
Let him go, Gertrude. Do not fear our° person.
There's such divinity doth hedge a king
That treason can but peep to what it would,°   140
Acts little of his will.° Tell me, Laertes,
Why thou art thus incens'd. Let him go, Gertrude.
Speak, man.

Laertes:　　　Where is my father?

King:　　　　　　Dead.   145

Queen:　But not by him.

King:　　　　　Let him demand his fill.

Laertes:　How came he dead? I'll not be juggled with.
To hell, allegiance! Vows, to the blackest devil!
Conscience and grace, to the profoundest pit!   150
I dare damnation. To this point I stand,
That both the worlds I give to negligence,°
Let come what comes, only I'll be reveng'd
Most throughly° for my father.

King:　Who shall stay you?   155

Laertes:　　　　My will, not all the world's.°
And for my means, I'll husband them so well,
They shall go far with little.

King:　　　　　　Good Laertes,
If you desire to know the certainty   160
Of your dear father, is 't writ in your revenge
That, swoopstake,° you will draw both friend and foe,
Winner and loser?

Laertes:　None but his enemies.

King:　　　　　Will you know them then?   165

Laertes:　To his good friends thus wide I'll ope my arms,
And, like the kind life-rend'ring pelican,°
Repast° them with my blood.

King:　　　　　Why, now you speak
Like a good child and a true gentleman.   170
That I am guiltless of your father's death,
And am most sensibly° in grief for it,
It shall as level° to your judgment 'pear

---

138 *fear our:* Fear for my.　　140 *can . . . would:* Can only glance; as from far off or through a
barrier, at what it would intend.　　141 *Acts . . . will:* (But) performs little of what it intends.
152 *both . . . negligence:* Both this world and the next are of no consequence to me.
154 *throughly:* Throughly.　　156 *My will . . . world's:* I'll stop (*stay*) when my will is accomplished, not for anyone else's.　　162 *swoopstake:* Literally, taking all stakes on the gambling table
at once, i.e., indiscriminately; *draw* is also a gambling term.　　167 *pelican:* Refers to the belief
that the female pelican fed its young with its own blood.　　168 *Repast:* Feed.　　172 *sensibly:*
Feelingly.　　173 *level:* Plain.

As day does to your eye.

(A noise within:) "Let her come in."   175

Laertes: How now? What noise is that?

(Enter Ophelia.)

O heat, dry up my brains! Tears seven times salt
Burn out the sense and virtue° of mine eye!
By heaven, thy madness shall be paid with weight°   180
Till our scale turn the beam.° O rose of May!
Dear maid, kind sister, sweet Ophelia!
O heavens, is 't possible a young maid's wits
Should be as mortal as an old man's life?
[Nature is fine in° love, and where 'tis fine,   185
It sends some precious instance°of itself
After the thing it loves.°]

Ophelia: "They bore him barefac'd on the bier;

(Song.)

[Hey non nonny, nonny, hey nonny,]   190
And in his grave rain'd many a tear"—
Fare you well, my dove!

Laertes: Hadst thou thy wits, and didst persuade° revenge,
It could not move thus.

Ophelia: You must sing "A-down a-down,   195
And you call him a-down-a."
O, how the wheel° becomes it! It is the false steward°
That stole his master's daughter.

Laertes: This nothing's more than matter.°

Ophelia: There's rosemary,° that's for remembrance; pray you, love,   200
remember. And there is pansies,° that's for thoughts.

Laertes: A document° in madness, thoughts and remembrance fitted.

Ophelia: There's fennel° for you, and columbines.° There's rue° for
you, and here's some for me; we may call it herb of grace o' Sundays.
You may wear your rue with a difference.° There's a daisy.° I would   205

179 *virtue:* Faculty, power.   180 *paid with weight:* Repaid, avenged equally or more.
181 *beam:* Crossbar of a balance.   185 *fine in:* Refined by.   186 *instance:* Token.
187 *After . . . loves:* Into the grave, along with Polonius.   193 *persuade:* Argue cogently for.
197 *wheel:* Spinning wheel as accompaniment to the song, or refrain.   *false steward:* The story
is unknown.   199 *This . . . matter:* This seeming nonsense is more meaningful than sane utterance.   200 *rosemary:* Used as a symbol of remembrance both at weddings and at funerals.
201 *pansies:* Emblems of love and courtship; perhaps from French *pensées,* thoughts.   202 *document:* Instruction, lesson.   203 *fennel:* Emblem of flattery.   *columbines:* Emblems of un-
chastity (?) or ingratitude (?).   *rue:* Emblem of repentance; when mingled with holy water, it
was known as *herb of grace.*   205 *with a difference:* Suggests that Ophelia and the Queen have
different causes of sorrow and repentance; perhaps with a play on *rue* in the sense of ruth, pity.
daisy: Emblem of dissembling, faithlessness.

give you some violets,° but they wither'd all when my father died.
They say 'a made a good end—
[*Sings.*] "For bonny sweet Robin is all my joy."

Laertes: Thought° and affliction, passion, hell itself,
She turns to favor° and to prettiness.   210

Ophelia: "And will 'a not come again?   (*Song.*)
And will 'a not come again?
 No, no, he is dead,
 Go to thy death-bed,
He never will come again.   215

"His beard was as white as snow,
All flaxen was his poll.°
 He is gone, he is gone,
 And we cast away moan.
God 'a' mercy on his soul!   220
And of all Christians' souls, I pray God. God buy you.

              [Exit.]

Laertes: Do you see this, O God?
King: Laertes, I must commune with your grief,
Or you deny me right. Go but apart,   225
Make choice of whom your wisest friends you will,
And they shall hear and judge 'twixt you and me.
If by direct or by collateral° hand
They find us touch'd,° we will our kingdom give,
Our crown, our life, and all that we call ours,   230
To you in satisfaction; but if not,
Be you content to lend your patience to us,
And we shall jointly labor with your soul
To give it due content.

Laertes: Let this be so.   235
His means of death, his obscure funeral—
No trophy,° sword, nor hatchment° o'er his bones,
No noble rite nor formal ostentation°—
Cry to be heard, as 'twere from heaven to earth,
That I must call 't in question.   240

King: So you shall;
And where th' offense is, let the great ax fall.
I pray you go with me.

             (*Exeunt.*)

---

206 *violets:* Emblems of faithfulness.   209 *Thought:* Melancholy.   210 *favor:* Grace.
217 *poll:* Head.   228 *collateral:* Indirect.   229 *us touch'd:* Me implicated.   237 *trophy:*
Memorial.   *hatchment:* Tablet displaying the armorial bearings of a deceased person.   238 *ostentation:* Ceremony.

[Scene VI]°

(Enter Horatio and others.)

Horatio: What are they that would speak with me?
Gentleman: Seafaring men, sir. They say they have letters for you.

[Exit Gentleman.]

Horatio: Let them come in. I do not know from what part of the
world I should be greeted, if not from lord Hamlet.   5

(Enter Sailors.)

First Sailor: God bless you sir.
Horatio: Let him bless thee too.
First Sailor: 'A shall, sir an't please him. There's a letter for you, sir—
it came from th' ambassador that was bound for England—if your   10
name be Horatio, as I am let to know it is.

[Gives letter.]

Horatio [reads]:   "Horatio, when thou shalt have overlook'd this, give
these fellows some means° to the King; they have letters for him.
Ere we were two days old at sea, a pirate of very warlike   15
appointment° gave us chase. Finding ourselves too slow of sail, we
put on a compell'd valor, and in the grapple I boarded them. On
the instant they got clear of our ship, so I alone became their
prisoner. They have dealt with me like thieves of mercy,° but they
knew what they did: I am to do a good turn for them. Let the King   20
have the letters I have sent, and repair thou to me with as much
speed as thou wouldest fly death. I have words to speak in thine
ear will make thee dumb; yet are they much too light for the bore°
of the matter. These good fellows will bring thee where I am.
Rosencrantz and Guildenstern hold their course for England.   25
Of them I have much to tell thee. Farewell.

He that thou knowest thine, Hamlet." Come, I will give you
way for these your letters, and do 't the speedier that you may
direct me to him from whom you brought them.

(Exeunt.)

IV. VI. LOCATION: The castle.   14 *means:* Means of access.   16 *appointment:* Equipage.
19 *thieves of mercy:* Merciful thieves.   23 *bore:* Caliber, i.e., importance.

[Scene VII]°

(Enter King and Laertes.)

King: Now must your conscience my acquittance seal,°
And you must put me in your heart for friend,
Sith you have heard, and with a knowing ear,

IV. VII. LOCATION: The castle.   1 *my acquittance seal:* Confirm or acknowledge my innocence.

That he which hath your noble father slain
Pursued my life.   5
Laertes: It well appears. But tell me
   Why you proceeded not against these feats°
   So criminal and so capital° in nature,
   As by your safety, greatness, wisdom, all things else,
   You mainly° were stirr'd up.   10
King: O, for two special reasons,
   Which may to you, perhaps, seem much unsinew'd,°
   But yet to me th' are strong. The Queen his mother
   Lives almost by his looks, and for myself—
   My virtue or my plague, be it either which—   15
   She's so conjunctive° to my life and soul
   That, as the star moves not but in his sphere,°
   I could not but by her. The other motive,
   Why to a public count° I might not go,
   Is the great love the general gender° bear him,   20
   Who, dipping all his faults in their affection,
   Would, like the spring° that turneth wood to stone,
   Convert his gyves° to graces, so that my arrows,
   Too slightly timber'd° for so loud° a wind,
   Would have reverted to my bow again   25
   And not where I had aim'd them.
Laertes: And so have I a noble father lost,
   A sister driven into desp'rate terms,°
   Whose worth, if praises may go back° again,
   Stood challenger on mount° of all the age   30
   For her perfections. But my revenge will come.
King: Break not your sleeps for that. You must not think
   That we are made of stuff so flat and dull
   That we can let our beard be shook with danger
   And think it pastime. You shortly shall hear more.   35
   I lov'd your father, and we love ourself;
   And that, I hope, will teach you to imagine—

(Enter a Messenger with Letters.)

   [How now? What news?]

---

7 *feats:* Acts.   8 *capital:* Punishable by death.   10 *mainly:* Greatly.   12 *unsinew'd:* Weak.   16 *conjunctive:* Closely united.   17 *sphere:* The hollow sphere in which, according to Ptolemaic astronomy, the planets moved.   19 *count:* Account, reckoning.   20 *general gender:* Common people.   22 *spring:* A spring with such a concentration of lime that it coats a piece of wood with limestone, in effect gilding it.   23 *gyves:* Fetters (which, gilded by the people's praise, would look like badges of honor).   24 *slightly timber'd:* Light.   *loud:* Strong.   28 *terms:* State, condition.   29 *go back:* Recall Ophelia's former virtues.   30 *mount:* On high.

Messenger: [Letters, my lord, from Hamlet:]   40
  These to your Majesty, this to the Queen.

                                        [Gives letters.]

King: From Hamlet? Who brought them?
Messenger: Sailors, my lord, they say; I saw them not.
  They were given me by Claudio. He receiv'd them   45
  Of him that brought them.
King: Laertes, you shall hear them.
  Leave us.   *[Exit Messenger.]*
  [*Reads.*] "High and mighty, you shall know I am set naked° on
  your kingdom. Tomorrow shall I beg leave to see your kingly eyes,   50
  when I shall, first asking your pardon° thereunto, recount the
  occasion of my sudden and more strange return. Hamlet." What
  should this mean? Are all the rest come back? Or is it some abuse,°
  and no such thing?
Laertes: Know you the hand?   55
King: 'Tis Hamlet's character.° "Naked!"
  And in a postscript here, he says "alone."
  Can you devise° me?
Laertes: I am lost in it, my lord. But let him come.
  It warms the very sickness in my heart   60
  That I shall live and tell him to his teeth,
  "Thus didst thou."
King: If it be so, Laertes—
  As how should it be so? How otherwise?°—
  Will you be ruled by me?   65
Laertes: Ay, my lord,
  So° you will not o'errule me to a peace.
King: To thine own peace. If he be now returned,
  As checking at° his voyage, and that he means
  No more to undertake it, I will work him   70
  To an exploit, now ripe in my device,
  Under the which he shall not choose but fall;
  And for his death no wind of blame shall breathe,
  But even his mother shall uncharge the practice°
  And call it accident.   75
Laertes: My lord, I will be rul'd,
  The rather if you could devise it so
  That I might be the organ.°

49 *naked:* Destitute, unarmed, without following.   51 *pardon:* Permission.   53 *abuse:*
Deceit.   56 *character:* Handwriting.   58 *Devise:* Explain to.   64 *As . . . otherwise:* How
can this (Hamlet's return) be true? Yet how otherwise than true (since we have the evidence of
his letter)?   67 *So:* Provided that.   69 *checking at:* Turning aside from (like a falcon leaving
the quarry to fly at a chance bird).   74 *uncharge the practice:* Acquit the stratagem of being a
plot.   78 *organ:* Agent, instrument.

King: It falls right.
    You have been talk'd of since your travel much,   80
    And that in Hamlet's hearing, for a quality
    Wherein, they say, you shine. Your sum of parts°
    Did not together pluck such envy from him
    As did that one, and that, in my regard,
    Of the unworthiest siege.°   85
Laertes: What part is that, my lord?
King: A very riband in the cap of youth,
    Yet needful too, for youth no less becomes
    The light and careless livery that it wears
    Than settled age his sables° and his weeds,°   90
    Importing health° and graveness. Two months since
    Here was a gentleman of Normandy.
    I have seen myself, and serv'd against, the French,
    And they can well° on horseback, but this gallant
    Had witchcraft in 't; he grew unto his seat,   95
    And to such wondrous doing brought his horse
    As had he been incorps'd and demi-natured°
    With the brave beast. So far he topp'd° my thought
    That I, in forgery° of shapes and tricks,
    Come short of what he did.   100
Laertes: A Norman was 't?
King: A Norman.
Laertes: Upon my life, Lamord.
King: The very same.
Laertes: I know him well. He is the brooch° indeed   105
    And gem of all the nation.
King: He made confession° of you,
    And gave you such a masterly report
    For art and exercise in your defense,
    And for your rapier most especial,   110
    That he cried out, 'twould be a sight indeed,
    If one could match you. The scrimers° of their nation,
    He swore, had neither motion, guard, nor eye,
    If you oppos'd them. Sir, this report of his
    Did Hamlet so envenom with his envy   115
    That he could nothing do but wish and beg
    Your sudden coming o'er to play° with you.
    Now, out of this—

---

82 *Your . . . parts:* All your other virtues.   85 *unworthiest siege:* Least important rank.   90 *sables:* Rich robes furred with sable.   *weeds:* Garments.   91 *Importing health:* Indicating prosperity. 94 *can well:* Are skilled.   97 *incorps'd and demi-natur'd:* Of one body and nearly of one nature (like the centaur).   98 *topp'd:* Surpassed.   99 *forgery:* Invention.   105 *brooch:* Ornament. 107 *confession:* Admission of superiority.   112 *scrimers:* Fencers.   117 *play:* Fence.

Laertes: What out of this, my lord?
King: Laertes, was your father dear to you?   120
     Or are you like the painting of a sorrow,
     A face without a heart?
Laertes: Why ask you this?
King: Not that I think you did not love your father,
     But that I know love is begun by time,°   125
     And that I see, in passages of proof,°
     Time qualifies° the spark and fire of it.
     There lives within the very flame of love
     A kind of wick or snuff° that will abate it,
     And nothing is at a like goodness still,°   130
     For goodness, growing to a plurisy,°
     Dies in his own too much.° That° we would do,
     We should do when we would; for this "would" changes
     And hath abatements° and delays as many
     As there are tongues, are hands, are accidents,°   135
     And then this "should" is like a spendthrift's sigh,°
     That hurts by easing.° But, to the quick o' th' ulcer;
     Hamlet comes back. What would you undertake
     To show yourself your father's son in deed
     More than in words?   140
Laertes: To cut his throat i' th' church!
King: No place, indeed, should murder sanctuarize;°
     Revenge should have no bounds. But, good Laertes,
     Will you do this,° keep close within your chamber.
     Hamlet return'd shall know you are come home.   145
     We'll put on those° shall praise your excellence
     And set a double varnish on the fame
     The Frenchman gave you, bring you in fine° together,
     And wager on your heads. He, being remiss,°
     Most generous,° and free from all contriving,   150
     Will not peruse the foils, so that, with ease,
     Or with a little shuffling, you may choose

---

125 *begun by time:* Subject to change.   126 *passages of proof:* Actual instances.   127 *qualifies:* Weakens.   129 *snuff:* The charred part of a candlewick.   130 *nothing . . . still:* Nothing remains at a constant level of perfection.   131 *plurisy:* Excess, plethora.   132 *in . . . much:* Of its own excess.   *That:* That which.   134 *abatements:* Diminutions.   135 *accidents:* Occurrences, incidents.   136 *spendthrift's sigh:* An allusion to the belief that each sigh cost the heart a drop of blood.   137 *hurts by easing:* Costs the heart blood even while it affords emotional relief.   142 *sanctuarize:* Protect from punishment (alludes to the right of sanctuary with which certain religious places were invested).   144 *Will you do this:* If you wish to do this.   146 *put on those:* Instigate those who.   148 *in fine:* Finally.   149 *remiss:* Negligently unsuspicious.   150 *generous:* Nobleminded.

A sword unbated,° and in a pass of practice°
Requite him for your father.
Laertes: I will do 't.   155
And for that purpose I'll anoint my sword.
I bought an unction° of a mountebank°
So mortal that, but dip a knife in it,
Where it draws blood no cataplasm° so rare,
Collected from all simples° that have virtue   160
Under the moon, can save the thing from death
That is but scratch'd withal. I'll touch my point
With this contagion, that, if I gall° him slightly,
It may be death.
King: Let's further think of this,   165
Weigh what convenience both of time and means
May fit us to our shape.° If this should fail,
And that our drift look through our bad performance,°
'Twere better not assay'd. Therefore this project
Should have a back or second, that might hold   170
If this did blast in proof.° Soft, let me see.
We'll make a solemn wager on your cunnings—I ha 't!
When in your motion you are hot and dry—
As° make your bouts more violent to that end—
And that he calls for drink, I'll have prepar'd him   175
A chalice for the nonce,° whereon but sipping,
If he by chance escape your venom'd stuck,°
Our purpose may hold there. [*A cry within.*]
But stay, what noise?

(*Enter Queen.*)   180

Queen: One woe doth tread upon another's heel,
So fast they follow. Your sister's drowned, Laertes.
Laertes: Drown'd! O, where?
Queen: There is a willow grows askant° the brook,
That shows his hoar° leaves in the glassy stream;   185
Therewith fantastic garlands did she make
Of crow-flowers, nettles, daisies, and long purples°
That liberal° shepherds give a grosser name,
But our cold° maids do dead men's fingers call them.

---

153 *unbated:* Not blunted, having no button.   *pass of practice:* Treacherous thrust.
157 *unction:* Ointment.   *mountebank:* Quack doctor.   159 *cataplasm:* Plaster or poultice.
160 *simples:* Herbs.   163 *gall:* Graze, wound.   167 *shape:* Part that we propose to act.
168 *drift . . . performance:* I.e., intention be disclosed by our bungling.   171 *blast in proof:*
Burst in the test (like a cannon).   174 *As:* And you should.   176 *nonce:* Occasion.
177 *stuck:* Thrust (from *stoccado*, a fencing term).   184 *askant:* Aslant.   185 *hoar:* White
or gray.   187 *long purples:* Early purple orchids.   188 *liberal:* Free-spoken.   189 *cold:*
Chaste.

There on the pendent boughs her crownet° weeds   190
Clamb'ring to hang, an envious sliver° broke,
When down her weedy° trophies and herself
Fell in the weeping brook. Her clothes spread wide,
And mermaid-like awhile they bore her up,
Which time she chanted snatches of old lauds,°   195
As one incapable° of her own distress,
Or like a creature native and indued°
Unto that element. But long it could not be
Till that her garments, heavy with their drink,
Pull'd the poor wretch from her melodious lay   200
To muddy death.

Laertes: Alas, then she is drown'd?
Queen: Drown'd, drown'd.
Laertes: Too much of water hast thou, poor Ophelia,
And therefore I forbid my tears. But yet   205
It is our trick;° nature her custom holds,
Let shame say what it will. [*He weeps.*] When these are gone,
The woman will be out.° Adieu, my lord.
I have a speech of fire, that fain would blaze,
But that this folly drowns it.   (*Exit.*)   210
King: Let's follow, Gertrude.
How much I had to do to calm his rage!
Now fear I this will give it start again;
Therefore let's follow.   (*Exeunt.*)

190 *crownet:* Made into a chaplet or coronet.   191 *envious sliver:* Malicious branch.
192 *weedy:* I.e., of plants.   195 *lauds:* Hymns.   196 *incapable:* Lacking capacity to apprehend.   197 *indued:* Adapted by nature.   206 *It is our trick:* Weeping is our natural way
(when sad).   207–208 *When . . . out:* When my tears are all shed, the woman in me will be expended, satisfied.

[ACT V

Scene I]°

(*Enter two Clowns.° [with spades, etc.]*)

First Clown: Is she to be buried in Christian burial when she willfully
seeks her own salvation?
Second Clown: I tell thee she is; therefore make her grave straight.°
The crowner° hath sat on her, and finds it Christian burial.   5
First Clown: How can that be, unless she drown'd herself in her own
defense?
Second Clown: Why, 'tis found so.

V. I. LOCATION: A churchyard.   1 *Clowns:* Rustics.   4 *straight:* Straightway, immediately.
5 *crowner:* Coroner.

First Clown: It must be "se offendendo";° it cannot be else. For here
   lies the point: if I drown myself wittingly, it argues an act, and an   10
   act hath three branches—it is to act, to do, and to perform. Argal,°
   she drown'd herself wittingly.

Second Clown: Nay, but hear you, goodman delver—

First Clown: Give me leave. Here lies the water; good. Here stands
   the man; good. If the man go to this water, and drown himself, it   15
   is, will he,° nill he, he goes, mark you that. But if the water come
   to him and drown him, he drowns not himself. Argal, he that is
   not guilty of his own death shortens not his own life.

Second Clown: But is this law?

First Clown: Ay, marry, is 't—crowner's quest° law.   20

Second Clown: Will you ha' the truth on 't? If this had not been a
   gentlewoman, she should have been buried out o' Christian burial.

First Clown: Why, there thou say'st.° And the more pity that great
   folk should have count'nance° in this world to drown or hang
   themselves, more than their even-Christen.° Come, my spade.   25
   There is no ancient gentlemen but gard'ners, ditchers, and grave-
   makers. They hold up Adam's profession.

Second Clown: Was he a gentleman?

First Clown: 'A was the first that ever bore arms.

[*Second Clown:* Why, he had none.   30

First Clown: What, art a heathen? How dost thou understand the
   Scripture? The Scripture says "Adam digg'd." Could he dig
   without arms?] I'll put another question to thee. If thou answer-
   est me not to the purpose, confess thyself°—

Second Clown: Go to.   35

First Clown: What is he that builds stronger than either the mason,
   the shipwright, or the carpenter?

Second Clown: The gallows-maker, for that frame outlives a thousand
   tenants.

First Clown: I like thy wit well, in good faith. The gallows does well;   40
   but how does it well? It does well to those that do ill. Now thou
   dost ill to say the gallows is built stronger than the church. Argal,
   the gallows may do well to thee. To 't again, come.

Second Clown: "Who builds stronger than a mason, a shipwright, or
   a carpenter?"   45

First Clown: Ay, tell me that, and unyoke.°

Second Clown: Marry, now I can tell.

First Clown: To 't.

---

9 *se offendendo:* A comic mistake for *se defendendo,* term used in verdicts of justifiable homicide.
11 *Argal:* Corruption of *ergo,* therefore.   16 *will he, nill he:* Willy-nilly, whether he wants to or
not.   20 *quest:* Inquest.   23 *there you say'st:* That's right.   24 *count'nance:* Privilege.
25 *even-Christen:* Fellow Christian.   34 *confess thyself:* The saying continues, "and be hanged."
46 *unyoke:* After this great effort you may unharness the team of your wits.

Second Clown: Mass,° I cannot tell.

> *(Enter Hamlet and Horatio [at a distance].)*   50

First Clown: Cudgel thy brains no more about it, for your dull ass will
not mend his pace with beating; and, when you are ask'd this
question next, say "a grave-maker." The houses he makes lasts till
doomsday. Go, get thee in, and fetch me a stoup° of liquor.

> *[Exit Second Clown. First Clown digs.]*   55

> *(Song.)*

"In youth, when I did love, did love,°
  Methought it was very sweet,
To contract—O—the time for—a—my behove,°
  O, methought there—a—was nothing—a—meet."°   60

Hamlet: Has this fellow no feeling of his business, that a sings at grave-
making?

Horatio: Custom hath made it in him a property of easiness.°

Hamlet: 'Tis e'en so. The hand of little employment hath the
daintier sense.°   65

> *(Song.)*

First Clown: "But age, with his stealing steps,
  Hath claw'd me in his clutch,
And hath shipped me into the land,°
  As if I had never been such."   70

> *[Throws up a skull.]*

Hamlet: That skull had a tongue in it, and could sing once. How the
knave jowls° it to the ground, as if 'twere Cain's jaw-bone, that
did the first murder! This might be the pate of a politician,° which
this ass now o'erreaches,° one that would circumvent God, might   75
it not?

Horatio: It might, my lord.

Hamlet: Or of a courtier, which could say "Good morrow, sweet lord!
How dost thou, sweet lord?" This might be my Lord Such-a-one,
that prais'd my Lord Such-a-one's horse when 'a meant to beg it,   80
might it not?

Horatio: Ay, my lord.

---

49 *Mass:* By the Mass.   54 *stoup:* Two-quart measure.   57 *In . . . love:* This and the two following stanzas, with nonsensical variations, are from a poem attributed to Lord Vaux and printed
in *Tottel's Miscellany,* 1557. The *O* and *a* (for "ah") seemingly are the grunts of the digger.
59 *To contract . . . behove:* To make a betrothal agreement for my benefit (?).   60 *meet:* Suitable,
i.e., more suitable.   63 *property of easiness:* Something he can do easily and without thinking.
65 *daintier sense:* More delicate sense of feeling.   69 *into the land:* Toward my grave (?) (but
note the lack of rhyme in *steps, land*).   73 *jowls:* Dashes.   74 *politician:* Schemer, plotter.
75 *o'erreaches:* Circumvents, gets the better of (with a quibble on the literal sense).

Hamlet: Why, e'en so, and now my Lady Worm's, chapless,° and
knock'd about the mazzard° with a sexton's spade. Here's fine
revolution,° an° we had the trick to see 't. Did these bones cost   85
no more the breeding,° but to play at loggats° with them? Mine
ache to think on 't.

(Song.)

First Clown: "A pick-axe, and a spade, a spade,
　　For and° a shrouding sheet;
　O, a pit of clay for to be made   90
　　For such a guest is meet."

[Throws up another skull.]

Hamlet: There's another. Why may not that be the skull of a lawyer?
Where be his quiddities° now, his quillities,° his cases, his tenures,°   95
and his tricks? Why does he suffer this mad knave now to knock
him about the sconce° with a dirty shovel, and will not tell him of
his action of battery? Hum! This fellow might be in 's time a great
buyer of land, with his statutes, his recognizances,° his fines, his
double° vouchers,° his recoveries.° [Is this the fine of his fines, and   100
the recovery of his recoveries,] to have his fine pate full of fine
dirt?° Will his vouchers vouch him no more of his purchases, and
double [ones too], than the length and breadth of a pair of
indentures?° The very conveyances° of his lands will scarcely lie in
this box,° and must th' inheritor° himself have no more, ha?   105
Horatio: Not a jot more, my lord.
Hamlet: Is not parchment made of sheep-skins?
Horatio: Ay, my lord, and of calf-skins too.
Hamlet: They are sheep and calves which seek out assurance in that.°
I will speak to this fellow.—Whose grave's this, sirrah?°   110
First Clown: Mine, sir. [*Sings.*] "O, a pit of clay for to be made [For
such a guest is meet]."
Hamlet: I think it be thine, indeed, for thou liest in 't.

83 *chapless:* Having no lower jaw.   84 *mazzard:* Head (literally, a drinking vessel).
85 *revolution:* Change.   *an:* If.   86 *the breeding:* In the breeding, raising.   *loggats:* A game
in which pieces of hard wood are thrown to lie as near as possible to a stake.   90 *For and:* And
moreover.   95 *quiddities:* Subtleties, quibbles (from Latin *quid*, a thing).   *quillities:* Verbal
niceties, subtle distinctions (variation of *quiddities*).   *tenures:* The holding of a piece of property or office, or the conditions or period of such holding.   97 *sconce:* Head.   99 *statutes,
recognizances:* Legal documents guaranteeing a debt by attaching land and property.
99–100 *fines, recoveries:* Ways of converting entailed estates into "fee simple" or freehold.
100 *double:* Signed by two signatories.   *vouchers:* Guarantees of the legality of a title to real estate.   100–2 *fine of his fines . . . fine pate . . . fine dirt:* End of his legal maneuvers . . . elegant
head . . . minutely sifted dirt.   103–4 *pair of indentures:* Legal document drawn up in duplicate on a single sheet and then cut apart on a zigzag line so that each pair was uniquely matched.
(Hamlet may refer to two rows of teeth, or dentures.)   104 *conveyances:* Deeds.   105 *this
box:* The skull.   *inheritor:* Possessor, owner.   109 *assurance in that:* Safety in legal parch-
ments.   110 *sirrah:* Term of address to inferiors.

First Clown: You lie out on 't, sir, and therefore 'tis not yours. For
my part, I do not lie in 't, yet it is mine.   115

Hamlet: Thou dost lie in 't, to be in 't and say it is thine. 'Tis for the
dead, not for the quick;° therefore thou liest.

First Clown: 'Tis a quick lie, sir; 'twill away again from me to you.

Hamlet: What man dost thou dig it for?

First Clown: For no man, sir.   120

Hamlet: What woman, then?

First Clown: For none, neither.

Hamlet: Who is to be buried in 't?

First Clown: One that was a woman, sir, but, rest her soul, she's dead.

Hamlet: How absolute° the knave is! We must speak by the card,° or   125
equivocation° will undo us. By the Lord, Horatio, this three years
I have taken note of it: the age is grown so pick'd° that the toe
of the peasant comes so near the heel of the courtier, he galls his
kibe.° How long hast thou been a gravemaker?

First Clown: Of all the days i' th' year, I came to 't that day that our 130
last king Hamlet overcame Fortinbras.

Hamlet: How long is that since?

First Clown: Cannot you tell that? Every fool can tell that. It was that
very day that young Hamlet was born—he that is mad, and sent
into England.   135

Hamlet: Ay, marry, why was he sent into England?

First Clown: Why, because 'a was mad. 'A shall recover his wits there,
or, if 'a do not, 'tis no great matter there.

Hamlet: Why?

First Clown: 'Twill not be seen in him there. There the men are as   140
mad as he.

Hamlet: How came he mad?

First Clown: Very strangely, they say.

Hamlet: How strangely?

First Clown: Faith, e'en with losing his wits.   145

Hamlet: Upon what ground?

First Clown: Why, here in Denmark. I have been sexton here, man
and boy, thirty years.

Hamlet: How long will a man lie i' th' earth ere he rot?

First Clown: Faith, if 'a be not rotten before 'a die—as we have many   150
pocky° corses [now-a-days], that will scarce hold the laying in—
'a will last you some eight year or nine year. A tanner will last you
nine year.

Hamlet: Why he more than another?

---

117 *quick:* Living.   125 *absolute:* Positive, decided.   *by the card:* By the mariner's card on
which the points of the compass were marked, i.e., with precision.   126 *equivocation:*
Ambiguity in the use of terms.   127 *pick'd:* Refined, fastidious.   128–29 *galls his kibe:* Chafes
the courtier's chilblain.   151 *pocky:* Rotten, diseased (literally, with the pox, or syphilis).

First Clown: Why, sir, his hide is so tann'd with his trade that 'a will   155
keep out water a great while, and your water is a sore decayer of
your whoreson dead body. [*Picks up a skull.*] Here's a skull now
hath lain you° i' th' earth three and twenty years.

Hamlet: Whose was it?

First Clown: A whoreson mad fellow's it was. Whose do you think it   160
was?

Hamlet: Nay, I know not.

First Clown: A pestilence on him for a mad rogue! 'A pour'd a flagon
of Rhenish° on my head once. This same skull, sir, was Yorick's
skull, the King's jester.   165

Hamlet: This?

First Clown: E'en that.

Hamlet: [Let me see.] [*Takes the skull.*] Alas, poor Yorick! I knew
him, Horatio, a fellow of infinite jest, of most excellent fancy. He
hath borne me on his back a thousand times; and now, how   170
abhorr'd in my imagination it is! My gorge rises at it. Here hung
those lips that I have kiss'd I know not how oft. Where be your
gibes now? Your gambols, your songs, your flashes of merriment
that were wont to set the table on a roar? Not one now, to mock
your own grinning? Quite chap-fall'n?° Now get you to my lady's   175
chamber, and tell her, let her paint an inch thick, to this favor° she
must come; make her laugh at that. Prithee, Horatio, tell me one
thing.

Horatio: What's that, my lord?

Hamlet: Dost thou think Alexander look'd o' this fashion i' th' earth?   180

Horatio: E'en so.

Hamlet: And smelt so? Pah! [*Puts down the skull.*]

Horatio: E'en so, my lord.

Hamlet: To what base uses we may return, Horatio! Why may not
imagination trace the noble dust of Alexander, till a' find it   185
stopping a bung-hole?

Horatio: 'Twere to consider too curiously,° to consider so.

Hamlet: No, faith, not a jot, but to follow him thither with modesty°
enough, and likelihood to lead it. [As thus]: Alexander died,
Alexander was buried, Alexander returneth to dust; the dust is   190
earth; of earth we make loam;° and why of that loam, whereto he
was converted, might they not stop a beer-barrel?
Imperious° Caesar, dead and turn'd to clay,
Might stop a hole to keep the wind away.
O, that that earth which kept the world in awe   195

---

158 *lain you:* Lain.   164 *Rhenish:* Rhine wine.   175 *chap-fall'n:* (1) Lacking the lower jaw,
(2) dejected.   176 *favor:* Aspect, appearance.   187 *curiously:* Minutely.   188 *modesty:*
Moderation.   191 *loam:* Clay mixture for brickmaking or other clay use.   193 *Imperious:*
Imperial.

Should patch a wall t' expel the winter's flaw!°
But soft, but soft awhile! Here comes the King.

(Enter King, Queen, Laertes, and the Corse [of Ophelia, in procession, with Priest, Lords etc.].)

The Queen, the courtiers. Who is this they follow?   200
And with such maimed rites? This doth betoken
The corse they follow did with desp'rate hand
Fordo it° own life. 'Twas of some estate.°
Couch° we awhile, and mark.

> *[He and Horatio conceal themselves.   205*
> *Ophelia's body is taken to the grave.]*

Laertes: What ceremony else?
Hamlet [to Horatio]:   That is Laertes, a very noble youth. Mark.
Laertes: What ceremony else?
Priest: Her obsequies have been as far enlarg'd   210
   As we have warranty. Her death was doubtful,
   And, but that great command o'ersways the order,
   She should in ground unsanctified been lodg'd
   Till the last trumpet. For° charitable prayers,
   Shards,° flints, and pebbles should be thrown on her.   215
   Yet here she is allow'd her virgin crants,°
   Her maiden strewments,° and the bringing home
   Of bell and burial.°
Laertes: Must there no more be done?
Priest: No more be done.   220
   We should profane the service of the dead
   To sing a requiem and such rest to her
   As to peace-parted souls.
Laertes: Lay her i' th' earth,
   And from her fair and unpolluted flesh   225
   May violets° spring! I tell thee, churlish priest,
   A minist'ring angel shall my sister be
   When thou liest howling!
Hamlet [To Horatio]:   What, the fair Ophelia!
Queen [Scattering flowers]:   Sweets to the sweet! Farewell.   230
   I hoped thou shouldst have been my Hamlet's wife.
   I thought thy bride-bed to have deck'd, sweet maid,
   And not have strew'd thy grave.
Laertes: O, treble woe

---

196 *flaw:* Gust of wind.   203 *Fordo it:* Destroy its.   *estate:* Rank.   204 *Couch:* Hide, lurk.
214 *For:* In place of.   215 *Shards:* Broken bits of pottery.   216 *crants:* Garland.
217 *strewments:* Traditional stewing of flowers.   217–18 *bringing . . . burial:* Laying to rest
of the body in consecrated ground, to the sound of the bell.   226 *violets:* See IV. v. 187 and
note.

Fall ten times treble on that cursed head
Whose wicked deed thy most ingenious sense° 235
Depriv'd thee of! Hold off the earth awhile,
Till I have caught her once more in mine arms.

[Leaps into the grave and embraces Ophelia.]

Now pile your dust upon the quick and dead,
Till of this flat a mountain you have made 240
T' o'ertop old Pelion,° or the skyish head
Of blue Olympus.°

Hamlet [coming forward]: What is he whose grief
Bears such an emphasis, whose phrase of sorrow
Conjures the wand'ring stars,° and makes them stand 245
Like wonder-wounded hearers? This is I,
Hamlet the Dane.°

Laertes: The devil take thy soul!

[Grappling with him.]

Hamlet: Thou pray'st not well. 250
I prithee, take thy fingers from my throat;
For, though I am not splenitive° and rash,
Yet have I in me something dangerous,
Which let thy wisdom fear. Hold off thy hand.

King: Pluck them asunder. 255

Queen: Hamlet, Hamlet!

All: Gentlemen!

Horatio: Good my lord, be quiet.

[Hamlet and Laertes are parted.]

Hamlet: Why, I will fight with him upon this theme 260
Until my eyelids will no longer wag.

Queen: O my son, what theme?

Hamlet: I lov'd Ophelia. Forty thousand brothers
Could not with all their quantity of love
Make up my sum. What wilt thou do for her? 265

King: O, he is mad, Laertes.

Queen: For love of God, forbear him.

Hamlet: 'Swounds,° show me what thou't do.
Woo 't° weep? Woo 't fight? Woo 't fast? Woo 't tear thyself?
Woo 't drink up eisel?° Eat a crocodile? 270
I'll do 't. Dost thou come here to whine?
To outface me with leaping in her grave?

---

235 *ingenious sense:* Mind endowed with finest qualities. 241–42 *Pelion, Olympus:* Mountains
in the north of Thessaly; see also *Ossa,* at line 277. 245 *wand'ring stars:* Planets. 247 *the
Dane:* This title normally signifies the King; see I. i. 15 and note. 252 *splenitive:* Quick-tem-
pered. 268 *'Swounds:* By His (Christ's) wounds. 269 *Woo 't:* Wilt thou. 270 *eisel:*
Vinegar.

Be buried quick° with her, and so will I.
And, if thou prate of mountains, let them throw
Millions of acres on us, till our ground,   275
Singeing his pate° against the burning zone,°
Make Ossa° like a wart! Nay, an thou 'lt mouth,°
I'll rant as well as thou.
Queen: This is mere° madness,
And thus a while the fit will work on him;   280
Anon, as patient as the female dove
When that her golden couplets° are disclos'd,°
His silence will sit drooping.
Hamlet: Hear you, sir.
What is the reason that you use me thus?   285
I lov'd you ever. But it is no matter.
Let Hercules himself do what he may,
The cat will mew, and dog will have his day.°
King: I pray thee, good Horatio, wait upon him.

                                  (Exit Hamlet and Horatio.)   290

[*To Laertes.*] Strengthen your patience in° our last night's speech;
We'll put the matter to the present push.°—
Good Gertrude, set some watch over your son.—
This grave shall have a living° monument.
An hour of quiet shortly shall we see;   295
Till then, in patience our proceeding be.   *(Exeunt.)*

273 *quick:* Alive.   276 *his pate:* Its head, i.e., top.   *burning zone:* Sun's orbit.   277 *Ossa:*
Another mountain in Thessaly. (In their war against the Olympian gods, the giants attempted to
heap Ossa, Pelion, and Olympus on one another to scale heaven.)   *mouth:* Rant.   279 *mere:*
Utter.   282 *golden couplets:* Two baby pigeons, covered with yellow down.   *disclos'd:*
Hatched.   287–88 *Let . . . day:* Despite any blustering attempts at interference every person
will sooner or later do what he must do.   291 *in:* By recalling.   292 *present push:* Immediate
test.   294 *living:* Lasting; also refers (for Laertes's benefit) to the plot against Hamlet.

[Scene II]°

(Enter Hamlet and Horatio.)

Hamlet: So much for this, sir; now shall you see the other.°
     You do remember all the circumstance?
Horatio: Remember it, my lord!
Hamlet: Sir, in my heart there was a kind of fighting
     That would not let me sleep. Methought I lay   5
     Worse than the mutines° in the bilboes.° Rashly,°
     And prais'd be rashness for it—let us know,°

V. II.   LOCATION: The castle.   1 *see the other:* Hear the other news.   6 *mutines:* Mutineers.   *bil-*
boes: Shackles.   *Rashly:* On impulse (this adverb goes with lines 12 ff.).   7 *know:* Acknowledge.

Our indiscretion sometime serves us well
When our deep plots do pall,° and that should learn° us
There's a divinity that shapes our ends,   10
Rough-hew° them how we will—
Horatio: That is most certain.
Hamlet: Up from my cabin,
  My sea-gown scarf'd about me, in the dark
  Grop'd I to find out them, had my desire,   15
  Finger'd° their packet, and in fine° withdrew
  To mine own room again, making so bold,
  My fears forgetting manners, to unseal
  Their grand commission; where I found, Horatio—
  Ah, royal knavery!—an exact command,   20
  Larded° with many several sorts of reasons
  Importing° Denmark's health and England's too,
  With, ho, such bugs° and goblins in my life,°
  That, on the supervise,° no leisure bated,°
  No, not to stay the grinding of the axe,   25
  My head should be struck off.
Horatio: Is 't possible?
Hamlet: Here's the commission; read it at more leisure.

                                    [Gives document.]

  But wilt thou hear now how I did proceed?   30
Horatio: I beseech you.
Hamlet: Being thus benetted round with villainies,
  Or I could make a prologue to my brains,
  They had begun the play.° I sat me down,
  Devis'd a new commission, wrote it fair.°   35
  I once did hold it, as our statists° do,
  A baseness° to write fair, and labor'd much
  How to forget that learning, but, sir, now
  It did me yeoman's° service. Wilt thou know
  Th' effect° of what I wrote?   40
Horatio: Ay, good my lord.
Hamlet: An earnest conjuration from the King,
  As England was his faithful tributary,
  As love between them like the palm might flourish,
  As peace should still her wheaten garland° wear   45

---

9 *pall:* Fail.   *learn:* Teach.   11 *Rough-hew:* Shape roughly.   16 *Finger'd:* Pilfered, pinched.
in fine: Finally, in conclusion.   21 *Larded:* Enriched.   22 *Importing:* Relating to.   23 *bugs:*
Bugbears, hobgoblins.   *in my life:* To be feared if I were allowed to live.   24 *supervise:*
Reading.   *leisure bated:* Delay allowed.   33–34 *Or . . . play:* Before I could consciously turn my
brain to the matter, it had started working on a plan. (*Or* means *ere.*)   35 *fair:* In a clear hand.
36 *statists:* Statesmen.   37 *baseness:* Lower-class trait.   39 *yeoman's:* Substantial, workmanlike.
40 *effect:* Purport.   45 *wheaten garland:* Symbolic of fruitful agriculture, of peace.

And stand a comma° 'tween their amities,
And many such-like as's° of great charge,°
That, on the view and knowing of these contents,
Without debatement further, more or less,
He should those bearers put to sudden death,   50
Not shriving time° allow'd.
Horatio: How was this seal'd?
Hamlet: Why, even in that was heaven ordinant.°
I had my father's signet° in my purse,
Which was the model of that Danish seal;   55
Folded the writ up in the form of th' other,
Subscrib'd° it, gave 't th' impression,° plac'd it safely,
The changeling° never known. Now, the next day
Was our sea-fight, and what to this was sequent
Thou knowest already.   60
Horatio: So Guildenstern and Rosencrantz go to 't.
Hamlet: [Why, man, they did make love to this employment.]
They are not near my conscience. Their defeat
Does by their own insinuation° grow.
'Tis dangerous when the baser nature comes   65
Between the pass° and fell° incensed points
Of mighty opposites.
Horatio: Why, what a king is this!
Hamlet: Does it not, think thee, stand° me now upon—
He that hath killed my king and whor'd my mother,   70
Popp'd in between th' election° and my hopes,
Thrown out his angle° for my proper° life,
And with such coz'nage°—is 't not perfect conscience
[To quit° him with this arm? And is 't not to be damn'd
To let this canker° of our nature come in further evil?   75
Horatio: It must be shortly known to him from England
What is the issue of the business there.
Hamlet: It will be short. The interim is mine,
And a man's life's no more than to say "One."°
But I am very sorry, good Horatio,   80
That to Laertes I forgot myself,
For by the image of my cause I see

---

46 *comma:* Indicating continuity, link.   47 *as's:* (1) The "whereases" of formal document, (2) asses.   *charge:* (1) Import, (2) burden.   51 *shriving-time:* Time for confession and absolution.   53 *ordinant:* Directing.   54 *signet:* Small seal.   57 *Subscrib'd:* Signed.   *impression:* With a wax seal.   58 *changeling:* The substituted letter (literally, a fairy child substituted for a human one).   64 *insinuation:* Interference.   66 *pass:* Thrust.   *fell:* Fierce.   69 *stand:* Become incumbent.   71 *election:* The Danish monarch was "elected" by a small number of high-ranking electors.   72 *angle:* Fishing line.   *proper:* Very.   73 *coz'nage:* Trickery.   74 *quit:* Repay.   75 *canker:* Ulcer.   79 *a man's . . . "One":* To take a man's life requires no more than to count to one as one duels.

The portraiture of his. I'll court his favors.
But, sure, the bravery° of his grief did put me
Into a tow'ring passion.   85

Horatio: Peace, who comes here?]

(Enter a Courtier [Osric].)

Osric: Your lordship is right welcome back to Denmark.

Hamlet: I humbly thank you, sir. [*To Horatio.*] Dost know this
water-fly?   90

Horatio: No, my good lord.

Hamlet: Thy state is the more gracious, for 'tis a vice to know him.
He hath much land, and fertile. Let a beast be lord of beasts, and
his crib shall stand at the King's mess.° 'Tis a chough,° but, as I
say, spacious in the possession of dirt.   95

Osric: Sweet lord, if your lordship were at leisure, I should impart a
thing to you from his Majesty.

Hamlet: I will receive it, sir, with all diligence of spirit. Put your
bonnet to his right use; 'tis for the head.

Osric: I thank your lordship, it is very hot.   100

Hamlet: No, believe me, 'tis very cold; the wind is northerly.

Osric: It is indifferent° cold, my lord, indeed.

Hamlet: But yet methinks it is very sultry and hot for my
complexion.°

Osric: Exceedingly, my lord; it is very sultry, as 'twere—I cannot tell   105
how. My lord, his Majesty bade me signify to you that 'a has laid
a great wager on your head. Sir, this is the matter—

Hamlet: I beseech you, remember—

[Hamlet moves him to put on his hat.]

Osric: Nay, good my lord; for my ease,° in good faith. Sir, here is   110
newly come to court Laertes—believe me, an absolute gentleman,
full of most excellent differences,° of very soft society° and great
showing.° Indeed, to speak feelingly° of him, he is the card° or
calendar° of gentry,° for you shall find in him the continent of
what part° a gentleman would see.   115

Hamlet: Sir, his definement° suffers no perdition° in you, though, I
know, to divide him inventorially° would dozy° th' arithmetic of

---

84 *bravery:* Bravado.   93–94 *Let . . . mess:* If a man, no matter how beastlike, is as rich in possessions as Osric, he may eat at the King's table.   94 *chough:* Chattering jackdaw.   102 *indifferent:* Somewhat.   104 *complexion:* Temperament.   110 *for my ease:* A conventional reply declining the invitation to put his hat back on.   112 *differences:* Special qualities.   *soft
society:* Agreeable manners.   112–13 *great showing:* Distinguished appearance.   113 *feelingly:* With just perception.   *card:* Chart, map.   114 *calendar:* Guide.   *gentry:* Good
breeding.   114–15 *the continent . . . part:* One who contains in him all the qualities (a *continent* is that which contains).   116 *definement:* Definition. (Hamlet proceeds to mock Osric
by using his lofty diction back at him.)   *perdition:* Loss, diminution.   117 *divide him in-
ventorially:* Enumerate his graces.   *dozy:* Dizzy.

memory, and yet but yaw° neither° in respect of° his quick sail.
But, in the verity of extolment,° I take him to be a soul of great
article,° and his infusion° of such dearth and rareness,° as, to make 120
true diction° of him, his semblable° is his mirror, and who else
would trace° him, his umbrage,° nothing more.

Osric: Your lordship speaks most infallibly of him.

Hamlet: The concernancy,° sir? Why do we wrap the gentleman in
our more rawer breath?° 125

Osric: Sir?

Horatio: Is 't not possible to understand in another tongue?° You will
do 't,° sir, really.

Hamlet: What imports the nomination° of this gentleman?

Osric: Of Laertes? 130

Horatio [to Hamlet]: His purse is empty already; all 's golden words
are spent.

Hamlet: Of him, sir.

Osric: I know you are not ignorant—

Hamlet: I would you did, sir; yet, in faith, if you did, it would not 135
much approve° me. Well, sir?

Osric: You are not ignorant of what excellence Laertes is—

Hamlet: I dare not confess that, lest I should compare° with him in
excellence; but to know a man well were to know himself.°

Osric: I mean, sir, for his weapon; but in the imputation laid on him 140
by them,° in his meed° he's unfellow'd.°

Hamlet: What's his weapon?

Osric: Rapier and dagger.

Hamlet: That's two of his weapons—but well.

Osric: The King, sir, hath wager'd with him six Barbary horses, against 145
the which he has impawn'd,° as I take it, six French rapiers and
poniards, with their assigns,° as girdle, hangers,° and so. Three of

---

118 *yaw:* To move unsteadily (said of a ship). *neither:* For all that. *in respect of:* In comparison with. 119 *in . . . extolment:* In true praise (of him). 120 *article:* Moment or importance. *infusion:* Essence, character imparted by nature. *dearth and rareness:* Rarity. 120–21 *make true diction:* Speak truly. 121 *semblable:* Only true likeness. 121–22 *who . . . trace:* Any other person who would wish to follow. 122 *umbrage:* Shadow. 124 *concernancy:* Import, relevance. 125 *breath:* Speech. 127 *to understand . . . tongue:* For Osric to understand when someone else speaks in his manner. (Horatio twits Osric for not being able to understand the kind of flowery speech he himself uses when Hamlet speaks in such a vein.) 127–28 *You will do 't:* You can if you try. 129 *nomination:* Naming. 136 *approve:* Commend. 138 *compare:* Seem to compete. 139 *but . . . himself:* For, to recognize excellence in another man, one must know oneself. 140–41 *imputation . . . them:* Reputation given him by others. 141 *meed:* Merit. *unfellow'd:* Unmatched. 146 *impawn'd:* Staked, wagered. 147 *assigns:* Appurtenances. *hangers:* Straps on the sword belt (*girdle*) from which the sword hung.

the carriages,° in faith, are very dear to fancy,° very responsive° to
the hilts, most delicate° carriages, and of very liberal conceit.°

Hamlet: What call you the carriages?   150

Horatio [to Hamlet]: I knew you must be edified by the margent° ere
you had done.

Osric: The carriages, sir, are the hangers.

Hamlet: The phrase would be more germane to the matter if we could
carry a cannon by our sides; I would it might be hangers till then.   155
But, on: six Barb'ry horses against six French swords, their assigns,
and three liberal-conceited carriages; that's the French bet against
the Danish. Why is this impawn'd, as you call it?

Osric: The King, sir, hath laid,° sir, that in a dozen passes° between
yourself and him, he shall not exceed you three hits. He hath laid   160
on twelve for nine, and it would come to immediate trial, if your
lordship would vouchsafe the answer.

Hamlet: How if I answer no?

Osric: I mean, my lord, the opposition of your person in trial.

Hamlet: Sir, I will walk here in the hall. If it please his Majesty, it is the 165
breathing time° of day with me. Let the foils be brought, the
gentleman willing, and the King hold his purpose, I will win for him
an I can; if not, I will gain nothing but my shame and the odd hits.

Osric: Shall I deliver you so?

Hamlet: To this effect, sir—after what flourish your nature will.   170

Osric: I commend my duty to your lordship.

Hamlet: Yours, yours. [*Exit Osric.*] He does well to commend it
himself; there are no tongues else for 's turn.

Horatio: This lapwing ° runs away with the shell on his head.

Hamlet: 'A did comply, sir, with his dug,° before 'a suck'd it. Thus   175
has he—and many more of the same breed that I know the drossy°
age dotes on—only got the tune° of the time and, out of an habit
of encounter,° a kind of yesty° collection,° which carries them
through and through the most fann'd and winnow'd° opinions;
and do but blow them to their trial, the bubbles are out.°   180

---

148 *carriages:* An affected way of saying *hangers,* literally, gun-carriages. *dear to fancy:*
Fancifully designed, tasteful. *responsive:* Corresponding closely, matching. 149 *delicate:*
I.e., in workmanship. *liberal conceit:* Elaborate design. 151 *margent:* Margin of a book,
place for explanatory notes. 159 *laid:* Wagered. *passes:* Bouts. (The odds of the betting are
hard to explain. Possibly the King bets that Hamlet will win at least five out of twelve, at which
point Laertes raises the odds against himself by betting he will win nine.) 166 *breathing time:*
Exercise period. 174 *lapwing:* A bird that draws intruders away from its nest and was thought
to run about when newly hatched with its head in the shell; a seeming reference to Osric's hat.
175 *comply . . . dug:* Observe ceremonious formality toward his mother's teat. 176 *drossy:*
Frivolous. 177 *tune:* Temper, mood, manner of speech. 177–78 *habit of encounter:*
Demeanor of social intercourse. 178 *yesty:* Yeasty, frothy. *collection:* I.e., of current phrases.
179 *fann'd and winnow'd:* Select and refined. 180 *blow . . . out:* Put them to the test, and
their ignorance is exposed.

(Enter a Lord.)

Lord: My lord, his Majesty commended him to you by young Osric, who brings back to him that you attend him in the hall. He sends to know if your pleasure hold to play with Laertes, or that you will take longer time.   185

Hamlet: I am constant to my purposes; they follow the King's pleasure. If his fitness speaks,° mine is ready; now or whensoever, provided I be so able as now.

Lord: The King and Queen and all are coming down.

Hamlet: In happy time.°   190

Lord: The Queen desires you to use some gentle entertainment° to Laertes before you fall to play.

Hamlet: She well instructs me.   *[Exit Lord.]*

Horatio: You will lose, my lord.

Hamlet: I do not think so. Since he went into France, I have been in   195
continual practice; I shall win at the odds. But thou wouldst not think how ill all's here about my heart; but it is no matter.

Horatio: Nay, good my lord—

Hamlet: It is but foolery, but it is such a kind of gain-giving,° as would perhaps trouble a woman.   200

Horatio: If your mind dislike anything, obey it. I will forestall their repair hither, and say you are not fit.

Hamlet: Not a whit, we defy augury. There is special providence in the fall of a sparrow. If it be now, 'tis not to come; if it be not to come, it will be now; if it be not now; yet it will come. The   205
readiness is all. Since no man of aught he leaves knows what is 't to leave betimes,° let be.

(A table prepar'd. [Enter] trumpets, drums, and Officers with cushions; King, Queen, [Osric,] and all the State; foils, daggers, [and wine borne in;] and Laertes.)   210

King: Come, Hamlet, come, and take this hand from me.

>   *[The King puts Laertes' hand into Hamlet's.]*

Hamlet: Give me your pardon, sir. I have done you wrong,
But pardon 't, as you are a gentleman.
This presence° knows,   215
And you must needs have heard, how I am punish'd
With a sore distraction. What I have done
That might your nature, honor, and exception°
Roughly awake, I here proclaim was madness.
Was 't Hamlet wrong'd Laertes? Never Hamlet.   220

187 *If . . . speaks:* If his readiness answers to the time.   190 *In happy time:* A phrase of courtesy indicating acceptance.   191 *entertainment:* Greeting.   199 *gain-giving:* Misgiving.
206–7 *what . . . betimes:* What is the best time to leave it.   215 *presence:* Royal assembly.
218 *exception:* Disapproval.

If Hamlet from himself be ta'en away,
And when he's not himself does wrong Laertes,
Then Hamlet does it not, Hamlet denies it.
Who does it, then? His madness. If 't be so,
Hamlet is of the faction that is wrong'd;   225
His madness is poor Hamlet's enemy.
[Sir, in this audience,]
Let my disclaiming from a purpos'd evil
Free me so far in your most generous thoughts
That I have shot my arrow o'er the house   230
And hurt my brother.
Laertes: I am satisfied in nature,°
Whose motive in this case should stir me most
To my revenge. But in my terms of honor
I stand aloof, and will no reconcilement   235
Till by some elder masters of known honor
I have a voice° and precedent of peace
To keep my name ungor'd. But till that time,
I do receive your offer'd love like love,
And will not wrong it.   240
Hamlet: I embrace it freely,
And will this brothers' wager frankly play.
Give us the foils. Come on.
Laertes: Come, one for me.
Hamlet: I'll be your foil,° Laertes. In mine ignorance   245
Your skill shall, like a star i' th' darkest night,
Stick fiery off° indeed.
Laertes: You mock me, sir.
Hamlet: No, by this hand.
King: Give them the foils, young Osric. Cousin Hamlet,   250
You know the wager?
Hamlet: Very well, my lord.
Your Grace has laid the odds o' th' weaker side.
King: I do not fear it; I have seen you both.
But since he is better'd,° we have therefore odds.   255
Laertes: This is too heavy, let me see another.

[Exchanges his foil for another.]

Hamlet: This likes me well. These foils have all a length?

[They prepare to play.]

Osric: Ay, my good lord.   260

---

232 *in nature:* As to my personal feelings.   237 *voice:* Authoritative pronouncement.   245 *foil:*
Thin metal background which sets a jewel off (with pun on the blunted rapier for fencing).
247 *Stick fiery off:* Stand out brilliantly.   255 *is better'd:* Has improved; is the odds-on-favorite.

King: Set me the stoups of wine upon that table.
    If Hamlet give the first or second hit,
    Or quit° in answer of the third exchange,
    Let all the battlements their ordnance fire.
    The King shall drink to Hamlet's better breath,   265
    And in the cup an union° shall he throw,
    Richer than that which four successive kings
    In Denmark's crown have worn. Give me the cups,
    And let the kettle° to the trumpet speak,
    The trumpet to the cannoneer without,   270
    The cannons to the heavens, the heaven to earth,
    "Now the King drinks to Hamlet." Come, begin.

                                        (*Trumpets the while.*)

    And you, the judges, bear a wary eye.
Hamlet: Come on sir.   275
Laertes: Come, my lord.

                          [*They play. Hamlet scores a hit.*]

Hamlet: One.
Laertes: No.
Hamlet: Judgment.   280
Osric: A hit, a very palpable hit.

                          (*Drum, trumpets, and shot. Flourish.
                                        A piece goes off.*)

Laertes: Well, again.
King: Stay, give me drink. Hamlet, this pearl is thine.   285

            [*He throws a pearl in Hamlet's cup, and drinks.*]

    Here's to thy health. Give him the cup.
Hamlet: I'll play this bout first; set it by awhile. Come. [*They play.*]
    Another hit; what say you?
Laertes: A touch, a touch, I do confess 't.   290
King: Our son shall win.
Queen: He's fat,° and scant of breath.
    Here, Hamlet, take my napkin,° rub thy brows.
    The Queen carouses° to thy fortune, Hamlet.
Hamlet: Good madam!   295
King: Gertrude, do not drink.
Queen: I will, my lord; I pray you pardon me.

                                                    [*Drinks.*]

King [aside]: It is the pois'ned cup. It is too late.

---

263 *quit:* Repay (with a hit).   266 *union:* Pearl (so called, according to Pliny's *Natural History,*
IX, because pearls are *unique,* never identical.   269 *kettle:* Kettledrum.   292 *fat:* Not physically fit, out of training.   293 *napkin:* Handkerchief: 294 *carouses:* Drinks a toast.

Hamlet: I dare not drink yet, madam; by and by.   300
Queen: Come, let me wipe thy face.
Laertes [to King]:   My lord, I'll hit him now.
King: I do not think 't.
Laertes [aside]:   And yet it is almost against my conscience.
Hamlet: Come, for the third, Laertes. You do but dally.   305
    I pray you, pass with your best violence;
    I am afeard you make a wanton of me.°
Laertes: Say you so? Come on.   *[They play.]*
Osric: Nothing, neither way.
Laertes: Have at you now!   310

> *[Laertes wounds Hamlet; then, in scuffling,*
> *they change rapiers,° and Hamlet wounds Laertes.]*

King: Part them! They are incens'd.
Hamlet: Nay, come, again.

>   *[The Queen fails.]*   315

Osric: Look to the Queen there, ho!
Horatio: They bleed on both sides. How is it, my lord?
Osric: How is 't, Laertes?
Laertes: Why, as a woodcock° to mine own springe,° Osric;
    I am justly kill'd with mine own treachery.   320
Hamlet: How does the Queen?
King: She swoons to see them bleed.
Queen: No, no, the drink, the drink—O my dear Hamlet—
    The drink, the drink! I am pois'ned.   *[Dies.]*
Hamlet: O villainy! Ho, let the door be lock'd!   325
    Treachery! Seek it out.   *[Laertes falls.]*
Laertes: It is here, Hamlet. Hamlet, thou art slain.
    No med'cine in the world can do thee good;
    In thee there is not half an hour's life.
    The treacherous instrument is in thy hand,   330
    Unbated° and envenom'd. The foul practice
    Hath turn'd itself on me. Lo, here I lie,
    Never to rise again. Thy mother's pois'ned.
    I can no more. The King, the King's to blame.
Hamlet: The point envenom'd too? Then, venom, to thy work.   335

>   *[Stabs the King.]*

All: Treason! Treason!

---

307 *make . . . me:* Treat me like a spoiled child, holding back to give me an advantage.
311–12 *in scuffling, they change rapiers:* This stage direction occurs in the Folio. According to
a widespread stage tradition, Hamlet receives a scratch, realizes that Laertes's sword is unbated,
and accordingly forces an exchange.   319 *woodcock:* A bird, a type of stupidity or as a decoy.
springe: Trap, snare.   331 *Unbated:* Not blunted with a button.

King: O, yet defend me, friends; I am but hurt.
Hamlet: Here, thou incestuous, murd'rous, damned Dane,

> *[He forces the King to drink*   340
> *the poisoned cup.]*

    Drink off this potion. Is thy union° here?
    Follow my mother.   *[King dies.]*
Laertes: He is justly serv'd.
    It is a poison temper'd° by himself.   345
    Exchange forgiveness with me, noble Hamlet.
    Mine and my father's death come not upon thee,
    Nor thine on me!   *[Dies.]*
Hamlet: Heaven make thee free of it! I follow thee.
    I am dead, Horatio. Wretched Queen, adieu!   350
    You that look pale and tremble at this chance,
    That are but mutes° or audience to this act,
    Had I but time—as this fell° sergeant,° Death,
    Is strict in his arrest—O, I could tell you—
    But let it be. Horatio, I am dead;   355
    Thou livest. Report me and my cause aright
    To the unsatisfied.
Horatio: Never believe it.
    I am more an antique Roman° than a Dane.
    Here's yet some liquor left.   360

> *[He attempts to drink from the poisoned cup.*
> *Hamlet prevents him.]*

Hamlet: As th' art a man,
    Give me the cup! Let go! By heaven, I'll ha 't.
    O God, Horatio, what a wounded name,   365
    Things standing thus unknown, shall I leave behind me!
    If thou didst ever hold me in thy heart,
    Absent thee from felicity awhile,
    And in this harsh world draw thy breath in pain
    To tell my story.   370

> *(A march afar off [and a volley within].)*

Osric: What warlike noise is this?
    Young Fortinbras, with conquest come from Poland,
    To the ambassadors of England gives
    This warlike volley.   375
Hamlet: O, I die, Horatio!
    The potent poison quite o'ercrows° my spirit.

---

342 *union:* Pearl (see line 276; with grim puns on the word's other meanings: marriage, shared death?).   345 *temper'd:* Mixed.   352 *mutes:* Silent observers.   353 *fell:* Cruel   *sergeant:* Sheriff's officer.   359 *Roman:* It was the Roman custom to follow masters in death. 377 *o'ercrows:* Triumphs over.

I cannot live to hear the news from England,
But I do prophesy th' election lights
On Fortinbras. He has my dying voice.°   380
So tell him, with th' occurrents° more and less
Which have solicited°—the rest is silence.   *[Dies.]*
Horatio: Now cracks a noble heart. Good night, sweet prince;
And flights of angels sing thee to thy rest!

                                                        [March within.] 385

Why does the drum come hither?

(Enter Fortinbras, with the [English] Ambassadors [with
drum, colors, and attendants].)

Fortinbras: Where is this sight?
Horatio: What is it you would see?   390
If aught of woe or wonder, cease your search.
Fortinbras: This quarry° cries on havoc.° O proud Death,
What feast is toward° in thine eternal cell,
That thou so many princes at a shot
So bloodily hast struck?   395
First Ambassador: The sight is dismal;
And our affairs from England come too late.
The ears are senseless that should give us hearing,
To tell him his commandment is fulfill'd,
That Rosencrantz and Guildenstern are dead.   400
Where should we have our thanks?
Horatio: Not from his° mouth,
Had it th' ability of life to thank you.
He never gave commandment for their death.
But since, so jump° upon this bloody question,°   405
You from the Polack wars, and you from England,
Are here arriv'd, give order that these bodies
High on a stage° be placed to the view,
And let me speak to th' yet unknowing world
How these things came about. So shall you hear   410
Of carnal, bloody, and unnatural acts,
Of accidental judgments,° casual° slaughters,
Of deaths put on° by cunning and forc'd cause,
And, in this upshot, purposes mistook
Fall'n on th' inventors' heads. All this can I   415
Truly deliver.

---

380 *voice:* Vote.   381 *occurrents:* Events, incidents.   382 *solicited:* Moved, urged.
392 *quarry:* Heap of dead.   *cries on havoc:* Proclaims a general slaughter.   393 *toward:* In
preparation.   402 *his:* Claudius's.   405 *jump:* Precisely.   *question:* Dispute.   408 *stage:*
Platform.   412 *judgments:* Retributions.   *casual:* Occurring by chance.   413 *put on:*
Instigated.

Fortinbras: Let us haste to hear it,
  And call the noblest to the audience.
  For me, with sorrow I embrace my fortune.
  I have some rights of memory° in this kingdom,   420
  Which now to claim my vantage° doth invite me.
Horatio: Of that I shall have also cause to speak,
  And from his mouth whose voice will draw on more.°
  But let this same be presently° perform'd,
  Even while men's minds are wild, lest more mischance   425
  On° plots and errors happen.
Fortinbras: Let four captains
  Bear Hamlet, like a soldier, to the stage,
  For he was likely, had he been put on,°
  To have prov'd most royal; and, for his passage,°   430
  The soldiers' music and the rite of war
  Speak loudly for him.
  Take up the bodies. Such a sight as this
  Becomes the field,° but here shows much amiss.
  Go, bid the soldiers shoot.   435

(*Exeunt [marching, bearing off the dead bodies;*
a peal of ordnance is shot off].)

420 *of memory:* Traditional, remembered.   421 *vantage:* Presence at this opportune moment.
423 *voice . . . more:* Vote will influence still others.   424 *presently:* Immediately.   426 *On:*
On the basis of.   429 *put on:* Invested in royal office, and so put to the test.   430 *passage:*
Death.   434 *field:* I.e., of battle.

Sophocles   (c. 496–406 B.C.)

*Sophocles lived in Athens during the last Persian invasion and its defeat. The great
age of Athens began in 480 B.C. and before Sophocles died, Pericles and Phidias
had rebuilt the Acropolis and erected the Parthenon. Sophocles, unlike his
predecessors, was not an actor. He broke with tradition by writing plays but not
acting in them. Although we know he wrote at least ninety plays, only a few have
survived. We have the great Oedipus trilogy:* Antigone *(441 B.C.),* Oedipus Rex
(c. 430–27 B.C.), and Oedipus at Colonus *(401 B.C.). Besides these are* Ajax,
Philoctetes, Trachiniae, *and* Elektra.

*Sophocles' tragedies, like all Greek plays, were produced during great
celebrations. The audiences at the outdoor theaters numbered fifteen thousand
people, and the acoustics were designed so carefully that everyone in the theater
could hear the action on stage. The actors and the chorus, fifteen citizens of Thebes
in this play, held large masks in front of their faces. The masks identified their
characters and helped emphasize the text of the play by preventing charismatic
actors from distracting the audience.*

Aristotle considered Oedipus Rex *the masterpiece of Greek drama and used it to illustrate the perfection of tragedy. He praised its unities: it tells only one story and has no distracting subplot; the action takes place in the time it takes to perform the play, with no break for an intermission; and all the action takes place in front of Oedipus's palace. The tension of the play rises constantly until Oedipus realizes that he is responsible for the plague. At that moment the action falls sharply toward the conclusion. Aristotle felt that this combination—simultaneous recognition and reversal—made for perfection in tragedy.*

Oedipus Rex *is the story of a man who attempts to flee his fate. It was prophesied that he would kill his father, King Laios, and marry his mother, Iokaste. Knowing this, Laios had him left to die in a remote area, his feet pierced and bound. But the shepherd assigned this task took pity on the infant and gave him to a childless couple. When he grew up, Oedipus heard about the prophesy and determined to leave home to avoid hurting his parents. Ironically, however, he headed directly toward his true home, Thebes, murdering Laios along the way.*

When the play opens, Oedipus has married Iokaste and become king because he has solved the riddle of the Sphinx. But Thebes now suffers a plague brought on by the failure of the Thebans to solve the murder of Laios. Oedipus, the source of the plague, begins the action by vowing to find the murderer and punish him no matter who he is. The irony is that he has no way of knowing where that search will lead him. In pride, he demands that people tell him what they know no matter what the cost. But the closer he gets to the truth, the less his pride permits him to believe it. This prideful resistance builds both suspense and tension throughout the rising action. Finally, however, Oedipus displays his nobility by facing the truth squarely. The play does not end with his death—not all tragedies do—but he suffers the twin pains of blindness and exile. Blindness is emblematic of his inability to see the truth about himself, and exile is emblematic of his condition before he returned to Thebes. His ultimate fate, the humbling of his pride, is in some ways worse than death.

OEDIPUS REX   (c. 430 B.C.)

Translated by Dudley Fitts and Robert Fitzgerald

Characters

Oedipus, King of Thebes, supposed son of Polybos and Merope, King and Queen of Corinth

Iokaste, wife of Oedipus and widow of the late King Laios

Kreon, brother of Iokaste, a prince of Thebes

Teiresias, a blind seer who serves Apollo

Priest

Messenger, from Corinth

Shepherd, former servant of Laios

Second Messenger, from the palace

Chorus of Theban Elders

Choragos, leader of the Chorus

Antigone and *Ismene*, young daughters of Oedipus and Iokaste. They appear in the Exodos but do not speak.

Suppliants, Guards, Servants

(Scene: *Before the palace of Oedipus, King of Thebes. A central door and two lateral doors open onto a platform which runs the length of the facade. On the platform, right and left, are altars; and three steps lead down into the orchestra, or chorus-ground. At the beginning of the action these steps are crowded by suppliants who have brought branches and chaplets of olive leaves and who sit in various attitudes of despair. Oedipus enters.*)

PROLOGUE°

Oedipus: My children, generations of the living
    In the line of Kadmos,° nursed at his ancient hearth:
    Why have you strewn yourselves before these altars
    In supplication, with your boughs and garlands?
    The breath of incense rises from the city   5
    with a sound of prayer and lamentation.
                                  Children,
    I would not have you speak through messengers,
    and therefore I have come myself to hear you—
    I, Oedipus, who bear the famous name.   10
    (*To a Priest.*) You, there, since you are eldest in the company,
    Speak for them all, tell me what preys upon you,
    Whether you come in dread, or crave some blessing:
    Tell me, and never doubt that I will help you
    In every way I can; I should be heartless   15
    Were I not moved to find you suppliant here.
Priest: Great Oedipus, O powerful king of Thebes!
    You see how all the ages of our people
    Cling to your altar steps: here are boys
    Who can barely stand alone, and here are priests   20
    By weight of age, as I am a priest of God,
    And young men chosen from those yet unmarried;
    As for the others, all that multitude,
    They wait with olive chaplets in the squares,
    At the two shrines of Pallas,° and where Apollo°   25
    Speaks in the glowing embers.
                        Your own eyes
    Must tell you: Thebes is tossed on a murdering sea
    And cannot lift her head from the death surge.
    A rust consumes the buds and fruits of the earth;   30
    The herds are sick; children die unborn,
    And labor is vain. The god of plague and pyre

Prologue: Portion of the play explaining the background and current action.   2 *Kadmos:* Founder of Thebes.   25 *Pallas:* Pallas Athene, daughter of Zeus and goddess of wisdom. *Apollo:* Son of Zeus and god of the sun, of light and truth.

Raids like detestable lightning through the city,
And all the house of Kadmos is laid waste,
All emptied, and all darkened: Death alone   35
Battens upon the misery of Thebes.

You are not one of the immortal gods, we know;
Yet we have come to you to make our prayer
As to the man surest in mortal ways
And wisest in the ways of God. You saved us   40
From the Sphinx,° that flinty singer, and the tribute
We paid to her so long; yet you were never
Better informed than we, nor could we teach you:
A god's touch, it seems, enabled you to help us.

Therefore, O mighty power, we turn to you: 45
Find us our safety, find us a remedy,
Whether by counsel of the gods or of men.
A king of wisdom tested in the past
Can act in a time of troubles, and act well.
Noblest of men, restore   50
Life to your city! Think how all men call you
Liberator for your boldness long ago;
Ah, when your years of kingship are remembered,
Let them not say *We rose, but later fell—*
Keep the State from going down in the storm!   55
Once, years ago, with happy augury,
You brought us fortune; be the same again!
No man questions your power to rule the land:
But rule over men, not over a dead city!
Ships are only hulls, high walls are nothing,   60
When no life moves in the empty passageways.
Oedipus: Poor children! You may be sure I know
All that you longed for in your coming here.
I know that you are deathly sick; and yet,
Sick as you are, not one is as sick as I.   65
Each of you suffers in himself alone
His anguish, not another's; but my spirit
Groans for the city, for myself, for you.

I was not sleeping, you are not waking me.
No, I have been in tears for a long while   70
And in my restless thought walked many ways.
In all my search I found one remedy,

---

41 *Sphinx:* A winged monster with the body of a lion and the face of a woman, the Sphinx had tormented Thebes with her riddle, killing those who could not solve it. When Oedipus solved the riddle, the Sphinx killed herself.

And I have adopted it: I have sent Kreon,
Son of Menoikeus, brother of the queen,
To Delphi,° Apollo's place of revelation,   75
To learn there, if he can,
What act or pledge of mine may save the city.
I have counted the days, and now, this very day,
I am troubled, for he has overstayed his time.
What is he doing? He has been gone too long.   80
Yet whenever he comes back, I should do ill
Not to take any action the god orders.
Priest: It is a timely promise. At this instant
They tell me Kreon is here.
Oedipus: O Lord Apollo!   85
May his news be fair as his face is radiant!
Priest: Good news, I gather! he is crowned with bay,
The chaplet is thick with berries.
Oedipus: We shall soon know;
He is near enough to hear us now. (*Enter Kreon.*) O prince: 90
Brother: son of Menoikeus:
What answer do you bring us from the god?
Kreon: A strong one. I can tell you, great afflictions
Will turn out well, if they are taken well.
Oedipus: What was the oracle? These vague words   95
Leave me still hanging between hope and fear.
Kreon: Is it your pleasure to hear me with all these
Gathered around us? I am prepared to speak,
But should we not go in?
Oedipus: Speak to them all,   100
It is for them I suffer, more than for myself.
Kreon: Then I will tell you what I heard at Delphi.
In plain words
The god commands us to expel from the land of Thebes
An old defilement we are sheltering.   105
It is a deathly thing, beyond cure;
We must not let it feed upon us longer.
Oedipus: What defilement? How shall we rid ourselves of it?
Kreon: By exile or death, blood for blood. It was
Murder that brought the plague-wind on the city.   110
Oedipus: Murder of whom? Surely the god has named him?
Kreon: My Lord: Laios once ruled this land,
Before you came to govern us.
Oedipus: I know;
I learned of him from others; I never saw him.   115

75 *Delphi:* Site of the oracle, source of religious authority and prophecy, under the protection
of Apollo.

Kreon: He was murdered; and Apollo commands us now
   To take revenge upon whoever killed him.
Oedipus: Upon whom? Where are they? Where shall we find a clue
   To solve that crime, after so many years?
Kreon: Here in this land, he said. Search reveals   120
   Things that escape an inattentive man.
Oedipus: Tell me: Was Laios murdered in his house,
   Or in the fields, or in some foreign country?
Kreon: He said he planned to make a pilgrimage.
   He did not come home again.   125
Oedipus: And was there no one,
   No witness, no companion, to tell what happened?
Kreon: They were all killed but one, and he got away
   So frightened that he could remember one thing only.
Oedipus: What was that one thing? One may be the key   130
   To everything, if we resolve to use it.
Kreon: He said that a band of highwaymen attacked them,
   Outnumbered them, and overwhelmed the king.
Oedipus: Strange, that a highwayman should be so daring—
   Unless some faction here bribed him to do it   135
Kreon: We thought of that. But after Laios' death
   New troubles arose and we had no avenger.
Oedipus: What troubles could prevent your hunting down the killers?
Kreon: The riddling Sphinx's song
   Made us deaf to all mysteries but her own.   140
Oedipus: Then once more I must bring what is dark to light.
   It is most fitting that Apollo shows,
   As you do, this compunction for the dead.
   You shall see how I stand by you, as I should,
   Avenging this country and the god as well,   145
   And not as though it were for some distant friend,
   But for my own sake, to be rid of evil.
   Whoever killed King Laios might—who knows?—
   Lay violent hands even on me—and soon.
   I act for the murdered king in my own interest.   150

   Come, then, my children: leave the altar steps,
   Lift up your olive boughs!
              One of you go
   And summon the people of Kadmos to gather here.
   I will do all that I can; you may tell them that.   155

                     (Exit a Page.)

   So, with the help of God,
   We shall be saved—or else indeed we are lost.

Priest: Let us rise, children. It was for this we came,
  and now the king has promised it.   160
  Phoibos° has sent us an oracle; may he descend
  Himself to save us and drive out the plague.

> *(Exeunt° Oedipus and Kreon into the palace by the
> central door. The Priest and the Suppliants disperse
> right and left. After a short pause the Chorus enters
> the orchestra.)*

161 *Phoibos:* Apollo.   163 *Exeunt:* Latin for "they go out."

PARODOS°

Strophe° 1

Chorus: What is God singing in his profound
  Delphi of gold and shadow?
  What oracle for Thebes, the Sunwhipped city?
  Fear unjoints me, the roots of my heart tremble.
  Now I remember, O Healer, your power, and wonder: 5
  Will you send doom like a sudden cloud, or weave it
  Like nightfall of the past?
  Speak to me, tell me, O
  Child of golden Hope, immortal Voice.

Antistrophe° 1

  Let me pray to Athene, the immortal daughter of Zeus,   10
  And to Artemis° her sister
  Who keeps her famous throne in the market ring,
  And to Apollo, archer from distant heaven—
  O gods, descend! Like three streams leap against
  The fires of our grief, the fires of darkness;   15
  Be swift to bring us rest!
  As in the old time from the brilliant house
  Of air you stepped to save us, come again!

Strophe 2

  Now our afflictions have no end,
  Now all our stricken host lies down   20
  And no man fights off death with his mind;

Parodos: The song or ode chanted by the Chorus on their entry.   *Strophe:* Song sung by the Chorus as they danced from stage right to stage left.   *Antistrophe:* Song sung by the Chorus following the Strophe, as they danced back from stage left to stage right.   11 *Artemis:* The huntress, daughter of Zeus, twin sister of Apollo.

The noble plowland bears no grain,
And groaning mothers cannot bear—
See, how our lives like birds take wing,
Like sparks that fly when a fire soars,   25
To the shore of the god of evening.

Antistrophe 2

The plague burns on, it is pitiless,
Though pallid children laden with death
Lie unwept in the stony ways,
And old gray women by every path   30
Flock to the strand about the altars
There to strike their breasts and cry
Worship of Phoibos in wailing prayers:
Be kind, God's golden child!

Strophe 3

There are no swords in this attack by fire,   35
No shields, but we are ringed with cries.
Send the besieger plunging from our homes
Into the vast sea-room of the Atlantic
Or into the waves that foam eastward of Thrace—
For the day ravages what the night spares—   40
Destroy our enemy, lord of the thunder!
Let him be riven by lightning from heaven!

Antistrophe 3

Phoibos Apollo, stretch the sun's bowstring,
That golden cord, until it sing for us,
Flashing arrows in heaven!   45
                    Artemis, Huntress,
Race with flaring lights upon our mountains!
O scarlet god,° O golden-banded brow,
O Theban Bacchos in a storm of Maenads,°

(Enter Oedipus, center.)   50

Whirl upon Death, that all the Undying hate!
Come with blinding torches, come in joy!

48 *scarlet god:* Bacchus, god of wine and revelry; also called Dionysus.   49 *Maenads:* Female
worshipers of Bacchus (Dionysus).

SCENE 1

Oedipus: Is this your prayer? It may be answered. Come,
           Listen to me, act as the crisis demands,
           And you shall have relief from all these evils.

Until now I was a stranger to this tale,
As I had been a stranger to the crime. 5
Could I track down the murderer without a clue?
But now, friends,
As one who became a citizen after the murder,
I make this proclamation to all Thebans:
If any man knows by whose hand Laios, son of Labdakos, 10
Met his death, I direct that man to tell me everything,
No matter what he fears for having so long withheld it.
Let it stand as promised that no further trouble
Will come to him, but he may leave the land in safety.
Moreover: If anyone knows the murderer to be foreign, 15
Let him not keep silent: he shall have his reward from me.
However, if he does conceal it; if any man
Fearing for his friend or for himself disobeys this edict,
Hear what I propose to do:

I solemnly forbid the people of this country, 20
Where power and throne are mine, ever to receive that man
Or speak to him, no matter who he is, or let him
Join in sacrifice, lustration, or in prayer.
I decree that he be driven from every house,
Being, as he is, corruption itself to us: the Delphic 25
Voice of Apollo has pronounced this revelation.
Thus I associate myself with the oracle
And take the side of the murdered king.

As for the criminal, I pray to God—
Whether it be a lurking thief, or one of a number— 30
I pray that that man's life be consumed in evil and wretchedness.
And as for me, this curse applies no less
If it should turn out that the culprit is my guest here,
Sharing my hearth.
     You have heard the penalty. 35
I lay it on you now to attend to this
For my sake, for Apollo's, for the sick
Sterile city that heaven has abandoned.
Suppose the oracle had given you no command:
Should this defilement go uncleansed for ever? 40
You should have found the murderer: your king,
A noble king, had been destroyed!
     Now I,
Having the power that he held before me,
Having his bed, begetting children there 45
Upon his wife, as he would have, had he lived—
Their son would have been my children's brother,

If Laios had had luck in fatherhood!
(And now his bad fortune has struck him down)—
I say I take the son's part, just as though   50
I were his son, to press the fight for him
And see it won! I'll find the hand that brought
Death to Labdakos' and Polydoros' child,
Heir of Kadmos' and Agenor's line.°
And as for those who fail me,   55
May the gods deny them the fruit of the earth,
Fruit of the womb, and may they rot utterly!
Let them be wretched as we are wretched, and worse!

For you, for loyal Thebans, and for all
Who find my actions right, I pray the favor   60
Of justice, and of all the immortal gods.
Choragos:° Since I am under oath, my lord, I swear
I did not do the murder, I cannot name
The murderer. Phoibos ordained the search;
Why did he not say who the culprit was?   65
Oedipus: An honest question. But no man in the world
Can make the gods do more than the gods will.
Choragos: There is an alternative, I think—
Oedipus: Tell me.
Any or all, you must not fail to tell me.   70
Choragos: A lord clairvoyant to the lord Apollo,
As we all know, is the skilled Teiresias.
One might learn much about this from him, Oedipus.
Oedipus: I am not wasting time:
Kreon spoke of this, and I have sent for him—   75
Twice, in fact; it is strange that he is not here.
Choragos: The other matter—that old report—seems useless.
Oedipus: What was that? I am interested in all reports.
Choragos: The king was said to have been killed by highwaymen.
Oedipus: I know. But we have no witnesses to that.   80
Choragos: If the killer can feel a particle of dread,
Your curse will bring him out of hiding!
Oedipus: No.
The man who dared that act will fear no curse.

(*Enter the blind seer Teiresias, led by a Page.*)   85

Choragos: But there is one man who may detect the criminal.
This is Teiresias, this is the holy prophet
In whom, alone of all men, truth was born.

53–54 *Labdakos, Polydoros, Kadmos, and Agenor:* Father, grandfather, great-grandfather, and great-great-grandfather of Laios.   62 *Choragos:* Leader of the Chorus.

Oedipus: Teiresias: seer: student of mysteries,
      Of all that's taught and all that no man tells,   90
      Secrets of Heaven and secrets of the earth:
      Blind though you are, you know the city lies
      Sick with plague; and from this plague, my lord,
      We find that you alone can guard or save us.

      Possibly you did not hear the messengers?   95
      Apollo, when we sent to him,
      Sent us back word that this great pestilence
      Would lift, but only if we established clearly
      The identity of those who murdered Laios.
      They must be killed or exiled.   100
                                    Can you use
      Birdflight° or any part of divination
      To purify yourself, and Thebes, and me
      From this contagion? We are in your hands.
      There is no fairer duty   105
      Than that of helping others in distress.
Teiresias: How dreadful knowledge of the truth can be
      When there's no help in truth! I knew this well,
      But did not act on it; else I should not have come.
Oedipus: What is troubling you? Why are your eyes so cold?   110
Teiresias: Let me go home. Bear your own fate, and I'll
      Bear mine. It is better so: trust what I say.
Oedipus: What you say is ungracious and unhelpful
      To your native country. Do not refuse to speak.
Teiresias: When it comes to speech, your own is neither temperate   115
      Nor opportune. I wish to be more prudent.
Oedipus: In God's name, we all beg you—
Teiresias: You are all ignorant.
      No; I will never tell you what I know.
      Now it is my misery; then, it would be yours.   120
Oedipus: What! You do know something, and will not tell us?
      You would betray us all and wreck the State?
Teiresias: I do not intend to torture myself, or you.
      Why persist in asking? You will not persuade me.
Oedipus: What a wicked old man you are! You'd try a stone's   125
      Patience! Out with it! Have you no feeling at all?
Teiresias: You call me unfeeling. If you could only see
      The nature of your own feelings . . .
Oedipus: Why,
      Who would not feel as I do? Who could endure   130
      Your arrogance toward the city?

---

102 *Birdflight:* Prophets used the flight of birds to predict the future.

Teiresias: What does it matter?
Whether I speak or not, it is bound to come.
Oedipus: Then, if "it" is bound to come, you are bound to tell me.
Teiresias: No, I will not go on. Rage as you please. 135
Oedipus: Rage? Why not!
And I'll tell you what I think:
You planned it, you had it done, you all but
Killed him with your own hands: if you had eyes,
I'd say the crime was yours, and yours alone. 140
Teiresias: So? I charge you, then,
Abide by the proclamation you have made:
From this day forth
Never speak again to these men or to me;
You yourself are the pollution of this country. 145
Oedipus: You dare say that! Can you possibly think you have
Some way of going free, after such insolence?
Teiresias: I have gone free. It is the truth sustains me.
Oedipus: Who taught you shamelessness? It was not your craft.
Teiresias: You did. You made me speak. I did not want to. 150
Oedipus: Speak what? Let me hear it again more clearly.
Teiresias: Was it not clear before? Are you tempting me?
Oedipus: I did not understand it. Say it again.
Teiresias: I say that you are the murderer whom you seek.
Oedipus: Now twice you have spat out infamy. You'll pay for it! 155
Teiresias: Would you care for more? Do you wish to be really angry?
Oedipus: Say what you will. Whatever you say is worthless.
Teiresias: I say you live in hideous shame with those
Most dear to you. You cannot see the evil.
Oedipus: Can you go on babbling like this for ever? 160
Teiresias: I can, if there is power in truth.
Oedipus: There is:
But not for you, not for you,
You sightless, witless, senseless, mad old man!
Teiresias: You are the madman. There is no one here 165
Who will not curse you soon, as you curse me.
Oedipus: You child of total night! I would not touch you;
Neither would any man who sees the sun.
Teiresias: True: it is not from you my fate will come.
That lies within Apollo's competence, 170
As it is his concern.
Oedipus: Tell me, who made
These fine discoveries? Kreon? or someone else?
Teiresias: Kreon is no threat. You weave your own doom.
Oedipus: Wealth, power, craft of statemanship! 175
Kingly position, everywhere admired!

What savage envy is stored up against these,
If Kreon, whom I trusted, Kreon my friend,
For this great office which the city once
Put in my hands unsought—if for this power   180
Kreon desires in secret to destroy me!

He has bought this decrepit fortune-teller, this
Collector of dirty pennies, this prophet fraud—
Why, he is no more clairvoyant than I am!
                                        Tell us: 185
Has your mystic mummery ever approached the truth?
When that hellcat the Sphinx was performing here,
What help were you to these people?
Her magic was not for the first man who came along:
It demanded a real exorcist. Your birds—   190
What good were they? or the gods, for the matter of that?
But I came by,
Oedipus, the simple man, who knows nothing—
I thought it out for myself, no birds helped me!
And this is the man you think you can destroy,   195
That you may be close to Kreon when he's king!
Well, you and your friend Kreon, it seems to me,
Will suffer most. If you were not an old man,
You would have paid already for your plot.
Choragos: We cannot see that his words or yours   200
    Have been spoken except in anger, Oedipus,
    And of anger we have no need. How to accomplish
    The god's will best: that is what most concerns us.
Teiresias: You are a king. But where argument's concerned
    I am your man, as much a king as you.   205
    I am not your servant, but Apollo's.
    I have no need of Kreon or Kreon's name.

    Listen to me. You mock my blindness, do you?
    But I say that you, with both your eyes, are blind:
    You cannot see the wretchedness of your life,   210
    Nor in whose house you live, no, nor with whom.
    Who are your father and mother? Can you tell me?
    You do not even know the blind wrongs
    That you have done them, on earth and in the world below.
    But the double lash of your parents' curse will whip you   215
    Out of this land some day, with only night
    Upon your precious eyes.
    Your cries then—where will they not be heard?
    What fastness of Kithairon° will not echo them?

219 *Kithairon:* The mountain where Oedipus was abandoned as an infant.

And that bridal-descant of yours—you'll know it then,   220
The song they sang when you came here to Thebes
And found your misguided berthing.
All this, and more, that you cannot guess at now,
Will bring you to yourself among your children.

Be angry, then. Curse Kreon. Curse my words.   225
I tell you, no man that walks upon the earth
Shall be rooted out more horribly than you.
Oedipus: Am I to bear this from him?—Damnation
Take you! Out of this place! Out of my sight!
Teiresias: I would not have come at all if you had not asked me.   230
Oedipus: Could I have told that you'd talk nonsense, that you'd come
here to make a fool of yourself, and of me?
Teiresias: A fool? Your parents thought me sane enough.
Oedipus: My parents again!—Wait: who were my parents?
Teiresias: This day will give you a father, and break your heart.   235
Oedipus: Your infantile riddles! Your damned abracadabra!
Teiresias: You were a great man once at solving riddles.
Oedipus: Mock me with that if you like; you will find it true.
Teiresias: It was true enough. It brought about your ruin.
Oedipus: But if it saved this town?   240
Teiresias (to the Page):   Boy, give me your hand.
Oedipus: Yes, boy; lead him away.—
                                    While you are here
We can do nothing. Go; leave us in peace.
Teiresias: I will go when I have said what I have to say.   245
How can you hurt me? And I tell you again:
The man you have been looking for all this time,
The damned man, the murderer of Laios,
That man is in Thebes. To your mind he is foreign-born,
But it will soon be shown that he is a Theban,   250
A revelation that will fail to please.
                                    A blind man,
Who has his eyes now; a penniless man, who is rich now;
And he will go tapping the strange earth with his staff.
To the children with whom he lives now he will be   255
Brother and father—the very same; to her
Who bore him, son and husband—the very same
Who came to his father's bed, wet with his father's blood.
Enough. Go think that over.
If later you find error in what I have said,   260
You may say that I have no skill in prophecy.

(Exit Teiresias, led by his Page. Oedipus goes into the palace.)

ODE° 1

Strophe 1

Chorus: The Delphic stone of prophecies
          Remembers ancient regicide
          And a still bloody hand.
          That killer's hour of flight has come.
          He must be stronger than riderless   5
          Coursers of untiring wind,
          For the son of Zeus° armed with his father's thunder
          Leaps in lightning after him;
          And the Furies° hold his track, the sad Furies.

Antistrophe 1

Holy Parnassos'° peak of snow   10
Flashes and blinds that secret man,
That all shall hunt him down:
Though he may roam the forest shade
Like a bull gone wild from pasture
To rage through glooms of stone.   15
Doom comes down on him; flight will not avail him;
For the world's heart calls him desolate,
And the immortal voices follow, for ever follow.

Strophe 2

But now a wilder thing is heard
From the old man skilled at hearing Fate in the wing-beat of a bird. 20
Bewildered as a blown bird, my soul hovers and cannot find
Foothold in this debate, or any reason or rest of mind.
But no man ever brought—none can bring
Proof of strife between Thebes' royal house,
Labdakos' line, and the son of Polybos;°   25
And never until now has any man brought word
Of Laios' dark death staining Oedipus the King.

Antistrophe 2

Divine Zeus and Apollo hold
Perfect intelligence alone of all tales ever told;
And well though this diviner works, he works in his own night;   30
No man can judge that rough unknown or trust in second sight,
For wisdom changes hands among the wise.

Ode: Song sung by the Chorus.   7 *son of Zeus:* Apollo.   9 *Furies:* Spirits called upon to avenge crimes, especially against kin.   10 *Parnassos:* Mountain sacred to Apollo.   25 *Polybos:* King who adopted Oedipus.

Shall I believe my great lord criminal
At a raging word that a blind old man let fall?
I saw him, when the carrion woman° faced him of old,   35
Prove his heroic mind. These evil words are lies.

SCENE 2

Kreon: Men of Thebes:
   I am told that heavy accusations
   Have been brought against me by King Oedipus.

   I am not the kind of man to bear this tamely.   40

   If in these present difficulties
   He holds me accountable for any harm to him
   Through anything I have said or done—why, then,
   I do not value life in this dishonor.
   It is not as though this rumor touched upon   45
   Some private indiscretion. The matter is grave.
   The fact is that I am being called disloyal
   To the State, to my fellow citizens, to my friends.
Choragos: He may have spoken in anger, not from his mind.
Kreon: But did you not hear him say I was the one   50
   Who seduced the old prophet into lying?
Choragos: The thing was said; I do not know how seriously.
Kreon: But you were watching him! Were his eyes steady?
   Did he look like a man in his right mind?
Choragos: I do not know.   55
   I cannot judge the behavior of great men.
   But here is the king himself.

   (Enter Oedipus.)

Oedipus: So you dared come back.
   Why? How brazen of you to come to my house,   60
   You murderer!
   Do you think I do not know
   That you plotted to kill me, plotted to steal my throne?
   Tell me, in God's name: am I coward, a fool,
   That you should dream you could accomplish this?   65
   A fool who could not see your slippery game?
   A coward, not to fight back when I saw it?
   You are the fool, Kreon, are you not? hoping
   Without support or friends to get a throne?
   Thrones may be won or bought: you could do neither.   70

---

35 *woman:* The Sphinx.

Kreon: Now listen to me. You have talked; let me talk, too.
    You cannot judge unless you know the facts.
Oedipus: You speak well: there is one fact; but I find it hard
    To learn from the deadliest enemy I have.
Kreon: That above all I must dispute with you.
Oedipus: That above all I will not hear you deny.   75
Kreon: If you think there is anything good in being stubborn
    Against all reason, then I say you are wrong.
Oedipus: If you think a man can sin against his own kind
    And not be punished for it, I say you are mad.   80
Kreon: I agree. But tell me: what have I done to you?
Oedipus: You advised me to send for that wizard, did you not?
Kreon: I did. I should do it again.
Oedipus: Very well. Now tell me:
    How long has it been since Laios—   85
Kreon: What of Laios?
Oedipus: Since he vanished in that onset by the road?
Kreon: It was long ago, a long time.
Oedipus: And this prophet,
    Was he practicing here then?   90
Kreon: He was; and with honor, as now.
Opdipus: Did he speak of me at that time?
Kreon: He never did,
    At least, not when I was present,
Oedipus: But . . . the enquiry?   95
    I suppose you held one?
Kreon: We did, but we learned nothing.
Oedipus: Why did the prophet not speak against me then?
Kreon: I do not know; and I am the kind of man
    Who holds his tongue when he has no facts to go on.   100
Oedipus: There's one fact that you know, and you could tell it.
Kreon: What fact is that? If I know it, you shall have it.
Oedipus: If he were not involved with you, he could not say
    That it was I who murdered Laios.
Kreon: If he says that, you are the one that knows it!—   105
    But now it is my turn to question you.
Oedipus: Put your questions. I am no murderer.
Kreon: First, then: You married my sister?
Oedipus: I married your sister.
Kreon: And you rule the kingdom equally with her?   110
Oedipus: Everything that she wants she has from me.
Kreon: And I am the third, equal to both of you?
Oedipus: That is why I call you a bad friend.
Kreon: No. Reason it out, as I have done.
    Think of this first: would any sane man prefer   115

Power, with all a king's anxieties,
To that same power and the grace of sleep?
Certainly not I.
I have never longed for the king's power—only his rights.
Would any wise man differ from me in this?   120
As matters stand, I have my way in everything
With your consent, and no responsibilities.
If I were king, I should be a slave to policy.
How could I desire a scepter more
Than what is now mine—untroubled influence?   125
No, I have not gone mad; I need no honors,
Except those with the perquisites I have now.
I am welcome everywhere; every man salutes me,
And those who want your favor seek my ear,
Since I know how to manage what they ask.   130
Should I exchange this ease for that anxiety?
Besides, no sober mind is treasonable.
I hate anarchy
And never would deal with any man who likes it.

Test what I have said. Go to the priestess   135
At Delphi, ask if I quoted her correctly.
And as for this other thing: if I am found
Guilty of treason with Teiresias,
Then sentence me to death. You have my word
It is a sentence I should cast my vote for—   140
But not without evidence!
                          You do wrong
When you take good men for bad, bad men for good.
A true friend thrown aside—why, life itself
Is not more precious!   145
                 In time you will know this well:
For time, and time alone, will show the just man,
Though scoundrels are discovered in a day.
Choragos: This is well said, and a prudent man would ponder it.
      Judgments too quickly formed are dangerous.   150
Oedipus: But is he not quick in his duplicity?
      And shall I not be quick to parry him?
      Would you have me stand still, hold my peace, and let
      This man win everything, through my inaction?
Kreon: And you want—what is it, then? To banish me?   155
Oedipus: No, not exile. It is your death I want,
      So that all the world may see what treason means.
Kreon: You will persist, then? You will not believe me?
Oedipus: How can I believe you?

| *Kreon:* | Then you are a fool. | 160 |

Kreon: Then you are a fool.   160
Oedipus: To save myself?
Kreon: In justice, think of me.
Oedipus: You are evil incarnate.
Kreon: But suppose that you are wrong?
Oedipus: Still I must rule.   165
Kreon: But not if you rule badly.
Oedipus: O city, city!
Kreon: It is my city, too!
Choragos: Now, my lords, be still. I see the queen,
    Iokaste, coming from her palace chambers;   170
    And it is time she came, for the sake of you both.
    This dreadful quarrel can be resolved through her.

   (Enter Iokaste.)

Iokaste: Poor foolish men, what wicked din is this?
    With Thebes sick to death, is it not shameful   175
    That you should rake some private quarrel up?
    (*To Oedipus.*) Come into the house.
                        — And you, Kreon, go now:
    Let us have no more of this tumult over nothing.
Kreon: Nothing? No, sister: what your husband plans for me   180
    Is one of two great evils: exile or death.
Oedipus: He is right.
                Why, woman I have caught him squarely
    Plotting against my life.
Kreon: No! Let me die   185
    Accurst if ever I have wished you harm!
Iokaste: Ah, believe it, Oedipus!
    In the name of the gods, respect this oath of his
    For my sake, for the sake of these people here!

   Strophe 1

Choragos: Open your mind to her, my lord. Be ruled by her, I beg you! 190
Oedipus: What would you have me do?
Choragos: Respect Kreon's word. He has never spoken like a fool,
    And now he has sworn an oath.
Oedipus: You know what you ask?
Choragos: I do.   195
Oedipus: Speak on, then.
Choragos: A friend so sworn should not be baited so,
    In blind malice, and without final proof.
Oedipus: You are aware, I hope, that what you say
    Means death for me, or exile at the least.   200

Strophe 2

Choragos: No, I swear by Helios, first in heaven!
　　May I die friendless and accurst,
　　The worst of deaths, if ever I meant that!
　　It is the withering fields
　　　　That hurt my sick heart: 205
　　Must we bear all these ills,
　　　　And now your bad blood as well?
Oedipus: Then let him go. And let me die, if I must,
　　Or be driven by him in shame from the land of Thebes.
　　It is your unhappiness, and not his talk,   210
　　That touches me.
　　　　　　　As for him—
　　Wherever he goes, hatred will follow him.
Kreon: Ugly in yielding, as you were ugly in rage!
　　Natures like yours chiefly torment themselves.   215
Oedipus: Can you not go? Can you not leave me?
Kreon:　　　　　　　　　　　　　I can.
　　You do not know me; but the city knows me,
　　And in its eyes I am just, if not in yours.

　　　　　　　　　　　　　　　　(Exit Kreon.)   220

Antistrophe 1

Choragos: Lady Iokaste, did you not ask the King to go to his chambers?
Iokaste: First tell me what has happened.
Choragos: There was suspicion without evidence; yet it rankled
　　As even false charges will.
Iokaste: On both sides?   225
Choragos:　　　　　　On both.
Iokaste:　　　　　　　　　　But what was said?
Choragos: Oh let it rest, let it be done with!
　　Have we not suffered enough?
Oedipus: You see to what your decency has brought you: 230
　　You have made difficulties where my heart saw none.

Antistrophe 2

Choragos: Oedipus, it is not once only I have told you—
　　You must know I should count myself unwise
　　To the point of madness, should I now forsake you—   235
　　You, under whose hand,
　　　　In the storm of another time,
　　　　　　Our dear land sailed out free.
　　But now stand fast at the helm!

Iokaste: In God's name, Oedipus, inform your wife as well:
    Why are you so set in this hard anger?   240
Oedipus: I will tell you, for none of these men deserves
    My confidence as you do. It is Kreon's work,
    His treachery, his plotting against me.
Iokaste: Go on, if you can make this clear to me.
Oedipus: He charges me with the murder of Laios.   245
Iokaste: Has he some knowledge? Or does he speak from hearsay?
Oedipus: He would not commit himself to such a charge,
    But he has brought in that damnable soothsayer
    To tell his story.
Iokaste: Set your mind at rest.   250
    If it is a question of soothsayers, I tell you
    That you will find no man whose craft gives knowledge
    Of the unknowable.
                 Here is my proof:
    An oracle was reported to Laios once   255
    (I will not say from Phoibos himself, but from
    His appointed ministers, at any rate)
    That his doom would be death at the hands of his own son—
    His son, born of his flesh and of mine!

    Now, you remember the story: Laios was killed   260
    By marauding strangers where three highways meet;
    But his child had not been three days in this world
    Before the king had pierced the baby's ankles
    And left him to die on a lonely mountainside.

    Thus, Apollo never caused that child   265
    To kill his father, and it was not Laios' fate
    To die at the hands of his son, as he had feared.
    This is what prophets and prophecies are worth!
    Have no dread of them.
                 It is God himself   265
    Who can show us what he wills, in his own way.
Oedipus: How strange a shadowy memory crossed my mind,
    Just now while you were speaking; it chilled my heart.
Iokaste: What do you mean? What memory do you speak of?
Oedipus: If I understand you, Laios was killed   275
    At a place where three roads meet.
Iokaste: So it was said;
    We have no later story.
Oedipus: Where did it happen?
Iokaste: Phokis, it is called: at a place where the Theban Way   280
    Divides into the roads toward Delphi and Daulia.
Oedipus: When?

Iokaste: We had the news not long before you came
  And proved the right to your succession here.
Oedipus: Ah, what net has God been weaving for me?   285
Iokaste: Oedipus! Why does this trouble you?
Oedipus: Do not ask me yet.
  First, tell me how Laios looked, and tell me
  How old he was.
Iokaste: He was tall, his hair just touched
  With white; his form was not unlike your own.   290
Oedipus: I think that I myself may be accurst
  By my own ignorant edict.
Iokaste: You speak strangely.
  It makes me tremble to look at you, my king.
Oedipus: I am not sure that the blind man cannot see.
  But I should know better if you were to tell me—   295
Iokaste: Anything—though I dread to hear you ask it.
Oedipus: Was the king lightly escorted, or did he ride
  With a large company, as a ruler should?
Iokaste: There were five men with him in all: one was a herald;
  And a single chariot, which he was driving.   300
Oedipus: Alas, that makes it plain enough!
                                 But who—
  Who told you how it happened?
Iokaste: A household servant,
  The only one to escape.   305
Oedipus: And is he still
  A servant of ours?
Iokaste: No; for when he came back at last
  And found you enthroned in the place of the dead king,
  He came to me, touched my hand with his, and begged   310
  That I would send him away to the frontier district
  Where only the shepherds go—
  As far away from the city as I could send him.
  I granted his prayer; for although the man was a slave,
  He had earned more than this favor at my hands.   315
Oedipus: Can he be called back quickly?
Iokaste: Easily.
  But why?
Oedipus: I have taken too much upon myself
  Without enquiry; therefore I wish to consult him.   320
Iokaste: Then he shall come.
                         But am I not one also
  To whom you might confide these fears of yours?
Oedipus: That is your right; it will not be denied you,
  Now least of all; for I have reached a pitch   325

Of wild foreboding. Is there anyone
To whom I should sooner speak?

Polybos of Corinth is my father.
My mother is a Dorian: Merope.
I grew up chief among the men of Corinth   330
Until a strange thing happened—
Not worth my passion, it may be, but strange.
At a feast, a drunken man maundering in his cups
Cries out that I am not my father's son!

I contained myself that night, though I felt anger   335
And a sinking heart. The next day I visited
My father and mother, and questioned them.
They stormed,
Calling it all the slanderous rant of a fool;
And this relieved me. Yet the suspicion   340
Remained always aching in my mind;
I knew there was talk; I could not rest;
And finally, saying nothing to my parents,
I went to the shrine at Delphi.

The god dismissed my question without reply;   345
He spoke of other things.
                              Some were clear,
Full of wretchedness, dreadful, unbearable:
As, that I should lie with my own mother, breed
Children from whom all men would turn their eyes;   350
And that I should be my father's murderer.

I heard all this, and fled. And from that day
Corinth to me was only in the stars
Descending in that quarter of the sky,
As I wandered farther and farther on my way   355
To a land where I should never see the evil
Sung by the oracle. And I came to this country
Where, so you say, King Laios was killed.

I will tell you all that happened there, my lady.
There were three highways   360
Coming together at a place I passed;
And there a herald came toward me, and a chariot
Drawn by horses, with a man such as you describe
Seated in it. The groom leading the horses
Forced me off the road at his lord's command;   365
But as this charioteer lurched over toward me
I struck him in my rage. The old man saw me
And brought his double goad down upon my head

As I came abreast.
                          He was paid back, and more!   370
Swinging my club in this right hand I knocked him
Out of his car, and he rolled on the ground.
                                    I killed him.

I killed them all.
Now if that stranger and Laios were—kin,   375
Where is a man more miserable than I?
More hated by the gods? Citizen and alien alike
Must never shelter me or speak to me—
I must be shunned by all.
                          And I myself   380
Pronounced this malediction upon myself!

Think of it: I have touched you with these hands,
These hands that killed your husband. What defilement!

Am I all evil, then? It must be so,
Since I must flee from Thebes, yet never again   385
See my own countrymen, my own country,
For fear of joining my mother in marriage
And killing Polybos, my father.
                          Ah,
If I was created so, born to this fate,   390
Who could deny the savagery of God?

O holy majesty of heavenly powers!
May I never see that day! Never!
Rather let me vanish from the race of men
Than know the abomination destined me!   395
Choragos: We too, my lord, have felt dismay at this.
     But there is hope: you have yet to hear the shepherd.
Oedipus: Indeed, I fear no other hope is left me.
Iokaste: What do you hope from him when he comes?
Oedipus: This much: 400
     If his account of the murder tallies with yours,
     Then I am cleared.
Iokaste: What was it that I said
     Of such importance?
Oedipus: Why, "marauders," you said,   405
     Killed the king, according to this man's story.
     If he maintains that still, if there were several,
     Clearly the guilt is not mine: I was alone.
     But if he says one man, singlehanded, did it,
     Then the evidence all points to me.   410
Iokaste: You may be sure that he said there were several;

And can he call back that story now? He cannot.
The whole city heard it as plainly as I.
But suppose he alters some detail of it:
He cannot ever show that Laios' death   415
Fulfilled the oracle: for Apollo said
My child was doomed to kill him; and my child—
Poor baby!—it was my child that died first.

No. From now on, where oracles are concerned,
I would not waste a second thought on any.   420
Oedipus: You may be right.
                                    But come: let someone go
For the shepherd at once. This matter must be settled.
Iokaste: I will send for him.
I would not wish to cross you in anything,   425
And surely not in this.—Let us go in.

                                    (*Exeunt into the palace.*)

ODE 2

Strophe 1

Chorus: Let me be reverent in the ways of right,
     Lowly the paths I journey on;
     Let all my words and actions keep
     The laws of the pure universe
     From highest Heaven handed down.   5
     For Heaven is their bright nurse,
     Those generations of the realms of light;
     Ah, never of mortal kind were they begot,
     Nor are they slaves of memory, lost in sleep:
     Their Father is greater than Time, and ages not.   10

Antistrophe 1

     The tyrant is a child of Pride
     Who drinks from his great sickening cup
     Recklessness and vanity,
     Until from his high crest headlong
     He plummets to the dust of hope.   15
     That strong man is not strong.
     But let no fair ambition be denied;
     May God protect the wrestler for the State
     In government, in comely policy,
     Who will fear God, and on his ordinance wait.   20

Strophe 2

Haughtiness and the high hand of disdain
Tempt and outrage God's holy law;
And any mortal who dares hold
No immortal Power in awe
Will be caught up in a net of pain: 25
The price for which his levity is sold.
Let each man take due earnings, then,
And keep his hands from holy things,
And from blasphemy stand apart—
Else the crackling blast of heaven   30
Blows on his head, and on his desperate heart.
Though fools will honor impious men,
In their cities no tragic poet sings.

Antistrophe 2

Shall we lose faith in Delphi's obscurities,
We who have heard the world's core   35
Discredited, and the sacred wood
Of Zeus at Elis° praised no more?
The deeds and the strange prophecies
Must make a pattern yet to be understood.
Zeus, if indeed you are lord of all,   40
Throned in light over night and day,
Mirror this in your endless mind:
Our masters call the oracle
Words on the wind, and the Delphic vision blind!
Their hearts no longer know Apollo,   45
And reverence for the gods has died away.

37 *Elis:* Ancient country where Olympia was reputed to have existed.

SCENE 3

(Enter Iokaste.)

Iokaste: Princes of Thebes, it has occurred to me
To visit the altars of the gods, bearing
These branches as a suppliant, and this incense.
Our king is not himself: his noble soul
Is overwrought with fantasies of dread,   5
Else he would consider
The new prophecies in the light of the old.
He will listen to any voice that speaks disaster,
And my advice goes for nothing. (*She
Approaches the altar, right.*)   10

To you, then, Apollo,
Lycean lord, since you are nearest, I turn in prayer.
Receive these offerings, and grant us deliverance
From defilement. Our hearts are heavy with fear
When we see our leader distracted, as helpless sailors   15
Are terrified by the confusion of their helmsman.

(Enter Messenger.)

Messenger: Friends, no doubt you can direct me:
Where shall I find the house of Oedipus,
Or, better still, where is the king himself?   20
Choragos: It is this very place, stranger; he is inside.
This is his wife and mother of his children.
Messenger: I wish her happiness in a happy house,
Blest in all the fulfillment of her marriage.
Iokaste: I wish as much for you: your courtesy   25
Deserves a like good fortune. But now, tell me:
Why have you come? What have you to say to us?
Messenger: Good news, my lady, for your house and your husband.
Iokaste: What news? Who sent you here?
Messenger: I am from Corinth.   30
The news I bring ought to mean joy for you,
Though it may be you will find some grief in it.
Iokaste: What is it? How can it touch us in both ways?
Messenger: The word is that the people of the Isthmus
Intend to call Oedipus to be their king.   35
Iokaste: But old King Polybos—is he not reigning still?
Messenger: No. Death holds him in his sepulchre.
Iokaste: What are you saying? Polybos is dead?
Messenger: If I am not telling the truth, may I die myself.
Iokaste (to a Maidservant):   Go in, go quickly; tell this to your master.   40
O riddlers of God's will, where are you now!
This was the man whom Oedipus, long ago,
Feared so, fled so, in dread of destroying him—
But it was another fate by which he died.

(Enter Oedipus, center.)   45

Oedipus: Dearest Iokaste, why have you sent for me?
Iokaste: Listen to what this man says, and then tell me
What has become of the solemn prophecies.
Oedipus: Who is this man? What is his news for me?
Iokaste: He has come from Corinth to announce your father's death!   50
Oedipus: Is it true, stranger? Tell me in your own words.
Messenger: I cannot say it more clearly: the king is dead.
Oedipus: Was it by treason? Or by an attack of illness?
Messenger: A little thing brings old men to their rest.

Oedipus: It was sickness, then?   55
Messenger: Yes, and his many years.
Oedipus: Ah!
   Why should a man respect the Pythian hearth,° or
   Give heed to the birds that jangle above his head?
   They prophesied that I should kill Polybos,   60
   Kill my own father; but he is dead and buried,
   And I am here—I never touched him, never,
   Unless he died of grief for my departure,
   And thus, in a sense, through me. No. Polybos
   Has packed the oracles off with him underground.   65
   They are empty words.
Iokaste: Had I not told you so?
Oedipus: You had; it was my faint heart that betrayed me.
Iokaste: From now on never think of those things again.
Oedipus: And yet—must I not fear my mother's bed?   70
Iokaste: Why should anyone in this world be afraid,
   Since Fate rules us and nothing can be foreseen?
   A man should live only for the present day.

   Have no more fear of sleeping with your mother:
   how many men, in dreams, have lain with their mothers!   75
   No reasonable man is troubled by such things.
Oedipus: That is true; only—
   If only my mother were not still alive!
   But she is alive. I cannot help my dread.
Iokaste: Yet this news of your father's death is wonderful.
Oedipus: Wonderful. But I fear the living woman.   80
Messenger: Tell me, who is this woman that you fear?
Oedipus: It is Merope, man; the wife of King Polybos.
Messenger: Merope? Why should you be afraid of her?
Oedipus: An oracle of the gods, a dreadful saying.
Messenger: Can you tell me about it or are you sworn to silence?   85
Oedipus: I can tell you, and I will.
   Apollo said through his prophet that I was the man
   Who should marry his own mother, shed his father's blood
   With his own hands. And so, for all these years
   I have kept clear of Corinth, and no harm has come—   90
   Though it would have been sweet to see my parents again.
Messenger: And is this the fear that drove you out of Corinth?
Oedipus: Would you have me kill my father?
Messenger: As for that   95
   You must be reassured by the news I gave you.

---

58 *Pythian hearth:* Delphi.

Oedipus: If you could reassure me, I would reward you.
Messenger: I had that in mind, I will confess: I thought
    I could count on you when you returned to Corinth.
Oedipus: No: I will never go near my parents again.   100
Messenger: Ah, son, you still do not know what you are doing—
Oedipus: What do you mean? In the name of God tell me!
Messenger: —If these are your reasons for not going home.
Oedipus: I tell you, I fear the oracle may come true.
Messenger: And guilt may come upon you through your parents?   105
Oedipus: That is the dread that is always in my heart.
Messenger: Can you not see that all your fears are groundless?
Oedipus: Groundless? Am I not my parents' son?
Messenger: Polybos was not your father.
Oedipus: Not my father?   110
Messenger: No more your father than the man speaking to you.
Oedipus: But you are nothing to me!
Messenger: Neither was he.
Oedipus: Then why did he call me son?
Messenger: I will tell you: 115
    Long ago he had you from my hands, as a gift.
Oedipus: Then how could he love me so, if I was not his?
Messenger: He had no children, and his heart turned to you.
Oedipus: What of you? Did you buy me? Did you find me by chance?
Messenger: I came upon you in the woody vales of Kithairon.   120
Oedipus: And what were you doing there?
Messenger: Tending my flocks.
Oedipus: A wandering shepherd?
Messenger: But your savior, son, that day.
Oedipus: From what did you save me?   125
Messenger: Your ankles should tell you that
Oedipus: Ah, stranger, why do you speak of that childhood pain?
Messenger: I pulled the skewer that pinned your feet together.
Oedipus: I have had the mark as long as I can remember.
Messenger: That was why you were given the name you bear.   130
Oedipus: God! Was it my father or my mother who did it?
    Tell me!
Messenger: I do not know. The man who gave you to me
    Can tell you better than I.
Oedipus: It was not you that found me, but another?   135
Messenger: It was another shepherd gave you to me.
Oedipus: Who was he? Can you tell me who he was?
Messenger: I think he was said to be one of Laios' people.
Oedipus: You mean the Laios who was king here years ago?
Messenger: Yes; King Laios; and the man was one of his herdsmen.   140
Oedipus: Is he still alive? Can I see him?

Messenger: These men here
  Know best about such things.
Oedipus: Does anyone here
  Know this shepherd that he is talking about?   145
  Have you seen him in the fields, or in the town?
  If you have, tell me. It is time things were made plain.
Choragos: I think the man he means is that same shepherd
  You have already asked to see. Iokaste perhaps
  Could tell you something.   150
Oedipus: Do you know anything
  About him, Lady? Is he the man we have summoned?
  Is that the man this shepherd means?
Iokaste: Why think of him?
  Forget this herdsman. Forget it all.   155
  This talk is a waste of time.
Oedipus: How can you say that,
  When the clues to my true birth are in my hands?
Iokaste: For God's love, let us have no more questioning!
  Is your life nothing to you?   160
  My own is pain enough for me to bear.
Oedipus: You need not worry. Suppose my mother a slave,
  And born of slaves: no baseness can touch you.
Iokaste: Listen to me, I beg you: do not do this thing!
Oedipus: I will not listen; the truth must be made known.   165
Iokaste: Everything that I say is for your own good!
Oedipus: My own good
  Snaps my patience, then; I want none of it.
Iokaste: You are fatally wrong! May you never learn who you are!
Oedipus: Go, one of you, and bring the shepherd here.   170
  Let us leave this woman to brag of her royal name.
Iokaste: Ah, miserable!
  That is the only word I have for you now.
  That is the only word I can ever have.

                                          (Exit into the palace.)   175

Choragos: Why has she left us, Oedipus? Why has she gone
  In such a passion of sorrow? I fear this silence:
  Something dreadful may come of it.
Oedipus: Let it come!
  However base my birth, I must know about it.   180
    The Queen, like a woman, is perhaps ashamed
    To think of my low origin. But I
    Am a child of Luck; I cannot be dishonored.
    Luck is my mother; the passing months, my brothers,
    Have seen me rich and poor.   185

                              If this is so,
     How could I wish that I were someone else?
     How could I not be glad to know my birth?

ODE 3

Strophe

Chorus: If ever the coming time were known
     To my heart's pondering,
     Kithairon, now by Heaven I see the torches
     At the festival of the next full moon,
     And see the dance, and hear the choir sing   5
     A grace to your gentle shade:
     Mountain where Oedipus was found,
     O mountain guard of a noble race!
     May the god° who heals us lend his aid,
     And let that glory come to pass   10
     For our king's cradling-ground.

Antistrophe

     Of the nymphs that flower beyond the years,
     Who bore you,° royal child,
     To Pan° of the hills or the timberline Apollo,
     Cold in delight where the upland clears,   15
     Or Hermes° for whom Kyllene's° heights are piled?
     Or flushed as evening cloud,
     Great Dionysos,° roamer of mountains,
     He—was it he who found you there,
     And caught you up in his own proud   20
     Arms from the sweet god-ravisher
     Who laughed by the Muses'° fountains?

9 *god:* Apollo.   13 *Who bore you:* The Chorus is asking if Oedipus is the son of an immortal nymph and a god: Pan, Apollo, Hermes, or Dionysus.   14 *Pan:* God of nature, forests, flocks, and shepherds, depicted as half-man and half-goat.   16 *Hermes:* Son of Zeus, messenger of the gods. *Kyllene:* Mountain reputed to be the birthplace of Hermes; also the center of a cult to Hermes.   18 *Dionysos:* (Dionysus) God of wine around whom wild, orgiastic rituals developed; also called Bacchus.   22 *Muses:* Nine sister goddesses who presided over poetry and music, art and sciences.

SCENE 4

Oedipus: Sirs: though I do not know the man,
     I think I see him coming, this shepherd we want:
     He is old, like our friend here, and the men
     Bringing him seem to be servants of my house.

But you can tell, if you have ever seen him.   5

(Enter Shepherd escorted by Servants.)

Choragos: I know him, he was Laios' man. You can trust him.
Oedipus: Tell me first, you from Corinth: is this the shepherd
   We were discussing?
Messenger: This is the very man.   10
Oedipus Answer *(to Shepherd):*   Come here. No, look at me. You must
   Everything I ask.—You belonged to Laios?
Shepherd: Yes: born his slave, brought up in his house.
Oedipus: Tell me: what kind of work did you do for him?
Shepherd: I was a shepherd of his, most of my life.   15
Oedipus: Where mainly did you go for pasturage?
Shepherd: Sometimes Kithairon, sometimes the hills nearby.
Oedipus: Do you remember ever seeing this man out there?
Shepherd: What would he be doing there? This man?
Oedipus: This man standing here. Have you ever seen him before?   20
Shepherd: No. At least, not to my recollection.
Messenger: And that is not strange, my lord. But I'll refresh
   His memory: he must remember when we two
   Spent three whole seasons together, March to September,
   On Kithairon or thereabouts. He had two flocks;   25
   I had one. Each autumn I'd drive mine home
   And he would go back with his to Laios' sheepfold.—
   Is this not true, just as I have described it?
Shepherd: True, yes; but it was all so long ago.
Messenger: Well, then: do you remember, back in those days,   30
   That you gave me a baby boy to bring up as my own?
Shepherd: What if I did? What are you trying to say?
Messenger: King Oedipus was once that little child.
Shepherd: Damn you, hold your tongue!
Oedipus: No more of that: 35
   It is your tongue needs watching, not this man's.
Shepherd: My king, my master, what is it I have done wrong?
Oedipus: You have not answered his question about the boy.
Shepherd: He does not know . . . He is only making trouble . . .
Oedipus: Come, speak plainly, or it will go hard with you.   40
Shepherd: In God's name, do not torture an old man!
Oedipus: Come here, one of you; bind his arms behind him.
Shepherd: Unhappy king! What more do you wish to learn?
Oedipus: Did you give this man the child he speaks of?
Shepherd: I did.   45
   And I would to God I had died that very day.
Oedipus: You will die now unless you speak the truth.
Shepherd: Yet if I speak the truth, I am worse than dead.
Oedipus (to Attendant):   He intends to draw it out, apparently—

Shepherd: No! I have told you already that I gave him the boy.   50
Oedipus: Where did you get him? From your house? From somewhere else?
Shepherd: Not from mine, no. A man gave him to me.
Oedipus: Is that man here? Whose house did he belong to?
Shepherd: For God's love, my king, do not ask me any more!
Oedipus: You are a dead man if I have to ask you again.   55
Shepherd: Then . . . Then the child was from the palace of Laios.
Oedipus: A slave child? or a child of his own line?
Shepherd: Ah, I am on the brink of dreadful speech!
Oedipus: And I of dreadful hearing. Yet I must hear.
Shepherd: If you must be told, then . . .   60

                                    they said it was Laios' child;
But it is your wife who can tell you about that.
Oedipus: My wife—Did she give it to you?
Shepherd: My lord, she did.
Oedipus: Do you know why?   65
Shepherd: I was told to get rid of it.
Oedipus: Oh heartless mother!
Shepherd: But in dread of prophecies . . .
Oedipus: Tell me.
Shepherd: It was said that the boy would kill his own father.   70
Oedipus: Then why did you give him over to this old man?
Shepherd: I pitied the baby, my king,
And I thought that this man would take him far away
To his own country.
                He saved him—but for what a fate!   75
For if you are what this man says you are,
No man living is more wretched than Oedipus.
Oedipus: Ah God! It was true!
               All the prophecies!—
                    Now,   80
O Light, may I look on you for the last time!
I, Oedipus,
Oedipus, damned in his birth, in his marriage damned,
Damned in the blood he shed with his own hand!

(He rushes into the palace.)   85

ODE 4

Strophe 1

Chorus: Alas for the seed of men.
What measure shall I give these generations
That breathe on the void and are void
And exist and do not exist?

Who bears more weight of joy   5
Than mass of sunlight shifting in images,
Or who shall make his thought stay on
That down time drifts away?
Your splendor is all fallen.
O naked brow of wrath and tears,   10
O change of Oedipus!
I who saw your days call no man blest—
Your great days like ghosts gone.

Antistrophe 1

That mind was a strong bow.
Deep, how deep you drew it then, hard archer,   15
At a dim fearful range,
And brought dear glory down!
You overcame the stranger°—
The virgin with her hooking lion claws—
And though death sang, stood like a tower   20
To make pale Thebes take heart.
Fortress against our sorrow!
True king, giver of laws,
Majestic Oedipus!
No prince in Thebes had ever such renown,   25
No prince won such grace of power.

Strophe 2

And now of all men ever known
Most pitiful is this man's story:
His fortunes are most changed; his state
Fallen to a low slave's   30
Ground under bitter fate.
O Oedipus, most royal one!
The great door° that expelled you to the light
Gave at night—ah, gave night to your glory:
As to the father, to the fathering son.   35
All understood too late.
How could that queen whom Laios won,
The garden that he harrowed at his height,
Be silent when that act was done?

Antistrophe 2

But all eyes fail before time's eye,   40
All actions come to justice there.

18 *stranger:* The Sphinx.   33 *door:* Iokaste's womb.

Though never willed, though far down the deep past,
Your bed, your dread sirings,
Are brought to book at last.
Child by Laios doomed to die,   45
Then doomed to lose that fortunate little death,
Would God you never took breath in this air
That with my wailing lips I take to cry:
For I weep the world's outcast.
I was blind, and now I can tell why: 50
Asleep, for you had given ease of breath
To Thebes, while the false years went by.

EXODOS°

(Enter, from the palace, Second Messenger.)

Second Messenger: Elders of Thebes, most honored in this land,
    What horrors are yours to see and hear, what weight
    Of sorrow to be endured, if, true to your birth,
    You venerate the line of Labdakos!
    I think neither Istros nor Phasis, those great rivers,   5
    Could purify this place of all the evil
    It shelters now, or soon must bring to light—
    Evil not done unconsciously, but willed.

    The greatest griefs are those we cause ourselves.
Choragos: Surely, friend, we have grief enough already;   10
    What new sorrow do you mean?
Second Messenger: The queen is dead.
Choragos: O miserable queen! But at whose hand?
Second Messenger: Her own.
    The full horror of what happened you cannot know,   15
    For you did not see it; but I, who did, will tell you
    As clearly as I can how she met her death.

    When she had left us,
    In passionate silence, passing through the court,
    She ran to her apartment in the house,   20
    Her hair clutched by the fingers of both hands.
    She closed the doors behind her; then, by that bed
    Where long ago the fatal son was conceived—
    That son who should bring about his father's death—
    We heard her call upon Laios, dead so many years,   25

Exodos: Final scene.

And heard her wail for the double fruit of her marriage,
A husband by her husband, children by her child.

Exactly how she died I do not know:
For Oedipus burst in moaning and would not let us
Keep vigil to the end: it was by him   30
As he stormed about the room that our eyes were caught.
From one to another of us he went, begging a sword,
Hunting the wife who was not his wife, the mother
Whose womb had carried his own children and himself.
I do not know: it was none of us aided him,   35
But surely one of the gods was in control!
For with a dreadful cry
He hurled his weight, as though wrenched out of himself,
At the twin doors: the bolts gave, and he rushed in.
And there we saw her hanging, her body swaying   40
From the cruel cord she had noosed about her neck.
A great sob broke from him, heartbreaking to hear,
As he loosed the rope and lowered her to the ground.

I would blot out from my mind what happened next!
For the king ripped from her gown the golden brooches   45
That were her ornament, and raised them, and plunged them down
Straight into his own eyeballs, crying, "no more,
No more shall you look on the misery about me,
The horrors of my own doing! Too long you have known
The faces of those whom I should never have seen,   50
Too long been blind to those for whom I was searching!
From this hour, go in darkness!" And as he spoke,
He struck at his eyes—not once, but many times;
And the blood spattered his beard,
Bursting from his ruined sockets like red hail.   55

So from the unhappiness of two this evil has sprung,
A curse on the man and woman alike. The old
Happiness of the house of Labdakos
Was happiness enough: where is it today?
It is all wailing and ruin, disgrace, death—all   60
The misery of mankind that has a name—
And it is wholly and for ever theirs.
Choragos: Is he in agony still? Is there no rest for him?
Second Messenger: He is calling for someone to open the doors wide
So that all the children of Kadmos may look upon   65
His father's murderer, his mother's—no,
I cannot say it!
        And then he will leave Thebes,

Self-exiled, in order that the curse
Which he himself pronounced may depart from the house.   70
He is weak, and there is none to lead him,
So terrible is his suffering.
                              But you will see:
Look, the doors are opening; in a moment
You will see a thing that would crush a heart of stone.   75

(The central door is opened; Oedipus, blinded, is led in.)

Choragos: Dreadful indeed for men to see.
      Never have my own eyes
      Looked on a sight so full of fear.

      Oedipus!   80
      What madness came upon you, what demon
      Leaped on your life with heavier
      Punishment than a mortal man can bear?
      No: I cannot even
      Look at you, poor ruined one.   85
      And I would speak, question, ponder,
      If I were able. No.
      You make me shudder.
Oedipus: God. God.
      Is there a sorrow greater?   90
      Where shall I find harbor in this world?
      My voice is hurled far on a dark wind.
      What has God done to me?
Choragos: Too terrible to think of, or to see.

      Strophe 1

Oedipus: O cloud of night,   95
      Never to be turned away: night coming on,
      I cannot tell how: night like a shroud!
      My fair winds brought me here.
                              O God. Again
      The pain of the spikes where I had sight,   100
      The flooding pain
      Of memory, never to be gouged out.
Choragos: This is not strange.
      You suffer it all twice over, remorse in pain,
      Pain in remorse.   105

      Antistrophe 1

Oedipus: Ah dear friend
      Are you faithful even yet, you alone?

Are you still standing near me, will you stay here,
Patient, to care for the blind?
                           The blind man!   110
Yet even blind I know who it is attends me,
By the voice's tone—
Though my new darkness hide the comforter.
Choragos: Oh fearful act!
What god was it drove you to rake black   115
Night across your eyes?

Strophe 2

Oedipus: Apollo. Apollo. Dear
Children, the god was Apollo.
He brought my sick, sick fate upon me.
But the blinding hand was my own!   120
How could I bear to see
When all my sight was horror everywhere?
Choragos: Everywhere; that is true.
Oedipus: And now what is left?
Images? Love? A greeting even,   125
Sweet to the senses? Is there anything?
Ah, no, friends: lead me away.
Lead me away from Thebes.
Lead the great wreck
And hell of Oedipus, whom the gods hate.   130
Choragos: Your misery, you are not blind to that.
Would God you had never found it out!

Antistrophe 2

Oedipus: Death take the man who unbound
My feet on that hillside
And delivered me from death to life! What life?   135
If only I had died,
This weight of monstrous doom
Could not have dragged me and my darlings down.
Choragos: I would have wished the same.
Oedipus: Oh never to have come here   140
With my father's blood upon me! Never
To have been the man they call his mother's husband!
Oh accurst! Oh child of evil,
To have entered that wretched bed—
                         the selfsame one!   145
More primal than sin itself, this fell to me.
Choragos: I do not know what words to offer you.
You were better dead than alive and blind.

Oedipus: Do not counsel me anymore. This punishment
    That I have laid upon myself is just.   150
    If I had eyes,
    I do not know how I could bear the sight
    Of my father, when I came to the house of Death,
    Or my mother: for I have sinned against them both
    So vilely that I could not make my peace   155
    By strangling my own life.
                Or do you think my children,
    Born as they were born, would be sweet to my eyes?
    Ah never, never! Nor this town with its high walls,
    Nor the holy images of the gods.   160
            For I,
    Thrice miserable!—Oedipus, noblest of all the line
    Of Kadmos, have condemned myself to enjoy
    These things no more, by my own malediction
    Expelling that man whom the gods declared   165
    To be a defilement in the house of Laios.
    After exposing the rankness of my own guilt,
    How could I look men frankly in the eyes?
    No, I swear it,
    If I could have stifled my hearing at its source,   170
    I would have done it and made all this body
    A tight cell of misery, blank to light and sound:
    So I should have been safe in my dark mind
    Beyond external evil.
               Ah Kithairon!   175
    Why did you shelter me? When I was cast upon you,
    Why did I not die? Then I should never
    Have shown the world my execrable birth.

    Ah Polybos! Corinth, city that I believed
    The ancient seat of my ancestors: how fair   180
    I seemed, your child! And all the while this evil
    Was cancerous within me!
              For I am sick
    In my own being, sick in my origin.

    O three roads, dark ravine, woodland and way   185
    Where three roads met; you, drinking my father's blood,
    My own blood, spilled by my own hand: can you remember
    The unspeakable things I did there, and the things
    I went on from there to do?
               O marriage, marriage!   190
    The act that engendered me, and again the act
    Performed by the son in the same bed—

Ah, the net
Of incest, mingling fathers, brothers, sons,
With brides, wives, mothers: the last evil   195
That can be known by men: no tongue can say
How evil!

        No. For the Love of God, conceal me
Somewhere far from Thebes; or kill me; or hurl me
Into the sea, away from men's eyes for ever.   200

Come, lead me. You need not fear to touch me.
Of all men, I alone can bear this guilt.

(Enter Kreon.)

Choragos: Kreon is here now. As to what you ask,
    He may decide the course to take. He only   205
    Is left to protect the city in your place.
Oedipus: Alas, how can I speak to him? What right have I
    To beg his courtesy whom I have deeply wronged?
Kreon: I have not come to mock you, Oedipus,
    Or to reproach you, either.—   210
    (To Attendants)   You, standing there:
    if you have lost all respect for man's dignity,
    At least respect the flame of Lord Helios:
    Do not allow this pollution to show itself
    Openly here, an affront to the earth   215
    And Heaven's rain and the light of day. No, take him
    Into the house as quickly as you can.
    For it is proper
    That only the close kindred see his grief.
Oedipus: I pray you in God's name, since your courtesy   220
    Ignores my dark expectation, visiting
    With mercy this man of all men most execrable:
    Give me what I ask—for your good, not for mine.
Kreon: And what is it that you turn to me begging for?
Oedipus: Drive me out of this country as quickly as may be   225
    To a place where no human voice can ever greet me.
Kreon: I should have done that before now—only,
    God's will had not been wholly revealed to me.
Oedipus: But his command is plain: the parricide
    Must be destroyed. I am that evil man.   230
Kreon: That is the sense of it, yes; but as things are,
    We had best discover clearly what is to be done.
Oedipus: You would learn more about a man like me?
Kreon: You are ready now to listen to the god.
Oedipus: I will listen. But it is to you   235
    That I must turn for help. I beg you, hear me.

The woman is there—
Give her whatever funeral you think proper:
She is your sister.
                    —But let me go, Kreon!   240
Let me purge my father's Thebes of the pollution
Of my living here, and go out to the wild hills,
To Kithairon, that has won such fame with me,
The tomb my mother and father appointed for me,
And let me die there, as they willed I should.   245
And yet I know
Death will not ever come to me through sickness
Or in any natural way: I have been preserved
For some unthinkable fate. But let that be.

As for my sons, you need not care for them.   250
They are men, they will find some way to live.
But my poor daughters, who have shared my table,
Who never before have been parted from their father—
Take care of them, Kreon; do this for me.

And will you let me touch them with my hands   255
A last time, and let us weep together?
Be kind, my lord,
Great prince, be kind!
                    Could I but touch them,
They would be mine again, as when I had my eyes.   260

(Enter Antigone and Ismene, attended.)

Ah, God!
Is it my dearest children I hear weeping?
Has Kreon pitied me and sent my daughters?
Kreon: Yes, Oedipus: I knew that they were dear to you   265
    In the old days, and know you must love them still.
Oedipus: May God bless you for this—and be a friendlier
    Guardian to you than he has been to me!

Children, where are you?
Come quickly to my hands: they are your brother's—   270
Hands that have brought your father's once clear eyes
To this way of seeing—
                    Ah dearest ones,
I had neither sight nor knowledge then, your father
By the woman who was the source of his own life!   275
And I weep for you—having no strength to see you—,
I weep for you when I think of the bitterness

That men will visit upon you all your lives.
What homes, what festivals can you attend
Without being forced to depart again in tears?   280
And when you come to marriageable age,
Where is the man, my daughters, who would dare
Risk the bane that lies on all my children?
Is there any evil wanting? Your father killed
His father; sowed the womb of her who bore him;   285
Engendered you at the fount of his own existence!
That is what they will say of you.

                            Then, whom
Can you ever marry? There are no bridegrooms for you,
And your lives must wither away in sterile dreaming.   290

O Kreon, son of Menoikeus!
You are the only father my daughters have,
Since we, their parents, are both of us gone for ever.
They are your own blood: you will not let them
Fall into beggary and loneliness;   295
You will keep them from the miseries that are mine!
Take pity on them; see, they are only children,
Friendless except for you. Promise me this,
Great prince, and give me your hand in token of it.

(Kreon clasps his right hand.)   300

Children:
I could say much, if you could understand me,
But as it is, I have only this prayer for you:
Live where you can, be as happy as you can—
Happier, please God, than God has made your father.   305
Kreon: Enough. You have wept enough. Now go within.
Oedipus: I must; but it is hard.
Kreon: Time eases all things.
Oedipus: You know my mind, then?
Kreon: Say what you desire.   310
Oedipus: Send me from Thebes!
Kreon: God grant that I may!
Oedipus: But since God hates me . . .
Kreon: No, he will grant your wish.
Oedipus: You promise?   315
Kreon: I cannot speak beyond my knowledge.
Oedipus: Then lead me in.
Kreon: Come now, and leave your children.
Oedipus: No! Do not take them from me!

Kreon: Think no longer   320
   That you are in command here, but rather think
   How, when you were, you served your own destruction.

   *(Exeunt into the house all but the Chorus; the Choragos chants directly to
   the audience.)*

Choragos: Men of Thebes: look upon Oedipus.   325

   This is the king who solved the famous riddle
   And towered up, most powerful of men.
   No mortal eyes but looked on him with envy,
   Yet in the end ruin swept over him.

   Let every man in mankind's frailty   330
   Consider his last day; and let none
   Presume on his good fortune until he find
   Life, at his death, a memory without pain.

August Strindberg   (1849–1912)

*Strindberg was one of Sweden's greatest writers. His plays were shocking in their
day because they frankly assessed life as he saw it, making little effort to spare the
feelings and proprieties of his audiences. He wrote in several styles, one of them
called naturalism, a form of realism that emphasizes the power of circumstances to
shape people's lives. His purpose was to be faithful to the way people lived as a way
of revealing the truths that lay beneath the surfaces of experience. But he also used
a symbolic style, which is more appropriately revealed in* Miss Julie, *in which not
only objects, such as the Count's boots, but people, such as the Count himself, take on
symbolic values.*

   *Strindberg was misogynistic—a woman-hater—throughout his life, yet he was
filled with contradictions. On one hand, he felt that women should be homemakers
and caregivers and refrain from public life. Yet he married a famous actress, Siri
von Essen. All his three marriages were unhappy. One of his books, a collection of
short stories called* Marriages *(1886), took a frank and sometimes shocking look at
the institution of marriage.*

   Miss Julie *(1888) portrays a powerful but discontented woman who tries to use
her elevated birth—she is the daughter of a Count—to seduce and control Jean, the
Count's valet. Jean is on one level faithful and obedient to his master the Count,
yet he is tempted by his lustful feelings toward Julie. Strindberg described Julie in
his foreword to the play as a "half-woman" "man-hater." The setting is
midsummer eve, a time thought in Scandinavia and elsewhere to hold special
meaning for lovers. Jean mentions brewing a "magic potion" that will help Julie
"prophesy" who her lover will be. Julie says it is a night to forget the distinctions
between people. But it is also the feast of St. John, who was beheaded by Salome
after she failed to seduce him. Thus Strindberg focuses on a theme of sexual
domination.*

MISS JULIE   1888

Translated by Harry G. Carlson

Characters

> *Miss Julie*, twenty-five years old
> *Jean*, her father's valet, thirty
>   years old
>
> *Kristine*, her father's cook,
>   thirty-five years old

(*The action takes place in the count's kitchen on midsummer eve.*)

(*Scene: A large kitchen, the ceiling and side walls of which are hidden by draperies. The rear wall runs diagonally from down left to up right. On the wall down left are two shelves with copper, iron, and pewter utensils; the shelves are lined with scalloped paper. Visible to the right is most of a set of large, arched glass doors, through which can be seen a fountain with a statue of Cupid, lilac bushes in bloom, and the tops of some Lombardy poplars. At down left is the corner of a large tiled stove; a portion of its hood is showing. At right, one end of the servants' white pine dining table juts out; several chairs stand around it. The stove is decorated with birch branches; juniper twigs are strewn on the floor. On the end of the table stands a large Japanese spice jar, filled with lilac blossoms. An ice box, a sink, and a washstand. Above the door is an old-fashioned bell on a spring; to the left of the door, the mouthpiece of a speaking tube is visible.*)

(*Kristine is frying something on the stove. She is wearing a light-colored cotton dress and an apron. Jean enters. He is wearing livery and carries a pair of high riding boots with spurs, which he puts down on the floor where they can be seen by the audience.*)

Jean: Miss Julie's crazy again tonight; absolutely crazy!

Kristine: So you finally came back?

Jean: I took the Count to the station and when I returned past the barn I stopped in for a dance. Who do I see but Miss Julie leading off the dance with the gamekeeper! But as soon as she saw me she rushed over to ask me for the next waltz. And she's been waltzing ever since—I've never seen anything like it. She's crazy!

Kristine: She always has been, but never as bad as the last two weeks since her engagement was broken off.

Jean: Yes, I wonder what the real story was there. He was a gentleman, even if he wasn't rich. Ah! These people have such romantic ideas. (*Sits at the end of the table.*) Still, it's strange, isn't it? I mean that she'd rather stay home with the servants on midsummer eve instead of going with her father to visit relatives?

Kristine: She's probably embarrassed after that row with her fiancé.

Jean: Probably! He gave a good account of himself, though. Do you know how it happened, Kristine? I saw it, you know, though I didn't let on I had.

Kristine: No! You saw it?

Jean: Yes, I did.—That evening they were out near the stable, and she was "training" him—as she called it. Do you know what she did? She made him jump over her riding crop, the way you'd teach a dog to jump. He jumped twice and she hit him each time. But the third time he grabbed the crop out of her hand, hit her with it across the cheek, and broke it in pieces. Then he left.

Kristine: So, that's what happened! I can't believe it!

Jean: Yes, that's the way it went!—What have you got for me that's tasty, Kristine?

Kristine (serving him from the pan): Oh, it's only a piece of kidney I cut from the veal roast.

Jean (smelling the food): Beautiful! That's my favorite *délice.*° (*Feeling the plate.*) But you could have warmed the plate!

Kristine: You're fussier than the Count himself, once you start! (*She pulls his hair affectionately.*)

Jean (angry): Stop it, leave my hair alone! You know I'm touchy about that.

Kristine: Now, now, it's only love, you know that. (*Jean eats. Kristine opens a bottle of beer.*)

Jean: Beer? On midsummer eve? No thank you! I can do better than that. (*Opens a drawer in the table and takes out a bottle of red wine with yellow sealing wax.*) See that? Yellow seal! Give me a glass! A wine glass! I'm drinking this *pur.*°

Kristine (returns to the stove and puts on a small saucepan): God help the woman who gets you for a husband! What a fussbudget.

Jean: Nonsense! You'd be damned lucky to get a man like me. It certainly hasn't done you any harm to have people call me your sweetheart. (*Tastes the wine.*) Good! Very good! Just needs a little warming. (*Warms the glass between his hands.*) We bought this in Dijon. Four francs a liter, not counting the cost of the bottle, or the customs duty.—What are you cooking now? It stinks like hell!

Kristine: Oh, some slop Miss Julie wants to give Diana.

Jean: Watch your language, Kristine. But why should you have to cook for that damn mutt on midsummer eve? Is she sick?

Kristine: Yes, she's sick! She sneaked out with the gatekeeper's dog—and now there's hell to pay. Miss Julie won't have it!

Jean: Miss Julie has too much pride about some things and not enough about others, just like her mother was. The Countess was most at home in the kitchen and the cowsheds, but a *one*-horse carriage wasn't

---

délice: Delight.   *pur:* Pure; the first drink from the bottle.

elegant enough for her. The cuffs of her blouse were dirty, but she had to have her coat of arms on her cufflinks.—And Miss Julie won't take proper care of herself either. If you ask me, she just isn't refined. Just now, when she was dancing in the barn, she pulled the gamekeeper away from Anna and made him dance with her. *We* wouldn't behave like that, but that's what happens when aristocrats pretend they're common people—they get *common*!—But she is quite a woman! Magnificent! What shoulders, and what—et cetera!

Kristine: Oh, don't overdo it! I've heard what Clara says, and she dresses her.

Jean: Ha, Clara! You're all jealous of each other! I've been out riding with her. . . . And the way she dances!

Kristine: Listen, Jean! You're going to dance with me, when I'm finished here, aren't you?

Jean: Of course I will.

Kristine: Promise?

Jean: Promise? When I say I'll do something, I do it! By the way, the kidney was very good. (*Corks the bottle.*)

Julie (in the doorway to someone outside):   I'll be right back! You go ahead for now! (*Jean sneaks the bottle back into the table drawer and gets up respectfully. Miss Julie enters and crosses to Kristine by the stove.*) Well? Is it ready? (*Kristine indicates that Jean is present.*)

Jean (gallantly):   Are you ladies up to something secret?

Julie (flicking her handkerchief in his face):   None of your business!

Jean: Hmm! I like the smell of violets!

Julie (coquettishly):   Shame on you! So you know about perfumes, too? You certainly know how to dance. Ah, ah! No peeking! Go away.

> *Jean (boldly but respectfully):*   Are you brewing up a magic potion for midsummer eve? Something to prophesy by under a lucky star, so you'll catch a glimpse of your future husband!

Julie (caustically):   You'd need sharp eyes to see him! (*To Kristine.*) Pour out half a bottle and cork it well.—Come and dance a schottische° with me, Jean . . .

Jean (hesitating):   I don't want to be impolite to anyone, and I've already promised this dance to Kristine . . .

Julie: Oh, she can have another one—can't you, Kristine? Won't you lend me Jean?

Kristine: It's not up to me, ma'am. (*To Jean.*) If the mistress is so generous, it wouldn't do for you to say no. Go on, Jean, and thank her for the honor.

Jean: To be honest, and no offense intended, I wonder whether it's wise for you to dance twice running with the same partner, especially since these people are quick to jump to conclusions . . .

---

schottische: A Scottish round dance resembling a polka.

Julie (flaring up):   What's that? What sort of conclusions? What do you
   mean?

Jean (submissively):   If you don't understand, ma'am, I must speak more
   plainly. It doesn't look good to play favorites with your servants. . . .

Julie: Play favorites! What an idea! I'm astonished! As mistress of the
   house, I honor your dance with my presence. And when I dance, I
   want to dance with someone who can lead, so I won't look ridiculous.

Jean: As you order, ma'am! I'm at your service!

Julie (gently):   Don't take it as an order! On a night like this we're all just
   ordinary people having fun, so we'll forget about rank. Now, take my
   arm!—Don't worry, Kristine! I won't steal your sweetheart! (*Jean
   offers his arm and leads Miss Julie out.*)

   Mime: (*The following should be played as if the actress playing
   Kristine were really alone. When she has to, she turns her back to the
   audience. She does not look toward them, nor does she hurry as if she were
   afraid they would grow impatient. Schottische music played on a fiddle
   sounds in the distance. Kristine hums along with the music. She clears the
   table, washes the dishes, dries them, and puts them away. She takes off her
   apron. From a table drawer she removes a small mirror and leans it against
   the bowl of lilacs on the table. She lights a candle, heats a hairpin over the
   flame, and uses it to set a curl on her forehead. She crosses to the door and
   listens, then returns to the table. She finds the handkerchief Miss Julie left
   behind, picks it up, and smells it. Then, preoccupied, she spreads it out,
   stretches it, smooths out the wrinkles, and folds it into quarters, and so forth.*)

Jean (enters alone):   God, she really *is* crazy! What a way to dance!
   Everybody's laughing at her behind her back. What do you make of it,
   Kristine?

Kristine: Ah! It's that time of the month for her, and she always gets
   peculiar like that. Are you going to dance with me now?

Jean: You're not mad at me, are you, for leaving . . . . ?

Kristine: Of course not!—Why should I be, for a little thing like that?
   Besides, I know my place . . .

Jean (puts his arm around her waist):   You're a sensible girl, Kristine, and
   you'd make a good wife . . .

Julie (entering; uncomfortably surprised; with forced good humor):   What a
   charming escort—running away from his partner.

Jean: On the contrary, Miss Julie. Don't you see how I rushed back to
   the partner I abandoned!

Julie (changing her tone):   You know, you're a superb dancer!—But why
   are you wearing livery on a holiday? Take it off at once!

Jean: Then I must ask you to go outside for a moment. You see, my black
   coat is hanging over here . . . (*Gestures and crosses right.*)

Julie: Are you embarrassed about changing your coat in front of me?
   Well, go in your room then. Either that or stay and I'll turn my back.

Jean: With your permission, ma'am! (*He crosses right. His arm is visible as he changes his jacket.*)

Julie (to Kristine):   Tell me, Kristine—you two are so close—. Is Jean your fiancé?

Kristine: Fiancé? Yes, if you wish. We can call him that.

Julie: What do you mean?

Kristine: You had a fiancé yourself, didn't you? So . . .

Julie: Well, we were properly engaged . . .

Kristine: But nothing came of it, did it? (*Jean returns dressed in a frock coat and bowler hat.*)

Julie: *Très gentil, monsieur Jean! Très gentil!*

Jean: *Vous voulez plaisanter, madame!*

Julie: *Et vous voulez parler français!*° Where did you learn that?

Jean: In Switzerland, when I was wine steward in one of the biggest hotels in Lucerne!

Julie: You look like a real gentleman in that coat! *Charmant!*° (*Sits at the table.*)

Jean: Oh, you're flattering me!

Julie (offended):   Flattering you?

Jean: My natural modesty forbids me to believe that you would really compliment someone like me, and so I took the liberty of assuming that you were exaggerating, which polite people call flattering.

Julie: Where did you learn to talk like that? You must have been to the theater often.

Jean: Of course. And I've done a lot of traveling.

Julie: But you come from here, don't you?

Jean: My father was a farmhand on the district attorney's estate nearby. I used to see you when you were little, but you never noticed me.

Julie: No! Really?

Jean: Sure. I remember one time especially . . . but I can't talk about that.

Julie: Oh, come now! Why not? Just this once!

Jean: No, I really couldn't, not now. Some other time, perhaps.

Julie: Why some other time? What's so dangerous about now?

Jean: It's not dangerous, but there are obstacles.—Her, for example. (*Indicating Kristine, who has fallen asleep in a chair by the stove.*)

Julie: What a pleasant wife she'll make! She probably snores, too.

Jean: No, she doesn't, but she talks in her sleep.

Julie (cynically):   How do *you* know?

Jean (audaciously):   I've heard her! (*Pause, during which they stare at each other.*)

Julie: Why don't you sit down?

Jean: I couldn't do that in your presence.

Très gentil . . . français!:   Very pleasing, Mr. Jean! Very pleasing. You would trifle with me, madam! And you want to speak French!   *Charmant:*   Charming.

Julie: But if I order you to?

Jean: Then I'd obey.

Julie: Sit down, then.—No, wait. Can you get me something to drink first?

Jean: I don't know what we have in the ice box. I think there's only beer.

Julie: Why do you say "only"? My tastes are so simple I prefer beer to wine. (*Jean takes a bottle of beer from the ice box and opens it. He looks for a glass and a plate in the cupboard and serves her.*)

Jean: Here you are, ma'am.

Julie: Thank you. Won't you have something yourself?

Jean: I'm not partial to beer, but if it's an order . . .

Julie: An order?—Surely a gentleman can keep his lady company.

Jean: You're right, of course. (*Opens a bottle and gets a glass.*)

Julie: Now, drink to my health! (*He hesitates.*) What? A man of the world—and shy?

Jean (in mock romantic fashion, he kneels and raises his glass): Skål to my mistress!

Julie: Bravo!—Now kiss my shoe, to finish it properly. (*Jean hesitates, then boldly seizes her foot and kisses it lightly.*) Perfect! You should have been an actor.

Jean (rising): That's enough now, Miss Julie! Someone might come in and see us.

Julie: What of it?

Jean: People talk, that's what! If you knew how their tongues were wagging just now at the dance, you'd . . .

Julie: What were they saying? Tell me!—Sit down!

Jean (sits): I don't want to hurt you, but they were saying things—suggestive things, that, that . . . well, you can figure it out for yourself! You're not a child. If a woman is seen drinking alone with a man—let alone a servant—at night—then . . .

Julie: Then what? Besides, we're not alone. Kristine is here.

Jean: Asleep!

Julie: Then I'll wake her up. (*Rising.*) Kristine! Are you asleep? (*Kristine mumbles in her sleep.*)

Julie: Kristine!—She certainly can sleep!

Kristine (in her sleep): The Count's boots are brushed—put the coffee on—right away, right away—uh, huh—oh!

Julie (grabbing Kristine's nose): Will you wake up!

Jean (severely): Leave her alone—let her sleep!

Julie (sharply): What?

Jean: Someone who's been standing over a stove all day has a right to be tired by now. Sleep should be respected . . .

Julie (changing her tone): What a considerate thought—it does you credit—thank you! (*Offering her hand.*) Come outside and pick some lilacs for me!

(During the following, Kristine awakens and shambles sleepily off right to bed.)

Jean: Go with you?

Julie: With me!

Jean: We couldn't do that! Absolutely not!

Julie: I don't understand. Surely you don't imagine . . .

Jean: No, I don't, but the others might.

Julie: What? That I've fallen in love with a servant?

Jean: I'm not a conceited man, but such things happen—and for these people, nothing is sacred.

Julie: I do believe you're an aristocrat!

Jean: Yes, I am.

Julie: And I'm stepping down . . .

Jean: Don't step down, Miss Julie, take my advice. No one'll believe you stepped down voluntarily. People will always say you fell.

Julie: I have a higher opinion of people than you. Come and see!— Come! *(She stares at him broodingly.)*

Jean: You're very strange, do you know that?

Julie: Perhaps! But so are you!—For that matter, everything is strange. Life, people, everything. Like floating scum, drifting on and on across the water, until it sinks down and down! That reminds me of a dream I have now and then. I've climbed up on top of a pillar. I sit there and see no way of getting down. I get dizzy when I look down, and I must get down, but I don't have the courage to jump. I can't hold on firmly, and I long to be able to fall, but I don't fall. And yet I'll have no peace until I get down, no rest unless I get down, down on the ground! And if I did get down to the ground, I'd want to be under the earth . . . Have you ever felt anything like that?

Jean: No. I dream that I'm lying under a high tree in a dark forest. I want to get up, up on top, and look out over the bright landscape, where the sun is shining, and plunder the bird's nest up there, where the golden eggs lie. And I climb and climb, but the trunk's so thick and smooth, and it's so far to the first branch. But I know if I just reached that first branch, I'd go right to the top, like up a ladder. I haven't reached it yet, but I will, even if it's only in a dream!

Julie: Here I am chattering with you about dreams. Come, let's go out! Just into the park! *(She offers him her arm, and they start to leave.)*

Jean: We'll have to sleep on nine midsummer flowers, Miss Julie, to make our dreams come true! *(They turn at the door. Jean puts his hand to his eye.)*

Julie: Did you get something in your eye?

Jean: It's nothing—just a speck—it'll be gone in a minute.

Julie: My sleeve must have brushed against you. Sit down and let me help you. *(She takes him by the arm and seats him. She tilts his head back and with the tip of a handkerchief tries to remove the speck.*) Sit still, absolutely still! (*She slaps his hand.*) Didn't you hear me?—Why, you're trembling; the big, strong man is trembling! (*Feels his biceps.*) What muscles you have!

Jean (warning): Miss Julie!

Julie: Yes, *monsieur* Jean.

Jean: Attention! *Je ne suis qu'un homme!*°

Julie: Will you sit still!—There! Now it's gone! Kiss my hand and thank me.

Jean (rising): Miss Julie, listen to me!—Kristine has gone to bed!—Will you listen to me!

Julie: Kiss my hand first!

Jean: Listen to me!

Julie: Kiss my hand first!

Jean: All right, but you've only yourself to blame!

Julie: For what?

Jean: For what? Are you still a child at twenty-five? Don't you know that it's dangerous to play with fire?

Julie: Not for me. I'm insured.

Jean (boldly): No, you're not! But even if you were, there's combustible material close by.

Julie: Meaning you?

Jean: Yes! Not because it's me, but because I'm young—

Julie: And handsome—what incredible conceit! A Don Juan perhaps! Or a Joseph!° Yes, that's it, I do believe you're a Joseph!

Jean: Do you?

Julie: I'm almost afraid so. (*Jean boldly tries to put his arm around her waist and kiss her. She slaps his face.*) How dare you?

Jean: Are you serious or joking?

Julie: Serious.

Jean: Then so was what just happened. You play games too seriously, and that's dangerous. Well, I'm tired of games. You'll excuse me if I get back to work. I haven't done the Count's boots yet and it's long past midnight.

Julie: Put the boots down!

Jean: No! It's the work I have to do. I never agreed to be your playmate, and never will. It's beneath me.

Julie: You're proud.

Jean: In certain ways, but not in others.

Julie: Have you ever been in love?

Jean: We don't use that word, but I've been fond of many girls, and once

---

Attention! Je ne suis qu'un homme!: Watch out! I am only a man!   *Don Juan . . . Joseph:* Don Juan in Spanish legend is a seducer of women; in Genesis, Joseph resists the advances of Potiphar's wife.

I was sick because I couldn't have the one I wanted. That's right, sick, like those princes in the Arabian Nights—who couldn't eat or drink because of love.

Julie: Who was she? (*Jean is silent.*) Who was she?

Jean: You can't force me to tell you that.

Julie: But if I ask you as an equal, as a—friend! Who was she?

Jean: You!

Julie (sits): How amusing . . .

Jean: Yes, if you like! It was ridiculous!—You see, that was the story I didn't want to tell you earlier. Maybe I will now. Do you know how the world looks from down below?—Of course you don't. Neither do hawks and falcons, whose backs we can't see because they're usually soaring up there above us. I grew up in a shack with seven brothers and sisters and a pig, in the middle of a wasteland, where there wasn't a single tree. But from our window I could see the tops of apple trees above the wall of your father's garden. That was the Garden of Eden, guarded by angry angels with flaming swords. All the same, the other boys and I managed to find our way to the Tree of Life.—Now you think I'm contemptible, I suppose.

Julie: Oh, all boys steal apples.

Jean: You say that, but you think I'm contemptible anyway. Oh well! One day I went into the Garden of Eden with my mother, to weed the onion beds. Near the vegetable garden was a small Turkish pavilion in the shadow of jasmine bushes and overgrown with honeysuckle. I had no idea what it was used for, but I'd never seen such a beautiful building. People went in and came out again, and one day the door was left open. I sneaked close and saw walls covered with pictures of kings and emperors, and red curtains with fringes at the windows— now you know the place I mean. I—(*Breaks off a sprig of lilac and holds it in front of Miss Julie's nose.*)—I'd never been inside the manor house, never seen anything except the church—but this was more beautiful. From then on, no matter where my thoughts wandered, they returned—there. And gradually I got a longing to experience, just once, the full pleasure of—*enfin,*° I sneaked in, saw, and marveled! But then I heard someone coming! There was only one exit for ladies and gentlemen, but for me there was another, and I had no choice but to take it! (*Miss Julie, who has taken the lilac sprig, lets it fall on the table.*) Afterwards, I started running. I crashed through a raspberry bush, flew over a strawberry patch, and came up onto the rose terrace. There I caught sight of a pink dress and a pair of white stockings—it was you. I crawled under a pile of weeds, and I mean under—under thistles that pricked me and wet dirt that stank. And I looked at you as you walked among the roses, and I thought: if it's true that a thief can enter

enfin: Finally.

heaven and be with the angels, then why can't a farmhand's son here on God's earth enter the manor house garden and play with the Count's daughter?

Julie (romantically):   Do you think all poor children would have thought the way you did?

Jean (at first hesitant, then with conviction):   If *all* poor—yes—of course. Of course!

Julie: It must be terrible to be poor!

Jean (with exaggerated suffering):   Oh, Miss Julie! Oh!—A dog can lie on the Countess's sofa, a horse can have his nose patted by a young lady's hand, but a servant—(*Changing his tone.*)—oh, I know—now and then you find one with enough stuff in him to get ahead in the world, but how often?—Anyhow, do you know what I did then?—I jumped in the millstream with my clothes on, was pulled out, and got a beating. But the following Sunday, when my father and all the others went to my grandmother's, I arranged to stay home. I scrubbed myself with soap and water, put on my best clothes, and went to church so that I could see you! I saw you and returned home, determined to die. But I wanted to die beautifully and pleasantly, without pain. And then I remembered that it was dangerous to sleep under an elder bush. We had a big one, and it was in full flower. I plundered its treasures and bedded down under them in the oat bin. Have you ever noticed how smooth oats are?—and soft to the touch, like human skin . . . ! Well, I shut the lid and closed my eyes. I fell asleep and woke up feeling very sick. But I didn't die, as you can see. What was I after?—I don't know. There was no hope of winning you, of course.—You were a symbol of the hopelessness of ever rising out of the class in which I was born.

Julie: You're a charming storyteller. Did you ever go to school?

Jean: A bit, but I've read lots of novels and been to the theater often. And then I've listened to people like you talk—that's where I learned most.

Julie: Do you listen to what we say?

Jean: Naturally! And I've heard plenty, too, driving the carriage or rowing the boat. Once I heard you and a friend . . .

Julie: Oh?—What did you hear?

Jean: I'd better not say. But I was surprised a little. I couldn't imagine where you learned such words. Maybe at bottom there isn't such a great difference between people as we think.

Julie: Shame on you! We don't act like you when we're engaged.

Jean (staring at her):   Is that true?—You don't have to play innocent with me, Miss . . .

Julie: The man I gave my love to was a swine.

Jean: That's what you all say—afterwards.

Julie: All?

Jean: I think so. I know I've heard that phrase before, on similar occasions.

Julie: What occasions?

Jean: Like the one I'm talking about. The last time . . .

Julie (rising):   Quiet! I don't want to hear any more!

Jean: That's interesting—that's what *she* said, too. Well, if you'll excuse me, I'm going to bed.

Julie (gently):   To bed? On midsummer eve?

Jean: Yes! Dancing with the rabble out there doesn't amuse me much.

Julie: Get the key to the boat and row me out on the lake. I want to see the sun come up.

Jean: Is that wise?

Julie: Are you worried about your reputation?

Jean: Why not? Why should I risk looking ridiculous and getting fired without a reference, just when I'm trying to establish myself. Besides, I think I owe something to Kristine.

Julie: So, now it's Kristine . . .

Jean: Yes, but you, too.—Take my advice, go up and go to bed!

Julie: Am I to obey you?

Jean: Just this once—for your own good! Please! It's very late. Drowsiness makes people giddy and liable to lose their heads! Go to bed! Besides—unless I'm mistaken—I hear the others coming to look for me. And if they find us together, you'll be lost!

(The Chorus approaches, singing.)

Chorus:

The swineherd found his true love
a pretty girl so fair,
The swineherd found his true love
but let the girl beware.

For then he saw the princess
the princess on the golden hill,
but then saw the princess,
so much fairer still.

So the swineherd and the princess
they danced the whole night through,
and he forgot his first love,
to her he was untrue.

And when the long night ended,
and in the light of day, of day,
the dancing too was ended,
and the princess could not stay.

Then the swineherd lost his true love,
and the princess grieves him still,
and never more she'll wander
from atop the golden hill.

Julie: I know all these people and I love them, just as they love me. Let them come in and you'll see.

Jean: No, Miss Julie, they don't love you. They take your food, but they spit on it! Believe me! Listen to them, listen to what they're singing!— No, don't listen to them!

Julie (listening): What are they singing?

Jean: It's a dirty song! About you and me!

Julie: Disgusting! Oh! How deceitful!—

Jean: The rabble is always cowardly! And in a battle like this, you don't fight; you can only run away!

Julie: Run away? But where? We can't go out—or into Kristine's room.

Jean: True. But there's my room. Necessity knows no rules. Besides, you can trust me. I'm your friend and I respect you.

Julie: But suppose—suppose they look for you in there?

Jean: I'll bolt the door, and if anyone tries to break in, I'll shoot!— Come! (*On his knees.*) Come!

Julie (urgently): Promise me . . . ?

Jean: I swear! (*Miss Julie runs off right. Jean hastens after her.*)

> **Ballet:** (*Led by a fiddler, the servants and farm people enter, dressed festively, with flowers in their hats. On the table they place a small barrel of beer and a keg of schnapps, both garlanded. Glasses are brought out, and the drinking starts. A dance circle is formed and "The Swineherd and the Princess" is sung. When the dance is finished, everyone leaves, singing.*)
>
> (*Miss Julie enters alone. She notices the mess in the kitchen, wrings her hands, then takes out her powder puff and powders her nose.*)

Jean (enters, agitated): There, you see? And you heard them. We can't possibly stay here now, you know that.

Julie: Yes, I know. But what can we do?

Jean: Leave, travel, far away from here.

Julie: Travel? Yes, but where?

Jean: To Switzerland, to the Italian lakes. Have you ever been there?

Julie: No. Is it beautiful?

Jean: Oh, an eternal summer—oranges growing everywhere, laurel trees, always green . . .

Julie: But what'll we do there?

Jean: I'll open a hotel—with first-class service for first-class people.

Julie: Hotel?

Jean: That's the life, you know. Always new faces, new languages. No time to worry or be nervous. No hunting for something to do—there's always work to be done: bells ringing night and day, train whistles blowing, carriages coming and going, and all the while gold rolling into the till! That's the life!

Julie: Yes, it sounds wonderful. But what'll I do?

Jean: You'll be mistress of the house: the jewel in our crown! With your looks . . . and your manner—oh—success is guaranteed! It'll be wonderful! You'll sit in your office like a queen and push an electric button to set your slaves in motion. The guests will file past your throne and timidly lay their treasures before you.—You have no idea how people tremble when they get their bill.—I'll salt the bills° and you'll sweeten them with your prettiest smile.—Let's get away from here—(*Takes a timetable out of his pocket.*)—Right away, on the next train!—We'll be in Malmö six-thirty tomorrow morning, Hamburg at eight-forty; from Frankfort to Basel will take a day, then on to Como by way of the St. Gotthard Tunnel, in, let's see, three days. Three days!

Julie: That's all very well! But Jean—you must give me courage!—Tell me you love me! Put your arms around me!

Jean (hesitating): I want to—but I don't dare. Not in this house, not again. I love you—never doubt that—you don't doubt it, do you, Miss Julie?

Julie (shy; very feminine): "Miss!"—Call me Julie! There are no barriers between us anymore. Call me Julie!

Jean (tormented): I can't! There'll always be barriers between us as long as we stay in this house.—There's the past and there's the Count. I've never met anyone I had such respect for.—When I see his gloves lying on a chair, I feel small.—When I hear that bell up there ring, I jump like a skittish horse.—And when I look at his boots standing there so stiff and proud, I feel like bowing! (*Kicking the boots.*) Superstitions and prejudices we learned as children—but they can easily be forgotten. If I can just get to another country, a republic, people will bow and scrape when they see my livery—*they'll* bow and scrape, you hear, not me! I wasn't born to cringe. I've got stuff in me, I've got character, and if I can only grab onto that first branch, you watch me climb! I'm a servant today, but next year I'll own my own hotel. In ten years I'll have enough to retire. Then I'll go to Rumania and be decorated. I could—mind you I said *could*—end up a count!

Julie: Wonderful, wonderful!

Jean: Ah, in Rumania you just buy your title, and so you'll be a countess after all. My countess!

Julie: But I don't care about that—that's what I'm putting behind me! Show me you love me, otherwise—otherwise, what am I?

Jean: I'll show you a thousand times—afterwards! Not here! And whatever you do, no emotional outbursts, or we'll both be lost! We must think this through coolly, like sensible people. (*He takes out a cigar, snips the end, and lights it.*) You sit there, and I'll sit here. We'll talk as if nothing happened.

---

salt the bills: Inflate or pad the bills.

Julie (desperately):   Oh, my God! Have you no feelings?

Jean: Me? No one has more feelings than I do, but I know how to control them.

Julie: A little while ago you could kiss my shoe—and now!

Jean (harshly):   Yes, but that was before. Now we have other things to think about.

Julie: Don't speak harshly to me!

Jean: I'm not—just sensibly! We've already done one foolish thing, let's not have any more. The Count could return any minute, and by then we've got to decide what to do with our lives. What do you think of my plans for the future? Do you approve?

Julie: They sound reasonable enough. I have only one question: for such a big undertaking you need capital—do you have it?

Jean (chewing on the cigar):   Me? Certainly! I have my professional expertise, my wide experience, and my knowledge of languages. That's capital enough, I should think!

Julie: But all that won't even buy a train ticket.

Jean: That's true. That's why I'm looking for a partner to advance me the money.

Julie: Where will you find one quickly enough?

Jean: That's up to you, if you want to come with me.

Julie: But I can't; I have no money of my own. (*Pause.*)

Jean: Then it's all off . . .

Julie: And . . .

Jean: Things stay as they are.

Julie: Do you think I'm going to stay in this house as your lover? With all the servants pointing their fingers at me? Do you imagine I can face my father after this? No! Take me away from here, away from shame and dishonor—Oh, what have I done! My God, my God! (*She cries.*)

Jean: Now, don't start that old song!—What have you done? The same as many others before you.

Julie (screaming convulsively):   And now you think I'm contemptible!— I'm falling, I'm falling!

Jean: Fall down to my level and I'll lift you up again.

Julie: What terrible power drew me to you? The attraction of the weak to the strong? The falling to the rising? Or was it love? Was this love? Do you know what love is?

Jean: Me? What do you take me for? You don't think this was my first time, do you?

Julie: The things you say, the thoughts you think!

Jean: That's the way I was taught, and that's the way I am! Now don't get excited and don't play the grand lady, because we're in the same boat now!—Come on, Julie, I'll pour you a glass of something special! (*He opens a drawer in the table, takes out a wine bottle, and fills two glasses already used.*)

Julie: Where did you get that wine?

Jean: From the cellar.

Julie: My father's burgundy!

Jean: That'll do for his son-in-law, won't it?

Julie: And I drink beer! Beer!

Jean: That only shows I have better taste.

Julie: Thief!

Jean: Planning to tell?

Julie: Oh, oh! Accomplice of a common thief! Was I drunk? Have I been walking in a dream the whole evening? Midsummer eve! A time of innocent fun!

Jean: Innocent, eh?

Julie (pacing back and forth): Is there anyone on earth more miserable than I am at this moment?

Jean: Why should you be? After such a conquest? Think of Kristine in there. Don't you think she has feelings, too?

Julie: I thought so awhile ago, but not anymore. No, a servant is a servant . . .

Jean: And a whore is a whore!

Julie (on her knees, her hands clasped): Oh, God in heaven, end my wretched life! Take me away from the filth I'm sinking into! Save me! Save me!

Jean: I can't deny I feel sorry for you. When I lay in that onion bed and saw you in the rose garden, well . . . I'll be frank . . . I had the same dirty thoughts all boys have.

Julie: And you wanted to die for me!

Jean: In the oat bin? That was just talk.

Julie: A lie, in other words!

Jean (beginning to feel sleepy): More or less! I got the idea from a newspaper story about a chimney sweep who curled up in a firewood bin full of lilacs because he got a summons for not supporting his illegitimate child . . .

Julie: So, that's what you're like . . .

Jean: I had to think of something. And that's the kind of story women always go for.

Julie: Swine!

Jean: Merde!°

Julie: And now you've seen the hawk's back . . .

Jean: Not exactly its *back* . . .

Julie: And I was to be the first branch . . .

Jean: But the branch was rotten . . .

Julie: I was to be the sign on the hotel . . .

Jean: And I the hotel . . .

Merde!: Excrement!

Julie: Sit at your desk, entice your customers, pad their bills . . .

Jean: That I'd do myself . . .

Julie: How can anyone be so thoroughly filthy?

Jean: Better clean up then!

Julie: You lackey, you menial, stand up, when I speak to you!

Jean: Menial's strumpet, lackey's whore, shut up and get out of here! Who are you to lecture me on coarseness? None of my kind is ever as coarse as you were tonight. Do you think one of your maids would throw herself at a man the way you did? Have you ever seen any girl of my class offer herself like that? I've only seen it among animals and streetwalkers.

Julie (crushed): You're right. Hit me, trample on me. I don't deserve any better. I'm worthless. But help me! If you see any way out of this, help me, Jean, please!

Jean (more gently): I'd be lying if I didn't admit to a sense of triumph in all this, but do you think that a person like me would have dared even to look at someone like you if you hadn't invited it? I'm still amazed . . .

Julie: And proud . . .

Jean: Why not? Though I must say it was too easy to be really exciting.

Julie: Go on, hit me, hit me harder!

Jean (rising): No! Forgive me for what I've said! I don't hit a man when he's down, let alone a woman. I can't deny though, that I'm pleased to find out that what looked so dazzling to us from below was only tinsel, that the hawk's back was only gray, after all, that the lovely complexion was only powder, that those polished fingernails had black edges, and that a dirty handkerchief is still dirty, even if it smells of perfume . . . ! On the other hand, it hurts me to find out that what I was striving for wasn't finer, more substantial. It hurts me to see you sunk so low that you're inferior to your own cook. It hurts like watching flowers beaten down by autumn rains and turned into mud.

Julie: You talk as if you were already above me.

Jean: I am. You see, I could make you a countess, but you could never make me a count.

Julie: But I'm the child of a count—something you could never be!

Jean: That's true. But I could be the father of counts—if . . .

Julie: But you're a thief. I'm not.

Jean: There are worse things than being a thief! Besides, when I'm working in a house, I consider myself sort of a member of the family, like one of the children. And you don't call it stealing when a child snatches a berry off a full bush. (*His passion is aroused again.*) Miss Julie, you're a glorious woman, much too good for someone like me! You were drinking and you lost your head. Now you want to cover up your mistake by telling yourself that you love me! You don't. Maybe there was a physical attraction—but then your love is no better than mine.—I could never be satisfied to be no more than an animal to you, and I could never arouse real love in you.

Julie: Are you sure of that?

Jean: You're suggesting it's possible—Oh, I could fall in love with you, no doubt about it. You're beautiful, you're refined—(*Approaching and taking her hand.*)—cultured, lovable when you want to be, and once you start a fire in a man, it never goes out. (*Putting his arm around her waist.*) You're like hot, spicy wine, and one kiss from you . . . (*He tries to lead her out, but she slowly frees herself.*)

Julie: Let me go!?—You'll never win me like that.

Jean: How then?—Not like that? Not with caresses and pretty speeches. Not with plans about the future or rescue from disgrace! *How* then?

Julie: How? How? I don't know!—I have no idea!—I detest you as I detest rats, but I can't escape from you.

Jean: Escape with me!

Julie (pulling herself together):   Escape? Yes, we must escape!—But I'm so tired. Give me a glass of wine. (*Jean pours the wine. She looks at her watch.*) But we must talk first. We still have a little time. (*She drains the glass, then holds it out for more.*)

Jean: Don't drink so fast. It'll go to your head.

Julie: What does it matter?

Jean: What does it matter? It's vulgar to get drunk! What did you want to tell me?

Julie: We must escape! But first we must talk, I mean I must talk. You've done all the talking up to now. You told about your life, now I want to tell about mine, so we'll know all about each other before we go off together.

Jean: Just a minute! Forgive me! If you don't want to regret it afterwards, you'd better think twice before revealing any secrets about yourself.

Julie: Aren't you my friend?

Jean: Yes, sometimes! But don't rely on me.

Julie: You're only saying that.—Besides, everyone already knows my secrets.—You see, my mother was a commoner—very humble background. She was brought up believing in social equality, women's rights, and all that. The idea of marriage repelled her. So, when my father proposed, she replied that she would never become his wife, but he could be her lover. He insisted that he didn't want the woman he loved to be less respected than he. But his passion ruled him, and when she explained that the world's respect meant nothing to her, he accepted her conditions.

But now his friends avoided him and his life was restricted to taking care of the estate, which couldn't satisfy him. I came into the world—against my mother's wishes, as far as I can understand. She wanted to bring me up as a child of nature, and, what's more, to learn everything a boy had to learn, so that I might be an example of how a woman can be as good as a man. I had to wear boy's clothes and learn to take care of horses, but I was never allowed in the cowshed. I had to groom and harness the horses and go hunting—and even had to watch them slaughter animals—that was disgusting! On the estate men were put on women's jobs and women on men's jobs—with the result that the property became run down and we became the laughingstock of the district. Finally, my father must have awakened from his trance because he rebelled and changed everything his way. My parents were then married quietly. Mother became ill—I don't know what illness it was—but she often had convulsions, hid in the attic and in the garden, and sometimes stayed out all night. Then came the great fire, which you've heard about. The house, the stables, and the cowshed all burned down, under very curious circumstances, suggesting arson, because the accident happened the day after the insurance had expired. The quarterly premium my father sent in was delayed because of a messenger's carelessness and didn't arrive in time. (*She fills her glass and drinks.*)

Jean: Don't drink any more!

Julie: Oh, what does it matter.—We were left penniless and had to sleep in the carriages. My father had no idea where to find money to rebuild the house because he had so slighted his old friends that they had forgotten him. Then my mother suggested that he borrow from a childhood friend of hers, a brick manufacturer who lived nearby. Father got the loan without having to pay interest, which surprised him. And that's how the estate was rebuilt.—(*Drinks again.*) Do you know who started the fire?

Jean: The Countess, your mother.

Julie: Do you know who the brick manufacturer was?

Jean: Your mother's lover?

Julie: Do you know whose money it was?

Jean: Wait a moment—no, I don't.

Julie: It was my mother's.

Jean: You mean the Count's, unless they didn't sign an agreement when they were married.

Julie: They didn't.—My mother had a small inheritance which she didn't want under my father's control, so she entrusted it to her—friend.

Jean: Who stole it!

Julie: Exactly! He kept it.—All this my father found out, but he couldn't bring it to court, couldn't repay his wife's lover, couldn't prove it was his wife's money! It was my mother's revenge for being forced into marriage against her will. It nearly drove him to suicide—there was a rumor that he tried with a pistol, but failed. So, he managed to live through it and my mother had to suffer for what she'd done. You can imagine that those were a terrible five years for me. I loved my father, but I sided with my mother because I didn't know the circumstances.

I learned from her to hate men—you've heard how she hated the whole male sex—and I swore to her I'd never be a slave to any man.

Jean: But you got engaged to that lawyer.

Julie: In order to make him my slave.

Jean: And he wasn't willing?

Julie: He was willing, all right, but I wouldn't let him. I got tired of him.

Jean: I saw it—out near the stable.

Julie: What did you see?

Jean: I saw—how he broke off the engagement.

Julie: That's a lie! I was the one who broke it off. Has he said that he did? That swine . . .

Jean: He was no swine, I'm sure. So, you hate men, Miss Julie?

Julie: Yes!—Most of the time! But sometimes—when the weakness comes, when passion burns! Oh, God, will the fire never die out?

Jean: Do you hate me, too?

Julie: Immeasurably! I'd like to have you put to death, like an animal . . .

Jean: I see—the penalty for bestiality—the woman gets two years at hard labor and the animal is put to death. Right?

Julie: Exactly!

Jean: But there's no prosecutor here—and no animal. So, what'll we do?

Julie: Go away!

Jean: To torment each other to death?

Julie: No! To be happy for—two days, a week, as long as we can be happy, and then—die . . .

Jean: Die? That's stupid! It's better to open a hotel!

Julie (without listening): —on the shore of Lake Como, where the sun always shines, where the laurels are green at Christmas and the oranges glow.

Jean: Lake Como is a rainy hole, and I never saw any oranges outside the stores. But tourists are attracted there because there are plenty of villas to be rented out to lovers, and that's a profitable business.—Do you know why? Because they sign a lease for six months—and then leave after three weeks!

Julie (naively): Why after three weeks?

Jean: They quarrel, of course! But they still have to pay the rent in full! And so you rent the villas out again. And that's the way it goes, time after time. There's never a shortage of love—even if it doesn't last long!

Julie: You don't want to die with me?

Jean: I don't want to die at all! For one thing, I like living, and for another, I think suicide is a crime against the Providence which gave us life.

Julie: You believe in God? *You?*

Jean: Of course I do. And I go to church every other Sunday.—To be honest, I'm tired of all this, and I'm going to bed.

Julie: Are you? And do you think I can let it go at that? A man owes
  something to the woman he's shamed.

Jean (taking out his purse and throwing a silver coin on the table): Here! I
  don't like owing anything to anybody.

Julie (pretending not to notice the insult): Do you know what the law
  states . . .

Jean: Unfortunately the law doesn't state any punishment for the woman
  who seduces a man!

Julie (as before): Do you see any way out but to leave, get married, and
  then separate?

Jean: Suppose I refuse such a *mésalliance?*°

Julie: *Mésalliance* . . .

Jean: Yes, for me! You see, I come from better stock than you. There's no
  arsonist in my family.

Julie: How do you know?

Jean: You can't prove otherwise. We don't keep charts on our ancestors—
  there's just the police records! But I've read about your family. Do
  you know who the founder was? He was a miller who let the king
  sleep with his wife one night during the Danish War. I don't have any
  noble ancestors like that. I don't have any noble ancestors at all, but I
  could become one myself.

Julie: This is what I get for opening my heart to someone unworthy, for
  giving my family's honor . . .

Jean: Dishonor!—Well, I told you so: when people drink, they talk, and
  talk is dangerous!

Julie: Oh, how I regret it!—How I regret it!—If you at least loved me.

Jean: For the last time—what do you want? Shall I cry; shall I jump over
  your riding crop? Shall I kiss you and lure you off to Lake Como for
  three weeks, and then God knows what . . . ? What shall I do? What do
  you want? This is getting painfully embarrassing! But that's what
  happens when you stick your nose in women's business. Miss Julie! I
  see that you're unhappy. I know you're suffering, but I can't
  understand you. We don't have such romantic ideas; there's not this
  kind of hate between us. Love is a game we play when we get time off
  from work, but we don't have all day and night, like you. I think
  you're sick, really sick. Your mother was crazy, and her ideas have
  poisoned your life.

Julie: Be kind to me. At least now you're talking like a human being.

Jean: Be human yourself, then. You spit on me, and you won't let me
  wipe myself off—

Julie: Help me! Help me! Just tell me what to do, where to go!

Jean: In God's name, if I only knew myself!

Julie: I've been crazy, out of my mind, but isn't there any way out?

---

mésalliance: Misalliance or mismatch, especially regarding relative social status.

Jean: Stay here and keep calm! No one knows anything!

Julie: Impossible! The others know and Kristine knows.

Jean: No they don't, and they'd never believe a thing like that!

Julie (hesitantly): But—it could happen again!

Jean: That's true!

Julie: And then?

Jean (frightened): Then?—Why didn't I think about that? Yes, there is only one thing to do—get away from here! Right away! I can't come with you, then we'd be finished, so you'll have to go alone—away—anywhere!

Julie: Alone?—Where?—I can't do that!

Jean: You must! And before the Count gets back! If you stay, you know what'll happen. Once you make a mistake like this, you want to continue because the damage has already been done. . . . Then you get bolder and bolder—until finally you're caught! So leave! Later you can write to the Count and confess everything—except that it was me! He'll never guess who it was, and he's not going to be eager to find out, anyway.

Julie: I'll go if you come with me.

Jean: Are you out of your head? Miss Julie runs away with her servant! In two days it would be in the newspapers, and that's something your father would never live through.

Julie: I can't go and I can't stay! Help me! I'm so tired, so terribly tired.—Order me! Set me in motion—I can't think or act on my own . . .

Jean: What miserable creatures you people are! You strut around with your noses in the air as if you were the lords of creation! All right, I'll order you. Go upstairs and get dressed! Get some money for the trip, and then come back down!

Julie (in a half-whisper): Come up with me!

Jean: To your room?—Now you're crazy again! (*Hesitates for a moment.*) No! Go, at once! (*Takes her hand to lead her out.*)

Julie (as she leaves): Speak kindly to me, Jean!

Jean: An order always sounds unkind—now you know how it feels. (*Jean, alone, sighs with relief. He sits at the table, takes out a notebook and pencil, and begins adding up figures, counting aloud as he works. He continues in dumb show until Kristine enters, dressed for church. She is carrying a white tie and shirt front.*)

Kristine: Lord Jesus, what a mess! What have you been up to?

Jean: Oh, Miss Julie dragged everybody in here. You mean you didn't hear anything? You must have been sleeping soundly.

Kristine: Like a log.

Jean: And dressed for church already?

Kristine: Of course! You remember you promised to come with me to communion today!

Jean: Oh, yes, that's right.—And you brought my things. Come on, then! (*He sits down. Kristine starts to put on his shirt front and tie. Pause. Jean begins sleepily.*) What's the gospel text for today?

Kristine: On St. John's Day?—the beheading of John the Baptist, I should think!

Jean: Ah, that'll be a long one, for sure.—Hey, you're choking me!—Oh, I'm sleepy, so sleepy!

Kristine: Yes, what have you been doing, up all night? Your face is absolutely green.

Jean: I've been sitting here gabbing with Miss Julie.

Kristine: She has no idea what's proper, that one! (*Pause.*)

Jean: You know, Kristine . . .

Kristine: What?

Jean: It's really strange when you think about it.—Her!

Kristine: What's so strange?

Jean: Everything! (*Pause.*)

Kristine (looking at the half-empty glasses standing on the table):   Have you been drinking together, too?

Jean: Yes.

Kristine: Shame on you!—Look me in the eye!

Jean: Well?

Kristine: Is it possible? Is it possible?

Jean (thinking it over for a moment):   Yes, it is.

Kristine: Ugh! I never would have believed it! No, shame on you, shame!

Jean: You're not jealous of her, are you?

Kristine: No, not of her! If it had been Clara or Sofie I'd have scratched your eyes out!—I don't know why, but that's the way I feel.—Oh, its disgusting!

Jean: Are you angry at her, then?

Kristine: No, at you! That was an awful thing to do, awful! Poor girl!— No, I don't care who knows it—I won't stay in a house where we can't respect the people we work for.

Jean: Why should we respect them?

Kristine: You're so clever, you tell me! Do you want to wait on people who can't behave decently? Do you? You disgrace yourself that way, if you ask me.

Jean: But it's a comfort to know they aren't any better than us.

Kristine: Not for me. If they're no better, what do we have to strive for to better ourselves.—And think of the Count! Think of him! As if he hasn't had enough misery in his life! Lord Jesus! No, I won't stay in this house any longer!—And it had to be with someone like you! If it had been that lawyer, if it had been a real gentleman . . .

Jean: What do you mean?

Kristine: Oh, you're all right for what you are, but there are men and gentlemen, after all!—No, this business with Miss Julie I can never forget. She was so proud, so arrogant with men, you wouldn't have believed she could just go and give herself—and to someone like you! And she was going to have poor Diana shot for running after the gatekeepers' mutt!—Yes, I'm giving my notice, I mean it—I won't stay here any longer. On the twenty-fourth of October, I leave!

Jean: And then?

Kristine: Well, since the subject has come up, it's about time you looked around for something since we're going to get married, in any case.

Jean: Where am I going to look? I couldn't find a job like this if I was married.

Kristine: No, that's true. But you can find work as a porter or as a caretaker in some government office. The state doesn't pay much, I know, but it's secure, and there's a pension for the wife and children . . .

Jean (grimacing): That's all very well, but it's a bit early for me to think about dying for a wife and children. My ambitions are a little higher than that.

Kristine: Your ambitions, yes! Well, you have obligations, too! Think about them!

Jean: Don't start nagging me about obligations. I know what I have to do! (*Listening for something outside.*) Besides, this is something we have plenty of time to think over. Go and get ready for church.

Kristine: Who's that walking around up there?

Jean: I don't know, unless it's Clara.

Kristine (going): You don't suppose it's the Count, who came home without us hearing him?

Jean (frightened): The Count? No, I don't think so. He'd have rung.

Kristine (going): Well, God help us! I've never seen anything like this before. (*The sun has risen and shines through the treetops in the park. The light shifts gradually until it slants in through the windows. Jean goes to the door and signals. Miss Julie enters, dressed in travel clothes and carrying a small bird cage, covered with a cloth, which she places on a chair.*)

Julie: I'm ready now.

Jean: Shh! Kristine is awake.

Julie (very nervous during the following): Does she suspect something?

Jean: She doesn't know anything. But my God, you look awful!

Julie: Why? How do I look?

Jean: You're pale as a ghost and—excuse me, but your face is dirty.

Julie: Let me wash up then.—(*She goes to the basin and washes her hands and face.*) Give me a towel!—Oh—the sun's coming up.

Jean: Then the goblins will disappear.

Julie: Yes, there must have been goblins out last night!—Jean, listen, come with me! I have some money now.

Jean (hesitantly): Enough?

Julie: Enough to start with. Come with me! I just can't travel alone on a day like this—midsummer day on a stuffy train—jammed in among crowds of people staring at me. Eternal delays at every station, while I'd wish I had wings. No, I can't, I can't! And then there'll be memories, memories of midsummer days when I was little. The church—decorated with birch leaves and lilacs; dinner at the big table with relatives and friends; the afternoons in the park, dancing, music, flowers, and games. Oh, no matter how far we travel, the memories will follow in the baggage car, with remorse and guilt!

Jean: I'll go with you—but right away, before it's too late. Right this minute!

Julie: Get dressed, then! (*Picking up the bird cage.*)

Jean: But no baggage! It would give us away!

Julie: No, nothing! Only what we can have in the compartment with us.

Jean (has taken his hat): What've you got there? What is it?

Julie: It's only my greenfinch. I couldn't leave her behind.

Jean: What? Bring a bird cage with us? You're out of your head! Put it down!

Julie: It's the only thing I'm taking from my home—the only living being that loves me, since Diana was unfaithful. Don't be cruel! Let me take her!

Jean: Put the cage down, I said!—And don't talk so loudly—Kristine will hear us!

Julie: No, I won't leave her in the hands of strangers! I'd rather you killed her.

Jean: Bring the thing here, then, I'll cut its head off!

Julie: Oh! But don't hurt her! Don't . . . no, I can't.

Jean: Bring it here! I can!

Julie (taking the bird out of the cage and kissing it): Oh, my little Serena, must you die and leave your mistress?

Jean: Please don't make a scene! Your whole future is at stake! Hurry up! (*He snatches the bird from her, carries it over to the chopping block, and picks up a meat cleaver. Miss Julie turns away.*) You should have learned how to slaughter chickens instead of how to fire pistols. (*He chops off the bird's head.*) Then you wouldn't feel faint at the sight of blood.

Julie (screaming): Kill me, too! Kill me! You, who can slaughter an innocent animal without blinking an eye! Oh, how I hate, how I detest you! There's blood between us now! I curse the moment I set eyes on you! I curse the moment I was conceived in my mother's womb!

Jean: What good does cursing do? Let's go!

Julie (approaching the chopping block, as if drawn against her will): No, I don't want to go yet. I can't . . . until I see . . . Shh! I hear a carriage— (*She listens, but her eyes never leave the cleaver and the chopping block.*) Do you think I can't stand the sight of blood? You think I'm so weak

. . . Oh—I'd like to see your blood and your brains on a chopping block!—I'd like to see your whole sex swimming in a sea of blood, like my little bird . . . I think I could drink from your skull! I'd like to bathe my feet in your open chest and eat your heart roasted whole!— You think I'm weak. You think I love you because my womb craved your seed. You think I want to carry your spawn under my heart and nourish it with my blood—bear your child and take your name! By the way, what is your family name? I've never heard it.—Do you have one? I was to be Mrs. Bootblack—or Madame Pigsty.—You dog, who wears my collar, you lackey, who bears my coat of arms on your buttons—do I have to share you with my cook, compete with my own servant? Oh! Oh! Oh!—You think I'm a coward who wants to run away! No, now I'm staying—and let the storm break! My father will come home . . . to find his desk broken open . . . and his money gone! Then he'll ring—that bell . . . twice for his valet—and then he'll send for the police . . . and then I'll tell everything! Everything! Oh, what a relief it'll be to have it all end—if only it will end!—And then he'll have a stroke and die . . . That'll be the end of all of us—and there'll be peace . . . quiet . . . eternal rest!—And then our coat of arms will be broken against his coffin—the family title extinct—but the valet's line will go on in an orphanage . . . win laurels in the gutter, and end in jail!

Jean: There's the blue blood talking! Very good, Miss Julie! Just don't let that miller out of the closet! (*Kristine enters, dressed for church, with a psalm-book in her hand.*)

Julie (rushing to Kristine and falling into her arms, as if seeking protection): Help, me Kristine! Help me against this man!

Kristine (unmoved and cold): What a fine way to behave on a Sunday morning! (*Sees the chopping block.*) And look at this mess!—What does all this mean? Why all this screaming and carrying on?

Julie: Kristine! You're a woman and my friend! Beware of this swine!

Jean (uncomfortable): While you ladies discuss this, I'll go in and shave. (*Slips off right.*)

Julie: You must listen to me so you'll understand!

Kristine: No, I could never understand such disgusting behavior! Where are you off to in your traveling clothes?—And he had his hat on.— Well?—Well?—

Julie: Listen to me, Kristine! Listen, and I'll tell you everything—

Kristine: I don't want to hear it . . .

Julie: But you must listen to me . . .

Kristine: What about? If it's about this silliness with Jean, I'm not interested, because it's none of my business. But if you're thinking of tricking him into running out, we'll soon put a stop to that!

Julie (extremely nervous): Try to be calm now, Kristine, and listen to me! I can't stay here, and neither can Jean—so we must go away . . .

Kristine: Hm, hm!

Julie (brightening):   You see, I just had an idea—What if all three of us go—abroad—to Switzerland and start a hotel together?—I have money, you see—and Jean and I could run it—and I thought you, you could take care of the kitchen . . . Wouldn't that be wonderful?—Say yes! And come with us, and then everything will be settled!—Oh, do say yes! (*Embracing Kristine and patting her warmly.*)

Kristine (coolly, thoughtfully):   Hm, hm!

Julie (presto tempo):°   You've never traveled, Kristine.—You must get out and see the world. You can't imagine how much fun it is to travel by train—always new faces—new countries.—And when we get to Hamburg, we'll stop off at the zoo—you'll like that.—and then we'll go to the theater and the opera—and when we get to Munich, dear, there we have museums, with Rubens and Raphael, the great painters, as you know.—You've heard of Munich, where King Ludwig lived— the king who went mad.—And then we'll see his castles—they're still there and they're like castles in fairy tales.—And from there it isn't far to Switzerland—and the Alps.—Imagine—the Alps have snow on them even in the middle of summer!—And oranges grow there and laurel trees that are green all year round—

(*Jean can be seen in the wings right, sharpening his razor on a strop which he holds with his teeth and his left hand. He listens to the conversation with satisfaction, nodding now and then in approval. Miss Julie continues tempo prestissimo.*)°

And then we'll start a hotel—and I'll be at the desk, while Jean greets the guests . . . does the shopping . . . writes letters.—You have no idea what a life it'll be—the train whistles blowing and the carriages arriving and the bells ringing in the rooms and down in the restaurant.—And I'll make out the bills—and I know how to salt them! . . . You'll never believe how timid travelers are when they have to pay their bills!—And you—you'll be in charge of the kitchen.— Naturally, you won't have to stand over the stove yourself.—And since you're going to be seen by people, you'll have to wear beautiful clothes.—And you, with your looks—no, I'm not flattering you—one fine day you'll grab yourself a husband!—You'll see!—A rich Englishman—they're so easy to—(*Slowing down.*)—catch—and then we'll get rich—and build ourselves a villa on Lake Como.—It's true it rains there a little now and then, but—(*Dully.*)—the sun has to shine sometimes—although it looks dark—and then . . . of course we could always come back home again—(*Pause.*)—here—or somewhere else—

Kristine: Listen, Miss Julie, do you believe all this?

Julie (crushed):   Do I believe it?

---

presto tempo: At a rapid pace.   *tempo prestissimo:* At a very rapid pace.

Kristine: Yes!

Julie (wearily): I don't know. I don't believe in anything anymore. (*She sinks down on the bench and cradles her head in her arms on the table.*) Nothing! Nothing at all!

Kristine (turning right to where Jean is standing): So, you thought you'd run out!

Jean (embarrassed; puts the razor on the table): Run out? That's no way to put it. You hear Miss Julie's plan, and even if she is tired after being up all night, it's still a practical plan.

Kristine: Now you listen to me! Did you think I'd work as a cook for that . . .

Jean (sharply): You watch what you say in front of your mistress! Do you understand?

Kristine: Mistress!

Jean: Yes!

Kristine: Listen to him! Listen to him!

Jean: Yes, you listen! It'd do you good to listen more and talk less! Miss Julie is your mistress. If you despise her, you have to despise yourself for the same reason!

Kristine: I've always had enough self-respect—

Jean: —to be able to despise other people!

Kristine: —to stop me from doing anything that's beneath me. You can't say that the Count's cook has been up to something with the groom or the swineherd! Can you?

Jean: No, you were lucky enough to get hold of a gentleman!

Kristine: Yes, a gentleman who sells the Count's oats from the stable.

Jean: You should talk—taking a commission from the grocer and bribes from the butcher.

Kristine: What?

Jean: And you say you can't respect your employers any longer. You, you, you!

Kristine: Are you coming to church with me, now? You could use a good sermon after your fine deed!

Jean: No, I'm not going to church today. You'll have to go alone and confess what you've been up to.

Kristine: Yes, I'll do that, and I'll bring back enough forgiveness for you, too. The Savior suffered and died on the Cross for all our sins, and if we go to Him with faith and a penitent heart, He takes all our sins on Himself.

Jean: Even grocery sins?

Julie: And do you believe that, Kristine?

Kristine: It's my living faith, as sure as I stand here. It's the faith I learned as a child, Miss Julie, and kept ever since. "Where sin abounded, grace did much more abound!"

Julie: Oh, if I only had your faith. If only . . .

Kristine: Well, you see, we can't have it without God's special grace, and that isn't given to everyone—

Julie: Who is it given to then?

Kristine: That's the great secret of the workings of grace, Miss Julie, and God is no respecter of persons, for the last shall be the first . . .

Julie: Then He does respect the last.

Kristine (continuing): . . . and it is easier for a camel to go through the eye of a needle, than for a rich man to enter the Kingdom of God. That's how it is, Miss Julie! Anyhow, I'm going now—alone, and on the way I'm going to tell the groom not to let any horses out, in case anyone wants to leave before the Count gets back!—Goodbye! (*Leaves.*)

Jean: What a witch!—And all this because of a greenfinch!—

Julie (dully): Never mind the greenfinch!—Can you see any way out of this? Any end to it?

Jean (thinking): No!

Julie: What would you do in my place?

Jean: In your place? Let's see—as a person of position, as a woman who had—fallen. I don't know—wait, now I know.

Julie (taking the razor and making a gesture): You mean like this?

Jean: Yes! But—understand—*I* wouldn't do it! That's the difference between us!

Julie: Because you're a man and I'm a woman? What sort of difference is that?

Jean: The usual difference—between a man and a woman.

Julie (with the razor in her hand): I want to, but I can't!—My father couldn't either, the time he should have done it.

Jean: No, he shouldn't have! He had to revenge himself first.

Julie: And now my mother is revenged again, through me.

Jean: Didn't you ever love your father, Miss Julie?

Julie: Oh yes, deeply, but I've hated him, too. I must have done so without realizing it! It was he who brought me up to despise my own sex, making me half woman, half man. Whose fault is what's happened? My father's, my mother's, my own? My own? I don't have anything that's my own. I don't have a single thought that I didn't get from my father, not an emotion that I didn't get from my mother, and this last idea—that all people are equal—I got that from my fiancé.— That's why I called him a swine! How can it be my fault? Shall I let Jesus take on the blame, the way Kristine does?—No, I'm too proud to do that and too sensible—thanks to my father's teachings.—And as for someone rich not going to heaven, that's a lie. But Kristine won't get in—how will she explain the money she has in the savings bank? Whose fault is it?—What does it matter whose fault it is? I'm still the one who has to bear the blame, face the consequences . . .

Jean: Yes, but . . . (*The bell rings sharply twice. Miss Julie jumps up. Jean changes his coat.*) The Count is back! Do you suppose Kristine—(*He goes to the speaking tube, taps the lid, and listens.*)

Julie: He's been to his desk!

Jean: It's Jean, sir! (*Listening; the audience cannot hear the Count's voice.*) Yes, sir! (*Listening.*) Yes, sir! Right away! (*Listening.*) At once, sir! (*Listening.*) I see, in half an hour!

Julie (desperately frightened):   What did he say? Dear Lord, what did he say?

Jean: He wants his boots and his coffee in half an hour.

Julie: So, in half an hour! Oh, I'm so tired. I'm not able to do anything. I can't repent, can't run away, can't stay, can't live—can't die! Help me now! Order me, and I'll obey like a dog! Do me this last service, save my honor, save his name! You know what I *should* do, but don't have the will to . . . You will it, you order me to do it!

Jean: I don't know why—but now I can't either—I don't understand.— It's as if this coat made it impossible for me to order you to do anything.—And now, since the Count spoke to me—I—I can't really explain it—but—ah, it's the damn lackey in me!—I think if the Count came down here now—and ordered me to cut my throat, I'd do it on the spot.

Julie: Then pretend you're he, and I'm you!—You gave such a good performance before when you knelt at my feet.—You were a real nobleman.—Or—have you ever seen a hypnotist in the theater? (*Jean nods.*) He says to his subject: "Take the broom," and he takes it. He says: "Sweep," and he sweeps—

Jean: But the subject has to be asleep.

Julie (ecstatically):   I'm already asleep.—The whole room is like smoke around me . . . and you look like an iron stove . . . shaped like a man in black, with a tall hat—and your eyes glow like coals when the fire is dying—and your face is a white patch, like ashes—(*The sunlight has reached the floor and now shines on Jean.*)—it's so warm and good— (*She rubs her hands as if warming them before a fire.*)—and bright—and so peaceful!

Jean (taking the razor and putting it in her hand):   Here's the broom! Go now while it's bright—out to the barn—and . . . (*Whispers in her ear.*)

Julie (awake):   Thank you. I'm going now to rest! But just tell me—that those who are first can also receive the gift of grace. Say it, even if you don't believe it.

Jean: The first? No, I can't—But wait—Miss Julie—now I know! You're no longer among the first—you're now among—the last!

Julie: That's true.—I'm among the very last. I'm the last one of all! Oh!— But now I can't go!—Tell me once more to go!

Jean: No, now I can't either! I can't!

Julie: And the first shall be the last!

Jean: Don't think, don't think! You're taking all my strength from me, making me a coward.—What was that? I thought the bell moved!—

No! Shall we stuff paper in it?—To be so afraid of a bell!—But it isn't just a bell.—There's someone behind it—a hand sets it in motion— and something else sets the hand in motion.—Maybe if you cover your ears—cover your ears! But then it rings even louder! rings until someone answers.—And then it's too late! And then the police come—and—then—(*The bell rings twice loudly. Jean flinches, then straightens up.*) It's horrible! But there's no other way!—Go! (*Miss Julie walks firmly out through the door.*)

WINDOW ON

Psychological Realism

Psychological realism—the portrayal of characters behaving in ways similar to what we observe in everyday life—has not always been of great importance in drama. Symbolic and improbable actions were central to Greek as well as medieval European plays, and ritual drama of many cultures ignores realism. Even contemporary dramas such as *The Glass Menagerie* mix symbolism with realistic actions.

Nonetheless, many modern plays ground themselves in the mode of psychological realism adopted by Henrik Ibsen in *Hedda Gabler* and *A Doll House*. In these plays Ibsen moved into a style of theater that was to become accepted throughout the late nineteenth and most of the twentieth centuries. We have the feeling as we watch Nora and Helmer in *A Doll House* that we are actually overhearing their conversation. Early commentators remarked that it was as if we were looking into a living room whose fourth wall had been removed for our convenience so we could witness events without being seen. The sets for such plays were usually so detailed and complete that even under the brilliance of direct lighting they seemed as real as the rooms in which the audience lived. In *A Doll House* the metaphor is especially appropriate: just as children who play with a doll house usually remove walls to get into the rooms to change furniture and move dolls about from room to room, so the theatrical audience enjoys similar powers of observation. Both children and audience are, in different senses, "at play." For each the play is of great significance, since for children it establishes patterns of a lifetime, and for adults watching *A Doll House* it may reveal otherwise unrecognized patterns of behavior. The realism in this play is of great importance because of the nature of its message, which hits harder because its reality and appropriateness are painfully clear.

Hedda Gabler is realistic as well, although Hedda's romantic compulsions tend to introduce mythic elements. For example, Hedda's romantic ambitions for Lovborg include his killing himself in a romantically satisfying way—quickly with one shot. However, the reality is gruesome and in some ways disgusting to her. He shoots himself, but in the bowels, and dies only after a painful, bloody, and totally unromantic agony. Therefore, one of the themes of this play is coming to terms with reality and its limitations while relinquishing romantic illusions.

Not all dramas are weighted with such a concern for realism. Woody Allen's *Death Knocks* may be set in a realistic room with all the trappings of middle-class comfort, but the situation is palpably unreal with a character who could not possibly exist. Yet we take Death more or less as he is, assuming him to be a reflection of Nat Ackerman; at the same time, we *cannot* take Nat Ackerman seriously in terms of psychological realism. Can you imagine yourself honestly playing gin rummy with Death? Can you imagine yourself being as composed as Nat is in the face of Death? Woody Allen depends on our **suspension of disbelief** for the drama to work. We often accord that suspension to plays, and willingly. In Marsha Norman's *Getting Out*, we easily accept the possibility of seeing the same character at different times in her life portrayed by two different actors—even confronting each other and discussing themselves (herself).

Shakespeare often asks us to suspend disbelief. He brings Hamlet's father back from the grave as a ghost and expects us to accept such a detail without complaint. August Wilson's *Fences* and Manuel Puig's *Kiss of the Spider Woman* depend on our accepting the actions and motivations of the characters as plausible, despite interruptions that may be termed nonrealistic because they represent memory or imaginative flights.

Expressionist drama distorts reality for the sake of expressing a strong mood or psychological state. Often such drama resorts to the device of the dream, or to dreamlike sequences that seem to waver between reality and unreality, almost like a waking dream. *Miss Julie* has been considered a dream-based drama, since the dreams Jean and Julie discuss are central to the play. Powerful symbolic elements, such as the Count's boots, bring us back to reality from time to time, but the overall structure of the play sometimes alludes to Nordic fairy tales, which again undermines our sense of reality. Much the same is true of Paula Vogel's *The Baltimore Waltz*, which takes on hallucinatory qualities—especially as the third man in the cast takes on more than eleven other roles, from the Munich Virgin to the Little Dutch Boy. Vogel also relies on allusions to dreamlike sequences in film, especially *The Third Man*, in which Joseph Cotten's character wanders in a nightmare landscape wondering what is and what is not real. Manuel Puig's *Kiss of the Spider Woman*, starting with its title, begins in the all too real nightmare world of a Latin American prison, and moves then into the unreality of melodramatic spy movies. Expressionist drama often grounds itself in what appears to be a realistic situation, but soon veers and blurs the lines of reality and dream.

Reading

Abbott, Anthony. *The Vital Lie: Reality and Illusion in Modern Drama.* Tuscaloosa: University of Alabama Press, 1989.

Brustein, Robert. *Theatre of Revolt.* Boston: Little, Brown, 1964.

Cohn, Ruby. *Currents in Contemporary Drama.* Bloomington: Indiana University Press, 1969.

Gilman, Richard. *The Making of Modern Drama.* New York: Farrar, 1974.

Whitaker, Thomas. *Fields of Play in Modern Drama.* Princeton: Princeton University Press, 1977.

Tennessee Williams   (1911–1983)

Born in Missisippi, Tennessee Williams was raised in St. Louis and attended the University of Missouri and Washington University in St. Louis. Eventually, he got his degree at the State University of Iowa. Some of his plays were produced while he was an undergraduate, but when his first commercially produced play, Battle of Angels *(1940), failed in Boston, he feared he had no future as a playwright. While living on foundation grants he wrote* The Glass Menagerie, *which opened in Chicago in 1944 and in New York in 1945. It was his first success, winning the New York Drama Critic's Circle Award for best play. It ran for 561 performances. A* Streetcar Named Desire *(1947) established him as one of the most important American postwar playwrights. The play ran for 855 performances and won the Pulitzer Prize. Williams was a poetic writer, and his stage directions have a special lyrical quality.*

Some circumstances in The Glass Menagerie *were drawn from Williams's own life. Laura Wingfield resembles his sister, Rose, who also took consolation from a collection of glass animals. She was a psychologically troubled woman whose condition worsened when Williams was young. The family decided to have Rose undergo a lobotomy—an operation in which a portion of the frontal lobe of the brain is cut away. The operation was unsuccessful, and Rose spent most of her life in an institution. Williams felt a lifelong sense of guilt and failure over his family's decision.*

Williams solidified his position as a major playwright with Summer and Smoke *(1948),* The Rose Tatoo *(1951),* Camino Real *(1953),* Cat on a Hot Tin Roof *(1955), and* Night of the Iguana *(1961).* The Glass Menagerie *is a "memory play," exploring complex psychological issues operating in the minds of all the characters. The production notes to this play explain many of the approaches to drama that characterize Williams's work. He thought carefully about all phases of the production, including the music.*

THE GLASS MENAGERIE   (1944)

Nobody, not even the rain, has such small hands.

—**E. E. Cummings**

Production Notes by Tennessee Williams

Being a "memory play," *The Glass Menagerie* can be presented with unusual freedom of convention. Because of its considerably delicate or tenuous material, atmospheric touches and subtleties of direction play a particularly important part. Expressionism and all other unconventional techniques in drama have only one valid aim, and this is a closer approach to truth. When a play employs unconventional techniques, it is not, or certainly shouldn't be, trying to escape its responsibility of dealing with reality, or interpreting experience, but is actually or should be attempting to find a closer approach, or more penetrating and vivid expression of things as they are. The straight realistic play with its genuine frigidaire and authentic ice cubes, its characters that speak exactly as its audience speaks, corresponds to the academic landscape and has the same virtue of a photographic likeness. Everyone should know nowadays the unimportance of the photographic in art: that truth, life, or reality is an organic thing which the poetic imagination can represent or suggest, in essence, only through transformation, through changing into other forms than those which were merely present in appearance.

These remarks are not meant as a preface only to this particular play. They have to do with a conception of a new, plastic theatre which must take the place of the exhausted theatre of realistic conventions if the theatre is to resume vitality as a part of our culture.

The Screen Device. *There is only one important difference between the original and acting version of the play* and that is the *omission* in the latter of the device which I tentatively included in my *original* script. This device was the use of a screen on which were projected magic-lantern slides bearing images or titles. I do not regret the omission of this device from the present Broadway production. The extraordinary power of Miss Taylor's° performance made it suitable to have the utmost simplicity in the physical production. But I think it may be interesting to some readers to see how this device was conceived. So I am putting it into the published manuscript. These images and legends, projected from behind, were cast on a section of wall between the front-room and dining-room areas, which should be indistinguishable from the rest when not in use.

The purpose of this will probably be apparent. It is to give accent to certain values in each scene. Each scene contains a particular point (or several) which is structurally the most important. In an episodic play, such as this, the basic structure or narrative line may be obscured from the audience; the effect may seem fragmentary rather than architectural. This may not be the fault of the play so much as a lack of attention in the audience. The legend or image upon the screen will strengthen the effect of what is merely allusion in the writing and allow the primary

---

Miss Taylor: The actress Laurette Taylor (1884–1946), who played Amanda.

point to be made more simply and lightly than if the entire responsibility were on the spoken lines. Aside from this structural value, I think the screen will have a definite emotional appeal, less definable but just as important. An imaginative producer or director may invent many other uses for this device than those indicated in the present script. In fact the possibilities of the device seem much larger to me than the instance of this play can possibly utilize.

The Music. Another extraliterary accent in this play is provided by the use of music. A single recurring tune, "The Glass Menagerie," is used to give emotional emphasis to suitable passages. This tune is like circus music, not when you are on the grounds or in the immediate vicinity of the parade, but when you are at some distance and very likely thinking of something else. It seems under those circumstances to continue almost interminably and it weaves in and out of your preoccupied consciousness; then it is the lightest, most delicate music in the world and perhaps the saddest. It expresses the surface vivacity of life with the underlying strain of immutable and inexpressible sorrow. When you look at a piece of delicately spun glass you think of two things: how beautiful it is and how easily it can be broken. Both of those ideas should be woven into the recurring tune, which dips in and out of the play as if it were carried on a wind that changes. It serves as a thread of connection and allusion between the narrator with his separate point in time and space and the subject of his story. Between each episode it returns as reference to the emotion, nostalgia, which is the first condition of the play. It is primarily Laura's music and therefore comes out most clearly when the play focuses upon her and the lovely fragility of glass which is her image.

The Lighting. The lighting in the play is not realistic. In keeping with the atmosphere of memory, the stage is dim. Shafts of light are focused on selected areas or actors, sometimes in contradistinction to what is the apparent center. For instance, in the quarrel scene between Tom and Amanda, in which Laura has no active part, the clearest pool of light is on her figure. This is also true of the supper scene, when her silent figure on the sofa should remain the visual center. The light upon Laura should be distinct from the others, having a peculiar pristine clarity such as light used in early religious portraits of female saints or madonnas. A certain correspondence to light in religious paintings, such as El Greco's, where the figures are radiant in atmosphere that is relatively dusky, could be effectively used throughout the play. (It will also permit a more effective use of the screen.) A free, imaginative use of light can be of enormous value in giving a mobile, plastic quality to plays of a more or less static nature.

Characters

Amanda Wingfield, the mother. A little woman of great but confused vitality clinging frantically to another time and place. Her characterization must be carefully created, not copied from type. She is not paranoiac, but her life is paranoia. There is much to admire in Amanda, and as much to love and pity as there is to laugh at. Certainly she has endurance and a kind of heroism, and though her foolishness makes her unwittingly cruel at times, there is tenderness in her slight person.

Laura Wingfield, her daughter. Amanda, having failed to establish contact with reality, continues to live vitally in her illusions, but Laura's situation is even graver. A childhood illness has left her crippled, one leg slightly shorter than the other, and held in a brace. This defect need not be more than suggested on the stage.

Stemming from this, Laura's separation increases till she is like a piece of her own glass collection, too exquisitely fragile to move from the shelf.

Tom Wingfield, her son. And the narrator of the play. A poet with a job in a warehouse. His nature is not remorseless, but to escape from a trap he has to act without pity.

Jim O'Connor, the gentleman caller. A nice, ordinary, young man.

Scene: An alley in St. Louis.
Part I: Preparation for a Gentleman Caller.
Part II: The Gentleman Calls.
Time: Now and the Past.

SCENE I

(*The Wingfield apartment is in the rear of the building, one of those vast hivelike conglomerations of cellular living-units that flower as warty growths in overcrowded urban centers of lower middle-class population and are symptomatic of the impulse of this largest and fundamentally enslaved section of American society to avoid fluidity and differentiation and to exist and function as one interfused mass of automatism.*)

(*The apartment faces an alley and is entered by a fire escape, a structure whose name is a touch of accidental poetic truth, for all of these huge buildings are always burning with the slow and implacable fires of human desperation. The fire escape is included in the set—that is, the landing of it and steps descending from it.*)

(*The scene is memory and is therefore nonrealistic. Memory takes a lot of poetic license. It omits some details; others are exaggerated, according to the emotional value of the articles it touches, for memory is seated predominantly in the heart. The interior is therefore rather dim and poetic.*)

(*At the rise of the curtain, the audience is faced with the dark, grim rear wall of the Wingfield tenement. This building, which runs parallel to the footlights, is flanked on both sides by dark, narrow alleys which run into murky canyons of tangled clotheslines, garbage cans, and the sinister latticework of neighboring fire escapes. It is up and down these side alleys that exterior entrances and exits are made, during the play. At the end of Tom's opening commentary, the dark tenement wall slowly reveals (by means of a transparency) the interior of the ground floor Wingfield apartment.)*

(Downstage is the living room, which also serves as a sleeping room for Laura, the sofa unfolding to make her bed. Upstage, center, and divided by a wide arch or second proscenium with transparent faded portieres (or second curtain), is the dining room. In an old-fashioned what-not in the living room are seen scores of transparent glass animals. A blown-up photograph of the father hangs on the wall of the living room, facing the audience, to the left of the archway. It is the face of a very handsome young man in a doughboy's First World War cap. He is gallantly smiling, ineluctably smiling, as if to say, "I will be smiling forever.")

(The audience hears and sees the opening scene in the dining room through both the transparent fourth wall of the building and the transparent gauze portieres of the dining room arch. It is during this revealing scene that the fourth wall slowly ascends, out of sight. This transparent exterior wall is not brought down again until the very end of the play, during Tom's final speech.)

(The narrator is an undisguised convention of the play. He takes whatever license with dramatic convention as is convenient to his purposes.)

(Tom enters dressed as a merchant sailor from alley, stage left, and strolls across the front of the stage to the fire escape. There he stops and lights a cigarette. He addresses the audience.)

Tom: Yes, I have tricks in my pocket, I have things up my sleeve. But I am the opposite of a stage magician. He gives you illusion that has the appearance of truth. I give you truth in the pleasant disguise of illusion. To begin with, I turn back time. I reverse it to that quaint period, the thirties, when the huge middle class of America was matriculating in a school for the blind. Their eyes had failed them, or they had failed their eyes, and so they were having their fingers pressed forcibly down on the fiery Braille alphabet of a dissolving economy. In Spain there was revolution. Here there was only shouting and confusion. In Spain there was Guernica.° Here there were disturbances of labor, sometimes pretty violent, in otherwise peaceful cities such as Chicago, Cleveland, Saint Louis. . . . This is the social background of the play.

(Music.)

The play is memory. Being a memory play, it is dimly lighted, it is sentimental, it is not realistic. In memory everything seems to happen

---

Guernica: Spanish town destroyed by aerial bombardment as an "experiment" during the Spanish Civil War.

to music. That explains the fiddle in the wings. I am the narrator of the play, and also a character in it. The other characters are my mother, Amanda, my sister, Laura, and a gentleman caller who appears in the final scenes. He is the most realistic character in the play, being an emissary from a world of reality that we were somehow set apart from. But since I have a poet's weakness for symbols, I am using this character also as a symbol; he is the long delayed but always expected something that we live for. There is a fifth character in the play who doesn't appear except in this larger-than-life photograph over the mantel. This is our father who left us a long time ago. He was a telephone man who fell in love with long distances; he gave up his job with the telephone company and skipped the light fantastic out of town . . . The last we heard of him was a picture postcard from Mazatlan, on the Pacific coast of Mexico, containing a message of two words—"Hello—Good-bye!" and no address. I think the rest of the play will explain itself. . . .

> (*Amanda's voice becomes audible through the portieres.*)
> (*Legend on Screen: "Où Sont les Neiges."*)°
> (*He divides the portieres and enters the upstage area.*)
> (*Amanda and Laura are seated at a drop-leaf table. Eating is indicated by gestures without food or utensils. Amanda faces the audience. Tom and Laura are seated in profile.*)
> (*The interior has lit up softly and through the scrim we see Amanda and Laura seated at the table in the upstage area.*)

Amanda (calling):   Tom?

Tom: Yes, Mother.

Amanda: We can't say grace until you come to the table!

Tom: Coming, Mother. (*He bows slightly and withdraws, reappearing a few moments later in his place at the table.*)   5

Amanda (to her son):   Honey, don't *push* with your *fingers*. If you have to push with something, the thing to push with is a crust of bread. And chew—chew! Animals have sections in their stomachs which enable them to digest food without mastication, but human beings are supposed to chew their food before they swallow it down. Eat food leisurely, son, and really enjoy it. A well-cooked meal has lots of delicate flavors that have to be held in the mouth for appreciation. So chew your food and give your salivary glands a chance to function!

(*Tom deliberately lays his imaginary fork down and pushes his chair back from the table.*)

Tom: I haven't enjoyed one bite of this dinner because of your constant directions on how to eat it. It's you that makes me rush through meals with your hawklike attention to every bite I take. Sickening—spoils my

---

Où Sont les Neiges: Where are the snows [of yesteryear]?

appetite—all this discussion of animals' secretion—salivary glands—mastication!

Amanda (lightly): Temperament like a Metropolitan° star! (*He rises and crosses downstage.*) You're not excused from the table.

Tom: I'm getting a cigarette.

Amanda: You smoke too much.

(*Laura rises.*)

Laura: I'll bring in the blancmange.

(*He remains standing with his cigarette by the portieres during the following.*)

Amanda (rising): No, sister, no, sister—you be the lady this time and I'll be the darky.

Laura: I'm already up.

Amanda: Resume your seat, little sister—I want you to stay fresh and pretty—for gentlemen callers!

Laura: I'm not expecting any gentlemen callers.

Amanda (crossing out to kitchenette. Airily): Sometimes they come when they are least expected! Why, I remember one Sunday afternoon in Blue Mountain—(*Enters kitchenette.*)

Tom: I know what's coming!

Laura: Yes. But let her tell it.

Tom: Again?

Laura: She loves to tell it.

(*Amanda returns with bowl of dessert.*)

Amanda: One Sunday afternoon in Blue Mountain—your mother received—*seventeen!*—gentlemen callers! Why, sometimes there weren't chairs enough to accommodate them all. We had to send the nigger over to bring in folding chairs from the parish house.

Tom (remaining at portieres): How did you entertain those gentlemen callers?

Amanda: I understood the art of conversation!

Tom: I bet you could talk.

Amanda: Girls in those days *knew* how to talk, I can tell you.

Tom: Yes?

(*Image: Amanda as a girl on a porch greeting callers.*)

Amanda: They knew how to entertain their gentlemen callers. It wasn't enough for a girl to be possessed of a pretty face and a graceful figure—although I wasn't slighted in either respect. She also needed to have a nimble wit and a tongue to meet all occasions.

Tom: What did you talk about?

Metropolitan: The Metropolitan Opera in New York City.

Amanda: Things of importance going on in the world! Never anything coarse or common or vulgar. (*She addresses Tom as though he were seated in the vacant chair at the table though he remains by portieres. He plays this scene as though he held the book.*) My callers were gentlemen— all! Among my callers were some of the most prominent young planters of the Mississippi Delta—planters and sons of planters!

> (*Tom motions for music and a spot of light on Amanda.*)
> (*Her eyes lift, her face glows, her voice becomes rich and elegiac.*)
> (*Screen legend: "Où Sont les Neiges."*)

There was young Champ Laughlin who later became vice-president of the Delta Planters Bank. Hadley Stevenson who was drowned in Moon Lake and left his widow one hundred and fifty thousand in Government bonds. There were the Cutrere brothers, Wesley and Bates. Bates was one of my bright particular beaux! He got in a quarrel with that wild Wainright boy. They shot it out on the floor of Moon Lake Casino. Bates was shot through the stomach. Died in the ambulance on his way to Memphis. His widow was also well-provided for, came into eight or ten thousand acres, that's all. She married him on the rebound—never loved her—carried my picture on him the night he died! And there was that boy that every girl in the Delta had set her cap for! That beautiful, brilliant young Fitzhugh boy from Greene County!

Tom: What did he leave his widow?

Amanda: He never married! Gracious, you talk as though all of my old admirers had turned up their toes to the daisies!

Tom: Isn't this the first you mentioned that still survives?

Amanda: That Fitzhugh boy went North and made a fortune—came to be known as the Wolf of Wall Street! He had the Midas touch, whatever he touched turned to gold! And I could have been Mrs. Duncan J. Fitzhugh, mind you! But—I picked your *father!*

Laura (rising):   Mother, let me clear the table.

Amanda: No, dear, you go in front and study your typewriter chart. Or practice your shorthand a little. Stay fresh and pretty!—It's almost time for our gentlemen callers to start arriving. (*She flounces girlishly toward the kitchenette.*) How many do you suppose we're going to entertain this afternoon?

(*Tom throws down the paper and jumps up with a groan.*)

Laura (alone in the dining room):   I don't believe we're going to receive any, Mother.

Amanda (reappearing, airily):   What? No one—not one? You must be joking! (*Laura nervously echoes her laugh. She slips in a fugitive manner through the half-open portieres and draws them gently behind her. A shaft of very clear light is thrown on her face against the faded tapestry of the curtains. Music: "The Glass Menagerie" under faintly. Lightly.*) Not one gentleman caller? It can't be true! There must be a flood, there must have been a tornado!

Laura: It isn't a flood, it's not a tornado, Mother. I'm just not popular like you were in Blue Mountain. . . . (*Tom utters another groan. Laura glances at him with a faint, apologetic smile. Her voice catching a little.*) Mother's afraid I'm going to be an old maid.

(*The scene dims out with "Glass Menagerie" music.*)

SCENE II

(*"Laura, Haven't You Ever Liked Some Boy?"*)
(*On the dark stage the screen is lighted with the image of blue roses.*)
(*Gradually Laura's figure becomes apparent and the screen goes out.*)
(*The music subsides.*)
(*Laura is seated in the delicate ivory chair at the small clawfoot table.*)
(*She wears a dress of soft violet material for a kimono—her hair tied back from her forehead with a ribbon.*)
(*She is washing and polishing her collection of glass.*)
(*Amanda appears on the fire escape steps. At the sound of her ascent, Laura catches her breath, thrusts the bowl of ornaments away and seats herself stiffly before the diagram of the typewriter keyboard as though it held her spellbound. Something has happened to Amanda. It is written in her face as she climbs to the landing: a look that is grim and hopeless and a little absurd.*)
(*She has on one of those cheap or imitation velvety-looking cloth coats with imitation fur collar. Her hat is five or six years old, one of those dreadful cloche hats that were worn in the late twenties, and she is clasping an enormous black patent-leather pocketbook with nickel clasp and initials. This is her full-dress outfit, the one she usually wears to the D.A.R.°*)
(*Before entering she looks through the door.*)
(*She purses her lips, opens her eyes wide, rolls them upward and shakes her head.*)
(*Then she slowly lets herself in the door. Seeing her mother's expression Laura touches her lips with a nervous gesture.*)

Laura: Hello, Mother, I was—(*She makes a nervous gesture toward the chart on the wall. Amanda leans against the shut door and stares at Laura with a martyred look.*)

Amanda: Deception? Deception? (*She slowly removes her hat and gloves, continuing the swift suffering stare. She lets the hat and gloves fall on the floor—a bit of acting.*)

D.A.R.: Daughters of the American Revolution, a conservative, patriotic organization for women whose ancestors were involved in the American Revolutionary War.

Laura (shakily):   How was the D.A.R. meeting? (*Amanda slowly opens her purse and removes a dainty white handkerchief which she shakes out delicately and delicately touches to her lips and nostrils.*) Didn't you go to the D.A.R. meeting, Mother?

Amanda (faintly, almost inaudibly):   —No.—No. (*Then more forcibly.*) I did not have the strength—to go to the D.A.R. In fact, I did not have the courage! I wanted to find a hole in the ground and hide myself in it forever! (*She crosses slowly to the wall and removes the diagram of the typewriter keyboard. She holds it in front of her for a second, staring at it sweetly and sorrowfully—then bites her lips and tears it in two pieces.*)

Laura (faintly):   Why did you do that, Mother? (*Amanda repeats the same procedure with the chart of the Gregg Alphabet.*) Why are you—

Amanda: Why? Why? How old are you, Laura?

Laura: Mother, you know my age.

Amanda: I thought that you were an adult; it seems that I was mistaken. (*She crosses slowly to the sofa and sinks down and stares at Laura.*)

Laura: Please don't stare at me, Mother.

(*Amanda closes her eyes and lowers her head. Count ten.*)

Amanda: What are we going to do, what is going to become of us, what is the future?

(*Count ten.*)

Laura: Has something happened, Mother? (*Amanda draws a long breath and takes out the handkerchief again. Dabbing process.*) Mother, has—something happened?

Amanda: I'll be all right in a minute. I'm just bewildered—(*Count five.*)—by life. . . .

Laura: Mother, I wish that you would tell me what's happened.

Amanda: As you know, I was supposed to be inducted into my office at the D.A.R. this afternoon. (*Image: a swarm of typewriters.*) But I stopped off at Rubicam's Business College to speak to your teachers about your having a cold and ask them what progress they thought you were making down there.

Laura: Oh. . . .

Amanda: I went to the typing instructor and introduced myself as your mother. She didn't know who you were. Wingfield, she said. We don't have any such student enrolled at the school! I assured her she did, that you had been going to classes since early in January. "I wonder," she said, "if you could be talking about that terribly shy little girl who dropped out of school after only a few days' attendance?" "No," I said, "Laura, my daughter, has been going to school every day for the past six weeks!" "Excuse me," she said. She took the attendance book out and there was your name, unmistakably printed, and all the dates you were absent until they decided that you had dropped out of school. I still said, "No, there must have been some mistake! There must have been some mix-up in the records!" And she said, "No—I remember her perfectly now. Her hands shook so that she couldn't hit the right keys! The first time we gave a speed test, she broke down completely—was sick at the stomach and almost had to be carried into the wash-room! After that morning she never showed up any more. We phoned the house but never got any answer"—while I was working at Famous and Barr, I suppose, demonstrating those—Oh! I felt so weak I could barely keep on my feet. I had to sit down while they got me a glass of water! Fifty dollars' tuition, all of our plans—my hopes and ambitions for you—just gone up the spout, just gone up the spout like that. (*Laura draws a long breath and gets awkwardly to her feet. She crosses to the victrola and winds it up.*) What are you doing?

Laura: Oh! (*She releases the handle and returns to her seat.*)

Amanda: Laura, where have you been going when you've gone out pretending that you were going to business college?

Laura: I've just been going out walking.

Amanda: That's not true.

Laura: It is. I just went walking.

Amanda: Walking? Walking? In winter? Deliberately courting pneumonia in that light coat? Where did you walk to, Laura?

Laura: All sorts of places—mostly in the park.

Amanda: Even after you'd started catching that cold?

Laura: It was the lesser of two evils, Mother. (*Image: winter scene in park.*) I couldn't go back up. I—threw up—on the floor!

Amanda: From half past seven till after five every day you mean to tell me you walked around in the park, because you wanted to make me think that you were still going to Rubicam's Business College?

Laura: It wasn't as bad as it sounds. I went inside places to get warmed up.

Amanda: Inside where?

Laura: I went in the art museum and the bird houses at the Zoo. I visited the penguins every day! Sometimes I did without lunch and went to the movies. Lately I've been spending most of my afternoons in the Jewel-box, that big glass house where they raise the tropical flowers.

Amanda: You did all this to deceive me, just for the deception? (*Laura looks down.*) Why?

Laura: Mother, when you're disappointed, you get that awful suffering look on your face, like the picture of Jesus' mother in the museum!

Amanda: Hush!

Laura: I couldn't face it.

(*Pause. A whisper of strings.*)
(*Legend: "The Crust of Humility."*)

Amanda (*hopelessly fingering the huge pocketbook*): So what are we going to do the rest of our lives? Stay home and watch the parades go by?

Amuse ourselves with the glass menagerie, darling? Eternally play those worn-out phonograph records your father left as a painful reminder of him? We won't have a business career—we've given that up because it gave us nervous indigestion! (*Laughs wearily.*) What is there left but dependency all our lives? I know so well what becomes of unmarried women who aren't prepared to occupy a position. I've seen such pitiful cases in the South—barely tolerated spinsters living upon the grudging patronage of sister's husband or brother's wife!— stuck away in some little mousetrap of a room—encouraged by one in-law to visit another—little birdlike women without any nest—eating the crust of humility all their life! Is that the future that we've mapped out for ourselves? I swear it's the only alternative I can think of! It isn't a very pleasant alternative, is it? Of course—some girls do *marry.*
(*Laura twists her hands nervously.*) Haven't you ever liked some boy?
Laura: Yes. I liked one once. (*Rises.*) I came across his picture a while ago.
Amanda (with some interest):   He gave you his picture?
Laura: No, it's in the yearbook.
Amanda (disappointed):   Oh—a high-school boy.

  (*Screen image: Jim as high school hero bearing a silver cup.*)

Laura: Yes. His name was Jim. (*Laura lifts the heavy annual from the clawfoot table.*) Here he is in *The Pirates of Penzance.*
Amanda (absently):   The what?
Laura: The operetta the senior class put on. He had a wonderful voice and we sat across the aisle from each other Mondays, Wednesdays, and Fridays in the Aud. Here he is with the silver cup for debating! See his grin?
Amanda (absently):   He must have had a jolly disposition.
Laura: He used to call me—Blue Roses.

  (*Image: blue roses.*)

Amanda: Why did he call you such a name as that?
Laura: When I had that attack of pleurosis—he asked me what was the matter when I came back. I said pleurosis—he thought that I said Blue Roses! So that's what he always called me after that. Whenever he saw me, he'd holler, "Hello, Blue Roses!" I didn't care for the girl that he went out with. Emily Meisenbach. Emily was the best-dressed girl at Soldan. She never struck me, though, as being sincere . . . It says in the Personal Section—they're engaged. That's—six years ago! They must be married by now.
Amanda: Girls that aren't cut out for business careers usually wind up married to some nice man. (*Gets up with a spark of revival.*) Sister, that's what you'll do!

  (*Laura utters a startled, doubtful laugh. She reaches quickly for a piece of glass.*)

Laura: But, Mother—
Amanda: Yes? (*Crossing to photograph.*)
Laura (*in a tone of frightened apology*):   I'm—crippled!

   (*Image: screen.*)

Amanda: Nonsense! Laura, I've told you never, never to use that word. Why, you're not crippled, you just have a little defect—hardly noticeable, even! When people have some slight disadvantage like that, they cultivate other things to make up for it—develop charm—and vivacity—and—*charm!* That's all you have to do! (*She turns again to the photograph.*) One thing your father had *plenty of*—was *charm!*

   (*Tom motions to the fiddle in the wings.*)
   (*The scene fades out with music.*)

SCENE III

   (*Legend on screen: "After the Fiasco—"*)
   (*Tom speaks from the fire escape landing.*)

Tom: After the fiasco at Rubicam's Business College, the idea of getting a gentleman caller for Laura began to play a more important part in Mother's calculations. It became an obsession. Like some archetype of the universal unconscious, the image of the gentleman caller haunted our small apartment. . . . (*Image: young man at door with flowers.*) An evening at home rarely passed without some allusion to this image, this specter, this hope. . . . Even when he wasn't mentioned, his presence hung in Mother's preoccupied look and in my sister's frightened, apologetic manner—hung like a sentence passed upon the Wingfields! Mother was a woman of action as well as words. She began to take logical steps in the planned direction. Late that winter and in the early spring—realizing that extra money would be needed to properly feather the nest and plume the bird—she conducted a vigorous campaign on the telephone, roping in subscribers to one of those magazines for matrons called *The Home-maker's Companion*, the type of journal that features the serialized sublimations of ladies of letters who think in terms of delicate cuplike breasts, slim, tapering waists, rich, creamy thighs, eyes like wood smoke in autumn, fingers that soothe and caress like strains of music, bodies as powerful as Etruscan sculpture.

   (*Screen image: glamor magazine cover.*)
   (*Amanda enters with phone on long extension cord. She is spotted in the dim stage.*)

Amanda: Ida Scott? This is Amanda Wingfield! We *missed* you at the D.A.R. last Monday! I said to myself: She's probably suffering with that sinus condition! How is that sinus condition? Horrors! Heaven have mercy!—You're a Christian martyr, yes, that's what you are, a Christian martyr! Well, I just now happened to notice that your subscription to the *Companion's* about to expire! Yes, it expires with the next issue, honey!—just when that wonderful new serial by Bessie Mae Hopper is getting off to such an exciting start. Oh, honey, it's something that you can't miss! You remember how *Gone With the Wind* took everybody by storm? You simply couldn't go out if you hadn't read it. All everybody *talked* was Scarlett O'Hara. Well, this is a book that critics already compare to *Gone With the Wind*. It's the *Gone With the Wind* of the post-World War generation!—What?—Burning?—Oh, honey, don't let them burn, go take a look in the oven and I'll hold the wire! Heavens—I think she's hung up!

> *(Dim out.)*
> *(Legend on screen: "You Think I'm in Love with Continental Shoemakers?")*
> *(Before the stage is lighted, the violent voices of Tom and Amanda are heard.)*
> *(They are quarreling behind the portieres. In front of them stands Laura with clenched hands and panicky expression.)*
> *(A clear pool of light on her figure throughout this scene.)*

Tom: What in Christ's name am I—

Amanda (shrilly):   Don't you use that—

Tom: Supposed to do!

Amanda: Expression! Not in my—

Tom: Ohhh!

Amanda: Presence! Have you gone out of your senses?

Tom: I have, that's true, *driven* out!

Amanda: What is the matter with you, you—big—big—IDIOT!

Tom: Look—I've got *no thing*, no single thing—

Amanda: Lower your voice!

Tom: In my life here that I can call my OWN! Everything is—

Amanda: Stop that shouting!

Tom: Yesterday you confiscated my books! You had the nerve to—

Amanda: I took that horrible novel back to the library—yes! That hideous book by that insane Mr. Lawrence.° (*Tom laughs wildly.*) I cannot control the output of diseased minds or people who cater to them—(*Tom laughs still more wildly.*) BUT I WON'T ALLOW SUCH FILTH BROUGHT INTO MY HOUSE! No, no, no, no, no!

Tom: House, house! Who pays rent on it, who makes a slave of himself to—

Amanda (fairly screeching):   Don't you DARE to—

Mr Lawrence: D. H. Lawrence (1885–1930), in this collection. His sexual explicitness was shocking to many.

Tom: No, no, *I* musn't say things! *I've* got to just—

Amanda: Let me tell you—

Tom: I don't want to hear any more! (*He tears the portieres open. The upstage area is lit with a turgid smoky red glow.*)

(*Amanda's hair is in metal curlers and she wears a very old bathrobe, much too large for her slight figure, a relic of the faithless Mr. Wingfield.*)

(*An upright typewriter and a wild disarray of manuscripts are on the dropleaf table. The quarrel was probably precipitated by Amanda's interruption of his creative labor. A chair lying overthrown on the floor.*)

(*Their gesticulating shadows are cast on the ceiling by the fiery glow.*)

Amanda: You *will* hear more, you—

Tom: No, I won't hear more, I'm going out!

Amanda: You come right back in—

Tom: Out, out out! Because I'm—

Amanda: Come back here, Tom Wingfield! I'm not through talking to you!

Tom: Oh, go—

Laura (desperately): Tom!

Amanda: You're going to listen, and no more insolence from you! I'm at the end of my patience! (*He comes back toward her.*)

Tom: What do you think I'm at? Aren't I supposed to have any patience to reach the end of, Mother? I know, I know. It seems unimportant to you, what I'm *doing*—what I *want* to do—having a little *difference* between them! You don't think that—

Amanda: I think you've been doing things that you're ashamed of. That's why you act like this. I don't believe that you go every night to the movies. Nobody goes to the movies night after night. Nobody in their right minds goes to the movies as often as you pretend to. People don't go to the movies at nearly midnight, and movies don't let out at two A.M. Come in stumbling. Muttering to yourself like a maniac! You get three hours' sleep and then go to work. Oh, I can picture the way you're doing down there. Moping, doping, because you're in no condition.

Tom (wildly): No, I'm in no condition!

Amanda: What right have you got to jeopardize your job? Jeopardize the security of us all? How do you think we'd manage if you were—

Tom: Listen! You think I'm crazy *about* the *warehouse*? (*He bends fiercely toward her slight figure.*) You think I'm in love with the Continental Shoemakers? You think I want to spend fifty-five *years* down there in that—*celotex interior!* with—*fluorescent—tubes!* Look! I'd rather somebody picked up a crowbar and battered out my brains—than go back mornings! I *go!* Every time you come in yelling that God damn *"Rise and Shine!" "Rise and Shine!"* I say to myself, "How *lucky dead* people are!" But I get up. I *go!* For sixty-five dollars a month I give up all that I dream of doing and being *ever!* And you say self—*self's* all I ever think of. Why, listen, if self is what I thought of, Mother, I'd be where he is—GONE! (*Pointing to father's picture.*) As far as the system of transportation reaches! (*He starts past her. She grabs his arm.*) Don't grab at me, Mother!

Amanda: Where are you going?

Tom: I'm going to the *movies!*

Amanda: I don't believe that lie!

Tom (*crouching toward her, overtowering her tiny figure. She backs away, gasping*):   I'm going to opium dens! Yes, opium dens, dens of vice and criminals' hangouts, Mother. I've joined the Hogan gang, I'm a hired assassin, I carry a tommy-gun in a violin case! I run a string of cathouses in the Valley! They call me Killer, Killer Wingfield, I'm leading a double life, a simple, honest warehouse worker by day, by night, a dynamic *czar* of the *underworld, Mother.* I go to gambling casinos, I spin away fortunes on the roulette table! I wear a patch over one eye and a false mustache, sometimes I put on green whiskers. On those occasions they call me—*El Diablo!*° Oh, I could tell you things to make you sleepless! My enemies plan to dynamite this place. They're going to blow us all sky-high some night! I'll be glad, very happy, and so will you! You'll go up, up on a broomstick, over Blue Mountain with seventeen gentlemen callers! You ugly—babbling old—*witch.* . . . (*He goes through a series of violent, clumsy movements, seizing his overcoat, lunging to the door, pulling it fiercely open. The women watch him, aghast. His arm catches in the sleeve of the coat as he struggles to pull it on. For a moment he is pinioned by the bulky garment. With an outraged groan he tears the coat off again, splitting the shoulders of it, and hurls it across the room. It strikes against the shelf of Laura's glass collection, there is a tinkle of shattering glass. Laura cries out as if wounded.*)

(*Music legend: "The Glass Menagerie."*)

Laura (*shrilly*):   My glass!—menagerie. . . . (*She covers her face and turns away.*)

(*But Amanda is still stunned and stupefied by the "ugly witch" so that she barely notices this occurrence. Now she recovers her speech.*)

Amanda (*in an awful voice*):   I won't speak to you—until you apologize! (*She crosses through portieres and draws them together behind her. Tom is left with Laura. Laura clings weakly to the mantel with her face averted. Tom stares at her stupidly for a moment. Then he crosses to shelf. Drops awkwardly to his knees to collect the fallen glass, glancing at Laura as if he would speak but couldn't.*)

(*"The Glass Menagerie" steals in as the scene dims out.*)

El Diablo: The devil (Spanish).

SCENE IV

> (*The interior is dark. Faint light in the alley.*)
>
> (*A deep-voiced bell in a church is tolling the hour of five as the scene commences.*)
>
> (*Tom appears at the top of the alley. After each solemn boom of the bell in the tower, he shakes a little noisemaker or rattle as if to express the tiny spasm of man in contrast to the sustained power and dignity of the Almighty. This and the unsteadiness of his advance make it evident that he has been drinking.*)
>
> (*As he climbs the few steps to the fire escape landing light steals up inside. Laura appears in nightdress, observing Tom's empty bed in the front room.*)
>
> (*Tom fishes in his pockets for the door key, removing a motley assortment of articles in the search, including a perfect shower of movie ticket stubs and an empty bottle. At last he finds the key, but just as he is about to insert it, it slips from his fingers. He strikes a match and crouches below the door.*)

Tom (bitterly): One crack—and it falls through!

> (*Laura opens the door.*)

Laura: Tom! Tom, what are you doing?

Tom: Looking for a door key.

Laura: Where have you been all this time?

Tom: I have been to the movies.

Laura: All this time at the movies?

Tom: There was a very long program. There was a Garbo picture and a Mickey Mouse and a travelogue and a newsreel and a preview of coming attractions. And there was an organ solo and a collection for the milk fund—simultaneously—which ended up in a terrible fight between a fat lady and an usher!

Laura (innocently): Did you have to stay through everything?

Tom: Of course! And, oh, I forgot! There was a big stage show! The headliner on this stage show was Malvolio the Magician. He performed wonderful tricks, many of them, such as pouring water back and forth between pitchers. First it turned to wine and then it turned to beer and then it turned to whiskey. I know it was whiskey it finally turned into because he needed somebody to come up out of the audience to help him, and I came up—both shows! It was Kentucky Straight Bourbon. A very generous fellow, he gave souvenirs. (*He pulls from his back pocket a shimmering rainbow-colored scarf.*) He gave me this. This is his magic scarf. You can have it, Laura. You wave it over a canary cage and you get a bowl of goldfish. You wave it over the goldfish bowl and they fly away canaries. . . . But the wonderfullest trick of all was the coffin trick. We nailed him into a coffin and he got

out of the coffin without removing one nail. (*He has come inside.*)
There is a trick that would come in handy for me—get me out of this
2 by 4 situation! (*Flops onto bed and starts removing shoes.*)

Laura: Tom—Shhh!

Tom: What you shushing me for?

Laura: You'll wake up Mother.

Tom: Goody, goody! Pay 'er back for all those "Rise an' Shines." (*Lies
down, groaning.*) You know it don't take much intelligence to get
yourself into a nailed-up coffin, Laura. But who in hell ever got
himself out of one without removing one nail?

> (*As if in answer, the father's grinning photograph lights up.*)
> (*Scene dims out.*)
> (*Immediately following: The church bell is heard striking six. At the
> sixth stroke the alarm clock goes off in Amanda's room, and after a few
> moments we hear her calling: "Rise and Shine! Rise and Shine! Laura,
> go tell your brother to rise and shine!"*)

Tom (sitting up slowly):   I'll rise—but I won't shine.

> (*The light increases.*)

Amanda: Laura, tell your brother his coffee is ready.

> (*Laura slips into front room.*)

Laura: Tom! it's nearly seven. Don't make Mother nervous. (*He stares at
her stupidly. Beseechingly.*) Tom, speak to Mother this morning. Make
up with her, apologize, speak to her!

Tom: She won't to me. It's her that started not speaking.

Laura: If you just say you're sorry she'll start speaking.

Tom: Her not speaking—is that such a tragedy?

Laura: Please—please!

Amanda (calling from kitchenette):   Laura, are you going to do what I
asked you to do, or do I have to get dressed and go out myself?

Laura: Going, going—soon as I get on my coat! (*She pulls on a shapeless
felt hat with nervous, jerky movement, pleadingly glancing at Tom.
Rushes awkwardly for coat. The coat is one of Amanda's, inaccurately
made over, the sleeves too short for Laura.*) Butter and what else?

Amanda (entering upstage):   Just butter. Tell them to charge it.

Laura: Mother, they make such faces when I do that.

Amanda: Sticks and stones may break my bones, but the expression on
Mr. Garfinkel's face won't harm us! Tell your brother his coffee is
getting cold.

Laura (at door):   Do what I asked you, will you, will you, Tom?

> (*He looks sullenly away.*)

Amanda: Laura, go now or just don't go at all!

Laura (rushing out):   Going—going! (*A second later she cries out. Tom springs up and crosses to the door. Amanda rushes anxiously in. Tom opens the door.*)

Tom: Laura?

Laura: I'm all right. I slipped, but I'm all right.

Amanda (peering anxiously after her):   If anyone breaks a leg on those fire escape steps, the landlord ought to be sued for every cent he possesses! (*She shuts door. Remembers she isn't speaking and returns to other room.*)

   (*As Tom enters listlessly for his coffee, she turns her back to him and stands rigidly facing the window on the gloomy gray vault of the areaway. Its light on her face with its aged but childish features is cruelly sharp, satirical as a Daumier° print.*)

   (*Music under: "Ave Maria."*)

   (*Tom glances sheepishly but sullenly at her averted figure and slumps at the table. The coffee is scalding hot; he sips it and gasps and spits it back in the cup. At his gasp, Amanda catches her breath and half turns. Then catches herself and turns back to window.*)

   (*Tom blows on his coffee, glancing sidewise at his mother. She clears her throat. Tom clears his. He starts to rise. Sinks back down again, scratches his head, clears his throat again. Amanda coughs. Tom raises his cup in both hands to blow on it, his eyes staring over the rim of it at his mother for several moments. Then he slowly sets the cup down and awkwardly and hesitantly rises from the chair.*)

Tom (hoarsely):   Mother, I—I apologize. Mother. (*Amanda draws a quick, shuddering breath. Her face works grotesquely. She breaks into childlike tears.*) I'm sorry for what I said, for everything that I said, I didn't mean it.

Amanda (sobbingly):   My devotion has made me a witch and so I make myself hateful to my children!

Tom: No, you *don't*.

Amanda: I worry so much, don't sleep, it makes me nervous!

Tom (gently):   I understand that.

Amanda: I've had to put up a solitary battle all these years. But you're my right-hand bower!° Don't fall down, don't fail!

Tom (gently):   I try, Mother.

Amanda (with great enthusiasm):   Try and you will SUCCEED! (*The notion makes her breathless.*) Why, you—you're just *full* of natural endowments! Both of my children—they're *unusual* children! Don't you think I know it? I'm so—*proud!* Happy and—feel I've—so much to be thankful for but—Promise me one thing, son!

Tom: What, Mother?

Daumier: Honoré Daumier (1808–1879), a French painter known for his satirical art.   *right-hand bower:* Reference to a card game in which the Jack of trump is the second-highest card.

Amanda: Promise, son, you'll—never be a drunkard!

Tom (turns to her grinning):   I will never be a drunkard, Mother.

Amanda: That's what frightened me so, that you'd be drinking! Eat a bowl of Purina!

Tom: Just coffee, Mother.

Amanda: Shredded wheat biscuit?

Tom: No, no, Mother, just coffee.

Amanda: You can't put in a day's work on an empty stomach. You've got ten minutes—don't gulp! Drinking too-hot liquids makes cancer of the stomach. . . . Put cream in.

Tom: No, thank you.

Amanda: To cool it.

Tom: No! No, thank you, I want it black.

Amanda: I know, but it's not good for you. We have to do all that we can to build ourselves up. In these trying times we live in, all that we have to cling to is—each other. . . . That's why it's so important to— Tom, I—I sent out your sister so I could discuss something with you. If you hadn't spoken I would have spoken to you. (*Sits down.*)

Tom (gently):   What is it, Mother, that you want to discuss?

Amanda: Laura!

> (*Tom puts his cup down slowly.*)
> (*Legend on screen: "Laura."*)
> (*Music: "The Glass Menagerie."*)

Tom: —Oh.—Laura . . .

Amanda (touching his sleeve):   You know how Laura is. So quiet but—still water runs deep! She notices things and I think she—broods about them. (*Tom looks up.*) A few days ago I came in and she was crying.

Tom: What about?

Amanda: You.

Tom: Me?

Amanda: She has an idea that you're not happy here.

Tom: What gave her that idea?

Amanda: What gives her any idea? However, you do act strangely. I— I'm not criticizing, understand *that!* I know your ambitions do not lie in the warehouse, that like everybody in the whole wide world— you've had to—make sacrifices, but—Tom—Tom—life's not easy, it calls for—Spartan endurance! There's so many things in my heart that I cannot describe to you! I've never told you but I—*loved your father.* . . .

Tom (gently):   I know that, Mother.

Amanda: And you—when I see you taking after his ways! Staying out late—and—well, you *had* been drinking the night you were in that— terrifying condition! Laura says that you hate the apartment and that you go out nights to get away from it! Is that true, Tom?

Tom: No. You say there's so much in your heart that you can't describe to me. That's true of me, too. There's so much in my heart that I can't describe to *you!* So let's respect each other's—

Amanda: But, why—*why*, Tom—are you always so *restless?* Where do you go to, nights?

Tom: I—go to the movies.

Amanda: Why do you go to the movies so much, Tom?

Tom: I go to the movies because—I like adventure. Adventure is something I don't have much of at work, so I go to the movies.

Amanda: But, Tom, you go to the movies *entirely* too *much!*

Tom: I like a lot of adventure.

> *(Amanda looks baffled, then hurt. As the familiar inquisition resumes he becomes hard and impatient again. Amanda slips back into her querulous attitude toward him.)*
> *(Image on screen: sailing vessel with Jolly Roger.°)*

Amanda: Most young men find adventure in their careers.

Tom: Then most young men are not employed in a warehouse.

Amanda: The world is full of young men employed in warehouses and offices and factories.

Tom: Do all of them find adventure in their careers?

Amanda: They do or they do without it! Not everybody has a craze for adventure.

Tom: Man is by instinct a lover, a hunter, a fighter, and none of those instincts are given much play at the warehouse!

Amanda: Man is by instinct! Don't quote instinct to me! Instinct is something that people have got away from! It belongs to animals! Christian adults don't want it!

Tom: What do Christian adults want, then, Mother?

Amanda: Superior things! Things of the mind and the spirit! Only animals have to satisfy instincts! Surely your aims are somewhat higher than theirs! Than monkeys—pigs—

Tom: I reckon they're not.

Amanda: You're joking. However, that isn't what I wanted to discuss.

Tom (rising): I haven't much time.

Amanda (pushing his shoulders): Sit down.

Tom: You want me to punch in red° at the warehouse, Mother?

Amanda: You have five minutes. I want to talk about Laura.

> *(Legend: "Plans and Provisions.")*

Tom: All right! What about Laura?

Amanda: We have to be making plans and provisions for her. She's older than you, two years, and nothing has happened. She just drifts along doing nothing. It frightens me terribly how she just drifts along.

Jolly Roger: The black flag with white skull and crossbones used by pirates.   *punch in red:* Be late.

Tom: I guess she's the type that people call home girls.

Amanda: There's no such type, and if there is, it's a pity! That is unless the home is hers, with a husband!

Tom: What?

Amanda: Oh, I can see the handwriting on the wall as plain as I see the nose in front of my face! It's terrifying! More and more you remind me of your father! He was out all hours without explanation—Then *left! Goodbye!* And me with a bag to hold. I saw that letter you got from the Merchant Marine. I know what you're dreaming of. I'm not standing here blindfolded. Very well, then. Then *do* it! But not till there's somebody to take your place.

Tom: What do you mean?

Amanda: I mean that as soon as Laura has got somebody to take care of her, married, a home of her own, independent—why, then you'll be free to go wherever you please, on land, on sea, whichever way the wind blows you! But until that time you've got to look out for your sister. I don't say me because I'm old and don't matter! I say for your sister because she's young and dependent. I put her in business college—a dismal failure! Frightened her so it made her sick to her stomach. I took her over to the Young People's League at the church. Another fiasco. She spoke to nobody, nobody spoke to her. Now all she does is fool with those pieces of glass and play those worn-out records. What kind of a life is that for a girl to lead!

Tom: What can I do about it?

Amanda: Overcome selfishness! Self, self, self is all that you ever think of! (*Tom springs up and crosses to get his coat. It is ugly and bulky. He pulls on a cap with earmuffs.*) Where is your muffler? Put your wool muffler on! (*He snatches it angrily from the closet and tosses it around his neck and pulls both ends tight.*) Tom! I haven't said what I had in mind to ask you.

Tom: I'm too late to—

Amanda (catching his arms—very importunately. Then shyly):   Down at the warehouse, aren't there some—nice young men?

Tom: No!

Amanda: There *must* be—*some* . . .

Tom: Mother—

(*Gesture.*)

Amanda: Find out one that's clean-living—doesn't drink and—ask him out for sister!

Tom: What?

Amanda: For *sister!* To *meet!* Get *acquainted!*

Tom (stamping to door):   Oh, my go-*osh!*

Amanda: Will you? (*He opens door. Imploringly.*) Will you? (*He starts down.*) Will you? *Will* you, dear?

Tom (calling back): YES!

> (*Amanda closes the door hesitantly and with a troubled but faintly hopeful expression.*)
> (*Screen image: glamor magazine cover.*)
> (*Spot° Amanda at phone.*)

Amanda: Ella Cartwright? This is Amanda Wingfield! How are you, honey? How is that kidney condition? (*Count five.*) Horrors! (*Count five.*) You're a Christian martyr, yes, honey, that's what you are, a Christian martyr! Well, I just happened to notice in my little red book that your subscription to the *Companion* has just run out! I knew that you wouldn't want to miss out on the wonderful serial starting in this new issue. It's by Bessie Mae Hopper, the first thing she's written since *Honeymoon for Three.* Wasn't that a strange and interesting story? Well, this one is even lovelier, I believe. It has a sophisticated society background. It's all about the horsey set on Long Island!

> (*Fade out.*)

Spot: Spotlight.

SCENE V

> (*Legend on screen: "Annunciation." Fade with music.*)
> (*It is early dusk of a spring evening. Supper has just been finished in the Wingfield apartment. Amanda and Laura in light colored dresses are removing dishes from the table, in the upstage area, which is shadowy, their movements formalized almost as a dance or ritual, their moving forms as pale and silent as moths.*)
> (*Tom, in white shirt and trousers, rises from the table and crosses toward the fire escape.*)

Amanda (as he passes her): Son, will you do me a favor?
Tom: What?
Amanda: Comb your hair! You look so pretty when your hair is combed! (*Tom slouches on sofa with evening paper. Enormous caption "Franco° Triumphs."*) There is only one respect in which I would like you to emulate your father.
Tom: What respect is that?
Amanda: The care he always took of his appearance. He never allowed himself to look untidy. (*He throws down the paper and crosses to fire escape.*) Where are you going?
Tom: I'm going out to smoke.
Amanda: You smoke too much. A pack a day at fifteen cents a pack. How much would that amount to in a month? Thirty times fifteen is how

Franco: Generalissimo Franco's Fascist army won the Spanish Civil War in 1939.

much, Tom? Figure it out and you will be astounded at what you
could save. Enough to give you a night school course in accounting at
Washington U! Just think what a wonderful thing that would be for
you, son!

(*Tom is unmoved by the thought.*)

Tom: I'd rather smoke. (*He steps out on landing, letting the screen door
slam.*)

Amanda (*sharply*): I know! That's the tragedy of it. . . . (*Alone, she turns
to look at her husband's picture.*)

(*Dance music: "All the World is Waiting for the Sunrise!"*)

Tom (*to the audience*): Across the alley from us was the Paradise Dance
Hall. On evenings in spring the windows and doors were open and the
music came outdoors. Sometimes the lights were turned out except for
a large glass sphere that hung from the ceiling. It would turn slowly
about and filter the dusk with delicate rainbow colors. Then the
orchestra played a waltz or a tango, something that had a slow and
sensuous rhythm. Couples would come outside, to the relative privacy
of the alley. You could see them kissing behind ash-pits and telephone
poles. This was the compensation for lives that passed like mine,
without any change or adventure. Adventure and change were
imminent in this year. They were waiting around the corner for all
these kids. Suspended in the mist over Berchtesgaden, caught in the
folds of Chamberlain's° umbrella—In Spain there was Guernica! But
here there was only hot swing music and liquor, dance halls, bars, and
movies, and sex that hung in the gloom like a chandelier and flooded
the world with brief, deceptive rainbows. . . . All the world was waiting
for bombardments!

(*Amanda turns from the picture and comes outside.*)

Amanda (*sighing*): A fire escape landing's a poor excuse for a porch. (*She
spreads a newspaper on a step and sits down, gracefully and demurely as
if she were settling into a swing on a Mississippi veranda.*) What are you
looking at?

Tom: The moon.

Amanda: Is there a moon this evening?

Tom: It's rising over Garfinkel's Delicatessen.

Amanda: So it is! A little silver slipper of a moon. Have you made a wish
on it yet?

Tom: Um-hum.

Amanda: What did you wish for?

Tom: That's a secret.

Berchtesgaden . . . Chamberlain: References to the approach of World War II in Europe.
Berchtesgaden was Hitler's summer home; Neville Chamberlain was the prime minister of
England who signed the Munich Pact, which was regarded as a capitulation to Hitler.

Amanda: A secret, huh? Well, I won't tell mine either. I will be just as mysterious as you.

Tom: I bet I can guess what yours is.

Amanda: Is my head so transparent?

Tom: You're not a sphinx.

Amanda: No, I don't have secrets. I'll tell you what I wished for on the moon. Success and happiness for my precious children! I wish for that whenever there's a moon, and when there isn't a moon, I wish for it, too.

Tom: I thought perhaps you wished for a gentleman caller.

Amanda: Why do you say that?

Tom: Don't you remember asking me to fetch one?

Amanda: I remember suggesting that it would be nice for your sister if you brought home some nice young man from the warehouse. I think I've made that suggestion more than once.

Tom: Yes, you have made it repeatedly.

Amanda: Well?

Tom: We are going to have one.

Amanda: *What?*

Tom: A gentleman caller!

> *(The annunciation is celebrated with music.)*
> *(Amanda rises.)*
> *(Image on screen: caller with bouquet.)*

Amanda: You mean you have asked some nice young man to come over?

Tom: Yep. I've asked him to dinner.

Amanda: You really did?

Tom: I did!

Amanda: You did, and did he—*accept?*

Tom: He did!

Amanda: Well, well—well, well! That's—lovely!

Tom: I thought that you would be pleased.

Amanda: It's definite, then?

Tom: Very definite.

Amanda: Soon?

Tom: Very soon.

Amanda: For heaven's sake, stop putting on and tell me some things, will you?

Tom: What things do you want me to tell you?

Amanda: *Naturally* I would like to know when he's *coming!*

Tom: He's coming tomorrow.

Amanda: *Tomorrow?*

Tom: Yep. Tomorrow.

Amanda: But, Tom!

Tom: Yes, Mother?

Amanda: Tomorrow gives me no time!

Tom: Time for what?

Amanda: Preparations! Why didn't you phone me at once, as soon as you asked him, the minute that he accepted? Then, don't you see, I could have been getting ready!

Tom: You don't have to make any fuss.

Amanda: Oh, Tom, Tom, Tom, of course I have to make a fuss! I want things nice, not sloppy! Not thrown together. I'll certainly have to do some fast thinking, won't I?

Tom: I don't see why you have to think at all.

Amanda: You just don't know. We can't have a gentleman caller in a pigsty! All my wedding silver has to be polished, the monogrammed table linen ought to be laundered! The windows have to be washed and fresh curtains put up. And how about clothes? We have to *wear* something, don't we?

Tom: Mother, this boy is no one to make a fuss over!

Amanda: Do you realize he's the first young man we've introduced to your sister? It's terrible, dreadful, disgraceful that poor little sister has never received a single gentleman caller! Tom, come inside! (*She opens the screen door.*)

Tom: What for?

Amanda: I want to ask you some things.

Tom: If you're going to make such a fuss, I'll call it off, I'll tell him not to come.

Amanda: You certainly won't do anything of the kind. Nothing offends people worse than broken engagements. It simply means I'll have to work like a Turk! We won't be brilliant, but we'll pass inspection. Come on inside. (*Tom follows, groaning.*) Sit down.

Tom: Any particular place you would like me to sit?

Amanda: Thank heavens I've got that new sofa! I'm also making payments on a floor lamp I'll have sent out! And put the chintz covers on, they'll brighten things up! Of course I'd hoped to have these walls repapered. . . . What is the young man's name?

Tom: His name is O'Connor.

Amanda: That, of course, means fish—tomorrow is Friday!° I'll have that salmon loaf—with Durkee's dressing! What does he do? He works at the warehouse?

Tom: Of course! How else would I—

Amanda: Tom, he—doesn't drink?

Tom: Why do you ask me that?

Amanda: Your father *did*!

Tom: Don't get started on that!

Amanda: He *does* drink, then?

---

fish . . . Friday: Until recent decades, Catholics were prohibited from eating meat on Fridays.

Tom: Not that I know of!

Amanda: Make sure, be certain! The last thing I want for my daughter's a boy who drinks!

Tom: Aren't you being a little premature? Mr. O'Connor has not yet appeared on the scene!

Amanda: But will tomorrow. To meet your sister, and what do I know about his character? Nothing! Old maids are better off than wives of drunkards!

Tom: Oh, my God!

Amanda: Be still!

Tom (leaning forward to whisper): Lots of fellows meet girls whom they don't marry!

Amanda: Oh, talk sensibly, Tom—and don't be sarcastic! (*She has gotten a hairbrush.*)

Tom: What are you doing?

Amanda: I'm brushing that cowlick down! What is this young man's position at the warehouse?

Tom (submitting grimly to the brush and the interrogation): This young man's position is that of a shipping clerk, Mother.

Amanda: Sounds to me like a fairly responsible job, the sort of a job *you* would be in if you just had more *get-up*. What is his salary? Have you got any idea?

Tom: I would judge it to be approximately eighty-five dollars a month.

Amanda: Well—not princely, but—

Tom: Twenty more than I make.

Amanda: Yes, how well I know! But for a family man, eighty-five dollars a month is not much more than you can just get by on. . . .

Tom: Yes, but Mr. O'Connor is not a family man.

Amanda: He might be, mightn't he? Some time in the future?

Tom: I see. Plans and provisions.

Amanda: You are the only young man that I know of who ignores the fact that the future becomes the present, the present the past, and the past turns into everlasting regret if you don't plan for it!

Tom: I will think that over and see what I can make of it.

Amanda: Don't be supercilious with your mother! Tell me some more about this—what do you call him?

Tom: James D. O'Connor. The D. is for Delaney.

Amanda: Irish on *both* sides! *Gracious!* And doesn't drink?

Tom: Shall I call him up and ask him right this minute?

Amanda: The only way to find out about those things is to make discreet inquiries at the proper moment. When I was a girl in Blue Mountain and it was suspected that a young man drank, the girl whose attentions he had been receiving, if any girl *was*, would sometimes speak to the minister of his church, or rather her father would if her father was living, and sort of feel him out on the young man's character. That is

the way such things are discreetly handled to keep a young woman
from making a tragic mistake!

Tom: Then how did you happen to make a tragic mistake?

Amanda: That innocent look of your father's had everyone fooled! He
smiled—the world was *enchanted!* No girl can do worse than put
herself at the mercy of a handsome appearance! I hope that Mr.
O'Connor is not too good-looking.

Tom: No, he's not too good-looking. He's covered with freckles and
hasn't too much of a nose.

Amanda: He's not right-down homely, though?

Tom: Not right-down homely. Just medium homely, I'd say.

Amanda: Character's what to look for in a man.

Tom: That's what I've always said, Mother.

Amanda: You've never said anything of the kind and I suspect you would
never give it a thought.

Tom: Don't be suspicious of me.

Amanda: At least I hope he's the type that's up and coming.

Tom: I think he really goes in for self-improvement.

Amanda: What reason have you to think so?

Tom: He goes to night school.

Amanda (beaming):   Splendid! What does he do, I mean study?

Tom: Radio engineering and public speaking!

Amanda: Then he has visions of being advanced in the world! Any young
man who studies public speaking is aiming to have an executive job
some day! And radio engineering? A thing for the future! Both of
these facts are very illuminating. Those are the sort of things that a
mother should know concerning any young man who comes to call on
her daughter. Seriously or—not.

Tom: One little warning. He doesn't know about Laura. I didn't let on
that we had dark ulterior motives. I just said, why don't you come
have dinner with us? He said okay and that was the whole
conversation.

Amanda: I bet it was! You're eloquent as an oyster. However, he'll know
about Laura when he gets here. When he sees how lovely and sweet
and pretty she is, he'll thank his lucky stars he was asked to dinner.

Tom: Mother, you mustn't expect too much of Laura.

Amanda: What do you mean?

Tom: Laura seems all those things to you and me because she's ours and
we love her. We don't even notice she's crippled anymore.

Amanda: Don't say crippled! You know that I never allow that word to
be used!

Tom: But face facts, Mother. She is and—that's not all—

Amanda: What do you mean "not all"?

Tom: Laura is very different from other girls.

Amanda: I think the difference is all to her advantage.

Tom: Not quite all—in the eyes of others—strangers—she's terribly shy and lives in a world of her own and those things make her seem a little peculiar to people outside the house.

Amanda: Don't say peculiar.

Tom: Face the facts. She is.

(*The dance-hall music changes to a tango that has a minor and somewhat ominous tone.*)

Amanda: In what way is she peculiar—may I ask?

Tom (gently):   She lives in a world of her own—a world of—little glass ornaments, Mother. . . . (*Gets up. Amanda remains holding brush, looking at him, troubled.*) She plays old phonograph records and—that's about all—(*He glances at himself in the mirror and crosses to door.*)

Amanda (sharply):   Where are you going?

Tom: I'm going to the movies. (*Out screen door.*)

Amanda: Not to the movies, every night to the movies! (*Follows quickly to screen door.*) I don't believe you always go to the movies! (*He is gone. Amanda looks worriedly after him for a moment. Then vitality and optimism return and she turns from the door. Crossing to portieres.*) Laura! Laura! (*Laura answers from kitchenette.*)

Laura: Yes, Mother.

Amanda: Let those dishes go and come in front! (*Laura appears with dish towel. Gaily.*) Laura, come here and make a wish on the moon!

Laura (entering):   Moon—moon?

Amanda: A little silver slipper of a moon. Look over your left shoulder, Laura, and make a wish! (*Laura looks faintly puzzled as if called out of sleep. Amanda seizes her shoulders and turns her at an angle by the door.*) Now! Now, darling, *wish!*

Laura: What shall I wish for, Mother?

Amanda (her voice trembling and her eyes suddenly filling with tears):   Happiness! Good Fortune!

(*The violin rises and the stage dims out.*)

SCENE VI

(*Image: high school hero.*)

Tom: And so the following evening I brought Jim home to dinner. I had known Jim slightly in high school. In high school Jim was a hero. He had tremendous Irish good nature and vitality with the scrubbed and polished look of white chinaware. He seemed to move in a continual spotlight. He was a star in basketball, captain of the debating club, president of the senior class and the glee club and he sang the male lead in the annual light operas. He was always running or bounding, never just walking. He seemed always at the point of defeating the law of gravity. He was shooting with such velocity through his adolescence that you would logically expect him to arrive at nothing short of the White House by the time he was thirty. But Jim apparently ran into more interference after his graduation from Soldan. His speed had definitely slowed. Six years after he left high school he was holding a job that wasn't much better than mine.

(Image: clerk.)

He was the only one at the warehouse with whom I was on friendly terms. I was valuable to him as someone who could remember his former glory, who had seen him win basketball games and the silver cup in debating. He knew of my secret practice of retiring to a cabinet of the washroom to work on poems when business was slack in the warehouse. He called me Shakespeare. And while the other boys in the warehouse regarded me with suspicious hostility, Jim took a humorous attitude toward me. Gradually his attitude affected the others, their hostility wore off and they also began to smile at me as people smile at an oddly fashioned dog who trots across their path at some distance.

I knew that Jim and Laura had known each other at Soldan, and I had heard Laura speak admiringly of his voice. I didn't know if Jim remembered her or not. In high school Laura had been as unobtrusive as Jim had been astonishing. If he did remember Laura, it was not as my sister, for when I asked him to dinner, he grinned and said, "You know, Shakespeare, I never thought of you as having folks!"

He was about to discover that I did. . . .

(Light up stage.)
(Legend on screen: "The Accent of a Coming Foot.")
(Friday evening. It is about five o'clock of a late spring evening which comes "scattering poems in the sky.")
(A delicate lemony light is in the Wingfield apartment.)
(Amanda has worked like a Turk in preparation for the gentleman caller. The results are astonishing. The new floor lamp with its rose-silk shade is in place, a colored paper lantern conceals the broken light fixture in the ceiling, new billowing white curtains are at the windows, chintz covers are on chairs and sofa, a pair of new sofa pillows make their initial appearance.)
(Open boxes and tissue paper are scattered on the floor.)
(Laura stands in the middle with lifted arms while Amanda crouches before her, adjusting the hem of the new dress, devout and ritualistic. The dress is colored and designed by memory. The arrangement of Laura's hair is changed; it is softer and more becoming. A fragile, unearthly prettiness has come out in Laura: she is like a piece of

translucent glass touched by light, given a momentary radiance, not actual, not lasting.)

Amanda (impatiently): Why are you trembling?

Laura: Mother, you've made me so nervous!

Amanda: How have I made you nervous?

Laura: By all this fuss! You make it seem so important!

Amanda: I don't understand you, Laura. You couldn't be satisfied with just sitting home, and yet whenever I try to arrange something for you, you seem to resist it. (*She gets up.*) Now take a look at yourself. No, wait! Wait just a moment—I have an idea!

Laura: What is it now?

(Amanda produces two powder puffs which she wraps in handkerchiefs and stuffs in Laura's bosom.)

Laura: Mother, what are you doing?

Amanda: They call them "Gay Deceivers"!

Laura: I won't wear them!

Amanda: You will!

Laura: Why should I?

Amanda: Because, to be painfully honest, your chest is flat.

Laura: You make it seem like we were setting a trap.

Amanda: All pretty girls are a trap, a pretty trap, and men expect them to be. (*Legend: "A Pretty Trap."*) Now look at yourself, young lady. This is the prettiest you will ever be! I've got to fix myself now! You're going to be surprised by your mother's appearance! (*She crosses through portieres, humming gaily.*)

(Laura moves slowly to the long mirror and stares solemnly at herself.)

(A wind blows the white curtains inward in a slow, graceful motion and with a faint, sorrowful sighing.)

Amanda (offstage): It isn't dark enough yet. (*She turns slowly before the mirror with a troubled look.*)

(Legend on screen: "This Is My Sister: Celebrate Her with Strings!" Music.)

Amanda (laughing, off): I'm going to show you something. I'm going to make a spectacular appearance!

Laura: What is it, Mother?

Amanda: Possess your soul in patience—you will see! Something I've resurrected from that old trunk! Styles haven't changed so terribly much after all. . . . (*She parts the portieres.*) Now just look at your mother! (*She wears a girlish frock of yellowed voile with a blue silk sash. She carries a bunch of jonquils—the legend of her youth is nearly revived. Feverishly.*) This is the dress in which I led the cotillion. Won the cakewalk twice at Sunset Hill, wore one spring to the Governor's ball in Jackson! See how I sashayed around the ballroom, Laura? (*She raises her skirt and does a mincing step around the room.*) I wore it on Sundays for my gentlemen callers! I had it on the day I met your father—I had malaria fever all that spring. The change of climate from East Tennessee to the Delta—weakened resistance—I had a little temperature all the time—not enough to be serious—just enough to make me restless and giddy! Invitations poured in—parties all over the Delta!—"Stay in bed," said Mother, "you have fever!"—but I just wouldn't.—I took quinine but kept on going, going!—Evenings, dances!—Afternoons, long, long rides! Picnics—lovely!—So lovely, that country in May.—All lacy with dogwood, literally flooded with jonquils!—That was the spring I had the craze for jonquils. Jonquils became an absolute obsession. Mother said, "Honey, there's no more room for jonquils." And still I kept on bringing in more jonquils. Whenever, wherever I saw them, I'd say, "Stop! Stop! I see jonquils!" I made the young men help me gather the jonquils! It was a joke, Amanda and her jonquils! Finally there were no more vases to hold them, every available space was filled with jonquils. No vases to hold them? All right, I'll hold them myself! And then I—(*She stops in front of the picture. Music.*) met your father! Malaria fever and jonquils and then—this—boy. . . . (*She switches on the rose-colored lamp.*) I hope they get here before it starts to rain. (*She crosses upstage and places the jonquils in bowl on table.*) I gave your brother a little extra change so he and Mr. O'Connor could take the service car home.

Laura (*with altered look*):   What did you say his name was?
Amanda: O'Connor.
Laura: What is his first name?
Amanda: I don't remember. Oh, yes, I do. It was—Jim!

> (*Laura sways slightly and catches hold of a chair.*)
> (*Legend on screen: "Not Jim!"*)

Laura (*faintly*):   Not—Jim!
Amanda: Yes, that was it, it was Jim! I've never known a Jim that wasn't nice!

> (*Music: ominous.*)

Laura: Are you sure his name is Jim O'Connor?
Amanda: Yes. Why?
Laura: Is he the one that Tom used to know in high school?
Amanda: He didn't say so. I think he just got to know him at the warehouse.
Laura: There was a Jim O'Connor we both knew in high school—(*Then, with effort.*) If that is the one that Tom is bringing to dinner—you'll have to excuse me, I won't come to the table.
Amanda: What sort of nonsense is this?

Laura: You asked me once if I'd ever liked a boy. Don't you remember I showed you this boy's picture?

Amanda: You mean the boy you showed me in the yearbook?

Laura: Yes, that boy.

Amanda: Laura, Laura, were you in love with that boy?

Laura: I don't know, Mother. All I know is I couldn't sit at the table if it was him!

Amanda: It won't be him! It isn't the least bit likely. But whether it is or not, you will come to the table. You will not be excused.

Laura: I'll have to be, Mother.

Amanda: I don't intend to humor your silliness, Laura. I've had too much from you and your brother, both! So just sit down and compose yourself till they come. Tom has forgotten his key so you'll have to let them in, when they arrive.

Laura (panicky): Oh, Mother—*you* answer the door!

Amanda (lightly): I'll be in the kitchen—busy!

Laura: Oh, Mother, please answer the door, don't make me do it!

Amanda (crossing into kitchenette): I've got to fix the dressing for the salmon. Fuss, fuss—silliness!—over a gentleman caller!

> (*Door swings shut. Laura is left alone.*)
>
> (*Legend: "Terror!"*)
>
> (*She utters a low moan and turns off the lamp—sits stiffly on the edge of the sofa, knotting her fingers together.*)
>
> (*Legend on screen: "The Opening of a Door!"*)
>
> (*Tom and Jim appear on the fire escape steps and climb to landing. Hearing their approach, Laura rises with a panicky gesture. She retreats to the portieres.*)
>
> (*The doorbell. Laura catches her breath and touches her throat. Low drums.*)

Amanda (calling): Laura, sweetheart! The door!

> (*Laura stares at it without moving.*)

Jim: I think we just beat the rain.

Tom: Uh-huh. (*He rings again, nervously. Jim whistles and fishes for a cigarette.*)

Amanda (very, very gaily): Laura, that is your brother and Mr. O'Connor! Will you let them in, darling?

> (*Laura crosses toward kitchenette door.*)

Laura (breathlessly): Mother—you go to the door!

> (*Amanda steps out of kitchenette and stares furiously at Laura. She points imperiously at the door.*)

Laura: Please, please!

Amanda (in a fierce whisper): What is the matter with you, you silly thing?

Laura (desperately):   Please, you answer it, *please!*

Amanda: I told you I wasn't going to humor you, Laura. Why have you chosen this moment to lose your mind?

Laura: Please, please, please, you go!

Amanda: You'll have to go to the door because I can't!

Laura (despairingly):   I can't either!

Amanda: *Why?*

Laura: I'm *sick!*

Amanda: I'm sick, too—of your nonsense! Why can't you and your brother be normal people? Fantastic whims and behavior! (*Tom gives a long ring.*) Preposterous goings on! Can you give me one reason— (*Calls out lyrically.*) COMING! JUST ONE SECOND!—why should you be afraid to open a door? Now you answer it, Laura!

Laura: Oh, oh, oh . . . (*She returns through the portieres. Darts to the victrola and winds it frantically and turns it on.*)

Amanda: Laura Wingfield, you march right to that door!

Laura: Yes—yes, Mother!

> (*A faraway, scratchy rendition of "Dardanella" softens the air and gives her strength to move through it. She slips to the door and draws it cautiously open.*)
>
> (*Tom enters with the caller, Jim O'Connor.*)

Tom: Laura, this is Jim. Jim, this is my sister, Laura.

Jim (stepping inside):   I didn't know that Shakespeare had a sister!

Laura (retreating stiff and trembling from the door):   How—how do you do?

Jim (heartily extending his hand):   Okay!

> (*Laura touches it hesitantly with hers.*)

Jim: Your hand's *cold,* Laura!

Laura: Yes, well—I've been playing the victrola. . . .

Jim: Must have been playing classical music on it! You ought to play a little hot swing music to warm you up!

Laura: Excuse me—I haven't finished playing the victrola. . . .

> (*She turns awkwardly and hurries into the front room. She pauses a second by the victrola. Then catches her breath and darts through the portieres like a frightened deer.*)

Jim (grinning):   What was the matter?

Tom: Oh—with Laura? Laura is—terribly shy.

Jim: Shy, huh? It's unusual to meet a shy girl nowadays. I don't believe you ever mentioned you had a sister.

Tom: Well, now you know. I have one. Here is the *Post Dispatch.* You want a piece of it?

Jim: Uh-huh.

Tom: What piece? The comics?

Jim: Sports! (*Glances at it.*) Ole Dizzy Dean° is on his bad behavior.

Tom (disinterest):   Yeah? (*Lights cigarette and crosses back to fire escape door.*)

Jim: Where are *you* going?

Tom: I'm going out on the terrace.

Jim (goes after him):   You know, Shakespeare—I'm going to sell you a bill of goods!

Tom: What goods?

Jim: A course I'm taking.

Tom: Huh?

Jim: In public speaking! You and me, we're not the warehouse type.

Tom: Thanks—that's good news. But what has public speaking got to do with it?

Jim: It fits you for—executive positions!

Tom: Awww.

Jim: I tell you it's done a helluva lot for me.

(*Image: executive at desk.*)

Tom: In what respect?

Jim: In every! Ask yourself what is the difference between you an' me and men in the office down front? Brains?—No!—Ability?—No! Then what? Just one little thing—

Tom: What is that one little thing?

Jim: Primarily it amounts to—social poise! Being able to square up to people and hold your own on any social level!

Amanda (offstage):   Tom?

Tom: Yes, Mother?

Amanda: Is that you and Mr. O'Connor?

Tom: Yes, Mother.

Amanda: Well, you just make yourselves comfortable in there.

Tom: Yes, Mother.

Amanda: Ask Mr. O'Connor if he would like to wash his hands.

Jim: Aw,—no—no—thank you—I took care of that at the warehouse. Tom—

Tom: Yes?

Jim: Mr. Mendoza was speaking to me about you.

Tom: Favorably?

Jim: What do you think?

Tom: Well—

Jim: You're going to be out of a job if you don't wake up.

Tom: I am waking up—

Jim: You show no signs.

Tom: The signs are interior.

(*Image on screen: the sailing vessel with Jolly Roger again.*)

Dizzy Dean: Baseball "bad boy" of the 1930s.

Tom: I'm planning to change. (*He leans over the rail speaking with quiet exhilaration. The incandescent marquees and signs of the first-run movie houses light his face from across the alley. He looks like a voyager.*) I'm right at the point of committing myself to a future that doesn't include the warehouse and Mr. Mendoza or even a night school course in public speaking.

Jim: What are you gassing about?

Tom: I'm tired of the movies.

Jim: Movies!

Tom: Yes, movies! Look at them—(*A wave toward the marvels of Grand Avenue.*) All of those glamorous people—having adventures—hogging it all, gobbling the whole thing up! You know what happens? People go to the *movies* instead of *moving!* Hollywood characters are supposed to have all the adventures for everybody in America, while everybody in America sits in a dark room and watches them have them! Yes, until there's a war. That's when adventure becomes available to the masses! *Everyone's* dish, not only Gable's! Then the people in the dark room come out of the dark room to have some adventures themselves—Goody, goody!—It's our turn now, to go to the South Sea Island—to make a safari—to be exotic, far-off!—But I'm not patient. I don't want to wait till then. I'm tired of the *movies* and I am *about* to *move!*

Jim (incredulously):   Move?

Tom: Yes.

Jim: When?

Tom: Soon!

Jim: Where? Where?

(*Theme three music seems to answer the question, while Tom thinks it over. He searches among his pockets.*)

Tom: I'm starting to boil inside. I know I seem dreamy, but inside—well, I'm boiling! Whenever I pick up a shoe, I shudder a little thinking how short life is and what I am doing!—Whatever that means. I know it doesn't mean shoes—except as something to wear on a traveler's feet! (*Finds paper.*) Look—

Jim: What?

Tom: I'm a member.

Jim (reading):   The Union of Merchant Seamen.

Tom: I paid my dues this month, instead of the light bill.

Jim: You will regret it when they turn the lights off.

Tom: I won't be here.

Jim: How about your mother?

Tom: I'm like my father. The bastard son of a bastard! See how he grins? And he's been absent going on sixteen years!

Jim: You're just talking, you drip. How does your mother feel about it?

Tom: Shhh!—Here comes Mother! Mother is not acquainted with my plans!

Amanda (enters portieres): Where are you all?

Tom: On the terrace, Mother.

> *(They start inside. She advances to them. Tom is distinctly shocked at her appearance. Even Jim blinks a little. He is making his first contact with girlish Southern vivacity and in spite of the night school course in public speaking is somewhat thrown off the beam by the unexpected outlay of social charm.)*
>
> *(Certain responses are attempted by Jim but are swept aside by Amanda's gay laughter and chatter. Tom is embarrassed but after the first shock Jim reacts very warmly. Grins and chuckles, is altogether won over.)*
>
> *(Image: Amanda as a girl.)*

Amanda (coyly smiling, shaking her girlish ringlets): Well, well, well, so this is Mr. O'Connor. Introductions entirely unnecessary. I've heard so much about you from my boy. I finally said to him, Tom—good gracious!—why don't you bring this paragon to supper? I'd like to meet this nice young man at the warehouse!—Instead of just hearing him sing your praises so much! I don't know why my son is so standoffish—that's not Southern behavior! Let's sit down and—I think we could stand a little more air in here! Tom, leave the door open. I felt a nice fresh breeze a moment ago. Where has it gone to? Mmm, so warm already! And not quite summer, even. We're going to burn up when summer really gets started. However, we're having—we're having a very light supper. I think light things are better fo' this time of year. The same as light clothes are. Light clothes an' light food are what warm weather calls fo'. You know our blood gets so thick during th' winter—it takes a while fo' us to *adjust* ou'selves!—when the season changes . . . It's come so quick this year. I wasn't prepared. All of a sudden—heavens! Already summer!—I ran to the trunk an' pulled out this light dress—Terribly old! Historical almost! But feels so good—so good an' co-ol, y'know. . . .

Tom: Mother—

Amanda: Yes, honey?

Tom: How about—supper?

Amanda: Honey, you go ask Sister if supper is ready! You know that Sister is in full charge of supper! Tell her you hungry boys are waiting for it. (*To Jim.*) Have you met Laura?

Jim: She—

Amanda: Let you in? Oh, good, you've met already! It's rare for a girl as sweet an' pretty as Laura to be domestic! But Laura is, thank heavens, not only pretty but also very domestic. I'm not at all. I never was a bit. I never could make a thing but angel food cake. Well, in the South we had so many servants. Gone, gone, gone. All vestiges of gracious living! Gone completely! I wasn't prepared for what the future brought me. All of my gentlemen callers were sons of planters and so of course I assumed that I would be married to one and raise my family on a large piece of land with plenty of servants. But man proposes—and woman accepts the proposal!—To vary that old, old saying a little bit—I married no planter! I married a man who worked for the telephone company!—That gallantly smiling gentleman over there! (*Points to the picture.*) A telephone man who—fell in love with long distance!—Now he travels and I don't even know where!—But what am I going on for about my—tribulations! Tell me yours—I hope you don't have any! Tom?

Tom (returning): Yes, Mother?

Amanda: Is supper nearly ready?

Tom: It looks to me like supper is on the table.

Amanda: Let me look—(*She rises prettily and looks through portieres.*) Oh, lovely!—But where is Sister?

Tom: Laura is not feeling well and she says that she thinks she'd better not come to the table.

Amanda: What?—Nonsense!—Laura? Oh, Laura!

Laura (offstage, faintly): Yes, Mother.

Amanda: You really must come to the table. We won't be seated until you come to the table! Come in, Mr. O'Connor. You sit over there, and I'll—Laura? Laura Wingfield! You're keeping us waiting, honey! We can't say grace until you come to the table!

> (*The back door is pushed weakly open and Laura comes in. She is obviously quite faint, her lips trembling, her eyes wide and staring. She moves unsteadily toward the table.*)
> (*Legend: "Terror!"*)
> (*Outside a summer storm is coming abruptly. The white curtains billow inward at the windows and there is a sorrowful murmur and deep blue dusk.*)
> (*Laura suddenly stumbles—she catches at a chair with a faint moan.*)

Tom: Laura!

Amanda: Laura! (*There is a clap of thunder.*) (*Legend: "Ah!"*) (*Despairingly.*) Why, Laura, you *are* sick, darling! Tom, help your sister into the living room, dear! Sit in the living room, Laura—rest on the sofa. Well! (*To the gentleman caller.*) Standing over the hot stove made her ill!—I told her that it was just too warm this evening, but—(*Tom comes back in. Laura is on the sofa.*) Is Laura all right now?

Tom: Yes.

Amanda: What *is* that? Rain? A nice cool rain has come up! (*She gives the gentleman caller a frightened look.*) I think we may—have grace—now . . . (*Tom looks at her stupidly.*) Tom, honey—you say grace!

Tom: Oh . . . "For these and all thy mercies—" (*They bow their heads,
Amanda stealing a nervous glance at Jim. In the living room Laura,
stretched on the sofa, clenches her hand to her lips, to hold back a
shuddering sob.*) God's Holy Name be praised—

(*The scene dims out.*)

SCENE VII

(*A Souvenir*)
(*Half an hour later. Dinner is just being finished in the upstage
area which is concealed by the drawn portieres.*)
(*As the curtain rises Laura is still huddled upon the sofa, her feet
drawn under her, her head resting on a pale blue pillow, her eyes wide
and mysteriously watchful. The new floor lamp with its shade of rose-
colored silk gives a soft, becoming light to her face, bringing out the
fragile, unearthly prettiness which usually escapes attention. There is a
steady murmur of rain, but it is slackening and stops soon after the scene
begins; the air outside becomes pale and luminous as the moon breaks
out.*)
(*A moment after the curtain rises, the lights in both rooms flicker
and go out.*)

Jim: Hey, there, Mr. Light Bulb!

(*Amanda laughs nervously.*)
(*Legend: "Suspension of a Public Service."*)

Amanda: Where was Moses when the lights went out? Ha-ha. Do you
know the answer to that one, Mr. O'Connor?
Jim: No, Ma'am, what's the answer?
Amanda: In the dark! (*Jim laughs appreciably.*) Everybody sit still. I'll
light the candles. Isn't it lucky we have them on the table? Where's a
match? Which of you gentlemen can provide a match?
Jim: Here.
Amanda: Thank you, sir.
Jim: Not at all, Ma'am!
Amanda: I guess the fuse has burnt out. Mr. O'Connor, can you tell a
burnt-out fuse? I know I can't and Tom is a total loss when it comes to
mechanics. (*Sound: getting up: voices recede a little to kitchenette.*) Oh, be
careful you don't bump into something. We don't want our gentleman
caller to break his neck. Now wouldn't that be a fine howdy-do?
Jim: Ha-ha! Where is the fuse box?
Amanda: Right here next to the stove. Can you see anything?
Jim: Just a minute.
Amanda: Isn't electricity a mysterious thing? Wasn't it Benjamin Franklin
who tied a key to a kite? We live in such a mysterious universe, don't

we? Some people say that science clears up all the mysteries for us. In my opinion it only creates more! Have you found it yet?

Jim: No, Ma'am. All these fuses look okay to me.

Amanda: Tom!

Tom: Yes, Mother?

Amanda: That light bill I gave you several days ago. The one I told you we got the notices about?

Tom: Oh.—Yeah.

(*Legend: "Ha!"*)

Amanda: You didn't neglect to pay it by any chance?

Tom: Why, I—

Amanda: Didn't! I might have known it!

Jim: Shakespeare probably wrote a poem on that light bill, Mrs. Wingfield.

Amanda: I might have known better than to trust him with it! There's such a high price for negligence in this world!

Jim: Maybe the poem will win a ten-dollar prize.

Amanda: We'll just have to spend the remainder of the evening in the nineteenth century, before Mr. Edison made the Mazda lamp!°

Jim: Candlelight is my favorite kind of light.

Amanda: That shows you're romantic! But that's no excuse for Tom. Well, we got through dinner. Very considerate of them to let us get through dinner before they plunged us into everlasting darkness, wasn't it, Mr. O'Connor?

Jim: Ha-ha!

Amanda: Tom, as a penalty for your carelessness you can help me with the dishes.

Jim: Let me give you a hand.

Amanda: Indeed you will not!

Jim: I ought to be good for something.

Amanda: Good for something? (*Her tone is rhapsodic.*) *You?* Why, Mr. O'Connor, nobody, *nobody's* given me this much entertainment in years—as you have!

Jim: Aw, now, Mrs. Wingfield!

Amanda: I'm not exaggerating, not one bit! But Sister is all by her lonesome. You go keep her company in the parlor! I'll give you this lovely old candelabrum that used to be on the altar at the church of the Heavenly Rest. It was melted a little out of shape when the church burnt down. Lightning struck it one spring. Gypsy Jones was holding a revival at the time and he intimated that the church was destroyed because the Episcopalians gave card parties.

Jim: Ha-ha.

Mazda lamp: The first incandescent lamp.

Amanda: And how about coaxing Sister to drink a little wine? I think it would be good for her! Can you carry both at once?
Jim: Sure. I'm Superman!
Amanda: Now, Thomas, get into this apron!

> (*The door of kitchenette swings closed on Amanda's gay laughter; the flickering light approaches the portieres.*)
> (*Laura sits up nervously as he enters. Her speech at first is low and breathless from the almost intolerable strain of being alone with a stranger.*)
> (*The legend: "I Don't Suppose You Remember Me at All!"*)
> (*In her first speeches in this scene, before Jim's warmth overcomes her paralyzing shyness, Laura's voice is thin and breathless as though she has just run up a steep flight of stairs.*)
> (*Jim's attitude is gently humorous. In playing this scene it should be stressed that while the incident is apparently unimportant, it is to Laura the climax of her secret life.*)

Jim: Hello, there, Laura.
Laura (faintly):   Hello. (*She clears her throat.*)
Jim: How are you feeling now? Better?
Laura: Yes. Yes, thank you.
Jim: This is for you. A little dandelion wine. (*He extends it toward her with extravagant gallantry.*)
Laura: Thank you.
Jim: Drink it—but don't get drunk! (*He laughs heartily. Laura takes the glass uncertainly; laughs shyly.*) Where shall I set the candles?
Laura: Oh—oh, anywhere . . .
Jim: How about here on the floor? Any objections?
Laura: No.
Jim: I'll spread a newspaper under to catch the drippings. I like to sit on the floor. Mind if I do?
Laura: Oh, no.
Jim: Give me a pillow?
Laura: What?
Jim: A pillow!
Laura: Oh . . . (*Hands him one quickly.*)
Jim: How about you? Don't you like to sit on the floor?
Laura: Oh—yes.
Jim: Why don't you, then?
Laura: I—will.
Jim: Take a pillow! (*Laura does. Sits on the other side of the candelabrum. Jim crosses his legs and smiles engagingly at her.*) I can't hardly see you sitting way over there.
Laura: I can—see you.
Jim: I know, but that's not fair, I'm in the limelights. (*Laura moves her pillow closer.*) Good! Now I can see you! Comfortable?

Laura: Yes.

Jim: So am I. Comfortable as a cow. Will you have some gum?

Laura: No, thank you.

Jim: I think that I will indulge, with your permission. (*Musingly unwraps it and holds it up.*) Think of the fortune made by the guy that invented the first piece of chewing gum. Amazing, huh? The Wrigley Building is one of the sights of Chicago.—I saw it summer before last when I went up to the Century of Progress. Did you take in the Century of Progress?

Laura: No, I didn't.

Jim: Well, it was quite a wonderful exposition. What impressed me most was the Hall of Science. Gives you an idea of what the future will be in America, even more wonderful than the present time is! (*Pause Smiling at her.*) Your brother tells me you're shy. Is that right, Laura?

Laura: I—don't know.

Jim: I judge you to be an old-fashioned type of girl. Well, I think that's a pretty good type to be. Hope you don't think I'm being too personal—do you?

Laura (hastily, out of embarrassment):   I believe I *will* take a piece of gum, if you—don't mind. (*Clearing her throat.*) Mr. O'Connor, have you— kept up with your singing?

Jim: Singing? Me?

Laura: Yes. I remember what a beautiful voice you had.

Jim: When did you hear me sing?

(*Voice offstage in the pause.*)

Voice (offstage):   O blow, ye winds, heigh-ho,
   A-roving I will go!
      I'm off to my love
      With a oxing glove—
   Ten thousand miles away!

Jim: You say you've heard me sing?

Laura: Oh, yes! Yes, very often . . . I—don't suppose you remember me—at all?

Jim (smiling doubtfully):   You know I have an idea I've seen you before. I had that idea soon as you opened the door. It seemed almost like I was about to remember your name. But the name that I started to call you—wasn't a name! And so I stopped myself before I said it.

Laura: Wasn't it—Blue Roses?

Jim (springs up. Grinning):   Blue Roses! My gosh, yes—Blue Roses! That's what I had on my tongue when you opened the door! Isn't it funny what tricks your memory plays? I didn't connect you with the high school somehow or other. But that's where it was; it was high school. I didn't even know you were Shakespeare's sister! Gosh, I'm sorry.

Laura: I didn't expect you to. You—barely knew me!

Jim: But we did have a speaking acquaintance, huh?

Laura: Yes, we—spoke to each other.

Jim: When did you recognize me?

Laura: Oh, right away!

Jim: Soon as I came in the door?

Laura: When I heard your name I thought it was probably you. I knew that Tom used to know you a little in high school. So when you came in the door—Well, then I was—sure.

Jim: Why didn't you *say* something, then?

Laura (breathlessly): I didn't know what to say, I was—too surprised!

Jim: For goodness' sakes! You know, this sure is funny!

Laura: Yes! Yes, isn't it, though . . .

Jim: Didn't we have a class in something together?

Laura: Yes, we did.

Jim: What class was that?

Laura: It was—singing—Chorus!

Jim: Aw!

Laura: I sat across the aisle from you in the Aud.

Jim: Aw.

Laura: Mondays, Wednesdays, and Fridays.

Jim: Now I remember—you always came in late.

Laura: Yes, it was so hard for me, getting upstairs. I had that brace on my leg—it clumped so loud!

Jim: I never heard any clumping.

Laura (wincing at the recollection): To me it sounded like—thunder!

Jim: Well, well, well, I never even noticed.

Laura: And everybody was seated before I came in. I had to walk in front of all those people. My seat was in the back row. I had to go clumping all the way up the aisle with everyone watching!

Jim: You shouldn't have been self-conscious.

Laura: I know, but I was. It was always such a relief when the singing started.

Jim: Aw, yes, I've placed you now! I used to call you Blue Roses. How was it that I got started calling you that?

Laura: I was out of school a little while with pleurosis. When I came back you asked me what was the matter. I said I had pleurosis—you thought I said Blue Roses. That's what you always called me after that!

Jim: I hope you didn't mind.

Laura: Oh, no—I liked it. You see, I wasn't acquainted with many—people. . . .

Jim: As I remember you sort of stuck by yourself.

Laura: I—I—never had much luck at—making friends.

Jim: I don't see why you wouldn't.

Laura: Well, I—started out badly.

Jim: You mean being—

Laura: Yes, it sort of—stood between me—

Jim: You shouldn't have let it!

Laura: I know, but it did, and—

Jim: You were shy with people!

Laura: I tried not to be but never could—

Jim: Overcome it?

Laura: No, I—I never could!

Jim: I guess being shy is something you have to work out of kind of gradually.

Laura (sorrowfully):   Yes—I guess it—

Jim: Takes time!

Laura: Yes—

Jim: People are not so dreadful when you know them. That's what you have to remember! And everybody has problems, not just you, but practically everybody has got some problems. You think of yourself as having the only problems, as being the only one who is disappointed. But just look around you and you will see lots of people as disappointed as you are. For instance, I hoped when I was going to high school that I would be further along at this time, six years later, than I am now—You remember that wonderful write-up I had in *The Torch*?

Laura: Yes! (*She rises and crosses to table.*)

Jim: It said I was bound to succeed in anything I went into! (*Laura returns with the annual.*) Holy Jeez! *The Torch!* (*He accepts it reverently. They smile across it with mutual wonder. Laura crouches beside him and they begin to turn through it. Laura's shyness is dissolving in his warmth.*)

Laura: Here you are in *Pirates of Penzance!*

Jim (wistfully):   I sang the baritone lead in that operetta.

Laura (rapidly):   So—*beautifully!*

Jim (protesting):   Aw—

Laura: Yes, yes—beautifully—beautifully!

Jim: You heard me?

Laura: All three times!

Jim: No!

Laura: Yes!

Jim: All three performances?

Laura (looking down):   Yes.

Jim: Why?

Laura: I—wanted to ask you to—autograph my program.

Jim: Why didn't you ask me to?

Laura: You were always surrounded by your own friends so much that I never had a chance to.

Jim: You should have just—

Laura: Well, I—thought you might think I was—

Jim: Thought I might think you was—what?

Laura: Oh—

Jim (with reflective relish): I was beleaguered by females in those days.

Laura: You were terribly popular!

Jim: Yeah—

Laura: You had such a—friendly way—

Jim: I was spoiled in high school.

Laura: Everybody—liked you!

Jim: Including you?

Laura: I—yes, I—I did, too—(*She gently closes the book in her lap.*)

Jim: Well, well, well!—Give me that program, Laura. (*She hands it to him. He signs it with a flourish.*) There you are—better late than never!

Laura: Oh, I—what a—surprise!

Jim: My signature isn't worth very much right now. But some day— maybe—it will increase in value! Being disappointed is one thing and being discouraged is something else. I am disappointed but I am not discouraged. I'm twenty-three years old. How old are you?

Laura: I'll be twenty-four in June.

Jim: That's not old age!

Laura: No, but—

Jim: You finished high school?

Laura (with difficulty): I didn't go back.

Jim: You mean you dropped out?

Laura: I made bad grades in my final examinations. (*She rises and replaces the book and the program. Her voice strained.*) How is—Emily Meisenbach getting along?

Jim: Oh, that kraut-head!

Laura: Why do you call her that?

Jim: That's what she was.

Laura: You're not still—going with her?

Jim: I never see her.

Laura: It said in the Personal Section that you were—engaged!

Jim: I know, but I wasn't impressed by that—propaganda!

Laura: It wasn't—the truth?

Jim: Only in Emily's optimistic opinion!

Laura: Oh—

> (*Legend: "What Have You Done since High School?"*)
> (*Jim lights a cigarette and leans indolently back on his elbows smiling at Laura with a warmth and charm which lights her inwardly with altar candles. She remains by the table and turns in her hands a piece of glass to cover her tumult.*)

Jim (after several reflective puffs on a cigarette): What have you done since high school? (*She seems not to hear him.*) Huh? (*Laura looks up.*) I said what have you done since high school, Laura?

Laura: Nothing much.

Jim: You must have been doing something these six long years.

Laura: Yes.

Jim: Well, then, such as what?

Laura: I took a business course at business college—

Jim: How did that work out?

Laura: Well, not very—well—I had to drop out, it gave me—indigestion—

(*Jim laughs gently.*)

Jim: What are you doing now?

Laura: I don't do anything—much. Oh, please don't think I sit around doing nothing! My glass collection takes up a good deal of my time. Glass is something you have to take good care of.

Jim: What did you say—about glass?

Laura: Collection I said—I have one—(*She clears her throat and turns away again, acutely shy.*)

Jim (abruptly):   You know what I judge to be the trouble with you? Inferiority complex! Know what that is? That's what they call it when someone low-rates himself! I understand it because I had it, too. Although my case was not so aggravated as yours seems to be. I had it until I took up public speaking, developed my voice, and learned that I had an aptitude for science. Before that time I never thought of myself as being outstanding in any way whatsoever! Now I've never made a regular study of it, but I have a friend who says I can analyze people better than doctors that make a profession of it. I don't claim that to be necessarily true, but I can sure guess a person's psychology, Laura! (*Takes out his gum.*) Excuse me, Laura. I always take it out when the flavor is gone. I'll use this scrap of paper to wrap it in. I know how it is to get it stuck on a shoe. Yep—that's what I judge to be your principal trouble. A lack of confidence in yourself as a person. You don't have the proper amount of faith in yourself. I'm basing that fact on a number of your remarks and also on certain observations I've made. For instance that clumping you thought was so awful in high school. You say that you even dreaded to walk into class. You see what you did? You dropped out of school, you gave up an education because of a clump, which as far as I know was practically nonexistent! A little physical defect is what you have. Hardly noticeable even! Magnified thousands of times by imagination! You know what my strong advice to you is? Think of yourself as *superior* in some way!

Laura: In what way would I think?

Jim: Why, man alive, Laura! Just look about you a little. What do you see? A world full of common people! All of 'em born and all of 'em going to die! Which of them has one-tenth of your good points! Or mine! Or anyone else's, as far as that goes—Gosh! Everybody excels in some one thing. Some in many! (*Unconsciously glances at himself in the mirror.*) All you've got to do is discover in *what!* Take me, for instance. (*He adjusts his tie at the mirror.*) My interest happens to lie in electrodynamics. I'm taking a course in radio engineering at night school, Laura, on top of a fairly responsible job at the warehouse. I'm taking that course and studying public speaking.

Laura: Ohhhh.

Jim: Because I believe in the future of television! (*Turning back to her.*) I wish to be ready to go up right along with it. Therefore I'm planning to get in on the ground floor. In fact, I've already made the right connections and all that remains is for the industry itself to get under way! Full steam—(*His eyes are starry.*) *Knowledge*—Zzzzzp! *Money*—Zzzzzzp!—*Power!* That's the cycle democracy is built on! (*His attitude is convincingly dynamic. Laura stares at him, even her shyness eclipsed in her absolute wonder. He suddenly grins.*) I guess you think I think a lot of myself!

Laura: No—o-o-o, I—

Jim: Now how about you? Isn't there something you take more interest in than anything else?

Laura: Well, I do—as I said—have my—glass collection—

(*A peal of girlish laughter from the kitchen.*)

Jim: I'm not right sure I know what you're talking about. What kind of glass is it?

Laura: Little articles of it, they're ornaments mostly! Most of them are little animals made out of glass, the tiniest little animals in the world. Mother calls them a glass menagerie! Here's an example of one, if you'd like to see it! This one is one of the oldest. It's nearly thirteen. (*He stretches out his hand.*) (*Music: "The Glass Menagerie."*) Oh, be careful—if you breathe, it breaks!

Jim: I'd better not take it. I'm pretty clumsy with things.

Laura: Go on, I trust you with him! (*Places it in his palm.*) There now—you're holding him gently! Hold him over the light, he loves the light! You see how the light shines through him?

Jim: It sure does shine!

Laura: I shouldn't be partial, but he is my favorite one.

Jim: What kind of a thing is this one supposed to be?

Laura: Haven't you noticed the single horn on his forehead?

Jim: A unicorn, huh?

Laura: Mmm-hmmm!

Jim: Unicorns, aren't they extinct in the modern world?

Laura: I know!

Jim: Poor little fellow, he must feel sort of lonesome.

Laura (smiling): Well, if he does he doesn't complain about it. He stays on a shelf with some horses that don't have horns and all of them seem to get along nicely together.

Jim: How do you know?

Laura (lightly):   I haven't heard any arguments among them!

Jim (grinning):   No arguments, huh? Well, that's a pretty good sign! Where shall I set him?

Laura: Put him on the table. They all like a change of scenery once in a while!

Jim (stretching):   Well, well, well, well—Look how big my shadow is when I stretch!

Laura: Oh, oh, yes—it stretches across the ceiling!

Jim (crossing to door):   I think it's stopped raining. (*Opens fire escape door.*) Where does the music come from?

Laura: From the Paradise Dance Hall across the alley.

Jim: How about cutting the rug a little, Miss Wingfield?

Laura: Oh, I—

Jim: Or is your program filled up? Let me have a look at it. (*Grasps imaginary card.*) Why, every dance is taken! I'll just have to scratch some out. (*Waltz music: "La Golondrina."*) Ahhh, a waltz! (*He executes some sweeping turns by himself then holds his arms toward Laura.*)

Laura (breathlessly):   I—can't dance!

Jim: There you go, that inferiority stuff!

Laura: I've never danced in my life!

Jim: Come on, try!

Laura: Oh, but I'd step on you!

Jim: I'm not made out of glass.

Laura: How—how—how do we start?

Jim: Just leave it to me. You hold your arms out a little.

Laura: Like this?

Jim: A little bit higher. Right. Now don't tighten up, that's the main thing about it—relax.

Laura (laughing breathlessly):   It's hard not to.

Jim: Okay.

Laura: I'm afraid you can't budge me.

Jim: What do you bet I can't? (*He swings her into motion.*)

Laura: Goodness, yes, you can!

Jim: Let yourself go, now, Laura, just let yourself go.

Laura: I'm—

Jim: Come on!

Laura: Trying!

Jim: Not so stiff—Easy does it!

Laura: I know but I'm—

Jim: Loosen th' backbone! There now, that's a lot better.

Laura: Am I?

Jim: Lots, lots better! (*He moves her about the room in a clumsy waltz.*)

Laura: Oh, my!

Jim: Ha-ha!

Laura: Oh, my goodness!

Jim: Ha-ha-ha! (*They suddenly bump into the table. Jim stops.*) What did we hit on?

Laura: Table.

Jim: Did something fall off it? I think—

Laura: Yes.

Jim: I hope that it wasn't the little glass horse with the horn!

Laura: Yes.

Jim: Aw, aw, aw. Is it broken?

Laura: Now it is just like all the other horses.

Jim: It's lost its—

Laura: Horn! It doesn't matter. Maybe it's a blessing in disguise.

Jim: You'll never forgive me. I bet that that was your favorite piece of glass.

Laura: I don't have favorites much. It's no tragedy, Freckles. Glass breaks so easily. No matter how careful you are. The traffic jars the shelves and things fall off them.

Jim: Still I'm awfully sorry that I was the cause.

Laura (smiling): I'll just imagine he had an operation. The horn was removed to make him feel less—freakish! (*They both laugh.*) Now he will feel more at home with the other horses, the ones that don't have horns . . .

Jim: Ha-ha, that's very funny! (*Suddenly serious.*) I'm glad to see that you have a sense of humor. You know—you're—well—very different! Surprisingly different from anyone else I know! (*His voice becomes soft and hesitant with a genuine feeling.*) Do you mind me telling you that? (*Laura is abashed beyond speech.*) I mean it in a nice way . . . (*Laura nods shyly, looking away.*) You make me feel sort of—I don't know how to put it! I'm usually pretty good at expressing things, but—This is something that I don't know how to say! (*Laura touches her throat and clears it—turns the broken unicorn in her hands. Even softer.*) Has anyone ever told you that you were pretty? (*Pause: Music. Laura looks up slowly, with wonder, and shakes her head.*) Well, you are! In a very different way from anyone else. And all the nicer because of the difference, too. (*His voice becomes low and husky. Laura turns away, nearly faint with the novelty of her emotions.*) I wish that you were my sister. I'd teach you to have some confidence in yourself. The different people are not like other people, but being different is nothing to be ashamed of. Because other people are not such wonderful people. They're one hundred times one thousand. You're one times one! They walk all over the earth. You just stay here. They're common as—weeds, but—you—well, you're—*Blue Roses!*

    (*Image on screen: blue roses.*)
    (*Music changes.*)

Laura: But blue is wrong for—roses . . .

Jim: It's right for you—You're—pretty!

Laura: In what respect am I pretty?

Jim: In all respects—believe me! Your eyes—your hair—are pretty! Your hands are pretty! (*He catches hold of her hand.*) You think I'm making this up because I'm invited to dinner and have to be nice. Oh, I could do that! I could put on an act for you, Laura, and say lots of things without being very sincere. But this time I am. I'm talking to you sincerely. I happened to notice you had this inferiority complex that keeps you from feeling comfortable with people. Somebody needs to build your confidence up and make you proud instead of shy and turning away and—blushing—Somebody ought to—Ought to—*kiss* you, Laura! (*His hand slips slowly up her arm to her shoulder. Music swells tumultuously. He suddenly turns her about and kisses her on the lips. When he releases her Laura sinks on the sofa with a bright, dazed look. Jim backs away and fishes in his pocket for a cigarette.*) (*Legend on screen: "Souvenir."*) Stumble-john! (*He lights the cigarette, avoiding her look. There is a peal of girlish laughter from Amanda in the kitchen. Laura slowly raises and opens her hand. It still contains the little broken glass animal. She looks at it with a tender, bewildered expression.*) Stumble-john! I shouldn't have done that—That was way off the beam. You don't smoke, do you? (*She looks up, smiling, not hearing the question. He sits beside her a little gingerly. She looks at him speechlessly—waiting. He coughs decorously and moves a little farther aside as he considers the situation and senses her feelings, dimly, with perturbation. Gently.*) Would you—care for a—mint? (*She doesn't seem to hear him but her look grows brighter even.*) Peppermint—Life Saver? My pocket's a regular drugstore—wherever I go . . . (*He pops a mint in his mouth. Then gulps and decides to make a clean breast of it. He speaks slowly and gingerly.*) Laura, you know, if I had a sister like you, I'd do the same thing as Tom. I'd bring out fellows and—introduce her to them. The right type of boys of a type to—appreciate her. Only—well—he made a mistake about me. Maybe I've got no call to be saying this. That may not have been the idea in having me over. But what if it was? There's nothing wrong about that. The only trouble is that in my case—I'm not in a situation to—do the right thing. I can't take down your number and say I'll phone. I can't call up next week and—ask for a date. I thought I had better explain the situation in case you misunderstood it and—hurt your feelings. . . . (*Pause. Slowly, very slowly, Laura's look changes, her eyes returning slowly from his to the ornament in her palm.*)

(*Amanda utters another gay laugh in the kitchen.*)

Laura (faintly):   You—won't—call again?

Jim: No, Laura, I can't. (*He rises from the sofa.*) As I was just explaining, I've—got strings on me, Laura, I've—been going steady!

I go out all the time with a girl named Betty. She's a home-girl like you, and Catholic, and Irish, and in a great many ways we—get along fine. I met her last summer on a moonlight boat trip up the river to Alton, on the *Majestic*. Well—right away from the start it was—love! (*Legend: Love!*) (*Laura sways slightly forward and grips the arm of the sofa. He fails to notice, now enrapt in his own comfortable being.*) Being in love has made a new man of me! (*Leaning stiffly forward, clutching the arm of the sofa, Laura struggles visibly with her storm. But Jim is oblivious, she is a long way off.*) The power of love is really pretty tremendous! Love is something that— changes the whole world, Laura! (*The storm abates a little and Laura leans back. He notices her again.*) It happened that Betty's aunt took sick, she got a wire and had to go to Centralia. So Tom— when he asked me to dinner—I naturally just accepted the invitation, not knowing that you—that he—that I—(*He stops awkwardly.*) Huh—I'm a stumble-john! (*He flops back on the sofa. The holy candles in the altar of Laura's face have been snuffed out! There is a look of almost infinite desolation. Jim glances at her uneasily.*) I wish that you would—say something. (*She bites her lip which was trembling and then bravely smiles. She opens her hand again on the broken glass ornament. Then she gently takes his hand and raises it level with her own. She carefully places the unicorn in the palm of his hand, then pushes his fingers closed upon it.*) What are you—doing that for? You want me to have him?—Laura? (*She nods.*) What for?

Laura: A—souvenir . . .

>   (*She rises unsteadily and crouches beside the victrola to wind it up.*)
>   (*Legend on screen: "Things Have a Way of Turning out so Badly."*)
>   (*Or Image: "Gentleman Caller Waving Good-bye!—Gaily."*)
>   (*At this moment Amanda rushes brightly back in the front room. She bears a pitcher of fruit punch in an old-fashioned cut-glass pitcher and a plate of macaroons. The plate has a gold border and poppies painted on it.*)

Amanda: Well, well, well! Isn't the air delightful after the shower? I've made you children a little liquid refreshment. (*Turns gaily to the gentleman caller.*) Jim, do you know that song about lemonade?
"Lemonade, lemonade
Made in the shade and stirred with a spade—
Good enough for any old maid!"

Jim (*uneasily*):   Ha-ha! No—I never heard it.

Amanda: Why, Laura! You look so serious!

Jim: We were having a serious conversation.

Amanda: Good! Now you're better acquainted!

Jim (*uncertainly*):   Ha-ha! Yes.

Amanda: You modern young people are much more serious-minded than my generation. I was so gay as a girl!

Jim: You haven't changed, Mrs. Wingfield.

Amanda: Tonight I'm rejuvenated! The gaiety of the occasion, Mr. O'Connor! (*She tosses her head with a peal of laughter. Spills lemonade.*) Oooo! I'm baptizing myself!

Jim: Here—let me—

Amanda (setting the pitcher down): There now. I discovered we had some maraschino cherries. I dumped them in, juice and all!

Jim: You shouldn't have gone to that trouble, Mrs. Wingfield.

Amanda: Trouble, trouble? Why it was loads of fun! Didn't you hear me cutting up in the kitchen? I bet your ears were burning! I told Tom how outdone with him I was for keeping you to himself so long a time! He should have brought you over much, much sooner! Well, now that you've found your way, I want you to be a very frequent caller! Not just occasional but all the time. Oh, we're going to have a lot of gay times together! I see them coming! Mmm, just breathe that air! So fresh, and the moon's so pretty! I'll skip back out—I know where my place is when young folks are having a—serious conversation!

Jim: Oh, don't go out, Mrs. Wingfield. The fact of the matter is I've got to be going.

Amanda: Going, now? You're joking! Why, it's only the shank of the evening, Mr. O'Connor!

Jim: Well, you know how it is.

Amanda: You mean you're a young workingman and have to keep workingmen's hours. We'll let you off early tonight. But only on the condition that next time you stay later. What's the best night for you? Isn't Saturday night the best night for you workingmen?

Jim: I have a couple of time clocks to punch, Mrs. Wingfield. One at morning, another one at night!

Amanda: My, but you *are* ambitious! You work at night, too?

Jim: No, Ma'am, not work but—Betty! (*He crosses deliberately to pick up his hat. The band at the Paradise Dance Hall goes into a tender waltz.*)

Amanda: Betty? Betty? Who's—Betty! (*There is an ominous cracking sound in the sky.*)

Jim: Oh, just a girl. The girl I go steady with! (*He smiles charmingly. The sky falls.*)

(*Legend: "The Sky Falls."*)

Amanda (a long-drawn exhalation): Ohhhh . . . Is it a serious romance, Mr. O'Connor?

Jim: We're going to be married the second Sunday in June.

Amanda: Ohhhh—how nice! Tom didn't mention that you were engaged to be married.

Jim: The cat's not out of the bag at the warehouse yet. You know how they are. They call you Romeo and stuff like that. (*He stops at the oval mirror to put on his hat. He carefully shapes the brim and the crown to give a discreetly dashing effect.*) It's been a wonderful evening, Mrs. Wingfield. I guess this is what they mean by Southern hospitality.

Amanda: It really wasn't anything at all.

Jim: I hope it don't seem like I'm rushing off. But I promised Betty I'd pick her up at the Wabash depot, an' by the time I get my jalopy down there her train'll be in. Some women are pretty upset if you keep 'em waiting.

Amanda: Yes, I know—The tyranny of women! (*Extends her hand.*) Good-bye, Mr. O'Connor. I wish you luck—and happiness—and success! All three of them, and so does Laura!—Don't you, Laura?

Laura: Yes!

Jim (taking her hand):   Good-bye, Laura. I'm certainly going to treasure that souvenir. And don't you forget the good advice I gave you. (*Raises his voice to a cheery shout.*) So long, Shakespeare! Thanks again, ladies—Good night!

> (*He grins and ducks jauntily out.*)
> (*Still bravely grimacing, Amanda closes the door on the gentleman caller. Then she turns back to the room with a puzzled expression. She and Laura don't dare to face each other. Laura crouches beside the victrola to wind it.*)

Amanda (faintly):   Things have a way of turning out so badly. I don't believe that I would play the victrola. Well, well—well—Our gentleman caller was engaged to be married! Tom!

Tom (from back):   Yes, Mother?

Amanda: Come in here a minute. I want to tell you something awfully funny.

Tom (enters with macaroon and a glass of the lemonade):   Has the gentleman caller gotten away already?

Amanda: The gentleman caller has made an early departure. What a wonderful joke you played on us!

Tom: How do you mean?

Amanda: You didn't mention that he was engaged to be married.

Tom: Jim? Engaged?

Amanda: That's what he just informed us.

Tom: I'll be jiggered! I didn't know about that.

Amanda: That seems very peculiar.

Tom: What's peculiar about it?

Amanda: Didn't you call him your best friend down at the warehouse?

Tom: He is, but how did I know?

Amanda: It seems extremely peculiar that you wouldn't know your best friend was going to be married!

Tom: The warehouse is where I work, not where I know things about people!

Amanda: You don't know things anywhere! You live in a dream; you manufacture illusions! (*He crosses to door.*) Where are you going?

Tom: I'm going to the movies.

Amanda: That's right, now that you've had us make such fools of ourselves. The effort, the preparations, all the expense! The new floor lamp, the rug, the clothes for Laura! All for what? To entertain some other girl's fiancé! Go to the movies, go! Don't think about us, a mother deserted, an unmarried sister who's crippled and has no job! Don't let anything interfere with your selfish pleasure! Just go, go, go—to the movies!

Tom: All right, I will! The more you shout about my selfishness to me the quicker I'll go, and I won't go to the movies!

Amanda: Go, then! Then go to the moon—you selfish dreamer!

(*Tom smashes his glass on the floor. He plunges out on the fire escape, slamming the door. Laura screams—cut by door.*)

(*Dance-hall music up. Tom goes to the rail and grips it desperately, lifting his face in the chill white moonlight penetrating the narrow abyss of the alley.*)

(*Legend on screen: "And so Good-bye . . ."*)

(*Tom's closing speech is timed with the interior pantomime. The interior scene is played as though viewed through soundproof glass. Amanda appears to be making a comforting speech to Laura who is huddled upon the sofa. Now that we cannot hear the mother's speech, her silliness is gone and she has dignity and tragic beauty. Laura's dark hair hides her face until at the end of the speech she lifts it to smile at her mother. Amanda's gestures are slow and graceful, almost dancelike, as she comforts the daughter. At the end of her speech she glances a moment at the father's picture—then withdraws through the portieres. At close of Tom's speech, Laura blows out the candles, ending the play.*)

Tom: I didn't go to the moon, I went much further—for time is the longest distance between two places—Not long after that I was fired for writing a poem on the lid of a shoebox. I left Saint Louis. I descended the steps of this fire escape for a last time and followed, from then on, in my father's footsteps, attempting to find in motion what was lost in space—I traveled around a great deal. The cities swept about me like dead leaves, leaves that were brightly colored but torn away from the branches. I would have stopped, but I was pursued by something. It always came upon me unawares, taking me altogether by surprise. Perhaps it was a familiar bit of music. Perhaps it was only a piece of transparent glass—Perhaps I am walking along a street at night, in some strange city, before I have found companions. I pass the lighted window of a shop where perfume is sold. The window is filled with pieces of colored glass, tiny transparent bottles in delicate colors, like bits of a shattered rainbow. Then all at once my sister touches my shoulder. I turn around and look into her eyes . . . Oh, Laura, Laura, I tried to leave you behind me, but I am more faithful than I intended to be! I reach for a cigarette, I cross the street, I run into the movies or a bar, I buy a drink, I speak to the nearest stranger—anything that can blow your candles out! (*Laura bends over the candles.*)—for nowadays the world is lit by lightning! Blow out your candles, Laura— and so good-bye. . . .

> (*She blows the candles out.*)
> (*The scene dissolves.*)

Paula Vogel

Paula Vogel directs Brown University's MFA Playwriting Program and has been a successful screenwriter as well as dramatist. She has won numerous awards for her work, including a National Endowment for the Arts prize and two fellowships to the MacDowell Colony, at which The Baltimore Waltz *was first written in 1989.* The Baltimore Waltz *(1991) won the Obie Award for best play in 1991–1992 and has been produced in numerous theaters throughout the United States. Among Vogel's plays are* The Oldest Profession *(1992),* And Baby Makes Seven *(1993), and* Hot 'N' Throbbing *(1994).* The Baltimore Waltz *is an imaginary trip to Europe, a trip that her brother Carl invited her to take in 1986. She turned down the chance because of time and money problems, but she did not know then that her brother was HIV positive. The doctors in the play are talking an unintelligible language of technical jargon, and the hospital is a cool, antiseptic environment in which the pleasures of Europe can only be imagined. The play is about languages, communication, and trips not taken. Much of it takes place in the imagination as mediated by popular films, such as* The Third Man. *The result is dreamlike expressionism, but completely within the realm of experience of a modern audience.*

Playwright's Note

In 1986, my brother Carl invited me to join him in a joint excursion to Europe. Due to pressures of time and money, I declined, never dreaming that he was HIV positive. This is the letter he wrote me after his first bout with pneumonia at Johns Hopkins Hospital in Baltimore, Maryland. He died on January 9, 1988.

As executor of his estate, I give permission to all future productions to reprint Carl's letter in the accompanying program. I would appreciate letting him speak to us in his own words.

The Baltimore Waltz—*a journey with Carl to a Europe that exists only in the imagination—was written during the summer of 1989 at the MacDowell Colony, New Hampshire.*

Paula Vogel

March 1987

Dear Paula:

I thought I would jot down some of my thoughts about the (shall we say) production values of my ceremony. Oh God—I can hear you groaning—everybody wants to direct. Well, I want a good show, even though my role has been reduced involuntarily from player to prop.

First, concerning the choice between a religious ceremony and a memorial service. I know the family considers my Anglican observances as irrelevant as Shinto. However, I wish prayers in some recognizably traditional form to be said, prayers that give thanks to the Creator for the gift of life and the hope of reunion. For reasons which you appreciate, I prefer a woman cleric, if possible, to lead the prayers. Here are two names: Phebe Coe, Epiphany Church; the Rev. Doris Mote, Holy Evangelists. Be sure to make a generous contribution from the estate for the cleric.

As for the piece of me I leave behind, here are your options:

(1) open casket, full drag.

(2) open casket, bum up (you'll know where to place the calla lilies, won't you?).

(3) closed casket, interment with the grandparents.

(4) cremation and burial of my ashes.

(5) cremation and dispersion of my ashes in some sylvan spot.

I would really like good music. My tastes in these matters run to the highbrow: Faure's "Pre Jesu" from his Requiem, Gluck's "Dance of the Blessed Spirits" from Orfeo, "La Virgina Dell'Angeli" from Verdi's Forza. But my favorite song is "I Dream of Jeannie," and I wouldn't mind a spiritual like "Steal Away." Also, perhaps, "Nearer My God to Thee." Didn't Jeannette MacDonald sing that di-vinely in "San Francisco"?

Finally, would you read or have read A.E. Housman's "Loveliest of Trees"?

Well, my dear, that's that. Should I be lain with Grandma and Papa Ben, do stop by for a visit from year to year. And feel free to chat. You'll find me a good listener.

Love, Brother

To the memory of Carl—because I cannot sew.

Ron Vawter:

"*. . . I always saw myself as a surrogate who, in the absence of anyone else, would stand in for him. And even now, when I'm in front of an audience and I feel good, I hearken back to that feeling, that I'm standing in for them.*"

Breaking the Rules, David Savran

Characters
  Anna
  Carl, her brother
  The Third Man/Doctor, who also plays:
      Harry Lime
      Public Health Official
      Airport Security Guard
      Garçon
      Customs Official
      The Little Dutch Boy at Age 50
      Munich Virgin
      Radical Student Activist
      Concierge
      Dr. Todesrocheln
      and all other parts.

  (Setting: The Baltimore Waltz takes place in a hospital [perhaps in a lounge, corridor or waiting room] in Baltimore, Maryland.)
  (Notes: The lighting should be highly stylized, lush, dark and imaginative, in contrast to the hospital white silence of the last scene. Wherever possible, prior to the last scene, the director is encouraged to score the production with music—every cliché of the European experience as imagined by Hollywood.)
  (ANNA might be dressed in a full slip/negligee and a trench coat. CARL is dressed in flannel pajamas and a blazer or jacket. The stuffed rabbit should be in every scene with CARL after Scene VI. THE THIRD MAN should wear latex gloves throughout the entire play.)

THE BALTIMORE WALTZ   1991

SCENE I

(Three distinct areas on stage: Anna, stage right, in her trench coat, clutching the Berlitz Pocket Guide to Europe; Carl, stage left, wearing pajamas and blazer; The Third Man/Doctor in his lab coat and with stethoscope, is center.)

Anna (reads from her book. Her accents are execrable):   "Help me please." Dutch: "Kunt U mij helpn, alstublieft?" "There's nothing I can do." French:—"I have no memory." *(Reading.)* "Il n'y a rien a faire." "Where are the toilets?" "Wo sind die Toiletten?" I've never been abroad. It's not that I don't want to—but the language terrifies me. I was traumatized by a junior high school French teacher and, after that, it was a lost cause. I think that's the reason I went into elementary education. Words like bureau, bidet, bildungsroman raise a sweat. Oh,

I want to go. Carl—he's my brother, you'll meet him shortly—he desperately wants to go. But then, he can speak six languages. He's the head librarian of literature and languages at the San Francisco Public. It's a very important position. The thought of eight-hundred-year-old houses perched on the sides of mountains and rivers whose names you've only seen in the Sunday Times crossword puzzles—all of that is exciting. But I'm not going without him. He's read so much. I couldn't possibly go without him. You see, I've never been abroad—unless you count Baltimore, Maryland.

Carl: Good morning, boys and girls. It's Monday morning, and it's time for "Reading Hour with Uncle Carl" once again, here at the North Branch of the San Francisco Public Library. This is going to be a special reading hour. It's my very last reading hour with you. Friday will be my very last day with the San Francisco Public as children's librarian. Why? Do any of you know what a pink slip is? (*Carl holds up a rectangle of pink.*) It means I'm going on a paid leave of absence for two weeks. Shelley Bizio, the branch supervisor, has given me my very own pink slip. I got a pink slip because I wear this—(*He points to a pink triangle on his lapel.*) A pink triangle. Now, I want you all to take the pink construction paper in front of you, and take your scissors, and cut out pink triangles. There's tape at every table, so you can wear them too! Make some for Mom and Dad, and your brothers and sisters. Very good, Fabio. Oh, that's a beautiful pink triangle, Tse Heng. Now before we read our last story together, I thought we might have a sing-along. Your parents can join in, if they'd like to. Oh, don't be shy. Let's do "Here we go round the Mulberry Bush." Remember that one? (*He begins to sing. He also demonstrates.*) "Here we go round the Mulberry Bush, the Mulberry Bush, the Mulberry Bush; Here we go round the Mulberry Bush, so early in the morning."

"This is the way we pick our nose, pick our nose, pick our nose; This is the way we pick our nose, so early in the morning."

Third verse! (*He makes a rude gesture with his middle finger.*)

"This is the way we go on strike, go on strike, go on strike; this is the way we go on strike, so early in the—"

What, Mrs. Bizio? I may leave immediately? I do not have to wait until Friday to collect unemployment? Why, thank you, Mrs. Bizio.

Well, boys and girls, Mrs. Bizio will take over now. Bear with her, she's personality-impaired. I want you to be very good and remember me. I'm leaving for an immediate vacation with my sister on the east coast, and I'll think of you as I travel. Remember to wear those pink triangles. (*To his supervisor.*) I'm going. I'm going. You don't have to be rude. They enjoyed it. We'll take it up with the union. (*Shouting.*) In a language you might understand, up-pay ours-yay!

Anna: It's the language that terrifies me.

Carl: Lesson Number One: Subject position. I. Je. Ich. Ik. I'm sorry. Je
   regrette. Es tut mir leid.°
Anna: But we decided to go when the doctor gave us his verdict.
Doctor: I'm sorry.
Carl: I'm sorry.
Doctor: There's nothing we can do.
Anna: But what?
Carl: How long?
Anna: Explain it to me. Very slowly. So I can understand. Excuse me,
   could you tell me again?
Doctor: There are exudative and proliferative inflammatory alterations of
   the endocardium, consisting of necrotic debris, fibrinoid material, and
   disintegrating fibroblastic cells.
Carl: Oh, sweet Jesus.
Doctor: It may be acute or subacute, caused by various bacteria:
   streptococci, staphylococci, enterococci, gonococci, gram negative
   bacilli, etc. It may be due to other micro-organisms, of course, but
   there is a high mortality rate with or without treatment. And there is
   usually rapid destruction and metastases.
Carl: Anna—
Anna: I'm right here, darling. Right here.
Carl: Could you explain it very slowly?
Doctor: Also known as Loffler's syndrome, i.e., eosinophilia, resulting in
   fibroblastic thickening, persistent tachycardia, hepatomegaly,
   splenomegaly, serious effusions into the pleural cavity with edema. It
   may be Brugia malayi or Wuchereria bancofti—also known as
   Weingarten's syndrome. Often seen with effusions, either exudate or
   transudate.
Anna: Carl—
Carl: I'm here, darling. Right here.
Anna: It's the language that terrifies me.

Es tut mir leid: I'm sorry.

SCENE II

Carl: Medical Straight Talk: Part One.
Anna: So you're telling me that you really don't know?
Doctor: I'm afraid that medical science has only a small foothold in this
   area. But of course, it would be of great benefit to our knowledge if
   you would consent to observation here at Johns Hopkins—
Carl: Why? Running out of laboratory rats?!
Anna: Oh, no. I'm sorry. I can't do that. Can you tell me at least how it
   was . . . contracted?

Doctor: Well—we're not sure, yet. It's only a theory at this stage, but one that seems in great favor at the World Health Organization. We think it comes from the old cultus ornatus—

Carl: Toilet seats?

Anna: Toilet seats! My God. Mother was right. She always said—

Carl: And never, ever, in any circumstances, in bus stations—

Anna: Toilet seats? Cut down in the prime of youth by a toilet seat?

Doctor: Anna—I may call you Anna?—you teach school, I believe?

Anna: Yes, first grade. What does that have—

Doctor: Ah, yes. We're beginning to see a lot of this in elementary schools. Anna—I may call you Anna? With assurances of complete confidentiality—we need to ask you very specific questions about the body, body fluids, and body functions. As mature adults, as scientists and educators. To speak frankly—when you needed to relieve yourself—where did you make wa-wa?

Anna: There's a faculty room. But why—how—

Doctor: You never, ever used the johnny in your classroom?

Anna: Well, maybe once or twice. There's no lock, and Robbie Matthews always tries to barge in. Sometimes I just can't get the time to—surely you're not suggesting that—

Doctor: You did use the facilities in your classroom? (*The Doctor makes notes from this.*)

Carl: Is that a crime? When you've got to go, you've got to—

Anna: I can't believe that my students would transmit something like this—

Doctor: You have no idea. Five-year-olds can be deadly. It seems to be an affliction, so far, of single schoolteachers. Schoolteachers with children of their own develop an immunity to ATD . . . Acquired Toilet Disease.

Anna: I see. Why hasn't anybody heard of this disease?

Doctor: Well, first of all, the Center for Disease Control doesn't wish to inspire an all-out panic in communities. Secondly, we think education on this topic is the responsibility of the NEA, not the government. And if word of this pestilence gets out inappropriately, the PTA is going to be all over the school system demanding mandatory testing of every toilet seat in every lavatory. It's kindling for a political disaster.

Anna (taking the Doctor aside):   I want to ask you something confidentially. Something that my brother doesn't need to hear. What's the danger of transmission?

Doctor: There's really no danger to anyone in the immediate family. You must use precautions.

Anna: Because what I want to know is . . . can you transmit this thing by . . . by doing—what exactly do you mean by precautions?

Doctor: Well, I guess you should do what your mother always told you. You know, wash your hands before and after going to the bathroom. And never lick paper money or coins in any currency.

Anna: So there's no danger to anyone by . . . what I mean, Doctor, is that I can't infect anyone by—

Doctor: Just use precautions.

Anna: Because, in whatever time this schoolteacher has left, I intend to fuck my brains out.

Doctor: Which means, in whatever time is left, she can fuck her brains out.

SCENE III Carl and the Doctor.

Carl (agitated):   I'll tell you what. If Sandra Day O'Connor sat on just one infected potty, the media would be clamoring to do articles on ATD. If just one grandchild of George Bush caught this thing during toilet training, that would have been the last we had heard about the space program. Why isn't someone doing something?! I'm sorry. I know you're one of the converted. You're doing . . . well, everything you can. I'd like to ask you something in confidence, something my sister doesn't need to hear. Is there any hope at all?

Doctor: Well, I suppose there's . . . always hope.

Carl: Any experimental drugs? Treatments?

Doctor: Well, they're trying all sorts of things abroad. Our hands are tied here by NIH and the FDA, you understand. There is a long-shot avenue to explore, nothing, you understand, that I personally endorse, but there is an eighty-year-old urologist overseas who's been working in this field for some time—

Carl: We'll try anything.

Doctor: His name is Dr. Todesrocheln. He's somewhat unorthodox, outside the medical community in Vienna. It's gonna cost you. Mind you, this is not an endorsement.

Anna: You hear the doctor through a long-distance corridor. Your ears are functioning, but the mind is numb. You try to listen as you swim toward his sentences in the fluorescent light in his office. But you don't believe it at first. This is how I'd like to die: with dignity. No body secretions—like Merle Oberon° in "Wuthering Heights." With a somewhat becoming flush, and a transcendental gaze. Luminous eyes piercing the veil of mortal existence. The windows are open to the fresh breeze blowing off the moors. Oh. And violins in the background would be nice, too. (*Music: violins playing Strauss swell in the background.*)

Merle Oberon: Popular actress in the 1940s.

SCENE IV The Phone Call.

The Third Man: Lesson Number Two: Basic dialogue. The phone call. Hello. I would like to speak to Mr. Lime, please.

Carl: Entschuldigen Sie, bitte°—operator? Operator? Hello? Guten Tag? Kann ich bitte mit Herrn Lime sprechen?° Harry? Harry? Wie geht es dir?!° Listen, I . . . can you hear . . . no, I'm in Baltimore . . . yeah, not since Hopkins . . . no, there's—well, there is something up. No, dear boy, seriously—it's my sister. ATD.

The Third Man: ATD? Jesus, that's tough, old man. You've got to watch where you sit these days. She's a sweet kid. Yeah. Yeah. Wait a second. (*Offstage.*) Inge? Inge, baby? Ein Bier, bitte,° baby. Ja. Ja. You too, baby. (*Pause.*) Okay. Dr. Todelsrocheln? Yeah, you might say I know him. But don't tell anybody I said that. There's also a new drug they've got over here. Black market. I might be able to help you. I said might. But it's gonna cost you. (*Cautiously, ominously.*) Do you still have the rabbit?

Carl: I'll bring the rabbit.

The Third Man: Good. A friend of mine will be in touch. And listen, old man . . . if anybody asks you, you don't know me. I'll see you in a month. You know where to find me.

The Third Man and Carl (simultaneously):   Click.

Entschuldigen Sie, bitte: I beg your pardon, please.   *Guten Tag? . . . sprechen?:* Good day. May I please speak with Harry Lime?   *Wie geht es dir?:* How are you?   *Ein Bier, bitte:* A beer, please.

SCENE V

The Third Man: Lesson Number Three: Pronouns and the possessive case. I, you, he, she and it. They and We. Yours, mine, and ours.

Voice of Anna: There's nothing I can do. There's nothing you can do. There's nothing he, she or it can do. There's nothing we can do. There's nothing they can do.

Anna: So what are we going to do?

Carl: Start packing, sister dear.

Anna: Europe? You mean it?

Carl: We'll mosey about France and Germany, and then work our way down to Vienna.

Anna: What about your job?

Carl: It's only a job.

Anna: It's a very important job! Head of the entire San Francisco Public—

Carl: They'll hold my job for me. I'm due for a leave.

Anna: Oh, honey. Can we afford this?

Carl: It's only money.

Anna: It's your money.

Carl: It's our money.

SCENE VI

The Third Man: Lesson Four: Present tense of faire. What are we going to
    do? Qu'est-ce qu'on va faire?
Anna: So what are we going to do?
Carl: We'll see this doctor in Vienna.
Anna: Dr. Todelsrocheln?
Carl: We have to try.
Anna: A urologist?
Carl: He's working on a new drug.
Anna: A European urologist?
Carl: What options do we have?
Anna: Wait a minute. What are his credentials? Who is this guy?
Carl: He was trained at the Allgemeines Krankenhaus during the Empire.
Anna: Yeah? Just what was he doing from, say, 1938 to 1945? Research?
Carl: It's best not to ask too many questions. There are people who
    swear by his work.
Anna: What's his specialty?
Carl: Well, actually, he's a practitioner of uriposia.
Anna: He writes poems about urine?
Carl: No. He drinks it.
Anna: I'm not going.
Carl: Let's put off judgment until we arrange a consultation . . . my god,
    you're so messy. Look at how neat my suitcase is in comparison. You'll
    never find a thing in there.
Anna: I refuse to drink my own piss for medical science. (*Carl grabs a
    stuffed rabbit and thrusts it in Anna's suitcase.*)
Anna: What are you doing?
Carl: We can't leave bunny behind.
Anna: What is a grown man like you doing with a stuffed rabbit?
Carl: I can't sleep without bunny.
Anna: I didn't know you slept with . . . stuffed animals.
Carl: There's a lot you don't know about me.

SCENE VII

The Third Man: Lesson Five: Basic dialogue. At the airport. We are going
    to Paris. What time does our flight leave? Nous allons a Paris. Quelle
    est l'heure de depart de notre vol? (*The Third Man becomes an Airport
    Security Guard.*)
Airport Security Guard: Okay. Next. Please remove your keys and all
    other metallic items. Place all belongings on the belt. Next. (*Carl and
    Anna carry heavy luggage. Carl halts.*)
Carl: Wait. I need your suitcase. (*He opens Anna's luggage and begins to
    rummage around.*)

Anna: Hey!

Carl: It was a mess to begin with. Ah—(*He retrieves the stuffed rabbit.*) There.

Anna: Are you having an anxiety attack?

Carl: You hold it. (*He and Anna stamp, sit and stand on the baggage. Carl manages to relock the bag.*)

Anna: What is wrong with you?

Carl: X-rays are bad for bunny.

Airport Security Guard: Next. Please remove all metallic objects. Keys. Eyeglasses. Gold Fillings. Metallic objects?

Carl: Go on. You first. (*Anna passes through, holding the stuffed rabbit. Carl sighs, relieved. Carl passes through. The Airport Security Guard stops him.*)

Airport Security Guard: One moment, please. (*The Airport Security Guard almost strip searches him. He uses a metallic wand which makes loud, clicking noises. Finally, he nods. He hands Anna and Carl their bags, still suspiciously looking at Carl.*)

Anna: Okay, bunny—Paris, here we come!

SCENE VIII

The Third Man (simultaneously with Carl's next lines):   Lesson Six. Direct pronouns. I am tired. And my sister looks at herself in the mirror.

Carl: Sixieme Leçon: Pronoms—complements directs. Je suis fatigué. Et ma soeur—elle se regarde dans la glace. (*Carl climbs into a double bed with the stuffed rabbit. Anna stares into a mirror. The Third Man, apart, stands in their bedroom.*)

The Third Man: The first separation—your first sense of loss. You were five—your brother was seven. Your parents would not let you sleep in the same bed anymore. They removed you to your own bedroom. You were too old, they said. But every now and then, when they turned off the lights and went downstairs—when the dark scared you, you would rise and go to him. And he would let you nestle under his arm, under the covers, where would fall to sleep, breathing in the scent of your own breath and his seven-year-old body.

Carl: Come to bed, sweetie. Bunny and I are waiting. We're going to be jetlagged for a while. (*Anna continues to stare in the mirror.*)

Anna: It doesn't show yet.

Carl: No one can tell. Let's get some sleep, honey.

Anna: I don't want anyone to know.

Carl: It's not a crime. It's an illness.

Anna: I don't want anybody to know.

Carl: It's your decision. Just don't tell anyone . . . what . . . you do for a living. (*Anna joins Carl in the bed. He holds her hand.*)

Anna: Well, there's one good thing about travelling in Europe . . . and about dying.
Carl: What's that?
Anna: I get to sleep with you again.

SCENE IX

Carl: Medical Straight Talk: Part Two. (*The Third Man becomes a Public Health Official.*)
Public Health Official: Here at the Department of Health and Human Services we are announcing Operation Squat. There is no known cure for ATD right now, and we are recognizing the urgency of this dread disease by recognizing it as our 82nd national health priority. Right now ATD is the fourth major cause of death of single schoolteachers, ages 24 to 40 . . . behind school buses, lockjaw and playground accidents. The best policy, until a cure can be found, is of education and prevention. (*Anna and Carl hold up posters of a toilet seat in a circle with a red diagonal slash.*) If you are in the high-risk category— elementary school teachers, classroom aides, custodians and playground drug pushers—follow these simple guides. (*Anna and Carl hold up copies of the educational pamphlets.*)
Public Health Official:
Do: Use the facilities in your own home before departing for school.
Do: Use the facilities in your own home as soon as you return from school.
Do: Hold it.
Don't: Eat meals in public restrooms.
Don't: Flush lavatory equipment and then suck your digits. If absolutely necessary to relieve yourself at work, please remember the Department of Health and Human Services ATD slogan: Don't sit, do squat.

SCENE X

(*Music: accordian playing "La vie en rose." Anna and Carl stroll.*)
Carl: Of course, the Left Bank has always been a haven for outcasts, foreigners and students, since the time that Abelard fled the Ile de La Cité to found the university here—
Anna: Oh, look. Is that the Eiffel Tower? It looks so . . . phallic.
Carl: And it continued to serve as a haven for the avant-garde of the Twenties, the American expatriate community that could no longer afford Montparnesse—
Anna: My god, they really do smoke Gauloises° here.

Gauloises: Brand of French cigarettes.

Carl: And, of course, the Dada and Surrealists who set up camp here after World War I and their return from Switzerland—(*The Third Man, in a trench coat and red beret, crosses the stage.*)

Anna: Are we being followed?

Carl: Is your medication making you paranoid? (*Pause.*) Now, over here is the famous spot where Gertrude supposedly said to her brother Leo—(*The Third Man follows them.*)

Anna: I know. God is the answer. What is the question?—I'm not imagining it. That man has been trailing us from the Boulevard St. Michel.

Carl: Are you getting hungry?

Anna: I'm getting tired.

Carl: Wait. Let's just whip around the corner to the Café St. Michel where Hemingway, after an all-night bout, threw up his shrimp heads all over Scott's° new suede shoes—which really was a movable feast. (*The Third Man is holding an identical stuffed rabbit and looks at them.*)

Anna: Carl! Carl! Look! That man over there!

Carl: So? They have stuffed rabbits over here, too. Let's go.

Anna: Why is he following us? He's got the same—

Carl: It's your imagination. How about a little déjeuner? (*Anna and Carl walk to a small table and chairs.*)

Hemingway . . . Scott: Ernest Hemingway (1899–1961) and F. Scott Fitzgerald (1896–1940), in this collection. They lived in Paris for a time, like many American artists.

SCENE XI

Garçon (with a thick Peter Sellers French accent):   It was a simple bistro affair by French standards. He had le Veau Prince Orloff, she le boeuf a la mode—a simple dish of haricots verts, and a Medoc to accompany it all. He barely touched his meal. She mopped the sauces with the bread. As their meal progressed, Anna thought of the lunches she packed back home. For the past ten years, hunched over in the faculty room at McCormick Elementary, this is what Anna ate: on Mondays, pressed chipped chicken sandwiches with mayonaise on white; on Tuesdays, soggy tuna sandwiches; on Wednesdays, Velveeta cheese and baloney; on Thursdays, drier pressed chicken on the now-stale white bread; on Fridays, Velveeta and tuna. She always had a small wax envelope of carrot sticks or celery, and a can of Diet Pepsi. Anna, as she ate in the bistro, wept. What could she know of love?

Carl: Why are you weeping?

Anna: It's just so wonderful.

Carl: You're a goose.

Anna: I've wasted over thirty years on convenience foods. (*The Garçon approaches the table.*)

Garçon: Is everything all right?

Anna: Oh God. Yes—yes—it's wonderful.

Carl: My sister would like to see the dessert tray. (*Anna breaks out in tears again. The Garçon shrugs and exits. He reappears a few minutes later as The Third Man, this time with a trench coat and blue beret. He sits at an adjacent table and stares in their direction.*)

Anna: Who is that man? Do you know him? (*Carl hastily looks at The Third Man.*)

Carl: No, I've never seen him before. (*The Third Man brings the stuffed rabbit out of his trench coat.*)

Anna: He's flashing his rabbit at you. (*Carl rises.*)

Carl: Excuse me. I think I'll go to les toilettes.

Anna: Carl! Be careful! Don't sit! (*Carl exits. The Third Man waits a few seconds, looks at Anna, and then follows Carl without expression.*) What is it they do with those rabbits? (*A split second later, the Garçon reenters with the dessert tray. Anna ogles him.*)

Garçon: Okay. We have la creme plombiere pralinée, un bavarois a l'orange, et ici we have une Charlotte Malakoff aux Framboises. Our specialite is le gateau de crepes a la Normande. What would mademoiselle like? (*Anna has obviously not been looking at the dessert tray.*)

Anna (sighing):   Ah, yes. (*The Garçon smiles.*)

Garçon: Vous êtes Americaine? This is your first trip to Paris?

Anna: Yes.

Garçon: And you do not speak at all French?

Anna: No. (*The Garçon smiles.*)

Garçon (suggestively):   Bon. Would you like la spécialité de la maison?°

Spécialité de la maison: Specialty of the house.

SCENE XII

Carl: Excercise: La Carte. La specialité de la maison. Back at the hotel, Anna sampled the Garçon's specialité de la maison while her brother browsed the Louvre. (*Anna and the Garçon are shapes beneath the covers of the bed. Carl clutches his stuffed rabbit.*) Jean Baptiste Camille Corot lived from 1796 to 1875. Although he began his career by studying in the classic tradition, his later paintings reveal the influence of the Italian style.

Anna (muffled):   Ah! Yes!

Garçon (also muffled):   Ah! Oui!

Carl: He traveled extensively around the world, and in the salon of 1827 his privately lauded techniques were displayed in public.

Anna: Yes—oh, yes, yes!

Garçon: Mais oui!

Carl: Before the Academy had accepted realism, Corot's progressive paintings, his clear sighted observations of nature, revealed a fresh almost spritely quality of light, tone and composition.

Anna: Yes—that's right—faster—

Garçon: Plus vite?

Anna: Faster—

Garçon: Encore! Plus vite!

Anna: Wait!

Garçon: Attends?

Carl: It was his simplicity, and his awareness of color that brought a fresh wind into the staid academy—

Garçon: Maintenant?

Anna: Lower—faster—lower—

Garçon: Plus bas—plus vite—plus bas—

Carl: He was particularly remembered and beloved for his championing the cause of younger artists with more experimental techniques, bringing the generosity of his advancing reputation to their careers.

Anna: Yes—I—I—I—I—!

Garçon: Je—je! Je!! Je! (*Pause.*)

Carl: In art, as in life, some things need no translation.

Garçon: Gauloise?

Carl: For those of you who are interested, in the next room are some stunning works by Delacroix.

SCENE XIII *Back at the Hotel.*

Carl: Lesson Seven: Basic vocabulary. Parts of the body. (*Carl, slightly out of the next scene, watches them. Anna sits up in bed. The Garçon is asleep beneath the sheet.*)

Anna: I did read one book once in French. Le Petit Prince. Lying here, watching him sleep, I look at his breast and remember the Rose with its single, pathetic thorn for protection. And here—his puckered red nipple, lying poor and vulnerable on top of his blustering breast plate. It's really so sweet about men. (*She kisses the Garçon's breast. The Garçon stirs.*)

Garçon: Encore?

Anna: What is the word—in French—for this? She fingers his breast.

Garçon: For un homme—le sein. For une femme—la mamelle.

Anna: Sein?

Garçon: Oui, sein.

Anna (she kisses his neck):   And this?

Garçon: Le cou.

Anna: Et ici?

Garçon: Bon. Decollette°—(*Anna begins to touch him under the sheet.*)
Anna: And this? (*The Garçon laughs.*)
Garçon: S'il vous plait . . . I am tickling there. Ah. Les couilles.°
Anna: Culle?
Garçon: Non. Couilles. Le cul° is something much different. Ici c'est le cul.
Anna: Oh, yes. That's very different.
Garçon (taking her hand under the sheet):   We sometimes call these also Le Quatrième Etat. The Fourth Estate.
Anna: Really? Because they enjoy being "scooped"?
Garçon: Bien sur.
Anna: And this?
Garçon: Ah. Ma Tour Eiffel. I call it aussi my Charles DeGalle.
Anna: Wow.
Garçon: My grandfather called his Napoleon.
Anna: I see. I guess it runs in your family.
Garçon (modestly):   Oui. Grand-mere—qu'est-ce que c'est le mot en anglais?° Her con—here—ici—do you know what I am meaning?
Anna: You're making yourself completely clear—
Garçon: We called hers the Waterloo de mon grand-pere—(*Anna digs under the sheet more.*)
Anna: And this? (*The Garçon is scandalized.*)
Garçon: Non. There is no word en francais. Pas du tout.°
Anna: For this? There must be—
Garçon: Non! Only the Germans have a word for that. (*Carl enters and casually converses with Anna. Startled, the Garçon covers himself with the sheet.*)
Carl: Hello, darling. Are you feeling better? (*Carl walks to the chair beside the bed and removes the Garçon's clothing.*)
Anna: Yes, much. I needed to lie down. How was the Louvre? (*The Garçon carefully rises from the bed and takes his clothing from Carl, who is holding them out. He creeps cautiously stage left and begins to pull on his clothes.*)
Carl: Oh, Anna. I'm so sorry you missed it. The paintings of David were amazing. The way his paintbrush embraced the body—it was just incredible to stand there and see them in the flesh.
Anna: Ah yes—in the flesh. (*She smiles at the confused Garçon.*)
Carl: Well, sweetie. It's been a thoroughly rewarding day for both of us. I'm for turning in. How about you? (*The Garçon is now fully dressed.*)
Anna: Yes, I'm tired. Here—I've warmed the bed for you. (*She throws back the sheet.*)
Carl: Garçon—l'addition!
Anna (to the Garçon):   Merci beaucoup. (*Anna blows him a kiss. The Garçon takes a few steps out of the scene as Carl climbs into bed.*)

Decollette: Cleavage.   *Couilles:* Ribs.   *Cul:* Backside.   *qu'est-ce que c'est le mot en anglais?:* What is the word in English?   *Pas du tout:* Not at all.

SCENE XIV

The Third Man: Anna has a difficult time sleeping. She is afflicted with night thoughts. According to Elizabeth Kubler-Ross,° there are six stages the terminal patient travels in the course of her illness. The first stage: Denial and Isolation. (*The Third Man stays in the hotel room and watches Carl and Anna in the bed. They are sleeping, when Anna sits upright.*)

Anna: I feel so alone. The ceiling is pressing down on me. I can't believe I am dying. Only at night. Only at night. In the morning, when I open my eyes, I feel absolutely well—without a body. And then the thought comes crashing in my mind. This is the last spring I may see. This is the last summer. It can't be. There must be a mistake. They mixed the specimens up in the hospital. Some poor person is walking around, dying, with the false confidence of my prognosis, thinking themselves well. It's a clerical error. Carl! I can't sleep. Do you think they made a mistake?

Carl: Come back to sleep—(*Carl pulls Anna down on the bed to him, and strokes her brow. They change position on the bed.*)

The Third Man: The second stage: Anger. (*Anna sits bolt upright in bed, angry.*)

Anna: How could this happen to me! I did my lesson plans faithfully for the past ten years! I've taught in classrooms without walls—kept up on new audio-visual aids—I read Summerhill! And I believed it! When the principal assigned me the job of the talent show—and nobody wants to do the talent show—I pleaded for cafeteria duty, bus duty—but no, I got stuck with the talent show. And those kids put on the best darn show that school has ever seen! Which one of them did this to me? Emily Baker? For slugging Johnnie MacIntosh? Johnnie MacIntosh? Because I sent him home for exposing himself to Susy Higgins? Susy Higgins? Because I called her out on her nosepicking? Or those Nader twins? I've spent the best years of my life giving to those kids—it's not—

Carl: Calm down, sweetie. You're angry. It's only natural to be angry. Elizabeth Kubler-Ross says that—

Anna: What does she know about what it feels like to die?! Elizabeth Kubler-Ross can sit on my face! (*Carl and Anna change positions on the bed.*)

The Third Man: The third stage: Bargaining.

Anna: Do you think if I let Elizabeth Kubler-Ross sit on my face I'll get well? (*Carl and Anna change positions on the bed.*)

The Third Man: The fourth stage: Depression. (*Carl sits on the side of the bed beside Anna.*)

Elizabeth Kubler-Ross: Author of several important books on dying.

Carl: Anna—honey—come on, wake up.

Anna: Leave me alone.

Carl: Come on, sweetie . . . you've been sleeping all day now, and you slept all yesterday. Do you want to sleep away our last day in France?

Anna: Why bother?

Carl: You've got to eat something. You've got to fight this. For me.

Anna: Leave me alone. (*Carl lies down beside Anna. They change positions.*)

The Third Man: The fifth stage: Acceptance. (*Anna and Carl are lying in bed, awake. They hold hands.*)

Anna: When I'm gone, I want you to find someone.

Carl: Let's not talk about me.

Anna: No, I want to. It's important to me to know that you'll be happy and taken care of after . . . when I'm gone.

Carl: Please.

Anna: I've got to talk about it. We've shared everything else. I want you to know how it feels . . . what I'm thinking . . . when I hold your hand, and I kiss it . . . I try to memorize what it looks like, your hand . . . I wonder if there's any memory in the grave?

The Third Man: And then there's the sixth stage: Hope. (*Anna and Carl rise from the bed.*)

Carl: How are you feeling?

Anna: I feel good today.

Carl: Do you feel like travelling?

Anna: Yes. It would be nice to see Amsterdam. Together. We might as well see as much as we can while I'm well—

Carl: That's right, sweetie. And maybe you can eat something—

Anna: I'm hungry. That's a good sign, don't you think?

Carl: That's a wonderful sign. You'll see. You'll feel better when you eat.

Anna: Maybe the doctor in Vienna can help.

Carl: That's right.

Anna: What's drinking a little piss? It can't hurt you.

Carl: Right. Who knows? We've got to try.

Anna: I'll think of it as . . . European lager.

Carl: Golden Heidelberg. (*Carl and Anna hum/sing the drinking song from "The Student Prince."*)

SCENE XV

The Third Man: And as Anna and Carl took the train into Holland, the seductive swaying of the TEE-train aroused another sensation. Unbeknownst to Elizabeth Kubler-Ross, there is a seventh stage for the dying. There is a growing urge to fight the sickness of the body with the health of the body. The seventh stage: lust. (*Anna and Carl*

*are seated in a train compartment. Carl holds the stuffed rabbit out to
   Anna.*)
Anna: Why?
Carl: Just take it. Hold it for me. Just through customs.
Anna: Only if you tell me why.
Carl: Don't play games right now. Or we'll be in deep, deep do-do.
   (*Anna reluctantly takes the stuffed rabbit and holds it.*)
Anna: You're scaring me.
Carl: I'm sorry, sweetie. You're the only one I can trust to hold my
   rabbit. Trust me. It's important.
Anna: Then why won't you tell me—?
Carl: There are some things you're better off not knowing.
Anna: Are you smuggling drugs? Jewels?
Carl (whispers): It's beyond measure. It's invaluable to me. That's all I'll
   say. (*In a louder tone.*) Just act normal now.
Customs Official: Uw paspoort, aistublieft. (*Anna and Carl give him their
   passports. Carl is nervous. Anna smiles at the Customs Official a bit
   lasciviously.*) Have you anything to declare?
Anna (whispering): Yes—captain, I'm smuggling contraband. I demand
   to be searched. In private. (*The Customs Official blushes.*)
Customs Official: Excuse me?
Anna: Yes. I said—waar is het damestoilet?
Customs Official: Oh . . . I thought . . . (*The Customs Official giggles.*)
Anna: Yes?
Customs Official: First left. (*The Customs Official returns their passports.*)
   Have a very pleasant stay. (*Anna waves bunny's arm goodbye. The
   Customs Official looks at her, blushes again and retreats. Carl relaxes.*)
Carl: You're good at this. Very good.
Anna: When in Holland, do like the Dutch . . . Mata Hari° was Dutch,
   you know.

Mata Hari: Margarethe Zelle (1876–1917), exotic dancer and famous spy for the Germans in
World War I.

SCENE XVI

Carl: Questions sur le Dialogue. Est-ce que les hommes Hollandais sont
   comme les Francais? Are Dutch men like the French? (*Anna and The
   Little Dutch Boy At Age 50. He wears traditional wooden shoes, trousers
   and vest. His Buster Brown haircut and hat make him look dissipated.*)
The Little Dutch Boy At Age 50: It was kermis-time, the festival in my
   village. And I had too much bier with my school friends, Piet and Jan.
   Ja. Soo—Piet thought we should go to the outer dyke with cans of
   spray paint, after the kermis. So we went.

Here in Noord Brabant there are three walls of defenses against the cruelty of the North Sea. The first dyke is called the Waker—the Watcher; the second dyke is de Slaper—the Sleeper; and the last dyke, which had never before been tested, is known as the Dromer—the Dreamer.

And when we got to the Dreamer, Piet said to me: "Willem, you do it." Meaning I was to write on the walls of the Dreamer. This is why I was always in trouble in school—Piet and Jan would say, "Willem, you do it," and whatever it was—I would do it.

Soo—I took up a can of the paint and in very big letters, I wrote in Dutch that our schoolmaster, Mijnheer Van Doorn, was a gas-passer. Everyone could read the letters from far away. And just as I was finishing this, and Piet and Jan were laughing behind me, I looked—I was on my knees, pressed up against the dyke—and I could see that the wall of the Dreamer was cracking its surface, very fine little lines, like a goose egg when it breaks from within.

And I yelled to my friends—Look! And they came a bit closer, and as we looked, right above my head, a little hole began to peck its way through the clay. And there was just a small trickle of water. And Jan said: "Willem, put your thumb in that hole." And by that time, the hole in the dyke was just big enough to put my thumb in. "Why?" I asked of Jan. "Just do it," he said. And so I did.

And once I put my thumb in, I could not get it out. Suddenly we could hear the waves crashing as The Sleeper began to collapse. Only the Dreamer remained to hold off the savage water. "Help me!" I yelled to Jan and Piet—but they ran away. "Vlug!" I cried—but no one could hear me. And I stayed there, crouching, with my thumb stuck into the clay. And I thought what if the Dreamer should give in, too. I thought how the waves would bear my body like a messenger to the Village. How no one would survive the Flood. Only the church steeple would remain to mark the place where we had lived. How young we were to die. (*Pause.*) Have you ever imagined what it would be like to be face to face with death?

Anna: Yes—yes, I have.

The Little Dutch Boy At Age 50:   And have you ever prayed for deliverance against all hope?

Anna: I—no. I haven't been able to get to that stage. Yet.

The Little Dutch Boy At Age 50:   But the Dreamer held. And finally there came wagons with men from the village, holding lanterns and sand and straw. And they found me there, strung up by my thumb, beside the big black letters: Mijnheer Van Doorn is een gas-passer. And they freed me and said I was a hero, and I became the boy who held back the sea with his thumb.

Anna: Golly. You were very brave.

The Little Dutch Boy At Age 50:   I was stupid. Wrong place, wrong time.

Anna: How long ago did this happen?

The Little Dutch Boy At Age 50 (sadly):   Let us just say it happened a long time ago.

Anna: You've faced death. I wish my brother were here to meet you.

The Little Dutch Boy At Age 50:   Where is he? Wo ist dein bruder?°

Anna: Oh, he stayed in Amsterdam to see the Rijksmuseum and the Van Gogh Museum.

The Little Dutch Boy At Age 50:   And you did not go? You should see them, they are really fantastic.

Anna: Why? What's the use? I won't remember them, I'll have no memory.

The Little Dutch Boy At Age 50:   So you are an American?

Anna: Yes.

The Little Dutch Boy At Age 50:   So, do you want to sleep with me? All the women touristen want to sleep with the little Dutch Boy who put his thumb in the dyke.

Anna: Do you mind so much?

The Little Dutch Boy At Age 50 (shrugs):   Nee. It's a way to make a living, is it niet?

Anna (quietly):   Let's go then.

Wo ist dein bruder?: Where is your brother?

SCENE XVII

Carl: Repetez. En Francais. Where is my brother going? Ou va mon frère? Bien.

Anna: I had just returned from my day trip and left the Central Station. The sun sparkled on the waters of the canal, and I decided to walk back to the hotel. . . . Just then I saw my brother. (*Carl enters in a trench coat, sunglasses, holding the stuffed rabbit.*) I tried to catch up with Carl, dodging bicycles and pedestrians. And then, crossing the Amstel on the Magere Brug, he appeared. (*The Third Man enters, in a trench coat, sunglasses, and with black gloves, holding a stuffed rabbit.*) I trailed them from a discreet distance. (*The Third Man and Carl walk rapidly, not glancing at each other. Carl stops; The Third Man stops a few paces behind. Carl walks; The Third Man walks. Carl stops; The Third Man stops. Finally, they face each other and meet. Quickly, looking surreptitiously around, Carl and The Third Man stroke each other's stuffed rabbits. They quickly part and walk off in opposite directions. Anna rushes to center stage, looking in both directions.*) I tried to follow the man in the trench coat, and crossed behind him over the Amstel, but I lost sight of him in the crowd of men wearing trench coats and sunglasses. I want some answers from my brother. Whatever trouble he's in, he has to share it with me. I want some answers back at the hotel. He's going to talk.

SCENE XVIII

Carl: Questions sur le dialogue. You must learn. Sie mussen lernen.
  (*Anna enters the empty hotel room. On the bed, propped up on pillows, lies
  a stuffed rabbit.*)

Anna: Carl? Carl? Are you back? Carl? (*Anna stops and looks at the stuffed
  rabbit.*)

Carl (from the side):   You were not permitted to play with dolls; dolls are
  for girls. You played with your sister's dolls until your parents found
  out. They gave you a stuffed animal—a thin line was drawn. Rabbits
  were an acceptable surrogate for little boys. You named him Jo-Jo.
  You could not sleep without him. Jo-Jo traveled with you to the
  seashore, to the hotel in New York City when you were seven, to your
  first summer camp. He did not have the flaxen plastic hair of your
  sister's Betsey-Wetsy, but he had long, furry ears, soft white on one
  side, pink satin inside. He let you stroke them. He never betrayed you.
  He taught you to trust in contact. You will love him always. (*Anna
  moves toward the stuffed rabbit.*)

Anna: My brother left you behind, did he? Alone at last. Okay, bunny,
  now you're going to talk. I want some answers. What have you got
  that's so important? (*Just as Anna reaches for the stuffed rabbit, The
  Third Man [in trench coat, sunglasses and black gloves] steps out into the
  room.*)

The Third Man (threateningly):   I wouldn't do that, if I were you. (*Anna
  screams in surprise.*) Now listen. Where is your brother? I have a
  message for him. Tell him he's running out of time. Do you
  understand? (*Anna, scared, nods.*) Good. He'd better not to try to
  dupe us. We're willing to arrange a swap—his sister for the rabbit. Tell
  him we're waiting for him in Vienna. And tell him he'd better bring
  the rabbit to the other side. (*The Third Man leaves. Anna, shaken, sits
  on the bed and holds the stuffed rabbit. She strokes it for comfort. Carl
  enters, in a frenzy. He carries his stuffed rabbit. Anna stares as Carl
  tosses the decoy rabbit away.*)

Carl: Don't ask me any questions. I can't tell you what's happening. Are
  you able to travel? Good. We have to leave Amsterdam tonight.
  There's a train in an hour. We'll go to Germany. Are you packed?

SCENE XIX

Anna and The Third Man (simultaneously):   Wann geht der nachste Zug
  nach Hamburg?° (*German band music swells as Anna and Carl sit in
  their railroad compartment, side by side. Anna, pale, holds the stuffed
  rabbit in her lap.*)

Wann geht der nachste Zug nach Hamburg?:   When is the next train to Hamburg?

Carl: Ah, Saxony, Bavaria, the Black Forest, the Rhineland . . . I love
them all. I think perhaps now would be a good time to show the
slides.

Anna: I'm so sorry. I hate it when people do this to me.

Carl: Nonsense. People like to see slides of other people's trips. These are
in no particular order. We'll only show a few, just to give a taste of the
German countryside.

Anna: Carl took over two hours' worth of slides.

Carl: If you'll just dim the lights, please. (*The Third Man wheels in the
projector and operates it throughout the travelogue.*) Well. Bonn's as
good a place to start as anywhere. This is the view from our snug little
hotel we stayed in. The gateway to the Rhine, the birthplace of
Beethoven, and the resting place of Schumann.
(*Slide: the view of downtown Baltimore from the Ramada Inn near
Johns Hopkins Hospital, overlooking the industrial harbor.*)

Anna: Looks a lot like Baltimore to me.

Carl: My sister jests. As you can see in the slide, one night we splurged
and stayed in a rather dear inn near the Drachenfels mountains, where
Lord Byron had sported.
(*Slide: a close-up of the balcony railing looking into the Ramada Inn
hotel room.*)

Anna (deadpan): This is the room I slept in while I stayed with my
brother Carl.
(*Slide: gutted ruins of inner-city Baltimore near the Jones-Fall
Expressway; rubble and obvious urban blight.*)

Carl: Alas, poor Koln. Practically wiped out by airplane raids during World
War II, and yet, out of this destruction, the cathedral of Koln managed
to survive—one of the most beautiful Gothic churches in the world,
with a superb altar painted by the master artist of Koln, Stefan Lochner.
(*Slide: an impoverished storefront church, a black evangelical sect in
Baltimore.*)
Let's see—what do we have next?
(*Slide: a Sabrett's? hot dog cart with its blue and orange umbrella in
front of Johns Hopkins Hospital.*)
Oh, yes. Let's talk about the food. Whereas I snapped mementos of
the regal pines of the Black Forest, Anna insisted on taking photos of
everything she ate.

Anna: I can remember things I feel.

Carl: Well, then, let's talk about the food. Germany has a more robust
gustatory outlook than the delicate palate of France. The Germans
positively celebrate the pig from snout to tail. I could not convince
Anna to sample the Sulperknochen, which is a Rheingau concoction of
ears, snout, tail and feet.

Sabrett's: Famous urban street-corner hotdog vendor.

Anna: Ugh.
   (Slide: a close-up of vender placing a hot dog on a bun and slathering it with mustard; there are canned sodas in a wide variety.)
Carl: And of course, everything is washed down with beer.
   (Slide: Anna sipping a Bud Lite.)
Anna: It was delicious.
Carl: Enough of food. May we talk about culture, sister, dear? Next slide, please.
   (Slide: the Maryland National Armory; the state penitentiary.)
   Ah, Heidelberg. Dueling scars and castles. Spectacular ruin which serves as the locale for open-air concerts and fireworks . . .
   (Slide: the Baltimore smokestack.)
   . . . and by a quaint cable car, you can reach the peak at Konigstuhl, 2,000 feet high, with its breathtaking view of the Neckar Valley.
   (Slide: the Bromo Seltzer tower in Baltimore.)
   (Slide: the interstate highways viewed from the tower.)
   Every cobblestoned street, every alleyway, was so pristine and clean.
   (Slide: the row-houses on Monument Street.)
   (Slide: a corridor of Hopkins Hospital, outside the basement laboratories.)
   Wasn't it, Anna?
Anna (deadpan): Yes. Sterile.
   (Slide: a hospital aide washing the floor.)
Carl: Even the Black Forest looked swept. We splurged once again and stayed at the Waldhorn Post here, outside of Wildbad.
   (Slide: exterior of Johns Hopkins Hospital.)
   The hotel dates back to 1145—the chef there is renowned for his game dishes.
   (Slide: Anna in front of a vending machine dispensing wrapped sandwiches in the Hopkins Hospital cafeteria.)
Anna: I wasn't too hungry.
Carl: I was ravenous.
   (Slides: Route 95 outside the harbor tunnel; the large toll signs are visible.) Let's see—the Romantic Road . . . Die Romantishe Strasse . . . a trek through picturebook Bavaria and the Allgau Alpen . . . Fussen to Wurzburg.
Anna: Honey, perhaps they've seen enough. It's hard to sit through this many—
Carl: Wait. Just one more. They've got to see Neuschwanstein, built by mad King Ludwig II. It's so rococco it's Las Vegas.
   (Slide: the castle at Disneyland.)
   I believe that Ludwig was reincarnated in the twentieth century as Liberace. Wait a moment, that's not the castle.
Anna: Yes, it is.

Carl (upset):   It looks like—how did that get in here?
Anna: I don't know which castle you're referring to, but it's definitely a castle.
   (*Slide: a close-up of the castle, with a large Mickey Mouse in the picture.*)
Carl: That's not funny, Anna! Are you making fun of me?
Anna: Don't get upset.
   (*Slide: Donald Duck has joined Mickey Mouse with tourists.*)
Carl: I went to Europe. I walked through Bavaria and the Black Forest. I combed through Neuschwanstein! I did these things, and I will remember the beauty of it all my life! I don't appreciate your mockery!
Anna: It's just a little—
Carl: You went through Germany on your back. All you'll remember are hotel ceilings. You can show them your Germany—

   (*He rushes off, angry.*)

Anna: Sometimes my brother gets upset for no apparent reason. Some wires cross in his brain and he—I'm sorry. Lights, please. (*The Third Man wheels the projector offstage.*) I would like to show you my impressions of Germany. They were something like this—

SCENE XX *In Munich.*

   (*Anna is under the sheet beside the Munich Virgin, who is very young.*)

Anna: Are you comfortable?
Munich Virgin: Ja, ja . . . danke.
Anna: Good. Have you been the bellhop here for a long time?
Munich Virgin: Not so very long a time. My vater owns the hotel, and says I must learn and work very hard. Soon I will be given the responsibility of the front desk.
Anna: My. That's exciting. (*Pause.*) Are you cold?
Munich Virgin: Nein. Just a . . . klein nervos. My English is not so very good.
Anna: Is this your first time? You always remember your first time. (*Pause.*) I'm very honored. (*Pause.*) Listen. I'm a schoolteacher. May I tell you something? A little lesson? When you're a much older man, and you've loved many women, you'll be a wonderful lover if you're just a little bit nervous . . . like you are right now. Because it will always be the first time.
Munich Virgin: You are a very nice woman.
Anna: The human body is a wonderful thing. Like yours. Like mine. The beauty of the body heals all the sickness, all the bad things that happen to it. And I really want you to feel this. Because if you feel it, you'll remember it. And then maybe you'll remember me.

SCENE XXI

(Anna and the Munich Virgin rise. Carl gets into the bed with his stuffed rabbit. Anna gets ready to leave.)

The Third Man: Conjugations of the verb "verlassen." To leave, to abandon, to forsake. The present tense.

Carl: Are you leaving me alone?

Anna: Yes. Just for a little while. I need to take a walk. I'm restless. It's perfectly safe.

Carl: Okay, sweetie. Don't be too long. Bunny and I are ready for bed.

Anna: I won't stay out long. I'll be right back.

The Third Man: The future tense of the verb "verlassen."

Carl: Will you be leaving me alone again tonight? I'm ready for bed.

Anna: I will be leaving you alone. Just for a little while.

Carl: Who will it be tonight? The bellhop? The desk clerk? Or the maitre d'?

Anna: Don't be mean. You said you didn't make judgments.

Carl: I don't. I just want to spend time with you.

Anna: I'll be back in time for a bedtime story.

The Third Man: The past tense of the verb "verlassen."

Carl: Again? Again? You left me alone last night. And the night before.

Anna: I can't help it. I've been a good girl for the past thirty years. Now I want to make up for lost time.

Carl: And what am I supposed to do while you're out traipsing around with every Thomas, Deiter und Heinrich?

Anna: Hug bunny.

The Third Man: There are three moods of the verb "verlassen": the indicative, the imperative, and the subjunctive. Anna and Carl are never in the same mood.

Carl: Leave me alone.

Anna: Carl, don't be like that.

Carl: Why? It doesn't matter what I want. You are going to leave.

Anna: I never stay out very long.

Carl: All I can say is if this establishment charges us for room service, they've got some nerve—

Anna: I've got to take what opportunities come along—

Carl: I wish you wouldn't go—

Anna: Please understand. I don't have much time. I spend as much time with you as I can, but while I still have my health . . . please?

SCENE XXII

The Third Man: As children they fought.

Carl: We never fought, really.

Anna: Not in a physical way. He was a sickly child.

Carl: She was very willful.

Anna: No roughhousing. But he knew all of my weak points. My secret openings. He could be ruthless.

Carl: She'd cry at the slightest thing.

Anna: He has a very sharp tongue.

Carl: But when one of you is very, very sick, you can't fight. It's not fair. You've got to hold it in. We never fight.

Anna: But we had a doozy in the hotel room in Berlin.

Carl: Well, my god, Anna, even though you're sick, I have the right to get angry.

Anna: We'd been traveling too long. We were cranky. The rooms were closing in.

Carl: I'm just saying that we should spend a little more time together. I don't get to see you alone enough. You're always restless.

Anna: Fine. You go out without me for a change.

Carl: I'm going out for a walk.

Anna (starting to weep):   I don't care.

Carl: When she was little, this would be the time I'd bribe her. With a comic book or an ice cream. I always had pennies saved up for these little contingencies.

Anna: But sometimes, for the sake of my pride, I would be inconsolable. I would rush off and then feel just awful alone. Why didn't I take the bribe? (*To Carl.*) I'm going out.

Carl: To fuck?

Anna: No, dear. The passive voice is used to emphasize the subject, to indicate the truth of the generalization. I'm going out. To get fucked.

SCENE XXIII

(Music: Kurt Weill.° Anna goes over to a small cabaret table. There is a telephone on the table. The Radical Student Activist sits at another identical table, smoking, watching her.)

Anna: I'm going to enjoy Berlin without him. I'll show him. I'm going to be carefree, totally without scruples. I'll pretend I've never taught first-graders. (*Beat.*) I'm going to have a perfectly miserable time. (*The Radical Student Activist picks up the telephone. The telephone at Anna's table rings.*) Oh my goodness. My miserable time is calling me. (*Anna picks up the phone.*) Yes?

Radical Student Activist: Are you alone, Fraulein?

Anna: Well, uh, actually—yes, I am.

Radical Student Activist: Gut. Du willst mal richtig durchgefickt werden, ja?

Kurt Weill: 1900–1950; U.S. composer, born in Germany.

Anna: I'm sorry. I don't speak a word of German. (*The Radical Student Activist laughs.*)

Radical Student Activist: Ja. Even better. I said, would you like to get fucked?

Anna: Do you always come on to single women like that?

Radical Student Activist: Would you like it better if I bought you tall drinks with umbrellas? Told to you the stories of how hard a time my parents had during the war? Tell you how exciting I find foreign women, how they are the real women, not like the pale northern madchen here at home? How absolutely bourgeois.

Anna: I see. Why do you come here?

Radical Student Activist: I don't come here for the overpriced drinks. I come here because of the bored western women who come here, who leave their tired businessmen husbands in the hotel rooms behind.

Anna: You're cute. In a hostile way.

Radical Student Activist: Fucking is a revolutionary act.

Anna: Your hovel or my hotel?

SCENE XXIV

(*In the hotel room. Anna, awake, lies in the middle of the bed. To her left, Carl sleeps, curled up. To her right, the Radical Student Activist, curled on her breast, slumbers. Anna is awake with an insomniacal desperation.*)

Anna (singing softly):   Two and two are four; four and four are eight; eight and eight are sixteen; sixteen and sixteen are thirty-two—

Radical Student Activist (groggy):   Wo ist die Toilette? (*The Radical Student Activist rises and stumbles stage left.*)

Anna: In lovemaking, he's all fury and heat. His North Sea pounding against your Dreamer. And when you look up and see his face, red and huffing, it's hard to imagine him ever having been tiny, wrinkled, and seven pounds. That is, until afterwards. When he rises from sleep and he walks into the bathroom. And there he exposes his soft little derriere, and you can still see the soft baby flesh. (*As the Radical Student Activist comes back into the room.*) I've got to put a name to that behind. What's your name? Wie heissen Sie? (*The Radical Student Activist starts dressing in a hurry.*)

Radical Student Activist: Auf Wiedersehn. Next thing you'll ask for my telephone number.

Anna: No, I won't. I was just curious—

Radical Student Activist: Ja, ja . . . und then my sign of the zodiac. I'll get cards from Hallmark und little scribblings like "I'll never forget the night we shared."

Anna: Forget it.

Radical Student Activist: There is something radical in two complete
strangers committing biological necessity without having to give into
bourgeois conventions of love, without breeding to produce workers
for a capitalist system, without the benediction of the church, the
family, the bosses—
Anna: I have something to confess to you. I lied to you.
Radical Student Activist: About what?
Anna: I'm not here on business. I don't specialize in corporate takeovers.
I don't work on Wall Street. I only told you that because I thought
that was what you wanted to hear.
Radical Student Activist: Okay. So you do estate planning? Income tax?
Anna: No. You just committed a revolutionary act with a first-grade
schoolteacher who lives in low-income housing. And I'm tired. I think
you should go.
Radical Student Activist: And your husband?
Anna: Not too loud. And he's not my husband. He's my brother. A
maiden librarian for the San Francisco Public. (*As the Radical Student
Activist starts to leave.*) And by the way—the missionary position does
not a revolution make. (*The Radical Student Activist leaves. Anna,
depressed, lies down. Carl rises from the bed.*)

SCENE XXV

Carl: And as she lay in the bed, sleepless, it swept over her—the way her
classroom smelled early in the morning, before the children came. It
smelled of chalk dust—
The Third Man: It smelled of Crayola wax, crushed purple and green—
Carl: The cedar of hamster cage shavings—
The Third Man: The sweet wintergreen of LePage's paste—
Carl: The wooden smell of the thick construction paper—
The Third Man: The spillings of sticky orange drink and sour milk—
The Third Man and Carl (simultaneously):   And the insidious smell of
first-grader pee.
Carl: It smelled like heaven.
Anna: And the first thing I did each morning was put up the weather
map for today on the board under the flag. A bright, smiling sun, or
Miss Cloud or Mr. Umbrella. On special days I put up Suzy
Snowflake. And when I opened my desk drawer, scattered like
diamonds on the bottom were red, silver and gold stars. (*Beat.*) I want
to go home. Carl, I want to go home.
Carl: Soon, sweetie. Very soon.
Anna: I've had enough. I've seen all of the world I want to see. I want to
wake up in my own bed. I want to sit with you at home and we'll
watch the weather. And we'll wait.

Carl: We've come so far. We have to at least go to Vienna. Do you think you can hold out long enough to meet Dr. Todelsrocheln? (*Anna, miserable and homesick, nods.*) That a girl. I promise you don't have to undertake his . . . hydrotherapy unless you decide to. I have a friend in Vienna, a college chum, who might be able to get us some of the black-market stuff. It's worth a shot.

Anna: Then you'll take me home?

Carl: Then I'll take you home.

SCENE XXVI

(*Music: the zither theme from "The Third Man." Carl and Anna stand, with their luggage, in front of a door buzzer.*)

Carl: First we'll just look up Harry and leave our bags here. Then we'll cab over to Dr. Todesrocheln. (*Carl rings the buzzer. They wait. Carl rings the buzzer again. They wait. An aging Concierge comes out.*) Entschuldigung. Wir suchen Harry Lime? Do you speak English?

Concierge: Nein. Ich spreche kein Englisch. (*Carl and the Concierge start to shout as if the other one was deaf.*)

Carl: Herr Lime? Do you know him? Herr Harry Lime?

Concierge: Ach. Ach. Ja, Herr Harry Lime. You come . . . too spat.

Carl: He's gone? Too spat?

Concierge: Funf minuten too spat. Er ist tot—°

Carl: What?

Concierge: Ja. Ein auto mit Harry splatz-machen auf der Strasse.° Splatz!

Anna: Splatz!?

Carl: Splatz! (*It dawns on Carl and Anna what the Concierge is saying.*)

Concierge: Ja, ja. Er geht uber die strasse, und cin auto . . . spppllaattz!°

Anna: Oh, my god!

Concierge (gesturing with hands): Ja. Er hat auch eine rabbit. Herr rabbit auch—sppllaattz! They are . . . diggen ein grab in den Boden. Jetz.°

Carl: Now? You saw this happen?

Concierge: Ja. I . . . saw it mit meinen own Augen. Splatz. (*As he exits.*) "Splatzen, splatzen, uber alles . . ."

Carl: Listen, darling. I want you to take a cab to the doctor's office.

Anna: Where are you going?

Carl: Ich verlasse. I'll find out what happened to Harry.

Anna: I wish you wouldn't leave . . .

Carl: I'll come back. Okay?

Funf minuten too spat. Er ist tot: Five minutes too late. He is dead.   *Ein . . . Strasse:* An auto killed Harry on the street. Splat!   *Er geht . . . spppllaattz:* He was walking down the street, and this car . . . splat!   *Er hat . . . Jetz:* He had a rabbit. Mr. Rabbit also—splat! They are digging a grave in the ground. Right now.

SCENE XXVII

(Anna climbs onto a table and gathers a white paper sheet around her. She huddles.)

Anna: Some things are the same in every country. You're scared when you see the doctor, here in Vienna just like in Baltimore. And they hand you the same paper cup to fill, just like in America. Then you climb up onto the same cold metal table, and they throw a sheet around you and you feel very small. And just like at home, they tell you to wait. And you wait. *(As Anna waits, dwarfed on the table, the scene with Harry Lime and Carl unfolds. "The Third Man" theme music up.)*

SCENE XXVIII *On the Ferris Wheel in the Prater.*

(Carl holds the stuffed rabbit closely.)

Carl: I just came from your funeral.

Harry Lime: I'm touched, old man. Was it a nice funeral?

Carl: What are you doing? Why are we meeting here?

Harry Lime: It's best not to ask too many questions. The police were beginning to do that. It's extremely convenient, now and then in a man's career, to die. I've gone underground. So if you want to meet me, you have to come here. No one asks questions here.

Carl: Can you help us? *(Harry Lime at first does not answer. He looks at the view.)*

Harry Lime: Where is your sister? She left you alone?

Carl: She's—she needs her rest.

Harry Lime: Have you looked at the view from up here? It's quite inspiring. No matter how old I get, I always love the ferris wheel.

Carl: You were my closest friend in college.

Harry Lime: I'll be straight with you. I can give you the drugs—but it won't help. It won't help at all. Your sister's better off with that quack Todesrocheln—we call him the Yellow Queen of Vienna—she might end up drinking her own piss, but it won't kill her.

Carl: But I thought you had the drugs—

Harry Lime: Oh, I do. And they cost a pretty penny. For a price, I can give them to you. At a discount for old times. But you have to know, we make them up in my kitchen.

Carl: Jesus.

Harry Lime: Why not? People will pay for these things. When they're desperate, people will eat peach pits, or aloe, or egg protein—they'll even drink their own piss. It gives them hope.

Carl: How can you do this?

Harry Lime: Listen, old man, if you want to be a millionaire, you go into real estate. If you want to be a billionaire, you sell hope. Nowadays the only place a fellow can make a decent career of it is in Mexico and Europe.

Carl: That's . . . disgusting.

Harry Lime: Look. I thought you weren't going to be . . . sentimental about this. It's a business. You have to have the right perspective. Like from up here . . . the people down on the street are just tiny little dots. And if you could charge 1,000 dollars, wouldn't you push the drugs? I could use a friend I can trust to help me.

Carl: When we were at Hopkins together, I thought you were God. You could hypnotize us into doing anything, and it would seem . . . charming. Carl, old man, you'd say, "Just do it." Cutting classes, cribbing exams, shop-lifting, stupid undergraduate things—and I would do it. Without knowing the consequences. I would do it.

The Third Man: Oh, you knew the consequences, old man. You knew. You chose not to think about them.

Carl: I've grown old before my time from the consequences. I'm turning you in.

Harry Lime: I wouldn't do that, old man. (*Harry Lime pats a bulge on the inside of his trench coat.*) By the time you hit the ground, you'll be just a tiny little dot. (*Carl and Harry Lime look at each other, waiting.*) And I think you have something I want. The rabbit, bitte.

Carl: No. You're not getting it. I'm taking it with me. (*Harry Lime puts his arms in position for a waltz and begins to sway, seductively.*)

Harry Lime: Come on, give it up. Come to my arms, my only one. Dance with me, my beloved, my sweet—(*Carl takes the stuffed rabbit and threatens to throw it out the window of the ferris wheel. A Strauss waltz plays very loudly, and Harry Lime and Carl waltz-struggle for the rabbit. Carl is pushed and Harry Lime waltzes off with the rabbit.*)

SCENE XXIX

(*Meanwhile, back at Doctor Todesrocheln.*)

Anna: You begin to hope that the wait is proportionate to the medical expertise. My God. My feet are turning blue. Where am I? An HMO? The problem with being an adult is that you never forget why you're waiting. When I was a child, I could wait blissfully unaware for hours. I used to read signs and transpose letters, or count tiles in the floor. And in the days before I could read, I would make up stories about my hands—Mr. Left and Mr. Right. (*Beat.*) Mr. Left would provoke Mr. Right. Mr. Right would ignore it. The trouble would escalate, until my hands were battling each other to the death. (*Beat. Anna demonstrates.*) Then one of them would weep. Finally, they became friends again, and they'd dance—(*Anna's two hands dance together; she is unaware that Dr. Todesrocheln has entered and is watching her. He clears his throat. He wears a very dirty lab coat with pockets filled with paper and a stale doughnut. He wears a white fright wig and glasses. He also wears one sinister black glove. With relish, he carries a flask of a golden liquid.*) Oh, thank goodness.

Dr. Todesrocheln: Ja. So happy to meet you. Such an interesting specimen. I congratulate you. Very, very interesting.

Anna: Thank you.

Dr. Todesrocheln: We must have many more such specimens from you— for the urinocryoscopy, the urinometer, the urinoglucosometer, the uroacidimeter, uroazotometer, and mein new acquirement in der laboratorium—ein urophosphometer.

Anna: My goodness. (*Dr. Todesrocheln has put the flask down on a table. Quietly, his left hand reaches for it; the right hand stops the left.*)

Dr. Todesrocheln: Ja. Nowadays, we have learned to discover the uncharted mysteries of the fluids discharged through the urethra. We have been so primitive in the past. Doctors once could only analyze by taste and smell—but thanks to the advancement of medical science, there are no limits to our thirst for knowledge.

Anna: Uh-huh. (*Dr. Todesrocheln's left hand seizes the flask. Trembling, with authority, his right hand replaces the flask on the table, and soothes the left hand into quietude.*)

Dr. Todesrocheln: So much data has been needlessly, carelessly destroyed in the past—the medical collections of Ravensbruck senselessly annihilated—and that is why, as a scientist, I must be exacting in our measurements and recordings.

Anna: What can I hope to find out from these . . . specimens?

Dr. Todesrocheln: Ah, yes—the layman must have his due! Too much pure research und no application makes Jack . . . macht Jack . . . (*Dr. Todesrocheln loses his train of thought.*) Fraulein Anna—I may call you Fraulein Anna?—Let us look at the body as an alchemist, taking in straw and mud und schweinefleisch and processing it into liquid gold which purifies the body. You might say that the sickness of the body can only be cured by the health of the body. To your health! (*His left hand seizes the flask in a salute, and raises the flask to his lips. In time, the right hand brings the flask down. A brief struggle. It appears the flask might spill, but at last the right hand triumphs.*)

Anna: You know, even though I really grew up in the suburbs of Baltimore, I like to think of myself as an open-minded person—

Dr. Todesrocheln: The ancient Greeks knew that the aromatic properties of the fluid could reveal the imbalances of the soul itself . . . (*The left hand sneaks toward the flask.*)

Anna: I'm always very eager to try new foods, or see the latest John Waters film—

Dr. Todesrocheln: —its use in the purification rites of the Aztecs is, of course, so well known that it need not be mentioned—(*The hand has grasped the flask and begins to inch it off the table.*)

Anna: And whenever I meet someone who cross-dresses, I always compliment him on his shoes or her earrings—

Dr. Todesrocheln: It is the first golden drop that marks the infant's identity separate from the womb—(*The hand has slipped the flask beneath the table; his right hand is puzzled.*)

Anna: But still, it's important to know where your threshold is . . . and I think we're coming dangerously close to mine . . .

Dr. Todesrocheln: Until the last precious amber releases the soul from the body—ashes to ashes, drop to drop—excuse me—(*His left hand, with the flask, swings in an arc behind his body; he swivels his body to the flask, his back turned to us; we can hear him drink in secrecy. With his back turned . . .*) Ahhh . . . (*He orders himself. Composed, he turns around to face Anna again, and demurely sets down the flask. Its level is noticeably lower. Anna is aghast.*) I can sense your concern. I have been prattling on without regard to questions you must surely have—

Anna: Is that your real hair?

Dr. Todesrocheln: Of course, I cannot promise results, but first we must proceed by securing more samples—

Anna: I don't believe that's your real hair.

Dr. Todesrocheln: I will need first of all twenty-four hours of your time for a urononcometry—

Anna (increasingly scared):   You look familiar to me—

Dr. Todesrocheln: Although I can tell you from a first taste—er, test, that your uroammonica level is high—not unpleasantly so, but full-bodied—

Anna: Oh, my god . . . I think I know who you are . . . you're . . . you're . . . (*Anna rises to snatch his toupee. Dr. Todesrocheln suddenly stands, menacing. And the lights change.*)

Dr. Todesrocheln: WO IST DEIN BRUDER? (*He takes off his wig and glasses and appears as the Doctor in the first scene, peeling off the black gloves to reveal latex gloves underneath.*) You fool! You left your brother in the room alone! WO IST DEIN BRUDER?

(*Music: "The Emperor Waltz" plays at a very loud volume. Anna, frightened, races from the doctor's office to the hotel room. We see Carl, lying stiff beneath a white sheet. To the tempo of the Strauss, Anna tries to wake him. He does not respond. Anna forces him into a sitting position, the stuffed rabbit clenched beneath his arm. Carl remains sitting, stiff, eyes open, wooden. Then he slumps. Anna raises him again. He remains upright for a beat, and begins to fall. Anna stops him, presses his body against hers, pulls his legs over the bed, tries to stand him up. Frozen, his body tilts against hers. She tries to make him cross the floor, his arms around her neck. She positions him in a chair, but his legs are locked in a*

*perpendicular angle and will not touch the floor. He mechanically springs
forward. Then, suddenly, like the doll in E.T.A. Hoffman,° the body of
Carl becomes animated, but with a strange, automatic life of its own,
and faltering, falls back to the bed. There is the sound of a loud alarm
clock; the Doctor enters, and covers Carl with a sheet. Then he pulls a
white curtain in front of the scene, as the stage lights become, for the first
time, harsh, stark and white.)*

doll in E.T.A. Hoffman: Reference to a wind-up singing doll in the opera *The Tales of Hoffman,*
by E.T.A. Hoffman (1776–1822).

SCENE XXX   *In the hospital lounge.*

*(The Doctor holds the stuffed rabbit and travel brochures in his hands. He
awkwardly peels off his latex gloves.)*

Doctor: I'm sorry. There was nothing we could do.

Anna: Yes. I know.

Doctor: I thought you might want to take this along with you. (*The
Doctor hands Anna the stuffed rabbit.*)

Anna (to the stuffed rabbit):   There you are! (*Anna hugs the stuffed rabbit
and sees the Doctor watching her.*) It's Jo-Jo. My brother's childhood
rabbit. I brought it to the hospital as a little surprise. I thought it
might make him feel better.

Doctor: Sometimes little things become important, when nothing else will
help—

Anna: Yes. (*They pause and stand together awkwardly.*) At least Carl went
in his sleep. I guess that's a blessing.

Doctor: If one has to die from this particular disease, there are worse ways
to go than pneumonia.

Anna: I never would have believed what sickness can do to the body.
(*Pause.*) Well, Doctor, I want to thank you for all you've done for my
brother.

Doctor: I wish I could do more. By the way, housekeeping found these
brochures in your brother's bedside table. I didn't know if they were
important. (*Anna takes the brochures.*)

Anna: Ah, yes. The brochures for Europe. I've never been abroad. We're
going to go when he gets—(*Anna stops herself. With control.*) I must
learn to use the past tense. We would have gone had he gotten better.

Doctor: Anna—may I call you Anna?—I, uh, if there's anything I can
do—

Anna: Thank you, but there's nothing you can do—

Doctor: I mean, I really would like it if you'd call me for coffee, or if you
just want to talk about all this—(*The Doctor trails off. Anna looks at
him. She smiles. He squirms.*)

Anna: You're very sweet. But no, I don't think so. Not now. I feel it's simply not safe for me right now to see anyone. Thanks again and goodbye.

(Anna starts to exit. The Doctor, wistful, watches her go. The lighting begins to change back to the dreamy atmosphere of the first scene. Softly, a Strauss waltz begins. Carl, in uniform, perfectly well, waits for Anna. They waltz off as the lights dim.)

WINDOW ON

Types, Stereotypes, and Archetypes

Dramatists often rely on the economy achieved by using quickly recognizable types. We all recognize the miser, the spoiled brat, the wallflower, the bully, the snob. Sometimes these types are gender specific, such as the shrew, the witch, the hysteric for women, and the braggart soldier, the drunk, the tough guy for men. However, dramatists usually use types only with minor characters. When a character such as Laura in *The Glass Menagerie* takes a central role, the limitations of type fall away, and we begin to see the wallflower developed into a complex human being.

Although most good drama develops central characters as individuals, not types, some plays are developed successfully around the concept of the type. *The Glass Menagerie* and *Hamlet* are both built on types: Amanda is the over ambitious mother, Laura is the wallflower, and Hamlet is the melancholy intellectual. Hamlet, however, develops far beyond any superficial concepts of the type. Although we sometimes call him the Melancholy Dane, we also recognize that such a term does not sum him up. The same may be said of both Amanda and Laura. In contrast, the minor characters in *Hamlet* sometimes do not develop beyond their type. Osric is the sleazy courtier who will say anything to please, Polonius is the fatherly busybody who keeps giving advice even when it is not welcome, Fortinbras is the warrior who lives to fight, Laertes is the rash young man, and Ophelia may be the hysteric.

A stereotype is even less complex than a type character. The differences may be a matter of degree. For example, Polonius, although a type character, is somewhat individuated. A stereotype, however, is usually an uncomplicated—and uninteresting—two-dimensional shadow of a person. Racial stereotypes are common in drama as well as in life: the greedy Jew, lazy black, mafia-owned Italian, drunken Irishman, dumb Polack, stingy Scot, and fanatical Arab are all popular stereotypes. They are oversimple, the product of prejudice. Woody Allen sometimes relies on stereotypes to get his drama going. Nat Ackerman is the stereotype of a New York Jew in the garment business. But Allen presses far beyond such a stereotype by developing the character sympathetically. Even Death is a type, with an allusion to the type established by Ingmar Bergman in his film *The Seventh Seal.*

Death Knocks also parodies the archetype of death as it appears in Poe's "The Masque of the Red Death" and in Bergman's film *The Seventh Seal.* An archetype, unlike a type or stereotype, always retains its psychological and thematic complexity and in addition takes on a larger-than-life quality and becomes a cross-cultural force. For example, Oedipus is the archetype of the tyrant. He meets his fate in part because he will not listen to others and demands that they bend to his will. He is an archetype because he models or establishes the pattern that others, no matter what their culture, follow. His "fault" is universal, something everyone struggles with.

Laura Wingfield is an archetypal smothering mother, the mother who lives her life through her children. All these characters have a complexity and dimension that makes them individuals, but at the same time they establish patterns that many others follow. Hedda Gabler establishes a modern archetype of the talented, frustrated woman—the woman who vaguely senses liberation but, unlike Nora in *A Doll House,* cannot find the door through which to pass to freedom. In some ways Troy Maxson becomes an archetypal father in August Wilson's *Fences.* His inability to communicate with his son will be recognizable to many young men in the audience. The same might be said for the Count in *Miss Julie,* although he never appears in the play.

Types, stereotypes, and archetypes work because they are recognizable. We respond to types and stereotypes in part because the playwright depends on our inbuilt prejudices and in part because experience has taught us that some aspects of types are reliable some of the time. Archetypes are more difficult to recognize as such, but once we do we see in them the patterns of behavior that we know guide many people. The archetypal father-figure, the archetypal mother, the archetypal adventurer and seeker—all these are patterns that many people will follow in their own lives. Types and stereotypes are reductive and simplifying. But archetypes, such as Oedipus or Hamlet, are complex and inclusive. Archetypes do not limit a range of behavior, they merely demonstrate its range so that we can tell when we—or others—take part in similar behavior.

Reading

Frye, Northrop. *Anatomy of Criticism.* Princeton: Princeton University Press, 1957.

August Wilson   (b. 1945)

August Wilson spent much of the period of the 1960s and 1970s in civil rights activities, during which time he described himself as a black nationalist. He began writing plays in his native Pittsburgh and continued when he moved to St. Paul to work for the Science Museum of Minnesota. Many of his dramatic skits were performed at the museum. He joined the Playwrights Center in Minneapolis and began a professional career writing plays for performance there. Jitney, about gypsy cabs, was produced in 1982. His first Broadway play was Ma Rainey's Black Bottom *(1984), which won the New York Drama Critics' Circle Award.* Fences *followed in 1985, winning the Drama Critics' Circle Award and the Pulitzer Prize. Wilson won the Drama Critics' Circle Award again in 1988 for* Joe Turner's Come and Gone. *These have been followed by two highly successful plays,* The Piano Lesson *(1987) and* Two Trains Running *(1992). The last five plays all premiered earlier at the Yale Repertory Theatre under the direction of Lloyd Richards, and then moved to Broadway. The plays are part of a large cycle projected by Wilson to cover the experience of African-Americans. Wilson has said, "I think the black Americans have the most dramatic story of all mankind to tell."* Seven Guitars *(1994) is his most recent play.*

FENCES   1987

Characters

Troy Maxson	Gabriel, Troy's brother
Jim Bono, Troy's friend	Cory, Troy and Rose's son
Rose, Troy's wife	Raynell, Troy's daughter
Lyons, Troy's oldest son by	
previous marriage	

(Setting: The setting is the yard which fronts the only entrance to the Maxson household, an ancient two-story brick house set back off a small alley in a big-city neighborhood. The entrance to the house is gained by two or three steps leading to a wooden porch badly in need of paint.)

(A relatively recent addition to the house and running its full width, the porch lacks congruence. It is a sturdy porch with a flat roof. One or two chairs of dubious value sit at one end where the kitchen window opens onto the porch. An old-fashioned icebox stands silent guard at the opposite end.)

(The yard is a small dirt yard, partially fenced, except for the last scene, with a wooden sawhorse, a pile of lumber, and other fence-building equipment set off to the side. Opposite is a tree from which hangs a ball made of rags. A baseball bat leans against the tree. Two oil drums serve as garbage receptacles and sit near the house at right to complete the setting.)

(The Play: Near the turn of the century, the destitute of Europe sprang on the city with tenacious claws and an honest and solid dream. The city devoured them. They swelled its belly until it burst into a thousand furnaces and sewing machines, a thousand butcher shops and bakers' ovens, a thousand churches and hospitals and funeral parlors and money-lenders. The city grew. It nourished itself and offered each man a partnership limited only by his talent, his guile, and his willingness and

capacity for hard work. For the immigrants of Europe, a dream dared and won true.)

(The descendants of African slaves were offered no such welcome or participation. They came from places called the Carolinas and the Virginias, Georgia, Alabama, Mississippi, and Tennessee. They came strong, eager, searching. The city rejected them and they fled and settled along the riverbanks and under bridges in shallow, ramshackle houses made of sticks and tarpaper. They collected rags and wood. They sold the use of their muscles and their bodies. They cleaned houses and washed clothes, they shined shoes, and in quiet desperation and vengeful pride, they stole, and lived in pursuit of their own dream. That they could breathe free, finally, and stand to meet life with the force of dignity and whatever eloquence the heart could call upon.)

(By 1957, the hard-won victories of the European immigrants had solidified the industrial might of America. War had been confronted and won with new energies that used loyalty and patriotism as its fuel. Life was rich, full, and flourishing. The Milwaukee Braves won the World Series, and the hot winds of change that would make the sixties a turbulent, racing, dangerous, and provocative decade had not yet begun to blow full.)

ACT I

Scene I

(It is 1957. Troy and Bono enter the yard, engaged in conversation. Troy is fifty-three years old, a large man with thick, heavy hands; it is this largeness that he strives to fill out and make an accommodation with. Together with his blackness, his largeness informs his sensibilities and the choices he has made in his life.)

(Of the two men, Bono is obviously the follower. His commitment to their friendship of thirty-odd years is rooted in his admiration of Troy's honesty, capacity for hard work, and his strength, which Bono seeks to emulate.)

(It is Friday night, payday, and the one night of the week the two men engage in a ritual of talk and drink. Troy is usually the most talkative and at times he can be crude and almost vulgar, though he is capable of rising to profound heights of expression. The men carry lunch buckets and wear or carry burlap aprons and are dressed in clothes suitable to their jobs as garbage collectors.)

Bono: Troy, you ought to stop that lying!

Troy: I ain't lying! The nigger had a watermelon this big. (*He indicates with his hands.*) Talking about . . . "What watermelon, Mr. Rand?" I liked to fell out! "What watermelon, Mr. Rand?" . . . And it sitting there big as life.

Bono: What did Mr. Rand say?

Troy: Ain't said nothing. Figure if the nigger too dumb to know he carrying a watermelon, he wasn't gonna get much sense out of him. Trying to hide that great big old watermelon under his coat. Afraid to let the white man see him carry it home.

Bono: I'm like you . . . I ain't got no time for them kind of people.

Troy: Now what he look like getting mad cause he see the man from the union talking to Mr. Rand?

Bono: He come to me talking about . . . "Maxson gonna get us fired." I told him to get away from me with that. He walked away from me calling you a troublemaker. What Mr. Rand say?

Troy: Ain't said nothing. He told me to go down the Commissioner's office next Friday. They called me down there to see them.

Bono: Well, as long as you got your complaint filed, they can't fire you. That's what one of them white fellows tell me.

Troy: I ain't worried about them firing me. They gonna fire me cause I asked a question? That's all I did. I went to Mr. Rand and asked him, "Why? Why you got the white mens driving and the colored lifting?" Told him, "what's the matter, don't I count? You think only white fellows got sense enough to drive a truck. That ain't no paper job! Hell, anybody can drive a truck. How come you got all whites driving and the colored lifting?" He told me "take it to the union." Well, hell, that's what I done! Now they wanna come up with this pack of lies.

Bono: I told Brownie if the man come and ask him any questions . . . just tell the truth! It ain't nothing but something they done trumped up on you cause you filed a complaint on them.

Troy: Brownie don't understand nothing. All I want them to do is change the job description. Give everybody a chance to drive the truck. Brownie can't see that. He ain't got that much sense.

Bono: How you figure he be making out with that gal be up at Taylors' all the time . . . that Alberta gal?

Troy: Same as you and me. Getting just as much as we is. Which is to say nothing.

Bono: It is, huh? I figure you doing a little better than me . . . and I ain't saying what I'm doing.

Troy: Aw, nigger, look here . . . I know you. If you had got anywhere near that gal, twenty minutes later you be looking to tell somebody. And the first one you gonna tell . . . that you gonna want to brag to . . . is gonna be me.

Bono: I ain't saying that. I see where you be eyeing her.

Troy: I eye all the women. I don't miss nothing. Don't never let nobody tell you Troy Maxson don't eye the women.

Bono: You been doing more than eyeing her. You done bought her a drink or two.

Troy: Hell yeah, I bought her a drink! What that mean? I bought you one, too. What that mean cause I buy her a drink? I'm just being polite.

Bono: It's all right to buy her one drink. That's what you call being polite. But when you wanna be buying two or three . . . that's what you call eyeing her.

Troy: Look here, as long as you known me . . . you ever known me to chase after women?

Bono: Hell yeah! Long as I done known you. You forgetting I knew you when.

Troy: Naw, I'm talking about since I been married to Rose?

Bono: Oh, not since you been married to Rose. Now, that's the truth, there. I can say that.

Troy: All right then! Case closed.

Bono: I see you be walking up around Alberta's house. You supposed to be at Taylors' and you be walking up around there.

Troy: What you watching where I'm walking for? I ain't watching after you.

Bono: I seen you walking around there more than once.

Troy: Hell, you liable to see me walking anywhere! That don't mean nothing cause you see me walking around there.

Bono: Where she come from anyway? She just kinda showed up one day.

Troy: Tallahassee. You can look at her and tell she one of them Florida gals. They got some big healthy women down there. Grow them right up out the ground. Got a little bit of Indian in her. Most of them niggers down in Florida got some Indian in them.

Bono: I don't know about that Indian part. But she damn sure big and healthy. Woman wear some big stockings. Got them great big old legs and hips as wide as the Mississippi River.

Troy: Legs don't mean nothing. You don't do nothing but push them out of the way. But them hips cushion the ride!

Bono: Troy, you ain't got no sense.

Troy: It's the truth! Like you riding on Goodyears!

(Rose enters from the house. She is ten years younger than Troy, her devotion to him stems from her recognition of the possibilities of her life without him: a succession of abusive men and their babies, a life of partying and running the streets, the Church, or aloneness with its attendant pain and frustration. She recognizes Troy's spirit as a fine and illuminating one and she either ignores or forgives his faults, only some of which she recognizes. Though she doesn't drink, her presence is an integral part of the Friday night rituals. She alternates between the porch and the kitchen, where supper preparations are under way.)

Rose: What you all out here getting into?

Troy: What you worried about what we getting into for? This is men talk, woman.

Rose: What I care what you all talking about? Bono, you gonna stay for supper?

Bono: No, I thank you, Rose. But Lucille say she cooking up a pot of pigfeet.

Troy: Pigfeet! Hell, I'm going home with you! Might even stay the night if you got some pigfeet. You got something in there to top them pigfeet, Rose?

Rose: I'm cooking up some chicken. I got some chicken and collard greens.

Troy: Well, go on back in the house and let me and Bono finish what we was talking about. This is men talk. I got some talk for you later. You know what kind of talk I mean. You go on and powder it up.

Rose: Troy Maxson, don't you start that now!

Troy (puts his arm around her):   Aw, woman . . . come here. Look here, Bono . . . when I met this woman . . . I got out that place, say, "Hitch up my pony, saddle up my mare . . . there's a woman out there for me somewhere. I looked here. Looked there. Saw Rose and latched on to her." I latched on to her and told her—I'm gonna tell you the truth— I told her, "Baby, I don't wanna marry, I just wanna be your man." Rose told me . . . tell him what you told me, Rose.

Rose: I told him if he wasn't the marrying kind, then move out the way so the marrying kind could find me.

Troy: That's what she told me. "Nigger, you in my way. You blocking the view! Move out the way so I can find me a husband." I thought it over two or three days. Come back—

Rose: Ain't no two or three days nothing. You was back the same night.

Troy: Come back, told her . . . "Okay, baby . . . but I'm gonna buy me a banty rooster and put him out there in the backyard . . . and when he see a stranger come, he'll flap his wings and crow . . ." Look here, Bono, I could watch the front door by myself . . . it was that back door I was worried about.

Rose: Troy, you ought not talk like that. Troy ain't doing nothing but telling a lie.

Troy: Only thing is . . . when we first got married . . . forget the rooster . . . we ain't had no yard!

Bono: I hear you tell it. Me and Lucille was staying down there on Logan Street. Had two rooms with the outhouse in the back. I ain't mind the outhouse none. But when that goddamn wind blow through there in the winter . . . that's what I'm talking about! To this day I wonder why in the hell I ever stayed down there for six long years. But see, I didn't know I could do no better. I thought only white folks had inside toilets and things.

Rose: There's a lot of people don't know they can do no better than they doing now. That's just something you got to learn. A lot of folks still shop at Bella's.

Troy: Ain't nothing wrong with shopping at Bella's. She got fresh food.

Rose: I ain't said nothing about if she got fresh food. I'm talking about what she charge. She charge ten cents more than the A & P.

Troy: The A&P ain't never done nothing for me. I spends my money where I'm treated right. I go down to Bella, say, "I need a loaf of bread, I'll pay you Friday." She give it to me. What sense that make when I got money to go and spend it somewhere else and ignore the person who done right by me? That ain't in the Bible.

Rose: We ain't talking about what's in the Bible. What sense it make to shop there when she overcharge?

Troy: You shop where you want to. I'll do my shopping where the people been good to me.

Rose: Well, I don't think it's right for her to overcharge. That's all I was saying.

Bono: Look here . . . I got to get on. Lucille going be raising all kind of hell.

Troy: Where you going, nigger? We ain't finished this pint. Come here, finish this pint.

Bono: Well, hell, I am . . . if you ever turn the bottle loose.

Troy (hands him the bottle):   The only thing I say about the A&P is I'm glad Cory got that job down there. Help him take care of his school clothes and things. Gabe done moved out and things getting tight around here. He got that job. . . . He can start to look out for himself.

Rose: Cory done went and got recruited by a college football team.

Troy: I told that boy about that football stuff. The white man ain't gonna let him get nowhere with that football. I told him when he first come to me with it. Now you come telling me he done went and got more tied up in it. He ought to go and get recruited in how to fix cars or something where he can make a living.

Rose: He ain't talking about making no living playing football. It's just something the boys in school do. They gonna send a recruiter by to talk to you. He'll tell you he ain't talking about making no living playing football. It's a honor to be recruited.

Troy: It ain't gonna get him nowhere. Bono'll tell you that.

Bono: If he be like you in the sports . . . he's gonna be all right. Ain't but two men ever played baseball as good as you. That's Babe Ruth and Josh Gibson.° Them's the only two men ever hit more home runs than you.

Troy: What it ever get me? Ain't got a pot to piss in or a window to throw it out of.

Rose: Times have changed since you was playing baseball, Troy. That was before the war. Times have changed a lot since then.

Josh Gibson: 1911–1947; powerful, black baseball player known in the 1930s as the Babe Ruth of the Negro leagues.

Troy: How in hell they done changed?

Rose: They got lots of colored boys playing ball now. Baseball and football.

Bono: You right about that, Rose. Times have changed, Troy. You just come along too early.

Troy: There ought not never have been no time called too early! Now you take that fellow . . . what's that fellow they had playing right field for the Yankees back then? You know who I'm talking about, Bono. Used to play right field for the Yankees.

Rose: Selkirk?

Troy: Selkirk! That's it! Man batting .269, understand? .269. What kind of sense that make? I was hitting .432 with thirty-seven home runs! Man batting .269 and playing right field for the Yankees! I saw Josh Gibson's daughter yesterday. She walking around with raggedy shoes on her feet. Now I bet you Selkirk's daughter ain't walking around with raggedy shoes on her feet! I bet you that!

Rose: They got a lot of colored baseball players now. Jackie Robinson was the first. Folks had to wait for Jackie Robinson.

Troy: I done seen a hundred niggers play baseball better than Jackie Robinson. Hell, I know some teams Jackie Robinson couldn't even make! What you talking about Jackie Robinson. Jackie Robinson wasn't nobody. I'm talking about if you could play ball then they ought to have let you play. Don't care what color you were. Come telling me I come along too early. If you could play . . . then they ought to have let you play.

(Troy takes a long drink from the bottle.)

Rose: You gonna drink yourself to death. You don't need to be drinking like that.

Troy: Death ain't nothing. I done seen him. Done wrassled with him. You can't tell me nothing about death. Death ain't nothing but a fastball on the outside corner. And you know what I'll do to that! Lookee here, Bono . . . am I lying? You get one of them fastballs, about waist high, over the outside corner of the plate where you can get the meat of the bat on it . . . and good god! You can kiss it goodbye. Now, am I lying?

Bono: Naw, you telling the truth there. I seen you do it.

Troy: If I'm lying . . . that 450 feet worth of lying! (*Pause.*) That's all death is to me. A fastball on the outside corner.

Rose: I don't know why you want to get on talking about death.

Troy: Ain't nothing wrong with talking about death. That's part of life. Everybody gonna die. You gonna die, I'm gonna die. Bono's gonna die. Hell, we all gonna die.

Rose: But you ain't got to talk about it. I don't like to talk about it.

Troy: You the one brought it up. Me and Bono was talking about baseball

. . . you tell me I'm gonna drink myself to death. Ain't that right, Bono? You know I don't drink this but one night out of the week. That's Friday night. I'm gonna drink just enough to where I can handle it. Then I cuts it loose. I leave it alone. So don't you worry about me drinking myself to death. 'Cause I ain't worried about Death. I done seen him. I done wrestled with him.

Look here, Bono . . . I looked up one day and Death was marching straight at me. Like Soldiers on Parade! The Army of Death was marching straight at me. The middle of July, 1941. It got real cold just like it be winter. It seem like Death himself reached out and touched me on the shoulder. He touch me just like I touch you. I got cold as ice and Death standing there grinning at me.

Rose: Troy, why don't you hush that talk.

Troy: I say . . . What you want, Mr. Death? You be wanting me? You done brought your army to be getting me? I looked him dead in the eye. I wasn't fearing nothing. I was ready to tangle. Just like I'm ready to tangle now. The Bible say be ever vigilant. That's why I don't get but so drunk. I got to keep watch.

Rose: Troy was right down there in Mercy Hospital. You remember he had pneumonia? Laying there with a fever talking plumb out of his head.

Troy: Death standing there staring at me . . . carrying that sickle in his hand. Finally he say, "You want bound over for another year?" See, just like that . . . "You want bound over for another year?" I told him, "Bound over hell! Let's settle this now!"

It seem like he kinda fell back when I said that, and all the cold went out of me. I reached down and grabbed that sickle and threw it just as far as I could throw it . . . and me and him commenced to wrestling.

We wrestled for three days and three nights. I can't say where I found the strength from. Every time it seemed like he was gonna get the best of me, I'd reach way down deep inside myself and find the strength to do him one better.

Rose: Every time Troy tell that story he find different ways to tell it. Different things to make up about it.

Troy: I ain't making up nothing. I'm telling you the facts of what happened. I wrestled with Death for three days and three nights and I'm standing here to tell you about it. (*Pause.*) All right. At the end of the third night we done weakened each other to where we can't hardly move. Death stood up, throwed on his robe . . . had him a white robe with a hood on it. He throwed on that robe and went off to look for his sickle. Say, "I'll be back." Just like that. "I'll be back." I told him, say, "Yeah, but . . . you gonna have to find me!" I wasn't no fool. I wan't going looking for him. Death ain't nothing to play with. And I know he's gonna get me. I know I got to join his army . . . his camp followers. But as long as I keep my strength and see him coming . . . as long as I keep up my vigilance . . . he's gonna have to fight to get me. I ain't going easy.

Bono: Well, look here, since you got to keep up your vigilance . . . let me have the bottle.

Troy: Aw hell, I shouldn't have told you that part. I should have left out that part.

Rose: Troy be talking that stuff and half the time don't even know what he be talking about.

Troy: Bono know me better than that.

Bono: That's right. I know you. I know you got some Uncle Remus° in your blood. You got more stories than the devil got sinners.

Troy: Aw hell, I done seen him too! Done talked with the devil.

Rose: Troy, don't nobody wanna be hearing all that stuff.

(Lyons enters the yard from the street. Thirty-four years old, Troy's son by a previous marriage, he sports a neatly trimmed goatee, sport coat, white shirt, tieless and buttoned at the collar. Though he fancies himself a musician, he is more caught up in the rituals and "idea" of being a musician than in the actual practice of the music. He has come to borrow money from Troy, and while he knows he will be successful, he is uncertain as to what extent his lifestyle will be held up to scrutiny and ridicule.)

Lyons: Hey, Pop.

Troy: What you come "Hey, Popping" me for?

Lyons: How you doing, Rose? *(He kisses her.)* Mr. Bono. How you doing?

Bono: Hey, Lyons . . . how you been?

Troy: He must have been doing all right. I ain't seen him around here last week.

Rose: Troy, leave your boy alone. He come by to see you and you wanna start all that nonsense.

Troy: I ain't bothering Lyons. *(Offers him the bottle.)* Here . . . get you a drink. We got an understanding. I know why he come by to see me and he know I know.

Lyons: Come on, Pop . . . I just stopped by to say hi . . . see how you was doing.

Troy: You ain't stopped by yesterday.

Rose: You gonna stay for supper, Lyons? I got some chicken cooking in the oven.

Lyons: No, Rose . . . thanks. I was just in the neighborhood and thought I'd stop by for a minute.

Troy: You was in the neighborhood all right, nigger. You telling the truth there. You was in the neighborhood cause it's my payday.

Uncle Remus: Black storyteller who recounts traditional black tales in the book by Joel Chandler Harris.

Lyons: Well, hell, since you mentioned it . . . let me have ten dollars.

Troy: I'll be damned! I'll die and go to hell and play blackjack with the devil before I give you ten dollars.

Bono: That's what I wanna know about . . . that devil you done seen.

Lyons: What . . . Pop done seen the devil? You too much, Pops.

Troy: Yeah, I done seen him. Talked to him too!

Rose: You ain't seen no devil. I done told you that man ain't had nothing to do with the devil. Anything you can't understand, you want to call it the devil.

Troy: Look here, Bono . . . I went down to see Hertzberger about some furniture. Got three rooms for two-ninety-eight. That what it say on the radio. "Three rooms . . . two-ninety-eight." Even made up a little song about it. Go down there . . . man tell me I can't get no credit. I'm working every day and can't get no credit. What to do? I got an empty house with some raggedy furniture in it. Cory ain't got no bed. He's sleeping on a pile of rags on the floor. Working every day and can't get no credit. Come back here—Rose'll tell you— madder than hell. Sit down . . . try to figure what I'm gonna do. Come a knock on the door. Ain't been living here but three days. Who know I'm here? Open the door . . . devil standing there bigger than life. White fellow . . . got on good clothes and everything. Standing there with a clipboard in his hand. I ain't had to say nothing. First words come out of his mouth was . . . "I understand you need some furniture and can't get no credit." I liked to fell over. He say, "I'll give you all the credit you want, but you got to pay the interest on it." I told him, "Give me three rooms worth and charge whatever you want." Next day a truck pulled up here and two men unloaded them three rooms. Man what drove the truck give me a book. Say send ten dollars, first of every month to the address in the book and everything will be all right. Say if I miss a payment the devil was coming back and it'll be hell to pay. That was fifteen years ago. To this day . . . the first of the month I send my ten dollars, Rose'll tell you.

Rose: Troy lying.

Troy: I ain't never seen that man since. Now you tell me who else that could have been but the devil? I ain't sold my soul or nothing like that, you understand. Naw, I wouldn't have truck with the devil about nothing like that. I got my furniture and pays my ten dollars the first of the month just like clockwork.

Bono: How long you say you been paying this ten dollars a month?

Troy: Fifteen years!

Bono: Hell, ain't you finished paying for it yet? How much the man done charged you.

Troy: Ah hell, I done paid for it. I done paid for it ten times over! The fact is I'm scared to stop paying it.

Rose: Troy lying. We got that furniture from Mr. Glickman. He ain't paying no ten dollars a month to nobody.

Troy: Aw hell, woman. Bono know I ain't that big a fool.

Lyons: I was just getting ready to say . . . I know where there's a bridge for sale.

Troy: Look here, I'll tell you this . . . it don't matter to me if he was the devil. It don't matter if the devil give credit. Somebody has got to give it.

Rose: It ought to matter. You going around talking about having truck with the devil . . . God's the one you gonna have to answer to. He's the one gonna be at the Judgment.

Lyons: Yeah, well, look here, Pop . . . let me have that ten dollars. I'll give it back to you. Bonnie got a job working at the hospital.

Troy: What I tell you, Bono? The only time I see this nigger is when he wants something. That's the only time I see him.

Lyons: Come on, Pop, Mr. Bono don't want to hear all that. Let me have the ten dollars. I told you Bonnie working.

Troy: What that mean to me? "Bonnie working." I don't care if she working. Go ask her for the ten dollars if she working. Talking about "Bonnie working." Why ain't you working?

Lyons: Aw, Pop, you know I can't find no decent job. Where am I gonna get a job at? You know I can't get no job.

Troy: I told you I know some people down there. I can get you on the rubbish if you want to work. I told you that the last time you came by here asking me for something.

Lyons: Naw, Pop . . . thanks. That ain't for me. I don't wanna be carrying nobody's rubbish. I don't wanna be punching nobody's time clock.

Troy: What's the matter, you too good to carry people's rubbish? Where you think that ten dollars you talking about come from? I'm just supposed to haul people's rubbish and give my money to you cause you too lazy to work. You too lazy to work and wanna know why you ain't got what I got.

Rose: What hospital Bonnie working at? Mercy?

Lyons: She's down at Passavant working in the laundry.

Troy: I ain't got nothing as it is. I give you that ten dollars and I got to eat beans the rest of the week. Naw . . . you ain't getting no ten dollars here.

Lyons: You ain't got to be eating no beans. I don't know why you wanna say that.

Troy: I ain't got no extra money. Gabe done moved over to Miss Pearl's paying her the rent and things done got tight around here. I can't afford to be giving you every payday.

Lyons: I ain't asked you to give me nothing. I asked you to loan me ten dollars. I know you got ten dollars.

Troy: Yeah, I got it. You know why I got it? Cause I don't throw my money away out there in the streets. You living the fast life . . . wanna be a musician . . . running around in them clubs and things . . . then, you learn to take care of yourself. You ain't gonna find me going and asking nobody for nothing. I done spent too many years without.

Lyons: You and me is two different people, Pop.

Troy: I done learned my mistake and learned to do what's right by it. You still trying to get something for nothing. Life don't owe you nothing. You owe it to yourself. Ask Bono. He'll tell you I'm right.

Lyons: You got your way of dealing with the world . . . I got mine. The only thing that matters to me is the music.

Troy: Yeah, I can see that! It don't matter how you gonna eat . . . where your next dollar is coming from. You telling the truth there.

Lyons: I know I got to eat. But I got to live too. I need something that gonna help me to get out of the bed in the morning. Make me feel like I belong in the world. I don't bother nobody. I just stay with my music cause that's the only way I can find to live in the world. Otherwise there ain't no telling what I might do. Now I don't come criticizing you and how you live. I just come by to ask you for ten dollars. I don't wanna hear all that about how I live.

Troy: Boy, your mamma did a hell of a job raising you.

Lyons: You can't change me, Pop. I'm thirty-four years old. If you wanted to change me, you should have been there when I was growing up. I come by to see you . . . ask for ten dollars and you want to talk about how I was raised. You don't know nothing about how I was raised.

Rose: Let the boy have ten dollars, Troy.

Troy (to Lyons): What the hell you looking at me for? I ain't got no ten dollars. You know what I do with my money. (*To Rose.*) Give him ten dollars if you want him to have it.

Rose: I will. Just as soon as you turn it loose.

Troy (handing Rose the money): There it is. Seventy-six dollars and forty-two cents. You see this, Bono? Now, I ain't gonna get but six of that back.

Rose: You ought to stop telling that lie. Here, Lyons. (*She hands him the money.*)

Lyons: Thanks, Rose. Look . . . I got to run . . . I'll see you later.

Troy: Wait a minute. You gonna say, "thanks, Rose" and ain't gonna look to see where she got that ten dollars from? See how they do me, Bono?

Lyons: I know she got it from you, Pop. Thanks. I'll give it back to you.

Troy: There he go telling another lie. Time I see that ten dollars . . . he'll be owing me thirty more.

Lyons: See you, Mr. Bono.

Bono: Take care, Lyons!

Lyons: Thanks, Pop. I'll see you again.

(*Lyons exits the yard.*)

Troy: I don't know why he don't go and get him a decent job and take care of that woman he got.

Bono: He'll be all right, Troy. The boy is still young.

Troy: The *boy* is thirty-four years old.

Rose: Let's not get off into all that.

Bono: Look here . . . I got to be going. I got to be getting on. Lucille gonna be waiting.

Troy (puts his arm around Rose):   See this woman, Bono? I love this woman. I love this woman so much it hurts. I love her so much . . . I done run out of ways of loving her. So I got to go back to basics. Don't you come by my house Monday morning talking about time to go to work . . . 'cause I'm still gonna be stroking!

Rose: Troy! Stop it now!

Bono: I ain't paying him no mind, Rose. That ain't nothing but gin-talk. Go on, Troy. I'll see you Monday.

Troy: Don't you come by my house, nigger! I done told you what I'm gonna be doing.

(The lights go down to black.)

Scene II

(The lights come up on Rose hanging up clothes. She hums and sings softly to herself. It is the following morning.)

Rose (sings):   Jesus, be a fence all around me every day
Jesus, I want you to protect me as I travel on my way.
Jesus, be a fence all around me every day.

(Troy enters from the house.)

Jesus, I want you to protect me
As I travel on my way.
(To Troy.) 'Morning. You ready for breakfast? I can fix it soon as I finish hanging up these clothes?

Troy: I got the coffee on. That'll be all right. I'll just drink some of that this morning.

Rose: That 651 hit yesterday. That's the second time this month. Miss Pearl hit for a dollar . . . seem like those that need the least always get lucky. Poor folks can't get nothing.

Troy: Them numbers don't know nobody. I don't know why you fool with them. You and Lyons both.

Rose: It's something to do.

Troy: You ain't doing nothing but throwing your money away.

Rose: Troy, you know I don't play foolishly. I just play a nickel here and a nickel there.

Troy: That's two nickels you done thrown away.

Rose: Now I hit sometimes . . . that makes up for it. It always comes in handy when I do hit. I don't hear you complaining then.

Troy: I ain't complaining now. I just say it's foolish. Trying to guess out of six hundred ways which way the number gonna come. If I had all the money niggers, these Negroes, throw away on numbers for one week—just one week—I'd be a rich man.

Rose: Well, you wishing and calling it foolish ain't gonna stop folks from playing numbers. That's one thing for sure. Besides . . . some good things come from playing numbers. Look where Pope done bought him that restaurant off of numbers.

Troy: I can't stand niggers like that. Man ain't had two dimes to rub together. He walking around with his shoes all run over bumming money for cigarettes. All right. Got lucky there and hit the numbers . . .

Rose: Troy, I know all about it.

Troy: Had good sense, I'll say that for him. He ain't throwed his money away. I seen niggers hit the numbers and go through two thousand dollars in four days. Man bought him that restaurant down there . . . fixed it up real nice . . . and then didn't want nobody to come in it! A Negro go in there and can't get no kind of service. I seen a white fellow come in there and order a bowl of stew. Pope picked all the meat out the pot for him. Man ain't had nothing but a bowl of meat! Negro come behind him and ain't got nothing but the potatoes and carrots. Talking about what numbers do for people, you picked a wrong example. Ain't done nothing but make a worser fool out of him than he was before.

Rose: Troy, you ought to stop worrying about what happened at work yesterday.

Troy: I ain't worried. Just told me to be down there at the Commissioner's office on Friday. Everybody think they gonna fire me. I ain't worried about them firing me. You ain't got to worry about that. (*Pause.*) Where's Cory? Cory in the house? (*Calls.*) Cory?

Rose: He gone out.

Troy: Out, huh? He gone out 'cause he know I want him to help me with this fence. I know how he is. That boy scared of work.

(*Gabriel enters. He comes halfway down the alley and, hearing Troy's voice, stops.*)

Troy (continues):   He ain't done a lick of work in his life.

Rose: He had to go to football practice. Coach wanted them to get in a little extra practice before the season start.

Troy: I got his practice . . . running out of here before he get his chores done.

Rose: Troy, what is wrong with you this morning? Don't nothing set right with you. Go on back in there and go to bed . . . get up on the other side.

Troy: Why something got to be wrong with me? I ain't said nothing
     wrong with me.
Rose: You got something to say about everything. First it's the numbers
     . . . then it's the way the man runs his restaurant . . . then you done
     got on Cory. What's it gonna be next? Take a look up there and see if
     the weather suits you . . . or is it gonna be how you gonna put up the
     fence with the clothes hanging in the yard.
Troy: You hit the nail on the head then.
Rose: I know you like I know the back of my hand. Go on in there and
     get you some coffee . . . see if that straighten you up. 'Cause you ain't
     right this morning.

*(Troy starts into the house and sees Gabriel. Gabriel starts singing. Troy's
brother, he is seven years younger than Troy. Injured in World War II, he
has a metal plate in his head. He carries an old trumpet tied around his
waist and believes with every fiber of his being that he is the Archangel
Gabriel. He carries a chipped basket with an assortment of discarded
fruits and vegetables he has picked up in the strip district and which he
attempts to sell.)*

Gabriel (singing):   Yes, ma'am, I got plums
     You ask me how I sell them
     Oh ten cents apiece
     Three for a quarter
     Come and buy now
     'Cause I'm here today
     And tomorrow I'll be gone

     (Gabriel enters.)

     Hey, Rose!
Rose: How you doing, Gabe?
Gabriel: There's Troy . . . Hey, Troy!
Troy: Hey, Gabe.

     (Exit into kitchen.)

Rose (to Gabriel):   What you got there?
Gabriel: You know what I got, Rose. I got fruits and vegetables.
Rose (looking in basket):   Where's all these plums you talking about?
Gabriel: I ain't got no plums today, Rose. I was just singing that. Have
     some tomorrow. Put me in a big order for plums. Have enough plums
     tomorrow for St. Peter and everybody. *(Troy reenters from kitchen,
     crosses to steps. To Rose.)* Troy's mad at me.
Troy: I ain't mad at you. What I got to be mad at you about? You ain't
     done nothing to me.
Gabriel: I just moved over to Miss Pearl's to keep out from in your way. I
     ain't mean no harm by it.

Troy: Who said anything about that? I ain't said anything about that.

Gabriel: You ain't mad at me, is you?

Troy: Naw . . . I ain't mad at you, Gabe. If I was mad at you I'd tell you about it.

Gabriel: Got me two rooms. In the basement. Got my own door too. Wanna see my key? (*He holds up a key.*) That's my own key! Ain't nobody else got a key like that. That's my key! My two rooms!

Troy: Well, that's good, Gabe. You got your own key . . . that's good.

Rose: You hungry, Gabe? I was just fixing to cook Troy his breakfast.

Gabriel: I'll take some biscuits. You got some biscuits? Did you know when I was in heaven . . . every morning me and St. Peter would sit down by the gate and eat some big fat biscuits? Oh, yeah! We had us a good time. We'd sit there and eat us them biscuits and then St. Peter would go off to sleep and tell me to wake him up when it's time to open the gates for the judgment.

Rose: Well, come on . . . I'll make up a batch of biscuits.

(Rose exits into the house.)

Gabriel: Troy . . . St. Peter got your name in the book. I seen it. It say . . . Troy Maxson. I say . . . I know him! He got the same name like what I got. That's my brother!

Troy: How many times you gonna tell me that, Gabe?

Gabriel: Ain't got my name in the book. Don't have to have my name. I done died and went to heaven. He got your name though. One morning St. Peter was looking at his book . . . marking it up for the judgment . . . and he let me see your name. Got it in there under M. Got Rose's name . . . I ain't seen it like I seen yours . . . but I know it's in there. He got a great big book. Got everybody's name what was ever been born. That's what he told me. But I seen your name. Seen it with my own eyes.

Troy: Go on in the house there. Rose going to fix you something to eat.

Gabriel: Oh, I ain't hungry. I done had breakfast with Aunt Jemimah. She come by and cooked me up a whole mess of flapjacks. Remember how we used to eat them flapjacks?

Troy: Go on in the house and get you something to eat now.

Gabriel: I got to go sell my plums. I done sold some tomatoes. Got me two quarters. Wanna see? (*He shows Troy his quarters.*) I'm gonna save them and buy me a new horn so St. Peter can hear me when it's time to open the gates. (*Gabriel stops suddenly. Listens.*) Hear that? That's the hellhounds. I got to chase them out of here. Go on get out of here! Get out! (*Gabriel exits singing.*)

Better get ready for the judgment
Better get ready for the judgment
My Lord is coming down

(Rose enters from the house.)

Troy: He gone off somewhere.

Gabriel (offstage): Better get ready for the judgment

Better get ready for the judgment morning

Better get ready for the judgment

My God is coming down

Rose: He ain't eating right. Miss Pearl say she can't get him to eat nothing.

Troy: What you want me to do about it, Rose? I done did everything I can for the man. I can't make him get well. Man got half his head blown away . . . what you expect?

Rose: Seem like something ought to be done to help him.

Troy: Man don't bother nobody. He just mixed up from that metal plate he got in his head. Ain't no sense for him to go back into the hospital.

Rose: Least he be eating right. They can help him take care of himself.

Troy: Don't nobody wanna be locked up, Rose. What you wanna lock him up for? Man go over there and fight the war . . . messin' around with them Japs, get half his head blown off . . . and they give him a lousy three thousand dollars. And I had to swoop down on that.

Rose: Is you fixing to go into that again?

Troy: That's the only way I got a roof over my head . . . cause of that metal plate.

Rose: Ain't no sense you blaming yourself for nothing. Gabe wasn't in no condition to manage that money. You done what was right by him. Can't nobody say you ain't done what was right by him. Look how long you took care of him . . . till he wanted to have his own place and moved over there with Miss Pearl.

Troy: That ain't what I'm saying, woman! I'm just stating the facts. If my brother didn't have that metal plate in his head . . . I wouldn't have a pot to piss in or a window to throw it out of. And I'm fifty-three years old. Now see if you can understand that!

(Troy gets up from the porch and starts to exit the yard.)

Rose: Where you going off to? You been running out of here every Saturday for weeks. I thought you was gonna work on this fence?

Troy: I'm gonna walk down to Taylors'. Listen to the ball game. I'll be back in a bit. I'll work on it when I get back.

(He exits the yard. The lights go to black.)

Scene III

(The lights come up on the yard. It is four hours later. Rose is taking down the clothes from the line. Cory enters carrying his football equipment.)

Rose: Your daddy like to had a fit with you running out of here this morning without doing your chores.

Cory: I told you I had to go to practice.

Rose: He say you were supposed to help him with this fence.

Cory: He been saying that the last four or five Saturdays, and then he don't never do nothing, but go down to Taylors'. Did you tell him about the recruiter?

Rose: Yeah, I told him.

Cory: What he say?

Rose: He ain't said nothing too much. You get in there and get started on your chores before he gets back. Go on and scrub down them steps before he gets back here hollering and carrying on.

Cory: I'm hungry. What you got to eat, Mama?

Rose: Go on and get started on your chores. I got some meat loaf in there. Go on and make you a sandwich . . . and don't leave no mess in there. (*Cory exits into the house. Rose continues to take down the clothes. Troy enters the yard and sneaks up and grabs her from behind.*) Troy! Go on, now. You liked to scared me to death. What was the score of the game? Lucille had me on the phone and I couldn't keep up with it.

Troy: What I care about the game? Come here, woman. (*He tries to kiss her.*)

Rose: I thought you went down Taylors' to listen to the game. Go on, Troy! You supposed to be putting up this fence.

Troy (attempting to kiss her again): I'll put it up when I finish with what is at hand.

Rose: Go on, Troy. I ain't studying you.

Troy (chasing after her): I'm studying you . . . fixing to do my homework!

Rose: Troy, you better leave me alone.

Troy: Where's Cory? That boy brought his butt home yet?

Rose: He's in the house doing his chores.

Troy (calling): Cory! Get your butt out here, boy! (*Rose exits into the house with the laundry. Troy goes over to the pile of wood, picks up a board, and starts sawing. Cory enters from the house.*) You just now coming in here from leaving this morning?

Cory: Yeah, I had to go to football practice.

Troy: Yeah, what?

Cory: Yessir.

Troy: I ain't but two seconds off you noway. The garbage sitting in there overflowing . . . you ain't done none of your chores . . . and you come in here talking about "Yeah."

Cory: I was just getting ready to do my chores now, Pop . . .

Troy: Your first chore is to help me with this fence on Saturday. Everything else come after that. Now get that saw and cut them boards.

(*Cory takes the saw and begins cutting the boards. Troy continues working. There is a long pause.*)

Cory: Hey, Pop . . . why don't you buy a TV?

Troy: What I want with a TV? What I want one of them for?

Cory: Everybody got one. Earl, Ba Bra . . . Jesse!

Troy: I ain't asked you who had one. I say what I want with one?

Cory: So you can watch it. They got lots of things on TV. Baseball games and everything. We could watch the World Series.

Troy: Yeah . . . and how much this TV cost?

Cory: I don't know. They got them on sale for around two hundred dollars.

Troy: Two hundred dollars, huh?

Cory: That ain't that much, Pop.

Troy: Naw, it's just two hundred dollars. See that roof you got over your head at night? Let me tell you something about that roof. It's been over ten years since that roof was last tarred. See now . . . the snow come this winter and sit up there on that roof like it is . . . and it's gonna seep inside. It's just gonna be a little bit . . . ain't gonna hardly notice it. Then the next thing you know, it's gonna be leaking all over the house. Then the wood rot from all that water and you gonna need a whole new roof. Now, how much you think it cost to get that roof tarred?

Cory: I don't know.

Troy: Two hundred and sixty-four dollars . . . cash money. While you thinking about a TV, I got to be thinking about the roof . . . and whatever else go wrong around here. Now if you had two hundred dollars, what would you do . . . fix the roof or buy a TV?

Cory: I'd buy a TV. Then when the roof started to leak . . . when it needed fixing . . . I'd fix it.

Troy: Where you gonna get the money from? You done spent it for a TV. You gonna sit up and watch the water run all over your brand new TV.

Cory: Aw, Pop. You got money. I know you do.

Troy: Where I got it at, huh?

Cory: You got it in the bank.

Troy: You wanna see my bankbook? You wanna see that seventy-three dollars and twenty-two cents I got sitting up in there.

Cory: You ain't got to pay for it all at one time. You can put a down payment on it and carry it on home with you.

Troy: Not me. I ain't gonna owe nobody nothing if I can help it. Miss a payment and they come and snatch it right out your house. Then what you got? Now, soon as I get two hundred dollars clear, then I'll buy a TV. Right now, as soon as I get two hundred and sixty-four dollars, I'm gonna have this roof tarred.

Cory: Aw . . . Pop!

Troy: You go on and get you two hundred dollars and buy one if ya want it. I got better things to do with my money.

Cory: I can't get no two hundred dollars. I ain't never seen two hundred dollars.

Troy: I'll tell you what . . . you get you a hundred dollars and I'll put the other hundred with it.

Cory: All right, I'm gonna show you.

Troy: You gonna show me how you can cut them boards right now.

(Cory begins to cut the boards. There is a long pause.)

Cory: The Pirates won today. That makes five in a row.

Troy: I ain't thinking about the Pirates. Got an all-white team. Got that boy . . . that Puerto Rican boy . . . Clemente. Don't even half-play him. That boy could be something if they give him a chance. Play him one day and sit him on the bench the next.

Cory: He gets a lot of chances to play.

Troy: I'm talking about playing regular. Playing every day so you can get your timing. That's what I'm talking about.

Cory: They got some white guys on the team that don't play every day. You can't play everybody at the same time.

Troy: If they got a white fellow sitting on the bench . . . you can bet your last dollar he can't play! The colored guy got to be twice as good before he get on the team. That's why I don't want you to get all tied up in them sports. Man on the team and what it get him? They got colored on the team and don't use them. Same as not having them. All them teams the same.

Cory: The Braves got Hank Aaron and Wes Covington. Hank Aaron hit two home runs today. That makes forty-three.

Troy: Hank Aaron ain't nobody. That's what you supposed to do. That's how you supposed to play the game. Ain't nothing to it. It's just a matter of timing . . . getting the right follow-through. Hell, I can hit forty-three home runs right now!

Cory: Not off no major-league pitching, you couldn't.

Troy: We had better pitching in the Negro leagues. I hit seven home runs off of Satchel Paige.° You can't get no better than that!

Cory: Sandy Koufax. He's leading the league in strikeouts.

Troy: I ain't thinking of no Sandy Koufax.

Cory: You got Warren Spahn and Lew Burdette. I bet you couldn't hit no home runs off of Warren Spahn.

Troy: I'm through with it now. You go on and cut them boards. (*Pause.*) Your mama tell me you done got recruited by a college football team? Is that right?

Cory: Yeah. Coach Zellman say the recruiter gonna be coming by to talk to you. Get you to sign the permission papers.

Troy: I thought you supposed to be working down there at the A&P. Ain't you suppose to be working down there after school?

Satchell Paige: 1906?–1982; legendary black pitcher in the Negro leagues.

Cory: Mr. Stawicki say he gonna hold my job for me until after the football season. Say starting next week I can work weekends.

Troy: I thought we had an understanding about this football stuff? You suppose to keep up with your chores and hold that job down at the A&P. Ain't been around here all day on a Saturday. Ain't none of your chores done . . . and now you telling me you done quit your job.

Cory: I'm gonna be working weekends.

Troy: You damn right you are! And ain't no need for nobody coming around here to talk to me about signing nothing.

Cory: Hey, Pop . . . you can't do that. He's coming all the way from North Carolina.

Troy: I don't care where he coming from. The white man ain't gonna let you get nowhere with that football noway. You go on and get your book-learning so you can work yourself up in that A&P or learn how to fix cars or build houses or something, get you a trade. That way you have something can't nobody take away from you. You go on and learn how to put your hands to some good use. Besides hauling people's garbage.

Cory: I get good grades, Pop. That's why the recruiter wants to talk with you. You got to keep up your grades to get recruited. This way I'll be going to college. I'll get a chance . . .

Troy: First you gonna get your butt down there to the A&P and get your job back.

Cory: Mr. Stawicki done already hired somebody else 'cause I told him I was playing football.

Troy: You a bigger fool than I thought . . . to let somebody take away your job so you can play some football. Where you gonna get your money to take out your girlfriend and whatnot? What kind of foolishness is that to let somebody take away your job?

Cory: I'm still gonna be working weekends.

Troy: Naw . . . naw. You getting your butt out of here and finding you another job.

Cory: Come on, Pop! I got to practice. I can't work after school and play football too. The team needs me. That's what Coach Zellman say . . . .

Troy: I don't care what nobody else say. I'm the boss . . . you understand? I'm the boss around here. I do the only saying what counts.

Cory: Come on, Pop!

Troy: I asked you . . . did you understand?

Cory: Yeah . . .

Troy: What?!

Cory: Yessir.

Troy: You go on down there to that A&P and see if you can get your job back. If you can't do both . . . then you quit the football team. You've got to take the crookeds with the straights.

Cory: Yessir. (*Pause.*) Can I ask you a question?

Troy: What the hell you wanna ask me? Mr. Stawicki the one you got the questions for.

Cory: How come you ain't never liked me?

Troy: Liked you? Who the hell say I got to like you? What law is there say I got to like you? Wanna stand up in my face and ask a damn fool-ass question like that. Talking about liking somebody. Come here, boy, when I talk to you. (*Cory comes over to where Troy is working. He stands slouched over and Troy shoves him on his shoulder.*) Straighten up, goddammit! I asked you a question . . . what law is there say I got to like you?

Cory: None.

Troy: Well, all right then! Don't you eat every day? (*Pause.*) Answer me when I talk to you! Don't you eat every day?

Cory: Yeah.

Troy: Nigger, as long as you in my house, you put that sir on the end of it when you talk to me!

Cory: Yes . . . sir.

Troy: You eat every day.

Cory: Yessir!

Troy: Got a roof over your head.

Cory: Yessir!

Troy: Got clothes on your back.

Cory: Yessir.

Troy: Why you think that is?

Cory: Cause of you.

Troy: Ah, hell I know it's 'cause of me . . . but why do you think that is?

Cory (hesitant):   Cause you like me.

Troy: Like you? I go out of here every morning . . . bust my butt . . . putting up with them crackers° every day . . . cause I like you? You about the biggest fool I ever saw. (*Pause.*) It's my job. It's my responsibility! You understand that? A man got to take care of his family. You live in my house . . . sleep you behind on my bed-clothes . . . fill you belly up with my food . . . cause you my son. You my flesh and blood. Not 'cause I like you! Cause it's my duty to take care of you. I owe a responsibility to you! Let's get this straight right here . . . before it go along any further . . . I ain't got to like you. Mr. Rand don't give me my money come payday cause he likes me. He gives me cause he owe me. I done give you everything I had to give you. I gave you your life! Me and your mama worked that out between us. And liking your black ass wasn't part of the bargain. Don't you try and go through life worrying about if somebody like you or not. You best be making sure they doing right by you. You understand what I'm saying, boy?

Cory: Yessir.

---

crackers: White people, often used to refer disparagingly to poor whites.

Troy: Then get the hell out of my face, and get on down to that A&P.

(*Rose has been standing behind the screen door for much of the scene. She enters as Cory exits.*)

Rose: Why don't you let the boy go ahead and play football, Troy? Ain't no harm in that. He's just trying to be like you with the sports.

Troy: I don't want him to be like me! I want him to move as far away from my life as he can get. You the only decent thing that ever happened to me. I wish him that. But I don't wish him a thing else from my life. I decided seventeen years ago that boy wasn't getting involved in no sports. Not after what they did to me in the sports.

Rose: Troy, why don't you admit you was too old to play in the major leagues? For once . . . why don't you admit that?

Troy: What do you mean too old? Don't come telling me I was too old. I just wasn't the right color. Hell, I'm fifty-three years old and can do better than Selkirk's .269 right now!

Rose: How's was you gonna play ball when you were over forty? Sometimes I can't get no sense out of you.

Troy: I got good sense, woman. I got sense enough not to let my boy get hurt over playing no sports. You been mothering that boy too much. Worried about if people like him.

Rose: Everything that boy do . . . he do for you. He wants you to say "Good job, son." That's all.

Troy: Rose, I ain't got time for that. He's alive. He's healthy. He's got to make his own way. I made mine. Ain't nobody gonna hold his hand when he get out there in that world.

Rose: Times have changed from when you was young, Troy. People change. The world's changing around you and you can't even see it.

Troy (slow, methodical):   Woman . . . I do the best I can do. I come in here every Friday. I carry a sack of potatoes and a bucket of lard. You all line up at the door with your hands out. I give you the lint from my pockets. I give you my sweat and my blood. I ain't got no tears. I done spent them. We go upstairs in that room at night . . . and I fall down on you and try to blast a hole into forever. I get up Monday morning . . . find my lunch on the table. I go out. Make my way. Find my strength to carry me through to the next Friday. (*Pause.*) That's all I got, Rose. That's all I got to give. I can't give nothing else.

(*Troy exits into the house. The lights go down to black.*)

Scene IV

(*It is Friday. Two weeks later. Cory starts out of the house with his football equipment. The phone rings.*)

Cory (calling):   I got it! (*He answers the phone and stands in the screen door talking.*) Hello? Hey, Jesse. Naw . . . I was just getting ready to leave now.

Rose (calling):   Cory!

Cory: I told you, man, them spikes is all tore up. You can use them if you want, but they ain't no good. Earl got some spikes.

Rose (calling):   Cory!

Cory (calling to Rose):   Mam? I'm talking to Jesse. (*Into phone.*) When she say that? (*Pause.*) Aw, you lying, man. I'm gonna tell her you said that.

Rose (calling):   Cory, don't you go nowhere!

Cory: I got to go to the game, Ma! (*Into the phone.*) Yeah, hey, look, I'll talk to you later. Yeah, I'll meet you over Earl's house. Later. Bye, Ma.

(*Cory exits the house and starts out the yard.*)

Rose: Cory, where you going off to? You got that stuff all pulled out and thrown all over your room.

Cory (in the yard):   I was looking for my spikes. Jesse wanted to borrow my spikes.

Rose: Get up there and get that cleaned up before your daddy get back in here.

Cory: I got to go to the game! I'll clean it up *when I get back.* (*Cory exits.*)

Rose: That's all he need to do is see that room all messed up.

(*Rose exits into the house. Troy and Bono enter the yard. Troy is dressed in clothes other than his work clothes.*)

Bono: He told him the same thing he told you. Take it to the union.

Troy: Brownie ain't got that much sense. Man wasn't thinking about nothing. He wait until I confront them on it . . . then he wanna come crying seniority. (*Calls.*) Hey, Rose!

Bono: I wish I could have seen Mr. Rand's face when he told you.

Troy: He couldn't get it out of his mouth! Liked to bit his tongue! When they called me down there to the Commissioner's office . . . he thought they was gonna fire me. Like everybody else.

Bono: I didn't think they was gonna fire you. I thought they was gonna put you on the warning paper.

Troy: Hey, Rose! (*To Bono.*) Yeah, Mr. Rand like to bit his tongue.

(*Troy breaks the seal on the bottle, takes a drink, and hands it to Bono.*)

Bono: I see you run right down to Taylors' and told that Alberta gal.

Troy (calling):   Hey Rose! (*To Bono.*) I told everybody. Hey, Rose! I went down there to cash my check.

Rose (entering from the house):   Hush all that hollering, man! I know you out here. What they say down there at the Commissioner's office?

Troy: You supposed to come when I call you, woman. Bono'll tell you that. (*To Bono.*) Don't Lucille come when you call her?

Rose: Man, hush your mouth. I ain't no dog . . . talk about "come when you call me."

Troy (puts his arm around Rose):   You hear this, Bono? I had me an old dog used to get uppity like that. You say, "C'mere, Blue!" . . . and he just lay there and look at you. End up getting a stick and chasing him away trying to make him come.

Rose: I ain't studying you and your dog. I remember you used to sing that old song.

Troy (he sings): Hear it ring! Hear it ring! I had a dog his name was Blue.

Rose: Don't nobody wanna hear you sing that old song.

Troy (sings): You know Blue was mighty true.

Rose: Used to have Cory running around here singing that song.

Bono: Hell, I remember that song myself.

Troy (sings): You know Blue was a good old dog. Blue treed a possum in a hollow log. That was my daddy's song. My daddy made up that song.

Rose: I don't care who made it up. Don't nobody wanna hear you sing it.

Troy (makes a song like calling a dog): Come here, woman.

Rose: You come in here carrying on, I reckon they ain't fired you. What they say down there at the Commissioner's office?

Troy: Look here, Rose . . . Mr. Rand called me into his office today when I got back from talking to them people down there . . . it come from up top . . . he called me in and told me they was making me a driver.

Rose: Troy, you kidding!

Troy: No I ain't, Ask Bono.

Rose: Well, that's great, Troy. Now you don't have to hassle them people no more.

(Lyons enters from the street.)

Troy: Aw hell, I wasn't looking to see you today. I thought you was in jail. Got it all over the front page of the *Courier* about them raiding Sefus' place . . . where you be hanging out with all them thugs.

Lyons: Hey, Pop . . . that ain't got nothing to do with me. I don't go down there gambling. I go down there to sit in with the band. I ain't got nothing to do with the gambling part. They got some good music down there.

Troy: They got some rogues . . . is what they got.

Lyons: How you been, Mr. Bono? Hi, Rose.

Bono: I see where you playing down at the Crawford Grill tonight.

Rose: How come you ain't brought Bonnie like I told you. You should have brought Bonnie with you, she ain't been over in a month of Sundays.

Lyons: I was just in the neighborhood . . . thought I'd stop by.

Troy: Here he come . . .

Bono: Your daddy got a promotion on the rubbish. He's gonna be the first colored driver. Ain't got to do nothing but sit up there and read the paper like them white fellows.

Lyons: Hey, Pop . . . if you knew how to read you'd be all right.

Bono: Naw . . . naw . . . you mean if the nigger knew how to *drive* he'd be all right. Been fighting with them people about driving and ain't even got a license. Mr. Rand know you ain't got no driver's license?

Troy: Driving ain't nothing. All you do is point the truck where you want it to go. Driving ain't nothing.

Bono: Do Mr. Rand know you ain't got no driver's license? That's what I'm talking about. I ain't asked if driving was easy. I asked if Mr. Rand know you ain't got no driver's license.

Troy: He ain't got to know. The man ain't got to know my business. Time he find out, I have two or three driver's licenses.

Lyons (going into his pocket): Say, look here, Pop . . .

Troy: I knew it was coming. Didn't I tell you, Bono? I know what kind of "Look here, Pop" that was. The nigger fixing to ask me for some money. It's Friday night. It's my payday. All them rogues down there on the avenue . . . the ones that ain't in jail . . . and Lyons is hopping in his shoes to get down there with them.

Lyons: See, Pop . . . if you give somebody else a chance to talk sometime, you'd see that I was fixing to pay you back your ten dollars like I told you. Here . . . I told you I'd pay you when Bonnie got paid.

Troy: Naw . . . you go ahead and keep that ten dollars. Put it in the bank. The next time you feel like you wanna come by here and ask me for something . . . you go on down there and get that.

Lyons: Here's your ten dollars, Pop. I told you I don't want you to give me nothing. I just wanted to borrow ten dollars.

Troy: Naw . . . you go on and keep that for the next time you want to ask me.

Lyons: Come on, Pop . . . here go your ten dollars.

Rose: Why don't you go on and let the boy pay you back, Troy?

Lyons: Here you go, Rose. If you don't take it I'm gonna have to hear about it for the next six months.

(*He hands her the money.*)

Rose: You can hand yours over here too, Troy.

Troy: You see this, Bono. You see how they do me.

Bono: Yeah, Lucille do me the same way.

(*Gabriel is heard singing offstage. He enters.*)

Gabriel: Better get ready for the Judgment! Better get ready for . . . Hey! . . . Hey! . . . There's Troy's boy!

Lyons: How are you doing, Uncle Gabe?

Gabriel: Lyons . . . The King of the Jungle! Rose . . . hey, Rose. Got a flower for you. (*He takes a rose from his pocket.*) Picked it myself. That's the same rose like you is!

Rose: That's right nice of you, Gabe.

Lyons: What you been doing, Uncle Gabe?

Gabriel: Oh, I been chasing hellhounds and waiting on the time to tell St. Peter to open the gates.

Lyons: You been chasing hellhounds, huh? Well . . . you doing the right thing, Uncle Gabe. Somebody got to chase them.

Gabriel: Oh, yeah . . . I know it. The devil's strong. The devil ain't no pushover. Hellhounds snipping at everybody's heels. But I got my trumpet waiting on the judgment time.

Lyons: Waiting on the Battle of Armageddon, huh?

Gabriel: Ain't gonna be too much of a battle when God get to waving that Judgment sword. But the people's gonna have a hell of a time trying to get into heaven if them gates ain't open.

Lyons (putting his arm around Gabriel):   You hear this, Pop. Uncle Gabe, you all right!

Gabriel (laughing with Lyons):   Lyons! King of the Jungle.

Rose: You gonna stay for supper, Gabe. Want me to fix you a plate?

Gabriel: I'll take a sandwich, Rose. Don't want no plate. Just wanna eat with my hands. I'll take a sandwich.

Rose: How about you, Lyons? You staying? Got some short ribs cooking.

Lyons: Naw, I won't eat nothing till after we finished playing. (*Pause.*) You ought to come down and listen to me play, Pop.

Troy: I don't like that Chinese music. All that noise.

Rose: Go on in the house and wash up, Gabe . . . I'll fix you a sandwich.

Gabriel (to Lyons, as he exits):   Troy's mad at me.

Lyons: What you mad at Uncle Gabe for, Pop.

Rose: He thinks Troy's mad at him cause he moved over to Miss Pearl's.

Troy: I ain't mad at the man. He can live where he want to live at.

Lyons: What he move over there for? Miss Pearl don't like nobody.

Rose: She don't mind him none. She treats him real nice. She just don't allow all that singing.

Troy: She don't mind that rent he be paying . . . that's what she don't mind.

Rose: Troy, I ain't going through that with you no more. He's over there cause he want to have his own place. He can come and go as he please.

Troy: Hell, he could come and go as he please here. I wasn't stopping him. I ain't put no rules on him.

Rose: It ain't the same thing, Troy. And you know it. (*Gabriel comes to the door.*) Now, that's the last I wanna hear about that. I don't wanna hear nothing else about Gabe and Miss Pearl. And next week . . .

Gabriel: I'm ready for my sandwich, Rose.

Rose: And next week . . . when that recruiter come from that school . . . I want you to sign that paper and go on and let Cory play football. Then that'll be the last I have to hear about that.

Troy (to Rose as she exits into the house):   I ain't thinking about Cory nothing.

Lyons: What . . . Cory got recruited? What school he going to?

Troy: That boy walking around here smelling his piss . . . thinking he's grown. Thinking he's gonna do what he want, irrespective of what I say. Look here, Bono . . . I left the Commissioner's office and went down to the A&P . . . that boy ain't working down there. He lying to me. Telling me he got his job back . . . telling me he working weekends . . . telling me he working after school . . . Mr. Stawicki tell me he ain't working down there at all!

Lyons: Cory just growing up. He's just busting at the seams trying to fill out your shoes.

Troy: I don't care what he's doing. When he get to the point where he wanna disobey me . . . then it's time for him to move on. Bono'll tell you that. I bet he ain't never disobeyed his daddy without paying the consequences.

Bono: I ain't never had a chance. My daddy came on through . . . but I ain't never knew him to see him . . . or what he had on his mind or where he went. Just moving on through. Searching out the New Land. That's what the old folks used to call it. See a fellow moving around from place to place . . . woman to woman . . . called it searching out the New Land. I can't say if he ever found it. I come along, didn't want no kids. Didn't know if I was gonna be in one place long enough to fix on them right as their daddy. I figured I was going searching too. As it turned out I been hooked up with Lucille near about as long as your daddy been with Rose. Going on sixteen years.

Troy: Sometimes I wish I hadn't known my daddy. He ain't cared nothing about no kids. A kid to him wasn't nothing. All he wanted was for you to learn how to walk so he could start you to working. When it come time for eating . . . he ate first. If there was anything left over, that's what you got. Man would sit down and eat two chickens and give you the wing.

Lyons: You ought to stop that, Pop. Everybody feed their kids. No matter how hard times is . . . everybody care about their kids. Make sure they have something to eat.

Troy: The only thing my daddy cared about was getting them bales of cotton in to Mr. Lubin. That's the only thing that mattered to him. Sometimes I used to wonder why he was living. Wonder why the devil hadn't come and got him. "Get them bales of cotton in to Mr. Lubin" and find out he owe him money . . .

Lyons: He should have just when on and left when he saw he couldn't get nowhere. That's what I would have done.

Troy: How he gonna leave with eleven kids? And where he gonna go? He ain't knew how to do nothing but farm. No, he was trapped and I think he knew it. But I'll say this for him . . . he felt a responsibility toward us. Maybe he ain't treated us the way I felt he should have . . . but without that responsibility he could have walked off and left us . . . made his own way.

Bono: A lot of them did. Back in those days what you talking about . . . they walk out their front door and just take on down one road or another and keep on walking.

Lyons: There you go! That's what I'm talking about.

Bono: Just keep on walking till you come to something else. Ain't you
never heard of nobody having the walking blues? Well, that's what you
call it when you just take off like that.

Troy: My daddy ain't had them walking blues! What you talking about? He
stayed right there with his family. But he was just as evil as he could be.
My mama couldn't stand him. Couldn't stand that evilness. She run off
when I was about eight. She sneaked off one night after he had gone to
sleep. Told me she was coming back for me. I ain't never seen her no
more. All his women run off and left him. He wasn't good for nobody.

When my turn come to head out, I was fourteen and got to
sniffing around Joe Canewell's daughter. Had us an old mule we
called Greyboy. My daddy sent me out to do some plowing and I tied
up Greyboy and went to fooling around with Joe Canewell's daughter.
We done found us a nice little spot, got real cozy with each other. She
about thirteen and we done figured we was grown anyway . . . so we
down there enjoying ourselves . . . ain't thinking about nothing. We
didn't know Greyboy had got loose and wandered back to the house
and my daddy was looking for me. We down there by the creek
enjoying ourselves when my daddy come up on us. Surprised us. He
had them leather straps off the mule and commenced to whupping me
like there was no tomorrow. I jumped up, mad and embarrassed. I was
scared of my daddy. When he commenced to whupping on me . . .
quite naturally I run to get out of the way. (*Pause.*) Now I thought he
was mad cause I ain't done my work. But I see where he was chasing
me off so he could have the gal for himself. When I see what the
matter of it was, I lost all fear of my daddy. Right there is where I
become a man . . . at fourteen years of age. (*Pause.*) Now it was my
turn to run him off. I picked up them same reins that he had used on
me. I picked up them reins and commenced to whupping on him. The
gal jumped up and run off . . . and when my daddy turned to face me,
I could see why the devil had never come to get him . . . cause he was
the devil himself. I don't know what happened. When I woke up, I
was laying right there by the creek, and Blue . . . this old dog we had
. . . was licking my face. I thought I was blind. I couldn't see nothing.
Both my eyes were swollen shut. I layed there and cried. I didn't know
what I was gonna do. The only thing I knew was the time had come
for me to leave my daddy's house. And right there the world suddenly
got big. And it was a long time before I could cut it down to where I
could handle it.

Part of that cutting down was when I got to the place where I
could feel him kicking in my blood and knew that the only thing that
separated us was the matter of a few years.

(*Gabriel enters from the house with a sandwich.*)

Lyons: What you got there, Uncle Gabe?

Gabriel: Got me a ham sandwich. Rose gave me a ham sandwich.

Troy: I don't know what happened to him. I done lost touch with everybody except Gabriel. But I hope he's dead. I hope he found some peace.

Lyons: That's a heavy story, Pop. I didn't know you left home when you was fourteen.

Troy: And didn't know nothing. The only part of the world I knew was the forty-two acres of Mr. Lubin's land. That's all I knew about life.

Lyons: Fourteen's kinda young to be out on your own. (*Phone rings.*) I don't even think I was ready to be out on my own at fourteen. I don't know what I would have done.

Troy: I got up from the creek and walked on down to Mobile. I was through with farming. Figured I could do better in the city. So I walked the two hundred miles to Mobile.

Lyons: Wait a minute . . . you ain't walked no two hundred miles, Pop. Ain't nobody gonna walk no two hundred miles. You talking about some walking there.

Bono: That's the only way you got anywhere back in them days.

Lyons: Shhh. Damn if I wouldn't have hitched a ride with somebody!

Troy: Who you gonna hitch it with? They ain't had no cars and things like they got now. We talking about 1918.

Rose (entering): What you all out here getting into?

Troy (to Rose): I'm telling Lyons how good he got it. He don't know nothing about this I'm talking.

Rose: Lyons, that was Bonnie on the phone. She say you supposed to pick her up.

Lyons: Yeah, okay, Rose.

Troy: I walked on down to Mobile and hitched up with some of them fellows that was heading this way. Got up here and found out . . . not only couldn't you get a job . . . you couldn't find no place to live. I thought I was in freedom. Shhh. Colored folks living down there on the riverbanks in whatever kind of shelter they could find for themselves. Right down there under the Brady Street Bridge. Living in shacks made of sticks and tarpaper. Messed around there and went from bad to worse. Started stealing. First it was food. Then I figured, hell, if I steal money I can buy me some food. Buy me some shoes too! One thing led to another. Met your mama. I was young and anxious to be a man. Met your mama and had you. What I do that for? Now I got to worry about feeding you and her. Got to steal three times as much. Went out one day looking for somebody to rob . . . that's what I was, a robber. I'll tell you the truth. I'm ashamed of it today. But it's the truth. Went to rob this fellow . . . pulled out my knife . . . and he pulled out a gun. Shot me in the chest. It felt just like somebody had taken a hot branding iron and laid it on me. When he shot me I jumped at him with my knife. They told me I killed him and they put me in the penitentiary and locked me up for fifteen years. That's where I met Bono. That's where I learned how to play baseball. Got out that place and your mama had taken you and went on to make life without me. Fifteen years was a long time for her to wait. But that fifteen years cured me of that robbing stuff. Rose'll tell you. She asked me when I met her if I had gotten all that foolishness out of my system. And I told here, "Baby, it's you and baseball all what count with me." You hear me, Bono? I meant it too. She say, "Which one comes first?" I told her, "Baby, ain't no doubt it's baseball . . . but you stick and get old with me and we'll both outlive this baseball." Am I right, Rose? And it's true.

Rose: Man, hush your mouth. You ain't said no such thing. Talking about, "Baby, you know you'll always be number one with me." That's what you was talking.

Troy: You hear that, Bono. That's why I love her.

Bono: Rose'll keep you straight. You get off the track, she'll straighten you up.

Rose: Lyons, you better get on up and get Bonnie. She waiting on you.

Lyons (gets up to go):   Hey, Pop, why don't you come on down to the Grill and hear me play?

Troy: I ain't going down there. I'm too old to be sitting around in them clubs.

Bono: You got to be good to play down at the Grill.

Lyons: Come on, Pop . . .

Troy: I got to get up in the morning.

Lyons: You ain't got to stay long.

Troy: Naw, I'm gonna get my supper and go on to bed.

Lyons: Well, I got to go. I'll see you again.

Troy: Don't you come around my house on my payday.

Rose: Pick up the phone and let somebody know you coming. And bring Bonnie with you. You know I'm always glad to see her.

Lyons: Yeah, I'll do that, Rose. You take care now. See you, Pop. See you, Mr. Bono. See you, Uncle Gabe.

Gabriel: Lyons! King of the Jungle!

   (*Lyons exits.*)

Troy: Is supper ready, woman? Me and you got some business to take care of. I'm gonna tear it up too.

Rose: Troy, I done told you now!

Troy (puts his arm around Bono):   Aw hell, woman . . . this is Bono. Bono like family. I done known this nigger since . . . how long I done know you?

Bono: It's been a long time.

Troy: I done known this nigger since Skippy was a pup. Me and him done been through some times.

Bono: You sure right about that.

Troy: Hell, I done know him longer than I known you. And we still standing shoulder to shoulder. Hey, look here, Bono . . . a man can't ask for no more than that. (*Drinks to him.*) I love you, nigger.

Bono: Hell, I love you too . . . but I got to get home see my woman. You got yours in hand. I got to go get mine.

(Bono starts to exit as Cory enters the yard, dressed in his football uniform. He gives Troy a hard, uncompromising look.)

Cory: What you do that for, Pop?

(He throws his helmet down in the direction of Troy.)

Rose: What's the matter? Cory . . . what's the matter?

Cory: Papa done went up to the school and told Coach Zellman I can't play football no more. Wouldn't even let me play the game. Told him to tell the recruiter not to come.

Rose: Troy . . .

Troy: What you Troying me for. Yeah, I did it. And the boy know why I did it.

Cory: Why you wanna do that to me? That was the one chance I had.

Rose: Ain't nothing wrong with Cory playing football, Troy.

Troy: The boy lied to me. I told the nigger if he wanna play football . . . to keep up his chores and hold down that job at the A&P. That was the conditions. Stopped down there to see Mr. Stawicki . . .

Cory: I can't work after school during the football season, Pop! I tried to tell you that Mr. Stawicki's holding my job for me. You don't never want to listen to nobody. And then you wanna go and do this to me!

Troy: I ain't done nothing to you. You done it to yourself.

Cory: Just cause you didn't have a chance! You just scared I'm gonna be better than you, that's all.

Troy: Come here.

Rose: Troy . . .

(Cory reluctantly crosses over to Troy).

Troy: All right! See. You done made a mistake.

Cory: I didn't even do nothing!

Troy: I'm gonna tell you what your mistake was. See . . . you swung at the ball and didn't hit it. That's strike one. See, you in the batter's box now. You swung and you missed. That's strike one. Don't you strike out!

(Lights fade to black).

ACT II

Scene I

(The following morning. Cory is at the tree hitting the ball with the bat. He tries to mimic Troy, but his swing is awkward, less sure. Rose enters from the house).

Rose: Cory, I want you to help me with this cupboard.

Cory: I ain't quitting the team. I don't care what Poppa say.

Rose: I'll talk to him when he gets back. He had to go see about your Uncle Gabe. The police done arrested him. Say he was disturbing the peace. He'll be back directly. Come on in here and help me clean out the top of this cupboard. (*Cory exits into the house. Rose sees Troy and Bono coming down the alley.*) Troy . . . what they say down there?

Troy: Ain't said nothing. I give them fifty dollars and they let him go. I'll talk to you about it. Where's Cory?

Rose: He's in there helping me clean out these cupboards.

Troy: Tell him to get his butt out here.

(*Troy and Bono go over to the pile of wood. Bono picks up the saw and begins sawing*).

Troy (to Bono): All they want is the money. That makes six or seven times I done went down there and got him. See me coming they stick out their *hands.*

Bono: Yeah. I know what you mean. That's all they care about . . . that money. They don't care about what's right. (*Pause.*) Nigger, why you got to go and get some hard wood? You ain't doing nothing but building a little old fence. Get you some soft pine wood. That's all you need.

Troy: I know what I'm doing. This is outside wood. You put pine wood inside the house. Pine wood is inside wood. This here is outside wood. Now you tell me where the fence is gonna be?

Bono: You don't need this wood. You can put it up with pine wood and it'll stand as long as you gonna be here looking at it.

Troy: How you know how long I'm gonna be here, nigger? Hell, I might just live forever. Live longer than old man Horsely.

Bono: That's what Magee used to say.

Troy: Magee's a damn fool. Now you tell me who you ever heard of gonna pull their own teeth with a pair of rusty pliers.

Bono: The old folks . . . my granddaddy used to pull his teeth with pliers. They ain't had no dentists for the colored folks back then.

Troy: Get clean pliers! You understand? Clean pliers! Sterilize them! Besides we ain't living back then. All Magee had to do was walk over to Doc Goldblum's.

Bono: I see where you and that Tallahassee gal . . . that Alberta . . . I see where you all done got tight.

Troy: What you mean "got tight"?

Bono: I see where you be laughing and joking with her all the time.

Troy: I laughs and jokes with all of them, Bono. You know me.

Bono: That ain't the kind of laughing and joking I'm talking about.

(*Cory enters from the house.*)

Cory: How you doing, Mr. Bono?

Troy: Cory? Get that saw from Bono and cut some wood. He talking
about the wood's too hard to cut. Stand back there, Jim, and let that
young boy show you how it's done.

Bono: He's sure welcome to it. (*Cory takes the saw and begins to cut the
wood.*) Whew-e-e! Look at that. Big old strong boy. Look like Joe
Louis. Hell, must be getting old the way I'm watching that boy whip
through that wood.

Cory: I don't see why Mama want a fence around the yard noways.

Troy: Damn if I know either. What the hell she keeping out with it? She
ain't got nothing nobody want.

Bono: Some people build fences to keep people out . . . and other people
build fences to keep people in. Rose wants to hold on to you all. She
loves you.

Troy: Hell, nigger, I don't need nobody to tell me my wife loves me,
Cory . . . go on in the house and see if you can find that other saw.

Cory: Where's it at?

Troy: I said find it! Look for it till you find it! (*Cory exits into the house.*)
What's that supposed to mean? Wanna keep us in?

Bono: Troy . . . I done known you seem like damn near my whole life.
You and Rose both. I done know both of you all for a long time. I
remember when you met Rose. When you was hitting them baseball
out the park. A lot of them old gals was after you then. You had the
pick of the litter. When you picked Rose, I was happy for you. That
was the first time I knew you had any sense. I said . . . My man Troy
knows what he's doing . . . I'm gonna follow this nigger . . . he might
take me somewhere. I been following you too. I done learned a whole
heap of things about life watching you. I done learned how to tell
where the shit lies. How to tell it from the alfalfa. You done learned
me a lot of things. You showed me how to not make the same
mistakes . . . to take life as it comes along and keep putting one foot in
front of the other. (*Pause.*) Rose a good woman, Troy.

Troy: Hell, nigger, I know she a good woman. I been married to her for
eighteen years. What you got on your mind, Bono?

Bono: I just say she a good woman. Just like I say anything. I ain't got to
have nothing on my mind.

Troy: You just gonna say she a good woman and leave it hanging out
there like that? Why you telling me she a good woman?

Bono: She loves you, Troy. Rose loves you.

Troy: You saying I don't measure up. That's what you trying to say. I
don't measure up cause I'm seeing this other gal. I know what you
trying to say.

Bono: I know what Rose means to you, Troy. I'm just trying to say I
don't want to see you mess up.

Troy: Yeah, I appreciate that, Bono. If you was messing around on Lucille
I'd be telling you the same thing.

Bono: Well, that's all I got to say. I just say that because I love you both.

Troy: Hell, you know me . . . I wasn't out there looking for nothing. You can't find a better woman than Rose. I know that. But seems like this woman just stuck onto me where I can't shake her loose. I done wrestled with it, tried to throw her off me . . . but she just stuck on tighter. Now she's stuck on for good.

Bono: You's in control . . . that's what you tell me all the time. You responsible for what you do.

Troy: I ain't ducking the responsibility of it. As long as it sets right in my heart . . . then I'm okay. Cause that's all I listen to. It'll tell me right from wrong every time. And I ain't talking about doing Rose no bad turn. I love Rose. She done carried me a long ways and I love and respect her for that.

Bono: I know you do. That's why I don't want to see you hurt her. But what you gonna do when she find out? What you got then? If you try and juggle both of them . . . sooner or later you gonna drop one of them. That's common sense.

Troy: Yeah, I hear what you saying, Bono. I been trying to figure a way to work it out.

Bono: Work it out right, Troy. I don't want to be getting all up between you and Rose's business . . . but work it so it come out right.

Troy: Ah hell, I get all up between you and Lucille's business. When you gonna get that woman that refrigerator she been wanting? Don't tell me you ain't got no money now. I know who your banker is. Mellon don't need that money bad as Lucille want that refrigerator. I'll tell you that.

Bono: Tell you what I'll do . . . when you finish building this fence for Rose . . . I'll buy Lucille that refrigerator.

Troy: You done stuck your foot in your mouth now! (*Troy grabs up a board and begins to saw. Bono starts to walk out the yard.*) Hey, nigger . . . where you going?

Bono: I'm going home. I know you don't expect me to help you now. I'm protecting my money. I wanna see you put that fence up by yourself. That's what I want to see. You'll be here another six months without me.

Troy: Nigger, you ain't right.

Bono: When it comes to my money . . . I'm right as fireworks on the Fourth of July.

Troy: All right, we gonna see now. You better get out your bankbook.

(*Bono exits, and Troy continues to work. Rose enters from the house.*)

Rose: What they say down there? What's happening with Gabe?

Troy: I went down there and got him out. Cost me fifty dollars. Say he was disturbing the peace. Judge set up a hearing for him in three weeks. Say to show cause why he shouldn't be recommitted.

Rose: What was he doing that cause them to arrest him?

Troy: Some kids was teasing him and he run them off home. Say he was howling and carrying on. Some folks seen him and called the police. That's all it was.

Rose: Well, what's you say? What'd you tell the judge?

Troy: Told him I'd look after him. It didn't make no sense to recommit the man. He stuck out his big greasy palm and told me to give him fifty dollars and take him on home.

Rose: Where's he at now? Where'd he go off to?

Troy: He's gone on about his business. He don't need nobody to hold his hand.

Rose: Well, I don't know. Seem like that would be the best place for him if they did put him into the hospital. I know what you're gonna say. But that's what I think would be best.

Troy: The man done had his life ruined fighting for what? And they wanna take and lock him up. Let him be free. He don't bother nobody.

Rose: Well, everybody got their own way of looking at it I guess. Come on and get your lunch. I got a bowl of lima beans and some cornbread in the oven. Come on get something to eat. Ain't no sense you fretting over Gabe.

(Rose turns to go into the house.)

Troy: Rose . . . got something to tell you.

Rose: Well, come on . . . wait till I get this food on the table.

Troy: Rose! (*She stops and turns around.*) I don't know how to say this. (*Pause.*) I can't explain it none. It just sort of grows on you till it gets out of hand. It starts out like a little bush . . . and the next thing you know it's a whole forest.

Rose: Troy . . . what is you talking about?

Troy: I'm talking, woman, let me talk. I'm trying to find a way to tell you . . . I'm gonna be a daddy. I'm gonna be somebody's daddy.

Rose: Troy . . . you're not telling me this? You're gonna be . . . what?

Troy: Rose . . . now . . . see . . .

Rose: You telling me you gonna be somebody's daddy? You telling your *wife* this?

(Gabriel enters from the street. He carries a rose in his hand.)

Gabriel: Hey, Troy! Hey, Rose!

Rose: I have to wait eighteen years to hear something like this.

Gabriel: Hey, Rose . . . I got a flower for you. (*He hands it to her.*) That's a rose. Same rose like you is.

Rose: Thanks, Gabe.

Gabriel: Troy, you ain't mad at me is you? Them bad mens come and put me away. You ain't mad at me is you?

Troy: Naw, Gabe, I ain't mad at you.

Rose: Eighteen years and you wanna come with this.

Gabriel (takes a quarter out of his pocket): See what I got? Got a brand new quarter.

Troy: Rose . . . it's just . . .

Rose: Ain't nothing you can say, Troy. Ain't no way of explaining that.

Gabriel: Fellow that give me this quarter had a whole mess of them. I'm gonna keep this quarter till it stop shining.

Rose: Gabe, go on in the house there. I got some watermelon in the frigidaire. Go on and get you a piece.

Gabriel: Say, Rose . . . you know I was chasing hellhounds and them bad mens come and get me and take me away. Troy helped me. He come down there and told them they better let me go before he beat them up. Yeah, he did!

Rose: You go on and get you a piece of watermelon, Gabe. Them bad mens is gone now.

Gabriel: Okay, Rose . . . gonna get me some watermelon. The kind with the stripes on it.

(Gabriel exits into the house.)

Rose: Why, Troy? Why? After all these years to come dragging this in to me now. It don't make no sense at your age. I could have expected this ten or fifteen years ago, but not now.

Troy: Age ain't got nothing to do with it, Rose.

Rose: I done tried to be everything a wife should be. Everything a wife could be. Been married eighteen years and I got to live to see the day you tell me you been seeing another woman and done fathered a child by her. And you know I ain't never wanted no half nothing in my family. My whole family is half. Everybody got different fathers and mothers . . . my two sisters and my brother. Can't hardly tell who's who. Can't never sit down and talk about Papa and Mama. It's your papa and your mama and my papa and my mama . . .

Troy: Rose . . . stop it now.

Rose: I ain't never wanted that for none of my children. And now you wanna drag your behind in here and tell me something like this.

Troy: You ought to know. It's time for you to know.

Rose: Well, I don't want to know, goddamn it!

Troy: I can't just make it go away. It's done now. I can't wish the circumstance of the thing away.

Rose: And you don't want to either. Maybe you want to wish me and my boy away. Maybe that's what you want? Well, you can't wish us away. I've got eighteen years of my life invested in you. You ought to have stayed upstairs in my bed where you belong.

Troy: Rose . . . now listen to me . . . we can get a handle on this thing. We can talk this out . . . come to an understanding.

Rose: All of a sudden it's "we." Where was "we" at when you was down there rolling around with some godforsaken woman? "We" should have come to an understanding before you started making a damn fool of yourself. You're a day late and a dollar short when it comes to an understanding with me.

Troy: It's just . . . She gives me a different idea . . . a different understanding about myself. I can step out of this house and get away from the pressures and problems . . . be a different man. I ain't got to wonder how I'm gonna pay the bills or get the roof fixed. I can just be a part of myself that I ain't never been.

Rose: What I want to know . . . is do you plan to continue seeing her. That's all you can say to me.

Troy: I can sit up in her house and laugh. Do you understand what I'm saying. I can laugh out loud . . . and it feels good. It reaches all the way down to the bottom of my shoes. (*Pause.*) Rose, I can't give that up.

Rose: Maybe you ought to go on and stay down there with her . . . if she's a better woman than me.

Troy: It ain't about nobody being a better woman or nothing. Rose, you ain't the blame. A man couldn't ask for no woman to be a better wife than you've been. I'm responsible for it. I done locked myself into a pattern trying to take care of you all that I forgot about myself.

Rose: What the hell was I there for? That was my job, not somebody else's.

Troy: Rose, I done tried all my life to live decent . . . to live a clean . . . hard . . . useful life. I tried to be a good husband to you. In every way I knew how. Maybe I come into the world backwards, I don't know. But . . . you born with two strikes on you before you come to the plate. You got to guard it closely . . . always looking for the curve ball on the inside corner. You can't afford to let none get past you. You can't afford a call strike. If you going down . . . you going down swinging. Everything lined up against you. What you gonna do. I fooled them, Rose. I bunted. When I found you and Cory and a halfway decent job . . . I was safe. Couldn't nothing touch me. I wasn't gonna strike out no more. I wasn't going back to the penitentiary. I wasn't gonna lay in the streets with a bottle of wine. I was safe. I had me a family. A job. I wasn't gonna get that last strike. I was on first looking for one of them boys to knock me in. To get me home.

Rose: You should have stayed in my bed, Troy.

Troy: Then when I saw that gal . . . she firmed up my backbone. And I got to thinking that if I tried . . . I just might be able to steal second. Do you understand after eighteen years I wanted to steal second.

Rose: You should have held me tight. You should have grabbed me and held on.

Troy: I stood on first base for eighteen years and I thought . . . well, goddamn it . . . go on for it!

Rose: We're not talking about baseball! We're talking about you going off to lay in bed with another woman . . . and then bring it home to me. That's what we're talking about. We ain't talking about no baseball.

Troy: Rose, you're not listening to me. I'm trying the best I can to explain it to you. It's not easy for me to admit that I been standing in the same place for eighteen years.

Rose: I been standing with you! I been right here with you, Troy. I got a life too. I gave eighteen years of my life to stand in the same spot with you. Don't you think I ever wanted other things? Don't you think I had dreams and hopes? What about my life? What about me. Don't you think it ever crossed my mind to want to know other men? That I wanted to lay up somewhere and forget about my responsibilities? That I wanted someone to make me laugh so I could feel good? You not the only one who's got wants and needs. But I held on to you, Troy. I took all my feelings, my wants and needs, my dreams . . . and I buried them inside you. I planted a seed and watched and prayed over it. I planted myself inside you and waited to bloom. And it didn't take me no eighteen years to find out the soil was hard and rocky and it wasn't never gonna bloom.

But I held on to you, Troy. I held you tighter. You was my husband. I owed you everything I had. Every part of me I could find to give you. And upstairs in that room . . . with the darkness falling in on me . . . I gave everything I had to try and erase the doubt that you wasn't the finest man in the world. And wherever you was going . . . I wanted to be there with you. Cause you was my husband. Cause that's the only way I was gonna survive as your wife. You always talking about what you give . . . and what you don't have to give. But you take too. You take . . . and don't even know nobody's giving!

(Rose turns to exit into the house; Troy grabs her arm.)

Troy: You say I take and don't give!

Rose: Troy! You're hurting me!

Troy: You say I take and don't give.

Rose: Troy . . . you're hurting my arm! Let go!

Troy: I done give you everything I got. Don't you tell that lie on me.

Rose: Troy!

Troy: Don't you tell that lie on me!

(Cory enters from the house.)

Cory: Mama!

Rose: Troy. You're hurting me.

Troy: Don't you tell me about no taking and giving.

(Cory comes up behind Troy and grabs him. Troy, surprised, is thrown off balance just as Cory throws a glancing blow that catches him on the chest and knocks him down. Troy is stunned, as is Cory.)

Rose: Troy. Troy. No! (*Troy gets to his feet and starts at Cory.*) Troy . . . no. Please! Troy!

(Rose pulls on Troy to hold him back. Troy stops himself.)

Troy (to Cory):   All right. That's strike two. You stay away from around me, boy. Don't you strike out. You living with a full count. Don't you strike out.

(Troy exits out the yard as the lights go down.)

Scene II

(It is six months later, early afternoon. Troy enters from the house and starts to exit the yard. Rose enters from the house.)

Rose: Troy, I want to talk to you.
Troy: All of a sudden, after all this time, you want to talk to me, huh? You ain't wanted to talk to me for months. You ain't wanted to talk to me last night. You ain't wanted no part of me then. What you wanna talk to me about now?
Rose: Tomorrow's Friday.
Troy: I know what day tomorrow is. You think I don't know tomorrow's Friday? My whole life I ain't done nothing but look to see Friday coming and you got to tell me it's Friday.
Rose: I want to know if you're coming home.
Troy: I always come home, Rose. You know that. There ain't never been a night I ain't come home.
Rose: That ain't what I mean . . . and you know it. I want to know if you're coming straight home after work.
Troy: I figure I'd cash my check . . . hang out at Taylors' with the boys . . . maybe play a game of checkers . . .
Rose: Troy, I can't live like this. I won't live like this. You livin' on borrowed time with me. It's been going on six months now you ain't been coming home.
Troy: I be here every night. Every night of the year. That's 365 days.
Rose: I want you to come home tomorrow after work.
Troy: Rose . . . I don't mess up my pay. You know that now. I take my pay and I give it to you. I don't have no money but what you give me back. I just want to have a little time to myself . . . a little time to enjoy life.
Rose: What about me? When's my time to enjoy life?
Troy: I don't know what to tell you, Rose. I'm doing the best I can.

Rose: You ain't been home from work but time enough to change your clothes and run out . . . and you wanna call that the best you can do?

Troy: I'm going over to the hospital to see Alberta. She went into the hospital this afternoon. Look like she might have the baby early. I won't be gone long.

Rose: Well, you ought to know. They went over to Miss Pearl's and got Gabe today. She said you told them to go ahead and lock him up.

Troy: I ain't said no such thing. Whoever told you that is telling a lie. Pearl ain't doing nothing but telling a big fat lie.

Rose: She ain't had to tell me. I read it on the papers.

Troy: I ain't told them nothing of the kind.

Rose: I saw it right there on the papers.

Troy: What it say, huh?

Rose: It said you told them to take him.

Troy: Then they screwed that up, just the way they screw up everything. I ain't worried about what they got on the paper.

Rose: Say the government send part of his check to the hospital and the other part to you.

Troy: I ain't got nothing to do with that if that's the way it works. I ain't made up the rules about how it work.

Rose: You did Gabe just like you did Cory. You wouldn't sign the paper for Cory . . . but you signed for Gabe. You signed that paper.

(The telephone is heard ringing inside the house.)

Troy: I told you I ain't signed nothing, woman! The only thing I signed was the release form. Hell, I can't read, I don't know what they had on that paper! I ain't signed nothing about sending Gabe away.

Rose: I said send him to the hospital . . . you said let him be free . . . now you done went down there and signed him to the hospital for half his money. You went back on yourself, Troy. You gonna have to answer for that.

Troy: See now . . . you been over there talking to Miss Pearl. She done got mad cause she ain't getting Gabe's rent money. That's all it is. She's liable to say anything.

Rose: Troy, I seen where you signed the paper.

Troy: You ain't seen nothing I signed. What she doing got papers on my brother anyway? Miss Pearl telling a big fat lie. And I'm gonna tell her about it too! You ain't seen nothing I signed. Say . . . you ain't seen nothing I signed.

(Rose exits into the house to answer the telephone. Presently she returns.)

Rose: Troy . . . that was the hospital. Alberta had the baby.

Troy: What she have? What is it?

Rose: It's a girl.

Troy: I better get on down to the hospital to see her.

Rose: Troy . . .

Troy: Rose . . . I got to go see her now. That's only right . . . what's the
matter . . . the baby's all right, ain't it?

Rose: Alberta died having the baby.

Troy: Died . . . you say she's dead? Alberta's dead?

Rose: They said they done all they could. They couldn't do nothing for her.

Troy: The baby? How's the baby?

Rose: They say it's healthy. I wonder who's gonna bury her.

Troy: She had family, Rose. She wasn't living in the world by herself.

Rose: I know she wasn't living in the world by herself.

Troy: Next thing you gonna want to know if she had any insurance.

Rose: Troy, you ain't got to talk like that.

Troy: That's the first thing that jumped out your mouth. "Who's gonna
bury her?" Like I'm fixing to take on that task for myself.

Rose: I am your wife. Don't push me away.

Troy: I ain't pushing nobody away. Just give me some space. That's all.
Just give me some room to breathe.

(Rose exits into the house. Troy walks about the yard.)

Troy (with a quiet rage that threatens to consume him): All right . . . Mr.
Death. See now . . . I'm gonna tell you what I'm gonna do. I'm gonna
take and build me a fence around this yard. See? I'm gonna build me a
fence around what belongs to me. And then I want you to stay on the
other side. See? You stay over there until you're ready for me. Then
you come on. Bring your army. Bring your sickle. Bring your wrestling
clothes. I ain't gonna fall down on my vigilance this time. You ain't
gonna sneak up on me no more. When you ready for me . . . when the
top of your list say Troy Maxson . . . that's when you come around
here. You come up and knock on the front door. Ain't nobody else
got nothing to do with this. This is between you and me. Man to man.
You stay on the other side of that fence until you ready for me. Then
you come up and knock on the front door. Anytime you want. I'll be
ready for you.

(The lights go down to black.)

Scene III

*(The lights come up on the porch. It is late evening three days later. Rose
sits listening to the ball game waiting for Troy. The final out of the game
is made and Rose switches off the radio. Troy enters the yard carrying an
infant wrapped in blankets. He stands back from the house and calls.)*

*(Rose enters and stands on the porch. There is a long, awkward
silence, the weight of which grows heavier with each passing second.)*

Troy: Rose . . . I'm standing here with my daughter in my arms. She ain't
but a wee bittie little old thing. She don't know nothing about
grownups' business. She innocent . . . and she ain't got no mama.

Rose: What you telling me for, Troy? (*She turns and exits into the house.*)

Troy: Well . . . I guess we'll just sit out here on the porch. (*He sits down on the porch. There is an awkward indelicateness about the way he handles the baby. His largeness engulfs and seems to swallow it. He speaks loud enough for Rose to hear.*) A man's got to do what's right for him. I ain't sorry for nothing I done. It felt right in my heart. (*To the baby.*) What you smiling at? Your daddy's a big man. Got these great big old hands. But sometimes he's scared. And right now your daddy's scared cause we sitting out here and ain't got no home. Oh, I been homeless before. I ain't had no little baby with me. But I been homeless. You just be out on the road by your lonesome and you see one of them trains coming and you just kinda go like this . . .
(*He sings as a lullaby.*) Please, Mr. Engineer let a man ride the line
Please, Mr. Engineer let a man ride the line
I ain't got no ticket please let me ride the blinds
(*Rose enters from the house. Troy hearing her steps behind him, stands and faces her.*) She's my daughter, Rose. My own flesh and blood. I can't deny her no more than I can deny them boys. (*Pause.*) You and them boys is my family. You and them and this child is all I got in the world. So I guess what I'm saying is . . . I'd appreciate it if you'd help me take care of her.

Rose: Okay, Troy . . . you're right. I'll take care of your baby for you . . . cause . . . like you say . . . she's innocent . . . and you can't visit the sins of the father upon the child. A motherless child has got a hard time. (*She takes the baby from him.*) From right now . . . this child got a mother. But you a womanless man.

(*Rose turns and exits into the house with the baby. Lights go down to black.*)

Scene IV

(*It is two months later. Lyons enters from the street. He knocks on the door and calls.*)

Lyons: Hey, Rose! (*Pause.*) Rose!

Rose (from inside the house): Stop that yelling. You gonna wake up Raynell. I just got her to sleep.

Lyons: I just stopped by to pay Papa this twenty dollars I owe him. Where's Papa at?

Rose: He should be here in a minute. I'm getting ready to go down to the church. Sit down and wait on him.

Lyons: I got to go pick up Bonnie over her mother's house.

Rose: Well, sit it down there on the table. He'll get it.

Lyons (enters the house and sets the money on the table): Tell Papa I said thanks. I'll see you again.

Rose: All right, Lyons. We'll see you.

(Lyons starts to exit as Cory enters.)

Cory: Hey, Lyons.

Lyons: What's happening, Cory. Say man, I'm sorry I missed your graduation. You know I had a gig and couldn't get away. Otherwise, I would have been there, man. So what you doing?

Cory: I'm trying to find a job.

Lyons: Yeah I know how that go, man. It's rough out here. Jobs are scarce.

Cory: Yeah, I know.

Lyons: Look here, I got to run. Talk to Papa . . . he know some people. He'll be able to help get you a job. Talk to him . . . see what he say.

Cory: Yeah . . . all right, Lyons.

Lyons: You take care. I'll talk to you soon. We'll find some time to talk.

(Lyons exits the yard. Cory wanders over to the tree, picks up the bat, and assumes a batting stance. He studies an imaginary pitcher and swings. Dissatisfied with the result, he tries again. Troy enters. They eye each other for a beat. Cory puts the bat down and exits the yard. Troy starts into the house as Rose exits with Raynell. She is carrying a cake.)

Troy: I'm coming in and everybody's going out.

Rose: I'm taking this cake down to the church for the bake sale. Lyons was by to see you. He stopped by to pay you your twenty dollars. It's laying in there on the table.

Troy *(going into his pocket):* Well . . . here go this money.

Rose: Put it in there on the table, Troy. I'll get it.

Troy: What time you coming back?

Rose: Ain't no use in you studying me. It don't matter what time I come back.

Troy: I just asked you a question, woman. What's the matter . . . can't I ask you a question?

Rose: Troy, I don't want to go into it. Your dinner's in there on the stove. All you got to do is heat it up. And don't you be eating the rest of them cakes in there. I'm coming back for them. We having a bake sale at the church tomorrow.

(Rose exits the yard. Troy sits down on the steps, takes a pint bottle from his pocket, opens it, and drinks. He begins to sing.)

Troy: Hear it ring! Hear it ring!
Had an old dog his name was Blue
You know Blue was mighty true
You know Blue as a good old dog
Blue trees a possum in a hollow log
You know from that he was a good old dog

(Bono enters the yard.)

Bono: Hey, Troy.

Troy: Hey, what's happening, Bono?

Bono: I just thought I'd stop by to see you.

Troy: What you stop by and see me for? You ain't stopped by in a month of Sundays. Hell, I must owe you money or something.

Bono: Since you got your promotion I can't keep up with you. Used to see you every day. Now I don't even know what route you working.

Troy: They keep switching me around. Got me out in Greentree now . . . hauling white folks' garbage.

Bono: Greentree, huh? You lucky, at least you ain't got to be lifting them barrels. Damn if they ain't getting heavier. I'm gonna put in my two years and call it quits.

Troy: I'm thinking about retiring myself.

Bono: You got it easy. You can *drive* for another five years.

Troy: It ain't the same, Bono. It ain't like working the back of the truck. Ain't got nobody to talk to . . . feel like you working by yourself. Naw, I'm thinking about retiring. How's Lucille?

Bono: She all right. Her arthritis get to acting up on her sometime. Saw Rose on my way in. She going down to the church, huh?

Troy: Yeah, she took up going down there. All them preachers looking for somebody to fatten their pockets. (*Pause.*) Got some gin here.

Bono: Naw, thanks. I just stopped by to say hello.

Troy: Hell, nigger . . . you can take a drink. I ain't never known you to say no to a drink. You ain't got to work tomorrow.

Bono: I just stopped by. I'm fixing to go over to Skinner's. We got us a domino game going over his house every Friday.

Troy: Nigger, you can't play no dominoes. I used to whup you four games out of five.

Bono: Well, that learned me. I'm getting better.

Troy: Yeah? Well, that's all right.

Bono: Look here . . . I got to be getting on. Stop by sometime, huh?

Troy: Yeah, I'll do that, Bono. Lucille told Rose you bought her a new refrigerator.

Bono: Yeah, Rose told Lucille you had finally built your fence . . . so I figured we'd call it even.

Troy: I knew you would.

Bono: Yeah . . . okay. I'll be talking to you.

Troy: Yeah, take care, Bono. Good to see you. I'm gonna stop over.

Bono: Yeah. Okay, Troy.

(*Bono exits. Troy drinks from the bottle.*)

Troy: Old Blue died and I dig his grave
Let him down with a golden chain
Every night when I hear old Blue bark
I know Blue treed a possum in Noah's Ark.
Hear it ring! Hear it ring!

(Cory enters the yard. They eye each other for a beat. Troy is sitting in the middle of the steps. Cory walks over.)

Cory: I got to get by.

Troy: Say what? What's you say?

Cory: You in my way. I got to get by.

Troy: You got to get by where? This is my house. Bought and paid for. In full. Took me fifteen years. And if you wanna go in my house and I'm sitting on the steps . . . you say excuse me. Like your mama taught you.

Cory: Come on, Pop . . . I got to get by.

(Cory starts to maneuver his way past Troy. Troy grabs his leg and shoves him back.)

Troy: You just gonna walk over top of me?

Cory: I live here too!

Troy *(advancing toward him)*: You just gonna walk over top of me in my own house?

Cory: I ain't scared of you.

Troy: I ain't asked if you was scared of me. I asked you if you was fixing to walk over top of me in my own house? That's the question. You ain't gonna say excuse me? You just gonna walk over top of me?

Cory: If you wanna put it like that.

Troy: How else am I gonna put it?

Cory: I was walking by you to go into the house cause you sitting on the steps drunk, singing to yourself. You can put it like that.

Troy: Without saying excuse me??? *(Cory doesn't respond.)* I asked you a question. Without saying excuse me???

Cory: I ain't got to say excuse me to you. You don't count around here no more.

Troy: Oh, I see . . . I don't count around here no more. You ain't got to say excuse me to your daddy. All of a sudden you done got so grown that your daddy don't count around here no more . . . Around here in his own house and yard that he done paid for with the sweat of his brow. You done got so grown to where you gonna take over. You gonna take over my house. Is that right? You gonna wear my pants. You gonna go in there and stretch out on my bed. You ain't got to say excuse me cause I don't count around here no more. Is that right?

Cory: That's right. You always talking this dumb stuff. Now, why don't you just get out my way.

Troy: I guess you got someplace to sleep and something to put in your belly. You got that, huh? You got that? That's what you need. You got that, huh?

Cory: You don't know what I got. You ain't got to worry about what I got.

Troy: You right! You one hundred percent right! I done spent the last seventeen years worrying about what you got. Now it's your turn, see?

I'll tell you what to do. You grown . . . we done established that. You a man. Now, let's see you act like one. Turn your behind around and walk out this yard. And when you get out there in the alley . . . you can forget about this house. See? 'Cause this is my house. You go on and be a man and get your own house. You can forget about this. 'Cause this is mine. You go on and get yours 'cause I'm through with doing for you.

Cory: You talking about what you did for me . . . what'd you ever give me?

Troy: Them feet and bones! That pumping heart, nigger! I give you more than anybody else is ever gonna give you.

Cory: You ain't never gave me nothing! You ain't never done nothing but hold me back. Afraid I was gonna be better than you. All you ever did was try and make me scared of you. I used to tremble every time you called my name. Every time I heard your footsteps in the house. Wondering all the time . . . what's Papa gonna say if I do this? . . . What's he gonna say if I do that? . . . What's Papa gonna say if I turn on the radio? And Mama, too . . . she tries . . . but she's scared of you.

Troy: You leave your mama out of this. She ain't got nothing to do with this.

Cory: I don't know how she stand you . . . after what you did to her.

Troy: I told you to leave your mama out of this!

(He advances toward Cory.)

Cory: What you gonna do . . . give me a whupping? You can't whup me no more. You're too old. You just an old man.

Troy (shoves him on his shoulder):   Nigger! That's what you are. You just another nigger on the street to me!

Cory: You crazy! You know that?

Troy: Go on now! You got the devil in you. Get on away from me!

Cory: You just a crazy old man . . . talking about I got the devil in me.

Troy: Yeah, I'm crazy! If you don't get on the other side of that yard . . . I'm gonna show you how crazy I am! Go on . . . get the hell out of my yard.

Cory: It ain't your yard. You took Uncle Gabe's money he got from the army to buy this house and then you put him out.

Troy (Troy advances on Cory):   Get your black ass out of my yard!

(Troy's advance backs Cory up against the tree. Cory grabs up the bat.)

Cory: I ain't going nowhere! Come on . . . put me out! I ain't scared of you.

Troy: That's my bat!

Cory: Come on!

Troy: Put my bat down!

Cory: Come on, put me out. (*Cory swings at Troy, who backs across the yard.*) What's the matter? You so bad . . . put me out! (*Troy advances toward Cory.*)

Cory (backing up):   Come on! Come on!

Troy: You're gonna have to use it! You wanna draw that bat back on me . . . you're gonna have to use it.

Cory: Come on! . . . Come on!

(Cory swings the bat at Troy a second time. He misses. Troy continues to advance toward him.)

Troy: You're gonna have to kill me! You wanna draw that bat back on me. You're gonna have to kill me. (*Cory, backed up against the tree, can go no farther. Troy taunts him. He sticks out his head and offers him a target.*) Come on! Come on!

(Cory is unable to swing the bat. Troy grabs it.)

Troy: Then I'll show you. (*Cory and Troy struggle over the bat. The struggle is fierce and fully engaged. Troy ultimately is the stronger and takes the bat from Cory and stands over him ready to swing. He stops himself.*) Go on and get away from around my house.

(Cory, stung by his defeat, picks himself up, walks slowly out of the yard and up the alley.)

Cory: Tell Mama I'll be back for my things.

Troy: They'll be on the other side of that fence. (*Cory exits.*) I can't taste nothing. Helluljah! I can't taste nothing no more. (*Troy assumes a batting posture and begins to taunt Death, the fastball on the outside corner.*) Come on! It's between you and me now! Come on! Anytime you want! Come on! I be ready for you . . . but I ain't gonna be easy.

(The lights go down on the scene.)

Scene V

(The time is 1965. The lights come up in the yard. It is the morning of Troy's funeral. A funeral plaque with a light hangs beside the door. There is a small garden plot off to the side. There is noise and activity in the house as Rose, Gabriel, and Bono have gathered. The door opens and Raynell, seven years old, enters dressed in a flannel nightgown. She crosses to the garden and pokes around with a stick. Rose calls from the house.)

Rose: Raynell!

Raynell: Mam?

Rose: What you doing out there?

Raynell: Nothing.

(Rose comes to the door.)

Rose: Girl, get in here and get dressed. What you doing?

Raynell: Seeing if my garden growed.

Rose: I told you it ain't gonna grow overnight. You got to wait.

Raynell: It don't look like it never gonna grow. Dag!

Rose: I told you a watched pot never boils. Get in here and get dressed.

Raynell: This ain't even no pot, Mama.

Rose: You just have to give it a chance. It'll grow. Now you come on and do what I told you. We got to be getting ready. This ain't no morning to be playing around. You hear me?

Raynell: Yes, mam.

(*Rose exits into the house. Raynell continues to poke at her garden with a stick. Cory enters. He is dressed in a Marine corporal's uniform, and carries a duffel bag. His posture is that of a military man, and his speech has a clipped sternness.*)

Cory (to Raynell):   Hi. (*Pause.*) I bet your name is Raynell.

Raynell: Uh huh.

Cory: Is your mama home?

(*Raynell runs up on the porch and calls through the screendoor.*)

Raynell: Mama . . . there's some man out here. Mama?

(*Rose comes to the door.*)

Rose: Cory? Lord have mercy! Look here, you all!

(*Rose and Cory embrace in a tearful reunion as Bono and Lyons enter from the house dressed in funeral clothes.*)

Bono: Aw, looka here . . .

Rose: Done got all grown up!

Cory: Don't cry, Mama. What are you crying about?

Rose: I'm just so glad you made it.

Cory: Hey Lyons. How you doing, Mr. Bono.

(*Lyons goes to embrace Cory.*)

Lyons: Look at you, man. Look at you. Don't he look good, Rose. Got them Corporal stripes.

Rose: What took you so long.

Cory: You know how the Marines are, Mama. They got to get all their paperwork straight before they let you do anything.

Rose: Well, I'm sure glad you made it. They let Lyons come. Your Uncle Gabe's still in the hospital. They don't know if they gonna let him out or not. I just talked to them a little while ago.

Lyons: A Corporal in the United States Marines.

Bono: Your daddy knew you had it in you. He used to tell me all the time.

Lyons: Don't he look good, Mr. Bono?

Bono: Yeah, he remind me of Troy when I first met him. (*Pause.*) Say, Rose, Lucille's down at the church with the choir. I'm gonna go down and get the pallbearers lined up. I'll be back to get you all.

Rose: Thanks, Jim.

Cory: See you, Mr. Bono.

Lyons (with his arm around Raynell):   Cory . . . look at Raynell. Ain't she precious? She gonna break a whole lot of hearts.

Rose: Raynell, come and say hello to your brother. This is your brother, Cory. You remember Cory.

Raynell: No, Mam.

Cory: She don't remember me, Mama.

Rose: Well, we talk about you. She heard us talk about you. (*To Raynell.*) This is your brother, Cory. Come on and say hello.

Raynell: Hi.

Cory: Hi. So you're Raynell. Mama told me a lot about you.

Rose: You all come on into the house and let me fix you some breakfast. Keep up your strength.

Cory: I ain't hungry, Mama.

Lyons: You can fix me something, Rose. I'll be in there in a minute.

Rose: Cory, you sure you don't want nothing. I know they ain't feeding you right.

Cory: No, Mama . . . thanks. I don't feel like eating. I'll get something later.

Rose: Raynell . . . get on upstairs and get that dress on like I told you.

(Rose and Raynell exit into the house.)

Lyons: So . . . I hear you thinking about getting married.

Cory: Yeah, I done found the right one, Lyons. It's about time.

Lyons: Me and Bonnie been split up about four years now. About the time Papa retired. I guess she just got tired of all them changes I was putting her through. (*Pause.*) I always knew you was gonna make something out yourself. Your head was always in the right direction. So . . . you gonna stay in . . . make it a career . . . put in your twenty years?

Cory: I don't know. I got six already, I think that's enough.

Lyons: Stick with Uncle Sam and retire early. Ain't nothing out here. I guess Rose told you what happened with me. They got me down the workhouse. I thought I was being slick cashing other people's checks.

Cory: How much time you doing?

Lyons: They give me three years. I got that beat now. I ain't got but nine more months. It ain't so bad. You learn to deal with it like anything else. You got to take the crooked with the straights. That's what Papa used to say. He used to say that when he struck out. I seen him strike out three times in a row . . . and the next time up he hit the ball over the grandstand. Right out there in Homestead Field. He wasn't satisfied hitting in the seats . . . he want to hit it over everything! After the game he had two hundred people standing around waiting to shake his hand. You got to take the crookeds with the straights. Yeah, Papa was something else.

Cory: You still playing?

Lyons: Cory . . . you know I'm gonna do that. There's some fellows down
    there we got us a band . . . we gonna try and stay together when we
    get out . . . but yeah, I'm still playing. It still helps me to get out of
    bed in the morning. As long as it do that I'm gonna be right there
    playing and trying to make some sense out of it.
Rose (calling):   Lyons, I got these eggs in the pan.
Lyons: Let me go on and get these eggs, man. Get ready to go bury Papa.
    (*Pause.*) How you doing? You doing all right?

(*Cory nods. Lyons touches him on the shoulder and they share a moment of
silent grief. Lyons exits into the house. Cory wanders about the yard.
Raynell enters.*)

Raynell: Hi.
Cory: Hi.
Raynell: Did you used to sleep in my room?
Cory: Yeah . . . that used to be my room.
Raynell: That's what Papa call it. "Cory's room." It got your football in
    the closet.

(*Rose comes to the door.*)

Rose: Raynell, get in there and get them good shoes on.
Raynell: Mama, can't I wear these. Them other one hurt my feet.
Rose: Well, they just gonna have to hurt your feet for a while. You ain't said
    they hurt your feet when you went down to the store and got them.
Raynell: They didn't hurt then. My feet done got bigger.
Rose: Don't you give me no backtalk now. You get in there and get them
    shoes on. (*Raynell exits into the house.*) Ain't too much changed. He
    still got that piece of rag tied to that tree. He was out here swinging
    that bat. I was just ready to go back in the house. He swung that bat
    and then he just fell over. Seem like he swung it and stood there with
    this grin on his face . . . and then he just fell over. They carried him on
    down to the hospital, but I knew there wasn't no need . . . why don't
    you come on in the house?
Cory: Mama . . . I got something to tell you. I don't know how to tell
    you this . . . but I've got to tell you . . . I'm not going to Papa's
    funeral.
Rose: Boy, hush your mouth. That's your daddy you talking about. I
    don't want hear that kind of talk this morning. I done raised you to
    come to this? You standing there all healthy and grown talking about
    you ain't going to your daddy's funeral?
Cory: Mama . . . listen . . .
Rose: I don't want to hear it, Cory. You just get that thought out of your
    head.
Cory: I can't drag Papa with me everywhere I go. I've got to say no to
    him. One time in my life I've got to say no.

Rose: Don't nobody have to listen to nothing like that. I know you and
your daddy ain't seen eye to eye, but I ain't got to listen to that kind
of talk this morning. Whatever was between you and your daddy . . .
the time has come to put it aside. Just take it and set it over there on
the shelf and forget about it. Disrespecting your daddy ain't gonna
make you a man, Cory. You got to find a way to come to that on your
own. Not going to your daddy's funeral ain't gonna make you a man.

Cory: The whole time I was growing up . . . living in his house . . . Papa
was like a shadow that followed you everywhere. It weighed on you
and sunk into your flesh. It would wrap around you and lay there until
you couldn't tell which one was you anymore. That shadow digging in
your flesh. Trying to crawl in. Trying to live through you. Everywhere
I looked, Troy Maxson was staring back at me . . . hiding under the
bed . . . in the closet. I'm just saying I've got to find a way to get rid
of that shadow, Mama.

Rose: You just like him. You got him in you good.

Cory: Don't tell me that, Mama.

Rose: You Troy Maxson all over again.

Cory: I don't want to be Troy Maxson. I want to be me.

Rose: You can't be nobody but who you are, Cory. That shadow wasn't
nothing but you growing into yourself. You either got to grow into it
or cut it down to fit you. But that's all you got to make life with.
That's all you got to measure yourself against that world out there.
Your daddy wanted you to be everything he wasn't . . . and at the
same time he tried to make you into everything he was. I don't know
if he was right or wrong . . . but I do know he meant to do more good
than he meant to do harm. He wasn't always right. Sometimes when
he touched he bruised. And sometimes when he took me in his arms
he cut.

When I first met your daddy I thought . . . Here is a man I can
lay down with and make a baby. That's the first thing I thought when
I seen him. I was thirty years old and had done seen my share of men.
But when he walked up to me and said, "I can dance a waltz that'll
make you dizzy," I thought, Rose Lee, here is a man that you can
open yourself up to and be filled to bursting. Here is a man that can
fill all them empty spaces you been tipping around the edges of. One
of them empty spaces was being somebody's mother.

I married your daddy and settled down to cooking his supper and
keeping clean sheets on the bed. When your daddy walked through the
house he was so big he filled it up. That was my first mistake. Not to
make him leave some room for me. For my part in the matter. But at
that time I wanted that. I wanted a house that I could sing in. And
that's what your daddy gave me. I didn't know to keep up his strength
I had to give up little pieces of mine. I did that. I took on his life as
mine and mixed up the pieces so that you couldn't hardly tell which

was which anymore. It was my choice. It was my life and I didn't have
to live it like that. But that's what life offered me in the way of being a
woman and I took it. I grabbed hold of it with both hands.

By the time Raynell came into the house, me and your daddy
had done lost touch with one another. I didn't want to make my
blessing off of nobody's misfortune . . . but I took on to Raynell like
she was all them babies I had wanted and never had. (*The phone rings.*)
Like I'd been blessed to relive a part of my life. And if the Lord see fit
to keep up my strength . . . I'm gonna do her just like your daddy did
you . . . I'm gonna give her the best of what's in me.

Raynell (entering, still with her old shoes):   Mama . . . Reverend Tollivier
on the phone. (*Rose exits into the house.*) Hi.

Cory: Hi.

Raynell: You in the Army or the Marines?

Cory: Marines.

Raynell: Papa said it was the Army. Did you know Blue?

Cory: Blue? Who's Blue?

Raynell: Papa's dog what he sing about all the time.

Cory (singing):   Hear it ring! Hear it ring!
   I had a dog his name was Blue
   You know Blue was mighty true
   You know Blue was a good old dog
   Blue treed a possum in a hollow log
   You know from that he was a good old dog.
   Hear it ring! Hear it ring!

   (*Raynell joins in singing.*)

Cory and Raynell: Blue treed a possum out on a limb
   Blue looked at me and I looked at him
   Grabbed that possum and put him in a sack
   Blue stayed there till I came back
   Old Blue's feets was big and round
   Never allowed a possum to touch the ground.
   Old Blue died and I dug his grave
   I dug his grave with a silver spade
   Let him down with a golden chain
   And every night I call his name
   Go on Blue, you good dog you
   Go on Blue, you good dog you

Raynell: Blue laid down and died like a man
   Blue laid down and died . . .

Both: Blue laid down and died like a man
   Now he's treeing possums in the Promised Land
   I'm gonna tell you this to let you know
   Blue's gone where the good dogs go

When I hear old Blue bark
When I hear old Blue bark
Blue treed a possum in Noah's Ark
Blue treed a possum in Noah's Ark.

(Rose comes to the screen door.)

Rose: Cory, we gonna be ready to go in a minute.

Cory (to Raynell):   You go on in the house and change them shoes like Mama told you so we can go to Papa's funeral.

Raynell: Okay, I'll be back.

(Raynell exits into the house. Cory gets up and crosses over to the tree. Rose stands in the screen door watching him. Gabriel enters from the alley.)

Gabriel (calling):   Hey, Rose!

Rose: Gabe?

Gabriel: I'm here, Rose. Hey Rose, I'm here!

(Rose enters from the house.)

Rose: Lord . . . Look here, Lyons!

Lyons: See, I told you, Rose . . . I told you they'd let him come.

Cory: How you doing, Uncle Gabe?

Lyons: How you doing, Uncle Gabe?

Gabriel: Hey, Rose. It's time. It's time to tell St. Peter to open the gates. Troy, you ready? You ready, Troy. I'm gonna tell St. Peter to open the gates. You get ready now.

(Gabriel, with great fanfare, braces himself to blow. The trumpet is without a mouthpiece. He puts the end of it into his mouth and blows with great force, like a man who has been waiting some twenty-odd years for this single moment. No sound comes out of the trumpet. He braces himself and blows again with the same result. A third time he blows. There is a weight of impossible description that falls away and leaves him bare and exposed to a frightful realization. It is a trauma that a sane and normal mind would be unable to withstand. He begins to dance. A slow, strange dance, eerie and life-giving. A dance of atavistic signature and ritual. Lyons attempts to embrace him. Gabriel pushes Lyons away. He begins to howl in what is an attempt at song, or perhaps a song turning back into itself in an attempt at speech. He finishes his dance and the gates of heaven stand open as wide as God's closet.)

That's the way that go!

HENRIK IBSEN IN DEPTH

The work of Henrik Ibsen (1828–1906) was not immediately successful. Among the reasons for his early failures was his inability to write verse plays in the accepted style of the time. His early life centered on the new National Theater in what is now Oslo, Norway, and by the 1850s he was writing and producing plays, most of which were generally unnoticed. His first success came in 1866 with Brand, *a verse play about a fiery preacher who rejected the New Testament god of love in favor of the Old Testament god of wrath. Brand is last seen on a mountaintop in his Ice Church facing an avalanche that will destroy him. Even though this play made Ibsen well known in Norway, it was not until 1877 that he began to have an important place in the world theater.*

Ibsen's great work began with The Pillars of Society *(1877), a study of the corruption of the merchant class. This was the first of his realistic plays. For Ibsen, realism meant showing his audience the problems they faced in their daily lives, both individually and as members of society. In an environment that preferred sentimental comedies and fluffy dramas, Ibsen's plays cut through like a cleaver. His work was shocking and thrilling. It was also difficult for many theatergoers to accept, and Europe took sides for and against Ibsen. In the early 1900s William Butler Yeats thought Ibsen damaging to all that was literary, but the younger approving James Joyce learned enough Dano-Norwegian to write Ibsen a letter proclaiming his genius. Realism seemed heartless and soulless to Yeats, but it was a breath of honesty to Joyce. Whatever it was, realism swept other dramatic styles aside, and Ibsen became known as the father of modern drama.*

Although A Doll House *(1879) established Ibsen as a critic of society, its feminist theme was acceptable in Norway in the late 1870s because a strong feminist movement was already in place. The rest of Europe found it shocking. Later,* Ghosts *(1881) shocked Norway and Europe because it discussed a subject never publicly mentioned: syphilis. The primary character, Oswald Alving, has inherited syphilis from his seagoing father. Moreover, Captain Alving's illegitimate daughter Regina falls in love with Oswald, raising the specter of incest. Such subject matter was so unusual and so shocking that Ibsen became ostracized and felt he had to go into temporary exile.* Hedda Gabler *(1890) continued his analysis of the European middle class, but added to it a rich psychological portrait of a woman dissatisfied with her role in society.*

Ibsen treated social issues with relentless honesty and directness. He was also a skilled dramatic craftsman and an interpreter of character, and his work has guided the major dramatists of the twentieth century. Arthur Miller paid homage to Ibsen by adapting An Enemy of the People *(original version 1882; Miller's version 1992) for the modern American stage.*

A DOLL HOUSE   1879

When Ibsen produced A Doll House, *Europe had begun to see a major movement toward women's rights. Women could not vote, nor could they exercise many of their political rights independently of their husband, who in most marriages expected to be served, to be patronized, and to make all the important decisions. But modern women, living in an age of rapid industrialization and change, saw opportunities for change and began to assert themselves in a variety of organizations.* A Doll House *has often been described as an important stimulus for change, and Nora's slamming of the household door at the end of the play has been regarded as resounding throughout the modern world.*

Torvald Helmer and his wife Nora are in many ways models of the comfortable upper middle class of Europe and the Americas. Their world is family centered, the house is a special protected environment, and as far as Torvald is concerned everything is perfect. Throughout the early part of the play, Nora is compared to a singing bird or a busy squirrel—a pet to amuse Torvald and to keep his life smooth and functioning. She seems to him an empty-headed woman, a decoration in his life. His own empty-headedness is at times almost overwhelming.

The problems begin when Nora tries to help her husband in a manifest way by borrowing money to take a trip to Italy to save Torvald's health. In order to pay back her loan, which she got by forging her father's signature, Nora has to take in work. She discovers that work is congenial, and it gives her an entirely new sense of her own worth. She now feels some of the pleasures that had been reserved only for men. For Ibsen, this was part of the crux of the play, since he was interested not only in the feminist question, but also in how people fulfill their talent. Unfortunately, these issues were not evident to the first critics in Copenhagen, and they were generally negative. However, audiences were curious and flocked to the theater, making the play a resounding success.

The play's ending, with Nora storming out of the house into a totally uncertain future, disturbed audiences and theater people alike. In some versions in 1880 and after, a "happy ending" was inserted into the play because actresses would not play the part as written, insisting that no woman would willingly leave her children as Nora did. Even today critics debate the degree to which the play is feminist and the extent to which Nora can be praised. Ibsen has left us with a great many challenging questions.

Henrik Ibsen   (1828–1906)
A DOLL HOUSE   1879

Translated by Eva LeGallienne

Characters
  Torvald Helmer, a lawyer
  Nora, his wife
  Doctor Rank
  Mrs. Kristine Linde
  Nils Krogstad, an attorney
  Helmer's Three Small Children
  Anne-Marie,° nurse at the Helmers'
  Helene, maid at the Helmers'
  A Porter

  The action takes place in the Helmer residence.

1 *Anne-Marie:* For stage purposes, often *Anna-Maria.*

ACT I

Scene: A comfortable room furnished with taste, but not expensively. In the back wall a door on the right leads to the hall; another door on the left leads to Helmer's study. Between the two doors a piano. In the left wall, center, a door; farther downstage a window. Near the window a round table with an armchair and a small sofa. In the right wall upstage a door, and further downstage a porcelain stove round which are grouped a couple of armchairs and a rocking chair. Between the stove and the door stands a small table. Engravings on the walls. A whatnot with china objects and various bric-a-brac. A small bookcase with books in fancy bindings. The floor is carpeted; a fire burns in the stove. A winter day.

Nora: Be sure and hide the Christmas tree carefully, Helene, the children mustn't see it till this evening, when it's all decorated. (*To the Porter, taking out her purse.*) How much?
Porter: Fifty, Ma'am.
Nora: Here you are. No—keep the change.
    (*The Porter thanks her and goes. Nora closes the door. She laughs gaily to herself as she takes off her outdoor things. Takes a bag of macaroons out of her pocket and eats a couple, then she goes cautiously to the door of her husband's study and listens.*) Yes—he's home. (*She goes over to the table right, humming to herself again.*)
Helmer (*from his study*): Is that my little lark twittering out there?
Nora (*busily undoing the packages*): Yes, it is.

Helmer: Is that my little squirrel bustling about?

Nora: Yes.

Helmer: When did my squirrel get home?

Nora: Just this minute. (*She puts the bag of macaroons back in her pocket and wipes her mouth.*) Oh, Torvald, do come in here! You must see what I have bought.

Helmer: Now, don't disturb me! (*A moment afterwards he opens the door and looks in—pen in hand.*) Did you say "bought"? That—all *that*? Has my little spendthrift been flinging money about again?

Nora: But, Torvald, surely this year we ought to let ourselves go a bit! After all, it's the first Christmas we haven't had to be careful.

Helmer: Yes, but that doesn't mean we can afford to *squander* money.

Nora: Oh, Torvald, we can squander a bit, can't we? Just a little tiny bit? You're going to get a big salary and you'll be making lots and lots of money.

Helmer: After the first of the year, yes. But remember there'll be three whole months before my salary falls due.

Nora: We can always borrow in the meantime.

Helmer: Nora! (*Goes to her and pulls her ear playfully.*) There goes my little featherbrain! Let's suppose I borrowed a thousand crowns today, you'd probably squander it all during Christmas week; and then let's suppose that on New Year's Eve a tile blew off the roof and knocked my brains out—

Nora (puts her hand over his mouth):   Don't say such frightful things!

Helmer: But let's suppose it happened—then what?

Nora: If anything as terrible as *that* happened, I shouldn't care whether I owed money or not.

Helmer: But what about the people I'd borrowed from?

Nora: Who cares about them? After all they're just strangers.

Helmer: Oh, Nora, Nora! What a little woman you are! But seriously, Nora, you know my feelings about such things. I'll have no borrowing—I'll have no debts! There can be no freedom—no, nor beauty either—in a home based upon loans and credit. We've held out bravely up to now, and we shall continue to do so for the short time that remains.

Nora (goes toward the stove):   Just as you like, Torvald.

Helmer (following her):   Come, come; the little lark mustn't droop her wings. Don't tell me my little squirrel is sulking! (*He opens his purse.*) Nora! Guess what I have here!

Nora (turns quickly):   Money!

Helmer: There you are! (*He hands her some notes.*) Don't you suppose I know that money is needed at Christmas time.

Nora (counts the notes):   Ten, twenty, thirty, forty. Oh thank you, thank you, Torvald—this'll last me a long time!

Helmer: Better see that it does!

Nora: Oh, it will—I know. But do come here. I want to show you everything I've bought, and all so cheap too! Here are some new clothes for Ivar, and a little sword—and this horse and trumpet are for Bob, and here's a doll for Emmy—and a doll's bed. They're not worth much, but she's sure to tear them to pieces in a minute anyway. This is some dress material and handkerchiefs for the maids. Old Anne-Marie really should have had something better.

Helmer: And what's in that other parcel?

Nora (with a shriek):   No, Torvald! You can't see that until this evening!

Helmer: I can't, eh? But what about you—you little squanderer? Have you thought of anything for yourself?

Nora: Oh, there's nothing I want, Torvald.

Helmer: Of course there is!—now tell me something sensible you'd really like to have.

Nora: But there's nothing—really! Except of course—

Helmer: Well?

Nora (she fingers the buttons on his coat; without looking at him):   Well—If you really want to give me something—you might—you might—

Helmer: Well, well, out with it!

Nora (rapidly):   You might give me some money, Torvald—just anything you feel you could spare; and then one of these days I'll buy myself something with it.

Helmer: But Nora—

Nora: Oh, please do, dear Torvald—I beg you to! I'll wrap it up in beautiful gold paper and hang it on the Christmas tree. Wouldn't that be fun?

Helmer: What's the name of the bird that eats up money?

Nora: The Spendthrift bird—I know! But do let's do as I say, Torvald!—it will give me a chance to choose something I really need. Don't you think that's a sensible idea? Don't you?

Helmer (smiling):   Sensible enough—providing you really *do* buy something for yourself with it. But I expect you'll fritter it away on a lot of unnecessary household expenses, and before I know it you'll be coming to me for more.

Nora: But, Torvald—

Helmer: You can't deny it, Nora dear. (*Puts his arm round her waist.*) The Spenthrift is a sweet little bird—but it costs a man an awful lot of money to support one!

Nora: How can you say such nasty things—I save all I can!

Helmer: Yes, I dare say—but that doesn't amount to much!

Nora (hums softly and smiles happily):   You don't know, Torvald, what expenses we larks and squirrels have!

Helmer: You're a strange little creature; exactly like your father. You'll go to any lengths to get a sum of money—but as soon as you have it, it just slips through your fingers. You don't know yourself what's become of it. Well, I suppose one must just take you as you are. It's in your blood. Oh, yes! such things are hereditary, Nora.

Nora: I only wish I had inherited a lot of Father's qualities.

Helmer: And I wouldn't wish you any different than you are, my own sweet little lark. But Nora, it's just occurred to me—isn't there something a little—what shall I call it—a little guilty about you this morning?

Nora: About me?

Helmer: Yes. Look me straight in the eye.

Nora (looking at him):   Well?

Helmer (wags a threatening finger at her):   Has my little sweet-tooth been breaking rules today?

Nora: No! What makes you think that?

Helmer: Are you sure the sweet-tooth didn't drop in at the confectioner's?

Nora: No, I assure you, Torvald—

Helmer: She didn't nibble a little candy?

Nora: No, really not.

Helmer: Not even a macaroon or two?

Nora: No, Torvald, I assure you—really—

Helmer: There, there! Of course I'm only joking.

Nora (going to the table right):   It would never occur to me to go against your wishes.

Helmer: Of course I know that—and anyhow—you've given me your word—(*Goes to her.*) Well, my darling, I won't pry into your little Christmas secrets. They'll be unveiled tonight under the Christmas tree.

Nora: Did you remember to ask Dr. Rank?

Helmer: No, it really isn't necessary. He'll take it for granted he's to dine with us. However, I'll ask him, when he stops by this morning. I've ordered some specially good wine. I am so looking forward to this evening, Nora, dear!

Nora: So am I—And the children will have such fun!

Helmer: Ah! How nice it is to feel secure; to look forward to a good position with an ample income. It's a wonderful prospect—isn't it, Nora?

Nora: It's simply marvelous!

Helmer: Do you remember last Christmas? For three whole weeks—you locked yourself up every evening until past midnight—making paper flowers for the Christmas tree—and a lot of other wonderful things you wanted to surprise us with. I was never so bored in my life!

Nora: I wasn't a bit bored.

Helmer (smiling):   But it all came to rather a sad end, didn't it, Nora?

Nora: Oh, do you have to tease me about that again! How could I help the cat coming in and tearing it all to pieces.

Helmer: Of course you couldn't help it, you poor darling! You meant to give us a good time—that's the main thing. But it's nice to know those lean times are over.

Nora: It's wonderful!

Helmer: Now I don't have to sit here alone, boring myself to death; and you don't have to strain your dear little eyes, and prick your sweet little fingers—

Nora (claps her hands): No, I don't—do I, Torvald! Oh! How lovely it all is. (*Takes his arm.*) I want to tell you how I thought we'd arrange things after Christmas. (*The doorbell rings.*) Oh there's the bell. (*Tidies up the room a bit.*) It must be a visitor—how tiresome!

Helmer: I don't care to see any visitors, Nora—remember that.

Helene (in the doorway): There's a lady to see you, Ma'am.

Nora: Well, show her in.

Helene (to Helmer): And the Doctor's here too, Sir.

Helmer: Did he go straight to my study?

Helene: Yes, he did, Sir.

(*Helmer goes into his study. Helene ushers in Mrs. Linde who is dressed in traveling clothes, and closes the door behind her.*)

Mrs. Linde (in subdued and hesitant tone): How do you do, Nora?

Nora (doubtfully): How do you do?

Mrs. Linde: You don't recognize me, do you?

Nora: No, I don't think—and yet—I seem to—(*With a sudden outburst.*) Kristine! Is it really you?

Mrs. Linde: Yes, it's really I!

Nora: Kristine! And to think of my not knowing you! But how could I when—(*More softly.*) You've changed so, Kristine!

Mrs. Linde: Yes I suppose I have. After all—it's nine or ten years—

Nora: Is it *that* long since we met? Yes, so it is. Oh, these last eight years have been such happy ones! Fancy your being in town! And imagine taking that long trip in midwinter! How brave you are!

Mrs. Linde: I arrived by the morning boat.

Nora: You've come for the Christmas holidays, I suppose—what fun! Oh, what a good time we'll have! Do take off your things. You're not cold, are you? (*Helping her.*) There; now we'll sit here by the stove. No, you take the armchair; I'll sit here in the rocker. (*Seizes her hands.*) Now you look more like yourself again. It was just at first—you're a bit paler, Kristine—and perhaps a little thinner.

Mrs. Linde: And much, much older, Nora.

Nora: Well, perhaps a *little* older—a tiny, tiny bit—not much, though. (*She suddenly checks herself; seriously:*) Oh, but, Kristine! What a thoughtless wretch I am, chattering away like that—Dear, darling Kristine, do forgive me!

Mrs. Linde: What for, Nora, dear?

Nora (softly): You lost your husband, didn't you, Kristine! You're a widow.

Mrs. Linde: Yes, my husband died three years ago.

Nora: Yes, I remember; I saw it in the paper. Oh, I *did* mean to write to

you, Kristine! But I kept on putting it off, and all sorts of things kept
coming in the way.

Mrs. Linde: I understand, dear Nora.

Nora: No, it was beastly of me, Kristine! Oh, you poor darling! What you
must have gone through!—And he died without leaving you anything,
didn't he?

Mrs. Linde: Yes.

Nora: And you have no children?

Mrs. Linde: No.

Nora: Nothing then?

Mrs. Linde: Nothing—Not even grief, not even regret.

Nora (looking at her incredulously):   But how is that possible, Kristine?

Mrs. Linde (smiling sadly and stroking her hair):   It sometimes happens,
Nora.

Nora: Imagine being so utterly alone! It must be dreadful for you,
Kristine! I have three of the loveliest children! I can't show them to
you just now, they're out with their nurse. But I want you to tell me
all about yourself—

Mrs. Linde: No, no; I'd rather hear about you, Nora—

Nora: No, I want you to begin. I'm not going to be selfish today. I'm
going to think only of you. Oh! but one thing I *must* tell you. You
haven't heard about the wonderful thing that's just happened to us,
have you?

Mrs. Linde: No. What is it?

Nora: My husband's been elected president of the Joint Stock Bank!

Mrs. Linde: Oh, Nora—How splendid!

Nora: Yes, isn't it? You see, a lawyer's position is so uncertain, especially if
he refuses to handle any cases that are in the least bit—shady; Torvald is
very particular about such things—and I agree with him, of course! You
can imagine how glad we are. He's to start at the Bank right after the
New Year; he'll make a big salary and all sorts of percentages. We'll be
able to live quite differently from then on—we'll have everything we
want. Oh, Kristine! I'm so happy and excited! Won't it be wonderful to
have lots and lots of money, and nothing to worry about!

Mrs. Linde: It certainly would be wonderful to have enough for one's
needs.

Nora: Oh, not just for one's *needs*, Kristine! But heaps and heaps of money!

Mrs. Linde (with a smile):   Nora, Nora, I see you haven't grown up yet! I
remember at school you were a frightful spendthrift.

Nora (quietly; smiling):   Yes; that's what Torvald always says. (*Holding up
her forefinger.*) But I haven't had much chance to be a spendthrift. We
have had to work hard—both of us.

Mrs. Linde: You too?

Nora: Oh yes! I did all sorts of little jobs: needlework, embroidery,
crochet—that sort of thing. (*Casually.*) And other things as well. I

suppose you know that Torvald left the Government service right after we were married. There wasn't much chance of promotion in his department, and of course he had to earn more money when he had me to support. But that first year he overworked himself terribly. He had to undertake all sorts of odd jobs, worked from morning till night. He couldn't stand it; his health gave way and he became deathly ill. The doctors said he absolutely *must* spend some time in the South.

Mrs. Linde: Yes, I heard you spent a whole year in Italy.

Nora: Yes, we did. It wasn't easy to arrange, I can tell you. It was just after Ivar's birth. But of course we had to go. It was a wonderful trip, and it saved Torvald's life. But it cost a fearful lot of money, Kristine.

Mrs. Linde: Yes, it must have.

Nora: Twelve hundred dollars! Four thousand eight hundred crowns! That's an awful lot of money, you know.

Mrs. Linde: You were lucky to have it.

Nora: Well, you see, we got it from Father.

Mrs. Linde: Oh, I see. Wasn't it just about that time that your father died?

Nora: Yes, it was, Kristine. Just think! I wasn't able to go to him—I couldn't be there to nurse him! I was expecting Ivar at the time and then I had my poor sick Torvald to look after. Dear, darling Papa! I never saw him again, Kristine. It's the hardest thing I have had to go through since my marriage.

Mrs. Linde: I know you were awfully fond of him. And after that you went to Italy?

Nora: Yes; then we had the money, you see; and the doctors said we must lose no time; so we started a month later.

Mrs. Linde: And your husband came back completely cured?

Nora: Strong as an ox!

Mrs. Linde: But—what about the doctor then?

Nora: How do you mean?

Mrs. Linde: Didn't the maid say something about a doctor, just as I arrived?

Nora: Oh, yes; Dr. Rank. He's our best friend—it's not a professional call; he stops in to see us every day. No, Torvald hasn't had a moment's illness since; and the children are strong and well, and so am I. (*Jumps up and claps her hands.*) Oh Kristine, Kristine! How lovely it is to be alive and happy! But how disgraceful of me! Here I am talking about nothing but myself! (*Seats herself upon a footstool close to Kristine and lays her arms on her lap.*) Please don't be cross with me—Is it really true, Kristine, that you didn't love your husband? Why did you marry him, then?

Mrs. Linde: Well, you see—Mother was still alive; she was bedridden: completely helpless; and I had my two younger brothers to take care of. I didn't think it would be right to refuse him.

Nora: No, I suppose not. I suppose he had money then?

Mrs. Linde: Yes, I believe he was quite well off. But his business was precarious, Nora. When he died it all went to pieces, and there was nothing left.

Nora: And then—?

Mrs. Linde: Then I had to struggle along as best I could. I had a small shop for a while, and then I started a little school. These last three years have been one long battle—but it is over now, Nora. My dear mother is at rest—She doesn't need me any more. And my brothers are old enough to work, and can look after themselves.

Nora: You must have such a free feeling!

Mrs. Linde: No—only one of complete emptiness. I haven't a soul to live for! (*Stands up restlessly.*) I suppose that's why I felt I had to get away. I should think here it would be easier to find something to do— something to occupy one's thoughts. I might be lucky enough to get a steady job here—some office work, perhaps—

Nora: But that's so terribly tiring, Kristine; and you look so tired already. What you need is a rest. Couldn't you go to some nice watering-place?°

Mrs. Linde (going to the window):   I have no father to give me the money, Nora.

Nora (rising):   Oh, please don't be cross with me!

Mrs. Linde (goes to her):   My dear Nora, you mustn't be cross with me! In my sort of position it's hard not to become bitter. One has no one to work for, and yet one can't give up the struggle. One must go on living, and it makes one selfish. I'm ashamed to admit it—but, just now, when you told me the good news about your husband's new position—I was glad—not so much for your sake as for mine.

Nora: How do you mean? Oh of course—I see! You think Torvald might perhaps help you.

Mrs. Linde: That's what I thought, yes.

Nora: And so he shall, Kristine. Just you leave it to me. I'll get him in a really good mood—and then bring it up quite casually. Oh, it would be such fun to help you!

Mrs. Linde: How good of you, Nora dear, to bother on my account! It's especially good of you—after all, you've never had to go through any hardship.

Nora: I? Not go through any—?

Mrs. Linde (smiling):   Well—Good Heavens—a little needlework, and so forth—You're just a child, Nora.

Nora (tosses her head and paces the room):   You needn't be so patronizing!

Mrs. Linde: No?

Nora: You're just like all the rest. You all think I'm incapable of being serious—

---

watering-place: A beach resort.

Mrs. Linde: Oh, come now—

Nora: You seem to think I've had no troubles—that I've been through nothing in my life!

Mrs. Linde: But you've just told me all your troubles, Nora dear.

Nora: I've only told you trifles! (*Softly.*) I haven't mentioned the important thing.

Mrs. Linde: Important thing? What do you mean?

Nora: I know you look down on me, Kristine; but you really shouldn't. You take pride in having worked so hard and so long for your mother.

Mrs. Linde: I don't look down on anyone, Nora; I can't help feeling proud and happy too, to have been able to make Mother's last days a little easier—

Nora: And you're proud of what you did for your brothers, too.

Mrs. Linde: I think I have a right to be.

Nora: Yes, so do I. But I want you to know, Kristine—that I, too, have something to be proud of.

Mrs. Linde: I don't doubt that. But what are you referring to?

Nora: Hush! We must talk quietly. It would be dreadful if Torvald overheard us! He must never know about it! No one must know about it, except you.

Mrs. Linde: And what is it, Nora?

Nora: Come over here. (*Draws her down beside her on sofa.*) Yes, I have something to be proud and happy about too. I saved Torvald's life, you see.

Mrs. Linde: Saved his life? But how?

Nora: I told you about our trip to Italy. Torvald would never have recovered if it hadn't been for that.

Mrs. Linde: Yes, I know—and your father gave you the necessary money.

Nora (smiling):   That's what everyone thinks—Torvald too; but—

Mrs. Linde: Well—?

Nora: Papa never gave us a penny. I raised the money myself.

Mrs. Linde: All that money! You?

Nora: Twelve hundred dollars. Four thousand eight hundred crowns. What do you think of that?

Mrs. Linde: But, Nora, how on earth did you do it? Did you win it in the lottery?

Nora (contemptuously):   The lottery! Of course not! Any fool could have done that!

Mrs. Linde: Where did you get it then?

Nora (hums and smiles mysteriously):   H'm; tra-la-la-la.

Mrs. Linde: You certainly couldn't have borrowed it.

Nora: Why not?

Mrs. Linde: A wife can't borrow without her husband's consent.

Nora (tossing her head):   Oh I don't know! If a wife has a good head on her shoulders—and has a little sense of business—

Mrs. Linde: I don't in the least understand, Nora—

Nora: Well, you needn't. I never said I borrowed the money. I may have got it some other way. (*Throws herself back on the sofa.*) Perhaps I got it from some admirer. After all when one is as attractive as I am—!

Mrs. Linde: What a mad little creature you are!

Nora: I'm sure you're dying of curiosity, Kristine—

Mrs. Linde: Nora, are you sure you haven't been a little rash?

Nora (sitting upright again):   Is it rash to save one's husband's life?

Mrs. Linde: But mightn't it be rash to do such a thing behind his back?

Nora: But I couldn't tell him—don't you understand that! He wasn't even supposed to know how ill he was. The doctors didn't tell him— they came to me privately, told me his life was in danger and that he could only be saved by living in the South for a while. At first I tried persuasion; I cried, I begged, I cajoled—I said how much I longed to take a trip abroad like other young wives; I reminded him of my condition and told him he ought to humor me—and finally, I came right out and suggested that we borrow the money. But then, Kristine, he was almost angry; he said I was being frivolous and that it was his duty as my husband not to indulge my whims and fancies—I think that's what he called them. Then I made up my mind he must be saved in spite of himself—and I thought of a way.

Mrs. Linde: But didn't he ever find out from your father that the money was not from him?

Nora: No; never. You see, Papa died just about that time. I was going to tell him all about it and beg him not to give me away. But he was so very ill—and then, it was no longer necessary—unfortunately.

Mrs. Linde: And you have never confided all this to your husband?

Nora: Good heavens, no! That's out of the question! He's much too strict in matters of that sort. And besides—Torvald could never bear to think of owing anything to me! It would hurt his self-respect—wound his pride. It would ruin everything between us. Our whole marriage would be wrecked by it!

Mrs. Linde: Don't you think you'll ever tell him?

Nora (thoughtfully; half-smiling):   Perhaps some day—a long time from now when I'm no longer so pretty and attractive. No! Don't laugh! Some day when Torvald is no longer as much in love with me as he is now; when it no longer amuses him to see me dance and dress up and act for him—then it might be useful to have something in reserve. (*Breaking off.*) Oh, what nonsense! That time will never come! Well— what do you think of my great secret, Kristine? Haven't I something to be proud of too? It's caused me endless worry, though. It hasn't been easy to fulfill my obligations. You know, in business there are things called installments, and quarterly interest—and they're dreadfully hard to meet on time. I've had to save a little here and there, wherever I could. I couldn't save much out of the housekeeping, for of course Torvald had to live well. And I couldn't let the children go about badly dressed; any money I got for them, I spent on them, the darlings!

Mrs. Linde: Poor Nora! I suppose it had to come out of your own allowance.

Nora: Yes, of course. But after all, the whole thing was my doing. Whenever Torvald gave me money to buy some new clothes, or other things I needed, I never spent more than half of it; I always picked out the simplest cheapest dresses. It's a blessing that almost anything looks well on me—so Torvald never knew the difference. But it's been hard sometimes, Kristine. It's so nice to have pretty clothes—isn't it?

Mrs. Linde: I suppose it is.

Nora: And I made money in other ways too. Last winter I was lucky enough to get a lot of copying to do. I shut myself up in my room every evening and wrote far into the night. Sometimes I was absolutely exhausted—but it was fun all the same—working like that and earning money. It made me feel almost like a man!

Mrs. Linde: How much have you managed to pay off?

Nora: Well, I really don't know exactly. It's hard to keep track of things like that. All I know is—I've paid every penny I could scrape together. There were times when I didn't know which way to turn! (*Smiles.*) Then I used to sit here and pretend that some rich old gentleman had fallen madly in love with me—

Mrs. Linde: What are you talking about? *What* old gentleman?

Nora: I'm just joking! And then he was to die and when they opened his will, there in large letters were to be the words: "I leave all my fortune to that charming Nora Helmer to be handed over to her immediately."

Mrs. Linde: But who *is* this old gentleman?

Nora: Good heavens, can't you understand? There never *was* any such old gentleman; I just used to make him up, when I was at the end of my rope and didn't know where to turn for money. But it doesn't matter now—the tiresome old fellow can stay where he is as far as I am concerned. I no longer need him nor his money; for now my troubles are over. (*Springing up.*) Oh, isn't it wonderful to think of, Kristine. No more troubles! No more worry! I'll be able to play and romp about with the children; I'll be able to make a charming lovely home for Torvald—have everything just as he likes it. And soon spring will be here, with its great blue sky. Perhaps we might take a little trip—I might see the ocean again. Oh, it's so marvelous to be alive and to be happy!

(*The hall doorbell rings.*)

Mrs. Linde (rising): There's the bell. Perhaps I had better go.

Nora: No, no; do stay! It's probably just someone for Torvald.

Helene (in the doorway):   Excuse me, Ma'am; there's a gentleman asking
  for Mr. Helmer—but the doctor's in there—and I didn't know if I
  should disturb him—
Nora: Who is it?
Krogstad (in the doorway):   It is I, Mrs. Helmer.

   (Mrs. Linde starts and turns away to the window.)

Nora (goes a step toward him, anxiously; in a low voice):   You? What is it?
  Why do you want to see my husband?
Krogstad: It's to do with Bank business—more or less. I have a small
  position in the Joint Stock Bank, and I hear your husband is to be the
  new president.
Nora: Then it's just—?
Krogstad: Just routine business, Mrs. Helmer; nothing else.
Nora: Then, please be good enough to go into his study.

   *(Krogstad goes. She bows indifferently while she closes the door into the
   hall. Then she goes to the stove and tends the fire.)*

Mrs. Linde: Who was that man, Nora?
Nora: A Mr. Krogstad—he's a lawyer.
Mrs. Linde: I was right, then.
Nora: Do you know him?
Mrs. Linde: I used to know him—many years ago. He worked in a law
  office in our town.
Nora: Yes, so he did.
Mrs. Linde: How he has changed!
Nora: He was unhappily married, they say.
Mrs. Linde: Is he a widower now?
Nora: Yes—with lots of children. There! That's better! (*She closes the door
  of the stove and moves the rocking chair a little to one side.*)
Mrs. Linde: I'm told he's mixed up in a lot of rather questionable business.
Nora: He may be; I really don't know. But don't let's talk about
  business—it's so tiresome.

   (Dr. Rank comes out of Helmer's room.)

Rank (still in the doorway):   No, no, I won't disturb you. I'll go in and see
  your wife for a moment. (*Sees Mrs. Linde.*) Oh, I beg your pardon. I
  seem to be in the way here, too.
Nora: Of course not! (*Introduces them.*) Dr. Rank—Mrs. Linde.
Rank: Well, well, I've often heard that name mentioned in this house;
  didn't I pass you on the stairs when I came in?
Mrs. Linde: Yes; I'm afraid I climb them very slowly. They wear me out!
Rank: A little on the delicate side—eh?
Mrs. Linde: No; just a bit overtired.
Rank: I see. So I suppose you've come to town for a good rest—on a
  round of dissipation!

Mrs. Linde: I have come to look for work.

Rank: Is that the best remedy for tiredness?

Mrs. Linde: One has to live, Doctor.

Rank: Yes, I'm told that's necessary.

Nora: Oh, come now, Dr. Rank! You're not above wanting to live yourself!

Rank: That's true enough. No matter how wretched I may be, I still want to hang on as long as possible. All my patients have that feeling too. Even the *morally* sick seem to share it. There's a wreck of a man in there with Helmer now—

Mrs. Linde (softly): Ah!

Nora: Whom do you mean?

Rank: A fellow named Krogstad, he's a lawyer—you wouldn't know anything about him. He's thoroughly depraved—rotten to the core— Yet even he declared, as though it were a matter of paramount importance, that he must live.

Nora: Really? What did he want with Torvald?

Rank: I've no idea; I gathered it was some Bank business.

Nora: I didn't know that Krog—that this man Krogstad had anything to do with the Bank?

Rank: He seems to have some sort of position there. (*To Mrs. Linde.*) I don't know if this is true in your part of the country—but there are men who make it a practice of prying about in other people's business, searching for individuals of doubtful character—and having discovered their secret, place them in positions of trust, where they can keep an eye on them, and make use of them at will. Honest men—men of strong moral fiber—they leave out in the cold.

Mrs. Linde: Perhaps the weaklings need more help.

Rank (shrugs his shoulders): That point of view is fast turning society into a clinic.

(*Nora, deep in her own thoughts, breaks into half-stifled laughter and claps her hands.*)

Rank: Why should that make you laugh? I wonder if you've any idea what "society" is?

Nora: Why should I care about your tiresome old "society"? I was laughing at something quite different—something frightfully amusing. Tell me, Dr. Rank—will all the employees at the Bank be dependent on Torvald now?

Rank: Is *that* what strikes you as so amusing?

Nora (smiles and hums): Never you mind! Never you mind! (*Walks about the room.*) What fun to think that we—that Torvald—has such power over so many people. (*Takes the bag from her pocket.*) Dr. Rank, how about a macaroon?

Rank: Well, well!—Macaroons, eh? I thought they were forbidden here.

Nora: These are some Kristine brought—

Mrs. Linde: What! I—

Nora: Now, you needn't be so frightened. How could you possibly know that Torvald had forbidden them? He's afraid they'll spoil my teeth. Oh, well—just for once! Don't you agree, Dr. Rank? There you are! (*Puts a macaroon into his mouth.*) You must have one too, Kristine. And I'll have just one—just a tiny one, or at most two. (*Walks about again.*) Oh dear, I am so happy! There's just one thing in all the world that would give me the greatest pleasure.

Rank: What's that?

Nora: It's something I long to say in front of Torvald.

Rank: What's to prevent you?

Nora: Oh, I don't dare; it isn't nice.

Mrs. Linde: Not nice?

Rank: It might be unwise, then; but you can certainly say it to us. What is it you so long to say in front of Torvald?

Nora: I'd so love to say "Damn!—damn!—damn it all!"

Rank: Have you gone crazy?

Mrs. Linde: Good gracious, Nora—

Rank: Go ahead and say it—here he comes!

Nora (hides the macaroons):   Hush—sh—sh.

(*Helmer comes out of his room; he carries his hat and overcoat.*)

Nora (going to him):   Well, Torvald, dear, did you get rid of him?

Helmer: He has just gone.

Nora: Let me introduce you—this is Kristine, who has just arrived in town—

Helmer: Kristine? I'm sorry—but I really don't—

Nora: Mrs. Linde, Torvald, dear—Kristine Linde.

Helmer: Oh yes! I suppose you're one of my wife's school friends?

Mrs. Linde: Yes; we knew each other as children.

Nora: Imagine, Torvald! She came all that long way just to talk to you.

Helmer: How do you mean?

Mrs. Linde: Well, it wasn't exactly—

Nora: Kristine is tremendously good at office work, and her great dream is to get a position with a really clever man—so she can improve still more, you see—

Helmer: Very sensible, Mrs. Linde.

Nora: And when she heard that you had become president of the Bank—it was in the paper, you know—she started off at once; you *will* try and do something for Kristine, won't you, Torvald? For my sake?

Helmer: It's by no means impossible. You're a widow, I presume?

Mrs. Linde: Yes.

Helmer: And you've already had business experience?

Mrs. Linde: A good deal.

Helmer: Then, I think it's quite likely I may be able to find a place for you.

Nora (clapping her hands):   There, you see! You see!

Helmer: You have come at a good moment, Mrs. Linde.

Mrs. Linde: How can I ever thank you—?

Helmer (smiling):   Don't mention it. (*Puts on his overcoat.*) But just now, I'm afraid you must excuse me—

Rank: I'll go with you. (*Fetches his fur coat from the hall and warms it at the stove.*)

Nora: Don't be long, Torvald, dear.

Helmer: I shan't be more than an hour.

Nora: Are you going too, Kristine?

Mrs. Linde (putting on her outdoor things): Yes; I must go and find a place to live.

Helmer: We can all go out together.

Nora (helping her):   How tiresome that we're so cramped for room, Kristine; otherwise—

Mrs. Linde: Oh, you mustn't think of that! Good-bye, dear Nora, and thanks for everything.

Nora: Goodbye for the present. Of course you'll come back this evening. And you too, Dr. Rank—eh? If you're well enough? But of course you'll be well enough! Wrap up warmly now! (*They go out talking, into the hall; children's voices are heard on the stairs*) Here they come! Here they come! (*She runs to the outer door and opens it. The nurse, Anne-Marie, enters the hall with the children.*) Come in, come in—you darlings! Just look at them, Kristine. Aren't they sweet?

Rank: No chattering in this awful draught!

Helmer: Come along, Mrs. Linde; you have to be a mother to put up with this!

(*Dr. Rank, Helmer, and Mrs. Linde go down the stairs; Anne-Marie enters the room with the children; Nora comes in too, shutting the door behind her.*)

Nora: How fresh and bright you look! And what red cheeks! Like apples and roses. (*The children chatter to her during what follows.*) Did you have a good time? Splendid! You gave Emmy and Bob a ride on your sled? Both at once? You *are* a clever boy, Ivar! Let me hold her for a bit, Anne-Marie. My darling little doll-baby. (*Takes the smallest from the nurse and dances with her.*) All right, Bobbie! Mama will dance with you too. You threw snowballs, did you? I should have been in on that! Never mind, Anne; I'll undress them myself—oh, do let me—it's such fun. Go on into the nursery, you look half-frozen. There's some hot coffee in there on the stove. (*The nurse goes into the room on the left. Nora takes off the children's things and throws them down anywhere, while the children all talk together.*) Not really! You were chased by a big dog? But he didn't bite you? No; dogs don't bite tiny little doll-babies! Don't touch the packages, Ivar. What's in them? Wouldn't you like to know! No. No! Careful! It might bite! Come on, let's play. What will we play? Hide-and-seek? Let's play hide-and-seek. Bob, you hide first! Do you want me to? All right! I'll hide first then.

(She and the children play, laughing and shouting, all over the room and in the adjacent room to the left. Finally Nora hides under the table; the children come rushing in, look for her, but cannot find her, hear her half-suppressed laughter, rush to the table, lift up the cover and see her. Loud shouts of delight. She creeps out, as though to frighten them. More shouts. Meanwhile there has been a knock at the door leading into the hall. No one has heard it. Now the door is half-opened and Krogstad appears. He waits a little—the game continues.)

Krogstad: I beg your pardon, Mrs. Helmer—

Nora (with a stifled scream, turns round and half jumps up):   Oh! What do you want?

Krogstad: Excuse me; the outer door was ajar—someone must have forgotten to close it—

Nora (standing up):   My husband is not at home, Mr. Krogstad.

Krogstad: I know that.

Nora: Then, what do you want here?

Krogstad: I want a few words with you.

Nora: With—? (*To the children, softly.*) Go in to Anne-Marie. What? No— the strange man won't do Mama any harm; when he's gone we'll go on playing. (*She leads the children into the right hand room, and shuts the door behind them; uneasy, in suspense.*) You want to speak to me?

Krogstad: Yes, I do.

Nora: Today? But it's not the first of the month yet—

Krogstad: No, it is Christmas Eve. It's up to you whether your Christmas is a merry one.

Nora: What is it you want? Today I can't possibly—

Krogstad: That doesn't concern me for the moment. This is about something else. You have a few minutes, haven't you?

Nora: I suppose so; although—

Krogstad: Good. I was sitting in the restaurant opposite, and I saw your husband go down the street—

Nora: Well?

Krogstad:—with a lady.

Nora: What of it?

Krogstad: May I ask if that lady was a Mrs. Linde?

Nora: Yes.

Krogstad: She's just come to town, hasn't she?

Nora: Yes. Today.

Krogstad: Is she a good friend of yours?

Nora: Yes, she is. But I can't imagine—

Krogstad: I used to know her too.

Nora: Yes, I know you did.

Krogstad: Then you know all about it. I thought as much. Now, tell me: is Mrs. Linde to have a place in the Bank?

Nora: How dare you question me like this, Mr. Krogstad—you, one of my husband's employees! But since you ask—you might as well know. Yes, Mrs. Linde is to have a position at the Bank, and it is I who recommended her. Does that satisfy you, Mr. Krogstad?

Krogstad: I was right, then.

Nora (walks up and down):   After all, one has a little influence, now and then. Even if one is only a woman it doesn't always follow that— people in subordinate positions, Mr. Krogstad, ought really to be careful how they offend anyone who—h'm—

Krogstad:—has influence?

Nora: Precisely.

Krogstad (taking another tone):   Then perhaps you'll be so kind, Mrs. Helmer, as to use your influence on *my* behalf?

Nora: What? How do you mean?

Krogstad: Perhaps you'll be good enough to see that I *retain* my subordinate position?

Nora: But, I don't understand. Who wants to take it from you?

Krogstad: Oh, don't try and play the innocent! I can well understand that it would be unpleasant for your friend to associate with me; and I understand too, whom I have to thank for my dismissal.

Nora: But I assure you—

Krogstad: Never mind all that—there is still time. But I advise you to use your influence to prevent this.

Nora: But, Mr. Krogstad, I *have* no influence—absolutely none!

Krogstad: Indeed! I thought you just told me yourself—

Nora: You misunderstood me—*really* you did! You must know my husband would never be influenced by me!

Krogstad: Your husband and I were at the University together—I know him well. I don't suppose he's any more inflexible than other married men.

Nora: Don't you dare talk disrespectfully about my husband, or I'll show you the door!

Krogstad: The little lady's plucky.

Nora: I'm no longer afraid of you. I'll soon be free of all this—after the first of the year.

Krogstad (in a more controlled manner):   Listen to me, Mrs. Helmer. This is a matter of life and death to me. I warn you I shall fight with all my might to keep my position in the Bank.

Nora: So it seems.

Krogstad: It's not just the salary; that is the least important part of it—It's something else—Well, I might as well be frank with you. I suppose you know, like everyone else, that once—a long time ago—I got into quite a bit of trouble.

Nora: I have heard something about it, I believe.

Krogstad: The matter never came to court; but from that time on, all doors were closed to me. I then went into the business with which you are familiar. I had to do something; and I don't think I've been among the worst. But now I must get away from all that. My sons are growing up, you see; for their sake I'm determined to recapture my good name. This position in the Bank was to be the first step; and now your husband wants to kick me back into the mud again.

Nora: But I tell you, Mr. Krogstad, it's not in my power to help you.

Krogstad: Only because you don't really want to; but I can compel you to do it, if I choose.

Nora: You wouldn't tell my husband that I owe you money?

Krogstad: And suppose I were to?

Nora: But that would be an outrageous thing to do! (*With tears in her voice.*) My secret—that I've guarded with such pride—such joy! I couldn't bear to have him find it out in such an ugly, hateful way—to have him find it out from you! I couldn't bear it! It would be too horribly unpleasant!

Krogstad: Only unpleasant, Mrs. Helmer?

Nora (vehemently):   But just you do it! You'll be the one to suffer; for then my husband will *really* know the kind of man you are—there'll be no chance of keeping your job then!

Krogstad: Didn't you hear my question? I asked if it were only unpleasantness you feared?

Nora: If my husband got to know about it, he'd naturally pay you off at once, and then we'd have nothing more to do with you.

Krogstad (takes a step towards her):   Listen, Mrs. Helmer: Either you have a very bad memory, or you know nothing about business. I think I'd better make the position clear to you.

Nora: What do you mean?

Krogstad: When your husband fell ill, you came to me to borrow twelve hundred dollars.

Nora: I didn't know what else to do.

Krogstad: I promised to find you the money—

Nora: And you did find it.

Krogstad: I promised to find you the money, on certain conditions. At that time you were so taken up with your husband's illness and so anxious to procure the money for your journey, that you probably did not give much thought to details. Perhaps I'd better remind you of them. I promised to find you the amount in exchange for a note, which I drew up.

Nora: Yes, and I signed it.

Krogstad: Very good. But then I added a clause, stating that your father would stand sponsor for the debt. This clause your father was to have signed.

Nora: Was to—? He did sign it.

Krogstad: I left the date blank, so that your father himself should date his signature. You recall that?

Nora: Yes, I believe—

Krogstad: Then I gave you the paper, and you were to mail it to your father. Isn't that so?

Nora: Yes.

Krogstad: And you must have mailed it at once; for five or six days later you brought me back the document with your father's signature; and then I handed you the money.

Nora: Well? Haven't I made my payments punctually?

Krogstad: Fairly—yes. But to return to the point: That was a sad time for you, wasn't it, Mrs. Helmer?

Nora: It was indeed!

Krogstad: Your father was very ill, I believe?

Nora: Yes—he was dying.

Krogstad: And he did die soon after, didn't he?

Nora: Yes.

Krogstad: Now tell me, Mrs. Helmer: Do you happen to recollect the date of your father's death: the day of the month, I mean?

Nora: Father died on the 29th of September.

Krogstad: Quite correct. I have made inquiries. Now here is a strange thing, Mrs. Helmer—(*Produces a paper.*) something rather hard to explain.

Nora: What do you mean? What strange thing?

Krogstad: The strange thing about it is, that your father seems to have signed this paper three days after his death!

Nora: I don't understand—

Krogstad: Your father died on the 29th of September. But look at this: his signature is dated October 2nd! Isn't that rather strange, Mrs. Helmer? (*Nora is silent.*) Can you explain that to me? (*Nora continues silent.*) It is curious, too, that the words "October 2nd" and the year are not in your father's handwriting, but in a handwriting I seem to know. This could easily be explained, however; your father might have forgotten to date his signature, and someone might have added the date at random, before the fact of your father's death was known. There is nothing wrong in that. It all depends on the signature itself. It is of course genuine, Mrs. Helmer? It was your father himself who wrote his name here?

Nora (*after a short silence, throws her head back and looks defiantly at him*):   No, it wasn't. *I* wrote father's name.

Krogstad: I suppose you realize, Mrs. Helmer, what a dangerous confession that is?

Nora: Why should it be dangerous? You will get your money soon enough!

Krogstad: I'd like to ask you a question: Why didn't you send the paper to your father?

Nora: It was impossible. Father was too ill. If I had asked him for his signature, he'd have wanted to know what the money was for. In his condition I simply could not tell him that my husband's life was in danger. That's why it was impossible.

Krogstad: Then wouldn't it have been wiser to give up the journey?

Nora: How could I? That journey was to save my husband's life. I simply couldn't give it up.

Krogstad: And it never occurred to you that you weren't being honest with me?

Nora: I really couldn't concern myself with that. You meant nothing to me—In fact I couldn't help disliking you for making it all so difficult—with your cold, businesslike clauses and conditions—when you knew my husband's life was at stake.

Krogstad: You evidently haven't the faintest idea, Mrs. Helmer, what you have been guilty of. Yet let me tell you that it was nothing more and nothing worse that made me an outcast from society.

Nora: You don't expect me to believe that you ever did a brave thing to save your wife's life?

Krogstad: The law takes no account of motives.

Nora: It must be a very bad law, then!

Krogstad: Bad or not, if I produce this document in court, you will be condemned according to the law.

Nora: I don't believe that for a minute. Do you mean to tell me that a daughter has no right to spare her dying father worry and anxiety? Or that a wife has no right to save her husband's life? I may not know much about it—but I'm sure there must be something or other in the law that permits such things. You as a lawyer should be aware of that. You don't seem to know very much about the law, Mr. Krogstad.

Krogstad: Possibly not. But business—the kind of business we are concerned with—I *do* know something about. Don't you agree? Very well, then; do as you please. But I warn you: if I am made to suffer a second time, you shall keep me company. (*Bows and goes out through the hall.*)

Nora (stands a while thinking, then tosses her head):   What nonsense! He's just trying to frighten me. I'm not such a fool as all that! (*Begins folding the children's clothes. Pauses.*) And yet—? No, it's impossible! After all—I only did it for love's sake.

Children (at the door, left):   Mamma, the strange man has gone now.

Nora: Yes, yes, I know. But don't tell anyone about the strange man. Do you hear? Not even Papa!

Children: No, Mamma; now will you play with us again?

Nora: No, not just now.

Children: But Mamma! You promised!

Nora: But I can't just now. Run back to the nursery; I have so much to do. Run along now! Run along, my darlings! (*She pushes them gently into the inner room, and closes the door behind them. Sits on the sofa, embroiders a few stitches, but soon pauses.)* No! (*Throws down the work, rises, goes to the hall door and calls out.*) Helene, bring the tree in to me, will you? (*Goes to table, right, and opens the drawer; again pauses.*) No, it's utterly impossible!

Helene (carries in the Christmas tree):   Where shall I put it, Ma'am?

Nora: Right there; in the middle of the room.

Helene: Is there anything else you need?

Nora: No, thanks; I have everything.

(*Helene, having put down the tree, goes out.*)

Nora (busy dressing the tree):   We'll put a candle here—and some flowers here—that dreadful man! But it's just nonsense! There's nothing to worry about. The tree will be lovely. I'll do everything to please you, Torvald; I'll sing for you, I'll dance for you—

(*Enter Helmer by the hall door, with a bundle of documents.*)

Nora: Oh! You're back already?

Helmer: Yes. Has somebody been here?

Nora: No. Nobody.

Helmer: That's odd. I just saw Krogstad leave the house.

Nora: Really? Well—as a matter of fact—Krogstad was here for a moment.

Helmer: Nora—I can tell by your manner—he came here to ask you to put in a good word for him, didn't he?

Nora: Yes, Torvald.

Helmer: And you weren't supposed to tell me he'd been here—You were to do it as if of your own accord—isn't that it?

Nora: Yes, Torvald; but—

Helmer: Nora, Nora! How could you consent to such a thing! To have dealings with a man like that—make him promises! And then to lie about it too!

Nora: Lie!

Helmer: Didn't you tell me that nobody had been here? (*Threatens with his finger.*) My little bird must never do that again! A song-bird must sing clear and true! No false notes! (*Puts arm around her.*) Isn't that the way it should be? Of course it is! (*Lets her go.*) And now we'll say no more about it. (*Sits down before the fire.*) It's so cozy and peaceful here! (*Glances through the documents.*)

Nora (busy with the tree, after a short silence):   Torvald!

Helmer: Yes.

Nora: I'm so looking forward to the Stenborgs' fancy dress party, day after tomorrow.

Helmer: And I can't wait to see what surprise you have in store for me.

Nora: Oh, it's so awful, Torvald!

Helmer: What is?

Nora: I can't think of anything amusing. Everything seems so silly, so
   pointless.
Helmer: Has my little Nora come to *that* conclusion?
Nora (behind his chair, with her arms on the back): Are you very busy,
   Torvald?
Helmer: Well—
Nora: What are all those papers?
Helmer: Just Bank business.
Nora: Already!
Helmer: The board of directors has given me full authority to do some
   reorganizing—to make a few necessary changes in the staff. I'll have to
   work on it during Christmas week. I want it all settled by the New
   Year.
Nora: I see. So that was why that poor Krogstad—
Helmer: H'm.
Nora (still leaning over the chair-back and slowly stroking his hair):   If you
   weren't so very busy, I'd ask you to do me a great, great favor,
   Torvald.
Helmer: Well, let's hear it! Out with it!
Nora: You have such perfect taste, Torvald; and I do so want to look well
   at the fancy dress ball. Couldn't you take me in hand, and decide what
   I'm to be, and arrange my costume for me?
Helmer: Well, well! So we're not so self-sufficient after all! We need a
   helping hand, do we?
Nora: Oh, please, Torvald! I know I shall *never* manage without your help!
Helmer: I'll think about it; we'll hit on something.
Nora: Oh, how sweet of you! (*Goes to the tree again; pause.*) Those red
   flowers show up beautifully! Tell me, Torvald; did that Krogstad do
   something very wrong?
Helmer: He committed forgery. Have you any idea of what that means?
Nora: Perhaps he did it out of necessity?
Helmer: Or perhaps he was just foolhardy, like so many others. I am not
   so harsh as to condemn a man irrevocably for one mistake.
Nora: No, of course not!
Helmer: A man has a chance to rehabilitate himself, if he honestly admits
   his guilt and takes his punishment.
Nora: Punishment—
Helmer: But that wasn't Krogstad's way. He resorted to tricks and
   evasions; became thoroughly demoralized.
Nora: You really think it would—?
Helmer: When a man has that sort of thing on his conscience his life
   becomes a tissue of lies and deception. He's forced to wear a mask—
   even with those nearest to him—his own wife and children even. And
   the children—that's the worst part of it, Nora.
Nora: Why?

Helmer: Because the whole atmosphere of the home would be contaminated. The very air the children breathed would be filled with evil.

Nora (closer behind him):   Are you sure of that?

Helmer: As a lawyer, I know it from experience. Almost all cases of early delinquency can be traced to dishonest mothers.

Nora: Why—only mothers?

Helmer: It usually stems from the mother's side; but of course it can come from the father too. We lawyers know a lot about such things. And this Krogstad has been deliberately poisoning his own children for years, by surrounding them with lies and hypocrisy—that is why I call him demoralized. (*Holds out both hands to her.*) So my sweet little Nora must promise not to plead his cause. Shake hands on it. Well? What's the matter? Give me your hand. There! That's all settled. I assure you it would have been impossible for me to work with him. It literally gives me a feeling of physical discomfort to come in contact with such people. (*Nora draws her hand away, and moves to the other side of the Christmas tree.*)

Nora: It's so warm here. And I have such a lot to do.

Helmer (rises and gathers up his papers):   I must try and look through some of these papers before dinner. I'll give some thought to your costume too. Perhaps I may even find something to hang in gilt paper on the Christmas tree! (*Lays his hand on her head.*) My own precious little songbird! (*He goes into his study and closes the door after him.*)

Nora (softly, after a pause):   It can't be—! It's impossible. Of course it's impossible!

Anne-Marie (at the door, left):   The babies keep begging to come in and see Mamma.

Nora: No, no! Don't let them come to me! Keep them with you, Anne-Marie.

Anne-Marie: Very well, Ma'am (*Shuts the door.*)

Nora (pale with terror): Harm my children!—Corrupt my home! (*Short pause. She throws back her head.*) It's not true! I know it's not! It could never, never be true!

ACT II

Scene: The same room. In the corner, beside the piano, stands the Christmas tree, stripped and with the candles burnt out. Nora's outdoor things lie on the sofa. Nora, alone, is walking about restlessly. At last she stops by the sofa, and picks up her cloak.

Nora (puts the cloak down again):   Did someone come in? (*Goes to the hall and listens.*) No; no one; of course no one will come today, Christmas Day; nor tomorrow either. But perhaps—(*Opens the door and looks out.*) No, there's nothing in the mailbox; it's quite empty. (*Comes forward.*) Oh nonsense! He only meant to frighten me. There won't be any trouble. It's all impossible! Why, I—I have three little children!

(*Anne-Marie enters from the left, with a large cardboard box.*)

Anne-Marie: Well—I found the box with the fancy dress clothes at last, Miss Nora.

Nora: Thanks; put it on the table.

Anne-Marie (does so):   I'm afraid they're rather shabby.

Nora: If I had my way I'd tear them into a thousand pieces!

Anne-Marie: Good gracious! They can be repaired—just have a little patience.

Nora: I'll go and get Mrs. Linde to help me.

Anne-Marie: I wouldn't go out again in this awful weather! You might catch cold, Miss Nora, and get sick.

Nora: Worse things might happen—How are the children?

Anne-Marie: The poor little things are playing with their Christmas presents; but—

Nora: Have they asked for me?

Anne-Marie: They're so used to having Mamma with them.

Nora: I know; but, you see, Anne-Marie, I won't be able to be with them as much as I used to.

Anne-Marie: Well, little children soon get used to anything.

Nora: You really think so? Would they forget me if I went away for good?

Anne-Marie: Good gracious!—for good!

Nora: Tell me something, Anne-Marie—I've so often wondered about it—how could you bear to part with your child—give it up to strangers?

Anne-Marie: Well, you see, I had to—when I came to nurse my little Nora.

Nora: Yes—but how could you *bear* to do it?

Anne-Marie: I couldn't afford to say "no" to such a good position. A poor girl who's been in trouble must take what comes. Of course *he* never offered to help me—the wicked sinner!

Nora: Then I suppose your daughter has forgotten all about you.

Anne-Marie: No—indeed she hasn't! She even wrote to me—once when she was confirmed and again when she was married.

Nora (embracing her):   Dear old Anne-Marie—you were a good mother to me when I was little.

Anne-Marie: But then my poor little Nora *had* no mother of her own!

Nora: And if ever my little ones were left without—you'd look after them, wouldn't you?—Oh, that's just nonsense! (*Opens the box.*) Go back to them. Now I must—Just you wait and see how lovely I'll look tomorrow!

Anne-Marie: My Miss Nora will be the prettiest person there! (*She goes into the room on the left.*)

Nora (takes the costume out of the box, but soon throws it down again):   I wish I dared go out—I'm afraid someone might come. I'm afraid something might happen while I'm gone. That's just silly! No one will come. I must try not to think—This muff needs cleaning. What pretty gloves—they're lovely! I must put it out of my head! One, two, three, four, five, six—(*With a scream.*) Ah! They're here!

(*Goes toward the door, then stands irresolute. Mrs. Linde enters from the hall, where she has taken off her things.*)

Nora: Oh, it's you, Kristine! There's no one else out there, is there? I'm so glad you have come!

Mrs. Linde: I got a message you'd been asking for me.

Nora: Yes, I just happened to be passing by. There's something I want you to help me with. Sit down here on the sofa. Now, listen: There's to be a fancy dress ball at the Stenborgs' tomorrow evening—they live just overhead—and Torvald wants me to go as a Neapolitan peasant girl, and dance the tarantella; I learned it while we were in Capri.

Mrs. Linde: So you're going to give a real performance, are you?

Nora: Torvald wants me to. Look, here's the costume; Torvald had it made for me down there. But it's all torn, Kristine, and I don't know whether—

Mrs. Linde: Oh, we'll soon fix that. It's only the trimming that has come loose here and there. Have you a needle and thread? Oh, yes. Here's everything I need.

Nora: It's awfully good of you!

Mrs. Linde (sewing): So you're going to be all dressed up, Nora—what fun! You know—I think I'll run in for a moment—just to see you in your costume—I haven't really thanked you for last night. I had such a happy time!

Nora (rises and walks across the room): Somehow it didn't seem as nice to me as usual. I wish you'd come to town a little earlier, Kristine. Yes—Torvald has a way of making things so gay and cozy.

Mrs. Linde: Well—so have you. That's your father coming out in you! But tell me—is Doctor Rank always so depressed?

Nora: No; last night it was worse than usual. He's terribly ill, you see—tuberculosis of the spine, or something. His father was a frightful man, who kept mistresses and all that sort of thing—that's why his son has been an invalid from birth—

Mrs. Linde (lets her sewing fall into her lap): Why, Nora! what do you know about such things?

Nora (moving about the room): After all—I've had three children; and those women who look after one at childbirth know almost as much as doctors; and they love to gossip.

Mrs. Linde (goes on sewing; a short pause): Does Doctor Rank come here every day?

Nora: Every single day. He's Torvald's best friend, you know—always has been; and he's *my* friend too. He's almost like one of the family.

Mrs. Linde: Do you think he's quite sincere, Nora? I mean—isn't he inclined to flatter people?

Nora: Quite the contrary. What gave you that impression?

Mrs. Linde: When you introduced us yesterday he said he had often heard my name mentioned here; but I noticed afterwards that your husband hadn't the faintest notion who I was. How could Doctor Rank—?

Nora: He was quite right, Kristine. You see Torvald loves me so tremendously that he won't share me with anyone; he wants me all to himself, as he says. At first he used to get terribly jealous if I even mentioned any of my old friends back home; so naturally I gave up doing it. But I often talk to Doctor Rank about such things—he likes to hear about them.

Mrs. Linde: Listen to me, Nora! In many ways you are still a child. I'm somewhat older than you, and besides, I've had much more experience. I think you ought to put a stop to all this with Dr. Rank.

Nora: Put a stop to what?

Mrs. Linde: To the whole business. You said something yesterday about a rich admirer who was to give you money—

Nora: One who never existed, unfortunately. Go on.

Mrs. Linde: Has Doctor Rank money?

Nora: Why yes, he has.

Mrs. Linde: And he has no one dependent on him?

Nora: No, no one. But—

Mrs. Linde: And he comes here every single day?

Nora: Yes—I've just told you so.

Mrs. Linde: It's surprising that a sensitive man like that should be so importunate.

Nora: I don't understand you—

Mrs. Linde: Don't try to deceive me, Nora. Don't you suppose I can guess who lent you the twelve hundred dollars?

Nora: You must be out of your mind! How could you ever think such a thing? Why, he's a friend of ours; he comes to see us every day! The situation would have been impossible!

Mrs. Linde: So it wasn't he, then?

Nora: No, I assure you. Such a thing never even occurred to me. Anyway, he didn't have any money at that time; he came into it later.

Mrs. Linde: Perhaps that was just as well, Nora, dear.

Nora: No—it would never have entered my head to ask Dr. Rank—Still— I'm sure that if I did ask him—

Mrs. Linde: But you won't, of course.

Nora: No, of course not. Anyway—I don't see why it should be necessary. But I'm sure that if I talked to Doctor Rank—

Mrs. Linde: Behind your husband's back?

Nora: I want to get that thing cleared up; after all, that's behind his back too. I must get clear of it.

Mrs. Linde: That's just what I said yesterday; but—

Nora (walking up and down):   It's so much easier for a man to manage things like that—

Mrs. Linde: One's own husband, yes.

Nora: Nonsense. (*Stands still.*) Surely if you pay back everything you owe—the paper is returned to you?

Mrs. Linde: Naturally.

Nora: Then you can tear it into a thousand pieces, and burn it up—the nasty, filthy thing!

Mrs. Linde (looks at her fixedly, lays down her work, and rises slowly):   Nora, you are hiding something from me.

Nora: You can see it in my face, can't you?

Mrs. Linde: Something's happened to you since yesterday morning, Nora, what is it?

Nora (going towards her):   Kristine—! (*Listens.*) Hush! Here comes Torvald! Go into the nursery for a little while. Torvald hates anything to do with sewing. Get Anne-Marie to help you.

Mrs. Linde (gathers the things together):   Very well; but I shan't leave until you have told me all about it. (*She goes out to the left, as Helmer enters from the hall.*)

Nora (runs to meet him):   Oh, I've missed you so, Torvald, dear!

Helmer: Was that the dressmaker—?

Nora: No, it was Kristine. She's helping me fix my costume. It's going to look so nice.

Helmer: Wasn't that a good idea of mine?

Nora: Splendid! But don't you think it was good of me to let you have your way?

Helmer: Good of you! To let your own husband have his way! There, there, you crazy little thing; I'm only teasing. Now I won't disturb you. You'll have to try the dress on, I suppose.

Nora: Yes—and I expect you've work to do.

Helmer: I have. (*Shows her a bundle of papers.*) Look. I've just come from the Bank—(*Goes towards his room.*)

Nora: Torvald.

Helmer (stopping):   Yes?

Nora: If your little squirrel were to beg you—with all her heart—

Helmer: Well?

Nora: Would you do something for her?

Helmer: That depends on what it is.

Nora: Be a darling and say 'Yes,' Torvald! Your squirrel would skip about and play all sorts of pretty tricks—

Helmer: Well—out with it!

Nora: Your little lark would twitter all day long—

Helmer: She does that anyway!

Nora: I'll pretend to be an elf and dance for you in the moonlight, Torvald.

Helmer: Nora—you're surely not getting back to what we talked about this morning?

Nora (coming nearer):   Oh, Torvald, dear, I do most humbly beg you—!

Helmer: You have the temerity to bring that up again?

Nora: You must give in to me about this, Torvald! You *must* let Krogstad keep his place!

Helmer: I'm giving his place to Mrs. Linde.

Nora: That's awfully sweet of you. But instead of Krogstad—couldn't you dismiss some other clerk?

Helmer: This is the most incredible obstinacy! Because you were thoughtless enough to promise to put in a good word for him, am I supposed to—?

Nora: That's not the reason, Torvald. It's for your own sake. Didn't you tell me yourself he writes for the most horrible newspapers? He can do you no end of harm. Oh! I'm so afraid of him—

Helmer: I think I understand; you have some unpleasant memories—that's why you're frightened.

Nora: What do you mean?

Helmer: Aren't you thinking of your father?

Nora: Oh, yes—of course! You remember how those awful people slandered poor father in the newspapers? If you hadn't been sent to investigate the matter, and been so kind and helpful—he might have been dismissed.

Helmer: My dear Nora, there is a distinct difference between your father and me. Your father's conduct was not entirely unimpeachable. But mine is; and I trust it will remain so.

Nora: You never know what evil-minded people can think up. We could be so happy now, Torvald, in our lovely, peaceful home—you and I and the children! Oh! I implore you, Torvald—!

Helmer: The more you plead his cause the less likely I am to keep him on. It's already known at the Bank that I intend to dismiss Krogstad. If I were to change my mind, people might say I'd done it at the insistence of my wife—

Nora: Well—what of that?

Helmer: Oh, nothing, of course! As long as the obstinate little woman gets her way! I'd simply be the laughingstock of the whole staff; they'd think I was weak and easily influenced—I should soon be made to feel the consequences. Besides—there is one factor that makes it quite impossible for Krogstad to work at the Bank as long as I'm head there.

Nora: What could that be?

Helmer: His past record I might be able to overlook—

Nora: Yes, you might, mightn't you, Torvald—?

Helmer: And I'm told he's an excellent worker. But unfortunately we were friendly during our college days. It was one of those impetuous friendships that subsequently often prove embarrassing. He's tactless

enough to call me by my first name—regardless of the circumstances—
and feels quite justified in taking a familiar tone with me. At any
moment he comes out with "Torvald" this, and "Torvald" that! It's
acutely irritating. It would make my position at the Bank intolerable.

Nora: You're surely not serious about this, Torvald?

Helmer: Why not?

Nora: But—it's all so petty.

Helmer: Petty! So you think I'm petty!

Nora: Of course not, Torvald—just the opposite; that's why—

Helmer: Never mind; you call my motives petty; so I must be petty too!
Petty! Very well!—We'll put an end to this now—once and for all.
(*Helmer goes to the door into the hall and calls Helene.*)

Nora: What do you want?

Helmer (searching among his papers):   I want this thing settled. (*Helene
enters.*) Take this letter, will you? Get a messenger and have him
deliver it at once! It's urgent. Here's some money.

Helene: Very good, Sir. (*Goes with the letter.*)

Helmer (putting his papers together):   There, little Miss Obstinacy.

Nora (breathless):   Torvald—what was in that letter?

Helmer: Krogstad's dismissal.

Nora: Call her back, Torvald! There's still time. Call her back! For my
sake, for your own sake, for the sake of the children, don't send that
letter! Torvald, do you hear? You don't realize what may come of this!

Helmer: It's too late.

Nora: Too late, yes.

Helmer: Nora, dear; I forgive your fears—though it's not exactly
flattering to me to think I could ever be afraid of any spiteful nonsense
Krogstad might choose to write about me! But I forgive you all the
same—it shows how much you love me. (*Takes her in his arms.*) And
that's the way it should be, Nora darling. No matter what happens,
you'll see—I have strength and courage for us both. My shoulders are
broad—I'll bear the burden.

Nora (terror-struck):   How do you mean?

Helmer: The whole burden, my darling. Don't you worry any more.

Nora (with decision):   No! You mustn't—I won't let you!

Helmer: Then we'll share it, Nora, as man and wife. That is as it should be.
(*Petting her.*) Are you happy now? There! Don't look at me like a
frightened little dove! You're just imagining things, you know—Now
don't you think you ought to play the tarantella through—and practice
your tambourine? I'll go into my study and close both doors, then you
won't disturb me. You can make all the noise you like! (*Turns round in
doorway.*) And when Rank comes, just tell him where I am. (*He nods to
her, and goes with his papers to his room, closing the door.*)

*Nora (bewildered with terror, stands as though rooted to the ground, and
whispers):*   He'd do it too! He'd do it—in spite of anything! But he

mustn't—never, never! Anything but that! There must be some way out! What shall I do? (*The hall bell rings.*) Dr. Rank—! Anything but that—anything, *anything* but that!

(*Nora draws her hands over her face, pulls herself together, goes to the door and opens it. Rank stands outside hanging up his fur coat. During the following scene, darkness begins to fall.*)

Nora: How are you, Doctor Rank? I recognized your ring. You'd better not go in to Torvald just now; I think he's busy.

Rank: How about you? (*Enters and closes the door.*)

Nora: You know I always have an hour to spare for you.

Rank: Many thanks. I'll make use of that privilege as long as possible.

Nora: What do you mean—as long as possible?

Rank: Does that frighten you?

Nora: No—but it's such a queer expression. Has anything happened?

Rank: I've been expecting it for a long time; but I never thought it would come quite so soon.

Nora: What is it you have found out? Doctor Rank, please tell me!

Rank (sitting down by the stove): I haven't much time left. There's nothing to do about it.

Nora (with a sigh of relief):   Oh! Then—it's about you—?

Rank: Of course. What did you think? It's no use lying to one's self. I am the most miserable of all my patients, Mrs. Helmer. These past few days I've been taking stock of my position—and I find myself completely bankrupt. Within a month, I shall be rotting in the churchyard.

Nora: What a ghastly way to talk!

Rank: The whole business is pretty ghastly, you see. And the worst of it is, there are so many ghastly things to be gone through before it's over. I've just one last examination to make, then I shall know approximately when the final dissolution will begin. There's something I want to say to you: Helmer's sensitive nature is repelled by anything ugly. I couldn't bear to have him near me when—

Nora: But Doctor Rank—

Rank: No, I couldn't bear it! I won't have him there—I shall bar my door against him—As soon as I am absolutely certain of the worst, I'll send you my visiting-card marked with a black cross; that will mean that the final horror has begun.

Nora: Doctor Rank—you're absolutely impossible today! And I did so want you to be in a good humor.

Rank: With death staring me in the face? And why should I have to expiate another's sins! What justice is there in that? Well—I suppose in almost every family there are some such debts that have to be paid.

Nora (her hands over her ears):   Don't talk such nonsense! Come along! Cheer up!

Rank: One might as well laugh. It's really very funny when you come to think of it—that my poor innocent spine should be made to suffer for my father's exploits!

Nora (at table, left):   He was much addicted to asparagustips and paté de foie gras, wasn't he?

Rank: Yes; and truffles.

Nora: Oh, of course—truffles, yes. And I suppose oysters too?

Rank: Oh, yes! Masses of oysters, certainly!

Nora: And all the wine and champagne that went with them! It does seem a shame that all these pleasant things should be so damaging to the spine, doesn't it?

Rank: Especially when it's a poor miserable spine that never had any of the fun!

Nora: Yes, that's the biggest shame of all!

Rank (gives her a searching look):   H'm—

Nora (a moment later):   Why did you smile?

Rank: No; you were the one that laughed.

Nora: No; you were the one that smiled, Doctor Rank!

Rank (gets up):   You're more of a rogue than I thought you were.

Nora: I'm full of mischief today.

Rank: So it seems.

Nora (with her hands on his shoulders):   Dear, dear Doctor Rank, don't go and die and leave Torvald and me.

Rank: Oh, you won't miss me long! Those who go away—are soon forgotten.

Nora (looks at him anxiously):   You really believe that?

Rank: People develop new interests, and soon—

Nora: What do you mean—new interests?

Rank: That'll happen to you and Helmer when I am gone. You seem to have made a good start already. What was that Mrs. Linde doing here last evening?

Nora: You're surely not jealous of poor old Kristine!

Rank: Yes, I am. She will be my successor in this house. When I'm gone she'll probably—

Nora: Sh—hh! She's in there.

Rank: She's here again today? You see!

Nora: She's just helping me with my costume. Good heavens, you *are* in an unreasonable mood! (*Sits on sofa.*) Now do try to be good, Doctor Rank. Tomorrow you'll see how beautifully I'll dance; and then you can pretend I'm doing it all to please you—and Torvald too, of course—that's understood.

Rank (after a short silence):   You know—sitting here talking to you so informally—I simply can't imagine what would have become of me, if I had never had this house to come to.

Nora (smiling):   You really *do* feel at home with us, don't you?

Rank (in a low voice—looking straight before him):   And to be obliged to leave it all—

Nora: Nonsense! You're not going to leave anything.

Rank (in the same tone):   And not to be able to leave behind one even the smallest proof of gratitude; at most a fleeting regret—an empty place to be filled by the first person who comes along.

Nora: And supposing I were to ask you for—? No—

Rank: For what?

Nora: For a great proof of your friendship.

Rank: Yes?—Yes?

Nora: No, I mean—if I were to ask you to do me a really tremendous favor—

Rank: You'd really, for once, give me that great happiness?

Nora: Oh, but you don't know what it is.

Rank: Then tell me.

Nora: I don't think I can, Doctor Rank. It's much too much to ask—it's not just a favor—I need your help and advice as well—

Rank: So much the better. I've no conception of what you mean. But tell me about it. You trust me, don't you?

Nora: More than anyone. I know you are my best and truest friend— that's why I can tell you. Well then, Doctor Rank, there is something you must help me prevent. You know how deeply, how intensely Torvald loves me; he wouldn't hesitate for a moment to give up his life for my sake.

Rank (bending towards her):   Nora—do you think he is the only one who—?

Nora (with a slight start):   Who—what?

Rank: Who would gladly give his life for you?

Nora (sadly):   I see.

Rank: I was determined that you should know this before I—went away. There'll never be a better chance to tell you. Well, Nora, now you know, and you must know too that you can trust me as you can no one else.

Nora (standing up; simply and calmly):   Let me get by—

Rank (makes way for her, but remains sitting):   Nora—

Nora (in the doorway):   Bring in the lamp, Helene. (*Crosses to the stove.*) Oh, dear Doctor Rank, that was really horrid of you.

Rank (rising):   To love you just as deeply as—as someone else does; is that horrid?

Nora: No—but the fact of your telling me. There was no need to do that.

Rank: What do you mean? Did you know—?

(*Helene enters with the lamp; sets it on the table and goes out again.*)

Rank: Nora—Mrs. Helmer—tell me, did you know?

Nora: Oh, how do I know what I knew or didn't know. I really can't say—How could you be so clumsy, Doctor Rank? It was all so nice.

Rank: Well, at any rate, you know now that I stand ready to serve you body and soul. So—tell me.

Nora (looking at him): After this?

Rank: I beg you to tell me what it is.

Nora: I can't tell you anything now.

Rank: But you must! Don't punish me like that! Let me be of use to you; I'll do anything for you—anything within human power.

Nora: You can do nothing for me now. Anyway—I don't really need help. I was just imagining things, you see. Really! That's all it was! (*Sits in the rocking chair, looks at him and smiles.*) Well—you're a nice one, Doctor Rank! Aren't you a bit ashamed, now that the lamp's been lit?

Rank: No; really not. But I suppose I'd better go now—for good?

Nora: You'll do no such thing! You must come here just as you always have. Torvald could never get on without you!

Rank: But how about *you?*

Nora: You know I always love to have you here.

Rank: Yes—I suppose that's what misled me. I can't quite make you out. I've often felt you liked being with me almost as much as being with Helmer.

Nora: Well—you see—There are the people one loves best—and yet there are others one would almost rather *be* with.

Rank: Yes—there's something in that.

Nora: When I was still at home, it was of course Papa whom I loved best. And yet whenever I could, I used to slip down to the servants' quarters. I loved being with them. To begin with, they never lectured me a bit, and it was such fun to hear them talk.

Rank: I see; and now you have me instead!

Nora (jumps up and hurries toward him): Oh, dear, darling Doctor Rank. I didn't mean it like that! It's just that now, Torvald comes first—the way Papa did. *You* understand—!

(*Helene enters from the hall.*)

Helene: I beg your pardon, Ma'am—(*Whispers to Nora, and gives her a card.*)

Nora (glancing at card): Ah! (*Puts it in her pocket.*)

Rank: Anything wrong?

Nora: No, nothing! It's just—it's my new costume—

Rank: Isn't that your costume—there?

Nora: Oh, that one, yes. But this is a different one. It's one I've ordered—Torvald mustn't know—

Rank: So *that's* the great secret!

Nora: Yes, of course it is! Go in and see him, will you? He's in his study. Be sure and keep him there as long as—

Rank: Don't worry; he shan't escape me. (*Goes into Helmer's room.*)

Nora (to Helene): He's waiting in the kitchen?

Helene: Yes, he came up the back stairs—

Nora: Why didn't you tell him I was busy?

Helene: I did, but he insisted.

Nora: He won't go away?

Helene: Not until he has spoken to you, Ma'am.

Nora: Very well, then; show him in; but quietly, Helene—and don't say a word to anyone; it's about a surprise for my husband.

Helene: I understand, Ma'am. (*She goes out.*)

Nora: It's coming! It's going to happen after all! No, no! It can't happen. It *can't!*

(*She goes to Helmer's door and locks it. Helene opens the hall door for Krogstad, and shuts it after him. He wears a traveling coat, boots, and a fur cap.*)

Nora (*goes towards him*):   Talk quietly; my husband is at home.

Krogstad: What's that to me?

Nora: What is it you want?

Krogstad: I want to make sure of something.

Nora: Well—what is it? Quickly!

Krogstad: I suppose you know I've been dismissed.

Nora: I couldn't prevent it, Mr. Krogstad. I did everything in my power, but it was useless.

Krogstad: So that's all your husband cares about you! He must realize what I can put you through, and yet, in spite of that, he dares to—

Nora: You don't imagine my husband knows about it?

Krogstad: No—I didn't really suppose he did. I can't imagine my friend Torvald Helmer showing that much courage.

Nora: I insist that you show respect when speaking of my husband, Mr. Krogstad!

Krogstad: With all due respect, I assure you! But am I right in thinking— since you are so anxious to keep the matter secret—that you have a clearer idea today than you had yesterday, of what you really did?

Nora: Clearer than *you* could ever give me!

Krogstad: Of course! I who know so little about the law—!

Nora: What do you want of me?

Krogstad: I just wanted to see how you were getting on, Mrs. Helmer. I've been thinking about you all day. You see—even a mere moneylender, a cheap journalist—in short, someone like me—is not entirely without feeling.

Nora: Then prove it; think of my little children.

Krogstad: Did you or your husband think of mine? But that's not the point. I only wanted to tell you not to take this matter too seriously. I shan't take any action—for the present, at least.

Nora: You won't, will you? I was sure you wouldn't!

Krogstad: It can all be settled quite amicably. It needn't be made public. It needn't go beyond us three.

Nora: But, my husband must never know.

Krogstad: How can you prevent it? Can you pay off the balance?

Nora: No, not immediately.

Krogstad: Have you any way of raising the money within the next few days?

Nora: None—that I will make use of.

Krogstad: And if you had, it would have made no difference. Even if you were to offer me the entire sum in cash—I still wouldn't give you back your note.

Nora: What are you going to do with it?

Krogstad: I shall simply keep it—I shall guard it carefully. No one, outside the three of us, shall know a thing about it. So, if you have any thought of doing something desperate—

Nora: I shall.

Krogstad: —of running away from home, for instance—

Nora: I shall!

Krogstad: —or perhaps even something worse—

Nora: How could you guess that?

Krogstad: —then put all such thoughts out of your head.

Nora: How did you know I had thought of *that*?

Krogstad: Most of us think of *that*, at first. I thought of it, too; but I didn't have the courage—

Nora (tonelessly):   I haven't either.

Krogstad (relieved):   No; you haven't the courage for it either, have you?

Nora: No! I haven't, I haven't!

Krogstad: Besides, it would be a very foolish thing to do. You'll just have to get through one domestic storm—and then it'll all be over. I have a letter for your husband, here in my pocket—

Nora: Telling him all about it?

Krogstad: Sparing you as much as possible.

Nora (quickly):   He must never read that letter. Tear it up, Mr. Krogstad! I will manage to get the money somehow—

Krogstad: Excuse me, Mrs. Helmer, but I thought I just told you—

Nora: Oh, I'm not talking about the money I owe you. Just tell me how much money you want from my husband—I will get it somehow!

Krogstad: I want no money from your husband.

Nora: What *do* you want then?

Krogstad: Just this: I want a new start; I want to make something of myself; and your husband shall help me do it. For the past eighteen months my conduct has been irreproachable. It's been a hard struggle—I've lived in abject poverty; still, I was content to work my way up gradually, step by step. But now I've been kicked out, and now I shall not be satisfied to be merely reinstated—taken back on sufferance. I'm determined to make something of myself, I tell you. I intend to continue working in the Bank—but I expect to be promoted. Your husband shall create a new position for me—

Nora: He'll never do it!

Krogstad: Oh, yes he will; I know him—he'll do it without a murmur; he wouldn't dare do otherwise. And then—you'll see! Within a year I'll be his right hand man. It'll be Nils Krogstad, not Torvald Helmer, who'll run the Joint Stock Bank.

Nora: That will never happen.

Krogstad: No? Would you, perhaps—?

Nora: Yes! I have the courage for it now.

Krogstad: You don't frighten me! A dainty, pampered little lady such as you—

Nora: You'll see, you'll see!

Krogstad: Yes, I dare say! How would you like to lie there under the ice—in that freezing, pitch-black water? And in the spring your body would be found floating on the surface—hideous, hairless, unrecognizable—

Nora: You can't frighten me!

Krogstad: You can't frighten me either. People don't do that sort of thing, Mrs. Helmer. And, anyway, what would be the use? I'd still have your husband in my power.

Nora: You mean—afterwards? Even if I were no longer—?

Krogstad: Remember—I'd still have your reputation in my hands! (*Nora stands speechless and looks at him.*) Well, I've given you fair warning. I wouldn't do anything foolish, if I were you. As soon as Helmer receives my letter, I shall expect to hear from him. And just remember this: I've been forced back into my former way of life—and your husband is responsible. I shall never forgive him for it. Good-bye, Mrs. Helmer.

(*Goes out through the hall. Nora hurries to the door, opens it a little, and listens.*)

Nora: He's gone. He didn't leave the letter. Of course he didn't—that would be impossible! (*Opens the door further and further.*) What's he doing? He's stopped outside the door. He's not going down the stairs. Has he changed his mind? Is he—? (*A letter falls into the box. Krogstad's footsteps are heard gradually receding down the stairs. Nora utters a suppressed shriek, and rushes forward toward the sofa table; pause.*) It's in the letter-box! (*Slips shrinkingly up to the hall door.*) It's there!—Torvald, Torvald—now we are lost!

(*Mrs. Linde enters from the left with the costume.*)

Mrs. Linde: There, I think it's all right now. If you'll just try it on—?

Nora (hoarsely and softly):   Come here, Kristine.

Mrs. Linde (throws down the dress on the sofa):   What's the matter with you? You look upset.

Nora: Come here. Do you see that letter? Do you see it—in the letter-box?

Mrs. Linde: Yes, yes, I see it.

Nora: It's from Krogstad—

Mrs. Linde: Nora—you don't mean Krogstad lent you the money!

Nora: Yes; and now Torvald will know everything.

Mrs. Linde: It'll be much the best thing for you both, Nora.

Nora: But you don't know everything. I committed forgery—

Mrs. Linde: Good heavens!

Nora: Now, listen to me, Kristine; I want you to be my witness—

Mrs. Linde: How do you mean "witness"? What am I to—?

Nora: If I should go out of my mind—that might easily happen—

Mrs. Linde: Nora!

Nora: Or if something should happen to me—something that would prevent my being here—!

Mrs. Linde: Nora, Nora, you're quite beside yourself!

Nora: In case anyone else should insist on taking all the blame upon himself—the whole blame—you understand—

Mrs. Linde: Yes, but what makes you think—?

Nora: Then you must bear witness to the fact that that isn't true. I'm in my right mind now; I know exactly what I'm saying; and I tell you nobody else knew anything about it; I did the whole thing on my own. Just remember that.

Mrs. Linde: Very well—I will. But I don't understand at all.

Nora: No—of course—you couldn't. It's the wonderful thing—It's about to happen, don't you see?

Mrs. Linde: What "wonderful thing"?

Nora: The wonderful—wonderful thing! But it must never be allowed to happen—never. It would be too terrible.

Mrs. Linde: I'll go and talk to Krogstad at once.

Nora: No, don't go to him! He might do you some harm.

Mrs. Linde: There was a time—he would have done anything in the world for me.

Nora: He?

Mrs. Linde: Where does he live?

Nora: How do I know—? Yes—(*Feels in her pocket.*) Here's his card. But the letter, the letter—!

Helmer (from his study; knocking on the door):   Nora!

Nora (shrieks in terror):   Oh! What is it? What do you want?

Helmer: Don't be frightened! We're not coming in; anyway, you've locked the door. Are you trying on?

Nora: Yes, yes, I'm trying on. I'm going to look so pretty, Torvald.

Mrs. Linde (who has read the card):   He lives just round the corner.

Nora: But it won't do any good. It's too late now. The letter is in the box.

Mrs. Linde: I suppose your husband has the key?

Nora: Of course.

Mrs. Linde: Krogstad must ask for his letter back, unread. He must make up some excuse—

Nora: But this is the time that Torvald usually—

Mrs. Linde: Prevent him. Keep him occupied. I'll come back as quickly as I can. (*She goes out hastily by the hall door.*)

Nora (opens Helmer's door and peeps in): Torvald!

Helmer (in the study): Well? May one venture to come back into one's own living room? Come along, Rank—now we shall see—(*In the doorway.*) Why—what's this?

Nora: What, Torvald, dear?

Helmer: Rank led me to expect some wonderful disguise.

Rank (in the doorway): That's what I understood. I must have been mistaken.

Nora: Not till tomorrow evening! Then I shall appear in all my splendor!

Helmer: But you look quite tired, Nora, dear. I'm afraid you've been practicing too hard.

Nora: Oh, I haven't practiced at all yet.

Helmer: You ought to, though—

Nora: Yes—I really should, Torvald! But I can't seem to manage without your help. I'm afraid I've forgotten all about it.

Helmer: Well—we'll see what we can do. It'll soon come back to you.

Nora: You will help me, won't you, Torvald? Promise! I feel so nervous— all those people! You must concentrate on me this evening—forget all about business. *Please*, Torvald, dear—promise me you will!

Helmer: I promise. This evening I'll be your slave—you sweet, helpless little thing—! Just one moment, though—I want to see—(*Going to hall door.*)

Nora: What do you want out there?

Helmer: I just want to see if there are any letters.

Nora: Oh, don't, Torvald! Don't bother about that now!

Helmer: Why not?

Nora: *Please* don't, Torvald! There aren't any.

Helmer: Just let me take a look—(*Starts to go.*)

(*Nora, at the piano, plays the first bars of the tarantella.*)

Helmer (stops in the doorway): Aha!

Nora: I shan't be able to dance tomorrow if I don't rehearse with you!

Helmer (going to her): Are you really so nervous, Nora, dear?

Nora: Yes, I'm terrified! Let's rehearse right away. We've plenty of time before dinner. Sit down and play for me, Torvald, dear; direct me— guide me; you know how you do!

Helmer: With pleasure, my darling, if you wish me to. (*Sits at piano.*)

(*Nora snatches the tambourine out of the box, and hurriedly drapes herself in a long parti-colored shawl; then, with a bound, stands in the middle of the floor and cries out.*)

Nora: Now play for me! Now I'll dance!

(Helmer plays and Nora dances. Rank stands at the piano behind Helmer and looks on.)

Helmer (playing):   Too fast! Too fast!
Nora: I can't help it!
Helmer: Don't be so violent, Nora!
Nora: That's the way it *should* be!
Helmer (stops):   No, no; this won't do at all!
Nora (laughs and swings her tambourine):   You see? What did I tell you?
Rank: I'll play for her.
Helmer (rising):   Yes, do—then I'll be able to direct her.

(Rank sits down at the piano and plays; Nora dances more and more wildly. Helmer stands by the stove and addresses frequent corrections to her; she seems not to hear. Her hair breaks loose, and falls over her shoulders. She does not notice it, but goes on dancing. Mrs. Linde enters and stands spellbound in the doorway.)

Mrs. Linde: Ah—!
Nora (dancing):   We're having such fun, Kristine!
Helmer: Why, Nora, dear, you're dancing as if your life were at stake!
Nora: It is! It is!
Helmer: Rank, stop! This is absolute madness. Stop, I say!

(Rank stops playing, and Nora comes to a sudden standstill.)

Helmer (going toward her):   I never would have believed it. You've forgotten everything I ever taught you.
Nora (throws the tambourine away):   I told you I had!
Helmer: This needs an immense amount of work.
Nora: That's what I said; you see how important it is! You must work with me up to the very last minute. Will you promise me, Torvald?
Helmer: I most certainly will!
Nora: This evening and all day tomorrow you must think of nothing but me. You mustn't open a single letter—mustn't even *look* at the mail box.
Helmer: Nora! I believe you're still worried about that wretched man—
Nora: Yes—yes, I am!
Helmer: Nora—Look at me—there's a letter from him in the box, isn't there?
Nora: Maybe—I don't know; I believe there is. But you're not to read anything of that sort now; nothing must come between us until the party's over.
Rank (softly, to Helmer):   Don't go against her.
Helmer (putting his arm around her):   Very well! The child shall have her way. But tomorrow night, when your dance is over—
Nora: Then you'll be free.

(Helene appears in the doorway, right.)

Helene: Dinner is served, Ma'am.

Nora: We'll have champagne, Helene.

Helene: Very good, Ma'am. (*Goes out.*)

Helmer: Quite a feast, I see!

Nora: Yes—a real feast! We'll stay up till dawn drinking champagne! (*Calling out.*) Oh, and we'll have macaroons, Helene—lots of them! Why not—for once?

Helmer (seizing her hand):   Come, come! Not so violent! Be my own little lark again.

Nora: I will, Torvald. But now—both of you go in—while Kristine helps me with my hair.

Rank (softly, as they go):   Is anything special the matter? I mean anything—?

Helmer: No, no; nothing at all. It's just this childish fear I was telling you about. (*They go out to the right.*)

Nora: Well?

Mrs. Linde: He's gone out of town.

Nora: I saw it in your face.

Mrs. Linde: He'll be back tomorrow evening. I left a note for him.

Nora: You shouldn't have bothered. You couldn't prevent it anyway. After all, there's a kind of joy in waiting for the wonderful thing to happen.

Mrs. Linde: I don't understand. What *is* this thing you're waiting for?

Nora: I can't explain. Go in and join them. I'll be there in a moment.

(*Mrs. Linde goes into the dining room. Nora stands for a moment as though pulling herself together; then looks at her watch.*)

Nora: Five o'clock. Seven hours till midnight. Twenty-four hours till the next midnight and then the tarantella will be over. Twenty-four and seven? I've thirty-one hours left to live.

(*Helmer appears at the door, right.*)

Helmer: Well! What has become of the little lark?

Nora (runs to him with open arms):   Here she is!

ACT III

Scene: The same room. The table, with the chairs around it, has been moved to stage-center. A lighted lamp on the table. The hall door is open. Dance music is heard from the floor above. Mrs. Linde sits by the table absent-mindedly turning the pages of a book. She tries to read, but seems unable to keep her mind on it. Now and then she listens intently and glances towards the hall door.

Mrs. Linde (looks at her watch):   Where can he be? The time is nearly up. I hope he hasn't—(*Listens again.*) Here he is now. (*She goes into the hall and cautiously opens the outer door; cautious footsteps are heard on the stairs; she whispers.)* Come in; there is no one here.

Krogstad (in the doorway):   I found a note from you at home. What does it mean?

Mrs. Linde: I simply *must* speak to you.

Krogstad: Indeed? But why here? Why in this house?

Mrs. Linde: I couldn't see you at my place. My room has no separate entrance. Come in; we're quite alone. The servants are asleep, and the Helmers are upstairs at a party.

Krogstad (coming into the room):   Well, well! So the Helmers are dancing tonight, are they?

Mrs. Linde: Why shouldn't they?

Krogstad: Well—why not!

Mrs. Linde: Let's have a talk, Krogstad.

Krogstad: Have we two anything to talk about?

Mrs. Linde: Yes. A great deal.

Krogstad: I shouldn't have thought so.

Mrs. Linde: But then, you see—you have never really understood me.

Krogstad: There wasn't much to understand, was there? A woman is heartless enough to break off with a man, when a better match is offered; it's quite an ordinary occurrence.

Mrs. Linde: You really think me heartless? Did you think it was so easy for me?

Krogstad: Wasn't it?

Mrs. Linde: You really believed that, Krogstad?

Krogstad: If not, why should you have written to me as you did?

Mrs. Linde: What else could I do? Since I was forced to break with you, I felt it was only right to try and kill your love for me.

Krogstad (clenching his hands together):   So that was it! And you did this for money!

Mrs. Linde: Don't forget I had my mother and two little brothers to think of. We couldn't wait for you, Krogstad; things were so unsettled for you then.

Krogstad: That may be; but, even so, you had no right to throw me over—not even for their sake.

Mrs. Linde: Who knows? I've often wondered whether I did right or not.

Krogstad (more softly):   When I had lost you, I felt the ground crumble beneath my feet. Look at me. I'm like a shipwrecked man clinging to a raft.

Mrs. Linde: Help may be nearer than you think.

Krogstad: Help was here! Then you came and stood in the way.

Mrs. Linde: I knew nothing about it, Krogstad. I didn't know until today that I was to replace *you* at the Bank.

Krogstad: Very well—I believe you. But now that you do know, will you withdraw?

Mrs. Linde: No; I'd do you no good by doing that.

Krogstad: "Good" or not—I'd withdraw all the same.

Mrs. Linde: I have learnt to be prudent, Krogstad—I've had to. The bitter necessities of life have taught me that.

Krogstad: And life has taught me not to believe in phrases.

Mrs. Linde: Then life has taught you a very wise lesson. But what about deeds? Surely you must still believe in them?

Krogstad: How do you mean?

Mrs. Linde: You just said you were like a shipwrecked man, clinging to a raft.

Krogstad: I have good reason to say so.

Mrs. Linde: Well—I'm like a shipwrecked *woman* clinging to a raft. I have no one to mourn for, no one to care for.

Krogstad: You made your choice.

Mrs. Linde: I *had* no choice, I tell you!

Krogstad: What then?

Mrs. Linde: Since we're both of us shipwrecked, couldn't we join forces, Krogstad?

Krogstad: You don't mean—?

Mrs. Linde: Two people on a raft have a better chance than one.

Krogstad: Kristine!

Mrs. Linde: Why do you suppose I came here to the city?

Krogstad: You mean—you thought of me?

Mrs. Linde: I can't live without work; all my life I've worked, as far back as I can remember; it's always been my one great joy. Now I'm quite alone in the world; my life is empty—aimless. There's not much joy in working for one's self. You could help me, Nils; you could give me something and someone to work for.

Krogstad: I can't believe all this. It's an hysterical impulse—a woman's exaggerated craving for self-sacrifice.

Mrs. Linde: When have you ever found me hysterical?

Krogstad: You'd really be willing to do this? Tell me honestly—do you quite realize what my past has been?

Mrs. Linde: Yes.

Krogstad: And you know what people think of me?

Mrs. Linde: Didn't you just say you'd have been a different person if you'd been with me?

Krogstad: I'm sure of it.

Mrs. Linde: Mightn't that still be true?

Krogstad: You really mean this, Kristine, don't you? I can see it in your face. Are you sure you have the courage—?

Mrs. Linde: I need someone to care for, and your children need a mother. We two need each other, Nils. I have faith in your fundamental goodness. I'm not afraid.

Krogstad (seizing her hands):   Thank you—thank you, Kristine. I'll make others believe in me too—I won't fail you! But—I'd almost forgotten—

Mrs. Linde (listening): Hush! The tarantella! You must go!

Krogstad: Why? What is it?

Mrs. Linde: Listen! She's begun her dance; as soon as she's finished dancing, they'll be down.

Krogstad: Yes—I'd better go. There'd have been no need for all that— but, of course, you don't know what I've done about the Helmers.

Mrs. Linde: Yes, I do, Nils.

Krogstad: And yet you have the courage to—?

Mrs. Linde: I know you were desperate—I understand.

Krogstad: I'd give anything to undo it!

Mrs. Linde: You can. Your letter's still in the mail box.

Krogstad: Are you sure?

Mrs. Linde: Quite, but—

Krogstad (giving her a searching look): Could that be it? You're doing all this to save your friend? You might as well be honest with me! Is that it?

Mrs. Linde: I sold myself once for the sake of others, Nils; I'm not likely to do it again.

Krogstad: I'll ask for my letter back unopened.

Mrs. Linde: No, no.

Krogstad: Yes, of course. I'll wait till Helmer comes; I'll tell him to give me back the letter—I'll say it refers to my dismissal—and ask him not to read it—

Mrs. Linde: No, Nils; don't ask for it back.

Krogstad: But wasn't that actually your reason for getting me to come here?

Mrs. Linde: Yes, in my first moment of fear. But that was twenty-four hours ago, and since then I've seen incredible things happening here. Helmer must know the truth; this wretched business must no longer be kept secret; it's time those two came to a thorough understanding; there's been enough deceit and subterfuge.

Krogstad: Very well, if you like to risk it. But there's one thing I can do, and at once—

Mrs. Linde (listening): You must go now. Make haste! The dance is over; we're not safe here another moment.

Krogstad: I'll wait for you downstairs.

Mrs. Linde: Yes, do; then you can see me home.

Krogstad: Kristine! I've never been so happy! (*Krogstad goes out by the outer door. The door between the room and the hall remains open.*)

Mrs. Linde (arranging the room and getting her outdoor things together): How different things will be! Someone to work for, to live for; a home to make happy! How wonderful it will be to try!—I wish they'd come—(*Listens.*) Here they are! I'll get my coat—(*Takes bonnet and cloak. Helmer's and Nora's voices are heard outside, a key is turned in the lock, and Helmer drags Nora almost by force into the hall. She wears the Italian costume with a large black shawl over it. He is in evening dress and wears a black domino, open.*)

Nora (*struggling with him in the doorway*):   No, no! I don't want to come home; I want to go upstairs again; I don't want to leave so early!

Helmer: Come—Nora dearest!

Nora: I beg you, Torvald! Please, *please*—just one hour more!

Helmer: Not one single minute more, Nora darling; don't you remember our agreement? Come along in, now; you'll catch cold. (*He leads her gently into the room in spite of her resistance.*)

Mrs. Linde: Good evening.

Nora: Kristine!

Helmer: Why, Mrs. Linde! What are you doing here so late?

Mrs. Linde: Do forgive me. I did so want to see Nora in her costume.

Nora: Have you been waiting for me all this time?

Mrs. Linde: Yes; I came too late to catch you before you went upstairs, and I didn't want to go away without seeing you.

Helmer (*taking Nora's shawl off*):   And you *shall* see her, Mrs. Linde! She's worth looking at I can tell you! Isn't she lovely?

Mrs. Linde: Oh, Nora! How perfectly—!

Helmer: Absolutely exquisite, isn't she? That's what everybody said. But she's obstinate as a mule, is my sweet little thing! I don't know what to do with her! Will you believe it, Mrs. Linde, I had to drag her away by force?

Nora: You'll see—you'll be sorry, Torvald, you didn't let me stay, if only for another half-hour.

Helmer: Do you hear that, Mrs. Linde? Now, listen to this: She danced her tarantella to wild applause, and she deserved it, too, I must say— though, perhaps, from an artistic point of view, her interpretation was a bit too realistic. But never mind—the point is, she made a great success, a phenomenal success. Now—should I have allowed her to stay on and spoil the whole effect? Certainly not! I took my sweet little Capri girl—my capricious little Capri girl, I might say—in my arms; a rapid whirl round the room, a low curtsey to all sides, and—as they say in novels—the lovely apparition vanished! An exit should always be effective, Mrs. Linde; but I can't get Nora to see that. Phew! It's warm here. (*Throws his domino on a chair and opens the door to his room.*) Why—there's no light on in here! Oh no, of course—Excuse me— (*Goes in and lights candles.*)

Nora (*whispers breathlessly*):   Well?

Mrs. Linde (*softly*):   I've spoken to him.

Nora: And—?

Mrs. Linde: Nora—you must tell your husband everything—

Nora (*tonelessly*):   I knew it!

Mrs. Linde: You have nothing to fear from Krogstad; but you must speak out.

Nora: I shan't.

Mrs. Linde: Then the letter will.

Nora: Thank you, Kristine. Now I know what I must do. Hush—!

Helmer (coming back): Well, have you finished admiring her, Mrs. Linde?

Mrs. Linde: Yes, and now I must say good night.

Helmer: Oh—must you be going already? Does this knitting belong to you?

Mrs. Linde (takes it): Oh, thank you; I almost forgot it.

Helmer: So you knit, do you?

Mrs. Linde: Yes.

Helmer: Why don't you do embroidery instead?

Mrs. Linde: Why?

Helmer: Because it's so much prettier. Now watch! You hold the embroidery in the left hand—so—and then, in the right hand, you hold the needle, and guide it—so—in a long graceful curve—isn't that right?

Mrs. Linde: Yes, I suppose so—

Helmer: Whereas, knitting can never be anything but ugly. Now, watch! Arms close to your sides, needles going up and down—there's something Chinese about it!—That really was splendid champagne they gave us.

Mrs. Linde: Well, good night, Nora; don't be obstinate any more.

Helmer: Well said, Mrs. Linde!

Mrs. Linde: Good night, Mr. Helmer.

Helmer (accompanying her to the door): Good night, good night; I hope you get home safely. I'd be only too glad to—but you've such a short way to go. Good night, good night. (*She goes; Helmer shuts the door after her and comes forward again.*) Well—thank God we've got rid of her; she's a dreadful bore, that woman.

Nora: You must be tired, Torvald.

Helmer: I? Not in the least.

Nora: But, aren't you sleepy?

Helmer: Not a bit. On the contrary, I feel exceedingly lively. But what about you? You seem to be very tired and sleepy.

Nora: Yes, I am very tired. But I'll soon sleep now.

Helmer: You see! I was right not to let you stay there any longer.

Nora: Everything you do is always right, Torvald.

Helmer (kissing her forehead): There's my sweet, sensible little lark! By the way, did you notice how gay Rank was this evening?

Nora: Was he? I didn't get a chance to speak to him.

Helmer: I didn't either, really; but it's a long time since I've seen him in such a jolly mood. (*Gazes at Nora for a while, then comes nearer her.*) It's so lovely to be home again—to be here alone with you. You glorious, fascinating creature!

Nora: Don't look at me like that, Torvald.

Helmer: Why shouldn't I look at my own dearest treasure?—at all this loveliness that is mine, wholly and utterly mine—mine alone!

Nora (goes to the other side of the table):   You mustn't talk to me like that tonight.

Helmer (following):   You're still under the spell of the tarantella—and it makes you even more desirable. Listen! The other guests are leaving now. (*More softly.*) Soon the whole house will be still, Nora.

Nora: I hope so.

Helmer: Yes, you do, don't you, my beloved? Do you know something— when I'm out with you among a lot of people—do you know why it is I hardly speak to you, why I keep away from you, and only occasionally steal a quick glance at you; do you know why that is? It's because I pretend that we love each other in secret, that we're secretly engaged, and that no one suspects there is anything between us.

Nora: Yes, yes; I know your thoughts are always round me.

Helmer: Then, when it's time to leave, and I put your shawl round your smooth, soft, young shoulders—round that beautiful neck of yours—I pretend that you are my young bride, that we've just come from the wedding, and that I'm taking you home for the first time—that for the first time I shall be alone with you—quite alone with you, in all your tremulous beauty. All evening I have been filled with longing for you. As I watched you swaying and whirling in the tarantella—my pulses began to throb until I thought I should go mad; that's why I carried you off—made you leave so early—

Nora: Please go, Torvald! Please leave me. I don't want you like this.

Helmer: What do you mean? You're teasing me, aren't you, little Nora? Not want me—! Aren't I your husband—?

(*A knock at the outer door.*)

Nora (starts):   Listen—!

Helmer (going toward the hall):   Who is it?

Rank (outside):   It is I; may I come in a moment?

Helmer (in a low tone, annoyed):   Why does he have to bother us now! (*Aloud.*) Just a second! (*Opens door.*) Well! How nice of you to look in.

Rank: I heard your voice, and I thought I'd like to stop in a minute. (*Looks round.*) These dear old rooms! You must be so cozy and happy here, you two!

Helmer: I was just saying how gay and happy you seemed to be, upstairs.

Rank: Why not? Why shouldn't I be? One should get all one can out of life; all one can, for as long as one can. That wine was excellent—

Helmer: Especially the champagne.

Rank: You noticed that, did you? It's incredible how much I managed to get down.

Nora: Torvald drank plenty of it too.

Rank: Oh?

Nora: It always puts him in such a jolly mood.

Rank: Well, why shouldn't one have a jolly evening after a well-spent day?

Helmer: Well-spent! I'm afraid mine wasn't much to boast of!

Rank (slapping him on the shoulder): But mine was, you see?

Nora: Did you by any chance make a scientific investigation, Doctor Rank?

Rank: Precisely.

Helmer: Listen to little Nora, talking about scientific investigations!

Nora: Am I to congratulate you on the result?

Rank: By all means.

Nora: It was good then?

Rank: The best possible, both for the doctor and the patient—certainty.

Nora (quickly and searchingly): Certainty?

Rank: Absolute certainty. Wasn't I right to spend a jolly evening after that?

Nora: You were quite right, Doctor Rank.

Helmer: I quite agree! Provided you don't have to pay for it, tomorrow.

Rank: You don't get anything for nothing in this life.

Nora: You like masquerade parties, don't you, Dr. Rank?

Rank: Very much—when there are plenty of amusing disguises—

Nora: What shall we two be at our next masquerade?

Helmer: Listen to her! Thinking of the next party already!

Rank: We two? I'll tell you. You must go as a precious talisman.

Helmer: How on earth would you dress that!

Rank: That's easy. She'd only have to be herself.

Helmer: Charmingly put. But what about you? Have you decided what you'd be?

Rank: Oh, definitely.

Helmer: Well?

Rank: At the next masquerade party I shall be invisible.

Helmer: That's a funny notion!

Rank: There's a large black cloak—you've heard of the invisible cloak, haven't you? You've only to put it around you and no one can see you any more.

Helmer (with a suppressed smile): Quite true!

Rank: But I almost forgot what I came for. Give me a cigar, will you, Helmer? One of the dark Havanas.

Helmer: Of course—with pleasure. (*Hands cigar case.*)

Rank (takes one and cuts the end off): Thanks.

Nora (striking a wax match): Let me give you a light.

Rank: I thank you. (*She holds the match. He lights his cigar at it.*) And now, I'll say good-bye!

Helmer: Good-bye, good-bye, my dear fellow.

Nora: Sleep well, Doctor Rank.

Rank: Thanks for the wish.

Nora: Wish me the same.

Rank: You? Very well, since you ask me—Sleep well. And thanks for the light. (*He nods to them both and goes out.*)

Helmer (in an undertone): He's had a lot to drink.

Nora (absently): I dare say. (*Helmer takes his bunch of keys from his pocket and goes into the hall.*) Torvald! What do you want out there?

Helmer: I'd better empty the mail box; it's so full there won't be room for the papers in the morning.

Nora: Are you going to work tonight?

Helmer: No—you know I'm not.—Why, what's this? Someone has been at the lock.

Nora: The lock—?

Helmer: Yes—that's funny! I shouldn't have thought that the maids would—Here's a broken hairpin. Why—it's one of yours, Nora.

Nora (quickly): It must have been the children—

Helmer: You'll have to stop them doing that—There! I got it open at last. (*Takes contents out and calls out towards the kitchen.*) Helene?—Oh, Helene; put out the lamp in the hall, will you? (*He returns with letters in his hand, and shuts the door to the hall.*) Just look how they've stacked up. (*Looks through them.*) Why, what's this?

Nora (at the window): The letter! Oh, Torvald! No!

Helmer: Two visiting cards—from Rank.

Nora: From Doctor Rank?

Helmer (looking at them): Doctor Rank, physician. They were right on top. He must have stuck them in just now, as he left.

Nora: Is there anything on them?

Helmer: There's a black cross over his name. Look! What a gruesome thought. Just as if he were announcing his own death.

Nora: And so he is.

Helmer: What do you mean? What do you know about it? Did he tell you anything?

Nora: Yes. These cards mean that he has said good-bye to us for good. Now he'll lock himself up to die.

Helmer: Oh, my poor friend! I always knew he hadn't long to live, but I never dreamed it would be quite so soon—! And to hide away like a wounded animal—

Nora: When the time comes, it's best to go in silence. Don't you think so, Torvald?

Helmer (walking up and down): He'd become so a part of us. I can't imagine his having gone for good. With his suffering and loneliness he was like a dark, cloudy background to our lives—it made the sunshine of our happiness seem even brighter—Well, I suppose it's for the best—for him at any rate. (*Stands still.*) And perhaps for us too, Nora. Now we are more than ever dependent on each other. (*Takes her in his arms.*) Oh, my beloved wife! I can't seem to hold you close enough.

Do you know something, Nora. I often wish you were in some great
danger—so I could risk body and soul—my whole life—everything,
everything, for your sake.

Nora (tears herself from him and says firmly):   Now you must read your
letters, Torvald.

Helmer: No, no; not tonight. I want to be with you, my beloved wife.

Nora: With the thought of your dying friend—?

Helmer: Of course—You are right. It's been a shock to both of us. A
hideous shadow has come between us—thoughts of death and decay.
We must try and throw them off. Until then—we'll stay apart.

Nora (her arms round his neck):   Torvald! Good night! Good night!

Helmer (Kissing her forehead):   Good night, my little songbird; Sleep well!
Now I'll go and read my letters. (*He goes with the letters in his hand
into his room and shuts the door.*)

*Nora (with wild eyes, gropes about her, seizes Helmer's domino, throws it
round her, and whispers quickly, hoarsely, and brokenly):*   I'll never see
him again. Never, never, never. (*Throws her shawl over her head.*) I'll
never see the children again. I'll never see them either—Oh the
thought of that black, icy water! That fathomless—! If it were only
over! He has it now; he's reading it. Oh, not yet—please! Not yet!
Torvald, good-bye—! Good-bye to you and the children!

*(She is rushing out by the hall; at the same moment Helmer flings his door
open, and stands there with an open letter in his hand.)*

Helmer: Nora!

Nora (shrieks):   Ah—!

Helmer: What does this mean! Do you know what is in this letter?

Nora: Yes, yes, I know. Let me go! Let me out!

Helmer (holds her back):   Where are you going?

Nora (tries to break away from him):   Don't try to save me, Torvald!

Helmer (falling back):   So it's true! It's true what he writes? It's too
horrible! It's impossible—it can't be true.

Nora: It *is* true. I've loved you more than all the world.

Helmer: Oh, come now! Let's have no silly nonsense!

Nora (a step nearer him):   Torvald—!

Helmer: Do you realize what you've done?

Nora: Let me go—I won't have you suffer for it! I won't have you take
the blame!

Helmer: Will you stop this play-acting! (*Locks the outer door.*) You'll stay
here and give an account of yourself. Do you understand what you
have done? Answer me! Do you understand it?

Nora (looks at him fixedly, and says with a stiffening expression):   I think
I'm beginning to understand for the first time.

Helmer (walking up and down):   God! What an awakening! After eight
years to discover that you who have been my pride and joy—are no

better than a hypocrite, a liar—worse than that—a criminal! It's too horrible to think of! (*Nora says nothing, and continues to look fixedly at him.*) I might have known what to expect. I should have foreseen it. You've inherited all your father's lack of principle—be silent!—all of your father's lack of principle, I say!—no religion, no moral code, no sense of duty. This is my punishment for shielding him! I did it for your sake; and this is my reward!

Nora: I see.

Helmer: You've destroyed my happiness. You've ruined my whole future. It's ghastly to think of! I'm completely in the power of this scoundrel; he can force me to do whatever he likes, demand whatever he chooses; order me about at will; and I shan't dare open my mouth! My entire career is to be wrecked and all because of a lawless, unprincipled woman!

Nora: If I were no longer alive, then you'd be free.

Helmer: Oh yes! You're full of histrionics! Your father was just the same. Even if you "weren't alive," as you put it, what good would that do me? None whatever! He could publish the story all the same; I might even be suspected of collusion. People might say I was behind it all— that I had prompted you to do it. And to think I have you to thank for all this—you whom I've done nothing but pamper and spoil since the day of our marriage. Now do you realize what you've done to me?

Nora (with cold calmness):   Yes.

Helmer: It's all so incredible, I can't grasp it. But we must try and come to some agreement. Take off that shawl. Take it off, I say! Of course, we must find some way to appease him—the matter must be hushed up at any cost. As far as we two are concerned, there must be no change in our way of life—in the eyes of the world, I mean. You'll naturally continue to live here. But you won't be allowed to bring up the children—I'd never dare trust them to you—God! to have to say this to the woman I've loved so tenderly—There can be no further thought of happiness between us. We must save what we can from the ruins—we can save appearances, at least—(*A ring; Helmer starts.*) What can that be? At this hour! You don't suppose he—! Could he—? Hide yourself, Nora; say you are ill.

(*Nora stands motionless. Helmer goes to the door and opens it.*)

Helene: (*Half dressed, in the hall*): It's a letter for Mrs. Helmer.

Helmer: Give it to me. (*Seizes the letter and shuts the door.*) It's from him. I shan't give it to you. I'll read it myself.

Nora: Very well.

Helmer (by the lamp):   I don't dare open it; this may be the end—for both of us. Still—I must know. (*Hastily tears the letter open; reads a few lines, looks at an enclosure; with a cry of joy.*) Nora! (*Nora looks inquiringly at him.*) Nora!—I can't believe it—I must read it again. But it's true—it's really true! Nora, I am saved! I'm saved!

Nora: What about me?

Helmer: You too, of course; we are both of us saved, both of us. Look!—he's sent you back your note—he says he's sorry for what he did and apologizes for it—that due to a happy turn of events he— Oh, what does it matter what he says! We are saved, Nora! No one can harm you now. Oh, Nora, Nora—; but let's get rid of this hateful thing. I'll just see—(*Glances at the I.O.U.*) No, no—I won't even look at it; I'll pretend it was all a horrible dream. (*Tears the I.O.U. and both letters in pieces. Throws them into the fire and watches them burn.*) There! Now it's all over—He said in his letter you've known about this since Christmas Eve—you must have had three dreadful days, Nora!

Nora: Yes. It's been very hard.

Helmer: How you must have suffered! And you saw no way out but— No! We'll forget the whole ghastly business. We'll just thank God and repeat again and again: It's over; all over! Don't you understand, Nora? You don't seem to grasp it: It's over. What's the matter with you? Why do you look so grim? My poor darling little Nora, I understand; but you mustn't worry—because I've forgiven you, Nora; I swear I have; I've forgiven everything. You did what you did because you loved me—I see that now.

Nora: Yes—that's true.

Helmer: You loved me as a wife should love her husband. You didn't realize what you were doing—you weren't able to judge how wrong it was. Don't think this makes you any less dear to me. Just you lean on me; let me guide you and advise you; I'm not a man for nothing! There's something very endearing about a woman's helplessness. And try and forget those harsh things I said just now. I was frantic; my whole world seemed to be tumbling about my ears. Believe me, I've forgiven you, Nora—I swear it—I've forgiven everything.

Nora: Thank you for your forgiveness, Torvald. (*Goes out, to the right.*)

Helmer: No! Don't go. (*Looking through the doorway.*) Why do you have to go in there?

Nora (inside): I want to get out of these fancy-dress clothes.

Helmer (in the doorway):   Yes, do, my darling. Try to calm down now, and get back to normal, my poor frightened little song-bird. Don't you worry—you'll be safe under my wings—they'll protect you. (*Walking up and down near the door.*) How lovely our home is, Nora! You'll be sheltered here; I'll cherish you as if you were a little dove I'd rescued from the claws of some dreadful hawk. You'll see—your poor fluttering little heart will soon grow calm again. Tomorrow all this will appear in quite a different light—things will be just as they were. I won't have to keep on saying I've forgiven you—you'll be able to sense it. You don't really think I could ever drive you away, do you? That I could even so much as reproach you for anything? You'd understand if you could see into my heart. When a man forgives his wife whole-heartedly—as I have you—it fills him with such tenderness, such peace. She seems to belong to him in a double sense; it's as though he'd brought her to life again; she's become more than his wife—she's become his child as well. That's how it will be with us, Nora—my own bewildered, helpless little darling. From now on you mustn't worry about anything; just open your heart to me; just let me be both will and conscience to you. (*Nora enters in everyday dress.*) What's all this? I thought you were going to bed. You've changed your dress?

Nora: Yes, Torvald; I've changed my dress.

Helmer: But what for? At this hour?

Nora: I shan't sleep tonight.

Helmer: But, Nora dear—

Nora (looking at her watch):   It's not so very late—Sit down, Torvald; we have a lot to talk about. (*She sits at one side of the table.*)

Helmer: Nora—what does this mean? Why that stern expression?

Nora: Sit down. It'll take some time. I have a lot to say to you.

(*Helmer sits at the other side of the table.*)

Helmer: You frighten me, Nora. I don't understand you.

Nora: No, that's just it. You don't understand me; and I have never understood you either—until tonight. No, don't interrupt me. Just listen to what I have to say. This is to be a final settlement, Torvald.

Helmer: How do you mean?

Nora (after a short silence):   Doesn't anything special strike you as we sit here like this?

Helmer: I don't think so—why?

Nora: It doesn't occur to you, does it, that though we've been married for eight years, this is the first time that we two—man and wife—have sat down for a serious talk?

Helmer: What do you mean by serious?

Nora: During eight whole years, no—more than that—ever since the first day we met—we have never exchanged so much as one serious word about serious things.

Helmer: Why should I perpetually burden you with all my cares and problems? How could you possibly help me to solve them?

Nora: I'm not talking about cares and problems. I'm simply saying we've never once sat down seriously and tried to get to the bottom of anything.

Helmer: But, Nora, darling—why should you be concerned with serious thoughts?

Nora: That's the whole point! You've never understood me—A great injustice has been done me, Torvald; first by Father, and then by you.

Helmer: What a thing to say! No two people on earth could ever have loved you more than we have!

Nora (shaking her head):   You never loved me. You just thought it was
fun to be in love with me.

Helmer: This is fantastic!

Nora: Perhaps. But it's true all the same. While I was still at home I used
to hear Father airing his opinions and they became my opinions; or if I
didn't happen to agree, I kept it to myself—he would have been
displeased otherwise. He used to call me his doll-baby, and played
with me as I played with my dolls. Then I came to live in your house—

Helmer: What an expression to use about our marriage!

Nora (undisturbed):   I mean—from Father's hands I passed into yours.
You arranged everything according to your tastes, and I acquired the
same tastes, or I pretended to—I'm not sure which—a little of both,
perhaps. Looking back on it all, it seems to me I've lived here like a
beggar, from hand to mouth. I've lived by performing tricks for you,
Torvald. But that's the way you wanted it. You and Father have done
me a great wrong. You've prevented me from becoming a real person.

Helmer: Nora, how can you be so ungrateful and unreasonable! Haven't
you been happy here?

Nora: No, never. I thought I was; but I wasn't really.

Helmer: Not—not happy!

Nora: No; only merry. You've always been so kind to me. But our home
has never been anything but a play-room. I've been your doll-wife, just
as at home I was Papa's doll-child. And the children in turn, have been
my dolls. I thought it fun when you played games with me, just as
they thought it fun when I played games with them. And that's been
our marriage, Torvald.

Helmer: There may be a grain of truth in what you say, even though it is
distorted and exaggerated. From now on things will be different. Play-
time is over now; tomorrow lessons begin!

Nora: Whose lessons? Mine, or the children's?

Helmer: Both, if you wish it, Nora, dear.

Nora: Torvald, I'm afraid you're not the man to teach me to be a real
wife to you.

Helmer: How can you say that?

Nora: And I'm certainly not fit to teach the children.

Helmer: Nora!

Nora: Didn't you just say, a moment ago, you didn't dare trust them to me?

Helmer: That was in the excitement of the moment! You mustn't take it
so seriously!

Nora: But you were quite right, Torvald. That job is beyond me; there's
another job I must do first: I must try and educate myself. You could
never help me to do that; I must do it quite alone. So, you see—that's
why I'm going to leave you.

Helmer (jumping up):   What did you say—?

Nora: I shall never get to know myself—I shall never learn to face
reality—unless I stand alone. So I can't stay with you any longer.

Helmer: Nora! Nora!

Nora: I am going at once. I'm sure Kristine will let me stay with her tonight—

Helmer: But, Nora—this is madness! I shan't allow you to do this. I shall forbid it!

Nora: You no longer have the power to forbid me anything. I'll only take a few things with me—those that belong to me. I shall never again accept anything from you.

Helmer: Have you lost your senses?

Nora: Tomorrow I'll go home—to what *was* my home, I mean. It might be easier for me there, to find something to do.

Helmer: You talk like an ignorant child, Nora—!

Nora: Yes. That's just why I must educate myself.

Helmer: To leave your home—to leave your husband, and your children! What do you suppose people would say to that?

Nora: It makes no difference. This is something I *must* do.

Helmer: It's inconceivable! Don't you realize you'd be betraying your most sacred duty?

Nora: What do you consider that to be?

Helmer: Your duty towards your husband and your children—I surely don't have to tell you that!

Nora: I've another duty just as sacred.

Helmer: Nonsense! What duty do you mean?

Nora: My duty towards myself.

Helmer: Remember—before all else you are a wife and mother.

Nora: I don't believe that anymore. I believe that before all else I am a human being, just as you are—or at least that I should try and become one. I know that most people would agree with you, Torvald—and that's what they say in books. But I can no longer be satisfied with what most people say—or what they write in books. I must think things out for myself—get clear about them.

Helmer: Surely your position in your home is clear enough? Have you no sense of religion? Isn't that an infallible guide to you?

Nora: But don't you see, Torvald—I don't really know what religion is.

Helmer: Nora! How *can* you!

Nora: All I know about it is what Pastor Hansen told me when I was confirmed. He taught me what he thought religion was—said it was *this* and *that*. As soon as I get away by myself, I shall have to look into that matter too, try and decide whether what he taught me was right—or whether it's right for *me*, at least.

Helmer: A nice way for a young woman to talk! It's unheard of! If religion means nothing to you, I'll appeal to your conscience; you must have some sense of ethics, I suppose? Answer me! Or have you none?

Nora: It's hard for me to answer you, Torvald. I don't think I know—all these things bewilder me. But I *do* know that I think quite differently from you about them. I've discovered that the law, for instance, is quite different from what I had imagined; but I find it hard to believe it can be right. It seems it's criminal for a woman to try and spare her old, sick, father, or save her husband's life! I can't agree with that.

Helmer: You talk like a child. You have no understanding of the society we live in.

Nora: No, I haven't. But I'm going to try and learn. I want to find out which of us is right—society or I.

Helmer: You are ill, Nora; you have a touch of fever; you're quite beside yourself.

Nora: I've never felt so sure—so clear-headed—as I do tonight.

Helmer: "Sure and clear-headed" enough to leave your husband and your children?

Nora: Yes.

Helmer: Then there is only one explanation possible.

Nora: What?

Helmer: You don't love me any more.

Nora: No; that is just it.

Helmer: Nora!—What are you saying!

Nora: It makes me so unhappy, Torvald; for you've always been so kind to me. But I can't help it. I don't love you any more.

Helmer (mastering himself with difficulty):   You feel "sure and clear-headed" about this too?

Nora: Yes, utterly sure. That's why I can't stay here any longer.

Helmer: And can you tell me how I lost your love?

Nora: Yes, I can tell you. It was tonight—when the wonderful thing didn't happen; I knew then you weren't the man I always thought you were.

Helmer: I don't understand.

Nora: For eight years I've been waiting patiently; I knew, of course, that such things don't happen every day. Then, when this trouble came to me—I thought to myself: Now! Now the wonderful thing will happen! All the time Krogstad's letter was out there in the box, it never occurred to me for a single moment that you'd think of submitting to his conditions. I was absolutely convinced that you'd defy him—that you'd tell him to publish the thing to all the world; and that then—

Helmer: You mean you thought I'd let my wife be publicly dishonored and disgraced?

Nora: No. What I thought you'd do, was to take the blame upon yourself.

Helmer: Nora—!

Nora: I know! You think I never would have accepted such a sacrifice. Of course I wouldn't! But my word would have meant nothing against yours. That was the wonderful thing I hoped for, Torvald, hoped for with such terror. And it was to prevent that, that I chose to kill myself.

Helmer: I'd gladly work for you day and night, Nora—go through suffering and want, if need be—but one doesn't sacrifice one's honor for love's sake.

Nora: Millions of women have done so.

Helmer: You think and talk like a silly child.

Nora: Perhaps. But you neither think nor talk like the man I want to share my life with. When you'd recovered from your fright—and you never thought of me, only of yourself—when you had nothing more to fear—you behaved as though none of this had happened. I was your little lark again, your little doll—whom you would have to guard more carefully than ever, because she was so weak and frail. (*Stands up.*) At that moment it suddenly dawned on me that I had been living here for eight years with a stranger and that I'd borne him three children. I can't bear to think about it! I could tear myself to pieces!

Helmer (sadly):   I see, Nora—I understand; there's suddenly a great void between us—Is there no way to bridge it?

Nora: Feeling as I do now, Torvald—I could never be a wife to you.

Helmer: But, if I were to change? Don't you think I'm capable of that?

Nora: Perhaps—when you no longer have your doll to play with.

Helmer: It's inconceivable! I *can't* part with you, Nora. I can't endure the thought.

Nora (going into room on the right):   All the more reason it should happen. (*She comes back with outdoor things and a small traveling-bag, which she places on a chair.*)

Helmer: But not at once, Nora—not now! At least wait till tomorrow.

Nora (putting on cloak):   I can't spend the night in a strange man's house.

Helmer: Couldn't we go on living here together? As brother and sister, if you like—as friends.

Nora (fastening her hat):   You know very well that wouldn't last, Torvald. (*Puts on the shawl.*) Good-bye. I won't go in and see the children. I know they're in better hands than mine. Being what I am—how can I be of any use to them?

Helmer: But surely, some day, Nora—?

Nora: How can I tell? How do I know what sort of person I'll become?

Helmer: You are my wife, Nora, now and always!

Nora: Listen to me, Torvald—I've always heard that when a wife deliberately leaves her husband as I am leaving you, he is legally freed from all responsibility towards her. At any rate, I release you now from all responsibility. You mustn't feel yourself bound, any more than I shall. There must be complete freedom on both sides. Here is your ring. Now give me mine.

Helmer: That too?

Nora: That too.

Helmer: Here it is.

Nora: So—it's all over now. Here are the keys. The servants know how to run the house—better than I do. I'll ask Kristine to come by tomorrow, after I've left town; there are a few things I brought with me from home; she'll pack them up and send them on to me.

Helmer: You really mean it's over, Nora? *Really* over? You'll never think of me again?

Nora: I expect I shall often think of you; of you—and the children, and this house.

Helmer: May I write to you?

Nora: No—never. You mustn't! Please!

Helmer: At least, let me send you—

Nora: Nothing!

Helmer: But, you'll let me help you, Nora—

Nora: No, I say! I can't accept anything from strangers.

Helmer: Must I always be a stranger to you, Nora?

Nora (taking her traveling bag):   Yes. Unless it were to happen—the most wonderful thing of all—

Helmer: What?

Nora: Unless we both could change so that—Oh, Torvald! I no longer *believe* in miracles, you see!

Helmer: Tell me! Let *me* believe! Unless we both could change so that—?

Nora: —So that our life together might truly be a marriage. Good-bye.

(*She goes out by the hall door.*)

Helmer (sinks into a chair by the door with his face in his hands):   Nora! Nora! (*He looks around the room and rises.*) She is gone! How empty it all seems! (*A hope springs up in him.*) The most wonderful thing of all—?

(*From below is heard the reverberation of a heavy door closing.*)

HEDDA GABLER

Critics attacked Hedda Gabler *savagely in its first performances. More than his other plays, it was denounced as a vulgar "escape of moral sewage gas." Part of the reason was that the setting of the play was unrelievedly depressing to its first audiences. Hedda was herself not a likeable character. She revealed emotions that were thought to be inappropriate for a woman of her station, and the ultimate feeling of many in the audience was that she was a horrid human being. Audiences felt the play was a wholesale condemnation of Scandinavian society. Because they could not feel sympathy toward Hedda, critics rejected the play.*

Hedda Gabler *fascinates us today. Hedda is a powerful woman in a world entirely dominated by men, most of whom are hardly a match for her in terms of intellect or imagination. Her father was a general, a man of action, and her sense of herself is reflected in her sense of him. His guns are left behind for her to use.*

When the play opens, Hedda has returned from her honeymoon, having married Jörgen Tesman, an academic man with prospects of a solid job in a

professorship at the university. The man whom she really loves, Ejlert Lövborg,
wrote a book while she was away, and it turns out that he, after all, may have a
chance at Tesman's professorship. To a large extent the contrast between Tesman
and Lövberg powers the play. Hedda's efforts to regain Lövborg's affection are
tragic in outcome but fascinating to watch. Hedda is jealous of her old friend Mrs.
Elvsted, who spent time nurturing Lövborg's talent and helping him write his book,
which Mrs. Elvsted refers to as their "child." Once she has the opportunity, Hedda
sets about to destroy the book and Lövborg along with it.

The men in the play are weak or corrupt. Tesman is almost helpless and has
been babied by the women in his life; Lövborg, although brilliant and imaginative,
is unable to control himself; and Judge Brack is an opportunist who will do almost
anything for power. The largest character in the play is Hedda, whose stature looms
above the rest. But is she a good character or not? Does she do what she does because
circumstances are against her, or is her character deeply flawed? (Or both?)
Should we admire or condemn her? These are questions that have long been asked,
but rarely answered successfully. Some psychoanalytic critics have seen Hedda as a
portrayal of an aspect of Ibsen himself. Critic Arne Duve has called her a portrait
of Ibsen's "repressed and crippled emotional life."

Hedda Gabler *is worth examining from many points of view, and most of the*
critical strategies we have discussed are fruitful. The complexity and richness of the
play—along with its smashing portrayal of a dynamic personality—make this one
of modern drama's most durable dramatic experiences.

Henrik Ibsen   (1828–1906)
HEDDA GABLER   1890

Translated by Eva Le Gallienne

Characters

> Jörgen Tesman,° holder of a
> scholarship for research
> in the History of
> Civilization
> Mrs. Hedda Gabler Tesman,
> his wife
> Miss Juliane Tesman, his
> aunt

> Mrs. Thea Rysing Elvsted
> Judge Brack
> Ejlert Lövborg
> Berte, maid at the Tesmans'

> *The action takes place in*
> *Tesman's villa on the*
> *west side of the city*

ACT I

Scene: A large handsomely furnished drawing room, decorated in dark
colors. In the back wall a wide opening with portieres that are drawn
back. This opening leads to a smaller room decorated in the same style as

---

Jörgen Tesman: In performance, the form *George* is always used.

the drawing room. In the right-hand wall of the front room is a folding door leading to the hall. In the wall opposite, on the left, a glass door, its hangings also drawn back. Through the panes can be seen part of a veranda and trees covered in autumn foliage. Standing well forward is an oval table, with a cover on it and surrounded by chairs. By the wall on the right stands a wide stove of dark porcelain, a high-backed armchair, an upholstered footstool and two tabourets.° A small sofa fits into the right-hand corner with a small round table in front of it. Down left, standing slightly away from the wall, another sofa. Above the glass door, a piano. On either side of the opening in the back wall two étagères° with terra-cotta and majolica ornaments. Against the back wall of the inner room a sofa, a table, and a couple of chairs. Above the sofa hangs the portrait of a handsome elderly man in the uniform of a general. Over the table a hanging lamp with an opalescent glass shade. A number of bouquets of flowers are arranged about the drawing room, in vases and glasses. Others lie on the various tables. The floors in both rooms are covered with thick carpets. It is morning. The sun shines through the glass door.

Miss Juliane Tesman, wearing a hat and carrying a parasol, enters from the hall followed by Berte, who carries a bouquet wrapped in paper. Miss Tesman is a good and pleasant-looking lady of about sixty-five. Simply but nicely dressed in a gray tailor-made suit. Berte is a maid getting on in years, plain and rather countrified in appearance.

Miss Tesman (stops just inside the door, listens, and says softly):   Good gracious! They're not even up—I do believe!

Berte (also speaks softly):   That's what I told you, Miss Juliane. The steamer got in so late last night; and the young mistress had such a lot of unpacking to do before she could get to bed.

Miss Tesman: Well—let them sleep as long as they like. But when they do get up, they'll certainly need a breath of fresh air. (*She goes to the glass door and opens it wide.*)

Berte (at the table, uncertain what to do with the bouquet in her hand):   There's not a bit of room left anywhere. I'll just put them down here, Miss Juliane. (*Puts the bouquet down on the piano.*)

Miss Tesman: So now you have a new mistress, Berte. Heaven knows it was hard enough for me to part with you.

Berte (on the verge of tears):   Don't think it wasn't hard for me too, Miss Juliane; after all those happy years I spent with you and Miss Rina.

Miss Tesman: We'll just have to make the best of it, Berte. Master Jörgen needs you—he really does. You've looked after him ever since he was a little boy.

Berte: That's true, Miss Juliane; but I can't help worrying about Miss

---

tabourets: Backless stool for sitting.   *étagères:*   Cabinets with shelves.

Rina lying there helpless, poor thing; how *will* she manage? That new maid will never learn to take proper care of an invalid!

Miss Tesman: I'll soon be able to train her; and until then, I'll do most of the work myself—so don't you worry about my poor sister, Berte.

Berte: But, there's something else, Miss Juliane—you see, I'm so afraid I won't be able to please the young mistress.

Miss Tesman: Well—there may be one or two things, just at first—

Berte: She'll be very particular, I expect—

Miss Tesman: That's only natural—after all, she's General Gabler's daughter. She was used to being spoiled when her father was alive. Do you remember how we used to see her galloping by? How smart she looked in her riding clothes!

Berte: Indeed I do remember, Miss Juliane! Who would ever have thought that she and Master Jörgen would make a match of it!

Miss Tesman: God moves in mysterious ways—! But, by the way, Berte—before I forget—you mustn't say Master Jörgen any more—it's Doctor Tesman!

Berte: I know, Miss Juliane. That was one of the very first things the young mistress told me last night. So it's really true, Miss Juliane?

Miss Tesman: Yes, it is indeed! He was made a doctor by one of the foreign universities while he was abroad. It was a great surprise to me; I knew nothing about it until he told me last night on the pier.

Berte: Well—he's clever enough for anything, he is! But I never thought he'd go in for doctoring people!

Miss Tesman: It's not *that* kind of a doctor, Berte! (*Nods significantly.*) But later on, you may have to call him something even grander!

Berte: Really, Miss Juliane? Now what could that be?

Miss Tesman (smiles):   Wouldn't you like to know! (*Moved.*) I wonder what my poor brother would say if he could see what a great man his little boy has become. (*Looking around.*) But, what's this, Berte? Why have you taken all the covers off the furniture?

Berte: The young mistress told me to. She said she couldn't bear them.

Miss Tesman: Perhaps she intends to use this as the living room?

Berte: I think maybe she does, Miss Juliane; though Master Jörgen—I mean the Doctor—said nothing about it.

(*Jörgen Tesman enters the inner room from right, singing gaily. He carries an unstrapped empty suitcase. He is a young-looking man of thirty-three, medium height. Rather plump, a pleasant, round, open face. Blond hair and beard, wears spectacles. Rather carelessly dressed in comfortable lounging clothes.*)

Miss Tesman: Good morning—good morning, my dear Jörgen!

Tesman (at the opening between the rooms):   Aunt Juliane! Dear Aunt Juliane! (*Goes to her and shakes her warmly by the hand.*) Way out here—so early in the morning—eh?

Miss Tesman: I had to come and see how you were getting on.

Tesman: In spite of going to bed so late?

Miss Tesman: My dear boy—as if that mattered to me!

Tesman: You got home all right from the pier—eh?

Miss Tesman: Quite all right, dear, thank you. Judge Brack was kind enough to see me safely to my door.

Tesman: We were so sorry we couldn't give you a lift—but Hedda had such a fearful lot of luggage—

Miss Tesman: Yes—she did seem to have quite a bit!

Berte (to Tesman):   Should I ask the Mistress if there's anything I can do for her, sir?

Tesman: No thank you, Berte—there's no need. She said she'd ring if she wanted anything.

Berte (starting right):   Very good, sir.

Tesman (indicates suitcase):   You might just take that suitcase with you.

Berte (taking it):   Yes, sir. I'll put it in the attic. (*She goes out by the hall door.*)

Tesman: Do you know, Aunt Juliane—I had that whole suitcase full of notes? It's unbelievable how much I found in all the archives I examined; curious old details no one had any idea existed.

Miss Tesman: You don't seem to have wasted your time on your wedding trip!

Tesman: Indeed I haven't!—But do take off your hat, Aunt Juliane—let me help you—eh?

Miss Tesman (while he does so):   How sweet of you! This is just like the old days when you were still with us!

Tesman (he turns the hat round in his hands, looking at it admiringly from all sides):   That's a very elegant hat you've treated yourself to.

Miss Tesman: I bought that on Hedda's account.

Tesman: On Hedda's account—eh?

Miss Tesman: Yes—I didn't want her to feel ashamed of her old aunt—in case we should happen to go out together.

Tesman (patting her cheek):   What a dear you are, Aunt Juliane—always thinking of everything! (*Puts the hat down on a chair near the table.*) And now let's sit down here on the sofa and have a cozy little chat till Hedda comes. (*They sit down. She leans her parasol in the corner of the sofa.*)

Miss Tesman (takes both his hands and gazes at him):   I can't tell you what a joy it is to have you home again, Jörgen.

Tesman: And it's a joy for me to see you again, dear Aunt Juliane. You've been as good as a father and mother to me—I can never forget that!

Miss Tesman: I know, dear—you'll always have a place in your heart for your poor old aunts.

Tesman: How *is* Aunt Rina—eh? Isn't she feeling a little better?

Miss Tesman: No, dear. I'm afraid she'll never be any better, poor thing! But I pray God I may keep her with me a little longer—for now that I haven't you to look after any more, I don't know what will become of me when she goes.

Tesman (pats her on the back):   There, there, there!

Miss Tesman (with a sudden change of tone):   You know, I can't get used to thinking of you as a married man, Jörgen. And to think that you should have been the one to carry off Hedda Gabler—the fascinating Hedda Gabler—who was always surrounded by so many admirers!

Tesman (hums a little and smiles complacently):   Yes—I wouldn't be surprised if some of my friends were a bit jealous of me—eh?

Miss Tesman: And then this wonderful wedding trip! Five—nearly six months!

Tesman: Of course you must remember the trip was also of great value to me in my research work. I can't begin to tell you all the archives I've been through—and the many books I've read!

Miss Tesman: I can well believe it! (*More confidentially, lowering her voice.*) But, Jörgen dear, are you sure you've nothing—well—nothing *special* to tell me?

Tesman: About our trip?

Miss Tesman: Yes.

Tesman: I can't think of anything I didn't write you about. I had a doctor's degree conferred on me—but I told you that last night.

Miss Tesman: Yes, yes—you told me about that. But what I mean is—haven't you any—well—any expectations?

Tesman: Expectations?

Miss Tesman: Yes, Jörgen. Surely you can talk frankly to your old aunt?

Tesman: Well, of course I have expectations!

Miss Tesman: Well?

Tesman: I have every expectation of becoming a professor one of these days!

Miss Tesman: A professor—yes, yes, I know dear—but—

Tesman: In fact, I'm certain of it. But you know that just as well as I do, Aunt Juliane.

Miss Tesman (chuckling):   Of course I do, dear—you're quite right. (*Changing the subject.*) But we were talking about your journey—it must have cost a great deal of money, Jörgen!

Tesman: Well, you see, the scholarship I had was pretty ample—that went a good way.

Miss Tesman: Still—I don't see how it could have been ample enough for two—especially traveling with a lady—they say that makes it ever so much more expensive.

Tesman: It does make it a bit more expensive—but Hedda simply had to have this trip—she really had to—it was the fashionable thing to do.

Miss Tesman: I know—nowadays it seems a wedding has to be followed by a wedding trip. But tell me, Jörgen—have you been over the house yet?

Tesman: I have indeed! I've been up since daybreak!

Miss Tesman: What do you think of it?

Tesman: It's splendid—simply splendid! But it seems awfully big—what on earth shall we do with all those empty rooms?

Miss Tesman (laughingly):   Oh, my dear Jörgen—I expect you'll find plenty of use for them—a little later on.

Tesman: Yes, you're right, Aunt Juliane—as I get more and more books—eh?

Miss Tesman: Of course, my dear boy—it was your books I was thinking of!

Tesman: I'm especially pleased for Hedda's sake. She had her heart set on this house—it belonged to Secretary Falk, you know—even before we were engaged, she used to say it was the one place she'd really like to live in.

Miss Tesman: But I'm afraid you'll find all this very expensive, my dear Jörgen—very expensive!

Tesman (looks at her a little despondently):   Yes, I suppose so. How much do you really think it will cost? I mean approximately—eh?

Miss Tesman: That's impossible to say until we've seen all the bills.

Tesman: Judge Brack wrote Hedda that he'd been able to secure very favorable terms for me.

Miss Tesman: But you mustn't worry about it, my dear boy—for one thing, I've given security for all the furniture and the carpets.

Tesman: Security? You, dear Aunt Juliane? What sort of security?

Miss Tesman: A mortgage on our annuity.

Tesman (jumps up):   What!

Miss Tesman: I didn't know what else to do.

Tesman (standing before her):   You must be mad, Aunt Juliane—quite mad. That annuity is all that you and Aunt Rina have to live on!

Miss Tesman: Don't get so excited about it! It's only a matter of form, Judge Brack says. He was kind enough to arrange the whole matter for me.

Tesman: That's all very well—but still—!

Miss Tesman: And from now on you'll have your own salary to depend on—and even if we should have to help out a little, just at first—it would only be the greatest pleasure to us!

Tesman: Isn't that just like you, Aunt Juliane! Always making sacrifices for me.

Miss Tesman (rises and places her hands on his shoulders):   The only happiness I have in the world is making things easier for you, my dear boy. We've been through some bad times, I admit—but now we've reached the goal and we've nothing to fear.

Tesman (sits down beside her again):   Yes—it's amazing how everything's turned out for the best!

Miss Tesman: Now there's no one to stand in your way—even your most dangerous rival has fallen. Well, he made his bed—let him lie on it, poor misguided creature.

Tesman: Has there been any news of Ejlert—since I went away, I mean?

Miss Tesman: They say he's supposed to have published a new book.

Tesman: Ejlert Lövborg! A new book? Recently—eh?

Miss Tesman: That's what they say—but I shouldn't think any book of his would be worth much. It'll be a very different story when *your* new book appears. What's it to be about, Jörgen?

Tesman: It will deal with the Domestic Industries of Brabant during the Middle Ages.

Miss Tesman: Fancy being able to write about such things!

Tesman: Of course it'll be some time before the book is ready—I still have to arrange and classify all my notes, you see.

Miss Tesman: Yes—collecting and arranging—no one can compete with you in that! You're not your father's son for nothing!

Tesman: I can't wait to begin! Especially now that I have my own comfortable home to work in.

Miss Tesman: And best of all—you have your wife! The wife you longed for!

Tesman (embracing her):   Yes, you're right, Aunt Juliane—Hedda! She's the most wonderful part of it all! (*Looks toward opening between the rooms.*) But here she comes—eh?

(*Hedda enters from the left through the inner room. She is a woman of twenty-nine. Her face and figure show breeding and distinction. Her complexion is pale and opaque. Her eyes are steel-gray and express a cold, unruffled repose. Her hair is an agreeable medium-brown, but not especially abundant. She wears a tasteful, somewhat loose-fitting negligee.*)

Miss Tesman (goes to meet Hedda):   Good morning, Hedda dear—and welcome home!

Hedda (gives her her hand):   Good morning, my dear Miss Tesman. What an early visitor you are—how kind of you!

Miss Tesman (seems slightly embarrassed):   Not at all. And did the bride sleep well in her new home?

Hedda: Thank you—fairly well.

Tesman (laughing):   Fairly well! I like that, Hedda! You were sleeping like a log when I got up!

Hedda: Yes—fortunately. You know, Miss Tesman, one has to adapt oneself gradually to new surroundings. (*Glancing toward the left.*) Good heavens—what a nuisance! That maid's opened the window and let in a whole flood of sunshine!

Miss Tesman (starts towards door):   Well—we'll just close it then!

Hedda: No, no—don't do that! Jörgen, dear, just draw the curtains, will you? It'll give a softer light.

Tesman (at the door):   There, Hedda! Now you have both shade and fresh air!

Hedda: Heaven knows we need some fresh air, with all these stacks of flowers! But do sit down, my dear Miss Tesman.

Miss Tesman: No—many thanks! Now that I know everything's all right here, I must be getting home to my poor sister.

Tesman: Do give her my best love, Aunt Juliane—and tell her I'll drop in and see her later in the day.

Miss Tesman: Yes, dear, I'll do that. . . . Oh! I'd almost forgotten. (*Feeling in the pocket of her dress.*) I've brought something for you!

Tesman: What can that be, Aunt Juliane—eh?

Miss Tesman (produces a flat parcel wrapped in newspaper and presents him with it):   Look, dear!

Tesman (opens the parcel):   Oh, Aunt Juliane! You really kept them for me! Isn't that touching, Hedda—eh?

Hedda (by the étagère *on the right):*   Well, what is it, dear?

Tesman: My slippers, Hedda! My old bedroom slippers!

Hedda: Oh, yes—I remember. You often spoke of them on our journey.

Tesman: I can't tell you how I've missed them! (*Goes up to her.*) Do have a look at them, Hedda—

Hedda (going toward stove):   I'm really not very interested, Jörgen—

Tesman (following her):   Dear Aunt Rina embroidered them for me during her illness. They have so many memories for me—

Hedda (at the table):   Scarcely for me, Jörgen.

Miss Tesman: Of course not, Jörgen! They mean nothing to Hedda.

Tesman: I only thought, now that she's one of the family—

Hedda (interrupting):   We shall never get on with this servant, Jörgen!

Miss Tesman: Not get on with Berte?

Tesman: Hedda dear, what do you mean?

Hedda (pointing):   Look! She's left her old hat lying about on the table.

Tesman (flustered—dropping the slippers on the floor):   Why—Hedda—!

Hedda: Just imagine if someone were to come in and see it!

Tesman: But, Hedda! That's Aunt Juliane's hat!

Hedda: Oh! Is it?

Miss Tesman (picks up the hat):   Yes, indeed it is! And what's more it's not old—little Mrs. Tesman!

Hedda: I really didn't look at it very closely, Miss Tesman.

Miss Tesman (puts on the hat):   This is the very first time I've worn it!

Tesman: And it's a lovely hat, too—quite a beauty!

Miss Tesman: Oh, it isn't as beautiful as all that. (*Looking round.*) Where's my parasol? (*Takes it.*) Ah—here it is! (*Mutters.*) For this is mine too—not Berte's.

Tesman: A new hat and a new parasol—just think, Hedda!

Hedda: Most handsome and lovely, I'm sure!

Tesman: Yes—isn't it, eh? But do take a good look at Hedda—see how lovely *she* is!

Miss Tesman: Hedda was always lovely, my dear boy—that's nothing new. (*She nods and goes toward the right.*)

Tesman (following her):   But don't you think she's looking especially well? I think she's filled out a bit while we've been away.

Hedda (crossing the room): Oh, do be quiet . . . !

Miss Tesman (who has stopped and turned toward them): Filled out?

Tesman: Of course, you can't notice it so much in that loose dress—but I have certain opportunities—

Hedda (stands at the glass door—impatiently): You have no opportunities at all, Jörgen—

Tesman: I think it must have been the mountain air in the Tyrol—

Hedda (curtly interrupting): I'm exactly as I was when we left!

Tesman: That's what you say—but I don't agree with you! What do you think, Aunt Juliane?

Miss Tesman (gazing at her with folded hands): Hedda is lovely—lovely! (*Goes to her, takes her face in her hands and gently kisses the top of her head.*) God bless and keep you, Hedda Tesman, for Jörgen's sake!

Hedda (quietly freeing herself): Please! Oh, please let me go!

Miss Tesman (with quiet emotion): I shan't let a day pass without coming to see you!

Tesman: That's right, Aunt Juliane!

Miss Tesman: Good-bye, dearest Hedda—good-bye!

(*She goes out by the hall door. Tesman sees her out. The door remains half open. Tesman can be heard repeating his greetings to Aunt Rina and his thanks for the bedroom slippers. Meanwhile, Hedda paces about the room, raises her arms and clenches her hands as though in desperation. She flings back the curtains of the glass door and stands gazing out. In a moment Tesman returns and closes the door behind him.*)

Tesman (picking up the slippers from the floor): What are you looking at, Hedda?

Hedda (once more calm and controlled): I'm just looking at the leaves—they're so yellow—so withered.

Tesman (wraps up the slippers and puts them on the table): Well, we're well into September now.

Hedda (again restless): God, yes! September—September already!

Tesman: Didn't you think Aunt Juliane was a little strange? Almost solemn, I thought. What do you suppose was the matter with her—eh?

Hedda: Well, you see, I scarcely know her. Isn't she always like that?

Tesman: No, not as she was today.

Hedda (leaving the glass door): Perhaps she was annoyed about the hat.

Tesman: Oh, not specially—perhaps just for a moment—

Hedda (crosses over toward the fireplace): Such a peculiar way to behave—flinging one's hat about in the drawing room—one doesn't do that sort of thing.

Tesman: I'm sure Aunt Juliane won't do it again.

Hedda: I shall manage to make my peace with her. When you see her this afternoon, Jörgen, you might ask her to come and spend the evening here.

Tesman: Yes, I will, Hedda. And there's another thing you could do that would give her so much pleasure.

Hedda: Well—what's that?

Tesman: If you could only be a little more affectionate with her—just for my sake—eh?

Hedda: I shall try to call her Aunt—but that's really all I can do.

Tesman: Very well. I just thought, now that you belong to the family—

Hedda: I really don't see why, Jörgen—(*She goes up toward the center opening.*)

Tesman (after a short pause):   Is there anything the matter with you, Hedda, eh?

Hedda: No, nothing. I'm just looking at my old piano. It doesn't seem to fit in with the rest of the furniture.

Tesman: The first time I draw my salary, we'll see about exchanging it.

Hedda: Exchange it! Why exchange it? I don't want to part with it. Why couldn't we put it in the inner room and get a new one for here? That is, of course, when we can afford it.

Tesman (slightly taken back):   Yes, I suppose we could do that.

Hedda (takes up the bouquet from the piano):   These flowers weren't here last night when we arrived.

Tesman: I expect Aunt Juliane brought them for you.

Hedda (examines the bouquet):   Here's a card. (*Takes out a card and reads it.*) "Shall return later in the day." Can you guess who it's from?

Tesman: No. Tell me.

Hedda: From Mrs. Elvsted.

Tesman: Really! Sheriff Elvsted's wife. The former Miss Rysing.

Hedda: Exactly. The girl with that irritating mass of hair—she was always showing off. I've heard she was an old flame of yours, Jörgen?

Tesman (laughs):   Oh, that didn't last long, and it was before I met you, Hedda. Fancy her being in town.

Hedda: Funny that she should call on us. I haven't seen her for years. Not since we were at school together.

Tesman: I haven't seen her, either, for ever so long. I wonder how she can stand living in that remote, dreary place.

Hedda: I wonder! (*After a moment's thought, says suddenly*): Tell me, Jörgen, doesn't Ejlert Lövborg live somewhere near there?

Tesman: Yes, I believe he does. Somewhere in that neighborhood.

Berte (enters by the hall door):   That lady, ma'am, who left some flowers a little while ago is back again. (*Pointing.*) The flowers you have in your hand, ma'am.

Hedda: Oh, is she? Very well, ask her to come in.

(*Berte opens the door for Mrs. Elvsted and exits. Mrs. Elvsted is a fragile woman with soft, pretty features. Her large, round, light-blue eyes are slightly prominent and have a timid, questioning look. Her hair is unusually fair, almost white-gold and extremely thick and wavy. She is a couple of years younger than Hedda. She wears a dark visiting dress, in good taste but not in the latest fashion.)*

Hedda (graciously goes to meet her):   How do you do, my dear Mrs. Elvsted? How delightful to see you again after all these years.

Mrs. Elvsted (nervously, trying to control herself):   Yes, it's a very long time since we met.

Tesman (gives her his hand):   And we haven't met for a long time, either, eh?

Hedda: Thank you for your lovely flowers.

Mrs. Elvsted: Oh, don't mention it. I would have come to see you yesterday, but I heard you were away.

Tesman: Have you just arrived in town, eh?

Mrs. Elvsted: Yes, I got here yesterday morning. I was so upset not to find you at home.

Hedda: Upset! But why, my dear Mrs. Elvsted?

Tesman: But, my dear Mrs. Rysing—eh, Mrs. Elvsted, I mean—

Hedda: I hope you're not in any trouble.

Mrs. Elvsted: Well, yes, I am, and I know no one else in town that I could possibly turn to—

Hedda (puts the bouquet down on the table):   Come, let's sit down here on the sofa—

Mrs. Elvsted: I'm really too nervous to sit down.

Hedda: Of course you're not. Come along now—(*She draws Mrs. Elvsted down to the sofa and sits beside her.*)

Tesman: Well, Mrs. Elvsted?

Hedda: Has anything gone wrong at home?

Mrs. Elvsted: Well, eh—yes, and no. I do hope you won't misunderstand me.

Hedda: Perhaps you'd better tell us all about it, Mrs. Elvsted.

Tesman: I suppose that's what you've come for, eh?

Mrs. Elvsted: Yes, of course. Well, first of all—But perhaps you've already heard—Ejlert Lövborg is in town, too.

Hedda: Lövborg!

Tesman: What! Ejlert Lövborg has come back! Think of that, Hedda!

Hedda: Good heavens, yes, I heard it!

Mrs. Elvsted: He's been here for a week. A whole week. I'm so afraid he'll get into trouble—

Hedda: But, my dear Mrs. Elvsted, why should you be so worried about him?

Mrs. Elvsted (gives her a startled look and speaks hurriedly):   Well, you see— he's the children's tutor.

Hedda: Your children's?

Mrs. Elvsted: No. My husband's. I have none.

Hedda: Oh, your stepchildren's then?

Mrs. Elvsted: Yes.

Tesman (with some hesitation): Was he—I don't quite know how to put it—was he dependable enough to fill such a position, eh?

Mrs. Elvsted: For the last two years his conduct has been irreproachable.

Tesman: Has it, really? Think of that, Hedda!

Hedda: Yes, yes, yes! I heard it.

Mrs. Elvsted: Irreproachable in every respect, I assure you, but still I know how dangerous it is for him to be here in town all alone, and he has quite a lot of money with him. I can't help being worried to death about him.

Tesman: But why did he *come* here? Why didn't he stay where he was? With you and your husband, eh?

Mrs. Elvsted: After his book was published he felt too restless to stay on with us.

Tesman: Oh, yes, of course. Aunt Juliane told me he had published a new book.

Mrs. Elvsted: Yes, a wonderful book. A sort of outline of civilization. It came out a couple of weeks ago. It's sold marvelously. Made quite a sensation.

Tesman: Has it really? Then I suppose it's something he wrote some time ago—during his better years.

Mrs. Elvsted: No, no. He's written it all since he's been with us.

Tesman: Well, isn't that splendid, Hedda? Think of that!

Mrs. Elvsted: Yes, if only he'll keep it up.

Hedda: Have you seen him here in town?

Mrs. Elvsted: Not yet. I had great trouble finding out his address, but this morning I got it at last.

Hedda (gives her a searching look): But doesn't it seem rather odd of your husband to—

Mrs. Elvsted (with a nervous start): Of my husband—what?

Hedda: Well—to send you on such an errand. Why didn't he come himself to look after his friend?

Mrs. Elvsted: Oh, no. My husband is much too busy. And besides, I had some shopping to do.

Hedda (with a slight smile): Oh, I see!

Mrs. Elvsted (rising quickly and uneasily): I implore you, Mr. Tesman, be good to Ejlert Lövborg if he should come to see you. I'm sure he will. You were such great friends in the old days, and after all, you're both interested in the same studies. You specialize in the same subjects—as far as I can understand.

Tesman: Yes, we used to, at any rate.

Mrs. Elvsted: That's why I'd be so grateful if you too would—well—keep an eye on him. You will do that, won't you, Mr. Tesman?

Tesman: I'd be delighted to, Mrs. Rysing.

Hedda: Elvsted!

Tesman: I'd be delighted to do anything in my power to help Ejlert. You can rely on me.

Mrs. Elvsted (presses his hands): Oh, how very kind of you! I can't thank you enough. . . . (*Frightened.*) You see, my husband is so very fond of him.

Hedda (rises): Yes—I see. I think you should write to him, Jörgen. He may not care to come of his own accord.

Tesman: Perhaps that would be the right thing to do, Hedda, eh?

Hedda: Yes. The sooner the better. Why not at once?

Mrs. Elvsted (imploringly): Oh, yes, please do!

Tesman: I'll write him this minute. Have you his address, Mrs. Ry— Elvsted?

Mrs Elvsted (takes a slip of paper from her pocket and gives it to him): Here it is.

Tesman: Splendid. Then I'll go in. (*Looks around.*) Oh—I mustn't forget my slippers. Ah! Here they are. (*Takes the parcel and starts to go.*)

Hedda: Mind you write him a nice friendly letter, Jörgen, and a good long one, too.

Tesman: I most certainly will.

Mrs. Elvsted: But don't let him know that I suggested it!

Tesman: Of course not! That goes without saying, eh? (*He goes out right, through the inner room.*)

Hedda (smilingly goes to Mrs. Elvsted and says in a low voice): There! Now we've killed two birds with one stone.

Mrs. Elvsted: What do you mean?

Hedda: Couldn't you see that I wanted to get rid of him?

Mrs. Elvsted: Yes, to write the letter.

Hedda: And so that I could talk to you alone.

Mrs. Elvsted (bewildered): About the same thing?

Hedda: Precisely.

Mrs. Elvsted (apprehensively): But there's nothing else to tell, Mrs. Tesman. Absolutely nothing.

Hedda: Of course there is. I can see that. There's a great *deal* more to tell. Come along. Sit down. We'll have a nice friendly talk. (*she forces Mrs. Elvsted down into the armchair by the stove and seats herself on one of the tabourets.*)

Mrs. Elvsted (anxiously looking at her watch): But, really, Mrs. Tesman, I was just thinking of going—

Hedda: Oh, you can't be in such a hurry. Come along, now—I want to know all about your life at home.

Mrs. Elvsted: I prefer not to speak about that.

Hedda: But to me, dear! After all, we went to school together.

Mrs. Elvsted: Yes, but you were in a higher class, and I was always so dreadfully afraid of you then.

Hedda: Afraid of me!

Mrs. Elvsted: Yes, dreadfully. When we met on the stairs you always used to pull my hair.

Hedda: Did I, really!

Mrs. Elvsted: Yes. And once you said you were going to burn it all off.

Hedda: I was just teasing you, of course!

Mrs. Elvsted: I was so silly in those days, and afterwards we drifted so far apart. We lived in such different worlds. . . .

Hedda: Well, then we must drift together again. At school we always called each other by our first names. Why shouldn't we now?

Mrs. Elvsted: I think you're mistaken—

Hedda: Of course not. I remember it distinctly. We were *great* friends! (*Draws her stool near to Mrs. Elvsted and kisses her on the cheek.*) So you must call me Hedda.

Mrs. Elvsted (pressing her hands and patting them): You're so kind and understanding. I'm not used to kindness.

Hedda: And I shall call you my darling little Thora.

Mrs. Elvsted: My name is Thea.

Hedda: Yes, yes, of course, I meant Thea! (*Looking at her compassionately.*) So my darling little Thea—you mean they're not kind to you at home?

Mrs. Elvsted: If only I had a home! But I haven't. I never had one.

Hedda (gives her a quick look): I suspected something of the sort.

Mrs. Elvsted (gazing helplessly before her): Ah!

Hedda: Tell me, Thea—I'm a little vague about it. When you first went to the Elvsteds', you were engaged as housekeeper, weren't you?

Mrs. Elvsted: I was supposed to go as governess, but Mrs. Elvsted—the first Mrs. Elvsted, that is—was an invalid, and rarely left her room, so I had to take charge of the house as well.

Hedda: And, eventually, you became mistress of the house?

Mrs. Elvsted (sadly): Yes, I did.

Hedda: How long ago was that?

Mrs. Elvsted: That I married him?

Hedda: Yes.

Mrs. Elvsted: Five years ago.

Hedda: Yes, that's right.

Mrs. Elvsted: Oh, those five years, especially the last two or three of them—If only you knew, Mrs. Tesman!

Hedda (slaps her lightly on the hand): Mrs. Tesman! Thea!

Mrs. Elvsted: I'll try—You have no idea, Hedda—

Hedda (casually): Ejlert Lövborg's lived near you about three years, hasn't he?

Mrs. Elvsted (looks at her doubtfully): Ejlert Lövborg? Why, yes, he has.

Hedda: Had you met him before, here in town?

Mrs. Elvsted: No, not really—I knew him by his name, of course.

Hedda: But I suppose up there you saw a good deal of him.

Mrs. Elvsted: Yes, he came to our house every day. He gave the children lessons, you see. I had so much to do; I couldn't manage that, as well.

Hedda: No. Of course not. And I suppose your husband's away from home a good deal.

Mrs. Elvsted: Yes. Being sheriff, he often has to travel about his district.

Hedda (leans against the arm of the chair):   Now, my dear darling little Thea, I want you to tell me everything—exactly as it is.

Mrs. Elvsted: Well, then you must question me.

Hedda: Tell me—what sort of a man is your husband, Thea? To live with, I mean. Is he kind to you?

Mrs. Elvsted (evasively):   He probably thinks he is.

Hedda: But isn't he much too old for you, dear? There must be at least twenty years between you.

Mrs. Elvsted (irritably):   Yes, that makes it all the harder. We haven't a thought in common. Nothing, in fact.

Hedda: But, I suppose he's fond of you in his own way.

Mrs. Elvsted: Oh, I don't know. I think he finds me useful. And then it doesn't cost much to keep me. I'm not expensive.

Hedda: That's stupid of you.

Mrs. Elvsted (shakes her head):   It couldn't be otherwise. Not with him. I don't believe he really cares about anyone but himself. And perhaps a little for the children.

Hedda: And for Ejlert Lövborg, Thea?

Mrs. Elvsted (looking at her):   Ejlert Lövborg? What makes you say that?

Hedda: Well, it's obvious!—After all, he's sent you all this way into town, simply to look for him!—(*With the trace of a smile.*) Wasn't that what you told Jörgen?

Mrs. Elvsted (with a nervous twitch):   Yes, I suppose I did. (*Vehemently but in a low voice.*) Oh, I might as well tell you the truth. It's bound to come out sooner or later.

Hedda: What—?

Mrs. Elvsted: Well, then—my husband knew nothing about my coming here.

Hedda: Your husband didn't know!

Mrs. Elvsted: No, of course not. He was away himself at the time. I couldn't stand it any longer, Hedda. I simply couldn't. I felt so alone, so deserted—

Hedda: Yes, yes—well?

Mrs. Elvsted: So I packed a few of my things—just those I needed most— I didn't say a word to anyone. I simply left the house.

Hedda: Just like that!

Mrs. Elvsted: Yes, and took the next train to town.

Hedda: But, Thea, my darling! How did you dare do such a thing?

Mrs. Elvsted (rises and walks about the room):   What else could I possibly do?

Hedda: But what will your husband say when you go home again?

Mrs. Elvsted (at the table, looks at her): Back to him!

Hedda: Well, of course.

Mrs. Elvsted: I shall never go back to him again.

Hedda (rises and goes toward her): You mean you've actually left your home for *good?*

Mrs. Elvsted: I saw nothing else to do.

Hedda: But to leave like that, so openly—

Mrs. Elvsted: You can't very well *hide* a thing like that!

Hedda: But what will people say about you, Thea?

Mrs. Elvsted: They can say whatever they like. (*Sits on the sofa wearily and sadly.*) I only did what I had to do.

Hedda (after a short silence): What are your plans now?

Mrs. Elvsted: I don't know yet. All I know is that I must live near Ejlert Lövborg, if I'm to live at all.

Hedda (takes a chair from the table, sits down near Mrs. Elvsted and strokes her hands): Tell me, Thea—how did this friendship start between you and Ejlert Lövborg?

Mrs. Elvsted: It grew gradually. I began to have a sort of power over him.

Hedda: Really?

Mrs. Elvsted: Yes. After a while he gave up his old habits. Oh, not because I asked him to—I never would have dared do that. But I suppose he realized how unhappy they made me, and so he dropped them.

Hedda (concealing a scornful smile): So, my darling little Thea, you've actually reformed him!

Mrs. Elvsted: Well, *he* says so, at any rate, and in return he's made a human being out of me. Taught me to think and understand so many things.

Hedda: Did he give you lessons, too, then?

Mrs. Elvsted: Not lessons, exactly, but he talked to me, explained so much to me—and the most wonderful thing of all was when he finally allowed me to share in his work. Allowed me to help him.

Hedda: He did, did he?

Mrs. Elvsted: Yes. He wanted me to be a part of everything he wrote.

Hedda: Like two good comrades!

Mrs. Elvsted (brightly): Comrades! Why, Hedda, that's exactly what *he* says! I ought to be so happy, but somehow I'm not. I'm so afraid it may not last.

Hedda: You're not very sure of him, then?

Mrs. Elvsted (gloomily): I sometimes feel a shadow between Lövborg and me—a woman's shadow.

Hedda (looks at her intently): Who could that be?

Mrs. Elvsted: I don't know. Someone he knew long ago. Someone he's never been able to forget.

Hedda: Has he told you anything about her?

Mrs. Elvsted: He spoke of her once—quite vaguely.

Hedda: What did he say?

Mrs. Elvsted: He said that when they parted she threatened to shoot him.

Hedda (with cold composure):   What nonsense! No one does that sort of thing here!

Mrs. Elvsted: I know. That's why I think it must have been that red-haired cabaret singer he was once—

Hedda: Very likely.

Mrs. Elvsted: They say she used to go about with loaded pistols.

Hedda: Then of course it must have been she.

Mrs. Elvsted (wringing her hands):   But, Hedda, they say she's here now—in town, again! I'm so worried I don't know what to do!

Hedda (with a glance toward inner room):   Sh! Here comes Tesman. Not a word to him. All this is between us.

Mrs. Elvsted (jumps up):   Yes, yes, of course.

(*Jörgen Tesman, a letter in his hand, enters from the right through the inner room.*)

Tesman: Well, here is the letter signed and sealed!

Hedda: Splendid! Mrs. Elvsted was just leaving, Jörgen. Wait a minute! I'll go with you as far as the garden gate.

Tesman: Do you think Berte could post this for me, dear?

Hedda (takes the letter):   I'll tell her to.

(*Berte enters from the hall.*)

Berte: Judge Brack wishes to know if you will see him, ma'am.

Hedda: Yes. Show him in. And post this letter, will you?

Berte (taking the letter):   Certainly, ma'am.

(*She opens the door for Judge Brack and goes out. The Judge is a man of forty-five. Thick-set but well-built and supple in his movements. His face is rounded and his profile aristocratic. His short hair is still almost black and carefully dressed. His eyes are bright and sparkling. His eyebrows thick. His mustache also thick with short-cut ends. He wears a smart walking suit, slightly youthful for his age. He uses an eyeglass, which he lets drop from time to time.*)

Brack (bowing, hat in hand):   May one venture to call so early in the day?

Hedda: Of course one may.

Tesman (shakes hands with him):   You know you're always welcome. (*Introduces him.*) Judge Brack, Miss Rysing.

Hedda: Ah!

Brack (bows):   Delighted.

Hedda (looks at him and laughs):   What fun to have a look at you by daylight, Judge.

Brack: Do you find me—altered?

Hedda: A little younger, I think.

Brack (laughs and goes down to fireplace): I thank you, most heartily.

Tesman: But what do you say to Hedda, eh? Doesn't she look flourishing? She's positively—

Hedda: For heaven's sake, leave me out of it, Jörgen! You'd far better thank Judge Brack for all the trouble he's taken.

Brack: Oh, don't mention it. It was a pleasure, I assure you.

Hedda: Yes, you're a loyal soul; but I mustn't keep Mrs. Elvsted waiting. Excuse me, Judge. I'll be back directly.

(Exchange of greetings. Mrs. Elvsted and Hedda go out through the hall door.)

Brack: Well, I hope your wife's pleased with everything.

Tesman: We really can't thank you enough. Of course she wants to rearrange things a bit, and she talks of buying a few additional trifles.

Brack: Is that so?

Tesman: But you needn't bother about that. Hedda will see to that herself. Why don't we sit down, eh?

Brack (sits at table): Thanks. Just for a moment—There's something I must talk to you about, my dear Tesman.

Tesman: Yes, the expenses, eh? (*Sits down.*) I suppose it's time we got down to business.

Brack: Oh, that's not so very pressing. Though perhaps it would have been wiser to be a bit more economical.

Tesman: But that would have been out of the question. You know Hedda, Judge. After all, she's been used to a certain standard of living—

Brack: Yes, that's just the trouble.

Tesman: Fortunately, it won't be long before I receive my appointment.

Brack: Well, you see—such things sometimes hang fire.

Tesman: Have you heard anything further, eh?

Brack: Nothing really definite. (*Interrupts himself.*) But, by the way, I have one bit of news for you.

Tesman: Well?

Brack: Your old friend Ejlert Lövborg is back in town.

Tesman: I've heard that already.

Brack: Really? Who told you?

Tesman: That lady who went out with Hedda.

Brack: Oh, yes, what was her name? I didn't quite catch it.

Tesman: Mrs. Elvsted.

Brack: Oh, yes, the sheriff's wife. Of course. Lövborg's been living near them these past few years.

Tesman: And, just think, I'm delighted to hear he's quite a reformed character.

Brack: Yes, so they say.

Tesman: And he's published a new book, eh?

Brack: Indeed he has.

Tesman: I hear it's made quite a sensation.

Brack: A most unusual sensation.

Tesman: Think of that. I'm delighted to hear it. A man of such extraordinary gifts. I felt so sorry to think he'd gone completely to wrack and ruin!

Brack: Well—everybody thought so.

Tesman: I wonder what he'll do now—how on earth will he manage to make a living?

(During these last words Hedda has re-entered by the hall door.)

Hedda (to Brack with a scornful laugh):   Isn't that just like Tesman, Judge? Always worrying about how people are going to make their living.

Tesman: We were just talking about Ejlert Lövborg, dear.

Hedda (giving him a quick glance. Seats herself in the armchair by the stove and asks casually):   What's the matter with him?

Tesman: That money he inherited—he's undoubtedly squandered that long ago. And he can't very well write a new book every year, eh? So why shouldn't I wonder what's to become of him?

Brack: Perhaps I can give you some information on the subject.

Tesman: Indeed?

Brack: You must remember that his relatives have a great deal of influence.

Tesman: But they washed their hands of him long ago.

Brack: At one time he was considered the hope of the family.

Tesman: At one time, perhaps. But he soon put an end to that.

Hedda: Who knows? (*With a slight smile.*) I hear they've quite reformed him up at the Elvsteds'.

Brack: And then there's his new book, of course.

Tesman: Yes, that's true. Let's hope things will turn out well for him. I've just written him a note. I asked him to come and see me this evening, Hedda dear.

Brack: But you're coming to my stag party this evening. You promised me last night on the pier.

Hedda: Had you forgotten, Tesman!

Tesman: Yes, I really had.

Brack: In any case, I think you can be pretty sure he won't come.

Tesman: Why shouldn't he?

Brack (with a slight hesitation, rises and leans against the back of the chair):   My dear Tesman, and you, too, Mrs. Tesman, I think it's only right that I should inform you of something that—

Tesman: That concerns Ejlert, eh?

Brack: Yes, you as well as him.

Tesman (jumps up anxiously):   But, my dear Judge, what is it?

Brack: I think you should be prepared to find your appointment deferred—rather longer than you desired or expected.

Tesman: Has anything happened to prevent it, eh?

Brack: The nomination may depend on the result of a competition.

Tesman: A competition! Think of that, Hedda. But who would my competitor be? Surely not—?

Brack: Yes. Ejlert Lövborg. Precisely. (*Hedda leans further back in the armchair with an ejaculation.*)

Tesman: No, no! It's impossible! It's utterly inconceivable, eh?

Brack: It may come to that, all the same.

Tesman: But, Judge Brack, this would be incredibly unfair to me. (*Waving his arms.*) Just think, I'm a married man! We married on these prospects, Hedda and I. Think of the money we've spent, and we've borrowed from Aunt Juliane, too! Why, they practically promised me the appointment, eh?

Brack: Don't get so excited. You'll probably get the appointment all the same, only you'll have to compete for it.

Hedda (sits motionless in the armchair):   Just think, Jörgen, it will have quite a sporting interest.

Tesman: Dearest Hedda, how can you be so indifferent about it?

Hedda (as before):   Indifferent! I'm not in the least indifferent. I can hardly wait to see which of you will win.

Brack: In any case, I thought it better to warn you, Mrs. Tesman! Perhaps under the circumstances, you'd better go easy on those "additional trifles" you're thinking of buying.

Hedda: I don't see how this could possibly make any difference, my dear Judge.

Brack: Really? Then I've no more to say. Good-bye. I'll call for you later on my way back from my afternoon walk.

Tesman: Yes, yes—I'm so upset—my head's in a whirl!

Hedda (still reclining, holds out her hand to him):   I shall hope to see you later, Judge.

Brack: Thank you, Mrs. Tesman. Good-bye.

Tesman (accompanies him to the door):   Good-bye, my dear Judge. You really must excuse me—

(*Judge goes out by the hall door.*)

Tesman (pacing the room):   Oh, Hedda, Hedda, one should never rush into adventures, eh?

Hedda (looks at him and smiles):   Do you do that, Jörgen?

Tesman: What else can you call it? To get married and settle down on mere expectations, eh?

Hedda: You may be right.

Tesman: Well, at least we have our lovely home, Hedda, eh? The home we both dreamt of.

Hedda (rises slowly and wearily):   I'd counted on doing a lot of entertaining. That was part of the agreement, I thought. We were to keep open house.

Tesman: I'd been so looking forward to it, Hedda dear. To see you, a brilliant hostess, surrounded by distinguished guests—Well, we'll just have to make the best of it for the time being, dear—Be happy in one another—We can always invite Aunt Juliane in now and then. But I wanted it to be so different for you, Hedda. So very different.

Hedda: I suppose this means I'll have to do without my butler.

Tesman: Yes, I'm afraid a butler is quite out of the question!

Hedda: You promised me a saddle-horse, remember? I suppose *that's* out of the question, too?

Tesman: I'm afraid so, Hedda.

Hedda (walks about the room):   Well, at least I have one thing to amuse myself with.

Tesman (beaming):   Thank heaven for that. What is it, Hedda, eh?

Hedda (at center opening—looks at him with suppressed scorn):   My pistols, Jörgen.

Tesman: Your pistols!

Hedda (with cold eyes):   General Gabler's pistols. (*She goes out through the inner room to the left.*)

Tesman (rushes to the center opening and calls after her):   Oh, Hedda, darling, please don't touch those dangerous things. For my sake, Hedda, eh?

ACT II

Scene: The room at the Tesman's as in the first act. Only the piano has been removed and replaced by an elegant little writing table with bookshelves. A smaller table has been placed by the sofa left. Most of the bouquets have been removed. Mrs. Elvsted's bouquet stands on the large table downstage. It is afternoon.

Hedda, dressed to receive callers, is alone in the room. She stands by the open glass door loading a pistol. The matching pistol lies in an open pistol case on the writing table.

Hedda (looks down into the garden and calls out):   Welcome back, Judge!

Brack (is heard calling below at a distance):   Thank you, Mrs. Tesman.

Hedda (raises the pistol and takes aim):   Now, I'm going to shoot you, Judge!

Brack (from below):   No, no, don't aim at me like that!

Hedda: That's what you get for sneaking in the back way.

(She fires.)

Brack (nearer):   Have you gone quite mad?

Hedda: So sorry. Did I hit you by any chance?

Brack (still from outside):   I wish you'd stop all this nonsense.

Hedda: Come along, Judge, I'll let you pass.

(Judge Brack, dressed as for a men's party, comes in through the glass door. Over his arm he carries a light overcoat.)

Brack: So you're still fooling with those pistols. What are you shooting at?

Hedda: Just killing time. Shooting up into the blue.

Brack (gently takes the pistol out of her hand):   Allow me. (*Examines it.*) Hm . . . I know this pistol . . . I've seen it before. (*Looks around.*) Where's the case for it? Ah, here! (*Places the pistol in its case and closes it.*) So that game is finished for today.

Hedda: What in heaven's name am I to do with myself all day long!

Brack: Haven't you had any visitors?

Hedda (closing the glass door):   Not one. I suppose all our friends are still out of town.

Brack: Isn't Tesman home?

Hedda (at the writing table, putting the pistol case away in a drawer):   No. He rushed off to his aunts' directly after lunch. He didn't expect you so early, Judge.

Brack: Fancy my not thinking of that—That was stupid of me.

Hedda (turns her head and looks at him):   Why stupid?

Brack: Because I should have come even earlier.

Hedda (crossing the room):   Then you'd have found no one to receive you, for I've been dressing ever since lunch.

Brack: But isn't there a little crack in the door through which one might converse?

Hedda: No. You forgot to provide one, Judge.

Brack: Again stupid of me.

Hedda: We must just sit here and wait until Tesman comes—He may not be back for some time.

Brack: Never mind. I shan't be impatient.

(Hedda sits in the corner of the sofa. Brack lays his overcoat over the back of the nearest chair and sits down, but keeps his hat in his hand. A short pause. They look at each other.)

Hedda: Well?

Brack (in the same tone):   Well?

Hedda: I spoke first.

Brack (slightly bending forward):   Let's have a really pleasant little talk, Mrs.—Hedda.

Hedda (leaning farther back on the sofa):   It seems ages since our last one, doesn't it, Judge? Of course, I don't count the few words we had last night and this morning.

Brack: I know—you mean a *real* talk. Just a "twosome."

Hedda: Yes, that's it.

Brack: Every single day I've wished you were home again.

Hedda: I've wished that, too.

Brack: You have? Really, Mrs. Hedda? And I thought you were having such a good time on your journey.

Hedda: Ha!

Brack: Tesman's letters led me to think so.

Hedda: Oh, well, Tesman! You know Tesman, my dear Judge! His idea of bliss is grubbing about in a lot of dirty bookshops and making endless copies of antiquated manuscripts.

Brack (with a touch of malice):   Well, after all, that's his vocation in life, you know. Or a large part of it.

Hedda: Yes, if it's one's vocation, I suppose that makes it different, but as for me! Oh, my dear Judge, I can't tell you how bored I've been!

Brack (sympathetically):   Are you really serious?

Hedda: Of course. Surely you can understand? How would *you* like to spend six whole months without meeting a soul you could really talk to?

Brack: I shouldn't like it at all.

Hedda: But the most unendurable thing of all was—

Brack: What?

Hedda: To be everlastingly with one and the same person.

Brack (with a nod of agreement):   Morning, noon, and night, at all possible times.

Hedda: I said "everlastingly."

Brack: But with our good Tesman, I should have thought one might—

Hedda: Tesman is a specialist, my dear Judge.

Brack: Undeniably.

Hedda: And specialists are not amusing traveling companions—Not for long, at any rate.

Brack: Not even the specialist you happen to love?

Hedda: Ugh! Don't use that revolting word!

Brack (startled):   What? What's that, Mrs. Hedda?

Hedda (half laughing, half in irritation):   Just you try it! Nothing but the history of civilization morning, noon, and night.

Brack: Everlastingly.

Hedda: And then all this business about the domestic industries of Brabant during the Middle Ages. That's the most maddening part of it all.

Brack (looks at her searchingly):   But, tell me, in that case, how did it happen that you—?

Hedda: Married Tesman, you mean? Is there anything so very odd in that?

Brack: Both yes and no, Mrs. Hedda.

Hedda: I had danced myself tired, my dear Judge—and I wasn't getting any younger. (*With a slight shudder.*) But I won't talk about that. I won't even think about it.

Brack: You certainly have no cause.

Hedda (watching him intently):   And one must admit that Jörgen Tesman is a thoroughly worthy man.

Brack: A worthy, dependable man. There can be no question of that.

Hedda: And I don't see anything especially—*funny* about him, do you?

Brack: Funny? No—o—not really. No, I wouldn't say that.

Hedda: After all, he's a distinguished scholar. Who knows? He may still go far.

Brack (looks at her uncertainly):   I thought you believed like everyone else that some day he'd become a really famous man.

Hedda (in a tired voice):   Yes, so I did. And then since he was so absolutely bent on supporting me, I really didn't see why I shouldn't accept his offer.

Brack: No, if you look at it from that point of view—

Hedda: Well, that was more than some of my other admirers were prepared to do, my dear Judge.

Brack (laughs):   I can't answer for the others, of course. You know that, generally speaking, I have a great respect for the state of matrimony, but I confess, that as an individual—

Hedda (jokingly):   I never had any hopes as far as you were concerned.

Brack: All I ask of life is to know a few people intimately. A few nice people whom I can help and advise, in whose houses I can come and go as a trusted friend.

Hedda: Of the—master of the house, you mean?

Brack (with a bow):   Well, preferably, of the mistress. But of the master, too, of course! I find such a triangular friendship, if I may call it so, a great convenience to all concerned.

Hedda: Yes, God knows, a third person would have been welcome on our journey. Oh, those infernal tête-à-têtes!

Brack: Cheer up! Your wedding trip is over now.

Hedda (shaking her head):   Not by a long shot. No, we've only stopped at a station on the line.

Brack: Then the thing to do is to jump out and stretch oneself a bit, Mrs. Hedda.

Hedda: I never jump out.

Brack: Why not?

Hedda: There's always someone there waiting to—

Brack (laughing):   Stare at your legs, you mean?

Hedda: Precisely.

Brack: Well, good heavens—

Hedda (with a gesture of distaste):   I don't like that sort of thing. I'd rather keep my seat and continue to tête-à-tête.

Brack: But if a third person were to jump *in* and join the couple?

Hedda: Ah! But *that's* quite a different thing!

Brack: A trusted, understanding friend.

Hedda: Gay and entertaining in a variety of ways?

Brack: And not a bit of a specialist.

Hedda (with an audible sigh):   That would certainly be a great relief!

Brack (hears the front door open and glances in that direction): The triangle is completed.

Hedda (in a half-tone): And on goes the train.

(*Jörgen Tesman enters from the hall. He wears a gray walking suit and a soft felt hat. He carries a great number of paperbound books under his arm and in his pockets.*)

Tesman (goes up to the table beside the corner sofa): Pooh! It's a warm job to carry all these books, Hedda. (*Puts them down.*) I'm positively perspiring! (*Hedda makes a scarcely audible ejaculation: "How charming, Jörgen!" Tesman puts some of the books down on the table.*) Oh, you're here already, Judge. Berte didn't tell me.

Brack (rising): I came in through the garden.

Hedda: What are all those books, Jörgen?

Tesman (thumbing through the books): They're some new books on my special subject. I simply had to have them.

Hedda: Your special subject, Jörgen?

Brack: On his special subject, Mrs. Tesman. (*He and Hedda exchange a confidential smile.*)

Hedda: Do you need still more books on your special subject, Jörgen?

Tesman: One can never have too many, Hedda. One *must* keep up with all the new publications.

Hedda: Yes, I suppose one must.

Tesman (searching among the books): Look, I got Ejlert Lövborg's new book, too. (*Offers it to her.*) Would you care to have a look at it, Hedda, eh?

Hedda: No, thank you—Well, perhaps a little later, Jörgen.

Tesman: I glanced through it on my way home.

Brack: What do you think of it? As a specialist, I mean.

Tesman: He handles his subject with the greatest restraint. That is what struck me most—It's quite remarkable. He never wrote like that before. (*Gathers the books together.*) I'll just take these into my study. I'm longing to cut the leaves.° And then I suppose I'd better change, though we needn't go just yet, eh?

Brack: Oh, no. There's not the slightest hurry.

Tesman: Then I'll take my time. (*Starts to go out with the books but stops and turns at center opening.*) Oh, by the way, Hedda, Aunt Juliane is afraid she can't come to see you this evening.

Hedda: Oh? Why not? Is she still annoyed about the hat?

Tesman: Of course not. That wouldn't be a bit like her! No, but you see, Aunt Rina's very ill.

Hedda: She always is.

---

cut the leaves: Books were published with the pages gathered and folded. When the owners read them they cut the edges so as to read each side.

Tesman: Yes, but today she's worse than ever, poor thing!

Hedda: Then she'll need her sister with her. That's only natural. I shall have to try and bear it.

Tesman: I can't tell you how delighted Aunt Juliane was to see you looking so well, so positively flourishing.

Hedda (in a half-tone, rising):   Oh, those eternal aunts!

Tesman: What did you say, dear?

Hedda (going to the glass door):   Nothing—nothing—nothing!

Tesman: Very well, Hedda—eh? (*He goes out right, through the inner room.*)

Brack: What was that you said about a hat?

Hedda: Oh, it was just something that happened this morning. Miss Tesman had taken off her hat and put it down on the table. (*Looks at him and smiles.*) And I pretended to think it was the servant's.

Brack (shakes his head):   Why, my dear Mrs. Hedda. How could you do such a thing to that nice old lady?

Hedda (walks nervously about the room):   My dear Judge, I really don't know. I suddenly get impulses like that and I simply can't control them. (*Flings herself down in the armchair by the stove.*) I don't know how to explain it myself.

Brack (behind the armchair):   You're not really happy. I think that's the explanation.

Hedda (gazing straight before her):   I can't imagine why I should be—happy? Can you tell me?

Brack: Well, to begin with; here you are, in the very house you always longed to live in.

Hedda (looks up at him and laughs):   You really believe in that fairy tale?

Brack: Wasn't it true, then?

Hedda: I'll tell you how it happened: last summer I made use of Tesman to see me home from parties.

Brack: Unfortunately, my way lay in a different direction.

Hedda: Yes, you were going in a different direction then, weren't you, Judge?

Brack (laughs):   Shame on you, Mrs. Hedda! And so you and Tesman—?

Hedda: Well, one evening we happened to pass by this house. Tesman, poor thing, was turning and twisting and couldn't think of anything to say. I really felt sorry for the poor learned wretch.

Brack (smiles skeptically):   Sorry! You!

Hedda: Yes, I really did. I felt sorry for him. And so just to make conversation, to help him out a bit, I was foolish enough to say what a charming house this was, and how I should love to live in it.

Brack: No more than that?

Hedda: Not *that* evening.

Brack: But afterwards?

Hedda: Afterwards! Afterwards my foolishness was not without consequences, my dear Judge.

Brack: Yes—Unfortunately, that happens all too often.

Hedda: Thanks! So, you see it was this fictitious enthusiasm for Secretary Falk's Villa that really brought Tesman and me together. It was the immediate cause of our engagement, our wedding, our wedding journey, and all the rest of it. Well, my dear Judge, they say, as you make your bed, so you must lie.

Brack: This is really priceless! So I suppose you didn't really care a rap about the house?

Hedda: No, God knows, I didn't!

Brack: Still, now that we've made it so attractive and comfortable for you—

Hedda: To me it smells of lavender and dried rose leaves. What might be called the "Aunt Juliane atmosphere."

Brack (laughs): No. That's probably a legacy from the late Mrs. Falk.

Hedda: Yes! Yes, you're right! There is a touch of decay about it. (*She clasps her hands behind her head, leans back in the chair and looks at him.*) Oh, my dear Judge, my dear Judge! How incredibly I shall bore myself here!

Brack: Why shouldn't you, too, find some sort of vocation in life, Mrs. Hedda?

Hedda: A vocation—that would attract me?

Brack: Preferably, yes.

Hedda: God only knows what kind of a vocation that would be! I often wonder whether— (*Breaks off.*) But that wouldn't be any good, either.

Brack: What? Tell me.

Hedda: I was wondering whether I could get Jörgen to go into politics.

Brack (laughs): Tesman? No, really! I'm afraid political life would be the last thing in the world for him.

Hedda: I know you're probably right; but I could try and get him into it all the same.

Brack: But what satisfaction would it be to you unless he were successful at it? Why should you want to drive him into it?

Hedda: Because I'm *bored*, I tell you. (*After a pause.*) So you think it quite out of the question for Jörgen ever to become—let's say— Secretary of State?

Brack: Ha, ha! Mrs. Hedda. You must remember, apart from anything else, to become anything of that sort he'd have to be a fairly rich man.

Hedda (rises impatiently): There you are. Money! Always money! (*Crosses the room.*) It's this genteel poverty that makes life so hideous, so utterly ludicrous.

Brack: Now I should say the fault lies elsewhere.

Hedda: Where then?

Brack: I don't believe you've ever really been stirred by anything in life.

Hedda: Anything serious, you mean?

Brack: If you like. But I expect it will come.

Hedda (tossing her head): If you're thinking about that ridiculous professorship, that's Jörgen's own affair. I assure you I shan't give a thought to that!

Brack: I dare say. But suppose you should suddenly find yourself faced with what's known in solemn language, as a grave responsibility— (*Smiling.*) a *new* responsibility, Mrs. Hedda.

Hedda (angrily): Be quiet! Nothing of that sort will ever happen to me.

Brack (cautiously): We'll talk of this again a year from now, at the very latest.

Hedda (curtly): That sort of thing doesn't appeal to me, Judge. I'm not fitted for it. No responsibilities for me!

Brack: What makes you think you're less fitted than the majority of women? Why should you deliberately turn away from duties—?

Hedda (at the glass door): Be quiet, I tell you! I sometimes think there's only one thing in this world I'm really fitted for.

Brack (nearer to her): What's that, if I may ask?

Hedda (looking out): Boring myself to death! Now you know it. (*Turns, looks toward the inner room, and laughs.*) Ah! I thought so—here comes the professor!

Brack (softly, warningly): Now, now! Mrs. Hedda!

(*Jörgen Tesman, dressed for the party, his gloves and hat in his hands, enters from the right through the inner room.*)

Tesman: Oh, Hedda, has any message come from Ejlert, eh?

Hedda: No.

Tesman: Then he'll be here presently, you'll see.

Brack: You really think he'll come?

Tesman: I'm almost sure of it. What you told us this morning was probably just a rumor.

Brack: Do you think so?

Tesman: At any rate, Aunt Juliane didn't believe for a moment that he would ever stand in my way again. Think of that!

Brack: Well, then, there's nothing to worry about.

Tesman (puts his hat and gloves down on a chair, right): I'd like to wait for him as long as possible, though.

Brack: We've plenty of time. My guests won't arrive before seven or half-past.

Tesman: Meanwhile, we can keep Hedda company and see what happens, eh?

Hedda (puts Brack's overcoat and hat on the corner sofa): And if the worst comes to the worst, Mr. Lövborg can spend the evening with me.

Brack: What do you mean by "the worst"?

Hedda: I mean—if he refuses to go with you and Tesman.

Tesman (looks at her dubiously): But, Hedda dear, do you think it would be quite the thing for him to stay here with you, eh? Remember, Aunt Juliane isn't coming.

Hedda: No, but Mrs. Elvsted is. We three can have a cup of tea together.

Tesman: Oh, well, then it would be *quite* all right.

Brack (smiling):   It might perhaps be the best thing for him, too.

Hedda: Why the "best thing," Judge?

Brack: Well, you know how rude you are about my stag parties, Mrs. Tesman. You always say they're only safe for men of the strictest principles.

Hedda: I'm sure Mr. Lövborg's principles are strict enough now. A converted sinner—

(Berte appears at the hall door.)

Berte: There's a gentleman asking to see you, ma'am.

Hedda: Oh, yes—show him in.

Tesman (softly):   It must be Ejlert. Think of that! (*Ejlert Lövborg enters from the hall. He is slim and lean. The same age as Tesman, he looks older, as though worn out by life. Hair and beard dark-brown; a long, pale face, but with patches of color on the cheekbones; he wears a well-cut black visiting suit, obviously new. He carries dark gloves and a silk hat. He stands near the door and makes a rapid bow. He seems slightly embarrassed. Tesman goes to him and shakes him by the hand.*) Welcome, my dear Ejlert. So at last we meet again!

Lövborg (speaks in a hushed voice):   Thanks for your letter, Jörgen. (*Approaches Hedda.*) May I shake hands with you, too, Mrs. Tesman?

Hedda (takes his hand):   How do you do, Mr. Lövborg, I'm delighted to see you. (*She motions with her hand.*) I don't know if you two gentlemen—

Lövborg (with a slight bow):   Judge Brack, I believe.

Brack (bows likewise):   Yes, I've had the pleasure, some years ago.

Tesman (to Lövborg, with his hands on his shoulders):   And now, Ejlert, you must make yourself at home, mustn't he, Hedda? I hear you're going to settle in town again, eh?

Lövborg: Yes, I am.

Tesman: Well, that's splendid. I just got your new book, Ejlert, but I haven't had time to read it yet.

Lövborg: I wouldn't bother to, if I were you.

Tesman: Why, what do you mean?

Lövborg: It's pretty thin stuff.

Tesman: Just think! How can you say that?

Brack: It's been enormously praised, I hear.

Lövborg: That was exactly what I wanted, so I put nothing in it that anyone could take exception to.

Brack: Very wise of you.

Tesman: But, my dear Ejlert—

Lövborg: You see, I'm determined to make a fresh start; to win a real position for myself.

Tesman (slightly embarrassed): Oh, so that's what you plan to do, eh?

Lövborg (smiles, puts down his hat, and takes a parcel wrapped in paper from his coat pocket): But when this one appears, Jörgen Tesman, you'll have to read it, for this is a real book. Every ounce of my true self is in this.

Tesman: Really! What's it about?

Lövborg: It's the sequel.

Tesman: Sequel? Sequel of what?

Lövborg: Of the other book.

Tesman: You mean, the new one?

Lövborg: Yes, of course.

Tesman: But, my dear Ejlert, surely that comes right down to our time, doesn't it?

Lövborg: Yes, but this deals with the future.

Tesman: With the future. But good heavens, we know nothing about the future!

Lövborg: There's a thing or two to be said about it all the same. (*Opens the parcel.*) Look here—

Tesman: That's not your handwriting.

Lövborg: No, I dictated it. (*Thumbs through the pages.*) It falls into two sections. The first deals with the civilizing forces of the future and the second—(*turning to the pages toward the end.*) forecasts the probable lines of development.

Tesman: How remarkable! I should never have thought of writing anything of that sort.

Hedda (at the glass door, drumming on the pane): No, I daresay not.

Lövborg (puts the manuscript back in its wrapping and lays it on the table): I brought it with me; I thought I might read you a bit of it this evening.

Tesman: That was very kind of you, Ejlert, but this evening— (*Glancing at Brack.*) I don't see how we can manage it—

Lövborg: Well, then, some other time. There's no hurry.

Brack: The fact is, Mr. Lövborg, I'm giving a little party this evening to celebrate Tesman's return.

Lövborg (looking for his hat): Oh, then I mustn't detain you.

Brack: No, but wait. I'd be delighted if you would give me the pleasure of your company.

Lövborg (curtly and decisively): I'm sorry. I can't. Thank you very much.

Brack: Oh, nonsense! Do, come. We shall be quite a select little circle, and I can assure you, we shall have a "jolly time," as Mrs. Hed—Mrs. Tesman puts it.

Lövborg: I don't doubt that, but nevertheless—

Brack: And you could bring your manuscript with you and read it to Tesman at my house. I could give you a room all to yourselves.

Tesman: Yes, think of that, Ejlert. Why shouldn't you do that, eh?

Hedda (interposing): But, Jörgen dear, if Mr. Lövborg says he doesn't want to go, I'm sure Mr. Lövborg would much prefer to stay here and have supper with me.

Lövborg (looking at her):   With you, Mrs. Tesman?

Hedda: Mrs. Elvsted will be here, too.

Lövborg: Oh—(*Casually.*) I saw her for a moment today.

Hedda: Oh, did you? Well, she's spending the evening here. So you see, you're almost obliged to stay, Mr. Lövborg. Otherwise, Mrs. Elvsted will have no one to see her home.

Lövborg: That's true. Many thanks. In that case, I will stay, Mrs. Tesman.

Hedda: Splendid! I'll just give one or two orders to the servant. (*She goes to the hall door and rings. Berte enters. Hedda talks to her in a whisper and points to the inner room. Berte nods and goes out.*)

Tesman (during the above, to Ejlert Lövborg):   Tell me, Ejlert, is it this new subject, the future, that you are going to lecture about?

Lövborg: Yes.

Tesman: They told me at the bookstore that you were planning a series of lectures.

Lövborg: Yes, I am. you've no objection.

Tesman: No, of course not, but—

Lövborg: I can quite see that it might interfere with your plans.

Tesman (depressed):   I can't very well expect you, out of consideration for *me*, to—

Lövborg: But, of course, I'll wait until you receive your appointment.

Tesman: What! You'll wait! Then—then you're not going to compete with me, eh?

Lövborg: No. I only want people to realize that I *could* have—a sort of moral victory, if you like.

Tesman: Why, bless my soul, then Aunt Juliane was right after all! I was sure of it. Hedda, just think, Ejlert is not going to stand in our way!

Hedda (curtly):   Our way! Do please leave me out of it, Jörgen. (*She goes up toward the inner room where Berte is arranging a tray with decanters and glasses on the table. Hedda nods approvingly and comes forward again. Berte goes out.*)

Tesman (during the above):   What do you say to this, Judge, eh?

Brack: Well, I say a moral victory may be all very fine but—

Tesman: Yes, certainly, but all the same—

Hedda (looks at Tesman with a cold smile):   You stand there looking absolutely thunderstruck, Jörgen.

Tesman: Well, you know, I almost believe I am.

Hedda (pointing to the inner room):   And now, gentlemen, won't you have a glass of cold punch before you go?

Brack (looks at his watch):   A sort of stirrup cup, you mean. Yes, that's not a bad idea.

Tesman: A capital idea, Hedda. Just the thing. Now that a heavy weight has been lifted off my mind—

Hedda: You'll join them, Mr. Lövborg?

Lövborg (with a gesture of refusal):   No, thank you, nothing for me.

Brack: Why, surely, cold punch is not poison.

Lövborg: Perhaps not for everyone.

Hedda: Well, then, you two go in and I'll sit here and keep Mr. Lövborg company.

Tesman: Yes, do, Hedda, dear.

(*Tesman and Brack go into the inner room, sit down, drink punch, smoke cigarettes, and carry on an animated conversation during the following. Ejlert Lövborg remains standing by the stove. Hedda goes to the writing table.*)

Hedda (in a raised voice):   Perhaps you'd like to look at some snapshots, Mr. Lövborg. You know, Tesman and I did some sightseeing in the Tyrol, on our way home. I'd so love to show you— (*She brings over an album which she lays on the table by the sofa, in the further corner of which she seats herself. Ejlert Lövborg approaches, then stops and stands looking at her. He then takes a chair and sits on her left with his back to the inner room. She opens the album.*) Do you see this group of mountains, Mr. Lövborg? It's the Ortlar group—Oh, yes, Tesman has written the name underneath. "The Ortlar group near Meran."

Lövborg (who has never taken his eyes off her, says softly and slowly):   Hedda Gabler—

Hedda (gives him a hasty look):   Sh!

Lövborg (repeats softly):   Hedda Gabler—

Hedda (looking at the album):   That was my name in the old days, when you and I knew each other.

Lövborg: Then I must learn never to say Hedda Gabler again? Never as long as I live?

Hedda (turning over the pages):   Yes, I'm afraid you must.

Lövborg (in an indignant tone):   Hedda Gabler married! And married to Jörgen Tesman!

Hedda: Such is life!

Lövborg: Oh, Hedda, Hedda, how could you throw yourself away like that?

Hedda (looks at him sharply):   I won't have you say such things.

Lövborg: Why shouldn't I?

(*Tesman comes into the room and goes toward the sofa.*)

Hedda (hears him coming and says in a casual tone):   And this, Mr. Lövborg, is a view from the Ampezzo Valley. Just look at those peaks. (*Looks up at Tesman affectionately.*) Oh, Jörgen dear, what's the name of these curious peaks?

Tesman: Let me see—oh, those are the Dolomites.

Hedda: Oh, yes, those are the Dolomites, Mr. Lövborg.

Tesman: Hedda dear, are you sure you wouldn't like me to bring some
  punch. For yourself, at any rate, eh?
Hedda: Yes, I think I will have some, dear. And perhaps a few biscuits.
Tesman: A cigarette?
Hedda: No, I think not, dear.
Tesman: Very well.

  *(He goes into the inner room again and out to the right. Brack sits in the
  inner room, occasionally keeping an eye on Hedda and Lövborg.)*

Lövborg (softly as before):   Answer me, Hedda. How could you do it?
Hedda (apparently absorbed in the album):   If you go on calling me
  Hedda, I won't talk to you.
Lövborg: Can't I say Hedda even when we're alone?
Hedda: No. You may think it, but you mustn't say it.
Lövborg: I understand. It offends your love for Jörgen Tesman.
Hedda (glances at him and smiles):   Love? How funny you are!
Lövborg: It's not love, then?
Hedda: All the same, no unfaithfulness, remember.
Lövborg: Hedda, answer me just one thing.
Hedda: Sh!

  (Tesman comes from the inner room carrying a small tray.)

Tesman: Here you are! Doesn't this look tempting? *(He puts the tray
  down on the table.)*
Hedda: Why do you bring it yourself, Jörgen?
Tesman (filling the glasses):   I think it's such fun to wait on you, Hedda.
Hedda: But you've poured out two glasses. Mr. Lövborg said he
  wouldn't have any.
Tesman: I know. But Mrs. Elvsted will be here soon, won't she?
Hedda: Oh, yes, of course, Mrs. Elvsted—
Tesman: Had you forgotten her, eh?
Hedda: Yes, you know we were so engrossed in these photographs. Oh,
  Jörgen dear, do you remember this little village?
Tesman: Yes, of course I do. It's the one just below the Brenner Pass.
  Don't you remember? We spent the night there.
Hedda: Oh, yes. And met that gay party of tourists.
Tesman: Yes, that was the place. Just think, if only we could have had you
  with us, Ejlert, eh? *(He goes back to the inner room and sits down with
  Judge Brack.)*
Lövborg: Answer me this one thing, Hedda.
Hedda: Well?
Lövborg: Was there no love in your feeling for *me*, either? Not the
  slightest touch of love?
Hedda: I wonder—To me it seems that we were just two good comrades,
  two thoroughly intimate friends. *(Smiles.)* You especially were
  exceedingly frank!

Lövborg: It was you who made me so.

Hedda: You know, as I look back on it all, I realize there was something very beautiful, something fascinating, something daring—yes, daring—in that secret intimacy, that comradeship no living soul suspected.

Lövborg: Yes, there was, wasn't there, Hedda? Do you remember when I used to come to your home in the afternoon and the General sat over at the window reading his paper, with his back toward us—

Hedda: We two sat on the corner sofa—

Lövborg: Always the same illustrated paper before us—

Hedda: For want of an album, yes!

Lövborg: Do you remember, Hedda, all those wild things I confessed to you? Things no one suspected at the time—my days and nights of passion and frenzy, of drinking and madness—How did you make me talk like that, Hedda? By what power?

Hedda: Power?

Lövborg: Yes. How else can one explain it? And all those devious questions you used to ask—

Hedda: Questions you understood so perfectly—

Lövborg: How could you bring yourself to ask such questions? So candidly, so boldly?

Hedda: In a devious way, if you please.

Lövborg: Yes, but boldly, all the same.

Hedda: How could you bring yourself to answer them, Mr. Lövborg?

Lövborg: That's just what I can't understand. There must have been love at the bottom of it. Perhaps you felt that by making me confess like that you were somehow washing away my sins.

Hedda: No, not quite.

Lövborg: What was your motive, then?

Hedda: Isn't it quite easy to understand, that a young girl, especially if it can be done in secret—

Lövborg: Well?

Hedda: Should be tempted to investigate a forbidden world? A world she's supposed to know nothing about?

Lövborg: So that was it.

Hedda: That had a lot to do with it, I think.

Lövborg: I see; we were both greedy for life. That made us comrades. But why did it end?

Hedda: You were to blame for that!

Lövborg: You broke with me.

Hedda: I realized the danger; you wanted to spoil our intimacy—to drag it down to reality. You talk of my boldness, my candor—why did you try to abuse them?

Lövborg (clenching his hands):   Why didn't you do as you said? Why didn't you shoot me?

Hedda: Because . . . I have such a fear of scandal.

Lövborg: Yes, Hedda, you are a coward at heart.

Hedda: A terrible coward. (*With a change of tone.*) But after all, it was a lucky thing for you. You found ample consolation at the Elvsteds'.

Lövborg: I know Thea has confided in you.

Hedda: And I suppose you've confided in her—about us?

Lövborg: Not a word. She's too stupid to understand that.

Hedda: Stupid?

Lövborg: About that sort of thing—yes.

Hedda: And I am a coward. (*Leans toward him, without looking him in the eye, says softly:*) Now I'll confide something to you.

Lövborg (intensely):   Well?

Hedda: My not daring to shoot you—

Lövborg: Yes?

Hedda: That was not my greatest cowardice that evening.

Lövborg (looks at her a moment, understands, and whispers passionately): Oh, Hedda, Hedda Gabler! I begin to understand the real meaning of our comradeship. You and I!—You see, it *was* your craving for life—

Hedda (softly, with a keen look):   Be careful! Believe nothing of the sort. (*It has begun to get dark. The hall door is opened by Berte. Hedda closes the album with a bang and calls out smilingly:*) At last! Thea darling!— (*Mrs. Elvsted enters from the hall. She is in evening dress. The door is closed behind her. Hedda, still on the sofa, stretches out her arms toward her.*) Darling little Thea, I thought you were never coming!

(*In passing, Mrs. Elvsted lightly greets the gentlemen in the inner room, then goes to the table and gives Hedda her hand. Ejlert Lövborg rises. He and Mrs. Elvsted greet each other with a silent nod.*)

Mrs. Elvsted: Shouldn't I go and say good evening to your husband?

Hedda (puts her arm around Mrs. Elvsted and leads her toward sofa):   No, we needn't bother about them. I expect they'll soon be off.

Mrs. Elvsted: Are they going out?

Hedda: Yes. To a wild party!

Mrs. Elvsted (quickly. To Lövborg):   You're not going, are you?

Lövborg: No.

Hedda: No. Mr. Lövborg is staying here with us.

(*Lövborg sits down again on the sofa.*)

Mrs. Elvsted (takes a chair and starts to sit beside him):   Oh, how nice it is to be here!

Hedda: No, no, little Thea, not there! You be a good girl and sit here, next to me. I'll sit between you.

Mrs. Elvsted: Just as you like. (*She goes round the table and sits on the sofa to Hedda's right. Lövborg sits down again.*)

Lövborg (to Hedda, after a short pause):   Isn't she lovely to look at?

Hedda (lightly stroking her hair):   Only to look at?

Lövborg: We're two real comrades, she and I. We have absolute faith in each other. We can talk with perfect frankness.

Hedda: Not in a devious way, Mr. Lövborg.

Lövborg: Well—

Mrs. Elvsted (softly, clinging to Hedda): Oh, I'm so happy, Hedda! You know—he actually says I've inspired him in his work.

Hedda (looks at her and smiles): Does he really, dear?

Lövborg: And then she has such courage, Mrs. Tesman.

Mrs. Elvsted: Good heavens, courage!

Lövborg: Tremendous courage where your comrade is concerned.

Hedda: God, yes, courage! If one only had that!

Lövborg: What then?

Hedda: Then life might perhaps be endurable, after all. . . . (*With a sudden change of tone.*) Now, my darling little Thea, you must have a nice glass of cold punch.

Mrs. Elvsted: No, thank you. I never take anything like that.

Hedda: Then how about you, Mr. Lövborg?

Lövborg: I don't either, thank you.

Mrs. Elvsted: No, he doesn't either.

Hedda (looks at him intently): But if I want you to.

Lövborg: It makes no difference.

Hedda (laughs): Poor me! Have I no power over you at all, then?

Lövborg: Not in that respect.

Hedda: No, but seriously. I really think you ought to take it for your own sake.

Mrs. Elvsted: Why, Hedda—

Lövborg: How do you mean?

Hedda: People might begin to suspect that you weren't quite sure, quite confident of yourself.

Mrs. Elvsted (softly): Don't, Hedda.

Lövborg: People may suspect whatever they like.

Mrs. Elvsted (happily): Yes, let them.

Hedda: You should have seen Judge Brack's face a moment ago. . . .

Lövborg: Indeed?

Hedda: His contemptuous smile when you didn't dare join them in there.

Lövborg: Didn't dare! I simply preferred to stay here and talk to you.

Mrs. Elvsted: That's natural enough, Hedda.

Hedda: That's not what Judge Brack thought. You should have seen him smile and look at Tesman when you didn't dare go to his ridiculous little party.

Lövborg: Didn't dare! You say I didn't dare!

Hedda: No, *I* don't say it—but that's how Judge Brack looks at it.

Lövborg: Well, let him.

Hedda: So you're not going with them?

Lövborg: No, I'm staying here with you and Thea.

Mrs. Elvsted: Yes, Hedda, of course, he is.

Hedda (smiles and nods approvingly to Lövborg): There, you see! Firm as a rock. Faithful to all good principles now and forever. That's how a man should be. (*Turns to Mrs. Elvsted and says with a caress:*) What did I tell you this morning, Thea? Didn't I tell you not to be upset?

Lövborg (amazed): Upset?

Mrs. Elvsted (terrified): Hedda—! *Please*, Hedda.

Hedda: You see? Now are you convinced? You haven't the slightest reason to be so anxious and worried. . . . . There! Now we can all three enjoy ourselves.

Lövborg (with a start): What does all this mean, Mrs. Tesman?

Mrs. Elvsted: Oh, God! What are you doing, Hedda?

Hedda: Be careful! That horrid Judge is watching you.

Lövborg: So you were anxious and worried on my account?

Mrs. Elvsted (softly, miserably): Oh, Hedda, you've ruined everything.

Lövborg (looks at her intently for a moment. His face is distorted): Well, my comrade! So that's all your faith amounts to!

Mrs. Elvsted (imploringly): You *must* listen to me, Ejlert—

Lövborg (takes one of the glasses of punch, raises it, and says in a low, hoarse voice): Your health, Thea! (*He empties the glass, puts it down, and takes the second one.*)

Mrs. Elvsted (softly): Hedda, Hedda, how could you do this?

Hedda: I do it? I? Are you crazy?

Lövborg: And your health, too, Mrs. Tesman. Thanks for the truth. Long live the truth! (*He empties the glass and is about to fill it again.*)

Hedda (lays her hand on his arm): There, there! No more for the present. You're going to the party, remember.

Lövborg (putting down the glass): Now, Thea, be honest with me.

Mrs. Elvsted: Yes?

Lövborg: Did your husband know you came after me?

Mrs. Elvsted (wringing her hands): Ejlert . . .

Lövborg: It was arranged between you, wasn't it, that you should come to town and keep an eye on me. I dare say the old man suggested it himself. No doubt he needed my help in the office. Or perhaps it was at the card table he missed me.

Mrs. Elvsted (softly, in great distress): Ejlert! Ejlert!

Lövborg (seizes the glass and is about to fill it): Let's drink to the old sheriff, too!

Hedda (preventing him): No more now. Remember you're going to read your manuscript to Jörgen.

Lövborg (calmly, putting down the glass): I'm behaving like a fool, Thea. Try and forgive me, my dear, dear comrade. You'll see—I'll prove to you—I'll prove to everyone, that I'm all right again. I'm back on my feet. Thanks to you, Thea.

Mrs. Elvsted (Radiant): Oh, thank God!

(In the meantime Brack has looked at his watch. He and Tesman rise and come into the drawing room.)

Brack (Takes up his hat and overcoat): Well, Mrs. Tesman, it's time to go.
Hedda: I suppose it is, Judge.
Lövborg (rising): I've decided to join you, Judge.
Mrs. Elvsted (softly, imploringly): Oh, Lövborg, don't!
Hedda (pinching her arm): Sh! They'll hear you.
Lövborg (to Brack): Since you were kind enough to invite me.
Brack: You've changed your mind?
Lövborg: Yes, if you don't mind.
Brack: I'm delighted.
Lövborg (putting the manuscript in his pocket, to Tesman): I should like to show you one or two things before the manuscript goes to press.
Tesman: Just think, how delightful! But, Hedda, dear, in that case, how is Mrs. Elvsted to get home?
Hedda: Oh, we shall manage, somehow.
Lövborg (looking toward the ladies): Mrs. Elvsted? Of course, I'll come back and fetch her. (*Comes nearer.*) Around ten o'clock, Mrs. Tesman. Will that do?
Hedda: That will be splendid, Mr. Lövborg.
Tesman: Well, then, that's settled. But you mustn't expect me so early, Hedda.
Hedda: Oh, you can stay as long as you like, Jörgen.
Mrs. Elvsted (with suppressed anxiety): Well, then, Mr. Lövborg, I'll wait here till you come.
Lövborg (with his hat in his hand): That's understood, Mrs. Elvsted.
Brack: Well, gentlemen, shall we start? I hope we're going to have a very jolly time, as a certain fair lady puts it.
Hedda: If only the fair lady could be there, unseen, Judge.
Brack: Why unseen?
Hedda: So as to share a little in your unbridled fun.
Brack (laughs): I shouldn't advise the fair lady to try it.
Tesman (also laughing): Come. You're a nice one, Hedda. Think of that!
Brack: Well, good-bye. Good-bye, ladies!
Lövborg (bowing): About ten o'clock then.
Hedda: Yes, Mr. Lövborg!

(Brack, Lövborg, and Tesman go out by the hall door. Simultaneously, Berte comes in from the inner room with a lighted lamp which she puts on the drawing room table; she goes out again through the inner room.)

Mrs. Elvsted (who has risen and paces restlessly about the room): Hedda, what will come of all this!
Hedda: At ten o'clock he will be here, with vine leaves in his hair. Flushed and fearless!
Mrs. Elvsted: If I could only believe that—

Hedda: And then, you see, he will have regained confidence in himself. He'll be a free man forever and ever.

Mrs. Elvsted: Pray God you may be right.

Hedda: I am right! It will be as I say. (*Rises and approaches her.*) Doubt him as much as you like. I believe in him. Now we shall see—

Mrs. Elvsted: You have some hidden reason for all this, Hedda.

Hedda: Yes, I have. For once in my life I want the power to shape a human destiny.

Mrs. Elvsted: But surely, you have that!

Hedda: I haven't. I never have had.

Mrs. Elvsted: But what about your husband?

Hedda: Do you think he's worth bothering about! If you could only understand how poor I am; and that you should be allowed to be so rich!—(*She flings her arms round her passionately.*) I think I shall have to burn your hair off, after all!

Mrs. Elvsted: Let me go! Let me go! I'm afraid of you, Hedda!

Berte (at the center opening):   Supper's ready, ma'am.

Hedda: Very well, we're coming.

Mrs. Elvsted: No, no! I'd rather go home alone. Now—at once!

Hedda: Nonsense! You'll do nothing of the sort, you silly little thing. You'll have some supper and a nice cup of tea and then at ten o'clock Ejlert Lövborg will be here with vine leaves in his hair— (*She almost drags Mrs. Elvsted toward the doorway.*)

ACT III

Scene: The room at the Tesmans'. The curtains of the center doorway are closed as well as the curtains of the glass door. The shaded lamp on the table is turned low. In the stove, of which the door stands open, there has been a fire which is now nearly burnt out.

Mrs. Elvsted, wrapped in a large shawl, reclines in the armchair close to the stove with her feet on a footstool. Hedda lies asleep on the sofa, covered with a rug.

Mrs. Elvsted (after a pause, suddenly straightens up in her chair and listens eagerly. Then she sinks back wearily and says softly and plaintively): Not yet—Oh God!—Oh God!—Not yet—

(Berte slips cautiously in by the hall door. She has a letter in her hand.)

Mrs. Elvsted (turns and whispers eagerly):   Did someone come?

Berte (softly):   A girl just brought this letter, ma'am.

Mrs. Elvsted (quickly, stretching out her hand):   A letter! Give it to me!

Berte: It's for Dr. Tesman, ma'am.

Mrs. Elvsted: Oh.

Berte: Miss Tesman's maid brought it. I'll just put it on the table.

Mrs. Elvsted: Yes, do.

Berte (puts down the letter): I think I'd better put out the lamp, ma'am.

Mrs. Elvsted: You might as well—it must be nearly daylight.

Berte (puts out the lamp): It *is* daylight, ma'am.

Mrs. Elvsted: So it is! Broad daylight—and no one's come home yet!

Berte: Lord bless you, ma'am—I thought something like this would happen.

Mrs. Elvsted: You did?

Berte: Yes—when I saw them go off with a—certain gentleman, last night—we used to hear plenty about him in the old days.

Mrs. Elvsted: Sh! Not so loud! You'll wake Mrs. Tesman—

Berte (looks toward the sofa and sighs): Yes, you're right—let her sleep, poor thing. Shall I make up the fire, ma'am?

Mrs. Elvsted: Thank you—you needn't trouble—

Berte: Very well, ma'am. (*She goes out softly by the hall door.*)

Hedda (wakes at the closing of the door and looks up): What—what was that?

Mrs. Elvsted: It was just the maid—

Hedda (looks round her): What are we doing in here? Oh yes! Now I remember! (*She sits up on the sofa, stretches herself, and rubs her eyes.*) What's the time, Thea?

Mrs. Elvsted (looks at her watch): It's past seven.

Hedda: When did Jörgen get home?

Mrs. Elvsted: He hasn't come.

Hedda: Not home yet?

Mrs. Elvsted (rising): No one has come.

Hedda: And we were fools enough to sit up half the night—watching and waiting!

Mrs. Elvsted (wringing her hands): And waiting in such terrible anxiety!

Hedda (yawns, and says with her hand in front of her mouth): Well—we might have spared ourselves the trouble.

Mrs. Elvsted: Did you manage to get a little sleep?

Hedda: Yes, I believe I slept quite well—didn't you?

Mrs. Elvsted: I couldn't, Hedda—I couldn't possibly!

Hedda (rises and goes toward her): There, there! There's nothing to worry about! It's easy to see what's happened.

Mrs. Elvsted: What—tell me!

Hedda: Brack's party probably dragged on for hours—

Mrs. Elvsted: I expect that's true, but still—

Hedda: —and probably Tesman didn't want to come home and wake me up in the middle of the night—perhaps he was in no condition to show himself, after the famous party.

Mrs. Elvsted: But where could he have gone?

Hedda: To his aunts', of course!—I expect he went there to sleep it off. They always keep his old room ready for him.

Mrs. Elvsted: No, he can't be there. That letter just came for him, from Miss Tesman.

Hedda: Letter? (*looks at the address*) Oh, yes! It's from Aunt Juliane. Well—then I suppose he stayed at Judge Brack's. As for Ejlert Lövborg—he is sitting with vine leaves in his hair, reading his manuscript.

Mrs. Elvsted: You're talking nonsense, Hedda! You know you don't believe a word of it—

Hedda: What a little ninny you are, Thea!

Mrs. Elvsted: Yes, I'm afraid I am—

Hedda: And how dreadfully tired you look!

Mrs. Elvsted: I am—dreadfully tired.

Hedda: Now you do exactly as I tell you! You go into my room—lie down on the bed—and get a little rest.

Mrs. Elvsted: No, no!—I'd never be able to sleep.

Hedda: Of course you would.

Mrs. Elvsted: Besides, your husband should be back soon; I must find out at once—

Hedda: I'll tell you the moment he arrives—

Mrs. Elvsted: You promise, Hedda?

Hedda: Yes—you can count on me—Go on in now, and have a good sleep.

Mrs. Elvsted: Thanks—I will try. (*She goes out through the inner room.*)

(*Hedda goes to the glass door and opens the curtains. Bright daylight streams into the room. She takes a small mirror from the writing table, looks at herself in it, and tidies her hair. Then she goes to the hall door and rings the bell. A few moments later Berte appears at the hall door.*)

Berte: Did you ring, ma'am?

Hedda: Yes—do something to the fire—I'm absolutely frozen.

Berte: Certainly, ma'am—I'll make it up at once. (*She rakes the embers together and puts on a piece of wood. She stops and listens.*) That was the front door, ma'am.

Hedda: See who it is—I'll look after the fire.

Berte: It'll soon burn up, ma'am.

(*She goes out by the hall door. Hedda kneels on the footstool and puts several pieces of wood in the stove. After a short pause Jörgen Tesman comes in from the hall. He looks tired and rather serious. He tiptoes up toward the center opening and is about to slip through the curtains.*)

Hedda (At the stove, without looking up): Good morning, Jörgen!

Tesman (Turns): Hedda! (*Approaches her*) Good heavens—are you up so early, eh?

Hedda: Yes, I'm up very early today, Jörgen.

Tesman: And I was sure you'd still be sound asleep—think of that, Hedda!

Hedda: Sh! Don't talk so loud. You'll wake Mrs. Elvsted.

Tesman: Did Mrs. Elvsted stay here all night?

Hedda: Naturally—since no one came to call for her.

Tesman: No—I suppose not—

Hedda (closes the stove door and rises):   Well—did you enjoy yourselves?

Tesman: Were you worried about me, Hedda, eh?

Hedda: That would never occur to me—I asked if you'd enjoyed yourselves?

Tesman: Yes, we really did, Hedda. Especially at first—you see, Ejlert read me part of his book. We got there quite early, think of that—and Brack had all sorts of arrangements to make, so Ejlert read to me.

Hedda (sits to the right of table):   Yes?—Well?

Tesman (sits on a stool near the stove):   Hedda, you can't conceive what a book it will be! I believe it's one of the most remarkable things that has ever been written. Think of that!

Hedda: I'm really not very interested, Jörgen.

Tesman: I've something to confess, Hedda—after he'd finished reading, I had such a horrid feeling—

Hedda: A horrid feeling, Jörgen?

Tesman: Yes. I felt quite jealous of Ejlert, because he'd been able to write such a book. Just think, Hedda.

Hedda: Yes, yes! I *am* thinking!

Tesman: It's really appalling, that he, with all his great gifts, should be so utterly incorrigible!

Hedda: Because he has more daring than any of the rest of you?

Tesman: It's not that, Hedda—he's utterly incapable of moderation.

Hedda: Well—tell me what happened.

Tesman: There's only one word to describe it, Hedda—it was an orgy!

Hedda: Did he have vine leaves in his hair?

Tesman: Vine leaves? No, I didn't see any vine leaves—but he made a long incoherent speech in honor of the woman who had inspired him in his work—that was the phrase he used.

Hedda: Did he mention her name?

Tesman: No, he didn't. But I can't help thinking he meant Mrs. Elvsted—just you see!

Hedda: Where did you part?

Tesman: When the party finally broke up, there were only a few of us left—so we came away together. Brack came with us too—he wanted a breath of fresh air; and then we decided we had better take Ejlert home—he was in pretty bad shape, you see.

Hedda: Yes, I dare say.

Tesman: And then, the strangest thing happened, Hedda—the most tragic thing! I'm really almost ashamed to tell you about it—for Ejlert's sake—

Hedda: Oh, do go on, Jörgen!

Tesman: Well—as we were nearing town, you see—I happened to drop a little behind the others—only for a minute or two—think of that!

Hedda: Yes, yes!—Well?

Tesman: And then, as I hurried after them, what do you think I found on the sidewalk, eh?

Hedda: How should I know?

Tesman: You mustn't say a word about it to anyone, Hedda—do you hear? Promise me—for Ejlert's sake.

Hedda: Yes, Jörgen!

Tesman (takes a parcel wrapped in paper from his pocket): Just think, dear—I found this.

Hedda: Isn't that the parcel he had with him yesterday?

Tesman: Yes. It's his precious, irreplaceable manuscript. He had lost it, and hadn't even noticed it. Isn't it tragic, Hedda, that—?

Hedda: Why didn't you give it back to him at once?

Tesman: I didn't dare trust him with it, in the condition he was in.

Hedda: Did you tell any of the others you'd found it?

Tesman: Certainly not! I didn't want them to know—for Ejlert's sake, you see.

Hedda: Then no one knows that Ejlert Lövborg's manuscript is in your possession?

Tesman: No—and no one must know it.

Hedda: What did you say to him afterwards?

Tesman: I didn't get a chance to talk to him again; he and two or three of the others gave us the slip and disappeared—think of that!

Hedda: I suppose they took him home then.

Tesman: Yes, I suppose they did—and Brack went home too.

Hedda: And where have you been gallivanting ever since?

Tesman: Someone suggested we should go back to his house and have an early breakfast there—or perhaps it should be called a late supper—eh? And now—as soon as I have had a little rest and poor Ejlert has had a chance to recover himself a bit—I must take this back to him.

Hedda (stretching out her hand for the parcel): No, Jörgen—don't give it back to him—not right away, I mean. Let me read it first.

Tesman: No, dearest Hedda, I daren't do that. I really dare not.

Hedda: You dare not, Jörgen?

Tesman: Think of the state he'll be in when he wakes up and can't find his manuscript! There's no copy of it, Hedda—think of that! He told me so himself.

Hedda (looks at him searchingly): Tell me, Jörgen—would it be quite impossible to write such a thing over again?

Tesman: Oh, I should think so, Hedda. You see, it's the inspiration—

Hedda: Yes, of course—the inspiration. . . . I suppose it depends on that. (*Lightly.*) By the way, Jörgen, here's a letter for you.

Tesman: Just think—

Hedda (hands it to him):   It came just a little while ago.

Tesman: It's from Aunt Juliane, Hedda! What can it be? (*He puts the parcel down on the other stool, opens the letter, glances through it, and jumps up.*) Oh, Hedda—she says Aunt Rina is dying, poor thing.

Hedda: Well—we were expecting that.

Tesman: And that I must hurry, if I want to see her again—I'll just run over and see them at once.

Hedda (suppressing a smile):   Will you run, Jörgen?

Tesman: Oh, my dearest Hedda—if you could only bring yourself to come with me! Just think!

Hedda (rising. Rejects the idea wearily):   No, no! Don't ask me to do that! I'll have nothing to do with sickness or death. I loathe anything ugly.

Tesman: Well then, in that case—(*Rushing about.*) My hat?—My overcoat?—Oh, in the hall. I do hope I won't be too late, Hedda—eh?

Hedda: Well, after all—if you run, Jörgen—!

(*Berte enters by the hall door.*)

Berte: Judge Brack is here, sir—and wishes to know if you'll see him?

Tesman: At this hour? No, no! I can't possibly—

Hedda: But I'll see him. (*To Berte.*) Ask him to come in, Berte. (*Berte goes. Rapidly, in a whisper.*) Jörgen!— The manuscript! (*She snatches it up from the stool.*)

Tesman: Yes, give it to me!

Hedda: No, no. I'll keep it here till you come back. (*She goes over to the writing table and puts it in the bookcase. Tesman in a frenzy of haste can't get his gloves on. Brack enters from the hall.*)

Hedda (nodding to him):   You're certainly an early bird, Judge.

Brack: I am, aren't I? (*To Tesman.*) Where are you off to in such a hurry?

Tesman: I must rush off to my aunts'. Just think, Aunt Rina is dying, poor thing.

Brack: Dear me, is she? Then don't let me detain you; every moment may be precious.

Tesman: Yes, I really must run—good-bye, good-bye, Hedda—(*He rushes out by the hall door.*)

Hedda (approaching Brack):   I hear the party was more than usually jolly last night, Judge.

Brack: Yes, I've been up all night—haven't even changed my clothes.

Hedda: So I see—

Brack: What has Tesman told you of last night's adventures?

Hedda: Oh, nothing much; some dreary tale about going to someone's house and having breakfast.

Brack: Yes, I've heard about that breakfast party—but Ejlert Lövborg wasn't with them, was he?

Hedda: No—he'd been escorted home.

Brack: By Tesman, you mean?

Hedda: No—by some of the others.

Brack (smiling):   Jörgen Tesman is certainly a naïve creature, Mrs. Hedda.

Hedda: Yes, God knows he is! But, you're very mysterious—what else happened last night?

Brack: Oh, a number of things—

Hedda: Do sit down, Judge, and tell me all about it! (*She sits to the left of the table. Brack sits near her, at the long side of the table.*)—Well?

Brack: I had special reasons for keeping an eye on my guests—or rather some of my guests—last night.

Hedda: One of them being Ejlert Lövborg, I suppose.

Brack: Frankly—yes.

Hedda: This sounds quite thrilling, Judge!

Brack: Do you know where he and some of the others spent the rest of the night?

Hedda: No. Do tell me—if it's not quite unmentionable!

Brack: No. It's by no means unmentionable. Well—they turned up at an extremely gay party.

Hedda: A *very* jolly party, Judge?

Brack: An excessively jolly one!

Hedda: Do go on!

Brack: Lövborg, as well as the others, had been invited some time ago. I knew all about it. But he had refused the invitation, for he had become a reformed character, as you know—

Hedda: At the Elvsteds', yes. But he went all the same?

Brack: Well, you see, Mrs. Hedda, he became somewhat inspired at my place last night—

Hedda: Yes. I heard he was . . . inspired.

Brack: Rather violently inspired, in fact—and so, he changed his mind. We men are not always as high-principled as perhaps we should be.

Hedda: I'm sure you are an exception, Judge. But to get back to Ejlert Lövborg—

Brack: So—to make a long story short—he did finally turn up at Mlle. Diana's residence.

Hedda: Mlle. Diana?

Brack: Yes, it was she who was giving the party—to a very select circle of her friends and admirers.

Hedda: Is she that red-haired woman?

Brack: Precisely.

Hedda: A sort of . . . singer?

Brack: Yes—in her leisure moments. She is also a mighty huntress—of men. You must have heard of her, Mrs. Hedda. In the days of his glory Ejlert Lövborg was one of her most enthusiastic protectors.

Hedda: But how did all this end, Judge?

Brack: In a none-too-friendly fashion, it seems. After greeting him most tenderly, Mlle. Diana finally proceeded to tear his hair out!

Hedda: What?—Lövborg's?

Brack: Yes. It seems he accused her, or her friends, of having robbed him. He kept insisting some valuable notebook had disappeared—as well as various other things. In short, he raised quite a terrific row.

Hedda: What did all this lead to?

Brack: It led to a general free-for-all, in which the women as well as the men took part. Fortunately the police at last appeared on the scene.

Hedda: The police?

Brack: Yes. I'm afraid it may prove an expensive amusement for Ejlert Lövborg—crazy lunatic that he is!

Hedda: How?

Brack: They say he made a violent resistance—half killed one policeman, and tore another one's coat off his back. So they marched him off to the police station.

Hedda: Where did you hear all this?

Brack: From the police themselves.

Hedda (gazing straight before her):   So that's what happened! Then, after all, he had no vine leaves in his hair!

Brack: Vine leaves, Mrs. Hedda?

Hedda (with a change of tone):   Tell me, Judge—why should you be so interested in spying on Lövborg in this way?

Brack: In the first place—I am not entirely indifferent to the fact that during the investigation it will be known that he came directly from my house.

Hedda: You mean, the case will go to court?

Brack: Naturally. However—be that as it may. But I felt it my duty, as a friend of the family, to give you and Tesman a full account of his nocturnal exploits.

Hedda: For what reason, Judge?

Brack: Because I have a shrewd suspicion that he means to use you as a sort of . . . screen.

Hedda: Whatever makes you think that?

Brack: After all—we're not completely blind, Mrs. Hedda. You watch! This Mrs. Elvsted—she'll be in no great hurry to leave town.

Hedda: Well—supposing there were something between them—there must be plenty of other places where they could meet.

Brack: Not a single *home*. From now on, every respectable house will be closed to Ejlert Lövborg.

Hedda: And mine ought to be too, you mean?

Brack: Yes. I admit it would be more than painful to me if he should be welcome here. If this undesirable and superfluous person should be allowed to force his way into the—

Hedda: —the Triangle?

Brack: Precisely. It would simply mean that I should find myself homeless.

Hedda (looks at him with a smile):   I see. So you want to be cock-of-the-walk, Judge. That is your aim.

Brack (nods slowly and speaks in a low voice):   Yes—that is my aim; and for that I will fight with every weapon I can command.

Hedda (her smile vanishing):   I wonder, Judge, now one comes to think of it, if you're not rather a dangerous person.

Brack: Do you think so?

Hedda: I'm beginning to think so. And I'm exceedingly glad that you have no sort of hold over me.

Brack (laughs ambiguously):   Well, well, Mrs. Hedda—perhaps you're right. If I had, who knows what I might be capable of.

Hedda: Come now! Come, Judge! That sounds almost like a threat.

Brack (rising):   Not at all! For the Triangle, it seems to me, ought, if possible, to be based on mutual understanding.

Hedda: There I entirely agree with you.

Brack: Well—now I've said all I had to say—I'd better be off. Good-bye, Mrs. Hedda. (*Crossing toward the glass door.*)

Hedda (rising):   Are you going through the garden, Judge?

Brack: Yes, it's a short cut for me.

Hedda: Yes—and then it's the back way, isn't it?

Brack: Very true; I've no objection to back ways. They are rather intriguing at times.

Hedda: When there's shooting going on, you mean?

Brack (at the glass door, laughingly):   People don't shoot their tame poultry, I fancy.

Hedda (also laughing):   And certainly not the cock-of-the-walk, Judge! Good-bye!

(*They exchange laughing nods of farewell. He goes. She closes the glass door after him. Hedda, now serious, stands looking out. She goes up and peeps through the portieres into the inner room. Then goes to the writing table, takes Lövborg's parcel from the bookcase, and is about to examine it. Berte is heard speaking loudly in the hall. Hedda turns and listens. She hurriedly locks the parcel in the drawer and puts the key on the inkstand. Ejlert Lövborg, wearing his overcoat and carrying his hat in his hand, tears open the hall door. He looks somewhat confused and excited.*)

Lövborg (turns toward the hall):   I will go in, I tell you! (*He closes the door, turns, sees Hedda, at once controls himself and bows.*)

Hedda (at the writing table):   Well, Mr. Lövborg! Isn't it rather late to call for Thea?

Lövborg: And rather early to call on you—forgive me.

Hedda: How do you know Thea's still here?

Lövborg: They told me at her lodgings she'd been out all night.

Hedda (goes to the table):   Did you notice anything odd in their manner when they told you that?

Lövborg (looks at her inquiringly):   Anything odd?

Hedda: Didn't they seem to think it—a little—queer?

Lövborg (suddenly understanding):   Oh, of course! I see what you mean. I suppose I'm dragging her down with me—However, I didn't notice anything. I suppose Tesman isn't up yet?

Hedda: No—I don't think so—

Lövborg: When did he get home?

Hedda: Oh, very late.

Lövborg: Did he tell you anything?

Hedda: He just said it had all been very jolly at Judge Brack's.

Lövborg: Nothing else?

Hedda: No, I don't believe so. In any case, I was so dreadfully sleepy—

(*Mrs. Elvsted comes in through the portieres from the inner room. She goes to him.*)

Mrs. Elvsted: Ejlert! At last!

Lövborg: Yes—at last—and too late!

Mrs. Elvsted (looks at him anxiously):   What is too late?

Lövborg: Everything's too late now—it's all up with me.

Mrs. Elvsted: No, no! You mustn't say that!

Lövborg: You'll say the same when you hear—

Mrs. Elvsted: I don't want to hear anything!

Hedda: Perhaps you'd rather talk to her alone? I'll leave you.

Lövborg: No! Stay, please—I beg of you!

Mrs. Elvsted: But I don't want to hear anything, I tell you.

Lövborg: I don't intend to talk about last night, Thea—

Mrs. Elvsted: No?

Lövborg: No. I just want to tell you that now we must part.

Mrs. Elvsted: Part?

Hedda (involuntarily):   I knew it!

Lövborg: I no longer have any use for you, Thea.

Mrs. Elvsted: How can you say that! No more use for me? You'll let me go on helping you—we'll go on working together, Ejlert?

Lövborg: I shall do no more work, from now on.

Mrs. Elvsted (despairingly):   Then, what shall I have to live for?

Lövborg: You must try and live as though you'd never known me.

Mrs. Elvsted: But you know I can't do that!

Lövborg: You must try, Thea. You must go home again.

Mrs. Elvsted (protesting vehemently):   Never! I won't leave you! I won't allow you to drive me away. We must be together when the book appears.

Hedda (whispers, in suspense):   Ah, yes—the book!

Lövborg (looks at her):   My book and Thea's—for that's what it is.

Mrs. Elvsted: Yes—that's true; I feel that. That's why we must be together when it's published. I want to see you showered with praise and honors—and, the joy! I want to share that with you too!

Lövborg: Our book will not be published, Thea.

Mrs. Elvsted: Not published?

Lövborg: No. It never can be.

Mrs. Elvsted (anxiously, with foreboding):   Lövborg—what have you done with the manuscript?

Hedda (watches him intently):   Yes—the manuscript?

Mrs. Elvsted: Where is it?

Lövborg: Thea! Don't ask me about it!

Mrs. Elvsted: Yes—I must know—I have a right to know.

Lövborg: Very well, then!—I've torn it into a thousand pieces!

Mrs. Elvsted (cries out):   No—no!

Hedda (involuntarily):   But that's not—

Lövborg (looks at her):   Not true, you think?

Hedda (controlling herself):   Of course it must be—if you say so! But it sounds so utterly incredible!

Lövborg: It's true all the same.

Mrs. Elvsted (wringing her hands):   Torn his own work to pieces!—Oh, God, Hedda!

Lövborg: I've torn my life to pieces—why shouldn't I tear up my work as well!

Mrs. Elvsted: And you did this last night?

Lövborg: Yes. I tore it into a thousand pieces. I scattered them far out on the fjord. I watched them drift on the cool sea water—drift with the current and the wind. In a little while they'll sink, deeper and deeper—just as I shall, Thea.

Mrs. Elvsted: Lövborg—this thing you've done to the book—it's as though you'd killed a little child.

Lövborg: You're right—it was child-murder.

Mrs. Elvsted: Then—how could you?—it was my child too.

Hedda (almost inaudibly):   The child—

Mrs. Elvsted (breathes heavily):   It's all over then—I'll go now, Hedda.

Hedda: But you won't be leaving town?

Mrs. Elvsted: I don't know what I'll do—there's nothing but darkness before me. (*She goes out by the hall door.*)

Hedda (stands waiting a moment):   Then—you're not going to see her home, Mr. Lövborg?

Lövborg: I?—Do you want people to see her with *me*?

Hedda: Of course, I don't know what else may have happened last night—but is it so utterly irreparable?

Lövborg: It won't end with last night—I know that only too well; and the trouble is, that kind of life no longer appeals to me. I have no heart to start it again—she's somehow broken my courage—my defiant spirit!

Hedda (gazes before her):   To think that that pretty little fool should have influenced a man's destiny! (*Looks at him.*) Still, I don't see how you could be so heartless.

Lövborg: Don't say that!

Hedda: What do you expect me to say! You've destroyed her whole purpose in life—isn't that being heartless?

Lövborg: Hedda—to you I can tell the truth.

Hedda: The truth?

Lövborg: First, promise me—give me your word—that Thea will never know.

Hedda: I give you my word.

Lövborg: Good. There was no truth in what I said just now—

Hedda: You mean—about the manuscript?

Lövborg: Yes. I didn't tear it to pieces or scatter it on the fjord—

Hedda: Where is it then?

Lövborg: But I have destroyed it, Hedda—utterly destroyed it!

Hedda: I don't understand.

Lövborg: Just now, Thea said I had killed our child—

Hedda: Yes—so she did—

Lövborg: One can do worse things to a child than kill it—I wanted to spare Thea the truth—

Hedda: What do you mean?

Lövborg: I couldn't bring myself to tell her; I couldn't say to her: Thea, I spent last night in a frenzy of drinking—I took our child with me, dragged it round with me to all sorts of obscene and loathsome places—and I lost our child—lost it! God only knows what's become of it—or who's got hold of it!

Hedda: But, when you come right down to it, this was only a book—

Lövborg: Thea's pure soul was in that book.

Hedda: Yes—so I understand.

Lövborg: Then you must also understand why no future is possible for us.

Hedda: What will you do now?

Lövborg: Nothing. I want to make an end of it. The sooner the better.

Hedda (takes a step toward him):   If you do make an end of it, Ejlert Lövborg—let it be beautiful!

Lövborg (smiles):   Beautiful! Shall I put vine leaves in my hair, as you wanted me to in the old days?

Hedda: No—I don't believe in vine leaves any more. But—for once—let it be beautiful! Good-bye—you must go now—you mustn't come here any more.

Lövborg: Good-bye, Mrs. Tesman. Remember me to Jörgen Tesman.
    (*He's on the point of going.*)

Hedda: No, wait!—I want you to take something of mine with you—as a token—(*She goes to the writing table, opens the drawer, and the pistol case. Goes back to Lövborg, carrying one of the pistols.*)

Lövborg (looks at her):   This? Is this the token?
Hedda (nods slowly):   Do you remember it? It was aimed at you once.
Lövborg: You should have used it then.
Hedda: Take it!—Use it now!
Lövborg (puts the pistol in his inner pocket):   Thanks.
Hedda: But let it be—beautiful, Ejlert Lövborg! Promise me that!
Lövborg: Good-bye, Hedda Gabler.

> (*He goes out by the hall door. Hedda listens at the door a moment. Then she goes to the writing table and takes out the parcel with the manuscript, peeps inside the cover, half takes out a few sheets of paper and looks at them. Then she takes the parcel over to the armchair by the stove and sits down. She has the parcel in her lap. In a moment she opens the stove door, then opens the parcel.*)

Hedda (she throws part of the manuscript in the fire and whispers to herself):
Your child, Thea—your child and Ejlert Lövborg's. Darling little
Thea, with the curly golden hair. (*Throws more of the manuscript into
the stove.*) I'm burning your child, Thea. (*Throws in the rest of the
manuscript.*) I'm burning it—burning it—

ACT IV

> *Scene: The same room at the Tesmans'. It is evening. The drawing room
> is dark. In the inner room the hanging lamp over the table is lighted. The
> curtains are drawn over the glass doors. Hedda, dressed in black, paces
> back and forth in the dark room. Then she goes up into the inner room
> and off left. A few chords are heard on the piano. She appears again and
> returns to the drawing room. Berte enters from the right, through the
> inner room, carrying a lighted lamp which she puts down on the table by
> the corner sofa in the drawing room. Her eyes are red with weeping and
> she has black ribbons on her cap. She goes out right, quietly and
> circumspectly. Hedda goes to the glass door, pulls the curtains aside a
> little, and peers out into the darkness. After a moment Miss Tesman
> comes in from the hall. She is in mourning and wears a hat and veil.
> Hedda goes toward her and holds out her hand.*

Miss Tesman: Well, Hedda, here I am, all dressed in black! My poor sister
has found rest at last!
Hedda: As you see, I have heard already. Tesman sent me a note.
Miss Tesman: He promised he would. I wish Rina hadn't left us just
now—this is not the time for Hedda's house to be a house of
mourning.
Hedda (changing the subject):   It is good to know she died peacefully,
Miss Tesman.
Miss Tesman: Yes, her end was so calm, so beautiful. And thank heaven,

she had the joy of seeing Jörgen once more—and bidding him good-bye.—He is not home yet?

Hedda: No. He wrote me he might be detained. But do sit down, Miss Tesman.

Miss Tesman: No, thank you, my dearest Hedda. I should like nothing better, but I have so much to do. I must prepare my darling sister for her burial. She must look her very sweetest when they carry her to her grave.

Hedda: Can I do anything to help?

Miss Tesman: Oh, no, you mustn't think of that! This is no time for Hedda Tesman to take part in such sad work. Nor let her thoughts dwell on it either—

Hedda: H'm—one's! thoughts—!

Miss Tesman (continuing the theme):   How strange life is! At home we shall be sewing a shroud; and soon I expect there will be sewing here, too—but of a different kind, thank God!

(Jörgen Tesman enters by the hall door.)

Hedda: Well! Here you are at last!

Tesman: You here, Aunt Juliane? With Hedda? Think of that!

Miss Tesman: I am just going, my dear boy. Did you get everything done?

Tesman: I'm afraid I forgot half of it. I'll have to run over and see you in the morning. Today my brain's in a whirl! I can't keep my thoughts together.

Miss Tesman: But, my dear Jörgen, you mustn't take it so much to heart.

Tesman: How do you mean?

Miss Tesman: We must be glad for her sake—glad that she has found rest at last.

Tesman: Oh, yes, of course—you are thinking of Aunt Rina.

Hedda: I'm afraid it will be very lonely for you now, Miss Tesman.

Miss Tesman: It will be at first—but I won't let poor Rina's room stay empty for long.

Tesman: Really? Who will you put in it—eh?

Miss Tesman: One can always find some poor invalid who needs to be taken care of.

Hedda: Would you really take such a burden on yourself again?

Miss Tesman: A burden? Heaven forgive you, child, it has been no burden to me.

Hedda: But it's different with a stranger!

Miss Tesman: I simply must have someone to live for—and one soon makes friends with sick folks; and perhaps some day there may be something in this house to keep an old aunt busy.

Hedda: Oh, please don't trouble about us!

Tesman: Just think! What a wonderful time we three might have together if—

Hedda: If—?

Tesman (uneasy):   Nothing. Let's hope things will work out for the best—eh?

Miss Tesman: Well, well, I daresay you two want to have a little talk. (*Smiling.*) And perhaps Hedda may have something to tell you, Jörgen. Good-bye! I must go home to poor Rina. (*Turning at the door.*) How strange it is to think that now Rina is with my poor brother, as well as with me.

Tesman: Yes, think of that, Aunt Juliane! Eh?

(*Miss Tesman goes out by the hall door.*)

Hedda (gives Tesman a cold, searching look):   Aunt Rina's death seems to affect you more than it does Aunt Juliane.

Tesman: Oh, it's not that alone. It's Ejlert I am so terribly upset about.

Hedda (quickly):   Have you heard anything new?

Tesman: I called on him this afternoon. I wanted to tell him the manuscript was safe.

Hedda: Did you see him?

Tesman: No, he wasn't home. But later, I met Mrs. Elvsted and she said he had been here, early this morning.

Hedda: Yes, directly after you had left.

Tesman: And he said that he had torn his manuscript to pieces, eh?

Hedda: That is what he said.

Tesman: Good heavens, he must have gone completely mad! I suppose in that case you didn't dare give it back to him, Hedda.

Hedda: No, he didn't get it.

Tesman: But of course you told him that we had it?

Hedda: No. Did you tell Mrs. Elvsted?

Tesman: No, I thought I had better not. But you ought to have told him. Just think—he might do himself some injury. Give me the manuscript. I'll run over with it at once. Where is it, Hedda? Eh?

Hedda (cold and motionless, leaning against the armchair):   I haven't got it any longer.

Tesman: Haven't got it? What in the world do you mean?

Hedda: I've burnt it—every word of it.

Tesman (starts up in terror):   Burnt! Burnt Ejlert's manuscript!

Hedda: Don't shout so loud. The servant might hear you.

Tesman: Burnt! Why, good God—! No, no, no! It's utterly impossible!

Hedda: It's true, all the same.

Tesman: Do you realize what you have done, Hedda? It is unlawful appropriation of lost property. Think of that! Just ask Judge Brack, he will tell you what that means.

Hedda: It would be wiser not to speak of it—either to Judge Brack or to anyone else.

Tesman: But how could you do anything so unheard of? What put it into your head? What possessed you? Do answer me—

Hedda (suppressing a scarcely perceptible smile):   I did it for your sake,
Jörgen!

Tesman: For my sake!

Hedda: This morning when you told me that he had read it to you—

Tesman: Yes, yes—what then?

Hedda: You admitted that you were jealous of his work.

Tesman: Of course, I didn't mean that literally.

Hedda: All the same—I couldn't bear the thought of anyone putting you
in the shade.

Tesman (in an outburst of mingled doubt and joy):   Hedda? Is this true?
But—but—I have never known you to show your love like that before.
Think of that!

Hedda: Then—perhaps I'd better tell you that—just now—at this time—
(*Violently breaking off.*) No, no; ask Aunt Juliane. She'll tell you all
about it.

Tesman: Oh, I almost think I understand, Hedda. (*Clasping his hands
together.*) Great heavens! Do you really mean it, eh?

Hedda: Don't shout so loud. The servants will hear—

Tesman (laughing with irrepressible joy):   The servants—? Why, how
absurd you are, Hedda! It's only my dear old Berte! Why, I'll run out
and tell her myself!

Hedda (Clenching her hands in despair):   Oh God, I shall die—I shall die
of all this—!

Tesman: Oh what, Hedda? What is it? Eh?

Hedda (coldly, controlling herself):   It's all so ludicrous—Jörgen!

Tesman: Ludicrous! That I should be overjoyed at the news? Still, after
all, perhaps I had better not tell Berte.

Hedda: Why not that—with all the rest?

Tesman: No, no, I won't tell her yet. But I must certainly tell Aunt
Juliane. Oh, she will be so happy—so happy!

Hedda: When she hears that I've burnt Ejlert Lövborg's manuscript—
four your sake?

Tesman: No, of course not—nobody must know about the manuscript.
But I will certainly tell her how dearly you love me, Hedda. She must
share that joy with me. I wonder, now, whether this sort of thing is
usual in young wives? Eh?

Hedda: Why not ask Aunt Juliane that, too?

Tesman: I will, indeed, some time or other. (*Again agitated and
concerned.*) But the manuscript. Good God—the manuscript! I can't
bear to think what poor Ejlert will do now! (*Mrs. Elvsted, dressed as on
her first visit, wearing a hat and coat, comes in from the hall door.*)

Mrs. Elvsted (greets them hurriedly, and says in evident agitation):   Hedda,
dear—please forgive my coming back so soon.

Hedda: What is it, Thea? What has happened?

Tesman: Is it something to do with Ejlert Lövborg, eh?

Mrs. Elvsted: Yes, I am terribly afraid he has met with some accident.

Hedda (seizes her arm):   Ah!—You think so?

Tesman: Why should you think that, Mrs. Elvsted?

Mrs. Elvsted: When I got back to my lodgings—I heard them talking about him. There are all sorts of strange rumors—

Tesman: Yes, I've heard them too! And yet I can bear witness that he went straight home last night. Think of that!

Hedda: What sort of things did they say?

Mrs. Elvsted: Oh, I couldn't quite make it out. Either they knew nothing definite or—in any case, they stopped talking the moment I came in, and I didn't dare question them.

Tesman (moving about the room uneasily):   We must only hope you misunderstood them, Mrs. Elvsted.

Mrs. Elvsted: No, I am sure they were talking about him—they said something about a hospital or—

Tesman: Hospital?

Hedda: No, no! That's impossible!

Mrs. Elvsted: Oh, I am so terribly afraid for him. I finally went to his house to ask after him!

Hedda: You went there yourself, Thea?

Mrs. Elvsted: What else could I do? I couldn't bear the suspense any longer.

Tesman: But you didn't find him—eh?

Mrs. Elvsted: No. And the people there knew nothing about him. They said he hadn't been home since yesterday afternoon.

Tesman: Yesterday! Just think—how could they say that?

Mrs. Elvsted: I am sure something terrible must have happened to him!

Tesman: Hedda dear—supposing I run over and make some inquiries—?

Hedda: No, no! Please don't mix yourself up in this affair.

(*Judge Brack, hat in hand, enters by the hall door which Berte opens and closes behind him. He looks grave and bows silently.*)

Tesman: Oh, it's you, my dear Judge—eh?

Brack: Yes, it's imperative that I see you at once.

Tesman: I can see you have heard the news about Aunt Rina?

Brack: Yes, that among other things.

Tesman: Isn't it sad? Eh?

Brack: Well, my dear Tesman, that depends on how you look at it.

Tesman (looks at him doubtfully):   Has anything else happened?

Brack: Yes.

Hedda (intensely):   Anything sad, Judge?

Brack: That, too, depends on how you look at it, Mrs. Tesman.

Mrs. Elvsted (in an involuntary outburst):   Oh! It's something about Ejlert Lövborg!

Brack (glancing at her):   What makes you think that, Mrs. Elvsted? Perhaps you have already heard something—?

Mrs. Elvsted (confused):   No, no, nothing at all—but—

Tesman: Well, for heaven's sake, tell us. What is it?

Brack (shrugging his shoulders):   Well, I am sorry to say, Ejlert Lövborg has been taken to the hospital—they say he is dying.

Mrs. Elvsted (cries out):   Oh, God! God!

Tesman: To the hospital!! And dying—

Hedda (involuntarily):   So soon then—

Mrs. Elvsted (tearfully):   And we parted in anger, Hedda!

Hedda (in a whisper):   Thea—Thea—be careful!

Mrs. Elvsted (not heeding her):   I must go to him! I must see him alive!

Brack: I'm afraid it is useless, Mrs. Elvsted. No one is allowed to see him.

Mrs. Elvsted: But at least tell me what happened to him? What is it?

Tesman: He didn't try to kill himself—eh?

Hedda: Yes—I am sure he did!

Tesman: Hedda, how can you—?

Brack (not taking his eyes off her):   Unfortunately, you have guessed quite correctly, Mrs. Tesman.

Mrs. Elvsted: Oh, how horrible!

Tesman: Killed himself!—Think of that!

Hedda: Shot himself!

Brack: You are right again, Mrs. Tesman.

Mrs. Elvsted (trying to control herself):   When did it happen, Judge Brack?

Brack: This afternoon—between three and four.

Tesman: But, where did it happen? Eh?

Brack (with a slight hesitation):   Where? Well—I suppose at his lodgings.

Mrs. Elvsted: No, it couldn't have been there—for I was there myself between six and seven.

Brack: Well, then, somewhere else—I don't know exactly. I only know that he was found—he had shot himself . . . through the heart.

Mrs. Elvsted: How horrible! That he should die like that!

Hedda (to Brack):   Through the heart?

Brack: Yes—as I told you.

Hedda: Through the heart—

Tesman: It's absolutely fatal, you say?

Brack: Absolutely! Most likely it is already over.

Mrs. Elvsted: Over—all over—oh, Hedda!

Tesman: You're quite positive of this? Who told you—eh?

Brack (curtly):   One of the police.

Hedda (loudly):   At last, a deed worth doing!

Tesman (terrified):   Good heavens, what are you saying, Hedda?

Hedda: I say, there is beauty in this.

Brack: H'm, Mrs. Tesman—

Tesman: Beauty! Think of that!

Mrs. Elvsted: Oh, Hedda, how can you talk of beauty in such a case?

Hedda: Ejlert Lövborg has made up his own account with life. He had the courage to do—the one right thing.

Mrs. Elvsted: No; no! You mustn't believe that! He did it in delirium!

Tesman: In despair.

Hedda: No! No! He didn't—I'm sure of that!

Mrs. Elvsted: I tell you he must have been delirious—as he was when he tore up our manuscript!

Brack (with a start):   The manuscript? He tore up the manuscript?

Mrs. Elvsted: Yes. Last night.

Tesman (in a low whisper):   Oh, Hedda, we'll never get over this!

Brack: H'm—how very extraordinary.

Tesman (pacing the room):   To think of Ejlert dead! And his book destroyed too—his book that would have made him famous!

Mrs. Elvsted: If only there were some way of saving it—

Tesman: Yes, if only there were!—There's nothing I wouldn't give—

Mrs. Elvsted: Perhaps there is a way, Mr. Tesman.

Tesman: What do you mean?

Mrs. Elvsted (searches in the pocket of her dress):   Look! I have kept all the notes he used to dictate from—

Hedda (takes a step toward her):   Ah—!

Tesman: You have, Mrs. Elvsted?—Eh?

Mrs. Elvsted: Yes. I took them with me when I left home—they're here in my pocket—

Tesman: Do let me see them!

Mrs. Elvsted (hands him a bundle of scraps of paper):   I'm afraid they are dreadfully mixed up—

Tesman: Perhaps, together, we might be able to sort them out—just think!

Mrs. Elvsted: We could try at any rate—

Tesman: We'll do it—we *must* do it—I'll devote my life to it!

Hedda: You, Jörgen? Your life?

Tesman: Or at least, all the time I can spare. My own work will simply have to wait—I owe this to Ejlert's memory . . . you understand, Hedda, eh?

Hedda: You may be right.

Tesman: Now, my dear Mrs. Elvsted, we must pull ourselves together—it is no good brooding over what has happened. Eh? We must try and control our grief as much as possible—

Mrs. Elvsted: Yes, you're right, Mr. Tesman, I *will* try—

Tesman: That's splendid! Now then, let's see—we must go through the notes at once—Where shall we sit? Here? No, no, we'd better go in there—Excuse me, Judge—Come along, Mrs. Elvsted!

Mrs. Elvsted: Oh! If only it were possible—

(Tesman and Mrs. Elvsted go into the inner room. She takes off her hat

*and coat. They sit at the table under the hanging lamp and become
absorbed in examining the papers. Hedda goes toward the stove and sits
down in the armchair. After a moment Brack joins her.)*

Hedda (In a low voice):   Oh, what a sense of freedom there is in this act of
  Ejlert Lövborg's.
Brack: Freedom, Mrs. Hedda? Of course, it is freedom for him.
Hedda: I mean for me. It gives a sense of freedom to know that an act of
  deliberate courage is still possible in this world—an act of spontaneous
  beauty.
Brack (smiles):   H'm—my dear Mrs. Hedda—
Hedda: Oh, I know what you are going to say. For you're a specialist,
  too, in a way—just like—well, you know.
Brack (looks at her intently):   Ejlert Lövborg meant more to you than you
  are willing to admit—even to yourself. Or am I mistaken?
Hedda: I don't answer such questions. I know that Ejlert Lövborg had
  the courage to live his life as he saw it—and to end it in beauty. He
  had the strength and the will to break with life—while still so young.
Brack: It pains me to do so, Mrs. Hedda—but I fear I must rob you of
  this beautiful illusion.
Hedda: Illusion?
Brack: It would soon be destroyed, in any case.
Hedda: What do you mean?
Brack: He did not shoot himself—of his own accord.
Hedda: Not of his own—?
Brack: No, the thing did not happen exactly as I told it.
Hedda (in suspense):   You've concealed something? What is it?
Brack: For poor Mrs. Elvsted's sake, I slightly changed the facts.
Hedda: What are the facts, then?
Brack: First, that he is already dead.
Hedda: At the hospital.
Brack: Yes—without regaining consciousness.
Hedda: What else have you concealed?
Brack: That—the tragedy did not happen at his lodgings—
Hedda: That makes no difference—
Brack: Doesn't it? Not even if I tell you that Ejlert Lövborg was found
  shot in—in Mademoiselle Diana's boudoir?
Hedda (attempts to jump up but sinks back again):   That is impossible,
  Judge. He couldn't have gone there again today.
Brack: He was there this afternoon. He went there to claim something he
  said they had taken from him—talked wildly about a lost child—
Hedda: Ah—that was why—
Brack: I thought he must have meant the manuscript. But now I hear he
  destroyed that himself. So I suppose it must have been his pocketbook.
Hedda: Yes—probably. So, he was found—there.

Brack: Yes. With a discharged pistol in his breast pocket. He had wounded himself mortally.

Hedda: Through the heart!—Yes!

Brack: No—in the bowels.

Hedda (looks at him with an expression of loathing):   How horrible! Everything I touch becomes ludicrous and despicable!—It's like a curse!

Brack: There is something else, Mrs. Hedda—something rather ugly—

Hedda: What is that?

Brack: The pistol he carried—

Hedda (breathless):   What of it?

Brack: He must have stolen it.

Hedda (leaps up):   That is not true! He didn't steal it!

Brack: No other explanation is possible. He *must* have stolen it—hush!

(Tesman and Mrs. Elvsted have risen from the table in the inner room and come into the drawing room.)

Tesman (his hands full of papers):   Hedda dear, it is almost impossible to see under that lamp. Just think!

Hedda: Yes, I am thinking.

Tesman: Do you think you'd let us use your desk, eh?

Hedda: Of course—no, wait! Just let me clear it first.

Tesman: Oh, you needn't trouble, Hedda. There's plenty of room.

Hedda: No, no! Let me do as I say. I'll put all these things in on the piano.

(She has taken something covered with sheet music from under the bookcase, puts some added pieces of music on it, and carries the whole lot into the inner room and off left. Tesman arranges the scraps of paper on the writing table and moves the lamp from the corner table over to it. He and Mrs. Elvsted sit down and resume their work. Hedda returns.)

Hedda (stands behind Mrs. Elvsted's chair, gently ruffling her hair):   Well, darling little Thea—how are you getting on with Ejlert Lövborg's memorial?

Mrs. Elvsted (looks up at her with a disheartened expression):   I'm afraid it's all very difficult—

Tesman: We *must* manage it. We've simply got to do it! And you know sorting out and arranging other people's papers—that's something I'm particularly good at—

(Hedda crosses to the stove and sits down on one of the stools. Brack stands over her, leaning on the armchair.)

Hedda (in a whisper):   What was that you said about the pistol?

Brack (softly):   That he must have stolen it.

Hedda: Why stolen?

Brack: Because any other explanation ought to be out of the question, Mrs. Hedda.

Hedda: Indeed?

Brack (glancing at her): Of course, Ejlert Lövborg was here this morning. Was he not?

Hedda: Yes.

Brack: Were you alone with him?

Hedda: Yes—for a little while.

Brack: Did you leave the room while he was here?

Hedda: No.

Brack: Try to remember. Are you *sure* you didn't leave the room—even for a moment?

Hedda: I might have gone into the hall—just for a moment—

Brack: And where was your pistol case?

Hedda: It was put away in—

Brack: Well, Mrs. Hedda?

Hedda: It was over there on the desk.

Brack: Have you looked since to see if both pistols are there?

Hedda: No.

Brack: Well, you needn't. I saw the pistol Lövborg had with him, and I recognized it at once as the one I had seen yesterday—and before that too.

Hedda: Have you got it by any chance?

Brack: No, the police have it.

Hedda: What will the police do with it?

Brack: Search until they find the owner.

Hedda: Do you think they will succeed?

Brack (bends over her and whispers): No, Hedda Gabler, not so long as I keep silent.

Hedda (gives him a frightened look): And if you do *not* keep silent—what then?

Brack (shrugs his shoulders): One could always declare that the pistol was stolen.

Hedda (firmly): It would be better to die!

Brack (smiling): One *says* such things—but one doesn't *do* them.

Hedda (without answering): And if the pistol were not stolen and the police find the owner? What then?

Brack: Well, Hedda—then—think of the scandal!

Hedda: The scandal!

Brack: The scandal, yes—of which you are so terrified. You'd naturally have to appear in court—both you and Mademoiselle Diana. She would have to explain how the thing happened—whether it was an accident or murder. Did he threaten to shoot her, and did the pistol go off then—or did she grab the pistol, shoot him, afterwards putting it back into his pocket. She might have done that, for she is a hefty woman, this—Mademoiselle Diana.

Hedda: What have I to do with all this repulsive business?

Brack: Nothing. But you will have to answer the question: Why did you give Ejlert Lövborg the pistol? And what conclusion will people draw from the fact that you did give it to him?

Hedda (bowing her head):   That is true. I didn't think of that.

Brack: Well, fortunately, there is no danger as long as I keep silent.

Hedda (looks up at him):   That means you have me in your power, Judge! You have me at your beck and call from now on.

Brack (whispers softly):   Dearest Hedda—believe me—I shall not abuse my advantage.

Hedda: I am in your power, all the same. Subject to your commands and wishes. No longer free—not free! . . . (*Rises impetuously.*) No, I won't endure that thought. Never!

Brack (looks at her half mockingly):   People manage to get used to the inevitable.

Hedda (returns his look):   Yes, perhaps. (*She crosses to the writing table. Suppressing an involuntary smile and imitating Tesman's intonations.*) Well? How's it going, Jörgen, eh?

Tesman: Heaven knows, dear. In any case, it will take months to do.

Hedda (as before):   Think of that! (*She runs her fingers softly through Mrs. Elvsted's hair.*) Doesn't it seem strange to you, Thea? Here you are working with Tesman—as you used to work with Ejlert Lövborg?

Mrs. Elvsted: If I could only inspire your husband in the same way!

Hedda: Oh, no doubt that will come—in time.

Tesman: You know, Hedda—I'm really beginning to feel something of the sort! Why don't you go and talk to Judge Brack again?

Hedda: Is there nothing at all—I can do to help?

Tesman: No, thank you. Not a thing. (*Turning his head.*) You'll have to keep Hedda company from now on, my dear Judge.

Brack (with a glance at Hedda):   It will give me the greatest of pleasure!

Hedda: Thanks. But this evening I feel a little tired. I'll go and lie down on the sofa for a little while.

Tesman: Yes, do that dear—eh?

(*Hedda goes into the inner room and closes the portieres after her. A short pause. Suddenly she is heard playing a wild dance tune on the piano.*)

Mrs. Elvsted (starts up from her chair):   Oh—what's that?

Tesman (runs to the center opening):   Dearest Hedda, don't play dance music tonight! Think of Aunt Rina! And of poor Ejlert!

Hedda (sticks her head out between the curtains):   And of Aunt Juliane. And of all the rest of them—Never mind—From now on, I promise to be quiet. (*She closes the curtains again.*)

Tesman (at the writing table):   I don't think it is good for her to see us at this distressing work; I have an idea, Mrs. Elvsted. You can move over to Aunt Juliane's and then I'll come over in the evenings and we'll work there. Eh?

Mrs. Elvsted: Perhaps that would be the best thing to do.

Hedda (from the inner room):   I can hear what you are saying, Tesman. What am I to do with all those long evenings—here—by myself?

Tesman (turning over the papers):   Oh, I am sure Judge Brack will be kind enough to drop in and see you.

Brack (in the armchair, calls out gaily):   Every single evening, with the very greatest of pleasure, Mrs. Tesman! I'm sure we'll have a very jolly time together, we two.

Hedda (In a loud, clear voice):   Yes, that's what you hope, Judge, isn't it?—Now that you are cock-of-the-walk—

(A shot is heard within. Tesman, Mrs. Elvsted, and Brack leap to their feet.)

Tesman: Now she is playing with those pistols again.

(He throws back the portieres and runs in, followed by Mrs. Elvsted. Hedda lies stretched out on the sofa, dead. Confusion and cries. Berte, alarmed, comes in from the right.)

Tesman (cries out, to Brack):   Shot herself! Shot herself in the temple! Think of that!

Brack (sinks into the armchair, half fainting):   Good God—but—people don't *do* such things!

Research Materials

Henrik Ibsen
NOTES ON *A DOLL HOUSE*   1878

Ibsen's journals and notes give us insight into some of his key beliefs. In his notes to A Doll House, for example, he says that men and women are very different and that a woman cannot be herself because she lives in a masculine society. This selection also shows how Ibsen planned the play, thus giving us a glimpse of the creative process at work. Note that Nora and Torvald first had the name of Stenborg.

NOTES FOR THE MODERN TRAGEDY

There are two kinds of spiritual law, two kinds of conscience, one in man and another, altogether different, in woman. They do not understand each other; but in practical life the woman is judged by man's law, as though she were not a woman but a man.

The wife in the play ends by having no idea of what is right or wrong; natural feeling on the one hand and belief in authority on the other have altogether bewildered her.

A woman cannot be herself in the society of the present day, which is an exclusively masculine society, with laws framed by men and with a judicial system that judges feminine conduct from a masculine point of view.

She has committed forgery, and she is proud of it; for she did it out of love for her husband, to save his life. But this husband with his commonplace principles of honor is on the side of the law and looks at the question from the masculine point of view.

Spiritual conflicts. Oppressed and bewildered by the belief in authority, she loses faith in her moral right and ability to bring up her children. Bitterness. A mother in modern society, like certain insects who go away and die when she has done her duty in the propagation of the race. Love of life, of home, of husband and children and family. Now and then a womanly shaking off of her thoughts. Sudden return of anxiety and terror. She must bear it all alone. The catastrophe approaches, inexorably, inevitably. Despair, conflict, and destruction.

(Krogstad has acted dishonorably and thereby become well-to-do; now his prosperity does not help him, he cannot recover his honor.)

SCENARIO: FIRST ACT

A room comfortably, but not showily, furnished. A door to the right in the back leads to the hall; another door to the left in the back leads to the room or office of the master of the house, which can be seen when the door is opened. A fire in the stove. Winter day.

She enters from the back, humming gaily; she is in outdoor dress and carries several parcels, has been shopping. As she opens the door, a porter is seen in the hall, carrying a Christmas tree. She: Put it down there for the present. (Taking out her purse) How much? Porter: Fifty öre. She: Here is a crown. No, keep the change. The porter thanks her and goes. She continues humming and smiling contentedly as she opens several of the parcels she has brought. Calls off to find out if he is home. Yes! At first, conversation through the closed door; then he opens it and goes on talking to her while continuing to work most of the time, standing at his desk. There is a ring at the hall door; he does not want to be disturbed; shuts himself in. The maid opens the door to her mistress's friend, just arrived in town. Happy surprise. Mutual explanation of the state of affairs. He has received the post of manager in the new joint-stock bank and is to begin at New Year's; all financial worries are at an end. The friend has come to town to look for some small employment in an office or whatever may present itself. Mrs. Stenborg encourages her, is certain that all will turn out well. The maid opens the front door to the debt collector. Mrs. Stenborg terrified; they exchange a few words; he is shown into the office. Mrs. Stenborg and her friend; the circumstances of the collector are touched upon. Stenborg enters in his overcoat; has sent the collector out the other way. Conversation about the friend's affairs; hesitation on his part. He and the friend go out; his wife follows them into the hall; the Nurse enters with the children. Mother and children play. The collector enters. Mrs. Stenborg sends the children out to the left. Big scene between her and him. He goes. Stenborg enters; has met him on the stairs; displeased; wants to know what he came back for? Her support? No intrigues. His wife cautiously tries to pump him. Strict legal answers. Exit to his room. *She*: (repeating her words when the collector went out) But that's impossible. Why, I did it from love!

SECOND ACT

The last day of the year. Midday. Nora and the old Nurse. Nora, driven by anxiety, is putting on her things to go out. Anxious random questions of one kind and another intimate that thoughts of death are in her mind. Tries to banish these thoughts, to make light of it, hopes that something or other may intervene. But what? The Nurse goes off to the left. Stenborg enters from his room. Short dialogue between him and Nora. The Nurse re-enters; looks for Nora; the youngest child is crying. Annoyance and questioning on Stenborg's part; exit the Nurse; Stenborg is going in to the children. Doctor enters. Scene between him and Stenborg. Nora soon re-enters; she has turned back; anxiety has driven her home again. Scene between her, the Doctor, and Stenborg. Stenborg goes into his room. Scene between Nora and the Doctor. The Doctor goes out. Nora alone. Mrs. Linde enters. Scene between her and Nora. Lawyer Krogstad enters. Short scene between him, Mrs. Linde, and Nora. Mrs. Linde in to the children. Scene between Krogstad and Nora. She entreats and implores him for the sake of her little children; in vain. Krogstad goes out. The letter is seen to fall from outside into the letter box. Mrs. Linde re-enters after a short pause. Scene between her and Nora. Half confession. Mrs. Linde goes out. Nora alone. Stenborg enters. Scene between him and Nora. He wants to empty the letter box. Entreaties, jests, half-playful persuasion. He promises to let business wait till after New Year's Day; but at 12 o'clock midnight . . . ! Exit. Nora alone. *Nora:* (looking at the clock) It is five o'clock. Five; seven hours till midnight. Twenty-four hours till the next midnight. Twenty-four and seven—thirty-one. Thirty-one hours to live.

THIRD ACT

A muffled sound of dance music is heard from the floor above. A lighted lamp on the table. Mrs. Linde sits in an armchair and absently turns the pages of a book, tries to read, but seems unable to fix her attention; once or twice she looks at her watch. Nora comes down from the party; so disturbed she was compelled to leave; surprise at finding Mrs. Linde, who pretends that she wanted to see Nora in her costume. Helmer, displeased at her going away, comes to fetch her back. The Doctor also enters, to say good-by. Meanwhile Mrs. Linde has gone into the side room on the right. Scene between the Doctor, Helmer, and Nora. He is going to bed, he says, never to get up again; they are not to come and see him; there is ugliness about a deathbed. He goes out. Helmer goes upstairs again with Nora, after the latter has exchanged a few words of farewell with Mrs. Linde. Mrs. Linde alone. Then Krogstad. Scene and explanation between them. Both go out. Nora and the children. Then she alone. Then Helmer. He takes the letters out of the letter box. Short scene; good night; he goes into his room. Nora in despair prepares for the final step, is already at the door when Helmer enters with the open letter in his hand. Big scene. A ring. Letter to Nora from Krogstad. Final scene. Divorce. Nora leaves the house.

From *Playwrights on Playwrighting*, edited by Toby Cole

Janet Achurch

ON BEING NORA   1889

In this interview, actress Janet Achurch compares the part of Nora with that of Hamlet in terms of its demands on her talent. She also reveals that she likes the role of Nora better than any other she has played. Interestingly, the interviewer's concerns for the children parallel those of the general audience. Janet Achurch feels the children will be taken care of and disregards the charge of "reckless abandonment."

It is not often that any young actress achieves the phenomenal success with which Miss Janet Achurch has brought to a temporary close her dramatic career in the old country. Before *A Doll House* was brought out at the Novelty Theatre almost every one predicted that the attempt would result in disastrous failure. Ibsen as a dramatist had never been brought before the London playgoer, and it was a somewhat daring experiment to begin with such a dish of strong meat as the drama in which the Norwegian poet laid the axe to the root of the conventional idea of matrimonial fine-ladyism. You will be fortunate, very fortunate, said sympathizing friends, if you can keep it running a week, and no doubt but for Miss Achurch's brilliant rendering of the arduous role of the heroine the play would have been numbered among the numerous failures which make up so large a part of the history of the attempts to acclimatize the higher drama on the London stage. Thanks, however, to the extraordinary fidelity with which Miss Achurch represented Ibsen's Nora, the play has had a run of three weeks, and has only been withdrawn because it was impossible to postpone any longer the departure of Miss Achurch and Mr. Charrington for Australia. They start to-day for Brindisi, where they meet the *Ballarat* and take ship for Melbourne. Seldom has any actress had a more brilliant "send off" than that which the creation as the English Nora Helmer has supplied to Miss Achurch; and the following interview will be read with interest by many who usually regard with supreme indifference the sayings and doings of the stars of the London stage.

"Yes," said Miss Achurch, in reply to a question from our representative, "*A Doll House* has been a great success. But it has taken a great deal out of me, and if it had gone on much longer I should have broken down. It is the hardest part I have ever played. Nora is never off the stage for a single moment during the whole of the first and second acts, and in the third act she is only absent for five minutes. The part is heavier than that of Hamlet, and to go through it eight times a week is too great a strain."

"Eight times a week?"

"Yes. We had a morning performance every Wednesday and Saturday, and to go through such a piece twice a day twice a week has told somewhat seriously on me. I shall be delighted to get rest on the voyage out, before beginning again on the Australian boards. As soon as we land in Melbourne we have four months' engagement before us in that city. Then we go to Adelaide and Sydney and perhaps to Brisbane. It will be eighteen months at the least, and two years at the most, before we return home."

"But Nora, how do you like the character?"

"I like Nora better than about 200 roles I have filled since I first appeared on the stage. After Nora I think on the whole I prefer Lady Macbeth. But Nora is a wonderful conception, into the realization of which one can throw one's whole soul."

"Tell me, what is your reading of what Nora will do afterwards?"

"Ibsen leaves every one to form their own idea as to the sequel of his play. It is left an interrogation which every one can answer as he pleases. I think she will come back after a time and try again the experiment of living with Helmer. But it will fail. That man is impossible, utterly impossible. She did right to leave him."

"But the children?"

"Ah! that is another matter. I don't think that was right, but you should remember that it was partly for the sake of the children she went away. She felt herself so utterly unworthy of undertaking their education, and she left them in the hands of a very good nurse."

"At the same time don't you think it was a mistake, the last and crowning illustration of the extent to which her doll-like upbringing worked out its dismal harvest of wrongdoing? Even when she caught a glimpse of a higher ideal and aspired after a nobler life, at that very moment the impulsive weaknesses of the untrained mind asserted itself, and her frantic plunge at the last was as natural an outcome of the moral atmosphere of a doll's house as her forgery or any other of her heedless acts of impulsive ignorance."

"Possibly you are right, but the moral is plain enough in any case. For men the play can hardly be accused of being anything but good. To open their eyes to the consequences of ignoring the moral and intellectual nature of the human being with whom they have allied themselves is surely excellent. For the women, if I may judge from the letters I have received, it has been also useful, nor do I think that it will tend, as some say, to more easy divorce and reckless abandonment of home. What it ought to do is to make them much less reckless about marrying, by showing that a plunge into matrimony in the mere fever of a passionate attachment, without any similarity of taste or common interest in the serious work of life, is to prepare for yourself a terrible awakening."

From The Pall Mall Gazette, 1889

Bernard Shaw   (1856–1950)

HEDDA GABLER   1890

The modern playwright George Bernard Shaw was also an important critic. His work on Ibsen is justifiably famous and his insights are still of value. This discussion of Hedda Gabler concentrates on the qualities Shaw finds difficult to accept in her character. His critical approach is essentially to describe the action of the drama, and while doing so to comment on the motives and morals of the characters. His deepest concerns center on the political and economic issues in the play.

Hedda Gabler has no ethical ideals at all, only romantic ones. She is a typical nineteenth century figure, falling into the abyss between the ideals which do not impose on her and the realities she has not yet discovered. The result is that though she has imagination, and an intense appetite for beauty, she has no conscience, no conviction: with plenty of cleverness, energy, and personal fascination she remains mean, envious, insolent, cruel in protest against others' happiness, fiendish in her dislike of inartistic people and things, a bully in reaction from her own cowardice. Hedda's father, a general, is a widower. She has the traditions of the military caste about her; and these narrow her activities to the customary hunt for a socially and pecuniarily eligible husband. She makes the acquaintance of a young man of genius who, prohibited by an ideal-ridden society from taking his pleasures except where there is nothing to restrain him from excess, is going to the bad in search of his good, with the usual consequences. Hedda is intensely curious about the side of life which is forbidden to her, and in which powerful instincts, absolutely ignored and condemned in her circle, steal their satisfaction. An odd intimacy springs up between the inquisitive girl and the rake. Whilst the general reads the paper in the afternoon, Lövborg and Hedda have long conversations in which he describes to her all his disreputable adventures. Although she is the questioner, she never dares to trust him: all the questions are indirect; and the responsibility for his interpretations rests on him alone. Hedda has no conviction whatever that these conversations are disgraceful; but she will not risk a fight with society on the point: it is easier to practise hypocrisy, the homage that truth pays to falsehood, than to endure ostracism. When he proceeds to make advances to her, Hedda has again no conviction that it would be wrong for her to gratify his instinct and her own; so that she is confronted with the alternative of sinning against herself and him, or sinning against social ideals in which she has no faith. Making the coward's choice, she carries it out with the utmost bravado, threatening Lövborg with one of her father's pistols, and driving him out of the house with all that ostentation of outraged purity which is the instinctive defence of women to whom chastity is not natural, much as libel actions are mostly brought by persons concerning whom libels are virtually, if not technically, justifiable.

Hedda, deprived of her lover, now finds that a life of conformity without faith involves something more terrible than the utmost ostracism: to wit, boredom. This scourge, unknown among revolutionists, is the curse which makes the security of respectability as dust in the balance against the unflagging interest of rebellion, and which forces society to eke out its harmless resources for killing time by licensing gambling, gluttony, hunting, shooting, coursing, and other vicious distractions for which even idealism has no disguise. These licenses, being expensive, are available only for people who have more than enough money to keep up appearances; and as Hedda's father, being in the army instead of in commerce, is too poor to leave her much more than the pistols, her boredom is only mitigated by dancing, at which she gains much admiration, but no substantial offers of marriage.

At last she has to find somebody to support her. A good-natured mediocrity of a professor is the best that is to be had; and though she regards him as a member of an inferior class, and despises almost to loathing his family circle of two affectionate old aunts and the inevitable general servant who has helped to bring him up, she marries him *faute de mieux*, and immediately proceeds to wreck this prudent provision for her livelihood by accommodating his income to her expenditure instead of accommodating her expenditure to his income. Her nature so rebels against the whole sordid transaction that the prospect of bearing a child to her husband drives her almost frantic, since it will not only expose her to the intimate solicitude of his aunts in the course of a derangement of her health in which she can see nothing that is not repulsive and humiliating, but will make her one of his family in earnest.

To amuse herself in these galling circumstances, she forms an underhand alliance with a visitor who belongs to her old set, an elderly gallant who quite understands how little she cares for her husband, and proposes a *ménage à trois* to her. She consents to his coming there and talking to her as he pleases behind her husband's back; but she keeps her pistols in reserve in case he becomes seriously importunate. He, on the other hand, tries to get some hold over her by placing her husband under pecuniary obligations, as far as he can do it without being out of pocket.

Meanwhile Lövborg is drifting to disgrace by the nearest way: drink. In due time he descends from lecturing at the university on the history of civilization to taking a job in an out-of-the-way place as tutor to the little children of Sheriff Elvsted. This functionary, on being left a widower with a number of children, marries their governess, finding that she will cost him less and be bound to do more for him as his wife. As for her, she is too poor to dream of refusing such a settlement in life. When Lövborg comes, his society is heaven to her. He does not dare tell her about his dissipations; but he tells her about his unwritten books, which he never discussed with Hedda. She does not dare to remonstrate with him for drinking; but he gives it up as soon as he sees that it shocks her. Just as Mr. Fearing,° in Bunyan's story, was in a way the bravest of the pilgrims, so this timid and unfortunate Mrs. Elvsted trembles her way to a point at which Lövborg, quite reformed, publishes one book which makes him celebrated for the moment, and completes another, fair-copied in her handwriting, to which he looks for a solid position as an original thinker. But he cannot now stay tutoring Elvsted's children; so off he goes to town with his pockets full of the money the published book has brought him. Left once more in her old lonely plight, knowing that without her, Lövborg will probably relapse into dissipation, and that without him her life will not be worth living, Mrs. Elvsted must either sin against herself and him or against the institution of marriage under which Elvsted purchased his housekeeper. It never occurs to her that she has any choice. She knows that her action will count as "a dreadful thing"; but she sees that she must go; and accordingly Elvsted finds himself without a wife and his children without a governess, and so disappears unpitied from the story.

Now it happens that Hedda's husband, Jörgen Tesman, is an old friend and competitor (for academic honors) of Lövborg, and also that Hedda was a schoolfellow of Mrs. Elvsted, or Thea, as she had better now be called. Thea's first business is to find out where Lövborg is; for hers is no preconcerted elopement: she has hurried to town to keep Lövborg away from the bottle, a design she dare not hint at to himself. Accordingly, the first thing she does in town is to call on the Tesmans, who have just returned from their honeymoon, to beg them to invite Lövborg to their house so as to keep him in good company. They consent, with the result that the two pairs are brought together under the same roof, and the tragedy begins to work itself out.

Hedda's attitude now demands a careful analysis. Lövborg's experience with Thea has enlightened his judgment of Hedda; and as he is, in his gifted way, an arrant *poseur* and male coquet, he immediately tries to get on romantic terms with

---

Mr. Fearing: A character in *A Pilgrim's Progress*.

her (for have they not "a past"?) by impressing her with the penetrating criticism that she is and always was a coward. She admits that the virtuous heroics with the pistol were pure cowardice; but she is still so void of any other standard of conduct than conformity to the conventional ideals, that she thinks her cowardice consisted in not daring to be wicked. That is, she thinks that what she actually did was the right thing; and since she despises herself for doing it, and feels that he also rightly despises her for doing it, she gets a passionate feeling that what is wanted is the courage to do wrong. This unlooked-for reaction of idealism, this monstrous but very common setting-up of wrong-doing as an ideal, and of the wrongdoer as hero or heroine *qua* wrongdoer, leads Hedda to conceive that when Lövborg tried to seduce her he was a hero, and that in allowing Thea to reform him he has played the recreant. In acting on this misconception she is restrained by no consideration for any of the rest. Like all people whose lives are valueless, she has no more sense of the value of Lövborg's or Tesman's or Thea's lives than a railway shareholder has of the value of a shunter's. She gratifies her intense jealousy of Thea by deliberately taunting Lövborg into breaking loose from her influence by joining a carouse at which he not only loses his manuscript, but finally gets into the hands of the police through behaving outrageously in the house of a disreputable woman whom he accuses of stealing it, not knowing that it has been picked up by Tesman and handed to Hedda for safe keeping. Now Hedda's jealousy of Thea is not jealousy of her bodily fascination: at that Hedda can beat her. It is jealousy of her power of making a man of Lövborg, of her part in his life as a man of genius. The manuscript which Tesman gives to Hedda to lock up safely is in Thea's handwriting. It is the fruit of Lövborg's union with Thea: he himself speaks of it as "their child." So when he turns his despair to romantic account by coming to the two women and making a tragic scene, telling Thea that he has cast the manuscript, torn into a thousand pieces, out upon the fiord; and then, when she is gone, telling Hedda that he has brought "the child" to a house of ill-fame and lost it there, she, deceived by his posing, and thirsting to gain faith in the beauty of her own influence over him from a heroic deed of some sort, makes him a present of one of her pistols, only begging him to "do it beautifully," by which she means that he is to kill himself in some manner that will make his suicide a romantic memory and an imaginative luxury to her forever. He takes it unblushingly, and leaves her with the air of a man who is looking his last on earth. But the moment he is out of sight of his audience, he goes back to the house where he still supposes the manuscript to lie stolen, and there renews the wrangle of the night before, using the pistol to threaten the woman, with the result that he gets shot in the abdomen, leaving the weapon to fall into the hands of the police. Meanwhile Hedda deliberately burns "the child." Then comes her elderly gallant to disgust her with the unromantically ugly details of the deed which Lövborg promised her to do so beautifully, and to make her understand that he himself has now got her into his power by his ability to identify the pistol. She must either be the slave of this man, or else face the scandal of the connection of her name at the inquest with a squalid debauch ending in a murder. Thea, too, is not crushed by Lövborg's death. Ten minutes after she has received the news with a cry of heartfelt loss, she sits down with Tesman to reconstruct "the child" from the old notes she has piously preserved. Over the congenial task of collecting and arranging another man's ideas Tesman is perfectly happy, and forgets his beautiful Hedda for the first time. Thea the trembler is still mistress of the situation, holding the dead Lövborg, gaining Tesman, and leaving Hedda to her elderly admirer, who smoothly remarks that he will answer for Mrs. Tesman not being bored whilst her husband is occupied with Thea in putting the pieces of the book together. However, he has again reckoned without General Gabler's second pistol. She shoots herself then and there; and so the story ends.

From *The Quintessence of Ibsenism*

Jan Kott   (b. 1914)

ON *HEDDA GABLER*   1984

Kott's analysis of the play concentrates on the various levels of sexual symbolism found especially in Hedda's pistols. Kott raises the possibility of a sexual neurosis in the drama. His approach is somewhat Freudian, especially in the way in which he interprets the symbols, the neuroses, and the sexual overtones throughout the drama. Kott examines one production for its exploration of lesbian themes. He also explores other questions relative to the inversion of libido and its effect on sexual drives.

Chekhov wrote: "If in the first act a gun hangs on the wall, in the last act it must go off." In laying down this dramatic precept, he must surely have had *Hedda Gabler* in mind. Hedda inherits two pistols from her father. She fires the first one over Judge Brack's head when he approaches the house from the garden; and again at the end, when she shoots herself. The other pistol is fired offstage. It kills Eilert Lövborg. But the two pistols in *Hedda Gabler* are not only props exploited by Ibsen with iron-clad dramatic logic and preordained consequences; they also have sexual undertones. A Scandinavian Madame Bovary, well read in romantic novels, gives Lövborg a pistol: "use it now . . . and beautifully." But the fatal shot wounds him "in the stomach—more or less," and is fired in the parlor of the red-haired Mademoiselle Diana.

Ibsen's setting for *Hedda Gabler* is striking. The action takes place in a spacious salon with French windows which open out on a veranda and a garden in the "fashionable part of town," not a fjord. The windows are curtained; the theater had already learned the advantages of gaslight.

In the first scene, Hedda orders the curtains drawn. She can't stand sunlight. This is our first glimpse of her character. The salon is spacious and the furniture arrangement makes it possible for two separate conversations to be carried on at the same time. The old-fashioned *a parte*° is no longer necessary. Chekhov borrowed this "contrapuntal" dialogue from Ibsen and masterfully refined it.

The crucial part of the stage design is the room in the background, with a huge portrait of "a handsome, elderly man in a general's uniform" hanging on the wall behind the sofa. In the last scene Hedda will enter this room, draw the curtains, and shoot herself in front of her father's portrait. Hedda Tesman, two months pregnant, kills Hedda Gabler. The inner room, whose only exit leads to the salon in the foreground, is at once the concrete and the symbolic setting of the conflict between the Father/superego and the id. By shooting herself, Hedda kills the shadow of her Father and the child she never wanted. The "shadow" of

---

a parte: Keeping different conversations separate from one another as if in different spaces.

the father kills the daughter. In contrast to the earlier dramas [by Ibsen], *Lady from the Sea* and *Rosmersholm*, where the prehistory of the conflicts, traumas, and sexual complexes festers beneath the surface, and though continuing to grow they are never seen, in *Hedda Gabler* nothing remains unspoken.

In this case study of a neurosis, the mother's place is left empty. Hedda was raised by her father, who would have preferred a son. She rode horses and learned to shoot guns. In school, like a tomboy, she pulled her girlfriends' hair. She can barely resist pulling Thea's blond locks in Act II. In the last *Hedda Gabler* I saw, in Bochum in 1977, Peter Zadek directed the scene of Hedda's and Thea's drinking bout with distinct lesbian undertones. It is an extreme though not arbitrary reading of the text. In this record of sexual neurosis, the inversion and displacement of libido are intended. Thirty-year-old Hedda Gabler is frigid.

General Gabler's daughter not only wants to rule in a man's world. Unable to assume her female sexual role, she escapes by playing out the male one in her imagination. She demands that Lövborg initiate her into masculine rites and describe his visits to the red-haired Diana. Imaginary sex is vicarious. Hedda, rejecting the traditional roles of wife and mother, is condemned to live vicariously, full of the frustration and sense of emptiness which she calls deadly boredom. Madame Bovary's love affairs with shallow men were substitutions for the romantic ecstasies she read about in contemporary novels. For General Gabler's daughter these flights and escapes are ruled out. She has only her inner room "with its heavy curtains and her father's portrait."

It is not only sexual fulfillment that Hedda strives for through imagination. Until the very last scene, all her passions and hatreds are realized only by acts of substitution. The manuscript of Lövborg's new book is twice called his and Thea's "child"; Hedda commits a substitute "infanticide" by burning it in the fireplace. The pistol shot above Judge Brack's head was a substitute murder and a substitute sexual act. Fear paralyzed her twice before: once when she was afraid to shoot Lövborg for his aggressive advances, and then a second time when she was afraid to sleep with him. Handing the pistol to Lövborg is murder by intent: The shot that kills him, in keeping with the logic of the dramaturgy, symbolically castrates him as well.

In coded messages, myths, dreams, and unconscious acts, opposite terms are interchangeable: They assume the guise of their antitheses. As in Racine and Chekhov (although in Chekhov it is deeply hidden), the appeal of death in Ibsen disguises itself as the pulse of life, the instinct toward self-destruction is masked as libido. *Hedda Gabler* appears to return to the realistic technique of the earlier dramas, but along with *Rosmersholm*, it marks the beginning of Ibsen's last cycle of plays, from *Little Eyolf* to *When We Dead Awaken*, each of which repeats the theme of sexual frustration leading to self-destruction. With the exception of his final masterpiece, *John Gabriel Borkman*, in all these plays the balance between the realistic world and its symbolic projection is broken.

In his biography of Ibsen (1957), Michael Meyer entitled his chapter on *Hedda Gabler* "Portrait of the Dramatist as a Young Woman." "*Madame Bovary— c'est moi*," Flaubert once wrote, and Hedda Gabler is in some sense Ibsen's alter ego. The psychoanalysis of Hedda would no doubt become the merciless psychoanalysis of her author. But in psychoanalytic interpretations of the author or of his work Ibsen's invention and artistic discoveries are usually neglected, and what is even more important, the historical context, the customs and atmospheric realism of the *fin de siècle*, are altogether lost.

Ibsen never read a page of Freud. Neither did Strindberg. In the early 1890s Freud began his first methodical studies of hysteria; in 1895 he announced his first analysis of dreams; and he used the term "psychoanalysis" for the first time in 1896. The Scandinavian Miss Julies and Heddas were finding their dramatists in Strindberg and Ibsen while the Viennese Julies and Heddas were finding their analyst in Freud.

From *The Theatre of Essence and Other Essays*

Joan Templeton (contempo)

THE *DOLL HOUSE* BACKLASH: CRITICISM, FEMINISM, AND IBSEN 1989

In this excerpt from a longer article, Joan Templeton gives us insight into the range of negative criticism of Nora Helmer's actions. Critics of Nora, both men and women, have seen her as problematic not only because of her problems with her role in society, but also because of her psychological instability, her "hysteria." Their responses have often been quite personal.

A *Doll House* is no more about women's rights than Shakespeare's *Richard II* is about the divine right of kings, or *Ghosts* about syphilis. . . . Its theme is the need of every individual to find out the kind of person he or she is and to strive to become that person.

(M. Meyer 457)

Ibsen has been resoundingly saved from feminism, or, as it was called in his day, "the woman question." His rescuers customarily cite a statement the drama-tist made on 26 May 1898 at a seventieth-birthday banquet given in his honor by the Norwegian Women's Rights League:

I thank you for the toast, but must disclaim the honor of having consciously worked for the women's rights movement. . . . True enough, it is desirable to solve the woman problem, along with all the others; but that has not been the whole purpose. My task has been the description of humanity.

(Ibsen, *Letters* 337)

Ibsen's champions like to take this disavowal as a precise reference to his pur-pose in writing A *Doll House* twenty years earlier, his "original intention," ac-cording to Maurice Valency. Ibsen's biographer Michael Meyer urges all review-ers of *Doll House* revivals to learn Ibsen's speech by heart, and James McFarlane, editor of *The Oxford Ibsen*, includes it in his explanatory material on A *Doll House*, under "Some Pronouncements of the Author," as though Ibsen had been speak-ing of the play. Whatever propaganda feminists may have made of A *Doll House*,

Ibsen, it is argued, never meant to write a play about the highly topical subject of women's rights; Nora's conflict represents something other than, or something more than, woman's. In an article commemorating the half century of Ibsen's death, R. M. Adams explains, "*A Doll House* represents a woman imbued with the idea of becoming a person, but it proposes nothing categorical about women becoming people; in fact, its real theme has nothing to do with the sexes." Over twenty years later, after feminism had resurfaced as an international movement, Einar Haugen, the doyen of American Scandinavian studies, insisted that "Ibsen's Nora is not just a woman arguing for female liberation; she is much more. She embodies the comedy as well as the tragedy of modern life." In the Modern Language Association's *Approaches to Teaching* A Doll House, the editor speaks disparagingly of "reductionist views of [*A Doll House*] as a feminist drama." Summarizing a "major theme" in the volume as "the need for a broad view of the play and a condemnation of a static approach," she warns that discussions of the play's "connection with feminism" have value only if they are monitored, "properly channeled and kept firmly linked to Ibsen's text."

Removing the woman question from *A Doll House* is presented as part of a corrective effort to free Ibsen from his erroneous reputation as a writer of thesis plays, a wrongheaded notion usually blamed on Shaw, who, it is claimed, mistakenly saw Ibsen as the nineteenth century's greatest iconoclast and offered that misreading to the public as *The Quintessence of Ibsenism*. Ibsen, it is now de rigueur to explain, did not stoop to "issues." He was a poet of the truth of the human soul. That Nora's exit from her dollhouse has long been the principal international symbol for women's issues, including many that far exceed the confines of her small world, is irrelevant to the essential meaning of *A Doll House*, a play, in Richard Gilman's phrase, "pitched beyond sexual difference." Ibsen, explains Robert Brustein, "was completely indifferent to [the woman question] except as a metaphor for individual freedom." Discussing the relation of *A Doll House* to feminism, Halvdan Koht, author of the definitive Norwegian Ibsen life, says in summary, "Little by little the topical controversy died away; what remained was the work of art, with its demand for truth in every human relation."

Thus, it turns out, the *Uncle Tom's Cabin* of the women's rights movement is not really about women at all. "Fiddle-faddle," pronounced R. M. Adams, dismissing feminist claims for the play. Like angels, Nora has no sex. Ibsen meant her to be Everyman.

THE DEMON IN THE HOUSE

> [Nora is] a daughter of Eve. . . . [A]n irresistibly bewitching piece of femininity. . . . [Her] charge that in all the years of their marriage they have never exchanged one serious word about serious things is incorrect: she has quite forgotten how seriously Torvald lectured her on the subjects of forgery and lying less than three days ago.

The a priori dismissal of women's rights as the subject of *A Doll House* is a gentlemanly backlash, a refusal to acknowledge the existence of a tiresome reality, "the hoary problem of women's rights," as Michael Meyer has it; the issue is decidedly *vieux jeu*,° and its importance has been greatly exaggerated. In Ibsen's timeless world of Everyman, questions of gender can only be tedious intrusions.

But for over a hundred years, Nora has been under direct siege as exhibiting the most perfidious characteristics of her sex; the original outcry of the 1880s is swollen now to a mighty chorus of blame. She is denounced as an irrational and frivolous narcissist; an "abnormal" woman, a "hysteric"; a vain, unloving egoist who abandons her family in a paroxysm of selfishness. The proponents of the last view would seem to think Ibsen had in mind a housewife Medea, whose cruelty to husband and children he tailored down to fit the framed, domestic world of realist drama.

The first attacks were launched against Nora on moral grounds and against Ibsen, ostensibly, on "literary" ones. The outraged reviewers of the premiere claimed that *A Doll House* did not have to be taken as a serious statement about women's rights because the heroine of Act III is an incomprehensible transformation of the heroine of Acts I and II. This reasoning provided an ideal way to dismiss Nora altogether; nothing she said needed to be taken seriously, and her door slamming could be written off as silly theatrics.

The argument for the two Noras, which still remains popular, has had its most determined defender in the Norwegian scholar Else Høst, who argues that Ibsen's carefree, charming "lark" could never have become the "newly fledged feminist." In any case it is the "childish, expectant, ecstatic, broken-hearted Nora" who makes *A Doll House* immortal; the other one, the unfeeling woman of Act III who coldly analyzes the flaws in her marriage, is psychologically unconvincing and wholly unsympathetic.

The most unrelenting attempt on record to trivialize Ibsen's protagonist, and a favorite source for Nora's later detractors, is Hermann Weigand's. In a classic 1925 study, Weigand labors through forty-nine pages to demonstrate that Ibsen conceived of Nora as a silly, lovable female. At the beginning, Weigand confesses, he was, like all men, momentarily shaken by the play: "Having had the misfortune to be born of the male sex, we slink away in shame, vowing to mend our ways." The chastened critic's remorse is short-lived, however, as a "clear male voice, irreverently breaking the silence," stuns with its critical acumen: " 'The meaning of the final scene,' the voice says, 'is epitomized by Nora's remark: "Yes, Torvald. Now I have changed my dress." ' " With this epiphany as guide, Weigand spends the night poring over the "little volume." Dawn arrives, bringing with it the return of "masculine self-respect." For there is only one explanation for the revolt of "this winsome little woman" and her childish door slamming: Ibsen meant *A Doll House* as comedy. Nora's erratic behavior at the curtain's fall leaves us laughing heartily, for there is no doubt that she will return home to "revert, imperceptibly, to her role of songbird and charmer." After all, since Nora is

> an irresistibly bewitching piece of femininity, an extravagant poet and romancer, utterly lacking in sense of fact, and endowed with a natural gift for play-acting which makes her instinctively dramatize her experiences: how can the settlement fail of a fundamentally comic appeal?

The most popular way to render Nora inconsequential has been to attack her morality; whatever the vocabulary used, the arguments have remained much

---

vieux jeu: Old hat.

the same for over a century. Oswald Crawford, writing in the *Fortnightly Review* in 1891, scolded that while Nora may be "charming as doll-women may be charming," she is "unprincipled." A half century later, after Freudianism had produced a widely accepted "clinical" language of disapproval, Nora could be called "abnormal." Mary McCarthy lists Nora as one of the "neurotic" women whom Ibsen, she curiously claims, was the first playwright to put on stage. For Maurice Valency, Nora is a case study of female hysteria, a willful, unwomanly woman: "Nora is a carefully studied example of what we have come to know as the hysterical personality—bright, unstable, impulsive, romantic, quite immune from feelings of guilt, and, at bottom, not especially feminine."

More recent assaults on Nora have argued that her forgery to obtain the money to save her husband's life proves her irresponsibility and egotism. Brian Johnston condemns Nora's love as "unintelligent" and her crime as "a trivial act which nevertheless turns to evil because it refused to take the universal ethical realm into consideration at all"; Ibsen uses Torvald's famous pet names for Nora—lark, squirrel—to give her a "strong 'animal' identity" and to underscore her inability to understand the ethical issues faced by human beings. Evert Sprinchorn argues that Nora had only to ask her husband's kindly friends (entirely missing from the play) for the necessary money: " . . . any other woman would have done so. But Nora knew that if she turned to one of Torvald's friends for help, she would have had to share her role of savior with someone else."

Even Nora's sweet tooth is evidence of her unworthiness, as we see her "surreptitiously devouring the forbidden [by her husband] macaroons," even "brazenly offer[ing] macaroons to Doctor Rank, and finally lying in her denial that the macaroons are hers"; eating macaroons in secret suggests that "Nora is deceitful and manipulative from the start" and that her exit thus "reflects only a petulant woman's irresponsibility." As she eats the cookies, Nora adds insult to injury by declaring her hidden wish to say "death and damnation" in front of her husband, thus revealing, according to Brian Downs, of Christ's College, Cambridge, "something a trifle febrile and morbid" in her nature.

Much has been made of Nora's relationship with Doctor Rank, the surest proof, it is argued, of her dishonesty. Nora is revealed as *la belle dame sans merci*[o] when she "suggestively queries Rank whether a pair of silk stockings will fit her"; she "flirts cruelly with [him] and toys with his affection for her, drawing him on to find out how strong her hold over him actually is."

Nora's detractors have often been, from the first, her husband's defenders. In an argument that claims to rescue Nora and Torvald from "the campaign for the liberation of women" so that they "become vivid and disturbingly real." Evert Sprinchorn pleads that Torvald "has given Nora all the material things and all the sexual attention that any young wife could reasonably desire. He loves beautiful things, and not least his pretty wife." Nora is incapable of appreciating her husband because she "is not a normal woman. She is compulsive, highly imaginative, and very much inclined to go to extremes." Since it is she who has acquired the money to save his life, Torvald, and not Nora, is really the "wife in the family," although he "has regarded himself as the breadwinner . . . the main support of his wife and children, as any decent husband would like to regard himself." In another defense, John Chamberlain argues that Torvald deserves our sympathy be-

---

la belle dame sans merci: The beautiful lady without mercy.

cause he is no "mere common or garden chauvinist." If Nora were less the actress Weigand has proved her to be, "the woman in her might observe what the embarrassingly naive feminist overlooks or ignores, namely, the indications that Torvald, for all his faults, is taking her at least as seriously as he can—and perhaps even as seriously as she deserves."

From *PMLA*, January 1989

Acknowledgments–*Continued from copyright page–*

Suzanne Jacob. "Two Cents" from *Life After All*, Tr. by Susanna Finnell. Reprinted by permission of Press Gang Publishers.

Jamaica Kincaid. "Lucy" from *Lucy* by Jamaica Kincaid. Copyright ©1990 by Jamaica Kincaid. Reprinted by permission of Farrar, Straus & Giroux, Inc.

Mary Lavin. "Happiness" from *Happiness*. Copyright ©1969 by Mary Lavin. Reprinted by permission of the author's daughter, Caroline Walsh.

D.H. Lawrence. "The Horse Dealer's Daughter" from *Complete Short Stories of D.H. Lawrence* by D.H. Lawrence. Copyright 1922 by Thomas B. Seltzer, Inc., renewed 1950 by Frieda Lawrence. Used by permission of Viking Penguin, a division of Penguin Books USA Inc.

Ursula K. Le Guin. "Sur" by Ursula K. Le Guin first appeared in *The New Yorker*. Copyright ©1982 by Ursula K. Le Guin. Reprinted by permission of the author and the author's agent, Virginia Kidd.

Doris Lessing. "To Room 19" from *The Doris Lessing Reader* by Doris Lessing. Copyright ©1988 by Doris Lessing. Reprinted by permission of Alfred A. Knopf, Inc. and Jonathan Clowes, Ltd, London on behalf of Doris Lessing (Copyright ©1963 Doris Lessing).

Katherine Mansfield. "The Garden Party" from *The Short Stories of Katherine Mansfield* by Katherine Mansfield. Copyright 1922 by Alfred A. Knopf, Inc. and renewed 1950 by J. Middleton Murry. Reprinted by permission of Alfred A. Knopf, Inc.

Gabriel Garcia Marquez. "Eyes of a Blue Dog" from *Innocent Erendira and Other Stories* by Gabriel Garcia Marquez. Copyright ©1978 by Harper & Row, Publishers, Inc. Reprinted by permission of HarperCollins, Publishers, Inc. This story originally appeared in *The New Yorker*.

Bharati Mukerjee. "Jasmine" from the book *The Middleman & Other Stories* by Bharati Mukerjee, Copyright ©1988 by Bharati Mukerjee. Used with the permission of Grove/Atlantic Monthly Press. To order call 800-937-5557.

Alice Munro. "The Moons of Jupiter" from *The Moons of Jupiter and Other Stories* by Alice Munro. Copyright ©1982 by Alice Munro. Reprinted by permission of Alfred A. Knopf, Inc. and Virginia Barber Literary Agency.

Joyce Carol Oates. "Where Are You Going, Where Have You Been?" from *The Wheel of Love and Other Stories* by Joyce Carol Oates. Copyright ©1970 by Joyce Carol Oates. Reprinted by permission of John Hawkins & Associates, Inc.

Tim O'Brien. "Sweetheart of the Song Tra Bong" from *The Things They Carried* by Tim O'Brien. Copyright ©1990 by Tim O'Brien. Reprinted by permission of Houghton Mifflin Company/Seymour Lawrence. All rights reserved.

Flannery O'Connor. "A Good Man is Hard to Find" from *A Good Man Is Hard to Find and Other Stories*, copyright 1953 by Flannery O'Connor and renewed 1981 by Regina O'Connor. Reprinted by permission of Harcourt Brace & Company.

Sean O'Faolain. "Falling Rocks, Narrowing Road, Cul-de-Sac, Stop" by Sean O'Faolain. Copyright ©1971 by Sean O'Faolain. First published in PLAYBOY. Reprinted by permission of Curtis Brown Ltd.

Katherine Anne Porter. "The Jilting of Granny Weatherall" from *Flowering Judas and Other Stories*, copyright 1930 and renewed 1958 by Katherine Anne Porter, reprinted by permission of Harcourt Brace & Company.

James Thurber. "The Secret Life of Walter Mitty" Copyright ©1942 by James Thurber. Copyright ©1970 by Helen Thurber and Rosemary A. Thurber. From *My World—and Welcome to It*, published by Harcourt Brace Jovanovich, Inc. Reprinted by permission of Rosemary A. Thurber.

William Trevor. "The Ballroom of Romance" from *The Ballroom of Romance* by William Trevor. Copyright ©1965, 1966, 1969, 1971, 1972 by William Trevor. Used by permission of Viking Penguin, a division of Penguin Books USA Inc.

Alice Walker. "Everyday Use" from *In Love & Trouble: Stories of Black Women*, copyright ©1973 by Alice Walker, reprinted by permission of Harcourt Brace & Company.

Fay Weldon. "Weekend" from *Watching Me, Watching You*. Copyright ©Fay Weldon 1981. Reprinted by permission of Sheil Land Associates Ltd.

Eudora Welty. "Lily Daw and the Three Ladies" from *A Curtain of Green and Other Stories*, copyright 1937 and renewed 1965 by Eudora Welty. "A Worn Path" from *A Curtain of Green and Other Stories*, copyright 1941 and renewed 1969 by Eudora Welty. "Livvie" from *The Wide Net and Other Stories*, copyright 1942 and renewed 1970 by Eudora Welty. All reprinted by permission of Harcourt Brace & Company.

Patrick Kavanagh. "To the Man After the Harrow" from *Patrick Kavanagh–The Complete Poems.* Copyright 1972 by the Peter Kavanagh Hand Press, New York. Reprinted by permission of Peter Kavanagh.

Denise Levertov. "Cancion" from *The Freeing of the Dust* by Denise Levertov. Copyright ©1975 by Denise Levertov. First published in *Poetry.* Reprinted by permission of New Directions Publishing Corporation.

John Masefield. "Cargoes". Copyright 1912 by The Macmillan Company, renewed 1940 by John Masefield. Reprinted by permission of The Society of Authors as the literary representative of the Estate of John Masefield.

Walter McDonald. "The Food Pickers of Saigon" from *After the Noise of Saigon* by Walter McDonald (Amherst: University of Massachusetts Press, 1988). Copyright ©1988 by Walter McDonald. Reprinted by permission of University of Massachusetts Press.

Peter Meinke. "Miss Arbuckle" by Peter Meinke from *The Educational Forum*, Volume 33, Number 1, Nov. 1968, Page 26. Reprinted by permission of of Kappa De Pi, an International Honor Society in Education. "The Poet, Trying to Surprise" from *Trying to Surprise God*, by Peter Meinke, by permission of the University of Pittsburg ©1981 by Peter Meinke.

W. S. Merwin. "Fly" from *The Lice* by W. S. Merwin. Copyright ©1967 by W. S. Merwin. Reprinted by permission of Georges Borchardt, Inc.

Howard Nemerov. "Because You Asked About The Line Between Prose and Poetry" from *Sentence.* Reprinted by permission of Margaret Nemerov, Trustee of the Howard Nemerov Trust.

Ezra Pound. "In a Station of the Metro" from *Ezra Pound: Personae.* Copyright 1926 by Ezra Pound. Reprinted by permission of New Direction Publishing Corporation.

Ishmael Reed. "Beware: Do Not Read This Poem" by Ishmael Reed. Reprinted by permission of Whitman, Breed, Abbot & Morgan.

Judith Rodriguez. "Eskimo occasion" by Judith Rodriguez from *Judith Rodriguez: New and Selected Poems*, published by University of Queensland Press, 1989. Reprinted by permission of University of Queensland Press.

Carol Rumens. "An Easter Garland" from *Star Whisper* by Carol Rumens. Published by Martin Secker & Warburg. Copyright ©1983 by Carol Rumens. Reprinted by permission of Martin Secker & Warburg Ltd.

Anne Sexton. "All My Pretty Ones" from *All My Pretty Ones* by Anne Sexton. Copyright ©1962 by Anne Sexton, ©renewed 1990 by Linda G. Sexton. Reprinted by permission of Houghton Mifflin Co. All rights reserved.

Edith Sitwell. "Sir Beelzebub" from *Collected Poems* by Edith Sitwell, published by Sinclair Stevenson. Reprinted by permission of David Higham Associates.

Stevie Smith. "Mother Among the Dustbins" from *Collected Poems of Stevie Smith* by Stevie Smith. Copyright ©1972 by Stevie Smith. Reprinted by permission of New Directions Publishing Corporation.

James Stephens. "A Glass of Beer" from *Collected Poems of James Stephens.* Reprinted by permission of The Society of Authors as the literary representative of the Estate of James Stephens.

Anne Stevenson. "The Fiction-Makers" ©Anne Stevenson 1987. Reprinted from Anne Stevenson's *Selected Poems 1956–1986* (1987) by permission of Oxford University Press.

Dylan Thomas. "Do Not Go Gentle Into That Good Night" from *Poems of Dylan Thomas* by Dylan Thomas. Copyright 1939 by New Direction Publishing Corporation, 1945 by The Trustees for the Copyrights of Dylan Thomas, 1952 by Dylan Thomas. Reprinted by permission of New Direction Publishing Corporation and David Higham Associates.

Derek Walcott. "A Far Cry from Africa" from *Collected Poems* by Derek Walcott. Copyright ©1986 by Derek Walcott. Reprinted by permission of Farrar, Straus & Giroux, Inc.

ALBUM OF POEMS

Diane Ackerman. "Patrick Ewing Takes a Foul Shot," "Letter to Wallace Stevens," "On Looking into Sylvia Plath's Copy of Goethe's FAUST," and "Anne Donne to Her

Husband" from *Jaguar of Sweet Laughter* by Diane Ackerman. Copyright ©1991 by Diane Ackerman. Reprinted by permission of Random House, Inc.

Bella Akhmadulina. "Volcanoes" II, Bella Akhmadulina, 32 11 from *About the House* by W. H. Auden. Copyright ©1963 by W. H. Auden. Reprinted by permission of Random House, Inc.

Ann Akhmatova. "Lot's Wife" from *Walking to Sleep, New Poems and Translations* by Richard Wilbur. Reprinted by permission of Harcourt Brace & Company.

Agha Shahid Ali. "Homage to Faiz Ahmed Faiz" from *The Half Inch Himalayas*, Copyright 1987 by Agha Shahid Ali. Reprinted by permission of Wesleyan University Press, University Press of New England.

Alurista. "fire and earth," "with," "who are we? . . . somos aztlan: a letter to 'el jefe corky'," and "urban prison" by Alurista from *Return, Poems Collected and New*. Reprinted by permission of Bilingual Press.

Maya Angelou. "The Yet To Be United States" from *I Shall Not Be Moved* by Maya Angelou. Copyright ©1990 by Maya Angelou. Reprinted by permission of Random House, Inc.

W. H. Auden. "In Memory of W. B. Yeats" and "Musee Des Beaux Arts" from W. H. Auden, edited by E. Mendelson. Copyright 1940 and renewed 1968 by W. H. Auden. Reprinted by permission of Random House, Inc. and Faber and Faber Ltd.

Imamu Amiri Baraka. "In Memory of Radio" from *Preface to a Twenty Volume Suicide Note* by Amiri Baraka. Copyright ©by Amiri Baraka. Reprinted by permission of Sterling Lord Literistic, Inc.

Grace Bauer. "Eve Recollecting The Garden" from *Poetry*, April 1990. Copyright 1990 by The Modern Poetry Association. Reprinted by permission of the Editor of *Poetry* and Grace Bauer.

Patricia Beer. "Jane Austen at the Window" from *Selected Poems* by Patrica Beer. Reprinted by permission of Carcanet Press Limited, Manchester.

Marvin Bell. "Icarus Thought" from Virginia Quarterly Review, Vol. 66, #3, Summer 1990. Reprinted by permission of Virginia Quarterly Review.

Elizabeth Bishop. "Poem," "Seascape" and "The Fish" from *The Complete Poems 1927–1979* by Elizabeth Bishop. Copyright ©1979,1983 by Alice Helen Methfessel. Reprinted by permission of Farrar, Straus & Giroux, Inc.

Peter Blue Cloud. "Wolf" from *Voices of the Rainbow*, edited by Kenneth Rosen. Copyright ©1975 by Kenneth Rosen. Reprinted by permission of Seaver Books, New York, NY.

Louise Bogan. "Medusa" and "Women" from *The Blue Estuaries* by Louise Bogan. Copyright ©1968 by Louise Bogan. Reprinted by permission of Farrar, Straus & Giroux, Inc.

Arna Bontemps. "A Black Man Talks of Reaping". Reprinted by permission of Harould Ober Associates Incorporated. Copyright ©1963 by Arna Bontemps.

Anne Bradstreet. "To My Dear and Loving Husband" and "The Author to Her Book" from *Poems of Anne Bradstreet*, edited by Robert Hutchinson. Reprinted by permission of Dover Publications.

Gwendolyn Brooks. "the mother" and "We Real Cool" from *Blacks* by Gwendolyn Brooks. Copyright ©1991 by Gwendolyn Brooks. Published by Third World Press, Chicago, 1991. Reprinted by permission of the author.

Christopher Buckley. "Serenade in Blue" from *Dark Matter*, Copper Beech Press, 1993, ©Christopher Buckley. First appeared in *The Iowa Review*, Spring/Summer 1990. Reprinted by permission of Christopher Buckley.

Jose Antonio Burciaga. "Bicentennial Recipe" and "World Premiere" from *Restless Serpents*. Reprinted by permission of the author. Kathleen Stripling Byer. "Chestnut Flat Mine" from *Wildwood Flower* by Kathleen Stripling Byer, published by LSU Press, Baton Rouge, LA. Copyright ©Kathryn Stripling Byer, 1992.

Juanita Casey. "Pegasus" from *Horse by the River*. Reprinted by permission of Colin Smythe, Ltd.

Marilyn Chin. "How I Got That Name" from *The Iowa Review*, Spring/Summer 1990. Reprinted by permission of Marilyn Chin.

Amy Clampitt. "Beach Glass" from *The Kingfisher* by Amy Clampitt. Copyright ©1983 by Amy Clampitt. Reprinted by permission of Alfred A. Knopf, Inc.

John Cotton. "Report Back" from *Old Movies and Other Poems* by John Cotton. Reprinted by permission of the author.

Robert Creeley. "Ballad of the Despairing Husband" from *Collected Poems of Robert Creeley*, 1945–1975. Reprinted by permission of University of California Press.

Countee Cullen. "Heritage" from Color by Countee Cullen. Copyright © 1925 by Harper & Brothers; copyright renewed 1953 by Ida M. Cullen. Reprinted by permission of GRM Associates, Inc., Agents for the Estate of Ida M. Cullen.

E. E. Cummings. "Buffalo Bill's Defunct" and "my sweet old etcetera" reprinted from *Complete Poems, 1904–1962*, by E. E. Cummings, Edited by George J. Firmage, by permission of Liveright Publishing Corporation. Copyright © 1923, 1925, 1926, 1931, 1935, 1938, 1939, 1940, 1944, 1945, 1946, 1947, 1948, 1949, 1950, 1951, 1952, 1953, 1954, 1955, 1956, 1957, 1958, 1959, 1960, 1961, 1962 by E. E. Cummings. Copyright ©1961, 1963, 1966, 1967, 1968 by Marion Morehouse Cummings. Copyright ©1972, 1973, 1974, 1975, 1976, 1977, 1978, 1979, 1980, 1981, 1982, 1983, 1984, 1985, 1986, 1987, 1988, 1989, 1990, 1991 by the Trustees for the E. E. Cummings Trust.

Philip Dacey. "Jack and Afterwards" and "Jill Afterwards" from *How I Escaped From the Labyrinth and Other Poems* by Philip Dacey. Reprinted by permission of Carnegie Mellon University Press ©1977 by Philip Dacey.

Bernard Dadié. "In Memoriam" and "I Thank You, Lord" from *The Negritude Poets*, Edited by Ellen Conroy Kennedy. Reprinted by permission of Thunder's Mouth Press.

Carl Dennis. "Oedipus the King" from *Meetings With Time* (Viking Penguin, 1992). Reprinted by permission of Carl Dennis.

James Dickey. "On the Hill Below the Lighthouse" from *Poems: 1957–1967*. Copyright 1967 by James Dickey. Reprinted by permission of Wesleyan University Press/University Press of New England.

Emily Dickinson. "Poem #341" from *The Complete Poems of Emily Dickinson*, edited by Thomas H. Johnson. Copyright 1929 by Martha Dickinson Bianchi; Copyright ©renewed 1957 by Mary L. Hampson. By permission of Little, Brown and Company. "Success is Counted Sweetest," "I Taste a Liquor Never Brewed," "I Felt a Funeral in My Brain," "Tell the Truth, but Tell it Slant," "A Narrow Fellow in the Grass," "Because I Could Not Stop for Death," "I Heard a Fly Buzz When I Died," from *Final Harvest: Emily Dickinson's Poems* published by Harvard University Press. Reprinted by permission of the publishers and the Trustees of Amherst College from *The Poems of Emily Dickinson*, Thomas H. Johnson, ed., Cambridge, Mass.: The Belknap Press of Harvard University Press, Copyright ©1951, 1955, 1979, 1983 by the President and Fellows of Harvard College.

Sheila Dietz. "The Baby in the Basket I," and "Not Remembering More" by Sheila Dietz. Reprinted by permission of the author.

Birago Diop. "Viaticum" from *The Negritude Poets*, edited by Ellen Conroy Kennedy. Reprinted by permission of Thunder's Mouth Press.

Thomas Disch. "The Rapist's Villanelle" from *ABCDEFG HIJKLM NOPQRST UVWXYZ*. Reprinted by permission of Thomas M. Disch and the Karpfinger Agency.

H. D. (Hilda Doolittle). "Heat" and "Helen" from *Collected Poems 1912–1914* by H. D.. Copyright ©1982 by The Estate of Hilda Doolittle. Reprinted by permission of New Directions Publishing Corporation.

Rita Dove. "Used" was first published in *The Atlantic Monthly*. Copyright 1989 by Rita Dove. Reprinted by permission of the author.

James Doyle. "The Village" by James Doyle first appeared in POETRY, July 1990. Copyright ©1990 by The Modern Poetry Association. Reprinted by permission of the Editor of POETRY and the author, James Doyle.

T. S. Eliot. "V. Lines for Cuscuscaraway and Mirza Murad Ali Beg," "The Love Song of J. Alfred Prufrock," and "The Hollow Men" from *Collected Poems* by T. S. Eliot, copyright 1936 by Harcourt Brace & Company, copyright ©1964, 1963 by T. S. Eliot. All reprinted by permission of Harcourt Brace & Company and Faber and Faber Limited.

Gretel Ehrlich. "The Orchard" ©Gretel Ehrlich. Published in 1980 by Ahsahta Press, Boise State University, Boise, Idaho. Reprinted by permission of Gretel Ehrlich and Ahsahta Press.

Lynn Emanuel. "The Sleeping" from the two book volume, *The Dig and Hotel Fiesta*, published by The University of Illinois Press. Reprinted by permission of Lynn Emanuel.

Faiz Ahmed Faiz. "Before You Came" by Faiz Ahmed Faiz, translated by Agha Shahid Ali. Published in the new renaissance, Vol. VIII, No. 2—Spring 1988. Reprinted by permission of the new renaissance.

Carolyn Forché. "The Colonel" from *The Country Between Us* by Carolyn Forché. Copyright ©1982 by Carolyn Forché. Reprinted by permission of HarperCollins, Publishers, Inc.

Robert Frost. "Mending Wall," "Home Burial," "After Apple Picking,"."The Road Not Taken," "The Oven Bird," "Out, Out—," "Stopping by Woods on a Snowy Evening," "Acquainted with the Night," "West-Running Brook," "Neither Out Far Nor In Deep," "Provide, Provide," and "Auspex" from *The Poetry of Robert Frost*, Edited by Edward Connery Lathem. Copyright 1916, 1923, 1934, 1939, ©1969 by Henry Holt and Company, Inc. Copyright 1936, 1944, 1951, ©1956, 1958, 1960, 1962 by Robert Frost. Copyright ©1964, 1967 by Lesley Frost Ballantine. Reprinted by permission of Henry Holt and Company, Inc.

Margaret Gibson. "Out in the Open" from *Out in the Open* by Margaret Gibson. Copyright ©1989 by Margaret Gibson. "Unborn Child" from *Long Walks in The Afternoon* by Margaret Gibson. Copyright © 1982 by Margaret Gibson. Both reprinted by permission of Louisiana State University Press.

Allen Ginsberg. "Howl" from *Collected Poems 1947–1980* by Allen Ginsberg. Copyright ©1955 by Allen Ginsberg. Originally from HOWL. Reprinted by permission of HarperCollins, Publishers, Inc.

Louise Glück. "Brown Circle" ©1990 by Louise Glück. From *Ararat* by Louise Glück. "Palais des Arts" and "The Mirror" ©1976, 1977, 1978, 1979, 1980 by Louise Glück. From *Descending Figure* by Louise Glück. "Brooding Likeness" ©1985 by Louise Gluck. From *The Triumph of Achilles* by Louise Glück. "Matins" and "Vespers" ©1992 by Louise Glück. From *The Wild Iris* by Louise Glück. All were published by The Ecco Press and reprinted by permission.

Lorna Goodison. "Jamaica 1980" and "My Last Poem" from *I Am Becoming My Mother* by Lorna Goodison, published by New Beacon Books 1986; "My Last Poem (Again)" from *Heartease* by Lorna Goodison, published by New Beacon Books 1988. Reprinted by permission of New Beacon Books.

Jorie Graham. "The Hiding Place" ©1991 by Jorie Graham. From *Region of Unlikeness* by Jorie Graham, published by The Ecco Press. Reprinted by permission. "History" by Jorie Graham from *Erosion*, Copyright ©1983 by Princeton University Press. Reprinted by permission of Princeton University Press.

Linda Gregg. "Whole and Without Blessing" Copyright 1981 by Linda Gregg. Reprinted from *Too Bright to See* with the permission of Graywolf Press, Saint Paul.

Marilyn Hacker. "Sonnet Ending with a Film Subtitle" from *Taking Notice* by Marilyn Hacker. Copyright © 1980 by Marilyn Hacker. "Elektra on Third Avenue from *Presentation Piece* by Marilyn Hacker. Copyright © 1972, 1973, 1974 by Marilyn Hacker. "Le Manuscrit" and "Did you love well what very soon you left" from *Love, Death and the Changing of The Seasons* by Marilyn Hacker. Copyright © 1986 by Marilyn Hacker. All reprinted by permission of the author.

Joy Harjo. "Santa Fe", "Crossing Water," and "Nine Lives" reprinted from *In Mad Love and War* ©1990 by Joy Harjo, Wesleyan University Press. By permission of University Press of New England.

Michael Harper. "Last Affair: Bessie's Blues Song" is reprinted from *Song: I Want a Witness* by Michael S. Harper, by permission of the University of Pittsburgh Press. ©1972 by Michael S. Harper.

Robert Hayden. "Middle Passage" by Robert Hayden from *Collected Poems of Robert Hayden*, edited by Frederick Glaysher, is reprinted with the permission of Liveright Publishing Corporation. Copyright ©1962 by Robert Hayden, renewed 1990 by Erma Hayden.

Seamus Heaney. "Punishment," "The Grauballe Man," "Digging," and "The Tollund Man" from *Selected Poems 1966–1987* by Seamus Heaney. Copyright ©1990 by Seamus Heaney. Reprinted by permission of Farrar, Straus & Giroux, Inc. and Faber and Faber Limited.

Geoffrey Hill. "September Song" from *Collected Poems* by Geoffrey Hill. Copyright ©1959, 1968, 1971, 1978, 1983, 1985. Reprinted by permission of Oxford University Press, Inc.

Christine Holbo. "Gomorrah," originally in *The New Yorker*, ©1992 by Christine Holbo. Reprinted by permission of *The New Yorker*, All rights reserved.

Langston Hughes. "Dream Deferred" (Harlem) from *The Panther and The Lash* by Langston Hughes. Copyright 1951 by Langston Hughes. "The Negro Speaks of Rivers" from *Selected Poems* by Langston Hughes. Copyright 1926 by Alfred A. Knopf, Inc. and renewed 1954 by Langston Hughes. "The Weary Blues" from *Selected Poems* by Langston Hughes. Copyright 1926 by Alfred A. Knopf, Inc. and renewed 1954 by Langston Hughes. "Madam and the Rent Man" from *Selected Poems* by Langston Hughes. Copyright 1948 by Alfred A. Knopf, Inc. All are reprinted by permission of Alfred A. Knopf, Inc. "Ballad of the Landlord" and "Theme for English B" from *Montage of a Dream Deferred* by Langston Hughes. Copyright 1951 by Langston Hughes. Copyright renewed 1979 by George Houston Bass. Reprinted by permission of Harold Ober Associates, Incorporated.

Ted Hughes. "Crow's First Lesson" Copyright ©1971 by Ted Hughes. Originally appeared in *Crow* by Ted Hughes. "Examination at the Womb Door" Copyright ©1971 by Ted Hughes. Originally appeared in *Crow* by Ted Hughes. "Pike" Copyright ©1959 by Ted Hughes. Copyright renewed. Originally appeared in *Lupercal* by Ted Hughes. "Skylarks" Copyright ©1967 by Ted Hughes. Originally appeared in *Wodwo* by Ted Hughes. All from *New Selected Poems* by Ted Hughes. Reprinted by permission of HarperCollins Publishers, Inc. and Ted Hughes.

Lynda Hull. "Midnight Reports" by Lynda Hull reprinted from *Star Ledger* by Lynda Hull by permission of the University of Iowa Press. Copyright 1991 by Lynda Hull.

T. R. Hummer. "The Rural Carrier Stops to Kill a Nine-Foot Cottonmouth" by T. R. Hummer. Reprinted by permission of Louisiana State University Press from *The Angelic Orders* by T. R. Hummer. Copyright ©1982 by T. R. Hummer. "The Rural Carrier Discovers That Love is Everywhere" by T. R. Hummer, Copyright ©Commonweal 1980. Reprinted by permission of *Commonweal.*

Richard Jackson. "Benediction" from *Prairie Schooner*. Copyright 1990 University of Nebraska Press. Reprinted by permission of the University of Nebraska Press and the author.

Elizabeth Jennings. "Fragment for the Dark," "The Child's Story," and "Wonder" from *Collected Poems* by Elizabeth Jennings, published by Carcanet Press Ltd. Reprinted by permission of David Higham Associates.

June Jordan. "Letter to the Local Police" and "A Right-to Lifer in Grand Forks, North Dakota" from *Passion: New Poems 1977–1980* by June Jordan. Reprinted by permission of June Jordan.

Jenny Joseph. "Warning" from *Selected Poems* published by Bloodaxe Books. ©Jenny Joseph 1992. Reprinted by permission of the author and the author's agent, John Johnson Ltd.

Donald Justice. "A Map of Love" from *The Summer Anniversaries*, copyright 1981 by Donald Justice. Reprinted by permission of Wesleyan University Press, University Press of New England.

Brigit Pegeen Kelly. "Young Wife's Lament" reprinted from *To the Place of Trumpets* by permission of Yale University Press. *To the Place of Trumpets* copyright 1983.

Dolores Kendrick. "Leah: in Freedom" from *The Women of Plums: Poems in the Voices of Slave Women*, Copyright ©1989 by Dolores Kendrick, William Morrow and Company, Inc., N.Y., Publisher, Phillips Exeter Academy Press Edition, Exeter, N.H. 1991. Reprinted by permission of the author.

Galway Kinnell. "When One Has Lived A Long Time Alone" from *When One Has Lived a Long Time Alone* by Galway Kinnell. Copyright ©1990 by Galway Kinnell. Reprinted by permission of Alfred A. Knopf, Inc.

Rachel Korn. "Keep Hidden From Me" by Rachel Korn, translated by Carolyn Kizer, from *A Treasury of Yiddish Poetry*, edited by Irving Howe and Eliezer Greenberg. Copyright © 1969 by Irving Howe and Eliezer Greenberg. Reprinted by permission of Henry Holt and Company, Inc.

Mazisi Kunene. "From the Ravages of Life We Create," "The Political Prisoner" and "Place of Dreams" from *Zulu Poems* by Mazisi Kunene (New York: Africana Publishing Co., 1970). Copyright © 1970 by Mazisi Kunene. Reprinted by permission of the Publisher, Africana Publishing Co., a division of Holmes & Meier Publishers, Inc.

Philip Larkin. "Faith Healing" from *Collected Poems* by Philip Larkin, edited by Anthony

Thwaite. Reprinted by permission of Faber and Faber Ltd and Farrar, Straus & Giroux, Inc. "Church Going" by Philip Larkin is reprinted from *The Less Deceived* by permission of The Marvell Press, England and Australia.

Denise Levertov. "O Taste and See" and "Matins" from *Denise Levertov: Poems 1960–1967*. Copyright © 1961, 1964 by Denise Levertov Goodman. Reprinted by permission of New Directions Publishing Corporation.

Jan Heller Levi. "Sex is not Important" by Jan Heller Levi. Copyright ©1990 by *The Antioch Review, Inc.* First appeared in *The Antioch Review*, Vol. 48, No. 1 (Winter, 1990). Reprinted by permission of the Editors.

Amy Lowell. "Venus Transiens" from *The Complete Works of Amy Lowell*. Copyright ©1955 Houghton Mifflin Co., ©renewed 1983 by Houghton Mifflin Co., Brinton P. Roberts and G. D'Andelot Belin, Esquire. Reprinted by permission of Houghton Mifflin Co. All rights reserved.

Robert Lowell. "Robert Frost" and "Skunk Hour" from *Selected Poems* by Robert Lowell. Copyright ©1976 by Robert Lowell. Reprinted by permission of Farrar, Straus & Giroux, Inc.

Wing Tek Lum. "At a Chinaman's Grave" and Minority Poem" by Wing Tek Lum from *Expounding Doubtful Points*. Reprinted by permission of the author.

George Ella Lyon. "Salvation" Copyright 1982 by Appalachian State University/Appalachian Journal. "Progress" Copyright 1984 by Appalachian State University/Appalachian Journal. Both used with permission of Appalachian Journal.

Mekeel McBride. "If I'd Been Born in Tennessee" reprinted from *Red Letter Days* by Mekeel McBride by permission of Carnegie Mellon University Press, ©1986 by Mekeel McBride.

J. D. McClatchy. "The Window" from *The Rest of the Way* by J. D. McClatchy. Copyright ©1990 by J. D. McClatchy. Reprinted by permission of Alfred A. Knopf, Inc.

Walter McDonald. "Father's Straight Razor" first appeared in *Poetry*, June 1990. Copyright ©1990 by The Modern Poetry Association. Reprinted by permission of the Editor of POETRY and Walter McDonald.

Claude McKay. "The Harlem Dancer" by Claude McKay from *Selected Poems of Claude McKay*. Reprinted by permission of the Archives of Claude McKay, Carl Cowl, Administrator. Originally published by Harcourt Brace, 1979.

Naomi Long Madgett. "Midway" and "The Race Question" from *Star by Star* by Naomi Long Madgett, 1965, 1970. By permission of the author.

W. S. Merwin. "For a Coming Extinction" from *The Lice*. ©1967 by W. S. Merwin. Reprinted by permission of Georges Borchardt, Inc.

Edna St. Vincent Millay. "Childhood is the Kingdom Where Nobody Dies" and "Apostrophe to Man" by Edna St. Vincent Millay. From *Collected Poems*, HarperCollins. Copyright 1934, 1962 by Edna St. Vincent Millay and Norma Millay Ellis. Reprinted by permission of Elizabeth Barnett, literary executor.

Cheng Min. "Student" from *Women Poets of China* by Kenneth Rexroth. Copyright ©1972 by Kenneth Rexroth and Ling Chung. Reprinted by permission of New Directions Corporation.

N. Scott Momaday. "Comparatives" from *The Gourd Dancer* by N. Scott Momaday. Reprinted by permission of the author.

Marianne Moore. "Poetry" from *Collected Poems of Marianne Moore*. Copyright 1935 by Marianne Moore, renewed 1963 by Marianne Moore and T. S. Eliot. Reprinted by permission of Macmillan Publishing Company.

Larry Neal. "Ghost Poem #1" from the book, *Vision of a Liberated Future* by Larry Neal. Copyright ©1989 by Evelyn Neal. Used by permission of the publisher, Thunder's Mouth Press.

Sharon Olds. "The Death of Marilyn Monroe," "Things That Are Worse Than Death" and "The One Girl at the Boy's Party" from *The Dead and the Living* by Sharon Old. Copyright ©1983 by Sharon Olds. Reprinted by permission of Alfred A. Knopf, Inc.

Mary Oliver. "Marengo," "The Summer Day," and "Some Questions You Might Ask" from *New and Selected Poems* by Mary Oliver. Copyright ©1992 by Mary Oliver. Reprinted by permission of Beacon Press.

Simon Ortiz. "Juanita, Wife of Manuelito" by Simon J. Ortiz from *Going for the Rain*. Reprinted by permission of the author, Simon J. Ortiz.

Wilfred Owen. "Spring Offensive," "Arms and the Boy," and "Dulce et Decorum Est" from *Wilfred Owen: Poems of Wilfred Owen*. Copyright ©1963 by Chatto & Windus Ltd. Reprinted by permission of New Directions Publishing Corporation and Chatto & Windus Ltd.

Dorothy Parker. "General Review of the Sex Situation", copyright 1926, renewed ©1954 by Dorothy Parker, "Men", copyright 1928, renewed ©1956 by Dorothy Parker, "Now At Liberty", copyright 1928, renewed ©1956 by Dorothy Parker, "Observation", copyright 1928, renewed ©1956 by Dorothy Parker, "Symptom Recital", copyright 1926, renewed ©1954 by Dorothy Parker, "Incurable", copyright 1928, renewed ©1956 by Dorothy Parker, from *The Portable Dorothy Parker* by Dorothy Parker, Introduction by Brendan Gill. Used by permission of Viking Penguin, a division of Penguin Books USA Inc.

Marge Piercy. "Secretary Chant" from *Circles on the Water* by Marge Piercy. Copyright ©1982 by Marge Piercy. Reprinted by permission of Alfred A. Knopf, Inc.

Donald Platt. "Aria For This Listening Area" from *Fresh Peaches, Fireworks, & Guns* (Purdue University Press, 1994). Copyright ©1994 by Donald Platt. Originally appeared in POETRY, April 1990. Reprinted by permission of Author.

Katha Pollitt. "Old Neighbors" by Katha Pollitt. Originally published in *Southwest Review*, Winter 1990. "In Memory" from *Antarctic Traveller* by Katha Pollitt. Copyright ©1981 by Katha Pollitt. Reprinted by permission of Alfred A. Knopf, Inc.

Alexander Pope. "Ode on Solitude" from *Poems of Alexander Pope*. Reprinted by permission of Methuen & Co.

Ezra Pound. "Ancient Music," "The Return," and "The River Merchant's Wife, A Letter" from *Personae* by Ezra Pound. Copyright 1926 by Ezra Pound. Reprinted by permission of New Diretions Publishing Corporation.

Henry Reed. "The Naming of Parts" from *A Map of Verona* by Henry Reed. Copyright Henry Reed, reproduced by permission of Curtis Brown Ltd, London.

Carter Revard. "What the Eagle Fan Says" from *Cowboys and Indians*. Also, reprinted in *An Eagle Nation*. Reprinted by permission of Carter Revard.

Adrienne Rich. "Snapshots of a Daughter-In-Law," "Song," "Diving Into the Wreck," and "Trying to Talk with a Man" from *The Fact of a Doorframe*, Poems Selected and New, 1950–1984 by Adrienne Rich, reprinted by permission of W. W. Norton & Company, Inc. Copyright ©1984 by Adrienne Rich. Copyright ©1975, 1978, by W. W. Norton & Company, Inc. Copyright ©1981 by Adrienne Rich.

Edwin Arlington Robinson. "Richard Cory" from *The Children of the Nigh* by Edwin Arlington Robinson (New York: Charles Scribner's Sons, 1897). Reprinted by permission of Macmillan Publishing Company.

Muriel Rukeyser. "From Letter to the Front: To Be A Jew in the Twentieth Century" and "Myth" from *Out of Silence* by Muriel Rukeyser, 1992, TriQuarterly Books, Evanston, IL, ©William L. Rukeyser.

Theodore Roethke. "Dolor", copyright 1943 by Modern Poetry Association, Inc. "Elegy for Jane", copyright 1950 by Theodore Roethke. "My Papa's Waltz", copyright 1942 by Hearst Magazines, Inc. from *The Collected Poems of Theodore Roethke* by Theodore Roethke. Used by permission of Doubleday, a division of Bantam Doubleday Dell Publishing Group, Inc.

Leopold Senghor. "Night of Sine" from *The Negritude Poets*, edited by Ellen Conroy Kennedy. Reprinted by permission of Thunder's Mouth Press.

Anne Sexton. "Her Kind" and "Ringing the Bells" from *To Bedlam and Part Way Back* by Anne Sexton, Copyright ©1960 by Anne Sexton, © renewed 1988 by Linda G. Sexton. "For My Lover, Returning to His Wife" from *Love Poems* by Anne Sexton. Copyright ©1967, 1968, 1969 by Anne Sexton. "Red Riding Hood" and "Snow White and the Seven Dwarfs" from *Transformation* by Anne Sexton. Copyright ©1971 by Anne Sexton. All reprinted by permission of Houghton Mifflin Co. All rights reserved.

Leslie Marmon Silko. "Four Mountain Wolves" from *Voices of the Rainbow* edited by Kenneth Rosen. Copyright ©1975 by Kenneth Rosen. Reprinted by permission of Seaver Books, New York, New York.

Louis Simpson. "New Lines for Cuscuscaraway and Mirza Murad Ali Beg" by Louis Simpson. Reprinted from *At the End of the Open Road*, ©1963 by Louis Simpson, Wesleyan University Press. By permission of University Press of New England.

Fily-Dabo Sissoko. "Brush Fire" from *The Negritude Poets*, edited by Ellen Conroy Kennedy. Reprinted by permission of Thunder's Mouth Press.

Dave Smith. "On a Field Trip at Fredericksburg" from *Cumberland Station* by Dave Smith. Reprinted by permission of the author.

Stevie Smith. "The Galloping Cat," "Scorpion," and "Away, Melancholy" from *Collected Poems of Stevie Smith* by Stevie Smith. Copyright ©1972 by Stevie Smith. Reprinted by permission of New Directions Publishing Corporation.

Gary Snyder. "Riprap" from *Riprap and Cold Mountain Poems* by Gary Snyder. Copyright ©1958, 1959, 1965 by Gary Snyder. Reprinted by permission of North Point Press, a division of Farrar, Straus & Giroux, Inc.

Cathy Song. "The Youngest Daughter" from *Picture Bride* by Cathy Song. Copyright ©1983 by Cathy Song. Reprinted by permission of the publisher, Yale University Press.

Marcia Southwick. "Owning a Dead Man" and "Dusk" from *The Night Won't Save Anyone* by Marcia Southwick. Copyright 1980 by the University of Georgia Press. Reprinted by permission of the University of Georgia Press.

Maura Stanton. "Childhood" by Maura Stanton first appeared in POETRY, Copyright ©1982 by The Modern Poetry Association. "Biography" by Maura Stanton first appeared in *Poetry*, Copyright ©1982 by The Modern Poetry Association. "Childhood" and "Biography" are reprinted from *Crier of Swimmers* by permission of Carnegie Mellon University Press. ©1984 by Maura Stanton.

Georgre Starbuck. "On First Looking in on Blodgett's Keat's Chapman's Homer" from *Bone Thoughts* by George Starbuck, Copyright ©1960 by George Starbuck. Reprinted by permission of Yale University Press.

Wallace Stevens. "The Emperor of Ice-Cream", Copyright 1923 and renewed 1951 by Wallace Stevens. "Thirteen Ways of Looking at a Blackbird," Copyright 1923 and renewed 1951 by Wallace Stevens. "The Idea of Order at Key West", Copyright 1936 by Wallace Stevens and renewed 1964 by Holly Stevens. All are from *Collected Poems* by Wallace Stevens. Reprinted by permission of Alfred A. Knopf, Inc.

Anne Stevenson. "Cain" and "By the Boat House, Oxford", © Anne Stevenson 1987. Reprinted from Anne Stevenson's *Selected Poems 1956–1986* (1987) by permission of Oxford University Press.

Ruth Stone. "Where I Come From," Copyright © 1987 by Ruth Stone. Reprinted by permission of Yellow Moon Press, P.O. Box 3816, Cambridge, MA 02238.

Mark Strand. "Where are the Waters of Childhood" from *Selected Poems* by Mark Strand. Copyright ©1979, 1980 by Mark Strand. Reprinted by permission of Alfred A. Knopf, Inc.

Dylan Thomas. "Fern Hill" and "Poem in October" from *Poems of Dylan Thomas* by Dylan Thomas. Copyright 1939 by New Directions Publishing Corporation, 1945 by the Trustees for the Copyrights of Dylan Thomas, 1952 by Dylan Thomas. "Poem in October" was first published in *Poetry*. Reprinted by permission of New Directions Publishing Corporation and David Higham Associates.

David Wagoner. "The Shooting of John Dillinger Outside the Biograph Theater, July 22, 1934" from *New and Selected Poems* by David Wagoner. Copyright ©1976 by David Wagoner. Reprinted by permission of the author.

Diane Wakoski. "Sestina to the Common Glass of Beer: I Do Not Drink Beer", Copyright ©1976 by Diane Wakoski. Reprinted from *Waiting for the King of Spain* with the permission of Black Sparrow Press.

Marilyn Nelson Waniek. "Emily Dickinson's Defunct" by Marilyn Nelson Waniek. Reprinted by permission of Louisiana State University Press from *For the Body* by Marilyn Nelson Waniek. Copyright ©1978 by Marilyn Nelson Waniek.

Belle Waring. "What Hurts" and "Children Must Have Manners" are reprinted from *Refuge* by Belle Waring. ©1990 by Belle Waring. Reprinted by permission of the University of Pittsburgh Press.

Cand ice Warne. "Blackbird Sestina" by Candice Warne. Reprinted by permission of the author.

John Wieners. "The Eagle Bar" Copyright ©1967 by John Wieners. Reprinted from *Selected Poems 1958–1984* with the permission of Black Sparrow Press.

William Carlos Williams. "The Red Wheelbarrow" and "Danse Russe" from *Collected Poems of William Carlos Williams, 1909–1939*, Vol. 1 by William Carlos Williams. Copyright 1938 by New Directions Publishing Corporation. Reprinted by permission of New Directions Publishing Corporation.

SYLVIA PLATH IN DEPTH

DRAMA

HENRIK IBSEN IN DEPTH

ndex

Index of Authors, Titles, First Lines, and Critical Windows

Alphabetical arrangement is letter-by-letter.
Author's names are in **bold** type, titles are in *italic* type, first lines and critical windows in roman type.